W9-AEO-500

Webster's New Explorer Crossword Puzzle Dictionary

Webster's New Explorer Crossword Puzzle Dictionary

Third Edition

Created in Cooperation with the Editors of
MERRIAM-WEBSTER

A division of Merriam-Webster, Incorporated
Springfield, Massachusetts

Federal Street Press books are available for bulk purchase for sales promotion and premium use. For details, write the manager of special sales, Federal Street Press, P.O. Box 281, Springfield, MA 01102.

This edition published by
Federal Street Press
A Division of Merriam-Webster, Incorporated
P.O. Box 281
Springfield, MA 01102

ISBN 978-1-59695-177-8

1st Printing LSC, Crawfordsville, IN 9/2018

Printed in the United States of America

Preface

This dictionary has been thoroughly reviewed and updated from the Second Edition with over 10,000 additional entries. It contains more than 335,000 answer words and includes many terms and names that have only recently entered the general English vocabulary: recent slang (*plotz*, *himbo*, *crunk*, *bubkes*), sports stars (*A-Rod*, *Zidane*), computer languages (*SQL*), automobiles (*Mini*, *Prius*), Nobel Prize winners (*Pamuk*, *Yunus*), national currencies (*kroon*, *som*, *manat*), actors and actresses (*Alba*, *Falco*)—not to mention all the familiar words and names that show up with enough frequency in contemporary puzzle grids to have earned the name of "crosswordese": *asea*, *Oreo*, *aloe*, *A-one*, *espy*, *ciao*, *ta-ta*, *e'er*, *erose*, *amah*, *etui*, *Odie*, *tec*, *Tey*, *olio*, *ern*, *ASAP*, *Opie*, *ad-in*, *ecru*, *luau*, and a legion of others.

As crossword constructors continue to aim for ever fresher and cleverer clues and answers, we hope this updated reference will prove to be the indispensable tool for filling in those final few elusive letters in crosswords of all kinds for puzzlers of every ability and age.

Using This Book

The book is organized to make it easy to find answer words with a specific number of letters. Every answer word follows a numeral indicating the number of letters it contains. The answer words generally run up to 13 letters; an exception to this limit is made for multiword titles of works, to allow for those clues that omit one or two words from a title, perhaps enough for a five- or ten-letter answer.

As in any crossword dictionary, a single list of answer words will often include words representing various parts of speech. Thus, the entry for **fast** includes synonyms for the adjective (*rapid*), the noun (*diet*), and the verb (*abstain*), all in a continuous list. Puzzle clues are often intentionally ambiguous as to which meaning is intended, and listing all possible synonyms together represents the ideal format for the puzzle solver.

Since puzzle creators rarely provide a clue whose answer word shares the clue's root, such root-related words have generally been omitted from the answer lists. Thus, *singular* does not appear at **single**, *basal* does not appear at **basic**, and *papa* does not appear at **pop**. However, since clues do occasionally share a standard prefix (such as *re-* or *un-*) with an answer word, we have retained a number of clue/answer-word pairs of this kind (**redo**/*remodel*, **unsettle**/*unnerve*, etc.).

When one entry word simply adds a suffix to another entry word, as when **shared** follows **share**, the answer list for the suffixed entry word will usually omit any words that merely add the same suffix to a word in the un-suffixed word's list. For example, since **share** includes such answer words as *divide* and *prorate*, the list at **shared** omits *divided* and *prorated*. Therefore, the user who encounters a clue with a familiar suffix will occasionally want to look at a neighboring entry to be sure of finding all the possible synonyms.

When a personal name is entered as an answer term, the first name generally appears in parentheses and is ignored in the letter count. In cases where the first name is the one normally encountered—e.g., for historical figures such as *Napoleon* and *Galileo*, or fictional characters such as *Atticus* and *Scout Finch*—the last name is generally parenthesized instead. When a title begins with an article (*A*, *An*, or *The*), the article is parenthesized and omitted from the letter count. In a list of geographic entities (**river**, **bay**, **peak**, **mountain**, etc.), any generic term that forms part of a proper name (*River*, *Bay*, *Peak*, *Mount*, etc.) is similarly omitted from the letter count. If none of the answers as listed fits the blanks for a given clue, you should naturally check to see if adding a parenthesized or omitted element might produce the desired answer.

In the many entries that are broken into subentries, the subheadings often consist of a single word, which should usually be read as either preceding or following the main entry word. Thus, at **liquor**, the subheadings include **inferior** (which should be read as "inferior liquor") and **measure** (which should be read as "liquor measure"). The subentry **combining form** lists the kinds of word fragments, usually Greek or Latin in origin, that are commonly called roots (*omni*, *derm*, *giga*, etc.).

The dictionary is best used somewhat imaginatively. If you fail to find a clue word at its own entry, look up a synonym; only rarely will you fail to find one. If a clue takes a form such as *Basque game*, *white wine*, or *Italian tenor* and the dictionary provides no such entry, check at the entry for the generic term—**game**, **wine**, **tenor**, etc.

Webster's New Explorer Crossword Puzzle Dictionary

A1 **4** best, tops **5** prime **6** tip-top **7** optimal, perfect **8** splendid, superior, top-notch **9** excellent, first-rate, front-rank, matchless, top-drawer **10** blue-ribbon, first-class

Aaron ***brother:*** **5** Moses ***father:*** **5** Amram ***sister:*** **6** Miriam

aback **7** unaware **8** suddenly, unawares **10** by surprise **12** unexpectedly

abaft **4** back **5** after **6** astern, behind **8** rearward **9** sternward

abalone **7** mollusc, mollusk **9** gastropod

abandon **4** cede, drop, dump, ease, jilt, junk, play, quit **5** cease, chuck, ditch, leave, let go, scrap, yield **6** desert, disown, give up, laxity, maroon, reject, resign, strand, vacate **7** back out, bail out, cast off, discard, drop out, forsake, freedom, liberty, license, pull out, retreat **8** abdicate, give over, hand over, renounce, wildness, withdraw **9** looseness, repudiate, surrender, throw over **10** enthusiasm, exuberance, relinquish, wantonness **11** discontinue, leave behind, spontaneity, unrestraint **12** carelessness, heedlessness, intemperance, recklessness, unconstraint **13** impulsiveness

abandoned **4** free, lewd, lorn, wild **5** loose **6** gave up, jilted, vacant, wanton **7** cast off, corrupt, given up, outcast, uncouth **8** cast away, depraved, derelict, desolate, forsaken **9** cast aside, debauched, destitute, dissolute, lecherous, neglected, reprobate, shameless **10** degenerate, dissipated, friendless, lascivious, left behind, licentious, profligate, unoccupied **11** uninhibited **12** incorrigible, uncontrolled, unrestrained

abase **5** lower, shame **6** defame, demean, demote, grovel, humble, lessen, reduce **7** cheapen, degrade, devalue, put down **8** belittle **9** denigrate, discredit, disparage, downgrade, humiliate **10** depreciate, undervalue

abash **4** faze **5** mix up, shame, upset **6** dismay, puzzle, rattle **7** confuse, mortify, mystify **8** confound **9** discomfit, embarrass **10** discompose, disconcert

abashment **6** unease **7** chagrin **8** disquiet **9** confusion **12** discomfiture, discomposure

abate **3** ebb, end **4** ease, fade, fall, omit, slow, void, stem, wane **5** allay, annul, close, let up, quash, taper **6** deduct, lessen, negate, recede, reduce, relent, weaken **7** abolish, decline, deprive, die down, dwindle, ease off, nullify, slacken, subside **8** decrease, diminish, mitigate, moderate **9** alleviate, eradicate **10** invalidate

abatement **6** ebbing, rebate, waning **8** decrease, discount **9** declining, deduction, dwindling, exemption, lessening, reduction, shrinkage **10** diminution, subsidence **11** subtraction

abattoir **8** shambles

Abba ____ **4** Eban

abbey **6** friary **7** convent **8** cloister **9** monastery

abbot ***female:*** **6** abbess

abbreviate **3** cut **4** clip, trim **5** prune **6** cut out, reduce **7** abridge, curtail, cut back, shorten **8** compress, condense, contract, cut short, truncate

abbreviation **5** brief **6** digest, précis, sketch **7** acronym, cutting, outline **8** abstract, clipping, synopsis, trimming **10** abridgment, shortening **11** curtailment **12** condensation

ABC island **5** Aruba **7** Baranof, Bonaire, Curaçao **9** Admiralty, Chichagof

abdicate **4** cede, drop, quit **5** evade, forgo, leave, waive, yield **6** abjure, give up, reject, resign **7** abandon, cast off, discard **8** abnegate, disclaim, hand over, renounce, withdraw **9** repudiate, surrender **10** relinquish

abdomen **3** gut, pot **5** belly, tummy **6** middle, paunch **7** midriff, stomach **8** potbelly **9** bay window **10** midsection **11** breadbasket ***depression:*** **5** navel

abduct **4** grab, take **5** seize **6** kidnap, remove, snatch **8** carry off, draw away, take away **9** carry away, steal away **10** spirit away **11** make off with

Abduction from the Seraglio ***character:*** **5** Osmin, Selim **8** Belmonte, Pedrillo **9** Konstanze ***composer:*** **6** Mozart (Wolfgang Amadeus)

abecedarian **4** tyro **6** novice **7** amateur, dabbler, learner **8** beginner, initiate, neophyte **9**

beginning, smatterer **10** apprentice, dilettante, elementary **11** rudimentary **12** alphabetical

Abel ***brother:*** **4** Cain, Seth ***father:*** **4** Adam ***mother:*** **3** Eve ***slayer:*** **4** Cain

Abelard ***son:*** **9** Astrolabe ***wife:*** **7** Heloise

abele 6 poplar

aberrant 3 odd **7** deviant, strange, unusual **8** abnormal, atypical, peculiar, straying **9** anomalous, deviating, different, eccentric, irregular, unnatural, untypical **11** exceptional, nonstandard

aberration 4 slip **5** quirk **6** change, oddity **7** anomaly, mistake **8** mutation, straying **9** curiosity, deviation, exception, wandering **10** deflection, difference, distortion, divergence **11** abnormality, peculiarity **12** eccentricity, irregularity

abet 3 aid, egg **4** ally, back, help, prod, spur, urge **5** boost, egg on **6** assist, exhort, foment, incite, second, stir up **7** condone, endorse, forward, promote, support **8** advocate **9** encourage, instigate **11** countenance

abettor 4 aide, ally **6** backup, cohort, helper **7** inciter, partner **8** fomenter **9** accessory, supporter **10** accomplice, instigator **11** confederate, conspirator **12** collaborator

abeyance 4 lull, rest **5** break, lapse, pause **6** recess **7** respite, time-out, waiting **8** breather, interval **10** inactivity, quiescence, suspension **12** intermission, interruption

abeyant 7 dormant **8** deferred, inactive, recessed **9** postponed, quiescent, suspended **11** interrupted

abhor 4 hate **5** scorn **6** detest, loathe, reject, revile, vilify **7** contemn, despise, disdain, dislike **8** execrate **9** abominate, excoriate, repudiate

abhorrence 4 evil, hate **6** hatred, horror **7** disgust **8** aversion, distaste, loathing **9** repulsion, revulsion **10** repugnance **11** abomination, detestation

abhorrent 4 base, foul, vile **5** awful **6** horrid, odious **7** beastly, hateful, heinous **8** damnable, horrible, horrific **9** atrocious, execrable, invidious, loathsome, monstrous, obnoxious, repellent, repugnant, repulsive, revolting **10** abominable, deplorable, despicable, detestable, disgusting **12** contemptible **13** reprehensible

abide 4 bear, last, live, stay, wait **5** await, brook, dwell, exist, stand, tarry **6** accede, accept, comply, endure, keep on, linger, remain, reside, stay on, suffer **7** consent, hang out, inhabit, persist, sojourn, stomach, subsist, swallow, wait for **8** continue, live with, stand for, tolerate **9** put up with, withstand

abiding 4 fast, firm, sure **6** steady **7** durable, eternal, lasting, staying **8** constant, enduring, timeless **9** complying, perpetual, steadfast **10** continuing, persistent, persisting, unchanging **11** everlasting, unfaltering

abigail 4 maid

Abigail ***brother:*** **5** David ***husband:*** **5** David, Nabal ***mother:*** **5** Amasa ***son:*** **7** Chileah

ability 4 bent, gift **5** craft, flair, knack, might, savvy, skill **6** talent **7** aptness, command, faculty, know-how, mastery, prowess **8** aptitude, capacity, facility **9** adeptness, dexterity, expertise, handiness, ingenuity, potential **10** adroitness, capability, cleverness, competence, efficiency **11** proficiency **12** skillfulness **13** qualification

abject 3 low **4** base, mean, poor, vile **5** lowly, sorry **6** dismal, humble, shabby, sordid **7** debased, fawning, forlorn, ignoble, pitiful, servile **8** cast down, degraded, dejected, downcast, hopeless, pathetic, pitiable, rejected, resigned, wretched **9** afflicted, destitute, groveling, miserable, worthless **10** deplorable, obsequious, spiritless, submissive **11** deferential, downtrodden, subservient **12** contemptible, dishonorable, ingratiating

abjure 4 cede, deny **5** avoid, spurn **6** desert, disown, recall, recant, reject, refuse, revoke **7** abandon, disavow, decline, forsake, retract **8** disclaim, forswear, renounce, take back, withdraw **9** repudiate, surrender **10** relinquish **11** abstain from

ablaze 5 afire, aglow, fiery **6** aflame, alight, on fire **7** burning, flaming, excited, flaring, ignited, radiant

able 3 apt, fit **4** keen **5** adept, alert, sharp, smart **6** adroit, clever, expert, facile, suited **7** capable, skilled **8** skillful, talented **9** competent, effective, effectual, efficient, qualified **10** proficient **11** intelligent, resourceful **12** accomplished, enterprising

able-bodied 3 fit **4** hale **5** hardy, lusty, sound, stout **6** brawny, hearty, robust, strong, sturdy **7** capable **8** stalwart, vigorous **9** strapping

ablution 4 bath **6** laving **7** bathing, washing **8** lavation **9** cleansing, immersion **12** purification

abnegate 4 cede, deny, drop **5** forgo, waive, yield **6** abjure, give up, recant, revoke, vacate **7** disavow, gainsay **8** disallow, disclaim, forswear, renounce, withdraw **9** repudiate, surrender **10** contradict, contravene, relinquish

abnegation 6 denial **9** surrender **10** abstinence, self-denial **12** renouncement, renunciation

Abner ***cousin:*** **4** Saul ***father:*** **3** Ner ***slayer:*** **4** Joab

abnormal **3** odd **5** freak, outré, undue, weird **6** off-key **7** bizarre, deviant, strange, unusual **8** aberrant, atypical, freakish, peculiar **9** anomalous, divergent, eccentric, irregular, unnatural **11** heteroclite **13** preternatural

abnormality **4** flaw **6** oddity **7** anomaly **8** deviance **9** deviation, exception **10** aberration, difference **12** irregularity

abode **3** hut **4** home, nest, tent **5** house **7** address, lodging, sojourn **8** domicile, dwelling **9** residence **10** habitation ***conical:*** **5** tepee **6** teepee

abolish **3** end **4** undo, kill, void **5** abate, annul, erase, quash **6** cancel, negate, recall, repeal, revoke, vacate **7** destroy, nullify, rescind, retract, reverse, wipe out **8** abrogate, disallow, dissolve, overturn, prohibit **9** eliminate, eradicate, terminate **10** do away with, extinguish, invalidate

abolitionist **4** Mott (Lucretia), Weld (Theodore) **5** Brown (John), Child (Lydia), Lundy (Benjamin), Smith (Gerrit), Stowe (Harriet Beecher) **6** Birney (James), Lowell (James Russell), Parker (Theodore), Tappan (Arthur), Tubman (Harriet) **7** Lincoln (Abraham) **8** Douglass (Frederick), Garrison (William Lloyd), Phillips (Wendell), Whittier (John Greenleaf)

abominable **5** awful, nasty **6** cursed, horrid, odious **7** hateful, heinous **8** horrible, shocking, terrible, wretched **9** abhorrent, loathsome, offensive, repellent, repugnant, repulsive, revolting **10** deplorable, despicable, detestable, disgusting **12** contemptible

abominable snowman **4** yeti

abominate **4** damn, hate **5** abhor, curse, scorn **6** detest, loathe, revile **7** despise **8** execrate **9** repudiate

abomination **4** evil, hate **5** scorn **6** hatred, horror, plague **7** disdain, disgust, dislike **8** anathema, aversion, contempt, distaste, loathing **9** repulsion, revulsion **10** abhorrence, repugnance, repugnancy **11** detestation

aboriginal **5** first **6** native **7** ancient, endemic, primary **8** earliest, original, primeval **9** primitive **10** indigenous, primordial **13** autochthonous

aborigine **6** native **7** ancient **8** indigene **10** autochthon

abort **4** drop, halt, stop **5** check, expel, scrap, scrub **6** arrest, cancel **7** abandon, call off **8** cut short **9** interrupt, terminate

abortive **4** vain **5** empty **6** futile, unripe **7** failing, useless **9** fruitless, worthless **10** unavailing, unfruitful **11** ineffective, ineffectual **12** unproductive, unsuccessful

abound **4** flow, teem **5** burst, crawl, crowd, flood, swarm, swell **6** throng **8** overflow

abounding **4** full, rife **5** laden **6** filled, full of, jammed, packed **7** copious, profuse, replete, stuffed, teeming **8** abundant, swarming, thronged **9** alive with, bristling, plenteous, plentiful **11** overflowing

about **4** as to, back, in re, near, nigh, over, some **5** again, anent, circa, round **6** almost, around, nearby, nearly **7** apropos, close to, roughly **8** backward **9** as regards, in general, in reverse, regarding **10** as concerns, concerning, in regard to, more or less, relating to, relative to, respecting **11** dealing with, practically, referring to **12** with regard to **13** approximately, concerned with, in reference to, with respect to

about-face **4** turn **7** reverse **8** reversal **9** turnabout

above **3** o'er **4** atop, over, past **5** aloft, supra **6** beyond **8** overhead **9** exceeding ***prefix:*** **4** over **5** hyper, super, supra

above all **7** chiefly **9** primarily **10** especially **11** principally **12** particularly

aboveboard **4** free, open **5** frank **6** candid, honest, openly **7** frankly, up front **8** candidly, honestly, straight, truthful **10** truthfully, forthright, scrupulous

abracadabra **5** charm, magic **6** babble, jargon **9** gibberish **10** double talk, mumbo jumbo **11** incantation **12** gobbledygook **13** mystification

abrade **3** bug, irk, rub **4** burn, fret, gall, rasp, wear **5** annoy, chafe, erode, grate, graze, upset, weary **6** bother, ruffle, scrape **7** corrode, eat away, perturb, provoke, roughen **8** irritate, wear away, wear down **9** aggravate, grind down

Abraham ***brother:*** **5** Haran, Nahor ***concubine:*** **5** Hagar ***father:*** **5** Terah ***grandfather:*** **5** Nahor ***grandson:*** **4** Esau ***nephew:*** **3** Lot ***son:*** **5** Isaac, Medan, Shuah **6** Midian, Zimran **7** Ishmael ***well:*** **9** Beer-Sheba ***wife:*** **5** Sarah **7** Keturah

abrasion **5** chafe, scuff **6** scrape **7** chafing, erosion, grating, rubbing, scratch **8** friction, grinding, scraping, scuffing **10** irritation, scratching

abrasive **5** emery, rough, sharp **6** biting, pumice **7** wearing **8** annoying **9** smoothing, polishing **10** irritating **11** Carborundum, garnet paper

abreast 6 beside, next to, versed, with-it **7** versant **8** familiar, informed, up-to-date **9** au courant **10** acquainted, conversant

abridge 3 cut **4** pare, trim **5** limit, prune **6** lessen, narrow, reduce **7** curtail, cut back, shorten **8** boil down, compress, condense, cut short, diminish, restrict, truncate **9** summarize **10** abbreviate

abridgment 5 brief **6** digest **7** capsule, cutting, summary **8** abstract, synopsis **9** lessening, reduction, short form **10** diminution, shortening **11** compression, contraction, curtailment, restriction **12** abbreviation, condensation

abroad 4 afar, away **5** about **6** afield, astray, widely **7** touring **8** overseas **9** elsewhere, traveling

abrogate 3 end **4** undo, void **5** abate, annul, quash **6** cancel, negate, repeal, revoke, vacate **7** abolish, blot out, nullify, rescind, reverse **8** dissolve **9** discharge **10** extinguish, invalidate, obliterate

abrupt 4 curt **5** bluff, blunt, brief, brisk, gruff, hasty, sharp, sheer, short, steep **6** cut off, snippy, sudden **7** brusque, hurried **8** headlong **9** broken off, impetuous **10** unexpected **11** precipitate, precipitous **13** unceremonious

abruptness 10 brusquerie **12** precipitance

Absalom *commander:* 5 Amasa ***father:* 5** David ***mother:* 7** Maachah ***sister:* 5** Tamar ***slayer:* 4** Joab

abscess 4 boil, sore **5** botch, ulcer **6** lesion, pimple, trauma **7** blister, pustule **8** furuncle **9** carbuncle

abscond 4 bolt, flee, quit, skip **5** break, leave **6** decamp, escape, run off **7** run away, take off **8** slip away, sneak off **9** disappear, sneak away, steal away

absence 4 AWOL, lack, need, void, want **6** dearth, defect, vacuum **7** default, drought, failure, sick-out, vacancy **9** privation **10** deficiency, inadequacy **11** absenteeism, inattention **13** insufficiency

absent 4 away, AWOL, gone, lost **6** no-show **7** bemused, faraway, lacking, missing, omitted, wanting, without **8** distrait, heedless **9** elsewhere, forgetful **10** abstracted, distracted **11** inattentive, preoccupied

absentminded 4 lost **7** bemused, faraway **8** distrait, dreaming, heedless, unseeing **9** forgetful, oblivious, unheeding, unmindful **10** abstracted, distracted, unnoticing **11** inattentive, inconscient, preoccupied, unconscious, unobserving

absolute 4 full, pure, real, true **5** ideal, sheer, total, utter **6** actual, entire, simple, strict **7** eternal, factual, genuine, perfect, supreme, unmixed **8** autarkic, complete, despotic, flawless, infinite, outright, positive, ultimate, simplest, thorough, unflawed **9** arbitrary, autarchic, boundless, downright, embodying, imperious, masterful, sovereign, unalloyed, undiluted, unlimited **10** autocratic, autonomous, consummate, impeccable, monocratic, tyrannical **11** categorical, dictatorial, domineering, fundamental, independent, unequivocal, unmitigated, unqualified **12** indisputable, totalitarian, unrestrained, unrestricted **13** authoritarian, unconditional

absolutely 5 fully **6** wholly **7** utterly **8** entirely **9** doubtless, perfectly **10** completely, definitely, positively, thoroughly **11** doubtlessly **13** unequivocally

absolution 6 pardon **7** amnesty, freeing, release **9** releasing, remission **10** letting off **11** exculpation, exoneration, forgiveness **12** dispensation

absolutism 9 Caesarism, despotism **12** dictatorship

absolve 4 free **5** clear, let go, remit, spare **6** acquit, excuse, exempt, let off, pardon **7** forgive, release, relieve, set free **8** dispense **9** discharge, exculpate, exonerate, vindicate

absorb 4 bear, blot **5** imbue, learn, sop up, use up **6** assume, embody, endure, engage, imbibe, infuse, ingest, soak up, sponge, suck up, take in, take up **7** acquire, consume, drink in, engross, immerse, involve, receive, sustain **8** permeate **9** preoccupy, transform **10** assimilate **11** incorporate

absorbed 4 deep, into, lost, rapt **6** intent **7** engaged, wrapped **8** caught up, immersed, involved **9** engrossed, wrapped up **10** captivated, fascinated **11** preoccupied

absorbing 9 arresting, consuming **10** engrossing, intriguing **11** captivating, fascinating, interesting **12** monopolizing, preoccupying

abstain 4 curb, deny, diet, fast, keep, pass, stop **5** avoid, forgo, spurn **6** abjure, eschew, give up, pass up, refuse, reject **7** decline, forbear, refrain **8** abnegate, forswear, hold back, keep from, renounce, swear off, teetotal, withhold **9** constrain, do without **11** deny oneself

abstemious 5 sober **6** chaste, strict **7** ascetic, austere, sparing **9** abstinent, continent, temperate **10** restrained **11** self-denying

abstinence 6 denial **7** fasting **8** chastity, sobriety **9** soberness **10** continence, self-denial, temperance **12** renunciation **13** self-restraint

abstract 5 brief, ideal **6** detach, digest, précis **7** epitome, neutral, outline, shorten, summary, utopian **8** academic, breviary, condense, detached, notional, separate, synopsis **9** disengage, summarize **10** abridgment, conceptual, conspectus, disconnect, dissociate, impersonal **11** appropriate, impractical, speculative, theoretical **12** condensation, hypothetical, transcendent **13** disinterested

abstracted 4 lost, rapt **6** absent, intent **7** bemused, faraway **8** absorbed, distrait, heedless **9** engrossed, oblivious, unheeding, unmindful, unminding, withdrawn **11** inattentive, inconscient, preoccupied, unconscious **12** absentminded

abstruse 4 deep **5** heavy **6** knotty, occult **7** complex **8** esoteric, hermetic, involved, profound **9** difficult, intricate, recondite **11** complicated

absurd 5 balmy, comic, crazy, droll, inane, loony, potty, silly, wacky **6** insane **7** asinine, fatuous, foolish, idiotic **8** farcical **9** illogical, laughable, ludicrous **10** irrational, ridiculous **11** harebrained **12** preposterous, unreasonable

absurdity 5 farce, folly **7** inanity **8** nonsense **9** craziness, dottiness, silliness **11** foolishness, incongruity, witlessness **13** ludicrousness, senselessness

abundance 6 bounty, excess, plenty, riches, wealth **9** affluence, profusion **10** lavishness, prosperity **11** prodigality ***Scottish:*** **5** routh

abundant 4 full, lush, rich, rife **5** ample **6** filled, galore, lavish, plenty **7** aplenty, copious, crammed, crowded, liberal, profuse, replete **8** fruitful, prolific **9** abounding, bounteous, bountiful, extensive, luxuriant, plenteous, plentiful

abuse 3 mar **4** harm, hurt, rail **5** anger, decry, shame, spoil, wrong **6** damage, debase, deride, impair, injure, misuse, revile, vilify **7** calumny, corrupt, cursing, exploit, obloquy, oppress, profane **8** belittle, berating, derision, derogate, disgrace, ill-treat, maltreat, mistreat, swearing **9** blaspheme, contumely, desecrate, disparage, harshness, invective, manhandle, mishandle, persecute, profanity **10** defamation, depreciate, malignment, revilement, scurrility **11** disapproval **12** billingsgate, denunciation, vilification, vituperation

abusive 5 dirty, harsh **6** odious **7** corrupt **8** scurrile **9** injurious, insulting, invective, offending, offensive, truculent **10** calumnious, defamatory, scurrilous **11** blasphemous, castigating, opprobrious **12** calumniating, contumelious, sharp-tongued, vituperative, vituperatory

abut 4 join, link **5** flank, touch, verge **6** adjoin, border, butt on **8** border on, neighbor **9** lie beside **11** butt against, communicate

abutting 4 next **6** beside, joined, next to **7** joining, verging **8** adjacent, next door, touching **9** adjoining, bordering, impinging **10** connecting, contiguous, juxtaposed **11** bordering on, coextensive, coterminous, neighboring **12** conterminous

abysmal 4 deep, vast **7** endless **8** infinite, profound, unending, wretched **9** boundless, cavernous, plumbless, soundless, unplumbed **10** bottomless, fathomless, unmeasured **11** illimitable, measureless **12** immeasurable, unfathomable

abyss 3 pit **4** gulf, hell, hole, void **5** abysm, chasm, depth, gorge, hades, Sheol **6** Tophet **7** fissure, Gehenna, inferno **8** crevasse, deepness **9** perdition **10** underworld

academia 10 university **12** professoriat

academic 3 don **5** pupil, tutor **6** closet, fellow, master **7** bookish, learned, scholar, student **8** abstract, gownsman, lecturer, pedantic **9** professor, scholarly **10** scholastic **11** book-learned, conjectural, impractical, speculative, theoretical **12** conventional, hypothetical

academic period 4 term **7** quarter **8** semester **9** trimester

academy 5 lycée **6** lyceum **7** college, society **9** institute **10** prep school **12** conservatory

Academy Award winner

picture:

1927-28: 5 Wings **1928-29: 14** Broadway Melody **1929-30: 25** All Quiet on the Western Front **1930-31: 8** Cimarron **1931-32: 10** Grand Hotel **1932-33: 9** Cavalcade **1934: 18** It Happened One Night **1935: 17** Mutiny on the Bounty **1936: 16** The Great Ziegfeld **1937: 15** Life of Emile Zola **1938: 20** You Can't Take It with You **1939: 15** Gone with the Wind **1940: 7** Rebecca **1941: 19** How Green Was My Valley **1942: 10** Mrs. Miniver **1943: 10** Casablanca **1944: 10** Going My Way **1945: 11** Lost Weekend (The) **1946: 19** Best Years of Our Lives (The) **1947: 19** Gentleman's Agreement **1948: 6** Hamlet **1949: 14** All the King's Men **1950: 11** All About Eve **1951: 15** American in Paris (An) **1952: 19** Greatest Show on Earth (The) **1953: 18** From Here to Eternity **1954: 15** On the Waterfront **1955: 5** Marty **1956: 26** Around the World in Eighty Days **1957: 20** Bridge on the River Kwai (The) **1958:**

4 Gigi **1959: 6** Ben-Hur **1960: 9** Apartment (The) **1961: 13** West Side Story **1962: 16** Lawrence of Arabia **1963: 8** Tom Jones **1964: 10** My Fair Lady **1965: 12** Sound of Music (The) **1966: 16** Man for All Seasons (A) **1967: 19** In the Heat of the Night **1968: 6** Oliver **1969: 14** Midnight Cowboy **1970: 6** Patton **1971: 16** French Connection (The) **1972: 9** Godfather (The) **1973: 5** Sting (The) **1974: 9** Godfather (Part Two, The) **1975: 25** One Flew over the Cuckoo's Nest **1976: 5** Rocky **1977: 9** Annie Hall **1978: 10** Deer Hunter (The) **1979: 14** Kramer vs. Kramer **1980: 14** Ordinary People **1981: 14** Chariots of Fire **1982: 6** Gandhi **1983: 17** Terms of Endearment **1984: 7** Amadeus **1985: 11** Out of Africa **1986: 7** Platoon **1987: 11** Last Emperor (The) **1988: 7** Rain Man **1989: 16** Driving Miss Daisy **1990: 16** Dances with Wolves **1991: 17** Silence of the Lambs (The) **1992: 10** Unforgiven **1993: 14** Schindler's List **1994: 11** Forrest Gump **1995: 10** Braveheart **1996: 14** English Patient (The) **1997: 7** Titanic **1998: 17** Shakespeare in Love **1999: 14** American Beauty **2000: 9** Gladiator **2001: 13** Beautiful Mind (A) **2002: 7** Chicago **2003: 14** Lord of the Rings (The) **2004: 17** Million Dollar Baby **2005: 5** Crash **2006: 8** Departed (The) **2007: 18** No Country for Old Men **2008: 18** Slumdog Millionaire **2009: 10** Hurt Locker (The)

actor:

1927-28: 8 Jannings (Emil) **1928-29: 6** Baxter (Warner) **1929-30: 6** Arliss (George) **1930-31: 9** Barrymore (Lionel) **1931-32: 5** Beery (Wallace), March (Fredric) **1932-33: 8** Laughton (Charles) **1934: 5** Gable (Clark) **1935: 8** McLaglen (Victor) **1936: 4** Muni (Paul) **1937: 5** Tracy (Spencer) **1938: 5** Tracy (Spencer) **1939: 5** Donat (Robert) **1940: 7** Stewart (James) **1941: 6** Cooper (Gary) **1942: 6** Cagney (James) **1943: 5** Lukas (Paul) **1944: 6** Crosby (Bing) **1945: 7** Milland (Ray) **1946: 5** March (Fredric) **1947: 6** Colman (Ronald) **1948: 7** Olivier (Laurence) **1949: 8** Crawford (Broderick) **1950: 6** Ferrer (José) **1951: 6** Bogart (Humphrey) **1952: 6** Cooper (Gary) **1953: 6** Holden (William) **1954: 6** Brando (Marlon) **1955: 8** Borgnine (Ernest) **1956: 7** Brynner (Yul) **1957: 8** Guinness (Alec) **1958: 5** Niven (David) **1959: 6** Heston (Charlton) **1960: 9** Lancaster (Burt) **1961: 6** Schell (Maximilian) **1962: 4** Peck (Gregory) **1963: 7** Poitier (Sidney) **1964: 8** Harrison (Rex) **1965: 6** Marvin (Lee) **1966: 8** Scofield (Paul) **1967: 7** Steiger (Rod) **1968: 9** Robertson (Cliff) **1969: 5** Wayne (John) **1970: 5** Scott (George C.) **1971: 7** Hackman (Gene) **1972: 6** Brando (Marlon) **1973: 6** Lemmon (Jack) **1974: 6** Carney (Art) **1975: 9** Nicholson (Jack) **1976: 5** Finch (Peter) **1977: 8** Dreyfuss (Richard) **1978: 6** Voight (Jon) **1979: 7** Hoffman (Dustin) **1980: 6** De Niro (Robert) **1981: 5** Fonda (Henry) **1982: 8** Kingsley (Ben) **1983: 6** Duvall (Robert) **1984: 7** Abraham (F. Murray) **1985: 4** Hurt (William) **1986: 6** Newman (Paul) **1987: 7** Douglas (Michael) **1988: 7** Hoffman (Dustin) **1989: 8** Day-Lewis (Daniel) **1990: 5** Irons (Jeremy) **1991: 7** Hopkins (Anthony) **1992: 6** Pacino (Al) **1993: 5** Hanks (Tom) **1994: 5** Hanks (Tom) **1995: 4** Cage (Nicholas) **1996: 4** Rush (Geoffrey) **1997: 9** Nicholson (Jack) **1998: 7** Benigni (Roberto) **1999: 6** Spacey (Kevin) **2000: 5** Crowe (Russell) **2001: 10** Washington (Denzel) **2002: 5** Brody (Adrien) **2003: 4** Penn (Sean) **2004: 4** Foxx (Jamie) **2005: 7** Hoffman (Philip Seymour) **2006: 8** Whitaker (Forest) **2007: 8** Day-Lewis (Daniel) **2008: 4** Penn (Sean) **2009: 7** Bridges (Jeff)

actress:

1927-28: 6 Gaynor (Janet) **1928-29: 8** Pickford (Mary) **1929-30: 7** Shearer (Norma) **1930-31: 8** Dressler (Marie) **1931-32: 5** Hayes (Helen) **1932-33: 7** Hepburn (Katharine) **1934: 7** Colbert (Claudette) **1935: 5** Davis (Bette) **1936: 6** Rainer (Luise) **1937: 6** Rainer (Luise) **1938: 5** Davis (Bette) **1939: 5** Leigh (Vivien) **1940: 6** Rogers (Ginger) **1941: 8** Fontaine (Joan) **1942: 6** Garson (Greer) **1943: 5** Jones (Jennifer) **1944: 7** Bergman (Ingrid) **1945: 8** Crawford (Joan) **1946: 11** de Havilland (Olivia) **1947: 5** Young (Loretta) **1948: 5** Wyman (Jane) **1949: 11** de Havilland (Olivia) **1950: 8** Holliday (Judy) **1951: 5** Leigh (Vivien) **1952: 5** Booth (Shirley) **1953: 7** Hepburn (Audrey) **1954: 5** Kelly (Grace) **1955: 7** Magnani (Anna) **1956: 7** Bergman (Ingrid) **1957: 8** Woodward (Joanne) **1958: 7** Hayward (Susan) **1959: 8** Signoret (Simone) **1960: 6** Taylor (Elizabeth) **1961: 5** Loren (Sophia) **1962: 8** Bancroft (Anne) **1963: 4** Neal (Patricia) **1964: 7** Andrews (Julie) **1965: 8** Christie (Julie) **1966: 6** Taylor (Elizabeth) **1967: 7** Hepburn (Katharine)

1968: 7 Hepburn (Katharine) **9** Streisand (Barbra) **1969: 5** Smith (Maggie) **1970: 7** Jackson (Glenda) **1971: 5** Fonda (Jane) **1972: 8** Minnelli (Liza) **1973: 7** Jackson (Glenda) **1974: 7** Burstyn (Ellen) **1975: 8** Fletcher (Louise) **1976: 7** Dunaway (Faye) **1977: 6** Keaton (Diane) **1978: 5** Fonda (Jane) **1979: 5** Field (Sally) **1980: 6** Spacek (Sissy) **1981: 7** Hepburn (Katharine) **1982: 6** Streep (Meryl) **1983: 8** MacLaine (Shirley) **1984: 5** Field (Sally) **1985: 4** Page (Geraldine) **1986: 6** Matlin (Marlee) **1987: 4** Cher **1988: 6** Foster (Jodie) **1989: 5** Tandy (Jessica) **1990: 5** Bates (Kathy) **1991: 6** Foster (Jodie) **1992: 8** Thompson (Emma) **1993: 6** Hunter (Holly) **1994: 5** Lange (Jessica) **1995: 8** Sarandon (Susan) **1996: 9** McDormand (Frances) **1997: 4** Hunt (Helen) **1998: 7** Paltrow (Gwyneth) **1999: 5** Swank (Hilary) **2000: 7** Roberts (Julia) **2001: 5** Berry (Halle) **2002: 6** Kidman (Nicole) **2003: 6** Theron (Charlize) **2004: 5** Swank (Hilary) **2005: 11** Witherspoon (Reese) **2006: 6** Mirren (Helen) **2007: 9** Cotillard (Marion) **2008: 7** Winslet (Kate) **2009: 7** Bullock (Sandra)

accede 3 let **5** admit, agree, allow, grant, yield **6** accept, assent, comply, concur, give in, permit **7** agree to, approve, concede, consent **9** acquiesce, cooperate, subscribe

accelerando 6 faster **7** speed up **10** speeding up

accelerate 3 gun, rev **4** grow, roll **5** hurry, impel, rev up, speed **6** hasten, open up, step up **7** quicken, speed up **8** expedite, increase **9** fast-track **10** peel rubber

acceleration 7 speedup **8** hurrying, spurring **9** hastening, revving up **10** increasing, quickening, speeding up, stepping up

accent 4 beat, lilt, tone **5** acute, grave, meter, pulse, throb **6** rhythm, stress, weight **7** cadence **8** emphasis **9** diacritic, pulsation **10** inflection, intonation ***Irish:* 6** brogue ***Scottish:* 4** burr ***Southern:* 5** drawl

accept 3 bow, buy, see **4** bear, gain, okay, take **5** admit, adopt, agree, catch, favor, go for, grasp, yield **6** accede, admire, affirm, assent, endure, follow, take in, take on **7** agree to, approve, believe, receive, respect, swallow, welcome **8** assent to, bear with, hold with, live with, stand for, tolerate **9** acquiesce, agree with, undertake **10** capitulate, comprehend, concur with, understand **11** acknowledge, countenance, subscribe to

acceptable 4 good, okay **6** decent, worthy **7** average, welcome **8** adequate, all right, bearable, ordinary, passable, pleasing, standard, suitable **9** endurable, tolerable **10** sufficient **11** commonplace, respectable, supportable **12** satisfactory **13** unexceptional, unimpeachable

acceptably 4 well **5** amply **7** capably **8** properly, suitably **9** fittingly, tolerably **10** becomingly **11** competently **13** appropriately

acceptant 4 open **8** amenable, friendly, swayable **9** favorable, receptive, recipient, welcoming **10** open-minded, responsive **11** persuadable, persuasible, susceptible

acceptation 4 gist **5** point, sense **6** import **7** meaning, message, purport **9** intention **10** intendment **12** significance, significancy **13** signification, understanding

accepted 5 usual **6** common, normal, proper **7** correct, regular, routine **8** approved, everyday, expected, habitual, ordinary, orthodox, received **9** customary **10** accustomed, recognized, sanctioned **11** established, traditional **12** conventional

access 3 fit, way **4** adit, door, gust, pang, path, road, turn **5** burst, entry, get at, onset, route, sally, spell, throe **6** attack, avenue, entrée **7** contact, flare-up, ingress, passage, seizure **8** approach, entrance, eruption, increase, outburst **9** admission, explosion **10** admittance

accessible 4 near, open **5** handy **6** public, usable **8** possible **9** available, operative, reachable **10** attainable, employable, obtainable **11** practicable **12** approachable, unrestricted

accession 4 rise **5** raise **8** addition, approach, increase, outburst, taking on **9** accretion, adherence, increment, induction **10** admittance, assumption, attainment, succession **11** acquisition **12** augmentation, inauguration

accessory 3 aid **4** aide, prop, trim **5** extra, frill **6** helper **7** abettor, adjunct, fitting, insider, partner **8** addition, adjuvant, appendix **9** accretion, adornment, ancillary, appendage, assistant, associate, auxiliary, increment, secondary, tributary **10** accomplice, coincident, collateral, concurrent, decoration, incidental, subsidiary **11** appurtenant, concomitant, confederate, conspirator, subordinate, subservient **12** appurtenance, contributory **13** accompaniment, coconspirator, supplementary

accident 3 hap, lot **4** fate, luck, odds **5** fluke **6** chance, gamble, hazard, kismet, mishap **7** bad luck, destiny **8** calamity, casualty, fortuity, incident **9** mischance **10** misfortune **12** misadventure

accidental **3** odd **4** flat **5** fluky, sharp **6** casual, chance, flukey, random **7** unmeant **8** by chance, careless **9** chromatic, dependent, extempore, impromptu, unplanned, unwitting **10** coincident, contingent, fortuitous, unexpected, unforeseen, unintended **11** conditional, inadvertent **12** coincidental, uncalculated **13** unintentional

acclaim **4** hail, clap, laud **5** cheer, éclat, exalt, extol, glory, honor, kudos, roose **6** homage, praise, salute **7** applaud, approve, commend, glorify, magnify, ovation, root for **8** applause, plaudits **10** compliment

acclimate **5** adapt **6** adjust, change, harden, season **7** toughen **9** condition, habituate

accolade **4** bays, fame **5** award, badge, honor, kudos **6** praise **7** laurels, tribute **8** approval **10** decoration **11** distinction

accommodate **3** fit **4** hold, rent, suit **5** adapt, alter, board, defer, favor, house, humor, lodge, put up, yield **6** adjust, attune, bestow, billet, change, encase, harbor, modify, oblige, please, submit, tailor, take in **7** cater to, conform, contain, enclose, furnish, indulge, quarter, receive, shelter **8** accustom, allow for, domicile **9** entertain, harmonize, integrate, reconcile **11** domiciliate, make room for

accommodating **7** amiable, helpful, willing **8** gracious, obliging **9** adaptable **10** hospitable, solicitous, thoughtful **11** considerate, cooperative

accommodations **3** inn **4** digs, keep, room **5** hotel, lodge, motel **6** hostel **7** housing, lodging, shelter **8** hostelry, lodgment, quarters **9** residence **12** room and board

accompaniment **6** backup **7** adjunct **8** addition **9** accessory, associate, attendant, corollary **10** supplement **11** concomitant, enhancement **12** augmentation

accompany **4** join **5** bring, guide, pilot **6** attend, convoy, escort, go with **7** combine, conduct, consort **8** chaperon, come with **9** associate **10** appear with, go together **11** perform with

accompanying **8** incident **9** accessory, ancillary, attendant, attending, secondary **10** associated, coincident, collateral **11** concomitant

accomplice **4** aide, ally **5** aider **6** flunky, helper, stooge **7** abettor, partner **9** accessory, assistant, associate **11** confederate, conspirator, subordinate **13** coconspirator

accomplish **3** win **4** gain **5** reach, score **6** attain, effect, fulfil, rack up **7** achieve, execute, fulfill, perfect, pull off, realize, succeed **8** bring off, carry out, complete **9** discharge **10** bring about

accomplished **4** able **5** adept **6** expert **7** skilled **8** finished, masterly, skillful, talented **9** practiced **10** proficient

accomplishment **3** act, art **4** deed, feat **5** craft, doing, skill **7** ability **9** adeptness, expertise **10** attainment, capability, completion **11** achievement, acquirement, proficiency

accord **4** deal, fuse, give, jibe, pact **5** agree, award, blend, chime, fit in, grant, match, merge, tally, union **6** affirm, assent, concur, confer, treaty **7** compact, concert, conform, empathy, entente, harmony, rapport **8** affinity, coincide, dovetail, sympathy **9** agreement, harmonize, reconcile **10** attraction, conformity, consonance, correspond, solidarity **11** concordance **13** understanding

accordant **8** agreeing **9** congruous, consonant **10** conforming, harmonious **13** correspondent

accordingly **2** so **4** duly, ergo, then, thus **5** hence **9** therefore, thereupon **12** consequently

accost **3** dog **4** call, dare, face, hail **5** annoy, beard, cross, front, hound, worry **6** bother, call to **7** affront, outface, outrage **8** approach, confront **9** challenge **10** buttonhole

accouchement **7** lying-in **8** childbed, delivery **10** childbirth **11** confinement, parturition

account **3** tab, use **4** bill, deem, note, rate, view **5** avail, basis, favor, score, story, track, value, worth **6** assess, client, esteem, reason, reckon, record, regard, report, repute **7** analyze, explain, expound, justify, recital, version **8** appraise, consider, customer, estimate **9** chronicle, narrative, rationale, reckoning, statement **11** explanation **13** consideration ***book:*** **6** ledger

accountable **6** liable **8** amenable **10** answerable **11** explainable, responsible

accounting **11** bookkeeping ***method:*** **4** FIFO, FILO, LIFO

accoutre **3** arm, rig **4** deck, gear **5** adorn, dress, equip, fix up, ready **6** attire, fit out, outfit, supply **7** appoint, furnish, prepare, provide, turn out **9** provision

accoutrement **3** kit **4** gear **6** outfit, tackle **7** regalia **8** tackling **9** accessory, apparatus, equipment, machinery, trappings **10** provisions **11** furnishings, habiliments **12** appointments **13** paraphernalia

accredit **2** OK **3** lay **4** okay **5** refer **6** assign, attest, charge, credit, enable **7** approve, ascribe, certify, commend, empower, endorse, license, warrant **8** sanction, validate, vouch for **9** attribute, authorize, recognize, recommend **10** commission, credential

accretion 4 rise **5** raise **6** growth **7** buildup **8** addition, increase **9** accession, appendage, increment **10** attachment **11** enlargement **12** accumulation, augmentation

accrue 4 grow **5** amass **6** gather, pile up **7** build up, collect, compile **8** increase **10** accumulate, amalgamate **11** agglomerate

accumulate 4 heap, grow, mass, pile **5** add to, amass, hoard, lay by, lay in, lay up, stock, store **6** accrue, garner, gather, pile up, rack up, roll up **7** acquire, backlog, collect, compile, lay down, stack up, store up **8** assemble, increase **9** stockpile

accumulation 4 bank, heap, mass, pile **5** hoard, stock, store, trove **6** growth **7** backlog, buildup, reserve **8** increase **9** accretion, amassment **10** collection **11** aggregation, enlargement

accumulative 6 heaped **7** growing **8** additive, additory **9** summative **10** collective, increasing **11** aggregative **12** augmentative

accuracy 8 veracity **9** certainty, exactness, precision **10** definition, exactitude **11** correctness, preciseness **12** definiteness

accurate 4 just, nice, true **5** exact, right **6** actual, dead on, proper, spot on **7** certain, correct, factual, precise **8** definite, reliable, rigorous **9** authentic, error-free, errorless **10** dependable

accursed 4 vile **6** odious **7** hateful **8** damnable **9** abhorrent, execrable, loathsome, offensive, repugnant, revolting **10** abominable, despicable, detestable

accusation 3 rap **6** charge **9** complaint **10** allegation, indictment **12** denunciation ***false:*** **7** calumny

accuse 3 tax **5** blame, brand **6** allege, charge, delate, finger, impute, indict **7** arraign, ascribe, censure, impeach **8** admonish, denounce, reproach **9** criminate, criticize, inculpate, reprobate **10** denunciate **11** incriminate

accustom 3 use **4** wont **5** adapt, inure **6** adjust, harden, season **7** conform **9** habituate **11** acclimatize, familiarize

accustomed 3 set **5** usual **6** normal **7** chronic, regular, routine **8** accepted, everyday, familiar, habitual, ordinary, standard **9** customary **10** habituated **11** commonplace, established, traditional **12** conventional

ace 3 bit, jot, pip, top **4** atom, hair, iota, mite, star **5** crumb, minim, pilot, point, score, speck **6** Bishop (Billy), bullet, defeat, master, winner **7** whisker **8** molecule, particle, Red Baron **9** first rate, hole in one **10** Richthofen (Manfred von) **11** hairbreadth, tennis score **12** Rickenbacker (Eddie)

ace and face card 7 natural **9** blackjack

acedia 5 ennui **6** apathy **7** boredom, languor **8** lethargy

acerbate 3 vex **5** anger, annoy, peeve **6** madden **7** incense, inflame **8** embitter, irritate **9** aggravate **10** exasperate

acerbic 4 acid, sour, tart **5** acrid, harsh, rough, sharp **7** caustic, cutting, satiric **8** stinging **9** acidulous, corrosive, sarcastic **10** astringent

acerbity 7 acidity, sarcasm **8** acrimony, asperity, sourness, tartness **9** harshness, roughness, surliness **10** bitterness, causticity

Achates' companion 6 Aeneas

ache 3 yen **4** hurt, long, pain, pang, pine, pity, sigh **5** crave, smart, throb, yearn **6** hanker, hunger, stitch, suffer, thirst, twinge **8** yearning **11** commiserate ***Scottish:*** **6** stound

Achebe novel 15 Things Fall Apart

Acheron 5 Hades, river

achieve 2 do **3** get, win **4** gain **5** reach, score **6** attain, effect, finish, obtain, rack up, secure **7** acquire, execute, fulfill, get done, perform, realize, succeed **8** carry out, complete, conclude **9** actualize **10** accomplish

achievement 4 deed, feat **6** finish **7** exploit, success **10** attainment, completion **11** acquisition, tour de force

Achilles *adviser:* 6 Nestor ***companion:*** **9** Patroclus ***father:*** **6** Peleus ***horse:*** **7** Xanthus ***lover:*** **7** Briseis ***mother:*** **6** Thetis ***slayer:*** **5** Paris ***victim:*** **6** Hector ***vulnerable part:*** **4** heel

aching 4 hurt, sore **6** in pain **7** hurtful, hurting, painful **8** yearning **9** disturbed **10** afflictive, distressed **13** compassionate

acicular 5 acute, peaky, piked, sharp **6** peaked, pointy, spiked **7** pointed

acid 4 sour, tart **5** acerb **7** acerbic, acetose, caustic **8** stinging **9** corrosive, sarcastic, vitriolic ***bleaching:*** **6** oxalic ***fatty:*** **6** capric **7** caproic, stearic **8** caprylic ***found in apples:*** **5** malic ***found in cranberries:*** **7** benzoic ***found in grapes:*** **8** tartaric ***found in lemons:*** **6** citric ***found in rhubarb:*** **6** oxalic ***found in sour milk:*** **6** lactic ***indicator:*** **6** litmus ***kind:*** **5** amino, boric, iodic, malic, oleic **6** acetic, bromic, formic, nitric, oxalic, tannic **7** nitrous, silicic **8** carbolic, carbonic, muriatic, sulfuric **9** aqua regia **12** hydrochloric ***neutralizer:*** **4** base **6** alkali ***tanning:*** **6** tannic **8** catechin ***vinegar:*** **6** acetic

acidulous 3 dry **4** sour, tart **5** acerb, harsh, sharp **6** biting **7** acerbic, acetose, cutting, piquant, pungent **9** sarcastic

Acis ***lover:*** **7** Galatea ***slayer:*** **10** Polyphemus

acknowledge 3 own **4** avow, deem, tell, view **5** admit, agree, allow, grant, let on, own up **6** accede, accept, fess up, reveal **7** concede, confess, declare, divulge, profess **8** announce, consider, disclose, proclaim **9** recognize

acknowledgment 6 assent, avowal, credit, notice **9** admission **10** confession **11** affirmation, declaration, recognition

acme 3 cap, top **4** apex, peak **6** apogee, climax, summit, tiptop, vertex, zenith **8** capstone, pinnacle, ultimate **9** high point **10** perfection **11** culmination

acorn tree 3 oak

acoustic 5 aural **6** audile **8** auditory **9** unplugged

acquaint 4 clue, tell, warn **6** advise, fill in, inform, notify, orient, reveal **7** apprise, present **8** accustom, disclose **9** enlighten, introduce **11** familiarize

acquaintance 4 mate **5** amigo, crony, grasp **6** friend **7** comrade, contact **9** associate, colleague, companion **10** cognizance, experience **11** familiarity

acquainted 6 versed **7** abreast, in touch **8** familiar, informed, up-to-date **9** au courant **10** conversant

acquiesce 3 bow, yes **5** agree, allow, bow to, yield **6** accede, accept, assent, comply, concur, give in, submit **7** consent, go along **9** reconcile, subscribe

acquiescence 6 assent **7** consent **8** giving in, yielding **9** deference **10** acceptance, compliance, conformity, submission **11** resignation

acquiescent 6 docile **7** passive **8** resigned, yielding **10** submissive **11** unresistant, unresisting **12** nonresistant, nonresisting

acquire 3 add, buy, get, win **4** earn, form, gain, land **5** amass, annex **6** garner, obtain, pick up, secure, take on **7** bring in, collect, develop, procure **10** accumulate

acquirement 8 addition **9** accretion **11** acquisition

acquisition 4 gain **5** prize **7** winning **8** addition, learning, property, purchase **9** accretion

acquisitive 5 eager, itchy **6** grabby, greedy **8** covetous, desirous, grasping **10** avaricious

acquit 3 act **4** bear, free **5** carry, clear, let go **6** behave, deport, let off **7** absolve, comport, conduct, perform, release, set free **8** liberate **9** discharge, exculpate, exonerate, vindicate

acres 4 area, land **5** lands **6** estate **7** demesne, expanse, holding **8** property

acrid 4 acid, sour **5** harsh, nasty, sharp **6** biting, bitter **7** austere, burning, caustic, cutting, pungent **8** stinging **9** trenchant **10** astringent, irritating **11** acrimonious

acrimonious 3 mad **5** angry, cross, irate, sharp, testy **6** biting, bitter, cranky, ireful **7** acerbic, caustic, cutting **9** indignant, irascible, rancorous **11** belligerent, contentious, quarrelsome

acrimony 5 anger, spite **6** animus, malice, rancor **7** ill will **8** acerbity, asperity, mordancy **9** animosity, antipathy, harshness, virulence **10** bitterness **11** malevolence

Acrisius ***daughter:*** **5** Danaë ***slayer:*** **7** Perseus

acrobat 7 gymnast **9** aerialist, trapezist **11** funambulist

across 4 over **6** beyond **7** athwart **12** transversely ***prefix:*** **5** trans

act 3 law, run **4** bear, bill, deed, fake, feat, mime, play, pose, sham, work **5** bluff, feign, front, put-on, serve, stunt **6** affect, appear, behave, shtick **7** exploit, operate, perform, portray, pretend, routine, statute **8** function, pretense, simulate **9** officiate **10** masquerade **11** counterfeit, impersonate ***wrongful:*** **3** sin **4** tort **5** crime, error, fault **7** default, misdeed, offense

acting 6 pro tem **7** interim, playing **9** ad interim, dramatics, imitating, portrayal, temporary **10** pro tempore **12** entertaining

actinium symbol 2 Ac

action 4 case, deed, move, step, stir, suit, work **5** cause, doing **6** battle, bustle, combat **7** lawsuit, process, service **8** activity, behavior, conflict, fighting, function **9** execution, operation, procedure **10** engagement, proceeding **11** performance

action painter 5 Kline (Franz) **7** Pollock (Jackson) **9** de Kooning (Willem)

action painting 7 tachism

activate 4 stir, wake **5** rally, rouse, set up, waken **6** arouse, awaken, call up, turn on **8** energize, mobilize, motivate, vitalize **9** stimulate

active 4 busy, live, spry **5** agile, alert, alive, brisk, going **6** at work, in play, lively, moving **7** driving, dynamic, flowing, on the go, running, working **8** animated, bustling, emitting, erupting, spirited, vigorous **9** effective, energetic, operating, operative, sprightly **11** functioning, industrious **12** enterprising

activity 6 action, bustle, motion **7** process, pursuit, venture **8** exercise, exertion **10** exercising, liveliness **11** undertaking

actor 4 mime, star **5** mimic **6** mummer, player **7** artiste, trouper **8** thespian **9** performer **11** participant **12** impersonator ***name:* 3** Cox (Wally), Fox (James, Michael J.), Lee (Bruce), Lom (Herbert), Mix (Tom), Ray (Aldo) **4** Alda (Alan, Robert), Bean (Orson), Blue (Ben), Bond (Ward), Caan (James), Cage (Nicholas), Cobb (Lee J.), Coco (James), Culp (Robert), Dean (James), Depp (Johnny), Dern (Bruce), Duff (Howard), Egan (Richard), Falk (Peter), Ford (Glenn, Harrison), Foxx (Redd), Geer (Will), Gere (Richard), Grey (Joel), Hill (Arthur), Hope (Bob), Hurt (John, William), Ives (Burl), Kaye (Danny), Kean (Edmund), Keel (Howard), Ladd (Alan), Lahr (Bert), Lord (Jack), Lowe (Rob), Lunt (Alfred), Marx (Chico, Groucho, Harpo, Zeppo), Muni (Paul), Ngor (Haing S.), Peck (Gregory), Penn (Sean), Pitt (Brad), Raft (George), Reid (Wallace), Roth (Tim), Ryan (Robert), Shaw (Robert), Tati (Jacques), Tone (Franchot), Torn (Rip), Tune (Tommy), Wahl (Ken), Webb (Clifton, Jack), Wynn (Ed, Keenan), York (Michael) **5** Adler (Luther), Allen (Fred, Tim, Woody), Arkin (Adam, Alan), Asner (Ed), Autry (Gene), Ayres (Lew), Bacon (Kevin), Barry (Gene), Bates (Alan), Beery (Wallace), Benny (Jack), Berle (Milton), Boone (Richard), Booth (Edwin), Boyer (Charles), Brand (Neville), Burns (George), Caine (Michael), Candy (John), Chase (Chevy), Clift (Montgomery), Cosby (Bill), Dafoe (Willem), Davis (Clifton, Ossie, Sammy Jr.), Delon (Alain), Donat (Robert), Evans (Maurice), Ewell (Tom), Finch (Peter), Firth (Colin, Peter), Flynn (Errol), Fonda (Henry, Peter), Franz (Dennis), Gabin (Jean), Gable (Clark), Gould (Elliot), Grant (Cary, Hugh), Gwenn (Edmund), Hanks (Tom), Hardy (Oliver), Hauer (Rutger), Hawke (Ethan), Hayes (Gabby), Hogan (Paul), Irons (Jeremy), Jaffe (Sam), Jones (Dean, James Earl, Tommy Lee), Kazan (Elia), Keach (Stacy), Keith (Brian, David), Kelly (Gene), Kiley (Richard), Kline (Kevin), Kotto (Yaphet), Lamas (Fernando, Lorenzo), Lanza (Mario), Lewis (Jerry, Richard), Lloyd (Harold), Lorre (Peter), Lukas (Paul), Lynde (Paul), March (Fredric), Mason (James), McCoy (Tim), Mills (John), Mineo (Sal), Moore (Dudley, Roger, Victor), Neill (Sam), Nimoy (Leonard), Niven (David), Nolte (Nick), Olmos (Edward James), O'Neal (Patrick, Ryan), O'Shea (Milo), Payne (John), Perry (Luke, Matthew), Pesci (Joe), Power (Tyrone), Price (Vincent), Pryce (Jonathan), Quaid (Dennis, Randy), Quinn (Aidan, Anthony), Rains (Claude), Reeve (Christopher), Scott (Campbell, George C., Randolph), Segal (George), Sheen (Charlie, Martin), Smits (Jimmy), Stack (Robert), Stamp (Terence), Sydow (Max von), Tracy (Spencer), Wayne (John), Wilde (Cornel), Wills (Chill), Woods (James), Young (Gig, Robert) **6** Abbott (Bud), Albert (Eddie), Ameche (Don), Arness (James), Backus (Jim), Balsam (Martin), Barker (Lex), Baxter (Warner), Beatty (Ned, Warren), Begley (Ed), Blades (Ruben), Bogart (Humphrey), Bolger (Ray), Brando (Marlon), Brooks (Albert, Mel), Burton (Richard), Caesar (Sid), Cagney (James), Cantor (Eddie), Cariou (Len), Carney (Art), Carrey (Jim), Carvey (Dana), Chaney (Lon), Cleese (John), Coburn (Charles, James), Colman (Ronald), Conrad (Robert, William), Conway (Tim, Tom), Coogan (Jackie), Cooper (Gary), Cotten (Joseph), Coward (Noël), Crabbe (Buster), Crenna (Richard), Cronyn (Hume), Crosby (Bing), Cruise (Tom), Culkin (Macaulay), Curtis (Tony), Dailey (Dan), Dalton (Timothy), Danson (Ted), Danton (Ray), Darren (James), De Niro (Robert), de Sica (Vittorio), De Vito (Danny), Dillon (Matt), Downey (Robert), Dullea (Keir), Duryea (Dan), Duvall (Robert), Ferrer (José, Mel), Fields (W.C.), Finney (Albert), Garcia (Andy), Garner (James), Gibson (Hoot, Mel), Glover (Danny), Graves (Peter), Greene (Lorne), Grodin (Charles), Harris (Ed, Richard), Harvey (Laurence), Hayden (Sterling), Heflin (Van), Heston (Charlton), Hingle (Pat), Holden (Bill), Hopper (Dennis, William), Howard (Leslie, Ron, Trevor), Hudson (Rock), Hunter (Jeffrey, Tab), Huston (John, Walter), Hutton (Jim, Timothy), Irving (Henry), Jacobi (Derek, Lou), Jagger (Dean), Keaton (Buster, Michael), Keitel (Harvey), Kilmer (Val), Knotts (Don), Landau (Martin), Landon (Michael), Laurel (Stan), Lemmon (Jack), Liotta (Ray), Lugosi (Bela), MacRae (Gordon), Malden (Karl), Martin (Dean, Steve), Marvin (Lee), Massey (Raymond), Mature (Victor), McCrea (Joel), Meeker (Ralph), Menjou (Adolphe), Mifune (Toshiro), Modine (Matthew), Morley (Robert), Mostel (Zero), Murphy (Audie, Eddie), Murray (Bill, Don), Neeson (Liam), Nelson (Ozzie), Newley (Anthony), Newman (Paul), O'Brian (Hugh), O'Brien (Edmund,

Pat), Oldman (Gary), O'Toole (Peter), Pacino (Al), Parker (Fess), Poston (Tom), Powell (Dick), Quayle (Anthony), Reeves (Keanu, Steve), Reiner (Carl, Rob), Reiser (Paul), Rennie (Michael), Ritter (John, Tex), Rogers (Roy, Wayne, Will), Romero (Cesar), Rooney (Mickey), Rourke (Mickey), Schell (Maximilian), Seagal (Steven), Sharif (Omar), Slezak (Walter), Snipes (Wesley), Spacey (Kevin), Spader (James), Swayze (Patrick), Taylor (Robert, Rod), Thomas (Danny, Richard), Turpin (Ben), Vallee (Rudy), Vaughn (Robert), Voight (Jon), Wagner (Robert), Walker (Robert), Warden (Jack), Wayans (Damon, Keenen Ivory), Weaver (Dennis, Fritz), Welles (Orson), Werner (Oskar), Wilder (Gene), Willis (Bruce) **7** Abraham (F. Murray), Andrews (Dana), Astaire (Fred), Aykroyd (Dan), Baldwin (Alec, Daniel, Stephen, William), Bellamy (Ralph), Bogarde (Dirk), Branagh (Kenneth), Bridges (Beau, Jeff, Lloyd), Bronson (Charles), Brosnan (Pierce), Brynner (Yul), Burbage (Richard), Bushman (Francis X.), Buttons (Red), Calhern (Louis), Calhoun (Rory), Cameron (Rod), Carroll (Leo G.), Chaplin (Charlie), Clooney (George), Connery (Sean), Connors (Chuck), Conried (Hans), Costner (Kevin), Crystal (Billy), Daniels (Jeff), da Silva (Howard), DeLuise (Dom), Dennehy (Brian), Donahue (Troy), Donlevy (Brian), Douglas (Kirk, Melvyn, Michael, Paul), Durante (Jimmy), Edwards (Vince), Feldman (Marty), Fiennes (Ralph), Freeman (Morgan), Garrick (David), Gazzara (Ben), Gielgud (John), Gleason (Jackie), Goodman (John), Gosling (Ryan), Gossett (Lou), Grammer (Kelsey), Granger (Farley, Stewart), Gulager (Clu), Hackman (Gene), Henreid (Paul), Hoffman (Dustin), Homolka (Oscar), Hopkins (Anthony), Hoskins (Bob), Janssen (David), Johnson (Ben, Don, Van), Jourdan (Louis), Jurgens (Curt), Karloff (Boris), Kennedy (Arthur, George), Klugman (Jack), Lawford (Peter), Leonard (Robert Sean, Sheldon), Lithgow (John), MacLane (Barton), Maharis (George), Mathers (Jerry), Matthau (Walter), McCarey (Leo), McGavin (Darren), McQueen (Steve), Milland (Ray), Mitchum (Robert), Montand (Yves), Morales (Esai), Navarro (Ramon), Newhart (Bob), O'Connor (Carroll, Donald), Olivier (Laurence), Palance (Jack), Paulsen (Pat), Peppard (George), Perkins (Anthony), Pickens (Slim), Pidgeon (Walter), Poitier (Sidney), Preston (Robert), Randall (Tony), Redford (Robert), Rickman (Alan), Robards (Jason), Robbins (Tim), Robeson (Paul), Roberts (Pernell, Tony), Sanders (George), Savalas (Telly), Scourby (Alexander), Selleck (Tom), Sellers (Peter), Shatner (William), Shepard (Sam), Silvers (Phil), Sinatra (Frank), Skelton (Red), Skinner (Otis), Steiger (Rod), Stewart (James, Patrick), Stooges (Three), Tamblyn (Russ), Ustinov (Peter), Van Dyke (Dick, Jerry), Wallach (Eli), Widmark (Richard), Wilding (Michael), Winters (Jonathan), Woolley (Monty) **8** Banderas (Antonio), Barrault (Jean-Louis), Basehart (Richard), Belmondo (Jean-Paul), Berenger (Tom), Blackmer (Sidney), Borgnine (Ernest), Buchanan (Edgar), Buchholz (Horst), Chandler (Jeff), Costello (Lou), Crawford (Broderick, Michael), Cummings (Robert), Day-Lewis (Daniel), DiCaprio (Leonardo), Dreyfuss (Richard), Eastwood (Clint), Forsythe (John), Garfield (John), Goldblum (Jeff), Griffith (Andy), Guinness (Alec), Harrison (Noel, Rex), Hemmings (David), Holbrook (Hal), Holloway (Stanley), Houseman (John), Jannings (Emil), Kingsley (Ben), Langella (Frank), Laughton (Charles), Marshall (E.G., Herbert), McDowall (Roddy), McDowell (Malcolm), McGregor (Ewan), McLaglen (Victor), Meredith (Burgess), Rathbone (Basil), Redgrave (Michael), Reynolds (Burt), Ritchard (Cyril), Robinson (Edward G.), Sarrazin (Michael), Scofield (Paul), Seinfeld (Jerry), Stallone (Sylvester), Stroheim (Erich von), Sullivan (Barry), Travolta (John), Turturro (John), Van Damme (Jean-Claude), Von Sydow (Max), Whitaker (Forest), Whitmore (James), Williams (Robin) **9** Amsterdam (Morey), Barrymore (John, Lionel), Brandauer (Klaus Maria), Broderick (Matthew), Carnovsky (Morris), Carradine (David, John, Keith, Robert), Courtenay (Tom), Depardieu (Gérard), Fairbanks (Douglas), Fishburne (Larry), Franciosa (Anthony), Hardwicke (Cedric), Harrelson (Woody), Hyde-White (Wilfrid), Lancaster (Burt), MacMurray (Fred), Malkovich (John), Montalban (Ricardo), Nicholson (Jack), Pleasance (Donald), Robertson (Cliff, Dale), Strasberg (Lee), Tarantino (Quentin), Valentino (Rudolph), Zimbalist (Efrem) **10** Fitzgerald (Barry), Hasselhoff (David), Montgomery (Robert), Richardson (Ralph), Sutherland (Donald, Kiefer), Washington (Denzel)

11 Chamberlain (Richard), Greenstreet (Sydney), Mastroianni (Marcello), Trintignant (Jean-Louis) **13** Kristofferson (Kris)

actor's *quest:* **4** part, role ***signal:*** **3** cue

actress 3 Bow (Clara), Cox (Courtney), Day (Doris), Dee (Ruby, Sandra), Dru (Joanne), Gam (Rita), Loy (Myrna), May (Elaine), Rae (Charlotte) **4** Alba (Jessica), Ball (Lucille), Bara (Theda), Barr (Roseanne), Cass (Peggy), Cher, Coca (Imogene), Cruz (Penelope), Dahl (Arlene), Daly (Tyne), Dern (Laura), Diaz (Cameron), Dors (Diana), Down (Lesley-Ann), Duke (Patty), Duse (Eleonora), Eden (Barbara), Foch (Nina), Garr (Teri), Gish (Dorothy, Lillian), Grey (Jennifer), Gwyn (Nell), Hawn (Goldie), Holm (Celeste), Hunt (Helen, Linda, Marsha), Hurt (Mary Beth), Hyer (Martha), Ivey (Judith), Kahn (Madeline), Kerr (Deborah), Lake (Veronica), Lisi (Virna), Long (Nia, Shelley), Main (Marjorie), Mayo (Virginia), Neal (Patricia), Olin (Lena), Page (Geraldine), Raye (Martha), Rigg (Diana), Ross (Diana, Katharine), Rush (Barbara), Ryan (Meg, Peggy), Shue (Elisabeth), Weld (Tuesday), West (Mae), Wood (Natalie, Peggy), Wray (Fay), York (Susannah) **5** Adams (Maude), Aimee (Anouk), Allen (Joan, Gracie, Karen, Nancy), Alley (Kirstie), Arden (Eve), Astor (Mary), Bates (Kathy), Berry (Halle), Black (Karen), Bloom (Claire), Blyth (Ann), Booth (Shirley), Brice (Fanny), Britt (May), Bruce (Virginia), Buzzi (Ruth), Caron (Leslie), Close (Glenn), Crain (Jeanne), Danes (Claire), Davis (Bette, Geena, Judy), Dench (Judi), Derek (Bo), Dunne (Irene), Eggar (Samantha), Evans (Edith), Falco (Edie), Field (Sally), Fonda (Bridget, Jane), Gabor (Eva, Zsa Zsa), Garbo (Greta), Gless (Sharon), Grant (Lee), Greer (Jane), Grier (Pam), Hagen (Uta), Hasso (Signe), Hayek (Salma), Hayes (Helen), Heche (Anne), Henie (Sonja), Howes (Sally Ann), Jones (Cherry, Jennifer, Shirley), Kazan (Lainie), Kelly (Grace, Patsy), Kurtz (Swoosie), Lahti (Christine), Lange (Hope, Jessica), Leigh (Janet, Jennifer Jason, Vivien), Lenya (Lotte), Lewis (Juliette), Loren (Sophia), Mason (Marsha, Pamela), Meara (Anne), Miles (Sarah, Vera), Moore (Demi, Julianne, Mary Tyler, Terry), Naldi (Nita), North (Sheree), Novak (Kim), O'Hara (Maureen), Olson (Nancy), O'Neal (Tatum), Perez (Rosie), Picon (Molly), Pitts (Zasu), Reese (Della), Ricci (Christina), Roman (Ruth), Ruehl (Mercedes), Ryder (Winona), Saint (Eva Marie), Scott (Lizbeth, Martha), Shire (Talia), Smith (Alexis, Maggie), Stone (Sharon), Storm (Gale), Swank (Hilary), Tandy (Jessica), Terry (Ellen), Tomei (Marisa), Tyler (Liv), Tyson (Cicely), Watts (Naomi), Welch (Raquel), Wiest (Dianne), Wyatt (Jane), Wyman (Jane), Young (Sean, Loretta) **6** Adjani (Isabelle), Angeli (Pier), Arthur (Beatrice, Jean), Ashley (Elizabeth), Bacall (Lauren), Bardot (Brigitte), Barkin (Ellen), Barrie (Wendy), Baxter (Anne), Bening (Annette), Bergen (Candice, Polly), Bisset (Jacqueline), Blaine (Vivian), Brooks (Louise), Bujold (Genevieve), Butler (Brett), Cannon (Dyan), Carter (Dixie, Lynda, Nell), Cooper (Gladys), Crouse (Lindsay), Curtin (Jane), Curtis (Jamie Lee), Danner (Blythe), Davies (Marion), Del Rio (Dolores), Dennis (Sandy), Diller (Phyllis), Draper (Ruth), Driver (Minnie), Dumont (Margaret), Duncan (Sandy), Durbin (Deanna), Duvall (Shelley), Ekberg (Anita), Ekland (Britt), Fabray (Nanette), Farmer (Frances), Farrow (Mia), Feldon (Barbara), Fisher (Carrie), Foster (Jodie), Garner (Peggy Ann), Garson (Greer), Gaynor (Mitzi), Gordon (Ruth), Grable (Betty), Grimes (Tammy), Hannah (Daryl), Harlow (Jean), Harper (Jessica, Tess, Valerie), Harris (Barbara, Julie, Rosemary), Hedren (Tippi), Hiller (Wendy), Hunter (Holly, Kim), Hussey (Ruth), Huston (Anjelica), Hutton (Betty), Irving (Amy), Keaton (Diane), Keeler (Ruby), Kidman (Nicole), Kinski (Nastassja), Knight (Shirley), Lamarr (Hedy), Lamour (Dorothy), Lasser (Louise), Laurie (Piper), Lillie (Beatrice), Louise (Tina), Lupino (Ida), MacRae (Sheila), Malone (Dorothy), Martin (Mary), Matlin (Marlee), McGraw (Ali), Merkel (Una), Merman (Ethel), Midler (Bette), Miller (Ann), Mirren (Helen), Monroe (Marilyn), Moreau (Jeanne), Moreno (Rita), Oberon (Merle), O'Brien (Margaret), Oliver (Edna May), Palmer (Lili), Paquin (Anna), Parker (Eleanor, Mary-Louise, Sarah Jessica, Suzy), Peters (Bernadette), Powers (Stephanie), Prowse (Juliet), Rainer (Luise), Rashad (Phylicia), Remick (Lee), Ritter (Thelma), Rivera (Chita), Rogers (Ginger), Scales (Prunella), Seberg (Jean), Sidney (Sylvia), Somers (Suzanne), Sommer (Elke), Spacek (Sissy), Streep (Meryl), Taylor (Elizabeth), Temple (Shirley), Theron (Charlize), Thomas (Marlo),

Tiffin (Pamela), Tomlin (Lily), Turner (Kathleen, Lana), Walker (Nancy), Warren (Lesley Ann), Watson (Emily), Weaver (Sigourney), Wilson (Marie), Winger (Debra), Wright (Teresa), Wynter (Dana) **7** Allyson (June), Andress (Ursula), Andrews (Julie), Aniston (Jennifer), Bassett (Angela), Bennett (Constance, Joan), Bergman (Ingrid), Binoche (Juliette), Blethyn (Brenda), Buckley (Betty), Bullock (Sandra), Burnett (Carol), Burstyn (Ellen), Colbert (Claudette), Collins (Joan, Pauline), Cornell (Katherine), Cushman (Charlotte), Darnell (Linda), DeCarlo (Yvonne), Delaney (Dana), Deneuve (Catherine), Dukakis (Olympia), Dunaway (Faye), Dunnock (Mildred), Fawcett (Farrah), Fleming (Rhonda), Fricker (Brenda), Gardner (Ava), Garland (Judy), Gershon (Gina), Gingold (Hermione), Goddard (Paulette), Grahame (Gloria), Grayson (Kathryn), Hayward (Susan), Heckart (Eileen), Hepburn (Audrey, Katharine), Hershey (Barbara), Jackson (Anne, Glenda, Kate), Langtry (Lillie), Learned (Michael), Lombard (Carole), MacGraw (Ali), Madonna, Magnani (Anna), Mangano (Silvana), McGuire (Dorothy), McKenna (Siobhan), McQueen (Butterfly), Meadows (Audrey, Jayne), Mimieux (Yvette), Miranda (Carmen), Mulgrew (Kate), Natwick (Mildred), Parsons (Estelle), Perlman (Rhea), Perrine (Valerie), Plummer (Amanda), Podesta (Rosanna), Portman (Natalie), Roberts (Julia), Russell (Jane, Rosalind, Theresa), Scacchi (Greta), Sevigny (Chloë), Shearer (Norma), Shields (Brooke), Siddons (Sarah), Simmons (Jean), Sorvino (Mira), Sothern (Ann), Stevens (Connie, Stella), Stritch (Elaine), Swanson (Gloria), Swinton (Tilda), Thaxter (Phyllis), Thurman (Uma), Tierney (Gene), Ullmann (Liv), Verdugo (Elena), Winfrey (Oprah), Winslet (Kate), Winters (Shelley), Withers (Jane), Woodard (Alfre) **8** Anderson (Judith, Loni, Melissa Sue), Arquette (Patricia, Rosanna), Ashcroft (Peggy), Bancroft (Anne), Bankhead (Tallulah), Basinger (Kim), Blondell (Joan), Byington (Spring), Caldwell (Zoe), Campbell (Mrs. Patrick), Channing (Carol, Stockard), Charisse (Cyd), Christie (Julie), Crawford (Joan), DeMornay (Rebecca), Dewhurst (Colleen), Dietrich (Marlene), Dressler (Marie), Fletcher (Louise), Fontaine (Joan), Fontanne (Lynn), Goldberg (Whoopi), Griffith (Melanie), Hayworth (Rita), Holliday (Judy), Lansbury (Angela), Lawrence (Gertrude), Leachman (Cloris), Leighton (Margaret), Lindfors (Viveca), Lockhart (June), Lovelace (Linda), MacLaine (Shirley), McDaniel (Hattie), Mercouri (Melina), Minnelli (Liza), Nelligan (Kate), Neuwirth (Bebe), O'Donnell (Rosie), Pfeiffer (Michelle), Pickford (Mary), Prentiss (Paula), Redgrave (Lynn, Vanessa), Reynolds (Debbie), Roseanne, Rowlands (Gena), Sarandon (Susan), Shepherd (Cybill), Signoret (Simone), Spelling (Tori), Stanwyck (Barbara), Straight (Beatrice), Sullavan (Margaret), Talmadge (Norma), Thompson (Emma, Sada), Van Doren (Mamie), Vardalos (Nia), Williams (Esther), Woodward (Joanne) **9** Alexander (Jane), Barrymore (Drew, Ethel), Bernhardt (Sarah), Blanchett (Cate), Cardinale (Claudia), Christian (Linda), Clayburgh (Jill), Dandridge (Dorothy), DeGeneres (Ellen), Dickinson (Angie), Fairchild (Morgan), Henderson (Florence), Kellerman (Sally), Mansfield (Jayne), McDonnell (Mary), Moorehead (Agnes), O'Sullivan (Maureen), Pleshette (Suzanne), Plowright (Joan), Schneider (Romy), Singleton (Penny), Stapleton (Jean, Maureen), Strasberg (Susan), Streisand (Barbra), Struthers (Sally), Thorndike (Sybil), Vera-Ellen, Zellweger (Renée) **10** Ann-Margret, Lanchester (Elsa), Montgomery (Elizabeth), Richardson (Miranda, Natasha), Rossellini (Isabella), Rutherford (Margaret), Tushingham (Rita) **11** de Havilland (Olivia), McCambridge (Mercedes), Riefenstahl (Leni), Silverstone (Alicia), Steenburgen (Mary) **12** Bonham-Carter (Helena), Lollabrigida (Gina), Mastrantonio (Mary Elizabeth)

actual 4 echt, hard, live, real, true **5** exact **6** extant, living **7** certain, current, de facto, factual, genuine **8** absolute, bona fide, concrete, definite, existent, existing, material, physical, positive, tangible **9** authentic, objective, veritable **10** legitimate, phenomenal **12** indisputable

actuality 4 fact **5** being, truth **7** reality **9** existence, substance **10** embodiment **11** incarnation, materiality

actually 4 very **5** truly **6** indeed, in fact, really **7** de facto, no doubt **9** genuinely, in reality, veritably **10** absolutely

actuate 4 move, spur, stir **5** drive, impel, rouse **6** arouse, excite, propel, set off, turn on **7** provoke, trigger **8** activate, energize, mobilize, motivate, vitalize

act up 5 cut up **7** show off **9** misbehave **11** misfunction

acumen **3** wit **6** acuity, vision, wisdom **7** insight **8** keenness **9** acuteness, sharpness **10** astuteness, perception, shrewdness **11** discernment, penetration, percipience **12** perspicacity

acute **4** dire, keen **5** sharp **6** urgent **7** crucial, exigent, intense, pointed **8** critical, incisive, piercing, shooting, stabbing **9** knifelike, observant, trenchant **10** perceptive **11** penetrating, quick-witted, sharp-witted

ad ____ **3** hoc, lib, rem **7** hominem, interim, nauseam **9** infinitum

adage **3** saw **4** rule **5** axiom, maxim, motto **6** byword, saying, truism **7** proverb **8** aphorism, apothegm

adagio **4** slow **5** tempo

Adah ***husband:*** **4** Esau **6** Lamech ***son:*** **5** Jabal, Jubal **7** Eliphaz

Adam ***grandson:*** **4** Enos **5** Enoch ***rib:*** **3** Eve ***son:*** **4** Abel, Cain, Seth ***wife:*** **3** Eve **6** Lilith

Adam ____ **4** Bede **5** Smith

adamant **3** set **4** firm, hard **5** rigid, stiff, stone, tough **6** flinty **8** immobile, obdurate, resolute **9** immovable, unbending, unswaying **10** determined, inflexible, unbendable, unyielding **11** unbreakable

adapt **3** fit **4** suit **5** alter, shape, yield **6** adjust, change, modify, revise, square, tailor **7** arrange, conform, remodel **9** acclimate, habituate, reconcile **11** acclimatize, accommodate

adaptable **6** mobile, pliant, supple **7** ductile, plastic, pliable **8** flexible, moldable **9** malleable, versatile

adaptation **6** change **8** revision **9** reworking **10** adjustment, alteration **12** modification

ad astra per ____ **6** aspera

add **3** sum, tot **4** cast, foot, join, tote **5** affix, annex, count, tally, total, unite **6** append, attach, figure, reckon, tack on, take on **7** augment, compute, count up, enlarge, improve, include **8** compound, increase, totalize **9** build onto, calculate **10** supplement

Addams family **5** Gomez **7** Pugsley **8** Morticia **9** Grandmama, Wednesday **11** Uncle Fester ***servants:*** **5** Lurch, Thing

added **3** new **4** else, more **5** extra, fresh, other **7** another, farther, further **9** accessory **10** additional **13** supplementary

addendum **5** extra, rider **8** addition **10** supplement

adder **5** snake, viper **10** calculator **12** hognose snake

addict **3** fan, nut **4** bias, buff **5** hound, lover **6** abuser, devote, junkie, zealot **7** booster, devotee, fanatic, groupie, habitué **9** habituate, surrender **10** aficionado, enthusiast

addition **4** plus, rise **5** annex, extra, raise, rider **7** accrual, adjunct **8** addendum, appendix, increase **9** accession, accessory, accretion, extension, increment **10** supplement **11** enlargement **12** appurtenance, augmentation

additional see **added**

additionally **3** too **4** also, more, then **5** again **6** as well **7** besides, further **8** likewise, moreover **11** furthermore

additive **5** extra **8** extender **9** summative, substance

addle **5** mix up, spoil **6** muddle, puzzle **7** confuse, fluster, nonplus, perplex **8** befuddle, bewilder, confound, distract, throw off **9** dumbfound

add-on **3** ell **7** adjunct **9** accessory **11** enhancement

address **3** aim, air, set, URL **4** hail, send, tact, talk **5** apply, court, grace, greet, level, place, point, poise, remit, route, skill, speak, treat **6** call to, devote, direct, pursue, relate, salute, speech **7** bearing, consign, deliver, forward, know-how, lecture, oration, speak to, write to **8** appeal to, approach, converse, deal with, deftness, delivery, demeanor, dispatch, identify, location, petition, position, presence, transmit **9** attention, dexterity, diplomacy, expertise **10** adroitness, competence, directions, efficiency **11** comportment, designation, proficiency, savoir faire

adduce **3** lay **4** cite **5** claim, offer **6** allege, submit, tender **7** advance, present, proffer, propose, refer to, suggest **8** document **9** exemplify **10** illustrate

add up **3** sum **5** count, tally, total **6** amount, reckon **7** compute **9** make sense

add up to **4** mean **5** spell **6** amount, denote, import, intend **7** compute, connote, express, signify

adept **3** pro **4** able, deft, whiz **5** crack, savvy **6** adroit, expert, master, wizard **7** skilled **8** masterly, skillful, virtuoso **9** dexterous, masterful **10** proficient **11** crackerjack **12** professional

adequacy **5** might **6** enough **7** ability **8** capacity **10** capability, competence, sufficient **11** sufficiency **13** qualification

adequate **6** common, decent, enough **8** all right, passable, pleasing, standard, suitable **9** competent, sufficing **10** acceptable, sufficient **11** comfortable **12** satisfactory **13** unexceptional, unimpeachable

adequately **4** well **5** amply, right **6** enough **8** all right, passably, properly, suitably **9** fittingly, tolerably **12** sufficiently **13** appropriately

adhere 4 bond, glue **5** cling, paste, stick **6** attach, bind to, cement, cleave, cohere, fasten **7** stick to **8** hold fast

adherence 4 bond **5** cling **7** loyalty **8** adhesion, clinging, cohesion, fidelity, sticking **9** constancy **10** attachment **12** faithfulness

adherent 3 fan, ist **6** cohort, votary **7** devotee, sectary **8** disciple, follower, henchman, partisan, stalwart **9** satellite, supporter **10** aficionado

adhering 6 clingy, sticky **7** binding

adhesive 4 glue **5** epoxy, gluey, gooey, gummy, stamp, tacky **6** cement, clingy, gummed, sticky **7** holding, stickum **8** adhering, fastener, mucilage, sticking **9** attaching

adieu 3 bye **4** ciao, ta-ta **5** congé **6** bye-bye, so long **7** cheerio, good-bye, parting, toodles **8** farewell, toodle-oo **11** leave-taking

ad interim 6 acting, pro tem **9** temporary **10** pro tempore **11** temporarily

adios 4 by-by, ciao, ta-ta **5** adieu, later **6** bye-bye, so long **7** cheerio, goodbye, toodles **8** farewell, toodle-oo **10** hasta luego

adipose 3 fat **4** oily **5** fatty **6** greasy **7** fatlike

adit 3 way **4** door **5** entry **6** access, entrée, tunnel **7** ingress, passage **8** entrance **9** mine entry **10** passageway **12** mine entrance

adjacent 4 near **5** close **6** beside, nearby, next to **8** abutting, next door, touching **9** adjoining, alongside, bordering **10** contiguous, juxtaposed, near-at-hand **11** close-at-hand, neighboring **12** conterminous

adjoin 3 add **4** abut, link, line, meet **5** annex, touch, verge **6** append, attach, border, butt on, couple **7** connect, impinge **8** neighbor **11** communicate

adjourn 4 move, rise, stay **5** defer, delay **6** hold up, put off, recess, shelve **7** hold off, suspend **8** dissolve, hold over, postpone, prorogue **9** prorogate

adjudge 4 deem, rule **5** award, grant **6** decide, settle, umpire **7** mediate, referee **9** arbitrate

adjunct 5 added, affix **6** joined **8** addendum, addition, appanage, appendix, attached **9** accessory, accretion, appendage, assistant, associate, auxiliary **10** attachment **12** appurtenance

adjure 3 beg, bid **4** urge **6** exhort **7** beseech, entreat, command, implore, require **9** importune **10** supplicate

adjust 3 fit, fix, rig **4** suit, tune **5** adapt, order, right **6** accord, attune, modify, orient, settle, square, tailor, tune up **7** arrange, conform, correct, rectify, resolve **8** modulate, regulate **9** habituate, harmonize, reconcile **11** accommodate

adjutant 4 aide **6** deputy

adjuvant 4 aide **6** aiding, helper **8** enhancer, modifier **9** accessory, ancillary, assisting, auxiliary **10** collateral, subsidiary **11** appurtenant **12** contributory

ad-lib 9 extempore, improvise, impromptu **10** improvised, off-the-cuff, unprepared **11** extemporize, spontaneous, unrehearsed

Admetus ***father:*** **6** Pheres ***wife:*** **8** Alcestis

administer 3 run **4** boss, deal, give, head **5** issue **6** direct, govern, head up, manage **7** conduct, control, deal out, deliver, dole out, execute, give out, mete out, oversee, perform, provide **8** carry out, dispense, share out **9** apportion, supervise **10** distribute, portion out

administration 6 regime **7** control **9** direction **10** governance, presidency ***system of:*** **11** bureaucracy

administrator 4 boss, exec, head **5** chief **7** manager, officer **8** director, official, overseer **9** executive **10** supervisor

admirable 6 august, worthy **8** laudable **9** deserving, estimable, excellent, meritable **11** commendable, meritorious, outstanding **12** praiseworthy

admiral ***American:*** **4** Byrd (Richard), Sims (William) **5** Dewey (George), Stark (Harold) **6** Halsey (Bull), Nimitz (Chester) **7** Zumwalt (Elmo) **8** Farragut (David), Rickover (Hyman), Spruance (Raymond) ***Chinese:*** **7** Zheng He ***Confederate:*** **6** Semmes (Raphael) ***Dutch:*** **5** Tromp (Maarten) ***English:*** **5** Drake (Francis) **6** Nelson (Horatio), Rodney (George), Vernon (Edward) **7** Hawkins (John) **8** Beaufort (Francis), Jellicoe (John), Villiers (George) **11** Mountbatten (Louis) ***fictional:*** **10** Hornblower (Horatio) ***French:*** **10** Villeneuve (Pierre-Charles) ***German:*** **4** Spee (Graf Maximilian von) **6** Dönitz (Karl), Raeder (Erich) **7** Doenitz (Karl), Tirpitz (Alfred von) ***Japanese:*** **4** Togo (Hideki) **5** Yonai (Mitsumasa) **8** Yamamoto (Isoroku) ***Spanish:*** **8** Menéndez (Pedro)

admiration 5 favor **6** esteem, praise, regard **7** account, delight, respect **8** applause, approval, pleasure **9** affection **10** estimation **11** approbation **12** appreciation

admire 5 adore, honor, prize, value **6** esteem, praise, regard, relish, revere **7** adulate, applaud, approve, cherish, commend, respect **8** consider, treasure **9** delight in **10** appreciate

admirer 3 fan **4** beau, buff **7** booster, devotee, fancier **8** believer, follower, partisan **9** supporter **10** enthusiast

admission 3 way **4** door, gate **5** entry **6** access, assent, entrée **7** ingress **8** entrance **10** admittance, concession, confession **11** affirmation

admit 3 own **4** avow, take **5** agree, allow, enter, grant, let in, let on, lodge, own up **6** accept, fess up, harbor, permit, suffer, take in **7** concede, confess, receive, shelter, welcome **9** entertain, introduce, recognize **11** acknowledge

admix 5 blend, merge **6** mingle **7** combine **8** comingle, compound, immingle **9** commingle **11** intermingle

admixture 5 alloy, blend, combo **6** fusion **7** amalgam **8** compound **9** aggregate, composite **12** amalgamation

admonish 4 warn **5** alert, chide **6** lesson, monish, rebuke, talk to **7** caution, counsel, reprove, speak to **8** call down, forewarn, reproach **9** criticize, reprimand

admonition 3 tip **6** caveat, rebuke **7** caution, chiding, reproof, warning **8** reproach **9** criticism, reprimand **11** disapproval, forewarning

ado 4 fuss, stir **5** tizzy, whirl, worry **6** bother, bustle, flurry, hubbub, pother **7** concern, problem, trouble, turmoil **9** commotion, confusion **10** difficulty

adolescence 5 youth **7** puberty **8** minority **9** greenness **10** juvenility, pubescence **12** youthfulness

adolescent 4 teen **5** minor **6** teener **7** teenage **8** immature, preadult, teenager, youthful **9** pubescent

Adonai 3 God **4** YHWH **6** Elohim, Yahweh

Adonijah *brother:* 5 Amnon **7** Absalom, Chileab ***father:* 5** David ***mother:* 7** Haggith ***slayer:* 7** Benaiah

Adonis *lover:* 5 Venus **9** Aphrodite ***mother:* 5** Myrrh **6** Myrrha ***slayer:* 4** boar

adopt 4 pick, take **5** raise **6** accept, affect, assume, choose, select, take on, take up **7** care for, embrace, endorse, espouse

adoption 6 choice **7** raising, support **8** espousal, taking in **9** embracing, selection **11** embracement

adorable 4 cute, dear **7** darling, lovable, winsome **8** charming, pleasing, precious **9** appealing **10** attractive, delightful

adoration 4 love **5** ardor, honor **6** esteem, praise **7** passion, worship **8** devotion, idolatry **9** adulation, affection, reverence **10** admiration **11** idolization

adore 4 love **5** honor, prize **6** admire, dote on, esteem, revere **7** cherish, idolize, respect, worship **8** dote upon, treasure, venerate **9** affection, delight in, reverence

adorn 4 deck, trim **5** fix up, grace **6** bedeck, enrich, pretty **7** dress up, enhance, enliven, furbish, garnish, smarten **8** beautify, decorate, ornament, prettify **9** embellish

adornment 5 decor, frill **6** finery **7** garnish **8** ornament, trimming **9** accessory, caparison **10** decoration **13** embellishment

ad rem 3 apt **7** apropos, fitting, germane **8** apposite, material, relevant **9** pertinent **10** applicable, relevantly, to the point **11** applicative, applicatory

adrift 4 asea, lost **5** at sea, loose **6** afloat **7** aimless, mixed up **8** confused, floating, unmoored **10** anchorless, bewildered **11** disoriented, purposeless

adroit 3 apt **4** able, deft **5** adept, canny, handy, savvy, smart **6** astute, clever, expert, nimble, shrewd **7** cunning, skilled **8** skillful, talented **9** dexterous, ingenious **11** intelligent, quick-witted, resourceful **13** perspicacious

adroitness 3 art **4** gift **5** craft, flair, knack, savvy, skill **7** address, cunning, know-how, prowess **8** deftness **9** adeptness, dexterity, expertise, ingenuity, readiness **10** cleverness, expertness **12** intelligence

adulation 7 acclaim, baloney, blarney, fawning, tribute, worship **8** applause, flattery, soft soap **10** overpraise **11** hero-worship **12** blandishment

adulatory 7 buttery, fawning **8** unctuous **9** kowtowing **10** flattering, obsequious, oleaginous **11** bootlicking, sycophantic

adult 4 aged, ripe **5** grown **6** mature **7** grown-up, matured, ripened **9** full-blown, full-grown **11** full-fledged

adulterate 3 cut **4** thin **5** alloy, dirty, taint, water **6** debase, defile, dilute, doctor, dope up, impair, weaken **7** cheapen, corrupt, defiled, degrade, devalue, diluted, falsify, pollute, tainted, thinned **8** degraded, denature, impurify, polluted, spurious **9** water down **10** tamper with **11** contaminate

adumbrate 3 dim, fog **4** bode, call, hint, mist, veil **5** augur, cloud **6** darken, shadow, sketch **7** becloud, bespeak, betoken, obscure, outline, portend, predict, presage, suggest **8** block out, disclose, forebode, forecast, foretell, indicate, intimate, prophesy **9** obfuscate, prefigure **10** foreshadow, overshadow **11** prefigurate **12** characterize

adumbration 4 hint, sign **5** shade, umbra **6** shadow **7** outline **8** penumbra **10** indication, intimation, suggestion

advance 3 aid **4** cite, help, lend, loan, move, rise **5** get on, march, money, raise, serve **6** assist, course, foster, mature, prefer, supply, uplift **7** deposit, develop, elevate, forward, furnish, further, headway, ongoing, present, proceed, promote, propose, upgrade **8** approach, get along, heighten, increase, progress **9** encourage, evolution, provision **10** accelerate, bring about **11** development, furtherance, improvement, progression **12** breakthrough
advanced 3 old **5** first **6** far out **7** forward, in front, leading, liberal, radical **8** far ahead, foremost **9** developed **10** precocious **11** broad-minded, progressive
advancement 4 gain, rise **5** boost **6** growth **7** headway **8** progress **9** elevation, promotion **10** betterment, preference **11** improvement, progression
advantage 4 boon, edge, gain, good, help, lead, odds **5** asset, avail, serve **6** better, profit **7** account, benefit, mastery **8** blessing, interest, leverage **9** allowance, head start, upper hand **10** ascendancy, domination, leadership, prosperity **11** superiority **12** running start
advantageous 4 good **6** timely, toward, useful **7** benefic, gainful, helpful **8** favoring, salutary **9** conducive, desirable, expedient, favorable, fortunate, promising **10** beneficial, profitable, propitious, worthwhile
advent 5 onset **6** coming **7** arrival **8** approach **9** beginning
adventitious 5 fluky **6** casual, chance, flukey **8** by chance **9** unplanned **10** accidental, contingent, fortuitous, incidental, unexpected
adventure 3 try **4** feat, risk, trip **5** quest, wager **6** chance, gamble, hazard **7** exploit **8** escapade **9** undertake **10** enterprise, experience
adventurous 4 bold, rash **5** brash, risky **6** daring **8** intrepid, reckless **9** audacious, dangerous, daredevil, foolhardy, hazardous, impetuous, imprudent **10** innovative **12** enterprising
adversary 3 con, foe **4** anti **5** enemy, rival **7** opposer **8** opponent, opposing **10** antagonist, competitor
adverse 3 bad **4** anti **7** counter, harmful, hostile, hurtful, opposed **8** contrary, damaging, negative, opposing, opposite **9** injurious **11** deleterious, detrimental, obstructive, unfavorable **12** antagonistic, antipathetic
adversity 4 dole **5** trial **6** misery, mishap **7** bad luck, bad news, trouble **8** bad break, distress, hard time, hardship **9** mischance, suffering **10** difficulty, ill fortune, misfortune
advert 4 cite, note **5** refer **6** allude, notice, remark **7** bring up, mention, observe **8** indicate, point out
advertent 5 aware **7** heedful, mindful **9** attentive, intentive, observant, regardful
advertise 4 drum, hype, plug, puff, push, tout **5** boost, pitch **6** blazon, herald, inform, notify, report **7** advance, apprise, build up, declare, promote, publish, sponsor **8** announce, ballyhoo, proclaim **9** broadcast, publicize **10** annunciate, promulgate
advertisement 4 bill, plug, sign **5** blurb, flyer, promo **6** notice, poster, want ad **7** affiche **8** circular **9** billboard, broadcast, promotion, publicity **10** commercial **11** declaration, publication **12** announcement, proclamation
advertising award 4 Clio
advice 3 aid, tip **4** help, news, view, word **5** input **6** notice **7** caution, counsel, opinion, tidings, warning **8** guidance, teaching **10** admonition, suggestion **11** information, instruction **12** intelligence
advisable 4 wise **5** sound **6** seemly **7** politic, prudent **8** sensible, suitable, tactical **9** desirable, expedient, practical **10** worthwhile **11** recommended **12** advantageous
advise 3 tip **4** tell, tout, urge, warn **5** guide **6** clue in, confer, enjoin, fill in, inform, notify, tip off, wise up **7** apprise, caution, consult, counsel, suggest **8** acquaint, forewarn, instruct, point out **9** encourage, prescribe, recommend
advised 7 studied, weighed **8** designed, intended **10** calculated, considered, deliberate, thought out **11** intentional **12** premeditated
adviser 5 coach, guide **6** mentor **7** counsel, tipster **9** counselor **10** consultant, instructor
advisory 7 guiding, helping **9** educative **10** counseling **12** consultative **13** informational
advocacy 3 aid **6** urging **7** backing, defense, support **9** promotion
advocate 4 back, push, tout, urge **5** favor **6** backer, defend, preach, uphold **7** promote, propose, support **8** argue for, backstop, champion, exponent, plump for, side with **9** encourage, expounder, proponent, recommend, spokesman, supporter **11** countenance
Aeacus ***father:*** **4** Zeus ***mother:*** **6** Aegina ***son:*** **6** Peleus **7** Telamon
Aedon ***brother:*** **7** Amphion ***sister-in-law:*** **5** Niobe ***son (victim):*** **6** Itylus
Aeëtes ***daughter:*** **5** Medea ***father:*** **6** Helios
aegis 4 care, ward **5** armor, guard **6** charge,

shield **7** backing, control, defense, support **8** auspices, guidance, security **9** influence, patronage, safeguard **10** protection **11** sponsorship

Aegisthus ***father:*** **8** Thyestes ***lover:*** **12** Clytemnestra ***mother:*** **7** Pelopia ***slayer:*** **7** Orestes ***victim:*** **6** Atreus **9** Agamemnon

Aeneas ***companion:*** **7** Achates ***father:*** **8** Anchises ***lover:*** **4** Dido ***mother:*** **5** Venus **9** Aphrodite ***son:*** **5** Iulus **8** Ascanius ***wife:*** **6** Creusa **7** Lavinia

Aeneid ***author:*** **6** Vergil, Virgil ***first words:*** **16** arma virumque cano ***hero:*** **6** Aeneas

Aeolus ***daughter:*** **7** Alcyone **8** Halcyone ***father:*** **8** Poseidon

aeon **3** age **4** time **6** period **8** blue moon, duration

aerate **7** lighten, freshen, refresh **9** oxygenate, ventilate

aerial **4** high **5** lofty **6** flying, vapory **7** antenna, soaring **8** birdlike, elevated, ethereal, fanciful, towering, vaporous **9** pneumatic **10** impalpable **11** atmospheric, forward pass

aerie **4** nest **7** citadel, lookout **9** penthouse ***resident:*** **5** eagle **6** eaglet

aeroembolism **5** bends

aeronaut **4** Fogg (Phileas) **5** pilot **7** aviator **8** Zeppelin (Ferdinand, Graf von) **10** balloonist

Aerope ***husband:*** **6** Atreus ***lover:*** **8** Thyestes ***son:*** **8** Menelaus **9** Agamemnon

aery see **aerial**

Aesculapius ***daughter:*** **6** Hygeia **7** Panacea ***father:*** **6** Apollo ***slayer:*** **4** Zeus **7** Jupiter ***teacher:*** **6** Chiron ***wife:*** **6** Epione

Aeson ***brother:*** **6** Pelias ***son:*** **5** Jason

aesthete **4** buff **6** expert **7** devotee **9** authority **10** dilettante **11** appreciator, cognoscente, connoisseur

aesthetic **6** artful **8** artistic, creative, pleasing **9** beautiful, sensitive **10** attractive, harmonious

afar **5** apart **6** remote **7** distant

affable **4** kind, open, warm **6** at ease, genial, gentle, kindly, polite **7** amiable, cordial **8** friendly, gracious, obliging, pleasant, sociable **9** congenial, courteous

affair **4** case, love **5** amour, fling, worry **6** action, matter **7** concern, liaison, palaver, romance **8** business, function, interest, intrigue, occasion **9** dalliance, happening, procedure **10** proceeding **12** relationship

affect **3** act **4** fake, move, sham, stir, sway **5** act on, adopt, alter, bluff, fancy, feign, haunt, put on, touch **6** assume, change, strike **7** act upon, disturb, impress, inspire, pretend **8** frequent, simulate **9** cultivate, influence

affectation **3** air **4** airs, pose, sham, show **6** facade **8** pretense **9** mannerism **10** pretension **13** artificiality

affected **5** apish, false, moved, phony, put-on **6** phoney **7** altered, assumed, changed, feigned, stilted **8** disposed, inclined, involved, mannered, precious, spurious **9** concerned, conscious, contrived, insincere, pretended, unnatural **10** artificial **11** overrefined, pretentious **13** self-conscious

affecting **3** sad **6** lively, moving **7** pitiful **8** exciting, poignant, touching **9** thrilling **10** disturbing, impressive **11** distressing, influential

affection **4** bias, love **5** trait **6** doting, liking, malady, virtue, warmth **7** ailment, concern, disease, emotion, feature, feeling, illness, leaning, passion, quality **8** devotion, disorder, fondness, interest, penchant, property, sickness, sympathy **9** attention, attribute, character, complaint, condition, sentiment **10** attachment, propensity, tenderness **12** predilection

affectionate **4** dear, fond, warm **6** caring, doting, loving, tender **7** devoted **8** friendly **11** sympathetic

affective **6** moving **7** emotive **8** stirring, touching **9** emotional

affectivity **7** emotion, feeling, passion **9** sentiment

affianced **7** engaged, pledged **8** intended, plighted, promised **9** betrothed, committed **10** contracted

affiche **4** bill, list **6** notice, poster **7** placard **8** handbill

affidavit **4** oath **9** testimony **11** affirmation, declaration

affiliate **4** ally, join **5** annex, unite **6** branch **7** combine, connect, partner **9** associate

affiliated **4** akin **5** bound **6** allied, joined, linked **7** kindred, related **9** connected, dependent **10** associated

affiliation **4** club **5** tie-in, union **6** hookup, league **7** cahoots, company, joining **8** alliance **10** connection, fellowship **11** association, combination, conjunction, partnership

affinity **6** simile **7** analogy, kinship, rapport **8** likeness, relation, sympathy **9** alikeness **10** attraction, similarity, similitude **11** resemblance **13** compatibility

affirm **3** say, yes **4** aver, avow, okay **5** state, swear, vouch **6** assent, assert, attest, depose, ratify, uphold **7** certify, confirm, declare, profess, protest, testify, witness **8** dedicate, validate **9** guarantee

affirmative **3** A-OK, aye, yea, yes **4** yeah **5** roger **6** assent, aye-aye, yessir **7** right on **8** approval, positive **9** affirming, approving, asserting, assertion, endorsing, favorable, ratifying **10** confirming, supporting **11** affirmation

affix **3** add, tag **4** bind, glue, join, nail, tack **5** annex, paste, put on, rivet, stick, tag on **6** append, attach, fasten, tack on **7** impress, stick on, subjoin **8** addition **9** appendage **10** attachment

afflict **3** try, vex **4** pain, rack **5** annoy, beset, harry, press, smite, worry, wound, wring **6** bother, burden, harass, harrow, injure, martyr, pester, plague, strike, suffer **7** agonize, anguish, torment, torture, trouble **8** distress

afflicted **6** pained, rueful, woeful **7** doleful, injured, unhappy, worried **8** dolorous, stricken, troubled, wretched **9** disturbed, miserable, sorrowful, tormented **10** distressed

affliction **3** woe **4** care **5** cross, grief, trial **6** ordeal, plague, sorrow **7** anguish, illness, scourge, torment, trouble **8** distress, hardship, sickness **9** adversity, heartache, infirmity **10** misfortune **11** tribulation

afflictive **3** sad **4** dire, sore **6** aching, bitter, woeful **7** galling, hurtful, hurting, painful **8** grievous, mournful **9** sorrowful **10** calamitous, deplorable, lamentable **11** distasteful, distressing, regrettable, troublesome, unfortunate, unpalatable **13** heartbreaking

affluence **5** means, worth **6** bounty, influx, plenty, riches, wealth **8** opulence, property, richness **9** abundance, plenitude, profusion, resources **10** prosperity

affluent **4** full, rich **5** flush **6** loaded **7** copious, flowing, moneyed, opulent, upscale, wealthy, well-off **8** abundant, well-to-do **9** bountiful, plentiful, tributary, well-fixed **10** prosperous, well-heeled

afford **4** able, bear, give **5** allow, grant, incur, offer, spare, stand **6** bestow, confer, donate, impart, manage, supply **7** furnish, present, support, sustain

affordable **5** cheap **6** modest **7** low-cost **8** bearable **10** manageable, reasonable **11** inexpensive

affray **3** row **5** clash, fight, melee, scrap **6** fracas, rumpus **7** dispute, quarrel, ruction, scuffle **8** disorder, skirmish

affront **3** vex **4** face, meet, slap, slur **5** abuse, anger, annoy, wrong **6** injury, insult, offend, slight **7** offense, outrage, put down **8** contempt, rudeness **9** aspersion, criticize, encounter, indignity

Afghanistan ***capital:*** **5** Kabul ***city:*** **5** Herat **8** Kandahar **12** Mazar-i-Sharif ***ethnic group:*** **7** Pashtun ***language:*** **4** Dari **6** Pashto ***monetary unit:*** **7** Afghani ***neighbor:*** **4** Iran **5** China **8** Pakistan **10** Tajikistan, Uzbekistan **12** Turkmenistan

aficionado **3** fan **4** buff **5** hound, lover **6** expert **7** admirer, devotee, habitué **10** enthusiast **11** appreciator

afield **4** afar, away, awry **5** amiss, badly, wrong **6** abroad, astray **8** straying **9** elsewhere, off course

afire **3** hot **5** aglow, fiery **6** ablaze, aflame, alight, red-hot **7** blazing, burning, excited, flaming, flaring, ignited, kindled **8** inflamed, in flames **9** energized, excitable **10** passionate **11** conflagrant

afloat **4** asea **5** at sea **6** adrift, buoyed **9** supported, sustained

afraid **4** wary **5** chary, jumpy, loath, scary, sorry, timid **6** averse, scared, trepid **7** anxious, fearful, uneager, worried **8** cautious, hesitant, skittish, timorous **9** concerned, regretful, reluctant, unwilling **10** frightened **11** disinclined **12** apprehensive

afresh **3** new **4** anew, over **5** again, newly **6** de novo, encore **8** once more, repeated **9** once again

Africa ***country:*** **4** Chad, Mali, Togo **5** Benin, Congo, Egypt, Gabon, Ghana, Kenya, Libya, Niger, Sudan, Zaire **6** Angola, Gambia, Guinea, Malawi, Rwanda, Uganda, Zambia **7** Algeria, Burundi, Comoros, Eritrea, Lesotho, Liberia, Morocco, Namibia, Nigeria, Senegal, Somalia, Tunisia **8** Botswana, Cameroon, Djibouti, Ethiopia, Tanzania, Zimbabwe **9** Cape Verde, Mauritius, Swaziland **10** Ivory Coast, Madagascar, Mauritania, Mozambique, Seychelles **11** Burkina Faso, Côte d'Ivoire, Sierra Leone, South Africa **12** Guinea-Bissau ***ethnic group:*** **3** Ibo **4** Akan, Arab, Baya, Boer, Copt, Fula, Issa, Jebu, Moor, Zulu **5** Bantu, Fulah, Galla, Hausa, Kongo, Mande, Pygmy, Swazi, Wolof, Xhosa **6** Berber, Fulani, Hamite, Herero, Kikuyu, Nubian, Somali, Tuareg, Ubangi, Yoruba **7** Ashanti, Bedouin, Bushman, Malinke, Swahili, Touareg **8** Egyptian, Mandingo **9** Hottentot ***language:*** **3** Ibo **4** Taal **5** Bantu, Galla, Hausa, Xhosa **6** Arabic, Berber, Somali, Yoruba **7** Amharic, Bambara, Swahili **8** Malagasy **9** Afrikaans

aft **6** astern **8** rearmost, rearward **9** sternward

after **4** back, hind, next, past, rear **5** below, later, since **6** astern, back of, behind, beyond, hinder **7** ensuing **8** hindmost **9** following, posterior, sternward **10** subsequent

after all 3 yet **5** still **6** at last, though **7** finally, however **8** in the end **11** nonetheless **12** nevertheless
aftereffect 5 issue **6** result, upshot **7** fallout, outcome **11** consequence, eventuality
afterlife 6 beyond **8** eternity **9** hereafter
aftermath 4 wake **6** effect, result, upshot **12** consequences, repercussion
afterward 4 next, soon, then **5** later **6** behind **7** by and by, thereon **8** latterly **9** hereafter **10** thereafter **12** subsequently
afterword 5 envoi **6** epilog **8** epilogue
Agag ***kingdom:*** **6** Amalek ***slayer:*** **6** Samuel
again 3 bis **4** also, anew, back, over **6** afresh, de novo, encore **8** once more
again and again 3 oft **4** much **5** often **8** ofttimes **10** frequently, oftentimes, repeatedly **11** continually
against 3 con **4** anti **6** contra, facing, versus **7** vis-à-vis **8** fronting, opposite, touching ***prefix:*** **4** anti **6** contra **7** counter
Agamemnon ***avenger:*** **7** Orestes ***brother:*** **8** Menelaus ***daughter:*** **7** Electra **9** Iphigenia ***father:*** **6** Atreus ***slayer:*** **9** Aegisthus ***son:*** **7** Orestes ***wife:*** **12** Clytemnestra
agape 4 love, open **6** amazed **7** yawning **8** wide open **9** astounded, love feast **10** astonished, confounded **11** dumbfounded, overwhelmed **13** thunderstruck
agate 3 taw **4** type **6** marble, quartz **7** shooter **8** type size
agave 4 aloe **5** yucca ***drink:*** **6** mescal, pulque ***product:*** **4** hemp **5** sisal
Agave ***father:*** **6** Cadmus ***husband:*** **6** Echion ***mother:*** **8** Harmonia ***sister:*** **3** Ino **6** Semele **7** Autonoë ***son:*** **8** Pentheus
age 3 eon, era **4** aeon, grow, span, time **5** epoch, ripen, stage **6** grow up, mature, mellow, period **7** develop **8** blue moon, division, interval, lifetime, majority, maturate **10** generation
aged 3 old **4** ripe, worn **5** cured, hoary, olden **6** mellow, senior **7** ancient, antique, elderly, matured, ripened **8** grown old, timeworn **9** developed, senescent, venerable **11** patriarchal **12** antediluvian
ageless 7 endless, eternal, lasting **8** dateless, enduring, immortal, timeless **9** immutable **11** everlasting
agency 4 firm **5** cause, force, means, organ, power **6** action, bureau, medium, office **7** company, channel, vehicle **8** activity, auspices, business, division, function, ministry **9** mechanism, operation **10** department, instrument **12** organization **13** establishment
agenda 5 slate **6** docket, lineup **7** program **8** calendar, schedule, to-do list **9** timetable ***entry:*** **4** item
Agenor ***brother:*** **5** Belus ***daughter:*** **6** Europa ***father:*** **7** Antenor, Neptune **8** Poseidon ***mother:*** **5** Libya ***son:*** **6** Cadmus
agent 3 fed, spy **4** G-man, narc, T-man, tool **5** actor, means, organ, proxy, spook **6** broker, deputy, factor, medium **7** channel, proctor, steward, vehicle **8** assignee, attorney, executor, minister, ministry **9** activator, go-between, middleman, operative **10** instrument, procurator
age-old 7 ancient, antique **9** venerable **10** immemorial **11** traditional
agglomerate 4 heap, mass, pile, rock **6** gather **7** cluster, collect **9** aggregate **10** collection **11** aggregation
agglomeration 4 heap **5** hoard, trove **7** cluster **9** aggregate, amassment, gathering **10** collection, cumulation **11** aggregation
aggrandize 4 hype **5** boost **6** beef up, expand, extend, praise **7** augment, build up, enhance, enlarge, ennoble, glorify, inflate, magnify **8** heighten, increase, multiply **11** distinguish
aggravate 3 vex **4** gall **5** anger, annoy, grate, mount, peeve, pique, rouse, upset **6** burn up, deepen, nettle, worsen **7** bedevil, disturb, enhance, inflame, magnify, perturb, provoke **8** heighten, increase, irritate **9** intensify **10** exacerbate
aggravation 4 pain **5** worry **6** bother **9** annoyance, worsening **11** provocation
aggregate 3 all, sum **4** body, bulk, floc **5** add up, gross, total, whole **6** amount, gather **7** collect **8** entirety, quantity, totality **9** composite **10** cumulative **11** agglomerate **12** conglomerate **13** agglomeration
aggregation 4 body, mass **5** crowd, group, hoard, total, trove **7** cluster, company **8** assembly **9** amassment, gathering **10** assemblage, collection, cumulation **11** agglomerate **12** accumulation
aggression 4 push, raid **5** fight, onset **6** attack **7** assault, offense **8** invasion **9** hostility, incursion, offensive, onslaught, pugnacity **10** assailment **12** belligerence **13** combativeness
aggressive 5 pushy **6** fierce, severe **7** hostile, scrappy, vicious, warlike **8** emphatic, forceful, militant **9** assertive, attacking, combative, energetic, intrusive, offensive **11** belligerent, contentious, domineering, hard-hitting **12** enterprising
aggrieve 4 hurt, pain **5** annoy, harry, upset, worry, wrong **6** harass, injure, plague **7** af-

flict, oppress, torment, trouble **8** distress **9** constrain, persecute

aghast 4 agog, awed **6** afraid, amazed, scared **7** anxious, fearful, shocked, stunned **8** appalled, dismayed, startled **9** awestruck, horrified, terrified **10** astonished, confounded, frightened **11** dumbfounded, overwhelmed **13** thunderstruck

agile 4 deft, spry **5** alert, brisk, catty, lithe, quick, zippy **6** active, adroit, limber, lively, nimble, supple **7** lissome **9** adaptable, dexterous, sprightly

agitate 4 move, rile, roil, rock, stir, toss **5** argue, churn, peeve, shake, upset **6** arouse, bother, excite, flurry, joggle, ruffle, stir up **7** discuss, dispute, disturb, fluster, perturb, provoke, tempest, trouble, unhinge **8** disquiet, irritate, unsettle **9** thrash out **10** discompose

agitation 4 flap, fuss, stir, to-do **5** clash **6** bustle, clamor, debate, flurry, lather, tumult **7** dispute, ferment, tempest, turmoil **9** commotion, confusion **10** turbulence **11** disturbance

agitator 5 rebel **6** shaker **7** inciter, stirrer **8** fomenter, inflamer **9** disrupter **10** instigator **11** provocateur

Aglaia see **Graces**

Aglauros *father:* 7 Cecrops ***sister:* 5** Herse **9** Pandrosos

aglow 4 warm **5** afire **6** bright, aflame, alight **7** excited, radiant, shining **8** gleaming, luminous

agnate 4 akin, like **5** alike **6** allied, joined, linked **7** cognate, connate, kindred, kinsman, related, similar **8** relation, relative **9** analogous **10** affiliated **11** consanguine **13** corresponding

agnostic 7 doubter, skeptic **8** doubting **10** questioner, undogmatic **11** uncommitted **12** noncommittal

Agnus ____ 3 Dei

ago 4 back, gone, past, yore **5** since **6** before

agog 4 avid, keen **5** eager **6** roused **7** excited, fervent **8** desirous **9** expectant, impatient **12** enthusiastic

agon 5 clash **6** battle, strife **7** contest **8** conflict, struggle

agonize 4 fret, gall, hurt, pain, rack **5** chafe **6** harrow, squirm, suffer, writhe **7** afflict, torment, torture, trouble **8** distress, stew over, struggle **10** excruciate

agonizing 6 fierce **7** extreme, intense, painful, racking, tearing **9** harrowing, suffering, torturing, torturous **10** tormenting **12** excruciating

agony 4 pain **5** dolor, pangs **6** misery **7** anguish, passion, torment, torture **8** distress, outburst, struggle **9** suffering **10** affliction

agora 6 market **11** marketplace **12** meeting place

agrarian 5 rural **6** rustic **8** pastoral **10** campestral **12** agricultural

agree 3 buy, set, yes **4** jibe, okay, suit **5** admit, check, equal, fit in, match, tally **6** accede, accept, accord, assent, concur, settle, square **7** comport, concede, concert, concord, conform, consent **8** check out, coincide, dovetail **9** acquiesce, harmonize, recognize, subscribe **10** correspond **11** acknowledge

agreeable 4 nice, open **5** ready **7** affable, welcome, willing **8** amenable, in accord, pleasant, pleasing **9** approving, congenial, congruous, consonant, favorable, receptive **10** acceptable, compatible, concurring, consenting, consistent **11** pleasurable, sympathetic

agreed 3 aye, yea, yep, yes **4** okay **8** all right, of course **9** certainly **10** definitely, positively

agreement 4 bond, deal, pact **6** accord, assent, treaty **7** bargain, compact, concord, consent, entente, harmony **8** contract, covenant **9** concordat **10** acceptance, consonance **11** arrangement, concordance, concurrence

agree with 3 fit **4** suit **5** befit **6** assist, become **7** support **10** go together

agricultural 5 rural **7** bucolic **8** agrarian, pastoral

agriculture 7 farming, tillage **8** agronomy, ranching **9** husbandry **11** cultivation, soil culture

Agrippina *brother:* 8 Caligula ***husband:* 8** Claudius ***son:* 4** Nero

aground 5 stuck **6** ashore **7** beached **8** disabled, stranded ***run:* 3** sew

ague 3 flu **5** chill, fever **7** malaria, shivers **9** influenza, shivering **10** blackwater

Ahab *daughter:* 8 Athaliah ***father:* 4** Omri ***prey:* 8** Moby-Dick ***ship:* 6** Pequod ***wife:* 7** Jezebel

Ahasuerus *kingdom:* 6 Persia ***wife:* 6** Esther, Vashti

Ahaz *kingdom:* 5 Judah ***son:* 8** Hezekiah ***wife:* 3** Abi

Ahaziah *father:* 4 Ahab **5** Joram **7** Jehoram ***kingdom:* 5** Judah **6** Israel ***mother:* 7** Jezebel **8** Athaliah ***sister:* 9** Jehosheba **11** Jehosobeath

ahead 4 ante, fore,on top **6** before, dormie, onward **7** earlier, forward, in front, leading, onwards **8** foremost, forwards, previous **9** in advance **10** beforehand

Ahinoam ***father:*** **7** Ahimaaz ***husband:*** **4** Saul **5** David ***son:*** **5** Amnon

Ah, Wilderness! author 6 O'Neill (Eugene)

aid 4 abet, care, hand, help, lift **6** assist, helper, relief, rescue, succor **7** backing, comfort, help out, support, sustain **8** befriend **9** assistant, attendant, subsidize **10** assistance, benefactor, mitigation **11** alleviation

Aida ***composer:*** **5** Verdi (Giuseppe) ***father:*** **8** Amonasro ***lover:*** **7** Radames ***rival:*** **7** Amneris

aide 4 ass't **6** deputy, helper, second **7** orderly **8** adjutant, sidekick **9** assistant, attendant, coadjutor **10** coadjutant, lieutenant

aikido 10 martial art

ail 4 ache, hurt, pain **5** upset, worry **6** bother **7** afflict, disturb, trouble **8** distress

ailing 3 ill, low **4** down, sick, weak **6** in pain, poorly, sickly, unwell **8** below par, diseased **9** enfeebled **10** indisposed **11** debilitated

ailment 6 malady, unrest **7** disease, ferment, illness, turmoil **8** disorder, disquiet, sickness, syndrome **9** affection, complaint, condition, infirmity **10** inquietude, uneasiness **11** disquietude, restiveness **12** restlessness

aim 3 end, try **4** cast, goal, head, mark, mean, plan, want, wish **5** angle, essay, focus, level, point, slant, train **6** aspire, design, desire, direct, intend, intent, object, strive, target, zero in **7** address, attempt, propose, purpose **8** ambition, endeavor **9** objective **11** contemplate

aimless 6 random **7** wayward **8** goalless **9** desultory, haphazard, hit-or-miss, irregular, pointless, unplanned **10** designless **11** purposeless

air 3 sky **4** aura, mien, mood, song, tune, vent **5** style **6** manner, melody, reveal, strain **7** bearing, divulge, express, feeling, quality **8** demeanor **9** broadcast, character, ventilate **10** atmosphere, deportment

aircraft 5 blimp, drone, plane **6** glider **7** airship, balloon, chopper **8** aerodyne, aerostat, airplane, jetliner, zeppelin **9** dirigible **10** helicopter ***carrier:*** **7** flattop ***designer:*** **6** Fokker (Anthony), Martin (Glenn) **7** Junkers (Hugo), Tupolev (Andrei) **8** Northrop (Jack), Sikorsky (Igor), Yakovlev (Alexander) **13** Messerschmitt (Willy)

airless 5 close **6** stuffy, sultry **8** stagnant, stifling **11** suffocating

airline 3 JAL, KLM, LOT, TWA **4** BOAC, El Al **5** Delta, Pan Am, USAir, Varig **6** Iberia, Qantas, Sabena, United, Virgin **7** Eastern, JetBlue, Olympic **8** Aeroflot, Alitalia, American, Swissair **9** Aer Lingus, Air France, Lufthansa, Northwest, Southwest, U.S. Airways **11** Continental, Pan American

airman 3 ace **5** flier, flyer, pilot **6** flyboy **7** aviator **8** aeronaut

air movement 4 gust, wind **5** draft **6** breath, breeze **7** updraft **9** downdraft

air navigation system 5 loran, navar, radar

airplane 3 jet **5** avion **6** bomber **7** fighter **8** autogiro, autogyro **9** transport ***A-bomb-dropper:*** **8** Enola Gay ***battle:*** **8** dogfight ***body:*** **8** fuselage ***engine:*** **3** jet **6** fanjet **7** propjet **8** turbofan, turbojet **9** turboprop ***engine casing:*** **7** nacellc ***engineless:*** **6** glider ***instrument:*** **5** radar, radio **7** compass **9** altimeter, gyroscope **10** tachometer **11** transponder ***maneuver:*** **4** buzz, dive, loop, roll **8** nosedive **9** chandelle **10** barrel roll ***movement:*** **3** yaw **4** bank, spin **5** pitch **8** tailspin ***part:*** **3** fin **4** flap, nose, prop, tail, wing **5** cabin, wheel **6** engine, rudder **7** aileron **8** airscrew, elevator **9** empennage, propeller **10** stabilizer ***pilotless:*** **5** drone ***safety machine:*** **6** deicer ***shelter:*** **6** hangar ***supersonic:*** **3** SST ***target:*** **6** drogue ***vapor:*** **8** contrail

air plant 6 orchid **8** epiphyte **9** bromeliad, kalanchoe **11** Spanish moss **12** strangler fig

airport 5 field **7** helipad **8** heliport **9** aerodrome ***abbreviation:*** **3** ETA, ETD ***building:*** **8** terminal ***flag:*** **8** windsock
name:
Atlanta: 10 Hartsfield **Boston: 5** Logan **Chicago: 5** O'Hare **6** Midway **Dublin: 7** Shannon **London: 7** Gatwick **8** Heathrow **Los Angeles: 3** LAX **New York: 3** JFK **7** Kennedy **9** La Guardia **Paris: 4** Orly **8** DeGaulle **9** Le Bourget **Rome: 7** Da Vinci **Washington: 6** Dulles, Reagan **8** National
part: **5** apron, tower **6** runway **7** taxiway

Airport author 6 Hailey (Arthur)

airs 4 pose, show **5** front **6** vanity **7** hauteur **8** pretense **9** loftiness, mannerism, vainglory **10** pretension **11** affectation, insincerity, ostentation **13** artificiality

airship 3 jet **5** blimp, plane **8** zeppelin **9** dirigible

airtight 4 shut **6** closed, sealed **7** certain **8** hermetic, ironclad **10** impervious **11** impermeable, irrefutable **12** indisputable, invulnerable **13** incontestable

airy 4 open, rare, thin **5** blowy, fresh, gusty, light, lofty, proud, windy **6** aerial, bouncy, breezy, dainty, unreal **7** buoyant, gaseous, soaring, tenuous **8** affected, animated, delicate, ethereal, graceful, illusory, rarefied, spirited, towering, vaporous, volatile **9** expansive, frivolous, pneumatic, resilient, sprightly, vivacious **10** diaphanous, ventilated **11** atmospheric, skyscraping **12** effervescent, high-spirited

Ajax **4** hero **5** Greek **7** warrior ***father:*** **6** Oileus **7** Telamon ***opponent:*** **6** Hector ***participant:*** **9** Trojan War

akin **4** like, same **5** alike **6** allied **7** kindred, related, similar, uniform **8** parallel **9** analogous, consonant **10** affiliated, comparable, compatible **11** consanguine **13** corresponding

Alabama ***capital:*** **10** Montgomery ***city:*** **5** Selma **6** Mobile **10** Birmingham, Huntsville, Tuscaloosa **12** Muscle Shoals ***college, university:*** **6** Auburn **8** Tuskegee ***mountain:*** **6** Cheaha ***nickname:*** **6** Cotton (State) **12** Heart of Dixie ***river:*** **6** Mobile **7** Alabama **9** Tombigbee ***state bird:*** **12** yellowhammer ***state flower:*** **8** camellia ***state tree:*** **12** longleaf pine

alacrity **8** dispatch **9** briskness, eagerness, quickness, readiness **10** enthusiasm, expedition, liveliness, promptness **11** promptitude, willingness **12** cheerfulness

Alamo ***city:*** **10** San Antonio ***hero:*** **5** Bowie (Jim) **6** Travis (William) **8** Crockett (Davy)

alamo **6** poplar **10** cottonwood

à la mode **4** chic, tony **6** trendy **7** dashing, stylish **8** up-to-date **9** exclusive **11** fashionable **12** with ice cream

alarm **3** SOS **4** bell, fear, horn **5** alert, dread, panic, scare, siren, spook, upset **6** dismay, excite, fright, signal, terror, tocsin **7** anxiety, disturb, red flag, startle, terrify, unnerve, warning **8** distress, frighten **9** terrorize **11** forewarning, trepidation **12** apprehension **13** consternation

alas **3** heu, woe **4** darn, drat **5** alack, oy vey **7** woe is me

Alaska ***capital:*** **6** Juneau ***city:*** **4** Nome **5** Sitka **6** Barrow **9** Anchorage, Fairbanks **10** Prudhoe Bay ***island group:*** **6** Kodiak **8** Aleutian, Pribilof ***mountain, range:*** **6** Brooks, Denali **8** McKinley, Wrangell ***nickname:*** **12** Last Frontier ***park:*** **6** Denali, Katmai ***river:*** **5** Yukon ***state bird:*** **9** ptarmigan ***state flower:*** **11** forget-me-not ***state tree:*** **11** sitka spruce

alb **4** gown **8** vestment

Albania ***capital:*** **6** Tirana, Tiranë ***city:*** **5** Korçë, Vlorë **6** Durrës **7** Shkodër ***ethnic group:*** **4** Gheg, Tosk ***monetary unit:*** **3** lek ***neighbor:*** **6** Greece **9** Macedonia **10** Montenegro ***part of:*** **7** Balkans ***peninsula:*** **6** Balkan ***sea:*** **8** Adriatic

albatross **5** check, goony, worry **6** burden, gooney **7** anxiety, seabird **9** hindrance, millstone, restraint **11** encumbrance

Albee play **7** Sandbox (The) **8** Seascape, Zoo Story (The) **9** Tiny Alice **13** American Dream (The) **14** Three Tall Women **16** A Delicate Balance **25** Who's Afraid of Virginia Woolf?

albeit **5** still, while **6** even if, much as, though **7** despite, whereas **8** although **10** even though

Alberta ***capital:*** **8** Edmonton ***city:*** **5** Banff **7** Calgary ***lake:*** **6** Claire, Louise **9** Athabasca ***mountain, range:*** **7** Rockies **8** Columbia ***provincial flower:*** **8** wild rose ***river:*** **4** Milk **5** Peace **9** Athabasca

Albion **7** England

album **3** ana **4** book **6** jacket, record **7** garland, omnibus **8** notebook, pictures, register **9** anthology, portfolio, scrapbook **10** collection, miscellany

Alcestis ***father:*** **6** Pelias ***husband:*** **7** Admetus ***rescuer:*** **8** Heracles, Hercules

alchemist **5** Faust **10** Paracelsus

alchemy **5** charm, magic **7** panacea, sorcery **8** wizardry **9** conjuring **10** necromancy

Alcina ***sister:*** **7** Morgana **10** Logistilla ***victim:*** **6** Rogero **8** Astolpho, Ruggiero

Alcinous ***daughter:*** **8** Nausicaa ***wife:*** **5** Arete

Alcmaeon ***father:*** **10** Amphiaraus ***mother:*** **8** Eriphyle ***wife:*** **10** Callirrhoe

Alcmene ***husband:*** **10** Amphitryon ***son:*** **8** Heracles, Hercules

alcohol **4** grog **5** booze, hooch, juice, sauce **6** hootch, liquor, red-eye, rotgut, tipple **7** spirits **8** home brew **9** aqua vitae, firewater, moonshine ***name:*** **4** amyl **5** butyl, cetyl, ethyl **6** glycol, methyl, sterol **7** butanol, ethanol, mannite, menthol **8** glycerin, glycerol, inositol, mannitol, methanol **9** isopropyl **11** cholesterol ***used in perfumes:*** **5** nerol **7** borneol **8** geraniol, linalool

alcoholic **4** hard **5** dipso, drunk **6** brewed **8** drunkard **9** distilled, fermented, inebriant, inebriate, spiritous **10** spirituous **11** dipsomaniac, inebriating **12** intoxicating

alcoholic drink see under **beverage**

Alcott novel **7** Jo's Boys **9** Little Men **11** Little Women

alcove **4** nook **5** niche **6** gazebo, recess **9** belvedere **11** summerhouse ***Japanese:*** **8** tokonoma

Alcyone ***father:*** **5** Atlas **6** Aeolus ***husband:*** **4** Ceyx ***mother:*** **7** Pleione ***sisters:*** **8** Pleiades

ale **3** nog **4** beer, brew, nogg

aleatory **4** iffy **5** dicey, risky, shaky **6** chancy **9** hazardous, uncertain **10** contingent, pre-

carious, vulnerable **11** problematic, speculative **13** unpredictable
alehouse 3 bar, pub **6** bistro, saloon, tavern **7** taproom **8** beer hall **10** beer garden **11** rathskeller
alembic 5 still **6** filter **9** distiller
alert 3 SOS **4** keen, warn **5** alarm, quick, ready, sharp, smart **6** brainy, bright, clever, lively, notify, tip off, tocsin **7** heedful, mindful, on guard, red flag, wakeful **8** animated, forewarn, open-eyed, vigilant, watchful **9** attentive, mercurial, sprightly, wide-awake **10** perceptive **11** intelligent, quick-witted ***Scottish:* 4** gleg **8** wakerife
Aleutian island 3 Fox **4** Adak, Atka, Attu, Near **5** Amlia, Kiska **6** Unimak **8** Unalaska **9** Andreanof ***town:* 11** Dutch Harbor
alewife 4 fish **7** herring **8** menhaden
Alexander *birthplace:* 5 Pella ***conquest:* 4** Tyre **5** Egypt, Issus **6** Greece, Persia **7** Parthia **8** Granicus ***father:* 6** Philip ***general:* 9** Antipater ***horse:* 10** Bucephalus ***kingdom:* 9** Macedonia ***mother:* 8** Olympias ***teacher:* 9** Aristotle ***wife:* 6** Roxana
alfalfa 3 hay **6** forage, legume **7** lucerne
alfresco 7 open-air, outdoor, outside **8** outdoors **9** out-of-door **10** out-of-doors
alga 6 desmid, diatom **7** seaweed ***blue-green:* 6** nostoc ***brown:* 4** kelp **5** fucus **8** rockweed ***green:* 9** chlorella ***red:* 4** nori
algebra term 4 root **6** factor **8** binomial, equation, monomial, variable **9** quadratic **10** polynomial
Algeria *capital:* 7 Algiers ***city:* 4** Bône, Oran **6** Annaba **11** Constantine ***coast:* 7** Barbary ***desert:* 6** Sahara ***ethnic group:* 4** Arab **6** Berber ***language:* 6** Arabic, Berber ***monetary unit:* 5** dinar ***mountain range:* 5** Atlas **12** Saharan Atlas ***neighbor:* 4** Mali **5** Libya, Niger **7** Morocco, Tunisia **10** Mauritania
Algren novel 17 Walk on the Wild Side (A) **19** Man with the Golden Arm (The)
Ali *son:* 5 Hasan **6** Husayn ***wife:* 6** Fatima
alias 3 AKA **6** anonym, handle **7** moniker, pen name **8** nickname **9** false name, pseudonym, stage name **10** also called, nom de plume **11** nom de guerre
Ali Baba's spell 10 Open Sesame
alibi 4 plea **5** clear, cover, proof **6** answer, excuse **7** account, cover up, defense, pretext **9** assertion, exonerate **11** explanation
alien 6 exotic **7** foreign, opposed, strange **8** estrange, outsider, stranger, transfer **9** estranged, extrinsic, foreigner, outlander **10** extraneous, outlandish **12** incompatible
alienate 4 part **5** repel **6** assign, convey, divide, offend, oppose **7** break up, turn off **8** disunify, disunite, estrange, separate, sign over, transfer **9** disaffect
alienation 5 break **6** breach **7** discord, divorce, rupture **8** division **10** conveyance, separation **12** disaffection, estrangement
alight 4 land **5** fiery **6** arrive, bright, on fire, settle **7** blazing, burning, deplane, descend, detrain, flaming, flaring, get down, glowing, ignited, shining **8** dismount **9** touch down **11** conflagrant
align 4 ally, join, line, true **5** agree, array, order, range **6** adjust, follow, line up **8** regulate **9** affiliate, associate **10** straighten
alike 4 akin, same **7** similar **8** parallel **9** analogous, consonant **10** comparable **13** corresponding
alikeness 6 simile **7** analogy **8** affinity, alliance, relation **9** closeness, semblance **10** comparison, connection, similarity, similitude **11** resemblance
aliment 4 eats, fare, feed, food, grub **7** nourish, nurture, sustain **9** nutriment **10** sustenance **11** nourishment
alimentary 9 nutritive **10** nourishing, sustaining **11** nutritional ***canal:* 7** enteron
alimony 4 keep **5** bread **6** living, upkeep **7** support **9** allowance, provision **10** livelihood, sustenance **11** maintenance, subsistence
alive 4 rife, spry **5** alert, awake, aware, brisk, fresh, quick, ready, vital **6** active, extant, living, moving, viable **7** animate, dynamic, knowing, replete, running, teeming, working, zestful **8** animated, existent, existing, sensible, sentient, swarming, thronged **9** abounding, breathing, cognizant, conscious, energetic, operative, sensitive, wide-awake **11** functioning, overflowing
alkali 4 base, salt **9** substance **11** soluble salt ***metal:* 6** cesium, sodium **7** lithium **8** francium, rubidium **9** potassium **10** monovalent ***opposite:* 4** acid
alkaline 5 acrid, basic, salty **6** bitter **7** antacid, caustic, soluble **8** chemical ***substance:* 3** lye **4** lime, soda **5** borax **6** potash **7** ammonia, antacid **8** pearl ash, saltwort **11** caustic soda
alkaloid 4 base ***medicinal:* 5** ergot **7** codeine, emetine, eserine, quinine **8** atropine, caffeine, lobeline, morphine **9** ephedrine, quinidine, reserpine **11** scopolamine ***narcotic:* 6** heroin **7** cocaine, codeine **8** morphine ***poisonous:* 8** atropine, nicotine, solanine **11** scopolamine
all 3 sum **4** each **5** every, gross, total, whole **6** entire, in toto, purely, wholly **7** exactly, totally, utterly **8** complete, entirety, everyone,

outright, totality **9** aggregate, everybody **10** altogether, everything ***combining form:*** **3** pan **4** omni, pant

all-around 7 general, overall, skilled **8** complete, sweeping, synoptic **9** adaptable, competent, many-sided, panoramic, universal, versatile **10** consummate, proficient **11** wide-ranging **12** encompassing **13** comprehensive

allay 4 balm, calm, ease, lull **5** abate, quell, quiet, still **6** lessen, reduce, settle, soothe, subdue **7** assuage, compose, lighten, mollify, quieten, relieve **8** decrease, diminish, mitigate, moderate **9** alleviate **11** tranquilize

all but 4 most, much, nigh **5** about **6** almost, nearly **8** as much as, in effect **9** just about, virtually **11** essentially, practically

All Creatures Great and Small author 7 Herriot (James)

allegation 5 claim **6** charge, report **9** assertion, statement **10** contention, profession **11** declaration

allege 3 say **4** avow, cite **5** claim, offer, state **6** adduce, assert, attest, charge, submit **7** advance, contend, declare, present, profess **8** maintain **10** put forward

alleged 7 accused, dubious, reputed, suspect **8** doubtful, so-called, supposed **9** described, pretended, purported, soi-disant **10** ostensible, self-styled **12** questionable

allegiance 4 duty **5** ardor, piety **6** fealty, homage **7** loyalty **8** devotion, fidelity **9** adherence, constancy, obedience **10** dedication, obligation **11** devotedness **12** faithfulness

allegiant 4 firm, true **5** liege, loyal **6** ardent, steady **7** devoted, dutiful, staunch **8** constant, faithful, resolute **9** steadfast **10** dependable

allegorical 5 moral **6** fabled **8** mythical, symbolic **9** legendary, spiritual **10** emblematic, exegetical, fictitious, figurative **12** iconographic, illustrative, metaphorical

allegory 4 myth, tale **5** fable, story **6** emblem, symbol **7** parable **8** apologue **9** symbolism **10** figuration **12** typification

allegro 4 fast **5** brisk **6** bouncy, lively **8** animated, spirited **9** sprightly

Allende novel 17 House of the Spirits (The)

allergy 5 dread **6** hatred **7** disgust, dislike **8** aversion, distaste, hay fever **9** antipathy, disliking, rejection, repulsion

alleviate 4 cure, ease **5** allay **6** lessen, reduce, remedy **7** assuage, lighten, mollify, relieve **8** decrease, diminish, mitigate

alleviation 4 ease **6** relief **7** decline **8** decrease, easement **9** lessening, reduction **10** diminution, mitigation

alley 4 lane, walk **6** marble, street **7** passage **10** backstreet

all-fired 7 totally, utterly **9** extremely **10** absolutely, completely **11** excessively

alliance 3 tie **4** axis, bloc, bond, pact **5** union **6** accord, league, treaty **7** compact, concord **8** affinity, relation **9** coalition **10** connection, federation **11** affiliation, association, combination, confederacy, conjunction, partnership, unification **12** relationship **13** confederation ***international:*** **3** CIS, OAS **4** APEC, EFTA, NATO, OECD, OPEC **5** ASEAN, CENTO, NORAD, SEATO **7** CARICOM **8** Interpol **10** Warsaw Pact

allied 4 akin **5** bound **6** agnate, joined, linked, united **7** cognate, connate, kindred, related, unified **8** in league **9** connected **10** affiliated, associated, connatural **11** consanguine

alligator 11 crocodilian ***relative:*** **4** croc **6** caiman, cayman **9** crocodile

alligator pear 7 avocado

all in 4 dead, used, worn **5** spent, tired **6** bushed, done in, used up **7** drained, fargone, worn-out **8** depleted **9** dead tired, exhausted, washed-out

all in all 5 in all **6** mainly **7** en masse, largely **9** generally **10** altogether, by and large, on the whole

All in the Family *character:* **5** Edith (Bunker) **6** Archie (Bunker), Gloria **7** Michael ***creator:*** **4** Lear (Norman) ***nickname:*** **7** Dingbat **8** Meathead ***setting:*** **6** Queens **7** Astoria ***star:*** **6** Reiner (Rob) **7** O'Connor (Carroll) **9** Stapleton (Jean), Struthers (Sally) ***theme song:*** **16** Those Were the Days

allocate 4 give **5** allot, slice **6** assign, divide **7** dish out, divvy up, dole out, earmark, mete out, prorate **8** set apart **9** admeasure, apportion, designate **10** distribute

allocution 4 talk **5** spiel **6** sermon, speech **7** address, lecture, oration, oratory, pep talk **11** exhortation

allot 4 give **5** grant, share **6** accord, assign **7** deal out, divvy up, dole out, mete out **8** allocate, dispense, set aside **9** admeasure, apportion **10** distribute

allotment 3 cut, lot **4** bite, part **5** chunk, piece, quota, share, slice **6** ration **7** measure, portion **9** allowance, provision **13** apportionment

all-out 4 full **5** total **6** entire, utmost **7** maximum **8** absolute, complete, thorough **9** full-blown, full-scale, unlimited **12** totalitarian **13** thoroughgoing

all over 8 wherever **9** all around **10** everyplace, everywhere, far and near, far and wide, high and low, thoroughly, throughout

allow 3 let, lot, own **4** avow, give **5** admit, allot, brook, grant, leave, let on, stand **6** assign, endure, permit, suffer **7** concede, confess, consent, entitle, forbear, mete out **8** allocate, tolerate **9** apportion **11** acknowledge

allowance 3 aid, cut, lot, pay, sum **4** bite, edge, help, part, tare, tret **5** grant, leave, piece, quota, share, slice **6** amount, permit, ration **7** consent, measure, partage, portion, quantum, subsidy, vantage **8** handicap, pittance, quantity, sanction **9** advantage, allotment, head start, reduction **10** adjustment, allocation, assistance, concession, permission, sufferance, toleration **13** accommodation, apportionment, authorization

alloy 5 blend **6** fusion **7** amalgam, mixture **8** compound **9** admixture, composite **10** adulterant **11** interfusion **12** amalgamation, intermixture ***brass-like:*** **6** latten ***copper-sulfur:*** **6** niello ***copper-tin:*** **6** bronze ***copper-zinc:*** **5** brass **6** tombac ***enamel-like:*** **6** niello ***gold-like:*** **6** ormolu ***gold-silver:*** **8** electrum ***iron-carbon:*** **5** steel ***iron-nickel:*** **5** invar ***mercury:*** **7** amalgam ***tin-lead:*** **5** terne **6** pewter, solder ***used in jewelry:*** **6** tombac

all-powerful 6 mighty **7** supreme **8** absolute, almighty **10** invincible, omnipotent **11** controlling

all right 3 A-OK, aye, yea, yep, yes **4** good, okay, safe, well **5** A-okay **6** agreed, decent, proper, surely **7** average **8** adequate, of course, passable, passably, pleasing, standard, very well **9** agreeable, certainly, tolerable, tolerably **10** acceptably, adequately, definitely, positively, sufficient, well enough **12** satisfactory

all round see **all-around**

All the King's Men author 6 Warren (Robert Penn)

allude 4 hint **5** imply, point, refer **7** bring up, suggest **8** indicate, intimate

allure 4 draw, pull **5** charm, tempt **6** appeal, entice, lead on, seduce **7** attract, beguile, enchant, glamour, win over **8** charisma, inveigle, persuade **9** captivate, fascinate, magnetism, magnetize **10** attraction **11** enchantment, fascination

alluring 4 sexy **6** lovely **7** winning, winsome **8** charming, inviting, pleasing **9** appealing, beguiling, glamorous, seductive **10** appetizing, attractive, bewitching, enchanting **11** captivating, fascinating

ally 4 join **5** unite **6** friend, helper **7** comrade, partner **8** federate **9** accessory, affiliate, associate, auxiliary, bedfellow, colleague, supporter **10** accomplice **11** confederate **12** collaborator

almighty 4 very **6** hugely, mighty **7** awfully, godlike, supreme **8** absolute **9** extremely **10** invincible, omnipotent **11** all-powerful, exceedingly

almost 4 nigh **5** about **6** all but, nearly **8** as good as, as much as, not quite, well-nigh **9** just about, virtually **11** essentially, practically **13** approximately ***Scottish:*** **6** feckly

alms 4 gift **6** relief **7** present **8** donation, offering **10** assistance **11** benefaction, beneficence **12** contribution

aloe 9 emollient, succulent

Aloeus ***father:*** **7** Neptune **8** Poseidon ***mother:*** **6** Canace ***son:*** **4** Otus **9** Ephialtes ***wife:*** **9** Iphimedia

aloft 4 high, over **5** above **6** on high, upward **7** skyward **8** in flight, overhead

aloha 4 by-by, ciao, hail **5** hello, howdy **6** bye-bye, good-by, so long **7** good-bye, welcome **8** farewell, greeting **9** greetings ***State:*** **6** Hawaii

alone 4 only, sole, solo, stag **5** apart **6** singly, solely, unique, wholly **7** isolate, removed **8** detached, entirely, isolated, peerless, singular, solitary **9** matchless, unequaled, unmatched, unrivaled **10** nothing but, unequalled, unexampled, unexcelled **11** exclusively, unsurpassed **12** incomparable, unparalleled, unrepeatable **13** unaccompanied

aloneness 8 solitude **9** isolation, seclusion **10** uniqueness

along 3 too, yet **4** also, near, with **5** forth, there **6** as well, at hand, on hand, onward **7** besides, forward **8** likewise, moreover **11** furthermore **12** accompanying, additionally

alongside 6 beside, next to **8** touching **9** adjoining, bordering

aloof 3 shy **4** cold, cool **5** apart, proud **6** casual, chilly, frigid, offish, remote **7** distant, haughty, removed, stuck up **8** arrogant, detached, reserved, reticent, solitary **9** incurious, unbending, uncurious, withdrawn **10** disdainful, restrained, unfriendly, unsociable **11** constrained, indifferent, standoffish, unconcerned **12** uninterested **13** disinterested

alopecia 8 baldness

alp 4 peak **5** mount **8** mountain

alpaca 4 wool **5** cloth **6** mammal ***habitat:*** **4** Peru **5** Andes **7** Bolivia

alpha 4 dawn **5** first, start **6** outset **7** dawning, genesis, opening **9** beginning **12** commencement

alphabet **4** ABC's **7** letters ***Arabic:*** **2** ba, fa, ha, ra, ta, ya, za **3** ayn, dad, dal, gaf, jim, kaf, kha, lam, mim, nun, qaf, sad, sin, tha, waw, zay **4** alif, dhal, shin **5** ghayn ***Greek:*** **2** mu, nu, pi, xi **3** chi, eta, phi, psi, rho, tau **4** beta, iota, zeta **5** alpha, delta, gamma, kappa, omega, sigma, theta **6** lambda **7** epsilon, omicron, upsilon ***Hebrew:*** **2** he, pe **3** mem, nun, sin, taw, tet, vav, waw, yod **4** alef, ayin, beth, heth, kaph, koph, qoph, resh, shin, teth **5** aleph, gimel, lamed, sadhe, tsade, zayin **6** daleth, samekh ***Old Irish:*** **4** ogam **5** ogham ***runic:*** **7** futhark

Alpheus ***beloved:*** **8** Arethusa ***father:*** **7** Oceanus ***form:*** **5** river ***mother:*** **6** Tethys

Alpine ***animal:*** **4** ibex **7** chamois ***dress:*** **6** dirndl ***house:*** **6** chalet ***lake:*** **4** Como, Iseo **5** Garda **6** Geneva **7** Lucerne **8** Bodensee, Maggiore **9** Constance, Neuchâtel ***pass:*** **3** col **5** Cenis **7** Brenner, Simplon **9** St. Bernard ***peak:*** **5** Blanc, Eiger **7** Bernina **8** Jungfrau **10** Matterhorn ***plant:*** **9** edelweiss ***primrose:*** **8** auricula ***resort:*** **5** Davos **7** Bolzano, Zermatt **8** Chamonix, Grenoble, St. Moritz **9** Innsbruck **10** Interlaken **11** Saint Moritz ***river:*** **5** Rhine, Rhône ***snowfield:*** **4** firn, névé ***staff:*** **10** alpenstock ***state:*** **5** Tirol, Tyrol ***tunnel:*** **5** Blanc, Cenis **7** Arlberg, Simplon **10** St. Gotthard ***wind:*** **4** bora, föhn **5** foehn

already **4** even, once **5** by now, prior **6** before, by then **7** earlier, just now **8** formerly **9** before now **10** by this time, heretofore, previously

also **3** and, too **4** more, plus **5** again, along **6** as well **7** besides, further **8** likewise, moreover **9** along with, including, similarly **10** in addition **11** furthermore **12** additionally

also-ran **3** dud **5** loser **7** failure, wannabe, washout **8** defeated, runner-up

altar **6** shrine ***boy:*** **6** server **7** acolyte ***cloth:*** **4** pall **7** frontal ***constellation:*** **3** Ara ***hanging:*** **6** dorsal, dossal ***platform:*** **8** predella ***screen:*** **7** reredos ***shelf:*** **7** retable ***site:*** **4** apse, bema ***vessel:*** **5** cruet, paten **7** chalice **8** ciborium **10** monstrance

alter **3** fix **4** geld, spay, turn, vary **5** adapt **6** adjust, change, doctor, modify, mutate, neuter, revamp **7** remodel **8** castrate, moderate, modulate **9** refashion

alteration **4** turn **5** shift **6** change **8** mutation, revision **9** variation **10** adaptation, adjustment, changeover, conversion, remodeling, transition **12** modification

altercate **4** spat, tiff **5** argue, scrap **6** bicker, hassle **7** dispute, quarrel, wrangle **8** squabble **9** caterwaul

altercation **3** row **4** beef, flap, spat, tiff **5** brawl **6** blowup, combat, fracas, hassle **7** contest, dispute, quarrel, rhubarb, wrangle **8** argument, squabble **9** bickering **10** falling-out **11** controversy, embroilment

alternate **3** sub **5** proxy **6** backup, by turn, change, fill-in, rotate, second **7** another, relieve, stand-in **8** periodic, rotating **9** change off, fluctuate, recurrent, recurring, replacing, surrogate **10** equivalent, every other, periodical, substitute **11** every second, pinch hitter, replacement **12** intermittent

alternately **6** in lieu, rather **7** instead **10** preferably

alternative **5** other, proxy **6** backup, choice, option, second **7** another **8** atypical, druthers, election **9** different, selection, surrogate **10** preference, substitute **11** contingency, nonstandard, possibility

Althaea ***father:*** **8** Thestius ***husband:*** **6** Oeneus ***son (victim):*** **8** Meleager

although **4** when **5** still, while **6** albeit, even if, much as **7** despite, howbeit, whereas

altitude **6** height **8** eminence **9** elevation, high level

altitudinous **4** high, tall **7** eminent **8** elevated

alto **3** Day (Doris), Lee (Peggy) **4** Cher, Kitt (Eartha), Piaf (Edith) **5** Baker (Janet), Lenya (Lotte) **6** London (Julie), Merman (Ethel) **7** Clooney (Rosemary), Ferrier (Kathleen), Vaughan (Sarah) **8** Anderson (Marian), Dietrich (Marlene) **9** Forrester (Maureen) **10** Chookasian (Lili) **13** Schumann-Heink (Ernestine)

altogether **4** nude, well **5** fully, in all, quite **6** in toto, wholly **7** all told, en masse, exactly, totally, utterly **8** all in all, entirely **9** generally, perfectly **10** absolutely, by and large, completely, on the whole, thoroughly

altruism **7** charity **8** sympathy **10** compassion, generosity **11** benevolence **12** philanthropy, selflessness **13** unselfishness

altruistic **3** big **6** humane **8** generous **9** unselfish **10** benevolent, bighearted, charitable, open-handed **11** considerate, magnanimous, noble-minded **12** humanitarian **13** philanthropic

alum **4** grad **6** emetic **7** styptic **8** graduate **10** astringent

aluminum ***source:*** **7** bauxite ***symbol:*** **2** Al

always **3** e'er **4** ever **7** forever **8** evermore, for keeps **9** at any rate, endlessly, eternally **10** at all times, constantly, in any event, invariably **11** continually, forevermore, in perpetuum, perpetually, unceasingly **12** consistently, continuously

Amahl and the Night Visitors composer 7 Menotti (Gian Carlo)
amalgamate 3 mix **4** ally, fuse, meld, pool **5** admix, alloy, merge, unify, unite **6** mingle **7** combine **8** coalesce, compound, intermix **9** commingle, integrate **11** consolidate, intermingle
amalgamation 5 alloy, blend, union **6** fusion, merger **7** joining, melding, merging, mixture, uniting **8** alliance, compound **9** admixture, coalition, composite **10** commixture **12** intermixture **13** consolidation
Amalthea ***form:*** **4** goat ***horn:*** **10** cornucopia ***nursling:*** **4** Zeus
amanita 8 death cap, mushroom **9** fly agaric **10** death angel
amanuensis 6 scribe **7** copyist **9** scrivener, secretary **11** transcriber **12** stenographer
amass 4 bulk, heap, make, pile **5** hoard, lay up, store, uplay **6** accrue, garner, gather, pile up, roll up **7** acquire, collect, compile, round up, store up **8** assemble, cumulate **9** aggregate, stockpile **10** accumulate **12** come together
amassment 4 pile **5** clump, group, hoard, stack, stock, store, trove **7** cluster **8** assembly, quantity **9** gathering, stockpile **10** assemblage, collection, cumulation **11** aggregation **12** accumulation **13** agglomeration
amateur 4 tyro **6** layman, novice, tinker, votary **7** admirer, dabbler, devotee, learner **8** aspirant, beginner, neophyte, putterer **9** greenhorn, smatterer **10** apprentice, dilettante, enthusiast, uninitiate **11** abecedarian
amateurish 3 raw **5** green **6** simple **7** artless **8** dabbling, inexpert **9** deficient, unskilled, untutored **10** dilettante, unfinished, unpolished, unskillful **12** dilettantist, unproficient **13** inexperienced
amative see **amorous**
amatory 6 ardent, erotic, loving, tender **7** sensual **8** romantic **9** erogenous, seductive **10** passionate **11** aphrodisiac
amaze 4 daze **5** floor **6** wonder **7** astound, nonplus, perplex, startle **8** astonish, bewilder, blow away, bowl over, confound, surprise **9** dumbfound **10** admiration **11** flabbergast
amazement 3 awe **6** marvel, wonder **8** surprise **9** marveling **10** admiration, perplexity, wonderment **12** astonishment, bewilderment, confoundment
amazing 7 awesome **8** striking, stunning, wondrous **9** marvelous, startling, wonderful **10** astounding, impressive, miraculous, stupendous, surprising **11** astonishing, bewildering, spectacular **12** breathtaking
Amazon 6 parrot **8** giantess **12** woman warrior ***tributary:*** **5** Negro (Rio)
ambassador 5 agent, envoy **6** legate **8** diplomat, emissary **9** messenger ***papal:*** **6** nuncio
amber 5 ocher, ochre, resin, rosin **6** orange, yellow **7** saffron
ambience 4 aura, mood, tone **6** flavor, medium, milieu **7** climate **10** atmosphere **11** environment **12** surroundings
ambient 5 music **6** milieu **7** general, setting **8** everyday **9** prevalent **10** atmosphere, prevailing **11** atmospheric, environment, mise-en-scène **12** encompassing, surroundings **13** environmental
ambiguity 5 doubt **6** enigma, puzzle **7** evasion **9** equivoque, obscurity, vagueness **11** incertitude, uncertainty **12** doubtfulness, equivocality, equivocation **13** double meaning
ambiguous 5 vague **6** opaque, unsure **7** cryptic, dubious, inexact, obscure, unclear **8** doubtful, puzzling, two-edged **9** enigmatic, equivocal, tenebrous, uncertain, unsettled **10** indefinite, inexplicit **11** problematic **12** inconclusive, questionable
ambit 4 area, room **5** field, limit, orbit, range, reach, scope, space, sweep **6** border, bounds, extent, limits, radius, sphere **7** breadth, circuit, compass, expanse, purview **8** boundary, confines **9** extension, perimeter, periphery **13** circumference
ambition 3 aim **4** goal, hope, itch, push, wish, zeal **5** ardor, dream, drive, vigor **6** desire, energy, hunger, spirit, target, thirst **7** avidity, craving, purpose **8** appetite, striving, yearning **9** eagerness, intention, objective **10** aspiration, enterprise, enthusiasm, get-up-and-go, initiative, pretension
ambitious 4 avid, bold, keen **5** eager, pushy **6** driven, hungry, intent **7** driving, zealous **8** aspiring, desirous, striving **9** energetic **10** aggressive **11** hard-working **12** enterprising, enthusiastic
ambivalent 5 mixed **6** unsure **7** warring **8** clashing, wavering **9** equivocal, uncertain, undecided **10** unresolved **11** fluctuating, vacillating **13** contradictory
amble 4 gait, walk **5** dally, drift, mosey **6** dawdle, linger, stroll, wander **7** meander, saunter
ambrosia 6 dainty, regale **7** dessert, perfume **8** delicacy, ointment
ambrosial 5 balmy, spicy, sweet **6** savory **7** scented **8** aromatic, fragrant, heavenly, luscious, perfumed, pleasing, redolent **9** deli-

cious **10** delectable, delightful **11** scrumptious
ambulate 4 hoof, move, pace, step, walk **5** tread, troop **6** foot it, hoof it **7** traipse
ambulatory 6 moving, on foot, roving **7** nomadic, roaming, walking **8** vagabond **9** itinerant **11** peripatetic
ambush 4 jump, lurk, trap **5** snare **6** assail, attack, entrap, lay for, waylay **7** assault, ensnare **8** surprise **9** ambuscade **11** concealment
ameliorate 3 fix **4** help, lift, mend **5** amend, raise **6** better, perk up, remedy, reform **7** elevate, enhance, improve, lighten, relieve, upgrade **8** mitigate **9** alleviate **10** convalesce, recuperate
amenable 4 open, tame **6** docile, liable, pliant, suited **7** plastic, pliable, subdued, subject, willing **8** biddable, in accord, obedient, yielding **9** adaptable, agreeable, complying, malleable, receptive, tractable **10** answerable, consenting, responsive, submissive **11** accountable, acquiescent, cooperative, responsible
amend 3 fix **4** help **5** alter, right **6** better, change, modify, reform, remedy, repair, revise, square **7** correct, improve, rectify **8** put right **9** meliorate **10** ameliorate
amendment 5 rider **6** change **7** codicil **8** addendum, revision **10** alteration, attachment, correction **11** enhancement, improvement **12** modification
amends 7 redress **8** reprisal **9** indemnity, quittance **10** recompense, reparation **11** restitution **12** compensation
amenities 5 mores **6** polish **7** decorum, manners **8** civility, courtesy **9** etiquette, propriety **12** social graces
amenity 5 charm, frill **6** luxury **7** comfort, quality **8** civility, courtesy, facility **9** advantage, etiquette, geniality, pleasance **10** affability, amiability, betterment, cordiality, enrichment, pleasantry, politeness **11** convenience, enhancement, improvement, sociability **12** agreeability, graciousness, pleasantness
ament 6 catkin
amerce 3 tax **4** dock, fine, levy **5** exact, mulct **6** punish **7** hit with, make pay **8** penalize
amercement 4 fine **5** mulct **7** damages, forfeit, penalty **10** assessment, punishment, reparation
American League *Baltimore:* 7 Orioles ***Boston:* 6** Red Sox ***Los Angeles:* 6** Angels (of Anaheim) ***Chicago:* 8** White Sox ***Cleveland:* 7** Indians ***Detroit:* 6** Tigers ***Kansas City:* 6** Royals ***Minnesota:* 5** Twins ***New York:* 7** Yankees ***Oakland:* 9** Athletics ***Seattle:* 8** Mariners ***Tampa Bay:* 9** Rays ***Texas:* 7** Rangers ***Toronto:* 8** Blue Jays
American Samoa *capital:* 8 Pago Pago ***island, island group:* 4** Rose **5** Aunuu, Manua **6** Swains **7** Tutuila ***language:* 6** Samoan
America's Cup winner 6 Ranger **7** Alinghi, Freedom **8** Columbia, Intrepid **9** Weatherly **10** Black Magic, Courageous
America, the Beautiful *music:* 4 Ward (Samuel Augustus) ***words:* 5** Bates (Katherine Lee)
americium symbol 2 Am
Amfortas *father:* 7 Titurel ***opera:* 8** Parsifal
amiability 7 amenity **9** geniality, pleasance **10** cordiality **11** sociability **12** complaisance, congeniality, friendliness, pleasantness, sociableness **13** agreeableness, enjoyableness
amiable 4 kind, warm **6** genial, gentle, kindly **7** affable, cordial, likable **8** cheerful, friendly, gracious, likeable, obliging, sociable **9** agreeable, congenial, courteous **10** responsive **11** complaisant, good-humored, good-natured, warmhearted
amicable 7 cordial, pacific **8** empathic, friendly, peaceful, sociable **9** congenial, peaceable **10** harmonious, like-minded, neighborly **11** sympathetic **13** understanding
amid 4 over **5** among, midst **6** during **7** amongst, between **10** throughout
amigo 3 pal **4** chum, mate, pard **6** friend **7** comrade, partner **8** sidekick **9** companion, confidant **12** acquaintance
amino acid 4 dopa **6** leucin, lysine, serine, toluid, valine **7** cystein, cystine, glycine, leucine, proline, toluide **8** cysteine, dopamine, histidin, thyroxin, toluidin, tyrosine
Amis, Kingsley *novel:* 8 Lucky Jim ***son:* 6** Martin
Amis, Martin *father:* 8 Kingsley ***novel:* 5** Money **10** Time's Arrow **11** Information (The) **12** London Fields
amiss 3 bad **4** awry, poor **5** badly, wrong **6** afield, astray, faulty, flawed **7** wrongly **8** erringly, faultily **9** defective, imperfect **10** improperly, mistakenly, out of place **11** erroneously, imperfectly, incorrectly, unfavorably **12** inaccurately **13** inappropriate
amity 5 union **6** accord, comity, unison **7** concert, concord, harmony **8** alliance, goodwill **9** agreement **10** cordiality, friendship, kindliness **11** concurrence **12** friendliness
Ammonite 6 Semite ***god:* 6** Molech, Moloch
ammunition 4 ammo, shot **5** bombs **6** rounds,

shells **7** charges **8** armament, grenades, missiles, ordnance **10** cartridges **11** projectiles

Amneris's rival 4 Aïda

amnesty 6 pardon **7** freeing, release **8** immunity, reprieve **9** discharge **10** absolution **11** forgiveness **12** dispensation

Amnon *father:* 5 David ***half sister:* 5** Tamar ***mother:* 7** Ahinoam

amoeba 4 blob **8** rhizopod **9** protozoan

Amon *father:* 8 Manasseh ***son:* 6** Josiah

Amonasro's daughter 4 Aïda

among 3 mid **4** amid **5** midst **6** amidst, within **7** between ***other things:* 9** inter alia ***prefix:* 5** inter

amorist 4 rake, wolf **5** lover, Romeo **7** Don Juan, gallant, playboy **8** Casanova, lothario, paramour **9** womanizer **12** heartbreaker

amorous 6 ardent, erotic, in love **7** amative, amatory, lustful **8** enamored, romantic **10** infatuated, passionate **11** aphrodisiac, impassioned

amorousness 4 love, lust **5** amour, ardor **6** desire **7** passion **9** eroticism

amorphous 7 unclear **8** formless, inchoate, nebulous, unformed, unshaped **9** shapeless, undefined **10** indistinct **11** nondescript **12** disorganized **13** characterless ***mass:* 4** blob

amortize 5 repay **6** pay off, reduce **7** pay down **8** write off

amount 4 bulk, dose **5** add up, equal, price, total **6** dosage, matter, number, upshot **7** purport, quantum **8** quantity **9** aggregate, substance ***owed:* 4** debt ***small:* 3** bit, jot **4** atom, drop, iota, mite, whit **5** minim, spark, speck, trace **7** modicum, smidgen **8** molecule, particle **9** scintilla

amour 4 love **5** fling, lover **6** affair **7** liaison, passion, romance **8** intimacy, intrigue **9** dalliance **10** love affair **12** entanglement, relationship

amour propre 5 pride **6** egoism, vanity **7** conceit, egotism **8** self-love, vainness **9** vainglory **10** narcissism, self-esteem, self-regard **11** self-conceit, self-respect **12** pridefulness **13** conceitedness

amphetamines 5 speed **6** dexies, hearts, uppers **7** bennies, Dexoxyn **8** greenies, pep pills, Preludin **9** Dexedrine **10** Benzedrine, Methedrine

amphibian *burrowing:* 9 caecilian ***genus:* 4** Hyla, Rana ***legless:* 9** caecilian ***tailed:* 3** eft **4** newt **10** salamander ***tailless:* 4** frog, toad **8** bullfrog, tree toad **10** batrachian ***wormlike:* 9** caecilian ***young:* 7** tadpole **8** polliwog

Amphion *brother:* 6 Zethus ***conquest:* 6** Thebes ***father:* 4** Zeus ***mother:* 7** Antiope ***sister:* 5** Aedon ***wife:* 5** Niobe

amphitheater 4 bowl **5** arena **7** stadium **8** coliseum **10** auditorium, hippodrome

Amphitrite *father:* 6 Nereus ***husband:* 7** Neptune **8** Poseidon ***mother:* 5** Doris ***son:* 6** Triton

Amphitryon's wife 7 Alcmene

amphora 3 jar, jug, urn **4** ewer, vase **5** crock, flask **6** carafe, flagon, vessel

ample 4 wide **5** buxom, great, large, roomy **6** lavish, plenty, portly **7** copious, liberal, profuse **8** abundant, generous, handsome, spacious **9** bounteous, bountiful, capacious, expansive, extensive, plenteous, plentiful **10** commodious, sufficient **11** substantial

amplify 5 boost, raise, swell **6** dilate, expand, extend, jack up **7** augment, develop, distend, enhance, enlarge, inflate, magnify **8** increase **9** elaborate, intensify **10** supplement

amplitude 4 size **5** range, scale, scope, space **6** amount, extent, spread **7** bigness, breadth, expanse, stretch **8** distance, fullness, wideness **9** abundance, expansion, greatness, largeness, magnitude, roominess **12** spaciousness **13** capaciousness

amulet 4 juju, luck **5** charm **6** fetish, grigri, mascot **7** periapt **8** gris-gris, talisman **10** lucky piece, phylactery **11** rabbit's-foot

amuse 4 wile **5** charm, cheer **6** appeal, divert, engage, occupy, please, regale, tickle **7** animate, beguile, delight, enchant, enliven, gladden **8** distract, interest, recreate **9** entertain, fascinate

amusement 3 fun **4** play **7** delight, pastime **8** pleasure **9** diversion, enjoyment **10** recreation **11** distraction

amusing 3 fun **5** droll, funny **7** comical, risible **8** engaging, humorous, pleasing **9** diverting, enjoyable **9** laughable **12** entertaining

Amycus *father:* 7 Neptune **8** Poseidon ***friend:* 8** Heracles, Hercules ***mother:* 5** Melia

ana 5 album, varia **7** sayings **9** anecdotes, anthology **10** collection, miscellany **11** memorabilia, miscellanea

anabasis 5 march **7** advance, headway, retreat **8** progress **11** advancement, progression

anagogic 6 arcane, hidden, mystic, occult, secret **7** obscure **8** esoteric, mystical, telestic **9** spiritual **10** symbolical **11** allegorical

analects 5 album **6** digest **7** garland, omnibus **8** treasury **9** anthology, selection **10** compendium, miscellany **11** compilation, florilegium

analgesic **6** opiate **7** anodyne **10** anesthetic, painkiller
analogous **4** akin, like **5** alike **7** kindred, similar, related, uniform **8** parallel **9** consonant **10** comparable, equivalent, resembling
analogue **5** match **7** cognate **8** parallel **9** correlate **10** similarity **11** correlation, counterpart, equivalence **13** correspondent
analogy **6** simile **8** affinity, likeness, metaphor, parallel, relation **9** agreement, alikeness, semblance **10** comparison, similarity, similitude **11** correlation, equivalence, resemblance
analysis **5** assay, audit, proof, study **6** method, review, report, survey **7** finding, inquiry **8** division **9** breakdown, partition, statement **10** dissection, inspection, resolution, separation **11** examination **13** clarification
analytic **6** cogent, subtle **7** logical, testing **8** studious **9** organized **10** diagnostic, scientific, systematic **11** proposition, questioning **13** investigative, ratiocinative
analyze **4** part, test **5** assay, parse, study **6** divide **7** dissect, examine, inspect, resolve **8** classify, consider, separate **9** anatomize, break down, decompose, interpret **10** decompound, scrutinize **11** deconstruct, distinguish, investigate
Ananias **4** liar **9** falsifier **12** prevaricator ***father:*** **9** Nedebaeus ***wife (coconspirator):*** **8** Sapphira
anarchism **4** riot **6** theory **7** misrule **8** disorder **9** distemper, rebellion **11** lawlessness
anarchist **5** rebel **6** rioter **8** agitator, mutineer, provoker, revolter **9** dissident, insurgent **10** malcontent **11** provocateur **13** revolutionary ***famous:*** **6** Tucker (Benjamin), Zerzan (John) **7** Bakunin (Mikhail), Chomsky (Noam), Goldman (Emma), Stirner (Max) **8** Christie (Stuart), Proudhon (Pierre-Joseph) **9** Kropotkin (Peter)
anarchy **4** riot **5** chaos **7** misrule, mob rule, turmoil **8** disarray, disorder **9** confusion, distemper, mobocracy, rebellion **10** ochlocracy, revolution **11** lawlessness **13** nongovernment
anathema **3** ban **4** bane **5** curse, enemy, odium, taboo **6** pariah **7** bugbear, censure, malison, outcast, reproof **8** loathing **9** damnation, bête noire **10** black beast, execration **11** abomination, commination, detestation, imprecation, malediction **12** condemnation, denunciation
anathematize **3** ban **4** damn, oust **5** curse, expel **6** banish **7** condemn **8** denounce, execrate **9** objurgate, proscribe **13** excommunicate
anatomical depression **5** fossa, fovea
anatomical tube **3** vas **4** duct **5** canal
anatomist **5** Wolff (Kaspar) **6** Harvey (William) **8** Vesalius (Andreas)
anatomize **5** cut up **7** analyze, dissect **8** separate **9** break down, decompose
anatomy **5** frame, mummy **6** makeup **8** analysis, division, skeleton **9** framework, histology, structure **10** dissection, morphology, physiology **11** examination
Anaxo ***brother:*** **10** Amphitryon ***daughter:*** **7** Alcmene ***father:*** **7** Alcaeus ***husband:*** **9** Electryon
ancestor **8** forebear, foregoer **9** ascendant, precursor, prototype **10** antecedent, antecessor, forefather, forerunner, progenitor **11** predecessor **12** primogenitor
ancestral **6** family, inborn, inbred, lineal **7** genetic **8** familial **9** inherited **10** bequeathed, hereditary **11** consanguine, patrimonial ***sequence:*** **8** pedigree **9** bloodline, genealogy
ancestry **4** line, race **5** blood, breed, stock **6** family, origin, source **7** descent, history, kindred, lineage **8** heritage, pedigree **9** parentage **10** derivation, extraction
Anchises' son **6** Aeneas
anchor **4** moor **5** kedge **6** secure **7** grapnel, mooring **8** mainstay ***network news:*** **4** Daly (John), Hume (Brit) **5** Chung (Connie) **6** Brokaw (Tom), Couric (Katie), Gibson (Charles), Koppel (Ted), Lehrer (Jim), Murrow (Edward R.), Rather (Dan), Sawyer (Diane), Swayze (John Cameron) **7** Edwards (Douglas), Huntley (Chet), Walters (Barbara) **8** Brinkley (David), Cronkite (Walter), Jennings (Peter), Reasoner (Harry), Reynolds (Frank), Williams (Brian) **10** Chancellor (John) ***part:*** **3** arm **4** bill, ring **5** crown, fluke, shank, stock
anchorage **4** port **5** haven, roads **6** harbor, refuge, riding **7** mooring, shelter **9** harborage, roadstead
anchorite **5** loner **6** hermit **7** recluse **8** solitary
anchors ____ **6** aweigh
ancient **3** old **4** aged **5** hoary, olden **6** age-old, primal **7** antique, archaic, elderly **8** Noachian, old-timer, primeval, timeworn **9** venerable **10** primordial **12** antediluvian
ancient capital **4** Susa **5** Aksum, Balkh, Calah, Isker, Kalhu, Ninus, Pella, Petra, Sibir **6** Angkor, Bactra, Nimrud, Sardis **7** Babylon, Knossos, Memphis, Nineveh, Samaria, Shushan **10** Persepolis

ancient city ***Asia Minor:*** **4** Nice, Teos **5** Tyana **6** Edessa, Nicaea **7** Antioch **13** Halicarnassus ***Babylonia:*** **4** Sura **5** Agade, Akkad, Eridu, Larsa **7** Ellasar ***Bengal:*** **4** Gaur **9** Lakhnauti ***Canaan:*** **5** Gezer ***Cyprus:*** **7** Salamis ***Egypt:*** **5** Tanis **6** Thebes **7** Memphis **10** Heliopolis ***Etruria:*** **4** Veii ***Euphrates River:*** **7** Babylon ***Greece:*** **5** Crisa **6** Athens, Sparta **7** Calydon **10** Lacedaemon ***Ionia:*** **4** Myus, Teos **5** Chios, Samos **6** Priene **7** Ephesus, Lebedos, Miletus, Phocaea **8** Colophon, Erythrae **10** Clazomenae ***Italy:*** **5** Locri **7** Pompeii **8** Siracusa, Syracuse **11** Herculaneum ***Latium:*** **5** Gabii **9** Alba Longa ***Mayan:*** **4** Cobá **5** Tikal, Tulum, Uxmal **8** Palenque **11** Chichén Itzá ***Nile River:*** **5** Meroë ***North Africa:*** **5** Utica **8** Carthage ***Palestine:*** **4** Gaza **5** Ekron, Endor, Sodom **6** Beroea, Bethel, Gilead, Hebron **7** Jericho, Samaria **8** Ashkelon **9** Capernaum, Jerusalem ***Peloponnesus:*** **5** Tegea **6** Sparta **7** Corinth ***Sumeria:*** **4** Kish, Uruk **5** Erech, Larsa **6** Lagash ***Turkey:*** **5** Assos, Assus **9** Byzantium

ancient country ***Adriatic coast:*** **7** Illyria ***Africa:*** **10** Mauretania ***Arabian Peninsula:*** **5** Sheba ***Asia:*** **4** Aram **5** Media, Minni, Syria **7** Armenia, Ash Sham, Bactria ***Asia Minor:*** **5** Lydia, Mysia **6** Aeolis, Pontus **7** Cilicia, Phrygia **8** Bithynia ***Balkan:*** **7** Macedon **9** Macedonia ***Black Sea:*** **7** Colchis ***Dead Sea:*** **4** Edom ***Euphrates River:*** **9** Babylonia ***Europe:*** **4** Gaul **5** Dacia **6** Gallia ***gold-rich:*** **5** Ophir ***Italy:*** **6** Latium **7** Etruria ***Nile valley:*** **4** Cush ***Peloponnesus:*** **4** Elis **7** Arcadia ***Syria:*** **9** Phoenicia

ancient empire **6** Median **7** Hittite, Persian **8** Assyrian, Athenian, Chaldean, Seleucid **9** Ptolemaic **10** Babylonian

ancient kingdom ***Anglo-Saxon:*** **6** Wessex ***Asia:*** **4** Ghor, Ghur ***Celtic:*** **7** Cumbria ***China:*** **3** Shu ***Euphrates valley:*** **4** Hira **7** Al-Hirah ***Greece:*** **8** Pergamon, Pergamum ***North Of Assyria:*** **3** Van **6** Ararat, Urartu ***Palestine:*** **5** Judah **6** Israel ***Persian Gulf:*** **4** Elam ***Portugal:*** **7** Algarve ***Spain:*** **4** Leon **6** Aragon **7** Castile, Galicia, Granada, Navarre ***Syria:*** **4** Moab ***Welsh:*** **5** Powys ***West Sahara:*** **4** Gana **5** Ghana

ancient monument **6** sphinx **7** obelisk, pyramid

ancient royal forest **4** Dean **8** Sherwood

ancient town ***Africa:*** **4** Zama ***Armenia:*** **4** Dwin, Tvin ***Asia Minor:*** **4** Soli **5** Derbe, Issus, Soloi ***Attica:*** **6** Icaria ***Black Sea:*** **5** Olbia **9** Apollonia ***Greece:*** **4** Abae, Opus **8** Marathon ***Italy:*** **4** Elea, Luna **5** Cumae, Velia ***Latium:*** **5** Ardea, Cures ***Macedonia:*** **5** Pydna, Stobi **9** Apollonia ***Peloponnesus:*** **5** Asine ***Persia:*** **6** Hormuz **8** Harmozia ***Sicily:*** **5** Hybla ***Spain:*** **5** Munda ***Tatar:*** **5** Isker, Sibir ***Wendish:*** **5** Julin

ancilla **3** aid **4** aide, ally, hand, help **6** helper **9** assistant, attendant, supporter

ancillary **5** extra **8** adjuvant, incident **9** accessory, attendant, attending, auxiliary, satellite, secondary **10** additional, coincident, collateral, subsidiary, supporting **11** appurtenant, concomitant, subordinate, subservient **12** accompanying, contributory **13** supplementary

andante **4** slow **5** tempo **7** relaxed, walking **8** moderate

Anderson play **7** High Tor **8** Key Largo **9** Winterset **11** Valley Forge **14** What Price Glory

Anderson book **9** Poor White **12** Dark Laughter **13** Winesburg Ohio

Andes ***grazer:*** **5** llama **6** alpaca, guemal, huemal, vicuña **7** camelid, guanaco ***native:*** **4** Inca ***peak:*** **9** Aconcagua, Huascarán

andiron **7** firedog

Andorra ***capital:*** **7** Andorra ***language:*** **7** Catalan ***liberator:*** **11** Charlemagne ***monetary unit:*** **4** euro ***monetary unit, former:*** **6** peseta **11** French franc ***mountain range:*** **8** Pyrenees ***neighbor:*** **5** Spain **6** France ***river:*** **6** Valira

Andrea ____ **5** Doria **8** del Sarto

androgynous **7** epicene **8** bisexual **9** unisexual

android **5** robot **9** automaton

Andromache ***husband:*** **6** Hector ***son:*** **8** Astyanax, Molossus

Andromeda ***father:*** **7** Cepheus ***husband:*** **7** Perseus ***mother:*** **10** Cassiopeia ***rescuer:*** **7** Perseus

Andy Griffith Show ***actor:*** **6** Bavier (Francis), Howard (Ron), Knotts (Don), Nabors (Jim) ***character:*** **4** Opie (Taylor) **5** Gomer (Pyle) **6** Barney (Fife) **7** Aunt Bee

anecdote **4** tale, yarn **5** story **7** account, episode, recital **8** relation **9** narration, narrative **12** recollection, reminiscence

anemic **3** wan **4** pale, thin, weak **5** pasty **6** feeble, pallid, sickly, watery **7** insipid **8** ischemic **9** bloodless, colorless **10** spiritless

anemone **9** buttercup **10** windflower

anent **4** as to, in re **5** about, as for **7** apropos **8** touching **9** as regards **10** concerning **13** with respect to

anesthetic **6** opiate **7** anodyne **9** analgesic **10** painkiller, palliative ***medical:*** **5** ether **6** spinal **8** morphine, procaine **9** halothane, novocaine **10** benzocaine, chloroform, tetracaine **11** scopolamine ***suffix:*** **5** caine

anesthetize **4** numb, stun **6** benumb, deaden **8** etherize, knock out **9** narcotize **11** desensitize

anesthetized **4** dead, numb **5** inert **6** asleep, torpid **10** insensible **11** insensitive, unconscious

anew **4** over **5** again **6** afresh, de novo, lately, of late **8** once more, recently

angel **6** backer, cherub, patron, seraph, surety **7** sponsor **8** backer-up, guardian **9** celestial, guarantor, supporter **10** benefactor **11** underwriter ***biblical:*** **5** Uriel **7** Gabriel, Michael, Raphael ***fallen:*** **7** Lucifer ***hierarchy:*** **6** powers **7** thrones, virtues **8** cherubim, seraphim **9** dominions ***Mormon:*** **6** Moroni ***of death:*** **6** Azrael

Angel Clare's bride **4** Tess

angelic **4** holy, pure **5** godly **6** divine **7** saintly **8** cherubic, ethereal, heavenly **9** celestial **11** beneficient

Angelica ***father:*** **9** Galaphron ***husband:*** **6** Medoro ***lover:*** **7** Orlando

Angelou work **13** Heart of a Woman (The) **25** I Know Why the Caged Bird Sings

anger **3** ire, vex **4** bile, boil, burn, fume, fury, gall, huff, rage, rant, rave, rile **5** storm, upset, wrath **6** choler, dander, enrage, madden, nettle, offend, seethe **7** affront, bristle, dudgeon, incense, outrage, provoke, steam up, umbrage **8** acrimony **9** animosity, infuriate **10** antagonism, antagonize, exasperate

angle **3** aim, bow **4** axil, bend, bias, fish, hand, skew, turn **5** facet, slant **6** aspect, corner, crotch, dogleg **7** flexure, outlook, turning **9** direction, viewpoint **10** standpoint

angler **6** fisher **8** monkfish **9** fisherman, goosefish

Anglo-Saxon ***assembly:*** **4** moot **5** gemot **6** gemote ***council:*** **9** heptarchy ***county:*** **5** shire ***court:*** **4** moot **5** gemot **6** gemote ***crown tax:*** **4** geld ***epic:*** **7** Beowulf ***free servant:*** **5** thane, thegn ***god:*** **3** Ing ***goddess of fate:*** **4** Wyrd ***historian:*** **4** Bede ***king:*** **3** Ine, Ini **4** Edwy **5** Edgar, Edred **6** Alfred, Edmund, Edward, Egbert **8** Ethelred ***kingdom:*** **4** Kent **5** Essex **6** Mercia, Sussex, Wessex **10** East Anglia **11** Northumbria ***king's council:*** **5** witan ***letter:*** **3** edh, eth, wen, wyn **4** rune, wynn **5** thorn ***nobleman:*** **4** earl ***poet:*** **4** scop ***prince:*** **8** atheling ***sheriff:*** **5** reeve ***slave:*** **4** esne ***warrior:*** **5** thane, thegn

Angola ***capital:*** **6** Luanda ***city:*** **6** Huambo **7** Lubango **8** Benguela ***exclave:*** **7** Cabinda ***language:*** **10** Portuguese ***monetary unit:*** **6** kwanza ***neighbor:*** **5** Congo **6** Zambia **7** Namibia **11** South Africa ***river:*** **5** Congo

angora **3** cat **4** goat, hair, wool, yarn **6** mohair, rabbit

angry **3** hot, mad **4** sore **5** irate, riled, riley, upset, vexed, wroth **6** fuming, heated, ireful, wrathy **7** enraged, furious, riled up, teed off **8** choleric, incensed, inflamed, maddened, wrathful **9** indignant, irritated **10** aggravated, infuriated **11** acrimonious, exasperated

angst **4** fear **5** agita, worry **6** unease **7** anxiety, concern **8** disquiet, distress **10** insecurity **11** disquietude, fretfulness **12** apprehension

Anguilla ***island, island group:*** **3** Dog **4** Seal **5** Scrub **7** Leeward ***location:*** **10** West Indies ***territory of:*** **7** Britain

anguish **3** rue, woe **4** ache, care, dole, hurt, pain, pang **5** agony, dread, grief, throe, worry **6** misery, regret, sorrow, throes **7** anxiety, torment, torture **8** distress, hardship **9** heartache, suffering **10** affliction, heartbreak **12** wretchedness

angular **4** bony, edgy, lank, lean, thin **5** gaunt, lanky, spare, stiff **6** forked, skinny, zigzag **7** pointed, scraggy, scrawny **8** cornered, rawboned, ungainly **9** roughhewn **10** unfinished, ungraceful, unpolished

ani **6** cuckoo

anima **4** soul **6** psyche, spirit

animadversion **4** slam, slur **7** censure, obloquy **9** aspersion, criticism **10** accusation, imputation, reflection **11** insinuation **12** reprehension

animadvert **6** notice **7** observe **9** criticize

animal **5** beast, brute, feral **6** brutal, carnal, ferine **7** beastly, bestial, brutish, critter, fleshly, sensual, swinish, wilding **8** creature, wildling ***antlered:*** **3** elk **4** axis, deer **5** moose **7** caribou **8** reindeer ***aquatic:*** **3** eel **4** fish, frog, seal **5** otter, whale **6** dugong, sea cow, walrus **7** dolphin, manatee, octopus **8** bryozoan, porpoise **9** alligator, crocodile ***arboreal:*** **2** ai **4** bird **5** chimp, coati, koala, lemur, sloth **6** gibbon, monkey **7** opossum, tarsier **8** kinkajou, marmoset, squirrel **9** orangutan ***burrowing:*** **4** mole **5** brock, ratel **6** badger, gopher, marmot, rabbit **7** echidna **9** armadillo, groundhog, woodchuck ***castrated:*** **2** ox **5** capon, steer **6** barrow, wether **7** gelding ***coat:*** **3** fur **4** hair, hide **6** pelage ***draft:*** **2** ox **3** yak **4** mule, oxen (plural) **5** horse **6** donkey **8** elephant ***exhibit:*** **3** zoo ***extinct:*** **3** moa **4** dodo, urus **6** quagga **7** mammoth **8** dinosaur, eohippus, mastodon **9** trilobite ***female:*** **3** cow, dam, doe, ewe, hen, pen, roe, sow **4** mare, puss **5** bitch, goose, jenny, nanny, vixen **6** jennet **7** lioness ***four-footed:*** **9** quadruped ***four-limbed:*** **8** tetrapod ***free-swimming:*** **6** nekton ***hibernating:*** **4** bear, frog, toad **5** skunk, snake **7** polecat **8** chipmunk **9** groundhog, woodchuck ***horned:*** **2** ox **3** ram, yak **4** bull, goat, ibex, kudu **5** addax, bison, eland, rhino **6** cattle, koodoo **7** buffalo, gazelle, giraffe, unicorn **8** antelope ***humped:*** **2** ox **3** elk, yak **4** zebu **5** bison, camel, moose ***imaginary:*** **5** snark **6** Harvey **10** hippogriff ***male:*** **3** cob, ram, tom **4** boar, buck, bull, cock, stag, stud **5** billy, steer **6** gander **7** gobbler, rooster **8** bachelor, stallion ***many-celled:*** **8** metazoan ***many-footed:*** **9** centipede, millipede ***meat-eating:*** **9** carnivore ***mythical:*** **5** Hydra **6** dragon, kraken, sphinx **7** centaur, griffin, mermaid, Pegasus, unicorn **8** basilisk, Cerberus, Minotaur ***one-celled:*** **9** protozoan ***Peruvian:*** **5** llama **6** alpaca, vicuña ***plant-eating:*** **9** herbivore ***skin disease:*** **5** mange ***spotted:*** **4** axis, paca **6** calico, jaguar, ocelot **7** cheetah, leopard, piebald **8** skewbald **9** dalmatian ***striped:*** **4** kudu **5** tiger, zebra **6** koodoo, quagga ***tender:*** **8** herdsman ***trail:*** **3** pug **4** foil, slot **5** spoor ***tusked:*** **6** walrus **7** warthog **8** elephant ***two-footed:*** **5** biped ***web-footed:*** **4** duck, frog, toad **5** goose, otter **6** beaver **8** duckbill, platypus ***young:*** **3** cub, kid, kit, pup **4** calf, colt, fawn, foal, joey, lamb **5** bunny, chick, kitty, poult, shoat, stirk, whelp **6** cygnet, farrow, heifer, kitten, piglet **7** bullock, gosling, lambkin **8** suckling, yeanling, yearling **9** fledgling

animal behavior ***study of:*** **8** ethology

animal fat **4** suet **6** tallow

animalism **4** lust **7** abandon **8** vitality **9** carnality **10** sensualism, sensuality **11** lustfulness, physicality, unrestraint

animalize **4** warp **6** debase **7** corrupt, deprave, pervert, vitiate **9** brutalize **10** bestialize, demoralize

animal life **5** fauna

animal sound **3** arf, baa, bay, caw, coo, low, mew, moo **4** bark, bray, buzz, crow, hiss, hoot, howl, meow, purr, roar, yelp **5** bleat, chirp, croak, drone, growl, grunt, miaow, neigh, quack **6** bellow, gibber, gobble, warble **7** screech, twitter

animate **4** fire, live, move, spur, stir, urge **5** alert, alive, cheer, drive, exalt, impel, liven, nerve, spark, steel, vital **6** active, arouse, excite, inform, kindle, lively, living, moving, viable, vivify **7** actuate, chirk up, dynamic, enliven, hearten, inspire, quicken, refresh **8** activate, embolden, energize, inspirit, motivate, spirited, vitalize **9** breathing, encourage, energized, enhearten, make alive, stimulate **10** invigorate

animated **3** gay **4** keen **5** alert, alive, peppy, quick, vivid, vital **6** lively, living **7** dynamic, excited, vibrant, zestful **8** spirited, vigorous **9** activated, energetic, energized, exuberant, sprightly, vitalized, vivacious **12** high-spirited

animation **3** pep, vim, zip **4** brio, dash, élan, life, toon, zing **5** oomph, verve **6** energy, esprit, gaiety, spirit **7** cartoon, dynamic **8** dynamism, vitality, vivacity **10** liveliness ***unit:*** **3** cel **4** cell

animato **5** brisk, tempo **6** lively **8** spirited **9** energetic, sprightly

animosity **4** hate **5** venom **6** animus, enmity, hatred, rancor **7** dislike, ill will **8** acrimony **9** antipathy, hostility **10** antagonism, resentment

animus **4** plan, soul **6** design, enmity, intent, pneuma, psyche, rancor, spirit **7** dislike, ill will, meaning, purpose **9** antipathy, élan vital, hostility, intention **10** antagonism, intendment, opposition, vital force **11** disposition, malevolence

Anjou **4** pear ***capital:*** **6** Angers ***native:*** **7** Angevin

ankle **5** talus **6** tarsus

Anna Karenina ***author:*** **7** Tolstoy (Leo) ***character:*** **5** Dolly, Kitty, Levin (Konstantin), Stiva **6** Andrei (Karenin) **7** Vronsky (Count Alexei) **8** Ivanovna (Countess Lidia), Seriozha ***film star:*** **4** Bean (Sean) **5** Bloom (Claire), Garbo (Greta), Leigh (Vivien), March (Fredric), Reeve (Christopher) **6** Bisset (Jacqueline) **7** Connery (Sean), Marceau (Sophie) **10** Richardson (Ralph) ***radio star:*** **4** Peck (Gregory) **7** Bergman (Ingrid)

annals **6** record **7** account, history **8** archives, register **9** chronicle

annelid **4** worm **5** leech **9** earthworm

annex **3** add, arm, cop, ell, win **4** gain, hook, join, land, take, wing **5** add on, affix, seize, tag on **6** adjoin, append, attach, fasten, obtain, pick up, secure, tack on, take on **7** acquire, connect, preempt, procure, subjoin **8** accroach, addition, appendix, arrogate, superadd, take over **9** extension **10** attachment, commandeer, subsidiary, supplement **11** appropriate, expropriate, incorporate

Annie Oakley **4** comp, pass **10** free ticket, markswoman

annihilate **4** do in, kill, raze, rout, ruin, undo **5** abate, annul, crush, erase, quash, quell, wrack, wreck **6** murder, negate, quench, rub out, squash, uproot, vanish **7** abolish, blot out, destroy, expunge, nullify, put down, root out, vitiate, wipe out **8** abrogate, demolish, massacre, suppress, vanquish **9** eradicate, extirpate, liquidate, slaughter **10** extinguish, invalidate, obliterate **11** exterminate

annihilation 7 killing **8** massacre **9** abolition **11** destruction, elimination, liquidation, termination **12** obliteration **13** extermination

anniversary *hundredth:* 9 centenary **10** centennial ***tenth:* 9** decennial ***thousandth:* 10** millennial

Anno ____ 6 Domini

annotate 5 gloss **6** remark **7** comment, explain **8** footnote **9** elucidate, interpret **10** commentate

announce 4 call, tell **5** augur, issue, sound, state **6** attest, blazon, herald, impart, report, reveal, signal **7** bespeak, declare, divulge, forerun, give out, portend, predict, presage, present, publish, release, signify, trumpet **8** disclose, forecast, foreshow, foretell, indicate, proclaim **9** advertise, broadcast, harbinger, make known, publicize **10** give notice, make public, promulgate **11** preindicate

announcement 4 news **5** promo **6** notice, report **7** message, release **8** briefing, bulletin **9** broadcast, statement **10** communiqué, disclosure **11** declaration, publication **12** proclamation, promulgation **13** advertisement, communication

announcer 2 DJ **5** emcee **6** deejay, herald, veejay **9** anchorman, voice-over **10** disc jockey, disk jockey, newscaster **11** anchorwoman, broadcaster, commentator **12** anchorperson, sportscaster

annoy 3 bug, irk, vex **4** bait, fret, gall, miff **5** chafe, chivy, harry, peeve, tease, upset, worry **6** badger, bother, harass, heckle, hector, molest, needle, nettle, pester, plague, ruffle **7** agitate, bedevil, disturb, hagride, perturb, provoke, tick off **8** distress, irritate **9** beleaguer ***Scottish:* 4** fash

annoyance 4 drag, to-do **5** trial, upset, worry **6** bother, nettle, plague, strain **7** problem, trouble **8** distress, headache, irritant, nuisance, vexation **10** affliction, harassment, irritation **11** aggravation, botheration, disturbance, indignation, provocation **12** exasperation

annoying 5 pesky **8** tiresome **9** troubling, vexatious **10** disturbing, irritating **11** aggravating, distressing, troublesome **12** exasperating

annual 5 plant **6** flower, yearly **7** almanac **8** each year, yearbook, yearlong **9** every year

annul 4 undo, void **5** abate, erase, quash **6** cancel, delete, efface, negate, revoke, vacate **7** abolish, blot out, expunge, nullify, redress, rescind, retract, reverse, vitiate, wipe out **8** abrogate, dissolve **9** cancel out, discharge, frustrate **10** annihilate, counteract, extinguish, invalidate, neutralize, obliterate **11** countermand

annunciate see **announce**

anodyne 4 balm **5** bland **6** opiate, relief, remedy **7** soother **8** narcotic, nepenthe, painless, sedative **9** analgesic, calmative, innocuous, soporific **10** anesthetic, depressant, pain-killer, palliative **11** inoffensive, unoffending **12** tranquilizer

anoint 3 rub **4** daub, laud, name **5** anele, apply, bless, honor, smear **6** choose, hallow, ordain **7** confirm, massage **8** dedicate, sanctify, set apart, venerate **9** designate **10** consecrate

anomalous 3 odd **6** off-key **7** deviant, strange, unusual **8** aberrant, abnormal, atypical, peculiar **9** deviating, deviatory, divergent, irregular, unnatural, untypical **10** unexpected **11** heteroclite, incongruous, paradoxical **12** inconsistent **13** nonconforming, preternatural

anomaly 5 freak, quirk **6** oddity **7** paradox **9** departure, deviation, exception **10** aberration, divergence **11** abnormality, incongruity, peculiarity **12** idiosyncrasy, irregularity **13** inconsistency

anomie 4 flux **6** unrest **7** anxiety, inertia **10** alienation, insecurity **11** disquietude, instability, uncertainty **12** disaffection, estrangement, indifference, restlessness

anon 4 soon **5** later **7** by and by, shortly **8** directly, in a while **9** presently **10** before long **11** after a while

anonym 5 alias **6** handle **7** pen name **8** nickname **10** nom de plume **11** assumed name, nom de guerre

anonymous 7 unknown, unnamed **8** nameless, not named, unsigned **9** incognito **11** unspecified **12** unidentified, unrecognized

anorak 5 parka

another 3 new **4** else, more **5** added, fresh **7** farther, further, one more **9** different **10** additional **11** alternative, someone else **13** something else

anschluss 5 union **6** league **8** alliance **9** coalition **10** federation **11** confederacy **13** confederation

answer 4 fill, meet, plea, RSVP **5** atone, plead, rebut, reply, serve, solve **6** come in, refute, rejoin, result, retort, return **7** conform, defense, explain, fulfill, respond, satisfy **8** antiphon, rebuttal, response, solution **9** rejoinder **10** refutation **11** recriminate **13** countercharge

answerable 5 bound **6** liable **7** obliged, subject **8** amenable **9** compelled, duty-bound, obligated **11** accountable, constrained, responsible

ant 5 emmet **9** carpenter ***relating to:*** **6** formic

Antaean 4 huge **5** giant **6** heroic **7** mammoth, titanic **8** colossal, enormous, gigantic **9** cyclopean **10** gargantuan

Antaeus *father:* 7 Neptune **8** Poseidon ***mother:*** **4** Gaea ***slayer:*** **8** Heracles, Hercules

antagonism 3 con **6** animus, enmity, hatred, rancor **7** discord **8** conflict, friction **9** animosity, antipathy, hostility **10** antithesis, contention, dissension, opposition, resistance **11** contrariety **12** disagreement

antagonist 3 con, foe **4** anti **5** enemy, match **6** muscle **7** opposer **8** chemical, opponent **9** adversary, contender

antagonistic 4 anti **6** averse **7** adverse, hostile, opposed **8** clashing, contrary, inimical, opposing **9** bellicose, combative, rancorous, truculent **11** belligerent, conflicting, contentious **12** antipathetic

Antarctica sea 4 Ross **7** Weddell **8** Amundsen

ante 3 bet, pay, pot **4** cost, risk **5** level, pay up, price, put up, stake, wager **6** stakes **7** produce

anteater 8 aardvark, pangolin, tamandua

antecede 7 forerun, precede, predate **8** foredate, go before

antecedence 8 priority **10** precedence, precession, preference

antecedent 4 fore, line **5** cause, prior **6** former, reason **7** earlier **8** ancestor, anterior, forebear, foregoer, occasion, previous **9** condition, foregoing, precedent, preceding, precursor, prototype **10** forerunner, progenitor **11** determinant, predecessor

antedate 7 forerun, precede **11** anachronize

antediluvian 3 old **4** aged, fogy **5** hoary, passé **6** age-old, fogram, fossil, square **7** ancient, antique, archaic **8** mossback, Noachian, obsolete, outdated, outmoded, primeval, timeworn **9** out-of-date, primitive **10** antiquated, fuddy-duddy **12** old-fashioned **13** stick-in-the-mud

antelope 3 gnu, kob **4** guib, kudu, oryx, poku, puku, topi, tora **5** addax, bongo, eland, nyala, oribi, serow **6** dik-dik, duiker, impala, koodoo, lechwe, nilgai **7** blesbok, chamois, gazelle, gemsbok, gerenuk, sassaby **8** bushbuck, reedbuck, steinbok **9** springbok, waterbuck **10** hartebeest ***female:*** **3** doe ***genus:*** **4** Oryx ***male:*** **4** buck ***young:*** **3** kid (see also **gazelle**)

antenna 4 wire **6** aerial, device, dipole, sensor **8** monopole, receiver

antennae 4 ears **11** sensitivity **13** receptiveness

anterior 4 past **5** prior **6** former **8** previous **9** foregoing, precedent, preceding **10** antecedent

anteroom 5 entry, foyer, lobby **6** alcove **9** vestibule

Anteros *brother:* 4 Eros ***father:*** **4** Ares, Mars ***mother:*** **5** Venus **9** Aphrodite ***opposite:*** **4** Eros

anthem 4 hymn, song **5** chant, paean, psalm **8** canticle

anthology 3 ana **5** album **6** digest, reader **7** garland, omnibus **8** analects, treasury **9** selection **10** assortment, collection, compendium, miscellany **11** compilation, florilegium

anthropoid 3 ape **4** saki, titi **5** biped **6** bonobo, gibbon, monkey, uakari **7** bipedal, gorilla, macaque, manlike, primate, tamarin, tarsier **8** capuchin, hominoid, humanoid, marmoset **9** orangutan **10** chimpanzee

anthropologist 4 Boas (Franz), Dart (Raymond), Mead (Margaret) **5** Sapir (Edward), Tylor (Edward Burnett) **6** Frazer (James George), Geertz (Clifford), Leakey (Louis), Morgan (Lewis Henry) **7** Bateson (Gregory), Kroeber (Alfred Louis) **8** Benedict (Ruth) **10** Malinowski (Bronisław) **11** Lévi-Strauss (Claude)

anti 3 con **6** averse **7** adverse, against, counter, opposed, opposer **8** contrary, opponent, opposing **9** adversary, opposed to **10** antagonist **12** antagonistic, antipathetic, in opposition

antiaircraft fire 4 flak

antibiotic 7 colicin **8** neomycin, viomycin **9** polymyxin **10** bacitracin, novobiocin, penicillin **11** bacteriocin, tyrothricin **12** streptomycin, tetracycline

antic 3 gag **4** dido, joke, lark, romp **5** caper, comic, prank, trick **6** frisky, frolic, lively **7** comical, foolish, playful **8** escapade, farcical, prankish, spirited **9** high jinks, laughable, ludicrous, sprightly **10** frolicsome, rollicking, shenanigan, tomfollery **11** mischievous, monkeyshine **12** monkeyshines **13** practical joke

anticipate 3 see **4** wait **5** await, check **6** divine, expect **7** counter, count on, foresee, prepare, presage, prevent, wait for **8** forecast, foreknow, foretell **9** apprehend, forestall, prevision, visualize **10** prepare for

anticipation **7** inkling, outlook, promise **8** awaiting, forecast, prospect **9** awareness, foresight, foretaste **10** expectancy **11** expectation, realization **12** apprehension **13** visualization

Anticlea ***father:*** **9** Autolycus ***husband:*** **7** Laertes ***son:*** **7** Ulysses **8** Odysseus

antidote **4** cure, drug **6** remedy **7** negator **8** medicine **9** nullifier **10** corrective, counteract, preventive **11** counterstep, neutralizer **12** counteragent **13** counteractant, counteractive

Antigone ***brother:*** **9** Polynices **10** Polyneices ***father:*** **7** Oedipus ***mother:*** **7** Jocasta ***sister:*** **6** Ismene ***uncle:*** **5** Creon

Antigua and Barbuda ***capital:*** **7** St. Johns ***island:*** **7** Antigua, Barbuda, Redonda

Antilochus ***father:*** **6** Nestor ***friend:*** **8** Achilles ***slayer:*** **6** Memnon

antimony symbol **2** Sb

Antiope ***father:*** **6** Asopus ***husband:*** **5** Lycus **7** Theseus ***queen of:*** **7** Amazons ***son:*** **6** Zethus **7** Amphion **10** Hippolytus

antipasto **9** appetizer **11** hors d'oeuvre **12** hors d'oeuvres

antipathetic **5** loath **6** averse, loathe **7** adverse, hostile, opposed **8** aversive, clashing, contrary, inimical, opposing, opposite **9** abhorrent, loathsome, repellent, repugnant, repulsive **10** discordant, unfriendly **11** conflicting, distasteful, ill-disposed, uncongenial **12** antagonistic **13** contradictory

antipathy **4** hate **6** animus, enmity, hatred, rancor **7** allergy, dislike, ill will **8** aversion, distaste, loathing **9** animosity, hostility **10** abhorrence, antagonism, opposition, repellency

antiphon **5** psalm, reply, verse **6** answer, anthem, return **7** respond **8** response

antipodal **5** polar **7** adverse, counter, opposed, reverse **8** contrary, converse, opposite **9** diametric **11** conflicting, contrasting, diametrical **12** antithetical **13** contradictory

antipode **6** contra **7** counter, reverse **8** contrary, converse, flip side, opposite **9** other side **11** counterpole

antiquate **7** outdate, outmode **8** obsolete **9** obsolesce **12** superannuate

antiquated **3** old **4** aged **5** dated, fusty, hoary, moldy, passé **6** bygone, old hat **7** ancient, antique, archaic **8** obsolete, old-timey, outmoded **9** out-of-date **10** oldfangled, out-of-style **11** discredited, obsolescent **12** antediluvian, old-fashioned **13** inappropriate, superannuated

antique **3** old **4** aged **5** dated, hoary, olden, passé, relic **6** age-old, bygone, rarity **7** ancient, archaic, vintage **8** artifact, heirloom, old-timey, outdated, outmoded, timeworn **9** ancestral, objet d'art, out-of-date, venerable **10** antiquated, oldfangled **12** antediluvian, old-fashioned

antiseptic **6** iodine **7** alcohol, sterile **8** hygienic, peroxide, sanitary **9** boric acid, carvacrol, germicide, merbromin **10** gramicidin, sterilized **12** carbolic acid, disinfectant ***pioneer:*** **6** Lister (Joseph)

antisocial **7** ascetic, austere, hostile **8** eremitic, solitary **9** alienated, reclusive, withdrawn **10** unfriendly **11** standoffish **12** antagonistic, misanthropic

antithesis **3** con **6** contra **7** counter, reverse **8** antipode, antipole, contrary, contrast, converse, opposite **10** antagonism, opposition **11** counterpole

antithetical **5** polar **6** contra **7** counter, reverse **8** contrary, converse, opposite **9** antipodal, diametric **10** antipodean **11** diametrical **13** contradictory

antitoxin **4** sera (plural) **5** serum **11** neutralizer

antiwar **6** irenic **8** pacifist **10** nonviolent, pacifistic

Antony, Mark ***defeat:*** **6** Actium ***friend:*** **6** Caesar ***lover:*** **9** Cleopatra ***wife:*** **7** Octavia

anxiety **4** care, fear **5** agita, doubt, dread, panic, worry **6** unease **7** concern **8** distress, mistrust, suspense **9** self-doubt, suffering **10** uneasiness **11** disquietude, uncertainty **12** apprehension

anxious **4** avid, keen **5** eager **6** afraid, ardent, scared, uneasy **7** alarmed, fearful, worried **8** agitated, desirous, troubled, worrying **9** impatient, perturbed, terrified **10** breathless, disquieted, frightened **12** apprehensive

any **3** all **4** a bit, some **5** every **7** a little, several **8** whatever

anyhow **6** random **7** however **8** at random, randomly **9** hit-or-miss **10** carelessly, regardless **11** haphazardly **13** helter-skelter

anymore **3** now **5** today **8** nowadays **9** presently, these days

anyone **3** all **9** everybody

anything **5** aught

anytime **4** ever **8** whenever

anyway **4** ever, once **5** at all **7** however **12** nevertheless

anywise **5** at all

apace **4** fast **6** versed **7** abreast, flat-out, hastily, quickly, rapidly, swiftly **8** informed, up-to-date, speedily **9** posthaste **12** lickety-split **13** expeditiously

Apache ***chief:*** **7** Cochise **8** Geronimo ***subgroups:*** **7** Cibecue **9** Jicarilla, Mescalero **10** Chiricahua

apart **5** alone, aside **6** singly **7** asunder, removed **8** detached, isolated, one by one **9** severally **10** separately **12** individually **13** independently, unaccompanied ***prefix:*** **3** dis

apart from **3** bar, but **4** save **6** except, saving **7** barring, besides **9** except for, excepting, excluding, other than, outside of **11** exclusive of

apartheid **8** division **9** partition **10** separation, separatism **11** segregation **12** separateness

apartment **4** flat, room **5** rooms, suite **6** rental **7** chamber, housing, lodging **8** building, dwelling **9** residence **10** maisonette **13** accommodation

apathetic **4** dull, flat, limp **5** inert **6** stolid, torpid **7** languid, passive, unmoved **8** sluggish **9** impassive, untouched **10** anesthetic, insensible, phlegmatic, spiritless **11** emotionless, indifferent, insensitive **12** unresponsive **13** disinterested

apathy **6** torpor **8** coldness, dullness, lethargy, obduracy, stoicism **9** aloofness, disregard, inertness, lassitude, passivity, stolidity, torpidity, unconcern **10** detachment, dispassion **11** callousness, disinterest, impassivity **12** heedlessness, indifference, listlessness **13** insensibility, insensitivity

ape **4** copy, mime, mock **5** mimic **6** bonobo, gibbon, parody, pongid, simian **7** copycat, emulate, gorilla, imitate, siamang, take off **8** simulate, travesty **9** burlesque, orangutan **10** anthropoid, caricature, chimpanzee **11** impersonate

aperçu **5** brief **6** digest, précis, sketch, survey **7** insight, outline **8** syllabus **10** compendium, impression

aperitif **3** kir **4** whet **5** drink **6** Pastis, Pernod, sherry **7** Campari, Cinzano **8** cocktail **9** appetizer

aperture **3** gap **4** hole, vent **5** chink **6** outlet **7** opening, orifice, pinhole

apery **7** mimicry **9** imitation

apex **3** cap, tip, top **4** acme, cusp, peak, roof **5** crest, crown, limit, point **6** apogee, climax, summit, vertex, zenith **8** capstone, pinnacle, ultimate **9** crescendo, sublimity **11** culmination, ne plus ultra **12** quintessence

aphorism **3** saw **4** rule **5** adage, axiom, maxim, moral **6** dictum, saying, truism **7** precept, proverb **8** apothegm

aphrodisiac **6** erotic **7** amative, amatory, amorous, lustful **8** excitant **10** passionate

Aphrodite ***Roman counterpart:*** **5** Venus ***consort:*** **4** Ares **6** Vulcan **10** Hephaestus ***father:*** **4** Zeus **7** Jupiter ***goddess of:*** **4** love ***mother:*** **5** Dione ***sister:*** **6** Athena **7** Artemis ***son:*** **4** Eros **6** Aeneas **7** Priapus

apiarist **9** beekeeper

apical **3** top **7** highest, topmost **8** loftiest **9** uppermost

apiculture **10** beekeeping

apiece **3** per **4** a pop, each **6** singly, to each **7** for each **8** one by one **9** per capita, severally **10** separately **12** individually, respectively

apish **5** phony, silly **6** phoney **7** slavish **8** affected **9** emulative, imitative **10** artificial

aplenty **4** full **5** ample **6** galore, indeed **7** copious, greatly **8** abundant, very much **9** extremely

aplomb **4** ease **5** poise **6** polish **8** coolness, easiness **9** assurance, certainty, certitude, composure **10** confidence, equanimity **11** nonchalance, savoir faire **12** self-reliance **13** self-assurance

apocalypse **6** augury, oracle, vision **8** disaster, prophecy **10** Armageddon, prediction, revelation

apocalyptic **4** dire **5** awful **7** baleful, baneful, fateful, fearful, ominous **8** Delphian, dreadful, oracular, terrible **9** appalling, climactic, grandiose, prophetic **10** foreboding, predicting **11** foretelling, prophetical, threatening **12** inauspicious ***book:*** **10** Revelation **11** Revelations

apocryphal **5** false, wrong **6** untrue **7** dubious **8** doubtful, spurious **9** incorrect, ungenuine **10** fictitious, inaccurate, unverified **11** unauthentic **12** questionable

apogee **4** acme, apex, peak **6** climax, summit, zenith **8** capstone, meridian, pinnacle **9** high point **11** culmination

Apollo **6** Helios **7** Phoebus ***beloved:*** **6** Cyrene, Daphne **8** Calliope ***birthplace:*** **5** Delos ***father:*** **4** Zeus **7** Jupiter ***mother:*** **4** Leto **6** Latona ***oracle:*** **6** Delphi ***sister:*** **5** Diana **7** Artemis ***son:*** **3** Ion **7** Orpheus ***temple:*** **6** Delphi

apologetic **5** sorry **6** rueful **8** contrite, penitent **9** regretful, repentant **10** remorseful **11** penitential **12** compunctious

apologia **4** plea **6** excuse, reason **7** defense **8** argument **11** elucidation, explanation **13** clarification, justification

apologize **5** atone **6** lament, regret, repent **7** confess **9** beg pardon **10** make amends

apologue **4** myth, tale **5** fable, story **7** parable **8** allegory

apology **4** plea **6** amends, excuse **7** redress,

regrets **8** mea culpa **9** admission, makeshift **10** concession, confession
apoplexy 4 esca **6** stroke
apostasy 7 perfidy **9** defection, desertion, disavowal, falseness, rejection **11** abandonment, repudiation **12** disaffection, renunciation
apostate 7 heretic, traitor **8** defector, deserter, recreant, renegade, turncoat **9** turnabout
apostatize 4 turn **6** defect, desert **7** abandon, forsake, sell out **8** renounce **9** repudiate
a posteriori 9 inductive
apostle 4 John, Jude, Paul **5** James, Judas, Peter, Silas, Simon **6** Andrew, Philip, Thomas **7** Matthew **8** Barnabas, disciple, follower, Matthias, preacher **9** missioner **10** colporteur, evangelist, missionary **11** Bartholomew **12** propagandist ***of Germany:* 8** Boniface ***of Ireland:* 7** Patrick ***of the English:* 9** Augustine ***of the French:* 5** Denis ***of the Gauls:* 8** Irenaeus ***of the Gentiles:* 4** Paul ***of the Goths:* 7** Ulfilas ***to the Indians:* 9** John Eliot
apothecary 7 chemist **8** druggist, pharmacy **9** drugstore **10** pharmacist
apothegm see **aphorism**
apotheosis 6 height **7** epitome **8** exemplar, ultimate **9** archetype, elevation **10** embodiment, exaltation **11** deification, ennoblement, idolization, lionization **12** enshrinement, quintessence **13** glorification
appall 3 awe **4** faze **5** alarm, shake, shock **6** dismay **7** horrify, outrage, overawe, perturb **8** confound, distress **10** disconcert **11** consternate
appalled 6 aghast **11** dumbfounded
appalling 5 awful **6** horrid **7** fearful **8** daunting, dreadful, horrible, horrific, shocking, terrible **9** atrocious, dismaying, frightful, loathsome **10** disgusting, formidable, horrifying
appanage 5 grant, right **7** adjunct **8** property **9** endowment, privilege **10** birthright, perquisite **11** prerogative
apparatus 4 gear, tool **5** gismo, gizmo **6** device, gadget, outfit, tackle, widget **7** utensil **8** matériel, tackling **9** equipment, implement, machinery **10** instrument **11** contraption **13** accouterments, accoutrements, paraphernalia
apparel 4 clad, duds, garb, gear, robe, suit, togs **5** adorn, array, dress, getup, habit **6** attire, clothe, livery, outfit **7** clothes, costume, garment, raiment, threads, vesture **8** clothing, enclothe, glad rags, vestment **9** embellish **11** habiliments
apparent 5 clear, overt, plain **6** patent **7** evident, obvious, seeming, visible **8** distinct, manifest, palpable **9** succedent **10** noticeable, observable **11** discernible, perceivable, perceptible
apparition 5 ghost, shade, umbra **6** shadow, spirit, vision, wraith **7** fantasm, phantom, specter **8** illusion, phantasm **10** appearance, phenomenon **13** hallucination
appeal 3 ask, beg, bid **4** call, lure, plea, pray, pull, suit, urge **5** apply, brace, charm, crave, plead **6** accuse, allure, charge, excite, invoke, sue for **7** attract, beseech, entreat, glamour, implore, request **8** call upon, charisma, entreaty, interest, intrigue, petition **9** fascinate, importune, magnetism, seduction **10** allurement, attraction, supplicate **11** application, fascination, imploration **12** drawing power, solicitation, supplication
appealing 8 alluring, charming, pleading, pleasant, pleasing **9** agreeable **10** attractive, bewitching, enchanting **11** captivating, fascinating
appear 4 look, loom, rise, seem, show **5** arise, issue, occur **6** arrive, emerge, show up, turn up **7** emanate **8** resemble **9** come forth **11** materialize
appearance 3 air **4** face, form, look, mien, pose, show **5** debut, dress, front, guise, image **6** advent, aspect, facade, manner **7** arrival, bearing, display, seeming **8** attitude, demeanor, illusion **9** semblance **10** impression, occurrence, simulacrum **11** countenance **13** manifestation
appease 4 calm, ease **5** allay, quiet **6** buy off, pacify, soothe **7** assuage, concede, content, gratify, mollify, placate, relieve, satisfy, sweeten **10** conciliate, propitiate
appellation 4 name **5** brand, label, nomen, style, title **7** moniker **8** cognomen **10** identifier **11** designation **12** denomination
append 3 add **5** add on, affix, annex, tag on **6** adjoin, attach, tack on **7** subjoin **10** supplement
appendage 3 arm, fin, leg, tab, tag **4** barb, flap, horn, limb, seta, tail, wing **5** extra **6** cercus, member **7** adjunct, antenna, elytron, stipule **8** pedipalp, pendicle, tentacle **9** accessory, auxiliary, extremity **10** attachment, collateral, incidental, projection, supplement **12** appurtenance, nonessential, protuberance
appendix 5 notes, rider **7** adjunct, codicil **8** addendum, addition **9** accessory, appendage **10** attachment, supplement **12** appurtenance
apperception 5 grasp **9** awareness **10** cognizance **11** realization, recognition **12** appre-

hension, assimilation **13** comprehension, introspection, understanding
appertain 4 bear **5** apply, refer **6** bear on, belong, relate **8** bear upon **10** be relevant **11** be connected, be pertinent
appetence 3 yen **5** taste **6** desire, hunger, relish, thirst **7** craving, longing, stomach **8** fondness
appetent 4 agog, avid, keen **5** eager **6** ardent **7** anxious, craving, lusting, thirsty **8** desirous, yearning **9** impatient **10** breathless
appetite 3 yen **4** bent, itch, lust, urge **5** taste **6** desire, hunger, liking, relish **7** craving, leaning, longing, passion, stomach **8** cupidity, fondness, gluttony, penchant, soft spot, voracity, weakness, yearning **9** hankering **10** preference, proclivity, propensity **11** inclination
appetizer 4 whet **5** snack **6** canapé, savory, tidbit **7** starter **8** aperitif, cocktail, stimulus **9** antipasto **11** amuse-bouche, hors d'oeuvre
appetizing 5 tasty **6** savory **8** saporous, tempting **9** agreeable, appealing, aperitive, flavorful, palatable, relishing, toothsome **10** delectable, flavorsome **11** scrumptious, tantalizing **13** mouth-watering
applaud 4 clap, hail, laud, root **5** bravo, cheer, extol **6** praise, rise to **7** acclaim, approve, commend **9** recommend **10** compliment
applause 4 hand **5** round **6** bravos, cheers, praise **7** acclaim, hurrahs, ovation, rooting **8** accolade, approval, cheering, clapping, plaudits **11** acclamation **12** commendation
apple 4 crab, Fuji, Gala, pome **6** Empire, Macoun, pippin, russet **7** Baldwin, costard, Duchess, Winesap **8** Braeburn, Cortland, greening, Jonagold, Jonathan, McIntosh **9** Delicious **10** Rome Beauty **11** Granny Smith, Gravenstein, Northern Spy, Transparent ***dessert:*** **5** crisp ***juice:*** **5** cider ***sugar:*** **4** ates **8** sweetsop
applejack 5 cider **6** brandy, liquor **8** calvados **9** hard cider
apple knocker see **rustic**
apple-polish 4 fawn **5** toady **6** kowtow **7** cater to, flatter, honey up, truckle **8** butter up **10** curry favor, ingratiate
apple-polisher 5 toady **6** yes-man **8** bootlick, groveler, lickspit **9** flatterer, sycophant **11** lickspittle
applesauce 5 hooey **6** bunkum **7** baloney, rubbish, twaddle **8** malarkey, nonsense **9** poppycock
appliance 6 device **7** utensil **9** implement **10** instrument **11** application ***kitchen:*** **4** oven **5** mixer, range, stove **6** fridge **7** blender, toaster **9** can opener, microwave **10** dishwasher **12** refrigerator
applicability 3 use **7** account, fitness, utility **9** advantage, relevance **10** usefulness
applicable 3 apt, fit **4** just, meet **5** ad rem **6** seemly, suited, useful **7** apropos, fitting, germane **8** apposite, material, relevant, suitable **9** befitting, pertinent **10** felicitous **11** appropriate
applicant 6 seeker **7** hopeful **8** aspirant, inquirer **9** candidate, job-hunter, job-seeker
application 3 use **4** form, heed, plea, suit **5** study **6** appeal, debate, effort, letter **7** request **8** entreaty, exercise, exertion, industry, petition **9** assiduity, attention, diligence, operation, treatment **10** dedication **11** requisition, utilization
appliqué 5 decal
apply 3 dab, use **4** bend, give, turn, urge **5** press, put on, refer **6** accost, affect, appeal, assign, bear on, bestow, devote, direct, employ, engage, handle, relate, resort, take on **7** address, beseech, concern, entreat, execute, implore, involve, pertain, utilize **8** approach, bear upon, exercise, petition, set about **9** appertain, implement, importune, undertake **10** administer, buckle down
appoint 3 arm, fix, rig, set, tap **4** gear, name **5** equip **6** assign, decide, fit out, outfit, supply **7** dress up, furbish, furnish, provide, turn out **8** accouter, accoutre, accredit, delegate, nominate **9** authorize, designate, determine, embellish, provision **10** commission
appointment 3 job **4** date, meet, post, spot **5** berth, place, tryst **6** billet, choice, office **7** meeting **8** election, position **9** equipment, selection, situation **10** assignment, connection, engagement, rendezvous **11** arrangement, assignation, designation
appointments 7 fitting **8** equipage **9** equipment, trappings **11** furnishings **13** accouterments, accoutrements
apportion 3 cut, lot **4** give, mete, part **5** allot, allow, cut up, divvy, quota, serve, share, slice, split **6** assign, bestow, divide, parcel, ration **7** deal out, dish out, divvy up, dole out, measure, mete out, prorate, split up **8** allocate, dispense, separate, share out **9** admeasure, partition **10** administer, distribute
apportionment 3 cut, lot **4** part **5** piece, quota, share, slice, split **6** ration **7** measure, quantum **9** allotment, allowance **10** allocation, assignment
apposite 3 apt **4** just **5** ad rem **6** proper, suited, timely **7** apropos, fitting, germane, right on **8** material, on target, relevant, suit-

able **9** pertinent **10** applicable **11** appropriate

appositeness 7 aptness, fitness **9** relevance **10** pertinence, timeliness **11** suitability

appraisal 5 stock **6** rating, survey **7** pricing **8** estimate, judgment **9** valuation **10** assessment, estimation, evaluation

appraise 3 eye, fix, set **4** rate, size **5** assay, audit, gauge, judge, price, set at, value **6** assess, figure, size up, survey **7** adjudge, examine, inspect, measure, valuate **8** estimate, evaluate, look over **9** calculate, figure out

appreciable 5 clear, plain **6** marked **7** evident, obvious **8** apparent, clear-cut, concrete, manifest, material, palpable, sensible, tangible **10** detectable, measurable, noticeable, observable **11** discernible, perceptible, substantial **12** considerable

appreciate 4 gain, go up, grow, know, like, love, rise **5** enjoy, grasp, judge, prize, savor, value **6** admire, esteem, fathom, regard, relish **7** apprize, cherish, cognize, enhance, improve, inflate, realize, respect **8** evaluate, increase, treasure **9** apprehend, delight in, recognize **10** comprehend, understand

appreciation 4 gain, rise **6** growth, regard, thanks **7** tribute **8** increase, judgment **9** awareness, gratitude, inflation **10** evaluation, perception **11** recognition, sensitivity, testimonial **12** gratefulness

apprehend 3 nab **4** bust, fear, grab, know, nail, read, twig **5** catch, grasp, run in, seize, sense **6** absorb, accept, arrest, collar, detain, divine, fathom, pick up, take in **7** capture, catch on, cognize, compass, foresee, make out, preknow, realize **8** conceive **9** recognize, visualize **10** anticipate, appreciate, understand

apprehensible 5 clear, lucid, plain **7** evident, obvious **8** distinct, explicit, knowable, luminous **9** graspable **10** fathomable

apprehension 3 ken **4** care, fear, idea **5** alarm, angst, dread, grasp, pinch, worry **6** arrest, notion, pickup, unease **7** anxiety, capture, concern, seizure, thought **8** disquiet, judgment **9** agitation, awareness, detention, knowledge, misgiving, suspicion **10** conception, foreboding, perception, solicitude, uneasiness **11** disquietude, premonition **13** understanding

apprehensive 5 alive, awake, aware, sharp **6** afraid, astute, scared, uneasy **7** anxious, fearful, knowing, worried **8** sensible, sentient, troubled **9** cognizant, conscious, observant, sensitive **10** discerning, disquieted, insightful, perceptive

apprentice 4 bind, tiro, tyro **5** pupil **6** novice, rookie **7** learner, starter, student, trainee **8** beginner, freshman, neophyte, newcomer **9** novitiate **10** tenderfoot

apprenticed 5 bound **7** obliged, pledged **8** articled **9** obligated **10** indentured

apprise 4 clue, post, tell, warn **6** advise, clue in, fill in, impart, inform, notify, reveal, wise up **7** let know **8** acquaint, announce, describe, disclose **9** make known **11** communicate

apprize 5 value **6** admire, esteem, regard, relish **7** cherish **8** hold dear, treasure **10** appreciate, rate highly

approach 4 near, nigh **5** reach, rival, verge **6** avenue, border, gain on **7** address, advance, apply to, attempt, descent **8** draw near, overture **11** approximate

approachable 7 affable **8** friendly, sociable **9** agreeable, congenial, reachable, receptive **10** accessible, attainable

approaching 6 coming **7** nearing **8** expected, imminent, oncoming, upcoming **11** forthcoming

approbate 4 back, like **5** favor **6** accept, assent, praise **7** applaud, approve, commend, consent, endorse, support **8** sanction **9** recommend **11** countenance

approbation 2 OK **3** nod **4** euge, okay **5** bravo, favor **6** esteem, praise **7** acclaim, consent, support **8** applause, approval, sanction **10** admiration, permission **11** endorsement, recognition **12** commendation

appropriate 3 apt, cop, due, fit **4** grab, just, lift, meet, take, true **5** allot, annex, claim, exact, filch, grasp, pinch, right, seize, steal, swipe, usurp **6** assign, assume, budget, devote, pilfer, proper, snatch, snitch, suited, timely, useful, worthy **7** apropos, desired, earmark, fitting, germane, merited, preempt, purloin **8** accroach, apposite, arrogate, deserved, eligible, entitled, relevant, rightful, set apart, set aside, suitable **9** befitting, opportune, pertinent, requisite **10** acceptable, admissible, applicable, commandeer, compatible, confiscate, convenient, felicitous, seasonable

appropriately 4 well **5** amply, aptly, right **8** properly, suitably **9** fittingly **10** acceptably, adequately, becomingly

appropriateness 3 use **5** order **7** account, aptness, fitness, service, utility **8** meetness **9** advantage, propriety, relevance, rightness **10** expediency, usefulness **13** applicability

appropriation 5 grant **7** funding, stipend, subsidy **9** allotment, allowance **10** allocation, assignment, earmarking, subvention

approval 2 OK **3** nod **4** okay **5** favor, leave,

say-so **6** assent **7** consent, go-ahead, license, support **8** applause, blessing, sanction, suffrage **10** acceptance, compliment, green light, permission **11** approbation, benediction, concurrence, endorsement **12** commendation, confirmation, ratification **13** authorization

approve 2 OK **4** okay **5** clear, favor, go for **6** accept, back up, praise, ratify, uphold **7** applaud, certify, commend, condone, confirm, endorse, initial, mandate, stand by, support, sustain **8** accredit, hold with, sanction **9** approbate, authorize, encourage **10** compliment **11** countenance

approximate 4 near **5** close, rough, touch **6** almost **7** similar, verge on **8** approach, ballpark, come near **10** resembling

approximately 4 most, nigh, or so **5** about, circa **6** all but, almost, nearly **7** close to **8** well-nigh **9** just about **10** more or less **11** practically

approximation 8 likeness, nearness **9** closeness **10** similarity **11** resemblance

appurtenance 7 adjunct **8** addition, appendix, ornament **9** accessory, apparatus, appendage **10** attachment **11** furnishings **13** accompaniment

appurtenant 5 extra **8** adjuvant **9** accessory, ancillary, auxiliary **10** additional, collateral, subsidiary **11** subordinate, subservient **12** accompanying, contributory

apricot 3 ume **4** ansu

a priori 8 provable, reasoned **9** deducible, deductive, derivable, inferable **11** inferential, presumptive

apron 5 stage **6** shield **7** garment **8** pinafore **9** extension

apropos 3 apt **4** as to, in re, meet **5** about, ad rem, anent, aptly, as for **6** proper, timely **7** fitting, germane, related **8** apposite, material, relevant, suitable, suitably, touching **9** as regards, opportune, pertinent, regarding **10** applicable, concerning, respecting **11** applicative, in respect to

apt 3 fit **4** just **5** alert, given, prone, quick, ready, savvy, smart **6** bright, clever, liable, likely, prompt, proper **7** apropos, fitting, germane, tending **8** apposite, disposed, inclined, relevant, suitable **9** befitting, pertinent, qualified **10** felicitous, responsive **11** appropriate, intelligent

aptitude 4 bent, gift **5** flair, knack, savvy **6** genius, liking, talent **7** ability, faculty, fitness **8** capacity, tendency **10** capability, cleverness, proclivity, propensity **11** disposition, inclination, suitability **12** predilection

aptness 4 bent, gift **5** flair, knack, skill **6** genius, talent **7** ability, faculty, fitness **8** tendency **9** propriety, readiness **10** capability, cleverness, expediency, likelihood **11** inclination, suitability **12** intelligence

aquanaut 5 diver **10** scuba diver

aquarium 4 tank **8** fish tank

aqua vitae 4 grog **5** booze, drink, hooch **6** brandy, cognac, liquor, tipple **7** alcohol, spirits **8** schnapps

aqueduct 5 canal **6** course **7** channel, conduit, passage **8** waterway **11** watercourse

aqueous 5 fluid **6** liquid, watery **9** liquefied

Aquila 5 eagle **13** constellation ***star:* 6** Altair

Aquitaine 7 Guienne ***queen:* 7** Eleanor

aquiver 5 shaky **7** quaking, shaking, trembly **9** shivering, trembling, tremulant, tremulous

Arab *chief:* 4 emir **5** sheik **6** sheikh, sultan ***country:* 4** Iraq, Oman **5** Egypt, Libya, Qatar, Sudan, Syria, Yemen **6** Jordan, Kuwait **7** Algeria, Bahrain, Lebanon, Morocco, Tunisia **11** Saudi Arabia

arable 7 fertile **8** fruitful, tillable **10** cultivable, productive

Arachne *father:* 5 Idmon ***form:* 6** spider ***mother:* 6** Cyrene ***rival:* 6** Athena **7** Minerva

arachnid 4 mite, tick **6** acarus, spider **8** scorpion **9** arthropod, phalangid, tarantula **10** harvestman **13** daddy longlegs

arbiter 3 ump **5** judge **6** expert, umpire **7** referee **8** mediator **9** authority, moderator **11** adjudicator

arbitrary 4 rash **6** chance, random **7** erratic, offhand, wayward, willful **8** fanciful, heedless **9** frivolous, impetuous, whimsical **10** capricious, subjective **10** irrational **12** unreasonable **13** discretionary

arbitrate 5 judge **6** settle, umpire **7** adjudge, mediate, referee **9** intervene **10** adjudicate **12** intermediate

arbitrator 5 judge **6** umpire **7** referee, settler **8** mediator **9** moderator **11** adjudicator

arbor 4 axle, beam **5** bower, frame, shaft **7** pergola, shelter, spindle

arc 3 bow, lob **4** arch, bend, path **5** curve, round **7** rainbow **9** curvation, curvature **11** measurement, progression

arcade 6 arches, loggia **7** gallery **10** passageway ***game:* 8** Skee-Ball ***pioneer:* 5** Atari

arcadia 4 Eden, Zion **6** heaven, utopia **7** Elysium, nirvana **8** paradise **9** fairyland, Shangri-la **10** wonderland

arcane 6 hidden, mystic, occult, opaque, secret **7** obscure, unknown **8** abstruse, esoteric **9** recondite **10** cabalistic, mysterious, unknowable **11** inscrutable **12** impenetrable **13** unaccountable

Arcas ***father:*** **4** Zeus **7** Jupiter ***mother:*** **8** Callisto

arch **3** bow, coy, sly **4** bend, hump, pert **5** curve, fresh, saucy, vault **6** camber, cheeky, impish **7** playful, roguish, waggish **8** flippant, malapert **9** curvature **10** coquettish **11** mischievous ***inner curve:*** **6** soffit **8** intrados ***kind:*** **4** ogee **5** ogive, round, Tudor **6** lancet **7** rampart, trefoil **9** horseshoe, primitive, segmental **10** shouldered **11** equilateral **12** basket-handle ***outer curve:*** **8** extrados ***part:*** **6** impost **8** keystone, springer, voussoir

archaeological site ***Africa:*** **8** Zimbabwe **13** Great Zimbabwe ***Britain:*** **7** Avebury **9** Skara Brae, Sutton Hoo **10** Stonehenge ***Cambodia:*** **6** Angkor **9** Angkor Wat ***Crete:*** **7** Knossos ***Egypt:*** **4** Giza **5** Luxor **6** Abydos, Karnak, Naqada, Thebes **7** Memphis **9** El-Bahnasa **11** Oxyrhynchus ***Greece:*** **6** Delphi **7** Mycenae, Olympia ***Guatemala:*** **5** Tikal ***Honduras:*** **5** Copán ***Indonesia:*** **9** Borobudur ***Iran:*** **10** Persepolis ***Iraq:*** **4** Isin, Nuzi **6** Nimrud **7** Babylon, Nineveh, Samarra ***Israel:*** **7** Jericho ***Italy:*** **7** Pompeii **11** Herculaneum ***Lebanon:*** **6** Byblos **7** Baalbek ***Mexico:*** **5** Mitla, Tulum, Uxmal **8** Palenque **10** Monte Albán **11** Chichén Itzá ***Peru:*** **11** Machu Picchu ***Syria:*** **7** Palmyra ***Tunisia:*** **8** Carthage, Kairouan ***Turkey:*** **4** Troy **6** Knidos **8** Hisarlik, Pergamon **9** Hissarlik ***Uzbekistan:*** **9** Samarkand

archaeologist **4** Bell (Gertrude), Dart (Raymond) **5** Evans (Arthur) **6** Carter (Howard), Childe (V. Gordon), Kidder (Alfred), Petrie (Flinders) **7** Thomsen (Christian), Woolley (Leonard), Worsaae (Jens) **8** Breasted (James Henry), Goodyear (William) **10** Schliemann (Heinrich) **11** Champollion (Jean-François), Winckelmann (Johann)

archaic **3** old **5** dated, olden, passé **6** bygone **7** ancient, antique **8** obsolete, outdated **9** out-of-date, primitive, unevolved **10** antiquated **11** undeveloped **12** old-fashioned

archangel **5** Uriel **7** Gabriel, Michael, Raphael

arched **4** bent **5** bowed, round **6** curved **7** curving, rounded

archer **4** Tell (William) **5** Cupid **6** bowman **9** Robin Hood **11** Sagittarius

archery **9** toxophily

archetypal **5** ideal, model **7** classic, perfect, typical **9** classical, exemplary **10** consummate **12** paradigmatic, prototypical

archetype **4** idea **5** ideal, model **6** mirror **7** epitome, essence, example, pattern **8** exemplar, original, paradigm, standard **9** beau ideal, prototype **10** apotheosis, embodiment, protoplast **12** quintessence

archfiend **5** demon, devil, Satan **6** diablo **7** Lucifer

Archie ***character:*** **5** Betty, Lodge (Hiram) **6** Archie, Reggie **7** Andrews (Fred, Mary), Jughead **8** Veronica ***creator:*** **7** Montana (Bob) ***Jughead's pet:*** **6** Hot Dog ***school:*** **9** Riverdale ***school staff:*** **6** Grundy (Geraldine), Kleats (Coach) **7** Beazley (Miss), Clayton (Coach), Svenson (Mr.) **10** Flutesnoot (Prof.), Weatherbee (Mr. Waldo) ***shop owner:*** **7** Pop Tate

Archimedes **5** Greek **8** inventor ***cry:*** **6** eureka ***discovery:*** **5** screw **8** buoyancy **9** principle **11** water raiser

archipelago ***Asian:*** **5** Malay ***Canada:*** **6** Arctic ***Japan:*** **4** Goto **9** Gotoretto ***Norway:*** **11** Spitsbergen ***Papua New Guinea:*** **8** Bismarck **9** Louisiade ***Philippines:*** **4** Sulu ***off Scotland:*** **7** Orcades, Orkneys ***United States:*** **9** Alexander

architect **5** maker **7** creator **8** designer, inventor **9** generator **10** originator ***American:*** **3** Pei (I. M.) **4** Hood (Raymond), Kahn (Louis) **5** Gehry (Frank), McKim (Charles), Meier (Richard), Roche (Kevin), Stone (Edward Durell), Weese (Harry), White (Stanford) **6** Breuer (Marcel), Fuller (Buckminster), Graves (Michael), Morgan (Julia), Neutra (Richard), Rogers (Isaiah), Soleri (Paolo), Upjohn (Richard), Walter (Thomas), Warren (William), Wright (Frank Lloyd) **7** Burnham (Daniel), Gilbert (Cass), Johnson (Philip), Latrobe (Benjamin), Olmsted (Frederick Law), Renwick (James), Sturgis (John Hubbard), Venturi (Robert) **8** Bulfinch (Charles), Saarinen (Eero, Eliel), Sullivan (Louis), Thornton (William), Yamasaki (Minoru) **10** Richardson (Henry Hobson) ***Austrian:*** **4** Loos (Adolf) **6** Wagner (Otto) ***Brazilian:*** **8** Niemeyer (Oscar) ***Canadian:*** **6** Safdie (Moshe) ***Dutch:*** **8** Koolhaas (Rem), Rietveld (Gerrit) ***English:*** **4** Nash (John), Shaw (Richard), Wood (John), Wren (Christopher) **5** Jones (Inigo), Scott (George Gilbert), Wyatt (James) **6** Foster (Norman), Rogers (Richard), Street (George Edmund), Voysey (Charles) **7** Lutyens (Edwin) **8** Vanbrugh (John) ***Finnish:*** **5** Aalto (Alvar) **8** Saarinen (Eero, Eliel) ***French:*** **6** Perret (Auguste) **7** Garnier (Tony), L'Enfant (Pierre-Charles) **11** Le Corbusier **12** Viollet-le-Duc (Eugène) ***German:*** **7** Gropius (Walter) **8** Schinkel

(Karl) **10** Mendelsohn (Erich) ***Israeli:*** **6** Safdie (Moshe) ***Italian:*** **5** Nervi (Pier Luigi), Piano (Renzo) **6** Romano (Giulio), Soleri (Paolo) **7** Alberti (Leon Battista), Bernini (Gian Lorenzo), da Vinci (Leonardo), Orcagna, Peruzzi (Baldassare), Raphael, Vignola (Giacomo da) **8** Bramante (Donato), Leonardo (da Vinci), Palladio (Andrea), Sangallo (Giuliano da), Terragni (Giuseppe) **9** Borromini (Francesco), Sansovino (Jacopo) **12** Michelangelo ***Japanese:*** **5** Tange (Kenzo) **8** Yamasaki (Minoru) ***Roman:*** **9** Vitruvius ***Scottish:*** **10** Mackintosh (Charles Rennie) ***Spanish:*** **5** Gaudí (Antonio) ***Swedish:*** **7** Asplund (Erik Gunnar)

architecture 6 design, makeup **9** formation **11** composition **12** constitution, construction ***ornament:*** **4** boss, fret **5** gutta **6** finial, volute **7** cabling, console, crocket, diglyph **8** triglyph, vignette **9** arabesque, modillion ***style:*** **5** Doric, Ionic, Tudor **6** Gothic, Norman, Rococo **7** Baroque **8** Colonial, Georgian **9** Byzantine, Victorian **10** Corinthian, Romanesque

archive 4 file **6** record **7** collect, history, library, records **8** document, register **9** chronicle **10** collection, repository

archon 10 magistrate

arctic 3 icy **4** cold **5** chill, gelid **6** chilly, frigid, frosty, wintry **7** glacial, numbing **8** freezing, hibernal **11** hyperborean ***animal:*** **3** auk, fox **4** bear, hare, seal, vole **5** sable, whale **6** ermine, marten **7** caribou, lemming **8** reindeer **9** polar bear, ptarmigan ***base:*** **4** Etah **5** Thule **6** Barrow **11** Point Barrow ***bird:*** **3** auk ***cetacean:*** **7** narwhal ***current:*** **8** Labrador ***dog:*** **5** husky **7** Samoyed **8** malamute ***explorer:*** **4** Byrd (Richard), Cook (Frederick) **5** Bylot (Robert), Davis (John), Peary (Robert) **6** Baffin (William), Bering (Vitus), Henson (Matthew), Hudson (Henry), Nansen (Fridtjof), Nobile (Umberto) **7** Barents (Willem), Bennett (Floyd), Wilkins (George), Wrangel (Ferdinand) **8** Amundsen (Roald) **9** Ellsworth (Lincoln), Mackenzie (Alexander), MacMillan (Donald) **10** Stefansson (Vilhjalmus) ***forest:*** **5** taiga ***jacket:*** **5** parka **6** anorak ***people:*** **4** Lapp **5** Aleut, Inuit, Yakut **6** Eskimo, Tungus **7** Chukchi, Samoyed ***sea:*** **4** Kara **6** Laptev **7** Barents, Chukchi **8** Beaufort ***transport:*** **7** dogsled ***treeless plains:*** **6** tundra

ardent 3 hot **4** agog, avid, keen, true **5** eager, fiery, loyal **6** fervid, fierce, heated, intent, red-hot, strong, torrid **7** blazing, burning, devoted, earnest, fervent, flaming, glowing, intense, shining, staunch, zealous **8** constant, desirous, faithful, powerful, resolute, sizzling, vehement, white-hot **9** allegiant, impatient, impetuous, impulsive, perfervid, scorching, steadfast **10** breathless, hot-blooded, passionate **11** impassioned **12** enthusiastic

ardor 4 élan, fire, heat, zeal, zest, zing **5** gusto, verve, vigor **6** energy, fealty, fervor, spirit, warmth **7** avidity, loyalty, passion **8** devotion, fidelity **9** eagerness, intensity, vehemence **10** allegiance, enthusiasm, excitement **12** faithfulness

arduous 4 hard **5** harsh, rough, sheer, steep, tight, tough **6** severe, taxing, tiring, trying, uphill **7** labored **8** grueling, rigorous, toilsome **9** difficult, effortful, gruelling, laborious, punishing, strenuous **10** formidable **11** precipitate, precipitous

area 4 belt, turf, zone **5** field, place, range, realm, scene, space, tract **6** domain, locale, region, sector, sphere **7** expanse, stretch **8** district, locality, province, vicinity **9** bailiwick, territory **12** neighborhood ***unit:*** **3** ure **4** acre **7** hectare

arena 5 field, scene, stage **6** sphere **7** stadium, theater **8** activity, building, coliseum, province **10** hippodrome **12** amphitheater ***level:*** **4** tier

Ares *Roman counterpart:* **4** Mars ***consort:*** **9** Aphrodite ***father:*** **4** Zeus ***mother:*** **4** Enyo, Hera ***sister:*** **4** Eris ***son:*** **5** Remus **7** Romulus

arête 5 crest, ridge

Arethusa 5 nymph **6** spring **9** wood nymph ***pursuer:*** **7** Alpheus

argent 6 silver **7** silvern, silvery **9** whiteness

Argentina *capital:* **11** Buenos Aires ***city:*** **6** Paraná **7** Córdoba, La Plata, Rosario, Santa Fe **11** Mar del Plata ***desert:*** **9** Patagonia ***language:*** **7** Spanish ***leader:*** **5** Perón (Juan) ***monetary unit:*** **4** peso ***mountain, range:*** **5** Andes **9** Aconcagua ***neighbor:*** **5** Chile **6** Brazil **7** Bolivia, Uruguay **8** Paraguay ***plain:*** **6** Pampas ***river:*** **5** Plata (Río de la) **6** Paraná **8** Colorado **12** Río de la Plata ***volcano:*** **5** Maipo **9** Tupungato

Arges 7 Cyclops ***brother:*** **7** Brontes **8** Steropes ***father:*** **6** Uranus ***mother:*** **4** Gaea

argon symbol 2 Ar

Argonaut 4 hero **10** adventurer **13** paper nautilus ***leader:*** **5** Jason

argosy 4 ship **5** fleet **6** armada, supply **8** flotilla

argot 4 cant **5** idiom, lingo, slang **6** jargon, patois, patter **7** dialect **10** vernacular

arguable 4 moot **7** dubious **8** doubtful **9** debatable, in dispute, uncertain **10** disputable **11** contestable, problematic **12** questionable

argue 5 claim, clash, prove **6** assert, attest, bicker, debate, differ, induce, object, reason **7** agitate, canvass, contend, discuss, dispute, dissent, justify, protest, quarrel, quibble, stickle, testify, witness, wrangle **8** announce, conflict, consider, disagree, indicate, maintain, persuade, polemize, squabble **9** thrash out **10** polemicize **11** expostulate, remonstrate

argument 3 row **4** case, feud, flap, fuss **5** claim, proof, set-to, theme, topic **6** debate, dustup, hassle, motive, reason, rumpus, thesis **7** defense, dispute, polemic, sorites, subject, summary, wrangle **8** abstract, evidence, rebuttal **9** amplitude, assertion, discourse **10** contention, discussion, dissension, squabbling **11** controversy, disputation, embroilment **12** disagreement

argumentation 6 debate **7** dispute, oratory **8** forensic, rhetoric **9** dialectic, reasoning **10** discussion **11** controversy, disputation

argumentative 4 moot **9** in dispute, litigious, polemical **11** contentious, quarrelsome **12** disputatious, questionable **13** controversial

Argus *father:* 4 Zeus ***mother:* 5** Niobe ***slayer:* 6** Hermes

Argus-eyed 5 alert **8** watchful **9** all-seeing

argyle 4 sock **6** design **7** diamond, pattern **8** Campbell

aria 3 air, lay **4** hymn, lied, solo, song, tune **5** ditty **6** melody **7** descant

Ariadne *father:* 5 Minos ***husband:* 7** Theseus ***island home:* 5** Naxos ***mother:* 8** Pasiphaë

arid 3 dry **4** drab, dull, sere **5** dusty, vapid **6** barren, boring, desert, dreary, jejune **7** bone-dry, insipid, parched, sterile, tedious, thirsty **8** droughty, lifeless, weariful **9** dryasdust, infertile, unwatered, waterless, wearisome **10** lackluster, spiritless, unfruitful **12** moistureless **13** uninteresting

Ariel 6 spirit ***master:* 8** Prospero

Aries 3 ram **13** constellation

aright 4 well **5** fitly **6** justly, nicely **8** decently, properly **9** correctly, fittingly, precisely **10** accurately, decorously

Ariosto epic 14 Orlando Furioso

arise 4 go up, lift, soar, wake **5** awake, begin, get up, issue, mount, occur, start **6** appear, ascend, aspire, come up, crop up, emerge, spring, uprear, wake up **7** emanate, proceed **8** commence **9** originate

Aristaeus *father:* 6 Apollo ***mother:* 6** Cyrene ***son:* 7** Actaeon ***wife:* 7** Autonoë

aristocracy 5 elite, state **6** gentry, jet set **7** who's who **8** nobility, noblesse **9** beau monde, blue blood, gentility, haut monde **10** government, patricians, patriciate, upper class, upper crust

aristocrat 9 blue blood, gentleman, patrician ***ancient Greek:* 8** eupatrid ***Russian:* 5** boyar **6** boyard

aristocratic 5 aloof, elite, noble **6** lordly **7** courtly, elegant, genteel, haughty, refined, stately **8** highborn, well-born, well-bred **9** dignified, exclusive, patrician **10** privileged, upper-class, upper-crust **11** blue-blooded

Aristophanes play 5 Birds (The), Frogs (The), Wasps (The) **6** Clouds (The), Plutus **10** Lysistrata

arithmetic 4 math **8** addition, counting, figuring **9** ciphering, reckoning **10** estimation **11** calculation, computation, mathematics

Arizona *capital:* 7 Phoenix ***city:* 4** Mesa, Yuma **5** Tempe **6** Bisbee, Sedona, Tucson **8** Glendale, Prescott **9** Flagstaff **10** Scottsdale ***mountain:* 9** Humphreys (Peak) ***nickname:* 11** Grand Canyon (State) ***park:* 15** Petrified Forest ***river:* 4** Gila, Salt **8** Colorado ***state bird:* 10** cactus wren ***state flower:* 7** saguaro (cactus) ***state tree:* 9** palo verde

ark 3 den **4** ship **5** chest, haven **6** adytum, asylum, refuge **7** convent, retreat, shelter **8** hideaway **9** safe house, sanctuary **10** repository, Torah chest ***landfall:* 6** Ararat ***wood:* 6** gopher **7** cypress

Arkansas *capital:* 10 Little Rock ***city:* 4** Hope **9** Fort Smith, Pine Bluff **10** Hot Springs **11** Bentonville **12** Fayetteville ***mountain, range:* 5** Ozark **8** Magazine ***nickname:* 17** Land of Opportunity ***river:* 3** Red ***state bird:* 11** mockingbird ***state flower:* 12** apple blossom ***state tree:* 12** loblolly pine

arm 3 bay, ell, gun, rig **4** cove, gear, gulf, limb, wing **5** annex, bayou, equip, firth, force, inlet, power **6** fit out, harbor, muscle, outfit, slough, weapon **7** appoint, furnish, turn out **8** accouter, strength **9** extension ***bone:* 4** ulna **6** radius **7** humerus ***combining form:* 6** brachi **7** brachio ***muscle:* 6** biceps **7** triceps

armada 4 navy **5** boats, fleet, force, group, ships **7** vessels **8** flotilla, warships

armadillo 4 apar, peba, tatu ***relative:* 5** sloth **8** anteater, tamandua

armament 4 arms **5** armor **6** weapon **7** defense **8** ordnance, security, weaponry **9** munitions, safeguard **10** ammunition, protection

armamentarium 4 fund **5** stock, store **6** supply **9** inventory

armchair 6 remote **8** fauteuil **9** vicarious **11** theoretical

armed forces **4** army, navy **6** troops **7** marines **8** air force, military **10** servicemen
Armenia ***capital:*** **7** Yerevan ***city:*** **6** Gyumri **8** Vanadzor ***lake:*** **5** Sevan ***monetary unit:*** **4** dram ***mountain, range:*** **7** Aragats **8** Caucasus ***neighbor:*** **4** Iran **6** Turkey **7** Georgia **10** Azerbaijan ***river:*** **5** Araks
armistice **5** truce **9** agreement, cease-fire **10** suspension
armor **4** mail **5** aegis, cover, guard **6** shield **7** buckler **8** security **9** safeguard **10** protection ***arm:*** **8** brassard ***body:*** **7** cuirass ***armpit:*** **8** pallette ***buttocks:*** **5** culet ***coat:*** **7** hauberk **10** brigandine ***face:*** **5** visor **6** beaver ***flexible:*** **4** mail ***foot:*** **8** solleret ***hand:*** **7** gantlet **8** gauntlet ***head:*** **6** helmet ***horse:*** **4** bard **5** barde **8** chamfron ***leg:*** **6** greave **7** jambeau ***mail:*** **4** coif **7** hauberk ***suit:*** **7** panoply ***thigh:*** **4** tace **5** tasse **6** cuisse, tuille ***throat:*** **6** gorget
armory **4** dump **5** depot, plant, range, store **7** arsenal, factory **8** magazine **10** collection, storehouse
armpit **6** axilla **8** underarm ***Scottish:*** **5** oxter
arms **7** ensigns, warfare **8** weaponry
army **4** host **5** flock, horde **6** legion **7** militia **9** multitude ***combat arm:*** **5** armor **8** infantry **9** artillery ***commission:*** **6** brevet **7** reserve ***Fort:*** **3** Dix, Lee, Ord **4** Drum, Hood, Knox, Myer, Polk, Sill **5** Bliss, Bragg, Irwin, Lewis, McCoy, Meade, Riley, Story **6** Carson, Eustis, Gillem, Gordon, Greely, McNair, Monroe, Rucker **7** Belvoir, Benning, Detrick, Jackson, Ritchie, Shafter, Stewart **8** Buchanan, Campbell, Hamilton, Holabird, Huachuca, Monmouth **9** McClellan, McPherson **10** Richardson, Sam Houston, Wainwright **11** Leavenworth ***law enforcer:*** **2** MP ***mascot:*** **4** mule ***meal:*** **3** MRE **4** chow, mess ***mine layer:*** **6** sapper ***NCO:*** **8** corporal, sergeant ***officer:*** **5** major **7** captain, colonel, general, warrant **10** lieutenant ***post:*** **4** base, camp, fort ***postal abbreviation:*** **3** APO ***ration:*** **3** MRE ***relating to:*** **7** martial **8** military ***school:*** **3** OCS, OTS **7** academy **9** West Point ***signaler:*** **6** bugler ***store:*** **2** PX **10** commissary **12** post exchange ***unit:*** **5** corps, squad, troop **7** brigade, cavalry, company, platoon **8** division, regiment **9** battalion ***vehicle:*** **4** jeep, tank **6** Abrams, Humvee **7** Bradley **9** half-track
Arnaz, Desi ***character:*** **5** Ricky (Ricardo) ***company:*** **6** Desilu ***mentor:*** **6** Cougat (Xavier) ***signature song:*** **6** Babalu ***star of:*** **9** I Love Lucy ***wife:*** **4** Ball (Lucille), Lucy
aroma **4** balm, odor **5** scent, smell, spice **6** flavor **7** bouquet, incense, perfume **9** fragrance, redolence
aromatic **5** balmy, spicy, sweet **6** savory **7** odorous, perfumy, pungent, scented **8** fragrant, perfumed, redolent **9** ambrosial
around **4** near, nigh **5** about, circa **6** nearby **7** through ***prefix:*** **4** ambi, peri **5** amphi **6** circum
around-the-clock **8** constant, unending **9** ceaseless, continual, incessant, perpetual, unceasing **10** continuous **11** unremitting **13** uninterrupted
arouse **4** fire, stir, wake, whet **5** alert, awake, pique, rally, waken **6** awaken, bestir, excite, fire up, foment, incite, kindle, work up **7** agitate, inflame **9** challenge, stimulate
arraign **3** tax, try **5** blame **6** accuse, charge, indict, summon **9** criminate, inculpate **11** incriminate
arrange **4** plan, sort **5** adapt, array, chart, order, score, unify **6** assort, codify, deploy, design, devise, lay out, line up, map out, scheme, set out, settle **7** dispose, marshal, prepare, work out **8** organize, sequence **9** blueprint, harmonize, integrate, methodize **10** bring about, categorize, instrument, symphonize, synthesize **11** choreograph, orchestrate, systematize
arrangement **5** array, order, setup **6** format, layout, lineup, series **8** grouping, ordering, sequence **9** structure **10** adaptation, deployment **11** disposition **12** distribution ***floral:*** **4** posy **7** bouquet, garland
arrant **4** rank **5** gross, total, utter **6** brassy, brazen **7** blatant, extreme, flat-out **8** absolute, complete, impudent, infernal, overbold **9** barefaced, downright, egregious, out-and-out, shameless, unabashed **10** immoderate, unblushing
arras **6** screen **7** drapery **8** curtains, tapestry
array **3** lot **4** clad, garb, pomp, show **5** adorn, batch, bunch, clump, dress, group, order **6** attire, bundle, clothe, draw up, finery, lineup, parade **7** apparel, arrange, cluster, display, dispose, garment, marshal, militia, panoply, raiment, variety **8** clothing, decorate, enclothe, organize, spectrum **9** formation **10** assortment **11** systematize
arrears **3** due **4** debt **5** claim, debit **7** deficit **9** liability **10** balance due, obligation **12** indebtedness
arrest **3** nab, tab, tag **4** bust, grab, halt, hold, jail, slow, snag, stay, stem, stop **5** block, catch, check, pinch, run in, seize, stall **6** collar, detain, haul in, lock up, pick up, pull in, retard, take in **7** capture, contain, seizure **8** imprison, obstruct, restrain **9** apprehend,

detention, interrupt **11** incarcerate **12** apprehension

arresting 6 marked, signal **7** salient **8** striking **9** affective, appealing, prominent **10** attractive, compelling, enchanting, impressive, noticeable, remarkable **11** conspicuous, eye-catching, outstanding

arrival 6 advent, coming **7** landing, success **8** entrance, incoming **9** emergence **10** appearance

arrive 4 come, land, show **5** get in, get to, reach **6** appear, show up, thrive, turn up **7** prosper, succeed **8** flourish

arriviste 7 parvenu, upstart **8** roturier **12** nouveau riche

arrogance 3 ego **4** airs, gall **5** brass, cheek, pride **6** hubris **7** conceit, disdain, hauteur **8** self-love **9** loftiness **11** haughtiness

arrogant 5 cocky, proud **6** lordly, snooty **7** haughty, pompous **8** cavalier, fastuous, insolent, superior **9** egotistic **10** disdainful, high-handed, peremptory **11** domineering, magisterial, overbearing **12** supercilious **13** high-and-mighty, self-important

arrogate 4 grab, take **5** annex, claim, seize, usurp **6** assume, demand **7** ascribe, preempt **8** accroach, take over **9** sequester **10** commandeer, confiscate **11** appropriate, expropriate

arrow 4 dart **5** shaft ***poison:*** **4** inée, upas **6** curare

arrowroot 5 plant, tuber **6** starch **7** coontie

Arrowsmith's wife 5 Leora

arroyo 3 gap **4** draw **5** brook, chasm, cleft, clove, creek, gorge, gulch, gully **6** coulee, ravine **7** channel **11** watercourse

Ars Amatoria poet 4 Ovid

arsenal 4 dump **5** depot, stock, store **6** armory, supply **7** factory, weapons **8** magazine, ordnance **9** stockpile **10** depository, repertoire, repository, storehouse

arsenic symbol 2 As

arson 6 firing **8** torching **9** pyromania **12** incendiarism

arsonist 5 firer, torch **7** firebug **10** incendiary

art 5 craft, skill **6** métier **7** finesse, know-how **8** artifice, painting, vocation **9** dexterity, expertise, sculpture **10** handicraft ***botanical:*** **6** bonsai ***faddish:*** **6** kitsch ***style:*** **2** op **3** pop **4** dada **6** cubist, rococo **7** fauvist, realist, surreal **8** abstract, futurist **9** classical **10** naturalist, surrealist **12** naturalistic, surrealistic **13** expressionist, impressionist

art deco 5 style **6** design ***designer:*** **4** Erté

Artemis *Roman counterpart:* **5** Diana ***birthplace:*** **5** Delos ***brother:*** **6** Apollo ***father:*** **4** Zeus ***mother:*** **4** Leto ***priestess:*** **9** Iphigenia

artery 3 way **4** duct, line, path, road, tube **5** aorta, track **6** avenue, course, street, vessel **7** carotid, channel, conduit, highway, passage, pathway **8** coronary **9** boulevard **12** thoroughfare

artful 3 sly **4** foxy, wily **5** adept, sharp, slick, smart, suave **6** adroit, astute, clever, crafty, shrewd, smooth, tricky **7** cunning **8** guileful, skillful **9** dexterous, ingenious **10** artificial, diplomatic

arthropod 3 bee, fly **4** crab, mite, moth, tick **6** beetle, insect, shrimp, spider **7** lobster **8** arachnid, barnacle, diplopod, myriapod, scorpion **9** butterfly, centipede, cockroach, millipede, trilobite **10** crustacean ***body segment:*** **6** somite, telson **8** metamere

Arthur see **King Arthur**

article 2 an **3** the **4** bind, item, part **5** essay, paper, piece, point, theme, thing **6** matter, object **7** element, feature, passage, section **10** particular **11** composition, stipulation ***French:*** **3** les, une ***German:*** **3** das, dem, den, der, des, die, ein **4** eine ***Spanish:*** **2** un **3** las, los, una

articled 5 bound **10** indentured

articulate 3 say **4** join, link, oral, talk **5** clear, hinge, joint, lucid, shape, speak, state, utter, vocal, voice **6** couple, fluent, prolix, relate, spoken, voiced **7** connect, express, jointed **8** coherent, definite, distinct, eloquent, vocalize **9** effective, enunciate, harmonize, integrate, pronounce, verbalize **10** coordinate, expressive **11** concatenate **12** intelligible, smooth-spoken

artifact 5 curio, relic **6** legacy, rarity, trophy **7** remnant, spin-off, vestige **8** creation, heirloom **9** by-product, handcraft, handiwork **10** handicraft **11** contrivance, fabrication

artifice 4 play, ploy, ruse, wile **5** craft, feint, guile, skill, trick **6** deceit, device, gambit **7** cunning, slyness **8** facility, foxiness, trickery, wiliness **9** adeptness, canniness, chicanery, duplicity, ingenuity, stratagem **10** adroitness, artfulness, cleverness, craftiness

artificial 4 fake, faux, mock, sham **5** bogus, dummy, faked, false, phony, put-on **6** ersatz, forced, hollow, unreal **7** assumed, feigned, in vitro, labored, man-made, plastic, pretend **8** affected, mannered, spurious **9** contrived, imitation, insincere, simulated, synthetic, unnatural **10** fabricated, factitious, fictitious, substitute

artillery 4 arms **5** canon, force **6** rocket **7** battery, bazooka, gunnery, weapons **8** cannonry, howitzer, ordnance, weaponry **9** munitions

artisan 6 worker **7** builder, workman **8** producer **9** carpenter, craftsman **12** craftsperson

artist 7 painter **8** sculptor, virtuoso ***garb:* 5** smock ***knife:* 7** spatula ***medium:* 3** oil **5** paint **6** pastel **7** tempera **8** charcoal **10** watercolor ***pigment board:* 7** palette ***stand:* 5** easel ***workshop:* 6** studio **7** atelier (see also **painter**)

artless 4 free, open, pure, true **5** crude, naive, plain **6** direct, honest, simple **7** genuine, natural, sincere, unaware **8** trusting **9** childlike, guileless, ingenuous, unstudied **10** aboveboard, forthright, unaffected, uncultured, unschooled **12** unartificial, unsuspicious

Art of Love poet 4 Ovid

arty 5 showy **6** pseudo **8** affected, imposing **9** overblown **11** pretentious **12** high-sounding

Aruba *capital:* 10 Oranjestad ***language:* 5** Dutch **10** Papiamento ***monetary unit:* 6** florin ***part of:* 11** Netherlands

as 3 for, who **4** coin, like, that, when **5** being, since, which, while **6** though **7** because **11** considering, for instance

ASAP 4 stat **6** at once **11** immediately

as a rule 6 mainly, mostly **7** usually **8** commonly **9** generally **10** frequently, ordinarily

Ascanius 5 Iulus ***father:* 6** Aeneas

ascend 4 go up, lift, rise, soar **5** arise, climb, crest, mount, scale **6** aspire, move up, occupy **7** lift off, take off **8** escalade, escalate, surmount

ascendancy 4 rule **5** power, reign **7** command, control, mastery **8** dominion **9** authority, dominance, influence, supremacy **10** domination, prepotency **11** preeminence, sovereignty **13** preponderance

ascendant 6 master, rising **7** regnant **8** ancestor, dominant, forebear, relative, superior **9** paramount, precursor, prevalent, sovereign **10** commanding, forefather, forerunner, prevailing, progenitor **11** controlling, overbearing, predecessor, predominant, predominate **12** preponderant, primogenitor

ascension 4 rise **6** rising **7** going up, scaling **8** climbing, mounting

ascent 4 ramp, rise **5** climb, grade, slope **6** rising **7** advance, incline **8** gradient, progress **9** acclivity, elevation, uplifting

ascertain 5 learn **7** catch on, find out, unearth **8** discover, make sure **9** determine, establish, figure out

ascetic 5 stoic **6** hermit, severe **7** austere, eremite, recluse **9** abstinent, anchoress, anchorite, mortified **10** abstemious, astringent, forbearing, restrained **11** disciplined, self-denying ***ancient Hebrew:* 6** Essene ***Buddhist:* 5** bonze ***early Christian:* 7** stylite ***Hindu:* 4** yogi **5** fakir, sadhu, Yogin ***Muslim:* 4** Sufi

Asclepius see **Aesculapius**

ascribe 3 lay **4** cite **5** infer, refer **6** assign, charge, credit, impute **7** chalk up **8** accredit **9** attribute, reference **10** conjecture

Asenath *husband:* 6 Joseph ***son:* 7** Ephraim **8** Manasseh

aseptic 4 cool, flat **5** clean **7** sterile **8** germfree, hygienic, sanitary **9** unfeeling **10** restrained, sterilized **11** emotionless, unemotional

asexual 6 agamic

as for 4 in re **5** about, anent **7** apropos **9** regarding **10** concerning, respecting **12** with regard to

as good as 4 nigh **6** all but, almost, nearly **8** in effect, well-nigh **9** basically, in essence, just about, virtually **11** essentially, practically

ash 4 soot, tree, wood **7** cinders, residue **8** clinkers

ashamed 6 abased, abject, guilty **7** abashed, humbled **8** contrite, penitent **9** chagrined, mortified, repentant **10** humiliated **11** discomfited, embarrassed

ashen 3 wan **4** gray, pale **5** faded, pasty, waxen **6** doughy, pallid, sallow, sickly **7** ghostly **8** blanched, bleached **9** bloodless, colorless **10** corpselike

Asher *daughter:* 5 Serah ***father:* 5** Jacob ***mother:* 6** Zilpah ***son:* 4** Isui **6** Beriah, Ishuah, Jimnah

ashes 5 ruins **6** pallor **7** remains

ashy 3 wan **4** drab, pale **5** livid, waxen **6** doughy, leaden, pallid **7** ghastly, greyish **8** blanched **9** bloodless, colorless, washed-out **10** cadaverous

Asia *country:* 4 Laos **5** Burma, China, India, Japan, Korea, Nepal **6** Bhutan, Russia, Taiwan **7** Armenia, Georgia, Myanmar, Vietnam **8** Cambodia, Malaysia, Mongolia, Pakistan, Sri Lanka, Thailand **9** Indonesia, Kampuchea, Kazakstan, Singapore **10** Azerbaijan, Bangladesh, Kazakhstan, Kyrgyzstan, North Korea, South Korea, Tajikistan, Uzbekistan **11** Afghanistan, Philippines **12** Turkmenistan ***ethnic group:* 3** Han, Lao, Tai **4** Arab, Kurd, Moor, Shan **5** Karen, Khmer, Malay, Tajik, Tamil, Uzbek **6** Burman, Lepcha, Manchu, Mongol, Sindhi **7** Baluchi, Bengali, Persian, Punjabi, Tibetan **8** Armenian, Assyrian, Javanese **9** Dravidian, Indo-Aryan, Sinhalese **10** Circassian, Montagnard, Singhalese ***language:* 3** Lao **4** Ainu, Urdu **5** Hindi, Malay, Tamil,

Uzbek **6** Arabic, Bahasa, Korean, Nepali **7** Bengali, Burmese, Khalkha, Kurdish, Persian, Tibetan, Turkish **8** Armenian, Japanese, Javanese, Mandarin **9** Cambodian **10** Vietnamese

Asia Minor 8 Anatolia ***country:*** **6** Turkey ***region:*** **5** Ionia

Asian inland sea 4 Aral

Asian Sasquatch 4 yeti

aside 4 away **5** apart **7** tangent **8** away from **9** in reserve, privately **10** digression, discursion **11** parenthesis

aside from 3 bar, but **4** save **6** bating, except **7** barring, besides **9** excepting, excluding, other than, outside of

Asimov, Isaac ***forte:*** **5** sci-fi ***work:*** **6** I Robot **9** Nightfall **10** Foundation (Trilogy)

asinine 5 crazy, daffy, silly **6** absurd, simple **7** fatuous, foolish, idiotic, puerile, witless **8** mindless **9** brainless **10** irrational, ridiculous **11** nonsensical

ask 3 beg, bid **4** pray, quiz, seek **5** crave, exact, grill, plead, query **6** appeal, demand, desire, invite **7** beseech, call for, canvass, consult, enquire, entreat, examine, implore, inquire, request, require, solicit **8** petition, question **9** catechize, importune **10** supplicate **11** interrogate ***Scottish:*** **5** speer, speir

askance 8 sidelong, sideways **9** cynically, obliquely **10** critically, doubtfully, doubtingly, scornfully **11** skeptically **12** suspiciously **13** distrustfully, mistrustfully

asker 6 beggar, prayer, suitor **7** speaker **9** suppliant **10** petitioner, questioner, supplicant **11** supplicator

askew 4 awry **6** turned **8** cockeyed **9** crookedly

aslant 4 awry **5** askew **7** crooked **8** cockeyed, sideways, sidewise **9** obliquely

asleep 4 dead, idle, numb **5** inert **6** dozing, numbed **7** defunct, dormant, napping **8** benumbed, deadened, inactive, in repose, not alert, sluggish **9** senseless, unfeeling **10** insensible, slumbering, unanimated **11** indifferent, unconscious **12** anesthetized

as long as 3 for **5** since **6** seeing **7** because, whereas **8** provided **11** considering **12** provided that

as much as 6 all but, almost **8** well-nigh **11** essentially, practically

aspect 3 air **4** look, mien, side **5** angle, facet, phase, scene, slant **6** regard, status **7** bearing, seeming **8** exposure, position **9** direction **10** appearance **11** perspective

aspen 4 tree **6** poplar

asperity 5 rigor **8** acerbity, acrimony, grimness, hardness, hardship, mordancy, severity, tartness **9** harshness, roughness, sharpness **10** bitterness, difficulty, unevenness **12** irregularity, irritability

asperse 4 slur **5** libel, smear, sully **6** attack, defame, insult, malign, vilify **7** baptize, slander, tarnish, traduce **8** bad mouth, dishonor, sprinkle **9** denigrate, insinuate **10** calumniate

aspersion 4 muck, slam, slur **5** abuse **7** calumny, obloquy, slander **9** invective, stricture **10** defamation, detraction **11** denigration **12** vilification, vituperation **13** animadversion

asphalt 4 pave **7** bitumen, surface **8** blacktop, pavement

asphyxiate 4 kill **5** choke, drown **6** stifle **7** smother **8** strangle, throttle **9** suffocate

aspirant 6 seeker **7** hopeful, seeking **9** applicant, candidate, contender

aspiration 3 aim **4** goal, urge, wish **5** dream **6** desire, intent, object **7** craving, longing, passion, pursuit **8** ambition, striving, yearning **9** breathing, objective **10** pretension **13** ambitiousness

aspire 3 aim, try **4** long, pant, rise, seek, soar, want, wish **5** arise, mount, yearn **6** ascend, desire, hunger, strive, thirst

aspiring 7 longing, seeking, wanting, wishful **8** striving, vaulting, yearning **9** ambitious

as regards 4 in re **7** apropos **8** touching **10** concerning, respecting

ass 4 dolt, fool, jerk, moke, mule **5** burro, dunce, idiot **6** donkey, nitwit **8** bonehead, imbecile **10** nincompoop ***female:*** **5** jenny ***male:*** **4** jack ***wild Asian:*** **5** kiang **6** onager

assai 4 very

assail 4 bash, beat **5** abuse, beset, blast, pound, storm **6** attack, berate, buffet, charge, fall on, malign, oppugn, pummel, revile, strike, vilify **7** assault, bombard **8** fall upon, lambaste **9** break down

assassin 3 gun **5** bravo **6** gunman, hit man, killer **7** torpedo **8** murderer **9** cutthroat **10** hatchet man, triggerman ***of Caesar:*** **6** Brutus **7** Cassius ***of Garfield:*** **7** Guiteau (Charles Julius) ***of J. F. Kennedy:*** **6** Oswald (Lee Harvey) ***of M. L. King:*** **3** Ray (James Earl) ***of Lincoln:*** **5** Booth (John Wilkes) ***of Marat:*** **6** Corday (Charlotte) ***of McKinley:*** **8** Czolgosz (Leon) ***of R. F. Kennedy:*** **6** Sirhan (Sirhan)

assassinate 4 do in, kill, slay **6** finish, murder, rub out **7** bump off, execute, gun down, put away, take out **8** dispatch, knock off **9** eliminate, liquidate

assault 3 mug, war **4** raid **5** beset, fight, onset, set-to, storm **6** assail, attack, charge, fall on, strike, threat **7** aggress, besiege, mugging, offense **8** fall upon, invasion, storming **9** incursion, offensive, onslaught, violation **10** aggression

assay 3 try **4** rate, seek, test **5** judge, offer, prove, trial, value, weigh **6** assess, result, rating, strive, survey **7** analyze, attempt, examine, inspect, measure, valuate, venture **8** analysis, appraise, endeavor, estimate, evaluate, struggle **9** appraisal, undertake, valuation **10** assessment, evaluation, inspection **11** examination, measurement

assemblage 5 crowd, group **6** muster **7** company, turnout **8** audience **9** gathering **10** collection **11** aggregation, composition, convergence **12** congregation

assemble 4 call, form, make, mass, meet, mold **5** amass, build, clump, group, shape, unite **6** gather, muster, summon **7** cluster, collect, convene, convoke, fashion, marshal, produce, round up **8** congress, contrive **9** aggregate, forgather **10** accumulate, congregate **11** fit together, manufacture, put together **12** call together, come together **13** bring together

assembly 4 bevy **5** bunch, covey, crowd, flock, group, party, plena (plural), rally, setup **6** muster, plenum, troupe **7** cluster, meeting **8** conclave **9** congeries, gathering **10** collection **11** association, fabrication, get-together, manufacture **12** congregation, construction ***American Indian:*** **6** powwow ***ancient Greek:*** **8** ecclesia ***ancient Roman:*** **7** comitia ***Anglo-Saxon:*** **4** moot **5** gemot **6** gemote **8** folkmoot, folkmote ***ecclesiastical:*** **5** synod **10** consistory ***legislative:*** **4** diet **6** senate **8** congress **10** parliament ***place:*** **4** hall, room **5** agora **10** auditorium ***Russian:*** **4** duma ***witches':*** **6** sabbat **7** sabbath

assent 2 OK **3** nod, yes, yup **4** okay, yeah **5** agree, uh-huh **6** accede, accord, concur, say yes **7** approve, consent, embrace **8** approval, sanction, thumbs-up **9** accession, acquiesce, admission, agreement, subscribe **10** acceptance, permission **11** affirmation, concurrence **12** acquiescence

assert 3 say **4** aver, avow **5** argue, claim, posit, state, utter, voice **6** adduce, affirm, allege, attest, avouch, defend, depose, insist, submit **7** advance, contend, declare, express, justify, profess, protest, publish, warrant **8** announce, maintain, proclaim **9** broadcast, postulate, predicate **10** promulgate

assertion 6 avowal **8** averment **9** affidavit, statement **10** allegation, avouchment, contention, deposition, disclosure, insistence, profession **11** affirmation, attestation, declaration **12** asseveration **13** pronouncement

assertive 4 firm, sure **5** pushy **6** strong **7** assured, certain, decided, pushing **8** cocksure, emphatic, forceful, positive **9** confident, energetic, insistent **10** aggressive, resounding **11** affirmative, distinctive, self-assured **13** self-confident

assess 3 fix, tax **4** deem, levy, rate **5** assay, exact, judge, put on, set at, value, weigh **6** charge, figure, impose, reckon, survey **7** account, compute, subject, valuate **8** appraise, consider, estimate, evaluate **9** determine

assessment 3 fee, tax **4** duty, levy, toll **6** charge, impost, rating, tariff **8** estimate, judgment **9** appraisal, valuation **10** estimation, evaluation **12** appraisement

asset 4 boon, good, plus **5** merit **6** credit **7** benefit **8** blessing, resource **9** advantage **11** distinction ***opposite:*** **9** liability

assets 5 items, means, money **6** wealth **7** capital **8** bankroll, holdings, property **9** resources, valuables **11** possessions

asseverate 4 aver, avow **5** state **6** affirm, assert, attest, avouch, depose, insist **7** certify, contend, declare, profess **8** maintain, proclaim **9** pronounce

assiduous 4 busy **5** eager **6** active **7** moiling, zealous **8** diligent, sedulous, tireless **9** attentive, laborious **10** persistent, unflagging **11** hard-working, industrious **13** indefatigable

assiduously 4 hard **6** busily **9** earnestly, intensely **10** diligently, thoroughly **11** intensively **12** exhaustively, meticulously, persistently **13** painstakingly, unremittingly

assign 3 fix, lay, set **4** cede, deed, give, name **5** allot, allow, refer **6** charge, convey, credit, define, impute, remise, settle **7** appoint, ascribe, chalk up, earmark, lay down, mete out, specify, station **8** accredit, allocate, delegate, make over, relegate, sign over, transfer **9** admeasure, apportion, attribute, designate, establish, prescribe **10** pigeonhole

assignation 4 date **5** tryst **7** meeting **9** allotment **10** engagement, rendezvous **11** appointment, get-together

assignee 5 agent, proxy **6** deputy, factor **7** officer **8** attorney, delegate

assignment 3 job **4** beat, duty, post, task, work **5** chore, stint **6** office **8** homework, position, transfer **9** allotment **10** allocation, delegation, obligation **11** designation

assimilate 5 adapt, adopt, grasp, learn, liken, match **6** absorb, adjust, digest, equate, imbibe, soak up, take in, take up **7** blend in, compare, conform **8** parallel **10** comprehend, understand **11** incorporate

assimilation 8 taking in **9** awareness **10** absorption, conversion **11** mindfulness, recognition **12** apperception **13** consciousness, incorporation

assist 3 aid **4** abet, back, help, lift **5** boost, do for, serve, stead **6** relief, succor **7** backing, benefit, comfort, help out, secours, service, support, work for **8** benefact, work with **9** accompany, cooperate, open doors

assistance 3 aid **4** hand, help, lift **5** boost **6** relief, succor **7** backing, benefit, comfort, secours, service, subsidy, support **8** abetment **9** upholding **10** subvention, supporting **11** cooperation

assistant 3 aid **4** aide, ally, help **5** aider **6** backer, backup, deputy, flunky, helper, second **7** acolyte, ancilla, orderly **8** adjutant, henchman **9** attendant, auxiliary, coadjutor **10** accomplice, aide-de-camp, coadjutant, lieutenant **12** right-hand man

assistive 6 aiding, useful **7** helpful **10** beneficial **11** serviceable

assize 3 law **4** rule, writ **5** canon, edict **6** decree **7** finding, inquest, precept, statute, verdict **8** standard **9** ordinance, prescript **10** regulation

associate 3 pal **4** ally, chum, join, link, mate, pair, yoke **5** blend, buddy, crony, group, match, merge, unite **6** cohort, comate, couple, fellow, friend, hobnob, relate, worker **7** bracket, combine, compeer, comrade, conjoin, connect, consort, partner **8** confrere, coworker, employee, familiar, federate, identify, intimate **9** affiliate, bedfellow, colleague, companion, confidant, copartner, secondary **10** accomplice, amalgamate, compatriot, complement, confidante **11** concomitant, confederate, correlative **12** acquaintance **13** accompaniment

association 3 tie **4** band, bloc, bond, clan, club, crew, hint, tong **5** group, guild, order, tie-up, union **6** hookup, league **7** circuit, concert, linkage, linking, society **8** alliance, congress, overtone, relation, sodality, teamwork **9** coalition, undertone **10** conference, connection, federation, fellowship, fraternity, mental link, suggestion **11** affiliation, brotherhood, combination, conjunction, connotation, cooperation, implication, partnership **12** conjointment, organization, relationship, togetherness **13** collaboration

assort 5 class, group, order **6** codify, divide **7** arrange **8** classify, stratify **9** associate, designate, harmonize, methodize **10** categorize, distribute, pigeonhole **11** systematize

assorted 4 like **5** mixed **6** fitted, motley, suited, sundry, varied **7** adapted, diverse, matched, similar, various **9** different **11** diversified, conformable **12** conglomerate, multifarious **13** heterogeneous, miscellaneous

assortment 4 olio **5** array, group **6** choice, jumble, medley **7** mélange, mixture, variety **8** mishmash, mixed bag, pastiche **9** diversity, potpourri, selection **10** collection, hodgepodge, miscellany **11** gallimaufry

assuage 4 calm, cool, ease **5** allay, quiet **6** lessen, pacify, quench, reduce, soften, soothe, temper **7** appease, lighten, mollify, placate, relieve, sweeten **8** decrease, mitigate, moderate **9** alleviate **10** conciliate, propitiate

as such 5 per se **8** by itself **9** in essence, virtually **11** essentially **13** fundamentally, intrinsically

assumably 6 likely, surely **7** no doubt **8** probably **9** doubtless **10** most likely, presumably

assume 3 act, don **4** fake, sham, take **5** adopt, bluff, feign, posit, put on, seize, usurp **6** affect, draw on, expect, reckon, slip on, take in, take on, take up **7** believe, imagine, preempt, premise, presume, pretend, receive, suppose, suspect **8** accroach, arrogate, shoulder, simulate, take over **9** postulate, undertake **10** commandeer, presuppose, understand **11** appropriate, counterfeit

assumed 4 fake, sham **5** bogus, false, given, put on, tacit **6** made-up, phoney **7** feigned **8** affected, delusory, putative, spurious, supposed **9** deceptive, pretended, simulated **10** artificial, fictitious

assumption 5 posit **6** belief, thesis **7** conceit, premise, seizure, surmise **8** takeover **9** arrogance, postulate **10** acceptance, arrogation, conjecture, pretension, usurpation **11** expectation, supposition, undertaking **13** appropriation

assurance 3 say **4** oath, word **5** nerve, say-so, troth **6** aplomb, parole, pledge, safety, surety **7** promise, support, warrant **8** audacity, boldness, safeness, security, sureness, temerity, warranty **9** assertion, brashness, certainty, certitude, cockiness, composure, guarantee, hardiness, self-trust **10** brazenness, confidence, conviction, equanimity, profession **11** affirmation, presumption

assure 4 aver **5** bet on, cinch, swear **6** affirm, attest, ensure, insure, pledge, secure, soothe **7** certify, comfort, confirm, promise, satisfy **8** convince, persuade **9** guarantee **11** make certain

assured **3** set **4** cool **5** fixed **6** secure **7** certain, decided, settled **8** clear-cut, composed, definite, positive, sanguine **9** assertive, collected, confident, undoubted, unruffled **10** guaranteed, pronounced **11** beyond doubt, made certain, unflappable **13** imperturbable, self-confident, self-satisfied

assuredly **9** certainly, doubtless **10** positively **11** confidently, undoubtedly, without fail

assuredness **6** surety **9** certainty, certitude **10** confidence, conviction

Assyria ***capital:*** **5** Calah **7** Nineveh ***city:*** **5** Ashur, Assur ***god:*** **3** Sin **4** Asur, Nabu **5** Ashur, Nusku **6** Tammuz **7** Ninurta ***goddess:*** **6** Ishtar ***king:*** **3** Pul **6** Sargon **11** Sennacherib, Shalmaneser **12** Ashurbanipal ***language:*** **7** Aramaic ***queen:*** **9** Semiramis ***river:*** **6** Tigris ***writing:*** **9** cuneiform

astatine symbol **2** At

asterisk **4** star **6** symbol **9** character

astern **3** aft **4** baft, rear, tail **5** abaft **6** back of, behind **8** backward, rearmost, rearward

asteroid **5** Ceres

Asterope ***father:*** **5** Atlas ***mother:*** **7** Pleione ***sisters:*** **8** Pleiades

asthma **7** allergy **8** disorder

as to **4** in re **5** about, anent **7** apropos **9** regarding **10** concerning, respecting **11** according to

astonish **4** daze, stun **5** amaze, floor, shock **7** astound, stagger, startle, stupefy **8** blow away, bowl over, confound, dumfound, surprise **9** dumbfound, take aback **11** flabbergast

astonishing **7** amazing **8** stunning, wondrous **9** marvelous, startling, wonderful **10** astounding, miraculous, prodigious, staggering, stupendous, surprising **11** spectacular **12** breathtaking

astonishment **3** awe **5** shock **6** wonder **8** surprise **9** amazement, confusion **10** perplexity, wonderment **12** bewilderment, stupefaction **13** consternation

astound **4** daze, stun **5** amaze, shock **7** confuse **8** astonish, bewilder, confound, dumfound, surprise **9** dumbfound, overwhelm, take aback **11** flabbergast

Astraea ***father:*** **4** Zeus **7** Jupiter ***mother:*** **6** Themis

astral **6** dreamy, starry **7** exalted, highest, stellar **8** elevated, sidereal **9** celestial, top-drawer, unworldly, visionary **10** top-ranking **11** high-ranking **12** otherworldly

astray **4** awry **5** amiss, badly, wrong **6** adrift, afield **7** in error **9** off course ***lead:*** **6** seduce

astride **8** bridging, spanning **10** on each side, straddling

astringent **4** acid, keen **5** acerb, acrid, harsh, sharp, stern **6** biting, bitter, severe, strict **7** acerbic, ascetic, austere, caustic, cutting, puckery, pungent, styptic **8** incisive, stinging **10** irritating **11** contracting **12** constrictive

astrolabe successor **7** sextant

astrologer **5** Dixon (Jeane), Faust **9** stargazer, Zoroaster **11** horoscopist, Nostradamus

astrological aspect **5** trine **7** sextile **8** quartile **10** opposition **11** conjunction

astronaut **4** Ride (Sally) **5** Glenn (John), White (Edward), Young (John) **6** Aldrin (Buzz), Cooper (Gordon), Lovell (James), Worden (Alfred) **7** Bluford (Guion), Collins (Michael), Gagarin (Yuri), Grissom (Gus), Jemison (Mae), Schirra (Walter), Shepard (Alan), Yegorov (Boris) **8** Stafford (Thomas) **9** Armstrong (Neil), Carpenter (Scott), McAuliffe (Christa) **10** Tereshkova (Valentina)

astronomer ***American:*** **3** See (Thomas Jefferson) **5** Sagan (Carl) **6** Hubble (Edwin), Lowell (Percival) **7** Langley (Samuel), Newcomb (Simon), Shapley (Harlow) **8** Bowditch (Nathaniel), Mitchell (Maria), Tombaugh (Clyde) **9** Pickering (Edward) **11** Schlesinger (Frank) ***Austrian:*** **13** Schwarzschild (Karl) ***Danish:*** **5** Brahe (Tycho) ***Dutch:*** **4** Oort (Jan Hendrik) **6** Sitter (Willem de) **7** Huygens (Christiaan) ***English:*** **4** Ryle (Martin), Wren (Christopher) **6** Halley (Edmond), Lovell (Bernard) **7** Lockyer (Joseph), Parsons (William) **8** Herschel (Caroline, John, William) ***French:*** **6** Picard (Jean) **7** Laplace (Pierre-Simon de), Messier (Charles) ***German:*** **4** Wolf (Maximilian) **5** Vogel (Hermann) **6** Bessel (Friedrich), Kepler (Johannes), Müller (Johann), Struve (Otto) ***Greek:*** **12** Eratosthenes ***Italian:*** **7** Galileo (Galilei) **12** Schiaparelli (Giovanni) ***Persian:*** **11** Omar Khayyám ***Polish:*** **10** Copernicus (Nicolaus) ***Swedish:*** **7** Celsius (Anders) ***Swiss:*** **6** Zwicky (Fritz)

astute **3** sly **4** cagy, deep, foxy, keen, wily **5** cagey, canny, heady, quick, savvy, sharp **6** artful, clever, crafty, shrewd, tricky **7** cunning, knowing **8** guileful **9** insidious, sagacious **11** calculating **13** perspicacious

astuteness **3** wit **6** acumen **8** wiliness **9** canniness **10** craftiness **11** discernment, percipience **12** perspicacity

Astyanax ***father:*** **6** Hector ***mother:*** **10** Andromache

asunder **4** torn **5** apart, split **7** divided **9** into parts, separated

as usual **8** normally, wontedly **9** routinely **10**

habitually, ordinarily **11** customarily **12** consistently

as well 3 and, too, yet **4** also, even, just, more, plus **7** besides, further **8** likewise, moreover **9** along with, including, similarly **10** in addition **11** furthermore **12** additionally

as well as 3 and **4** plus **7** besides **9** along with **11** not counting **12** in addition to, together with

as yet 5 so far, to now **7** earlier, thus far **8** hitherto, until now **10** to this time **12** to the present

asylum 4 home, port **5** cover, haven **6** covert, harbor, refuge **7** retreat, shelter **8** hospital, security **9** harborage, safe house, sanctuary **10** protection, sanatorium **11** institution

asymmetric 6 uneven **7** not even, unequal **8** lopsided **9** irregular **10** unbalanced **12** overbalanced

Atalanta ***husband:*** **8** Melanion ***suitor:*** **10** Hippomenes

at all 4 ever, once **6** anyway **7** anytime **10** whatsoever

atavism 9 reversion, throwback **10** recurrence

ataxia 5 chaos, snarl **6** huddle, muddle **7** clutter **8** disarray, disorder **9** confusion

atelier 6 studio **8** workroom, workshop

Athamas ***daughter:*** **5** Helle ***father:*** **6** Aeolus ***son:*** **7** Phrixos, Phrixus **8** Learchus ***wife:*** **3** Ino **7** Nephele

Athena ***Roman counterpart:*** **7** Minerva ***attribute:*** **3** owl **5** Aegis **7** serpent ***city:*** **6** Athens ***father:*** **4** Zeus ***names:*** **4** Nike **6** Pallas **9** Parthenos ***shield:*** **5** Aegis ***statue:*** **9** Palladium ***temple:*** **9** Parthenon

athenaeum 6 museum **7** library **8** archives **10** repository

Athens ***citadel:*** **9** Acropolis ***founder:*** **7** Cecrops ***last king:*** **6** Codrus ***lawgiver:*** **5** Solon ***marketplace:*** **5** agora ***rival:*** **6** Sparta ***senate:*** **5** boule ***temple:*** **9** Parthenon

athirst 4 avid, keen **5** eager **6** ardent **7** anxious **8** desiring, desirous, yearning **9** impatient

athlete 4 jock **5** sport **6** player **7** acrobat, gymnast, tumbler **9** sportsman **10** competitor **11** sportswoman

athlete's foot 8 ringworm **10** tinea pedis

athletic 6 brawny, robust, sinewy **8** sporting, vigorous **9** strapping, strenuous ***contest:*** **4** agon, game **5** match ***field:*** **4** oval, ring, rink **5** arena, court **7** diamond, stadium **8** gridiron ***prize:*** **3** cup **5** medal **6** trophy, wreath

athletics 5 games, races **6** events, sports **7** contest **8** exercise **9** exercises **10** gymnastics, recreation **12** calisthenics

athwart 4 over **5** cross **6** across, beyond **9** crossways, crosswise, opposed to **12** transversely

Atlanta's civic center 4 Omni

Atlas ***brother:*** **10** Prometheus ***daughter:*** **5** Hyads **6** Hyades **8** Pleiades **10** Atlantides ***father:*** **7** Iapetus ***mother:*** **7** Clymene ***race:*** **5** Titan ***wife:*** **7** Pleione

at last 7 finally

Atli ***wife (slayer):*** **6** Gudrun

atmosphere 3 air **4** aura, mood, tone **6** medium, milieu **7** ambient, climate, feeling, quality **8** ambiance, ambience **11** environment, mise-en-scène **12** surroundings ***stratum:*** **9** exosphere **10** ionosphere, mesosphere **11** chemosphere, ozonosphere, troposphere **12** stratosphere, thermosphere ***sun's:*** **12** chromosphere

atmospheric 4 airy **6** aerial **8** ethereal

atoll 6 island ***equatorial area:*** **5** Baker ***Indian Ocean:*** **4** Male ***Kiribati:*** **4** Beru ***Marshall Islands:*** **6** Bikini **8** Eniwetok ***Tuamotu:*** **4** Anaa **5** Chain ***Tuvalu:*** **8** Funafuti

atom 3 bit, jot **4** iota, mite, whit **5** minim, speck, touch, trace **6** tittle **7** modicum, smidgen **8** particle **9** scintilla ***charged:*** **3** ion **5** anion ***group:*** **7** radical

atomic particle 3 ion **4** beta, muon, pion **5** alpha, boson, meson **6** baryon, hadron, lepton, proton **7** fermion, hyperon, neutron, nucleon **8** electron, mesotron, neutrino, positron, thermion ***hypothetical:*** **5** quark **6** parton

atomic weapon 5 A-bomb, H-bomb **6** Fat Man **9** Little Boy

atomize 4 nuke, ruin **5** smash, wreck **6** divide, rub out **7** break up, destroy, shatter **8** demolish, destruct, disperse, dynamite, fragment, nebulize **9** break down, devastate, pulverize **10** disconnect

at once 3 now, PDQ **4** ASAP, away, both, stat **6** pronto **8** directly, first off, right now, together **9** forthwith, instanter, instantly, right away **11** immediately, straightway **12** concurrently, straightaway

atone 3 pay **6** redeem, repair, repent **7** correct, expiate, rectify, redress, satisfy **10** compensate, make amends, recompense

atoner 8 penitent

atop 4 upon

Atossa ***father:*** **5** Cyrus ***husband:*** **6** Darius **7** Smerdes **8** Cambyses ***son:*** **6** Xerxes

at random 5 about **6** anyhow **7** anywise **8** by chance **9** aimlessly, haphazard **10** carelessly **11** any which way, haphazardly **12** accidentally **13** helter-skelter

at rest 4 dead **5** still **8** inactive, lifeless, reposing, sleeping, tranquil, unmoving **9** quiescent **10** motionless, stationary, untroubled **11** trouble-free

Atreus ***brother:*** **8** Thyestes ***father:*** **6** Pelops ***mother:*** **10** Hippodamia ***slayer:*** **9** Aegisthus ***son:*** **8** Menelaus **9** Agamemnon **11** Pleisthenes ***victim:*** **11** Pleisthenes ***wife:*** **6** Aerope

atrium **5** court, patio

atrocious **4** foul, vile **5** awful, cruel **6** brutal, horrid, odious, savage, wicked **7** heinous, noisome, obscene **8** barbaric, horrible, shocking, terrible **9** appalling, desperate, execrable, loathsome, monstrous, offensive, repulsive, revolting, sickening **10** abominable, despicable, detestable, disgusting, horrifying, outrageous, scandalous **12** contemptible

atrocity **4** evil **5** crime **6** horror, infamy **7** cruelty, outrage **8** enormity, savagery **9** barbarity, brutality **11** abomination, heinousness **13** monstrousness

atrophy **7** decline, wasting **9** decadence, waste away **10** devolution **11** declination **12** degeneration **13** deterioration

attach **3** fix, tie **4** bind, hook, link **5** affix, annex, latch, rivet, stick, unite **6** adhere, append, assign, fasten, secure **7** ascribe, connect **8** make fast **9** associate, attribute

attached **5** bound, fixed **7** sessile

attachment **3** tag, tie **4** bond, link, love **6** fealty **7** loyalty, seizure **8** addition, adhesion, devotion, fastener, fidelity, fondness **9** accessory, adherence, affection, connector, constancy **10** allegiance, connection **12** faithfulness

attack **4** bout, jump, raid, rush **5** beset, blitz, drive, fight, foray, onset, sally, siege, spasm, spell, storm, throe **6** access, ambush, assail, banzai, battle, charge, fall on, harass, have at, invade, irrupt, onrush, sortie, strike, tackle **7** aggress, assault, barrage, besiege, bombard, lay into, offense, seizure **8** fall upon, invasion, outbreak, paroxysm **9** beleaguer, incursion, offensive, onslaught, pugnacity **10** aggression, blitzkrieg

attain **3** get, win **4** gain **5** reach, score **6** arrive, come to, effect, make it, obtain, rack up **7** achieve, fulfill, pull off, realize, succeed **8** bring off, complete **10** accomplish

attainment **4** feat **6** finish **7** arrival **10** completion **11** achievement, acquirement, acquisition, fulfillment, realization

attempt **3** bid, try **4** seek, shot, stab **5** assay, crack, essay, offer, trial **6** attack, effort, strive, tackle **7** assault, venture **8** endeavor, striving, struggle **9** undertake **11** undertaking **12** make an effort

attend **3** aid, see **4** be at, go to, hear, heed, help, mark, mind, note **5** apply, catch, nurse, see to, serve, visit, watch **6** assist, convoy, doctor, drop in, escort, go with, harken, listen, notice, show up, turn up, wait on **7** be there, care for, conduct, hearken, oversee, pay heed, work for **8** chaperon, stay with, wait upon **9** accompany, chaperone, companion, look after, supervise **11** concentrate

attendant **4** aide, page **5** valet **6** escort, helper, lackey **7** orderly, servant **9** ancillary, assistant **10** bridesmaid, coincident **11** chamberlain, concomitant **12** accompanying ***ancient Roman:*** **6** lictor ***in court:*** **7** bailiff **8** tipstaff

attendants **5** suite, train **7** cortege, retinue **9** entourage

attendee **4** goer

attention **4** care, heed, mark, note **5** study **6** notice, regard, remark **7** amenity, command, concern, respect, service, thought **8** civility, courtesy, industry, scrutiny **9** assiduity, awareness, deference, diligence, gallantry, spotlight, treatment **10** absorption, cognizance, observance, politeness **11** application, mindfulness, observation, sensibility **12** deliberation **13** concentration, consciousness, consideration

attention getter **4** ahem **5** gavel

attentive **4** kind **5** alert, awake, aware, civil **6** intent, polite **7** all ears, devoted, gallant, heedful, mindful **8** gracious, obliging, open-eyed **9** advertent, courteous, observant, regardful **10** interested, respectful, solicitous, thoughtful **11** considerate **13** concentrating

attenuate **3** sap **4** rare, slim, thin **5** abate, blunt, reedy **6** lessen, rarefy, shrink, slight, stalky, subtle, twiggy, weaken **7** cripple, deflate, disable, reduced, slender, squinny, subtile, tenuous, unbrace **8** contract, enfeeble, mitigate, rarefied, tapering, wiredraw **9** constrict, dissipate, undermine **10** become thin, become fine, become less, debilitate

attest **4** aver, show **5** argue, prove, swear, vouch **6** adjure, affirm, assert, verify **7** certify, confirm, declare, display, exhibit, point to, support, sustain, swear to, testify, warrant, witness **8** announce, indicate, manifest **9** establish **10** asseverate **11** bear witness, demonstrate **12** authenticate

attestation **5** proof **7** witness **8** evidence **9** testament, testimony **10** validation **11** declaration, testimonial **12** confirmation

attic **4** loft, room **6** garret **7** storage **8** cockloft

Attica **6** Greece ***division:*** **4** deme

at times 9 sometimes **10** now and then, on occasion **11** now and again **12** occasionally
attire 4 clad, duds, garb, gear, togs, wear **5** array, drape, dress, getup, habit, tog up **6** clothe, enrobe, fit out, outfit **7** apparel, clothes, costume, garment, raiment, threads **8** clothing, garments, glad rags **11** habiliments
attitude 4 pose, view **5** angle, stand **6** manner, stance **7** bearing, mind-set, outlook, posture **8** carriage, demeanor, position, pretense **10** standpoint **11** inclination, perspective, point of view
attitudinize 4 mask, pose, sham **6** affect **7** pass for, pass off, posture, pretend, show off **10** masquerade
attorney 5 agent, proxy **6** deputy, factor, lawyer **7** counsel **8** advocate, assignee **9** barrister, counselor, solicitor **10** counsellor, legal eagle, mouthpiece
attract 4 draw, lure, wile **5** charm, court, tempt **6** allure, appeal, beckon, draw in, entice, invite, seduce **7** beguile, bewitch, enchant, solicit **8** appeal to, interest, intrigue, inveigle **9** captivate, fascinate, influence, magnetize
attraction 4 bait, call, draw, lure, pull **5** charm **6** allure, appeal, liking **8** affinity, cynosure, sympathy **9** affection, chemistry, magnetism, seduction **10** allurement **12** drawing power
attractive 4 cute, fair, sexy **5** bonny, dishy **6** comely, lovely, luring, pretty **7** Circean, likable, winsome **8** alluring, charming, engaging, enticing, fetching, handsome, inviting, magnetic, mesmeric, tempting **9** appealing, beauteous, beautiful, beckoning, glamorous, seductive **10** bewitching, enchanting **11** captivating, fascinating, good-looking, tantalizing **13** prepossessing
attractiveness 5 charm **6** appeal, beauty, glamor **7** glamour
attribute 3 lay **4** mark, sign **5** apply, facet, pin on, point, refer, trait **6** aspect, assign, charge, credit, emblem, impute, symbol, virtue **7** ascribe, connect, earmark, explain, feature, quality **8** accredit, classify, property **9** adjective, character, designate
attrition 3 rue **4** ruth, wear **6** sorrow **7** erosion, penance, remorse, rubbing, wearing **8** abrasion, friction, grinding **9** penitence, penitency, reduction, weakening **10** repentance **12** contriteness
attritional 5 sorry **6** rueful **8** contrite, penitent **9** regretful, repentant **10** apologetic, remorseful **11** penitential
attune 6 accord, adjust **7** balance, conform **9** harmonize, integrate, reconcile **10** coordinate, proportion **11** accommodate
Atwood novel 7 Cat's Eye **12** Oryx and Crake **13** Handmaid's Tale (The)
atypical 3 odd **5** queer **7** deviant, strange, unusual **8** aberrant, abnormal, peculiar **9** anomalous, deviative, different, divergent, irregular, unnatural **11** exceptional, heteroclite, nonstandard **13** preternatural
auberge 3 inn **5** hotel, lodge **6** hostel, tavern **7** hospice **8** hostelry **9** roadhouse **11** caravansary, public house
Auber opera 10 Fra Diavolo
auburn 4 rust **5** henna **6** russet **8** chestnut **11** burnt sienna **12** reddish-brown
Auchincloss novel 9 Embezzler (The) **13** East Side Story **14** Rector of Justin (The)
au courant 3 mod **4** up on **5** awake, aware, hep to, hip to, savvy **6** modern, modish, versed **7** abreast, current, in touch, knowing, stylish, versant, witting **8** familiar, informed, sentient, up-to-date **9** cognizant, conscious, plugged in **10** acquainted, conversant **11** fashionable **12** contemporary **13** up-to-the-minute
auction 4 sale, sell
audacious 4 bold, rash **5** brash, brave, cocky, risky, saucy **6** brazen, cheeky, daring **7** valiant **8** arrogant, fearless, impudent, insolent, intrepid, reckless, unafraid, uncurbed **9** daredevil, dauntless, foolhardy, shameless, undaunted, venturous **10** courageous, ungoverned, unhampered **11** adventurous, impertinent, temerarious, uninhibited, untrammeled, venturesome **12** unrestrained **13** adventuresome
audacity 4 gall **5** brass, cheek, moxie, nerve, spunk **6** mettle, spirit **7** courage **8** boldness, chutzpah, rashness, temerity **9** assurance, arrogance, brashness, cockiness, disregard, hardihood, hardiness, impudence, insolence **10** brazenness, effrontery **12** recklessness
audible 5 aural, clear, heard **8** distinct **9** auricular
audibly 5 aloud **7** aurally, clearly, out loud
audience 5 crowd, group, house **6** public **7** hearing, gallery, hearers, meeting **8** admirers, assembly, audition, devotees **9** clientele, following, gathering, interview, listeners **10** assemblage, spectators
audile see **auditory**
audio 5 sound
audit 4 scan **5** check, probe **6** go over, report, review, survey, verify **7** analyze, balance, checkup, examine, inspect **8** analysis, scrutiny **10** inspection, scrutinize **11** examination **13** investigation

audition 4 test **5** trial **6** tryout **7** hearing, reading

auditor 8 examiner, listener **9** inspector **10** accountant, controller **11** comptroller

auditory 5 aural **8** acoustic

Auel, Jean ***novel:*** **17** Clan of the Cave Bear (The) ***series:*** **14** Earth's Children

au fait 4 able **5** right **6** decent, proper, versed **7** abreast, capable, correct, versant **8** becoming, decorous, familiar, informed, relevant **9** befitting, competent, qualified **10** acquainted, conforming, conversant, to the point

au fond 8 at bottom **9** basically, in essence **11** essentially **13** fundamentally

Augean 9 difficult **10** formidable **11** distasteful ***stable:*** **3** sty **4** sink **5** filth, Sodom **7** cesspit **8** cesspool

auger 3 bit **5** borer, drill, screw **6** gimlet, trepan, wimble **9** corkscrew

Auge's son 8 Telephus

aught 3 all, nil, nix, zip **4** nada, zero **5** zilch **6** cipher **7** nothing **8** anything, goose egg **10** everything

augment 3 wax **4** grow, hike, rise **5** add to, boost, build, exalt, mount, raise **6** beef up, expand, extend **7** amplify, build up, develop, enhance, enlarge, magnify **9** intensify, reinforce **8** compound, heighten, increase, multiply **10** aggrandize, supplement **11** make greater

augmentation 4 rise **5** annex, extra, raise **7** adjunct, buildup **8** addition, increase **9** accession, accretion, increment **10** complement, enrichment **11** enhancement, enlargement

augur 4 bode, seer **6** herald, oracle **7** betoken, diviner, portend, predict, presage, promise, prophet, suggest **8** forebode, forecast, foreshow, foretell, indicate, prophesy, soothsay **9** adumbrate, foretoken, harbinger, predictor, prefigure **10** forecaster, foreshadow, foreteller, prophesier, soothsayer, vaticinate **11** Nostradamus **13** prognosticate

augury 4 omen, sign **5** token **6** herald **7** auspice, portent, presage, warning **8** bodement, forecast, prophecy **9** foretoken, harbinger **10** divination, forerunner, prediction, prognostic **11** forewarning

august 5 grand, noble, regal **6** lordly **7** eminent, stately **8** baronial, imposing, majestic, princely, splendid **9** dignified, grandiose **11** magnificent

auk 5 alcid **7** seabird ***genus:*** **4** Alca

au naturel 3 raw **4** nude **5** naked, plain **6** unclad **8** stripped **9** unclothed, undressed **10** stark naked

aunt ***French:*** **5** tante ***German:*** **5** Tante ***Italian:*** **3** zia ***Japanese:*** **6** obasan ***Spanish:*** **3** tía

aura 3 air **4** feel, glow, halo, mood, tone, vibe **5** aroma, vibes **6** nimbus **7** aureole, feeling, quality **8** ambience, mystique, radiance, stimulus **9** emanation, semblance, sensation **10** atmosphere

aural 6 audile **7** audible **8** acoustic, auditory **9** auricular

aureate 6 florid, golden **7** flowery, orotund **8** sonorous **9** bombastic, grandiose, overblown **10** euphuistic, rhetorical **11** declamatory **13** grandiloquent

aureole 4 aura, halo, ring **5** crown, light **6** circle, corona, nimbus **8** radiance

au revoir 4 by-by, ciao, ta-ta **5** adieu, adios **6** bye-bye, so long **7** good-bye **8** farewell **11** arrivederci

auricular see **aural**

Auriga star 7 Capella

aurora 4 dawn, morn **7** dawning, morning, sunrise **8** cockcrow, daybreak

Aurora ***Roman counterpart:*** **3** Eos ***goddess of:*** **4** dawn ***husband:*** **8** Tithonus ***son:*** **6** Memnon

auslander 5 alien **7** inconnu **8** outsider, stranger **9** foreigner

auspice 4 omen, sign **10** divination

auspices 5 aegis **6** charge **7** backing, support **8** guidance **9** influence, patronage **11** sponsorship, supervision

auspicious 5 lucky **6** bright, timely **7** hopeful **9** favorable, fortunate, opportune, promising, well-timed **10** propitious, prosperous **11** encouraging

Austen, Jane ***novel:*** **4** Emma **10** Persuasion **13** Mansfield Park **15** Northanger Abbey **17** Pride and Prejudice **19** Sense and Sensibility

Auster see **Notus**

austere 4 bare, cold, dour, firm, grim, hard **5** acrid, bleak, grave, harsh, plain, rigid, sharp, spare, stern **6** bitter, severe, simple, somber, strict **7** ascetic, serious, spartan **8** exacting **9** stringent, unadorned, unfeeling **10** astringent, restrained **11** self-denying

austerity 5 rigor **6** thrift **7** economy **8** acerbity, asperity, coldness, grimness, hardness, rigidity, severity **9** harshness, parsimony, privation, solemnity, spareness, sternness, stiffness **10** self-denial, simplicity, strictness, stringency **11** unadornment **13** self-restraint

Australia ***capital:*** **8** Canberra ***city:*** **5** Perth **6** Darwin, Sydney **8** Adelaide, Brisbane **9** Melbourne, Newcastle ***desert:*** **10** Great Sandy **13** Great Victoria ***ethnic group:*** **9**

Aborigine ***island:*** **6** Fraser **8** Kangaroo, Melville, Tasmania ***lake:*** **4** Eyre ***monetary unit:*** **6** dollar ***mountain, range:*** **9** Ayers Rock **9** Kosciusko **13** Great Dividing ***reef:*** **12** Great Barrier ***river:*** **4** Swan **6** Murray **7** Darling **8** Flinders **11** Cooper Creek **12** Coopers Creek ***strait:*** **4** Bass **6** Torres

Austria ***capital:*** **6** Vienna ***city:*** **4** Graz, Linz **8** Salzburg **9** Innsbruck **10** Klagenfurt ***lake:*** **10** Neusiedler ***monetary unit:*** **4** euro ***monetary unit, former:*** **9** schilling ***mountain:*** **13** Grossglockner ***mountain range:*** **4** Alps ***neighbor:*** **5** Italy **7** Croatia, Germany, Hungary **8** Slovakia, Slovenia **11** Switzerland **13** Czech Republic, Liechtenstein ***river:*** **3** Ems **6** Danube

autarchy see **autocracy**

autarkic **4** free **8** separate **9** sovereign **10** autonomous, self-ruling **11** independent, self-reliant **13** self-governing

autarky **7** freedom **8** autonomy **12** independence, self-reliance

authentic **4** real, true **5** legit, pukka, right, solid, sound, valid **6** actual, trusty **7** certain, factual, for real, genuine **8** accurate, bona fide, credible, faithful, reliable **9** undoubted, veritable **10** convincing, dependable, legitimate, sure-enough **11** indubitable, trustworthy **12** questionless

authenticate **5** prove, vouch **6** adduce, attest, verify **7** bear out, certify, confirm, justify, voucher, warrant **8** accredit, notarize, validate **11** corroborate **12** substantiate

author **5** maker **6** penman, scribe, writer **7** creator **8** inventor, novelist, prosaist **9** generator **10** originator ***American:*** **3** Bly (Robert), Fox (Paula), Nin (Anaïs), Poe (Edgar Allan), Tan (Amy) **4** Agee (James), Baum (L. Frank), Buck (Pearl S.), Cain (James M.), Cook (Robin), Dana (Richard Henry), Fast (Howard), Ford (Richard), Grey (Zane), Jong (Erica), Mann (Thomas), Puzo (Mario), Rand (Ayn), Rice (Anne), Roth (Philip), Shaw (Irwin), Uris (Leon), West (Nathanael), Wouk (Herman) **5** Aiken (Conrad), Alger (Horatio), Banks (Russell), Barth (John), Benét (Stephen Vincent), Blume (Judy), Boyle (T. Coraghessan), Brown (Rita Mae), Clark (Mary Higgins), Crane (Hart, Stephen), Dunne (Dominick, John Gregory), Elkin (Stanley), Ellis (Bret Easton), Foote (Horton), Haley (Alex), Harte (Bret), Henry (O.), Jaffe (Rona), Jakes (John), James (Henry), Levin (Ira), Lewis (Sinclair), Lurie (Alison), Mason (Bobbie Ann), Oates (Joyce Carol), O'Hara (John), Ozick (Cynthia), Paine (Thomas), Paley (Grace), Potok (Chaim), Price (Reynolds, Richard), Steel (Danielle), Stein (Gertrude), Stone (Irving), Stout (Rex), Stowe (Harriet Beecher), Turow (Scott), Twain (Mark), Tyler (Anne), Vidal (Gore), Welty (Eudora), White (Edmund, E. B., T. H.), Wolfe (Thomas, Tom), Wylie (Elinor) **6** Alcott (Louisa May), Asimov (Isaac), Auster (Paul), Bellow (Saul), Berger (Thomas), Bierce (Ambrose), Bowles (Paul), Cabell (James Branch), Capote (Truman), Cather (Willa), Chopin (Kate), Clancy (Tom), Conroy (Pat), Cooper (James Fenimore), Dickey (James), Didion (Joan), Ellroy (James), Ferber (Edna), French (Marilyn), Gaddis (William), Gaines (Ernest J.), Gilroy (Frank), Godwin (Gail), Hailey (Arthur), Harris (Frank, Joel Chandler), Hawkes (John), Heller (Joseph), Hersey (John), Hinton (S. E.), Holmes (Oliver Wendell), Hughes (Langston), Hunter (Evan), Irving (John, Washington), Jewett (Sarah Orne), Kidder (Tracy), Koontz (Dean), Krantz (Judith), L'Amour (Louis), L'Engle (Madeleine), Le Guin (Ursula K.), London (Jack), Mailer (Norman), McBain (Ed), Miller (Arthur, Henry, Joaquin, May), Morley (Christopher), Morris (Wright), Mosley (Walter), Norris (Frank), Parker (Dorothy), Piercy (Marge), Porter (Katherine Anne, William Sydney), Proulx (E. Annie), Runyon (Damon), Sarton (May), Sheehy (Gail), Singer (Isaac Bashevis), Smiley (Jane), Styron (William), Taylor (Peter), Updike (John), Walker (Alice), Waller (Robert James), Warren (Robert Penn), Wilder (Laura Ingalls, Thornton), Wilson (August, Edmund, Harriet, Lanford), Wister (Owen), Wright (James, Richard) **7** Baldwin (Faith, James), Beattie (Ann), Cheever (John), Clavell (James), Clemens (Samuel Langhorne), Collins (Jackie), Connell (Evan), Cozzens (James Gould), DeLillo (Don), Dreiser (Theodore), Ellison (Ralph), Erdrich (Louise), Farrell (James T.), Francis (Dick), Franzen (Jonathan), Gardner (Erle Stanley), Garland (Hamlin), Glasgow (Ellen), Goldman (William), Grafton (Sue), Grisham (John), Hammett (Dashiell), Heyward (DuBose), Howells (William Dean), Hurston (Zora Neale), Jackson (Shirley), Jarrell (Randall), Johnson (Diane, James), Keillor (Garrison), Kennedy (William), Kerouac (Jack), Kincaid (Jamaica), Lardner (Ring), Leonard (Elmore), Malamud (Bernard), Marquis (Don), Masters (Edgar Lee), McCourt

(Frank), Mumford (Lewis), Nabokov (Vladimir), O'Connor (Flannery), Pynchon (Thomas), Rexroth (Kenneth), Richter (Conrad), Roberts (Elizabeth Madox, Kenneth, Nora), Saroyan (William), Sheehan (Neil), Sheldon (Sidney), Theroux (Paul), Thoreau (Henry David), Thurber (James), Wallace (Lew), Wharton (Edith) **8** Anderson (Maxwell, Poul, Regina, Sherwood), Benchley (Peter), Bradbury (Ray), Bradford (Barbara Taylor), Caldwell (Erskine), Chandler (Raymond), Cornwell (Patricia), Crichton (Michael), Doctorow (E. L.), Faulkner (William), Kingston (Maxine Hong), Marquand (John P.), McCarthy (Cormac, Mary), McMillan (Terry), McMurtry (Larry), Melville (Herman), Michener (James), Mitchell (Donald Grant, Margaret, S. Weir), Morrison (Toni), Remarque (Erich Maria), Rinehart (Mary Roberts), Salinger (J. D.), Sandburg (Carl), Sinclair (Upton), Spillane (Mickey), Stockton (Frank R.), Vonnegut (Kurt), Wambaugh (Joseph) **9** Burroughs (Edgar Rice, John, William S.), Dos Passos (John), Hawthorne (Nathaniel), Hemingway (Ernest), Hillerman (Tony), Isherwood (Christopher), McCullers (Carson), Steinbeck (John), Wodehouse (P. G.), Woollcott (Alexander) **10** Cunningham (Michael), Fitzgerald (F. Scott), Kingsolver (Barbara), Tarkington (Booth) **11** Auchincloss (Louis), Matthiessen (Peter) ***Argentinian:*** **6** Borges (Jorge Luis) ***Australian:*** **4** West (Morris L.) **5** Stead (Christina), White (Patrick) **7** Clavell (James), Idriess (Ion) **8** Keneally (Thomas) **10** McCullough (Colleen), Richardson (Henry Handel) ***Austrian:*** **5** Kafka (Franz) **6** Handke (Peter) **7** Jelinek (Elfriede), Suttner (Bertha) **8** Bernhard (Thomas) **10** Schnitzler (Arthur) ***Brazilian:*** **6** Coelho (Paulo) ***Canadian:*** **3** Roy (Camille, Gabrielle) **5** Kirby (William), Moore (Brian), Munro (Alice) **6** Atwood (Margaret), Davies (Robertson) **7** Leacock (Stephen), Raddall (Thomas), Richler (Mordecai), Service (Robert), Shields (Carol) **8** Woodcock (George) **9** de la Roche (Mazo), MacLennan (Hugh) ***Chilean:*** **6** Donoso (José) **7** Allende (Isabel) ***Chinese:*** **5** Han Yu ***Colombian:*** **7** Márquez (Gabriel García) ***Czech:*** **5** Capek (Karel), Hasek (Jaroslav) **7** Kundera (Milan) ***Danish:*** **4** Rode (Helge), Wied (Gustav) **6** Jensen (Johannes Vilhelm) **7** Dinesen (Isak), Holberg (Ludwig) ***Dutch:*** **6** Vondel (Joost van den) ***Egyptian:*** **7** Mahfouz (Naguib) ***English:*** **4** Amis (Kingsley, Martin), Dahl (Roald), Ford (Ford Madox, John), Lyly (John), Saki, Snow (C. P.), Ward (Mrs. Humphry), West (Rebecca) **5** Byatt (A. S.), Defoe (Daniel), Doyle (Authur Conan), Eliot (George, Thomas Stearns), Evans (Mary Ann), Frayn (Michael), Hardy (Thomas), James (Henry, P. D.), Lewis (C. S., Monk, Wyndham), Lowry (Malcolm), Milne (A. A.), Munro (H. H.), Powys (John Cowper, Llewelyn, Theodore Francis), Reade (Charles), Spark (Muriel), Waugh (Alec, Evelyn), Wells (Charles Jeremiah, H. G.), White (T. H.), Wilde (Oscar), Woolf (Leonard, Virginia), Young (Arthur, Edward, Francis Brett) **6** Ambler (Eric), Archer (Jeffrey), Austen (Jane), Belloc (Hilaire), Brontë (Anne, Charlotte, Emily), Bunyan (John), Butler (Samuel), Clarke (Arthur C.), Conrad (Joseph), Fowles (John), Graves (Robert), Greene (Graham, Robert), Hilton (James), Hudson (W. H.), Huxley (Aldous), Malory (Thomas), McEwan (Ian), O'Brian (Patrick), Orwell (George), Potter (Beatrix), Powell (Anthony), Sayers (Dorothy L.), Sterne (Laurence), Stoker (Bram), Storey (David), Walton (Izaak) **7** Ballard (J. G.), Burgess (Anthony), Burnett (Frances Hodgson), Carroll (Lewis), Clavell (James), Collins (Wilkie), Dickens (Charles), Dodgson (Charles), Durrell (Lawrence), Fleming (Ian), Follett (Ken), Forster (E. M.), Forsyth (Frederick), Golding (Louis, William), Kipling (Rudyard), Le Carré (John), Lessing (Doris), Lofting (Hugh), Maugham (Robin, W. Somerset), Murdoch (Iris), Naipaul (V. S.), Rendell (Ruth), Rowling (J. K.), Sassoon (Siegfried), Shelley (Mary Wollstonecraft, Percy Bysshe), Sitwell (Edith, Osbert, Sacheverell), Southey (Robert), Stewart (Mary), Surtees (Robert Smith), Tolkien (J. R. R.), Walpole (Horace, Hugh), Wyndham (John) **8** Christie (Agatha), Fielding (Henry), Forester (C. S.), Koestler (Arthur), Lawrence (D. H., T. E.), Macaulay (Rose, Thomas Babington), Meredith (George), Sillitoe (Alan), Smollett (Tobias), Strachey (Lytton), Trollope (Anthony), Zangwill (Israel) **9** De Quincey (Thomas), Du Maurier (Daphne, George), Goldsmith (Oliver), Isherwood (Christopher), Mansfield (Katherine), Masefield (John), Priestley (J. B.), Radcliffe (Ann), Stevenson (Robert Louis), Thackeray (William Makepeace), Wodehouse (P. D.) **10** Chesterton (Gilbert Keith), Galsworthy

(John), Richardson (Dorothy, Samuel) **12** Quiller-Couch (Arthur Thomas) ***Finnish:*** **7** Waltari (Mika) **9** Sillanpää (Frans Eemil) ***French:*** **3** Nin (Anaïs) **4** Gide (André), Hugo (Victor), Kock (Charles-Paul de), Sade (Marquis de), Sand (George), Zola (Emile) **5** Beyle (Marie Henri), Camus (Albert), Dumas (Alexandre), Genet (Jean), Sagan (Françoise), Staël (Germaine de), Verne (Jules), Vigny (Alfred-Victor) **6** Balzac (Honoré de), Daudet (Alphonse), France (Anatole), Lesage (Alain-René, Proust (Marcel), Sartre (Jean-Paul) **7** Cocteau (Jean), Colette, Gautier (Léon, Théophile), Malraux (André), Mauriac (Claude, François), Maurois (André), Merimée (Prosper), Rolland (Romain), Romains (Jules), Simenon (Georges) **8** Beauvoir (Simone de), Flaubert (Gustave), Marivaux (Pierre), Rabelais (François), Stendhal, Voltaire **9** Giraudoux (Jean) **10** Maupassant (Guy de), Saint-Simon (Duke de) **12** Robbe-Grillet (Alain), Saint-Exupéry (Antoine de) ***German:*** **4** Böll (Heinrich), Mann (Thomas) **5** Grass (Gunter), Hesse (Hermann), Kafka (Franz), Storm (Theodor), Tieck (Ludwig), Zweig (Stefan) **6** Goethe (Johann Wolfgang von), Toller (Ernst) **7** Fontane (Theodor), Richter (Jean Paul), Wieland (Christoph Martin) **8** Hoffmann (E. T. A., Heinrich), Remarque (Erich Maria), Schlegel (August Wilhelm von, Friedrich von, Johann Elias) **9** Hauptmann (Gerhart), Sudermann (Hermann) **10** Wassermann (Jakob) ***Greek:*** **5** Homer **6** Hesiod, Lucian, Pindar, Sappho **7** Plautus, Terence **8** Xenophon **9** Aeschylus, Euripedes, Herodotus, Sophocles **10** Thucydides **11** Kazantzakis (Nikos) ***Hungarian:*** **5** Jókai (Mór) ***Icelandic:*** **7** Laxness (Halldór) ***Indian:*** **7** Rushdie (Salman) ***Irish:*** **5** Behan (Brendan), Doyle (Roddy), Joyce (James), Moore (Brian), Synge (J. M.), Wilde (Oscar) **6** O'Brien (Edna), Stoker (Bram) **7** Beckett (Samuel), O'Connor (Frank), Russell (George William) **8** O'Faolain (Julia, Sean), Stephens (James) **9** O'Flaherty (Liam) ***Italian:*** **3** Eco (Umberto) **5** Verga (Giovanni) **6** Silone (Ignazio) **7** Calvino (Italo), Manzoni (Alessandro), Moravia (Alberto) **9** Boccaccio (Giovanni), Vittorini (Elio) **10** Pirandello (Luigi), Straparola (Gianfrancesco) ***Japanese:*** **7** Mishima (Yukio) **8** Kawabata (Yasunari), Murakami (Haruki), Murasaki (Shikibu) **9** Yokomitsu (Richi), Yoshikawa (Eiji) ***Lebanese:*** **6** Gibran (Khalil) ***Mexican:*** **7** Fuentes (Carlos) ***Nigerian:*** **6** Achebe (Chinua) **7** Soyinka (Wole), Tutuola (Amos) ***Norwegian:*** **3** Lie (Jonas) **6** Hamsun (Knut), Undset (Sigrid) **7** Rolvaag (Ole) **8** Bjornson (Bjornstjerne), Kielland (Alexander) ***Peruvian:*** **11** Vargas Llosa (Mario) ***Polish:*** **3** Lem (Stanislaw) **7** Reymont (Wladyslaw) **8** Zeromski (Stefan) **10** Gombrowicz (Witold) **11** Sienkiewicz (Henryk) ***Portuguese:*** **6** Pessoa (Fernando) **8** Saramago (José) ***Roman:*** **4** Livy **5** Pliny, Varro (Marcus Terentius) **7** Tacitus **8** Apuleius **9** Petronius ***Russian:*** **5** Gogol (Nikolai), Gorki (Maxim), Gorky (Maxim) **7** Chekhov (Anton), Pushkin (Alexander), Tolstoy (Leo) **8** Andreyev (Leonid), Turgenev (Ivan), Zamyatin (Yevgeny) **9** Ehrenburg (Ilya), Lermontov (Mikhail), Pasternak (Boris), Sholokhov (Mikhail) **10** Dostoevsky (Fyodor) **11** Dostoyevsky (Fyodor), Yevtushenko (Yevgeny) **12** Solzhenitsyn (Alexander) ***Scottish:*** **3** Tey (Josephine) **4** Lang (Andrew) **5** Scott (Alexander, Walter) **6** Barrie (James M.), Buchan (John) **8** Urquhart (Thomas) **9** Stevenson (Robert Louis) ***South African:*** **5** Paton (Alan) **6** Fugard (Athol) **7** Coetzee (J. M.) **8** Gordimer (Nadine) ***Spanish:*** **6** Baroja (Pio) **7** Alarcón (Pedro Antonio de) **9** Cervantes (Miguel de) ***Swedish:*** **7** Johnson (Eyvind), Rydberg (Viktor) **8** Lagerlöf (Selma) **10** Lagerkvist (Pär), Strindberg (August) ***Swiss:*** **4** Wyss (Johann Rudolf) **5** Spyri (Johanna) **6** Frisch (Max) **9** Spitteler (Carl) ***Trinidadian:*** **7** Naipaul (V. S.) ***Welsh:*** **4** Owen (Alun, Daniel, Goronwy, John) **5** Evans (David, Evan), Wynne (Ellis) ***Yiddish:*** **4** Asch (Sholem) **6** Singer (Isaac Bashevis) **8** Aleichem (Sholem)

authoritarian **5** harsh, rigid **6** despot, severe, strict, tyrant **8** absolute, autocrat, despotic, dictator, dogmatic **9** imperious, stringent **10** absolutist, autocratic, oppressive, totalistic, tyrannical **11** dictatorial, doctrinaire, domineering, magisterial **12** totalitarian

authoritative **4** sure, true **5** legal, legit, sound **6** lawful, proven **7** factual **8** accepted, accurate, approved, attested, dogmatic, official, orthodox, reliable, verified **9** canonical, cathedral, confirmed, imperious, trustable, validated **10** autocratic, commanding, definitive, dependable, documented, dominating, ex cathedra, legitimate, sanctioned **11** dictatorial, doctrinaire, domineering, irrefutable, magisterial, overbearing, trustworthy **12** indisputable

authority **4** rule, sway **5** clout, force, power, right, say-so **6** agency, charge, credit, expert, master, weight **7** command, control, grounds, license, mastery, warrant **8** citation, decision, dominion, prestige **9** influence, testimony **10** domination, governance, government, management **12** jurisdiction

authorization 4 okay, word **5** leave **6** permit **7** consent, go-ahead, license, mandate **8** approval, sanction **9** agreement, allowance, clearance **10** green light, permission, sufferance **11** approbation

authorize 3 let **4** okay, vest **5** allow **6** affirm, enable, invest, permit **7** approve, confirm, empower, endorse, entitle, license, qualify, warrant **8** accredit, sanction, vouch for **9** give leave, recognize **10** commission **11** countenance

auto see **automobile**

autobahn 7 highway **8** turnpike **10** expressway **12** superhighway

autobiography 4 life, vita **5** diary **6** memoir **7** account, journal **9** life story **11** confessions **13** reminiscences

autochthonous 6 native **7** endemic **8** original **10** aboriginal, indigenous

autocracy 7 czarism, tyranny **8** monarchy **9** despotism, monocracy **12** absolute rule, dictatorship

autocrat 4 czar, duce, emir, lord, raja, shah, tsar, tzar **5** mogul, rajah, ruler **6** caliph, despot, sultan, tyrant **7** magnate, monarch **8** dictator, oligarch, overlord **9** potentate, sovereign **10** absolutist

autocratic 7 haughty **8** absolute, arrogant, despotic **9** arbitrary, imperious, tyrannous **10** monocratic, tyrannical **11** dictatorial, domineering, overbearing

autodidactic 10 self-taught **12** self-educated

autograph 3 ink, pen **4** sign **5** write **7** endorse **8** original **9** signature, subscribe **11** endorsement, John Hancock

Autolycus ***daughter:*** **8** Anticlea ***father:*** **6** Hermes **7** Mercury

automated 7 robotic **9** by machine, motorized **10** electrical, electronic, mechanical, mechanized, programmed **12** computerized

automatic 6 reflex **8** habitual **9** impulsive, reflexive **10** mechanical, self-acting, unprompted **11** instinctive, involuntary, perfunctory, spontaneous, unmeditated ***prefix:*** **4** self

automaton 5 droid, golem, robot **7** android, machine **9** mechanism

automobile 3 bus, car **5** buggy, coupe, racer, sedan **6** beater, jalopy, tourer, wheels **7** clunker, flivver, hardtop, machine **8** dragster, motorcar, roadster, runabout **9** hatchback, limousine **10** rust bucket **11** convertible ***American:*** **3** Geo, Reo **4** Cord, Dart, Ford, Fury, Jeep, Nash, Neon, Olds, Vega **5** Buick, Dodge, Eagle, Edsel, Essex, Focus, Pinto, T-bird **6** Cougar, DeSoto, Duster, Fraser, Hudson, Hummer, Impala, Kaiser, Model A, Model T, Saturn, Tucker, Willys **7** Charger, Cutlass, LaSalle, LeBaron, LeSabre, Lincoln, Maxwell, Mercury, Mustang, Packard, Pontiac, Rambler, Seville **8** Cadillac, Chrysler, Corvette, Eldorado, Franklin, Plymouth **9** Barracuda, Chevrolet, Hupmobile **10** Duesenberg, Oldsmobile, Studebaker **11** Continental, Pierce-Arrow, Thunderbird ***British:*** **2** MG **3** Jag **4** Mini **5** Lotus **6** Anglia, Arnage, Austin, Cooper, DeSoto, Jaguar, Morris **7** Bentley, Daimler, Hillman, Phantom, Sunbeam, Triumph **8** Vauxhall **9** Land Rover **10** Range Rover, Rolls-Royce **11** Aston Martin, Silver Ghost **12** Austin-Healey ***French:*** **5** Simca **7** Citroën, Peugeot, Renault ***German:*** **3** BMW **4** Audi, Benz, Golf, Opel **6** Beetle **7** Daimler, Maybach, Porsche, Quattro **8** Mercedes **10** Volkswagen **12** Mercedes-Benz ***Italian:*** **4** Fiat **6** Lancia **7** Bugatti, Ferrari **8** Maserati **9** Alfa-Romeo **11** Lamborghini ***Japanese:*** **5** Acura, Civic, Honda, Isuzu, Lexus, Mazda, Prius **6** Datsun, Altima, Maxima, Nissan, Subaru, Toyota **7** Corolla **8** Infiniti **10** Mitsubishi ***Korean:*** **3** Kia **6** Daewoo **7** Hyundai ***Russian*** **4** Lada ***Serbian:*** **4** Yugo ***Swedish:*** **4** Saab **5** Volvo

automobile safety device 3 ABS **6** air bag **8** seat belt

automotive pioneer 4 Benz (Carl Friedrich), Ford (Henry), Olds (Ransom), Otto (Nikolaus), Pope (Albert) **5** Evans (Oliver), Rolls (Charles), Roper (Sylvester) **6** Cugnot (Nicholas Joseph), Duryea (Charles E., J. Frank), Lenoir (Etienne), Winton (Alexander) **7** Bugatti (Ettore), Citroën (André-Gustave), Daimler (Gottlieb), Peugeot (Armand), Stanley (Francis, Freelan) **8** Morrison (William) **10** Lanchester (Frederick William)

Autonoë ***father:*** **6** Cadmus ***husband:*** **9** Aristaeus ***mother:*** **8** Harmonia ***sister:*** **5** Agave ***son:*** **7** Actaeon

autonomous 4 free **8** autarkic, separate **9** sovereign **10** self-ruling **11** independent, self-reliant **12** self-governed, uncontrolled **13** self-contained, self-governing

autonomy 7 autarky, freedom **8** home rule, self-rule **11** sovereignty **12** independence

autopsy 6 assess **7** examine **8** evaluate,

necropsy **10** assessment, dissection, evaluation, postmortem **11** examination

auto racer 4 Foyt (A. J.), Hill (Graham) **5** Clark (Jim), Mears (Rick), Petty (Richard), Unser (Al, Bobby) **6** Carter (Pancho), Fangio (Juan), Vogler (Rich) **7** Brabham (Jack), Stewart (Jackie) **8** Andretti (Mario, Michael), Johncock (Gordon) **9** Earnhardt (Dale) **10** Rutherford (Johnny)

autumn 4 fall **6** season **8** maturity

auxiliary 4 aide **5** spare **6** backup, helper **7** reserve **8** adjutant, adjuvant **9** accessory, ancillary, assistant, coadjutor, secondary **10** accomplice, additional, collateral, subsidiary **11** appurtenant, subservient **12** contributory **13** complementary, supplementary ***verb:*** **3** are, can, did, had, has, may, was **4** been, does, have, must, were, will **5** could, might, ought, shall, would **6** should

avail 3 aid, use **4** gain, good, help **5** asset, serve **6** profit **7** account, benefit, fitness, satisfy, service **9** advantage, relevance **10** usefulness **13** applicability

available 5 handy, on tap, ready, valid **6** at hand, on hand, usable **7** present, willing **8** prepared **9** qualified **10** accessible, attainable, convenient, obtainable, procurable **11** purchasable

avalanche 4 mass, rush **5** drown, flood, slide **6** deluge **7** overrun, smother **8** inundate, mudslide, overflow, rockfall **9** landslide, overwhelm, rockslide, snowslide **10** inundation **12** accumulation

Avalon 8 paradise

avant-garde 7 radical **8** advanced, contempo **10** innovative, pioneering **11** cutting-edge, leading-edge, progressive **12** experimental **13** up-to-the-minute

avarice 5 greed **7** avidity **8** cupidity, rapacity, voracity **10** greediness **12** covetousness

avaricious 6 grabby, greedy, stingy **7** miserly **8** covetous, esurient, grasping, ravenous **9** mercenary, rapacious **11** acquisitive

avatar 4 type **5** image **7** epitome **8** exemplar **9** archetype **10** apotheosis, embodiment, expression **11** incarnation, reification **13** manifestation ***of Vishnu:*** **4** Rama

avaunt 4 away **5** hence, leave, scram **6** beat it, depart, get out

ave 4 hail **8** farewell, greeting

avenge 5 repay, right **6** punish **7** get even, pay back, redress, requite **9** fight back, retaliate, vindicate

avenue 3 way **4** path, road **5** drive, means, route, track **6** access, artery, course, street **7** channel, parkway, pathway **8** approach **9** boulevard **10** passageway **12** thoroughfare

aver 4 avow **5** prove, state, swear **6** affirm, allege, assert, attest, avouch, depose, insist, verify **7** declare, profess, protest, testify, warrant **8** maintain **9** guarantee, predicate

average 3 par **4** fair, mean, norm, so-so **5** usual **6** common, divide, equate, figure, median, medium, middle, normal **7** balance, even out, typical **8** everyday, midpoint, moderate, ordinary **12** intermediate

averagely 4 so-so **6** enough, fairly, rather **8** passably **9** tolerably **10** moderately

averse 5 balky, loath **6** afraid **7** hostile, opposed, uneager **8** allergic, hesitant **9** reluctant, resistant, unwilling **10** indisposed **11** disinclined **12** antipathetic

aversion 4 fear, hate **5** dread **6** hatred, horror **7** allergy, disgust, dislike **8** disfavor, distaste, loathing **9** antipathy, disliking, repulsion, revulsion **10** abhorrence, antagonism, repugnance **11** abomination, detestation, displeasure **13** indisposition

aversive 8 ungenial **9** repellent, repugnant **11** uncongenial **12** antipathetic **13** unsympathetic

avert 4 foil, halt, turn, veer, ward **5** avoid, check, deter **6** thwart **7** deflect, fend off, forfend, obviate, prevent, rule out, ward off **8** go around, stave off, turn away **9** forestall, turn aside

avian 6 flying, winged **8** birdlike, ornithic

aviary 4 cage **8** birdcage, dovecote **9** birdhouse, enclosure

aviator 3 ace **4** Post (Wiley) **5** flier, pilot **6** airman, Cessna (Clyde), flyboy, Wright (Orville, Wilbur), Yeager (Chuck) **7** birdman, Earhart (Amelia) **8** aeronaut **9** bush pilot, Lindbergh (Charles) **10** Richthofen (Manfred von) **12** Rickenbacker (Eddie)

avid 4 agog, keen **5** eager **6** ardent, greedy, hungry **7** anxious, athirst, craving, fervent, thirsty, zealous **8** appetent, covetous, desirous, grasping **9** impatient **10** breathless, insatiable **12** enthusiastic

avidity 4 zeal **5** greed **6** fervor, thirst **7** avarice, craving **8** cupidity, keenness, rapacity **9** eagerness **10** greediness

Avis competitor 5 Hertz

____ avis 4 rara

avocation 5 hobby **7** pastime, pursuit **8** sideline **9** amusement, diversion **10** recreation

avoid 4 bilk, duck, miss, shun, snub **5** annul, avert, dodge, elude, evade, shirk, skirt **6** bypass, divert, escape, eschew, pass up **7** abstain, prevent, refrain **8** preclude, sidestep, stay away, withdraw **9** keep clear **11** refrain from **12** keep away from

avoidance 5 dodge **6** escape **7** dodging, elu-

sion, evasion **8** escaping, escapism, eschewal, shirking, shunning **9** runaround **10** abstinence
avouch 3 own **4** aver, avow **5** admit, claim, state, swear **6** affirm, assert, depose, insist **7** certify, confess, confirm, declare, profess, testify **9** predicate, pronounce **11** acknowledge, corroborate
avow 3 own **4** aver **5** admit, allow, grant, let on, own up, state, swear **6** affirm, assert, avouch, depose **7** concede, confess, declare, profess, protest **8** disclose, maintain, proclaim **9** predicate **11** acknowledge
avowal 6 assent **9** admission, assertion, statement **10** profession **11** affirmation, attestation, declaration
avowedly 6 openly **7** frankly **8** candidly **9** allegedly **10** apparently, ostensibly, supposedly
await 4 bide, hope, stay **5** abide **6** expect **7** count on, look for **8** watch for **10** anticipate, hang around
awake 4 stir **5** alert, alive, aware, rouse **6** active, arouse, bestir, excite, revive, roused, stir up **7** animate, aroused, excited, on guard **8** activate, sensible, sentient, vigilant, watchful **9** attentive, cognizant, conscious, observant, stimulate, stirred up
award 4 gift, give, kudo **5** allot, badge, endow, grant, honor, kudos, medal, prize **6** accord, bestow, confer, donate, ribbon, trophy **7** concede, laurels, tribute **8** accolade, citation, donation **9** vouchsafe **10** blue ribbon, decoration, distribute **11** distinction ***advertising:*** **4** Addy, Andy, Clio ***broadcasting:*** **7** Peabody ***cable:*** **5** Telly ***cartooning:*** **6** Ignatz, Reuben ***comic books:*** **6** Eisner, Harvey ***computing:*** **6** Turing ***horror writing:*** **10** Bram Stoker ***Internet:*** **5** Webby ***motion picture:*** **5** Annie, Oscar **6** Razzie, Saturn **7** Academy **11** Golden Globe ***mystery novel:*** **5** Edgar **6** Agatha ***record:*** **6** Grammy ***remodeling:*** **9** Chrysalis ***romance novel:*** **4** Rita ***science & technology:*** **11** Enrico Fermi ***science-fiction:*** **4** Hugo **6** Nebula ***software:*** **5** Codie ***television:*** **4** Emmy ***theater:*** **4** Obie, Tony
aware 4 onto **5** alert, alive, awake **7** heedful, knowing, mindful, tuned in, witting **8** informed, sensible, sentient, vigilant **9** attentive, au courant, cognizant, conscious, observant **10** conversant, perceptive **12** apprehensive **13** knowledgeable
awash 4 full **6** afloat, filled, jammed, loaded, packed **7** brimful, covered, crammed, crowded, flooded, run-over, stuffed **8** brimming, chockful **9** chock-full **11** overflowing
away 3 far, fro, now, off, out **4** afar, gone **5** along, apart, aside, forth, hence **6** abroad, absent, afield, far off **7** distant, lacking, missing, not here **9** elsewhere **11** incessantly **12** continuously
away from 6 beyond
awe 5 alarm, amaze, scare **6** wonder **7** inspire, startle **8** astonish **9** amazement, reverence **10** veneration, wonderment **11** flabbergast **12** astonishment
aweless 4 bold **5** brave **7** valiant **8** fearless, intrepid, unafraid **9** dauntless, undaunted **10** courageous
awesome 3 rad **6** august **7** amazing, sublime **8** imposing, terrific, wondrous **10** formidable, impressive **11** astonishing **12** breathtaking **13** extraordinary
awful 3 bad **4** dire, very **5** nasty **6** odious **7** hateful, heinous **8** dreadful, horrible, horrific, shocking, terrible, terrific **9** appalling, atrocious, extremely, frightful, loathsome, offensive **10** deplorable, disgusting, formidable
awfully 4 much, very **6** hugely, vastly **7** greatly **8** terribly, whopping **9** extremely, immensely **10** dreadfully, enormously **11** exceedingly
awhile 7 briefly **8** for a time **11** temporarily
awkward 5 gawky, inept, messy, nerdy, splay **6** clumsy, gauche, klutzy, wooden **7** artless, gawkish, halting, lumpish, unhandy, unhappy **8** bumbling, bungling, tactless, ungainly **9** graceless, ham-handed, ill-chosen, inelegant, lumbering, maladroit **10** blundering, ungraceful, unskillful **11** heavy-handed, unfortunate **12** embarrassing, incommodious, inconvenient, infelicitous
awl 4 tool **7** piercer
awning 6 canopy **7** marquee **8** sunshade ***ancient Roman:*** **8** velarium
awry 5 amiss, askew, atilt, wrong **6** astray **7** askance, crooked **8** cockeyed **9** cock-a-hoop, crookedly ***Scottish:*** **5** agley
ax, axe 3 adz, can, hew **4** adze, boot, chop, fire, sack **6** bounce **7** boot out, chopper, cleaver, dismiss, hatchet, kick out **8** tomahawk **9** discharge, terminate ***blade:*** **3** bit ***handle:*** **5** helve
axillary 4 alar
axiom 3 law **4** rule **5** adage, maxim, moral, truth **6** dictum, truism **7** precept, theorem **8** aphorism, apothegm **9** postulate, principle **10** principium **11** fundamental
axiomatic 5 given **7** assumed, certain, obvious **8** accepted, absolute, manifest, provable **10** aphoristic, understood **11**

fundamental, indubitable, self-evident **12** unquestioned
axis 4 line, pole, stem **5** point, pivot **8** alliance **9** continuum, plant stem **11** partnership **12** straight line, turning point
axle 3 bar, pin, rod **4** beam **5** bogie, shaft **7** spindle, support
aye 3 yea, yep, yes **4** amen, okay, ever, vote **6** agreed, always **8** all right **11** affirmative, continually
Azerbaijan ***capital:*** **4** Baku ***city:*** **5** Gäncä **8** Sumqayit ***exclave:*** **8** Naxçivan **11** Nakhichevan ***monetary unit:*** **5** manat ***neighbor:*** **4** Iran **6** Russia **7** Armenia, Georgia ***river:*** **4** Kura **5** Araks ***sea:*** **7** Caspian
Azores ***capital:*** **12** Ponta Delgada ***city:*** **5** Horta ***island:*** **4** Pico **5** Corvo, Faial, Lajes **6** Flores **8** São Jorge, Terceura **9** São Miguel **10** Santa Maria ***part of:*** **8** Portugal
Aztec ***capital:*** **12** Tenochtitlán ***conqueror:*** **6** Cortés, Cortéz ***emperor:*** **9** Moctezuma, Montezuma ***god:*** **4** Xipe **6** Tlaloc **9** Xipetotec **12** Quetzalcoatl ***hero:*** **4** Nata ***language:*** **7** Nahuatl ***temple:*** **8** teocalli
azure 3 sky **4** blue **5** color **7** sky blue

B

baa 5 bleat
Babbitt 10 conformist, middlebrow, philistine ***author:*** **5** Lewis (Sinclair)
babble 3 gab, jaw, yak, yap **4** blab, chat, go on, gush, rant, rave **5** clack, prate, run on **6** burble, drivel, gibber, gossip, jabber, murmur, patter, piffle, rattle, yammer **7** blabber, blather, chatter, maunder, palaver, prattle, twaddle **8** nonsense, idle talk **9** gibberish **11** jabberwocky
babe 3 cub, tot **4** doll, girl **5** bairn, child, chick, cutie, toots, woman **6** infant, hottie **7** bambino, papoose, neonate, newborn **8** bantling, nursling
babel 3 ado, din, row **4** to-do **5** hoo-ha **6** bedlam, clamor, hubbub, jangle, outcry, racket, ruckus, tumult, uproar **7** clangor, discord, ferment, turmoil **8** brouhaha, clangour, foofaraw **9** cacophony, commotion, confusion **10** dissonance, hullabaloo, hurly-burly, turbulence **11** pandemonium **12** vociferation
baboon 3 oaf **4** clod, dolt, goon, lout **6** chacma, galoot, simian **7** palooka **8** lunkhead, mandrill, meathead **9** hamadryas
babushka 6 granny **7** bandana **8** bandanna, kerchief
baby 3 pet, tot **4** tiny **5** bairn, sissy, spoil **6** cocker, coddle, cosset, dote on, infant, pamper **7** bambino, cater to, indulge, neonate, newborn, papoose, toddler **8** bantling, dote upon, nursling, suckling, weanling **11** mollycoddle ***ailment:*** **5** colic, croup ***bed:*** **4** crib **6** cradle **8** bassinet ***bedroom:*** **7** nursery ***breechcloth:*** **6** diaper ***cap:*** **6** biggin, bonnet ***carriage:*** **4** pram **5** buggy **8** stroller **12** perambulator ***doctor:*** **12** pediatrician ***food:*** **3** pap **4** milk **6** pablum **7** pabulum ***garment:*** **7** rompers ***Italian:*** **7** bambino ***napkin:*** **3** bib ***outfit:*** **7** layette ***powder:*** **4** talc ***shoe:*** **6** bootee ***Spanish:*** **4** bebé, nene
baby grand 5 piano
babyhood 7 infancy **10** diaper days, immaturity
babyish 5 petty **7** foolish, puerile, spoiled **8** childish, immature, juvenile **9** infantile, infantine
Babylonian 6 lavish **9** luxurious ***abode of the dead:*** **5** Aralu ***capital:*** **7** Babylon ***chaos:*** **4** Apsu ***city:*** **5** Akkad **6** Cunaxa ***crown prince:*** **10** Belshazzar ***division:*** **5** Akkad, Sumer ***first ruler:*** **6** Nimrod ***god:*** **3** Bel **4** Adad, Addu, Enki, Enzu, Irra, Nabu, Nebo **6** Marduk, Tammuz **7** Shamash ***goddess:*** **4** Erua, Gula **5** Belit **6** Ishtar ***hero:*** **9** Gilgamesh ***king:*** **6** Sargon **9** Hammurabi **12** Ashurbanipal ***priest:*** **2** en ***river:*** **6** Tigris **9** Euphrates ***tower:*** **5** Babel **8** ziggurat ***waters:*** **4** Apsu **6** Tiamat ***winged dragon:*** **6** Tiamat
baccalaureate 6 degree **9** bachelor's **10** graduation
bacchanal 6 maenad see also **bacchanalia**
bacchanalia 4 bash, orgy **5** binge, revel, spree **6** bender, excess **7** blowout, carouse, debauch, revelry, wassail **8** carnival, festival, wingding **11** celebration, dissipation, merrymaking
bacchanalian 4 wild **7** drunken, riotous **8**

frenzied **9** debauched, orgiastic **12** intoxicating ***cry*** **4** evoe **5** evohe

Bacchus 8 Dionysus ***attendant:*** **6** maenad **9** bacchante ***father:*** **4** Zeus **7** Jupiter ***lover:*** **5** Venus **9** Aphrodite ***mother:*** **6** Semele ***son:*** **7** Priapus ***staff:*** **7** thyrsus

Bach, Johann Sebastian ***birthplace:*** **8** Eisenach ***genre:*** **5** fugue, motet, suite **6** sonata **7** cantata, chorale, partita, prelude, toccata **8** concerto, fantasia, oratorio, sinfonia ***home:*** **7** Leipzig ***instrument:*** **5** organ **11** harpsichord ***musical style:*** **7** baroque ***religion:*** **8** Lutheran

back 3 aft, aid **4** abet, fund, help, hind, rear **5** abaft, about, bet on, dorsa (plural), spine, stake, stern **6** assist, astern, dorsum, hinder, recede, uphold **7** endorse, finance, promote, retract, retreat, reverse, sponsor, support **8** advocate, bankroll, champion, rearward, side with **9** in reverse, posterior, retrocede, subsidize **10** retrograde ***ailment:*** **7** lumbago **10** rheumatism ***muscle:*** **3** lat **4** trap **8** rhomboid **9** trapezius ***of an arthropod:*** **6** tergum ***of an insect:*** **5** notum ***of the neck:*** **4** nape **6** scruff ***prefix:*** **4** post **5** retro ***relating to:*** **6** dorsal

back answer 3 lip **6** retort **7** riposte **8** comeback, repartee **9** rejoinder, wisecrack **10** return shot **11** parting shot

backbite 4 slam, slur **5** abuse, decry, knock, libel, smear, sully, taint **6** defame, defile, malign, vilify **7** asperse, put down, run down, slander, traduce **8** bad-mouth, belittle, besmirch, derogate, diminish **9** denigrate, discredit

backbiter 6 gossip **7** defamer, traitor **9** detractor, slanderer **10** talebearer

backbiting 5 abuse, smear, spite **6** gossip **7** abusing, calumny, obloquy, scandal, slander **8** libelous, smearing **9** aspersion, cattiness, gossiping, invective, maligning, traducing, vilifying **10** calumnious, defamation, defamatory, scandalous, slandering, slanderous **11** denigration **12** belittlement, depreciation, spitefulness, vituperation **13** disparagement

backbone 4 base, grit, guts, will **5** basis, moxie, nerve, spine, spunk **6** mettle, pillar, rachis **7** resolve, support **8** mainstay, tenacity **9** character, fortitude, framework, toughness, vertebrae **10** foundation, moral fiber, resolution **12** spinal column **13** determination, steadfastness

backbreaking 6 taxing, tiring **7** arduous, onerous **8** grueling, toilsome **9** fatiguing, gruelling, laborious, punishing, strenuous, torturous, wearisome **10** burdensome, exhausting

backchat 6 banter, gossip **10** persiflage

backcomb 5 tease

backcountry 4 bush **6** sticks **7** boonies, outback **8** frontier, interior **9** boondocks **10** hinterland

backcourtman 5 guard

back down 4 balk **5** admit, demur, welsh, yield **6** beg off, bow out, cry off, give in, give up, recall, recant, renege **7** concede, disavow, retract, retreat **8** take back, withdraw **9** surrender, weasel out **10** chicken out

backdrop 6 milieu **7** climate, context, scenery, setting **8** stage set **10** atmosphere, background **11** environment, mise-en-scène **12** surroundings

backer 4 ally **5** angel **6** patron, surety **7** sponsor **8** advocate, defender, exponent, follower, investor, promoter **9** auxiliary, guarantor, proponent, supporter **10** bankroller, benefactor, meal ticket

backfire 4 fail **5** blast **6** fizzle, go awry **7** go amiss, go wrong **8** miscarry, ricochet **9** boomerang, discharge, explosion **10** disappoint, spring back **11** fall through **13** counteraction

backgammon ***board section:*** **5** table ***piece:*** **5** stone ***wedge:*** **5** point

background 4 base, tone **6** milieu **7** history, scenery, setting **8** heritage, training **9** education **10** experience, supporting **13** circumstances, qualification

backhanded 7 devious, oblique **8** indirect, derisive, sneering **9** insulting, sarcastic **10** roundabout **12** disingenuous **13** condescending ***compliment:*** **6** insult, slight **7** putdown **9** aspersion

backing 3 aid **4** help **5** aegis, funds **7** harmony, support **8** auspices **9** patronage, promotion **10** assistance **11** endorsement, sponsorship **13** accompaniment, encouragement

backland see **backcountry**

backlash 5 slack **6** recoil **8** kickback, reaction, response, ricochet **11** retaliation **12** repercussion

backlog 4 pile **5** hoard, stock, store **6** pile up, supply **7** nest egg, reserve **9** inventory, reservoir, stockpile **12** accumulation

back of 5 abaft **6** behind **9** following

back off see **back down**

back out 4 quit **5** leave, welsh, yield **6** beg off, desert, give up, renege **7** forsake **8** withdraw **9** surrender

backpack 4 gear, hike **5** tramp **6** duffel, ramble **8** knapsack, rucksack **9** haversack

backpedal see **back down**
backset see **setback**
backside 3 bum **4** butt, rear, rump, seat, tail, tush **5** fanny, hiney, stern **6** behind, bottom, breech, far end, heinie **8** buttocks, derriere, haunches **9** fundament, posterior **12** hindquarters
backslide 4 fall, sink, slip **5** lapse **6** return, revert **7** go wrong, regress, relapse **9** retrovert **10** degenerate, go downhill, recidivate **11** deteriorate
backstabbing 4 slur **5** smear **6** malice **7** calumny, scandal, slander **8** betrayal **9** treachery **10** defamation, detraction, traitorous **11** treacherous **12** belittlement, depreciation, vilification **13** disparagement
backstairs 6 covert, secret, sneaky, sordid **7** furtive **8** hush-hush **9** secretive **10** scandalous **11** clandestine, underhanded **13** surreptitious
backstop 5 fence **6** screen, uphold **7** bolster, support **8** advocate, champion, side with
back talk 3 lip **4** guff, sass **5** cheek, mouth, sauce **9** freshness, impudence, insolence **12** impertinence
backtrack 7 regress, retrace, retreat, reverse **8** turn tail
backward 4 dull, slow, rear **5** abaft, dense **6** averse, astern, behind, stupid **7** awkward, delayed, moronic **8** ignorant, inverted, rearward, retarded, reversed, stagnant **9** benighted, dim-witted, in reverse **10** half-witted, retrograde, slow-witted, uncultured **11** thickheaded, undeveloped **12** feebleminded, simpleminded, uncultivated **13** unprogressive
backwoods see **backcountry**
backwoodsman 4 hick, rube **5** swain, yokel **6** rustic **7** bumpkin, hayseed **9** hillbilly **10** clodhopper, country boy, provincial **11** mountaineer
bacon ***side:*** **6** flitch, gammon ***slice:*** **6** rasher
Bacon, Francis ***work:*** **12** Novum Organum
bacteria 5 cocci **6** coccus **7** bacilli, vibrios **8** bacillus, spirilla **9** spirillum ***culture medium:*** **4** agar ***destroyer:*** **10** antibiotic ***pathogenic:*** **5** E. coli
bacterial disease 6 plague, typhus **7** anthrax, leprosy, tetanus, typhoid **8** botulism, syphilis **9** gonorrhea, infection, pneumonia **10** diphtheria, meningitis **11** shigellosis
bacteriologist ***American:*** **6** Enders (John Franklin) **7** Noguchi (Hideyo), Theiler (Max) ***British:*** **7** Fleming (Alexander) ***French:*** **5** Widal (Fernand) **7** Nicolle (Charles-Jean-Henri), Pasteur (Louis) ***German:*** **4** Cohn (Ferdinand Julius), Koch (Robert) **5** Klebs (Edwin) **7** Behring (Emil von), Ehrlich (Paul), Löffler (Friedrich) **10** Wassermann (August von) ***Japanese:*** **8** Kitasato (Shibasaburo) ***Russian:*** **11** Metchnikoff (Elie) ***Swiss:*** **6** Yersin (Alexandre-Emile-John)
bad 3 ill, low **4** evil, foul, sour **5** amiss, awful, lousy, wrong **6** crummy, putrid, rancid, rotten, sinful, wicked **7** harmful, hateful, hurtful, immoral, naughty, noisome, noxious, spoiled, tainted, vicious **8** damaging, dreadful, inferior, perverse, terrible, wretched **9** abhorrent, defective, execrable, injurious, loathsome, obnoxious, offensive, putrefied, reprobate, repulsive, sickening **10** disgusting, iniquitous **11** deleterious, detrimental, distasteful, intolerable **12** unacceptable **13** objectionable ***comparative:*** **5** worse ***prefix:*** **3** dys, mis ***superlative:*** **5** worst
bad blood 7 ill will **10** bitterness, ill feeling
Badebec ***husband:*** **9** Gargantua ***son:*** **10** Pantagruel
Baden 3 spa **6** resort **9** hot spring
badge 3 pin **4** arms, logo, mark, seal, sign **5** award, honor, kudos, medal, token **6** button, emblem, ensign **7** laurels **8** accolade, hallmark, insignia **10** coat of arms, decoration **11** distinction, purple heart
badger 3 bug, nag **4** bait, goad, ride **5** annoy, brock, chivy, harry, hound, ratel **6** chivvy, harass, hassle, heckle, hector, needle, pester, plague **7** torment **8** bullyrag **9** importune
Badger State 9 Wisconsin
badinage 4 play **6** banter, joking **7** jesting, joshing, kidding, ribbing, teasing **8** backchat, chitchat, repartee **9** cross talk **10** persiflage
badland 4 wild **5** waste, wilds **6** barren, desert **7** outback **8** wildness **10** wilderness **11** hill country
bad mark 3 gig **7** demerit
bad-tempered 4 dour, sour **5** cross, sulky, surly, testy **6** crabby, cranky, crusty, grumpy, ornery, sullen, touchy **7** grouchy, peevish **8** choleric, petulant **9** crotchety, dyspeptic, irascible, irritable, splenetic **10** ill-humored, ill-natured, unpleasant **11** quarrelsome **12** cantankerous, curmudgeonly, disagreeable, misanthropic
Baedeker 5 guide **6** manual **8** handbook **9** guidebook, vade mecum **10** compendium **11** enchiridion, travel guide
baffle 4 balk, foil **5** addle, block, floor, mix up, stump **6** bemuse, hinder, impede, muddle, puzzle, thwart **7** barrier, confuse, flummox, mystify, nonplus, perplex **8** befuddle,

bewilder, confound **9** deflector, dumbfound, frustrate **10** circumvent, disappoint, disconcert
bafflement 9 confusion **10** bemusement, perplexity **12** bewilderment
bag 3 cop, nab, kit, net, sag, win **4** flop, grip, hook, kill, land, nail, poke, sack, tote, trap **5** biddy, bulge, catch, crone, forgo, pouch, purse, seize, shoot, snare, steal, udder **6** beldam, collar, duffel, duffle, give up, secure, valise **7** abandon, acquire, capture, satchel **8** backpack, knapsack, reticule, suitcase **9** apprehend, haversack **12** protuberance
bagatelle 6 trifle, whimsy **9** plaything
baggage 4 gear **5** hussy, stuff, tramp, trull, wench **6** burden, things, wanton **7** carry-on, effects, jezebel, luggage, parcels, trollop **8** obstacle, matériel, slattern, strumpet **9** equipment, hindrance **10** impediment, prostitute **11** impedimenta **13** paraphernalia
baggy 5 loose
Baghdad *founder:* 6 Mansur ***river:* 6** Tigris
bagnio 4 crib, stew **7** brothel, lupanar **8** bordello, cathouse **10** bawdy house, whorehouse
bagpipe *part:* 5 drone **7** bourdon, chanter ***sound:* 5** skirl
Bahamas *capital:* 6 Nassau ***island:* 3** Cat **5** Abaco **6** Andros, Inagua **7** Watling **9** Eleuthera, Mayaguana **11** Grand Bahama, San Salvador **13** New Providence ***neighbor:* 4** Cuba
Bahrain *capital:* 6 Manama ***island:* 6** Sitrah **7** Bahrain **10** Al Muharraq ***language:* 6** Arabic ***monetary unit:* 5** dinar ***ruler:* 4** amir, emir **5** ameer, hakim
bail 3 bar, dip **4** bond, flee, lade **5** ladle, scoop **6** handle, pledge, surety **7** release **8** guaranty, security, warranty **9** guarantee **10** collateral **12** recognizance
bailiwick 4 area, turf, zone **5** field, realm **6** domain, sphere **7** demesne, purview, terrain **8** district, dominion, province **9** champaign, specialty, territory **10** discipline **12** jurisdiction
bailout 3 aid **6** relief, rescue **7** subsidy **11** benefaction, deliverance
bairn 3 kid, tot **4** babe, baby, tyke **5** child **6** infant
bait 3 nag, try, vex **4** lure, ride, trap **5** abuse, chase, chivy, decoy, harry, hound, leger, snare, taunt, tease, tempt, worry **6** allure, badger, come-on, entice, entrap, harass, heckle, hector, lead on, molest, pester, seduce **7** beguile, torment, torture **8** bullyrag, inveigle, ridicule **9** persecute, seduction, sweetener **10** attraction, allurement, enticement, temptation ***and switch:* 4** lure **5** trick **8** inveigle **10** substitute
bake 4 burn, char, cook, fire, kiln **5** broil, roast, toast **6** scorch **7** scallop, scollop, swelter
baked clay 7 ceramic
baker's dozen 8 thirteen
bakers' yeast 6 leaven **9** leavening
baking 3 hot **5** fiery **6** red-hot, torrid **7** burning **8** broiling, scalding, sizzling, white-hot **9** scorching ***chamber:* 4** kiln, oven
baksheesh 3 tip **4** alms **5** bribe, favor **6** grease, reward **7** payment **8** gratuity **9** emolument **12** compensation
Balaam *beast:* 3 ass **6** donkey ***father:* 4** Beor
balance 4 rest **5** level, poise, scale, weigh **6** adjust, excess, make up, offset, set off, square, stasis **7** harmony, remains, remnant, residue **8** atone for, equalize, outweigh, residual, residuum, symmetry **9** composure, congruity, equipoise, harmonize, remainder, stability **10** compensate, counteract, difference, equanimity, neutralize, proportion, steadiness **11** consistency, countervail, equilibrium, self-control **12** counterpoise
balanced 4 fair **5** equal **6** offset, stable, steady **7** equable, weighed **9** equitable, impartial **10** evenhanded, harmonized, stabilized
balcony 6 piazza **7** catwalk, gallery **8** platform **9** mezzanine ***section:* 4** loge
bald 4 bare, nude **5** blunt, naked, plain, stark **6** barren, severe, shaven, smooth **8** glabrous, hairless, palpable, treeless **9** depilated, unadorned, uncovered **10** deforested, forthright **11** undisguised, unvarnished
baldachin 4 silk **6** canopy, fabric
Balder, Baldur *father:* 4 Odin ***mother:* 5** Frigg **6** Frigga ***slayer:* 3** Höd **4** Hoth, Loke, Loki **5** Hoder, Hothr ***wife:* 5** Nanna
balderdash 3 rot **4** bosh, bull, bunk **5** bilge, crock, hooey **6** blague, bunkum, drivel **7** baloney, eyewash, garbage, hogwash, palaver, rubbish, twaddle **8** buncombe, claptrap, malarkey, nonsense, tommyrot **9** poppycock **10** tomfoolery **11** foolishness **13** horsefeathers
bald-faced 4 bold **6** arrant, brazen **7** blatant, defiant **8** impudent, insolent **9** audacious, shameless, unabashed **11** impertinent
baldness 8 alopecia **12** hairlessness
baldpate 7 widgeon **8** skinhead
Baldwin, James *essay:* 17 Nobody Knows My Name, Notes of a Native Son ***novel:* 12** Fire Next Time (The) **13** Giovanni's Room

14 Another Country 21 Go Tell It on the Mountain ***play:*** 21 Blues for Mister Charlie

balefire 6 beacon

baleful 4 dire, evil 6 deadly, malign 7 direful, fateful, harmful, hostile, malefic, ominous 8 menacing, sinister 9 ill-boding, ill-omened, malignant 10 maleficent, malevolent, pernicious 11 apocalyptic, threatening 12 unpropitious

balk 3 bar, gag, jib, shy 4 beam, dash, foil, ruin 5 block, check, demur, plank, stall 6 baffle, boggle, desist, flinch, hinder, rafter, refuse, thwart 7 prevent, scruple, stumble 8 hang back, hesitate, obstruct 9 frustrate, hindrance 10 circumvent, disappoint

balky 5 loath 6 averse, ornery, mulish, unruly 7 froward, restive, wayward, willful 8 contrary, hesitant, perverse, stubborn 9 immovable, obstinate, reluctant 10 unreliable 11 intractable, wrongheaded 12 cross-grained, recalcitrant 13 uncooperative, unpredictable

ball 3 orb, wad 4 prom 5 dance, globe, round 6 sphere 8 spheroid ***batted high:*** 3 fly ***batted straight:*** 5 liner ***high-arching:*** 3 lob ***of thread or yarn:*** 4 clew ***ornamental:*** 6 pompom, pompon ***tiny:*** 7 globule

ballad 3 lay 4 poem, song ***singer:*** 8 minstrel 10 troubadour

ballast 4 load 5 poise 6 steady 7 balance, freight 8 balancer 9 stabilize, weigh down 10 dead weight, stabilizer 12 counterpoise 13 counterweight

ballerina 6 dancer 8 coryphée, danseuse 9 toe dancer 11 dancing girl ***skirt:*** 4 tutu see also **dancer**

ballet 4 Agon 6 Apollo, Jewels, Sylvia 7 Giselle, Orpheus 8 Bayadère (La), Coppélia, Firebird (The), Raimonda, Raymonda, Swan Lake, Sylphide (La) 9 Fancy Free, Petrushka, Sylphides (Les) 10 Don Quixote, Nutcracker (The), Petrouchka 12 Rite of Spring (The) ***company:*** 5 Kirov 7 Joffrey 8 Imperial ***costume:*** 4 tutu 6 tights 7 leotard ***dancer:*** 7 danseur 8 coryphée, danseuse 9 ballerina ***for two:*** 9 pas de deux ***handrail:*** 5 barre ***jump:*** 4 jeté 9 entrechat ***knee bend:*** 4 plié ***position:*** 6 pointe 8 attitude 9 arabesque ***step:*** 3 pas 8 glissade ***turn:*** 6 chaîné 9 pirouette

Ballets ____ 6 Russes

ball game see at **game**

Ballo in Maschera composer 5 Verdi (Giuseppe)

balloon sail 9 spinnaker

ball-shaped 7 globoid, globose 8 globular, spheroid 9 globulous, spherical

ball up 4 clew, daze 5 addle 6 fuddle, jumble, muddle, puzzle, tangle 7 confuse, fluster 8 befuddle, bewilder, bollix up, confound, distract, throw off 9 disorient

ballyhoo 4 hype, tout 6 blazon, herald, hoopla, hubbub, tumult 7 promote, trumpet 8 brouhaha 9 commotion, publicity 12 extravaganza

balm 4 lull 5 aroma, cream, quiet, salve, scent, spice 6 chrism, relief, remedy, solace 7 anodyne, bouquet, comfort, incense, perfume, soother, unction, unguent 8 easement, ointment 9 emollient, fragrance, redolence 10 palliative 11 consolation, restorative

balmacaan 8 overcoat

balm of Gilead 6 poplar 7 soother 8 restorer 9 balsam fir 11 restorative 12 balsam poplar

balmy 4 calm, daft, mild, nuts, soft 5 crazy, loony, nutty, potty, silly, sweet, wacky 6 gentle, insane, smooth 7 cracked, foolish, lenient, summery 8 aromatic, deranged, fragrant, perfumed, peaceful, pleasant, pleasing, redolent, soothing, tropical 9 agreeable, ambrosial, temperate

baloney 3 rot 4 bosh, bull, bunk 5 bilge, hokum, hooey 6 bunkum, humbug 7 hogwash, rubbish 8 buncombe, claptrap, nonsense 9 poppycock 10 balderdash 11 foolishness

balsam poplar 9 tacamahac 12 balm of Gilead

Balthazar's gift 5 myrrh

Baltic *city:* 4 Riga 7 Tallinn 8 Helsinki 9 Stockholm ***native:*** 4 Lett, Sorb, Wend 7 Latvian 8 Estonian, Prussian 10 Lithuanian ***state:*** 6 Latvia 7 Estonia 9 Lithuania

Baltimore team 5 Blast, Colts 6 Ravens 7 Orioles

balustrade 4 rail 5 fence 7 railing 8 banister, handrail

Balzac character 4 Pons (Cousin) 5 Bette (Cousin) 6 Goriot (Père), Vidocq 7 Chabert (Colonel), Eugénie (Grandet), Grandet, Vautrin 8 Rubempré (Lucien de) 9 Birotteau, Rastignac (Eugène de) 13 Henri de Marsay

Bambi author 6 Salten (Felix)

bambino 3 kid, tot 4 babe, baby, tyke 5 bairn, child 6 cherub, Christ, infant, moppet, nipper 7 toddler

bamboozle 3 con 4 bilk, dupe, fool, gull, hoax, hose, scam 5 stump, trick 6 baffle, befool, diddle, puzzle 7 chicane, confuse, deceive, defraud, mislead, perplex, swindle 8 befuddle, confound, flimflam, hoodwink, throw off 9 frustrate 11 hornswoggle

ban 3 bar 5 curse, taboo 6 enjoin, forbid, outlaw 7 censure, exclude 8 anathema, prohibit, suppress **9** damnation, interdict, proscribe **10** injunction **11** forbiddance, malediction, prohibition, suppression **12** denunciation, interdiction, proscription

Ban ***ally:*** **6** Arthur ***son:*** **8** Lancelot

banal **4** blah, dull, flat **5** bland, corny, ho-hum, tired, trite, usual, vapid **6** common, jejune, stupid **7** clichéd, humdrum, insipid, prosaic, sapless, trivial **8** ordinary **9** hackneyed, quotidian, wearisome **10** namby-pamby, pedestrian, uninspired, wishy-washy **11** commonplace

banality **5** ennui **6** cliché, old saw, truism **7** bromide, inanity, old song **8** chestnut, monotony, prosaism **9** platitude **10** dreariness, shibboleth, triviality **11** commonplace, old chestnut, tediousness

banana **3** fei

banana-like fruit **8** plantain

banausic **4** blah, drab, dull, poky **6** dreary, earthy, stodgy **7** humdrum, mundane, routine, secular, sensual, tedious, worldly **8** everyday, material, plodding, temporal, workaday **9** practical, pragmatic **10** monotonous, pedestrian **11** acquisitive, utilitarian **13** materialistic, uninteresting

band **4** belt, bevy, club, crew, gang, gird, sash, tape **5** bunch, corps, covey, group, horde, party, strap, strip, troop, unite **6** concur, fillet, girdle, league, outfit, ribbon, team up, troupe **7** cluster, combine, company, coterie **8** cincture, engirdle, ensemble, symphony **9** cooperate, orchestra **10** federation ***horizontal:*** **4** fess ***Mexican:*** **8** mariachi ***neck:*** **6** torque ***small:*** **5** combo

bandage **4** bind **5** cover, dress, gauze, truss **6** swathe **7** plaster, swaddle **8** compress, dressing

bandanna **8** babushka, kerchief **9** headscarf **11** neckerchief

bandeau **3** bra **5** strip **6** fillet, ribbon, stripe **7** tube top **8** swimwear **9** brassiere

banderilla **4** dart

banderole **4** flag, jack **6** banner, burgee, colors, ensign, pennon, scroll **7** pennant **8** bannerol, standard, streamer

bandicoot **3** rat

bandit **6** outlaw, raider, robber, sacker **7** brigand, cateran, forager, ravager **8** marauder, pillager **9** cutthroat, desperado, holdup man, plunderer **10** freebooter, highwayman **11** bushwhacker

bandleader **7** maestro **9** conductor ***famous:*** **3** Rey (Alvino) **4** Shaw (Artie), Ward (Hedley), Welk (Lawrence) **5** Basie (Count), Brown (Les), Cugat (Xavier), Faith (Percy), Heath (Ted), James (Harry), Jones (Spike), Kyser (Kay), Lewis (Ted), Lopez (Vincent), Owens (Buck), Prado (Pérez), Sousa (John Philip) **6** Cotton (Billy), Dorsey (Jimmy, Tommy), Duchin (Eddie, Peter), Herman (Woody), Hylton (Jack), Kenton (Stan), Miller (Glenn), Mingus (Charles), Waring (Fred) **7** Goodman (Benny), Trotter (John Scott) **8** Calloway (Cab), Giordano (Vince), Lombardo (Guy), Whiteman (Paul) **9** Ellington (Duke), Henderson (Fletcher), Mantovani

bandolier **4** belt, sash

bandwagon **3** fad **4** chic, mode, rage **5** craze, style, trend, vogue **7** fashion

bandy **3** bat **4** flip, swap, toss **5** argue, bowed **6** banter **7** discuss, shuffle **8** exchange **9** bowlegged, pass about **11** interchange

bane **3** woe **4** pest, ruin **5** curse, death, venom, virus **6** blight, burden, plague, poison **7** bugaboo, bugbear, scourge, torment, undoing **8** anathema, calamity, downfall, nuisance **9** bête noire, contagion, destroyer, ruination **10** affliction, pestilence **11** destruction

baneful **4** dire, evil **5** fatal **6** deadly **7** fateful, harmful, hurtful, malefic, noxious, ominous **9** ill-boding, ill-omened, injurious, malignant, pestilent, unhealthy **10** disastrous, pernicious **11** apocalyptic, deleterious, pestiferous, threatening **12** pestilential, unpropitious

bang **3** bat, box, hit, pop, rap **4** bash, beat, belt, blow, boom, bump, clap, peal, push, rape, shot, slam, sock, wham, whop **5** blast, burst, crack, crash, noise, pound, punch, smack, smash, sound, vigor, whack **6** fringe, report, strike, thrill, wallop **7** collide, exactly, resound **8** smack-dab, squarely **9** explosion **10** detonation

banger **7** athlete, sausage

Bangkok native **4** Thai

Bangladesh ***capital:*** **5** Dacca, Dhaka ***city:*** **6** Khulna **10** Chittagong ***former name:*** **6** Bengal ***language:*** **7** Bengali ***monetary unit:*** **4** taka ***neighbor:*** **5** Burma, India **7** Myanmar ***river:*** **5** Padma **6** Ganges, Jamuna **11** Brahmaputra

bangle **4** disk **5** charm **6** anklet, bauble **7** pendant, trinket **8** bracelet, wristlet

bang-up **3** ace **4** fine **5** dandy, primo, super **6** far-out, superb **7** capital **8** champion, fabulous, five-star, splendid, top-notch **9** excellent, first-rate **10** first-class **11** spectacular

banish **3** ban **4** oust **5** debar, eject, evict, exile, expel **6** deport, dispel, put out, run out **7** cast out, dismiss, exclude, shut out, turn out **8** drive out, relegate, send away **9** dis-

charge, ostracize, rusticate, transport **10** expatriate **13** excommunicate
banishment 5 exile **7** banning **8** eviction **9** discharge, expulsion, ostracism **10** dispelling, relegation **11** deportation, dissolution **12** displacement
banister 3 bar **4** rail **7** railing **10** balustrade
bank 3 row **4** edge, heap, hill, mass, pile, rank, save, tier, tilt **5** amass, array, beach, coast, group, hoard, levee, marge, mound, pitch, shoal, shore, slope, stack, stash **6** coffer, dealer, invest, margin, rivage, strand **7** deposit, incline, lay away, pyramid **8** lakeside, lay aside, salt away, seafront, set aside, sock away, squirrel, treasury **9** riverside **10** repository, storehouse **11** credit union **12** squirrel away ***machine:* 3** ATM
bank on 5 trust **7** believe
bankroll 4 back, fund **5** endow, funds, stake **6** pay for **7** capital, finance, sponsor, support **9** grubstake, subsidize **10** capitalize, underwrite
bankrupt 4 bare, bust, do in, ruin **5** break, drain, empty, strip, spent, use up, wreck **6** broken, divest, failed, fold up **7** deplete, deprive, exhaust, lacking, sterile **8** depleted, indebted **9** destitute, exhausted, pauperize, penniless **10** impoverish **12** impoverished
bankruptcy 4 lack, ruin **6** penury **7** failure **9** depletion, ruination, sterility, total loss **10** barrenness, exhaustion, insolvency **11** destitution, liquidation
banned 5 taboo **6** barred **7** illegal, illicit, tabooed **8** enjoined, verboten **9** forbidden **10** contraband, disallowed, prohibited, proscribed **11** interdicted
banner 4 flag, jack **6** burgee, ensign, pennon **7** pendant, pennant **8** banderol, gonfalon, standard, streamer **9** banderole ***Roman:* 7** labarum **8** vexillum
bannerol see **banderole**
banquet 4 feed **5** feast, roast **6** dinner, regale, repast, spread
banquette 4 seat, sofa **5** bench, shelf **8** platform, sidewalk
Banquo 5 ghost ***murderer:* 7** Macbeth
banshee 6 keener, wailer
bantam 3 wee **4** arch, fowl, mini, pert, runt, tiny **5** dwarf, saucy, small **6** cheeky, little, petite **8** insolent, malapert **9** combative, undersize **10** diminutive, undersized
banter 3 fun, kid, rag, rib, wit **4** fool, jest, jive, joke, josh, razz **5** chaff, dally, jolly, tease **7** jesting, joshing, kidding, mockery, ragging, razzing, ribbing, teasing **8** backchat, back talk, badinage, chitchat, drollery, exchange, repartee **9** challenge, small talk **10** persiflage, pleasantry **11** give-and-take
bantling 4 babe, baby **5** bairn **6** infant **7** bambino, newborn, papoose
baptize 3 dip, dub **4** call, name, soak **5** douse, title **6** anoint, drench, purify **7** asperse, cleanse, entitle, immerse **8** christen, dedicate, initiate, sprinkle **9** designate **10** consecrate, denominate, regenerate
bar 3 ban, dam, pub, rod, tap **4** curb, dive, fess, halt, save, stop **5** block, court, estop, ingot, limit, stick, strip **6** bistro, except, impede, lounge, saloon, tavern **7** barrier, cantina, delimit, exclude, gin mill, rule out, taproom **8** alehouse, blockade, count out, obstacle, obstruct, restrict, tribunal **9** barricade, eliminate, honky-tonk, nightclub, roadhouse **11** obstruction, rathskeller **12** circumscribe, watering hole ***type:* 3** raw **4** cash, fern, open, roll, tiki **6** sports
barb 3 dig **4** dart, hook **5** quill, shaft, thorn **6** zinger
Barbados *capital:* 10 Bridgetown ***location:* 10** West Indies
barbarian 3 Hun **4** Goth, lout, rude, wild **5** beast, crude, brute **6** savage, Vandal **7** lowbrow, uncouth **8** Visigoth **9** foreigner, Ostrogoth, primitive **10** uncultured **11** uncivilized **12** uncultivated
barbaric 4 wild **5** crude, rough **6** brutal, coarse, savage **7** beastly, boorish, brutish, loutish, uncouth **8** churlish **9** atrocious, monstrous, primitive, unrefined **11** uncivilized
barbarism 8 malaprop, rudeness, solecism **9** vulgarism, vulgarity **10** coarseness, corruption **11** impropriety, malapropism **12** backwardness, unseemliness
barbarity 7 cruelty **8** atrocity, savagery **9** brutality, depravity **10** inhumanity, savageness **11** viciousness **12** ruthlessness **13** monstrousness
barbarous 4 base, fell, grim, rude, vile, wild **5** cruel, harsh **6** brutal, fierce, Gothic, savage, unholy, vulgar, wicked **7** brutish, Hunnish, inhuman, lowbrow, uncivil, ungodly, vicious, wolfish **8** backward, fiendish, inhumane, ruthless, sadistic **9** benighted, ferocious, graceless, heartless, merciless, monstrous, primitive, tasteless, truculent **10** abominable, outlandish, outrageous, philistine, unmerciful **11** unchristian, uncivilized **12** uncultivated
Barbary state 5 Tunis **7** Algiers, Morocco, Tripoli
barbecue 5 grill, roast **7** cookout, roaster
barber 3 bob, cut **4** clip, crop, trim **5** shave,

shear **6** shaver, tonsor **7** clipper, cropper **8** coiffeur **9** coiffeuse **10** beautician, haircutter **11** hairdresser, hair stylist

Barber of Seville ***author:*** **12** Beaumarchais (Pierre-Augustin de) ***character:*** **6** Figaro, Rosina, Rosine **7** Bartolo, Basilio **8** Almaviva, Bartholo ***composer:*** **7** Rossini (Gioacchino) **9** Paisiello (Giovanni)

bard 4 muse, poet, scop **5** skald **8** jongleur, minstrel **9** balladist **10** Parnassian, troubadour ***fictitious:*** **6** Ossian

Bard of Avon 11 Shakespeare (William)

bare 4 bald, mere, nude, void **5** empty, naked, shorn, stark, strip **6** barren, denude, devoid, expose, peeled, reveal, unclad, unveil, vacant **7** denuded, disrobe, emptied, exposed, uncover **8** bankrupt, disclose, stripped **9** unclothed, uncovered, undressed

barefaced 4 bald, bold, open **5** blunt, naked **6** arrant, brassy, brazen **7** blatant, glaring, obvious **8** flagrant, impudent, overbold **9** audacious, beardless, shameless, unabashed **10** unblushing **11** temerarious, unconcealed

barefoot 6 unshod **8** shoeless **9** discalced

bareheaded 7 hatless

barely 4 just **6** hardly, scarce **7** faintly **8** meagerly, scarcely

bargain 3 buy **4** bond, deal, pact, swap **5** agree, steal, trade, truck, value **6** barter, confer, dicker, haggle, higgle, palter, pledge **7** chaffer, compact, savings, traffic **8** closeout, contract, covenant, exchange, giveaway, good deal, huckster, markdown, transact **9** agreement, good value, negotiate, reduction **10** compromise, convention, loss leader, pennyworth **11** arrangement, transaction **13** understanding

barge 3 hoy **4** scow **5** clump, stump **6** lumber **7** galumph, stumble

baritone 4 Prey (Hermann) **5** Gobbi (Tito) **6** Bailey (Norman), London (George), Milnes (Sherrill), Terfel (Bryn), Warren (Leonard) **7** Hampson (Thomas), MacNeil (Cornell), Merrill (Robert), Tibbett (Lawrence) **8** Raimondi (Ruggero), Warfield (William)

barium symbol 2 Ba

bark 3 arf, bay, yap, yip **4** snap, woof, yelp **5** snarl **6** bellow ***mulberry:*** **4** tapa

barkeeper see **bartender**

barker 4 tout **5** shill **6** hawker **8** pitchman

Barlow epic 9 Columbiad

barman see **bartender**

Barmecidal 5 empty, false **6** unreal **7** fictive **8** apparent, illusive, illusory **9** imaginary **10** chimerical, ostensible **13** insubstantial

barn 6 stable ***area of:*** **4** loft **7** hayloft

barnacle 5 leech **7** sponger **8** hanger-on, nuisance, parasite **9** dependent, free rider **10** crustacean, freeloader

barnstorm 8 campaign

Barnum ***elephant:*** **5** Jumbo ***midget:*** **8** Tom Thumb ***partner:*** **6** Bailey

barnyard 4 foul, rude **5** crass, crude, dirty, nasty **6** coarse, earthy, filthy, ribald, smutty, vulgar **7** obscene, raunchy, uncouth **8** indecent **9** tasteless **10** indelicate **12** scatological

baron 4 lord, peer **5** mogul, noble **6** tycoon **7** kingpin, magnate **8** overlord **13** industrialist

baronial 5 ample, grand, noble **6** august, lordly **7** stately **8** imposing, majestic, princely **9** grandiose **10** commanding, impressive **11** magnificent, resplendent

baroque 6 florid, ornate, rococo **7** complex **8** dramatic **9** excessive, grotesque, irregular **10** flamboyant, ornamented **11** embellished, extravagant **12** ostentatious **13** overdecorated

Baroque ***architect:*** **4** Wren (Christopher) **7** Bernini (Gian Lorenzo), Guarini (Guarino), Maderno (Carlo) **9** Borromini (Francesco) ***composer:*** **4** Bach (Johann Sebastian) **5** Lully (Jean-Baptiste) **6** Handel (George Frideric), Rameau (Jean-Philippe), Schütz (Heinrich) **7** Corelli (Arcangelo), Purcell (Henry), Vivaldi (Antonio) **8** Albinoni (Tommaso), Couperin (François), Telemann (Georg Philipp) **9** Pachelbel (Johann), Scarlatti (Alessandro, Domenico) **10** Monteverdi (Claudio) ***painter:*** **4** Hals (Frans) **5** Steen (Jan) **6** Claude (Lorrain), Rubens (Peter Paul) **7** El Greco, Holbein (Hans), Poussin (Nicolas), Van Dyck (Anthony), Vermeer (Jan) **8** Carracci (Agostino, Annibale, Lodovico), Ter Borch (Gerard) **9** Rembrandt (van Rijn), Velázquez (Diego) **10** Caravaggio ***sculptor:*** **5** Puget (Pierre) **7** Bernini (Gian Lorenzo), Coustou (Guillaume, Nicholas), Pigalle (Jean-Baptiste) **8** Coysevox (Antoine), Girardon (François)

barrack 4 jeer, root **5** cheer, scoff, taunt **6** billet, casern, deride, hector **7** caserne **8** quarters

barrage 3 dam **4** fire, hail, mass **5** blitz, burst, salvo, storm, surge **6** deluge, shower, stream, volley **7** gunfire, torrent **8** drumfire, shelling **9** broadside, cannonade, crossfire, fusillade, onslaught **11** bombardment

barranca 4 bank **5** bluff, gully **6** arroyo

barrel 3 keg, tun, vat **4** butt, cask, drum, peck, race, rush, tear **5** hurry **6** firkin, hasten **8** hogshead ***maker:*** **6** cooper ***part:*** **4** hoop **5** stave ***stopper:*** **4** bung ***support:*** **6** gantry

barrelhouse 4 dive **5** hurry, joint **7** hangout **9** honky-tonk

barren 3 dry **4** arid, bare, poor **5** bleak, empty, stark, stony, waste **6** desert, devoid, effete, futile, fallow **7** badland, lacking, parched, sterile, wanting **8** desolate, heirless, impotent **9** childless, fruitless, infertile, unbearing, unfertile, wasteland **10** unfruitful, untillable **11** unrewarding **12** hardscrabble, unproductive, unprofitable

barricade 5 block, fence **7** barrier **8** blockade **9** roadblock ***of trees:*** **6** abatis

Barrie character 4 Hook (Capt.), John, Nana, Smee **5** Peter, Tommy, Wendy **7** Michael **8** Crichton **9** Tiger Lily **10** Tinker Bell **11** Captain Hook

barrier see **barricade**

barring 3 but **4** save **6** bating, except, saving **7** besides, without **9** aside from, excluding, excepting, outside of **11** exclusive of

barrio 4 slum, turf, ward **6** ghetto **7** quarter, section **8** district, precinct **12** neighborhood

barrister 6 lawyer **7** counsel **8** advocate, attorney **9** counselor

barroom 3 pub **6** lounge, saloon, tavern **7** gin mill, rum room, taproom **8** alehouse, beer hall, dramshop, drinkery, groggery, grogshop **9** beer joint, roadhouse **12** watering hole

bartender 7 tapster **8** boniface **10** mixologist **12** saloonkeeper

barter 4 swap **5** trade, truck **7** bargain, traffic **8** exchange

Bartered Bride composer 7 Smetana (Bedrich)

Barth novel 7 Chimera **12** Giles Goat-Boy **13** Sot-Weed Factor (The)

Baruch *father:* **6** Neriah, Zabbai ***occupation:*** **6** scribe

basal 5 basic, vital **6** bottom, lowest **7** minimal, primary, radical **8** simplest **9** beginning, essential, undermost **10** bottommost, elementary, primordial, underlying **11** fundamental, preliminary, rudimentary **12** foundational ***layer:*** **4** sima

base 3 bad, bed, fix, key, low **4** camp, evil, foot, fort, foul, home, mean, poor, post, prop, rest, root, seat, site, ugly, vile **5** build, cheap, dirty, found, hinge, lousy, lowly, nadir, plant, set up, sorry, stand **6** bottom, coarse, common, depend, derive, filthy, ground, humble, menial, origin, paltry, scurvy, shoddy, sleazy, sordid, source, trashy, wicked **7** bedrock, caitiff, essence, footing, ignoble, lowborn, low-down, pitiful, servile, squalid, support **8** beggarly, buttress, cowardly, garrison, inferior, pedestal, plebeian, recreant, unwashed, unworthy, wretched **9** construct, dastardly, degrading, establish, framework, loathsome, low-minded, predicate, principle **10** abominable, despicable, foundation, groundwork, substratum, unennobled **11** disgraceful, humiliating, ignominious **12** contemptible, meanspirited, substructure, underpinning

baseball *abbreviation:* **2** AB, AL, BA, BB, BI, CF, DH, DP, ER, FA, HR, IP, LF, LP, NL, RF, SB, SO, SS, WP **3** ERA, LOB, MVP, RBI ***reputed founder:*** **9** Doubleday (Abner) ***glove:*** **4** mitt ***official:*** **3** ump **6** umpire ***pitch:*** **4** drop, heat **5** curve, smoke **6** change, heater, sinker, slider, slurve **7** spitter **8** change-up, fadeaway, fastball, fork ball, knuckler, palm ball, spitball **9** brushback, screwball **11** knuckleball **12** change of pace, knuckle curve ***player:*** **6** batter **7** baseman, catcher, fielder, pitcher **9** infielder, shortstop **10** base runner, outfielder **11** left fielder **12** right fielder **13** center fielder ***term:*** **3** bag, bat, box, fan, fly, out, run, tag, tap, tip **4** balk, ball, base, bean, bunt, cage, deck, foul, hook, line, mitt, no-no, pill, pole, save, walk **5** alley, apple, bench, bloop, clout, count, drive, error, flare, fungo, glove, homer, liner, mound, pop-up, slide, swing **6** assist, clutch, double, dugout, groove, ground, inning, inside, pop fly, pop-out, powder, putout, relief, rubber, runner, single, strike, triple, windup **7** battery, blooper, bullpen, cleanup, diamond, floater, fly ball, home run, infield, manager, outside, pickoff, rhubarb, sidearm, squeeze, stretch **8** baseline, beanball, delivery, foul ball, grounder, keystone, no-hitter, outfield, pinch-hit, rosin bag, southpaw **9** full count, home plate, hot corner, line drive, sacrifice, strikeout, two-bagger **10** double play, frozen rope, ground ball, scratch hit, strike zone **11** knuckleball, pinch hitter, squeeze play, three-bagger (see also **American League, National League**)

baseballer 3 Ott (Mel) **4** Alou (Felipe, Jesús, Matty, Moises), A-Rod, Bell (George), Cobb (Ty), Cone (David), Dean (Dizzy), Fisk (Carlton), Ford (Whitey), Foxx (Jimmy), Kaat (Jim), Mays (Willie), Rice (Jim), Rose (Pete), Ruth (Babe), Ryan (Nolan), Sosa (Sammy) **5** Aaron (Henry), Anson (Cap), Banks (Ernie), Belle (Albert), Bench (Johnny), Berra (Yogi), Boggs (Wade), Bonds (Barry), Brett (George), Brock (Lou), Brown (Kevin), Carew (Rod), Clark (Will), Damon (Johnny), Davis

(Mark), Green (Shawn), Grove (Lefty), Gwynn (Tony), Henke (Tom), Jeter (Derek), Kiner (Ralph), Maris (Roger), Mauer (Joe), Paige (Satchel), Perez (Tony), Perry (Gaylord), Smith (Lee), Spahn (Warren), Staub (Rusty), Tiant (Luis), Viola (Frank), Weeks (Rickie), Young (Cy), Yount (Robin) **6** Dawson (Andre), Feller (Bob), Foster (George), Franco (John), Garvey (Steve), Gehrig (Lou), Gibson (Bob, Josh, Kirk), Gooden (Dwight), Herzog (Whitey), Hunter (Catfish), Koufax (Sandy), Lajoie (Nap), Maddux (Greg), Mantle (Mickey), Morgan (Joe), Murphy (Dale), Murray (Eddie), Musial (Stan), Palmer (Jim), Piazza (Mike), Pujols (Albert), Raines (Tim), Ripken (Cal), Seaver (Tom), Sisler (George), Sutter (Bruce), Sutton (Don), Thomas (Frank), Vaughn (Mo), Wagner (Honus), Walker (Larry) **7** Bagwell (Jeff), Canseco (José), Carlton (Steve), Clemens (Roger), Coleman (Vince), Collins (Eddie), Delgado (Carlos), Fingers (Rollie), Griffey (Ken), Hornsby (Roger), Hubbell (Carl), Jackson (Joe, Reggie), Johnson (Randy, Walter), Justice (David), Leonard (Buck), McGwire (Mark), Mondesi (Raul), Puckett (Kirby), Ramirez (Manny), Reardon (Jeff), Schmidt (Mike), Simmons (Al), Speaker (Tris) **8** Anderson (Sparky), Blyleven (Bert), Clemente (Roberto), DiMaggio (Joe), Guerrero (Vladimir), Martinez (Pedro), Mitchell (Kevin), Righetti (Dave), Robinson (Brooks, Frank, Jackie), Williams (Bernie, Ted), Winfield (Dave) **9** Alexander (Grover), Eckersley (Dennis), Gehringer (Charlie), Greenberg (Hank), Henderson (Rickey), Hernandez (Willie), Hershiser (Orel), Killebrew (Harmon), Mathewson (Christy), Mattingly (Don), Rodriguez (Alex), Sheffield (Gary) **10** Campanella (Roy), Conigliaro (Tony), Strawberry (Darryl), Valenzuela (Fernando) **11** Garciaparra (Nomar), Yastrzemski (Carl)

baseball team see **American League; National League**

baseboard 7 molding **8** skirting

baseless 4 idle, thin, vain **5** empty, false, wrong **6** feeble, flimsy **9** frivolous, pointless, senseless, unfounded, untenable **10** fallacious, gratuitous, groundless, inadequate, incredible, ungrounded **11** uncalled-for, unconfirmed, unnecessary, unsupported, unsustained, unwarranted **12** indefensible, contemptible, unpersuasive **13** unjustifiable

basement 6 bottom, cellar, ground **7** bedrock **10** foundation, groundwork, substratum **12** substructure

base on balls 4 walk

bash 3 bat, hit **4** belt, blow, fete, gala, slam, whop **5** blast, crack, crash, party, pound, smack, smash, thump, whack **6** attack, pummel, soiree, strike, wallop **7** blowout, shindig **8** wingding

Bashemath ***father:*** **7** Ishmael ***husband:*** **4** Esau ***sister:*** **8** Nebaioth

bashful 3 coy, shy **5** chary, mousy, timid **6** demure, modest **7** abashed, nervous **8** blushing, reserved, retiring, timorous **9** diffident, reluctant, shrinking, unassured **11** unassertive

basic 3 key **4** main **5** chief **6** bottom, innate, simple **7** capital, central, element, minimum, primary, radical **8** cardinal, inherent, rudiment **9** beginning, elemental, essential, intrinsic, primitive, principal, unadorned **10** elementary, underlying **11** fundamental **12** foundational

basically 6 au fond, mainly, mostly **7** at heart, chiefly, firstly, overall **8** in effect **9** generally, in essence, primarily

basic point 4 crux, gist, pith **5** heart **6** kernel **7** essence

basilica 6 church **7** minster **9** cathedral

basics 4 ABCs

basin 3 dip, pan, sag **4** bowl, sink **6** cirque, hollow **7** sinkage **8** sinkhole, washbowl **9** concavity **10** depression ***liturgical:*** **5** stoup **7** piscina

basis 3 bed **4** crux, root, seat, seed **5** heart, nexus **6** bottom, ground, reason **7** bedrock, essence, footing, grounds, nucleus, premise, support, warrant **9** authority, postulate, principle **10** assumption, foundation, groundwork, substratum **11** fundamental, presumption **12** substructure, underpinning **13** justification

bask 3 sun **4** loll **5** glory, revel, relax **6** lounge, wallow, welter **7** indulge **8** sunbathe **9** luxuriate

basket 6 bushel, gabion **7** pannier ***angler's:*** **5** creel ***material:*** **5** osier **6** raffia

basketball ***inventor:*** **8** Naismith (James) ***official:*** **6** umpire **7** referee ***player:*** **5** cager, guard **6** center **7** forward **8** hoopster, swingman **10** point guard ***team:*** **4** five **7** quintet ***term:*** **3** gun, jam, key **4** cage, dunk, pass **5** board, hoops, lay-up, press, shoot, tip-in **6** freeze, screen, tap-off, tip-off, travel **7** dribble, keyhole, rebound, throw-in, time-out **8** alley-oop, jump ball, slam dunk **9** backboard, backcourt, field goal, free throw **11**

ball control (see also **National Basketball Association**)

basketballer 3 Bol (Manute) **4** Bird (Larry), Ming (Yao), Nash (Steve), Redd (Michael), Reed (Willis), West (Jerry, Mark) **5** Allen (Ray), Barry (Rick), Brand (Elton), Cousy (Bob), Davis (Baron), Ewing (Patrick), James (LeBron), Mikan (George), O'Neal (Shaq, Shaquille), Price (Mark) **6** Baylor (Elgin), Blount (Mark), Boozer (Carlos), Bryant (Kobe), Carter (Vince), Cowens (Dave), Duncan (Tim), Erving (Julius), Gervin (George), Jordan (Michael), Malone (Jeff, Karl, Moses), McAdoo (Bob), McHale (Kevin), Miller (Brad, Reggie), Parish (Robert), Pierce (Paul, Ricky), Pippin (Scottie), Rodman (Dennis), Skiles (Scott), Thomas (Kenny), Thorpe (Otis), Walton (Bill), Worthy (James) **7** Barkley (Charles), Billups (Chauncey), Dampier (Erick), Dawkins (Darryl), Edwards (James), Frazier (Walt), Garnett (Kevin), Hilario (Nene), Houston (Allan), Iverson (Allen), Jackson (Lauren), Jamison (Antawn), Johnson (Magic), McGrady (Tracy), Russell (Bill), Rollins (Tree), Taurasi (Diana), Wallace (Ben), Wilkins (Dominique) **8** Auerbach (Red), Cardinal (Brian), Havlicek (John), Magloire (Jamaal), Nowitzki (Dirk), Olajuwon (Akeem), Randolph (Zach), Robinson (David), Stockton (John), Thompson (Tina), Williams (Buck) **9** Donaldson (James), Ferdinand (Marie), Holdsclaw (Chamique), Robertson (Oscar) **10** Stojakovic (Predrag), Williamson (Corliss) **11** Abdul-Jabbar (Kareem), Chamberlain (Wilt)

Basmath's father 7 Solomon

Basque 6 bodice ***cap:* 5** beret ***game:* 6** pelota **7** jai alai ***mountains:* 8** Pyrenees ***province:* 5** Alava **7** Vizcaya **9** Guipúzcoa

bass 3 low **4** deep **6** singer **8** cabrilla ***famous:* 5** Hines (Jerome), Pinza (Ezio), Ramey (Samuel), Siepi (Cesare), Tozzi (Giorgio) **6** Hotter (Hans), London (George), Morris (James) **7** Plishka (Paul), Robeson (Paul), Talvela (Martti) **8** Flagello (Ezio), Ghiaurov (Nicolai), Raimondi (Ruggero) **9** Chaliapin (Fyodor), Christoff (Boris)

Bassanio's beloved 6 Portia

bassinet 6 cradle, basket

bastard 5 cross **6** by-blow, hybrid **7** mongrel **9** love child **12** natural child ***combining form:* 4** noth **5** notho

bastardize 4 warp **5** taint **6** debase, defile **7** corrupt, debauch, degrade, deprave, pervert, pollute, vitiate **9** brutalize **10** adulterate, bestialize, demoralize, depreciate **11** contaminate

baste 3 sew **4** beat, drub, lash, mill, pelt, rail, tack, whip **5** paste, scold **6** batter, berate, larrup, pummel, revile, stitch, thrash, wallop **7** bawl out, belabor, chew out, clobber, moisten, tell off, trounce, upbraid **8** bless out, chastise **9** dress down **10** tongue-lash

bastille 4 jail **6** prison **9** bridewell

bastinado 3 bat, rod **4** bash, beat, blow, cane, club **5** birch, crack, pound, smack, smash, stick, whack **6** cudgel, paddle, strike, switch, thwack, wallop **8** bludgeon **9** truncheon

bastion 5 tower **7** bulwark, citadel, parapet, rampart, redoubt **8** fastness, fortress **10** breastwork, stronghold **13** fortification

bat 3 bag, bop, hag **4** belt, biff, blow, bust, club, slam, sock, swat, whop, wink **5** biddy, blink, crone, smack **6** cudgel, thwack **7** meander **8** bludgeon **9** flying fox, truncheon **10** knobkerrie, shillelagh **11** pipistrelle

batch 3 lot, set **5** array, bunch, clump, crowd, group **6** bundle, clutch, parcel **7** cluster **8** quantity, shipment **10** assemblage, assortment, collection **11** aggregation **12** accumulation

bate 3 bar **4** omit **5** check **6** deduct, except, reduce **7** cut back, exclude, suspend **8** diminish, moderate, restrain, subtract

bateau 4 boat, dory **5** craft, skiff **6** dinghy, launch **7** shallop

bath 3 spa, tub **4** soak, wash **5** hydro, wells **6** shower **7** springs **8** ablution **13** watering place

bathe 3 dip, lap, lip, sop, tub, wet **4** bask, lave, soak, soap, swim, wash **5** clean, douse, flood, rinse, flush, souse, steep **6** shower **7** cleanse, immerse, pervade, suffuse **8** irrigate

bathetic 5 mushy, soppy, stale, tired, trite **6** drippy **7** clichéd, cloying, gushing, maudlin, mawkish **9** emotional, hackneyed, schmaltzy **10** lachrymose **11** commonplace, sentimental, stereotyped, tear-jerking **13** anticlimactic, overemotional, stereotypical

bathhouse 5 sauna **6** cabana

bathing suit 6 bikini, trunks **7** bandeau, maillot

bathos 7 letdown **8** banality, comedown **9** triteness **10** anticlimax

bathroom 3 lav, loo **4** john **5** privy **6** toilet **8** lavatory, outhouse

Bathsheba *father:* 5 Eliam ***husband:* 5** David, Uriah ***son:* 7** Solomon

bathtub gin 5 hooch **6** rotgut **7** bootleg **8** homebrew **9** moonshine **11** mountain dew

Batman ***alias:*** **13** Matches Malone ***bat-signal:*** **11** searchlight ***butler:*** **6** Alfred ***creator:*** **4** Kane (Bob) ***film director:*** **5** Nolan (Christopher) **6** Burton (Tim) ***film star:*** **4** Bale (Christian), West (Adam) **6** Carrey (Jim), DeVito (Danny), Keaton (Michael), Kilmer (Val) **7** Clooney (George), Thurman (Uma) **8** Meredith (Burgess), Pfeiffer (Michelle) **9** Nicholson (Jack) ***secret identity:*** **10** Bruce Wayne ***setting:*** **6** Gotham ***sidekick:*** **5** Robin ***TV star:*** **4** Ward (Burt), West (Adam) **8** McDowall (Roddy) ***villain:*** **5** Chill (Joe), Joker **7** Penguin, Riddler, Two-Face **8** Catwoman, Clayface, Deadshot, Mr. Freeze **9** Mad Hatter, Poison Ivy, Scarecrow

baton **3** rod **4** club, mace, wand **5** billy, staff, stick **6** cudgel **7** war club **8** bludgeon **9** billy club, truncheon **10** nightstick

____ Bator **4** Ulan

batrachian **4** frog, toad **9** amphibian

battalion **4** army, host, unit **5** force, horde **6** legion, throng, troops **8** squadron **10** contingent, detachment

batter **4** bash, beat, drub, hurt, maul, mush **5** baste, break, dough, paste, pound, wreck **6** bruise, buffet, bung up, hitter, mangle, pommel, pummel, thrash, wallop **7** assault, belabor, bombard, clobber, coating, contuse, cripple, lambast **8** demolish, lambaste

battery **3** lot, set **4** body, guns **5** abuse, array, batch, bunch, clump, group, suite **6** bundle, cannon, series **7** assault, beating, cluster **8** thumping **9** artillery, onslaught **10** energy cell **11** gunnery unit ***terminal:*** **5** anode **7** cathode

battle **4** fray **5** brush, clash, fight **6** action, assail, attack, combat, sortie **7** assault, contend, contest **8** conflict, skirmish, struggle **9** encounter, onslaught, scrimmage **10** engagement **11** hostilities

battle-ax **5** harpy, scold, shrew **6** virago **8** harridan **9** termagant, Xanthippe

Battle Born State **6** Nevada

battle cry **6** banzai

battlement **4** wall **7** barrier, bastion, bulwark, parapet, rampart **10** protection

battling **5** at war

batty **3** mad **4** daft, nuts, zany **5** barmy, crazy, kooky, loony, nutty, potty, wacky **6** crazed, cuckoo, insane, maniac, screwy, whacko **7** bananas, bonkers, cracked, idiotic, lunatic **8** deranged **9** bedlamite

bauble **3** toy **5** curio **6** gewgaw, trifle **7** bibelot, novelty, trinket, whatnot **8** gimcrack, ornament **9** objet d'art, plaything **10** knickknack

Baucis's husband **8** Philemon

Bavaria **6** Bayern ***capital:*** **6** Munich ***city:*** **8** Augsburg, Bayreuth, Würzburg **9** Nuremberg ***king:*** **6** Ludwig ***patron saint:*** **6** Rupert

bawd **4** drab, moll, tart **5** madam, tramp, whore **6** floozy, harlot, hooker **7** trollop **8** strumpet **10** prostitute **11** nightwalker **12** streetwalker

bawdy **4** blue, lewd **5** crude, dirty **6** coarse, erotic, ribald, risqué, smutty, vulgar **7** obscene **8** indecent, prurient **9** lecherous, offensive, salacious **10** lascivious, libidinous, licentious, suggestive

bawdy house **4** crib, stew **6** bagnio **7** brothel, lupanar **8** bordello

bawl **3** cry, sob **4** howl, roar, rout, wail, weep, yell, yowl **5** shout **6** bellow, berate, boohoo, clamor, holler, outcry, scream, shriek, squall **7** blubber, bluster

bawl out **3** wig **4** lash **5** baste, scold **6** berate, rebuke **7** censure, chew out, condemn, tell off, upbraid **8** bless out, denounce, tear into **9** castigate, dress down, reprimand **10** tongue-lash

bay **3** arm **4** cove, gulf, howl, loch, nook, wail **5** award, bight, crown, firth, honor, inlet, niche **6** harbor, laurel, recess **7** garland, laurels **8** accolade **10** decoration ***Aegean Sea:*** **5** Anzac ***Africa:*** **6** Walvis ***Alaska:*** **7** Glacier ***Antarctica:*** **3** Ice **8** Amundsen ***Argentina:*** **6** Blanca ***Atlantic Ocean:*** **6** Baffin ***Australia:*** **5** Anson, Shark **6** Botany, Sharks **7** Repulse **9** Discovery ***Baltic:*** **4** Hano, Kiel **6** Danzig, Kieler **9** Pomerania **10** Pomeranian, Pommersche ***Beaufort Sea:*** **7** Prudhoe **9** Mackenzie ***Brazil:*** **9** Guanabara ***Bristol Channel:*** **10** Carmarthen ***California:*** **5** Morro **8** Monterey, San Diego ***Canada:*** **5** Fundy **6** Hudson **7** Repulse ***Capetown:*** **5** Table ***Caribbean Sea:*** **5** Limón **8** Chetumal ***Central America:*** **7** Fonseca ***Cuba:*** **10** Guantánamo ***East River:*** **8** Flushing ***Egypt:*** **6** Abu Qir ***Eire:*** **4** Clew **7** Brandon ***English Channel:*** **3** Tor **4** Lyme ***Europe:*** **6** Biscay ***Florida:*** **8** Biscayne ***Greenland:*** **6** Baffin **8** Melville ***Gulf of Alaska:*** **12** Resurrection ***Gulf of California:*** **5** Adair ***Gulf of Guinea:*** **5** Benin **6** Biafra ***Gulf of Mexico:*** **5** Tampa **6** Mobile **7** Aransas **8** Campeche, Sarasota **9** Matagorda, Pensacola **10** San Antonio, Terrebonne **11** Atchafalaya, Ponce de Leon **12** Apalachicola **13** Corpus Christi ***Gulf of St. Lawrence:*** **5** Bonne, Gaspé ***Hawaii:*** **5** Koloa, Lawai ***Hong Kong:*** **4** Deep ***Honshu:*** **3** Ise **5** Mutsu, Osaka, Owari, Tokyo **6** Atsuta, Sagami ***Indian Ocean:*** **6** Bengal ***Indonesia:*** **8** Humboldt ***Irish Sea:*** **4** Luce **7** Dundalk ***Jamaica:*** **4** Long ***Japan:*** **4** Tosa

Java Sea: **7** Batavia **8** Djakarta ***Lake Erie:*** **8** Sandusky ***Lake Huron:*** **7** Saginaw, Thunder ***Lake Michigan:*** **5** Green **13** Grand Traverse ***Lake Ontario:*** **11** Irondequoit ***Lake Superior:*** **5** Huron **8** Keweenaw **9** Whitefish ***Long Island Sound:*** **6** Oyster ***Maine:*** **5** Casco **7** Machias **9** Penobscot ***Maryland-Virginia:*** **10** Chesapeake **12** Chincoteague ***Massachusetts:*** **6** Boston **7** Cape Cod **8** Buzzards, Plymouth ***New Brunswick:*** **13** Passamaquoddy ***Newfoundland:*** **4** Hare **5** White **7** Fortune ***New Jersey:*** **5** Great **6** Newark **7** Raritan **8** Barnegat ***New York:*** **7** Jamaica ***North Carolina:*** **6** Onslow ***Northwest Territories:*** **5** Wager **7** Repulse **8** Franklin **9** Frobisher ***Oregon:*** **4** Coos ***Puerto Rico:*** **5** Sucia ***Quebec:*** **6** Ungava ***Rhode Island:*** **12** Narragansett ***Sea of Japan:*** **13** Peter the Great ***South Carolina:*** **4** Bull, Long ***South China Sea:*** **5** Subic, Subig **7** Camranh ***Spain:*** **5** Cadiz ***Strait of Gibraltar:*** **7** Tangier ***Sydney:*** **6** Botany ***Tasmania:*** **5** Storm ***Texas:*** **7** Trinity ***Tyrrhenian Sea:*** **6** Naples **7** Paestum ***Wales:*** **10** Caernarfon, Caernarvon ***Washington:*** **5** Dabob **6** Skagit ***West Indies:*** **5** Coral

bayou 5 creek, marsh **6** slough **9** everglade, tributary ***Louisiana:*** **5** Macon **9** Barataria, Lafourche **10** Terrebonne ***Mississippi:*** **9** Chickasaw

Bay State 13 Massachusetts

bay window 3 gut, pot **5** oriel, tummy **6** paunch **8** potbelly **9** beer belly, spare tire **11** corporation, breadbasket

bazaar 4 fair, mall, mart, souk **6** market **7** benefit **8** emporium, exchange **11** marketplace

bazooka's target 4 tank

be 4 live **5** exist

beach 4 bank **5** Cocoa, coast, Omaha, shore **6** Malibu, Pebble, strand, Venice **7** seaside, shingle, Waikiki **8** cast away, lakeside, littoral, seashore **9** lakeshore **10** Clearwater, Copacabana, oceanfront, run aground ***resort:*** **4** lido

____ **Beach 3** Amy **4** Long, Palm, Vero **5** Dover, Miami, Omaha **6** Delray, Myrtle, Ormond **7** Daytona, Riviera, Waikiki **8** Imperial, Virginia

beached 6 ashore **7** aground **8** grounded, marooned, stranded **9** abandoned

beachhead 8 foothold

beachwear see **bathing suit**

beacon 4 buoy, sign **5** flare, guide **6** pharos, signal **7** bonfire, lantern **8** balefire **9** watchfire **10** lighthouse, signal fire **11** inspiration, transmitter **12** guiding light

bead 3 dab, dot, pea **4** blob, drop **6** bubble **7** driblet, globule **8** spherule

beak 3 neb, nib **4** bill, nose **5** snoot, snout, spout **6** pecker, schnoz **7** schnozz **8** mandible **9** proboscis, schnozzle

beaker 3 cup **6** carafe, goblet, vessel **8** decanter

beaklike part 7 rostrum

be-all and end-all 3 sum **4** pith, root, soul **5** total, whole **6** bottom **7** essence **8** entirety, sum total, totality **9** aggregate, substance **10** prime cause **12** quintessence

beam 3 bar, ray **4** balk, boom, burn, glow, grin, I-bar, spar **5** flare, flash, gleam, joist, plank, shaft, shine, shoot, smile, strut **6** girder, lintel, rafter, signal, streak, stream, timber **7** radiate **8** transmit **9** broadcast

beaming 6 bright, joyful, lucent **7** fulgent, lambent, radiant **8** animated, cheerful, luminous **9** brilliant, effulgent, refulgent **12** incandescent

bean 3 soy, wax **4** bush, conk, dome, fava, head, lima, mung, navy, pate, pole, poll, snap, soya **5** baked, brain, broad, horse, jelly, pinto **6** belfry, coffee, frijol, kidney, legume, noddle, noggin, noodle, string **7** jumping **9** headpiece **10** stringless ***curd:*** **4** tofu ***of India:*** **3** urd

beanery 4 café **5** diner, grill **9** hash house **10** coffee shop, restaurant **11** greasy spoon **12** luncheonette

beano 5 bingo

Bean Town 6 Boston

bear 3 lug **4** tote **5** abide, allow, beget, bring, brook, bruin, carry, stand, touch **6** accept, behave, convey, deport, endure, permit, suffer **7** comport, condone, conduct, deliver, stomach, support, sustain, swallow, undergo **8** engender, generate, shoulder, tolerate **9** procreate, propagate, reproduce, transport **10** bring forth **11** countenance ***Alaskan:*** **5** polar **6** Kodiak ***Australian:*** **5** koala ***constellation:*** **4** Ursa **9** Ursa Major, Ursa Minor ***genus:*** **5** Ursus ***kind:*** **3** sun **5** black, brown, honey, koala, polar, sloth **6** Kodiak **7** grizzly **10** spectacled ***Kipling:*** **5** Baloo **7** Adam-zad ***relating to:*** **6** ursine ***young:*** **3** cub

bearable 7 livable, tenable **8** adequate, passable **9** allowable, endurable, tolerable **10** acceptable, admissible, good enough, manageable, sufferable **11** supportable, sustainable

bearcat 5 panda

beard 4 dare, defy, face, fuzz **5** brave, front **6** goatee **7** outface, stubble, Vandyke **8** confront, imperial, whiskers **9** challenge, soul patch ***on grain:*** **3** awn

bearded **5** bushy, fuzzy, hairy **6** shaggy, tufted **7** bristly, goateed, hirsute, stubbly **8** unshaven **9** whiskered **11** bewhiskered

bear down **4** rout **5** crush, quell **6** burden, defeat, reduce, subdue **7** conquer, overrun, trample **8** overcome, vanquish **9** emphasize, overpower, overwhelm, subjugate

bearer **4** mule **5** envoy **6** coolie, porter, runner **7** carrier, courier **8** conveyor, emissary **9** go-between, messenger **11** internuncio

bear hug **6** clinch

bearing **3** air, set **4** look, mien, pose **5** poise **6** aspect, manner, stance **7** address, conduct, display, posture **8** attitude, behavior, carriage, delivery, demeanor, presence, relation **9** demeanour, direction **10** connection, deportment **11** comportment

bearish **4** curt **5** gruff, rough, terse, surly **6** cranky, ornery **7** anxious, dubious, prickly, uncouth **8** cautious, vinegary **9** crotchety, irascible **10** ill-humored **11** pessimistic **12** cantankerous

bearlike **6** ursine

bear out **4** show **5** prove **6** attest, uphold, verify **7** certify, confirm, justify **8** validate, vouch for **9** vindicate **11** corroborate, demonstrate **12** authenticate, substantiate

bear up **4** cope, fare, prop **5** brace, get by **6** endure, uphold **7** bolster, support, sustain **8** buttress, get along, maintain, underpin

beast **5** brute **6** animal **7** critter, monster, varmint **8** behemoth, creature, gargoyle

beastly **4** foul, mean, vile **5** awful, brute, feral, nasty **6** animal, brutal, odious **7** bestial, brutish, inhuman, ogreish, swinish **8** horrible, terrible **9** barbarous, revolting **10** abominable, detestable

beat **3** box, get, gyp, hit, lam, rap, tan, top **4** balk, belt, best, cane, dash, drub, drum, dump, flap, flog, foil, lash, lick, maul, pelt, rout, ruin, stir, tick, trim, whip, whop **5** baste, cheat, cozen, excel, forge, lay on, meter, outdo, paste, pound, pulse, punch, rhyme, route, scoop, scour, smear, spent, stick, stump, swing, throb, tread, tromp, whack, whisk **6** baffle, batter, better, buffet, cudgel, defeat, diddle, exceed, forage, hammer, larrup, muss up, patrol, pummel, rhythm, rounds, strike, thrash, thresh, thwart, wallop **7** belabor, clobber, circuit, conquer, exhaust, fashion, fatigue, lambast, lay down, prevail, pulsate, ransack, rough up, shellac, surpass, swindle, triumph, trounce **8** bewilder, bludgeon, Bohemian, lambaste, outshine, outsmart, outstrip, overcome, precinct **9** exhausted, frustrate, palpitate, pulsation, shattered, transcend, vibration **10** circumvent, pistol-whip **11** oscillation

beating **4** rout **5** lumps **6** defeat, hiding, mayhem **7** assault, setback **9** hammering, pulsation, throbbing **11** palpitation, shellacking

beatitude **3** joy **5** bliss **7** delight, ecstasy, rapture **8** euphoria, gladness, rhapsody **9** happiness, transport **10** exaltation, joyfulness **11** blessedness **12** blissfulness

Beatles **4** John (Lennon), Paul (McCartney) **5** Ringo (Starr) **6** George (Harrison) **7** Fab Four ***album:*** **8** Revolver **9** Abbey Road, Sgt. Pepper **10** Rubber Soul ***early:*** **4** Best (Pete) **9** Quarrymen (The), Sutcliffe (Stuart) ***manager:*** **5** Klein (Allen) **7** Epstein (Brian) ***producer:*** **6** Martin (George) ***wife:*** **5** Linda **7** Yoko Ono

beatnik **5** rebel **6** hippie **7** radical **8** Bohemian **9** dissident **11** flower child **13** nonconformist

beat-up **6** shabby **7** rickety, worn-out **8** decrepit, tattered **9** crumbling **10** broken-down, ramshackle, tumble-down **11** dilapidated

beau **5** dandy, flame, lover, swain, wooer **6** steady, suitor **7** admirer, beloved **8** paramour, truelove, young man **9** boyfriend **10** sweetheart

Beau Brummell **3** fop **5** dandy, swell **7** coxcomb, gallant **8** macaroni **11** petit-maître **12** lounge lizard

beau ideal **5** guide, model **6** mirror **7** epitome, example, paragon, pattern **8** exemplar, paradigm, standard **9** archetype **12** quintessence

Beaumarchais hero **6** Figaro

beau monde **5** elite **6** gentry, jet set **7** society **8** smart set **10** glitterati, upper crust

beauteous see **beautiful**

beautiful **4** fair **5** bonny **6** comely, lovely, pretty **7** radiant **8** glorious, gorgeous, handsome, splendid, stunning **9** exquisite **10** attractive **11** good-looking, resplendent, well-favored

beautiful people **6** jet set **8** smart set **9** haut monde **10** glitterati **11** high society

beautify **4** deck, gild, trim **5** adorn, array, fix up, grace, prank, primp **6** bedeck, doll up **7** dress up, festoon, garland, garnish, gussy up, enhance, improve **8** decorate, ornament, prettify, spruce up **9** embellish, glamorize

beauty **5** asset, belle, dream, merit, peach **6** appeal, eyeful, looker, lovely **7** charmer, dazzler, stunner **8** knockout **9** eye-opener, good looks **10** good-looker, loveliness ***mark:*** **4** mole

beaver 6 castor, rodent ***home:*** **5** lodge ***project:*** **3** dam ***skin:*** **4** plew ***young:*** **3** kit, pup

Beaver State 6 Oregon

becalm 4 hush, lull, stop **5** allay, quiet, stall, still **6** arrest, pacify, sedate, settle, soothe, steady, subdue **7** assuage, compose, quieten **11** tranquilize

because 3 for, now **4** that **5** since **7** being as, whereas **8** being how, as long as, seeing as **10** inasmuch as

because of 4 over **5** due to **7** owing to, through **8** thanks to **10** by reason of **11** on account of

Beckett work 4 Not I, Play, Watt **6** Molloy, Murphy **7** Endgame **9** Happy Days, Unnamable (The) **10** Eleutheria, Malone Dies **14** Krapp's Last Tape **15** Waiting for Godot

beckon 3 bid, nod **4** lure, wave **6** allure, entice, invite, motion, signal, summon **7** attract

becloud 3 dim, fog **4** blur, hide, veil **5** addle, bedim, befog, cloak, muddy **6** impair, darken, muddle, puzzle, shroud **7** confuse, eclipse, obscure, perplex **8** befuddle **9** obfuscate **10** overshadow

become 3 fit, get, wax **4** grow, suit **5** befit **6** go with **7** enhance, flatter **8** turn into

becoming 3 apt **5** right **6** decent, proper, seemly **7** correct, fitting **8** decorous, suitable, tasteful **9** befitting **10** attractive, flattering, well-chosen **11** appropriate, comme il faut

bed 3 cot **4** base, bunk, crib, doss, sack, twin **5** basis, berth, layer **6** bottom, cradle, double, ground, Murphy, pallet **7** bedrock, stratum, trundle **8** rollaway **10** foundation, substratum ***of India:*** **7** charpoy

bedaub 4 coat **5** cover, smear **6** smudge **7** overlay, plaster

bedazzle 4 daze **5** blind

bedcover 5 duvet, quilt **6** afghan, spread **7** blanket **8** coverlet **9** comforter **11** counterpane

bedeck 4 trim **5** adorn, array, prank **6** attire, bedaub, jazz up **7** appoint, bedizen, dress up, festoon, furbish, garland, garnish, gussy up **8** accouter, accoutre, beautify, decorate, ornament, prettify **9** embellish

bedevil 5 annoy, harry, spoil, tease, worry **6** harass, needle, nettle, pester, plague **7** hagride, provoke, torment, trouble **8** bewilder **10** exasperate

bedevilment 6 bother **7** torment, trouble **8** disorder, vexation **9** annoyance, confusion **10** irritation **11** aggravation **12** bewilderment

bedfellow 4 ally **5** crony **7** comrade **9** associate, colleague **10** compatriot **11** confederate **12** collaborator

bedim 3 fog **4** blur, mask, veil **5** befog, blear, cloud, gloom, shade **6** darken, muddle, shadow, shroud **7** becloud, confuse, eclipse, obscure **9** obfuscate

bedizen 4 deck, garb, gild **5** adorn, array, endue **6** doll up, dude up, invest, outfit, rig out **7** costume, dandify, dress up, garnish, gussy up, turn out **8** beautify, ornament **9** caparison, embellish

bedlam 3 ado **5** chaos, furor **6** asylum, clamor, furore, hubbub, tumult, uproar, welter **7** turmoil **8** foofaraw, madhouse, upheaval **9** commotion, maelstrom **10** hurly-burly **11** pandemonium

bedlamite 3 mad, nut **4** loon, nuts **5** batty, crazy, loony **6** insane, madman, maniac **7** cracked, lunatic **8** demented, deranged

bedouin 4 Arab **5** nomad

bedraggled 5 faded, seedy **6** shabby, ragtag, untidy **7** muddied, rundown, unkempt **8** decrepit, dripping, slovenly, tattered **10** disheveled, disarrayed, disordered, down-at-heel, ramshackle, threadbare **11** dilapidated

bedridden 6 laid up, shut-in **8** confined **12** hospitalized

bedrock 4 base, core, foot, root **5** axiom, basic, basis, floor, nadir **6** bottom, depths, ground **7** footing, support **10** foundation, groundwork, substratum **11** fundamental **12** substructure, underpinning

bedroom 7 boudoir, chamber

bedspread 8 coverlet **11** counterpane

bed-wetting 8 enuresis

bee ***food:*** **6** nectar ***genus:*** **4** Apis ***glue:*** **8** propolis ***group:*** **5** swarm **6** colony ***house:*** **4** hive **6** apiary ***kind:*** **5** drone, mason, queen **6** mining, sewing, worker **8** quilting, spelling **9** carpenter ***nest:*** **4** hive, skep ***product:*** **3** wax **5** honey ***relating to:*** **8** apiarian ***wax cells:*** **9** honeycomb

beechnuts 4 mast

beef 4 crab, fuss, meat, veal **5** bitch, brawn, gripe **6** grouse, muscle **7** grumble **9** bellyache, complaint, grievance ***cut:*** **3** rib **4** loin, rump, side **5** chuck, flank, plate, round, shank **7** brisket, sirloin **10** tenderloin **11** porterhouse ***grade:*** **5** prime **6** choice **7** utility **8** standard **10** commercial ***order:*** **4** rare **6** medium **8** well-done

beefcake 4 hunk, stud **5** himbo

beefeater 5 guard **6** sentry, warder, yeoman

beefy 5 bulky, burly, hefty, husky, meaty **6** brawny, fleshy, robust, stocky, sturdy **7**

massive **8** muscular, thickset **9** strapping **11** substantial

Beehive State 4 Utah

beekeeper 8 apiarist **12** apiculturist

beekeeping 10 apiculture

beeline 3 fly, nip, zip **4** race, whiz **5** hurry, speed **6** bullet, hasten, hustle, rocket **7** hotfoot **8** expedite, highball **10** make tracks **12** shortest path

Beelzebub 5 devil, fiend, Satan **6** diablo **7** Evil One, Lucifer, Old Nick, serpent **8** Apollyon **9** adversary, archfiend

beer 3 ale, IPA **4** bock, brew, suds **5** draft, lager, stout, weiss **6** porter **7** brewski, cerveza, pilsner **8** pilsener ***vessel:* 3** mug **4** toby **5** stein **6** flagon, seidel **7** tankard **8** schooner **9** blackjack ***drinking place:* 3** bar, inn, pub **6** saloon, tavern **7** taproom **8** alehouse **11** public house, rathskeller ***ingredient:* 4** hops, malt **5** yeast **6** barley ***maker:* 6** brewer ***mythical inventor:* 9** Gambrinus ***plant:* 7** brewery ***Russian:* 5** kvass ***Scottish:* 10** barley-bree

Beeri *daughter:* 6 Judith ***son:* 5** Hosea

beet 5 chard **6** mangel, wurzel **10** Swiss chard ***family:* 9** goosefoot

Beethoven, Ludwig van *birthplace:* 4 Bonn ***opera:* 7** Fidelio ***overture:* 6** Egmont **7** Leonore **10** Coriolanus ***sonata:* 7** Tempest **8** Kreutzer **9** Moonlight, Waldstein **10** Pathétique **12** Appassionata ***symphony:* 6** Choral, Eroica **8** Pastoral

beetle 3 bug, jut **5** bulge **6** insect, scarab, scurry **7** project **8** overhang, protrude, stand out, stick out ***click:* 6** elater **7** firefly ***dung:* 6** scarab **9** tumblebug ***front wing:* 6** elytra (plural) **7** elytron ***fruit-eating:* 8** curculio ***insect-eating:* 7** ladybug **8** ladybird ***kind:* 4** bean, dung, fire, June, stag **5** click, flour, grain, tiger, water **6** carpet, chafer, ground, May bug, museum **7** blister, cadelle, carabid, firefly, goldbug, goliath, June bug, vedalia **8** ambrosia, Japanese **9** longicorn, potato bug **10** cockchafer, rhinoceros ***order:* 10** Coleoptera ***ornament:* 6** scarab ***snouted:* 6** weevil **7** billbug **8** curculio **9** wood borer ***young:* 4** grub **5** larva **6** larvae (plural) **8** wireworm

beet soup 6 borsch **7** borscht

befall 3 hap **5** ensue, occur **6** betide, chance, follow, happen **7** come off, develop, fall out **8** happen to **9** come about, eventuate, transpire

befit 4 meet, suit **6** become, go with **9** agree with, chime with **10** accord with, be right for **11** be proper for

befitting 3 apt **4** just, meet **5** happy, right **6** decent, proper, seemly **7** correct **8** becoming, decorous, suitable **10** conforming, felicitous **11** appropriate, comme il faut

befog 3 dim **4** blur, hide, veil **5** bedim, blear, cloak, cloud, muddy **6** darken, puzzle **7** becloud, confuse, eclipse, envelop, obscure, perplex **8** bewilder, confound **9** obfuscate, overcloud **10** overshadow

befool 4 dupe, gull, hoax, play **5** cozen, trick **6** delude **7** chicane, deceive, mislead **8** hoodwink **9** bamboozle, victimize **11** hornswoggle

before 3 ere **4** ante, once, till, up to **5** ahead, until **6** facing, sooner, up till **7** ahead of, already, earlier, prior to **8** formerly **9** in advance, in front of, preceding **10** previously **11** in advance of ***prefix:* 3** pre, pro **4** ante, fore

befoul 3 mar, tar **4** slur, soil **5** dirty, smear, spoil, sully, taint **6** defame, defile, malign, smudge **7** blacken, pollute, profane, spatter, tarnish, traduce **8** besmirch **9** bespatter, denigrate **10** adulterate **11** contaminate

befuddle 4 daze **5** addle, mix up **6** ball up, baffle, bemuse, muddle **7** confuse, fluster, perplex, stupefy **8** bewilder, confound, distract, throw off **9** disorient

befuddlement 3 fog **4** daze, haze, maze **5** mix-up **6** muddle, stupor **9** confusion **10** perplexity, puzzlement **11** distraction

beg 3 ask, bum, dun, nag, sue **4** pray, urge **5** apply, brace, cadge, crave, evade, hit on, mooch, plead, press, worry **6** adjure, appeal, call on, demand, invoke, pester **7** beseech, besiege, conjure, entreat, implore, request, solicit **8** petition, sidestep **9** importune, panhandle **10** supplicate

beget 4 bear, sire **5** breed, bring, cause, forge, hatch, spawn, yield **6** create, effect, father **7** produce **8** engender, generate, multiply, result in **9** procreate, propagate, reproduce **10** bring about

beggar 4 hobo, defy, ruin **5** tramp **6** bummer, cadger, fellow, pauper, prayer, sponge, suitor **7** moocher, sponger **8** bankrupt, deadbeat, vagabond **9** overwhelm, pauperize, schnorrer, suppliant **10** down-and-out, freeloader, impoverish, panhandler, petitioner, supplicant **11** bindle stiff, supplicator **12** street person

beggared 4 flat, poor **5** broke, needy **6** ruined **7** drained **8** bankrupt, dirt poor, indigent, strapped, wiped out **9** destitute, insolvent, penniless, penurious, tapped out **10** pauperized **11** impecunious, overwhelmed **12** dispossessed, impoverished

beggarly 3 low **4** base, mean, poor **5** cheap,

lowly, nasty, petty, sorry **6** cheesy, meager, measly, paltry, scanty, scurvy, shabby, shoddy, trashy **7** ignoble, miserly, pitiful, squalid **8** pitiable, inferior, wretched **9** miserable, niggardly **10** despicable, despisable **11** ignominious **12** contemptible, parsimonious

Beggar's Opera ***music:*** **7** Pepusch (John) ***painting:*** **7** Hogarth (William) ***text:*** **3** Gay (John)

beggarweed 6 dodder **9** knotgrass **11** tick trefoil

beggary 4 need, want **6** penury **7** bumming, cadging, poverty **8** mooching, pleading **9** indigence, neediness, pauperism, privation **10** meagerness, mendicancy **11** destitution, panhandling

begin 4 dawn, open, rise **5** arise, cause, dig in, enter, found, mount, set to, start **6** appear, attack, be born, broach, create, effect, emerge, get off, induce, invent, launch, spring, sprout, tackle, take up, tee off **7** break in, emanate, jump off, kick off, lead off, prepare, usher in **8** activate, commence, embark on, engender, initiate **9** establish, instigate, institute, introduce, originate **10** embark upon, inaugurate, issue forth **11** break ground

beginner 4 colt, tiro, tyro **6** newbie, new kid, novice, rookie **7** recruit, starter, student, trainee **8** freshman, neophyte, newcomer **9** fledgling, greenhorn, novitiate **10** apprentice, catechumen, tenderfoot **11** abecedarian

beginning 4 dawn, font, rise, root **5** alpha, basal, birth, fount, get-go, onset, start **6** day one, origin, outset, primal, source, spring **7** dawning, genesis, infancy, initial, kickoff, nascent, opening **8** creation, exordium, outstart, prologue, rudiment, simplest **9** elemental, emergence, inception, incipient **10** appearance, elementary, incipiency, initiative, initiatory, opening gun, rudimental **11** origination, rudimentary **12** commencement, inauguration, introductory

begird 3 hem **4** belt, bind, ring **5** beset, fence, hem in, round **6** circle, corral, girdle, immure **7** confine, enclose, wreathe **8** encircle, engirdle, surround **9** encompass **12** circumscribe

beg off 5 demur, welsh **6** bow out, cop out, opt out, pass up, refuse, renege **7** back out, bail out, decline, drop out, pull out **8** back down, withdraw

begone 5 leave, scram, split **6** beat it, decamp, depart, get out **7** buzz off, get lost, skiddoo, take off, vamoose **8** clear out, hightail, shove off **9** skedaddle **10** make tracks

begrime 3 tar **4** foul, soil, spot **5** dirty, muddy, smear, spoil, sully, taint **6** defile, mess up, muck up, smirch, smooch, smudge, smutch **7** blacken, corrupt, pollute, tarnish **8** besmirch **11** contaminate

begrudge 4 envy **6** resent

beguile 3 con **4** draw, dupe, fool, hoax, lure, play, snow, wile **5** bluff, charm, fleet, trick **6** allure, beckon, betray, delude, divert, entice, humbug, lead on, seduce, take in **7** attract, bewitch, deceive, enchant, engross, exploit, finesse, mislead **8** distract, hoodwink, intrigue, maneuver **9** captivate, fascinate, while away **10** manipulate **11** double-cross

beguiling 4 wily **5** false **6** artful, subtle **8** alluring, deluding, delusive, delusory **9** deceitful, deceiving, deceptive, insidious, seductive **10** bewitching, chimerical, enchanting, fallacious, misleading **11** enthralling

Behan's autobiography 10 Borstal Boy

behave 3 act, run **5** carry, react **6** acquit, be good, deport, direct, manage **7** comport, conduct, disport, perform **8** function

behavior 3 act, air, way **4** mien, tone, ways **6** action, aspect, custom, habits, manner **7** bearing, conduct **8** demeanor, presence, response **10** deportment **11** comportment

behead 4 head, kill **7** execute **9** decollate **10** decapitate, guillotine

beheaded noblewoman 8 Jane Grey (Lady) **9** Catherine (Howard) **10** Anne Boleyn

behemoth 5 giant, jumbo, whale **7** goliath, mammoth, monster **8** colossus **9** leviathan **11** monstrosity

behemothic 4 huge **5** jumbo **7** mammoth, massive, titanic **8** colossal, gigantic, towering **9** Herculean, monstrous **10** gargantuan **11** elephantine

behest 3 say **4** will, wish, word, writ **5** edict, order **6** charge, demand, urging **7** bidding, command, dictate, mandate, precept, request **9** direction, enjoinder, ordinance, prescript, prompting **10** injunction **11** commandment, exhortation, instruction **12** solicitation

behind 3 can **4** late, next, rump **5** after, fanny **6** back of, bottom, heinie **7** backing **8** backside, buttocks, derriere, trailing **9** following, posterior **10** supporting **12** subsequent to ***prefix:*** **4** post **5** retro

behindhand 3 lax **4** late, slow **5** slack, tardy **6** in debt, remiss **7** belated, delayed, laggard, overdue **8** backward, careless, derelict **9** in arrears, negligent, unmindful **10** delinquent, neglectful, unpunctual **11** undeveloped

behold 3 see **4** espy, note, view **6** descry, notice **7** discern, observe, witness ***French:* 5** voilà ***Latin:* 4** ecce

beholden 5 bound **7** obliged **8** grateful, indebted **9** duty-bound, obligated

beholder 4 seer **6** gawker, viewer **7** watcher, witness **8** observer, onlooker, passerby **9** bystander, spectator **10** eyewitness **12** rubbernecker

beige 3 tan **4** buff, ecru **7** vanilla

being 3 ens, man **4** body, esse, life, self, soul **5** human, stuff, thing **6** entity, matter, mortal, nature, object, person, spirit **7** essence **8** creature, existent, material **9** actuality, character, existence, personage, something, substance **10** individual **11** personality **12** essentiality **13** individuality ***celestial:* 6** cherub, seraph

bejeweled 7 studded **8** sequined, spangled **9** encrusted **10** bespangled, gem-studded, ornamented

Bel *Sumerian counterpart:* 5 Enlil ***wife:* 5** Belit **6** Beltis

Bel ____ 3 Air **5** Paese

bel ____ 5 canto **6** esprit

Bela *father:* 4 Beor **8** Benjamin ***son:* 3** Ard

belabor 4 beat, drub, flog **5** baste, pound, scold **6** batter, berate, buffet, pummel, thrash, wallop **7** lambast, scourge, tell off, upbraid **8** chastise, lambaste, tear into **9** criticize, fulminate, overstate **10** flagellate **11** overexplain

Belarus *capital:* 5 Minsk ***city:* 6** Homyel **7** Vitebsk **8** Mahilyow **9** Vitsyebsk ***language:* 7** Russian **10** Belarusian **11** Belarussian ***monetary unit:* 5** rubel, ruble **7** kapeyka ***neighbor:* 6** Latvia, Poland, Russia **7** Ukraine **9** Lithuania ***river:* 3** Bug **5** Neman **7** Dnieper, Pripyat

belated 4 late, slow **5** tardy **6** remiss **7** delayed, laggard, overdue **10** behindhand, behind time, unpunctual

Belau see **Palau**

belch 4 burp, emit, gush, spew, vent, void **5** eject, eruct, erupt, expel, issue, spout, spurt, vomit **6** hiccup, irrupt **7** explode, extrude **8** disgorge **10** eructation **11** expectorate

beldam 3 hag **5** crone **8** old woman

beleaguer 3 bug, dog, hem, nag, vex **4** gnaw **5** annoy, beset, harry, hound, siege, storm, tease, worry **6** assail, attack, badger, bother, fall on, harass, invest, pester, plague **7** bedevil, besiege, hagride, put upon, set upon, trouble **8** blockade, fall upon

belfry 7 steeple **8** carillon **9** bell tower, campanile ***dweller:* 3** bat

Belgium *capital:* 8 Brussels ***city:* 4** Gent **5** Ghent, Liège **7** Antwerp **9** Charleroi ***ethnic group:* 7** Fleming, Flemish, Walloon ***language:* 5** Dutch **7** Flemish ***monetary unit:* 4** euro ***monetary unit, former:* 5** franc ***neighbor:* 6** France **7** Germany **10** Luxembourg **11** Netherlands ***plain:* 8** Flanders ***port:* 7** Antwerp **8** Oostende ***river:* 4** Yser **5** Meuse **7** Schlede ***sea:* 5** North ***sleuth:* 6** Poirot (Hercule), Suchet (David)

belie 4 deny, hide, warp **5** color, twist **6** expose, doctor, garble **7** conceal, confute, distort, falsify, gainsay, pervert, trump up **8** confront, denounce, disagree, disguise, disprove, miscolor, misstate, negative **9** disaffirm, gloss over, repudiate **10** contradict, contravene, controvert **11** dissimulate **12** misrepresent

belief 3 ism **4** idea, mind, view **5** axiom, credo, creed, dogma, faith, hunch, tenet, trust **6** assent, avowal, credit, surety, theory, thesis **7** concept, feeling, opinion, precept, surmise, theorem **8** credence, doctrine, firmness, religion, sureness **9** assurance, certainty, certitude, intuition, postulate, principle, sentiment **10** acceptance, assumption, confidence, contention, conviction, hypothesis, impression, persuasion **11** supposition

believable 5 solid, sound, valid **6** cogent, likely **7** logical, tenable **8** credible, possible, probable, reliable **9** authentic, colorable, plausible **10** convincing, creditable, persuasive, reasonable **11** conceivable, trustworthy

believe 3 buy **4** deem, hold, know **5** lap up, think, trust **6** accept, affirm, assume, credit, expect, reckon **7** fall for, imagine, profess, suppose, suspect, swallow **8** conceive, consider **10** conjecture, presuppose, understand

belittle 3 cut, pan **5** abuse, decry, knock, scorn **6** deride, insult, jeer at, revile **7** cut down, put down, run down, sneer at **8** badmouth, derogate, diminish, discount, minimize, write off **9** criticize, discredit, disparage, dispraise, downgrade, underrate **10** depreciate, undervalue **13** underestimate

belittlement 5 abuse, scorn **7** calumny, jeering, scandal, slander **8** derision, ridicule **9** aspersion **10** backbiting, defamation, detraction **11** denigration **12** backstabbing, depreciation

Belize *capital:* 8 Belmopan ***city:* 10** Belize City ***ethnic group:* 4** Maya **5** Mayan ***moun-***

tain: **8** Victoria ***neighbor:*** **6** Mexico **9** Guatemala ***river:*** **5** Hondo ***sea:*** **9** Caribbean

bell **4** peal **5** chime, knell **6** tocsin

belle **5** siren **6** beauty, eyeful **7** charmer **8** knockout, ornament **11** enchantress, femme fatale

Bellerophon ***father:*** **7** Glaucus **8** Poseidon ***grandfather:*** **8** Sisyphus ***horse:*** **7** Pegasus ***victim:*** **7** Chimera

belles lettres **10** literature

belletrist **8** novelist **4** poet **6** author, writer **9** dramatist **10** playwright

bellflower **9** campanula

____ belli **5** casus

bellicose **6** ornery **7** hawkish, hostile, martial, scrappy, warlike **8** factious, fighting, militant **9** assertive, combative, truculent **10** aggressive, pugnacious, rebellious **11** belligerent, contentious, hot-tempered, quarrelsome **12** disputatious, gladiatorial

belligerence **5** fight **6** attack, enmity, rancor, spleen **7** ill will **9** hostility, militancy, petulance, pugnacity **10** aggression, antagonism, truculence **11** bellicosity **12** churlishness **13** combativeness

belligerent **6** ardent, fierce **7** fighter, hostile, scrappy, soldier, warlike, warring, warrior **8** battling, churlish, fighting, invading, militant, opponent, petulant **9** aggressor, attacking, bellicose, combatant, combative, disputant, splenetic, truculent **10** aggressive, antagonist, pugnacious **11** contentious, hot-tempered, quarrelsome **12** antagonistic, disputatious

Bellini ***opera:*** **5** Norma **6** Pirata (Il) **8** Puritani (I) **10** Sonnambula (La) ***sleepwalker:*** **5** Amina

Bell Jar author **5** Plath (Sylvia)

bell metal **6** bronze

bellow **3** bay, cry, moo **4** bark, bawl, bray, howl, roar, rout, yowl **5** shout **6** clamor, holler **7** bluster

Bellow character **4** Rose (Billy) **5** Chick **6** Herzog (Moses E.) **7** Citrine (Charlie), Sammler (Arthur) **8** Humboldt, Fonstein (Harry) **9** Henderson **10** Ravelstein (Abe), Augie March

bell ringer **6** toller **9** Quasimodo **12** carillonneur **13** campanologist

bell ringing **11** campanology

bell-shaped **11** campanulate

bell sound **4** bong, boom, ding, dong, peal, ring, ting, toll **5** chime, clang, knell **6** tinkle

bell tower **6** belfry **7** clocher **8** carillon **9** campanile

____ bellum **4** ante, post

bellwether **4** dean, lead **5** doyen, guide, pilot **6** leader **7** pioneer **8** lodestar **9** harbinger **10** forerunner **11** trend setter

belly **3** gut, pot **5** tummy **6** paunch, venter **7** abdomen, midriff, stomach **9** bay window **10** front porch, midsection **11** breadbasket ***Scottish:*** **4** wame

bellyache **4** beef, carp, crab, fret, fuss, moan, yawp **5** bitch, bleat, colic, gripe, whine **6** grouse, snivel, squawk, yammer **7** grumble **8** complain **11** let off steam **12** collywobbles

bellyacher **4** crab **5** crank **6** griper, grouch, whiner **7** grouser **8** grumbler, sourpuss **10** complainer, crosspatch, malcontent **11** faultfinder

belly button **5** navel

belong **3** fit, set **4** suit, vest **5** agree, apply, befit, chime, fit in, match, tally **6** accord, attach, become, reside **7** pertain **9** correlate, harmonize **10** correspond

belongings **3** kit **4** gear **5** goods, stuff **6** assets, estate, legacy, things **7** baggage, effects **8** chattels, movables, property **9** patrimony **11** attachments, impedimenta, inheritance, possessions **13** appurtenances

beloved **3** gra, pet **4** baby, beau, dear, idol, love **5** flame, honey, lover, swain, sweet **6** adored, steady **7** darling, dearest, dear one, doted on, sweetie **8** favorite, idolized, ladylove, old flame, precious, truelove **9** boyfriend, cherished, inamorata, treasured **10** girlfriend, heartthrob, sweetheart, sweetie pie

below **5** infra, 'neath, under **7** beneath **10** underneath ***prefix:*** **3** sub **5** infra

belt **3** bat, bop **4** area, band, bash, biff, blow, gird, loop, ring, sash, slam, slug, sock, whap, whop, zone **5** smack, smash, strap, strip **6** begird, cestus, circle, engird, girdle, region, wallop **7** baldric, clobber, stretch **8** begirdle, ceinture, cincture, encircle, engirdle **9** bandoleer, bandolier, territory, waistband **10** cummerbund ***celestial:*** **6** zodiac

beltway **8** ring road

Belus ***brother:*** **6** Agenor ***daughter:*** **4** Dido ***father:*** **7** Neptune **8** Poseidon ***mother:*** **5** Libya ***son:*** **6** Danaus **7** Cepheus, Phineus **8** Aegyptus

belvedere **6** alcove, cupola, gazebo, pagoda **7** balcony, terrace **10** widow's walk **11** garden house, summerhouse, observatory

bemedaled **9** decorated **10** beribboned

bemired **4** miry, oozy **5** boggy, dirty, grimy, gummy, gunky, muddy, stuck **6** filthy, soiled, swampy **7** swamped

bemoan **3** rue **4** wail, weep **6** bewail, grieve, lament, oppose, regret **7** deplore **8** complain, object to **10** sorrow over **12** disapprove of

bemuse 4 daze **5** addle **6** absorb, muddle, puzzle **7** confuse, mystify, nonplus, perplex **8** bewilder, distract **10** disconcert

bemused 3 wry **4** lost **6** absent, remote **7** faraway **8** distrait **9** distraite **10** abstracted, distracted **11** preoccupied **12** absentminded **13** lost in thought

bench 5 court **6** settee, settle, thwart **7** counter **8** platform **9** worktable ***church:*** **3** pew ***outdoor:*** **6** exedra ***upholstered:*** **9** banquette

benchmark 4 norm **5** basis, gauge, guide, model, scale **7** measure **8** exemplar, paradigm, standard **9** criterion, guideline, milestone, yardstick **10** touchstone

benchwarmer 5 scrub

bend 3 arc, bow, sag **4** arch, bank, cave, curl, flex, hang, hook, lean, mold, sway, tend, tilt, turn, veer, warp **5** angle, crook, curve, round, shape, shift, stoop, twist, yield **6** compel, corner, buckle, direct, double, fasten, kowtow, subdue, submit, zigzag **7** deflect, dispose, distort, flexure, turning **8** lean over **9** curvature, deviation, genuflect **10** compromise, predispose

bendable 5 lithe **6** limber, pliant, supple **7** elastic, plastic, pliable **8** flexible, moldable **9** malleable, tractable **11** manipulable

bender see **binge**

____ **bene 4** nota

beneath 5 below, under ***prefix:*** **3** hyp, sub **4** hypo **5** infra

____ **Benedict 4** eggs

benediction 4 boon, okay **5** favor, grace **6** orison, thanks **7** benefit, benison, godsend **8** approval, blessing **9** advantage **11** approbation **12** consecration, thanksgiving

benefaction 4 alms, care, fund, gift, help **5** favor, grant **6** relief **7** charity, comfort, handout, largess, service, subsidy **8** donation, largesse, oblation, offering, windfall **9** endowment, patronage **10** assistance **12** contribution, ministration

benefactor 5 angel, donor **6** backer, patron **7** grantor, sponsor **9** supporter, sustainer **11** contributor, underwriter

beneficence see **benefaction**

beneficent 4 kind **6** benign, caring, giving **8** generous **10** altruistic, bighearted, charitable, ungrudging **11** kindhearted, magnanimous **13** compassionate, philanthropic

beneficial 4 good **5** brave, tonic **6** benign, toward, useful **7** helpful **8** favoring, salutary, valuable **9** favorable, healthful, nurturing, wholesome **10** profitable, propitious, salubrious **12** advantageous, constructive

beneficiary 4 heir **5** donee, payee **7** grantee, heiress, legatee **8** assignee **9** inheritor, recipient

beneficiate 5 treat **6** reduce **7** prepare, process

benefit 3 aid **4** boon, gain, good, help, perk, sake **5** avail, extra, favor, serve **6** assist, behalf, better, profit, relief, succor **7** account, advance, charity, further, godsend, improve, promote, relieve, welfare **8** blessing, interest **9** advantage, well-being **10** ameliorate, fund-raiser, prosperity **11** good fortune **12** contribute to

benevolence 4 boon, gift, help **5** amity, favor, grant **6** comity, relief **7** caritas, charity **8** altruism, clemency, goodness, goodwill, humanity, kindness **10** compassion, compliment, kindliness **11** magnanimity

benevolent 4 good, kind, warm **6** caring, do-good, humane, kindly **7** helpful, liberal **8** generous, tolerant **10** altruistic, beneficent, bighearted, charitable, openhanded **11** considerate, magnanimous, warmhearted **12** eleemosynary, humanitarian **13** compassionate, philanthropic, tenderhearted

Ben Hur author 7 Wallace (Lew)

benighted 6 obtuse, unread **8** backward, ignorant, untaught **9** untutored, unwitting **10** illiterate, uneducated, uninformed, unlettered, unschooled **11** know-nothing **12** un cultivated **13** unenlightened, unprogressive

benign 4 kind, mild **6** genial, gentle, humane, kindly, mellow **7** amiable, clement **8** gracious, harmless, merciful, pleasant **9** favorable, fortunate, healthful, temperate, wholesome **10** auspicious, benevolent, charitable, forbearing, propitious, remediable **11** good-hearted **12** noncancerous

Benin *capital:* **9** Porto-Novo ***city:*** **7** Cotonou ***coast:*** **5** Slave ***ethnic group:*** **3** Fon **6** Fulani, Yoruba ***former name:*** **7** Dahomey ***language:*** **3** Fon **6** French ***monetary unit:*** **5** franc ***neighbor:*** **4** Togo **5** Niger **7** Nigeria **11** Burkina Faso ***river:*** **5** Ouémé

benison 5 grace **8** blessing **11** benediction **12** consecration

Benjamin *brother:* **6** Joseph ***father:*** **5** Jacob ***mother:*** **6** Rachel

bent 3 set **4** bias, gift **5** arced, bowed, flair, knack **6** arched, curved, intent, talent **7** decided, faculty, leaning **8** aptitude, capacity, penchant, resolute, resolved, tendency **10** determined, proclivity, propensity **11** disposition, inclination **12** predilection

benumb 4 daze, dull, stun **5** blunt, chill **6**

deaden, freeze **7** petrify, stupefy **8** etherize, paralyze **10** immobilize **11** desensitize

benumbed **4** cold **6** frozen **9** unfeeling **10** insensible **11** insensitive **12** anesthetized

Beowulf ***drink:*** **4** mead ***monster:*** **7** Grendel

bequeath **4** gift, will **5** endow, grant, leave **6** bestow, commit, confer, devise, hand on, impart, legate, pass on **7** furnish, present **8** hand down, make over, transmit

bequest **3** lot **4** gift **5** share, trust **6** devise, estate, legacy **7** portion **8** heritage **10** settlement **11** inheritance

berate **3** jaw **4** rail, rate **5** chide, scold **6** rail at, rebuke, revile **7** bawl out, blister, chew out, condemn, reprove, tell off, upbraid **8** admonish, chastise, reproach **9** castigate, criticize, reprimand **10** tongue-lash, vituperate

berceuse **7** lullaby **10** cradlesong

bereave **3** rob **4** lose **5** seize, strip **6** divest, remove **7** deprive **8** take away **10** confiscate, disinherit, dispossess **11** appropriate, requisition

bereaved **8** mourning **9** sorrowful, sorrowing **10** distressed **11** heartbroken **13** grief-stricken

bereavement **3** rue, woe **4** loss **5** dolor, grief **6** misery, pining, regret, sorrow **7** anguish, despair, remorse, sadness **8** grieving, mourning **9** dejection, heartache **10** affliction, depression, desolation **11** deprivation, despondency, lamentation, tribulation

bereft **4** lorn **5** shorn **6** devoid, robbed **7** fleeced, forlorn, wanting **8** beggared, deprived, desolate, divested, stricken, stripped **9** destitute **10** despondent **12** disconsolate, dispossessed, impoverished

Bergen's dummy **7** Charlie (McCarthy) **8** Mortimer (Snerd)

Berger novel **12** Little Big Man

Bergman role **4** Ilsa

berkelium symbol **2** Bk

berm **4** path **5** ledge, mound, shelf **8** shoulder

Bermuda ***capital:*** **8** Hamilton ***territory of:*** **7** Britain

Bernice ***brother:*** **7** Agrippa ***father:*** **5** Herod ***husband:*** **6** Polemo ***lover:*** **5** Titus **9** Vespasian

berry **3** haw **5** cubeb, fruit, grape **7** currant, madrona, madrone **8** allspice **9** saskatoon

berserk **3** ape **4** amok **5** amuck, crazy **6** crazed, insane **7** bonkers, lunatic **8** demented, deranged, frenzied

berth **3** bed, cot **4** dock, moor, pier, port, post, quay, slip, spot **5** cabin, jetty, levee, place, wharf **6** billet, office **8** position **9** anchorage, situation **10** connection **11** appointment, compartment **13** accommodation

beryllium symbol **2** Be

beseech see **beg**

beset **3** dog, hem, try, vex **4** gird, ring **5** harry, hem in, storm, worry **6** assail, attack, badger, circle, fall on, harass, infest, pester, plague, strike **7** assault, besiege, overrun, trouble, torture **8** blockade, encircle, fall upon, surround **9** beleaguer, encompass, overswarm

besetment **3** nag **4** bane, pain, pest **5** curse, trial **6** blight, bother, gadfly, pester, plague **7** torment **8** irritant, nuisance, vexation **9** annoyance **10** affliction, botherment, holy terror **11** aggravation, botheration

besetting **6** urgent **7** driving **8** dominant **9** obsessive **10** compelling, persistent **11** omnipresent **12** overwhelming

beside **4** near, nigh **6** next to

besides **3** too **4** also, else, plus, save **5** added, extra **6** and all, as well, beyond, except, to boot **7** barring, farther, further, without **8** as well as, likewise, moreover, more than **9** aside from, along with, exceeding, excluding, other than, otherwise, outside of **10** in addition **11** exclusive of, furthermore, not counting **12** additionally, together with

besiege **3** nag **4** ring, trap **5** beset, hem in, hound **6** assail, attack, circle, girdle, harass, pester, plague **7** assault, confine, environ, trouble **8** blockade, encircle, surround **9** beleaguer, encompass

besmear see **smear**

besmirch **4** blot, foul, slur, soil **5** dirty, libel, stain, sully, taint **6** defile, damage, impugn, malign **7** asperse, slander, tarnish **8** disgrace, dishonor

besom **5** broom

besotted **5** dotty, drunk **7** charmed, muddled, smitten **8** enamored **9** enchanted **10** captivated, fascinated, infatuated, spellbound **11** intoxicated

bespatter see **spatter**

bespeak **3** ask **4** book, hire, show **5** imply **6** accost, attest, desire, evince, reveal **7** address, apply to, betoken, connote, lecture, portend, request, reserve, signify, solicit, suggest, testify, witness **8** announce, approach, foretell, indicate, intimate, petition **9** preengage **10** prearrange

bespoke **8** tailored **10** custom-made

best **3** gem, top **4** beat, pick, tops **5** cream, elite, excel, model, one-up, outdo, pride, prime, prize **6** choice, defeat, exceed, finest **7** conquer, leading, optimal, optimum, paragon, premium, supreme, surpass **8** exemplar, foremost, greatest, nonesuch, outshine, outstrip, overcome **9** matchless, nonpareil, number-one, paramount, transcend, unequaled **11** outstanding **12** incomparable ***combining form:*** **6** aristo

bestial **4** vile, wild **5** brute, cruel, feral **6** animal, brutal, carnal, fierce, malign, savage **7** beastly, brutish, inhuman, swinish, vicious **8** depraved, inhumane **9** ferocious **10** degenerate

bestialize **4** ruin, warp **5** abase **6** debase, defile **7** corrupt, debauch, degrade, deprave, pervert, pollute, subvert, vitiate, violate **9** brutalize **10** bastardize, demoralize

bestir **3** fly, rip **4** dash, flit, goad, race, rush, spur, stir, tear, urge, wake, whet **5** rally, rouse, scoot, waken, whirl **6** arouse, awaken, hasten, hustle, kindle **8** get going, scramble **9** challenge

bestow **4** give **5** apply, award, grant **6** confer, devote, donate, lavish **7** hand out, present **8** bequeath, give away ***Scottish:*** **7** propine

bestower **5** donor, giver **6** patron **7** donator **8** altruist **9** conferrer, patroness, presenter **10** benefactor **12** benefactress **13** good Samaritan

bestrew **3** dot, sow **6** pepper, shower **7** diffuse, disject, scatter, speckle, stipple **8** disperse, sprinkle **9** broadcast, interlard **10** distribute **11** disseminate

bestride **5** mount, tower **8** dominate, loom over, straddle **9** stand over

bet **3** pot **4** ante, game, play, risk, shot **5** put on, stake, wager **6** gamble, hazard, parlay, pledge **7** lay odds, venture ***racing:*** **6** exacta **8** perfecta, quinella, quiniela ***taker:*** **6** bookie

Betelgeuse **4** star ***constellation:*** **5** Orion

betel palm **5** areca

bête noire **4** bane, hate, ruin **5** trial **6** animus, horror **7** bugbear, nemesis, scourge, torment, undoing **8** anathema, aversion, downfall **9** ruination **10** black beast

bethink **4** cite, mind **6** call up, recall, remind, retain, review, revive **7** flash on **8** hark back, look back, remember, summon up **9** conjure up, recollect, reminisce **10** call to mind, retrospect

Bethuel ***daughter:*** **7** Rebekah ***father:*** **5** Nahor ***mother:*** **6** Milcah ***son:*** **5** Laban ***uncle:*** **7** Abraham

betide **4** fall **5** break, ensue, occur **6** befall, chance, happen **7** come off, develop, fall out **8** commence **9** come about, transpire

betimes **4** anon, soon **5** early **6** pronto, seldom, timely **7** too soon **8** directly, far ahead, fitfully, promptly **9** presently **10** before long, now and then, on occasion, seasonably **11** prematurely **12** occasionally, sporadically

betoken **4** bode, omen, show, warn **5** argue, augur **6** attest, denote, hint at **7** bespeak, point to, portend, presage, promise, signify, suggest, testify, witness **8** announce, forebode, evidence, foreshow, foretell, indicate, intimate, prophesy **9** prefigure **10** foreshadow **13** prognosticate

betray **4** dupe, jilt, trap **5** rat on, snare, spill, split **6** desert, entrap, evince, finger, inform, reveal, seduce, take in, tattle, tell on, turn in, unveil **7** abandon, beguile, deceive, divulge, forsake, let down, let slip, sell out, traduce **8** blurt out, denounce, disclose, discover, evidence, give away, manifest **10** apostatize, break faith **11** double-cross

betrayal **4** leak **7** perfidy, sellout, treason **8** exposure **9** duplicity, falseness, Judas kiss, treachery **10** disclosure, infidelity, revelation **13** faithlessness

betrayer **3** rat **4** fink, nark **5** Judas **6** snitch **7** stoolie, tattler, traitor **8** apostate, defector, informer, quisling, renegade, squealer, turncoat **10** talebearer, tattletale **11** backstabber, stool pigeon

betroth **3** wed **5** marry **6** pledge **7** espouse **8** affiance

betrothal **6** pledge **8** espousal **10** engagement

betrothed **6** fiancé **7** engaged, fiancée, pledged **8** intended, plighted, promised, wife-to-be **9** affianced, bride-to-be, spoken for **10** contracted **11** husband-to-be

better **3** fix, top, win **4** beat, help, mend, more, well **5** amend, cured, elder, excel, finer, outdo **6** exceed, fitter, repair **7** advance, correct, enhance, further, greater, improve, largest, mending, rectify, success, surpass, triumph, victory **8** greatest, improved, outshine, outstrip, stronger, superior, whip hand, worthier **9** advantage, desirable, excellent, healthier, improving, meliorate, preferred, transcend, upper hand **10** ameliorate, preferable, preferably, recovering, surpassing

bettor **7** gambler, wagerer

between **4** amid **5** among, twixt **6** within **7** betwixt ***prefix:*** **5** inter, intra

betweentimes **11** at intervals

bevel **4** bias, cant **5** angle, grade, slant, slope **7** chamfer, incline, oblique **8** diagonal

beverage **3** ade, nog, pop, tea **4** chai, cola, kava, maté, milk, soda **5** cider, cocoa, drink, juice, mocha, shake **6** coffee, eggnog, frappe, malted, nectar **7** potable, soda pop **8** lemonade, libation, potation **9** drinkable, milk shake ***alcoholic:*** **3** ale, gin, rum **4** beer, grog, mead, nipa, wine **5** cider, julep, negus, punch, stout, toddy, vodka **6** bishop, brandy, caudle, cooler, liquor, rickey, shandy, sherry, whisky **7** liqueur, martini, sangria, tequila, whiskey **8** cocktail, highball, sillabub, syllabub, vermouth ***Arab:*** **4** arak **6** arrack ***Australasian:*** **4** kava ***Balkan:*** **9** slivovitz ***British:*** **5** perry, stout **6** porter ***carbonated:*** **4** cola, soda **5** tonic **6** rickey **7** Perrier, seltzer, soda pop **8** club soda, root beer **9** ginger ale ***central Asian:*** **6** kumiss **7** koumiss ***Dutch:*** **7** schnaps **8** schnapps ***from milk:*** **5** kefir **6** kumiss **7** koumiss ***Greek:*** **4** ouzo **7** retsina ***Hawaiian:*** **3** ‘ava ***Irish:*** **6** poteen **10** usquebaugh ***Japanese:*** **4** sake ***medicinal:*** **6** elixir, tisane ***Mexican:*** **6** pulque **7** tequila ***of the gods:*** **6** nectar ***Oriental:*** **4** arak, sake, saki **6** arrack ***Russian:*** **5** kefir, kvass, vodka ***Scottish:*** **6** scotch ***South American:*** **4** maté **5** yerba **9** yerba maté ***Swedish:*** **5** glogg ***Turkish:*** **4** raki ***West Indies:*** **3** rum see also **cocktail**

bevy 3 mob **4** band, club, crew, gang, herd, knot, pack **5** bunch, covey, crowd, drove, flock, group, horde, party, swarm **6** clutch, gaggle, troupe **7** cluster, company, coterie **8** assembly **9** menagerie, multitude **10** assemblage, collection

bewail 3 rue **4** keen, moan, weep **5** mourn **6** bemoan, grieve, lament, regret **7** deplore

beware 4 heed, mark, mind, note, shun **5** avoid, watch **6** attend, notice **7** look out **8** take heed, watch out

bewhiskered 5 bushy **7** bearded, goateed, hirsute, stubbly **8** unshaven

bewilder 3 fog **4** daze, stun **5** addle, amaze, befog, mix up, stump **6** baffle, ball up, bemuse, fuddle, muddle, puzzle, rattle **7** confuse, fluster, mystify, nonplus, perplex, stumble **8** befuddle, confound, distract **9** disorient, dumbfound **10** disconcert

bewilderment 3 awe **4** daze **6** wonder **8** surprise **9** amazement, confusion **10** perplexity, puzzlement **11** distraction **12** astonishment, discomfiture, stupefaction **13** consternation

bewitch 3 hex **4** draw, pull, snow, take, wile **5** charm, spell, trick **6** allure, dazzle, seduce, voodoo **7** attract, bedevil, beguile, control, delight, enchant, possess **8** demonize, ensorcel, enthrall, entrance, intrigue, overlook **9** captivate, enrapture, ensorcell, fascinate, hypnotize, magnetize, mesmerize, spellbind

Bewitched *character:* 6 Darrin, Endora **7** Maurice, Tabitha **8** Samantha **9** Aunt Clara ***creator:*** **4** Saks (Sol) ***film director:*** **6** Ephron (Nora) ***film star:*** **5** Caine (Michael) **6** Kidman (Nicole) **7** Ferrell (Will) **8** MacLaine (Shirley) ***TV star:*** **4** York (Dick) **7** Sargent (Dick) **9** Moorehead (Agnes) **10** Montgomery (Elizabeth)

bewitching 4 foxy **5** siren **7** magical **8** alluring, charming, engaging, enticing, magnetic, mesmeric **9** seductive **10** attractive **12** irresistible

bewitchment 3 hex **4** jinx **5** charm, magic, spell **6** trance **7** evil eye, sorcery **8** black art, wizardry **9** conjuring **10** necromancy **11** conjuration, enchantment, incantation, thaumaturgy

beyond 4 over, past **5** above, after **6** across, beside, yonder **7** besides, further, outside **8** as well as **9** afterlife, hereafter, otherwise **10** afterworld **12** over and above ***prefix:*** **4** meta, over, para **5** extra, hyper, super, trans, ultra **6** preter

Bhutan *capital:* 7 Thimphu ***ethnic group:*** **6** Bhutia **8** Assamese, Nepalese **9** Mongolian, Sharcrops ***language:*** **8** Dzongkha ***monetary unit:*** **8** ngultrum ***mountain range:*** **8** Himalaya **13** Great Himalaya ***neighbor:*** **5** China, India, Tibet ***plain:*** **5** Duars

bias 4 bend, bent, skew, sway, tilt, turn **5** angle, bevel, slant **7** beveled, bigotry, dispose, distort, incline, leaning, oblique, slanted **8** diagonal, penchant, slanting, tendency **9** crosswise, inclining, influence, prejudice, proneness, viewpoint **10** diagonally, favoritism, partiality, propensity, predispose, prepossess, proclivity, standpoint, transverse **11** disposition, inclination **12** one-sidedness, predilection **13** preconception

biased 6 racist, swayed, unfair, warped **7** bigoted, colored, partial, slanted **8** disposed, inclined, one-sided, partisan, slanting **9** jaundiced, sectarian, unneutral **10** influenced, interested, prejudiced **11** opinionated, predisposed, tendentious

bibelot 5 curio **6** bauble, gewgaw, trifle **7** memento, novelty, trinket, whatnot **8** gimcrack, ornament **9** objet d'art **10** knickknack

Bible *abbreviation:* 3 Col, Cor, Dan, Eph, Gal, Gen, Hab, Heb, Hos, Jas, Jer, Jon, Lam, Lev, Mal, Mic, Neh, Num, Pet, Rev, Rom, Sam, Tim, Tit **4** Deut, Ezek, Josh, Judg, Obad, Phil, Prov, Zech, Zeph **5** Chron, Thess **6** Eccles, Philem ***Apocrypha book:*** **5** Tobit **6** Baruch, Esdras, Esther, Judith **7** Susanna **8** Manasseh, Manasses **9** Maccabees ***New Testament book:*** **4** Acts, John, Jude, Luke, Mark **5** James, Peter, Titus **6** Romans **7** Hebrews, Matthew, Timothy **8** Philemon **9** Ephesians, Galatians **10** Colossians, Revelation **11** Corinthians, Philippians **13** Thessalonians ***Old Testament book:*** **3** Job **4** Amos, Ezra, Joel, Ruth **5** Hosea, Jonah, Kings, Micah, Nahum **6** Daniel, Esther, Exodus, Haggai, Isaiah, Joshua, Judges, Psalms, Samuel **7** Ezekiel, Genesis, Malachi, Numbers, Obadiah **8** Habakkuk, Jeremiah, Nehemiah, Proverbs **9** Leviticus, Zechariah, Zephaniah **10** Chronicles **11** Deuteronomy **12** Ecclesiastes, Lamentations **13** Song of Solomon ***part:*** **4** book **5** verse **7** chapter **9** testament ***translator:*** **4** Knox (Ronald Arbuthnott) **5** Eliot (John) **6** Jerome, Luther (Martin) **7** Erasmus (Desiderius), Tyndale (William), Zwingli (Huldrych) **8** Andrewes (Lancelot), Wycliffe (John) **9** Coverdale (Miles) ***version:*** **5** Douay **6** Coptic, Gothic, Syriac **7** Vulgate **9** Jerusalem, King James, Masoretic **10** New English, Septuagint

Biblical ***animal:*** **8** behemoth ***ascetic order:*** **6** Essene ***battle:*** **7** Jericho ***battle site:*** **10** Armageddon ***charioteer:*** **4** Jehu ***city, town:*** **4** Cana, Gaza, Tyre, Zoar **5** Endor, Golan, Haifa, Joppa, Sidon, Sodom **6** Asshur, Bethel, Emmaus, Gilgal, Hebron, Mizpah, Shiloh, Smyrna, Tarsus **7** Antioch, Baalbec, Bethany, Corinth, Ephesus, Ephraim, Jericho, Magdala, Nineveh, Samaria **8** Caesarea, Damascus, Gomorrah, Nazareth, Philippi, Tiberias **9** Beersheba, Bethlehem, Capernaum, Jerusalem ***coin:*** (see at **Hebrew**) ***desert:*** **5** Sinai ***garden:*** **4** Eden **8** Paradise ***giant:*** **7** Goliath ***giant slayer:*** **5** David ***hill:*** **4** Zion **7** Calvary ***hunter:*** **6** Nimrod ***judge:*** **3** Eli **4** Ehud **6** Gideon, Samson, Samuel **7** Deborah, Jephtha **8** Jephthah ***king:*** **3** Asa **4** Ahab, Amon, Elah, Jehu, Saul **5** David, Herod, Hiram **6** Josiah **7** Azariah, Menahem, Solomon **8** Hezekiah, Jeroboam, Manasseh, Rehoboam, Zedekiah **9** Zechariah **11** Jehoshaphat ***land:*** **3** Nod **4** Aram, Elam, Moab, Seba **5** Judah, Judea, Magog **6** Canaan, Goshen, Israel, Judaea **7** Chaldea, Galilee, Samaria **9** Palestine ***land of plenty:*** **6** Goshen ***measure:*** (see at **Hebrew**) ***mountain:*** **4** Nebo **5** Horeb, Sinai, Tabor **6** Ararat, Carmel, Gilboa, Gilead, Hermon, Moriah, Olivet, Pisgah **7** Lebanon ***name:*** **3** Asa, Bel, Dan, Eli, Eve, Gad, Ham, Ira, Job, Lot, Uri **4** Abel, Adam, Ahab, Amon, Boaz, Cain, Elam, Enos, Esau, Jael, Jehu, Joel, John, Lael, Leah, Levi, Mark, Mary, Mica, Moab, Noah, Omar, Onan, Paul, Reba, Ruth, Sara, Saul, Seth, Shem **5** Aaron, Abner, Amram, Asher, Caleb, David, Dinah, Elias, Enoch, Ethan, Hagar, Heman, Herod, Hosea, Isaac, Jacob, James, Jared, Jesse, Jonah, Jubal, Judah, Judas, Laban, Micah, Moses, Naomi, Peter, Rufus, Sarah, Sheba, Simon, Tamar, Tubal, Uriah, Uriel, Zadok **6** Ashhur, Balaam, Baruch, Canaan, Daniel, Elijah, Elisha, Esther, Gideon, Gilead, Hannah, Hebron, Isaiah, Israel, Jeshua, Jethro, Joanna, Joseph, Joshua, Josiah, Judith, Martha, Miriam, Nathan, Nimrod, Pasach, Philip, Pilate, Rachel, Reuben, Salome, Samson, Samuel, Simeon, Thomas, Tobias ***patriarch:*** (see at **Hebrew**) ***people:*** **6** Kenite, Levite **7** Amorite, Edomite, Elamite, Moabite **9** Israelite ***plains:*** **6** Sharon **7** Jericho ***plotter:*** **5** Haman ***poem:*** **5** psalm ***pool:*** **8** Bethesda ***priest:*** **3** Eli **4** Levi **5** Aaron, Annas **8** Caiaphas ***Promised Land:*** **6** Canaan ***pronoun:*** **2** ye **3** thy **4** thee, thou **5** thine ***prophet:*** (see **prophet**) ***Psalmist:*** **5** David ***punishment:*** **7** stoning ***queen:*** **5** Sheba **6** Esther **7** Jezebel ***quotation:*** **4** text ***river:*** **4** Nile **6** Jordan ***sacred object:*** **4** urim **7** thummin ***scribe:*** **6** Baruch ***sea:*** **3** Red **4** Dead **7** Galilee ***sea monster:*** **9** Leviathan ***spice:*** **5** aloes, myrrh **6** cassia **7** calamus **8** cinnamon **12** frankincense ***spy:*** **5** Caleb ***strongman:*** **6** Samson ***temptress:*** **3** Eve **7** Delilah ***text set to music:*** **8** oratorio ***thief:*** **8** Barabbas ***tree:*** **5** cedar ***twin:*** **4** Esau **5** Jacob ***valley:*** **4** Baca, Elah **6** Hinnon, Kidron, Shaveh, Siddim ***weed:*** **4** tare ***witch's home:*** **5** Endor

bibliography **4** list **7** catalog, history **8** book list **13** reference list

bibliopole **7** bookman **10** book dealer, bookseller

bibulous **6** spongy **7** thirsty **8** drinking **9** absorbent **10** absorptive

bicker **3** row **4** spar, spat, tiff **5** argue, clack, fight, scrap **6** gurgle, hassle **7** brabble, clatter, contend, dispute, fall out, flicker, quarrel, quibble, wrangle **8** squabble

bickering **3** row **4** at it, spat **5** brawl, run-in **6** blowup, fracas, hassle, ruckus, rumpus, strife **7** discord, dispute, quarrel, rhubarb, wrangle **8** squabble **11** altercation, embroilment

bicycle **4** bike ***brake:*** **7** caliper, coaster ***for two:*** **6** tandem ***gear shift:*** **10** derailleur ***rider:*** **6** cycler **7** cyclist ***track:*** **9** velodrome

bid **3** ask, say, try **4** call, tell, warn, wish **5** essay, greet, offer, order **6** amount, charge, direct, effort, enjoin, invite, render, summon, tender **7** attempt, command, proffer, request, require, venture **8** endeavor, instruct, proposal **10** invitation, submission **11** proposition

biddable **4** mild **6** docile, pliant **7** amiable,

pliable, willing **8** amenable, obedient, obliging **9** malleable, tractable **10** governable, manageable **11** acquiescent, cooperative, good-natured **13** accommodating

bidding **4** call, word **5** offer, order **6** behest, charge, demand, notice, tender **7** auction, command, dictate, mandate, request, summons **9** ordinance, summoning **10** injunction, invitation **11** commandment, instruction **12** proclamation

biddy **3** bag, bat, hag, hen **4** drab, trot **5** crone, witch **6** beldam **7** chicken

bide **4** live, stay, wait **5** await, dwell, tarry **6** hang in, linger, remain, reside **7** hang out, sojourn **8** continue, sit tight, tolerate **10** hang around **11** stick around

bier **10** catafalque

biff **3** bop, box, hit, jab, zap **4** bash, belt, blow, clip, ding, nail, slam, slug, sock, swat, whop **5** blast, catch, clout, pound, slosh, smack, thump, whack **6** strike, thwack, wallop

bifurcate **3** cut **4** fork **5** halve, split **6** bisect, branch, cleave, divide **8** separate **9** branch out **11** dichotomize, dichotomous

bifurcation **4** fork **6** branch **8** division **9** dichotomy, partition, radiation **10** separation

big **3** fat **4** full, hard, huge, main, mega, tall, vast **5** adult, ample, chief, great, grown, heavy, hefty, husky, large, lofty, major, proud, roomy **6** bumper, hugely **7** capital, copious, crammed, crowded, eminent, grown-up, hulking, leading, liberal, mammoth, massive, monster, notable, popular, replete, sizable, stuffed, swollen, weighty **8** colossal, enormous, generous, gracious, imposing, inflated, material, oversize, princely, spacious, swelling **9** capacious, chock-full, distended, extensive, heavy duty, humongous, important, momentous, overblown, paramount, ponderous, principal, prominent, unselfish **10** commodious, large-scale, preeminent, prodigious, voluminous **11** heavyweight, magnanimous, major-league, overflowing, significant, substantial **12** considerable **13** comprehensive, consequential ***prefix:*** **4** mega

big bang theorist **5** Gamow (George)

Big Bertha **6** cannon **8** howitzer ***birthplace:*** **5** Essen ***manufacturer:*** **5** Krupp

Big ____, Cal. **3** Sur

Big Dipper ***constellation:*** **9** Ursa Major ***star:*** **5** Alcor, Dubhe, Merak, Mizar

bigfoot **9** Sasquatch

biggety **4** bold, vain, wise **5** fresh, nervy, sassy **6** cheeky, snippy, snooty, uppity **7** forward, stuck-up **8** impudent, insolent, puffed up, snobbish **9** conceited **11** smart-alecky **13** self-important

bighearted **6** giving **7** liberal **8** generous **9** forgiving **10** altruistic, benevolent, charitable, munificent, openhanded **11** magnanimous **13** compassionate

big house **3** can, jug, pen **4** coop, jail **5** clink, joint **6** cooler, lockup, prison **7** slammer **8** bastille, hoosegow, stockade **9** bridewell **11** reformatory **12** penitentiary

bight **3** arm, bay **4** cove, gulf **6** harbor

bigmouthed **4** loud, rude **8** boastful **10** boisterous

bigness **4** size **5** scale, scope **6** extent, volume **9** amplitude, immensity, magnitude **10** dimensions, importance

bigot **6** racist **8** jingoist **9** extremist, racialist **10** chauvinist **11** supremacist

bigoted **6** biased, narrow, unfair **9** hidebound, illiberal, sectarian **10** brassbound, intolerant, prejudiced **11** small-minded **12** narrow-minded

bigotry **4** bias **6** racism **9** apartheid, prejudice **10** xenophobia **11** intolerance

big shot **3** VIP **4** czar **5** celeb, mogul, nabob **6** fat cat, tycoon **7** kingpin, notable, pooh-bah **8** higher-up, luminary, top brass **9** celebrity, dignitary, personage **13** high-muck-a-muck

Big Ten team **4** Iowa (Hawkeyes) **6** Purdue (Boilermakers) **7** Indiana (Hoosiers) **8** Illinois (Fighting Illini), Michigan (Wolverines) **9** Minnesota (Golden Gophers), Ohio State (Buckeyes), Penn State (Nittany Lions), Wisconsin (Badgers) **12** Northwestern (Wildcats) **13** Michigan State (Spartans)

big-time **5** major **7** eminent, greatly, leading **8** renowned **9** high-level, important, paramount, prominent **10** large-scale **11** influential, major-league

big top **4** tent **6** circus

bigwig **3** VIP **5** heavy, mogul, nabob **6** honcho, kahuna **7** kingpin, magnate, notable **8** luminary, somebody **9** dignitary, personage **11** heavy hitter, muckety-muck **13** high-muck-a-muck

bijou **3** gem **5** jewel **8** gemstone

bijouterie **6** jewels **7** jewelry **8** trinkets **10** decoration

bike **5** cycle **7** scooter **10** motorcycle **12** motorscooter

bilge **3** rot **4** bull, bunk, guff **5** hooey, trash **6** bunkum **7** baloney, garbage, hogwash, malarky, rubbish, twaddle **8** claptrap, nonsense **9** poppycock, silliness **10** balderdash **11** foolishness

bilk **3** con, gyp **4** balk, beat, dash, duck, dupe,

foil, fool, hoax, hose, kite, milk, rook, ruin, scam, take **5** avoid, cheat, cozen, dodge, elude, evade, shake, shaft, skirt, stiff, trick **6** baffle, chisel, chouse, diddle, double, escape, eschew, fleece, rip off, sucker, thwart **7** deceive, defraud, prevent, swindle **8** flimflam, hoodwink, sidestep, stave off **9** frustrate **10** circumvent

bill 3 dun, fin, neb, nib, one, tab, ten **4** beak, bone, buck, chit, list, note, skin **5** check, fiver, score, visor **6** charge, damage, dollar, notice, poster, roster, tenner **7** account, charges, invoice, placard, program, sawbuck, smacker, ten-spot **8** Hamilton, mandible **9** greenback, reckoning, smackeroo, statement ***part:*** **4** cere

billet 3 bar, bed, gig, hut, job, rod **4** post, slab, spar, spot **5** berth, board, house, ingot, lodge, place, put up, stick, strip **6** bestow, canton, harbor, office **7** quarter **8** domicile, position, quarters, vocation **9** entertain, situation **10** assignment, connection, employment, encampment, livelihood, profession, occupation **11** appointment

billet-doux 8 mash note **10** love letter

billfold 6 wallet

billiards term 3 cue **4** foot, head, jaws, kiss, long, peas, pool, race, rack, spot **5** break, carom, chalk, count, masse **6** bridge, cannon, corner, crotch, inning, miscue, nurses, pocket, stance, string **7** bricole, cue ball, cushion, ferrule, kitchen, pyramid, scratch, shooter, snooker **8** apex ball, balkline, bank shot, cue stick, dead ball, jump shot, rotation, triangle **9** clean bank, eight ball **10** chuck nurse, head string, object ball **12** balance point

billingsgate 5 abuse **6** tirade **7** obloquy **9** contumely, invective **10** revilement, scurrility **12** vilification, vituperation

billion *British:* 8 milliard ***combining form:*** **4** giga

billionth *combining form:* **4** nano

bill of fare 4 menu **7** program **11** carte du jour

billow 4 mass, wave **5** bulge, cloud, surge, swell **6** puff up, roller **7** balloon, upsurge

Billy Budd *author:* **8** Melville (Herman) ***character:*** **4** Vere (Captain) **8** Claggert (John)

billy club 4 cane **5** baton **6** cudgel, paddle **8** bludgeon **9** bastinado, truncheon **10** knobkerrie, nightstick

bin 4 crib **5** frame, stall **6** bunker, hamper, trough **9** container **10** receptacle

binary 4 twin, dual **5** duple **6** double, duplex, paired **7** coupled, matched, twofold **9** dualistic

bind 3 tie **4** frap, gird, tape, wrap **5** chain, cinch, strap, tie up, truss **6** cement, commit, fasten, fetter, ligate, pinion **7** bandage, confine, enchain, shackle, trammel **8** enfetter, restrain **9** constrain, constrict, indenture

binder 4 file **5** cover **6** folder, jacket **7** wrapper **9** harvester

binding 8 required **9** mandatory, requisite **10** obligatory

bindlestiff 4 hobo

binge 3 jag **4** orgy, riot, soak, tear, time, toot **5** blast, booze, fling, party, revel, souse, spree, stint **6** bender **7** blowoff, blowout, carouse, debauch, rampage, revelry, shindig, splurge, surfeit, wassail **8** carousal, gluttony **9** bacchanal, brannigan **10** debauchery, indulgence **11** bacchanalia, celebration **12** intemperance

bingo 3 yes **5** beano **7** correct

biographer *American:* **5** Weems (Parson) **6** Parton (James) **7** Freeman (Douglas) **8** Bradford (Gamaliel), Sandburg (Carl) **10** McCullough (David) ***English:*** **6** Aubrey (John), Morley (John), Walton (Izaak) **8** Strachey (Lytton) ***French:*** **7** Maurois (André) ***German:*** **6** Ludwig (Emil) ***Greek:*** **8** Plutarch ***Italian:*** **6** Vasari (Giorgio) ***Roman:*** **9** Suetonius ***Scottish*** **7** Boswell (James)

biography 3 bio **4** life, obit, vita **5** diary, story **6** memoir **7** history, profile **8** obituary **11** confessions

biological category 5 class, genus, order **6** family, phylum **7** kingdom, species, variety **10** subspecies

bionomics 7 ecology

Bip's creator 7 Marceau (Marcel)

bird 2 io **3** ani, auk, daw, eme, emu, ern, iwa, jay, kea, mew, moa, owl, poe, tit, tui **4** Alca, Anas, chat, Chen, coot, crow, dove, duck, erne, guan, gull, hawk, ibis, iiwi, kite, kiwi, knot, koko, lark, loon, loro, lory, mina, moho, myna, Olor, Pavo, Pica, rail, rhea, rook, ruff, shag, skua, smew, sora, Sula, swan, teal, tern, Uria, wren, Xema **5** booby, brant, buteo, cahow, crake, crane, eagle, egret, finch, galah, goose, grebe, heron, junco, macaw, merle, murre, mynah, noddy, ousel, ouzel, owlet, pewee, pewit, pipit, quail, raven, robin, stilt, snipe, stork, swift, veery, vireo **6** avocet, barbet, bulbul, canary, chough, chukar, condor, corbie, cuckoo, curlew, drongo, dunlin, falcon, fulmar, gannet, godwit, grouse, hoopoe, jabiru, jacana, jaeger, kakapo, linnet, magpie, martin, merlin, mud hen, oriole, osprey, parrot, peahen, peewit, petrel, phoebe, plover, puffin, raptor, ratite, redleg, scoter, shrike, takahe, thrush, tomtit, toucan, towhee, trogon, turaco, turkey, verdin, wigeon, willet **7** anhinga, apteryx, bittern, blue jay, bunting, bustard, buzzard, catbird, chicken, courser, creeper, dovekie, flicker, goshawk, grackle, harrier, jacamar, jackdaw, kestrel, kinglet, lapwing, limpkin, mallard, marabou, moorhen, oilbird, ostrich, peacock, pelican, penguin, pintail, quetzal, redwing, sawbill, skimmer, skylark, sparrow, swallow, tanager, tattler, titlark, touraco, vulture, wagtail, warbler, waxbill, waxwing, widgeon **8** baldpate, bellbird, blackcap, bobolink, bobwhite, brantail, caracara, cardinal, cockatoo, curassow, dabchick, dotterel, flamingo, guacharo, hornbill, killdeer, lorikeet, lyrebird, marsh hen, moorfowl, murrelet, nightjar, nuthatch, oxpecker, parakeet, pheasant, Philomel, redshank, redstart, screamer, shoebill, shoveler, starling, thrasher, throstle, titmouse, tragopan, troupial, wheatear, whimbrel, wildfowl, woodcock, woodlark **9** accipiter, albatross, broadbill, cassowary, chaffinch, chickadee, cormorant, crossbill, francolin, gallinule, guillemot, gyrfalcon, kittiwake, merganser, nighthawk, owl parrot, partridge, phalarope, ptarmigan, razorbill, sandpiper, snakebird, spoonbill, stonechat, trumpeter, turnstone **10** bufflehead, chiffchaff, flycatcher, goatsucker, kingfisher, shearwater, sheathbill **11** lammergeier, nightingale **12** whippoorwill ***class:*** **4** Aves ***colony:*** **5** roost **7** rookery ***combining form:*** **5** ornis **6** ornith **7** ornitho **8** ornithes (plural) ***extinct:*** **3** moa **4** dodo **9** aepyornis, solitaire ***mythical:*** **3** roc **7** phoenix ***relating to:*** **5** avian **8** ornithic ***sound:*** **3** caw, coo **4** chip, crow, honk, hoot, peep **5** cheep, chirp, cluck, croak, quack, trill, tweet **6** squawk **7** screech, twitter ***unfledged:*** **4** eyas **5** chick **8** nestling

birdbrain 4 clod, dodo, dolt, goof, loon **5** dummy, dunce, idiot, moron, ninny **6** nitwit **7** airhead, dullard, halfwit **8** dumbbell, imbecile, meathead, numskull **9** dumb bunny, ignoramus, numbskull, simpleton **10** nincompoop **11** featherhead

birdcage 6 aviary

birdlife 8 avifauna

bird pepper 9 chiltepin

birds' eggs *study of:* 6 oology

birth 4 dawn, stem **5** arise, issue, onset, start **6** create, outset, spring **7** emanate, genesis, lineage, opening **8** delivery, generate, geniture, nascence, nascency, nativity, pedigree **9** beginning, originate **10** extraction **11** parturition **12** commencement

birth-control leader 6 Sanger (Margaret)

birth flower *April:* 5 daisy ***August:* 9** gladiolus ***December:* 10** poinsettia ***February:* 8** primrose ***January:* 9** carnation ***July:* 8** sweet pea ***June:* 4** rose ***March:* 6** violet ***May:* 15** lily of the valley ***November:* 13** chrysanthemum ***October:* 6** dahlia ***September:* 5** aster

birthmark 4 mole **5** nevus, point, trait **7** feature **13** discoloration

Birth of a Nation director 8 Griffith (D. W.)

birthright 3 due, lot **6** legacy **7** bequest, portion **8** appanage, heirloom, heritage **9** patrimony **11** entitlement, inheritance

birthroot 8 trillium

birthstone *April:* 7 diamond **8** sapphire ***August:* 7** peridot **8** sardonyx ***December:* 6** zircon **9** turquoise ***February:* 8** amethyst ***January:* 6** garnet ***July:* 4** ruby ***June:* 5** agate, pearl **11** alexandrite ***March:* 6** jasper **10** aquamarine, bloodstone ***May:* 7** emerald ***November:* 5** topaz ***October:* 4** opal **10** tourmaline ***September:* 8** sapphire **10** chrysolite

biscotti flavor 5 anise

biscuit 4 rusk, snap **6** cookie **7** cracker **8** cracknel, hardtack

bishop *district:* 7 diocese ***headdress:* 5** miter, mitre ***seat of office:* 3** see ***skullcap:* 9** zucchetto ***staff:* 7** crosier, crozier ***throne:* 8** cathedra

bishopric 3 see **7** diocese

bismuth symbol 2 Bi

bison *European:* 6 wisent **7** aurochs ***family:* 7** Bovidae ***North American:* 7** buffalo

bistered 4 dark **5** brown, dusky, swart, tawny **6** brunet, tanned **7** swarthy **8** brunette **11** dark-skinned

bistro 3 bar, pub **4** café **5** joint **6** nitery, tavern **7** barroom, cabaret, hot spot, niterie, taproom **8** snack bar **9** coffee bar, nightclub, night spot **10** coffee shop **11** rathskeller **13** watering place

bit 3 dab, dot, end, jot, tad **4** atom, dash, drop, iota, lump, mite, part, rein, tick, time, whet **5** borer, flake, grain, minim, pinch, scrap, shard, shred, slice, space, speck, spell, trace, while **6** minute, moment, morsel, rather, second **7** portion, segment, smidgen, stretch, trickle **8** fraction, fragment, molecule, mouthful, particle, somewhat

bit by bit 6 evenly **9** by degrees, gradually, piecemeal **12** continuously **13** slow and steady

bitch goddess 7 success

bite 3 cut, eat, lot, nip **4** chaw, chew, edge, etch, food, gnaw, kick, meal, nosh, pain, part, rust, snap, tang, tapa, zest **5** champ, chomp, erode, munch, piece, quota, share, slice, snack, stink, taste, tooth **6** crunch, morsel, nibble **7** corrode, eat away, eat into, engrave, portion **8** mouthful **9** masticate, occlusion

biting 3 raw **4** cold **5** bleak, crisp, harsh, nippy, sharp **6** bitter, severe **7** acerbic, caustic, cutting, mordant, satiric **8** freezing, incisive, piercing, scathing **9** sarcastic, trenchant **11** penetrating

bitter 4 acid, tart **5** acerb, acrid, harsh, sharp **6** severe **7** acerbic, caustic, galling, hostile, painful **8** grievous, virulent **9** rancorous, vitriolic **11** acrimonious

bitterness 4 gall **6** rancor **7** ill will **8** acridity, acrimony, asperity, coldness **9** animosity, antipathy **10** resentment

bittersweet 4 vine **8** poignant **10** nightshade

bitumen 3 tar **5** pitch **7** asphalt **8** blacktop

bivalve 4 clam, spat **6** cockle, mussel, oyster **7** geoduck, mollusc, mollusk, piddock, scallop **9** lampshell **10** brachiopod

bivouac 4 camp, tent **6** billet, encamp, laager, maroon **7** shelter, sojourn **10** encampment

bizarre 3 odd **5** antic, outré, queer, weird **7** curious, oddball, strange, uncanny, unusual **8** abnormal, atypical, freakish, peculiar, quixotic, singular **9** anomalous, eccentric, fantastic, grotesque, unearthly, unnatural **10** outlandish, outrageous **11** extravagant

bizarrerie 5 freak **6** oddity **7** anomaly, caprice, oddness **9** curiosity, weirdness **10** aberration

Bizet opera 6 Carmen

blab 3 gab, gas, jaw, yak **4** chat, leak, sing, talk, tell **5** run on, spill **6** babble, betray, burble, gabble, gossip, inform, jabber, reveal, snitch, squeal, tattle, tell on, yammer **7** blather, chatter, divulge, let slip, palaver, prattle **8** blurt out, disclose, give away, go public

blabber 3 gab, rat **4** chat, fink **5** clack, drool, prate **6** babble, canary, drivel, gabber, gabble, gossip, jabber, magpie, prater, ramble **7** blather, chatter, palaver, prattle, twaddle **8** idle talk, jabberer, prattler **9** chatterer **10** chatterbox, tattletale

blabbermouth 3 rat **4** fink **5** yenta **6** canary, gabber, gossip, magpie, prater, snitch **7** windbag **8** busybody, jabberer, prattler **10** chatterbox, talebearer, tattletale **11** stool pigeon

black 3 jet **4** ebon, inky, noir, onyx **5** ebony, raven, sable **6** pitchy **8** charcoal, funereal **9** pitch-dark ***combining form:*** **3** mel **4** atro, mela, melo **5** melam, melan **6** melano

blackball 3 bar **4** veto, shun, snub **5** block, spurn **6** ice out, refuse, reject, strike **7** boycott, exclude, keep out, rule out **9** interdict, ostracize **11** vote against

black bass 7 sunfish

black beast see **bête noire**

Black Beauty author 6 Sewell (Anna)

black cohosh 7 bugbane

black crappie 7 sunfish **10** calico bass

black death 6 plague **13** bubonic plague

black diamond 4 coal **8** hematite **9** carbonado

blacken 3 dim, fog, ink **4** blot, burn, char, sear, slur, soil, soot **5** cloud, libel, shade, singe, smear, sully, taint **6** bruise, darken, defame, defile, malign, scorch, vilify **7** asperse, cloud up, eclipse, slander, traduce **8** besmirch, dishonor **10** calumniate

black eye 4 blot, onus, slur **5** stain **6** bruise, defeat, shiner, stigma **7** setback

blackfish 5 whale **6** tautog **10** pilot whale

Black Forest 11 Schwarzwald ***city:*** **10** Baden-Baden ***peak:*** **8** Feldberg ***product:*** **11** cuckoo clock ***river:*** **5** Rhein, Rhine **6** Danube, Neckar

black gold 3 oil **9** petroleum

blackguard 4 heel, punk **5** abuse, cheat, knave, rogue **6** rascal **7** hoodlum, lowlife, ruffian, villain **8** hooligan, scalawag **9** charlatan, miscreant, reprobate, scoundrel **10** delinquent, mountebank **11** rapscallion

blackhead 3 zit **4** spot **5** sebum **6** pimple **10** larval clam

blackjack 3 oak, sap **4** bash, club, cosh **6** coerce **7** pontoon, tankard **8** bludgeon **9** twenty-one, vingt-et-un **10** sphalerite

black lead 8 graphite

black letter 6 Gothic **7** Fraktur **10** Old English

blacklist 3 bar **4** oust **5** expel, purge, smear **6** banish, impugn **7** boycott, condemn, exclude, shut out **8** denounce **9** ostracize, proscribe **10** stigmatize

blackmail 5 bleed **6** extort, payoff **7** milking, squeeze **8** chantage, coercion **9** extortion, hush money, shake down

Blackmore novel 10 Lorna Doone

black out 4 edit, wipe **5** annul, erase, faint, swoon **6** cancel, censor, cut off, darken, delete, efface, excise **7** conceal, eclipse, expunge **8** collapse, make dark, sanitize, suppress **9** eradicate, expurgate **10** blue-pencil, obliterate

blackpoll 7 warbler

Black Prince 6 Edward

Black Sea *arm:* 4 Azov ***city:*** **5** Yalta **6** Odessa **9** Constanta ***peninsula:*** **6** Crimea **7** Crimean

Blackshirt 7 fascist

blacksmith 6 forger **7** farrier, striker **10** horseshoer
blacktail 8 mule deer
blackthorn 4 plum, sloe
black widow 6 spider
bladder 3 sac **4** cyst **5** pouch **7** blister, vacuole **7** vesicle ***gall:*** **9** cholecyst
blade 4 beau, buck, dude, edge, leaf, shiv **5** knife, sword **6** runner **9** swordsman
blah 4 bosh, dull, flat, tame **5** ho-hum, hooey, tired, vapid **6** boring, bunkum, dreary, humbug, stodgy **7** humdrum **8** banausic, lifeless, mediocre, nonsense, plodding **10** balderdash, lackluster, monotonous, pedestrian **11** indifferent, uninspiring **13** uninteresting
Blake work 5 Tiger (The), Tyger (The) **10** Book of Thel (The) **16** Songs of Innocence **17** Songs of Experience
blamable see **blameworthy**
blame 3 rap **4** onus **5** fault, guilt, knock **6** accuse, charge, finger, indict **7** censure, condemn **8** denounce, reproach **9** criticize, liability, reprehend, reprobate **10** accusation, imputation **11** culpability **12** condemnation, denunciation, reprehension ***Scottish:*** **4** wite, wyte **6** dirdum
blameless 4 good, pure **5** clean, moral **7** perfect, upright **8** innocent, unguilty, virtuous **9** crimeless, exemplary, faultless, guiltless, honorable, lily-white, righteous, unsullied **10** immaculate, impeccable, inculpable **13** unimpeachable
blameworthy 3 lax **5** amiss **6** guilty, liable, sinful **7** at fault **8** criminal, culpable, derelict **9** negligent **10** answerable, censurable, delinquent, indictable, punishable **11** disgraceful, inexcusable, responsible **12** dishonorable **13** reprehensible, objectionable
blanch 4 fade, pale **5** quail, scald, start **6** bleach, shrink, whiten **7** decolor, lighten, parboil **8** etiolate
blanched 3 wan **4** ashy, pale **5** ashen, faded, livid, peaky, waxen, white **6** anemic, doughy, pallid, peaked **7** ghostly **9** bloodless, colorless, washed out **10** cadaverous
Blancheflor's beloved 6 Flores, Floris
bland 4 dull, flat, blah, mild, soft **5** balmy, banal, vapid **6** boring, gentle, pablum **7** insipid, restful, sapless **8** soothing **9** calmative **10** complacent, flavorless, monotonous, namby-pamby, wishy-washy **12** ingratiating **13** nonirritating
blandish 3 con, woo **4** coax, fawn, urge **5** cozen **6** cajole, stroke **7** blarney, flatter, wheedle **8** butter up, inveigle, soft-soap **9** importune, sweet-talk **10** curry favor
blandishment 3 oil **5** honey **7** blarney, eyewash, incense, promise **8** flattery, soft soap **9** adulation, seduction, sweet talk **10** allurement, compliment, inducement, sycophancy, temptation
blank 3 gap **4** bare, dull, seal, skip, void **5** chasm, dazed, empty, space **6** stupid, vacant, virgin **7** deadpan, obscure, vacuous **8** complete, omission, outright, spotless, unfilled **9** impassive **10** empty space, interstice, obliterate **11** featureless **12** inexpressive, unexpressive
blanket 4 bury, hide **5** cover, quilt, throw **6** afghan, stroud **7** overlay **8** coverlet, mackinaw, sweeping **9** comforter **10** overspread
blankness 6 vacuum **7** nullity, vacancy, vacuity **9** emptiness **10** desolation
blare 4 roar **5** blast, shout **6** clamor, jangle **7** trumpet
blaring 4 loud **5** sharp **6** brassy, shrill **7** clarion, jarring, roaring **8** blinding, piercing, strident **9** deafening, dissonant **10** stentorian **11** ear-piercing, penetrating, stentorious **12** earsplitting
blarney 3 con, oil **4** coax, bunk **5** charm, honey, hooey **6** bunkum, cajole, humbug **7** baloney, incense, wheedle **8** blandish, buncombe, cajolery, flattery, inveigle, nonsense, soft soap **9** adulation, sweet-talk **11** compliments **12** blandishment, inveiglement
blasé 4 cool **5** bored, jaded, sated **6** breezy **7** knowing, offhand, unmoved, worldly **9** apathetic, incurious, surfeited, unexcited **10** world-weary **11** indifferent, unconcerned, worldly-wise **12** disenchanted, uninterested **13** disillusioned, sophisticated
blaspheme 4 cuss **5** abuse, curse, swear **6** revile **7** pollute, profane **8** denounce, execrate **9** castigate, excoriate
blasphemous 6 coarse, sinful **7** godless, impious, obscene, profane, ungodly **10** irreverent **12** sacrilegious **13** disrespectful
blasphemy 3 sin **5** abuse, error **6** heresy **7** cursing, cussing, impiety, mockery **8** swearing **9** profanity, sacrilege, violation **10** execration, heterodoxy, iconoclasm **11** desecration, imprecation, irreverence, malediction, profanation
blast 3 din **4** bang, beat, blow, boom, clap, dash, gale, gust, kill, peal, ruin, slam, toot **5** blare, burst, crack, crash, salvo, shoot, smash, wreck **6** attack, blight, blow up, damage, squall, wallop **7** destroy, lambast, shatter, shrivel, trumpet **8** dynamite, lam-

baste, outburst **9** explosion, castigate, discharge, overwhelm, shock wave **10** annihilate, detonation

blat 4 bray **5** blurt **6** cry out **7** exclaim **8** blurt out

blatant 4 bald, loud **5** brash, clear, gaudy, naked, noisy, overt, saucy **6** arrant, brassy, brazen, crying, flashy, garish, patent, tawdry, vulgar **7** glaring, jarring, obvious **8** flagrant, immodest, impudent, insolent, manifest, overbold, strident **9** barefaced, clamorous, obtrusive, shameless, unabashed **10** boisterous, outrageous, scurrilous, unblushing, vociferous **11** conspicuous, loudmouthed, transparent **12** ear-splitting, obstreperous

blather 3 gab, gas, jaw, rot, yak **4** bosh, gush, rave, stir **5** bleat, drool, hokum, prate **6** babble, bunkum, drivel, effuse, gabble, jabber, natter, yammer **7** blabber, chatter, enthuse, palaver, prattle, rubbish, twaddle **8** chitchat, claptrap, idle talk, nonsense **9** commotion **10** balderdash, double-talk, flapdoodle **12** gobbledygook

blaze 4 burn, fire **5** burst, flame, flare, glare, shine **7** flare up **8** eruption, outburst **10** incandesce **13** conflagration ***Scottish:*** **3** low **4** lowe

blazer 6 marker, reefer **9** sport coat **10** sports coat **12** sports jacket

blazes 4 hell **5** abyss, Hades, Sheol **6** Tophet **7** Gehenna, inferno **9** perdition **11** netherworld

blazing 4 keen **5** afire, fiery **6** aflame, alight, ardent, fervid, on fire, red-hot **7** burning, fervent, flaming, flaring, furious, glowing, ignited, intense, lighted **8** dazzling, feverish, powerful, speeding, white-hot **9** brilliant, perfervid **11** conflagrant, impassioned **12** incandescent **13** scintillating

blazon 4 deck **5** adorn, sound **7** declare, display, publish, trumpet **8** announce, proclaim **9** advertise, broadcast **10** coat of arms, promulgate **11** ostentation

bleach 3 dim **4** fade, pale **5** white **6** blanch, blench, purify, whiten **7** decolor, launder, wash out **8** etiolate, peroxide, sanitize **9** whitewash

bleak 3 raw, sad **4** bare, cold, dour, drab, grim, wild **5** chill, drear, empty, harsh, stark **6** barren, chilly, dismal, dreary, gloomy, lonely, severe, somber, wintry **7** austere, exposed, joyless **8** blighted, desolate, funereal, hopeless **9** cheerless, windswept, woebegone **10** depressing, despondent, oppressive, melancholy

blear 3 dim, fog **4** blur, dull, mist, murk, veil **5** bedim, faint, vague **6** hidden, shroud **7** becloud, obscure, shadowy, unclear **10** indistinct

bleary 3 dim **5** all in, faint, filmy, fuzzy, milky, spent, tired, vague **6** pooped, sapped, used-up, wasted **7** blurred, drained, obscure, shadowy, unclear, worn-out **8** depleted **9** enervated, exhausted, washed-out **10** indistinct

bleat 3 baa **4** blat, carp, crab, fuss, yawp **5** gripe, whine **6** bellow, grouse, squawk, yammer **7** blather, grumble, whimper **8** complain **9** bellyache

bleed 3 sap, run **4** milk, ooze, pity, seep **5** drain, exude, leech, mulct **6** extort, fleece **7** diffuse, extract **9** blackmail **10** hemorrhage

blemish 3 mar **4** blot, flaw, harm, mark, maim, mole, scar, spot, vice, wart **5** fault, nevus, spoil, stain **6** blotch, damage, deface, defect, impair, injure, pimple, stigma **7** blacken, distort, freckle, pervert, tarnish, vitiate **8** impurity, mutilate, pockmark **9** birthmark **12** imperfection **13** disfigurement

blench 3 shy **4** balk, duck, fade **5** blink, cower, quail, quake, start, wince **6** flinch, purify, recoil, shrink, whiten **7** launder, shy away, squinch, tremble **8** draw back, etiolate **9** whitewash

blend 3 fit, mix **4** brew, fuse, meld, weld **5** admix, alloy, merge, unify, union, unite **6** commix, fusion, go with, hybrid, mingle **7** amalgam, combine, mélange, mixture **8** beverage, coalesce, compound, conflate, immingle, infusion, intermix, mishmash **9** admixture, commingle, composite, harmonize, integrate **10** amalgamate, commixture, concoction, synthesize **12** adulteration, amalgamation, intermixture

blender setting 3 mix **4** chop, whip **5** grate, mince, puree **7** liquefy

blesbok 8 antelope

bless 4 laud **5** exalt, extol, endow, favor, grace **6** anoint, bestow, hallow, praise, uphold **7** approve, beatify, glorify, magnify **8** enshrine, eulogize, make holy, sanctify **10** consecrate

blessed 4 holy **5** happy, lucky **6** joyous, sacred **7** saintly **8** beatific, hallowed **9** beatified, fortunate, venerated **10** inviolable, sacrosanct, sanctified **11** consecrated

blessedness 5 bliss **8** felicity, sanctity **9** beatitude, godliness, happiness **12** blissfulness

blessing 4 boon, good, okay **5** asset, favor, grace **6** assent, bounty, thanks **7** benefit, benison, consent, fortune, godsend, support **8** approval, good luck, windfall **9** advantage **10** invocation, permission **11** approbation, benediction, endorsement, good fortune, valediction **12** commendation, consecration, thanksgiving **13** encouragement

"____ bleu!" **5** Sacré

blight **3** mar, nip **4** bane, dash, ruin **5** blast, decay, spoil, wreck **6** canker, wither **7** disease, scourge, shrivel **9** withering **10** pestilence **13** deterioration

blimp **7** airship **8** zeppelin **9** dirigible

blind **4** boma, daze, dull **5** decoy, front, shade, shill **6** dazzle **7** eyeless, muddled, shutter **8** bedazzle, jalousie, unseeing **9** enclosure, sightless **10** visionless

blind alley **6** pocket **7** dead end, impasse **8** cul-de-sac, deadlock **9** stone wall **10** standstill **11** obstruction

blind god **4** Eros, Hodr, Hoth **5** Cupid, Hoder, Hodur, Hothr

blindworm **8** slowworm

blink **3** bat **4** wink **5** flash, yield **6** give in, squint **7** flicker, flutter, nictate, twinkle **9** nictitate **11** scintillate

blink at **4** omit **5** clear, let go **6** bypass, excuse, forget, ignore, slight **7** condone, connive, let pass, neglect **8** discount, overlook, pass over **9** disregard, exonerate, whitewash

blip **6** censor, screen **9** deviation, expurgate, radar spot **10** bowdlerize

bliss **3** joy **4** Zion **6** Canaan, heaven **7** ecstasy, elation, elysium, nirvana, rapture **8** empyrean, euphoria, paradise **9** beatitude, cloud nine, happiness **10** exaltation **11** blessedness

blissful **5** happy **6** divine, elated, joyful, joyous **8** beatific, ecstatic, euphoric **9** ambrosial, delighted, entranced, rapturous **10** delightful, entrancing

blissfulness **3** joy **7** ecstasy **8** euphoria **9** beatitude, happiness **10** exaltation **11** contentment

blister **4** bleb, flay, lash **5** blain, bulla, slash **6** assail, canker, scathe, scorch **7** lambast, scarify, scourge, vesicle **8** lambaste **9** castigate, excoriate

blithe **3** gay **4** boon **5** happy, jolly, merry, sunny **6** bouncy, casual, cheery, chirpy, jaunty, jocund, jovial **7** gleeful **8** carefree, careless, cheerful, chirrupy, gladsome, heedless, mirthful **9** lightsome, sprightly, unworried, vivacious **10** untroubled **11** thoughtless **12** lighthearted

blitz **4** raid, rush **6** attack **7** air raid, bombard, bombing **8** shelling **9** offensive, onslaught **10** mass attack **11** bombardment

blitzkrieg **6** attack **7** assault, bombing **9** offensive, onslaught **11** bombardment

blizzard **4** gale **6** squall **8** whiteout **9** snowstorm

bloat **5** bulge, swell **6** billow, expand, fatten, puff up **7** balloon, distend, enlarge, inflate **10** distension

bloated **5** puffy, tumid **6** puffed **7** pompous, swollen **8** arrogant, enlarged, inflated **9** distended, overblown, overlarge **11** pretentious **13** self-important

bloc **4** band, ring **5** cabal, party, union **6** clique, league **7** combine, faction **8** alliance **9** coalition **10** consortium, contingent, federation **11** association, combination **13** confederation

block **3** bar **4** clog, fill, hunk, Lego, plug, slab, stop, wall, wing **5** brick, choke, chunk, close, ingot **6** cut off, hinder, impede **7** barrier, congest, occlude, stopper **8** obstacle, obstruct **9** barricade, hindrance, intercept

blockade **3** bar **4** stop, wall **5** beset, hem in, siege **6** shut in **7** barrier, besiege **8** close off, encircle, obstruct, stoppage **9** barricade, beleaguer, blank wall, hindrance, roadblock **10** impediment **11** obstruction

blockage **3** bar **4** clog, halt **7** barrier **8** obstacle, stoppage **10** impediment **11** obstruction

blockbuster **4** bomb **11** spectacular

blockhead **3** oaf **4** clod, dolt, dope, fool **5** clunk, dummy, dunce, idiot, moron, ninny **6** nitwit **7** halfwit, jackass **8** clodpole, clodpoll, dumbbell, imbecile, numskull **9** ignoramus, lamebrain, numbskull, simpleton **10** nincompoop **12** featherbrain

blockheaded **4** dull, dumb **5** dense, thick **6** obtuse, stupid **7** doltish **9** brainless, dimwitted **10** slow-witted

block out **4** mark **5** chart, close, draft, frame **6** hinder, screen, sketch **7** obscure, outline, prepare, repress, shut off **8** indicate, obstruct **9** adumbrate, formulate

block up **3** dam **4** clog, fill, plug, stop **5** choke **7** congest

bloke **3** guy, man **4** chap, gent **6** fellow **9** gentleman

blond **4** fair, gold, pale **5** light, sandy, straw, tawny **6** flaxen, golden **7** towhead **8** platinum **9** champagne, towheaded **10** fair-haired **11** sandy-haired **12** honey-colored

blood **4** gore **7** descent, kindred, kinship, lineage **8** ancestry **10** extraction ***cancer of:*** **8** leukemia ***cell:*** **3** red **5** white **8** hemocyte, monocyte, platelet **9** corpuscle, leukocyte **10** lymphocyte **11** erythrocyte, granulocyte ***clot:*** **8** thrombus ***coloring matter:*** **10** hemoglobin ***combining form:*** **3** hem **4** hemo ***dis-***

ease: **6** anemia **8** leukemia **10** hemophilia *factor:* **2** Rh *fluid part:* **5** serum **6** plasma *of the gods:* **5** ichor *particle in:* **7** embolus *poisoning:* **6** pyemia **7** toxemia **10** septicemia *pressure:* **8** systolic **9** diastolic *relating to:* **5** hemic *serum:* **6** plasma *study of:* **10** hematology *sugar:* **7** glucose

bloodbath 7 carnage, slaying **8** butchery, massacre **9** slaughter **10** decimation **12** annihilation **13** extermination

bloodless 3 wan **4** ashy, dull, pale, weak **5** ashen, waxen **6** anemic, feeble, pallid, sallow, torpid **8** listless **9** insensate, unfeeling **10** insensible, nonviolent **11** coldhearted, passionless, unemotional

bloodletting 4 gore **7** carnage, killing **8** butchery, shambles, violence **9** slaughter **10** phlebotomy **11** venesection

bloodline 6 family, strain **7** descent, lineage **8** ancestry, pedigree **10** family tree

bloodroot 7 puccoon

bloodshed 4 gore **7** carnage, killing **8** butchery **9** slaughter

bloodstained 4 gory **6** grisly **7** imbrued, wounded **8** sanguine **10** sanguinary **11** ensanguined, sanguineous

bloodstone 10 chalcedony

bloodsucker 3 ked **4** tick **5** lamia, leech **6** lizard, sponge **7** sponger, vampire **8** hanger-on, parasite, sheep ked **10** freeloader **12** lounge lizard

bloodthirsty 5 rabid **8** ravening, sanguine **9** cutthroat, homicidal, murdering, murderous, predatory, voracious **10** sanguinary **11** sanguineous

blood vessel 4 vein **5** aorta **6** artery **7** jugular **9** capillary *combining form:* **3** vas **4** angi, vasi, vaso **5** angio

bloody 4 gory, grim, very **5** cruel **6** damage, damned, deadly, grisly **7** blasted, hateful, imbrued, wounded **8** accursed, infernal, sanguine **9** cutthroat, homicidal, murdering, murderous **10** detestable, sanguinary **11** ensanguined, sanguineous **12** death-dealing, slaughtering

bloom 4 blow, glow, open, posy **5** blush **6** floret, flower, thrive, unfold **7** blossom, burgeon, coating, develop, dusting, prosper **8** flourish, rosiness **10** cloudiness, effloresce **13** discoloration

blooper 4 goof, slip, trip **5** boner, break, error, fluff, gaffe, lapse **6** boo-boo, bungle, howler, slipup **7** blunder, faux pas, fly ball, misstep, mistake, offense **8** solecism **9** indecorum, false step **11** impropriety **12** indiscretion

blossom 3 bud, wax **4** blow, glow, grow, open, posy **5** bloom, blush, flush **6** expand, flower, mature, thrive, unfold **7** burgeon, develop, prosper **8** flourish, floweret, progress **10** effloresce, peak period **13** efflorescence

blot 4 blur, mark, onus, slur, smut, soil, spot **5** brand, odium, smear, speck, stain, sully **6** absorb, smudge, stigma **7** bestain, blemish, spatter, tarnish **8** black eye, discolor, disgrace **9** bespatter, moral flaw

blotch 4 mark, spot **5** stain **6** macula, macule, mottle, smudge **7** blemish, splotch **12** imperfection

blot out 4 raze, void **5** annul, crush, erase, quash, quell, scrub **6** cancel, delete, efface, squash **7** abolish, destroy, expunge **9** eliminate, eradicate, extirpate **10** annihilate, extinguish, obliterate **11** exterminate

blotto see **drunk**

blouse 5 middy, shell, shirt, smock, tunic **6** guimpe

bloviate 4 rail, rant, rave **5** mouth, orate, spout **7** bluster, carry on, declaim, inveigh, soapbox, talk big **8** harangue, perorate, sound off, splutter **9** hold forth **10** vociferate

blow 3 bop, fan, hit, jar **4** bang, bash, belt, biff, bump, cuff, damn, fail, gasp, gust, huff, pipe, puff, slam, slug, swat, toot, whop, wind **5** boast, botch, crack, drive, erupt, leave, pound, punch, shock, slosh, smack, smash, sound, spend, waste, whack **6** buffet, depart, impact, mishap, thwack, wallop **7** assault, breathe, chagrin, consume, debacle, explode, flutter, fritter, trumpet **8** calamity, disaster, flounder, knockout, squander **9** bombshell, collision, dissipate, throw away **10** concussion, misfortune, trifle away **11** catastrophe

blow-by-blow 4 full **5** fussy **6** minute **7** careful, precise **8** detailed, itemized, thorough **10** exhaustive, meticulous, scrupulous **13** thoroughgoing

blowhard see **boaster**

blow in 4 land **5** pop by **6** appear, arrive, drop by, show up, turn up **7** hit town **11** materialize

blowout 4 bash, fete, gala, riot, tear **5** binge, blast, break, party, split, spree **6** frolic, shindy **7** shindig, victory **8** carousal, flat tire **9** festivity

blowsy 5 dingy, ruddy **6** florid, frowsy, sloppy, untidy **7** flushed, healthy, unkempt **8** blooming, blushing **10** bedraggled

blow up 4 bomb, burn, fume, rage **5** bloat, burst, erupt, flare, go off, storm, swell **6** expand, lose it, seethe **7** bristle, distend, enlarge, explode, inflate, magnify, rupture, shatter **8** boil over, demolish, detonate, dynamite, heighten, mushroom **9** discredit, fulminate, overstate **10** aggrandize

blowy 4 airy, wild **5** fresh, gusty, windy **6** breezy, stormy **7** squally **8** blustery **9** windswept **11** tempestuous

blubber 3 cry, fat, sob **4** bawl, flab, keen, lard, pipe, wail, weep **5** flesh **6** snivel **7** carry on **8** whale fat

bludgeon 3 bat **4** club **5** baton, billy, bully **6** attack, cudgel, hector **7** bluster, war club **8** browbeat, bulldoze, bullyrag **9** bastinado, billy club, blackjack, strong-arm, truncheon **10** intimidate, nightstick ***British:*** **4** cosh

blue 3 low, sad, sea **4** cyan, down, glum, lewd, navy, racy **5** bawdy, ocean, royal, salty, spicy **6** cobalt, gloomy, risqué **7** naughty, profane, unhappy **8** dejected, downcast, indecent, off-color **9** depressed, woebegone **10** despondent, dispirited, melancholy, suggestive **11** downhearted ***combining form:*** **4** cyan **5** cyano ***dark:*** **4** anil **5** perse **6** indigo ***dye:*** **4** woad ***grayish:*** **5** merle, slate ***greenish:*** **4** aqua, cyan, teal **5** beryl **6** cobalt **7** azurite **9** turquoise ***reddish:*** **5** smalt **6** marine, purple, violet **7** cyanine, gentian, lobelia ***sky:*** **5** azure **8** cerulean

____ Blue 3 Ben **9** Little Boy

blue blood 4 lady, lord, peer **5** elite, noble **6** aristo **7** royalty **8** nobleman **9** gentility, gentleman, patrician **10** aristocrat, noblewoman **11** gentle birth, gentlewoman

bluebonnet 4 Scot **11** Texas lupine

Blue Boy painter 12 Gainsborough (Thomas)

bluecoat 3 cop, law **4** fuzz **5** bobby **6** copper **9** constable, patrolman, policeman

Bluegrass State 8 Kentucky

Blue Grotto site 5 Capri

bluejacket 4 mate, salt, swab **5** limey **6** sailor, seaman **7** swabbie **9** sailorman

blue jeans 5 Levis **6** denims

blue moon 3 age, eon, era **4** aeon **5** epoch **7** dog's age **8** eternity, lifetime **10** generation

bluenose 4 prig, snob **5** prude **7** puritan **9** Mrs. Grundy, nice Nelly **10** goody-goody

bluenosed 4 prim **5** rigid **6** prissy, proper, square, stuffy **7** prudish **8** overnice, priggish **9** Victorian **10** scrupulous, tight-laced **11** puritanical, straitlaced

blue-pencil 3 cut **4** edit, trim **5** emend **6** cut out, delete, excise, remove, revise **7** clean up **8** boil down, cross out **9** strike out, tighten up

bluepoint 6 oyster

blueprint 3 map **4** cast, plan, plot **5** chart, draft, frame, model, trace **6** design, devise, rubric, scheme, set out, sketch **7** arrange, diagram, outline, picture, project **8** game plan, strategy **9** delineate **10** conception, rough draft **11** description

blue-ribbon 3 top **4** A-one **5** prime, prize **6** Grade A, tip-top **7** capital, premier, stellar **8** five-star, top-notch, superior **9** excellent, first-rate, top-drawer **10** first-class, top-quality, world-class **11** outstanding **12** prize-winning

blues 4 funk **5** dumps, gloom, grief **6** lament **7** sadness, trouble **8** doldrums, glumness **9** dejection, pessimism **10** depression, desolation, low spirits, melancholy, woefulness **11** despondency, melancholia, unhappiness **12** hopelessness, mournfulness

blues musician 3 Guy (Buddy) **4** Cray (Robert), King (Albert, B. B.), Wolf (Howlin') **5** Bland (Bobby "Blue"), Brown (Clarence "Gatemouth"), Dixon (Willie), Foley (Sue), Handy (W. C.), James (Elmore), Myers (Sam), Smith (Bessie), Wells (Junior) **6** Hooker (John Lee), Rainey (Gertrude "Ma"), Taylor (Koko), Turner (Joe), Walker (T-Bone), Waters (Ethel, Muddy) **7** Broonzy (Big Bill), Diddley (Bo), Collins (Albert), Hammond (John), Hopkins (Sam "Lightnin' "), Johnson (Robert), Rushing (Jimmy) **8** Burnside (R. L.), Copeland (Johnny) **9** Jefferson (Blind Lemon), Leadbelly, Ledbetter (Huddie) **10** Williamson (John Lee, Sonny Boy)

bluff 3 act, con **4** curt, fake, fool, jive, ruse, sham, show **5** blunt, cliff, feign, frank, gruff, rough, trick **6** abrupt, betray, candid, crusty, delude, direct, hearty, humbug **7** beguile, brusque, deceive, fake out, mislead, playact, pretend **8** headland, pretense **9** deception, outspoken, precipice, steep bank **10** escarpment, forthright, no-nonsense, promontory, subterfuge **11** counterfeit, double-cross, plainspoken, short-spoken **13** unceremonious

blunder 3 err **4** bull, gaff, goof, mess, muff, slip, trip **5** boner, botch, error, fluff, gaffe, gum up, lapse, lurch, misdo, snafu **6** bobble, bollix, bumble, bungle, foul up, fumble, goof up, howler, mess up, wander **7** balls-up, blooper, failure, faux pas, louse up, misstep, mistake, screw up, stumble **8** disaster, flounder **12** indiscretion, misadventure

blunderbuss 3 gun **4** dolt **5** klutz **6** galoot, lummox **7** bungler, firearm **8** bonehead, numskull **9** blockhead, numbskull **10** stumblebum **13** butterfingers

blunt 4 bald, calm, curt **5** allay, bluff, brief,

frank, gruff, plain, rough, terse **6** abrupt, benumb, candid, crusty, deaden, direct, lessen, obtuse **7** brusque, rounded, uncivil **8** enfeeble, not sharp, snippety **10** forthright **11** desensitize, insensitive, plainspoken, unvarnished **12** discourteous **13** unceremonious

blur 3 dim, fog **4** blot, dull, mist **5** befog, blear, cloud, muddy, smear, stain, taint **6** smudge, stigma **7** becloud, besmear, confuse, obscure, tarnish **8** besmirch, discolor ***in printing:*** **6** mackle

blurb 2 ad **4** hype, plug, puff **5** press, promo **6** notice **7** write-up **8** good word **9** promotion **12** commendation

blurry 4 hazy **5** vague **6** cloudy **7** clouded, unclear **9** undefined, unfocused **10** indistinct

blurt 4 blab, blat, bolt **5** spill **6** cry out, let out **7** divulge, exclaim, let slip, spit out **8** disclose, give away **9** ejaculate

blush 4 burn, glow, rose, view **5** bloom, color, flame, flush, rouge **6** mantle, pinken, redden, ruddle **7** blossom, crimson, redness, turn red **8** mantling, rosiness

bluster 4 bawl, crow, gust, huff, rage, roar, rout **5** blast, bully, prate, storm, strut, vaunt **6** bellow, clamor, hector, lean on **7** bombast, bravado, dragoon, roister, swagger, talk big **8** boasting, browbeat, bulldoze, bullyrag, domineer **9** gasconade **10** grandstand, intimidate **11** braggadocio

blustery 4 wild **5** blowy, gusty, rough **6** drafty, raging, raving, stormy **7** furious, squally, violent **9** truculent, turbulent **10** boisterous, tumultuous **11** tempestuous

boa 5 scarf, snake

Boadicea clan 5 Iceni

boar 3 pig **4** male **5** swine

board 4 fare, feed, food, lath, slab, slat **5** catch, get on, hop on, house, lodge, meals, panel, plank, put up, table **6** billet, embark **7** emplane, entrain, quarter **9** directors **11** directorate ***artist's:*** **7** palette ***mystic:*** **5** Ouija

boarder 5 guest **6** lodger, renter, roomer, tenant

board game see at **game**

boarding house 6 hostel **7** hospice, lodging, pension **8** pensione

boardwalk 7 gangway **9** esplanade, promenade

boast 3 own **4** blow, brag, crow, have, puff **5** exalt, exult, glory, mouth, prate, preen, strut, vaunt **6** parade **7** bluster, bombast, bravado, contain, enlarge, exhibit, inflate, possess, show off, swagger, talk big **9** gasconade **10** exaggerate, grandstand **11** rodomontade **12** exaggeration

boaster 6 gascon **7** egotist, peacock, show-off **8** big mouth, blowhard, braggart **11** braggadocio, rodomontade

boastful 4 vain **5** cocky **6** braggy **8** arrogant, braggart, puffed-up, vaunting **9** bigheaded, conceited, egotistic **11** egotistical, pretentious, swellheaded **12** vainglorious **13** swelled-headed ***Scottish:*** **6** vaunty

boat 3 ark, hoy, tug **4** dhow, dory, junk, pram, prau, proa, punt, scow, ship, yawl **5** balsa, barge, canoe, coble, ferry, kayak, ketch, scull, shell, skiff, sloop, smack, umiak, yacht **6** bateau, bugeye, caïque, cutter, dinghy, hooker, lateen, lugger, packet, sampan, vessel, wherry **7** caravel, coracle, cruiser, currach, curragh, gondola, inboard, lighter, pinnace, pirogue, pontoon, shallop, steamer, trawler, vedette, vidette **8** outboard, runabout, schooner, trimaran **9** catamaran, hydrofoil ***bottom projection:*** **4** keel ***captain:*** **5** pilot **6** master **7** skipper ***dock, basin:*** **6** marina ***front end of:*** **3** bow **4** fore, prow ***on a ship:*** **3** gig **6** launch **7** pinnace ***race:*** **7** regatta ***rear end of:*** **3** aft **5** stern ***song:*** **6** chanty, shanty **7** chantey **9** barcarole **10** barcarolle

boatman 3 tar **4** mate, swab **5** limey **6** Charon, sailor **7** mariner, oarsman, paddler **8** deckhand, water dog **9** gondolier, navigator

boat-shaped 8 scaphoid **9** navicular

Boaz's wife 4 Ruth

bob 3 jig, nod, rap, tap **4** buff, clip, crop, dock, trim **5** bunch, float **6** bounce, curtsy, jiggle, jounce, polish, trifle, wobble **7** cluster, curtsey, nosegay **8** shilling **9** genuflect

bobbery 3 ado, din, row **4** fray, riot **5** babel, noise **6** bedlam, hubbub, racket, ruckus, rumpus **7** ferment, ruction **9** commotion, confusion **10** hullabaloo, hurly-burly **11** disturbance, pandemonium

bobbin 4 pirn **5** quill, spool, wheel **7** spindle **8** cylinder

bobble 3 bob, dud **4** flub, goof, mess, muff **5** botch, error, fluff, gum up **6** ball up, bollix, bumble, bungle, flub up, fumble, goof up, muff up **7** blooper, failure, louse up, mistake

bobby 3 law **6** copper, peeler **7** officer **9** constable, patrolman, policeman

bobwhite 5 quail **9** partridge

Boccaccio *beloved:* **9** Fiammetta ***tales:*** **9** Decameron

bode 4 hint **5** augur **6** signal, warn of **7** betoken, portend, presage, promise, signify, suggest **8** foreshow, indicate **9** foretoken, prefigure **10** foreshadow

bodega 3 bar, pub **6** saloon **7** barroom, grocery **8** wineshop **12** general store

bodement 4 omen, sign **5** hunch **6** augury **7** portent, presage **8** prophecy **9** foretoken, harbinger **10** foreboding, intimation, prediction, prognostic **11** premonition **12** presentiment

bodiless 7 ghostly **8** ethereal, spectral **9** unfleshly **10** discarnate, immaterial, unphysical **11** disembodied, incorporeal, nonmaterial **12** apparitional **13** insubstantial

bodily 6 carnal **7** en masse, earthly, fleshly, sensual, somatic, totally **8** corporal, entirely, physical, visceral **9** corporeal **10** altogether, completely **11** unspiritual

bodkin 4 shiv **5** blade, knife, shank **6** dagger, lancet, needle **7** poniard **8** stiletto

____ **bodkins 4** odds

body 4 bulk, core, form, hull, mass, soma **5** frame, stiff, stock, torso **6** corpse, corpus **7** anatomy, cadaver, carcass, chassis, corpora (plural), remains **8** physique **9** aggregate, substance ***combining form:*** **4** dema, soma, some, somi (plural) **5** somat, somia, somus **6** somata (plural), somato ***human:*** **4** clay

body cavity 5 cecum, sinus **6** coelom **7** abdomen **8** hemocoel

body check 5 block

bodyguard 7 retinue **9** attendant, protector

body of water 3 bay, sea **4** cove, gulf, lake, pond, pool **5** bight, brook, creek, fiord, firth, fjord, inlet, ocean, river **6** harbor, lagoon, puddle, stream **7** channel, estuary **9** reservoir

body passage 4 duct, vein **5** canal **6** artery, meatus, ureter, vagina, venule, vessel **7** trachea, urethra **8** bronchus **9** arteriole, capillary, esophagus, intestine **10** bronchiole **13** bronchial tube, fallopian tube

body politic 5 state **6** nation **11** nation-state

boffo 3 gag, gas, hit **4** wild **5** laugh **6** scream **7** sold-out **8** smash-hit, smashing **10** successful **11** sensational

bog 3 fen **4** mire, quag **5** delay, marsh, swamp **6** impede, morass, muskeg, slough, slow up **8** quagmire **9** swampland

boggy 4 miry **5** mucky **6** marshy, quaggy, swampy **7** sloughy

Bogart, Humphrey ***film:*** **6** Sahara **7** Dead End, Sabrina **8** Big Sleep (The), Key Largo **10** Casablanca, High Sierra **11** Caine Mutiny (The) **12** African Queen (The) **13** Maltese Falcon (The) **15** Petrified Forest (The) **16** To Have and Have Not **24** Treasure of the Sierra Madre (The) ***wife:*** **6** Bacall (Lauren)

bog down 4 flag, mire **5** choke, delay, stall **6** detain, falter, hang up, hinder, impede, retard, slow up **7** embroil, set back, slacken **8** encumber, keep back, obstruct, slow down **9** lose steam **10** decelerate

bogey 5 ghost, haunt, shade, spook **6** scarer, shadow, spirit, wraith **7** phantom, specter **8** phantasm, revenant **10** apparition

bogeyman 5 spook **7** bugbear, chimera, monster, phantom, specter, spectre **10** apparition

boggle 4 balk, mess, muff, stun **5** amaze, botch, fudge, gum up, shock, wreck **6** bollix, bungle, cobble, goof up, mess up, strain **7** astound, louse up, nonplus, stagger, stumble, stupefy **8** astonish, bewilder, bowl over, confound **9** dumbfound, mishandle, mismanage, overwhelm, take aback **11** flabbergast

boggy 4 miry **5** mucky **6** marshy, quaggy, swampy **7** sloughy

bogus 4 fake, mock, sham **5** false, phony, pseud, snide **6** ersatz, forged, pseudo **7** fictive, pretend **8** invented, specious, spurious **9** brummagem, concocted, imitation, pinchbeck, simulated, trumped up **10** artificial, fabricated, fraudulent, mendacious **11** counterfeit

Bohème, La ***character:*** **4** Mimi **7** Rodolfo ***composer:*** **7** Puccini (Giacomo) ***setting:*** **5** Paris

bohemian 4 arty, boho **5** artsy, gypsy, hippy **6** hippie **7** beatnik, dropout, oddball, offbeat **8** maverick, vagabond, wanderer **9** eccentric **10** avant-garde, free spirit, iconoclast, unorthodox **13** nonconformist

boil 3 jet **4** bolt, brew, burn, cook, dash, foam, fume, gush, moil, race, rage, rush, spew, spot, stew, vent **5** anger, churn, erupt, fling, froth, poach, shoot, storm, swirl **6** blow up, bubble, charge, canker, coddle, decoct, pimple, seethe, simmer **7** abscess, agitate, bristle, ferment, flare up, pustule, smolder **8** furuncle **9** carbuncle, discharge **10** effervesce **11** excrescence

boil down 4 pare, trim **6** amount, decoct, reduce **7** distill **8** compress, condense, simplify, truncate **9** summarize, synopsize **10** streamline **11** concentrate, encapsulate

boiler suit 8 coverall

boiling 3 hot **5** fiery **6** baking, red-hot, sultry, torrid **7** burning, febrile **8** agitated, roasting, scalding, sizzling, tropical **9** scorching **10** blistering

boil over 4 burn, fume, rage **5** erupt **6** blow up, bridle, see red, seethe **7** bristle, flare up

boisterous 4 loud, wild **5** noisy, rowdy **6** lively, stormy, unruly **7** blatant, raucous, riotous **8** strident **9** clamorous, convivial, turbulent **10** disorderly, disruptive, rollicking, tumultuous, uproarious, vociferous **11** loud-mouthed, tempestuous **12** high-spirited, obstreperous, rambunctious, ungovernable, unrestrained

Boito opera 11 Mefistofele

bold 4 edgy, free, pert, rude **5** bluff, brave, fresh, gutsy, nervy, sassy, saucy, sheer, showy, steep **6** arrant, brassy, brazen, bright, cheeky, daring, heroic **7** doughty, forward, glaring, obvious, valiant **8** cocksure, fearless, impudent, insolent, intrepid, resolute, unafraid, valorous **9** audacious, dauntless, intrusive, prominent, shameless, undaunted **10** courageous, pronounced **11** adventurous, impertinent, smart-alecky, venturesome **12** enterprising, presumptuous

boldness 4 gall, grit **5** drive, nerve, valor **6** aplomb, mettle, spirit **8** audacity, backbone, chutzpah, temerity **9** arrogance, challenge, hardihood, impudence, insolence **10** brazenness, disrespect, effrontery **11** discourtesy **12** impertinence

Bolero composer 5 Ravel (Maurice)

Bolivia *ancient culture:* 4 Inca **10** Tiahuanaco ***capital:* 5** La Paz, Sucre ***city:* 6** El Alto **9** Santa Cruz **10** Cochabamba ***conqueror:* 7** Pizarro (Hernando) ***Indian people:* 6** Aymara **7** Quechua ***lake:* 5** Poopó **8** Titicaca ***language:* 6** Aymara **7** Quechua, Spanish ***monetary unit:* 9** boliviano ***mountain, range:* 5** Andes **6** Sajama ***neighbor:* 4** Peru **5** Chile **6** Brazil **8** Paraguay **9** Argentina ***river:* 4** Beni **5** Abuna **6** Mamoré **7** Guaporé **9** Pilcomayo

bollix 4 flub, mess, muff, ruin **5** botch, gum up, mix-up, snafu, spoil, upset **6** bobble, bumble, bungle, foul up, fumble, goof up, jumble, mess up, muck up, muddle, muff up **7** balls-up, confuse, louse up, screw up **8** dishevel, disorder, scramble, unsettle **9** mishandle, mismanage

bolo 5 knife **7** machete

Bolshevik 3 Red **6** commie **7** comrade **8** Leninist, tovarich, tovarish **9** communist

bolshevism 7 Marxism **8** Leninism **9** communism

bolster 3 aid **4** buoy, gird, help, husk, prop **5** boost, brace, carry, cheer **6** assist, bear up, buoy up, pillow, upbear, uphold **7** bulwark, cushion, fortify, hearten, shore up, support, sustain **8** backstop, buttress, maintain **9** encourage, reinforce **10** strengthen **12** underpinning **13** reinforcement

bolt 3 bar, fly, rod, run **4** cram, dash, dart, flee, gulp, jump, lock, race, rush, tear, wolf **5** arrow, blurt, bound, chase, dowel, flush, rivet, scarf, scoot, shoot, skirr, slosh, start **6** charge, decamp, devour, gobble, guzzle, secure, spring **7** abscond, exclaim, hotfoot, make off, missile, rigidly, scamper, startle, take off **8** blurt out, hightail **9** skedaddle **10** make tracks, take flight **11** ingurgitate **13** thunderstroke

bomb 3 dud, hit **4** bust, dull, fail, flop, sink, zero **5** blast, blitz, lemon, loser, pound, shell **6** blow up **7** debacle, destroy, failure, home run, success, washout, wipe out **8** detonate, disaster, fall flat, long pass, long shot, spray can

bombard 4 pelt **5** blast, blitz, shell, storm **6** attack, assail, cannon, hammer, pepper, shower, strafe, strike **7** assault, barrage **8** catapult **9** cannonade

bombardment 4 hail **5** burst, salvo **6** attack, shower, volley **7** barrage, battery **8** drumfire **9** broadside, cannonade, fusillade, onslaught

bombardon 4 bass **8** bass tuba

bombast 4 rant **6** hot air **7** bluster, fustian, oration **8** rhapsody, tumidity **9** fancy talk, pomposity, turgidity **10** pretension **11** rodomontade

bombastic 5 wordy **6** prolix, turgid **7** aureate, flowery, orotund, pompous, swollen **8** inflated, puffed-up **9** overblown **10** euphuistic, rhetorical **11** declamatory, overwrought **12** magniloquent **13** grandiloquent

____ Bombeck 4 Erma

bombed 4 high **5** drunk, fried, stiff, tight **6** blotto, stoned, wasted **8** comatose, tanked up **9** plastered **10** inebriated **11** intoxicated

bombinate 3 hum **4** buzz, purr, whir **5** drone, strum, thrum **6** bumble, rumble **7** grumble

bombshell 4 blow, jolt **5** shock **6** marvel **8** surprise **9** curveball, sensation **10** revelation **11** thunderbolt

Bonaduce role 5 Danny

bona fide 4 real, sure, true **5** valid **6** actual **7** earnest, genuine, sincere **8** sterling **9** authentic, undoubted, veritable **10** legitimate, sure-enough **11** indubitable, in good faith **13** authenticated

bona fides 6 candor **7** probity **8** goodwill **9** good faith, sincerity **10** reputation **11** reliability, sincereness

bonanza 4 mine **5** catch, hoard **7** pay dirt **8** Golconda, gold mine, treasure, treasury, windfall **12** extravaganza **13** treasure trove

bonbon 5 candy, sweet **7** fondant **9** sweetmeat, sugarplum **10** confection

bond **3** tie **4** bail, fuse, knot, link, pact, yoke **5** nexus **6** cement, fetter, pledge, surety **7** bargain, compact, linkage, promise, shackle, warrant **8** adhesive, affinity, cohesion, contract, covenant, guaranty, ligament, ligature, security, vinculum, warranty **9** adherence, agreement, coherence, guarantee **10** attachment, connection, connective, obligation

bondage **4** yoke **6** chains, thrall **7** durance, fetters, helotry, peonage, serfage, serfdom, slavery **9** captivity, detention, servitude, thralldom, vassalage, villenage **10** subjection **11** enslavement, subjugation **12** imprisonment

bondman **4** peon, serf **5** helot, slave **6** vassal

bondsman **4** peon, serf **5** helot, slave **6** surety **7** chattel

bone ***ankle:*** **4** tali (plural) **5** talus, tarsi (plural) **6** tarsus ***arm:*** **4** ulna **5** radii (plural), ulnae (plural) **6** radius **7** humerus ***back:*** **5** spine **8** vertebra **9** vertebrae (plural) ***breast:*** **7** sternum ***calf:*** **6** fibula ***cavity:*** **5** fossa ***change into:*** **6** ossify ***cheek:*** **5** malar **6** zygoma ***chest:*** **3** rib ***collar:*** **8** clavicle ***combining form:*** **4** oste **5** osteo ***face:*** **5** malar, nasal **7** frontal ***finger:*** **7** phalanx **8** phalange ***foot:*** **5** tarsi (plural) **6** tarsus **9** calcaneum, calcaneus **10** astragalus, metatarsus ***hand:*** **10** metacarpus ***head:*** **5** skull, vomer **7** cranium **8** parietal, sphenoid **9** occipital ***heel:*** **9** calcaneum, calcaneus ***hip:*** **5** ilium, pubis **6** pelvis **7** ischium ***jaw:*** **7** maxilla **8** mandible ***kneecap:*** **7** patella ***leg:*** **5** femur, tibia **6** fibula **7** patella ***lower back:*** **6** coccyx, sacrum ***middle ear:*** **5** anvil, incus **6** hammer, stapes **7** malleus, stirrup ***pelvis:*** **5** ilium ***projection:*** **7** mastoid ***relating to:*** **6** osteal ***shin:*** **5** tibia **6** tibiae (plural) ***shoulder blade:*** **7** scapula **8** scapulae (plural) ***small:*** **7** ossicle ***substance:*** **6** ossein ***temporal process:*** **7** mastoid ***thigh:*** **5** femur ***toe:*** **7** phalanx **8** phalange ***U-shaped:*** **5** hyoid ***wrist:*** **5** carpi (plural) **6** carpus

bonehead **4** clod **5** dunce, moron **6** cretin, dimwit, nitwit **7** halfwit **8** clodpole, clodpoll, lunkhead, numskull **9** ignoramus, lamebrain, numbskull **12** featherbrain

bonelike **7** osseous, osteoid

boner see **blooper**

bone up **4** cram **5** study **6** review, revise **8** pore over

bong **4** bell, dong, peal, ring, toll **5** chime, knell, sound **6** hookah, strike **7** resound **9** water pipe **11** reverberate

boniface **7** barkeep **8** publican, taverner **9** barkeeper, innkeeper **12** saloonkeeper

Bonjour Tristesse author **5** Sagan (Françoise)

bonkers **3** ape, mad, off **4** daft, loco, nuts, wild **5** batty, crazy, dotty, giddy, loony, potty **6** cuckoo, insane **7** bananas, haywire **8** demented, deranged, unhinged

bon mot **4** jest, quip **5** crack, sally **6** zinger **7** epigram, riposte **8** one-liner, repartee **9** witticism

bonny **4** fair, fine **6** comely, lovely, pretty **7** winsome **8** pleasing **9** beauteous, beautiful, excellent **10** attractive, delightful **11** good-looking

bon ton **4** élan **5** flair, style **6** gentry, jet set **7** fashion, society **8** elegance, smart set **9** haut monde, propriety **11** high society

bonus **4** gift, plus **6** reward **7** benefit, payment, premium **8** dividend **12** compensation **13** fringe benefit

bon vivant **7** epicure, flaneur, gourmet, trifler **8** aesthete, gourmand **10** aficionado, dilettante, gastronome **11** cognoscente, connoisseur **12** boulevardier, gastronomist, man-about-town

bony **4** lank, lean, thin **5** gaunt, lanky, spare **6** barren, skinny, twiggy **7** angular, osseous, scraggy, scrawny, starved **8** rawboned, skeletal, underfed **9** emaciated **10** cadaverous

boo **4** hiss, hoot, jeer, razz **6** bellow, deride, heckle, revile **7** catcall **9** raspberry, shout down

boob **3** oaf **4** dolt, dope, goof, goon, boor **5** chump, dunce, goose, ninny **6** breast, dumb ox **7** blunder, fathead, mistake, tomfool **8** lunkhead **9** simpleton **10** dunderhead, philistine

boo-boo see **blooper**

booby hatch **6** asylum, bedlam **8** bughouse, loony bin, madhouse, nuthouse **9** funny farm **11** institution

booby trap **4** mine **5** snare **6** hazard **7** pitfall, springe **8** deadfall, land mine

boodle **3** wad **4** bilk, haul, heap, loot, mint, perk, take **5** booty, prize, spoil **6** bundle, packet, payola, spoils **7** fortune, plunder, present **8** kickback **9** incentive **10** bribe money, inducement

book **4** list, text, tome **5** album, bible, codex, enter, folio, novel, tract **6** charge, engage, enroll, folder, line up, manual, octavo, quarto, record, script, volume **7** catalog, edition, reserve **8** hardback, inscribe, register, schedule, softback, treatise **9** hardcover, monograph, paperback, preengage **10** compendium **11** publication ***binding:*** **4** case, sewn, tape, Yapp **5** cloth **7** leather, perfect **9** hardcover ***combining form:*** **6** biblio ***of***

hours: 5 Horae *of Mass:* 6 missal *of psalms:* 7 psalter *part:* 4 head, mull, tail 5 board, cover, crash, envoy, hinge, joint, spine 6 gutter, lining 7 chapter, flyleaf, preface 8 appendix, fore edge, foreword 9 text block 10 dedication

bookie see **bookmaker**

bookish 5 nerdy 6 formal 7 erudite, learned 8 academic, cerebral, literary, pedantic, studious, well-read 9 scholarly 10 longhaired 12 intellectual, professorial

bookkeeping term 4 loss 5 asset, audit, check, debit, entry, yield 6 budget, credit, equity, income, ledger, margin, profit, return 7 account, accrual, balance, expense, invoice, revenue, voucher 8 discount, dividend, interest, write off 9 inventory, liability 10 appreciate, depreciate, fiscal year 11 double entry 12 amortization, appreciation, balance sheet, depreciation, variable cost

booklet 8 brochure, opuscule, pamphlet

bookmaker 6 binder, bookie, editor 7 printer 9 bet holder, oddsmaker, publisher

book of account 6 ledger, record 7 journal 8 register

bookplate 5 label 8 ex libris

bookstall 5 booth, kiosk 9 newsstand

boom 3 wax 4 bang, clap, grow, rise, slam, spar, wham 5 blast, boost, burst, crack, crash, sound, smash, swell 6 do well, expand, growth, rumble, thrive 7 explode, prosper, resound, thunder 8 flourish, kick hard, long beam 9 expansion 10 bull market, detonation, prosperity 11 reverberate *opposite:* 4 bust

boomerang 6 recoil 7 rebound 8 backfire, backlash, come back, kick back, ricochet 10 bounce back

booming 4 bass, deep 6 robust 7 roaring 8 affluent, resonant, sonorous, thriving 9 deafening 10 prospering, prosperous, successful 11 flourishing

boon 3 aid, gay 4 gift, good, help 5 asset, grant, favor, jolly, merry, token 6 blithe, bounty, jocund, jovial 7 benefit, festive, gleeful, godsend, largess, present 8 blessing, largesse, mirthful, windfall 9 advantage, convivial, privilege 10 indulgence 11 benediction, benefaction

boondocks 5 wilds 6 sticks 7 outback 8 backland, frontier 9 backwater, backwoods, provinces, rural area 10 hinterland 11 backcountry, countryside 12 back of beyond

boondoggle 4 cord, hoax, scam 5 fraud, hokum 6 hustle 7 fast one, hatband, lanyard, swindle 8 flimflam 10 fool around, mess around 11 horse around

boor 3 cad, oaf 4 lout, hick, rube 5 brute, chuff, churl, clown, yahoo, yokel 6 lummox, rustic 7 buffoon, bumpkin, hayseed, peasant 9 ignoramus, vulgarian 10 clodhopper, philistine, provincial

boorish 4 rude 5 crass, crude, rough 6 coarse, common, rugged, vulgar 7 apelike, ill-bred, loutish, lowbred, lumpish, uncivil, uncouth 8 churlish, cloddish, clownish, impolite, insolent, lubberly, swainish 9 graceless, offensive, tasteless, unrefined 10 philistine, provincial, robustious, uncultured, ungracious, unmannerly, unpolished, unsociable 11 bad-mannered, clodhopping, ill-mannered, uncivilized 12 discourteous, uncultivated 13 disrespectful

boost 3 aid 4 hike, lift, jump, plug, push, rise 5 raise, steal 6 assist, beef up, expand, extend, foster, jack up 7 advance, amplify, augment, elevate, magnify, promote, support 8 heighten, increase, shoplift 9 advertise, encourage, expansion, promotion 10 assistance 11 helping hand 13 encouragement

booster 3 fan 4 hypo, shot 6 backer, Jaycee, patron, rocket, rooter 7 vaccine 8 champion, defender, promoter, upholder 9 amplifier, expositor, injection, proponent, supporter 10 shoplifter 11 inoculation

boot 2 ax 3 axe, can 4 bang, fire, kick, sack 5 chuck, eject, evict, expel, start 6 bounce, thrill 7 dismiss, kick out, start up 8 throw out 9 discharge, dismissal, terminate *kind:* 5 wader 6 arctic, chukka, gaiter, galosh, mukluk 7 jodhpur, shoepac 8 balmoral, cothurni (plural), overshoe, shoepack 9 cothurnus 10 Wellington

Boötes star 8 Arcturus

booth 4 nook 5 berth, bower, kiosk, stall, stand 6 carrel 9 enclosure 11 compartment

bootleg 3 hot, run 5 hooch 6 pirate 7 illicit, smuggle 9 irregular, moonshine 10 bathtub gin, contraband 11 black market, mountain dew 12 unauthorized

bootless 4 vain 5 empty 6 futile, hollow 7 useless 8 abortive, impotent, nugatory 9 fruitless, valueless, worthless 10 profitless, unavailing 11 ineffective, ineffectual 12 unproductive, unprofitable, unsuccessful

bootlick 4 fawn 5 cower, crawl, creep, toady 6 cringe, grovel, kowtow, stroke 7 cater to, flatter, truckle 8 blandish 9 brownnose, importune, seek favor 10 curry favor 11 apple-polish 12 bow and scrape

bootlicker 4 toad 5 toady 6 lackey, lapdog, minion, yes-man 7 doormat, spaniel 8 hanger-on 9 sycophant 11 lickspittle

booty 4 haul, lift, loot, pelf, swag, take **5** prize, spoil, yield **6** spoils **7** pillage, plunder, rear end, seizure, takings **8** buttocks

booze 4 brew, grog, swig **5** binge, drink, hooch, juice, quaff, sauce, souse, swill **6** guzzle, imbibe, liquor, rotgut, tank up, tipple **7** alcohol, carouse, put away, spirits, swizzle **8** cocktail, liquor up **9** aqua vitae, firewater, knock back, moonshine

boozehound 3 sot **4** lush, wino **5** drunk, hoser, souse **7** guzzler **8** drunkard **9** alcoholic, inebriate **11** dipsomaniac

bop 3 bat, box, hit, jab, pop, rap **4** bash, bean, belt, biff, boff, blow, clip, cuff, jive, slug, sock, swat, whop **5** clock, pound, smack, thump, whack **8** plant one

borax 4 junk

Bordeaux wine *district:* 5 Médoc **6** Graves ***grape:* 6** Malbec, Merlot **8** Cabernet ***name:* 5** Arsac, Ludon, Macau **6** Moulis **7** Labarde, Margaux, Pomerol **8** Cantenac, St. Julien, Pauillac **9** St. Emilion, St. Estèphe, St. Laurent ***red:* 6** claret

bordello see **brothel**

border 3 hem, lip, rim **4** abut, brim, edge, join, line, pale, trim **5** bound, brink, flank, frame, limit, march, skirt, touch, verge **6** adjoin, bounds, butt on, define, fringe, limbus, margin, trench **7** contour, outline, selvage **8** approach, boundary, frontier, neighbor, sideline, surround **9** marchland, perimeter, periphery **11** butt against, communicate ***heraldry:* 4** orle ***inlaid:* 8** purfling ***raised:* 7** coaming

bordereau 4 note **6** record **7** account **10** memorandum

bordering 4 nigh **5** close **6** almost, next to **7** meeting, verging **8** abutting, adjacent, touching **9** adjoining, alongside, close upon, impinging **10** approximal, contiguous, juxtaposed **11** coterminous, neighboring, practically

borderland 5 march **6** fringe, margin **8** frontier **9** marchland

borderline 4 pale **6** almost, nearly **7** dubious, unclear **8** boundary, doubtful, marginal, unstable **9** ambiguous, debatable, dubitable, equivocal, perimeter, uncertain, undecided, unsettled **11** demarcation, problematic **12** intermediate **13** indeterminate

border state 8 Delaware, Kentucky, Maryland, Missouri, Virginia

bore 3 irk **4** drag, drip, mine, peer, pill, ream, sink, tire, yawn **5** auger, drill, drone, gouge, prick, punch **6** burrow, pierce, tunnel **7** bromide, caliber, fatigue **8** diameter, puncture **9** penetrate, perforate, soporific **10** dullsville

boreal 3 icy **4** cold, cool **5** chill, gelid, polar **6** arctic, bitter, chilly, frosty, frigid, tundra **7** glacial, wintery **8** freezing, northern **9** northerly

Boreas *beloved:* 8 Orithyia ***brother:* 5** Notus **8** Hesperus, Zephyrus ***father:* 8** Astraeus ***mother:* 3** Eos ***son:* 5** Zetes **6** Calais

boredom 5 blahs, ennui **6** apathy, stupor, tedium, torpor **7** fatigue **8** doldrums, dullness, flatness, monotony **9** lassitude, weariness **11** incuriosity, tediousness **12** indifference

Borges work 5 Aleph (The) **10** Labyrinths

Borgia 4 Juan **6** Alonso, Cesare **7** Alfonso, Rodrigo **8** Lucrezia

boring 3 dry **4** arid, drab, dull, flat, zero **5** ho-hum, vapid **6** dreary, stodgy, tiring **7** humdrum, tedious **8** bromidic, drudging, lifeless, tiresome **9** wearisome **10** lackluster, lacklustre, monotonous, pedestrian, unexciting **13** uninteresting

boring tool 5 drill, auger **6** trepan

Boris Godunov composer 10 Mussorgsky (Modest) **11** Moussorgsky (Modest)

born 3 née **6** innate, native **8** destined, inherent **9** intrinsic **10** congenital, deep-seated ***combining form:* 3** gen **4** gene **6** genous **7** genetic

borne by the wind 6 aeolic, eolian **7** aeolian

Borneo *ethnic group:* 4 Dyak **5** Dayak ***mountain:* 8** Kinabalu ***nation:* 6** Brunei ***river:* 6** Rabang

Born Free *author:* 7 Adamson (Joy) ***lion:* 4** Elsa

Borodin opera 10 Prince Igor

borough 4 town **5** burgh **7** village **8** township

bosh see **bunkum**

Bosnia-Herzegovina *capital:* 8 Sarajevo ***language:* 7** Serbian **8** Croatian **13** Serbo-Croatian ***monetary unit:* 4** mark **5** dinar ***neighbor:* 6** Serbia **7** Croatia ***part of:* 7** Balkans ***sea:* 8** Adriatic

bosom 4 bust, core, soul, teat **5** chest, close, heart **6** breast **7** embrace **8** feelings, intimate **10** affections, conscience

bosomy 5 built, busty, buxom, curvy **6** chesty, zaftig **7** shapely, stacked **9** Junoesque **11** full-figured

boss 4 capo, head, stud **5** chief, neato **6** direct, honcho, leader, manage, master, survey, worthy **7** command, foreman, headman, oversee **8** director, employer, overlook, overseer, superior **9** chieftain, excellent, first-rate, supervise **10** supervisor, taskmaster **11** superintend ***African:* 5** bwana

bossy 3 cow **4** calf **7** studded **8** despotic, imperial **9** arbitrary, assertive, imperious, masterful **10** autocratic, high-handed, imperative, oppressive, peremptory, tyrannical **11** controlling, dictatorial, domineering, magisterial, overbearing

botanist ***American:*** **4** Gray (Asa) **5** Sears (Paul B.) **6** Bailey (Liberty), Bessey (Charles), Carver (George Washington) **7** Bartram (John, William), Burbank (Luther) **9** Fairchild (David) ***Austrian:*** **6** Mendel (Gregor) ***British:*** **6** Sloane (Sir Hans) ***Danish:*** **7** Warming (Johannes) ***Dutch:*** **7** De Vries (Hugo) ***French:*** **7** Lamarck (Chevalier de) ***German:*** **4** Cohn (Ferdinand), Mohl (Hugo von) **5** Sachs (Julius von) ***Irish:*** **6** Harvey (William) ***Scottish:*** **5** Brown (Robert) ***Swedish:*** **8** Linnaeus (Carolus) ***Swiss:*** **6** Nägeli (Karl) **8** Candolle (Augustin)

botany branch **7** ecology **8** algology, bryology, mycology **9** phycology **10** morphology, palynology, physiology **11** hydroponics, paleobotany, pteridology, systematics **12** bacteriology

botch **4** blow, flop, flub, foul, goof, mess, muck, muff, ruin **5** fluff, gum up, misdo, mix-up, snafu, snarl, spoil **6** bobble, boggle, bollix, bumble, bungle, fiasco, fumble, goof up, mess up, muddle **7** balls-up, blunder, confuse, louse up, washout **8** bugger up, disaster, disorder, dishevel, mishmash, shambles **9** mishandle, mismanage, patchwork **10** discompose, hodgepodge, misconduct

botchy **5** messy **6** blowsy, blowzy, frowsy, frowzy, sloppy, untidy **7** chaotic **8** careless, confused, slapdash, slipshod, slovenly

both ***combining form:*** **3** bis ***prefix:*** **4** ambi, amph **5** amphi

bother **3** ado, bug, irk, nag, vex **4** drag, fret, fuss, gall, pest, pain **5** annoy, eat at, harry, trial, upset **6** badger, flurry, harass, needle, pester, plague, ruffle **7** afflict, agitate, anxiety, bedevil, concern, disturb, fluster, perturb, provoke, torment, trouble **8** disquiet, headache, irritant, nuisance, vexation **9** aggravate, annoyance **10** discompose, exasperate, irritation **11** aggravation, intrude upon **12** exasperation **13** inconvenience

botheration **4** damn, pain, pest **5** trial **6** plague **7** torment **8** headache, irritant, nuisance, vexation **9** annoyance **10** difficulty, irritation **11** aggravation, provocation **12** exasperation **13** inconvenience

Botswana ***capital:*** **8** Gaborone ***city:*** **11** Francistown ***desert:*** **8** Kalahari ***former name:*** **12** Bechuanaland ***language:*** **6** Tswana ***monetary unit:*** **4** pula ***neighbor:*** **7** Namibia **8** Zimbabwe **11** South Africa ***river:*** **5** Chobe **6** Molopo **7** Limpopo **8** Okavango

bottle **4** vial **5** cruet, cruse, flask, phial **6** ampule, carafe, fiasco, flacon, magnum, vessel **7** ampoule **8** decanter, jeroboam **9** container

bottle gourd **8** calabash

bottleneck **5** choke **6** hinder, impede, narrow **7** impasse **8** obstacle, obstruct, paralyze, slowdown, throttle **9** hindrance **10** choke point, congestion, traffic jam **11** obstruction

bottom **3** bum **4** base, boat, core, foot, root, pith, rump, seat, ship, sole, soul, tail, tush **5** basal, basic, basis, fanny, found, nadir **6** behind, breech, heinie, lowest, source **7** bedrock, essence, footing, primary, rear end **8** backside, buttocks, derriere, pedestal, pediment **9** establish, fundament, lowermost, posterior, predicate, principle, underbody, undermost, underside **10** foundation, nethermost, underbelly, underlying, underneath **11** fundamental, lowest point **12** undersurface

bottomless **4** deep, vast **7** abysmal, endless **8** baseless, enduring, profound, unending **9** boundless, unlimited **10** groundless, unfillable, ungrounded **11** everlasting, inestimable, never-ending **12** immeasurable, incalculable, unfathomable **13** inexhaustible

bottommost **4** last **5** least **6** lowest **7** deepest

bough **3** arm **4** limb **5** shoot **6** branch **8** offshoot

boulder **4** rock

boulevard **4** road **6** artery, avenue, street **7** terrace **8** main drag **9** esplanade, promenade **10** high street **12** thoroughfare

boulevardier **7** flaneur, trifler **9** bon vivant **10** aficionado, dilettante **11** cognoscente, connoisseur **12** man-about-town

bounce **2** ax **3** axe, can, hop, pep, vim, zip **4** fire, jump, leap, oust, sack, zest **5** expel, vault, verve, vigor **6** energy, hurdle, spirit, spring **7** bluster, boot out, dismiss, kick out, rebound, saltate, sparkle **8** buoyancy, ricochet, vitality **9** animation, discharge, eliminate, terminate **10** ebullience, elasticity, liveliness

bounce back **5** rally **6** perk up, pick up, recoil, return, revive **7** cheer up, improve, rebound, recover **8** backfire **9** boomerang **10** recuperate, turn around

bounce off **5** carom **7** rebound **8** ricochet

bouncer **4** goon **5** guard **8** houseman, sentinel, watchman **9** muscleman

bouncing ball game **5** jacks

bouncy **3** gay **4** airy **5** peppy, perky **6** blithe, cheery, jaunty, jocund, lively **7** buoyant, elastic **8** animated, volatile **9** ebullient, energetic, expansive, exuberant, resilient, sprightly **10** unsinkable **12** effervescent, high-spirited **13** irrepressible

bound 3 end, hem, hop, rim **4** bolt, edge, jump, leap, term, skip **5** caper, frisk, hem in, limit, skirt, vault, verge **6** border, bounce, define, demark, driven, finite, fringe, gambol, hurdle, margin, spring, sprint **7** confine, delimit, enclose, hotfoot, limited, mark out, obliged, pledged, rebound, saltate **8** articled, beholden, confined, confines, enslaved, resolved, restrain, surround **9** compelled, demarcate, obligated **10** determined, indentured, limitation **11** apprenticed, responsible **12** circumscribe

boundary 3 hem **4** mete, pale **5** ambit, limit **6** limits, margin **7** compass, outline **8** confines, environs, purlieus **9** perimeter, precincts **10** borderline **11** demarcation **13** circumference

bounder 3 cad, cur, dog **4** boor, worm **5** knave, louse, rogue **6** rascal, rotter

boundless 4 vast **5** great **7** endless **8** infinite **9** excessive, limitless, unbounded, unlimited **10** indefinite, unconfined, unmeasured **11** illimitable, measureless **12** immeasurable, unrestricted **13** inexhaustible, unsurpassable

bounteous 5 ample **6** benign, lavish **7** copious, liberal, profuse **8** abundant, generous, handsome, prodigal **9** bountiful, capacious, expansive, extensive, plenteous, plentiful, unsparing **10** beneficent, big-hearted, freehanded, munificent, openhanded, voluminous **11** magnanimous, overflowing

bountiful see **bounteous**

bounty 5 grant, prize, yield **6** deluge, plenty, reward, wealth **7** payment, premium **8** plethora, richness **9** abundance, affluence, plenitude, profusion **10** cornucopia, generosity, inducement, liberality, luxuriance, prosperity **11** benevolence, copiousness **12** compensation

Bounty ***captain:*** **5** Bligh (William) ***event:*** **6** mutiny ***first mate:*** **9** Christian (Fletcher) ***letters:*** **3** HMS

bouquet 4 balm, kudo, odor, posy **5** aroma, kudos, scent, spice, spray **6** eulogy, medley **7** acclaim, corsage, essence, garland, incense, nosegay, perfume **8** accolade, encomium **9** fragrance, redolence **10** compliment **11** arrangement, boutonniere **12** commendation

bourgeois 7 burgher **8** ordinary **10** conformist, philistine **11** middle-class **12** conventional

bourgeoisie 11 middle class, third estate

Bourne Identity author 6 Ludlum (Robert)

bout 3 jag, run **4** game, meet, term, tour, turn **5** match, round, shift, siege, spell, spasm, spree, stint, throe, trick **6** attack **7** contest, session **8** outbreak **9** smackdown **10** engagement

boutique 4 shop **8** emporium

bovine 2 ox **3** cow, yak **4** anoa, bull, calf, gaur, neat, zebu **5** bison, steer, stirk **6** heifer, placid, torpid, wisent **7** aurochs, banteng, buffalo, bullock, cowlike **8** longhorn ***genus:*** **3** Bos ***sound:*** **3** low, moo

bow 3 arc, bob, dip, nod **4** arch, bend, knot, lout, prow, turn **5** angle, crook, curve, debut, defer, hunch, round, stoop, yield **6** archer, congee, curtsy, give in, kowtow, relent, salaam, salute, submit **7** concede, curtsey, flexure, incline, rainbow, succumb, turning **9** curvation, curvature, genuflect, obeisance, surrender **10** capitulate **11** buckle under **12** knuckle under ***ornament:*** **10** figurehead

Bow, Clara 6 It girl

bowdlerize 4 blip, edit **6** censor, excise, purify, screen **7** abridge, cleanse, distort, launder **8** sanitize **9** expurgate **10** adulterate, blue-pencil

bowed 4 bent **5** arced, bandy **6** arched, curved **11** bandy-legged, curvilinear

bowel 3 gut **6** paunch **9** intestine

bower 5 arbor **6** anchor **7** enclose, pergola, retreat **9** apartment

bowery 7 skid row

bowfin 4 amia **7** mudfish

bowl 5 arena, basin, jorum, mazer, stade, tazza **6** tureen, vessel **7** stadium **8** coliseum **12** amphitheater

bowlegged 5 bandy

bowler 3 hat **5** derby **6** kegler

Bowl game 5 Super ***Abilene:*** **5** Pecan ***Anaheim:*** **7** Freedom ***Atlanta:*** **5** Peach ***Dallas:*** **6** Cotton ***El Paso:*** **3** Sun ***Fresno:*** **10** California ***Honolulu:*** **5** Aloha ***Houston:*** **10** Bluebonnet ***Jacksonville:*** **5** Gator ***Memphis:*** **7** Liberty ***Miami:*** **6** Orange **8** Carquest ***Mobile:*** **6** Senior ***New Orleans:*** **5** Sugar ***Orlando:*** **13** Florida Citrus ***Pasadena:*** **4** Rose ***San Diego:*** **7** Holiday ***Shreveport:*** **12** Independence ***Tampa:*** **10** Hall of Fame ***Tempe:*** **6** Fiesta ***Tucson:*** **6** Copper

bowling 7 kegling ***British:*** **8** skittles ***Italian:*** **5** bocce, bocci **6** boccie ***term:*** **3** pin **4** hook, lane, spot **5** curve, frame, spare, split **6** gutter, strike, string, turkey **7** duckpin **9** candlepin

bowl over 3 awe, wow **4** daze, fell, stun **5** floor, shock, throw **6** boggle, dismay **7** astound, flatten, impress, stupefy **8** blow away, surprise **9** bring down, dumbfound, knock down, overwhelm **10** disconcert

bow out 4 exit, fold, quit **5** leave, welsh **6** beg off, give up, retire **8** withdraw **9** surrender

box 3 bin **4** case, cell, chop, cuff, duke, inro, loge, slap, sock, spar **5** booth, chest, clout, crate, fight, punch, smack, stall, trunk **6** buffet, carton, casket, coffer, coffin, encase, hopper, packet **7** confine, enclose, package **9** container, enclosure, rectangle **10** pigeonhole, receptacle **11** compartment

boxer 7 fighter, palooka **8** pugilist **9** flyweight **11** heavyweight, lightweight **12** bantamweight, middleweight, welterweight **13** featherweight ***champ:*** **3** Ali (Muhammad) **4** Bowe (Riddick) **5** Bruno (Frank), Jones (Roy), Lewis (Lennox), Louis (Joe), Moore (Archie), Tyson (Mike) **6** Hagler (Marvin), Hearns (Thomas), Holmes (Larry), McCall (Oliver), Moorer (Michael), Seldon (Bruce), Spinks (Leon, Michael), Tunney (Gene), Walker (Mickey) **7** Charles (Ezzard), Corbett (James), Dempsey (Jack), Douglas (Buster), Foreman (George), Frazier (Joe), Johnson (Jack), LaMotta (Jake), Leonard (Sugar Ray), Sharkey (Jack), Walcott (Joe), Willard (Jess) **8** de la Hoya (Oscar), Marciano (Rocky), Robinson (Sugar Ray), Sullivan (John L.) **9** Armstrong (Henry), Holyfield (Evander), Klitschko (Vitali, Wladimir), Patterson (Floyd), Schmeling (Max)

boxing 8 pugilism **10** fisticuffs **13** prizefighting ***term:*** **2** KO **3** jab, TKO **4** blow, bout, duck, foul, hook, kayo, ring, rope, spar **5** break, count, feint, glove, match, parry, punch, round, swing **6** bucket, canvas, corner **7** low blow, referee **8** heavy bag, knockout, uppercut **9** knockdown **11** punching bag

boy 3 lad, son, tad **5** gamin, puppy, sonny **6** laddie, nipper, shaver **9** shaveling, stripling, youngster ***combining form:*** **3** ped **4** paed, paid, pedo **5** paedo, paido ***errand:*** **5** gofer **8** lobbygow ***French:*** **6** garçon ***Italian:*** **7** ragazzo ***Latin:*** **4** puer ***mischievous:*** **6** urchin ***Spanish:*** **4** niño **8** muchacho

boyfriend 4 beau **5** swain **6** fiancé, old man, suitor **7** main man **9** inamorato

Boy Scout ***founder:*** **11** Baden-Powell (Robert) ***gathering:*** **8** jamboree ***motto:*** **10** be prepared ***rank:*** **4** Life (Scout), Star (Scout) **5** Eagle (Scout) **10** Tenderfoot ***unit:*** **5** troop **6** patrol

Boys Town ***founder:*** **8** Flanagan (Edward) ***star:*** **6** Crosby (Bing) ***state:*** **8** Nebraska

bozo 3 oaf **4** boob, clod, dodo, dolt, dope, fool, goof, jerk, mutt, simp, yo-yo **5** chump, dummy, dunce, idiot, moron, ninny, noddy, stupe **6** dimwit, donkey, dum-dum, nitwit, noodle **7** airhead, dullard, pinhead **8** bonehead, clodpoll, dumbbell, dumbhead, imbecile, lunkhead, meathead, numskull **9** birdbrain, blockhead, ignoramus, lamebrain, numbskull, simpleton, thickhead **10** dunderhead, hammerhead, nincompoop **11** chowderhead, chucklehead, knucklehead

B.P.O.E. member 3 Elk

Brabantio's daughter 9 Desdemona

brabble 3 row **4** beef, feud, flap, riot, spat, tiff **5** argue, scrap, set to **6** bicker, blowup, fracas, grouse **7** dispute, fall out, palaver, quarrel, rhubarb, scuffle, wrangle **8** argument, squabble **9** altercate, bickering, brannigan, caterwaul, wrangling **10** falling-out **11** altercation, disputation, embroilment

brace 3 arm, bar, duo, tie **4** dyad, gird, pair, prop, stay **5** clamp, ready, shore, steel, strut, truss **6** accost, bear up, column, couple, demand, splint, steady, uphold **7** bolster, bracket, enliven, fortify, freshen, prepare, refresh, shore up, support, sustain, tighten, twosome **8** buttress **9** reinforce **10** cantilever, exhilarate, invigorate, strengthen **12** underpinning **13** underpropping

bracelet 6 bangle **7** manacle **8** wristlet

bracing 4 keen **5** brisk, crisp, fresh, nippy, sharp, tonic **6** biting, chilly **7** rousing **8** stirring **9** animating **10** energizing, quickening **11** restorative, stimulating, stimulative **12** exhilarating, invigorating

bracken 4 fern **5** brake, brush, scrub **11** undergrowth

bracket 3 arm **4** join, link, omit **5** brace **6** couple, relate, remove **7** combine, compare, conjoin, connect, embrace, enclose, include, support **8** buttress, encircle, leave out, put aside, set aside **9** associate, encompass **11** parenthesis **12** strengthener

brackish 4 sour **5** acrid, briny, salty **6** saline, salted **9** repulsive, sickening **10** nauseating

bract 4 leaf **5** glume **6** paleat, spathe **8** phyllary

brad 4 nail

Bradamant ***brother:*** **7** Rinaldo ***husband:*** **6** Rogero **8** Ruggiero

Bradbury, Ray ***forte:*** **5** sci-fi **7** fantasy ***work:*** **13** Dandelion Wine **14** Illustrated Man (The) **17** Martian Chronicles (The)

Brady Bunch ***actor:*** **4** Reed (Robert) **5** Davis (Ann B.), Olsen (Susan), Plumb (Eve) **6** Knight (Christopher) **8** Williams (Barry) **9** Henderson (Florence), McCormick (Maureen) **10** Lookinland (Mike) ***character:*** **3**

Jan **4** Greg **5** Alice, Bobby, Cindy, Peter, Tiger **6** Marcia **9** Mike Brady ***creator:*** **8** Schwartz (Sherwood)

brae 4 bank, hill **5** slope **8** hillside

brag 3 gas **4** blow, crow, puff **5** boast, mouth, prate, vaunt **7** show off, swagger, talk big **9** cockiness, gasconade **10** grandstand **11** rodomontade

braggadocio 6 hot air **7** boaster, bombast, bravado, conceit, puffery, swagger, windbag **8** blowhard, boasting, braggart, bragging **9** arrogance, cockiness, pomposity **10** cockalorum, pretension, swaggering **11** fanfaronade

braggart 6 blower **7** boaster, egotist, vaunter, windbag **8** big mouth, blowhard **9** big talker, know-it-all, swaggerer, vulgarian **11** braggadocio

Brahmin 8 highbrow **9** blueblood, patrician **10** aristocrat

braid 4 plat **5** plait, queue **7** galloon, pigtail **8** soutache **9** interlace **10** intertwine, interweave

brain 3 wit **4** bean, conk, mind **7** concuss **9** intellect **10** gray matter **12** intelligence ***bone:*** **5** skull **7** cranium ***channel:*** **4** iter ***clot:*** **10** thrombosis ***gland:*** **6** pineal **9** pituitary ***layer:*** **6** cortex ***lobe:*** **6** limbic, vermis **7** frontal **8** parietal, temporal **9** occipital ***membrane:*** **3** pia **4** dura **6** meninx **8** pia mater **9** arachnoid, dura mater ***part:*** **4** lobe **6** fornix **7** medulla **8** cerebrum, thalamus **9** sensorium, ventricle **10** cerebellum, hemisphere **12** diencephalon ***relating to:*** **8** cerebral **10** encephalic ***ridge:*** **4** gyri (plural) **5** gyrus ***scan:*** **3** EEG, MEG, MRI, PET ***vertebrate:*** **10** encephalon ***wave record:*** **3** EEG

brainchild 4 idea, opus, work **6** animus, scheme, theory **7** coinage **9** handiwork, invention **10** hypothesis, innovation **11** achievement, chef-d'oeuvre, contrivance

brainiac 3 wiz **4** whiz **6** genius **7** prodigy

brainless 3 dim **5** dense, silly, thick **6** simple, stupid **7** asinine, foolish, idiotic, moronic, vacuous, witless **9** dim-witted, nitwitted **10** acephalous **12** feebleminded

brainpower 3 wit **5** sense **6** smarts **8** aptitude, capacity, sagacity **9** intellect, mentality, mother wit **10** perception **11** discernment, penetration **12** intelligence **13** comprehension

brains 4 mind **6** smarts **9** intellect **12** intelligence

brainsick 3 mad **4** daft **5** batty, crazy, manic, potty **6** crazed, insane, mental **7** cracked, haywire, lunatic **8** aberrant, demented, deranged, maniacal, unhinged **9** bedlamite, delirious, disturbed **10** disordered, incoherent, irrational, unbalanced

brainstorm 3 rap, jaw **4** idea **6** confer, huddle **7** discuss, dream up, think up **8** cogitate, mull over **9** mental fit **10** groupthink, kick around, toss around **11** inspiration, put together

brainteaser 5 poser, rebus **6** puzzle, riddle **7** stumper **9** conundrum **10** cryptogram

brainwashing 10 propaganda **11** mind control, reeducation

brainy 4 keen **5** quick, savvy, sharp, smart **6** adroit, astute, bright, clever **9** eggheaded, brilliant, sagacious **10** discerning, precocious **11** intelligent, quick-witted, ready-witted **13** knowledgeable, perspicacious

brake 4 curb, slow, stop **5** block **6** damper, hinder, impede, retard, slough **7** barrier, bracken, slacken **8** blockade, obstacle, obstruct, slow down **9** deterrent, hindrance **10** constraint, decelerate **11** bracken fern

bramble 4 burr **5** brier, furze, gorse, hedge, shrub, thorn **6** nettle **7** thistle

branch 3 arm, leg **4** fork, limb, rami (plural), spur, wing **5** bough, ramus **6** office, ramify **7** chapter, diverge, outpost **8** division **9** tributary **10** subsidiary

branched 6 ramate, ramose

brand 4 blot, blur, logo, make, mark, onus, sear, slur, sort, spot, type **5** badge, class, odium, stain, stamp, sword, taint, torch **6** accuse, charge, impute, stigma, stripe **7** species, variety **8** black eye, disgrace, insignia, logotype **9** trademark **10** stigmatize

brandish 4 wave **5** flash, shake, sport, swing, wield **6** flaunt, parade **7** display, exhibit, show off **8** flourish

brand-new 4 mint **5** fresh **6** latest, unused, virgin **8** up-to-date **9** untouched **11** cutting-edge **13** inexperienced

brandy 4 marc, ouzo, raki **5** Pisco **6** cognac, grappa, kirsch, Metaxa **7** liqueur **8** Armagnac, calvados, digestif, eau-de-vie **9** applejack, framboise, slivovitz ***cocktail:*** **7** sidecar, stinger **9** Alexander

brannigan 3 row **4** bust, flap, spat, tiff **5** binge, fight, set-to, spree **6** bender, blowup, hassle, ruckus **7** brabble, discord, dispute, quarrel, wassail, wrangle **8** squabble **10** falling-out **11** altercation

brash 4 bold, flip, pert **5** cocky, gutsy, hasty, nervy, saucy **6** brassy, brazen, cheeky, madcap, uppish, uppity **7** brittle, forward **8** arrogant, cocksure, flippant, impudent, insolent, reckless, tactless **9** audacious, bumptious, ebullient, energetic, exuberant, hot-headed, impetuous, impolitic, maladroit, unabashed, untactful **10** ill-advised, incautious **11** overweening, thoughtless **12** high-spirited, presumptuous, undiplomatic, unrestrained **13** disrespectful, inconsiderate, irrepressible, self-assertive

brashness 4 gall, grit, guts **5** brass, cheek, crust, nerve, pluck **6** aplomb, daring, mettle, spirit **8** audacity, chutzpah, temerity **9** assurance **10** confidence, effrontery **11** presumption

brass 4 gall **5** cheek, nerve **8** audacity, chutzpah **9** brashness, impudence, insolence **10** confidence, effrontery **11** presumption **12** impertinence

brassbound 3 set **5** brash, rigid **6** brazen, narrow **7** adamant, bigoted, forward **8** obdurate **9** illiberal, presuming, obstinate, unbending **10** implacable, inflexible, intolerant, relentless, unswayable, unyielding **11** opinionated, small-minded, unrelenting **12** narrow-minded, presumptuous, single-minded **13** dyed-in-the-wool, self-asserting, self-assertive

brasserie 10 restaurant

brass hat 3 VIP **4** boss **5** elder **6** better, senior **7** big shot **8** big whell, higher-up, superior

brassica 4 kale, rape **5** colza **6** turnip **7** cabbage, mustard **8** broccoli, collards, kohlrabi, rutabaga **11** cauliflower

brass tacks 5 facts **7** details **11** nitty-gritty, particulars

brass worker 7 brazier

brassy see **brazen**

brat 3 imp **4** punk **6** urchin **10** holy terror

bravado 5 bluff **6** hot air **7** bluster, bombast **8** audacity, boasting, boldness, bragging, defiance, vaunting **9** gasconade **10** blustering, pretension, swaggering **11** braggadocio, grandiosity **12** boastfulness

brave 4 bold, dare, defy, face, game, meet, risk **5** beard, gutsy, hardy, manly, nervy, noble, stout **6** daring, heroic, manful, plucky, spunky, take on **7** defiant, doughty, gallant, valiant, venture **8** confront, face down, fearless, intrepid, reckless, resolute, spirited, splendid, stalwart, unafraid, valorous **9** audacious, challenge, dauntless, excellent, steadfast, undaunted, withstand **10** courageous **11** boldhearted, indomitable, lionhearted, undauntable, unflinching, venturesome **12** stouthearted **13** adventuresome

Brave New World author 6 Huxley (Aldous)

bravery 4 grit, guts **5** nerve, pluck, valor **6** daring, mettle, spirit **7** courage, heroism **8** audacity, boldness, temerity **9** derring-do, fortitude, gallantry **11** intrepidity **12** fearlessness, intrepidness ***false:*** **7** bravado

bravo 3 olé **4** euge, rave, thug **5** cheer **6** encore, gunman, hit man, killer **7** ovation, plaudit, villain **8** applause, assassin **9** desperado

bravura 4 bold **5** showy **6** daring, florid, ornate **8** dazzling, skillful, virtuoso **9** brilliant

brawl 3 row **4** feud, flap, fray, fuss, maul, riot, spar, spat, tiff **5** clash, broil, fight, melee, scrap, set-to **6** affray, battle, bicker, dustup, fracas, rumble, tussle **7** bobbery, brabble, contend, quarrel, rhubarb, ruction, scuffle, wrangle **8** dogfight, skirmish, slugfest **9** fistfight, imbroglio, scrimmage **10** donnybrook, fisticuffs, free-for-all **11** altercation, disturbance

brawn 4 beef, meat, thew **5** clout, flesh, might, power, sinew **6** muscle **8** strength **9** puissance **10** headcheese

brawny 5 beefy, burly, husky, lusty, tough **6** robust, sinewy, stocky, strong, sturdy **8** athletic, muscular, powerful, thickset, vigorous **9** strapping, well-built **10** able-bodied

bray 4 mill **5** crush, grind, pound **6** bellow, hee-haw, pestle, powder **7** atomize, trumpet **9** pulverize

brazen 4 bold, loud **5** brash, gaudy, noisy, showy **6** arrant, brassy, cheeky **7** blatant, defiant, forward, glaring, jarring **8** flagrant, impudent, insolent **9** audacious, barefaced, obtrusive, shameless, unabashed **10** outrageous, procacious, unblushing **11** conspicuous, impertinent **12** contumelious, presumptuous **13** disrespectful

Brazil *capital:* 8 Brasília ***city:* 5** Belém **6** Recife **8** Salvador, São Paulo **12** Rio de Janeiro **13** Belo Horizonte ***discoverer:* 6** Cabral (Pedro) ***island:* 6** Marajó **7** Caviana ***language:* 10** Portuguese ***monetary unit:* 4** real ***neighbor:* 4** Peru **6** Guyana **7** Bolivia, Uruguay **8** Colombia, Paraguay, Suriname **9** Argentina, Venezuela **12** French Guiana ***river:* 4** Pará **6** Amazon **8** Parnaíba **10** Alto Paraná **12** São Francisco ***state:* 4** Acre, Pará **5** Amapá, Bahia, Ceará, Goiás, Piauí **6** Paraná

breach 3 gap **4** gash, hole, leap, open, rent, rift, slit **5** break, chasm, cleft, crack, split **6** hiatus, lacuna, schism **7** break in, discord, disrupt, fissure, infract, interim, opening, rupture, violate **8** aperture, disunity, division, fracture, infringe, interval, trespass **9** disregard, severance, violation **10** alienation, contravene, infraction, separation, transgress **11** delinquency, dereliction **12** disaffection, disobedience, estrangement, infringement, interruption **13** contravention, discontinuity, noncompliance, nonobservance, transgression

bread 3 bun **4** food, pita, rusk, wrap **5** bagel, money, scone, toast **6** living, muffin, sippet **7** biscuit, crouton, edibles, stollen **8** victuals, zwieback **9** provender **10** livelihood, provisions, sustenance **11** comestibles, maintenance, subsistence ***communion:*** **4** host **5** wafer **9** Eucharist ***from heaven:*** **5** manna ***ingredient:*** **4** meal **5** flour, yeast **6** leaven ***Jewish:*** **5** matzo **6** hallah, matzoh **7** challah ***maker:*** **5** baker ***Scottish:*** **7** bannock ***spread:*** **3** jam **4** oleo **5** jelly **6** butter **9** margarine ***unleavened:*** **5** matzo **6** matzoh

bread and butter 4 keep, work **6** basics, living **7** support **8** mainstay, victuals **10** employment, livelihood, occupation, sustenance **9** nutriment **11** maintenance, necessities, subsistence **12** alimentation

breadbasket 3 gut **5** belly, tummy **6** paunch **7** abdomen, stomach **8** potbelly **9** bay window, beer belly

breadth 4 area, size, span **5** range, reach, scope, space, sweep, width **6** extent, spread **7** compass, expanse, stretch **8** distance, fullness, latitude, vastness, wideness **9** amplitude, expansion, magnitude **10** liberality

break 3 gap **4** bust, dash, halt, knap, leak, luck, rest, rift, ruin, tame **5** burst, clear, crack, inure, sever, solve, spell **6** breach, chance, decode, divide, escape, exceed, hiatus, impair, lacuna, refute, relief, reveal **7** destroy, divulge, fall out, interim, lighten, opening, respite, rupture, shatter, surpass, suspend, take ten, time-out, violate **8** accustom, bankrupt, breather, decipher, disclose, division, downtime, fracture, good luck, interval, moderate, take five **9** interlude, interrupt **10** annihilate, controvert, impoverish **11** discontinue, disjunction, dislocation, opportunity, suspensions **12** intermission, interruption **13** discontinuity

breakable 4 weak **5** frail **6** flimsy **7** brittle, fragile, friable **8** delicate **9** frangible

breakaway 4 prop **7** escapee **8** offshoot, renegade, seceding

break down 4 fail, fold, sort, wilt **5** class, decay, index **6** cave in, digest, give in **7** analyze, crumble, crumple, give out, give way, go crazy, succumb **8** classify, collapse, dissolve **9** anatomize, decompose, fall apart **12** disintegrate

breakdown 5 crash, decay, smash, study, wreck **6** mishap **7** crack-up, debacle, failure, smashup **8** analysis, collapse, taxonomy **9** cataclysm, partition **10** disruption, dissection, resolution **11** dysfunction, examination, prostration

breaker 4 wave **6** billow, comber, roller

Breakfast at Tiffany's author 6 Capote (Truman)

breakfront 7 cabinet **8** bookcase

break in 4 tame **5** train **6** breach, burgle, gentle, invade **7** intrude **8** initiate **9** condition, habituate, interfere, interpose, interrupt

breakneck 4 fast **5** fleet, hasty, quick, rapid, swift **6** racing, speedy, unsafe **8** meteoric **10** harefooted **11** precipitous

break off 3 end **4** drop, halt, kill, stop **5** abort, cease, scrub, sever **6** cancel, detach **7** curtail, scratch, suspend **8** cut short **9** terminate **11** discontinue

break out 4 bolt, flee **5** arise, erupt, flare **6** emerge, escape **7** explode **8** mushroom, separate

break through 5 burst **6** breach, emerge, pierce **7** rupture, surface **8** overcome **9** penetrate

breakthrough 4 find, gain, hike, leap, rise **5** boost **7** advance, radical, upgrade **8** advanced, increase, landmark **9** invention, milestone **10** avant-garde, innovation **11** cutting-edge, development, exceptional, progressive, quantum leap

break up 3 end **4** halt, knap, part **6** divide, sunder **7** destroy, disband, disjoin, disrupt, rupture, scatter, shatter **8** disperse, dissever, dissolve, disunite, separate **9** decompose, dismantle, pulverize, terminate **12** disintegrate

breakup 4 rift **5** split **7** divorce, parting **8** analysis **9** dispersal **10** dissection, separation **11** dissolution

breakwater 5 groin, jetty **7** seawall

breast 5 bosom, chest, heart ***animal:*** **7** brisket ***combining form:*** **3** maz **4** mast, mazo **5** masto, stern, steth **6** mastia (plural), sterno, stetho

breastbone 7 sternum

breast-feed 5 nurse **6** suckle **7** nourish

breastwork 7 barrier, bastion, bulwark, defense, parapet, rampart **9** barricade, earthwork **10** embankment **13** fortification, reinforcement

breath 4 gasp, gust, hint, puff **5** let-up, pause, trace, whiff **6** breeze **7** respite **10** exhalation, inhalation, suggestion

breathe 4 emit, sigh **5** exude, utter, voice **6** endure, exhale, expire, inhale, murmur **7** confide, express, give off, inspire, persist, radiate, respire, subsist, survive, whisper

breather 4 lull, rest, stay, vent **5** break, let-up, pause, spell **6** hiatus, recess **7** caesura, respite **8** downtime **9** remission **12** interruption

breathing ***labored:*** **7** dyspnea ***normal:*** **6** eupnea ***rapid:*** **8** polypnea

breathing apparatus 10 respirator ***underwater:*** **5** scuba

breathing orifice 4 nose **5** mouth **8** blowhole, spiracle

breathless 4 agog, avid, keen **5** eager **6** ardent **7** anxious, gasping, intense **8** gripping **9** expectant, impatient **11** short-winded **13** on tenterhooks

breathtaking 6 moving **7** awesome **8** dramatic, exciting, imposing, stunning, wondrous **9** panoramic, thrilling **10** impressive, staggering **11** astonishing, magnificent, spectacular **12** awe-inspiring, overwhelming **13** heart-stirring

Brecht play 4 Baal **13** Life of Galileo (The), Mother Courage **15** Seven Deadly Sins (The), Threepenny Opera (The) **20** Caucasian Chalk Circle (The)

breech 3 bum **4** duff, rear, rump, seat, tail **5** fanny **6** behind, bottom, heinie **7** keester, keister, rear end **8** backside, buttocks, derriere, haunches **9** fundament, posterior **12** hindquarters

breechclout 5 dhoti **9** loincloth

breed 3 ilk **4** bear, grow, kind, make, mate, race, rear, sire, sort, type **5** beget, brand, cause, class, cross, genus, hatch, likes, raise, stock, yield **6** couple, create, father, induce, nature, strain, stripe **7** bring up, develop, educate, lineage, nurture, produce, species, variety **8** copulate, engender, generate, mate with, multiply **9** cultivate, procreate, propagate, reproduce **10** discipline, extraction, give rise to, impregnate, inseminate

breeding 4 line **5** grace, taste **6** polish **7** culture, decorum, lineage, manners **8** ancestry, civility, courtesy, pedigree **9** genealogy, gentility, propriety **10** refinement, upbringing **11** cultivation

breeding ground 6 hotbed, origin **8** hothouse **10** forcing bed, mating spot **12** forcing house

breeze 3 zip **4** flit, sail, snap, waft **5** cinch, draft, waltz **6** zephyr **8** duck soup, kid stuff **10** child's play

breezy 4 airy, cool **5** fresh, gusty, windy **6** blithe, casual, drafty **7** offhand, relaxed **8** carefree, careless, detached, informal **9** easygoing **10** insouciant, nonchalant **11** unconcerned **12** devil-may-care, lighthearted

Breton 4 Celt

____ **breve 4** alla

breviary 5 brief **6** digest, précis **7** epitome, essence, outline, rundown, summary **8** abstract, boildown, synopsis **9** reduction **10** abridgment, conspectus, prayer book **11** abridgement **12** condensation, divine office

brevity 7 economy **8** laconism **9** briefness, concision, crispness, pithiness, shortness, terseness **10** transience

brew 3 ale, tea **4** beer, loom, mull, plan, plot, suds **5** drink, lager, stout **6** cook up, foment, gather, impend, infuse, porter, scheme, stir up **7** concoct, ferment **8** contrive

briar 4 burr, pipe **5** furze, gorse, shrub, thorn **6** nettle **7** bramble, thistle

Briareus 7 Aegaeon ***father:*** **6** Uranus ***mother:*** **4** Gaea

bribe 3 buy, fix, sop **6** buy off, payoff, payola, square, suborn **7** corrupt **9** incentive **10** enticement, inducement, tamper with

bric-a-brac 6 curios **8** trinkets **9** ornaments **10** objets d'art **11** gingerbread, knickknacks **13** embellishment

brick 5 block, gaffe **7** blunder ***layer:*** **5** mason ***laying:*** **7** masonry ***material:*** **4** clay, marl ***oven:*** **4** kiln ***row:*** **6** course ***sun-dried:*** **5** adobe ***toy:*** **4** Lego ***trough for carrying:*** **3** hod

bridal 7 nuptial, spousal **8** conjugal **9** connubial **11** matrimonial ***path:*** **5** aisle

bridal wreath 6 spirea

bridewell 3 can, jug, pen **4** coop, jail **5** clink, joint **6** lockup, prison **7** slammer **8** bastille **12** penitentiary

bridge 4 join, link, span **5** unite **7** connect **8** overpass, traverse ***great:*** **8** Brooklyn **10** Golden Gate ***kind:*** **4** arch, draw, rope **5** swing, truss **7** bascule, covered, natural, pontoon, trestle, viaduct **10** cantilever, suspension ***term:*** **3** bid **4** book, east, pass, ruff, slam, suit, void, west **5** bonus, dummy, north, raise, south, trick, trump **6** double, renege, rubber **7** auction, finesse, no-trump, overbid **8** contract, jump call, redouble **9** grand slam, overtrick, singleton **10** little slam, undertrick, vulnerable

bridgelike game 5 whist **6** hearts

bridle 3 bit **4** curb, fume, rein, rule **5** check, flare, quell **6** govern, halter, hold in, manage, master, rein in, ruffle, seethe, subdue **7** bristle, control, flare up, inhibit, repress **8** hold back, moderate, restrain, suppress, withhold **9** constrain, deterrent, hackamore, restraint

brief 4 curt **5** pithy, short, terse **6** abrupt, digest, inform **7** brusque, concise, epitome, laconic, outline, passing, summary **8** abstract, breviary, fleeting, succinct, synopsis

9 momentary, transient 10 abridgment, conspectus 11 abridgement, compendious 12 condensation 13 short and sweet

briefs alternative 6 boxers

brig 3 can, jug, pen 4 coop, jail 5 clink 6 cooler, lockup, prison 7 slammer 8 stockade 9 guardroom 10 guardhouse

brigade 4 army, unit 5 force, group 6 troops 10 contingent, detachment

brigand 6 bandit, bummer, looter, pirate, raider 7 cateran, corsair, forager, rustler 8 marauder, pillager 9 buccaneer, plunderer 10 freebooter, highwayman

brigandage 7 pillage, sacking 10 despoiling, ransacking 11 depredation

bright 4 fair, keen 5 aglow, alert, clear, light, lucid, quick, shiny, smart, sunny, vivid 6 brainy, cheery, clever, lively, lucent 7 beaming, blazing, flaming, fulgent, glowing, lambent, lighted, radiant, shining 8 cheerful, dazzling, gleaming, luminous, lustrous, sunshiny 9 brilliant, effulgent, favorable, refulgent, sparkling 10 auspicious, glittering, precocious, propitious, shimmering 11 illuminated, intelligent, quick-witted 12 incandescent 13 scintillating

brighten 4 buoy 5 cheer, clear, shine 6 look up, perk up, polish, revive, solace 7 burnish, cheer up, clear up, enhance, enliven, furbish, gladden, hearten, improve 8 illumine 10 illuminate

brightness 5 éclat, shine 6 luster, lustre 8 radiance, splendor 10 brilliance, effulgence, luminosity ***measure of:*** 3 lux 5 lumen 6 candle 7 candela 10 foot-candle

brilliance see **brightness**

brilliant 6 ablaze, brainy, genius, lucent, superb 7 beaming, fulgent, lambent, radiant, shining, stellar 8 dazzling, luminous, masterly, striking 9 effulgent, ingenious, refulgent, sparkling 10 glittering 11 exceptional 12 incandescent

brilliantine 6 pomade 9 hair cream

brim 3 hem, lip, rim 4 edge, fill, well 5 brink, skirt, verge, visor 6 border, fill up, fringe, margin 7 run over 8 overflow, well over 9 perimeter, periphery 13 circumference

brimming 4 full 5 awash, flush 6 filled, jammed, loaded, packed 7 crammed, crowded, replete, stuffed, teeming, welling 8 bursting, overfull, suffused, swarming, swelling 9 chock-full, jam-packed 11 chockablock, running over

brimstone 6 sulfur

brine 3 sea 4 deep, main 5 ocean 8 seawater 9 salt water

bring 3 lug 4 lead, pack, tote 5 carry, fetch, gross, yield 6 convey 7 attract, produce 9 transport

bring about 3 win 5 beget, cause 6 create, draw on, effect, secure 7 procure, produce, trigger 8 engender, generate, result in 10 accomplish, effectuate, give rise to

bring around 4 hook, sway, turn 7 convert, win over 8 convince, persuade, talk into 9 argue into, prevail on, sweet-talk 11 prevail upon

bring back 5 renew 6 recall, recoup, return, revive 7 recover, reprise, restore, salvage 8 retrieve, revivify 9 reinstate 10 repatriate 11 reestablish

bring down 3 bag, hew 4 drop, fell, raze 5 floor, level, shoot 6 defeat, depose, ground, humble, lay low, reduce 7 depress, flatten 8 demolish, overturn 9 humiliate, overthrow, prostrate, undermine

bring forth 4 bear 5 beget, yield 6 create, elicit, invent 7 deliver, produce 8 generate 9 propagate, reproduce 10 give rise to

bring forward 6 adduce, submit, tender, unveil 7 advance, present, produce, proffer 9 introduce

bring in 3 pay, net, win 4 draw, earn, gain, make, sell 5 fetch, gross, yield 6 garner, return, secure 7 acquire, be worth, realize 9 introduce

bring off 6 effect, finish, rescue 7 achieve, execute, realize, succeed 8 carry out 9 discharge, implement 10 accomplish, consummate, effectuate 12 carry through

bring out 4 cull 5 educe, utter, voice 6 elicit, reveal 7 declare, enhance, explain, extract 8 disclose, showcase 9 elucidate, highlight, introduce

bring together 3 mix, wed 4 herd, join, link, yoke 5 amass, batch, blend, group, marry, merge, rally, unify, unite 6 corral, muster 7 collect, compact, compile, convene, round up 8 assemble 9 aggregate, integrate, reconcile, stockpile 10 synthesize 11 consolidate

bring up 4 moot, rear 5 breed, raise, refer, teach, train, vomit 6 advert, allude, broach, foster, school 7 advance, educate, mention, nurture, propose, suggest, touch on 8 point out, instruct 9 cultivate, introduce 10 put forward 11 regurgitate

brink 3 hem, rim 4 bank, brim, edge 5 point, skirt, verge 6 border, fringe, margin 9 extremity, perimeter, periphery, threshold

briny 5 salty 6 saline

brio 3 pep, vim, zip 4 dash, élan, fire, life, zest, zing 5 ardor, flair, gusto, oomph, style, verve, vigor 6 bounce, esprit, fervor, spirit

7 panache, passion, sparkle 8 dynamism, vivacity 9 animation
brioche 4 roll
Briseis' lover 8 Achilles
brisk 4 busy, fast, keen, spry, yare 5 agile, fresh, nippy, quick, sharp, zippy 6 lively, nimble, snappy, speedy 7 bracing 8 animated, bustling, vigorous 9 energetic, sprightly 10 refreshing 11 stimulating 12 invigorating
bristle 4 boil, burn, fume, seta 5 anger, quill, setae (plural), spine 6 arista, chaeta, seethe 7 chaetae (plural) ***Scottish:*** 5 birse
bristle-like appendage 3 awn 4 seta 6 arista
British ***air force:*** 3 RAF ***cathedral city:*** 3 Ely 4 York 5 Ripon, Truro, Wells 6 Durham, Exeter 7 Chester, Lincoln 8 Coventry, Hereford, St. David's 9 Lichfield, Salisbury, Wakefield, Worcester 10 Canterbury, Gloucester ***Channel Island:*** 4 Sark 6 Jersey 8 Alderney, Guernsey ***coin, current:*** 5 pence (plural), penny, pound ***coin, old:*** 3 bob 5 crown, groat, noble 6 bawbee, florin, George, guinea, tanner, teston 8 farthing, shilling 9 halfcrown, halfpenny, sovereign 10 threepence ***colony, former:*** 4 Aden, Cape 5 Adana, Kenya, Malta, Natal 6 Ceylon, Cyprus, Gambia 7 Jamaica, Sarawak 9 Gold Coast, Singapore, Transvaal 10 Basutoland, New Zealand 11 Orange River, Sierra Leone 12 Bechuanaland ***county:*** 4 Avon, Kent, York 5 Derby, Devon, Essex, Gwent 6 Dorset, Durham, Oxford, Surrey, Sussex 7 Bedford, Cumbria, Norfolk, Rutland, Suffolk, Warwick 8 Cheshire, Cornwall, Hereford, Hertford, Somerset, Stafford 9 Berkshire, Cleveland, Hampshire, Lancaster, Leicester, Wiltshire, Worcester 10 Cumberland, Gloucester, Humberside, Lancashire, Merseyside, Shropshire 11 Westmorland 12 Lincolnshire ***court, local:*** 8 hustings ***court, medieval:*** 4 eyre ***era:*** 9 Edwardian, Victorian 11 Elizabethan ***forest:*** 5 Arden, weald 8 Sherwood ***king, legendary:*** 3 Lud 4 Beli, Bran 6 Arthur 7 Artegal, Belinus, Elidure 8 Brannius ***language, ancient:*** 6 Celtic, Cymric 9 Brythonic ***legislature:*** 10 Parliament ***medical system:*** 3 NHS ***news agency:*** 7 Reuters ***nobleman:*** 4 duke, earl, peer 5 baron 6 prince 8 marquess, viscount ***order:*** 6 Garter ***people, early:*** 5 Celts, Iceni, Jutes, Picts 6 Angles, Saxons ***political party:*** 4 Tory, Whig 6 Labour 12 Conservative ***pope:*** 8 Adrian IV ***prince:*** 5 Harry 6 Andrew, Edward 7 Charles, William ***princess:*** 4 Anne 5 Diana 8 Margaret ***prison:*** 5 Tower (of London) 7 Newgate 8 Dartmoor ***queen, ancient:*** 8 Boadicea, Boudicca ***resort:*** 4 Bath 7 Margate 8 Brighton 9 Blackpool ***royal house:*** 4 York 5 Tudor 6 Stuart 7 Hanover, Windsor 9 Lancaster 11 Plantagenet ***royal residence:*** 7 Windsor 8 Balmoral 10 Buckingham ***school:*** 4 Eton 5 Rugby 6 Harrow 10 Winchester ***school, military:*** 9 Sandhurst ***spa:*** 4 Bath 5 Epsom 6 Buxton 7 Malvern, Matlock 8 Brighton 9 Harrogate 10 Cheltenham
British Columbia ***capital:*** 8 Victoria ***city:*** 6 Surrey 7 Burnaby 8 Richmond 9 Vancouver ***mountain:*** 11 Fairweather ***provincial flower:*** 7 dogwood (Pacific)
British Honduras 6 Belize
brittle 4 curt 5 crisp, frail, stiff 6 infirm 7 crumbly, fragile, friable 9 breakable, frangible, inelastic, irritable, sensitive 10 perishable, transitory
broach 3 tap 4 moot 6 open up 7 bring up, mention, propose, suggest 8 initiate 9 introduce 10 put forward
broad 4 wide 7 general, liberal 8 extended, generous, spacious, sweeping, tolerant 9 expansive, extensive ***combining form:*** 4 eury, lati, plat 5 platy
broadcast 3 air, sow 4 beam, show 5 radio, strew 6 blazon, report, spread 7 bestrew, declare, publish, scatter 8 announce, proclaim, televise, transmit 9 advertise, publicize 10 bruit about, promulgate 11 communicate, declaration, disseminate, publication 12 announcement, proclamation, promulgation, transmission
broaden 4 open 5 swell, widen 6 dilate, expand, extend, fatten, spread 7 amplify, augment, distend, enlarge, thicken 8 increase 10 supplement
broadloom 6 carpet
broad-minded 4 open 7 liberal 8 catholic, eclectic, flexible, tolerant, unbiased 9 accepting, indulgent, unbigoted 10 forbearing, undogmatic 11 progressive 12 unjudgmental, unprejudiced
broadsheet 7 tabloid 9 newspaper
broadside 4 hail 5 burst, salvo, sheet, storm 6 shower, volley 7 barrage, torrent 8 at random 9 cannonade, fusillade, laterally, obliquely 11 bombardment
broadtail 4 hawk 5 sheep 7 karakul 8 lambskin
Broadway backer 5 angel
Brobdingnagian 4 huge 5 giant, jumbo 7 hulking, immense, mammoth, massive, titanic 8 colossal, gigantic, towering 9 cyclopean, humongous, monstrous 10 gargantuan, prodigious 11 elephantine

brochette **4** spit **6** skewer
brochure **5** flier, flyer **7** booklet **8** pamphlet
brogue **4** lilt, shoe **6** accent, oxford **7** dialect
broil **3** row **4** bake, burn, char, cook, fray, riot, sear **5** brawl, clash, fight, grill, melee, roast, run-in, toast **6** affray, fracas, scorch, tumult **7** bobbery, rhubarb, ruction, swelter, wrangle **8** disorder, squabble **10** donnybrook, free-for-all **11** disturbance
broiling **3** hot **5** fiery **6** baking, red-hot, torrid **7** blazing, burning **8** ovenlike, scalding, sizzling, white-hot **9** scorching **10** blistering, oppressive, sweltering
broke **4** poor **5** needy, spent **6** busted, ruined **7** drained **8** bankrupt, beggared, dirt poor, indigent, strapped, wiped out **9** destitute, insolvent, out of cash, penniless, penurious, played out **10** cleaned out **11** impecunious
broke-in **4** tame **5** tamed **6** docile
broken **4** shot **5** tamed **6** beaten, busted, cut off, faulty **7** crushed, haywire, humbled, subdued **8** bankrupt, defeated, violated, weakened **9** depressed, disrupted, fractured, heartsick, shattered, sorrowful **11** discouraged, demoralized, interrupted **12** disconnected, disheartened **13** discontinuous
broken-down **7** rickety **8** battered, decaying, decrepit **9** crumbling, neglected **10** threadbare, ramshackle **11** debilitated, dilapidated **12** deteriorated
brokenhearted **7** crushed, unhappy **8** dejected, dolorous, hopeless, wretched **9** depressed, heartsick, sorrowful **10** despairing, despondent **12** inconsolable **13** grief-stricken
broker **5** agent **6** factor **8** diplomat, mediator **9** financier, go-between, middleman **10** interagent, interceder, matchmaker, negotiator **11** intercessor **12** intermediary **13** intermediator
brolly **8** umbrella **11** bumbershoot
bromide **4** bore, drip, lump, pill, yawn **5** drone, grind **6** cliché, old saw, truism **7** proverb **8** banality, chestnut, prosaism, sedative **9** platitude, soporific **10** shibboleth, triviality **11** commonplace, rubber stamp
bromidic **3** dry **4** arid, dull **5** banal, bland, dusty, stale, trite **6** boring **7** humdrum, insipid, tedious **8** shopworn, tiresome **9** dryasdust, moth-eaten, wearisome **10** monotonous, pedestrian, unoriginal **11** commonplace **13** unimaginative, uninteresting
bromine symbol **2** Br
bronco **5** horse **6** cayuse **7** mustang ***Australian:*** **6** brumby
Brontë ***character:*** **9** Catherine, Rochester **10** Heathcliff ***novel:*** **7** Shirley **8** Jane Eyre, Villette **16** Wuthering Heights ***sisters:*** **4** Anne **5** Emily **9** Charlotte
Bronx cheer **3** boo **4** hoot, jeer, razz **5** taunt **7** catcall **9** raspberry
brooch **3** pin **4** clip **5** clasp **8** fastener
brood **3** set, sit **4** fret, mope, muse, stew, sulk **5** cover, flock, gloom, hatch, worry **6** litter, ponder, repine **7** despond, progeny **8** children, meditate, ruminate **9** offspring
brook **4** bear, burn, gill, race, rill **5** abide, creek, stand **6** arroyo, endure, rillet, runnel, stream, suffer **7** rivulet, stomach, swallow **8** stand for, tolerate ***Scottish:*** **6** burnie
Brookner novel **10** Hotel du Lac
broom **5** besom, brush, shrub, sweep, whisk **7** heather
broth **5** stock **8** bouillon, consommé
brothel **4** crib, stew **6** bagnio **7** lupanar **8** bordello, cathouse **9** call house **10** bawdy house, whorehouse
brother **3** kin **4** monk **5** friar **7** comrade, sibling ***French:*** **5** frère ***Italian:*** **3** fra **5** frate **8** fratello ***Latin:*** **6** frater ***relating to:*** **9** fraternal ***Spanish:*** **7** hermano
brotherhood **4** club, gang **5** amity, guild, order, union **6** league **7** kinship, society **8** alliance, sodality **10** fellowship, fraternity, friendship **11** association, camaraderie, comradeship, confederacy **12** togetherness **13** consanguinity, secret society
brotherly **9** fraternal
Brothers Karamazov **4** Ivan **5** Mitya **6** Alexei, Alexey, Dmitri, Dmitry **7** Alyosha **10** Smerdyakov
brought up **4** bred **6** raised, reared
brouhaha **3** din **4** coil, flap, fuss, riot, to-do **5** babel, broil, hoo-ha, whirl **6** bedlam, clamor, fracas, furore, hubbub, hurrah, jangle, pother, racket, ruckus, rumpus, shindy, tumult, uproar **7** ferment **8** foofaraw **9** agitation, commotion **10** excitement, hullabaloo, hurly-burly **11** pandemonium
brow **3** top **4** mien **5** front, crest, crown **8** forehead **9** gangplank **10** expression **11** countenance
browbeat **3** cow **5** beset, bully, harry, press **6** badger, carp at, coerce, harass, hector, lean on **7** bluster, dragoon **8** bludgeon, bulldoze, bullyrag, domineer, overbear, pressure **9** tyrannize **10** intimidate
brown **4** sear **5** dusky, toast **6** scorch, tanned **7** swarthy ***dark:*** **5** mocha, sepia, umber **9** chocolate ***grayish:*** **3** dun **6** bister, bistre ***light:*** **3** tan **4** ecru, fawn **5** beige, hazel, khaki, tawny ***moderate:*** **4** teak **6** sienna ***reddish:*** **3** bay **4** roan **5** henna **6** auburn,

russet, sorrel, titian **8** chestnut ***yellowish:*** **6** bronze **12** butterscotch

Brown Bomber 5 Louis (Joe)

brown coal 7 lignite

brownie 3 elf, fay **5** fairy, pixie **6** sprite

Browning poem 8 Prospice, Sordello **11** Aurora Leigh, Pippa Passes **12** Rabbi Ben Ezra **13** Fra Lippo Lippi, My Last Duchess **14** How Do I Love Thee?

brown recluse 6 spider

brownshirt 4 Nazi **12** storm trooper

browse 4 crop, feed, scan, shop, skim **5** graze, munch **6** forage, nibble, peruse **7** dip into, pasture **8** glance at, look over **10** glance over **11** flip through, leaf through, look through, skim through **12** thumb through

Broz, Josip 4 Tito

bruin 4 bear

bruise 5 pound, wound **6** batter, damage, injure, injury **7** contuse **8** abrasion, discolor **9** contusion **13** discoloration

bruit about 6 blazon, gossip, report, spread **7** declare, publish **8** announce, proclaim **9** advertise, broadcast, circulate **10** annunciate, pass around, promulgate **11** blaze abroad

brume 3 fog **4** film, haze, mist, murk **5** vapor **6** miasma **8** haziness **11** obscuration

brummagem 4 fake, sham **5** bogus, false, gaudy, phony, showy **6** ersatz, pseudo, shoddy, tinsel, tawdry **7** chintzy **8** spurious **9** imitation, pinchbeck, tasteless **10** fabricated, fictitious **11** counterfeit, make-believe

brunch cocktail 5 shrub **6** mimosa **7** bellini **10** Bloody Mary **11** screwdriver

Brunei *capital:* 17 Bandar Seri Begawan ***island:*** **6** Borneo ***language:*** **5** Malay ***neighbor:*** **8** Malaysia ***sea:*** **10** South China

brunet 3 jet **4** dark, onyx **5** dusky, ebony, raven, sable, sooty, swart **6** swarth **7** swarthy **8** bistered, obsidian **10** dark-haired **11** brown-haired

Brunhild 5 queen **7** heroine **8** Valkyrie ***husband:*** **6** Gunnar **7** Gunther ***lover:*** **9** Siegfried

brunt 4 jolt **5** shock **6** burden, impact

brush 4 clip, kiss, skim **5** broom, clash, graze, run-in, scrap, scrub, shave, sweep, whisk **6** glance, scrape, tussle **7** contact, thicket **8** skirmish **9** encounter, shrubbery, sideswipe **11** undergrowth

brusque 4 curt, tart **5** bluff, blunt, brief, gruff, rough, short, surly, terse **6** abrupt, crusty, snippy **7** uncivil **8** impolite, snippety, succinct **10** peremptory, ungracious **11** ill-mannered **12** discourteous

brutal 4 hard **5** cruel, feral, harsh **6** rugged, savage, severe **7** beastly, bestial, callous, inhuman, swinish, vicious **8** barbaric, pitiless, ruthless, sadistic **9** barbarous, ferocious, merciless **10** relentless **11** cold-blooded, remorseless **12** bloodthirsty

brutalize 5 abuse **6** debase, harden **7** corrupt, debauch, deprave, pervert, roughen, subvert, vitiate **8** maltreat, mistreat **9** manhandle **10** bestialize

brute 4 ogre **5** beast, cruel, feral **6** animal, savage **7** beastly, bestial, inhuman, piggish, swinish, varmint **8** creature **10** troglodyte **11** instinctive

brutish 3 low **4** base, vile **5** crude, feral, gross, rough, stony **6** animal, carnal, coarse, scurvy, strong **7** beastly, bestial, boorish, inhuman, obscene, piggish, swinish, uncivil, uncouth **8** barbaric, degraded, depraved, inhumane, physical, sadistic **9** primitive, truculent, unrefined **11** animalistic, uncivilized

bryophyte 4 moss **8** hornwort **9** liverwort

Brythonic see **Cymric**

bubble 3 sac **4** blob, boil, dome, fizz, foam, moil **5** churn, froth, slosh, spume, swash **6** burble, gurgle, seethe, simmer **7** ferment, globule, vesicle **10** effervesce

bubbly 5 alive, fizzy, foamy, jolly, perky, sudsy **6** cheery, frothy, lively **7** buoyant, excited **8** animated, effusive **9** champagne, ebullient, exuberant, sparkling **10** carbonated

buccaneer 5 rover **6** cowboy, pirate, sea dog **7** corsair, sea wolf **8** picaroon, sea rover **9** sea robber **10** freebooter

buck 3 fop, guy, lad, lug **4** balk, bear, bill, chap, clam, dude, jerk, load, male, move, note, oner, pack, stag, tote, trip **5** cadet, carry, dandy, ferry, fight, money, pitch, repel, stark, throw, token **6** combat, dollar, fellow, oppose, resist, unseat **7** coxcomb, trestle **8** antelope, bank note, sawhorse, traverse **9** greenback, withstand, workhorse **10** completely **11** Beau Brummel

bucket 3 fly, run **4** pail, rush, whiz **5** hurry, speed **6** barrel, basket, hasten, hustle, vessel **9** clamshell **10** receptacle

Buckeye State 4 Ohio

buckle 4 bend, clip, fold, hasp, kink, warp **5** catch, clamp, clasp, heave, yield **6** cave in, fasten **7** contort, crumple, harness **8** collapse **9** fastening **10** coffee cake

buckle under 3 bow **4** cave, fold, give **5** defer, yield **6** cave in, submit **7** concede, succumb **8** collapse **9** surrender **10** capitulate **11** admit defeat

Buck novel 9 Good Earth (The)
buckram 4 taut **5** stiff **6** wooden **8** starched **9** cardboard, unbending **10** inflexible **11** interlining
bucks 4 kale **5** bread, dough, money, moola **6** dinero, do-re-mi, moolah **7** lettuce **10** greenbacks
buck up 4 buoy, lift **5** cheer, rally **6** solace **7** comfort, console, gladden, improve, refresh, smarten **8** brighten **9** encourage **10** strengthen
____ buco 4 osso
bucolic 5 rural **6** rustic **7** georgic, halcyon, idyllic **8** agrarian, arcadian, pastoral **10** campestral, provincial **11** countrified, picturesque
bud 4 germ, seed **5** gemma, spark **6** sprout **7** burgeon **9** pullulate **10** primordium ***combining form:*** **5** blast **6** blasto
Buddha 7 Gautama **10** Siddhartha ***dialogues:*** **5** sutra ***disciple:*** **6** Ananda ***enemy:*** **4** Mara ***Japanese:*** **5** Amida, Amita ***mother:*** **4** Maya ***son:*** **6** Rahula ***teachings:*** **6** dharma ***wife:*** **9** Yasodhara
Buddhist *chant:* **6** mantra ***dialogues:*** **5** sutra ***enlightenment:*** **6** satori ***evil spirit:*** **4** Mara ***fate:*** **5** karma ***language:*** **4** Pali **8** Sanskrit ***monk:*** **4** lama **5** arhat, bonze ***sacred city:*** **5** Lhasa ***saint:*** **5** arhat ***scripture:*** **5** sutra **6** sutras **9** Pali canon ***sect, tradition:*** **3** Son, Zen **4** Chan **5** Kegon **6** Huayan, Tendai **7** Tiantai **8** Hinayana, Mahayana, Nichiren, Pure Land **9** Theravada, Vajrayana ***shrine:*** **4** tope **5** stupa **7** chorten ***spell:*** **6** mantra ***spiritual leader:*** **4** guru **9** Dalai Lama ***state of happiness:*** **7** nirvana ***temple:*** **6** pagoda ***title:*** **7** mahatma ***tree of enlightenment:*** **2** bo **5** bodhi, pipal
buddy 3 mac, pal **4** chum, mate **5** crony **6** comate, fellow, friend **7** compeer, comrade, partner **8** coworker, playmate, sidekick **9** associate, companion **10** accomplice **11** confederate
buddy-buddy 5 close, pally, thick, tight **6** chummy **8** intimate **10** palsy-walsy **11** inseparable
budge 4 move **5** shift, yield **7** give way
budgerigar 6 parrot **8** parakeet
budget 5 funds, means **6** amount, ration, supply **8** allocate, estimate **9** allowance, apportion, resources
buff 3 fan, fit, nut, rub, tan **4** ecru, fawn, sand, wipe **5** beige, brush, fiend, freak, glaze, gloss, lover, shine, toned **6** addict, expert, polish, votary **7** admirer, burnish, devotee, fanatic, fancier, furbish, groupie, habitué **8** follower **9** yellowish **10** aficionado, altogether, enthusiast **11** connoisseur, yellow-brown
buffalo 4 anoa, arna, bilk, faze **5** bison, bovid, stump **6** baffle, muddle, rattle **7** carabao, confuse, defraud, flummox, fluster, nonplus, perplex, swindle **8** befuddle, bewilder, confound, hoodwink **9** bamboozle, dumbfound
buffalo grass 5 grama
buffer 6 screen, shield **7** buckler, bulwark, cushion **8** absorber, mediator, polisher **9** safeguard **10** protection **12** intermediary
buffet 3 box, hit, rap **4** beat, blip, blow, bump, chop, cuff, drub, jolt, move, poke, slap, sock **5** clout, drive, force, pound, punch, smack, spank **6** batter, hammer, pummel, thrash, wallop **7** belabor, clobber, counter, lambast **8** lambaste, salad bar **9** sideboard
buffoon 3 wag **4** dolt, fool, goof, lout, zany **5** antic, clown, comic, droll, dunce, joker, yokel **6** jester **7** bumpkin, dullard **8** bonehead **9** blockhead, harlequin **10** clodhopper **11** merry-andrew
bug 3 fad, fan, irk, nag, nut, spy, tap, vex **4** buff, flaw, fret, gall, germ, rage **5** annoy, bulge, craze, fiend, freak, mania, peeve **6** badger, bother, defect, insect, malady, needle, nettle, pester, plague, zealot **7** disease, fanatic, microbe, provoke, wiretap **8** irritate, listen in, protrude, sickness **9** eavesdrop, infection, obsession **10** enthusiast **12** imperfection **13** microorganism
bugaboo see **bugbear**
bugbear 4 bane, bogy, fear, ogre **5** bogey, bogie, poser **6** goblin, teaser **7** bugaboo, problem, specter, spectre **8** anathema, bogeyman, phantasm **9** bête noire, boogerman, boogeyman, hobgoblin **10** black beast **11** abomination
buggy 4 cart, tram **6** go-cart, jalopy **8** carriage
bugle *call:* **4** mess, taps **5** drill **6** sennet, tattoo **7** fanfare, retreat, tantara **8** assembly, reveille ***relative:*** **6** cornet **7** trumpet **10** flugelhorn ***sound:*** **5** blare
build 3 wax **4** body, form, make, mode, mold, rise **5** boost, erect, forge, frame, habit, mount, put up, raise, set up, shape, swell **6** expand, figure **7** amplify, augment, compose, enlarge, fashion, magnify, produce, upsurge **8** assemble, compound, engineer, escalate, heighten, increase, multiply, physique **9** construct, establish, fabricate, institute, intensify, originate **10** accelerate, inaugurate, strengthen **11** fit together, manufacture **12** conformation, constitution

builder 5 mason **9** carpenter **10** bricklayer, contractor
builder's knot 10 clove hitch
building 3 hut **5** house **7** edifice **8** dwelling **9** structure ***addition:*** **3** ell **4** wing **5** annex ***block:*** **4** Lego **5** brick ***compartment:*** **3** bay **4** room **6** office ***connector:*** **9** breezeway ***farm:*** **4** barn, crib, shed, silo ***for apartments:*** **8** tenement ***for arms:*** **7** arsenal ***for gambling:*** **6** casino ***for grain:*** **4** silo **7** granary **8** elevator ***for horses:*** **6** stable ***for manufacture:*** **4** shop **5** plant **7** factory ***for music:*** **10** auditorium ***for sports:*** **3** gym **4** bowl **5** arena **7** stadium **8** coliseum **9** gymnasium **10** hippodrome ***material:*** **4** iron, wood **5** adobe, brick, glass, steel, stone **6** cement **8** concrete ***projection:*** **3** bay, ell **4** wing **5** annex **6** dormer **7** cornice ***round:*** **7** rotunda
building kit 5 Legos **10** Erector set **11** Lincoln Logs
build up 4 hype, plug, puff **5** boost, brace, erect **6** accrue, expand, extend, praise **7** collect, develop, enhance, fortify, improve, promote **8** buttress, heighten, increase **9** advertise, construct, establish, intensify, publicize **10** accumulate, aggrandize, strengthen
buildup 4 hype, puff, to-do **6** growth, hoopla **8** increase, ballyhoo **9** accretion, expansion, promotion, publicity **10** escalation **11** development, enhancement, enlargement **12** accumulation, augmentation **13** strengthening
built-in 6 inborn, inbred, innate **8** included, inherent **9** essential, ingrained, intrinsic **10** congenital, deep-seated, indwelling **11** established, fundamental **12** constitutive, incorporated
bulb 4 leek, lily, sego **5** onion, tulip **6** allium, dahlia, garlic, squill **8** daffodil, hyacinth **9** amaryllis, narcissus ***segment:*** **5** clove
bulb-like bud 4 corm **5** tuber **7** rhizome
Bulgaria *capital:* **5** Sofia ***city:*** **4** Ruse **5** Stara, Varna **6** Burgas, Pleven, Zagora **7** Plovdiv ***monetary unit:*** **3** lev ***mountain, range:*** **6** Balkan, Musala **7** Rhodope ***neighbor:*** **6** Greece, Serbia, Turkey **7** Romania **9** Macedonia ***part of:*** **7** Balkans ***river:*** **6** Danube **7** Maritsa ***sea:*** **5** Black
bulge 3 bag, jut, sac, sag **4** blob, bump, edge, lump, poke **5** bloat, pouch, swell **6** beetle, billow, bubble, bug out, dilate, excess, expand **7** balloon, distend, inflate, project, puff out **8** overhang, protrude, stand out, stick out, swelling **9** allowance, head start **10** distension, projection, promontory, protrusion **11** excrescence, protuberate **12** protuberance
bulk 4 body, core, heft, loom, mass **5** fiber, swell, total **6** amount, corpus, expand, volume **7** bigness, quantum **8** majority, quantity, stand out **9** aggregate, magnitude, substance
bulky 3 fat **5** beefy, hefty, husky, large, obese, stout **7** massive **8** cumbrous, unwieldy **9** corpulent, ponderous **10** cumbersome, overweight **11** substantial
bull 4 bunk, male, slip, toro, trip **5** boner, edict, error, fluff, force, hooey, lapse **6** bovine, bungle, decree, el toro **7** baloney, blooper, blunder, hogwash, mistake **8** nonsense **9** detective ***combining form:*** **4** taur **5** tauri, tauro
bulldoze 3 cow **4** move, push, raze **5** abash, bully, clear, cream, elbow, force, level, press, scare, shove **6** coerce, hector, hustle, jostle, lean on, menace, propel, thrust **7** bluster, clobber, dragoon, flatten, oppress, trounce **8** bludgeon, browbeat, bullyrag, demolish, domineer, restrain, shoulder **9** terrorize, tyrannize **10** intimidate, obliterate
bullet 3 ace **4** slug **6** dumdum, tracer **9** cartridge **10** projectile ***size:*** **7** caliber, calibre
bulletin 4 news **5** flash, scoop **6** notice, report **7** account, catalog, gazette, message, missive, release **8** briefing, calendar, dispatch, magazine, register **9** catalogue, statement **10** communiqué, periodical **12** announcement
bull fiddle 10 contrabass, double bass
bullfighter 6 torero **7** matador, picador **8** toreador **11** cuadrillero **12** banderillero ***famous:*** **6** Arruza **7** Ordóñez **8** Belmonte, Joselito, Manolete **9** Dominguin **10** El Cordobés
bullfighting *arena:* **5** plaza ***cheer:*** **3** olé ***hero:*** **6** torero **7** matador **8** toreador ***lancer:*** **7** picador ***red cloth:*** **6** muleta ***Spanish:*** **7** corrida ***team:*** **9** cuadrilla
bullheaded 6 mulish **7** adamant, willful **8** contrary, obdurate, perverse, stubborn **9** insistent, obstinate, pigheaded **10** headstrong, refractory, self-willed, unyielding **11** intractable, stiff-necked **12** intransigent, pertinacious, strong-willed
bullish 4 rosy **6** brawny, rising, upbeat **7** booming **9** advancing, expanding, favorable **10** optimistic
bully 3 cow **4** goon, pimp, punk, thug **5** abuse, heavy, meany, tease, tough **6** harass, hector, meanie, menace, pander, pick on, rascal **7** bluster, buffalo, dragoon, harrier, oppress, ruffian, torment, torture **8** bludgeon, browbeat, bulldoze, bullyrag, ha-

rasser, threaten **9** bulldozer, persecute, victimize, tormenter, tyrannize **10** browbeater, corned beef, intimidate, persecutor **11** intimidator

bullyrag see **bulldoze**

bulrush 4 reed, tule **5** sedge **7** cattail, papyrus

bulwark 4 wall **6** screen, shield **7** barrier, bastion, parapet, rampart, seawall **8** buttress, fortress, palisade **9** earthwork, safeguard **10** breakwater, breastwork, embankment, stronghold **13** fortification

bum 3 beg, vag **4** bust, hobo, idle, laze, lazy, loaf, loll, slug, wino **5** binge, cadge, drunk, hit up, idler, mooch, tramp **6** bottom, dawdle, loafer, loiter, lounge, slouch, unfair **7** depress, drifter, feel low, goof off, rear end, vagrant, wheedle **8** buttocks, derelict, fainéant, slugabed, sluggard, vagabond **9** do-nothing, goldbrick, importune, lazybones, panhandle, transient

bumbershoot 6 brolly **8** umbrella

bumble 3 mar **4** blow, flub, muff **5** botch, fluff, gum up, lurch **6** bobble, bollix, bungle, falter, fumble, mess up, muck up, rumble, slip up, teeter, totter **7** blunder, screw up, stagger, stumble **8** flounder

bumbling 5 inept, gawky **6** clumsy, gauche, klutzy **7** awkward, halting, unhandy **8** ungainly **9** all thumbs, graceless, ham-handed, incapable, maladroit, unskilled **11** heavy-handed, incompetent **13** butterfingers, uncoordinated

bummer 3 dud **4** drag, flop, hobo **5** tramp **6** beggar, cadger, downer, sponge, too bad **7** failure, forager, moocher, sponger **8** deadbeat, vagabond **9** tough luck **10** freebooter, panhandler, rotten luck, wet blanket

bump 3 bop, hit, jar, ram, rap, wen **4** bang, bash, bust, jolt, knot, lump, oust, slam **5** break, carom, clash, crack, crash, gnarl, knock, prang, shift, shock, shove, wound **6** demote, growth, impact, injury, jostle, jounce, nodule, remove, strike, wallop **7** collide, degrade, demerit, pothole, run into **8** demotion, dislodge, displace, swelling **9** carbuncle, collision, contusion, convexity **10** concussion, projection, protrusion **12** protuberance

bumpkin 3 oaf **4** boor, hick, lout, rube **5** clown, swain, yokel **6** rustic **7** hayseed, peasant **9** chawbacon, hillbilly, simpleton **10** clodhopper, country boy, countryman, provincial

bump off 3 ice **4** do in, kill, slay **5** erase, snuff **6** murder, rub out **7** butcher, execute, take out **8** knock off **9** eliminate, liquidate **11** assassinate

Bumppo, Natty ***alias:*** **7** Hawkeye **10** Deerslayer, Pathfinder ***creator:*** **6** Cooper (James Fenimore)

bumptious 5 cocky, pushy **8** arrogant, impudent **9** audacious, obnoxious, obtrusive, officious **13** self-assertive

bumpy 5 jerky, nubby, ridgy, rough **6** bouncy, jouncy, knobby, knotty, patchy, pimply, uneven **7** jolting, nodular **9** difficult, irregular

bun 4 load, roll **6** pastry

bunch 3 lot, set, wen **4** band, bevy, bump, clot, crew, knot, lump, mass, push, slew **5** batch, clump, covey, crowd, flock, group, party, spray, stack, swell **6** bundle, circle, clutch, gather, huddle, parcel, throng **7** bouquet, collect, cluster **8** assembly, protrude, swelling **9** gathering **10** assemblage, assortment, collection, congregate **11** aggregation **12** accumulation

bunco steerer 3 gyp **6** con man **7** cheater, diddler, grifter, sharper **8** swindler **9** defrauder, trickster **12** double-dealer **13** confidence man

bundle 3 lot, pot, set, wad **4** bale, body, heap, mint, pack, pile, wrap **5** array, batch, bunch, clump, group, sheaf, truss **6** fardel, packet, parcel **7** cluster, fortune **8** fascicle **10** assortment

bung 4 plug **5** cecum, spile **7** stopper

bungalow 5 cabin, lodge **6** chalet **7** cottage

bungle 3 err **4** flub, goof, mess, muff, slip, trip **5** boner, botch, error, fluff, gum up, lapse, misdo, mix up, spoil **6** bollix, bumble, fiasco, foozle, foul up, fumble, goof up, mess up, muck up, muddle **7** blooper, blunder, failure, louse up, misstep, mistake, stumble **9** mishandle, mismanage

bungler 3 oaf **4** clod, dolt, goof **5** klutz **7** screw-up, tomfool **8** bonehead, goofball, shlemiel **9** blunderer, schlemiel **10** stumblebum **11** blunderbuss, incompetent **13** butterfingers

bunglesome 6 clumsy, klutzy **7** awkward **8** bumbling **9** all thumbs **13** uncoordinated

bung up 4 beat, hurt **5** abuse, pound **6** batter, bruise, injure **7** contuse, disable **9** disfigure, manhandle

bunion 4 lump **8** swelling **10** protrusion, tumescence **11** enlargement

bunk 3 bed, cot, kip, rot **4** bosh, bull, guff, jazz **5** bilge, board, crash, hokum, hooey, house, lodge, put up **6** humbug, pallet, piffle **7** eyewash, baloney, hogwash, rubbish, twaddle **8** claptrap, domicile, flimflam, malarkey, nonsense, tommyrot **9** poppycock **10** balderdash

bunker 3 bin **6** dugout **7** bastion, chamber **8**

sand trap **10** embankment, stronghold **11** compartment
bunkum 3 rot **4** bosh, bull, guff, jazz **5** bilge, hokum, hooey **6** humbug, piffle **7** baloney, hogwash, rubbish, twaddle **8** claptrap, flimflam, malarkey, nonsense, tommyrot **9** poppycock **10** balderdash
bunting 5 finch, flags **8** songbird **9** streamers
Bunyanesque 4 huge **5** giant, jumbo **7** mammoth, massive, titanic **8** behemoth, colossal, gigantic, towering **9** Herculean **10** gargantuan, prodigious
Bunyan's ox 4 Babe
buoy 4 lift, prop **5** boost, cheer, float, raise **6** assist, beacon, bear up, buck up, signal, solace, uphold, uplift **7** bolster, comfort, gladden, hearten, support, sustain **9** encourage
buoyancy 6 bounce, levity **7** jollity **8** airiness **10** ebullience, exuberance, exuberancy, liveliness, resilience **12** floatability **13** effervescence
buoyant 3 gay **4** airy **5** sunny **6** afloat, bouncy **7** elastic **8** cheerful, floating, volatile **9** expansive, floatable, resilient **10** unsinkable, weightless **12** effervescent, lighthearted
burble 3 gas, yak **4** blab, chat, gush, talk, wash **5** clack, plash, run on, slosh, swash **6** babble, bubble, gabble, gurgle, murmur, rattle, splash, yammer **7** chatter, prattle, sparkle
burden 3 tax, try **4** care, clog, core, duty, gist, haul, lade, load, onus, pile, pith, task, text **5** brunt, cargo, press, theme, weigh **6** amount, charge, chorus, cumber, hamper, lading, lumber, saddle, strain, stress, thrust, upshot, weight **7** afflict, anxiety, freight, oppress, payload, refrain, purport **8** encumber, handicap, obligate, overload, shiralee **9** millstone, substance, weigh down **10** deadweight **11** encumbrance
burdensome 5 tough **6** taxing, trying **7** arduous, exigent, irksome, onerous, weighty **8** crushing, exacting, grievous **9** demanding, difficult, fatiguing, ponderous **10** exhausting, oppressive **11** troublesome **12** backbreaking, unmanageable
bureau 4 unit **5** chest **6** agency **7** dresser, section **8** ministry **10** department, chiffonier **11** writing desk
bureaucrat 8 mandarin, minister, official **11** functionary **12** civil servant, officeholder
burg 4 city, town **7** borough **8** fortress **10** metropolis, walled town **12** municipality
burgee 4 flag **6** banner, ensign, pennon **7** pendant, pennant **8** standard, streamer
burgeon 4 blow, boom, open **5** bloom, build, mount, run up **6** emerge, expand, flower, sprout, thrive, unfold **7** augment, blossom, develop, enlarge, fill out, prosper, run riot **8** flourish, heighten, increase, multiply, mushroom, snowball **9** germinate **10** burst forth, effloresce
Burgess novel 7 Enderby **13** Earthly Powers **15** Clockwork Orange (A)
burghal 5 civic, urban **8** citified **9** municipal **12** metropolitan
burgher 7 citizen, denizen **8** townsman
burglar 4 yegg **5** thief ***loot:* 4** swag
burglarize see **burgle**
burglary 5 heist, theft **7** larceny
burgle 3 rob **4** lift, loot **5** heist, steal, strip **6** rip off, thieve **7** despoil, plunder, ransack **9** break into, knock over **10** housebreak
burgomaster 5 mayor **10** magistrate
Burgundy wine *grape:* 5 Gamay **9** Pinot Noir **10** Chardonnay ***red:* 8** Mercurey **10** Beaujolais ***white:* 5** Rully **6** Chagny **7** Chablis **10** Montrachet **13** Pouilly-Fuissé
burial 4 tomb **5** grave **7** funeral **9** interment, obsequies, sepulcher, sepulchre, sepulture **10** entombment, inhumation ***box:* 6** casket, coffin ***ceremony:* 7** funeral, obsequy **9** obsequies ***mound:* 6** barrow **7** tumulus ***tomb:* 9** mausoleum, sepulcher, sepulchre
burial ground 8 boot hill, cemetery **8** boneyard, God's acre **9** graveyard **10** churchyard, necropolis **12** memorial park, potter's field ***early Christian:* 8** catacomb
Burkina Faso *capital:* 11 Ouagadougou ***ethnic group:* 3** Gur **5** Mossi **7** Voltaic ***former name:* 10** Upper Volta ***language:* 4** Moré **5** Dyula **6** French ***monetary unit:* 5** franc ***neighbor:* 4** Mali, Togo **5** Benin, Ghana, Niger **10** Ivory Coast ***river:* 5** Volta (Black, Red) **6** Nazion **7** Mouhoun, Nakanbe **8** Red Volta **10** Black Volta
burlap 5 gunny **6** fabric **7** bagging, sacking ***fiber:* 4** hemp, jute
burlesque 3 ape **4** mock, sham **5** farce, spoof **6** parody, satire, send-up **7** lampoon, mockery, mocking, takeoff **8** pastiche, skin show, travesty **10** caricature, distortion, girlie show, lampoonery
burly 4 hale **5** beefy, hefty, husky, tough **6** brawny, robust, strong, stocky **8** athletic, heavyset, muscular, powerful, stalwart, thickset, vigorous **9** strapping
Burma see **Myanmar**
burn 4 bake, char, cook, fire, fume, rage, sear **5** anger, blaze, broil, creek, flame, flare, gleam, roast, scald, singe, smart, smoke, sting, toast **6** ignite, kindle, scorch, seethe **7** bristle, combust, consume, cremate, flare up,

inflame, radiate, smolder, swelter **8** smoulder **9** carbonize, cauterize **10** incinerate
burnable 8 volatile **9** flammable, ignitable **10** incendiary **11** combustible, inflammable
burned-out 4 beat, shot **5** spent, weary **6** sapped **7** drained, worn-out **8** consumed, fatigued **9** destroyed, exhausted, played-out **10** broken-down **11** debilitated **12** extinguished
burner 3 hob **4** ring
burning 3 hot **5** afire, aglow, fiery **6** ablaze, aflame, alight, ardent, fervid, heated, hectic, red-hot, torrid, urgent **7** blazing, fervent, fevered, glowing, ignited, kindled, searing **8** broiling, feverish, pressing, sizzling, white-hot **9** scorching **10** imperative, passionate **11** conflagrant, impassioned **12** incandescent ***combining form:*** **4** igni ***malicious:*** **5** arson
burnish 3 rub, wax **4** buff **5** glaze, gloss, scour, sheen, shine **6** luster, patina, polish, smooth **7** furbish, varnish **8** brighten
burnished 5 shiny **6** glossy, satiny, sheeny **7** lambent, radiant, shining **8** gleaming, lustrous, polished **9** brilliant **10** glistening **11** resplendent
burnsides 8 whiskers **9** sideburns **10** sideboards **11** dundrearies, muttonchops **12** side-whiskers
burp 5 belch, eruct, expel
burro 3 ass **6** donkey **7** jackass
Burroughs hero 6 Tarzan
burrow 3 den, dig **4** hole, lair, mine, nook, snug **5** delve, gouge, lodge **6** cavity, cuddle, nestle, nuzzle, tunnel **7** snuggle **10** excavation
burst 3 pop, run **4** bang, boom, clap, gush, gust, rive, rush, slam, wham **5** blast, crack, crash, erupt, flare, go off, lunge, sally, salvo, smash, spasm, split, storm, surge **6** access, blow up, emerge, irrupt, launch, plunge, shiver, spring, shower, volley **7** assault, barrage, dehisce, explode, flare-up, fly open, rupture, shatter, torrent **8** detonate, drumfire, eruption, fragment, outbreak, splinter, splitter **9** broadside, cannonade, explosion, fusillade, onslaught **11** bombardment
Burundi *capital:* 9 Bujumbura ***ethnic group:*** **4** Hutu **5** Tutsi ***former name:*** **6** Urundi ***lake:*** **10** Tanganyika ***language:*** **5** Rundi **6** French **7** Kirundi ***monetary unit:*** **5** franc ***neighbor:*** **5** Congo **6** Rwanda **8** Tanzania
bury 4 hide, sink, stow **5** cache, cover, embed, inter, plant, stash **6** absorb, entomb, inhume, mantle, shroud **7** blanket, conceal, cover up, implant, lay away, overlay, put away, secrete **8** ensconce, submerge
bus 5 clear **6** jitney **7** missile, trolley, vehicle **9** hand truck **10** spacecraft
bush 4 rose **5** lilac, shrub, wahoo **6** azalea, cassis, privet **7** currant, thicket, weigela **8** backland, barberry, hazelnut **9** backwater, backwoods, forsythia, manzanita **10** gooseberry, hinterland, wilderness **11** pussy willow **12** rhododendron
bushel 3 ton **4** heap, load, pile **6** basket, hamper **7** pannier
bush-league 5 minor **6** junior, two-bit **8** inferior, mediocre, small-fry **9** small-time **10** inadequate, second-rate **11** lightweight **13** insignificant
bushranger 6 outlaw **8** woodsman **12** frontiersman
bushwhack 4 trap **6** ambush, assail, attack, entrap, waylay **7** assault **8** surprise **9** blindside
bushwhacker 6 bandit, outlaw, raider, sniper **8** guerilla, woodsman **9** guerrilla **10** highwayman
bushy 5 bosky, fuzzy, hairy, leafy **6** fluffy, woolly **7** hirsute, unkempt **9** bristling, luxuriant, overgrown **10** disordered **11** flourishing
business 3 job **4** firm, line, work **5** trade **6** affair, custom, matter, métier, office, outfit, racket **7** calling, company, concern, pursuit, traffic **8** commerce, function, industry **9** patronage **10** employment, enterprise, livelihood, occupation **11** corporation **13** establishment ***course:*** **7** finance **8** modeling **9** marketing **10** accounting ***expense:*** **8** overhead ***syndicate:*** **6** cartel
businesslike 6 formal **7** orderly, serious **8** diligent, thorough **9** competent, efficient, practical, pragmatic **10** impersonal, methodical, no-nonsense, purposeful, systematic **11** disciplined, hardworking **12** professional
businessman 6 broker, dealer, trader, tycoon **7** magnate **8** investor, merchant **9** bourgeois, financier, tradesman, executive **10** capitalist, trafficker **12** entrepreneur, merchandiser **13** industrialist
busker 8 minstrel, musician **11** entertainer
buss 4 kiss, peck **5** smack **6** smooch **8** osculate
bust 3 bag, cop, dud, hit, jag, nab, net **4** bomb, bump, fail, flop, fold, raid, ruin, slug, sock, tear, tour **5** binge, bosom, break, broke, burst, catch, chest, crash, lemon, loser, punch, smash, spell, spree, stint, torso, trash **6** arrest, bender, breast, collar, demote, pick up **7** break up, carouse, degrade, demerit, destroy, exhaust, failure, rupture, wear out **8** bankrupt, demolish, fracture **9** apprehend, break down, destitute, downgrade, penniless **10** impoverish, police raid ***opposite:*** **4** boom

bustle **3** ado, fly, run **4** flit, fuss, rush, stir, tear, teem, to-do **5** hurry, whirl, whisk **6** action, be busy, bestir, clamor, flurry, furore, hassle, hasten, hubbub, hustle, motion, pother, scurry, tumult, uproar **7** ferment, turmoil **8** activity, to-and-fro **9** commotion, whirlpool, whirlwind **10** hurly-burly, excitement, liveliness

bustling **4** busy, rife **5** brisk, fussy, peppy **6** active, hectic, lively **7** dynamic, festive, hopping, humming, jumping **8** animated, swarming, vigorous **9** energetic **10** tumultuous **11** hard-working, industrious

busty **5** ample, buxom, curvy **6** bosomy, chesty, zaftig **7** shapely, stacked **10** curvaceous, voluptuous **11** full-bosomed, well-rounded

busy **5** brisk, fussy, in use **6** active, at work, lively, on duty, tied up **7** crowded, engaged, hopping, humming, swamped, teeming, working **8** bustling, diligent, employed, hustling, meddling, occupied, overdone, sedulous **9** assiduous, congested, elaborate, energetic, intrusive, obtrusive, officious **10** meddlesome **11** distracting, impertinent, industrious, unavailable

busybody **5** prier, pryer, snoop, yenta **6** butt-in, gossip, old hen **7** meddler **8** informer, kibitzer, quidnunc **9** pragmatic **10** chatterbox, newsmonger, pragmatist, talebearer, tattletale **11** nosey parker, rumormonger **12** gossipmonger, rubbernecker, troublemaker

but **3** bar, yet **4** just, only, save **5** alone **6** except, merely, saving, unless **7** barring, besides, however **8** entirely **9** aside from, excepting, excluding, outside of **13** on the contrary

butcher **4** ruin, slay **5** botch, carve, clean, spoil, wreck **6** bollix, killer, mess up, slayer **7** cut meat, destroy, meat man **8** mutilate **9** slaughter **11** slaughterer

butcher-bird **6** shrike

butcherly **5** cruel **6** bloody, clumsy, savage **7** awkward **8** sadistic **9** ferocious, merciless **10** unskillful

butchery **7** carnage **8** abattoir, genocide, massacre **9** bloodbath, bloodshed, holocaust, slaughter **10** mass murder **12** annihilation **13** extermination

buteo **4** hawk **7** buzzard

butler **5** valet **7** steward **10** manservant

Butler, Samuel ***novel:*** **7** Erewhon **13** Way of All Flesh (The) ***poem:*** **8** Hudibras

butt **3** end, keg, tip, ram, tun, vat **4** base, cask, drum, dupe, join, push, rump, stub, tail **5** chump, fanny, patsy, stump, touch, verge **6** adjoin, barrel, border, bottom, firkin, pigeon, sucker, target, thrust, victim **7** collide, fall guy, rear end, run into **8** derriere, hogshead, neighbor **9** cigarette, fundament, lie beside, pilgarlic, posterior, remainder **11** communicate, sitting duck **12** hindquarters **13** laughingstock

butter ***artificial:*** **4** oleo **9** margarine **13** oleomargarine ***Indian:*** **4** ghee ***piece:*** **3** pat ***semi-fluid:*** **4** ghee ***tree:*** **4** shea

butterball **5** blimp, whale **8** dumpling, elephant **10** bufflehead

butterfish **6** gunnel

butterfly **4** blue **5** diana, satyr, zebra **6** copper, morpho **7** admiral, buckeye, monarch, satyrid, skipper, sulphur, vanessa, viceroy **8** crescent, grayling, milkweed, victoria **9** aphrodite, metalmark, nymphalid, wood nymph **10** fritillary, hairstreak **11** swallowtail ***bush:*** **8** buddleia ***fish:*** **6** blenny, chiton **7** gurnard ***larva:*** **11** caterpillar ***lily:*** **8** mariposa ***order:*** **11** Lepidoptera ***plant:*** **8** oncidium ***pupa:*** **9** chrysalis ***scientist:*** **13** lepidopterist

butter up **4** coax **5** charm **6** cajole, kowtow, praise, stroke **7** adulate, beguile, blarney, flatter, massage, wheedle **8** blandish, bootlick, soft-soap **9** brownnose, sweet-talk **10** overpraise

butt in **6** kibitz, meddle **7** intrude, obtrude **8** busybody, overstep **9** interfere, interlope, interpose, interrupt

buttinsky **7** meddler **8** busybody, kibitzer, quidnunc **9** loudmouth **10** trespasser **12** troublemaker

buttocks **4** rear, rump, seat, tail **5** fanny, nates **6** behind, bottom, breech, heinie **7** hind end, hunkers, keister, rear end, tail end **8** backside, derriere, haunches **9** fundament, posterior

buttonball **8** sycamore **9** plane tree

button-down **6** square, stuffy **8** decorous, orthodox, straight **10** restrained **11** straitlaced, traditional **12** conservative, conventional

buttonhole **5** lobby **6** accost, chat up, detain, waylay **8** confront

buttonwood **8** sycamore **9** plane tree

buttress **4** pier, prop, stay **5** brace, carry, shore, strut, truss **6** back up, bear up, hold up, column, uphold **7** bolster, bulwark, fortify, shore up, support, sustain **9** reinforce, stanchion **10** strengthen **12** underpinning **13** fortification, reinforcement

buxom **5** ample, busty, curvy **6** bosomy, chesty, zaftig **7** shapely, stacked **10** curvaceous, voluptuous **11** full-bosomed, full-figured, well-rounded

buy 5 bribe **6** obtain, ransom, redeem **7** acquire, bargain, believe **8** purchase
buy back 6 ransom, recoup, redeem, regain **8** retrieve **10** repurchase
buyer 6 client, patron, vendee **7** shopper **8** consumer, customer **9** purchaser
buy off 3 fix, sop **5** bribe **6** settle **7** corrupt, silence **9** influence **10** manipulate, tamper with
buzz 3 fad, hum **4** call, fizz, high, hiss, news, purr, ring, talk, whir, whiz **5** craze, drone, hurry, rumor, strum, thrum, whirr, whish **6** bumble, fizzle, gossip, murmur, natter, report, rumble, sizzle, summon, wheeze, whoosh **7** chatter, scandal, whisper **8** sibilate **9** bombinate **11** reverberate, scuttlebutt
buzzard 5 buteo **7** vulture **13** turkey vulture
by 3 per, via **4** away, near, nigh, past **5** along, aside **6** at hand, beside, next to **7** through **9** alongside **10** incidental **11** according to **12** not later than
by and by 4 anon, soon **5** after, later **7** ere long, shortly **8** directly, latterly **9** afterward, presently **10** before long **12** subsequently
by and large 7 all told, broadly, en masse, overall, usually **8** all in all, normally **9** generally, typically **10** altogether, on the whole, ordinarily **11** principally
by dint of see **by means of**
bye-bye 4 ciao, ta-ta **5** adieu, adios **6** so long **7** cheerio, toodles **8** au revoir, farewell, sayonara, toodle-oo
bygone 3 old **4** dead, late, lost, once, past **5** dated, of old, olden **6** former, fossil, of yore, remote, whilom **7** antique, archaic, belated, defunct, extinct, old-time, onetime, quondam, vintage **8** departed, sometime, obsolete, outdated, outmoded, vanished **9** erstwhile, out-of-date **10** antiquated, old-fangled **12** antediluvian, old-fashioned
by means of 3 per, via **4** with **5** using **7** through **9** employing, utilizing
byname 6 handle **7** epithet, moniker **8** cognomen **9** sobriquet **10** diminutive, hypocorism **11** appellation
bypass 4 omit, skip **5** avoid, burke, shunt, skirt **6** detour, ignore **7** highway **8** go around, outflank, ring road, sidestep **10** circumvent, pass around **11** deviate from
by-product 5 yield **6** effect, result **7** outcome, residue, spin-off **8** offshoot **9** outgrowth **10** derivative, descendant **11** aftereffect, consequence **12** repercussion
Byron work 4 Cain, Lara **5** Beppo **6** Giaour (The), Werner **7** Corsair (The), Don Juan, Manfred **12** Childe Harold
bystander 6 gawker, viewer **7** watcher, witness **8** beholder, observer, onlooker, passerby **9** spectator **10** eyewitness **12** rubbernecker
by stealth 5 slyly **7** sub rosa **8** covertly, in secret, secretly **9** furtively, privately **10** under cover **11** insidiously **13** clandestinely
by virtue of see **by means of**
by way of see **by means of**
byword 3 saw **5** adage, axiom, maxim, motto, nomen **6** dictum, phrase, saying, slogan, truism **7** epigram, epithet, precept, proverb, refrain **8** aphorism, cognomen, nickname **9** platitude, prescript, sobriquet **10** hypocorism, shibboleth **11** catchphrase, commonplace, rallying cry
Byzantine 6 daedal, knotty **7** complex, devious **8** involved **9** elaborate, intricate **10** convoluted **11** complicated **12** labyrinthine **13** sophisticated, surreptitious ***emperor:*** **3** Leo **4** Zeno **5** Basil **6** Bardas, Justin, Phocas **7** Michael, Romanus **9** Heraclius, Justinian **10** Nicephorus, Theodosius ***empress:*** **3** Zoe **5** Irene **8** Theodora

C

cab 4 hack, taxi **6** jitney **7** hackney **8** carriage
cabal 3 mob **4** clan, club, plot, ring **5** coven, group, junta, mafia **6** cartel, circle, clique **7** coterie, faction, in-group **8** intrigue **9** camarilla **10** conspiracy **11** machination
cabaletta 4 aria, song
cabalistic 6 arcane, mystic, occult **8** esoteric **9** recondite **10** mysterious **11** inscrutable **12** impenetrable
caballero 6 knight **7** paladin **8** cavalier, horseman **9** chevalier
cabana 3 hut **5** shack **7** shelter

cabaret 4 café **6** bistro, nitery **7** hot spot **9** nightclub, nightspot **10** supper club **12** watering hole

cabbage 3 nab, nip **4** cash, hook, lift, palm **5** bread, dough, filch, kraut, money, moola, pinch, steal, swipe **6** dinero, do-re-mi, moolah, pilfer **7** purloin, scratch **10** greenbacks, sauerkraut ***disease of:*** **6** mildew, mosaic **7** root rot, yellows **8** blackleg, club root ***family:*** **4** cole, kale, rape **5** colza, savoy **6** turnip **7** collard, mustard **8** broccoli, colewort, kohlrabi, rutabaga **11** cauliflower ***sliced:*** **4** slaw

cabdriver 4 hack **5** cabby **6** cabbie

cabin 3 hut **4** camp, shed **5** berth, hovel, lodge, shack **6** cabana, chalet, lean-to, shanty **7** bivouac, cottage **9** stateroom

cabin cruiser 5 yacht **9** motorboat, powerboat

cabinet 4 case **6** bureau **7** armoire, chamber, commode, console, council, dresser **8** advisers, advisors, cupboard, ministry **9** presidium **10** chiffonier, collection, counselors

cabinetmaker *American:* 5 Eames (Charles, Ray), Phyfe (Duncan) **6** Belter (John Henry) **7** Goddard (John, Stephen, Thomas) **8** McIntire (Samuel), Townsend (Christopher, Edmund, James, Job, John) ***English:*** **4** Adam (James, Robert), Hope (Thomas), Kent (William) **8** Sheraton (Thomas) **11** Chippendale (Thomas), Hepplewhite (George) ***French:*** **6** Boulle (André-Charles) **8** Caffieri (Jacques, Jean-Jacques, Philippe), Cressent (Charles) ***German:*** **10** Weisweiler (Adam)

cable 4 rope, wire **5** braid, chain **6** stitch **8** transmit **9** telegraph

cabriolet 5 coupe **8** carriage

cache 4 bury, hide **5** cover, plant, stash, store, trove **6** memory, wealth **7** arsenal, conceal, lay away, nest egg, put away, reserve, secrete **8** ensconce, treasure **9** stockpile **10** accumulate **11** hiding place

cachet 4 rank, seal **5** motto, state **6** slogan, status **7** dignity, stature **8** approval, position, prestige, standing **11** consequence

cachinnate 4 crow, howl, roar **5** laugh, whoop **6** guffaw, shriek

cackle 3 gab, jaw **4** blab, chat, crow **5** clack, cluck **6** babble, burble, gabble, gaggle, gobble **7** blabber, blatter, chatter, prattle

cacoëthes 4 zeal **5** mania **6** desire **9** obsession

cacomistle 5 civet **7** raccoon **8** civet cat, ringtail

cacophonic 5 harsh **8** tuneless **9** dissonant, unmusical **10** discordant **11** unmelodious **12** unharmonious

cacophony 5 babel, noise **9** confusion, harshness **10** dissonance

cactus 5 nopal **6** cereus, cholla, mescal, peyote **7** opuntia, saguaro **11** prickly pear

cad 3 cur, dog, rat **4** boor, heel, lout, rake **5** creep, knave, louse, rogue **6** rascal, rotter **7** bounder **9** conductor, scoundrel

cadaver 4 body, mort **5** stiff **6** corpse **7** carcass, remains **8** deceased

cadaverous 5 ashen, gaunt, livid **6** pallid, wasted **7** deathly, ghastly, ghostly, shadowy **8** skeletal, spectral **9** deathlike, emaciated, ghostlike **10** corpselike

caddy 3 bin, box **4** aide **5** toter **6** casket **8** canister, tea chest

cadence 4 beat, flow, lilt **5** meter, pulse **6** rhythm **9** pulsation **10** conclusion, inflection, intonation

cadet 4 pimp **5** plebe **7** student, trainee **10** midshipman

cadge 3 beg, bum **5** mooch **6** hustle, sponge **8** freeload, scrounge **9** panhandle

cadmium symbol 2 Cd

Cadmus *daughter:* 3 Ino **5** Agave **6** Semele **7** Autonoë ***father:*** **6** Agenor ***sister:*** **6** Europa ***victim:*** **6** dragon ***wife:*** **8** Harmonia

cadre 4 cell, core **5** frame, staff **6** cohort **7** ingroup **9** framework

caducity 3 age **6** dotage, old age **8** senility **10** senescence **11** senectitude

Caesar *assassin:* 6 Brutus (Marcus Junius) **7** Cassius (Gaius) ***battle:*** **4** Zela **9** Pharsalus ***conquest:*** **4** Gaul **7** Britain ***death date:*** **4** Ides **11** Ides of March ***eulogist:*** **6** Antony (Marc) **7** Anthony (Mark) **8** Antonius (Marcus) ***message:*** **12** Veni vidi vici ***river:*** **7** Rubicon ***utterance:*** **4** Et tu **9** Et tu Brute ***wife:*** **7** Pompeia **8** Cornelia **9** Calpurnia

Caesarism 7 tyranny **9** authority, autocracy, despotism **10** absolutism **12** dictatorship

caesura 5 break, pause **12** interruption

café 5 diner **6** bistro, nitery **7** barroom, beanery, cabaret, hot spot **8** cookshop **9** lunchroom, nightclub, nightspot **10** coffee shop, restaurant, supper club **12** luncheonette, watering hole **13** watering place

café ____ 4 noir **5** latte **6** au lait, filtre **7** society

caftan 4 gown, robe **6** muumuu **12** dressing gown

cage 3 hem, pen **4** cell, coop, jail **5** score **6** aviary, corral, immure, lock up, shut in **7** close in, enclose, impound **8** imprison **9** enclosure **11** incarcerate

cagey 3 sly **4** foxy, wary, wily **5** canny, sharp **6** astute, clever, crafty, shrewd

cahier 6 record, report, review **7** journal **8** notebook
cahoots 6 hookup, league **8** alliance **9** collusion **10** complicity **11** partnership
caiman 9 crocodile **11** crocodilian
Cain *brother:* 4 Abel, Seth ***father:* 4** Adam ***land:* 3** Nod ***mother:* 3** Eve ***nephew:* 4** Enos ***son:* 5** Enoch ***victim:* 4** Abel
Caine Mutiny *author:* 4 Wouk (Herman) ***character:* 5** Keith (Willie), Maryk (Steve), Queeg (Capt. Francis)
Cain novel 8 Serenade **13** Mildred Pierce **23** Postman Always Rings Twice (The)
cajole 3 con **4** coax, dupe **6** entice, seduce **7** beguile, blarney, deceive, wheedle **8** blandish, inveigle, maneuver, persuade, softsoap **9** sweet-talk
cake 3 dry, set **4** coat, loaf, rime **5** cover, crust, torte **6** gâteau, harden, pastry **7** congeal, encrust, incrust **8** solidify ***almond:* 8** macaroon ***flat:* 5** cooky **6** cookie ***oatmeal:* 4** farl **5** scone **7** bannock ***ring-shaped:* 5** donut **6** jumble **8** doughnut ***rum-soaked:* 4** baba ***Scottish:* 4** farl **5** scone ***shell-shaped:* 9** madeleine ***topping:* 5** icing **8** frosting, streusel ***twisted:* 7** cruller ***without shortening:* 6** sponge
Cakes and Ale author 7 Maugham (W. Somerset)
cakewalk 4 romp, rout, snap **5** cinch, dance, strut **6** breeze, prance **8** pushover, walkover
calaboose 3 can **4** brig, coop, jail, tank **5** clink, pokey **6** cooler, lockup, prison **7** slammer **8** hoosegow **9** jailhouse
calamitous 4 dire **5** fatal **6** woeful **7** ruinous **8** grievous **10** disastrous, lamentable **11** cataclysmic, devastating, unfortunate **12** catastrophic **13** heartbreaking
calamity 4 ruin **5** wreck **7** tragedy **8** disaster, downfall **9** cataclysm **11** catastrophe, tribulation
calcium symbol 2 Ce
calculate 4 rely **5** assay, count, gauge, judge, solve, tally, tot up, value **6** assess, cipher, figure, intend, reckon **7** compute, measure, work out **8** appraise, estimate, evaluate, forecast **9** ascertain, determine, figure out
calculated 6 likely **7** planned **8** intended **9** worked out **10** deliberate **12** aforethought, premeditated
calculating 3 sly **4** wary, wily **5** canny, chary, sharp **6** artful, crafty, shrewd **7** careful, cunning, devious, politic **8** cautious, discreet, guileful, scheming **9** designing **11** circumspect
calculating device 6 abacus ***Peruvian:* 5** quipu
calculation 8 analysis, counting, estimate, figuring, prudence **9** ciphering, reckoning **10** arithmetic, estimation, prediction **11** computation
Caledonia 8 Scotland
calendar 3 log **4** card, sked **6** agenda, docket **7** almanac, program **8** schedule **9** timetable ***abbreviation:* 3** Apr, Aug, Dec, Feb, Fri, Jan, Mar, Mon, Nov, Oct, Sat, Sep, Sun, Tue, Wed **4** Sept **5** Thurs ***ecclesiastical:* 4** ordo ***unit:* 3** day **4** week, year **5** month
calenture 4 fire, zeal **5** ardor, fever **6** fervor **7** passion **10** enthusiasm
calf *hide:* 3 kip ***leather:* 3** elk ***meat:* 4** veal ***stray:* 5** dogie ***unbranded:* 8** maverick
Caliban 5 slave ***master:* 8** Prospero ***witch-mother:* 7** Sycorax
caliber 4 bore **5** class, gauge, grade, merit, value, worth **6** virtue **7** ability, quality, stature **8** diameter
calibrate 3 set **6** adjust, polish **7** measure **8** fine-tune, regulate **9** ascertain **11** standardize
California *capital:* 10 Sacramento ***city:* 4** Napa **6** Fresno, Sonoma **7** Anaheim, Oakland, San Jose **8** San Diego, Santa Ana **9** Long Beach, Santa Cruz **10** Los Angeles **12** San Francisco ***college, university:* 3** USC **4** UCLA **5** Mills **6** Pomona **8** Berkeley, Stanford, Whittier **9** Loma Linda **10** Golden Gate, Occidental, Pepperdine, Santa Clara ***desert:* 6** Mohave ***fault zone:* 10** San Andreas ***lake:* 5** Owens, Tahoe **9** Salton Sea ***lowest spot:* 11** Death Valley ***motto:* 6** Eureka ***mountain, range:* 5** Coast **6** Lassen (Peak), Shasta **7** Whitney **12** Sierra Nevada ***nickname:* 6** Golden (State) ***park:* 7** Sequoia **8** Yosemite **11** Kings Canyon **14** Channel Islands ***river:* 10** Sacramento, San Joaquin ***state bird:* 5** quail ***state flower:* 11** golden poppy ***state tree:* 7** redwood, sequoia ***wine region:* 4** Napa **6** Sonoma
californium symbol 2 Cf
caliginous 3 dim **4** dark, dusk **5** dusky, foggy, misty, murky **6** gloomy **7** obscure, sunless **8** nebulous **9** lightless, tenebrous
Caligula *mother:* 9 Agrippina ***predecessor:* 8** Tiberius ***successor:* 8** Claudius
caliph's name 3 Ali **7** Abu Bakr
Calista's seducer 8 Lothario
calisthenics 7 workout **9** exercises
call 3 bid, cry **4** buzz, hail, lure, name, page, ring, yell **5** phone, pop in, shout, visit **6** bellow, come by, drop by, drop in, holler, salute, stop by, stop in, summon **7** convene, convoke, summons **8** estimate **9** designate, telephone

calla 4 lily
call down 5 chide, scold **6** rebuke **7** censure, reprove **8** admonish, reproach **9** reprimand
called 5 named **6** chosen, picked, yclept **7** ycleped **8** selected
caller 5 guest **6** suitor **7** visitor
call for 3 ask, beg **4** page, seek **5** crave, plead **6** demand, entail, pick up **7** beseech, entreat, implore, involve, require **11** necessitate
call forth 5 awake, educe, evoke, rouse **6** arouse, elicit **7** conjure, provoke **9** conjure up
calligrapher 6 penman, scribe **7** copyist **9** engrosser, scrivener
calligraphy 4 hand **6** script **7** writing **8** longhand **10** penmanship **11** handwriting
call in 5 phone **6** summon **7** convene, reclaim **8** retrieve, withdraw **9** repossess, telephone
calling 3 job **4** duty, work **5** craft, trade **6** career, métier **7** mission, pursuit, yelling **8** business, lifework, shouting, vocation **10** employment, obligation, occupation, profession
call in sick 7 book off
Calliope 4 Muse ***father:*** **4** Zeus **7** Jupiter ***mother:*** **9** Mnemosyne ***son:*** **7** Orpheus
Callisto *lover:* **4** Zeus **7** Jupiter ***son:*** **5** Arcas
Call It Sleep author 4 Roth (Henry)
call off 4 halt **5** abort, scrub **6** cancel, divert **8** distract
Call of the Wild *author:* **6** London (Jack) ***dog:*** **4** Buck
call on 5 visit **6** oblige **7** require
callosity 8 hardness **9** thickness
callous 5 stony **8** hardened, obdurate, uncaring **9** heartless, indurated, unfeeling **10** hard-bitten, hard-boiled **11** coldhearted, hardhearted, insensitive, unemotional **12** case-hardened, stonyhearted **13** unsympathetic
callow 3 raw **5** fresh, green, naive, young **7** puerile **8** immature, juvenile, youthful **9** unfledged **10** unseasoned **13** inexperienced, unexperienced
call up 5 draft, evoke **6** summon **8** mobilize, retrieve **9** conscript
calm 4 cool, ease, hush, lull **5** allay, peace, quiet, relax, salve, still **6** hushed, pacify, placid, poised, repose, sedate, serene, settle, smooth, soothe, stable, steady, stilly **7** appease, assuage, compose, halcyon, mollify, pacific, placate, restful, resting **8** composed, inactive, peaceful, reposing, serenity, tranquil **9** collected, composure, easygoing, impassive, possessed, quiescent, unruffled **10** phlegmatic, untroubled **11** tranquility, tranquilize, unflappable **12** even-tempered, self-composed, tranquillity **13** imperturbable, self-possessed
calmative 8 quietive, relaxing, sedative **9** soporific **12** tranquilizer
calmness 4 lull **5** quiet **6** phlegm **8** coolness, serenity **9** composure, placidity, sangfroid **10** equanimity **11** tranquility **12** tranquillity
calumet 4 pipe **9** peace pipe
calumniate 5 libel, smear **6** defame, malign, vilify **7** asperse, slander, tarnish, traduce **8** besmirch **9** denigrate **10** scandalize
calumnious 8 libelous **9** maligning, traducing, vilifying **10** backbiting, defamatory, detracting, scandalous, slanderous
calumny 7 scandal, slander **9** aspersion **10** backbiting, defamation, detraction **11** denigration **12** backstabbing, belittlement, depreciation **13** disparagement
calvados 6 brandy **9** applejack
calvary 5 agony, cross, trial **6** misery, ordeal **7** anguish **8** distress **9** suffering **10** affliction, visitation **11** tribulation ***inscription:*** **4** INRI
Calvino work 11 Cosmicomics **15** Invisible Cities
Calypso *beloved:* **7** Ulysses **8** Odysseus ***island:*** **6** Ogygia
calyx part 3 cup **5** sepal
camaraderie 5 cheer **7** jollity **10** affability, fellowship **12** conviviality
camarilla 3 mob **4** camp, clan, ring **5** cabal, mafia **6** circle, clique **7** coterie, ingroup
Cambodia 9 Kampuchea ***capital:*** **9** Phnom Penh ***city:*** **10** Battambang **11** Kompong Cham ***ethnic group:*** **8** Mon-Khmer ***lake:*** **8** Tonle Sap ***language:*** **5** Khmer ***leader:*** **6** Pol Pot ***monetary unit:*** **4** riel ***neighbor:*** **4** Laos **7** Vietnam **8** Thailand ***river:*** **6** Mekong ***ruin:*** **9** Angkor Wat
camel *one-humped:* **9** dromedary ***two-humped:*** **8** Bactrian
camel-hair fabric 3 aba
camelopard 7 giraffe
Camelot 6 palace ***lord:*** **6** Arthur
Camembert 6 cheese
cameo 6 brooch, relief, walk-on **8** portrait
camera type 3 SLR, spy, TLR **5** video **7** digital, folding, pinhole **9** autofocus, single-use **10** viewfinder **11** rangefinder
cameraman 6 photog **7** lensman **12** photographer
Cameroon *capital:* **7** Yaoundé ***ethnic group:*** **4** Fang **5** Duala, Pygmy **6** Fulani **8** Bamileke ***largest city:*** **6** Douala ***monetary unit:*** **5** franc ***neighbor:*** **4** Chad **5** Congo, Gabon **7** Nigeria ***river:*** **5** Nyong **6** Sanaga

Camille's creator **5** Dumas (Alexandre)

Camino ____ **4** Real

camouflage **4** mask **5** cloak **7** conceal, deceive **8** disguise **9** dissemble **11** dissimulate

camp **3** hut **4** bloc, shed **5** cabin, lodge, shack **6** clique, shanty **7** bivouac, coterie, cottage, faction **10** settlement

campaign **4** push, race **5** blitz, drive, fight, lobby, stump **6** attack **7** agitate, canvass, crusade **8** movement, politick **9** barnstorm, offensive **10** engagement, expedition **11** electioneer, whistle-stop

campaigner **8** activist **9** candidate

campanile **6** belfry **8** carillon **9** bell tower

campesino **6** farmer **7** peasant

campestral **5** rural **6** rustic, sylvan **7** bucolic, country, idyllic **8** agrarian, pastoral **10** provincial **11** countrified

campus see **college**

Camus work **4** Fall (The) **5** Rebel (The) **6** Plague (The) **8** Caligula, Stranger (The)

can **3** may, tin **4** boot, fire, sack **5** let go, put up **7** dismiss **8** preserve **9** container, discharge **10** receptacle

Canaan **4** Zion **12** Promised Land ***father:*** **3** Ham ***grandfather:*** **4** Noah

Canaanite god **3** Mot **4** Baal **6** Molech, Moloch

Canada ***bay:*** **5** Fundy, James **6** Baffin, Hudson, Ungava **8** Georgian **9** Frobisher ***capital:*** **6** Ottawa ***city:*** **6** London, Oshawa, Quebec, Regina, Surrey **7** Burnaby, Calgary, Halifax, Moncton, Toronto, Windsor **8** Edmonton, Hamilton, Montreal, Moose Jaw, Victoria, Winnipeg **9** Longueuil, North York, Saskatoon, Vancouver **10** Lethbridge, Thunder Bay **11** Fredericton, Scarborough **13** Charlottetown, Mississisauga ***district:*** **6** riding ***explorer:*** **6** Hudson (Henry) **7** Cartier (Jacques) **9** Champlain (Samuel de) ***Indian people:*** **4** Cree, Inuk **5** Blood, Haida, Huron, Inuit, Métis, Niska, Slave **6** Abnaki, Beaver, Eskimo, Micmac, Mohawk, Nootka, Ojibwa, Ojibwe, Ottawa, Piegan, Seneca, Stoney **7** Kutenai, Naskapi, Ojibway, Siksika, Wyandot **8** Algonkin, Chippewa, Iroquois, Kootenai, Kootenay, Kwakiutl, Salishan, Tsattine **9** Algonkian, Algonquin, Blackfeet, Blackfoot, Chipewyan, Tsimshian **10** Algonquian, Athapascan, Gros Ventre, Montagnais **11** Assiniboine ***island, island group:*** **5** Banks, Devon **6** Baffin **7** Belcher **8** Melville, Victoria **9** Anticosti, Ellesmere, Vancouver **10** Cape Breton **11** Southampton **12** Newfoundland, Prince Edward ***lake:*** **6** Louise **7** Nipigon **8** Reindeer, Winnipeg **9** Athabasca, Champlain, Great Bear **10** Great Slave ***language:*** **6** French **7** English ***monetary unit:*** **6** dollar ***mountain, range:*** **5** Coast, Logan, Rocky **10** Laurentian ***national park:*** **5** Banff, Fundy **6** Jasper **7** Glacier, Nahanni **8** Kootenay **9** Gros Morne **10** Grasslands, Point Pelee **11** Georgian Bay, Wood Buffalo ***peninsula:*** **5** Bruce, Gaspé **6** Ungava **8** Labrador ***prime minister:*** **4** King (W. L. Mackenzie) **5** Clark (Joe) **6** Abbott (John), Borden (Robert Laird), Bowell (Mackenzie), Harper (Stephen), Martin (Paul), Tupper (Charles), Turner (John) **7** Bennett (Richard Bedford), Laurier (Wilfrid), Meighen (Arthur), Pearson (Lester), Trudeau (Pierre Elliott) **8** Campbell (Kim), Chrétien (Jean), Mulroney (Brian), Thompson (John) **9** MacDonald (John), Mackenzie (Alexander), St. Laurent (Louis) **11** Diefenbaker (John) ***province:*** **3** Man., NWT, Ont., PEI, Que. **4** Alta, Sask. **6** Quebec **7** Alberta, Nunavut, Ontario **8** Manitoba **10** Nova Scotia **12** New Brunswick, Newfoundland (and Labrador), Saskatchewan **15** British Columbia **18** Prince Edward Island ***provincial park:*** **3** Gas **7** Rondeau **9** Garibaldi ***river:*** **3** Red **5** Liard, Slave, Yukon **6** Albany, Fraser, Nelson, Ottawa, Severn **8** Columbia, Saguenay **9** Athabasca, Churchill, Mackenzie **10** St. Lawrence ***sea:*** **8** Beaufort, Labrador ***symbol:*** **9** maple leaf ***territory:*** **5** Yukon **9** Northwest

Canadian insurgent **4** Riel (Louis)

canaille **3** mob **6** masses, rabble **8** riffraff, unwashed **9** hoi polloi **11** proletarian, proletariat

canal **4** duct **6** course **7** channel, conduit **8** aqueduct **11** watercourse ***Africa:*** **4** Suez **8** Ismailia ***Belgium:*** **6** Albert ***Canada:*** **7** Welland ***Central America:*** **6** Panama ***China:*** **7** Da Yunhe ***Florida:*** **10** Saint Lucie ***Germany:*** **4** Kiel **10** Nord-Ostsee ***Greece:*** **7** Corinth ***Michigan:*** **3** Soo ***New York:*** **4** Erie **6** Oswego **9** Champlain ***Ontario:*** **6** Rideau ***Venice:*** **5** Grand

canapé **6** morsel **9** appetizer **11** hors d'oeuvre ***spread:*** **4** paté ***topper:*** **3** roe **6** caviar

canard **3** fib, lie **4** tale, yarn **5** fraud, rumor, spoof **6** deceit **7** falsity, untruth **8** chestnut **9** falsehood

canary **3** rat **4** fink, wine **5** finch **6** snitch **7** rat fink, stoolie **8** informer, squealer **11** stool pigeon

Canary Islands **5** Ferro, Lobos, Palma **6** Gomera, Hierro **7** Inferno **8** Graciosa, Tenerife **9** Alegranza, Lanzarote

cancel **3** end **4** drop, lift, undo, x out **5** abort, annul, erase, scrub **6** delete, efface, negate, offset, repeal, revoke **7** blot out, call off, destroy, expunge, nullify, rescind, wipe out **8** black out, deletion **9** terminate **10** invalidate, neutralize, obliterate

cancer 5 tumor **9** carcinoma **10** malignancy ***treatment:*** **5** chemo, X rays **9** radiation **12** chemotherapy

cancer-causing 12 carcinogenic ***substance:*** **10** carcinogen

candescent 7 glowing **8** dazzling **9** refulgent

Candia 5 Crete

candid 4 fair, just, open **5** blunt, frank, plain **6** honest **7** sincere **8** unbiased **9** equitable, guileless, impartial, objective **10** aboveboard, forthright, scrupulous, unreserved **11** openhearted, unconcealed, undisguised **12** unprejudiced **13** dispassionate

candidate 6 seeker **7** hopeful, nominee, stumper **8** aspirant **9** applicant, contender **10** campaigner, contestant ***unlisted:*** **7** write-in

Candide *author:* **8** Voltaire ***lover:*** **9** Cunegonde ***tutor:*** **8** Pangloss (Dr.) ***valet:*** **7** Cacambo

candle 5 taper **6** bougie ***holder:*** **6** sconce **7** menorah, pricket **9** girandole **10** candelabra **11** candelabrum ***material:*** **3** wax **4** wick **6** tallow **7** beeswax, stearin **8** paraffin ***religious:*** **6** votive **7** paschal

candlefish 8 eulachon ***relative:*** **5** smelt

candlelit service 5 vigil

candlepins 7 bowling

candor 7 honesty **8** fairness, openness **9** frankness, sincerity, whiteness **11** artlessness **13** guilelessness

candy 7 sweeten **9** sugarcoat **10** confection ***kind:*** **4** rock **5** fudge, lolly, sweet, taffy **6** bonbon, comfit, dragée, jujube, nougat, toffee **7** brittle, caramel, fondant, gumdrop, penuche, praline **8** licorice, lollipop, lollypop, marzipan, sourball **9** chocolate, jelly bean, nonpareil, sweetmeat **10** confection **12** butterscotch ***medicated:*** **7** lozenge **9** cough drop

cane 3 rod **4** beat, drub, flog, lash, reed, stem, swat **5** flail, grass, spank, staff, stave, stick, weave, whale **6** batter, buffet, cudgel, larrup, paddle, rattan, thrash, wallop **7** lambast, sorghum **8** lambaste **12** walking stick

Canea's land 5 Crete

canine 3 dog **4** tyke **5** hound, pooch

caning material 5 istle

Canis Major star 6 Sirius

Canis Minor star 7 Procyon

canker 4 rust, sore **5** stain **6** debase, infect **7** corrupt, debauch, deprave, pervert, vitiate **8** necrosis **10** demoralize

cankered 8 infested, infected

canker sore 5 ulcer **6** lesion **10** ulceration

cannabis 3 pot **4** hemp **5** bhang, ganja, grass **7** hashish **9** marijuana

canned 5 drunk, fired **6** potted **11** prerecorded

Cannery Row author 9 Steinbeck (John)

canniness 7 caution, cunning, slyness **8** prudence, wiliness **9** cageyness, foresight **10** artfulness, cleverness, craftiness, discretion, precaution, providence, shrewdness **11** forethought

cannon 6 pom-pom **8** howitzer, ordnance **9** artillery ***part:*** **5** chase **6** breech **8** cascabel, trunnion

cannonade 4 bomb **5** blitz, burst, salvo, shell **6** shower, volley **7** barrage, bombard **8** drumfire, shelling **9** broadside, fusillade **11** bombardment

cannonball 4 dive **5** speed **7** missile

cannoneer 6 gunner

cannon fodder 6 troops **8** infantry, soldiers

canny 3 sly **4** wary, wise **5** acute, cagey, chary, quick, sharp, smart **6** adroit, clever, frugal, saving, shrewd **7** cunning, knowing, prudent, thrifty **9** ingenious, provident **10** economical **11** quick-witted, sharp-witted **12** nimble-witted

canoe 6 dugout **7** pirogue ***ancient:*** **7** coracle ***Eskimo:*** **5** kayak, umiak

canon 3 law **4** list, rule **5** dogma, edict, round, tenet **6** decree **7** precept, statute **8** doctrine, standard **9** clergyman, criterion, ordinance **10** regulation

canonical 5 sound **6** lawful **7** classic **8** accepted, approved, official, orthodox, received **10** authorized, recognized, sanctioned **13** authoritative

canonical hour 4 none, sext **5** lauds, prime, terce **6** matins, tierce **7** vespers **8** compline

canonicals 9 vestments

canoodle 3 hug, pet **5** spoon **6** caress, cuddle, fondle

can opener 9 church key

canopy 5 cover, shade **6** awning, tester **7** marquee, shelter **8** covering, sunshade **9** baldachin **10** baldachino ***canvas:*** **4** tilt

cant 3 tip **4** heel, lean, list, tilt **5** angle, argot, bevel, idiom, lingo, piety, slang, slant, slope **6** humbug, jargon, patois, patter, speech **7** dialect, diction, incline, lexicon, palaver, recline **8** language, singsong **9** hypocrisy **10** dictionary, pharisaism, sanctimony, vernacular **11** inclination, insincerity **12** pecksniffery

cantaloupe 5 melon **9** muskmelon

cantankerous 4 dour, sour **5** cross, huffy, testy, waspy **6** crabby, cranky, crusty, grumpy, morose, ornery **7** bearish, crabbed, grouchy, peevish, prickly, waspish **8** cankered, liverish, petulant, snappish, stubborn, vinegary **9** crotchety, difficult, dyspeptic, irascible, irritable, obstinate **10** ill-natured, irritating, vinegarish **12** cross-grained

canter 3 bum **4** gait, hobo, lope **5** tramp **6** beggar **7** drifter, vagrant **8** derelict, vagabond **11** bindle stiff

Canterbury ***Archbishop:*** **3** Oda **6** Anselm, Becket (Thomas á), Parker (Matthew) **7** Cranmer (Thomas), Dunstan **9** Augustine

Canterbury Tales ***author:*** **7** Chaucer (Geoffrey) ***character:*** **4** host, monk **5** clerk, friar, reeve **6** knight, miller, parson, squire, yeoman **7** plowman, shipman **8** franklin, Griselda, manciple, merchant, pardoner, prioress, summoner **9** physician **10** wife of Bath ***inn:*** **6** Tabard

canticle 3 ode **4** hymn, song **6** Te Deum **10** Benedicite, Benedictus, Magnificat **12** Nunc Dimittis

canticles 11 Song of Songs **13** Song of Solomon

cantilever 4 beam **6** bridge **7** bracket, support

cantillate 4 sing **5** chant **6** intone, recite

cantina 3 bar, pub **6** saloon, tavern **7** barroom

canton 5 state **6** billet **7** quarter, section **8** district, division

cantor 5 hazan **6** singer **9** precentor

canvas 4 duck, sail, tarp, tent **7** tenting **8** painting **9** sailcloth, tarpaulin

canvasback 4 duck

canvass 3 con, vet **5** argue, study **6** debate, survey **7** discuss, dispute, examine, inspect, solicit **8** campaign **9** check over **10** scrutinize **11** electioneer **12** authenticate

canyon 4 Glen, Zion **5** Bryce, chasm, gorge, Grand, gulch, Hells **6** Copper, coulee, ravine, valley

cap 3 tam, top **4** best, coif **5** beret, cover, crest, crown, limit, trump **6** beanie, exceed, top off **7** calotte **9** culminate ***clergyman's:*** **7** biretta **9** zucchetto ***hoodlike:*** **4** coif ***hunter's:*** **7** montero ***jester's:*** **7** coxcomb **9** cockscomb ***Jewish:*** **8** yarmulke ***knitted:*** **5** toque, tuque **9** balaclava ***military:*** **4** kepi ***mushroom:*** **6** pileus ***part:*** **4** bill, brim, flap, peak **5** visor **7** earflap ***Roman:*** **6** pileus ***Scottish:*** **3** tam **8** balmoral **9** glengarry **11** tam-o'-shanter ***Turkish:*** **3** fez **6** calpac **7** calpack

capability 5 craft, means, skill **7** ability, potency **8** adequacy, aptitude, capacity, efficacy, facility **9** potential **10** competence, efficiency **12** potentiality **13** effectiveness, qualification

capable 3 apt **4** able **5** adept **6** adroit, au fait **9** competent, efficient, qualified **10** proficient **11** susceptible

capacious 4 wide **5** ample, roomy **7** sizable **8** abundant, spacious **9** extensive **10** commodious **11** substantial

capacitance ***unit of:*** **5** farad

capacity 4 bent, gift, rank, role, room **5** knack, range, reach, scope, skill, space **6** output, status, talent **7** ability, caliber, faculty **8** adequacy, aptitude, facility, position, standing **10** capability, competence **11** proficiency **13** qualification ***unit of:*** **4** gill, peck, pint **5** liter, litre, minim, quart **6** bushel, gallon **10** fluid ounce, milliliter

Capaneus ***slayer:*** **4** Zeus ***wife:*** **6** Evadne

caparison 5 adorn **6** finery **7** apparel, panoply, raiment **9** adornment, trappings

cape 4 cope, ness **5** cloak, point, talma **6** capote, mantle, tabard, tippet **7** manteau, pelisse **8** foreland, headland, mantelet, mantilla, pelerine **9** peninsula **10** promontory ***clergyman's:*** **8** mozzetta ***papal:*** **5** fanon, orale

Cape ***Africa:*** **4** Juby, Yubi **5** Blanc **6** Blanco **7** Agulhas ***Alaska:*** **3** Icy **4** Nome **11** Krusenstern ***Algeria:*** **3** Fer ***Antarctica:*** **3** Ann **4** Dart **5** Adare ***Arctic:*** **8** Nordkaap ***Asia:*** **5** Aniva ***Australia:*** **5** Byron, Otway, Sandy, Smoky **6** Arnhem **9** Van Diemen ***Baffin Island:*** **4** Dyer ***Black Sea:*** **5** Yasun ***Borneo:*** **4** Datu **6** Datoek ***Brazil:*** **4** Frio, Raso ***California:*** **9** Mendocino ***Colombia:*** **5** Aguja ***Costa Rica:*** **5** Velas ***Crete:*** **5** Plaka ***Croatia:*** **5** Ploca **6** Planka ***Cuba:*** **4** Cruz **5** Maisi ***Denmark:*** **4** Skaw **6** Skagen ***Desolación Island:*** **5** Pilar **6** Pillar ***Djibouti:*** **3** Bir ***Egypt:*** **5** Banas ***England:*** **8** Bolerium, Lands End ***Florida:*** **5** Sable **7** Kennedy **9** Canaveral ***Greece:*** **4** Busa **5** Gallo, Malea, Papas, Vouxa **6** Araxos, Maleas **7** Akritas ***Guinea:*** **5** Verga ***Gulf of California:*** **5** Lobos ***Gulf of Guinea:*** **5** Lopez ***Gulf of Mexico:*** **4** Rojo ***Hawaii:*** **5** Ka Lae **10** South Point **11** Diamond Head ***Hispaniola:*** **5** Beata ***Honshu:*** **3** Iro, Oma **5** Inubo, Kyoga, Nyudo ***Indonesia:*** **4** Vals **5** False ***Japan:*** **4** Esan, Nomo, Sata, Soya **5** Erimo, Kamui ***Libya:*** **3** Tin **4** Milh ***Long Island Sound:*** **10** Throgs Neck ***Malay Peninsula:*** **5** Bulat ***Malaysia:*** **4** Piai **5** Sirik ***Massachusetts:*** **3** Ann, Cod ***Mediterranean:*** **5** Ajdir ***Mexico:*** **4** Buey ***Morocco:*** **3** Sim **4** Guir, Rhir ***Namibia:*** **4** Fria ***Newfoundland:*** **5** Bauld ***New Jersey:*** **3** May

New Zealand: **5** Brett ***North Carolina:*** **4** Fear **7** Lookout **8** Hatteras ***Northwest Territories:*** **8** Bathurst ***Nova Scotia:*** **5** Canso **6** Breton ***Oman:*** **3** Nus **4** Hadd ***Ontario:*** **4** Hurd, Rich ***Pakistan:*** **5** Monze, Muari ***Portugal:*** **4** Roca ***Puerto Rico:*** **4** Rojo ***Quebec:*** **5** Gaspé ***Red Sea:*** **5** Kasar ***Sicily:*** **4** Boeo, Faro **7** Lilibeo, Passero, Pelorus ***Solomon Islands:*** **5** Zelee ***Somalia:*** **4** Asir **5** Assir, Hafun ***South Africa:*** **8** Good Hope ***South America:*** **4** Horn ***Spain:*** **3** Nao **4** Gata **5** Creus, Penas ***Syria:*** **5** Basit ***Taiwan:*** **5** O-Iuan **7** Garam Bi ***Tierra del Fuego:*** **5** Penas ***Tunisia:*** **5** Blanc ***Turkey:*** **3** Boz **4** Baba, Ince, Kara, Krio **6** Lectum **8** Bozburun **9** Inceburun, Karaburun ***Vancouver Island:*** **5** Scott ***Virginia:*** **5** Henry ***Washington:*** **5** Alava

Čapek, Karel ***coinage:*** **5** robot ***play:*** **3** R.U.R.

caper **4** dido, lark, leap, romp **5** antic, frisk, heist, prank, revel, shine, theft, trick **6** cavort, frolic, gambol, prance **7** roguery, rollick **8** escapade, mischief **10** shenanigan, tomfoolery **11** monkeyshine

Cape Verde ***capital:*** **5** Praia ***city:*** **7** Mindelo ***island:*** **3** Sal **4** Fogo, Maio **5** Brava **8** Boa Vista, São Tiago **10** São Vicente, São Nicolau, Santa Luzia, Santo Antão ***language:*** **7** Crioulo **10** Portuguese ***monetary unit:*** **6** escudo

capillary **4** tube **6** tubule **8** hairlike **11** blood vessel

capital **4** main **5** basic, chief, funds, major, prime **6** assets, lethal, wealth **8** cardinal **9** essential, excellent, financing, first-rate, principal, resources **10** first-class, investment, preeminent, underlying **11** fundamental, outstanding, predominant, wherewithal ***Afghanistan:*** **5** Kabul ***Albania:*** **6** Tirana, Tiranë ***Alberta:*** **8** Edmonton ***Algeria:*** **7** Algiers ***Angola:*** **6** Luanda ***Antigua and Barbuda:*** **7** St. John's **10** Saint John's ***Argentina:*** **11** Buenos Aires ***Armenia:*** **7** Yerevan ***Assam:*** **6** Dispur ***Australia:*** **8** Canberra ***Austria:*** **4** Wien **6** Vienna ***Azerbaijan:*** **4** Baku ***Bahamas:*** **6** Nassau ***Bahrain:*** **6** Manama ***Bangladesh:*** **5** Dacca, Dhaka ***Barbados:*** **10** Bridgetown ***Belarus:*** **5** Minsk ***Belgium:*** **8** Brussels ***Belize:*** **8** Belmopan ***Benin:*** **9** Porto-Novo ***Bhutan:*** **7** Thimphu ***Bolivia:*** **5** La Paz, Sucre ***Bosnia and Herzegovina:*** **8** Sarajevo ***Botswana:*** **8** Gaborone ***Brazil:*** **8** Brasília ***Bulgaria:*** **5** Sofia ***Burkina Faso:*** **11** Ouagadougou ***Burma:*** **6** Yangon **7** Rangoon ***Burundi:*** **9** Bujumbura ***Cambodia:*** **9** Phnom Penh ***Cameroon:*** **7** Yaoundé ***Canada:*** **6** Ottawa ***Cape Verde:*** **5** Praia ***Central African Republic:*** **6** Bangui ***Chad:*** **8** N'Djamena ***Chile:*** **8** Santiago ***China:*** **6** Peking **7** Beijing ***Colombia:*** **6** Bogotá ***Comoros:*** **6** Moroni ***Congo (Zaire):*** **8** Kinshasa ***Costa Rica:*** **7** San José ***Côte d'Ivoire:*** **7** Abidjan **12** Yamoussoukro ***Croatia:*** **6** Zagreb ***Cuba:*** **6** Havana ***Cyprus:*** **7** Nicosia ***Czech Republic:*** **6** Prague ***Denmark:*** **10** Copenhagen ***Dominica:*** **6** Roseau ***Dominican Republic:*** **12** Santo Domingo ***East Timor:*** **4** Dili ***Ecuador:*** **5** Quito ***Egypt:*** **5** Cairo ***El Salvador:*** **11** San Salvador ***Equatorial Guinea:*** **6** Malabo ***Eritrea:*** **6** Asmara ***Estonia:*** **7** Tallinn ***Ethiopia:*** **10** Addis Ababa ***Faeroe Islands:*** **8** Tórshavn ***Falkland Islands:*** **7** Stanley ***Fiji:*** **4** Suva ***Finland:*** **8** Helsinki ***France:*** **5** Paris ***French Guiana:*** **7** Cayenne ***Gabon:*** **10** Libreville ***Galápagos Islands:*** **12** San Cristóbal ***Gambia:*** **6** Banjul ***Georgia, Republic of:*** **6** Tiflis **7** Tbilisi ***Germany:*** **6** Berlin ***Ghana:*** **5** Accra ***Greece:*** **6** Athens ***Greenland:*** **8** Godthaab ***Grenada:*** **9** St. George's **12** Saint George's ***Guam:*** **5** Agana ***Guinea:*** **7** Conakry ***Guyana:*** **10** Georgetown ***Haiti:*** **12** Port-au-Prince ***Honduras:*** **11** Tegucigalpa ***Hungary:*** **8** Budapest ***Iceland:*** **9** Reykjavík ***India:*** **8** New Delhi ***Indonesia:*** **7** Jakarta **8** Djakarta ***Iran:*** **6** Tehran **7** Teheran ***Iraq:*** **7** Baghdad ***Ireland:*** **4** Tara **6** Dublin ***Israel:*** **7** Tel-Aviv **9** Jerusalem ***Italy:*** **4** Rome ***Jamaica:*** **8** Kingston ***Japan:*** **5** Tokyo ***Jordan:*** **5** Amman ***Kazakhstan:*** **6** Astana **7** Alma-Ata ***Kenya:*** **7** Nairobi ***Kiribati:*** **6** Tarawa **11** South Tarawa ***Korea, North:*** **9** Pyongyang ***Korea, South:*** **5** Seoul ***Kuwait:*** **10** Kuwait City ***Kyrgyzstan:*** **7** Bishkek ***Laos:*** **9** Vientiane ***Latvia:*** **4** Riga ***Lebanon:*** **6** Beirut ***Lesotho:*** **6** Maseru ***Libya:*** **7** Tripoli ***Liechtenstein:*** **5** Vaduz ***Lithuania:*** **7** Vilnius ***Macedonia:*** **6** Skopje ***Madagascar:*** **12** Antananarivo ***Malawi:*** **8** Lilongwe ***Malaysia:*** **11** Kuala Lumpur ***Maldives:*** **4** Male ***Mali:*** **6** Bamako ***Malta:*** **8** Valletta ***Manitoba:*** **8** Winnipeg ***Marshall Islands:*** **6** Majuro ***Mauritania:*** **10** Nouakchott ***Mauritius:*** **9** Port Louis ***Micronesia:*** **7** Palikir ***Moldova:*** **8** Chişinău, Kishinev ***Mongolia:*** **9** Ulan Bator **11** Ulaanbaatar ***Montenegro:*** **7** Cetinje **9** Podgorica ***Montserrat:*** **8** Plymouth ***Morocco:*** **5** Rabat ***Mozambique:*** **6** Maputo ***Myanmar:*** **6** Yangon **7** Rangoon ***Namibia:*** **8** Windhoek ***Nauru:*** **5** Yaren ***Nepal:*** **8** Katmandu **9** Kathmandu ***Netherlands:*** **9** Amsterdam ***Newfoundland:*** **10** Saint Johns ***New Zealand:*** **10** Wellington ***Nicaragua:*** **7** Managua ***Niger:*** **6** Niamey ***Nigeria:*** **5** Abuja ***Northern Ireland:*** **7** Belfast

Northern Territory: **6** Darwin ***North-West Frontier Province:*** **8** Peshawar ***Northwest Territories:*** **11** Yellowknife ***Norway:*** **4** Oslo ***Nova Scotia:*** **7** Halifax ***Oman:*** **6** Muscat ***Pakistan:*** **9** Islamabad ***Palau:*** **5** Koror **10** Babelthuap ***Papua New Guinea:*** **11** Port Moresby ***Paraguay:*** **8** Asunción ***Peru:*** **4** Lima ***Philippines:*** **6** Manila ***Poland:*** **6** Warsaw ***Portugal:*** **6** Lisbon ***Prince Edward Island:*** **13** Charlottetown ***Puerto Rico:*** **7** San Juan ***Qatar:*** **4** Doha ***Queensland:*** **8** Brisbane ***Réunion:*** **7** St. Denis **10** Saint Denis ***Romania:*** **9** Bucharest ***Russia:*** **6** Moscow ***Rwanda:*** **6** Kigali ***Saint Helena:*** **9** Jamestown ***Saint Kitts and Nevis:*** **10** Basseterre ***Saint Lucia:*** **8** Castries ***Samoa:*** **4** Apia ***Saskatchewan:*** **6** Regina ***Saudi Arabia:*** **6** Riyadh ***Scotland:*** **9** Edinburgh ***Senegal:*** **5** Dakar ***Serbia:*** **8** Belgrade ***Seychelles:*** **8** Victoria ***Shetland:*** **7** Lerwick ***Sicily:*** **7** Palermo ***Sierra Leone:*** **8** Freetown ***Sikkim:*** **7** Gangtok ***Sind:*** **7** Karachi ***Slovakia:*** **10** Bratislava ***Slovenia:*** **9** Ljubljana ***Solomon Islands:*** **7** Honiara ***Somalia:*** **9** Mogadishu ***South Africa:*** **8** Cape Town, Pretoria **12** Bloemfontein ***South Australia:*** **8** Adelaide ***South-West Africa:*** **8** Windhoek ***Spain:*** **6** Madrid ***Sri Lanka:*** **7** Colombo ***Sudan:*** **8** Khartoum ***Suriname:*** **10** Paramaribo ***Swaziland:*** **7** Mbabane ***Sweden:*** **9** Stockholm ***Switzerland:*** **4** Bern **5** Berne ***Syria:*** **8** Damascus ***Tahiti:*** **7** Papeete ***Taiwan:*** **6** Taipei ***Tajikistan:*** **8** Dushanbe ***Tanzania:*** **6** Dodoma **11** Dar es Salaam ***Tasmania:*** **6** Hobart ***Thailand:*** **7** Bangkok ***Tibet:*** **5** Lhasa ***Tirol:*** **9** Innsbruck ***Togo:*** **4** Lomé ***Tonga:*** **9** Nuku'alofa ***Trinidad and Tobago:*** **11** Port-of-Spain ***Tunisia:*** **5** Tunis ***Turkey:*** **6** Ankara ***Turkmenistan:*** **8** Ashgabat **9** Ashkhabad ***Tuvalu:*** **8** Funafuti ***Uganda:*** **7** Kampala ***Ukraine:*** **4** Kiev ***United Arab Emirates:*** **8** Abu Dhabi ***United Kingdom:*** **6** London ***Uruguay:*** **10** Montevideo ***Uttar Pradesh:*** **7** Lucknow ***Uzbekistan:*** **8** Tashkent ***Vanuatu:*** **4** Vila ***Venezuela:*** **7** Caracas ***Victoria:*** **9** Melbourne ***Vietnam:*** **5** Hanoi ***Wales:*** **7** Cardiff ***Western Australia:*** **5** Perth ***Yemen:*** **4** Sana **5** Sanaa ***Yugoslavia:*** **8** Belgrade ***Yukon:*** **10** Whitehorse ***Zambia:*** **6** Lusaka ***Zimbabwe:*** **6** Harare

capitalist 6 backer, tycoon **7** magnate **8** investor **9** bourgeois, financier, plutocrat **12** entrepreneur

capitalistic 9 bourgeois

capitalize 4 back, fund **5** stake **6** profit **7** convert, finance, promote, sponsor, support **8** bankroll **9** grubstake, subsidize

capital sin see **deadly sin**

capitation 3 tax **7** payment, poll tax

Capitol Hill sound 3 aye, nay

capitulate 3 bow **4** cave **5** defer, yield **6** cave in, give in, give up, relent, submit **7** concede, succumb **9** acquiesce, surrender **12** knuckle under

capitulation 9 surrender **10** submission

capo 3 bar **4** boss, head **5** chief **9** godfather

capote 4 cope **5** cloak **6** mantle, tabard **7** manteau, pelisse **8** overcoat

Capote work 11 In Cold Blood **19** Breakfast at Tiffany's

capper 4 lure **5** blind, decoy, shill **6** climax, finale **8** clincher

capriccio 4 whim **5** caper, fancy, prank **6** notion, vagary, whimsy **7** impulse

caprice 3 bee **4** mood, vein, whim **5** fancy, freak, humor **6** foible, maggot, megrim, notion, vagary, whimsy **7** conceit **8** crotchet

capricious 4 iffy **5** flaky, moody **6** chancy, fickle **7** erratic, flighty, wayward **8** fanciful, unstable, variable, volatile **9** arbitrary, impulsive, mercurial, uncertain, whimsical **10** changeable, inconstant **12** effervescent, incalculable **13** temperamental, unpredictable

caprid 4 goat

capriole 4 leap **5** caper

capsize 4 keel, roll, sink **5** upset **7** founder, tip over **8** collapse, overturn, turn over

capstone 4 acme, apex, peak **6** apogee, climax, coping, summit, zenith **8** pinnacle **9** high point **11** culmination

capsule 6 canned, pocket, potted **7** compact, outline **9** condensed

capsulize 6 reduce **7** enclose **8** compress, condense **9** summarize, synopsize

captain 6 master **7** skipper ***fictional:*** **4** Ahab, Hook, Kirk, Nemo **5** Queeg **10** Hornblower ***historical:*** **4** Cook (James) **5** Bligh (William) ***pirate:*** **4** Kidd (William) **6** Morgan (Henry)

Captains Courageous author 7 Kipling (Rudyard)

caption 5 title **6** legend, rubric **7** cutline, heading **8** subtitle **9** underline

captious 5 testy **7** carping, peevish **8** caviling, contrary, critical, exacting, petulant, snappish **9** demanding, irritable **10** censorious, nit-picking **12** faultfinding, overcritical **13** hypercritical

captivate 4 draw, grip, hold, take **5** charm **6** allure, dazzle, enamor, please, ravish, seduce **7** attract, beguile, bewitch, delight, enamour, enchant, gratify **8** enthrall **9** enrapture, fascinate, hypnotize, infatuate, magnetize, mesmerize, spellbind

captivating 8 charming, enticing, fetching, magnetic, riveting **9** appealing, glamorous, seductive **10** bewitching, engrossing, intriguing **11** enthralling, fascinating
captive 5 bound, caged, taken **6** jailed **7** hostage **8** confined, detainee, internee, prisoner **10** enthralled, hypnotized, imprisoned
captivity 7 bondage, custody, slavery **9** detention **10** internment **11** confinement **12** imprisonment
capture 3 bag, get, nab, net, win **4** nail, take, trap **5** catch, lasso, prize, seize, snare **6** arrest, collar, entrap, occupy, secure **7** conquer, ensnare **8** preserve
Capuan 4 lush **5** plush **6** deluxe **7** opulent **8** luscious, palatial **9** luxuriant, luxurious, sumptuous **11** upholstered
car 4 auto, heap **5** buggy, coach, crate, sedan, wreck **6** beater, jalopy, junker, wheels **7** clunker, flivver **8** roadster **10** automobile, rattletrap, rust bucket ***city:*** **4** Aygo, Lupo **5** Matiz, Panda, Prime **6** Twingo **7** Picanto (see also **automobile**)
carafe 4 ewer **5** cruet **6** bottle, flacon, flagon **8** decanter
caravan 6 convoy, safari
caravansary 3 inn **4** khan **5** hotel, lodge, serai **6** hostel, tavern **10** campground
carbohydrate 5 sugar **6** starch **7** amylose, glucose, lactose, maltose, sucrose **8** fructose, glycogen **9** cellulose, galactose
carbolic acid 6 phenol
carbon 4 coal, coke, soot **8** charcoal, graphite, plumbago **9** lampblack
carbonate 6 aerate
carbon copy 4 dupe, twin **5** clone, ditto, mimeo, repro, Xerox **7** replica **8** knockoff **9** duplicate, facsimile **10** dead ringer **11** replication **12** reproduction
carbonize 4 burn, char, sear **5** singe, toast **6** scorch
carbuncle 4 boil, sore **5** ulcer **6** garnet, pimple **7** abscess, pustule **8** cabochon
carcass 4 body, hulk, mort **5** frame, shell, stiff **6** corpse **7** cadaver, remains **8** skeleton
carcinoid 5 tumor **8** neoplasm
carcinoma 5 tumor **6** cancer **8** neoplasm
card 3 wag, wit **4** menu, sked **5** joker **6** agenda, docket **7** program **8** calendar, comedian, humorist, schedule **9** timetable ***fortune-telling:*** **5** tarot ***game:*** **3** gin, loo, Uno, war **4** faro, fish, skat, solo, stud **5** monte, ombre, pitch, poker, rummy, whist **6** Boston, bridge, casino, écarté, euchre, fan-tan, hearts, piquet **7** auction, bezique, canasta, cooncan, old maid, primero **8** baccarat, Canfield, conquian, cribbage, gin rummy, pinochle **9** blackjack, solitaire, twenty-one, vingt-et-un **11** chemin de fer ***game authority:*** **5** Hoyle (Edmond) ***high:*** **3** ace ***low:*** **5** deuce ***performer's:*** **3** cue ***spot:*** **3** pip ***wild:*** **5** deuce, joker
cardboard 5 stiff **6** unreal, wooden **7** bristol, buckram, stilted **8** lifeless **10** unlifelike **11** stereotyped, unrealistic
card-carrying 4 true **7** genuine **8** bona fide **9** authentic, certified **11** full-fledged
cardiac stimulant 7 ouabain **9** digitalis
cardinal 3 key **4** main **5** basic, chief, prime, vital **6** ruling **7** central, leading, pivotal, primary **9** essential, important, principal **10** overriding, overruling **11** fundamental **12** constitutive ***point:*** **4** east, west **5** north, south ***suffix:*** **4** teen ***title:*** **8** Eminence ***virtue:*** **7** justice **8** prudence **9** fortitude **10** temperance
care 4 fear, heed, mind, tend, ward **5** alarm, nurse, serve, trust, worry **6** attend, charge, effort, regard, regret, strain, stress, unease, wait on **7** anguish, anxiety, concern, custody, keeping **8** disquiet, handling **9** attention, curiosity, misgiving, oversight **10** management, solicitude **11** maintenance, safekeeping, supervision **12** guardianship **13** consideration
careen 4 race, sway, tilt **5** lurch, pitch, speed, swing, weave **6** repair, wobble **7** stagger
career 3 job **4** race, rush, tear, work **5** chase, speed **6** charge, course **7** calling, passage **8** lifework, vocation **9** encounter **10** livelihood, profession
care for 4 like, love, mind, tend **5** nurse, treat **6** attend, foster **7** cherish, nurture **8** preserve **9** cultivate, look after
carefree 4 wild **6** blithe, breezy, jaunty **8** reckless **10** insouciant, untroubled **12** happy-go-lucky, lighthearted **13** irresponsible
careful 4 safe, wary **5** chary, exact, fussy **7** dutiful, guarded, precise, prudent, studied **8** accurate, cautious, critical, discreet, gingerly, thorough **9** attentive, provident **10** deliberate, meticulous, particular, scrupulous **11** calculating, circumspect, considerate, foresighted, painstaking, punctilious **13** conscientious
carefully 6 warily **8** gingerly **10** cautiously, discreetly **12** meticulously, scrupulously **13** painstakingly, punctiliously
careless 3 lax **5** hasty, messy, slack **6** casual, remiss, sloppy, untidy **7** cursory, offhand, unkempt **8** feckless, heedless, reckless, slapdash, slipshod, slovenly **9** forgetful, negligent, oblivious, unheeding, unmindful,

unstudied **10** disheveled, inaccurate, incautious, neglectful, unthinking, untroubled **11** inadvertent, inattentive, indifferent, perfunctory, spontaneous, thoughtless, unconcerned **12** uninterested, unreflective **13** irresponsible

caress 3 pat, pet, toy **4** kiss, love **5** dally, touch **6** coddle, cosset, cuddle, dandle, fondle, nuzzle, pamper, stroke **7** cherish, indulge **8** canoodle **10** endearment

caressive 7 calming **8** soothing

caretaker 6 warden **7** curator, janitor **9** custodian

careworn 3 wan **5** drawn, faded, jaded **7** haggard, pinched, wearied **8** fatigued, troubled **9** exhausted **10** distressed

cargo 4 haul, load **6** burden, lading **7** freight, payload **8** shipload, shipment **11** consignment

Caribbean country 4 Cuba **5** Haiti **7** Bahamas, Grenada, Jamaica **8** Dominica **10** Saint Lucia

caribe 7 piranha

caribou 4 deer **8** reindeer ***kin:*** **3** elk **6** wapiti

caricature 4 mock, sham **5** farce, phony **6** parody **7** cartoon, lampoon, mockery, takeoff **8** travesty **9** burlesque **10** distortion, pasquinade **12** exaggeration

Carlsbad feature 4 cave **6** cavern

Carmen *author:* **7** Mérimée (Prosper) ***composer:*** **5** Bizet (Georges) ***lover:*** **7** Don José **9** Escamillo

carnage 4 gore **8** butchery, hecatomb, massacre **9** bloodbath, bloodshed, slaughter

carnal 4 lewd **6** animal, bodily, coarse, earthy, sexual, vulgar, wanton **7** earthly, fleshly, lustful, mundane, obscene, sensual, worldly **8** corporal, material, physical, sensuous, temporal **9** corporeal **10** lascivious

carnation 4 pink **5** color **6** flower

carnival 4 fair, fete **6** fiesta ***attraction:*** **4** ride **6** midway **8** sideshow **10** concession ***character:*** **5** shill **6** barker, hawker **7** grifter, spieler ***game:*** **8** Skee-Ball ***New Orleans:*** **9** Mardi Gras ***performer:*** **4** geek

carnivore 9 meat-eater **10** flesh-eater

carol 4 song **6** ballad ***Christmas:*** **4** noel

carom 6 bounce, glance **7** rebound **8** ricochet

Caron role 4 Gigi, Lili **5** Fanny

carotid's relative 5 aorta

carousal 3 bat, jag **4** bash, tear **5** binge, booze, drunk, fling, revel, spree **6** bender, frolic **7** blowout, debauch, shindig **8** wingding **9** brannigan ***Scottish:*** **6** splore

carouse 5 revel **6** cavort, frolic **7** roister ***Scottish:*** **4** birl

carp 3 nag **4** crab, fuss **5** bream, cavil, scold **6** peck at, pester **7** henpeck **8** complain, cyprinid, sea bream **9** complaint, criticize, find fault

carpe ____ 4 diem

carpenter 3 ant, bee **6** joiner, wright **7** builder, workman **10** woodworker

carpentry 7 joinery **10** timberwork ***tool:*** **3** saw **5** drill, plane **6** chisel, hammer **11** brace and bit, screwdriver

carper 6 critic, nagger **7** caviler, knocker **9** nitpicker **10** complainer, criticizer **11** faultfinder

carpet 3 mat, rug **4** Agra **5** Herat, Heriz, Koula, Ladik, Sarok, tapis **6** Herati, Kerman, Keshan, Kirman, Sarouk, Tabriz, Wilton **8** moquette **9** Axminster, broadloom

carpet beetle 10 buffalo bug

carping 7 blaming, railing **8** captious, critical **10** censorious **11** reproachful **12** faultfinding, overcritical

carrageen 7 seaweed **9** Irish moss

carrefour 5 plaza **6** square **10** crossroads

carriage 3 gig, rig **4** pose **5** coach **6** stance **7** posture, transit **8** attitude **9** transport **10** conveyance, deportment ***American:*** **5** buggy **8** rockaway **9** buckboard ***attendant:*** **6** flunky **7** footman ***baby:*** **4** pram **5** buggy **8** stroller **12** perambulator ***driver:*** **4** hack **5** cabby **8** coachman ***folding top:*** **6** calash ***four-wheeled:*** **4** trap **5** buggy, coupe **6** berlin, calash, fiacre, landau, surrey **7** droshky, hackney, phaeton **8** barouche, brougham, carryall, clarence, rockaway, sociable, stanhope, victoria **9** buckboard ***Indian:*** **6** gharry ***man-drawn:*** **8** rickshaw **10** jinricksha, jinrikisha ***Russian:*** **6** troika **7** droshky ***stately:*** **7** caroche ***three-horse:*** **6** troika ***two-wheeled:*** **3** gig **4** shay, trap **5** buggy, sulky, tonga **6** chaise, dennet, hansom **7** calèche, dogcart, tilbury **8** curricle **9** cabriolet ***with attendants:*** **8** equipage

carriage trade 5 elite **6** gentry **7** quality **9** blue blood, gentility **10** upper class, upper crust **11** aristocracy

carrick bend 4 knot

carrier 4 mule **5** envoy **6** bearer, porter, runner, vector **7** airline, courier, shipper, vehicle **8** conveyor, emissary **9** go-between, messenger, stretcher **11** internuncio, transporter

Carroll character 5 Alice, Bruno, snark **6** boojum, Sylvie **8** Dormouse, Red Queen **9** Mad Hatter, March Hare **10** Mock Turtle **11** White Rabbit **12** Humpty Dumpty

carrot 5 prize **6** reward **9** incentive **10** inducement

carry 3 get, lug **4** bear, haul, have, hump,

keep, move, pack, send, take, tote, wear **5** bring, ferry, fetch, range, stock **6** affect, bear up, convey, uphold **7** comport, conduct, portage, possess, support, sustain **8** buttress, transfer, transmit **9** influence, transport
carryall 4 tote **7** tote bag
carrying case 7 holdall, satchel
carry off 4 kill **6** abduct, kidnap, remove **7** achieve, destroy, execute, perform, realize **8** complete, conclude, dispatch, shanghai **10** accomplish, spirit away
carry on 3 run **4** go on, keep, rant, rave, wage **6** direct, endure, manage, ordain **7** conduct, operate, persist, prattle, proceed **8** continue, sound off **9** persevere
carry out 6 effect, govern, render **7** achieve, execute, fulfill, oversee, perform, realize **8** bring off, complete, finalize, transact **9** discharge, prosecute **10** accomplish, administer, effectuate **12** administrate
carry over 6 deduct **7** persist **8** postpone, transfer
carry through 4 last **5** abide **6** effect, endure **7** execute, perdure, perform, persist, survive **8** bring off, complete, continue **10** accomplish, effectuate
Carson work 11 Sea Around Us (The) **12** Silent Spring
cart 3 gig **4** dray, haul **5** buggy, carry **6** barrow, convey, schlep **7** schlepp, trundle, tumbrel, tumbril **8** carriage **9** transport **11** wheelbarrow ***Indian:* 5** tonga ***racing:* 5** sulky
____ **carte 3** à la
____ **Carte 5** D'Oyly
carte blanche 3 say **5** power, right, say-so **7** freedom, license **8** free hand, free rein **9** authority **10** blank check **11** prerogative
carte du jour 4 menu
cartel 4 bloc, OPEC, pool **5** trust **7** combine **9** syndicate **10** consortium **12** conglomerate
Carthaginian *goddess of the moon:* 5 Tanit **6** Tanith ***queen:* 4** Dido **6** Elissa
cartilage 7 gristle
cartographer *English:* 5 Smith (William) ***Flemish:* 6** Kremer (Gerhard) **8** Mercator (Gerardus), Ortelius ***German:* 13** Waldseemüller (Martin) ***Greek:* 7** Ptolemy ***Italian:* 8** Vespucci (Amerigo)
cartography 9 mapmaking
carton 3 box **4** pack
cartoon 5 anime, manga **10** comic strip (see also **comic strip**)
cartoonist 3 Lee (Stan) **4** Arno (Peter), Auth (Tony), Capp (Al), Kane (Bob), Nast (Thomas), Szep (Paul) **5** Adams (Scott), Block (Herbert), Booth (George), Chast (Roz), Crumb (R.), Davis (Jim), Gould (Chester), Hanna (Bill), Jones (Chuck), Kelly (Walt), Steig (William), Toles (Tom), Young (Chic) **6** Addams (Charles), Caniff (Milton), Conrad (Paul), Disney (Walt), Larson (Gary), Martin (Don), Peters (Mike), Schulz (Charles), Walker (Mort) **7** Barbera (Joe), Feiffer (Jules), Ketcham (Hank), Mauldin (Bill), Thurber (James), Trudeau (Garry) **8** Goldberg (Rube), Groening (Matt), Herblock, Hokinson (Helen), MacNelly (Jeff), Oliphant (Pat) **9** Fleischer (Max) **10** Hirschfeld (Al)
cartouche 5 frame **6** shield **9** cartridge
cartridge 4 case, tube **5** shell **8** cassette, cylinder **9** cartouche, container
cartwheel 4 coin **6** dollar, tumble **10** handspring
carve 3 cut, hew **4** chip, etch, form, hack **5** shape, slice **6** chisel, cleave, incise, sculpt **7** dissect, engrave, whittle **9** sculpture
Casablanca *actor:* 5 Lorre (Peter), Rains (Claude) **6** Bogart (Humphrey) **7** Bergman (Ingrid), Henreid (Paul) **11** Greenstreet (Sydney) ***character:* 4** Ilsa (Lund), Rick (Blaine) **6** Laszlo (Victor) ***director:* 6** Curtiz (Michael)
Casanova 4 rake, roué, wolf **5** Romeo **6** lecher, masher, tomcat **7** amorist, Don Juan, gallant, playboy, seducer **8** lothario, paramour **9** adulterer, ladies' man, libertine, womanizer **10** lady-killer, voluptuary **11** philanderer
cascade 4 fall, gush, lace, pour, spew **5** chute, falls, flood, spill **6** deluge, plunge, rapids, shower, tumble **7** Niagara, torrent **8** cataract **9** avalanche, waterfall **10** outpouring
Cascade Mountains peak 6 Lassen, Shasta **7** Rainier
case 3 box, con, vet **4** etui, hull, husk, skin, suit **5** cause, event, shell, trunk **6** action, sample, sheath **7** episode, examine, example, inspect, lawsuit **8** argument, covering, incident, instance, sampling, specimen **9** check over, condition, situation **10** occurrence, proceeding, scrutinize **11** eventuality **12** circumstance ***grammatical:* 6** dative **8** ablative, genitive, vocative **9** objective **10** accusative, nominative, possessive
casebearer 5 larva **11** caterpillar
case-hardened 5 tough **7** callous **8** obdurate **9** indurated, insensate, toughened, unfeeling **11** insensitive **12** thick-skinned
casement 4 sash **6** window

Casey at the Bat poet **6** Thayer (Ernest Lawrence)

cash **4** coin, jack **5** bread, dough, money, scrip **6** dinero, redeem, wampum **7** cabbage, lettuce, scratch **8** currency **10** greenbacks, ready money **11** legal tender ***machine:*** **3** ATM

cashier **2** ax **3** axe, can **4** boot, fire, oust, sack **5** clerk, eject, expel, scrap **6** banker, bounce, bursar, reject, teller **7** boot out, discard, dismiss, kick out **8** jettison, throw out **9** discharge, eliminate, terminate, throw away **10** bookkeeper **11** bean counter, comptroller

cash in **3** die **4** conk, drop **5** croak **6** expire, pop off, redeem, retire **7** kick off, succumb **8** check out, drop dead, pass away, settle up **9** liquidate

casing **4** hull, husk, pipe, rind, skin, tire **5** frame, shell, space **7** wrapper **8** membrane

casino ***attendant:*** **6** dealer **8** croupier ***game:*** **4** faro **5** craps, monte, poker **6** tierce **8** baccarat, roulette **9** blackjack

cask **3** keg, tun **4** butt, drum, pipe **6** barrel, firkin **8** hogshead

casket **3** box **5** chest **6** coffer, coffin **8** jewel box

Caspian Sea ***city:*** **4** Baku ***feeder:*** **4** Kura, Ural **5** Volga

Cassandra **4** seer **7** prophet, seeress **8** doomster **9** doomsayer, pessimist, worrywart **10** prophetess ***brother:*** **7** Helenus ***father:*** **5** Priam ***lover:*** **9** Agamemnon ***mother:*** **6** Hecuba ***slayer:*** **12** Clytemnestra

cassava **4** yuca **5** yucca **6** manioc **7** tapioca

casserole **4** dish **5** crock **6** tureen

Cassiopeia **13** constellation ***daughter:*** **9** Andromeda ***husband:*** **7** Cepheus

Cassio's mistress **6** Bianca

cassock **4** robe **7** soutane **8** vestment

cassowary kin **3** emu, moa

cast **3** add, hue, sum, tot **4** drop, face, fire, form, hurl, kind, look, mold, shed, sort, tint, tone, toss, turn, type **5** color, fling, heave, leave, pitch, range, shade, shape, strew, throw, tinge, total, touch **6** actors, design, devise, direct, figure, nature, reject, slough, troupe, visage **7** arrange, company, quality, replica, scatter **8** abdicate, disperse, jettison, sprinkle **9** character, prognosis, throw away **10** appearance, conjecture, distribute, expression, prediction, strabismus, suggestion **11** countenance ***a spell on:*** **3** hex **5** charm **7** beguile, bewitch **8** enthrall **9** captivate, enrapture, fascinate, hypnotize, infatuate, mesmerize, spellbind ***overboard:*** **7** deep-six **8** jettison

cast about **4** hunt, seek **5** grope **6** search **7** seek out **8** contrive **9** search for, search out

castaway **5** leper, tramp **6** beggar, maroon, pariah **7** Ishmael, outcast, vagrant **8** deadbeat, derelict **10** Ishmaelite

cast down see **downcast**

caste **5** class **6** degree, estate, status **7** station **8** division, prestige

cast head **4** bust

castigate **4** beat, flay, rail, whip **5** baste, chide, scold, slash **6** berate, pummel, punish, rebuke, scorch, thrash **7** belabor, blister, chasten, chew out, lambast, reprove, scarify, scourge, upbraid **8** chastise, lambaste, penalize **9** criticize, dress down, excoriate, reprimand **10** discipline, tongue-lash

castigation **3** rod **6** rebuke **7** reproof **8** punition, scolding **10** correction, discipline, punishment **12** chastisement

castle **5** manor, villa **7** alcazar, château, citadel, mansion **8** fortress **10** stronghold ***adjunct:*** **4** moat ***gate:*** **10** portcullis ***ledge:*** **7** rampart ***structure:*** **6** turret ***tower:*** **4** keep **6** donjon ***wall:*** **6** bailey **10** battlement

cast off **5** fling, flung, let go, loose, untie **6** jilted, untied **7** unhitch **8** cut loose, forsaken, rejected, unfasten, unmoored **9** discarded, unhitched **10** left behind, unfastened

Castor ***brother:*** **6** Pollux **10** Polydeuces ***constellation:*** **6** Gemini ***father:*** **4** Zeus **9** Tyndareus ***mother:*** **4** Leda ***sister:*** **5** Helen ***slayer:*** **4** Idas

castor oil **8** laxative **9** cathartic, lubricant, purgative

cast out **4** oust **5** egest, eject, evict, exile, expel **6** banish, deport **7** discard **9** eliminate, ostracize

castrate **3** fix **4** geld, spay **5** alter, unman, unsex **6** neuter **7** unnerve **8** enervate, mutilate **9** sterilize **10** emasculate **11** desexualize

castrato singer **9** Farinelli

casual **5** light, minor **6** breezy, chance, random, remote **7** natural, offhand, relaxed, trivial, unfussy **8** detached, informal, laidback **9** easygoing, impromptu, irregular, uncurious, unplanned, unserious **10** accidental, contingent, fortuitous, improvised, incidental, insouciant, nonchalant, occasional **11** indifferent, low-pressure, spontaneous, unconcerned, unimportant **12** uninterested **13** disinterested, insignificant

casualty **4** prey **5** death **6** mishap, victim **8** accident, calamity, disaster, fatality **9** mischance **10** misfortune **11** catastrophe **12** misadventure

casuistry **7** sophism **9** deception, sophistry

12 equivocation, speciousness **13** deceptiveness

casus ____ 5 belli

cat 4 eyra, lion, lynx, pard, puma, puss **5** felid, kitty, liger, moggy, ounce, pussy, tabby, tiger, tigon **6** cougar, feline, jaguar, margay, mouser, ocelot, serval **7** caracal, cheetah, leopard, panther **10** jaguarundi **12** mountain lion ***Alice's:* 5** Dinah ***Born Free:* 4** Elsa ***combining form:* 5** ailur **6** ailuro ***disease:* 9** distemper ***domestic:* 3** Mau, Rex **4** Manx **5** tabby **6** Angora, Birman, calico, exotic, Ocicat, Somali **7** bobtail, Burmese, Persian, Ragdoll, Siamese **8** longhair, Wirehair **9** Himalayan, Maine coon, shorthair, Tonkinese **10** Abyssinian ***extinct:* 10** saber-tooth ***fastest:* 7** cheetah ***female:* 5** queen **7** lioness, tigress **9** grimalkin ***genus:* 5** Felis ***grinning:* 8** Cheshire ***hybrid:* 5** liger, tigon **6** Bengal, Safari **7** Chausie **8** Savannah ***lookalike:* 5** civet, genet **7** linsang ***male:* 3** gib, tom ***relating to:* 6** feline ***sound:* 3** mew **4** hiss, meow, purr, roar **5** miaou, miaow **9** caterwaul ***tailless:* 4** Manx ***young:* 6** kitten

cataclysm 5 flood **6** deluge **7** Niagara, torrent, tragedy **8** calamity, cataract, disaster, flooding **10** inundation **11** catastrophe, devastation

cataclysmic 5 fatal **7** ruinous **10** calamitous, disastrous **11** devastating **12** catastrophic

catacomb 5 crypt, vault **8** cemetery **10** necropolis, undercroft

catafalque 4 bier

catalepsy 6 trance

catalog 4 list, roll **5** enter, index, tally **6** enroll, roster **7** itemize, program **8** classify, inscribe, register, roll call, schedule, syllabus **9** enumerate, inventory **10** prospectus ***of books:* 11** bibliotheca ***of saints:* 9** hagiology

catalyst 4 goad, spur **7** impetus, impulse **8** stimulus **9** incentive, stimulant **10** incitation, incitement, motivation

catamaran 4 boat, raft

catamount 4 lynx, puma **6** bobcat, cougar **7** panther, wildcat **12** mountain lion

cataract 5 falls, flood, rapid **6** deluge, rapids **7** cascade, Niagara, torrent **8** downpour **9** waterfall **10** inundation

catastrophe 3 woe **6** deluge, fiasco **7** debacle, tragedy **8** calamity, disaster, meltdown **9** cataclysm, emergency **11** devastation

catastrophic 5 fatal **6** deadly, tragic **7** ruinous **10** calamitous, disastrous **11** cataclysmic

Catawba 4 wine **5** river **6** Indian

catcall 3 boo **4** hiss, hoot, jeer, razz **9** criticism, raspberry **10** Bronx cheer

catch 3 bag, get, nab, net, see, wed **4** dupe, find, fool, grab, grip, gull, haul, hoax, hook, nail, snag, sock, spot, take, trap **5** block, clasp, clout, grasp, hit on, marry, reach, round, seize, smite, snare, stick, stump, trick, watch, whack **6** accept, anchor, arrest, clutch, collar, cut off, descry, detect, engage, entrap, fasten, flurry, follow, put out, rattle, secure, snatch, strike, take in, tangle, turn up **7** capture, confuse, deceive, disturb, ensnare, grapple, hit upon, perplex, receive **8** confound, contract, entangle, flimflam, fragment, hoodwink, kick over, meet with, overhaul, overtake **9** apprehend, bamboozle, embarrass, encounter, intercept **10** comprehend, understand **12** come down with

Catch-22 author 6 Heller (Joseph)

catchall term 3 etc. **4** et al. **5** and/or **7** and so on **10** and so forth

Catcher in the Rye *author:* 8 Salinger (J. D.) ***character:* 9** Caulfield (Holden)

catcher's glove 4 mitt

catching 10 contagious, infectious **12** communicable

catch on 3 see **4** hear **5** learn **7** find out **8** discover **9** ascertain, determine, figure out

catchphrase see **catchword**

catch up 4 hold **6** gain on **7** close in, ensnare **8** entangle, enthrall **9** fascinate, mesmerize, spellbind

catchword 5 maxim, motto **6** slogan **10** shibboleth

catchy 6 fitful, spotty, tricky **7** erratic **8** sporadic **9** appealing, desultory, irregular, memorable, spasmodic

catechist 7 teacher

catechize 3 ask **4** quiz **5** grill, query, train **7** examine, inquire **8** instruct, question **9** inculcate **11** interrogate

catechumen 6 novice **7** convert, student, trainee **8** initiate, neophyte

categorical 7 certain, decided, express **8** absolute, clear-cut, definite, emphatic, explicit, positive **9** downright **10** definitive, forthright **11** unambiguous, unequivocal, unqualified

categorize 3 peg **4** sort **5** class, group **7** put down **8** classify, identify **10** pigeonhole

category 4 rank, tier **5** class, genre, grade, group, taxon **6** league **7** section **8** division, grouping **10** pigeonhole

catenation 4 link **5** chain **6** series, string **7** linkage **10** connection, succession

catercorner 9 obliquely, slantways, slantwise **10** cornerwise, diagonally

caterpillar **5** larva **7** cutworm, webworm **8** armyworm, silkworm **10** casebearer

cater to **5** humor **6** pamper, supply **7** furnish, gratify, indulge

caterwaul **4** howl, meow, yowl **5** miaow **6** squall

catfish see **fish**

catharsis **5** purge, tonic **7** purging **8** curative **9** cleansing, purgation, purgative **10** lustration **11** expurgation, restorative **12** purification

cathartic **5** purge, tonic **8** curative **9** castor oil, purgative **11** restorative, therapeutic

Cathay **5** China

cathedral **5** duomo **6** church **8** basilica ***feature:*** **4** apse, nave **5** altar **6** chapel **7** chancel **10** clerestory **8** buttress, transept

cathedral city **3** Ely **4** Bath, York **5** Wells **6** Durham, Exeter, London, Oxford **7** Bristol, Chester, Lincoln, Norwich **8** Carlisle, Coventry, Hereford **9** Lichfield, Liverpool, Salisbury, Worcester **10** Canterbury, Chichester, Gloucester, Winchester **11** Westminster **12** Peterborough

Cather novel **8** Lost Lady (A) **9** My Antonia, One of Ours, O Pioneers **13** Song of the Lark **15** Professor's House (The) **16** Shadows on the Rock

catholic **5** broad **6** global **7** general, liberal **8** eclectic, tolerant **9** expansive, inclusive, undivided, universal, worldwide **10** ecumenical **12** cosmopolitan **13** comprehensive

catholicity **7** breadth **9** tolerance **10** liberality **11** magnanimity **12** universality

catholicon **6** elixir **7** cure-all, nostrum, panacea

catkin **5** ament

catlike **6** feline **7** furtive **8** stealthy

catnap **3** nap **4** doze **6** siesta, snooze **10** forty winks

catnip **3** nep

Cato ***title:*** **6** aedile, censor, consul **7** praetor, tribune **8** quaestor

cat's-paw **4** dupe, knot, pawn, tool **5** patsy **6** puppet, stooge

cattail **4** reed, rush

cattle **4** cows, kine, neat, oxen **7** bovines **9** livestock ***breed:*** **5** Angus, Devon, Kerry **6** Durham, Jersey, Sussex **7** Brahman, Hariana, Red Poll **8** Ayrshire, Galloway, Guernsey, Hereford, Highland, Holstein, Limousin, Longhorn **9** Charolais, Red Polled, Shorthorn, Simmental **10** Brown Swiss **11** Dutch Belted ***catching rope:*** **5** lasso **6** lariat ***cry:*** **3** low, moo ***dehorn:*** **4** poll ***disease:*** **4** loco **5** bloat **6** mad cow, nagana **7** anthrax, locoism, measles, murrain **8** blackleg, lumpy jaw, mastitis, staggers **10** rinderpest, Texas fever **11** brucellosis ***dung:*** **4** tath ***extinct breed:*** **9** Teeswater ***family:*** **7** Bovidae ***feed:*** **6** fodder, silage, stover ***genus:*** **3** Bos ***goddess:*** **6** Bubona ***grazing land:*** **5** range **6** meadow **7** pasture ***group:*** **4** herd **5** drove ***herdsman:*** **6** cowboy, drover, gaucho **7** vaquero **8** neatherd, wrangler **10** cowpuncher ***identification:*** **5** brand ***pen:*** **6** corral ***round up:*** **7** wrangle ***stable:*** **4** barn, byre ***steal:*** **6** rustle ***wild flight:*** **8** stampede

catty **4** mean **5** nasty **6** barbed, bitchy, feline **7** furtive, vicious **8** spiteful, stealthy **9** malicious **10** backbiting, malevolent

Caucasian ***capital:*** **4** Baku **6** Tiflis **7** Tbilisi, Yerevan ***republic:*** **7** Armenia, Georgia **10** Azerbaijan

Caucasus ***peak:*** **6** Elbrus ***people:*** **5** Osset

caucus **4** bloc, sect **5** cabal, lobby **6** parley, powwow **7** faction

caudal appendage **4** tail

caudillo **6** despot, tyrant **8** dictator **9** strongman

cauldron **3** pot **6** boiler, kettle **8** crucible

cause **4** case, make, root **5** evoke, hatch **6** compel, effect, elicit, induce, motive, origin, reason, source, spring **7** produce, provoke **8** engender, generate, movement **9** necessity, principle **10** antecedent, bring about, inducement, originator **11** determinant, precipitate **13** consideration

cause ____ **7** célèbre

causerie **4** chat **5** essay **6** column **7** article, feature **8** colloquy, dialogue **12** conversation

caustic **4** acid, keen, tart **5** acerb, acrid, sharp **6** biting, bitter, ironic **7** acerbic, cutting, mordant, pungent **8** scathing, stinging **9** corrosive, sarcastic, trenchant **10** astringent ***solution:*** **3** lye

cauterize **4** burn, numb, sear **6** deaden **11** anesthetize

caution **4** warn **6** caveat **7** warning **8** forewarn, monition, prudence **9** canniness, chariness, foresight, vigilance **10** admonition, discretion, providence **11** carefulness, forethought, forewarning **12** admonishment, discreetness

cautionary **7** warning **8** monitory **10** admonitory

cautious **4** wary **5** alert, cagey, canny, chary, leery **6** shrewd **7** careful, guarded, politic, prudent **8** discreet, gingerly, vigilant, watchful **9** judicious, provident **11** circumspect, considerate, foresighted

cavalcade **6** parade, series **7** cortege **8** sequence **10** procession, succession

cavalier 5 lofty, proud **6** casual, knight, lordly **7** gallant, haughty, offhand **8** arrogant, debonair, horseman, scornful, superior **9** caballero, gentleman **10** disdainful, dismissive, insouciant, nonchalant **12** aristocratic, supercilious

cavalryman 6 lancer **7** dragoon, trooper ***Algerian:*** **5** spahi ***horse:*** **5** waler ***Prussian:*** **5** uhlan ***Russian:*** **7** cossack ***Turkish:*** **5** spahi ***weapon:*** **5** lance, saber **7** carbine

cave 3 bow, den **4** bend, drop, give, grot, lair **5** antre, break, defer, yield **6** fold up, grotto, hollow, submit **7** crumple, knuckle, succumb **8** collapse **9** break down **10** capitulate, subterrane **11** buckle under **12** knuckle under, subterranean ***dweller:*** **3** bat **4** bear, lion **6** hermit **9** Cro-Magnon **10** troglodite **11** Neanderthal ***explorer:*** **9** spelunker ***formation:*** **10** stalactite, stalagmite ***France:*** **7** Lascaux **10** Rouffignac ***Iceland:*** **7** Singing ***Indiana:*** **9** Wyandotte ***Iraq:*** **8** Shanidar ***Kentucky:*** **7** Mammoth ***New Zealand:*** **7** Waitomo ***rock:*** **8** dolomite **9** limestone ***Scotland:*** **7** Fingal's ***South Africa:*** **5** Cango ***Spain:*** **8** Altamira ***study of:*** **10** speleology

caveat 6 notice **7** caution, warning **8** monition **10** admonition **11** explanation, forewarning

caveat ____ 6 emptor

caveman 5 brute **6** savage **9** barbarian, Cro-Magnon **10** troglodyte

cavern 6 grotto **12** subterranean ***Capri:*** **10** Blue Grotto ***Montana:*** **13** Lewis and Clark ***New Mexico:*** **8** Carlsbad ***Tennessee:*** **10** Cumberland ***Virginia:*** **5** Luray

cavernous 4 vast **6** gaping, hollow **7** yawning

caviar 3 roe **4** eggs **6** relish ***source:*** **6** beluga **8** sturgeon

cavil 4 carp **7** nitpick, quibble **9** criticize, find fault

caviler 6 carper, critic **7** knocker **8** quibbler **10** criticizer **11** faultfinder

caviling 5 fussy **7** carping, finicky, nagging **8** captious, contrary, critical, exacting, niggling **10** censorious, nitpicking **12** faultfinding **13** hairsplitting

cavity 3 pit **4** bore, hole, void **5** decay, fossa **6** caries, hollow **7** vacuity **10** depression, interstice ***body:*** **5** antra (plural), sinus **6** antrum **8** follicle, hemocoel

cavort 4 leap, romp **5** caper, cut up, frisk, sport **6** frolic, gambol, prance **7** carry on, rollick **10** roughhouse **11** horse around

cavy 4 paca **6** rodent **9** guinea pig

caw 4 crow, yawp **6** squall, squawk

cay 3 key **4** isle, reef **5** islet **6** island

cayenne 6 pepper ***genus:*** **8** Capsicum

cayman see **caiman**

Cayman Islands *capital:* **10** George Town ***discoverer:*** **8** Columbus (Christopher) ***territory of:*** **7** Britain

Cayuga chief 5 Logan (James)

cease 3 die, end **4** halt, quit, stop **5** close **6** desist, ending, finish **8** conclude, give over, knock off, leave off **9** terminate **10** conclusion **11** discontinue, termination

cease-fire 5 truce **9** armistice **10** suspension

ceaseless 7 endless, eternal, nonstop **8** constant, immortal, unending **9** continual, incessant, perennial, perpetual, sustained, unabating **10** continuing, continuous **11** everlasting, never-ending, unremitting **12** interminable **13** uninterrupted

Cecrops' daughter 5 Herse **8** Aglauros, Aglaurus **9** Pandrosos, Pandrosus

cede 4 deed **5** grant, leave, yield **6** assign, convey, give up **7** abandon, concede **8** alienate, hand over, make over, part with, renounce, sign over, transfer **9** surrender, vouchsafe **10** relinquish

ceinture 4 belt, sash **6** girdle **9** waistband

Celaeno *father:* **5** Atlas ***mother:*** **7** Pleione ***sisters:*** **8** Pleiades

celebrate 4 fete, hold, hymn, keep, laud **5** bless, cry up, exalt, extol, honor, party, revel **6** praise **7** carouse, glorify, maffick, observe, perform, rejoice **8** eulogize **9** solemnize **11** commemorate

celebrated 5 famed, great, noted **6** famous **7** eminent, notable, partied **8** caroused, rejoiced, renowned **9** prominent, well-known **11** illustrious **13** distinguished

celebration 4 bash, fete, gala **5** beano, party **6** fiesta **7** blowout, jubilee, revelry **8** ceremony, festival, jamboree, wingding **10** observance

celebrity 3 VIP **4** fame, hero, lion, name, star **5** éclat, glory **6** renown, repute **7** notable **8** eminence, luminary, prestige, somebody **9** notoriety, personage, superstar **10** notability, prominence, reputation

celerity 4 pace **5** speed **8** alacrity, dispatch, rapidity, velocity **9** briskness, fleetness, quickness, swiftness **10** speediness

celestial 6 divine **7** blessed, elysian, sublime **8** beatific, empyreal, empyrean, ethereal, heavenly, Olympian, supernal **9** unearthly **12** otherworldly

celestial body 3 sun **4** moon, star **5** comet **6** meteor, nebula, planet **8** asteroid **9** satellite

Celestial Empire 5 China

celibate 5 unwed **6** chaste, single, virgin **8** virginal, virtuous **9** abstinent, continent

cell 4 room **5** cubby, zooid **6** alcove **7** chamber, cubicle **9** corpuscle, cubbyhole **11** compartment ***blood:*** **8** hemocyte ***disease:*** **6** cancer ***division:*** **7** meiosis, mitosis ***fertilized egg:*** **6** zygote ***material:*** **3** DNA, RNA **7** protein **9** chromatin, cytoplasm **10** protoplasm ***nerve:*** **6** neuron ***part:*** **4** gene **7** nucleus, vacuole **8** ribosome **9** centriole **10** chromosome ***reproductive:*** **3** egg **4** germ, ovum **5** sperm **6** gamete **8** gonidium

cellar 5 store **7** shelter **8** basement

cellist *American:* **2** Ma (Yo-Yo) **4** Rose (Leonard) **6** Lesser (Laurence), Parnas (Leslie) **7** Nelsova (Zara), Parisot (Aldo), Starker (Janos) **8** Schuster (Joseph) **10** Greenhouse (Bernard) ***English:*** **5** du Pré (Jacqueline) ***French:*** **8** Fournier (Pierre) ***Russian:*** **11** Piatigorsky (Gregor) **12** Rostropovich (Mstislav) ***Spanish:*** **6** Casals (Pablo)

cellophane 4 wrap **7** wrapper **8** wrapping **9** packaging

cell-phone sound 8 ringtone

celluloid 4 film **7** plastic

Celt 4 Gael, Scot **6** Breton **8** Irishman, Welshman **10** Cornishman, Highlander

Celtic *deity:* **4** Bran **5** Epona, Lugus, Macha **6** Brigit **8** Rhiannon **9** Cernunnos ***festival:*** **7** Beltane, Samhain ***queen:*** **8** Boadicea, Boudicca

cement 4 bind, glue, join **5** grout, unify, unite **6** mortar, secure **8** concrete ***ingredient:*** **4** lime **6** silica **7** alumina **8** magnesia, pozzolan **9** iron oxide, pozzolana

cemetery 8 boneyard, boot hill **8** God's acre **9** graveyard **10** churchyard, necropolis **12** burial ground, memorial park, potter's field ***underground:*** **8** catacomb

cenacle 7 coterie **9** Upper Room **12** retreat house

cenotaph 4 tomb **6** marker **8** memorial, monument

censer 8 thurible ***carrier:*** **8** thurifer

censor 3 ban, cut **4** blip, edit **5** bleep, purge **6** cut out, delete, excise, purify, screen **7** clean up **8** black out, restrict, suppress, withhold **9** expurgate, red-pencil **10** blue-pencil, bowdlerize

censorious 6 severe **7** carping **8** captious, critical **10** accusatory, condemning **11** reproachful **12** condemnatory, denunciatory, disapproving, faultfinding, overcritical, reprehending **13** hypercritical

censurable 5 wrong **6** guilty, sinful **7** heinous **8** blamable, blameful, culpable, improper, wrongful **9** incorrect **10** deplorable, despicable, detestable **11** blameworthy, disgraceful, impeachable **12** unacceptable **13** discreditable, objectionable, reprehensible

censure 5 blame, chide, scold **6** berate, rebuke, strafe **7** condemn, reprove, upbraid **8** chastise, denounce, disallow, reproach **9** castigate, criticize, reprehend, reprimand, reprobate **10** disapprove

centaur 6 Chiron, Nessus

Centaurus star 4 Beta **5** Alpha

Centennial State 8 Colorado

center 3 hub, mid **4** axis, core, crux, mean, pith, root, seat **5** focus, heart, midst, pivot **6** inside, medial, median, middle, source **7** central, essence **8** interior, midpoint, omphalos **10** focal point **11** equidistant **12** intermediary, intermediate

centerboard 4 keel

centerfold 7 foldout **8** gatefold

centerpiece 7 epergne

central 3 hub, key, mid **4** main, mean **5** basic, chief, focal **6** medial, median, middle **7** leading, pivotal, primary, salient **8** cardinal, dominant, exchange, foremost, moderate **9** essential, paramount, principal **10** overriding **11** fundamental, outstanding, predominant **12** intermediate

Central African Republic *capital:* **6** Bangui ***former name:*** **11** Ubangi-Shari ***language:*** **5** Sango, Zande **6** French ***monetary unit:*** **5** franc ***neighbor:*** **4** Chad **5** Congo, Sudan **8** Cameroon

Central America *country:* **6** Belize, Panama **8** Honduras **9** Costa Rica, Guatemala, Nicaragua **10** El Salvador ***language:*** **7** Nahuatl, Spanish

centralize 5 focus, unify **11** concentrate, consolidate

centripetal 8 afferent, focusing, unifying **10** converging **11** integrative **12** centralizing **13** concentrating, consolidating

centurion 7 officer **9** commander

century plant 5 agave

cephalopod 5 squid **7** mollusc, mollusk, octopus **10** cuttlefish

Cepheus *daughter:* **9** Andromeda ***kingdom:*** **8** Ethiopia ***wife:*** **10** Cassiopeia

cerate 4 balm **5** cream, salve **6** chrism **7** unction, unguent **8** dressing, liniment, ointment **9** demulcent, emollient

Cerberus 5 guard **8** guardian, sentinel, watchdog ***father:*** **6** Typhon ***form:*** **3** dog ***mother:*** **7** Echidna

cereal 4 meal, mush, samp **5** gruel **6** farina **7** oatmeal **8** cornmeal, porridge ***disease:*** **4** bunt, smut **5** ergot ***fungus:*** **5** ergot ***grass:*** **3** rye **4** corn, oats, ragi, rice, teff **5** emmer,

maize, spelt, wheat **6** barley, millet **7** sorghum **9** buckwheat ***Russian:*** **5** kasha
cerebral 6 mental **7** bookish **8** highbrow **9** scholarly **10** highbrowed **12** intellectual
cerebrate 5 think **6** reason **7** reflect **8** cogitate **9** speculate **10** deliberate
cerebration 7 thought **9** brainwork **10** cogitation, reflection **11** speculation **12** deliberation
ceremonial 6 august, formal, ritual, solemn **7** courtly, stately, studied **8** mannered, stylized **10** liturgical **11** ritualistic **12** conventional
ceremonious 6 formal, proper, seemly, solemn **7** courtly, stately **8** decorous, imposing, majestic **9** dignified, grandiose **10** impressive **11** punctilious **12** conventional
ceremony 4 form, pomp, rite **6** ritual **7** decorum, liturgy, service **8** protocol **9** formality **10** observance ***Jewish:*** **8** habdalah, havdalah **10** bar mitzvah, bat mitzvah ***university:*** **8** encaenia
Ceres *Greek counterpart:* **7** Demeter ***daughter:*** **10** Persephone, Proserpina, Proserpine ***father:*** **6** Cronus, Saturn ***mother:*** **3** Ops **4** Rhea
cerium symbol 2 Ce
certain 3 set **4** firm, sure, true **5** fixed **6** stated **7** assured, settled **8** credible, definite, destined, positive, provable, reliable, specific, surefire **9** authentic, confident, convinced **10** conclusive, dependable, guaranteed, inarguable, inevitable, infallible, stipulated, undeniable, verifiable **11** confirmable, indubitable, unavoidable **12** demonstrable, indisputable, well-grounded **13** incontestable, uncontestable
certainty 5 faith **6** surety **8** sureness **9** assurance, sure thing **10** confidence, conviction **12** definiteness
certificate 7 diploma, license, voucher **8** contract, document **9** affidavit **10** credential
certifier 6 notary **7** auditor **9** registrar
certify 2 OK **4** aver, avow, okay **5** state, swear, vouch **6** assert, assure, attest, verify **7** approve, confirm, endorse, license, testify, warrant, witness **8** accredit, guaranty, notarize **9** authorize, guarantee, recognize **10** commission **12** authenticate
Cervantes character 10 Don Quixote **11** Sancho Panza
cervid 3 elk **4** deer **5** moose **6** wapiti **7** caribou **8** reindeer
cesium symbol 2 Cs
cessation 3 end **4** halt, rest, stop **5** break, cease, close, letup, pause **6** ending, finish, freeze, hiatus, period, recess **7** respite **10** conclusion, suspension **11** termination **12** interruption
cesspool 3 den, pit, sty **4** sink **5** sewer, Sodom **6** cloaca, gutter, pigsty **8** Gomorrah **12** Augean stable
cetacean 5 whale **7** dolphin **8** porpoise
Cetus star 4 Mira
Ceylon see **Sri Lanka**
cgs unit 3 erg **4** dyne, gram, phot **5** gauss, poise, stilb **6** second, stokes **7** lambert, maxwell, oersted **10** centimeter
Chablis 4 wine **8** Burgundy **9** white wine
Chad *capital:* **8** N'Djamena ***city:*** **4** Sarh **6** Abéché **7** Moundou ***language:*** **6** Arabic, French ***monetary unit:*** **5** franc ***neighbor:*** **5** Libya, Niger, Sudan **7** Nigeria **8** Cameroon ***river:*** **5** Chari **6** Logone
chafe 3 irk, rub, vex **4** fret, gall, peel, rage, skin, wear **5** annoy, erode **6** abrade, bother, scrape **7** provoke **8** irritate, vexation
chaff 3 kid, rag, rib **4** jest, joke, josh, razz **5** dregs, husks, tease **6** banter, debris, refuse **7** remains **8** detritus **9** sweepings
chaffer 6 barter, dicker, haggle, higgle, palter **7** bargain, chatter **8** exchange, huckster
chagrin 3 ire, irk, vex **5** abash, annoy, peeve, pique, upset **6** dismay **7** perturb **8** disquiet, distress, unsettle, vexation **9** annoyance, discomfit, displease, embarrass, humiliate, petulance **10** disappoint, discompose, disconcert, irritation **11** frustration, humiliation **12** discomfiture
chagrined 4 hurt **5** upset, vexed **6** shamed **7** ashamed **8** dismayed **9** disturbed, mortified, perturbed, unsettled **10** distressed, humiliated **11** discomposed, embarrassed **12** disappointed, disconcerted
chain 3 row **4** bind, bond, gyve **5** group, train, trust **6** cartel, catena, fetter, hobble, series, string, tether **7** combine, manacle, shackle **8** handcuff, sequence **9** syndicate **10** succession **11** concatenate, progression **12** conglomerate **13** concatenation ***adjunct:*** **8** sprocket ***collar:*** **6** torque ***gang:*** **6** coffle ***ornamental:*** **10** chatelaine ***sound:*** **5** clank
chain ____ 3 saw **4** gang, mail **5** store **6** letter **8** reaction
Chained Lady 9 Andromeda
chain store 6 big box
chair 4 seat **5** stool **6** rocker, settee, settle **7** preside ***back:*** **5** splat ***bishop's:*** **8** cathedra ***designer:*** **5** Eames (Charles, Ray) **6** Breuer (Marcel) ***maker:*** **5** caner ***portable:*** **5** sedan ***reclining:*** **6** chaise **12** chaise longue, chaise lounge ***royal:*** **6** throne ***type:*** **4** club, easy **6** morris **7** rocking **8** captain's, electric **9** di-

rector's, reclining **10** Adirondack, ladder-back

chaise 4 sofa **5** chair, coach, divan **8** carriage

chalcedony 4 onyx, sard **5** agate, chert **6** jasper, quartz **9** carnelian, cornelian **10** bloodstone **11** chrysoprase

chalet 3 hut **4** camp **5** lodge **7** cottage

chalice 3 cup **5** grail **6** goblet ***veil:*** **3** aer

chalk out 5 draft **6** sketch **7** outline **8** block out, rough out **11** skeletonize **12** characterize

chalk up 3 get, win **4** gain **6** attain, credit, impute, obtain, secure **7** achieve, acquire, ascribe, procure, realize **9** attribute

challenge 3 try **4** dare, defy, face, stir, wake **5** brave, claim, demur, doubt, exact, rouse, waken **6** arouse, awaken, demand, impugn, invite, kindle **7** calling, dispute, protest, require, solicit, venture **8** confront, defiance, demurral, demurrer, question, struggle **9** objection, postulate, stimulate **10** difficulty, insistence **12** remonstrance

challenger 5 rival **8** aspirant, opponent **9** adversary, contender **10** antagonist, competitor, contestant

chamber 4 cell, hall, room **5** haven, house **7** cubicle **9** apartment, enclosure **11** compartment ***burial:*** **4** cist ***ceremonial:*** **4** kiva ***underground:*** **8** hypogeum

chambered seashell 8 nautilus

chamberlain 6 priest **7** officer, servant **9** attendant, treasurer

chameleon 6 lizard

chameleonic 6 fickle **7** protean **9** mercurial **10** changeable, inconstant

chamfer 5 bevel **6** groove

chamois 5 izard **6** shammy **7** leather **8** antelope, ruminant ***habitat:*** **4** Alps ***Old Testament:*** **6** aoudad

chamois-like animal 4 goat, ibex

champ 3 gum **4** bite, chew, mash **5** gnash, munch **7** trample **8** macerate, ruminate **9** masticate

champagne 4 wine **6** bubbly ***bucket:*** **4** icer ***center:*** **5** Reims **6** Rheims ***type:*** **3** sec **4** brut

Champagne capital 6 Troyes

champaign 5 field, plain **7** expanse, terrain **11** battlefield

champignon 6 fungus **8** mushroom

champion 4 back, hero **5** first, prime **6** uphold, victor, winner **7** capital, contend, leading, paladin, premier, support, titlist **8** advocate, defender, exponent, fight for, foremost, medalist, unbeaten **9** excellent, nonpareil, number one, principal, proponent, protector, supporter **11** illustrious, outstanding, titleholder, white knight

championship 5 crown, title **6** laurel, trophy **7** contest, defense, laurels, pennant **8** advocacy **10** blue ribbon

chance 3 hap, hit, lot, odd **4** fate, luck, meet, odds, risk, shot **5** break, fluke, light, wager **6** befall, casual, gamble, happen, hazard **7** fortune, offhand, stumble, venture **8** accident, fortuity, occasion, prospect **9** advantage, transpire **10** accidental, fortuitous, incidental, likelihood **11** contingency, opportunity, possibility, probability ***even:*** **6** toss-up

chancellor 5 judge **8** minister **9** secretary ***German:*** **4** Kohl (Helmut) **6** Brandt (Willy), Erhard (Ludwig), Hitler (Adolf), Merkel (Angela) **7** Schmidt (Helmut) **8** Adenauer (Konrad), Bismarck (Otto von) **9** Schroeder (Gerhard)

chancy 4 iffy **5** dicey, fluky, hairy, risky **6** touchy, tricky **8** perilous, ticklish **9** dangerous, haphazard, hazardous, uncertain **10** capricious, precarious **11** speculative, treacherous **12** incalculable **13** unpredictable

Chandler, Raymond *character:* **7** Marlowe (Philip) ***novel:*** **8** Big Sleep (The) **11** Long Good-Bye (The) **13** Murder My Sweet **16** Farewell My Lovely ***screenplay:*** **10** Blue Dahlia (The) **15** Double Indemnity

Chanel, ____ 4 Coco

change 3 fix **4** swap, turn, vary **5** add-on, alter, coins, money, morph, shift, trade **6** adjust, evolve, modify, mutate, reform, remake, revamp, revert, revise, switch **7** commute, convert, novelty, replace, reverse **8** exchange, mutation, revision, transfer **9** alternate, deviation, diversify, fluctuate, refashion, transform, transmute, transpose, variation **10** alteration, conversion, divergence, innovation, substitute **11** interchange, permutation, transfigure, vicissitude **12** metamorphose, modification, transmogrify **13** metamorphosis, transmutation ***sudden:*** **8** peripety **10** peripeteia

changeable 5 fluid **6** fickle, labile, pliant, shifty **7** flighty, mutable, plastic, protean, unfixed, varying **8** restless, shifting, slippery, ticklish, unstable, unsteady, variable, volatile **9** adaptable, alterable, impulsive, mercurial, uncertain, unsettled, whimsical **10** capricious, inconstant **11** chameleonic, fluctuating, vacillating **13** kaleidoscopic, temperamental, unpredictable

changeless 5 fixed **6** steady **7** abiding, regular, uniform **8** constant, enduring, resolute **9** immutable, perpetual, steadfast, unvarying **10** invariable

change off 6 rotate **9** alternate

change of heart 8 reversal
change of life 9 menopause **11** climacteric
change of pace 5 pitch, shift **9** slow pitch
changeover 5 shift **10** alteration, conversion, transition
channel 3 way **4** band, duct, kyle, pass, path, pipe **5** agent, canal, carry **6** agency, convey, course, funnel, groove, gutter, medium, siphon, strait, trough, tunnel **7** conduct, conduit, passage, vehicle **8** aqueduct, pipeline, transmit **10** instrument **11** watercourse ***Africa-Madagascar:*** **10** Mozambique ***Atlantic-Nantucket Sound:*** **8** Muskeget ***Atlantic-North Sea:*** **7** English ***Ellesmere-Greenland:*** **7** Robeson ***Ganges:*** **5** Hugli **7** Hooghly ***Hawaii:*** **5** Kaiwi, Kauai ***Japan:*** **5** Bungo ***Northwest Territories:*** **9** M'Clintock ***Pakistan:*** **4** Nara ***Scotland:*** **5** Minch ***Tierra del Fuego:*** **6** Beagle ***Tigris-Euphrates:*** **11** Shatt al Arab ***Virginia:*** **12** Hampton Roads ***West Indies:*** **9** Old Bahama
channel bass 4 drum **7** red drum, redfish
Channel Islands *capital:* 8 St. Helier **11** St. Peter Port ***dependency of:*** **7** Britain ***island:*** **4** Herm, Sark **6** Jersey **8** Alderney, Guernsey
chanson 4 song
"Chanson ____" 6 Triste
chanson de ____ 5 geste
chant 4 sing, tune **5** drone **6** intone **8** vocalize **10** cantillate ***Gregorian:*** **9** plainsong **12** cantus firmus ***Jewish:*** **6** Hallel
chanteuse 6 singer **7** artiste **10** cantatrice
chanticleer 4 cock **7** rooster
chaos 5 havoc, snafu **6** bedlam, muddle **7** anarchy, clutter, entropy, turmoil **8** disarray, disorder **9** confusion **11** lawlessness, pandemonium
Chaos *daughter:* 3 Nox, Nyx **4** Gaea ***son:*** **6** Erebus
chaotic 7 jumbled, lawless **8** anarchic, confused, formless **9** amorphous, haphazard, scrambled **10** disordered, disorderly, topsy-turvy, tumultuous **11** harum-scarum, unorganized **12** disorganized **13** helter-skelter, unpredictable
chap 3 guy **4** gent **5** bloke **6** fellow
chaparral 5 scrub **7** thicket
chaparral cock 10 roadrunner
chapeau 3 hat **6** topper
chapel 6 bethel, church, shrine **7** chantry **9** sanctuary
chaperone 5 guide **6** attend, duenna, escort, matron **7** oversee **9** accompany, companion, supervise **11** superintend
chapfallen see **crestfallen**
chaplain 5 padre **6** pastor **8** minister, sky pilot
chaplet 5 crown **6** anadem, laurel, rosary, wreath **7** coronal, coronet, garland
chapter 4 unit **5** phase, stage **6** branch, period **7** episode, section **8** division **9** affiliate
char 4 burn, sear **6** scorch **9** carbonize
character 3 ilk **4** bent, case, cast, kind, mark, mind, name, rank, role, rune, sign, sort, type **5** ethos, state, trait **6** cipher, device, letter, makeup, nature, repute, status, symbol, temper, virtue **7** oddball, persona, quality, variety **8** eminence, identity, standing **9** attribute, eccentric, rectitude **10** reputation **11** disposition, personality, temperament ***chief:*** **4** hero **11** protagonist ***defect:*** **8** hamartia
character assassination 5 libel **7** calumny, scandal, slander **10** backbiting, defamation **12** backstabbing
characteristic 4 mark, sign **5** badge, point, token, trait **6** aspect, innate, normal, proper **7** feature, natural, quality, special, typical **8** especial, peculiar, property, specific, tendency **9** attribute, birthmark, component, mannerism, trademark **10** diagnostic, emblematic, individual, particular **11** distinction, distinctive, peculiarity, singularity **12** idiosyncrasy **13** idiosyncratic
characterize 4 mark **5** draft **6** define, sketch, typify **7** outline, portray **8** describe, identify **10** constitute, pigeonhole **11** distinguish, individuate, personalize **12** discriminate **13** differentiate, individualize
characterless 4 flat **5** mousy **7** humdrum, insipid, vacuous **8** mediocre **9** colorless **10** namby-pamby, wishy-washy **11** nondescript
charade 4 sham **5** farce, put-on **6** parody **8** disguise, pretense, travesty **9** deception **11** make-believe
chare see **chore**
charge 3 ask, bid, fee, lay, tab, tax **4** bill, care, cost, duty, fill, heap, kick, load, onus, race, rate, rush, task, tell, toll, warn **5** choke, debit, order, place, price, refer, trust **6** accuse, assign, attack, burden, credit, direct, enjoin, exhort, impugn, impute, indict, saddle, thrill **7** arraign, ascribe, bidding, command, conduct, entrust, expense, impeach, mandate, request, solicit **8** accredit, handling, instruct, price tag, reproach, stampede **9** attribute, committal, electrify, inculpate **10** accusation, allegation, commitment, injunction, management, obligation **11** incriminate, instruction, requirement, supervision
chargeable 6 liable **7** subject **11** accountable, responsible
chargeless 4 free **6** gratis **8** costless **10** gratuitous **13** complimentary

charger 5 horse, mount, steed **6** salver **7** courser, platter **8** trencher, warhorse
chariness 7 caution **8** prudence **9** integrity **10** discretion
chariot 8 carriage ***four-horse:* 8** quadriga
charioteer 6 Auriga, driver
charisma 5 charm **6** allure, appeal, duende **7** glamour **9** magnetism **10** attraction **11** fascination
charitable 6 benign, giving, humane, kindly **7** clement, lenient, liberal **8** generous, merciful, obliging, tolerant **9** forgiving, indulgent **10** altruistic, beneficent, benevolent, forbearing, thoughtful **11** considerate, kindhearted, sympathetic **12** eleemosynary, humanitarian **13** philanthropic
charity 4 alms, love **5** grace, mercy **6** lenity, relief **7** caritas **8** altruism, clemency, donation, goodwill, leniency, offering **10** generosity, humaneness, kindliness **11** benefaction, beneficence, benevolence **12** contribution
charivari 5 babel, melee **6** jangle, jumble, medley, racket, ruckus, uproar **7** farrago **8** serenade, shivaree **9** cacophony, confusion **10** hodgepodge **11** celebration
charlatan 4 sham **5** bluff, faker, fraud, quack **6** con man **8** imposter, impostor, swindler **10** mountebank **11** quacksalver **13** confidence man
Charlemagne *brother:* 8 Carloman ***capital:* 3** Aix **6** Aachen ***father:* 5** Pepin ***knight:* 6** Oliver, Roland **7** Olivier, Orlando, paladin **8** douzeper ***nephew:* 6** Roland **7** Orlando ***sword:* 7** Joyeuse ***traitor:* 4** Gano **7** Ganelon
Charles's Wain 9 Big Dipper, Ursa Major
charleston 5 dance
Charlie and the Chocolate Factory author 4 Dahl (Roald)
Charlie Brown see **Peanuts**
Charlie McCarthy 5 dummy **6** stooge ***friend:* 5** Snerd (Mortimer) ***voice:* 6** Bergen (Edgar)
charm 3 hex **4** juju, lure, mojo, rune, take, wile **5** grace, quark, spell **6** allure, amulet, appeal, disarm, enamor, fetish, mascot, seduce, voodoo **7** attract, beguile, bewitch, enchant, glamour **8** enthrall, entrance, talisman, witchery **9** captivate, enrapture, ensorcell, fascinate, hypnotize, magnetism, mesmerize **10** allurement, attraction, phylactery, witchcraft **11** fascination, incantation **13** agreeableness
charmed 5 lucky **7** blessed **8** enamored **9** bewitched, enchanted, entranced, fortunate **10** captivated, fascinated, infatuated
charmer 4 roué **5** magus **6** wizard **7** seducer, warlock **8** conjurer, lothario, magician, sorcerer **9** enchanter **11** spellbinder
charming 7 winsome **8** adorable, alluring, inviting, magnetic **9** appealing, glamorous, seductive **10** attractive, delightful, enchanting, entrancing **11** captivating
Charon 7 boatman **8** ferryman ***father:* 6** Erebus ***mother:* 3** Nox ***river:* 4** Styx
Charpentier opera 5 Médée **6** Louise
charpoy 3 bed, cot
chart 3 map **4** plan, plat, plot **5** graph, table **6** design, lay out, map out, sketch **7** arrange, diagram, outline, project **9** blueprint **10** tabulation
charter 3 let **4** deed, hire, rent **5** grant, lease **10** conveyance **12** constitution
Chartreuse 7 liqueur
chary 4 wary **5** cagey, canny **6** frugal, stingy **7** careful, guarded, miserly, prudent, sparing, thrifty **8** cautious, discreet, gingerly, hesitant **9** provident, reluctant **10** economical, restrained, suspicious, unwasteful **11** calculating, circumspect, constrained, disinclined
Charybdis 9 whirlpool ***rock associated with:* 6** Scylla
chase 3 run **4** bolt, dash, game, hunt, prey, race, rush, tear **5** chivy, drive, eject, evict, hound, shoot, speed, trail **6** career, charge, course, follow, hasten, pursue, quarry **7** boot out, hunting, kick out, pursuit **8** run after, throw out
chase away 4 rout, shoo
chaser 4 wolf **6** masher **7** Don Juan **8** Casanova **9** ladies' man, womanizer **10** ladykiller **11** philanderer
chasm 3 gap **4** gulf, rift **5** abyss, cleft, clove, flume, gorge, gulch, split **6** ravine **8** crevasse
chasmal 6 gaping **7** echoing, yawning **9** cavernous
chassepot 5 rifle
chaste 4 pure **5** clean, moral **6** decent, modest, proper, seemly, vestal, virgin **7** austere, prudish **8** celibate, decorous, innocent, maidenly, platonic, spotless, virginal, virtuous **9** abstinent, continent, stainless, undefiled, unsullied **10** immaculate **11** unblemished
chasten 5 abase, scold **6** humble, punish, rebuke, refine, subdue **7** correct, upbraid **8** chastise **9** castigate, humiliate, reprimand **10** discipline
chastise 4 beat, flog, whip **5** scold **6** punish, rebuke, thrash **7** belabor, censure, chasten, correct, reprove, scourge, upbraid **9** castigate **10** discipline

chastisement 3 rod **7** reproof **8** punition **10** correction, discipline, punishment **11** castigation

chastity 6 purity, virtue **7** modesty **8** celibacy **9** innocence, integrity, virginity **10** abstention, continence, maidenhood

chasuble 8 vestment

chat 3 gab, jaw, rap, yak, yap **4** blab, gush, talk **5** prate, visit **6** babble, confab, gossip, jabber, natter, parley, patter, yak-yak **7** chatter, palaver, prattle, twaddle **8** causerie, colloquy, converse, dialogue, schmooze **9** tête-à-tête, yakety-yak **11** confabulate **12** conversation, tittle-tattle **13** confabulation

château 5 manor, villa **6** castle, estate **7** mansion **8** fortress **12** country house

chateaubriand 5 steak **10** tenderloin

Chateaubriand novel 4 René **5** Atala

chatelain 6 warden **8** governor **9** castellan

chatelaine 4 hook, wife **5** clasp **8** mistress

chattel 4 serf **5** slave **7** bondman **8** bondsman, property

chatter 3 gab, jaw, yak **4** blab, bull **5** prate **6** babble, gabble, gibber, gossip, jabber, natter, patter, yak-yak, yammer **7** blabber, blather, palaver, prattle, vibrate **9** small talk, yakety-yak **12** tittle-tattle

chatterbox 5 yenta **6** gabber, gossip, magpie, prater **7** blabber **8** jabberer, prattler **12** blabbermouth

chatty 5 gabby **7** voluble **9** garrulous, talkative **10** loquacious

Chaucer pilgrim 4 Cook, Monk **5** Clerk, Friar, Reeve **6** Miller, Parson, Squire **8** Franklin, Manciple, Merchant, Summoner **10** Nun's Priest, Wife of Bath

chauffeur 5 drive **6** driver **9** transport

chauvinism 6 sexism **8** jingoism **10** patriotism **11** nationalism

cheap 4 mean, poor **5** junky, tight **6** cheesy, common, cruddy, flashy, measly, paltry, shabby, shoddy, sleazy, stingy, tawdry, trashy **7** chintzy, cut-rate, low-cost, reduced, thrifty **8** inferior, trifling, uncostly **9** brummagem, low-priced **10** economical **11** inexpensive **12** contemptible, meretricious

cheapen 5 decry, lower **6** debase, reduce **7** devalue **8** mark down **9** devaluate, downgrade **10** depreciate, undervalue

cheapjack 5 junky **6** hawker, cheesy, cruddy, shoddy, sleazy, tawdry, trashy **7** haggler, higgler, packman, peddler **8** huckster, inferior, rubbishy **9** worthless

cheapskate 5 miser **7** niggard, scrooge **8** tightwad **9** skinflint **11** cheeseparer

cheat 3 con, gyp **4** bilk, burn, dupe, fool, gull, hoax, hose, milk, ream, rook, scam **5** bunco, cozen, crook, fraud, fudge, gouge, hocus, put-on, screw, shaft, short, slick **6** chisel, chouse, con man, deceit, delude, diddle, extort, fleece, humbug, rip-off, sucker, take in **7** beguile, chicane, deceive, defraud, diddler, mislead, sharper, shyster, swindle, two-time **8** flimflam, hoodwink, swindler, trickery **9** bamboozle, chicanery, deception, defrauder, imposture, overreach, trickster **11** double-cross **12** double-dealer **13** confidence man ***on a check:*** **4** kite

check 3 tab, try **4** bill, curb, halt, jibe, stay, stop, test, tick **5** block, brake, draft, prove, score, stall **6** accord, arrest, baffle, bridle, damage, desist, hold in, square, thwart, verify **7** compare, conform, control, examine, inhibit, repress, setback **8** dovetail, hold back, hold down, preclude, restrain, reversal, suppress **9** constrain, criterion, interrupt, restraint **10** correspond, inspection **11** examination **13** investigation

checkered 5 plaid **6** motley **7** mutable, spotted **9** patchwork, patterned **10** variegated **11** diversified

checklist 7 catalog **9** catalogue, inventory **11** enumeration

checkmate 4 beat **6** corner, defeat **7** outplay **8** vanquish **9** finish off

check out 3 die, eye **4** case **5** leave **6** assess **7** examine, inspect **8** appraise, evaluate, look over

check over 3 con, vet **4** scan **5** audit, study **6** review, survey **7** analyze, canvass, examine, inspect **10** scrutinize

checkup 4 exam **8** physical **10** inspection **11** examination

cheek 4 gall **5** brass, nerve **8** audacity, chutzpah, temerity **9** brashness, impudence, insolence **10** confidence, effrontery **11** presumption **12** impertinence

cheekbone 5 malar

cheeky 4 bold, flip, pert, wise **5** brash, cocky, fresh, nervy, sassy, saucy, smart **6** brazen **7** forward **8** flippant, impudent, insolent **11** impertinent, smart-alecky **12** presumptuous

cheep 4 peep **5** chirp, tweet **7** chirrup, chitter, twitter

cheer 3 olé, rah, yay **4** buoy, hail, root **5** bravo, huzza, nerve **6** buck up, gaiety, hoorah, hooray, hurrah, hurray, huzzah, rahrah, solace, spirit **7** animate, applaud, comfort, console, enliven, gladden, hearten **8** embolden, inspirit **9** animation, encourage **10** strengthen

cheerful 3 gay **4** glad, rosy **5** jolly, merry, perky, riant, sunny **6** blithe, bouncy, bright, chirpy, hearty, jaunty, jocund, lively **7**

beamish, buoyant, radiant **8** animated, carefree, chirrupy **9** vivacious **12** lighthearted

cheerio 3 bye **4** ciao, ta-ta **5** adieu **6** bye-bye, good-by, so long **7** good-bye, toodles **8** farewell, toodle-oo

cheerless 4 dour, drab, grim **5** bleak **6** dismal, dreary, gloomy, somber, sombre **7** forlorn, joyless **8** desolate, dolorous, funereal, mournful **9** dejecting **10** depressing, melancholy, oppressive, tenebrific **11** dispiriting

cheers 5 salud, skoal **6** cincin, l'chaim, prosit **7** l'chayim, sláinte **8** applause, approval, chinchin **9** bottoms up **10** jubilation **11** acclamation, approbation

Cheers ***actor:*** **4** Long (Shelley) **5** Alley (Kirstie), Wendt (George) **6** Danson (Ted) **7** Grammer (Kelsey), Perlman (Rhea) **8** Neuwirth (Bebe) **9** Harrelson (Woody) ***character:*** **3** Sam **4** Norm **5** Carla, Cliff, Diane, Ernie, Woody **6** Lilith **7** Frasier, Rebecca ***creator:*** **7** Burrows (James), Charles (Glen, Les)

cheery 5 happy, jolly, merry, sunny **6** blithe, bouncy, chirpy, lively, upbeat **7** buoyant, chipper, festive, gleeful **8** animated, carefree, gladsome **9** convivial, sparkling **12** lighthearted

cheese 3 pot **4** bleu, blue, jack **5** brick, cream **6** farmer **7** cottage, process, ricotta **9** smearcase ***American:*** **8** Longhorn **11** Liederkranz **12** Monterey Jack ***Belgian:*** **9** Limburger ***curdling agent:*** **6** rennet, rennin ***Danish:*** **7** Havarti ***dish:*** **6** fondue **7** rarebit, soufflé ***Dutch:*** **4** Edam **5** Gouda **6** Leyden ***English:*** **7** cheddar, Stilton **8** Cheshire **10** Lancashire ***French:*** **4** Brie **7** fromage, Livarot **9** Camembert, Reblochon, Roquefort **10** Neufchâtel **11** Pont l'Évêque, Port du Salut ***German:*** **6** Tilsit **7** Munster **8** Muenster, Tilsiter ***Greek:*** **4** feta ***green:*** **7** sapsago ***Italian:*** **6** Asiago, Romano **7** fontina, ricotta **8** Bel Paese, Parmesan, pecorino **9** provolone **10** Gorgonzola, mozzarella ***lover:*** **9** turophile ***main ingredient:*** **6** casein ***Norwegian:*** **9** Jarlsberg ***pickled:*** **4** feta **5** Ezine **8** Halloumi ***protein:*** **6** casein ***Scottish:*** **6** Dunlop, Orkney **7** kebbock, kebbuck ***Swiss:*** **6** Saanen **7** Gruyère, sapsago **8** Vacherin **10** Emmentaler **11** Emmenthaler ***uncured:*** **7** cottage ***Welsh:*** **10** Caerphilly

cheesecloth 5 gauze

cheeselike 6 caseic **7** caseous

cheeseparer 5 miser **7** niggard, scrooge **8** tightwad **9** skinflint **10** cheapskate, pinchpenny

cheeseparing 4 mean **5** chary, cheap, mingy, tight **6** frugal, shabby, stingy **7** chintzy, miserly, thrifty **8** grudging, skimping **9** niggardly, penurious **11** closefisted, tightfisted **12** parsimonious **13** penny-pinching

cheesy 4 poor **5** cheap **6** common, shabby, shoddy, sleazy, tawdry, trashy **7** caseous **8** rubbishy

Cheever, John ***family:*** **7** Wapshot ***novel:*** **8** Falconer **14** Wapshot Scandal (The) **16** Wapshot Chronicle (The) ***story:*** **7** Swimmer (The)

chef 4 cook

chef d'oeuvre 7 classic **9** showpiece **10** magnum opus, masterwork **11** masterpiece, tour de force

Chekhov, Anton ***play:*** **6** Ivanov **7** Seagull (The) **10** Uncle Vanya **12** Three Sisters **13** Cherry Orchard (The) ***story:*** **9** Black Monk (The)

chelonian 6 turtle **8** tortoise

chemical ***agent:*** **8** catalyst ***combining power:*** **7** valence ***compound:*** **4** acid, base, diol, enol, imid, oxim, salt, tepa, urea **5** amide, amine, diene, ester, imide, imine, indol, orcin, oxime, purin, pyran, salol, tolan, triol **6** alkali, benzin, benzol, diamin, emodin, guanin, halide, hydrid, indole, inulin, ionone, isatin, isolog, isomer, ketone, lactam, maltol, metepa, natron, nitril, pterin, purine, pyrone, pyrrol, quinol, retene, silane, skatol, tannin, tetryl, thiram, thymol, tolane, triene, trimer, uracil, ureide, yttria, zeatin **7** barilla, benzene, benzole, cumarin, diamide, diamine, diazine, diazole, diester, flavone, guanine, heptose, hydride, indamin, indican, indoxyl, isatine, levulin, metamer, monomer, naphtol, nitrile, orcinol, oxazine, phytane, picolin, polyene, polymer, pyrrole, quinoid, quinone, salicin, skatole, steroid, taurine, terpene, thiazin, thiazol, thymine, tolidin, triazin, urethan, uridine, vitamer, xylidin **8** cephalin, cyanamid, disulfid, elaterin, fluorene, furfural, guaiacol, hematein, hexamine, indamine, isologue, kephalin, lichenin, limonene, melamine, naloxone, naphthol, palmitin, phenazin, phosphid, phthalin, picoline, piperine, pristane, quinolin, resorcin, salicine, santonin, siloxane, sodamide, sorbitol, spermine, squalene, stilbene, strontia, tautomer, thiazine, thiazole, thiophen, thiotepa, thiourea, tolidine, triazine, triazole, triptane, tyramine, urethane, vanillin, warfarin, xanthene, xanthine, xanthone, xylidine, ytterbia, zaratite, zirconia (see also **element**) ***quantity:*** **4** mole ***radical:*** **4** acyl, amyl, aryl, cyan **5** allyl, butyl, ethyl, tolyl **6** acetyl, formyl, methyl, oxalic, phenyl, propyl, toluyl **7** benzoyl ***reaction:*** **5** redox ***salt:*** **5** niter, nitre, urate, ziram **6** haloid, humate, malate, oleate, phytin **7** ferrate, formate, gallate, maleate, pectate, persalt, picrate, tannate, toluate, zincate **8** fumarate, pyruvate, racemate, selenate, silicate, stearate, tartrate, thionate, titanate, valerate, vanadate, xanthate ***suffix:*** **3** ane, ase, ate, ein, ene, ide, ile, ine, ite, ium, oic, oin, one, ose, ous, yne **4** eine, idin, itol, oate, olic, onic **5** idine, onium, oside, ylene ***warfare agent:*** **7** tear gas **8** vesicant **10** mustard gas

chemin de fer **5** train **7** railway **8** railroad

chemise **4** slip

chemist **7** analyst **8** druggist **10** apothecary, pharmacist ***American:*** **4** Urey (Harold) **6** Remsen (Ira), Sumner (James) **7** Onsager (Lars), Pauling (Linus), Seaborg (Glenn) **8** Hoffmann (Roald), Langmuir (Irving), Mulliken (Robert), Richards (Theodore), Woodward (Robert) ***Austrian:*** **4** Kuhn (Richard) **5** Pregl (Fritz) ***British:*** **4** Abel (Frederick), Davy (Humphry), Todd (Alexander) **5** Boyle (Robert), Soddy (Frederick) **6** Dalton (John), Ramsay (William) **7** Faraday (Michael) **8** Smithson (James) **9** Priestley (Joseph), Wollaston (William) **10** Williamson (Alexander) ***Dutch:*** **8** van't Hoff (Jacobus) ***French:*** **5** Curie (Irene, Marie, Pierre) **7** Moissan (Henri), Pasteur (Louis) **8** Sabatier (Paul) **9** Gay-Lussac (Joseph), Lavoisier (Antoine), Berthelot (Marcellin) ***German:*** **5** Haber (Fritz) **6** Bunsen (Robert), Liebig (Justus von), Nernst (Walther), Wittig (Georg), Wohler (Friedrich) **7** Fischer (Emil, Ernst, Hans), Hofmann (August), Ostwald (Friedrich), Wallach (Otto), Wieland (Heinrich), Windaus (Adolf), Ziegler (Karl) **9** Zsigmondy (Richard) **10** Erlenmeyer (Richard), Staudinger (Hermann) **11** Willstatter (Richard) ***Italian:*** **5** Natta (Giulio) **8** Avogadro (Amedeo) ***Russian:*** **8** Semyonov (Nikolay), Zelinsky (Nikolay) **10** Mendeleyev (Dmitry) ***Swedish:*** **8** Svedberg (The, Theodor) **9** Berzelius (J. J.) ***Swiss:*** **6** Karrer (Paul), Werner (Alfred) (see also under **Nobel Prize winner**)

chemist's vessel **4** vial **5** flask, phial **6** ampule, beaker, mortar, retort **7** ampoule **8** crucible, test tube

chemoreceptor **8** taste bud

cheongsam **5** dress

Cheops **5** Khufu

cherish **4** keep, save **5** adore, guard, honor, nurse, prize, value **6** admire, cosset, defend, dote on, esteem, foster, harbor, relish, revere, shield **7** apprize, care for, nourish, nurture, shelter, worship **8** conserve, hold dear, preserve, treasure, venerate **9** cultivate, delight in, entertain, reverence, safeguard **10** appreciate

Cherokee ***chief:*** **4** Ross (John) ***historian:*** **7** Sequoia, Sequoya **8** Sequoyah

cherry ***dark:*** **4** bing ***family:*** **4** rose **8** Rosaceae ***genus:*** **6** Prunus ***hybrid:*** **4** Duke ***sour:*** **7** morello ***sweet:*** **4** bing **7** mazzard, oxheart ***wild:*** **7** mazzard **10** maraschino

cherry bomb **11** firecracker

Cherry Orchard author **7** Chekhov (Anton)

cherrystone **4** clam **6** quahog

Chersonese **9** peninsula

cherub **4** babe, baby **5** angel, child, cupid, putto **6** infant **7** bambino **8** amoretto, innocent

cherubic **4** cute, rosy **6** chubby **7** angelic **8** adorable, innocent

chess ***champion:*** **3** Tal (Mikhail) **4** Euwe (Max) **6** Karpov (Anatoly), Lasker (Emanuel) **7** Fischer (Bobby), Kramnik (Vladimir), Smyslov (Vassily), Spassky (Boris) **8** Alekhine (Alexander), Kasparov (Garry), Steinitz (Wilhelm) **9** Botvinnik (Mikhail), Petrosian (Tigran) **10** Capablanca (José) ***draw game:*** **9** stalemate ***goal:*** **4** mate **9** checkmate ***move:*** **6** castle, gambit ***opening:*** **6** gambit ***piece:*** **4** king, pawn, rook **5** queen **6** bishop, knight ***risk:*** **6** gambit ***term:*** **3** pin **4** draw, FIDE, file, fork, luft, rank **5** check **6** skewer **7** battery, capture, endgame**8** blockade, castling, diagonal **9** promotion

chest **3** box **4** arca, cist, kist **5** bosom, torso, trunk **6** breast, bureau, coffer, thorax **7** cabinet **8** cupboard, treasury **9** exchequer ***combining form:*** **5** stern **6** sterno, thorac

chesterfield **4** sofa **5** divan **8** overcoat **9** davenport

chestnut **4** tree **5** color, horse **6** cliché, marron **10** chinquapin ***extract:*** **6** tannin ***water:*** **4** ling

cheval glass **6** mirror

chevalier **5** noble **6** knight **8** horseman **9** caballero, gentleman

chevet **4** apse

chevron **6** stripe

chew **3** eat, gum **4** bite, gnaw **5** champ, chomp, munch **6** crunch, devour, nibble **7** consume **8** ruminate **9** masticate

chewing gum **6** chicle

chew out **3** jaw **5** scold **6** rebuke, revile **7** bawl out, reprove, tell off, upbraid **8** lambaste, reproach **9** castigate, criticize, reprimand **10** tongue-lash, vituperate

Chiang ____ **7** Kai-shek

chic **4** mode, rage, tony **5** nobby, smart, style, swank, swish, vogue **6** modish, trendy, with-it **7** dashing, elegant, fashion, stylish **8** elegance **10** dernier cri **11** fashionable

Chicago **7** Chi-Town **9** Windy City **10** Second City ***newspaper:*** **4** Trib **7** Tribune ***team:*** **4** Cubs **5** Bears, Bulls **8** White Sox **10** Black Hawks

chicane **4** dupe, fool, gull, hoax, ploy, ruse, wile **5** cavil, cheat, feint, fraud, trick **6** gambit **8** artifice, flimflam, hoodwink, trickery **9** bamboozle, deception, duplicity, stratagem, victimize **10** dishonesty, hanky-panky **13** double-dealing

chicanery **4** plot, ruse **5** fraud, trick **6** gambit **8** intrigue, trickery **9** deception, duplicity **10** subterfuge **11** machination, skulduggery

chichi **4** arty **5** gaudy, showy, swank **6** dressy, frills, frilly, la-di-da **7** splashy **8** affected, précieux, precious **10** flamboyant, preciosity **11** affectation, fashionable, overrefined, pretentious **12** ostentatious

chick **3** kid, tot **4** girl **5** child **6** moppet, nipper, pullet **7** toddler **8** juvenile **9** youngster

chickadee **8** titmouse ***family:*** **7** Paridae

chicken **4** fowl, funk **5** sissy, timid **6** coward, craven **7** dastard, gutless **8** cowardly, poltroon **11** lily-livered, yellowbelly **13** pusillanimous ***breed:*** **4** Java **6** Cochin **7** Cornish, Leghorn **9** Dominique, Orpington, Wyandotte **11** Jersey Giant, Rock Cornish ***castrated:*** **5** capon ***cooking:*** **5** fryer **7** broiler, roaster ***disease:*** **8** avian flu, pullorum **11** coccidiosis ***female:*** **3** hen **6** pullet ***genus:*** **6** Gallus ***male:*** **4** cock **7** rooster **8** cockerel ***pen:*** **4** coop **7** hennery **10** chick house ***small:*** **6** bantam ***sound:*** **6** cackle

chicken feed **6** bubkes, bupkes, bupkus **7** peanuts **8** pittance **11** chump change

chicken pox **9** varicella

chickpea **4** gram **8** garbanzo

chickweed **4** pink **7** potherb

chicle **3** gum **10** chewing gum

chicory **6** endive **7** witloof **9** radicchio

chide **3** kid **5** scold **6** berate, rebuke **7** chew out, lecture, reprove, upbraid **8** admonish, call down, reproach **9** castigate, reprimand

chiding **6** rebuke **7** reproof **8** reproach **9** reprimand **10** admonition **12** admonishment

chief **3** key **4** arch, boss, duce, emir, head, jefe, lion, main, star **5** first, major, prime **6** führer, honcho, leader, master, primal, ruling, sachem **7** fuehrer, headman, highest, leading, premier, primary **8** cardinal, champion, dictator, dominant, eminence, foremost **9** number-one, principal, prominent **10** preeminent **11** outstanding, predominant ***prefix:*** **4** arch

Chief Justice **3** Jay (John) **4** Taft (William Howard) **5** Chase (Salmon), Stone (Harlan Fiske), Taney (Roger), Waite (Morrison), White (Edward) **6** Burger (Warren), Fuller (Melville), Hughes (Charles Evans), Vinson (Fred), Warren (Earl) **7** Roberts (John) **8** Marshall (John), Rutledge (John) **9** Ellsworth (Oliver), Rehnquist (William)

chiefly **6** mainly, mostly **7** largely, notably, overall **9** generally, primarily **10** especially **11** principally **12** preeminently **13** predominantly

chief priest **7** primate

chiffchaff **4** bird **7** warbler

chiffonier **5** chest **6** bureau **7** armoire, dresser

chigger **4** mite **6** chigoe, red bug

chignon **3** bun **4** knot

chilblain **4** sore **8** swelling **12** inflammation

child **3** kid **4** brat **5** gamin, minor, youth **6** cherub, infant, moppet, nipper, shaver, urchin **7** bambino, toddler **8** juvenile, small fry **9** youngling, youngster ***combining form:*** **3** ped **4** paed, pedo **5** paedo ***gifted:*** **7** prodigy ***homeless:*** **4** waif ***parentless:*** **6** orphan ***Scottish:*** **5** bairn ***spoiled:*** **4** brat ***young:*** **3** tot **4** baby, tike, tyke **6** infant, kiddie, rug rat **8** bantling, weanling

childish **5** naive **7** puerile **8** arrested, immature, juvenile **9** infantile

childless **6** barren **7** sterile

childlike **5** naive **6** docile, filial **7** natural, puerile **8** innocent, trustful, trusting **9** ingenuous

children **4** kids, seed **5** brood, heirs, issue **6** scions **7** progeny **9** offspring, posterity **11** descendants

child's play **4** snap **5** cinch, setup **6** breeze, picnic **8** cakewalk, duck soup, kid stuff, pushover **11** piece of cake

Chile ***capital:*** **8** Santiago ***city:*** **6** Temuco **10** Concepción, Talcahuano, Valparaíso, Viña del Mar **11** Antofagasta ***conqueror:*** **7** Almagro (Diego de) **8** Valdivia (Pedro de) ***desert:*** **7** Atacama ***island:*** **6** Easter **13** Juan Fernández ***lake:*** **10** Llanquihue ***language:*** **7** Spanish ***leader:*** **7** Allende (Salvador) **8** Pinochet (Augusto) ***monetary unit:*** **4** peso ***mountain range:*** **5** Andes ***neighbor:*** **4** Peru **7** Bolivia **9** Argentina ***passage:*** **5** Drake ***poet:*** **6** Neruda (Pablo) **7** Mistral (Gabriela) ***river:*** **6** Bío-Bío ***strait:*** **8** Magellan

Chileab ***father:*** **5** David ***mother:*** **7** Abigail

chili con ____ **5** carne

Chilion ***father:*** **9** Elimelech ***mother:*** **5** Naomi

chill **3** ice, icy, raw **4** ague, cold, cool, hang **5**

algid, gelid, nippy **6** arctic, formal, freeze, frigid, frosty, wintry **7** distant, glacial, hostile **8** dispirit, freezing **10** demoralize, discourage, dishearten **11** emotionless, refrigerate

chiller 7 shocker **8** thriller

chilling 5 frore, gelid, scary **6** frigid, frosty **8** alarming **9** unnerving **10** disturbing, terrifying **11** distressing, frightening

chilly 3 raw **4** cold **5** algid, brisk, crisp, nippy **6** frigid **7** bracing, coldish, hostile **10** unfriendly

chilopod 9 centipede

chime 4 bell, bong, dong, peal, ring, toll, tune **5** agree, clang, knell, sound **6** accord, strike **7** concord, harmony **8** carillon **9** agreement, harmonize **10** consonance, correspond

chime in 3 say **4** tell **5** state, utter **6** inject **7** break in, declare **9** interrupt

chimera 5 dream, fancy **7** fantasy, figment, monster, specter, spectre **8** illusion, phantasy **9** nightmare, pipe dream

Chimera *father:* 6 Typhon ***mother:* 7** Echidna ***slayer:* 11** Bellerophon

chimerical 6 absurd, unreal **7** fictive, utopian **8** delusive, delusory, fabulous, fanciful, illusory, mythical, spurious **9** ambitious, beguiling, deceptive, fantastic, fictional, imaginary, visionary **10** far-fetched, fictitious, improbable, outlandish **11** extravagant, unrealistic **12** preposterous, suppositious

chiming 8 harmonic **9** consonant **10** harmonious

chimney 3 lum **4** flue, tube, vent **5** stack **10** smokestack ***corner:* 8** fireside **9** inglenook ***output:* 4** soot **5** fumes, smoke

chimpanzee 3 ape **7** primate **10** anthropoid ***kin:* 6** bonobo, gibbon **7** gorilla **9** orangutan

chin 3 gab, jaw, rap, yak **4** blab, chat, talk **8** converse ***hair:* 5** beard **6** goatee **7** Vandyke **9** soul patch

china 6 dishes **7** ceramic **8** crockery **9** porcelain, tableware **11** earthenware ***maker:* 3** Bow **5** Hizen, Imari, Spode **6** Doccia, Sèvres **7** Bristol, Chelsea, Dresden, Limoges, Meissen **8** Caughley, Haviland, Wedgwood

China *bay:* 8 Hangzhou ***capital:* 7** Beijing ***city:* 4** Sian, Xi'an **5** Wuhan **6** Canton, Harbin, Mukden **7** Nanjing, Nanking, Tianjin **8** Shanghai, Shenyang, Tientsin **9** Chongqing, Guangzhou ***desert:* 4** Gobi **10** Taklimakan ***dynasty:* 3** Ch'i, Han, Qin, Sui, Wei, Yin **4** Ch'en, Ch'in, Chou, Hsia, Ming, Qing, Song, Sung, T'ang, Tsin, Yüan **5** Ch'ing, Liang, Shang **6** Manchu, Mongol, Shu Han ***emperor, legendary:* 7** Huangdi, Huang-ti ***ethnic group:* 3** Han ***feudal state:* 3** Wei ***gulf:* 5** Bo Hai ***heritage site:* 9** Great Wall ***island:* 6** Hainan **8** Hong Kong ***lake:* 5** Tai Hu **8** Hongze Hu, Poyang Hu **10** Dongting Hu ***language:* 3** Han **8** Mandarin ***leader:* 3** Mao (Tse-tung, Zedong) **8** Hu Jintao **9** Kubla Khan, Mao Zedong, Sun Yat-sen **10** Kublai Khan, Mao Tse-tung **12** Deng Xiaoping **13** Chiang Kai-shek, Teng Hsiao-p'ing ***monetary unit:* 4** jiao, yuan **8** renminbi ***monetary unit, former:* 4** tael ***mountain, range:* 6** Kunlun **8** Himalaya **9** Altai Shan, Altay Shan, Himalayan **10** Gongga Shan ***old name:* 6** Cathay ***peninsula:* 7** Leizhou **8** Liaodong, Shandong ***province:* 5** Anhui, Gansu, Hevei, Henan, Hubei, Hunan, Jilin **6** Fujian, Shanxi, Yunnan **7** Guizhou, Jiangsu, Jiangxi, Qinghai, Shaanxi, Sichuan **8** Liaoning, Shandong, Szechuan, Szechwan, Zhejiang **9** Guangdong **12** Heilongjiang ***region:* 5** Macao, Tibet **6** Xizang **8** Hong Kong **10** Nei Monggol **12** Ningxia Huizu **13** Inner Mongolia, Xinjiang Uygur ***river:* 4** Amur **5** Chang, Huang, Tarim **6** Mekong, Yellow, Zangbo **7** Salween, Yangtze

china clay 6 kaolin

chinchilla 3 fur **6** rodent

chine 5 crest, ridge, spine **7** hogback **8** backbone

Chinese *aromatic root:* 7 ginseng ***bamboo:* 7** whangee ***boat:* 4** junk **6** sampan ***bow:* 6** kowtow ***broadsword:* 3** dao ***cabbage:* 7** bok choy, pak choi ***calculator:* 6** abacus ***card game:* 6** fan-tan ***cauterizing agent:* 4** moxa ***conveyance:* 7** pedicab **8** rickshaw **10** jinricksha, jinrikisha ***date:* 6** jujube ***dialect:* 4** Amoy **8** Mandarin **9** Cantonese, Pekingese ***distance unit:* 2** li ***dog:* 4** chow, Peke **8** chow chow **9** Pekingese ***fabric:* 6** pongee, tussah **8** shantung ***feminine principle:* 3** yin ***food:* 6** dim sum, lo mein, mantou, subgum, wonton **8** chop suey, chow mein **9** fried rice **10** egg foo yong, egg foo yung, Peking duck **11** egg foo young ***fruit:* 6** lichee, litchi, lychee, loquat **7** kumquat **8** mandarin ***gambling game:* 6** fan-tan ***gong:* 6** tam-tam ***gruel:* 6** congee ***healing art:* 6** qigong ***herb:* 5** ramie **7** ginseng ***idol:* 4** joss ***laborer:* 6** coolie ***mandarin's residence:* 5** yamen ***masculine principle:* 4** yang ***money, silver:* 5** sycee ***musical instrument:* 3** kin **4** pipa ***nurse:* 4** amah ***official:* 8** mandarin ***official seal:* 4** chop ***oil:* 4** tung ***ox:* 4** zebu ***pagoda:* 2** ta ***penal system:* 6** laogai ***porcelain:* 4** Ming **7**

celadon, Nankeen **8** mandarin **9** cloisonné ***pottery:*** **4** Kuan, Ming **5** Chien ***prefix:*** **4** Sino ***puzzle:*** **7** tangram ***race:*** **9** Mongoloid ***religion:*** **6** Taoism **8** Buddhism **12** Confucianism ***sauce:*** **3** soy ***secret society:*** **4** tong ***sheep:*** **5** urial ***silkworm:*** **6** tussah ***tea:*** **5** bohea, hyson **6** congou, oolong **8** souchong ***temple:*** **2** ta **6** pagoda **9** joss house ***tree:*** **4** tung **6** ginkgo, loquat **7** kumquat ***unicorn:*** **3** lin ***vine:*** **5** kudzu ***vital energy:*** **3** chi

chink **4** rift, slit **5** caulk, cleft, crack, split **6** cranny **7** crevice, fissure, opening **8** aperture

chinquapin **3** nut **8** chestnut

chintzy **5** cheap, gaudy, showy, tacky **6** flashy, garish, stingy, tawdry, vulgar **9** tasteless **12** meretricious

chip **4** flaw, nick **5** flake, notch, shard, slice, split, wafer, wedge **6** chisel, defect, paring, sliver **7** counter

chip in **6** ante up, kick in **7** pitch in **10** contribute **11** come through

chipper **4** spry **5** alert, brisk, perky, zesty **6** bright, lively, nimble **8** animated, spirited **9** sprightly, vivacious

chirk **4** buoy **5** cheer **7** animate, enliven, hearten **8** energize, inspirit **9** encourage **10** strengthen

chirography **6** script **8** longhand **10** penmanship **11** calligraphy, handwriting

chiromancy **9** palmistry

Chiron **7** centaur ***father:*** **6** Cronus ***mother:*** **7** Philyra ***pupil:*** **5** Jason **8** Achilles, Heracles, Hercules **9** Asclepius **11** Aesculapius

chiropody **8** podiatry

chiropractic founder **6** Palmer (Daniel)

chirp **4** chip, peep, sing **5** cheep, trill, tweet **6** warble **7** chirrup, twitter

chirpy **3** gay **5** sunny **6** blithe, cheery, sparky **7** buoyant, sparkly **8** cheerful, sunbeamy **9** lightsome

chirrup **4** chip, peep, sing **5** cheep, tweet **6** warble **7** chipper, twitter

chisel **3** gad, gyp, hew **4** beat, bilk, scam **5** carve, cheat, cozen, cut in, gouge, trick **6** butt in, diddle, fleece, horn in, sculpt **7** defraud, engrave, intrude, swindle

chit **3** IOU, kid **4** memo, note, slip **5** child **6** moppet **7** invoice, voucher **8** notation **9** youngster **10** memorandum

chitchat **3** gab **5** chaff **6** babble, banter, gossip **7** chatter, palaver, prattle **8** badinage **9** small talk **12** tittle-tattle

Chi-Town **7** Chicago

chitter **4** chip, peep, sing **5** cheep, chirp, tweet **6** warble **7** chatter, chirrup, twitter

chivalric see **chivalrous**

chivalrous **5** lofty, manly, noble **7** courtly, gallant, valiant **8** generous, gracious, knightly **9** honorable **10** benevolent, courageous **11** considerate, gentlemanly, magnanimous

chivy, chivvy **4** bait, ride **5** annoy, tease **6** badger, heckle, hector **7** torment **8** bullyrag

Chloe **11** shepherdess ***beloved:*** **7** Daphnis

chlordane **11** insecticide

chlorine symbol **2** Cl

Chloris ***father:*** **7** Amphion ***husband:*** **6** Neleus **8** Zephyrus ***mother:*** **5** Niobe ***son:*** **6** Nestor

chloroform **7** anodyne, solvent **10** anesthetic **11** anaesthetic

chockablock **4** full **6** jammed, loaded, packed **7** brimful, crammed, crowded, stuffed **9** jam-packed

chocolate **5** brown, cacao, cocoa

Chocolate Soldier composer **6** Straus (Oscar)

chocolate tree **5** cacao

choice **3** top **4** best, pick, rare, vote **5** cream, elite, prime, prize **6** chosen, dainty, option, rating, select **7** elegant, verdict **8** decision, delicate, druthers, election, judgment, selected, superior, volition **9** exquisite, selection **9** selection **10** preference **11** alternative **13** determination ***even:*** **6** toss-up

choir **6** chorus **7** chorale ***area:*** **4** loft **7** chancel, gallery ***leader:*** **6** cantor **8** choragus **9** precentor ***member:*** **9** chorister ***section:*** **4** alto, bass **5** tenor **7** soprano ***vestment:*** **4** gown, robe **5** cotta **8** surplice

choke **3** gag **4** clog, plug, stop **5** block, close **6** stifle **7** congest, occlude, silence, smother **8** obstruct, strangle, throttle **9** constrict, suffocate **10** asphyxiate

choking **8** quashing, stifling **10** repression, smothering, squelching, strangling **11** suppression

choleric **5** angry, fiery, irate **6** fierce, heated **7** enraged **8** incensed, wrathful **9** irascible, splenetic **10** infuriated **11** hot-tempered **13** quick-tempered

cholla **6** cactus **7** opuntia

Chomolungma **7** Everest (Mt.)

chomp **4** bite, chaw, chew **5** munch **6** crunch **9** masticate

choose **3** opt **4** cull, mark, pick, take, want **5** adopt, elect, favor **6** decide, desire, opt for, prefer, select **7** embrace, pick out **8** decide on, handpick **9** single out

choosy **5** fussy, picky **7** finical, finicky **9** finicking, selective **10** fastidious, particular, pernickety **11** persnickety

chop **3** cut, hew **4** dice, fell, hack, hash, seal, veer **5** cut up, grade, mince **7** quality

chop-chop **4** fast **5** quick **6** presto, pronto **7** quickly, rapidly **8** promptly, speedily **9** posthaste **12** lickety-split

chophouse **10** restaurant

Chopin, Frédéric ***birthplace:*** **6** Poland ***instrument:*** **5** piano ***lover:*** **4** Sand (George) ***work:*** **5** étude **7** mazurka, prelude **8** nocturne **9** polonaise **11** Minute Waltz

chopper **10** motorcycle

choppy **4** wavy **5** jerky, rough **6** ripply, stormy, uneven **7** erratic **8** variable **9** turbulent, unsettled

choral section **5** altos **6** basses, tenors **8** sopranos

choral work **5** motet **6** anthem **7** cantata, passion **8** oratorio

chord **5** triad **6** tetrad **7** harmony ***sequence:*** **7** cadence **11** progression

chore **3** job **4** duty, task **5** stint, trial **6** devoir, effort **7** routine **10** assignment, obligation **11** tribulation

choreograph **6** devise, direct, map out **7** arrange, compose **11** orchestrate

choreographer ***American:*** **4** Feld (Elliot), Holm (Hanya), Lang (Pearl) **5** Ailey (Alvin), Fosse (Bob), Limón (José), Shawn (Ted), Tharp (Twyla) **6** Duncan (Isadora), Dunham (Katherine), Fokine (Michel), Graham (Martha), Morris (Mark), Taylor (Paul), Tetley (Glen) **7** de Mille (Agnes), Jamison (Judith), Joffrey (Robert), Martins (Peter), Massine (Leonide), Robbins (Jerome), St. Denis (Ruth), Tamiris (Helen), Weidman (Charles) **8** Champion (Gower, Marge), Humphrey (Doris), Nikolais (Alwin), Villella (Edward) **10** Balanchine (George), Cunningham (Merce) ***Australian:*** **8** Helpmann (Robert) ***Cuban:*** **6** Alonso (Alicia) ***Danish:*** **5** Bruhn (Erik) **7** Martins (Peter) **12** Bournonville (August) ***English:*** **5** Dolin (Anton), Tudor (Antony) **6** Ashton (Frederick), Weaver (John) **7** Markova (Alicia), Rambert (Marie) **8** de Valois (Ninette), Helpmann (Robert) **9** MacMillan (Kenneth) ***French:*** **5** Lifar (Serge) **6** Béjart (Maurice), Perrot (Jules), Petipa (Marius) **7** Camargo (Marie), Massine (Léonide), Noverre (Jean-Georges) ***German:*** **5** Jooss (Kurt) ***Hungarian:*** **5** Laban (Rudolf) ***Mexican:*** **5** Limón (José) ***Russian:*** **5** Lifar (Serge) **6** Fokine (Michel), Petipa (Marius) **8** Nijinska (Bronislava), Nijinsky (Vaslav)

chorography **3** map **7** mapping **8** features **9** mapmaking

chortle **5** laugh **6** giggle, guffaw, hee-haw, titter **7** chuckle, snicker

chorus **5** choir **7** refrain

chorus girl **7** chorine

chosen **4** pick **5** elect, elite, named **6** called, marked, pegged, picked, select **7** blessed **8** selected **9** appointed, delegated, exclusive

Chou ____ **5** En-lai

chouse **3** gyp **4** bilk, clip, dupe, herd **5** cheat, cozen, drive, trick **6** diddle, fleece **7** defraud, swindle **8** flimflam

chow **4** eats, feed, food, grub, meal, mess

chowchow **6** medley, relish **7** mélange

chowderhead **4** boob, clod, dodo, dolt, dope, fool **5** chump, dunce, idiot, noddy **6** dimwit, nitwit, noodle **7** halfwit, schnook **8** dumbbell, numskull **9** lamebrain, numbskull

chowhound **7** glutton **8** gourmand

chrism **3** oil **4** balm **5** cream, salve **6** cerate **7** unction, unguent **8** ointment

christen **3** dub **4** call, name, term **5** title **7** asperse, baptize, immerse **8** dedicate, sprinkle **9** designate

christening **7** baptism

Christian ***denomination:*** **6** Mormon, Quaker **7** Baptist, Friends **8** Anglican, Catholic, Lutheran, Moravian, Nazarene, Reformed **9** Calvinist, Episcopal, Mennonite, Methodist, Unitarian **10** Anabaptist **11** Pentecostal **12** Episcopalian, Presbyterian, Universalist ***Eastern rite:*** **5** Uniat **6** Uniate ***Egyptian:*** **4** Copt ***love feast:*** **5** agape ***martyr, first:*** **7** Stephen ***symbol:*** **3** IHS **4** fish, rood **5** cross **6** Chi-Rho **7** ichthus

Christiania **4** Oslo

Christian Science founder **4** Eddy (Mary Baker)

Christie, Agatha ***character:*** **6** Marple (Jane), Poirot (Hercule) ***novel:*** **14** Death on the Nile **16** Ten Little Indians **24** Murder on the Orient Express ***play:*** **9** Mousetrap (The) **24** Witness for the Prosecution

Christina's World painter **5** Wyeth (Andrew)

Christmas **4** Noel, Yule **8** Nativity, yuletide ***crumpet:*** **7** pikelet ***song:*** **4** noel **5** carol ***symbol:*** **7** Yule log

Christmas Carol, A ***author:*** **7** Dickens (Charles) ***character:*** **7** Scrooge (Ebenezer), Tiny Tim **8** Cratchit (Bob)

Christogram **6** Chi-Rho

Christopher Robin creator **5** Milne (A. A.)

chromatic **8** colorful **10** accidental

chromatin thread **7** spireme

chromium symbol **2** Cr

chromosome component **3** DNA **4** gene **8** telomere **10** centromere, chromomere

chronic **5** usual **6** wonted **7** routine **8** constant, enduring, habitual **9** ceaseless, confirmed, continual, customary, incessant, perennial, perpetual, recurrent, recurring **10** accustomed, continuing, habituated, inveterate, persisting **11** unrelenting

chronicle 4 list, tale **6** annals, record, relate, report **7** account, history, narrate, recital, recount **8** describe **9** narration, narrative

chronicler 8 annalist, narrator, recorder, reporter **9** historian

chronograph 5 clock, watch **9** timepiece

chronology 5 annal **6** annals, record **7** history **8** calendar, register, schedule **9** timetable

chronometer 5 clock, watch **9** timepiece

chrysalis 4 pupa **8** covering

Chryseis ***captor:*** **9** Agamemnon ***father:*** **7** Chryses

Chrysippus ***father:*** **6** Pelops ***slayer:*** **6** Atreus **8** Thyestes

chthonic 6 Hadean, nether **7** hellish, satanic **8** accursed, infernal, plutonic **9** plutonian, Tartarean **10** sulphurous

chubby 5 hefty, husky, plump, podgy, pudgy, round, tubby **6** chunky, fleshy, portly, rotund, stocky, zaftig **8** plumpish, roly-poly

chuck 3 pat, tap **4** beef, cast, hurl, junk, oust, shed, toss **5** ditch, fling, heave, nudge, pitch, scrap, throw **6** give up, reject **7** abandon, boot out, discard, dismiss, kick out **8** jettison, throw out **9** throw away

chucker 7 bouncer

chuckle 5 laugh **6** giggle, guffaw, hee-haw, titter **7** chortle, snicker

chucklehead see **chowderhead**

chuff 3 oaf **4** boor, lout, rube **5** churl, clown, yahoo, yokel **7** bumpkin, hayseed **10** clodhopper

chum 3 pal **4** mate, pard **5** buddy, crony **6** friend, salmon **7** comrade **8** sidekick **9** companion

chummy 4 cozy **5** close, pally, palsy, thick **8** familiar, intimate **10** buddy-buddy, palsy-walsy

chump 3 oaf, sap **4** boob, dolt, dope, dupe, fool, goof, goon, gull, mark **5** booby, dummy, dunce, loser, patsy **6** pigeon, sucker, turkey **7** failure, fall guy, fathead **8** dolthead, lunkhead

chunk 3 sum, wad **4** clod, hunk, lump, slab **5** clump **6** nugget

chunky 5 beefy, dumpy, hefty, husky, plump, pudgy, squat, stout **6** chubby, fleshy, portly, rotund, stocky, stubby, stumpy **8** heavyset, thickset

church 4 cult, fane, kirk, sect **5** creed, faith **6** temple **7** minster **8** basilica, religion **9** cathedral, communion **10** tabernacle **12** denomination ***adjunct:*** **6** belfry **7** steeple **9** bell tower ***basin:*** **4** font **5** stoup ***bench:*** **3** pew ***bishop's:*** **9** cathedral ***Buddhist:*** **2** ta ***calendar:*** **4** ordo ***caretaker:*** **6** sexton ***chapel:*** **7** oratory ***code:*** **8** canon law ***council:*** **5** synod ***court:*** **4** rota **10** consistory ***creed:*** **6** Nicene **8** Apostles' ***district:*** **6** parish **7** diocese ***father:*** **5** Basil **6** Jerome, Justin, Origen **7** Ambrose, Clement **8** Ignatius **9** Augustine **10** Chrysostom, Tertullian, theologian ***fund-raiser:*** **5** bingo **6** bazaar, raffle ***governing body:*** **5** curia **7** classis **10** consistory, presbytery ***head:*** **4** pope **7** pontiff ***law:*** **5** canon ***member:*** **11** communicant ***of a monastery:*** **7** minster ***officer:*** **5** elder, vicar **6** beadle, deacon, sexton, verger, warden **9** presbyter, sacristan ***part:*** **4** apse, bema, loft, nave **5** aisle, altar, choir **6** vestry **7** chancel, gallery, narthex, steeple **8** sacristy, transept **9** baptistry, sanctuary **10** baptistery, clerestory ***porch:*** **6** parvis **7** galilee ***reader:*** **6** lector ***recess:*** **4** apse ***response:*** **4** amen ***revenue:*** **5** tithe ***room:*** **6** vestry **8** sacristy ***Scottish:*** **4** kirk ***seats for clergy:*** **7** sedilia ***service:*** **4** mass **6** matins **7** vespers **8** evensong **9** communion ***small:*** **6** chapel ***tribunal:*** **4** rota ***vault:*** **5** crypt

Churchill, Winston ***daughter:*** **4** Mary **5** Diana, Sarah ***estate:*** **8** Checkers ***father:*** **8** Randolph ***gesture:*** **5** V-sign ***mother:*** **6** Jennie (Jerome) ***phrase:*** **11** Iron Curtain ***son:*** **8** Randolph ***trademark:*** **5** cigar ***wife:*** **10** Clementine

church key 9 can opener

churchman 6 bishop, cleric, divine, parson, pastor, priest **8** minister, preacher, reverend **9** clergyman **12** ecclesiastic

churl 3 oaf **4** boor, clod, lout, rube **5** chuff, clown, yahoo, yokel **6** mucker **7** bumpkin, hayseed **10** clodhopper

churlish 4 base, curt, dour, rude **5** blunt, crude, gruff, surly **6** coarse, crusty, oafish, vulgar **7** boorish, brusque, loutish, lowbred, uncivil **8** cloddish, clownish **10** unmannerly **11** clodhopping, uncivilized **12** discourteous

churn 4 boil, foam, roil, stir **5** froth, swirl **6** bubble, seethe, simmer, stir up **7** agitate, ferment, smolder

chute 4 fall, ramp **5** falls, rapid, slide, spout **6** rapids **7** cascade, channel, descent **8** cataract **9** spinnaker, waterfall

chutzpah 4 gall **5** brass, cheek, moxie, nerve, spunk **8** audacity, temerity **10** effrontery

CIA predecessor 3 OSS

ciao 4 by-by, ta-ta **5** adieu, adios, aloha, hello, howdy **6** bye-bye, good-by, so long **7** cheerio, good-bye, toodles **8** farewell, toodle-oo **9** greetings

cicatrix 4 scar **13** scarification

Cicero ***forte:*** **7** oratory ***speech:*** **9** philippic ***target:*** **8** Catiline **10** Mark Antony
cicerone **4** guru **5** coach, guide, tutor **6** docent, escort, mentor **7** adviser **9** counselor, tour guide
Cid, El (Le) **4** epic, hero, play, poem **5** opera ***composer:*** **8** Massenet (Jules) ***meaning:*** **4** lord ***name:*** **4** Díaz (Rodrigo, Ruy) **5** Bivar ***playwright:*** **9** Corneille (Pierre) ***sword:*** **6** Colada, Tizona ***wife:*** **6** Jimena, Ximena
cigar **5** claro, stogy **6** corona, Havana, stogie **7** cheroot **8** panatela, perfecto ***case:*** **7** humidor ***color:*** **5** claro **6** maduro **8** colorado
cigarette **3** fag **4** butt **5** smoke **6** gasper **10** coffin nail
cilium **4** hair, lash **7** eyelash
Cimmerian **4** dark **5** dusky, murky **6** gloomy **7** hellish, shadowy, stygian **8** infernal, plutonic **9** plutonian
cinch **4** snap **5** girth, setup **6** assure, breeze, ensure, fasten, insure, picnic, secure, shoo-in **8** duck soup, kid stuff, pushover **9** certainty **10** child's play
cinchona bark extract **7** quinine
cincture **4** band, belt, sash **6** girdle **9** waistband
cinders **3** ash **4** coal, lava, slag **5** ashes, dross **6** embers **8** clinkers
cinema **4** film, nabe, show **5** flick, movie **6** movies **7** picture, theater, theatre **12** silver screen **13** motion picture
cinereous **4** ashy, gray, grey **5** ashen **7** ashlike
cinnabar **3** ore **7** mineral, pigment **9** vermilion ***color:*** **3** red
cinnamon bark **6** cassia
cinnamon stone **6** garnet **8** essonite
cipher **4** code, zero **5** aught, count, digit **6** figure, naught, nobody, number, reckon, symbol **7** compute, integer, numeral **8** estimate, monogram **9** calculate, nonentity **11** whole number
ciphering **8** figuring **9** computing, reckoning **10** arithmetic **11** calculation, computation
circa **4** near, nigh **5** about **6** approx., around **7** roughly **13** approximately
circadian **5** daily **6** cyclic **7** diurnal, regular **9** quotidian
Circe **5** siren, witch **9** sorceress **11** enchantress ***brother:*** **6** Aeëtes ***father:*** **3** Sol **6** Helios ***home:*** **5** Aeaea ***lover:*** **7** Ulysses **8** Odysseus ***niece:*** **5** Medea ***son:*** **5** Comus **9** Telegonus
Circean **6** luring **8** alluring, enticing, fetching, tempting **10** bewitching
circinate **6** coiled **7** rounded
circle **4** belt, gyre, hoop, loop, ring **5** crowd, cycle, group, orbit, wheel, whorl **6** clique, corona, girdle, gyrate, rotary, rotate **7** compass, coterie, cronies, friends, revolve, rondure **8** surround **9** encompass **10** associates, companions, revolution ***bisector:*** **8** diameter ***colored:*** **6** areola ***combining form:*** **3** gyr **4** cycl, gyro **5** cyclo ***graph:*** **8** pie chart ***luminous:*** **4** aura, halo **6** corona, nimbus **7** aureole ***part:*** **3** arc **6** sector **8** quadrant ***small:*** **4** disk **7** annulet
circlet **4** band, ring **6** bangle, diadem **8** bracelet, headband ***for head or helmet:*** **7** coronal
circuit **3** lap, way **4** loop, tour, trip, turn **5** ambit, cycle, orbit, round, route, track **6** course, hookup, league **7** compass, journey, pathway, travels **8** district, rotation **9** perimeter, periphery, round trip **10** revolution, roundabout **11** association, circulation **13** circumference
circuitous **7** devious, oblique, winding **8** circular, indirect, tortuous **10** collateral, convoluted, meandering, roundabout
circuit rider **5** judge **8** minister, preacher **9** clergyman
circular **4** bill **5** flier, flyer, round **7** annular, cycloid, discoid, handout, leaflet **8** handbill **9** throwaway ***file:*** **11** wastebasket ***fort:*** **8** martello ***motion:*** **4** eddy, gyre, spin **5** whirl **8** gyration, rotation **10** revolution ***plate:*** **4** disc, dish, disk
circularize **4** poll **6** survey **7** canvass **9** advertise, publicize
circulate **4** flow **6** rotate, spread **7** diffuse, radiate, revolve **8** disperse **9** propagate **10** distribute **11** disseminate
circulation **4** flow **6** spread **8** currency **9** diffusion **11** propagation **12** transmission **13** dissemination
circumciser **5** mohel
circumcision, Jewish **4** bris **9** Brit Milah
circumference **3** rim **5** ambit **6** border, bounds, limits, margin **7** circuit, compass **8** boundary, confines **9** perimeter, periphery
circumflex **9** diacritic
circumjacent **11** surrounding
circumlocution **8** pleonasm, verbiage **9** euphemism, loquacity, prolixity, verbosity, wordiness **10** redundancy **11** periphrasis, verboseness
circumnavigate **5** skirt **6** bypass, detour **8** sidestep
circumnavigator **4** Cook (James) **5** Drake (Francis) **8** Magellan (Ferdinand), van Noort (Olivier) **9** Cavendish (Thomas)
circumscribe **5** cramp, limit **6** fetter, hamper **7** confine, delimit, enclose, mark off, out-

line, trammel **8** restrict, surround **9** constrict

circumscribed 5 bound, fixed **6** finite, narrow, strait **7** bounded, cramped, limited, precise **8** confined, definite, hampered **10** restrained, restricted **11** determinate

circumscription 5 cramp, limit, stint **6** border, margin **8** boundary **9** perimeter, restraint, stricture **10** constraint, definition, limitation **11** confinement, restriction **12** ball and chain, delimitation

circumspect 4 safe, wary **5** chary **7** careful, guarded, prudent **8** cautious, discreet, gingerly **11** calculating

circumstance 4 fact, item **5** event, thing **6** detail, factor **7** adjunct, element, episode, feature **8** accident, incident, occasion **9** component, condition, happening **10** occurrence, particular **11** concomitant, constituent, eventuality ***unforeseen:* 8** exigency **9** emergency

circumstantial 4 full **5** close, exact **6** strict **7** precise, replete **8** accurate, complete, detailed, thorough **9** elaborate, pertinent **10** blow-by-blow, ceremonial, exhaustive, incidental, particular

circumvent 5 avoid, dodge, elude, evade, hem in, skirt **6** bypass, detour **8** outflank, sidestep

circumvolution 4 gyre, turn **5** wheel, whirl **8** gyration, rotation **10** revolution

circus 4 ring **5** arena **6** big top **9** spectacle **12** amphitheater ***animal:* 4** bear, flea, lion, seal **5** horse, tiger **8** elephant ***attraction:* 5** freak **8** sideshow ***owner:* 6** Bailey (James), Barnum (P. T.) **8** Ringling (Bros.) ***performer:* 5** clown, tamer **7** acrobat, athlete, juggler, tumbler **9** aerialist, fire eater, strong man ***worker:* 10** roustabout

Cisco Kid 9 caballero ***actor:* 4** Beck (Jackson) **6** Baxter (Warner), Roland (Gilbert), Romero (Cesar) **7** Renaldo (Duncan) ***horse:* 6** Diablo ***sidekick:* 6** Pancho **7** Gordito

citadel 4 fort **7** redoubt **8** fastness, fortress **10** stronghold ***of Carthage:* 5** Bursa, Byrsa ***Russian:* 7** kremlin

citation 5 quote **6** eulogy **7** excerpt, mention, summons, tribute **8** accolade, encomium **9** panegyric, quotation, reference **12** commendation

cite 4 name, tell **5** offer, quote **6** adduce, recall, summon **7** arraign, mention, present, refer to, specify **8** point out, remember **9** recollect

citizen 7 burgess, burgher, subject **8** civilian, national, resident, townsman **10** inhabitant

Citizen Kane director 6 Welles (Orson)

citron 4 tree **5** melon

citrus *family:* 3 rue **8** Rutaceae ***fruit:* 4** lime, ugli **5** lemon **6** citron, orange, pomelo **7** kumquat, tangelo **8** bergamot, mandarin, shaddock **9** tangerine **10** grapefruit

city 4 burg **5** urban **7** burghal **9** municipal **10** metropolis ***combining form:* 5** polis ***Eternal:* 4** Rome ***fortress:* 7** citadel ***French:* 5** ville ***heavenly:* 4** Sion, Zion ***Latin:* 4** urbs ***Motor:* 7** Detroit ***of Bells:* 10** Strasbourg ***of Bridges:* 6** Bruges ***of Brotherly Love:* 12** Philadelphia ***of David:* 9** Jerusalem ***official:* 5** mayor **7** manager **8** alderman **10** councilman ***of God:* 6** heaven **8** paradise ***of Gold:* 8** Eldorado ***of Kings:* 4** Lima ***of Lights:* 5** Paris ***of Lilies:* 8** Florence ***of Masts:* 6** London ***of Rams:* 6** Canton ***of Refuge:* 6** Medina ***of Saints:* 8** Montreal ***of Seven Hills:* 4** Rome ***of the dead:* 10** necropolis ***of Victory:* 5** Cairo ***planner:* 8** urbanist ***section:* 4** slum, ward **5** block, plaza **6** barrio, ghetto, square, uptown **8** business, downtown, red-light **11** residential ***slicker:* 4** dude ***windy:* 7** Chicago

city-state, Greek 5 Argos, polis **6** Athens, Delphi, poleis (plural), Sparta, Thebes **7** Corinth

city, town, village (see also **capital**) ***Afghanistan:* 5** Balkh, Farah, Herat, Kushk **6** Konduz **8** Kandahar, Qandahar **9** Jalalabad ***Alabama:* 3** Opp **4** Arab, Boaz, Elba **5** Selma **6** Athens, Dothan, Mobile **7** Decatur, Florala **8** Prichard **10** Birmingham, Huntsville, Scottsboro, Tuscaloosa **12** Muscle Shoals ***Alaska:* 4** Nome **5** Kenai, Sitka **6** Barrow, Bethel, Kodiak, Valdez **9** Anchorage, Fairbanks, Ketchikan **11** Point Barrow ***Albania:* 4** Fier **5** Berat, Korçë, Kukës, Vlorë ***Alberta:* 4** Olds **5** Hanna, Leduc, Taber **7** Calgary **10** Lethbridge **11** Medicine Hat ***Algeria:* 4** Bône, Oran **5** Batna, Blida, Médéa, Saïda, Sétif **6** Annaba, Bechar **11** Constantine ***Angola:* 6** Huambo **7** Lubango **8** Benguela ***Argentina:* 4** Azul, Goya **5** Junin, Lanus, Lujan, Merlo, Salta, Tigre **6** Parana **7** Córdoba, La Plata, La Rioja, Mendoza, Rosario, San Juan, Santa Fe **9** Catamarca **11** Bahía Blanca, Mar del Plata ***Arizona:* 3** Ajo **4** Eloy, Mesa, Yuma **5** Globe, Tempe **6** Tucson **7** Sun City, Winslow **8** Glendale, Prescott **9** Flagstaff, Tombstone **10** Casa Grande, Scottsdale ***Arkansas:* 4** Mena **5** Beebe, Cabot, Earle, Ozark, Wynne **9** Fort Smith, Pine Bluff, Texarkana **10** Hot Springs ***Armenia:* 6** Gyumri **8** Vanadzor ***Australia:* 3** Ayr **5** Dalby, Dubbo, Perth, Unley **6** Darwin, Sydney **8** Adelaide, Brisbane, Randwick **9** Bankstown, Blacktown, Gold Coast, Melbourne, Newcastle **10** Kalgoorlie, Parramatta, Sutherland, Wollongong **12** Alice Springs ***Austria:*** **4** Enns, Graz, Linz, Wels **5** Steyr, Traun **8** Salzburg **9** Innsbruck **10** Klagenfurt ***Azerbaijan:*** **5** Gäncä **8** Sumqayit **9** Kirovabad ***Bahamas:*** **8** Freeport ***Bangladesh:*** **5** Bogra, Pabna **6** Khulna, Sylhet **7** Barisal, Comilla, Jessore, Rangpur, Saidpur **10** Chittagong ***Belarus:*** **5** Brest, Gomel, Mozyr, Pinsk **6** Grodno, Homyel', Hrodna **7** Mogilev, Vitebsk **8** Babruysk, Mahilyow **9** Vitsyebsk ***Belgium:*** **3** Ath, Hal, Huy, Mol **4** Amay, Dour, Geel, Genk, Gent, Hoei, Luik, Mons, Vise **5** Aalst, Arlon, Diest, Evere, Ghent, Halle, Ieper, Jumet, Leuze, Liège, Namur, Ronse, Theux, Wavre, Ypres **6** Bruges, Brugge **7** Antwerp, Hasselt, Louvain **8** Oostende **9** Charleroi ***Benin:*** **5** Kandi **6** Abomey **7** Parakou ***Bolivia:*** **5** Oruro, Uyuni **6** Potosí **9** Santa Cruz **10** Cochabamba ***Bosnia and Herzegovina:*** **5** Bihac, Brcko, Jajce, Tuzla **6** Mostar, Zenica **9** Banja Luka ***Botswana:*** **4** Maun **5** Kanye **11** Francistown ***Brazil:*** **4** Codo, Pará **5** Bahia, Bauru, Belém, Ceara, Natal **6** Campos, Canoas, Caxias, Ilheus, Maceio, Manaus, Olinda, Recife, Santos **7** Aracaju, Caruaru, Goiania, Jundiai, Marilia, Niteroi, Pelotas, São Luis, Uberaba, Vitória **8** Campinas, Colatina, Curitiba, Londrina, Salvador, Santarém, São Paulo, Sorocaba, Teresina **9** Caratinga, Fortaleza, Guarulhos, Rio Grande **10** Guarapuava, Joao Pessoa, Juiz de Fora, Nova Iguaçu, Pernambuco, Petropolis, Piracicaba, Pôrto Velho, Santa Maria, Santo André, São Gonçalo, Uberlândia **11** Campo Grande, Caxias do Sul, Ponta Grossa, Pôrto Alegre **12** Montes Claros, Rio de Janeiro, Teófilo Otoni, Volta Redonda **13** Belo Horizonte ***British Columbia:*** **5** Comox **6** Surrey **7** Burnaby **8** Richmond **9** Vancouver ***Bulgaria:*** **3** Lom **4** Ruse **5** Varna, Vidin **6** Burgas **7** Plovdiv **11** Stara Zagora ***Burma:*** see **Myanmar** ***California:*** **4** Brea, Galt, Lodi, Ojai **5** Arvin, Azusa, Ceres, Chico, Chino, Dixon, Hemet, Indio, Norco, Ripon, Ukiah, Wasco, Yreka **6** Downey, Encino, Fresno, Oxnard, Pomona, Sonoma **7** Anaheim, Burbank, Compton, Fremont, Hayward, Modesto, Oakland, San Jose, Seaside, Soledad, Van Nuys **8** Berkeley, Glendale, Palo Alto, Pasadena, San Diego, Santa Ana, Stockton, Torrance, Yuba City **9** El Segundo, Hollywood, Long Beach, Menlo Park, Riverside, Sausalito **10** Chula Vista, Culver City, Los Angeles, San Leandro, Santa Clara **11** Bakersfield, Laguna Beach, Pebble Beach, Redwood City, San Clemente, Santa Monica **12** Beverly Hills, Mission Viejo, Redondo Beach, San Francisco, Santa Barbara **13** San Bernardino, San Luis Obispo ***Cambodia:*** **8** Siem Reap **10** Battambang **11** Kompong Cham ***Cameroon:*** **4** Buea, Edea **5** Kribi, Lomie **6** Douala **7** Bamenda, Foumban **9** Bafoussam ***Canada:*** **4** York **5** Banff **6** London, Oshawa, Regina, St. John **7** Brandon, Burnaby, Calgary, Halifax, Iqaluit, Red Deer, St. John's, Sudbury, Toronto, Windsor **8** Hamilton, Montreal, Moose Jaw, North Bay, Victoria, Winnipeg **9** Dartmouth, Kitchener, Longueuil, North York, Saint John, Saskatoon, Vancouver **10** Lethbridge, Saint John's, Sherbrooke, Thunder Bay, Whitehorse **11** Fredericton, Medicine Hat, Mississauga, Scarborough, Yellowknife **12** Peterborough, Prince Albert, Prince George **13** Charlottetown, Trois-Rivières ***Central African Republic:*** **5** Bouar **7** Bambari ***Chad:*** **4** Sarh **6** Abéché ***Chile:*** **4** Lebu, Lota, Tomé **5** Ancud, Angol, Arica, Maipu, Penco, Rengo, Talca **6** Temuco **7** Copiapó, Iquique **8** Rancagua **10** Concepción, Talcahuano, Valparaíso **11** Antofagasta ***China:*** **4** Amoy, Jian, Luan, Xi'an, Yaan **5** Hefei, Jilin, Jinan, Lhasa, Qinan, Ssuan, Wuhan, Yibin, Yumen **6** Andong, Anqing, Anshan, Anshun, Anyang, Beihai, Canton, Dalian, Datong, Foshan, Fushun, Fuzhou, Guilin, Haikou, Handan, Harbin, Hohhot, Hoihao, Jilong, Luzhou, Mukden, Ningbo, Pengbu, Suzhou, Ürümqi, Xiamen, Xining, Xuzhou, Yanggu, Yichun, Yining, Zhangi, Zhaoan **7** Baoding, Changan, Chengdu, Dandong, Guiyang, Huainan, Jiamusi, Jiaxing, Kaifeng, Kunming, Lanzhou, Luoshan, Luoyang, Nanking, Nanjing, Nanning, Shantou, Tianjin, Taiyuan **8** Changchi, Changsha, Hangzhou, Hanzhong, Huangshi, Jiangmen, Shanghai, Shaoyang, Shenyang, Shenzhen, Zhenjing **9** Changchun, Chenjiang, Chongqing, Chungking, Guangzhou, Zhengzhou, Zhenjiang ***Colombia:*** **4** Buga, Cali **5** Bello, Mocoa, Neiva, Ocaña, Pasto, Tuluá, Tunja **6** Cúcuta, Ibagué **7** Ciénaga, Palmira, Pereira, Popayán **8** Medellín, Montería **9** Cartagena, Manizales **10** Santa Marta **11** Bucaramanga **12** Barranquilla ***Colorado:*** **6** Arvada, Aurora, Golden, Salida **7** Alamosa, Boulder, Durango, Greeley, La Junta **8** Brighton, Gunnison, Lakewood, Longmont, Loveland, Montrose, Thornton

9 Englewood, Estes Park, Leadville, Littleton, Rocky Ford, Telluride 10 Broomfield, Castle Rock 11 Fort Collins 13 Grand Junction ***Congo (Zaire):*** 4 Boma 6 Bukavu 7 Kolwezi 8 Bandundu 9 Kisangani 10 Lubumbashi 12 Stanleyville ***Congo-Brazzaville:*** 11 Pointe-Noire ***Connecticut:*** 6 Darien, Granby, Groton, Haddam 7 Danbury, Enfield, Meriden, Milford, Newtown, Norwalk, Norwich, Old Lyme, Pomfret, Windham 8 Guilford, New Haven, Simsbury, Stamford, Suffield, Westport 9 Greenwich, New Canaan, New London, Waterbury, Waterford 10 Bridgeport, Farmington, Kensington, Litchfield, New Britain, Ridgefield, Stonington, Torrington ***Costa Rica:*** 8 Alajuela 10 Puntarenas 11 Puerto Limón ***Croatia:*** 4 Pula 5 Sisak, Split, Zadar 6 Osijek, Rijeka 9 Dubrovnik ***Cuba:*** 5 Banes, Bauta 6 Bayamo 7 Holguín 8 Camagüey, Marianao, Matanzas, Santiago 10 Cienfuegos, Guantánamo 11 Pinar del Río ***Cyprus:*** 7 Kyrenia, Larnaca 8 Limassol 9 Famagusta ***Czech Republic:*** 4 Brno, Zlín 5 Plzen 7 Liberec, Olomouc, Ostrava 10 Bratislava ***Delaware:*** 5 Lewes 7 Seaford 10 Harrington, Wilmington, Winterthur ***Denmark:*** 5 Arhus, Skive, Vejle 6 Alborg, Odense, Viborg 13 Frederiksberg ***Dominican Republic:*** 4 Azua, Bani, Moca 5 Bonao, Nagua 8 Barahona, Santiago ***Ecuador:*** 4 Loja 5 Canar, Daule, Manta, Pinas 7 Machala 8 Riobamba 9 Guayaquil ***Egypt:*** 4 Giza, Idfu, Isna, Qena 5 Aswan, Asyut, Benha, Disuq, Girga, Luxor, Minuf, Tahta, Tanta 6 Helwan 7 El Arish, Zagazig 8 Damanhur, Damietta, El Faiyum, Ismailia, Port Said 10 Alexandria ***Eire:*** see **Ireland,** below ***El Salvador:*** 7 La Unión 8 Santa Ana 9 Sonsonate ***England:*** 4 Bath, Eton, Hove, Ryde, York 5 Brent, Brigg, Colne, Corby, Cowes, Derby, Dover, Egham, Eling, Esher, Eston, Goole, Leeds, Leigh, Lewes, Luton, Poole, Ryton, Wigan 6 Bexley, Bolton, Dudley, Durham, Exeter, Merton, Oldham, Oxford, Torbay, Warley, Welwyn 7 Bristol, Bromley, Croydon, Hackney, Ipswich, Malvern, Norwich, Salford, Seaford, Walsall 8 Abingdon, Basildon, Bradford, Brighton, Coventry, Hastings, Hatfield, Havering, Hertford, Kingston, Lewisham, Plymouth, Wallsend 9 Aylesbury, Blackpool, Cambridge, Islington, Leicester, Liverpool, Newcastle, Sheffield, Stratford 10 Birkenhead, Birmingham, Canterbury, Colchester, Manchester, Nottingham, Portsmouth, Sunderland 11 Bournemouth, Northampton, Southampton 12 Peterborough, Stoke-on-Trent, West Bromwich 13 Southend-on-Sea, Wolverhampton ***Estonia:*** 5 Narva, Pärnu, Tartu ***Ethiopia:*** 5 Aksum, Harer 6 Nazret 8 Dire Dawa ***Finland:*** 4 Kemi, Oulu, Pori 5 Espoo, Hango, Kotka, Lahti, Rauma, Turku, Vaasa 6 Vantaa 7 Tampere ***Florida:*** 5 Largo, Miami, Ocala, Ocoee, Oneco, Tampa 6 DeLand, Naples 7 Hialeah, Key West, Orlando, Sebring 8 Gulfport, Key Largo, Lakeland, Opa-Locka, Sarasota 9 Boca Raton, Bradenton, Fort Myers, Kissimmee, Palm Beach, Pensacola, Vero Beach 10 Clearwater, Cocoa Beach, Miami Beach, Punta Gorda, Titusville 11 Coral Gables, Gainesville, Key Biscayne, St. Augustine, Winter Haven 12 Apalachicola, Daytona Beach, Ft. Lauderdale, Jacksonville, Pompano Beach, St. Petersburg 13 Chattahoochee ***France:*** 3 Dax, Pau 4 Agde, Agen, Albi, Ales, Auch, Caen, Gien, Laon, Lyon, Metz, Nice, Orly, Rezé, Sens, Sète, Vire 5 Arles, Arras, Auray, Auton, Avion, Berck, Blois, Bondy, Brest, Creil, Digne, Dijon, Douai, Dreux, Flers, Gagny, Laval, Le Puy, Lille, Lunel, Lyons, Mâcon, Meaux, Melun, Muret, Nîmes, Niort, Noyon, Reims, Revin, Rodez, Rouen, Royan, Tours, Tulle, Vichy, Vitre 6 Amiens, Angers, Calais, Cannes, Dieppe, Evreux, Le Mans, Nantes, Nevers, Rennes, Rheims, Thiers, Toulon, Troyes 7 Ajaccio, Antibes, Avignon, Béthune, Bourges, Le Havre, Limoges, Lorient, Lourdes, Orléans, Roubaix 8 Beauvais, Besançon, Biarritz, Bordeaux, Chartres, Gentilly, Grenoble, Nanterre, Poitiers, Toulouse 9 Cherbourg, Dunkerque, Marseille, Perpignan 10 Marseilles, Strasbourg, Versailles 11 Carcassonne, Montpellier 13 Aix-en-Provence ***Gabon:*** 4 Oyem 5 Bitam 10 Port-Gentil 11 Franceville ***Gambia:*** 9 Serekunda ***Georgia:*** 4 Adel, Alma, Arco 5 Jesup, Macon, McRae 6 Albany, Athens 7 Augusta, Calhoun 8 Americus, Columbus, Marietta, Savannah, Valdosta 9 Brunswick ***Georgia, Republic of:*** 6 Batumi 7 Kutaisi, Rustavi, Sukhumi ***Germany:*** 3 Aue, Hof, Ulm 4 Bonn, Gera, Goch, Hamm, Jena, Kehl, Kiel, Köln, Marl, Suhl 5 Aalen, Ahlen, Borna, Bruhl, Calbe, Celle, Düren, Emden, Essen, Forst, Fulda, Furth, Gotha, Greiz, Hagen, Halle, Hanau, Herne, Hurth, Kleve, Lemgo, Lobau, Mainz, Trier 6 Aachen, Bremen, Coburg, Dachau, Dessau, Erfurt, Kassel, Lübeck, Munich 7 Cologne, Cottbus, Dresden, Hamburg, Hanover, Koblenz, Krefeld, Leipzig, München, Mun-

ster, Potsdam, Rostock, Zwickau **8** Augsburg, Bayreuth, Chemnitz, Cuxhaven, Dortmund, Duisburg, Freiburg, Hannover, Mannheim, Nürnberg, Würzburg **9** Bielefeld, Brunswick, Darmstadt, Frankfurt, Göttingen, Karlsruhe, Magdeburg, Nuremberg, Stuttgart, Wiesbaden, Wuppertal **10** Baden-Baden, Düsseldorf, Heidelberg, Regensburg **11** Brandenburg, Bremerhaven, Saarbrücken **12** Braunschweig **13** Gelsenkirchen ***Ghana:*** **4** Axim, Keta, Tema **5** Lawra, Yendi **6** Kumasi ***Greece:*** **3** Kos **4** Arta **5** Argos, Lamia, Nemea, Volos **6** Sparta, Thebes **7** Corinth, Khalkis, Larissa, Piraeus, Tríkala **8** Salonika **12** Thessaloniki ***Guatemala:*** **5** Cobán **13** Quezaltenango ***Guinea:*** **4** Labé **6** Kankan, Kindia ***Haiti:*** **8** Gonaïves **10** Cap Haitien ***Hawaii:*** **4** Aiea, Hilo, Laie **5** Kapaa, Lihue, Maili **6** Kailua **7** Kaneohe, Waikiki, Wailuku ***Honduras:*** **5** Danlí **7** La Ceiba **12** San Pedro Sula ***Hong Kong:*** **7** Kowloon ***Hungary:*** **3** Ozd **4** Eger, Györ, Pécs **5** Abony, Bekes **6** Szeged **7** Miskolc **8** Debrecen ***Idaho:*** **4** Buhl **5** Nampa **6** Dubois, Moscow **7** Gooding, Payette, Rexburg **8** Caldwell **9** Blackfoot, Pocatello, Sandpoint, Sun Valley, Twin Falls **11** Coeur d' Alene, Grangeville ***Illinois:*** **6** DeKalb, Galena, Hardin, Joliet, Macomb, Moline, Paxton, Peoria, Skokie, Urbana **7** Chicago, Decatur, Glencoe, Oak Lawn, Oak Park, Tuscola, Watseka, Wheaton **8** Carthage, Evanston, Kankakee, La Grange, Monmouth, Rockford, Vandalia, Waukegan **9** Belvidere, Effingham, Galesburg, Park Ridge, Yorkville **10** Belleville, Carbondale, Carrollton, Des Plaines, Northbrook, Rock Island ***India:*** **3** Mau **4** Agra, Ahwa, Bhuj, Durg, Gaya, Kota, Mhow, Pune, Puri, Rewa, Tonk, Ziro **5** Adoni, Aimer, Akola, Alwar, Arcot, Arrah, Banda, Barsi, Bidar, Bihar, Churu, Damoh, Delhi, Dewas, Eluru, Gonda, Jalna, Jammu, Karur, Miraj, Morvi, Nasik, Patan, Patna, Poona, Sagar, Satna, Sikar, Simla, Surat, Thana **6** Baroda, Bhopal, Bombay, Cochin, Guntur, Howrah, Indore, Jaipur, Jhansi, Kanpur, Madras, Meerut, Mysore, Nagpur, Raipur, Rajkot, Ranchi, Ujjain **7** Aligarh, Asansol, Belgaum, Bikaner, Burdwan, Cuttack, Gauhati, Gwalior, Jodhpur, Kurnool, Lucknow, Madurai, Mathura, Nellore, Patiala, Vellore **8** Amritsar, Bhatpara, Calcutta, Dehra Dun, Kolhapur, Ludhiana, Sholapur, Srinagar, Varanasi **9** Ahmadabad, Allahabad, Bangalore, Hyderabad **10** Ahmadnagar, Chandigarh, Trivandrum **11** Pondicherry ***Indiana:*** **4** Gary **5** Berne, Paoli, Vevay **6** Delphi, Kokomo, Marlon, Muncie, Tipton **7** Bedford, Corydon, Elkhart, La Porte, Winamac **8** Bluffton, Kentland **9** Boonville, Fort Wayne, New Albany, Rushville, South Bend, Vincennes **10** Crown Point, Evansville, Logansport, Scottsburg, Terre Haute, Valparaiso **11** Bloomington ***Indonesia:*** **4** Pati **5** Ambon, Bogor, Garut, Kudus, Medan, Tegal, Turen **6** Batang, Kediri, Madiun, Malang, Manado, Padang **7** Bandung, Kendari **8** Semarang, Surabaja, Surabaya, Tjirebon **9** Palembang, Pontianak, Surakarta **10** Pekalongan **11** Tasikmalaja **12** Bandjarmasin ***Iowa:*** **5** Onawa, Pella **6** Eldora, Harlan, Keokuk, Le Mars, Red Oak **7** Allison, Anamosa, Carroll, Clinton, Corydon, Denison, Dubuque, Marengo, Osceola, Waverly **8** Clarinda, Ida Grove, Waterloo **9** Davenport, Fort Dodge, Indianola, Mason City, Muscatine, Oskaloosa, Sioux City, Storm Lake, West Union, Winterset **10** Emmetsburg, Rock Rapids, Spirit Lake **11** Cedar Rapids, Fort Madison **13** Council Bluffs ***Iran:*** **3** Qom, Qum **4** Amul, Arak, Khoi, Sari, Yazd, Yezd **5** Ahvaz, Ahwaz, Babol, Rasht **6** Abadan, Meshed, Shiraz, Tabriz **7** Esfahan, Hamadan, Isfahan, Mashhad **9** Bakhtaran ***Iraq:*** **3** Ana, Kut **4** Kufa **5** Al Kut, Amara, Basra, Erbil, Hilla, Mosul, Najaf, Rutba **6** Amarah, Hillah, Kirkuk, Ramadi, Rutbah **7** Falluja, Samarra **8** Fallujah, Nasiriya **9** Nasiriyah ***Ireland:*** **4** Athy, Birr, Cobh, Cork, Naas, Tuam **5** Ennis, Sligo **6** Carlow, Galway, Tralee **7** Dundalk, Kildare, Wexford, Wicklow **8** Drogheda, Kilkenny, Limerick, Monaghan **9** Castlebar, Killarney, Tipperary, Waterford **10** Balbriggan ***Israel:*** **5** Afula, Haifa, Holon, Jaffa **7** Rehovot **8** Ashqelon, Nazareth, Ramat Gan **9** Beersheba ***Italy:*** **4** Acri, Alba, Asti, Bari, Enna, Este, Fano, Gela, Iesi, Lodi, Lugo, Pisa **5** Adria, Agira, Anzio, Aosta, Arola, Cantù, Capua, Carpi, Crema, Cuneo, Eboli, Fermo, Fondi, Forli, Gaeta, Genoa, Imola, Ivrea, Lecce, Lecco, Lucca, Massa, Melfi, Menfi, Milan, Monza, Padua, Parma, Prato, Siena, Turin **6** Ancona, Assisi, Foggia, Mantua, Milano, Modena, Naples, Napoli, Rimini, Torino, Venice, Verona **7** Bergamo, Bologna, Bolzano, Brescia, Catania, Firenze, Leghorn, Messina, Palermo, Perugia, Pescara, Potenza, Ravenna, Salerno, San Remo, Taranto, Trieste, Venezia **8** Brindisi, Cagliari, Florence, La Spezia, Piacenza, Siracusa, Syracuse ***Ivory Coast:*** **6**

Bouaké ***Jamaica:*** **6** May Pen **10** Montego Bay ***Japan:*** **3** Ina, Ise, Ito, Ota, Tsu, Ube, Uji, Yao **4** Ageo, Anan, Gifu, Hagi, Himi, Hofu, Iida, Joyo, Kaga, Kobe, Kofu, Kure, Miki, Mito, Naha, Nara, Noda, Oita, Otsu, Saga, Saku, Soka, Tosu, Ueda, Yono **5** Akita, Atami, Beppu, Chiba, Imari, Itami, Iwaki, Iwata, Izumi, Izumo, Kiryu, Kochi, Kyoto, Minoo, Odate, Ogaki, Okawa, Okaya, Omiya, Omuta, Osaka, Otaru, Oyama, Sabae, Saiki, Sakai, Sanjo, Suita, Tenri, Urawa **6** Akashi, Aomori, Himeji, Kadoma, Kurume, Matsue, Mitaka, Nagano, Nagoya, Numazu, Sasebo, Sendai, Suzuka, Toyama, Yonago **7** Fukuoka, Hitachi, Ibaraki, Imabari, Muroran, Niigata, Niihama, Nobeoka, Obihiro, Odawara, Okayama, Okazaki, Sapporo **8** Ashikaga, Fujisawa, Fukuyama, Hirakata, Hirosaki, Ichihara, Ichikawa, Kakogawa, Kamakura, Kanazawa, Kawasaki, Miyazaki, Nagasaki, Onomichi, Shizuoka, Takasaki, Toyonaka, Wakayama, Yamagata, Yokohama, Yokosuka **9** Hiroshima ***Jordan:*** **5** Aqaba, Irbid ***Kansas:*** **4** Gove, Iola **5** Colby, Hoxie, Lakin, Leoti, Paola, Pratt **6** Atwood, Beloit, Girard, Holton, Salina **7** Abilene, Emporia, Garnett, Kinsley, Wichita **8** Cimarron, Goodland, La Crosse, Sublette **9** Coldwater, Fort Scott, Great Bend, Oskaloosa **10** Hutchinson **11** Leavenworth **12** Council Grove, Overland Park **13** Medicine Lodge ***Kazakhstan:*** **5** Semey **6** Almaty, Aqtöbe, Guryev, Uralsk **7** Alma-Ata, Zhambyl **8** Balkhash, Chimkent, Dzhambul, Kyzl Orda, Pavlodar, Shymkent **9** Karaganda **10** Aktyubinsk ***Kentucky:*** **4** Inez **5** Cadiz, Hyden, McKee **6** Elkton, Harlan **7** Ashland, Campton, Greenup, Hindman, Paducah, Stanton **8** Fort Knox, Mayfield **9** Bardstown, Covington, Cynthiana, Lexington, Maysville, Owensboro, Pikeville, Pineville, Southgate, Vanceburg **10** Booneville, Hawesville, Louisville, Whitesburg **12** Bowling Green ***Kenya:*** **4** Embu **5** Nyeri **6** Kisumu, Nakuru **7** Mombasa ***Kyrgyzstan:*** **3** Osh **5** Naryn ***Laos:*** **5** Pakse **11** Savannakhet ***Latvia:*** **7** Jelgava, Liepaja **9** Ventspils **10** Daugavpils ***Lebanon:*** **4** Tyre **5** Sidon, Zahlé **7** Juniyah, Tripoli ***Libya:*** **4** Homs **5** Derna, Zawia **6** Tobruk **8** Benghazi, Misratah ***Lithuania:*** **6** Kaunas **8** Klaipeda ***Louisiana:*** **4** Jena **5** Amite, Arabi, Houma, Mamou, Norco, Rayne **6** Colfax, Edgard, Gretna, Minden, Ruston **7** Arcadia, Bastrop, Marrero, Oberlin **8** Bogalusa, De Ridder, Metairie, New Roads, Oak Grove, Westwego **9** Abbeville, Chalmette, Hahnville, Leesville, New Iberia, Opelousas, Port Allen, Thibodaux, Winnfield, Winnsboro **10** New Orleans, Plaquemine, Shreveport **11** Lake Charles **12** Natchitoches ***Macedonia:*** **6** Bitola, Prilep, Tetovo ***Maine:*** **4** Saco **5** Orono **6** Auburn, Bangor, Gorham **7** Berwick, Kittery, Machias, Rumford **8** Lewiston, Portland, Rockland **9** Bar Harbor, Biddeford, Brunswick, Ellsworth, Kennebunk, Skowhegan, Wiscasset **11** Millinocket, Presque Isle **13** Kennebunkport ***Malawi:*** **5** Mzuzu, Zomba **8** Blantyre ***Malaysia:*** **4** Ipoh **5** Gemas, Klang **6** Kelang, Penang, Pinang **11** Johore Bahru ***Mali:*** **5** Kayes, Mopti, Ségou **7** Sikasso ***Malta:*** **10** Birkirkara ***Maryland:*** **5** Bowie **6** Denton, Elkton, Towson **8** Bethesda, Landover, Snow Hill **9** Baltimore, Rockville **10** Beltsville, Hagerstown **11** Chestertown, College Park, Leonardtown **12** Havre de Grace, Silver Spring ***Massachusetts:*** **5** Lenox, Salem **6** Boston, Dedham, Lowell, Malden, Monson, Natick, Saugus, Woburn **7** Amherst, Duxbury, Holyoke, Hyannis, Methuen, Needham, Swansea, Taunton, Walpole, Waltham, Wareham **8** Brockton, Chicopee, Falmouth, Plymouth, Rockport, Yarmouth **9** Brookline, Cambridge, Edgartown, Fall River, Fitchburg, Haverhill, Lexington, Nantucket, Worcester **10** Framingham, Gloucester, Greenfield, Leominster, New Bedford, North Adams, Pittsfield, Somerville **11** Northampton **11** Springfield **12** Provincetown, Williamstown ***Mauritania:*** **4** Atar **5** Kaedi **6** Dakhla ***Mexico:*** **4** León **5** Ameca, Choix, Tepic **6** Cancún, Celaya, Colima, Jalapa, Juárez, Mérida, Oaxaca, Puebla, Toluca, Tuxtla **7** Durango, Guasave, Morelia, Obregón, Reynosa, Tampico, Tijuana, Tlalpán, Torreón, Uruapan, Zapopan **8** Chetumal, Coyoacán, Culiacán, Ensenada, Mazatlan, Mexicali, Saltillo, Tuxtepec **9** Chihuahua, Fresnillo, Ixtacalco, Monterrey, Querétaro, Salamanca, Tapachula, Zacatecas **10** Cuernavaca, Hermosillo, Ixtapalapa, Xochimilco **11** Guadalajara, Nuevo Laredo **13** San Luis Potosí ***Michigan:*** **4** Alma, Holt **5** Flint, Ionia, L'Anse, Niles **6** Otsego, Paw Paw, Warren **7** Allegan, Corunna, Detroit, Gladwin, Livonia, Midland, Saginaw **8** Ann Arbor, Bessemer, Dearborn, Escanaba, Grayling, Hastings, Houghton, Muskegon, Sandusky **9** Cheboygan, Coldwater, Kalamazoo, Menominee, Port Huron, Ypsilanti **10** Charlevoix, Grand Haven **11** Battle Creek,

Grand Rapids ***Minnesota:*** **3** Ely **4** Mora **5** Anoka, Edina, Osseo **6** Aitkin, Benson, Duluth, Waseca, Windom, Winona **7** Glencoe, Hibbing, Mankato, Red Wing, St. Cloud, Wabasha **8** Brainerd, Elk River, Moorhead, Shakopee **9** Caledonia, Crookston, Faribault, Pipestone, Rochester, Saint Paul, Silver Bay **10** Park Rapids, Saint Cloud, Saint James, Saint Peter, Stillwater, Two Harbors **11** Bloomington, Fergus Falls, Long Prairie, Minneapolis, Worthington **12** Breckenridge, Granite Falls, Redwood Falls ***Mississippi:*** **4** Iuka **5** Amory **6** Biloxi, Leland, McComb, Purvis, Sardis, Sumner, Tupelo, Winona **7** Belzoni, Brandon, Okolona, Quitman, Wiggins **8** Gulfport, Hernando, Meridian, Paulding, Rosedale, Walthall **9** Greenwood, Indianola, New Albany, Pittsboro, Vicksburg **10** Batesville, Booneville, Brookhaven, Clarksdale, Ellisville, Greenville, Hazlehurst, Pascagoula, Port Gibson, Starkville, Waynesboro **11** Hattiesburg **12** Holly Springs ***Missouri:*** **3** Ava **4** Linn **5** Eldon, Hayti, Ladue, Rolla **6** Galena, Neosho, Potosi **7** Hermann, Ironton, Kennett, Linneus, Osceola, Palmyra, Sedalia, St. Louis **8** Gallatin, Hannibal **9** Boonville, Hartville, Hillsboro, Maryville, Pineville, Tuscumbia, Warrenton **10** Kansas City, Kirksville, Marble Hill, Marshfield, Perryville, Saint Louis, Springfield **11** Saint Joseph **12** Independence, Saint Charles ***Moldova:*** **5** Balti **7** Tighina **8** Tiraspol ***Mongolia:*** **5** Kobdo **6** Darhan **10** Choybalsan ***Montana:*** **5** Butte, Havre, Libby **6** Hardin, Polson **7** Bozeman **8** Billings, Missoula, Red Lodge **10** Great Falls ***Montenegro:*** **8** Titograd ***Morocco:*** **3** Fès **4** Safi, Salé, Taza **5** Nador, Oujda **6** Agadir, Meknès **7** Kenitra, Tangier **9** Marrakech, Marrakesh **10** Casablanca ***Mozambique:*** **5** Beira **7** Chimoio, Nampula **9** Quelimane, Quilimane ***Myanmar:*** **3** Pyu **4** Paan **5** Akyab, Bhamo, Chauk, Katha, Magwe, Minbu, Mogok, Tavoy **7** Bassein **8** Mandalay, Moulmein ***Namibia:*** **5** Outjo **6** Tsumeb **8** Oshakati **12** Keetmanshoop ***Nebraska:*** **3** Ord **5** Cozad, Omaha, Ponca, Tryon, Wahoo **6** Elwood, Gering, McCook, Minden, Wilber **7** Burwell, Fremont, Kearney, Kimball, Osceola, Tekamah **8** Beatrice, Fairbury, Hastings, Ogallala, Red Cloud, Schuyler, Tecumseh, Thedford **9** Fullerton, Papillion **10** Springview, Stockville **11** Grand Island, Hayes Center, North Platte, Plattsmouth ***Netherlands:*** **3** Ede, Epe, Oss **4** Echt, Tiel, Uden **5** Aalst, Assen, Breda, Delft, Emmen, Hague, Soest, Vaals, Venlo, Vught, Weert, Weesp, Zeist **6** Arnhem **7** Haarlem, Tilburg, Utrecht **8** Enschede, Nijmegen, The Hague **9** Apeldoorn, Eindhoven, Groningen, Rotterdam, Zandvoort **10** Maastricht ***Nevada:*** **3** Ely **4** Elko, Reno **6** Fallon, Minden, Pioche **7** Tonopah **8** Las Vegas, Lovelock **9** Goldfield, Yerington **10** Winnemucca ***New Brunswick:*** **5** Minto **6** St. John **7** Moncton **9** Dalhousie, Saint John **10** Edmundston, Richibucto **12** Hopewell Cape, Perth Andover, Saint Andrews ***Newfoundland:*** **5** Burin **6** Wabana **10** Mount Pearl **11** Corner Brook ***New Hampshire:*** **5** Derry, Dover, Keene **6** Berlin, Exeter, Gorham, Nashua **7** Hanover, Laconia, Lebanon, Ossipee **8** Hinsdale, Seabrook **9** Littleton, Merrimack **10** Manchester, Portsmouth, Woodsville ***New Jersey:*** **4** Atco, Lodi **6** Camden, Newark, Nutley, Rahway, Rumson **7** Bayonne, Cape May, Clifton, Hoboken, Paramus, Passaic, Raritan, Teaneck **8** Freehold, Metuchen, Paterson, Vauxhall, Woodbury **9** Elizabeth, Glassboro, Lakehurst, Menlo Park, Montclair, Princeton, Riverside, Toms River **10** Asbury Park, Bloomfield, Cherry Hill, Hackensack, Jersey City, Morristown, Mount Holly, Perth Amboy, Piscataway, Plainfield, Somerville **11** Mays Landing **12** Atlantic City, New Brunswick **13** Palisades Park ***New Mexico:*** **4** Taos **5** Belen, Hobbs, Raton **6** Clovis, Deming, Grants **7** Roswell, Socorro **8** Estancia, Los Lunas, Portales **9** Carrizozo, Las Cruces, Los Alamos, Lovington, Tucumcari **10** Alamogordo, Bernalillo, Fort Sumner **11** Albuquerque ***New York:*** **4** Elma, Ovid, Troy **5** Depew, Ilion, Islip, Le Roy, Nyack, Olean, Owego, Utica **6** Attica, Cohoes, Delmar, Elmira, Hudson, Ithaca, Oneida **7** Batavia, Buffalo, Corning, Geneseo, Katonah, Mineola, Yonkers **8** Bay Shore, Cortland, Hyde Park, Kingston, Lockport, Ossining, Syracuse, **9** Greenport, Hempstead, Patchogue, Rochester, Scarsdale, Schoharie **10** Binghamton, Glens Falls, Huntington, Lackawanna, Lake George, Lake Placid, Mamaroneck, Massapequa, Mount Kisco, **11** Cooperstown, Plattsburgh, Port Chester, Saint George, Schenectady, Southampton, Watkins Glen, White Plains **12** Poughkeepsie ***New Zealand:*** **4** Hutt, Tawa **5** Levin, Taupo, Waihi **7** Dunedin, Manukau **8** Auckland **12** Christchurch ***Nicaragua:*** **4** León **5** Boaco, Rivas **6** Masaya **7** Granada ***Nigeria:*** **3** Aba, Ado, Ede, Ife, Ila, Iwo, Jos, Owo, Oyo **4** Kano, Ondo **5** Akure, Enugu, Gusau, Lagos, Okene, Zaria

6 Ibadan, Ilesha, Ilorin, Kaduna, Mushin, Sokoto **7** Onitsha, Oshogbo **8** Abeokuta **9** Maiduguri, Ogbomosho **12** Port Harcourt ***North Carolina:*** **4** Dunn **5** Ayden, Elkin, Erwin, Oteen, Sylva **6** Dobson, Durham, Lenoir, Manteo, Marlon, Shelby, Winton **7** Bayboro, Brevard, Edenton, Roxboro, Sanford, Tarboro **8** Asheboro, Beaufort, Gastonia, Hatteras, Snow Hill **9** Albemarle, Asheville, Charlotte, Kitty Hawk, Morganton **10** Chapel Hill, Greensboro, Smithfield, Wilkesboro **12** Murfreesboro, Winston-Salem ***North Dakota:*** **4** Mott **5** Cando, Fargo, Minot, Rolla **6** Amidon, Ashley, Bowman, Formon, Lakota, Linton, Medora, Mohall **8** Wahpeton, Washburn **9** Dickinson, Williston **10** Devils Lake, Grand Forks ***Northern Ireland:*** **5** Derry, Larne, Newry, Omagh **6** Antrim, Armagh **9** Bally-mena, Coleraine, Craigavon, Dungannon **10** Ballymoney **11** Ballycastle, Downpatrick, Enniskillen, Londonderry **13** Carrickfergus ***North Korea:*** **5** Haeju, Nampo **6** Wonsan **7** Hamhung, Kaesong, Sinuiju **8** Ch'ongjin, Kimchaek ***Northwest Territories:*** **6** Dawson **10** Whitehorse ***Norway:*** **4** Bodo **5** Hamar, Skien, Vardo **6** Bergen, Tromso **8** Kirkenes **9** Stavanger, Trondheim **10** Hammerfest **12** Kristiansand ***Nova Scotia:*** **5** Digby **6** Pictou **7** Arichat, Baddeck **8** Port Hood **9** Dartmouth, Kentville, Lunenburg, Shelburne, Westville **10** Antigonish **11** Guysborough ***Ohio:*** **4** Kent **5** Akron, Berea, Bryan, Carey, Eaton, Heath, Logan, Niles, Parma, Piqua, Solon, Xenia **6** Canton, Celina, Dayton, Elyria, Euclid, Kenton, Lorain, Marion, Medina, Sidney, Tiffin, Toledo **7** Ashland, Batavia, Bucyrus, Chardon, Findlay, Ironton, Oakwood, Pomeroy, Ravenna, Wauseon, Wooster **8** Conneaut, Marietta, Sandusky **9** Ashtabula, Cleveland, Coshocton, Mansfield **10** Cincinnati, Gallipolis, Zanesville **11** Chillicothe, Mount Gilead, Port Clinton **12** Steubenville ***Oklahoma:*** **3** Ada **4** Alva, Enid **5** Altus, Atoka, Sayre, Tulsa **6** Durant, El Reno, Guymon, Idabel, Lawton, Okemah, Poteau, Wewoka **7** Antlers, Ardmore, Cordell, Eufaula, Newkirk, Purcell, Sapulpa, Watonga **8** Anadarko, Okmulgee, Pawhuska, Sallisaw, Stilwell **9** Chickasha, Claremore, Frederick, McAlester, Wilburton **10** Stillwater, Tishomingo ***Oman:*** **3** Sur **6** Matrah **7** Salalah ***Ontario:*** **4** Ajax, Wawa, York **6** Barrie, Guelph, Kenora, London, Oshawa, Sarnia, Simcoe **7** Cobourg, Markham, Napanee, Sudbury, Windsor **8** Brampton, Cochrane, Goderich, Hamilton, North Bay, Pembroke, Prescott **9** Brantford, Etobicoke, Kitchener, L'Original, Newmarket, North York, Owen Sound, Walkerton **10** Belleville, Brockville, Burlington, Haileybury, Parry Sound, Thunder Bay **11** Bracebridge, Fort Frances, Mississauga, Scarborough **12** Peterborough, St. Catharines ***Oregon:*** **5** Canby, Nyssa **6** Eugene **8** Coquille, La Grande, Portland, Roseburg **9** Clackamas, Corvallis, Gold Beach, Pendleton, The Dalles, Tillamook **10** Grants Pass **12** Klamath Falls ***Pakistan:*** **5** Bannu, Bhera, Kasur, Kohat **6** Gujrat, Lahore, Mardan, Multan, Quetta, Sukkur **7** Karachi, Sialkot **8** Lyallpur, Peshawar, Sargodha **9** Hyderabad **10** Bahawalpur, Faisalabad, Gujranwala, Rawalpindi ***Papua New Guinea:*** **3** Lae **10** Mount Hagen, Popondetta ***Paraguay:*** **3** Itá **4** Yuty **5** Luque, Pilar **7** Caacupé, Caazapa **9** Paraguarí **10** San Lorenzo ***Pennsylvania:*** **4** Erie, York **5** Avoca, Darby, Muncy, Paoli **6** Easton **7** Altoona, Bedford, Clarion, Hanover, Hershey, Latrobe, Reading, Ridgway, Sunbury **8** Carlisle, Edinboro, Hazleton, Montrose, Scranton, Somerset **9** Allentown, Ebensburg, Honesdale, Jim Thorpe, Lancaster, Lewisburg, Lock Haven, Meadville, New Castle, Wellsboro **10** Bloomsburg, Brookville, Carbondale, Clearfield, Gettysburg, McKeesport, Middleburg, Pittsburgh, Pottsville, Waynesburg **11** Valley Forge, Wilkes-Barre **12** Philadelphia, State College ***Peru:*** **3** Ica, Ilo **5** Ancon, Cuzco, Jauja, Junin, Lamas, Pisco, Piura, Tacna **6** Callao **8** Arequipa, Chiclayo, Chimbote, Trujillo ***Philippines:*** **3** Iba **4** Bago, Bais, Boac, Bogo, Cebu, Daet, Jolo, Lipa, Mati **5** Basco, Bulan, Cadiz, Danao, Davao, Digos, Gapan, Gubat, Iriga, Laoag, Ormoc, Pasay, Silay, Tagum, Vigan **6** Butuan, Iloilo, Quezon **7** Angeles, Bacolod, Basilan **8** Batangas, Calbayog, Caloocan **9** Zamboanga **10** Quezon City ***Poland:*** **4** Lodz, Nysa, Pila, Zary **5** Bytom, Bytow, Chelm, Kutno, Lomza, Luban, Lubin, Plock, Radom, Torun, Tychy **6** Elblag, Gdansk, Gdynia, Kalisz, Kielce, Krakow, Lublin, Poznan, Rybnik, Zabrze **7** Chorzow, Dabrowa, Gliwice, Rzeszow, Wroclaw **8** Gornicza, Katowice, Szczecin **9** Bialystok, Bydgoszcz, Sosnowiec, Walbrzych **11** Czestochowa ***Portugal:*** **4** Faro **5** Braga, Evora, Porto **6** Almada, Oporto, Queluz **7** Amadora **8** Barreiro, Santarém ***Prince Edward Island:*** **10** Summerside ***Puerto Rico:*** **5** Ponce **6** Caguas **7** Arecibo, Bayamón **8** Carolina,

Guaynabo, Mayagüez ***Quebec:*** **4** Alma **5** Amqui, Anjou, Gaspé, Laval, Lévis, Magog, Percé, Rouyn **6** Granby, Ham Sud, Matane, Ste.-Foy, Val d'Or **7** Bedford, Lachute **8** Beauport, Cap Santé, Joliette, Lac Brome, Maniwaki, Montreal, Rimouski, Roberval, Sept-Iles, Waterloo **9** Bécancour, Cookshire, Iberville, Inverness, La Malbaie, La Prairie, Longueuil, Montmagny, Sainte-Foy, Saint Jean, Tadoussac, Vaudreuil **10** Baie-Comeau, Chicoutimi **11** Beauharnois, Louiseville, Mont-Laurier **12** Charlesbourg **13** Trois-Rivières ***Rhode Island:*** **7** Newport, Rumford, Warwick **8** Apponaug, Coventry, Cranston, Tiverton, Westerly **9** Hopkinton, Pawtucket **10** Woonsocket **12** Narragansett ***Romania:*** **3** Dej **4** Aiud, Arad, Cluj, Deva, Husi, Iasi **5** Anina, Bacau, Buzau, Carei, Lugoj, Sibiu, Turda **6** Braila, Brasov, Galati, Oradea **7** Craiova **8** Ploiesti **9** Constanta, Timisoara **10** Cluj-Napoca ***Russia:*** **3** Kem, Ufa **4** Inta, Luga, Okha, Omsk, Orel, Orsk, Perm, Tula, Tura, Zima **5** Aldan, Artem, Chita, Ishim, Kansk, Kazan, Lysva, Onega, Penza, Pskov, Rzhev, Salsk, Serov, Sochi, Sokol, Tomsk, Tulun, Volsk, Yurga **6** Bratsk, Grozny, Kaluga, Kovrov, Kurgan, Rostov, Ryazan, Samara, Syzran, Tambov, Tyumen, Vyborg, Yelets **7** Irkutsk, Ivanovo, Izhevsk, Kalinin, Kolomna, Lipetsk, Magadan, Norilsk, Rybinsk, Saransk, Saratov, Shakhty, Vologda, Yakutsk, Zhdanov **8** Belgorod, Kemerovo, Kostroma, Murmansk, Nakhodka, Novgorod, Orenburg, Smolensk, Taganrog, Vladimir, Volzhski, Voronezh **9** Archangel, Astrakhan, Krasnodar, Stavropol, Ulyanovsk, Volgograd, **10** Dzerzhinsk **11** Arkhangel'sk, Chelyabinsk, Kaliningrad, Krasnoyarsk, Novosibirsk, Vladivostok **12** St. Petersburg **13** Yekaterinburg ***Saskatchewan:*** **8** Moose Jaw **9** Saskatoon **10** Assiniboia **12** Prince Albert ***Saudi Arabia:*** **4** Jauf, Taif **5** Jedda, Jidda, Mecca, Tabuk **6** Jeddah, Jiddah, Medina **8** Buraydah ***Scotland:*** **3** Ayr **4** Alva, Caol, Dyce, Oban **5** Alloa, Annan, Beith, Cowie, Cupar, Dalry, Ellon, Kelso, Kelty, Largs, Leven, Nairn, Patna, Troon **6** Dundee **7** Glasgow, Paisley **8** Aberdeen, Greenock, Hamilton **9** Inverness, Lockerbie **10** Kilmarnock **11** Dunfermline, John o' Groats ***Senegal:*** **5** Thiès **6** Kaolak **7** Kaolack **10** Saint-Louis ***Serbia:*** **3** Bor, Nis, Pec **4** Ruma **5** Becej, Cacak, Pirot, Sabac, Senta, Vrbas, Vrsac **7** Novi Sad **8** Subotica **10** Kragujevac ***Slovakia:*** **5** Nitra **6** Kosice, Presov, Zilina ***Slovenia:*** **4** Bled **5** Celje, Koper, Kranj **7** Maribor ***Somalia:*** **3** Eil **5** Afgoi, Alula, Brava, Burao, Marka, Obbia **7** Berbera, Kismayu **8** Hargeysa, Kismaayo ***South Africa:*** **5** Brits, Ceres, De Aar, Nigel, Paarl **6** Benoni, Durban, Soweto **7** Springs **8** Boksburg, Mafeking **9** Germiston, Kimberley, Ladysmith, Uitenhage **10** East London **11** Krugersdorp, Vereeniging **12** Johannesburg **13** Port Elizabeth ***South Carolina:*** **5** Aiken, Cayce, Saxon **6** Sumter **7** Gaffney, Laurens, Manning, Pickens **8** Beaufort, Newberry, Rock Hill, Walhalla **9** Abbeville, Allendale, Greenwood, Kingstree, McCormick, Winnsboro **10** Charleston, Darlington, Greenville, Hilton Head, Orangeburg, Walterboro **11** Myrtle Beach, Spartanburg ***South Dakota:*** **7** Sturgis, Yankton **8** Deadwood, Elk Point **9** Brookings, Rapid City **10** Sioux Falls ***South Korea:*** **3** Iri **4** Yosu **5** Cheju, Masan, Mokpo, Pusan, Suwon, Taegu, Ulson, Wonju **6** Chinju, Chonju, Inchon, Kunsan, Taejon **7** Kwangju ***Spain:*** **4** Adra, Baza, Elda, Jaca, Jaén, León, Loja, Lugo, Olot, Reus, Vich, Vigo **5** Albox, Alcoy, Alora, Avila, Baena, Cádiz, Ceuta, Cieza, Ecija, Eibar, Elche, Gijón, Ibiza, Jodar, Lorca, Mahon, Oliva, Osuna, Palma, Ronda, Soria, Ubeda **6** Bilbao, Burgos, Cuenca, Huelva, Lérida, Málaga, Mérida, Murcia, Oviedo, Toledo **7** Almadén, Almería, Cáceres, Córdoba, Durango, Granada, Segovia, Sevilla, Seville, Tarrasa, Vitoria **8** Albacete, Alicante, La Coruña, Pamplona, Sabadell, Valencia, Zaragoza **9** Algeciras, Barcelona, Salamanca, Santander, Saragossa, Tarragona **10** Hospitalet, Valladolid **12** San Sebastián ***Sri Lanka:*** **5** Galle, Kandy **6** Jaffna **8** Dehiwala, Moratuwa **10** Batticaloa ***Sudan:*** **4** Juba **5** Kodok, Kosti **7** El Obeid, Kassala **8** Omdurman ***Sweden:*** **4** Lund, Täby, Umea **5** Falun, Gävle, Lulea, Malmö, Växjö, Visby **6** Orebro **7** Uppsala **8** Göteborg, Halmstad **9** Jönköping, Linköping **12** Kristianstad ***Switzerland:*** **3** Zug **4** Biel, Chur, Sion, Thun **5** Aarau, Arbon, Baden, Basel, Koniz **6** Geneva, Lugano, St. Gall, Zürich **7** Lucerne, Zermatt **8** Lausanne, Montreux, St. Moritz **9** Neuchâtel, Saint Gall **11** Saint Moritz ***Syria:*** **4** Hama, Homs **5** Idlib **6** Aleppo, Tartus **7** Latakia ***Taiwan:*** **5** Chia-i **6** T'ai-nan **7** Chi-lung, Hsin-chu **8** Feng-shan, Panch'iao, San-ch'ung, T'ai-chung **9** Kaohsiung ***Tanzania:*** **5** Lindi, Mbeya, Tanga **6** Arusha, Kigoma, Mwanza **8** Morogoro, Zanzibar **11** Dar es Salaam ***Tennessee:*** **5** Alcoa, Erwin, Rives **6** Loudon, Ripley, Selmer **7** Memphis, Waverly **8** Gallatin, Oak Ridge, Rutledge, Tazewell, Wartburg **9** Dandridge, Dyersburg, Jacksboro, Jonesboro, Knoxville, Lewisburg, Maryville **10** Cookeville, Crossville, Somerville, Waynesboro **11** Blountville, Chattanooga, Clarksville, Greeneville, McMinnville, Rogersville, Sevierville, Shelbyville **12** Elizabethton, Lawrenceburg, Madisonville, Murfreesboro ***Texas:*** **4** Azle, Waco **5** Alvin, Anson, Baird, Bowie, Bryan, Clute, Cuero, Emory, Ennis, Freer, Hondo, Marfa, Mexia, Olney, Pampa, Pecos, Pharr, Plano, Sealy, Vidor, Wylie **6** Belton, Boerne, Bonham, Burnet, Dallas, Denton, El Paso, Lamesa, Laredo, Linden, Lufkin, Odessa, Seguin **7** Abilene, Bandera, Denison, Houston, Kaufman, Lubbock, Midland, Wharton **8** Amarillo, Angleton, Beaumont, Eastland, Giddings, Gonzales, Granbury, Groveton, Hemphill, La Grange **9** Fort Worth, Galveston **10** Brownfield, Port Arthur, San Antonio, Sweetwater, Waxahachie **11** Brownsville, Littlefield, Nacogdoches, Weatherford **12** New Braunfels **13** Corpus Christi ***Thailand:*** **3** Nan, Tak **5** Phrae, Roi Et, Surin **8** Songkhla **9** Chiang Mai **10** Nonthaburi ***Tunisia:*** **4** Béja, Sfax **5** Gabès, Gafsa, Susah **6** Ariana **7** Bizerte, Safaqis ***Turkey:*** **5** Adana, Bursa, Izmir, Konya, Sivas **6** Edirne, Erzurm, Samsun **7** Antakya, Antalya, Antioch, Kayseri, Malatya **8** Istanbul **9** Eskisehir, Gallipoli, Gaziantep **10** Diyarbakir ***Turkmenistan:*** **8** Nebit Dag **9** Chardzhou, Dashhowuz ***Uganda:*** **5** Jinja, Mbale **7** Entebbe ***Ukraine:*** **4** Lviv, Lvov, Sumy **5** Lutsk, Rovno, Yalta **6** Odessa **7** Donetsk, Kharkiv, Kharkov, Kherson, Luhansk, Poltava **8** Mariupol, Vinnitsa, Zhitomir **9** Chernigov, Chernobyl, Krivoy Rog, Krivyy Rih, Nikolayev **10** Kirovograd, Sebastopol, Sevastopol, Simferopol, Zaporozhye ***United Arab Emirates:*** **5** Ajman, Dubai **6** Dubayy **8** Fujairah, Fujayrah ***Uruguay:*** **4** Melo **5** Minas, Pando, Rocha, Salto **6** Rivera **8** Paysandú **10** Las Piedras ***Utah:*** **3** Loa **4** Lehi, Orem **5** Manti, Ogden, Provo, Sandy **6** Dugway, Tooele **7** Parowan **8** Duchesne **9** Coalville **11** Saint George ***Uzbekistan:*** **5** Nukus **6** Kokand **7** Bukhara, Fergana **8** Andizhan, Chirchik, Namangan **9** Samarkand, Samarqand ***Venezuela:*** **4** Coro **5** Anaco, Cagua **6** Cumaná, Mérida, Petare **7** Cabimas, Guayana, Maracay **8** Valencia **9** Maracaibo **12** Barquisimeto, San Cristóbal ***Vermont:*** **5** Barre **7** Rutland **8** St. Albans **10** Bennington, Burlington, Middlebury **11** Brattleboro, Saint Albans, St. Johnsbury ***Vietnam:*** **3** Hue **4** Vinh **5** Da Lat, Hoi An, My Tho **6** Can Tho, Da Nang, Saigon **7** Bien Hoa, Nam Dinh, Qui Nhon **8** Haiphong, Nha Trang, Thanh Hoa **9** Long Xuyen ***Virginia:*** **4** Tabb **5** Luray **6** Grundy **7** Accomac, Boydton, Fairfax, Hampton, New Kent, Norfolk **8** Abingdon, Culpeper, Leesburg, Manassas, Montross, Nottoway, Powhatan, Tazewell **9** Arlington, Clintwood, Courtland, Eastville, Farmville, Lunenburg, Lynchburg **10** Alexandria, Appomattox, Front Royal, Hillsville, King George, Portsmouth, Rocky Mount **11** King William, Newport News **12** Prince George, Spotsylvania, Williamsburg ***Wales:*** **4** Rhyl **5** Neath, Risca, Tenby, Tywyn **7** Cwmbran, Denbigh, Harlech, Newport, Swansea **8** Aberdare, Bridgend **10** Caernarfon, Caernarvon, Llangollen **11** Aberystwyth ***Washington:*** **4** Omak **5** Brier, Camas, Kelso, Lacey, Pasco, Selah **6** Asotin, Colfax, Tacoma, Yakima **7** Ephrata, Everett, Prosser, Redmond, Seattle, Spokane **8** Bellevue, Chehalis, Colville, Okanogan **9** Montesano, Ritzville, Snohomish, Wenatchee **10** Bellingham, Coupeville, Ellensburg, Goldendale, Walla Walla, Waterville **11** Port Angeles ***West Virginia:*** **5** Nitro, Welch **6** Elkins, Hamlin, Hinton, Keyser, Ripley **7** Beckley, Weirton **8** Kingwood, Philippi, Wheeling **9** Pineville, Wellsburg **10** Buckhannon, Clarksburg, Huntington, Moorefield, Morgantown, Petersburg, Williamson **11** Harrisville, Martinsburg, Moundsville, Parkersburg **12** Harpers Ferry ***Wisconsin:*** **4** Kiel **5** Ripon, Tomah **6** Antigo, Barron, Oconto, Racine, Wausau **7** Baraboo, Chilton, Elkhorn, Hayward, Kenosha, Mauston, Merrill, Oshkosh, Shawano, Viraqua, Waupaca, Wautoma **8** Appleton, Green Bay, Kewaunee, La Crosse, Washburn, Waukesha, West Bend **9** Eau Claire, Ellsworth, Fond du Lac, Green Lake, Manitowoc, Marinette, Menomonie, Milwaukee, Sheboygan, Whitehall **10** Balsam Lake, Darlington, Dodgeville **12** Stevens Point ***Wyoming:*** **6** Casper, Lander **7** Laramie, Rawlins **8** Gillette, Kemmerer, Sheridan **10** Green River **11** Rock Springs ***Yemen:*** **4** Aden **5** Taizz **7** Hodeida, Mukalla **8** Hudaydah ***Zambia:*** **5** Kabwe, Kitwe, Mansa, Mbala, Mongu, Ndola **6** Kasama **7** Chipata ***Zimbabwe:*** **5** Gweru **6** Hwange, Kadoma, Kwekwe, Mutare, Umtali **7** Mashava **8** Bulawayo, Masvingo

civet 3 cat **5** rasse ***Madagascar:* 5** fossa ***relative:* 5** genet
civic 5 urban **6** public, social **8** communal, national, societal **9** municipal
civil 6 polite, public, seemly, urbane **7** affable, cordial, courtly, genteel, refined **8** decorous, gracious, mannerly, national, obliging, well-bred **9** courteous, political **10** diplomatic **12** well-mannered **13** accommodating
civilian clothes 5 mufti
civility 6 comity **7** amenity, decency, decorum, manners **8** courtesy **9** etiquette, gentility, propriety **10** politeness **11** correctness
civilization 7 culture
civilized 6 decent, proper, urbane **7** genteel, refined **8** decorous, mannerly, tasteful **9** courteous **10** cultivated **13** sophisticated
civil rights *organization:* 4 CORE, SCLC **5** NAACP ***pioneer:* 4** King (Martin Luther) **5** Evers (Medgar), Parks (Rosa) **6** Du Bois (W. E. B.), Garvey (Marcus) **7** Jackson (Jesse) **8** Malcolm X, Marshall (Thurgood) **10** Washington (Booker T.)
Civil War *admiral:* 8 Buchanan (Franklin), Farragut (David) ***battle:* 6** Shiloh **7** Bull Run **8** Antietam, Manassas **9** Mobile Bay, Nashville, Vicksburg **10** Cold Harbor, Gettysburg **11** Chattanooga, Chickamauga ***general:* 3** Lee (Robert E.) **4** Hood (John Bell), Pope (John) **5** Bragg (Braxton), Buell (Don Carlos), Ewell (Richard Stoddart), Grant (Ulysses S.), Meade (George), Sykes (George) **6** Hooker (Joseph) **7** Forrest (Nathan Bedford), Jackson (Thomas "Stonewall"), Sherman (Thomas West, William Tecumseh) **8** Burnside (Ambrose), Johnston (Albert Sidney, Joseph Eggleston), Sheridan (Philip) **9** McClellan (George Brinton), Rosecrans (William), Schofield (John) **10** Beauregard (Pierre) ***ship:* 7** Monitor **9** Merrimack ***soldier:* 3** reb **4** yank **9** Billy Yank, Johnny Reb
civil wrong 4 tort
clabber 5 curds
clack 3 gab, jaw, yak **4** blab, chat **5** prate **6** babble, cackle, gabble, gossip, jabber, rattle **7** blabber, chatter, clatter, palaver, prattle **9** yakety-yak
clad 4 face, side, skin **5** dress, faced **6** clothe, decked, garbed, outfit **7** attired, clothed, covered, dressed, overlay, sheathe **8** costumed, overlaid, sheathed **9** outfitted
claim 4 call, dibs, hold, lien, plea, take **5** argue, exact, right, share, stake, title **6** adduce, allege, assert, defend, demand, insist **7** advance, call for, contend, declare, justify, profess, purport, require, solicit, warrant **8** interest, maintain **9** assertion, challenge, postulate, privilege **10** allegation, birthright **11** affirmation, declaration, prerogative, requisition **12** protestation
clairvoyance 3 ESP **7** insight **9** intuition, telepathy **10** sixth sense **11** penetration, second sight **12** precognition
clairvoyant 4 seer **5** sibyl **7** diviner **8** telepath **10** soothsayer
clam 4 buck **5** razor **6** dollar, quahog **7** bivalve, coquina, geoduck, mollusc, mollusk, smacker, steamer **11** cherrystone ***genus:* 3** Mya
clamant 4 dire **6** crying, urgent **7** blatant, burning, exigent **8** pressing **9** insistent **10** compelling, imperative
clamber 5 climb, crawl, scale, swarm **8** scrabble, scramble, struggle
clammy 4 cool, dank, damp **5** close, moist, slimy **6** sticky
clamor 3 cry, din, row **4** bawl, roar, to-do **5** babel, hoo-ha, noise **6** bellow, demand, hoo-hah, hubbub, jangle, outcry, racket, ruckus, tumult, uproar **7** agitate, dispute, ferment, protest, turmoil **8** brouhaha, foofaraw, shouting **9** agitation, commotion **10** hullabaloo, hurly-burly **11** pandemonium
clamorous 5 noisy, vocal **6** crying, shrill, urgent **7** blatant, exigent, raucous, voluble **8** strident, vehement **9** insistent **10** boisterous, imperative, tumultuous, vociferous **11** importunate **12** obstreperous
clamp 4 grip, hold, vise **5** clasp, grasp **6** clench, clinch, clutch, fasten, secure **7** grapple
clamshell 6 bucket **7** grapple
clan 3 mob **4** camp, folk, ring, sept **5** cabal, house, stock, tribe **6** circle, clique, family **7** coterie, kindred, lineage **9** camarilla ***emblem:* 5** totem
Clancy novel 12 Patriot Games **13** Sum of All Fears (The) **17** Hunt for Red October (The) **21** Clear and Present Danger
clandestine 6 covert, secret, sneaky **7** furtive, illicit, sub rosa **8** hush-hush, stealthy **10** undercover, under wraps **11** underhanded **12** hugger-mugger, illegitimate **13** surreptitious, under-the-table
clang 3 cry, din **4** ding, peal, slam **6** jangle **8** ding-dong
clangor 3 din **5** noise **6** clamor, jangle, racket, rattle, tumult, uproar **7** clatter, ringing **9** stridency **13** reverberation
clangorous 5 noisy **7** booming, rackety, ringing **8** clattery, sonorous **9** deafening **12** ear-splitting

Clan of the Cave Bear author 4 Auel (Jean M.)

clap 3 pat **4** bang, blow, boom, slam, slap **5** blast, burst, crack, crash, whack **6** strike **7** applaud **8** applause

claptrap 4 bull, bunk **5** cheap, hokum, showy, trash, tripe **6** bunkum, drivel, humbug, vulgar **7** baloney, eyewash, hogwash, twaddle **8** malarkey, nonsense **9** poppycock **10** balderdash, flapdoodle

Clara Bow 6 It girl

claret 3 red **4** wine **8** Bordeaux

clarify 5 clean, clear **6** define, filter, purify **7** analyze, cleanse, clear up, explain, resolve **8** simplify **9** elucidate **10** illuminate **13** straighten out

clarion 5 clear **7** ringing, rousing, trumpet **8** gleaming, stirring **9** brilliant

clarity 6 purity **8** accuracy, lucidity **9** clearness, limpidity, precision **10** exactitude, simplicity **12** transparency

Clarke novel 10 Earthlight **13** Childhood's End **19** Fountains of Paradise (The)

clash 4 bump, jolt **5** brawl, crash, melee, set-to, smash **6** battle, fracas, impact, jangle **7** collide **8** conflict, mismatch, skirmish **9** collision, encounter **10** engagement **11** embroilment

clasp 3 hug, pin **4** clip, grip, hold **5** clamp, grasp, press **6** brooch, buckle, clench, clinch, clutch, enfold **7** embrace, grapple, squeeze **10** chatelaine

class 3 ilk **4** hold, kind, mark, part, rank, rate, sort, tier, type **5** allot, brand, caste, gauge, genre, genus, grade, grain, group, judge, order, score, stamp, style **6** assess, assign, assort, branch, course, league, nature, reckon, regard, stripe **7** bracket, caliber, quality, section, species, variety **8** appraise, category, consider, division, evaluate, grouping, separate **10** categorize, pigeonhole **11** description **12** denomination ***middle:* 11** bourgeoisie ***school:* 6** junior, senior **8** freshman **9** sophomore ***working:* 11** proletariat

classic 5 ideal, model, prime **7** capital, typical, vintage **8** champion, enduring, standard, superior, top-notch **9** authentic, canonical, classical, excellent, exemplary, memorable, tradition **10** magnum opus, masterwork **11** chef d'oeuvre, masterpiece, tour de force, traditional **12** paradigmatic, prototypical **13** authoritative

classical 4 pure **5** Attic, Greek, ideal, Latin, Roman **7** ancient, fitting, Grecian, perfect, typical, vintage **8** Hellenic, standard, sterling **9** canonical, exemplary **10** consummate **11** traditional **13** authoritative

classical musician 4 Böhm (Karl), Hess (Myra), Lind (Jenny), Muti (Riccardo), Pons (Lily), Shaw (Robert) **5** Arrau (Claudio), Biggs (E. Power), Borge (Victor), Boult (Adrian), Davis (Colin), du Pré (Jacqueline), Gould (Glenn), Masur (Kurt), Mehta (Zubin), Melba (Nellie), Ozawa (Seiji), Patti (Adelina), Pinza (Ezio), Price (Leontyne), Ramey (Samuel), Sills (Beverly), Stern (Isaac), Szell (George) **6** Abbado (Claudio), Battle (Kathleen), Boulez (Pierre), Callas (Maria), Caruso (Enrico), Casals (Pablo), Galway (James), Levine (James), Maazel (Lorin), Midori, Norman (Jessye), Peters (Roberta), Previn (André), Rampal (Jean-Pierre), Rattle (Simon), Reiner (Fritz), Serkin (Peter, Rudolf), Terfel (Bryn), Tucker (Richard), Upshaw (Dawn), Walter (Bruno) **7** Bartoli (Cecilia), Beecham (Thomas), Bocelli (Andrea), Brendel (Alfred), Cliburn (Van), Corelli (Franco), Domingo (Plácido), Farrell (Eileen), Fiedler (Arthur), Fleming (Renée), Glennie (Evelyn), Haitink (Bernard), Heifetz (Jascha), Karajan (Herbert von), Menuhin (Yehudi), Nilsson (Birgit), Ormandy (Eugene), Perlman (Itzhak), Pollini (Maurizio), Sargent (Malcolm), Segovia (Andrés), Tebaldi (Renata) **8** Anderson (Marian), Argerich (Martha), Bergonzi (Carlo), Carreras (José), Flagstad (Kirsten), Horowitz (Vladimir), Kreisler (Fritz), Marriner (Neville), Oistrakh (David), Schnabel (Artur), Te Kanawa (Kiri), Zukerman (Pinchas) **9** Barenboim (Daniel), Bernstein (Leonard), Chaliapin (Feodor), Klemperer (Otto), Landowska (Wanda), Pavarotti (Luciano), Stokowski (Leopold), Toscanini (Arturo) **10** Rubinstein (Arthur), Sutherland (Joan), Tetrazzini (Luisa) **11** Furtwängler (Wilhelm), Kostelanetz (André), Schwarzkopf (Elisabeth) **12** Rostropovich (Mstislav)

classification 4 sort, type **5** genre, genus, grade, order **6** family, phylum, rating **7** sorting, species **8** category, division, grouping, ordering, taxonomy, typology **11** arrangement, cataloguing

classified 6 secret, sorted **7** divided, ordered **9** top secret **11** categorized **12** confidential

classified-ad abbreviation 3 ABS, AKC, APR, apt, brm, CDL, CPA, EDP, EOE, est, exc, exp, flr, FSH, FWD, gar, gdn, GWO, ISO, kit, LPN, lux, lwd, max, mgr, min, MLS, neg, OBO, opp, pkg, PWO, rec, ref, rep, sal, sep, sig, spd, TLC, wgn **4** appl, bldg, bdrm, bsmt, demo, flex, frpl, furn, HVAC, pass, pref, priv, prof, prop, temp, util, vacc, warr **5** specs (see also **real estate term**)

classify 4 rank, rate, sort **5** grade, group **6** assort **7** arrange **9** break down **10** categorize, pigeonhole

classy 4 chic, tony **5** swank **6** modish **7** dashing, elegant, refined, stylish **8** gracious, tasteful, well-bred **9** courteous **11** fashionable

clatter 4 to-do **6** clamor, hubbub, pother, rattle, tumult, uproar **7** turmoil **9** commotion **10** hurly-burly ***Scottish:* 7** brattle

clattery 5 noisy **7** rackety **10** clangorous

Claudia's husband 6 Pilate

Claudio's beloved 4 Hero

Claudius *nephew:* 6 Hamlet ***predecessor:* 8** Caligula ***slayer:* 6** Hamlet **9** Agrippina ***successor:* 4** Nero ***wife:* 8** Gertrude **9** Agrippina

Clavell novel 6 Gai-Jin, Shogun, Tai-Pan **7** King Rat

claw 3 dig **4** nail, rake, tear **5** chela, talon, uncus **6** pincer, scrape, ungula **7** scratch

clay 3 cob **4** loam, lute, marl **5** argil, brick, earth, gault, loess, ocher, ochre **6** kaolin **10** terra-cotta ***baked:* 4** tile **5** adobe, brick ***box:* 6** saggar, sagger ***building:* 5** adobe ***ceramic:* 10** terra-cotta ***constituent:* 6** silica **8** feldspar, silicate **9** kaolinite ***in glass:* 4** tear ***made of:* 7** fictile ***porcelain:* 6** kaolin ***red:* 8** laterite ***rock:* 5** shale ***tobacco pipe:* 6** dudeen ***watery mixture:* 4** slip ***white:* 6** kaolin

clay pigeon 6 target

clean 4 dust, fair, pure, swab, tidy, wash, wipe **5** bathe, fresh, groom, purge, scour, scrub, sweep **6** bright, chaste, decent, neaten, purify, spruce, vacuum, washed **7** clarify, launder, sinless **8** hygienic, innocent, sanitary, sanitize, spotless, unsoiled **9** blameless, faultless, sparkling, stainless, undefiled, unsullied, untainted, wholesome **10** antiseptic, immaculate **11** unblemished **12** spick-and-span

clean-cut 4 trim **7** defined, precise **8** definite, explicit, specific **9** wholesome **10** definitive **11** categorical, unambiguous, well-groomed

cleaner see **cleanser**

cleanhanded 8 innocent **9** blameless

clean-limbed 4 trim **7** shapely **8** handsome **10** statuesque

cleanse 4 lave, wash **5** purge, rinse **6** purify, refine **7** clarify, deterge, launder **8** lustrate, sanitize **9** disinfect, expurgate, sterilize

cleanser 3 lye **4** soap **9** detergent **10** antiseptic **12** disinfectant

cleansing 7 purging **8** ablution **9** catharsis, purgation **10** lustration **11** expurgation **12** purification

clear 4 earn, fair, fine, pure **5** lucid, overt, plain, repay, solve, stark, sunny **6** acquit, limpid, secure, settle, simple **7** absolve, audible, clarify, clarion, defined, evident, legible, obvious, precise **8** apparent, definite, distinct **9** authorize, cloudless, elucidate, exculpate, exonerate, liquidate, meliorate, unblurred, unclouded, vindicate **10** ameliorate, illuminate, see-through **11** disentangle, open-and-shut, perceptible, transparent, unambiguous, unequivocal **12** unmistakable

clearance 3 gap **4** sale **7** go-ahead, removal **8** approval **10** green light, permission **13** authorization

clear away 6 remove **7** take out

clear-cut 5 crisp, exact, plain **7** decided, precise **8** definite, distinct, explicit, manifest **10** definitive, pronounced, undisputed **11** categorical, indubitable, unambiguous, unequivocal **12** unquestioned

clear-eyed 6 astute **9** judicious, observant **10** discerning, perceptive

clearheaded 4 calm, cool **10** perceptive

clearing 3 gap **5** field, glade **7** opening **10** settlement

clear out 5 scoot, scram, split **6** beat it, begone, bug off, decamp, depart **7** buzz off, skiddoo, take off, vamoose **8** shove off **9** drive away, skedaddle **10** hightail it

clear-sightedness 6 acuity, acumen **8** keenness, sagacity **10** astuteness, shrewdness **11** discernment, penetration, percipience **12** perspicacity

clear up 5 solve **6** cipher, unfold **7** clarify, dope out, explain, resolve, unravel **8** decipher **9** elucidate, figure out **10** illuminate

clearwing 4 moth

cleat 4 bitt **5** chock **6** batten **7** bollard, dolphin

cleavage 4 rift **5** chasm, cleft, split **6** schism **7** fissure **8** crevasse **9** splitting

cleave 3 cut, hew **4** chop, join, link, rend, rive **5** carve, cling, sever, slice, split, stick, unite **6** adhere, divide, sunder **7** combine **8** dissever, separate

cleft 3 gap **4** rift **5** chasm, chink, clove, crack, gorge, gulch, split **6** clough, ravine, schism **7** crevice, divided, fissure **8** cleavage

clemency 5 grace, mercy **6** lenity **7** caritas, charity **8** kindness, lenience, leniency, mildness **9** tolerance **10** compassion, gentleness, indulgence, sufferance, toleration **11** forbearance

clement 4 fair, kind, mild **5** balmy **6** benign,

humane, kindly **7** lenient **8** merciful, tolerant **9** indulgent **10** benevolent, charitable, forbearing **13** compassionate

clench 4 grip, grit, hold **5** clamp, clasp, grasp **6** clutch **7** grapple

Cleopatra *attendant:* 4 Iras **8** Charmian ***brother:* 7** Ptolemy ***husband:* 7** Ptolemy ***killer:* 3** asp ***lover:* 6** Antony (Marc), Caesar (Julius) **7** Anthony (Mark) ***river:* 4** Nile

Cleopatra's Needle 7 obelisk

clepsydra 9 timepiece **10** water clock

clerestory 7 gallery

clergy 7 canonry **8** ministry **9** churchmen, diaconate, pastorate, rabbinate **10** priesthood **11** cardinalate **13** ecclesiastics

clergyman 5 clerk, padre, vicar **6** bishop, cleric, curate, divine, father, parson, pastor, priest, rector **7** dominie, prelate **8** chaplain, clerical, minister, preacher, reverend, shepherd, sky pilot **9** churchman, pulpiteer **10** evangelist, missionary, sermonizer **12** ecclesiastic ***American:* 4** Hale (Edward Everett), King (Martin Luther, Thomas Starr) **5** Eliot (John), Moody (Dwight), Stone (Barton Warren), Weems (Parson) **6** Dwight (Timothy), Finney (Charles), Graham (Billy), Holmes (John Haynes), Hooker (Thomas), Mather (Cotton, Increase, Richard), Merton (Thomas), Parker (Samuel, Theodore), Sunday (Billy), Taylor (Edward, Graham, Nathaniel William) **7** Beecher (Henry Ward, Lyman), Edwards (Jonathan), Harvard (John), Russell (Charles Taze) **10** Muhlenberg (Frederick Augustus, Henry Melchior, John Peter Gabriel) ***English:* 4** Ward (Nathaniel, Seth, William George) **5** Donne (John), Paley (William), Smith (Henry "Silver-Tongued," John "The Sebaptist," Sidney) **6** Cotton (John), Fuller (Andrew, Thomas), Taylor (Jeremy, Rowland), Wesley (Charles, John) **7** Cranmer (Thomas), Parsons (Robert) **8** Kingsley (Charles) **10** Whitefield (George) ***home:* 5** manse **6** priory **7** rectory **8** vicarage **9** monastery, parsonage ***traveling:* 12** circuit rider

cleric see **clergyman**

clerisy 8 literati **10** illuminati **13** intellectuals

clerk 7 cashier **8** salesman **9** secretary **10** accountant, bookkeeper **11** salesperson **12** stenographer

clever 3 apt, sly **4** able, deft, good, keen **5** adept, alert, canny, funny, handy, quick, savvy, sharp, smart, witty **6** adroit, astute, brainy, bright, crafty, expert, shrewd, tricky **7** amusing, capable, cunning, knowing, skilled **8** fanciful, humorous, pleasing, skillful, talented **9** competent, dexterous, ingenious **10** proficient **11** intelligent, quick-witted, resourceful **12** entertaining

cliché 3 saw **6** truism **7** bromide **8** banality, buzzword, chestnut **9** platitude **10** shibboleth, stereotype **11** commonplace

clichéd 5 banal, bland, musty, stale, tired, trite, vapid **6** old-hat **7** humdrum, insipid, worn-out **8** bromidic, shopworn, timeworn **9** hackneyed **10** pedestrian, unoriginal **11** stereotyped **13** platitudinous, unimaginative

click 3 fit **4** snap, tick, work **5** agree, match **6** go over, pan out **7** come off, succeed

client 6 patron **7** patient, protégé **8** customer **9** dependent

clientele 4 fans **5** trade, train **6** custom, market, public **7** patrons, traffic **8** audience, patients, regulars, shoppers **9** customers **10** purchasers, supporters **12** constituency

cliff 4 crag **5** bluff, scarp **8** headland, palisade **9** precipice **10** escarpment

climacteric 4 apex, crux, cusp **5** acute **6** crisis **7** crucial **8** critical **9** menopause **11** culmination **12** change of life, turning point

climactic 4 peak **7** crucial, pivotal **8** critical, decisive, dramatic **9** momentous **10** definitive **11** culminating, determining

climate 6 medium, milieu **7** ambient **8** ambience **10** atmosphere **11** environment **12** surroundings

climax 3 cap **4** acme, apex, peak **5** crown **6** apogee, summit, top off **8** capstone, meridian, pinnacle **9** culminate **11** culmination

climb 4 go up, rise, soar **5** mount, scale, slope **6** ascend, ascent **7** clamber **8** escalate, increase

climbing 8 scandent

climbing device 3 cam, nut **5** biner, cinch, piton **7** crampon **9** carabiner

clinch 3 hug, ice **4** grip, hold, seal **5** clamp, clasp, grasp, sew up **6** clutch, decide, ensure, lock up **7** confirm, embrace, grapple, squeeze **8** nail down

clincher 4 tire **5** proof **6** kicker **7** quietus **9** deathblow **10** smoking gun **11** affirmation, attestation, coup de grâce **12** confirmation **13** corroboration

cling 4 bond **5** stick **6** adhere, cleave, clutch, hold on, linger **8** adhesion **9** adherence

clingstone 5 peach

clink 3 can, jug, pen **4** brig, cell, coop, jail, stir **5** pokey, pound **6** cooler, jingle, lockup, prison, tingle, tinkle **7** slammer **8** hoosegow **9** calaboose

clinker 3 dud **4** bomb, bust, flop, goof, slag **5** botch, brick, error, lemon, loser **6** bummer,

bungle, fiasco, howler, turkey **7** bloomer, blunder, failure, faux pas, mistake
clinkers 3 ash **4** slag **5** ashes **7** cinders
clinquant 5 gaudy **6** flashy, garish, tawdry, tinsel **8** specious **10** glittering **11** superficial
Clio see **Muse**
clip 3 bob, cut, mow, pin **4** crop, hasp, pare, snip, sock, trim **5** block, clasp, prune, punch, shave, shear, slash **6** broach, brooch, fleece, reduce **7** curtail, cut back, cut down, shorten **8** magazine, truncate **10** abbreviate, overcharge
clipped 3 cut, hit **4** curt, taut **5** brief, crisp, shorn, short, terse **6** abrupt, cut off, docked, pruned **7** blocked, clasped, cropped, trimmed **8** cut short, fastened **9** curtailed, shortened, truncated
clique 3 set **4** camp, clan, club, gang, ring **5** cabal, crowd, mafia **6** circle **7** coterie, faction, in-group **9** camarilla
cloak 4 cape, mask, robe, veil, wrap **5** cover, guise, talma **6** domino, facade, joseph, mantle, screen, shroud, veneer **7** blanket, conceal, curtain, dress up, manteau, obscure **8** disguise **9** dissemble, semblance **10** camouflage **11** dissimulate ***ancient Greek:*** **7** chlamys ***ancient Roman:*** **7** pallium ***Arab:*** **3** aba ***fur:*** **7** pelisse ***hooded:*** **6** capote **7** burnous **8** burnoose ***liturgical:*** **4** cope ***Moroccan:*** **8** djellaba ***over armor:*** **6** tabard **7** surcoat ***Spanish:*** **5** manta
clobber 4 belt, drub, flay, lick, slam, slug, sock, whip, whup **5** blast, brain, clout, cream, pound, smash **6** hammer, thrash, wallop **7** lambast, shellac, trounce **8** demolish, lambaste
clochard 3 bum, vag **4** hobo **5** tramp **6** beggar, canter **7** drifter, floater, moocher, vagrant **8** deadbeat, derelict, vagabond **9** transient **10** freeloader, panhandler **11** bindle stiff
cloche 3 hat **5** cover, toque, tuque
clock 4 time **9** timepiece **11** chronometer ***water:*** **9** clepsydra
clocklike 5 exact **6** minute, prompt, strict, timely **7** precise, regular **8** accurate, punctual, reliable, thorough **9** assiduous **10** dependable, meticulous, scrupulous **11** painstaking **13** conscientious
clockmaker 10 horologist
clockwise 6 deasil **7** dextral **11** right-handed
Clockwork Orange author 7 Burgess (Anthony)
clod 3 gob, wad **4** boob, dolt, dope, hunk, lump, soil **5** chump, chunk, clump, dummy, dunce, earth **6** dimwit **8** dumbbell **9** blockhead, lamebrain
cloddish 7 boorish, ill-bred, loutish, uncouth **8** churlish, clownish **9** unrefined **10** uncultured, unpolished **11** uncivilized
clodhopper 4 boor, boot, hick, lout **5** chuff, churl, clown, yokel **6** rustic **7** bumpkin, hayseed, redneck **9** chawbacon
clog 3 gum, jam, tax **4** fill, glut, load, plug, stop **5** block, choke, close, stuff **6** hamper, hinder **7** congest **8** encumber, obstruct, overload **10** impediment **11** encumbrance
cloisonné 6 enamel
cloister 5 abbey, court **6** arcade, garden **7** convent, retreat, seclude, shelter **9** courtyard, monastery, sequester
Cloister and the Hearth author 5 Reade (Charles)
cloistered 7 recluse **8** confined, hermetic, secluded **9** seclusive, withdrawn **11** sequestered
cloistered one 3 nun **4** monk
clone 4 copy **5** ditto **6** double, carbon **7** replica **9** duplicate, facsimile, replicate, reproduce **10** carbon copy, simulacrum **12** reproduction
Clorinda *beloved:* 7 Tancred ***father:*** **6** Senapo ***guardian:*** **6** Arsete ***slayer:*** **7** Tancred
close 3 end **4** near, nigh, shut, slam **5** block, cease, choke, humid, muggy, tight **6** ending, finale, finish, narrow, nearby, stuffy, sultry, windup, wrap up **7** airless, compact, crowded, stopper **8** adjacent, complete, conclude, finalize, intimate, obstruct, stifling **9** adjoining, cessation, condensed, terminate **10** conclusion, consummate, convenient, near-at-hand **11** constricted, neighboring, termination **12** confidential
closed-minded 4 deaf **6** narrow **8** obdurate **9** hidebound, obstinate, pigheaded, unbending **10** bullheaded, hardheaded **11** intractable
closefisted 5 cheap, mingy **6** frugal, stingy **7** miserly, thrifty **9** niggardly, penurious **13** penny-pinching
close in 3 hem **4** cage **5** fence, hedge **6** corral, immure **7** advance, confine, enclose, envelop, impound **8** approach, converge, encircle, enshroud, imprison, surround
close-knit 8 intimate
close match 6 toss-up
closemouthed 3 mum **4** mute **6** silent **7** laconic **8** reserved, reticent, taciturn **12** tight-mouthed
closeness 8 intimacy
close off 4 clog, plug **5** block **6** stop up **7** isolate, occlude **8** insulate **9** segregate, sequester
closet 6 covert, inside, office, secret **7** cabinet, chamber, furtive, private **8** wardrobe

closing 3 end **4** last, stop **5** final **6** ending, finish, latest, period, windup, wrap-up **7** curtain **8** eventual, terminal, ultimate **9** cessation **10** concluding **11** termination
closure 3 cap, end, lid **6** ending, finish **8** fastener **9** cessation
clot 3 gel, set **4** curd, glob, jell, lump **5** clump **6** curdle, gelate **7** congeal **8** coagulum, thrombus **9** coagulate **10** gelatinize ***combining form:*** **6** thromb **7** thrombo
cloth see **fabric**
clothe 3 tog **4** deck, do up, garb, robe **5** array, cloak, couch, drape, dress, endow, endue, equip **6** attire, bedeck, outfit, swathe **7** apparel, costume, dress up **8** accouter
clothes 3 rig **4** duds, garb, rags, togs **5** array, dress, getup, habit **6** attire, outfit, things **7** apparel, costume, raiment, rigging, threads, toggery, vesture **8** garments, glad rags **9** vestments **11** habiliments ***basket:*** **6** hamper ***civilian:*** **5** mufti
clothes-moth genus 5 Tinea
clothespress 7 armoire **8** wardrobe
cloud 3 dim, fog, tar **4** blur, haze, mist, murk **5** addle, befog, brume, gloom, muddy, plume, smear, sully, taint **6** muddle, nebula, puzzle, shadow, smudge **7** besmear, confuse, obscure, perplex, tarnish **8** befuddle, besmirch, discolor, distract, overcast **9** obfuscate ***type:*** **4** nine **6** cirrus, nimbus **7** cumulus, stratus **11** altocumulus, altostratus **12** cirrocumulus, cirrostratus, cumulonimbus, interstellar, nimbostratus **13** stratocumulus
cloudburst 6 deluge, shower **7** monsoon, torrent **8** downpour, drencher, rainfall **10** outpouring
clouded 5 dusky, murky, shady **6** dreary, gloomy, somber, sombre **7** dubious, ominous, sunless, unclear **8** doubtful, overcast **9** ambiguous, equivocal, uncertain, unsettled **11** problematic
cloudless 4 fair, fine **5** clear, sunny **7** clarion **8** pleasant, rainless, sunshiny
cloud-like mass 6 nebula
cloud nine 5 bliss **6** heaven **7** ecstasy, elation, nirvana, rapture **8** euphoria
cloudy 4 dull, hazy **5** dusky, foggy, heavy, misty, murky, vague **6** gloomy, opaque, somber, sombre **7** louring, obscure, tainted, unclear **8** confused, darkened, lowering, nebulous, overcast, vaporous **10** indistinct
clout 3 box, hit, rag **4** blow, cuff, poke, pull, slam, slap, slug, sock, swat, sway **5** paste, power, punch, smack, smite, whack **6** strike **9** influence
clove 4 bulb **5** spice **7** chopped, severed
clove hitch 4 knot
clover 5 lotus **6** alsike, ladino, lucern **7** alfalfa, berseem, lucerne, melilot, trefoil **8** four-leaf, shamrock **9** lespedeza ***family:*** **3** pea ***genus:*** **9** Trifolium
clown 3 wag **4** bozo, mime, zany **5** cutup, joker, Punch **6** jester, mummer **7** buffoon **8** comedian, jokester **9** harlequin, prankster **11** merry-andrew ***French:*** **7** Pierrot ***operatic:*** **5** buffo ***Spanish:*** **8** gracioso
clownish 4 rude **6** clumsy, gauche, oafish **7** awkward, boorish, ill-bred, loutish, lumpish, uncouth **8** churlish, cloddish **9** unrefined
cloy 4 fill, glut, jade, pall, sate **5** gorge **6** sicken **7** satiate, surfeit **8** overfill
cloying 4 icky **5** gushy, mushy, sappy, soppy **6** sticky, sugary **7** fulsome, gushing, maudlin, mawkish **9** excessive, schmaltzy, sickening **10** disgusting, lovey-dovey, nauseating, saccharine **11** distasteful, sentimental
club 3 bat, sap **4** beat, cosh, frat, iron, mace **5** baton, billy, guild, lodge, order, union **6** cudgel, league **7** society **8** bludgeon, sodality, sorority **9** blackjack, truncheon **10** fellowship, fraternity, knobkerrie, nightstick **11** association, brotherhood ***Australian:*** **5** waddy ***Irish:*** **10** shillelagh ***Maori:*** **4** patu
clubfoot 7 talipes
cluck 4 dodo, dolt, dope, fool **5** dunce **6** dimwit, nitwit **7** pinhead
clue 3 cue **4** hint, idea, lead, sign, tell, warn **6** advise, inform, notify, notion, tip-off **7** inkling **8** evidence, telltale **10** indication, intimation, suggestion
Clue character 4 Plum (Prof.) **5** Green (Mr., Rev.) **7** Mustard (Col.), Peacock (Mrs.) **8** Scarlett (Miss)
clueless 4 lost **10** out to lunch
clump 3 gob, wad **4** clod, hunk, lump, mass, mess, plod **5** batch, bunch, chunk, group, stomp, tramp **6** bumble, bundle, lumber, parcel **7** cluster, galumph, stumble ***of grass:*** **4** tuft **6** tuffet **7** tussock
clumsy 5 bulky, gawky, inept, splay **6** clunky, gauche, klutzy, wooden **7** awkward, hulking, lumpish, uncouth, unhandy **8** bumbling, bungling, tactless, ungainly, unsubtle, unwieldy **9** all thumbs, graceless, ham-handed, inelegant, lumbering, maladroit **11** heavy-handed, inefficient ***person:*** **3** oaf **4** clod, goon, lout, slob **5** klutz **6** baboon, galoot, lummox **7** bumpkin, bungler, palooka **13** butterfingers
clunk 4 thud **5** clout, thump, whack **6** thwack, wallop

clunker 3 car **4** bomb, heap **5** crate, lemon, wreck **6** beater, jalopy, junker **7** stinker **10** rattletrap, rust bucket
cluster 3 lot, set **4** band, bevy, crew, knot, pack **5** array, batch, bunch, clump, covey, group **6** bundle, clutch, gather **7** collect, package **8** assemble, assembly **9** aggregate, associate, gathering **10** accumulate
cluster bean 4 guar
clutch 4 grab, grip, hold, keep **5** catch, clamp, clasp, grasp, pinch, seize **6** bundle, clench, clinch, snatch **7** cluster, grapple
clutter 4 hash, mash, mess, muss, ruck **5** chaos, snarl, strew **6** jumble, litter, muddle **7** mélange, rummage **8** disarray, disorder, mishmash, shambles **9** confusion **10** hodgepodge, hotchpotch
Clydesdale 5 horse **10** draft horse
Clymene *father:* 7 Oceanus ***husband:* 7** Iapetus ***mother:* 6** Tethys ***son:* 5** Atlas **10** Epimetheus, Prometheus
Clytemnestra *brother:* 6 Castor, Pollux **10** Polydeuces ***daughter:* 7** Electra **9** Iphigenia ***father:* 9** Tyndareus ***husband:* 9** Agamemnon ***lover:* 9** Aegisthus ***mother:* 4** Leda ***slayer:* 7** Orestes ***son:* 7** Orestes ***victim:* 9** Agamemnon, Cassandra
Clytle *beloved:* 6 Apollo ***form:* 9** sunflower **10** heliotrope
coach 3 bus, car, pro **5** drill, stage, train, tutor **6** chaise, mentor **7** prepare, trainer **8** carriage, instruct **10** instructor
coadjutor 3 aid **4** aide **6** bishop, deputy **9** assistant **10** aide-de-camp, lieutenant
coagulate 3 gel, set **4** clot, jell **6** curdle **7** congeal, jellify, thicken **8** coalesce, condense, solidify **10** gelatinize, inspissate **11** concentrate, consolidate
coal *carrier:* 3 hod **7** scuttle ***distillate:* 3** tar ***dust:* 4** culm, smut, soot **5** slack ***element:* 6** carbon ***fused leavings:* 4** slag **7** clinker ***glowing:* 5** ember, gleed ***hard:* 10** anthracite ***lump:* 3** cob ***miner:* 7** collier ***region:* 4** Saar ***residue:* 4** coke ***soft:* 6** cannel **10** bituminous
coalesce 3 mix **4** fuse, join, link **5** blend, merge, unite **6** mingle **7** combine, conjoin **10** amalgamate
coalition 4 bloc, ring **5** party, union **6** fusion, league, merger **7** combine, melding, merging **8** alliance **9** anschluss **10** federation **11** affiliation, association, combination, confederacy, integration, unification **13** confederation, consolidation
coarse 3 raw **4** rude **5** bawdy, crass, crude, dirty, gross, harsh, rough, tacky **6** common, filthy, grainy, ribald, smutty, vulgar **7** boorish, obscene, raffish, raunchy, uncouth **8** granular, indecent **9** inelegant, roughneck, unrefined **10** uncultured **11** particulate **12** uncultivated
coast 4 bank **5** beach, drift, shore, slide **6** strand **7** seaside **8** littoral, seashore **9** freewheel ***of Antarctica:* 4** Knox
coastal 7 seaside **8** littoral, riverine
coaster 4 sled, tray **6** trader
coat 5 crust, glaze, gloss, layer, parka, plate, tunic **6** blazer, duster, finish, jacket, patina, raglan, reefer, ulster, veneer **7** cutaway **8** covering, mackinaw, tegument **9** newmarket, redingote **10** integument, mackintosh **11** windbreaker **12** Prince Albert ***animal:* 3** fur **4** hide, pelt, wool **6** pelage ***fur-lined:* 7** pelisse ***kind:* 3** pea, top **5** frock **6** trench ***Levantine:* 6** caftan ***of arms:* 5** crest **6** blazon, emblem, shield, tabard **8** blazonry **10** escutcheon ***of egg white:* 5** glair **6** glaire ***of mail:* 7** hauberk ***soldier's:* 5** frock, tunic **6** capote ***waterproof:* 7** slicker **10** mackintosh
coating 4 film, leaf, scum, skin **5** glaze, gloss, layer **6** finish, patina, veneer **7** dusting, lacquer, overlay, surface, varnish **8** covering ***winter:* 3** ice **4** snow **5** sleet
coat rack part 3 leg, peg **4** base, hook **5** stand **6** hanger
coax 4 lure, urge **5** cable, press, tempt **6** cajole, entice, induce **7** blarney, wheedle **8** blandish, butter up, inveigle, persuade, softsoap **9** importune, sweet-talk
cob 3 ear **4** swan **5** adobe, horse
cobalt symbol 2 Co
cobble 4 make, mend **5** patch, stone **6** repair **11** paving stone
cobbler 3 pie **5** drink **8** cocktail **9** shoemaker ***form:* 4** last ***tool:* 3** awl
cobelligerent 4 ally
cobweb 3 net **4** mesh, trap **8** gossamer **9** confusion, spiderweb **12** entanglement
coccyx 8 tailbone
cochineal 3 dye **6** insect
cock 3 tap **4** boss, head, heap, hill, lord, mass, pile, rick, tilt **5** chief, mound, stack, strut, valve **6** faucet, honcho, leader, master, spigot **7** headman, hydrant, rooster, swagger **11** chanticleer
cock-a-hoop 4 awry **5** askew **7** askance, crooked **8** boastful, exultant, exulting, jubilant **9** triumphal **10** triumphant
Cockaigne 6 utopia **7** arcadia **9** Shangri-la **10** wonderland
cockalorum 7 bluster, bombast, bravado **8** blowhard, boasting, braggart, leapfrog **11** braggadocio
cockamamy 5 batty, crazy, daffy, flaky,

kooky, loony, nutty, wacky **6** absurd **9** ludicrous **10** incredible, ridiculous **11** harebrained
cock-and-bull story 5 crock **6** canard **7** whopper **9** fairy tale
cockcrow 4 dawn, morn **5** sunup **7** morning, sunrise **8** daybreak, daylight
cocker 4 baby **5** humor, spoil **6** coddle, cosset, pamper **7** indulge, spaniel **11** mollycoddle
cockeyed 4 awry **5** askew **8** lopsided **11** harebrained
cockle 5 shell **6** dimple, furrow, groove, pucker, ripple **7** bivalve, mollusc, mollusk, wrinkle
cockleshell 4 boat
cockscomb see **coxcomb**
cocksure 5 brash **6** cheeky **9** bumptious **13** overconfident
cocktail 5 Bronx, drink, julep **6** Gibson, gimlet, mai tai, mimosa, mojito, Rob Roy, zombie **7** gin fizz, martini, sidecar, stinger **8** aperitif, daiquiri, pink lady, salty dog, sombrero **9** Cuba libre, manhattan, margarita, mint julep, rusty nail **10** Bloody Mary, Tom Collins, wallbanger **11** grasshopper, screwdriver, whiskey sour **12** black russian, cosmopolitan, old-fashioned ***fruit:*** **9** macedoine ***gasoline:*** **7** Molotov
Cocktail Party author 5 Eliot (T. S.)
cocky 4 bold, sure **5** brash, pushy, sassy, saucy **6** brassy, cheeky, jaunty **8** arrogant, impudent, insolent **9** conceited **10** swaggering **11** self-assured **12** enterprising **13** overconfident, self-confident
coconspirator 7 abettor **9** accessory **10** accomplice **11** confederate
coconut ***husk fiber:*** **4** coir ***meat:*** **5** copra
coda 5 envoi, envoy **6** ending, finale **7** summary **8** epilogue, follow-up **9** afterword **10** conclusion
coddle 4 baby **5** humor, spoil **6** cosset, pamper **7** cater to, indulge
code 6 cipher, symbol **7** encrypt **8** encipher ***kind:*** **3** PIN, zip **4** area **5** Morse, legal, penal ***message in:*** **10** cryptogram **11** cryptograph
code word see **communications code word**
codger 4 coot, fogy **5** fogey **6** duffer, fellow, fossil, geezer **7** old coot, old fogy **8** old fogey
codicil 5 rider **8** addendum, addition, appendix **10** postscript, supplement
codswallop see **nonsense**
coefficient 6 factor **7** measure **8** constant
coelenterate 5 coral **7** anemone, hydroid **9** cnidarian, jellyfish **10** sea anemone
coerce 3 cow **5** bully, force, impel, press **6** compel, menace, oblige **8** browbeat, bulldoze, dominate, pressure, threaten **9** blackjack, constrain, strong-arm, terrorize **10** intimidate
coercion 5 force **6** duress, menace, threat **8** pressure **10** compulsion, constraint
Coetzee novel 8 Disgrace
Coeur d'____ 5 Alene
coeval see **contemporary**
coexistent see **contemporary**
coffee 3 joe, mud **4** java **6** jamoke ***alkaloid:*** **8** caffeine ***bean:*** **3** nib ***cake:*** **6** kuchen ***cup:*** **9** demitasse ***French:*** **4** café ***grinder:*** **4** mill ***kind:*** **4** drip, java **5** decaf, latte, mocha **7** arabica, instant **8** espresso **9** Americano, macchiato **10** café au lait, cappuccino ***maker:*** **10** percolator ***pot:*** **3** urn
coffee shop 4 café **5** diner **8** snack bar **9** cafeteria, hash house, lunchroom **11** greasy spoon **12** luncheonette
coffer 5 chest **6** casket **8** treasury **9** exchequer, strongbox
coffin 3 box **4** kist **6** casket ***carrier:*** **6** hearse **10** pallbearer ***nail:*** **9** cigarette ***stand:*** **4** bier **10** catafalque
cogency 5 force, point, power, punch **7** potency **8** strength, validity **9** relevance **10** conviction, pertinence **13** effectiveness
cogent 5 solid, sound, valid **6** potent **7** telling, weighty **8** forceful, powerful, relevant **9** pertinent **10** compelling, convincing, meaningful, persuasive **11** influential, well-founded **12** well-grounded **13** consequential
cogitate 4 muse **5** think **6** ponder, reason **7** reflect **8** conceive, consider, meditate, mull over, ruminate **9** cerebrate, speculate **10** deliberate
cogitation 7 thought **10** meditation, reflection, rumination **11** cerebration, speculation **12** deliberation **13** consideration
cogitative 7 pensive **10** meditative, reflective, ruminative, thoughtful **11** speculative **13** contemplative
Cogito ____ sum 4 ergo
cognac 6 brandy
cognate 4 akin, like **5** alike **6** allied, common **7** kindred, related, similar **8** parallel **10** affiliated, associated
cognition 9 awareness, knowledge, sentience **10** perception
cognizance 4 heed, note **6** notice **9** attention, awareness, knowledge **12** jurisdiction
cognizant 5 aware **7** knowing, mindful **8** informed, sensible **9** conscious **13** knowledgeable
cognize 4 know **5** grasp **6** fathom **7** realize **8**

perceive **9** apprehend **10** appreciate, comprehend, understand

cognomen **4** name **5** alias, title **7** epithet, moniker, surname **8** nickname **11** appellation, appellative, designation **12** denomination

cognoscente **5** judge **6** critic, expert **7** epicure **8** aesthete **9** authority **10** specialist **11** connoisseur

cognoscible **8** knowable **10** fathomable **13** apprehensible

cogwheel **4** gear

cohere **4** fuse, join **5** agree, blend, cling, merge, stick, unite **6** accord **7** combine, comport, conform, connect **8** coalesce, dovetail **10** correspond **11** consolidate

coherence **4** bond **5** union, unity **8** adhesion, cohesion **9** agreement, congruity, integrity **10** conformity, connection, consonance, solidarity **11** consistency, integration

coherent **5** sound **7** logical, ordered, unified **8** rational **10** consistent, integrated, meaningful **11** coordinated

cohesion see **coherence**

coho **6** salmon **12** silver salmon

cohort **3** pal **4** ally, band, chum, crew, mate **5** buddy, crony, group **6** fellow, friend **7** comrade, partner **8** adherent, confrere, disciple, follower, henchman, sidekick **9** assistant, associate, colleague, companion, supporter **10** accomplice **11** demographic **12** collaborator

coif **3** cap, cut **4** hood, perm **6** hairdo **7** haircut **8** skullcap

coiffeur **6** barber **10** haircutter **11** hairdresser, hairstylist

coiffure **6** hairdo ***aid:*** **3** net, rat **5** snood

coil **4** curl, loop, ring, turn, wind **5** helix, twine, twist **6** rotate, spiral **7** entwine, revolve, wreathe **8** curlicue **9** corkscrew

coiled **6** spiral, volute **7** helical, voluted, whorled **9** circinate

coin **4** mint **6** invent, make up, strike ***Afghanistan:*** **3** pul **7** afghani ***Albania:*** **3** lek **9** quindarka ***Algeria:*** **5** dinar **7** centime ***ancient Greek:*** **4** obol ***ancient Muslim:*** **5** dinar ***ancient Roman:*** **8** denarius ***Argentina:*** **4** peso **7** centavo ***Austria:*** **4** euro **8** groschen **9** schilling ***Bahrain:*** **4** fils **5** dinar ***Belgium:*** **4** euro **5** franc **7** centime ***Benin:*** **5** franc **7** centime ***Bhutan:*** **7** chetrum **8** ngultrum ***Bolivia:*** **7** centavo **9** boliviano ***Botswana:*** **4** pula **5** thebe ***Brazil:*** **4** real **7** centavo **8** cruzeiro ***Bulgaria:*** **3** lev **8** stotinka ***Burma:*** **4** kyat ***Burundi:*** **5** franc **7** centime ***Cameroon:*** **5** franc **7** centime ***Canada:*** **6** loonie, toonie, twonie ***Cape Verde Islands:*** **6** escudo **7** centavo ***Chile:*** **4** peso **7** centavo ***China:*** **3** fen **4** jiao, yuan ***Colombia:*** **4** peso **7** centavo ***Costa Rica:*** **5** colón **7** centimo ***Cuba:*** **4** peso **7** centavo ***Czech Republic:*** **5** haler **6** koruna ***defective:*** **4** fido ***Denmark:*** **3** ore **5** krone ***Dominican Republic:*** **4** peso **7** centavo ***Ecuador:*** **5** sucre **7** centavo ***edge:*** **7** milling ***Egypt:*** **7** piastre ***European gold:*** **5** ducat ***Finland:*** **4** euro **5** penni **6** markka ***former:*** **3** ecu, mil, pie, sol, sou **4** anna, besa, doit, duit, fels, kran, para, pice, reis (plural) **5** fanam, litas, mohur, paisa, rupia, shahi, soldo, taler, toman **6** besant, centas, denier, heller, macuta, pagoda, tangka **7** santims, sapeque **8** maravedi, skilling **9** rigsdaler **10** Indian head, reichsmark **13** reichspfennig ***France:*** **3** ecu, sou **4** euro **5** franc **7** centime ***Gambia:*** **5** butut **6** dalasi ***Germany:*** **4** euro, mark **7** pfennig ***Ghana:*** **4** cedi **6** pesewa ***Great Britain:*** **3** bob **4** quid **5** crown, penny, pound **6** guinea **7** ha'penny **8** farthing, shilling, sixpence **9** halfpenny, sovereign **10** threepence ***Greece:*** **4** euro **6** lepton **7** drachma ***Guatemala:*** **7** centavo, quetzal ***Guinea-Bissau:*** **4** peso ***Guyana:*** **3** bit ***Haiti:*** **6** gourde **7** centime ***Honduras:*** **7** centavo, lempira ***Hungary:*** **5** pengo **6** filler, forint ***Iceland:*** **5** aurar (plural), eyrir, krona ***India:*** **3** pie **4** anna **5** paisa, rupee ***Indonesia:*** **3** sen **6** rupiah ***Iran:*** **4** rial **5** dinar ***Iraq:*** **4** fils **5** dinar ***Ireland:*** **4** euro **5** penny **8** farthing ***Israel:*** **5** agora **6** shekel ***Italy:*** **4** euro, lira **5** scudo ***Japan:*** **3** rin, sen, yen ***Jordan:*** **4** fils **5** dinar ***Kenya:*** **8** shilling ***Korea, North and South:*** **3** won **4** chon ***Kuwait:*** **4** fils **5** dinar ***large:*** **9** cartwheel ***Lebanon:*** **5** livre **7** piastre ***Lesotho:*** **4** loti **7** licente, lisente ***Libya:*** **5** dinar **6** dirham ***Luxembourg:*** **4** euro **5** franc ***Macao:*** **3** avo ***Madagascar:*** **5** franc ***Malawi:*** **6** kwacha **7** tambala ***Mauritania:*** **5** khoum **7** ouguiya ***Mauritius:*** **5** rupee ***Mexico:*** **4** peso **7** centavo ***Moldova:*** **3** leu ***Monaco:*** **4** euro **5** franc ***Morocco:*** **6** dirham ***Mozambique:*** **7** metical ***Nepal:*** **5** paisa, rupee ***Netherlands:*** **4** euro **6** florin, gulden **7** guilder ***Nicaragua:*** **7** centavo, córdoba ***Nigeria:*** **4** kobo **5** naira ***Norway:*** **3** ore **5** krone ***Oman:*** **4** rial **5** baiza ***Pakistan:*** **4** anna **5** paisa, rupee ***Palestine:*** **3** mil ***Panama:*** **6** balboa **9** centesimo ***Papua New Guinea:*** **4** kina, toea ***Paraguay:*** **7** centimo, guarani ***Peru:*** **3** sol **7** centimo ***Philippines:*** **4** peso, piso **7** sentimo ***Poland:*** **5** grosz, zloty ***Portugal:*** **4** euro **6** escudo **7** centavo ***Qatar:*** **5** riyal **6** dirham ***Roman:*** **6** aureus, bezant **7** solidus ***Romania:*** **3** ban, leu ***Russia:*** **5** kopek, ruble **6** kopeck ***Samoa:*** **4** sene, tala ***San Marino:*** **4** lira ***Saudi Arabia:*** **4** rial **6** halala ***Scandinavia:*** **3** ore

Seychelles: **5** rupee ***Siam:*** **3** att ***side of a:*** **7** obverse ***Slovakia:*** **5** haler **6** koruna ***South Africa:*** **4** rand **10** Krugerrand ***Spain:*** **4** euro **6** peseta **7** centimo ***Sri Lanka:*** **5** rupee ***stamping metal:*** **8** planchet ***Suriname:*** **6** florin, gulden **7** guilder ***Swaziland:*** **9** lilangeni ***Sweden:*** **3** ore **5** krona **8** skilling ***Switzerland:*** **5** franc **6** rappen ***Syria:*** **7** piastre ***Tanzania:*** **8** shilling ***Thailand:*** **4** baht **5** tical **6** satang ***Timor:*** **3** avo ***Tonga:*** **6** pa'anga, seniti ***Tunisia:*** **5** dinar ***Turkey:*** **4** lira, para **5** kurus ***Uganda:*** **8** shilling ***United Arab Emirates:*** **6** dirham ***United Kingdom:*** see **Great Britain** ***United States:*** **4** dime **5** penny **6** dollar, nickel **7** quarter **10** half-dollar ***Uruguay:*** **4** peso **9** centesimo ***Vatican City:*** **4** lira ***Venezuela:*** **7** bolivar ***Virgin Islands:*** **3** bit ***Zambia:*** **5** ngwee **6** kwacha

coinage 7 new word **8** creation, currency **9** invention, neologism **10** brainchild **11** contrivance

coincide 4 jibe **5** agree, equal, match, tally **6** accord, concur, square **7** comport, conform **8** dovetail **9** harmonize **10** correspond

coincident 7 similar **9** consonant **10** concurrent **11** concomitant, synchronous **12** accompanying, contemporary, simultaneous

coincidentally 8 by chance, together **12** accidentally, concurrently, fortuitously

coin-shaped 8 nummular

col 4 pass **5** ridge **6** saddle

____ colada 4 piña

colander's cousin 5 sieve **6** sifter **8** strainer

cold ____ 3 war **4** call, cash, cuts, feet, fish, sore, wave **5** cream, frame, front, patch, steel, sweat, water **6** turkey **7** comfort, storage **8** shoulder

cold 3 icy, raw **4** cool, dead, iced **5** aloof, chill, crisp, frore, gelid, nippy, polar **6** arctic, biting, chilly, frigid, frosty, frozen, wintry **7** bracing, glacial, shivery **8** chilling, comatose, freezing, lifeless **11** emotionless, passionless, unconscious, unemotional **12** unresponsive ***combining form:*** **4** cryo, kryo ***common:*** **6** coryza ***symptom:*** **5** cough, fever **6** sneeze **7** catarrh

cold-blooded 5 cruel **6** brutal **7** callous **8** hardened, obdurate, pitiless, ruthless **9** heartless, impassive, unfeeling **10** hard-boiled, impersonal **11** ectothermic, emotionless, hard-hearted **12** matter-of-fact, stonyhearted **13** dispassionate, unimpassioned

cold feet 4 fear **5** alarm, doubt, dread, panic, worry **6** dismay, fright, terror **7** anxiety, jitters **8** timidity **9** cowardice **11** trepidation **12** apprehension

coldhearted see **cold-blooded**

cold-shoulder 3 cut **4** snub **6** ignore, slight **9** ostracize

cold storage 8 abeyance, dormancy **10** quiescence, suspension **12** intermission, interruption

cole 4 kale, rape **7** cabbage **8** brassica, broccoli, kohlrabi **11** cauliflower

Coleridge poem 9 Dejection, Kubla Khan **10** Christabel

Colette character 4 Gigi **5** Chéri **8** Claudine

colewort 4 kale **7** cabbage

colic 5 gripe **9** bellyache **11** stomachache **12** collywobbles

coliseum 4 bowl **5** arena, stade **6** circus **7** stadium

collaborate 6 team up **7** collude **8** conspire **9** cooperate

collaborator 4 ally **6** helper **7** abettor, partner, traitor **8** coworker, henchman, quisling **9** accessory, assistant, associate, auxiliary, colleague **10** accomplice **11** confederate, conspirator

collapse 4 cave, drop, fail, ruin **5** break, crash, plotz, smash, wreck **6** buckle, cave in, fold up **7** breakup, crack-up, crumple, debacle, deflate, failure, founder, give out, give way, pass out, shatter, smashup, succumb **8** condense, downfall **9** breakdown, cataclysm, fall apart, ruination **10** disruption **11** catastrophe, destruction, prostration **12** disintegrate

collar 3 bag, nab **4** grab, hook, nail, take **5** catch, seize **6** arrest, secure **7** capture **9** apprehend ***armor:*** **6** gorget ***boy's:*** **4** Eton ***chain:*** **4** torc **6** torque ***jeweled:*** **8** carcanet ***lace-edged:*** **6** rebato ***metal:*** **4** torc **6** torque ***pleated:*** **4** ruff

collarbone 8 clavicle

collate 5 group, order **7** arrange, collect, compare, compile **8** assemble, contrast, organize **9** integrate

collateral 4 bond **6** allied, lineal, pledge, surety **7** cognate, kindred, oblique, related, subject **8** indirect, parallel, security **9** accessory, ancillary, attendant, auxiliary, dependent, secondary, tributary **10** coincident, coordinate, reciprocal, subsidiary **11** concomitant, subordinate, subservient **12** accompanying, confirmatory, contributory **13** complementary, corresponding, corroborative

colleague 4 aide **6** cohort, fellow, helper **7** partner **8** confrere, coworker, teammate **9** assistant, associate, companion **10** compatriot **11** confederate **12** collaborator

collect 4 draw **5** amass, glean, group, infer,

raise **6** deduce, derive, gather, muster, prayer **7** build up, compile, compose, convene, dispose, marshal, round up **8** assemble, conclude, converge **10** accumulate, congregate, rendezvous

collected 4 calm, cool **5** quiet, still **6** poised, serene **7** assured **8** complete, composed, sanguine, tranquil **9** assembled, confident, unruffled **11** unflappable **13** imperturbable, self-possessed

collection 3 ana, kit, lot **4** band, bevy, crew, olio, ruck **5** bunch, crowd, hoard, trove **6** medley, muster **7** cluster, variety **8** assembly, caboodle **9** aggregate, anthology, congeries, gathering, stockpile **10** assemblage, assortment, cumulation, miscellany **11** aggregation **12** accumulation, congregation **13** agglomeration ***miscellaneous:* 4** hash, olio **6** jumble, medley **7** mélange, mixture **8** mishmash, pastiche **9** potpourri **10** hodgepodge, hotchpotch, salmagundi **11** olla podrida ***of anecdotes:* 3** ana ***of animals:* 3** zoo **9** menagerie ***of artistic works:* 6** museum **7** gallery ***of clothes:* 8** wardrobe ***of dried plants:* 9** herbarium ***of literary pieces:* 8** analects **9** anthology ***of reports:* 4** file **7** dossier ***of trinkets:* 10** bijouterie

collective 5 joint **7** commune, kibbutz, kolkhoz **11** cooperative

collector *of bird's eggs:* 8 oologist ***of books:* 11** bibliophile ***of coins:* 11** numismatist ***of fares:* 9** conductor ***of phonograph records:* 10** discophile ***of stamps:* 11** philatelist

colleen 4 girl, lass **6** maiden ***country:* 4** Eire, Erin **7** Ireland

college 9 alma mater ***building:* 3** gym, lab **4** dorm, hall ***campus area:* 4** quad **10** quadrangle ***class meeting:* 3** lab **7** lecture, seminar **8** tutorial, workshop ***climber:* 3** ivy ***degree:* 2** AA, AB, BA, BD, BS, CE, DD, MA, MM, MS **3** BLS, DST, MBA, MEd, MFA, MLS, PhD **5** LittD ***graduate:* 6** alumna, alumni (plural) **7** alumnae (plural), alumnus ***official:* 4** dean **5** prexy **6** bursar, regent **7** proctor, provost **9** registrar ***oldest in U.S.:* 7** Harvard ***oldest women's in U.S.:* 12** Mount Holyoke ***relating to:* 8** academic **10** collegiate ***social group:* 4** frat **8** sorority **10** fraternity ***song:* 9** alma mater ***student class:* 4** soph **5** frosh **6** junior, senior **8** freshman **9** sophomore ***teacher:* 3** don **4** prof **8** academic **9** professor ***term:* 7** quarter, session **8** semester **9** trimester ***VIP:* 4** BMOC ***woman:* 4** coed

college team *Air Force:* 7 Falcons ***Alabama:* 11** Crimson Tide ***Arizona:* 8** Wildcats ***Arizona State:* 9** Sun Devils ***Arkansas:* 10** Razorbacks ***Arkansas State:* 7** Indians ***Army:* 6** Cadets ***Auburn:* 6** Tigers ***Baylor:* 5** Bears ***Boston College:* 6** Eagles ***Boston University:* 8** Terriers ***Brigham Young:* 7** Cougars ***Brown:* 5** Bears ***California:* 11** Golden Bears ***Central Michigan:* 9** Chippewas ***Cincinnati:* 8** Bearcats ***Citadel:* 8** Bulldogs ***Clemson:* 6** Tigers ***Colgate:* 10** Red Raiders ***Colorado:* 9** Buffaloes ***Colorado State:* 4** Rams ***Columbia:* 5** Lions ***Connecticut:* 7** Huskies ***Cornell:* 6** Big Red ***Dartmouth:* 8** Big Green ***Davidson:* 8** Wildcats ***Delaware State:* 7** Hornets ***Drake:* 8** Bulldogs ***Duke:* 10** Blue Devils ***Eastern Kentucky:* 8** Colonels ***Eastern Michigan:* 6** Eagles ***Florida:* 6** Gators ***Florida State:* 9** Seminoles ***Fresno State:* 8** Bulldogs ***Furman:* 8** Palidans ***Georgia:* 8** Bulldogs ***Georgia Tech:* 13** Yellow Jackets ***Harvard:* 7** Crimson ***Hawaii:* 15** Rainbow Warriors ***Holy Cross:* 9** Crusaders ***Houston:* 7** Cougars ***Howard:* 6** Bisons ***Idaho:* 7** Vandals ***Idaho State:* 7** Bengals ***Illinois:* 14** Fighting Illini ***Illinois State:* 8** Redbirds ***Indiana:* 8** Hoosiers ***Indiana State:* 9** Sycamores ***Iowa:* 8** Hawkeyes ***Iowa State:* 8** Cyclones ***Kansas:* 8** Jayhawks ***Kansas State:* 8** Wildcats ***Kent State:* 13** Golden Flashes ***Kentucky:* 8** Wildcats ***Lehigh:* 9** Engineers ***Louisiana State:* 6** Tigers ***Louisiana Tech:* 8** Bulldogs ***Maine:* 10** Black Bears ***Maryland:* 5** Terps **9** Terrapins ***Massachusetts:* 9** Minutemen ***Miami (Florida):* 10** Hurricanes ***Miami (Ohio):* 8** Redskins ***Michigan:* 10** Wolverines ***Michigan State:* 8** Spartans ***Minnesota:* 7** Gophers ***Mississippi:* 6** Rebels ***Mississippi State:* 8** Bulldogs ***Missouri:* 6** Tigers ***Montana:* 9** Grizzlies ***Montana State:* 7** Bobcats ***Navy:* 10** Midshipmen ***Nebraska:* 11** Cornhuskers ***Nevada:* 6** Rebels **8** Wolfpack ***New Hampshire:* 8** Wildcats ***New Mexico:* 5** Lobos ***New Mexico State:* 6** Aggies ***North Carolina:* 8** Tar Heels ***North Carolina State:* 8** Wolfpack ***Northeastern:* 7** Huskies ***Northwestern:* 8** Wildcats ***Notre Dame:* 13** Fighting Irish ***Ohio State:* 8** Buckeyes ***Ohio University:* 7** Bobcats ***Oklahoma:* 7** Sooners ***Oklahoma State:* 7** Cowboys ***Oregon:* 5** Ducks ***Oregon State:* 7** Beavers ***Pennsylvania:* 7** Quakers ***Pennsylvania State:* 12** Nittany Lions ***Pittsburgh:* 8** Panthers ***Princeton:* 6** Tigers ***Purdue:* 12** Boilermakers ***Rhode Island:* 4** Rams ***Rice:* 4** Owls ***Rutgers:* 14** Scarlet Knights ***San Diego State:* 6** Aztecs ***San Jose State:* 8** Spartans ***South Carolina:* 9** Gamecocks ***South Carolina State:* 8** Bulldogs ***Southern California:***

7 Trojans ***Southern Illinois:*** **7** Salukis ***Southern Methodist:*** **8** Mustangs ***Stanford:*** **9** Cardinals ***Syracuse:*** **9** Orangemen ***Temple:*** **4** Owls ***Tennessee:*** **10** Volunteers ***Tennessee State:*** **6** Tigers ***Tennessee Tech:*** **12** Golden Eagles ***Texas:*** **9** Longhorns ***Texas A&M:*** **6** Aggies ***Texas Christian:*** **11** Horned Frogs ***Texas Southern:*** **6** Tigers ***Texas Tech:*** **10** Red Raiders ***Toledo:*** **7** Rockets ***Tulane:*** **9** Green Wave ***UCLA:*** **6** Bruins ***UNLV:*** **12** Runnin' Rebels ***Utah:*** **4** Utes ***Utah State:*** **6** Aggies ***Vanderbilt:*** **10** Commodores ***Villanova:*** **8** Wildcats ***Virginia:*** **9** Cavaliers ***VMI:*** **7** Keydets ***VPI:*** **8** Gobblers ***Wake Forest:*** **12** Demon Deacons ***Washington:*** **7** Huskies ***Washington State:*** **7** Cougars ***West Virginia:*** **12** Mountaineers ***William & Mary:*** **5** Tribe ***Wisconsin:*** **7** Badgers ***Wyoming:*** **7** Cowboys ***Yale:*** **4** Elis **8** Bulldogs

collide 3 hit, ram **4** bump **5** clash, crash, smash **6** impact, strike **7** impinge **8** conflict

collier 4 ship **5** miner **6** choker

Collins novel 9 Moonstone (The) **12** Woman in White (The)

collision 4 bump, jolt **5** clash, crash, shock, smash, wreck **6** impact **7** crack-up, smashup **10** concussion

collocate 7 arrange **8** position **9** juxtapose

collogue 6 confer, huddle, parley, powwow **7** consult

colloid 3 gel, sol **4** agar **7** mixture **8** hydrogel, hydrosol

colloquial 6 casual, vulgar **7** demotic **8** familiar, informal **9** idiomatic **10** vernacular

colloquium 5 forum **7** palaver, seminar **9** symposium **10** conference, roundtable

colloquy 4 chat, talk **5** forum **6** debate, parley **7** palaver, seminar **8** dialogue **9** symposium **10** conference, discussion, roundtable **12** conversation **13** confabulation

collude 4 plot **6** devise, scheme **7** connive **8** conspire, contrive, intrigue **9** machinate

collusion 4 plot **8** intrigue, skin game **10** conspiracy

collywobbles 5 colic, gripe **9** bellyache **11** stomachache

Colombia *capital:* 6 Bogotá ***city:*** **4** Cali **6** Ibagué **8** Medellín **9** Cartagena **12** Barranquilla ***language:*** **7** Spanish ***liberator:*** **7** Bolivar (Simón) ***monetary unit:*** **4** peso ***mountain, range:*** **5** Andes, Chita **6** Puracé, Tolima **9** Cristóbal ***neighbor:*** **4** Peru **6** Brazil, Panama **7** Ecuador **9** Venezuela ***river:*** **6** Chauca **7** Orinoco **9** Magdalena ***sea:*** **9** Caribbean

Colonel Blimp 4 fogy, Tory **5** fogey **6** fossil **7** old fogy **8** mossback, old fogey **10** fuddy-duddy **11** reactionary

colonist 6 émigré, nester **7** evacuee, pilgrim, pioneer, settler **8** emigrant, squatter **9** immigrant **10** expatriate **11** homesteader

colonnade 4 stoa **9** peristyle

colony 7 outpost **9** satellite **10** settlement

color 3 dun, dye, hue, red, tan **4** aqua, blue, cast, ecru, glow, gold, gray, grey, jade, lime, navy, pink, puce, rose, teal, tint, tone **5** amber, azure, beige, belie, black, blush, brown, coral, ebony, flush, green, hazel, henna, ivory, khaki, lilac, mauve, ocher, ochre, olive, paint, peach, rouge, shade, stain, taupe, tinge, umber **6** auburn, bronze, canary, copper, indigo, maroon, orange, purple, redden, salmon, sienna, silver, violet, yellow **7** crimson, emerald, magenta, pigment, saffron, scarlet **8** chestnut, dyestuff, lavender, tincture **9** embellish, embroider, turquoise, vermilion **10** aquamarine, exaggerate, vermillion **12** pigmentation ***band:*** **5** facia, vitta **6** fascia ***combining form:*** **5** chrom **6** chromo **7** chromat **8** chromato ***primary:*** **3** red **4** blue **6** yellow ***relating to:*** **9** chromatic ***secondary:*** **5** green **6** orange, purple ***soft:*** **6** pastel

Colorado *capital:* 6 Denver ***city:*** **4** Vail **5** Aspen **6** Aurora, Pueblo **7** Boulder **8** Lakewood **11** Fort Collins ***college, university:*** **5** Regis **9** Fort Lewis ***mountain, range:*** **5** Longs (Peak), Pikes (Peak), Rocky **6** Elbert **7** Rockies ***nickname:*** **10** Centennial (State) ***park:*** **9** Mesa Verde ***river:*** **8** Arkansas **9** Rio Grande ***state bird:*** **11** lark bunting ***state flower:*** **9** columbine ***state tree:*** **10** blue spruce

colorant 3 dye **5** stain **7** pigment **8** dyestuff, tincture

colored 6 biased, warped **8** one-sided, partisan **9** jaundiced **10** prejudiced **11** tendentious

colorful 3 gay **5** gaudy, showy, vivid **6** bright, flashy, florid, garish, motley **7** splashy

coloring 4 cast, tint **5** front, tinge **6** facade, nuance **7** pigment **8** overtone **10** camouflage, complexion **12** embroidering **13** embellishment

colorless 3 wan **4** ashy, drab, dull, flat, pale **5** ashen, pasty, prosy, waxen, white **6** albino, doughy, pallid **7** insipid, neutral, prosaic **8** abstract, blanched, bleached **10** achromatic, lackluster

Color Purple author 6 Walker (Alice)

colossal 4 huge, vast **7** immense, mammoth, massive, titanic **8** enormous, gigantic, towering **9** cyclopean, monstrous **10** gargan-

tuan, stupendous **11** astonishing, elephantine
colossus 5 giant, titan **6** statue **7** goliath, mammoth, monster **8** behemoth **9** leviathan
Colossus of ____ 6 Rhodes
colporteur 10 evangelist, missionary **12** propagandist
colt 4 foal, tyro **6** novice, rookie **8** beginner, freshman, neophyte, newcomer **9** fledgling **10** tenderfoot
coltish 6 frisky, impish **7** playful **10** frolicsome
Columbine *beloved:* 9 Harlequin ***father:* 9** Pantaloon
columbium symbol 2 Cb
Columbus, Christopher *birthplace:* 5 Genoa ***patron:* 8** Isabella **9** Ferdinand ***ship:* 4** Niña **5** Pinta **10** Santa Maria ***son:* 5** Diego ***starting point:* 5** Palos
column 3 row **4** pier **5** shaft, stela **6** pillar **7** obelisk **8** pilaster ***angle:* 5** arris ***base:* 4** dado, ordo **5** socle **6** plinth **9** stylobate ***bulge:* 7** entasis ***female figure:* 8** caryatid ***male figure:* 5** atlas **7** telamon **8** atlantes (plural) ***style:* 5** Doric, Ionic **10** Corinthian ***top:* 7** capital **8** chapiter
coma 6 stupor, torpor **8** blackout, hebetude, lethargy **9** lassitude
comate 3 pal **4** chum **5** buddy, crony **7** comrade, partner **9** associate, colleague, companion
comatose 5 dopey **6** stupid, torpid **7** out cold **8** sluggish **9** lethargic **10** insensible **11** unconscious
comb 4 rake, sift, sort **5** crest, curry, probe, scour, sweep, tease **6** search, winnow **7** ransack **8** untangle **10** straighten **11** investigate
combat 3 war **4** buck, duel, fray **5** fight, repel **6** action, battle, oppose, resist, strife **7** contend, contest, dispute **8** skirmish, struggle **9** withstand **11** controversy
combatant 7 battler, fighter, soldier, warrior **8** militant, opponent **9** adversary, aggressor, assailant, contender, disputant, mercenary **10** antagonist, challenger, competitor, contestant **11** belligerent
combative 6 feisty **7** scrappy, warlike **8** militant **9** agonistic, bellicose, truculent **10** aggressive, pugnacious **11** belligerent, contentious, quarrelsome **12** disputatious, militaristic
combativeness 9 pugnacity **10** aggression, truculence **11** bellicosity **12** belligerence
combe 4 dale, dell, glen, vale **6** dingle, valley
combination 3 mix **4** bloc, pool, ring **5** blend, union **6** fusion, hookup, merger **7** melding, merging **8** alliance **9** aggregate, coalition, composite, synthesis **10** connection **11** affiliation, association, conjunction, partnership, unification **13** consolidation
combine 3 add, mix, wed **4** band, bloc, fuse, join, link, pool, ring **5** blend, chain, group, marry, merge, trust, unify, union, unite **6** cartel, league, mingle **7** bracket, conjoin, connect, faction **8** coadjute, coalesce **9** associate, coalition, commingle, cooperate, integrate, syndicate **10** amalgamate **11** consolidate, incorporate **12** conglomerate ***Japanese:* 8** keiretsu, zaibatsu ***Korean:* 7** chaebol, jaebeol
combined action 7 synergy **9** synergism
combo 4 band, trio **5** group, nonet, octet **6** septet, sextet **7** quartet, quintet **8** ensemble
combust 4 burn **6** ignite, kindle **10** incinerate
combustible 4 edgy, fuel **8** burnable, volatile **9** excitable, flammable, ignitable **11** inflammable ***material:* 3** gas, oil **4** coal, peat, wood **6** tinder
combustion 4 riot **7** burning **8** eruption, ignition, kindling **9** explosion, oxidation **13** thermogenesis
come 4 flow, hail, stem **5** arise, issue, occur **6** arrive, derive, show up, spring, turn up **7** advance, emanate, proceed **8** approach **9** originate ***a cropper:* 4** fail, fall ***across:* 4** find, meet **8** discover **9** encounter ***apart:* 12** disintegrate ***at:* 6** attack ***away:* 5** leave **6** depart ***before:* 7** precede ***clean:* 7** confess ***forth:* 5** issue **6** appear, emerge ***forward:* 7** advance **9** volunteer ***into:* 5** enter **7** acquire ***near:* 5** verge **8** approach ***round:* 5** rally **7** get well, recover ***to pass:* 5** occur **6** happen ***up:* 5** arise ***upon:* 4** find, meet **8** discover **9** encounter
comeback 5 rally **6** answer, retort, return **7** rebound, revival, riposte **8** rebuttal, recovery, repartee, response **11** improvement **12** counterclaim, recuperation
come by 4 call **5** pop in, visit **6** drop in, look in **7** acquire, collect, inherit
comedian 3 wag, wit **4** card **5** clown, comic, droll, joker **6** jester **7** farceur **8** funnyman, humorist, jokester, quipster **11** entertainer ***famous:* 3** Cho (Margaret), Fey (Tina), Nye (Louis) **4** Ball (Lucille), Chan (Jackie), Coca (Imogene), Cook (Peter), Dana (Bill), Foxx (Redd), Hope (Bob), Idle (Eric), Kaye (Danny), Leno (Jay), Marx (Chico, Groucho, Gummo, Harpo, Zeppo), Rock (Chris), Sahl (Mort), Wise (Ernie), Wood (Victoria) **5** Abbot (Bud), Allen (Gracie, Steve, Woody), Benny (Jack), Berle (Milton), Borge (Victor), Bruce (Lenny), Burns (George), Candy (John), Chase (Chevy),

Cosby (Bill), David (Larry), Guest (Christopher), Hardy (Oliver), Lewis (Jerry), Lloyd (Harold), Lopez (George), Maher (Bill), Meara (Anne), Moore (Dudley), Myers (Mike), Palin (Michael), Pearl (Minnie), Pryor (Richard), Rogen (Seth), Sales (Soupy) **6** Caesar (Sid), Carell (Steve), Carlin (George), Carrey (Jim), Carson (Johnny), Cleese (John), DeVito (Danny), Diller (Phyllis), Fields (W. C.), Gosden (Freeman), Izzard (Eddie), Keaton (Buster), Knotts (Don), Kovacs (Ernie), Laurel (Stan), Lehrer (Tom), Lemmon (Jack), Little (Rich), Martin (Dean, Steve), Midler (Bette), Murphy (Eddie), Murray (Bill), O'Brien (Conan), Radner (Gilda), Reiner (Carl), Rivers (Joan), Rogers (Will), Thomas (Danny), Tomlin (Lily), Turpin (Ben), Wayans (Damon, Keenan Ivory, Marlon, Shawn) **7** Aykroyd (Dan), Belushi (Jim, John), Buttons (Red), Burnett (Carol), Chaplin (Charlie), Colbert (Stephen), Crystal (Billy), Durante (Jimmy), Feldman (Marty), Freberg (Stan), Gleason (Jackie), Grammer (Kelsey), Hackett (Buddy), Keillor (Garrison), Matthau (Walter), Moranis (Rick), Newhart (Bob), Nielsen (Leslie), Paulsen (Pat), Rickles (Don), Russell (Mark), Sandler (Adam), Sedaris (Amy, David), Sellers (Peter), Silvers (Phil), Skelton (Red), Stewart (Jon), Stiller (Ben, Jerry), Winters (Jonathan) **8** Atkinson (Rowan), Costello (Lou), Goldberg (Whoopi), Grenfell (Joyce), Mulligan (Spike), O'Donnell (Rosie), Seinfeld (Jerry), Smothers (Dick, Tom), Williams (Robin), Youngman (Henny) **9** Carrot Top, DeGeneres (Ellen), Leguizamo (John), Letterman (David), Morecambe (Eric) **10** Poundstone (Paula) **11** Dangerfield (Rodney)

comedo **9** blackhead

comedown **4** dive, fall, ruin **5** crash **7** decline, descent, failure, setback **8** collapse **9** ruination

come down with **3** get **5** catch **7** develop **8** contract

comedy **5** farce, humor **6** levity **8** drollery, hilarity **9** drollness, slapstick, wittiness *show:* **3** SNL **6** Hee-Haw **7** Laugh-In **9** Daily Show (The)

come forth **4** grow, rise **5** arise **6** appear **7** emanate

come in **5** enter, reply **6** answer **7** respond

comely **4** fair **5** bonny, sonsy **6** lovely, pretty, proper, sonsie **7** winsome **8** becoming, decorous, handsome, pleasing **9** beauteous, beautiful, befitting **10** attractive **11** good-looking

come off **4** fare, seem **5** click, occur **6** appear, go over, happen, pan out **7** develop, succeed **8** prove out **9** transpire

come-on **4** bait, lure, trap **5** decoy, snare **9** seduction **10** allurement, enticement, inducement, invitation, temptation **12** blandishment, inveiglement, solicitation

come out **4** leak **5** break, debut, end up **6** emerge **9** transpire

come out with **3** say **4** tell **5** state, utter **6** report **7** declare, deliver, publish, release **8** announce, proclaim

comestible **6** edible **7** eatable **8** esculent

comestibles **4** feed, food **6** viands **7** edibles **8** victuals **9** provender **10** provisions

comet **4** West **7** Halley's **8** Hale-Bopp, Kohoutek, McNaught **9** Hyakutake

come through **6** chip in, endure **7** pitch in, prevail, survive **8** transmit **10** contribute

come together **4** mass, meet **5** merge, swarm **6** gather, huddle **7** cluster, collect, combine, convene **8** assemble, converge **10** congregate

come upon **4** find **7** run into, uncover, unearth **8** bump into, discover, trip over **9** encounter, run across

comeuppance **3** due **5** lumps **7** deserts

comfort **3** aid **4** ease, help **5** cheer **6** assist, buck up, luxury, relief, solace, soothe, succor **7** amenity, cheer up, console, relieve, support **8** reassure, sympathy **10** assistance, sympathize **11** commiserate, consolation, contentment

comfortable **4** cozy, easy, homy, snug, soft **5** ample, cushy, homey, roomy **7** content, easeful, restful, well-off **8** adequate, homelike, pleasant, pleasing, spacious, well-to-do **9** agreeable, satisfied, well-fixed **10** commodious, prosperous, sufficient, well-heeled **11** substantial **12** satisfactory

comforter **4** down, pouf, puff **5** duvet, quilt **9** eiderdown

comfy **4** cozy, homy, snug **5** cushy, homey

comic **3** wag, wit **5** antic, droll, funny, joker **6** jester **7** risible **8** comedian, farcical, funnyman, humorist, jokester, quipster **9** laughable, ludicrous **10** ridiculous

comical **4** zany **5** droll, funny, goofy, silly **6** absurd **7** amusing, foolish, risible, waggish **8** farcical **9** laughable, ludicrous **10** ridiculous

comic strip **4** Pogo, Shoe **5** Hazel, Henry, Nancy **6** Archie, Popeye **7** Blondie, Dilbert, Far Side (The), Peanuts **8** Alley Oop, Andy Capp, Garfield, Krazy Kat, Li'l Abner, Superman **9** Betty Boop, Dick Tracy, Marmaduke, Mary Worth, Spider-Man, Yellow Kid

(The) **10** Doonesbury, Joe Palooka, Little Nemo **11** Bloom County, Brenda Starr, Flash Gordon, Hogan's Alley, Mutt and Jeff, Rex Morgan M.D., Steve Canyon **12** Beetle Bailey **13** Captain Marvel, Gasoline Alley, Prince Valiant ***character:*** **3** Arn, Jon, Kim, Liz, Owl, Roz **4** Asok, Elmo, Flip, Herb, Irma, Lizz, Loon, Lucy, Odie, Opus, Otto, Phil, Rube, Tess, Thun, Zero **5** Aleta, Alice, Bella, Betty, Carol, Cosmo, Foozy, Honey, Itchy, Lacey, Linus, Mammy, Ooola, Pappy, Patty, Percy, Phred, Plato, Porky, Rerun, Rocky, Rollo, Sally, Shmoo, Spike, Wally **6** Albert, Arlene, Belfry, Cookie, Doc Boy, Dottie, Frieda, Joanie, Junior, Lt. Flap, Lt. Fuzz, Marcie, Nermal, Pig-Pen, Reggie, Skyler, Sluggo, Snoopy, Vultan, Zipper, Zonker **7** Aunt May, Boopsie, Chalkie, Churchy, Dagwood, Dithers, Flattop, Florrie, Jughead, Mr. Butts, Mumbles, Phyllis, Portnoy, Skeezix, Tootsie, Wolf Gal **8** Black Cat, B. O. Plenty, Bull Pupp, Daisy Mae, Dr. Sivana, June Gale, Lana Lang, Lois Lane, Olive Oyl, Pete Ross, Shroeder, Veronica **9** Alexander, Brilliant, Chip Gizmo, Clark Kent, Dale Arden, Diet Smith, Gwen Stacy, Pat Patton, Pruneface, Uncle Duke **10** Aunt Fritzi, Betty Brant, Bill the Cat, Cutter John, Dragon Lady, Hans Zarkov, Hodge-Podge, Jimmy Olsen, Joe Btfsplk, Louise Lugg, Marryin' Sam, Miss Buxley, Perry White, Sam Catchem, Scott Sloan, Sgt. Snorkel, Walt Wallet **11** Happy Easter, Harry Osborn, Ignatz Mouse, Lola Granola, Mickey Dugan, Peter Parker, Steve Dallas, Summer Olson **12** Charlie Brown, Felicia Hardy, Gen. Halftrack, Gravel Gertie

coming **3** due **4** next **5** fated, onset **6** advent, future **7** arrival, ensuing, nearing **8** approach, expected, foreseen, imminent **9** following, impending **11** approaching ***forth:*** **7** issuant

comity **5** amity **7** concord, harmony **8** goodwill **10** friendship **11** benevolence, camaraderie **12** friendliness

comma **4** lull **5** pause **8** interval

command **3** bid **4** rule, sway **5** order **6** adjure, behest, charge, compel, direct, enjoin **7** bidding, conduct, control, dictate, mandate, mastery, precept **9** authority, direction, directive, expertise, ordinance **10** domination, imperative, injunction **11** instruction **12** jurisdiction ***to go:*** **4** mush **6** avaunt, begone **7** giddyap, giddyup ***to stop:*** **4** whoa **5** avast

commandeer **4** take **5** annex, seize, usurp **6** assume, hijack **7** preempt **8** accroach, arrogate **9** conscript, sequester **10** confiscate **11** appropriate, expropriate, requisition

commander **4** boss, head **6** honcho, leader, master **7** captain, general, headman, officer

commandment **3** law **4** fiat, rule **5** edict, order **6** decree **7** mitzvah, precept, statute

commedia dell' ____ **4** arte

comme il faut **6** decent, polite, proper, seemly **7** correct **8** becoming, decorous, suitable

commemorate **4** keep **7** observe **8** eulogize, monument **9** celebrate, solemnize **11** memorialize **13** monumentalize

commemorative **8** memorial **10** dedicatory **11** celebratory

commence **5** begin, start **6** launch, set out **7** kick off **8** embark on, initiate **10** embark upon, inaugurate

commencement **4** dawn **5** birth, onset, start **6** outset **7** dawning, genesis, opening **9** beginning, inception **10** graduation **12** inauguration

commend **4** hail, laud **5** extol **6** commit, kudize, praise, salute, tender **7** acclaim, applaud, approve, consign, entrust **8** hand over, relegate, turn over **10** compliment

commendable **6** worthy **8** laudable **9** admirable, deserving, estimable, meritable, venerable **10** creditable **11** meritorious **12** praiseworthy

commensurable see **commensurate**

commensurate **4** even **5** equal **10** comparable **11** coextensive **12** proportional **13** corresponding, proportionate

comment **4** note **5** opine **6** remark **7** mention, observe **8** critique, point out **9** criticism, interject **10** animadvert **11** observation **12** obiter dictum

commentary **5** gloss **6** review **8** analysis, critique, exegesis **9** editorial, narration, voice-over **10** annotation, exposition **11** explanation, observation **12** appreciation, obiter dictum

commerce **5** trade **7** contact, traffic **8** business, congress, dealings, exchange, industry **9** communion **11** interchange **13** communication

commercial **2** ad **6** advert **8** economic **10** mercantile **13** advertisement

commie **3** Red **5** pinko **6** bolshy **7** bolshie **9** Bolshevik

commination **5** curse **8** anathema **10** accusation, execration **11** imprecation, malediction **12** denunciation

commingle **3** mix **4** meld **5** blend, merge, unify **8** compound, intermix **9** integrate **10** amalgamate

comminute 4 bray **5** crush, grind **9** granulate, pulverize
commiserate 4 pity **7** condole, feel for **9** empathize **10** sympathize **13** compassionate
commiseration 4 pity, ruth **7** empathy **8** sympathy **10** compassion, condolence
commission 3 bid, fee **4** name **5** board, order, panel **6** agency, assign, charge, enable, engage, enjoin, enlist **7** appoint, command, council, empower, license, warrant **8** accredit, delegate, deputize **9** authorize, designate **10** delegation, deputation, percentage **11** certificate
commit 4 bind **5** allot, grant, refer **6** assign, convey, invest, ordain, pledge, record, reveal **7** achieve, consign, deposit, entrust, execute, perform, promise, pull off, trustee **8** allocate, carry out, hand over, obligate, relegate, turn over **10** accomplish, perpetrate
commitment 3 vow **4** bond, deal, duty **6** charge, devoir, pledge **7** promise **8** contract **9** agreement, assurance, guarantee **10** obligation **11** undertaking
committal see **commitment**
commixture 5 blend **6** fusion **7** amalgam, melange **8** compound, mingling **9** composite
commodious 4 wide **5** ample, roomy **8** spacious **9** capacious, expansive, luxurious **11** comfortable
commodities 5 goods, items, wares **8** articles, products **9** vendibles **11** merchandise
common 4 park **5** banal, daily, joint, plaza, trite, usual **6** mutual, normal, shared **7** general, generic, prosaic, regular, routine, typical **8** adequate, communal, conjoint, conjunct, déclassé, everyday, familiar, frequent, habitual, ordinary, standard, workaday **9** customary, prevalent, tolerable, universal **10** collective, pedestrian, prevailing, unexciting, widespread **12** conventional, run-of-the-mill, satisfactory **13** unexceptional, uninteresting
commonalty 3 mob **5** plebs **6** masses, people, plebes, public, rabble **7** commune **8** populace **9** hoi polloi, multitude, plebeians **11** proletariat, rank and file, third estate
commoners see **commonalty**
commonplace 5 banal, stale, tired, trite, usual **6** cliché, normal, truism **7** bromide, clichéd, humdrum, mundane, obvious, prosaic, regular, routine, typical **8** banality, bromidic, chestnut, everyday, habitual, mediocre, ordinary, well-worn, workaday **9** hackneyed, platitude, prevalent **10** pedestrian, shibboleth, stereotype, uneventful **11** stereotyped **12** conventional, run-of-the-mill, unremarkable **13** stereotypical, unexceptional, uninteresting
common sense 6 wisdom **8** judgment, prudence **10** shrewdness
Common Sense author 5 Paine (Thomas)
commotion 3 ado, din, row **4** flap, fuss, moil, riot, stew, stir, to-do **5** hoo-ha, storm, whirl **6** bustle, clamor, dither, flurry, fracas, furore, hoo-hah, hoopla, hubbub, hurrah, lather, outcry, pother, racket, ruckus, rumpus, shindy, tumult, uproar, upturn **7** ferment, tempest, turmoil **8** brouhaha, foofaraw **9** agitation, confusion **10** convulsion, hullabaloo, hurly-burly, turbulence **11** pandemonium
commove 5 rouse **6** excite **7** agitate, inspire, provoke **9** electrify, galvanize, stimulate
communal 5 civil, joint **6** common, mutual, public, shared **10** collective **11** socialistic
commune 10 collective ***Israeli:*** **7** kibbutz ***Russian:*** **3** mir **7** kolkhoz
communicable 8 catching **10** contagious, infectious **13** transmissible, transmittable
communicate 4 tell **6** convey, impart, inform, pass on, relate, reveal, signal **7** connect, contact, divulge **8** disclose, transmit **9** make known
communication 4 talk **7** contact, message, missive, talking **8** converse, exchange **9** directive **10** discussing, discussion **11** interchange, intercourse **12** conversation ***means:*** **2** IM, TV **3** Web **4** drum, mail, note **5** e-mail, media, phone, radio **6** letter, medium, pigeon, speech **8** Internet **9** telegraph, telephone **10** television
communications code word 4 Alfa, Echo, Golf, Kilo, Lima, Mike, Papa, Xray, Zulu **5** Alpha, Bravo, Delta, Hotel, India, Oscar, Romeo, Tango **6** Quebec, Sierra, Victor, Yankee **7** Charlie, Foxtrot, Juliett, Uniform, Whiskey **8** November
communicative 5 vocal **6** fluent, prolix **7** verbose, voluble **8** eloquent **9** expansive, garrulous, talkative **10** articulate, expressive, loquacious
communion 7 rapport, sharing **9** Eucharist, sacrament **10** connection, fellowship ***cloth:*** **8** corporal ***cup:*** **7** chalice ***plate:*** **5** paten
communism 7 Marxism **8** Leninism **10** bolshevism **12** collectivism
Communist 3 red **5** lefty, pinko **6** bolshy, Maoist **7** bolshie, comrade, Marxist **8** Leninist **9** Bolshevik, Stalinist **10** Bolshevist, Trotskyist
Communist leader *Chinese:* 3 Mao **4** Deng **5** Jiang **8** Hu Jintao **9** Mao Zedong **10** Jiang Zemin, Mao Tse-tung **12** Deng Xiaoping **13**

Teng Hsiao-p'ing ***Cuban:*** **6** Castro (Fidel) ***Russian:*** **5** Lenin (Vladimir Ilyich) **6** Stalin (Joseph) **7** Kosygin (Aleksey), Trotsky (Leon) **8** Andropov (Yuri), Brezhnev (Leonid) **9** Chernenko (Konstantin), Gorbachev (Mikhail) **10** Khrushchev (Nikita)

community 4 town **7** enclave, society **12** neighborhood ***closed:*** **5** abbey **6** priory **7** convent, nunnery **8** cloister **9** monastery ***ecological:*** **10** biocenosis **11** biocoenosis

commute 5 alter **6** change, make up, modify, soften, travel **7** convert, curtail, shorten, shuttle **8** decrease, exchange, mitigate, transfer **9** transform, translate, transmute, transpose **10** compensate, substitute **11** interchange

Comoros *capital:* **6** Moroni ***island:*** **6** Mohéli **7** Anjouan **12** Grande Comore ***language:*** **6** Arabic, French **8** Comorian ***monetary unit:*** **5** franc ***volcano:*** **8** Karthala

compact 4 bond **5** close, dense, unify **7** bargain, bunched, crowded, pressed **8** compress, condense, contract, covenant **9** agreement, concordat **10** convention **11** concentrate, consolidate, transaction

compadre 3 pal **4** chum, mate **5** amigo, buddy, crony **6** cohort, friend **7** comrade, partner **8** confrere, sidekick, intimate **9** associate, colleague, companion

companion 3 pal **4** chum, mate **5** buddy, crony **6** cohort, escort, fellow **7** comrade, consort, partner **8** sidekick **9** associate, attendant, colleague

companionable 6 genial, social **7** affable, amiable **8** outgoing, sociable **9** agreeable, congenial, convivial **10** gregarious **11** good-natured

companionship 7 company, society **8** intimacy **10** fellowship **11** camaraderie

company 4 band, club, crew, firm, gang, team **5** corps, group, party, troop **6** circle, clique, guests, outfit, troupe **7** concern, coterie, retinue, society, visitor **8** assembly, business, ensemble, visitors **9** gathering **10** assemblage, enterprise, fellowship **11** association, camaraderie, corporation **12** congregation **13** companionship, establishment

comparable 4 akin, like **5** alike **6** agnate **7** similar, uniform **8** parallel **9** analogous **10** equivalent, homologous **12** commensurate **13** corresponding

comparative 4 near **8** relative **11** approximate

compare 5 liken, match **6** equate, relate **7** collate **8** contrast, parallel **9** correlate **10** assimilate

comparison 6 simile **7** analogy **8** affinity, contrast, likeness **9** collation, semblance **10** similarity, similitude **11** correlation, resemblance

compartment 3 bay **4** cell, nook, part, slot **5** berth, booth, niche, stall **6** alcove, carrel, locker **7** chamber, cubicle, section **8** division **9** cubbyhole **10** pigeonhole **11** subdivision

compass 3 hem **4** ring **5** ambit, field, grasp, orbit, range, reach, scope, sweep **6** bounds, circle, domain, extent, girdle, limits, radius, sphere **7** circuit, environ, purview **8** boundary, confines, environs **9** enclosure, extension, perimeter, periphery **13** circumference ***kind:*** **4** gyro **5** solar **8** magnetic ***stand:*** **8** binnacle

compassion 4 pity, ruth **5** mercy **7** charity, empathy **8** clemency, humanity, kindness, sympathy **10** condolence, humaneness **11** benevolence **13** commiseration, fellow feeling

compassionate 4 pity, warm **6** humane, tender **7** clement **8** merciful **10** benevolent, charitable, solicitous **11** commiserate, kind-hearted, softhearted, sympathetic, warm-hearted

compassionless 5 stony **7** callous **8** obdurate **9** heartless, unfeeling **11** coldblooded, hard-hearted, ironhearted **12** stonyhearted

compass point 3 ENE, ESE, NNE, NNW, SSE, SSW, WNW, WSW **4** east, west **5** north, rhumb, south **7** bearing ***Scottish:*** **4** airt

compatible 6 proper **8** suitable **9** agreeable, congenial, congruous, consonant **10** consistent, harmonious, like-minded **11** appropriate, sympathetic

compatriot 7 paesano **8** confrere **9** associate, colleague, companion

compel 4 hale, urge **5** drive, force **6** coerce, impose, oblige **7** enforce **9** constrain

compelling 4 dire **5** acute **6** cogent, crying, urgent **7** clamant, exigent, telling, weighty **8** forceful, pressing **10** convincing, persuasive **11** importunate**12** well-grounded

compendious 5 brief, pithy, short **7** compact, concise, summary **8** succinct **9** condensed **11** abbreviated

compendium 4 list **5** brief, guide **6** aperçu, digest, manual, précis, sketch, survey **7** epitome, summary **8** abstract, Baedeker, handbook, overview, syllabus, synopsis **9** anthology, guidebook, vade mecum **10** abridgment, collection, conspectus **11** abridgement, compilation, enchiridion

compensate 3 pay **5** atone, repay **6** make up, offset, pay off, redeem, set off **7** balance, guerdon, requite, satisfy **8** outweigh **9** indemnify, reimburse **10** counteract, neutralize, recompense, remunerate **11** countervail

compensation 6 amends, reward, salary **7** damages, payment, redress **8** earnings, reprisal, requital, solatium **9** atonement, indemnity, quittance, repayment **10** recompense, reparation **11** restitution **12** remuneration ***unexpected:*** **4** gift **5** bonus **8** windfall

compete 3 vie **4** spar **5** fight **6** battle, strive **7** contend, contest **8** struggle

competence 5 skill **7** ability, know-how **8** adequacy, aptitude, capacity, facility **9** expertise **10** capability **11** proficiency, sufficiency **13** qualification

competent 3 fit **4** able **5** adept **6** au fait, decent, proper **7** capable, skilled **8** adequate **9** efficient, qualified **10** proficient, sufficient **12** satisfactory

competition 4 bout, game, meet, race **5** clash, fight, match, rival **6** strife **7** contest, matchup, rivalry **8** concours, conflict, striving, struggle, tug-of-war **10** antagonism, contention, tournament

competitor 5 enemy, rival **7** entrant **8** opponent **9** adversary **10** antagonist, contestant, opposition

compile 4 edit **5** amass **6** gather, select **7** build up, collate, collect **8** assemble **9** construct **10** accumulate **11** anthologize

complacency 5 pride **7** conceit **8** smugness **10** narcissism

complacent 4 smug **6** serene **7** assured **9** conceited, confident **11** self-assured, unconcerned **13** self-confident, self-contented, self-possessed, self-satisfied

complain 3 nag **4** beef, carp, crab, fret, fuss, moan, wail **5** gripe, grump, whine **6** grouch, grouse, lament, repine, yammer **7** grizzle, grumble, protest **9** bellyache

complainer 4 crab **5** crank **6** griper, grouch **7** grouser **8** grumbler, sourpuss **10** malcontent **11** faultfinder

complaint 4 beef **5** gripe **6** grouse, lament, malady **7** ailment, disease, protest **8** disorder, sickness, syndrome **9** condition, criticism, grievance, infirmity, objection **10** affliction, allegation **12** protestation

complaisant 4 easy, mild **7** amiable, lenient **8** generous, obliging **9** agreeable, compliant, easygoing, indulgent **11** deferential, good-humored, good-natured **12** good-tempered **13** accommodating

complement 4 crew, rest **9** correlate, remainder **10** supplement **11** counterpart

complete 3 end **4** done, full, halt **5** close, ended, total, utter, whole **6** entire, finish, intact, wind up, wrap up **7** achieve, fulfill, perfect, perform, plenary **8** absolute, conclude, finalize, finished, integral, round out, thorough **9** concluded, out-and-out, terminate **10** accomplish, consummate, exhaustive, unabridged **11** categorical, unmitigated **13** thoroughgoing

completed 4 done, over **5** ended **7** through **8** done with, executed, finished **9** concluded, fulfilled **10** terminated **11** consummated **12** accomplished

completely 4 A to Z**5** fully**6** wholly **7** totally, utterly **8** entirely **9** inside out, up and down **10** thoroughly

completion 3 end **6** finish, windup, wrap-up **8** fruition **10** conclusion

complex 6 daedal, knotty, system, varied **7** chelate, gordian, network **8** abstruse, compound, involved, syndrome, tortuous **9** aggregate, Byzantine, composite, elaborate, intricate **10** convoluted **11** complicated **12** conglomerate, labyrinthine **13** heterogeneous, sophisticated

complexion 3 hue **4** cast, tint, tone **5** color, humor, tinge **6** aspect, makeup, nature, temper **8** tincture **9** character **10** appearance, coloration **11** disposition, temperament **12** pigmentation **13** individuality

compliance 7 consent **8** docility **9** agreement, deference, obedience **10** acceptance, conformity, submission **11** amenability, flexibility, resignation **12** acquiescence, tractability

complicate 5 mix up, ravel, snarl **6** jumble, muddle, tangle **7** confuse, involve **8** confound, disorder, entangle **9** aggravate, convolute **10** disarrange, exacerbate

complicated 6 daedal, knotty **7** complex, gordian, tangled **8** abstruse, involved, tortuous **9** Byzantine, elaborate, intricate, recondite **10** convoluted **12** labyrinthine **13** heterogeneous, sophisticated

complicity 8 abetment **9** collusion **10** connivance **11** involvement

compliment 4 hail, kudo, laud **5** extol, honor, kudos **6** praise, salute **7** acclaim, applaud, bouquet, commend, regards, tribute **8** accolade, encomium **9** laudation, recommend **11** recognition **12** appreciation, commendation, congratulate

complimentary 4 free **6** gratis **8** costless **9** favorable, laudatory **10** chargeless, gratuitous **12** appreciative

comply 4 obey **5** yield **6** accede, submit **7** conform **9** acquiesce

component 4 part **5** piece **6** factor **7** element, segment **10** ingredient **11** constituent

comport **4** bear, jibe **5** agree, carry, fit in, match, tally **6** accord, acquit, behave, demean, square **7** conduct **8** coincide, dovetail **9** harmonize **10** correspond

comportment **3** air **4** mien **7** address, bearing, conduct **8** attitude, behavior, carriage, demeanor, presence

compose **4** calm, cool, form, lull, make **5** forge, quiet, relax, still, write **6** becalm, create, devise, draw up, indite, invent, make up, settle, solace, soothe **7** collect, console, contain, control **8** comprise **9** construct, fabricate, formulate, originate **10** constitute ***type:*** **3** set

composed **4** calm, cool **5** staid **6** poised, sedate, serene **9** collected, unruffled **11** unflappable **13** imperturbable, self-possessed

composer **6** scorer **8** melodist **9** balladist, songsmith, tunesmith **10** songwriter ***American:*** **3** Kay (Hershy, Ulysses) **4** Ager (Milton), Bock (Jerry), Cage (John), Hill (Edward Burlingame), Ives (Charles), Kern (Jerome), King (Carole), Lane (Burton), Monk (Thelonious), Work (Henry Clay) **5** Adams (John), Arlen (Harold), Beach (Amy), Blake (Eubie), Bland (James A.), Bloch (Ernest), Cohan (George M.), Friml (Rudolf), Glass (Philip), Gould (Morton), Grofé (Ferde), Handy (W. C.), Loewe (Frederick), Mason (Daniel Gregory, Lowell), Moore (Douglas), Reich (Steve), Rorem (Ned), Sousa (John Philip), Still (William Grant), Styne (Jule), Zappa (Frank) **6** Barber (Samuel), Berlin (Irving), Carter (Elliott), Cowell (Henry), Emmett (Daniel), Foster (Stephen), Hanson (Howard), Harris (Roy), Herman (Jerry), Joplin (Scott), Kander (John), McHugh (Jimmy), McKuen (Rod), Menken (Alan), Morton ("Jelly Roll"), Oliver ("King"), Parker (Charlie "Bird," Horatio), Piston (Walter), Porter (Cole), Previn (André), Seeger (Pete), Taylor (Deems), Varèse (Edgard), Warren (Harry) **7** Babbitt (Milton), Brubeck (Dave), Copland (Aaron), Gilbert (Henry F.), Gilmore (Patrick), Goldman (Edwin Franko), Herbert (Victor), Loesser (Frank), Mancini (Henry), Menotti (Gian Carlo), Rodgers (Richard), Romberg (Sigmund), Schuman (William), Thomson (Virgil), Tiomkin (Dimitri), Willson (Meredith), Youmans (Vincent) **8** Anderson (Leroy), Billings (William), Burleigh (Henry Thacker), Damrosch (Leopold, Walter), Gershwin (George), Hamlisch (Marvin), Herrmann (Bernard), Korngold (Erich Wolfgang), Kreisler (Fritz), Marsalis (Wynton), Schifrin (Lalo), Schuller (Gunther), Sessions (Roger), Sondheim (Stephen), Williams (John) **9** Bacharach (Burt), Bernstein (Elmer, Leonard), Donaldson (Walter), Ellington (Duke), Hovhaness (Alan), MacDowell (Edward) **10** Blitzstein (Marc), Carmichael (Hoagy), Gottschalk (Louis Moreau) ***Argentinian:*** **9** Ginastera (Alberto) ***Australian:*** **8** Grainger (Percy) ***Austrian:*** **4** Berg (Alban), Wolf (Hugo) **5** Haydn (Franz Joseph) **6** Czerny (Karl), Mahler (Gustav), Mozart (Leopold, Wolfgang Amadeus), Straus (Oscar), Webern (Anton) **7** Strauss (Eduard, Johann, Josef) **8** Bruckner (Anton), Schubert (Franz) **10** Schoenberg (Arnold) ***Belgian:*** **5** Ysaÿe (Eugène) **6** Franck (César) ***Brazilian:*** **5** Jobim (Antonio Carlos) **10** Villa-Lobos (Heitor) ***Czech:*** **3** Suk (Josef) **5** Friml (Rudolf) **6** Dvořák (Antonín) **7** Janáček (Leoš), Martinu (Bohuslav), Smetana (Bedřich) ***Danish:*** **7** Nielsen (Carl) ***Dutch:*** **9** Sweelinck (Jan Pieterszoon) ***English:*** **4** Arne (Thomas Augustine), Byrd (William) **5** Elgar (Edward), Holst (Gustav) **6** Delius (Frederick), Morley (Thomas), Tallis (Thomas), Walton (William), Wesley (Charles, Samuel) **7** Britten (Benjamin), Dowland (John), Gibbons (Orlando), Purcell (Henry), Tippett (Michael), Weelkes (Thomas) **8** Sullivan (Arthur) **9** Dunstable (John) **11** Lloyd Webber (Andrew) ***Finnish:*** **8** Palmgren (Selim), Sibelius (Jean) ***Flemish:*** **5** Dufay (Guillaume), Lasso (Orlando di) **6** Lassus (Orlande de) **8** Willaert (Adriaan) ***French:*** **4** Indy (Vincent d'), Lalo (Edouard) **5** Auber (Esprit), Bizet (Georges), Dukas (Paul), Fauré (Gabriel), Ibert (Jacques), Jarre (Maurice), Lully (Jean-Baptiste), Ravel (Maurice), Satie (Erik), Widor (Charles-Marie) **6** Boulez (Pierre), Campra (André), Franck (César), Gounod (Charles), Rameau (Jean-Philippe), Thomas (Ambroise) **7** Berlioz (Hector), Debussy (Claude), Delibes (Léo), Machaut (Guillaume de), Milhaud (Darius), Poulenc (Francis) **8** Chabrier (Emmanuel), Couperin (François, Louis), Honegger (Arthur), Massenet (Jules), Messiaen (Olivier) **9** Meyerbeer (Giacomo), Offenbach (Jacques) **10** Saint-Saëns (Camille) ***German:*** **4** Bach (C. P. E., Johann Christian, Johann Sebastian, Wilhelm Friedemann), Orff (Carl) **5** Bruch (Max), Gluck (Christoph Willibald von), Reger (Max), Spohr (Louis, Ludwig), Weber (Carl Maria von), Weill (Kurt) **6** Brahms (Johannes), Handel (George Frideric), Schütz (Heinrich), Vogler (Abt), Wagner (Richard) **7** Hassler (Hans Leo), Strauss (Richard) **8** Korngold (Erich Wolfgang), Schumann (Robert), Telemann (Georg Philipp) **9** Beethoven (Ludwig van), Buxtehude (Dietrich), Hindemith (Paul), Meyerbeer (Giacomo), Pachelbel (Johann) **10** Praetorius (Michael) **11** Humperdinck (Engelbert), Mendelssohn (Felix), Stockhausen (Karlheinz) ***Hungarian:*** **5** Léhar (Franz), Liszt (Franz) **6** Bartók (Béla), Kodály (Zoltán), Ligeti (György) **8** Dohnányi (Erno) ***Italian:*** **4** Peri (Jacopo), Rota (Nino) **5** Berio (Luciano), Boito (Arrigo), Verdi (Giuseppe) **6** Busoni (Ferruccio) **7** Bellini (Vincenzo), Caccini (Giulio), Corelli (Arcangelo), Martini (Padre), Puccini (Giacomo), Rossini (Gioacchino), Salieri (Antonio), Tartini (Giuseppe), Vivaldi (Antonio) **8** Albinoni (Tomaso), Clementi (Muzio), Gabrieli (Andrea, Giovanni), Mascagni (Pietro), Paganini (Niccolò), Respighi (Ottorino) **9** Cherubini (Luigi), Donizetti (Gaetano), Pergolesi (Giovanni Battista), Scarlatti (Alessandro, Domenico), Tommasini (Vincenzo) **10** Boccherini (Luigi), Monteverdi (Claudio), Palestrina (G. P. da), Ponchielli (Amilcare), Zingarelli (Niccolò) **11** Frescobaldi (Girolamo), Leoncavallo (Ruggero) **12** Dallapiccola (Luigi) ***Japanese:*** **4** Taki (Rentaro) **5** Satoh (Somei) **6** Tomita (Isao) **7** Ifukube (Akira) **9** Katsuhisa (Hattori), Takemitsu (Toru) ***Mexican:*** **6** Chávez (Carlos) ***Norwegian:*** **5** Grieg (Edvard) ***Polish:*** **6** Chopin (Frédéric) **7** Gorecki (Henryk) **10** Paderewski (Ignacy Jan), Penderecki (Krzysztof), Wieniawski (Henryk) **11** Lutoslawski (Witold), Szymanowski (Karol) ***Romanian:*** **6** Enescu (Gheorghe, George) **7** Xenakis (Iannis) ***Russian:*** **6** Glinka (Mikhail) **7** Borodin (Aleksandr) **8** Glazunov (Aleksandr), Scriabin (Aleksandr) **9** Balakirev (Mily), Prokofiev (Sergey), Schnittke (Alfred) **10** Kabalevsky (Dmitri), Mussorgsky (Modest), Rubinstein (Anton), Stravinsky (Igor), Tcherepnin (Nikolay) **11** Tchaikovsky (Pyotr Ilich) **12** Khachaturian (Aram), Rachmaninoff (Sergey), Shostakovich (Dmitry) ***Spanish:*** **5** Falla (Manuel de) **7** Albéniz (Isaac), Rodrigo (Joaquin) **8** Granados (Enrique), Victoria (Tomas Luis de) ***Swiss:*** **5** Bloch (Ernest) **6** Martin (Frank) **8** Honegger (Arthur) (see also **songwriter**)

composite **3** mix **5** blend **6** fusion, hybrid **7** amalgam, complex, mixture **8** compound **11** combination **12** amalgamation

composition **4** opus **5** essay, paper, theme **6** design, layout, makeup **7** article **9** formation **11** arrangement **12** architecture, constitution, construction ***choral:*** **4** mass **5** motet **7** cantata, passion **8** oratorio ***for eight:*** **5** octet ***for five:*** **7** quintet ***for four:*** **7** quartet ***for nine:*** **5** nonet ***for one:*** **4** aria, solo ***for seven:*** **6** septet ***for six:*** **6** sextet ***for three:*** **4** trio ***for two:*** **3** duo **4** duet ***instrumental:*** **3** jig **4** reel **5** étude, fugue, gigue, march, rondo, suite **6** sonata **7** caprice, partita, prelude, scherzo **8** concerto, fantasia, overture, rhapsody, saraband, sinfonia, symphony, tone poem **9** allemande, capriccio, sarabande **10** intermezzo ***vocal:*** **4** aria, lied, mass, song **5** carol, chant, motet, opera, round **6** arioso, ballad, chanty **7** cantata, chanson, chantey, chorale, lullaby, requiem **8** berceuse, madrigal, oratorio **9** plainsong, spiritual **10** plainchant

compos mentis **4** sane **5** lucid, sound **6** normal

composure **4** calm **5** poise **7** balance, dignity **8** calmness, coolness, evenness, serenity, sobriety **9** sangfroid **10** equanimity **11** equilibrium

compound **3** mix **4** join, link **5** admix, alloy, blend, union, unite **6** expand, extend, fusion, make up, mingle **7** amalgam, augment, complex, compost, enlarge, magnify, mixture **8** coalesce, comingle, heighten, increase, intermix, multiply **9** admixture, aggravate, associate, commingle, composite, intensify, synthesis **10** commixture, exacerbate **11** intermingle **12** amalgamation ***aroma:*** **5** neral **6** citral **7** menthol **8** vanillin ***chemical:*** (see at **chemical**) ***protein:*** **7** peptone

comprehend **4** know **5** catch, grasp **6** absorb, accept, embody, fathom, take in **7** cognize, compass, contain, discern, embrace, include, involve, subsume **8** comprise, perceive **9** encompass **10** appreciate, understand

comprehensible **8** knowable **9** graspable **10** fathomable **12** intelligible

comprehension **3** ken **5** grasp **6** uptake **9** awareness, knowledge **10** cognizance, conception, perception **11** discernment **12** apperception **13** understanding

comprehensive **4** full, wide **5** broad **6** global **7** general, overall **8** catholic, complete, sweeping **9** all-around, extensive, inclusive, universal **10** exhaustive **12** all-inclusive, encyclopedic

comprehensiveness **5** range, reach, scope **7** breadth **8** entirety, fullness, totality **9** amplitude

compress 3 jam **4** cram, push **5** crush, press **6** reduce, shrink, squash, squish, shrink **7** bandage, compact, squeeze **8** condense, contract **11** concentrate
comprise 4 form **6** make up **7** compose, contain, embrace, include, subsume **10** comprehend, constitute
compromise 4 mean, pact, risk **6** settle **7** bargain, compact **8** contract, endanger, trade off **9** agreement, middle way **10** concession, golden mean, jeopardize, settlement **12** middle ground
compulsion 4 itch, need, urge **5** drive, force **6** duress **8** coercion **9** necessity **10** constraint
compulsive 6 driven **7** driving **9** besetting, obsessive **12** irresistible, overwhelming
compulsory 7 binding **8** coercive, enforced, required **9** mandatory, requisite **10** imperative, obligatory
compunction 4 pang **5** demur, qualm **6** regret, unease **7** remorse, scruple **8** distress **9** hesitancy, misgiving **10** conscience, hesitation
compunctious 5 sorry **8** contrite, penitent **9** regretful, repentant **10** apologetic, remorseful **11** penitential
computation 8 figuring **9** ciphering, reckoning **10** arithmetic, estimation **11** calculation
compute 5 tally, total **6** cipher, figure, reckon **8** estimate **9** calculate, determine
computer 6 abacus, laptop **7** desktop **9** mainframe **10** calculator ***code:*** **5** ASCII ***component:*** **3** CPU **4** chip **5** mouse, tower **7** monitor **8** keyboard **9** hard drive ***early:*** **5** Eniac **6** Univac ***expert:*** **4** geek **6** techie ***graphics application:*** **3** CGI, FMV ***information:*** **4** data ***instruction:*** **5** macro ***inventor:*** **7** Babbage (Charles) ***key:*** **3** Alt, Esc, Tab **4** Ctrl **5** Enter, Shift ***language:*** **3** Ada, APL, SQL **4** Java, Lisp, Perl **5** ALGOL, BASIC, COBOL **6** Pascal **7** FORTRAN see also **programming language** ***type:*** **6** analog **7** digital
computer-game genre 3 FPS, RPG, RTS **6** action, puzzle, racing, sports **8** fighting, platform **9** adventure **10** simulation
comrade 3 pal **4** ally, chum, mate **5** buddy, crony **6** cohort, comate, fellow **7** consort **8** sidekick, tovarich, tovarish **9** associate, colleague, companion
con 3 gyp, vet **4** anti, bilk, coax, dupe, fool, hoax, rook, scam **5** cheat, fraud, learn, study, trick **6** cajole, fleece, gammon, inmate, survey **7** against, blarney, canvass, chicane, convict, deceive, defraud, examine, inspect, swindle, wheedle **8** blandish, flimflam, hoodwink, inveigle, jailbird, memorize, negative, opponent, persuade, prisoner, soft-soap **9** bamboozle, check over, sweet-talk **10** antithesis, manipulate, scrutinize **11** hornswoggle **12** tuberculosis
concatenate 4 join, link **5** unite **7** connect
concavity 3 dip, sag **4** bowl, dent, sink **5** basin **6** crater, hollow, trough **7** sinkage **8** sinkhole **10** depression
conceal 4 bury, hide, mask, veil **5** cache, cloak, cover, stash **6** screen **7** obscure, secrete **8** ensconce, enshroud, palliate **10** camouflage
concealed 3 hid **5** privy **6** buried, covert, hidden, secret **8** obscured, shrouded, ulterior **11** clandestine
concede 3 own **4** avow, fold **5** admit, allow, award, grant, yield **6** accept, accord **7** confess **9** surrender, vouchsafe **10** capitulate, relinquish **11** acknowledge
conceit 4 idea, whim **5** fancy, pride **6** egoism, megrim, notion, vagary, vanity **7** caprice, egotism, thought **8** crotchet, metaphor, self-love, smugness, snobbery **9** self-pride, vainglory **10** narcissism, self-esteem **11** complacence, complacency, self-opinion, swelled head
conceited 4 vain **6** snobby, snooty, uppish, uppity **7** pompous, stuck-up **8** immodest, puffed up, snobbish **12** narcissistic, vainglorious
conceitedness 6 vanity **8** self-love **9** vainglory **10** narcissism
conceivable 8 possible **9** plausible, thinkable **10** imaginable, supposable
conceive 4 form **5** beget, fancy, grasp, think **6** devise, expect, ideate, ponder **7** dream up, feature, imagine, realize, suppose, suspect, think up **8** envisage, envision **9** formulate, originate, speculate, visualize **10** excogitate, mastermind
concentrate 4 mass **5** focus **6** gather, shrink **7** collect, compact **8** assemble, compress, condense, contract, converge **10** accumulate **11** consolidate
concentrated 5 thick **6** intent, strong **7** focused, intense **8** vehement **9** intensive, undiluted, undivided **12** undistracted
concentration 5 field, major, study **9** attention **10** absorption **11** application
concept 4 idea **5** image **6** notion, theory **7** conceit, thought **10** impression, perception
conception 4 idea **5** birth, image, start **6** notion, origin, outset, theory **7** conceit, genesis, thought **9** beginning **10** impression, perception
conceptual 5 ideal **8** abstract, notional **9**

imaginary, visionary **10** ideational **11** theoretical **12** hypothetical, intellectual
concern 4 care, firm, heed **5** doubt, worry **6** affair, bear on, bother, engage, gadget, matter, occupy, outfit, regard, unease **7** anxiety, company, disturb, involve, perturb, trouble **8** business, deal with, disquiet, interest, mistrust **9** attention, curiosity, misgiving, suspicion **10** enterprise, skepticism, solicitude, uneasiness **11** carefulness, contrivance, uncertainty **12** apprehension **13** consciousness, consideration, establishment
concerned 7 anxious, worried **8** affected, involved **10** implicated, interested
concerning 4 as to, in re **5** about, anent, as for **7** apropos **9** as regards, regarding **10** relating to, relative to, respecting
concert 5 agree, union **6** accord, concur, settle, soiree **7** arrange, concord, harmony, recital **8** coincide, musicale **9** agreement, cooperate, harmonize, negotiate **11** performance
concerted 5 joint **6** mutual, united **7** unified **8** combined **11** coordinated **13** collaborative
concert hall 5 arena, odeum **7** theater, theatre **10** auditorium
concession 5 favor, grant **8** giveback **9** admission, allowance, privilege **10** compromise **12** acquiescence
conch 5 shell **7** mollusc, mollusk
concierge 6 porter, warden **7** doorman, janitor **9** custodian **10** doorkeeper
conciliate 4 calm, ease **6** disarm, pacify, soothe **7** appease, assuage, mollify, placate, sweeten, win over **9** reconcile **10** propitiate
concise 5 brief, pithy, short, terse **7** compact, laconic, summary **8** abridged, succinct **9** condensed **10** compressed, contracted **11** compendious **13** short and sweet
conclave 5 synod **6** caucus, powwow **7** meeting, session **8** assembly **9** gathering **10** conference, consistory, convention **11** convocation
conclude 3 end **4** halt, stop **5** close, infer, judge **6** decide, deduce, derive, effect, figure, finish, gather, reason, settle, wind up, wrap up **7** collect, resolve **8** complete **9** determine, terminate
concluding 4 last **5** final **6** latest, latter **7** closing **8** eventual, terminal, ultimate
conclusion 3 end **4** stop **5** cease, close **6** ending, epilog, finale, finish, period, result, windup **7** closing, closure, outcome, verdict **8** decision, epilogue, judgment, sequitur **9** cessation, deduction, inference, summation **10** completion, denouement, resolution, settlement **11** culmination, termination **13** determination ***musical:* 4** coda ***poetic:* 5** envoi
conclusive 4 last **5** final **6** cogent **8** deciding, decisive, ultimate **9** clinching **10** compelling, convincing, definitive, undeniable **11** determinant, determinate, irrefutable **12** irrefragable, unanswerable **13** determinative
concoct 3 mix **4** brew, cook **5** frame, hatch **6** cook up, create, devise, invent **7** dream up **8** conceive, contrive **9** fabricate, formulate, originate
concoction 4 brew, plan **5** blend **7** mixture, project **8** compound, creation **9** invention **11** combination, contrivance, fabrication, preparation
concomitant 7 adjunct **8** adjuvant **9** accessory, ancillary, associate, attendant, attending, companion, satellite **10** coincident, collateral **12** accompanying **13** accompaniment, supplementary
concord 4 pact **5** amity, peace, unity **6** accord, comity, treaty, unison **7** concert, entente, harmony, rapport **8** goodwill **9** agreement **10** consonance
concordant 8 agreeing **9** congruous, consonant **10** compatible, consistent, harmonious **11** appropriate
concourse 5 foyer **6** throng **7** joining, meeting **8** junction **9** gathering **10** confluence, crossroads
concrete 5 solid **6** actual **8** specific, tangible **10** particular **11** substantial ***component:* 4** sand **5** water **6** gravel
concubine 7 hetaera, hetaira **8** mistress **9** courtesan, odalisque
concupiscence 4 lust **5** ardor **6** desire **7** lechery, passion **9** prurience, pruriency **11** lustfulness **13** lickerishness
concupiscent 3 hot **7** aroused, goatish, lustful **8** prurient **9** lecherous, lickerish, salacious **10** lascivious, libidinous, lubricious, passionate
concur 4 jibe **5** agree, unite **6** accord, assent **7** approve, combine, concord, consent, go along **8** coincide **9** cooperate, harmonize
concurrent 6 coeval **8** parallel **10** coexistent, coexisting, convergent, synchronic **11** synchronous **12** contemporary, simultaneous
concurrently 6 at once **8** together **12** coincidently
concuss 3 jar **4** rock, stun **5** shake, shock **7** agitate
concussion 3 jar **4** bump, jolt **5** clout, crash, shock **6** impact **7** jarring, jolting, shaking **8** pounding **9** agitation, collision
condemn 3 rap **4** damn, doom **5** blame, decry, knock, seize **7** censure, convict, de-

plore **8** denounce, sentence **9** criticize, deprecate, proscribe, reprehend, reprobate **10** denunciate

condensation 3 dew **5** brief **6** digest, précis **7** epitome, outline, summary **8** abstract, synopsis **9** reduction **10** abridgment, conspectus **11** abridgement

condense 5 sum up **6** digest, reduce, shrink **7** abridge, compact, shorten **8** boil down, compress, contract **9** constrict, epitomize, summarize, synopsize **10** abbreviate **11** concentrate, consolidate, precipitate

condensed 7 concise, summary **10** boiled down **11** compendious

condenser 9 capacitor

condescend 5 deign, stoop **6** unbend

condescending 5 lofty **6** lordly, snobby, snooty, uppish, uppity **7** haughty, pompous **8** affected, arrogant, cavalier, snobbish, superior **10** disdainful **11** patronizing, pretentious **12** supercilious

condign 3 apt, due, fit **4** fair, just **5** right **6** proper **7** fitting, merited **8** deserved, rightful, suitable **9** equitable, justified **11** appropriate

condiment 5 curry, sauce, spice **6** catsup, relish, tamari **7** chutney, ketchup, mustard **8** dressing, soy sauce **9** seasoning **10** mayonnaise

____ con Dios! 4 Vaya

condition 5 shape, state, terms **6** fettle, malady, status **7** ailment, disease, fitness, proviso **8** syndrome **9** complaint, essential, exception, necessity, provision, requisite, situation **10** limitation, sine qua non **11** requirement, reservation, stipulation **12** prerequisite **13** qualification

conditional 7 reliant **8** relative **9** dependent, provisory, qualified, tentative, uncertain **10** contingent, restricted **11** provisional

condolence 3 rue **4** pity, ruth **6** solace **7** comfort **8** sympathy **10** compassion **13** commiseration

condonable 7 tenable **9** excusable, tolerable **10** acceptable, defensible, pardonable **11** justifiable

condone 5 remit **6** excuse, pardon **7** forgive **8** overlook

conduce 4 lead, tend **7** redound **10** contribute

conducive 7 helpful, leading, tending **9** favorable **10** beneficial, salubrious **11** efficacious, serviceable, stimulating **12** advantageous, contributory, instrumental **13** accommodating

conduct 3 act, run **4** bear, head, lead, show **5** guide, pilot, steer, usher **6** attend, behave, charge, convey, demean, deport, direct, escort, handle, manage **7** arrange, bearing, comport, control, manners, operate, oversee **8** behavior, demeanor, handling, shepherd, transmit **9** accompany, oversight, supervise **10** administer, deportment, management **11** comportment, supervision

conductor 5 guide **6** escort, leader **7** maestro **8** motorman **10** bandleader ***American:* 4** Shaw (Robert) **5** Stock (Frederick), Szell (George) **6** Levine (James), Maazel (Lorin), Previn (André), Reiner (Fritz), Thomas (Theodore, Michael Tilson), Walter (Bruno) **7** Fennell (Frederick), Fiedler (Arthur), Monteux (Pierre), Ormandy (Eugene), Schwarz (Gerard), Slatkin (Leonard) **8** Damrosch (Leopold, Walter), Williams (John) **9** Bernstein (Leonard), Leinsdorf (Erich), Rodzinski (Artur), Steinberg (William), Stokowski (Leopold) **11** Kostelanetz (André), Mitropoulos (Dimitri) ***Argentinian:* 7** Kleiber (Carlos) **9** Barenboim (Daniel) ***Australian:* 7** Bonynge (Richard) ***Austrian:* 4** Böhm (Karl) **6** Mahler (Gustav) **7** Karajan (Herbert von) **11** Weingartner (Felix) ***Belgian:* 5** Ysaÿe (Eugene) ***Canadian:* 6** Dutoit (Charles) **9** MacMillan (Ernest) ***Czech:* 7** Kubelik (Jan, Rafael) ***Dutch:* 7** Haitink (Bernard) **10** Mengelberg (Willem) ***English:* 4** Wood (Henry) **5** Boult (Adrian), Davis (Colin) **6** Rattle (Simon) **7** Beecham (Thomas), Leppard (Raymond), Malcolm (George), Pinnock (Trevor), Sargent (Malcolm) **8** Goossens (Eugene), Marriner (Neville) **9** Mackerras (Charles) **10** Barbirolli (John) ***Finnish:* 7** Salonen (Esa-Pekka) ***French:* 5** Munch (Charles) **6** Boulez (Pierre), Prêtre (Georges) **7** Monteux (Pierre) ***German:* 4** Muck (Carl, Karl) **5** Masur (Kurt) **6** Jochum (Eugen) **7** Kleiber (Erich) **9** Klemperer (Otto), Scherchen (Hermann) **10** Sawallisch (Wolfgang) **11** Furtwängler (Wilhelm), Mendelssohn (Felix) ***Greek:* 11** Mitropoulos (Dimitri) ***Hungarian:* 5** Seidl (Anton), Solti (Georg), Szell (George) **6** Doráti (Antal), Reiner (Fritz) **7** Nikisch (Arthur), Ormandy (Eugene), Richter (Hans) ***Indian:* 5** Mehta (Zubin) ***Italian:* 4** Muti (Riccardo) **6** Abbado (Claudio) **7** Chailly (Riccardo), Giulini (Carlo Maria) **8** Cantelli (Guido), Sinopoli (Giuseppe) **9** Toscanini (Arturo) ***Japanese:* 5** Ozawa (Seiji) ***Polish:* 9** Rodzinski (Artur) ***Russian:* 7** Gergiev (Valery) **10** Temirkanov (Yuri) **12** Koussevitzky (Serge) ***Spanish:* 6** Iturbi (José) ***Swiss:* 8** Ansermet (Ernest) ***Venezuelan:* 7** Dudamel (Gustavo) ***stick:* 5** baton

conduit 4 duct, main, pipe **5** canal **6** course **7** channel **8** aqueduct, penstock, pipeline **11** watercourse
coney 4 pika **5** hyrax, lapin **6** rabbit **10** butterfish
confab 4 chat, talk **6** confer, huddle, parley, powwow **7** consult **8** collogue, colloquy, dialogue **10** conference, discussion **12** conversation, deliberation
confabulate see **confab**
confabulation see **confab**
confection see **candy**
confederacy 5 cabal, union **6** league **7** compact **8** alliance **9** coalition, syndicate **10** conspiracy, federation
confederate 3 reb **4** ally **5** rebel, unite **6** fellow **7** abettor, partner **9** accessory, associate, colleague, Johnny Reb **10** accomplice **11** conspirator **12** collaborator **13** coconspirator ***admiral:* 6** Semmes ***capital:* 8** Richmond ***color:* 4** gray ***general:* 3** Lee (Robert E.) **4** Hill (Ambrose), Hood (John Bell) **5** Bragg (Braxton), Ewell (Richard Stoddart), Price (Sterling), Smith (Edmund Kirby) **6** Morgan (John Hunt), Stuart (J. E. B.) **7** Forrest (Nathan Bedford), Hampton (Wade), Jackson (Thomas Jonathan "Stonewall"), Pickett (George) **8** Johnston (Albert Sidney, Joseph Eggleston) **9** Pemberton (John Clifford) **10** Beauregard (Pierre G. T.), Longstreet (James) ***president:* 5** Davis (Jefferson) ***soldier:* 9** butternut ***spy:* 4** Boyd (Belle) ***vice-president:* 8** Stephens (Alexander)
confederation see **confederacy**
confer 4 give, meet, talk **5** allot, award, grant, speak **6** accord, advise, bestow, confab, donate, huddle, parley, powwow **7** consult, discuss, present **8** collogue, converse **10** deliberate **11** confabulate
conference 4 talk **5** forum, synod **6** caucus, league, parley, powwow **7** meeting, palaver, seminar **8** assembly, colloquy, congress **9** symposium **10** colloquium, discussion, round-robin, roundtable **11** association, convocation **12** consultation, deliberation **13** confabulation
confess 3 own **4** avow, sing **5** admit, allow, grant, let on, own up **6** reveal **7** concede, divulge, profess **8** disclose **9** come clean **11** acknowledge
confession 5 creed **6** avowal **7** peccavi **9** admission, statement **10** disclosure
confidant 8 familiar, intimate
confide 4 tell **5** trust **6** bestow, commit, reveal **7** commend, consign, entrust, whisper **8** hand over, relegate, turn over
confidence 5 faith, poise, stock, trust **6** aplomb, surety **8** credence, reliance, sureness **9** assurance, certainty, certitude **10** conviction, equanimity ***game:* 4** scam **5** bunco, bunko, grift, sting **7** swindle **8** flimflam
confidence man 3 gyp **5** shark **7** diddler, grifter, scammer, sharper, sharpie **8** swindler **9** charlatan, defrauder, trickster **11** bunco artist
confident 4 bold, sure **5** brash, brave, cocky **6** secure **7** assured, certain **8** cocksure, fearless, intrepid, positive, sanguine, unafraid **9** dauntless, undaunted **10** courageous, undoubtful **11** self-assured, self-reliant **13** self-assertive, self-possessed
confidential 5 close, privy **6** hushed, inside, secret **7** private **8** familiar, hush-hush, intimate **9** auricular **10** classified
configuration 4 cast, form **5** shape **6** figure, layout, makeup **7** contour, gestalt, outline, pattern **9** structure **12** conformation
confine 3 box, mew, pen **4** cage, coop, crib, jail, term **5** bound, cramp, hem in, limit **6** immure, intern, lock up, shut in, shut up **7** delimit, enclose, impound, put away **8** encircle, imprison, localize, restrict **9** constrain **11** incarcerate **12** circumscribe
confinement 7 custody, lying-in **8** childbed **9** captivity, detention, restraint **10** constraint **12** accouchement, imprisonment **13** incarceration
confines 6 bounds, limits **7** borders, compass **8** boundary, environs, purlieus **9** precincts **10** boundaries
confirm 3 fix, set **5** check, prove, vouch **6** attest, ratify, uphold, verify **7** approve, bear out, certify, concede, endorse, justify, support **8** buttress, check out, validate **9** ascertain, reinforce **10** strengthen **11** corroborate **12** authenticate, substantiate
confirmation 5 proof **7** support, witness **8** approval, evidence **9** testimony **10** validation **11** attestation, endorsement, testimonial **12** ratification, verification **13** certification, corroboration
confirmed 3 set **5** fixed, sworn **6** proven **7** chronic, settled **8** deep-dyed, definite, habitual, hardened, ratified **10** accustomed, deep-rooted, deep-seated, entrenched, habituated, inveterate, persistent **13** bred-in-the-bone, dyed-in-the-wool
confiscate 4 grab, take **5** annex, seize, usurp **7** escheat, impound, preempt **8** arrogate **9** sequester **10** commandeer **11** appropriate, expropriate
confiture 3 jam **8** conserve, preserve **9** marmalade, preserves

conflagrant **5** afire, fiery **6** ablaze, aflame, alight **7** blazing, burning, flaming
conflagration **3** war **4** fire **5** blaze **7** inferno **8** conflict **9** holocaust
conflate **3** mix **4** fuse, join, meld, weld **5** blend, merge, mix up **6** mingle, muddle **7** combine, confuse, mistake **8** coalesce, confound **9** commingle
conflict **3** row, war **4** bout, duel, rift, vary **5** brawl, clash, fight, melee, set-to **6** battle, combat, differ, fracas, strife **7** contend, contest, discord, dispute, rivalry, warfare **8** argument, disagree, mismatch, struggle, tug-of-war, variance **9** encounter, rencontre **10** contention, engagement **11** competition
conflicting **6** at odds **7** opposed, warring **8** clashing, contrary, opposing **9** dissonant **10** contending, discordant, discrepant **11** incongruent, incongruous, inconsonant **12** antagonistic, antipathetic, incompatible, inconsistent, inharmonious **13** contradictory
confluence **6** merger **7** joining, meeting, merging **8** junction **9** concourse, gathering **11** convergence
conform **3** fit **4** jibe, obey, suit **5** adapt, agree, fit in, match, yield **6** accord, adjust, attune, comply, follow, square, submit, tailor **8** dovetail **9** acquiesce, harmonize, reconcile **10** coordinate, correspond, proportion **11** accommodate
conformable **6** fitted, suited **7** adapted, matched **8** amenable, obedient, suitable **9** agreeable, compliant, congenial, consonant **10** submissive
conformation **4** cast, form **5** shape **6** figure **7** anatomy **9** structure **10** adaptation **11** arrangement **13** configuration
conforming **3** apt **6** decent, proper, seemly **7** correct, uniform **8** becoming, decorous, suitable **9** befitting, civilized **10** compatible, consistent **11** comme il faut
conformity **6** accord **7** decorum, harmony **9** agreement, coherence, congruity, obedience, orthodoxy **10** accordance, allegiance, compliance, consonance, observance, submission **11** consistency **12** acquiescence
confound **4** damn, faze **5** befog, mix up, stump **6** baffle, puzzle, rattle, refute **7** confuse, mistake, mystify, nonplus, perplex, stupefy **8** befuddle, bewilder, disprove **9** discomfit, dumbfound, embarrass, frustrate **10** controvert, disconcert **11** misidentify
confounded **5** utter **6** blamed, cursed, cussed, damned **7** blasted, blessed, doggone, shocked **8** absolute, accursed, dismayed, infernal, outright **9** consarned, dad-blamed, execrable, out-and-out **11** dumbfounded, overwhelmed, unmitigated **13** thunderstruck
confrere see **colleague**
confront **4** defy, face, meet **5** beard, brave, cross **6** accost, breast, oppose, take on **9** challenge, encounter
confuse **3** fog **4** blur, daze, faze **5** abash, addle, befog, cloud, dizzy, mix up, muddy, stump, upset **6** baffle, ball up, bemuse, flurry, foul up, fuddle, garble, jumble, mess up, muddle, puzzle, rattle **7** agitate, becloud, derange, disrupt, distort, flummox, fluster, mislead, mistake, mystify, nonplus, perplex, perturb, snarl up **8** bedazzle, befuddle, bewilder, confound, disorder, disquiet, distract, throw off, unsettle **9** discomfit, disorient, embarrass **10** complicate, disarrange, discompose, disconcert **11** disorganize, misidentify **12** misrepresent
confused **4** lost **5** dazed, messy, muddy, muzzy, vague **6** addled **7** at a loss, chaotic, mixed up, muddled, puzzled **9** flustered, perplexed, unsettled **10** bewildered, nonplussed, topsy-turvy **11** disoriented **12** disconcerted
confusion **3** ado, din **4** flap, mess, stew **5** babel, chaos, havoc, mix-up, snafu, snarl **6** bedlam, dither, foul-up, hubbub, huddle, jumble, lather, muddle, tumult, unease **7** anarchy, clutter, turmoil **8** disarray, disorder, shambles **9** abashment, agitation, commotion, imbroglio **10** hullabaloo, perplexity, puzzlement, turbulence, uneasiness **11** derangement, disturbance, pandemonium **12** bewilderment **13** embarrassment
confute **4** deny **5** evert, rebut **6** defeat, negate **8** confound, disprove, puncture **10** controvert, disconfirm
congé **3** bow **5** adieu **6** good-by **7** good-bye, molding, parting, sendoff **8** farewell **9** dismissal **11** leave-taking
congeal **3** dry, gel, set **4** clot, jell **5** jelly **6** curdle, harden **7** stiffen, thicken **8** solidify **9** coagulate **10** gelatinize
congener **6** agnate **7** cognate, sibling **8** relation, relative
congenial **4** nice **6** social **7** affable, amiable, cordial, kindred, welcome **8** amicable, friendly, gracious, pleasant, pleasing, sociable, suitable **9** agreeable, congruous, consonant, favorable **10** compatible, consistent, gratifying, harmonious **11** cooperative, pleasurable, sympathetic **13** companionable
congenital **6** inborn, inbred, innate, native **7** natural **8** inherent **9** essential, ingrained, intrinsic **10** deep-seated, indigenous, indwelling

conger 3 eel
congeries 5 group **7** company **8** assembly **9** gathering **10** assemblage, collection **11** aggregation **12** congregation
congest 3 jam **4** clog, fill, plug, stop **5** block, choke, close, crowd **6** plug up **7** occlude **8** obstruct
conglobate 4 ball **6** sphere **8** ensphere **9** spherical
conglomerate 4 mass, pool **5** chain, group, mixed, trust **6** cartel, motley **7** chaebol, combine **8** keiretsu, zaibatsu **9** aggregate, syndicate **11** aggregation **12** multifarious **13** heterogeneous
conglomeration 5 hoard, trove **8** mishmash **9** aggregate **10** collection, cumulation, hodgepodge, miscellany **11** agglomerate, aggregation **12** accumulation
Congo, Democratic Republic of the *capital:* 8 Kinshasa ***city:* 7** Kolwezi **9** Kisangani, Mbuji-Mayi **10** Lubumbashi ***explorer:* 7** Stanley (Henry Morton) ***former name:* 5** Zaire **12** Belgian Congo ***lake:* 4** Kivu **5** Mweru **6** Albert, Edward **10** Tanganyika ***language:* 6** French **7** English ***monetary unit:* 5** franc ***neighbor:* 5** Sudan **6** Angola, Rwanda, Uganda, Zambia **7** Burundi **8** Tanzania ***river:* 4** Uele
Congo, Republic of *capital:* 11 Brazzaville ***city:* 11** Pointe-Noire ***former name:* 11** Middle Congo ***language:* 6** French ***monetary unit:* 5** franc ***neighbor:* 5** Gabon **6** Angola **7** Cabinda **8** Cameroon
congratulate 4 laud **6** salute **10** compliment, felicitate
congregate 4 meet **5** swarm **6** gather, muster **7** collect, convene **8** assemble, converge **9** forgather **10** foregather, rendezvous
congregation 4 mass **5** crowd, flock, group **7** meeting **8** assembly, audience **9** gathering **10** assemblage, collection **11** churchgoers **12** parishioners
congress 4 diet **5** synod **6** league **7** meeting, society **8** assembly, conclave **10** convention, parliament **11** association, Capitol Hill, legislature
congressman 5 solon **7** senator **8** delegate, lawmaker **10** legislator
congruity 9 agreement, coherence **10** conformity **11** consistency
congruous 3 apt, fit **7** fitting **9** agreeable, befitting, congenial, consonant **10** compatible, concordant, consistent, harmonious **11** appropriate, sympathetic
conifer 3 fir, yew **4** pine **5** cedar, larch **6** spruce **7** cypress, hemlock, juniper **8** softwood **9** evergreen **10** arborvitae
conjectural 7 reputed **8** putative, supposed **11** speculative, theoretical **12** hypothetical, suppositious **13** suppositional
conjecture 5 guess, infer **6** assume, theory **7** presume, suppose, surmise, suspect **8** theorize **9** inference, speculate **11** hypothesize, proposition, speculation, supposition
conjoin 3 wed **4** band, link, yoke **5** unite **6** couple **7** combine, connect **8** federate **9** affiliate, associate, cooperate **11** consolidate
conjoint 6 common, mutual, public, shared, united **7** unified **8** combined, communal **9** concerted **10** collective **11** coefficient, cooperative, intermutual
conjointly 8 mutually, together
conjugal 6 wedded **7** marital, married, nuptial, spousal **8** hymeneal **9** connubial **11** matrimonial
conjugality 7 wedlock **8** marriage **9** matrimony
conjugate 4 fuse, join, link, pair, yoke **5** yoked **6** couple, joined, linked **7** bracket, combine, conjoin, connect, coupled **9** associate, connected
conjunct 5 joint **6** common, joined, mutual, shared, united
conjunction 2 as, if, or, so **3** and, but, for, nor, yet **4** lest, once, than, then, when **5** after, since, union, until, where, which, while **6** before, either, though, unless **7** because, however, neither, whereas, whether **8** alliance, although, moreover, whenever **9** therefore **10** connection **11** affiliation, association, combination, concurrence
conjuration 4 oath **5** charm, spell, trick **7** sorcery **10** adjuration, hocus-pocus, invocation **11** abracadabra, incantation
conjure 3 beg **4** urge **6** appeal, invoke, summon **7** beseech, entreat, imagine, implore **8** contrive **9** importune **10** supplicate
conjurer 4 mage, seer **5** magus **6** Magian, wizard **7** warlock **8** magician, sorcerer **9** enchanter, trickster **11** illusionist, necromancer
conjuring 5 magic **7** sorcery **8** wizardry **10** hocus-pocus, necromancy **11** abracadabra, legerdemain, thaumaturgy
conk 3 die, hit, rap **4** belt, swat **5** croak, faint, knock, thump, whack **8** knock out
con man see **confidence man**
connate 4 akin **6** allied, inborn, native **7** kindred, related **8** inherent **9** congenial, elemental, essential, ingrained, inherited, intrinsic **10** affiliated, congenital, indigenous, indwelling **11** consanguine
connect 3 tie, wed **4** ally, bind, join, link, yoke **5** marry, unite **6** attach, bridge, cou-

ple, fasten, relate **7** combine, conjoin **8** transfer **9** affiliate, associate, interlock

Connecticut ***capital:*** **8** Hartford ***city:*** **4** Avon **6** Darien **8** New Haven, Stamford **9** Greenwich, New London, Waterbury **10** Bridgeport ***college, university:*** **4** Yale **7** Trinity **8** Wesleyan **9** Fairfield **10** Quinnipiac ***nickname:*** **6** Nutmeg (State) **12** Constitution (State) ***river:*** **6** Thames **10** Housatonic **11** Connecticut ***state bird:*** **5** robin (American) ***state flower:*** **14** mountain laurel ***state tree:*** **8** white oak

connection **3** tie **4** bond, link **5** joint, nexus, tie-in, union **6** hookup, splice **7** joining, kinship, network **8** affinity, alliance, coupling, junction, juncture **9** coherence, communion, fastening **10** attachment, catenation, continuity **11** affiliation, association, combination, conjunction, partnership **12** relationship

connective **2** or **3** and, nor, not **4** then **6** either **7** neither **8** syndetic **11** conjunction, conjunctive

conniption **3** fit **4** bout, snit **5** furor, spasm, spate, spell, throe **6** attack, frenzy **7** seizure, tantrum **8** outburst, paroxysm **10** convulsion

connivance **8** intrigue **9** collusion **10** complicity, conspiracy

connive **4** plot, wink **5** blink **6** devise, scheme, wink at **7** blink at, collude **8** conspire, contrive, intrigue **9** machinate

connoisseur **4** buff **6** expert **7** epicure, gourmet **8** aesthete, gourmand, highbrow **9** authority, bon vivant **10** dilettante, gastronome **11** cognoscente

connotation **4** hint **7** meaning **8** overtone **9** undertone **10** intimation, suggestion **11** association, implication **13** signification

connote **4** hint, mean **5** imply, spell **6** hint at, intend **7** betoken, express, signify, suggest **8** indicate, intimate **9** insinuate

connubial **6** wedded **7** marital, married, nuptial, spousal **8** conjugal, hymeneal **11** matrimonial

connubiality **7** wedlock **8** marriage **9** matrimony **11** conjugality

conquer **4** beat, best, lick, tame, whip **5** crush **6** defeat, master, subdue **8** overcome, surmount, vanquish **9** checkmate, overpower, overthrow, overwhelm, subjugate

conquest **3** win **4** rout **7** triumph, victory **9** overthrow, seduction **11** subjugation

Conrad, Joseph ***character:*** **3** Jim **4** Axel, Lena **5** Flora, Kurtz **6** Marlow, Verloc **7** Almayer **8** MacWhirr, Nostromo ***work:*** **5** Youth **6** Chance **7** Lord Jim, Typhoon, Victory **8** Nostromo **11** Secret Agent (The) **13** Almayer's Folly **15** Heart of Darkness

Conroy novel **10** Beach Music **11** Water Is Wide (The) **12** Great Santini (The) **13** Prince of Tides (The) **17** Lords of Discipline (The)

consanguineous **4** akin **6** agnate **7** cognate, connate, kindred, related

conscience **5** demur, honor, qualm **6** ethics, virtue **7** decency, remorse, scruple **8** morality, scruples, superego **9** integrity **10** contrition **11** compunction

conscienceless **6** amoral **7** immoral **9** unethical **12** unprincipled, unscrupulous

conscientious **4** fair, just, true **5** exact **6** honest **7** careful, dutiful, upright **8** diligent, reliable, studious **9** honorable **10** high-minded, meticulous, principled, scrupulous **11** hard-working, painstaking, punctilious

conscious **5** alive, awake, aware **7** knowing, mindful, witting **8** sensible, sentient **9** attentive, cognizant **10** deliberate, perceptive

consciousness **4** heed, mind **6** regard **7** concern **9** alertness, awareness, knowledge **10** cognizance, perception **11** realization, recognition

conscribe **5** draft, limit **6** call up, enlist, enroll, muster **7** recruit

conscript **5** draft, elect **6** called, choose, chosen, enlist, enroll, induct, select **7** drafted, dragoon, impress, recruit, soldier **8** selected

consecrate **5** bless **6** anoint, devote, hallow, ordain, pledge **8** dedicate, sanctify

consecrated **4** holy **6** sacred **7** blessed **8** hallowed **10** sanctified ***oil:*** **6** chrism

consecution see **sequence**

consecutive **4** next **5** later **6** serial **7** ensuing, ordered, sequent **9** following, succedent **10** sequential, subsequent, succeeding, successive **11** progressive **12** successional

consent **3** yes **4** okay **5** agree, allow, leave, yield **6** accede, accord, assent, comply, concur, permit **7** approve, go-ahead **8** approval, sanction **9** acquiesce, agreement, allowance, subscribe **10** compliance, permission **12** acquiescence **13** authorization, understanding

consequence **4** fame, note, rank **5** issue, state **6** cachet, effect, import, moment, renown, repute, result, sequel, status, upshot, weight **7** account, conceit, fallout, outcome, stature **8** eminence, position, prestige, reaction **9** aftermath, magnitude **10** importance, reputation **11** aftereffect, weightiness **12** repercussion, significance

consequent **5** later, sound **7** ensuing, logical **8** rational **9** deduction, following, resulting

consequential **3** big **5** major **7** serious, weighty **8** egoistic, indirect, material **9** conceited, egotistic, important, momentous **10** collateral, incidental, meaningful, subsidiary **11** significant, substantial **12** considerable **13** self-important

consequently **4** ergo, thus **5** hence **9** as a result, therefore, thereupon **10** inevitably **11** accordingly

conservation **4** care **7** control **9** attention, husbandry **10** management, protection **11** safekeeping **12** guardianship, preservation

conservative **4** tory **6** proper **7** diehard, oldline **8** cautious, discreet, old-guard, orthodox, rightist, standpat **9** right-wing, temperate **10** restrained **11** circumspect, reactionary, right-winger, standpatter, traditional

conservatory **6** school **7** academy, nursery **8** hothouse **10** greenhouse **11** music school

conserve **3** can, jam **4** keep, save **5** hoard, lay up, put up, skimp, store **6** keep up **7** husband, protect, support, sustain **8** maintain, set aside, withhold **9** confiture, economize, safeguard, sweetmeat

consider **3** see **4** deem, feel, mind, muse, note, rate, view **5** fancy, judge, sense, study, think, weigh **6** credit, look at, notice, ponder, reason, reckon, regard **7** account, believe, examine, imagine, inspect, reflect, respect, suppose **8** appraise, cogitate, conclude, envisage, meditate, mull over, ruminate **9** speculate, think over **10** deliberate, excogitate, scrutinize, think about **11** contemplate

considerable **3** big **5** ample, hefty, large, major **7** notable, sizable, weighty **8** material, sensible, sizeable **9** extensive, important, momentous, plentiful **10** large-scale, meaningful **11** respectable, significant, substantial **13** consequential

considerably **3** far **4** well **5** quite **6** rather **7** notably **8** somewhat **10** noticeably **11** appreciably **13** significantly, substantially

considerate **4** kind **6** kindly, polite, tender **7** amiable, careful, patient, tactful **8** discreet, generous, obliging **9** attentive **10** chivalrous, forbearing, solicitous, thoughtful **11** circumspect, complaisant, sympathetic, warmhearted **13** compassionate

consideration **3** fee **4** heed, tact **5** cause, favor, issue, study **6** esteem, factor, motive, reason, regard **7** account, concern, payment, respect, thought **8** kindness **9** attention, awareness **10** admiration, cogitation, discussion, reflection, solicitude **11** application, forbearance, mindfulness **12** deliberation

considered **7** advised, studied, weighed **8** studious **10** deliberate, thought-out **11** intentional **12** aforethought, premeditated

consign **4** give, send, ship **5** agree, allot, award, remit, yield **6** commit, convey, devote, submit **7** address, commend, confide, deliver, entrust, forward **8** dispatch, hand over, relegate, transmit, turn over **9** surrender

consist **3** lie **4** rest **5** abide, agree, dwell, exist, fit in **6** accord, inhere, reside **7** comport, conform, consort, subsist **8** dovetail **10** correspond

consistency **7** aptness, concord, density, fitness, harmony, texture **8** evenness, firmness, likeness **9** agreement, coherence, congruity, thickness, viscosity **10** conformity, consonance, similarity **11** suitability

consistent **4** even, true **6** steady **7** regular, uniform **8** constant **9** accordant, agreeable, congenial, congruous, consonant, unfailing, unvarying **10** compatible, conforming, dependable, invariable, unchanging **11** homogeneous, sympathetic, undeviating

consistently **8** wontedly **9** regularly, routinely **10** habitually, invariably **11** customarily

console **4** calm, case **5** cheer **6** buck up, solace **7** cabinet, comfort, hearten **9** sideboard

consolidate **3** mix, set **4** fuse, join, meld, pool **5** blend, merge, unify, unite **6** firm up, secure **7** compact, fortify **8** compress, condense, federate, solidify **9** integrate **10** amalgamate, strengthen **11** concentrate

consolidation **5** union **6** merger **7** melding, merging **9** coalition **11** combination, integration, unification **12** amalgamation

consonance **6** accord **7** concord, harmony **9** agreement, congruity, resonance **10** congruence

consonant **4** akin, like **6** agnate **7** musical, similar **8** blending, harmonic, resonant **9** congruous **10** compatible, harmonious **11** conformable **13** corresponding ***kind:*** **4** stop, surd **5** nasal, velar **6** atonic, voiced **7** lateral, palatal, spirant **8** alveolar, bilabial, unvoiced **9** fricative, voiceless

consort **3** set **4** mate, wife **5** agree, group, tally, unite **6** accord, attend, fellow, spouse, square, troupe **7** company, comport, conform, husband, partner **8** assembly, chaperon, dovetail **9** accompany, associate, companion, harmonize **10** correspond

consortium **4** bloc, club, ring **5** guild, trust, union **6** cartel, league **7** combine, society **8** alliance, congress **9** coalition, syndicate **10** federation **11** association **12** conglomerate

conspectus **5** brief **6** digest, précis, sketch,

survey **7** epitome, outline, summary **8** abstract, overview, synopsis **9** reduction **10** abridgment **11** abridgement **12** condensation

conspicuous **5** clear, overt, showy **6** marked, patent, signal **7** blatant, evident, glaring, notable, obvious, pointed, salient **8** apparent, distinct, flagrant, manifest, striking **9** arresting, egregious, notorious, obtrusive, prominent **10** celebrated, noticeable, pronounced, remarkable **11** eye-catching, illustrious, outstanding **12** ostentatious

conspiracy **4** plan, plot **5** cabal **6** scheme **8** intrigue **11** machination

conspirator **7** abettor, plotter, schemer **9** accessory, intriguer **10** accomplice **11** confederate

conspire **4** plot **5** cabal **6** scheme **7** collude, connive **8** intrigue **9** machinate

constable **6** deputy, lawman, warden **7** marshal, sheriff

constancy **5** faith **6** fealty **7** loyalty, resolve **8** adhesion, devotion, fidelity, firmness **9** adherence, diligence, endurance, fortitude **10** allegiance, attachment, dedication, resolution, steadiness **11** staunchness **12** faithfulness, perseverance **13** dependability, steadfastness

constant **4** even, fast, firm, true **5** fixed, loyal **6** dogged, stable, steady, trusty **7** abiding, chronic, endless, equable, lasting, nonstop, staunch, uniform **8** enduring, faithful, habitual, resolute, unending **9** ceaseless, confirmed, continual, immovable, immutable, incessant, obstinate, perpetual, steadfast, sustained, unceasing, unfailing, unmovable, unvarying **10** changeless, consistent, continuous, dependable, inflexible, invariable, inveterate, persistent, persisting, unchanging, unwavering **11** everlasting, inalterable, unalterable, unrelenting, unremitting **12** interminable, unchangeable

Constantine ***birthplace:*** **4** Nish ***mother:*** **6** Helena ***son:*** **7** Crispus ***victim:*** **6** Fausta **7** Crispus ***wife:*** **6** Fausta

constantly **4** ever **5** often **6** always **7** forever **9** eternally **10** frequently, invariably, repeatedly **11** incessantly, perpetually **12** continuously

constellation **5** group **7** pattern **10** assemblage, collection **11** arrangement ***Altar:*** **3** Ara ***Archer:*** **11** Sagittarius ***Arrow:*** **7** Sagitta ***Balance:*** **5** Libra ***Bear, Great:*** **9** Ursa Major ***Bear, Little:*** **9** Ursa Minor ***Big Dipper:*** **9** Ursa Major ***Bird of Paradise:*** **4** Apus ***Bull:*** **6** Taurus ***Centaur:*** **9** Centaurus ***Chained Lady:*** **9** Andromeda ***Chameleon:*** **10** Chamaeleon ***Champion:*** **7** Perseus ***Charioteer:*** **6** Auriga ***Clock:*** **10** Horologium ***Colt:*** **8** Equuleus ***Crab:*** **6** Cancer ***Crane:*** **4** Grus ***Cross:*** **4** Crux ***Crow:*** **6** Corvus ***Crown:*** **6** Corona ***Cup:*** **6** Crater ***Dolphin:*** **9** Delphinus ***Dove:*** **7** Columba ***Dragon:*** **5** Draco ***Eagle:*** **6** Aquila ***Fishes:*** **6** Pisces ***Fly:*** **5** Musca ***Flying Fish:*** **6** Volans ***Furnace:*** **6** Fornax ***Graving Tool:*** **6** Caelum ***Great Bear:*** **9** Ursa Major ***Greater Dog:*** **10** Canis Major ***Hare:*** **5** Lepus ***Herdsman:*** **6** Boötes ***Horned Goat:*** **11** Capricornus ***Hunter:*** **5** Orion ***Indian:*** **5** Indus ***Keel:*** **6** Carina ***Lady in the Chair:*** **10** Cassiopeia ***Larger Bear:*** **9** Ursa Major ***Larger Dog:*** **10** Canis Major ***Lesser Dog:*** **10** Canis Minor ***Lion:*** **3** Leo ***Little Bear:*** **9** Ursa Minor ***Little Dipper:*** **9** Ursa Minor ***Little Fox:*** **9** Vulpecula ***Lizard:*** **7** Lacerta ***Lyre:*** **4** Lyra ***Mariner's Compass:*** **5** Pyxis ***Monarch:*** **7** Cepheus ***Net:*** **9** Reticulum ***Painter's Easel:*** **6** Pictor ***Pair of Compasses:*** **8** Circinus ***Peacock:*** **4** Pavo ***Pump:*** **6** Antlia ***Ram:*** **5** Aries ***Rescuer:*** **7** Perseus ***River Po:*** **8** Eridanus ***Sails:*** **4** Vela ***Scorpion:*** **8** Scorpius ***Serpent:*** **7** Serpens ***Serpent Holder:*** **9** Ophiuchus ***Sextant:*** **7** Sextans ***Shield:*** **6** Scutum ***Smaller Bear:*** **9** Ursa Minor ***Square:*** **5** Norma ***Stern:*** **6** Puppis ***Swan:*** **6** Cygnus ***Table:*** **5** Mensa ***Toucan:*** **6** Tucana ***Triangle:*** **10** Triangulum ***Twins:*** **6** Gemini ***Unicorn:*** **9** Monoceros ***Virgin:*** **5** Virgo ***Water Carrier:*** **8** Aquarius ***Water Monster:*** **5** Hydra ***Water Snake:*** **6** Hydrus ***Whale:*** **5** Cetus ***Winged Horse:*** **7** Pegasus ***Wolf:*** **5** Lupus

consternate **5** alarm, daunt, shake, shock **6** appall, dismay **7** horrify, unnerve **8** distress

consternation **4** fear **5** alarm, dread, panic, shock **6** dismay, fright, horror, terror **11** trepidation **12** bewilderment

constituent **4** part **5** piece, voter **6** factor, member **7** element, portion **8** division, fraction **9** component, elemental, principal **10** ingredient

constitute **4** form, make **5** enact, found, set up, start **6** create, embody, make up **7** appoint, compose **8** complete, comprise, organize **9** establish, institute, represent

constitution **3** law **4** code **5** build, canon **6** design, makeup, nature **7** charter **8** physique **9** formation, structure **11** composition **12** architecture, construction

constitutional **4** walk **6** inborn, inbred, innate, lawful **7** built-in, organic **8** inherent **9** essential, ingrained, intrinsic **10** congenital, deep-seated

Constitution State **11** Connecticut

Constitution, U.S.S. **12** Old Ironsides

constitutive **5** vital **8** cardinal **9** essential **11** fundamental **12** constructive

constrain **3** bar **4** curb, deny, jail **5** chain, check, crush, force, impel, limit, press **6** bridle, coerce, compel, enjoin, oblige, secure, squash, squish **7** confine, deprive, inhibit, refrain, squeeze **8** compress, hold back, hold down, imprison, restrain, restrict **11** incarcerate

constraint **4** bond **5** check, force **6** duress **8** coercion, pressure **9** captivity, detention, restraint **10** compulsion, diffidence, inhibition, limitation, repression **11** confinement, restriction, suppression **13** embarrassment

constrict **4** curb **5** cramp, limit, pinch, strap **6** hamper, narrow, shrink **7** confine, inhibit, squeeze, tighten **8** compress, condense, contract, restrain, strangle, stultify **9** constrain **12** circumscribe

constrictor **3** boa **5** snake **6** muscle **8** anaconda **9** sphincter, strangler

construct **4** form, make **5** build, erect, forge, frame, put up, raise, set up, shape **6** create, devise **7** build up, compile, fashion, produce **8** assemble, engineer **9** establish, fabricate **11** manufacture, put together

construction **6** design, makeup **7** edifice, shaping **8** assembly, building **9** formation **10** fashioning **11** arrangement, engineering, fabrication, manufacture **12** architecture, constitution

constructive **6** useful **7** helpful, implied, virtual **8** implicit, positive, valuable **9** practical **10** beneficial

construe **5** educe, gloss, parse **6** induct **7** analyze, explain, expound **9** explicate, interpret **10** paraphrase, understand

consuetude **5** habit, usage **6** custom, manner **8** practice **10** convention

consult **3** ask **6** advise, confer, huddle, parley **7** examine, refer to **8** collogue, consider **11** confabulate

consume **3** eat, use **4** down, gulp, ruin **5** drain, drink, eat up, gorge, spend, use up, waste **6** absorb, devour, expend, finish, ingest, obsess, take up **7** deplete, destroy, engross, exhaust, put away, put down, swallow **8** squander **9** dissipate, finish off, polish off **10** annihilate, extinguish, monopolize, run through

consumer **4** user **5** buyer **6** client **7** shopper, end user **8** customer **9** purchaser

consumer advocate **5** Nader (Ralph)

consuming **6** ardent **7** fervent, intense **8** gripping, riveting **9** absorbing **10** engrossing **11** enthralling **12** monopolizing

consummate **3** end **4** ripe **5** close, crown, ideal, utter **6** finish, superb, wind up, wrap up **7** achieve, perfect, supreme **8** absolute, complete, conclude, finished, flawless, peerless, ultimate **9** faultless, matchless, perfected, virtuosic **10** accomplish, impeccable, inimitable **11** superlative **12** accomplished **13** thoroughgoing

consumption **2** TB **3** use **5** decay, waste **6** intake **7** wasting **8** phthisis **9** depletion, ingestion **10** absorption **11** dissipation **12** tuberculosis

contact **4** meet **5** reach, touch **8** tangency, touching **9** closeness, communion, proximity **10** connection, contiguity **11** association, contingence **13** communication

contagion **3** pox **4** bane, meme **5** taint, venom, virus **6** miasma, plague, poison **7** disease, scourge **8** epidemic **9** infection, pollution **10** corruption, pestilence **13** contamination

contagious **6** catchy **8** catching, epidemic **9** spreading **10** infectious **12** communicable, pestilential **13** transmissible, transmittable

contain **4** hold, keep **5** check, house **6** embody, take in **7** collect, control, embrace, enclose, include, receive, repress, subsume **8** comprise, restrain **9** encompass **10** comprehend **11** accommodate

container **3** bag, bin, box, can, cup, jar, keg, mug, pod, pot, tin, tub, urn, vat **4** cage, case, cask, drum, etui, ewer, pail, sack, silo, tank, vase, vial, well **5** chest, crate, cruet, flask, glass, gourd, phial, pouch **6** basket, bottle, carafe, carton, casket, coffin, cooler, goblet, hamper, hatbox, holder, inkpot, shaker **7** bandbox, capsule, chalice, inkwell, package, pitcher, thermos **8** canister, catchall, decanter, envelope, hogshead, jerrican, puncheon **10** receptacle ***liturgical:*** **3** pyx **7** chalice **8** ciborium

contaminate **4** foul, soil **5** dirty, spoil, stain, sully, taint **6** befoul, debase, defile, infect, injure, poison **7** corrupt, deprave, pervert, pollute, profane, tarnish, vitiate **9** desecrate **10** adulterate

conte **4** tale **5** story **9** narrative

contemn **4** snub **5** abhor, scorn, spurn **6** deride **7** deplore, despise, disdain **8** ridicule **10** look down on

contemplate **3** eye **4** mull, muse, view **5** study, think, weigh **6** behold, debate, gaze at, intend, look at, ponder, regard **7** examine, inspect, propose, reflect **8** consider, gaze upon, look upon, meditate, mull over, ruminate, think out **9** think over **10** deliberate, excogitate, scrutinize

contemplation **5** study **6** musing **7** thought **8**

thinking **9** intention, pondering **10** cogitation, meditation, reflection, rumination **11** cerebration, expectation, speculation **12** deliberation **13** consideration

contemplative 6 musing **7** pensive **10** cogitative, meditative, reflecting, reflective, ruminative, thoughtful **11** speculative **13** introspective

contemporary 3 new **6** coeval, extant, modern, recent **7** current, present, topical **8** existent, existing, up-to-date **9** au courant **10** coexistent, coexisting, coincident, concurrent, present-day, synchronic **11** synchronous **12** simultaneous

contempt 5 scorn, shame **7** despite, disdain, mockery **8** aversion, defiance, disfavor, disgrace, dishonor, distaste, ignominy **9** antipathy, discredit, disesteem, disrepute **10** disrespect, opprobrium, repugnance **12** disobedience, stubbornness

contemptible 3 low **4** base, mean, poor, vile **5** cheap, sorry **6** abject, odious, paltry, scummy, scurvy, shabby, sordid **7** hateful, ignoble, pitiful, squalid **8** inferior, pitiable, shameful, unworthy, wretched **9** abhorrent, loathsome **10** despicable, detestable, disgusting **11** ignominious **12** dishonorable

contemptuous 7 haughty **8** arrogant, derisive, scornful **10** disdainful **12** supercilious **13** condescending, disrespectful

contend 3 vie, war **4** aver, avow, cope, face, urge **5** argue, brawl, claim, fight **6** affirm, allege, assert, battle, charge, combat, debate, defend, insist, oppose, report, strive **7** compete, contest **8** confront, maintain, struggle **9** encounter, withstand

contender 5 match, rival **6** player **8** opponent **9** adversary, candidate, combatant **10** antagonist, challenger, competitor, contestant

____ contendere 4 nolo

content 4 cozy, gist **5** happy **6** at ease, serene **7** appease, gratify, meaning, placate, satisfy **9** gratified, satisfied, substance **11** comfortable **12** significance

contention 3 war **4** beef, feud **6** combat, rumpus, strife, thesis **7** discord, dispute, dissent, quarrel, rivalry, wrangle **8** argument, conflict, disunity, squabble **10** difference, dissension, dissidence **11** altercation, competition, controversy ***Scottish:*** **5** sturt

contentious 5 fiery **7** carping, froward, peppery, scrappy, warlike **8** captious, caviling, contrary, militant, perverse **9** bellicose, combative, hotheaded, litigious, polemical, truculent **10** pugnacious **11** belligerent, quarrelsome **12** disputatious, faultfinding **13** argumentative, controversial

conterminous 10 coincident **11** coextensive

contest 3 vie **4** bout, duel, feud, fray, game, meet, race, tilt **5** clash, fight, match, repel, rival, trial **6** battle, combat, debate, oppose, resist, strife, strive **7** compete, dispute, rivalry, warfare **8** argument, conflict, endeavor, skirmish, struggle, tug-of-war **9** challenge, encounter, rencontre **10** engagement, tournament **11** competition

contestant 5 rival **7** also-ran, entrant, opposer, wannabe **8** opponent **9** adversary, contender **10** challenger, competitor

contiguity 9 adjacency, immediacy, proximity **11** propinquity

contiguous 4 next **8** abutting, adjacent, touching **9** adjoining, bordering **10** juxtaposed

continence 6 purity, virtue **8** chastity, sobriety **9** austerity **10** abnegation, abstinence, asceticism, chasteness, moderation, temperance **11** forbearance **12** renunciation **13** self-restraint

continent 4 Asia, mass **5** sober **6** Africa, chaste, Europe **8** celibate, mainland **9** abstinent, Australia, temperate **10** abstemious, Antarctica, restrained **11** abstentious **12** North America, South America ***lost:*** **8** Atlantis

contingence 5 touch **7** contact **8** tangency, touching

contingency 4 pass **5** event, pinch **6** chance, crisis **8** exigency, juncture, occasion **9** emergency **10** likelihood **11** opportunity, possibility, probability, uncertainty

contingent 3 odd **4** band **5** group, party, troop **6** casual, chance, likely **7** reliant **8** possible, probable, relative **9** dependent, empirical, entourage, uncertain **10** accidental, delegation, deputation, detachment, fortuitous, incidental, unforeseen **11** conditional **13** unanticipated, unforeseeable, unpredictable

continual 6 steady **7** abiding, endless, nonstop, regular, running **8** constant, enduring, timeless, unbroken, unending **9** ceaseless, incessant, perpetual, perennial, recurrent, recurring, unceasing, unfailing, unvarying **10** persistent, persisting, relentless, unchanging, unflagging **11** everlasting, unremitting **12** interminable **13** uninterrupted

continually 4 ever **5** on end **6** always **7** forever **8** steadily, together **9** endlessly **10** constantly **11** incessantly, night and day **12** interminably, persistently, relentlessly, successively **13** consecutively

continuance 3 run **4** stay **5** delay **6** sequel **8** duration, survival **9** longevity **10** permanence **11** adjournment, persistence **12** postponement, prolongation

continuation 3 run **4** coda **6** sequel **8** appendix, duration, epilogue **9** endurance, extension **10** resumption **11** persistence, protraction **12** prolongation

continue 4 go on, last, stay **5** abide, renew, run on, segue **6** endure, hang in, keep at, keep on, keep up, pick up, push on, remain, reopen, resume, retain, take up **7** carry on, persist, press on, proceed, prolong, restart, survive **8** maintain, postpone **9** carry over, persevere **10** recommence

continuing 5 fixed **6** steady **7** abiding, chronic, durable, eternal, lasting, ongoing **8** constant, enduring, lifelong, stubborn **9** long-lived, obstinate, perennial, prolonged, steadfast, tenacious, unabating **10** inveterate, persistent, persisting **11** long-lasting

continuity 4 flow **6** script **8** duration, scenario, sequence **9** endurance **11** persistence, progression

continuous see **continual**

continuously see **continually**

contort 4 knot, warp **5** twist, wring **6** deform, wrench, writhe **7** distort, grimace, torture **9** convolute, corkscrew, disfigure

contortionist 7 acrobat

contour 4 form, line **5** curve, lines, shape **6** figure **7** outline, pattern, profile **9** lineament, lineation **10** silhouette **11** delineation

contra 6 facing, toward **7** against, counter, reverse, vis-à-vis **8** converse, fronting, opposite **10** conversely

contraband 3 hot **5** taboo **6** banned **7** bootleg, illegal, illicit, smuggle **8** unlawful **9** forbidden **10** prohibited, proscribed **11** black market, bootlegging, trafficking

contract 4 bond, hire, pact, sink **5** catch, incur, lease **6** engage, induce, lessen, reduce, shrink, treaty, weaken **7** abridge, acquire, afflict, bargain, decline, dwindle, shorten, shrivel **8** compress, condense, covenant, decrease, diminish **9** agreement, constrict, succumb to **11** concentrate, transaction **12** come down with ***part:*** **6** clause **7** article, proviso

contraction 3 he'd, he's, I'll, it's, I've, tic **4** ain't, can't, don't, flex, he'll, isn't, let's, she'd, she's, won't, you'd **5** aren't, cramp, didn't, hadn't, hasn't, she'll, spasm, they'd, wasn't, you'll, you're, you've **6** haven't, mustn't, needn't, they'll, they've, weren't **7** couldn't, elision, mightn't, wouldn't **8** shouldn't **9** reduction, shrinkage **10** abridgment **11** abridgement **12** abbreviation ***heart's:*** **7** systole ***poetic:*** **3** e'en, e'er, o'er, 'tis **4** ne'er, 'twas **5** 'twere, 'twill

contradict 4 deny **5** belie, cross, rebut **6** impugn, negate, refute, take on **7** confute, dispute, gainsay **8** negative, traverse **9** challenge, disaffirm

contradiction 6 denial **7** paradox **8** antinomy, negation, rebuttal, variance **9** disparity **10** gainsaying, opposition, refutation **11** discrepancy, incongruity **12** disagreement, protestation **13** inconsistency

contradictory 7 counter, reverse **8** contrary, converse, negating, opposite **9** antipodal **10** antipodean, antithesis, nullifying **12** antithetical

contraption 3 rig **5** gizmo **6** device, doodad, gadget **7** machine **9** apparatus, doohickey **11** contrivance

contrariety 10 antagonism, antithesis, opposition, perversity, unlikeness

contrariwise 9 vice versa **10** conversely, oppositely

contrary 5 balky **6** averse, ornery, unruly **7** adverse, counter, froward, reverse, wayward **8** converse, opposite, perverse, stubborn **9** antipodal, diametric, dissident, obstinate, vice versa **10** conversely, discordant, headstrong, oppositely, rebellious, refractory **11** conflicting, intractable, wrongheaded **12** antagonistic, antipathetic, antithetical, contumacious, cross-grained, recalcitrant ***prefix:*** **7** counter

contrast 6 differ **7** collate, compare, diverge **8** conflict, disagree **9** disparity **10** comparison, difference, divergence **11** distinction, distinguish

contravene 4 defy, deny **5** break, cross, fight **6** abjure, breach, disown, impugn, negate, offend, oppose, reject **7** disobey, gainsay, violate **8** disclaim, infringe, renege on **9** disaffirm, go against, repudiate **10** contradict, transgress

contravention 6 breach **7** offense **8** trespass **9** violation **10** infraction **12** infringement **13** nonobservance, transgression

contretemps 3 row **4** slip, tiff **5** clash, run-in **6** dustup, mishap, slip-up **7** dispute, quarrel **8** argument **9** mischance **10** falling-out, misfortune

contribute 3 add **4** give, help, tend **5** grant **6** chip in, donate, kick in, submit, supply **7** conduce, pitch in, redound **9** subscribe **11** come through

contribution 4 alms, gift **5** input, share, tithe **7** charity, payment, present **8** donation, offering **11** benefaction, beneficence

contributory 8 adjuvant **9** accessory, ancillary, auxiliary **10** collateral, subsidiary, supporting **11** appurtenant, subservient

contrite 5 sorry **8** penitent **9** regretful, repentant **10** apologetic, remorseful **11** penitential

contrition 3 rue **4** ruth **6** regret **7** penance, remorse **9** penitence **10** repentance **11** compunction **12** self-reproach

contrivance 4 ruse **6** device, gadget **7** gimmick **8** artifice **9** apparatus, expedient, invention, stratagem **10** brainchild **11** contraption

contrive 3 rig **4** fake, make, move, plan, plot **5** frame, hatch **6** cook up, devise, invent, make up, manage, scheme, vamp up, wangle **7** arrange, concoct, connive, develop, dream up, fashion, project, work out **8** cogitate, conspire, engineer, intrigue **9** construct, elaborate, fabricate, formulate, machinate

contrived 5 hokey **6** forced **7** labored **8** strained **9** concocted, insincere **10** artificial, engineered, fabricated, factitious

control 3 run **4** curb, rein, rule, sway **5** guide, power, steer **6** bridle, direct, govern, handle, manage, master, rein in, subdue **7** command, conduct, mastery, oversee, repress, reserve **8** dominate, dominion, regulate, restrain **9** authority, direction, restraint, supervise, supremacy **10** discipline, domination, management **11** supervision **12** jurisdiction

controlled 8 discreet, reserved **9** temperate **10** restrained

controversial 5 risky **6** touchy **7** awkward, charged, eristic **8** delicate, disputed, ticklish **9** explosive, litigious, polemical **11** contentious, problematic **12** disputatious **13** argumentative

controversy 3 row **5** clash **6** debate, rumpus, strife **7** dispute, quarrel, wrangle **8** argument, squabble **10** contention, falling-out **11** altercation, disputation, embroilment

controvert 4 deny **5** rebut **6** debate, oppose, oppugn, refute **7** confute, counter, dispute, gainsay **8** disprove, question **9** challenge, repudiate

contumacious 7 froward **8** contrary, insolent, mutinous, obdurate, perverse **9** obstinate **10** rebellious, refractory **11** disobedient, intractable **12** recalcitrant **13** insubordinate

contumacy 8 contempt, defiance **9** insolence **10** perversity **12** stubbornness **13** recalcitrance

contumelious 7 abusive **8** derisive, insolent, scornful **9** insulting, truculent **10** disdainful, scurrilous **11** opprobrious **12** vituperative

contumely 5 abuse **6** insult **7** affront, mockery, obloquy **8** contempt, ridicule, sneering **9** aspersion, invective **10** scurrility **12** vituperation

contuse 6 batter, bruise, injure **7** blacken

conundrum 5 poser **6** enigma, puzzle, riddle **7** baffler, mystery, problem, puzzler, stumper **10** puzzlement **13** Chinese puzzle

convalesce 4 heal, mend **7** improve, recover **10** recuperate

convene 4 call, meet **6** call in, gather, muster, summon **7** convoke, summons **8** assemble **9** forgather **10** congregate **12** come together

convenience 4 ease **7** amenity, benefit, comfort, leisure **8** facility **9** handiness **10** assistance **13** accessibility

convenient 3 fit **4** near **5** close, handy, ready **6** at hand, nearby, proper, useful **7** close by, helpful **8** suitable **9** available, immediate, opportune **10** accessible **11** appropriate, comfortable **12** advantageous

convent 5 abbey **6** priory **7** nunnery **8** cloister **9** monastery, sanctuary

convention 3 law **4** bond, code, pact, rule **5** canon, usage **6** accord, custom, treaty **7** compact, meeting, precept **8** assembly, congress, contract, covenant, practice, protocol **9** agreement, concordat, formality, gathering, propriety, tradition **11** convocation

conventional 5 trite, usual **6** formal, normal, proper, seemly, solemn, square **7** correct, regular, routine, typical **8** everyday, habitual, moderate, ordinary, orthodox, standard, straight **9** bourgeois, customary **10** button-down, conforming, prevailing, restrained, unoriginal **11** commonplace, traditional **12** conservative

conventionalize 5 adapt **7** conform **9** normalize

converge 4 join, meet **5** focus, merge, unite **11** concentrate **12** come together

conversant 8 familiar **9** au courant **10** acquainted **11** experienced

conversation 4 chat, talk **6** confab, debate, parley **7** palaver, talking **8** causerie, colloquy, dialogue, duologue, exchange, repartee **9** discourse, tête-à-tête **10** discussion **13** confabulation

conversation piece 5 curio **6** oddity **9** curiosity

converse 3 gab **4** chat, chin, talk **5** speak, visit **6** confer, contra, parley **7** chatter, counter, reverse **8** antipode, contrary, opposite **9** antipodal, diametric **10** antithesis **12** antithetical **13** contradictory

conversely 9 vice versa **10** oppositely **12** contrariwise

conversion 5 shift **6** change, switch **7** novelty, rebirth, turning **8** metanoia, mutation, reversal **9** about-face **10** alteration, changeover **11** permutation **12** modification, regeneration **13** metamorphosis, transmutation

convert **4** sway **5** alter **6** change, modify, redeem, reform, switch **7** commute, remodel **8** persuade, renovate **9** proselyte, transform, translate, transmute, transpose **11** transfigure **12** metamorphose, transmogrify ***Christian:*** **10** catechumen

convex **5** bowed, toric **6** arched, curved **7** bulging, curving, gibbous, rounded

convexity **4** arch **6** camber

convey **3** lug **4** bear, cart, cede, deed, pack, send, tell, tote **5** bring, carry, ferry **6** assign, impart, pass on **7** channel, conduct, consign, deliver, express, project **8** make over, sign over, transfer, transmit **9** transport **11** communicate

conveyance **3** car **4** auto, cart, deed, sled **5** coach, sedan, stage, title, wagon **7** charter, trailer, transit, vehicle **8** carriage, carrying **9** transport **10** automobile **12** transporting ***public:*** **3** bus, cab **4** taxi, tram **5** plane, train **6** subway **7** trolley **8** airplane, monorail, railroad, rickshaw **9** streetcar **10** jinricksha, jinrikisha

convict **5** felon, lifer **6** inmate, send up **7** condemn, put away **8** criminal, jailbird, prisoner, sentence, yardbird **10** find guilty

conviction **4** view **5** creed, faith **6** belief, surety **7** opinion **8** doctrine, sentence, sureness **9** assurance, certainty, certitude, sentiment **10** confidence, persuasion **12** condemnation

convince **6** assure, induce, prompt **7** satisfy, win over **8** persuade, talk into **9** influence, prevail on **11** bring around, prevail upon

convincing **5** solid, sound, valid **6** cogent **8** credible, faithful **9** plausible **10** believable, conclusive, persuasive, satisfying **11** trustworthy

convivial **3** gay **5** jolly, merry **6** hearty, jocund, jovial, lively, social **7** festive **8** mirthful, sociable **9** fun-loving, vivacious **10** gregarious **13** companionable

convocation **5** synod **7** council, meeting **8** assembly, conclave **9** gathering **10** assemblage **12** congregation

convoke **4** call **6** gather, invite, muster, summon **7** collect, convene **8** assemble **12** call together

convoluted **6** coiled **7** complex, tangled, winding **8** involved, tortuous **9** intricate **10** circuitous **11** anfractuous, complicated **12** labyrinthine

convoy **6** attend, escort **7** conduct **9** accompany

convulse **4** rock **5** shake **7** agitate, concuss **8** tetanize

convulsion **3** fit **5** spasm **6** attack, tumult, uproar **7** quaking, rocking, seizure, shaking **8** disaster, paroxysm, upheaval **9** commotion, trembling

cook **3** fix, fry **4** bake, boil, chef, heat, melt, stew **5** broil, grill, poach, roast, sauté, steam **6** braise, doctor, simmer **7** falsify, parboil, prepare, swelter

cookbook ***abbreviation:*** **3** tsp **4** tbsp ***term:*** **3** cup, fry, mix **4** bake, beat, boil, chop, pare, peel, roux, sift, stew, stir, toss, whip, zest **5** baste, blend, broil, cream, glaze, grate, grind, knead, mince, pinch, poach, roast, sauté, scald, steam, stock **6** blanch, braise, fillet, season, simmer **7** al dente, deglaze, parboil **8** dissolve, emulsify, julienne, marinate, meringue **10** caramelize

cooked **4** done, sham **5** bogus, faked, phony **6** made-up **7** altered **8** doctored, spurious **10** fictitious

cookery **7** cuisine ***expert:*** **3** Ray (Rachael), Yan (Martin) **4** Chen (Joyce), Kerr (Graham), Puck (Wolfgang), Root (Waverley) **5** Beard (James), Child (Julia), David (Elizabeth), Hines (Duncan), Pépin (Jacques), Smith (Jeff) **6** Bocuse (Paul), Carême (Marie-Antoine), Farmer (Fannie), Fisher (M. F. K.), Franey (Pierre), Waters (Alice) **7** Crocker (Betty), Ducasse (Alain), Stewart (Martha) **8** Bourdain (Anthony), Rombauer (Irma) **9** Claiborne (Craig), Escoffier (Auguste), Prudhomme (Paul)

cookie **4** Oreo, snap **5** wafer **7** biscuit, brownie **10** gingersnap

cooking ***appliance:*** **4** oven **5** mixer, range, stove **7** blender, toaster **9** microwave **10** rotisserie ***implement:*** **3** cup, pan, pot, wok **4** olla **5** ladle, sieve, spoon, whisk **6** grater, masher, sifter, tureen **7** griddle, skillet, spatula, steamer **8** colander, teaspoon **9** eggbeater, frying pan **10** rolling pin, tablespoon **12** measuring cup ***measure:*** **3** cup, tsp **4** tbsp **8** teaspoon **10** tablespoon ***room:*** **6** galley **7** kitchen

Cook Islands ***capital:*** **6** Avarua ***dependency of:*** **10** New Zealand ***island:*** **9** Rarotonga

cool **3** hep, hip, icy, rad **4** calm, cold, phat **5** abate, aloof, chill, funky, gelid, nippy **6** arctic, chilly, frigid, frosty, with-it **7** assured, compose, control, decline, distant, dwindle, repress, subside **8** composed, decrease, detached, diminish, reserved, suppress **9** collected, confident, impassive, unruffled **10**

nonchalant, phlegmatic, unsociable **11** indifferent, standoffish, unflappable **13** dispassionate, imperturbable, self-possessed

cooler 3 fan, jug, pen **4** brig, coop, jail **5** clink, pokey **6** fridge, icebox, lockup, prison **7** freezer, slammer **9** calaboose **11** refrigerant **12** refrigerator

cooling device 3 fan **6** fridge, icebox **7** freezer **12** refrigerator

coolness 5 chill, poise **6** aplomb, phlegm **7** reserve **9** composure, frigidity, sangfroid **10** dispassion, equanimity **11** nonchalance, self-control

coop 3 hem, jug, mew, pen **4** brig, cage, jail **5** cramp, fence, pokey **6** cooler, corral, lockup, prison, shut in **7** close in, confine, enclose, slammer **9** calaboose, enclosure

cooperate 5 agree, unite **6** concur, league **7** combine, conjoin, pitch in **8** coincide, conspire **11** collaborate, participate **12** work together

cooperation 8 alliance, teamwork **13** confederation

cooperative 5 joint **6** common, mutual, shared **8** coactive, conjoint, obliging **9** collegial, concerted **10** collective, synergetic **11** coordinated **13** accommodating, collaborative, uncompetitive ***craft society:*** **5** artel

Cooper hero 7 Hawkeye **10** Deerslayer, Pathfinder **11** Natty Bumppo

coordinate 4 mate, mesh **5** align, equal, match, order **6** adjust, relate **7** coequal, conform **8** organize, parallel **9** companion, correlate, harmonize, integrate, reconcile **10** proportion, reciprocal **11** accommodate, correlative, counterpart ***system:*** **9** Cartesian

coot 4 bird, fogy **5** fogey **6** codger, dotard, duffer, fellow, oddity, scoter, weirdo **7** oddball **9** character, eccentric

cootie 5 louse **9** body louse

cop 3 nab **4** lift, take **5** adopt, catch, filch, pinch, steal, swipe **6** pilfer **7** capture, officer **8** bluecoat **9** patrolman, policeman

copacetic 3 A-OK **4** fine, jake, okay **5** dandy, great, nifty **8** all right **9** excellent **12** satisfactory

cope 4 cape, hack **5** cloak, cover, get by, match, vault **6** canopy, endure, make do, manage, mantle **7** carry on, survive **8** vestment

copestone 5 crown

copious 4 lush, rich **5** ample **6** lavish, plenty **7** liberal, profuse, replete **8** abundant, generous **9** abounding, bounteous, bountiful, exuberant, luxuriant, plenteous, plentiful

Copland work 5 Rodeo **11** Billy the Kid **17** Appalachian Spring

cop-out 5 dodge **6** excuse **7** evasion, pretext, retreat

copper 4 cent, coin **5** metal, penny, token **9** butterfly, policeman ***coating:*** **6** patina ***item:*** **4** cent **5** penny **6** kettle ***sulfate:*** **7** vitriol **9** bluestone **11** blue vitriol ***symbol:*** **2** Cu

copperhead 5 snake, viper **8** pit viper

coppice 4 bosk, wood **5** copse, grove, woods **6** bosque, forest, growth **7** thicket **9** brushwood, underwood

copse see **coppice**

Copt 8 Egyptian

copula 4 bond, link **5** joint, union **7** coupler

copy 3 ape **4** echo, fake, mock, sham **5** clone, ditto, forge, mimic, model, repro **6** carbon, parrot, repeat **7** emulate, forgery, imitate, replica, takeoff **8** knockoff, likeness, simulate **9** duplicate, facsimile, imitation, replicate, reproduce **10** impression, simulacrum, simulation, transcribe, transcript **11** counterfeit, counterpart, reduplicate, replication **12** reproduction

copycat 3 ape **4** aper **5** mimic **6** parrot **8** imitator

copyist 5 clerk **6** scribe **8** imitator **9** engrosser **10** plagiarist **11** transcriber

copyread 4 edit

coquet 3 toy **4** fool, vamp **5** dally, flirt, tease **6** trifle

coquette 4 vamp **5** flirt, tease

coquettish 3 coy **6** fickle **9** frivolous, kittenish **11** flirtatious

coral 3 red **4** pink, rosy **5** polyp **9** limestone

coral reef 3 cay, key **5** atoll ***off Australia:*** **5** Wreck ***world's largest:*** **12** Great Barrier

cord 3 tie **4** band, lace, pile, rope, whip, yarn **5** cable, nerve, stack **6** strand, string, tendon ***twisted:*** **7** torsade

cordage 4 rope **5** ropes **7** rigging ***fiber:*** **4** bast, hemp, jute, pita **5** sisal

Corday's victim 5 Marat (Jean-Paul)

Cordelia ***father:*** **4** Lear ***sister:*** **5** Regan **7** Goneril

cordial 4 warm **6** genial, hearty, jovial, tender **7** affable, liqueur, sincere **8** cheerful, friendly, gracious, sociable **9** congenial, convivial, heartfelt **10** hospitable **11** sympathetic, warmhearted **12** wholehearted

cordiality 6 warmth **7** amenity **9** geniality **10** amiability **12** agreeability, friendliness

cordon 4 lace, line, ring **5** braid **6** circle, ribbon **7** barrier **8** espalier ***bleu:*** **4** chef, cook **6** ribbon **10** blue ribbon, decoration, master chef

core 3 hub, nub **4** base, crux, gist, meat, pith, root **5** basis, focus, heart, midst **6** center, depths, kernel, middle, upshot **7** essence, nucleus **8** interior, midpoint **9** substance **10** foundation

corium 5 cutis **6** dermis

cork 4 bark, plug, seal, stop **5** float **6** bobber **7** stopper, stopple

corker 4 lulu **5** beaut, dandy, dilly, doozy **6** doozie, killer **8** jim-dandy, knockout **9** humdinger **11** crackerjack **12** lollapalooza

corkscrew 4 coil, wind **5** helix, twist **6** spiral

cormorant 4 bird, shag **7** glutton

corn 5 grain, maize **6** hominy **9** granulate ***bread:*** **4** pone **7** bannock, hoecake ***Indian:*** **5** maize **6** mealie ***kind:*** **3** pop **5** flint, flour, sweet **6** Indian ***pest:*** **5** borer ***piece:*** **3** cob, ear **5** spike **6** kernel, nubbin

Corncracker State 8 Kentucky

corner 3 box, fix, jam, nab **4** hole, nook, trap, tree **5** angle, catch, coign, niche, seize **6** collar, cranny, dogleg, pickle, plight, recess, scrape **7** capture, dilemma, impasse, trouble **8** bottle up, monopoly **10** bring to bay **11** predicament **12** intersection ***of eye:*** **7** canthus

cornerstone 4 base **5** basis **7** support **8** rudiment **10** foundation, groundwork

cornet 4 cone, horn **7** officer, trumpet **10** instrument

Cornhusker State 8 Nebraska

cornice 3 cap **4** band, eave **5** crown **7** molding

cornmeal 4 masa, mush, samp **5** grits **6** hominy **7** hoecake ***mush:*** **7** polenta

cornucopia 4 cone, horn **6** bounty, plenty, wealth **9** abundance, profusion **12** horn of plenty

Cornwallis, Charles *adversary:* 6 Greene (Nathanael) ***surrender site:*** **8** Yorktown

corny 5 banal, sappy, stale, trite **6** old hat **7** clichéd, mawkish **8** shopworn **9** hackneyed, schmaltzy **11** sentimental, stereotyped

corollary 6 effect, result, sequel, upshot **8** parallel, sequence **9** resulting **10** associated, end product, equivalent **11** aftereffect, consequence ***logical:*** **9** inference

corona 4 aura, glow, halo **5** cigar, crown, glory **6** circle, nimbus **7** aureola, aureole

coroner 8 examiner

coronet 5 crown, tiara **6** anadem, circle, diadem, wreath **7** chaplet, circlet, garland **8** headband

Coronis *form:* 4 crow ***son:*** **9** Asclepius **11** Aesculapius

corporal 3 NCO **6** bodily, carnal **7** fleshly, somatic **8** physical

corporate 7 unified **8** combined **9** aggregate

corporeal 6 bodily, carnal, mortal **7** fleshly, somatic **8** material, physical, tangible **9** objective **10** phenomenal **11** substantial

corposant 11 St. Elmo's fire

corps 4 band, body **5** group, party, troop **6** outfit, troupe **7** company

corpse 4 body **5** bones, stiff **7** cadaver, carcass, carrion, remains ***combining form:*** **4** necr **5** necro

corpselike 4 ashy, dead **5** ashen, gaunt **6** wasted **7** deathly, ghastly, macabre **8** lifeless, skeletal **10** cadaverous

corpulence 7 fatness, obesity **9** adiposity, rotundity **10** fleshiness, overweight, portliness

corpulent 3 fat **5** bulky, gross, heavy, obese, plump, stout **6** fleshy, portly, rotund **7** porcine, weighty **9** overblown **10** overweight

corpus 4 body, bulk, core, mass **6** oeuvre **9** principal, substance **10** collection **11** compilation

corpuscle 4 cell **8** hemocyte, monocyte **9** blood cell, leukocyte **10** lymphocyte **11** erythrocyte, granulocyte

corral 3 mew, pen **5** fence **6** gather, shut in **7** close in, collect, confine, enclose, round up **8** surround **9** enclosure

correct 3 fit, fix **4** edit, just, mend, true **5** amend, emend, exact, right **6** adjust, dead on, decent, proper, punish, reform, remedy, repair, revise, seemly, spot on **7** chasten, fitting, improve, perfect, precise, rectify, redress **8** accurate, becoming, chastise, decorous, flawless, set right **9** castigate, faultless **10** conforming, discipline, impeccable, legitimate, meticulous, scrupulous **11** appropriate, comme il faut, punctilious **12** conventional ***combining form:*** **4** orth **5** ortho

correction 3 rod **6** rebuke **7** reproof **8** revision **9** amendment **10** adjustment, discipline, emendation, punishment **11** castigation

corrective 4 cure **6** remedy **8** antidote, punitive, remedial **10** beneficial **11** counterstep, restorative **12** counteragent **13** counteractive

correctness 7 decorum **8** accuracy, fidelity **9** precision, propriety **10** exactitude

correlate 5 match **6** analog **7** pendant **8** analogue, coincide, dovetail, parallel **9** harmonize **10** complement, correspond **11** counterpart

correlative 2 if, or **3** and, nor **4** both, then **6** either **7** neither, related **10** complement, reciprocal **11** counterpart **13** complementary, corresponding

correspond 4 jibe **5** agree, equal, match, write **6** accord, concur **7** comport, conform **8** dovetail **9** harmonize **11** communicate

correspondence 4 mail **7** analogy, letters **8** symmetry **9** agreement, congruity **10** conformity, similarity **11** consistency, correlation ***mathematical:*** **7** mapping **8** function

correspondent 5 match **6** analog, pen pal, writer **7** fitting **8** analogue, parallel, reporter, suitable **9** correlate **10** conforming, journalist **11** commentator, contributor, counterpart

corresponding 4 akin, like **5** alike **6** agnate **7** related, similar **8** matching, parallel **9** analogous, consonant **10** comparable **11** correlative

correspondingly 4 also **7** equally **8** likewise **9** similarly **11** analogously

corrida 9 bullfight ***shout:* 3** olé

corridor 4 hall, lane, path **5** aisle, route, strip **6** artery, avenue **7** hallway, passage **10** passageway

corroborate 5 prove **6** uphold, verify **7** approve, bear out, certify, confirm, endorse, justify, support **8** document, validate **9** vindicate **12** authenticate, substantiate

corroborative 9 ancillary, auxiliary **10** collateral, supporting, supportive **12** confirmatory

corrode 4 rust **7** eat away, eat into, oxidize **8** wear away **9** undermine

corrosive 4 acid **5** acerb **6** biting **7** acerbic, caustic, cutting **9** sarcastic

corrosiveness 7 sarcasm **8** acerbity

corrugation 4 fold, ruck **5** plica, ridge **6** crease, furrow, groove **7** crinkle, wrinkle

corrupt 3 rot **5** bribe, decay, spoil, stain, taint, venal **6** befoul, debase, defile, molder, rotten, smirch **7** crooked, debauch, degrade, deprave, pervert, putrefy, tarnish, vitiate **8** bribable, degraded, depraved, infected, perverse **9** decompose, dishonest, miscreant, reprobate, unethical **10** bastardize, degenerate **12** unprincipled, unscrupulous **13** untrustworthy

corruptible 5 venal **7** buyable **8** bribable

corruption 4 vice **5** decay, fraud, graft **7** bribery, jobbery **9** barbarism, depravity, turpitude **10** immorality, wickedness **11** impropriety

corsair 5 rover **6** pirate **8** picaroon, sea rover **9** buccaneer, pickaroon, privateer **10** freebooter

corset 5 stays **6** bodice, girdle **7** support

Corsica *city:* 6 Bastia **7** Ajaccio ***hero:* 8** Napoleon (Bonaparte) ***patriot:* 5** Paoli (Pasquale)

cortege 5 train **6** parade **7** retinue **9** entourage **10** attendants, procession

cortex 4 bark, husk, peel, rind **6** casing **8** peridium

Cortland 5 apple

corundum 4 ruby **5** emery, topaz **7** emerald **8** abrasive, amethyst, sapphire

coruscate 5 flash, gleam, glint, shine **7** glisten, glitter, sparkle, twinkle **11** scintillate

corvid 3 jay **4** crow **5** raven **6** magpie **9** passerine

Corvino's wife 5 Celia

corybantic 3 mad **4** wild **5** rabid **6** crazed **7** frantic, furious **8** ecstatic, frenetic, frenzied **9** delirious

coryphée 6 dancer **8** danseuse **9** ballerina

Cosí Fan Tutte composer 6 Mozart (Wolfgang Amadeus)

cosine reciprocal 6 secant

cosmetic 4 kohl **5** blush, rouge **6** ceruse, lotion, makeup, powder **7** blusher, bronzer, mascara **8** lip gloss, lipstick **9** eye shadow **10** decorative, nail polish, ornamental **11** beautifying, superficial

cosmetologist 10 beautician

cosmic 4 huge, vast **7** immense **8** infinite **9** planetary, spiritual, unbounded, universal **12** astronomical, metaphysical

cosmopolitan 6 global, urbane **7** worldly **8** catholic, cultured, polished **9** civilized, universal, worldwide **10** cultivated, ecumenical **11** worldly-wise **13** sophisticated

cosmos 6 flower **8** creation, universe

Cossack *army:* 3 Don **4** Ural **5** Kuban ***land:* 7** Ukraine ***leader:* 5** Razin (Stenka) **6** ataman, hetman, Mazepa (Ivan) **7** Bulavin (Kondraty) **8** Pugachov (Yemelyan) ***novel:* 10** Taras Bulba

cosset 3 pet **4** baby, lamb, love **5** humor, spoil **6** caress, cocker, coddle, cuddle, dandle, dote on, fondle, pamper **7** cater to, indulge **11** mollycoddle

cost 3 tab **4** rate, toll **5** price **6** charge, damage, outlay, tariff **7** expense, payment **8** price tag **9** sacrifice **11** expenditure **12** disbursement ***business:* 8** overhead

Costa Rica *bay:* 8 Coronado ***capital:* 7** San José ***city:* 8** Alajuela **10** Puntarenas **11** Puerto Limón ***discoverer:* 8** Columbus (Christopher) ***language:* 7** Spanish ***leader:* 5** Arias (Oscar) ***monetary unit:* 5** colón ***neighbor:* 6** Panama **9** Nicaragua ***peninsula:* 3** Osa **6** Nicoya ***river:* 7** San Juan ***volcano:* 5** Barba, Irazú **9** Turrialba

costermonger 6 hawker **7** peddler **9** barrow boy

costive 4 mean, slow **5** bound, close, tight **6** frugal, stingy **7** miserly **9** penurious **10** hardfisted, pinchpenny **11** closefisted **12** cheeseparing, parsimonious

costless 4 free **6** gratis **10** gratuitous **13** complimentary

costly 4 dear, rich **5** fancy **6** lavish, pricey **7** opulent, premium **8** precious, splendid, valuable **9** expensive, luxurious, priceless **10** exorbitant, high-priced, invaluable **11** extravagant

costume 3 rig **4** duds, garb, mode **5** dress, getup, guise, habit, style **6** attire, outfit **7** apparel, clothes, fashion, threads, turnout, uniform **8** disguise, ensemble, garments **9** trappings

cot 3 bed, hut **4** camp **5** cabin, lodge, shack **6** shanty ***wheeled:*** **6** gurney

coterie 4 band, camp, clan, club, ring **5** cabal **6** circle, clique **7** in-group **9** camarilla

cotillion 4 ball, prom **5** dance ***girl:*** **3** deb **9** debutante

cottage 3 hut **4** camp **5** cabin, lodge, shack **6** shanty **8** bungalow ***Russian:*** **5** dacha ***Swiss:*** **6** chalet

cotton *cleaner:* **3** gin **6** linter ***cloth:*** **4** duck, jean, mull **5** baize, chino, denim, drill, khaki, scrim, terry, wigan **6** calico, canvas, chintz, dimity, muslin, oxford, sateen, velour **7** batiste, etamine, fustian, gingham, jaconet, nankeen, organdy, percale **8** corduroy, dungaree, moleskin, nainsook, tarlatan **9** grenadine, percaline, stockinet, swansdown **10** balbriggan **11** stockinette ***cloth, Indian:*** **5** surah **6** madras **7** dhurrie, khaddar ***comb:*** **4** card ***fuzz remover:*** **6** linter ***high-grade:*** **4** pima ***measure:*** **4** hank, pick, yard **5** count, skein ***pad:*** **7** pledget ***pod:*** **4** boll ***refuse:*** **5** flock ***seed separator:*** **3** gin ***sheet:*** **4** batt ***thread:*** **5** lisle

Cotton State 7 Alabama

cottonwood 5 alamo **6** poplar

cottony 4 soft **6** fluffy

____ Coty 4 René

couch 3 den, put **4** lair, sofa, word **5** divan, lodge **6** burrow, chaise, daybed, lounge, phrase **7** express, lie down, recline **9** davenport, formulate **12** chesterfield

couch potato 7 slacker

cougar 3 cat **4** puma **7** panther **9** catamount **12** mountain lion

cough 4 hack, hawk

cough drop 6 troche **7** lozenge

cough up 3 pay **5** spend **6** lay out, pay out **7** deliver, dole out, fork out **8** fork over, hand over, shell out

couloir 5 chasm, gorge, gulch, gully **6** ravine

council 4 diet **5** board, junta **6** powwow, senate **7** cabinet, meeting **8** assembly, conclave, congress, ministry **10** conference, federation **12** consultation ***ancient Greek:*** **5** boule ***church:*** **5** synod **10** consistory ***medieval English:*** **4** moot **5** gemot **6** gemote **8** hustings ***Muslim:*** **5** divan ***Russian:*** **4** duma **6** soviet ***secret:*** **5** cabal, junto **9** camarilla ***Spanish:*** **7** cabildo

counsel 4 rede, urge, warn **6** advice, advise, charge, direct, enjoin, lawyer **7** consult, suggest **8** advocate, attorney **9** prescribe, recommend **10** advisement **12** deliberation ***British:*** **9** barrister, solicitor

count 3 add, sum, tot **4** bank, earl, mean, rely, tote **5** issue, score, tally, total, tot up, weigh **6** census, charge, depend, expect, figure, matter, number, reckon, result, tote up **7** compute, signify **8** estimate, militate, numerate, quantify **9** calculate, enumerate **10** allegation

countenance 3 mug **4** back, cast, face, look, mien, phiz **5** favor, go for **6** accept, aspect, visage **7** approve, commend, condone, endorse, support **8** advocate, features, hold with, sanction, tolerate **9** approbate, composure, encourage **10** expression **11** physiognomy

counter 3 bar, pit, vie **4** anti, desk **5** asset, check, match, polar, shelf, table **6** contra, offset, oppose **7** adverse, against, hostile, obverse, opposed, reverse **8** antipode, contrary, converse, opposing, opposite **9** antipodal, diametric **10** antipodean, antithesis, contravene **12** antagonistic, antipathetic, antithetical **13** contradictory

counteract 3 fix **4** foil **5** annul **6** cancel, negate, oppose, resist, thwart **7** balance, correct, nullify, prevent, rectify, redress **8** negative **9** cancel out, frustrate **10** balance out, neutralize

counteragent 4 cure **6** remedy **8** antidote **9** antitoxin, antivenin **10** corrective

counterbalance 6 cancel, make up, offset, redeem, set off **7** ballast, correct, even out, rectify, redress **8** equalize, outweigh **10** compensate

counterblow 7 revenge **8** reprisal, requital, revanche **9** vengeance **11** retaliation, retribution

counterclockwise 4 levo **12** levorotatory

counterfeit 4 copy, fake, hoax, sham **5** bluff, bogus, dummy, false, feign, forge, fraud, mimic, phony **6** affect, assume, deceit, ersatz, forged, pseudo **7** feigned, imitate, pretend **8** delusive, delusory, knock off, simulate, spurious **9** brummagem, deception, deceptive, fabricate, imitation, imposture, insincere, pinchbeck, pretended, simulated **10** fraudulent, misleading, simulacrum ***prefix:*** **5** pseud **6** pseudo

counterpane 4 pouf, puff **5** duvet **6** spread **8** bedcover, coverlet **9** bedspread, comforter, eiderdown

counterpart 4 like, twin **5** equal, match **6** analog, double **7** vis-à-vis **8** alter ego, analogue, parallel **9** correlate, duplicate **10** complement, coordinate, equivalent **11** correlative **13** correspondent

counterpoise 6 make up, offset, redeem, set off **7** balance, ballast **8** outweigh **9** stabilize **10** compensate

countersign 8 password **9** watchword

countervail 4 foil **6** cancel, offset, oppose, redeem, set off, thwart **7** balance, correct, nullify, rectify **8** outweigh **9** frustrate **10** compensate, neutralize

countless 6 legion, myriad, untold **7** umpteen **11** innumerable

Count of Monte Cristo 6 Dantès (Edmond) ***author:*** **5** Dumas (Alexandre)

count out 5 expel **6** except **7** exclude **9** disregard, eliminate

countrified 5 rural **6** rustic **7** bucolic **8** homespun, pastoral **10** campestral

country 4 home, land, soil **5** rural **6** nation, region, rustic, sticks **7** boonies, bucolic, outland **8** homeland, pastoral **9** backwoods, boondocks **10** campestral, fatherland, motherland, provincial ***dance:*** **3** jig **4** reel **10** strathspey ***home:*** **5** dacha, manor, ranch, villa **8** hacienda ***music:*** **9** bluegrass ***road:*** **4** lane, path **5** byway (see also **nation**)

country-music star 4 Cash (Johnny), Ford (Tennessee Ernie), Gill (Vince), Lynn (Loretta), Rich (Charlie), Tubb (Ernest) **5** Acuff (Roy), Autry (Gene), Black (Clint), Cline (Patsy), Davis (Skeeter), Jones (George), Owens (Buck), Pearl (Minnie), Pride (Charley), Swift (Taylor), Twain (Shania), Urban (Keith), Wells (Kitty), Wills (Bob) **6** Arnold (Eddy), Atkins (Chet), Brooks (Garth), Carter (A. P., June, Maybelle, Sara), Harris (Emmylou), Miller (Roger), Monroe (Bill), Nelson (Willie), Parton (Dolly), Ritter (Tex), Rogers (Kenny, Roy), Skaggs (Ricky), Travis (Randy), Tucker (Tanya), Twitty (Conway) **7** Haggard (Merle), Millsap (Ronnie), Paisley (Brad), Robbins (Marty), Rodgers (Jimmie), Wynette (Tammy) **8** Jennings (Waylon), McEntire (Reba), Williams (Hank) **9** Underwood (Carrie)

coup 4 blow, feat **5** upset **6** putsch, stroke **8** takeover **9** overthrow

coup de ____ 5 grâce

couple 3 duo, twa, two **4** bond, dyad, fuse, item, join, link, mate, pair, span, team, yoke **5** brace, hitch, marry, merge, unite **6** hook up, link up **7** bracket, combine, conjoin, connect, doublet, harness, twosome

coupler 4 link, ring **5** hitch, joint **6** hookup **7** shackle **8** ligature ***railroad:*** **7** drawbar

couplet 3 duo **4** dyad, pair **5** twins **7** distich, doublet, twosome

coupling 4 link, seam **5** joint, union **6** yoking **7** joining, pairing **8** junction, juncture **9** connector **10** connection

courage 4 dash, grit, guts **5** heart, moxie, nerve, pluck, spunk, valor **6** daring, mettle, spirit **7** bravery, heroism **8** audacity, backbone, boldness, firmness, temerity, tenacity, valiance, valiancy **9** assurance, fortitude, gallantry **10** resolution **11** doughtiness, intrepidity **12** fearlessness **13** dauntlessness

courageous 4 bold **5** brave, gutsy, nervy, stout **6** daring, heroic, manful, plucky, spunky, strong **7** doughty, gallant, valiant **8** fearless, intrepid, resolute, stalwart, unafraid, valorous **9** audacious, dauntless, tenacious, undaunted **11** venturesome **12** stouthearted

courier 5 envoy, gofer **6** legate, runner **8** emissary **9** go-between, messenger **11** internuncio

course 3 row, run, way **4** dart, dash, duct, flow, line, path, plan, race, road, rush, tack, tear **5** canal, chain, chase, class, hurry, orbit, order, range, route, scoot, scope, speed, surge, track, trend **6** career, design, hasten, hustle, manner, policy, polity, scheme, sequel, series, string, system **7** advance, channel, circuit, conduit, passage, pattern, program, regimen, routine, seminar **8** aqueduct, duration, progress, sequence, syllabus **9** procedure, racetrack **10** curriculum, succession **11** progression ***curving:*** **4** coil, curl, turn, wind **5** swing, twist **6** spiral **9** corkscrew ***dinner:*** **4** soup **5** salad **6** entrée **7** dessert **9** appetizer, blue plate

courser 4 bird **5** horse **7** charger **8** huntsman, warhorse

court 3 bar, woo **4** date, quad, yard **5** atria (plural), charm, motel, spark, suite, tempt **6** allure, atrium, homage, invite, palace, pursue **7** address, flatter, justice, retinue, romance, solicit **8** assembly, cloister, tribunal **9** captivate, curtilage, enclosure, entourage **10** magistrate, parliament, quadrangle **11** legislature ***action:*** **4** suit **5** trial **6** appeal, assize **7** hearing, inquest, lawsuit **10** proceeding ***calendar:*** **6** docket ***call to:*** **7** summons **8** subpoena **11** arraignment ***circuit:*** **4** eyre ***crier's call:*** **4** oyez ***decision:*** **6** assize **7** finding, verdict **8** judgment ***ecclesiastical:*** **4** rota **5** Curia **10** consistory ***Indian:*** **6** durbar ***kind:*** **4** moot **5** civil **6** county, family **7** circuit, customs, federal, supreme **8** chancery, criminal, district, juvenile, kangaroo, superior **9** appellate, municipal **11** territorial ***medieval English:*** **4** eyre, moot **5** gemot **6** gemote **8** hustings ***of equity:*** **8** chancery ***officer:*** **2** DA **5** clerk, crier, judge **7** bailiff, justice, marshal, sheriff **10** prosecutor ***order:*** **4** writ **5** edict **6** decree **7** summons **8** mandamus, subpoena ***panel:*** **4** jury ***relating to:*** **8** judicial **9** juridical ***session:*** **6** assize **7** sitting **8** sederunt

courteous 5 civil **6** polite **7** courtly, gallant, genteel **8** mannerly, well-bred **9** attentive **10** chivalrous, thoughtful **11** considerate **12** well-mannered

courtesy 7 amenity, decorum, manners, service **8** chivalry, civility **9** attention, etiquette, gallantry **10** cordiality, indulgence **11** courtliness **12** graciousness **13** attentiveness, consideration

court game see under **game**

courtly 5 noble **6** august, formal, urbane **7** elegant, gallant, refined, stately **8** gracious **9** dignified **10** chivalrous, flattering **11** ceremonious

courtship 4 suit **6** dating, wooing **7** romance **10** flirtation ***former custom of:*** **8** bundling

courtyard 4 quad **5** atria (plural), garth, patio **6** atrium **9** curtilage **10** quadrangle

cousin 3 kin **7** kinsman **8** relative

Cousteau, Jacques *ship:* **7** Calypso ***vehicle:*** **11** bathysphere

couturier 8 clothier, costumer, designer **10** dressmaker

cove 3 arm, bay **4** nook **5** bight, firth, inlet, niche **6** harbor, recess **9** concavity

covenant 3 vow **4** bond, pact **5** agree, swear **6** pledge, treaty **7** compact, promise **8** contract **9** agreement **10** convention

Covent Garden offering 5 opera **6** ballet

cover 3 cap, lid **4** bury, hide, hood, mask, veil, wrap **5** alibi, cloak, front, guise, stash, track **6** clothe, enfold, enwrap, facade, hiding, insure, refuge, screen, secure, shield, shroud, sleeve, travel **7** blanket, conceal, embrace, enclose, envelop, obscure, overlay, protect, secrete, shelter, write up **8** disguise, ensconce, enshroud, traverse **9** encompass, safeguard, sanctuary, superpose **10** overspread **11** concealment, superimpose ***rooflike:*** **6** awning, canopy ***the eyes:*** **4** loup **9** blindfold ***the face:*** **4** mask, veil ***the head:*** **4** hood ***the mouth:*** **6** muzzle ***with asphalt:*** **4** pave ***with cloth:*** **5** drape ***with dirt:*** **7** begrime, blacken **8** besmirch ***with straw:*** **6** thatch

coverall 8 jumpsuit **10** boilersuit

covered wagon 9 Conestoga

covering *anatomical:* **5** theca, velum **6** tegmen **7** velamen **8** tegument **10** integument ***apex of roof:*** **3** épi ***close-fitting:*** **6** sheath **9** sheathing ***cloth:*** **5** sheet ***flap:*** **9** operculum ***for a book:*** **4** case **6** jacket ***for a cigar:*** **7** wrapper ***for a coffin:*** **4** pall ***for a corpse:*** **6** shroud **8** cerement ***for a package:*** **7** wrapper ***for concealment:*** **10** camouflage ***for food:*** **4** cosy, cozy ***for soil:*** **5** mulch ***metal:*** **4** mail **5** armor ***of a diatom:*** **6** lorica ***of a plant ovary:*** **8** pericarp ***of a seed:*** **4** aril, case **5** testa ***of fruits:*** **4** peel, rind ***of gloom:*** **4** pall ***of grain:*** **4** hull, husk **5** chaff ***shell-like:*** **7** testudo **8** carapace ***thin:*** **4** film **6** patina, veneer ***waterproof:*** **4** tarp **9** tarpaulin

coverlet 4 pouf, puff **5** duvet **6** spread **8** bedcover **9** bedspread, comforter **11** counterpane

covert 4 lair **5** haven, privy **6** hidden, masked, refuge, secret, veiled **7** feather, furtive, retreat, shelter, sub-rosa, thicket **8** hush-hush, shrouded, stealthy **9** concealed, disguised, sanctuary, sheltered **10** undercover **11** camouflaged, clandestine, hiding place, underhanded **12** hugger-mugger **13** surreptitious, under-the-table

covertly 7 sub-rosa **9** by stealth **12** hugger-mugger

covet 4 want **5** crave **6** desire

covetous 4 avid, keen **5** itchy **6** grabby, greedy **7** envious **8** desirous, esurient, grasping, ravenous **9** rapacious, voracious **10** avaricious, gluttonous **11** acquisitive

covey 4 band, bevy, crew, nest **5** brood, bunch, flock, group, party, troop **6** gaggle, troupe **7** cluster, company

cow (see also **cattle**) **4** faze, kine (plural), neat **5** abash, bossy, bully, daunt **6** appall, bovine, dismay, hector, rattle **7** bluster, dragoon **8** bludgeon, browbeat, bulldoze, bullyrag **9** discomfit, embarrass, strong-arm **10** disconcert, intimidate ***cud:*** **5** rumen ***French:*** **5** vache ***hornless:*** **5** muley **7** pollard ***mammary gland:*** **5** udder ***pen:*** **6** corral ***shed:*** **4** barn, byre ***Spanish:*** **4** vaca ***young:*** **4** calf **5** stirk **6** heifer

coward 6 craven **7** caitiff, chicken, dastard, milksop, nebbish **8** poltroon, recreant **9** jellyfish **10** scaredy-cat **11** yellowbelly

____ **Coward 4** Noël

cowardly 5 timid, wimpy **6** afraid, craven, yellow **7** caitiff, chicken, fearful, gutless **8** poltroon, recreant, timorous **9** dastardly **11** lily-livered, milk-livered, poltroonish **12** apprehensive, fainthearted, poor-spirited, white-livered **13** pusillanimous

cowboy 5 rogue, waddy **6** drover, herder,

waddie **7** puncher, rancher **8** buckaroo, herdsman, maverick, wrangler **9** cattleman, ranch hand **10** cowpuncher **12** broncobuster ***contest:*** **5** rodeo ***gear:*** **5** cuffs, quirt, spurs **6** duster **7** bedroll, slicker, Stetson ***legendary:*** **9** Pecos Bill ***leggings:*** **5** chaps ***movie:*** **3** Mix (Tom) **4** Hart (William S.) **5** Autry (Gene), Wayne (John) **6** Gibson (Hoot), McCrea (Joel), Murphy (Audie), Ritter (Tex), Rogers (Roy, Will) **8** Cisco Kid, Eastwood (Clint) ***rope:*** **5** lasso, reata, riata **6** lariat ***Spanish-American:*** **6** charro, gaucho **7** vaquero

cowcatcher **5** pilot

cower **5** quail, wince **6** blench, cringe, flinch, recoil, shrink

cowfish **6** dugong, sea cow **7** grampus, manatee **8** sirenian

cowl **4** cape, hood **5** cloak **6** capote, domino, mantle **7** capuche

cowpox **8** vaccinia

cowpuncher see **cowboy**

coxcomb **3** fop **4** beau, buck, dude, fool **5** blood, dandy, swell **7** peacock **8** macaroni **9** exquisite **11** Beau Brummel **12** clotheshorse, fashion plate, lounge lizard

coy **3** shy **4** arch, cute, pert **5** saucy, timid **6** demure, modest **7** bashful, evasive, playful **8** blushing, decorous, skittish **9** diffident, kittenish **10** capricious, coquettish **11** flirtatious, mischievous **12** noncommittal

Coyote State **11** South Dakota

coypu **6** rodent ***fur:*** **6** nutria

cozen **3** gyp **4** bilk, scam **5** cheat, trick **6** diddle, fleece, take in **7** beguile, deceive, defraud, swindle, wheedle **8** flimflam **9** bamboozle **11** double-cross

cozy **4** safe, snug, soft **5** comfy, cushy, pally, tight **6** chummy, secure **8** familiar, intimate **11** comfortable

CPR expert **3** EMT

crab **3** nag **4** beef, fuss, yawp **5** gripe, sidle **6** grinch, griper, grouch, kvetch, squawk, yammer **7** decapod, grouser, growler **8** arthopod, complain, grumbler, sourpuss **9** bellyache, shellfish **10** bellyacher, complainer, crosspatch, crustacean, curmudgeon **11** faultfinder ***claw:*** **5** chela **6** nipper ***constellation:*** **6** Cancer ***genus:*** **3** Uca **6** Birgus **7** Limulus, Pagurus ***kind:*** **3** pea **4** blue, king, pine, rock **5** ghost, purse **6** hermit, spider **7** fiddler **9** Dungeness, horseshoe ***king, horseshoe:*** **7** limulus

crabbed **4** dour, glum, grim, sour **5** gruff, surly **6** crusty, gloomy, morose, sullen **9** illegible, irascible, saturnine, splenetic

crablike **8** cancroid

crabwise **8** sidelong, sideward, sideways **9** laterally

crack **3** gag, gap, rap, try **4** bang, barb, bash, belt, blow, boom, clap, flaw, jest, joke, open, peal, quip, rift, roll, shot, slam, slap, snap, stab, wham, whop **5** adept, break, burst, chink, cleft, crash, craze, knock, smack, smash, solve, split, whack, whirl, wreck **6** breach, cranny, decode, expert, master, moment, thwack, zinger **7** break up, crevice, decrypt, destroy, fissure, instant, shatter, skilled **8** crevasse, decipher, disorder, interval, masterly, skillful, superior **9** break into, excellent, interrupt, masterful, witticism **10** percussion, proficient

crackbrain **3** nut **4** kook **5** crank, wacko **6** cuckoo **7** dingbat, lunatic **9** ding-a-ling, fruitcake, screwball

crackdown **5** purge **8** quashing **10** repression **11** suppression

cracked **3** mad **4** daft, nuts **5** balmy, batty, crazy, daffy, loony, nutty **6** broken, crazed, cuckoo, insane, screwy **7** bonkers, lunatic, smashed **8** demented, deranged

cracker **5** wafer **6** hacker, rustic **7** biscuit, saltine, snapper **8** Georgian **9** Floridian

crackerjack **3** ace **4** lulu **5** dandy, nifty, sharp **6** corker, killer **8** jim-dandy, knockout **9** humdinger **12** lollapalooza

crackle **4** snap **7** glitter, sparkle, twinkle **9** crepitate **10** effervesce **13** effervescence

crackpot **3** nut **4** case, kook, loon **5** crank, loony, wacko **6** cuckoo, madman **7** dingbat, lunatic, oddball **9** ding-a-ling, eccentric, fruitcake, harebrain, screwball

crack-up, crack up **5** crash, smash, wreck **6** fiasco **7** debacle **8** accident, collapse, disaster **9** breakdown **11** catastrophe

cradlesong **7** lullaby **8** berceuse

craft **3** art, job **4** boat **5** guile, knack, skill, trade, wiles **6** career, deceit, métier **7** ability, calling, cunning, know-how, slyness **8** artifice, caginess, foxiness, vocation, wiliness **9** adeptness, canniness, dexterity, duplicity, expertise, ingenuity, technique **10** adroitness, artfulness, competence, occupation, profession, shrewdness **11** proficiency (see also **boat**)

craftiness **5** guile **7** cunning **8** artifice, subtlety

craftsman **5** smith **6** carter, carver, potter, weaver, wright **7** artisan, builder, cobbler, jeweler **9** carpenter **10** blacksmith

crafty **3** sly **4** foxy, keen, wily **5** acute, cagey, canny, sharp, slick **6** adroit, artful, astute, clever, shrewd, tricky **7** cunning, devious, fawning, vulpine **8** guileful, scheming, skillful, slippery **9** deceitful, designing, ingenious, insidious **11** calculating, duplicitous ***Scottish:*** **7** sleekit

crag 3 tor **4** hill **5** cliff

craggy 5 erose, harsh, rocky, rough **6** jagged, rugged, uneven

cram 3 jam, ram **4** bolt, fill, gulp, heap, load, pack, wolf **5** crowd, crush, drive, force, press, shove, study, stuff, wedge **6** gobble, review, squash, thrust **7** jam-pack, overeat, squeeze

crammed 4 full **5** awash, flush **7** brimful **8** brimming **9** chock-full

cramp 4 kink, pain, pang **5** crick, limit, spasm **6** hamper, stitch **7** confine, inhibit, shackle **8** confined, restrain, restrict **9** restraint, stricture **10** constraint, limitation **11** confinement, restriction

cramped 5 close, tight **6** narrow **9** confining, two-by-four

crane 4 bird, boom, rail **5** heron **7** derrick, stretch ***arm:*** **3** jib ***genus:*** **4** Grus ***ship's:*** **5** davit

Crane hero 12 Henry Fleming

cranium 5 skull **9** braincase

crank 3 nut **4** crab, kook **5** fancy **6** griper, grouch, notion, rotate, turn up, vagary **7** caprice, conceit, fanatic, grouser, oddball **8** crackpot, crotchet, grumbler, sourpuss **9** eccentric, screwball **10** bellyacher, crosspatch

cranky 5 cross, testy **6** crabby, crusty, cussed, grumpy, morose, ornery, tetchy, touchy **7** bearish, crabbed, peevish, prickly **8** contrary, petulant, tortuous, vinegary **9** crotchety, irascible, irritable, obstinate **10** bad-humored, ill-humored **12** cantankerous, disagreeable **13** unpredictable

cranny 3 gap **4** nook, slit **5** chink, crack, niche **6** corner **7** crevice

crash 3 din, jar, ram **4** bang, boom, bump, bust, clap, fail, fold, jolt, peal, slam, wham **5** blast, break, burst, crack, shock, smash, wreck **6** impact, pileup **7** collide, crack-up, debacle, decline, failure, smashup **8** accident, collapse **9** breakdown, collision **10** concussion

crass 4 rude **5** crude, gross **6** coarse, vulgar **7** boorish, loutish, uncouth **8** churlish **9** unrefined **13** materialistic

crate 3 box **4** heap **5** wreck **6** jalopy, junker **7** clunker

crater 3 pit **4** dent, hole, pock **5** crash **6** cavity, dimple, hollow, trough **7** caldera **8** collapse **10** depression ***Hawaiian:*** **7** Kilauea

cravat 3 tie **4** band **5** ascot, scarf **7** necktie

crave 3 ask, beg **4** need, want, wish **5** covet **6** demand, desire **7** call for, entreat, implore, long for, require **8** yearn for

craven 4 funk **6** abject, coward **7** caitiff, chicken, dastard, fearful, gutless, ignoble **8** cowardly, cringing, poltroon, recreant **9** dastardly **11** lily-livered, poltroonish, yellowbelly **13** pusillanimous, yellowbellied

craving 4 itch, lust, urge **6** desire, hunger, thirst **7** longing, passion **8** appetite, yearning **9** hankering

crawl 4 flow, inch, teem **5** creep, swarm **6** abound, grovel **7** slither, wriggle **9** pullulate

crawling 6 repent

craze 3 fad **4** chic, rage **5** crack, fever, furor, mania, trend, vogue **6** dement, enrage, frenzy, furore, madden **7** derange, fashion, unhinge **9** unbalance **10** dernier cri, enthusiasm

craziness 5 folly, mania **6** lunacy **8** hysteria, insanity **9** absurdity

crazy 3 fey, mad **4** amok, bats, daft, gaga, loco, nuts, wild, zany **5** balmy, barmy, batty, daffy, dotty, goofy, kooky, loony, loopy, nutty, rabid, silly, wacko, wacky **6** absurd, cuckoo, fruity, insane, mental, psycho, screwy, teched, whacky **7** berserk, bonkers, cracked, foolish, frantic, lunatic, meshuga, smitten, tetched, touched, unsound **8** cockeyed, crackpot, demented, deranged, frenetic, frenzied, maniacal, meshugge, unhinged **9** bedlamite, delirious, eccentric, fanatical, foolhardy, ludicrous, possessed, screwball, senseless **10** crackbrain, moonstruck, ridiculous, unbalanced **11** harebrained, nonsensical **12** preposterous ***British:*** **5** potty **6** scatty ***Scottish:*** **3** wud

creak 4 rasp **5** grate, grind **6** scrape, squeak, squeal **7** grating, screech **9** squeaking

creaky 4 aged **5** rusty **7** rickety, run-down, squeaky, unsound, worn-out **8** decrepit **9** tottering **10** broken-down, ramshackle

cream 3 top **4** balm, beat, best, drub, pick, whip, whup **5** blast, elite, prime, salve **6** cerate, choice, defeat, finest, thrash **7** clobber, destroy, trounce, unguent **8** lambaste, liniment, ointment

crease 4 fold, ruck **5** graze, plica, ridge **6** furrow, groove, rumple **7** crinkle, wrinkle

create 3 dub **4** form, make, sire **5** beget, build, cause, forge, found, hatch, set up, spawn, start **6** author, design, devise, father, invent **7** compose, concoct, develop, fashion, produce **8** conceive, engender, generate, occasion **9** construct, establish, fabricate, formulate, institute, originate **10** constitute

creation 5 birth, world **6** cosmos, nature **7**

genesis **8** universe **9** inception, macrocosm **10** conception **11** macrocosmos

creative 7 fertile **8** artistic, inspired, original **9** deceptive, demiurgic, ingenious, inventive **10** innovative, innovatory **11** imaginative **12** innovational

creator 3 god **6** author **8** inventor **9** architect, generator, patriarch **10** originator, progenitor

creature 3 man **5** beast, being, brute, human **6** animal, mortal, person **7** critter, varmint ***fabled:*** **3** elf, imp, orc, roc **4** ogre, puck, yeti **5** dwarf, fairy, ghost, giant, gnome, harpy, nymph, pixie, troll **6** dragon, goblin, gorgon, kraken, merman, Nessie, sphinx, sprite, wyvern **7** bigfoot, brownie, bugbear, centaur, chimera, gremlin, griffin, mermaid, monster, unicorn, vampire, wendigo, windigo **8** chimaera, minotaur, werewolf **9** hobgoblin, manticore, sasquatch **10** cockatrice, hippogriff, leprechaun (see also **monster**)

credence 5 faith, trust **6** belief, credit **8** reliance **9** sideboard **10** acceptance, confidence

credentials 6 papers **9** documents **10** references **12** certificates, testimonials **13** documentation

credenza 6 buffet **7** console **8** bookcase **9** sideboard

credible 5 solid, sound, valid **6** trusty **8** reliable **9** authentic, colorable, plausible **10** believable, convincing, persuasive, reasonable **11** trustworthy **12** satisfactory

credit 4 deem, feel **5** asset, faith, honor, refer, sense, think, trust **6** accept, assign, belief, charge, impute, notice, weight **7** ascribe, believe **8** consider, credence, prestige, reliance **9** attribute, authority, influence **10** confidence, reputation **11** recognition

creditable 6 worthy **8** laudable, reliable **9** colorable, deserving, estimable, plausible, reputable **10** believable **11** commendable, meritorious, respectable **12** praiseworthy

credo 5 canon, creed, dogma, tenet **6** belief, tenets **7** beliefs, precept **8** doctrine, ideology **9** catechism, principle

credulous 5 naive **6** unwary **8** gullible, trustful, trusting **9** believing **12** unsuspecting, unsuspicious **13** unquestioning

creed 4 sect **5** canon, dogma, faith, tenet **6** belief, church, tenets **7** beliefs, precept **8** doctrine, ideology, religion **9** catechism, communion, principle **12** denomination

creek 3 ria **4** burn, rill **5** brook **6** arroyo, rillet, runlet, runnel, stream **7** freshet, rivulet **8** brooklet **9** streamlet

creep 4 drag, edge, inch, jerk, lurk, slip **5** crawl, freak, glide, schmo, shirk, sicko, skulk, slide, slink, snake, sneak, steal **6** shmuck, sickie, spread, tiptoe, weirdo **7** gumshoe, oddball, pervert, schmuck, slither, wriggle **9** pussyfoot

creeping 6 repent **7** gradual **9** prostrate

creepy 5 eerie, weird **6** spooky **7** anxious, macabre, ominous, strange, uncanny **8** ghoulish, menacing, sinister **9** unnerving **10** disturbing, unpleasant, unsettling **11** hair-raising

crème de la crème 4 best **5** elect, elite **6** finest

Cremona family 5 Amati **8** Guarneri **10** Stradivari **12** Stradivarius

Creole *dish:* 5 gumbo **9** andouille, dirty rice, jambalaya ***music:*** **6** zydeco

Creon *daughter:* 6 Creusa, Glauce, Glauke ***sister:*** **7** Jocasta ***son:*** **6** Haemon ***victim:*** **8** Antigone

crescendo 4 acme, apex, peak, rise **5** crest, surge, swell **6** apogee, climax, growth, height, zenith **8** increase, pinnacle **9** high point **11** culmination

crescent-shaped 5 bowed **6** lunate, sickle **7** falcate ***body or surface:*** **4** lune **8** meniscus

crest 3 cap, top **4** acme, apex, comb, noon, peak, roof, tuft **5** arête, chine, crown, plume, ridge **6** apogee, climax, summit, vertex **7** hogback **8** pinnacle, surmount **9** high point **10** coat of arms, prominence **11** culmination ***of a wave:*** **8** whitecap

crestfallen 3 low **4** blue, down **6** droopy **8** dejected, downcast, drooping **9** depressed **10** dispirited **11** discouraged, downhearted **12** disappointed, disconsolate, disheartened

Crete *ancient city:* 7 Cnossus, Knossos **8** Phaistos ***ancient name:*** **6** Candia ***capital:*** **5** Canea ***goddess:*** **8** Dictynna **11** Britomartis ***guard:*** **5** Talos ***king:*** **5** Minos **9** Idomeneus ***maze:*** **9** labyrinth ***monster:*** **8** Minotaur ***mountain:*** **3** Ida ***princess:*** **7** Ariadne

cretin 3 oaf **4** boob, clod, dolt, dope, fool, lout **5** dumbo, dummy, dunce, idiot, moron **6** dimwit, nitwit **7** half-wit **8** imbecile, lunkhead, numskull **9** lamebrain, numbskull, simpleton

Creusa *brother:* 6 Haemon ***father:*** **5** Priam ***husband:*** **6** Aeneas ***mother:*** **6** Hecuba ***sister:*** **6** Glauce, Glauke ***son:*** **3** Ion **8** Ascanius

crevice 3 gap **4** seam, slit **5** chink, cleft, crack **6** cranny **7** fissure **8** cleavage **10** interstice

crew 4 band, bevy, gang, team **5** bunch, covey, group, party **6** rowers, rowing **7** company, sailors ***leader:*** **3** cox **8** coxswain

crib 3 bed, bin, box, hut, key **4** pony, trot **5** cheat, crate, hovel, shack, stall, steal, theft

6 cradle, crèche, manger, pilfer **7** barrier, brothel **8** bassinet, bedstead, bordello **9** enclosure **10** plagiarism, plagiarize

Crichton novel 11 Terminal Man (The) **12** Jurassic Park **15** Andromeda Strain (The)

cricket ***period of play:*** **7** innings ***team:*** **6** eleven ***term:*** **3** leg, off, rot **4** bowl **5** pitch **6** bowler, wicket, yorker **7** batsman, striker **9** fieldsman ***turn at bat:*** **4** over

crime 3 sin **4** evil, tort, vice **5** caper **6** breach, delict, felony **7** misdeed, offense **8** atrocity, iniquity **9** diablerie, violation **10** corruption, illegality, infraction, wrongdoing **11** misdemeanor **13** transgression ***instructor:*** **5** Fagin

Crimea ***city:*** **5** Kerch, Yalta **10** Sebastopol, Sevastopol, Simferopol ***river:*** **4** Alma ***sea:*** **4** Azov **5** Black ***strait:*** **5** Kerch

criminal 4 hood, thug **5** crook, felon, shady **6** outlaw **7** convict, corrupt, crooked, hoodlum, illegal, illicit, lawless, mobster **8** culpable, fugitive, gangster, jailbird, offender, scofflaw, unlawful, wrongful **9** desperado, felonious, miscreant, nefarious, racketeer, wrongdoer **10** delinquent, lawbreaker, malefactor, trespasser **12** illegitimate, transgressor ***habitual:*** **8** repeater **10** recidivist ***intent:*** **7** mens rea

criminate see **incriminate**

crimp 4 bend, curb, wave **5** frizz **6** crease, hamper, hold in **7** crinkle, inhibit, wrinkle **8** hold back, obstacle, restrain **9** constrain, restraint **10** impediment **11** obstruction

crimson 3 red **4** rose **5** blush, color, flush **6** redden

cringe 4 duck **5** cower, hunch, quail, wince **6** blench, flinch, recoil, shrink

crinkle 4 ruck **5** crimp, plica, ridge **6** crease, furrow, pucker, ruck up, rumple, rustle **7** crackle, crumple, scrunch, wrinkle **11** corrugation

crinkly 5 crepy **6** crepey, frizzy **7** frizzed **8** wrinkled

cripple 4 lame, maim **6** mangle **7** disable **8** mutilate, paralyze **9** hamstring, undermine **10** debilitate **12** incapacitate

crippled 4 halt, lame **6** maimed **7** gnarled, mangled **8** battered, deformed, disabled, weakened **9** enfeebled, misshapen, mutilated, paralyzed **11** debilitated, handicapped

crisis 4 crux, pass **5** pinch **6** climax, crunch, height, strait **7** impasse, straits **8** disaster, exigency, juncture, zero hour **9** emergency, extremity **10** crossroads **11** catastrophe, contingency **12** turning point

crisp 4 cold, cool, curl, deft, keen, neat, wavy **5** brisk, clean, crimp, curly, fresh, nippy, pithy, sharp, short **6** biting, chilly, lively, ripple, spruce **7** bracing, brittle, crunchy, cutting, wrinkle **8** clean-cut, clear-cut, incisive **9** trenchant **11** stimulating **12** invigorating

crisscross 3 net **4** grid, mesh **5** weave **7** network, overlap **8** reticule **9** confusion, decussate, intersect, reticular **10** reticulate

criterion 4 norm **5** canon, gauge, ideal, model, tenet **7** measure, precept **8** exemplar, paradigm, standard **9** benchmark, yardstick **10** touchstone

critic 5 judge **6** carper, pundit **7** arbiter, caviler **8** caviller, censurer, quibbler, reviewer **9** belittler, nitpicker **10** disparager, mudslinger **11** commentator, connoisseur, faultfinder

critical 4 dire **5** acute, fussy **7** carping, crucial, finicky, pivotal, weighty **8** captious, caviling, decisive **9** desperate, important, momentous **10** belittling, censorious, conclusive, precarious **11** disparaging, significant **12** faultfinding **13** consequential, determinative, hairsplitting ***study:*** **6** examen **8** exegesis

criticism 4 flak, slap **5** blame, cavil, swipe **6** rebuke, review **7** censure, comment, opinion, reproof **8** analysis, judgment, reproach **9** appraisal, objection **10** assessment, commentary, evaluation, nitpicking **11** examination, observation **12** faultfinding

criticize 3 pan, rap **4** bash, carp, flay **5** blame, blast, cavil, chide, fault, judge, knock, roast, scold **6** assess, rebuke, review, scathe **7** blister, censure, condemn, nitpick, reprove **8** appraise, badmouth, chastise, denounce, evaluate, lambaste **9** castigate, disparage, dress down, excoriate, find fault, reprehend, reprimand, reprobate

critique see **criticism**

critter 5 beast **6** animal **7** varmint

Crius ***father:*** **6** Uranus ***mother:*** **4** Gaea ***son:*** **8** Astraeus

croak 3 die **6** cackle, cash in, expire, go west, squawk **7** go south, grumble, snuff it **8** check out

croaker 4 drum, fish, frog **6** doctor

croaky 5 gruff, husky, raspy **6** hoarse **8** gravelly

Croatia ***capital:*** **6** Zagreb ***city:*** **5** Split, Zadar **6** Osijek, Rijeka **9** Dubrovnik ***monetary unit:*** **4** kuna ***neighbor:*** **6** Bosnia, Serbia **7** Hungary **8** Slovenia ***part of:*** **7** Balkans ***region:*** **8** Dalmatia, Slavonia

crock 3 jar, lie, pot **4** tale **6** tureen **7** cripple, disable, fiction **9** break down **11** fabrication

crocked 3 lit **4** high **5** drunk, lit up, oiled, tipsy **6** bashed, blotto, bombed, juiced, potted, soaked, soused, stewed, stoned, tanked, wasted, zonked **7** drunken, pickled, pie-eyed, sloshed, smashed **9** plastered **10** inebriated, liquored up **11** intoxicated

crocodile 7 reptile ***bird:*** **6** plover ***Indian:*** **6** gavial **7** gharial ***relative:*** **9** alligator ***South American:*** **6** caiman, cayman ***Southeast Asian:*** **6** mugger

Croesus' kingdom 5 Lydia

croft 4 farm **5** field

crofter 4 hind **6** farmer

Cromwell, Oliver 13 lord protector ***battle:*** **6** Naseby **11** Marston Moor ***party:*** **10** Roundheads ***regiment:*** **9** Ironsides ***son:*** **7** Richard ***victim:*** **7** Charles (I)

crone 3 hag **4** trot **5** biddy, witch **6** beldam **7** beldame

Cronus 5 Titan **6** Saturn ***daughter:*** **4** Hera **6** Hestia **7** Demeter ***father:*** **6** Uranus ***mother:*** **4** Gaea ***sister:*** **4** Rhea **6** Cybele, Tethys ***son:*** **4** Zeus **5** Hades **7** Jupiter, Neptune **8** Poseidon ***wife:*** **4** Rhea **6** Cybele

crony 3 pal **4** chum **5** buddy **6** cohort **7** comrade **8** sidekick **9** associate, companion **10** accomplice **11** confederate

crook 3 bow **4** bend, flex, hook, wind **5** angle, curve, staff, thief **6** bandit, robber **7** burglar, crosier, hoodlum, pothook **8** criminal

crooked 4 awry **5** askew, lying, shady, venal **6** curved, errant, jagged, shifty, skewed, zigzag **7** bending, corrupt, devious, illegal, illicit, slanted **8** cockeyed, criminal, ruthless, tortuous, twisting **9** deceitful, dishonest, nefarious, underhand, unethical **10** fraudulent, mendacious, untruthful **11** duplicitous, underhanded **12** unscrupulous **13** double-dealing

croon 4 sing **6** murmur, warble

crooner 4 Cole (Nat "King"), Como (Perry) **5** Laine (Frankie), Tormé (Mel) **6** Crosby (Bing), Martin (Dean), singer, Vallee (Rudy) **7** Bennett (Tony), Sinatra (Frank) **8** Eckstine (Billy), vocalist, Williams (Andy)

crop 3 bob, cut, hew, lop, mow **4** chop, clip, pare, snip, trim **5** prune, shave, shear, stock, yield **6** gullet, handle, output **7** harvest, produce **8** fruitage, truncate **10** collection

croquet 5 roque

crosier 5 crook, staff

cross 3 mad **4** mule, rood, span **5** angry, surly, testy, trial **6** betray, bridge, crabby, cranky, grumpy, hybrid, negate, oppose, tetchy, touchy **7** athwart, calvary, grouchy, mongrel, peevish **8** captious, choleric, traverse **9** half blood, half-breed, hybridize, intersect, irascible, irritable, querulous, splenetic **10** affliction, contradict, interbreed, transverse **12** cantankerous ***a river:*** **4** ford ***bearer:*** **8** crucifer ***decoration:*** **4** Iron **8** Victoria ***kind:*** **3** tau **4** ankh **5** Greek, Latin, papal **6** Celtic, fleury, formée, moline, pommée, potent **7** avellan, botonée, Calvary, Maltese, saltire **8** crucifix, fourchée, Lorraine, quadrate **11** patriarchal **12** Saint Andrew's **13** Saint Anthony's ***section:*** **5** slice

crossbow 8 arbalest, arbalist

crossbreed 4 mule **6** hybrid **7** bastard, mongrel **9** half blood, hybridize

cross-eye 6 squint **10** strabismus

crossing 8 junction, overpass, traverse **9** traversal, underpass **10** transverse **11** decussation, interchange, transversal **12** intersection

cross out 5 erase **6** cancel, delete, efface, excise **7** expunge

crosspatch 4 crab **5** crank, grump **6** griper, grouch **7** grouser **8** grumbler, sorehead, sourpuss **10** complainer, curmudgeon

crossroads 4 crux, pass **5** pinch **6** crisis, strait **8** exigency, juncture, zero hour **9** carrefour, emergency **11** contingency **12** intersection, turning point ***goddess:*** **6** Hecate, Hekate, Trivia

cross-shaped 8 cruciate **9** cruciform

crossways 6 aslant **7** athwart, oblique **8** diagonal **9** obliquely **10** diagonally, transverse **11** catercorner, cattycorner, kitty-corner **12** transversely

crotchet 3 bee **4** whim **5** fancy, freak, quirk, trick **6** foible, megrim, notion, vagary **7** caprice, conceit **11** quarter note **12** eccentricity

crotchety 5 testy **6** crabby, cranky, crusty, ornery, tetchy, touchy **7** bearish, peevish, prickly **8** contrary, snappish, vinegary **9** difficult, eccentric, irascible **10** vinegarish **11** ill-tempered **12** cantankerous, cross-grained

crouch 4 bend, duck **5** cower, hunch, squat, stoop **6** cringe, huddle, shrink **10** hunker down

croup 3 bum **4** butt, hack, rear, rump, seat, tail **5** cough, edema, whoop **6** behind **7** keister, rear end, tail end **8** backside, buttocks, derriere, haunches **9** posterior

croupier tool 4 rake

crow 4 blow, brag, puff **5** boast, exult, gloat, prate, vaunt **6** cackle **7** bluster **9** gasconade, humble pie ***colony:*** **7** rookery ***cry:*** **3** caw ***family:*** **6** corvid **8** Corvidae ***genus:*** **6** Corvus ***relating to:*** **7** corvine, corvoid ***relative:*** **3** daw, jay **4** rook **5** raven **6** chough, magpie **7** jackdaw, jaybird

crowbar 3 pry **5** jimmy, lever

crowd **3** jam, mob **4** army, bear, cram, fill, herd, host, mass, pack, pile, push, rout, ruck **5** bunch, crush, drove, flock, flood, group, horde, hurry, press, serry, shove, surge, swarm, troop **6** circle, clique, gaggle, huddle, jostle, legion, rabble, squash, squish, stream, throng **7** cluster, collect, company, coterie, squeeze **8** assembly **9** gathering, multitude **10** assemblage, collection **11** aggregation **12** congregation

crowded **4** full **5** awash, close, dense, thick, tight **6** loaded **7** brimful, compact, teeming **8** brimming, populous, swarming **9** chock-full, congested, jam-packed

crown **3** cap, top **4** acme, apex, peak, roof **5** cover, crest, tiara **6** climax, diadem, laurel, summit, top off, vertex, wreath, zenith **7** chaplet, coronal, coronet, garland, overlay, perfect **8** pinnacle, round off, surmount **9** culminate, finish off **10** consummate **11** culmination

crucial **4** dire **5** acute, vital **6** urgent **7** central, pivotal **8** critical, deciding, decisive **9** desperate, essential, important, momentous, necessary **10** imperative **11** climacteric, significant

crucible **4** test **5** trial **6** ordeal **8** acid test **10** melting pot

crucifix **4** rood **5** cross

crucifixion site **7** Calvary **8** Golgotha

crucify **4** rack **6** impale, martyr **7** mortify, pillory, torment, torture **10** excruciate

crud **3** goo **4** glop, gook, gunk, junk, muck **5** dreck, filth, slime, trash **6** debris, sludge **7** deposit, garbage, rubbish **12** incrustation

crude **3** raw **4** poor **5** crass, dirty, gross, rough **6** coarse, earthy, gauche, impure, ribald, risqué, vulgar **7** boorish, ill-bred, loutish, lowbred, obscene, obvious, raunchy, uncivil, uncouth **8** backward, cloddish, homespun, ignorant, indecent, inferior **9** elemental, graceless, inelegant, makeshift, primitive, rough-hewn, unrefined **10** amateurish, unfinished, unpolished

cruel **4** fell, grim, mean **5** harsh **6** brutal, fierce, savage **7** bestial, brutish, callous, heinous, vicious **8** inhumane, ruthless, sadistic **9** atrocious, barbarous, ferocious, heartless, merciless, monstrous, truculent **12** bloodthirsty

cruise **4** roam, rove, sail, surf, tour **5** drift, jaunt **6** junket, voyage **9** excursion

cruiser **4** boat **5** yacht **7** warship **8** squad car **9** patrol car, powerboat

crumb **3** bit, ort **4** iota **5** ounce, scrap, shred **6** morsel, sliver **7** smidgen **8** fragment, particle

crumble **5** decay **8** collapse **9** break down, decompose **11** deteriorate **12** disintegrate

crumbly **7** friable

crummy **4** poor **5** dingy, lousy, seedy, tacky **6** cruddy, flimsy, shoddy, sleazy **8** inferior

crumple **3** wad **4** cave **5** crimp **6** buckle, cave in, ruck up **7** crinkle, scrunch, wrinkle **8** collapse

crunch **4** chew **5** champ, chomp, grind, munch, sit-up **6** crisis **7** compute, process, squeeze **8** shortage, showdown

crusade **5** cause, drive **6** appeal **7** holy war **8** campaign, movement **9** offensive **10** expedition **11** undertaking

Crusader ***English:*** **7** Richard (Lionheart) ***foe:*** **7** Saladin, Saracen ***French:*** **5** Louis (IX) **6** Philip, Robert **7** Baldwin, Charles, Godfrey, Raymond, Raymund **8** Boniface, Montfort, Philippe, Theobald ***German:*** **6** Conrad **9** Frederick, Friedrich **10** Barbarossa ***Norman:*** **7** Tancred **8** Bohemund ***preacher:*** **5** Peter (the Hermit), Urban (II) **7** Adhémar, Bernard **8** Innocent (III), Pelagius

crusading **11** evangelical **12** evangelistic

crush **3** jam, mob **4** cram, mash, pulp, push, ruin **5** crowd, drove, grind, horde, pound, press, quash, quell, smash, wreck **6** bruise, burden, defeat, reduce, squash, squish, subdue, throng **7** conquer, destroy, mortify, oppress, passion, put down, repress, scrunch, squeeze, squelch, squoosh, trample **8** bear down, beat down, demolish, overcome, suppress, vanquish **9** humiliate, multitude, overpower, overwhelm, pulverize, puppy love, subjugate **10** annihilate, extinguish, obliterate **11** infatuation

crust **4** cake, coat, rime, scab **7** coating, deposit **8** covering

crustacean **4** crab, flea **5** louse, prawn **6** isopod, shrimp, slater, sow bug **7** copepod, daphnia, decapod, lobster, pill bug **8** amphipod, barnacle, crawfish, crayfish, ostracod, sand flea **9** arthropod, beach flea, shellfish, water flea, wood louse **10** hermit crab, stomatopod, whale louse **11** branchiopod, fiddler crab ***aggregate of:*** **5** krill ***appendage:*** **7** pleopod ***body segment:*** **6** somite, telson **8** metamere ***claw:*** **5** chela **6** pincer ***covering substance:*** **6** chitin ***larva:*** **8** nauplius

crusty **4** curt **5** bluff, blunt, gross, gruff, short, surly **6** cranky **7** brusque, crabbed, prickly **8** choleric **9** irascible, irritable, saturnine, splenetic

crux **3** nub **4** core, gist, meat, pith **5** focus, heart **6** kernel, thrust **7** essence, purport **9** substance

cry (see also **exclamation**) **3** sob **4** bawl, blub, call, howl, keen, mewl, moan, pule, wail, weep, yawp, yell, yelp, yowl **5** bleat, motto, mourn, shout, whine, whoop **6** boohoo, furore, holler, lament, scream, snivel, squall, squawk, squeak, squeal **7** blubber, screech, ululate, whimper **10** vociferate ***bacchanals':*** **4** evoe ***calf:*** **5** bleat ***cat:*** **3** mew **4** meow **5** miaow ***cattle:*** **3** low, moo ***chick:*** **4** peep **5** cheep ***court:*** **4** oyez ***crane:*** **5** clang ***crow:*** **3** caw ***dog:*** **3** arf **4** bark, woof ***donkey:*** **4** bray **6** hee-haw ***duck:*** **5** quack ***frog:*** **5** croak ***goat:*** **5** bleat ***goose:*** **4** honk **5** clang ***hen:*** **6** cackle ***horse:*** **5** neigh **6** nicker, whinny **7** whicker ***lion:*** **4** roar ***owl:*** **4** hoot ***pig:*** **4** oink **5** grunt ***raven:*** **3** caw **5** croak ***rook:*** **3** caw ***sheep:*** **5** bleat ***songbird:*** **5** chirp, tweet ***turkey:*** **6** gobble

cry down **5** decry **6** defame, deride, malign, revile, vilify **7** condemn **8** belittle, denounce, derogate, diminish **9** denigrate, deprecate, discredit, disparage **10** calumniate, depreciate **11** detract from, opprobriate

crying **4** dire **5** acute, vital **6** urgent **7** blatant, burning, clamant, exigent, heinous **8** flagrant, pressing, shocking **9** atrocious, clamorous, desperate, monstrous, notorious **10** compelling, imperative, outrageous, scandalous **11** importunate

crypt **5** vault **7** chamber **8** catacomb **9** mausoleum **10** undercroft

cryptic **5** vague **6** arcane, occult, opaque, secret **7** Delphic, obscure, unclear **8** abstruse, Delphian, esoteric, puzzling **9** ambiguous, enigmatic, recondite, tenebrous **10** mysterious, mystifying **12** unfathomable

crystal **4** lens **5** clear, lucid **6** limpid, lucent, quartz **8** clear-cut, luminous, pellucid **9** glassware, unblurred **11** translucent, transparent **12** transpicuous ***gazer:*** **4** seer **7** psychic **11** clairvoyant ***set:*** **5** radio

cry up **4** laud, puff **5** boost, extol **6** praise **7** acclaim

cub **3** pup **4** baby, tyro **6** novice, rookie **8** neophyte **9** offspring, youngster **10** apprentice

Cuba ***capital:*** **6** Havana ***city:*** **7** Holguín **8** Camagüey, Santiago **10** Guantánamo, Santa Clara ***discoverer:*** **8** Columbus (Christopher) ***language:*** **7** Spanish ***leader:*** **6** Castro (Fidel) **7** Batista (Fulgencio), Guevara (Che) ***monetary unit:*** **4** peso ***sea:*** **9** Caribbean

cubbyhole **5** niche **6** alcove, recess **7** cubicle

cube **4** dice **5** mince

Cub Scout ***rank:*** **4** Bear, Lion, Wolf **6** Bobcat **7** Webelos ***unit:*** **3** den **4** pack

Cuchulain ***father:*** **3** Lug **4** Lugh **5** Lugus ***foe:*** **4** Medb **5** Maeve ***kingdom:*** **6** Ulster ***lord:*** **9** Conchobar ***mother:*** **8** Dechtire ***son:*** **8** Conlaoch ***victim:*** **8** Conlaoch ***wife:*** **4** Emer

cuckoo **3** mad, nut **4** daft, kook, nuts **5** batty, crank, crazy, daffy, loony, loopy, nutty, potty, silly, wacko, wacky **6** crazed, fruity, insane, screwy, whacky **7** bonkers, cracked, idiotic, lunatic, nutcase **8** crackpot, demented **9** ding-a-ling, harebrain, screwball **12** crackbrained ***bird:*** **3** ani **8** keelbill

cucumber **4** pepo **7** gherkin

cuddle **3** hug, pet **4** neck, snug **5** spoon **6** burrow, caress, clinch, cosset, dandle, fondle, nestle, nuzzle **7** embrace, snuggle, squeeze **8** canoodle

cuddly **7** lovable, snuggly **8** huggable **11** embraceable

cudgel **3** bat, sap **4** club, cosh, mace **5** baton, billy **7** war club **8** bludgeon **9** bastinado, billy club, blackjack, truncheon **10** knobkerrie, nightstick, shillelagh

cue **3** key, nod, rod, tip **4** clue, hint, lead, prod, sign **5** alert **6** insert, notion, prompt, signal, tip-off **7** heads-up, inkling, warning **8** high sign, reminder, telltale **10** indication, intimation, suggestion

cuff **3** box, hit **4** belt, blip, clip, poke, slap, sock **5** clout, fight, punch, smack, whack **6** bangle, buffet, wallop **7** clobber, scuffle **8** bracelet, wristlet

cul-de-sac **5** pouch **6** pocket **7** dead end, impasse **10** blind alley **12** diverticulum

cull **4** pick, sift, thin **5** elect, glean **6** choose, garner, gather, select, winnow **7** extract, thin out

culminate **4** peak **5** crest **6** climax

culmination **3** top **4** acme, apex, peak **6** apogee, capper, climax, height, payoff, summit, zenith **8** capstone, pinnacle **11** ne plus ultra **12** consummation

culpability **4** onus **5** blame, fault, guilt

culpable **6** guilty, liable, sinful **7** at fault **8** blamable, blameful **10** censurable, delinquent **11** blameworthy, impeachable, responsible **13** reprehensible

cult **3** fad **4** sect **5** creed, faith **6** church **8** religion **10** persuasion **12** denomination

cultivable **6** arable **8** tillable

cultivate **4** farm, grow, tend, till **5** breed, nurse, raise **6** enrich, foster, refine **7** cherish, develop, further, improve, nourish, nurture, produce, promote **9** encourage, propagate

cultivated **6** urbane **7** genteel, refined **8** cultured, polished, well-bred

cultivation 6 polish **7** culture, tillage **8** breeding **10** refinement **11** development
culture 4 grow **5** taste **6** foster **7** nurture **9** cultivate, erudition, gentility **10** refinement **11** cultivation **12** civilization **13** enlightenment
cultured 6 urbane **7** erudite, genteel, learned, refined **8** educated, highbrow, literate, polished, well-bred **9** civilized **10** cultivated **11** enlightened
culture medium 4 agar
cum ____ salis 5 grano
cumber 4 clog, lade, load **6** burden, hinder, hobble, impede, saddle **7** clutter **8** handicap **9** hindrance
cumbersome 5 bulky, heavy, hefty **6** clumsy **7** awkward **8** unwieldy **9** lumbering, ponderous **10** slow-moving
cumshaw 3 fee, tip **5** bribe **6** payoff **7** present **8** gratuity, largesse **9** baksheesh, lagniappe, pourboire **10** perquisite
cumulate 4 heap **5** amass, hoard, lay up, store **6** garner, gather, pile up **7** collect, combine, store up **9** stockpile
cumulation 4 heap, mass, pile **5** cache, hoard, trove **9** stockpile **10** collection **11** aggregation **13** agglomeration
cumulative 8 additive, compound **9** summative **10** compounded, increasing
cunning 3 sly **4** cute, foxy, keen, wary, wily **5** acute, cagey, canny, craft, guile, savvy, sharp, skill, slick, smart **6** adroit, artful, astute, clever, crafty, deceit, shifty, tricky **7** finesse, know-how, slyness **8** artifice, caginess, deftness, facility, foxiness, guileful, slippery, subtlety, wiliness **9** adeptness, cageyness, canniness, dexterity, dexterous, duplicity, ingenious, ingenuity, insidious, sharpness, slickness **10** adroitness, artfulness, cleverness, craftiness, shiftiness, shrewdness, trickiness
cup 3 mug **4** toby **5** grail, jorum, stein **6** beaker, goblet, seidel **7** chalice, tankard **8** schooner ***handle:*** **3** ear, lug ***holder:*** **6** saucer ***liturgical:*** **3** ama **5** calix **7** chalice ***Scottish:*** **4** tass ***small:*** **6** noggin **8** cannikin, pannikin **9** demitasse ***sports:*** **5** Davis, Ryder, World **6** Curtis, Nextel **7** Stanley **8** America's, Wightman
cupbearer of the gods 4 Hebe **8** Ganymede
cupboard 5 ambry, cuddy **6** buffet, closet, larder, pantry **7** armoire, cabinet **8** credence, credenza **9** sideboard
Cupid 4 Amor, Eros **5** putto **6** cherub **8** amoretto ***beloved:*** **6** Psyche ***brother:*** **7** Anteros ***father:*** **6** Hermes **7** Mercury ***mother:*** **5** Venus **9** Aphrodite ***title:*** **3** Dan
cupidity 4 lust **5** greed **6** desire **7** avarice, avidity, craving, lechery, passion **8** rapacity, voracity **9** eagerness, esurience **10** greediness **11** infatuation **12** covetousness **13** rapaciousness
cupola 4 dome **5** vault **6** turret **7** furnace, lookout
cur 3 dog **4** mutt **7** mongrel
curate 6 cleric, priest **9** churchman, clergyman
curative 4 pill **5** tonic **6** elixir, relief, remedy **7** healing, nostrum, panacea, therapy **8** antidote, remedial, salutary, sanative, solution **9** healthful, medicinal, remedying, treatment, wholesome **10** beneficial, corrective **11** restorative, therapeutic **12** health-giving
curator 6 keeper, warden **9** caretaker, custodian **11** conservator
curb 3 bit **4** deny, rein **5** check, frame, leash, tie up **6** border, bridle, edging, fetter, hamper, hobble, hold in, rein in, subdue **7** abstain, contain, control, inhibit, refrain, repress **8** hold back, hold down, restrain, suppress, withhold **9** constrain, entrammel, restraint ***British:*** **4** kerb
curdle 4 clot, sour, turn **5** spoil **7** clabber, congeal, thicken **9** coagulate
curdling substance 6 rennet
cure 3 age, spa **4** heal, mend **5** treat **6** elixir, kipper, physic, pickle, relief, remedy **7** rectify, relieve, restore, therapy **8** antidote, medicant, medicine, preserve, recovery, solution **10** ameliorate, corrective **12** counteragent **13** counteractive
cure-all 6 elixir **7** nostrum, panacea **10** catholicon
curio 6 oddity, whimsy **7** novelty, whatsit **9** objet d'art
curiosity 5 freak **6** marvel, oddity, rarity, whimsy, wonder **7** anomaly, concern, novelty **8** interest, nonesuch
curious 3 odd **4** nosy **5** nosey, novel, queer, weird **6** exotic, prying, quaint, snoopy **7** bizarre, oddball, strange, unusual **8** meddling, peculiar, puzzling, singular **9** inquiring, intrusive **11** inquisitive, questioning
curium symbol 2 Cm
curl 4 coil, kink, wind **5** frizz, twine, twist **6** spiral **7** contort, crinkle, entwine, frizzle, ringlet, wreathe **9** corkscrew
curling *match:* **8** bonspiel ***period of play:*** **3** end ***team:*** **4** four ***term:*** **3** tee **4** hack, rink **5** house, stone
curly 4 wavy **5** kinky **6** frizzy
currency 4 cash, coin **5** dough, lucre, money, scrip **7** coinage **8** banknote **10** acceptance,

prevalence **11** legal tender ***unit:*** see individual country

current 4 eddy, flow, flux, race, rush, tide **5** drift, flood, spate, tenor, trend **6** extant, modern, strain, stream **7** instant, ongoing, popular, present, regnant, topical **8** accepted, existent, existing, tendency, up-to-date **9** prevalent **10** present-day, prevailing, widespread **11** fashionable **12** contemporary ***air:* 4** gale, gust, wind **5** blast, draft **6** breeze, squall, zephyr **7** cyclone, indraft, updraft **9** downdraft **10** slipstream ***ocean:* 7** riptide **8** undertow **9** maelstrom, whirlpool ***unit:* 3** amp **6** ampere

Currier's partner 4 Ives (James)

curry 4 beat, comb, seek, whip **5** groom **6** thrash

curse 3 hex, pox **4** bane, cuss, damn, evil, jinx, oath **5** swear **6** blight, plague, whammy **7** afflict, damning, malison, scourge, torment **8** anathema, cussword, execrate **9** bête noire, blaspheme, blasphemy, expletive, imprecate, profanity, swearword **10** affliction, execration, misfortune, pestilence **11** commination, imprecation, malediction, profanation **12** anathematize, denunciation

cursed 6 damned **7** blasted, dratted **8** damnable, infernal **9** execrable **10** confounded **13** blankety-blank

cursive 6 fluent, smooth **7** flowing, running

cursory 5 hasty, quick, rapid **6** casual **7** hurried, shallow, sketchy **8** careless **10** uncritical **11** perfunctory, superficial

curt 4 rude **5** bluff, blunt, brief, gruff, short, terse **6** abrupt, crusty **7** brusque, concise **8** succinct **10** peremptory

curtail 3 cut **4** clip, dock, trim **5** prune, slash **6** lessen, reduce **7** abridge, cut back, shorten **8** diminish, pare down, retrench, truncate **10** abbreviate

curtain 4 drop, veil **5** drape **6** screen **7** barrier ***doorway:* 8** portiere ***holder:* 3** rod ***Indian:* 6** purdah ***material:* 4** lace, silk **5** gauze **6** damask, velvet **8** chenille, jacquard ***rod concealer:* 7** valance ***sash:* 7** tieback ***stage:* 4** drop **5** scrim **8** backdrop

curtains 3 end **4** ruin **5** death **6** demise, finish **7** decease **8** disaster

curtilage 4 quad, yard **5** court **8** cloister **9** courtyard, enclosure **10** quadrangle

curvaceous 5 buxom **7** rounded, shapely **9** Junoesque **10** statuesque, voluptuous **13** well-developed

curvature *of the spine:* 8 kyphosis, lordosis **9** scoliosis

curve 3 arc, bow **4** arch, bend, coil, curl, turn, veer, wind **5** crook, round, swing, swirl, twist **6** convex, spiral, swerve **7** concave, flexure, rondure **9** corkscrew ***of an arch:* 8** extrados, intrados ***pitcher's:* 4** hook ***plane:* 7** cycloid, limaçon **8** parabola, sinusoid, trochoid **9** hyperbola ***S-shaped:* 3** ess **4** ogee **7** sigmoid

curved 4 bent **5** arced, bowed, round **6** arched, convex **7** arcuate, bending, embowed, falcate, rounded, sigmoid, sinuous, twisted ***implement:* 6** sickle ***molding:* 4** ogee ***sword:* 5** kukri, saber, sabre **7** cutlass **8** scimitar

curvilinear see **curved**

curvy see **curvaceous; curved**

Cush *father:* 3 Ham ***son:* 6** Nimrod

cushion 3 mat, pad **5** squab **6** absorb, buffer, pillow, soften **7** bolster, hassock, pillion **8** palliate, woolsack

cushy 4 cozy, easy, soft **11** comfortable, undemanding

cusp 3 tip **4** apex, edge, peak **5** point, verge **12** turning point

cuspid 6 canine **8** eyetooth

cuspidate 5 sharp **6** peaked, pointy **7** pointed

cuss 3 guy, man **4** chap, damn, dude, oath **5** curse, swear **6** fellow **9** expletive

cussed 4 dour **5** crude, gruff **6** crusty, cursed, grumpy, ornery **7** boorish, brusque, grouchy **8** churlish **9** obstinate **10** unyielding **11** contentious **12** antagonistic, cantankerous

cussword 4 oath **5** curse **9** expletive, swearword

custard 4 flan **7** pudding

custodian 5 super **6** keeper, porter, warden **7** curator, steward **8** guardian, overseer, watchdog, watchman **9** caretaker, concierge, protector **10** supervisor **11** conservator

custody 4 care, ward **5** guard, trust **6** charge **7** keeping **9** captivity, detention **10** caretaking, management, protection **11** confinement, safekeeping, supervision **12** guardianship

custom 3 use **4** norm **5** habit, mores (plural), trade, usage **6** groove, manner, praxis, ritual **7** folkway, precept, routine, traffic **8** business, habitude, practice **9** patronage **10** consuetude, convention

customary 5 usual **6** common, normal, wonted **7** general, regular, routine **8** accepted, everyday, familiar, frequent, habitual, ordinary, orthodox, standard **10** accustomed **11** established, traditional **12** conventional

custom-built 7 bespoke **10** tailor-made **11** made-to-order

customer **5** buyer **6** client, patron **7** shopper **8** consumer **9** purchaser ***frequent:*** **7** habitué
customized see **custom-built**
custom-made see **custom-built**
cut **3** bob, hew, lop, mow, saw **4** bite, chop, clip, crop, dice, dock, fell, gash, hack, nick, pare, reap, sawn, skip, slit, snip, snub, trim **5** carve, filet, lathe, lower, mince, notch, piece, prune, quota, sawed, sever, share, shave, shear, slash, slice, split, wound **6** cleave, delete, dilute, divide, excise, fillet, incise, reduce, scythe, sickle, sunder **7** abridge, curtail, dissect, portion, section, segment, shorten **8** division, separate, truncate **9** allotment, allowance, reduction **10** abbreviate ***of beef:*** **3** rib **4** loin, rump **5** chine, chuck, flank, roast, shank, steak, T-bone **6** saddle **7** brisket, sirloin **9** aitchbone **11** porterhouse
cut across **6** bisect **8** transect **9** transcend
cut-and-dried **5** stock **7** routine **9** formulaic **10** unoriginal **11** predictable **13** unimaginative
cutaneous **6** dermal
cutaway **4** coat, dive **5** tails
cut back **3** zag **4** clip, curb, dock, pare, trim **5** lower, prune, shave, slash **6** lessen, reduce **7** abridge, curtail, shorten **8** decrease, retrench, truncate **10** abbreviate
cut down **3** axe **4** chop, clip, fell, pare **5** lower, shave, slash **6** digest, reduce **7** abridge, shorten **10** abbreviate
cute **4** twee **6** dainty, pretty **7** cunning **8** affected **10** attractive **11** impertinent, smart-alecky
cut in **7** include, intrude, obtrude **9** introduce
cutlass **5** saber, sabre, sword **7** machete **8** scimitar
cut off **2** ax **3** axe, bar, end, lop **4** halt, kill, stop **5** abort, block, sever **6** disown **7** curtail, destroy, isolate, suspend **8** amputate, obstruct, renounce, separate, truncate **9** intercept, interrupt, terminate **10** disinherit **11** discontinue
cut out **3** end **4** halt **5** cease, leave, scram, usurp **6** beat it, delete, depart, escape, excise, remove, resect **7** defraud, deprive, take off **8** displace, supplant **9** eliminate, extirpate **10** disconnect
cutpurse **5** thief **10** pickpocket
cut short **3** bob **4** clip, crop, dock, halt, poll **5** abort, check, scrub, shear **7** abridge, curtail **8** break off **9** interrupt, terminate **10** abbreviate
cuttable **7** sectile **8** scissile
cutthroat **5** bravo **6** gunman, hit man, killer **7** torpedo **8** assassin, murderer **10** hatchet man, triggerman
cutting **5** acerb **7** acerbic **8** incisive, piercing **9** sarcastic, trenchant **11** penetrating ***edge:*** **5** blade ***remark:*** **3** dig **4** barb **5** taunt ***tool:*** **2** ax **3** axe, hob, saw **4** adze **5** knife, lathe, mower, plane, razor **6** reaper, scythe, shears, sickle **7** hatchet **8** scissors, tomahawk
cuttlefish **7** mollusc, mollusk **10** cephalopod ***ink:*** **5** sepia ***relative:*** **5** squid **7** octopus
cut up **4** dice, hash, romp **5** caper, clown, mince, slash **6** cavort **7** carry on, show off **9** misbehave **10** roughhouse
cutup **3** wag **4** zany **5** clown, joker **6** madcap **7** buffoon, farceur **8** jokester
cyan **4** blue
Cybele **4** Rhea ***beloved:*** **5** Attis ***brother:*** **6** Cronus ***father:*** **6** Uranus ***husband:*** **6** Cronus ***mother:*** **4** Gaea ***son:*** **4** Zeus **7** Jupiter, Neptune **8** Poseidon
cyber **5** wired **10** electronic
cybernetics founder **6** Wiener (Norbert)
cycle **3** age, lap, set **4** bike, loop, ring **5** chain, orbit, recur, round, wheel **6** course, period, series **7** circuit **8** rotation, sequence **9** vibration **10** revolution, succession, two-wheeler, velocipede **11** oscillation
cycle track **9** velodrome
cyclic **7** regular **8** periodic, repeated, rhythmic **9** iterative, recurring, repeating **10** isochronal **12** intermittent
cyclone **7** tornado, twister
cyclopean **4** huge **7** immense, mammoth, massive, titanic **8** colossal, enormous, gigantic **9** monstrous **10** gargantuan, tremendous **11** elephantine
Cyclops **5** Arges **7** Brontes **8** Steropes **10** Polyphemus
Cycnus ***father:*** **4** Ares, Mars ***slayer:*** **8** Heracles, Hercules
cygnet **4** swan ***dam (mother):*** **3** pen ***sire (father):*** **3** cob
Cygnus ***form:*** **4** swan ***friend:*** **7** Phaeton ***star:*** **5** Deneb
cylinder **4** drum, pipe, tube **5** spool **6** barrel, bobbin, platen, roller
cylindrical **6** terete **7** tubular **8** tubelike
Cymbeline ***daughter:*** **6** Imogen ***son:*** **9** Arviragus, Guiderius ***son-in-law:*** **9** Posthumus
Cymric **5** Welsh **6** Celtic **9** Brythonic ***bard:*** **8** Taliesin ***Elysium:*** **6** Annwfn
god: **5** Lludd **of Elysium:** **5** Arawn **of the dead:** **5** Pwyll **of the seas:** **3** Ler **4** Llyr **5** Dylan **of the sky:** **7** Gwydion **of the sun:** **4** Lleu, Llew **of the underworld:** **4** Gwyn

goddess: 3 Don 9 Arianrhod *magician:* 6 Merlin

Cymru 5 Wales

cynical 8 derisive, sardonic, scornful 12 misanthropic

Cynthia 4 Luna, moon 5 Diana 7 Artemis

cyprian 4 bawd, jade, slut, tart 5 hussy, tramp 6 floozy, harlot, hooker, wanton 7 jezebel, trollop 8 slattern, strumpet 10 prostitute

Cyprus *capital:* 7 Nicosia 8 Lefkosia *city:* 7 Larnaca 8 Limassol *language:* 5 Greek 7 Turkish *monetary unit:* 4 lira 5 pound *mountain:* 7 Olympus *port:* 9 Famagusta *sea:* 13 Mediterranean

Cyrano de Bergerac 4 poet 7 duelist 8 duellist *author:* 7 Rostand (Edmond) *beloved:* 6 Roxane 7 Roxanne *feature:* 4 nose *rival:* 9 Christian

Cyrus *conquest:* 5 Lydia, Media 7 Babylon *daughter:* 6 Atossa *empire:* 7 Persian *father:* 8 Cambyses *son:* 8 Cambyses

cyst 3 sac, wen 4 sore 5 pouch, spore 6 growth 7 abscess, blister, capsule, vesicle 8 swelling

Cytherea 4 isle 5 Venus 6 island 9 Aphrodite

czar 5 chief, mogul 6 despot, honcho, tycoon, tyrant 7 emperor, kingpin, magnate 8 autocrat *Russian:* 4 Ivan 5 Basil, Boris, Peter 6 Alexis, Dmitry, Feodor, Fyodor, Vasily 7 Dimitri, Michael, Romanov 8 Nicholas, Romanoff, Theodore 9 Alexander 12 Boris Godunov *son:* 10 czarevitch *wife:* 7 czarina

czar's wife 7 czarina

Czech Republic *capital:* 6 Prague *city:* 4 Brno 7 Ostrava *monetary unit:* 6 koruna *neighbor:* 6 Poland 7 Austria, Germany 8 Slovakia *region:* 7 Bohemia, Moravia *river:* 4 Labe, Oder 5 March 6 Morava

D

dab 3 bit, pat 4 blob, blow, daub, peck, poke, spot 5 smear, touch 6 bedaub 7 besmear, plaster, splotch 8 flatfish

dabble 3 dip, dot, toy 4 fool, stud 5 fleck 6 dampen, fiddle, monkey, pepper, putter, splash, tinker 7 freckle, spatter, stipple 8 sprinkle 9 bespeckle, muck about 10 muck around

dabbler 4 duck, tyro 7 amateur 8 putterer, tinkerer 9 smatterer 10 dilettante

dabchick 5 grebe

dacha 5 villa 7 cottage 12 country house

dad 3 pop 4 papa 5 padre, pater 6 father, old man, parent

Dadaist 3 Arp (Jean), Ray (Man) 4 Ball (Hugo) 5 Ernst (Max), Grosz (George), Tzara (Tristan) 7 Duchamp (Marcel), Picabia (Francis) 10 Schwitters (Kurt)

daedal 6 knotty 7 complex 8 artistic, involved, skillful 9 elaborate, intricate 11 complicated 12 labyrinthine 13 sophisticated

Daedalus 7 builder 9 architect, artificer *construction:* 9 Labyrinth *father:* 6 Metion *son:* 6 Icarus *victim:* 5 Talos 6 Perdix

daffy see **daft**

daft 3 mad 4 loco, nuts 5 balmy, crazy, dopey, flaky, loony, nutty, potty, silly, wacko, wacky 6 absurd, crazed, cuckoo, insane, screwy 7 cracked, foolish, idiotic, lunatic, witless 8 demented 10 unbalanced 11 harebrained

Dag *father:* 7 Delling *horse:* 9 Skinfaksi *mother:* 4 Nott

Dagda *chief god of the:* 5 Gaels, Irish *daughter:* 6 Brigit *instrument:* 4 harp *son:* 6 Aengus *wife:* 5 Boann

dagger 4 dirk, snee 5 skean, skene 6 bodkin, stylet 7 dudgeon, poniard 8 stiletto *handle:* 4 hilt *Malay:* 4 kris

____ **Dahl** 5 Roald 6 Arlene

daikon 6 radish

daily 7 diurnal 8 everyday 9 circadian, quotidian *grind:* 7 rat race

dainty 5 goody, tasty, treat 6 choice, morsel, select, tidbit 7 elegant, fragile 8 delicacy, delicate, ethereal, graceful, kickshaw 9 exquisite, recherché 10 delightful

dairy 8 creamery

dais 5 stage 6 podium 7 rostrum 8 platform

daisy 5 oxeye 6 Shasta *British:* 10 moonflower *Scottish:* 5 gowan

Daisy Miller author 5 James (Henry)

Dakota dialect 5 Teton

Daksha's father 6 Brahma

dale 4 dell, glen, vale 6 dingle, valley

Dallas series ***character:*** **3** Liz, Ray **4** Jack, Jock, Lucy **5** April, Bobby, Cally, Cliff, Donna, James, Jenna **6** Carter **7** Clayton, J. R. Ewing, Kristin **8** Michelle, Sue Ellen **9** Miss Ellie ***family:*** **5** Ewing ***ranch home:*** **9** Southfork ***star:*** **4** Gray (Linda), Keel (Howard), Reed (Donna) **5** Davis (Jim), Duffy (Patrick), Rambo (Dack) **6** Crosby (Mary), Hagman (Larry), Howard (Susan), Kanaly (Steve), Tilton (Charlene), Wilson (Sheree) **7** Presley (Priscilla) **9** Bel Geddes (Barbara), Kercheval (Ken), Principal (Victoria)

dally **3** lag, pet, toy **4** drag, idle, play **5** delay, flirt, tarry **6** coquet, dawdle, diddle, linger, loiter, trifle **8** lollygag **9** hang about, waste time **10** fool around

dam **4** weir **5** block, check **7** barrier **8** hold back, restrain ***major:*** **4** Oahe **6** Hoover **7** San Luis **8** Fort Peck, Garrison, Oroville **10** Bonneville, Glen Canyon **11** Grand Coulee

damage **3** mar **4** blot, harm, hurt, loss, maim, ruin **5** abuse, burst, cloud, spoil, stain, wound **6** blight, deface, impair, injure, injury, mangle, ravage, scathe **7** blemish, destroy, marring, tarnish, vitiate **8** maltreat, mischief, mistreat, mutilate, sabotage **9** devastate, vandalism **10** impairment **11** devastation

damaged **4** hurt, rent **6** broken, busted, dinged, flawed, marred **7** injured, spoiled, totaled **8** battered, impaired, ruptured **9** blemished, fractured, imperfect, shattered **10** fragmented

damaging **6** nocent **7** harmful, hurtful, nocuous **9** injurious **11** deleterious, detrimental, prejudicial

dame **4** lady **5** woman **6** gammer, matron **7** dowager **9** matriarch

Damien's island **7** Molokai

Damkina's son **6** Marduk

damn **4** cuss, darn, doom, drat **5** curse, swear **7** condemn, doggone **8** execrate, sentence **9** imprecate **10** vituperate **12** anathematize

damnable **6** blamed, cursed, cussed **7** blasted, dratted **8** accursed, infernal **9** abhorrent, execrable **10** abominable, detestable

damned **5** utter **6** blamed, cursed, cussed, darned, dashed, doomed **7** awfully, blasted, doggone, dratted, goldarn **8** accursed, infernal **9** condemned **10** confounded **13** anathematized

Damocles' ____ **5** sword

Damon's friend **7** Pythias

damp **3** wet **4** dank, dewy **5** check, choke, humid, moist, musty **6** clammy **7** bedewed **8** humidify, humidity

dampen **4** cool, curb **5** chill **6** deaden **7** depress, moisten **8** diminish

damsel **3** gal **4** girl, lass, maid, miss **5** filly, wench **6** lassie, maiden

Dan ***father:*** **5** Jacob ***mother:*** **6** Bilhah ***son:*** **6** Hushim

Danaë ***father:*** **8** Acrisius ***lover:*** **4** Zeus ***son:*** **7** Perseus

Danaus ***brother:*** **8** Aegyptus ***daughters:*** **7** Danaïds **8** Danaïdes ***father:*** **5** Belus ***founder of:*** **5** Argos ***grandfather:*** **7** Neptune **8** Poseidon

dance **3** dip, hop, jig, tap **4** ball, flit, foot, heel, hoof, hula, juba, leap, lope, reel, step, trip **5** bamba, brawl, galop, gigue, hover, lindy, mambo, mixer, polka, rumba, stomp, swing, tread **6** ballet, bolero, boogie, Boston, cancan, chassé, foot it, formal, frolic, German, hoof it, rhumba, shimmy **7** beguine, coranto, courant, flicker, flitter, flutter, hoedown, one-step, shuffle **8** cakewalk, flamenco, galliard, glissade, rigadoon, rigaudon **9** allemande, cotillion, jitterbug, pas de deux ***Argentinian:*** **5** tango ***art of:*** **12** choreography ***Austrian:*** **7** ländler ***ballroom:*** **5** rumba, tango **6** cha-cha, rhumba **7** foxtrot, mazurka, two-step **8** merengue **9** cotillion **10** Charleston ***Bohemian:*** **5** polka ***Brazilian:*** **5** samba **6** maxixe **7** carioca, lambada **8** capoeira **9** bossa nova ***combining form:*** **5** chore **6** choreo, chorio ***country:*** **3** hay **4** reel **8** hornpipe ***couple:*** **5** polka **9** cotillion, malaguena **11** square dance ***court:*** **6** canary, pavane **8** saraband **9** allemande, sarabande ***Cuban:*** **5** conga, mambo, rumba **6** rhumba **8** habanera ***designer:*** **13** choreographer ***English:*** **6** morris ***formal:*** **4** ball, prom **9** cotillion ***French:*** **6** cancan **7** bourrée, gavotte **9** allemande **10** carmagnole ***garment:*** **4** tutu **7** leotard ***Haitian:*** **4** juba **8** merengue ***Hawaiian:*** **4** hula ***Hungarian:*** **7** czardas ***Indian:*** **6** nautch **7** bhangra ***instrument:*** **8** castanet ***Israeli:*** **4** hora ***Italian:*** **10** saltarello, tarantella, villanella **11** passacaglia ***lively:*** **3** jig **4** reel, trot **5** galop, gigue, polka, rumba **6** rhumba **7** bourrée **8** fandango, hornpipe, rigadoon, rigaudon **9** farandole, shakedown **10** Charleston, saltarello, tarantella ***Maori:*** **4** haka ***movement:*** **4** plié, step **8** capriole, glissade **9** pirouette ***Muse of:*** **11** Terpsichore ***1920's:*** **10** Charleston ***Polish:*** **5** polka **7** mazurka **9** polonaise ***Polynesian:*** **4** hula ***ragtime:*** **10** turkey trot ***Scottish:*** **3** bob **4** reel **5** fling **10** strathspey **11** schottische **13** Highland fling ***shoes:*** **5** pumps **8** slippers ***slipper:*** **7** toeshoe ***slow:*** **6** adagio, minuet, pavane **8** habanera ***Spanish:*** **4** jota **6** bolero **7** zapateo **8** cachucha, chaconne, fandango, flamenco, saraband **9** malaguena, sarabande **10** seguidilla ***spectator:*** **10** wallflower ***springy:*** **3** jig ***square:*** **7** hoedown, lancers **9** cotillion, quadrille ***stately:*** **5** pavan **6** pavane **8** saraband **9** polonaise, sarabande ***step:*** **3** pas ***woman's:*** **6** cancan

dancer 6 hoofer **7** chorine, clogger, danseur, stepper **8** coryphée, danseuse **9** ballerina, chorus boy **10** cakewalker, chorus girl ***American:*** **4** Feld (Elliot), Holm (Hanya), Lang (Pearl), Tune (Tommy) **5** Ailey (Alvin), Fosse (Bob), Kelly (Gene), Shawn (Ted), Tharp (Twyla), Watts (Heather) **6** Castle (Irene, Vernon), Duncan (Isadora), Dunham (Katherine), Graham (Martha), Morris (Mark), Taylor (Paul), Verdon (Gwen) **7** Astaire (Adele, Fred), Bujones (Fernando), de Mille (Agnes), Farrell (Suzanne), Gregory (Cynthia), Jamison (Judith), Joffrey (Robert), Kistler (Darci), Martins (Peter), Massine (Leonide), McBride (Patricia), Robbins (Jerome), St. Denis (Ruth), Tamiris (Helen) **8** Champion (Gower, Marge), d'Amboise (Jacques), Humphrey (Doris), Kirkland (Gelsey), LeClercq (Tanaquil), Mitchell (Arthur), Nikolais (Alwin), Villella (Edward) **9** Tallchief (Maria) **10** Cunningham (Merce) ***Cuban:*** **6** Alonso (Alicia) ***Danish:*** **5** Bruhn (Erik) **7** Martins (Peter) **8** Tomasson (Helgi) ***English:*** **5** Dolin (Anton), Somes (Michael), Tudor (Antony) **7** Fonteyn (Margot), Markova (Alicia), Rambert (Marie) **8** de Valois (Ninette), Helpmann (Robert) ***French:*** **5** Lifar (Serge) **6** Béjart (Maurice), Perrot (Jules), Petipa (Marius) **7** Camargo (Marie), Massine (Leonide) ***German:*** **5** Jooss (Kurt) ***Italian:*** **5** Grisi (Carlotta) ***Mexican:*** **5** Limón (José) ***Russian:*** **5** Lifar (Serge) **6** Fokine (Michel), Petipa (Marius) **7** Massine (Leonide), Nureyev (Rudolf), Pavlova (Anna), Ulanova (Galina) **8** Danilova (Aleksandra), Makarova (Natalia), Nijinska (Bronislava), Nijinsky (Vaslav), Vaganova (Agrippina) **9** Karsavina (Tamara), Semyonova (Marina) **11** Baryshnikov (Mikhail), Plisetskaya (Maya) ***Scottish:*** **7** Shearer (Moira)

dancing 6 ballet **12** choreography ***mania:*** **9** tarantism

dandle 3 pet **4** play **6** caress, cosset, cradle, cuddle, pamper

dandruff 5 scall, scurf

dandy 3 fop, pip **4** beau, buck, dude, fine, lulu, toff **5** dilly, doozy, nifty, swell **6** doozie, peachy **7** coxcomb, foppish **8** terrific **9** excellent, first-rate, humdinger, hunky-dory **11** Beau Brummel, crackerjack **12** lounge lizard

dang 4 damn, darn **6** cursed, cussed, damned, darned **7** blasted, dratted, goldarn **8** infernal **10** confounded

danger 4 risk **5** peril **6** crisis, hazard, menace, plight, threat **7** pitfall, trouble **8** distress, jeopardy **9** emergency ***signal:*** **4** bell **5** alarm, siren **6** tocsin

dangerous 5 risky **6** unsafe **7** parlous **8** insecure, menacing, perilous, unstable **9** hazardous **10** precarious **11** threatening

dangle 4 hang **5** droop, swing **6** depend **7** suspend

Daniel ____ *pioneer:* **5** Boone ***statesman:*** **7** Webster

Danish *hero:* **5** Ogier ***king:*** **9** Christian, Frederick ***queen:*** **9** Margrethe

dank 3 wet **4** damp **5** humid, moist **6** clammy **8** dripping

Dante *beloved:* **8** Beatrice ***birthplace:*** **8** Florence ***daughter:*** **7** Antonia ***deathplace:*** **7** Ravenna ***party:*** **6** Guelph **7** Bianchi ***patron:*** **5** Scala ***teacher:*** **6** Latini ***wife:*** **5** Gemma ***work:*** **5** canto **7** Inferno **8** Commedia, Paradiso **9** Vita Nuova **10** Purgatorio **12** Divine Comedy (The)

Danton's colleague 5 Marat (Jean-Paul) **11** Robespierre (Maximilien)

Danzig 6 Gdańsk

Daphne *father:* **5** Ladon **6** Peneus ***form:*** **6** laurel **10** laurel tree ***pursuer:*** **6** Apollo **9** Leucippus

Daphnis' lover 5 Chloe

dapper 4 neat, trim **5** doggy, natty, sassy, smart, swank **6** classy, jaunty, rakish, snazzy, spiffy, spruce, sprucy **7** bandbox, dashing, doggish, foppish, stylish **11** well-groomed

dapple 4 spot **5** fleck, patch **6** mottle **7** speckle, stipple

dappled 4 pied **6** motley **7** flecked, mottled, patched, piebald, spotted **8** brindled **10** variegated **11** varicolored

Dardanelles 10 Hellespont

Dardanus *descendants:* **7** Trojans ***father:*** **4** Zeus **7** Jupiter ***mother:*** **7** Electra

dare 3 try **4** defy, risk **5** beard, brave **6** hazard **7** attempt, venture **8** confront, defiance **9** challenge

daredevil see **daring**

darer 4 hero **6** risker

daring 4 bold, guts, rash **5** brash, brave, gutsy, moxie, nerve, nervy, pluck, valor **6** heroic, plucky **7** bravery, courage, heroism

8 audacity, boldness, fearless, reckless **9** audacious, derring-do, fortitude, venturous **10** courageous **11** adventurous, venturesome **13** adventuresome

Darius ***battle:*** **8** Marathon ***father:*** **9** Hystaspes ***country:*** **6** Persia **7** Parthia ***son:*** **6** Xerxes ***wife:*** **6** Atossa

Darjeeling 3 tea

dark 3 dim **4** dusk, inky, murk **5** black, blind, cloud, dingy, dusky, ebony, murky, night, sable, shady, sooty, swart, umber, unlit, vague **6** brunet, cloudy, dismal, gloomy, opaque, somber, sombre, wicked **7** obscure, ominous, rayless, satanic, shadowy, stygian, subfusc, sunless, swarthy, unclear **8** bistered, brunette, infernal, sinister **9** enigmatic, lightless, secretive, tenebrous, unlighted **10** caliginous, indistinct, mysterious, mystifying, pitch-black **11** crepuscular **13** unilluminated ***poetic:*** **4** ebon

darken 3 dim **5** bedim, cloud, gloom, lower, shade, sully, umber **6** shadow **7** becloud, blacken, eclipse, obscure, tarnish **8** melanize, overcast **9** obfuscate, overcloud **10** overshadow ***Scottish:*** **5** gloam

dark-haired ***female:*** **8** brunette ***male:*** **6** brunet

darkness 4 dusk, evil, murk **5** black, gloom, night, shade **6** shadow **8** blackout **9** nightfall, obscurity

darkroom liquid 3 fix **8** emulsion, hardener

darling 3 gra, hon, pet **4** dear, duck, love **5** angel, deary, ducky, flame, honey, loved, sugar, sweet **7** beloved, dearest, sweetie **8** adorable, charming, favorite, precious **10** sweetheart, sweetie pie

darn 4 drat, knit, mend **5** patch **6** blamed, cursed, cussed, damned, shucks **7** blasted, doggone, dratted **8** infernal **9** embroider **10** confounded ***French:*** **3** zut

Darrow client 4 Debs (Eugene), Loeb (Richard) **6** Scopes (John) **7** Haywood (William), Leopold (Nathan)

dart 3 fly, run, zip **4** barb, bolt, buzz, dash, flit, leap, rush, sail, scud, skim, tear **5** arrow, bound, hurry, lance, pitch, scamp, scoot, shaft, shoot, skirr, spear, speed, spurt **6** glance, hasten, scurry, spring, sprint **7** javelin, missile, scamper ***barbed:*** **10** banderilla

D'Artagnan's friends 5 Athos **6** Aramis **7** Porthos **10** musketeers

Dartmouth location 5 Devon **7** Hanover **12** New Hampshire

darts term 3 leg **4** bust **5** split **6** double, flight, hockey, treble **8** bull's-eye

Darwin, Charles ***colleague:*** **7** Wallace (Alfred Russel) ***ship:*** **6** Beagle ***theory:*** **9** evolution, selection

dash 3 fly, nip, run **4** bolt, brio, cast, damn, dart, élan, foil, hurl, race, ruin, rush, slam, tear, zing **5** break, chase, flair, fling, pinch, smash, style, trace **6** esprit, hyphen, pizazz, scurry, splash, sprint, thrust, thwart **7** bravura, depress, destroy, pizzazz, shatter, smidgen, spatter **8** confound **9** animation, frustrate

dashboard reading 4 fuel **5** speed **7** mileage **8** pressure **11** temperature

dashing 4 bold **5** smart **6** dapper, jaunty, lively, modish **7** gallant, stylish **8** animated, spirited **11** adventurous, fashionable

Das Kapital author 4 Marx (Karl)

dassie 4 pika **5** coney, hyrax

dastard 6 coward, craven **7** chicken, quitter **8** poltroon, recreant **9** scoundrel

dastardly 3 low **4** base, mean **6** craven, yellow **8** cowardly, shameful, skulking **11** treacherous, underhanded **13** pusillanimous

data 4 info **5** facts, input **7** figures **9** documents **11** information ***numerical:*** **5** stats **10** statistics

date 3 age, era, woo **5** court, epoch, tryst **6** cutoff, escort **7** take out **8** deadline **9** accompany **10** engagement, rendezvous **11** anniversary, appointment, assignation

dated 3 old **5** passé **6** démodé, old hat **7** archaic, outworn **8** obsolete, outmoded **10** antiquated **12** old-fashioned **13** unfashionable ***fashionably:*** **5** retro

datum 4 fact

daub 4 blob, blot, spot **5** fleck, paint, smear **6** dapple, smudge, splash **7** besmear, dribble, plaster, speckle, splotch

daughter ***Blythe Danner's:*** **7** Paltrow (Gwyneth) ***Bruce Dern's:*** **5** Laura ***Bush's:*** **5** Jenna **7** Barbara ***Carter's:*** **3** Amy ***Cash's:*** **7** Rosanne ***Cher's:*** **8** Chastity (Bono) ***Clinton's:*** **7** Chelsea ***Cole's:*** **7** Natalie ***Coppola's:*** **5** Sofia ***Danny Thomas's:*** **5** Marlo ***Debbie Reynolds's:*** **6** Carrie (Fisher) ***Eddie Fisher's:*** **6** Carrie ***Elizabeth II's:*** **4** Anne ***Elvis's:*** **9** Lisa Marie ***Fonda's:*** **4** Jane ***Ford's (Gerald):*** **5** Susan ***Freud's:*** **4** Anna ***Garland's:*** **4** Liza (Minnelli) ***Goldie Hawn's:*** **10** Kate Hudson ***Ingrid Bergman's:*** **8** Isabella (Rossellini) ***Janet Leigh's:*** **8** Jamie Lee (Curtis) ***Joel Grey's:*** **8** Jennifer ***Johnson's (Lyndon):*** **4** Lucy **5** Linda ***Jon Voight's:*** **8** Angelina (Jolie) ***Kennedy's (John F.):*** **8** Caroline ***Klaus Kinski's:*** **9** Nastassja ***Maureen O'Sullivan's:*** **3** Mia (Farrow) ***Naomi Judd's:*** **7** Wynonna ***Nat King Cole's:*** **7** Natalie ***Nixon's:*** **5** Julie **6** Tricia ***Pat Boone's:*** **5** Debby ***Ravi Shankar's:*** **10** Norah Jones ***Reagan's:*** **5** Patti **7** Maureen ***Richard Bur-***

ton's: 4 Kate *Ryan O'Neal's:* 5 Tatum *Sinatra's:* 5 Nancy *Tony Curtis's:* 8 Jamie Lee
Daughter of the Moon 7 Nokomis
daunt 3 cow 5 alarm, deter 6 dismay, subdue 7 terrify 8 frighten 10 disconcert, discourage, dishearten, intimidate
daunting 7 awesome 8 imposing 9 dismaying, unnerving 10 forbidding, formidable 11 dispiriting 12 discouraging, intimidating, overwhelming
dauntless 4 bold, game 5 brave 6 daring 7 gallant, valiant 8 fearless, unafraid 9 unfearful, unfearing 10 courageous 11 lionhearted 12 stouthearted
dauntlessness 4 guts 5 heart, nerve, pluck, spunk, valor 6 daring, mettle, spirit 7 bravery, cojones, courage 8 boldness 10 resolution 12 fearlessness
davenport 4 desk, sofa 5 couch, divan 6 daybed 12 chesterfield
David *commander:* 4 Joab 5 Amasa *companion:* 8 Jonathan *daughter:* 5 Tamar *father:* 5 Jesse *rebuker:* 6 Nathan *son:* 5 Amnon 7 Absalom, Solomon 8 Adonijah *song of:* 5 psalm *wife:* 6 Michal 7 Abigail, Ahinoam 9 Bathsheba
____ **David** 4 Camp 5 Magen, Mogen 6 Star of
David Copperfield *author:* 7 Dickens (Charles) *character:* 4 Dora, Heep 5 Uriah 6 Barkis 8 Micawber, Peggotty 9 Murdstone 10 Steerforth
Da Vinci Code author 5 Brown (Dan)
davit 5 crane
dawdle 3 lag 4 idle, laze, loaf, loll 5 dally, delay, tarry 6 diddle, linger, loiter, lounge 8 lollygag 10 dillydally
dawn 4 morn 5 onset, sunup 6 aurora 7 morning, sunrise 8 cockcrow, daybreak, daylight 9 beginning 10 first light *goddess:* 3 Eos 6 Aurora *pertaining to:* 4 eoan
day *abbreviation:* 3 Fri, Mon, Sat, Sun, Thu, Tue, Wed 4 Thur, Tues 5 Thurs *before:* 3 eve *church calendar:* 5 feria *French:* 4 jour *German:* 3 Tag *holy:* 5 feast *hour:* 4 noon *Latin:* 4 dies *Spanish:* 3 día
daybreak 4 dawn, morn 5 sunup 6 aurora 7 dawning, morning, sunrise 8 cockcrow, daylight
daydream 4 muse 5 fancy 6 vision 7 fantasy, reverie 8 phantasy 9 fantasize 10 woolgather 13 woolgathering
daystar 3 Sol, sun 5 Venus 7 phoebus
daze 3 fog 4 haze, stun 5 amaze, blind 6 dazzle, stupor, trance 7 astound, confuse, stupefy 8 astonish, bedazzle, befuddle, confound 9 dumbfound
dazed 5 woozy 6 groggy, punchy 7 dazzled, stunned 8 confused 9 stupefied 10 punch-drunk
____ **d'Azur** 4 Côte
dazzle 3 wow 4 stun 5 amaze, blind, éclat, glitz, shine 7 impress 8 astonish, bewilder, confound, outshine 9 overpower
dazzling 6 flashy, garish 7 radiant 8 splendid, stunning 9 brilliant 11 confounding, resplendent 12 overpowering
deacon 6 clergy, cleric, layman 8 reverend 9 churchman
dead 4 cold, gone, late 5 passé, slain, stiff 6 buried, fallen 7 defunct, done for, expired, extinct 8 deceased, departed, lifeless 9 senseless 10 corpselike 11 unconscious 12 extinguished
deadbeat 3 bum 5 idler 6 debtor, loafer, slouch 7 lounger, shirker, slacker 10 delinquent, malingerer
dead duck 5 goner 8 casualty, fatality
deaden 4 dull, kill, mute, numb, stun 5 blunt, quiet 6 benumb, dampen, lessen, muffle, obtund, reduce, stifle 7 smother, stupefy 8 suppress 11 anesthetize, desensitize
dead end 4 halt, stop 6 pocket, unruly 7 impasse 8 cul-de-sac, standoff 9 stalemate, terminate 10 blind alley, bottleneck, standstill
deadened 4 numb 6 asleep, dulled, killed, numbed 7 blunted 8 benumbed, impaired 12 anesthetized
deadeye 5 block 8 marksman 12 sharpshooter
deadfall 4 trap 7 springe 9 booby trap, mousetrap
deadliness 8 fatality 9 lethality, mortality
deadlock 3 tie 4 draw 7 impasse 8 standoff, stoppage 9 checkmate, stalemate 10 standstill
deadly 5 fatal, toxic 6 lethal, mortal 7 capital, killing 8 lethally, unerring 10 implacable 11 destructive, internecine 12 pestilential
deadpan 5 blank, empty 6 vacant 9 impassive 10 poker-faced 11 inscrutable 12 inexpressive, unexpressive
Dead Souls author 5 Gogol (Nikolay)
dead to rights 9 red-handed
deadweight 4 load 6 weight
deal 4 dole, sale, sell 5 allot, serve, shake, share, trade, treat 6 barter, dicker, parcel 7 bargain, deliver, dish out, dole out, mete out, package, portion, traffic, wrestle 8 contract, disburse, dispense, share out 9 agreement, apportion, negotiate 10 administer, compromise, distribute, measure out 11 arrangement, transaction 13 understanding

great: **4** gobs, heap, lots, tons **5** heaps, horde, loads, scads **6** oodles, plenty, stacks ***out:*** **8** disburse, dispense **9** apportion **10** administer, distribute ***with:*** **5** serve, treat **6** handle, regard **7** concern, involve

dealer 5 agent **6** broker, seller, trader, vendor **8** chandler, merchant, operator **9** tradesman **10** negotiator, trafficker **11** businessman, distributer, distributor **12** merchandiser ***British:*** **5** coper **6** draper, jobber, mercer **7** chapman

dealings 5 trade, truck **7** affairs, matters, traffic **8** business, commerce, concerns **11** intercourse **12** interactions, transactions, undertakings

dean 4 head **5** chief, doyen, elder **6** leader

dear 3 gra, pet **4** fond, lamb, love **5** honey, loved, sugar, sweet **6** costly, doting, loving, prized, scarce **7** beloved, darling, devoted, lovable, machree, querida, tootsie **8** favorite, precious, valuable **9** cherished, expensive, heartfelt, treasured **10** fair-haired, honeybunch, sweetheart **12** affectionate ***French:*** **4** cher **5** chère **6** chérie ***Scottish:*** **2** jo

dearth 4 lack, want **6** famine **7** absence, default, paucity **8** scarcity, shortage, sparsity **9** privation, scantness **10** deficiency, meagerness, scantiness

death 3 end **4** exit **6** demise, ending, expiry **7** decease, passing, quietus **8** casualty, curtains, fatality, necrosis, thanatos **9** bloodshed, departure **10** expiration, extinction, grim reaper **11** dissolution, termination **12** annihilation ***after:*** **10** posthumous ***combining form:*** **6** thanat **7** thanato ***music:*** **5** dirge, elegy **8** threnody ***notice:*** **4** obit **8** obituary **9** necrology ***of tissue:*** **8** gangrene ***personification:*** **10** grim reaper ***put to:*** **3** gas, hit, ice, zap **4** do in, hang, kill, slay **5** drown, lynch, snuff, waste **6** murder, poison, rub out **7** bump off, butcher, execute, smother, wipe out **8** blow away, dispatch, immolate, knock off, strangle, throttle **9** slaughter, suffocate **10** asphyxiate **11** assassinate, electrocute ***rate:*** **9** mortality ***rites:*** **7** funeral **8** exequies **9** interment, obsequies

Death in the Family author 4 Agee (James)

deathless 7 abiding, eternal, lasting, undying **8** enduring, immortal **11** everlasting **12** imperishable

deathlike see **deathly**

deathly 5 fatal **6** lethal, mortal **7** macabre, stygian **12** pestilential

debacle 4 rout **6** defeat, fiasco **7** breakup, failure **8** collapse, disaster **9** breakdown, cataclysm **10** disruption

debar 3 ban **4** stop **6** forbid, outlaw **7** exclude, prevent, rule out **8** preclude, prohibit **9** interdict

debark 4 land **6** alight, get off **11** decorticate

debase 3 mar **4** harm **5** lower, stain **6** damage, defile, demean, dilute, impair, reduce, weaken **7** cheapen, corrupt, degrade, devalue, pervert, pollute, vitiate **8** dishonor **9** undermine **10** adulterate, depreciate **11** contaminate

debatable 4 iffy, moot **7** dubious **8** arguable, doubtful **9** contested, uncertain, undecided **10** disputable, unresolved **11** problematic **12** questionable

debate 4 moot **5** argue, bandy, plead **7** contend, contest, discuss, dispute, quarrel, wrangle **8** argument, consider, forensic, question **9** dialectic, thrash out **10** controvert, toss around **11** application, controversy, disputation **12** deliberation **13** argumentation ***again:*** **6** rehash ***art of:*** **9** forensics ***expert:*** **7** eristic ***place for:*** **5** forum ***side:*** **3** con, pro

debauch 4 orgy, warp **6** seduce **7** corrupt, deprave, pervert, vitiate **9** bacchanal, brutalize **10** lead astray, saturnalia **11** bacchanalia

debauched 6 wanton **8** degraded, depraved, vitiated **9** corrupted, dissolute, libertine, perverted **10** degenerate, licentious

debilitate 3 sap **6** impair, weaken **7** cripple, disable **8** enfeeble **9** attenuate, undermine **10** devitalize

debilitated 4 weak **6** feeble, infirm, sapped **7** run-down, worn-out **8** weakened **9** enfeebled

debility 7 disease, malaise **8** weakness **9** infirmity **10** feebleness, infirmness, sickliness **11** decrepitude

Debir *kingdom:* **5** Eglon ***slayer:*** **6** Joshua

debit 4 bill, levy **6** charge **7** deficit **8** drawback **9** liability **11** encumbrance, shortcoming

debonair 5 suave **6** smooth, urbane **7** dashing, elegant **10** nonchalant **12** lighthearted

Deborah's husband 9 Lappidoth

debouch 5 empty, issue **6** emerge

debris 4 junk, slag **5** trash, waste **6** litter, refuse, rubble, spilth **7** garbage, rubbish **8** detritus, riffraff, wreckage ***rock:*** **5** scree, talus **8** colluvia **9** colluvium

debt 3 due, sin **6** arrear, red ink **7** arrears, default, deficit **8** mortgage, trespass **9** arrearage, liability **10** obligation **11** delinquency ***acknowledgment:*** **3** IOU **4** bill **5** check

debtless 7 solvent

debunk 6 expose, reveal, show up, unmask **7**

lay bare, lay open, uncloak, uncover, undress **8** unshroud **9** demystify, discredit

Debussy's La ____ 3 Mer

debut 3 bow **5** entry **6** entree **7** come out, opening, present **8** entrance, premiere **9** beginning, coming out, introduce **12** introduction, presentation

decadence 5 decay **7** decline **10** degeneracy, regression **11** degradation **12** degeneration **13** deterioration

decadent 6 effete **7** debased **8** decaying, degraded, depraved **9** debauched, declining, dissolute **10** degenerate **13** self-indulgent

Decalogue 12 Commandments ***verb:*** **5** shalt

Decameron, The *author:* **9** Boccaccio (Giovanni) ***heroine:*** **8** Griselda

decamp 4 blow, bolt, exit, flee **5** leave, scram, split **6** beat it, begone, cut out, escape, get out, retire **7** abscond, make off, pull out, run away, skiddoo, take off, vamoose **8** clear out, withdraw **9** skedaddle

decant 4 pour **7** draw off, pour out **8** transfer

decanter 5 cruet, flask **6** bottle, carafe, flagon, vessel

decapitate 4 head **6** behead **9** decollate **10** guillotine

decapod 7 mollusc, mollusk **10** crustacean

decathlon champ 6 Jenner (Bruce), Morris (Glenn), O'Brien (Dan), Schenk (Christian), Sebrle (Roman), Toomey (Bill), Zmelik (Robert) **7** Doherty (Ken), Johnson (Rafer), Mathias (Bob) **8** Campbell (Milton), Thompson (Daley)

decay 3 rot **4** ruin, wane **5** spoil, waste **6** molder, wither **7** atrophy, crumble, decline, putrefy, rotting **8** putresce, spoilage **9** decompose **11** deteriorate **12** dilapidation, putrefaction **13** deterioration

decayed 6 putrid, rotted, rotten, ruined **7** carious, spoiled **8** decadent, moldered, overripe **9** putrefied **10** decomposed, degenerate

decease 3 die, end **4** fail, pass **5** death, dying, sleep **6** demise, depart, expire, finish, pass on, perish **7** passing, quietus, release, succumb **8** pass away **9** departure **10** expiration

deceased 4 body, dead, late **6** corpse **7** cadaver, carcass, expired, remains **8** departed, lifeless **9** inanimate

deceit 3 gyp **4** hoax, ruse, sham **5** fraud, guile, trick **6** humbug **7** swindle **8** artifice, flimflam, trickery **9** chicanery, deception, duplicity, imposture **10** dishonesty **13** double-dealing

deceitful 3 sly **4** wily **5** false, lying **6** crafty, sneaky, tricky **7** cunning, knavish, roguish **8** guileful, two-faced **9** deceptive, dishonest, underhand **10** mendacious **11** underhanded **13** double-dealing

deceive 3 con **4** bilk, dupe, fool, gull, hoax **5** bluff, cozen, lie to, trick **6** delude, humbug, palter, take in **7** beguile, mislead, sandbag, two-time **8** flimflam, hoodwink **9** bamboozle, four-flush **11** double-cross

deceiving 5 false **6** tricky **8** deluding, delusive, delusory, guileful, two-faced **9** beguiling, deceptive **10** fallacious, misleading **11** duplicitous, underhanded

decelerate 4 slow **5** delay **6** retard, slow up **7** slacken **8** slow down

decency 7 decorum, dignity, fitness, modesty **8** civility **9** etiquette, propriety **10** conformity, seemliness

decennium 6 decade

decent 4 fair, good **5** right **6** honest, modest, proper, seemly **7** correct, fitting, upright **8** adequate, all right **9** competent, honorable, tolerable **10** acceptable, conforming, sufficient **11** comme il faut, presentable, respectable **12** satisfactory

deception 3 gyp, lie **4** gaff, hoax, hype, ruse, scam, sham, wile **5** cheat, feint, fraud, guile, put-on, trick **6** deceit, dupery, humbug, mirage **7** chicane, cunning, fallacy, fantasm, knavery, sophism **8** flimflam, illusion, intrigue, phantasm, trickery, trumpery, wiliness **9** casuistry, chicanery, duplicity, imposture, sophistry, treachery **10** dishonesty, hanky-panky, subterfuge

deceptive 5 false, phony **6** tricky **8** deluding, delusory, illusory, specious **9** beguiling, deceitful, deceiving **10** fallacious, misleading

decide 3 opt **4** rule, will **5** judge **6** settle **7** adjudge, resolve **8** conclude **9** determine **10** adjudicate

decided 3 set **4** firm **5** fixed **6** intent **7** assured, certain, obvious, settled **8** definite, resolute, resolved **10** determined, pronounced **11** established, unequivocal

decimate 4 raze, ruin **5** wreck **7** abolish, destroy, wipe out **8** demolish, massacre **9** slaughter **10** annihilate, obliterate **11** exterminate

decipher 4 read **5** break, crack, solve **6** decode, reveal **7** decrypt, resolve, unravel **8** unriddle **9** figure out, interpret, puzzle out, translate **12** cryptanalyze

decision 4 fiat **6** choice, ruling **7** finding, resolve, verdict **8** firmness, judgment, sentence **9** selection **10** conclusion, resolution, settlement **13** determination ***rabbinical:*** **9** responsum

decisive 3 set **7** crucial, settled **8** critical, resolute **10** conclusive, convincing, determined, imperative, peremptory **11** determining **12** unmistakable

deck 4 trim **5** adorn, array, dress, equip, floor, level, porch, prank **6** attire, blazon, clothe **7** apparel, appoint, festoon, furnish, garland, garnish, terrace **8** accouter, accoutre, beautify, decorate, emblazon, ornament, platform **9** embellish ***chief:*** **4** bos'n **9** boatswain ***high:*** **4** poop ***lowest:*** **5** orlop ***out:*** **5** array, fix up, slick, spiff, tog up **6** clothe, doll up **7** dress up, gussy up **8** spruce up ***part:*** **7** scupper

deckhand 3 gob **4** jack, swab **6** sailor, seaman **7** jack-tar, rouster, swabbie **10** bluejacket

declaim 4 rant **5** mouth, orate, speak **6** recite **7** deliver, lecture **8** bloviate, harangue, perorate **9** hold forth

declamatory 5 tumid, windy, wordy **6** florid, turgid **7** aureate, flowery, fustian, orotund, pompous, ranting, verbose **8** sonorous **9** bombastic, high-flown, overblown **10** euphuistic, oratorical, rhetorical **12** magniloquent **13** grandiloquent

declaration 5 edict **6** avowal, notice, report **7** promise **8** document, pleading **9** affidavit, manifesto, statement, testimony **10** confession, deposition, disclosure, expression, profession **11** affirmation, attestation **12** announcement, notification, proclamation **13** advertisement, pronouncement

declare 3 say, vow **4** aver, avow, tell, vent **5** claim, sound, state, swear, utter, voice **6** affirm, allege, assert, avouch, blazon, depone, depose, herald, insist, ordain, report, reveal **7** certify, confirm, deliver, divulge, express, profess, signify, testify **8** announce, disclose, indicate, maintain, manifest, proclaim, propound **9** advertise, broadcast, enunciate, predicate, pronounce **10** annunciate, asseverate, promulgate **11** come out with, disseminate ***a saint:*** **8** canonize ***in cards:*** **3** bid **4** meld ***invalid:*** **5** annul

declass 4 bump, bust **5** abase, lower **6** demote, reduce **7** degrade, set back **9** downgrade

déclassé 4 mean, poor **6** common, vulgar **7** ignoble, lowered **8** inferior, lowgrade, mediocre, middling **10** second-rate **11** second-class

declension 5 class, slope **7** decline, descent **8** downfall **9** downgrade **10** inflection **12** dégringolade **13** deterioration

declination 3 ebb **5** slant, slide **6** ebbing **7** refusal, incline **8** downturn **9** downgrade **10** deflection **12** dégringolade, turning aside **13** deterioration

decline 3 dip, ebb, jib, rot, sag, set **4** balk, dive, drop, fade, fail, fall, flag, loss, sink, slip, wane **5** abate, avoid, demur, droop, lapse, lower, say no, slide, slope, slump, spurn **6** ebbing, go down, recede, refuse, reject, renege, waning, weaken, worsen **7** abstain, atrophy, descend, descent, devolve, dismiss, drop-off, dwindle, failure, falloff, forbear, refrain, relapse, sell-off, sinkage, subside **8** comedown, decrease, downfall, downturn, languish, lowering, turn down **9** backslide, decadence, downgrade, downslide, downswing, downtrend, reprobate, repudiate, weakening **10** degeneracy, degenerate, depression, devolution, disapprove, falling off **11** backsliding, deteriorate **12** degeneration, dégringolade **13** deterioration

declivitous 5 steep **6** sloped **7** pitched, sloping **8** inclined **9** inclining **10** descending

declivity 3 dip **4** drop, fall **5** slope **7** decline, descent **8** downturn, gradient **9** downgrade **11** inclination

decode see **decipher**

decollate 4 head, kill **6** behead **10** decapitate, guillotine

decolor 6 blanch, bleach, blench, whiten **7** wash out **11** achromatize

decompose 3 rot **5** decay, spoil, taint **6** fester, molder **7** analyze, break up, crumble, putrefy, resolve **8** dissolve, separate **9** anatomize, break down **12** disintegrate

decor 7 setting **8** backdrop, stage set **11** furnishings **13** ornamentation

decorate 4 do up, pink, trim **5** adorn, dress, frill **6** bedeck **7** bedizen, dress up, enhance, festoon, furnish, garnish **8** appliqué, beautify, emblazon, ornament **9** embellish ***a border:*** **6** purfle

decorated 6 ornate **7** adorned, honored, wrought **9** bemedaled, decked out, garnished **10** beribboned, ornamented **11** embellished

decoration 4 bays **5** award, badge, honor, kudos, medal **6** doodad, plaque **7** garnish, laurels **8** accolade, filigree, fretting, fretwork, frippery, furbelow, ornament, trimming, vignette **11** distinction ***cutout:*** **8** appliqué ***furniture:*** **4** buhl **6** boulle

decorous 3 fit **4** meet, prim **5** right **6** au fait, comely, decent, proper, seemly **7** correct, elegant, fitting **8** becoming, mannerly, suitable, tasteful **9** befitting, civilized, de rigueur, dignified **10** conforming **11** appropriate, respectable, well-behaved

decorously 5 fitly **7** rightly **8** decently, properly, suitably **9** correctly, fittingly **11** befittingly, respectably

decorousness 7 decency **8** civility **9** propriety, rightness **10** seemliness **11** correctness, orderliness **12** correctitude
decorticate 4 bare, bark, flay, hull, husk, pare, peel, skin **5** scale, scalp, shell, shuck, strip **6** denude **7** lay bare, pull off
decorum 5 order **7** decency, dignity, fitness, modesty **8** protocol **9** etiquette, propriety **10** properness, seemliness **11** correctness, orderliness **12** correctitude
decoy 4 bait, fake, lure **5** plant, shill, tempt **6** allure, capper, delude, entice, lead on, pigeon, seduce **7** deceive, mislead **8** inveigle **10** red herring
decrease 3 cut, ebb **4** batc, drop, ease, fall, loss, wane **5** allay, lower **6** lessen, reduce, shrink **7** abridge, curtail, cut back, cutback, cut down, decline, die down, drop off, dwindle, fall off, lighten, shorten, slacken, subside **8** diminish, downturn, moderate, rollback, taper off **9** abatement, alleviate, reduction **10** abbreviate, depreciate, diminution, falling off
decree 4 fiat, rule **5** canon, edict, enact, judge, order, ukase **6** behest, charge, dictum, impose, ordain, ruling **7** adjudge, appoint, bidding, command, declare, dictate, lay down, mandate, precept, statute **8** judgment, proclaim, sentence **9** directive, judgement, ordinance, prescribe, prescript, pronounce **10** adjudicate, injunction, regulation **11** declaration **12** adjudication, announcement, proclamation, promulgation **13** pronouncement ***Muslim:*** **5** fatwa
decrepit 4 aged, weak, worn **5** frail, seedy, tacky **6** creaky, feeble, infirm, senile, shabby, wasted, weakly **7** fragile, rundown, worn-out **8** battered, impaired, weakened **10** bedraggled, broken-down, down-at-heel, ramshackle **11** dilapidated
decrepitude 4 ruin **5** decay **7** frailty, wasting **8** collapse, debility, weakness **9** disrepair, infirmity **10** exhaustion, feebleness, infirmness **12** dilapidation, enfeeblement **13** deterioration
decretal 4 fiat, writ **5** edict, order, ukase **6** assize, dictum, letter, ruling **7** dictate **8** dcci-sion, judgment **11** declaration **13** pronouncement
decry 3 boo **4** bash, slam, slur **5** abuse **6** berate, malign, vilify **7** asperse, censure, condemn, degrade, devalue, put down **8** bad-mouth, belittle, denounce, derogate, reproach **9** criticize, deprecate, discredit, disparage, dispraise, reprehend, reprobate **10** depreciate, disapprove **11** rail against
decrypt see **decipher**
decumbent 4 flat **5** prone **6** supine **9** lying down, prostrate, reclining **10** horizontal
decussate 5 cross **8** crosscut **9** intersect **10** crisscross, intercross
dedicate 3 vow **5** bless **6** commit, devote, hallow, pledge **7** address **8** inscribe, restrict, set apart **10** consecrate
deduce 5 infer, judge, trace **6** derive, evolve, gather, reason, reckon **7** discern, make out, surmise **8** conclude **9** figure out
deduct 4 bate **5** abate, infer, judge **6** gather, remove **7** make out, take off, take out **8** conclude, knock off, perceive, subtract, take away
deduction 3 cut **4** tare **8** discount, illation, judgment, sequitur, write-off **9** abatement, inference, reasoning **10** conclusion **11** subtraction
deductive 7 a priori **8** dogmatic, illative, provable, reasoned **9** derivable, inferable **10** consequent **11** inferential **13** ratiocinative
deed 3 act **4** cede, fact, feat, pact **5** doing, title **6** action, assign, convey, escrow, remise **7** charter, exploit **8** alienate, contract, covenant, make over, sign over, transfer **9** adventure **10** conveyance, enterprise **11** achievement, performance, tour de force ***brutal:*** **8** atrocity ***evil:*** **3** sin **11** malefaction ***good:*** **7** mitzvah
deem 4 feel, hold **5** judge, think **7** account, adjudge, believe **8** consider
de-emphasize 8 downplay, minimize, play down **9** gloss over, soft-pedal, underplay **13** underestimate
deep 3 low **4** bass, rapt, sunk **5** abyss, grave, ocean **6** occult, orphic, secret **7** abyssal, obscure **8** abstruse, esoteric, hermetic, profound **9** engrossed, recondite **10** bottomless, fathomless, mysterious ***combining form:*** **5** bathy
deepen 6 darken, worsen **7** enhance, enlarge, magnify, thicken **8** heighten **9** aggravate, intensify **10** strengthen
deepness 5 abyss **9** intensity **10** profundity
deep-seated 6 inborn, inbred, innate **7** settled **8** inherent, lifelong, profound, stubborn **9** confirmed, ingrained, intrinsic **10** congenital, entrenched, indwelling, inveterate **11** established **12** long-standing **13** bred-in-the-bone, dyed-in-the-wool, thoroughgoing
deep-six 4 dump, toss **5** chuck, scrap **6** unload **7** discard **8** jettison **9** eliminate
deep water 7 trouble **8** distress **10** difficulty
deer 3 elk, roe **4** buck, musk, stag **5** moose **6** wapiti **7** caribou, venison ***Asian:*** **4** axis, maha **6** sambar **7** muntjac ***British:*** **4** hart ***female:*** **3** doe **4** hind ***Japanese:*** **4** sika ***male:***

4 buck, hart, stag 7 roebuck ***meat:*** 5 jerky 7 venison ***path:*** 3 run 5 trail ***red:*** 7 brocket ***relating to:*** 7 cervine ***track:*** 4 slot 5 spoor ***young:*** 3 kid 4 fawn

Deere rival 4 Case, Ford, Toro 6 Kubota 7 Farmall

Deerslayer, The ***author:*** 6 Cooper (James Fenimore) ***character:*** 5 Harry (Hurry) 6 Hutter (Thomas), Judith (Hutter) 11 Natty Bumppo 12 Chingachgook

deface 3 mar 4 harm, ruin 6 damage, deform, impair, injure 9 disfigure, vandalize

de facto 6 actual, really 8 actually, existing

defalcation 7 default, failing, failure 10 embezzling, inadequacy, negligence 12 embezzlement

defamation 5 libel, smear 7 calumny, obloquy, slander 10 backbiting 11 traducement 12 backstabbing 13 disparagement

defamatory 8 libelous 9 maligning, traducing, vilifying 10 backbiting, calumnious, slanderous 11 denigrating

defame 5 abase, libel, smear 6 malign, vilify 7 asperse, blacken, blemish, slander, traduce 8 dishonor 9 denigrate, discredit 10 calumniate

default 4 fail 5 welsh 7 absence, exclude, failure, forfeit, neglect 9 selection

defeasance 4 deed 6 defeat 9 overthrow 11 termination

defeat 3 tan 4 beat, best, down, drub, edge, foil, lick, loss, rout, sink, undo, whip, whup 5 crush, outdo, skunk, swamp, upset, waste, whomp 6 outgun, reduce, subdue, wallop 7 beating, conquer, destroy, failure, licking, mow down, nose out, nullify, outplay, overrun, setback, shellac, trounce, wipe out 8 confound, knock out, outfight, outflank, overcome, vanquish, waterloo 9 frustrate, overpower, overthrow, overtrump, subjugate, thrashing, trouncing 10 obliterate 11 shellacking

defeatist 8 doomster 9 doomsayer, Gloomy Gus, pessimist, worrywart

defect 3 bug 4 flaw, lack, vice, want 5 botch, error, fault 6 damage, dearth, desert, foible, injury 7 blemish, default, failing 8 drawback, weakness 9 birthmark, deformity 10 apostatize, deficiency 11 shortcoming 12 imperfection, tergiversate ***timber:*** 4 knot ***visual:*** 6 myopia, squint 9 amblyopia, hyperopia 10 presbyopia, strabismus

defection 8 apostasy 9 desertion, forsaking, recreancy 10 disloyalty 11 abandonment

defective 5 amiss 6 broken, faulty, flawed 7 damaged, lacking, unsound, wanting 8 impaired 9 corrupted, deficient, imperfect 10 inaccurate, inadequate, incomplete 12 insufficient

defector 5 Judas 7 traitor 8 apostate, quisling, recreant, renegade, turncoat 9 turnabout 13 double-crosser

defend 4 back, hold, save 5 argue, cover, guard 6 screen, secure, shield, uphold 7 contend, justify, protect, support 8 advocate, champion, maintain, plead for, preserve 9 safeguard

defendable see **defensible**

defendant 7 accused, libelee 8 libellee

defender 7 paladin, tribune 8 advocate, champion, guardian 9 protector 11 white knight

defense 4 fort, ward 5 aegis, alibi, armor, guard 6 excuse, sconce, shield 7 bulwark, rampart, shelter 8 apologia, armament, fastness, fortress, muniment, security 9 safeguard 10 protection, stronghold 11 exculpation, explanation 13 justification ***organization:*** 4 NATO 5 ANZUS, NORAD, SEATO 10 Warsaw Pact

defenseless 4 open 7 exposed, unarmed 8 helpless, wide open 9 unguarded 10 vulnerable 11 unprotected

defensible 5 valid 7 tenable 8 passable 9 excusable, plausible 10 condonable, reasonable 11 justifiable

defer 3 bow 4 stay, wait 5 delay, remit, stall, table, yield 6 accede, hold up, put off, shelve, submit 7 hold off, lay over, put over, suspend 8 hold over, postpone, prorogue 9 acquiesce 13 procrastinate

deference 5 honor 6 esteem, homage, regard 7 respect 8 courtesy 9 obeisance 11 recognition

deferential 8 obliging 9 disarming, regardful 10 respectful 11 complaisant

defiance 4 dare 5 moxie 7 bravado 8 audacity, contempt 9 challenge, contumacy, impudence, insolence 10 brazenness, effrontery 12 contrariness, stubbornness

defiant 4 bold 5 brash, gutsy, sassy, saucy 6 brazen, cheeky, daring 8 arrogant, impudent, insolent 9 audacious, obstinate, resistant 10 refractory 12 recalcitrant

deficiency 4 flaw, lack, want 5 fault, minus 6 dearth 7 absence, blemish, demerit, failing, failure, paucity 8 scarcity, shortage, weakness 9 privation 10 inadequacy, scantiness 11 defalcation, shortcoming 12 imperfection ***mental:*** 6 idiocy 7 amentia ***pigmentation:*** 8 albinism

deficient 3 shy 5 minus, scant, short 6 faulty, flawed, meager, meagre, measly, scanty, scarce 7 failing, lacking, unsound, wanting

8 exiguous, impaired **9** defective, imperfect **10** inadequate, incomplete

deficit 4 lack, loss **6** red ink **8** shortage **10** impairment, inadequacy **12** disadvantage **13** insufficiency

defile 3 tar **4** foul, pass, rape, soil **5** dirty, gorge, march, shame, smear, spoil, stain, sully, taint **6** befoul, debase, ravish **7** besmear, corrupt, pollute, profane, tarnish, violate **8** deflower, dishonor **9** desecrate **11** contaminate

defiled 5 raped **6** impure **7** stained, unclean **8** profaned, polluted, ravished, violated **9** corrupted **10** deflowered, desecrated **12** contaminated

define 3 fix, hem, rim, set **4** edge **5** limit **6** assign, border, detail **7** clarify, delimit, lay down, mark off, mark out, outline, specify **9** delineate, demarcate, determine, establish **11** distinguish **12** characterize

definite 3 set **4** sure **5** clear, final, fixed, sharp, solid **7** certain, decided, express, precise, settled **8** clear-cut, distinct, explicit, specific **10** conclusive, pronounced **11** unambiguous, unequivocal **12** unmistakable

definiteness 8 accuracy, sureness **9** certainty, certitude, exactness, precision **10** exactitude

definitive 5 final **7** express **8** clear-cut, complete, explicit, settling, specific, ultimate **10** concluding, conclusive, exhaustive **11** categorical, determining, unambiguous **13** authoritative

deflate 4 dash **6** humble, reduce, shrink **7** devalue, put down **8** contract, ridicule **9** humiliate, shoot down

deflect 5 avert, parry **6** divert **7** deviate, diverge, hold off **9** turn aside

deflection 3 yaw **4** bend, tack, turn, veer **5** carom, curve, shift **6** double, swerve **7** bending, rebound, turning, veering **8** swerving **9** departure, deviation, diversion **10** divergence

deflower 4 rape **5** spoil **6** defile, ravish **7** despoil, violate **9** desecrate

Defoe, Daniel ***character:*** **6** Crusoe (Robinson), Friday, Roxana **12** Moll Flanders

deform 4 warp **5** spoil **6** deface **7** contort, distort **8** misshape **9** disfigure

deformed 4 awry, bent **5** askew, bowed **6** warped **7** buckled, crooked **8** crippled **9** contorted, misshapen, unshapely

deformity 4 flaw **6** defect **7** blemish **11** abnormality **12** imperfection, irregularity, malformation **13** disfigurement

____ de France 3 Île

defraud 3 con, gyp **4** bilk, dupe, rook, scam **5** cheat, cozen, mulct, trick **6** fleece, rip off **7** swindle **8** flimflam **9** bamboozle

deft 3 apt **4** able **5** adept, agile, handy **6** adroit, clever **7** skilled **8** dextrous, skillful **9** dexterous

deftness 5 knack, skill **7** address, prowess **8** facility **9** adeptness, dexterity **10** capability

defunct 4 cold, dead, late **5** kaput **7** extinct **8** deceased, departed, lifeless, vanished

defy 4 dare, face, gibe, jeer, mock **5** beard, brave, flout, stump **6** resist **7** affront, outdare, outface **8** confront **9** challenge, disregard, withstand

dégagé 6 breezy, casual **7** relaxed, unfussy **8** informal **9** easygoing **10** nonchalant, unreserved **13** unconstrained

degeneracy see **degeneration**

degenerate 4 sink **6** rotten, sunken, worsen **7** corrupt, debased, decayed, decline, descend, immoral, pervert, vicious, vitiate **8** decadent, degraded, depraved **9** backslide, dissolute **11** deteriorate

degeneration 7 atrophy, decline **8** downfall, lowering **9** decadence, depravity, downgrade **10** debasement, perversion, regression **12** dégringolade

degradation 4 fall **7** decline, descent **8** demotion **9** abasement, decadence, depravity, downgrade, reduction **10** corruption, debasement, degeneracy, perversion **11** downgrading **12** degeneration

degrade 4 bump, bust **5** abase, break, decry, lower **6** debase, demean, demote, impair, lessen, reduce **7** corrupt, declass, pervert, put down **8** belittle, cast down, derogate, diminish **9** decompose, discredit, disparage, downgrade, humiliate

degree 3 peg **4** heat, rank, rate, rung, step, term, tier **5** grade, honor, notch, order, pitch, point, ratio, scale, shade, stage, stair **6** amount, extent, status **7** measure, station **8** standing **9** dimension, gradation, intensity, magnitude **10** proportion ***academic:*** **2** BA, BS, MA, MD, MS **3** BFA, BSc, DDS, LLB, LLD, LLM, MBA, MFA, MSc, PhD **5** MPhil **7** master's **9** bachelor's, doctorate ***highest:*** **5** magna, summa **8** cum laude **13** magna cum laude, summa cum laude ***seeker:*** **9** candidate

dégringolade see **degeneration**

____ de guerre 3 nom

dehydrate 3 dry **4** sear **5** parch **9** desiccate, exsiccate

Deianira ***brother:*** **8** Meleager ***father:*** **6** Oeneus ***husband:*** **8** Heracles, Hercules ***mother:*** **7** Althaea ***victim:*** **8** Heracles, Hercules

deific 5 godly **6** divine **7** godlike
deification 8 idolatry **10** apotheosis, glorifying **13** glorification
deify 5 exalt **7** glorify, idolize, worship **8** sanctify, venerate **11** apotheosize
deign 5 stoop **7** descend **9** vouchsafe **10** condescend
Deiphobus *brother:* 5 Paris **6** Hector ***father:* 5** Priam ***mother:* 6** Hecuba ***wife:* 5** Helen
Deirdre *beloved:* 5 Noisi ***father:* 5** Felim
deity 3 god **4** Lord **7** goddess, godhead, godhood **8** Almighty, divinity **12** supreme being (see also *god* and *goddess* at **Greek; Hindu; Norse; Roman**)
deject 5 chill, cloud, daunt **6** dampen, dismay **7** depress **8** dispirit **9** disparage **10** demoralize, discourage, dishearten
dejected 3 low, sad **4** blue, down, glum, sunk **6** bummed, gloomy, morose, somber, sombre **7** doleful, hangdog, humbled, unhappy **8** downcast, wretched **9** cheerless, depressed, woebegone **10** despondent, spiritless **11** crestfallen, downhearted **12** disconsolate, disheartened
dejection 5 dumps, gloom **7** despair, sadness **10** melancholy **11** despondency, unhappiness **12** mournfulness
Delaware *capital:* 5 Dover ***city:* 10** Wilmington ***nickname:* 5** First (State) **7** Diamond (State) ***state bird:* 14** blue hen chicken ***state flower:* 12** peach blossom ***state tree:* 13** American holly
delay 3 lag **4** drag, hold, slow, stay, wait **5** dally, defer, stall, tarry, trail **6** dawdle, detain, hang up, hinder, holdup, impede, linger, loiter, put off, retard, slow up **7** bog down, hold off, respite, set back, slacken, suspend **8** hesitate, hold over, postpone, prorogue, reprieve, slow down **10** dillydally, moratorium, suspension **13** procrastinate
delaying 8 dawdling, dilatory **10** postponing, putting off
delectable 5 tasty, yummy **6** choice, savory **8** charming, heavenly, luscious, pleasing **9** ambrosial, delicious, enjoyable, exquisite, toothsome **10** delightful, enchanting **11** scrumptious **13** mouthwatering
delectation 3 fun, joy **4** zest **5** gusto **6** relish **7** delight **8** gladness, pleasure **9** enjoyment
delegate 4 name, send **5** agent, envoy, proxy **6** assign, depute, deputy, legate **7** appoint, consign, entrust **8** deputize, emissary, transfer **9** authorize, catchpole, designate, spokesman **10** commission, mouthpiece, procurator
delete 4 drop, omit, x out **5** erase, purge **6** cancel, censor, cut out, efface, excise, remove **7** blot out, destroy, expunge, take out, wipe out **8** black out, cross out **9** eliminate, eradicate, strike out **10** blue-pencil, obliterate
deleterious 3 bad **6** nocent **7** baneful, harmful, hurtful, nocuous, noxious, ruinous **8** damaging **9** injurious **10** pernicious **11** destructive, detrimental, mischievous, prejudicial
deletion 7 erasure, voiding **9** canceling **10** deficiency **11** elimination **12** cancellation
deliberate 4 chaw, cool, muse, pore, slow **5** chary, meant, study, think, weigh **6** chew on, ponder, reason **7** careful, heedful, planned, reflect, studied, willful, willing, witting **8** cautious, cogitate, consider, intended, measured, meditate, mull over, ruminate, talk over **9** cerebrate, conscious, unhurried **10** calculated, considered, purposeful, thought-out **11** circumspect, intentional **12** premeditated
deliberately 9 knowingly, on purpose, purposely, willfully, wittingly **11** consciously **12** purposefully **13** intentionally
deliberation 5 study **6** debate **7** thought **10** conference, discussion, reflection **13** consideration
Delibes, Léo *ballet:* 6 Sylvia **8** Coppélia, La Source ***opera:* 5** Lakmé ***waltz:* 5** Naila
delicacy 5 goody, treat **6** dainty, luxury, morsel, nicety, tidbit **7** frailty **8** kickshaw, fineness **9** fragility, precision **10** daintiness, difficulty, indulgence, stickiness **11** awkwardness **12** ticklishness
delicate 4 fine, lacy, twee, weak **5** frail **6** choice, dainty, flimsy, petite, queasy, sickly, slight, subtle, tender, touchy, tricky **7** elegant, fragile, refined, tactful, tenuous **8** ethereal, feathery, finespun, gossamer, graceful, pleasing, ticklish **9** exquisite, sensitive, squeamish **10** precarious
delicatessen 11 charcuterie
delicious 5 tasty, yummy **6** choice, divine, savory **8** heavenly, luscious **9** ambrosial, exquisite, toothsome **10** delectable, delightful **11** scrumptious **13** mouthwatering
delight 3 joy **4** glee **5** amuse, bliss, charm, enjoy, exult, glory, mirth, revel **6** divert, please, regale, relish **7** ecstasy, enchant, gladden, gratify, jollity, rapture, rejoice **8** enravish, entrance, fruition, hilarity, pleasure **9** delectate, enjoyment, enrapture, entertain **11** delectation ***in:* 4** love **5** adore, enjoy, savor **6** admire, relish **7** cherish **10** appreciate
delighted 4 glad **5** happy **6** joyful **8** ecstatic, euphoric
delightful 5 yummy **6** dreamy, lovely **8**

charming, heavenly, luscious, pleasant, pleasing **9** congenial, enjoyable **10** delectable, enchanting, satisfying **11** captivating, fascinating, pleasurable, scrumptious **12** entertaining

Delilah's victim 6 Samson

DeLillo novel 5 Libra, Mao II **10** Underworld, White Noise

delimit 3 bar **5** bound, hem in **6** demark, define **7** confine, enclose **8** restrict **9** demarcate, determine **12** circumscribe

delineate 3 map **4** etch, limn **5** chart, image, trace **6** define, depict, detail, render **7** outline, picture, portray **8** describe, spell out **9** elucidate, interpret, represent **10** illustrate

delineation 5 draft, story **6** report **7** account, contour, drawing, outline, picture, profile **9** depiction, rendering **11** presentment

delinquency 4 debt **5** crime, fault, lapse **7** default, failure, misdeed, neglect, offense **8** omission **9** oversight **10** misconduct, nonpayment, wrongdoing **11** dereliction, misbehavior

delinquent 3 lax **5** slack **6** debtor **7** overdue **8** careless, offender **9** defaulter, in arrears, negligent **10** behindhand, neglectful

deliquesce 3 rot, run **4** flux, fuse, melt, thaw **5** decay **6** render, soften **7** liquefy, putrefy **8** dissolve, fluidize **9** decompose, disappear, waste away **12** disintegrate

delirious 3 mad **4** wild **5** crazy **6** crazed, insane, raving **7** frantic, lunatic **8** confused, demented, deranged, ecstatic, frenetic, frenzied, rambling **9** rapturous **10** bewildered, corybantic, distracted, irrational **11** lightheaded, overexcited, overwrought

delirium 5 furor, mania **6** fervor, frenzy **7** ecstasy, jimjams, rapture, seizure **8** dementia, hysteria **13** hallucination

delirium ____ 7 tremens

deliver 4 bear, deal, feed, find, give, hand, save, send, ship, sing, take **5** bring, serve, speak, state, throw, utter **6** convey, redeem, rescue, strike, supply **7** consign, present, produce, provide, set free, release **8** hand over, liberate, turn over **9** pronounce, surrender **10** bring forth, emancipate **11** come out with, come through

deliverance 6 rescue **7** freeing, opinion, release, verdict **8** decision **9** acquittal, discharge, salvation **10** absolution, liberation

Deliverance author 6 Dickey (James)

delivery 4 drop **5** birth, labor **6** rescue **7** address, bearing **8** birthing, shipment **9** elocution, rendition, salvation **10** childbirth, conveyance, liberation **11** consignment, parturition, transferral **12** childbearing, transmission

dell 4 dale, glen, vale **6** dingle, hollow, valley

Delphic 4 dark **5** vatic **6** arcane, hidden, mantic, mystic, occult, veiled **7** cryptic, obscure **8** auguring, divining, esoteric, mystical, oracular **9** ambiguous, enigmatic, equivocal, prophetic, recondite, sibylline, vaticinal **10** mystifying, portentous **11** prophesying, prophetical

delta 5 plain **6** letter, symbol **7** deposit **8** triangle **9** increment

delude 3 con **4** dupe, fool, gull, hoax **5** bluff, cozen, trick **6** betray, humbug, juggle, take in **7** beguile, deceive, mislead **8** flimflam, hoodwink **11** double-cross

deluge 5 drown, flood, swamp **6** drench, engulf **7** Niagara, torrent **8** cataract, downpour, drencher, flooding, inundate, overflow **9** cataclysm, overwhelm **10** cloudburst, outpouring, inundation

delusion 4 hoax, sham **5** dream, fancy, snare **6** mirage **7** chimera, fallacy, fantasy, figment, phantom, specter **8** daydream, phantasm **9** deception **10** apparition **11** ignis fatuus **13** hallucination

delusive 5 false **8** fanciful, illusory, specious **9** beguiling, deceiving, deceptive, imaginary **10** chimerical, fallacious, misleading

delusory see **delusive**

deluxe 4 lush, posh **5** grand, plush, ritzy, swank **6** choice, costly, swanky **7** elegant, opulent **8** luscious, splendid **9** expensive, exquisite, luxuriant, luxurious, sumptuous **10** first class

delve 3 dig, dip **4** mine **5** probe **6** dredge, fathom, hollow, quarry, search, shovel **7** inquire **8** excavate ***into:*** **4** sift **5** probe **7** explore **8** prospect **11** investigate

delving 6 asking **7** inquest, inquiry, probing **8** research **9** inquiring, searching

demagnetize 7 degauss

demagogue 6 leader **7** inciter **8** agitator, fomenter **9** firebrand **10** instigator **11** provocateur **12** rabble-rouser

demand 3 ask, use **4** call, need, urge, want **5** claim, crave, exact, force, order **6** compel, direct, expect, insist **7** call for, request, require **11** requirement, requisition

demanding 4 hard **5** pushy, tough **6** taxing, trying **7** exigent, onerous, weighty **8** exacting, forceful, rigorous **9** assertive, difficult, insistent, strenuous, stringent **10** aggressive, burdensome, oppressive **11** challenging

demarcate 5 bound, limit **6** define, set off **7** delimit, mark off, outline **8** separate, set

apart **9** delineate, determine **11** distinguish **12** circumscribe **13** differentiate
demarcation 9 outlining **10** border line, separation **11** distinction **12** delimitation
démarche 4 plan, ploy, ruse **5** feint **6** action, device, gambit, scheme, tactic **7** protest **8** artifice, maneuver, petition **9** stratagem **10** initiative **11** contrivance, machination
demean 4 bear **5** abase, carry, decry, lower **6** acquit, behave, debase, deport, humble **7** comport, conduct, degrade, detract **8** badmouth, belittle **9** disparage, humiliate
demeanor 3 air **4** look, mien **6** aspect, manner **7** address, bearing, conduct **8** behavior, carriage, presence **10** deportment **11** comportment
demented 3 mad **5** crazy, loony, nutty, wacko **6** crazed, insane, psycho **7** lunatic, unsound **8** deranged, frenzied, maniacal **9** delirious **10** hysterical, unbalanced **12** psychopathic
____ de mer 3 mal
demerit 4 mark **5** fault, stain **6** defect **7** blemish, penalty **9** downgrade **10** deficiency, punishment **11** shortcoming **12** imperfection
demesne 5 field, realm **6** domain, estate, region, sphere **7** terrain **8** dominion, province **9** bailiwick, champaign, territory ***house:* 5** manor
Demeter see **Ceres**
demigod 4 diva, idol **8** superman **9** superstar
demise 3 die, end **4** drop, pass **5** death, dying, sleep **6** cash in, depart, ending, expire **7** decease, passing, quietus, release, silence, succumb **8** pass away **9** cessation, departure **10** expiration, extinction
demit 4 quit **6** bow out, give up, resign **8** abdicate, renounce, step down, withdraw
demiurgic 8 creative, original **9** formative, inventive **10** innovative **11** originative
demobilize 7 break up, disband, dismiss, scatter **8** disperse, separate **9** discharge, disengage, muster out
democratic 7 popular **8** populist **10** self-ruling **11** egalitarian **13** self-governing
Democrats' symbol 6 donkey
démodé 5 dated, passé **7** antique, archaic **8** old-timey, outdated **9** out-of-date **12** old-fashioned
demoiselle 6 damsel, lassie, maiden **10** damselfish
demolish 4 raze, ruin **5** crush, level, smash, total, wrack, wreck **7** destroy, flatten, wipe out **8** decimate, tear down **9** finish off **10** annihilate, obliterate
demolition 6 razing **8** leveling, wrecking **10** bulldozing **11** destruction **12** annihilation
demolition bomb 11 blockbuster
demon 3 imp **4** jinn **5** devil, fiend, genie, ghoul, jinni, Satan **7** hellion, incubus **9** archfiend ***Arabic:* 5** afrit **6** afreet ***female:* 5** lamia **7** succuba, succubi (plural) **8** succubae (plural), succubus
demonic 6 wicked **7** satanic **8** devilish, diabolic, fiendish, infernal **9** possessed **10** diabolical
demonize 6 malign, revile, vilify **7** bedevil, censure, slander **8** denounce **9** diabolize
demonstrate 3 try **4** mark, show, test **5** prove, rally **7** confirm, display, exhibit, explain, make out, protest **8** evidence, manifest, proclaim, validate **9** determine, establish **10** illustrate **12** authenticate
demonstration 4 expo, show, test **5** march, proof, rally, trial **6** picket **7** display, protest **9** spectacle **10** exhibition, exposition, validation **12** presentation **13** corroboration, manifestation
demonstrative 4 open **8** effusive, outgoing, specific **9** emotional, expansive, exuberant, outspoken **10** outpouring, unreserved, validating **12** affectionate, unrestrained **13** unconstrained
demoralize 5 chill, daunt, shake, unman, upset **6** dampen, debase, deject, rattle, weaken **7** corrupt, debauch, deprave, unnerve, vitiate **8** dispirit, psych out **9** undermine **10** discourage, dishearten
Demosthenes 6 orator ***oration:* 9** Philippic
demote 4 bump, bust **5** lower **6** reduce **7** declass, degrade **9** downgrade
demulcent 4 balm **5** jelly, salve **7** unguent **8** liniment, ointment, soothing **9** softening
demur 5 qualm **6** object, oppose, resist **7** dispute, protest **8** hesitate, question **9** challenge, hesitancy, objection **10** hesitation, indecision, reluctance **11** compunction, remonstrate
demure 3 coy, shy **5** timid **6** modest **7** bashful **8** reserved, reticent, retiring **9** diffident **11** unassertive **12** self-effacing
demurral 7 protest **9** challenge, objection **12** remonstrance **13** remonstration
demurrer see **demurral**
den 4 base, cave, home, lair, nest, room **5** study **6** burrow, cavern, hollow **7** dayroom, hideout, sanctum **8** hideaway, playroom ***rabbit:* 6** warren
denial 2 no **3** nay, nix **6** heresy **7** refusal **8** disproof, negation, rebuttal **9** disavowal, rejection **10** abnegation, gainsaying, refutation **11** repudiation **12** renunciation
denigrate 5 decry, libel, smear, stain, sully **6** darken, defame, defile, impugn, malign,

vilify **7** asperse, devalue, put down, slander, tarnish, traduce **8** belittle, dishonor, tear down **9** discredit, disparage **10** calumniate, scandalize

denims 5 jeans **8** overalls **9** blue jeans, dungarees

denizen 5 liver **6** native **7** dweller, habitué, haunter, resider **8** habitant, occupant, resident **9** indweller, inhabiter **10** frequenter, inhabitant

Denmark ***capital:*** **10** Copenhagen ***city:*** **5** Århus **6** Ålborg, Odense **11** Helsingborg **13** Frederiksberg ***island:*** **3** Fyn **7** Falster, Zealand **8** Bornholm **9** Sjaelland ***monetary unit:*** **5** krone ***neighbor:*** **6** Sweden **7** Germany ***part of:*** **11** Scandinavia ***peninsula:*** **7** Jutland ***possession:*** **9** Greenland **12** Faroe Islands **13** Faeroe Islands ***sea:*** **5** North **6** Baltic ***strait:*** **5** Lille, Store **9** Langeland

denominate 3 dub **4** call, name, term **5** label, style, title **7** baptize, entitle **8** christen **9** designate

denomination 4 cult, name, sect **5** creed, faith, style, title **6** church **8** category, cognomen, religion **9** communion **10** persuasion ***religious:*** **5** Amish **6** Mormon **7** Baptist **8** Lutheran, Moravian, Reformed **9** Adventist, Episcopal, Mennonite, Methodist, Unitarian **11** Pentecostal **12** Presbyterian, Universalist **13** Roman Catholic

denotation 4 name, sign **5** sense **6** import **7** meaning **10** indication, signifying **11** designation **13** signification, specification

denote 4 mark, mean, name, show **5** spell **6** import **7** add up to, betoken, express **8** announce, indicate **9** designate, represent

denouement 6 effect, result, upshot **7** outcome **10** conclusion **11** consequence, culmination

denounce 3 rap **4** skin **5** blame, blast, decry, knock **6** rebuke, scathe **7** censure, condemn, upbraid **8** derogate, reproach **9** castigate, criticize, dress down, excoriate, reprehend, reprobate **10** denunciate, vituperate **11** incriminate **12** anathematize

de novo 4 anew, over **5** again, newly **6** afresh **8** once more **9** over again **11** from scratch

dense 4 dull, dumb **5** close, heavy, solid, thick, tight **6** obtuse, opaque, stupid **7** compact, crammed, crowded, doltish, serried **9** fatheaded, jam-packed **10** numskulled **11** blockheaded, numbskulled, thickheaded **12** impenetrable

dent 4 bash, ding, flaw, nick **5** tooth **6** dimple, hollow **10** depression, impression

dental addition 5 inlay, plate **6** braces, bridge **7** filling

denticulate 6 ridged **7** dentate, notched, serrate, serried, toothed **8** saw-edged, sawtooth, serrated **10** saw-toothed

dentin 6 enamel

dentine 5 ivory

denude 4 bare **5** strip **6** divest **7** disrobe, uncover, undress **8** unclothe

denunciate see **denounce**

deny 5 cross, rebut **6** disown, forbid, negate, refuse, refute, reject, renege **7** disavow, gainsay **8** abnegate, disallow, disclaim, forswear, renounce, traverse, withhold **9** disaffirm **10** contradict, contravene

depart 2 go **3** die **4** exit, flee, pass, quit **5** leave, scram, split **6** begone, decamp, demise, desert, escape, expire, go away, move on, pass on, perish, skidoo **7** decease, deviate, go forth, move out, pull out, skiddoo, take off, vamoose **8** pass away, shove off, slip away, withdraw **9** skedaddle, take leave

departing 6 egress, exodus **7** good-bye **8** farewell **9** desertion **11** leave-taking, valedictory

department 5 arena **6** branch, domain, sphere **7** section **8** category, division, province **9** bailiwick, territory **11** subdivision

departure 4 exit **5** adieu, break, congé, going **6** egress, exodus, flight **7** leaving **8** farewell **9** deviation, diversion **10** aberration, decampment, deflection, divergence, embarkment, setting-out, withdrawal **11** embarkation, leave-taking ***of a ship:*** **6** sortie ***point:*** **7** outport

dependable 4 sure, true **5** loyal, solid, tried **6** secure, steady, trusty **7** certain, staunch **8** accurate, constant, faithful, reliable, surefire **9** authentic, steadfast, unfailing **11** responsible, trustworthy **12** tried and true **13** authoritative ***Scottish:*** **6** sicker

dependence 4 need **5** faith, habit, stock, trust **8** reliance **9** addiction **11** contingency, habituation

dependent 5 child **6** minion, vassal **7** reliant, relying **9** secondary **10** contingent, equivalent **11** conditional, subordinate

depend on 5 bet on, trust **6** bank on, hang on, look to, rely on, turn on **7** build on, count on, hinge on, stand on, swear by

depict 4 draw, limn, show **5** image, paint **6** relate, render, sketch **7** express, picture, portray **8** describe **9** delineate, represent **10** illustrate

depiction 5 image **6** sketch **7** drawing, picture **9** portrayal, rendering **11** delineation, portraiture, presentment **12** illustration, presentation

deplete 3 sap **4** milk **5** bleed, drain, eat up,

empty, leech, use up **6** expend, lessen, reduce **7** consume, draw off, exhaust **8** decrease, diminish, draw down **9** undermine **10** run through

depleted **6** sapped, used up **7** drained, reduced **8** consumed, expended **9** exhausted, washed-out

deplorable **5** awful **6** rotten, woeful **8** dreadful, god-awful, grievous, terrible, wretched **9** execrable, miserable, sickening **10** calamitous, disastrous, lamentable **11** distressing, intolerable **12** contemptible, disreputable, heartrending **13** heartbreaking, reprehensible

deplore **3** rue **5** abhor, mourn **6** bemoan, bewail, grieve, lament, regret **7** condemn **8** denounce, object to **9** deprecate **10** disapprove

deploy **3** use **5** array **6** muster, unfold **7** arrange, display, dispose, marshal, utilize **8** position

____ **de plume** **3** nom

depone **5** state, swear **6** affirm, assert, attest **7** certify, confirm, declare, testify, warrant **11** corroborate **12** authenticate

deport **3** act **4** bear **5** carry, exile, expel **6** acquit, banish, behave, demean **7** conduct **8** displace, relegate **10** expatriate

deportee **2** DP **5** exile **8** expellee

deportment **3** air, set **4** mien, port **6** aspect, manner **7** address, bearing, conduct, manners **8** behavior, carriage, demeanor, presence

depose **4** aver, avow, oust **5** state, swear **6** affirm, assert, avouch, remove, topple, unmake **7** declare, profess, testify, uncrown **8** dethrone, displace, throw out, unthrone **9** overthrow

deposit **3** lay **4** bank, drop, dump, fund, lees, pawn, save, stow **5** cache, chest, dregs, place, put by, stash, store **6** settle **7** consign, grounds, lay away **8** put aside, security, sediment, sock away **9** settlings **11** precipitate **13** precipitation ***alluvial:*** **5** delta ***black:*** **4** soot ***calcium carbonate:*** **10** stalactite, stalagmite ***containing gold:*** **6** placer ***eggs:*** **5** spawn ***geologic:*** **7** horizon ***glacial:*** **4** till **5** drift, esker **7** moraine ***loam:*** **5** loess ***mineral:*** **4** lode **10** concretion ***muddy:*** **6** sludge ***sand:*** **4** bank **5** beach ***sedimentary:*** **4** silt ***skeletal:*** **5** coral ***stream:*** **8** alluvium, sediment ***tooth:*** **6** tartar

deposition **6** avowal **7** ousting, placing **9** affidavit, dismissal, testimony **10** testifying **11** attestation, declaration

depository **4** bank, dump, safe **5** attic, cache, depot, store, vault **7** archive, arsenal **8** magazine **9** warehouse **10** storehouse ***for bones:*** **7** ossuary

depot **4** dump **5** cache, store **6** armory, garage **7** arsenal, station **8** magazine, terminal, terminus **9** warehouse **10** depository, repository, storehouse **12** station house

deprave **4** warp **6** debase **7** corrupt, debauch, pervert, vitiate **9** brutalize **10** bastardize, bestialize, demoralize

depraved **3** bad, low **4** base, evil, ugly, vile **6** putrid, rotten, wanton, warped, wicked **7** bestial, corrupt, debased, immoral, twisted, vicious **8** degraded, perverse, vitiated **9** corrupted, debauched, miscreant, nefarious, perverted, reprobate **10** degenerate

depravity **4** vice **8** baseness **9** abasement, decadence **10** corruption, debasement, debauchery, degeneracy, immorality, perversion **12** degeneration

deprecate **7** frown on, put down **8** belittle, derogate, disfavor, object to, play down, pooh-pooh **9** disparage **10** disapprove **12** disapprove of

depreciate **4** drop, fall **5** abate, decry, erode, lower **6** lessen, reduce, slight **7** cheapen, devalue, put down **8** belittle, decrease, derogate, diminish, discount, mark down, write off **9** devaluate, disparage, downgrade, underrate **10** devalorize, undervalue **11** detract from

depreciation **8** discount **11** denigration **12** belittlement **13** disparagement

depreciative **9** slighting **10** derogatory, detracting, pejorative **11** disparaging, underrating **12** undervaluing

depredate **4** sack **5** waste **6** ravage **7** despoil, pillage, plunder **8** desolate, lay waste, prey upon, spoliate **9** desecrate, devastate, vandalize

depredation **4** sack **5** havoc **7** pillage, plunder, sacking **8** ravaging **9** marauding, ruination **10** spoliation **11** desecration, destruction, devastation **12** despoliation

depredator **6** looter, raider, vandal **7** forager, spoiler **8** marauder **9** plunderer **10** freebooter

depress **4** damp, dash, dent **5** chill, daunt, lower **6** dampen, deject, dismay, sadden **7** afflict, trouble **8** dispirit, enfeeble **9** disparage, weigh down **10** discourage, dishearten

depressed **3** low, sad **4** blue, down, glum, sunk **6** broody, gloomy, glumpy, lonely, somber **8** cast down, dejected, downcast **9** bummed out, flattened, woebegone **10** dispirited, lugubrious, melancholy, spiritless **11** crestfallen, downhearted, melancholic **12** disconsolate **13** disadvantaged

depressing **3** sad **5** bleak **6** dismal, dreary, gloomy, somber, sombre **7** joyless **8** funereal, mournful **9** saddening **10** melancholy, oppressive **11** melancholic **13** disheartening

depression 3 dip, low, pit, sag **4** bust, drop, funk, glen, hole, sink, vale **5** basin, blues, dolor, dumps, ennui, gloom, scoop, slump **6** cavity, crater, hollow, pocket, valley **7** cyclone, decline, sadness, sinkage **8** downturn, sinkhole **9** concavity, dejection **10** desolation, melancholy **11** melancholia, unhappiness ***anatomical:*** **5** fossa, fovea **6** foveae (plural) ***geographic:*** **7** Qattara ***in ridge:*** **3** col ***in snow:*** **8** sitzmark ***small:*** **4** dent **6** dimple

depressive 4 blue, dour, glum **6** woeful **7** doleful **8** downbeat, downcast, mournful **9** miserable, woebegone **10** despondent, melancholy **11** low-spirited

deprivation 4 lack, loss **6** denial **7** forfeit, removal **10** forfeiture **11** bereavement, divestiture **13** dispossession

deprive 3 rob **5** strip **6** divest **8** disseise, disseize **10** disinherit, dispossess ***of brilliancy:*** **4** dull **6** deaden ***of courage:*** **7** unnerve ***of sensation:*** **6** benumb

depth 4 base, drop, gulf **5** abyss, chasm, gorge **7** lowness **10** profundity ***measure:*** **6** fathom ***of water:*** **5** draft **7** draught

depthless 7 cursory, shallow, sketchy **10** uncritical **11** superficial

Dept. of ____ 5 Labor, State **6** Energy **7** Defense, Justice **8** Commerce, Interior, Treasury **9** Education **11** Agriculture

deputize 4 name **6** assign **7** appoint, empower, warrant **8** delegate **9** authorize, designate **10** commission

deputy 4 aide **5** agent, proxy **6** backup, factor **8** delegate **9** assistant, catchpole, surrogate

derange 4 muss **5** craze, upset **6** madden, mess up **7** confuse, perturb, unhinge **8** confound, disarray, disorder, distract, unsettle **9** interrupt, unbalance **10** discompose **11** disorganize

deranged 3 mad **4** loco **5** crazy, wacko **6** crazed, insane, maniac **7** berserk, bonkers, cracked, haywire, lunatic, unsound **8** demented, maniacal, unhinged **9** disturbed **10** disordered, flipped out, unbalanced

derangement 4 mess **5** chaos, mania **6** lunacy, muddle **7** madness **8** dementia, disorder, insanity **9** confusion, unbalance **10** hodgepodge **11** distraction, disturbance, psychopathy

derby 3 hat **4** race **7** contest **9** horse race

derelict 3 bum **4** hobo, lorn **5** tramp **6** remiss, shabby **7** drifter, outcast, run-down, uncouth, vagrant **8** careless, deserted, vagabond **9** abandoned, negligent **10** neglectful **11** dilapidated **12** disregardful, undependable **13** irresponsible

dereliction 5 fault **7** default, failure, neglect **9** deviation, disregard, oversight **11** abandonment, delinquency, shortcoming

deride 3 rag, rap **4** gibe, jeer, jibe, lout, mock, quiz, razz, twit **5** fleer, rally, scoff, scout, sneer, taunt **6** dump on, insult **7** catcall **8** ridicule

de rigueur 5 right **6** au fait, decent, proper **7** correct **8** becoming, decorous, required **9** essential, mandatory, requisite **10** compulsory, obligatory, prescribed **11** comme il faut

derision 5 abuse, scorn **7** disdain, mockery, ribbing **8** contempt, raillery, ridicule, scoffing **9** contumely, invective

derisive 7 abusive, jeering, mocking **8** sardonic, scoffing, scornful, taunting **9** insulting, sarcastic **10** disdainful **12** contemptuous

derivable 7 a priori **9** deducible, deductive, traceable **10** obtainable **11** extractable **12** attributable, determinable

derivation 4 root **6** origin, source **7** descent **8** ancestry **9** etymology **10** provenance, wellspring **11** origination, provenience

derivative 5 banal **7** spin-off **8** acquired, borrowed, offshoot **9** by-product, imitative, outgrowth, secondary **10** descendant, unoriginal

derive 3 get **4** draw, flow, rise, stem, take **5** adapt, arise, educe, infer, issue, trace **6** deduce, deduct, evolve, gather, obtain **7** descend, emanate, extract, proceed, work out **8** arrive at, conclude **9** formulate, originate

dernier cri 3 fad **4** chic, rage **5** craze, vogue **8** last word

derogate 5 decry **6** berate, dump on, insult **7** put down **8** bad-mouth, belittle, diminish, minimize, write off **9** disparage, dispraise **10** depreciate **11** detract from

derogatory 5 snide **8** decrying, scornful, spiteful **9** degrading, demeaning, maligning, slighting **10** belittling, detracting, disdainful, pejorative **11** disparaging **12** contumelious, depreciative

derrick 5 crane, davit, hoist

derriere 3 bum **4** beam, butt, rear, rump, seat, tail **5** fanny **6** behind, bottom **7** rear end **8** backside, buttocks **9** posterior

derring-do 4 guts **5** nerve, pluck, spunk, valor **6** daring, mettle **7** bravado, bravery, bravura, courage **8** boldness **9** gallantry **12** fearlessness **13** dauntlessness

dervish 4 monk, Sufi **9** mendicant ***in Arabian***

Nights: 4 Agib *practice:* 7 dancing 8 whirling *wandering:* 5 fakir 8 calender

descant 4 sing 6 melody, remark, treble 7 comment, discuss, melisma, melodia, oration, soprano 9 discourse, expatiate 12 counterpoint

Descartes's axiom 13 cogito ergo sum

descend 4 dive, drop, fall, pass, sink 5 slide, stoop, swoop 6 alight, derive, go down, plunge, worsen 7 decline 8 come down, dismount 9 originate 10 degenerate, retrograde *by rope:* 6 rappel

descendant 4 heir 5 scion 7 progeny, spin-off 8 offshoot, relative 9 by-product, offspring, outgrowth 10 derivative

descendants 4 seed 5 brood, heirs, issue, spawn 6 litter 7 progeny 8 children 9 offspring, posterity 11 progeniture

descent 3 dip 4 drop, fall 5 birth, blood, slide, slope 6 origin, plunge, tumble 7 decline, drop-off, incline, lineage, sinkage 8 ancestry, comedown, gradient, pedigree 9 declivity, downgrade 10 derivation, devolution, extraction *airplane:* 8 approach *parachute:* 4 jump 7 bailout

describe 4 limn 6 denote, depict, recite, relate, render, report 7 explain, express, mark out, narrate, outline, picture, portray, recount 9 delineate, represent 10 illustrate 12 characterize

description 3 ilk 4 kind, sort, type 6 nature, report 7 account, picture, species 9 character, depiction, narrative, portrayal 10 recounting

descry 3 see 4 espy, spot 6 behold, detect, spy out, turn up 7 discern, find out, hit upon 8 discover, meet with, perceive 9 encounter, recognize

Desdemona *father:* 9 Brabantio *husband:* 7 Othello *slanderer:* 4 Iago *slayer:* 7 Othello

desecrate 4 sack 5 stain, sully, waste 6 befoul, debase, defile, ravage 7 corrupt, degrade, despoil, pillage, pollute, profane, violate 8 spoliate 9 depredate, devastate

desecration 5 abuse 7 impiety 9 blasphemy, sacrilege 10 debasement, defilement, spoliation 11 profanation 12 despoliation

desensitize 4 dull, numb 5 blunt 6 benumb, dampen, deaden, freeze, sedate 11 anesthetize

desert 4 flee, quit 5 leave, waste 6 barren, betray, decamp, defect, escape, go AWOL, maroon, strand 7 abandon, abscond, badland, forsake 8 renounce 9 repudiate, wasteland 10 apostatize, wilderness 12 tergiversate *African:* 5 Namib 6 Libyan, Nubian, Sahara 7 Arabian 8 Kalahari *Arizona:* 7 Painted *Asian:* 4 Gobi, Thar 6 Syrian 7 Kara-Kum 8 Kyzyl Kum, Qizilkum 10 Great Sandy *Australian:* 6 Gibson, Tanami 7 Simpson *basin bottom:* 5 playa *beast:* 5 camel 9 dromedary *California:* 6 Mohave, Mojave *Chilean:* 7 Atacama *clay:* 5 adobe *dweller:* 4 bedu 5 nomad 6 Beduin, Berber, Nubian 7 bedouin 8 Maghrebi, Maghribi *Egyptian:* 7 Arabian *fertile area:* 5 oases (plural), oasis *garb:* 3 aba 7 burnous 8 burnoose *hallucination:* 6 mirage *Israeli:* 5 Negev *region:* 3 erg *Saudi Arabia:* 7 Al-Nafud, An Nafud 10 Rub Al-Khali *travel group:* 7 caravan *wind:* 7 sirocco 8 scirocco

deserted 4 bare, lorn 6 barren, vacant 8 derelict, desolate, forsaken, solitary 9 abandoned, neglected 11 uninhabited

deserter 3 rat 4 AWOL 6 bolter 7 runaway 8 apostate, defector, fugitive, renegade, runagate, turncoat

desertion 7 perfidy 8 apostasy 9 defection, forsaking 11 abandonment, dereliction

deserts 3 due 6 reward 8 requital 9 reckoning 10 recompense 11 comeuppance

deserve 3 win 4 earn, gain, rate 5 merit 6 demand 7 justify, warrant

deserved 3 apt, due 4 just 5 right 7 fitting, merited 8 rightful, suitable 9 befitting 11 appropriate 13 rhadamanthine

deserving 3 due 6 worthy 8 laudable 9 admirable, estimable 10 creditable 11 commendable, meritorious, thankworthy 12 praiseworthy

desiccate 3 dry 5 dry up, parch, wizen 6 wither 7 shrivel 9 dehydrate 10 devitalize

desiderate 4 want, wish 5 covet, crave 6 desire 7 long for, wish for 8 yearn for

design 3 aim 4 cast, draw, form, mean, mind, plan, plot, will 5 chart, draft, frame, model, motif 6 create, device, devise, figure, intend, intent, invent, lay out, makeup, map out, motive, scheme, set out, sketch, tailor 7 arrange, diagram, drawing, execute, fashion, meaning, outline, pattern, prepare, project, propose, tracing 8 contrive, creation, game plan, intrigue, strategy, thinking 9 blueprint, construct, delineate, direction, formation, intention, invention 10 decoration, figuration 11 arrangement, composition 12 architecture, construction *book:* 8 vignette *carpet:* 3 gul 9 medallion *incised:* 8 intaglio *Indonesian:* 5 batik *inlaid:* 6 mosaic *intricate:* 9 arabesque *of squares:* 5 check *openwork:* 8 filigree *perforated:* 7 stencil *raised:* 8 repoussé *skin:* 6 tattoo *textile:* 8 polka dot *velvety:* 8 flocking

designate 3 dub, tap 4 call, name, pick, term

5 allot, elect, label, style, title 6 assign, choose, denote, depute, select 7 appoint, declare, earmark, reserve, signify, specify 8 allocate, christen, delegate, identify, set aside, stand for 9 apportion, stipulate 10 decide upon 11 appropriate 12 characterize

designation 4 name, sign 5 class, nomen, style, title 6 naming 8 cognomen, monicker 11 appellation

designed 7 devised, planned 8 intended, resolved 9 contrived, patterned 10 considered, deliberate, determined, thought-out 12 premeditated

designedly 9 expressly, knowingly, on purpose, purposely, willfully, wittingly 11 consciously, purposively 12 deliberately 13 intentionally

desirable 8 enviable, fetching 9 advisable, agreeable, preferred 10 attractive, beneficial 12 advantageous

desire 3 aim, yen 4 envy, eros, itch, lust, want, wish 5 covet, crave, fancy, go for, greed 6 pining, thirst 7 avarice, craving, long for, longing, passion 8 appetite, cupidity, petition, yearn for, yearning 9 eroticism, hankering, prurience, pruriency 10 aphrodisia, attraction, preference 11 inclination, lustfulness 13 concupiscence, lickerishness

desired 6 wanted 8 hoped-for 9 preferred, requested

desirous 4 avid 6 greedy 7 athirst, craving, envious, longing, wishful, wishing 8 covetous, grasping 10 solicitous

desist 4 halt, quit, stop 5 cease, yield 7 forbear, hold off, refrain 8 knock off, leave off, surcease 11 discontinue

desistance 3 end 4 halt, stop 5 cease, close 6 ending, finish, period 8 stoppage, stopping 9 cessation 10 conclusion 11 termination

desk 5 booth, stand, table 7 counter, lectern, rolltop 8 lapboard 9 secretary 10 escritoire ***adjunct:*** 8 inkstand, standish ***item:*** 3 pad 7 blotter, inkwell ***library:*** 6 carrel

desolate 4 bare, lorn, sack 5 alone, bleak, drear, stark, waste 6 barren, devoid, dismal, dreary, gloomy, ravage 7 despoil, forlorn, joyless, pillage, plunder 8 dejected, derelict, deserted, desolate, downcast, forsaken, lay waste, lifeless, lonesome, solitary, spoliate 9 abandoned, cheerless, depredate, desecrate, destitute, devastate, sorrowful 10 despondent 11 dilapidated 12 inconsolable 13 disheartening

desolation 3 woe 4 ruin 5 gloom, grief, waste 6 misery, sorrow 7 anguish, despair, sadness 8 bareness 9 bleakness, dejection, wasteland 10 loneliness 11 abandonment, devastation 12 wretchedness

despair 6 give up 8 lose hope

despairing 7 anxious, doleful, forlorn 8 dejected, desolate, hopeless, wretched 9 depressed 10 despondent 11 downhearted 12 disconsolate 13 brokenhearted

desperado 6 bandit, gunman, outlaw 7 bandito, brigand, convict, ruffian 8 criminal 9 cutthroat 10 gunslinger, highwayman, lawbreaker

desperate 4 bold, dire, rash 5 acute, risky 6 daring, futile 7 crucial, forlorn, frantic, useless, violent 8 critical, headlong, hopeless, reckless, shocking 9 foolhardy, impetuous 10 despondent, frustrated, outrageous, scandalous 11 climacteric, precipitate 12 overpowering 13 irretrievable

Desperate Housewives ***actress:*** 5 Cross (Marcia) 7 Hatcher (Teri), Huffman (Felicity) 8 Longoria (Eva), Sheridan (Nicollette) ***creator:*** 6 Cherry (Marc) ***character:*** 4 Bree (Van De Kamp), Edie (Britt), Mike (Delfino) 5 Betty (Applewhite), Orson (Hodge), Susan (Mayer) 7 Lynette (Scavo) 9 Gabrielle (Solis) ***narrator:*** 6 Strong (Brenda) ***setting:*** 8 Fairview 12 Wisteria Lane

desperation 5 agony 7 anguish, despair 8 distress 11 distraction 12 hopelessness, wretchedness

despicable 3 low 4 base, foul, grim, mean, ugly, vile 5 awful, cheap, gross, sorry 6 abject, scurvy, shabby, sordid 7 beastly, hateful, ignoble, pitiful 8 pitiable, shameful, wretched 9 degrading, loathsome 10 deplorable, detestable, disgusting 11 disgraceful, ignominious 12 contemptible, disreputable 13 reprehensible

despise 4 hate, shun, snub 5 abhor, avoid, scorn, spurn 6 detest, loathe, reject 7 contemn 8 execrate 9 abominate

despised one 6 pariah 7 outcast

despisement 4 hate 5 scorn 6 hatred, malice 7 disdain, ill will 8 aversion, contempt, loathing 9 antipathy, contumely 10 abhorrence 11 detestation

despite 8 although 11 in the face of 12 regardless of

despiteful 4 evil, mean 5 catty 6 bitchy, horrid, malign, odious, wicked 7 baleful, baneful, hostile, vicious 8 vengeful 9 malicious, rancorous, repellent 10 despicable, malevolent

despoil 4 sack 5 blast, strip, waste, wreck 6 denude, devour, maraud, ravage 7 pillage, plunder 8 desolate, spoliate 9 depredate, desecrate, devastate, strip away, vandalize **10** wreak havoc

despoiler 6 looter, sacker, vandal **7** ravager, wrecker **8** marauder, pillager **9** plunderer, spoliator **10** depredator, freebooter

despond 4 fret, mope, wilt **5** brood, droop, worry **6** give up, sorrow **8** languish **9** dejection **12** hopelessness

despondency 5 blues, dumps, gloom **6** misery, sorrow **7** anguish, despair, sadness **8** glumness **9** dejection **10** depression, melancholy **11** desperation, unhappiness **12** hopelessness

despondent 3 low, sad **4** blue, down, glum **7** doleful, forlorn **8** cast down, dejected, downcast, grieving, hopeless, mourning **9** depressed, desperate, heartsick, heartsore, sorrowful, woebegone **10** dispairing, dispirited, melancholy **11** discouraged, downhearted **12** disconsolate, disheartened

despot 4 czar, duce, tsar, tzar **5** ruler **6** tyrant **7** autarch, emperor **8** autocrat, dictator **9** oppressor, strong man

despotic 8 absolute **9** arbitrary, autarchic, imperious, tyrannous **10** autocratic, monocratic, tyrannical **11** dictatorial **12** totalitarian

despotism 7 czarism, tsarism, tyranny, tzarism **8** autarchy **9** autocracy **10** absolutism, domination **12** dictatorship

desquamate 4 pare, peel **5** scale **7** peel off **8** flake off, scale off **9** exfoliate

dessert 3 ice, pie **4** cake, flan, fool, tart **5** Betty, bombe, crepe, crisp, fruit, grunt, halva, Jell-O, melba, s'more, sweet, torte **6** afters, blintz, Danish, éclair, fondue, frappe, gâteau, halvah, hermit, junket, kuchen, mousse, pastry, sorbet, sundae, trifle **7** brownie, cobbler, compote, custard, gelatin, parfait, pudding, sabayon, sherbet, soufflé, spumoni, strudel **8** ambrosia, Bismarck, clafouti, crostata, flummery, ice cream, macaroon, meringue, napoleon, pandowdy, streusel, tiramisu, turnover **9** charlotte, cream puff, fruitcake, petit four, shortcake **10** blancmange, brown Betty, cheesecake, frangipane, icebox cake, peach Melba, zabaglione **11** baked Alaska, banana split, crème brûlée, gingerbread **12** hasty pudding, zuppa inglese ***French:*** **5** bombe **6** éclair, frappe, gâteau, mousse **7** parfait, sabayon **9** petit four **10** blancmange, frangipane ***frozen:*** **5** bombe **7** parfait, sherbet ***German:*** **6** kuchen **7** strudel ***Italian:*** **7** cannoli, spumoni **8** tiramisu **10** zabaglione **12** zuppa inglese ***Turkish:*** **5** halva **6** halvah

destination 3 aim, end, use **6** object, target **7** purpose **8** terminus **9** objective **10** appointing

destine 4 fate **6** assign, direct, intend **8** dedicate, set aside **9** designate, determine, preordain **10** foreordain **12** predetermine

destiny 3 lot **4** doom, fate **5** karma **6** design, future, kismet, Moirai **7** fortune, portion **8** prospect **9** hereafter **12** circumstance

destitute 4 bare, poor, void **5** broke, empty, needy **6** bereft, devoid, ruined **7** drained, lacking **8** bankrupt, depleted, dirt poor, divested, indigent, strapped, stripped **9** deficient, exhausted, penurious **10** bankrupted, stone-broke **11** impecunious **12** impoverished

destitution 6 penury **7** poverty **9** indigence, privation

destroy 3 axe, zap **4** doom, down, kill, nuke, raze, ruin, sack, slay, undo **5** crush, erase, quash, quell, smash, total, trash, waste, wrack, wreck **6** finish, lay low, mangle, ravage, rubble, rub out **7** abolish, atomize, despoil, expunge, nullify, pillage, shatter, wipe out **8** decimate, demolish, dispatch, dynamite, lay waste, pull down, snuff out, stamp out, tear down **9** devastate, dismantle, eradicate, extirpate, liquidate, pulverize **10** annihilate, extinguish, obliterate **11** exterminate

destroyer 4 bane, ruin **6** tin can, vandal **7** undoing, warship **8** downfall

destruction 4 loss, ruin **5** havoc **7** killing, sacking, undoing **8** downfall **9** ruination **10** extinction **11** devastation, liquidation **12** annihilation

destructive 7 baneful, harmful, ruinous **8** damaging **9** corrosive, injurious **10** shattering **11** deleterious, detrimental

desuetude 6 disuse **7** closure, neglect **9** cessation **11** abandonment

desultory 6 casual, chance, fitful, random, spotty **7** aimless, erratic, offhand, vagrant **8** shifting, slipshod, sporadic, wavering **9** haphazard, hit-or-miss, unplanned **10** capricious, digressive, disjointed **11** purposeless **12** unmethodical, unsystematic

detach 4 free, part, undo, wean **5** sever **6** cut off, remove, sunder **7** disjoin, divorce, release **8** separate, uncouple, withdraw **9** disengage **10** disconnect **12** disaffiliate

detached 5 alone, aloof, apart **6** remote **7** distant, neutral, removed, severed **8** abstract, isolated, separate, unbiased **9** incurious, withdrawn **10** impersonal **11** indifferent, unconcerned, unconnected **12** uninterested **13** disinterested, dispassionate, unaccompanied

detachment 5 squad **7** divorce, rupture **8** disunion, division **9** partition **10** neutrality, separation **11** dissolution

detail 4 item, list, part **5** point **6** assign, nicety, relate, report **7** appoint, article, element, itemize, listing, minutia, specify **8** allocate, spell out **9** enumerate, stipulate **10** assignment, particular **12** circumstance **13** particularize

detailed 4 full **6** minute **8** itemized, complete, thorough **10** blow-by-blow, exhaustive, meticulous, particular **13** thoroughgoing

detain 3 nab **4** bust, curb, hold, keep, mire, snag **5** check, delay, run in **6** arrest, collar, hang up, hinder, hold up, impede, pick up, retard, slow up **7** bog down, reserve, set back **8** hold back, keep back, restrain, slow down, withhold **9** apprehend **10** buttonhole ***in conversation:*** **10** buttonhole

detect 4 espy, find, spot **5** catch, dig up, hit on, scent, smell **6** descry, notice, turn up **7** discern, hit upon, uncover, unearth **8** discover, meet with **9** ascertain, encounter, ferret out, track down

detectable 6 patent **7** evident, visible **8** sensible, tangible **10** noticeable, observable **11** discernible, perceptible

detection 9 discovery **10** unearthing ***system:*** **5** radar, sofar

detective 3 tec **4** dick, G-man **6** shamus, sleuth **7** gumshoe **8** hawkshaw, informer, sherlock **9** inspector **10** private eye **12** investigator ***fictional:*** **3** Pym (Lucy) **4** Chan (Charlie), Gray (Cordelia), Moto (Mr.) **5** Banks (Alan), Bosch (Harry), Brown (Father), Dupin (Auguste), Lecoq, Lupin (Arsène), McGee (Travis), Morse (Inspector), Queen (Ellery), Rebus (John), Saint, Spade (Sam), Trent (Philip), Vance (Philo), Wolfe (Nero) **6** Alleyn (Roderick), Archer (Lew), Carter (Nick), Hammer (Mike), Holmes (Sherlock), Marple (Miss Jane), McCone (Sharon), Poirot (Hercule), Wimsey (Peter) **7** Cadfael (Brother), Campion (Albert), Charles (Nick, Nora), Maigret (Jules), Marlowe (Philip) **8** Drummond (Bulldog), Millhone (Kinsey) **9** Dalgliesh (Adam) **10** Robicheaux (Dave), Warshawski (V. I.) **11** Father Brown

detective-story writer 3 Poe (Edgar Allan), Tey (Josephine) **4** Carr (John Dickson), Knox (Ronald) **5** Blake (Nicholas), Block (Lawrence), Cross (Amanda), Doyle (Arthur Conan), Green (Anna Katherine), Innes (Michael), James (P. D.), Marsh (Ngaio), Queen (Ellery), Stout (Rex) **6** Bramah (Ernest), Buchan (John), Dexter (Colin), Hansen (Joseph), McBain (Ed), Mosley (Walter), Parker (Robert), Peters (Ellis), Sayers (Dorothy L.) **7** Bentley (E. C.), Biggers (Earl Derr), Collins (Wilkie), Francis (Dick), Freeman (Austin), Gardner (Erle Stanley), Grafton (Sue), Hammett (Dashiell), Hiaasen (Carl), Hornung (E. W.), Leonard (Elmore), Rendell (Ruth), Simenon (Georges), Van Dine (S. S.), Wallace (Edgar) **8** Chandler (Raymond), Christie (Agatha), Cornwell (Patricia), Gaboriau (Emile), Marquand (John), Mortimer (John), Paretsky (Sara), Rinehart (Mary Roberts), Spillane (Mickey) **9** Allingham (Margery), Highsmith (Patricia), Hillerman (Tony), Lockridge (Frances, Richard), Macdonald (John, Ross) **10** Chesterton (Gilbert Keith)

detent 4 pawl

detention 6 arrest **7** holding **10** internment **11** confinement **12** imprisonment

deter 5 avert, block **6** divert, hamper, hinder, impede, thwart **7** forfend, inhibit, obviate, prevent, rule out, shut out, ward off **8** dissuade, preclude, restrain, stave off **9** forestall, turn aside **10** discourage

deterge 4 wash **7** cleanse, wash off

detergent 4 soap **8** cleanser

deteriorate 3 rot **4** fade, fail, flag, sink, wear **5** decay, lapse, slide, spoil **6** weaken, worsen **7** decline, regress **8** languish **9** decompose, fall apart **10** debilitate, degenerate, depreciate, go downhill, retrograde, retrogress **12** disintegrate

deterioration 4 ruin **5** decay **6** ebbing, waning **7** atrophy, decline, erosion, failing, rotting **8** decaying, spoiling **9** crumbling, decadence, downgrade **10** debasement, degeneracy **12** degeneration, dégringolade

determinant 4 gene **5** agent, basis, cause, trait **6** factor, ground, reason **7** epitope, radical **9** attribute, influence

determinate 5 fixed **6** cymose **7** limited, precise, settled **8** constant, definite **10** definitive, restricted **11** established **13** circumscribed

determination 5 drive, spunk **6** fixing, mettle **7** finding, opinion, purpose, resolve, verdict **8** decision, firmness, judgment, tenacity **9** assurance, hardihood, impulsion, intention, resolving, willpower **10** conclusion, dedication, definition, doggedness, resolution, settlement **11** decidedness, intrepidity **12** perseverance, resoluteness, stubbornness **13** purposiveness

determine 3 fix, set **4** rule **5** bound, limit, prove **6** decide, figure, ordain, settle **7** control, delimit, find out, mark out, measure, preform, unearth **8** conclude, discover, regulate **9** ascertain, demarcate, establish, preordain, resolve on **10** delimitate, foreordain, predestine, predispose

determined 3 set **4** bent **5** fixed **6** driven, intent **7** decided, earnest, serious, settled **8** decisive, hellbent, resolute, resolved, stubborn **9** tenacious **10** persistent, purposeful, unwavering **11** established, persevering, unfaltering **12** foreordained, unhesitating

detest 4 hate **5** abhor, spurn **6** loathe **7** despise, dislike **8** execrate **9** abominate, repudiate

detestable 4 foul, vile **6** damned, horrid, odious **7** hateful, heinous **9** abhorrent, execrable, loathsome **10** abominable, despicable **12** contemptible

detestation 4 hate **6** hatred **8** anathema, aversion, loathing **9** repulsion, revulsion **10** abhorrence, execration, repugnance

dethrone 4 oust **6** depose **7** uncrown **8** displace

detonate 5 blast, burst, go off, spark **6** blow up, set off **7** explode **8** touch off

detonator 3 cap **4** fuse **9** explosive **11** blasting cap

detour 5 avoid, skirt **6** bypass **8** side trip **9** diversion

detract 6 divert, lessen, reduce **8** decrease, diminish, minimize **10** depreciate

detraction 9 aspersion, maligning, traducing **10** backbiting, belittling, derogation, slandering **11** denigration, deprecation, traducement **12** backstabbing, belittlement **13** disparagement

detractive 9 maligning, slighting, traducing, vilifying **10** defamatory, derogatory, pejorative **11** denigrating, disparaging **12** depreciative, depreciatory

detriment 4 harm, loss **6** damage, injury **7** marring **8** drawback **10** impairment **12** disadvantage

detrimental 3 bad, ill **7** adverse, harmful, hurtful, nocuous **8** damaging, negative **9** injurious **11** deleterious, unfavorable

detritus 4 tufa, tuff **5** scree, talus **6** debris, rubble **7** remains **11** odds and ends

Detroit ***county:*** **5** Wayne ***founder:*** **8** Cadillac (Sieur de) ***lake:*** **4** Erie **10** Saint Clair ***sobriquet:*** **6** Motown **9** Motor City

de trop 5 extra, spare **7** too much, surplus **9** excessive, redundant **10** gratuitous **11** superfluous **13** supernumerary

Deucalion ***father:*** **10** Prometheus ***kingdom:*** **6** Phthia ***mother:*** **7** Clymene ***son:*** **6** Hellen ***wife:*** **6** Pyrrha

deuce 3 tie, two **4** card, draw **5** devil **7** dickens **10** even-steven

Deutschland über ____ 5 alles

Devaki's son 7 Krishna

____ De Valera 5 Eamon

devaluate 5 abase, decry, lower **6** reduce, weaken **7** cheapen, degrade **8** mark down, write off **9** undermine, underrate, write down **10** depreciate

devaluation 7 decline **10** debasement, declension **11** declination

devalue see **depreciate**

devastate 4 raze, ruin, sack **5** waste **6** ravage **7** despoil, pillage, plunder **8** demolish, desolate, lay waste, overcome, spoliate **9** depredate, desecrate, overpower, overwhelm

devastation 4 loss, ruin **5** chaos, havoc, waste **6** ravage **7** pillage, plunder **8** disorder **9** confusion, ruination **10** demolition, desolation, spoliation **11** depredation

develop 3 age **4** form, grow **5** occur, reach, ripen **6** attain, dilate, emerge, evolve, expand, grow up, happen, mature, mellow, open up, thrive, unfold, unfurl **7** achieve, acquire, advance, burgeon, enlarge, expound, promote **8** flourish **9** actualize, elaborate, establish, transpire **11** come to light, materialize

development 5 phase **6** growth, result, spread **7** advance, buildup, outcome **8** ontogeny, progress, ripening **9** evolution, expansion, flowering, phylogeny, unfolding **10** maturation **11** elaboration, progression ***of life:*** **10** biogenesis

Devi 7 goddess ***consort:*** **5** Shiva ***father:*** **7** Himavat ***name:*** **3** Uma **4** Kali **5** Durga, Gauri **6** Chandi **7** Parvati

deviant 4 bent **5** kinky, queer **6** off-key **7** twisted, wayward **8** aberrant, abnormal, atypical, perverse **9** anomalous, different, divergent, irregular, unnatural **11** heteroclite

deviate 3 err, yaw **4** turn, vary, veer **5** sheer, stray **6** depart, swerve, wander **7** digress, diverge **8** aberrant **9** eccentric, turn aside

deviation 3 yaw **4** bend, tack, turn **5** error, shift **6** change **7** anomaly, turning, veering **8** variance **9** departure, diversion **10** aberration, alteration, deflection, divergence

device 4 ploy, tool **5** feint, gizmo, means, motif, motto, shift, thing, trick **6** dingus, doodad, emblem, figure, gadget, gambit, hickey, jigger, medium, motive, symbol, widget **7** gimmick, machine, utensil, whatnot, whatsit **8** artifice, creation, insignia **9** apparatus, appliance, doohickey, expedient, implement, invention, makeshift, mechanism, thingummy **10** instrument **11** contraption, contrivance, inclination, thingamabob, thingamajig, thingumajig ***automatic:*** **5** servo ***binding:*** **5** clamp ***fastening:*** **6** zipper ***grasping:*** **4** tong ***heating:*** **8** radiator ***hoisting:*** **5** crane, lewis **8** windlass ***holding:*** **4**

vise **5** clamp ***paging:*** **6** beeper ***suction:*** **4** pump

devil 3 imp **5** beast, cloot, demon, fiend, rogue, Satan, scamp **6** Belial, diablo, dybbuk, rascal, spirit **7** Clootie, dickens, Lucifer, Old Nick, serpent, tempter, villain **8** Apollyon, Mephisto, scalawag, succubus **9** archfiend, Beelzebub, cacodemon, scoundrel, skeezicks **10** blackguard, Old Scratch **11** rapscallion

devilfish 3 ray **5** manta **7** octopus **8** manta ray **10** cephalopod

devilish 3 bad **4** evil **6** cursed, wicked **7** demonic, hellish, roguish, satanic **8** accursed, damnable, diabolic, fiendish, infernal, sinister **9** nefarious **10** diabolical, iniquitous, villainous **11** mischievous

devil-may-care 4 rash, wild **6** rakish, sporty **7** raffish **8** rakehell, reckless **9** easygoing

devilry 7 knavery, roguery, sorcery, waggery **8** mischief **9** diablerie **10** wickedness, witchcraft **11** roguishness, waggishness **12** sportiveness

devious 3 sly **4** foxy, wily **6** artful, crafty, errant, erring, roving, shifty, sneaky, tricky **7** bending, crooked, cunning, curving, erratic, winding **8** aberrant, guileful, indirect, scheming, sneaking, twisting **9** deceptive, underhand, wandering **10** roundabout **11** out-of-the-way, underhanded

devise 4 form, plan, plot, will **5** chart, forge, frame, shape **6** cook up, create, design, invent, legacy, legate, scheme **7** arrange, bequest, concoct, connive, dope out, dream up, hatch up, project **8** bequeath, property **9** determine, formulate **11** inheritance

devitalize 3 sap **5** drain **6** deaden, weaken **7** exhaust **8** enfeeble, etiolate **9** desiccate **10** eviscerate

devoid of 7 lacking, wanting **8** free from

devoir 3 job **4** duty, task, work **5** chore, stint **6** charge **9** committal **10** assignment, commitment, obligation

devolution 5 decay **7** decline, passing **8** receding, transfer **9** conferral, decadence, recession, surrender **10** conveyance, declension, degeneracy, regression, relegation, transferal **11** degradation **12** degeneration, dégringolade, retrograding, transference **13** retrogression

devolve 4 give, pass **6** pass on **8** hand down, hand over, relegate, transfer **10** degenerate

devote 5 apply **6** commit, direct, donate, hallow **7** reserve **8** dedicate, give over, sanctify **9** confirm in, habituate **10** consecrate

devoted 4 dear, fond, true **5** loyal **6** ardent, caring, doting, fervid, loving **7** dutiful, fervent, zealous **8** constant, faithful **9** dedicated **10** thoughtful **12** affectionate ***religiously:*** **6** oblate

devotee 3 fan, nut **4** buff **5** hound, lover **6** addict, votary, zealot **7** admirer, amateur, fanatic, fancier, habitué **8** follower **9** supporter **10** aficionado, enthusiast

devotion 4 love, zeal **5** ardor, piety **6** fealty, fervor, prayer, Rosary **7** loyalty, passion **8** fidelity, fondness **9** adherence, adoration, reverence **10** allegiance, attachment, dedication, enthusiasm **12** faithfulness

devour 3 eat **5** eat up, enjoy **6** absorb, feed on **7** consume, destroy, feast on, pillage **8** prey upon, wolf down **9** delight in, feast upon, polish off, swallow up **10** annihilate

devouring 4 avid **6** greedy **8** esurient, ravenous **9** voracious **10** gluttonous

devout 4 holy **5** godly, loyal, pious **6** ardent **7** earnest, fervent, serious, sincere, zealous **8** faithful, reverent **9** pietistic, prayerful, religious

devoutness 4 zeal **5** ardor, piety **9** reverence **10** commitment

dew 5 sweat, tears **8** moisture **11** precipitate **12** perspiration **13** precipitation

dewy 3 wet **4** damp, pure **5** fresh, moist, naive **7** artless, natural **8** innocent, wide-eyed **9** credulous, guileless, ingenuous, unworldly

dexter 5 right

dexterity 4 ease **5** craft, grace, skill **7** ability, aptness, know-how, prowess, sleight **8** deftness, facility **9** adeptness, expertise, readiness **10** adroitness, nimbleness, smoothness **12** skillfulness

dexterous 3 apt **4** able, deft **5** adept, agile, handy **6** adroit, artful, facile, nimble, smooth **7** skilled **8** masterly, skillful **10** proficient

____ **Dhabi 3** Abu

diablerie 7 devilry, roguery, sorcery, waggery **8** deviltry, iniquity, mischief, satanism **9** devilment **10** black magic, wickedness, witchcraft, wrongdoing

diabolical 4 evil **5** awful **6** impish, wicked **7** beastly, demonic, heinous, hellish, puckish, roguish, satanic **8** demoniac, devilish, dreadful, fiendish, god-awful, hellborn, infernal, rascally, sinister **9** execrable, malicious, monstrous, nefarious **10** degenerate, demoniacal, horrendous, iniquitous, scandalous, villainous **11** mischievous

diabolism see **diablerie**

diacritic 5 acute, breve, grave, haček, tilde **6** accent, macron, umlaut **7** cedilla **8** dieresis **9** diaeresis **10** circumflex ***Arabic:*** **5** hamza **6** hamzah

diadem **5** crown, tiara **6** wreath **7** chaplet, coronal, coronet **8** headband
diagnose **4** spot **5** place **8** identify, pinpoint **9** determine, interpret, recognize **11** distinguish
diagnostic **8** analytic **10** analytical, expository, indicating, indicative **11** explanatory, exploratory **12** interpretive
diagonal **4** bias **5** bevel **6** biased **7** beveled, oblique, slanted **8** inclined, slanting **9** inclining, slantways, slantwise
diagonally **7** athwart **9** slantways, slantwise **10** cornerwise **11** catercorner, kitty-corner
diagram **3** map **5** chart, graph **6** design, layout, sketch **7** drawing, isotype **9** represent
dial **4** call, face, knob, tune, turn **5** phone **6** rotate **7** control **10** manipulate
dialect **4** cant, jive **5** argot, idiom, koine, lingo, slang **6** creole, jargon, patois, patter, pidgin, speech, tongue **8** language, localism **10** vernacular **11** regionalism, terminology **13** provincialism ***Georgia:*** **6** Gullah ***London:*** **7** cockney
dialectic **5** logic **6** debate **8** dialogue, forensic **9** reasoning **10** discussion **11** disputation **13** argumentation, investigation
dialogue **4** chat, talk **6** confer, parley, script **8** colloquy, converse **12** conversation **13** confabulation
diameter **4** bore **5** chord, width **7** breadth, caliber **8** bisector, wideness **9** broadness
diametric **7** counter, opposed **8** contrary, converse, opposite **12** antithetical **13** contradictory
diamond **3** gem **5** field, stone **7** rhombus ***element:*** **6** carbon ***famous:*** **4** Hope, Pitt **5** Sancy **6** Orloff, Regent **8** Braganza, Cullinan, Kohinoor **9** Excelsior **10** Great Mogul ***holder:*** **3** dop ***inferior:*** **4** bort ***oval:*** **9** briolette ***pattern:*** **6** argyle ***playing card:*** **7** lozenge ***state:*** **8** Delaware ***surface:*** **5** facet
Diana see **Artemis**
diapason **4** peal, stop **5** range, scale, scope **7** compass, measure **8** spectrum **10** tuning fork
diaper **5** nappy **7** pattern **8** ornament
diaphanous **5** filmy, gauzy, sheer, vague **6** flimsy **8** ethereal, gossamer **11** transparent **13** insubstantial
diaphragm **4** stop **6** septum **8** membrane **9** partition
diarist **4** Gide (André), Mann (Thomas) **5** Frank (Anne), Inman (Arthur Crew), Kahlo (Frida), Pepys (Samuel), Plath (Sylvia), Rorem (Ned), Scott (Walter), Swift (Jonathan), Woolf (Virginia) **6** Burney (Fanny), Evelyn (John) **7** Boswell (James), Thoreau (Henry David) **8** Robinson (Henry Crabb) **9** Lindbergh (Anne Morrow) **10** chronicler, journalist
diary **3** log **6** record **7** daybook, diurnal, journal, logbook **8** notebook, register **9** chronicle
diastase **6** enzyme **8** catalyst, reactant
diatribe **4** rant, rave **6** tirade **7** polemic **8** harangue, jeremiad **9** criticism, philippic **11** castigation **12** denunciation
dibs **4** gelt **5** claim, dough, money, title **6** rights **11** reservation
dice **4** cast, cube **5** bones, cubes, ivory, mince **11** devil's-bones ***game:*** **5** craps ***losing throw:*** **7** missout ***singular:*** **3** die ***throw:*** **7** boxcars **9** snake eyes
dicer **5** loser **6** risker **7** gambler
dicey **4** iffy **5** risky **6** chancy, tricky **8** ticklish **9** uncertain, whimsical **10** precarious **11** problematic, speculative **13** unpredictable
dichotomize **5** halve **7** dissect **8** hemisect **9** bifurcate
dichotomous **5** split **6** forked **7** pronged **9** bifurcate **10** bifurcated
dichotomy **7** forking **8** division **9** bisection, branching, splitting **11** bifurcation **13** contradiction
Dickens, Charles ***birthplace:*** **10** Portsmouth ***captain:*** **6** Cuttle ***character:*** **3** Ada (Clare), Pip, Tim **4** Dick (Mr.), Dora, Gamp (Sairey), Heep (Uriah), Nell **5** Drood (Edwin), Emily, Fagin, Lucie (Manette), Sikes (Bill) **6** Barkis, Bumble (Mr.), Carton (Sydney), Cuttle (Capt.), Darnay (Charles), Dombey (Fanny, Florence, Paul), Dorrit (Amy), Oliver (Twist) **7** Barnaby (Rudge), Dedlock (Lady), Defarge, Gargery (Joe), Manette (Dr.), Scrooge (Ebenezer), Tiny Tim **8** Cratchit (Bob), Havisham (Miss), Jarndyce (John), Magwitch (Abel), Micawber (Mr.), Nickleby (Nicholas), Peggotty (Clara, Daniel, Ham), Pickwick (Mr.) **9** Bill Sikes, Gradgrind (Mr.), Murdstone (Mr.), Pecksniff (Mr.), Uriah Heep **10** Chuzzlewit (Anthony, Jonas, Martin), Steerforth **11** Copperfield (David) ***hero:*** **6** Carton (Sydney) ***nationality:*** **7** English ***pen name:*** **3** Boz ***villain:*** **5** Fagin ***work:*** **9** Hard Times **10** Bleak House **11** Oliver Twist **12** Barnaby Rudge, Dombey and Son, Little Dorrit **14** Christmas Carol (A), Pickwick Papers (The) **15** Our Mutual Friend, Tale of Two Cities (A) **16** David Copperfield, Martin Chuzzlewit, Nicholas Nickleby **17** Great Expectations
dicker **4** deal, swap **5** argue, trade **6** barter,

haggle, higgle, palter **7** bargain, chaffer **8** contract, huckster **9** negotiate
dickey 10 shirtfront
Dickey novel 11 Deliverance
dictate 3 set **4** lead, rule, word **5** edict, order, tenet **6** behest, decree, direct, enjoin, govern, impose, ordain, recite **7** bidding, command, control, lay down, mandate, read off, summons **9** determine, direction, directive, prescribe, principle, pronounce, verbalize **10** injunction **12** prescription
dictative 5 bossy **8** despotic, dogmatic **9** imperious **10** peremptory **11** doctrinaire, magisterial **13** authoritarian
dictator 4 czar, duce, tsar, tzar **6** caesar, despot, tyrant **8** autocrat, martinet **9** oppressor, strongman ***Chinese:*** **3** Mao **9** Mao Zedong **10** Mao Tse-tung ***German:*** **6** Hitler (Adolf) ***Italian:*** **9** Mussolini (Benito) ***military:*** **8** caudillo ***Russian:*** **6** Stalin (Joseph) ***Spanish:*** **6** Franco (Francisco)
dictatorial 5 bossy **8** despotic, dogmatic **9** arbitrary, imperious, masterful **10** autocratic, iron-handed, peremptory, tyrannical **11** doctrinaire, domineering, overbearing **12** totalitarian **13** authoritarian
dictatorship 7 tyranny **9** autocracy, Caesarism, despotism, supremacy **10** absolutism
diction 6 phrase, speech **7** wordage, wording **8** delivery, language, parlance, phrasing, rhetoric, verbiage **9** elocution, verbalism **11** enunciation, phraseology
dictionary 7 lexicon **8** glossary, wordbook **10** repository **13** reference book ***compiler:*** **7** Johnson (Samuel), Webster (Noah) **13** lexicographer ***geographical:*** **9** gazetteer ***of synonyms:*** **8** thesauri (plural) **9** thesaurus
dictum 4 fiat **5** adage, axiom, edict, maxim, moral **6** ruling **7** mandate, opinion, precept, proverb **11** declaration **13** pronouncement
didactic 5 moral **6** teachy **7** donnish, preachy **8** advisory, edifying, pedantic, sermonic, teaching **9** hortative, pedagogic, teacherly **10** moralizing **11** informative, instructive
diddle 3 con, gyp, toy **4** beat, bilk, dupe, hoax, fool, idle, laze, loaf, loll, rook, scam **5** cheat, cozen, delay, drone, trick **6** chisel, chouse, dabble, dawdle, delude, fiddle, fleece, loiter, lounge, rope in, take in **7** deceive, defraud, goof off, mislead, swindle **8** flimflam, fool with, hoodwink, lollygag **9** bamboozle, overreach, victimize, waste time **10** dilly-dally, fool around, hang around
diddler 3 gyp **4** sham **5** cheat, faker, fraud, rogue **6** con man **7** grifter, shammer, sharper **8** swindler **9** con artist, defrauder, trickster **11** flimflammer **12** double-dealer **13** confidence man
dido 4 jest, lark **5** antic, caper, curio, frill, prank **6** bauble, frolic, gewgaw, trifle, whimsy **7** bibelot, novelty, trinket **8** furbelow, gimcrack, kickshaw, mischief **9** bagatelle, plaything **10** knickknack, tomfoolery
Dido 6 Elissa ***brother:*** **9** Pygmalion ***city founded by:*** **8** Carthage ***father:*** **5** Belus **6** Mutton ***husband:*** **7** Acerbas **8** Sichaeus ***lover:*** **6** Aeneas
Dido and Aeneas composer 7 Purcell (Henry)
die 4 drop, fall, mold, pass, stop, wane **5** cease, croak **6** cash in, demise, expire, go west, matrix, pass on, peg out, perish, pop off **7** decease, go south, kick off, snuff it, succumb **8** cash it in, check out, drop dead, pass away **9** disappear **10** buy the farm **12** join the choir **13** kick the bucket ***from hunger:*** **6** starve ***loaded:*** **6** fulham
____ die 4 sine
diehard 7 devoted, fanatic **8** true-blue **9** dogmatist **10** determined **11** bitter-ender, doctrinaire, reactionary, standpatter **12** conservative, intransigent **13** stick-in-the-mud
____ diem 3 per **5** carpe
Dies ____ 4 Irae
diet 4 bant, eats, fare, fast, feed, menu **6** ration, reduce, regime **7** regimen **8** assembly, victuals **10** parliament **11** legislature, nourishment
Diet of ____ 5 Worms **6** Speyer, Spires **8** Augsburg
Dieu ____ (British motto) 10 et mon droit
____-dieu 4 prie
differ 4 vary **5** demur **7** deviate **8** disagree
difference 3 gap **7** discord, dispute, dissent **8** conflict, contrast, variance **9** departure, deviation, disparity, otherness, variation **10** dissension, divergence, unlikeness **11** controversy, discrepancy, distinction **12** disagreement **13** dissimilarity
different 5 other **6** divers, single, sundry, unlike, varied **7** another, deviant, distant, diverse, several, special, unalike, unequal, unusual, various **8** discrete, distinct, peculiar, separate **9** disparate, divergent **10** dissimilar, individual, particular **11** contrasting, distinctive
differentiate 4 vary **5** adapt **6** change, modify **8** contrast, separate **9** diversify, transform **11** distinguish, individuate **12** characterize, discriminate
difficult 4 hard **5** tight, tough **6** thorny, uphill **7** arduous, awkward, labored, obscure,

operose **8** exacting, perverse, puzzling, stubborn **9** demanding, effortful, herculean, laborious, strenuous **10** refractory **11** problematic

difficulty 3 ado, fix, jam **4** beef **4** pass, snag **5** hitch, nodus, pinch, rigor, worry **6** hang-up, hassle, pickle, plight, scrape, strait **7** dilemma, pitfall, problem, trouble **8** distress, hardship, hot water, obstacle, quandary, quagmire, question **9** adversity, challenge **10** impediment **11** aggravation, arduousness, predicament, vicissitude

diffidence 7 modesty, reserve, shyness **8** distrust, meekness, timidity **9** quietness, restraint, timidness **10** hesitation **11** bashfulness

diffident 3 shy **4** meek **5** timid **7** bashful **8** hesitant, reserved, retiring, timorous **9** reluctant, unassured **11** unassertive **12** self-effacing

diffuse 5 strew, vague, wordy **6** prolix, spread **7** scatter, verbose **8** disperse, rambling **9** broadcast, dispersed, propagate, scattered, spreading, spread out **10** distribute, long-winded, widespread **11** disseminate, distributed

diffusion 6 spread **7** osmosis **9** broadcast, dispersal, prolixity, spreading **10** dispersion, scattering **11** circulation, propagation **12** broadcasting, promulgation

dig 3 jab **4** barb, grub, hole, like, mine, poke, prod, root, site, stab **5** delve, ditch, enjoy, gouge, nudge, probe, scoop, spade, taunt **6** burrow, plunge, quarry, relish, rootle, shovel, thrust, trench, tunnel **7** explore, root out, unearth **8** excavate, prospect **10** excavation **11** investigate ***up:*** **6** exhume **7** unearth

digest 5 sum up **6** absorb, codify, précis **7** consume, stomach, summate, swallow **8** abstract, boil down, classify, compress, condense, syllabus, synopsis **9** summarize, summation, synopsize **10** abridgment **12** condensation

digger 4 plow **5** miner **6** shovel **7** soldier

digit 3 toe **5** thumb **6** cipher, figure, finger, number, pinkie **7** integer, numeral **9** character **11** whole number

dignified 4 prim **6** august, formal, proper, seemly **7** courtly, elegant, stately **8** cultured, decorous, ennobled, polished **9** distingué, patrician

dignify 5 adorn, exalt, grace, honor **7** ennoble, elevate, glorify, sublime **11** distinguish

dignitary 3 VIP **4** lion **5** chief, nabob **6** leader, worthy **7** notable **8** eminence, luminary **9** personage **10** notability **11** muckety-muck **13** high-muck-a-muck

dignity 4 rank **5** honor, merit, poise, pride, worth **6** cachet, status, virtue **7** address, decorum, gravity, hauteur, majesty, stature **8** grandeur, nobility, position, prestige, standing **9** propriety **10** augustness, seemliness **11** consequence, self-respect

digress 5 stray **6** depart, ramble, swerve, wander **7** deviate, diverge **8** divagate

digression 5 aside **7** episode, tangent **8** drifting, excursus, rambling, straying **9** deviation, wandering **10** deflection, divagation, divergence **11** parenthesis

dig up 4 find **6** expose, reveal **7** nose out, root out, uncover, unearth **8** discover **9** ferret out, run across, search out, track down

dik-dik 8 antelope

dike 3 dam **4** bank **5** ditch, drain, levee **7** barrier **8** causeway **10** embankment **11** watercourse

dilapidate 4 ruin **5** decay, wreck **7** break up, crumble, decline, neglect **9** break down, decompose, disregard **10** deliquesce **12** disintegrate

dilapidated 5 dingy, seedy **6** beat-up, ragtag, ruined, shabby **7** decayed, run-down **8** battered, crumbled, decrepit **9** crumbling **10** broken-down, down-at-heel, ramshackle **12** deteriorated

dilapidation 4 ruin **5** decay **7** atrophy **8** collapse, decaying **9** crumbling, decadence, disrepair **11** decrepitude **13** decomposition, deterioration

dilate 5 swell, widen **6** expand, extend **7** distend, enlarge, expound **9** discourse, expatiate

dilatory 4 idle, slow **5** slack, tardy **7** laggard **8** dallying, delaying, sluggish **9** leisurely, lingering, unhurried **11** time-wasting

dilemma 3 box, fix, jam **4** bind, hole, spot **6** choice, corner, pickle, plight, scrape **7** catch-22, problem **8** argument, quandary **10** difficulty **11** predicament

dilettante 4 tyro **7** amateur, dabbler **8** aesthete, putterer **9** smatterer

dilettantish see **amateurish**

diligence 4 zeal **8** industry **9** assiduity **10** commitment **11** application, persistence **12** perseverance, sedulousness **13** assiduousness

diligent 8 sedulous **9** assiduous **10** persistent, persisting, unflagging **11** hardworking, industrious, painstaking, persevering

dilly 3 pip **4** lulu **5** dandy, doozy, peach **6** corker, doozie, pippin, ripper, rouser **8** jim-dandy, knockout **9** humdinger **10** ripsnorter **11** crackerjack

dillydally see **delay**

dilute 3 cut **4** thin, weak **5** water **6** watery,

weaken **8** diminish, weakened **9** attenuate, water down **11** watered-down
dim 4 dull, dumb, hazy, pale, slow **5** befog, blear, blind, cloud, dense, dusky, faint, muddy, murky, muted, thick, vague **6** bleary, gloomy, stupid **7** becloud, low beam, obscure, shadowy, subdued, unclear **9** tenebrous **10** ill-defined, indistinct, lack-luster, lusterless **11** unpromising
dime novel 4 pulp **7** chiller, shocker **8** dreadful, thriller **12** bloodcurdler **13** penny dreadful
dimension 4 size **5** reach, scale, scope, width **6** aspect, extent, spread **7** compass, expanse, measure, quality **9** amplitude, magnitude
diminish 3 ebb **4** bate, wane **5** abate, peter, quell, taper **6** lessen, recede, reduce, subdue, temper, weaken **7** curtail, decline, dwindle, subside **8** belittle, decrease, minimize, moderate, restrain, taper off **9** attenuate, disparage, dispraise **10** depreciate **11** detract from
diminutive 3 wee **4** tiny **5** bitsy, dwarf, pygmy, small, teeny, weeny **6** bantam, little, midget, minute, peewee, petite, teensy **9** miniature, pint-sized, undersize **10** teeny-weeny **11** lilliputian **12** teensy-weensy
____ dimittis 4 Nunc
dimple 3 pit **4** dent, dint, fret, nick **5** notch **6** ripple **8** pockmark **10** depression **11** indentation
dimwit 3 oaf **4** clod, dodo, dolt, dope, fool, simp, yo-yo **5** booby, chump, cluck, dummy, dunce, idiot, moron, stupe **6** dum-dum **7** airhead, dullard, fathead, pinhead **8** bonehead, dumbbell, imbecile, lunkhead, meathead, numskull **9** birdbrain, blockhead, dumb bunny, dumb cluck, ignoramus, lamebrain, numbskull, simpleton **10** dunderhead, nincompoop **11** featherhead, knucklehead **12** featherbrain
dim-witted 4 dull, dumb, slow **6** stupid **7** doltish, foolish, idiotic, moronic **8** backward, imbecile, retarded **9** brainless, half-baked, imbecilic **11** birdbrained, lamebrained **12** feebleminded, simpleminded
din 3 row **4** roar **5** babel, clash, noise **6** bedlam, clamor, deafen, hubbub, racket, rattle, tumult, uproar **7** clangor, clatter, resound **8** brouhaha **9** commotion, stridency **10** hullabaloo, hurly-burly **11** pandemonium **13** clamorousness
Dinah ***brother:*** **4** Levi **6** Simeon ***father:*** **5** Jacob ***mother:*** **4** Leah
dine 3 eat, sup **4** feed **5** feast **6** eat out **7** banquet, nourish
diner 4 café **5** eater **6** eatery **7** canteen **8** snack bar **9** hash house **10** coffee shop, restaurant **11** greasy spoon **12** lunch counter, luncheonette, sandwich shop
Dinesen, Isak 6 Blixen (Karen) ***work:*** **11** Out of Africa **12** Winter's Tales **16** Seven Gothic Tales
ding 3 mar **4** dent, nick **5** clang **7** blemish
ding-a-ling 3 nut **4** kook, yo-yo **5** flake, loony, wacko **6** cuckoo, nitwit, weirdo **7** lunatic **8** crackpot **9** fruitcake, harebrain, lamebrain, screwball **10** crackbrain **12** scatterbrain
dinghy 5 skiff **7** rowboat, shallop **8** lifeboat, life raft, sailboat
dingle 4 dale, dell, glen, vale **6** ravine, valley
dingus 5 gizmo **6** doodad, gadget, jigger, widget **7** whatsit **9** doohickey, thingummy **11** thingamabob, thingamajig, thingumajig
dingy 4 foul, mean **5** dirty, seedy, tacky **6** filthy, grubby, grungy, scuzzy, shabby, soiled, sordid **7** run-down, squalid, sullied, unclean **8** begrimed
dinky 3 toy **4** tiny **5** small, teeny **9** undersize **10** locomotive
dinner 4 meal **5** feast **6** regale, repast, spread, supper **7** banquet **8** luncheon **9** collation **10** table d'hôte ***course:*** **4** meat, soup **5** salad **6** entrée **7** dessert **9** appetizer ***jacket:*** **3** tux **6** tuxedo
dinosaur 6 fossil **7** has-been **8** theropod **11** anachronism ***fictional:*** **8** Godzilla
dinosauric 4 huge **5** passé **6** bygone **7** extinct, mammoth **8** colossal, enormous, obsolete, outmoded **9** cyclopean, leviathan, out-of-date **10** antiquated, behemothic, fossilized, gargantuan, mastodonic, oldfangled **11** elephantine **12** antediluvian, old-fashioned, out-of-fashion **13** anachronistic
dint 4 nick **5** force, might, power **6** dimple, virtue **7** drive in, impress **10** impression **11** indentation
diocese 3 see **9** bishopric ***Eastern Orthodox:*** **7** eparchy ***subdivision:*** **6** parish
diode 9 rectifier **10** vacuum tube **12** electron tube ***component:*** **5** anode **7** cathode **9** electrode
Diomedes ***city founded by:*** **4** Arpi ***father:*** **4** Ares, Mars **6** Tydeus ***foe:*** **6** Aeneas, Hector ***slayer:*** **8** Heracles, Hercules ***victim:*** **6** Rhesus
Dione 5 Titan ***cult partner:*** **4** Zeus ***daughter:*** **5** Venus **9** Aphrodite ***father:*** **7** Oceanus ***lover:*** **4** Zeus ***mother:*** **6** Tethys
Dionysus see **Bacchus**
Dionyza's husband 5 Cleon
Dioscuri 5 twins **6** Castor, Gemini, Pollux ***father:*** **4** Zeus **9** Tyndareus ***mother:*** **4** Leda ***sister:*** **5** Helen

dip 3 sag **4** bail, draw, drop, duck, dunk, fall, lade, sink, skid, slip, slue, swim **5** basin, ladle, lower, pitch, sauce, scoop, slope, slump, spoon, stoop **6** go down, hollow, plunge **7** decline, descend, descent, falloff, immerse, sinkage **8** decrease, downturn, sinkhole, submerge, submerse **9** concavity, declivity, downswing, downtrend, immersion **10** depression

diphthong 7 digraph **8** ligature

diploma 6 degree **7** charter **8** document **9** sheepskin **10** credential

diplomacy 4 tact **7** address, finesse **8** delicacy **10** artfulness, discretion, statecraft **11** negotiation, savoir faire, tactfulness

diplomatic 4 deft **5** bland, suave **6** artful, astute, polite, smooth, urbane **7** courtly, politic, tactful **8** delicate, discreet **9** courteous **12** conciliating, conciliatory, paleographic **13** accommodating

diplomat's office 7 embassy, mission

diplopod 9 millipede

dipper 3 cup **4** bird **5** ladle, ouzel, scoop, stars **6** bucket **10** pickpocket, water ouzel

dippy 4 daft, zany **5** crazy, daffy, flaky, goofy, kooky, loony, nutty, silly, wacky **6** stupid **7** doltish, foolish, witless **9** half-baked **11** harebrained **12** preposterous

dipsomania 10 alcoholism

dire 4 grim **5** acute, awful **6** dismal, horrid, tragic, urgent, woeful **7** baleful, baneful, crucial, extreme, fateful, ominous, ruinous **8** alarming, critical, dreadful, grievous, horrible, horrific, menacing, shocking, sinister, terrible **9** appalling, desperate, frightful, illboding **10** calamitous, deplorable, depressing, foreboding, malevolent, oppressing, oppressive, pernicious **11** apocalyptic, distressing, threatening

direct 4 head, lead, show **5** apply, frank, guide, label, level, order, pilot, plain, point, route, steer, train **6** assign, charge, define, devote, divert, enjoin, escort, extend, govern, lineal, linear, manage, ordain, settle **7** address, carry on, command, conduct, control, genuine, nonstop, operate, oversee, preside, project, request **8** dispatch, instruct, regulate, shepherd, straight, unbroken, verbatim **9** determine, firsthand, immediate, prescribe **10** administer, contiguous, continuous, inevitable **11** categorical, undeviating, unequivocal, word for word ***a helmsman:* 4** conn ***proceedings:* 7** preside

direction 3 way **4** east, line, path, side, west **5** angle, north, point, south, trend **6** course, design **7** bearing, channel, command, purpose **8** guidance, tendency **9** clockwise, oversight, viewpoint **10** management, standpoint, trajectory **11** instruction, supervision ***blowing:* 7** leeward **8** windward ***horizontal:* 7** azimuth ***main line of:* 4** axis (see also **compass point**)

directive 4 fiat, memo, word, writ **5** edict, order, ukase **6** charge, decree, dictum, notice, ruling **7** bidding, command, dictate, mandate **8** deciding, managing **9** presiding **10** assignment, injunction, memorandum **11** instruction, supervising, supervisory **12** policy-making **13** communication, pronouncement

directly 3 due **4** anon, soon **5** right, spang **6** at once, pronto **7** bluntly, by and by, shortly **8** first off, in person, promptly, squarely, straight, verbatim **9** forthwith, instanter, instantly, presently, right away **10** face-to-face **11** immediately, straight off, straightway, word for word **12** contiguously, straightaway

director 4 boss, head **5** chief **6** leader, top dog **7** manager **8** overseer **9** conductor, organizer **10** head honcho, supervisor

directory 4 list **5** guide, index **6** folder **7** catalog **8** register **9** catalogue **11** compilation

dirge 6 lament **7** requiem **8** threnody **11** lamentation ***Gaelic:* 8** coronach

dirigible 5 blimp **7** airship **8** zeppelin **9** steerable

dirk 4 shiv, stab **5** skean, skene, sword **6** bodkin, dagger, stylet **7** poniard

dirt 3 mud **4** clay, dust, land, loam, mire, muck, porn, smut, soil, spot **5** earth, filth, fraud, grime, stain **6** gossip, ground **7** chicane, squalor **9** chicanery, excrement, indecency **10** corruption, hanky-panky **11** pornography

dirt-poor 4 bust **5** broke **8** beggared, indigent **9** destitute, flat broke, penniless, penurious **10** stone-broke **12** impoverished

dirty 3 low, tar **4** base, foul, lewd, racy, smut, soil **5** bawdy, foggy, grimy, messy, mucky, muddy, murky, nasty, smear, sooty, stain, sully, taint **6** basely, befoul, coarse, debase, defile, filthy, grubby, impure, smudge, smutty, soiled, sordid, vulgar **7** begrime, corrupt, defiled, hateful, immoral, naughty, obscene, raunchy, smutchy, spotted, squalid, squally, sullied, tainted, tarnish, unclean, unkempt **8** begrimed, besmirch, indecent, off-color, polluted, unchaste, unwashed **9** ill-gotten, uncleanly **10** abominable, scandalous, scurrilous **11** distasteful, unlaundered **12** contaminated, scatological

Dis see **Pluto**

disability 7 ailment **8** drawback, handicap **9**

detriment, hindrance, infirmity, unfitness **10** affliction, impairment, impediment, incapacity **11** restriction, shortcoming **12** disadvantage

disable 3 sap **4** maim **5** spoil **6** hobble, weaken **7** cripple **8** enfeeble, handicap, paralyze, sabotage **9** hamstring, undermine **10** debilitate, immobilize **12** incapacitate ***a racehorse:*** **6** nobble

disabled 7 hobbled **8** crippled **9** arthritic, paralyzed, rheumatic **11** handicapped **13** incapacitated

disabuse 4 free **5** emend, purge **7** correct, deliver, rectify, redress, release, relieve **8** liberate, unburden **9** enlighten, undeceive **10** illuminate **11** disencumber, disillusion

disaccharide 7 lactose, maltose, sucrose

disaccord 3 jar, war **4** vary **5** brawl, clash **6** combat, debate, differ **7** contest, contend, dispute, dissent, quarrel **8** conflict, disagree **12** disharmonize

disadvantage 3 bar **4** harm, loss **6** burden, damage, hamper **7** barrier, setback **8** drawback, handicap, obstacle **9** detriment, hindrance, liability, prejudice **10** impairment, impediment, imposition, limitation **11** deprivation, obstruction

disadvantaged 7 lacking **8** deprived **11** handicapped

disaffect 4 wean **5** alien, repel **8** alienate, disquiet, disunite, estrange **10** antagonize

disaffirm 4 deny **5** annul, belie, cross **6** abjure, impugn, negate, refute, reject **7** confute, explode, gainsay, reverse **8** disclaim, disprove, negative, traverse **9** repudiate **10** contradict, contravene

disagree 4 vary **5** argue, clash **6** bicker, differ, divide, haggle **7** contend, contest, dispute, dissent **8** conflict

disagreeable 4 ugly **7** peevish **8** annoying, petulant **9** offensive **10** unpleasant **11** disobliging, distressing, ill-tempered

disagreement 5 clash **6** debate **7** discord, dispute, quarrel, wrangle **8** argument, conflict, squabble, variance **9** disparity **10** contention, difference, dissension, divergence, unlikeness **11** altercation, controversy, discrepancy, incongruity

disallow 4 deny, veto **5** debar **6** enjoin, forbid, refuse, reject **7** disavow, dismiss, exclude, rule out, shut out **8** disclaim, prohibit **9** interdict, proscribe, repudiate

disallowance 4 veto **5** taboo **6** denial **7** refusal **9** disavowal, dismissal, exclusion, rejection **11** prohibition, repudiation **12** interdiction, proscription

____-disant 3 soi

disappear 3 die **5** clear, leave **6** depart, die out, vanish **8** evanesce, fade away, melt away, pass away, slip away **9** evaporate, sneak away, steal away **13** dematerialize

disappoint 4 dash, foil, ruin **6** baffle, defeat, thwart **7** let down **9** frustrate **10** discourage, dishearten

disappointment 4 blow **6** bummer, defeat, downer **7** failure, letdown **8** comedown **9** bringdown **11** frustration

disapproval 4 veto **6** rebuke **7** censure, dislike, obloquy, reproof **8** reproach **9** criticism, objection, rejection ***expression of:*** **3** boo **4** hiss, hoot, jeer **7** catcall **9** raspberry **10** Bronx cheer, thumbs-down

disapprove 4 veto **6** oppose, reject, tut-tut **7** decline, dislike, dismiss, frown on **8** disfavor, turn down **9** dispraise

disarm 5 charm **6** allure **7** win over **8** sideline **9** captivate **10** neutralize

disarming 7 amiable, likable, winning, winsome **8** likeable **9** endearing **10** convincing, persuasive **11** insinuating **12** ingratiating

disarrange 4 mess **5** mix up, upset **6** jumble, mess up, mislay, muddle, muss up **7** confuse, disturb **8** disorder, displace, misplace, unsettle **10** discompose **11** disorganize

disarray 5 chaos **6** bedlam, jumble, mess up, muddle **7** clutter, undress **8** disorder, shambles, unsettle **9** confusion **10** discompose, dishabille

disassemble 6 detach **7** scatter **8** dismount, disperse, separate, take down, tear down **9** break down, come apart, dismantle, dismember, take apart

disassociate 5 sever, unfix **6** detach, sunder **7** back off **8** abstract, alienate, back down, disunite, liberate, separate, uncouple, withdraw **9** disengage **10** disconnect

disaster 3 woe **6** fiasco **7** debacle, failure, tragedy **8** calamity **9** cataclysm, ruination **11** catastrophe, devastation

disastrous 4 dire **5** fatal **6** tragic **7** fateful, ruinous **8** terrible **10** calamitous, horrendous **11** cataclysmic, destructive, devastating **12** catastrophic

disavow 4 deny **6** abjure, disown, impugn, negate, recant, reject **7** forsake, gainsay, retract **8** abnegate, disclaim, forswear, negative, renounce **9** repudiate

disband 3 end **4** part **5** sever **6** divide, sunder **7** break up, dissect, divorce, scatter **8** disperse, dissolve, separate

disbelieve 5 doubt, scorn, scout **6** eschew, reject **7** scoff at, suspect **8** discount, distrust, mistrust, question **9** discredit, repudiate

disbeliever 5 cynic **7** doubter, sceptic,

scoffer, skeptic **9** dissenter **10** questioner **11** freethinker

disbelieving 4 wary **5** leery **6** show-me **7** cynical, dubious **8** doubting **9** quizzical, skeptical **11** incredulous, mistrustful, questioning, unconvinced

disburden 4 shed **6** unlade, unload, unship, unstow **7** off-load, relieve **8** disgorge **9** discharge

disburse 3 pay **5** allot, issue **6** lay out, pay out, supply **7** deliver, dole out, furnish, mete out, provide **8** dispense, disperse **9** apportion, partition **10** distribute, measure out

disbursement 4 cost **5** funds **6** outlay **7** expense, payment **9** allotment **11** expenditure **12** distribution

discard 4 cast, drop, dump, junk, shed, toss, waif **5** chuck, ditch, eject, let go, scrap **6** reject **7** cast off, castoff, deep-six, wash out **8** get rid of, jettison, shuck off, throw out **9** throw away, toss aside

discarnate 8 bodiless, ethereal, spectral **9** asomatous, unfleshly **10** immaterial, unembodied, unphysical, wraithlike **11** disembodied, incorporeal, nonphysical **12** otherworldly **13** insubstantial

discern 3 see **4** espy, know, note **5** grasp, sense **6** behold, detect, divine, notice **7** glimpse, observe **8** identify, perceive **9** apprehend, ascertain, recognize **10** comprehend **11** distinguish **12** discriminate **13** differentiate

discernible 7 visible **8** apparent, palpable **10** detectable, noticeable, observable **11** appreciable, perceivable **12** recognizable

discerning 4 keen **5** acute, aware **6** astute **7** knowing **9** clear-eyed, insighted, observant, sagacious **10** insightful, perceptive **12** clear-sighted **13** knowledgeable, perspicacious

discernment 6 acuity, acumen **7** insight **8** keenness, sagacity **9** intuition **10** astuteness, perception, shrewdness **11** penetration, percipience **12** perspicacity **13** comprehension, sagaciousness

discharge 2 ax **3** axe, can, pay **4** drop, emit, fire, free, gush, oust, quit, sack, spew, vent, void **5** annul, clear, demob, egest, eject, empty, expel, exude, let go, loose, pay up, quash, salvo, shoot, utter **6** bounce, excuse, exempt, let fly, let off, loosen, outlet, remove, settle, unbind, unload, vacate **7** absolve, boot out, barrage, cashier, deliver, dismiss, exclude, excrete, execute, fulfill, give off, kick out, manumit, off-load, release, relieve, removal, satisfy, unchain **8** abrogate, aquittal, dispense, displace, dissolve, ejection, emission, get rid of, liberate, separate, throw off **9** acquittal, dismissal, eliminate, explosion, expulsion, muster out, pour forth, send forth, terminate, unshackle **10** deactivate, demobilize **11** exoneration, fulfillment ***electrical:*** **5** spark **6** leader **8** streamer **9** lightning

disciple 3 fan **6** minion **7** apostle, devotee, learner **8** adherent, follower, henchman, partisan, retainer **9** supporter **10** enthusiast

disciplinarian 8 enforcer, martinet **10** taskmaster **11** slave driver

disciplinary 8 punitive **9** punishing **10** corrective

discipline 4 curb, rule, will **5** check, drill, field, guide, order, teach, train **6** bridle, direct, ferule, method, punish, school, subdue **7** chasten, conduct, control, correct, educate **8** approach, chastise, instruct, penalize, restrain, training **9** castigate, obedience, subjugate, will-power **10** correction, punishment **11** castigation, self-control, self-mastery **12** chastisement **13** self-restraint

disclaim 4 deny **6** abjure, reject **7** disavow, gainsay, retract **8** disallow, forswear, renounce, traverse **9** repudiate **10** contradict

disclose 3 own **4** avow, tell **5** admit, spill **6** expose, impart, relate, report, reveal, unmask, unveil **7** display, divulge, uncover **8** discover, give away, unclothe **9** make known

disclosure 6 exposé **8** exposure **9** admission **10** revelation **11** declaration

discolor 3 tar **4** blot, dull, fade, smut, soil **5** smear, stain, sully, taint, tinge **6** defile, smudge **7** besmear, bestain, tarnish **8** besmirch

discoloration 4 spot **5** stain, taint **6** blotch, bruise, smudge **7** blemish **9** birthmark

discomfit 3 irk, vex **4** faze **5** abash, annoy, upset **6** baffle, bother, defeat, rattle, thwart **7** fluster, nonplus, perturb, unnerve **8** confound **9** embarrass **10** discompose, disconcert

discomfiture 5 upset **6** unease **8** disquiet **9** abashment, agitation, confusion **10** uneasiness **11** frustration **12** discomposure, perturbation **13** embarrassment, inconvenience

discomfort 3 irk, vex **4** ache, pain **5** annoy **6** bother, unease **7** malaise **8** vexation **9** annoyance **10** uneasiness **13** embarrassment

discommend 5 decry **7** censure, frown on, put down **8** admonish, disfavor, object to **9** criticize, deprecate, disesteem, disparage, reprehend **10** disapprove

discommode 3 irk, vex **5** annoy, upset **6** bother, burden, flurry, put out **7** disturb, fluster, perturb, trouble **8** encumber **9** aggravate, disoblige **13** inconvenience

discompose 3 irk, vex **5** annoy, harry, upset, worry **6** bother, dismay, flurry, harass, pester, plague, ruffle, untune **7** agitate, disturb, fluster, perturb, unhinge **8** disarray, disorder, unsettle **9** embarrass **10** disarrange **11** disorganize

discomposure 5 upset, worry **6** bother, unease **8** vexation **9** abashment, agitation, annoyance, confusion **10** discomfort, irritation, perplexity, uneasiness **11** disquietude **12** discomfiture, perturbation **13** consternation, embarrassment

disconcert 4 faze **5** abash, upset, worry **6** bemuse, bother, puzzle, rattle, ruffle **7** confuse, disturb, nonplus, perplex, perturb, trouble **8** bewilder, confound, disquiet **9** discomfit, embarrass, frustrate

disconfirm 4 deny **5** rebut **6** refute, negate **7** gainsay **8** abnegate, confound, disclaim, disprove **10** contradict, controvert

disconnect 3 cut, gap **5** break, sever, unfix **6** cut off, detach **7** disjoin **8** separate, uncouple **9** disengage **10** dissociate

disconnected 7 muddled **8** detached, separate **10** disjointed, incoherent, unattached **11** fragmentary, unorganized **13** discontinuous

disconsolate 3 low, sad **4** blue, down **5** bleak, drear **6** abject, dreary, gloomy, woeful **7** doleful, forlorn, joyless, unhappy **8** dejected, downcast, wretched **9** cheerless, depressed, miserable, sorrowful, woebegone **10** dispirited, melancholy **11** comfortless, crestfallen, downhearted

discontent 4 envy **7** malaise, unhappy **9** dysphoria **10** depression, inquietude, uneasiness **12** restlessness

discontented 5 upset **6** uneasy **7** annoyed, fretful, unhappy **8** restless **9** disturbed, irritated, perturbed **10** displeased **11** complaining, disgruntled, ungratified, unsatisfied **12** dissatisfied

discontinuation 3 end **4** stop **5** cease, close, pause **6** ending, finish **7** closing **8** abeyance **9** cessation **10** conclusion, desistance, moratorium, suspension **12** postponement

discontinue 3 end **4** halt, quit, stay, stop **5** cease, close, sever **6** desist, give up, wind up, wrap up **8** break off, close out, conclude, knock off, leave off, shut down, surcease **9** terminate

discontinuity 3 gap **4** hole, rent, rift **5** break, cleft, crack, split **6** breach, lacuna **7** fissure, opening, rupture

discontinuous 6 fitful **7** muddled **8** discrete, separate **9** spasmodic **10** incoherent, incohesive **11** unconnected **12** disconnected, intermittent **13** nonsequential

discord 5 clash **6** enmity, rancor, strife **7** rupture **8** conflict, contrast, disunity, division, friction, mismatch, variance **9** animosity, antipathy, hostility **10** antagonism, contention, difference, dissension, dissidence, dissonance, opposition **12** inconsonance, polarization **13** inconsistency ***goddess:* 3** Ate **4** Eris

discordant 5 harsh **6** at odds **7** grating, jarring **8** clashing, contrary, jangling, strident **9** dissonant, out of tune **10** cacophonic, unpleasant **11** cacophonous, conflicting, disagreeing, inconsonant, quarrelsome, unmelodious **12** unharmonious

discotheque 6 bistro, nitery **7** hot spot **9** dance club, nightclub, night spot

discount 4 agio **5** doubt, lower **6** deduct, ignore, rebate, reduce, slight **7** neglect, take off **8** belittle, derogate, decrease, diminish, knock off, mark down, markdown, minimize, overlook, roll back, rollback, subtract, take away **9** abatement, deduction, disregard, reduction, substract, underrate **13** underestimate

discountenance 4 faze **5** abash **6** rattle **7** frown on **8** confound, disfavor **9** deprecate, discomfit, embarrass **10** disapprove, disconcert, discourage

discourage 4 damp **5** daunt, check, chill, deter **6** dampen, deject, divert, hinder, impede **7** depress, inhibit, trouble **8** disfavor, dissuade, suppress **10** demoralize, dishearten

discouraging 5 bleak **7** unhappy **8** daunting **9** deterring, troubling **10** depressing **11** unfavorable, unpromising **12** unpropitious **13** disappointing, disheartening

discourse 4 talk **5** argue, essay, orate, speak, spiel, voice **6** sermon, speech, thesis **7** amplify, descant, enlarge, explain, expound, lecture **8** converse, harangue, perorate, rhetoric, speaking, treatise **9** expatiate, hold forth, monograph, sermonize, utterance **10** expression **11** interchange **12** conversation **13** verbalization ***art of:* 8** rhetoric ***religious:* 6** homily, sermon

discourteous 4 rude **6** unkind **7** boorish, brusque, ill-bred, uncivil, uncouth **8** impolite **10** ungracious, unmannerly **11** ill-mannered, impertinent **13** disrespectful

discover 4 espy, find, spot **5** learn **6** betray, detect, expose, reveal, unmask **7** divulge, find out, observe, unearth **8** come upon, perceive, proclaim, unshroud **9** ascertain, determine, encounter, make known **10** come across

discovery **4** find **5** trove **6** espial, strike **7** finding **8** locating, sighting **9** detection **10** revelation, unearthing

discredit **4** slur, ruin **5** doubt, shame **6** defame, malign, show up **7** asperse, degrade, put down, run down, slander, traduce **8** disgrace, ignominy **9** disparage, disrepute **10** disbelieve, opprobrium

discreditable **5** shady **6** shabby, shoddy **8** shameful, unworthy **9** degrading **10** inglorious **11** blameworthy, disgraceful, ignominious **12** contemptible, dishonorable, disreputable

discreet **4** wary **5** chary, muted, plain **6** modest, simple **7** careful, guarded, prudent, tactful **8** cautious, moderate **9** unadorned **10** controlled, reasonable, restrained **11** circumspect, considerate, unelaborate, unobtrusive **12** unnoticeable **13** unpretentious

discrepancy **3** gap **8** alterity, conflict, variance **9** disparity, otherness, variation **10** difference, divergence, divergency, unlikeness **12** disagreement **13** inconsistency

discrepant **6** unlike **7** diverse, varying **8** contrary **9** different, differing, disparate, divergent **11** conflicting, disagreeing **12** incompatible, inconsistent **13** contradictory

discrete **8** detached, distinct, separate **9** countable, different **10** individual **12** disconnected **13** discontinuous, noncontinuous

discretion **4** care, tact **7** caution, reserve **8** delicacy, judgment, prudence, wariness **9** canniness, chariness, restraint **13** judiciousness

discriminate **5** judge **6** assess **7** compare, discern, make out **8** contrast, disfavor, evaluate, perceive, separate **9** segregate, tell apart **11** distinguish **13** differentiate

discriminating **6** choosy, select **7** finical, finicky **8** eclectic **9** judicious, selective **10** discerning **11** prejudicial

discrimination **5** taste **6** acumen **7** bigotry, insight **8** inequity, judgment **9** prejudice **10** astuteness, favoritism, partiality, perception **11** discernment, intolerance, penetration

discriminatory **6** biased **7** partial, unequal **8** partisan **9** jaundiced **10** prejudiced **11** inequitable, predisposed

discursive **5** windy, wordy **6** chatty, prolix **7** diffuse, logical, verbose **8** rambling, tortuous **9** desultory **10** analytical, circuitous, digressive, long-winded, meandering **11** wide-ranging

discuss **4** moot **5** argue, weigh **6** debate, parley **7** canvass, expound **8** consider, converse, hash over, talk over **9** elucidate, expatiate, interpret, talk about, thrash out, ventilate **10** deliberate, toss around ***business:*** **8** talk shop ***lightly:*** **5** bandy ***thoroughly:*** **7** exhaust

discussion **3** rap **4** chat, talk **6** confab, debate, parley, powwow **7** canvass, palaver **8** argument, colloquy **10** conference, rap session **11** bull session, ventilation **12** conversation, deliberation **13** confabulation

discus thrower **6** Alekna (Virgilijus), Marten (Maritza), Oerter (Al) **10** discobolus **11** Rashchupkin (Viktor)

disdain **5** abhor, scorn, scout, spurn **6** deride, refuse, reject, slight **7** contemn, despise, despite, hauteur, put down **8** aversion, belittle, contempt, disprize, misprize **9** antipathy **10** repugnance, undervalue

disdainful **5** aloof, proud **6** averse, lordly, sniffy, snooty, uppity **7** haughty **8** arrogant, cavalier, derisive, insolent, scorning, snobbish, spurning, superior, toplofty **11** overbearing **12** antipathetic, contemptuous, supercilious **13** high and mighty

disease **3** bug, ill **5** upset, virus **6** blight, malady **7** ailment, anthrax, illness, malaise, mycosis, purpura **8** debility, epidemic, myxedema, pandemic, sickness, syndrome, zoonoses (plural), zoonosis **9** affection, black lung, contagion, ill health, infection, infirmity, sclerosis **10** affliction, blackwater, bronchitis, infirmness, sickliness ***animal:*** **5** mange, surra **6** rabies **7** bighead **8** enzootic, zoonosis **9** distemper, tularemia **10** rinderpest ***blood:*** **8** leukemia, leukoses (plural), leukosis ***cabbage:*** **8** clubroot ***cattle:*** **6** cowpox **7** foot rot, locoism, murrain **8** blackleg, vaccinia **9** vibriosis **10** rinderpest **11** brucellosis ***cereal grass:*** **4** bunt, smut **5** ergot ***children's:*** **5** mumps **7** measles, rubella **10** chicken pox **13** whooping cough ***citrus tree:*** **8** tristeza ***classification:*** **8** nosology ***combining form:*** **4** path **5** patho ***communicable:*** **3** flu **4** mono **5** mumps, polio **6** dengue, herpes, plague, rabies **7** bird flu, cholera, leprosy, malaria, measles, rubella, tetanus, typhoid **8** avian flu, impetigo **9** hepatitis, influenza **10** giardiasis **12** tuberculosis ***deficiency:*** **6** scurvy **7** rickets **8** beriberi, pellagra ***disseminator:*** **6** vector **7** carrier ***eye:*** **6** iritis **8** glaucoma, trachoma **9** retinitis ***hair follicle:*** **7** sycoses (plural), sycosis ***heart:*** **11** cardiopathy ***horse:*** **6** nagana, spavin **7** locosim, sarcoid **8** glanders **9** strangles ***identification of:*** **9** diagnosis ***industrial:*** **10** byssinosis ***infectious:*** **4** mono, yaws **6** dengue, typhus **7** leprosy, malaria, tetanus, typhoid **9** tularemia, vibriosis **10** rinderpest **13** whooping cough ***liver:*** **9** cirrhosis, hepatitis ***livestock:*** **7** locoism **9** vibriosis **10** rinderpest ***lung:*** **8** phthisic, phthisis **9** pneumonia **10** byssinosis **12** tuberculosis ***lymph glands:*** **8** scrofula ***metabolic:*** **4** gout ***nervous system:*** **4** kuru **6** rabies **10** diphtheria ***of beets:*** **8** heartrot ***of mammals:*** **6** rabies **7** malaria **9** distemper **10** babesiosis, rinderpest ***parasitic:*** **3** rot **4** smut **5** mange **7** malaria **8** hookworm, kala-azar **9** heartworm ***plant:*** **4** rust, scab, smut, wilt **5** blast, edema, scald, scurf, stunt **6** blight, blotch, canker, mosaic, streak **7** blister, crinkle, foot rot, frogeye, red leaf, root rot **8** clubroot, curly top, fusarium, gummosis, leaf curl, leaf roll, leaf rust, leaf spot, ring spot, root knot, stem rust **9** chlorosis, crown gall, white rust **10** blackheart, leaf scorch ***poultry:*** **8** leukosis ***respiratory:*** **6** asthma, coryza **10** byssinosis ***sheep:*** **3** gid **7** scrapie **9** vibriosis **10** bluetongue ***silkworm:*** **3** uji ***skin:*** **4** acne, yaws **5** favus, hives, lupus, mange, pinta, tinea **6** eczema, tetter **7** leprosy, prurigo, sarcoid, scabies, serpigo **8** impetigo, miliaria, pyoderma, ringworm, vitiligo **9** pemphigus, psoriasis **10** erysipelas **11** scleroderma ***syphilitic:*** **5** tabes ***throat:*** **5** croup, strep ***thyroid:*** **6** struma ***tropical:*** **4** yaws **5** pinta, sprue, surra **6** dengue **7** malaria **8** kala-azar ***venereal:*** **6** herpes **8** syphilis **9** chancroid, gonorrhea ***viral:*** **3** flu **4** AIDS, noma **5** Ebola, mumps, polio **6** dengue, grippe, herpes, rabies, zoster **7** bird flu, measles, rubella, rubeola, variola **8** avian flu, morbilli, shingles, smallpox **9** hepatitis, influenza, monkey pox, varicella **13** poliomyelitis

diseased 3 ill **6** ailing, infirm, sickly, unwell **7** fevered, unsound **8** feverish, infected

disembark 4 land **6** alight **7** deplane, detrain **8** go ashore

disembarrass 3 rid **4** free **7** release, relieve **8** liberate, unburden, untangle **9** extricate **11** disencumber, disentangle

disembodied 7 ghostly **8** ethereal, spectral **9** asomatous, unfleshly **10** immaterial, unphysical, wraithlike **11** incorporeal, nonmaterial, nonphysical **13** insubstantial

disembogue 4 flow, gush, pour, spew **5** empty **7** pour out **9** discharge

disembowel 3 gut **10** eviscerate, exenterate

disemploy 2 ax **3** axe, can **4** boot, fire, sack **7** cashier **9** discharge, terminate

disenchanted 5 blasé, jaded **6** soured **7** cynical **9** jaundiced **10** undeceived **11** worldly-wise **12** disappointed, dissatisfied **13** disenthralled, disillusioned

disencumber 3 rid **4** free **7** lighten, release, relieve, sort out **8** free from, liberate, unburden **9** alleviate, disburden, extricate

disengage 4 free, part **5** loose, unfix **6** detach, opt out, unbind **7** back out, drop out, release, unloose **8** cut loose, liberate, separate, uncouple, unfasten, unloosen, withdraw **10** disconnect

disentangle 5 untie **6** detach **7** resolve, sort out, unravel, unsnarl, untwine **8** separate **9** extricate **10** unscramble **11** disencumber **13** straighten out

disenthrall 4 free **7** manumit, release **8** liberate **10** emancipate

disfavor 7 dislike **8** aversion, distrust, mistrust **9** deprecate, disesteem, disregard, disrepute **10** disrespect **11** disapproval **12** disadvantage, unpopularity

disfigure 3 mar **4** maim, scar **6** deface, defile, deform, impair, injure, mangle **7** blemish, distort **8** mutilate

disfranchise 3 bar **7** exclude **8** take away **9** deprive of **10** disentitle

disgorge 4 barf, spew **5** belch, eject, eruct, erupt, expel, vomit **6** give up, irrupt, spit up **7** release, throw up, upchuck **9** discharge

disgrace 5 odium, shame **6** stigma **7** attaint, mortify, obloquy **8** black eye, contempt, dishonor, ignominy, reproach **9** discredit, disrepute, humiliate **10** opprobrium, stigmatize **11** degradation, humiliation

disgraceful 7 ignoble **8** shameful **9** degrading **10** deplorable, inglorious, unbecoming **11** humiliating, ignominious, reproachful **12** dishonorable, disreputable

disgruntled 5 vexed **6** cranky, put out **7** annoyed, beefing, griping **8** grousing **9** irritated **10** discontent, displeased, ill-humored, malcontent **11** ungratified **12** discontented, malcontented

disguise 4 hide, mask, sham, veil **5** belie, cloak, feign, put on **6** facade **7** conceal, falsify, obscure **8** artifice, pretense **9** deception **10** camouflage, false front, pretension **12** misrepresent

disguised 6 masked, veiled **7** cloaked, feigned **9** incognito **10** undercover **11** camouflaged

disguisement 4 mask, veil **5** cloak, front **6** facade **8** pretense **9** deception **10** false front, pretention

disgust 6 nausea, offend, revolt, sicken **8** aversion, gross out, loathing, nauseate **9** antipathy, repulsion, revulsion **10** abhorrence, repugnance **11** abomination **13** squeamishness

disgusted 5 fed up **8** offended, repelled, repulsed, revolted, sickened **9** nauseated, squeamish **10** grossed out

disgusting 4 foul, icky, vile **5** gross, nasty, yucky **7** noisome **9** loathsome, offensive, repellent, repugnant, repulsive, revolting, sickening **10** nauseating

dish 4 bowl, buzz, food, talk, tray **5** plate **6** course, gossip, tureen **7** chatter, hearsay, platter, scandal, slander **9** casserole, container **11** scuttlebutt ***baked:*** **7** soufflé ***baking:*** **7** cocotte, scallop **9** casserole **12** scallop shell ***cheese:*** **6** fondue **7** ramekin, rarebit **8** raclette, ramequin ***Chinese:*** **6** dim sum, lo mein, subgum, wonton **8** chop suey, chow mein **10** egg foo yong, egg foo yung **11** egg foo young ***deep:*** **9** casserole ***Hungarian:*** **7** goulash ***Italian:*** **5** pasta, penne, pesto, pizza **6** scampi **7** cannoli, lasagna, polenta, ravioli **8** calamari, linguine, linguini, osso buco, rigatoni **9** foccaccia, manicotti **10** cannelloni, scaloppine, tortellini **11** saltimbocca ***Japanese:*** **5** sushi **7** sashimi, tempura **8** sukiyaki ***Mexican:*** **4** taco **5** chili **6** fajita, flauta, nachos, tamale **7** burrito, chalupa **8** frijoles **9** enchilada, guacamole **10** carne asada **11** chimichanga **12** refried beans **13** chili con carne ***Middle Eastern:*** **5** kebab, kibbe, kibbi **6** hummus, kibbeh **7** falafel **8** couscous, moussaka **10** shish kebab **11** baba ghanouj **12** baba ghanoush ***principal:*** **6** entrée ***rice:*** **5** pilaf **7** risotto ***Scottish:*** **5** brose **6** haggis ***shallow:*** **6** saucer ***Thai:*** **7** pad thai

disharmonize 3 jar, war **5** clash **6** jangle **7** discord **8** conflict, mismatch **9** disaccord

disharmony 6 strife **7** discord **8** conflict, disunion, disunity, friction, variance **9** cacophony **10** contention, difference, dissension, dissonance

dishearten 3 cow **5** chill, crush, daunt, shake **6** dampen, deject, dismay, sadden **7** depress, unnerve **8** dispirit, distress **10** demoralize, discourage, intimidate

dishes 4 ware ***clay:*** **7** pottery ***porcelain:*** **5** china

dishevel 5 touse **6** muss up, rumple, tousle **8** disarray, disorder **10** disarrange, discompose

disheveled 5 messy **6** mussed **7** unkempt **8** ill-kempt, uncombed

dishonest 5 false, lying, rogue, snide **6** tricky, unfair **7** corrupt, crooked, knavish **8** cheating, cozening, two-faced **9** deceitful, deceiving, deceptive, swindling **10** defrauding, fraudulent, mendacious, untruthful **13** double-dealing, untrustworthy

dishonesty 5 fraud, guile **6** deceit **7** falsity, knavery, roguery **8** flimflam, pretense, trickery **9** chicanery, deception, duplicity, falsehood, hypocrisy **10** corruption **11** crookedness **13** double-dealing

dishonor see **disgrace**

dishonorable see **disgraceful**

dish out 5 ladle, serve **6** pile on, supply **7** deliver, present, serve up **8** allocate, disburse, dispense **10** distribute

disillusioned see **disenchanted**

disinclination 7 dislike **8** aversion, distaste **9** antipathy, objection **10** reluctance **13** indisposition, unwillingness

disinclined 5 loath **6** averse **7** opposed **8** hesitant **9** reluctant, resistant, unwilling **10** indisposed

disinfect 6 purify **8** sanitize **9** autoclave, sterilize **13** decontaminate

disingenuous 3 sly **4** foxy, wily **5** false **6** artful, crafty, tricky **7** cunning, devious, feigned **8** delusive, guileful, indirect, specious **9** deceitful, deceiving, deceptive, dishonest, insidious, insincere, sophistic **10** misleading **11** calculating, casuistical, sophistical

disinherit 6 cut off **7** bereave, exclude **9** deprive of, repudiate **10** dispossess

disintegrate 3 rot **4** turn **5** break, burst, decay, spoil, taint **6** molder **7** crumble, scatter, shatter **8** splinter **9** break down, decompose, fall apart **10** deliquesce

disinter 5 dig up **6** exhume, unbury **7** unearth **8** exhumate **9** resurrect

disinterest 6 apathy **7** neglect **8** coolness, lethargy **9** aloofness, disregard, unconcern **10** detachment, dispassion, neutrality **11** impassivity, inattention, insouciance, nonchalance, objectivity **12** indifference

disinterested 4 fair, just **5** aloof **6** candid **7** neutral **8** detached, unbiased **9** impartial, impassive, incurious, objective **10** evenhanded, impersonal, neglectful, nonchalant **11** inattentive, indifferent, unconcerned

disjoin 4 part **5** sever, unfix **6** detach, divide, sunder, unlink **7** break up, divorce **8** disunite, separate, uncouple, unfasten **9** disengage, take apart **10** dissociate **12** disaffiliate, disassociate

disjointed 7 jumbled, muddled **8** confused, inchoate, rambling **9** displaced **10** disordered, incoherent, incohesive **11** unconnected, unorganized **13** discontinuous

disk 4 puck **5** wafer **6** record ***metal:*** **4** slug ***ornamental:*** **6** bangle, sequin

dislike 4 shun **5** scorn, spurn **6** animus, oppose, reject, resent **7** deplore, frown on **8** aversion, disfavor, distaste **9** animosity, antipathy **10** alienation, disapprove, repugnance **11** disapproval

dislimn 3 dim **5** bedim **6** darken **7** becloud, obscure **9** obfuscate

dislocate 5 break **7** disrupt, unhinge **9** disengage **10** disconnect **13** disarticulate

dislodge 4 oust **5** eject, evict, expel **6** remove, uproot **8** displace, drive out, force out

disloyal 5 false **6** untrue **8** apostate, recreant **9** alienated, faithless **10** perfidious, traitorous, unfaithful **11** disaffected, treacherous

disloyalty 7 falsity, perfidy, treason **8** apostasy **9** falseness, recreancy, treachery **10** alienation, infidelity **12** disaffection **13** faithlessness

dismal 4 grim **5** bleak, drear **6** dreary, gloomy, horrid, somber, sombre **7** joyless **8** desolate, dreadful, funereal, lowering **9** atrocious, cheerless, depressed, tenebrous **10** depressing, depressive **11** dispiriting **12** discouraging **13** disheartening

dismantle 4 raze, undo **5** strip, unrig, wreck **6** denude, divest **7** break up, destroy **8** demolish, pull down, take down **9** break down, knock down, take apart **11** disassemble

dismay 4 faze, fear **5** abash, alarm, daunt, dread, panic, scare, shake, upset **6** appall, fright, horror, rattle **7** agitate, fluster, horrify, perturb, unnerve **8** affright, bewilder, confound, dispirit, distress, frighten **9** discomfit, dumbfound, embarrass **10** discompose, disconcert, discourage, dishearten **11** trepidation **12** perturbation **13** consternation

dismayed 5 upset **6** afraid, aghast, scared, shaken **7** fearful, shocked **9** disturbed

dismember 4 maim **5** cut up **7** disjoin, dissect **8** mutilate **9** dismantle, take apart

dismiss 2 ax **3** axe, can **4** drop, fire, oust, sack, shed **5** chuck, eject, evict, let go, scorn, spurn **6** bounce, depose, deride, lay off, reject, remove, retire, shelve, unseat **7** boot out, cashier, contemn, decline, disband, kick out, kiss off, turn off **8** displace, furlough, pooh-pooh, ridicule, throw out, turn away, turn down **9** discharge, repudiate, terminate **11** send packing

dismissal 5 congé **6** firing, layoff, ouster **7** removal **8** brush-off, bum's rush **9** discharge, expulsion **10** cashiering

dismount 6 alight, debark, get off **7** deplane, detrain **9** disembark **10** alight from **11** descend from

Disney, Walt 10 cartoonist ***character:*** **4** Gyro, Huey, Lady, Nemo **5** Ariel, Bambi, Daisy, Dewey, Dumbo, Goofy, Louie, Mulan, Pluto, Simba, Tramp **6** Beauty, Donald, Mickey, Minnie, Mowgli **7** Aladdin, Scrooge **9** Gladstone, Pinocchio, Snow White **10** Beagle Boys, Clarabelle, Pocahontas ***classic:*** **5** Bambi, Dumbo **8** Fantasia **9** Pinocchio **10** Jungle Book (The) **15** Lady and the Tramp

disobedient 6 unruly **7** naughty, wayward, willful **8** contrary **10** headstrong, ill-behaved, rebellious, refractory **11** misbehaving, uncompliant **12** contumacious, noncompliant, obstreperous, recalcitrant **13** insubordinate

disoblige 5 annoy **6** bother, offend, put out **7** affront, disturb, trouble **9** displease, incommode **10** discommode **13** inconvenience

disorder 3 ill **4** mess, riot **5** chaos, havoc, mix up, snarl, upset **6** ataxia, hubbub, jumble, malady, mess up, muddle, muss up, ruckus, rumple, tumble, tumult, unrest, uproar **7** ailment, anarchy, clutter, confuse, disease, embroil, illness, misdeed, shuffle, turmoil **8** disarray, sickness, syndrome, unsettle, upheaval **9** affection, agitation, commotion, complaint, confusion, infirmity **10** affliction, turbulence, untidiness ***mental:*** **5** mania **8** delirium, insanity, neurosis, paranoia **9** psychosis **11** psychopathy **13** schizophrenia

disordered 6 roiled **7** chaotic, jumbled, muddled **8** confused, inchoate, shuffled **9** displaced **10** disjointed, dislocated, incoherent, incohesive **11** disarranged, unconnected, unorganized **13** discontinuous

disorderly 5 rowdy **6** unruly, untidy **7** jumbled, raucous, unkempt **8** confused **9** cluttered, offensive, turbulent **10** boisterous, topsy-turvy, tumultuous **12** disorganized, rambunctious, unsystematic

disorganize 5 upset **6** jumble, mess up **7** break up, confuse, derange, disband, disrupt **8** disorder, disperse, unsettle **10** disarrange

disoriented 4 lost **7** mixed up **8** confused **9** displaced, perplexed, unsettled **10** bewildered

disown 4 deny, dump **6** desert, reject **7** cast off, disavow **8** disclaim, renounce **9** repudiate

disparage 5 decry **6** defame, slight **7** condemn, degrade, devalue, dismiss, put down, run down **8** bad-mouth, belittle, derogate, discount, downplay, minimize, pooh-pooh **9** denigrate, deprecate, discredit, dispraise, downgrade, underrate **10** demoralize, depreciate, undervalue **11** detract from

disparagement 5 scorn **7** calumny, censure, despite, scandal, slander **8** contempt, despisal, reproach **9** aspersion, discredit, stricture **10** backbiting, defamation, derogation, detraction, diminution **11** degradation **12** backstabbing, depreciation **13** animadversion

disparate 6 at odds, divers, unlike, varied **7** diverse, unalike, unequal, various, varying **8** discrete, distinct, separate **9** different, divergent, unsimilar **10** dissimilar **11** distinctive, incongruous, inconsonant **12** incompatible, inconsistent

disparity 3 gap **8** contrast **9** imbalance **10** difference, divergence, divergency, inequality **11** discrepancy **13** disproportion, dissimilarity

dispassionate 4 calm, fair, just **7** neutral **8** composed, detached, unbiased **9** equitable, impartial, objective, unruffled **10** impersonal **11** unemotional **12** unprejudiced **13** disinterested

dispatch 4 kill, send, ship, slay **5** haste, hurry, scrag, speed **6** defeat, murder **7** bump off, execute, forward, killing, message, put away **8** alacrity, get rid of, shipment, transmit **9** dispose of, eliminate, swiftness **10** expedition, put to death, speediness **11** assassinate, promptitude

dispel 6 banish **7** cast out, scatter **8** disperse **9** clear away, dissipate, drive away

dispensable 5 minor **7** trivial **8** needless, unneeded **10** disposable, expendable, unrequired **11** superfluous, unessential, unimportant, unnecessary **12** nonessential

dispensary 6 clinic

dispensation 4 plan **5** favor, share **7** license, portion, service **8** bestowal, courtesy, kindness, ordering **9** allotment, exception, exemption, privilege, remission **10** indulgence, management **12** disbursement, distribution **13** apportionment, authorization

dispense 5 allot, apply, wield **6** assign, divide, excuse, exempt, ration, supply **7** absolve, deal out, deliver, dish out, dole out, furnish, give out, mete out, portion, provide, release **8** allocate, carry out, disburse, share out, transfer **9** apportion, discharge, partition **10** administer, distribute, measure out, portion out

disperse 3 sow **5** spray, strew **6** dispel, divide, spread, vanish **7** break up, diffuse, disband, radiate, scatter **9** broadcast, dissipate, partition, propagate **10** distribute

dispersion 6 spread **7** breakup, colloid **9** diffusion, spreading **10** scattering **11** dissipation **12** distribution **13** dissemination

dispirit 3 cow **5** chill, daunt **6** deject, dismay, sadden **7** depress, oppress **8** distress **10** demoralize, discourage, dishearten

dispirited 3 low, sad **4** blue, down, glum **5** cowed **6** morose **7** daunted **8** cast down, dejected, dismayed, downcast, saddened **9** bummed out, depressed, oppressed, woebegone **10** distressed, melancholy **11** crestfallen, demoralized, discouraged, downhearted **12** disconsolate, disheartened

dispiriting 4 blue **6** dismal, dreary, gloomy **8** daunting, dolorous, funereal **9** cheerless, dismaying, saddening **10** depressing, oppressive **12** demoralizing, disconsolate, discouraging **13** disheartening

displace 4 oust, sack **5** exile, expel, usurp **6** banish, deport, depose, remove **7** succeed **8** dethrone, supplant **9** supersede, transport **10** expatriate, substitute

display 4 pomp, show **5** array, model **6** evince, expose, flaunt, lay out, parade, reveal, spread, unfold, unfurl, unveil **7** exhibit, panoply, present, showing, show off, trot out, uncover **8** brandish, evidence, manifest, showcase **9** showiness, spectacle **10** exhibiting, exhibition **11** demonstrate, ostentation **13** demonstration, manifestation

displeasing 6 vexing **7** irksome **8** annoying **10** bothersome, unpleasant **12** disagreeable **13** objectionable

displeasure 5 anger **8** aversion, disfavor, vexation **9** annoyance **10** discomfort, discontent, irritation, uneasiness **11** indignation, unhappiness **13** indisposition

disport 4 show **5** amuse **6** acquit, behave, divert, expose, flaunt, frolic, parade **7** conduct, display, exhibit, show off, trot out **9** entertain

disposal 5 order **7** removal **8** bestowal, chucking, jettison, ordering, transfer **9** clearance **10** allocation, assignment, demolition, discarding, regulation, relegation **11** arrangement, consignment, destruction, disposition **12** distribution, transference

dispose 4 bend, bias, rank **5** array, order, range **6** settle **7** arrange, incline, marshal, prepare **8** organize, regulate **9** make ready **11** systematize ***of:*** **4** dump, junk, sell **5** chuck, scrap **6** finish, handle, unload **7** deep-six, destroy, discard **8** deal with, throw out, transfer **9** eighty-six, eliminate **10** distribute

disposed 3 apt **4** fain, game **5** prone, ready **6** biased, minded **7** partial, willing **8** arranged, inclined **9** persuaded

disposition 4 bent, cast, mood, tone, type, vein **5** being, order, stamp **6** makeup, nature, temper **7** control, leaning, mind-set **8**

ordering, penchant, riddance, sequence, tendency, transfer **9** character, direction **10** management, proclivity, propensity, settlement **11** arrangement, inclination, personality, temperament **12** constitution, predilection **13** individuality ***favorable:*** **8** optimism ***unfavorable:*** **9** pessimism

dispossess 3 rob **4** oust **5** eject, evict, strip **6** divest **7** bereave, deprive

dispossession 4 loss **6** ouster **7** seizure **9** privation **10** divestment **11** deprivation, divestiture **13** expropriation

dispraise 3 pan **5** decry **6** censor, deride, dump on **7** put down, run down **8** badmouth, belittle, derogate **9** criticize, deprecate, discredit, disparage **10** depreciate, disapprove **11** detract from **12** depreciation

disproportion 8 imparity, mismatch **9** disparity **10** inequality, unevenness **12** lopsidedness

disproportionate 6 uneven **7** unequal **8** lopsided **10** unbalanced

disprove 5 belie, rebut **6** refute, negate **7** confute, explode **8** confound, overturn, puncture, traverse **9** discredit, overthrow **10** invalidate

disputable 4 iffy, moot **7** dubious **8** arguable, doubtful **9** debatable, uncertain, unsettled **10** unresolved **11** problematic **12** questionable **13** controversial

disputation 6 debate **8** argument, forensic, polemics **9** dialectic **11** controversy **13** argumentation

dispute 4 buck, duel, moot, tiff **5** argue, fight, rebut, repel **6** bicker, combat, debate, hassle, impugn, negate, oppose, refute, resist, rumpus, strife **7** confute, contend, contest, discuss, gainsay, quarrel, quibble, wrangle **8** argument, conflict, question, squabble **9** bickering, challenge, thrash out, withstand **10** contention, controvert, falling-out **11** altercation, controversy, embroilment

disputed 7 debated **8** arguable **9** contested, uncertain **12** questionable **13** controversial

disqualified 5 unfit **8** unfitted **10** ineligible, unequipped

disqualify 3 bar **5** debar **6** except **7** exclude, rule out, suspend **9** eliminate ***as judge:*** **6** recuse

disquiet 5 alarm, angst, upset, worry **6** bother, flurry, unease, unrest **7** agitate, anxiety, concern, disturb, ferment, fluster, perturb, trouble, turmoil **10** discompose, uneasiness **11** disturbance, restiveness **12** restlessness **13** Sturm und Drang

disquietude 4 care **5** worry **6** unease, unrest **7** anxiety, concern, ferment, turmoil **9** agitation, misgiving **10** foreboding, uneasiness **11** nervousness, restiveness **12** apprehension, restlessness **13** Sturm und Drang

Disraeli, Benjamin *novel:* 5 Sybil **7** Lothair, Tancred **8** Endymion **9** Coningsby ***opponent:*** **4** Peel (Robert) **9** Gladstone (William) ***queen:*** **8** Victoria

disregard 4 skip **6** forget, ignore, slight **7** neglect, tune out **8** overlook **9** unconcern **12** heedlessness, indifference

disregardful 3 lax **5** slack **6** remiss **8** careless, derelict, heedless **9** forgetful, unheeding, negligent, unmindful **10** neglectful, regardless, unthinking **11** indifferent, unconcerned **12** absent-minded

disremember 6 forget

disreputable 4 base **5** dingy, seamy, seedy, shady **6** scurvy, shabby, shoddy, sordid **7** run-down **8** decrepit, infamous, shameful **10** inglorious **11** dilapidated, disgraceful, ignominious **12** contemptible, unprincipled **13** discreditable, unrespectable

disrepute 5 odium, shame **7** obloquy **8** disfavor, disgrace, dishonor, ignominy **9** disesteem **10** opprobrium

disrespect 6 insult **7** disdain **8** boldness, contempt, rudeness **9** disregard, flippancy, impudence, insolence **10** incivility **11** discourtesy, presumption **12** impertinence, impoliteness

disrespectful 4 flip, rude **5** sassy, saucy **7** ill-bred, uncivil **8** flippant, impolite, impudent, insolent **10** ungracious **11** ill-mannered, impertinent **12** contemptuous, discourteous

disrobe 4 bare, peel **5** strip **6** denude, divest **7** undress **8** unclothe

disrupt 5 upset **6** mess up **7** break up, rupture **8** disorder, unsettle

dissatisfaction 6 dismay **9** annoyance, complaint **10** discontent, irritation, uneasiness **11** displeasure, frustration

dissatisfied 5 irked, vexed **7** annoyed, unhappy **8** bothered **10** begrudging, discontent, displeased, malcontent **11** complaining, disaffected, unfulfilled **12** disappointed, discontented, malcontented

dissect 5 probe, study **7** analyze, examine, inspect **9** anatomize, break down, take apart **10** scrutinize

dissection 7 autopsy **8** analysis, necropsy ***of animals:*** **7** zootomy

dissemble 4 hide, mask **5** cloak, feign **7** conceal, cover up, dress up, falsify **8** disguise, simulate **9** whitewash **10** camouflage **11** counterfeit

dissembler 4 fake **5** faker, fraud, phony **8** deceiver, imposter, impostor, pharisee **9** hypocrite, pretender

disseminate 3 sow **5** strew **6** blazon, spread **7** bestrew, diffuse, pass out, publish, scatter, send out **8** announce, disperse, proclaim **9** advertise, broadcast, circulate, propagate, publicize **10** promulgate

dissension 5 fight **6** strife **7** discord, dispute, faction, quarrel, wrangle **8** argument, clashing, conflict, disunity, friction, variance **9** bickering **10** contention, difference, quarreling **11** altercation, controversy **12** disagreement

dissent 5 demur **6** differ, heresy, object **7** protest **8** conflict, variance **9** misbelief **10** contention, difference, heterodoxy, opposition, resistance **11** unorthodoxy **12** nonagreement **13** nonconformism, nonconformity

dissenter 7 heretic **8** apostate, defector, deserter, partisan, recreant **10** schismatic, separatist **11** misbeliever, schismatist **13** nonconformist

dissertation 6 thesis **8** tractate, treatise **9** discourse, monograph **10** commentary, exposition **11** disputation **12** disquisition **13** argumentation

dissever 3 cut, hew **4** hack, part **5** carve, slice, split **6** cleave, detach, divide, sunder **7** disjoin, divorce **8** disjoint, disunite, separate, uncouple **10** disconnect

dissidence 6 heresy, schism, strife **7** discord, dispute, dissent, faction **8** conflict, friction, variance **10** contention, disharmony, dissension, heterodoxy, opposition **11** discordance, unorthodoxy **12** disagreement **13** nonconformism, nonconformity

dissident 7 heretic **8** partisan, recusant **9** differing, dissenter, heretical, heterodox, protestor **10** schismatic, separatist, unorthodox **11** contentious, disagreeing, misbeliever, nonbeliever, quarrelsome, schismatist **12** disputatious, unharmonious **13** nonconformist

dissimilar 6 unlike **7** diverse, unalike, unequal, various **8** distinct **9** different, disparate, divergent **13** heterogeneous

dissimilarity 8 contrast, variance **9** disparity, diversity, variation **10** difference, divergence, divergency, unlikeness **11** incongruity **13** heterogeneity, inconsistency

dissimulate see **dissemble**

dissimulation 5 fraud, guile, lying **6** deceit **7** cunning **8** artifice, flimflam, pretense **9** deception, duplicity, hypocrisy, mendacity, sophistry **10** craftiness, pharisaism **11** beguilement, smoke screen

dissipate 4 blow **5** use up, waste **6** burn up, spread, vanish **7** break up, scatter **8** disperse, evanesce, melt away, misspend, squander **9** evaporate, throw away **11** fritter away

dissipated 6 rakish, wanton, wasted **8** depraved **9** debauched, reprobate **10** degenerate, licentious, profligate **11** intemperate

dissociate 4 part **5** unfix **6** cut off, detach **7** disband, disjoin **8** alienate, disunite, estrange, separate, uncouple **9** disengage **10** disconnect

dissolute 3 lax **4** fast, wild **5** loose, slack **6** rakish, wanton **7** raffish, wayward **8** decadent, depraved **9** abandoned, debauched, indulgent, reprobate **10** degenerate, dissipated, licentious, profligate **12** unprincipled, unrestrained

dissolution 5 death, decay, split **6** demise **7** breakup, divorce, rupture, split-up **8** division **9** dispersal, partition **10** detachment, disbanding, profligacy **11** evaporation **12** liquefaction

dissolvable 7 soluble **8** meltable

dissolve 3 end **4** flux, melt, thaw, undo, void **5** annul, quash **6** recess, vacate, vanish **7** adjourn, break up, diffuse, liquefy **8** abrogate, disperse, evanesce, fade away, get rid of, melt away, prorogue, separate **9** decompose, dissipate, evaporate, prorogate, terminate, waste away **10** deliquesce, do away with **12** disintegrate

dissonance 6 strife **7** discord **8** clashing, conflict **9** cacophony, harshness **10** contention, difference, disharmony **11** incongruity **12** disagreement **13** inconsistency

dissonant 5 harsh **7** grating, jarring, raucous **8** strident **9** unmusical **10** cacophonic, discordant, inharmonic **11** cacophonous, conflicting, incongruous **12** incompatible, inharmonious

dissuade 5 deter **7** turn off **10** discourage, disincline

distaff 6 female **8** maternal

distance 4 area **5** ambit, lapse, orbit, range, reach, scope, space, sweep **6** course, degree, extent, length, radius, remove, spread **7** breadth, compass, expanse, horizon, mileage, reserve, spacing, stretch **8** interval **9** amplitude, disparity, expansion, extension **10** divergence, divergency, remoteness, separation **11** distinction ***between levels:*** **4** drop ***between rails:*** **4** gage ***between supports:*** **4** span ***from bottom to top:*** **6** height ***geometric:*** **8** altitude ***greatest perpendicular:*** **6** camber ***measuring instrument:*** **8** odometer **9** pedometer, telemeter **11** range finder ***perpendicular:*** **5** depth ***shortest:*** **7** beeline **12** straight line

distant 3 far, shy **4** afar, cold, cool **5** aloof, apart **6** absent, far-off, remote **7** faraway, haughty, obscure, removed, spacial, spatial **8** far-flung, isolated, outlying, reserved, secluded, solitary **9** separated, unsimilar, withdrawn **10** unsociable **11** out-of-the-way, sequestered, standoffish ***combining form:*** **3** tel **4** tele, telo

distaste 7 disgust, dislike **8** aversion, loathing **9** antipathy, hostility, revulsion **10** abhorrence, repugnance **13** indisposition

distasteful 8 unsavory **9** loathsome, obnoxious, offensive, repellent, repugnant, repulsive **10** abominable, unpleasant **11** displeasing, unpalatable **12** disagreeable, unappetizing **13** objectionable

distemper 6 malady **7** ailment, disease **8** disorder **9** contagion, strangles **10** affliction **11** derangement **13** panleucopenia

distend 5 bloat, bulge, swell, widen **6** dilate, expand, extend, puff up **7** amplify, augment, enlarge, inflate, stretch **8** increase, lengthen **10** stretch out

distill 6 refine **7** extract **8** boil down **11** concentrate, precipitate

distinct 4 sole **5** clear, lucid, plain **6** marked, patent, single, unique **7** audible, defined, diverse, evident, express, notable, obvious, special, unusual **8** apparent, clear-cut, definite, discrete, especial, explicit, manifest, palpable, peculiar, separate, specific **9** different, divergent **10** individual, noticeable, particular **11** categorical, unambiguous, unequivocal **12** unmistakable

distinction 4 bays, rank **5** award, badge, grade, honor, kudos **6** nicety, renown **7** laurels **8** accolade, eminence, prestige **10** difference, divergence, divergency, prominence, unlikeness **11** differentia, peculiarity, preeminence, recognition **12** significance **13** dissimilarity

distinctive 6 proper, single, unique **7** special, unusual **8** peculiar, separate, singular **10** individual **13** idiosyncratic

distingué 6 classy, urbane **7** courtly, elegant, eminent, genteel, refined **8** cultured, decorous, highbrow, mannerly, polished, well-bred **9** dignified, high-class **10** cultivated **13** sophisticated

distinguish 4 mark, note, spot, view **5** honor, place **6** descry, notice, set off **7** dignify, make out, mark off, observe, pick out **8** classify, identify, perceive, separate **9** recognize, single out **10** categorize **12** characterize, discriminate **13** differentiate, individualize

distinguished 5 famed, noted **6** famous **7** eminent, notable, stately **8** esteemed, imposing, renowned **9** dignified, prominent **10** celebrated **11** illustrious

distort 4 bend, skew, warp, wind **5** alter, color, twist **6** deform, garble **7** contort, falsify, pervert, torture **8** misstate **11** misconstrue **12** misinterpret, misrepresent

distortion 8 twisting **9** deformity

distract 5 addle, mix up **6** ball up, bemuse, divert, puzzle **7** confuse, fluster, mislead, perplex **8** befuddle, bewilder, confound, throw off **9** sidetrack, unbalance

distracted 8 confused, deranged, maddened, troubled **9** oblivious **10** nonplussed **11** disoriented, inattentive, preoccupied **12** absent-minded

distraction 5 upset **9** agitation, amusement, confusion, diversion **10** perplexity **12** interruption **13** entertainment

distrait 5 upset **7** anxious, bemused, faraway, worried **8** confused, deranged, harassed, maddened, troubled **9** tormented, withdrawn **10** abstracted, distracted, distraught **11** inattentive, preoccupied **12** absent-minded, apprehensive

distraught 5 upset **6** addled, crazed **7** anxious, frantic, muddled, rattled, shook up, unglued, worried **8** agitated, confused, demented, deranged, frenzied, harassed, troubled, worked up **9** flustered, perturbed, tormented, wigged-out **10** distressed, bewildered, freaked out, nonplussed **11** overwrought

distress 3 ail, irk, mar, try, vex, woe **4** ache, care, hurt, pain, pang, rack **5** agony, annoy, cross, dolor, grief, rigor, throe, trial, upset, worry **6** bother, grieve, harass, misery, pester, plague, sorrow, strain, strait, twinge **7** afflict, anguish, anxiety, exhaust, torment, torture, trouble **8** aggrieve, calamity, exigency, hardship **9** adversity, constrain, hard times, suffering **10** affliction, difficulty, heartbreak, misfortune, visitation **11** tribulation, vicissitude ***call:*** **6** Mayday ***signal:*** **3** SOS **5** alarm

distressing 4 dire **6** woeful **8** alarming, grievous, shocking **9** offensive **10** deplorable, lamentable **11** dispiriting, regrettable, unfortunate **13** heartbreaking

distribute 4 deal, mete **5** allot, place, strew **6** assign, assort, divide, donate, parcel, ration, spread **7** deal out, deliver, diffuse, dish out, divvy up, dole out, dribble, give out, hand out, mete out, prorate, radiate, scatter, slice up **8** allocate, classify, disburse, dispense, deposition, separate **9** apportion, circulate, partition, propagate, spread out **10** administer, measure out **11** disseminate

distribution 7 density **8** delivery, dividend, grouping, ordering, sequence **9** allotment, allotting, diffusion, dispersal, marketing, placement, spreading **10** dispersion, scattering **11** arrangement, probability, propagation **12** apportioning, dispensation **13** apportionment, dissemination

distributor 5 agent **6** broker, jobber **7** carrier **9** middleman **10** wholesaler **12** intermediate

district 4 area, ward **5** tract **6** barrio, locale, parcel, region, sector **7** borough, quarter, section **8** division, locality, precinct, vicinage, vicinity **11** subdivision **12** neighborhood ***Danish:*** **3** amt ***ecclesiastical:*** **5** synod **6** parish **7** diocese ***Greek:*** **4** deme ***Indian:*** **6** tahsil ***judicial:*** **7** circuit ***London:*** **4** Soho **7** Chelsea, Mayfair **9** Docklands, Greenwich, Southwark **10** Kensington, Piccadilly **11** Canary Wharf, Notting Hill **13** Knightsbridge ***New York:*** **4** Soho **7** Chelsea, Tribeca ***theater:*** **6** rialto

District of Columbia *college, university:* 6 Howard **8** American, Catholic **9** Gallaudet **10** Georgetown ***motto:*** **13** E Pluribus Unum ***official bird:*** **10** wood thrush ***official flower:*** **18** American Beauty rose

distrust 5 doubt **7** suspect **8** question, wariness **9** disbelief, discredit, misgiving, suspicion **10** disbelieve

distrustful 4 wary **5** chary, leery **7** cynical, dubious, jealous **8** doubtful, doubting **10** suspicious **12** questionable

disturb 4 faze **5** alarm, daunt, rouse, upset, worry **6** bother, harass, meddle, mess up, pester, stir up **7** agitate, break up, disrupt, fluster, perplex, trouble, unnerve **8** bewilder, distress, unsettle **9** incommode, interrupt **10** discompose, disconcert, tamper with **13** inconvenience, interfere with

disturbance 4 flap, fuss, stir, to-do **5** stink **6** clamor, hubbub, rumpus, tumult, unrest, uproar **7** bobbery, turmoil **8** disorder **9** agitation, commotion, confusion **10** alteration, disruption, turbulence **11** derangement, distraction **12** interruption ***atmospheric:*** **5** storm **7** cyclone, tornado **9** hurricane ***mental:*** **6** frenzy **8** delirium, neurosis **9** psychosis

disturbed 5 upset **6** insane, shaken **7** anxious, puzzled, rattled, worried **8** bothered, demented, deranged, troubled **9** concerned, psychotic, unsettled **10** distracted, distressed **12** disconcerted

disunion 7 divorce, rupture, split-up **8** division, severing, variance **9** partition **10** detachment, difference, separation **13** disconnection

disunite 4 part **6** divide, sunder **7** break up, disjoin, divorce, split up **8** dissever, separate, uncouple **9** disengage, fall apart **10** disconnect **12** disaffiliate

disunity 6 strife, schism **7** discord **8** conflict, division, variance **10** alienation, contention, disharmony, dissension **12** disaffection, disagreement, estrangement

disused 5 passé **8** obsolete, outdated, outmoded **9** abandoned, discarded **10** antiquated, superseded

ditch 3 dig, pit **4** drop, dump, foss, ha-ha, junk, moat **5** chuck, fosse, leave, scrap, swale **6** reject, trench, trough **7** abandon, cashier, discard, dismiss, forsake, foxhole **8** jettison, throw out **9** crash-land, dispose of, throw away **10** excavation

dither 4 fuss, stew **5** quake, shake, tizzy, waver **6** falter, flurry, quaver, shiver **7** flutter, tremble, twitter, whiffle **8** hesitate **9** agitation, commotion, confusion, vacillate **10** excitement, turbulence **12** shilly-shally

dithyramb 4 hymn, poem **5** chant

dithyrambic 6 ardent, fervid **9** perfervid, rhapsodic **10** boisterous, passionate **11** impassioned

ditto 4 copy, idem, same **5** clone, me too, mimeo, repro, Xerox **6** carbon, repeat **7** replica, reprint, similar **9** duplicate, facsimile, photocopy **10** carbon copy, mimeograph **11** replication **12** reproduction **13** reduplication

ditty 3 air, lay **4** song, tune **5** carol, chant **6** ballad

diurnal 5 daily **7** daytime **8** daylight **9** circadian, ephemeral, quotidian

diva 7 goddess **10** prima donna **11** leading lady

divagate 4 turn, veer **5** drift, stray **6** depart, ramble, wander **7** digress, diverge

divan 4 sofa **5** couch **6** settee **7** chamber, council **9** davenport **12** chesterfield

dive 3 bar, pub **4** dash, dump, hole, jump, leap **5** joint, lunge, pitch, sound, swoop **6** header, lounge, plunge, saloon, tavern **7** barroom, decline, descend, descent, hangout, plummet, taproom **8** submerge **9** honky-tonk, roadhouse **10** cannonball ***type:*** **4** pike, swan, tuck **6** gainer **7** cutaway **9** belly flop, jackknife

diver 4 loon

diverge 4 part, vary **5** stray **6** depart, differ, swerve **7** deflect, deviate, digress **8** disagree, separate **9** bifurcate, branch off, draw apart

divergence 7 parting **9** departure, deviation, differing **10** aberration, deflection, difference, digression, separation **11** disagreeing, discrepancy, distinction **12** disagreement
divergent 6 unlike **8** aberrant, abnormal, atypical **9** anomalous, different, differing, disparate, irregular **10** dissimilar
divers 6 sundry **7** several, various **8** assorted **9** different, disparate **13** miscellaneous
diverse 5 mixed **6** motley, sundry, unlike, varied **7** several, unalike, unequal, various, varying **8** assorted, discrete, distinct, manifold, separate **9** different, differing, disparate, multiform, multiplex, unsimilar **10** contrasted, dissimilar **11** contrasting, contrastive **12** multifarious **13** contradictory, miscellaneous ***combining form:*** **4** vari **5** vario ***meanings:*** **8** polysemy
diversion 5 sport **7** pastime, turning **8** pleasure, sideshow **9** amusement, deviation, enjoyment **10** aberration, deflection, recreation, red herring **11** distraction **13** entertainment
diversity 7 variety **10** assortment, difference, unlikeness **11** variegation **12** multiformity **13** dissimilarity, heterogeneity
divert 4 turn, veer **5** amuse **6** regale, swerve **7** beguile, deflect, delight, deviate, digress **8** distract, redirect **9** entertain, turn aside
divest 3 rid, rob **4** free **5** spoil, strip **6** denude **7** bereave, deprive, despoil, disrobe, undress **8** take away **9** dismantle **10** disinherit, dispossess
divide 3 cut **4** fork, part **5** allot, cut up, sever, share **6** assign, cleave, parcel, ration, schism, sunder **7** break up, dissect, divorce, dole out, isolate, prorate, quarter, share in, split up **8** allocate, classify, dispense, disunite, separate **9** apportion, branch out, partition, watershed **10** distribute, measure out **11** dichotomize, distinguish ***into four parts:*** **7** quarter ***into three parts:*** **7** trisect ***into two parts:*** **5** halve **6** bisect **9** bifurcate
divided 4 rent **5** cleft, riven, split **6** cloven **7** asunder, partite **8** ruptured
dividend 5 bonus, share **6** return, reward **7** benefit, guerdon, portion, premium **9** allotment **12** dispensation
divider 6 border, screen **9** partition
divination 6 augury **7** insight **8** prophecy **11** foretelling, soothsaying ***by communication with the dead:*** **10** necromancy ***by figures:*** **8** geomancy ***by lots:*** **9** sortilege ***by numbers:*** **10** numerology ***by rods:*** **7** dowsing **11** rhabdomancy ***by stars:*** **9** astrology
divine 4 holy **5** clerk, godly, infer **6** cleric, deduce, deific, intuit, parson, priest, sacred, superb **7** foresee, godlike **8** clerical, foreknow, foretell, heavenly, luscious, minister, preacher, prophesy, reverend **9** apprehend, churchman, clergyman, marvelous, religious, visualize **10** anticipate, conjecture, sanctified, superhuman, theologian **11** scrumptious **12** ecclesiastic
Divine Comedy *guide:* **6** Vergil, Virgil ***poet:*** **5** Dante (Alighieri) ***section:*** **5** canto **7** Inferno **8** Paradiso **10** Purgatorio
diviner 4 seer **5** augur, sibyl **6** oracle **7** palmist, prophet **8** haruspex **10** forecaster, prophetess, soothsayer
divinity 3 god **5** deity, fudge **7** goddess, godhead, godhood **8** theology
division 3 cut **4** part, unit **5** class, piece, slice, split **6** branch, moiety, parcel, schism, sector **7** breakup, discord, dissent, divorce, parting, portion, rupture, section, segment, split-up **8** category, conflict, district, disunion, disunity, variance **9** partition **10** detachment, difference, disharmony, dissidence, separation **11** dissolution **12** disagreement **13** apportionment ***Bible:*** **5** verse ***book:*** **7** chapter ***British territorial:*** **5** shire ***building:*** **4** wing ***cell:*** **7** meiosis, mitosis ***city:*** **4** ward **7** borough **8** precinct ***contest:*** **4** heat **6** inning, period ***corolla:*** **5** petal ***country:*** **5** state **6** canton **8** province **10** department, prefecture ***family:*** **4** side **6** branch ***geologic time:*** **3** eon, era **5** epoch **6** period ***hospital:*** **4** ward, wing ***into two:*** **9** bisection **11** bifurcation, bipartition ***meal:*** **6** course ***music:*** **3** bar **4** beat **7** measure **8** movement ***opera, play:*** **3** act **5** scena, scene ***poem:*** **5** canto, verse **6** stanza ***population:*** **7** segment, stratum ***race:*** **3** lap **4** heat ***social:*** **5** caste, class, tribe ***state:*** **6** county, parish ***term:*** **8** quotient ***time:*** **3** day, eon **4** week, year **5** month **6** decade, minute, moment, second **7** century, weekend **9** fortnight **10** millennium ***tribal:*** **4** clan ***word:*** **8** syllable ***zodiac:*** **4** sign
divisive 8 factious **11** disunifying
divorce 4 part **5** sever, split **6** divide, sunder **7** break up, breakup, disjoin, rupture **8** disjoint, dissever, disunion, disunite, separate **9** partition, severance **10** detachment, separation **11** dissolution
divot 3 sod **4** turf **5** clump
divulge 4 blab, leak, tell **5** spill **6** betray, expose, gossip, reveal, tattle **7** let slip, uncover **8** disclose, give away
Dixie composer 6 Emmett (Daniel D.)
dizziness 7 vertigo **9** giddiness
dizzy 5 addle, dazed, giddy, mix up, silly, tipsy **6** addled **7** confuse, dazzled, flighty,

foolish, fuddled, muddled, puzzled, reeling **8** confused, swimming, whirling **9** befuddled, confusing **10** bewildered, confounded, distracted, exorbitant, immoderate, inordinate **11** extravagant, light-headed, vertiginous

Djibouti ***language:*** **6** Arabic, French ***monetary unit:*** **5** franc ***neighbor:*** **7** Eritrea, Somalia **8** Ethiopia ***sea:*** **3** Red

DNA ***component:*** **7** adenine, guanine, thymine **8** cytosine **10** nucleotide **11** deoxyribose ***segment:*** **4** exon, gene **7** cistron

doable 8 feasible, possible, workable **9** realistic **10** achievable, attainable **11** performable

do away with 3 end, nix, zap **4** kill, slay **5** annul, erase, whack **6** cancel, finish, murder, remove, repeal, revoke, rub out **7** abolish, bump off, deep-six, destroy, discard, expunge, rescind, squelch, wipe out **8** abrogate, blow away, demolish, dispatch, dissolve, massacre, stamp out **9** dispose of, eliminate, eradicate, extirpate, finish off, liquidate, slaughter **10** extinguish, obliterate **11** discontinue, exterminate

docent 5 guide **6** leader **7** teacher **8** lecturer **10** instructor

docile 4 tame **6** pliant **7** ductile, pliable **8** amenable, biddable, obedient, yielding **9** adaptable, compliant, teachable, tractable **10** submissive **11** acquiescent

dock 3 bob, cut **4** crop, fine, pier, quay, rump, slip **5** berth, jetty, levee, tie up, wharf **6** anchor, hangar, lessen, marina, reduce **7** abridge, landing, shorten **8** cut short, platform, truncate ***worker:*** **6** lumper **9** stevedore **12** longshoreman

docket 4 card **6** agenda, lineup, record **7** program **8** abstract, calendar, caseload, register, schedule **9** timetable

doctor 3 fix, vet **4** mend **5** adapt, alter, medic, treat **6** medico, repair **7** croaker, dentist, falsify, scholar, surgeon **8** sawbones **9** clinician, internist, physician **10** adulterate, specialist **11** medicine man, recondition, reconstruct ***animal:*** **3** vet **12** veterinarian ***children's:*** **12** pediatrician ***famous:*** **4** Koop (C. Everett), Weil (Andrew) **5** Galen, Spock (Benjamin) **6** Atkins (Robert), Chopra (Deepak), Ornish (Dean) **9** Kevorkian (Jack) **10** Schweitzer (Albert) **11** Hippocrates, Livingstone (David) ***foot:*** **10** podiatrist **11** chiropodist ***heart:*** **12** cardiologist ***organization:*** **3** AMA ***teeth:*** **7** dentist **10** exodontist ***women's:*** **12** gynecologist

Doctor of the Church 5 Basil **6** Jerome **7** Ambrose, Gregory **9** Augustine **10** Athanasius

Doctorow novel 7 Ragtime **9** City of God (The) **10** Waterworks, World's Fair **12** Book of Daniel (The) **13** Billy Bathgate **18** Welcome to Hard Times

Doctor Zhivago ***author:*** **9** Pasternak (Boris) ***character:*** **4** Lara **7** Larissa ***film director:*** **4** Lean (David) ***film star:*** **6** Sharif (Omar) **8** Christie (Julie)

doctrinaire 5 rigid **8** dogmatic **9** obstinate **10** unyielding **11** domineering, magisterial **13** authoritarian

doctrine 3 ism **5** axiom, basic, canon, credo, creed, dogma, faith, tenet **7** precept **8** teaching **9** principle **11** fundamental

document 4 deed **5** paper **6** record **8** evidence, monument **9** testimony **10** instrument **11** certificate ***travel:*** **8** passport

dodder 4 limp **5** shake **6** falter, hobble, totter **7** shamble, shuffle, stagger, tremble **12** morning glory

doddering 5 shaky **6** doting, feeble, senile **7** fragile **8** unsteady, weakened **9** faltering

dodge 4 duck, jink, ploy, ruse, slip **5** avert, avoid, elude, evade, fence, parry, shirk, skirt, slide, trick **6** escape, scheme, weasel **7** evasion **8** sidestep **9** avoidance, deception, expedient

Dodger 5 Davis (Tommy) **6** Garvey (Steve), Karros (Eric), Koufax (Sandy), Piazza (Michael), Snider (Duke), Sutton (Don) **8** Newcombe (Don), Robinson (Jackie) **9** Hershiser (Orel) **10** Campanella (Roy) ***field:*** **7** Ebbetts ***home:*** **8** Brooklyn **10** Los Angeles ***manager:*** **6** Alston (Walter) **7** Lasorda (Tommy)

dodger 6 outlaw, screen **7** escapee **8** circular, deceiver, deserter, fugitive, handbill, runagate **9** throwaway

dodgy 4 iffy **5** fishy, vague **6** tricky **7** cryptic, obscure **8** doubtful, unproven **9** ambiguous, enigmatic, uncertain **10** indefinite, suspicious, unreliable **11** problematic **12** questionable **13** controversial

dodo 3 oaf **4** bird, boob, clod, dolt, dope, goof, yo-yo **5** chump, dummy, dunce, idiot, moron, ninny, noddy, stupe **6** dimwit, dumdum, nitwit **7** airhead, dullard, pinhead **8** bonehead, dumbbell, imbecile, lunkhead, meathead, numskull **9** birdbrain, blockhead, ignoramus, lamebrain, numbskull, simpleton **10** dunderhead, nincompoop **11** chowderhead, chucklehead

doe 4 deer **6** female, rabbit **8** kangaroo

doff 4 shed **6** remove **7** take off

dog 3 cur, pom, pug, pup, tag **4** alan, bird,

chow, fice, mutt, peke, puli, tail, tyke **5** Akita, boxer, canid, corgi, dhole, dingo, feist, frank, hound, husky, lemon, pooch, puppy, spitz, trail **6** Afghan, beagle, borzoi, bowwow, briard, canine, collie, detent, poodle, pursue, rascal, saluki, setter, shadow, Talbot, vizsla, wiener, wretch **7** andiron, basenji, harrier, Maltese, mastiff, mongrel, pointer, redbone, Samoyed, Scottie, shar-pei, spaniel, terrier, whippet **8** Airedale, Brittany, elkhound, foxhound, inferior, keeshond, komondor, malamute, malemute, papillon, Pekinese, pinscher, sheepdog, Shiba Inu, spurious, wirehair **9** Chihuahua, dachshund, dalmation, deerhound, Great Dane, greyhound, Lhasa apso, Pekingese, retriever, schnauzer, wolfhound **10** bloodhound, Pomeranian, rottweiler, Weimaraner **11** basset hound, bullmastiff, frankfurter, wienerwurst **12** border collie, Newfoundland, Saint Bernard **13** cocker spaniel ***Bush's:*** **6** Millie ***Buster Brown's:*** **4** Tige ***Charlie Brown's:*** **6** Snoopy ***command:*** **3** sit **4** heel, stay ***Dagwood's:*** **5** Daisy ***Dorothy's:*** **4** Toto ***family:*** **7** Canidae ***FDR's:*** **4** Fala ***fictional:*** **3** Max **4** Buck, Lady **5** Astro, Pluto, Scamp, Tramp **6** Big Red **8** McBarker **9** Marmaduke, Old Yeller, Scooby-Doo, White Fang ***"Garfield":*** **4** Odie ***genus:*** **5** Canis ***Grinch's:*** **3** Max ***L.B.J.'s:*** **3** Her ***monster:*** **8** Barghest ***movie:*** **4** Asta, Lady, Toto **5** Benji, Tramp **6** Lassie **9** Beethoven, Old Yeller, Rin Tin Tin ***name:*** **4** Fido, Spot **5** Rover **6** Bowser ***Nixon's:*** **8** Checkers ***Odysseus's:*** **5** Argos ***of Hades:*** **8** Cerberus ***Orphan Annie's:*** **5** Sandy ***RCA:*** **6** Nipper ***Roy Rogers's:*** **6** Bullet ***Sgt. Snorkel's:*** **4** Otto ***sled command:*** **4** mush ***space traveler:*** **5** Laika ***Steinbeck's:*** **7** Charley ***television:*** **4** King **5** Eddie, Tramp **6** Lassie, Murray **8** Wishbone **9** Rin Tin Tin ***three-headed:*** **8** Cerberus ***tooth:*** **4** fang ***treat:*** **4** bone ***two-headed:*** **6** Orthos ***Wallace's:*** **6** Gromit ***Welsh:*** **5** corgi ***Wendy's:*** **4** Nana ***wild:*** **5** dingo ***young:*** **3** pup **5** puppy, whelp

dog days 6 August **9** canicular

dogfight 3 row **4** fray **5** brawl, broil, melee, set-to **6** fracas, ruckus **7** ruction **10** donnybrook, free-for-all

dogfish 6 bowfin, burbot **8** mud puppy

dogged 7 adamant **8** obdurate, resolute, stubborn **9** insistent, steadfast, obstinate, tenacious, unbending **10** bullheaded, determined, hardheaded, persistent, persisting, unshakable, unyielding **11** persevering, unremitting **12** pertinacious

doggone 4 damn, dang, darn, rank **5** utter **6** cursed, damned, darned **7** blasted, blessed, dratted **8** absolute, accursed, infernal, outright **9** out-and-out **10** confounded **11** unmitigated **13** blankety-blank

dogma 4 code, rule **5** canon, credo, creed, tenet **6** belief, gospel **7** precept **8** doctrine, ideology **9** orthodoxy, postulate, teachings **10** conviction, persuasion

dogmatic 8 oracular, orthodox **9** assertive, canonical, doctrinal **11** dictatorial, doctrinaire, magisterial, opinionated

Dog of Flanders author 5 Ouida

dog-paddle 4 swim

dog's age 3 eon **4** aeon **8** blue moon, eternity

Dog Star 6 Sirius

dogwood 6 cornel, Cornus **8** red osier

do in 4 kill, ruin, slay **5** cheat, wreck **6** defeat, finish, murder, rub out **7** blot out, bump off, destroy, execute, exhaust, frazzle, take out, wear out, wipe out **8** dispatch, knock off, knock out **9** eliminate, liquidate, prostrate, run ragged, shipwreck **11** assassinate

doing 3 act **6** action **8** activity ***good:*** **10** beneficent ***evil:*** **10** maleficent

doit 3 bit, jot **4** coin, damn, dram, drop, hoot, iota, mite, whit **6** trifle **8** particle

doldrums 5 blahs, blues, dumps, ennui, gloom, slump **6** apathy, tedium, torpor **7** boredom **9** dejection **10** depression, inactivity, quiescence, stagnation **12** listlessness

doleful 3 sad **4** down **7** forlorn, ruthful **8** cast down, dejected, dolorous, downcast, grieving, mournful, mourning **9** afflicted, cheerless, depressed, miserable, plaintive, sorrowful, sorrowing, woebegone **10** dispirited, lamentable, lugubrious, melancholy **11** crestfallen, downhearted **12** disconsolate

dole out 4 deal **5** allot **6** divide, parcel, ration **7** divvy up **8** disburse, dispense, disperse **9** apportion, partition **10** administer, distribute

doll 3 Ken **6** Barbie, figure, Kewpie, puppet **7** kachina **10** Betsy Wetsy, Raggedy Ann **11** Raggedy Andy ***grotesque:*** **8** golliwog

dollar 3 one **4** bill, buck, clam, oner, peso **5** taler **6** single **7** ringgit, smacker **8** simoleon **9** cartwheel, greenback

dollop 4 blob, glob, lump **7** portion

Doll's House, A *author:* **5** Ibsen (Henrik) ***heroine:*** **4** Nora

dolly 4 cart **7** stirrer **8** platform **10** locomotive

dolomite 6 marble **9** limestone

dolor 5 agony, grief **6** misery, sorrow **7** anguish, passion **8** distress **9** suffering **10** affliction

dolorous 6 rueful, woeful **7** ruthful **8** grievous, mournful, wretched **9** afflicted, anguished, miserable, plaintive, sorrowful **10** lamentable, lugubrious, melancholy **13** heartbreaking

dolphin 5 whale **7** bollard **8** porpoise

dolt 3 ass, oaf **4** boob, clod, dodo, dork, fool, goof, goon, lout, yo-yo **5** booby, chump, dunce, idiot **6** nitwit **7** dullard, fathead, halfwit, jughead, saphead, schnook **8** bonehead, dumbbell, dummkopf, imbecile, lunkhead, meathead, numskull **9** blockhead, lamebrain, numbskull, simpleton **11** chowderhead

doltish 4 dull, dumb **5** dense, thick **6** oafish, obtuse, stupid **7** idiotic, moronic **8** ignorant, mindless **9** dim-witted, fatheaded, imbecilic

domain 4 fief, land, rule, turf **5** field, realm **6** estate, sphere **7** fiefdom, kingdom, terrain **8** dominion, province **9** bailiwick, territory

dome 4 head, hill, roof **5** mound **6** cupola **7** ceiling, stadium **8** mountain ***shape:*** **4** cone **5** onion

domestic 4 help, home, maid, tame **6** butler, family, native **7** servant **8** houseboy, internal, national **9** charwoman, household **10** indigenous **11** chambermaid

domesticate 4 tame **5** adapt, adopt, train **10** housebreak

domicile 3 pad **4** home **5** abode, house, lodge, put up **6** bestow, billet, harbor **7** quarter **8** dwelling, quarters **9** residence, residency **10** habitation

domiciliate 4 bunk, tame **5** house, lodge, put up **6** billet, harbor, reside **7** quarter

dominance 4 rule, sway **5** power **7** command, control **7** mastery **9** supremacy **10** ascendancy, prepotency **11** preeminence, sovereignty

dominant 4 main **5** chief, first, major **6** ruling **7** leading, supreme **8** foremost, powerful, reigning **9** ascendant, governing, number-one, paramount, prevalent, principal **10** commanding, preeminent, prevailing, surpassing **11** controlling, overbearing **12** preponderant

dominate 4 rule **5** reign **6** direct, govern, obsess **7** control, prevail, repress **8** bestride, hold sway, look down, loom over, overlook **9** subjugate, tower over, tyrannize **10** tower above

domination 4 rule, sway **5** might, power **7** command, control, mastery **9** authority, supremacy **10** ascendancy, prepotency, suzerainty **11** preeminence, sovereignty **13** preponderancy

dominator 4 boss, head **5** chief, ruler **6** honcho, leader, master, top dog **7** headman **8** director, hierarch, kingfish **9** chieftain, commander

domineer 5 bully **6** hector **7** swagger **8** browbeat, bulldoze **9** tyrannize **10** intimidate

domineering 5 bossy **6** lordly **8** arrogant, despotic **9** imperious, masterful **10** autocratic, high-handed, oppressive, tyrannical **11** dictatorial, magisterial, overbearing

Dominica *capital:* **6** Roseau ***discoverer:*** **8** Columbus (Christopher) ***location:*** **10** West Indies ***sea:*** **9** Caribbean

Dominican Republic *capital:* **12** Santo Domingo ***island:*** **10** Hispaniola ***language:*** **7** Spanish ***location:*** **10** West Indies ***monetary unit:*** **4** peso ***mountain:*** **6** Duarte ***neighbor:*** **5** Haiti ***sea:*** **9** Caribbean

dominion 3 raj **4** rule, sway, turf **5** realm, power **6** domain, empery, empire, regnum, sphere **7** demesne, kingdom, terrain **8** province **9** ascendant, ownership, supremacy, territory **10** ascendancy, possession **11** preeminence, sovereignty

domino 4 bone, cape, mask **5** amice, cloak, visor **6** vizard **8** disguise ***spot:*** **3** pip

don 3 sir **4** lord **5** get on, put on, tutor **6** assume, fellow, take on **9** professor, undertake

Donalbain *brother:* **7** Malcolm ***father:*** **6** Duncan

donate 4 give **5** grant **6** bestow, chip in, supply **7** dish out, hand out, present, provide **8** give away, shell out, transfer **10** contribute

donation 3 aid **4** alms, gift **5** grant **7** bequest, handout **8** offering **9** endowment **11** benefaction, beneficence **12** contribution, philanthropy

Don Carlos *author:* **8** Schiller (Friedrich von) ***composer:*** **5** Verdi (Giuseppe) ***father:*** **6** Philip

done 4 over **5** all in, ended, ready, spent **6** bushed, gone by, used up **7** drained, dressed, far-gone, settled, through, worn-out **8** complete, depleted, finished, washed-up **9** completed, concluded, exhausted **10** terminated **12** accomplished ***poetic:*** **3** o'er

donee 7 grantee **8** receiver **9** recipient **11** beneficiary

done for 4 gone, sunk **5** kaput **6** beaten, doomed, ruined **7** wrecked **8** finished, stricken

done in 5 spent **6** bushed, effete, used up **7** drained, far gone, worn-out **8** depleted **9** exhausted, shattered, washed out

Don Giovanni *composer:* **6** Mozart (Wolfgang Amadeus) ***conquest:*** **4** Anna (Donna) **6** Elvira (Donna) **7** Zerlina ***servant:*** **9** Leporello

Donizetti, Gaetano ***hero:*** **7** Roberto (Devereux) ***opera:*** **5** Lucia (di Lammermoor) **10** Anna Bolena, La Favorita **11** Don Pasquale **12** Maria Stuarda

Don Juan **4** rake, roué, wolf **5** Romeo **6** chaser, masher **7** amorist, gallant, playboy, seducer **8** Casanova, lothario, paramour **9** ladies' man, libertine, womanizer **10** ladykiller, profligate **11** philanderer ***drama:*** **10** Stone Guest (The) ***home:*** **7** Seville ***mother:*** **4** Inez ***poet:*** **5** Byron (Lord) **7** Pushkin (Alexander)

donkey **3** ass **4** mule **5** burro **7** jackass ***female:*** **5** jenny **6** jennet

donkeywork **4** moil, toil **5** grind, labor **7** travail **8** drudgery

donnybrook **3** row **4** fray, riot **5** brawl, broil, fight, melee, set-to **6** fracas, ruckus, rumpus, tumult, uproar **7** dispute, quarrel, rhubarb, ruction **10** free-for-all **11** altercation

donor **5** giver, Type O **6** patron **7** granter, grantor **8** bestower **9** conferrer, presenter **10** benefactor **11** contributor

do-nothing **3** bum **4** slug **5** idler **6** loafer, slouch **7** goof-off, slacker **8** deadbeat, fainéant, layabout, slugabed, sluggard **9** lazybones, vegetable **11** couch potato

Don Pasquale composer **9** Donizetti (Gaetano)

Don Quixote ***author:*** **9** Cervantes (Miguel de) ***beloved:*** **8** Dulcinea ***companion (squire):*** **11** Sancho Panza ***giant:*** **8** windmill ***home:*** **8** La Mancha ***horse:*** **9** Rocinante, Rosinante, Rozinante

doodad **5** gizmo, thing **6** bauble, dingus, entity, gadget, gewgaw, jigger, widget **7** trinket, whatsit **8** gimcrack **9** doohickey, thingummy **10** attachment, decoration, knickknack **11** thingamabob, thingamajig, thingumajig

doodle **6** dabble, dawdle, fiddle, potter, putter, sketch, tinker, trifle **7** cartoon, drawing **8** scribble **10** mess around

doodlebug **7** ant lion, missile **8** buzz bomb

doohickey see **doodad**

doom **4** damn, fate, ruin **5** death **6** decree, demise, kismet **7** condemn, destiny, tragedy **8** calamity, disaster, judgment, sentence **11** catastrophe **12** annihilation, last judgment

doomful **4** dire **7** baleful, baneful, direful, fateful, malefic, ominous, unlucky **8** dreadful, ill-fated, sinister **10** foreboding, portentous **11** apocalyptic

doomsayer **7** killjoy **9** Cassandra, defeatist, Gloomy Gus, pessimist

____ **Doone** **5** Lorna

door **3** way **4** adit, exit **5** entry **6** access, egress, entrée, portal **7** gateway, ingress, opening **8** entrance, entryway **9** admission **10** admittance **11** entranceway ***rear:*** **7** postern

doorkeeper **5** usher **6** porter **7** ostiary

doorway **5** entry **6** portal **8** entrance, entryway **11** entranceway

doozy **3** ace, pip **4** lulu **5** beaut, dandy, dilly, peach **6** corker **7** paragon **8** standout **9** humdinger **10** ripsnorter **10** phenomenon **11** crackerjack

dope **3** oaf **4** bozo, clod, dodo, dolt, drug, goof, info, news, yo-yo **5** chump, drugs, dummy, dunce, facts, idiot, moron, ninny, noddy, stupe **6** dimwit, doofus, dum-dum, heroin, nitwit, opiate, sedate, skinny **7** airhead, cocaine, details, dullard, lowdown, pinhead **8** bonehead, dumbbell, imbecile, lunkhead, meathead, narcotic, numskull **9** birdbrain, blockhead, ignoramus, lamebrain, marijuana, narcotize, numbskull, simpleton **10** dunderhead, nincompoop **11** anesthetize, chowderhead, chucklehead, information, preparation

doped **4** high **5** dazed **6** stoned, zonked **7** drugged, tuned-in **8** hopped-up, tripping, turned on, wiped out **9** spaced-out, strung out, stupefied **10** narcotized

dopey **4** dumb **5** silly **6** dulled, stupid, torpid **7** fatuous, fuddled, muddled **8** comatose, sluggish **9** lethargic, senseless, stupefied

Doris ***brother:*** **6** Nereus ***daughters:*** **7** Nereids ***father:*** **7** Oceanus ***husband:*** **6** Nereus

dormancy **5** sleep **6** repose **7** latency, slumber **8** abeyance, diapause, doldrums, downtime **9** torpidity **10** inactivity, quiescence, suspension **11** cold storage **12** intermission, interruption

dormant **5** inert **6** asleep, drowsy, fallow, latent, torpid **7** abeyant **8** comatose, inactive, sluggish **9** lethargic, potential, quiescent, suspended **10** slow-moving, slumbering

dormer **3** bay **4** nook **5** niche **6** window

dorsal **6** aboral **7** abaxial

____ **d'Orsay** **4** Quai

dorsum **4** back

Dorus ***brother:*** **6** Aeolus ***father:*** **6** Hellen

dory **4** bark, boat **5** craft, skiff **6** barque, bateau **7** shallop **8** lifeboat

dose **3** fix, hit **4** dram, shot, slug **7** measure, portion **8** medicate, quantity

Dos Passos trilogy **3** U.S.A.

dossier **4** file **6** folder **9** portfolio

dot **4** mark, mote, stud **5** dower, dowry, point, speck **6** bestud, pepper, period **7** freckle, speckle, stipple **8** flyspeck, sprinkle **9** bespeckle **12** decimal point

dotage 8 senility **11** decrepitude, senectitude
dote on 5 adore, enjoy, fancy, prize **7** cherish, idolize **8** treasure **9** delight in
doting 4 dear, fond, gaga **6** loving **7** adoring, devoted **12** affectionate
dotted 4 semé, sown **6** spotty, strewn **8** punctate, stippled
dotty 4 gaga **5** crazy, loony, wacky **6** absurd, insane **7** foolish, smitten **8** enamored **9** eccentric **10** captivated, enraptured, infatuated **12** preposterous
double 4 copy, dual, fold, mate, tack, twin **5** clone, duple, image, match, twice **6** bifold, binary, duplex, paired, ringer **7** dualize, enlarge, magnify, replica, twofold **8** alter ego, geminate, increase **9** companion, dualistic, duplicate, look-alike, replicate **10** dead ringer, reciprocal, simulacrum, understudy **13** spitting image
double-barreled 4 dual **5** duple **6** bifold, binary, duplex, paired **7** twofold **9** dualistic
double bass 10 bull fiddle
double-cross 3 con **4** dupe **5** cheat, rat on, trick **6** betray, delude, humbug, juggle, take in **7** beguile, deceive, sell out, two-time **8** flimflam, hoodwink **9** four-flush
double dagger 6 diesis
double-dealer 3 gyp **5** cheat, knave **6** con man **7** cozener, diddler, sharper **8** deceiver, swindler **9** defrauder **11** flimflammer **13** confidence man
double-dealing 5 fraud **6** deceit **7** chicane **8** flimflam, trickery **9** chicanery, deceitful, deception, duplicity, two-timing **10** hanky-panky **11** duplicitous
double-dome 7 egghead **8** Einstein, highbrow **10** pointy-head **12** intellectual
double-faced 9 deceitful, deceptive, equivocal, insincere **10** reversible **12** hypocritical **13** untrustworthy
doublet 3 duo **4** dyad, pair, span **5** brace **6** couple, jacket **7** twosome
double-talk 4 bosh, bunk **5** hokum, hooey **6** babble, bunkum, drivel, jabber **7** blather, hogwash, twaddle **8** flimflam, nonsense **9** gibberish, poppycock **10** balderdash **12** gobbledygook
double vision 8 diplopia
doubt 5 qualm **7** concern, dispute, dubiety, suspect **8** distrust, mistrust, question **9** challenge, disbelief, misgiving, suspicion **10** skepticism **11** dubiousness, incertitude, incredulity, uncertainty
doubtable 4 hazy, iffy, moot **7** dubious, suspect **8** arguable **9** ambiguous, debatable, equivocal, uncertain, undecided **10** disputable, borderline, indefinite **11** problematic **12** questionable
doubter 5 cynic **6** Thomas **7** sceptic, skeptic **8** agnostic **10** Pyrrhonist, questioner, unbeliever **11** freethinker
doubtful 4 hazy, iffy, moot **5** fishy, shady, shaky **6** chancy, unsure **7** clouded, dubious, obscure, suspect, unclear **8** arguable, unlikely **9** ambiguous, debatable, dubitable, equivocal, uncertain, undecided, unsettled **10** borderline, disputable, improbable **11** problematic, speculative **12** questionable
doubtfulness 7 concern, dubiety **8** mistrust **9** ambiguity, misgiving, suspicion **10** indecision, skepticism, uneasiness **11** dubiousness, incertitude, uncertainty **13** indeterminacy
doubting Thomas see **doubter**
doubtless 6 likely, surely **7** certain, clearly **8** of course, probably **10** absolutely, definitely, positively, presumably **11** indubitably **12** indisputably **13** presumptively, unequivocally
douceur 3 tip **4** gift **5** bribe **7** present **8** gratuity **9** baksheesh
dough 4 cash **5** bread, money **6** dinero, moolah **7** cabbage, lettuce, scratch **8** currency **11** legal tender ***inflator:*** **5** yeast
doughboy 7 dogface **11** infantryman
doughty 4 bold **5** brave, gutsy, manly, stout **6** daring, heroic, plucky, spunky, strong **7** gallant, valiant **8** fearless, intrepid, resolved, stalwart, unafraid, valorous **9** dauntless, undaunted **10** courageous **12** stouthearted
doughy 3 wan **4** pale **5** pasty, waxen **6** pallid **8** blanched **9** colorless
do up 3 can, fix **4** mend, wash, wrap **5** clean, patch **6** clothe, doctor, fasten, repair, revamp **7** exhaust, festoon, launder, package, prepare, rebuild, wear out **8** decorate, gift wrap, ornament, overhaul **9** embellish **11** recondition, reconstruct
dour 4 glum, grim **5** bleak, harsh, rigid, stern, surly **6** gloomy, morose, severe, strict, sullen **7** austere, crabbed, peevish **9** obstinate, saturnine, stringent **10** forbidding, unyielding
douse 3 sop **4** duck, dunk, soak **5** bathe, drown, plash, slosh, souse **6** drench, put out, quench, splash, strike **7** immerse, slacken **8** inundate, saturate, snuff out, submerge, submerse **10** extinguish
dove 6 culver, pigeon **8** pacifist ***call:*** **3** coo ***genus:*** **7** Columba ***pen:*** **4** cote
dovecote 6 aviary **9** birdhouse
dovetail 3 fit **4** jibe, mesh **5** agree, match, tally **6** accord, splice, square **7** comport,

conform **8** check out **9** harmonize, interlock, intermesh **10** correspond
dovish 4 mild **6** gentle **7** antiwar, pacific **8** pacifist **9** peaceable **10** nonviolent, pacifistic **11** peace-loving **12** conciliatory
dowager 4 dame **5** widow **6** matron **9** matriarch **10** grande dame **11** grandmother
dowdy 4 drab **5** dated, frump, passé, seedy, tacky **6** blowsy, bygone, démodé, frowsy, frowzy, frumpy, old hat, shabby **7** rundown, unkempt **8** frumpish, outdated, outmoded, slattern, slovenly **9** out-of-date, unstylish **10** antiquated, bedraggled, slatternly **11** draggletail **12** old-fashioned **13** draggletailed
dowel 3 bar, peg, pin, rod **5** stick
dower 4 gift **5** endow, endue **6** legacy, talent **8** bequeath
dowitcher 5 snipe **9** sandpiper
do without 5 forgo, waive **6** abjure, eschew, give up, pass up **8** renounce
down 3 eat, fur, ill, low, off, sad **4** blue, fell, fuzz, lint, pile, sick **5** below, ended, floor, floss, fluff, level, lower, under **6** defeat, fallen, finish, lay low, nether **7** conquer, consume, destroy, flatten, swallow, unhappy **8** bowl over, complete, defeated, dejected, dispatch, feathers, finished, inferior, overcome, sluggish, surmount **9** completed, concluded, depressed, earthward, miserable **10** dispirited, groundward
down-and-out 5 broke, needy **6** hard-up, ruined **8** beggared, derelict, homeless **9** destitute, penniless, penurious **12** impoverished
down-and-outer 3 bum **6** beggar, pauper, wretch **7** have-not **9** mendicant **10** supplicant
down-at-heels 4 mean **5** dingy, ratty, seedy, tacky **6** ragged, ragtag, shabby, shoddy **7** ignoble, run-down, worn-out **8** decrepit, tattered **10** bedraggled, threadbare **11** dilapidated **12** deteriorated, disreputable
downbeat 3 low, sad **4** blue, glum **6** droopy, gloomy, morose **7** decline, doleful **8** dejected **9** depressed **10** dispirited, melancholy **11** discouraged, pessimistic **12** disconsolate, disheartened, heavyhearted
downcast 3 low, sad **4** blue, glum, sunk **5** moody, mopey **6** droopy, gloomy, morose **7** doleful, forlorn, unhappy **8** dejected, dismayed, listless, soul-sick, troubled **9** depressed, heartsick, heartsore, miserable, oppressed, woebegone **10** chapfallen, despondent, dispirited, distressed, melancholy, spiritless **11** crestfallen, discouraged, low-spirited **12** disconsolate, disheartened
downfall 4 bane, ruin **6** demise **7** decline, undoing **8** collapse, Waterloo **9** ruination **10** devolution **11** declination, destruction **12** degeneration, dégringolade **13** deterioration
downgrade 4 bump, bust **5** abase, lower **6** demote **7** decline, demerit, descent, devalue **8** belittle, diminish, discount, minimize, relegate **9** denigrate, deprecate, devaluate, discredit, disparage, humiliate **10** depreciate, undervalue **12** degeneration, dégringolade **13** deterioration
downhearted see **downcast**
down-in-the-mouth see **downcast**
down payment 5 token **6** pledge **7** advance, deposit, earnest
downplay 8 belittle, discount, minimize, pooh-pooh **11** de-emphasize
downpour 6 deluge **7** monsoon **8** drencher **9** drenching, rainstorm **10** cloudburst, inundation **11** gully washer
downright 5 blunt, gross, total, truly, utter **7** blatant, flat-out **8** absolute, complete, explicit, positive, thorough **9** out-and-out **10** absolutely, sure-enough **11** indubitable, unequivocal, unmitigated, unqualified **13** thoroughgoing
downslide 3 dip, sag **4** drop, slip **5** slump **7** decline, drop-off, falloff **8** decrease **9** declivity, reduction
downstairs 6 cellar **8** basement
down-to-earth 8 rational **9** practical, pragmatic, realistic **10** hard-boiled, hardheaded, no-nonsense, reasonable **11** common-sense, plain-spoken **12** matter-of-fact **13** unpretentious, unsentimental
downtrend see **downslide**
downtrodden 6 abject, abused **9** oppressed **10** maltreated, mistreated, persecuted, tyrannized
downturn see **downslide**
downward 8 dropping **9** declining **10** descending
downy 4 soft **5** fuzzy **6** fleecy, fluffy **7** velvety **8** feathery ***filler:*** **5** eider
dowry 4 gift **6** talent ***French:*** **3** dot
doxy 4 bawd, drab, moll, slut, tart **5** wench **6** floozy, harlot **7** trollop **8** mistress, slattern **10** prostitute
doyen 4 dean, head **5** chief, maven **6** expert, leader, master, wizard **7** maestro **8** virtuoso **9** authority, patriarch **10** past master
Doyle's detective 6 Holmes (Sherlock)
D'Oyly Carte offering 8 operetta
doze 3 nap **5** sleep **6** catnap, drowse, nod off, snooze **7** drop off, slumber **8** drift off **10** forty winks
dozy see **drowsy**
DP 5 exile **6** émigré **7** evacuee, outcast, refu-

gee **8** deportee, emigrant, fugitive **10** expatriate

drab 4 dull, flat **5** bleak, brown, dingy, faded, mousy, muddy, olive, vapid **6** dismal, dreary, mousey **7** subfusc **8** lifeless **9** cheerless, colorless **10** lackluster **11** dispiriting

draconian 5 cruel, harsh, rigid **6** severe, strict **7** callous **8** ironclad, rigorous, ruthless **9** merciless, stringent **10** inflexible, ironfisted, ironhanded

Dracula author 6 Stoker (Bram)

draft 3 tap **4** dose, haul, plan, plot, pull, pump, swig **5** check, claim, drink, frame, press, swill **6** breeze, call up, demand, design, devise, enlist, enroll, induct, potion, scheme, select, siphon, sketch **7** compose, concoct, current, outline, portion, prepare, project, recruit **8** block out, contrive, rough out, skeleton, traction **9** adumbrate, allowance, blueprint, conscribe, conscript, fabricate, formulate, muster out **11** delineation, skeletonize ***avoider:*** **6** dodger ***of a law:*** **4** bill

drag 3 lug, tow, tug **4** bore, haul, puff, pull, swig **5** dally, delay, draft, shlep, tarry, trail **6** burden, dawdle, harrow, loiter, schlep, search, sledge **7** schlepp **8** friction, straggle **9** lag behind **13** procrastinate

dragging 4 beat, long **5** all in, spent, weary **6** pooped **7** drained, lengthy, tedious **8** drawn-out, extended, fatigued, overlong, sluggish, wiped out **9** exhausted, lethargic, long-drawn, pooped out, prolonged, washed-out, wearisome **10** protracted, slow-moving **12** interminable, long-drawn-out

draggle 3 lag **4** rove **5** stray, trail **8** straggle, trail off **10** fall behind

draggle-tail 4 bawd, drab, slut **5** wench, whore **6** harlot **8** slattern **10** prostitute **11** nightwalker **12** streetwalker

draggletailed 6 blowsy, frowsy, frowzy, sordid, untidy **8** slattern, sluttish **10** slatternly

dragnet 4 trap **5** snare, trawl **7** network

drag off 4 cart, haul

dragon 5 beast **8** basilisk **10** cockatrice ***biblical:*** **5** Rahab ***Canaanite:*** **3** Yam **4** Yamm **5** Lotan ***Chinese:*** **4** lung ***French:*** **8** Tarasque ***genus:*** **5** Draco ***Greek:*** **5** Ladon **9** Eurythion ***slayer:*** **4** Baal, Enki, Zeus **5** Indra **6** Cadmus, George (St.), Marduk, Sigurd **7** Beowulf, Jupiter, Michael (St.), Ninurta, Perseus **8** Margaret (St.) ***Sumerian:*** **3** Kur ***Wagnerian:*** **6** Fafnir

dragoon 3 cow **5** bully **6** badger, coerce, harass, hector **8** bludgeon, browbeat, bulldoze, bullyrag, threaten **9** persecute, strong-arm, terrorize **10** cavalryman, intimidate

drain 3 dry, sap, tap **4** pump, sink, sump, swig, tire, vent, wear **5** bleed, draft, drink, empty, leech, sewer, swill, use up, weary **6** burden, gutter, siphon, trench **7** conduit, culvert, deplete, dwindle, draw off, exhaust, fatigue, outflow **8** bankrupt, draw down, wear down **9** discharge **10** impoverish **11** watercourse

drain away 3 ebb **4** drop, sink, wane **5** abate **6** lessen, reduce, remove **7** draw off, dwindle, retreat, subside **8** decrease, diminish, draw back, taper off, withdraw

drained 4 beat **5** all-in, spent, weary **6** bleary, pooped, used up **7** far-gone, worn-out **8** depleted, dragging, weakened, wiped out **9** exhausted, pooped out, washed-out

drainpipe 4 duct **5** sewer, spout **7** conduit **9** downspout

dram 3 bit, dab, nip, tot **4** atom, dash, drop, iota, jolt, mite, shot, slug, spot, swig, whit **5** crumb, grain, ounce, pinch, scrap, shred, snort, speck **6** morsel, sliver **7** modicum, smidgen, snifter, snippet, soupçon **8** particle

drama 4 play **7** pageant, theater, theatre, tragedy ***award:*** **4** Tony ***former English:*** **6** masque ***Japanese:*** **3** Noh ***main part:*** **8** epitasis ***musical:*** **5** opera **8** operetta, zarzuela ***suspenseful:*** **11** cliff-hanger

dramatic 5 vivid **8** striking, thespian **10** histrionic, theatrical ***conflict:*** **4** agon

dramatis personae 4 cast **5** parts, roles **6** actors, troupe **7** company **10** characters

dramatist 10 playwright ***American:*** **4** Hart (Moss), Inge (William), Rabe (David), Rice (Elmer), Uhry (Alfred) **5** Albee (Edward), Barry (Philip), Foote (Horton), Guare (John), Hecht (Ben), Mamet (David), Odets (Clifford), Parks (Suzan-Lori), Payne (John Howard), Simon (Neil) **6** Ferber (Edna), Gurney (A. R.), Henley (Beth), Miller (Arthur), Norman (Marsha), O'Neill (Eugene), Thomas (Augustus), Wilder (Thornton), Wilson (August, Lanford, Robert) **7** Hellman (Lillian), Kaufman (George S.), Kushner (Tony), Shanley (John Patrick), Shepard (Sam) **8** Anderson (Maxwell, Robert), Caldwell (Erskine), Connolly (Marc), Sherwood (Robert), Williams (Tennessee) **9** Chayefsky (Paddy), Fierstein (Harvey), Hansberry (Lorraine) **11** Hammerstein (Oscar), Wasserstein (Wendy) ***Austrian:*** **10** Schnitzler (Arthur) ***Belgian:*** **11** Maeterlinck (Maurice) ***Czech:*** **5** Havel (Vaclav) ***English:*** **3** Fry (Christopher), Gay (John) **4**

Gray (Simon), Hare (David), Rowe (Nicholas), Tate (Nahum) **5** Frayn (Michael), Milne (A. A.), Orton (Joe), Peele (George), Wilde (Oscar) **6** Barrie (James), Coward (Nöel), Dryden (John), Jonson (Ben), Pinero (Arthur Wing), Pinter (Harold), Steele (Richard), Storey (David) **7** Bennett (Alan), Delaney (Shelagh), Marlowe (Christopher), Marston (John), Osborne (John), Shaffer (Anthony, Peter), Webster (John) **8** Congreve (William), Rattigan (Terrence), Shadwell (Thomas), Stoppard (Tom), Tourneur (Cyril), Vanbrugh (John), Zangwill (Israel) **9** Ayckbourn (Alan), Churchill (Caryl), Goldsmith (Oliver), Middleton (Thomas), Wycherley (William) **11** Shakespeare (William) ***French:*** **5** Camus (Albert), Genet (Jean) **6** Musset (Alfred de), Racine (Jean), Sardou (Victorien), Sartre (Jean-Paul), Scribe (Eugène) **7** Anouilh (Jean), Ionesco (Eugène), Labiche (Eugène), Molière, Rostand (Edmond) **8** Marivaux (Pierre) **9** Corneille (Pierre), Crébillon, Giraudoux (Jean) **12** Beaumarchais (P. A. Caron de) ***German:*** **5** Weiss (Peter) **6** Brecht (Bertolt), Goethe (Johann Wolfgang von), Kleist (Heinrich von) **8** Schiller (Friedrich von) **9** Hauptmann (Gerhart), Zuckmayer (Carl) ***Greek:*** **8** Menander **9** Aeschylus, Euripides, Sophocles **12** Aristophanes ***Hindu:*** **8** Kalidasa ***Irish:*** **4** Shaw (George Bernard) **5** Behan (Brendan), Friel (Brian), Synge (John Millington), Yeats (William Butler) **6** O'Casey (Sean) **7** Beckett (Samuel), Gregory (Lady Augusta) **8** Sheridan (Richard Brinsley) ***Italian:*** **5** Gozzi (Carlo), Verga (Giovanni) **7** Alfieri (Vittorio), Ariosto (Ludovico), Giacosa (Giuseppe), Goldoni (Carlo) **8** Trissino (Gian Giorgio) **9** D'Annunzio (Gabriele) **10** Metastasio (Pietro), Pirandello (Luigi) ***Japanese:*** **5** Zeami ***Nigerian:*** **7** Soyinka (Wole) ***Norwegian:*** **5** Ibsen (Henrik) **8** Bjornson (Bjornstjerne) ***Roman:*** **6** Seneca **7** Plautus, Terence ***Romanian:*** **7** Ionesco (Eugene) ***Russian:*** **7** Chekhov (Anton) **8** Zamyatin (Yevgeny) ***South African:*** **6** Fugard (Athol) ***Spanish:*** **4** Vega (Lope de) **5** Lorca (Federico García) **7** Alberti (Rafael), Arrabal (Fernando) **8** Quintero (Serafín, Joaquín) **9** Benavente (Jacinto) **11** García Lorca (Federico), Valle-Inclán (R. M. del) ***Swedish:*** **5** Sachs (Nelly) **10** Strindberg (August) ***Swiss:*** **6** Frisch (Max)

drape 4 fold, hang, roll **5** adorn, array, cloak, cover **6** clothe, enfold, enwrap, swathe, wrap up **7** curtain, swaddle **8** enswathe, envelope, swathe in

drapery 7 curtain, hanging **8** curtains, hangings

drastic 4 dire **5** harsh **6** severe **7** extreme, radical **9** desperate **10** exorbitant

drat 4 damn, dang, darn **6** phooey, shucks **7** doggone

draw 3 gut, tie, tow, tug **4** etch, haul, limn, lure, puff, pull, pump **5** draft, drain, infer, judge, trace **6** allure, appeal, deduce, depict, derive, elicit, entice, extend, gather, indite, inhale, pencil, siphon, sketch **7** attract, deplete, exhaust, extract, outline, portray, prolong, spin out, win over **8** conclude, contract, convince, dead heat, deadlock, lengthen, protract, standoff **9** delineate, formulate, represent, stalemate **10** allurement, attraction, disembowel, eviscerate, exenterate ***forth:*** **5** educe **6** elicit **7** extract ***from:*** **4** milk, pump **5** bleed ***together:*** **3** tie **4** join, lace

draw back 4 duck **5** cower, quail, wince **6** blench, cringe, flinch, recoil, shrink **7** back off, retreat, take off **9** turn aside

drawback 4 flaw, snag **5** fault, hitch **6** defect, refund **7** failing, trouble **8** weakness **9** detriment, hindrance **10** deficiency, difficulty, impediment **11** shortcoming **12** disadvantage

draw down 4 milk **5** drain, spend, use up **6** expend, reduce **7** deplete, exhaust **8** decrease, diminish **9** reduction, siphon off

drawer 9 draftsman ***for money:*** **4** till

drawers 5 pants **6** undies **8** knickers, trousers **10** underpants

draw in 6 enmesh, entice, induce, prompt **7** involve, retract, win over **8** convince, persuade, pull back **9** prevail on **11** bring around, prevail upon

drawing 6 doodle, sketch **7** cartoon, outline

drawing power 4 lure, pull **6** allure, appeal **9** magnetism **10** attraction

drawn 4 taut, worn **6** peaked **7** fraught, haggard, pinched **8** careworn, fatigued, pictured, strained, stressed **9** attracted **10** delineated

drawn-out 4 long **7** lengthy, tedious **8** extended, overlong **9** prolonged **10** protracted

draw off 3 tap **4** pump **5** bleed, draft, drain **6** siphon

draw out 6 extend **7** prolong, stretch **8** elongate, lengthen, protract

draw up 4 balk, halt, lift, make, stop **5** array, draft, frame, order, raise, write **6** deploy, map out **7** compose, concoct, dispose, marshal, prepare, set down **8** organize, write out **9** formulate

dray 4 cart, drag **5** wagon **6** barrow, sledge **7** travois **9** stoneboat

dread 4 fear **5** alarm, panic **6** dismay, fright, horror, phobia, terror **7** anxiety **10** foreboding **11** trepidation **12** apprehension **13** consternation

dreadful 4 dire **5** awful **6** tragic **7** awesome, extreme, fearful, ghastly, heinous, hideous, ominous **8** alarming, horrible, horrific, shocking, terrible **9** appalling, frightful, revolting **11** distressing, frightening

dreadnought 10 battleship

dream 4 ache, long, wish **5** crave, fancy, ideal **6** aspire, bubble, desire, hanker, vision **7** chimera, fantasy, imagine, rainbow, reverie, specter, spectre **8** ambition, delusion, illusion, phantasm, phantasy **9** fantasize, nightmare **10** aspiration ***divination by:* 11** oneiromancy ***god:* 8** Morpheus ***sleep:* 3** REM

dreamer 7 utopian **8** idealist **9** visionary **10** Don Quixote, lotus-eater **13** castle-builder

dreamlike 5 ideal, vague **6** unreal **7** shadowy, surreal **8** fanciful, illusory, nebulous **9** imaginary, visionary **12** otherworldly

Dream of Gerontius composer 5 Elgar (Edward)

dream up 5 frame, hatch **6** cook up, create, devise, invent **7** concoct, imagine **8** conceive, contrive, envisage, envision **9** formulate, visualize

dreamy 7 pensive **9** unworldly, visionary **10** idealistic **11** impractical **12** otherworldly

dreary 4 blah, drab, dull **5** bleak **6** boring, dismal, gloomy, somber, sombre **7** forlorn, humdrum, joyless, tedious **8** banausic, tiresome, wretched **9** cheerless **10** depressing, depressive, monotonous, oppressive, pedestrian **11** dispiriting

dreck 3 mud **4** junk, muck, slop **5** offal, swill, trash, waste **6** litter, refuse, sewage **7** garbage, rubbish **9** sweepings

dredge 3 dig **5** barge, scoop **6** deepen, dig out, gather **8** excavate, scoop out **9** hollow out, scrape out

dregs 4 lees, scum **5** trash **6** grouts **7** deposit, grounds, remains, residue **8** sediment **9** settlings **11** precipitate

drei 5 three

dreidel 3 top

Dreiser, Theodore *character:* 5 Clyde (Griffiths) **6** Carrie (Meeber), Eugene (Witla), Sondra (Finchley) **7** Roberta (Alden) **9** Hurstwood (George) **10** Cowperwood (Frank) ***novel:* 5** Stoic (The), Titan (The) **6** Genius (The) **9** Financier (The) **12** Sister Carrie **14** Jennie Gerhardt **15** American Tragedy (An)

drench 3 sop **4** dunk, soak **5** douse, souse, steep, swill **6** deluge, seethe **7** immerse **8** inundate, saturate, submerge, waterlog

dress 3 gut **4** bind, clad, deck, doll, duds, garb, gown, sack, togs **5** adorn, align, A-line, array, frock, getup, guise, habit, smock, weeds **6** attire, bedeck, caftan, clothe, dirndl, enrobe, outfit, sacque **7** apparel, bandage, bedizen, chemise, clothes, costume, garment, garnish, raiment, threads, turnout, uniform **8** beautify, clothing, covering, decorate, ensemble, ornament, wardrobe **9** embellish, make ready **11** habiliments ***a wound:* 7** bandage ***designer:* 4** Dior (Christian), Erté, Head (Edith) **5** Blass (Bill), Bohan (Marc), Karan (Donna), Klein (Calvin), Prada (Miuccia), Pucci (Emilio), Quant (Mary), Worth (Charles Frederick) **6** Armani (Giorgio), Cardin (Pierre), Jacobs (Marc), Lauren (Ralph), Miyake (Issey), Poiret (Paul) **7** Balmain (Pierre), Cassini (Oleg), Halston, Lacroix (Christian), Mizrahi (Isaac), Versace (Gianni) **8** Galliano (John), Givenchy (Hubert) **9** Courrèges (André), de la Renta (Oscar), Gernreich (Rudi), Lagerfeld (Karl), St.-Laurent (Yves), Valentino **10** Balenciaga (Cristóbal) **12** Saint-Laurent (Yves), Schiaparelli (Elsa) ***line:* 3** hem ***mode of:* 5** habit ***ordinary:* 5** mufti ***oriental:* 9** cheongsam ***part:* 5** skirt **6** bodice ***South Seas:* 6** sarong

dress down 5 chide, scold **6** berate, rail at, rebuke, revile **7** bawl out, reprove, tell off, upbraid **8** admonish, chastise, reproach **9** castigate, reprimand **10** tongue-lash

dresser 5 chest **6** bureau **7** commode, highboy **10** chiffonier ***gaudy:* 9** butterfly

dressing 5 sauce **6** catsup **7** bandage, catchup, ketchup **8** stuffing ***salad:* 5** ranch **6** French **7** Italian, Russian **10** blue cheese **11** vinaigrette **12** green goddess

dressing room 6 vestry **8** vestiary

dressmaker 7 modiste **9** couturier **10** couturiere, seamstress

dress up 6 attire, clothe, rig out, tog out **7** apparel, deck out **8** beautify, disguise, prettify, trick out **9** embellish **10** camouflage

dressy 4 chic **5** showy, smart **6** classy, formal, frilly, ornate **7** duded up, elegant, stylish **9** rigged out

Dreyfus's defender 4 Zola (Emile) **6** Proust (Marcel)

dribble 4 drip, leak, weep **5** drool **6** bounce,

drivel, slaver **7** distill, drizzle, slobber, trickle **8** salivate, sprinkle
driblet 4 drop **6** gobbet **7** globule, smidgen **8** particle, pittance
dried grape 6 raisin
dried meat 5 jerky
dried plum 5 prune
drift 3 bat, gad **4** flow, flux, gist, roam, sail, skim, tide, waft, wash **5** amble, coast, creep, float, mosey, range, slide, stray, trend **6** bummel, linger, ramble, stream, stroll, wander **7** current, maunder, meander, meaning, saunter **8** movement, penchant, sideslip, tendency **9** deviation **10** propensity **11** disposition, inclination, progression **12** predilection
drifter 3 bum, vag **4** hobo **5** gypsy, nomad, tramp **7** floater, migrant, vagrant **8** derelict, vagabond **9** transient **11** beachcomber **12** rolling stone
drill 3 bit, dig **4** bore **5** auger, borer, punch, train **6** pierce, trepan, wimble **7** routine, wildcat, workout **8** exercise, practice, practise, rehearse **9** penetrate, rehearsal **10** discipline ***command:*** **6** at ease **8** left face **9** about face, attention, right face
drink 3 ade, lap, nip, sea, sip, tea **4** belt, brew, chug, deep, down, grog, gulp, soak, swig, tope, toss **5** booze, draft, drain, ocean, quaff, slurp, snort, swill, toast **6** absorb, brandy, cassis, cognac, embibe, guzzle, imbibe, jigger, liquid, liquor, pledge, potion, tank up, tipple, tisane **7** consume, potable, schnaps, spirits, swallow, swizzle, toss off **8** aperitif, beverage, libation, liquor up, schnapps **9** aqua vitae ***after-dinner:*** **6** frappé **7** cordial, liqueur ***drugged:*** **6** Mickey **10** Mickey Finn ***honey:*** **4** mead ***hot:*** **5** negus, toddy ***liquor:*** **5** booze, hooch **6** red-eye **9** firewater, moonshine ***mixed:*** **3** kir, nog **5** julep **6** Gibson, gimlet, mai tai, mimosa, mojito, rickey, Rob Roy, zombie **7** gin fizz, martini, sidecar, stinger **8** daiquiri, pink lady **9** alexander, Cuba libre, manhattan, margarita, mint julep, rusty nail **10** Bloody Mary, piña colada, Tom Collins **11** gin and tonic, grasshopper, screwdriver, whiskey sour **12** black Russian, old-fashioned ***mixer:*** **7** swirler ***noisily:*** **5** slurp ***of liquor:*** **4** dram, shot, slug **5** snort **6** bracer **8** highball ***of the gods:*** **6** nectar ***soft:*** **3** pop **4** cola, soda **5** tonic **7** soda pop **8** root beer **9** ginger ale **12** sarsaparilla ***stimulating:*** **6** bracer ***Vedic ritual:*** **4** soma (see also **beverage**)
drinkable 6 liquor **7** potable **8** beverage, libation, potation
drinking 8 potation ***fountain:*** **7** bubbler ***glass:*** **6** rummer **7** tumbler ***horn:*** **6** rhyton ***spree:*** **3** jag **4** tear, toot **5** binge, spree **6** bender **7** carouse **8** carousal
drip 4 leak, plop, weep **7** dribble, droplet, trickle **8** sprinkle
dripping 3 wet **5** runny, soppy **6** soaked, soused **7** drizzly, soaking, sopping **8** drenched **9** saturated **11** wringing-wet
drippy 5 mushy, rainy, sappy, sobby, soppy, soupy, teary, weepy **6** slushy, syrupy **7** drizzly, maudlin, mawkish, soaking, sopping, tearful **9** schmaltzy **11** sentimental
drive 3 pep, ram **4** goad, herd, push, spur, taxi, trip, urge **5** chase, force, guide, impel, jaunt, lunge, motor, moxie, oomph, pilot, pound, spunk, steer, surge, vigor **6** compel, convey, exhort, hammer, outing, plunge, propel, strike, thrust **7** actuate, impetus, operate, produce **8** ambition, mobilize, momentum, navigate, shepherd, vitality **9** chauffeur, excursion, urge along **10** enterprise, get-up-and-go, initiative, motivation ***away:*** **4** shoo **5** exile
drive away see **expel**
drivel 3 rot **4** bosh, bunk **5** drool, hokum, hooey, prate **6** babble, bunkum, gabble, jabber, slaver **7** baloney, blabber, blather, dribble, hogwash, prattle, rubbish, slobber, twaddle **8** claptrap, flimflam, nonsense, salivate **9** gibberish, poppycock **10** balderdash, double-talk, flapdoodle **12** blatherskite, gobbledygook
driver 4 hack, jehu **5** cabby **6** cabbie, cabman, hackie, mallet **7** hackman **8** coachman, motorist, muleteer, operator **9** chauffeur, dowitcher **10** taskmaster **11** tamping iron ***of an elephant:*** **6** mahout ***Roman:*** **10** charioteer ***truck:*** **8** teamster
driving 7 dynamic, powered **8** forceful, vigorous **9** energetic, inspiring **10** compelling
drizzle 4 mist, rain **7** dribble, spatter **8** droplets, sprinkle **10** sprinkling **13** precipitation
Dr. Jekyll and Mr. ____ 4 Hyde
droll 3 odd **5** comic, funny, nutty, witty **7** comical, risible **8** farcical, humorous **9** eccentric, laughable, ludicrous, whimsical
drollery 5 humor **6** comedy, joking, whimsy **7** jesting
dromedary 5 camel
drone 3 bee, hum **4** buzz, idle, laze, loaf, loll **5** idler **6** drudge, loiter, lounge, murmur, worker **7** bagpipe **8** aircraft, parasite **9** bombinate **10** pedal point
drool 4 gush, rave **5** froth **6** dote on, drivel, saliva, slaver **7** blather, dribble, enthuse, slobber **8** salivate **10** rhapsodize
droop 3 sag **4** fall, flag, hang, loll, sink, swag,

wilt **5** slump **6** dangle, slouch, weaken **7** decline, let down, subside **8** languish

droopy 4 blue, down, limp, weak **5** baggy **6** gloomy **7** doleful, languid, sagging, slouchy, wilting **8** cast down, dejected, downcast **9** depressed **10** dispirited **11** downhearted

drop 3 dip, nip, sag, tot **4** down, drib, dump, fall, fell, jilt, jolt, lose, omit, slip, slug, tear **5** cease, depth, lapse, lower, pitch, plump, scrub, slide, snort, speck, spend **6** cancel, cave in, demise, depart, expire, fumble, give up, go down, ground, plunge, reduce, smitch, topple, unload, vanish **7** abandon, decease, decline, deposit, descend, descent, distill, dribble, driblet, fall off, forfeit, give out, globule, pendant, plummet, trickle **8** bowl over, break off, collapse, comedown, downturn, keel over, nose-dive **9** declivity, discharge, downslide, downswing, downtrend, prostrate, reduction, terminate **10** depository

drop by 4 call **5** pop in, visit **6** stop in **8** come over

droplet 4 bead, drib, tear **7** globule

drop off 3 nap, sag **4** doze, fall, slip **5** slide, slump **6** catnap, drowse, lessen, snooze **7** decline, deliver, deposit, slacken **8** diminish, fall away, hand over **10** fall asleep

dropsical 5 puffy, tumid **6** turgid **7** swollen **8** inflated **9** edematous, tumescent

dropsy 5 edema **8** anasarca

dross 4 junk, scum, slag **5** dregs, offal, waste **6** debris, scoria **7** remains, residue, schlock **8** detritus, impurity, leavings

drossy 4 base **6** impure, scummy **7** trivial **8** inferior, unworthy **9** worthless

drought 4 lack, need, want **6** dearth **7** aridity, dryness **8** scarcity, shortage **10** deficiency

droughty 3 dry **4** arid, sere **7** bone-dry, dried up, parched, thirsty **10** desiccated

drove 3 mob **4** army, herd, host, mass, pack **5** crowd, flock, horde, troop **6** myriad, pushed, school, throng **7** phalanx **9** multitude

drover 6 cowboy **8** shepherd

drown 4 sink, soak **5** douse, flood, souse, swamp **6** deluge, drench, engulf **7** immerse, repress, smother **8** inundate, submerge **9** overpower, overwhelm, suffocate **10** asphyxiate, extinguish

drowse 3 nod **4** doze **5** sleep **6** catnap, snooze **7** doze off, drop off, shut-eye, slumber **10** forty winks

drowsy 4 dozy **5** dopey **6** droopy, sleepy, torpid **7** languid **8** indolent, sluggish **9** lethargic, somnolent, soporific **10** slumberous **13** lackadaisical

Dr. Seuss 6 Geisel (Theodor Seuss) ***book:*** **11** Cat in the Hat (The) **15** Green Eggs and Ham, Yertle the Turtle **19** Horton Hatches the Egg **26** How the Grinch Stole Christmas

drub 3 tan, wax, zap **4** bash, beat, club, deck, drum, flay, flog, lash, lick, mash, maul, pelt, trim, whip **5** baste, cream, crush, paste, pound, score, slash, smash, smear, spank, stamp, thump, wreck **6** batter, berate, bruise, buffet, deface, hammer, master, pummel, punish, revile, scorch, thrash, thresh, wallop **7** belabor, blister, censure, clobber, cripple, lambast, scourge, shatter, shellac, trounce **8** bulldoze, lambaste, lash into, outclass, outshine **9** castigate, excoriate, overwhelm

drubbing 4 loss, rout **6** defeat **7** setback **10** defeasance **11** shellacking

drudge 4 grub, hack, moil, peon, plod, slog **5** grind, slave **6** menial, slavey **7** grubber, plodder **8** dogsbody

drudgery 4 moil, toil **5** chore, grind **7** travail **9** grunt work **10** donkeywork **11** backbreaker

drudging 6 boring, tiring **7** irksome, tedious **8** dragging, tiresome **9** fatiguing, laborious, wearisome **10** monotonous

drug 4 dope, lull **5** sulfa **6** downer, ipecac, opiate, physic, poison, potion, remedy, statin **7** fen-phen, generic, stupefy **8** biologic, medicine, narcotic, nepenthe, relaxant, sedative **9** ibuprofen, medicinal, methadone **10** antibiotic, medicament, medication **11** thalidomide ***addict:*** **6** junkie ***agent:*** **4** narc ***calming:*** **8** sedative ***experience:*** **4** trip ***illicit:*** **3** ice, kif, LSD, pot **4** acid, coke, dope, hash, meth, scag, snow, weed **5** crack, grass, opium, smack, speed **6** heroin, peyote **7** cocaine, crystal, hashish **8** cannabis, goofball **9** mescaline **10** methadrine, psilocybin ***seller:*** **10** pharmacist ***sleep-inducing:*** **8** hypnotic **9** soporific **11** barbiturate

drugged 4 high **5** dazed, doped, dopey **6** flying, loaded, stoned, zonked **8** benumbed, hopped-up, turned on **9** spaced-out, stupefied **10** narcotized

druggist 7 chemist **10** apothecary, pharmacist

drugstore 8 pharmacy **10** apothecary

druid 4 Celt **6** priest **7** prophet ***sacred object:*** **3** oak **9** mistletoe

drum 3 keg, vat **4** beat, cask **5** conga, naker, tabor, thrum **6** barrel, tom-tom, tympan **7** tambour, timpani (plural), tympani (plural) **8** cylinder, timbales (plural) ***Indian:*** **5** tabla **8** mridanga ***Irish:*** **7** bodhran ***large:*** **4** bass ***small:*** **5** bongo, tabor **7** timbrel ***string:*** **5** snare

drumbeat 4 flam, roll, tuck **6** ruffle, tattoo **7** booming, pit-a-pat, rat-a-tat **8** rataplan
drumfire 5 salvo **6** volley **7** barrage, booming **9** broadside, cannonade, fusillade **11** bombardment
drumhead 4 skin **7** summary
drummer 4 Rich (Buddy) **5** Krupa (Gene), Roach (Max), Starr (Ringo), Watts (Charlie) **6** Blakey (Art), hawker, Puente (Tito), vendor **7** peddler **8** pitchman, salesman
drum up 6 invent **7** canvass, solicit **9** originate ***interest:*** **4** plug, tout **8** ballyhoo
drunk 3 lit, sot **4** lush, soak, wino **5** dipso, lit up, oiled, souse, tight, tipsy **6** blotto, boozer, juiced, soused, stewed, stinko, tiddly, wasted, zonked **7** crocked, guzzler, pie-eyed, sloshed, smashed, squiffy, tippler, tosspot **8** squiffed **9** inebriate, plastered **10** boozehound, inebriated **11** intoxicated
drunkard 3 sot **4** lush, soak, wino **5** dipso, rummy, souse, stiff, toper **6** bibber, boozer, soaker **7** guzzler, swiller, tippler, tosspot **9** alcoholic, inebriate, juicehead **10** boozehound **11** dipsomaniac
Drusilla *brother:* 8 Caligula ***father:* 5** Herod **10** Germanicus ***husband:* 5** Felix ***mother:* 9** Agrippina ***sister:* 8** Berenice **9** Agrippina
dry 3 set **4** arid, brut, dull, sere, sour, tart **5** baked, dusty, parch, stale, wizen **6** barren, desert, harden, stolid, thirst, wither **7** congeal, deadpan, parched, Saharan, shrivel, sterile, thirsty **8** rainless, solidify, tearless, teetotal, withered **9** anhydrous, dehydrate, desiccate, evaporate, unwatered **10** dehydrated, desiccated **11** unemotional **12** matter-of-fact **13** uninteresting ***combining form:* 3** xer **4** xero ***goods:* 6** linens, napery **8** clothing, textiles ***out:* 5** sober **8** soberize ***period:* 7** drought ***wine:* 3** sec **4** brut
dryasdust 4 arid, dull **5** banal, inane, vapid **6** boring, stodgy **7** insipid, prosaic, tedious **9** wearisome **10** uninspired **13** uninteresting
dry measure 4 peck, pint **5** quart **6** bushel
Dryope *form:* 5 lotus ***husband:* 9** Andraemon ***sister:* 4** Iole
dry up 4 wilt **5** wizen **6** wither **7** deplete, exhaust, mummify, shrivel **9** desiccate, disappear, evaporate
dual 3 two **4** twin **5** duple **6** bifold, binary, double, duplex, paired **7** coupled, matched, twofold **8** matching **9** duplicate
dualistic 5 duple **6** bifold, binary, double, duplex, paired **7** twofold **9** Manichean **10** Manichaean
dualize 4 copy, dupe **5** clone **6** double **9** duplicate, replicate, reproduce
dub 4 call, name, term, trim **5** style, title **6** duffer **7** baptize, bungler, entitle, fumbler **8** christen, nickname, rerecord **9** blunderer, designate **10** denominate
dubiety 5 doubt **7** concern **8** mistrust **9** confusion, suspicion **10** skepticism **11** incertitude, incredulity, uncertainty **12** doubtfulness
dubious 4 iffy **5** fishy **6** unsure **7** suspect, unclear **8** doubtful, hesitant, unlikely **9** equivocal, sceptical, skeptical, uncertain, undecided **10** improbable, unreliable **11** mistrustful, problematic, questioning, unconvinced, unpromising **12** questionable, undependable, undetermined
dubitable 5 fishy **7** suspect **8** doubtful, marginal **9** ambiguous, uncertain, unsettled **10** borderline **11** problematic **13** indeterminate
duce 5 ruler **6** despot, leader, tyrant **8** dictator **9** Mussolini (Benito), strongman
duck 3 bob, bow, dip, shy **4** bend, dive, dunk, shun **5** avoid, dodge, douse, elude, evade, fence, parry, shirk, stoop **6** escape, plunge **7** back out, immerse **8** sidestep, submerge, submerse **10** canvasback ***Asian:* 5** Pekin **8** mandarin ***dabbling:* 7** gadwall, mallard ***diving:* 4** smew **7** pochard **9** merganser **10** bufflehead ***Eurasian:* 4** smew ***European:* 8** shelduck ***genus:* 3** Aix **4** Anas ***group:* 4** team **5** brace, flock, skein **6** flight ***hunter's screen:* 5** blind ***male:* 5** drake ***red-wattled:* 7** Muscovy ***river:* 4** teal **6** wigeon **7** pintail, widgeon ***scaup:* 8** bluebill ***sea:* 5** eider, scaup **6** scoter
duckbill 8 platypus **9** hadrosaur, monotreme
duck soup 4 easy, snap **5** cinch **6** breeze, picnic, simple **8** kid stuff, painless, pushover **10** child's play **11** piece of cake
ducky 4 cute **5** swell **6** lovely, peachy **7** darling **9** hunky-dory **10** peachy-keen
duct 4 flue, pipe, tube **5** canal **6** course, runway **7** channel, conduit **11** watercourse ***anatomical:* 3** vas **4** vasa (plural)
ductile 6 pliant, supple **7** plastic, pliable **8** flexible, moldable **9** adaptable, compliant, malleable, tractable ***metal:* 4** wire
ductless gland see **endocrine gland**
dud 3 dog **4** bomb, bust, flop **5** lemon, loser **6** bummer, misfit, turkey **7** debacle, failure, washout **8** abortion
dude 3 fop, guy **4** beau, buck, rake **5** blood, dandy **6** fellow **7** coxcomb **8** macaroni **9** exquisite **12** Beau Brummell, lounge lizard
dudgeon 3 ire **4** fury, huff, miff, rage **5** anger, pique, wrath **7** chagrin, offense, outrage, umbrage **8** vexation **10** resentment **11** indignation **12** exasperation
duds 3 rig **4** garb, gear, rags, togs **5** dress,

getup, weeds **6** attire, things **7** apparel, clothes, raiment, threads, toggery **8** clothing, garments **9** trappings, vestments **11** habiliments

due 4 debt, just, owed **5** lumps, owing **6** direct, earned, lawful, proper, unpaid **7** arrears, condign, deserts, merited, payable, payment, regular **8** adequate, deserved, expected, rightful, suitable **9** deserving, equitable, requisite, scheduled **10** obligatory, receivable, sufficient **11** appropriate, outstanding

duel 4 tilt **5** fight, joust **6** combat **7** contest, dispute **8** conflict **9** smackdown

duenna 8 chaperon **9** chaperone, companion, governess

duet ***dancer's:*** **9** pas de deux

due to 4 over **7** owing to, through **9** because of **11** considering

duff 3 can **4** buns, butt, rear, rump, tail, tush **5** fanny, slack **6** bottom **7** keester, keister, pudding, rear end **8** backside, buttocks, coal dust, derriere **10** leaf litter

duffer 4 boob, clod, dolt, dope, yo-yo **5** chump, dunce, klutz **6** dimwit, dum-dum, lubber, nitwit **7** dullard, fumbler, peddler, pinhead **8** bonehead, dumbbell, lunkhead, numskull **9** blockhead, ignoramus, numbskull, simpleton **10** nincompoop, stumblebum **11** incompetent

dugout 5 canoe **6** trench **7** piragua, pirogue, shelter

duiker 8 antelope

dukedom 5 duchy **6** domain

dulcet 5 sweet **7** melodic, tuneful **8** charming, cheerful, engaging, euphonic, pleasant, pleasing, soothing **9** agreeable, melodious **10** euphonious **11** mellifluous

dulcimer 6 zither **8** psaltery ***Hungarian:*** **8** cimbalom ***Persian:*** **6** santir **7** santour

dull 3 dim, dun, mat **4** arid, blah, blur, drab, flat, numb **5** blunt, dense, dusty, faded, ho-hum, inert, matte, muddy, muted **6** benumb, blurry, boring, deaden, dreary, gloomy, leaden, obtuse, stodgy, stupid **7** blunted, humdrum, insipid, muffled, prosaic, stupefy, subdued, tarnish, tedious **8** banausic, bromidic, deadened, discolor, lifeless, listless, monotone, plodding, sluggish **9** colorless, dim-witted, dryasdust, ponderous, wearisome **10** indistinct, lackluster, lusterless, monotonous, pedestrian **11** commonplace, desensitize, insensitive, thickheaded, thick-witted, unsharpened **12** simpleminded **13** uninteresting

dullard 3 oaf **4** bird, boob, bore, clod, dolt, dope, yo-yo **5** chump, dummy, dunce, idiot, moron, ninny, noddy, stupe **6** dimwit, dum-dum, nitwit **7** airhead, pinhead **8** bonehead, dumbbell, imbecile, lunkhead, meathead, numskull **9** birdbrain, blockhead, ignoramus, lamebrain, numbskull, simpleton **10** dunderhead **11** chowderhead, chucklehead

dullness 5 ennui **6** apathy, stupor, tedium, torpor **7** boredom, languor **8** hebetude, lethargy, monotony **9** bluntness, denseness, lassitude, stupidity, torpidity **12** indifference, listlessness, sluggishness

duly 8 properly, suitably **9** correctly, regularly **12** sufficiently **13** appropriately

duma 7 council **8** assembly, congress **11** legislature

Dumas character 5 Athos **6** Aramis, Dantès (Edmond) **7** Camille, Porthos **9** D'Artagnan

dumb 3 mum **4** dull, mute **5** dense, quiet, thick **6** deaden, obtuse, silent, stupid **7** doltish, foolish, idiotic, moronic **8** ignorant, taciturn, wordless **9** dim-witted, fatheaded, voiceless **10** speechless, tongue-tied **11** blockheaded, thick-witted **12** close-mouthed, inarticulate, simple-minded

dumbbell see **dullard**

dumbfound 5 amaze **6** boggle, puzzle **7** astound, nonplus, perplex, stagger **8** astonish, bewilder, bowl over, confound, distract, surprise **9** take aback **11** flabbergast

dumbfounded 5 agape **6** amazed **7** puzzled, shocked **8** startled **9** astounded, perplexed, staggered, surprised **10** astonished, bewildered, bowled over, confounded, distracted, nonplussed, taken aback **13** thunderstruck

dummkopf 3 oaf **4** boob, clod, dodo, dolt, dope, fool, goof, jerk, mutt, simp, yo-yo **5** chump, dunce, idiot, moron, ninny, noddy, stupe **6** dimwit, donkey, nitwit, noodle **7** airhead, dullard, pinhead, schnook **8** bonehead, clodpoll, dumbbell, dumbhead, imbecile, lunkhead, meathead, numskull **9** birdbrain, blockhead, ignoramus, lamebrain, numbskull, simpleton, thickhead **10** dunderhead, hammerhead, nincompoop **11** chowderhead, chucklehead, knucklehead

dummy 4 boob, clod, dodo, dolt, mock, sham, yo-yo **5** chump, dunce, false, idiot, model, moron, ninny, noddy, stupe **6** dimwit, dum-dum, effigy, ersatz, layout, mock-up, nitwit, puppet, stooge **7** airhead, dullard, manikin, pinhead, stand-in **8** bonehead, dumbbell, imbecile, lunkhead, mannekin, meathead, numskull **9** birdbrain, blockhead, ignoramus, imitation, lamebrain, numbskull, simpleton, simulated **10** artificial, dunderhead, fictitious, nincompoop, substitute **11** chowderhead, chucklehead

dump 4 drop, junk **5** chuck, depot, ditch, scrap **6** armory, midden, pigpen, pigsty, plunge **7** abandon, arsenal, deep-six, discard **8** jettison, landfill, magazine, throw out **9** stockpile, throw away **10** depository

dumpling 5 dough **8** quenelle **10** butterball

dumps 4 funk **5** blues, dolor, gloom, mopes, slump **7** sadness **8** doldrums **9** dejection **10** depression, gloominess, melancholy **11** despondency, unhappiness

dumpy 5 dingy, seedy, squat, stout **6** chubby, chunky, shabby, slummy, stocky, stubby, stumpy **7** run-down **8** heavyset, thickset **9** shapeless

dun 3 dim, fly **4** dull, drab, gray **5** annoy, brown, dusky, horse, murky, press **6** demand, gloomy, mayfly, needle, pester, plague, somber, sombre **9** ephemerid, importune

Duncan's slayer 7 Macbeth

dunce 3 oaf **4** boob, clod, dodo, dolt, dope, goof, mutt, simp, yo-yo **5** booby, chump, dummy, idiot, moron, ninny, noddy, stupe **6** dimwit, donkey, duffer, dum-dum, nitwit, noodle, stupid **7** airhead, dullard, fathead, pinhead **8** bonehead, clodpoll, dumbbell, imbecile, lunkhead, meathead, numskull **9** birdbrain, blockhead, ignoramus, lamebrain, numbskull, simpleton **10** dunderhead, hammerhead, nincompoop **11** chowderhead, chucklehead, knucklehead

Dunciad author 4 Pope (Alexander)

dundrearies 9 burnsides, sideburns **11** muttonchops **12** side-whiskers

dune 8 sandbank ***area:*** **3** erg **5** beach, shore **6** desert

dung 4 muck **6** manure, ordure **9** excrement ***beetle:*** **6** scarab **9** tumblebug

dungeon 4 jail **5** vault **6** prison **9** black hole, oubliette

dunghill 6 midden

dunk 3 dip, sop **4** soak **5** douse, drown, souse **6** drench **7** immerse **8** saturate, submerge, submerse

dunlin 9 sandpiper

duo 4 dyad, pair **5** brace **6** couple **7** doublet, twosome

dupe 3 con, kid, sap **4** butt, fool, gull, hoax, mark **5** cheat, chump, cozen, patsy, spoof, trick **6** befool, delude, double, outwit, pigeon, sucker **7** chicane, deceive, defraud, mislead **8** flimflam, hoodwink **9** bamboozle, victimize **11** double-cross, hornswoggle

dupery 3 con **4** scam, sham **5** cheat, fraud **6** deceit, humbug, hustle **7** chicane **8** cheating, flimflam, trickery **9** chicanery, deception, duplicity, imposture, swindling **10** dishonesty, hanky-panky **11** hoodwinking **13** double-dealing, sharp practice

duple 4 dual, twin **6** bifold, binary, double, paired **7** coupled, doubled, twofold **9** dualistic

duplex see **duple**

duplicate 4 copy, fake, mate, redo, same, twin **5** clone, ditto, equal, match, mimeo, repro, Xerox **6** carbon, double **7** dualize, imitate, replica **8** knockoff **9** companion, facsimile, identical, imitation, look-alike, photocopy, replicate, reproduce **10** carbon copy, dead ringer, equivalent, reciprocal **11** counterfeit, counterpart, replication **12** reproduction

duplicitous 5 phony **6** shifty, sneaky **7** devious **8** delusive, guileful, scheming, sneaking, two-faced **9** deceitful, deceiving, deceptive, dishonest, underhand **10** fraudulent **11** underhanded **12** disingenuous **13** double-dealing

duplicity 5 fraud, guile **6** deceit **7** cunning, perfidy **8** scheming, trickery **9** chicanery, deception, treachery **10** dishonesty, doubleness **11** skulduggery **12** dissemblance, skullduggery **13** dissimulation, double-dealing

durability 4 wear **8** firmness **9** endurance, longevity, stability **10** permanence

durable 5 stout **6** stable, strong, sturdy **7** lasting **8** enduring **9** permanent, tenacious **10** dependable **11** long-lasting

durance 7 bondage **9** captivity, detention, restraint **11** confinement **12** enthrallment, imprisonment **13** incarceration

duration 3 run **4** term, time **6** extent, period **7** interim **8** interval **11** persistence

duress 5 force **6** menace, threat **8** bullying, coercion, menacing, pressure **9** restraint **10** compulsion, constraint **11** restriction **12** intimidation

during 4 amid **10** throughout

durra 7 sorghum **12** grain sorghum

Durrell work 4 Cleo **7** Justine **9** Balthazar **10** Mountolive **17** Alexandria Quartet

durum 5 wheat

dusk 4 dark **7** evening **8** darkness, eventide, gloaming, twilight **9** nightfall **12** semidarkness

dusky 3 dim **4** dark **5** murky, swart **6** brunet, gloomy, opaque, twilit **7** obscure, shadowy, swarthy **8** funereal, nubilous, overcast, twilight **9** tenebrous **10** caliginous **11** dark-skinned

dust 4 grit, sand, sift, soot **5** ashes, grime **6** powder **8** sprinkle **10** besprinkle, sprinkling

dust-bowl victim 4 Okie

dustup 3 row **4** spat **5** fight, melee, run-in,

set-to **6** battle, fracas, hassle, tussle **7** dispute, quarrel, rhubarb, scuffle **8** argument, skirmish **9** bickering, brannigan **10** falling-out **11** altercation

dusty 3 dry **4** arid, dull **5** stale **7** parched, powdery, tedious, unswept

Dutch 7 trouble **8** hot water ***African:*** **9** Afrikaans ***ceramics:*** **5** delft ***cheese:*** **4** Edam **5** Gouda ***dog breed:*** **7** griffon **8** keeshond ***painter:*** **3** Dou (Gerrit, Gerard) **4** Cuyp (Aelbert Jacobsz), Gogh (Vincent van), Hals (Frans) **5** Bosch (Hieronymus), Hooch (Pieter de), Steen (Jan) **6** Rubens (Peter Paul) **7** de Hooch (Pieter), Hobbema (Meindert), van Gogh (Vincent), Vermeer (Jan) **8** Mondrian (Piet), Ruysdael (Jacob van, Salomon van), Terborch (Gerard) **9** de Kooning (Willem), Honthorst (Gerrit van), Rembrandt (van Rijn) ***philosopher:*** **7** Spinoza (Benedict de) ***scholar:*** **7** Erasmus (Desiderius)

Dutch South African 4 Boer

dutiful 7 devoted **8** faithful **9** compliant **10** respectful **13** conscientious

duty 3 job, tax, use **4** levy, onus, role, task, work **5** chare, chore, stint **6** burden, charge, devoir, impost, office, tariff **7** respect, service **8** function **10** allegiance, assessment, assignment, commitment, dedication, obligation

dwarf 4 runt **5** gnome, pygmy, stunt, troll **6** midget, peewee **7** manikin **8** Tom Thumb **9** miniature **10** diminutive, homunculus ***in Snow White:*** **3** Doc **5** Dopey, Happy **6** Grumpy, Sleepy, Sneezy **7** Bashful ***Scottish:*** **7** blastie

dwarfish 5 pygmy, small **6** midget **7** minikin, stunted **8** inferior, pint-size **9** miniature, pint-sized **10** diminutive, undersized

dweeb 4 dork, drip, geek, nerd, wimp, wuss **5** loser **7** nebbish

dwell 3 lie **4** bide, live, stay **5** abide, exist **6** locate, remain, repose, reside, settle **7** hang out

dweller 7 citizen, denizen, settler **8** habitant, occupant, resident **10** inhabitant

dwelling 3 pad **4** casa, digs, home, nest **5** abode, haunt, house **7** address, habitat, lodging **8** domicile, quarters **9** residence **10** brownstone, habitation ***American Indian:*** **4** tipi **5** hogan, tepee **6** pueblo, teepee, wigwam ***clergyman's:*** **5** manse **7** rectory **8** vicarage **9** parsonage ***crude:*** **3** hut **4** camp **5** cabin, hovel, shack **6** cabana, shanty **7** barrack **8** barracks ***Eskimo:*** **5** igloo ***grand:*** **5** manor, manse, villa **6** palace **7** château, mansion ***Hindu:*** **6** ashram ***Navajo:*** **5** hogan ***Russian:*** **5** dacha ***small:*** **3** cot, hut **5** cabin, hovel, shack **6** shanty **7** cottage **8** bungalow

dwindle 3 ebb **4** fade, fall, wane **5** abate, taper **6** lessen, recede, reduce, shrink, weaken, wither **7** decline, die away, die down, shrivel, slacken, subside **8** decrease, diminish, taper off **9** attenuate, drain away

dyad 3 duo, two **4** pair, yoke **5** brace, twins **6** couple **7** doublet, twosome

dye 4 tint **5** color, stain, tinge **7** pigment **8** colorant, pyronine, tincture ***blue:*** **4** woad **6** indigo **7** cyanine ***plant:*** **4** woad **5** sumac **6** madder ***red:*** **5** eosin, henna **6** kermes, ruddle **7** cudbear, fuchsin, magenta **8** alizarin, fuchsine, amaranth, safranin **9** cochineal, rhodamine, safranine **10** erythrosin ***violet:*** **6** archil ***yellow:*** **7** flavine **8** orpiment ***yellowish red:*** **7** annatto

dyed-in-the-wool 5 loyal, sworn **7** devoted, die-hard, old-line, settled, staunch **8** faithful, hard-core, orthodox, standpat, true-blue **9** confirmed, hard-shell, steadfast **10** deep-rooted, deep-seated, entrenched, inveterate, unwavering **11** established **13** bred-in-the-bone, thoroughgoing

dyewood 6 fustic **10** brazilwood

dying 6 demise **7** done for, quietus **8** moribund **9** departure **10** extinction, in extremis **12** annihilation

dynamic 7 driving, intense **8** forceful, forcible, powerful, vigorous **9** energetic, strenuous **10** compelling, energizing

dynamite 4 raze **5** blast **6** blow up **7** destroy, explode, shatter **8** demolish **9** explosive **10** annihilate ***inventor:*** **5** Nobel (Alfred)

dynamo 8 go-getter, live wire **9** generator **10** ball of fire **11** self-starter

dynasty *Chinese:* **3** Han, Qin, Sui **4** Hsia, Ming, Qing, Sung, Tang ***Mongol:*** **4** Yuan

Dynasty series *character:* **3** Ben, Dex **4** Adam, Dana **5** Blake, Sable **6** Alexis, Amanda, Fallon, Leslie, Monica, Steven **7** Claudia, Jeffery, Krystie **8** Samantha **9** Dominique ***family:*** **5** Colby **10** Carrington ***setting:*** **6** Denver ***spin-off:*** **6** Colbys (The) ***star:*** **5** Evans (Linda), James (John), Nader (Michael), Samms (Emma) **6** Corley (Al), Garber (Terri), Hunley (Leann), Martin (Pamela Sue) **7** Beacham (Stephanie), Carroll (Diahann), Cellini (Karen), Coleman (Jack), Collins (Joan), Thomson (Gordon) **8** Bellwood (Pamela), Cazenove (Christopher), Forsythe (John), Locklear (Heather), Oxenberg (Catherine), Scoggins (Tracy)

dysentery 4 flux **6** scours **8** diarrhea

dyslogistic 7 adverse **10** derogatory, pejorative **11** deleterious, disparaging, prejudicial, unfavorable

dyspepsia **5** gloom **6** dismay **7** chagrin, pyrosis **8** glumness **9** dejection, heartburn **10** gloominess **11** frustration, indigestion
dyspeptic **5** cross, surly **6** crabby, morose, ornery **9** irritable **10** ill-humored, ill-natured **11** disgruntled, ill-tempered
dysphoria **4** funk **5** blues, dumps, gloom, mopes **6** sorrow **7** sadness **9** dejection **10** depression, gloominess, melancholy **11** unhappiness **12** mournfulness, wretchedness **13** cheerlessness
dysprosium symbol **2** Dy

E

each **3** all, per **4** a pop **5** every **6** apiece **8** everyone **9** per capita, everybody
eager **4** avid, keen **5** antsy, hyper, itchy, ready**6** ardent, fervid, gung ho, intent, raring **7** anxious, athirst, earnest, fervent, restive **8** appetent, aspiring, desirous, restless, yearning **9** ambitious, hankering, impatient **10** breathless **12** enthusiastic
eagerness **4** urge, zeal, zest, zing **5** ardor, gusto **6** desire, fervor, spirit, thirst **7** avidity, craving, itching, longing **8** alacrity, ambition, appetite, fervency **9** intensity **10** enthusiasm, impatience
eagle **4** hawk **9** accipiter ***nest:*** **4** aery **5** aerie, eyrie ***North American:*** **4** bald **6** golden ***sea:*** **3** ern **4** erne **6** osprey
eagle-eyed **8** vigilant, watchful **9** attentive, observant **10** perceptive **12** sharp-sighted
ear **6** notice **7** auricle **9** attention ***bone:*** **5** anvil, incus **6** hammer, stapes **7** malleus, stirrup ***canal:*** **5** scala ***combining form:*** **3** aur, oto **4** auri, otic ***doctor:*** **9** otologist ***inner:*** **9** labyrinth ***middle:*** **8** tympanum ***outer:*** **5** pinna ***part:*** **4** drum, lobe **5** canal **6** tragus **7** cochlea ***relating to:*** **5** aural **9** auricular ***science:*** **7** otology
eardrum **8** tympanum
____ **Earhart** **6** Amelia
earl **4** lord, peer **5** count, noble **8** nobleman, seigneur **9** patrician **10** aristocrat
earlier **3** ere, yet **4** once **5** as yet, so far **6** before, sooner **7** already, thus far **8** formerly, hitherto, previous **9** erstwhile, preceding **10** beforehand, heretofore, previously
earlier than **3** pre **6** before ***Latin:*** **4** ante
earliest **5** first, prime **6** maiden, primal **7** initial, pioneer, primary **8** original, primeval, pristine **10** aboriginal, primordial
earlike projection **3** lug
early **3** old **5** first, prior **6** primal, timely **7** ancient, betimes **8** original, previous, primeval, pristine, untimely **9** preceding, premature, primitive **10** antecedent, antiquated, precocious, primordial **11** prematurely ***prefix:*** **5** paleo
earn **3** bag, get, net, win **4** gain, make, rate, reap **5** amass, clear, gross, merit, score **6** attain, come by, obtain, pick up, rack up, secure, wangle **7** acquire, bring in, collect, deserve, harvest, procure, produce, realize, receive **8** pull down **9** bring home, knock down
earnest **3** vow **4** bond, busy, firm, keen, pawn, true, warm **5** grave, sober, token **6** active, ardent, intent, pledge, solemn, somber, surety **7** deposit, genuine, intense, serious, sincere, up front, warrant, zealous **8** contract, covenant, diligent, interest, security, sedulous, studious **9** assiduous, heartfelt **10** determined, no-nonsense, passionate, sobersided, thoughtful, unaffected **11** industrious **12** enthusiastic, wholehearted
earnestly **5** madly **7** for real, like mad
earnings **3** net, pay **4** gain **5** lucre, wages **6** EBITDA, income, profit, return, salary **7** profits **8** proceeds, take-home **9** emolument **10** bottom line
earring type **4** cuff, hook, hoop, stud **5** huggy, slave **6** clip-on, dangle **7** barbell, stick-on
ear shell see **abalone**
earshot **5** range, sound **7** hearing
earsplitting **4** loud **6** shrill **7** blaring, grating, raucous, roaring **8** piercing, strident **9** deafening, dissonant **10** screeching, stentorian **11** fullmouthed
earth **3** orb, sod **4** dirt, land, soil, turf **5** globe, world **6** ground, planet, sphere **7** dry land, terrain **8** creation **10** terra firma ***brick:*** **4** pisé **5** tapia ***combining form:*** **3** geo **4** geog **6** tellur **7** telluro ***core:*** **12** centrosphere ***crust:*** **4** sial, sima **11** lithosphere ***god:*** **3**

Geb, Keb, Seb **5** Dagan ***goddess:*** **4** Erda, Gaea **5** Ceres, Nintu **6** Kishar **7** Demeter, Nerthus ***pigment:*** **5** ocher, ochre, umber **6** sienna ***relating to:*** **8** telluric **11** terrestrial ***satellite:*** **4** moon ***science:*** **7** geology **9** geography

earthenware 4 clay **5** china, delft **7** biscuit, faience, pottery **8** clayware, crockery, majolica **9** porcelain, stoneware **10** terra-cotta

earthlike 11 terrestrial

earthling 6 Terran

earthly 6 mortal **7** mundane, worldly **8** material, physical, temporal **9** corporeal **11** terrestrial

earthquake 5 shake, shock **6** tremor **7** temblor ***measuring device:*** **11** seismograph, seismometer ***relating to:*** **7** seismic ***science:*** **10** seismology **11** seismometry

earthwork 4 bank, berm, wall **7** bulwark, rampart **10** embankment **13** fortification

earthworm 7 annelid **12** night crawler

earthy 3 low **4** base, real **5** crude, dirty, dusty, gross, muddy, ocher, ochre, sandy **6** clayey, coarse, common, simple **7** mundane, worldly **8** temporal **9** corporeal, inelegant, practical, pragmatic, realistic, unrefined **10** hard-boiled, hardheaded, indelicate, uncultured, unpolished **11** terrestrial **12** matter-of-fact

earwax 7 cerumen

ease 3 aid **4** bate, calm, dull, free, help, rest **5** allay, loose, peace, poise, relax, slack **6** assist, deaden, loosen, relief, repose, soften **7** assuage, comfort, fluency, improve, leisure, lighten, mollify, relieve, slacken **8** calmness, deftness, diminish, dispatch, facility, idleness, mitigate, moderate, pleasure, serenity **9** abundance, affluence, alleviate, expertise, reduction, untighten, well-being **10** ameliorate, efficiency, facilitate, inactivity, moderation, prosperity, relaxation, smoothness **11** alleviation, contentment, nonchalance, spontaneity ***off:*** **3** ebb **4** bate, fade, fall, flag, wane **5** abate, let up, loose, relax, slack **6** lessen, loosen, relent, unbend, unwind **7** die away, die down, slacken, subside **8** diminish, loosen up, moderate **9** untighten

easel 4 desk **5** frame, stand **7** support **9** workbench, worktable

easement 6 relief **7** comfort **10** mitigation, palliative **11** alleviation, consolation, restorative **13** mollification

easily 6 simply **7** handily, lightly, readily **8** facilely, smoothly **11** dexterously, efficiently **12** effortlessly

East 4 Asia **6** Levant, Orient

Easter 5 Pasch ***relating to:*** **7** paschal ***symbol:*** **3** egg **4** lamb, lily **5** bunny **6** rabbit

Easter Island 7 Rapa Nui

eastern 8 oriental **9** Levantine ***countries:*** **6** Orient ***European:*** **4** Slav

East Indies *country:* **8** Malaysia **9** Indonesia, Singapore ***plant:*** **2** da

East Timor *capital:* **4** Dili ***neighbor:*** **9** Indonesia

easy 3 lax **4** calm, cozy, mild, soft, snug **5** basic, clear, comfy, cushy, light, loose, naive, plain **6** facile, fluent, placid, polite, secure, serene, simple, smooth **7** amiable, evident, lenient, obvious, patient, relaxed **8** apparent, composed, familiar, graceful, gullible, informal, obliging, peaceful, pleasant, sociable, tolerant, trusting **9** collected, forgiving, indulgent **10** charitable, effortless, elementary **13** uncomplicated

easygoing 3 lax **4** calm, cool, lazy **5** quiet **6** breezy, casual, dégagé, folksy **7** affable, offhand, patient, relaxed, unfussy **8** amenable, carefree, down home, flexible, indolent, informal, laid-back, together, tranquil **9** apathetic, indulgent, unhurried **10** nonchalant, permissive, unaffected **11** comfortable, complaisant, low-pressure, pococurante, unconcerned, unflappable **12** devil-may-care, even-tempered, happy-go-lucky

easy mark 3 sap **4** butt, dupe, fool, gull **5** chump, patsy, sport **6** pigeon, softie, sucker, turkey, victim **7** fall guy **8** pushover **9** soft touch **11** sitting duck

eat 3 sup, vex **4** bite, chow, dine, gnaw, meal, nosh, pick, take, wolf **5** erode, feast, gorge, graze, lunch, mouth, munch, scarf, scoff, scour, snack, use up **6** devour, feed on, gobble, ingest, inhale, nibble, pester, pick at, pig out, take in **7** banquet, consume, corrode, gorge on, swallow, torment **8** chow down, dissolve, take food, wear away **9** breakfast, decompose, masticate, partake of, polish off **10** break bread, gormandize, nibble away

eatable 6 edible **8** esculent, harmless **9** palatable **10** comestible, digestible

eatery 4 café **5** diner, grill **10** coffee shop, restaurant **11** greasy spoon **12** luncheonette

eating place 3 pub **4** café, mess **5** diner, grill, joint **6** bistro, tavern **7** automat, beanery, canteen, commons, dinette, tearoom **8** cookshop, messroom, pizzeria, snack bar **9** brasserie, cafeteria, chophouse, hash house, lunchroom, trattoria **10** coffee shop, restaurant, steak house **11** greasy spoon **12** luncheonette

eavesdrop 3 bug, tap **4** lurk **5** snoop **7** monitor **8** listen in, overhear

ebb 4 drop, fade, fall, flag, tide, wane **5**

abate, droop, let up **6** lessen, recede, reduce, relent, shrink, wither **7** decline, descent, die away, die down, ease off, retreat, slacken, subside **8** decrease, diminish, languish, moderate, withdraw **10** retrograde

Eblis 5 Satan ***son:*** **3** Tir **4** Awar **5** Dasim **8** Zalambur

ebon, ebony 3 jet **4** inky **5** black, jetty, raven, sable **6** brunet **8** brunette, jet-black **9** pitch-dark **10** pitch-black

ebullience 3 vim, zip **4** brio, élan, zing **5** gusto **6** gaiety **7** abandon, elation **8** buoyancy, vitality, vivacity **9** animation **10** enthusiasm, exuberance, liveliness **11** high spirits **13** effervescence

ebullient 5 brash, zingy, zippy **6** bouncy, bubbly, elated, frothy, geeked, pumped, raring **7** boiling, excited, gleeful, gushing, vibrant **8** hopped-up **9** sprightly, vivacious **11** exhilarated **12** enthusiastic, high-spirited **13** irrepressible

eccentric 3 odd, nut **4** coot, kook **5** crank, crazy, droll, flaky, freak, funky, funny, goofy, kooky, nutty, outré, queer, wacky, weird **6** far out, oddity, quaint, quirky, screwy, weirdo, whacko, whacky **7** bizarre, deviant, erratic, heretic, oddball, offbeat, strange, unusual **8** aberrant, abnormal, bohemian, cockeyed, crackpot, goofball, maverick, peculiar, singular, uncommon **9** anomalous, character, deviating, fantastic, fruitcake, grotesque, irregular, off-center, screwball, whimsical **10** elliptical, off-balance, unbalanced, uncentered **11** exceptional **13** idiosyncratic, nonconformist

eccentricity 4 kink **5** quirk, twist **8** crotchet, quiddity **9** deviation, weirdness **10** aberration **11** strangeness **12** idiosyncrasy

ecclesiastic see **clergyman**

ecclesiastical 4 holy **5** papal **6** church, sacred **8** churchly, clerical, pastoral, priestly **9** apostolic, canonical, episcopal, spiritual, synagogal **10** churchlike, pontifical, rabbinical, sacerdotal **11** ministerial, patriarchal, theological **12** episcopalian, evangelistic, tabernacular

ecdysiast see **stripteaser**

echelon 3 row **4** file, line, rank, tier **5** grade, group, level, order, queue **6** string **7** chevron **9** formation

echidna 8 anteater **9** monotreme **13** spiny anteater

Echidna *father:* 7 Phorcys **8** Chrysaor ***mother:*** **4** Ceto **10** Callirrhoë ***offspring:*** **5** Hydra **6** dragon, Orthus, Sphinx **7** Chimera **8** Cerberus, Chimaera

echinoderm 6 urchin **7** crinoid, sea star **8** starfish **9** coelomate, sea urchin **11** sea cucumber

echo 3 ape **4** mime, ring **5** evoke, mimic, trace **6** mirror, parrot, repeat, result, reverb, second **7** imitate, iterate, reflect, resound, revoice, vestige **8** resonate, response **9** duplicate, imitation, reiterate **10** reflection, repetition **11** reverberate **12** repercussion **13** reverberation

Echo 5 nymph, oread ***beloved:*** **9** Narcissus

echoic 7 mimetic **9** imitative **10** derivative **12** onomatopoeic **13** onomatopoetic

éclat 4 bang, dash, fame, pomp **5** glory, honor, kudos **6** luster, lustre, praise, renown, repute **7** acclaim, display, laurels, stardom, success **8** applause, eminence, prestige, standing **9** celebrity, notoriety, publicity **10** brilliance, brilliancy, exaltation, prominence, reputation **11** distinction, ostentation

eclectic 5 broad, fussy, mixed, picky **6** choosy, select, varied **7** diverse, finicky, mingled **8** assorted, catholic, elective **9** inclusive, selective **10** discerning, fastidious, particular **11** diversified **12** dilettantish, multifarious **13** heterogeneous

eclipse 3 dim **5** bedim, cloud, cover, excel, outdo, shade **6** darken, exceed, shadow **7** becloud, decline, obscure, surpass **8** downfall, outshine **9** adumbrate, obfuscate, overcloud **10** extinguish, overshadow ***phenomenon:*** **5** umbra **6** corona, shadow **7** annulus **8** penumbra **11** Diamond Ring **12** Bailey's Beads

eclogue 3 ode **4** idyl, poem **5** idyll, lyric **8** pastoral

ecological 5 green **8** bionomic ***community:*** **5** biome

ecology 9 bionomics **11** environment

economic 6 fiscal **8** material, monetary **9** budgetary, financial, pecuniary **10** mercantile, profitable ***doctrine:*** **12** laissez-faire ***system:*** **9** communism, socialism **10** capitalism **11** syndicalism **12** mercantilism

economical 4 mean **5** canny, close, spare, tight **6** frugal, saving, stingy **7** careful, miserly, prudent, sparing, thrifty **8** skimping **9** efficient, niggardly, penny-wise, penurious, provident, scrimping **10** unwasteful **12** cheeseparing, parsimonious **13** penny-pinching

economist *American:* 5 Arrow (Kenneth), Simon (Herbert, Julian), Solow (Robert), Tobin (James) **6** Becker (Gary), George (Henry), Thurow (Lester), Veblen (Thorstein), Walker (Amasa), Weaver (Robert) **7** Krugman (Paul), Kuznets (Simon), Stigler

(George), Volcker (Paul) **8** Friedman (Milton), Stiglitz (Joseph) **9** Galbraith (John Kenneth), Greenspan (Alan), Samuelson (Paul) **10** Schumpeter (Joseph) ***Austrian:*** **5** Hayek (Friedrich von), Mises (Ludwig von) ***Canadian:*** **7** Leacock (Stephen) ***Dutch:*** **9** Tinbergen (Jan) ***English:*** **3** Sen (Amartya) **4** Mill (John Stuart) **5** Coase (Ronald), Hayek (Friedrich von), Pigou (Arthur) **6** Engels (Friedrich), Keynes (John Maynard) **7** Bagehot (Walter), Malthus (Thomas), Ricardo (David) ***French:*** **3** Say (Jean-Baptiste) **6** Monnet (Jean), Turgot (Anne-Robert-Jacques), Walras (Léon) **7** Quesnay (François) ***German:*** **4** Marx (Karl) **5** Weber (Max) **6** Engels (Friedrich) **7** Schacht (Hjalmar) ***Indian:*** **3** Sen (Amartya) ***Scottish:*** **4** Mill (James) **5** Smith (Adam) ***Swedish:*** **6** Myrdal (Gunnar) ***Swiss:*** **8** Sismondi (Simonde de)

economize **4** save **5** skimp, stint **6** manage, scrimp **7** husband **8** conserve **10** cut corners **12** pinch pennies

economy **6** saving, thrift **8** prudence, skimping **9** concision, frugality, husbandry, parsimony, restraint, scrimping **10** discretion, efficiency, providence, stinginess **11** carefulness, conciseness, miserliness, thriftiness **13** niggardliness

Eco novel **9** Baudolino **13** Name of the Rose (The) **17** Foucault's Pendulum

ecru see **beige**

ecstasy **3** joy **5** bliss **6** frenzy, heaven, trance **7** delight, elation, madness, rapture **8** euphoria, paradise, rhapsody **9** beatitude, transport **10** exaltation, joyfulness **11** blessedness, derangement, enchantment, high spirits, inspiration **12** blissfulness, exhilaration, intoxication **13** seventh heaven

ecstatic **6** elated, joyful **7** gleeful **8** euphoric, exultant, jubilant, thrilled **9** delirious, delighted, entranced, overjoyed, rapturous, rhapsodic **11** exhilarated, transported

ectothermic **11** cold-blooded

Ecuador ***capital:*** **5** Quito ***city:*** **6** Ambato, Cuenca **7** Machala **9** Guayaquil ***Indian people:*** **7** Quechua ***island group:*** **9** Galápagos ***language:*** **7** Spanish ***monetary unit:*** **5** sucre ***mountain range:*** **5** Andes ***neighbor:*** **4** Peru **8** Colombia ***volcano:*** **6** Sangay **7** Cayambe **8** Cotopaxi **10** Chimborazo

ecumenical **6** cosmic, global **7** general, generic **8** catholic **9** inclusive, planetary, universal, worldwide **12** all-inclusive, cosmopolitan **13** comprehensive

ecumenical council **4** Lyon **5** Basel, Lyons, Trent **6** Nicene **7** Ephesus, Ferrara, Lateran, Vatican **8** Florence **9** Chalcedon, Constance

eczema **6** tetter

edacious see **voracious**

eddy **4** purl **5** swirl, twirl, whirl, whorl **6** vortex **8** backwash **9** backwater, maelstrom, whirlpool **11** counterflow

edema **5** croup, tumor **6** dropsy **8** anasarca, swelling ***treatment:*** **8** diuretic

Eden **6** heaven, utopia **7** arcadia, elysium **8** paradise ***river:*** **5** Gihon **6** Pishon **8** Hiddekel **9** Euphrates

edentate **5** sloth **8** aardvark, anteater, pangolin **9** armadillo, toothless

Edessa's king **5** Abgar

edge **3** cut, end, hem, lip, rim **4** bank, bite, brim, cusp, draw, ease, hone, inch, lead, limb, line, pink, side, whet, worm **5** arris, bound, brink, bulge, force, ledge, picot, point, ridge, sidle, skirt, sting, strop, verge **6** border, fringe, margin, nosing **7** acidity, contour, chamfer, outline, serrate, sharpen, vantage **8** acerbity, acridity, boundary, emborder, handicap, keenness, surround, thinness **9** acuteness, advantage, extremity, harshness, head start, perimeter, periphery, sharpness, threshold, upper hand **10** causticity, shrillness, stringency **11** astringency **12** incisiveness **13** effectiveness

edge city **5** exurb **6** suburb

edged **4** acid, tart **5** acerb, acute, sharp **6** barbed, strong **7** acerbic, cutting **8** incisive, piercing

edge in **6** inject **9** interject, interpose, insinuate **10** infiltrate **11** interpolate

edging **3** hem **4** lace **5** braid, frill, limit **6** border, fringe, lacing, margin, piping **7** flounce, selvage **8** rickrack, selvedge, trimming

edgy **3** hip **5** funky, nervy, sharp, tense, testy, wired **6** daring, touchy, uneasy **7** excited, keyed up, offbeat, restive, uptight **8** Bohemian, out-there, renegade, restless, skittery, skittish, volatile **9** excitable, impatient, irascible, irritable **10** high-strung, outlandish **11** provocative

edible **8** esculent **9** palatable **10** comestible ***root:*** **3** oca, yam **4** beet, taro, yuca **6** carrot, daikon, ginger, jicama, potato, radish, turnip, wasabi **7** burdock, cassava, ginseng, malanga, parsnip, salsify **8** celeriac, galangal, kohlrabi, rutabaga **11** horseradish, sweet potato ***seed:*** **3** nut, pea **4** bean **6** peanut

edibles **4** chow, eats, feed, food, grub **6** viands **7** aliment, goodies, nurture **8** victuals

9 provender 10 provisions, sustenance 11 comestibles

edict 3 law 4 bull, fiat, rule 5 canon, order, ukase 6 decree, dictum, ruling 7 command, dictate, mandate, precept, statute 9 directive, manifesto, ordinance, prescript 10 injunction, regulation 12 proclamation 13 pronouncement ***Islamic:*** 5 fatwa ***papal:*** 4 bull 8 decretal

Edict of ____ 5 Milan, Worms 6 Nantes

edifice 4 pile 8 building, erection 9 structure

edify 5 teach 6 better, fill in, illume, inform, update, uplift 7 educate, elevate, enhance, improve 8 illumine, instruct 9 elucidate, enlighten 10 illuminate

edit 3 cut 4 cull, omit 5 adapt, alter, amend, emend, fix up 6 delete, doctor, excise, polish, redact, refine, review, revise, reword, select 7 abridge, compile, correct, rewrite 8 annotate, assemble, condense, copyread, fine-tune 9 proofread, rearrange 10 blue-pencil, bowdlerize

editing term 4 dele, stet 5 caret 7 jump cut

edition 4 copy, form 5 issue, print 7 reissue, reprint, version 8 printing, variorum 10 impression, reprinting 12 reproduction

editor 8 redactor 9 scrivener, wordsmith 10 copyreader 11 proofreader

Edmonton player 5 Oiler

Edomite's ancestor 4 Esau

educate 4 rear 5 brief, coach, drill, edify, nurse, teach, train, tutor 6 inform, school 7 explain, nurture 8 instruct 9 brainwash, enlighten 10 discipline 12 indoctrinate

education 7 culture, tuition 8 breeding, coaching, guidance, learning, literacy, pedagogy, teaching, training, tutelage, tutorage, tutoring 9 erudition, knowledge, schooling, tutorship 11 instruction, learnedness, scholarship 13 enlightenment

educational 11 informative, instructive 13 informational, instructional ***institution:*** 6 school 7 academy, college 10 university 12 conservatory

educator 5 tutor 7 teacher 9 professor 10 instructor ***American:*** 4 Mann (Horace) 5 Dewey (John) 6 Butler (Nicholas Murray), Conant (James Bryant), Harris (William Torrey) 7 Barnard (Henry), Beecher (Catharine), Peabody (Elizabeth) 8 Hutchins (Robert Maynard), McGuffey (William) 10 Washington (Booker T.) ***Czech:*** 8 Comenius (John Amos) ***English:*** 6 Arnold (Thomas) 7 Spencer (Herbert) ***German:*** 7 Froebel (Friedrich), Herbart (Johann) ***Italian:*** 10 Montessori (Maria) ***Swiss:*** 10 Pestalozzi (Johann Heinrich)

educe 4 drag, draw, milk, pull 5 evoke, wrest, wring 6 derive, elicit, evince, evolve, extort, obtain, secure 7 distill, draw out, extract, procure 8 bring out 10 excogitate

eel 5 moray, siren 6 conger 7 hagfish, lamprey, sniggle ***young:*** 5 elver

eelpout 6 blenny, burbot 10 muttonfish

eely 5 slimy 6 slippy, wiggly 7 elusive, wriggly 8 slippery, slithery 9 wriggling

eerie 5 scary, weird 6 creepy, spooky 7 bizarre, strange, uncanny 8 chilling, spectral 9 fantastic, grotesque, unearthly 10 mysterious 11 frightening, hair-raising 12 otherworldly

efface 4 dele, x out 5 annul, erase 6 cancel, delete, rub out 7 blot out, destroy, expunge, scratch, wipe out 8 black out, wear away 9 eliminate, eradicate, extirpate 10 obliterate

effect 3 end 4 make 5 cause, enact, event, fruit 6 create, draw on, induce, intent, invoke, render, result, upshot 7 achieve, execute, fulfill, outcome, perform, produce, realize, turn out 8 bring off, carry out, conceive, generate 9 actualize, aftermath, discharge, implement, outgrowth 10 accomplish, bring about, conclusion, denouement 11 consequence 12 carry through, ramification, repercussion

effective 4 able 5 sound, valid 6 causal, cogent, direct, potent, useful 7 capable, operant 8 adequate 9 competent, operative 10 compelling, convincing, productive

effectiveness 5 clout, force, point, power, vigor 6 weight 7 cogency, potency 8 strength, validity 10 capability

effects 4 gear 5 goods, stuff 6 things 8 chattels, movables, property 9 equipment, moveables, trappings 10 belongings 11 impedimenta, possessions 13 accoutrements

effectual 5 sound, valid 6 potent, strong, useful 7 capable 8 decisive, powerful, workable 10 conclusive, fulfilling, productive 11 influential, practicable 13 authoritative, determinative

effectuate see **effect**

effeminate 5 sissy 6 swishy 7 epicene 9 sissified 10 old-maidish

effervescence 5 giddy 7 fizzing, foaming, sparkle 8 bubbling, buoyancy, vivacity 9 animation 10 ebullience, ebullition, exuberance, exuberancy, liveliness 12 exhilaration

effervescent 3 gay 4 airy 5 jolly 6 bouncy, bubbly, lively 7 boiling, buoyant, excited 8 animated, mirthful, volatile 9 sparkling, sprightly, vivacious 10 carbonated 12 high-spirited 13 irrepressible

effete 4 soft, weak 5 frail, spent 6 barren 6

sickly **7** decayed, drained, sterile, worn-out **8** decadent, decaying, delicate, depleted, fatigued, pampered **9** declining, dissolute, enfeebled, exhausted, infertile, washed-out **10** degenerate, unfruitful **11** debilitated

efficacious 6 active, potent, strong **8** forceful, powerful, puissant **9** operative **10** productive **11** influential

efficacy see **effectiveness**

efficiency see **effectiveness**

efficient 4 able **5** adept **6** expert **7** capable, elegant, skilled **8** economic, masterly, skillful **9** competent **10** economical, productive

effigy 3 guy **4** icon, idol **5** dummy, image **6** figure **7** waxwork **8** likeness

effloresce 4 blow **5** bloom, burst **6** flower, sprout **7** blossom, burgeon **9** bear fruit

effluvium 3 air **4** odor, reek **5** smell, vapor, waste **6** miasma **7** exhaust **8** effusion, emission **9** by-product, discharge, emanation **10** exhalation

efflux see **effluvium**

effort 3 job, try **4** feat, push, task, toil, work **5** chore, essay, force, labor, might, nisus, pains, sweat, while **6** energy, strain **7** attempt, travail, trouble, venture **8** endeavor, exertion, industry, struggle **11** application, elbow grease

effortful 4 hard **6** tiring, uphill **7** arduous, labored, operose **8** exacting, toilsome **9** ambitious, difficult, laborious, strenuous **11** challenging

effortless 4 easy **5** adept, light, ready **6** expert, facile, fluent, simple, smooth **8** masterly, skillful **10** proficient **11** undemanding

effrontery 4 face, gall **5** brass, cheek, nerve **8** audacity, boldness, chutzpah, temerity **9** arrogance, assurance, brashness, hardihood, impudence, insolence **10** brazenness **11** presumption **12** impertinence

effulgence 4 glow **5** blaze, glory **6** luster, lustre **8** radiance, splendor **9** splendour **10** brightness, brilliance, brilliancy, luminosity

effulgent 5 vivid **6** bright, lucent **7** beaming, glowing, lambent, radiant, shining **8** dazzling, glorious, luminous, lustrous, splendid **9** brilliant **11** resplendent **12** incandescent

effuse 4 flow, gush, pour, shed **5** exude, issue **6** stream **7** emanate, enthuse, flow out, radiate

effusive 5 gushy **6** lavish, sloppy, smarmy **7** cloying, fulsome, gushing, profuse, verbose **9** expansive, exuberant **10** loquacious, outpouring, unreserved **11** extravagant **12** enthusiastic, unrestrained **13** demonstrative, unconstrained

eft 4 newt **6** triton **10** salamander

e.g. 3 say **10** for example **11** for instance **13** exempli gratia

egad 6 zounds **7** criminy **8** gadzooks **11** odds bodkins

egg 3 ova (plural) **4** ovum, seed **5** ovule ***case:* 5** shell **7** ootheca ***combining form:* 3** ovi, ovo ***dish:* 6** omelet **8** omelette ***fertilized:* 6** zygote **7** oospore ***fish:* 3** roe **6** caviar ***French:* 4** oeuf ***immature:* 6** oocyte ***louse:* 3** nit ***part:* 4** yolk **5** glair, shell, white ***shaped:* 5** ovate, ovoid ***white:* 5** glair **7** albumen

egghead 6 pundit **8** highbrow **10** doubledome **12** intellectual

egg on 4 goad, prod, spur, urge **5** prick, rally **6** arouse, exhort, excite, incite, prompt, stir up **7** agitate **9** instigate, stimulate

eggplant 6 purple **9** aubergine **10** nightshade

egg-shaped 4 oval **5** ovate, ovoid **7** oviform

Eglah *husband:* 5 David ***son:* 7** Ithream

eglantine 7 dog rose **10** sweetbriar, sweetbrier

Eglantine *father:* 5 Pepin ***husband:* 9** Valentine

Eglon *king:* 5 Debir ***slayer:* 4** Ehud

ego 4 self **5** pride **6** vanity **7** conceit **10** self-esteem

egocentric 7 selfish **9** conceited **10** self-loving **11** self-seeking **12** narcissistic, self-absorbed, self-affected, self-centered, self-involved, vainglorious **13** individualist, self-conceited, self-concerned, self-indulgent

egoism 5 pride **6** vanity **7** conceit **8** self-love **9** self-glory, self-pride, vainglory **10** narcissism, self-regard **11** selfishness, self-opinion

egoistic 4 smug, vain **7** selfish **9** conceited **12** self-absorbed, self-centered **13** self-concerned, self-contented, self-satisfied

egomaniacal 12 self-exalting, vainglorious

egotism 5 pride **6** vanity **7** conceit **8** boasting, bragging, self-love, vainness, vaunting **9** arrogance, pomposity, self-glory, self-pride, vainglory **10** narcissism, self-esteem **11** megalomania, self-opinion **12** boastfulness **13** conceitedness

egotistic 4 vain **5** cocky, proud **7** selfish, stuck-up **8** arrogant, boastful, inflated, puffed-up **9** conceited **11** pretentious, self-serving **12** self-absorbed, self-centered, self-involved **13** self-concerned, self-satisfied

egregious 4 rank **5** gross, stark **6** arrant, brazen **7** blatant, glaring, heinous **8** flagrant, infamous, outright, shocking **9** atrocious, notorious, shameless **10** deplorable, outrageous **11** conspicuous

egress, egression 4 door, exit **5** issue, leave **6** depart, escape, exodus, outlet **7** doorway, exiting, opening, passage **9** departure, emergence

egret 5 heron, wader

Egypt *ancient city:* 6 Thebes **7** Memphis ***capital:* 5** Cairo ***city:* 4** Giza **8** Port Said **10** Alexandria ***dam:* 5** Aswan ***desert:* 6** Libyan **7** Arabian, Western ***gulf:* 4** Suez **5** Aqaba ***lake:* 6** Nasser ***language:* 6** Arabic ***leader:* 5** Sadat (Anwar el-) **6** Nasser (Gamal Abdul) **7** Mubarak (Hosni) ***monetary unit:* 5** pound ***neighbor:* 5** Libya, Sudan **6** Israel ***oasis:* 4** Siwa **6** Dakhla, Kharga **7** Farafra ***peninsula:* 5** Sinai ***river:* 4** Nile ***sea:* 3** Red **13** Mediterranean

Egyptian *burial jar:* 7 canopic ***Christian:* 4** Copt ***cross:* 4** ankh ***dynasty:* 5** Saite, Xoite **6** Hyksos, Tanite, Theban **7** Persian, Thinite **8** Memphite **9** Bubastite, Ethiopian **10** Diospolite ***flower:* 5** lotus

god:

chief: **6** Amen-Ra **crocodile-headed: 5** Sebek **falcon-headed: 4** Ment **5** Horus, Mentu **6** Sokari **7** Sokaris **ibis-headed: 5** Thoth **6** Dhouti **jackal-headed: 6** Anubis **of creation: 4** Ptah **5** Phtha **of day: 5** Horus **of death: 6** Anubis **of earth: 3** Geb, Keb, Seb **of evil: 3** Set **4** Seth **5** Sebek **of life: 4** Amen, Amon **5** Ammon **of magic: 5** Thoth **6** Dhouti **of Memphis: 4** Ptah **5** Phtha **6** Sokari **7** Sokaris **of the heavens: 5** Horus **of the morning sun: 5** Horus **7** Khepera **of the sun: 4** Aten, Aton **6** Amen-Ra **of Thebes: 4** Amen **6** Khensu, Khonsu **of the underworld: 6** Osiris **of war: 4** Ment **5** Mentu **of wisdom: 5** Thoth **6** Dhouti **ram-headed: 4** Amen, Amon **5** Ammon, Khnum **6** Khnemu **snake: 4** Apep **5** Apepi

goddess:

cat-headed: **4** Bast **5** Pakht **cow-headed: 5** Athor **6** Hathor **lioness-headed: 4** Bast **5** Pakht **6** Sekhet **of fertility: 4** Isis **of love and mirth: 5** Athor **6** Hathor **of motherhood: 4** Apet, Isis **of Thebes: 3** Mut **of the heavens: 3** Nut **queen of the gods: 4** Sati **vulture-headed: 3** Mut **7** Nekhebt **8** Nekhebet ***king:*** (see **king** entry) ***language:* 6** Arabic, Coptic ***native:* 4** Arab, Copt **5** Nilot ***queen:* 9** Cleopatra, Nefertiti ***sacred bird:* 4** ibis **5** bennu ***sacred bull:* 4** Apis ***solar disk:* 4** Aten ***sultan:* 7** Saladin ***symbol of life:* 4** ankh ***talisman:* 6** scarab ***underworld:* 4** Aaru, Duat **6** Amenti ***wind:* 7** khamsin, sirocco

eider 4 down, duck **7** sea duck

eidetic 5 exact, vivid **7** perfect, precise **8** absolute, lifelike

eidolon 4 icon **5** ghost, ideal, image, model, shade **6** mirage, vision, wraith **7** epitome, fantasm, figment, paragon, phantom, specter, spectre **8** exemplar, illusion, paradigm, phantasm **9** archetype, prototype **10** apparition

eight *combining form:* 4 octa, octo ***group of:* 5** octad, octet **6** octave

eight bells 4 noon

eighteen-wheeler 3 rig **4** semi **11** semitrailer

eighth note 6 quaver

eighty-six 4 boot, junk, toss **5** chuck, eject, evict, scrap **6** bounce **7** discard, kick out **8** get rid of, jettison, throw out

Einstein, Albert *birthplace:* 3 Ulm ***theory:* 10** relativity

einsteinium symbol 2 Es

Eire see **Ireland**

Eisenhower, Dwight 3 Ike ***home:* 7** Abilene ***wife:* 5** Mamie

eject 4 boot, bump, dump, fire, oust, sack, spew **5** chuck, evict, expel **6** banish, bounce **7** boot out, cast out, dismiss, kick out **8** disgorge, throw out **9** discharge

eke out 6 extend **7** augment, enhance, fill out, squeeze, stretch **8** increase **10** supplement

elaborate 4 busy **5** fancy, showy **6** daedal, dressy, evolve, expand, knotty, minute, ornate, refine, unfold **7** amplify, build up, careful, clarify, comment, complex, develop, discuss, elegant, enlarge, explain, expound, profuse, work out **8** detailed, involved, overdone, thorough **9** Byzantine, decorated, embellish, extensive, interpret, intricate **10** overworked **11** complicated, embellished, extravagant, painstaking **12** labyrinthine

Elaine *father:* 6 Pelles ***lover:* 8** Lancelot **9** Launcelot ***son:* 7** Galahad

Elam *capital:* 4 Susa **7** Shushan ***father:* 4** Shem ***king:* 12** Chedorlaomer

élan 3 pep, vim, zip **4** brio, dash, fire, life, zeal, zest, zing **5** ardor, flair, gusto, oomph, verve, vigor **6** energy, esprit, fervor, spirit **7** impetus **8** vivacity **9** animation, eagerness, intensity **10** enthusiasm

élan vital 4 soul **5** anima **6** animus, pneuma, psyche, spirit

elapse 4 go by, pass **6** expire, run out, slip by **8** pass away

elastic 6 bouncy, limber, pliant, rubber, supple **7** ductile, pliable, rubbery, springy **8** animated, flexible, moldable, stretchy, volatile **9** adaptable, expansive, malleable, resilient

10 extendable, extensible, rubber band, rubberlike 11 stretchable

elate 4 buoy 5 cheer, exalt, flush, set up 6 excite, perk up, uplift 7 cheer up, delight, enliven, gladden, gratify, hearten, inspire, overjoy 8 brighten, embolden, inspirit, spirit up 9 encourage 10 exhilarate, invigorate

elated 4 glad, high 5 happy 7 exalted, excited 8 ecstatic, euphoric, exultant, gladsome, jubilant 9 overjoyed 10 enraptured 11 exhilarated, intoxicated, on cloud nine 12 high-spirited

elation 3 joy 4 glee 7 delight, ecstasy, rapture 8 buoyancy, euphoria 9 happiness, transport 10 exaltation, excitement, jubilation 12 exhilaration, intoxication

Elbe tributary 4 Eger, Iser, Ohre 5 Saale 6 Moldau, Vltava

elbow 4 push 5 joint, nudge, shove 6 hustle, jostle

eld 4 yore 6 old age 8 old times

elder 6 senior 8 old-timer 9 patriarch, presbyter 10 golden-ager

elderliness 3 age 6 dotage, old age 8 caducity 10 senescence 11 senectitude

elderly 3 old 4 aged, gray 5 aging, hoary 7 ancient 9 declining, venerable

eldritch 5 eerie, weird 6 creepy, spooky 7 uncanny

Eleanor's husband 7 Henry II 8 Franklin

elect 3 opt, tap 4 name, pick 5 co-opt, saved 6 choice, choose, chosen, decide, opt for, ordain, picked, vote in 7 resolve, vote for 8 destined, nominate, ordained, redeemed 9 delivered, designate, determine, exclusive, single out 10 designated, singled out

election 6 ballot, choice, voting 7 primary 8 choosing, decision 9 balloting 10 preference, referendum 11 alternative

electioneer 5 stump 7 canvass 8 campaign, politick 9 barnstorm

elective 6 chosen 8 optional 9 voluntary 11 sympathetic 13 discretionary, noncompulsory, nonobligatory

Electra ***brother:*** 7 Orestes ***father:*** 9 Agamemnon ***husband:*** 7 Pylades ***mother:*** 12 Clytemnestra ***sister:*** 9 Iphigenia ***victim:*** 9 Aegisthus 12 Clytemnestra

electric ***appliance:*** 3 fan 4 iron, oven 5 clock, drier, dryer, mixer, range, stove 6 stereo, washer 7 blender, freezer, toaster 10 dishwasher, television 12 refrigerator ***coil:*** 5 tesla 8 solenoid ***device:*** 4 coil, fuse, plug 6 dynamo, magnet, switch 7 battery 8 resistor, rheostat, varistor 9 amplifier, capacitor, condenser, generator 11 transformer ***generator:*** 6 dynamo ***particle:*** 3 ion ***unit:*** 3 amp, ohm 4 volt, watt 5 farad, henry, joule 6 ampere 7 coulomb, faraday 8 kilowatt

electric current ***kind:*** 2 AC, DC 4 AC/DC 6 direct 11 alternating ***power:*** 7 wattage ***strength:*** 8 amperage

electricity 5 juice, spark 7 current 9 galvanism, lightning ***kind:*** 6 static 7 current

electrify 3 jar 4 jolt, stun 5 amaze, power, shock 6 charge, excite, thrill 7 astound, enthuse, inflame, provoke, stagger, startle 8 astonish, energize

electrode 6 dynode ***negative:*** 7 cathode ***positive:*** 5 anode

electron 3 ion 7 polaron ***stream:*** 10 cathode ray ***tube:*** 6 triode 7 tetrode 8 dynatron, klystron

Electryon ***brother:*** 6 Mestor ***daughter:*** 7 Alcmene ***father:*** 7 Perseus ***mother:*** 9 Andromeda ***wife:*** 5 Anaxo

eleemosynary 6 humane 8 generous 10 altruistic, beneficent, benevolent, charitable, munificent, openhanded 12 humanitarian 13 philanthropic

elegance 4 chic, pomp, tone 5 charm, grace, style, taste 6 luxury, polish 7 culture, dignity 8 chicness, poshness, richness, splendor, urbanity 9 gentility, precision 10 ornateness, refinement 11 cultivation 12 tastefulness

elegant 4 chic, fine, posh 5 fancy, grand, noble, swank 6 choice, classy, dainty, lovely, modish, ornate, swanky, urbane 7 courtly, genteel, opulent, refined, stately, stylish 8 cultured, polished, splendid, tasteful 9 exquisite, luxurious, recherché, sumptuous 10 cultivated 11 fashionable

elegiac 7 pensive 8 dactylic 9 lamenting, sorrowful 10 melancholy

elegy 4 poem, song 5 dirge 6 lament, monody 8 threnody

____ eleison 5 Kyrie

Elektra composer 7 Strauss (Richard)

element 4 item, part 5 basic, facet, piece, point 6 aspect, detail, factor, member, sector 7 article, feature, portion, section 8 division, particle, rudiment 9 component, essential, principle 10 ingredient, particular 11 constituent, fundamental ***chemical:*** 3 tin 4 gold, iron, lead, neon, zinc 5 argon, boron, radon, xenon 6 barium, carbon, cerium, cesium, cobalt, copper, curium, erbium, helium, indium, iodine, nickel, osmium, oxygen, radium, silver, sodium 7 arsenic, bismuth, bohrium, bromine, cadmium, calcium, dubnium, fermium, gallium, hafnium, hassium, holmium, iridium, krypton, lithium, mercury, niobium, rhenium, rhodium, silicon, sulphur, terbium, thorium, thulium, uranium, yttrium **8** actinium, aluminum, antimony, astatine, chlorine, chromium, europium, fluorine, hydrogen, illinium, lutecium, masurium, nitrogen, nobelium, platinum, polonium, rubidium, samarium, scandium, selenium, tantalum, thallium, titanium, tungsten, vanadium **9** americium, berkelium, beryllium, columbium, germanium, lanthanum, magnesium, manganese, neodymium, neptunium, palladium, plutonium, potassium, ruthenium, strontium, tellurium, virginium, ytterbium, zirconium **10** dysprosium, gadolinium, lawrencium, meitnerium, molybdenum, seaborgium **11** californium, einsteinium, mendelevium, phosphorous **12** darmstadtium, praseodymium **13** rutherfordium, protoactinium

elemental 3 key **4** pure **5** basal, basic, crude, prime **6** inborn, innate, primal, simple **7** central, connate, primary, radical **8** cardinal, inherent, integral, intimate, simplest **9** beginning, essential, ingrained, intrinsic, primitive **10** deep-seated, primordial, underlying **11** fundamental **13** uncomplicated

elementary 4 easy **5** basal, basic **6** simple **7** initial **9** beginning, essential, primitive **10** rudimental, underlying **11** fundamental, preliminary, rudimentary **12** introductory

elemi 5 resin **9** oleoresin

elephant 5 Babar **6** Horton, tusker **9** pachyderm ***boy:*** **4** Sabu ***driver:*** **6** mahout ***enclosure:*** **5** kraal ***extinct:*** **7** mammoth **8** mastodon ***female:*** **3** cow ***group:*** **4** herd ***keeper:*** **6** mahout ***male:*** **4** bull ***maverick:*** **5** rogue ***nose:*** **5** trunk **9** proboscis ***seat:*** **6** howdah ***sound:*** **6** bellow **7** trumpet ***tooth:*** **4** tusk ***tusk:*** **5** ivory ***young:*** **4** calf

elephant-headed god 6 Ganesa, Ganesh **7** Ganesha

elephantine 4 huge **6** clumsy **7** awkward, hulking, mammoth, massive **8** colossal, enormous, gigantic **9** graceless, humongous, monstrous, ponderous **10** gargantuan, mastodonic, prodigious, ungraceful **11** heavy-footed

Elephant Man 7 Merrick (Joseph)

elevate 4 lift, rear, rise **5** boost, elate, erect, exalt, hoist, raise **6** buoy up, jack up, lift up, pick up, uplift **7** advance, dignify, ennoble, glorify, hearten, improve, inspire, promote, upgrade **8** heighten **10** exhilarate

elevated 4 high **5** grand, lofty, moral, noble **6** aerial, formal, superb **7** ethical, refined, soaring, stately, sublime **8** eloquent, majestic, virtuous **9** dignified, grandiose, highflown, honorable, righteous

elevation 4 hill, rise **5** boost **6** ascent, height, uplift **7** advance, raising **8** altitude, mountain **9** acclivity, promotion, upgrading **10** apotheosis, preference, preferment **11** advancement, ennoblement ***indication:*** **9** benchmark

elevator 4 cage, lift, silo **5** hoist ***maker:*** **4** Otis

elf 3 fay, imp **4** peri, puck **5** fairy, gnome, pixie, troll **6** goblin, sprite **7** brownie, gremlin **10** leprechaun

elfin 5 antic **6** frisky, impish **7** implike, playful, puckish **8** pixieish **11** mischievous

Elgin ____ 7 Marbles

Eli 4 Yale **5** Yalie

Eli ____ 4 Yale **5** Lilly **7** Whitney

Elia 4 Lamb (Charles)

Eliab *brother:* **5** David ***daughter:*** **7** Abihail ***father:*** **5** Helon, Pallu ***son:*** **6** Abiram, Dathan

Eliada *father:* **5** David ***son:*** **5** Rezon

Eliam's daughter 9 Bathsheba

elicit 5 educe, evoke **6** derive, evince, extort **7** extract, provoke **8** bring out **9** call forth, draw forth

elide 4 fail, omit, skip **6** cut off, excise, forget, ignore, remove, slight **7** abridge, curtail, neglect **8** condense, cross out, discount, overlook, pass over, suppress **9** disregard, strike out

eligible 3 fit **6** fitted, likely, nubile, seemly, suited, worthy **7** capable **8** entitled, suitable **9** desirable, qualified **10** acceptable **11** appropriate **12** marriageable

Elihu ____ 4 Root, Yale

Elijah 5 Elias **7** prophet **8** Tishbite ***father:*** **5** Harim **7** Jeroham

Elimelech's wife 5 Naomi

eliminate 3 bar **4** bate, drop, oust, void **5** debar, egest, eject, erase, evict, expel, purge **6** delete, except, remove **7** abolish, discard, dismiss, exclude, expunge, obviate, rule out, take out **8** count out **9** clear away, eradicate, liquidate **11** exterminate

Eliot, George *lover:* **5** Lewes (George Henry) ***novel:*** **6** Romola **8** Adam Bede **11** Middlemarch, Silas Marner **13** Daniel Deronda **14** Mill on the Floss (The) ***pseudonym of:*** **5** Evans (Mary Ann)

Eliot, T. S. *character:* **8** Prufrock (J. Alfred) ***play:*** **13** Cocktail Party (The) **20** Murder in the Cathedral ***poem:*** **9** Gerontion, Hollow Men (The), Waste Land (The) **12** Ash Wednesday, Four Quartets

Eliphaz ***father:*** **4** Esau ***mother:*** **4** Adah ***son:*** **5** Teman

Elisabeth ***husband:*** **9** Zacharias ***son:*** **4** John (the Baptist)

Elisha ***father:*** **7** Shaphat ***servant:*** **6** Gehazi

Elisheba ***brother:*** **7** Nahshon ***father:*** **9** Amminadab ***husband:*** **5** Aaron ***son:*** **5** Abihu, Nadab **7** Eleazar, Ithamar

elite **3** top **4** best, pick **5** A-list, cream, elect, pride, prime, prize **6** choice, flower, gentry, select **7** quality, society **9** exclusive, gentility, patrician **10** upper class, upper crust **11** aristocracy **12** aristocratic

elixir **4** balm, cure **6** potion **7** arcanum, cure-all, nostrum, panacea, philter, philtre **10** catholicon

Elizabeth I **6** Oriana **8** Gloriana

elk **4** deer **5** moose **6** sambar, wapiti **7** red deer

ell **3** arm **4** wing **5** annex, elbow, joint **8** addition **9** extension

ellipse **4** oval **5** curve, orbit

elliptical **5** brief, ovate, short **6** gnomic **7** concise, cryptic, laconic, obscure, summary **9** condensed, enigmatic **11** abbreviated

Ellison work **10** Juneteenth **12** Invisible Man

elm **5** wahoo

elocution **7** diction, oratory **8** delivery, rhetoric **11** declamation, speechcraft

elongate **4** draw **6** extend **7** draw out, lengthy, spin out, stretch **8** extended, lengthen **10** lengthened

elope **4** flee **6** escape, run off **7** abscond, run away **9** steal away

eloquence **5** force, power **6** fervor, spirit **7** fluency, oratory, passion **8** rhetoric **10** expression **12** expressivity, forcefulness

eloquent **5** lofty **6** ardent, fervid, fluent, moving **7** fervent, voluble **8** elevated, forceful, powerful, stirring **9** affecting **10** articulate, expressive, impressive, meaningful, passionate, persuasive, rhetorical **11** impassioned, sententious **12** smooth-spoken **13** silver-tongued

El Salvador ***capital:*** **11** San Salvador ***city:*** **8** Santa Ana **9** San Miguel ***ethnic group:*** **5** Pipil ***lake:*** **8** Ilopango ***language:*** **7** Spanish ***monetary unit:*** **5** colón **6** dollar ***neighbor:*** **8** Honduras **9** Guatemala ***river:*** **5** Lempa

else **5** if not **7** besides, further **9** otherwise **10** additional **11** differently **12** additionally

elucidate **7** clarify, clear up, explain, expound **8** annotate, spell out **9** exemplify, explicate, interpret **10** illuminate, illustrate

elude **4** defy, duck, flee, foil **5** avert, avoid, dodge, evade **6** baffle, escape, outwit, thwart **8** confound **9** frustrate **10** circumvent

elusive **6** subtle, tricky **7** evasive, phantom **8** baffling, fleeting, fugitive, slippery **10** evanescent, intangible, mysterious **13** insubstantial

elute **7** extract

elver **3** eel

elvish see **elfin**

Elysium **5** bliss **6** heaven **7** nirvana **8** empyrean, paradise

elytron **4** wing

emaciated **4** bony, lean, thin **5** gaunt **6** skinny, wasted **7** scrawny, starved, wizened **8** skeletal, underfed **10** cadaverous

emaciation **5** tabes **7** atrophy **8** marasmus **10** starvation **11** attenuation

e-mail abbreviation **3** AKA, BAK, BBL, BRB, BTW, FYI, HTH, IMO, IOW, KIT, LOL, NRN, OBO, POV, PDQ, TIA, UKW **4** ASAP, BCNU, BION, FWIW, GMTA, GTGB, IMHO, TTYL, YMMV

emanate **4** emit, flow, rise, stem **5** arise, exude, issue **6** derive, emerge, spring **7** come out, give off, give out, proceed, radiate **9** come forth, originate **10** derive from

emanation **4** aura, flow **6** efflux **8** effusion, emission **9** effluence

emancipate **4** free **5** let go, loose **6** loosen, redeem, unbind **7** manumit, release, set free, unchain **8** liberate, unfetter **9** discharge, unshackle **11** enfranchise

emancipation **7** release **10** liberation **11** deliverance

emancipator **5** Moses **7** Lincoln (Abraham) **9** deliverer, liberator

emasculate **3** fix **4** geld **5** alter, unman **6** neuter, soften, weaken **7** unnerve **8** castrate, enervate, unstring **10** debilitate, devitalize

embalm **7** mummify, perfume **8** preserve

embankment **4** berm, bund, dike, quay **5** levee, mound **6** escarp

embargo **3** ban, bar **5** edict, order **8** blockade, stoppage **10** impediment **11** prohibition

embark **5** board, enter, start **6** set out **7** set sail **8** commence

embarrass **4** faze **5** abash, upset **6** flurry, hamper, hinder, impede, rattle **7** confuse, flummox, fluster, mortify, nonplus, perturb **8** confound, distress **9** discomfit, humiliate **10** complicate, discomfort, discompose, disconcert

embarrassment **5** shame, upset **7** chagrin **8** distress **9** confusion **10** discomfort **11** humiliation **12** discomfiture, perturbation **13** mortification

embassy **5** envoy **7** mission **8** legation **10** ambassador, delegation, deputation

embay **4** trap **5** catch, seize **7** capture **8** encircle, surround

embed **3** fix, set **4** bury, root **5** infix, inlay, lodge **7** implant, ingrain **8** entrench

embellish **3** pad **4** deck, gild, trim **5** adorn, color **6** bedeck, blazon, emboss, enrich **7** amplify, dress up, enhance, festoon, garnish **8** beautify, decorate, ornament **9** elaborate, embroider **10** exaggerate **11** romanticize

embellishment **7** garnish, gilding, melisma, mordent **8** coloring, ornament **9** fioritura, floridity, hyperbole **10** decoration **11** elaboration **12** embroidering, exaggeration **13** ornamentation

ember **3** ash **4** coal **6** cinder

embezzle **4** loot **5** filch, steal **6** pilfer **7** purloin **8** peculate **9** defalcate

embitter **4** sour **6** poison **7** envenom **9** acidulate

emblazon **4** laud **5** extol **7** glorify **8** inscribe **9** celebrate

emblem **4** arms, flag, logo, mace, seal, sign **5** badge, brand, crest, image, token **6** banner, device, symbol **7** pennant **8** colophon, hallmark, insignia, monogram, standard **9** attribute, trademark **10** coat of arms

emblematic **8** symbolic **10** figurative, indicative **11** allegorical **12** illustrative, metaphorical

embodiment **6** avatar **7** epitome **8** exemplar **9** archetype **11** incarnation **13** manifestation

embody **5** reify **6** evince, mirror, typify **7** compose, contain, exhibit, realize, subsume **8** manifest **9** actualize, encompass, epitomize, exemplify, incarnate, integrate, objectify, personify, represent, symbolize **10** constitute, illustrate **11** emblematize, externalize, hypostatize, incorporate, materialize **12** substantiate

embolden **5** steel **7** fortify, hearten, inspire **8** inspirit **9** encourage **10** strengthen

embolus **4** clog, clot

embosom **3** hug **7** embrace, enclose, envelop, shelter

embouchure **10** mouthpiece

embowel **3** gut **4** draw **10** eviscerate, exenterate

embrace **3** hug **4** hold, lock, love, wrap **5** admit, adopt, clasp, cling, press **6** accept, cradle, cuddle, embody, enfold, fondle, nuzzle, take in, take on, take up **7** bear hug, cherish, contain, embosom, enclose, entwine, envelop, espouse, include, receive, snuggle, squeeze, subsume, welcome **8** comprise, encircle **9** encompass **10** comprehend **11** accommodate, incorporate **12** encirclement

embrangle see **embroil**

embrocation **5** salve **7** unguent **8** liniment

embroider **3** pad, sew, tat **4** gild **5** color **6** expand, overdo, play up, stitch **7** amplify, build up, enhance, garnish, magnify, stretch **8** decorate, ornament **9** dramatize, elaborate, embellish **10** exaggerate **11** hyperbolize, romanticize

embroidery **6** crewel **7** cutwork, orphrey **8** bargello, couching, smocking, tapestry **10** crewelwork, needlework **11** needlepoint

embroil **4** mire **6** tangle **7** confuse, ensnare, involve **8** disorder, entangle **9** implicate

embroilment **4** tiff **6** fracas **7** dispute, quarrel, wrangle **8** squabble **9** bickering **10** falling-out **11** altercation, controversy

embryo **3** bud **4** germ, seed **5** fetus, spark **7** nucleus **8** blastula, gastrula

emend **4** edit **5** alter, right **6** polish, revise **7** correct, improve, rectify, retouch

emerald **3** gem **5** beryl, green, stone **8** gemstone

Emerald Isle **4** Eire, Erin **7** Ireland

emerge **4** flow, loom, rise, stem **5** arise, issue **6** appear, derive, evolve, spring **7** come out, debouch, develop, emanate, proceed, surface **9** originate, transpire **11** come to light, materialize

emergency **3** fix **4** hole, pass **5** pinch **6** climax, clutch, crisis, crunch, strait **7** squeeze **8** accident, exigency

emeritus **7** retired

Emerson, Ralph Waldo ***essay:*** **12** Self-Reliance ***forte:*** **5** essay ***friend:*** **7** Thoreau (Henry David) ***home:*** **7** Concord

emery **6** powder **8** abrasive, corundum

emetic **8** vomitive **9** cathartic, purgative

émeute **4** riot **6** mutiny, revolt, rising, tumult **8** outbreak, upheaval, uprising **9** rebellion **12** insurrection

emigrant **7** pioneer, settler **8** colonist **10** expatriate

émigré **2** DP **5** alien, exile, expat **7** evacuee, migrant, refugee **8** colonist **10** expatriate

Emilia ***husband:*** **4** Iago **7** Palamon ***slayer:*** **4** Iago

eminence **3** VIP **4** fame, peak, rise **5** honor, power **6** bigwig, esteem, height, leader, renown, repute **7** dignity, notable **8** altitude, big-timer, luminary, prestige, standing **9** authority, dignitary, elevation, greatness, loftiness **10** importance, projection, prominence, promontory, reputation **11** distinction, superiority

eminent **4** high **5** famed, grand, great, large, lofty, noble, noted **6** august, famous **7** exalted, notable **8** esteemed, renowned, towering **9** important, well-known **10** celebrated, noteworthy, projecting **11** conspicuous, illustrious, outstanding, prestigious **13** distinguished

eminently 4 very **6** highly **7** notably **9** extremely **10** remarkably, strikingly **11** exceedingly **12** surpassingly **13** exceptionally

emir 5 chief, ruler, sheik, title **6** sheikh **9** chieftain, commander

emissary see **envoy**

emission 4 flow **7** venting **9** discharge, effluvium, emanation, radiation

emit 4 beam, glow, ooze, pour, shed, spew, vent, void **5** eject, expel, exude, issue, loose, utter **6** exhale, let out **7** emanate, excrete, extrude, give off, give out, radiate, release, secrete, send out **8** evacuate, throw off **9** circulate, discharge

emmer 5 grain, spelt, wheat

emmet 3 ant **7** pismire

emollient 4 aloe, balm **5** salve **7** lenient, unguent **8** aloe vera, lenitive, liniment, ointment, sedative, soothing **9** analgesic, softening **10** mollifying

emolument 3 fee, pay **4** wage **5** wages **6** income, reward, salary **7** guerdon, stipend **8** earnings **10** recompense **11** pay envelope **12** compensation

emotion 3 ire, joy **4** fear, glee, hate, love **5** agony, ardor, grief, shame **6** affect, hatred, relief, sorrow, warmth **7** ardency, despair, disgust, ecstasy, feeling, passion, sadness **8** jealousy, surprise **9** affection, agitation, happiness, sentiment

emotional 4 warm **6** ardent, fervid, heated, moving **7** feeling, fervent, intense, soulful, zealous **8** effusive, stirring, touching, vehement **9** affecting, affective, excitable, heartfelt, impetuous, rhapsodic, sensitive **10** hysterical, passionate **11** impassioned, overwrought, rhapsodical, softhearted, susceptible, sympathetic

emotionless 3 icy **4** cold, cool **5** chill, staid, stoic, stony **6** frigid, remote, torpid **7** callous, deadpan, distant, glacial **8** detached, reserved **9** apathetic, immovable, impassive, unfeeling **10** impersonal **11** cold-blooded, indifferent **12** matter-of-fact **13** dispassionate, unimpassioned

empathy 4 pity **6** lenity, warmth **7** rapport **8** affinity, sympathy **9** communion **10** compassion **12** congeniality **13** compatibility, comprehension, fellow feeling, understanding

emperor 4 czar, shah, tsar, tzar **5** ruler **6** caesar, kaiser **7** monarch **8** autocrat, dictator **9** potentate, sovereign ***French:*** **8** Napoleon (Bonaparte) **9** Bonaparte (Napoleon) **11** Charlemagne ***Indian:*** **5** Babur ***Japanese:*** **6** mikado **7** Akihito **8** Hirohito ***Mexican:*** **8** Iturbide (Agustín de) **10** Maximilian ***Roman:*** **4** Nero, Otho **5** Galba, Nerva, Titus **6** Decius, Julian, Trajan **7** Gratian, Hadrian, Severus **8** Augustus, Aurelian, Caligula, Claudius, Commodus, Domitian, Honorius, Tiberius, Valerian **9** Antoninus, Caracalla, Justinian, Vespasian, Vitellius **10** Diocletian, Elagabalus **11** Constantine

emphasis 5 focus, force **6** accent, stress, weight **9** attention, intensity **10** insistence, prominence **12** accentuation

emphasize 6 accent, play up, stress **7** feature **8** pinpoint **9** highlight, italicize, spotlight, underline **10** accentuate, underscore

emphatic 4 firm **6** marked **7** decided, earnest, pointed **8** accented, decisive, forceful, positive, stressed, vigorous **9** assertive, energetic, insistent **10** resounding, underlined **11** accentuated

empire 5 realm **6** domain **7** demesne, kingdom **8** dominion ***ancient:*** (see **ancient empire**)

Empire State 7 New York

empirical 7 factual **9** fact-based, pragmatic **12** experiential, experimental **13** observational

emplacement 7 battery **8** position

employ 3 job, use **4** busy, hire, work **5** apply, avail **6** devote, engage, occupy, retain, secure, take on **7** exploit, utilize **8** exercise, practice **9** make use of **10** occupation

employee 4 hand, help **5** agent **6** worker **7** servant **8** factotum **9** underling ***bank:*** **5** clerk, guard **6** teller ***hotel:*** **7** bellboy, bellhop, doorman **9** concierge, desk clerk **11** chambermaid

employer 4 boss **6** master **10** supervisor

employment 3 job, use **4** line, post, task, toil, work **5** trade, usage **6** hiring, métier, office **7** calling, mission, purpose, pursuit **8** business, exercise, function, position, vocation **9** appliance, operation, situation **10** engagement, occupation **11** application, recruitment, utilization **12** exploitation

emporium 4 mall, mart, shop **5** store **6** bazaar, market **8** exchange **11** marketplace

empower 5 endow **6** charge, enable, invest **7** entitle, entrust, license **8** accredit, delegate, deputize, sanction **9** authorize, privilege **10** commission

empress 5 queen ***Byzantine:*** **3** Zoe ***French:*** **7** Eugénie **9** Josephine ***Japanese:*** **5** Suiko ***of India:*** **8** Victoria ***Mexican:*** **7** Carlota ***Roman:*** **6** Fausta ***Russian:*** **4** Anna **7** czarina, tsarina, tzarina **9** Alexandra, Catherine, Elizabeth

empressement 6 fervor, warmth **10** cordiality
emprise 4 feat, gest **5** geste **7** exploit, venture **9** adventure **11** undertaking
emptiness 4 void **5** blank **6** hunger, vacuum **7** inanity, vacancy, vacuity
emptor 5 buyer **6** vendee **8** consumer, customer **9** purchaser
____ **emptor 6** caveat
empty 3 rid **4** bare, dump, pour, vain, void **5** blank, clear, drain **6** barren, devoid, hollow, unload, vacant, vacate **7** deplete, drained, exhaust, vacated, vacuous **8** depleted, deserted, evacuate, forsaken **9** abandoned, destitute **10** unoccupied, untenanted ***Scottish:*** **4** toom
empty-headed 6 simple, vacant **7** vacuous, witless **8** ignorant, untaught **9** benighted, brainless, frivolous **10** illiterate, uneducated, unlettered, unschooled **11** know-nothing **12** uninstructed **13** rattlebrained
empyreal 4 airy, holy **6** aerial, divine **7** sublime **8** beatific, ethereal, heavenly **9** celestial, spiritual, unearthly **12** transcendent
empyrean 3 sky **4** Zion **5** bliss, ether **6** heaven, welkin **7** Elysium, heavens, nirvana **8** paradise **9** firmament
EMT's skill 3 CPR
emu 4 bird, rhea **6** ratite **9** cassowary
emulate 3 ape **4** copy **5** equal, mimic, rival **6** follow, mirror **7** compete, imitate **9** challenge
emulation 7 rivalry **8** striving, tug-of-war **9** imitation **10** contention **11** competition
emulous 5 vying **8** aspiring, striving, vaulting **9** ambitious **11** competitive
emulsifier 4 soap **5** algin
enable 3 fit, let **5** allow, ready **6** permit **7** empower, entitle, license, prepare, qualify **8** accredit, sanction **9** authorize, condition **10** commission, facilitate **12** make possible
enact 4 pass, play **6** decree, depict, effect, ordain, ratify **7** execute, perform, portray **8** proclaim **9** authorize, discourse, establish, institute, legislate, represent **10** accomplish, bring about, constitute, effectuate **11** impersonate
enactment 3 law **6** action, decree **7** statute **9** depiction, ordinance, portrayal **11** legislation, performance **12** ratification
enamel 5 glaze, gloss, japan, paint **7** lacquer
enamored 4 fond **6** loving **7** devoted, smitten **8** besotted **9** bewitched, enchanted, entranced, infatuate **10** captivated, infatuated
encamp 4 tent **6** settle **7** bivouac
encampment 6 billet, laager **7** bivouac, hutment
encase 3 box **4** pack **7** confine, enclose, envelop, sheathe
enceinte 6 gravid **8** pregnant **9** expectant, expecting **10** parturient
enchain 4 bind **6** fetter **7** manacle, shackle
enchant 3 hex **4** lure, wile **5** charm, spell, witch **6** allure, enamor, seduce, thrill, voodoo **7** attract, beguile, bewitch, delight **8** ensorcel, enthrall **9** captivate, enrapture, ensorcell, fascinate, hypnotize, magnetize, mesmerize, spellbind
enchanter 4 mage **5** magus **6** wizard **7** charmer, warlock **8** conjurer, conjuror, magician, sorcerer **11** necromancer, spellbinder
enchanting 5 siren **9** glamorous, seductive **10** attractive, delectable, delightful, intriguing
enchantment 3 hex **5** charm, magic, spell **6** allure **7** glamour, sorcery **8** witchery, wizardry **9** conjuring, seduction **10** necromancy, witchcraft **11** incantation
enchantress 3 hex **5** bruja, Circe, lamia, Medea, siren, witch **9** sorceress
enchiridion 4 text **5** guide **6** manual **8** Baedeker, handbook **9** guidebook, vade mecum
encipher 4 code
encircle 3 hem **4** band, gird, halo, hoop, ring **5** girth **6** begird, engird, enlace, girdle **7** compass, embrace, enclose, environ, wreathe **8** surround **9** encompass **12** circumscribe
enclave 6 colony, ghetto, sector **7** quarter **8** district, homeland
enclose 3 box, hem, mew, pen, rim **4** cage, coop, mure, wall, wrap **5** bound, fence, hedge, limit **6** circle, closet, corral, hold in, immure, shroud, shut in, wall in **7** compass, confine, contain, embosom, include **8** fence off, imprison, surround **9** capsulize **12** circumscribe
enclosed 6 obtect
enclosure 3 box, mew, pen, sty **4** boma, cage, camp, cell, coop, cote, fold, jail, pale, quad, SΛSE, tank, trap, wall, weir, yard **5** court, fence, kraal, pound, stall **6** aviary, corral, cowpen, kennel, paling, prison **7** chamber, enclave, paddock **8** cloister, stockade **9** courtyard **10** quadrangle
encomiast 7 praiser **8** eulogist **10** panegyrist
encomiastic 9 adulatory, laudative, laudatory **10** eulogistic **11** panegyrical
encomium 4 laud **5** kudos, paean **6** eulogy, homage, praise **7** acclaim, plaudit, tribute **8** accolade, citation, plaudits **9** laudation, panegyric **10** compliment, salutation **11** acclamation **12** commendation
encompass 3 hem **4** belt, gird, ring **5** bound

6 begird, circle, girdle, take in 7 contain, embrace, enclose, include, subsume 8 encircle, surround 10 accomplish, bring about, comprehend

encore 6 recall, repeat, return 10 repetition

encounter 4 face, find, fray, meet 5 brush, clash, fight, run-in, scrap, set-to 6 battle, engage, take on 7 collide, contest, meeting, quarrel, run into 8 argument, bump into, come upon, conflict, confront, meet with, skirmish, struggle 10 contention, experience

encourage 3 egg 4 abet, back, buoy, push, spur, stir, urge 5 boost, cheer, egg on, rally, rouse, serve, steel 6 assist, assure, buck up, excite, foster, incite, induce, praise, spur on 7 advance, animate, approve, bolster, cheer up, endorse, fortify, further, hearten, improve, inspire, promote, provoke, quicken, support, sustain 8 advocate, embolden, energize, inspirit, reassure, sanction 9 enhearten, galvanize, instigate, patronize, reinforce, stimulate, subsidize 10 invigorate, strengthen

encouragement 4 lift, push 5 boost 7 backing, support 8 approval 11 inspiration

encouraging 4 rosy 6 bright, likely 7 hopeful 9 favorable, promising 10 auspicious, propitious

encroach 5 poach 6 invade, meddle, trench 7 impinge, intrude 8 entrench, infringe, overstep, trespass

encrypt 4 code 6 cipher, encode 7 convert 8 disguise, encipher

encumber 4 lade, load 6 burden, charge, fetter, hamper, hinder, impede, saddle, weight 7 freight, oppress 8 handicap, obstruct, overload 9 weigh down 10 overburden

encumbrance 4 lien, load, onus 5 claim 6 burden 7 baggage 8 easement, handicap, mortgage 9 albatross, millstone 10 impediment

encyclical 6 letter 7 general 8 circular

encyclopedic 5 broad 7 general 8 complete, thorough 9 extensive, inclusive, universal 11 compendious, wide-ranging 12 all-embracing, all-inclusive 13 comprehensive

encyclopedist 7 Diderot (Denis)

end 3 aim, tip 4 coda, doom, goal, halt, quit, stop, tail, term 5 cease, close, death, finis, lapse, limit 6 demise, expire, finale, finish, object, period, result, scotch, windup, wrap up 7 abolish, closing, closure, extreme, lineman, outcome, purpose 8 complete, conclude, curtains, surcease, terminal, terminus 9 cessation, extremity, objective, terminate 10 completion, conclusion, denouement, expiration 11 culmination, discontinue, termination 12 consummation

endanger 4 risk 5 peril 6 expose 7 imperil 8 threaten 10 compromise, jeopardize

endearment ***term:*** 3 hon, pet 4 baby, dear, duck, lamb 5 bubby, bunny, honey, romeo, sugar 6 kitten, poopsy, poppet, sparky 7 darling, dearest, gumdrop, ladybug, lambkin, pumpkin, sweetie 8 cutie pie, doll-face, gorgeous, honey-bun, lady-love, lover-boy, precious, princess, pussycat, snookums, snuggles, sunshine, sweet pea, sweetums 9 angel-face, babycakes, buttercup, sugar-lips 10 heartthrob, honey bunch, honeychild, love-muffin, sweetheart, sweetie pie, tootsie pie

endeavor 3 aim, try 4 push, seek, toil, work 5 assay, essay, labor, trial 6 effort, intend, strain, strive 7 attempt, purpose, travail, venture 8 exertion, striving, struggle 9 determine, undertake 10 enterprise 11 undertaking

ended 4 done, over, past 7 through 8 complete

endemic 5 local 6 innate, native 8 homebred, inherent, primeval 9 homegrown, prevalent 10 aboriginal, indigenous, native-born

ending 4 stop 5 close 6 finale, finish, period, windup 7 closing, closure 8 terminus 9 cessation 10 completion, conclusion, denouement 11 termination

endive 7 lettuce, witloof 8 escarole

endless 7 eternal, undying 8 constant, enduring, immortal, infinite, unending 9 ceaseless, continual, incessant, limitless, perpetual, unbounded, unceasing, unlimited 10 continuous, indefinite, unmeasured 11 everlasting, illimitable, measureless 12 immeasurable, interminable

endmost 4 last 5 final 8 farthest, furthest, ultimate 10 concluding

endocrine gland 5 gonad, ovary 6 pineal, testis, thymus 7 adrenal, thyroid 8 pancreas 9 pituitary 11 parathyroid 12 hypothalamus

endomorphic 5 beefy, heavy, husky, plump, pudgy, stout 6 chubby, portly, pyknic, rotund

endorse 2 OK 4 back, okay, sign 5 bless, vouch 6 attest, ratify, second, uphold 7 approve, certify, command, confirm, stand by, support, witness 8 accredit, advocate, champion, inscribe, make over, notarize, sanction 9 autograph, recommend 10 underwrite 12 authenticate

endorsement 2 OK 4 okay 7 backing, support 8 approval, sanction, thumbs-up 9 signature 10 green light 12 confirmation, ratification 13 authorization

endow 4 back, fund 5 found 6 bestow, confer, enrich, supply 7 empower, enhance, fi-

nance, furnish, promote, provide, sponsor, support **8** bequeath **9** subsidize
endowment 4 fund, gift **5** award, dower, dowry, grant, power, skill **6** legacy, talent **7** ability, bequest **8** appanage, aptitude, bestowal, capacity, donation **11** benefaction
end product 5 fruit, issue **6** effect, payoff, result, upshot **7** outcome **11** consequence
endue 3 don **4** vest **5** dower, equip, imbue, put on **6** clothe, invest, outfit **7** furnish, provide **8** accouter **9** crown with, transfuse
endurance 4 grit, guts, wind **5** moxie, pluck **6** mettle **7** stamina **8** patience, strength, tenacity **9** fortitude **10** permanence, resolution **11** persistence **12** perseverance
endure 4 bear, bide, go on, last **5** abide, brook, stand **6** accept, hold on, linger, pocket, remain, suffer **7** carry on, persist, ride out, stomach, survive, sustain, swallow, undergo, weather **8** continue, submit to, tolerate, tough out **9** withstand
enduring 3 old **4** fast, firm, sure **6** steady **7** abiding, durable, eternal, lasting, staunch **8** constant, lifelong **9** long-lived, perennial, permanent, steadfast **10** continuing, inveterate, persistent **11** long-lasting, unfaltering **12** never-failing
Endymion *father:* 8 Aethlius ***lover:* 5** Diana **6** Selene ***author:* 5** Keats (John)
enemy 3 foe **5** rival **8** attacker, opponent **9** adversary, assailant **10** antagonist, competitor
energetic 4 spry **5** brisk, fresh, hardy, lusty, peppy, zippy **6** active, lively **7** driving, dynamic, vibrant **8** spirited, tireless, vigorous **9** sprightly, strenuous, vivacious **13** indefatigable
energize 3 pep **4** fuel, stir **5** liven, pep up, rouse, spark **6** enable, excite, stir up, turn on **7** empower, enliven, fortify, inspire, juice up **8** activate, inspirit, vitalize **9** electrify, galvanize, stimulate **10** invigorate, strengthen
energy 2 qi **3** chi, pep, vim, zip **4** dash, life, tuck **5** drive, force, juice, moxie, pluck, power, steam, verve, vigor **6** effort, muscle, spirit **7** current, potency, stamina, voltage **8** activity, dynamism, exertion, strength, vitality **9** animation, puissance **10** enterprise, get-up-and-go, initiative ***unit:* 3** erg **4** dyne, volt **5** joule **7** quantum **10** horsepower
enervate 3 sap **4** jade, tire **5** weary **6** soften, weaken **7** disable, exhaust, fatigue, unnerve **8** enfeeble, unstring **10** debilitate, devitalize
enfant terrible 3 imp **5** scamp **6** bad boy, urchin **7** skeezix **9** skeezicks
enfeeble 3 sap **6** soften, weaken **7** deplete, disable, exhaust, fatigue **8** enervate **9** attenuate, undermine **10** debilitate, devitalize
enfold 3 hug **4** wrap **5** clasp, cover, press **6** shroud, swathe **7** contain, embrace, squeeze **8** surround
enforce 5 exact, impel **6** compel, effect, impose, invoke, oblige **7** execute, fulfill **8** carry out **9** constrain, discharge, implement, prosecute **10** accomplish, administer, strengthen
enfranchise 4 free **6** rescue **7** deliver, manumit, release, set free **8** liberate **10** emancipate
engage 4 bind, grip, hire, mesh **5** fight, tie up, troth **6** absorb, attack, battle, commit, employ, enlist, pledge, take on **7** assault, betroth, engross, immerse, involve, promise **8** affiance, interact **9** captivate, encounter, interlace, interlock, intermesh, interplay, preoccupy, undertake
engaged 4 busy, rapt **6** intent **7** working **8** absorbed, employed, immersed, intended, occupied, plighted **9** affianced, betrothed, committed, engrossed, wrapped up **10** contracted **11** preoccupied ***person:* 6** fiancé **7** fiancée
engage in 4 wage **5** enter **6** pursue, tackle, take up **7** conduct **8** embark on, practice **9** prosecute, undertake
engagement 3 gig **4** date, fray, word **5** fight, troth, tryst **6** action, battle, combat, hiring, pledge, plight **7** booking, meeting, promise **8** espousal, skirmish **9** betrothal, encounter **10** commitment, employment, rendezvous **11** appointment, assignation
engaging 7 likable, winning, winsome **8** charming, pleasant, pleasing **9** appealing **10** attractive **13** prepossessing
engender 4 sire, stir **5** beget, breed, cause, hatch, rouse, spawn **6** arouse, create, excite, father, induce, lead to, work up **7** develop, produce, provoke **8** generate **9** originate, procreate, stimulate
engine 5 motor, turbo **7** turbine **10** locomotive ***fluid:* 7** coolant **10** antifreeze ***kind:* 3** gas, jet **5** steam **6** diesel **7** turbine **8** gasoline **9** hydraulic ***jet:* 8** turbofan, turbojet ***part:* 3** cam, rod **4** gear, plug, pump **5** choke **6** filter, piston, tappet **8** cylinder, manifold, throttle **9** condenser, crankcase **10** carburetor **12** transmission ***siege:* 3** ram **6** onager **8** ballista, catapult **9** trebuchet **12** battering ram ***sound:* 4** chug, roar **6** rattle
engineer 4 plan, plot **5** set up, swing **6** devise, driver, manage, scheme, wangle **7** arrange, finagle **8** contrive, intrigue, maneuver, motorman **9** machinate, negoti-

ate **10** manipulate, mastermind **11** orchestrate ***kind:*** **5** civil **6** mining **8** chemical, sanitary **10** electrical, mechanical **12** aeronautical ***military:*** **6** sapper

engineers' group **4** ASME, IEEE

England **6** Albion **7** Britain **9** Britannia **12** Great Britain see also **United Kingdom**

English **7** British ***cathedral city:*** **3** Ely **4** York **5** Wells **6** Durham, Exeter **7** Lincoln, Norwich **8** Coventry, Hereford **9** Salisbury, Worcester **10** Canterbury, Winchester ***coin:*** **5** crown, groat, pence **6** florin, guinea **8** farthing, shilling, sixpence, twopence **9** fourpence, half crown, halfpenny, sovereign **10** threepence ***combining form:*** **5** Anglo ***farm:*** **5** croft ***forest:*** **5** Arden **8** Sherwood ***letter:*** **3** zed ***measure:*** **3** rod, tun **4** gill, hand, peck, span **5** chain **6** barrel, bushel, fathom, firkin **7** furlong **8** hogshead **10** barleycorn ***military college:*** **9** Sandhurst ***patron saint:*** **6** George ***person:*** **4** chap, mate **5** bloke **6** Briton ***pirate:*** **4** Kidd (Capt. William) **5** Avery (Henry), Teach (Edward) **6** Morgan (Henry) **7** Dampier (William) **10** Blackbeard ***prince:*** **5** Harry **6** Andrew, Edward, Philip **7** Charles, William ***princess:*** **4** Anne **5** Diana **8** Margaret ***professor:*** **3** don ***royal family:*** **5** Tudor **6** Stuart **7** Hanover, Windsor **11** Plantagenet ***saint:*** **7** Dunstan **8** Cuthbert ***school:*** **4** Eton **6** Harrow ***spa:*** **4** Bath ***sport:*** **5** darts, rugby **7** cricket ***tavern:*** **3** pub ***university:*** **5** Leeds **6** Oxford **9** Cambridge ***weight:*** **5** stone **6** firkin **7** quintal **8** quartern

English Channel ***French:*** **6** Manche (La) ***swimmer:*** **6** Ederle (Gertrude)

engrave **3** cut, fix **4** etch **5** carve, chase **6** incise, scrive **7** instill **8** inscribe

engraver **6** chaser, etcher ***German:*** **5** Dürer (Albrecht) **10** Schongauer (Martin) ***Italian:*** **8** Raimondi (Marcantonio)

engraving **7** etching, linecut, woodcut **8** drypoint, intaglio **9** xylograph

engross **4** bury, busy, copy, grip **5** apply, write **6** absorb, engage, indite, occupy, scribe **7** consume, immerse, involve **8** enthrall, inscribe **9** captivate, preoccupy **10** transcribe

engrossed **4** rapt **6** intent **7** engaged, riveted **8** absorbed, immersed **9** attentive **10** enraptured **11** preoccupied **12** concentrated

engrosser **6** scribe **7** copyist **9** scrivener **12** calligrapher **13** calligraphist

engulf **4** bury **5** drown, flood, swamp, whelm **6** deluge, devour **7** immerse, overrun, swallow **8** flow over, inundate, overflow, submerge **9** overwhelm, swallow up

enhance **4** lift **5** add to, adorn, exalt, raise **6** deepen **7** amplify, augment, build up, elevate, enlarge, flatter, improve, magnify **8** beautify, heighten, increase **9** aggravate, embellish, embroider, intensify, reinforce **10** exaggerate, strengthen

enigma **4** crux, knot **5** poser, rebus **6** puzzle, riddle, sphinx, teaser **7** mystery, problem, puzzler **9** conundrum **10** closed book, perplexity, puzzlement **12** question mark **13** Chinese puzzle, mystification

enigmatic **6** mystic **7** cryptic, Delphic, obscure **8** Delphian, oracular, puzzling **9** ambiguous **10** mysterious, mystifying, perplexing **11** inscrutable

enisle **6** cut off **7** isolate **8** insulate, separate **9** segregate, sequester

enjoin **3** ban, bid **4** deny, rule, tell, urge, warn **5** order, taboo **6** adjure, charge, decree, direct, forbid, impose, outlaw **7** caution, command, counsel, dictate, inhibit **8** admonish, disallow, forewarn, instruct, prohibit **9** interdict, prescribe, proscribe

enjoy **4** like, love **5** eat up, fancy, savor **6** relish **9** delight in **10** appreciate

enjoyable **3** fun **8** pleasant, pleasing **9** agreeable **10** delightful, satisfying **11** pleasurable **12** entertaining

enjoyment **4** zest **5** gusto, savor **6** relish **7** benefit, delight **8** felicity, fruition, pleasure **9** diversion **10** indulgence, recreation, relaxation **11** delectation **12** satisfaction **13** gratification

Enki ***consort:*** **5** Nintu ***son:*** **6** Ninsar

enkindle **4** fire **5** flame, light **6** ignite **7** inflame **8** touch off **9** set fire to

enlarge **3** wax **4** grow, rise **5** add to, boost, build, mount, widen **6** beef up, dilate, expand, extend **7** amplify, augment, broaden, develop, greaten, inflate, magnify, stretch **8** heighten, increase, multiply **9** elaborate, embroider **10** exaggerate

enlargement **4** node **5** tumor **6** blowup, growth, nodule **7** buildup **8** addition, increase, swelling **9** accretion, expansion, extension **12** augmentation **13** amplification

enlighten **5** edify, guide, teach **6** advise, illume, inform, uplift **7** educate, improve **8** illumine, instruct **10** illuminate

enlist **4** join **5** draft, enter **6** employ, enroll, join up, muster, sign on, sign up **7** attract, recruit **8** register **9** volunteer **11** participate

enliven **3** pep **4** buoy, fire, warm **5** amuse, cheer, pep up, renew, rouse **6** excite, jazz up, perk up, vivify, wake up **7** animate, cheer up, inspire, quicken, refresh, restore, spice up **8** energize, recreate **9** entertain, galvanize, stimulate **10** exhilarate, invigorate, rejuvenate

en masse 5 as one **6** bodily **8** together **12** collectively

enmesh 4 hook, mire, trap **5** catch, snare **6** draw in, tangle **7** embroil, ensnarl, involve, trammel **8** drag into, entangle **9** embrangle, implicate

enmity 4 hate **6** animus, hatred, rancor, spleen **7** ill will **8** aversion, bad blood, loathing **9** animosity, antipathy, hostility **10** abhorrence, antagonism **11** detestation

ennoble 5 exalt, honor, raise **6** uplift, uprear **7** dignify, elevate, glorify, magnify, sublime **10** aggrandize **11** distinguish

ennui 6 apathy, tedium **7** boredom, fatigue, languor **8** doldrums, dullness, lethargy **9** jadedness, lassitude, tiredness, weariness **11** languidness **12** listlessness

Enoch *father:* 4 Cain ***son:* 10** Methuselah

Enoch Arden author 8 Tennyson (Alfred)

enormity 6 infamy **7** outrage **8** atrocity, hugeness, rankness, savagery, vastness **9** barbarity, depravity, flagrancy, graveness, greatness, grossness, immensity, magnitude **11** abomination, heinousness, massiveness, monstrosity, seriousness, weightiness

enormous 4 huge, vast **5** great **7** immense, mammoth, massive, titanic **8** colossal, gigantic **9** humongous, monstrous **10** astronomic, gargantuan, prodigious, stupendous, tremendous **12** astronomical

Enos *father:* 4 Seth ***grandfather:* 4** Adam ***grandmother:* 3** Eve ***uncle:* 4** Abel, Cain

enough 5 ample **6** fairly, plenty **8** adequate, decently, passably **9** competent, tolerably **10** acceptably, adequately, sufficient **11** comfortable, sufficiency **12** satisfactory, sufficiently ***poetic:* 4** enow

enounce 3 say **5** state, utter **6** intone **8** proclaim, set forth **10** articulate

enrage 3 ire **4** rile **5** anger **6** madden **7** incense, inflame, steam up **9** infuriate

enrapture 5 charm, elate **6** ravish, trance **7** delight, enchant, rejoice **8** enthrall, entrance **9** captivate, transport

enraptured 6 elated **7** charmed **8** ecstatic, thrilled **9** bewitched, delighted, enchanted, entranced **10** captivated, enthralled, mesmerized, spellbound **11** transported

enrich 5 adorn, endow **6** fatten **7** enhance, improve **8** beautify, ornament **9** embellish, fertilize **10** supplement

enroll 4 book, file, join, list **5** draft, enter **6** enlist, induct, join up, muster, record, sign on, sign up, wrap up **7** catalog, engross, recruit **8** inscribe, register **9** conscript, subscribe **10** transcribe **11** matriculate

ensconce 4 bury, hide **5** cache, cover, place, plant, stash **6** hole up, locate, settle **7** conceal, install, secrete, shelter **9** establish

ensemble 3 duo **4** band, crew, suit, trio **5** choir, combo, decor, group, octet, suite, troop, whole **6** chorus, outfit, septet, sextet, troupe **7** chorale, company, costume, en masse, quartet, quintet **8** together **9** aggregate, orchestra

enshrine 6 hallow, revere **7** cherish **8** dedicate, preserve, sanctify, treasure **10** consecrate **11** memorialize

enshroud 4 hide, veil, wrap **5** cloak **6** clothe, enfold, enwrap, invest **7** blanket, conceal, envelop, obscure

ensign 4 flag, jack, sign **5** badge, crest **6** banner, colors, emblem, pennon **7** officer, pennant **8** gonfalon, insignia, standard, streamer **9** oriflamme

enslave 4 yoke **5** chain **6** fetter, thrall **7** enchain, oppress, shackle, subject **8** dominate, enthrall **9** indenture, subjugate **12** disfranchise

enslavement 4 yoke **6** thrall **7** bondage, helotry, peonage, serfdom, slavery **9** servitude, thralldom

ensnare 3 bag, net **4** hook, lure, mesh, snag, trap **5** benet, catch, decoy **6** enmesh, entrap, tangle **7** capture **8** entangle, inveigle

ensnarl 4 mire **6** enmesh, tangle **7** embroil, perplex, trammel **8** entangle **9** embrangle

ensorcell 3 hex **5** charm, spell, witch **6** allure, voodoo **7** beguile, bewitch, enchant **8** enthrall **9** captivate, enrapture, hypnotize, magnetize, mesmerize, spellbind

ensorcellment 5 magic **7** sorcery **8** witchery, wizardry **9** conjuring **10** necromancy, witchcraft **11** bewitchment, enchantment

ensphere 4 ball **8** conglobe **10** conglobate

ensue 4 stem **5** issue **6** attend, derive, follow, result **7** emanate, proceed, succeed **9** supervene

ensuing 4 next **5** later **9** resultant **10** consequent, subsequent, succeeding

ensure 5 cinch **6** clinch, secure **7** certify, confirm, warrant **9** establish, guarantee

enswathe 4 roll, wrap **5** cloak, drape **6** bundle, enwrap, shroud, wrap up **7** envelop, swaddle

entail 5 imply **6** assign, confer, demand, impose, lead to **7** call for, involve, require **8** occasion, restrict, result in, transmit **11** necessitate

entangle 4 mesh, mire, trap **5** catch, ravel, snare, snarl, tie up, twist **6** enmesh, entrap **7**

capture, catch up, embroil, ensnare, ensnarl, involve, perplex, trammel **10** complicate, intertwine, interweave

entanglement 3 web **4** knot, mesh, mess, toil **5** skein, snare **6** affair, cobweb, muddle **8** intrigue **9** confusion, imbroglio **11** embroilment, involvement **12** complication

entente 4 pact **6** league, treaty **7** compact **8** alliance, covenant **9** agreement, coalition, concordat **13** understanding

enter 4 go in, join, list, open **5** admit, begin, key in, start **6** come in, enlist, enroll, go into, insert, join up, muster, record, sign on, sign up **7** intrude **8** come into, embark on, inscribe, register **9** introduce, penetrate **10** embark upon

enterprise 4 deed, feat, firm, push, task **5** cause, drive, pluck, vigor **6** action, daring, effort, energy, hustle, outfit, scheme **7** attempt, company, concern, courage, exploit, project, pursuit, venture **8** activity, ambition, audacity, boldness, business, campaign, endeavor, gumption, industry **9** adventure, eagerness **10** enthusiasm, get-up-and-go, initiative **11** corporation, undertaking **12** organization, self-reliance **13** establishment

enterprising 4 bold **5** eager **6** daring, hungry **7** driving, go-ahead **8** aspiring, hustling **9** ambitious, audacious, energetic **10** aggressive **11** adventurous, hardworking, industrious, up-and-coming, venturesome

entertain 4 host **5** amuse **6** divert, regale **7** delight, receive **8** consider

entertainer 4 mime **5** actor, clown, comic **6** busker, dancer, jester, singer **7** actress, artiste, diseuse, trouper **8** comedian, minstrel **10** comedienne

entertaining 6 lively **7** amusing **8** engaging **9** diverting, enjoyable

entertainment 4 fete, play, show, skit **5** revue, sport **6** circus **7** banquet, concert, pastime, ridotto **8** pleasure **9** amusement, diversion, enjoyment **10** recreation **11** distraction, performance

enthrall 4 grip **5** charm **6** absorb, subdue **7** beguile, bewitch, enchant, engross, enslave **9** fascinate, hypnotize, mesmerize, spellbind, subjugate

enthralling 8 exciting, gripping, riveting **9** absorbing, arresting **10** enchanting, engrossing, entrancing **11** captivating, charismatic, provocative **12** spellbinding

enthuse 4 gush, rave **6** excite, thrill **7** animate, delight, inspire **8** energize **10** rhapsodize

enthusiasm 4 élan, fire, zeal, zest **5** ardor, craze, fever, mania, verve **6** fervor, spirit **7** ardency, passion, rapture **9** eagerness, intensity **10** ebullience, excitement, fanaticism

enthusiast 3 bug, fan, nut **4** buff **5** fiend, freak, lover, maven **6** addict, junkie, maniac, votary, zealot **7** booster, devotee, fanatic, groupie, habitué **8** believer, partisan **9** extremist **10** aficionado

enthusiastic 4 avid, gaga, keen **5** eager, rabid **6** ardent, fervid, gung ho, hearty, hipped, rah-rah, raring **7** devoted, excited, fervent, intense, zealous **8** hopped-up, obsessed, spirited, vascular **9** fanatical **10** passionate

entice 4 bait, coax, draw, lure, toll, wile **5** charm, decoy, tempt **6** allure, cajole, entrap, invite, lead on, seduce **7** attract, wheedle **8** inveigle, persuade

enticement 4 bait, lure, trap **5** decoy, snare **6** allure, come-on **9** seduction **10** allurement, attraction, seducement, temptation **12** blandishment, inveiglement

enticer 4 bait, vamp **5** Circe, decoy, siren **7** Lorelei **9** attractor, temptress **10** attraction, seductress **11** enchantress, femme fatale

enticing 5 siren **8** fetching, witching **9** seductive **10** attractive, bewitching, intriguing **11** captivating, fascinating

entire 3 all **4** full **5** gross, total, whole **6** intact **7** perfect, plenary, unified **8** complete, integral, outright **10** integrated **12** consolidated ***combining form:*** **3** hol, pan **4** holo

entirely 5 fully, quite **6** wholly **7** utterly **9** perfectly **10** altogether, completely, thoroughly **11** exclusively

entirety 3 sum **5** total, whole **8** sum total, totality **9** aggregate, wholeness **10** everything **12** completeness, universality

entitle 3 dub, let **4** call, name, term **5** allow **6** enable, permit **7** baptize, empower, license, qualify **8** christen **9** authorize, designate **10** denominate

entity 3 sum **4** body, item, unit **5** being, thing, whole **6** object **7** article, integer **8** quiddity, totality **9** existence, something, substance **10** individual

entomb 4 bury **5** inter, inurn **6** immure, inhume, shrine **7** mummify **8** enshrine **9** sepulcher, sepulchre

entombment 6 burial **7** funeral, obsequy **9** obsequies, sepulture **10** inhumation

entourage 5 staff, suite, train **6** escort, milieu **7** cortege, coterie, retinue **8** henchmen **9** courtiers, followers, following, hangers-on, retainers **10** associates, attendants **12** surroundings

entr'acte **8** interval **9** interlude **12** intermission

entrails **4** guts **5** pluck, tripe **6** bowels, tripes, umbles, vitals **7** giblets, innards, insides, viscera **8** stuffing **10** intestines

entrance **4** adit, door, gate, port **5** charm, foyer, inlet, lobby, mouth **6** access, portal, ravish **7** arrival, attract, bewitch, delight, doorway, enchant, gateway, ingress, opening **8** aperture, enthrall, open door **9** admission, captivate, enrapture, fascinate, hypnotize, mesmerize, spellbind, threshold, transport, vestibule **10** admittance, ingression **11** penetration

entrant **7** starter **10** competitor, contestant **11** participant

entrap **3** bag, net **4** bait, lure, toll **5** catch, decoy, snare, tempt **6** allure, ambush, entice, entoil, lead on, seduce, tangle **7** beguile, catch up, ensnare **8** entangle, inveigle

entre ____ **4** nous

entreat **3** ask, beg, bid **4** pray, urge **5** crave, plead, press **6** adjure, appeal **7** beseech, implore, wheedle **8** blandish **9** importune **10** supplicate

entreaty **4** plea, suit **6** appeal, orison, prayer **7** request **8** petition **11** application, importunity **12** supplication

entrechat **4** leap

entrée **6** access **7** ingress **8** main dish **9** admission **10** admittance, main course

entrench **3** fix **4** root **5** embed, lodge **6** define, furrow, ground, hole up, invade, settle **7** confirm, impinge, implant, intrude **8** encroach, ensconce, infringe, trespass **9** establish **10** strengthen

entrenched **3** set **4** firm **5** rigid, sworn **8** accepted, deep-dyed **9** hard-shell **10** deep-rooted, deep-seated, inveterate **13** bred-in-the-bone, dyed-in-the-wool

entrepôt **3** hub **4** mart **5** depot **6** bazaar, market **8** emporium, exchange **9** concourse, warehouse **10** depository, storehouse **11** marketplace

entrepreneur **10** capitalist, contractor, impresario

entresol **9** mezzanine

entropy **5** chaos, decay **7** decline **8** disorder **10** randomness **11** degradation

entrust **4** give **5** allot, leave **6** assign, charge, commit, confer, impose **7** commend, confide, consign, deliver, deposit **8** allocate, delegate, hand over, relegate, turn over

entry **3** way **4** adit, door, gate, item, port **5** debit, foyer, inlet, lobby **6** access, credit, portal, record **7** doorway, ingress, opening **8** headword **9** admission, threshold, vestibule **10** admittance, enlistment, enrollment, ingression

entryway **4** door, gate **5** foyer, lobby **6** portal **7** ingress, narthex, portico **9** vestibule

entwine **4** coil, wind **5** braid, plait, twist **6** enmesh **7** wreathe **8** entangle **9** interlace **10** interweave

enumerate **3** sum, tot **4** cite, list, tell, tote **5** add up, count, tally, total, tot up **6** detail, number, recite, reckon, tote up **7** compute, itemize, recount, specify, tick off **8** identify **9** calculate, inventory **13** particularize

enunciate **3** say **5** speak, state, utter, voice **6** affirm, intone **7** declare, express, lay down **8** announce, proclaim, propound, vocalize **9** formulate, postulate, pronounce, verbalize **10** articulate

envelop **3** hem **4** hide, roll, veil, wrap **5** cloak, cover, drape **6** cocoon, enfold, engulf, enwrap, invest, sheath, shield, shroud, swathe, wrap up **7** blanket, embrace, enclose, swaddle **8** encircle, enshroud, enswathe, surround **10** circumfuse

envelope abbreviation **4** ADSR, ATTN

envenom **6** poison **8** embitter **10** exacerbate

envious **7** jealous **8** coveting, covetous, grudging **9** green-eyed, invidious, resentful **10** begrudging

environment **6** medium, milieu **7** ambient, climate, context, habitat, setting, terrain **8** ambiance, ambience, backdrop **9** situation **10** atmosphere, background **11** mise-en-scène **12** surroundings ***science:*** **7** ecology

environmentalist **4** Gore (Al), Muir (John) **6** Brower (David), Carson (Rachel), Nelson (Gaylord), Wilson (Edward O.) **7** Ehrlich (Paul), Thoreau (Henry David) **8** Commoner (Barry), Cousteau (Jacques-Yves) **9** Burroughs (John), ecologist, Roosevelt (Theodore)

environs **4** nabe **6** bounds, limits **7** compass, fringes, suburbs **8** boundary, confines, locality, purlieus, vicinity **9** districts, outskirts, precincts **12** neighborhood, surroundings

envisage **4** view **5** dream, fancy, grasp, image, think **6** ideate, regard, vision **7** dream up, feature, foresee, imagine, picture, realize **8** conceive, look upon, summon up **9** conjure up, objectify, visualize

envoy **5** agent **6** bearer, consul, deputy, legate, nuncio **7** attaché, carrier, courier **8** diplomat, emissary, minister **9** messenger **10** ambassador **11** internuncio **12** intermediary

envy **5** covet **6** grudge **8** begrudge, grudging, jealousy **10** resentment **12** covetousness **13** invidiousness

enwrap **4** roll, veil **5** clasp, drape **6** enfold, invest, shroud, swathe **7** enclose, engross, envelop, sheathe, swaddle **8** enshroud, enswathe

enzyme **3** ase **5** ficin, lyase, renin, urase **6** kinase, ligase, lipase, mutase, papain, pepsin, rennin, urease, zymase **7** amidase, amylase, cyclase, enolase, guanase, hydrase, inulase, isozyme, lactase, maltase, oxidase, pectase, pepsine, plasmin, ptyalin, rennase, sucrase, trypsin, zymogen **8** aldolase, diastase, elastase, esterase, fumarase, lyzozyme, nuclease, protease, steapsin, thrombin, zymogene **9** cellulase, invertase

eon see **aeon**

Eos see **Aurora**

épée **5** blade, sword **6** rapier

epergne **5** stand **11** centerpiece

ephemeral **5** brief, short **7** passing **8** episodic, fleeting, fugitive, volatile **9** fugacious, momentary, temporary, transient **10** evanescent, short-lived, transitory **11** impermanent

Ephialtes **5** giant ***brother:*** **4** Otus ***father:*** **6** Aloeus **8** Poseidon ***mother:*** **9** Iphimedia ***slayer:*** **6** Apollo

Ephraim ***brother:*** **8** Manasseh ***father:*** **6** Joseph ***grandfather:*** **5** Jacob ***mother:*** **7** Asenath

epic **4** Edda, poem, saga **5** grand, Iliad **6** Aeneid, heroic **7** Beowulf, Odyssey **8** imposing, sweeping **9** Gilgamesh, narrative **12** Heimskringla

epicene **10** effeminate **11** intersexual **13** hermaphrodite

epicure **7** gourmet **8** aesthete, hedonist, sybarite **9** bon vivant **10** gastronome **11** connoisseur **12** gastronomist

epicurean **7** gourmet, sensual **8** aesthete, hedonist, sensuous, sybarite **9** bon vivant, luxurious **10** gastronome, voluptuous **11** connoisseur **12** gastronomist, sensualistic

epidemic **3** flu **4** rash, wave **6** plague **7** rampant, scourge **8** catching, outbreak **9** contagion, prevalent **10** contagious, pestilence

epidermis **4** skin **7** cuticle **10** integument

epigram **3** saw **4** poem **5** adage, axiom, maxim **6** bon mot, dictum, saying, truism **7** proverb **8** aphorism, apothegm

epigrammatic **5** meaty, pithy, terse, witty **6** cogent **7** compact, concise, marrowy, piquant, pointed

epigraph **5** motto **9** quotation **11** inscription

epilogue **4** coda **5** close **6** ending, finale, windup **7** closing **8** postlude **9** afterword **10** conclusion, postscript

Epimetheus ***brother:*** **10** Prometheus ***father:*** **7** Iapetus ***wife:*** **7** Pandora

epiphany **6** aperçu, vision **7** insight **9** discovery, intuition **10** appearance, disclosure, revelation **11** inspiration, realization **13** manifestation

episode **5** event, phase **7** passage **8** incident, occasion **9** happening, interlude **10** occurrence **12** circumstance

episodic **5** brief **7** passing **8** fleeting, sporadic **9** ephemeral, irregular, temporary, transient **10** evanescent, occasional, short-lived **12** intermittent

epistaxis **9** nosebleed

epistle **4** note **6** letter **7** lection, missive **13** communication

epitaph **3** R.I.P. **5** elegy **6** eulogy **8** hic jacet **11** inscription

epithet **4** name **5** label, title **7** agnomen, moniker **8** cognomen, nickname **9** sobriquet **11** appellation

epitome **3** sum **4** acme, type **5** brief, short **6** digest, précis, résumé **7** essence, example, outline, summary **8** abstract, breviary, exemplar, synopsis, ultimate **9** archetype, summation, summing-up **10** abridgment, apotheosis, conspectus, embodiment **11** abridgement **12** condensation, quintessence

epitomize **5** sum up **6** digest, embody, mirror, typify **7** abridge, outline, summate **8** abstract, boil down, condense, manifest, tabulate **9** capsulize, exemplify, incarnate, inventory, objectify, personify, represent, summarize, symbolize, synopsize **10** abbreviate, illustrate **11** concentrate, emblematize, incorporate, personalize

epoch **3** age, eon, era **4** aeon, term, time **6** period **8** interval, time span

equable **4** calm, even, just **6** serene, stable, steady **7** orderly, regular, stabile, uniform **8** composed, constant **9** immutable, temperate, unvarying **10** consistent, invariable, unchanging **12** unchangeable

equal **3** tie **4** even, fair, like, mate, peer, same, twin **5** agree, alike, match **7** uniform **8** alter ego, amount to, parallel **9** duplicate, identical, impartial, objective **10** fifty-fifty **11** counterpart, symmetrical **12** commensurate, correspond to, proportional **13** commensurable, proportionate ***combining form:*** **3** iso **4** equi, pari ***French:*** **4** égal

equality **3** par **6** equity, parity **7** balance, égalité **8** evenness, fairness, sameness **10** uniformity

Equality State **7** Wyoming

equalize **4** even **5** level **6** square **7** balance **9** harmonize

equalizer **3** gun **6** pistol **8** handicap **10** tying score

equally 10 fifty-fifty **11** impartially
equanimity 4 calm, cool **5** poise **6** aplomb, phlegm **7** balance **8** calmness, coolness, evenness, serenity **9** assurance, composure, equipoise, placidity, sangfroid **10** detachment, steadiness **11** tranquility **12** tranquillity
equate 4 even **5** liken, match, treat **6** adjust, regard, relate, square **7** compare **8** consider, equalize, parallel **10** assimilate
Equatorial Guinea ***capital:*** **6** Malabo ***island, island group:*** **5** Bioko **6** Elobey, Pagulu **7** Corisco ***language:*** **5** Bantu **6** French **7** Spanish ***mainland:*** **5** Mbini **7** Río Muni ***monetary unit:*** **5** franc ***neighbor:*** **5** Gabon **8** Cameroon
equestrian 5 rider **6** horsey **8** horseman, knightly **10** horsewoman
equidistant 3 mid **6** medial, median, middle, midway **7** central, halfway, midmost
equilibrium 5 poise **6** aplomb, stasis **7** balance **8** evenness, symmetry **9** composure, stability **10** steadiness **12** counterpoise **13** stabilization
equine 4 colt, mare **5** filly, horse, steed **6** horsey **8** stallion **9** horselike
equip 3 arm, fit, rig **5** array, dress, endow, rig up **6** attire, fit out, outfit, rig out, supply **7** appoint, furnish, prepare, provide **8** accouter, accoutre **9** provision
equipment 3 rig **4** gear **5** traps **6** attire, outfit, tackle, things **7** baggage, panoply **8** fittings, material, matériel, ordnance, supplies, tackling **9** apparatus, endowment, machinery, trappings **10** provisions **11** accessories, attachments, habiliments, impedimenta **12** accouterment, accoutrement, provisioning **13** accouterments, accoutrements, appurtenances, paraphernalia
equitable 4 even, fair, just **5** level **6** proper, square **7** condign **8** balanced, deserved, unbiased **9** identical, impartial, objective, uncolored **10** evenhanded, impersonal **12** unprejudiced **13** dispassionate
equity 3 law, par **7** justice **8** equality, interest, justness
equivalence 3 par **6** parity, simile **7** analogy **8** equality, identity, likeness, sameness **10** conformity **11** correlation
equivalent 4 akin, copy, like, peer, same, twin **5** alike, match **6** agnate **7** identic, similar **8** parallel **9** analogous, duplicate, identical **10** comparable, homologous, substitute, tantamount **11** convertible, correlative, counterpart **12** commensurate **13** corresponding, proportionate
equivocal 4 hazy **5** fishy, vague **6** unsure **7** clouded, dubious, obscure, suspect, unclear **8** doubtful **9** ambiguous, debatable, enigmatic, uncertain, undecided **10** ambivalent, indecisive, indistinct, irresolute, unresolved **11** problematic **12** disreputable, inconclusive, questionable **13** indeterminate
equivocate 3 fib, lie **5** cavil, dodge, evade, fudge, hedge **6** palter, waffle, weasel **7** shuffle **8** sidestep **9** pussyfoot **11** prevaricate **12** tergiversate
equivocation 3 fib **7** evasion, fibbing, hedging, sophism **8** waffling **9** ambiguity, casuistry, duplicity, sophistry **12** speciousness
equivoque 3 pun **8** wordplay
era 3 age, day, eon **4** aeon, date, term, time **5** epoch, stage **6** period
eradicate 4 dele, raze **5** abate, erase, purge **6** delete, efface, remove, uproot **7** abolish, blot out, destroy, expunge, root out, weed out, wipe out **8** demolish, stamp out **9** eliminate, extirpate, liquidate **10** annihilate, do away with, extinguish, obliterate **11** exterminate
erase 4 dele, void, x out **6** cancel, delete, efface, excise, remove, rub out **7** abolish, blot out, expunge, nullify, scratch, take out, wipe out **8** black out, blank out, cross off, cross out **9** eliminate, extirpate, sponge out, strike out **10** extinguish, obliterate
Erato see **Muse**
Erbin ***father:*** **9** Custennin ***nephew:*** **6** Arthur ***son:*** **7** Geraint
erbium symbol 2 Er
ere 6 before
Erebus ***daughter:*** **3** Day **6** Hemera ***father:*** **5** Chaos ***home:*** **5** Hades ***sister, wife:*** **3** Nox, Nyx ***son:*** **6** Aether, Charon
Erec et ____ 5 Enide
Erechteus ***daughter:*** **8** Chthonia ***father:*** **6** Vulcan **10** Hephaestus ***mother:*** **4** Gaea ***slayer:*** **4** Zeus **7** Jupiter
erect 4 form **5** build, put up, raise, set up **6** create, raised **7** build up, stand-up, upright **8** assemble, elevated, standing, straight, vertical **9** construct, establish **10** upstanding **13** perpendicular
eremite 6 hermit **7** ascetic, recluse, stylite **9** anchoress, anchorite
Erewhon 6 utopia **7** nowhere ***author:*** **6** Butler (Samuel)
ergo 4 then, thus **5** hence **9** therefore **11** accordingly **12** consequently
Erichthonius ***father:*** **8** Dardanus ***son:*** **4** Tros
Eridanus star 8 Achernar
Erin see **Ireland**
Erinyes 6 Alecto, Furies **7** Megaera **9** Eumenides, Tisiphone

Eris ***brother:*** **4** Ares, Mars ***daughter:*** **3** Ate ***fruit:*** **5** apple ***goddess of:*** **6** strife **7** discord ***mother:*** **3** Nox, Nyx

Eritrea ***archipelago:*** **6** Dahlak ***capital:*** **6** Asmara ***island:*** **5** Zuqar ***language:*** **8** Tigrinya ***monetary unit:*** **5** nakfa ***neighbor:*** **5** Sudan **8** Djibouti, Ethiopia ***river:*** **6** Baraka ***sea:*** **3** Red

ermine **3** fur **5** stoat **6** weasel

erode **3** eat, mar, rot, rub **4** rust, wear **5** decay, scour **6** abrade, rub off **7** consume, corrade, crumble, eat away, oxidize, rub away **8** wear away **9** scrape off **10** scrape away **11** deteriorate **12** disintegrate

Eroica composer **9** Beethoven (Ludwig van)

Eros see **Cupid**

erose **6** craggy, jagged, uneven **9** irregular

erotic **4** lewd, racy, sexy **5** bawdy, spicy **6** carnal, earthy, ribald, risqué **7** fleshly, obscene, profane, sensual **8** off-color, prurient, sensuous **9** salacious **10** voluptuous **11** aphrodisiac, titillating

err **3** sin **4** goof, slip, trip **5** lapse, stray **6** bollix, bungle, foul up, fumble, mess up, slip up **7** balls-up, blunder, deviate, screw up, stumble **8** trespass **10** transgress

errand **3** job **4** task **5** chore **7** mission **10** assignment

errand boy **4** page **5** gofer **7** bellboy, bellhop, courier **9** go-between

errant **5** stray **6** fickle, roving **7** aimless, deviant, erratic, naughty, ranging, roaming, wayward, willful **8** drifting, fallible, rambling, shifting, straying **9** deviating, itinerant, traveling, wandering **10** meandering, unreliable **11** mischievous

erratic **5** flaky **6** fitful, spotty **7** wayward **8** freakish, shifting, unstable, variable, volatile **9** arbitrary, desultory, eccentric, fluctuant, irregular, mercurial, spasmodic, uncertain, wandering, whimsical **10** capricious, changeable, inconstant, meandering **12** inconsistent **13** idiosyncratic, unpredictable

erring see **errant**

erroneous **3** off **4** awry **5** amiss, askew, false, wrong **6** untrue **7** unsound **8** mistaken, specious, spurious **9** defective, incorrect, misguided **10** fallacious, inaccurate, misleading

error **4** flub, goof, muff, slip, trip **5** boner, botch, fault, fluff, gaffe, lapse, snafu **6** booboo, bungle, fumble, howler, miscue, slipup **7** blooper, blunder, fallacy, falsity, faux pas, misdeed, misstep, mistake, screwup, stumble, untruth **8** delusion, illusion, screamer **9** falsehood, indecorum, oversight **10** inaccuracy, misreading **11** impropriety, misjudgment ***printing:*** **4** typo **6** errata (plural) **7** erratum

ersatz **4** copy, fake, sham **5** bogus, dummy, faked, false, phony, pseud **6** phoney, pseudo **8** spurious **9** imitation, simulated, synthetic **10** artificial, factitious, simulacrum, substitute **11** counterfeit

Erse **5** Irish **6** Celtic, Gaelic

erstwhile **3** old **4** late, once, past **5** prior **6** before, bygone, former, whilom **7** already, earlier, onetime, quondam **8** formerly, previous **10** heretofore, previously

eruct **4** burp, emit, gush, spew **5** belch, eject, expel **7** explode **8** detonate, disgorge

erudite **7** bookish, learned **8** lettered, literate, studious, well-read **9** scholarly **10** scholastic

erudition **7** culture **8** learning, literacy **9** knowledge **11** bookishness, cultivation, learnedness, scholarship **12** studiousness **13** scholarliness

erupt **3** jet **4** spew **5** belch, burst, eject, expel, go off, spout, spurt **7** explode **8** break out, burst out, detonate **9** discharge **10** break forth, burst forth

eruption **4** gust, rush **5** blast, burst, flare, sally **6** access **7** flare-up **8** outbreak, outburst **9** commotion, explosion ***skin:*** **3** zit **4** rash **6** pimple

Esau ***brother:*** **5** Jacob ***country:*** **4** Edom ***descendant:*** **7** Edomite ***father:*** **5** Isaac ***father-in-law:*** **4** Elon ***grandson:*** **6** Amalek ***mother:*** **7** Rebecca, Rebekah ***new name:*** **4** Edom ***son:*** **5** Korha, Reuel **7** Eliphaz ***wife:*** **4** Adah **10** Aholibamah

escalade **5** climb, mount, scale **6** ascend **7** scaling

escalate **4** grow, rise, soar **5** boost, climb, mount, widen **6** expand, extend, spread, step up **7** amplify, augment, broaden, enlarge, inflate **8** heighten, increase, multiply **9** intensify **11** proliferate

escapade **4** lark, romp **5** antic, caper, fling, folly, prank, spree, stunt **6** frolic, vagary **7** roguery, rollick **8** mischief **9** adventure

escape **3** fly, lam **4** bolt, duck, flee, shun, skip, slip **5** avoid, break, dodge, elude, evade, shake **6** bypass, depart, eschew, flight, hegira, outlet **7** abscond, duck out, evasion, get away, make off, release, run away, skip out **8** breakout **9** avoidance, desertion, disappear, steal away **10** circumvent, liberation **11** deliverance, evasiveness ***artist:*** **7** Houdini (Harry) ***narrow:*** **9** close call **10** close shave

escargot **5** snail

escarole **6** endive

escarpment **5** bluff, cliff, slope

eschar 4 scab **5** crust **6** lesion
eschew 4 shun **5** avoid, elude, evade, forgo, spurn **6** abjure, forego, pass up, refuse, reject **7** decline **8** turn down
eschewal 7 elusion, evasion, refusal **8** shunning, spurning **9** avoidance, rejection
escort 4 beau, date, lead, show **5** guard, guide, pilot, steer, usher **6** attend, convoy, direct, gigolo, squire **7** company, conduct, consort, retinue **8** cavalier, chaperon, henchman, shepherd **9** accompany, bodyguard, chaperone, companion, entourage, safeguard **13** accompaniment
escritoire 4 desk **9** secretary **11** writing desk
escrow 4 bond, deed, fund **7** deposit
esculent 6 edible **7** eatable **10** comestible, digestible
escutcheon 6 flange, shield
Eshcol ***ally:*** **7** Abraham ***brother:*** **4** Aner **5** Mamre
esker 2 os **4** kame **5** mound, ridge
Eskimo 4 Inuk **5** Aleut, Inuit ***boat:*** **5** kayak, umiak ***boot:*** **6** mukluk ***dog:*** **5** husky **8** malamute, malemute ***dwelling:*** **5** igloo ***outer garment:*** **5** parka **6** anorak ***sledge:*** **7** komatik
esophagus 6 gullet
esoteric 5 inner **6** arcane, mystic, occult, orphic, secret **7** cryptic, private **8** abstruse, hermetic, profound **9** recondite **10** cabalistic, mysterious **12** confidential
ESP 9 telepathy **10** sixth sense **12** clairvoyance, precognition
espadrille 4 shoe **6** sandal
espalier 7 lattice, railing, trellis
esparto 5 grass
especial 4 main **5** close **7** express, notable, unusual **8** dominant, intimate, peculiar, singular, specific, uncommon **9** paramount **10** individual, particular **11** exceptional
especially 7 notably **8** markedly **9** expressly, primarily, unusually **10** peculiarly, remarkably, singularly **11** principally **12** particularly, specifically **13** distinctively, exceptionally
espial 6 notice **9** detection, discovery **11** observation
espionage 6 spying **9** sleuthing **12** surveillance
espousal 5 troth, union **6** mating **7** embrace, support, wedding **8** adoption, advocacy, approval, ceremony, marriage **9** betrothal, embracing, matrimony, promotion **10** acceptance
espouse 3 wed **4** back **5** adopt, marry **6** accept, take on, take up **7** approve, embrace, support **8** advocate
esprit 3 vim, wit **4** brio, dash, élan, zest, zing **5** oomph, verve, vigor **6** fervor, gaiety, mettle, morale, spirit **7** courage, loyalty, panache, passion, sparkle **8** devotion, vibrancy, vitality **9** animation **10** brightness, enthusiasm, fellowship **11** camaraderie
esprit de corps see **morale**
espy 3 see **4** mark, spot **5** sight **6** descry, detect, notice **7** discern, make out **9** recognize
____ es Salaam 3 Dar
essay 3 try **4** seek, test **5** labor, paper, piece, study, theme, tract, trial **6** effort, strive, thesis **7** article, attempt, venture **8** endeavor, treatise **9** undertake **10** discussion, exposition **11** composition, undertaking **12** dissertation
essayist ***American:*** **4** Agee (James), Will (George) **5** Baker (Russell), Cooke (Alistair), Gould (Stephen Jay), White (E. B.) **6** Brooks (Cleanth), Fisher (M. F. K.), Holmes (Oliver Wendell), Lowell (James Russell), Sontag (Susan), Thomas (Lewis) **7** Buckley (William F.), Cousins (Norman), Emerson (Ralph Waldo), Mencken (Henry Louis), Thoreau (Henry David) **8** Benchley (Robert), Lippmann (Walter), Repplier (Agnes) **10** Crèvecoeur (Jean de) ***English:*** **4** Elia, Lamb (Charles) **5** Bacon (Francis), Cecil (Lord David), Pater (Walter), Smith (Sydney) **6** Arnold (Matthew), Cowley (Abraham), Morris (Jan), Ruskin (John), Steele (Richard) **7** Addison (Joseph), Hazlitt (William) **8** Beerbohm (Max) **9** De Quincey (Thomas) **12** Chesterfield (Lord) ***French:*** **9** Montaigne (Michel de) ***Scottish:*** **7** Carlyle (Thomas)
essence 3 nub **4** base, core, crux, gist, odor, pith, root, soul **5** attar, basis, being, fiber, fibre, point, stuff **6** center, entity, kernel, marrow, nature, spirit **7** extract, perfume, quality **9** substance **10** distillate **12** distillation, significance
essential 4 main, must, need **5** basal, basic, chief, prime, vital **6** inborn, inbred, innate, primal **7** connate, crucial, element, primary **8** cardinal, foremost, inherent, required, rudiment **9** condition, elemental, intrinsic, necessary, necessity, principal, requisite, substance **10** congenital, deep-seated, elementary, idiopathic, imperative, sine qua non, underlying **11** fundamental, requirement **12** precondition, prerequisite **13** indispensable, part and parcel
essentially 6 almost, au fond, really **7** largely **8** actually, as good as, as much as, well-nigh **9** basically, virtually **11** practically **13** fundamentally, substantially

essonite **6** garnet **13** cinnamon stone
establish **3** fix, lay, put, set **4** base, form, root, show **5** build, enact, endow, erect, found, place, prove, set up, start **6** attest, create, decree, effect, ground, impose, secure, settle, verify **7** build up, certify, clarify, confirm, find out, implant, install, instill, provide, set down **8** document, ensconce, organize **9** authorize, construct, determine, formulate, institute, legislate, originate, prescribe **10** bring about, constitute, inaugurate **11** corroborate, demonstrate **12** authenticate, substantiate
establishment **4** firm **6** outfit **7** company, concern **8** business, old guard **9** institute, workplace **10** enterprise, foundation **11** institution, ruling class
estate **4** farm, land **5** manor, ranch, villa **6** domain, legacy, quinta **7** demesne **8** dominion, hacienda, property **10** plantation ***agent:*** **7** Realtor ***feudal:*** **4** fief **7** fiefdom ***first:*** **6** clergy ***fourth:*** **5** press ***manager:*** **7** steward **8** executor, guardian ***second:*** **6** nobles **8** nobility ***third:*** **7** commons
esteem **4** deem **5** favor, honor, prize, think, value **6** admire, liking, regard, revere **7** account, believe, cherish, idolize, respect, worship **8** approval, consider, treasure, venerate **9** valuation **10** admiration, appreciate **12** appreciation **13** consideration
ester **6** oleate **7** acetate **8** compound **9** phosphate
Esther ***cousin:*** **8** Mordecai ***enemy:*** **5** Haman ***father:*** **7** Abihail ***festival:*** **5** Purim ***Hebrew name:*** **8** Hadassah ***husband:*** **6** Xerxes **9** Ahasuerus
estimable **5** noble **6** august, valued, worthy **7** admired **8** laudable, sterling **9** admirable, deserving, honorable, reputable, respected, venerable **10** creditable **11** commendable, meritorious, respectable **12** praiseworthy
estimate **3** put **4** call, rank, rate **5** assay, gauge, guess, infer, judge, price, set at, value **6** assess, deduce, figure, rating, reckon, survey **7** imagine, opinion, project, suppose, surmise **8** appraise, conclude, discover, evaluate, forecast, judgment, round off **9** appraisal, calculate, determine, reckoning, valuation **10** assessment, conjecture, evaluation, impression, projection **11** approximate, calculation, measurement
estimation **4** fame **5** favor, honor, stock **6** esteem, regard **7** account, opinion, respect **8** figuring, judgment **9** appraisal, reckoning, valuation **10** admiration, assessment, evaluation, impression **11** calculation **13** consideration
Estonia ***capital:*** **7** Tallinn ***city:*** **5** Tartu ***gulf:*** **4** Riga **7** Finland ***inhabitant:*** **4** Balt ***island:*** **4** Muhu **6** Vormsi **7** Hiiumaa **8** Saaremaa ***lake:*** **5** Pskov **6** Peipus **9** Vorts-Jarv ***monetary unit:*** **5** kroon ***neighbor:*** **6** Latvia, Russia ***river:*** **5** Narva, Pärnu **6** Kasari ***sea:*** **6** Baltic
estop **3** bar **6** enjoin, forbid **7** prevent **8** disallow, preclude, prohibit, restrain
estrange **4** part **5** split **7** break up, divorce **8** alienate, disunite, separate **9** disaffect
estrangement **4** rift **5** split **6** breach, schism **7** breakup, cooling, divorce, rupture **8** disunity, division **10** alienation, falling-out, withdrawal **12** disaffection
estuary **5** firth, frith, mouth **10** tidal river
esurient **4** avid **6** greedy, hungry **8** covetous, grasping, ravening, ravenous **9** rapacious, voracious **10** avaricious, gluttonous **11** acquisitive
étagère **7** cabinet, whatnot
Etats-____ **4** Unis
etch **3** cut **5** carve, stamp **6** depict, incise **7** engrave, impress, imprint, portray **8** inscribe **9** delineate, represent
etcher ***American:*** **7** Pennell (Joseph) **8** Whistler (James McNeil) ***Dutch:*** **9** Rembrandt (van Rijn) ***French:*** **5** Redon (Odilon) **6** Villon (Jacques) ***Italian:*** **8** Piranesi (Giambattista) ***Spanish:*** **6** Ribera (José) ***Swiss:*** **4** Zorn (Anders)
Eteocles ***brother:*** **9** Polynices **10** Polyneices ***father:*** **7** Oedipus ***mother:*** **7** Jocasta ***slayer:*** **9** Polynices **10** Polyneices
eternal **7** abiding, ageless, endless, lasting, undying **8** constant, enduring, immortal, infinite, timeless, unending **9** ceaseless, continual, deathless, immutable, incessant, permanent, perpetual, unceasing **10** immemorial, unchanging **11** amaranthine, everlasting, illimitable, inalterable, never-ending, unalterable, unremitting **12** imperishable, interminable
Eternal City **4** Rome
eternally **3** e'er **4** ever **6** always **7** forever **8** evermore, for keeps **11** forevermore, in perpetuum **12** in perpetuity
eternity **3** age, eon **4** aeon **7** dog's age **8** blue moon, coon's age, infinity **9** afterlife **10** infinitude, perpetuity **11** endlessness, immortality **12** infiniteness, timelessness
Etesian **4** wind **6** annual
Ethan ____ **5** Allen, Brand, Frome
Ethbaal's daughter **7** Jezebel
ether **3** air, gas, sky **6** heaven **7** heavens **8** airwaves, empyrean **10** anesthetic, atmosphere
ethereal **4** aery, airy **5** filmy, light **6** aerial **7**

fragile **8** delicate, empyreal, empyrean, gossamer, heavenly, rarefied, vaporous **9** celestial, spiritual, unearthly, unworldly **10** immaterial, intangible **13** unsubstantial

ethical **4** good **5** moral, noble **6** decent **7** upright, virtual **8** elevated, virtuous **9** righteous **10** principled, upstanding **11** right-minded **13** conscientious

ethics **5** mores **6** morals, values **8** morality **9** moral code, standards **10** principles

Ethiopia ***battle site:*** **5** Adowa ***biblical name:*** **4** Cush ***capital:*** **10** Addis Ababa ***city:*** **6** Gonder **8** Dire Dawa ***desert:*** **4** Haud **7** Danakil ***emperor:*** **7** Menelik, Menilek **8** Selassie **9** Ras Tafari **13** Haile Selassie ***former name:*** **9** Abyssinia ***language:*** **5** Oromo **7** Amharic ***monetary unit:*** **4** birr ***mountain:*** **9** Ras Dashen ***neighbor:*** **5** Kenya, Sudan **7** Eritrea, Somalia **8** Djibouti ***region:*** **5** Tigre **6** Ogaden, Tigray **7** Danakil ***river:*** **4** Abay **5** Awash **6** Tekeze **8** Blue Nile

ethnic **6** racial, tribal **8** minority

etiolate **4** fade, pale **6** bleach, weaken **7** lighten, wash out **8** enfeeble

etiquette **4** code, form **5** mores **7** conduct, customs, decency, decorum, manners **8** behavior, protocol **9** amenities, propriety **10** civilities, convention, deportment, seemliness **11** conventions, formalities, proprieties

Etruscan ***city, town:*** **4** Roma, Veii **5** Caere, Vulci **6** Arezzo **7** Clusium, Felsina, Perugia **8** Volsinii **9** Florentia, Tarquinia, Vetulonia ***deity:*** **3** Tin, Tiv, Uni **4** Turm, Usil **5** Tinia, Turan, Turms **6** Menfra, Menrva, Nethun, Trithn **7** Velchan **8** Sethlans, Voltumna ***king:*** **7** Porsena, Tarquin **10** Tarquinius **11** Lars Porsena ***kingdom:*** **7** Etruria

étude **5** study **8** exercise **11** composition

etui **4** case

etymology **11** word history

etymon **4** root **5** radix **6** source **8** morpheme

eucalyptus eater **5** koala

Eucharist ***container:*** **3** pyx ***plate:*** **5** paten ***service:*** **4** Mass **9** Communion ***vessel:*** **8** ciborium ***wafer:*** **4** host **8** viaticum

Euclid ***subject:*** **8** geometry ***work:*** **8** Elements

____ Eulenspiegel **4** Till, Tyll

eulogistic **9** adulatory, laudative, laudatory **11** encomiastic, panegyrical **12** commendatory **13** complimentary

eulogize **4** hymn, laud **5** cry up, exalt, extol **6** praise **7** acclaim, applaud, commend, glorify, magnify **9** celebrate **10** panegyrize

eulogy **5** paean **6** praise **7** oration, tribute **8** accolade, citation, encomium **9** laudation, panegyric **10** salutation **12** commendation **13** glorification

Eumenides see **Erinyes**

eunuch **7** gelding **8** castrate, castrato

euphony **7** harmony **8** lyricism **9** sweetness **10** consonance

euphoria **3** joy **4** glee **5** bliss **7** ecstasy, elation, rapture **9** transport **10** exaltation, jubilation **11** high spirits **12** exhilaration, intoxication

Euphrosyne see **Graces**

euphuistic **5** fancy, tumid **6** florid, ornate, prolix, purple, turgid **7** elegant, flowery, fustian, orotund, verbose **8** colorful, elevated, inflated, sonorous **9** bombastic, elaborate, high-flown, overblown **10** figurative, flamboyant, rhetorical **11** highfalutin, overwrought **12** magniloquent **13** grandiloquent

eureka **3** aha

Euridice's husband **7** Orpheus

Euripides play **3** Ion **5** Helen, Medea **6** Hecuba **7** Bacchae (The), Cyclops, Electra, Orestes **8** Alcestis **10** Andromache, Hippolytus, Suppliants (The) **11** Trojan Women (The)

Europa ***brother:*** **6** Cadmus ***father:*** **6** Agenor **7** Phoenix ***husband:*** **8** Asterius ***son:*** **5** Minos **8** Sarpedon

Europe **9** continent ***country:*** **4** Eire **5** Italy, Malta, Spain **6** Cyprus, France, Greece, Latvia, Monaco, Norway, Poland, Russia, Serbia, Sweden, Turkey **7** Albania, Andorra, Armenia, Austria, Belarus, Belgium, Croatia, Denmark, Estonia, Finland, Georgia, Germany, Hungary, Iceland, Ireland, Moldova, Romania, Rumania, Ukraine **8** Bulgaria, Portugal, Slovakia, Slovenia **9** Lithuania, Macedonia, San Marino **10** Azerbaijan, Luxembourg, Montenegro **11** Netherlands, Switzerland, Vatican City **13** Czech Republic, Liechtenstein, United Kingdom ***ethnic group:*** **4** Celt, Finn, Lapp, Lett, Pole, Serb, Sorb, Turk, Wend **5** Croat, Czech, Dutch, Greek, Gypsy, Irish, Latin, Swede, Swiss, Welsh **6** Basque, Celtic, French, German, Magyar, Polish, Scotch, Slovak **7** Bosnian, Catalan, English, Finnish, Fleming, Italian, Lettish, Maltese, Russian, Slovene, Spanish, Swedish, Walloon **8** Albanian, Andorran, Armenian, Croatian, Romanian **9** Belarusan, Bulgarian, Hungarian, Ukrainian **10** Belarusian, Macedonian, Monegasque, Phoenician **11** Belarussian **12** Byelorussian, Scandinavian ***language:*** **4** Lapp **5** Czech, Dutch, Greek, Irish, Latin, Welsh **6** Basque, Breton, Danish, French, Gaelic, German, Magyar, Polish, Slovak **7** Catalan, English, Finnish, Flemish, Italian, Maltese, Romansh, Russian, Serbian, Slovene, Spanish, Swedish, Turkish, Wendish **8** Albanian, Croatian, Lusatian, Romanian, Rumanian **9** Bulgarian, Hungarian, Icelandic, Norwegian **10** Macedonian, Portuguese **13** Serbo-Croatian ***mountain range:*** **4** Alps **8** Pyrenees **11** Carpathians

European Union member **5** Italy, Malta, Spain **6** Cyprus, France, Greece, Latvia, Poland, Sweden **7** Austria, Belgium, Denmark, Estonia, Finland, Germany, Hungary, Ireland, Romania, Rumania **8** Bulgaria, Portugal, Slovakia, Slovenia **9** Lithuania **10** Luxembourg **11** Netherlands **13** Czech Republic, United Kingdom

europium symbol **2** Eu

Euryale see **Gorgon**

Eurytus ***daughter:*** **4** Iole ***slayer:*** **8** Hercules

Euterpe see **Muse**

evacuate **4** exit, void **5** clear, empty, expel, leave **6** decamp, depart, remove, vacate **7** abandon, excrete, exhaust, pull out, retreat **8** clear out, pull back, withdraw **9** eliminate

evacuee **2** DP **6** émigré **7** refugee **8** fugitive

evade **4** duck, flee, foil **5** avoid, dodge, elude, hedge, parry, shirk, skirt **6** baffle, bypass, escape, eschew, outwit, thwart, weasel **7** shuffle **8** sidestep, slip away **9** pussyfoot, turn aside **10** circumvent, equivocate **11** prevaricate **12** tergiversate

evaluate **4** rank, rate **5** assay, class, gauge, grade, set at, weigh **6** assess, figure, reckon, size up, survey **7** eyeball **8** appraise, classify, estimate **9** calculate, criticize

evaluation **6** rating **7** judging, opinion **8** estimate, judgment **9** appraisal **10** assessment **12** appreciation

Evander ***father:*** **6** Hermes **7** Mercury ***mother:*** **8** Carmenta **9** Carmentis ***son:*** **6** Pallas

evanesce **4** fade **5** clear **6** vanish **7** scatter **8** disperse, dissolve, melt away **9** disappear, dissipate, evaporate **13** dematerialize

evanescent **6** fading **7** elusive, melting, passing **8** fleeting, fugitive, volatile **9** ephemeral, fugacious, momentary, transient, vanishing **10** dissolving, short-lived, transitory **12** disappearing

evangelical **6** ardent, fervid **7** fanatic, fervent, zealous **8** militant **9** crusading **10** missionary **13** proselytizing

Evangeline ***author:*** **10** Longfellow (Henry Wadsworth) ***beloved:*** **7** Gabriel ***home:*** **6** Acadia

evangelist **4** John, Luke, Mark **5** Moody (Dwight) **6** Bakker (Jim, Tammy Faye), Dobson (James), Graham (Billy, Franklin), Sunday (Billy), Warren (Rick), Wesley (John) **7** apostle, Edwards (Jonathan), Falwell (Jerry), Matthew, Roberts (Oral) **8** Schuller (Robert), Swaggart (Jimmy) **9** McPherson (Aimee Semple), missioner, Robertson (Pat) **10** colporteur, missionary, revivalist, Whitefield (George)

evangelistic **9** crusading, reforming **10** missionary, revivalist **13** proselytizing

evangelize **6** preach **7** convert **9** sermonize

evaporate **4** fade, melt **5** clear **6** vanish **8** diminish, disperse, dissolve, evanesce, melt away, vaporize **9** disappear, dissipate

evasion **5** dodge, fudge **6** escape, excuse **7** dodging, elusion, fudging **8** escaping **9** avoidance **13** circumvention

evasive **3** sly **5** cagey, dodgy, vague **6** shifty **7** elusive **8** slippery **9** ambiguous, equivocal

Eve ***home:*** **4** Eden ***husband:*** **4** Adam ***son:*** **4** Abel, Cain, Seth ***temptation:*** **5** apple, fruit

even **3** tie **4** fair, flat, just, same, tied **5** align, equal, exact, flush, grade, level, plane, still, truly **6** as well, equate, smooth, square, stable, steady **7** balance, equable, flatten, uniform **8** balanced, constant, equalize, smoothen, straight **9** equitable, expressly, identical, precisely, unvarying **10** absolutely, comparable, consistent, continuous, fifty-fifty, unchanging **13** fair and square, proportionate

evening **4** dusk **6** soiree, sunset, vesper **7** sundown **8** gloaming, twilight **9** nightfall ***French:*** **4** soir ***Italian:*** **4** sera ***service:*** **7** vespers ***star:*** **5** Venus **6** Vesper **8** Hesperus

evenness **6** equity, parity **7** balance **8** equality **9** stability **10** equanimity, uniformity **11** consistency, equilibrium

event **3** act **4** case, deed, fact, feat, meet **5** issue, match **6** action, affair, chance, effect, result, upshot **7** contest, episode, outcome, product **8** accident, function, incident, occasion **9** aftermath, happening **10** occurrence, phenomenon **11** achievement, competition, consequence, eventuality **12** circumstance, happenstance

eventful **4** busy **6** lively **9** important, momentous

eventual **4** last **5** final **6** ending **7** closing, endmost, ensuing **8** terminal, ultimate **9** resulting **10** concluding, consequent, inevitable, succeeding

eventuality **4** case **6** effect, result **7** outcome **11** consequence, contingency, possibility

eventually **6** at last, in time, one day **7** finally, someday **8** sometime **9** hereafter **10** ultimately **13** sooner or later

eventuate **5** ensue, occur **6** befall, follow, happen, result **9** come about, take place

ever **4** once **5** at all **6** always **7** forever **9** at any time, eternally, regularly **10** constantly, invariably **11** perpetually **12** consistently, continuously ***poetic:*** **3** e'er

evergreen 3 fir, ivy, yew **4** ilex, pine, tree **5** cedar, holly, savin **6** laurel, myrtle, spruce **7** conifer, cypress, hemlock, juniper, lasting, redwood, sequoia, undying **8** magnolia, mangrove, timeless, unfading **9** mistletoe, perennial **10** arborvitae **12** rhododendron

Evergreen State 10 Washington

everlasting 7 abiding, endless, eternal, forever, lasting, undying **8** constant, immortal, infinite, termless, timeless, unending **9** boundless, ceaseless, continual, deathless, limitless, permanent, perpetual, unceasing **10** continuous, perdurable **11** amaranthine, never-ending, unremitting **12** imperishable

evermore 6 always **7** for good **8** for keeps **9** eternally **12** in perpetuity

every 3 all **4** each ***prefix:*** **3** pan

everybody 3 all **4** each

everyday 5 banal, plain, usual **6** common, normal **7** mundane, prosaic, routine **8** familiar, habitual, ordinary **9** customary, quotidian **11** commonplace **12** conventional, run-of-the-mill, unremarkable

everything 3 all ***French:*** **4** tout ***German:*** **5** alles ***Spanish:*** **4** todo

everywhere 7 all over, overall **8** all round, wherever **9** all around **10** far and near, far and wide, high and low, throughout

evict 3 out **4** boot, oust **5** eject, expel **6** bounce, put out **7** boot out, dismiss, extrude, kick out **8** dislodge, force out, throw out **10** dispossess

evidence 4 clue, mark, show, sign **5** goods, proof, prove **6** attest, evince, expose, reveal **7** confirm, display, exhibit, symptom, testify, witness **8** indicate **9** testament, testimony **10** indication, smoking gun **11** attestation, demonstrate, testimonial **12** confirmation **13** documentation

evident 5 clear, overt, plain **6** marked, patent **7** obvious, visible **8** apparent, distinct, manifest, palpable, tangible **9** prominent **10** noticeable, pronounced **11** conspicuous, perceptible, unambiguous

evidently 9 outwardly, seemingly **10** officially, ostensibly

evil 3 bad, sin **4** foul, vice, vile **5** black **6** infamy, malice, sinful, wicked **7** badness, baleful, baneful, devilry, hateful, heinous, malefic, satanic, vicious **8** damnable, iniquity, satanism, villainy **9** atrocious, diablerie, diabolism, execrable, loathsome, malicious, malignant, nefarious **10** flagitious, iniquitous, maleficent, malevolent, pernicious, sinfulness, wickedness **11** maleficence ***combining form:*** **3** mal

evildoer 6 sinner **7** villain **8** criminal **9** miscreant **10** malefactor

evil spirit 3 imp **5** demon, devil, fiend, Satan **6** daemon

evince 4 mark, show **5** educe, evoke, prove **6** attest, betray, elicit, expose, reveal **7** bespeak, betoken, confirm, display, exhibit, signify **8** evidence, indicate, manifest, proclaim **10** illustrate **11** demonstrate

eviscerate 3 gut **4** draw **5** bowel **7** embowel **8** protrude **10** disembowel, exenterate

evocative 6 moving **8** redolent, stirring **9** affecting, emotional, nostalgic **10** expressive, meaningful, suggestive **11** stimulating

evoke 4 cite, stir **5** educe, raise, waken **6** arouse, awaken, call up, elicit, evince, excite, induce, recall **7** conjure **8** recreate, summon up **9** call forth, conjure up, stimulate **11** summon forth

evolution 6 change, growth **8** progress, upgrowth **9** flowering, phylogeny, unfolding **10** biogenesis, maturation **11** development, progression

evolve 4 grow **5** educe, ripen **6** change, derive, emerge, mature, open up, unfold **7** advance, develop, work out **8** progress **9** elaborate

ewe 5 sheep

ewer 3 jug **4** olpe, vase **7** pitcher

ex 4 from, past **5** out of, prior **6** former **7** earlier, without **9** erstwhile

exacerbate 6 worsen **7** envenom, inflame, provoke **8** embitter, heighten **9** aggravate, intensify

exact 4 levy, true **5** claim, force, gouge, pinch, screw, wrest, wring **6** coerce, compel, dead-on, demand, extort, spot-on, strict **7** correct, extract, literal, precise, require, solicit, squeeze **8** accurate, rigorous, selfsame **9** identical, postulate, shake down **10** meticulous, scrupulous **11** painstaking, punctilious, requisition

exacting 5 fussy, rigid, stern, tough **6** severe, strict, taxing, trying **7** exigent, finicky, onerous **8** critical, rigorous **9** demanding, stringent **10** fastidious, nitpicking, particular, scrupulous **11** persnickety **13** hypercritical

exactitude 5 rigor **8** accuracy **9** precision **10** definitude **11** correctness, preciseness **12** definiteness

exactly 4 bang, just **5** quite, right, sharp, spang **6** bang on, square, to a tee, wholly **7** totally, utterly **8** entirely, on the dot, smack-dab, squarely **9** on the nose, precisely **10** absolutely, accurately, altogether, completely, positively **12** specifically

exaggerate 6 overdo **7** amplify, enlarge, inflate, magnify, overact, romance **8** overdraw, overrate **9** embellish, embroider, overstate **11** hyperbolize **13** overemphasize

exaggeration 8 travesty **9** hyperbole **10** caricature, stretching **11** enlargement, overdrawing **12** embroidering **13** embellishment, overstatement

exalt 4 fete, laud, lift **5** boost, elate, extol, honor, raise **6** praise, uplift **7** acclaim, adulate, build up, dignify, elevate, enhance, ennoble, glorify, inspire, magnify, promote **8** eulogize, heighten, inspirit **9** intensify **10** aggrandize **11** apotheosize

exaltation 3 joy **5** bliss, glory **6** homage, praise **7** delight, ecstasy, elation, rapture, tribute **8** euphoria, rhapsody **9** panegyric, transport, uplifting **10** apotheosis, jubilation **11** deification **12** exhilaration, intoxication **13** glorification

exalted 4 high **5** grand, lofty, noble **6** august **7** eminent, highest, sublime **9** venerable **11** high-ranking, illustrious, outstanding, prestigious

examination 4 oral, quiz, scan, test **5** assay, final, probe, trial **6** review, survey **7** canvass, checkup, hearing, inquest, inquiry, perusal, sifting, testing **8** analysis, scrutiny **9** breakdown, check-over, diagnosis **10** dissection, inspection **11** inquisition **13** catechization, investigation, perlustration ***kind:*** **3** bar **4** oral **5** final **7** medical, midterm **8** physical ***of accounts:*** **5** audit ***of a corpse:*** **7** autopsy **10** postmortem

examine 3 con, vet **4** pump, quiz, scan, sift, test **5** audit, check, grill, probe, query, study **6** go over, look at, peruse, survey **7** canvass, check up, inquire, inspect, observe **8** check out, look into, look over, question **9** catechize, check over **10** scrutinize **11** interrogate, investigate

examiner 6 censor **7** auditor, coroner **9** inspector **10** inquisitor, prosecutor **12** investigator

example 4 case **5** ideal, model **7** paragon, pattern **8** instance, paradigm, specimen, standard **9** archetype, precedent, prototype **11** case history **12** illustration

exanimate 4 dead **5** inert **8** lifeless, listless, sluggish, stagnant **9** lethargic **10** spiritless

exasperate 3 irk, vex **4** gall, rile, roil **5** anger, annoy, peeve, pique, upset **6** enrage, madden, nettle, rankle **7** agitate, incense, inflame, provoke **8** irritate **9** aggravate, infuriate

exasperation 8 vexation **9** annoyance **10** irritation **11** aggravation

ex cathedra 8 official **9** ex officio **13** authoritative

excavate 3 dig **4** grub **5** scoop, spade **6** dig out, dredge, expose, hollow, quarry, shovel **7** unearth **8** gouge out, scoop out **9** hollow out, scrape out

excavation 3 dig, pit **4** hole, mine **5** ditch, stope **6** dugout, hollow, quarry, trench, trough

exceed 3 cap, top **4** beat, best, pass **5** break, excel, outdo **6** better, outrun, overdo **7** eclipse, outpace, overrun, surpass **8** go beyond, outreach, outshine, outstrip, outweigh, overstep, overtake **9** overreach, transcend

exceedingly 4 very **6** hugely, vastly **7** awfully, notably, vitally **9** extremely **10** remarkably, strikingly **12** surpassingly **13** exceptionally ***prefix:*** **5** ultra

excel 3 cap, top **4** beat, best, pass **5** outdo, shine **6** better, exceed, outrun, overdo **7** eclipse, outpace, overrun, surpass **8** go beyond, outclass, outreach, outshine, outstrip, outweigh, overstep, overtake **9** overreach, transcend

excellence 5 class, merit, value, worth **6** virtue **7** quality **8** fineness **9** greatness **10** perfection **11** distinction, superiority

excellent 3 top **4** A-one, boss, fine **5** bully, model, neato, prime **6** bang-up, banner, famous, Grade A, superb, tip-top, worthy **7** capital, premium, supreme **8** champion, five-star, splendid, stunning, superior, terrific, top-notch **9** classical, exemplary, first-rate, high-class, high-grade, marvelous, number one, top-drawer, wonderful **10** blue-ribbon, first-class **11** exceptional, magnificent, meritorious, sensational, superlative, unsurpassed **12** incomparable

except 3 bar, but, yet **4** omit, only, save **6** beside, exempt, object, reject, unless **7** barring, besides, exclude, however, outside, rule out, suspend **8** pass over **9** apart from, aside from, eliminate, excluding, outside of **11** exclusive of

exception 5 demur **7** anomaly, dissent **8** question **9** allowance, deviation, exclusion, objection **10** aberration

exceptionable 8 unwanted **9** unwelcome **10** unsuitable **11** regrettable, undesirable **12** unacceptable **13** objectionable

exceptional 4 rare **6** scarce, unique **7** notable, special, unusual **8** abnormal, atypical, distinct, singular, superior, uncommon, unwonted **9** anomalous, excellent, marvelous, wonderful **10** infrequent, noteworthy, phenomenal, remarkable **11** outstanding, uncustomary **13** extraordinary

exceptionally 4 very **6** hugely **7** notably **9** extremely **10** especially, remarkably, strikingly **11** exceedingly **12** particularly, stupendously
excerpt 4 cite, clip, cull, pick **5** glean, quote **6** choose, sample, select **7** extract, passage, pick out, portion, snippet **8** fragment **9** quotation
excess 3 fat **4** glut, rest **5** extra, flood, spare, waste **7** nimiety, overage, surfeit, surplus **8** leavings, leftover, overflow, overkill, overmuch **9** indulgent, overstock, redundant, remainder **10** oversupply, surplusage **11** dissipation, prodigality, superfluity, superfluous, unessential **12** extravagance, immoderation, intemperance **13** overabundance, supernumerary
excessive 4 over **5** dizzy, steep, super, undue **6** de trop, too-too **7** extreme, sky-high **8** overmuch, prodigal **10** exorbitant, immoderate, inordinate, profligate **11** extravagant, intemperate, overweening, superfluous **12** supernatural, unrestrained
excessively 3 too **6** overly, unduly **8** overmuch ***prefix:* 5** hyper
exchange 4 swap, swop **5** bandy, trade, truck **6** barter, market, switch **7** bargain, commute, convert, pay back, replace, traffic **8** displace **9** transpose **10** conversion, substitute **11** reciprocate
exchangerate premium 4 agio
exchequer 5 funds **8** treasury
excise 3 fee, tax **4** toll **5** elide, slash **6** cut out, delete, remove, resect **9** expurgate, extirpate, strike out, surcharge
excision 3 cut **7** removal, surgery **8** deletion **9** resection **11** extirpation
excitable 4 rash **8** volatile **9** impetuous **10** high-strung
excite 4 fire, goad, move, spur, stir **5** elate, evoke, key up, pique, prime, rouse, waken **6** appeal, arouse, elicit, fire up, induce, kindle, stir up, thrill, turn on **7** agitate, animate, commove, inflame, inspire, provoke, quicken **8** activate, charge up, energize, motivate **9** galvanize, impassion, innervate, stimulate **10** exhilarate
excited 3 hot **4** avid **5** eager **6** aflame **7** fevered **8** aflutter, worked up **10** passionate **12** enthusiastic
excitement 3 ado **4** buzz, stir, to-do **5** fever, furor **6** flurry, frenzy, furore, hubbub, thrill **7** turmoil **8** delirium, hysteria **9** agitation, commotion **10** enthusiasm, hullabaloo **11** disturbance, pandemonium **12** exhilaration
exclaim 4 blat, bolt **5** blurt **6** cry out **8** blurt out, burst out **9** ejaculate
exclamation 2 ha, hi, ho, lo **3** aah, aha, bah, boo, cry, eek, feh, fie, gee, hah, hey, huh, oho, ooh, pah, tsk, tut, ugh, wow **4** ahem, alas, amen, damn, dang, darn, drat, egad, gosh, heck, hell, oops, ouch, phew, pish, posh, rats, whew, yell **5** alack, bravo, faugh, golly, humph, pshaw, shout **6** clamor, hurrah, indeed, outcry, phooey, shucks **7** doggone, gee whiz, hosanna, jeepers, whoopee **9** expletive **10** hallelujah **12** interjection ***of disappointment:* 4** damn, darn, rats ***of disapproval:* 3** tsk **6** tsk-tsk ***of discovery:* 3** aha **6** eureka ***of disgust:* 3** bah, boo, feh, fie, ugh **4** yech, yuck **5** faugh, yecch **6** phooey ***of dismay:* 4** oh no, uh-oh **5** yikes ***of enthusiasm:* 4** whee **5** wahoo **7** whoopie ***of fear:* 3** eek ***of pain:* 2** ow **4** ouch ***of relief:* 4** phew ***of sorrow:* 3** woe **4** alas **5** alack ***of surprise:* 2** ah, oh **3** wow **4** gosh **5** golly ***of triumph:* 3** aha, hah **5** yahoo **6** eureka (see also **interjection**)
exclude 3 ban, bar **4** oust **5** block, debar **6** banish, disbar, reject **7** keep out, lock out, obviate, prevent, rule out, shut out, suspend **8** count out, preclude, prohibit **9** blackball, blacklist, eliminate, ostracize
excluding 3 bar, but **4** less, save **6** except **7** barring, besides **9** apart from, aside from, other than, outside of
exclusion 3 bar **6** ouster **7** barring, lockout, removal **8** ejection, eviction, omission **9** blackball, expulsion, ostracism **10** banishment **12** blackballing, nonadmission
exclusive 4 lone, only, sole **5** elect, elite, prime, scoop, smart, swank, swish **6** choice, chosen, picked, select, single **7** cliquey, high-hat, stylish **8** clannish, cliquish, selected, snobbish **9** preferred, undivided **10** privileged **11** fashionable, prohibitive, restrictive **12** aristocratic, concentrated, preferential
exclusively 4 only **5** alone **6** wholly **8** entirely **10** completely **12** particularly
excogitate 6 derive, devise, invent **7** develop, think up **8** contrive, think out
excommunicate 7 cast out **8** unchurch
excoriate 4 flay, lash, skin **5** roast, slash **6** abrade, scathe, scorch **7** blister, censure, scarify, scourge **8** chastise, lambaste, lash into **9** castigate
excrement 6 ordure ***of animals:* 4** dung, muck **6** manure ***of sea birds:* 5** guano
excrescence 4 blot, lump, mole, wart **5** tumor **6** growth, nodule, pimple **7** blemish, process **9** by-product, outgrowth
excrete 4 emit, spew **5** eject, expel, exude **9** discharge

excruciate **4** rack **6** martyr **7** afflict, crucify, torment, torture **9** martyrize
excruciating **5** acute, sharp **6** severe **7** extreme, intense **8** piercing, shooting, stabbing **9** agonizing, harrowing, torturous **10** unbearable **11** unendurable
exculpate **4** free **5** clear, remit **6** acquit, excuse, let off, pardon **7** absolve, amnesty, condone, forgive, justify **9** exonerate, vindicate **11** rationalize
excursion **4** ride, tour, trek, trip, walk **5** aside, drive, jaunt, paseo, sally, tramp **6** cruise, junket, outing, ramble, safari **7** day trip, journey **9** round trip **10** digression, divagation, expedition **11** parenthesis **12** pleasure trip
excusable **6** venial
excuse **3** out **4** plea **5** alibi, clear, remit **6** acquit, cop-out, defend, exempt, let off, pardon, reason, wink at **7** absolve, apology, condone, defense, forgive, justify, pretext, regrets, relieve **8** mitigate, overlook, palliate, pass over, shrug off, tolerate **9** discharge, exculpate, exonerate, extenuate, gloss over, makeshift, vindicate, whitewash **10** substitute **11** explanation, rationalize **13** justification
execrable **4** base, foul, vile **7** heinous **8** accursed, damnable, horrific, infernal, wretched **9** abhorrent, atrocious, loathsome, monstrous, repulsive, revolting **10** abominable, deplorable, despicable, detestable, horrifying
execrate **4** damn, hate **5** abhor, curse **6** detest, loathe, revile, vilify **7** censure, condemn, despise **8** denounce **9** abominate, imprecate **12** anathematize
execute **2** do **3** act **4** do in, kill, play, slay **5** cause, lynch **6** effect, finish, murder, render **7** achieve, bump off, conduct, enforce, fulfill, perform, realize **8** carry out, complete, dispatch, knock off, transact **9** discharge, eliminate, implement, liquidate **10** accomplish, administer, bring about, put through, put to death **11** assassinate **12** administrate
execution **6** murder **7** killing **11** performance
executioner **7** hangman, headman **8** headsman
executive **4** dean, suit **6** leader **7** manager **8** director, governor **9** president **10** supervisor **13** administrator ***ineffective:*** **9** empty suit
exegesis **5** gloss **8** analysis **9** construal **10** commentary, exposition **11** elucidation, explanation, explication **12** construction
exemplar **4** copy **5** ideal, model **7** epitome, paragon, pattern **8** instance, paradigm, specimen, standard **9** archetype, criterion, prototype **12** illustration
exemplary **4** pure **5** ideal, model **7** classic, typical **8** laudable, monitory, virtuous **9** admirable, blameless, classical, estimable, faultless, honorable, righteous **10** impeccable, inculpable, prototypal **11** commendable, meritorious **12** illustrative, paradigmatic, praiseworthy, prototypical
exemplify **4** copy **6** embody, mirror, typify **7** clarify **9** enlighten, epitomize, personify, represent, symbolize **10** concretize, illuminate, illustrate
exempt **4** free **5** spare **6** except, excuse, let off, spared **7** absolve, excused, relieve **8** dispense **9** discharge
exemption **7** freedom, release **8** immunity, impunity **9** discharge, exception
exenterate **3** gut **4** draw **7** embowel **10** disembowel, eviscerate
exercise **3** use, vex **4** fret, gall, hone **5** alarm, annoy, apply, drill, étude, exert, sit-up, train, upset, wield **6** chin-up, crunch, employ, pull-up, push-up **7** agitate, develop, exploit, improve, prepare, problem, provoke, utilize, work out **8** activity, maneuver, practice, rehearse **9** athletics, condition, cultivate, discharge, operation **10** employment **11** application **12** calisthenics
exert **3** use **5** apply, wield **6** employ, expend, put out, strain **8** exercise, put forth
exertion **4** toil, work **5** labor, pains **6** effort, strain **7** trouble **8** activity, exercise, striving **11** application, elbow grease
exfoliate **4** peel, shed **5** scale **7** cast off, leaf out **8** flake off **10** desquamate
exhalation **6** breath **8** emission **9** breathing, effluvium, emanation
exhale **4** blow, emit **6** expire, let out **7** breathe, respire **10** breathe out ***audibly:*** **4** sigh
exhaust **3** fag, sap **4** do in, tire **5** drain, eat up, empty, spend, use up, waste, weary **6** expend, finish, tucker, wash up, weaken **7** burn out, consume, deplete, fatigue, frazzle, tire out, wear out **8** draw down, enervate, squander, wear down **9** discharge, dissipate, prostrate, tucker out **10** debilitate, overextend, run through
exhausted **4** beat, limp, weak **5** all in, spent, tired **6** bushed **7** run-down, worn out **8** dog-tired
exhaustion **7** burnout, fatigue **8** collapse **9** lassitude, tiredness, weariness **11** prostration
exhaustive **8** complete, sweeping, thorough **9** full-blown, full-scale, intensive **10** scrupulous **11** painstaking **13** comprehensive, thoroughgoing
exhibit **4** fair, show **6** evince, expose, flaunt, parade, reveal **7** display, feature, show off **8**

evidence, manifest, proclaim, showcase **10** exposition **11** demonstrate
exhibition 4 expo, fair, show **5** rodeo **7** display, pageant, showing **9** trade show **12** presentation **13** demonstration, manifestation
exhibitionist 3 fop **4** toff **6** hot dog **7** peacock, show-off **8** showboat **12** grandstander
exhilarate 4 buoy, lift **5** boost, cheer, elate, exalt, pep up **6** buck up, excite, thrill, uplift **7** animate, cheer up, commove, delight, enliven, gladden, inspire, refresh **8** inspirit, vitalize **9** stimulate **10** invigorate
exhilaration 3 joy **4** glee **7** ecstasy, elation **8** euphoria, gladness **10** exaltation, excitement **11** inspiration **12** vitalization, vivification **13** galvanization
exhort 4 goad, prod, spur, urge, warn **5** egg on, plead, press, prick **6** adjure, call on, incite, prompt, propel **7** beseech, entreat **8** admonish, call upon **9** stimulate
exhortation 4 plea **6** advice, urging **7** caution, warning **8** entreaty, jeremiad **10** admonition, incitement, injunction **11** inspiration **13** encouragement
exhume 5 dig up **6** redeem **7** reclaim, recover, unearth **8** disinter **9** resurrect
exigency 3 fix, jam **4** need, pass **5** pinch, rigor **6** crisis, demand, pickle, plight, strait **7** urgency **8** juncture, pressure, zero hour **9** extremity, necessity **10** compulsion, constraint, crossroads, difficulty, insistence **11** predicament, requirement
exigent 5 acute, vital **6** crying, taxing **7** burning, clamant, instant, onerous **8** exacting, grievous, pressing **9** clamorous, demanding, insistent, necessary **10** burdensome, imperative **11** importunate
exiguous 4 poor, puny, thin, tiny **5** scant, spare, token **6** meager, meagre, measly, paltry, scanty, shabby, skimpy, slight, sparse **7** minimal, scrimpy **9** miserable **10** inadequate, straitened
exile 4 oust **5** eject, expel **6** banish, deport, emigré **7** cast out, outcast, refugee **8** diaspora, displace, drive out, evacuate, expellee **9** exclusion, expulsion, extradite, migration, ostracism, ostracize **10** banishment, dispossess, expatriate, scattering **11** deportation, extradition **12** displacement, expatriation ***place of:*** **4** Elba **7** Siberia **8** St. Helena
exist 2 am, be, is **3** are, lie **4** live **5** occur
existence 4 esse, life **5** being **7** reality **8** duration **9** actuality
existent 4 live, real **5** being, thing **6** actual, entity, extant, living **7** current, instant, present **10** present-day **12** contemporary
existentialist writer 5 Buber (Martin), Camus (Albert) **6** Marcel (Gabriel), Sartre (Jean-Paul) **7** Jaspers (Karl) **8** Beauvoir (Simone de) **9** Heidegger (Martin), Nietzsche (Friedrich) **11** Kierkegaard (Søren)
existing 5 alive, being, ontic **6** extant, living ***from birth:*** **6** innate **10** congenital ***Latin:*** **6** in esse
exit 2 go **3** die **4** door, gate, quit **5** death, going, leave, scram, split **6** depart, egress, escape, outlet, portal, retire **7** doorway, get away, off-ramp **8** withdraw **9** departure, egression **10** withdrawal
____ ex machina 4 deus
exodus 6 flight **9** migration **10** emigration
Exodus author 4 Uris (Leon)
exonerate 4 free **5** clear, remit **6** acquit, excuse, exempt, let off, pardon **7** absolve **8** reprieve **9** exculpate, vindicate
exorbitant 5 undue **7** extreme **9** excessive **10** immoderate, inordinate, outrageous **11** extravagant, unwarranted **12** preposterous
exordium 5 intro, proem **6** lead-in **7** opening, preface, prelude **8** foreword, overture, preamble, prologue **12** introduction, prolegomenon
exotic 4 rare **5** alien **7** bizarre, foreign, strange, unusual **8** alluring, enticing, imported, romantic **9** different, glamorous, nonnative **10** introduced, mysterious **11** fascinating
expand 3 wax **4** grow, open, rise **5** boost, mount, swell, widen **6** beef up, bulk up, dilate, pad out, spread, unfold **7** amplify, augment, bolster, develop, distend, enlarge, inflate, magnify, prolong, stretch **8** escalate, increase, lengthen, multiply, mushroom, protract **9** discourse, elaborate, expatiate, spread out
expanse 4 area, room **5** field, ocean, range, reach, scope, space, sweep, tract **6** domain, extent, sphere, spread **7** breadth, stretch **8** distance **9** territory
expansion 6 growth, spread **8** increase **9** unfolding **11** enlargement **12** augmentation
expansive 3 big **4** wide **5** ample, broad, large, roomy **6** lavish **7** buoyant, elastic, liberal, sizable **8** effusive, extended, generous, outgoing, spacious **9** capacious, garrulous, talkative **10** gregarious, openhanded, unreserved **11** extroverted **13** demonstrative
expatiate 6 ramble, wander **7** dissert, enlarge **8** dilate on, perorate **9** discourse, elaborate, sermonize **10** dilate upon, dissertate
expatriate 5 exile, expel **6** banish, deport, émigré **8** displace, expellee, relegate
expect 4 feel, hope, take **5** await, sense, think, trust **6** assume, divine, gather, look to **7** believe, count on, foresee, imagine, look

for, predict, presume, suppose, surmise **8** forecast, foreknow **9** apprehend, count upon **10** anticipate, presuppose

expectant 5 alert **6** gravid **7** anxious, hopeful **8** enceinte, pregnant, vigilant, watchful **10** breathless, parturient **12** anticipatory, apprehensive

expectation 4 hope **5** hunch **8** prospect **9** assurance, intuition **10** assumption, likelihood **11** presumption, probability **12** anticipation, presentiment

expectorate 4 spit

expediency 5 means **6** resort, tactic **7** aptness, fitness, measure, stopgap **8** meetness, recourse, resource, strategy **9** makeshift, propriety, rightness **11** opportunism, suitability **12** appositeness, practicality, suitableness

expedient 3 fit **5** ad hoc, means, shift **6** resort, timely, useful **7** fitting, politic, prudent, stopgap **8** feasible, recourse, resource, suitable, tactical **9** advisable, judicious, makeshift, opportune, practical, pragmatic, well-timed **10** convenient **11** appropriate, practicable, utilitarian **12** advantageous

expedite 4 send **5** hurry, issue, speed **6** hasten **7** quicken, speed up **8** dispatch **10** accelerate, facilitate

expedition 4 trek, trip **5** hurry, speed **6** voyage **7** journey **8** campaign, dispatch **9** excursion, swiftness **10** efficiency, speediness **11** punctuality

expeditious 4 fast **5** brisk, quick, rapid, swift **6** prompt, speedy **9** efficient **11** efficacious

expeditiousness 5 hurry, speed **6** hustle **8** dispatch

expel 4 boot, oust, spew **5** egest, eject, evict, exile **6** banish, bounce, deport, disbar **7** cast out, dismiss, drum out, kick out, turn out **8** disgorge, displace, throw out **9** discharge, eliminate **10** expatriate

expellee 5 exile **6** émigré **7** outcast **8** deportee, emigrant

expend 3 pay, sap **4** blow **5** drain, spend, use up, waste **6** lay out, outlay, pay out **7** consume, deplete, dig into, dole out, exhaust, fork out, utilize **8** disburse, dispense, shell out, squander **9** dissipate **10** run through

expendable 10 disposable **11** dispensable, inessential, replaceable **12** nonessential

expenditure 4 cost **5** outgo **6** outlay, payoff, payout **12** disbursement

expense 4 cost, loss, toll **5** debit, price **6** burden, charge, outlay **7** forfeit, payment **8** overhead **9** decrement, sacrifice **10** forfeiture **12** disbursement

expensive 4 dear, high, posh **5** fancy, pricy, ritzy, steep, stiff **6** costly, deluxe, lavish, pricey **7** upscale **8** precious, valuable, wasteful **9** big-ticket, luxurious **10** exorbitant, high-priced, overpriced **11** extravagant **12** uneconomical

experience 4 know, live **5** event, savor, skill, trial **6** ordeal, suffer, wisdom **7** episode, know-how, sustain, undergo **8** incident, practice **9** encounter, go through **10** background **11** familiarity, savoir faire ***anew:*** **6** relive

experienced 4 wise **6** mature, versed **7** old-line, veteran, worldly **8** broken in, seasoned **9** practiced, qualified **12** accomplished

experiential see **empirical**

experiment 3 try **4** test **5** assay, probe, trial **6** try out **7** test out **8** research, trial run **13** trial and error

experimental 9 empirical, tentative **10** innovative **11** exploratory, preliminary, preparatory, provisional **13** developmental, trial-and-error

experimentation 4 test **5** trial **7** testing **8** research, trial run **13** trial and error

expert 3 ace, pro, wiz **4** deft, whiz **5** adept, crack, doyen, maven **6** adroit, master, wizard **7** skilled **8** masterly, skillful, virtuoso **9** authority, dexterous, masterful, virtuosic **10** past master, proficient, specialist **11** crackerjack **12** passed master, professional

expertise 5 craft, skill **7** ability, command, know-how, mastery **8** facility **10** adroitness, competence **11** proficiency **12** skillfulness

expiate 6 offset, pay for, redeem **7** redress **8** atone for

expiation 9 atonement, indemnity **10** recompense, reparation **11** restitution **12** satisfaction

expiatory 7 atoning, lustral **9** purgative **11** penitential, purgatorial **12** propitiatory

expiration 3 end **5** death **10** exhalation **11** termination

expire 3 die, end **4** pass **5** lapse **6** elapse, exhale, pass on, perish, run out **7** decease **8** pass away **9** terminate **10** breathe out

explain 5 gloss, solve **7** analyze, clarify, clear up, condone, expound, justify, resolve, unravel **8** construe, decipher, spell out, unriddle, untangle **9** break down, elucidate, interpret **10** account for, illuminate, illustrate, unscramble **11** disentangle, rationalize

explain away 6 excuse **7** justify **8** minimize **9** extenuate **10** account for **11** rationalize

explanation 3 key **5** gloss **6** excuse, motive, reason **7** account, example, grounds, meaning **8** exegesis **9** construal, rationale **11** elucidation **12** significance **13** clarification

explanatory 10 discursive, exegetical **12** enlightening, illuminating, illustrative, interpretive

expletive 4 cuss, oath **5** curse, swear **8** cussword **9** swearword **12** interjection (see also **exclamation**)

explicate 7 amplify, develop, explain, expound **8** construe, spell out **9** elucidate, interpret

explication 5 gloss **8** exegesis **9** construal **10** commentary **11** development

explicative 10 discursive, exegetical, scholastic **12** interpretive **13** hermeneutical

explicit 4 open, sure **5** clear, exact, frank, lucid, overt, plain **7** certain, correct, express, obvious, precise **8** clear-cut, definite, distinct, specific **10** definitive **11** categorical, perspicuous, unambiguous, unequivocal

explode 3 pop **4** fire **5** blast, burst, erupt, go off **6** blow up, debunk, negate, refute **7** burgeon, deflate **8** break out, burst out, detonate, disprove, dynamite, mushroom, puncture **9** discharge, discredit **10** burst forth **11** proliferate

exploit 3 act, use **4** coup, deed, feat, gest, play **5** abuse, geste, stunt **6** bestow, effort, employ, parlay, play on **7** emprise, utilize, venture **8** escapade, exercise **9** adventure, cultivate **10** enterprise, manipulate **11** achievement, performance, tour de force

explore 5 probe, scout **6** burrow, go into, search **7** dig into, examine **8** look into, prospect, traverse **9** delve into **11** inquire into, investigate

explorer ***African:*** **3** Cam, Cão (Diogo) **4** Park (Mungo) **5** Grant (James), Laird (Macgregor), Speke (John Hanning) **6** Akeley (Carl, Mary), Burton (Richard), Lander (John, Richard) **7** Covilhâ (Pero da), Stanley (Henry) **8** Covilhâo (Pero da) **10** Clapperton (Hugh) **11** Livingstone (David) ***American:*** **4** Byrd (Richard), Hall (Charles Francis), Kane (Elisha Kent), Pike (Zebulon) **5** Beebe (Charles William), Clark (William), Lewis (Meriwether), Peary (Robert) **6** Henson (Matthew), Powell (John Wesley), Wilkes (Charles) **7** Ballard (Robert), Frémont (John Charles) ***Antarctic:*** **4** Byrd (Richard), Cook (Frederick), Ross (James Clark) **5** Fuchs (Vivian), Ronne (Finn), Scott (Robert Falcon) **6** Palmer (Nathaniel), Rymill (John Riddoch), Wilkes (Charles) **7** Weddell (James), Wilkins (George) **8** Amundsen (Roald), d'Urville (Dumont) **9** Ellsworth (Lincoln) **10** Shackleton (Ernest) ***Arctic:*** **3** Rae (John) **4** Byrd (Richard), Cook (Frederick) **5** Davis (John), Peary (Robert) **6** Baffin (William), Bering (Vitus), Henson (Matthew), Hudson (Henry), Nansen (Fridtjof), Nobile (Umberto) **7** Barents (Willem), Bennett (Floyd), Wilkins (George), Wrangel (Ferdinand von) **8** Amundsen (Roald) **9** Mackenzie (Alexander), MacMillan (Donald) **10** Stefansson (Vilhjalmur) ***Australian:*** **7** Wilkins (George) ***Austrian:*** **9** Weyprecht (Carl) ***Canadian:*** **9** Mackenzie (Alexander) **10** Stefansson (Vilhjalmur) ***Danish:*** **9** Rasmussen (Knud) ***Dutch:*** **6** Tasman (Abel Janszoon) ***English:*** **4** Cook (James) **5** Cabot (John, Sebastian), Drake (Francis), Scott (Robert Falcon), Smith (John) **6** Baffin (William), Burton (Richard), Hudson (Henry) **7** Raleigh (Walter), Stanley (Henry) **9** Vancouver (George) **10** Shackleton (Ernest) **12** Younghusband (Francis) ***French:*** **7** Cartier (Jacques), La Salle (Sieur de), Nicolet (Jean) **8** Cousteau (Jacques-Yves) **9** Champlain (Samuel de), La Perouse (Comte de), Marquette (Jacques) ***French Canadian:*** **6** Joliet (Louis) **7** Jolliet (Louis) **9** Iberville (Sieur d') ***German:*** **6** Peters (Carl) **8** Humboldt (Alexander von) ***Italian:*** **5** Cabot (John) **6** Nobile (Umberto) **8** Vespucci (Amerigo) ***New Zealand:*** **7** Hillary (Edmund) ***Norwegian:*** **6** Nansen (Fridtjof) **8** Amundsen (Roald), Sverdrup (Otto) **9** Heyerdahl (Thor) ***Portuguese:*** **4** Gama (Vasco da) **5** Cunha (Tristão da) **6** Cabral (Pedro) **8** Cabrilho (João Rodrigues), Magellan (Ferdinand) ***Scottish:*** **3** Rae (John) **4** Park (Mungo), Ross (James Clark) **7** Thomson (Joseph) **11** Livingstone (David) ***Spanish:*** **6** Balboa (Vasco Núñez de), Cortés (Hernán, Hernando), de Soto (Hernando), Pinzón (Martín Alonso, Vicente Yáñez) **7** Mendoza (Pedro de), Pizarro (Francisco) **8** Bastidas (Rodrigo de), Coronado (Francisco de) **11** Ponce de León (Juan)

explosion 3 pop, pow **4** bang, boom, clap **5** blast, burst, crack, crash, sally, salvo, storm **6** report, volley **7** barrage, blowout, torrent **8** eruption, outburst, paroxysm **9** discharge **10** detonation ***cosmic:*** **7** big bang

explosive 3 TNT **5** nitro, tense **6** charge, napalm, petard, powder **7** cordite, violent **8** dynamite **9** gunpowder **13** nitroglycerin ***device:*** **3** cap **4** bomb, mine **5** shell **6** petard **7** grenade **8** firework ***inventor:*** **5** Maxim (Hudson), Nobel (Alfred) ***sound:*** **3** pop, pow **4** bang, blam, boom **5** crack

exponent 6 backer **7** booster **8** advocate, champion, defender, partisan, promoter, upholder **9** supporter **12** practitioner

expose 3 air **4** bare, open, show **5** dig up, flash **6** debunk, flaunt, parade, reveal, show up, unmask, unveil **7** abandon, display, exhibit, lay open, publish, show off, subject, uncover, undress **8** brandish, disclose, discover, endanger, unclothe
exposé 10 disclosure, revelation, uncovering
exposed 4 bare, open **5** naked **6** liable **7** evident, subject, visible **8** manifest, stripped, unhidden **9** uncovered **11** susceptible, unconcealed, unprotected
exposition 4 fair, show **6** bazaar **7** display, exhibit **9** trade show
expostulate 5 argue **6** debate, reason **7** discuss, dispute
exposure 4 risk **5** peril **6** airing, baring, danger **8** betrayal, jeopardy, openness **9** liability, publicity **10** revelation **12** helplessness **13** vulnerability
expound 5 state **6** defend **7** clarify, comment, explain, present **8** construe, set forth, spell out **9** discourse, explicate, interpret
expounder 7 teacher **8** advocate, champion, defender, promoter **9** proponent, supporter
express 3 air, say **4** mean, tell, vent **5** couch, crush, frame, state, utter, voice **6** broach, convey, denote, impart, intend, voiced **7** connote, declare, signify, special, uttered **8** announce, clear-cut, definite, disclose, explicit, intended, proclaim, specific **9** enunciate, formulate, high-speed, pronounce, symbolize, ventilate **10** definitive, particular **11** categorical, communicate, intentional, unambiguous ***gratitude:*** **5** thank ***regret:*** **9** apologize
expression 4 cast, face, form, look, mien, sign, vent, word **5** idiom, issue, motto, token, voice **6** symbol, visage **7** diction, gesture **8** locution **9** eloquence, statement, utterance, verbalism, vividness **10** embodiment, indication **11** countenance, enunciation, observation **13** demonstration, manifestation ***facial:*** **4** grin, phiz, pout **5** frown, scowl, smile, smirk, sneer, wince **7** grimace ***of assent:*** **3** aye, nod, yea, yes **4** okay ***of sorrow:*** **4** alas, tear ***trite:*** **6** cliché **7** bromide **8** banality ***witty:*** **4** quip **5** sally **6** bon mot
expressionless 5 blank **6** stolid, vacant, wooden **7** deadpan **9** impassive **10** poker-faced **11** inscrutable
expressive 5 vivid **7** graphic **8** eloquent **9** revealing **10** meaningful, passionate
expressly 9 precisely, purposely **10** explicitly **12** particularly, specifically **13** intentionally
expressway 4 road **7** freeway, highway, parkway **8** turnpike **12** thoroughfare
expropriate 4 take **5** annex, seize **7** impound, preempt **8** arrogate **9** sequester **10** commandeer, confiscate, dispossess
expulsion 5 exile, purge **6** ouster **7** ousting, removal **8** ejection, eviction **9** ostracism **10** banishment, relegation **11** deportation **12** displacement
expunge 4 dele, x out **5** annul, erase **6** cancel, delete, efface **7** blot out, destroy, exclude, wipe out **8** black out **9** eliminate, eradicate, strike out **10** annihilate, obliterate
expurgate 4 blip **5** bleep, purge **6** censor, purify, screen **7** cleanse **8** sanitize **10** bowdlerize
expurgation 8 ablution **9** catharsis, cleansing **10** lustration **12** purification
exquisite 3 fop **4** fine, keen, rare **5** acute, dandy **6** choice, dainty, select, superb **7** coxcomb, elegant, extreme, intense, refined **8** delicate, finished, flawless, macaroni **9** recherché **10** fastidious, immaculate, impeccable
exsiccate 3 dry **4** sear **5** parch **6** wither **7** shrivel **9** dehydrate
extant 4 live **5** alive **6** actual, living **7** current, present **9** surviving **10** present-day **12** contemporary
extemporaneous 5 ad-lib **6** casual **7** offhand **8** ad-libbed, informal **9** impromptu, impulsive, makeshift, unplanned **10** improvised, unprepared, unscripted **11** spontaneous, unrehearsed **12** unthought-out
extempore see **extemporaneous**
extemporize 5 ad-lib **6** wing it **7** dash off, toss off **8** knock off **9** improvise
extend 4 draw, span, vary **5** award, offer, range, reach **6** bestow, spread, unbend, unfold **7** advance, augment, broaden, drag out, draw out, enlarge, further, hold out, proceed, proffer, project, prolong, spin out, stretch **8** continue, elongate, increase, lengthen, protract **10** outstretch, stretch out
extension 3 arm, ell **4** wing **5** add-on, annex, delay, range, reach, scope, sweep **6** radius, spread **7** adjunct, compass, purview **8** addition, increase **9** appendage, magnitude **10** broadening, elongation **11** enlargement, lengthening, protraction **12** augmentation, continuation, postponement, prolongation
extensity 5 ambit, orbit, range, reach, scope, sweep **6** radius **7** compass, purview
extensive 3 big **4** long, vast, wide **5** broad, large, major **7** general, immense, lengthy, sizable **8** far-flung, sizeable, spacious, sweeping, thorough **9** wholesale **10** large-scale, widespread **11** far-reaching, wide-ranging **12** considerable

extent **4** size **5** ambit, limit, orbit, range, reach, scope, sweep, width **6** amount, degree, domain, radius **7** breadth, compass, measure, purview **8** vicinity **9** magnitude **10** dimensions, proportion

extenuate **6** dilute, excuse, lessen, soften, temper, weaken **7** explain, justify, qualify, varnish **8** diminish, enervate, mitigate, moderate, palliate **9** gloss over **11** rationalize

exterior **4** skin **5** outer, shell **6** facade **7** outmost, outside, outward, surface **8** apparent **9** outermost **11** superficial

exterminate **4** kill **6** rub out **7** destroy, wipe out **8** massacre **9** eliminate, eradicate, finish off, liquidate, slaughter **10** annihilate, extinguish, obliterate

external **3** out **4** over **5** outer **7** foreign, outside, outward, surface **9** outermost **10** peripheral **11** superficial

externalize **4** show **6** embody, evince, excuse, expose, reveal **7** exhibit, justify **8** manifest **9** extenuate, incarnate, objectify, personify **11** rationalize **12** substantiate

extinct **4** cold, dead, gone, late **5** passé **6** bygone **7** archaic, defunct **8** deceased, departed, obsolete, perished, vanished **10** superseded

extinction **3** end **4** doom **5** death **6** demise **11** destruction, eradication, liquidation **12** annihilation, obliteration **13** disappearance, extermination

extinguish **3** end **5** crush, douse, erase, quash, quell, snuff **6** put out, quench, squash, stifle **7** abolish, blot out, blow out, destroy, eclipse, expunge, nullify, put down, wipe out **8** snuff out, stamp out, suppress **9** eliminate, eradicate, extirpate **10** annihilate, obliterate

extirpate **5** erase **6** cut out, efface, excise, resect, uproot **7** abolish, blot out, destroy, expunge, kill off, root out, wipe out **8** demolish **9** eliminate, eradicate **10** annihilate, deracinate, extinguish

extol **4** hymn, laud **5** cry up, exalt **6** praise **7** acclaim, applaud, commend, glorify, magnify **8** eulogize **9** celebrate **10** panegyrize

extort **5** wrest, wring **7** extract

extortion **8** exaction **9** blackmail

extra **3** odd **4** more, over, perk, plus **5** added, add-on, bonus, spare **6** de trop, rarely **7** reserve, surplus **8** leftover **9** lagniappe, redundant, unusually **10** additional, especially, perquisite **11** superfluous **12** particularly, supplemental **13** supernumerary, supplementary

extract **4** pull, yank **5** evoke, glean, quote, wring **6** derive, eke out, elicit, remove **7** abridge, distill, essence, excerpt, passage, pull out, squeeze, take out **8** citation, condense, infusion **9** quotation, selection **11** concentrate

extraction **5** birth, blood, stock **6** origin **7** descent, essence, lineage **8** ancestry, pedigree **9** parentage **10** derivation **12** distillation

extraneous **5** alien, outer **6** exotic **7** foreign, outside **8** external **9** unrelated **10** immaterial, inapposite, incidental, irrelevant, peripheral **11** impertinent, inessential, superfluous, unessential **12** adventitious, inapplicable, nonessential

extraordinary **3** odd **4** rare **6** unique **7** amazing, notable, special, unusual **8** abnormal, atypical, singular, terrific, uncommon, unwonted **9** wonderful **10** noteworthy, phenomenal, remarkable, stupendous, tremendous **11** exceptional, outstanding

extravagance **5** frill, waste **6** excess, luxury **9** hyperbole, profusion **10** indulgence, lavishness **11** ostentation, prodigality, superfluity **12** immoderation, wastefulness

extravagant **4** wild **5** outré, undue **6** lavish **7** bizarre, extreme, profuse **8** overdone, prodigal, reckless, wasteful **9** elaborate, excessive, fantastic, grandiose, overblown **10** exorbitant, hyperbolic, immoderate, inordinate, profligate **11** exaggerated, implausible, intemperate, nonsensical **12** ostentatious, preposterous, unrestrained

extreme **3** max, top **4** apex, dire, last, peak, wild **5** crown, final, limit, ultra, undue **6** climax, excess, height, summit, utmost, zenith **7** drastic, fanatic, intense, maximal, maximum, outmost, radical, violent **8** farthest, furthest, pinnacle, remotest, ultimate **9** desperate, excessive, outermost, uttermost **10** immoderate, inordinate, outlandish, outrageous **11** furthermost, unwarranted **12** unmeasurable, unreasonable **13** revolutionary
degree: **3** nth

extremely **4** mega, most, unco, very **5** ultra **6** highly, hugely, mighty, overly, plenty, wildly **7** acutely, awfully, greatly, utterly **8** severely, terribly **9** immensely, seriously, unusually **10** remarkably, strikingly **11** exceedingly **12** terrifically

extremist **5** rabid, ultra **6** zealot **7** die-hard, fanatic, radical **8** militant, ultraist **9** fanatical **10** monomaniac, ultraistic **11** reactionary **13** revolutionary

extremity **3** arm, end, leg, tip **4** acme, apex, foot, hand, tail **5** limit, verge **6** apogee, vertex, zenith **8** terminal, terminus

extricate **4** free **5** loose **6** detach, redeem, rescue **7** bail out, deliver, resolve, set free, untwine **8** liberate, untangle **9** disengage **11** disencumber, disentangle, distinguish, individuate **12** discriminate, disembarrass **13** differentiate

extrinsic 5 alien, outer **6** exotic **7** foreign, outside, outward **8** exterior, external, imported **10** incidental, extraneous

extrude 4 spew **5** eject **7** push out **8** press out **10** squeeze out

exuberance 4 glee, life, zest **5** ardor **6** gaiety, spirit **7** abandon **8** buoyancy, hilarity, vivacity **9** profusion **10** ebullience, enthusiasm, friskiness, liveliness **11** flamboyance, high spirits, zestfulness **12** exhilaration **13** effervescence, sprightliness

exuberant 3 gay **4** lush, rank **5** happy **6** bouncy, elated, fecund, lavish, lively **7** buoyant, profuse, rampant, riotous, zestful **8** fruitful, prodigal, prolific, spirited **9** ebullient, luxuriant, sprightly, vivacious **10** flamboyant **11** exhilarated **12** effervescent, enthusiastic, high-spirited

exude 4 emit, leak, ooze, seep, shed **5** issue **7** diffuse, display, emanate, excrete, exhibit, give off, ooze out, radiate, secrete **9** discharge

exult 4 crow **5** cheer, gloat, glory, revel **7** delight, rejoice **8** jubilate **9** celebrate

exultant 6 elated, joyful, joyous **7** gleeful **8** ecstatic, euphoric, jubilant **9** cock-a-hoop, overjoyed, rejoicing, triumphal **10** triumphant

exultation 3 joy **4** glee **7** delight, ecstasy, elation, rapture, triumph **8** euphoria, gloating **9** jubilance, rejoicing **10** jubilation

eye 3 orb **4** lamp, ogle, scan, view **5** sight, watch **6** behold, goggle, look at, ocular, oculus, peeper, regard, size up, vision **7** inspect, observe **8** check out, consider, gaze upon, scrutiny **9** headlight **10** scrutinize ***combining form:*** **4** ocul **5** oculo **8** ophthalm **9** ophthalmo ***defect:*** **6** myopia **9** hyperopia **10** emmetropia, presbyopia **11** astigmatism ***disease:*** **8** cataract, glaucoma, trachoma ***doctor:*** **7** oculist **11** optometrist ***opening:*** **5** pupil ***part:*** **4** iris, lens, uvea **5** pupil **6** cornea, retina, sclera ***relating to:*** **5** optic **7** optical ***socket:*** **5** orbit ***Spanish:*** **3** ojo ***test:*** **10** Amsler Grid **12** Snellen Chart

eyeball 4 scan **5** check, study **6** go over, look at, peruse, survey **7** examine, inspect, observe **8** appraise, check out, evaluate, pore over **10** scrutinize

eye-catching 4 bold **5** gaudy, showy **6** flashy **7** salient **8** striking **9** arresting, prominent **10** noticeable, remarkable **11** conspicuous

eyeful 6 looker **7** stunner **8** knockout

eyeglass 7 monocle

eyeglasses 5 specs **6** lenses **7** lorgnon **8** bifocals, pince-nez **9** lorgnette **10** spectacles

eyelash 6 cilium **11** hairbreadth

eyelet 4 hole **7** grommet **8** loophole, peephole

eyelid growth 3 sty **4** cyst, stye **5** nevus **9** chalazion, hordeolum

eyepiece 4 lens **6** ocular

eye-popping 7 amazing **8** exciting, stirring **9** thrilling **10** astounding **11** astonishing, mind-blowing, spectacular **12** breathtaking

eyesore 4 blot, dump, mess **6** blight **7** blemish **8** atrocity **11** monstrosity

eyespot 6 blight, fungus **7** ocellus

eyetooth 6 canine

eyewash 3 rot **4** bunk **5** bilge, hooey, tripe **6** bunkum **7** baloney, garbage, hogwash, rubbish, twaddle **8** malarkey, nonsense **9** poppycock **10** balderdash **13** horsefeathers

eyewitness 8 observer, onlooker **9** bystander, spectator

eyrie see **aerie**

F

Fabergé product 3 egg **9** Easter egg

Fabian 4 Shaw (George Bernard), Webb (Beatrice, Sidney) **7** politic **8** cautious, dilatory **9** socialist **11** circumspect, calculating

fable 4 myth, tale, yarn **5** story **6** legend **7** fantasy, fiction, figment, parable **8** allegory, tall tale ***animal:*** **8** bestiary

fabled 5 famed **6** famous, unreal **7** storied **8** fanciful, mythical, renowned **9** fictional, imaginary, legendary, pretended **10** fictitious **11** make-believe **12** mythological

fabric 3 aba, rep, web **4** lamé, repp **5** cloth, fiber, grain **7** texture **8** building, material, shirting **9** structure ***coarse:*** **4** tapa **5** crash, gunny **6** burlap, linsey, ratiné **7** cheviot, hopsack **8** homespun ***colorer:*** **4** dyer ***corded:*** **3** rep **4** repp **5** piqué **6** calico, moreen, poplin **7** pinwale **8** corduroy, paduasoy **9** bengaline ***cotton:*** **4** jean, leno **5** baize, chino, denim, domet, drill, lisle, scrim, wigan **6** chintz, dimity, faille, madras, muslin, sateen **7** etamine, gingham, nankeen, percale, ticking **8** chambray, dungaree, nainsook, tarlatan **9** crinoline **10** seersucker ***cotton and linen:*** **4** huck **7** fustian **9** huckaback ***crepe:*** **8** marocain ***dealer:*** **6** draper, mercer ***durable:*** **4** huck, jean **5** chino, denim, drill, scrim **6** frieze, moreen **7** lasting, ticking **8** cretonne, dungaree ***embroidered:*** **9** baldachin **10** baldachino ***finishing process:*** **8** lustring **9** mercerize ***flag material:*** **7** bunting ***glazed:*** **4** ciré **6** chintz **7** cambric, holland ***knitted:*** **6** tricot **10** balbriggan ***linen:*** **7** cambric, lockram ***looped:*** **6** bouclé ***lustrous:*** **4** silk **5** moiré, satin, surah **6** sateen **7** taffeta **12** brilliantine ***metallic:*** **4** lamé ***net:*** **5** tulle **8** bobbinet, illusion ***openwork:*** **4** lace **8** filigree ***ornamental:*** **4** lace **5** braid **6** ribbon **7** bunting ***pebbly-surface:*** **8** barathea ***pile-surface:*** **5** panne, plush, terry **6** velour, velvet **7** duvetyn, velours **8** chenille, moleskin **9** velveteen ***plaid:*** **6** tartan ***pleated:*** **5** ruche ***printed:*** **5** batik, toile **6** calico, chintz, damask **7** allover, challis **8** cretonne, jacquard **11** toile de Jouy ***puckered:*** **6** plissé **10** seersucker ***raised pattern:*** **4** lamé **7** brocade **10** brocatelle ***satin weave:*** **5** panne ***sheer:*** **4** lawn, mull **5** gauze, ninon, voile **6** dimity **7** batiste, chiffon, organdy, organza, tiffany **8** tarlatan ***silk:*** **6** faille, pongee, samite **7** foulard, grogram **8** paduasoy, sarcenet, sarsenet, shantung **9** bombazine ***striped:*** **3** aba **7** ticking **8** bayadere ***synthetic:*** **5** Arnel, ninon, nylon, Orlon, rayon **6** Dacron ***trim:*** **5** ruche ***twill:*** **4** jean **5** chino, drill, serge **7** foulard, nankeen, ticking **8** dungaree, shalloon **9** bombazine **10** broadcloth ***unfinished:*** **6** greige ***waterproof:*** **7** oilskin ***wool:*** **5** baize, loden, tweed **6** alpaca, caddis, camlet, duffel, duffle, melton, merino, wadmal, wadmel, wadmol, woolen **7** woollen **8** mackinaw, prunella **9** cassimere ***wool, poor quality:*** **5** mungo **6** shoddy ***wool mixture:*** **6** saxony **7** drugget, ratteen **8** moquette, shalloon, zibeline **9** zibelline ***woven:*** **4** weft **7** textile

fabricate **4** form, make **5** build, erect, frame, set up, shape **6** cook up, create, devise, invent, make up **7** concoct, dream up, fashion, produce, think up **8** assemble, contrive **9** construct, structure **11** manufacture, put together

fabrication **3** fib, lie **4** bull, jive **6** canard, deceit **7** fiction, figment, hogwash, product, untruth **8** assembly, building, creation **9** deception, fairy tale, falsehood, invention **10** concoction, production **11** manufacture **12** construction

fabulist **4** liar ***French:*** **10** La Fontaine (Jean de) ***Greek:*** **5** Aesop ***Roman:*** **8** Phaedrus ***Russian:*** **6** Krylov (Ivan)

fabulous **5** super **7** amazing **8** mythical, terrific, wondrous **9** fantastic, legendary, marvelous, wonderful **10** astounding, fictitious, incredible, outrageous, phenomenal, prodigious, remarkable, stupendous **11** astonishing, extravagant, spectacular **12** mythological ***animal:*** **6** dragon **7** centaur, unicorn ***bird:*** **3** roc ***serpent:*** **8** basilisk **10** cockatrice

facade **4** face, mask **5** color, front, guise, put-on **6** veneer **8** disguise, exterior, frontage, pretense **10** appearance, camouflage, false front

face **3** mug, pan **4** dare, defy, dial, meet, phiz, puss, show, side **5** abide, brave, front, guise, honor, image, nerve **6** endure, facade, kisser, makeup, mazard, oppose, resist, suffer, take on, visage **7** compete, contend, dignity, surface **8** confront, cope with, deal with, disguise, features, prestige, war paint **9** assurance, encounter, lineament, semblance, withstand **10** appearance, confidence, experience, expression, maquillage, reputation **11** countenance, self-respect

face-off **5** clash, set-to **13** confrontation

facet **4** edge, item, part, side **5** angle, bezel, front, phase, plane, point, trait **6** aspect, detail **7** element, feature, surface **9** attribute, component **10** appearance, particular

facetious **4** flip **5** comic, droll, jokey, smart, witty **6** blithe, breezy, joking **7** amusing, comical, jesting, jocular, joshing, kidding, risible, waggish **8** flippant, humorous **9** ludicrous, unserious, whimsical **10** irreverent, ridiculous **12** wisecracking **13** tongue-in-cheek

face-to-face **6** direct **7** contact, present, vis-à-vis **8** directly, in person, personal **10** personally

facile **4** deft, easy, glib, snap **5** light, quick, ready **6** adroit, expert, fluent, poised, simple, smooth **7** assured, cursory, offhand, shallow, voluble **8** skillful, untaxing **9** dexterous **10** effortless, simplistic **13** uncomplicated

facilitate **3** aid **4** abet, ease, help **6** assist, enable, smooth **7** advance, forward, further, promote **8** expedite, make easy, simplify

facility 3 aid, wit **4** bent, ease **5** knack, privy, skill **6** talent, toilet **7** ability, amenity, comfort, fluency, leaning **8** aptitude, bathroom, building, capacity, lavatory, washroom **9** advantage, dexterity **10** adroitness, competence, smoothness **11** convenience, institution, proficiency **12** installation **13** accommodation, establishment

facing 5 front, panel **6** contra, lining, toward, veneer **7** surface, vis-à-vis **8** covering, opposite, paneling **11** over against ***down:*** **5** prone ***up:*** **6** supine

facsimile 4 copy, dupe, fake, twin **5** clone, ditto, match, mimeo, repro, Xerox **6** carbon, double **7** replica **8** knockoff, likeness **9** duplicate, imitation, photocopy **10** carbon copy, dead ringer, similitude **11** counterpart, duplication, replication **12** reproduction

fact 4 dope **5** datum, event, truth **6** detail, gospel, truism, verity **7** episode, reality **8** evidence, incident **9** actuality **10** occurrence, particular, phenomenon **11** information **12** circumstance, intelligence

faction 4 band, bloc, camp, part, ring, sect, side, wing **5** cabal, group, party **6** caucus, circle, clique, sector, strife **7** combine, coterie, discord, section **8** alliance, disunity, splinter **10** contingent

factious 7 warring **8** contrary, divisive, partisan **9** dissident, insurgent, sectarian, seditious, turbulent **10** contending, malcontent **11** contentious, disaffected, dissentious, quarrelsome **12** disputatious **13** troublemaking

factitious 4 sham **5** bogus, false, phony **6** ersatz, forced, made-up, unreal **7** assumed, created, feigned, man-made, shammed **8** affected, invented, spurious **9** concocted, contrived, fashioned, pretended, simulated, synthetic, unnatural **10** artificial, fabricated **11** constructed, counterfeit **12** manufactured **13** counterfeited

____ facto 4 ipso **6** ex post

factor 4 gene, item **5** agent, cause, proxy **6** broker, lender, number, symbol **7** divisor, element, exclude, include, resolve **8** attorney, emissary, quantity **9** component, majordomo, substance **10** antecedent, ingredient, multiplier **11** determinant **12** intermediary

factory 4 mill, shop **5** plant, works **8** workshop **9** sweatshop **11** machine shop

factotum 4 grub **5** gofer **6** drudge **7** servant **9** assistant, gal Friday, man Friday, operative **11** functionary

factual 4 real, true **5** exact, valid **6** actual **7** certain, genuine, literal **8** absolute, positive **9** authentic, undoubted **10** undisputed **12** indisputable

faculty 4 bent, body, gift **5** flair, knack, power **6** talent **7** ability, college **8** aptitude, capacity, facility, function, instinct **9** educators, lecturers **10** department, professors **11** instructors

fad 4 chic, kick, mode, rage, whim **5** craze, furor, mania, style, trend **6** furore, latest, whimsy **7** caprice, fashion **9** bandwagon **10** dernier cri

faddish 3 hot **4** chic **5** today **6** modish, red-hot, trendy, with-it **7** stylish, voguish **8** contempo **9** au courant **11** cutting-edge, fashionable

fade 3 die, dim, ebb **4** fail, pale, wane, wilt **6** lessen, vanish, weaken, wither **7** decline, lighten, wash out **8** decrease, discolor, diminish **9** disappear, evaporate

faded 3 dim, wan **4** drab, dull, pale **6** pallid **8** bleached, vanished, withered **9** etiolated, washed-out

Faerie Queene, The ***author:*** **7** Spenser (Edmund) ***character:*** **3** Ate, Una **4** Alma **5** Guyon, Talus **6** Abessa, Amavia, Amoret, Arthur, Cambel, Duessa, Palmer **7** Artegal, Corceca, Fidessa, Maleger, Sansloy **8** Calidore, Florimel, Fradubio, Gloriana, Lucifera, Orgoglio, Satyrane **9** Archimago, Britomart **11** Britomartis

Faeroes whirlwind 2 oe

Fafnir 6 dragon ***brother:*** **5** Regin **6** Fasolt, Reginn ***father:*** **8** Hreidmar ***slayer:*** **6** Sigurd **9** Siegfried ***victim:*** **6** Fasolt **8** Hreidmar

fag 4 do in, moil, tire, toil **5** serve, smoke, stick, weary **6** drudge, overdo, tucker **7** exhaust, fatigue, servant, wear out **8** drudgery, knock out **9** cigarette

fag end 4 butt, edge, fray **7** remnant

faience 7 pottery **11** earthenware

fail 3 die, end **4** bomb, fade, lack, lose, miss, sink, slip, stop, wane **5** break, flunk **6** fizzle, forget, ignore, lessen, weaken **7** decline, default, founder, give out, go under, neglect **8** fall flat, languish, miscarry **9** break down, fall short **10** disappoint, go bankrupt **11** deteriorate

failing 4 flaw, vice **5** fault **6** defect **8** weakness **9** weak point **10** deficiency **11** shortcoming **12** imperfection

failure 3 bum, dud **4** bomb, bust, flop, miss **5** decay, loser **6** fiasco, fizzle, no-good, outage **7** default, washout **8** collapse, fracture, omission **9** breakdown, cessation, oversight, unconcern **10** bankruptcy, deficiency, insolvency, negligence **11** defalcation, dysfunction, miscarriage **12** interruption **13** deterioration

fain 3 apt **5** eager, prone, ready **6** gladly, minded **7** willing **8** amenable, inclined **9** agreeable

fainéant 3 bum **4** idle, lazy **5** idler, sloth **6** loafer, torpid **7** goof-off, slacker **8** deadbeat, inactive, indolent, layabout, slothful, sluggard, sluggish **9** do-nothing, lazybones, shiftless **11** couch potato, ineffectual **13** lackadaisical

faint 3 dim, low, wan **4** hazy, pale, soft, weak, wilt **5** dizzy, light, plotz, swoon, vague, woozy **6** feeble, subtle **7** conk out, obscure, pass out, shadowy, syncope, unclear **8** black out, collapse, keel over **9** undefined **10** ill-defined, indistinct

fair 2 OK **3** due **4** even, expo, fine, join, just, mild, okay, open, so-so **5** blond, bonny, clear, equal, fresh, light, sunny **6** bazaar, blonde, comely, decent, honest, kermis, lovely, market, pretty, square **7** cricket **8** adequate, all right, balanced, carnival, festival, mediocre, middling, pleasant, pleasing, rational, sunshiny, unbiased **9** beautiful, cloudless, equitable, favorable, fortunate, impartial, objective, tolerable, trade show, unclouded **10** acceptable, attractive, evenhanded, exhibition, exposition, openminded, reasonable **11** indifferent, nonpartisan, respectable **12** satisfactory, unprejudiced **13** disinterested, dispassionate, sportsmanlike

fair food 10 candy apple, candy floss, fried dough, funnel cake **11** cotton candy, elephant ear

fair-haired 3 pet **5** blond **6** blonde **7** beloved, darling, favored **8** favorite **9** fortunate

fairly 5 quite **6** nearly, rather **7** plainly **8** passably, properly, somewhat **9** tolerably **10** acceptably, deservedly, distinctly, moderately, reasonably **11** practically

fairness 6 candor, equity **7** honesty **8** justness **9** good faith **12** impartiality

fairy 3 elf, imp, nix **4** peri, puck **5** elfin, nixie, nymph, pixie, sylph **6** goblin, kobold, sprite **7** brownie, gremlin **10** leprechaun ***king:*** **6** Oberon ***queen:*** **3** Mab **7** Titania **8** Gloriana ***shoemaker:*** **10** leprechaun

fairy tale *author:* **4** Lang (Andrew) **5** Grimm (Jacob, Wilhelm), Wilde (Oscar) **7** Kipling (Rudyard) **8** Andersen (Hans Christian), Perrault (Charles) ***character:*** **4** Jack, Puck **6** Gretel, Hansel **8** Rapunzel, Tom Thumb **9** Snow White **10** Cinderella, Goldilocks, Thumbelina

faith 4 cult, sect **5** credo, creed, stock, troth, trust **6** belief, church, credit **8** credence, reliance, religion **9** certainty, certitude, communion, credulity **10** confidence, persuasion **12** denomination ***article of:*** **5** tenet

faithful 4 fast, just, true **5** liege, loyal, pious, tried **6** steady, trusty **7** devoted, dutiful, staunch **8** constant, follower, reliable, resolute, true-blue **9** religious, steadfast **10** dependable, scrupulous, unwavering **11** truehearted, trustworthy

faithfulness 5 piety, troth **6** fealty **7** loyalty **8** devotion, fidelity **9** adherence, constancy **10** allegiance, attachment

faithless 5 false, Punic **6** fickle, untrue **8** disloyal, recreant **10** perfidious, traitorous **11** treacherous **13** untrustworthy

faithlessness 7 perfidy, treason **8** betrayal **9** falseness, treachery **10** disloyalty, infidelity

fake 3 act, gyp **4** hoax, mock, sham **5** bluff, bogus, false, feign, fraud, phony, pseud, put on, spoof **6** affect, doctor, ersatz, forged, framed, humbug, pseudo **7** falsify, pretend **8** impostor, invented, simulate, spurious **9** brummagem, charlatan, concocted, fabricate, imitation, imposture, pinchbeck, pretended, simulated **10** artificial, fabricated, fictitious, fraudulent, simulation **11** counterfeit ***combining form:*** **5** pseud **6** pseudo

faker 4 sham **5** fraud, phony, quack **6** con man, hoaxer **8** deceiver, impostor **9** charlatan, con artist, pretender **10** mountebank **11** four-flusher **12** double-dealer **13** confidence man

fakir 7 ascetic, dervish **9** mendicant

falafel holder 4 pita, wrap **5** pitta

falcon 4 hawk **5** hobby, saker **6** lanner, merlin **7** kestrel **9** peregrine ***eye cover:*** **4** seel ***male:*** **4** jack **6** tercel **7** tiercel **8** lanneret ***mature:*** **7** haggard ***young:*** **4** eyas

falcon-headed god see at **Egyptian**

falconry 7 hawking ***equipment:*** **4** bell, hood, jess, lure ***procedure:*** **3** imp **4** cope, seel

Falkland Islands *capital:* **7** Stanlcy ***claimant:*** **9** Argentina ***colony of:*** **7** Britain

fall 3 dip, ebb, sag **4** dive, drip, drop, dump, hang, plop, sink, slip, trip, wane **5** abate, crash, lapse, slide, slump, spill **6** autumn, drowse, give up, go down, header, plunge, sprawl, tumble **7** cascade, decline, descend, descent, devolve, go under, plummet, scatter, stumble, subside **8** collapse, decrease, diminish, keel over, nose-dive **9** hairpiece **10** depreciate **11** precipitate

fallacious 6 untrue **7** invalid **8** delusive, delusory **9** deceitful, deceptive, erroneous, sophistic **10** fraudulent

fallacy 5 error **6** canard **7** falsity, sophism, untruth **8** delusion **9** falsehood **11** non sequitur **13** misconception

fall apart 6 lose it **7** crumble **9** break down, decompose **10** go to pieces **11** come unglued, deteriorate **12** disintegrate

fall back 6 recede, recoil, retire **7** retract, retreat **8** withdraw **9** disengage, retrocede **10** retrograde

fall behind 3 lag **4** drag **5** delay, tarry, trail **6** dawdle, linger, loiter

fall flat 4 bomb, fail, flop, miss **6** fizzle

fall guy 4 dupe, fool, goat, gull **5** chump, front, patsy **6** stooge, sucker **8** front man **9** scapegoat **11** whipping boy

fallible 4 iffy, weak **5** dicey, frail, human **6** errant, erring, faulty **9** imperfect **10** unreliable

falling-out 3 row **4** beef, feud, fuss, spat, tiff **5** break, run-in, words **6** bicker, fracas, hassle **7** dispute, quarrel, rhubarb, wrangle **8** argument, conflict, squabble **9** brannigan **11** altercation, controversy **12** disagreement, estrangement

falloff 3 sag **4** drop, slip **5** slump **7** decline **8** downturn **9** downslide, downswing, downtrend **13** deterioration

fall out 5 argue, break, leave, occur **6** bicker **7** brabble, quarrel, wrangle **8** disagree, squabble

fallow 4 idle **5** inert **6** unsown **7** dormant, resting **8** inactive, unseeded, untilled **9** neglected, quiescent, unplanted **12** uncultivated

false 4 fake, mock, sham **5** bogus, dummy, hokey, lying, phony, wrong **6** ersatz, forged, hollow, pseudo, untrue **7** crooked, devious, feigned, seeming, unloyal **8** apostate, apparent, deluding, delusive, delusory, disloyal, recreant, specious, spurious **9** brummagem, deceitful, deceiving, deceptive, dishonest, distorted, erroneous, faithless, illogical, imitation, incorrect, pinchbeck, simulated **10** artificial, fictitious, fraudulent, inaccurate, misleading, perfidious, traitorous, unfaithful, untruthful **11** counterfeit, treacherous ***combining form:*** **5** pseud **6** pseudo

falsehood 3 fib, lie **5** fable **6** canard **7** fallacy, fiction, untruth, whopper **8** roorback **9** mendacity **11** fabrication **12** misstatement **13** prevarication

falseness 7 fallacy, perfidy **8** apostasy **9** treachery **10** disloyalty, infidelity **11** insincerity

false teeth 8 dentures

falsify 3 fib, lie **4** cook, deny **5** belie, fudge, slant **6** doctor, refute **7** deceive, distort, mislead **8** disprove, misstate **10** contradict **11** prevaricate **12** misrepresent

falsity 3 fib, lie **4** tale, yarn **5** fable **6** canard **7** untruth, whopper **9** falsehood, mendacity **11** fabrication **13** prevarication

Falstaff ***companion:*** **3** Nym **4** Peto **6** Pistol **8** Bardolph ***composer:*** **5** Verdi (Giuseppe) ***creator:*** **11** Shakespeare (William) ***drink:*** **4** sack ***play:*** **7** Henry IV ***prince:*** **3** Hal ***tavern:*** **9** Boar's Head

Falstaffian 3 fat **6** jovial **7** roguish **8** boastful **9** convivial, dissolute

falter 4 halt, limp, reel, sway, trip **5** quail, waver **6** flinch, teeter, totter, wobble **7** give way, stagger, stammer, stumble **8** hesitate **9** vacillate **12** shilly-shally

fame 4 note **5** éclat, glory, honor, kudos **6** esteem, regard, renown, repute **7** acclaim, stardom **8** standing **9** celebrity, notoriety **10** popularity, prominence, reputation **11** acclamation, immortality, recognition

famed 5 noted **6** marked **7** eminent, notable **8** renowned **9** notorious, prominent, well-known **10** celebrated **11** illustrious **13** distinguished

familiar 4 cozy **6** common, folksy **8** domestic, everyday, frequent, informal, intimate, standard **10** accustomed **11** comfortable, commonplace **12** conventional, recognizable **13** garden-variety

familiarity 4 ease **8** intimacy **9** closeness, knowledge **11** informality **12** acquaintance

family 3 kin **4** clan, folk, home, line, race **5** brood, folks, house, issue, stirp, stock, tribe **6** ménage, strain **7** dynasty, kindred, lineage, progeny **8** pedigree **9** bloodline, household, offspring ***branch:*** **5** stirp ***lineage:*** **4** tree **6** stemma **8** pedigree **9** genealogy

famine 4 want **6** dearth, hunger **10** starvation

famished 6 hungry **7** starved **8** ravenous, starving

famous 5 famed, noble, noted **6** fabled **7** eminent, notable, popular **8** historic, renowned **9** legendary, notorious, prominent, well-known **10** celebrated **11** illustrious, prestigious, redoubtable

fan 3 bug, nut **4** blow, buff, open, wind **5** freak, lover, maven, rouse **6** addict, arouse, expand, extend, kindle, rooter, ruffle, spread, stir up, unfold, votary, whip up, winnow **7** admirer, devotee, habitué **8** adherent, enkindle, follower, railbird **9** stimulate **10** aficionado, enthusiast ***dance:*** **11** balletomane ***horseracing:*** **7** turfman ***India:*** **6** punkah ***movie:*** **7** cineast **8** cineaste **9** cinephile

fanatic 3 bug, nut **4** buff **5** fiend, freak, rabid **6** addict, maniac, votary, zealot **7** devotee, die-hard, habitué **10** aficionado, enthusiast

fanatical 5 fiery, rabid **6** ardent, fervid **7** extreme, fervent, zealous **8** frenetic, frenzied, maniacal, obsessed **9** perfervid **10** passionate **11** impassioned

fanaticism 4 zeal **5** mania **6** frenzy **8** zealotry **9** extremism, monomania, obsession

fancier 6 grower **7** amateur, admirer, breeder, devotee

fanciful 6 absurd, unreal **7** bizarre, fictive **8** fabulous, illusory, imagined, mythical, notional, romantic **9** fantastic, fictional, grotesque, imaginary **10** chimerical, fictitious **11** fantastical **12** preposterous

fancy 3 bee, fad **4** idea, like, posh, whim **5** dream, ritzy, shine, smart, taste **6** dressy, liking, megrim, notion, relish, snazzy, swanky, vision, whimsy **7** caprice, chimera, conceit, concept, dream up, elegant, fantasy, feature, imagine, picture **8** conceive, daydream, envision, fondness, judgment, velleity **9** capriccio, elaborate, intricate, inventive, visualize, whimsical **10** decorative, ornamental, partiality, propensity **11** extravagant, highfalutin, imagination, inclination

fandango 5 dance **9** malaguena

fanfare 4 pomp, show, ta-da **5** array, ta-dah **6** hoopla **7** display, hooplah, panoply **8** ballyhoo, flourish ***trumpet:*** **6** tucket **7** tantara

fanlike 7 plicate

fanny 3 bum, can **4** buns, butt, duff, moon, rear, rump, seat, tail, tush **5** booty, nates **6** behind, bottom, breech, heinie **7** caboose, hind end, keister, rear end, tail end **8** backside, buttocks, derriere **9** fundament, posterior

fantasia 6 vision **8** daydream, illusion, rhapsody **9** fairyland **10** apparition

fantasize 4 moon **5** dream, fancy **7** imagine **8** daydream **10** woolgather

fantastic 3 odd **4** wild **6** absurd, unreal **7** bizarre, surreal **8** fanciful, singular **9** eccentric, grotesque, imaginary, marvelous, monstrous, unearthly, whimsical **10** chimerical, far-fetched, improbable, incredible, outlandish, outrageous, prodigious, stupendous, tremendous **11** implausible, nonsensical, sensational, superlative **12** preposterous, unbelievable

fantasy 4 moon, whim **5** dream, fancy, freak **6** vagary, vision, whimsy **7** caprice, chimera, fiction, reverie **8** daydream, delusion, phantasm **9** imagining, invention, pipe dream **10** bizarrerie **11** imagination **12** grotesquerie

far 4 long **6** remote **7** distant **8** outlying ***combining form:*** **3** tel **4** tele, telo

far and wide 7 all over **10** everyplace, everywhere, throughout

faraway 4 lost **5** moony **6** absent, dreamy, remote **7** distant, removed **8** outlying **9** oblivious, unheeding **10** abstracted, distracted **11** preoccupied, inattentive **12** absentminded

farce 5 stuff **6** comedy, satire **7** mockery **8** travesty **9** burlesque, slapstick **10** caricature

farceur 5 clown, cutup, joker **7** buffoon

farcical 5 comic **6** absurd **7** comical, foolish, risible **9** laughable, ludicrous **10** ridiculous **12** preposterous

fare 4 diet, dine, food, pass, rate, toll **5** get on, price, track **6** manage, travel **7** come off, journey, make out, proceed, succeed **8** get along, progress, victuals **9** passenger, surcharge **10** provisions **11** comestibles

farewell 3 ave, bye **4** ciao, ta-ta, vale **5** adieu, adios, aloha, congé **6** bye-bye, pip-pip, shalom, so long **7** aloha oe, cheerio, good-bye, toodles **8** swan song, toodle-oo **9** bon voyage, departure **11** arrivederci, leave-taking, valediction, valedictory

far-fetched 5 fishy **6** absurd **7** dubious **8** doubtful, strained, unlikely **10** improbable, incredible **11** implausible, unrealistic **12** preposterous, unbelievable

far-flung 6 remote **7** distant, removed **8** outlying **10** widespread

farinaceous 5 mealy **6** floury **7** starchy ***food:*** **4** meal **5** flour, grits **6** cereal, hominy **7** polenta, pudding, tapioca

farm 4 till **5** croft, ranch **6** grange, rancho **7** hennery **8** estancia, hacienda, hatchery **9** cultivate, farmstead **10** plantation ***building:*** **4** barn, shed, silo ***Dutch:*** **6** bowery ***Israeli collective:*** **7** kibbutz ***Russian:*** **7** kolkhoz, sovkhoz

farmer 6 grower, tiller, yeoman **7** granger, planter, rancher **8** ranchero, ranchman **13** agriculturist ***Russian:*** **5** kulak ***South African:*** **4** Boer ***tenant:*** **6** cottar, cotter **7** crofter **12** sharecropper

farming 7 tillage **8** agronomy **9** husbandry **11** agriculture, cultivation

faro 5 monte ***bet:*** **7** sleeper ***card:*** **4** case, hock, soda

Faroes whirlwind 2 oe

far-off 6 remote **7** distant, removed **8** outlying

far-out 3 rad **4** cool **5** outré, weird **6** groovy **7** bizarre, offbeat, radical **9** eccentric **10** avant-garde, off-the-wall, outlandish

farrago 4 hash, mess, olio **5** gumbo **6** jumble, medley, muddle **7** goulash, mélange, mixture **8** mishmash, shambles **9** potpourri **10** hodgepodge, miscellany

far-reaching 5 broad **8** sweeping **9** extensive, momentous, pervasive **10** portentous, widespread **11** significant, wide-ranging **13** comprehensive, consequential

farrier 5 smith **10** blacksmith, horseshoer

farsighted 4 sage, wise **9** hyperopic, prescient, sagacious **10** discerning

farthest 6 utmost **7** apogean, extreme, outmost **8** remotest, ultimate **9** outermost, uttermost

Fasching 8 carnival

fascinate 4 draw, wile **5** charm **6** allure, enamor, entice, please **7** attract, beguile, bewitch, enchant **8** enthrall, intrigue, transfix **9** captivate, enrapture, magnetize, mesmerize, spellbind

fascination 5 charm **6** allure, appeal **7** glamour **8** charisma **9** magnetism **10** attraction, witchcraft **11** enchantment **12** enthrallment

Fascist 4 Nazi **6** despot, Hitler (Adolf), tyrant **8** autocrat **9** Falangist, Mussolini (Benito) **10** Blackshirt

fashion 3 fad, fit, ton, way **4** chic, form, mode, mold, suit, tone, vein, wear **5** craze, shape, style, trend, usage, vogue **6** create, custom, design, devise, manner, method, sculpt, tailor **7** compose, costume, pattern **8** contrive **9** bandwagon, construct, fabricate **10** dernier cri **12** haute couture ***magazine:* 3** WWD **4** Elle **5** Vogue **6** Hilary **7** Glamour, InStyle

fashionable 3 hip **4** chic, cool, posh, tony **5** fresh, ritzy, sharp, smart, swank, swish **6** chichi, du jour, modish, trendy, with-it **7** à la mode, current, dashing, faddish, popular, stylish, voguish **8** up-to-date **9** au courant, exclusive, happening **12** silk-stocking

fashionably nostalgic 5 retro

fashion designer *American:* 3 Sui (Anna) **4** Cole (Kenneth), Ford (Tom), Head (Edith), Kors (Michael), Wang (Vera) **5** Beene (Geoffrey), Blass (Bill), Daché (Lilly), Ellis (Perry), Karan (Donna), Klein (Anne, Calvin) **6** Jacobs (Marc), Lauren (Ralph), Mackie (Bob) **7** Galanos (James), Halston, Mizrahi (Isaac) **8** Galliano (John), Hilfiger (Tommy) **9** Claiborne (Liz), de la Renta (Oscar), Gernreich (Rudi) ***Anglo-French:* 5** Worth (Charles Frederick) ***Dominican:* 9** de la Renta (Oscar) ***English:* 5** Quant (Mary) **6** Bailey (Christopher) **7** McQueen (Alexander) **8** Westwood (Vivienne) **9** McCartney (Stella) ***French:* 4** Dior (Christian) **5** Bohan (Marc) **6** Cardin (Pierre), Chanel (Coco), Poiret (Paul) **6** Ungaro (Emanuel) **7** Balmain (Pierre), Lacroix (Christian), Montana (Claude) **8** Gaultier (Jean-Paul), Givenchy (Hubert de) **9** Courrèges (André), Lagerfeld (Karl) **12** Saint-Laurent (Yves), Schiaparelli (Elsa) ***German:* 9** Lagerfeld (Karl) ***Israeli:* 7** Mizrahi (Isaac) ***Italian:* 5** Ferrè (Gianfranco), Prada (Miuccia), Pucci (Emilio), Ricci (Nina), Zegna (Ermenegildo) **6** Armani (Giorgio) **7** Cassini (Oleg), Versace (Gianni) **9** Valentino **12** Schiaparelli (Elsa) ***Japanese:* 6** Miyake (Issey) ***Spanish:* 10** Balenciaga (Cristóbal)

fast 3 set **4** ASAP, diet, easy, firm, Lent, soon, sure, true, wild **5** apace, fixed, fleet, hasty, hitch, loose, loyal, quick, rapid, swift **6** firmly, presto, prompt, snappy, speedy, stable **7** abstain, hastily, hurried, lasting, quickly, rapidly, staunch, swiftly **8** chop-chop, constant, faithful, full tilt, immobile, promptly, resolute, speedily **9** breakneck, dissolute, immovable, libertine **10** abstinence, profligate, recklessly, stationary **11** expeditious, promiscuous **12** lickety-split **13** expeditiously

fasten 3 fix, peg, pin, set, sew, tie, zip **4** bind, bolt, clip, hook, join, lace, lash, link, lock, moor, nail, seal, shut, weld **5** affix, cable, catch, chain, cinch, clamp, clasp, close, cramp, dowel, girth, hitch, latch, rivet, screw, stake, stick, strap, tie up, truss **6** anchor, attach, batten, buckle, button, couple, secure, skewer, solder, staple, tether **7** connect, mortise **8** buckle up

fastener 3 nut, peg, pin, tie **4** bolt, brad, clip, cord, frog, hasp, link, lock, nail, rope, snap, stud, tack, tape **5** catch, clamp, clasp, dowel, girth, hinge, hitch, latch, rivet, screw, spike, stake, strap **6** buckle, button, cotter, skewer, staple, tether, toggle, Velcro, zipper **7** grommet, padlock, netsuke, shackle **8** coupling, cuff link, handcuff, seat belt, shoelace **9** connector, cotter pin, safety pin, thumbtack **10** clothespin

fastidious 5 fussy, picky **6** choosy, dainty, queasy **7** choosey, finical, finicky, refined **8** exacting **9** demanding, squeamish **10** meticulous, particular, pernickety **11** persnickety

fastness 4 fort, hold, keep **6** bunker, castle, refuge **7** alcazar, bastion, citadel, crannog, redoubt, sanctum **8** casemate, fortress, presidio **10** stronghold, tower house **11** strongpoint

fast-talking 4 glib **5** slick **6** facile **8** slippery **13** silver-tongued

fat 3 big, oil **4** flab, lard, suet, wide **5** beefy, broad, bulky, burly, cream, dumpy, gross, heavy, husky, large, lipid, obese, plump, pudgy, round, stout, thick, tubby **6** chunky, excess, fleshy, grease, portly, rotund, stocky, stubby, tallow **7** adipose, blubber, paunchy, pinguid, porcine, surfeit, surplus, weighty **8** heavyset, oversize, thickset **9** corpulent **10** full-bodied, overweight, pot-bellied **11** superfluity

fatal 6 deadly, lethal, mortal **7** deathly, ruinous **8** terminal **9** incurable, pestilent **10** pernicious **12** pestilential

fatality 4 doom **5** death **8** casualty **10** deadliness

fata morgana 6 mirage **8** illusion

fat cat 5 mogul, nabob **6** big gun, bigwig, tycoon **7** big shot, magnate, pooh-bah **8** big wheel **9** moneybags, plutocrat **11** mucketymuck **13** high-muck-a-muck

fate 3 end, lot **4** doom, luck, ruin **5** death, karma **6** chance, kismet, upshot **7** destiny, fortune, outcome, portion **13** inevitability

fateful 6 deadly **7** ominous, ruinous **8** decisive **9** momentous, prophetic **10** portentous

Fates see at **Greek; Norse; Roman**

fathead 3 ass, oaf **4** boob, clod, dodo, dope, dolt, gawk, goof, goon, jerk, lump, mutt, yo-yo **5** cluck, clunk, dummy, dunce, idiot, moron, stock, stupe, yahoo **6** cretin, dimwit, donkey, doofus, dum-dum, nitwit, noodle, schlub, turkey **7** buffoon, dullard, jackass, schnook **8** dumbbell, imbecile, numskull **9** birdbrain, ignoramus, lamebrain, numbskull, simpleton

fatheaded 4 dull, dumb **5** dense, dopey, thick **6** obtuse, simple, stupid **7** doltish, idiotic **8** gormless **9** brainless, dim-witted, imbecilic **10** numskulled **11** numbskulled, thick-witted

father 2 pa **3** dad, pop **4** dada, papa, père, sire **5** beget, breed, daddy, hatch, padre, pappy, pater, poppa, spawn **6** author, create, old man, parent, priest **7** builder, creator, founder, produce **8** ancestor, engender, generate, inventor, producer **9** architect, initiator, originate, patriarch, procreate **10** originator, prime mover ***combining form:*** **4** patr **5** patri, patro ***French:*** **4** père ***German:*** **5** Vater ***Italian:*** **5** padre ***Portuguese:*** **3** pai ***Spanish:*** **5** padre

Father Brown creator 10 Chesterton (Gilbert Keith)

fatherland 4 home, soil **7** country

Father Time's implement 6 scythe

fathom 4 know **5** probe, sound **7** discern, explore, measure **9** apprehend, figure out, penetrate **10** comprehend, understand **11** investigate

fathomless 7 abysmal, abyssal **8** profound **12** immeasurable

fatidic 5 vatic **6** mantic **7** Delphic, sibylic **8** Delphian, oracular, sibyllic **9** prophetic, prescient, sibylline, vaticinal **10** divinatory, predictive

fatigue 3 fag **4** poop, tire, wear **5** drain, weary **6** tucker **7** deplete, burn out, exhaust, frazzle, wear out **8** drudgery, wear down **9** tiredness, weariness **10** enervation, exhaustion ***combat:*** **7** frazzle **10** shell shock

Fatima ***father:*** **8** Mohammed, Muhammad ***husband:*** **9** Bluebeard ***son:*** **5** Hasan **6** Husayn ***stepbrother:*** **3** Ali

fatness 7 obesity **9** adiposity **10** corpulence, overweight

fatty 4 oily, rich **6** greasy **7** adipose **8** unctuous **10** oleaginous ***combining form:*** **4** lipo **5** adipo

fatuous 4 dumb, fond **5** inane, sappy, silly **6** jejune, simple **7** asinine, foolish, puerile, witless

faucet 3 tap **4** bung, cock, gate **5** valve **6** spigot **7** hydrant, petcock **8** stopcock

Faulkner, William ***character:*** **3** Ike (Snopes), Joe (Christmas) **4** Eula (Varner Snopes), Flem (Snopes), Mink (Snopes) **5** Benjy (Compson), Caddy (Compson), Gavin (Stevens), Henry (Sutpen), Jason (Compson), Lucas (Beauchamp) **6** Dilsey, Temple (Drake) **7** Candace (Compson), Quentin (Compson) **8** Benjamin (Compson) ***county:*** **13** Yoknapatawpha ***family:*** **6** Benbow, Snopes, Sutpen **7** Compson **8** McCaslin, Sartoris **9** Beauchamp ***novel:*** **4** Town (The) **6** Hamlet (The) **7** Mansion (The), Reivers (The) **8** Sartoris **9** Sanctuary, Wild Palms (The) **11** As I Lay Dying **13** Light in August **14** Absalom Absalom **15** Sound and the Fury (The) **17** Intruder in the Dust

fault 3 err, nag, sin **4** flaw, rift, slip, spot, vice, want **5** blame, break, knock, error, scold **6** accuse, defect, foible, miscue **7** censure, demerit, failing, fissure, frailty, mistake, upbraid **8** fracture, weakness **9** criticize, infirmity **10** San Andreas **11** culpability, dereliction, shortcoming **12** imperfection ***line:*** **4** rift **5** split **6** breach **7** fissure **8** crevasse

faultfinder 4 crab **5** grump **6** critic, griper, grouch, nagger, whiner **7** grouser **8** grumbler **10** bellyacher, complainer, criticizer, crosspatch

faultfinding 7 carping **8** captious, critical, nitpicky **9** criticism **10** censorious, nit-picking, pernickety **11** persnickety **12** overcritical **13** hypercritical

faultless 4 pure **7** perfect **8** innocent, unerring **9** guiltless **10** immaculate, impeccable, inculpable

faulty 4 awry **5** amiss, wrong **6** flawed, marred **7** botched, damaged, defaced, inexact, unsound **8** fallible, specious **9** blemished, defective, deficient, erroneous, imperfect, incorrect **10** fallacious, inaccurate ***prefix:*** **3** dys

faun 5 satyr

fauna 7 animals

Faunus *grandfather:* **6** Saturn ***son:*** **4** Acis **7** Latinus

Faust *author:* **6** Goethe (Johann Wolfgang von) ***beloved:*** **8** Gretchen ***composer:*** **6** Gounod (Charles)

faux 4 fake, mock, sham **5** bogus, false, phony **6** ersatz **9** imitation, pretended, simulated, synthetic **10** substitute

faux pas 4 flub, goof, slip **5** boner, error, gaffe **6** boo-boo, howler, miscue, slipup **7** blooper, blunder, misstep, mistake, stumble **8** pratfall, solecism **9** gaucherie **11** impropriety

favor 4 baby, back, bias, boon, gift, okay **5** bless, bribe, grace, mercy, token, value **6** accept, behalf, choose, oblige, pamper, prefer, regard **7** indulge, present, support, sustain **8** courtesy, goodwill, interest, keepsake, kindness, resemble, sanction, sympathy **9** attention, patronage, privilege, take after **10** admiration, facilitate, indulgence, partiality **11** approbation, benevolence, countenance

favorable 4 fair **5** lucky **6** benign, biased, golden, timely, toward, useful **7** helpful, partial **8** pleasant, pleasing, positive **9** agreeable, benignant, fortunate, promising **10** auspicious, benevolent, propitious, prosperous **11** affirmative **12** advantageous **13** complimentary

favoring 4 rosy **6** timely, toward, useful **7** helpful **9** opportune **10** auspicious, beneficial, propitious **12** advantageous ***prefix:*** **3** pro

favorite 3 pet **7** dearest, popular, special **8** precious **9** preferred, well-liked **10** fair-haired, preference **11** front-runner, teacher's pet, white-haired

favoritism 4 bias **8** cronyism, nepotism **10** partiality **12** one-sidedness

fawn 3 kid, tan **4** deer, ecru **5** beige, toady **6** bister, grovel, kowtow **7** flatter, truckle, wheedle **8** blandish, bootlick **9** sweet-talk **11** apple-polish

fawning 6 smarmy **8** unctuous **9** parasitic **10** obsequious **11** sycophantic

fay 3 elf, nix **4** puck **5** elfin, fairy, nixie, pixie **6** elfish, goblin, sprite **7** brownie **10** leprechaun

faze 3 cow **5** abash, daunt, throw **6** dismay, rattle **7** confuse, disturb, nonplus, perturb **8** befuddle, bewilder, confound, unsettle **9** discomfit, dumbfound, embarrass **10** disconcert **11** flabbergast

FBI director 5 Freeh (Louis) **6** Hoover (J. Edgar) **7** Mueller (Robert)

fealty 5 faith, troth **7** loyalty **8** devotion, fidelity **9** adherence, constancy, vassalage **10** allegiance, attachment **11** devotedness **12** faithfulness

fear 3 awe **5** alarm, angst, dread, panic, qualm, scare, worry **6** dismay, fright, horror, phobia, terror **7** anxiety, jitters **8** cold feet, disquiet, timidity **9** agitation, cowardice, misgiving **10** foreboding **11** disquietude, trepidation **12** apprehension, cowardliness, perturbation, presentiment, timorousness ***of animals:*** **9** zoophobia ***of being buried alive:*** **11** taphephobia ***of cats:*** **12** ailurophobia ***of crowds:*** **11** ochlophobia ***of darkness:*** **11** nyctophobia ***of dirt:*** **10** mysophobia ***of fire:*** **10** pyrophobia ***of heights:*** **10** acrophobia ***of men:*** **11** androphobia ***of new things:*** **9** neophobia ***of open areas:*** **11** agoraphobia ***of pain:*** **10** algophobia ***of strangers:*** **10** xenophobia ***of thunder:*** **12** brontophobia ***of water:*** **11** hydrophobia ***of women:*** **10** gynophobia

fearful 5 timid **6** afraid, aghast, scared, trepid **7** alarmed, anxious, jittery, panicky **8** alarmist, paranoid, timorous **9** terrified, tremulous **12** apprehensive

fearless 4 bold **5** brave **6** daring **7** gallant, valiant **8** intrepid, unafraid **9** dauntless **10** courageous **11** lionhearted **12** greathearted, stouthearted

fearmonger 8 alarmist

Fear of Flying author 4 Jong (Erica)

fearsome 3 shy **5** scary, timid **6** afraid **7** extreme, intense **8** daunting, timorous **9** frightful **10** terrifying **11** frightening **12** intimidating

feasible 6 doable, likely, viable **8** possible, suitable, workable **10** reasonable **11** practicable **12** tried-and-true

feast 3 eat **4** dine, meal **5** gorge **6** dinner, regale, repast, spread **7** banquet, indulge **8** potlatch ***Hawaiian:*** **4** luau ***Scottish:*** **3** foy

Feast of Lights 8 Chanukah, Hanukkah

Feast of Lots 5 Purim

Feast of Tabernacles 6 Sukkot **7** Sukkoth

feat 3 act **4** coup, deed, gest **5** stunt, trick **6** action **7** exploit **11** achievement, performance, tour de force

feather 3 ilk **4** down, kind, sort, type **5** breed, order, pinna, plume, quill **6** fledge, fletch, pinion **7** species, variety ***kind:*** **4** down **6** covert **7** contour, plumule, rectrix **8** scapular ***part:*** **3** web **4** barb, vane **5** shaft **7** barbule, calamus **8** barbicel

featherbrained 5 dizzy, giddy, silly **7** flighty, foolish **8** heedless **9** frivolous **11** lightheaded, thoughtless

feathered 7 plumose

feathers 4 down **7** plumage

feature 4 item, mark, part **5** add-on, trait **6** aspect, detail, factor **7** article, element, fixture, gimmick, quality **8** hallmark, property **9** attribute, component, lineament **10** attraction, ingredient **11** drawing card, peculiarity

febrile 3 hot **5** fiery **7** fevered, pyretic **8** feverish

feckless 4 weak **7** useless **8** carefree, impotent **11** incompetent, ineffective, ineffectual **12** undependable **13** irresponsible

fecund 4 rich **7** fertile **8** fruitful, prolific **9** inventive **10** productive

fecundity 9 abundance, fertility **11** prodigality **12** fruitfulness, productivity

Federalist writer 3 Jay (John) **7** Madison (James) **8** Hamilton (Alexander)

federation 5 union **6** league, nation **7** council **8** alliance **10** government **11** confederacy

fed up 4 sick **9** disgusted **11** exasperated

fee 3 cut, pay, tax **4** bill, cost, dues, hire, rate, toll, wage **5** price **6** charge **7** expense, payment, rake-off, stipend, tuition **8** retainer **9** emolument **10** commission, recompense ***minting:*** **10** seignorage **11** seigniorage ***wharf:*** **7** quayage

feeble 4 lame, puny, weak **5** anile, frail **6** infirm, senile, sickly, weakly **7** doddery **8** decrepit **9** doddering, unhealthy **10** inadequate

feebleminded 4 daft, dull, slow **5** dense, thick **6** stupid **7** doltish, foolish, idiotic, moronic, witless **8** imbecile, retarded **9** brainless, dim-witted, imbecilic **10** halfwitted, slow-witted **11** harebrained, thickheaded

feebleness 7 frailty **8** debility **9** fragility, infirmity **10** enervation, inadequacy **11** decrepitude

feed 3 eat **4** grub, hand, meal **5** feast, gorge, graze, stuff **6** browse, devour, fatten, fodder, ingest, regale, repast, supply, viands **7** banquet, consume, deliver, dish out, edibles, furnish, nourish, nurture, provide, sustain **8** bonemeal, dispense, hand over, victuals **9** partake of, provender, provision, refection **10** provisions

feedback 5 input **8** critique, reaction, response **9** criticism **10** evaluation

feed the kitty 4 ante

feel 5 grope, sense, touch **6** caress, fondle, handle, stroke **7** palpate

feeler 4 palp **5** probe **6** palpus **7** antenna **8** proposal, tentacle **12** trial balloon

feeling 3 air **4** aura, mood, vibe **5** hunch, sense, touch **6** notion, temper **7** emotion, inkling, opinion, outlook, passion, sensate **8** attitude, instinct, sentient **9** affection, emotional, intuition, sensation, sentiment, suspicion **10** atmosphere, impression, persuasion **11** sensibility, sensitivity

feign 3 act **4** fake, play, sham **5** bluff, put on **6** affect, assume **7** pretend **8** simulate **9** dissemble **11** counterfeit, make believe

feigned 4 fake, sham **5** false, phony, put-on **7** assumed **8** imagined **9** imitation, insincere, pretended, simulated **10** fabricated, fictitious **11** counterfeit

feint 4 fake, hoax, play, ploy, ruse, sham, wile **5** trick **6** gambit **8** maneuver **9** stratagem ***hockey:*** **4** deke

feisty 6 frisky, plucky, spunky, touchy **7** bristly, fidgety **8** petulant, snappish, spirited **9** fractious, irascible **10** aggressive **11** quarrelsome

feldspar 6 albite **8** andesine **9** anorthite, moonstone **10** microcline, orthoclase **11** plagioclase ***clay:*** **6** kaolin

felicitate 6 salute **7** commend **10** compliment **12** congratulate

felicitous 3 apt, fit **4** meet **5** happy **6** proper, timely **7** apropos, fitting **8** apposite, pleasant, suitable **9** agreeable **10** delightful **11** appropriate

feline 3 cat, sly, tom **4** lion, lynx, pard, puma, puss **5** catty, felid, pussy, sleek, tiger **6** bobcat, cougar, jaguar, margay, ocelot, serval, slinky, sneaky, tomcat **7** caracal, catlike, cheetah, furtive, leonine, leopard, lioness, panther, tigress, wildcat **8** pussycat, stealthy ***hybrid:*** **5** liger, tigon **6** tiglon

fell 3 cut, hew, mow **4** down, drop, kill, raze **5** floor **6** poleax **7** cut down, flatten **8** knock off **9** bring down, knock down

Fellini film 8 Amarcord, Casanova, La Strada **9** Satyricon **10** I Vitelloni **11** La Dolce Vita **15** Nights of Cabiria **18** Juliet of the Spirits

fellow 3 bub, guy, joe, lad, man **4** buck, chap, dude, gent, mate, peer, twin **5** bloke, match **6** codger, cohort, hombre, person **7** comrade, consort, partner **8** confrere **9** associate, companion, copartner, gentleman **10** coordinate, reciprocal

fellow feeling 5 agape **7** concern, empathy,

rapport **8** affinity, kindness, sympathy **9** affection **10** compassion, kindliness **11** consolation **13** understanding

fellowship 4 club **5** guild **6** league **7** coterie, society, stipend **8** sodality **9** communion, community **10** fraternity **11** association, brotherhood

felon 3 con **7** convict, whitlow **8** criminal **10** malefactor

felt 6 groped, sensed

felt hat 3 fez **5** derby, terai **6** fedora, trilby **7** homburg, stetson **8** snap-brim **9** wideawake

female 4 girl **5** woman **7** girlish, womanly **8** feminine ***suffix:* 3** ess **4** ette, trix

Feminine Mystique author 7 Friedan (Betty)

feminist 10 suffragist **11** suffragette

femme fatale 5 Circe, siren **6** Carmen, Salome **7** Delilah, Lorelei **8** Mata Hari **9** temptress **10** seductress **11** enchantress

femur 9 thighbone

fen 3 bog **4** mire, quag, wash **5** marsh, swale, swamp **6** morass, muskeg, slough **9** marshland

fence 3 bar, pen **4** cage, rail, pale, weir **5** hedge, parry **6** corral, paling, picket **7** barrier, enclose, railing **8** backstop, boundary, hoarding, palisade, receiver, sidestep, stockade **9** barricade, stone wall ***sunk:* 4** haha

fencer 7 duelist, épéeist **8** foilsman **9** swordsman

fencing 9 swordplay ***attack:* 5** lunge **6** thrust **7** reprise, riposte ***cry:* 6** touché **7** en garde ***defense:* 5** parry ***movement:* 4** volt ***term:* 4** jury **5** forte, lunge **6** flèche, foible, touché ***touch:* 3** cut, hit ***weapon:* 4** épée, foil **5** blade, guard, saber, sabre **6** pommel

fender 4 skid **5** guard **6** buffer, bumper, shield **7** cushion, railing **8** mudguard

fennec 3 fox

Fenrir *chain:* 8 Gleipnir ***father:* 4** Loki ***form:* 4** wolf ***mother:* 9** Angerboda **10** Angerbotha ***slayer:* 5** Vidar **6** Vithar ***victim:* 4** Odin **5** Woden

Fenway Park *fence:* 12 Green Monster ***site:* 6** Boston ***team:* 6** Red Sox

feral 4 wild **5** brute **6** brutal, savage **7** beastly, bestial, brutish, inhuman, untamed

Ferber novel 5 Giant, So Big **8** Cimarron, Show Boat **9** Ice Palace **13** Saratoga Trunk

Ferdinand *beloved:* 7 Miranda ***father:* 6** Alonso

Ferdinand, King *conquest:* 7 Granada ***daughter:* 6** Joanna ***wife:* 7** Isabela **8** Germaine, Isabella

fermata 4 hold **5** pause

ferment 4 boil, brew, stir **5** rouse, sweat **6** clamor, enzyme, excite, incite, leaven, seethe, simmer, unrest, work up **7** smolder, turmoil **9** agitation, commotion **12** restlessness

fermentation 7 zymosis **13** bioconversion

fern 4 tree **5** brake, holly, royal **6** Boston **7** bracken **8** polypody **10** maidenhair, spleenwort ***leaf:* 5** frond

ferocious 4 fell, grim, wild **5** brute, cruel **6** brutal, fierce, savage **7** bestial, extreme, inhuman, intense, vicious, violent **8** barbaric, inhumane, ruthless **9** barbarous, rapacious, truculent

ferret out 4 find **5** dig up, flush **6** elicit **7** unearth **8** discover **9** ascertain

ferrule 3 cap, tip **4** band, ring, virl **6** collet

ferry 5 carry **6** convey **7** shuttle **9** transport

ferryman 6 Charon **9** gondolier

fertile 4 lush, rich **6** fecund **8** abundant, creative, fruitful, pregnant, prolific **9** bountiful, ingenious, inventive, luxuriant, plenteous **10** productive **12** reproductive

fertilize 5 beget, breed **6** enrich **8** generate **9** fecundate, pollinate **10** impregnate, inseminate

fertilizer 4 dung **5** guano, mulch **6** manure **7** compost **8** bonemeal **9** plant food

ferule 3 rod **5** stick

fervent 3 hot **4** avid, keen **5** eager, fiery **6** ardent, devout, gung-ho **7** blazing, burning, earnest, glowing, intense, zealous **8** vehement **9** heartfelt **10** hot-blooded, passionate **11** impassioned, warm-blooded **12** enthusiastic, wholehearted

fervor 4 fire, heat, zeal **5** ardor **6** warmth **7** passion **8** devotion, violence **9** vehemence **10** devoutness, enthusiasm

fescennine 7 obscene **10** scurrilous

fess up 3 own **5** admit **9** come clean

fester 3 rot **6** rankle **7** inflame, putrefy **8** ulcerate **9** suppurate

festina ____ 5 lente

festival 4 fair, fete, gala **5** feast **6** fiesta **7** jubilee **8** carnival, jamboree **11** celebration, merrymaking

festive 3 gay **4** gala **5** jolly, merry **6** joyful, joyous **7** gleeful **8** mirthful **11** celebratory

festivity 4 bash, fair, fete, gala **5** feast, party, revel **6** affair, frolic, gaiety **7** blowout, revelry, whoopee **8** carnival, jamboree **9** rejoicing, merriment **11** celebration, merrymaking

festoon 4 deck, hang **5** adorn **6** bedeck **7** garland **8** decorate, ornament **9** embellish

fetch 3 get **4** draw, earn **5** bring, yield **6** take in **7** attract, bring in, realize **8** retrieve

fetching 4 fair **6** comely, lovely, pretty **7** winsome **8** alluring, charming, enticing, engaging, handsome, pleasing **9** appealing **10** attractive

fete **4** ball, bash, fair, gala **5** feast, honor, party **6** affair, fiesta, soiree **7** banquet, jubilee, shindig **8** carnival, festival, jamboree, wingding **9** celebrate, entertain **11** celebration, commemorate **13** entertainment

fetid **4** foul, high, rank **5** funky **6** putrid, rancid, smelly, strong **8** mephitic, stinking **10** malodorous

fetish **4** idol, juju, luck **5** charm **6** amulet **7** periapt **8** fixation, gris-gris, talisman **10** phylactery

fetor **4** odor, reek **5** stink **6** stench

fetter **3** tie **4** bind, bond, gyve **5** chain, check, irons **6** hobble, hog-tie, impede **7** enchain, manacle, shackle, trammel **8** handcuff, restrain **9** restraint

fettle **5** shape **6** health **7** fitness **9** condition **12** constitution

feud **6** enmity, strife **7** dispute, quarrel **8** argument, vendetta **9** hostility **11** controversy

feudal ***estate:*** **3** fee **4** feud, fief **6** domain ***jurisdiction:*** **4** soke ***laborer:*** **4** serf ***lord:*** **5** laird, liege, thane **8** suzerain ***status:*** **9** vassalage ***tax:*** **7** tallage ***tenant:*** **6** vassal **7** homager, socager, vavasor **8** vavasour ***tenure of land:*** **6** socage ***tribute:*** **6** heriot ***warrior:*** **5** bushi, ronin **7** samurai

feuilleton **5** essay

fever **4** ague, fire, heat **5** craze, flush, Lassa, mania **6** dengue, frenzy **7** ferment, passion, pyrexia **8** delirium **9** calenture ***recurrent:*** **7** malaria, quartan, tertian ***type:*** **3** hay **6** dengue, hectic **7** scarlet

fevered **6** crazed, heated **7** burning, febrile, flushed **8** agitated, frenetic, restless **9** delirious **10** distracted, overheated **11** overwrought

feverish **3** hot **5** fiery **6** hectic **7** burning, febrile, flushed, pyretic **8** frenetic, frenzied **10** passionate **11** overwrought

fever tree **6** acacia **7** blue gum

few **4** rare **5** scant **6** meager, meagre, scanty, scarce, sparse **7** handful, limited **8** sporadic **9** scattered **10** infrequent, occasional, scattering, smattering, spattering, sprinkling ***combining form:*** **4** olig **5** oligo

fey **4** daft **5** campy, crazy, vatic **7** touched **8** oracular, precious **9** pixilated, prophetic, sibylline, visionary **11** clairvoyant **12** otherworldly

fiasco **3** dud **4** bomb, flop **5** farce, flask **6** bottle, defeat **7** blunder, debacle, failure, washout **8** abortion, disaster **11** miscarriage **13** embarrassment

fiat **5** edict, order **6** decree **7** command, dictate, mandate, warrant **8** sanction **11** endorsement **12** proclamation **13** authorization

fib **3** lie **4** tale **5** story **7** falsify, falsity, untruth **8** white lie **9** falsehood, mendacity **10** taradiddle **11** fabrication, prevaricate

fiber **3** web **4** noil, pita **5** grain, istle **6** fabric, strand, thread **7** texture ***basketry:*** **5** istle ***brain:*** **4** pons ***coarse:*** **4** jute **8** piassava ***coconut husk:*** **4** coir ***rope:*** **4** bast, hemp **5** sisal **8** henequen ***silky:*** **5** kapok ***small:*** **6** fibril ***substructure:*** **7** micelle, spongin ***synthetic:*** **5** nylon, Orlon, rayon, saran, vinal **6** Dacron **7** spandex ***woody:*** **4** bast ***woollike:*** **7** lanital

fibrous **4** ropy, wiry **5** tough, woody **6** sinewy **7** stringy

fibula **4** bone **5** clasp

fichu **5** scarf **8** kerchief

fickle **7** flighty **8** unstable, variable, volatile **9** mercurial **10** capricious, changeable, inconstant, unfaithful, unreliable **12** undependable **13** temperamental, unpredictable

fiction **4** tale, yarn **5** fable, story **7** fantasy, figment **8** pretense **9** falsehood, fish story, invention, narrative **10** concoction **11** fabrication

fictional **6** made-up, unreal **8** notional **9** imaginary **11** make-believe **12** suppositious

fictitious **4** fake, mock, sham **5** bogus, faked, false, phony **6** ersatz, made-up, unreal, untrue **7** assumed, created **8** cooked-up, fanciful, illusory, imagined, invented, mythical, spurious **9** concocted, fantastic, imaginary, simulated, trumped-up **10** apocryphal, artificial, chimerical, fabricated **11** make-believe **12** suppositious

fiddle **3** toy **4** fool, play, rack **5** alter, cheat **6** dawdle, diddle, doodle, finger, meddle, monkey, potter, putter, tamper, tinker, trifle, violin **7** swindle **9** interfere **10** fool around, manipulate, mess around

fiddle-faddle **3** rot **4** bosh, bull, bunk, nuts **5** fudge, drool, hokum, hooey, pshaw **6** bunkum, drivel, hoodoo, humbug, piffle **7** baloney, blarney, hogwash, rubbish, twaddle **8** nonsense, pishposh, tommyrot **9** poppycock **10** applesauce, balderdash, flapdoodle **13** horsefeathers

____ **Fideles** **6** Adeste

Fidelio ***composer:*** **9** Beethoven (Ludwig van) ***hero:*** **9** Florestan ***heroine:*** **7** Leonora

fidelity **5** ardor, piety, troth **6** fealty **7** loyalty **8** devotion **9** adherence, constancy **10** allegiance, attachment **11** staunchness **12** faithfulness **13** dependability, steadfastness

Fidel's comrade **3** Che

fidget 6 fantod, fiddle, jitter, squirm, twitch **7** wriggle
fidgety 5 antsy, jumpy **6** uneasy **7** jittery, nervous, restive, squirmy, twitchy **8** restless
fiduciary 7 trustee
field 3 lea **4** area, mead, turf **5** green, major, milpa, orbit, range **6** domain, meadow, métier, region, sphere **7** demesne, pasture, purview, terrain **8** dominion, gridiron, precinct, vocation **9** bailiwick, champaign, specialty, territory **10** department, discipline, occupation
field crop 3 hay **4** corn, oats **5** grain, wheat **6** cotton **7** alfalfa **8** soybeans
field deity 3 Pan **4** Faun **5** Fauna **6** Faunus
field glasses 6 binocs **10** binoculars
field hand 4 hoer **5** sower **6** picker **7** laborer, planter
Fielding novel 6 Amelia **8** Tom Jones **13** Joseph Andrews
field marshal *Austrian:* 8 Radetzky (Joseph) ***British:* 6** Napier (Robert), Raglan (Baron), Wavell (Archibald), Wilson (Henry) **7** Roberts (Frederick) **8** Wolseley (Garnet) **9** Kitchener (Horatio) **10** Montgomery (Bernard) ***French:* 3** Ney (Michel) **4** Foch (Ferdinand) **6** Joffre (Joseph-Jacques-Césaire), Pétain (Philippe) ***German:* 6** Keitel (Wilhelm), Paulus (Friedrich), Rommel (Erwin), Rupert (Prince) **9** Mackensen (August von), Rundstedt (Karl von), Waldersee (Alfred von) **10** Kesselring (Albert) ***Japanese:* 8** Sugiyama (Hajime) ***Prussian:* 6** Moltke (Helmuth von) ***Russian:* 7** Kutuzov (Mikhail), Suvorov (Aleksandr) **8** Potemkin (Grigory)
field mouse 4 vole
field officer 5 major **7** colonel
fieldwork 5 redan
fiend 3 bug, imp, nut **5** demon, devil, freak, Satan **6** addict, Belial, diablo, maniac, zealot **7** devotee, fanatic, habitué, Lucifer, monster, Old Nick, serpent **8** Apollyon, succubus **9** Beelzebub **10** enthusiast, Old Scratch **13** Old Gooseberry
fiendish 3 bad **4** evil **5** cruel **6** malign, savage, wicked **7** baleful, demonic, hellish, inhuman, malefic, satanic, vicious **8** demoniac, devilish, diabolic, infernal, sinister **9** barbarous, difficult, ferocious, malicious, malignant **10** diabolical
fierce 4 fell, grim, wild **5** cruel **6** brutal, savage, wicked **7** brutish, hostile, inhuman, intense, vicious, violent, wolfish **8** inhumane, pitiless, ruthless, terrible, vehement **9** barbarous, bellicose, ferocious, merciless, truculent **10** aggressive, determined
fiery 3 hot, red **5** afire **6** ablaze, aflame, ardent, fervid, fierce, heated, red-hot, torrid **7** burning, febrile, fervent, flaming, flaring, igneous, intense, peppery **8** broiling, feverish, spirited, vehement, white-hot **9** flammable, hotheaded, irritable, perfervid **10** mettlesome, passionate **11** combustible, inflammable, impassioned
fiesta 4 fete **5** party **6** frolic **8** carnival, festival, jamboree **9** merriment
fife 4 pipe **5** flute
fifth *combining form:* 5 quint
fifth columnist 3 spy
fig *genus:* 5 Ficus ***sacred:* 5** pipal ***variety:* 5** elemi **6** Smyrna
fight 3 row, war **4** bout, buck, duel, feud, fray, spat, tiff **5** brawl, broil, clash, joust, match, melee, repel, scrap, set-to **6** affray, attack, battle, combat, fracas, oppose, oppugn, resist, rumble, scrape, tussle **7** contend, contest, dispute, quarrel, scuffle, wrangle, wrestle **8** conflict, skirmish, slugfest, squabble, struggle, traverse **10** aggression, donnybrook, free-for-all **11** altercation
fighter 2 GI **3** pug **4** swad **5** boxer **7** brawler, soldier, warrior **8** champion, pugilist, scrapper **9** combatant, gladiator, man-at-arms, mercenary **11** interceptor
fighter plane 3 MiG, Roc **4** Zero **5** Sabre **6** bomber, Fokker, Hawker, Mirage, Voodoo **7** Corsair, Harrier **8** Spitfire **11** interceptor
fighting fish 5 betta
figment 5 dream, fable, fancy **7** chimera, fiction **8** daydream, illusion, phantasm **9** invention, unreality **11** contrivance, fabrication
figure 3 add, sum, tot **4** cast, form, mold, rule, tote **5** count, digit, frame, image, model, motif, shape, total **6** cipher, decide, design, device, effigy, motive, number, reckon, settle, symbol **7** compute, integer, numeral, outline, pattern, resolve **8** conclude, estimate, physique **9** calculate, character, determine, enumerate ***geometric:* 4** cone, cube **5** rhomb **6** circle, isogon, square **7** decagon, ellipse, hexagon, nonagon, octagon, polygon, rhombus **8** pentacle, pentagon, rhomboid, tetragon, triangle **9** rectangle **10** hexahedron, octahedron **11** icosahedron **12** dodecahedron, rhombohedron ***human:* 4** nude **5** atlas **7** telamon **8** caryatid ***ornamental:* 6** statue **8** gargoyle
figurehead 4 pawn, tool **5** front **6** minion, puppet **7** cat's-paw **8** creature **10** instrument, mouthpiece
figure of speech 5 trope **6** aporia, simile **7** litotes **8** metaphor, metonymy **10** synecdoche

figure out 5 crack, learn, solve **6** decide, decode, fathom **7** resolve, unravel **8** decipher, discover, unriddle **9** ascertain, determine

figure skater see **ice skater**

figure skating ***jump:*** **4** axel, loop, lutz **5** split **6** rocker **7** bracket, counter, salchow **11** spreadeagle ***spin:*** **5** camel

figurine 9 statuette

Fiji ***capital:*** **4** Suva ***explorer:*** **4** Cook (Capt. James) **6** Tasman (Abel) ***island:*** **3** Gau **4** Koro **6** Ovalau **8** Viti Levu **9** Vanua Levu ***island group:*** **3** Lau **6** Yasawa ***language:*** **6** Fijian ***neighbor:*** **5** Samoa **7** Vanuatu

filch 3 cop, nip **4** crib, lift, take **5** boost, pinch, steal, swipe **6** pilfer, snitch **7** purloin

file 3 row, rub **4** line, rank, rasp, tier **5** lodge, march, place, queue **6** smooth **7** archive, arrange, corrupt, dossier **10** emery board

filial 5 sonly **7** duteous, dutiful

filibuster 5 delay, stall **10** adventurer

filigree 4 lace **6** design **7** pattern **8** fretwork, openwork, ornament **10** decoration **13** embellishment, ornamentation

fill 3 jam **4** clog, cloy, cram, glut, heap, lade, load, pack, pile, plug, sate, stop **5** block, choke, close, gorge, stock, stuff **6** charge, stodge **7** congest, engorge, inflate, occlude, pervade, satiate, satisfy, stopper, surfeit **8** permeate ***interstices:*** **4** calk **5** caulk, chink, putty

filled 5 awash, flush, sated **6** packed **7** replete **9** saturated

filler 5 squib **7** packing, padding, tobacco, wadding **8** stuffing

fillet 4 band **5** slice, snood, strip **6** ribbon, stripe **7** bandeau, banding **8** headband ***anatomical:*** **9** lemniscus ***architectural:*** **6** listel, reglet, taenia ***meat:*** **10** tenderloin

fill in 3 sub **4** clew, clue, post **6** advise, detail, insert, notify **7** apprise **8** acquaint, complete **10** substitute

fill-in 3 sub **4** temp **6** backup **7** stopgap **9** alternate, expedient, makeshift, surrogate, temporary **10** substitute **11** locum tenens, pinch hitter, replacement, succedaneum

filling 5 kapok

fillip 3 tap **4** goad, kick, spur **5** boost, tonic **6** buffet, strike **7** impetus, wrinkle **8** catalyst, stimulus **9** incentive, stimulant, stimulate **10** inducement, motivation **13** embellishment

film 4 coat, scum, skim, skin **5** glaze, layer, Mylar **6** lamina, patina **7** tarnish **8** membrane, pellicle (see also **movie**)

film director see **movie director**

film producer see **movie producer**

filmy 4 hazy **5** gauzy, misty, sheer, wispy **6** dainty **8** delicate, gossamer **10** diaphanous **11** transparent

fils 3 son

filter 4 sift **5** clean, leach, sieve **6** purify, refine, screen, strain **7** clarify, cleanse **9** percolate

filth 4 crud, dirt, dung, muck, slop, smut **5** dreck, grime, slime, trash **6** ordure, refuse, sludge **7** squalor **9** obscenity

filthy 4 base, foul, vile **5** black, dirty, grimy, gross, gunky, mucky, muddy, nasty **6** coarse, cruddy, grubby, ribald, scuzzy, skanky, smutty, sordid **7** obscene, raunchy, squalid, unclean **8** indecent **9** loathsome, offensive, repulsive, revolting **12** scatological

filthy lucre 4 cash, loot, pelf **5** bread, bucks, dough, money, moola **6** boodle, riches, moolah, wampum **7** cabbage, scratch **8** currency

fin 3 arm **4** bill **5** fiver, pinna **7** airfoil, flipper ***type:*** **6** caudal, dorsal **7** ventral **8** pectoral

finagle 5 cheat, trick **6** wangle **7** snaffle, swindle, wheedle **8** fast-talk, maneuver, scrounge **9** bamboozle, machinate

final 3 end **4** last **6** ending, latest **7** closing **8** hindmost, terminal, ultimate **10** concluding, conclusive, definitive **11** examination

finale 3 end **4** coda **5** close, finis **6** capper, climax, ending, payoff, windup, wrap-up **7** closing **10** conclusion, denouement **11** culmination, termination

finalize 3 end **5** close, sew up, tie up **6** decide, finish, wind up, wrap up **7** approve **8** complete, conclude, solidify **9** terminate **10** consummate

finally 6 at last, lastly **7** someday **8** at length **9** belatedly **10** at long last, eventually, ultimately **12** subsequently

finance 4 back, bank, fund **5** endow, funds, money, stake **6** credit **7** banking, promote, revenue, sponsor, support **8** bankroll **9** grubstake, patronize, subsidize **10** capitalize, investment, underwrite

financial 6 fiscal, pocket **8** business, economic, monetary **9** pecuniary **10** commercial ***plan:*** **6** budget ***statement:*** **12** balance sheet

financier ***American:*** **4** Hill (James Jerome), Ryan (Thomas Fortune), Sage (Russell) **5** Astor (John Jacob), Baker (George Fisher), Eaton (Cyrus), Field (Cyrus West), Gould (Jay), Grace (William Russell), Green (Hetty), Soros (George) **6** Biddle (Nicholas), Boesky (Ivan), Girard (Stephen), Mellon (Andrew), Morgan (John Pierpont, Junius Spencer), Morris (Robert), Rogers

(Henry Huttleston), Yerkes (Charles Tyson) **7** Buffett (Warren), Peabody (George) **10** Vanderbilt (Cornelius, William) ***British:*** **6** Baring (Alexander), Rhodes (Cecil) **7** Gresham (Thomas) ***French:*** **6** Necker (Jacques) **7** Colbert (Jean-Baptiste) ***German:*** **7** Schacht (Hjalmar) **10** Rothschild (Amschel, Jakob, Karl, Mayer, Nathan, Salomon)

finch 4 pape **5** junco, serin, zebra **6** canary, linnet, siskin, towhee **7** bunting, chewink, redpoll, sparrow **8** cardinal, grosbeak, longspur **9** crossbill, seedeater

find 3 gem **4** gain, meet, spot **5** catch, dig up, hit on, reach, sight **6** attain, detect, locate, supply, turn up **7** discern, furnish, scare up, uncover, unearth **8** bump into, come upon, discover, meet with, perceive, treasure **9** determine, discovery, encounter **10** experience **13** treasure trove

find out 4 hear **5** catch, learn **6** detect **7** catch on **8** discover, perceive **9** ascertain, determine

fine 3 A-OK, end, top **4** fair, keen, levy, pure, thin **5** bonny, close, clear, dandy, mulct, sheer **6** amerce, choice, minute, ornate, punish, purify, subtle **7** clarion, damages, elegant, forfeit, penalty **8** all right, delicate, penalize, pleasant, splendid, superior **9** beautiful, enjoyable, excellent, first-rate **10** punishment, reparation

finery 5 array **6** attire **7** apparel, regalia **8** clothing, frippery, glad rags, ornament **9** caparison, full dress, trappings, trimmings **10** decoration, Sunday best

finesse 5 dodge, evade, skill, skirt **6** jockey **7** beguile, cunning, exploit **8** maneuver, subtlety **9** dexterity **10** adroitness, artfulness, manipulate

fine-tune 4 true **5** tweak **6** adjust

Fingal's Cave *composer:* 11 Mendelssohn (Felix) ***island:*** **6** Staffa

finger 5 blame, digit, index, pinky, strum, touch **6** accuse, pinkie **7** palpate **8** identify, pinpoint ***bone:*** **7** phalanx ***combining form:*** **6** dactyl

finicky 5 fussy, picky **6** choosy, dainty, prissy **7** choosey **8** exacting **9** squeamish **10** fastidious, meticulous, particular, pernickety **11** persnickety

finis 3 end **5** close **6** finale **10** completion, conclusion

finish 3 end **4** do in, kill, slay, stop **5** cease, close, glaze, use up **6** cut off, ending, finale, murder, patina, polish, windup, wrap up **7** closing, consume, destroy, execute, exhaust, surface **8** complete, conclude, dispatch, finalize, terminus **9** cessation, liquidate, terminate **10** completion, conclusion, denouement, run through **11** termination ***dull:*** **3** mat **4** matt **5** matte ***second:*** **5** place ***third:*** **4** show

finished 4 done, over, ripe **5** ideal **7** done for, perfect, refined, through **8** achieved, complete, over with, polished, washed-up **9** perfected **10** consummate

finite 5 bound, fixed **7** bounded, limited, precise **9** definable **10** restricted **12** determinable

fink 3 rat **5** Judas **6** betray, snitch, squeal **7** traitor **8** betrayer, informer, quisling, snitcher **11** backstabber, stool pigeon **13** strikebreaker

Finland 5 Suomi ***Arctic region:*** **7** Lapland ***capital:*** **8** Helsinki ***city:*** **5** Espoo, Turku **6** Vantaa **7** Tampere ***ethnic group:*** **4** Lapp, Sami ***gulf:*** **7** Bothnia ***invader:*** **9** Alexander ***island:*** **5** Karlö **6** Kimito **9** Vallgrund ***island group:*** **5** Åland ***lake:*** **5** Inari **6** Saimaa **7** Keitele **8** Pielinen ***language:*** **7** Finnish, Swedish ***monetary unit:*** **4** euro ***monetary unit, former:*** **6** markka ***neighbor:*** **6** Norway, Russia, Sweden

Finlandia composer 8 Sibelius (Jean)

Finnigans Wake *author:* 5 Joyce (James) ***first word:*** **8** riverrun ***last word:*** **3** the

Finnish *bath:* 5 sauna ***epic:*** **8** Kalevala ***god:*** **6** Jumala

fir 4 pine **6** balsam, Fraser **7** conifer, Douglas **9** evergreen ***genus:*** **5** Abies

fire 2 ax **3** axe, can, pep, vim, zip **4** bake, brio, burn, cast, dash, hurl, sack, stir, toss, zeal, zest, zing **5** ardor, blaze, drive, flame, flare, fling, glare, ingle, light, pitch, rouse, salvo, shoot, spark, throw, torch, verve, vigor **6** arouse, energy, excite, fervor, flames, ignite, kindle, lay off, spirit **7** animate, boot out, dismiss, enthuse, inferno, inflame, inspire, kick out, passion, provoke **8** enkindle **9** calenture, discharge, holocaust, terminate **10** combustion, enthusiasm, liveliness **13** conflagration ***combining form:*** **3** pyr **4** igni, pyro ***god:*** **4** Agni, Loki **6** Vulcan **10** Hephaestus

firearm see **gun**

firebrand 8 agitator **10** incendiary, instigator

firebug 5 torch **8** arsonist **10** incendiary, pyromaniac

firecracker 5 squib **6** banger **9** explosive **10** cherry bomb, noisemaker

firedog 7 andiron

firedrake 6 dragon

firefly 12 lightning bug

fire opal 7 girasol

fireplace 5 grate, ingle ***equipment:* 6** fender, screen **7** andiron ***part:* 3** hob **6** hearth, mantel
fireplug 7 hydrant
fire up 5 anger, annoy, rouse, spark **6** excite, ignite, incite, kindle **7** enliven, inflame, inspire, provoke **8** enkindle, irritate
firework 6 petard, rocket **8** pinwheel, sparkler **11** pyrotechnic, Roman candle ***cluster:* 9** girandole
firkin 3 keg, tun, vat **4** butt, cask, pipe **6** barrel, vessel **8** hogshead
firm 3 set **4** fast, hard, sure **5** fixed, rigid, solid, sound, stiff, tight, tough **6** harden, outfit, secure, settle, stable, steady, strong, sturdy **7** abiding, adamant, certain, company, concern, improve, settled, staunch, unmoved **8** business, constant, definite, enduring, faithful, resolute, specific, vigorous **9** steadfast, tenacious **10** determined, enterprise, inflexible, stipulated, strengthen, unwavering, unyielding **11** established, partnership, substantial, unfaltering, well-founded **13** establishment
firmament 3 sky **5** vault **6** sphere, welkin **7** expanse, heavens **8** empyrean
firmness 7 resolve **8** decision, security, solidity, strength, tenacity **9** constancy, stability **10** durability, resolution **13** determination
first 4 arch, head **5** alpha, chief, prime **6** maiden, primal **7** highest, initial, leading, lead-off, opening, pioneer, premier, primary, supreme **8** champion, dominant, earliest, foremost, headmost, original **9** inaugural, initially, paramount, principal, sovereign **10** aboriginal, preeminent, primordial ***prefix:* 4** prot **5** proto
firstborn 4 heir **6** eldest, oldest
first-class 3 top **4** A-one, best, fine **5** prime, primo **6** tip-top **7** capital, supreme **8** five-star, superior, top-notch **9** excellent, top-drawer
firsthand 6 direct **7** primary **9** immediate
first man in space 7 Gagarin (Yury)
first showing 5 debut **7** opening **8** premiere
First State 8 Delaware
firth 3 arm, bay **4** cove, gulf **5** inlet **6** harbor, slough **7** estuary
fiscal 8 monetary **9** budgetary, financial
fish 3 aku, bob, cod, dab, eel, gar, koi, net, ray **4** barb, bass, carp, cast, cero, char, chub, chum, coho, cusk, dace, dory, drum, gata, gill, goby, hake, hint, jack, ling, mero, opah, parr, pike, rudd, scup, shad, sild, sisi, sole, spet, tuna, ulua **5** angle, betta, bream, brill, charr, cisco, cobia, danio, fluke, grunt, guppy, jurel, loach, moray, perch, platy, porgy, roach, scrod, seine, shark, skate, smelt, smolt, snook, sprat, tench, tetra, trawl, troll, trout, tunny, wahoo **6** blenny, bonito, burbot, caribe, conger, dorado, grilse, kipper, marlin, minnow, mullet, permit, plaice, pompon, puffer, remora, salmon, sauger, sebago, shiner, sucker, tarpon, tautog, tomcod, turbot, warsaw, wrasse **7** alewife, anchovy, buffalo, capelin, catfish, cavalla, chimera, chinook, cichlid, corbina, cowfish, crappie, dolphin, escolar, gillnet, gourami, grouper, grunion, haddock, hagfish, halibut, herring, hogfish, jewfish, lamprey, mudfish, oarfish, pigfish, pinfish, piranha, pollack, pollock, pompano, pupfish, rainbow, rasbora, sardine, sawfish, sculpin, sea carp, snapper, sniggle, sockeye, sunfish, tilapia, torpedo, whiting **8** albacore, blowfish, bluefish, bluegill, bocaccio, bonefish, brisling, bullhead, chimaera, crevalle, filefish, flounder, gambusia, goldfish, grayling, halfbeak, hornpout, kingfish, ladyfish, lionfish, lookdown, lumpfish, lungfish, mackerel, menhaden, moonfish, pickerel, pilchard, pipefish, porkfish, rock bass, rockfish, rosefish, sailfish, seahorse, sea trout, skipjack, stingray, sturgeon, tilefish, warmouth, weakfish, wolffish **9** amberjack, angelfish, barracuda, brandling, cutthroat, goosefish, greenling, pilotfish, spadefish, stargazer, swordfish, topminnow, trunkfish, whitebait, whitefish **10** butterfish, flying fish, needlefish, parrotfish, sheepshead, silverside, squeteague, tripletail, victorfish, yellowtail **11** Dolly Varden, hatchetfish, jacksmelt, killifish, lanternfish, mummichog, muskellunge, pumpkinseed, stickleback, triggerfish ***basket:* 5** creel ***character:* 4** Nemo **5** Wanda ***combining form:* 6** ichthy ***dish:* 7** ceviche, seviche **8** cioppino, matelote **13** bouillabaisse ***eggs:* 3** roe **5** spawn ***genus:* 4** Amia, Lota ***relating to:* 7** piscine ***spear:* 3** gig **7** harpoon, trident ***trap:* 4** weir ***young:* 3** fry **4** parr **5** larva, smolt **6** alevin, grilse
fisherman 6 angler
fish hawk 6 osprey
fishhook *adjunct:* 5 snell ***part:* 4** barb **5** shank
fishing line 4 trot **7** setline **8** longline, trotline ***float:* 3** bob **5** quill ***leader:* 5** snell
fishing lure 3 fly **4** bait **5** spoon **7** spinner
fishing net 5 seine, trawl
fishlike mammal 4 orca **5** whale **6** dugong, sea cow **7** dolphin, grampus, manatee, narwhal **8** cetacean, porpoise

fish story 3 fib, lie **4** bunk, yarn **11** fabrication **12** exaggeration **13** overstatement
fishwife 5 harpy, scold, shrew, vixen **6** virago **9** termagant, Xanthippe
fishy 7 dubious, suspect **8** doubtful, unlikely **9** ambiguous, dubitable, equivocal, uncertain **10** suspicious **11** problematic **12** questionable
fission element 7 uranium **9** plutonium
fissure 3 gap **4** gash, hole, part, rent, rift **5** break, chasm, chink, cleft, crack, split **6** breach, cleave, divide, schism **7** crevice, discord, opening, rupture **8** crevasse, fracture **10** disharmony, separation
fist 4 duke, grip, hand **5** clamp, grasp **6** clench, clinch, clutch
fit 3 apt, set **4** able, buff, hale, jibe, just, sane, suit, turn **5** adapt, agree, frame, ready, sound, spasm, spell, tally, throe, toned **6** access, accord, adjust, attack, become, belong, decent, go with, proper, seemly, square, tailor, useful **7** capable, conform, healthy, prepare, qualify, seizure, tantrum **8** assemble, decorous, dovetail, eligible, paroxysm, suitable **9** agree with, congruous, consonant, harmonize, reconcile **10** applicable, convenient, correspond, felicitous, go together **11** accommodate, appropriate
fitful 6 random, spotty **7** erratic **8** periodic, sporadic, variable **9** haphazard, hit-or-miss, irregular, spasmodic, uncertain **10** changeable, convulsive, herky-jerky, inconstant **12** intermittent
fitness 4 trim **5** order, shape **6** fettle, health, kilter, repair **7** account, decorum, service, utility **8** capacity **9** condition, propriety, relevance **11** eligibility, suitability **13** applicability
fit out 3 arm, rig **5** equip **6** outfit **7** appoint, furnish **8** accouter, accoutre
fitting 3 apt, due **4** able, just, meet, part, true **5** happy, right **6** proper, seemly **7** apropos, germane **8** apposite, relevant, suitable **9** accessory, befitting, pertinent, qualified **10** applicable, attachment, felicitous, harmonious **11** appropriate
fit together 4 hook, join, mesh **6** hook up **7** connect **8** dovetail **9** integrate
Fitzgerald novel 10 Last Tycoon (The) **11** Great Gatsby (The) **16** Tender Is the Night **17** Tales of the Jazz Age **18** This Side of Paradise **17** All the Sad Young Men **21** Beautiful and the Damned (The)
five *combining form:* 4 pent **5** penta **6** quinqu **7** quinque ***group of:* 6** pentad **7** quintet
five-dollar bill 3 fin
fivefold 9 quintuple
Five Nations 8 Iroquois ***member:* 7** Cayugas, Mohawks, Oneidas, Senecas **9** Onondagas
five-sided figure 8 pentagon
five-star 6 deluxe, superb **8** superior, top-notch **9** excellent, first-rate **10** first-class **11** outstanding
five-year period 6 luster, lustre **7** lustrum
fix 3 jam, rig, set **4** cook, cure, geld, mend, mess, moor, root, spay, spot, work **5** affix, alter, catch, patch, ready, renew, rivet, solve, state, stick **6** adjust, anchor, assign, attach, change, decide, doctor, fasten, neuter, pickle, plight, repair, revamp, scrape, secure, settle, square, steady **7** appoint, arrange, correct, dilemma, impress, ingrain, resolve, restore, specify, work out **8** castrate, discover, overhaul, position, renovate, solution **9** condition, establish, stabilize, sterilize **11** predicament
fixation 5 craze, mania **6** fetish **9** obsession **11** fascination, infatuation
____ **fixe 4** idée, prix
fixed 3 pat, set **4** fast, firm, sure **6** frozen, secure, stable, stated, steady **7** abiding, certain, limited, precise, settled **8** constant, definite, enduring, immobile, resolute **9** exclusive, immovable, immutable, permanent, steadfast, tenacious **10** inflexible, invariable, restricted, stationary, stipulated, unswerving, unwavering **11** determinate, unalterable **12** concentrated, unchangeable **13** circumscribed
fixture 9 appliance **10** attachment
fizz 4 buzz, foam, hiss **5** froth **6** bubble, spirit **7** bubbles, sparkle, sputter **10** effervesce, liveliness **13** effervescence
fizzle 4 bomb, fail, flop **6** fiasco **7** failure, misfire **8** miscarry, peter out **10** effervesce **11** fall through
fjord *Baffin Island:* 9 Admiralty ***Denmark:* 3** Ise, Lim **5** Lamme ***Iceland:* 4** Axar, Eyja **5** Horna, Skaga, Vopna ***Norway:* 3** Tys **4** Bokn, Nord, Salt, Stor, Tana, Vest **5** Lakse, Ranen, Sogne **9** Stavanger, Trondheim ***Spitsbergen:* 3** Ice ***Svalbard:* 4** Stor
flab 3 fat **4** bulk, lard **5** flesh **7** blubber, fatness **9** cellulite **10** corpulence **11** lovc handles
flabbergast 3 awe **4** stun **5** amaze, shock, throw **7** astound, nonplus **8** astonish, bowl over, dumfound, surprise **9** dumbfound, overwhelm
flabby see **flaccid**
flaccid 4 limp, soft, weak **6** feeble, flabby, floppy **8** flexible
flag 3 ebb, lag, sag, tag **4** fade, fail, hail, iris, jack, sign, swag, tail, tire, waft, wane,

wave, wilt **5** abate, color, droop, stone **6** banner, burgee, colors, ensign, falter, guidon, pennon, signal, weaken **7** bunting, decline, pendant, pennant **8** bannerol, gonfalon, languish, Old Glory, penalize, registry, standard, streamer, tricolor, vexillum **9** banderole, blue peter, oriflamme, Union Jack **10** Jolly Roger **11** deteriorate **12** Stars and Bars

flagellate 4 beat, flog, hide, lash, whip **5** whale **6** larrup, lather, stripe, switch, thrash **7** scourge **9** horsewhip

flagitious 4 evil **6** sinful, wicked **7** corrupt, vicious **8** criminal, depraved, infamous, perverse, shameful **9** miscreant, nefarious, perverted **10** degenerate, outrageous, scandalous, villainous **11** disgraceful

flagon 3 jug **4** ewer **5** stein, stoup **6** vessel **7** tankard

flagpole 4 mast **5** staff ***rope:*** **7** halyard

flag-raising site 7 Iwo Jima

flagrant 4 bold, rank **5** gross **6** wanton **7** blatant, glaring, heinous, obvious **8** striking **9** atrocious, egregious, monstrous **10** outrageous **11** conspicuous

flagstone 5 shale, slate

flag-waver 7 patriot **8** jingoist, loyalist **10** chauvinist **11** nationalist **12** superpatriot

flail 4 club, beat, flog, whip **6** strike, thrash, thresh **7** scourge **8** flounder, thresher

flair 4 bent, chic, élan, gift **5** knack, style **6** genius, talent **7** ability, aptness, faculty **8** aptitude, tendency **10** proclivity **11** inclination

flak 4 fire **5** abuse **6** shells **7** censure, vitriol **9** brickbats, criticism, hostility **10** opposition **11** disapproval **12** condemnation, fault-finding

flake 3 bit **4** chip, kook, peel **5** scale **6** lamina **7** oddball **8** crackpot, fragment **9** eccentric

flake off 4 chip, peel **5** scale **9** exfoliate **10** desquamate

flaky 3 odd **5** ditsy, ditzy, goofy, nutty, wacky, weird **6** fickle, screwy **7** bizarre, erratic, offbeat **9** eccentric

flambé 6 ablaze, aflame, alight **7** blazing, flaming

flamboyant 4 loud **5** gaudy, showy **6** flashy, florid, ornate, rococo **7** baroque, splashy **8** colorful, luscious **10** over-the-top **12** ostentatious

flame 4 beau, dear, fire, glow, love **5** ardor, blaze, flare, flash, honey, light, lover **7** beloved, darling, passion, sweetie **8** ladylove, truelove **9** boyfriend, inamorata, inamorato **10** brilliance, brightness, girlfriend, heartthrob, sweetheart

flamen 6 priest

flaming 5 afire, fiery **6** ablaze, alight, ardent, red-hot **7** blazing, burning, fervent, flaring, ignited, intense **10** hot-blooded, passionate **11** conflagrant, impassioned

flammable 8 burnable **9** ignitable **10** incendiary **11** combustible ***liquid:*** **3** gas, oil **7** acetone, alcohol, ethanol **8** gasoline, kerosene **9** petroleum **10** turpentine

Flanders *capital:* **5** Lille ***language:*** **7** Flemish

flaneur 5 idler **12** boulevardier, man-about-town

flank 4 abut, side **6** adjoin, border

flap 3 tab, tap **4** beat, flog, fold, slap, stew, wave, wing **5** fling, panel **6** crisis, dither, lather, pother, tumult, uproar **7** aileron, flutter, turmoil **9** agitation, commotion, confusion

flapdoodle 3 rot **4** bosh, bull, nuts **5** drool, fudge, hokum, hooey **6** bunkum, drivel **7** baloney, blarney, hogwash, rubbish **8** malarkey, nonsense, tommyrot **9** poppycock **10** applesauce, balderdash **12** blatherskite, fiddle-faddle, fiddlesticks

flapjack 7 hotcake, pancake **11** griddle cake

flare 4 burn **5** blaze, burst, flame, flash **6** signal **7** flicker **8** outburst ***type:*** **5** Hyder **9** air-assist **11** steam-assist

flare-up 5 blaze, burst, flame, flash, surge **8** eruption, outburst **9** explosion

flaring 5 afire, fiery **6** ablaze, aflame, alight **7** blazing, burning **11** conflagrant

flash 3 ray **4** beam, rush, snap, show **5** blaze, bling, blink, crack, flame, flare, glare, gleam, glint, jiffy, shake, shine, showy, spark, speed **6** dazzle, expose, flaunt, glance, minute, moment, second **7** display, disport, exhibit, flicker, glamour, glimmer, glisten, glitter, instant, pizzazz, shimmer, show off, spangle, sparkle, twinkle **8** brandish **9** coruscate **11** coruscation, scintillate, split second **13** scintillation

flashy 4 loud **5** gaudy, jazzy, showy **6** brazen, florid, garish, glitzy, ornate, snazzy, sporty, tawdry, tinsel **7** blatant, chintzy, glaring, insipid **9** sparkling **10** flamboyant, glittering **12** meretricious, ostentatious

flask 4 olpe, vial **6** bottle, fiasco, flacon **7** ampulla, canteen, costrel, thermos

flat 3 dim, mat **4** dead, drab, dull, even **5** banal, bland, exact, fixed, flush, level, muted, plane, prone, rooms, stale, vapid **7** insipid, prosaic **8** lodgings, tenement, unsavory **9** apartment, colorless, innocuous **10** flavorless, lackluster, monotonous

flatfish see at **fish**

flatland **4** mesa **5** plain **6** steppe, tundra **7** plateau **9** tableland

flat-out **8** absolute **9** downright **10** absolutely

flatten **4** deck, down, dull, even, fell, raze **5** crush, floor, level **6** smooth, squash **9** knock down, prostrate

flattened at the poles **6** oblate

flatter **4** coax, suit **5** toady **6** become, cajole, praise, stroke **7** adulate, blarney, gratify, wheedle **8** blandish, bootlick, butter up, soft-soap **9** sweet-talk

flattery **5** smarm **6** butter, praise **7** blarney **8** cajolery, soft soap, toadyism **9** adulation, sweet talk **10** sycophancy **11** compliments **12** blandishment, ingratiation, unctuousness

Flaubert, Gustave ***birthplace:*** **5** Rouen ***heroine:*** **4** Emma (Bovary) ***novel:*** **8** Salammbô **12** Madame Bovary

flaunt **4** show, wave **5** flash, flout, vaunt **6** expose, parade **7** display, disport, exhibit, show off **8** brandish, flourish

flavor **4** race, tang, zest, zing **5** sapor, savor, smack, spice, taste, tinge **6** relish, season **7** variety, version

flavorless **4** flat **5** bland, stale **7** insipid **8** unsavory **11** unpalatable

flavorsome **5** sapid, tasty, yummy **6** savory **9** delicious, palatable **10** appetizing, delectable **11** good-tasting

flaw **3** gap, rip, sin **4** blot, chip, tear, vice **5** crack, fault **6** defect **7** blemish **8** weakness **9** deformity **12** imperfection

flawed **5** amiss **6** faulty, marred **7** damaged, spoiled **8** impaired **9** defective, imperfect

flawless **4** pure **5** ideal, model **6** intact **7** perfect **8** seamless, unmarred **9** exquisite **10** immaculate, impeccable **11** unblemished

flax **5** linen ***fiber:*** **3** tow ***prepare:*** **3** ret **4** card **5** dress **6** hackle, scutch

flaxen **4** fair **5** blond, straw **6** blonde, golden, yellow **7** towhead

flay **4** beat, lash, peel, skin **7** blister, censure, lambast, upbraid **8** lambaste **9** castigate, criticize, excoriate

flea **6** chigoe, jigger **7** chigger ***water:*** **7** daphnid

Fleance's father **6** Banquo

flèche **5** spire

fleck **3** dot **4** mark, mote, spot **5** flake, speck **6** dapple, mottle, streak, stripe **7** spatter, speckle, stipple **8** particle **9** bespeckle

Fledermaus, Die **3** bat ***character:*** **5** Adele, Falke, Frank **6** Alfred **9** Rosalinde **10** Eisenstein ***composer:*** **7** Strauss (Johann)

fledge **4** rear **7** feather

fledgling **4** colt, tyro **6** novice, rookie **8** beginner, freshman, neophyte, newcomer **10** apprentice

flee **3** fly, lam, run **4** bolt, scat, skip **5** elude, scoot, scram, skirr, steal **6** decamp, escape **7** abscond, make off, run away, scamper, vamoose **8** stampede, turn tail **9** skedaddle **10** make tracks

fleece **3** rob **4** bilk, clip, gaff, milk, rook, skin, soak, wool **5** bleed, cheat, cozen, mulct, shear, stick, sweat **6** extort, hustle, rip off **7** defraud, swindle **8** flimflam **10** overcharge

fleecy **5** downy **6** fluffy, pilose, woolly **7** hirsute **9** whiskered **10** flocculent

fleer **4** gibe, gird, jeer, jest, mock, quip **5** flout, laugh, scoff, scout, sneer, taunt

fleet **4** fast, navy, spry **5** agile, brisk, group, hasty, quick, rapid, swift **6** argosy, armada, nimble, speedy **8** flotilla **9** breakneck **10** harefooted

fleeting **5** brief **7** passing **8** fugitive, volatile **9** ephemeral, fugacious, momentary, temporary, transient **10** evanescent, short-lived, transitory

Fleming, Ian see **James Bond**

flesh **4** beef, meat, skin **5** stock **7** kindred **9** offspring, relatives, substance

fleshly **5** obese **6** animal, bodily, carnal **7** lustful, profane, secular, sensual **8** corporal, physical, sensuous, temporal **9** corporeal, epicurean, luxurious, sybaritic **10** voluptuous

fleshy **3** fat **5** ample, beefy, burly, gross, heavy, hefty, husky, meaty, obese, plump, pudgy, stout, tubby **6** chubby, chunky, portly, rotund **7** porcine, weighty **9** corpulent **10** overweight, well-padded ***fruit:*** **4** plum, pome **5** berry, drupe, grape, mango, peach **6** cherry **8** cucumber

Fletcher's partner **8** Beaumont (Francis)

fleur-de-lis **4** iris

flex **4** bend **5** tense

flexible **5** lithe, loose **6** docile, floppy, limber, pliant, supple **7** elastic, pliable, springy, willowy **8** amenable, bendable, stretchy, yielding **9** adaptable, compliant, malleable, tractable

flexion **3** bow **4** bend, fold, turn **5** angle

flexuous **5** fluid, lithe, snaky **7** sinuous, winding **8** tortuous **10** circuitous, convoluted, meandering, serpentine **11** anfractuous

flick **4** film, show **5** movie **13** motion picture, moving picture

flicker **4** bird, film, flit, hint **5** flash, gleam, glint, movie, waver **6** quiver **7** twinkle **10**

woodpecker **13** motion picture, moving picture

flickering 7 lambent **8** unsteady

flier 3 ace **5** pilot **6** airman **7** aviator, birdman, handout **8** aviatrix, brochure, circular **9** throwaway

flight 3 hop, lam **4** rout, soar, slip, wing **5** flock, floor, flush, flyby, story **6** escape, flying, series **7** getaway **8** breakout ***formation:*** **7** echelon ***overnight:*** **6** redeye

flighty 5 dizzy, giddy, silly, swift **7** foolish **8** freakish, skittish, unstable, volatile **9** frivolous, mercurial, transient **10** capricious, changeable, inconstant **11** empty-headed, harebrained **13** irresponsible

flimflam 3 con, gyp **4** bilk, dupe, fake, fool, gull, hoax, jazz, sham **5** cheat, cozen, fraud, hokum, trick **6** chouse, deceit, diddle, humbug **7** chicane, deceive, defraud, swindle **8** hoodwink, trickery **9** bamboozle, deception, moonshine **10** balderdash, double-talk **11** hornswoggle

flimflammer 3 gyp **5** cheat **6** con man **7** diddler, sharper **8** swindler **9** defrauder **11** four-flusher **12** double-dealer

flimsy 4 limp, weak **5** cheap, filmy, frail, gauzy, sheer **6** feeble, flabby, sleazy, slight **7** flaccid, fragile, rickety, spindly, tenuous, unsound **8** decrepit, delicate, gossamer **10** diaphanous, improbable **11** implausible, transparent **12** unconvincing **13** insubstantial

flinch 5 quail, start, wince **6** blench, cringe, recoil, shrink

fling 3 peg **4** cast, emit, fire, flap, hurl, plop, rush, shot, slap, stab, tear, toss **5** binge, chuck, heave, pitch, shoot, spree, throw **6** affair, charge, hurtle, launch **7** splurge **8** catapult

Flintstones, The *character:* **4** Dino, Fred **5** Betty (Rubble), Wilma **6** Barney (Rubble) **8** Bamm-Bamm ***creator:*** **5** Hanna (Bill) **7** Barbera (Joe) ***setting:*** **7** Bedrock ***voice:*** **5** Blanc (Mel)

flip 4 glib, leaf, pert, riff, toss, wise **6** breezy, invert, riffle, ruffle **8** turn over **10** somersault **11** impertinent, smart-alecky

flip-flop 5 U-turn, waver **6** sandal, switch, waffle **7** reverse **8** reversal **9** about-face, turnabout, vacillate, volte-face **10** turnaround **11** vacillation

flippancy 5 cheek **6** levity **8** archness, pertness **9** cockiness, freshness, frivolity **10** cheekiness, impishness **11** roguishness

flippant 4 glib, pert **5** sassy, saucy **6** breezy, cheeky **11** impertinent, smart-alecky **13** disrespectful

flirt 3 toy **4** flit, fool, minx, ogle, vamp **5** dally, tease **6** coquet, trifle, wanton **8** coquette **10** experiment, mess around

flit 3 fly, zip **4** dart, pass, rush, sail, scud, whiz, wing **5** flash, hurry, scoot, speed **7** flicker, flutter, twinkle

flitter 4 dart, flap, wing **5** hover, waver **6** quiver **7** skitter **9** fluctuate

flivver 6 jalopy **9** tin lizzie

float 3 bob, fly **4** buoy, cork, hang, raft, ride, sail, scud, swim, waft **5** drift, hover **6** wander **7** pontoon, propose **8** levitate **9** negotiate

floater 3 bum, vag **4** hobo, raft **5** tramp **7** drifter, vagrant **8** derelict, vagabond **10** roustabout

floating 5 fluid, loose **6** adrift, natant **7** buoyant, movable **8** moveable, shifting, variable **10** adjustable **11** fluctuating

flocculent 5 flaky **6** fleecy, fluffy, woolly

flock 3 mob **4** army, bevy, herd, host, mass, pack, rout, wisp **5** brood, bunch, cloud, covey, crowd, drove, group **6** flight, gaggle, gather, legion, scores, throng **8** assemble, assembly, converge **9** multitude **11** aggregation **12** congregation

floe 3 ice **4** berg **7** glacier, iceberg **8** ice field

flog 3 tan **4** beat, cane, flap, hide, lash, slog, whip **5** birch, drive, flail, whale **6** larrup, lather, stripe, switch, thrash **7** cowhide, leather, scourge **10** flagellate

flood 4 fill, flow, flux, glut, pour, rush, tide **5** burst, drown, float, spate, swamp **6** deluge, engulf, stream **7** current, freshet, immerse, Niagara, torrent **8** alluvion, cataract, inundate, overflow, submerge **9** avalanche, cataclysm, overwhelm **10** inundation, outpouring

floor 3 awe **4** base, down, drop, fell, stun, tier **5** amaze, level, shock, story **6** ground **7** astound, flatten **8** astonish, audience, bowl down, bowl over, surprise **9** dumbfound, knock down **11** flabbergast

flop 3 dud **4** bomb, bust, fail, fall **5** lemon, loser **6** bummer, fizzle, turkey **7** clinker, failure

floppy 4 disk, limp **6** flimsy **7** flaccid **8** diskette, flexible

flora 6 plants **10** vegetation

flora and fauna 5 biota

Florence *bridge:* **12** Ponte Vecchio ***cathedral:*** **5** Duomo ***family:*** **6** Medici ***museum:*** **6** Uffizi **8** Bargello ***palace:*** **5** Pitti ***river:*** **4** Arno

florid 3 red **5** flush, gaudy, ruddy, showy **6** ornate, rococo **7** baroque, flowery, flushed, glowing **8** rubicund, sanguine, sonorous **9**

bombastic, elaborate, overblown **10** euphuistic, flamboyant, rhetorical **11** declamatory **12** magniloquent **13** grandiloquent

Florida ***capital:*** **11** Tallahassee ***city:*** **5** Miami, Tampa **6** Naples, Venice **7** Hialeah, Key West, Orlando **8** Sarasota **9** Palm Beach **11** St. Augustine **12** Jacksonville, St. Petersburg ***college, university:*** **7** Rollins, Stetson ***county:*** **3** Lee **4** Dade **6** Orange **7** Broward, Volusia **8** Pinellas, Sarasota ***key:*** **4** Long, Vaca, West **5** Largo **7** Big Pine **9** Matecumbe, Sugarloaf ***lake:*** **9** Kissimmee **10** Okeechobee ***nickname:*** **8** Sunshine (State) ***park:*** **10** Everglades ***race site:*** **7** Daytona ***river:*** **6** Indian **7** St. Johns **8** Suwannee **12** Apalachicola ***state bird:*** **11** mockingbird ***state flower:*** **13** orange blossom ***state tree:*** **9** sabal palm

florilegium **5** album **6** reader **7** garland, omnibus **8** analects **9** anthology **10** collection, miscellany

Florimel's husband **7** Marinel

floss **4** down, fuzz, lint **5** fluff **6** thread

flotilla **5** fleet **6** argosy, armada

Flotow opera **5** Indra **6** L'Ombre, Martha

flotsam **6** debris, jetsam **7** remains **8** wreckage **9** driftwood

flounce **5** frill, mince, strut, waltz **6** bounce, prance, ruffle, sashay

flounder **3** dab **5** slosh **6** fumble, muddle, splash, thrash, wallow **7** blunder, flounce **8** flatfish, struggle

flour **4** meal **6** pinole, powder ***beetle:*** **6** weevil ***merchant:*** **6** miller

flourish **3** wax **4** grow, wave **5** adorn, bloom **6** flower, stroke, thrive **7** blossom, burgeon, develop, fanfare, prosper, succeed **8** brandish, curlicue, ornament **13** embellishment, ornamentation

flout **4** defy, mock **5** scorn, spurn **6** deride, insult **7** scoff at

flow **4** emit, flux, gush, ooze, pour, rill, rise, rush, stem, tide, well **5** arise, drift, flood, issue, spate, spill, surge, swarm **6** course, deluge, onrush, sluice, spring, stream **7** cascade, current, emanate, give off, outflow, proceed **8** inundate, sequence **9** discharge, originate **10** continuity, inundation, succession **11** progression **12** continuation

flower **4** best, blow, pick, posy **5** bloom, cream, elite, pride, prime, prize **6** choice, thrive **7** blossom, burgeon, develop **10** effloresce **13** inflorescence ***buttonhole:*** **11** boutonniere ***cluster:*** **4** cyme **5** spike, umbel **6** corymb, floret, raceme, spadix **7** panicle **8** spikelet **9** capitulum, dichasium, glomerule **11** monochasium **13** inflorescence ***cup:*** **5** calyx ***garden:*** **4** iris, lily, pink, rose **5** aster, canna, daisy, oxlip, pansy, peony, phlox, poppy, tulip **6** azalia, cosmos, crocus, dahlia, orchid, violet **7** jonquil, petunia **8** camellia, daffodil, gardenia, geranium, gloxinia, hyacinth, larkspur, marigold, primrose **9** carnation, gladiolus, narcissus **10** delphinium, heliotrope **13** chrysanthemum ***necklace:*** **3** lei ***opening:*** **8** anthesis ***part:*** **5** bract, calyx, ovary, ovule, petal, sepal, style **6** anther, pistil, spathe, stamen, stigma **7** corolla, nectary, pedicel, petiole **8** calyptra, filament, peduncle, perianth ***spike:*** **5** ament **6** catkin, spadix ***stalk:*** **7** pedicel **8** peduncle ***type:*** **3** ray **4** disk **6** annual, simple **9** composite, perennial ***wild:*** **4** flag **5** bluet, daisy, vetch **6** lupine **7** anemone, arbutus, cowslip, gentian, vervain **8** bluebell, hepatica, trillium **9** buttercup, columbine, dandelion, saxifrage **10** cinquefoil **12** lady's slipper

flower arranging **7** ikebana

flowering **6** growth **8** progress **9** evolution **11** development, florescence, progression

flowerless plant **4** fern, moss **6** lichen **9** liverwort

flowery **5** wordy **6** florid, ornate, prolix **7** aureate, diffuse, verbose **8** sonorous **9** overblown **10** euphuistic, rhetorical **11** declamatory **12** magniloquent **13** grandiloquent

Flowery Kingdom **5** China

flowing **4** easy **5** fluid **6** fluent, liquid, smooth **7** cursive, running **10** effortless ***back:*** **6** reflux **8** refluent ***in:*** **6** influx **8** influent ***together:*** **7** conflux **9** confluent

flow regulator **4** cock, gate **5** valve **8** throttle

flu **6** grippe

flub **4** goof, mess, muff, slip **5** boner, botch, error, fluff, gaffe, lapse, snarl **6** bobble, bollix, bungle, foul up, goof up, mess up **7** blunder, faux pas, louse up

fluctuate **4** sway, yo-yo **5** swing, waver **6** seesaw **8** undulate **9** alternate, oscillate, vacillate

flue **4** duct, pipe, tube, vent **6** funnel, uptake **7** channel, chimney, outtake

fluent **4** easy, glib **5** fluid **6** facile, liquid, smooth, supple **7** cursive, flowing, voluble **8** eloquent, polished **10** articulate, effortless

fluff **4** down, flub, fuzz, goof, lint, mess, muff, slip, trip **5** boner, botch, error, floss, gaffe, lapse, whisk **6** bobble, bollix, bungle, goof up, mess up **7** blooper, blunder, faux pas, louse up, mistake

fluffy **5** downy **6** flossy **7** cursory, shallow **8**

puffed up **10** flocculent **11** superficial **13** unsubstantial

fluid 4 free, sera (plural) **5** lymph, serum, water **6** liquid, mobile, molten, serous, watery **7** mutable, protean **8** flexible, shifting, unstable, unsteady, variable **9** adaptable, changeful, unsettled **10** changeable ***excessive:*** **5** edema

fluke 3 hap **4** lobe, worm **5** quirk **6** chance **8** flatfish, fortuity **9** trematode

fluky 3 odd **6** casual, chance, chancy, random **9** arbitrary **10** accidental, fortuitous

flume 5 chute **6** sluice, stream **7** channel **8** aqueduct **11** watercourse

flummox 5 abash, addle **6** baffle, rattle, stymie **7** confuse, fluster, perplex **8** befuddle, bewilder, confound **9** discomfit, embarrass **10** disconcert

flunk 4 fail

flunky 4 peon **5** gofer, toady **6** drudge, lackey, stooge, yes-man **7** footman, servant, steward **8** factotum, follower

flurry 3 ado, fit **4** fuss, gust, spit, stir, to-do **5** haste, whirl **6** bother, bustle, furore, pother, tumult **7** barrage, flutter, turmoil **8** snowfall **9** agitation, commotion, confusion, whirlpool, whirlwind **10** excitement, turbulence

flush 4 even, flat, glow, pink, rich, rose, wash **5** bloom, color, level, plane, raise, rinse, rouge **6** florid, filled, mantle, redden, sluice **7** cleanse, crimson, glowing, inflame, opulent, suffuse, wealthy **8** abundant, abutting, irrigate, rubicund, sanguine, squarely **9** turn color

fluster 5 addle, dizzy, shake, upset **6** ball up, bother, fuddle, muddle, rattle, ruffle **7** agitate, confuse, disturb, nonplus, perturb, unhinge **8** befuddle, bewilder, confound, disquiet, distract **10** discompose

flustered 5 upset **7** abashed, anxious, rattled **8** agitated, confused, troubled **9** chagrined, disturbed, flummoxed, perplexed, perturbed **10** bewildered, disquieted, distracted, distraught, distressed, nonplussed **11** discomposed, embarrassed **12** disconcerted

flute 4 fife, roll **5** pleat **6** goffer, groove **7** chamfer, channel, piccolo **8** recorder **9** wineglass ***Japanese:*** **10** shakuhachi ***oval:*** **7** ocarina ***player:*** **5** piper **7** flutist **8** flautist

flutist *American:* **5** Baker (Julius), Baron (Samuel) **7** Robison (Paula) **8** Zukerman (Eugenia) ***French:*** **6** Rampal (Jean-Pierre) ***Irish:*** **6** Galway (James)

flutter 4 beat, flap, flit **5** hover, quake, shake **6** flurry, quaver, quiver, wobble **7** flicker, flitter, pulsate, tremble, vibrate **9** agitation, commotion, confusion, palpitate, vibration **11** fluctuation

flu type 4 bird **5** Asian, avian, swine

flux 3 run **4** flow, fuse, melt, rush, thaw, tide **5** drift, flood, spate **6** change, stream **7** current, flowing, outflow **8** dissolve

fly 3 zip **4** bolt, dart, dash, flee, flit, lure, scud, skip, soar, whiz, wing **5** fleet, float, glide, hover, hurry, pilot, scoot, shoot, skirr, sweep, whish, whisk **6** aviate, escape, hasten, hustle **7** abscond, flutter ***insect:*** **3** ked **4** gnat **5** midge **6** botfly, gadfly, mayfly, tsetse **7** deerfly, sandfly **8** blackfly, dipteron, horsefly, housefly, tachinid **10** bluebottle ***larva:*** **6** maggot

fly-by-night 5 shady **7** passing **9** transient **10** transitory, unreliable **12** disreputable, undependable **13** untrustworthy

flycatcher 5 pewee **6** phoebe, tyrant **8** bellbird, kingbird **9** passerine

flying 5 aloft **6** volant **8** airborne

Flying Dutchman, The *composer:* **6** Wagner (Richard) ***heroine:*** **5** Senta

flying fish 7 gurnard

flying fox 3 bat **8** fruit bat

flying horse 7 Pegasus **10** hippogriff

flying island 6 Laputa

flying lemur 6 colugo

flying mammal 3 bat

flying saucer 3 UFO

fly in the ointment 5 catch **8** drawback

foam 4 head, scud, scum, suds, surf **5** churn, froth, spume **6** bubble, lather, seethe **7** bubbles **10** effervesce

fob 4 seal **5** chain **6** pocket, ribbon **8** ornament

fob off 5 foist **6** put off **7** palm off, pass off

focus 3 fix, hub **4** node, zoom **5** heart, rivet **6** adjust, center, fixate, home in **8** converge, emphasis, meditate, polestar **9** concenter, epicenter **10** hypocenter **11** concentrate, nerve center

fodder 4 feed, food **6** forage, silage, stover **9** provender ***crop:*** **3** hay, oat, rye **4** corn **5** maize, vetch, wheat **6** barley, clover, millet **7** alfalfa, sorghum ***storage structure:*** **4** silo ***store:*** **6** ensile

foe 5 enemy, rival **8** opponent **9** adversary **10** antagonist

fog 4 blur, daze, foam, haze, mist, murk, soup **5** brume, cloud, vapor **6** miasma, muddle **7** pea soup, pogonip

foggy 4 hazy **5** dirty, grimy, misty, murky, soupy, vague **7** brumous, muddled, obscure, tenuous **8** confused, pea soupy, vaporous

fogy 6 dotard, fossil, square **7** diehard **8** mossback **10** fuddy-duddy **12** antediluvian, conservative **11** standpatter **13** stick-in-the-mud

fogyish 7 old-line **8** outmoded, standpat **9** hidebound, out-of-date **10** antiquated, fuddy-duddy, mossbacked **11** reactionary **12** conservative, old-fashioned

foible 4 vice **5** fault **6** defect **7** failing, frailty **8** weakness **11** shortcoming **12** imperfection

foil 4 balk, beat, curb, dash, faze **5** check, sword **6** baffle, defeat, rattle, thwart **7** buffalo **8** contrast, restrain **9** discomfit, embarrass, frustrate **10** circumvent, disappoint, disconcert **11** straight man

foist 6 fob off **7** palm off, pass off

fold 3 pen, ply **4** bend, fail, tuck **5** drape, flock, pleat, plica, ridge **6** crease, double, furrow, pucker **7** flexure, plicate **9** plication **11** corrugation ***skin:*** **4** ruga **5** plica, rugae (plural) **6** dewlap, plicae (plural)

folder 4 file **6** binder **9** portfolio

foliage 6 growth, leaves **7** verdure **8** greenery, lushness **10** vegetation

folk 4 race **6** people **9** community

folklore 4 myth, tale **5** fable **6** belief, custom, legend, mythos, wisdom **9** mythology, tradition **12** superstition

folks 6 family **7** parents **9** relatives

folksinger 4 Baez (Joan), Ives (Burl) **5** Dylan (Bob), Niles (John Jacob), White (Josh) **6** Odetta, Seeger (Pete) **7** Collins (Judy), Guthrie (Arlo, Woody), Robeson (Paul) **9** Belafonte (Harry), Ledbetter (Huddie)

folksy 5 homey **6** casual, earthy, mellow, rustic, simple **7** natural **8** down-home, familiar, informal, laid-back, sociable **9** easygoing, ingenuous **10** unaffected, unpolished **13** unpretentious

folktale 4 myth **5** fable **6** legend **7** märchen

follow 3 dog, spy, tag **4** hunt, keep, obey, seek, tail, walk **5** catch, chase, ensue, grasp, hound, trace, track, trail **6** accept, comply, convoy, pursue, search, shadow, travel **7** conform, imitate, proceed, replace, succeed **8** practice, supplant **9** supersede ***closely:*** **5** draft **10** slipstream

follower 3 fan **5** toady **6** addict, cohort, minion, sequel, votary **7** acolyte, apostle, devotee, groupie, habitué, sectary, trailer, wannabe **8** adherent, advocate, disciple, faithful, hanger-on, henchman, myrmidon, parasite, partisan, tagalong **9** dependent, satellite, supporter, sycophant **10** aficionado

following 4 next **5** after, below, later, since **6** behind, public **7** ensuing, retinue **8** audience **9** adherents, afterward, believers, disciples, entourage, partisans **10** afterwards, sequential, supporters, subsequent, succeeding, successive **12** subsequently, subsequent to

follow-up 6 sequel

folly 4 whim **6** lunacy, vanity **7** fatuity, foolery, inanity, madness **8** insanity, nonsense **9** absurdity, craziness, dottiness, silliness, stupidity **10** indulgence **11** foolishness **12** extravagance

foment 3 sow **4** brew, goad, spur **5** rouse, set on **6** arouse, excite, foster, incite, stir up, whip up **7** agitate, nurture, provoke **9** cultivate, encourage, instigate

fond 4 dear, warm **5** silly **6** doting, loving, tender **7** devoted, fatuous, foolish, partial **8** desirous, enamored, romantic **9** indulgent **10** infatuated **11** sentimental **12** affectionate

fondle 3 paw, pet **5** grope, touch **6** caress, cosset, dandle, stroke **7** embrace **8** canoodle

fondness 4 love **5** fancy, taste **6** liking, relish **8** appetite, devotion, penchant, soft spot, weakness **9** affection, tendresse **10** attachment, partiality, preference, propensity **11** inclination **12** predilection

font 4 root, type **6** origin, source **8** fountain **10** receptacle

food 3 pap **4** chow, diet, eats, fare, grub, meal, meat **5** bread, manna **6** fodder, viands **7** aliment, cuisine, edibles, nurture, pabulum, vittles **8** delicacy, victuals **9** nutriment, provender **10** provisions, sustenance **11** comestibles, nourishment ***disorder:*** **7** bulimia **8** anorexia ***divine:*** **8** ambrosia ***element:*** **5** fiber, fibre, sugar **6** starch **7** mineral, protein, vitamin **12** carbohydrate ***from heaven:*** **5** manna ***lover:*** **7** epicure, gourmet **8** gourmand ***provision:*** **4** mess **6** ration **7** serving ***scarcity:*** **6** famine ***waste:*** **7** garbage

foofaraw 3 ado **4** fuss, stir, to-do **5** hoo-ha, stink **6** bother, finery, frills, furore, hoohah, hurrah, pother, ruckus, rumpus **8** brouhaha **9** commotion **11** disturbance

fool 3 ass, kid, oaf, rag, rib, sap, toy **4** boob, butt, clod, dolt, dope, dupe, fish, gull, hoax, jerk, jest, joke, josh, mook, zany **5** chump, clown, comic, dally, dummy, dunce, goose, idiot, loser, moron, ninny, patsy, schmo, trick **6** banter, cretin, dawdle, delude, diddle, dimwit, doodle, galoot, gammon, jester, lead on, meddle, monkey, motley, nitwit, pigeon, schmoe, stooge, sucker, tamper, trifle, victim **7** beguile, buffoon, chicane, deceive, fake out, fall guy, fritter, half-wit, jackass, mislead, pinhead, saphead, schmuck **8** bonehead, comedian, dumbbell, flimflam, hoodwink, imbecile, lunkhead, numskull, pushover **9** bamboozle, birdbrain, blockhead, interfere, simpleton **10** nincompoop **11** hornswoggle, merry-andrew, string along **13** laughingstock ***around:*** **4** futz, idle, laze, loaf, loll **5** flirt **6** dawdle, diddle, lounge **8** lollygag, womanize **9** philander

foolhardy **4** bold, rash **6** daring, madcap **8** headlong, reckless **9** audacious, daredevil, impetuous **11** precipitate, temerarious

foolish **3** mad **4** daft, gaga, rash, zany **5** balmy, batty, crazy, dippy, dizzy, dorky, dotty, goofy, inane, inept, kooky, loony, loopy, nutty, sappy, silly, wacky **6** absurd, insane, simple, stupid, unwise **7** asinine, doltish, fatuous, idiotic, lunatic, meshuga, moronic, witless **8** clueless, meshugge, reckless, trifling **9** cockamamy, half-baked, brainless, fantastic, frivolous, half-baked, imbecilic, insensate, laughable, ludicrous, senseless **10** cockamamie, half-cocked, half-witted, irrational, ridiculous **11** harebrained, nonsensical

foolishness **4** bull, bunk **5** folly, fudge **6** bêtise, bunkum, lunacy **7** fatuity, inanity, rubbish **8** claptrap, drollery, insanity, nonsense, tommyrot **9** absurdity, craziness, silliness, stupidity **10** imbecility, imprudence **12** fiddle-faddle **13** horsefeathers

fool's gold **6** pyrite

foot **3** paw, pay **4** hoof ***ailment:*** **4** corn **6** bunion, callus ***animal:*** **3** pad, paw **4** hoof ***bones of:*** **5** talus, tarsi (plural) **6** cuboid, tarsal, tarsus **7** phalanx **9** calcaneus, cuneiform, navicular, phalanges (plural) **10** metatarsal ***combining form:*** **3** ped, pod **4** podo ***doctor:*** **10** podiatrist **11** chiropodist ***metric:*** **4** iamb **5** arsis, paeon **6** dactyl, thesis **7** anapest, pyrrhic, spondee, trochee ***part:*** **3** toe **4** arch, ball, claw, nail **5** ankle, digit, talon **6** hallux, instep

football **4** nerf **5** rugby **6** rugger, soccer **7** pigskin ***field:*** **8** gridiron ***foul:*** **7** holding, offside **8** clipping **12** interference ***official:*** **6** umpire **7** referee **8** linesman **9** back judge, line judge **10** field judge ***play:*** **4** dive, trap **5** sneak, sweep **6** option, screen **7** audible, counter, handoff, rollout, runback **8** dropback **9** crossbuck, off-tackle **10** buttonhook ***player position:*** **3** end **4** back, half, wing **5** guard **6** center, kicker, safety, tackle **7** flanker, lineman, wideout **8** defender, fullback, halfback, linesman, receiver, scatback, slotback, split end, tailback, tight end, wingback **9** noseguard **10** cornerback, linebacker, nose tackle **11** placekicker, quarterback, running back, snapper-back **12** defensive end, strong safety, wide receiver ***scoring:*** **6** safety **9** field goal, touchdown **10** conversion ***starting play:*** **7** kickoff ***team:*** **6** eleven ***term:*** **4** down, kick, pass, punt, rush, snap **5** blitz, block, squad **6** fumble, huddle, kicker, onside, option, player, safety, spiral **7** end zone, handoff, kickoff, offside, pigskin, quarter, spinner, tweener, yardage **8** clipping, crossbar, goal line, goalpost, gridiron, halftime **9** backfield, defensive, field goal, intercept, offensive, placekick, scrimmage, touchback, touchdown **11** ballcarrier, broken field **12** interception, triple threat (see also **National Football League**)

footballer **4** Kemp (Jack), Long (Howie), Lott (Ronnie), Levy (Marv), Monk (Art), Moon (Warren), Reed (Andre), Rice (Jerry) **5** Allen (Marcus), Baugh (Sammy), Berry (Raymond), Brady (Tom), Brown (Bob, Jim), Clark (Gary), Ditka (Mike), Elway (John), Eller (Carl), Favre (Brett), Gibbs (Joe), Groza (Lou), Jones (Bert, Deacon), Kelly (Jim), Kosar (Bernie), Leahy (Pat), Lomax (Neil), Muñoz (Anthony), Shula (Don), Simms (Phil), Smith (Emmitt), Starr (Bart), Stram (Hank), Swann (Lynn), Young (Steve) **6** Aikman (Troy), Blanda (George), Butkus (Dick), Carter (Chris, Ki-Jana), Csonka (Larry), Dawson (Len), Ellard (Henry), Graham (Otto), Grange (Red), Greene (Joe), Harris (Franco), Jaeger (Jeff), Joiner (Charlie), Lofton (James), Lowery (Nick), Marino (Dan), Murray (Eddie), Namath (Joe), Payton (Walter), Rypien (Mark), Sayers (Gale), Slater (Jackie), Taylor (Lawrence), Thorpe (Jim), Tittle (Y. A.), Turner (Jim), Unitas (Johnny), Walker (Herschel) **7** Bledsoe (Drew), Dorsett (Tony), Esiason (Boomer), Gifford (Frank), Hornung (Paul), Johnson (Norm), Largent (Steve), Luckman (Sid), Manning (Eli, Peyton), Montana (Joe), Newsome (Ozzie), Riggins (John), Rozelle (Pete), Sanders (Barry, Deion), Simpson (O. J.), Stabler (Ken), Thurman (Thomas) **8** Andersen (Morten), Anderson (Gary, Ottis), Bradshaw (Terry), Lombardi (Vince), Nagurski (Bronko), Plunkett (Jim), Staubach (Roger) **9** Dickerson (Eric), Jurgensen (Sonny), Hostetler (Jeff), Tarkenton (Fran) **10** Stallworth (John), Singletary (Mike), Stephenson (Dwight), Youngblood (Jack)

Foote play **15** Trip to Bountiful (The) **19** Young Man from Atlanta (The)

footfall **4** step **5** tread

footing **4** base, rank, seat, term **5** basis, place, state **6** bottom, ground, status **7** bedrock, seating, station, warrant **8** basement, capacity, pedestal, position, standing **9** character, situation **10** foundation, groundwork, substratum **12** underpinning

footless 4 dull, dumb **5** crass, dense, inept, unfit **6** apodal, stupid **7** foolish

foot lever 5 pedal **7** treadle

footman 7 servant **10** pedestrian **11** infantryman

footnote abbreviation 4 Ibid., Idem **5** op. cit. **6** loc. cit.

footpad 5 thief **6** mugger, robber **8** criminal **10** highwayman, pickpocket

footprint 3 pug **4** sign, step **5** spoor, trace, track, tract **7** pugmark, vestige

footslog 4 plod, slop, toil **5** tramp, tromp **6** trudge

footstone 6 ledger, marker **8** monument **11** grave marker

footstool 7 cricket, hassock, ottoman

fop 3 jay **4** beau **5** blade, blood, dandy, spark, swell **7** coxcomb, gallant **8** cavalier, macaroni, popinjay **9** exquisite, ladies' man, pretty boy **11** Beau Brummel, petit-maître **12** fashion plate, lounge lizard

foppish 6 chichi **8** dandyish, peacocky **10** peacockish

for 3 pro **7** in favor

forage 4 beat, comb, grub, prog, raid, rake, sack **5** scour **6** browse, fodder, ravage, rustle, search **7** plunder, ransack, rummage **8** finecomb, scrounge **9** pasturage ***crop:*** **5** grass **6** clover, kochia **7** alfalfa, sorghum (see also **fodder**)

foray 4 raid **6** inroad, sortie **8** invasion **9** incursion, irruption

forbear 4 shun **5** avoid, forgo, spare **6** endure, eschew, resist, suffer **7** abstain, decline, refrain **8** hold back, restrain, tolerate

forbearance 5 grace, mercy **6** lenity **7** charity **8** clemency, lenience, leniency, mildness, patience **9** restraint, tolerance **10** abstinence, toleration **13** consideration

forbearing 4 easy, kind, mild **6** gentle **7** clement, lenient, patient **8** merciful, tolerant **9** indulgent **10** charitable, thoughtful **11** considerate, magnanimous

Forbes hero 8 Tremaine (Johnny)

forbid 3 ban, bar, nix **4** curb, deny, halt, stop, veto **5** block, check, debar **6** enjoin, hinder, impede, outlaw, refuse **7** inhibit, prevent, rule out, shut out **8** disallow, obstruct, preclude, prohibit, restrain **9** interdict, proscribe

forbidden 5 taboo **6** banned, barred **7** illegal, illicit **8** verboten **10** prohibited

Forbidden City 5 Lhasa **6** Gu Gong **7** Beijing

forbidding 4 grim **5** drear, harsh **6** dreary, severe **8** daunting, menacing, sinister **9** repellent **10** formidable **11** threatening

force 2 od **3** jam **4** cram, dint, push **5** drive, foist, impel, might, power, press, vigor, wreak, wreck, wrest **6** coerce, compel, demand, duress, effort, energy, extort, impose, legion, muscle, oblige **7** command, impetus, inflict, potency, require, sandbag **8** coercion, manpower, momentum, obligate, pressure, shoehorn, strength, violence **9** constrain, intensity, puissance, strong-arm **10** compulsion, constraint ***apart:*** **5** wedge ***unit:*** **4** dyne

forced 8 strained **9** contrived, unnatural **10** artificial, compulsory **11** involuntary

forceful 5 stiff, stout **6** mighty, potent, punchy, strong, virile **7** dynamic **8** emphatic, powerful, puissant, vigorous **9** assertive **10** compelling

forceless 4 lame, weak **5** wimpy **6** feeble **8** impotent, nugatory **9** powerless **10** inadequate **11** ineffective, ineffectual

force out see **expel**

forcible 8 coercive **9** compelled **10** compulsory, obligatory, peremptory

ford 5 cross

Ford's folly 5 Edsel

for each 3 per **6** apiece

forearm bone 4 ulna **5** radii (plural), ulnae (plural) **6** radius

forebear 8 ancestor **9** precursor **10** antecedent, progenitor **11** predecessor **12** primogenitor

forebode 5 augur **7** betoken, portend, predict, presage **8** foretell, prophesy, soothsay **13** prognosticate

foreboding 4 omen, sign **5** dread **6** augury **7** anxiety, portent, presage, warning **10** prediction, prognostic **11** premonition **12** apprehension, presentiment

forecast 5 augur **6** divine **7** foresee, portend, predict, presage **8** estimate, foretell, indicate, prophecy, prophesy **9** adumbrate, calculate, prevision, prognosis **10** prediction **13** prognosticate

forecaster 4 seer **5** augur **6** oracle **7** diviner, prophet **8** haruspex **9** predictor **10** prophesier, soothsayer, weatherman **11** Nostradamus **13** meteorologist, weatherperson

foreclose 3 bar **5** debar **6** cut off, hinder **7** prevent, shut out **8** preclude

forefather see **forebear**

forefeel 6 divine **9** apprehend, prevision

forefinger 5 index

forefront 3 van **4** lead **8** vanguard **10** avant-garde, firing line **11** cutting edge

foregoer 6 herald **8** ancestor, forebear **9** harbinger, precursor, prototype **10** antecedent, antecessor, forerunner, progenitor **11** predecessor **12** primogenitor

foregoing 5 prior **6** former **7** earlier **8** anterior, previous **9** precedent, preceding **10** antecedent

forehanded 6 frugal **7** prudent, thrifty **8** sensible, well-to-do **9** provident **10** prosperous

forehead 4 brow **5** frons, front **8** sinciput **9** sincipita (plural)

foreign 5 alien **6** exotic **7** strange **8** external, offshore, overseas **9** extrinsic, nonnative **10** accidental, extraneous, immaterial, irrelevant **11** incongruous **12** adventitious, inapplicable, incompatible, inconsistent **13** inappropriate ***prefix:*** **4** xeno

foreigner 5 alien **8** outsider, stranger **9** outlander **10** tramontane

foreknow 6 divine **9** apprehend, prevision **10** anticipate

foreland 4 beak, cape, head, ness **5** point **10** promontory

forelock 5 bangs, quiff **7** cowlick

foreman 4 bos'n, boss **5** bosun, chief **6** gaffer, ganger, honcho, leader **7** captain, manager, steward **8** overseer **9** boatswain **10** supervisor

foremost 4 arch, head, high, main **5** chief, first, front, grand **7** leading, premier, supreme **9** number one, paramount, principal **10** preeminent **11** cutting-edge, outstanding

forenoon 4 morn **7** morning **12** ante meridiem

forensic 8 judicial **9** debatable **10** rhetorical **13** argumentative

foreordain 4 doom, fate **9** determine **10** predestine **12** predetermine

forerunner 4 omen, sign **5** envoy **6** augury, herald **7** pioneer, portent, presage, symptom, warning **8** ancestor, exemplar, outrider **9** announcer, harbinger, initiator, messenger **10** antecedent, originator, prognostic **11** anticipator, predecessor

foresee 6 divine **7** predict, presage **8** perceive, prophesy **9** apprehend, prefigure, prevision **10** anticipate **13** prognosticate

foreseer 5 augur **6** auspex, oracle **7** diviner, prophet **8** haruspex **9** predictor **10** soothsayer **11** Nostradamus

foreshadow 4 bode, hint **5** augur **6** herald **7** betoken, portend, predict, presage, promise, suggest **8** forecast, intimate **9** adumbrate, prefigure **13** prognosticate

foresight 6 vision **7** caution **8** prudence, sagacity **10** discretion, perception, precaution, prescience, providence

forest 4 bosk, wood **5** copse, grove, weald, woods **6** bosque **7** coppice, thicket, woodlot **8** wildwood, woodland **10** timberland, wilderness ***deity:*** **5** dryad **6** sylvan **8** Sylvanus ***English:*** **4** Dean **5** Arden **8** Sherwood ***German:*** **5** Black **11** Schwarzwald ***opening:*** **5** glade ***relating to:*** **6** sylvan ***subarctic:*** **5** taiga ***tropical:*** **5** selva **6** jungle

forestall 5 avert, block, deter **6** hinder **7** obviate, preempt, prevent, rule out, ward off **8** preclude, stave off **10** anticipate

Forester, C. S. ***hero:*** **10** Hornblower (Horatio) ***novel:*** **12** African Queen (The)

foretell 4 bode, warn **5** augur **6** divine **7** portend, predict, presage, promise **8** proclaim, prophesy, soothsay **9** adumbrate, apprehend, prefigure **10** anticipate, vaticinate **13** prognosticate

forethought 8 judgment, planning, prudence **10** discretion, precaution **12** deliberation **13** premeditation

foretoken 4 bode, hint, omen, sign, warn **5** augur **6** augury, herald **7** portend, portent, presage, promise, symptom, warning **8** forecast **9** harbinger, precursor **10** intimation

forever 3 aye **6** always **7** endless **8** eternity, evermore **9** endlessly, eternally **10** in aeternum **11** ad infinitum, ceaselessly, continually, everlasting, incessantly, permanently, perpetually, unceasingly **12** in perpetuity **13** everlastingly

forewarning 6 caveat, tip-off **7** caution **8** monition **11** premonition

foreword 5 intro, proem **7** preface, prelude **8** exordium, overture, preamble, prologue **12** introduction, prolegomenon

for example 3 say **6** such as

for fear that 4 lest

forfeit 4 fine, lose **5** mulct **6** give up **7** penalty **9** sacrifice **10** amercement

forfend 4 ward **5** avert, deter **6** secure **7** obviate, prevent, protect, rule out, ward off **8** preclude, preserve, stave off

forge 4 copy, fake, form, make **5** pound, shape **6** smithy **7** advance, fashion, imitate, produce, turn out **8** continue **9** construct, fabricate **11** counterfeit, manufacture

forget 4 fail, omit **6** ignore, slight **7** neglect **8** discount, overlook, pass over **9** disregard

forgetful 3 lax **5** slack **6** absent, remiss **7** amnesic **8** amnesiac, careless, heedless **9** negligent, oblivious, unwitting **10** abstracted, neglectful **11** inattentive, thoughtless **12** absentminded

forgetfulness 5 lethe **7** amnesia **8** oblivion **10** negligence **11** inattention

forgivable 6 venial **10** remissible

forgive 5 remit **6** excuse, pardon **7** absolve, condone **8** overlook
forgiveness 6 pardon **7** amnesty **9** remission **10** absolution
forgo 3 bag **5** leave, waive, yield **6** eschew, give up, resign **7** abandon **8** abnegate, jettison, renounce **9** sacrifice, surrender **10** relinquish
fork 6 bisect, branch, crotch **7** diverge, utensil **9** branch off ***prong:*** **4** tine
fork out 3 pay **5** spend **10** contribute
forlorn 5 alone **6** bereft, futile, lonely **8** desolate, forsaken, hopeless, lonesome, solitary, wretched **9** abandoned, depressed, destitute, miserable **10** despairing, despondent **12** disconsolate
form 3 way **4** body, cast, make, mode, mold **5** build, forge, found, frame, image, model, shape, style **6** create, design, devise, figure, make up, manner **7** compose, contour, develop, fashion, outline, process, produce, profile **8** comprise, organize, practice **9** construct, establish, fabricate, framework, procedure, structure, take shape **10** constitute, convention, regulation **11** materialize **13** configuration ***combining form:*** **5** morph ***set:*** **10** stereotype
formal 3 set **4** prim **5** exact, legal, rigid, stiff **6** dressy, lawful, proper, seemly, solemn **7** distant, orderly, regular, stately, starchy, stilted **8** abstract, black-tie, decorous, elevated, official, reserved **10** ceremonial, methodical, systematic **11** ceremonious, syntactical **12** conventional
formality 4 form, rite **6** ritual **7** liturgy, service **8** ceremony, insignia **10** ceremonial, convention, observance
formalize 6 codify **9** establish, normalize **10** regularize **11** standardize
format 4 plan, size **5** shape, style **6** makeup, method **11** arrangement **12** organization
formation 4 rank **6** design, makeup **9** structure **11** arrangement, composition, development **12** architecture, construction
former 3 old **4** late, once, past **5** prior **6** bygone, whilom **7** earlier, onetime, quondam **8** anterior, previous, sometime **9** erstwhile, precedent, preceding **10** antecedent
formerly 3 née **4** erst, once **6** before, whilom **7** already, earlier **9** erstwhile **10** heretofore, previously
formidable 8 daunting **9** difficult **10** impressive **11** redoubtable
formless 5 vague **7** chaotic, obscure, unclear **8** inchoate, nebulous, unshaped **9** amorphous, undefined, unordered **10** immaterial, indefinite, indistinct **11** unorganized
Formosa 6 Taiwan ***capital:*** **6** Taipei
formula 4 rite, rule **5** canon, maxim, tenet **6** method, recipe, ritual **7** precept, theorem **8** equation **9** algorithm, blueprint, principle, yardstick **10** touchstone **12** prescription
formulate 5 couch, draft, frame, hatch **6** codify, devise, invent, make up, phrase **7** concoct, dream up, express, prepare, work out **8** contrive
forsake 4 quit **5** avoid, leave, spurn **6** defect, depart, desert, give up, reject, resign **7** abandon **8** abdicate, renounce **9** throw over **10** relinquish
forsaken 4 lorn **6** bereft **7** forlorn **8** derelict, deserted, desolate, solitary **9** abandoned
Forseti *father:* 6 Balder, Baldur ***palace:*** **7** Glitnir
Forster work 7 Maurice **10** Howards End **13** Room with a View (A) **14** Passage to India (A)
forswear 4 deny **5** unsay **6** abjure, recall, recant, reject **7** perjure, retract **8** renounce, take back, withdraw
fort 4 base **6** castle **7** bastion, bulwark, citadel, redoubt **8** fastness, fortress, garrison, martello, stockade **10** stronghold ***Baltimore:*** **7** McHenry ***California:*** **3** Ord ***Kentucky:*** **4** Knox ***New Jersey:*** **3** Dix ***New York:*** **7** Niagara, Stanwix **8** Schuyler **11** Ticonderoga ***Ontario:*** **9** Frontenac ***San Antonio:*** **5** Alamo ***South Carolina:*** **6** Sumter ***Spanish:*** **7** alcazar **8** presidio
forte 3 bag **4** loud **5** thing **6** métier **8** long suit, strength **9** specialty **10** strong suit **11** strong point
forth 6 onward **7** forward
forthcoming 7 pending **8** imminent **9** impending, proximate **10** responsive **11** approaching
for the most part 9 generally, typically **10** on the whole
for the time being 3 now **6** pro tem **9** at present, currently, presently **10** pro tempore
forthright 4 open **5** blunt, frank, plain **6** candid, direct **7** up-front **8** straight **10** aboveboard, foursquare **11** openhearted, straight-out, undisguised, unvarnished
forthwith 3 now **6** at once **8** directly **9** instantly, right away, thereupon **11** immediately, straightway **12** straightaway
fortification 4 moat, wall **6** abatis, buffer, glacis **7** barrier, bastion, bulwark, citadel, parapet, rampart, redoubt **8** barbican, enceinte, fastness, garrison, palisade, presidio, stockade **9** barricade, earthwork **10** breastwork, stronghold ***part:*** **7** salient
fortify 3 arm **4** gird, stir **5** brace, rally, ready,

renew, rouse, steel **6** enrich, secure **7** hearten, prepare, protect, refresh, restore **8** embolden, energize **9** encourage, reinforce **10** invigorate, strengthen

fortitude 4 grit, guts, pith **5** fiber, heart, nerve, pluck, spunk, valor **6** mettle, phlegm, spirit **7** bravery, courage, stamina **8** backbone, boldness, strength, tenacity **9** constancy, endurance, tolerance **10** resolution **11** intrepidity **12** fearlessness, perseverance, resoluteness, staying power **13** dauntlessness, determination

fortress see **fort**

fortuitous 5 fluky, happy, lucky **6** casual, chance **10** accidental, auspicious **12** providential

fortuity 3 hap **4** luck **5** fluke **6** chance **8** accident **9** happening **10** occurrence

Fortuna 5 Tyche ***symbol:* 5** wheel **6** rudder

fortunate 5 happy, lucky **9** favorable **10** auspicious, propitious **12** providential

Fortunate Islands 8 Canaries

fortune 3 lot, pot, wad **4** doom, fate, luck, mint, pile, ship **5** worth **6** boodle, bundle, chance, happen, hazard, packet, riches, wealth **7** destiny, success, weather **8** property **9** resources

Fortune founder 4 Luce (Henry)

fortune-teller 4 seer **5** augur, sibyl **7** diviner, palmist **9** wisewoman **10** soothsayer (see also **foreseer**)

fortune-telling see **divination**

forty winks 3 nap **6** catnap, siesta, snooze **7** shut-eye

forum 5 court, panel **6** medium **8** congress, tribunal **9** symposium **10** colloquium, conference, roundtable **11** convocation, marketplace

forward 3 aid **4** abet, bold, send, ship **5** ahead, brash, eager, pushy, ready, relay, remit, sassy, saucy **6** cheeky, foster, onward, uphold **7** address, advance, consign, further, promote, support **8** advanced, champion, dispatch, impudent, transmit **9** encourage, in advance **11** smart-alecky **12** presumptuous **13** self-assertive ***prefix:* 4** ante

For Whom the Bell Tolls *author:* 9 Hemingway (Ernest) ***character:* 5** Maria, Pablo, Pilar **6** Jordan

Forza del Destino composer 5 Verdi (Giuseppe)

fossa 3 pit **5** fovea **6** cavity, groove **10** depression

fosse 4 dike, moat **5** canal, ditch **6** trench **7** acequia, channel

fossil 4 fogy **5** amber, fogey, relic **6** dotard **7** antique **8** calamite, conodont, mossback **10** antiquated, fuddy-duddy **12** antediluvian **13** stick-in-the-mud ***fuel:* 3** gas, oil **4** coal, peat **9** petroleum **10** natural gas

foster 4 back, help, rear, tend **5** nurse **6** assist, harbor, parent **7** advance, bring up, nourish, nurture, promote, support, sustain **8** champion **9** cultivate, encourage

fou 5 crazy, drunk

foul 4 base, rank, soil, vile **5** botch, dirty, fetid, funky, muddy, nasty, yucky **6** coarse, defile, filthy, grubby, horrid, impure, odious, putrid, rotten, scuzzy, smutty, stormy, turbid, vulgar, wicked **7** abusive, noisome, obscene, pollute, profane, raunchy, squalid, tarnish, unclean **8** indecent, obstruct, polluted, stinking, wretched **9** collision, loathsome, obnoxious, offensive, repellent, repugnant, repulsive, revolting **10** abominable, detestable, disgusting, malodorous **11** contaminate, treacherous **12** dishonorable, scatological

foul play 3 hit **5** blood **6** murder **7** killing, outrage **8** homicide, violence **12** manslaughter

found 4 base, cast, rear **5** begin, erect, raise, set up, start **6** bottom, create, invent **7** fashion, support **8** commence, initiate, organize **9** establish, institute, originate, predicate

foundation 3 bed **4** base, rock **5** basis **6** bottom, corset, makeup **7** bedding, footing, support **8** pedestal **9** endowment **10** groundwork, substratum **11** institution **12** organization, substructure, underpinning

foundational 5 basic **6** bottom **7** primary **10** supportive, underlying **11** fundamental

founder 4 fail, sink **5** wreck **6** author, father, go down **7** creator **8** collapse, inventor, submerge, submerse **9** architect, generator, patriarch, shipwreck **10** originator

foundling 6 infant, orphan

fountain 3 jet **4** head, root **5** spout **6** geyser, origin, source, spring **7** bubbler **8** wellhead **9** inception, reservoir **10** wellspring ***nymph:* 6** Egeria

four 6 tetrad **7** quartet **10** quaternion ***bagger:* 5** homer **7** home run ***combining form:* 4** tetr **5** quadr, tetra **6** quadri, quadru, quater, tessar **7** tessara, tessera ***gills:* 4** pint ***hundred:* 5** elite **10** upper crust ***inches:* 4** hand ***pecks:* 6** bushel ***quarts:* 6** gallon

four-flush 4 dupe **5** bluff **6** betray, delude, humbug, take in **7** beguile, deceive **11** doublecross

four-footed animal 8 tetrapod **9** quadruped

Four Horsemen 3 War **5** Death **6** Famine **8** Conquest **10** Pestilence

four-in-hand 3 tie **5** coach **7** necktie

fourpence 5 groat
four-poster 3 bed
fourscore 6 eighty
four-sided figure 5 rhomb **6** square **7** rhombus **9** rectangle **13** quadrilateral, parallelogram
foursquare 8 straight **10** forthright **13** quadrilateral
fourteen pounds 5 stone
fourth 7 quarter **8** quadrant, quartern ***combining form:*** **5** quadr, quart **6** quadri, quadru
fowl 3 hen **4** bird, cock, duck **5** chick, goose, poult **6** bantam, pullet, turkey **7** chicken, rooster (see also **chicken; poultry**)
Fowles novel 5 Magus (The) **9** Collector (The) **22** French Lieutenant's Woman (The)
fox 4 fool **5** trick **6** baffle, outwit **7** confuse, reynard **8** bewilder ***African:*** **4** asse ***female:*** **5** vixen ***kind:*** **3** kit, red **5** swift **6** arctic, fennec, silver **8** bat-eared ***Scottish:*** **3** tod ***young:*** **3** cub
foxglove 9 digitalis
fox grape 9 muscadine **11** scuppernong
foxiness 4 wile **5** craft, guile **7** cunning, slyness **8** wiliness **10** artfulness, craftiness, cleverness
foxlike 7 vulpine
foxy 3 sly **4** wily **5** canny, slick **6** artful, astute, clever, crafty, shrewd, tricky **7** cunning, vulpine **8** guileful **9** insidious
foyer 5 lobby **8** anteroom, entrance **9** vestibule
fracas 3 row **4** feud, fray, spat, to-do **5** brawl, broil, fight, melee, run-in, set-to **6** affray, hassle, shindy, uproar **7** dispute, quarrel, ruction **8** squabble **9** bickering **10** donnybrook, free-for-all **11** altercation
fraction 3 bit, cut **4** part **5** piece, scrap **6** divide, little **7** portion, section **8** fragment
fractious 4 wild **6** unruly **7** peevish, pettish, willful **8** contrary **9** bellicose, irritable **10** headstrong, pugnacious, refractory **11** belligerent, contentious, intractable, quarrelsome **12** recalcitrant, ungovernable, unmanageable
fracture 4 rent, rift, tear **5** break, cleft, crack, split **6** breach, schism **7** rupture
Fra Diavolo composer 5 Auber (Esprit)
fragile 4 weak **5** frail **6** feeble, flimsy, infirm **7** brittle, friable, tenuous, unsound **8** decrepit, delicate **9** breakable, frangible
fragment 3 bit **4** chip, iota, part, rive **5** burst, crumb, flake, grain, piece, scrap, shard, sherd, shred, smash **6** morsel, shiver, sliver **7** break up, flinder, shatter **8** fraction, particle, splinter **9** fall apart **12** disintegrate
fragmentary 6 broken **7** partial **10** fractional, incomplete, unfinished
fragrance 4 musk, nose, odor **5** aroma, attar, scent, smell, spice **7** bouquet, cologne, incense, perfume **9** redolence **11** eau de parfum, toilet water **13** eau de toilette
fragrant 7 odorous, scented **8** aromatic, perfumed, redolent **11** odoriferous
frail 4 puny, slim, thin, weak **5** petty, reedy, wispy **6** feeble, flimsy, infirm, sickly, slight **7** brittle, fragile, slender, spindly, tenuous, unsound **8** decrepit, delicate **9** breakable, frangible
frailty 4 vice **5** fault **6** foible **7** failing **8** delicacy, weakness **9** infirmity **10** feebleness
frame 4 body, form, mold, plan, sash **5** build, draft, erect, forge, mount, shape, shell **6** border, casing, cook up, devise, draw up, figure, invent, make up, sketch, system **7** arrange, chassis, concoct, fashion, imagine, prepare **8** assemble, casement, conceive, contrive, regulate, skeleton **9** cartouche, construct, fabricate, formulate, structure ***part:*** **4** sill, stud **5** joist, plate
framework 4 rack **5** shell, truss **7** trestle **8** cribbing, cribwork, scaffold, skeleton, studding, studwork, trussing **9** bare bones, structure ***of crossed strips:*** **7** lattice, trellis
France *bay:* **6** Biscay ***capital:*** **5** Paris ***channel:*** **6** Manche (La) **7** English ***city:*** **4** Caen, Lyon, Metz, Nice **5** Brest, Lyons **6** Amiens, Calais, Nantes, Rennes **8** Bordeaux, Grenoble, Toulouse **9** Marseille **10** Marseilles, Strasbourg, Versailles **11** Montpellier ***conqueror:*** **6** Caesar (Julius) ***department:*** **3** Var **4** Aude, Gard, Jura, Orne **5** Marne, Rhône, Somme **6** Savoie, Vosges **7** Bas-Rhin **8** Ardennes, Calvados ***emperor:*** **5** Pepin (III, the Short) **8** Napoleon (Bonaparte) **11** Charlemagne ***enclave:*** **6** Monaco ***former name:*** **4** Gaul **6** Gallia ***hero:*** **6** Clovis ***heroine:*** **9** Joan of Arc ***historic province:*** **4** Foix **5** Anjou, Aunis, Bearn, Berry, Maine **6** Alsace, Artois, Marche, Poitou, Vendée **7** Gascony, Guyenne, Picardy **8** Auvergne, Bretagne, Brittany, Burgundy, Dauphine, Flanders, Gascogne, Limousin, Lorraine, Lyonnais, Normandy, Picardie, Provence, Touraine **9** Angoumois, Bourgogne, Champagne, Languedoc, Nivernois, Orléanais, Saintonge, Venaissin **10** Roussillon **11** Bourbonnais, Île-de-France **12** Franche-Comté ***island:*** **3** Yeu **6** Hyères, Oléron, Ushant **7** Corsica **8** Belle-Île **11** Noirmoutier ***monarch:*** **5** Henri, Henry, Louis **6** Philip **7** Charles **8** Philippe ***monetary unit:*** **4** euro ***monetary unit, former:*** **3** sou **5** franc ***moun-***

tain, range: **4** Alps, Jura **6** Vosges **8** Auvergne, Pyrenees **9** Mont Blanc ***neighbor:*** **5** Italy, Spain **7** Andorra, Belgium, Germany **10** Luxembourg **11** Switzerland ***president:*** **6** Chirac (Jacques) **8** de Gaulle (Charles) **10** Mitterrand (François) ***region:*** **4** Midi **5** Corse **6** Alsace, Centre **7** Corsica, Picardy **8** Auvergne, Bretagne, Brittany, Burgundy, Limousin, Normandy, Picardie **9** Aquitaine, Bourgogne, Champagne, Languedoc, Normandie **10** Rhône-Alpes **11** Île-de-France **12** Franche-Comté, Midi-Pyrénées ***river:*** **4** Aire, Aude, Oise **5** Adour, Isère, Loire, Marne, Rhone, Saône, Seine, Somme, Yonne **7** Garonne ***sea:*** **13** Mediterranean ***spa city:*** **5** Evian ***strait:*** **5** Dover ***symbol:*** **8** Marianne

Francesca's lover 5 Paolo

franchise 4 vote **6** ballot **7** freedom, license **8** suffrage **9** privilege

frangible 7 brittle, fragile, friable **8** delicate **9** breakable

frank 3 dog **4** fair, free, open **5** blunt, plain **6** candid, direct, honest, hot dog, weenie, wiener, wienie **7** upright **8** man-to-man, out-front, straight **9** barefaced, outspoken **10** forthright, scrupulous, unreserved **11** openhearted, plainspoken, transparent, unconcealed, undisguised, uninhibited, unvarnished, wienerwurst **12** heart-to-heart, unmistakable

Frankenstein *author:* 7 Shelley (Mary) ***helper:*** **4** Igor

frankfurter 3 dog **6** hot dog, weenie, wiener, wienie **11** wienerwurst

Frankie's lover 6 Johnny

Frankish hero 6 Roland

Franklin, Benjamin *birthplace:* 6 Boston ***invention:*** **5** stove **8** bifocals ***pen name:*** **11** Poor Richard

frankness 6 candor **7** honesty

frantic 3 mad **4** wild **5** upset, wired **7** fraught, shook up, unglued **8** feverish, frenetic, frenzied, maniacal, worked up **10** distraught **11** overwrought

Franzen novel 11 Corrections (The)

frappe 7 chilled, liqueur **9** milk shake

fraternal 6 clubby **8** sociable **9** brotherly, comradely, dizygotic **10** like-minded

fraternal society 3 FOE, KOC, SAR **4** BPOE, Elks **5** Lions, Moose **6** Eagles, Masons, Rotary **7** Kiwanis, Woodmen **8** Shriners **10** Freemasons, Hibernians, Odd Fellows

fraternity 4 club **5** guild, order, union **6** league **7** company **8** sodality **10** fellowship **11** association, brotherhood **13** brotherliness

fraud 3 con, gyp **4** fake, gaff, hoax, scam, sham **5** cheat, faker, phony, quack, trick **6** deceit, dupery, humbug, hustle, phoney **7** chicane, con game, swindle **8** cozenage, flimflam, impostor, operator, trickery **9** charlatan, chicanery, deception, imposture, pretender, shell game, trickster **10** dishonesty, mountebank, subterfuge **11** counterfeit **12** double-dealer **13** double-dealing, sharp practice

fraudulence 6 deceit **8** quackery, trickery **9** chicanery, deception, phoniness **10** dishonesty

fraudulent 4 fake **5** false, phony **7** crooked **8** cheating, guileful **9** deceitful, deceptive, dishonest **10** fallacious **11** duplicitous

fraught 4 full **5** laden, tense **6** filled, uneasy **7** charged, replete, stuffed **8** pregnant **9** stressful

fräulein 4 maid, Miss **6** maiden **9** governess **12** mademoiselle

fray 3 row **4** fret **5** brawl, broil, brush, clash, fight, melee, ravel, shred **6** combat, fracas, strain, strife **7** dispute, frazzle, ruction, scuffle **8** irritate, skirmish, struggle **9** commotion, scrimmage **10** donnybrook **11** disturbance

frayed 4 worn **6** tatty **6** ragged, shabby **8** tattered **9** moth-eaten **10** threadbare

frazzle 4 do in, fray, poop, tire, wear **5** upset **6** tucker **7** exhaust, fatigue, wear out

frazzled 4 beat **5** upset **6** bushed, sapped **7** drained, rattled **8** agitated, confused, fatigued, tired out **9** exhausted, fagged out, unsettled **10** distressed **11** overwrought **12** disconcerted

freak 3 bug, nut **4** buff, geek, whim **5** go ape, fancy, fiend, maven **6** addict, hippie, maniac, megrim, oddity, vagary, weirdo, whimsy, zealot **7** anomaly, caprice, chimera, conceit, deviate, fanatic, monster **8** crotchet, flimflam **9** androgyne, curiosity **10** aberration, enthusiast **11** abnormality, monstrosity **12** lusus naturae, malformation

freakish 3 odd **5** kooky, outré, weird **6** far-out, quirky **7** bizarre, erratic, oddball, strange **8** aberrant, abnormal **9** arbitrary, eccentric, grotesque, whimsical **10** capricious, outlandish

freckle 3 dot **4** mole, spot **5** fleck **7** speckle, stipple

free 3 rid **4** comp, open **5** frank, loose, untie **6** acquit, exempt, gratis, loosen, unbind, untied **7** absolve, at large, donated, liberal, manumit, movable, pro bono, release, unbound, unchain, unleash, unloose **8** detached, generous, liberate, separate, unfasten, unloosen **9** at liberty, discharge, exculpate, exonerate, extricate, sovereign, unchained, unchecked, unimpeded, unshackle, unsparing, voluntary **10** autonomous, democratic, emancipate, gratuitous, unconfined, unfettered, unshackled **11** disentangle, emancipated, independent, spontaneous, untrammeled **12** unrestrained, unrestricted **13** complimentary, self-governing, unconstrained

freebie 4 comp, gift, pass **7** present **8** give-away

freebooter 5 rover **6** bandit, pirate, raider **7** brigand, corsair **8** marauder, picaroon, pillager, rapparee, sea rover **9** buccaneer, pickaroon, plunderer, ransacker

freedom 5 right **7** liberty, license, release **8** autonomy, immunity, latitude **9** exemption, franchise, privilege **11** prerogative **12** emancipation, independence **13** outspokenness ***Swahili:*** **5** uhuru

free-for-all 4 fray **5** brawl, broil, melee **6** affray, fracas, rumble **7** ruction **10** donnybrook

freehanded 7 liberal **8** generous **9** bounteous, bountiful **10** munificent

freeloader 3 bum **5** leech **6** cadger, sponge **7** moocher **8** barnacle, hanger-on, parasite **11** bloodsucker

Free State 8 Maryland

free ticket 4 pass **11** Annie Oakley

freeze 4 halt, stop **5** chill, stall **6** benumb **7** congeal **8** glaciate, solidify, stoppage **10** immobilize

freezing 3 icy **4** cold **5** chill, gelid, nippy, polar **6** arctic, bitter, chilly, frigid, frosty, wintry **7** glacial, shivery ***combining form:*** **4** cryo, kryo

freight 4 haul, lade, load **5** cargo **6** burden, charge, lading **7** payload **9** transport

freighter 4 scow, ship **7** carrier, shipper **9** cargo ship **11** bulk carrier

Freischütz composer 5 Weber (Carl Maria von)

French *article:* **2** la, le, un **3** les, une ***attendant:*** **9** concierge ***back:*** **3** dos ***bed:*** **3** lit **6** couche ***black:*** **4** noir ***born:*** **3** née ***boy:*** **6** garçon ***brother:*** **5** frère ***cap:*** **5** beret ***cardinal:*** **7** Mazarin (Jules) **9** Richelieu (Duc de) ***castle:*** **7** château ***cathedral city:*** **4** Albi **5** Paris, Reims, Rouen **6** Amiens, Nantes, Rheims **8** Chartres ***clergyman:*** **4** abbé, curé, père ***coin:*** **3** ecu ***cold:*** **5** froid ***combining form:*** **5** Gallo **6** Franco ***conjunction:*** **2** et, ou **4** mais ***daughter:*** **5** fille ***day:*** **5** jeudi, lundi, mardi **6** samedi **8** dimanche, mercredi, vendredi ***dear:*** **4** cher ***department head:*** **7** prefect ***direction:*** **3** est, sud **4** nord **5** ouest ***down with:*** **4** à bas ***dream:*** **4** rêve ***drink:*** **5** boire ***dynasty:*** **5** Capet **6** Valois **7** Bourbon ***egg:*** **4** oeuf ***emblem:*** **10** fleur-de-lis ***empress:*** **7** Eugénie **9** Joséphine ***evening:*** **4** soir ***exclamation:*** **3** zut **4** eheu, hein **9** sacrebleu ***eye:*** **4** oeil ***farewell:*** **5** adieu **8** au revoir ***farmhouse:*** **5** ferme ***father:*** **4** père ***forest:*** **7** Argonne, Belleau ***friend:*** **3** ami **4** amie ***game:*** **3** jeu **4** jeux (plural) ***God:*** **4** dieu ***good:*** **3** bon **5** bonne ***gray:*** **4** gris ***hat:*** **7** chapeau ***head:*** **4** tête ***here:*** **3** ici ***income:*** **5** rente ***island:*** **3** île ***king:*** **3** roi ***language:*** **9** Provençal ***leather:*** **4** cuir ***length:*** **4** aune ***mask:*** **4** loup ***milk:*** **4** lait ***month:*** **3** mai **4** août, juin, mars, mois **5** avril **7** février, janvier, juillet ***mother:*** **4** mère ***nail:*** **4** clou ***national anthem:*** **12** Marseillaise (La) ***nose:*** **3** nez ***nothing:*** **4** rien ***number:*** **3** dix, six **4** cinq, deux, huit, neuf, onze, sept **5** douze, trois **6** quatre ***opera:*** **5** Faust, Lakmé, Manon, Thaïs **6** Carmen, Mignon **7** Werther ***pancake:*** **5** crêpe ***pastry:*** **6** éclair **8** napoleon ***poem:*** **3** dit ***policeman:*** **4** flic **8** gendarme ***porcelain:*** **6** Sèvres **7** Limoges ***preposition:*** **2** de **3** par, sur **4** avec, dans, pour, sans, sous ***pretty:*** **4** joli **5** jolie ***prison:*** **8** Bastille ***pronoun:*** **2** il, je, te, tu, un **3** eux, ils, mes, moi, toi, une **4** elle, nous, vous ***Protestant:*** **6** Calvin (John) **8** Huguenot ***pupil:*** **5** élève ***queen:*** **5** reine ***quick:*** **4** vite ***rabbit:*** **5** lapin ***railroad station:*** **4** gare ***resort:*** **3** Pau **4** Nice **5** Vichy **6** Cannes, Menton **7** Antibes **8** Biarritz ***resort area:*** **7** Riviera ***restaurant:*** **6** bistro ***revolutionist:*** **5** Marat (Jean-Paul) **6** Danton (Georges) **11** Robespierre (Maximilien) ***Revolution party:*** **7** Gironde, Jacobin **8** Mountain ***Revolution song:*** **5** Ça Ira ***roasted:*** **4** rôti ***room:*** **5** salle ***saint:*** **4** Joan (of Arc) **5** Denis **6** Martin (of Tours) **7** Thérèse (of Lisieux) ***school:*** **5** école, lycée ***sea:*** **3** mer ***season:*** **3** été **5** hiver **7** automne **9** printemps ***servant:*** **5** valet ***sherry:*** **5** xérès ***shooting match:*** **3** tir ***shop:*** **8** boutique ***shrine:*** **7** Lourdes ***singer:*** **4** Piaf (Edith) **8** chanteur **9** chanteuse ***sister:*** **5** soeur ***small:*** **5** petit **6** petite ***soldier:*** **5** poilu **6** soldat, Zouave **8** chasseur ***son:*** **4** fils ***song:*** **3** dit **7** chanson ***soup:*** **6** potage ***star:*** **6** étoile ***state:*** **4** état ***stock exchange:*** **6** bourse ***street:*** **3** rue ***subway:*** **5** metro ***summer:*** **3** été ***there!:*** **5** voilà ***too much:*** **4** trop ***very:*** **4** très ***wartime capital:*** **5** Vichy ***water:*** **3** eau ***well:*** **4** bien ***wine:*** **3** vin ***wineshop:*** **6** bistro ***wood:*** **4** bois ***yes:*** **3** oui ***yesterday:*** **4** hier

French Guiana *capital:* **7** Cayenne ***ethnic***

group: **6** Creole ***island:*** **6** Devil's ***mountain range:*** **10** Tumac-Humac ***neighbor:*** **6** Brazil **8** Suriname ***river:*** **4** Mana **6** Maroni **7** Oyapock

French Polynesia ***archipelag:*** **7** Tuamotu ***capital:*** **7** Papeete ***island, island group:*** **6** Tahiti **7** Austral, Gambier, Society **9** Marquesas

frenetic 3 mad **4** loco, wild **5** crazy, wired **6** crazed, hectic **7** berserk, frantic **8** agitated, feverish, frenzied, maniacal **9** delirious, orgiastic **10** corybantic

frenzied see **frenetic**

frenzy 4 amok, fury, rage **5** amuck, craze, furor, mania **6** madden **7** derange, madness, unhinge **8** delirium, distract, hysteria, insanity, paroxysm **9** unbalance **11** derangement

frequency unit 5 hertz **7** fresnel **9** gigahertz

frequent 5 haunt, often, usual, visit **6** common, hourly **7** regular **8** everyday, familiar, habitual **9** customary

frequenter 7 denizen, habitué, haunter

frequently 4 a lot **5** often **8** commonly **9** routinely **10** oftentimes, repeatedly **11** customarily, recurrently

fresh 3 new, raw **4** rude **5** green, lippy, naive, novel, sassy, saucy, smart **6** callow, cheeky, recent, unused, vernal, virgin **8** brand-new, impudent, insolent, original **9** unspoiled **11** impertinent, smart-alecky **12** invigorating **13** inexperienced

freshet 5 flood, spate **6** influx

freshman 4 pleb, tyro **5** frosh, plebe **6** novice, rookie **8** beginner, neophyte, newcomer **10** apprentice, tenderfoot

fret 4 fume, fuss, stew **5** brood, chafe, worry **6** dither, pother

fretful 5 angry, cross **6** crabby, cranky **7** carping, chafing, peevish, pettish, whining **8** captious, caviling, critical, perverse, petulant, restless, snappish **9** fractious, impatient, irascible, irritable, querulous

Freudian term 2 id **3** ego **5** drive **6** denial, libido **7** complex, Oedipal **8** analysis, cathexis, fixation, neurosis, superego **9** analysand, disavowal, dreamwork, fetishism, psychosis **10** parapraxis, projection, regression, repression **11** association, sublimation, unconscious **12** condensation, displacement, preconscious, transference

Frey ***father:*** **5** Njörd **6** Njörth ***god of:*** **3** sun **4** rain **5** peace **9** fertility ***sister:*** **5** Freya ***wife:*** **4** Gerd **5** Gerda, Gerth

Freya ***brother:*** **4** Frey ***domain:*** **9** Folkvangr ***father:*** **5** Njörd **6** Njörth

friable 5 mealy **7** brittle, crumbly, fragile **9** frangible

friar 7 brother **8** cenobite **9** mendicant

fribble 3 toy **5** dally, flirt **6** coquet, trifle **7** trifler **8** trifling **9** dalliance, frivolity **10** dilly-dally, fool around

friction 4 drag **7** discord, rubbing **8** abrasion **9** animosity, attrition **10** disharmony, dissension, resistance **12** disagreement

friction match 5 vesta **7** lucifer **8** vesuvian

Friday's rescuer 6 Crusoe (Robinson)

friend 3 pal **4** ally, chum, mate, pard **5** buddy, crony, matey, serve **6** cohort **7** comrade, partner **8** alter ego, compadre, confrere, familiar, intimate, playmate, sidekick **9** colleague, companion, confidant **10** confidante ***French:*** **3** ami **4** amie ***Maori:*** **4** ehoa ***Spanish:*** **5** amiga, amigo

Friend 6 Quaker ***founder:*** **3** Fox (George)

friendly 5 happy **6** amical, chummy, folksy, genial **7** affable, amiable, cordial **8** amicable, cheerful, familiar, sociable **9** congenial, favorable **10** buddy-buddy, compatible, hospitable, neighborly **12** affectionate, well-disposed **13** accommodating

Friendly Islands 5 Tonga

Friends series ***character:*** **4** Joey, Ross **6** Monica, Phoebe, Rachel **8** Chandler ***setting:*** **9** Manhattan ***star:*** **3** Cox (Courteney) **5** Perry (Matthew) **6** Kudrow (Lisa) **7** Aniston (Jennifer), LeBlanc (Matt) **9** Schwimmer (David)

friends and neighbors 4 kith

friendship 5 amity **6** accord, comity **7** concord, empathy, harmony **8** affinity, alliance, goodwill

frigate bird 3 ioa, iwa **8** alcatras **11** man-o'-war bird ***genus:*** **7** Fregata

Frigga, Frigg ***husband:*** **4** Odin **5** Woden ***son:*** **6** Balder, Baldur

fright 4 fear **5** alarm, dread, panic, scare, shock **6** dismay, horror, terror **11** trepidation

frighten 3 cow **5** alarm, bully, daunt, scare, shock, spook **6** appall, dismay **7** horrify, perturb, scarify, startle, terrify, unnerve **9** terrorize **10** intimidate

frightful 4 ugly **5** awful, scary **6** horrid **7** fearful, ghastly, hideous **8** alarming, dreadful, fearsome, horrible, horrific, shocking, terrible, terrific **9** appalling, startling **10** formidable, horrendous, terrifying

frigid 3 icy **4** cold **5** chill **6** arctic, chilly, frosty **7** glacial **8** freezing **11** emotionless, indifferent, passionless, unemotional **12** unresponsive

frijoles 5 beans

frill 4 ruff **5** jabot, ruche **6** doodad, luxury,

ruffle **7** flounce, ruching **8** furbelow **11** affectation, superfluity **12** extravagance

fringe 3 hem, rim **4** brim, ruff **5** bound, brink, skirt, thrum, verge **6** border, edging, margin **7** fimbria **8** penumbra, trimming **9** perimeter, periphery **10** borderland

frippery 6 finery, frills, tawdry **7** regalia **8** foofaraw, trumpery **9** trappings **11** ostentation

frisée 6 endive **7** lettuce

frisk 4 leap, play, romp, skip **5** caper, dance **6** cavort, frolic, gambol, search **7** disport, pat down, rollick

frisky 3 gay **5** antic **6** feisty, lively **7** coltish, playful **8** animated, gamesome, sportive **9** sprightly, vivacious **10** frolicsome

fritter away 4 blow **5** spend, waste **7** consume **8** squander **9** dissipate

frivolity 3 fun **4** play **6** gaiety, levity, whimsy **8** nonsense **12** childishness

frivolous 3 gay **4** idle **5** ditsy, ditzy, dizzy, giddy, light, silly **6** breezy, frothy, yeasty **7** flighty, playful, shallow, trivial **8** carefree, careless, heedless, trifling **11** light-headed, superficial

frizzy 5 kinky **6** coiled, curled **7** twisted

frock 4 gown **5** dress, habit **6** jersey, mantle

Frodo's pal 3 Sam

frog 4 toad **5** ranid **6** anuran **7** croaker **9** amphibian **10** batrachian ***family:*** **7** Ranidae ***genus:*** **4** Rana ***kind:*** **4** hyla **5** coqui **6** peeper **7** leopard **8** bullfrog, tree toad ***larva:*** **7** tadpole

frolic 3 fun **4** lark, play, romp **5** antic, caper, dance, frisk, party, prank, revel, sport, spree **6** cavort, didoes, gaiety, gambol, prance **7** disport, skylark **8** escapade, hilarity **9** festivity, merriment **10** shenanigan, tomfoolery

frolicsome 3 gay **5** antic **6** frisky, impish **7** coltish, jocular, playful, roguish **8** sportful, sportive **9** sprightly **10** rollicking **11** mischievous

from *German:* **3** von ***Scottish:*** **4** frae

From Here to Eternity author 5 Jones (James)

frondeur 5 rebel **8** mutineer, renegade **9** anarchist, dissident, insurgent **10** malcontent

front 3 bow, van **4** face, fore, lend, look, mask, prow **5** beard **6** facade, facing **7** forward **8** anterior, disguise **9** challenge, encounter **10** appearance, figurehead **11** countenance

frontier 5 bound, field, march **6** border **8** backland, backwash, boundary **9** upcountry **10** borderland, hinterland **11** backcountry

frontiersman 5 Boone (Daniel), Clark (George Rogers, William) **6** Carson (Kit) **7** Frémont (J. C.), pioneer, settler **8** Crockett (Davy) **10** bushranger

fronton game 7 jai alai

frontward 8 anterior

frost 4 hoar, rime **6** freeze

frostfish 5 smelt **6** tomcod

frost heave 5 pingo

frosting 5 icing **7** topping **8** trimming

Frost poem 7 Birches **10** Fire and Ice **11** Mending Wall **12** Road Not Taken (The) **18** Death of the Hired Man (The) **30** Stopping By Woods on a Snowy Evening

frosty 3 icy **4** cold, rimy **5** chill, frore, hoary, nippy **6** chilly, frigid **7** glacial **8** freezing **10** unfriendly

Frosty's eyes 4 coal

froth 4 foam, head, suds **5** cream, spume, yeast **6** lather **8** airiness **9** frivolity, lightness

froufrou 6 frills **8** rustling

froward 5 balky **6** mulish, ornery **7** peevish, restive **8** contrary, perverse, petulant, stubborn **9** obstinate **10** headstrong, refractory **11** disobedient

frown 4 pout, sulk **5** glare, lower, scowl **6** glower

frowsy 5 dowdy, funky, fusty, messy, musty, stale **6** shabby, smelly, sordid, untidy **7** squalid, unkempt **8** slattern, slovenly **10** disheveled, disordered, slatternly **13** draggle-tailed

frozen 4 cold, hard **5** fixed, frore, rigid, stiff **6** frigid, iced up, numbed **7** chilled **8** benumbed, immobile **9** congealed, petrified

frugal 4 mean **5** canny, scant, spare **6** Scotch, stingy **7** careful, prudent, scrimpy, sparing, thrifty **8** discreet, stinting **9** niggardly, penurious, provident **10** economical, unwasteful **12** cheeseparing, parsimonious **13** penny-pinching

frugality 6 thrift **7** economy **8** prudence **9** husbandry **10** providence **11** thriftiness

fruit 3 fig, nut **4** ansu, date, lime, pear, pepo, plum, pome, seed, sloe **5** apple, berry, drupe, gourd, grape, guava, issue, lemon, mango, melon, olive, papaw, peach, prune, young **6** achene, banana, casaba, cherry, citron, durian, legume, loment, loquat, orange, papaya, pawpaw, pomelo, quince, result, samara **7** acerola, apricot, avocado, capsule, coconut, currant, kumquat, outcome, progeny, silique, syconia (plural), tangelo, utricle **8** bergamot, dewberry, mandarin, rambutan, shaddock, syconium, tamarind **9** blueberry, cherimoya, cranberry, muskmelon, nectarine, offspring, persimmon, pineapple, raspberry, tangerine **10** blackberry, calamondin, gooseberry, grapefruit, loganberry, mangosteen, strawberry **11** boysenberry, hesperidium, huckleberry, pomegranate ***dried:*** **5** prune **6** raisin ***drink:*** **3** ade **5** juice, punch ***residue:*** **4** marc **6** pomace ***seed:*** **3** pip ***study of:*** **8** pomology **9** carpology ***sugar:*** **7** glucose **8** fructose, levulose ***undeveloped:*** **6** nubbin

fruitful **6** fecund **7** copious, fertile **8** abundant, prolific **9** bountiful, fructuous, plenteous, plentiful **10** productive **11** proliferant

fruition **7** delight **8** pleasure **9** enjoyment **10** attainment, conclusion **11** achievement, delectation, fulfillment, realization

fruitless **4** vain **6** barren, futile **7** sterile, useless **8** abortive **10** unavailing **11** ineffective, ineffectual **12** unproductive, unsuccessful

frumpy **4** drab, dull **5** dated, dowdy, tacky **6** stodgy **8** outmoded **9** out-of-date, unstylish **12** old-fashioned

frustrate **4** balk, bilk, dash, foil, halt **5** block, check, stump **6** arrest, baffle, defeat, hinder, impede, stymie, thwart **7** inhibit, prevent **8** confound, obstruct, preclude, prohibit **9** discomfit, forestall, interrupt **10** disappoint

frustration **6** defeat, dismay **7** chagrin, letdown **8** vexation **9** annoyance, hindrance **10** impediment, irritation **11** displeasure, obstruction

fry **4** burn, sear **5** frizz, grill, sauté **6** fishes, picnic **7** frizzle **11** electrocute

frying pan **6** spider **7** griddle, skillet

fuddle **5** befog, booze **6** ball up, jumble, tipple **7** confuse, fluster, stupefy **8** bewilder **10** intoxicate

fuddy-duddy **4** fogy **5** fogey **6** fossil, square, stodgy **8** mossback, outdated, outmoded **12** antediluvian, Colonel Blimp, old-fashioned, stuffed shirt **13** stick-in-the-mud

fudge **3** pad **4** blur, bosh, fake **5** candy, cheat, color, dodge, hedge, hooey, welsh **6** bunkum **7** distort, falsify, hogwash, penuche **8** contrive, divinity, nonsense **9** embellish, embroider, overstate, poppycock **10** equivocate, flapdoodle **11** foolishness

fuel **3** gas, oil **4** coal, coke, fire, peat, wood **5** stoke **6** biogas, diesel, petrol, Sterno **7** ethanol, gasohol, inflame, propane **8** charcoal, gasoline, kerosene **9** biodiesel, petroleum, stimulate **10** natural gas **13** reinforcement ***jelled:*** **6** napalm

Fuentes novel **4** Aura **9** Old Gringo (The)

fugacious **7** brittle, passing **8** fleeting, fugitive, volatile **9** ephemeral, momentary, transient **10** evanescent, short-lived, transitory

fugitive **5** exile **6** outlaw **7** escapee, lamster, nomadic, passing, refugee, runaway **8** deserter, fleeting, runagate, vagabond **9** ephemeral, fugacious, momentary, transient, wandering **10** evanescent, short-lived, transitory

fugue master **4** Bach (Johann Sebastian)

Führer, der **6** Hitler (Adolf)

fulcrum **3** hub **4** axis, prop **5** hinge, nexus, pivot **7** support

fulfill **4** meet **5** honor **6** effect, finish, redeem **7** achieve, execute, perform, satisfy **8** complete **9** discharge, implement **10** accomplish

fulgent **6** bright **7** beaming, glowing, radiant, shining **8** luminous, lustrous **9** brilliant

fuliginous **4** dark **5** dingy, dusky, grimy, murky, sooty **7** obscure

full **5** sated, total, whole **6** entire, gorged, jammed, loaded, packed, utmost **7** crammed, crowded, glutted, maximum, plenary, replete, stuffed **8** brimming, complete, satiated **9** jam-packed, plentiful, surfeited **11** chockablock

full-blooded **4** rich **5** flush, ruddy **6** ardent, florid **7** flushed, genuine, glowing **8** forceful, purebred, rubicund, sanguine **9** pedigreed, pureblood **10** compelling **12** thoroughbred

full-blown **4** lush, ripe **5** adult, total **6** all-out, mature **7** grown-up

full-bodied **4** rich **5** husky, lusty, stout **6** potent, robust, strong **9** corpulent **10** meaningful **11** significant, substantial

full dress **6** finery **7** regalia **8** frippery, glad rags **10** Sunday best

full-figured **5** ample, buxom, plump **6** zaftig **10** curvaceous, Rubenesque, statuesque, voluptuous

full-fledged **4** ripe **5** adult, grown, total **6** mature **7** genuine, grown-up **8** complete **9** full-blown

full-grown **4** ripe **5** adult **6** mature

fullness **6** plenty **7** satiety **9** abundance, amplitude, repletion **10** perfection **12** completeness

full-scale **5** total **6** all-out **8** complete, life-size **9** unlimited

full tilt **7** flat-out, rapidly, swiftly **8** pell-mell, speedily **9** posthaste **12** lickety-split

fulminate **4** boil, burn, foam, fume, rage, rail, rave **5** curse, flare **7** bluster, explode, inveigh

fulsome **4** oily **5** plump, slick, soapy, suave **6** lavish, smarmy, smooth **7** buttery, cloying, copious, profuse **8** abundant, effusive, generous, overdone, unctuous **9** excessive **10** flattering, oleaginous **11** extravagant, pharisaical **12** ingratiating, Pecksniffian

Fulton's steamboat **8** Clermont

fumarole **4** vent

fumble **3** bob, err, paw **4** feel, flub, mess, muff **5** botch, grope **6** bobble, bollix, bungle, muddle **7** blunder, misplay **8** flounder

fume **3** gas **4** boil, burn, odor, rage, rant, rave, reek, snit, stew **5** smoke, vapor **6** seethe, swivet **7** sputter

fun **4** play **5** sport **6** frolic, gaiety **7** amusing, jollity, pastime, whoopee **8** hilarity, pleasant, ridicule **9** amusement, diversion, diverting, enjoyment, frivolity, horseplay, jocundity, joviality, merriment **10** pleasantry **12** entertaining **13** entertainment

function **3** act, job, run, use **4** duty, goal, mark, role, task, work **5** party, power, react, serve **6** affair, behave, object, office, target **7** concern, faculty, operate, perform, purpose, service **8** activity, behavior, business, capacity, ceremony, occasion, province **9** objective, officiate, operation, reception ***trigonometric:*** **4** sine **6** cosine, secant **7** tangent **8** cosecant **9** cotangent

functional **5** handy, utile **6** useful **7** working **9** practical **11** practicable, serviceable, utilitarian **12** occupational

functioning **6** active **7** dynamic **9** operative

fund **4** back, bank, pool **5** endow, stake, stock, store **6** coffer, supply **7** capital, finance, reserve, support **8** bankroll, treasury **9** inventory, subsidize **10** accumulate, capitalize

fundament **3** bum **4** butt, rear, rump, seat **5** basis, fanny **6** behind, bottom **8** backside, buttocks, derriere **9** posterior, principle **10** foundation, groundwork

fundamental **3** key **5** axiom, basal, basic, prime, vital **6** bottom, factor, primal, simple **7** bedrock, organic, primary, radical, theorem **8** absolute, cardinal, dominant, ultimate **9** component, essential, important, necessary, paramount, primitive, principal, principle, requisite **10** deep-rooted, elementary, grassroots, primordial, rock-bottom, underlying **11** constituent, irreducible, nitty-gritty **12** constitutive, foundational

fund-raiser **8** telethon

funeral **6** burial **7** obsequy **9** obsequies ***car:*** **6** hearse ***director:*** **9** mortician **10** undertaker ***oration:*** **6** eulogy **8** encomium **9** panegyric ***procession:*** **7** cortege ***service:*** **7** requiem **9** obsequies ***song:*** **5** dirge, elegy **8** threnody

funereal **3** sad **4** dark **5** black, bleak, grave **6** dismal, dreary, gloomy, solemn, somber, sombre **7** elegiac **8** mournful **9** deathlike, sorrowful **10** depressing, depressive, lugubrious, oppressive, sepulchral

fungus **4** conk, mold, rust, smut **5** ergot, yeast **6** agaric, dry rot, mildew **7** candida, truffle **8** mushroom, puffball **9** earthstar, stinkhorn, toadstool ***combining form:*** **4** myco **5** myces, mycet **6** mycete, myceto ***part:*** **3** cap **4** gill **5** ascus, hypha, stipe, volva **7** annulus **8** basidium, conidium, mycelium ***rust:*** **5** Uredo

fungus disease **3** rot **4** mold, rust, scab, smut **5** ergot, tinea **6** blight, mildew, thrush **7** mycosis **8** lumpy jaw, ringworm **12** athlete's foot

funk **4** odor, reek **5** blues, dolor, dumps, ennui, gloom, smell, stink, slump **6** recoil, stench **7** sadness **9** dejection **10** depression, melancholy

funky **3** hip, odd **4** foul, rank **5** fetid, reeky **6** earthy, frowsy, grungy, quaint, quirky, smelly, stinky **7** natural, noisome, oddball, offbeat **8** down-home **10** malodorous

funnel **4** flue, pipe **5** stack **6** hopper **7** channel, conduct, tornado, tundish, twister **8** transmit **10** smokestack

funny **3** odd **4** joke, zany **5** antic, comic, droll, fishy, queer **7** amusing, bizarre, comical, jocular, risible, strange **8** farcical, humorous, peculiar **9** facetious, fantastic, hilarious, laughable, ludicrous **10** ridiculous

Funny Girl **5** Brice (Fanny) ***composer:*** **5** Styne (Jule) ***star:*** **9** Streisand (Barbra)

funnyman **3** wag, wit **5** clown, comic, cutup, droll, joker **6** gagman, jester **8** comedian, humorist, jokester, quipster **10** comedienne

fur **4** down, hide, pelt, pile **5** floss, fluff, stole **6** pelage, peltry ***kind:*** **3** fox **4** mink, seal **5** coypu, fitch, otter, sable **6** ermine, fisher, marten, nutria, rabbit, tanuki **7** raccoon **10** chinchilla ***lamb:*** **7** caracul, karakul **9** broadtail ***medieval:*** **4** vair **7** miniver

furbelow **5** frill **7** flounce

furbish **4** buff **5** fix up, renew, shine **6** polish, revive **7** burnish, refresh, restore **8** renovate

Furies **6** Alecto **7** Erinyes, Megaera **9** Eumenides, Tisiphone

furious **3** mad **4** wild **5** angry, livid, irate, rabid, upset **6** crazed, fierce, insane, raging, stormy **7** enraged, excited, extreme, frantic, intense, violent **8** feverish, frenetic, frenzied, incensed, maddened, vehement, wrathful **9** impetuous, turbulent **10** boisterous, corybantic

furl **4** curl, fold, roll, wrap **6** take in

furlough **4** pass **5** leave **6** lay off **7** liberty **10** shore leave **13** authorization

furnace **4** kiln, oven **5** forge, stove **6** heater **7** smelter **8** tryworks **11** incinerator ***part:*** **4** port, vent **6** tuyere ***tender:*** **6** stoker

furnish **3** arm, rig **4** give, hand, lend **5** endow, endue, equip **6** fit out, outfit, supply **7** apparel, appoint, deliver, provide, turn out **8** accouter, accoutre, dispense, hand over, transfer **9** provision **10** contribute

furnishings 4 gear **5** decor **9** equipment, trappings **10** housewares **11** appointment **13** accouterments, accoutrements, paraphernalia

furniture designer *American:* 5 Eames (Charles, Ray), Phyfe (Duncan) **7** Goddard (John, Stephen, Thomas), Haldane (William) **8** Stickley (Gustav) ***British:* 6** Morris (William) **7** Gibbons (Grinling), Shearer (Thomas) **8** Sheraton (Thomas) **11** Chippendale (Thomas), Hepplewhite (George) ***French:* 5** Marot (Daniel) **6** Boulle (André-Charles) ***German:* 6** Breuer (Marcel) ***Scottish:* 4** Adam (James, Robert)

furniture style 4 Adam **6** Empire, Shaker **7** Bauhaus, Federal, Mission **8** Colonial, Georgian, Jacobean, Sheraton, Stickley **9** Queen Anne **11** chinoiserie, Chippendale, Duncan Phyfe, Hepplewhite **13** Arts and Crafts

furor 3 ado, cry, fad, wax **4** chic, mode, rage, stir, to-do **5** anger, craze, mania, style, vogue **6** flurry, frenzy, pother, ruckus, rumpus, uproar **7** fashion, madness **8** foofaraw **9** commotion **10** dernier cri, excitement **11** controversy

furrow 3 rut **4** ruck **5** plica, ridge, sulci (plural) **6** course, crease, groove, sulcus, trench **7** channel, crinkle, wrinkle **8** entrench **9** corrugate **11** corrugation

furrowed 5 lined **6** rugose **7** grooved, sulcate **8** wrinkled **10** corrugated

further 4 abet, also, help **5** again, fresh **6** beyond **7** advance, besides, forward, promote **8** engender, moreover **9** encourage, propagate **10** additional, in addition **12** additionally

furthermore 3 and, too **4** also **6** as well, withal **7** besides **8** likewise, moreover **9** what's more **12** additionally

furthermost 4 last **7** extreme **8** farthest, remotest, ultimate

furtive 3 sly **4** foxy, wary, wily **6** artful, covert, crafty, feline, masked, secret, shifty, sneaky, stolen, tricky **7** catlike, cunning, evasive, sub-rosa **8** guileful, hush-hush, scheming, stealthy **9** disguised, insidious **11** circumspect, clandestine **12** hugger-mugger **13** surreptitious, under-the-table ***look:* 4** peek, peep

fur trader 8 voyageur

furuncle 4 boil **7** abscess

fury 3 ire **4** burn, rage **5** anger, furor, wrath **6** frenzy **7** madness, passion **8** violence **9** vehemence **10** fierceness

furze 4 whin **5** gorse ***genus:* 4** Ulex **7** Genista

fuse 3 mix **4** flux, meld, melt, weld **5** blend, merge, smelt, unify, unite **6** anneal, solder **7** liquefy **8** coalesce, conflate, dissolve, intermix **9** commingle, integrate **10** amalgamate **11** consolidate, incorporate

fusillade 4 hail **5** burst, salvo **6** shower, volley **7** barrage **8** drumfire, outburst **9** broadside, cannonade **11** bombardment

fusion 5 alloy, blend, union **6** merger **7** amalgam, mixture **8** compound **9** coalition, immixture, synthesis

fuss 3 ado, nag, row **4** beef, crab, flap, fret, miff, stew, stir, to-do **5** gripe, stink, upset, whine, worry **6** bother, bustle, hassle, hurrah, pother, ruckus, rumpus, squawk **7** protest **8** complain, foofaraw, squabble **9** commotion, complaint, kerfuffle, objection **11** controversy

fussbudget 3 hen **6** granny **8** stickler **10** fuddy-duddy **13** perfectionist

fusspot 8 stickler **9** nitpicker, worrywart

fussy 5 picky **6** cranky, dainty, ornate **7** careful, finicky, fretful **9** crotchety, irritable, querulous **10** fastidious, meticulous, particular, pernickety, scrupulous **11** painstaking, persnickety, punctilious **13** conscientious

fustian 4 rant **7** bombast, pompous **8** affected, inflated **9** high-flown **11** exaggerated, highfalutin, pretentious **13** grandiloquent

fusty 4 rank **5** close, dated, fetid, moldy, passé, stale **6** bygone, old-hat, smelly **7** archaic **8** outdated **10** antiquated, malodorous **11** reactionary **12** old-fashioned

futhark letter 4 rune

futile 4 idle, vain **5** empty **6** hollow, otiose **7** useless **8** abortive, bootless, hopeless, nugatory **9** fruitless, worthless **10** unavailing **11** ineffective, ineffectual **12** unproductive, unsuccessful

future 5 later **6** mañana, offing, to come **7** by-and-by **8** oncoming, tomorrow **9** hereafter

Futurism *founder:* 9 Marinetti (Filippo Tommaso) ***painter:* 5** Balla (Giacomo), Carra (Carlo) **7** Russolo (Luigi) **8** Boccioni (Umberto), Severini (Gino) ***sculptor:* 8** Boccioni (Umberto)

fuzz 3 cop **4** down, lint **6** police

fuzzy 3 dim **5** faint, gauzy, linty, vague, woozy **6** bleary, blurry **7** blurred, muddled, obscure, shadowy, unclear **8** confused **9** distorted, undefined **10** ill-defined, incoherent, indefinite, indistinct

fylfot 8 swastika

G

gab 3 jaw, rap, yak **4** blab, chat, talk **5** clack, drool, prate, speak **6** babble, drivel, gibber, gossip, jabber, natter, yammer **7** blabber, blather, chatter, palaver, prattle, twaddle **8** chitchat, converse, idle talk **9** gibberish, small talk

gabber 5 yenta **6** gossip, magpie **7** blabber **9** chatterer **10** chatterbox **12** blabbermouth, gossipmonger

gabby 4 glib **5** talky, windy **6** chatty **7** voluble **8** effusive **9** garrulous, talkative **10** long-winded, loquacious **11** loose-lipped **12** loose-tongued

gaberdine 4 coat, suit **5** cloak, cloth **6** capote, fabric **7** garment, manteau **8** material

gable 4 wall **8** pediment ***ornament:*** **6** finial

Gabon *capital:* **10** Libreville ***city:*** **10** Port-Gentil ***ethnic group:*** **4** Fang **5** Bantu ***language:*** **6** French ***monetary unit:*** **5** franc ***neighbor:*** **5** Congo **8** Cameroon ***river:*** **6** Ogooué

gad 3 bat **4** flit, roam, rove **5** amble, drift, mooch, range, stray, tramp **6** chisel, ramble, wander **7** maunder, meander, traipse **9** gallivant

Gad *brother:* **5** Asher ***father:*** **5** Jacob ***mother:*** **6** Zilpah ***son:*** **3** Eri **5** Ezbon, Haggi

Gaddis novel 12 Recognitions (The) **14** Frolic of His Own (A) **16** Carpenter's Gothic

gadfly 3 nag **4** pest, pill **6** bother, critic, insect, nudnik **8** nuisance

gadget 4 tool **5** gizmo, thing **6** device, dingus, doodad, hickey, jigger, widget **7** concern, gimmick, utensil **9** apparatus, appliance, doohickey, implement, mechanism, thingummy **10** instrument **11** contraption, thingamabob, thingamajig, thingumajig

gadwall 4 bird, duck, fowl **9** waterfowl

gadzooks 4 drat, egad **6** crikey, zounds

Gaea *husband:* **6** Uranus ***offspring:*** **6** Furies, Giants, Titans, Typhon, Uranus **7** Erinyes **8** Cyclopes **9** Eumenides ***parent:*** **5** Chaos

Gaelic 4 Erse **5** Irish **6** Celtic **8** Scottish ***god:*** **3** Ler **5** Dagda ***hero:*** **5** Oisin **6** Cormac, Ossian **8** Diarmaid **11** Finn MacCool ***king:*** **9** Conchobar, Conchobor ***language:*** **4** Manx ***poet:*** **4** bard **6** Ossian ***queen:*** **4** Medb ***soldier:*** **4** kern **6** Fenian ***spirit:*** **7** banshee

gaff 3 fix, rig **4** hoax, hook, spar, spur **5** abuse, fraud, spear, trick **6** fleece, ordeal **7** deceive, gimmick **8** raillery **12** climbing iron

gaffe 4 flub, goof, muff **5** boner, error, fault, fluff, lapse **6** bollix, boo-boo, bungle, foul-up, howler, slipup **7** blooper, blunder, clinker, faux pas, misstep, mistake **8** solecism **9** gaucherie **11** impropriety, misjudgment **12** indiscretion

gag 4 balk, gasp, hoax, jape, jest, joke, quip **5** choke, crack, heave, prank, retch, trick **6** muffle, muzzle, shtick, stifle, strain **7** repress, silence, squelch **8** throttle **9** restraint, wisecrack, witticism

gaga 4 agog, wild **5** crazy, giddy, nutty, wacky **6** doting, fervid, gung ho **7** foolish, gushing, excited, smitten **8** animated, enamored, obsessed, thrilled **9** ebullient, exuberant **10** captivated, infatuated **12** enthusiastic

gage 3 vow **4** bond **5** token **6** pledge, surety **8** gauntlet, security (see also **gauge**)

gaggle 4 crew, gang, pack **5** array, bunch, flock, group **6** clutch, number **7** cluster **10** assemblage, collection **11** aggregation

Gaheris *brother:* **6** Gareth, Gawain ***father:*** **3** Lot ***mother:*** **8** Margawse, Morgause ***uncle:*** **6** Arthur ***victim:*** **8** Margawse, Morgause

gaiety 3 fun, joy **4** glee **5** mirth, revel **6** finery, frolic, hoopla **7** elation, jollity, revelry, whoopee **8** elegance, hilarity, reveling, vivacity **9** animation, festivity, happiness, joviality, merriment **10** ebullience, exuberance, hullabaloo, joyousness, jubilation, liveliness **11** high spirits, merrymaking **12** conviviality

gain 3 get, net, win **4** earn, land, make, reap **5** clear, cover, reach, score **6** attain, expand, obtain, pick up, profit, rack up, secure **7** achieve, acquire, advance, attract, augment, benefit, bring in, enlarge, procure **8** earnings, increase, persuade, proceeds, windfall **10** accomplish

gainful 6 paying **8** fruitful, generous **9** lucrative, rewarding **10** beneficial, productive, profitable, well-paying, worthwhile **12** advantageous, remunerative
gainsay 4 buck, defy, deny **6** impugn, negate, oppose, refute, resist **7** dispute **8** disclaim, disprove, negative, traverse **9** disaffirm, repudiate, withstand **10** contradict, contravene, controvert
Gainsborough painting 7 Blue Boy
gait 3 air, run **4** clip, dash, lope, pace, rate, step, trot, walk **5** amble, speed, strut, train, tread **6** canter, gallop, stride **7** bearing **8** demeanor
gaiter 4 boot, shoe, spat **7** legging **8** overshoe
gal 4 babe, doll **5** chick
gala 4 ball, bash, fete, prom **5** merry, party **6** lively **7** festive, jubilee, pageant, shindig **8** festival, jamboree, wingding **9** festivity, spectacle **11** celebration **13** entertainment
Galactica commander 5 Adama (Adm. William)
galago 5 lemur **8** bush baby
Galahad *father:* 8 Lancelot **9** Launcelot ***mother:* 6** Elaine ***quest:* 5** Grail **9** Holy Grail
Galatea *father:* 6 Nereus ***husband:* 9** Pygmalion ***lover:* 4** Acis ***mother:* 5** Doris
galaxy 6 nebula **8** Milky Way, universe
Galba *predecessor:* 4 Nero ***successor:* 4** Otho
gale 4 blow, gust, wind **5** blast, storm **6** squall **7** cyclone, tempest, typhoon **8** outburst **9** hurricane
galena 3 ore **4** lead
Galen's forte 7 healing **8** medicine
galilee 5 porch **6** chapel
Galilee town 4 Cana **7** Gergesa **8** Nazareth, Tiberias **9** Bethsaida, Capernaum
Galileo's birthplace 4 Pisa **5** Italy **7** Tuscany
gall 3 irk, nag, rub, vex **4** bile, fray, fret, rile, roil, sore, wear **5** annoy, brass, chafe, cheek, erode, grate, graze, nerve **6** abrade, bother, burn up, harass, pester, plague, rancor, ruffle, scrape **7** conceit, disturb, frazzle, inflame, provoke, scratch, torment **8** audacity, boldness, chutzpah, irritate, temerity **9** aggravate, arrogance, brashness, impudence, insolence **10** bitterness, effrontery ***bladder:* 9** cholecyst
gallant 3 fop **4** beau, bold, buck, dude, hero **5** blade, blood, brave, civil, dandy, lover, manly, Romeo, showy, suave, swain, wooer **6** daring, heroic, suitor, urbane **7** courtly, coxcomb, dashing, Don Juan, stately, valiant **8** Casanova, gracious, lothario, paramour, spirited, valorous **9** attentive, courteous, dauntless, ladies' man **10** chivalrous, courageous
gallantry 5 honor, poise, valor **6** daring, mettle, spirit **7** amenity, bravery, courage, heroism, prowess, suavity **8** boldness, chivalry, courtesy, urbanity, valiance, valiancy **9** attention, manliness **10** resolution **11** courtliness **12** fearlessness
galleon 7 warship **12** square-rigger
gallery 5 patio, porch, salon **6** arcade, loggia, museum, piazza **7** balcony, passage, portico, veranda **8** audience, corridor, showroom **9** colonnade, onlookers, promenade ***ancient Greek:* 4** stoa
galley 3 gig **4** boat, mess, ship, tray **5** cuddy, proof **6** bireme **7** canteen, kitchen, trireme, warship **8** scullery **9** cookhouse
Gallic 6 French
gallimaufry 3 mix **4** hash, mess, olio, stew **5** chaos **6** jumble, medley **7** clutter, goulash, mélange, mixture, variety **8** mishmash, pastiche **9** patchwork, potpourri **10** assortment, hodgepodge, hotchpotch, miscellany, salmagundi
gallinaceous bird 3 hen **5** quail **6** grouse, turkey **7** chicken, hoatzin, peacock **8** curassow, pheasant **9** partridge **10** guinea fowl
galling 6 bitter, vexing **8** rankling **9** upsetting, vexatious **10** afflictive, irritating, nettlesome **11** aggravating, distressing, troublesome **12** exasperating
gallivant 3 bat, bum, gad **4** flit, roam, rove **5** amble, drift, jaunt, mooch, range, stray **6** cruise, ramble, travel, wander **7** meander, traipse **8** vagabond **10** knock about
gallop 4 dash, race **6** sprint
gallows 6 gibbet ***bird:* 7** villain **8** criminal
galoot 3 ape, guy, oaf **4** dupe, goon, lout, slob **5** chump **6** fellow, lummox **7** palooka
galore 4 full, lush, rich **5** ample, great **6** lavish **7** aplenty, copious, endless, profuse **8** abundant, generous **9** bountiful, expansive, plentiful **11** overflowing
galosh 4 boot, shoe **6** rubber **8** overshoe
Galsworthy work 7 Justice **11** Forsyte Saga (The)
galumph 4 plod **5** barge, clomp, clump, stomp, stump, tramp **6** lumber, trudge
galvanize 3 jar, zap **4** coat, fire, jolt, stir, spur, stun **5** pep up, pique, prime, react, rouse, shock **6** arouse, excite, perk up, thrill **7** animate, enliven, immerse, inspire, provoke, quicken **8** activate, astonish, energize, motivate, vitalize **9** electrify, innervate, magnetize, stimulate **10** invigorate
gam 3 leg, pin, pod, rap **4** chat, flap, limb,

talk **5** visit **6** confab **9** drumstick **12** conversation

Gambia ***capital:*** **6** Banjul ***city:*** **9** Serekunda ***monetary unit:*** **6** dalasi ***neighbor:*** **7** Senegal

gambit 3 con, jig **4** move, play, ploy, ruse, wile **5** dodge, topic, trick **6** design, device, remark, tactic **7** gimmick **8** artifice, maneuver, trickery **9** expedient, stratagem **10** subterfuge

gamble 3 bet, lay, set **4** dare, game, play, punt, risk **5** put on, stake, wager **6** chance, hazard, plunge, raffle **7** imperil, lottery, venture **8** cast lots, long shot **9** crapshoot, speculate **10** jeopardize

gambler 5 dicer, shark, sharp **7** sharper **9** cardsharp **10** cardplayer **11** cardsharper

gambling place 3 den **4** club, dive, Reno **5** joint, Vegas **6** casino **8** Las Vegas, pool hall **9** roadhouse **10** Monte Carlo **12** Atlantic City, betting house

gambol 3 hop **4** jump, lark, leap, romp, skip **5** bound, caper, frisk, revel, sport **6** cavort, frolic, prance, spring **7** carry on, roister, rollick

Gambrinus' invention 3 ale **4** beer **5** lager

game 3 bet, fun, lay, RPG **4** bold, jest, joke, lark, play, prey, romp **5** brave, chase, eager, hardy, sport, stake, trick, wager **6** gamble, quarry, spunky **7** contest, pastime, valiant, willing **8** fearless, intrepid, resolute, unafraid, valorous **9** amusement, dauntless, diversion, undaunted **10** courageous, recreation ***arcade:*** **7** Gremlin **8** Carnival, Skee-Ball ***ball:*** **4** golf, polo, pool **5** fives, rogue, rugby **6** hockey, pelota, soccer, squash, tennis **7** cricket, croquet, jai alai **8** baseball, football, handball, hardball, lacrosse, racquets, rounders, softball **9** bagatelle, billiards **10** basketball, volleyball **11** racquetball ***Basque:*** **6** pelota **7** jai alai ***bird:*** **4** duck **5** quail **6** chukar, turkey **7** bustard **8** bobwhite, pheasant **9** partridge ***board:*** **4** Clue, Risk, wari **5** chess, chuba, oware, shogi **7** mancala, pachisi **8** checkers, Monopoly, Scrabble **9** crokinole, Parcheesi **10** backgammon ***child's:*** **3** tag **5** jacks **7** marbles, ringtaw **8** leapfrog, peekaboo **9** hopscotch, tic-tac-toe ***confidence:*** **4** scam **5** bunco, bunko, sting ***court:*** **5** roque **6** pelota, squash, tennis **7** jai alai **8** handball, racquets **9** badminton **10** basketball, volleyball **11** racquetball ***electric:*** **7** pinball ***English:*** **5** rugby **7** cricket **8** draughts ***Irish:*** **7** hurling ***of chance:*** **4** faro, keno **5** beano, bingo, boule, craps, lotto, rondo **6** fan-tan, hazard, policy, raffle **7** lottery, rondeau **8** roulette ***parlor:*** **8** Carnelli, charades ***piece:*** **3** die **4** tile **5** token **6** domino, marble, top hat **7** checker ***racket:*** **6** squash, tennis **8** lacrosse, ping-pong, racquets **9** badminton **11** racquetball, table tennis ***roulette-like:*** **5** boule ***rule maker:*** **5** Hoyle (Edmond) ***string:*** **10** cat's cradle ***table:*** **4** pool **5** craps **7** mah-jong, snooker **8** dominoes, mah-jongg, ping-pong, roulette **9** bagatelle, billiards **11** table tennis ***word:*** **5** rebus **6** crambo **7** anagram, hangman **8** acrostic, charades, Scrabble **9** crossword, logogriph (see also **card *game***)

game plan 6 scheme, tactic **8** scenario, strategy **9** blueprint **10** big picture

gamete 3 egg **4** ovum **5** sperm **8** germ cell

gamin 3 elf, imp, tad **4** brat, tyke, waif **5** scamp **6** monkey, rascal, urchin **11** guttersnipe **12** street urchin

gamine 3 elf, imp **4** brat, waif **5** scamp **6** hoyden, rascal, tomboy, urchin **11** guttersnipe **12** street urchin

gaming cubes 4 dice **5** bones

gammon 3 ham **4** dupe, fool, rook **5** bacon, feign **6** delude, fleece, humbug **7** deceive, pretend, swindle **8** flimflam, hoodwink **9** bamboozle **11** hornswoggle

gamut 4 A to Z **5** range, scale, scope, sweep **6** extent, series, spread **7** compass **8** diapason, spectrum

gamy 3 off **4** foul, racy, rank, vile **5** brave, fetid, funky **6** plucky, putrid, rancid, rotten, smelly, sordid, stinky, strong **7** corrupt, decayed, noisome, noxious, reeking **10** decomposed, malodorous, scandalous **12** disagreeable, disreputable

gander 4 look, peek **5** goose **6** glance **7** glimpse **9** simpleton, waterfowl

____ **Gandhi 5** Rajiv **6** Indira **7** Mahatma **8** Mohandas

gandy dancer 10 railroader, tracklayer

ganef 5 thief **6** rascal **9** scoundrel

Ganesa, Ganesh ***father:*** **4** Siva **5** Shiva ***head:*** **8** elephant ***mother:*** **7** Parvati

gang 3 lot, mob, set **4** band, clan, club, crew, pack, ring, team **5** bunch, crowd, group, horde **6** circle, clique, outfit **7** arrange, cluster, collect, combine, company, coterie **8** assemble **10** accumulate, assemblage **11** combination

gangling 4 bony, lean, slim **5** gaunt, lanky, rangy **6** meager, meagre, skinny **7** angular, scrawny, slender, spindly, stringy **8** rawboned **9** spindling

ganglion 5 tumor **7** nucleus

gangrene 3 rot **5** decay **7** mortify, putrefy **8** necrosis **9** decompose

gangster 4 goon, hood, thug **5** cholo, rough, thief, tough **6** bandit, gunman **7** hoodlum,

mafioso, mobster, ruffian **8** criminal **9** cutthroat, racketeer ***girlfriend:*** **4** moll
gangway **4** hall, path **5** aisle **7** passage, walkway **8** corridor **10** passageway
ganja **3** kef, kif, pot, tea **4** hemp, herb, weed **5** grass, smoke **7** hashish **8** cannabis, Mary Jane **9** marijuana
gannet **4** bird **5** booby **7** seabird
ganoid fish **3** gar **6** beluga, bowfin **7** dogfish, garfish, teleost **8** billfish, sturgeon **10** paddlefish
Ganymede ***abductor:*** **4** Zeus **7** Jupiter ***brother:*** **4** Ilus ***father:*** **4** Tros ***function:*** **9** cupbearer
gaol **3** jug, pen **4** jail **5** clink, joint, pokey **6** cooler, lockup, prison **7** slammer **8** bastille **9** calaboose, jailhouse **12** penitentiary
gap **3** cut, pit **4** gash, gulf, hole, lull, pass, rent, rift, skip, slit, slot, tear, vent, void, yawn **5** abyss, blank, break, chasm, chink, cleft, clove, crack, gorge, gulch, gully, pause, space, split **6** arroyo, breach, canyon, cavity, cranny, divide, hiatus, hollow, lacuna, ravine, recess, schism, vacuum **7** caesura, crevice, fissure, interim, lacunae (plural), opening, orifice, rupture, vacancy, vacuity **8** aperture, cleavage, division, fracture, interval **9** disparity, interlude **10** deficiency, difference, interstice, separation **12** intermission, interruption **13** discontinuity
gape **3** eye, yaw **4** bore, gawk, gawp, gaze, glom, leer, look, ogle, open, part, peer, yawn **5** crack, glare, gloat, space, split, stare **6** glance, goggle **7** eyeball **10** rubberneck
gaping **4** huge, open, vast, wide **5** broad, great **7** chasmal **9** cavernous
gar **4** fish, pike **8** billfish **10** needlefish
garage **4** shop **7** cabinet, car park, carport, shelter
Garand **5** rifle
garb **4** clad, duds **5** array, cover, dress, getup, style **6** attire, clothe, livery, outfit **7** apparel, clothes, garment, raiment, threads **9** trappings **10** appearance
garbage **4** junk, muck, slop **5** dreck, dregs, filth, offal, trash, waste **6** debris, litter, refuse, sewage **7** rubbish **8** detritus, riffraff ***heap:*** **6** midden
garble **4** sift, warp **5** alter, belie, color, twist **6** jumble, mangle, muddle **7** becloud, confuse, contort, distort, falsify, obscure, pervert **8** miscolor, misstate, mutilate **9** obfuscate **10** impurities **12** misrepresent
garçon **3** boy **6** waiter **7** servant
garden **4** Eden, park **7** nursery ***shelter:*** **5** arbor **6** arbour
gardener **6** grower **7** yardman **9** topiarist
garden house **6** alcove, gazebo **9** belvedere
Garden State **9** New Jersey
garden tool **3** hoe **4** claw, fork, rake **5** edger, mower, spade **6** dibble, pruner, scythe, shears, shovel, sickle, trowel, weeder **8** clippers
Gardner character **10** Perry Mason **11** Della Street
Gareth ***brother:*** **6** Gawain **7** Gaheris ***father:*** **3** Lot ***mother:*** **8** Margawse, Morgause ***slayer:*** **8** Lancelot **9** Launcelot ***uncle:*** **6** Arthur ***wife:*** **6** Liones
Garfield ***creator:*** **5** Davis (Jim) ***dog:*** **4** Odie
Gargamelle's son **9** Gargantua
Gargantua ***abbey:*** **7** Thélème ***author:*** **8** Rabelais (François) ***father:*** **12** Grandgousier ***first word:*** **5** drink ***mother:*** **10** Gargamelle ***son:*** **10** Pantagruel
gargantuan see **gigantic**
Garibaldi follower **8** redshirt
garish **4** loud **5** gaudy, showy, vivid **6** brassy, brazen, flashy, tawdry, tinsel, vulgar **7** blatant, chintzy, glaring, raffish **12** meretricious
garland **3** ana, lei **5** album, crown **6** anadem, digest, laurel, wreath **7** chaplet, coronal, coronet, laurels, omnibus **8** analects **9** anthology, selection **10** collection, compendium, miscellany **11** florilegium
garlic **4** moly, ramp **5** aglio, clove **6** allium ***mayonnaise:*** **5** aioli
garment **4** garb, gear **5** array, habit **6** attire **7** apparel, raiment **8** clothing, vestment **10** habiliment ***African:*** **6** kaross **7** dashiki ***Arab:*** **3** aba **4** haik ***British:*** **10** mackintosh ***clergy's:*** **3** alb **4** cope **7** cassock, soutane **8** vestment ***close-fitting:*** **6** girdle, tights **7** leotard ***for sleeping:*** **6** pajama **7** nightie **9** nightgown ***Greek:*** **5** tunic **6** chiton, peplos **7** chlamys **8** himation ***Hindu:*** **4** sari **6** patola ***hooded:*** **8** djellaba ***Japanese:*** **6** kimono ***lace:*** **10** chemisette ***Malay:*** **6** sarong ***Mexican:*** **6** sarape, serape ***outer:*** **4** cape, coat, robe, wrap **5** apron, cloak, parka, shawl, smock, stole **6** capote, jacket, kimono, poncho, sarong, ulster, wammus **7** overall, pelisse, surtout, sweater, topcoat **8** overcoat, pinafore, pullover, scapular **9** coveralls, gaberdine, polonaise ***Polynesian:*** **5** pareo, pareu ***rain:*** **6** poncho **7** oilskin, slicker ***Roman:*** **4** toga **5** tunic ***Scottish:*** **4** jupe, kilt **7** sporran ***sleeveless:*** **3** aba **4** cape **6** mantle, tabard ***Turkish:*** **6** dolman ***women's:*** **4** gown **5** dress, skirt, teddy **6** blouse, vestee **7** blouson, chemise, nightie, partlet **8** camisole, negligee, peignoir, pelerine

garner 4 cull, earn, hive, reap **5** amass, glean, hoard, lay up, store **6** gather, pick up, roll up **7** collect, extract, harvest, store up **8** cumulate, ingather **9** stockpile **10** accumulate

garnet 5 jewel, stone **6** pyrope **8** essonite **9** hessonite ***black:*** **8** melanite ***red:*** **9** almandine, almandite

garnish 4 deck, trim **5** adorn **6** bedeck **7** dress up, enhance **8** beautify, decorate, ornament **9** embellish

garret 4 loft, room **5** attic **8** cockloft

garrison 4 camp, fort, post **6** assign, billet, occupy, troops **7** station **8** fortress **10** stronghold

garrote 5 choke **8** strangle, throttle **11** strangulate

garrulous see **gabby**

garter 4 band, belt **5** strap **7** support **9** supporter

garth 4 yard **5** close **9** enclosure

gas 4 fuel, fume **5** fumes, steam, vapor **6** petrol **8** gasoline **9** petroleum ***atmospheric:*** **4** neon **5** argon, oxide, ozone, xenon **6** helium, oxygen **7** krypton, methane **8** hydrogen, nitrogen ***flammable:*** **6** butane, ethane, ethyne **7** methane, propane, propene **8** ethylene ***inert:*** **4** neon **5** argon, radon, xenon **6** helium **7** krypton ***mine:*** **8** firedamp **9** black damp ***oxygen:*** **5** ozone ***toxic:*** **5** sarin, soman, tabun **6** arsine, ketene **7** mustard **8** phosgene **9** phosphine

gasconade 4 brag **7** bravado **8** boasting, bragging **11** braggadocio

gash 3 cut, rip **4** rend, slit, tear **5** carve, cleft, gouge, slash, slice, split **6** incise **8** lacerate **10** depression, laceration

gasket 4 ring, seal **5** O-ring **6** sealer

gasoline 4 fuel **6** petrol ***rating:*** **6** octane

gasp 4 blow, huff, pant, puff **5** heave **6** wheeze **11** exclamation

Gaspar *companion:* **8** Melchior **9** Balthazar ***gift:*** **12** frankincense

gassy 5 windy **7** verbose **8** inflated, vaporous **9** flatulent

gastronome 7 epicure, gourmet **8** gourmand **9** bon vivant **11** connoisseur

gastropod 4 slug **5** conch, murex, snail, whelk **6** cowrie, limpet, volute **7** abalone, mollusc, mollusk, sea slug **8** pteropod, univalve **10** periwinkle

gat 3 gun, rod **6** pistol, roscoe **7** channel, firearm, handgun, passage **8** revolver

gate 3 tap **4** cock, door, exit, port **5** entry, hatch, toril, valve **6** faucet, portal, spigot, switch, wicket **7** hydrant, opening, petcock **8** entrance, entryway, stopcock **9** turnstile **10** attendance

gâteau 4 cake

gatefold 6 insert **7** foldout

Gates of Hercules 9 Gibraltar **12** promontories

gateway 4 arch, door, exit **5** pylon, toril **6** portal **7** archway, doorway, opening **8** entrance

gather 4 brew, cull, gain, grow, heap, herd, loom, mass, meet, pick, pile, pool, reap **5** amass, bunch, flock, glean, group, horde, infer, judge, pluck, shirr, swarm **6** assume, deduce, derive, expect, garner, muster, pick up, pucker, summon, take in **7** cluster, collect, convene, extract, harvest, marshal, round up, suppose, surmise, suspect **8** assemble, conclude, converge, increase **9** aggregate, intensify **10** accumulate, congregate, understand **11** concentrate

gathering 4 bevy, crew, gang, herd, mass, ruck **5** bunch, crowd, crush, drove, flock, group, horde, party, press, rally, swarm **6** caucus, klatch, muster, throng **7** company, harvest, klatsch, meeting, reunion, turnout **8** assembly, congress, junction **9** concourse, congeries **10** assemblage, collection, conference, confluence **11** aggregation, get-together **12** congregation

Gath's giant 7 Goliath **10** Philistine

gauche 5 crude, gawky, inept **6** clumsy **7** awkward, halting, loutish, uncouth **8** bumbling, tactless **9** graceless, ham-handed, inelegant, maladroit **10** blundering

gaucho 6 cowboy **8** herdsman ***weapon:*** **4** bola **5** bolas **7** machete

gaudeamus ____ 6 igitur

gaudy 4 loud **5** showy **6** brassy, brazen, coarse, flashy, garish, tawdry, tinsel, vulgar **7** blatant, chintzy, glaring **9** brummagem, tasteless **10** outlandish **12** meretricious, ostentatious

Gaugamela *loser:* **6** Darius, Persia ***victor:*** **9** Alexander (the Great)

gauge 4 bore, rule, size **5** check, judge, meter, scale, weigh, width **6** assess, degree **7** compute, measure **8** diameter, estimate, evaluate, quantify, standard **9** benchmark, criterion, dimension, thickness, yardstick **10** instrument, touchstone **11** measurement

Gauguin's island 6 Tahiti

Gaul 4 Celt **6** France **9** Frenchman ***ancient inhabitants:*** **4** Remi **6** Belgae

Gaulish 6 French ***god:*** **4** Esus **7** Taranis ***goddess:*** **8** Belisama ***priest:*** **5** druid

gaunt 4 bare, bony, grim, lank, lean, thin **5** harsh, lanky, spare **6** barren, gangly, skinny, wasted **7** angular, scraggy, scrawny **8** gangling, rawboned, skeletal **9** emaciated **10** cadaverous

gauntlet 4 dare, test **5** glove, trial **6** attack, ordeal **9** challenge, onslaught

Gautama 6 Buddha **10** Siddhartha ***mother:* 4** Maya **8** Mahamaya ***son:* 6** Rahula ***wife:* 9** Yasodhara

gauze 4 film, haze, leno, mesh, mist **5** cloth, crepe, tulle **6** fabric, tissue **7** bandage, chiffon, tiffany **8** compress, dressing **11** cheesecloth

gauzy 4 thin **5** filmy, fuzzy, sheer, vague **6** flimsy **8** delicate, pellucid **9** gossamery **10** diaphanous **11** transparent

gavel 6 hammer, mallet

gavial 7 gharial, reptile **9** crocodile

gavotte 4 tune **5** dance

Gawain *brother:* 6 Gareth **7** Gaheris ***father:* 3** Lot ***mother:* 8** Margawse, Morgause ***slayer:* 8** Lancelot **9** Launcelot ***uncle:* 6** Arthur ***victim:* 6** Uwayne **7** Lamerok **9** Pellinore

gawk 3 oaf **4** bore, gape, gaze, hick, look, lout, lump, peer, rube **5** churl, glare, gloat, klutz, looby, stare, yokel **6** goggle, lubber

gawky 5 inept, splay **6** clumsy, coarse, gauche, oafish **7** awkward, loutish, lumpish, uncouth **8** bumbling, bungling, lubberly, ungainly **9** graceless, ham-handed, lumbering, maladroit

gay 4 glad **5** happy, jolly, merry, queer, showy, sunny, vivid **6** blithe, bouncy, bright, cheery, festal, frisky, jocund, jovial, joyful, lively **7** excited, festive, gleeful, lesbian, playful, raffish **8** animated, cheerful, colorful, mirthful, spirited, sportive **9** exuberant, sparkling, vivacious **10** frolicsome, homosexual, insouciant, nonchalant **12** light-hearted

____ Gay 4 John **5** Enola

Gaza victor 7 Allenby (Edmund)

gaze 3 eye **4** bore, gape, gawk, leer, look, ogle, peer, pore, scan, view **5** glare, gloat, stare, watch **6** goggle **7** eyeball, observe **8** consider **10** rubberneck **11** contemplate

gazebo 6 alcove **8** pavilion **9** belvedere **11** garden house, summerhouse

gazelle 3 goa **4** cora, kudu, mohr, oryx **5** eland, nyala **6** koodoo **7** gemsbok **8** antelope

gazette 5 paper **6** record **7** journal, publish **9** newspaper **10** periodical **11** publication **12** announcement

gazetteer 5 atlas, guide, index

Ge see **Gaea**

gear 3 cam, cog, rig **5** dress, goods, shift, stuff, wheel **6** adjust, tackle, things **7** apparel, harness, rigging **8** clothing, cogwheel, garments, materiel, property, sprocket, tackling, trapping **9** apparatus, equipment, machinery **10** belongings **11** accessories, habiliments, possessions **13** accouterments, accoutrements, paraphernalia

Geats *king:* 7 Hygelac ***prince:* 7** Beowulf

Geb *daughter:* 4 Isis **8** Nephthys ***father:* 3** Shu ***mother:* 6** Tefnut ***sister:* 3** Nut ***son:* 3** Set **6** Osiris ***wife:* 3** Nut

gecko 6 lizard **7** reptile

Gedaliah *father:* 6 Ahikam **7** Pashhur **8** Jeduthun ***slayer:* 7** Ishmael

gee 3 wow **4** gosh, turn **5** golly, right **8** goodness, gracious **9** turn right

geek 4 buff, guru, nerd, whiz **5** carny, fiend, freak **6** carney, carnie, expert, pundit, weirdo **7** devotee, egghead, fanatic, oddball **9** authority, eccentric **10** enthusiast **12** intellectual

geezer 4 coot, fogy **5** bloke, crank, fogey **6** codger, dotard, fossil

Gehenna 3 pit **4** hell **5** abyss, hades, Sheol **6** Tophet **7** inferno **8** Tartarus **9** perdition **10** underworld **11** netherworld

Geisel pseudonym 7 Dr. Seuss

geisha wear 3 obi **6** kimono

gel 3 dry, set **4** agar, clot **6** harden, mousse **7** colloid, congeal, thicken **8** solidify **9** coagulate

gelatin 3 jam **4** agar **5** jelly **7** sericin

geld 3 cut, fix, tax **5** alter, desex, unsex **6** change, neuter **7** deprive **8** castrate, mutilate **9** sterilize **10** emasculate **11** desexualize

gelid 3 icy **4** cold **5** chill, nippy, polar **6** arctic, chilly, frigid, frosty, frozen, steely **7** glacial **8** freezing

gelt 5 money

gem 3 jet **4** jade, onyx, opal, rock, ruby, sard **5** agate, amber, beryl, bijou, coral, jewel, lapis, pearl, stone, topaz **6** amulet, garnet, jasper, scarab, sphene, spinel, zircon **7** bejewel, cat's-eye, citrine, diamond, emerald, enjewel, olivine, peridot **8** amethyst, corundum, diopside, fluorite, intaglio, lazurite, obsidian, sapphire, sardonyx, sparkler, tigereye **9** brilliant, carnelian, jadestone, moonstone, phenakite, scapolite, spodumene, tiger's-eye, turquoise **10** aquamarine, cordierite, tourmaline **11** alexandrite, chrysoberyl, chrysoprase, lapis lazuli, masterpiece ***blue:* 6** zircon **8** sapphire **9** turquoise **10** aquamarine **11** lapis lazuli ***carved:* 5** cameo **8** intaglio ***changeable:* 9** chatoyant ***cut:* 7** marquis **8** baguette, cabochon, marquise **9** brilliant ***face:* 5** culet, facet ***green:* 4** jade **7** emerald, peridot, smaragd **10** chrysolite **11** chrysoprase ***red:* 4**

ruby, sard **6** garnet, pyrope, spinel **9** carnelian ***support:*** **7** setting ***weight:*** **5** carat ***yellow:*** **5** amber, topaz **6** sphene **7** citrine

Gemini star 6 Castor, Pollux

gemmule 3 bud

gemsbok 4 oryx **8** antelope

Gem State 5 Idaho

gemütlich see **genial**

gendarme 3 cop **5** bobby **7** officer, soldier **8** flatfoot **9** constable, patrolman, policeman

gender 3 sex **4** kind, male, sort, type **5** class **6** female, neuter **8** feminine **9** masculine

genealogy 5 roots, stirp, stock **6** origin, stemma **7** descent, history, lineage **8** ancestry, heredity, pedigree **9** bloodline **10** family tree

general 4 wide **5** broad, usual, vague **6** common, global, normal, public **7** blanket, generic, overall, regular, routine, typical **8** catholic, everyday, sweeping **9** all-around, prevalent, universal **10** collective, prevailing, unspecific, widespread **11** commonplace **13** comprehensive ***American:*** **3** Lee (Robert E.) **4** Haig (Alexander), Pike (Zebulon), Wood (Leonard) **5** Clark (Mark, Wesley, William), Grant (Ulysses S.), Meade (George), Scott (Charles, Hugh, Winfield), Smith (Andrew Jackson, Giles, Holland, Morgan, Samuel, Walter, Bedell), Stark (John), Worth (William) **6** Abrams (Creighton), Custer (George Armstrong), Franks (Tommy), Hooker (Joseph), Kearny (Philip, Stephen), Patton (George S.), Porter (Fitz-John), Powell (Colin), Slocum (Henry), Spaatz (Carl), Taylor (Maxwell, Richard, Zachary) **7** Bradley (Omar), Frémont (John Charles), Houston (Samuel), Jackson (Andrew, Thomas "Stonewall"), Lejeune (John), Ridgway (Matthew B.), Sherman (William Tecumseh), Twining (Nathaniel), Wallace (Lewis), Wheeler (Joseph) **8** Burnside (Ambrose), Goethals (George Washington), Marshall (George), Mitchell (Billy), Pershing (John J.), Sheridan (Philip), Stilwell (Joseph) **9** MacArthur (Arthur, Douglas), McClellan (George), Rosecrans (William), Schofield (John), Wilkinson (James) **10** Beauregard (P. G. T.), Eisenhower (Dwight D.), Vandegrift (Alexander), Wainwright (Jonathan) **11** Schwarzkopf (Norman) **12** Westmoreland (William) ***American Revolutionary:*** **4** Knox (Henry), Ward (Artemas) **5** Gates (Horatio), Wayne ("Mad Anthony") **6** de Kalb (Baron), Greene (Nathanael), Morgan (Daniel), Putnam (Israel, Rufus) **8** Moultrie (William), Sullivan (John) **10** Washington (George) ***Austrian:*** **11** Wallenstein (Albrecht von) ***British:*** **4** Gage (Thomas), Howe (William) **5** Clive (Robert), Monck (George), Wolfe (James) **6** Rupert (Prince) **7** Amherst (Jeffery), Wingate (Orde Charles, Reginald) **8** Burgoyne (John), Cromwell (Oliver) **10** Abercromby (Ralph, Robert), Cornwallis (Charles), Wellington (Duke of) ***Carthaginian:*** **8** Hamilcar, Hannibal **9** Hasdrubal ***Chinese:*** **3** Tso, Yan (Xishan), Yen (Hsi-shan) **4** Feng (Guozhang, Kuo-chang, Yü-hsiang, Yuxiang) **5** Chang (Tso-lin), Zhang (Zuolin) ***Confederate:*** **3** Lee (Robert E.) **4** Hill (Ambrose), Hood (John Bell) **5** Bragg (Braxton), Ewell (Richard Stoddart), Price (Sterling), Smith (Edmund Kirby) **6** Morgan (John Hunt), Stuart (Jeb) **7** Forrest (Nathan Bedford), Hampton (Wade), Jackson (Thomas "Stonewall"), Pickett (George) **8** Johnston (Albert Sidney, Joseph Eggleston) **9** Pemberton (John) **10** Beauregard (Pierre G. T.), Longstreet (James) ***French:*** **3** Ney (Michel) **4** Foch (Ferdinand) **6** Moreau (Victor), Pétain (Philippe) **7** Weygand (Maxime) **8** de Gaulle (Charles), Lefebvre (Pierre), Montcalm (Marquis de), Saint-Cyr (Laurent de Gouvion-) **9** Frontenac (Comte de) **10** Rochambeau (Comte de) ***German:*** **4** Jodl (Alfred) **6** Kleist (Paul Ludwig von), Rommel (Erwin) **9** Rundstedt (Gerd von) **10** Kesselring (Albert), Ludendorff (Erich) ***Greek:*** **6** Nicias **9** Miltiades **10** Alcibiades **12** Themistocles ***Japanese:*** **4** Tojo (Hideki) **5** Koiso (Kuniaki) **6** Yasuda (Yoshisada) **8** Yamagata (Aritomo) **9** Yamashita (Tomoyuki) ***Mexican:*** **9** Santa Anna (Antonio López de) ***Prussian:*** **11** Scharnhorst (Gerhard von) ***Roman:*** **5** Sulla (Lucius Cornelius) **6** Caesar (Julius), Fabius (Quintus), Marius (Gaius), Pompey (the Great), Scipio (Gnaeus Cornelius, Publius Cornelius) **7** Regulus (Marcus Atilius), Ricimer (Flavius) **8** Agricola (Gnaeus Julius), Lucullus (Lucius Licinius), Stilicho (Flavius) **9** Marcellus (Marcus Claudius), Sertorius (Quintus) **10** Theodosius (the Great) **11** Cincinnatus (Lucius Quinctius) ***Russian:*** **6** Zhukov (Georgy) **7** Kutuzov (Mikhail), Trotsky (Leon), Wrangel (Pyotr), Zhdanov (Andrey) **9** Yeremenko (Andrey) ***Spanish:*** **4** Alba (Duke of), Alva (Duke of) **6** Franco (Francisco) ***Swedish:*** **7** Wrangel (Karl Gustav)

general assembly 4 diet **6** plenum **8** congress **10** parliament **11** legislature

generalize 5 infer, widen **6** derive, extend, induce, spread **7** broaden **8** conclude **12** universalize

generally 6 mainly, mostly, widely **7** all told, as a rule, broadly, chiefly, en masse, largely, overall, usually **8** all in all, commonly, normally **9** on average, primarily, typically **10** altogether, by and large, frequently, on the whole, ordinarily **11** customarily, principally

generate 4 bear, make, sire **5** beget, breed, cause, hatch, spawn, yield **6** create, effect, father, induce, work up **7** achieve, develop, produce, provoke **8** engender, initiate, multiply **9** originate, procreate, propagate, reproduce **10** bring about, bring forth

generic 5 broad **6** common, global **7** blanket **9** inclusive, unbranded, universal **10** indistinct **12** nonexclusive

____ **generis 3** sui

generosity 7 charity **8** altruism, kindness, largesse **9** abundance **10** liberality **11** beneficence, benevolence, magnanimity, munificence **12** philanthropy **13** unselfishness

generous 4 free, kind **5** ample **6** lavish **7** copious, helpful, liberal, profuse, willing **8** abundant **9** bounteous, bountiful, plenteous, plentiful, unselfish, unsparing **10** altruistic, benevolent, bighearted, charitable, munificent, openhanded, ungrudging, unstinting **11** considerate, kindhearted, magnanimous, overflowing **12** greathearted

genesis 4 dawn, root **5** alpha, birth, start **6** origin, outset, source **7** dawning, opening **8** creation **9** beginning, formation, inception **10** provenance **12** commencement

Genet play 5 Maids (The) **6** Blacks (The) **7** Balcony (The)

genetic 10 congenital, hereditary ***material:*** **3** DNA, RNA **7** cistron **9** chromatid **10** chromosome ***term:*** **8** synapsis **9** backcross

genial 4 kind, warm **5** jolly, merry **6** benign, blithe, hearty, jocund, jovial, kindly, mellow, social **7** affable, amiable, cordial **8** amicable, friendly, gracious, pleasant, sociable **9** agreeable, congenial, convivial, easygoing **10** neighborly **11** good-humored, good-natured, warmhearted

genie 3 imp **4** jann, jinn, puck **5** afrit **6** afreet, spirit, sprite

geniture 4 dawn **5** birth, start **6** origin **8** nativity **9** beginning, inception

genius 3 wiz **4** bent, gift, head, turn, whiz **5** flair, jinni, knack **6** acumen, brains, master, spirit, talent, wizard **7** aptness, faculty, prodigy **8** aptitude, brainiac, capacity, penchant **9** ingenuity, intellect **10** brilliance, creativity, mastermind, propensity **12** intelligence **13** inventiveness

Genoa's liberator 5 Doria (Andrea)

genre 3 ilk **4** kind, sort, type **5** class, style **6** family, stripe **7** species, variety **8** category, division

gens 3 kin **4** clan **5** group **6** family, people **7** kinfolk **9** relations, relatives

Genseric's subjects 7 Vandals

genteel 4 nice, prim **5** civil **6** formal, polite, prissy, strict, stuffy, urbane **7** courtly, elegant, prudish, refined, stilted, stylish **8** affected, cultured, graceful, gracious, ladylike, mannerly, polished, priggish, well-bred **9** courteous **10** cultivated **11** gentlemanly, pretentious, straitlaced, well-behaved

gentile 3 goy **5** pagan **7** heathen **9** Christian, non-Jewish

gentility 5 elite **6** gentry **7** decorum, manners, quality, society **8** breeding, courtesy, nobility **9** blue blood **10** aristocrat, refinement, upper class, upper crust **11** aristocracy

gentle 4 calm, easy, kind, meek, mild, soft, tame **5** balmy, quiet, tamed **6** benign, docile, genial, kindly, mellow, placid, serene, smooth, tender **7** amiable, lenient **8** delicate, peaceful, pleasant, soothing, tranquil **9** agreeable **11** softhearted, sympathetic, warmhearted **13** compassionate ***creature:*** **4** lamb

gentleman 3 sir **6** aristo, fellow, mister **8** cavalier **9** blue blood, chevalier, patrician **10** aristocrat ***English:*** **6** milord ***French:*** **8** monsieur ***Hindu:*** **4** babu ***Spanish:*** **3** don **5** señor

gentleman friend 4 beau **5** lover, swain **6** fiancé, squire, suitor **7** gallant

gentlemanly 5 civil, noble, suave **6** polite, urbane **7** elegant, gallant, genteel, refined **8** mannerly, well-bred **9** courteous, honorable **10** chivalrous, cultivated **11** considerate

Gentlemen Prefer Blondes author 4 Loos (Anita)

gentry 5 elite, folks **7** quality, society **8** nobility **9** gentility, patrician **10** gentlefolk, patriciate, upper class, upper crust **11** aristocracy, high society, ruling class

genuflect 3 bow **4** fawn **5** kneel **6** kowtow

genuine 4 echt, pure, real, true **5** plain, pucka, pukka, valid **6** actual, dinkum, honest, tested **7** factual, natural, sincere **8** absolute, bona fide, positive, trueborn **9** authentic, certified, unalloyed, undoubted, unfeigned, veritable **10** sure-enough, unaffected

genus 3 ilk **4** kind, mode, sort, type **5** class, group, order **6** family **7** species, variety **8** category ***amphibian:*** **4** Hyla, Rana ***antelope:*** **4** Oryx ***bee:*** **4** Apis ***bird:*** **4** Alca,

Anas, Chen, Olor, Pavo, Pica, Rhea, Sula, Uria, Xema **5** Sitta ***fish:*** **4** Amia, Lota ***herb:*** **4** Arum, Geum ***insect:*** **4** Nepa ***lily:*** **4** Aloe ***orchid:*** **4** Disa ***owl:*** **4** Bubo, Otus ***palm:*** **4** Nipa ***sheep:*** **4** Ovis ***shrub:*** **4** Ilex, Itea, Ulex ***snake:*** **4** Eryx ***tree:*** **4** Acer, Cola, Maba, Olea ***turtle:*** **4** Emys

geode **4** rock **5** stone **6** cavity, nodule

geoduck **4** clam

geographer ***American:*** **10** Huntington (Ellsworth) ***Flemish:*** **8** Mercator (Gerardus) ***German:*** **6** Ratzel (Friedrich) ***Greek:*** **6** Strabo **7** Ptolemy ***Italian:*** **8** Vespucci (Amerigo)

geologic period **5** azoic **6** Eocene, Hadean **7** Archean, Miocene, Permian **8** Cambrian, Cenozoic, Devonian, Holocene, Jurassic, Mesozoic, Pliocene, Silurian, Triassic **9** Oligocene, Paleocene, Paleozoic **10** Cretaceous, Ordovician **11** Phanerozoic, Pleistocene, Precambrian, Proterozoic **13** Mississippian, Pennsylvanian

geometer **6** Euclid **13** mathematician

geometric ***coordinate:*** **8** abscissa, ordinate ***curve:*** **3** arc **6** spiral **7** ellipse, evolute **8** parabola ***figure:*** **5** rhomb **6** circle, oblong, square **7** ellipse, hexagon, octagon, polygon, rhombus **8** heptagon, pentagon, rhomboid, triangle **9** rectangle ***solid:*** **4** cone, cube **5** prism **6** sphere **7** pyramid **8** cylinder, spheroid, spherule ***surface:*** **5** nappe, torus **6** toroid

geometry letters **3** QED

geophagy **4** pica

Georgia ***capital:*** **7** Atlanta ***city:*** **5** Macon **6** Albany, Athens **7** Augusta **8** Columbus, Marietta, Savannah ***college, university:*** **5** Clark, Emory **6** Mercer **7** Spelman **8** Valdosta **9** Morehouse ***founder:*** **10** Oglethorpe (James) ***nickname:*** **5** Peach (State) ***river:*** **8** Ocmulgee **13** Chattahoochee ***state bird:*** **13** brown thrasher ***state flower:*** **12** Cherokee rose ***state tree:*** **7** live oak ***swamp:*** **10** Okefenokee

Georgia, Republic of ***ancient kingdom:*** **6** Iberia **7** Colchis ***capital:*** **6** Tiflis **7** Tbilisi ***city:*** **7** Kutaisi, Rustavi ***includes:*** **6** Ajaria **8** Abkhazia, Adzharia **12** South Ossetia ***monarch:*** **6** Tamara (Queen) ***monetary unit:*** **4** lari ***mountain range:*** **8** Caucasus ***neighbor:*** **6** Russia, Turkey **7** Armenia **10** Azerbaijan ***river:*** **4** Kura **5** Rioni ***sea:*** **5** Black

Georgics author **6** Vergil, Virgil

Geraint's wife **4** Enid

Gerda's husband **4** Frey

geriatric **3** old **4** aged **5** aging **6** senior **7** elderly **8** outmoded **12** old-fashioned **13** superannuated

germ **3** bud, bug **4** seed **5** spark, spore, virus **6** embryo, origin, source **7** microbe, nucleus **8** pathogen **9** bacterium ***cell:*** **3** egg **4** ovum **5** sperm

German **3** Hun **4** Goth **6** Teuton ***after:*** **4** nach ***airport:*** **9** Flughafen ***always:*** **5** immer ***article:*** **3** das, der, des, die, ein **4** eine ***attention:*** **7** Achtung ***bad:*** **8** schlecht ***battle:*** **4** Kampf **8** Schlacht ***bomber:*** **5** Gotha, Stuka ***beneath:*** **5** unter ***border:*** **6** Grenze ***breakfast:*** **9** Frühstück ***cabbage:*** **5** Kraut ***child:*** **4** Kind ***city:*** **5** Stadt ***coin:*** **4** Mark **5** Taler **6** Thaler **7** Pfennig ***count:*** **4** Graf ***day:*** **3** Tag ***doctor:*** **4** Arzt ***dog:*** **4** Hund ***empire:*** **5** Reich ***entire, whole:*** **4** ganz ***fairy tale:*** **7** Märchen ***fast:*** **7** schnell ***forbidden:*** **8** verboten ***fruit:*** **4** Obst ***good:*** **3** gut **4** gute ***hardly, scarcely:*** **4** kaum ***head:*** **4** Kopf ***hero:*** **4** Held ***highway:*** **8** Autobahn ***history, story:*** **10** Geschichte ***honor:*** **4** Ehre ***hope:*** **8** Hoffnung ***horse:*** **5** Pferd ***I:*** **3** ich ***labor:*** **6** Arbeit ***leader:*** **6** Führer, Kaiser ***lightning:*** **5** Blitz ***liquor:*** **8** Schnapps ***little:*** **5** klein **6** kleine ***love:*** **5** Liebe ***measles:*** **7** rubella ***Miss:*** **8** Fräulein ***money:*** **4** Geld ***moon:*** **4** Mond ***mountain:*** **4** Berg ***musical:*** **9** Singspiel ***no:*** **4** nein ***Mr.:*** **4** Herr ***Mrs.:*** **4** Frau **4** nein ***nobleman:*** **6** Junker ***nothing:*** **6** nichts ***numbers:*** **3** elf **4** acht, drei, eins, fünf, neun, vier, zehn, zwei **5** sechs, zwölf **6** sieben ***over:*** **4** über ***picture:*** **4** Bild ***please:*** **5** bitte ***portion:*** **4** Teil ***prince:*** **5** Fürst ***pronoun:*** **2** du, er, es **3** ich, sie, wir **4** dich, mich, sich ***proud:*** **5** stolz ***railroad:*** **9** Eisenbahn ***rifle:*** **6** Gewehr, Mauser ***rule:*** **5** Regel ***silence:*** **4** Ruhe **6** Stille ***song:*** **4** Lied **6** Lieder (plural) ***space:*** **4** Raum ***spirit:*** **5** Geist ***strength, power*** **5** Kraft, Macht ***submarine:*** **5** U-boat, U-boot ***success:*** **6** Erfolg ***tank:*** **6** Panzer ***television:*** **9** Fernseher ***thank you:*** **5** danke ***today:*** **5** heute ***tomorrow:*** **6** morgen ***train:*** **3** Zug ***train station:*** **7** Bahnhof ***tree:*** **4** Baum ***truth:*** **8** Wahrheit ***valley:*** **3** Tal ***value:*** **4** Wert ***victory:*** **4** Sieg ***war:*** **5** Krieg ***weight:*** **3** Lot **5** Pfund, Stein **8** Vierling ***with:*** **3** mit ***work:*** **6** Arbeit ***world:*** **4** Welt ***woman:*** **4** Frau **8** Fräulein ***youth:*** **6** Jugend

germane **3** apt **5** ad rem **7** apropos, fitting, related **8** material, relevant **9** pertinent **10** applicable **11** appropriate

Germany **11** Deutschland ***capital:*** **6** Berlin ***city:*** **3** Ulm **4** Bonn, Jena, Kiel **5** Essen, Mainz **6** Bremen, Erfurt, Lübeck, Munich **7** Cologne, Dresden, Hamburg, Hanover, Leipzig, München, Potsdam **8** Augsburg,

Dortmund, Duisburg, Freiburg, Hannover, Schwerin **9** Frankfurt, Nuremberg, Stuttgart, Wiesbaden **10** Baden Baden, Düsseldorf ***leader:*** **4** Kohl (Helmut) **6** Brandt (Willy), Hitler (Adolf), Merkel (Angela) **7** Schmidt (Helmut), Wilhelm (Kaiser) **8** Bismarck (Otto) ***monetary unit:*** **4** euro ***monetary unit, former:*** **4** mark **5** taler **6** thaler **12** deutsche mark ***mountain, range:*** **4** Harz **7** Brocken ***neighbor:*** **6** France, Poland **7** Austria, Belgium, Denmark **10** Luxembourg **11** Netherlands, Switzerland **13** Czech Republic ***region:*** **4** Ruhr **6** Saxony **7** Bavaria **11** Black Forest ***river:*** **4** Eder, Elbe, Isar, Main, Oder, Ruhr, Saar **5** Fulda, Mosel, Rhein, Rhine, Weser **6** Danube **7** Moselle ***sea:*** **5** North **6** Baltic ***state:*** **5** Hesse **6** Saxony **7** Bavaria **8** Saarland **9** Thuringia **11** Brandenburg

germinate 3 bud **6** evolve, spring, sprout **7** blossom, develop **9** originate, pullulate

Gershom, Gershon *father:* 4 Levi ***son:*** **5** Libni **6** Shimei

Gershwin 3 Ira **6** George ***opera:*** **12** Porgy and Bess ***piece:*** **14** Rhapsody in Blue **15** American in Paris (An) ***show:*** **5** Oh Kay **9** Funny Face, Girl Crazy **10** Lady Be Good **11** Of Thee I Sing **15** Strike Up the Band ***song:*** **10** I Got Rhythm, Summertime

Gertrude *husband:* 8 Claudius ***son:*** **6** Hamlet

Gervaise's daughter 4 Nana

Geryon *dog:* 6 Orthus ***father:*** **8** Chrysaor ***mother:*** **10** Callirrhoë ***slayer:*** **8** Hercules

gestalt 4 form **5** shape **6** figure **7** pattern **9** structure **13** configuration

Gestapo chief 7 Himmler (Heinrich)

geste 4 deed, feat **7** emprise, exploit, romance, venture **9** adventure **10** enterprise **11** undertaking

gesticulate 3 nod **4** move, wave **6** beckon, motion, signal

gesticulation 4 wave **6** motion **7** gesture **8** high sign **9** pantomime **12** body language, sign language

gesture 3 nod **4** sign, wave **5** shrug, token **6** motion, salute, signal **8** reminder **9** signalize **10** expression, indication ***graceful:*** **9** beau geste

get 3 bag **4** draw, earn, gain, land **5** catch, cause, seize **6** access, attain, become, elicit, extort, obtain, pick up, secure **7** achieve, acquire, bring in, capture, chalk up, deliver, extract, procure, receive **8** contract **10** understand **12** come down with

get around 4 roam, rove, tour, trek, walk **5** avoid, dodge, elude, evade, skirt **6** cruise, detour, escape, ramble, travel, wander **8** ambulate, outflank, sidestep **10** circumvent

get away see **get out**

getaway 3 lam **4** exit, slip **6** escape, flight **7** retreat **8** breakout, vacation

get back 6 go home, recoup, regain, return, revert **7** recover, reclaim, revenge, revisit **8** retrieve **9** repossess, retaliate

get by 4 cope, fare, pass **5** slide **6** eke out, endure, manage **7** carry on, survive **8** maintain

get off 4 walk **5** leave **6** alight, depart, go free, launch **7** pull out **8** dismount **9** disembark **10** beat the rap

get out 2 go **4** exit, kite, leak **5** break, issue, leave, scram, split **6** alight, beat it, begone, decamp, depart, egress, escape **7** buzz off, publish, skiddoo, take off, vamoose **8** dispatch, hightail **9** circulate, skedaddle **10** make tracks

Gettysburg general 3 Lee (Robert E.) **5** Meade (George)

get up 4 gain **5** arise, breed, cause, dress, hatch, mount, raise, stand **6** create, induce, summon **7** acquire, prepare, produce **8** engender, generate **12** rise and shine

getup 3 rig **4** duds, garb, togs **5** array, dress, guise **6** outfit **7** costume, threads

get-up-and-go 3 pep, vim, zip **4** bang, push, snap, zeal, zest **5** drive, moxie, oomph, punch, spunk, steam, verve, vigor **6** energy, spirit, starch **8** ambition **10** enterprise, initiative

gewgaw 3 toy **4** dido **5** bijou, curio **6** bangle, bauble, doodad, trifle **7** bibelot, novelty, trinket, whatnot **8** gimcrack, kickshaw **9** bagatelle, objet d'art **10** knickknack

geyser 3 jet **5** fount, spout, spurt **6** gusher, spring **8** fountain **10** wellspring **11** Old Faithful

Ghana *capital:* 5 Accra ***city:*** **4** Tema **6** Kumasi, Tamale ***ethnic group:*** **4** Akan **5** Mossi ***former name:*** **9** Gold Coast ***gulf:*** **6** Guinea ***lake:*** **5** Volta ***monetary unit:*** **4** cedi ***neighbor:*** **4** Togo **10** Ivory Coast **11** Burkina Faso ***river:*** **5** Volta

ghastly 4 grim, pale **5** awful, lurid **6** grisly, horrid, pallid **7** ghostly, hideous, macabre **8** dreadful, ghoulish, gruesome, horrible, shocking, spectral, terrible **9** appalling, deathlike, frightful, ghostlike, repulsive, sickening **10** cadaverous, corpselike, disgustful, disgusting, horrifying, nauseating, terrifying **11** frightening

ghee 3 fat **6** butter

gherkin 4 vine **6** pickle **8** cucumber

ghetto 4 slum

ghost 4 soul **5** demon, haunt, shade, spook,

trace **6** kelpie, shadow, spirit, wraith, zombie **7** eidolon, phantom, specter **8** phantasm **10** apparition **11** poltergeist ***cartoon:*** **6** Casper

ghostly 5 eerie, scary **6** spooky **7** shadowy **8** ethereal, spectral **9** deathlike, spiritual, unearthly, unworldly **10** cadaverous, corpselike, phantasmal **12** supernatural

Ghosts author 5 Ibsen (Henrik)

ghoul 4 ogre **5** fiend **7** monster **11** grave robber

GI 5 grunt **7** dogface, fighter, soldier, warrior **8** doughboy **9** man-at-arms **10** serviceman

Gianni Schicchi composer 7 Puccini (Giacomo)

giant 4 huge, hulk, ogre, Otus, vast **5** gross, Gyges, Hymir, jumbo, titan, whale **6** Cottus, Typhon **7** Aloadae (plural), Antaeus, Cyclops, Goliath, immense, mammoth, monster, titanic, whopper **8** behemoth, Briareus, colossal, colossus, enormous, gigantic, Orgoglio **9** cyclopean, Enceladus, Ephialtes, Gargantua, humongous, leviathan, monstrous **10** gargantuan, prodigious **11** elephantine ***biblical:*** **4** Anak **7** Goliath ***cactus:*** **7** saguaro ***hundred-armed:*** **9** Enceladus ***hundred-eyed:*** **5** Argus ***killer:*** **4** Jack **5** David ***movie monster:*** **6** Mothra **8** Godzilla, King Kong ***one-eyed:*** **5** Arges **7** Cyclops **10** Polyphemus ***rime-cold:*** **4** Ymer, Ymir ***sea god:*** **5** Aegir

Giant author 6 Ferber (Edna)

giaour 7 infidel **10** unbeliever **11** nonbeliever

gib 3 tom **6** tomcat

gibber 3 gab, yak **4** blab **5** prate **6** babble, drivel, gabble, jabber, yammer **7** blabber, blather, chatter, palaver, prattle, twaddle

gibberish 3 gab **5** Greek, hokum **6** babble, bunkum, burble, drivel, gabble, jabber, yammer **7** blabber, blather, chatter, palaver, prattle, twaddle **8** claptrap, flimflam, nonsense **10** balderdash, double-talk, hocus-pocus, mumbo jumbo **11** abracadabra, jabberwocky **12** gobbledygook

gibbet 4 hang **5** lynch, noose, scrag **7** execute, gallows **8** string up

gibbon 3 ape, lar **7** primate, siamang **10** anthropoid

gibbous 6 arched, convex, humped **7** bulging, rounded, swollen **10** humpbacked **11** protuberant

gibe 4 gird, jape, jeer, jest, mock, quip, rail **5** fleer, flout, scoff, scorn, scout, sneer, taunt, tease **6** deride, insult **8** ridicule

Gibraltar *colony of:* 7 Britain, England ***conqueror:*** **5** Tarik, Tariq ***neighbor:*** **5** Spain ***opposite:*** **5** Ceuta

Gibran work 7 Prophet (The)

giddy 4 gaga **5** dizzy, inane, light, silly, woozy **6** elated, yeasty **7** flighty, foolish, vacuous **8** euphoric **9** frivolous, slaphappy **10** hoity-toity **11** empty-headed, harebrained, light-headed, vertiginous

____ Gide 5 André

Gideon *father:* 5 Joash ***servant:*** **5** Purah ***son:*** **9** Abimelech

gift 3 set, tip **4** alms, bent, boon, head, turn **5** award, bonus, endow, favor, flair, forte, grant, knack **6** genius, legacy, reward, talent **7** ability, aptness, cumshaw, faculty, freebie, handout, present, subsidy **8** aptitude, bestowal, capacity, donation, gratuity, largesse, oblation, offering **9** endowment, lagniappe **11** benefaction, benevolence **12** contribution, presentation

gifted 4 able **5** smart **6** expert **7** hotshot, skilled **8** masterly, skillful, talented **9** ingenious, masterful

gig 3 jab, job, top **4** boat, fool, goad, prod, spur **5** annoy, freak, rotor, spear **6** chaise, harass **7** booking, demerit, provoke, rowboat **8** carriage **10** engagement

gigantic 4 huge, vast **5** giant, jumbo **7** hulking, immense, mammoth, massive, titanic **8** behemoth, colossal, enormous, king-size, whopping **9** cyclopean, humongous, kingsized, monstrous, walloping **10** gargantuan, prodigious, stupendous **11** elephantine

giggle 5 laugh **6** guffaw, hee-haw, titter **7** chortle, chuckle, snicker, snigger, twitter

Gigi author 7 Colette

Gilbert and Sullivan opera 6 Mikado (The) **8** Iolanthe, Patience, Sorcerer (The) **9** Grand Duke (The), Ruddigore **10** Gondoliers (The) **11** H.M.S. Pinafore, Princess Ida, Trial by Jury

Gil Blas author 6 Lesage (Alain-René)

gild 4 coat, deck **5** adorn, cover, tinge **6** bedeck, tinsel **7** enhance, overlay **8** brighten, ornament **9** embellish, embroider

Gilda's father 9 Rigoletto

Gilead *father:* 6 Machir ***grandfather:*** **8** Manasseh ***son:*** **7** Jephtha **8** Jephthah

Gilgamesh 4 epic ***companion:*** **6** Eabani, Enkidu ***goddess:*** **5** Aruru **6** Ishtar, Siduri ***home:*** **4** Uruk **5** Erech ***mother:*** **6** Ninsun ***victim:*** **6** Huwawa **7** Humbaba

gill 4 race **5** brook, creek **6** runnel, stream, wattle **7** rivulet ***relating to:*** **9** branchial

gillyflower 4 pink **9** carnation, clove pink

Gilroy play 15 Subject Was Roses (The)

gilt 3 hog, pig, sow **4** bond, gold **5** swine **6** gilded, golden **10** brilliance

gimcrack 5 cheap **6** bauble, gewgaw, shoddy,

trifle **7** bibelot, chintzy, trinket **8** kickshaw **10** knickknack
gimlet 4 tool **5** drill, drink **8** cocktail ***ingredient:* 3** gin **5** vodka **9** lime juice
gimmick 3 con **4** ploy, ruse, wile **5** angle, catch, dodge, feint, gizmo, trick **6** device, gadget, gambit, jigger, scheme, widget **8** artifice, maneuver **9** stratagem **10** subterfuge
gimp 3 vim **4** cord, halt **5** braid, hitch **6** dodder, falter, hobble, spirit **7** cripple **8** lameness
gimpy 4 game, halt, lame **7** hobbled, limping **8** crippled
gin 3 net **4** sloe, trap **5** catch, rummy, snare **6** device, liquor **7** springe **8** beverage, generate, separatc
ginger 3 fig, pep, vim, zip **4** herb, stir, zing **5** liven, spice, verve, vigor **6** energy, mettle, revive, spirit **7** sparkle ***cookie:* 4** snap
gingerly 4 safe, wary **5** canny, chary **7** careful, guarded **8** cautious, delicate, discreet
gingery 4 tart **5** fiery, peppy, sharp, spicy, tangy, zesty **6** snappy, spunky **7** peppery, piquant, pungent **8** spirited **10** mettlesome **12** high-spirited
gingham 5 cloth **6** fabric **7** textile **8** material
gingiva 3 gum
gin mill 3 bar, pub **4** dive **5** joint **6** saloon, tavern **7** barroom, taproom **8** alehouse **9** roadhouse **11** public house **12** watering hole
Ginsberg poem 4 Howl **7** Kaddish
ginseng 4 herb, root
Gioconda, La 8 Mona Lisa ***composer:* 10** Ponchielli (Amilcare) ***painter:* 7** da Vinci (Leonardo) **8** Leonardo (da Vinci)
giraffe 8 ruminant **9** quadruped **10** camelopard
girandole 7 earring **10** candelabra **11** candelabrum, candlestick, composition
girasol 3 gem **4** opal **5** jewel, stone **7** mineral **8** fire opal **9** artichoke
gird 3 hem **4** band, belt, bind, ring, wrap **5** brace, equip, hem in, ready, round, steel **6** circle **7** bolster, enclose, fortify, prepare, provide, shore up, wreathe **8** buttress, cincture, encircle, surround **9** encompass, reinforce **10** strengthen
girder 4 beam **5** brace, I-beam **7** support **8** crossbar **9** crossbeam **10** crosspiece, transverse
girdle 4 band, belt, ring, sash **6** cestus, circle **8** ceinture, cincture, encircle, surround **9** encompass, waistband ***of Aphrodite:* 6** cestus
girl 4 babe, bird, coed, doll, lass, maid, miss **5** chick, filly, missy, wench **6** damsel, lassie, maiden **8** daughter **10** sweetheart
girth 4 band, belt, bind, size **5** brace, cinch, strap **6** circle, fasten, girdle **7** measure **8** cincture, encircle, surround **9** thickness **10** dimensions **13** circumference
Giselle composer 4 Adam (Adolphe)
gist 3 nub, sum **4** core, meat, pith **5** sense **6** burden, ground, kernel, marrow, matter, thrust, upshot **7** essence **9** main point, substance
give 3 pay **4** deal, hand **5** allot, allow, award, grant, issue, offer, remit **6** accord, afford, assign, bestow, commit, confer, convey, devote, direct, donate, extend, market, pony up, render, supply, tender **7** deliver, dish out, display, dole out, fall out, fork out, furnish, hand out, mete out, present, produce, proffer, provide **8** allocate, bequeath, disburse, dispense, give away, hand over, shell out, turn over **9** apportion, sacrifice **10** administer, contribute, distribute
give-and-take 6 banter **8** exchange, repartee, trade-off **10** compromise **11** cooperation, reciprocity
give away 4 blab, leak **5** award, grant, spill **6** bestow, betray, confer, devote, donate, expose, reveal, tattle **7** deliver, divulge, hand out, let slip, present **8** bequeath, disclose
giveaway 4 deal, gift, leak **5** steal, value **6** tip-off **7** bargain, freebee, freebie, premium, present, sellout **8** betrayal, exposure **10** disclosure, revelation
give back 6 refund, retire, return **7** replace, restore, retreat **8** withdraw **9** reinstate
give in 4 cave, fold, quit, stop **5** yield **6** assent, comply, desist, relent, submit **7** concede, deliver, indulge, succumb **8** back down, cry uncle **9** surrender **10** relinquish
given 5 prone **6** donnée **7** assumed, granted **8** inclined **9** presented, specified **10** particular **11** considering, susceptible
give off 4 beam, emit, flow, vent **5** exude, issue **6** effuse **7** emanate, radiate, release **9** discharge
give out 4 deal, dole, emit, fail, mete, vent **5** issue **6** cave in **7** declare, release, succumb **8** collapse, throw off **9** break down **10** distribute
giver 5 donor **7** donator, grantor
give up 4 cede, quit **5** allow, cease, forgo, waive, yield **6** abjure, devote, resign, vacate **7** abandon, despair **8** abdicate, hand over, renounce, withdraw **9** sacrifice, surrender **10** relinquish
give way 5 yield **6** buckle, cave in **7** retreat, succumb **8** collapse **9** surrender
gizmo see **gadget**
glabrous 4 bald, bare **6** shaven, smooth **8** hairless **9** beardless **10** bald-headed **12** smooth-shaven

glacial **3** icy, raw **5** chill, gelid, nippy, polar **6** arctic, biting, chilly, frigid, frosty, frozen, wintry **8** freezing **11** Pleistocene

glacier **3** ice **6** ice cap **8** ice field, ice sheet ***Alaska:*** **4** Muir, Taku **6** Bering **10** Mendenhall ***Antarctica:*** **9** Beardmore ***deposit:*** **4** kame **5** esker **6** placer **7** moraine ***fissure:*** **8** crevasse ***fragment:*** **4** berg **7** iceberg ***Greenland:*** **8** Humboldt ***hill:*** **7** drumlin ***Karakoram:*** **5** Biafo **7** Baltoro ***New Zealand:*** **6** Tasman ***pinnacle:*** **5** serac ***surface:*** **4** névé

glacis **5** grade, slope **7** incline **10** buffer zone **11** buffer state

glad **3** gay **4** fain **5** happy, jolly, merry **6** blithe, bright, cheery, genial, jocund, jovial, joyful, joyous **7** beaming, gleeful, pleased, radiant, tickled, willing **8** cheerful, mirthful, pleasant, rejoiced **9** delighted, gratified

gladden **4** buoy **5** cheer, elate **6** buck up, perk up, please, uplift **7** cheer up, delight, gratify, hearten

glade **6** meadow **8** clearing **9** open space

gladiator **7** fighter **9** combatant, Spartacus

gladly **4** fain, lief **6** freely **7** happily, readily **8** heartily **9** willingly **10** cheerfully, with relish **12** with pleasure

gladness **3** joy **4** glee **5** bliss, cheer, mirth **6** gaiety **7** delight, jollity **9** happiness, merriment

gladstone **3** bag **8** suitcase

glamorous **7** elegant **8** alluring, charming, dazzling, enticing, magnetic **9** seductive **10** attractive, bewitching, enchanting **11** captivating, fascinating **13** sophisticated

glamour **5** charm, magic, spell **6** allure, appeal **7** romance **8** charisma, witchery **9** magnetism, sex appeal **10** attraction, witchcraft **11** fascination **12** razzle-dazzle

glance **4** peek, peep, skim, skip **5** brush, carom, flash, glaze, graze, shine **6** bounce, careen **7** glimpse **8** ricochet ***lascivious:*** **4** leer

gland **5** gonad, liver, organ **6** pineal, thymus **7** adrenal, mammary, parotid, thyroid **8** exocrine, pancreas, prostate, salivary **9** endocrine, pituitary **11** parathyroid ***secretion:*** **7** hormone ***swelling:*** **4** bubo

glare **4** gaze, glow, peer **5** blaze, flame, flash, frown, gleam, light, lower, scowl, shine, stare **6** dazzle, glower **7** obtrude **8** stand out **10** garishness

glaring **4** loud, rank **5** gaudy, plain, vivid **6** brazen, flashy, garish, tawdry, tinsel **7** blatant, obvious **8** blinding, flagrant **9** audacious, egregious, obtrusive **10** noticeable **11** conspicuous, outstanding **12** ostentatious

glass **4** lens, pane **5** image, lense, prism **6** mirror **7** reflect **9** barometer, telescope ***combining form:*** **5** vitro ***container:*** **3** jar **6** beaker, bottle ***decorative:*** **7** schmelz **8** schmelze ***drinking:*** **4** pony **5** flute **6** goblet, jigger, rummer, seidel **7** snifter, tumbler **8** schooner, stemware ***gem:*** **5** paste **6** strass ***magnifying:*** **5** loupe ***milky:*** **7** opaline ***volcanic:*** **7** perlite **8** obsidian

glasses **5** specs **6** shades **7** goggles **8** bifocals, pince-nez, tumblers **9** lorgnette, trifocals **10** spectacles

glass-like **5** clear **6** glazed, limpid, smooth **8** pellucid, vitreous **9** vitrified **11** translucent, transparent

glassmaker **6** Blenko (William) **7** Lalique (René), Tiffany (Louis Comfort) **9** Waterford

glassmaking tool **5** punty **6** pontil **8** blowpipe

Glass Menagerie author **8** Williams (Tennessee)

glassy **5** blank, dazed, shiny **6** glazed, smooth, vacant **7** hyaloid **8** polished, vitreous **9** burnished

glaucous **4** waxy **7** frosted, powdery

Glaucus ***beloved:*** **6** Scylla ***father:*** **5** Minos **8** Sisyphus ***mother:*** **6** Merope **8** Pasiphaë ***son:*** **11** Bellerophon

glaze **3** rub **4** buff, coat, film **5** cover, glint, gloss, sheen, shine **6** enamel, finish, luster, patina, polish **7** burnish, coating, furbish, lacquer, overlay, varnish

glazed **5** blank **6** glassy

gleam **3** ray **4** beam, burn, glow **5** flare, flash, glint, sheen, shine **6** glance **7** glimmer, glisten, glitter, radiate, shimmer, sparkle, twinkle **8** radiance **11** coruscation, scintillate **13** scintillation

gleaming **5** aglow, shiny **6** glossy, sheeny **7** beaming, burning, glowing, lambent, radiant, shining **8** flashing, luminous, lustrous, polished **9** brilliant, burnished, refulgent, sparkling, twinkling **10** glimmering, glistening, glittering, shimmering **13** scintillating

glean **4** cull, reap, sift **5** amass, learn **6** garner, gather, pick up **7** extract, find out, harvest

glebe **4** land **5** field, tract **7** acreage **8** cropland, farmland

glee **3** joy **5** mirth **6** gaiety, levity **7** delight, elation, jollity **8** gladness, hilarity, partsong **9** enjoyment, festivity, good cheer, happiness, jocundity, joviality, merriment **10** exuberance, joyfulness, jubilation **12** exhilaration

gleeful **3** gay **5** jolly, merry **6** blithe, elated, jocund, jovial, joyous **8** cheerful, exultant, jubilant, mirthful **9** exuberant **12** lighthearted

glen 4 dale, vale **5** swale **6** dingle, valley ***deep:*** **5** gorge **6** ravine
glengarry 3 cap **6** bonnet
glib 4 easy **5** slick **6** facile, fluent, smooth **7** offhand, shallow, voluble **8** eloquent, flippant **10** articulate, nonchalant **11** superficial
glide 3 fly **4** flow, sail, skim, slip, soar, waft **5** coast, creep, drift, float, skate, skirr, skulk, slide, slink, sneak, steal **7** descend, slither **8** glissade, volplane **10** portamento
glimmer 4 glow, hint **5** blink, flash, gleam, glint, shine, spark, trace **6** glance **7** flicker, glisten, glitter, inkling, shimmer, sparkle, twinkle **9** coruscate **10** suggestion **11** coruscation, scintillate **13** scintillation
glimpse 4 espy, peek, peep **5** flash, glint, stime **6** glance
glint 3 ray **5** flash, glaze, gleam, sheen, shine, trace **6** glance, luster **7** glimmer, glisten, glitter, shimmer, sparkle, twinkle **9** coruscate **11** coruscation, scintillate **13** scintillation
glissade 4 skim, slip **5** glide, slide
glissando 3 run **5** slide **7** gliding, sliding
glisten 4 glow **5** flash, gleam, glint, shine **6** glance **7** flicker, glimmer, glitter, shimmer, spangle, sparkle, twinkle **9** coruscate **11** coruscation, scintillate **13** scintillation
glitch 3 bug **4** flaw, snag **5** fault, snafu **6** defect **7** failing, failure, gremlin, problem **8** obstacle **10** difficulty **11** malfunction
glitter 5 flash, gleam, glint, shine **7** glimmer, glisten, shimmer, spangle, sparkle, twinkle **9** coruscate **11** coruscation, scintillate **13** scintillation
glittering 5 gaudy, shiny, showy **6** flashy **7** fulgent **9** brilliant, clinquant, coruscant, effulgent **11** spectacular
gloaming 3 eve **4** dusk **5** gloom **7** evening **8** eventide, twilight **9** nightfall
gloat 4 crow **5** exult, revel, vaunt **6** relish **7** triumph **9** celebrate
glob 4 clot, lump **6** dollop
global 5 grand **6** cosmic **7** blanket, general, overall **8** all-round, catholic **9** inclusive, planetary, spherical, universal, worldwide **12** encyclopedic **13** comprehensive
globe 3 orb **4** ball **5** earth, round, world **6** planet, sphere **7** rondure ***half:*** **10** hemisphere
globule 4 ball, bead, drip, drop **6** gobbet, pellet **7** driblet, droplet **8** spherule
glom 4 grab, take **5** catch, latch, seize, steal
gloom 3 dim **4** dusk, funk, loom, murk **5** bedim, blues, cloud, dumps, frown, lower, mopes, scowl **6** darken, glower, shadow **7** becloud, despair, dimness, obscure, sadness **8** darkness, overcast, twilight **9** adumbrate, bleakness, dejection **10** blue devils, depression, melancholy, overshadow **11** despondency, unhappiness **12** mournfulness
gloomy 3 dim, dun, sad **4** cold, dark, dour, down, drab, dull, glum **5** black, bleak, drear, dusky, mopey, murky, muzzy, sulky, surly **6** dismal, dreary, morose, solemn, somber, sullen **7** forlorn, joyless, obscure, stygian, unhappy **8** dejected, desolate, downcast, funereal, mournful **9** cheerless, depressed, mirthless, oppressed, saturnine, tenebrous, woebegone **10** caliginous, chapfallen, depressing, depressive, dispirited, despondent, forbidding, lugubrious, melancholy, oppressive, tenebrific **11** dispiriting, pessimistic **12** disconsolate, discouraging
glorify 4 hymn, laud **5** bless, cry up, erect, exalt, extol, honor **6** admire, praise, revere **7** acclaim, dignify, elevate, ennoble, light up, lionize, magnify, sublime, worship **8** eulogize, venerate **9** celebrate **10** aggrandize
glorious 5 grand, great, noble, proud **6** august, divine, superb **7** eminent, exalted, radiant, sublime **8** esteemed, gorgeous, lustrous, majestic, renowned, splendid, stunning **9** beautiful, brilliant, effulgent, excellent, marvelous, ravishing, wonderful **11** illustrious, magnificent, resplendent, splendorous
glory 4 crow, fame, halo, pomp **5** exalt, exult, gloat, honor, revel **6** heaven, praise, relish, renown **7** acclaim, aureole, delight, majesty, rejoice, triumph **8** eminence, eternity, grandeur, jubilate, radiance, splendor **9** greatness, hereafter **10** effulgence, exaltation, exultation **11** distinction **12** magnificence, resplendence
gloss 4 buff **5** glaze, glint, sheen, shine **6** define, enamel, facade, finish, luster, patina, polish, veneer **7** burnish, comment, explain, furbish, varnish **8** annotate **9** interpret, sleekness, slickness, translate **10** annotation, appearance, brilliance, commentary, definition **11** elucidation, explanation, translation
glossary 7 lexicon **8** wordbook **9** word-hoard **10** dictionary, vocabulary
gloss over 4 mask **5** slant **6** veneer **7** conceal, cover up, distort, falsify, varnish **8** disguise, palliate **9** dissemble, extenuate, sugarcoat, whitewash **10** camouflage
glossy 5 glacé, shiny, sleek, slick **7** shining **8** gleaming, lustrous, polished **9** burnished **10** glistening ***fabric:*** **4** silk **5** satin ***paint:*** **6** enamel

glove 4 gage, mitt **5** catch, cover **6** mitten, sheath **8** covering, gauntlet
glow 4 burn, pink, rose **5** bloom, blush, flush, gleam, rouge, shine **6** mantle, redden **7** blossom, crimson, fox fire, glisten, glitter, radiate **8** brighten, radiance **10** brilliance, luminosity **13** incandescence
glower 5 frown, scowl, stare **11** look daggers
glowing 3 hot, red **4** avid **5** flush, ruddy, shiny **6** ardent, fervid, florid, heated, red-hot **7** beaming, burning, fervent, flushed, lambent, radiant, vibrant **8** blushing, dazzling, gleaming, luminous, lustrous, rubicund, sanguine, suffused **9** brilliant **10** candescent, hot-blooded, passionate **11** impassioned **12** enthusiastic, incandescent
Gluck opera 5 Orfeo **6** Armide **7** Alceste
glucose 5 sugar, syrup
glue 3 fix, gum **4** bind, join **5** epoxy, paste, stick **6** adhere, attach, cement, fasten **7** plaster, stickum **8** adhesive, mucilage
gluey 5 gummy, tacky **6** sticky, viscid **7** viscous **8** adhesive **12** mucilaginous
glum 3 sad **4** blue, dour, down **5** moody, sulky, surly **6** dismal, dreary, gloomy, morose, sullen, woeful **7** crabbed **8** brooding, dejected, downcast, taciturn **9** depressed, oppressed, saturnine, sorrowful, woebegone **10** despondent, dispirited, melancholy **11** downhearted, melancholic
glut 4 clog, cloy, cram, fill, pack, pall, sate **5** feast, flood, gorge, stuff **6** deluge, excess, stodge **7** satiate, surfeit, surplus, swallow **8** saturate **10** oversupply **13** overabundance
glutinous 4 ropy **5** gluey, gooey, gummy, pasty, tacky, thick **6** sticky, viscid **7** viscous **10** gelatinous **12** mucilaginous
glutton 3 hog, pig **8** gourmand **9** chowhound, wolverine **11** gormandizer
gluttonous 7 hoggish, piggish **8** edacious, ravening, ravenous **9** dissolute, indulgent, rapacious, voracious **10** insatiable **11** intemperate
gluttony 6 excess **7** edacity **8** gulosity, rapacity, voracity **11** piggishness
glyph 6 figure, groove, symbol **7** graphic **9** character
G-man 3 fed **4** narc, Ness (Eliot) **5** agent **6** Hoover (J. Edgar) **10** gangbuster
gnarl 4 bend, knot, warp **5** growl, snarl, twist **6** deform **7** contort, distort
gnash 4 bite **5** grind
gnat 3 bug, fly **4** pest **5** midge **6** insect, punkie **7** no-see-um
gnaw 3 eat, nag, vex **4** bite, chaw, chew **5** annoy, chomp, erode, munch, scour, tease, worry **6** bother, crunch, nibble, pester, plague, rankle **7** bedevil, corrode, eat away **8** irritate, wear away **9** masticate
gnome 3 elf, saw **4** rule **5** adage, axiom, dwarf, maxim, moral, troll, truth **6** dictum, goblin, saying, truism **7** proverb **8** aphorism, apothegm **10** shibboleth
gnostic 6 occult, secret **8** abstruse **10** mysterious
gnu 10 wildebeest
go ***against:*** **4** defy **5** fight **6** oppose, resist **7** counter, protest **10** contradict ***ahead:*** **4** lead **7** precede, proceed **8** continue, progress ***along:*** **5** agree, yield **6** accede, comply, concur **7** consent **9** acquiesce ***around:*** **5** avoid, skirt **6** bypass, detour **7** compass **8** outflank, sidestep **10** circumvent ***ashore:*** **6** debark **9** disembark ***at:*** **6** assail, attack, tackle **7** assault ***away:*** **3** git **4** exit, scat, shoo **5** leave, scram, split **6** beat it, begone, cut out, depart, move on, retire **7** buzz off, get lost, pull out, take off **8** clear out, run along, shove off, withdraw **9** skedaddle ***back:*** **6** recede, return, revert **7** regress, retreat ***back on:*** **6** betray, renege **7** abandon **8** abrogate ***back over:*** **6** rehash, review, rework **7** recheck, retrace ***before:*** **4** lead **7** precede, predate **8** antedate ***beyond:*** **4** pass **5** excel, outdo **6** exceed, outrun **7** eclipse, surpass **8** outshine, outstrip, overtake **9** transcend ***forward:*** **6** move on, push on **7** advance, press on, proceed **8** continue, progress ***in:*** **5** enter **9** penetrate ***out:*** **4** exit **5** leave **6** expire ***Scottish:*** **3** gae ***through:*** **4** bear **5** audit, brave, check, spend **6** endure, suffer **7** consume, deplete, examine, exhaust, ride out, survive, sustain, undergo **8** squander **9** penetrate, withstand **10** experience ***together:*** **3** fit **4** date, jibe, suit **5** agree, match, tally **6** accord, square **7** conform **8** dovetail **9** accompany, harmonize **10** correspond ***with:*** **4** suit **5** befit, match **9** accompany
goad 3 egg, rod, sic **4** prod, push, spur, urge **5** drive, egg on, impel, prick, thorn **6** coerce, exhort, incite, motive, needle, prompt, propel **7** impetus, impulse **8** catalyst, motivate, stimulus **9** encourage, impulsion, incentive, stimulant, stimulate **10** inducement
go-ahead 4 okay **7** consent **8** spirited **9** ambitious, authority, clearance, energetic **10** green light, permission **11** progressive, up-and-coming **12** enterprising **13** authorization
goal 3 aim, end, use **4** duty, hope, mark **5** score **6** design, intent, object, target **7** mission, purpose **8** ambition, function **9** intention, objective
goat 3 kid, ram **4** lech **5** billy, letch, nanny **6**

alpaca, angora, lecher, Saanen **8** cashmere **10** Toggenburg ***female:*** **3** doe **5** nanny ***genus:*** **5** Capra ***Himalayan:*** **4** tahr, thar ***male:*** **4** buck **5** billy ***neutered:*** **6** wether ***relating to:*** **7** caprine ***wild:*** **4** ibex ***wool:*** **6** mohair **8** cashmere, pashmina
goat antelope **5** serow **7** chamois
goatee **5** beard **7** Vandyke **8** imperial, whiskers
goatfish **6** mullet
goatish **3** hot **4** lewd **6** carnal **7** caprine, lustful, satyric **8** prurient **9** indulgent, lecherous, lickerish **10** lascivious, libidinous, passionate **12** concupiscent
goat-man deity **3** Pan **5** satyr **7** silenus
goat nut **6** jojoba, pignut
gob **3** wad **4** blob, clod, glob, hunk, lump, mass **5** chunk, mouth **6** nugget, sailor **7** extract
gobbet **4** drib, drip, drop, hunk, lump, mass **5** chunk, piece **7** driblet, droplet, globule, portion **8** fragment
gobble **3** eat **4** bolt, cram, grab, glut, gulp, slop, wolf **5** gorge **6** devour, guzzle **7** swallow **11** ingurgitate
gobbledygook see **gibberish**
go-between **5** agent, envoy, proxy **6** broker, deputy, factor **7** courier, liaison **8** emissary, mediator, procurer **9** middleman **10** arbitrator, interagent, interceder, matchmaker, negotiator, procurator **11** intercessor **12** intermediary, intermediate
goblet **3** cup **5** glass, grail **6** vessel **7** chalice
goblin **3** elf, fay, hob, imp **4** puck **5** bogey, bogle, fairy, ghost, gnome **6** sprite **7** brownie, bugbear **8** bogeyman
____ **go bragh** **4** Erin
gobs **4** lots, tons, wads **5** heaps, loads, lumps, piles, rafts, reams, scads **6** oodles **8** slathers **10** quantities
god **4** idol **5** deity **7** creator **8** Almighty, divinity, immortal ***combining form:*** **4** theo ***false:*** **4** baal ***French:*** **4** dieu ***Hebrew:*** **6** Elohim, Yahweh ***Latin:*** **4** deus ***Spanish:*** **4** dios see specific entries— **Greek, Roman,** etc.— for names of specific gods and goddesses
god-awful **4** foul **6** horrid, rotten **7** beastly **8** dreadful, horrible, shameful, shocking, terrible, wretched **9** appalling, atrocious, miserable **10** abominable, deplorable, despicable, detestable, disgusting, outrageous
God Bless America composer **6** Berlin (Irving)
goddess **4** idol **5** deity **8** divinity, immortal ***Italian:*** **4** diva ***Latin:*** **3** dea (see note at **god**)
godfather **3** don **4** boss, capo **6** leader **7** sponsor
Godfather, The **8** Corleone (Don) ***actor:*** **6** Brando (Marlon), De Niro (Robert), Pacino (Al) ***author:*** **4** Puzo (Mario) ***director:*** **7** Coppola (Francis Ford)
God-fearing **5** pious **6** devout **8** faithful, reverent **9** pietistic, religious, righteous
godforsaken **4** bare **5** bleak **6** barren, dismal, gloomy, remote **7** pitiful **8** deserted, desolate, pitiable, wretched **9** miserable, neglected **11** unfortunate
Godiva's husband **7** Leofric
godless **5** pagan **6** unholy, wicked **7** atheist, heathen, impious, infidel, profane **8** agnostic **9** atheistic **11** irreligious, unreligious
godlike **4** holy **6** divine **7** blessed, supreme **8** almighty, immortal **10** omniscient **11** all-powerful
godliness **5** piety **6** purity **8** devotion, divinity, holiness, sanctity **9** beatitude, reverence **10** devoutness, sacredness **11** religiosity, saintliness **12** spirituality, virtuousness
godly **4** holy **5** pious **6** devout, divine **7** angelic, blessed, saintly, supreme **8** almighty, hallowed, immortal, virtuous **9** pietistic, prayerful, religious **10** omniscient **11** all-powerful
go down **3** dip, set **4** drop, fall, fold, lose, sink **5** ensue, lower, occur, pitch, slide, slump **6** cave in, happen, plunge, settle, topple, tumble **7** crumple, decline, descend, founder, succumb **8** collapse, keel over, submerge, submerse **9** surrender, take place
God's acre **8** boneyard, catacomb, cemetery **9** graveyard **10** churchyard, necropolis **12** burial ground, memorial park, potter's field
godsend **4** boon, gift, good **5** manna **7** benefit **8** blessing, windfall **9** advantage **11** benevolence, serendipity
Goethe work **5** Faust **6** Egmont, Stella **7** Clavigo **10** Prometheus
gofer **4** aide, peon **5** toady **6** drudge, flunky, helper, lackey, menial **7** courier, servant **8** factotum **9** assistant, attendant
goffer **5** crimp, flute, pinch, plait, pleat
go-getter **6** dynamo **7** hustler, rustler **8** live wire **10** ball of fire, powerhouse **11** self-starter
goggle **3** eye **4** bore, gape, gawk, gaze, look, ogle, peer **5** glare, gloat, stare **10** rubberneck
goggles **5** specs **7** glasses **10** eyeglasses, spectacles
go-go **5** hyper **6** hectic **7** frantic **8** frenetic, frenzied
Gogol novel ***novel:*** **9** Dead Souls ***story:*** **8** Overcoat (The) **10** Taras Bulba **14** Diary of a Madman
goiter **6** struma **8** swelling

Golconda see **gold mine**
gold 4 gilt **5** money **6** riches, wealth, yellow **7** bullion **8** treasure ***bar:* 5** ingot ***combining form:* 4** auri, auro **5** chrys **6** chryso ***fool's:* 6** pyrite ***heraldic:* 2** or ***imitation:* 6** ormolu ***measure:* 5** carat, karat ***Spanish:* 3** oro ***symbol:* 2** Au
goldbrick 3 bum **4** idle, laze, lazy, loaf, loll **5** cheat, dally, dog it, idler, shirk, slack **6** dawdle, loafer, loiter, lounge **7** lounger, shirker, slacker, swindle **8** lollygag, malinger, sluggard **9** lazybones **10** dillydally, malingerer
Gold Bug author 3 Poe (Edgar Allan)
gold cloth 4 lamé
gold-covered 4 gilt **6** gilded
golden 4 gilt, rich **5** auric, blond, shiny, straw **6** blonde, flaxen, gilded, mellow, superb, yellow **7** aureate, honeyed, shining **8** glorious, lustrous, resonant **9** favorable **10** auspicious, prosperous **11** flourishing
golden-ager 5 elder **6** senior **7** ancient, oldster, retiree **8** old-timer **13** senior citizen
golden-apples guardian 5 Ithun **6** Ithunn
golden bough 9 mistletoe
Golden Bough author 6 Frazer (James George)
Golden Boy playwright 5 Odets (Clifford)
golden-crowned accentor 7 warbler **8** ovenbird
goldeneye 3 bug **4** duck, fowl **6** insect **8** lacewing
Golden Fleece seeker 5 Jason **8** Argonaut
Golden Hind captain 5 Drake (Francis)
Golden Horde 6 Tatars **7** Mongols ***leader:* 4** Batu
golden horse 7 Trigger **8** palomino
golden shiner 4 dace, fish
Golden State 10 California
goldfinch 4 bird **8** songbird **12** yellowhammer
Golding novel 14 Lord of the Flies
gold mine 7 bonanza, pay dirt **8** El Dorado, Golconda, treasure, treasury **13** treasure trove
golem 3 oaf **4** clod, dolt, dope **5** dunce, idiot, robot **6** nitwit **7** halfwit, machine **8** imbecile **9** automaton, blockhead **10** nincompoop **11** blunderhead
golf *assistant:* 5 caddy **6** caddie ***ball material:* 6** balata **11** gutta-percha ***club:* 4** iron, wood **5** billy, spoon, wedge **6** driver, mashie, putter **7** niblick, pitcher **9** metal wood, sand wedge ***club part:* 3** toe **4** face, grip, head, heel, neck, sole **5** hosel, shaft ***course:* 5** links ***cup:* 5** Ryder **6** Curtis, Walker ***hazard:* 4** trap **6** bunker **8** sand trap ***score:* 3** ace, par **5** bogey, eagle **6** birdie ***stroke:* 4** baff, chip, draw, fade, hook, putt **5** drive, pitch, shank, slice **6** sclaff ***target:* 3** cup, par, pin **4** flag **5** green **7** fairway ***term:* 3** lie, tee **4** club, fore, hole, loft **5** divot, rough, swing **6** dormie, hazard, marker, stance, stroke **8** foursome, handicap **9** backswing, downswing, flagstick
golfer 8 linksman ***man:* 3** Els (Ernie) **4** Aoki (Isao), Daly (John), Ford (Doug), Haas (Jay), Kite (Tom), Lyle (Sandy), Mize (Larry), Tway (Bob) **5** Boros (Julius), Faldo (Nick), Floyd (Ray), Grady (Wayne), Green (Hubert), Hagen (Walter), Hogan (Ben), Jones (Bobby), Irwin (Hale), North (Andy), Pavin (Corey), Peete (Calvin), Price (Nick), Shute (Denny), Singh (Vijay), Snead (Sam), Woods (Tiger) **6** Casper (Billy), Graham (David), Janzen (Lee), Langer (Bernhard), Miller (Johnny), Nelson (Byron, Larry), Norman (Greg), Ouimet (Francis), Palmer (Arnold), Player (Gary), Sluman (Jeff), Sutton (Hal), Vardon (Harry), Watson (Tom) **7** Azinger (Paul), Couples (Fred), Guldahl (Ralph), Mayfair (Billy), Sarazen (Gene), Simpson (Scott), Stewart (Payne), Strange (Curtis), Trevino (Lee), Woosnam (Ian), Zoeller (Fuzzy) **8** Crenshaw (Ben), Nicklaus (Jack), Olazabal (José), Weiskopf (Tom) **9** Mickelson (Phil), Rodriguez (Chi Chi), Elkington (Steve) **10** Middlecoff (Cary) **11** Ballesteros (Seve) ***woman:* 3** Pak (Se Ri) **4** Berg (Patty), King (Betsy) **5** Baker (Kathy), Lopez (Nancy), Rawls (Betsy), Stacy (Hollis), Suggs (Louise) **6** Alcott (Amy), Carner (Joanne), Daniel (Beth), Davies (Laura), Geddes (Jane), Mallon (Meg), Merten (Lauri), Wright (Mickey) **7** Bradley (Pat), Inkster (Juli), Mochrie (Dottie), Sheehan (Patty) **8** Zaharias (Babe) **9** Didrikson (Babe), Sorenstam (Annika), Whitworth (Kathy) **10** Stephenson (Jan)
Golgotha 7 Calvary
Goliath 5 giant **10** Philistine ***deathplace:* 4** Elah ***home:* 4** Gath ***slayer:* 5** David
Gollum creator 7 Tolkien (J. R. R.)
gonad 5 gland, ovary **6** testis **8** testicle
gondola 3 car **4** boat **7** ski lift **11** railroad car
gone 4 away, dead, left, lost, past **5** flown **6** absent **7** defunct, extinct, lacking, missing **8** departed, vanished
gonef see **ganef**
goner 8 dead duck **9** lost cause
Goneril *father:* 4 Lear (King) ***husband:* 6** Albany ***sister:* 5** Regan **8** Cordelia ***victim:* 5** Regan
Gone with the Wind *author:* 8 Mitchell (Mar-

garet) ***character:*** **5** Rhett (Butler) **6** Ashley (Wilkes) **7** Melanie (Wilkes) **8** Scarlett (O'Hara) ***plantation:*** **4** Tara
gonfalon 4 flag, jack **6** banner, ensign **7** pendant, pennant **8** banderol, standard **9** banderole
gong 6 cymbal, tam-tam
gonzo 6 far-out **7** bizarre, offbeat **9** wigged-out **10** outrageous
goo 4 crud, glop, guck, gunk, muck **5** slime
goober 6 peanut
good 4 pure **5** right, sound, whole **6** decent, humane, kindly, worthy **7** benefit, upright, welfare **8** innocent, virtuous **9** admirable, blameless, exemplary, favorable, honorable, righteous, well-being, wholesome **10** altruistic, beneficent, beneficial, benevolent, charitable, worthwhile **11** respectable, well-behaved ***French:*** **3** bon **5** bonne ***German:*** **3** gut **4** gute ***Spanish:*** **5** buena, bueno
good-bye 4 ciao, ta-ta **5** adieu, congé, later **6** so long **7** cheerio, parting, send-off, toodles **8** farewell, toodle-oo **9** departing, departure **11** leave-taking, valediction, valedictory ***French:*** **5** adieu **8** au revoir **9** bon voyage ***German:*** **8** lebe wohl ***Italian:*** **11** arrivederci ***Japanese:*** **8** sayonara ***Spanish:*** **5** adios **10** hasta luego **12** hasta la vista
Good Earth *author:* **4** Buck (Pearl S.) ***heroine:*** **4** O-lan
good-for-nothing 3 bum **6** rascal, waster **7** inutile, rounder, useless, wastrel **8** fainéant, feckless, rascally, unworthy **9** dissolute, scoundrel, valueless, worthless **10** ne'er-do-well, profligate, scapegrace **11** purposeless
good-looking 4 cute, fair, foxy **5** bonny, dishy, hunky **6** comely, lovely, pretty **8** alluring, drop-dead, fetching, handsome, stunning **9** beauteous, beautiful, bodacious, ravishing **10** attractive
goodly 4 fair, tidy **5** ample, hefty, large **7** sizable **8** generous **9** bountiful, plentiful **11** significant, substantial **12** considerable
good-natured 4 easy, kind, mild, warm **6** genial, jovial, mellow **7** affable, amiable, cordial, lenient **8** cheerful, friendly, laid-back, obliging, pleasant, pleasing, sanguine **9** agreeable, congenial, easygoing, gemütlich **10** altruistic, benevolent, charitable **11** complaisant
goodness 5 honor, merit, worth **6** purity, virtue **7** decency, honesty, probity, quality **8** morality **9** integrity, rectitude **11** benevolence
goods 4 gear **5** cargo, stock, stuff, wares **7** effects **8** chattels, movables, property **9** vendibles **10** belongings **11** commodities, merchandise, possessions **13** paraphernalia ***smuggled:*** **10** contraband ***stolen:*** **4** loot, swag **5** booty **6** boodle, spoils **7** plunder ***thrown overboard:*** **5** lagan **6** jetsam
good-tasting 5 sapid, yummy **6** delish, savory, toothy **8** luscious **9** delicious, palatable, relishing, toothsome **10** appetizing, delectable, flavorsome **11** scrumptious **13** mouthwatering
goodwill 5 amity, favor **6** comity **7** charity, rapport **8** altruism, kindness, sympathy **9** tolerance **10** compassion, friendship, generosity, kindliness **11** benevolence, helpfulness **12** friendliness
goody 5 candy, treat **6** bonbon, dainty, morsel, tidbit **8** delicacy, kickshaw
goody-goody 4 prig **5** prude **6** Grundy **7** prudish, puritan, uptight **8** bluenose, Comstock, priggish **9** Mrs. Grundy, nice-nelly **11** puritanical
gooey 5 gluey, gummy, mushy, sappy, soupy **6** cloggy, drippy, slushy, sticky, viscid **7** maudlin, viscous **8** adhesive **9** glutinous **11** sentimental **12** mucilaginous
goof 3 err, kid **4** boob, dolt, flub, fool, mess, muff, slip **5** boner, booby, botch, chump, dunce, error, fluff, gaffe, gum up, idiot, put on **6** bobble, boggle, bollix, boo-boo, bumble, bungle, fumble, mess up, slip-up **7** blooper, blunder, fathead, louse up, mistake **8** dolthead, lunkhead **9** blockhead
go off 4 blow **5** blast, burst, erupt, leave, sound **6** blow up, depart **7** explode **8** detonate
goofy 5 balmy, batty, crazy, daffy, dippy, loony, nutty, potty, silly **6** simple, stupid **7** foolish, idiotic **9** ludicrous **10** ridiculous **11** harebrained
gook 4 crud, glop, gunk, muck **5** gumbo, slime **6** debris, sludge
go on 4 last, stay **5** occur **6** endure, happen, keep up **7** persist, proceed **8** continue **9** persevere
goon 3 oaf, sap **4** boob, dodo, dolt, dope, fool, hood, thug **5** dummy, idiot **6** dimwit, hit man, nitwit **7** hoodlum **8** dumbbell, enforcer **10** triggerman
gooney 7 seabird **9** albatross
goop 4 crud, gunk, muck **5** gumbo, tripe
Goops author 7 Burgess (Gelett)
goose 4 poke, spur **9** stimulate ***cry:*** **4** honk **5** clang ***formation:*** **3** vee **5** skein, wedge **6** gaggle ***genus:*** **5** Anser ***Hawaiian:*** **4** nene ***male:*** **6** gander ***wild:*** **5** brant **7** greylag **8** barnacle ***young:*** **7** gosling
gooseberry 7 currant
Goosebumps author 5 Stine (R. L.)

goose egg 3 nil, nix, zip **4** nada, zero **5** aught, zilch **6** bubkes, bupkes, bupkus, cipher, naught, nought **7** no score, nothing
gooseflesh 5 bumps **7** pimples
go over 4 scan, skim **5** study **6** peruse, review **7** examine, inspect
gopher 6 rodent **8** tortoise
Gopher State 9 Minnesota
Gordian knot cutter 9 Alexander
Gordius' son 5 Midas
gore 3 jab **4** stab **5** blood, slime, wound **6** gusset, pierce **7** carnage **12** gruesomeness
gorge 3 gap **4** cloy, fill, glut, jade, pall, sate **5** abyss, chasm, cleft, clove, flume, gulch, stuff **6** arroyo, canyon, clough, defile, pig out, ravine **7** couloir, overeat, satiate, surfeit **11** overindulge ***Arizona:*** **11** Grand Canyon ***Colorado:*** **5** Royal
gorgeous 5 grand, plush **6** comely, lavish, lovely, pretty, superb **7** opulent, sublime **8** alluring, dazzling, glorious, splendid **9** beautiful, brilliant, exquisite, luxurious, sumptuous **10** attractive, glittering **11** magnificent, resplendent, splendorous
gorgon 3 hag **5** crone, harpy, witch **6** Medusa, ogress, virago **8** battle-ax, fishwife, harridan, slattern **9** battle-axe, termagant ***father:*** **7** Phorcus, Phorcys ***mother:*** **4** Ceto
gorilla 3 ape **4** goon, hood, thug **5** tough **6** simian **7** primate **8** gangster **10** anthropoid
Gorky drama 11 Lower Depths (The)
gormless 4 dumb, slow **6** stupid
gorse 4 whin **5** furze, shrub **6** legume
gory 5 lurid **6** bloody, grisly **8** gruesome, sanguine **10** sanguinary **11** ensanguined, sanguineous, sensational **12** bloodstained **13** bloodcurdling
gosh 3 gee, wow **4** dang, darn, drat, egad, geez, heck **5** golly **6** crikey, cripes, shucks **7** doggone **8** goodness, gracious
gospel 5 truth **6** truism **7** message **8** doctrine **9** scripture **11** evangelical
gossamer 4 airy, film, fine, webs **5** filmy, gauzy, sheer **6** flimsy **7** cobwebs, tenuous **8** delicate **10** diaphanous **11** transparent
gossip 4 blab, buzz, chat, dirt, dish, talk **5** clack, prate, rumor, yenta **6** babble, rumble, tattle **7** babbler, chatter, hearsay, prattle, tattler **8** bigmouth, busybody, informer, prattler, quidnunc, telltale **10** talebearer **11** rumormonger, scandalizer, scuttlebutt **12** blatherskite
gossipy 5 gabby, talky **6** chatty **8** babbling, blabbing **9** garrulous, talkative
Gotham 7 New York (City)
Gothic 4 dark, wild **5** crude **6** brutal, coarse, savage **7** uncouth **8** barbaric, Germanic, medieval, Teutonic **9** barbarian, barbarous, sans serif **11** black letter, uncivilized
Götterdämmerung composer 6 Wagner (Richard)
Gouda 6 cheese
gouge 3 dig **4** milk, ream, tool **5** cheat, exact, pinch, screw, wrest, wring **6** chisel, coerce, extort, groove, wrench **7** squeeze **8** scoop out **9** blackmail, extortion, shake down **10** overcharge
goulash 4 olio, stew **6** jumble, medley **7** mélange **8** mishmash **9** potpourri **10** bridge hand, hodgepodge, hotchpotch, salmagundi **11** gallimaufry
go under 4 fall, flop, fold, lose, sink **5** drown **6** plunge, submit **7** founder, immerse, succumb **8** collapse, submerge, submerse **9** surrender **10** capitulate
Gounod work 5 Faust **8** Ave Maria
gourd 4 pepo **5** fruit, melon **6** bottle, squash, vessel **7** chayote, gherkin, pumpkin **8** calabash, cucumber, cucurbit ***instrument:*** **6** maraca
gourmand see **glutton; gourmet**
gourmet 7 epicure **9** bon vivant, epicurean **10** gastronome **11** connoisseur **12** gastronomist
gout 4 blob, clot, gush **5** spurt **6** splash **7** disease, podagra **8** eruption, swelling
govern 4 head, lead, rule **5** guide, order, reign, steer **6** direct, manage, master **7** command, conduct, control, execute, oversee **8** dominate, hold sway, regulate **9** supervise **10** administer **11** superintend
governess 5 nanny, nurse **6** duenna **8** mistress **9** nursemaid **10** babysitter **11** Mary Poppins
government 4 rule **5** power **6** polity, regime **7** regency, regimen **8** monarchy, republic, Uncle Sam **9** authority, autocracy, democracy, hierarchy, oligarchy **10** Big Brother **11** aristocracy, sovereignty ***autocratic:*** **7** czarism, fascism, tyranny **9** despotism **10** absolutism **12** dictatorship ***by a few:*** **9** oligarchy ***by one:*** **8** monarchy ***by three:*** **8** triarchy **11** triumvirate ***by women:*** **8** gynarchy ***official:*** **10** bureaucrat **11** functionary ***without:*** **7** anarchy
government agency 3 ATF, BIA, BLM, CDC, CIA, DEA, EPA, FAA, FBI, FCC, FDA, FEC, FHA, GAO, GPO, HUD, ICC, INS, IRS, NBS, NEA, NIH, NRC, TVA **4** FDIC, FEMA, FEPC, NASA, NOAA, NTSB, OSHA
governor 3 bey, dey **4** head **5** chief, nabob, ruler **6** leader, regent **7** manager, viceroy **8** director **9** executive, regulator **10** commandant, magistrate ***Chinese:*** **6** tuchun ***of a***

fort: **7** alcaide, alcayde **9** castellan, chatelain ***Persian:*** **6** satrap
gown 4 robe, toga **5** dress, frock, habit, tunic **6** camise, kimono, kirtle, mantua **7** cassock, chemise **8** peignoir ***dressing:*** **8** bathrobe ***hospital:*** **6** johnny
goy 6 non-Jew **7** gentile
grab 3 nab **4** glom, grip, snag, take **5** catch, clasp, grasp, pluck, seize **6** clutch, collar, snatch, tackle **7** capture, grapple, seizure
grabby 6 greedy **8** covetous, desirous, grasping **9** rapacious **10** avaricious, prehensile **11** acquisitive
grace 4 ease **5** adorn, charm, favor, mercy, poise **6** allure, lenity, pardon, polish, prayer, thanks, virtue **7** charity, dignify, dignity, enhance **8** approval, blessing, clemency, easiness, elegance, goodness, kindness, leniency, petition, reprieve **9** embellish, privilege **10** indulgence, invocation, refinement **11** benediction, forbearance **12** thanksgiving
graceful 4 airy, deft, easy **5** lithe **6** nimble, poised, smooth **7** elegant, flowing **8** debonair, polished
graceless 4 rude **5** crude, gawky, inept **6** clumsy, coarse, gauche, klutzy, vulgar **7** awkward, boorish, uncouth **8** barbaric, ungainly **9** barbarian, barbarous **10** outlandish, unmannered **12** infelicitous
Graces 6 Charis **8** Charites (plural) ***brilliance:*** **6** Aglaia ***bloom:*** **6** Thalia ***joy:*** **10** Euphrosyne ***mother:*** **5** Aegle
gracious 4 kind **5** suave **6** benign, genial, kindly, urbane **7** affable, amiable, cordial, courtly, gallant, stately, tactful **8** charming, generous, mannered, merciful, obliging, sociable **9** congenial, courteous **11** complaisant, good-natured **13** compassionate
grackle 4 myna **5** mynah **7** jackdaw **8** starling **9** blackbird
gradation 4 rank, step **5** order, range, scale, shade, stage **6** ablaut, change, degree, nuance, series **8** ordering, position, spectrum **9** continuum, variation **10** difference, succession
grade 3 peg **4** cant, form, kind, lean, mark, rank, rate, rung, sort, step, tier, tilt **5** blend, class, group, level, notch, order, pitch, place, slant, slope, stage **6** assess, assort, degree, league, rating **7** arrange, caliber, echelon, incline, leaning, quality **8** appraise, category, classify, division, evaluate, grouping, position, standard **10** categorize **11** inclination
Grade A 3 ace, top **4** best, boss, fine, tops **5** grand, great, prime, primo, super **6** choice, tip-top **7** capital, supreme **8** five-star, superior, top-notch **9** excellent, first-rate, nonpareil, number one, top-drawer **10** first-class **11** outstanding **13** par excellence
gradient 4 lean, ramp, rise, tilt **5** angle, pitch, slant, slope **7** incline, leaning **9** acclivity, declivity **11** inclination
gradual 4 even, slow **6** Psalms, steady **7** ongoing **8** bit-by-bit, creeping **9** piecemeal, prolonged **10** continuous, developing, protracted, step-by-step **11** progressive
gradually 6 slowly **7** by steps **8** bit by bit **9** by degrees, piecemeal **10** step by step **12** deliberately **13** imperceptibly, incrementally
graduate 4 alum ***acquisition:*** **6** degree **7** diploma ***female:*** **6** alumna **7** alumnae (plural) ***male:*** **6** alumni (plural) **7** alumnus
Graeae, Graiae 4 Enyo **5** Deino **8** Pephredo ***father:*** **7** Phorcus, Phorcys ***mother:*** **4** Ceto ***sisters:*** **7** Gorgons
graffiti artist 6 tagger ***signature:*** **3** tag
graft 3 imp **4** join, mend, scam, skim **5** affix, crime, fraud, scion, unite **6** attach, boodle, fasten, payola, splice **7** implant, swindle, topwork **8** kickback **10** corruption
Grafton character 8 Millhone (Kinsey)
Grahame, Kenneth *character:* 3 Rat **4** Toad, Mole **6** Badger ***novel:*** **16** Wind in the Willows (The)
grail 3 cup, end **4** goal **6** goblet, object, target **7** chalice **9** objective ***seeker:*** **7** Galahad
grain 3 bit, jot, rye **4** corn, flax, iota, meal, mite, oats, rice **5** crumb, fiber, kamut, maize, speck, spelt, trace, wheat **6** barley, cereal, millet, quinoa, tittle **7** granule, smidgen, sorghum, texture **8** amaranth, molecule, particle **9** buckwheat, triticale ***beard:*** **3** awn ***bundle:*** **4** bale **5** sheaf ***chute:*** **6** hopper ***ear:*** **5** spike ***elevator:*** **4** silo ***mixture:*** **6** fodder ***row:*** **5** swath **7** windrow
grainy 5 rough **6** coarse **8** granular **10** unfinished, unpolished
grammarian 7 Donatus (Aelius)
grammatical case 6 dative **7** oblique **8** ablative, genitive, locative, vocative **9** objective **10** accusative, nominative, possessive, subjective
grampus 3 orc **5** whale **7** dolphin **8** cetacean, porpoise, scorpion **9** blackfish **12** whip scorpion
Granada *building:* 8 Alhambra ***citadel:*** **8** Alcazaba ***last Moorish king:*** **7** Boabdil
granary 3 bin **4** silo **10** repository, storehouse
grand 3 fab **4** epic, fine, huge, vast **5** gaudy, lofty, noble, regal, royal, showy, super **6** august, garish, lavish, lordly, mighty, ornate, superb **7** exalted, opulent, pompous, stately,

sublime **8** baronial, elevated, gorgeous, imposing, majestic, princely, splendid **9** first-rate, inclusive, luxurious, sumptuous, wonderful **10** first-class, impressive, monumental, prodigious, stupendous, tremendous **11** magnificent **12** ostentatious

Grand Canyon ***explorer:*** **6** Powell (John Wesley) ***state:*** **7** Arizona

grande dame **5** queen **6** matron **7** dowager, doyenne **9** matriarch

grandee **4** duke, earl, king, lord, peer **5** baron, noble, pasha **6** bashaw, prince **8** mandarin, marquess, nobleman, viscount **10** panjandrum **11** muckety-muck

grandeur **4** pomp **5** glory **7** dignity, majesty **8** nobility, opulence, splendor, vastness **9** greatness, immensity, largeness, loftiness, nobleness, sublimity **10** augustness **11** stateliness **12** magnificence

grandiloquent **5** lofty **7** aureate, bloated, fustian, orotund, pompous **8** inflated **9** bombastic, flatulent, high-flown, overblown **10** histrionic, portentous **11** declamatory, highfalutin, pretentious **12** magniloquent

grand inquisitor **10** Torquemada (Tomás de)

grandiose **4** epic, vast **5** lofty, noble, regal, royal, showy **6** august, cosmic, lavish, lordly **7** pompous, stately, sublime, utopian **8** affected, imposing, majestic, princely, splendid **9** ambitious, high-flown **11** extravagant, highfalutin, magnificent, pretentious **12** ostentatious

grand mal **7** seizure **8** epilepsy

grandmother **4** nana ***Russian:*** **8** babushka

grange **4** farm **9** farmhouse, farmstead

granite **3** ore **4** rock **5** stone **6** aplite **7** mineral **11** igneous rock

Granite State **12** New Hampshire

grant **3** aid **4** alms, avow, cede, dole, gift, give **5** admit, allow, award, endow, yield **6** accord, assert, assign, assume, bestow, confer, convey, donate, permit **7** charity, concede, consent, entitle, handout, present, subsidy, suppose **8** bequeath, donation, property, transfer **9** endowment, vouchsafe **10** assistance, concession, relinquish, subvention **11** acknowledge, benefaction **12** contribution **13** appropriation

granular **5** rough, sandy **6** coarse, grainy **7** powdery **8** powdered **10** unfinished, unpolished

granule **3** bit, jot **4** iota, pill, spot **5** grain **6** pellet **8** fragment, particle

grape **3** fox, uva **4** Bual **5** Gamay, Pinot, Syrah **6** Arinto, Burger, Gentil, merlot, muscat, Shiraz **7** Albillo, Aligote, Barbera, Catawba, Concord, Furmint, Niagara, sultana **8** Aleatico, Cabernet, Charbono, Delaware, Friularo, Grenache, Isabella, malvasia, muscadel, Muscadet, Nebbiolo, Riesling, Semillon, Sylvaner, Thompson, Traminer, vinifera, Viognier **9** Carmenère, Chasselas, Lambrusco, Malvoisie, muscadine, Pinot Gris, pinot noir, Sauvignon, Trebbiano, zinfandel **10** chardonnay, Grignolino, muscadelle, pinot blanc, Sangiovese, Verdicchio **11** Chenin Blanc, Petite Sirah, pinot grigio, scuppernong ***disease:*** **4** esca ***dried:*** **6** raisin ***drink:*** **4** wine ***pulp:*** **4** rape **6** pomace ***residue:*** **4** marc

grapefruit **6** pomelo

Grapes of Wrath, The ***author:*** **9** Steinbeck (John) ***family:*** **4** Joad ***people:*** **5** Okies

grapevine **4** buzz **5** rumor **6** gossip **7** hearsay **9** rumor mill **11** scuttlebutt

graph **3** map **4** plot **5** chart **6** sketch **7** diagram, outline **8** nomogram, pie chart

graphic **3** map **5** clear, lucid, photo, vivid **6** cogent, visual **7** picture, precise, telling, written **8** clear-cut, definite, detailed, explicit, incisive, striking **9** pictorial, realistic **10** compelling, photograph **11** descriptive, picturesque

graphite **4** lead **6** carbon **8** plumbago

grapnel **4** hook **6** anchor

grappa **6** brandy

grapple **3** nab **4** bind, cope, grab, grip, hold **5** catch, clamp, clasp, fight, grasp, seize **6** battle, bucket, clench, clinch, clutch, fasten, tackle, tussle **7** contest, scuffle, wrestle **8** struggle

grasp **3** dig, ken, see **4** glom, grip, hold, know, take **5** catch, clamp, clasp, cling, seize **6** accept, clench, clinch, clutch, fathom, follow, handle, take in, tenure **7** cognize, compass, control, embrace, grapple, realize **8** envisage, perceive **9** apprehend, awareness **10** appreciate, comprehend, take hold of, understand **12** apprehension **13** comprehension, understanding

graspable **5** clear, lucid **6** lucent **8** coherent, knowable, palpable **10** fathomable **11** perspicuous **12** intelligible **13** apprehensible

grasping **4** avid **6** grabby, greedy **8** covetous, desirous **9** rapacious **10** avaricious, prehensile **11** acquisitive

grass **3** Poa, pot, sod, tea, Zea **4** lawn, reed, turf, weed **6** redtop **7** herbage, panicum, pasture **8** cannabis, Mary Jane **9** cocksfoot, marijuana ***African:*** **6** imphee ***annual:*** **6** darnel **8** teosinte ***Asian:*** **7** vetiver, whangee ***Australian:*** **8** spinifex ***beach:*** **6** marram ***cereal:*** **3** oat, rye, Zea **4** milo, teff **5** kafir, maize, proso, sorgo, wheat **6** millet **7** sorghum **8** triticum ***clump:*** **4** tuft **7** tussock ***cover:*** **3** dew ***dried:*** **3** hay **5** straw ***European:*** **7** Bermuda, timothy ***fiber:*** **4** flax ***fragrant:*** **10** citronella ***meadow:*** **3** Poa ***pasture:*** **5** Bahia, grama ***perennial:*** **6** fescue, quitch, zoysia **7** esparto, galleta ***prairie:*** **8** bluestem ***second growth:*** **5** rowen ***tropical:*** **5** cogon **6** bamboo

grasshopper 6 locust **7** katydid **8** cocktail

grassland 3 lea **5** field **6** meadow **7** pasture, prairie ***African:*** **4** veld **5** veldt ***flat:*** **7** savanna **8** savannah ***South American:*** **5** pampa **6** pampas

Grass novel 7 Tin Drum (The) **8** Dog Years, Flounder (The) **11** Cat and Mouse

grate 3 irk, jar, rub, vex **4** file, fray, fret, gall, rasp, rile **5** annoy, chafe, gnash, grill, grind, peeve, pique **6** abrade, grille, nettle, rankle, scrape **7** provoke, scratch **8** irritate **9** aggravate, fireplace

grateful 7 obliged, pleased, restful, welcome **8** beholden, indebted, pleasant, pleasing, thankful **9** agreeable, congenial, favorable **10** refreshing **11** restorative **12** appreciative

Gratiano *brother:* 9 Brabantio ***friend:*** **7** Antonio **8** Bassanio ***niece:*** **9** Desdemona ***wife:*** **7** Nerissa

gratify 4 baby, sate **5** favor, humor, spoil **6** coddle, oblige, pamper, pander, please **7** appease, cater to, content, delight, gladden, indulge, satisfy

gratin 5 crust

grating 3 dry **4** grid, rasp **5** grill, harsh, rough **6** grille, hoarse **7** irksome, jarring, lattice, rasping, raucous **8** gridiron, strident **9** vexatious **10** stridulous

gratis 4 comp, free **6** comped **8** costless **10** chargeless **13** complimentary

gratitude 6 thanks **12** appreciation, gratefulness, thankfulness

gratuitous 6 wanton **8** baseless **9** unfounded, voluntary **10** groundless, reasonless, ungrounded **11** uncalled-for, unnecessary, unwarranted **12** indefensible

gratuity 3 tip **4** gift, perk **5** bonus **6** reward **7** cumshaw, douceur **8** donation, largesse, offering **9** baksheesh, lagniappe, pourboire **10** perquisite **11** benefaction **12** contribution

grave 3 pit, sad **4** dire, dour, fell, grim, tomb **5** acute, awful, crypt, fatal, heavy, major, sober, staid, vault **6** burial, deadly, gloomy, sedate, severe, solemn, somber, sombre, urgent **7** austere, ghastly, ominous, ossuary, serious, subdued, weighty **8** catacomb, critical, dreadful, perilous, pressing, terrible **9** dangerous, mausoleum, momentous, ponderous, saturnine, sepulcher, sepulchre, sepulture, unsmiling ***marker:*** **5** stela, stele **8** memorial, monument **9** footstone, headstone, tombstone **11** sarcophagus ***mound:*** **6** barrow **7** tumulus ***robber:*** **5** ghoul

gravel 4 dirt, grit, sand ***ridge:*** **5** esker

gravelly 5 raspy, rough **6** gritty, hoarse **7** rasping, grating **8** abrasive, granular, guttural, scratchy

graven image 4 icon, idol

graver 4 tool **5** burin **8** sculptor

graveyard 8 boot hill, catacomb, cemetery, God's acre **10** necropolis **12** burial ground, memorial park, potter's field

gravid 5 heavy **8** enceinte, pregnant **9** expectant, expecting, with child **10** parturient **12** childbearing

gravity 5 force **6** weight **7** dignity, urgency **8** sobriety **9** heaviness, solemnity **10** importance, somberness **11** consequence, seriousness **12** significance

gravlax 3 lox **6** salmon

gravy 4 perk **5** bonus, bribe, graft, juice, sauce **6** payola **8** dressing, windfall ***French:*** **3** jus

gray 3 ash, old **4** aged, ashy, blah, drab, dull **5** ashen, bleak, color, hoary, slate, slaty **6** dismal, gloomy, leaden **7** elderly, grizzly, neutral **8** grizzled, gunmetal, overcast **9** cinereous, colorless ***brownish:*** **3** dun **5** taupe **7** fuscous

gray duck 7 gadwall, pintail

grayfish 5 shark **7** dogfish

gray matter 3 wit **4** head, mind **5** brain **6** brains, noddle, noggin, noodle **8** cerebrum **9** intellect **10** encephalon **12** intelligence, neural tissue

graze 3 eat, rub **4** feed, gall, kiss, skim, skip, wear **5** brush, chafe, erode, shave, touch **6** abrade, browse, bruise, forage, glance, scrape **7** contuse, corrade, pasture **8** abrasion, ricochet

grazier 7 rancher

grease 3 fat, oil **4** lard **5** smear **6** smooth **7** lanolin **9** lubricant, lubricate ***combining form:*** **4** sebi, sebo

greasy 4 oily **5** fatty, slick **8** slippery, unctuous **10** lubricious, oleaginous

greasy spoon 4 café **5** diner, grill **6** eatery **7** beanery, hashery **9** chophouse, hash house, lunchroom **10** coffee shop **12** luncheonette

great 3 big, fat **4** huge, vast **5** boffo, grand, jumbo, large, noble, socko **6** famous, heroic **7** awesome, eminent, exalted, immense, mammoth, notable, sublime, supreme, titanic **8** colossal, enormous, gigantic, glorious, renowned, terrific, towering **9** excellent, fantastic, humongous, paramount, prominent, wonderful **10** celebrated, impressive, noteworthy, prodigious, remarkable, stupendous, tremendous **11** illustrious, magnificent, outstanding, superlative **13** distinguished ***combining form:*** **4** mega **6** megalo

Great Bear 9 Big Dipper, Ursa Major **13** constellation

Great Britain see **England, United Kingdom**

Great Commoner, the 4 Pitt (William) **5** Bryan (William Jennings) **7** Lincoln (Abraham)

Great Emancipator, the 7 Lincoln (Abraham)

greater 4 more **5** metro **6** better, bigger, higher, larger **8** superior **9** exceeding **10** surpassing **12** metropolitan

greatest 4 best, most **6** utmost **7** maximum, supreme **8** foremost

Great Expectations *author:* 7 Dickens (Charles) ***character:*** **3** Joe (Gargery), Pip **5** Biddy **7** Estella, Jaggers **8** Havisham (Miss), Magwitch (Abel)

greathearted 4 bold, kind **5** brave, lofty, noble **6** heroic **7** gallant **8** fearless, generous, princely **10** benevolent, chivalrous, courageous, high-minded **11** considerate, magnanimous

Great Lake 4 Erie **5** Huron **7** Ontario **8** Michigan, Superior ***acronym:*** **5** HOMES

Great Lake State 8 Michigan

greave 7 legging

grebe 4 bird, fowl **8** dabchick **10** diving bird

Greece 6 Hellas ***ancient city-state:*** **5** Argos **6** Athens, Sparta, Thebes **7** Corinth ***ancient town:*** **6** Delphi ***capital:*** **6** Athens ***city:*** **6** Patras **7** Larissa, Piraeus **8** Salonika **12** Thessaloníki ***conqueror:*** **6** Philip (of Macedonia) **9** Alexander (the Great) ***island, island group:*** **5** Crete **6** Aegean, Euboea, Ionian **8** Cyclades, Sporades ***monetary unit:*** **4** euro ***monetary unit, former:*** **6** lepton **7** drachma ***mountain, range:*** **3** Ida **4** Ossa **5** Athos **6** Pelion, Pindus **7** Olympus **9** Parnassus ***neighbor:*** **6** Turkey **7** Albania **8** Bulgaria **9** Macedonia ***part of:*** **7** Balkans ***peninsula:*** **6** Balkan **10** Chalcidice **11** Peloponnese ***region:*** **6** Attica, Epirus, Thrace **8** Thessaly ***sea:*** **6** Aegean, Ionian **13** Mediterranean ***vale:*** **5** Tempe

greed 4 lust **6** excess, hunger **7** avarice, avidity, craving **7** edacity, longing **8** cupidity, gluttony, rapacity, voracity **12** covetousness, ravenousness

greedy 4 avid **5** itchy **6** grabby **7** hoggish, miserly, selfish **8** covetous, desirous, edacious, esurient, grasping **10** avaricious, gluttonous **11** acquisitive

Greek 6 Argive, babble, drivel, jabber **7** Achaean, Hellene **8** Hellenic, nonsense **9** gibberish ***assembly:*** **5** agora, boule ***cheese:*** **4** feta ***coin:*** **4** obol **6** lepton, stater ***column:*** **5** Doric, Ionic **10** Corinthian ***contest:*** **4** agon ***counselor:*** **6** Nestor ***dictator:*** **7** Metaxas (Ioannis) ***dragon:*** **9** Eurythion ***drink:*** **4** ouzo ***epic:*** **5** Iliad **7** Odyssey ***Fates:*** **6** Clotho, Moirae **7** Atropos **8** Lachesis ***gift:*** **11** Trojan Horse

god:

chief: 4 Zeus **messenger: 6** Hermes **of agriculture: 6** Cronus **of death: 8** Thanatos **of dreams: 8** Morpheus **of fire: 10** Hephaestus **of healing: 9** Asclepius **11** Aesculapius **of love: 4** Eros **of marriage: 5** Hymen **of the sun: 6** Apollo **of physicians: 6** Hermes **of sleep: 6** Hypnos **of the sea: 6** Nereus, Triton **7** Oceanus **8** Poseidon **of the sun: 6** Helios **of the underworld: 5** Pluto **of the winds: 5** Eurus, Notus **6** Aeolus, Boreas **8** Zephyrus **of war: 4** Ares **of wine: 8** Dionysus **of woods: 3** Pan

goddess:

of agriculture: 7 Demeter **of beauty: 9** Aphrodite **of dawn: 3** Eos **of discord: 4** Eris **of fertility: 6** Cybele **of flowers: 7** Chloris **of fortune: 5** Tyche **of harvests: 4** Rhea **of hunting: 7** Artemis **of justice: 7** Astraea **of love: 9** Aphrodite **of marriage: 4** Hera **of night: 3** Nyx **of peace: 5** Irene **of retribution: 7** Nemesis **of ruin: 3** Ate **of the earth: 4** Gaea, Gaia **of the hearth: 6** Hestia **of magic: 6** Hecate, Hekate **of the moon: 6** Hecate, Hekate, Selena, Selene **7** Artemis, Astarte **of the rainbow: 4** Iris **of the seasons: 5** Horae **of the underworld: 6** Hecate, Hekate **10** Persephone **of vengeance: 7** Nemesis **of victory: 4** Nike **of wisdom: 6** Athena **of witchcraft: 6** Hecate, Hekate **of womanhood: 4** Hera **of youth: 4** Hebe ***hero:*** **4** Aias, Ajax **5** Jason **7** Theseus **8** Achilles, Argonaut, Heracles, Hercules, Odysseus **9** Achilleus ***historian:*** **8** Xenophon **9** Herodotus **10** Thucydides ***lawgiver:*** **5** Draco, Solon ***leader:*** **9** Agamemnon ***letter:*** **2** mu, nu, pi, xi **3** chi, eta, phi, psi, rho, tau **4** beta, iota, zeta **5** alpha, delta, gamma, kappa, omega, sigma, theta **6** lambda **7** epsilon, omicron, upsilon ***magistrate:*** **6** archon ***marketplace:*** **5** agora ***physician:*** **5** Galen ***porch:*** **4** stoa ***sandwich:*** **4** gyro ***soldier:*** **7** hoplite ***theater:*** **5** odeon, odeum ***underworld:*** **5** Hades ***war cry:*** **5** alala ***warrior:*** **4** Ajax **7** Ulysses **8** Achilles, Diomedes, Odysseus

9 Agamemnon, Palamedes ***weeper:*** **5** Niobe ***wine:*** **7** retsina

green 3 raw **4** jade, lime, moss **5** alive, fresh, kelly, leafy, naive, virid, young **6** callow, forest, unripe **7** avocado, celadon, emerald, envious, untried, verdant **8** immature, juvenile, unversed, youthful **9** unfledged **10** unseasoned **11** unpracticed **13** inexperienced ***bluish:*** **8** glaucous ***combining form:*** **4** verd **6** chloro ***grayish:*** **5** olive ***heraldry:*** **4** vert ***yellowish:*** **7** luteous **10** chartreuse

greenbacks 4 cash, jack, loot **5** bread, bucks, dough, lucre, money, moola **6** moolah, wampum **7** dollars, scratch **8** currency, smackers **11** legal tender

green beryl 7 emerald

greenery 7 foliage, leafage **8** verdancy

green-eyed 7 envious, jealous **9** invidious ***monster:*** **8** jealousy

greenfly 5 aphid

greengage 4 plum

greenhead 3 fly **8** horsefly

greenheart 6 laurel **9** evergreen

greenhorn 4 babe, hick, jake, naïf, rube, tiro, tyro **6** newbie, novice, rookie **7** ingenue **8** beginner, neophyte, newcomer **10** provincial

greenhouse 7 nursery **12** conservatory

Greenland *capital:* **4** Nuuk **7** Godthåb ***city:*** **5** Thule ***ethnic group:*** **5** Inuit **6** Eskimo ***explorer:*** **4** Eric (the Red), Erik (the Red), Leif (Eriksson) **9** Rasmussen (Knud) ***language:*** **6** Danish ***monetary unit:*** **5** krone ***possession of:*** **7** Denmark

green light 2 OK **3** nod **4** okay **5** leave **6** assent **7** consent, go-ahead, mandate **8** approval, blessing, sanction, thumbs-up **9** authority, clearance **10** permission **11** endorsement **13** authorization

Green Mansions *author:* **6** Hudson (W. H.) ***character:*** **4** Rima

green monkey 6 guenon, simian, vervet

Green Mountain State 7 Vermont

greenness 5 youth **6** spring **7** puberty **8** verdancy, viridity **9** youthhood **10** immaturity, juvenility, pubescence, springtide, springtime **11** adolescence **12** inexperience

green osier 6 willow **7** dogwood

green plover 7 lapwing **9** shorebird

greenroom 6 lounge

greenstone 4 jade **7** diabase **8** nephrite **9** tremolite **10** actinolite

greet 3 bow **4** hail, meet **6** accost, call to, salaam, salute **7** address, react to, receive, welcome

greeting 3 ave, bow, nod **4** ahoy, ciao, g'day, hail **5** aloha, hello, howdy **6** salaam, salute **7** address, welcome **9** handshake, reception **10** salutation

gregarious 6 clubby, genial, social **7** affable **8** outgoing, sociable **9** clubbable, congenial, convivial **11** extroverted **13** companionable

gremlin 3 bug, elf, imp **5** dwarf, gnome **6** defect, glitch **7** brownie

Grenada *capital:* **9** St. George's ***discoverer:*** **8** Columbus (Christopher) ***former name:*** **10** Concepción ***location:*** **10** West Indies ***nickname:*** **11** Isle of Spice

grenade 4 bomb **5** shell **7** missile **9** explosive, pineapple

grenadier 7 rattail, soldier

grenadine 4 pink, yarn **5** syrup **6** fabric **9** carnation

Grendel's slayer 7 Beowulf

Gretchen's lover 5 Faust

greylag 5 goose

grid 3 net **5** grate, grill **6** grille **7** grating, lattice, network, trellis

griddle 3 pan **5** grill

griddle cake 7 hotcake, pancake **8** flapjack

gridiron 3 net **5** field, grate, grill **7** grating, network

grief 3 rue, woe **4** care **5** agony, dolor, gloom, tears **6** mishap, regret, sorrow **7** anguish, chagrin, sadness, trouble **8** disaster, distress, hardship **9** adversity, heartache, suffering **10** affliction, heartbreak, misfortune **11** despondency

Grieg work 8 Peer Gynt

grievance 4 beef **5** cross, gripe, trial, wrong **6** burden, grouse, injury, squawk **8** hardship, jeremiad **9** complaint, injustice **10** affliction, allegation, unfairness **11** tribulation

grieve 3 cry **4** ache, keen, moan, wail, weep **5** mourn **6** burden, lament, sadden, sorrow, suffer **7** afflict, agonize **8** distress

grievous 3 sad **4** dire, fell, sore **5** cruel, grave, great, major **6** bitter, severe, taxing, tragic, woeful **7** galling, heinous, onerous, painful, serious, weighty **9** egregious **10** abominable, burdensome, calamitous, deplorable, lamentable, oppressive **11** distressing, regrettable, troublesome, unfortunate **12** heartrending

grift 3 con, gyp **4** bilk, rook **7** defraud, swindle **8** flimflam

grifter 3 gyp **5** cheat, crook, thief **6** con man, gouger **7** cheater, scammer, sharper, slicker **8** swindler **9** defrauder, trickster **13** confidence man

grill 3 fry, vex **4** cook, grid, pump, quiz **5** broil, grate, sauté, toast **6** eatery **7** afflict, debrief, grating, griddle, torment **8** gridiron, question **10** restaurant **11** interrogate **12** cross-examine

grilse 6 salmon

grim 3 set **4** cold, dour, fell, firm, hard **5** bleak, cruel, fixed, grave, harsh, rigid, stern **6** dismal, dogged, dreary, fierce, grisly, intent, savage, severe, somber **7** adamant, austere, inhuman, joyless, ominous **8** gruesome, inhumane, obdurate, resolute, ruthless, stubborn **9** merciless, offensive, truculent **10** determined, forbidding, implacable, inevitable, inexorable, inflexible, melancholy, relentless, unyielding, vindictive **11** unforgiving, unrelenting

grimace 3 mow, mug **4** face, moue, pout **5** frown, lower, mouth, scowl, sneer

grimalkin 3 cat **5** tabby **6** feline **9** female cat

grime 4 crud, dirt, gunk, muck, smut, soot **5** filth

grim reaper 5 death

grimy 5 dingy, dirty **6** filthy, grubby, grungy, soiled, scuzzy, smutty **10** besmirched

grin 4 beam **5** smile, smirk

grind 3 rut, vex **4** chew, grub, mill, moil, pace, plod, plug, rote, slog, toil, whet **5** crank, crush, gnash, grate, labor, slave, sweat **6** abrade, crunch, drudge, groove, harass, kibble, powder, rotate **7** oppress, routine, travail **8** drudgery, monotony, wear down **9** pulverize, treadmill **10** donkeywork

grinder 3 sub **4** gyro, hero **5** molar, tooth **6** hoagie **8** sandwich **9** submarine

grinding 5 harsh **6** severe **7** arduous, grating, wearing **9** fatiguing, strenuous ***stone:*** **4** mano **6** mortar, muller, pestle

griot 11 storyteller

grip 4 glom, hold, take **5** clamp, clasp, grasp, seize **6** clench, clinch, clutch, handle, tenure, valise **7** grapple **8** enthrall, suitcase **9** fascinate, mesmerize, restraint, spellbind, stagehand **10** constraint

gripe 3 bug, vex **4** beef, carp, crab, fuss, yawp **5** annoy, bitch, bleat, cavil, croak, groan, whine **6** bother, grouch, grouse, kvetch, murmur, mutter, object, squawk, yammer **7** afflict, grumble **8** complain, distress, irritate **9** bellyache, complaint, grievance, objection

griper see **grumbler**

grippe 3 flu **9** influenza

gripper 4 clip, hand, vise **5** clamp, clasp, tongs **6** pliers

gris-gris 4 juju **5** charm, spell **6** amulet, fetish **8** talisman **11** incantation

Grisham novel 4 Firm (The) **6** Broker (The), Client (The) **7** Chamber (The), Partner (The) **8** Brethren (The) **12** Pelican Brief (The)

grisly 4 gory, grim **5** awful, lurid **6** horrid **7** ghastly, hideous, macabre **8** fearsome, god-awful, gruesome, horrible, terrible **9** frightful, repellent, repulsive, sickening **10** disgusting, horrifying, terrifying

grist 3 lot **5** grain, input, stint **6** amount, output **7** product **8** quantity

gristle 9 cartilage

grit 4 guts, sand **5** grate, grind, heart, moxie, nerve, pluck, spunk **6** gravel, mettle, powder, smooth, spirit **7** bravery, courage, granule **8** backbone, tenacity **9** fortitude **10** doggedness **13** determination

gritty 4 game **5** dirty, gutsy, rough, sandy **6** dogged, plucky, spunky **8** abrasive, gravelly, resolute, spirited **9** steadfast, tenacious **10** courageous, determined

groan 4 beef, carp, moan **5** cavil, creak, gripe **6** bemoan, grouse, lament, object, repine **7** grumble **8** complain **9** bellyache

grocery 5 store **11** supermarket ***Spanish:*** **6** bodega

grog 3 rum **5** booze, drink, hooch, juice, sauce **6** liquor, tipple **7** alcohol, spirits **9** firewater

groggy 4 dull, hazy, logy, weak **5** dazed, dopey, foggy, muzzy, tired, woozy **6** dulled, sleepy **7** muddled **8** befogged, confused, sluggish **9** befuddled, slaphappy, stupefied **10** punch-drunk

groin 4 fold **6** crotch

grok 6 intuit

grommet 6 eyelet **7** cringle

groom 4 comb, tend, tidy **5** brush, clean, curry, primp, ready, shave **6** neaten, ostler, polish **7** hostler, prepare, servant **8** benedict **9** attendant ***Indian:*** **4** syce

groove 3 rut **4** dado, pace, rote, slot **5** canal, flute, glyph, gouge, grind, niche, score, stria **6** furrow, gutter, hollow, rabbet, rhythm **7** chamfer, channel, routine, top form **8** monotony **10** depression

groovy 3 hip **4** cool, neat **5** ducky, great, nifty, sharp, slick, super, swell **6** choice, gnarly, peachy **7** right-on **8** smashing **9** copacetic, excellent, hunky-dory, marvelous, wonderful **10** delightful, marvellous, peachy keen

grope 4 feel, grub, poke, root **6** fondle, fumble, search **7** grabble **8** scrabble

grosbeak 5 finch **8** hawfinch, songbird

gross 3 fat, raw, sum **4** earn, foul, mass, rude **5** brute, bulky, crude, obese, rough, utter, whole **6** carnal, coarse, entire, vulgar **7** blatant, boorish, capital, extreme, glaring, hulking, obscene, overall, porcine, uncouth **8** absolute, complete, flagrant, ignorant, improper, indecent, outright, sum total, tangible, totality **9** aggregate, before tax, corporeal, corpulent, downright, egregious, excessive, loathsome, offensive, out-and-out, repulsive, revolting, unrefined **10** disgusting, exorbitant, immoderate **11** twelve dozen

grotesque 6 absurd, rococo, unreal **7** baroque, bizarre, extreme **8** aberrant, abnormal, deformed, fanciful, freakish **9** distorted, fantastic, ludicrous, misshapen, monstrous **11** incongruous

grotto 4 cave, hole **5** crypt, vault **6** cavern ***Capri:*** **4** Blue

grouch 4 beef, carp, crab, kick, sulk, yawp **5** crank, croak, growl, grump, pique **6** carper, griper, grouse, grudge, kicker, kvetch, murmur, mutter, repine, squawk, whiner, yawper **7** crabber, grouser, growler, grumble **8** complain, grumbler, kvetcher, sorehead, sourpuss, squawker **9** bellyache, complaint **10** bellyacher, complainer, crosspatch, malcontent

ground 3 bed, sod **4** base, dirt, land, root, seat, soil, turf **5** basis, cause, earth, floor, proof **6** bottom, reason **7** bedrock, dry land, footing, support, sustain, terrain **8** argument, buttress, evidence **9** establish, testimony **10** foundation, terra firma

groundbreaking 10 innovative, innovatory, pioneering **11** cutting-edge, leading-edge

grounded 6 stable **7** beached **8** marooned, sensible, stranded **9** realistic **13** unpretentious

groundhog 6 marmot **9** woodchuck

grounding 8 practice, training, tutelage **11** instruction, preparation

groundless 4 idle **5** empty, false **6** hollow **8** baseless **9** causeless, unfounded **10** gratuitous **11** uncalled-for, unjustified, unwarranted

groundwork 3 bed **4** base, foot, root **5** basis **6** bottom **7** bedrock, footing, support **8** basement **10** foundation, substratum **11** cornerstone, preparation **12** substruction, substructure, underpinning

ground zero 5 focus, get-go **6** center, outset, target **8** bull's-eye **9** epicenter, square one

group 3 lot, set **4** band, bevy, body, club, crew, gang, pack, ruck, sect, team, tier **5** array, batch, bunch, class, clump, combo, covey, crowd, horde, panel, squad, taxon, troop **6** assort, bundle, cartel, circle, clique, clutch, huddle, klatch, league, passel **7** battery, brigade, cluster, combine, company, coterie, council, echelon, klatsch, platoon **8** assemble, assembly, category, classify, ensemble, organize **9** congeries, gathering, syndicate **10** assemblage, categorize, collection ***of angels:*** **4** host ***of ants:*** **6** colony ***of bees:*** **4** hive **5** swarm ***of birds:*** **6** flight ***of cats:*** **7** clowder, clutter ***of cattle:*** **5** drove ***of chicks:*** **5** brood **6** clutch ***of clams:*** **3** bed ***of crows:*** **6** murder ***of ducks:*** **5** brace ***of eight:*** **5** octad, octet ***of elephants:*** **4** herd ***of elks:*** **4** gang ***of fish:*** **5** shoal **6** school ***of five:*** **5** quint **6** pentad **7** quintet ***of four:*** **6** tetrad **7** quartet ***of foxes:*** **5** leash, skulk ***of geese:*** **5** flock, skein **6** gaggle ***of gnats:*** **5** cloud, horde ***of goats:*** **5** tribe ***of gorillas:*** **4** band ***of greyhounds:*** **5** leash ***of grouse:*** **5** covey ***of hares:*** **4** down, husk ***of hawks:*** **4** cast ***of hounds:*** **3** cry **4** mute, pack ***of kangaroos:*** **3** mob **5** troop ***of kittens:*** **6** litter ***of larks:*** **10** exaltation ***of lions:*** **5** pride ***of locusts:*** **6** plague ***of monkeys:*** **5** troop ***of mules:*** **4** span ***of nine:*** **5** nonet **6** ennead ***of oysters:*** **3** bed ***of partridges:*** **5** covey ***of peacocks:*** **6** muster ***of pheasants:*** **4** nest ***of plovers:*** **4** wing **12** congregation ***of quail:*** **4** bevy **5** covey ***of seals:*** **3** pod **5** patch ***of seven:*** **6** pleiad, septet ***of sheep:*** **5** drove, flock ***of six:*** **6** sextet ***of swans:*** **4** bevy ***of teals:*** **6** spring ***of ten:*** **6** decade ***of three:*** **4** trio **5** triad **7** ternary, trinity, triplet ***of vipers:*** **4** nest ***of whales:*** **3** gam, pod ***of wolves:*** **4** pack

grouper 8 rockfish

grouse 4 beef, carp, crab **5** croak, gripe, quail, scold **6** mutter, yammer **7** grumble **8** complain, pheasant **9** bellyache, blackcock, ptarmigan **12** capercaillie ***extinct:*** **8** heath hen ***red:*** **8** moorfowl ***strut:*** **3** lek

grout 4 lees, lute **5** dregs **6** cement, filler, mortar **7** grounds, plaster **8** concrete

grove 4 holt, wood **5** copse **7** boscage, coppice, orchard, thicket

grovel 4 fawn **5** abase, cower, crawl, creep, toady **6** cajole, cringe, kowtow, snivel, wallow **7** eat dirt, truckle **8** blandish, bootlick **9** brownnose **10** curry favor, ingratiate **11** apple-polish

grow 3 age, wax **4** flow, gain, rise, tend **5** amass, breed, nurse, raise, ripen, swell **6** abound, become, expand, foster, mature, sprout, thrive **7** burgeon, care for, develop, enlarge, gestate, nurture, produce **8** escalate, flourish, increase, multiply, mushroom, spring up **9** cultivate, propagate

growl 4 beef, carp, crab, fuss, gnar, roar **5** bitch, gripe, gnarr, groan, snarl **6** grouse,

kvetch, mutter, repine, rumble, yammer **7** grumble **8** complain **9** bellyache
growler 3 can **4** crab, floe **5** crank, grump **6** grouch, vessel **7** ice floe, iceberg, pitcher **8** sorehead, sourpuss **9** container **10** crosspatch, malcontent **11** faultfinder
grown-up 5 adult **6** mature **8** seasoned **9** developed **11** full-fledged
grow old 3 age **4** wane **5** ripen, wizen **6** mature, mellow
growth 4 gain, rise **5** surge, swell, tumor **7** buildup **8** increase, progress, swelling **9** accretion, evolution, expansion, flowering, unfolding **11** development, enlargement, progression ***malignant:* 6** cancer ***skin:* 3** tag, wen **4** corn, cyst, mole, wart **5** nevus **6** bunion, callus, keloid **7** verruca
grow up 3 age **5** ripen **6** evolve, mature, mellow **7** advance, develop **8** maturate **9** come of age
grub 3 dig **4** chow, comb, eats, feed, food, hack, moil, plod, poke, rake, root, slog, toil **5** grind, larva, scour, slave, spade, stump **6** burrow, drudge, forage, menial, shovel, slavey, uproot, viands **7** edibles, ransack, rummage, unearth, vittles **8** excavate, hireling, victuals **9** provender **11** comestibles
grubby 4 foul **5** dirty, grimy, messy, seedy **6** filthy, frowsy, frowzy, grungy, scuzzy, shabby, sloppy, soiled **7** scruffy, squalid, unclean, unkempt **8** slovenly, unwashed
grubstake 3 aid **4** back, fund, help, loan **5** funds **6** assist **7** backing, capital, finance, support **8** bankroll **9** financing **10** assistance, capitalize, underwrite
grudge 4 deny, envy **5** spite **6** refuse, spleen **7** ill will **9** grievance **10** resentment **12** hard feelings, spitefulness
gruel 4 mush **5** atole, kasha **6** burgoo, congee, sowens **8** flummery, loblolly, porridge **9** stirabout
gruesome see **grisly**
gruff 4 curt, dour **5** bluff, blunt, cross, harsh, husky, stern, surly **6** abrupt, crabby, crusty, hoarse, morose, sullen **7** bearish, brusque, crabbed, grating, grouchy **8** churlish, croaking, snappish, snippety **9** saturnine **10** ill-natured **11** bad-tempered
grumble 4 beef, carp, crab, fuss, moan, yawp **5** bitch, croak, gripe, groan, growl, snarl, whine **6** bemoan, grouch, grouse, murmur, mutter, repine, squawk **8** complain **9** bellyache
grumbler 4 crab **5** crank, grump **6** grouch **8** sorehead **10** crosspatch, malcontent
grump 3 pet **4** beef, carp, crab, pout, sulk **5** crank, gripe, growl **6** griper, grouch **7** growler, grumble **8** complain, sorehead, sourpuss **9** bellyache **10** bellyacher, malcontent
grumpy 4 dour, sour **5** cross, moody, sulky, surly, testy **6** crabby, cranky, sullen **7** crabbed, peevish **8** petulant, vinegary **9** crotchety, irascible **11** bad-tempered, ill-tempered **12** cantankerous
grunion 10 silverside
grunt 5 groan, growl, snort **7** dogface, draftee, soldier
G sharp 5 A flat
guacharo 7 oilbird
Guadeloupe *capital:* 10 Basse-Terre ***department of:* 6** France ***dependency:* 8** Désirade, St. Martin **12** Marie-Galante, St. Barthélemy ***discoverer:* 8** Columbus (Christopher) ***island:* 10** Basse-Terre **11** Grande-Terre ***location:* 10** West Indies ***volcano:* 9** Soufrière
Guam *capital:* 5 Agana ***ethnic group:* 8** Chamorro ***island group:* 7** Mariana
guanaco 5 llama **6** alpaca ***kin:* 5** camel
guano 6 manure **9** excrement
guarantee 3 vow **4** bail, bond, oath, seal, word **5** token, vouch **6** assert, assure, ensure, insure, pledge, surety **7** certify, earnest, promise, warrant **8** security, warranty **9** agreement, assurance, insurance, undertake **11** stand behind, undertaking
guarantor 5 angel **6** backer, patron, surety **7** ensurer, insurer, sponsor **8** bondsman **11** underwriter
guard 4 fend, mind, tend, ward **5** aegis, alert, armor, cover, watch **6** convoy, defend, escort, jailer, keeper, minder, patrol, picket, police, screen, secure, sentry, shield, warden, warder **7** bulwark, defense, lookout, oversee, protect, turnkey **8** chaperon, overseer, preserve, security, sentinel, shepherd, watchdog, watchman **9** chaperone, custodian, look after, patrolman, protector, watch over **10** protection
guarded 4 safe, wary **5** cagey, chary, leery **7** careful, politic, prudent **8** cautious, discreet, gingerly, reserved **11** circumspect, considerate
guardhouse 4 brig, jail, keep **5** clink **6** lockup, prison **8** stockade
guardian 6 escort, keeper, patron, warden, warder **7** curator, trustee **8** Cerberus, defender, overseer, watchdog **9** custodian, protector **10** genius loci **11** conservator
guardianship 4 care, keep, ward **5** aegis, trust **6** charge **7** custody, keeping **8** auspices **10** protection **11** safekeeping
Guare play 17 House of Blue Leaves (The) **22** Six Degrees of Separation

Guatemala ***capital:*** **9** Guatemala (City) ***ethnic group:*** **4** Maya **5** Mayan ***lake:*** **6** Izabal **7** Atitlán **9** Petén Itzá ***language:*** **7** Spanish ***monetary unit:*** **7** quetzal ***mountain, range:*** **6** Tacaná **9** Tajumulco **10** Acatenango, Santa María **11** Sierra Madre ***neighbor:*** **6** Belize, Mexico **8** Honduras **10** El Salvador ***peninsula:*** **7** Yucatán ***river:*** **7** Motagua **8** Polochic, Sarstoon **10** Usumacinta

guck 3 bog, goo, mud **4** clay, crud, dirt, glop, goop, mire, ooze, smut **5** filth, slime **7** stickum

gudgeon 3 pin **4** fish **5** pivot **6** socket **7** journal

Gudrun ***brother:*** **6** Gunnar **7** Gunther ***father:*** **5** Hetel ***husband:*** **4** Atli **5** Etzel **6** Sigurd **9** Siegfried

guerrilla 8 partisan **9** irregular ***Greek:*** **6** klepht

guess 4 call, shot, stab **5** fancy, hunch, infer **7** believe, predict, presume, suppose, surmise **8** estimate **9** speculate **10** conjecture, prediction **11** presumption, supposition, speculation

guest 6 caller, lodger, roomer **7** boarder, company, visitor **9** sojourner

guff 3 jaw, lip **4** bosh, sass **5** bilge, cheek, hokum, hooey, mouth, sauce, trash **6** bunkum, drivel, hot air, humbug **7** baloney, hogwash, palaver, twaddle **8** back talk, claptrap, malarkey, nonsense, tommyrot **9** poppycock **10** balderdash **13** horsefeathers

guffaw 6 cackle, hee-haw **7** chortle

guidance 6 advice **7** control, counsel **8** handling **9** direction, oversight **10** leadership, management **11** instruction, supervision

guide 4 dean, guru, help, lead, show **5** doyen, pilot, route, steer, usher **6** beacon, convoy, direct, docent, escort, handle, leader, manage, manual, mentor **7** adviser, conduct, control, marshal, oversee **8** Baedeker, chaperon, director, handbook, instruct, maneuver, navigate, shepherd, signpost **9** accompany, chaperone, conductor, vade mecum, Sacagawea **10** bellwether, compendium, instructor, pathfinder **11** enchiridion

guidebook 6 Fodor's, manual **8** Baedeker, Frommer's, handbook, Michelin **9** itinerary, vade mecum **10** compendium **11** enchiridion

guided missile 3 ABM **4** Hawk, ICBM, IRBM, Nike, Scud, Thor, Zuni **5** Atlas, drone, Snark, Titan **6** Bomarc, cruise, Exocet, Falcon, Navaho, rocket **7** Bullpup, Matador, Polaris, Regulus, Terrier **8** Redstone, Tomahawk **9** Minuteman **10** projectile, Sidewinder

Guiderius ***brother:*** **9** Arviragus ***father:*** **9** Cymbeline

guidon 4 flag **6** banner, burgee, ensign, pennon

guild 4 club **5** lodge, order, union **6** cartel, league **7** society **8** sodality **10** fellowship, fraternity **11** association, brotherhood ***medieval:*** **5** Hansa, Hanse

guile 4 wile **5** craft, fraud **6** deceit **7** cunning **8** artifice, trickery, wiliness **9** deception, duplicity, stratagem **10** cleverness **13** dissimulation

guileful 3 sly **4** foxy, wily **5** cagey, canny, slick **6** artful, astute, crafty, shifty, shrewd, sneaky, tricky **7** cunning, devious **8** indirect, slippery, sneaking **9** designing, insidious, underhand **11** calculating, duplicitous, underhanded

guileless 4 open **5** frank, naive **6** candid, direct, honest **7** genuine, natural, sincere, upfront **8** innocent, truthful **9** ingenuous **10** aboveboard, forthright

guillemot 3 auk **5** murre **7** seabird

guillotine 6 behead **9** decollate **10** decapitate

guilt 4 onus **5** blame, fault, shame **6** regret, stigma **7** offense, remorse **10** contrition **11** culpability **12** self-reproach

guiltless 4 pure **5** clean **6** chaste **8** innocent, virtuous **9** blameless, exemplary, faultless, righteous, stainless **10** immaculate, inculpable

guilty 6 liable, rueful, sinful **7** ashamed, at fault **8** blamable, contrite, culpable, indicted, penitent **9** impeached, regretful **10** answerable, remorseful **11** accountable, blameworthy, responsible

guimpe 6 blouse

Guinea ***capital:*** **7** Conakry ***city:*** **4** Labé **6** Kankan, Kindia ***ethnic group:*** **6** Fulani **7** Malinke ***island, island group:*** **3** Los **5** Tombo ***language:*** **6** French ***monetary unit:*** **5** franc ***mountain:*** **5** Nimba ***neighbor:*** **4** Mali **7** Liberia, Senegal **10** Ivory Coast **11** Sierra Leone **12** Guinea-Bissau ***river:*** **5** Niger **6** Gambia **7** Senegal

Guinea-Bissau ***archipelago:*** **7** Bijagós ***capital:*** **6** Bissau ***ethnic group:*** **6** Fulani **7** Malinke **8** Mandyako ***language:*** **10** Portuguese ***monetary unit:*** **5** franc ***neighbor:*** **6** Guinea **7** Senegal ***river:*** **4** Gêba

guinea fowl ***genus:*** **6** Numida ***young:*** **4** keet

guinea pig 4 cavy **6** rodent ***genus:*** **5** Cavia

Guinevere ***court:*** **7** Camelot ***husband:*** **6** Arthur ***lover:*** **8** Lancelot **9** Launcelot

guise 4 mask **5** cloak, cover, dress, getup **6** aspect, facade, outfit, veneer **7** costume, pretext **8** coloring, pretense **9** posturing, semblance **10** appearance, false front

guitar ***accessory:*** **4** capo ***Mexican:*** **5** tiple **6**

cuatro **8** charango ***part:*** **3** nut, peg **4** fret, neck **5** brace **6** bridge, string **7** peghead ***small:*** **3** uke **7** ukulele ***tool:*** **4** pick **8** plectrum

guitarist ***American:*** **3** Guy (Buddy) **4** Byrd (Charlie), King (Albert, B. B., Freddie), Page (Jimmy), Pass (Joe), Paul (Les) **5** Berry (Chuck), Ellis (Herb), Isbin (Sharon) **6** Allman (Duane), Atkins (Chet), Cooder (Ry), Garcia (Jerry), Kessel (Barney), Kottke (Leo), Watson (Doc) **7** Burrell (Kenny), Hendrix (Jimi), Johnson (Robert), Metheny (Pat), Santana (Carlos), Vaughan (Stevie Ray) **8** Van Halen (Eddie) **9** Christian (Charlie), Parkening (Christopher) **10** Montgomery (Wes), Pizzarelli (Bucky, John) ***Australian:*** **8** Williams (John) ***British:*** **4** Beck (Jeff) **5** Bream (Julian) **7** Clapton (Eric) **8** Richards (Keith) **9** Townshend (Pete) ***French:*** **9** Reinhardt (Django) ***Italian:*** **7** Ghiglia (Oscar) ***Spanish:*** **5** Yepes (Narciso) **6** Romero (Celedonio) **7** Segovia (Andrés)

guitarlike instrument **3** uke **4** lute, vina **5** banjo, sitar **7** bandore, pandora, samisen, ukulele **8** mandolin, shamisen

gulch **3** gap **4** glen **5** gorge, gully **6** arroyo, canyon, coulee, hollow, ravine, valley **7** couloir

gules **3** red

gulf **3** bay, pit **4** cove **5** abysm, abyss, bayou, bight, chasm, firth, gorge, gulch, inlet **6** cavity, harbor, hollow, ravine, slough **8** crevasse ***Adriatic Sea:*** **6** Venice ***Aegean Sea:*** **7** Saronic **8** Salonika ***Africa:*** **6** Guinea ***Arabian Sea:*** **4** Oman **7** Persian ***Australia:*** **9** Van Diemen **11** Carpentaria ***Baltic Sea:*** **4** Riga **6** Danzig, Gdansk **7** Bothnia, Finland ***Bering Sea:*** **6** Anadyr ***Canada:*** **13** Saint Lawrence ***Central America:*** **7** Fonseca ***Djibouti:*** **6** Tajura **8** Tadjoura ***Europe:*** **7** Bothnia, Gascony **8** Gascogne ***Greece:*** **7** Corinth, Lepanto ***Indian Ocean:*** **4** Aden ***Ionian Sea:*** **4** Arta **7** Taranto ***Iran:*** **7** Arabian ***Italy:*** **5** Genoa ***Mediterranean Sea:*** **5** Sidra, Tunis **8** Valencia **10** Khalij Surt **11** Syrtis Major ***Middle East:*** **7** Persian ***New Guinea:*** **5** Papua **7** McCluer ***New Zealand:*** **7** Hauraki ***North America:*** **6** Mexico ***Northwest Territories:*** **7** Boothia **8** Amundsen **9** Queen Maud ***Philippines:*** **4** Asid **5** Davao, Leyte, Panay, Ragay ***Red Sea:*** **4** Suez **5** Aqaba **11** Aelaniticus ***Russia:*** **8** Sakhalin ***Solomon Sea:*** **4** Huon, Kula **5** Vella ***South China Sea:*** **4** Siam **6** Tonkin **8** Lingayen ***Tyrrhenian Sea:*** **7** Paestum ***Yellow Sea:*** **6** Chihli

Gulf State **5** Texas **7** Alabama, Florida **9** Louisiana **11** Mississippi

gull **3** con, mew, sap **4** bird, dupe, fool, hoax, scam, Xema **5** chump, cozen **6** fleece, pigeon, stooge, sucker, take in **7** chicane, fall guy **8** flimflam, hoodwink **9** bamboozle **11** hornswoggle

gullet **3** maw **4** crop, tube **6** dewlap, throat **7** channel **9** esophagus

gullible **4** easy **5** green, naive **8** innocent, trusting **9** believing, credulous **11** susceptible **12** unsuspecting

Gulliver's Travels ***author:*** **5** Swift (Jonathan) ***horses:*** **10** Houyhnhnms ***land:*** **6** Laputa **8** Lilliput **11** Brobdingnag ***people:*** **6** Yahoos

gully **3** gap **4** glen, wadi, wash **5** gorge, gulch **6** arroyo, coulee, hollow, nullah, ravine, valley **7** couloir

gulp **4** bolt, chug, cram, glut, slop, swig, wolf **5** gorge, quaff, scarf, scoff, stuff, swill **6** devour, gobble, guzzle **7** swallow **8** mouthful **11** ingurgitate

gum **4** chew **5** botch **6** bobble, bollix, bungle, chicle, gluten, goof up, tupelo **7** exudate, gingiva, louse up **8** adhesive, mucilage **9** sapodilla **10** eucalyptus ***kind:*** **6** acacia, Arabic, balata, bubble **7** chewing, dextrin ***resin:*** **5** myrrh **7** gamboge **8** ammoniac, galbanum, scammony **9** asafetida **10** asafoetida **12** frankincense

gumbo **3** mud **4** okra, olio, soil, soup, stew **6** creole **7** mélange, mixture ***ingredient:*** **4** crab, duck, filé, okra **5** quail, tasso **6** shrimp **8** crawfish

gummy **5** gooey, pasty **6** cloggy, sticky, viscid **7** viscous **8** adhesive **9** glutinous **10** gelatinous **12** mucilaginous

gumption **5** drive, moxie, nerve, savvy **6** energy **8** industry **10** enterprise, get-up-and-go, initiative

gumshoe **3** cop, tec **4** bull, dick, fuzz, G-man, heat, narc **6** copper, peeler, shamus, sleuth **7** officer **8** flatfoot, hawkshaw, Sherlock **9** detective, policeman **10** bloodhound, private eye **12** investigator

gun **3** gat, rev, rod **4** Colt **5** rev up, rifle **6** cannon, Garand, heater, mortar, musket, pistol, weapon **7** bazooka, carbine, firearm **8** Browning, howitzer, revolver **9** derringer, Remington **10** Winchester **11** Springfield ***antiaircraft:*** **6** ack-ack, Bofors ***Austrian:*** **5** Glock ***British:*** **4** Sten ***French:*** **8** arquebus **9** harquebus ***German:*** **5** Luger ***Israeli:*** **3** Uzi ***Italian:*** **7** Beretta ***mount:*** **6** turret ***part:*** **3** pin **4** bolt, bore, butt, lock **5** sight, stock **6** barrel, breech, hammer, muzzle, safety **7**

chamber, trigger **8** cylinder, magazine **9** buttstock ***stun:*** **5** Taser

gunfire 4 shot **5** blast, salvo **6** volley **7** barrage **9** broadside, discharge, fusillade

gung ho 4 avid, keen **6** ardent, fervid, raring **7** fervent, zealous **9** exuberant **11** impassioned **12** enthusiastic

Guni's father 8 Naphtali

gunk 3 goo **4** crud, glop, gook, goop, muck **5** slime

gunman 5 bravo **6** hit man, killer **7** shooter, torpedo **8** assassin, enforcer

Gunnar *brother-in-law:* 6 Sigurd ***father:* 5** Hetel ***sister:* 6** Gudrun ***wife:* 8** Brunhild, Brynhild

gunner 6 sniper **7** shooter **8** marksman, rifleman **9** musketeer **11** infantryman **12** artilleryman

Gunther *sister:* 7 Gutrune **9** Kriemhild ***slayer:* 5** Hagen ***uncle:* 5** Hagen ***wife:* 8** Brunhild **9** Brynhilde

gurgle 3 lap **4** flow, purl, wash **5** plash, slosh, swash **6** babble, bubble, burble, ripple

Gurkha knife 5 kukri

gurney 3 cot **9** stretcher

guru 4 sage **5** guide, swami, tutor **6** expert, leader, master, mentor **7** teacher **9** maharishi

gush 3 jet **4** emit, flow, pour, rave, roll, rush, spew, teem, well **5** burst, flood, flush, issue, spout, spurt, surge **6** babble, effuse, sluice, spring, stream **7** cascade, emanate **10** effervesce, outpouring

gushy 5 gooey, mushy, sappy, soppy **6** sloppy, slushy, sticky **7** cloying, maudlin, mawkish, tearful **8** bathetic, effusive **9** schmaltzy, sickening **10** nauseating, saccharine **11** sentimental

gusset 4 fold, gore, tuck **5** armor, plate, pleat **6** insert **7** bracket

gussy up 5 adorn **6** bedeck **7** furbish **8** decorate, renovate

gust 3 fit **4** blow, gale, rush, wind **5** blast, burst, draft, sally, surge, whiff **6** breeze, flurry, squall **7** bluster, delight, flare-up **8** eruption, outburst, paroxysm

gusto 3 vim **4** brio, élan, zeal, zest **5** ardor, heart, oomph, taste, verve **6** fervor, palate, relish, spirit **7** delight, passion **9** enjoyment **10** enthusiasm

gusty 5 blowy, windy **6** breezy **8** blustery

gut 4 draw, loot, silk **5** belly, bowel, dress, empty, tummy **6** bowels, paunch **7** abdomen, ransack, stomach **8** clean out, entrails, visceral **9** intestine **10** disembowel, eviscerate, exenterate, intestines **11** instinctive

Gutenberg, Johannes *city:* 5 Mainz ***invention:* 11** movable type ***partner:* 4** Fust (Johann)

gutless 5 sissy, wimpy, wussy **6** coward, craven, yellow **7** chicken, unmanly **8** cowardly, timorous **9** spineless, spunkless, weak-kneed **11** lily-livered, poltroonish **12** faint-hearted **13** pusillanimous

guts 4 grit, sand **5** bowel, heart, moxie, nerve, pluck, spunk, tripe **6** bowels, mettle, spirit **7** bravery, courage, innards, insides, stamina, viscera **8** backbone, entrails, stuffing **9** fortitude, intestine **10** intestines, resolution

gutsy 4 bold **5** brave **6** plucky, spunky **7** valiant **8** intrepid, resolute **10** courageous, determined, mettlesome

gutter 5 chase, ditch, flume, gully **6** furrow, groove, trench, trough **7** channel, conduit

guttersnipe 3 bum **4** hobo, scum, waif **5** gamin **6** beggar, gamine, urchin **7** outcast, vagrant, wastrel **8** derelict, riffraff, vagabond **10** ragamuffin

guttural 4 deep **5** gruff, harsh, husky, rough, velar **6** croaky, hoarse **7** grating, palatal, rasping, throaty **8** gravelly ***warning:* 5** growl

guy 3 cat, joe, lad, man **4** buck, chap, dude, male, rope, stud, wire **5** bloke, brace, chain, guide **6** effigy, fellow, steady **7** support

Guyana *capital:* 10 Georgetown ***mountain range:* 9** Pacaraima ***neighbor:* 6** Brazil **8** Suriname **9** Venezuela ***river:* 9** Essequibo

Guys and Dolls *author:* 6 Runyon (Damon) ***character:* 3** Sky (Masterson) **6** Nathan (Detroit) **8** Adelaide (Miss) ***composer:* 7** Loesser (Frank)

guzzle 4 belt, chug, gulp, slop, soak, swig, toss, tope **5** booze, drink, quaff, slosh, swill **6** imbibe, tank up, tipple **7** consume, swizzle

Gwendolen's husband 7 Locrine

gymnast 7 acrobat, athlete, tumbler ***American:* 4** Hamm (Paul) **5** Rigby (Cathy) **6** Conner (Bart), Miller (Shannon), Retton (Mary Lou), Thomas (Kurt) ***Romanian:* 8** Comaneci (Nadia) ***Russian:* 3** Kim (Nelly) **6** Korbut (Olga) ***Ukrainian:* 5** Baiul (Oksana)

gymnastics 5 sport **8** exercise, tumbling **9** athletics **10** acrobatics **12** calisthenics ***apparatus:* 3** bar **4** bars, beam, buck, ring, rope **5** horse **11** balance beam ***feat:* 3** kip **4** flip **5** vault **6** tumble **9** handstand, headstand **10** handspring, headspring, somersault

gyp 3 con **4** bilk, dupe, fake, hoax, rook, scam, sham **5** bunco, cheat, cozen, cross, fraud, spoof, trick **6** chisel, chouse, con man, diddle, fleece, humbug, rip-off, rip off **7** cheater, deceive, defraud, diddler, finagle, sharper, swindle **8** chiseler, hoodwink, swindler **9** bamboozle, defrauder, imposture, trickster **10** mountebank **11** double-cross, flimflammer **12** double-dealer

gypsum 7 drywall, mineral **8** selenite **9** alabaster, wallboard

gypsy 3 Rom **5** caird, nomad, rover **6** roamer, Romany, tinker **7** drifter, tzigane **8** Bohemian, vagabond, wanderer ***Spanish:*** **6** gitano

gyrate 4 coil, purl, roll, spin, turn, wind **5** orbit, twirl, whirl **6** circle, rotate **7** revolve **9** oscillate, pirouette

gyration 4 coil, turn **5** cycle, orbit, twirl, wheel, whirl **6** circle **7** circuit, turning **8** rotation **10** revolution

gyre 4 coil, gird, ring, spin, wind **5** cycle, orbit, twirl, whirl **6** circle, girdle, rotate, spiral, vortex **7** circuit, revolve **8** rotation **10** revolution

gyro 8 sandwich

gyve 4 bond, iron **5** chain **6** fetter **7** shackle **8** restrain **9** restraint

Habakkuk 7 prophet

habeas corpus 4 writ **5** right **7** mandate

habiliments 4 gear **5** dress **6** attire, outfit **7** apparel, clothes **8** clothing **9** apparatus, equipment, trappings

habilitate 5 dress **6** clothe **7** qualify

habit 3 rut **4** bent, form, garb, mode, rote, wont **5** dress, quirk, style, usage **6** attire, clothe, custom, groove, manner, outfit **7** costume, fashion, pattern, routine **8** behavior, clothing, practice, tendency **9** addiction, mannerism **10** consuetude, convention, proclivity **11** disposition, inclination ***riding:*** **8** jodhpurs ***wearer:*** **3** nun **5** rider

habitable 7 livable

habitant 5 liver **7** denizen, dweller, resider **8** occupant, resident

habitat 4 home, site, turf **5** abode, haunt, range **6** locale, milieu **7** terrain **8** domicile **9** territory **11** environment **12** surroundings

habitation 3 pad **4** digs, flat, home, nest, seat **5** abode, haunt, haven, house, place, roost **7** housing, lodging, tenancy **8** domicile, dwelling, lodgment, quarters **9** homestead, residence, residency **10** settlement

habitual 3 set **5** fixed, usual **6** addict, inborn, native, normal, steady, wonted **7** chronic, regular, routine, settled **8** accepted, addicted, constant, familiar, frequent, inherent **9** automatic, confirmed, continual, customary, ingrained **10** accustomed, inveterate, persistent **11** established, instinctive, involuntary

habitually 8 commonly, normally, wontedly **9** generally, regularly, routinely **10** ordinarily **11** customarily **12** consistently

habituate 4 bear **5** inure, train **6** addict, adjust, endure, harden, school, season, take to **7** break in, prepare, support **8** accustom, tolerate **9** acclimate, condition **11** familiarize

habitué 3 fan **4** buff, user **5** hound, lover **6** addict, patron **7** denizen, devotee, haunter **8** adherent, customer **10** enthusiast, frequenter

hacienda 4 farm **5** ranch, villa **6** estate, quinta **8** estancia **10** plantation

hack 3 cab, cut, hew, try, vex **4** blow, chip, chop, dull, gash, grub, jade, loaf, mean, ride, taxi **5** annoy, cabby, cough, grind, horse, petty, sever, usual **6** cabbie, cliché, drudge, lackey, mangle, stroke, writer **7** clichéd, machine, plodder, taxicab, trivial **8** inferior, low-grade, mediocre, tolerate **9** cabdriver, mercenary, potboiler **10** second-rate, uninspired

hacker 4 geek, nerd **6** duffer

hackney 3 cab **4** taxi **5** horse **6** jitney **7** taxicab **8** carriage

hackneyed 4 dull, worn **5** banal, corny, stale, stock, tired, trite **6** cliché, common, old hat, old saw **7** archaic, clichéd, worn-out **8** everyday, obsolete, outdated, overused, outmoded, timeworn **9** out-of-date **10** antiquated, overworked, pedestrian

Hadad *father:* **5** Bedad **7** Ishmael ***victim:*** **6** Midian

Hades 4 Hell **5** Pluto, Sheol **6** blazes, Tophet **7** Gehenna, inferno **8** Tartarus **9** perdition **10** underworld **11** netherworld ***Babylonian:*** **5** Aralu ***god:*** **3** Dis **5** Orcus, Pluto ***goddess:***

10 Persephone ***guard:*** **8** Cerberus ***lake:*** **7** Avernus ***river:*** **4** Styx **5** Lethe **7** Acheron, Cocytus **10** Phlegethon

haft 4 grip, hilt, knob **5** helve **6** handle

hag 3 hex **5** biddy, crone, harpy, shrew, vixen, witch **6** beldam, gorgon, virago **8** battle-ax, fishwife, harridan, slattern **9** hobgoblin

Hagar 9 concubine ***lover:*** **7** Abraham ***rival:*** **5** Sarah, Sarai ***son:*** **7** Ishmael

Hagen *father:* 8 Alberich ***nephew:*** **7** Gunther ***slayer:*** **9** Kriemhild ***victim:*** **9** Siegfried

haggard 3 wan **4** hawk, lank, pale, thin, weak, wild, worn **5** ashen, drawn, faded, gaunt, tired **6** fagged, pallid, skinny, wasted **7** angular, pinched, scraggy, scrawny, starved, wearied **8** careworn, fatigued, shrunken, worn-down **9** emaciated, exhausted

Haggard, H. Rider *novel:* 3 She **17** King Solomon's Mines

Haggith *husband:* 5 David ***son:*** **8** Adonijah

haggle 4 deal **5** argue, cavil, trade **6** barter, bicker, dicker **7** bargain, chaffer, dispute, quibble, stickle, wrangle **8** squabble **10** horse-trade

hagiography subject 5 saint

hail 3 ave **4** ahoy, call **5** greet, salvo, shout, storm **6** accost, call to, holler, praise, salute, shower, volley **7** acclaim, address, applaud, barrage, call out, commend **8** greeting **9** broadside, cannonade, fusillade, originate, recommend **10** salutation **11** acclamation, bombardment

Haile Selassie 9 Ras Tafari ***follower:*** **11** Rastafarian ***nation:*** **8** Ethiopia

hair 3 bit, jot **4** hint, mite, wool **5** cilia (plural), pilus, trace **6** cilium, trifle **7** eyelash, whisker **8** fraction, particle ***animal:*** **3** fur **4** mane, pelt, wool **8** vibrissa **9** vibrissae (plural) ***braid:*** **5** plait, queue **7** pigtail ***clip:*** **8** barrette ***coarse:*** **7** bristle ***combining form:*** **3** pil **4** pili, pilo **5** trich **6** tricho ***covering of:*** **3** wig ***dressing:*** **3** gel **6** mousse **6** pomade **7** pomatum **8** macassar **12** brilliantine ***facial:*** **5** beard, patch **6** goatee **7** Vandyke **8** mustache, whiskers **9** burnsides, handlebar, moustache, sideburns, soul patch **11** muttonchops ***fine:*** **6** lanugo ***fringe:*** **5** bangs ***head of:*** **9** chevelure ***knot:*** **3** bun ***lock of:*** **4** curl **5** tress **7** cowlick ***loose roll:*** **4** pouf ***matted:*** **6** dreads **10** dreadlocks ***net:*** **5** snood ***ornament:*** **7** topknot ***preparation:*** **3** gel **6** mousse, pomade **12** brilliantine ***root:*** **6** fibril ***set:*** **4** perm ***stiff:*** **4** seta **5** setae (plural) ***tangled:*** **7** elflock ***tuft of:*** **5** quiff **7** cowlick, fetlock ***unruly:*** **3** mop ***without:*** **4** bald

haircutter 6 barber **7** stylist **8** coiffeur **9** coiffeuse

hairdo 2 DA **3** bob, bun **4** afro, flip, perm, pomp, shag, trim, updo **5** bangs, braid, butch, taper, wedge **6** Caesar, Mohawk, mullet **7** beehive, bowl cut, buzz cut, chignon, crew cut, flattop, pageboy, tonsure **8** brush cut, coiffure, cornrows, ducktail, pigtails, ponytail, razor cut **9** permanent, pompadour **10** dreadlocks

hairdresser see **haircutter**

hair-raising 5 eerie, scary **6** spooky **7** amazing, awesome **8** exciting **9** thrilling **10** terrifying **11** astonishing, fright ening

hairsplitting 7 finicky **8** exacting **9** quibbling **10** nit-picking **12** overcritical **13** hypercritical

hairstyle see **hairdo**

hairy 5 bushy, downy, furry, fuzzy, nappy, risky, rough **6** chancy, fleecy, fluffy, shaggy, tufted, woolly **7** bristly, hirsute, scraggy, unshorn, villous **8** perilous, strigose **9** dangerous, difficult, hazardous, tomentose, whiskered **11** treacherous

Haiti *capital:* 12 Port-au-Prince ***island:*** **7** Tortuga **10** Hispaniola ***language:*** **6** Creole, French ***leader:*** **8** Aristide (Jean-Bertrand), Duvalier (François, Jean-Claude) ***location:*** **10** West Indies ***monetary unit:*** **6** gourde ***passage:*** **8** Windward ***peninsula:*** **7** Tiburon ***river:*** **10** Artibonite

hajj 5 Umrah **10** pilgrimage ***site:*** **4** Mina **5** Mecca **6** Arafat **10** Muzdalifah

hake 4 fish, ling **7** codling, whiting ***relative:*** **3** cod

halcyon 4 calm **5** happy, lucky, quiet, still **6** golden, hushed, placid, serene **8** affluent, peaceful, tranquil **9** favorable **10** auspicious, felicitous, kingfisher, prosperous, untroubled

Halcyone *father:* 6 Aeolus ***husband:*** **4** Ceyx

hale 3 fit **4** sane, well **5** sound, stout **6** hearty, robust **7** healthy **8** vigorous **9** strapping, wholesome

Hale character 5 Nolan (Philip)

Haley epic 5 Roots

half 6 moiety ***prefix:*** **4** demi, hemi, semi

half-baked 8 slapdash, slipshod **9** imbecilic, senseless, underdone **11** harebrained, impractical, nonsensical, unrealistic **12** ill-conceived, shortsighted **13** irresponsible

half-cocked 4 rash **5** brash **8** reckless **9** foolhardy, imprudent, impulsive, misguided, premature **10** incautious, unprepared **11** precipitate

halfhearted 4 weak **5** tepid **6** feeble **8** lukewarm **12** uninterested

half-moon **4** arch **5** curve **6** lunule **8** crescent
halfway **3** mid **6** center, medial, median, middle **7** midmost **10** centermost **11** equidistant **12** intermediate
half-wit **4** dolt, dope, fool **5** dunce, idiot, moron **6** cretin **8** imbecile **9** blockhead, simpleton
half-witted **4** dull, slow **7** moronic **8** backward, imbecile **9** imbecilic **12** feebleminded, simpleminded
hall **4** dorm **5** foyer, lobby **6** lyceum **7** passage **8** corridor **9** dormitory **10** auditorium, passageway ***exhibition:*** **5** salon ***Salvation Army:*** **7** citadel
Halley's ____ **5** comet
hallmark **4** logo, seal, sign **5** badge, stamp, trait **6** device, emblem, symbol, virtue **7** feature, imprint, quality **8** logotype **9** attribute **11** distinction
hallow **5** bless, honor **6** anoint, devote, revere **8** dedicate, make holy, sanctify, venerate **10** consecrate
hallowed **4** holy **6** sacred
hallucination **4** trip **5** ghost **6** mirage, vision, wraith **7** fantasy, phantom, specter, spectre **8** delusion, illusion, phantasm **10** apparition **11** fata morgana, ignis fatuus
hallucinogen **3** LSD **9** mescaline **10** psilocybin **11** scopolamine
halo **4** aura, nimb **5** nimbi (plural) **6** corona, nimbus **7** aureole
halogen **6** iodine **7** bromine, element **8** astatine, chlorine, fluorine
halt **3** bar, end **4** lame, limp, quit, stay, stop **5** avast, cease, check, close, hitch, lapse, stall, waver **6** arrest, desist, dither, falter, finish, pull up **7** adjourn, bring up, stagger, suspend **8** conclude, cut short, hesitate, knock off, leave off **9** determine, interrupt, terminate, vacillate **10** standstill **11** discontinue
halter **3** bit **4** hang, rope **5** noose **6** blouse, bridle, hamper **8** restrain, trammels **9** hackamore, headstall, restraint
halvah base **6** sesame
ham **4** hock **5** bacon, emote, thigh **7** buttock, overact **8** overplay, strutter **10** scene-eater **13** exhibitionist
Ham ***brother:*** **4** Shem **7** Japheth ***father:*** **4** Noah ***son:*** **4** Cush, Phut **6** Canaan **7** Mizraim
Haman's adversary **6** Esther
ham-handed **5** inept **6** clumsy, gauche **8** bumbling **9** all thumbs, graceless, inelegant, maladroit **10** blundering, unskillful
Hamilcar ***conquest:*** **5** Spain ***home:*** **8** Carthage ***son:*** **8** Hannibal ***surname:*** **5** Barca
hamlet **4** dorp **7** village ***Irish, Scottish:*** **7** clachan
Hamlet ***author:*** **11** Shakespeare (William) ***beloved:*** **7** Ophelia ***castle:*** **8** Elsinore ***country:*** **7** Denmark ***friend:*** **7** Horatio ***mother:*** **8** Gertrude ***slayer:*** **7** Laertes ***uncle:*** **8** Claudius ***victim:*** **7** Laertes **8** Claudius, Polonius
Hamlet, The ***author:*** **8** Faulkner (William) ***family:*** **6** Snopes
hammer **4** drub, maul, peen **5** forge, gavel, pound **6** batter, mallet, pummel, sledge **7** malleus **8** lambaste ***end:*** **4** peen ***type:*** **3** air **4** claw, maul **6** sledge **8** ball-peen **9** pneumatic
hammerhead **4** dolt, dope, fool **5** dunce, idiot, shark **8** clodpoll, numskull **9** numbskull **10** thickskull
hamper **3** bin, tie **4** balk, curb, snag **5** block, check, cramp, crimp, leash, limit **6** baffle, basket, fetter, hinder, hobble, hold up, impede, retard, stymie, thwart **7** inhibit, manacle, pannier, prevent, trammel **8** encumber, handicap, obstacle, obstruct, restrain, restrict, slow down **9** frustrate
hamstring **4** lame **6** muscle, tendon **7** cripple, disable **10** immobilize **12** incapacitate
Hamutal ***father:*** **8** Jeremiah ***husband:*** **6** Josiah ***son:*** **8** Jehoahaz, Zedekiah
hand **3** aid, paw **4** fist, mitt, pass **5** manus **6** script, worker **7** deliver, dish out, laborer, workman **8** employee, transfer **10** assistance, penmanship **11** calligraphy, chirography ***clenched:*** **4** fist ***combining form:*** **4** chir **5** chiro ***counting zero:*** **8** baccarat ***covering:*** **5** glove **6** mitten ***down:*** **8** bequeath ***gesture:*** **5** mudra ***on hip:*** **6** akimbo ***part:*** **4** palm **5** thumb **6** finger ***poker:*** **5** flush **8** straight **9** full house ***protector:*** **5** glove **7** gantlet **8** gauntlet
handbag **4** grip **5** purse **6** clutch **8** reticule, suitcase **10** pocketbook
handbill **5** flier, flyer **6** poster **7** affiche, leaflet, placard **8** circular
handbook **5** guide **6** manual **8** Baedeker **9** vade mecum **10** compendium **11** enchiridion ***religious:*** **9** catechism
handcuff **6** fetter **7** manacle, shackle ***British:*** **7** darbies (plural)
hand down **4** will **6** bestow, pass on **7** deliver **8** bequeath, transmit
Handel, George Frideric ***aria:*** **5** Largo ***birthplace:*** **5** Halle **7** Germany ***opera:*** **4** Nero **5** Serse **6** Admeto, Alcina, Almira, Ottone, Xerxes **7** Arminio, Orlando, Rinaldo, Rodrigo **8** Berenice **9** Agrippina, Ariodante **12** Giulio Cesare, Julius Caesar ***oratorio:*** **4** Saul **6** Esther, Joshua, Samson, Semele **7** Athalia, Deborah, Jephtha, Messiah, Solomon **8** Theodora

handicap 4 edge, load, odds **6** burden, hamper, hinder, impede **8** drawback, encumber, restrict **9** advantage, allowance, detriment, head start, hindrance **10** disability, limitation **11** encumbrance **12** disadvantage

handicraft 5 skill **8** artefact, artifact

hand in 6 submit, tender **7** deliver, present

handkerchief 5 hanky **6** hankie **7** bandana **8** bandanna, mouchoir **9** accessory

handle 3 paw, use **4** ansa, feel, grip, haft, hilt, knob, name, test **5** crank, see to, touch, trade, treat, wield **6** manage **7** control, moniker, operate **8** deal with, doorknob, exercise, maneuver, nickname **10** manipulate ***scythe:*** **5** snath **6** snathe

handling 4 care **6** charge **9** packaging, treatment ***partner:*** **8** shipping

hand out 4 give, mete **6** bestow, donate **7** deliver, present, provide **8** disburse, dispense, give away **10** administer, distribute

hand over 4 cede, feed, give **5** leave, yield **6** commit, donate, fork up, give up, supply **7** commend, confide, consign, deliver, entrust, present **8** dispense, give back, relegate, transfer **9** deliver up, surrender **10** relinquish

handrail 8 banister

handsome 4 buff, cute, fair **5** hunky, noble **6** comely **7** dashing **10** attractive **11** good-looking

handspring 6 tumble ***lateral:*** **9** cartwheel

handwriting 6 script **8** longhand **10** autography, manuscript, penmanship **11** calligraphy, chirography, copperplate ***bad:*** **10** cacography ***study of:*** **10** graphology

handy 4 able, deft, near, yare **5** adept, close, utile **6** adroit, clever, nearby, nimble, useful **7** close-by, skilled **8** adjacent, skillful **9** adaptable, available, dexterous **10** accessible, convenient, proficient **11** practicable, within reach

handyman 6 helper **7** go-to guy **8** factotum

hang 3 jut, sag **4** hook, idle, loll **5** cling, drape, droop, float, hoist, knack, lynch, sling, swing **6** dangle, depend **7** suspend ***back:*** **3** lag **4** drag, poke **5** trail **6** dawdle, schlep **7** schlepp **8** straggle ***loosely:*** **3** sag **6** dangle

hang around 4 stay, wait **5** abide, dally, tarry **6** dawdle, linger, loiter **7** goof off **8** frequent

hangdog 3 sad **4** blue, glum **5** cowed **6** guilty **7** abashed, ashamed, pitiful, unhappy **8** dejected, sheepish **9** chagrined, depressed **11** embarrassed

hanger-on 5 leech **6** sponge, sucker **7** sponger **8** barnacle, follower, parasite **9** sycophant **10** freeloader **11** bloodsucker

hanging 5 arras, slope **7** curtain, drapery, pendant, pendent **8** covering, tapestry **9** declivity, execution, pendulous, suspended

Hanging Gardens site 7 Babylon

hang on 4 grip **5** grasp **6** clutch, endure, remain **7** persist, survive **8** continue, hold fast **9** persevere

hang out 4 idle, loaf **5** chill, dally, relax **6** loiter, lounge **7** goof off

hangout 5 haunt, joint **6** resort **7** purlieu, retreat **10** rendezvous **12** watering hole

hang up 4 mire, snag **5** delay **6** detain, impede, retard **7** bog down, set back, suspend **8** slow down

hang-up 5 block **7** dilemma, problem **9** obsession **10** difficulty, inhibition

hank 4 clip, coil, loop, ring **6** bundle

hanker 3 yen **4** ache, itch, long, lust, want, wish **5** covet, crave, yearn **6** desire, hunger, thirst

hankering 3 yen **4** ache, itch, lust, urge **5** ardor **6** desire, hunger, pining, thirst **7** craving, longing, passion **8** appetite, yearning

hanky-panky 5 fraud, trick **7** chicane **8** mischief, trickery **9** chicanery, dalliance, deception **13** double-dealing, sharp practice

Hannibal *defeat:* 4 Zama ***father:*** **8** Hamilcar ***home:*** **8** Carthage ***surname:*** **5** Barca ***vanquisher:*** **6** Scipio ***victory:*** **6** Cannae

Hansa 5 guild **6** league

Hans Brinker author 5 Dodge (Mary Mapes)

Hanseatic League city 6 Bremen, Lübeck, Wismar **7** Cologne, Hamburg, Rostock

Hänsel und Gretel composer 11 Humperdinck (Engelbert)

Hansen's disease 7 leprosy

hansom 3 cab **5** coach **8** carriage

haole 5 white **9** Caucasian

haphazard 6 casual, chance, random **7** aimless **8** at random, careless, slipshod **9** desultory, hit-or-miss, irregular, unplanned **10** accidental, willy-nilly **11** unorganized **12** unsystematic **13** helter-skelter

hapless 4 poor **6** woeful **7** unhappy, unlucky **8** ill-fated, wretched **9** miserable **10** ill-starred **11** star-crossed, unfortunate

happen 4 pass **5** occur **6** befall, betide **7** develop, fall out, turn out **8** bechance **9** transpire ***again:*** **5** recur ***together:*** **6** concur **8** coincide

happening 3 new **5** event, scene, thing **7** episode **8** incident, occasion **9** adventure **10** experience, occurrence, phenomenon **11** fashionable **12** circumstance

happen on 4 find **8** bump into, discover

happenstance 5 event **6** chance **8** incident,

occasion **9** condition, situation **11** coincidence

happiness 3 joy **4** glee **5** bliss, cheer, mirth **6** gaiety **7** aptness, content, delight, elation, jollity **8** felicity, gladness, pleasure **9** enjoyment, well-being **11** contentment **12** satisfaction

happy 4 glad **5** jolly, lucky, merry **6** joyful, joyous, upbeat **7** blessed, content, pleased **8** friendly, jubilant **9** contented, favorable, satisfied **12** enthusiastic, lighthearted

Happy Days *character:* 5 Chuck **6** Chachi, Fonzie, Howard, Joanie, Marion, Potsie, Richie ***family:* 10** Cunningham ***site:* 9** Milwaukee ***star:* 4** Baio (Scott), Ross (Marion) **5** Moran (Erin) **6** Bosley (Tom), Howard (Ron) **7** Winkler (Henry) **8** O'Herlihy (Gavan), Williams (Anson)

happy-go-lucky 4 easy **6** blithe, breezy, casual **8** carefree, careless, cheerful, heedless, laid-back, reckless **9** easygoing, unworried **10** insouciant, nonchalant **11** unconcerned **12** devil-may-care, light-hearted

hara-kiri 7 seppuku, suicide **8** felo-de-se

Haran *brother:* 7 Abraham ***daughter:* 5** Iscah **6** Milcah ***father:* 5** Terah **6** Shimei ***son:* 3** Lot

harangue 4 rant, rave **5** orate, spiel **6** exhort, hassle, tirade **7** declaim, lecture, oration **8** bloviate, diatribe, jeremiad **9** discourse, philippic **11** declamation, exhortation

harass 3 irk, vex **4** bait, raid, ride **5** annoy, beset, bully, chivy, harry, hound, tease, worry **6** badger, chivvy, hassle, heckle, hector, pester, plague, stress **7** bedevil, exhaust, fatigue, torment, trouble **8** bullyrag, distress **9** beleaguer, persecute

harbinger 4 omen, sign **5** augur **6** augury, herald **7** apostle, portent **9** messenger, precursor **10** forerunner, indication

harbor 3 bay **4** cove, port **5** haven, inlet, lodge, put up **6** billet, refuge, shield, take in **7** nurture, protect, seaport, shelter **9** anchorage, safeguard, sanctuary ***Hawaii:* 5** Pearl

hard 4 firm, iron **5** cruel, harsh, solid, tough **6** brutal, knotty, packed, rugged, tiring, trying **7** arduous, callous, onerous **8** absolute, concrete, exacting, granitic, grinding, indurate, pitiless, rigorous **9** demanding, difficult, fatiguing, intensely, intensive, laborious, unfeeling **10** adamantine, exhausting, spirituous, thoroughly, vigorously **11** complicated, intensively, intractable, troublesome, unrelenting, unremitting **12** backbreaking ***cover:* 5** crust ***to please:* 7** finicky

hard-boiled 4 grim **5** rough, stoic, tough **6** coarse **7** callous **8** seasoned **9** impassive, pragmatic, unfeeling **11** insensitive, unemotional **12** stonyhearted, thick-skinned **13** unsympathetic

harden 3 dry, set **5** enure, inure, steel **6** anneal, freeze, ossify, season, temper **7** calcify, compact, congeal, densify, lithify, petrify, stiffen, toughen **8** solidify **9** acclimate, fossilize, habituate **10** strengthen

hardfisted 4 mean **5** close, tight **6** stingy, strict **13** penny-pinching

hardheaded 5 sober, tough **6** mulish, shrewd **7** willful **8** obdurate, perverse, stubborn **9** obstinate, practical, pragmatic, realistic **10** determined **11** down-to-earth, intractable

hardhearted 4 cold **5** stony **8** pitiless, uncaring **9** merciless, unfeeling

hard-hitting 6 strong **8** emphatic, forceful, powerful **9** effective

hardihood 3 pep **4** gall, grit, guts **5** cheek, moxie, nerve, pluck, vigor **6** daring **7** courage **8** audacity, boldness, temerity **9** assurance, brashness, cockiness, fortitude, impudence, insolence **10** brazenness, robustness

hard-line 4 firm **5** fixed, rigid, tough **8** obdurate **9** obstinate, unbending **10** inflexible, unyielding **11** stiff-necked **12** intransigent

hardness 5 rigor **7** density **8** rigidity, severity **10** difficulty, resistance

hardscrabble 6 barren **8** marginal **9** infertile, unbearing, unfertile **12** impoverished, unproductive

hardship 4 need, toil **5** rigor, trial **6** burden **7** travail **8** asperity, distress, drudgery **9** adversity, privation, suffering **10** affliction, difficulty, discomfort, misfortune **11** tribulation

Hard Times author 7 Dickens (Charles)

hard up 4 poor **5** broke, needy **6** bad off **8** beggared, bankrupt, deprived, indigent, strapped **9** desperate, destitute, penniless **10** down-and-out **11** necessitous **12** impoverished

hardy 4 bold, hale **5** brave, tough **6** daring, robust, rugged, strong **7** healthy **8** intrepid, resolute **9** audacious

Hardy, Thomas *character:* 3 Sue (Bridehead) **4** Alec (D'Urberville), Clym (Yeobright), Jude (Fawley), Tess (Durbeyfield) **5** Angel (Clare) **7** Gabriel (Oak) **8** Arabella (Donn), Eustacia (Vye), Henchard (Michael) **9** Bathsheba (Everdene) ***novel:* 11** Woodlanders (The) **14** Jude the Obscure **17** Return of the Native (The) **19** Mayor of Casterbridge (The) **21** Tess of the D'Urbervilles **22** Far from the Madding Crowd ***setting:* 6** Wessex

Hardy Boys *author:* 5 Dixon (Franklin W.) **9**

McFarlane (Leslie) ***character:*** **3** Joe **4** Biff (Hooper), Chet (Morton), Iole **5** Frank, Laura **6** Callie, Fenton **12** Aunt Gertrude ***city:*** **7** Bayport ***jalopy:*** **5** Queen ***motorboat:*** **6** Napoli, Sleuth

hare **5** lapin **6** rabbit ***female:*** **3** doe ***genus:*** **5** Lepus ***male:*** **4** buck ***tail:*** **4** scut ***young:*** **7** leveret

harebrained **5** crazy, loony, silly, wacky **6** absurd, insane, stupid **7** asinine, foolish **9** frivolous **10** ridiculous **12** preposterous

harem **5** serai **6** zenana **8** seraglio ***attendant:*** **6** eunuch ***concubine:*** **9** odalisque

haricot **3** pod **4** bean **10** kidney bean

hark **4** hear, heed, mind, note **6** attend, listen, notice

harlequin **5** clown, joker **6** jester, mottle **7** buffoon **9** prankster

Harlequin ***beloved:*** **9** Columbine ***rival:*** **7** Pierrot

harm **3** mar **4** hurt, maim, ruin **5** abuse, spoil, wound, wrong **6** damage, ill-use, impair, injure, injury, misuse, molest **7** tarnish **8** ill-treat, maltreat, mischief, mistreat **9** undermine **10** disservice, misfortune

harmful **3** bad **4** evil **5** risky, toxic **6** malign, unsafe **7** noisome, noxious **8** damaging **9** dangerous, hazardous, injurious, malignant, unhealthy **10** pernicious **11** deleterious, detrimental, unhealthful

harmless **4** safe **6** benign **8** innocent, nontoxic **9** innocuous **11** inoffensive

Harmonia ***daughter:*** **3** Ino **5** Agave **6** Semele **7** Autonoë ***father:*** **4** Ares, Mars ***husband:*** **6** Cadmus ***mother:*** **5** Venus **9** Aphrodite ***son:*** **9** Polydorus

harmonious **5** sweet **7** chiming, chordal, musical, pacific **8** blending, friendly, in accord, peaceful, pleasing **9** agreeable, congenial, congruous, consonant, symphonic **10** compatible, concordant **11** cooperative, symmetrical, sympathetic

harmonize **3** fit **4** jibe, sing **5** agree, blend, match **6** accord, attune **7** arrange, concert, conform **8** coincide, dovetail **9** integrate **10** coordinate, correspond, synthesize **11** orchestrate

harmony **4** sync **5** grace, peace, unity **6** accord **7** balance, concert, concord, oneness, rapport **8** affinity, sonority, symmetry **9** agreement, congruity, polyphony **10** accordance, concinnity, conformity, consonance, proportion **11** concordance, consistency, cooperation ***lack of:*** **7** discord **10** dissonance ***of movement:*** **8** eurythmy

harness **4** curb, gear, yoke **5** hitch, leash **6** bridle, tackle **7** utilize **11** domesticate ***part:*** **3** bit **4** rein **5** girth, trace **6** collar **7** blinder, crupper **9** bellyband, breeching, checkrein **12** breast collar ***ring:*** **6** terret

harp **4** lyre **9** harmonica ***Greek:*** **7** cithara, kithara ***Japanese:*** **4** koto

harpsichord **7** cembalo **8** clavecin

harpsichordist ***American:*** **6** Fuller (Albert, David), Kipnis (Igor), Newman (Anthony) **7** Marlowe (Sylvia), Pinkham (Daniel), Valenti (Fernando) **11** Kirkpatrick (Ralph) ***Dutch:*** **9** Leonhardt (Gustav) ***English:*** **7** Malcolm (George), Pinnock (Trevor) ***German:*** **7** Richter (Karl) ***Italian:*** **7** Sgrizzi (Luciano) ***Polish:*** **9** Landowska (Wanda)

harpy **3** nag **5** leech, scold, shrew, vixen **6** virago **8** fishwife, harridan **9** termagant

Harpy **5** Aello **7** Celaeno, Ocypete ***father:*** **7** Thaumas ***mother:*** **7** Electra ***sister:*** **4** Iris

harridan **3** hag **4** fury **5** biddy, harpy, shrew, vixen, witch **6** dragon, gorgon, ogress, virago **7** hellcat **8** battle-ax, fishwife **9** battle-axe, termagant

harrier **3** dog **4** hawk **6** hector, runner **10** persecutor

Harris, Joel Chandler ***character:*** **7** Brer Fox **8** Brer Bear **10** Brer Rabbit ***narrator:*** **10** Uncle Remus

harrow **3** try, vex **4** bait, rack **5** devil, tease **6** badger, heckle, hector, needle, pester, suffer **7** afflict, bedevil, torment, torture, trouble **8** distress, irritate **9** cultivate **10** excruciate

harry **3** dog, irk, vex **4** gnaw, raid, ride, sack **5** annoy, tease, upset, worry **6** attack, badger, harass, hassle, maraud, pester, plague, ravage **7** assault, bedevil, despoil, perturb, pillage, plunder, torment **8** desolate, maltreat **9** beleaguer, depredate

harsh **5** cruel, gruff, rough, stern **6** biting, brutal, coarse, severe, uneven, unkind **7** austere, caustic, grating, jarring, painful, pungent, raucous, stubbly **8** exacting, grinding, jangling, scraping, scratchy, strident, unsmooth **9** dissonant, inclement **10** discordant, irritating, unpleasant

harshness **8** asperity **9** roughness

hart **4** deer, stag **7** red deer ***mate:*** **4** hind

hartebeest **4** tora **8** antelope ***family:*** **7** Bovidae

Harte story **17** Luck of Roaring Camp (The) **19** Outcasts of Poker Flat (The)

Hartford ***college:*** **7** Trinity ***specialty:*** **9** insurance

Hart, Moss ***autobiography:*** **6** Act One ***collaborator:*** **7** Kaufman (George S.) ***musical:*** **13** Lady in the Dark ***play:*** **15** Once in a Lifetime **18** Man Who Came to Dinner (The) **20** You Can't Take It with You

haruspex **4** seer **5** augur **7** diviner, prophet **8**

foreseer **9** predictor **10** forecaster, foreteller, soothsayer

harvest 4 crop, pick, reap **5** amass, cache, glean, hoard, stash, yield **6** garner, gather **7** collect, reaping, store up, vintage **8** ingather, squirrel, stow away **9** garnering, gathering ***bug:*** **4** mite **7** chigger ***fly:*** **6** cicada ***festival:*** **6** Lammas **7** Cerelia **10** Michaelmas **12** Thanksgiving ***god, goddess:*** **3** Ops **5** Ceres **6** Consus **7** Demeter

harvester 7 gleaner ***grain:*** **6** binder, header ***of grapes:*** **8** vintager

Harvey 5 pooka **6** rabbit ***author:*** **5** Chase (Mary) ***character:*** **6** Elwood (P. Dowd)

hash 4 chop, mess, stew **5** botch, mince, mix-up **6** jumble, medley, muddle, review **7** clutter, confuse, mélange, mixture **8** consider, shambles **9** patchwork **10** assortment, hodgepodge, miscellany

hash house 4 café **5** diner **6** bistro, eatery **7** beanery, pit stop **10** coffee shop **11** greasy spoon **12** luncheonette

hashish 5 bhang, ganja **6** charas **8** cannabis, narcotic ***plant:*** **4** hemp

hash out 6 review **7** discuss **8** talk over **9** talk about

hasp 5 catch **6** fasten **8** fastener **9** fastening

hassle 3 row **4** beef, to-do **5** annoy, argue, brawl, fight, run-in **6** bicker, clamor, harass, hubbub, tumult, uproar **7** dispute, problem, quarrel, rhubarb, turmoil, wrangle **8** argument, squabble, struggle **9** commotion **11** altercation, controversy

hassock 4 pouf **7** cushion, kneeler, ottoman **9** footstool

haste 3 hie, run **4** dash, rush **5** hurry, speed **6** barrel, bustle, flurry, hustle **7** beeline, hotfoot **8** celerity, dispatch, rapidity, velocity **9** fleetness, quickness, swiftness **10** speediness **11** hurriedness, impetuosity

hasten 3 fly, hie, run **4** rush, urge **5** hurry, press, speed **6** barrel, hustle, step up, urge on **7** hurry up, quicken, speed up **8** expedite **10** accelerate

hasty 4 fast, rash **5** brisk, eager, fleet, quick, rapid, swift **6** abrupt, rushed, speedy, sudden **7** cursory, hurried, rushing **8** careless, fleeting, headlong, heedless, reckless, slapdash **9** hotheaded, impatient, impetuous, irritable, quickened **10** ill-advised, incautious **11** expeditious, perfunctory, precipitate, precipitous, superficial, thoughtless

hat 5 derby, toque, tuque **6** boater, cloche, fedora, panama, topper **7** bicorne, chapeau, homburg, porkpie, Stetson, tricorn **8** sombrero, tricorne **9** headpiece **11** deerstalker ***ancient Greek:*** **7** petasos, petasus ***brimless:*** **7** pillbox ***close-fitting:*** **4** kufi **5** toque, tuque **6** cloche, turban ***felt:*** **5** busby, derby **6** bowler, trilby ***fur:*** **5** busby **6** castor ***helmet-like:*** **4** topi **5** topee ***maker:*** **7** modiste **8** milliner ***Middle Eastern:*** **3** fez ***military:*** **4** kepi **5** busby, shako **8** bearskin ***Muslim:*** **3** fez **6** turban **8** tarboosh ***Scottish:*** **3** tam **9** glengarry **11** tam-o'-shanter ***sheepskin:*** **6** calpac **7** calpack ***soft:*** **5** toque, tuque ***straw:*** **6** boater, panama, sailor **7** bangkok, leghorn, skimmer **8** sombrero ***sun:*** **5** terai ***tall:*** **9** stovepipe ***waterproof:*** **9** sou'wester ***woman's:*** **4** coif **5** toque, tuque **6** bonnet **7** pillbox

hatch 4 door, plan, plot **5** breed, brood, cover, inlay, spawn **6** cook up, create, design, devise, emerge, invent, make up, work up **7** concoct, dream up, opening, produce, think up **8** contrive, engender, generate, incubate, occasion **9** floodgate, formulate, give birth, give forth, originate, procreate **11** compartment

hatchet 3 axe **8** tomahawk

hatchet man 5 bravo **6** killer **7** torpedo **8** assassin, enforcer, murderer **9** attack dog, cutthroat **10** eliminator

hate 5 abhor, scorn **6** animus, detest, enmity, loathe, malice, rancor **7** despise **8** aversion, execrate, loathing **9** abominate, animosity, antipathy **10** abhorrence, repugnance

hateful 4 evil, foul, mean, vile **5** nasty **6** horrid, malign, odious, scurvy **7** vicious **8** accursed, damnable, infamous **9** abhorrent, execrable, malicious, obnoxious, repellent, repulsive **10** abominable, despicable, detestable, malevolent **11** blasphemous, opprobrious, unspeakable **13** reprehensible

Hatfields vs. ____ 6 McCoys

hatred 5 odium, spite **6** animus, enmity, rancor **7** dislike **8** aversion, loathing **9** animosity, antipathy, hostility, repulsion, revulsion **10** abhorrence, repugnance **11** abomination, detestation, malevolence ***of change:*** **9** misoneism ***of humankind:*** **11** misanthropy ***of marriage:*** **8** misogamy ***of men:*** **8** misandry ***of women:*** **8** misogyny

hats 9 millinery

hauberk 5 armor **9** chain mail, habergeon

haughtiness 4 airs **5** pride, scorn **7** conceit, disdain, hauteur **9** arrogance, insolence, pomposity **12** snobbishness

haughty 5 aloof, proud **6** lordly, sniffy **7** distant **8** arrogant, cavalier, scornful, snobbish, superior **9** egotistic **10** disdainful **11** overbearing **12** contemptuous, supercilious

haul 3 lug, tow, tug **4** cart, drag, draw, hump, lift, load, loot, pull, swag, take, tote **5** boost, booty, cargo, hoist, raise, truck **6**

burden, lading, schlep, spoils **7** freight, payload, schlepp ***with a tackle:*** **5** bowse
haul up 5 hoise, hoist ***with a rope:*** **5** trice
haunch 3 hip **11** hindquarter
haunches 4 butt, rump **7** hind end, rear end **8** backside, buttocks **9** posterior **12** hindquarters
haunt 4 site **5** spook **6** obsess, prey on **7** habitat, hang out, inhabit, torment, trouble **8** frequent **9** preoccupy **10** hang around, rendezvous, stay around, visit often
haunter 5 ghost **7** denizen, habitué
hautbois 4 oboe
hauteur see **haughtiness**
haut monde 5 elite **6** jet set **7** society, who's who **10** glitterati, upper crust **11** aristocracy, high society **13** carriage trade
have 3 own **4** hold **7** contain, include, possess
haven 4 port, roof **5** house, oases (plural), oasis **6** asylum, harbor, refuge **7** retreat, shelter **9** anchorage, sanctuary
haversack 3 bag **4** pack **8** backpack
havoc 4 loss, ruin, sack **5** chaos, waste **6** mayhem **8** calamity, disorder, ravaging **9** confusion, ruination **11** catastrophe, destruction, devastation, pandemonium
haw 4 left, tree **5** berry, fruit, shrub **8** turn left **10** equivocate
Hawaii *author:* 8 Michener (James A.) ***beach:*** **7** Waikiki ***capital:*** **8** Honolulu ***city:*** **4** Hilo ***coast:*** **4** Kona ***discoverer:*** **4** Cook (Capt. James) ***island:*** **4** Maui, Oahu **5** Kauai, Lanai **6** Niihau **7** Molokai ***mountain:*** **7** Kilauea **8** Mauna Kea, Mauna Loa ***nickname:*** **5** Aloha (State) ***park:*** **9** Haleakala ***state bird:*** **4** nene ***state flower:*** **8** hibiscus ***state tree:*** **5** kukui **9** candlenut
Hawaiian *dance:* 4 hula ***feast:*** **4** luau ***food:*** **3** poi ***god:*** **4** Kane, Lono **5** Wakea **7** Kanaloa ***goddess:*** **4** Pele ***goose:*** **4** nene ***gooseberry:*** **4** poha ***grass:*** **4** hilo ***instrument:*** **3** uke **7** ukulele ***lava:*** **2** aa ***neckwear:*** **3** lei ***nonnative:*** **5** haole **8** malihini ***resident:*** **8** kamaaina ***shaman:*** **6** kahuna ***soup:*** **6** saimin ***thrush:*** **4** omao ***tree:*** **3** koa
hawk 4 kite, sell, vend **5** buteo **6** falcon, monger, osprey, peddle **7** Cooper's, goshawk, haggard, harrier **8** caracara, huckster, roughleg **9** accipiter, red-tailed, warmonger **10** militarist **11** ferruginous, rough-legged ***Hawaiian:*** **2** io ***male:*** **6** tercel **7** tiercel ***young:*** **4** eyas
hawker 6 coster, monger, seller, vendor **7** packman, peddler **8** pitchman **12** costermonger
hawkeyed 11 keen-sighted **12** sharp-sighted
Hawkeye State 4 Iowa
hawkish 7 martial, warlike **9** combative **10** aggressive **11** belligerent **12** militaristic
____ Hawley Tariff 5 Smoot
Hawthorne, Nathaniel *birthplace:* 5 Salem ***character:*** **6** Hester (Prynne) **8** Clifford (Pyncheon), Hepzibah (Pyncheon), Pyncheon (Judge) **10** Dimmesdale (Rev. Arthur) **13** Chillingworth (Roger) ***novel:*** **10** Marble Faun (The) **13** Scarlet Letter (The) **21** House of the Seven Gables (The)
hay 3 bed **4** feed **5** grass **6** fodder, reward **7** herbage ***crops:*** **6** clover **7** alfalfa, timothy
Haydn oratorio 7 Seasons (The) **8** Creation (The)
hay fever 7 allergy **10** pollenosis, pollinosis ***cause:*** **6** pollen **7** ragweed
haying machine 5 baler
haymaker 3 box **4** blow, sock **5** clout, punch **6** wallop
hayseed see **hick**
haywire 4 amok, awry **5** amuck, crazy, upset **6** faulty **8** confused **10** out of order **12** out of control
hazard 3 bet, try **4** dare, game, luck, risk **5** peril, shoal, wager **6** chance, danger, gamble, menace **7** fortune, imperil, venture **8** accident, endanger, jeopardy, obstacle
hazardous 5 hairy, risky **6** chancy, unsafe **7** unsound **8** perilous **9** dangerous, unhealthy **10** precarious
haze 3 fog **4** film, mist, murk, smog **5** brume, cloud, drive, smoke, vapor **6** harass **7** dimness, obscure **8** dullness, initiate, overcast **9** mistiness, murkiness, vagueness **10** cloudiness
hazel 4 wood **5** birch, shrub **7** filbert
hazy 3 dim **5** faint, filmy, foggy, fuzzy, misty, murky, smoky, vague **6** cloudy, unsure **7** blurred, clouded, obscure, unclear **8** nebulous, vaporous **9** uncertain **10** indefinite, indistinct
head 3 nob, nut, top **4** bean, boss, capo, foam, john, main, mind, pate, poll **5** brain, caput, chief, first, gourd, poise, prime, privy, scalp, skull **6** honcho, leader, master, noggin, noodle, talent, toilet **7** cranium, faculty, latrine, premier, supreme **8** director, foremost, lavatory **9** chieftain, principal **10** promontory ***area:*** **5** crown **6** temple ***back part:*** **7** occiput ***bone:*** **5** skull **7** cranium **8** parietal ***combining form:*** **6** cranio **7** cephalo ***covering:*** **3** cap, hat **6** bonnet **8** kerchief ***monastery:*** **4** dean **5** abbot **8** superior ***nunnery:*** **6** abbess **8** superior ***of hair:*** **4** mane **6** fleece **9** chevelure ***relating to:*** **8** cephalic ***shaving of:*** **7** tonsure ***skin:*** **5** scalp ***top:*** **4** pate **5** crown

headache **4** pain **5** worry **6** bother, megrim **7** problem **8** migraine, nuisance, vexation **9** annoyance **10** irritation

headband **7** bandeau, circlet, coronal ***ancient Greek:*** **6** taenia **7** taeniae (plural)

headdress **7** topknot ***American Indian:*** **9** warbonnet ***Arab:*** **8** kaffiyeh, keffiyeh ***bishop's:*** **5** miter, mitre ***medieval:*** **4** barb ***Eastern:*** **6** turban ***nobleman's:*** **7** coronet ***royal:*** **5** crown, tiara **6** diadem ***Spanish women's:*** **8** mantilla ***women's:*** **6** bonnet (see also **hat**)

headland **4** cape **5** point **10** promontory

headline **6** banner **7** feature, promote **8** screamer **9** emphasize, publicize, spotlight **10** noteworthy

headlong **4** rash **5** brash, hasty **6** abrupt, daring, rashly, sudden **7** hurried, rushing **8** heedless, reckless **9** foolhardy, impetuous, impulsive **10** heedlessly, recklessly **11** precipitate, precipitous

headmaster **6** leader **9** principal

head off **4** stop **5** avert, block **6** thwart **7** deflect, obviate, prevent, ward off **8** stave off, turn back **9** forestall, intercept

headquarters **3** hub **4** base, seat **6** center

head start **4** edge, jump, lead, odds **5** boost **7** advance, vantage **8** handicap **9** advantage, allowance

headstone **6** marker **8** memorial, monument **11** grave marker

headstrong **6** dogged, mulish, unruly **7** willful **8** contrary, perverse, stubborn **9** obstinate **10** bullheaded, refractory, self-willed **11** intractable, stiff-necked

heads-up **5** alarm, alert **6** signal, tip-off **7** warning **8** high sign **11** resourceful

headway **4** gain **6** growth **7** advance **8** anabasis, progress **11** advancement, improvement

heady **4** rash, rich **5** giddy **6** elated, potent **7** willful **8** exciting **9** impetuous **11** exhilarated, intoxicated **12** intoxicating

heal **3** fix **4** cure, mend **5** sew up, treat **6** cement, remedy, repair **7** patch up, restore **8** make well

healer **6** doctor, shaman

healing **8** curative, remedial, salutary, sanative **9** vulnerary, wholesome **10** salubrious **11** restorative, therapeutic **12** convalescent ***goddess of:*** **3** Eir

health **7** fitness, welfare **8** haleness, vitality, wellness **9** soundness, well-being, wholeness ***club:*** **3** gym, spa

healthful **8** curative, hygienic, remedial, salutary **9** favorable, wholesome **10** beneficial, corrective, profitable, salubrious **11** restorative

healthy **3** fit **4** hale, spry, well **5** sound, tonic **6** benign, robust, strong, sturdy **7** chipper **8** blooming, hygienic, positive, salutary, thriving, vigorous **9** wholesome **10** able-bodied, beneficial, prosperous, salubrious **11** flourishing

Heaney work **5** North **9** Field Work **12** Wintering Out ***translation:*** **7** Beowulf

heap **3** lot **4** cock, fill, gobs, hill, load, lump, mass, much, pack, pile, rick, scad **5** amass, bunch, clump, crate, loads, mound, shock, stack, wreck **6** barrel, charge, gather, jalopy, junker, lumber, oodles **7** clunker, collect, deposit, jillion **8** assemble, mountain, slathers **9** abundance, profusion, stockpile

hear **4** heed, oyez **5** catch, learn **8** listen to, perceive **9** apprehend

hearing **4** oyer, test **5** trial **6** tryout **7** earshot, inquiry **8** audience, audition **9** interview **10** conference, discussion ***distance:*** **7** earshot

hearken **4** heed, mind, note **6** attend, listen, notice **7** observe

hearsay **4** buzz, news, talk **5** rumor **6** gossip, report **7** account, chatter **9** grapevine **11** scuttlebutt

heart **3** cor, hub **4** core, crux, gist, guts, love, pith, root, seat, soul, zest **5** ardor, bosom, focus, gusto, moxie, pluck, spunk **6** breast, center, kernel, mettle, relish, spirit, ticker **7** courage, resolve **8** feelings, sympathy **9** character, fortitude **10** compassion ***chart:*** **3** ECG, EKG ***combining form:*** **6** cardio ***contraction:*** **7** systole ***dilation:*** **8** diastole ***part:*** **5** valve **6** atrium, septum **9** ventricle

heartache **3** rue, woe **4** care, pain, pang **5** grief **6** regret, sorrow **7** anguish, sadness **8** distress **10** affliction

heartbeat **5** flash, jiffy, pulse, throb, trice **6** moment, second **9** pulsation ***irregular:*** **10** arrhythmia

heartbreak **3** rue, woe **5** agony, grief **6** misery, regret, sorrow **7** anguish, despair, torment, torture **9** suffering **10** desolation **12** wretchedness

heartbreaking **6** bitter, tragic **8** grievous **9** agonizing **10** calamitous, deplorable, lamentable **11** devastating, distressing

heartbroken **7** crushed, grieved **8** mournful, overcome, wretched **9** sorrowful **10** despairing, despondent **12** disconsolate

heartburn **7** pyrosis

hearten **4** buoy, stir **5** cheer, rally, rouse **6** arouse, buck up, buoy up, perk up **7** animate, cheer up, enliven, inspire **8** embolden, energize, inspirit **9** encourage

heartfelt **4** deep, true **6** honest **7** earnest, fervent, genuine, sincere **8** profound **9** unfeigned

hearth 4 home **5** abode **8** domicile, dwelling, fireside **9** fireplace, residence
heartily 6 wholly **9** sincerely, with gusto, zestfully **10** completely, thoroughly
heartless 4 cold, hard **5** cruel **6** unkind **7** callous **8** uncaring **9** unfeeling **10** hard-boiled **11** insensitive, unemotional **13** unsympathetic
Heart of Dixie 7 Alabama
heartsease 5 pansy, viola **6** violet **11** peace of mind, tranquility **12** johnny-jump-up, tranquillity
heart-shaped 7 cordate
heartsick 4 blue, down **8** dejected, desolate, dismayed, downcast **9** depressed **10** despondent, dispirited **11** demoralized **12** disconsolate
heartthrob 4 idol, love **5** flame, honey, sweet **7** beloved, darling, passion **9** dreamboat **10** sweetheart
heart-to-heart 4 open, talk **5** frank **6** candid, honest **7** sincere **8** truthful **12** conversation
hearty 4 hale, warm **5** ample **6** jovial, robust, sailor, strong **7** cordial, healthy, profuse, sincere **8** abundant, vehement, vigorous **9** approving, energetic, exuberant, flavorful, unfeigned **12** enthusiastic, unrestrained
heat 4 cook, rage, warm, zeal **5** ardor, fever **6** fervor, simmer, warmth **7** caloric, inflame, passion, swelter **8** pyrolyze ***combining form:*** **4** pyro **6** calori, thermo **7** thermia ***measuring device:*** **11** calorimeter, thermometer ***quantity:*** **3** BTU
heated 3 hot, mad **5** angry, fiery, irate **6** ardent, fervid, fierce, ireful, raging, steamy **7** boiling, burning, fevered, furious **8** broiling, feverish, scalding, sizzling, vehement, wrathful **9** indignant, scorching **10** passionate **11** acrimonious
heater 3 gun, rod **4** etna **5** stove **6** boiler, pistol **7** furnace, handgun **8** fastball, radiator
heath 4 ling, moor **5** broom, Erica, shrub **7** Calluna **9** crowberry, wasteland
heathen 5 pagan **7** infidel **8** barbaric **11** irreligious, uncivilized
heat-producing 9 calorific
heave 3 lob **4** cast, draw, fire, gasp, haul, heft, huff, hurl, lift, pant, puff, pull, push, toss **5** fling, hoist, labor, pitch, raise, retch, sling, surge, throw, vomit **6** launch
heave-ho 4 boot **6** ouster **8** bum's rush **9** dismissal
heaven 4 Eden, Zion **5** bliss, glory **6** utopia **7** arcadia, ecstasy, elysium, nirvana, rapture **8** empyrean, eternity, paradise **9** firmament, Shangri-la **10** wonderland **11** immortality, kingdom come **12** promised land
heavenly 4 lush **6** divine, sacred **7** blessed **8** beatific, empyreal, empyrean, ethereal **9** ambrosial, celestial, delicious **10** delectable, delightful, enchanting
heavy 3 big, fat **5** beefy, bulky, gross, hefty, obese, stout, thick **6** bad guy, chunky, fleshy, leaden, portly **7** labored, porcine, villain, weighty **8** cumbrous, sluggish, unwieldy **9** corpulent, laborious, lumbering, ponderous, strenuous **10** burdensome, cumbersome, oppressive, overweight
heavy-handed 5 crude, harsh, inept **6** clumsy, gauche, klutzy **7** awkward **8** bumbling, despotic **9** maladroit **10** oppressive **11** domineering, overbearing
heavyhearted 3 sad **4** glum **5** sorry **7** unhappy **8** dejected, downcast, mournful, saddened **9** depressed, miserable, sorrowful **10** despondent, dispirited, melancholy
heavyset 5 beefy, husky, stout, thick **6** chunky, portly, stocky **11** thick-bodied
heavyweight 3 VIP **4** lion **5** boxer, chief **6** big gun, bigwig, honcho, leader **7** big shot, notable **8** big-timer
Hebe ***father:*** **4** Zeus **7** Jupiter ***husband:*** **8** Hercules ***mother:*** **4** Hera, Juno ***successor:*** **8** Ganymede
hebetude 6 stupor, torpor **7** languor **8** dullness, lethargy **9** lassitude, torpidity **10** drowsiness
hebetudinous 4 dull, logy **5** dopey **6** drowsy, stupid, torpid **8** listless, sluggish **9** lethargic
Hebrew 3 Jew **6** Jewish ***coin:*** **6** lepton, shekel ***festival:*** **5** Purim **6** Pesach, Sukkot **7** Hanukah, Sukkoth **8** Chanukah, Lag b'Omer, Passover, Shabuoth **9** Tishah-b'Ab, Yom Kippur **12** Rosh Hashanah, Simchas Torah ***God:*** **6** Adonai, Elohim, Yahweh **7** Jehovah ***judge:*** **6** Gideon ***lawgiver:*** **5** Moses ***leader:*** **4** Saul **5** Moses **6** Joshua **7** Solomon ***letter:*** (see at **alphabet**) ***lyre:*** **6** kinnor ***measure:*** **4** beka, omer **5** bekah, cubit, ephah ***month:*** **2** Ab **4** Abib, Adar, Elul, Iyar **5** Nisan, Sivan, Tebet **6** Kislev, Shebat, Tammuz, Tishri **6** Veadar (in leap year) **7** Heshvan ***patriarch:*** **3** Dan, Gad **4** Cain, Levi, Seth **5** Asher, David, Isaac, Jacob, Judah **6** Joseph, Lamech, Reuben, Simeon **7** Abraham, Zebulun **8** Benjamin, Issachar, Naphtali ***sacred city:*** **5** Safad, Safed **6** Hebron **8** Tiberias **9** Jerusalem ***tribe:*** **3** Dan, Gad **4** Levi **5** Asher, Judah **6** Reuben, Simeon **7** Ephraim, Zebulon **8** Benjamin, Issachar, Manasseh, Naphtali (see also **Jewish**)
Hebrides island 4 Eigg, Rhum, Skye, Uist **5** Lewis **6** Harris

Hecate ***father:*** **6** Perses ***goddess of:*** **5** night **10** underworld, witchcraft ***mother:*** **7** Asteria

hecatomb **7** killing, slaying **8** butchery **9** bloodbath, sacrifice, slaughter

heck **4** darn, drat, geez, gosh, hell, jeez **5** golly **6** shucks

heckle **3** nag **4** bait, faze, gibe, ride **5** annoy, chivy, hound, tease, worry **6** badger, bother, harass, hassle, hector, molest, needle, pester, plague, rattle **7** disrupt, disturb, torment **9** interrupt **10** disconcert

hectic **3** red **6** fervid **7** burning, excited, fevered, flushed **8** confused, exciting, feverish, frenetic, restless **9** turbulent **10** persistent

hector **3** cow, nag **4** bait, ride **5** bully, chivy, hound **6** badger, harass, lean on **7** bedevil, swagger **8** browbeat, bullyrag, domineer **10** intimidate

Hector ***brother:*** **5** Paris **7** Helenus, Troilus **9** Deiphobus, Polydorus ***father:*** **5** Priam ***mother:*** **6** Hecuba ***sister:*** **6** Creusa **8** Polyxena **9** Cassandra ***slayer:*** **8** Achilles ***victim:*** **9** Patroclus ***wife:*** **10** Andromache

Hecuba ***daughter:*** **6** Creusa **8** Polyxena **9** Cassandra ***father:*** **5** Dymas ***husband:*** **5** Priam ***son:*** **5** Paris **6** Hector **7** Helenus, Troilus **9** Deiphobus, Polydorus ***victim:*** **11** Polymnestor

hedge **4** trim **5** avoid, evade, fence, guard, hem in, limit **6** hinder **7** barrier, defense, enclose, evasion, protect **8** boundary, encircle, restrict **9** shrubbery **10** protection

hedgehog **9** porcupine **10** stronghold

hedonist **4** rake **7** epicure, gourmet **8** gourmand, sybarite **9** bon vivant, epicurean, libertine **10** sensualist, voluptuary

heebie-jeebies **5** jumps **6** creeps, nerves, shakes **7** jitters, shivers, willies **11** nervousness

heed **4** care, hark, mark, mind, note, obey **5** watch **6** attend, harken, listen, notice, regard, remark **7** be aware, concern, hearing, hearken, observe, respect **8** consider, interest, listen to **9** attention **10** observance

heedful **5** alert, aware **7** on guard **8** vigilant **9** attentive, observant, observing **10** interested, meticulous, scrupulous **13** conscientious

heedless **9** negligent, oblivious, unmindful **10** unthinking **11** inadvertent, inattentive, unobservant **12** unreflective **13** inconsiderate

heedlessness **7** neglect **9** disregard, unconcern **11** disinterest, inattention, insouciance **12** indifference

hee-haw **4** bray **5** laugh **6** guffaw **10** horse laugh

heel **3** bum, cad, tip **4** cant, hock, lean, list, tilt **5** creep, knave, louse, rogue, skunk, slope **6** rascal, rotter **7** bounder, incline, lowlife, villain **9** scoundrel ***bone:*** **8** calcanea (plural), calcanei (plural) **9** calcaneum, calcaneus

heft **4** bulk, lift, load **5** hoist, raise, weigh **6** weight **7** heave up **9** heaviness, influence **10** importance

hefty **3** big **5** beefy, burly, bulky, heavy, husky, large, major **6** brawny, mighty, rugged, strong **7** massive, sizable **8** imposing, powerful **9** extensive, good-sized, plentiful, ponderous, strapping **11** substantial

hegira **6** escape, exodus, flight **7** journey **10** emigration, evacuation **11** deliverance

Heidi ***author:*** **5** Spyri (Johanna) ***goatherd:*** **5** Peter ***setting:*** **4** Alps

heifer **4** calf

____ **Heifetz** **6** Jascha

height **3** top **4** acme, apex, cusp, peak, rise **6** apogee, climax, heyday, summit, vertex, zenith **7** stature **8** altitude, pinnacle **9** elevation, loftiness **10** prominence ***combining form:*** **4** acro

heighten **3** wax **5** boost, mount, raise **6** beef up, expand, extend **7** amplify, augment, build up, elevate, enhance, enlarge, improve, magnify **8** increase **9** highlight, intensify **10** aggrandize

heinie **3** bum **4** butt, rear, rump, tush **5** fanny **6** bottom **7** hind end, rear end **8** backside

heinous **4** evil **6** odious **7** hateful **8** infamous, shocking **9** abhorrent, atrocious, execrable, monstrous **10** abominable, detestable, outrageous

heinousness **4** evil **6** horror, infamy **8** atrocity, enormity **13** monstrousness

heir **5** scion **7** grantee, heritor, legatee **9** inheritor, successor **11** beneficiary ***joint:*** **8** parcener **10** coparcener

heist **3** cop, rob **4** lift, loot **5** boost, caper, filch, pinch, steal, swipe, theft **6** holdup, rip off **7** larceny, purloin, robbery **8** burglary **9** strong-arm

Helen of Troy ***abductor:*** **5** Paris ***husband:*** **8** Menelaus

Helenus ***brother:*** **5** Paris **6** Hector **7** Troilus **9** Deiphobus, Polydorus ***father:*** **5** Priam ***mother:*** **6** Hecuba ***sister:*** **6** Creusa **8** Polyxena **9** Cassandra ***wife:*** **10** Andromache

Hel, Hela ***father:*** **4** Loki ***hall:*** **7** Niflhel **8** Niflheim ***mother:*** **9** Angerboda

helical **6** spiral

helicopter **7** chopper **9** eggbeater **10** whirlybird ***armed:*** **7** gunship **9** Black Hawk

blade: **5** rotor ***manufacturer:*** **8** Sikorsky (Igor)
Helios 6 Apollo ***daughter:*** **5** Circe **8** Pasiphaë ***father:*** **8** Hyperion ***mother:*** **5** Theia ***sister:*** **3** Eos **6** Aurora, Selene ***son:*** **8** Phaethon
heliotrope 4 herb **5** shrub **6** borage **10** bloodstone
helium symbol 2 He
hell 5 hades, Sheol **6** blazes, Tophet **7** Gehenna, inferno **9** perdition, tarnation **10** blue blazes
hell-bent 6 driven, intent **8** obsessed, resolved **10** determined
Hellen *father:* 9 Deucalion ***mother:*** **6** Pyrrha ***son:*** **5** Dorus **6** Aeolus, Xuthus
hellhole 3 pit **8** dystopia, snake pit **9** mare's nest
hellion 3 elf, imp **4** puck, punk **5** demon, rogue, scamp **6** rascal **7** gremlin
hellish 6 horrid **7** ghastly, hideous, satanic, stygian **8** damnable, diabolic, dreadful, gruesome, horrible, infernal, terrible **9** appalling, frightful, monstrous, plutonian **10** diabolical
Hellman play 11 Little Foxes (The) **13** Children's Hour (The) **15** Watch on the Rhine
hello 3 hey **4** ciao, hail **5** aloha, howdy **7** hi there, welcome **8** greeting **9** greetings
helm 4 head **5** wheel **7** cockpit **8** controls
helmet 6 casque, sallet, tin hat **7** morrion **8** burgonet, headgear ***medieval:*** **6** sallet **7** basinet ***part:*** **5** nasal **7** ventail **8** aventail ***sun:*** **4** topi **5** topee
helmsman 5 pilot
Heloïse *husband:* 7 Abelard (Peter) ***son:*** **9** Astrolabe
helot 4 peon, serf **5** slave **6** vassal **7** laborer, peasant, servant
helotry 4 yoke **6** thrall **7** bondage, peonage, serfdom, slavery **9** servitude, thralldom **11** enslavement
help 3 aid **4** abet, back, mend **5** avail, boost, guide, serve **6** assist, relief, remedy, succor **7** advance, benefit, bolster, further, promote, relieve, secours, service, support **8** mitigate, palliate **9** alleviate, meliorate **10** ameliorate, assistance, facilitate **11** cooperation ***forward:*** **7** further ***hired:*** **5** labor
helper 4 aide, ass't **6** deputy, server **7** ancilla, servant **8** employee **9** assistant, associate, attendant, auxiliary **10** apprentice **11** subordinate
helpful 5 of use **6** usable, useful **8** salutary, valuable **9** effective, favorable, practical **10** beneficial, profitable, propitious **11** encouraging **12** advantageous, constructive
helping 4 dose **5** share **7** portion, serving **9** auxiliary
helpless 4 weak **6** feeble, futile, unable **7** forlorn **8** desolate **9** abandoned, dependent **11** unprotected
helter-skelter 6 anyhow **7** anywise, flighty, hastily, turmoil **8** at random, disorder, pell-mell, randomly **9** confusion, haphazard, hit-or-miss **11** any which way, haphazardly, in confusion, precipitate
helve 4 haft **6** handle
Helvetian 5 Swiss
hem 3 pen, rim **4** brim, edge, gird, ring, seam, shut **5** bound, brink, fence, hedge, skirt, verge **6** border, circle, corral, edging, fringe, immure, margin, stitch **7** close in, enclose, selvage, shorten **8** encircle, surround **9** encompass, perimeter, periphery ***turned-back:*** **4** cuff
he-man 4 hunk, stud **5** macho
Heman *father:* 4 Joel ***grandfather:*** **6** Samuel
hematite 3 ore **7** mineral **12** black diamond
Hemingway, Ernest *work:* 9 In Our Time **12** Sun Also Rises (The) **13** Moveable Feast (A) **14** Farewell to Arms (A) **15** Old Man and the Sea (The) **16** To Have and Have Not **18** Islands in the Stream, Snows of Kilimanjaro (The) **19** For Whom the Bell Tolls ***sobriquet:*** **4** Papa
hemipterous insect 3 bug
hemlock 4 drug, herb, tree, wood **6** poison
hemophiliac 7 bleeder
hemp 3 kef, kif **7** hashish **8** cannabis **9** marijuana ***fiber:*** **5** oakum ***kind:*** **4** aloe
hen 5 biddy, layer ***broody:*** **6** sitter ***spayed:*** **8** poularde ***young:*** **6** pullet
hence 4 away, ergo, thus **5** since **6** hereat **9** as a result, from now on, therefore, thereupon **11** accordingly **12** consequently
henceforth 9 from now on, hereafter
henchman 6 cohort, lackey, minion, stooge **7** abettor **8** adherent, disciple, follower, partisan, retainer **9** attendant, supporter **10** accomplice
Henley poem 8 Invictus
henpeck 3 nag **4** carp, fuss **5** annoy **6** badger, carp at, harass, hector **8** domineer **9** find fault
Henry II *adversary:* 6 Becket (Thomas à) ***son:*** **4** John (Lackland) **7** Richard (Lionheart) ***surname:*** **5** Anjou **11** Plantagenet ***wife:*** **7** Eleanor
Henry IV 11 Bolingbroke ***surname:*** **9** Lancaster ***victim:*** **10** Richard III
Henry VIII *archbishop:* 7 Cranmer (Thomas) **10** Thomas More ***daughter:*** **9** Elizabeth ***son:*** **6** Edward ***surname:*** **5** Tudor ***victim:*** **4**

Anne (Boleyn) **9** Catherine (Howard) **10** Thomas More ***wife:*** **4** Anne (Boleyn, of Cleves), Jane (Seymour) **9** Catherine (Howard, of Aragon, Parr)

hepatic 9 liverwort

Hephaestus 6 Vulcan ***father:*** **4** Zeus **7** Jupiter ***mother:*** **4** Hera, Juno ***wife:*** **5** Venus **6** Charis **9** Aphrodite

Hephzibah *husband:* 8 Hezekiah ***son:*** **8** Manasseh

hepped up 5 eager **7** charged, excited, fervent **8** enthused **12** enthusiastic

Hera 4 Juno ***father:*** **6** Cronus, Saturn ***husband:*** **4** Zeus **7** Jupiter ***messenger:*** **4** Iris ***mother:*** **4** Rhea

Heracles *beloved:* **4** Iole ***brother:*** **8** Iphicles ***charioteer:*** **6** Iolaus ***father:*** **4** Zeus **7** Jupiter ***mother:*** **7** Alcmene ***son:*** **6** Hyllus ***victim:*** **5** Hydra, Ladon **6** Geryon, Megara, Orthus **10** Nemean lion ***wife:*** **4** Hebe **6** Megara **8** Deianira

herald 4 hail, tout **5** crier, greet **6** signal **7** courier, declare, portend, precede, presage, trumpet **8** announce, ballyhoo, exponent, outrider, proclaim **9** advertise, harbinger, messenger, precursor, publicize, spokesman **10** forerunner, foreshadow

heraldic *border:* **7** bordure ***cross:*** **6** fleury, formée, moline, pommée **8** fourchée ***term:*** **4** aile, bend, fess, orle, pale, semé, vair, vert **5** crest, flank, gules **6** argent, blazon, canton, charge, device, dexter, emblem, impale, manche, sejant, voided, volant **7** chevron, nombril, passant, purpure, rampant, saltire, statant, urinant **8** guardant, sinister, tincture **9** regardant **10** escutcheon

heraldry 6 armory **9** pageantry

herb 3 Iva, oca, pia, udo **4** arum, dill, flax, forb, geum, hemp, leek, mint, nard, sage, wort **5** basil, canna, chive, cumin, tansy, thyme **6** allium, arnica, borage, catnip, endive, eryngo, fat hen, fennel, garlic, hyssop, lovage, orpine, squill, yarrow **7** boneset, caraway, catmint, chervil, chicory, comfrey, episcia, ginseng, milfoil, mullein, oregano, parsley, pinesap, pussley, salsify, sanicle **8** angelica, camomile, capsicum, cardamom, centaury, cilantro, costmary, feverfew, freewort, hepatica, lungwort, mandrake, marjoram, origanum, pokeweed, purslane, rapeseed, selfheal, tarragon, turmeric, euphrasy, valerian, woodruff, wormwood **9** birthwort, bush basil, chamomile, goosefoot, patchouli, spikenard **10** basil thyme, cuckoo pint **12** balm of Gilead ***beverage:*** **6** tisane ***genus:*** **4** Arum, Geum ***mythical:*** **4** moly ***poisonous:*** **4** atis **7** aconite, dogbane, hemlock, henbane **8** veratrum **9** hellebore, monkshood

herbicide 6 dioxin, diquat, diuron **7** monuron **8** picloram, simazine **11** Agent Orange

Herculean 4 huge, vast **5** giant **7** arduous, immense, mammoth, titanic **8** colossal, enormous, gigantic, powerful **10** formidable, superhuman

Hercules see **Heracles**

herd 3 mob **4** bevy, lead **5** covey, crowd, drive, drove, flock, swarm **6** gather, throng **9** associate, multitude

herdsman 6 Boötes, cowboy **7** breeder **8** shepherd

here and there 6 passim **7** at times **9** sometimes **11** irregularly

hereditary 6 inborn, inbred, innate, lineal **7** genetic **9** ancestral, inherited **10** congenital **11** traditional, transmitted

heredity 7 lineage **8** ancestry **9** tradition **11** inheritance ***unit:*** **4** gene

heresy 6 schism **7** dissent, fallacy, impiety **9** defection, deviation, misbelief **10** dissidence, heterodoxy, infidelity, radicalism **11** revisionism, unorthodoxy **13** nonconformism, nonconformity

heretic 7 infidel **8** apostate, defector, recusant, renegade **9** dissenter, dissident **10** iconoclast, schismatic, separatist, unbeliever **11** misbeliever, nonbeliever, revisionist **13** nonconformist

heretical 7 infidel **8** apostate **9** dissident, heterodox, miscreant, sectarian **10** dissenting, schismatic, unorthodox **11** revisionist **12** misbelieving **13** nonconformist

heretofore 6 ere now **7** up to now

heritage 6 legacy **7** bequest **9** patrimony, tradition **10** birthright

Hermes 7 Mercury ***attribute:*** **7** petasos, petasus **8** caduceus ***father:*** **4** Zeus **7** Jupiter ***mother:*** **4** Maia

hermetic 6 arcane, closed, occult, sealed, secret **7** recluse **8** abstruse, airtight, profound, secluded, solitary **9** recondite **10** cloistered, impervious **11** sequestered

Hermia *beloved:* **8** Lysander ***father:*** **5** Egeus

Hermione *father:* **8** Menelaus ***husband:*** **7** Orestes, Pyrrhus **11** Neoptolemus ***mother:*** **5** Helen

hermit 5 loner **6** cookie **7** eremite, recluse **8** solitary **9** anchorite

hermitage 7 retreat **8** cloister, hideaway **9** monastery

hernia 6 breach **7** rupture **10** protrusion ***support:*** **5** truss ***type:*** **6** cystic, hiatal **7** femoral **9** umbilical **10** incisional

hero 4 idol, lion **6** knight **7** demigod, paladin

8 champion **11** protagonist ***American:*** **6** Bunyan (Paul) **8** Superman ***Armenian:*** **10** Skanderbeg ***Babylonian:*** **9** Gilgamesh ***Celtic-French:*** **7** Tristan **8** Tristram ***Crusades:*** **7** Tancred **8** Tancredi ***English:*** **6** Arthur **7** Beowulf **9** Robin Hood ***French:*** **6** Roland **11** Charlemagne ***German:*** **5** Etzel **8** Arminius **9** Siegfried ***Greek:*** **4** Ajax **5** Jason **7** Perseus, Ulysses **8** Achilles, Heracles, Hercules, Leonidas, Odysseus **11** Bellerophon ***Hebrew:*** **5** David **6** Daniel, Samson ***Hungarian:*** **5** Arpad **7** Hunyadi (János) ***Irish:*** **9** Cuchulain, Cuchulinn, Cuchullin ***Italian:*** **7** Orlando ***Roman:*** **7** Romulus **8** Horatius ***Scandinavian:*** **6** Sigurd **9** Siegfried ***Scottish:*** **5** Bruce (Robert) **6** Rob Roy ***Spanish:*** **3** Cid **5** El Cid ***Spartan:*** **8** Leonidas ***Trojan:*** **6** Aeneas, Hector

Herod ***daughter:*** **6** Salome ***father:*** **7** Antipas **9** Antipater ***kingdom:*** **5** Judea **6** Judaea ***mother:*** **6** Cyprus ***son:*** **5** Herod (Antipas) **6** Joseph **7** Pheroas **9** Phasaelus

Herodias ***daughter:*** **6** Salome ***father:*** **11** Aristobulus ***husband:*** **5** Herod (Antipas)

heroic **4** bold, epic **5** brave, noble **6** daring **7** drastic, extreme, radical, valiant **8** fearless, intrepid, unafraid, valorous **9** dauntless, Herculean, undaunted **10** courageous

heroin **4** gear, skag, snow **5** horse, smack **8** narcotic **11** diamorphine

heroism **5** valor **6** daring, spirit **7** bravery, courage, prowess **8** boldness, chivalry, nobility, valiance **9** gallantry **11** intrepidity

heron relative **5** egret **7** bittern

Hero's lover **7** Leander

herring **7** sardine **8** brisling, pilchard ***measure:*** **4** cran ***smoked:*** **7** bloater

Herse ***father:*** **7** Cecrops ***sister:*** **8** Aglauros ***son:*** **8** Cephalus

Hersey ***novel:*** **4** Wall (The) **12** Bell for Adano (A) ***town:*** **5** Adano

Hesione ***brother:*** **5** Priam ***father:*** **8** Laomedon ***husband:*** **7** Telamon ***rescuer:*** **8** Heracles, Hercules ***son:*** **6** Teucer

hesitant **4** slow **5** chary, loath, timid **6** afraid, averse, unsure **7** halting, uneager **9** faltering, reluctant, tentative, uncertain, unwilling **10** irresolute **11** disinclined, vacillating

hesitate **4** balk **5** delay, demur, hedge, pause, stall, stick, waver **6** dawdle, dither, falter, waffle **7** stammer, stutter **8** hang back, hold back **9** temporize, vacillate **12** shilly-shally

Hesperides **6** nymphs

Hesperus **5** Venus **11** evening star ***father:*** **8** Astraeus ***mother:*** **3** Eos

Hesse novel **6** Demian **10** Siddhartha **11** Steppenwolf **12** Magister Ludi

Hestia **5** Vesta ***father:*** **6** Cronus, Saturn ***mother:*** **4** Rhea

heterodox **9** dissident, heretical, sectarian **10** schismatic, unorthodox **13** nonconformist

heterodoxy **6** heresy, schism **7** dissent **9** misbelief **10** dissidence **13** nonconformism, nonconformity

heterogeneous **5** mixed **6** motley, sundry, varied **7** diverse, various **8** assorted **9** disparate **12** conglomerate

het up **5** irate, upset **7** excited **8** agitated

hew **3** axe, cut **4** chop, fell, form **5** shape, stick **6** adhere **7** conform, cut down

hex **4** jinx **5** charm, curse, spell, witch **6** voodoo, whammy **7** bad luck, bewitch, enchant **9** sorceress **11** enchantment, enchantress

hey **4** psst

heyday **4** acme, peak **5** prime **6** height, zenith **9** high point

Hezekiah ***father:*** **4** Ahaz **7** Neariah ***mother:*** **3** Abi ***son:*** **8** Manasseh ***wife:*** **9** Hephzibah

hiatus **3** gap **5** break, space **6** breach, lacuna **7** interim **8** aperture, downtime, interval **10** suspension **12** interruption **13** discontinuity

Hiawatha ***author:*** **10** Longfellow (Henry Wadsworth) ***craft:*** **5** canoe ***grandmother:*** **7** Nokomis ***mother:*** **7** Wenonah ***tribe:*** **6** Ojibwa, Ojibwe **8** Onondaga **7** Ojibway ***wife:*** **9** Minnehaha

hibernal **6** wintry **8** winterly

Hibernia **4** Eire, Erin **7** Ireland

hick **4** rube **5** yokel **6** rustic **7** bumpkin, hayseed **8** cornball **10** clodhopper, provincial

hidden **5** privy **6** buried, covert, occult, secret, veiled **7** obscure **8** obscured, shrouded, ulterior **9** concealed **11** undisclosed ***combining form:*** **6** crypto, krypto

hide **3** fur **4** bury, lurk, mask, pelt, skin, veil **5** cache, cloak, cover, inter, shade, stash **6** harbor, lie low, screen, shroud **7** conceal, cover up, leather, obscure, seclude, secrete, shelter **8** ensconce

hideaway see **hideout**

hidebound **8** obdurate **9** parochial **10** inflexible, provincial **11** reactionary, straitlaced **12** conservative, narrow-minded **13** straightlaced

hideous **4** ugly **5** awful, gross, lurid, nasty **6** grisly, horrid **7** ghastly, hateful **8** gruesome, horrible, shocking, terrible **9** appalling, dismaying, frightful, loathsome, monstrous, offensive, repellent, repugnant, repulsive, revolting, sickening **10** disgusting, horrifying

hideout **3** den **4** lair **5** cache, haven **6** covert, refuge **7** retreat, shelter **9** hermitage, safe house, sanctuary

hie 3 run **4** dash, push, trot **5** hurry, scoot **6** hasten, hustle

hierarch 4 boss, head **5** chief **6** honcho, leader, master **7** headman **9** chieftain **10** high priest

hierarchy 5 group, order, ranks **6** ladder, system **7** pyramid **9** food chain, structure **11** bureaucracy **12** pecking order

hieratic 6 formal **8** priestly, stylized **10** priestlike, sacerdotal

high 4 tall **5** drunk, giddy, grand, lofty, noble, tipsy **6** elated, raised, stoned, treble, zonked **7** drugged, keyed up, soaring, supreme **8** abstruse, elevated, eloquent, euphoric, hopped-up, piercing, towering **9** climactic, delirious, prominent, spaced-out **11** extravagant, intoxicated ***combining form:*** **4** alti

high ____ 3 hat, tea **4** card, five, noon, road, sign, tech, tide, time **5** chair, heels, hopes, jinks **6** priest, roller, school

high-and-mighty 5 bossy, proud **6** lordly **7** haughty **8** arrogant, cavalier, insolent, superior **9** imperious **10** disdainful **11** domineering, overbearing **12** supercilious

highball 3 fly, run **4** dash, rush, whiz **5** hurry, speed **6** barrel, hustle, signal **7** hotfoot **8** cocktail

highboy 5 chest **6** bureau **7** dresser **9** furniture

highbrow 4 snob **7** egghead **8** cerebral, cultured, educated **9** intellect **12** intellectual

high-class 7 elegant **8** five-star, superior **9** exclusive, exquisite, first-rate, patrician **11** fashionable **12** aristocratic **13** sophisticated

highest 3 top **5** chief **6** apical, upmost **7** exalted, supreme, topmost **9** top-drawer, uppermost **10** top-ranking ***point:*** **4** acme, apex **5** crest **6** summit, zenith **8** pinnacle

highfalutin 5 fancy, windy **6** florid **7** aureate, flowery, fustian, orotund, pompous **8** affected **9** bombastic, grandiose, overblown, rhapsodic **10** oratorical, rhetorical **11** declamatory, pretentious

high-flown 5 showy, tumid, windy **6** turgid **7** aureate, flowery, fustian, orotund, pompous, swollen **8** elevated, inflated, sonorous **9** bombastic, grandiose, overblown **10** flamboyant **11** declamatory, pretentious **12** magniloquent, ostentatious **13** grandiloquent

high-handed 5 bossy **8** arrogant, dogmatic, imperial **9** arbitrary, imperious **10** autocratic, disdainful, imperative, peremptory **11** dictatorial, domineering, magisterial, overbearing

high-hat 4 snub **6** slight, snobby, snooty **7** disdain, haughty **8** arrogant, snobbish **9** conceited, disregard **11** pretentious **12** supercilious

high jinks 3 fun **6** antics **7** fooling, revelry **9** horseplay, rowdiness, whoop-de-do

Highlander 4 Gael, Scot

highlight 4 mark **5** focus **6** accent, stress **7** feature **8** point out **9** emphasize, underline **10** accentuate, focal point

high-minded 5 lofty, moral, noble **7** ethical, upright **8** elevated **10** principled

high-muck-a-muck 3 VIP **5** nabob **6** bigwig **7** big shot, notable

high-pitched 6 shrill **7** excited **8** agitated, feverish, frenetic, piercing

high point 3 top **4** acme, peak **6** apogee, summit, zenith **8** best part, pinnacle

high-powered 6 driven, strong **7** dynamic **8** animated, forceful, vigorous **9** energetic, strenuous **10** aggressive, compelling **12** enterprising

high-pressure 7 intense **8** forceful **9** insistent, stressful **10** aggressive

high roller 7 gambler, spender, wastrel **8** prodigal **10** big spender, profligate, squanderer **11** spendthrift

high sign 3 nod, tip **4** wink **5** alarm **6** signal, tipoff **7** gesture, warning **8** thumbs-up

Highsmith novel 11 Ripley's Game **16** Talented Mr. Ripley (The)

high-sounding 7 fustian, pompous **8** affected, imposing, inflated, puffed-up **9** grandiose, overblown **11** pretentious

high-spirited 4 bold **5** brash, fiery, jolly, merry **6** bubbly, daring, joyful, lively, plucky, spunky **7** excited, gleeful **9** ebullient, energetic, exuberant, vivacious **12** effervescent, lighthearted

high-strung 4 edgy, taut **5** hyper, jumpy, nervy, tense, tight, wired **6** touchy **7** fidgety, jittery, keyed up, nervous, uptight **8** restless **9** excitable, sensitive

hightail it 3 run **4** bolt, dash, flee **5** scoot, scram **6** get out, run off **7** take off **8** clear out **9** skedaddle

highway 4 pike, road **5** track **6** artery **8** corridor, turnpike **10** interstate **12** thoroughfare ***German:*** **8** autobahn ***Italian:*** **10** autostrada

highwayman 5 thief **6** bandit, robber **7** brigand

hijack 5 seize, steal **6** abduct, kidnap **8** take over **10** commandeer **11** appropriate

hike 2 up **4** jump, rove, snap, trek, walk **5** boost, raise, tramp, tromp **6** jack up, rise up, travel **7** journey, traipse, upgrade **8** backpack, increase

hilarious 5 funny, merry **7** comical **8** humorous, mirthful **9** laughable, priceless **10** rollicking

hilarity 4 glee **5** cheer, mirth **6** gaiety **7** delight **8** jocosity, laughter **9** merriment **12** cheerfulness

hill 4 bank, brae, bump, cock, dune, heap, knob, pile, rick, rise **5** bluff, butte, knoll, mound, ridge, shock, slope, stack **6** cuesta, height **7** hummock, incline **8** mountain **9** elevation, monadnock ***African veld:* 5** kopje **6** koppie ***Boston:* 6** Bunker ***craggy:* 3** tor ***Cuba:* 7** San Juan ***D.C.:* 7** Capitol ***elongate:* 7** drumlin ***level-topped:* 4** mesa **5** butte ***of stratified drift:* 4** kame ***rounded:* 5** swell ***sand:* 4** dune ***small:* 5** knoll, kopje, mound **6** koppie ***surrounded by ice:* 7** nunatak

hillbilly 4 rube **5** yokel **6** rustic **7** bumpkin, hayseed **10** clodhopper **12** backwoodsman

hillock 4 rise **5** knoll, mound

hillside 5 slope ***Scottish:* 4** brae

hilt 4 grip, haft **6** handle **8** handgrip

Himalayan *country:* 5 Nepal **6** Bhutan ***creature:* 4** yeti ***peak:* 6** Makalu **7** Everest **9** Annapurna **10** Dhaulagiri **11** Nanga Parbat **13** Kangchenjunga

hind 3 doe **4** back, deer, rear **5** after **7** grouper **9** posterior ***mate:* 4** hart

hinder 4 balk, curb, mire **5** block, check, delay, deter **6** baffle, burden, fetter, hamper, hold up, impede, retard, thwart **7** inhibit, prevent, shackle, trammel **8** handicap, hold back, obstruct, restrain **9** frustrate, hamstring, interfere, interrupt

hindmost 3 end **4** back, last, rear **5** after, final **6** latter **7** closing **8** farthest, terminal, ultimate **9** posterior **10** concluding

hindquarters 8 haunches

hindrance 3 bar **4** snag **6** hurdle **7** barrier **8** obstacle **9** impedance **10** impediment **11** obstruction

Hindu *age:* 4 yuga ***ascetic:* 4** yogi **5** fakir, swami ***camel:* 4** oont ***caste (varna):* 5** Sudra **6** Vaisya **7** Brahman **9** Kshatriya ***class:* 5** caste, varna ***community:* 6** ashram ***demon:* 4** Rahu **6** Ravana ***essence:* 5** atman ***force:* 5** karma ***garment:* 4** sari ***gentleman:* 4** babu ***god:* 4** deva, Rama, Siva **5** Shiva **6** Brahma, Vishnu ***goddess:* 4** devi ***goddess of beauty:* 7** Lakshmi ***goddess of destruction:* 4** Kali ***goddess of speech:* 4** Vach ***god of destruction:* 4** Siva **5** Shiva ***god of fire:* 4** Agni ***god of love:* 4** Kama ***god of the heavens:* 7** Krishna ***god of the wind:* 4** Vayu ***god of war:* 6** Skanda **10** Karttikeya ***god of wisdom:* 6** Ganesa, Ganesh ***hell:* 6** Naraka ***holy man:* 5** sadhu ***honorific:* 3** Sri **5** Swami **6** Pandit ***hundred thousand:* 4** lakh ***instrument:* 5** sitar, tabla ***leader:* 6** Gandhi (Mahatma) ***lowest caste:* 5** Sudra ***nobleman:* 4** raja **5** rajah ***philosophy:* 7** Vedanta ***precept:* 5** sutra ***prince:* 4** raja **5** rajah **8** maharaja **9** maharajah ***queen:* 4** rani **5** ranee **8** maharani **9** maharanee ***salvation:* 7** nirvana ***scripture:* 4** Veda **6** Purana **12** Bhagavad Gita ***social group:* 5** caste, varna ***teacher:* 4** guru **5** swami **9** maharishi ***term of respect:* 5** sahib ***treatise:* 9** Upanishad ***twice-born:* 6** Vaisya **7** Brahman **9** Kshatriya ***weaver:* 5** tanti

hinge 4 pawl **5** joint, mount **12** turning point ***kind:* 4** butt **5** piano **10** hook-and-eye

hint 3 cue, tip **4** clue, dash, sign, wisp **5** imply, taste, tinge, touch, trace **6** allude, notion, shadow, tipoff **7** inkling, soupçon, suggest **8** allusion, indicate, innuendo, intimate **9** insinuate, scintilla, suspicion **10** indication, intimation, suggestion **11** implication, insinuation

hinterland 4 bush **6** sticks **8** frontier, interior **9** backwater, backwoods, boondocks, upcountry **10** wilderness **11** backcountry

hip 3 hot **4** chic, coxa **5** aware, savvy **6** haunch, trendy, with-it **7** tuned in **11** fashionable ***bone:* 5** ilium, pubis **6** pelvis **7** ischium ***cattle:* 5** thurl ***disorder:* 8** sciatica

hip-hop *star:* 3 DMC, DMX, Nas **4** Dash (Damon), Jay-Z, West (Kanye), Zola **5** Combs (Sean "Diddy"), Dr. Dre, Kelis **6** Eminem, Franti (Michael), Ja Rule, Lil' Kim **7** Ice Cube, LL Cool J, OutKast, Simmons (Russell) **8** Jadakiss, Ludacris **9** Biz Markie, Fifty Cent, Foxy Brown, Snoop Dogg **11** Busta Rhymes, Tupac Shakur ***term:* 3** dap, def, dip, dis **4** bima, simp, wack **5** busta, chill, crunk, floss, freak, homey, peeps, props, sherm, stilo, whodi **6** gaffle, hottie, nucker, step to **7** all that, be geese, down low, homeboy, hooptie, puff lye, shizzle, wangsta **9** dukey rope, freestyle, throw bows **10** bling bling, ghetto bird, scrap a lick **12** South Central

hippie 8 bohemian, longhair **11** flower child **13** nonconformist

Hippocratic ____ 4 oath

Hippodamia *father:* 8 Oenomaus ***husband:* 6** Pelops **9** Pirithous **10** Peirithous ***son:* 6** Atreus **8** Thyestes

Hippolytus *father:* 7 Theseus ***mother:* 7** Antiope **9** Hippolyte ***stepmother:* 7** Phaedra

hire 3 fee, let, pay **4** rent, wage **5** lease, wages **6** employ, engage, retain, sign on, take on **7** charter, payment, recruit **8** contract **10** employment **11** contract for

hireling 4 hack **6** worker **7** servant **8** employee **9** mercenary

Hirschfeld's daughter 4 Nina

hirsute 5 hairy **6** shaggy, woolly **9** whiskered

Hispania 6 Iberia **9** peninsula ***part:* 5** Spain **8** Portugal

Hispaniola country 5 Haiti

hiss 3 boo **4** hoot, jeer **5** decry **6** deride, revile, sizzle, wheeze **7** catcall, whisper, whistle **8** sibilate

historian 8 annalist **10** chronicler ***American:* 4** Webb (Charles Richard) **5** Adams (Brooks, Charles Kendall, Hannah, Henry, Herbert Baxter), Beard (Charles, Mary), Foote (Shelby) **6** Brooks (Van Wyck), Catton (Bruce), DeVoto (Bernard), Durant (Ariel, Will), Malone (Dumas), Miller (Perry), Muzzey (David), Nevins (Allen), Sarton (George Alfred), Shirer (William), Sparks (Jared), Turner (Frederick Jackson) **7** Ambrose (Stephen), Morison (Samuel Eliot), Parkman (Francis), Ridpath (John Clark), Tuchman (Barbara), Woodson (Carter G.) **8** Bancroft (George), Boorstin (Daniel), Channing (Edward), Commager (Henry Steele), Prescott (William H.), Robinson (James Harvey), Woodward (C. Vann) **10** McCullough (David) **11** Schlesinger (Arthur) ***Arab:* 10** Ibn Khaldun ***Danish:* 4** Saxo (Grammaticus) ***Dutch:* 8** Huizinga (Johan) ***English:* 4** Bede (Venerable), Stow (John), Ward (Adolphus) **5** Acton (Lord), Grote (George), Wells (Herbert George) **6** Camden (William), Gibbon (Edward), Keegan (John), Namier (Lewis Bernstein), Stubbs (William), Taylor (A. J. P.) **7** Hakluyt (Richard), Raleigh (Walter), Toynbee (Arnold), Whewell (William) **8** Geoffrey (of Monmouth), Macaulay (Thomas Babington) **9** Holinshed (Raphael), Trevelyan (George) ***French:* 5** Bloch (Marc), Renan (Ernest), Taine (Hippolyte) **6** Guizot (François), Thiers (Louis-Adolphe), Volney (Comte de) **7** Braudel (Ferdinand) **8** Hanotaux (Gabriel), Michelet (Jules) ***German:* 5** Ranke (Leopold von) **7** Mommsen (Theodor), Niebuhr (Barthold Georg) **8** Spengler (Oswald) ***Greek:* 8** Plutarch, Polybius, Xenophon **9** Dionysius, Herodotus **10** Thucydides ***Italian:* 4** Vico (Giovanni) **5** Croce (Benedetto) **9** Salvemini (Gaetano) ***Jewish:* 8** Josephus (Flavius) ***Roman:* 4** Livy **7** Sallust, Tacitus (Cornelius) **9** Suetonius ***Scottish:* 7** Carlyle (Thomas) **9** Robertson (William) ***Swiss:* 6** Müller (Johannes von) ***Welsh:* 7** Nennius

historical period 3 age, era **5** epoch

history 4 past, saga **5** diary **6** annals, memoir, record **7** account, done for, journal **9** chronicle, narrative, treatment **10** chronology

histrionic 5 showy, stagy **6** staged **8** affected, dramatic **10** artificial, theatrical

hit 3 bop, jab, rap **4** bang, bash, bean, biff, blow, bump, bunt, butt, conk, cuff, ding, lick, slap, slug, sock, swat **5** clout, knock, paste, pound, punch, smack, smash, smite, swipe, whack **6** batter, buffet, chance, larrup, strike, stroke, thwack, wallop **7** clobber, sellout, success **8** bludgeon, lambaste **9** collision, sensation ***baseball:* 5** homer, liner **6** double, single, triple **7** home run **9** line drive ***topposite:* 4** bomb, flop, miss ***golf ball:* 5** shank

hitch 4 jerk, join, halt, hook, knot, lift, limp, snag, yoke **5** delay, thumb, unite **6** attach, couple, fasten, hobble, tether **7** connect, harness **8** make fast, stoppage **10** connection, difficulty, impediment **11** obstruction **12** entanglement

Hitchcock, Alfred *film:* 4 Rope **5** Birds (The), Topaz **6** Frenzy, Marnie, Psycho **7** Rebecca, Vertigo **8** Lifeboat, Sabotage **9** Notorious, Suspicion **10** Rear Window, Spellbound **12** Lady Vanishes (The) **13** To Catch a Thief **14** Shadow of a Doubt **16** North by Northwest ***forte:* 8** suspense

hitchhike 5 thumb

hither 4 here **6** nearer **11** to this place

hitherto 5 as yet, so far **7** earlier, thus far, till now **8** formerly, until now **10** previously

Hitler, Adolf *follower:* 4 Nazi ***title:* 6** Führer **7** Fuehrer ***wife:* 5** Braun (Eva)

hit man 5 bravo **6** killer **7** torpedo **8** assassin, enforcer, hired gun, murderer **9** cutthroat

hit-or-miss 6 casual, chance, random **7** aimless, erratic **8** careless **9** desultory, haphazard, irregular, unplanned

hive 6 apiary, colony **7** cluster **9** stockpile

HMS Pinafore *composer:* 8 Sullivan (Arthur) ***librettist:* 7** Gilbert (W. S.)

hoagie 3 sub **4** hero **5** po'boy **7** grinder, torpedo **8** sandwich **9** submarine

hoar 4 rime **5** frost

hoard 4 save **5** amass, cache, lay by, lay up, stash, stock, store, trove **6** supply **7** collect, lay away, nest egg, reserve **8** squirrel, treasure **9** stockpile **10** accumulate, collection, cumulation **11** aggregation **12** accumulation

hoarder 5 miser **7** scrooge

hoarse 5 gruff, husky, raspy, rough, thick **6** croaky **7** grating, rasping, raucous, throaty **8** croaking, gravelly, guttural

hoary 3 old **4** aged **5** stale **6** age-old **7** ancient, antique, graying **8** grizzled, timeworn **9** venerable

hoax 3 con **4** dupe, fake, fool, gull, sham **5** fraud, phony, trick **6** befool, delude, humbug, take in **7** deceive, mislead **8** flimflam, hoodwink, trickery **9** bamboozle, deception, imposture

Hobbit creator 7 Tolkien (J. R. R.)

hobble 4 lame, limp **6** fetter, hamper, hinder, hog-tie, impede **7** cripple, trammel **8** handicap

hobby 6 falcon **7** pastime, pursuit **8** activity, sideline **9** avocation, diversion

hobgoblin ***4*** Puck **5** bogey **6** sprite **7** bugaboo

hobnob 3 mix **6** mingle **7** consort **9** associate, rub elbows, socialize **10** fraternize **11** get together

hobo 3 bum **5** gypsy, tramp **7** drifter, floater, swagman, vagrant **8** derelict, vagabond

hock 4 debt, pawn **5** ankle **6** prison

hockey 6 shinny ***arena:*** **4** rink ***cup:*** **7** Stanley ***implement:*** **4** puck **5** stick ***official:*** **7** referee **8** linesman ***player:*** **3** Orr (Bobby), Roy (Patrick) **4** Bure (Pavel), Fuhr (Grant), Hall (Glenn), Howe (Gordie), Hull (Bobby, Brett), Jagr (Jaromir), wing **5** Bossy (Mike), Bucyk (John), Hasek (Dominik), Kurri (Jari), Maruk (Dennis), Sakic (Joe), Shore (Eddie), Shutt (Steve) **6** center, Clarke (Bobby), Coffey (Paul), Dionne (Marcel), Dryden (Ken), goalie, Harvey (Doug), Juneau (Joe), Kariya (Paul), Leetch (Brian), Mikita (Stan), Morenz (Howie), Parent (Bernie), Plante (Jacques), Potvin (Denis), Recchi (Mark), Savard (Denis), Sundin (Mats) **7** Belfour (Ed), Bourque (Ray), Brodeur (Martin), Chelios (Chris), Fedorov (Sergei), forward, Francis (Ron), Gretzky (Wayne), Lafleur (Guy), Lemieux (Claude, Mario), Lindros (Eric), Messier (Mark), Mogilny (Alexander), Richard (Maurice), Richter (Mike), Sawchuk (Terry), Selanne (Teemu), Stastny (Peter), Yzerman (Steve) **8** Beliveau (Jean), Esposito (Phil, Tony), Forsberg (Peter), Nicholls (Bernie), pointman, Shanahan (Brendan), Trottier (Bryan), Ysebaert (Paul) **9** Hawerchuk (Dale) **10** Carbonneau (Guy), defenseman, goalkeeper ***term:*** **3** box **4** cage, deke, goal, puck, rink **5** bandy, bench, check, icing, stick **6** charge, crease, shinny **7** face-off, offside **8** blue line **9** back-check, body-check **10** center line, penalty box ***variation of:*** **9** broomball (see also **National Hockey League**)

hocus-pocus 4 sham **8** artifice, nonsense, trickery **9** conjuring, deception, imposture **10** mumbo jumbo **11** abracadabra, incantation, legerdemain **13** sleight of hand

hod 4 tray **6** trough **7** scuttle **11** coal scuttle

Hoder, Hoth ***brother:*** **6** Balder, Baldur ***slayer:*** **4** Vali ***victim:*** **6** Balder, Baldur

hodgepodge 4 hash, olio **6** jumble, medley **7** mélange, mixture **8** mishmash, mixed bag **9** patchwork, potpourri **10** assortment, miscellany, salmagundi **11** gallimaufry

hoe 4 till, weed **6** tiller, weeder **9** cultivate

hoedown 9 barn dance **11** contra dance, square dance

hog 3 pig, sow **4** boar, suid **5** swine ***family:*** **6** Suidae ***female:*** **3** sow **4** gilt ***genus:*** **3** Sus ***red:*** **5** duroc ***young:*** **5** shoat

hogback 5 crest, ridge

hogshead 3 keg, tun **4** butt, cask **6** barrel **9** container

hog-tie 4 bind **6** fetter **7** shackle, trammel

Hogwarts lesson 6 charms, spells **7** Muggles, potions

hogwash 3 rot **4** bosh, bunk, slop **5** bilge, hokum, hooey, swill **6** piffle **7** baloney, garbage, rubbish **8** nonsense, tommyrot **9** moonshine, poppycock **10** applesauce, balderdash, flapdoodle, taradiddle **12** gobbledygook

hog wild 5 crazy **6** crazed, madcap **7** berserk

ho-hum 4 dull **5** bored **6** boring **7** tedious **8** tiresome **10** unexciting **11** indifferent

hoi polloi 3 mob **5** horde **6** masses **8** populace **9** multitude **10** lower class **11** proletariat

hoist 4 lift **5** drink, raise, winch **6** lift up, pick up, take up **7** derrick, elevate **8** windlass

hoity-toity 4 smug **5** dizzy, giddy, silly **7** flighty, pompous **9** conceited, frivolous **11** highfalutin

hokey 4 fake, mock, sham **5** banal, bogus, corny, hammy, phony, stale, stagy, trite **6** ersatz, pseudo **7** clichéd **8** cornball, outdated **9** contrived, hackneyed **12** melodramatic

hokum 4 bosh **5** hooey **7** baloney, hogwash **8** malarkey, nonsense **9** moonshine, poppycock **10** applesauce, balderdash, flapdoodle, taradiddle **11** foolishness **12** gobbledygook

hold 3 own **4** bear, deem, grab, grip, keep **5** carry, clamp, clasp, cling, grasp, gripe, judge, sense, think, value **6** arrest, clench, clinch, clutch, detain, harbor, regard, retain **7** contain, convene, convoke, fermata, grapple, keep out, possess, reserve, support, sustain **8** keep back, maintain, preserve, restrict ***close:*** **6** cuddle ***dear:*** **7** cherish ***in check:*** **7** repress ***in common:*** **5** share ***out:*** **4** last **6** endure ***together:*** **4** bond **5** clamp **6** fasten ***wrestling:*** **6** nelson **8** headlock, scissors **10** full nelson, half nelson

hold back 4 curb, keep, stop **5** check, delay **6** bridle, detain, impede, retain **7** inhibit, keep

out, prevent, refrain, reserve **8** restrain, suppress, withhold **9** constrain
holder 3 cup, pot **4** bowl, cone, vase **5** owner **6** tenant **7** pitcher
hold forth 4 rant **5** orate, speak, spout **7** declaim, expound, lecture **8** harangue, proclaim **9** expatiate **10** dilate upon
hold off 4 stay, wait **5** defer, delay, pause, repel **6** rebuff, resist **7** abstain, adjourn, repulse, suspend **8** hesitate, postpone, prorogue **9** withstand **11** discontinue
holdup 5 heist, theft **7** mugging, robbery
hold up 3 rob **4** halt, lift, stay **5** check, defer, delay, raise **6** hinder, impede, put off, retard **7** support, suspend **8** postpone, prorogue, slow down
hole 3 den, gap, jam, pit **4** cave, flaw, lair, rent, spot, void **5** fault, niche **6** breach, burrow, cavity, cranny, defect, eyelet, lacuna, outlet **7** dilemma, opening, orifice **8** aperture, weakness **9** perforate **10** excavation, interstice **11** perforation, predicament
hole in one 3 ace
holiday 4 Xmas **5** leave **6** May Day **7** Flag Day **8** Labor Day, New Year's, vacation **9** Christmas, Hallowmas, Halloween **10** Father's Day, Mother's Day **11** Memorial Day, Veterans Day **12** All Saints' Day, Groundhog Day, Thanksgiving **13** Presidents' Day, St. Patrick's Day, Valentine's Day ***British:* 9** Boxing Day ***Canadian:* 11** Dominion Day, Victoria Day ***Jewish:* 8** Passover ***Vietnamese:* 3** Tet
holiness 5 piety **6** purity **8** devotion, divinity, sanctity **9** beatitude **11** religiosity **12** consecration, spirituality
Holland see **Netherlands**
holler 3 cry **4** call, yell **5** shout **6** bellow, clamor, cry out, outcry **7** call out **8** complain **9** complaint
hollow 3 dip, sag **4** void **5** basin, empty, false **6** cavity, ravine, sunken, vacant **7** concave, echoing, sinkage **8** sinkhole, thorough **9** cavernous, concavity **10** depression, sepulchral ***out:* 3** dig, gut **4** mine **5** gouge **8** excavate
holly 4 tree **5** shrub ***genus:* 4** Ilex
Hollywood 10 Tinseltown ***street:* 4** Vine
holocaust 4 fire **7** inferno **8** genocide **9** sacrifice **10** mass murder **11** destruction **13** conflagration
Holofernes' slayer 6 Judith
holy 6 adored, divine, sacred **7** angelic, blessed, revered, sainted, saintly, sublime **8** hallowed **9** glorified, religious, spiritual, venerated, worshiped **10** reverenced, sacrosanct, sanctified **11** consecrated ***combining form:* 5** hagio, hiero ***communion:* 9** Eucharist ***oil:* 6** chrism ***person:* 5** saint **6** zaddik **7** tzaddik ***Spirit:* 9** Paraclete ***vessel:* 5** grail **7** chalice **8** ciborium
holy place 6 church, shrine, temple **7** sanctum **9** sanctuary
Holy Roman Emperor 4 Karl, Otto **5** Adolf, Franz, Henry, Louis **6** Albert, Arnulf, Conrad, Joseph, Lothar, Ludwig, Philip, Rudolf, Rupert, Wenzel **7** Charles, Francis, Leopold, Lothair **8** Heinrich **9** Ferdinand, Frederick, Friedrich, Sigismund **10** Maximilian **11** Charlemagne
Holy Thursday 6 Maundy (Thursday) **9** Ascension (Day)
holy war 5 jihad **7** crusade
holy writ 5 Bible **9** Scripture
homage 5 honor **6** praise **7** respect, tribute **9** deference, obeisance, reverence
hombre 3 cat, guy, lad, man **4** buck, chap, dude, gent, stud **6** fellow, honcho **7** comrade
home 3 den **4** digs, lair, land, site **5** abode, haunt, house, range **6** family, hearth **7** country, habitat, housing **8** domicile, dwelling, locality **9** household, residence **10** fatherland, habitation, motherland **12** headquarters ***country:* 5** cabin **7** cottage **8** bungalow
homeless 5 stray **6** exiled **7** outcast, vagrant **8** derelict **9** abandoned, displaced, wandering **12** dispossessed
homely 4 cozy **5** plain **6** direct, modest, simple **7** natural **8** familiar, ordinary **11** comfortable, commonplace **12** unattractive **13** unpretentious
Homer epic 5 Iliad **7** Odyssey
homesickness 7 longing **9** nostalgia
homespun 5 plain **6** fabric, folksy, russet, simple **8** ordinary **9** practical **13** unpretentious
Home, Sweet Home *music:* 6 Bishop (Henry) ***words:* 5** Payne (John Howard)
homicidal 6 bloody **8** sanguine **9** murdering, murderous **10** sanguinary **11** sanguineous **12** bloodthirsty
homicide 5 blood **6** killer, murder, slayer **7** killing **8** foul play, murderer **9** manslayer **12** manslaughter
homily 6 sermon **7** lecture **9** discourse
homogeneous 7 uniform **10** consistent
Homo sapiens 3 man **7** mankind **8** humanity **9** humankind, human race
homunculus 5 dwarf, pygmy **6** midget, peewee **7** manikin **8** Tom Thumb
honcho 4 boss, head **5** chief, Mr. Big **6** bigwig, leader, master, top gun **7** big shot,

foreman, headman **8** hierarch, overseer **9** chieftain, Mister Big

Honduras ***capital:*** **11** Tegucigalpa ***city:*** **7** La Ceiba **9** Choluteca **10** El Progreso **12** San Pedro Sula ***coast:*** **8** Mosquito ***discoverer:*** **8** Columbus (Christopher) ***Indian people:*** **4** Maya **5** Mayan ***language:*** **7** Spanish ***monetary unit:*** **7** lempira ***neighbor:*** **9** Guatemala, Nicaragua **10** El Salvador ***river:*** **4** Coco, Ulúa **5** Aguán **6** Patuca ***sea:*** **9** Caribbean

hone 4 edge, whet **6** finish, polish, refine, smooth **7** perfect, sharpen **9** whetstone

honest 4 fair, just, open, real, true **5** frank, plain **6** candid **7** genuine, sincere, upright **8** innocent, reliable, truthful **9** objective, reputable, unfeigned, veracious **10** creditable, forthright, legitimate, scrupulous **13** conscientious, unimpeachable

honesty 4 herb **5** honor **6** candor, virtue **7** probity **8** fairness, goodness, justness, veracity **9** integrity, rectitude, sincerity **11** uprightness **12** truthfulness

honey ***combining form:*** **3** mel **4** meli, mell **5** melli ***drink:*** **4** mead

honeybee genus 4 Apis

honeycomb 3 pit **4** fill, fret **5** cells **6** impair, infest, riddle, weaken **7** subvert **9** perforate

honeydew 5 melon

honeyed 5 sweet **6** golden, liquid, mellow **9** sweetened **10** flattering **11** mellifluous

Honeymooners, The ***bus company:*** **6** Gotham ***character:*** **5** Alice (Kramden) **6** Trixie (Norton) **8** Ed Norton **12** Ralph Kramden ***lodge:*** **7** Raccoon ***setting:*** **8** Brooklyn **11** Bensonhurst ***star:*** **6** Carney (Art) **7** Gleason (Jackie), Meadows (Audrey) **8** Randolph (Joyce)

honeysuckle 6 azalea **9** columbine **13** pinxter flower

honk 4 blow, toot **5** blare, blast **7** trumpet

honky-tonk 4 dive **5** joint **7** hangout **9** juke joint, roadhouse **11** barrelhouse

honor 4 fete, laud **5** adorn, asset, award, badge, exalt, glory, kudos, medal **6** credit, esteem, homage, praise, purity, regard, trophy **7** commend, dignify, ennoble, fulfill, glorify, laurels, respect **8** accolade, approval, carry out, chastity, decorate, devotion, good name **9** adulation, deference, integrity, privilege, recognize, reverence **10** admiration, decoration, reputation, veneration **11** distinction, distinguish, recognition **12** commendation

honorable 4 just, true **5** moral, right **6** honest, worthy **7** ethical, upright **8** laudable **9** dignified **10** creditable, scrupulous **11** illustrious **13** conscientious

honorarium 7 payment **8** gratuity **10** recompense **12** compensation **13** consideration

hooch 6 liquor, rotgut **7** bootleg **8** dwelling, home brew **9** firewater, moonshine **10** bathtub gin

hood 4 cowl, thug **5** tough **6** bonnet, helmet **7** capuche **8** covering, gangster, hooligan **10** delinquent

hoodlum 4 punk, thug **5** bully **7** mobster, ruffian **8** criminal, gangster, hooligan **10** delinquent

hoodoo 3 hex **4** jinx, juju, rock **5** curse, haunt, hokum, magic, spell, spook **6** harass, whammy **7** bewitch, evil eye, sorcery, terrify, torment **8** nonsense **9** conjuring **10** black magic, hocus-pocus, mumbo jumbo, witchcraft

hoodwink 3 con **4** bilk, dupe, fool, gull, hoax, rook **5** trick **6** befool **7** deceive, mislead **8** flimflam **9** bamboozle

hooey 3 rot **4** bunk **5** bilge **6** bunkum **7** baloney, eyewash, hogwash **8** claptrap, malarkey, nonsense, tommyrot **10** balderdash

hoof 4 foot, walk **5** troop **6** ungula **7** traipse **8** ambulate ***cloven:*** **5** cloot ***sound:*** **4** clop **8** clip-clop

hoofer 6 dancer **7** danseur **8** coryphée, danseuse, showgirl **9** ballerina, tap dancer

hooflike 6 ungual

hook 3 nab, nip **4** gore, hasp **5** catch, curve, hitch, pinch, steal **6** anchor, fasten, pilfer **7** hamulus **8** crotchet ***a fish:*** **4** gaff, snag ***for keys:*** **10** chatelaine

hooklike 7 falcate **8** unciform, uncinate ***part:*** **5** uncus **7** hamulus

hookup 7 circuit, linkage **8** alliance **10** assemblage, connection **11** affiliation, association, combination, conjunction, partnership

hooky 6 truant **7** truancy **8** truantry

hooligan see **hoodlum**

hoop 4 band, ring **6** circle **7** circlet

hoopla 4 bash, fuss, stir, to-do **6** bustle, frolic **7** revelry, shindig, whoopee **8** ballyhoo, wingding **9** commotion, festivity, merriment, promotion

hoops 5 b-ball **10** basketball

hooray 3 rah, yay **5** cheer, huzza **6** huzzah, yippee **7** acclaim, whoopee **10** hallelujah

hoosegow 3 jug, pen **4** brig, cage, coop, jail, keep, stir **5** clink, pokey **6** cooler, lockup, prison **7** slammer **8** bastille, big house **9** calaboose, jailhouse **12** penitentiary

Hoosier State 7 Indiana

hoot 3 bit, boo, jot **4** hiss, iota, jeer, whit **5**

laugh, scrap, shout, whoop **6** assail, deride, heckle **7** catcall, modicum **8** particle

hooter 3 owl **5** owlet

Hoover Dam lake 4 Mead

hop 4 jump, leap, trip, vine **5** bound, dance **6** bounce, spring, wait on **7** rebound **8** jump over

hope 4 goal, wish **5** await, dream, faith, trust **6** aspire, desire, expect **7** count on, longing, promise **8** ambition, optimism, prospect **9** count upon **10** anticipate, aspiration, confidence ***loss of:*** **7** despair

hopeful 4 rosy **5** eager, sunny **6** bright, cheery, golden, seeker, upbeat **7** assured **8** aspirant, aspiring **9** candidate, confident, expectant, promising **10** auspicious, contestant, optimistic, propitious **11** encouraging **12** advantageous

hopeless 4 glum, lost, vain **6** futile, gloomy, morose **7** forlorn **8** downcast **9** desperate, incurable, insoluble **10** despairing, despondent, impossible **11** ineffectual, irreparable, pessimistic **12** incorrigible, irredeemable, irremediable

hoper 7 truster **8** optimist **9** expectant, Pollyanna

hopped-up 4 high **5** giddy **6** stoned, zonked **7** drugged, excited **9** delirious **12** enthusiastic

hopper 3 box, mix **4** frog, hare, tank, toad **5** bunny, chute **6** rabbit **7** cricket **10** freight car, receptacle

____ **Hopper 5** Grace (Murray), Hedda **6** Edward

hopping 4 busy **5** irate, livid **6** lively **7** furious **9** extremely, violently **10** infuriated

Horae 4 Dike **6** Eirene **7** Eunomia, seasons

Horam *kingdom:* 5 Gezer ***slayer:*** **6** Joshua

horde 3 mob **4** army **5** crowd, crush, drove, press, swarm **6** throng **9** multitude

horizon 4 goal **5** limit, range, reach, scope, vista **6** extent **7** purview, skyline **8** prospect **11** perspective

horizontal 4 flat **5** level **8** parallel

hormone 4 ACTH **5** kinin **6** estrin **7** estriol, estrone, gastrin, insulin, relaxin **8** autacoid, estrogen, glucagon, kallidin, secretin ***female:*** **8** estrogen ***insect:*** **8** ecdysone ***pituitary:*** **8** oxytocin

horn 4 toot **5** cornu **6** antler, klaxon, shofar **7** trumpet **10** cornucopia, projection ***ancient Greek:*** **5** rhyta (plural) **6** rhyton ***animal:*** **6** antler

Hornblower, Horatio *creator:* 8 Forester (C. S.) ***ship:*** **6** Le Reve **7** Atropos, Hotspur **10** Sutherland

horn in 6 meddle **7** intrude, obtrude **9** insinuate, interfere, interlope, interrupt

hornlike 8 corneous **10** keratinous

hornswoggle 3 con **4** dupe, fool, gull, hoax, hose **5** trick **7** deceive **8** flimflam, hoodwink **9** bamboozle

horrendous 5 awful **7** fearful, ghastly, heinous, hideous **8** alarming, dreadful, gruesome, horrible, horrific, shocking, terrible **9** abhorrent, appalling, execrable, frightful, repugnant, revolting **11** distressing, unspeakable

horrible 4 grim **5** awful, lurid **6** grisly **7** fearful, ghastly, hateful, hellish, hideous **8** dreadful, gruesome, shocking **9** abhorrent, appalling, frightful, loathsome, repellent, repugnant, repulsive, revolting **10** abominable, disgusting, terrifying

horrid 5 nasty **7** noisome **8** shocking **9** loathsome, offensive, repulsive, sickening **10** detestable, disgusting

horrific 5 awful **7** fearful **8** dreadful, shocking, terrible **9** appalling, dismaying, frightful, harrowing

horrified 6 aghast **8** appalled

horrify 5 daunt, shock **6** appall, dismay

horrifying 4 grim **5** awful, lurid **6** grisly **7** ghastly, hideous **8** gruesome, terrible **9** appalling, atrocious

horror 4 fear, hate, pain **5** alarm, dread, panic, shock **6** dismay, fright, hatred, terror **7** disgust **8** aversion, loathing **9** repulsion, revulsion **10** abhorrence, repugnance **11** abomination, detestation, trepidation

hors d'oeuvre 4 whet **5** snack **6** canape, tidbit **7** crudité **9** antipasto, appetizer

horse 3 nag **4** buck **5** bronc, mount, pacer, steed **6** bronco, brumby, equine **7** cavalry, palfrey, sawbuck, trestle, trotter **8** footrope, jackstay, stallion, traveler ***Australian-bred:*** **5** waler ***battle:*** **7** charger ***breed:*** **4** Arab **5** pinto **6** Morgan **7** Arabian, Belgian, Iceland **8** Palomino, Shetland **9** Appaloosa, Percheron **10** Lippizaner **12** standardbred, Thoroughbred ***champion:*** **7** Barbaro, Man o' War **8** Affirmed, Citation **10** Seabiscuit **11** Seattle Slew, Secretariat, Smarty Jones ***collar part:*** **4** hame ***color:*** **3** bay, dun **4** roan **6** grullo, sorrel **8** buckskin, chestnut, palomino ***combining form:*** **4** hipp **5** hippo ***covering:*** **8** trapping ***draft:*** **5** shire **10** Clydesdale ***extinct:*** **8** eohippus ***farm:*** **6** dobbin ***female:*** **4** mare **5** filly ***foot part:*** **7** pastern ***gait:*** **4** trot **6** canter, gallop ***gear:*** **3** bit **4** rein **6** saddle **7** harness **9** checkrein ***leg joint:*** **7** fetlock ***leg part:*** **6** gaskin **7** gambrel ***male:*** **4** colt **8** stallion ***mark:*** **5** blaze ***of the movies:*** **4** Fury **6** Flicka, Silver **7** Trigger **8** Champion **11** Black Beauty ***race:*** **5** Ascot, derby **7** Belmont **9** Preakness ***rump:*** **7** crupper ***small:*** **4** pony **6** garron, jennet ***spotted:*** **5** pinto **7** piebald ***talking:*** **4** Mr. Ed ***tan:*** **8** palomino ***thoroughbred:*** **8** hotblood ***tooth:*** **4** tush ***war:*** **8** destrier ***wild:*** **7** mustang

horsefeathers 3 rot **4** bull, bunk **5** bilge, hokum, hooey, trash **6** bunkum, drivel, piffle **7** baloney, garbage, hogwash, rubbish, twaddle **8** claptrap, flimflam, nonsense, tommyrot **9** poppycock **10** applesauce, balderdash

horseman 5 rider **6** cowboy **7** vaquero **8** cavalier **9** caballero, chevalier **10** equestrian

horsemanship 6 manège **10** equitation

horse opera 5 oater **7** western

horseplay 7 fooling **8** clowning, rowdyism **9** high jinks, rowdiness **10** buffoonery, roughhouse **11** shenanigans **12** roughhousing

horse-racing term 3 bug, cup **4** bolt, calk, gait, oaks, pill, prop, show, tack **5** float, place, purse, silks, washy **6** bobble, closer, exacta, impost, mudder, router, stayer **7** also-ran, blowout, clocker, paddock, spit box **8** breakage, claiming, climbing, dead heat, handicap, hand ride, off track, perfecta, post time, quiniela **9** hot walker **10** allowances, in the money, parimutuel, shadow roll **11** backstretch, daily double, morning line, triple crown **12** morning glory

horseshoer 6 smithy **10** blacksmith

hortative 8 advisory **9** exhorting, homiletic

horticulturist 6 Carver (George Washington) **7** Burbank (Luther)

Horus *brother:* 6 Anubis ***father:*** **6** Osiris ***mother:*** **4** Isis ***victim:*** **3** Set **4** Seth

hose 4 sock, tube, wash **5** cheat, spray, trick, water **6** tights **8** stocking

hoser 6 barfly, boozer **7** redneck

hospice see **hostel**

hospitable 4 kind, open **6** social **7** cordial **8** friendly, generous, gracious **9** convivial, receptive, welcoming **10** gregarious

hospital 6 clinic **7** lazaret **9** infirmary, lazaretto ***attendant:*** **7** orderly ***ship's:*** **7** sickbay

Hospitallers' island 5 Malta **6** Rhodes

host 2 MC **4** army **5** array, cloud, crowd, emcee, flock, horde **6** angels, legion, myriad, scores, server **7** compere, present, receive **8** assemble **9** innkeeper, introduce, moderator, multitude, presenter

hostage 4 pawn **5** token **6** pledge, surety **7** captive, earnest **8** guaranty, prisoner, security **9** guarantee

hostel 3 inn **4** stay **5** lodge **6** tavern, travel **7** auberge, lodging **11** caravansary, public house

hostile 4 anti, mean **5** enemy **6** bitter, fierce **7** adverse, opposed, warlike **8** contrary, inimical, opposite **9** bellicose, combative, resistant, resisting **10** malevolent, pugnacious, unfriendly **11** belligerent, contentious **12** antagonistic **13** argumentative

hostility 3 war **6** animus, enmity, hatred, rancor **7** ill will **8** conflict **9** antipathy **10** aggression, antagonism, opposition, resistance **12** belligerence

hot 3 new **4** fast, heat, sexy **5** angry, close, eager, fiery, lucky, spicy **6** ardent, baking, banned, heated, hectic, on fire, raging, stolen, sultry, torrid, urgent **7** boiling, burning, excited, fevered, illicit, lustful, peppery, popular, pungent, zealous **8** broiling, feverish, in demand, scalding, sizzling, tropical, vehement **9** energized, lecherous, scorching **10** blistering, contraband, passionate, sweltering **11** radioactive

hot air 4 bosh **6** bunkum **7** blather, prattle, twaddle **8** malarkey, nonsense **9** empty talk, poppycock **10** double-talk

hotbed 3 hub **4** core, seat **5** heart **6** center **7** nucleus **10** focal point **11** nerve center

hot-blooded 5 fiery **6** ardent **7** burning, fervent, flaming **9** excitable, impetuous, impulsive **10** passionate **11** impassioned **12** high-spirited

hotchpotch see **hodgepodge**

hot dog 5 frank **6** weenie, wiener, wienie **7** sausage, show-off **11** frankfurter, wienerwurst

hotel 3 inn **5** lodge **6** tavern **7** auberge, hospice, pension **8** motor inn **11** public house **12** lodging house, rooming house **13** boardinghouse ***chain:*** **5** Hyatt **6** Hilton, Ramada, Westin **7** Days Inn **8** Marriott, Radisson, Sheraton, Stouffer **10** Holiday Inn **11** Best Western, Four Seasons ***inferior:*** **7** fleabag **9** flophouse

hothead 5 rebel **7** fanatic, inciter, radical **8** agitator **9** demagogue, firebrand **10** incendiary **12** rabble-rouser, troublemaker **13** revolutionary

hotheaded 4 rash **5** brash, fiery, hasty **6** madcap **8** reckless **9** excitable, impetuous, imprudent, impulsive, irritable

hotshot 3 ace **4** star, whiz **5** comer **6** expert, master, wizard **8** virtuoso **10** powerhouse **11** heavyweight

hot-tempered see **quick-tempered**

hot water 3 box, fix, jam **4** bind, hole **6** corner, pickle **7** dilemma, trouble **9** tight spot **11** predicament ***in:*** **10** up the creek

____ Houdini 5 Harry

hound 3 dog, fan **4** bait, buff, ride **5** chivy **6** badger, basset, beagle, bowwow, canine, harass, hassle, heckle, hector, pester, pursue, Talbot **7** devotee **8** bullyrag **9** dachshund, persecute **10** aficionado ***Russian:*** **6** borzoi

hourglass 5 timer

house 3 cot, hut, ken **4** home, shed **5** abode, board, cabin, dwell, hovel, lodge, put up, shack **6** billet, chalet, harbor, shanty **7** contain, cottage, enclose, mansion, quarter, saltbox, shelter, theater **8** audience, bungalow, domicile, dwelling, quarters **9** residence ***clergyman's:*** **5** manse **7** rectory **9** parsonage ***country:*** **5** manor **7** cottage **8** bungalow ***dog:*** **6** kennel ***earth:*** **5** adobe ***Eskimo:*** **5** igloo ***mean:*** **5** hovel, shack ***of prostitution:*** **4** crib **6** bagnio **7** brothel **8** bordello ***religious:*** **5** abbey **6** priory **7** convent, nunnery **9** monastery ***rooming:*** **5** lodge ***Russian:*** **5** dacha ***small:*** **4** camp **5** cabin, shack **6** shanty **7** cottage **8** bungalow ***Spanish:*** **4** casa

housebreaker 4 yegg **5** thief **7** burglar, prowler **8** picklock

household 4 home **5** folks **6** family, ménage **8** domestic, familiar ***gods (Roman):*** **5** lares **7** penates

house of worship 6 bethel, chapel, church, mosque, pagoda, shrine, temple **7** chantry, minster, oratory **8** basilica **9** cathedral, sanctuary, synagogue **10** tabernacle **11** conventicle

housing 4 case, room **7** shelter **8** barracks, quarters **9** enclosure

hovel 3 hut, sty **4** dump, shed **5** hutch, shack **6** burrow, pigpen, pigsty, shanty **7** shelter

hover 4 flit, hang, loom **5** dance, drift, float, poise, waver **7** flitter, flutter, suspend **9** fluctuate, hang about

howbeit 3 yet **4** when **5** still, while **6** even if, much as, though **7** whereas **8** after all, although **11** nonetheless **12** nevertheless

however 3 but, yet **4** only **5** still **6** except, though **8** after all **11** nonetheless

howl 3 bay, cry **4** bark, keen, wail, yell, yelp **6** cry out **9** caterwaul

howler 4 flub, gaff, goof **5** boner, fluff, gaffe **6** boo-boo **7** blooper, blunder

huarache 6 sandal

hub 4 axis, core **5** focus, heart, pivot **6** center **8** polestar **10** focal point **11** nerve center ***opposite:*** **3** rim

hubbub 3 din **4** fuss, stir, to-do **5** babel, furor, hoo-ha, noise **6** clamor, furore, hassle, jangle, pother, racket, rumpus, tumult, uproar **7** turmoil **8** brouhaha, foofaraw **9** commotion, confusion **10** hullabaloo, hurly-burly **11** disturbance, pandemonium

hubris 3 ego **4** gall **5** brass, cheek, nerve, pride **7** conceit, hauteur, swagger **8** audacity, chutzpah **9** arrogance, cockiness, vainglory **11** braggadocio

hubristic 4 vain **5** cocky, proud **7** haughty **8** arrogant, insolent, superior **11** overbearing, overweening **13** overconfident

Huckleberry Finn *author:* **5** Twain (Mark) **7** Clemens (Samuel) ***character:*** **3** Jim, Tom (Sawyer) **4** Duke, King ***river:*** **11** Mississippi

huckster 4 hawk, plug, tout, vend **5** pitch **6** dicker, haggle, hawker, peddle, vendor **7** bargain, chaffer, haggler, packman, peddler, promote **8** pitchman

huddle 4 lump, mass **5** bunch, crowd, group, hunch **6** confab, confer, crouch, curl up, gather, parley, powwow **7** cluster, consult, meeting **8** assemble **10** conference, discussion

Hudson's ship 8 Half Moon

hue 4 cast, tint, tone **5** color, shade, shape, tinge, value **6** aspect, manner **8** coloring, tincture **10** coloration, complexion

huff 3 pet **4** blow, gasp, pant, rile, roil, snap, snit, tiff **5** annoy, grate, heave, peeve, pique, storm **6** nettle, put out **7** bluster, inflate **8** irritate

huffy 5 angry, proud, testy **6** piqued, touchy **7** annoyed, fretful, haughty, peevish, prickly, waspish **8** arrogant, petulant, snappish **9** irritable, irritated, querulous

hug 4 hold **5** clasp, press, prize, value **6** clinch, clutch, cuddle, enfold **7** cherish, embrace, envelop, squeeze **8** hold fast, hold onto **12** congratulate

huge 4 epic, vast, wide **5** bulky, giant, grand, great, jumbo, mondo **6** heroic, mighty, untold **7** immense, mammoth, massive, titanic **8** colossal, enormous, gigantic, whopping **9** extensive, monstrous **10** monumental, prodigious, stupendous, tremendous **11** magnificent, mountainous

hugeness 8 enormity **9** immensity, magnitude

hugger-mugger 4 hash **6** jumble, muddle, secret, tangle **7** clutter, furtive, jumbled, secrecy **8** confused, covertly, disorder, secretly **9** by stealth, confusion, furtively **10** disordered, disorderly, stealthily, undercover **11** clandestine **13** clandestinely

Hugo, Victor *character:* **6** Javert (Inspector) **7** Cosette, Fantine, Valjean (Jean) **9** Esmeralda, Quasimodo ***novel:*** **13** Les Misérables **20** Hunchback of Notre Dame (The)

Huguenot 10 Protestant ***leader:*** **5** Condé (Prince de), Rohan (Henri) **6** Mornay (Philippe) **7** Coligny (Gaspard II de)

Huguenots composer **9** Meyerbeer (Giacomo)

hulk **4** body, loom, ship **5** shell, wreck **8** skeleton **9** shipwreck

hulking **4** huge **5** beefy, bulky, burly, husky **7** immense, mammoth, massive **8** colossal, enormous, gigantic, oversize **9** humongous, lumbering, monstrous, ponderous, strapping **11** heavyweight

hull **3** pod **4** bark, body, case, husk, peel, rind, skin **5** chaff, frame, shell, shuck **6** casing **8** covering **11** decorticate

hullabaloo **3** ado, din **4** roar, to-do **5** hoo-ha, noise **6** clamor, hoo-hah, hubbub, jangle, pother, racket, tumult, uproar **8** ballyhoo, foofaraw **9** commotion, hue and cry **11** pandemonium

hum **4** buzz, purr, sing, zing **5** drone **6** murmur **7** vibrate

human **5** being, party **6** mortal, person **7** hominid **8** hominoid **10** individual ***race:*** **7** mankind

Human Comedy author **6** Balzac (Honoré de) **7** Saroyan (William)

humane **4** kind **6** gentle, kindly, tender **8** merciful **10** altruistic, benevolent, charitable **11** considerate, kindhearted, softhearted, sympathetic, warmhearted **13** compassionate, philanthropic

humanitarian **5** giver **8** generous **10** altruistic, benefactor, beneficent, benevolent, charitable **13** compassionate, philanthropic

humanity **6** people **7** mankind **8** kindness, sympathy **10** compassion, generosity **11** benevolence, Homo sapiens

humble **3** low **4** meek **5** abase, abash, crush, lowly, quiet **6** demean, modest, simple **7** chagrin, deflate, degrade, subdued **8** cast down, disgrace, ordinary **9** compliant, diffident, discomfit, embarrass, humiliate **10** submissive, unassuming **11** acquiescent, deferential **13** insignificant, unpretentious

humbug **3** con, rot **4** fake, fool, hoax, sham **5** faker, fraud, hokum, phony, spoof, trick **6** bunkum, delude, drivel, take in **7** beguile, deceive, mislead **8** flimflam, impostor, malarkey, nonsense, pretense, quackery **9** deception, hypocrite, imposture, pretender, trickster **10** balderdash

humdinger **3** ace, gem, pip **4** lulu **5** beaut, dandy, dilly, doozy, jewel, peach, prize **6** doozie **8** jim-dandy, knockout **11** crackerjack

humdrum **4** blah, dull, flat **6** boring, dreary, stodgy **7** prosaic, tedious **8** monotone, monotony, plodding, unvaried, workaday **10** monotonous, uneventful **13** uninteresting

humid **3** wet **4** damp, dank **5** close, moist, muggy, soggy **6** clammy, sodden, steamy, sticky, stuffy **10** oppressive

humidify **6** dampen **7** moisten

humiliate **5** abase, crush, lower, shame **6** bemean, debase, demean, humble **7** chagrin, degrade, mortify **8** belittle, cast down, disgrace **9** embarrass

humiliation **5** shame **7** chagrin, put-down **8** disgrace, ignominy, reproach **9** abasement, disrepute, indignity **11** degradation **13** embarrassment, mortification

humility **7** modesty, shyness **8** meekness **9** abasement, lowliness **10** diffidence, submission **12** subservience **13** self-abasement

humming **4** busy **5** brisk **6** active, lively **8** bustling, hustling **9** energetic

hummock **4** hump **5** couch, knoll, mound **7** hillock

humongous **4** huge, vast **5** giant, jumbo **7** immense, mammoth, massive, titanic **8** colossal, enormous, gigantic **9** monstrous **10** gargantuan, prodigious, tremendous

humor **3** wit **4** baby, bent, mind, mood, tone, vein, whim **5** fancy, fluid, spoil, yield **6** banter, coddle, comedy, cosset, esprit, joking, levity, nature, pamper, temper **7** caprice, cater to, conceit, gratify, indulge, jesting, kidding **8** crotchet, drollery, jocosity, repartee **9** character, drollness, flippancy, funniness, witticism, wittiness **10** complexion, jocularity, pleasantry **11** disposition, temperament

humorist **3** Ade (George), wag, wit **4** card, Nash (Ogden), Shaw (Henry Wheeler), Ward (Artemus, Edward) **5** Adams (Franklin Pierce), Allen (Fred), Barry (Dave), clown, comic, cutup, droll, Dunne (Finley Peter), joker, Twain (Mark), White (E. B.) **6** Blount (Roy), Browne (Charles Farrar), Diller (Phyllis), gagman, jester, kidder, Martin (Steve), Parker (Dorothy), Rogers (Will), Rourke (P. J.), Runyon (Damon), Thorpe (Thomas Bangs) **7** buffoon, Bombeck (Erma), Burgess (Gelett), Clemens (Samuel Langhorne), gagster, Hubbard (Kin), Keillor (Garrison), Marquis (Don), punster, Sedaris (David), Thurber (James), Trillin (Calvin) **8** Aleichem (Shalom), Benchley (Robert), comedian, funnyman, jokester, Perelman (S. J.), quipster **9** jokesmith, prankster, Wodehouse (P. G.) ***Canadian:*** **7** Leacock (Stephen)

humorous **5** comic, droll, funny, jokey, merry, witty **6** jocose **7** amusing, comical, jocular, risible, waggish **8** mirthful **9** facetious, laughable, whimsical

hump 3 lug **4** bump, race, tote **5** bulge, carry, hunch, mound, range **6** hustle, schlep **7** hummock, schlepp **8** mountain, obstacle, swelling **9** transport **10** protrusion

humpback 5 whale **8** kyphosis **10** pink salmon

humpbacked 6 convex, curved **7** gibbous

Humperdinck opera 15 Hansel and Gretel

humus 3 mor **4** mull, soil **7** compost **8** material

hunch 4 arch, clod, idea, lump, hump, push **5** chunk, clump, crook, squat, stoop **6** crouch, curl up, huddle, jostle, notion, nugget **7** feeling, inkling **9** intuition

Hunchback of Notre Dame *author:* 4 Hugo (Victor) ***character:* 9** Esmeralda, Quasimodo

hundred *combining form:* 5 centi, hecto ***dollar bill* 5** C-note

Hungary *capital:* 8 Budapest ***city:* 4** Pécs **6** Szeged **7** Miskolc **8** Debrecen ***ethnic group:* 6** Magyar ***lake:* 7** Balaton ***monetary unit:* 6** forint ***mountain range:* 10** Carpathian ***national hero:* 5** Árpád ***neighbor:* 6** Serbia **7** Austria, Croatia, Romania, Ukraine **8** Slovakia, Slovenia ***plain:* 11** Great Alföld ***river:* 4** Eger **5** Tisza **6** Danube

hunger 3 yen **4** ache, itch, long, lust, need, pine, want **5** crave, greed, yearn **6** desire, hanker, thirst **7** craving, longing

hungry 4 avid, keen, poor **5** eager **6** barren **7** craving, starved, thirsty **8** desirous, famished, ravenous, starving, underfed, yearning **9** hankering, motivated

hunk 3 gob, wad **4** clod, lump, stud **5** chunk, clump, himbo, piece, wedge **6** nugget **7** portion

hunker down 5 dig in, squat **6** crouch **8** settle in

hunky 4 buff **5** burly **6** buffed **8** athletic, muscular **9** strapping, well-built

hunky-dory 4 fine, okay **5** dandy, ducky, nifty, swell **6** peachy **10** peachy keen **12** satisfactory

Hunnish 4 rude, wild **6** savage **7** fearful, uncivil **9** barbarian, barbarous, ferocious **11** uncivilized

hunt 3 dog, run **4** hawk, seek **5** chase, hound, prowl, quest, shoot, snare, stalk, track, trail **6** battue, course, dig out, prey on, pursue, safari, search **7** explore, pursuit, rummage **9** ferret out, search for, search out ***birds:* 4** fowl ***illegally:* 5** poach

hunter 6 jaeger, nimrod **8** predator ***biblical:* 6** Nimrod ***cap:* 7** montero ***constellation:* 5** Orion ***mythological:* 5** Orion **7** Actaeon

hunting 5 chase **6** venery **7** gunning, hawking **8** coursing, falconry **9** predatory **10** predacious ***bird:* 6** falcon ***call:* 7** recheat ***cry:* 6** yoicks **7** tallyho **10** view halloo ***dog:* 5** hound **6** basset, beagle, borzoi, saluki, setter, vizsla **7** harrier, pointer, spaniel **9** ridgeback, wolfhound **10** bloodhound ***expedition:* 6** safari ***garb:* 4** camo **10** camouflage ***horn:* 5** bugle

huntress 5 Diana **7** Artemis **8** Atalanta

hurdle 3 bar **4** leap, snag **5** bound, clear, vault **6** hamper, spring **7** barrier **8** leap over, obstacle, overcome, overleap, surmount, traverse **9** negotiate **10** difficulty, impediment **11** obstruction

hurl 4 cast, fire **5** chuck, fling, heave, pitch, sling, throw, vomit **6** launch, thrust **8** catapult

hurly-burly 3 din **4** riot, to-do **5** melee **6** clamor, furore, hassle, hubbub, racket, rumpus, tumult, uproar **7** turmoil **8** confused **9** commotion, confusion

hurrah 3 olé, yay **4** fuss, to-do, zeal **5** cheer **6** fervor, rumpus **7** fanfare, ovation **8** approval **9** commotion **10** enthusiasm **11** acclamation

hurricane 7 typhoon

hurried 4 fast, sped **5** hasty, quick, swift **6** abrupt, rushed, sudden **7** cursory, rushing **8** headlong **9** impetuous **11** precipitant, precipitate

hurry 3 fly, hie, jog, run, zip **4** post, prod, push, rush **5** fleet, haste, scoot, speed, whirl, whish, whisk **6** barrel, breeze, bullet, bustle, hasten, hustle, rocket, rustle, step up, tumult **7** beeline, hotfoot, quicken, shake up, skelter, speed up, swiften **8** celerity, dispatch, expedite, highball, make time **9** commotion, make haste, swiftness **10** accelerate, speediness

hurt 3 mar **4** ache, blow, harm, pain **5** smart, wound, wrong **6** damage, grieve, hamper, harmed, impair, injure, injury, in pain, misuse, offend, pained, suffer **7** afflict, anguish, blemish, damaged, wounded **8** aggrieve, distress, mischief, mistreat **9** constrain, detriment, prejudice, resentful, suffering **10** resentment

hurtful 4 mean, sore **6** aching, unkind **7** harmful, painful **8** damaging, wounding **9** injurious **11** deleterious, destructive, detrimental, distressing, prejudicial

hurtle 3 fly **4** race, rush, tear **5** fling, shoot, speed, throw **6** charge, plunge, rocket

husband 3 man **4** mate, save **6** manage, mister, spouse **7** consort, partner **8** conserve, helpmate, helpmeet **9** economize, other half **10** bridegroom

husbandry 6 thrift **7** control, economy, farming **8** prudence **9** frugality **10** management **11** agriculture, thriftiness **12** conservation, preservation

hush 4 calm **5** quell, quiet **6** shut up, stifle **7** cover up, mollify, secrecy, silence **8** choke off, suppress **9** cessation, quietness, stillness

hush-hush 6 covert, secret **7** private, sub-rosa **9** top secret **11** clandestine **12** confidential **13** surreptitious, under-the-table

husk 3 pod **4** case, hull, peel, rind, skin **5** shell, shuck, strip **6** casing

husky 3 big, dog **5** beefy, burly, great, hefty, large, rough, stout **6** brawny, croaky, hoarse, mighty, robust, strong, sturdy **7** throaty **8** muscular, oversize, stalwart, thickset **9** strapping

hustings 5 stump

hustle 3 fly, rob, run **4** earn, move, push, rush, sell, urge, work **5** cheat, elbow, fraud, haste, hurry, press, shove, speed **6** hasten **7** hotfoot, promote, solicit, swindle **8** bulldoze, dispatch **9** deception, swiftness

hustler 4 doer **6** dynamo, vendor **8** go-getter, live wire **10** powerhouse

hustling 4 busy **5** eager **6** active, lively, speedy **7** hopping, humming **9** energetic **10** aggressive

hut 3 cot **4** camp, crib, shed **5** cabin, dacha, hooch, hovel, hutch, jacal, lodge, roost, shack **6** cabana, chalet, lean-to, shanty **7** cottage **8** bungalow ***American Indian:*** **6** wigwam **7** wickiup ***Scottish:*** **5** bothy, shiel **8** shieling

hutch 3 bin, pen **4** cage, coop **5** chest, shack **6** locker, shanty **8** cupboard **9** enclosure

Huxley novel 8 Antic Hay **11** Crome Yellow **13** Brave New World, Eyeless in Gaza

Hyacinthus *father:* **7** Amyclas ***slayer:*** **6** Apollo

hybrid 5 blend, cross, mixed, Prius, spork **7** amalgam, mixture **8** combined, compound **9** composite, crossbred **10** crossbreed **11** combination ***animal:*** **4** mule **5** hinny, liger, tigon ***fruit:*** **4** Ugli **7** tangelo

hybridize 4 join **5** blend, cross **7** combine **10** crossbreed, interbreed, intercross

Hydra 5 polyp **6** plague **7** monster, serpent **13** constellation ***father:*** **6** Typhon ***mother:*** **7** Echidna ***slayer:*** **8** Heracles, Hercules

hydrant 3 tap **4** pipe **5** valve **6** faucet, spigot **7** petcock **8** fireplug

hydraulic device 3 ram **4** jack, lift, pump **5** brake, press **8** elevator

hydrocarbon 5 xylol **6** dioxin, ethane, xylene **7** benzene, methane, styrene, toluene **8** biphenyl, butylene, ethylene, paraffin ***liquid:*** **6** octane **7** retinol, styrene **8** menthene

hydroid 5 polyp **6** medusa, obelia **9** jellyfish

hydrometer scale 4 Brix **5** Baumé

hydrophobia 5 lyssa **6** rabies

hyena 5 dingo **6** jackal **9** scavenger

Hygeia 5 Salus ***father:*** **9** Asclepius **11** Aesculapius ***goddess of:*** **6** health

hygiene 6 health **10** sanitation **11** cleanliness

hygienic 5 clean **7** aseptic, healthy, sterile **8** sanitary **9** healthful **10** antiseptic, unpolluted

Hyllus' father 8 Heracles, Hercules

hymeneal 6 bridal, wedded **7** marital, married, nuptial, spousal **8** conjugal **9** connubial **11** matrimonial

hymn 4 laud, song **5** bless, carol, chant, extol, paean, psalm **6** anthem, choral, praise, Te Deum **7** chorale, glorify **8** canticle, doxology, eulogize

hype 4 plug, tout **5** boost, thump **7** acclaim, enliven, glorify, promote, puffery, trumpet **8** ballyhoo, increase **9** advertise, excellent, publicity, publicize, stimulate **11** advertising

hyper 4 edgy **5** antsy, jumpy, wired **6** on edge **7** anxious, frantic **8** agitated, frenetic, hopped-up **9** excitable **10** high-strung, overactive **11** overwrought

hyperbole 6 excess **12** embroidering, exaggeration **13** embellishment, overstatement

hypercritical 6 severe **7** carping **8** captious, exacting **10** censorious, nit-picking **12** faultfinding

Hyperion *daughter:* **3** Eos **6** Aurora, Selene ***father:*** **6** Uranus ***mother:*** **4** Gaea ***son:*** **6** Helios ***wife:*** **5** Theia

hypnotic 6 opiate, sleepy **8** mesmeric, narcotic, sedative **9** somnolent, soporific **11** mesmerizing, somniferous **12** somnifacient, spellbinding

hypnotize 4 drug **5** charm **6** dazzle, trance **8** enthrall, entrance, overcome **9** captivate, fascinate, mesmerize, overpower, spellbind

hypocorism 7 pet name **8** nickname **9** sobriquet

hypocrisy 4 cant, sham **6** deceit, humbug **7** falsity, pietism **8** quackery **9** deception, duplicity, phoniness **10** sanctimony **11** insincerity, religiosity

hypocrite 4 fake, sham **5** actor, faker, fraud, phony, poser **6** humbug, poseur **7** bluffer, pietist **8** deceiver, impostor, pharisee **9** charlatan, pretender **10** dissembler **11** masquerader **12** dissimulator

hypocritical 5 false **7** canting **8** affected, specious, two-faced **9** deceitful, insincere, pietistic **10** Janus-faced **11** dissembling, double-faced, duplicitous **12** mealy-mouthed, pecksniffian **13** sanctimonious

hypothesis 6 belief, theory **7** premise **8** position, supposal **9** condition, inference **10** antecedent, assumption, conjecture **11** explanation, speculation, supposition

hypothetical 7 assumed **8** abstract, academic, supposed **10** assumptive **11** conditional, conjectural, suppositous, theoretical **12** suppositious **13** suppositional

hyrax 4 cony **5** coney **6** dassie, mammal **8** ungulate

hysteria 4 fear **5** craze, furor, mania, panic **6** excess, frenzy **7** madness **8** delirium

hysterical 5 rabid **6** crazed, raving **7** berserk, frantic **8** agitated, frenzied, neurotic **9** delirious, hilarious **10** convulsive, distraught, uproarious **11** overexcited, overwrought **13** side-splitting

I

Iago ***general:*** **7** Othello ***victim:*** **6** Cassio, Emilia **7** Othello **9** Desdemona ***wife:*** **6** Emilia

Iapetus ***father:*** **6** Uranus ***mother:*** **4** Gaea ***son:*** **5** Atlas **9** Menoetius **10** Epimetheus, Prometheus ***wife:*** **7** Clymene

Iasion ***brother:*** **8** Dardanus ***father:*** **4** Zeus **7** Jupiter ***lover:*** **5** Ceres **7** Demeter ***mother:*** **7** Electra ***son:*** **6** Plutus

ibex 4 tahr **8** wild goat ***family:*** **7** Bovidae ***genus:*** **5** Capra

Ibhar's father 5 David

ibis-headed god 5 Thoth

ibis relative 5 heron, stork

Ibsen, Henrik ***character:*** **3** Ase **4** Nora (Helmer) **5** Brack (Judge), Brand, Hedda (Gabler), Helen (Alving), Werle (Gergers) **6** Ejlert (Lovberg), Hedvig (Ekdal), Jorgen (Tesman), Oswald (Alving) **7** Solness (Halvard), Solveig, Torvald (Helmer) **8** Peer Gynt **9** Stockmann (Thomas) ***country:*** **6** Norway ***play:*** **6** Ghosts **8** Peer Gynt, Wild Duck (The) **10** Doll's House (A) **11** Hedda Gabler, Little Eyolf, Rosmersholm **13** Master Builder (The) **16** Enemy of the People (An)

Icarus' father 8 Daedalus

ICBM part 4 MIRV **7** booster, warhead

ice ***area:*** **4** rink ***dessert:*** **6** sorbet **7** sherbet ***floating:*** **4** berg, floe ***hanging:*** **6** icicle ***pinnacle:*** **5** serac ***sheet:*** **7** glacier

icebox 6 cooler, fridge **12** refrigerator

ice cream 6 gelato **7** spumoni, tortoni ***brand:*** **4** Edy's **7** Breyers **8** Klondike **9** Good Humor ***dish:*** **6** sundae **11** baked Alaska ***drink:*** **4** soda **6** frappe ***headache:*** **11** brain freeze ***holder:*** **4** cone

iced 5 glacé **6** glazed **7** chilled

ice field 4 floe **7** glacier

ice game 6 hockey **7** curling

ice house 5 igloo

Iceland ***capital:*** **9** Reykjavik ***monetary unit:*** **5** krona ***possession:*** **9** Greenalnd ***sea:*** **9** Norwegian ***snowfield:*** **11** Vatnajökull ***strait:*** **7** Denmark ***volcano:*** **5** Hekla

Icelandic ***epic:*** **4** Edda, saga ***hero:*** **5** Njáll **6** Gunnar **7** Grettir

ice skater ***figure skater:*** **4** Witt (Katarina) **5** Baiul (Oksana), Henie (Sonja), Kulik (Ilia) **6** Hughes (Sarah), Umanov (Alexei) **7** Arakawa (Shizuka), Cousins (Robin), Fleming (Peggy), Yagudin (Alexei) **8** Hamilton (Scott), Lipinski (Tara) **9** Plushenko (Evgeny) ***speed skater:*** **4** Koss (Johann Olav), Ohno (Apolo Anton), Yang (Yang) **5** Blair (Bonnie), Davis (Shani) **6** Heiden (Eric), Timmer (Marianne) **7** Hedrick (Chad), Klassen (Cindy), Zhurova (Svetlana) **9** Pechstein (Claudia)

ice smoother 7 Zamboni

Ichabod Crane's beloved 7 Katrina

icing 7 topping **8** frosting

icky 4 vile **5** awful, gross, nasty **9** loathsome, offensive, repellent, repulsive, revolting, sickening **10** disgusting **11** distasteful

icon 4 idol, sign **5** image **6** emblem, symbol

iconoclastic 9 dissident, heretical **10** rebellious, unorthodox **13** nonconformist

icy 4 cold **5** gelid, polar **6** arctic, chilly, frigid, frosty, frozen, steely **7** glacial **8** freezing **11** emotionless, unemotional

Idaho ***capital:*** **5** Boise ***city:*** **6** Moscow **9** Pocatello, Twin Falls **10** Idaho Falls **11** Coeur d'Alene ***mountain:*** **5** Borah (Peak) ***nickname:*** **3** Gem (State) ***river:*** **5** Snake **6** Salmon ***state bird:*** **8** bluebird ***state flower:*** **7** syringa ***state tree:*** **9** white pine

Idas ***brother:*** **7** Lynceus ***father:*** **8** Aphareus ***slayer:*** **4** Zeus ***victim:*** **6** Castor ***wife:*** **8** Marpessa

idea 4 whim **5** fancy, guess, motif **6** belief, notion, theory, thesis, vagary **7** caprice, conceit, concept, inkling, meaning, opinion, subject, surmise, thought **8** estimate **9** sentiment, suspicion **10** assumption, brainchild, brainstorm, conception, conclusion, conjecture, conviction, estimation, hypothesis, impression, perception, reflection **11** abstraction, formulation, supposition

ideal 4 best, goal **5** model **7** chimera, classic, epitome, paragon, perfect, utopian **8** absolute, ensample, exemplar, flawless, nonesuch, paradigm, standard, ultimate **9** archetype, classical, exemplary, nonpareil **10** archetypal, conceptual, consummate **11** theoretical

idealist 7 dreamer, quixote, utopian **9** ideologue, visionary

idealistic 6 dreamy **7** utopian **8** poetical, quixotic, romantic **9** visionary **10** starry-eyed **11** impractical, unrealistic

idealize 5 deify, exalt, extol **7** elevate, ennoble, glorify, worship **8** venerate

ideate 5 think **7** imagine **8** conceive, envisage, envision

idée fixe 5 mania **6** fetish, phobia **7** complex **8** fixation **9** obsession **13** preoccupation

identical 3 one **4** like, same, very **5** alike, equal, exact **8** selfsame **9** duplicate **10** equivalent, synonymous

identification mark 4 logo **5** badge, brand, label **6** emblem

identify 3 peg, tag **4** mark, name, spot **5** brand, place **6** finger, select **7** make out, pick out **8** pinpoint **9** determine, recognize **11** distinguish

identity 4 name, self **7** oneness **8** sameness, selfhood **9** character **10** congruence, uniformity, uniqueness **11** personality, singularity **13** individuality, particularity

ideological 8 notional **10** conceptual, ideational **11** speculative **13** philosophical

ideologue 8 believer, idealist, partisan, theorist

ideology 3 ism **5** credo, creed **7** beliefs **8** doctrine **10** philosophy, principles

idiocy 7 fatuity **9** cretinism, stupidity **10** imbecility **11** foolishness

idiomatic 7 demotic **8** peculiar **9** dialectal **10** colloquial, vernacular

idiosyncrasy 3 tic **5** quirk **6** oddity **7** anomaly **11** peculiarity, singularity **12** eccentricity

idiosyncratic 3 odd **5** kooky, queer, weird **6** quirky **7** erratic, oddball, offbeat, unusual **8** peculiar, singular **9** eccentric **11** distinctive

idiot 3 ass **4** dolt, fool, jerk, simp **5** dummy, dunce, moron, ninny **6** cretin, doofus, nitwit, stupid **7** airhead, dullard, half-wit, jackass, natural, tomfool **8** dumbbell, imbecile, numskull **9** ignoramus, numbskull, simpleton **10** nincompoop

idiotic 5 dopey **6** stupid **7** foolish, moronic **8** ignorant **9** brainless, imbecilic, senseless

idle 3 bum **4** laze, lazy, loaf, loll, rest, vain **5** dally, drone, empty, inert, slack, tarry **6** asleep, dawdle, diddle, fallow, futile, linger, loiter, lounge, otiose, unused, vacant **7** aimless, dormant, passive **8** inactive, indolent, slothful **9** shiftless **10** unoccupied

idleness 4 ease **5** sloth **6** vanity **7** leisure, loafing **8** lethargy **9** indolence **10** inactivity

idler 3 bum **4** slug **5** drone **6** loafer, slouch **7** dawdler **8** deadbeat, fainéant, loiterer, slugabed, sluggard **9** do-nothing, lazybones **11** couch potato

Idmon ***daughter:*** **7** Arachne ***father:*** **6** Apollo ***mother:*** **6** Cyrene

idol 3 god **4** hero, icon, star **5** deity, image, totem **6** fetish, minion, symbol **8** likeness ***Chinese:*** **4** joss

idolatry 7 worship **8** devotion **9** adoration **10** exaltation, veneration **11** deification **13** glorification

idolize 5 adore, deify, exalt **6** revere **7** glorify, worship **8** venerate

Idomeneo composer 6 Mozart (Wolfgang Amadeus)

Idyllic 5 ideal **6** rustic **7** bucolic, halcyon, perfect, utopian **8** arcadian, heavenly, pastoral, peaceful, romantic **9** idealized, unspoiled **11** picturesque, sentimental

Idylls of the King ***author:*** **8** Tennyson (Alfred) ***character:*** **4** Enid **6** Arthur, Elaine, Gareth, Merlin, Vivien **7** Geraint, Lynette **8** Lancelot

iffy 5 dicey, risky **6** chancy, unsure **7** dubious, erratic **8** doubtful **9** uncertain **10** unreliable **12** inconsistent **13** unpredictable

igneous rock 4 lava **5** magma **6** basalt, gabbro **7** diabase, granite **8** porphyry

ignis fatuus 6 mirage **7** chimera **8** delusion, illusion, phantasm **9** pipe dream **12** will-o'-the-wisp **13** hallucination

ignitable 8 burnable **9** excitable, flammable **10** incendiary **11** combustible, inflammable

ignite 4 fire **5** light, spark **6** excite, kindle **7** inflame **8** enkindle, touch off

ignited 3 lit **5** afire, fiery **6** ablaze, aflame, alight **7** blazing, burning, flaming, flaring **11** conflagrant

ignoble 3 low **4** base, mean, poor, vile **5** lowly **6** abject, coarse, common, scurvy, sordid, vulgar **7** lowborn, servile **8** baseborn, indecent, inferior, plebeian, shameful, unwashed, wretched **10** despicable, inglorious **11** disgraceful **12** contemptible, dishonorable

ignominious 6 odious **8** infamous, shameful **9** degrading **10** despicable, inglorious **11** disgraceful, humiliating, opprobrious **12** contemptible, dishonorable, disreputable **13** discreditable, unrespectable

ignominy 5 odium, shame **6** infamy **7** obloquy, scandal **8** disgrace, dishonor **9** discredit, disesteem, disrepute **10** opprobrium **11** humiliation **13** mortification

ignoramus 4 dolt **5** dummy, dunce, idiot, moron **6** dimwit, nitwit, stupid **7** airhead, dullard, half-wit **8** dumbbell, imbecile, numskull **9** numbskull, simpleton

ignorance 7 naiveté **9** innocence, nescience, stupidity **10** illiteracy, simpleness, simplicity **11** unawareness **12** incognizance

ignorant 5 naive **6** simple **7** unaware **8** clueless, nescient, untaught **9** benighted, ingenuous, oblivious, unknowing, unlearned, untutored, unwitting **10** illiterate, uncultured, uneducated, uninformed, unlettered, unschooled **11** incognizant, know-nothing **12** uninstructed **13** unenlightened

ignore 4 omit, snub **5** avoid **6** forget, reject, slight **7** neglect **8** overlook **9** disregard

Igraine ***husband:*** **5** Uther **7** Gorlois ***son:*** **6** Arthur

iguana 5 anole **6** lizard **8** basilisk **10** chuckwalla

ilex 4 maté **5** holly **6** yaupon **7** holm oak **8** inkberry

Iliad 4 epic ***author:*** **5** Homer ***character:*** **4** Ajax **5** Helen, Paris, Priam **6** Aeneas, Hector **8** Achilles, Diomedes, Odysseus **9** Agamemnon, Patroclus ***city:*** **4** Troy

Ilium 4 Troy

ilk 4 kind, sort, type **5** breed, class, genre **6** family, kidney, nature, stripe **7** variety

ill 4 sick **6** ailing, infirm, laid up, malady, peaked, queasy, unwell **7** ailment, disease, trouble, unlucky **8** diseased, disorder, distress, feverish, nauseous, scarcely, sickness, syndrome **9** afflicted, infirmity, nauseated, unhealthy **10** misfortune

ill-adapted 8 unfitted, unsuited **10** unsuitable

ill-advised 4 rash **5** brash, hasty **6** madcap, unwise **7** foolish **8** careless, heedless, reckless **9** foolhardy, impolitic, imprudent **10** incautious, indiscreet, unthinking **11** inexpedient, injudicious, thoughtless

ill at ease 3 shy **4** edgy **6** on edge **7** anxious, awkward, fidgety, nervous **8** insecure, restless **9** unsettled **11** discomfited **12** apprehensive **13** self-conscious, uncomfortable

ill-boding 4 dire **7** baleful, doomful, fateful, ominous, unlucky **8** sinister **10** portentous **11** apocalyptic **12** inauspicious, unpropitious

ill-bred 4 rude **5** crude **7** boorish, loutish, uncivil, uncouth **8** impolite **9** unrefined **10** uncultured, ungracious, unmannered, unmannerly, unpolished **11** uncivilized **12** discourteous

ill-defined 5 faint, fuzzy, vague **7** shadowy **10** indistinct

illegal 3 hot **6** banned **7** bootleg, illicit, lawless **8** criminal, outlawed, unlawful, wrongful **9** felonious, forbidden **10** actionable, prohibited, proscribed, unlicensed **12** illegitimate ***act:*** **5** crime **6** felony ***payment:*** **5** bribe **6** payola ***scheme:*** **4** scam

illegible 8 scrawled **10** unreadable **11** inscrutable

illegitimacy 8 bastardy **11** bar sinister **12** unlawfulness

illegitimate 7 bastard, bootleg, erratic, invalid, lawless, natural **8** criminal, improper, spurious, unlawful **11** misbegotten **12** unauthorized

ill-fated 6 cursed, doomed **7** unhappy, unlucky **8** accursed, luckless, untoward **10** disastrous **11** star-crossed, unfortunate

ill-favored 4 ugly **5** plain **6** homely **12** unattractive

ill-humored 4 dour, sour **5** cross, surly, testy **6** crabby, cranky, crusty, grumpy, morose, ornery, sullen, tetchy, touchy **7** crabbed, grouchy, peevish, prickly **8** choleric, churlish, snappish **9** dyspeptic, irascible, irritable, saturnine, splenetic **12** cantankerous, disagreeable, misanthropic

illiberal 6 biased, narrow **7** bigoted, insular **9** hidebound, parochial, penurious **10** intolerant, prejudiced, provincial **11** reactionary, small-minded **12** conservative, narrow-minded, uncharitable

illicit 7 bootleg, crooked, lawless **8** criminal, unlawful **9** forbidden **10** contraband, prohibited **11** black-market, clandestine **12** unauthorized

illimitable 7 endless **8** infinite, unending **9** boundless **11** measureless

Illinois ***capital:*** **11** Springfield ***city:*** **6** Aurora, Cicero, Joliet, Peoria **7** Chicago **8** Rockford ***college, university:*** **4** Knox **6** DePaul **7** Wheaton **12** Northwestern ***nickname:*** **7** Prairie (State) ***river:*** **6** Wabash ***state bird:*** **8** cardinal ***state flower:*** **6** violet ***state tree:*** **8** white oak

illiterate **6** unread **8** untaught **9** untutored **10** uneducated, unlettered, unschooled
ill-mannered **4** rude **6** coarse **7** boorish, loutish, uncivil, uncouth **8** churlish, impolite **10** ungracious **12** discourteous
ill-natured **4** sour **5** cross, huffy, surly, testy **6** bitchy, crabby, grumpy, ornery, tetchy **7** grouchy, peevish, waspish **8** choleric, churlish, snappish, spiteful **9** dyspeptic, fractious, irascible, irritable **10** malevolent **11** belligerent, contentious, quarrelsome **12** cantankerous, disagreeable
illness **6** malady **7** ailment, disease, malaise **8** cachexia, disorder, sickness **9** infirmity **10** affliction **13** indisposition
illogical **6** absurd **7** invalid, unsound **8** specious **9** plausible, senseless, sophistic **10** fallacious, irrational, unreasoned **11** nonrational **12** preposterous, unreasonable
ill-starred **6** cursed, doomed, malign **7** fateful, ominous, unhappy, unlucky **8** luckless, untoward **10** disastrous, foreboding, portentous **11** unfavorable, unfortunate, unpromising **12** inauspicious, unpropitious
ill-tempered **4** sour **5** cross, huffy, surly **6** crabby, bitchy, grumpy, ornery, snippy **7** grouchy, peevish, waspish **8** choleric, churlish, petulant, shrewish, snappish, spiteful **9** dyspeptic, fractious, irascible, irritable **11** belligerent, contentious, quarrelsome **12** cantankerous, disagreeable
ill-timed **11** inopportune **12** unseasonable
ill-treat **4** harm, hurt **5** abuse **6** injure, misuse, molest **7** torment **8** aggrieve **10** traumatize
illuminate **5** clear, edify, exalt, gloss, light **6** uplift **7** clarify, clear up, explain, lighten **8** brighten, decorate **9** elucidate, embellish, enlighten, highlight, irradiate, spotlight
illuminati **5** elite **7** clerisy, scholar **8** academic **11** academician **13** intellectuals
illumination **5** light **8** lighting ***unit of:*** **3** lux **4** phot **5** lumen **6** candle **7** candela **10** foot-candle
illusion **4** myth **5** dream, fancy, ghost **6** facade, mirage **7** chimera, fantasy **8** phantasm, phantasy **9** invention, pipe dream, semblance **11** ignis fatuus **12** will-o'-the-wisp **13** hallucination
illusionist **8** conjurer, magician **9** trickster
illusive see **illusory**
illusory **4** sham **6** unreal **7** seeming **8** apparent, fanciful **9** deceptive, fictional, imaginary, visionary **10** chimerical, fallacious, fictitious, misleading, ostensible
illustrate **4** mark, show **6** depict, evince, expose, reveal **7** clarify, display, exhibit, explain, picture, portray **8** decorate, describe, evidence, instance, manifest **9** elucidate, epitomize, exemplify **11** demonstrate
illustration **4** case **6** sample **7** diagram, drawing, example, picture, problem **8** instance
illustrative **7** graphic **9** pictorial **10** clarifying **11** descriptive **12** iconographic
illustrator ***American:*** **4** Kent (Rockwell), Pyle (Howard) **5** Abbey (Edwin Austin), Flagg (James Montgomery), Smith (Jessie Willcox), Wyeth (Newell Convers) **6** Gibson (Charles Dana) **7** Burgess (Gelett), Parrish (Maxwell) **8** Rockwell (Norman) **9** Remington (Frederic) ***English:*** **5** Crane (Walter) **6** Morris (William), Potter (Beatrix) **7** Nielsen (Kay), Rackham (Arthur), Tenniel (John) **9** Beardsley (Aubrey), Caldecott (Randolph), du Maurier (George), Greenaway (Kate) ***French:*** **4** Doré (Gustave) **5** Dulac (Edmund) ***German:*** **5** Dürer (Albrecht)
illustrious **5** famed, great, lofty, noted **6** famous **7** eminent, exalted, notable, sublime **8** glorious, renowned, splendid **9** acclaimed, prominent **10** celebrated, preeminent **11** outstanding, prestigious **13** distinguished
illustriousness **4** fame **5** glory **6** renown **8** eminence, prestige **9** celebrity **10** prominence **11** distinction, preeminence
ill will **5** spite, venom **6** animus, enmity, malice, rancor, spleen **7** despite, dislike **8** acrimony, aversion, bad blood **9** animosity, antipathy, hostility, malignity **10** resentment **11** malevolence **12** spitefulness **13** maliciousness
Ilus ***father:*** **4** Tros ***grandson:*** **5** Priam ***mother:*** **10** Callirrhoë ***son:*** **8** Laomedon
image **4** copy, form, icon, idea, idol, ikon **5** equal, match **6** double, effigy, figure, mirror, notion, ringer, vision **7** concept, fantasm, feature, picture **8** likeness, phantasm, portrait **9** facsimile, semblance **10** conception, equivalent, impression, reflection, simulacrum **12** illustration ***Polynesian:*** **4** tiki ***Semitic:*** **6** teraph **8** teraphim (plural)
imaginary **5** ideal **6** made-up, unreal **7** fancied, fictive **8** abstract, fabulous, fanciful, illusive, illusory, notional, quixotic **9** dreamlike, fantastic, fictional, legendary, visionary **10** apocryphal, chimerical, fictitious, phantasmal **11** make-believe **12** hypothetical, suppositious
imagination **5** fancy **7** fantasy **8** phantasy **9** invention **10** creativity **11** inspiration **13** inventiveness
imaginative **5** false **7** blue-sky, fictive **8** artistic, creative, fanciful, original, poetical **9**

ingenious, inventive, visionary, whimsical **11** resourceful **12** enterprising

imagine 5 dream, fancy **6** assume, invent, make up **7** dream up, feature, picture, suspect **8** conceive, envisage, envision **9** fabricate, visualize **10** conjecture

imbecile 4 dodo, dolt, dull, fool, jerk **5** dunce, idiot, moron, ninny **6** cretin, dimwit, nitwit **7** half-wit, jackass, moronic, pinhead, tomfool **8** numskull **9** birdbrain, blockhead, numbskull **10** dunderhead, nincompoop

imbibe 3 sip, sup **4** chug, soak, swig, tope, toss **5** booze, drink, quaff, swill **6** absorb, guzzle, tipple **7** consume, swallow, swizzle **10** assimilate

imbricate 3 lap **7** overlap, shingle **11** overlapping

imbroglio 3 row **4** maze, mess, spat, to-do **5** brawl, broil, mix-up **6** fracas, muddle, tangle **7** dispute, quarrel, rhubarb, scandal, wrangle **8** argument, disorder, squabble **9** confusion, intricacy **10** falling-out **11** altercation, predicament **12** complication, entanglement

imbrue 4 soil **5** stain **8** discolor

imbue 3 dye **4** soak **5** bathe, endow, steep, tinge **6** infuse, invest, leaven **7** ingrain, instill, pervade, suffuse **8** permeate, saturate **9** influence, inoculate

imitate 3 ape **4** copy, echo, mime, mock **5** forge, mimic, spoof **6** parody **7** emulate, take off **8** resemble, simulate, travesty **9** burlesque, duplicate, replicate, reproduce **11** counterfeit, impersonate

imitation 4 copy, fake, mock, sham **5** clone, ditto, dummy, false, match, phony **6** ersatz, parody, ringer **7** forgery, replica **8** likeness, parallel, spurious, travesty **9** duplicate, semblance, simulated **10** artificial, simulacrum, simulation, substitute **11** counterfeit, counterpart **12** reproduction, substitution

imitative 4 mock **5** apish **6** echoic **7** copycat, mimetic, parodic, slavish **11** counterfeit **12** onomatopoeic **13** onomatopoetic

imitator 4 aper, mime **5** mimic **6** parrot **7** copycat

immaculate 4 pure **5** clean **6** chaste, virgin **7** cleanly, perfect, sinless **8** flawless, spotless, unsoiled, virtuous **9** stainless, undefiled, unsullied **11** spic-and-span, unblemished **12** spick-and-span

immaterial 7 trivial **8** bodiless, ethereal **10** extraneous, inapposite, intangible, irrelevant **11** disembodied, incorporeal, nonphysical, unimportant **12** inapplicable **13** insignificant, insubstantial, unsubstantial

immature 3 raw **5** crude, green, young **6** callow, infant, unripe **7** puerile **8** childish, juvenile, youthful **9** infantile, primitive, unfledged **10** unfinished **11** undeveloped

immaturity 6 nonage **7** infancy **8** minority **9** childhood, salad days **11** adolescence **12** juvenescence

immeasurable 4 vast **6** untold **7** endless **8** infinite **9** boundless, extensive, limitless, unbounded, unlimited **11** illimitable, inestimable, uncountable **12** incalculable, unfathomable

immediate 4 next, nigh **5** close **6** at hand, direct, nearby, urgent **7** current, instant, ongoing, primary **9** firsthand, proximate **10** unmediated **12** straightaway **13** instantaneous

immediately 3 now, PDQ **4** anon, ASAP, stat **6** at once, presto, pronto **8** directly, promptly **9** forthwith, instanter, instantly, right away **11** straightway **12** straightaway

immense 4 huge, mega, vast **5** great, large, mondo **6** mighty **7** mammoth, massive, titanic **8** colossal, enormous, gigantic **9** humongous, monstrous **10** gargantuan, monumental, prodigious, tremendous **11** elephantine

immensely 4 a lot **8** terribly **9** extremely **11** exceedingly **12** inordinately

immensity 8 enormity, hugeness, vastness **9** greatness **12** enormousness

immerse 3 dip **4** duck, dunk, sink, soak **5** bathe, douse **6** drench, engage, plunge **7** baptize, engross, involve **8** saturate, submerge

immigrant 5 alien **7** settler **8** newcomer **10** transplant ***Japanese:*** **5** issei

imminent 4 near **6** at hand **6** coming **7** brewing, nearing, ominous, pending **8** upcoming **9** gathering, proximate **11** approaching, overhanging

immobile 3 set **5** fixed, inert, still **6** frozen, stable, static **9** unmovable **10** motionless, stationary

immobilize 5 still **7** cripple, disable **8** paralyze **9** hamstring **12** incapacitate

immoderate 5 undue **7** extreme **9** excessive **10** exorbitant, inordinate, untempered **11** extravagant, intemperate **12** unreasonable, unrestrained **13** extraordinary, overindulgent

immoderation 6 excess **11** exorbitance, prodigality **12** extravagance, intemperance

immodest 4 lewd, vain **7** stuck-up **8** arrogant, boastful, indecent, puffed-up, unchaste **9** conceited, egotistic **11** pretentious

immolate 4 burn, kill **7** destroy **9** sacrifice

immoral **4** evil, vile **5** dirty, wrong **6** sinful, wanton, wicked **7** corrupt, unclean, vicious **8** depraved, indecent, unchaste **9** dissolute, reprobate, uncleanly **10** degenerate, iniquitous, licentious

immorality **3** sin **4** vice **8** iniquity **9** depravity **10** corruption, unchastity, wickedness

immortal **7** endless, eternal, godlike, undying **8** timeless, unending **9** ceaseless, deathless, perpetual **11** amaranthine, everlasting, sempiternal

immotile **5** fixed, inert **6** rooted, static **9** paralyzed **10** stationary

immovable **3** pat, set **4** fast, firm **5** fixed, rigid **6** rooted, stable **7** adamant **8** constant, obdurate, stubborn **9** steadfast **10** inflexible, invariable, stationary, unyielding

immune **4** free, safe **6** exempt, secure **9** protected **10** impervious **12** invulnerable, unassailable

immunity **7** defense, freedom **9** exemption, privilege **10** protection

immure **3** pen **4** cage, coop, jail, wall **6** entomb, intern, shut in **7** confine, enclose **8** imprison **11** incarcerate

immutable **4** firm **5** fixed **8** constant **9** permanent, steadfast **10** changeless, inflexible, invariable, unchanging **11** inalterable, unalterable **12** unchangeable

Imogen ***father:*** **9** Cymbeline ***husband:*** **9** Posthumus

imp **3** elf **4** brat, puck **5** demon, devil, fiend, gamin, gnome, pixie, scamp **6** goblin, kobold, rascal, sprite, urchin **7** gremlin **9** hobgoblin

impact **3** hit, jar, rap **4** blow, bump, jolt, rock, slam, slap **5** brunt, embed, pound, punch, shock, smash, smite **6** affect, buffet, effect, strike, wallop **9** collision, influence **10** concussion, percussion

impair **3** mar, sap **4** harm, hurt **5** spoil **6** damage, injure, lessen, weaken, worsen **7** cripple, tarnish, vitiate **8** enfeeble **9** prejudice, undermine **10** debilitate

impala **8** antelope

impale **4** gore, spit, stab **5** lance, prick, spear, spike, stick **6** pierce, skewer **8** puncture, transfix **11** transpierce

impalpable **4** fine **7** powdery **8** ethereal **10** intangible **11** disembodied, incorporeal **12** imponderable **13** imperceptible, indiscernible

impart **4** cede, give, lend, tell **5** grant, share, yield **6** afford, bestow, confer, convey, pass on, relate, render **8** disclose, transmit **11** communicate ***knowledge:*** **5** teach **6** inform **7** educate **8** instruct

impartial **4** even, fair, just **5** equal **7** neutral **8** detached, unbiased **9** equitable, objective, uncolored **10** evenhanded **12** unprejudiced **13** disinterested, dispassionate

impassable **6** closed **7** blocked **10** obstructed **12** impenetrable

impasse **3** box, fix, jam **6** aporia, corner, logjam, pickle, pocket **7** dead end, dilemma **8** cul-de-sac, deadlock, standoff **9** stalemate **10** blind alley, bottleneck

impassioned **3** hot **5** fiery **6** ardent, fervid, fierce, heated, red-hot, torrid **7** burning, fervent, intense, zealous **8** feverish, romantic, vehement, white-hot **9** emotional, perfervid **10** hot-blooded, overheated **11** dithyrambic **12** melodramatic

impassive **4** calm, cold, cool **5** stoic **6** serene, stolid, vacant **7** deadpan **8** composed, hardened, reserved, reticent, taciturn **9** heartless **10** insensible, insentient, phlegmatic, poker-faced **11** cold-blooded, emotionless, insensitive, unconcerned, unemotional, unexcitable, unflappable **12** inexpressive, unexpressive, unresponsive **13** dispassionate, self-possessed

impassivity **6** apathy, phlegm **8** stoicism **9** sangfroid, stolidity **12** indifference **13** insensibility

impatient **4** edgy **5** antsy, eager, hasty **7** anxious, fretful, restive **8** restless

impeach **5** blame, doubt **6** accuse, charge, indict **7** censure **9** inculpate, reprehend **11** incriminate

impeccable **4** pure **5** exact **7** perfect, precise **8** absolute, accurate, flawless, unerring **9** blameless, errorless, faultless, guiltless **10** infallible **11** unblemished

impecunious **4** poor **5** broke, needy **7** pinched **8** bankrupt, beggarly, indigent **9** destitute, insolvent, penniless, penurious **10** down-and-out **11** necessitous

impecuniousness **4** need, want **6** penury **7** poverty **9** indigence, neediness, pauperism, privation **11** destitution

impedance **3** bar **4** clog **5** block **8** blockage, obstacle **9** hindrance **10** opposition **11** obstruction

impede **3** bar, dam **4** clog, slow **5** block, check, debar, delay, deter, stall **6** hinder, hang up, hold up, stymie, thwart **7** bog down **8** encumber, obstruct **9** embarrass, interfere, stonewall

impediment **3** bar **4** clog, snag **5** block, hitch **6** hurdle **7** barrier **8** obstacle **9** barricade, hindrance, roadblock **10** difficulty **11** encumbrance, obstruction

impel **4** goad, prod, push, spur, urge **5** drive,

force, rouse **6** excite, incite, prompt **7** actuate, inspire **8** mobilize, motivate **9** instigate, stimulate

impend 4 loom, near **6** menace **8** approach, overhang, threaten

impenetrable 5 dense **6** arcane **7** obscure **9** enigmatic, recondite **10** impervious, invincible, mysterious, unknowable **11** impermeable, bulletproof, inscrutable, ungraspable **12** unfathomable

imperative 4 duty, need, rule, writ **5** acute, vital **6** crying, urgent **7** burning, clamant, command, crucial, exigent **8** critical, pressing, required **9** clamorous, essential, insistent, mandatory, necessary, necessity, requisite **10** compulsory, obligation, obligatory **11** fundamental, necessitous **12** prerequisite

imperceptible 3 dim **5** faint, vague **6** slight, subtle **7** gradual **9** invisible **10** impalpable, indistinct, insensible, intangible, unapparent **12** undetectable, unnoticeable, unobservable **13** inappreciable, inconspicuous, indiscernible

imperceptive 4 dull **7** shallow, unaware **11** inattentive, insensitive

imperfect 6 faulty, flawed **9** defective, deficient, irregular **10** defeasible, inadequate

imperfection 3 sin **4** flaw, wart **5** fault **6** defect, foible **7** blemish, demerit, failing, frailty **8** weakness **10** deficiency **11** shortcoming

imperial 5 regal, royal **6** kingly, lordly **7** haughty **8** absolute, majestic **9** masterful, sovereign **10** high-handed, peremptory **11** domineering, magisterial, monarchical

imperil 4 risk **6** hazard, menace **7** venture **8** endanger, threaten **10** jeopardize

imperious 5 bossy **6** urgent **7** haughty **8** absolute, arrogant, despotic, dominant **9** arbitrary, masterful **10** autocratic, commanding, high-handed, oppressive, peremptory, tyrannical **11** dictatorial, domineering, heavy-handed, magisterial, overbearing

impermanent 7 passing **8** fleeting, fugitive **9** ephemeral, fugacious, momentary, temporary, transient **10** evanescent, short-lived, transitory

impersonal 4 cold **5** aloof **8** abstract, detached **11** cold-blooded, emotionless **13** dispassionate, unimpassioned

impersonate 3 ape **4** play **5** mimic **6** act out **7** imitate, playact, portray **9** represent **11** counterfeit

impersonator 3 ape **4** aper, mime **5** actor, mimic **6** mummer, player, ringer **7** actress, copycat **8** thespian ***female:*** **9** drag queen

impertinence 3 lip **4** gall, guff, sass **5** brass, cheek **8** audacity, boldness, chutzpah, rudeness, temerity **9** brashness, impudence, insolence **10** brazenness, effrontery, incivility **11** discourtesy, irrelevance

impertinent 4 bold, busy, rude **5** brash, fresh, sassy, saucy **6** brazen, cheeky **7** uncivil **8** insolent, meddling **9** audacious, intrusive, obtrusive, officious **10** inapposite, irrelative, irrelevant, meddlesome **11** ill-mannered **12** discourteous, inapplicable, presumptuous

imperturbability 5 poise **6** aplomb, phlegm **8** calmness, coolness, serenity, stoicism **9** composure, placidity, sangfroid **10** dispassion, equanimity **11** equilibrium, nonchalance, tranquility **12** tranquillity

imperturbable 4 calm, cool **5** stoic **6** placid, poised, serene, smooth, steady, stolid **7** unmoved **8** composed, tranquil **9** collected, unruffled **10** nonchalant, phlegmatic, unaffected **11** unflappable

impervious 4 safe **6** immune **8** hardened **10** inviolable **12** inaccessible, invulnerable

impetuous 3 hot **4** rash, wild **5** fiery, hasty **6** ardent, fervid, madcap, sudden **8** headlong, vehement, volatile **9** hotheaded, mercurial **10** irrational, passionate **11** precipitant, precipitate, precipitous, spontaneous **13** temperamental

impetus 4 goad, push, spur **5** force **6** motive **8** catalyst, momentum, stimulus **9** incentive, stimulant **10** incitement, motivation **13** encouragement

impinge 5 press **6** border **7** intrude, obtrude **8** encroach

impious 6 sinful, unholy, wicked **7** godless, infidel, profane, secular, ungodly **8** agnostic, apostate **9** atheistic **10** irreverent, unfaithful, unhallowed **11** blasphemous, irreligious, unrighteous **12** iconoclastic, sacrilegious **13** unconsecrated

impish 4 arch **5** elfin **6** elvish **7** playful, puckish, roguish, waggish **11** mischievous

impishness 7 devilry, roguery, waggery **8** deviltry, mischief **9** devilment **11** roguishness, waggishness

implacable 4 grim **8** ruthless **9** merciless **10** inexorable, unyielding **11** intractable **12** unappeasable

implant 3 fix **4** root **5** embed, graft, infix **6** enroot, infuse, insert **7** ingrain, inspire, instill **9** establish, inculcate, inoculate, introduce **10** inseminate **12** augmentation

implausible 5 fishy **6** flimsy **7** dubious, suspect **8** doubtful, fanciful, unlikely **10** far-fetched, incredible **12** questionable, unbelievable, unconvincing

implement **4** tool **6** device, effect, enable, gadget **7** enforce, execute, fulfill, perform, realize, utensil **8** carry out, complete, make good **9** actualize, apparatus, appliance **10** accomplish, instrument, supplement **11** contraption, contrivance ***carpentry:*** **3** adz, die, saw **4** adze, file **5** brace, clamp, drill, punch, tongs **6** chisel, hammer, pliers, reamer, sander, wrench **7** hacksaw, scraper **9** blowtorch **11** screwdriver ***cleaning:*** **3** mop **5** broom, brush, whisk **6** duster, vacuum **7** sweeper **10** whiskbroom ***cutting:*** **5** knife, mower, razor **6** scythe, shears, sickle **8** scissors ***digging:*** **5** spade **6** dibber, dibble, shovel ***drawing:*** **3** pen **6** eraser, pencil **7** compass **8** template ***eating:*** **4** fork **5** knife, spoon **9** chopstick ***engraving:*** **5** burin **6** graver ***farm:*** **4** plow **6** binder, harrow, plough, scythe, seeder, sickle **8** gangplow, reaphook, spreader, thresher **9** pitchfork **10** cultivator ***fireplace:*** **5** poker, tongs **7** andiron ***fishing:*** **3** rod **4** hook, lure, reel **6** sinker **7** harpoon, trident ***garden:*** **3** hoe **4** rake **5** edger, spade **6** dibber, dibble, digger, tiller, trowel **7** mattock ***grooming:*** **4** comb, file **5** brush, razor **7** clipper **8** clippers, nail file, tweezers **10** toothbrush ***kitchen:*** **3** pan, pot **4** mold **5** mixer, whisk **6** grater, kettle, mortar, pestle **7** blender, skillet, spatula **8** colander, saucepan, stockpot ***logging:*** **5** peavy **6** peavey **8** cant hook ***measuring:*** **3** cup **4** gage, rule **5** gauge, ruler, scale **7** caliper, divider, trammel, T-square **10** micrometer, protractor ***stone:*** **5** burin **7** neolith **9** paleolith

implicate **4** link, mire **5** blame **6** tangle **7** concern, embroil, entwine, include, involve **8** entangle, intimate **11** incriminate

implication **4** hint **8** allusion, overtone **9** inference, undertone **10** connection, intimation, suggestion **11** association, connotation **12** significance

implicit **5** tacit **6** unsaid **8** inherent, unspoken **9** doubtless, potential, unuttered **10** undeclared, understood **11** unexpressed

implied **5** tacit **6** unsaid **8** inherent, unspoken **9** suggested **10** undeclared, understood **11** unexpressed

implore **3** ask, beg **4** coax, pray **5** crave, plead **6** adjure, appeal **7** beseech, entreat, solicit **10** supplicate

imply **4** hint, mean **5** get at **7** connote, include, involve, signify, suggest **8** indicate, intimate **9** insinuate

impolite **4** rude **5** crude **7** ill-bred, uncivil, uncouth **10** ungracious, unladylike, unmannered, unmannerly **11** ill-mannered **12** discourteous **13** ungentlemanly

impolitic **5** brash **6** unwise **8** tactless **9** imprudent, maladroit, untactful **10** ill-advised, indiscreet **11** inadvisable, inexpedient, injudicious **12** shortsighted, undiplomatic

import **4** bear, gist, mean, pith **5** sense, value, worth **6** convey, denote, intend, intent, matter, moment, stress, thrust, weight **7** concern, connote, express, meaning, message, purpose, signify **8** emphasis, indicate, transfer **9** magnitude, substance **10** intendment **11** acceptation, consequence **12** significance **13** signification

importance **4** mark, note, pith **5** value, worth **6** moment, weight **7** account, gravity **8** eminence, priority, salience, standing **9** greatness, magnitude, substance **10** prominence, worthiness **11** consequence, distinction, seriousness, weightiness **12** significance

important **3** big **5** chief, grave, great, heavy, major, noted, vital **6** famous, marked, potent, urgent, worthy **7** big-time, capital, crucial, eminent, fateful, notable, salient, serious, telling, weighty **8** critical, eventful, foremost, material, powerful, pressing, valuable **9** essential, estimable, imperious, memorable, momentous, prominent **10** meaningful, noteworthy, preeminent, worthwhile **11** outstanding, significant, substantial **12** considerable **13** consequential, distinguished, indispensable

importune **3** beg **4** pray, urge **5** annoy, plead, worry **6** appeal, invoke, plague **7** beseech, besiege, entreat, solicit, trouble **8** petition

impose **3** fob **4** lade, levy **5** abuse, enact, exact, foist, force, order, place, put on, visit, wreak **6** assess, burden, charge, compel, decree, demand, enjoin, fob off, ordain, saddle **7** command, dictate, exploit, inflict, intrude, lay down, obtrude, palm off, pass off, require **8** encroach, encumber, infringe, trespass **9** authorize, constrain, establish

imposing **4** huge **5** grand, noble, regal, royal **6** august **7** awesome, massive, pompous, stately **8** baronial, majestic, towering **9** dignified **10** commanding, monumental **11** magnificent, outstanding **12** high-sounding **13** distinguished

imposition **3** tax **4** duty, fine, levy **6** burden, demand **7** penalty **9** deception **13** inconvenience

impossible **6** absurd **8** hopeless **10** infeasible, unfeasible, unworkable **11** unthinkable **12** preposterous, unacceptable, unattainable, unbelievable, unimaginable, unrealizable, unreasonable **13** inconceivable

impost **3** fee, tax **4** duty, levy, toll **6** charge, tariff **7** tribute **9** surcharge **10** assessment

impostor 4 fake, sham **5** actor, cheat, faker, fraud, mimic, phony, poser, quack **6** humbug, poseur **8** deceiver **9** charlatan, con artist, hypocrite, pretender **10** dissembler, mountebank **11** masquerader **12** impersonator
imposture 4 fake, hoax, sell, sham, wile **5** cheat, fraud **6** deceit, humbug **8** flimflam **9** deception, mare's nest, stratagem **11** counterfeit
impotence 8 weakness **9** sterility **10** inadequacy **12** helplessness **13** powerlessness
impotent 4 lame, weak **6** effete, feeble **7** sterile **8** helpless **9** forceless, incapable, powerless **11** ineffective, ineffectual **12** invertebrate
impound 5 seize **6** immure, lock up **7** confine, enclose, put away **8** imprison **10** confiscate
impoverish 4 bust, ruin **5** break **6** beggar **8** bankrupt **9** pauperize
impoverished 4 poor **5** broke, needy **8** bankrupt, indigent **9** destitute, penniless, penurious
impoverishment 4 need, want **6** penury **9** indigence, neediness, privation **11** destitution
impracticable 8 unusable **10** infeasible, unfeasible, unworkable **11** insuperable, unrealistic **12** inaccessible, unattainable
impractical 7 utopian **8** quixotic, romantic, unusable **9** visionary **10** idealistic, infeasible, ivory-tower, starry-eyed, unfeasible, unworkable **11** theoretical, unrealistic
imprecation 3 hex **4** cuss **5** curse **7** malison **8** anathema **11** malediction
imprecise 5 rough, vague **7** inexact **9** estimated **10** indefinite **11** approximate, unspecified
impregnable 4 safe **6** immune, secure **9** protected **10** invincible, inviolable, unbeatable **11** indomitable, insuperable **12** unassailable **13** unconquerable
impregnate 3 sop **4** fill, soak **5** imbue, souse, steep **6** drench, infuse **7** pervade **8** conceive, permeate, saturate **9** fecundate, fertilize, penetrate, transfuse **10** inseminate
impresario 4 Bing (Rudolf) **5** Carte (Richard D'Oyly), Hurok (Sol) **6** Pastor (Tony) **7** manager **8** director, Kirstein (Lincoln), producer, promoter **9** Diaghilev (Sergei) **10** D'Oyly Carte (Richard)
impress 3 fix, set **4** dent, etch, mark, move, seal, sway **5** brand, carry, drive, exert, force, grave, infix, print, stamp, touch **6** affect, effect, excite, strike **7** engrave, ingrain, inspire **8** inscribe, transfer, transmit **9** establish, influence, stimulate
impressible 8 gullible, immature, moldable **9** malleable, receptive, sensitive **10** affectable, susceptive, vulnerable **11** persuadable, suggestible, susceptible
impression 4 dent, idea, mark, sign **5** image, print, stamp, trace, track **6** effect, hollow, notion **7** concept, edition, feeling, reissue, thought, vestige **8** printing, reaction **9** influence
impressionable 8 sensible, sentient **9** malleable, receptive, sensitive **10** responsive **11** suggestible, susceptible
impressionist ***composer:*** **5** Ravel (Maurice) **7** Debussy (Claude) ***mimic:*** **6** Carvey (Dana), Little (Rich) ***painter:*** **5** Degas (Edgar), Manet (Edouard), Monet (Claude) **6** Renoir (Auguste), Sisley (Alfred) **7** Cassatt (Mary), Morisot (Berthe) **8** Pissarro (Camille) (see also **postimpressionist**)
impressive 5 grand, noble **6** moving, superb **7** amazing, awesome, notable, stately, sublime **8** dazzling, dramatic, gorgeous, majestic, powerful, splendid, stirring, striking, touching **9** admirable, affecting, arresting, inspiring **11** magnificent
imprimatur 6 permit **7** license **8** approval, sanction **10** permission **13** authorization
imprint 3 fix **4** dent, etch, mark **5** grave, press, stamp **6** dimple, effect **7** engrave **8** inscribe **9** engraving, influence **10** depression **11** indentation, inscription
imprison 3 jug **4** cage, jail **6** coop up, detain, immure, intern, send up **7** confine, enclose **8** restrain, restrict, stockade **9** constrain **11** incarcerate
improbable 5 fishy **7** dubious **8** doubtful, fanciful, unlikely **10** far-fetched **11** implausible
impromptu 5 ad-lib **7** offhand **9** extempore, makeshift, unplanned, unstudied **10** off-the-cuff, unprepared, unscripted **11** extemporary, spontaneous, unrehearsed
improper 5 inapt, inept, outré, undue, wrong **6** gauche, risqué **7** illicit, naughty **8** ill-timed, indecent, tactless, unseemly, untimely, untoward **9** incorrect, unethical, unfitting **10** inaccurate, inapposite, indecorous, indelicate, malapropos, unbecoming, undecorous, unsuitable **11** impertinent, unbefitting **12** illegitimate, inadmissible, inapplicable, infelicitous, unseasonable **13** inappropriate
impropriety 5 gaffe **7** blooper, blunder, faux pas **8** solecism **9** barbarism, gaucherie, indecorum, vulgarism **12** unseemliness **13** incorrectness
improve 4 edit, help, mend **5** amend, boost, edify, emend, raise **6** better, enrich, look up,

perk up, refine, reform, remedy, revise, revive, update, uplift **7** advance, amplify, augment, build up, correct, develop, enhance, enlarge, further, perfect, recover, rectify, upgrade **8** increase, progress **9** cultivate, intensify, meliorate **10** ameliorate, recuperate, strengthen

improvident 4 rash **6** lavish **8** careless, feckless, heedless, prodigal, reckless, wasteful **9** impetuous, negligent, unthrifty **10** profligate **11** extravagant, spendthrift **12** shortsighted

improvise 4 scat **5** ad-lib **6** cook up, invent, make up, wing it **7** concoct **8** contrive **9** fabricate **11** extemporize

improvised 7 offhand **9** extempore, unstudied **10** off-the-cuff, unprepared, unscripted **11** extemporary, unrehearsed

imprudent 4 rash **6** unwise **7** foolish **8** reckless **9** foolhardy **10** ill-advised, incautious, indiscreet **11** inadvisable, inexpedient, injudicious **12** shortsighted

impudence 4 gall **5** brass, cheek, nerve **8** audacity, boldness, chutzpah, temerity **9** brashness, cockiness, hardihood, insolence, nerviness **10** disrespect, effrontery **11** presumption

impudent 4 bold, flip, pert, rude, wise **5** brash, cocky, fresh, lippy, nervy, sassy, saucy, smart **6** brassy, brazen, cheeky **7** blatant, forward **8** flippant, insolent, overbold **9** audacious, barefaced, bold-faced **11** brazen-faced, smart-alecky **12** contumelious **13** disrespectful

impugn 5 cross **6** assail, attack, defame, malign, oppose, vilify **7** asperse, gainsay, impeach **8** chastise, reproach, traverse **9** castigate, denigrate, deprecate, disparage, reprehend **9** criticize, denigrate

impugnable 5 fishy, shady **6** guilty **7** suspect **8** doubtful **9** equivocal, uncertain **10** assailable, suspicious **11** problematic **12** disreputable

impulse 4 goad, push, spur, urge, whim **5** drive, force **6** motive, thrust, whimsy **7** caprice, passion **8** catalyst, excitant, stimulus **9** actuation, incentive, stimulant **10** incitation, incitement, motivation **11** inspiration, instigation ***conductor:*** **4** axon

impulsive 4 rash **5** brash, hasty **6** abrupt, fickle, sudden **7** erratic, flighty, offhand **8** headlong, volatile **9** extempore, mercurial, unplanned, whimsical **10** capricious **11** instinctive, precipitate, spontaneous

impunity 7 freedom, liberty, license **8** immunity **9** exception, exemption, indemnity, privilege **10** absolution, protection

impure 3 raw **5** mixed **6** soiled, sordid, unholy **7** alloyed, defiled, profane, sullied, unclean **8** indecent, polluted, unchaste **9** uncleanly, unrefined **10** desecrated, unhallowed **11** adulterated

impute 3 lay **4** cite **5** blame, refer **6** accuse, adduce, assign, charge, credit, indict **7** ascribe **8** accredit **9** attribute, implicate

inaccessible 5 aloof **6** arcane, closed, far-off, remote **7** cryptic, distant, faraway, obscure **8** abstruse, esoteric, hermetic **9** recondite **11** unavailable, unreachable **12** unattainable, unobtainable

inaccurate 5 false, wrong **6** all wet, faulty, untrue **7** unsound **8** specious **9** distorted, erroneous **10** fictitious

inaction 6 repose **7** latency **8** dormancy, idleness, lethargy **9** indolence, passivity, slackness, torpidity **10** quiescence

inactive 4 idle, lazy **5** inert, quiet, slack, still **6** asleep, latent, sleepy, static, torpid **7** abeyant, dormant, passive, resting **8** slothful, sluggish **9** do-nothing, lethargic, quiescent, sedentary

in addition 4 also **6** as well, to boot, withal **7** besides, further **8** moreover **11** furthermore

inadequacy 4 lack, want **6** dearth **7** deficit, failure, paucity **8** shortage, weakness **9** impotence **10** deficiency, scantiness **11** shortcoming

inadequate 3 shy **5** scant, short **6** meager, scanty, scarce, skimpy **7** lacking, scrimpy, wanting **8** impotent **9** defective, deficient

inadmissible 5 unapt, unfit **8** unusable, unworthy **9** unwelcome **10** unsuitable **11** unqualified **12** unacceptable

inadvertent 8 careless, heedless **9** negligent, unmindful, unplanned, unwitting **10** accidental, unintended, unthinking **13** unintentional

inadvisable 4 rash **6** unwise **7** foolish **8** careless, reckless **9** foolhardy, impolitic, imprudent, pointless **10** ill-advised **11** harebrained

inalterable 5 fixed **6** stable **8** constant **9** immovable, immutable, steadfast, unmovable, unvarying **12** unchangeable

inamorata, inamorato 4 beau, dear **5** flame, honey, lover **6** steady **7** beloved, darling, squeeze, sweetie **8** ladylove, mistress, paramour, truelove **9** boyfriend **10** girlfriend, heartthrob, sweetheart

inane 4 idle, vain **5** blank, dotty, empty, silly, vapid **6** absurd, jejune, vacant **7** asinine, fatuous, foolish, idiotic, insipid, trivial, vacuous, witless **8** mindless **9** frivolous, laughable, pointless, senseless

inanimate 4 dead, dull **5** inert **5** still **6** asleep, torpid **7** dormant **8** immotile, lifeless **9** quiescent **10** motionless **11** unconscious

inanity 5 folly **6** idiocy, lunacy **7** fatuity, vacuity **8** vapidity **9** absurdity, dottiness, emptiness, silliness **10** hollowness **11** foolishness, vacuousness, witlessness **13** senselessness

inappreciable 6 meager, scanty, skimpy, slight **10** impalpable, unapparent **13** imperceptible

inappropriate 5 amiss, undue, unfit **6** unmeet **8** improper, unseemly, untimely, untoward **9** ill-suited **10** malapropos, unsuitable **11** impertinent

inapt 5 unfit **6** clumsy, gauche, jejune, unmeet **7** awkward, unhandy **8** improper, unfitted, unsuited, untimely **9** maladroit, unfitting, unskilled **10** amateurish, irrelevant, malapropos, unskillful, unsuitable

inarticulate 4 dumb, mute **5** tacit **6** silent **7** halting, unvocal **8** mumbling, unspoken, wordless **9** voiceless **10** maundering, speechless, tongue-tied, undeclared **11** unexpressed

inasmuch as 5 since **7** because, whereas **11** considering

inattentive 6 absent, remiss **8** distrait, heedless **9** forgetful, negligent, unheeding, unmindful **10** abstracted, distracted, unthinking **12** absentminded

inaugural 5 first **6** maiden, speech **7** address, initial, leading, opening, premier **8** foremost **9** beginning

inaugurate 5 begin, set up, start **6** launch **7** kick off **8** commence, dedicate, initiate **9** establish, institute, originate **10** consecrate

inauspicious 4 dire **7** adverse, baleful, direful, fateful, ominous, unlucky **8** sinister **9** ill-boding **11** threatening, unfavorable, unpromising **12** unpropitious

inborn 6 innate, native **7** connate, natural **8** inherent **9** intrinsic **10** congenital, connatural, hereditary, unacquired

inbred 7 connate, genetic, natural **8** inherent **9** intrinsic **10** congenital, connatural, deep-seated, hereditary

Inca *capital:* 5 Cuzco ***conqueror:* 7** Pizarro (Francisco) ***god:* 4** Inti **9** Viracocha **10** Pachacamac ***language:* 7** Quechua ***record:* 5** quipu ***ruin:* 11** Machu Picchu ***ruler:* 9** Atahualpa, Pachacuti **10** Atahuallpa

incalculable 4 huge, iffy, vast **6** untold **8** enormous **9** boundless, countless, limitless, uncertain **10** tremendous, unnumbered **11** illimitable, measureless, uncountable **12** immeasurable, unmeasurable **13** unpredictable

in camera 7 privily, sub rosa **8** covertly, secretly **9** furtively, privately **10** stealthily **13** clandestinely

incandescent 3 hot **5** lucid **6** ardent, bright, lucent **7** beaming, fulgent, glowing, intense, lambent, radiant **8** dazzling, luminous **9** brilliant, effulgent, refulgent **11** resplendent

incantation 3 hex **4** rune **5** chant, charm, magic, spell **10** hocus-pocus, mumbo-jumbo, necromancy **11** abracadabra, conjuration, enchantment ***Buddhist, Hindu:* 6** mantra

incapable 5 unfit **6** unable **8** impotent, unexpert, unfitted **9** powerless, unskilled **10** unequipped, unskillful **11** unqualified **12** disqualified

incapacitate 6 disarm **7** cripple, disable **8** paralyze **10** debilitate, devitalize, disqualify, immobilize

incapacity 9 impotence, unfitness **10** impairment **11** disablement **12** fecklessness

incarcerate 3 jug **4** jail **6** coop up, immure, intern, send up **7** confine, enclose, impound **8** imprison

incarnadine 3 red **4** rosy **5** ruddy **6** redden **7** pinkish **8** bloodred

incarnate 5 human, reify **6** embody **7** realize **8** embodied, manifest **9** actualize, corporeal, personify **11** materialize, personalize **12** substantiate

incarnation 6 avatar **10** embodiment **11** reification ***of Christ:* 7** kenosis ***of Vishnu:* 4** Rama

incautious 4 rash **5** brash, hasty **6** daring, madcap, unwary **8** careless, heedless, reckless **9** daredevil, foolhardy, impetuous, imprudent, negligent, unmindful **10** ill-advised, neglectful, regardless **11** precipitate, thoughtless

incendiary 5 fiery, torch **7** firebug **8** agitator, arsonist, arsonous **9** explosive, firebrand, ignitable **10** pyromaniac **12** pyromaniacal

incense 3 ire, mad, oil **4** balm, burn, rile **5** anger, aroma, scent, spice **6** arouse, enrage, homage, incite, madden **7** inflame, provoke **8** irritate **9** infuriate ***vessel:* 6** censer **8** thurible

incentive 4 goad, spur **5** spark **6** motive **7** impetus, impulse **8** catalyst, stimulus **9** stimulant **10** inducement, motivation **11** provocation **13** encouragement

inception 4 root **5** birth, start **6** origin, outset, source **7** genesis, kickoff, opening **9** beginning **10** derivation, provenance **11** provenience **12** commencement

inceptive 7 initial, leadoff, nascent **9** beginning **10** initiatory

incertitude **5** doubt **7** dubiety **8** mistrust **9** suspicion **10** skepticism **11** dubiousness, uncertainty, vacillation **12** irresolution

incessant **6** steady **7** endless, eternal, nonstop **8** constant **9** ceaseless, continual, perpetual, unceasing **10** continuous **11** everlasting, unremitting **12** interminable **13** uninterrupted

inch **3** bit **5** crawl, creep **7** modicum

inchoate **8** formless, immature, unformed, unshaped **9** amorphous, embryonic, incipient, potential, shapeless **10** disjointed, incoherent **11** rudimentary, unorganized **12** disconnected

incident **5** event **7** episode **8** occasion **9** happening **10** affiliated, collateral, occurrence **11** concomitant

incidental **5** fluky, minor **6** casual, chance **9** accessory **10** contingent, fortuitous **11** subordinate **12** nonessential

incidentally **7** by the by **8** by the bye, by the way, casually **12** fortuitously

incinerate **4** burn **7** cremate

incipient **7** nascent **9** beginning, embryonic **10** commencing

incipit **5** start **7** opening **9** beginning

incise **3** cut **4** etch, gash, kerf, slit **5** carve **6** chisel **7** engrave

incision **3** cut **4** gash, slit **5** blaze, notch **10** laceration

incisive **4** keen **5** acute, crisp, sharp, terse **6** direct **7** cutting, mordant **8** clear-cut, piercing, slashing, succinct **9** trenchant **11** penetrating **13** perspicacious

incite **3** egg **4** abet, goad, prod, spur, urge **5** egg on, raise, rouse, set on **6** arouse, exhort, foment, kindle, set off, spur on, stir up, whip up **7** actuate, agitate, provoke, trigger **8** motivate **9** instigate, stimulate

incitement see **incentive**

inclement **3** raw **5** harsh, rough **6** bitter, brutal, severe, stormy **8** rigorous

inclination **3** bow, nod **4** bent, bias, lean, tilt, will **5** fancy, grade, pitch, slant, slope, taste, trend **6** ascent, liking **7** descent, incline, leaning **8** affinity, appetite, fondness, gradient, penchant, soft spot, tendency, velleity, weakness **9** affection **10** attachment, partiality, proclivity, propensity **11** disposition **12** predilection

incline **3** tip **4** bend, bias, cant, cast, heel, lean, list, sway, tend, tilt, turn **5** grade, impel, slant, slide, slope **6** affect, induce **7** dispose, leaning **8** gradient, persuade **9** influence, prejudice

inclined **3** apt **5** atilt, given, leant, prone, raked, ready **6** liable, likely, minded **7** dipping, leaning, oblique, sloping, tilting, willing **8** diagonal, pitching **11** predisposed
way: **4** ramp

include **5** admit, bound, cover **6** enfold, number, take in **7** confine, contain, embrace, enclose, receive, subsume **8** comprise, encircle **9** encompass **10** comprehend **11** accommodate

inclusive **5** all up, broad **6** global **7** general, overall **8** complete, sweeping **9** all-around, embracive **11** compendious **12** encompassing, encyclopedic **13** comprehensive

incognito **6** veiled **7** cloaked **9** anonymous, disguised **11** camouflaged

incognizant **7** unaware **8** ignorant **9** oblivious, unknowing, unmindful, unwitting **10** unfamiliar, uninformed **11** unconscious **12** unacquainted

incoherent **5** loose **6** broken, raving **7** muddled, unclear **8** confused **9** illogical **10** disjointed, disordered, irrational, maundering, tongue-tied **11** unconnected, unorganized **12** disconnected, disorganized **13** discontinuous

incombustible **9** fireproof **10** unburnable **12** nonflammable

income **4** gain, take **5** wages **6** profit **7** revenue **8** entrance, proceeds, receipts **9** emolument

incommode **3** irk, vex **5** annoy, upset **6** bother, burden, hinder, plague, put out **7** disturb, perturb, trouble **8** disquiet, distress, irritate **9** disoblige **10** disconcert

incommodious **7** awkward, cramped, crowded **8** confined **9** congested

incommunicable **8** reserved, taciturn **9** ineffable, withdrawn **11** unspeakable, unutterable **13** undescribable, unexpressible

incomparable **6** unique **7** supreme **8** peerless, singular, ultimate **9** matchless, nonpareil, paramount, unequaled, unmatched, unrivaled **10** preeminent, surpassing, unequalled, unrivalled **11** outstanding, superlative, unequalable, unmatchable **12** transcendent, unparalleled **13** unsurpassable

incompatible **7** adverse, counter **8** contrary, opposite **9** dissonant, unmixable **10** discordant, discrepant **11** conflicting, disagreeing, uncongenial, unfavorable **12** antagonistic, antithetical **13** contradictory, unsympathetic

incompetence **9** unfitness **10** disability, ineptitude **12** fecklessness

incompetent **5** inept, unfit **6** clumsy **8** helpless, inexpert, unfitted **9** incapable, maladroit, unskilled **10** unequipped **11** inefficient, unqualified

incomplete **4** part **5** short **6** broken, undone **7**

partial, sketchy **8** abridged, immature **9** truncated **10** unfinished **11** fragmentary

incompliant 5 rigid, stiff **6** mulish **7** defiant **8** perverse, stubborn **9** obstinate, pigheaded, resistant, unbending **10** bullheaded, headstrong, inflexible, self-willed, unyielding **11** intractable **12** pertinacious, recalcitrant

incomprehensible 7 cryptic, obscure, unclear **8** abstruse, baffling, esoteric **9** fantastic **10** fathomless, mysterious, mystifying, unknowable **11** ungraspable **12** impenetrable, unfathomable, unimaginable

inconceivable 10 improbable, unknowable **11** implausible, unthinkable **12** unbelievable, unconvincing, unimaginable

in conclusion 6 lastly **7** finally

inconclusive 4 open **9** equivocal, uncertain, undecided, unsettled **10** unfinished

incongruous 5 alien **6** absurd **7** foreign, variant **9** anomalous, dissonant **10** discordant, discrepant, unsuitable **11** conflicting, disagreeing **12** disconsonant

inconsequential 5 petty, small **6** measly, paltry **7** trivial **8** picayune, trifling **9** illogical, small-time **10** immaterial, irrelevant, negligible **11** impertinent, superficial, unimportant

inconsiderable 4 puny **5** minor, petty **6** meager, meagre, paltry, scanty, skimpy, slight **7** scrimpy, trivial **8** picayune, trifling **9** frivolous, small-beer **10** negligible **11** unimportant

inconsiderate 4 rash **5** brash, hasty **6** unkind **8** careless, heedless, impolite, reckless **9** hotheaded, impulsive **10** ill-advised, ungracious **11** precipitate, thoughtless **12** discourteous, uncharitable

inconsistent 6 fickle **8** contrary **9** dissonant, illogical, mercurial **10** capricious, changeable, discordant, discrepant **11** conflicting **13** contradictory

inconsolable 7 forlorn **8** desolate **9** heartsick **11** comfortless, heartbroken

inconspicuous 6 hidden, subtle **7** obscure **9** concealed **11** unobtrusive **12** unnoticeable

inconstant 6 fickle, untrue **7** erratic, mutable, protean, vagrant **8** unstable, unsteady, variable, volatile, wavering **9** changeful, faithless, fluctuant, irregular, mercurial, uncertain, unsettled **10** capricious, changeable, irresolute, perfidious, unfaithful **11** chameleonic, vacillating **13** temperamental

incontestable 4 sure **7** certain **8** absolute, clear-cut, ironclad, positive **9** apodictic, undoubted **10** conclusive, inarguable, undeniable **11** irrefutable, unequivocal **12** unassailable, undisputable **13** unimpeachable

incontinent 5 loose **6** wanton **9** dissolute **10** licentious, profligate **12** unrestrained

incontrovertible 4 sure **7** certain **8** absolute, clear-cut, definite, positive **10** conclusive, undeniable **11** irrefutable, unequivocal **12** undisputable

inconvenience 3 irk, vex **5** annoy **6** bother, meddle, put out **7** disrupt, disturb, trouble **8** handicap, vexation **9** annoyance **10** discomfort, discommode, disruption, exasperate **11** aggravation

inconvenient 7 awkward, unhandy **8** annoying **10** bothersome, unsuitable **11** pestiferous, troublesome

incorporate 3 mix **4** form, fuse, join **5** blend, merge, unite **6** absorb, embody, imbibe, mingle **7** combine **8** organize **9** establish **10** amalgamate, assimilate

incorporeal 8 bodiless, formless **9** spiritual **10** discarnate, immaterial, unphysical **11** disembodied, nonmaterial, nonphysical **12** metaphysical **13** unsubstantial

incorrect 5 false, wrong **6** faulty, untrue **7** unsound **8** improper, specious **9** erroneous, imprecise **10** fallacious, inaccurate, unbecoming

incorrigible 6 unruly **8** depraved **9** incurable **10** delinquent, inveterate **11** unalterable **12** irredeemable

increase 2 up **3** add, wax **4** gain, grow, hike, jump, plus, rise, soar, teem **5** add to, boost, build, mount, raise, run up, surge, swarm, swell **6** accrue, amount, beef up, dilate, expand, extend, growth, jack up, markup, step up **7** accrual, advance, amplify, augment, burgeon, enhance, enlarge, inflate, magnify, prolong, upsurge **8** addition, compound, escalate, flourish, heighten, lengthen, manifold, multiply, protract, snowball **9** accession, accretion, expansion, extension, increment, inflation, intensify, reinforce **10** accelerate, accumulate, aggrandize, appreciate **11** enlargement **12** augmentation **13** amplification

incredible 7 amazing, awesome **8** unlikely **9** cockamamy, fantastic **10** astounding, cockamamie, far-fetched, impossible, improbable, outlandish, phenomenal, remarkable **11** astonishing, implausible **12** preposterous, unbelievable, unconvincing, unimaginable **13** extraordinary

incredulity 7 unfaith **8** distrust, mistrust, unbelief **9** disbelief, nonbelief, suspicion **10** skepticism

incredulous 6 show-me **7** dubious **8** doubting **9** quizzical, sceptical, skeptical **10** suspicious **11** distrustful, mistrustful, questioning, unbelieving, unconvinced **12** disbelieving

increment **4** gain, hike, rise, step **5** raise **6** degree, growth **7** quantum **8** addition **9** accession, accretion **11** enlargement **12** augmentation

incriminate **6** accuse, charge **7** arraign, impeach **9** implicate

incrustation **4** film, rime, scab **5** scale **6** tartar **7** coating

incubate **5** hatch

incubus **5** demon, fiend **9** nightmare

inculcate **5** teach, train **6** impart **7** educate, implant, impress, instill

inculpable **4** pure **5** clean **8** innocent, spotless, virtuous **9** blameless, guiltless, righteous **10** impeccable

incumbent **7** leaning, resting **8** occupant, required **9** overlying **10** obligatory **12** officeholder

incur **7** acquire, bring on **8** contract

incurable **5** fatal **6** deadly, lethal **8** hopeless, terminal **9** immutable **11** immedicable, irreparable **12** irremediable, unchangeable **13** uncorrectable

incursion **4** raid **5** blitz, foray, sally **6** attack, sortie **7** assault **9** irruption

incus **4** bone **5** anvil

indebted **5** bound **7** obliged **8** beholden **9** obligated

indebtedness **3** due, IOU **7** arrears **9** arrearage, gratitude, liability **10** obligation **11** delinquency **12** thankfulness

indecent **4** blue, lewd, racy **5** bawdy, dirty, gross **6** coarse, filthy, impure, risqué, smutty, vulgar **7** obscene, profane, raunchy **8** immodest, improper, off-color, unseemly, untoward **9** offensive **10** scurrilous **13** objectionable

indecision **5** doubt **8** wavering **9** hesitancy **11** ambivalence, uncertainty, vacillation **12** equivocation, irresolution, shilly-shally

indecisive **5** vague **6** unsure **7** dubious, unclear **8** wavering **9** equivocal, tentative, uncertain, undecided, unsettled **10** irresolute **11** problematic, vacillating

indecorous **4** rude **5** gross, rough **6** coarse, vulgar **7** uncivil **8** impolite, improper, unseemly, untoward **9** graceless, irregular, offensive, tasteless, unrefined **10** unbecoming **11** ill-mannered, undignified **12** discourteous

indecorum **5** gaffe **6** breach **7** blooper, blunder, faux pas, offense **8** solecism **11** impropriety

indeed **4** amen **5** truly **6** really, surely, verily **8** forsooth, honestly **9** assuredly, certainly **10** positively, undeniably **11** doubtlessly, undoubtedly **13** unequivocally

indefatigable **6** dogged **8** tireless, untiring, vigorous **9** energetic, tenacious **10** persistent, relentless, unflagging, unwearying **11** unrelenting

indefensible **9** unguarded, untenable **10** assailable, vulnerable **11** unprotected **12** unforgivable, unpardonable **13** unjustifiable

indefinable **5** vague **7** elusive **9** uncertain **11** unspeakable, unutterable **13** undescribable

indefinite **4** wide **5** broad, loose, vague **7** endless, general, inexact, obscure, unclear, unfixed **8** infinite **9** ambiguous, boundless, imprecise, limitless, unbounded, uncertain, undefined, unlimited **10** indistinct, inexplicit, unmeasured, unspecific **12** inconclusive **13** indeterminate ***article:*** **2** an ***pronoun:*** **3** all, any, few **4** each, many, most, none, some **6** anyone, nobody **7** anybody, several, someone **8** everyone, somebody **9** everybody

indehiscent fruit **3** key, nut **4** pepo **5** berry, grain, grape, melon **6** achene, loment, samara, squash **7** pumpkin **8** cucumber **9** caryopsis **10** schizocarp

indelible **4** fast **5** fixed **7** lasting **8** enduring **9** memorable, permanent **13** unforgettable

indelicate **3** raw **4** lewd, rude **5** crude, gross, rough **6** coarse, vulgar **7** uncouth **8** impolite, immodest, improper, tactless, unseemly, untoward **9** unrefined **10** unbecoming

indemnify **5** repay **6** secure **7** redress, requite **9** reimburse **10** compensate, recompense, remunerate

indemnity **6** amends **7** redress **8** requital, security **9** exemption, quittance, reprisals **10** protection, recompense, reparation **11** restitution **12** compensation, remuneration **13** fee-for-service

indentation **4** dent, nick, pock **5** notch **6** dimple, recess **10** depression

indenture **4** nick **5** notch **8** contract **9** agreement **11** certificate

indentured **5** bound **10** controlled **11** apprenticed

independent **4** free **8** absolute, autarkic, separate **9** autarchic, sovereign **10** autonomous **11** self-reliant **13** self-contained

indescribable **11** unspeakable, unutterable **13** unexplainable

indestructible **7** lasting **8** enduring, immortal **9** permanent **12** imperishable, irrefragable, unperishable

indeterminate **5** vague **9** imprecise, uncertain, unlimited

index **4** list, mark, sign **5** ratio, table **7** catalog, symptom **8** classify, evidence, regulate **9** catalogue **11** systematize

India ***bay:*** **6** Bengal ***capital:*** **8** New Delhi ***city:*** **5** Delhi **6** Bombay, Kanpur, Madras, Mumbai, Nagpur **7** Benares, Chennai, Kolkata, Lucknow **8** Calcutta **9** Ahmadabad, Bangalore, Hyderabad ***coast:*** **7** Malabar **10** Coromandel ***European discoverer:*** **4** Gama (Vasco da) ***language:*** **5** Hindi ***leader:*** **3** Rao (P. V. N.) **5** Nehru (Jawaharlal) **6** Gandhi (Indira, Mohandas, Rajiv) ***monetary unit:*** **5** rupee ***mountain range:*** **7** Vindhya **9** Himalayas ***neighbor:*** **5** Burma, China, Nepal **6** Bhutan **7** Myanmar **8** Pakistan **10** Bangladesh ***pass:*** **5** Bolan, Gumal **6** Khyber ***plateau:*** **6** Deccan ***river:*** **5** Indus **6** Ganges, Yamuna **7** Krishna **11** Brahmaputra ***sea:*** **7** Arabian

Indian ***bread:*** **3** nan **4** naan **7** chapati ***butter:*** **3** ghi **4** ghee ***caste:*** **4** Bahr **5** Sudra **6** Vaisya **7** Brahman **9** Kshatriya ***cattle:*** **4** dhan ***cavalry commander:*** **8** risaldar ***crop-related:*** **4** rabi **6** kharif ***female dancer:*** **8** bayadere ***groom:*** **4** syce ***harem:*** **6** zenana ***instrument:*** **4** vina **5** sarod, sitar, tabla **7** tambura ***lady:*** **4** bibi **5** begum **8** memsahib ***musical term:*** **4** raga, tala ***musician:*** **7** Shankar (Ravi) ***nurse:*** **4** amah, ayah ***outcast:*** **6** pariah ***peasant:*** **4** ryot ***prince:*** **4** raja, rana **5** rajah **8** maharaja **9** maharajah ***princess:*** **5** begum ***queen:*** **4** rani **5** ranee ***scholar:*** **6** pandit, pundit ***screen:*** **6** purdah ***seal, stamp:*** **4** chop ***soldier:*** **4** peon **5** sepoy ***steps:*** **4** ghat ***teacher:*** **4** guru ***title:*** **5** sahib ***viceroy:*** **5** nabob, nawab ***weight unit:*** **3** ser **4** cash, dhan, pank, pice, powe, rati, tank, tola **5** adpao, fanam, hubba, masha, maund, pally, pouah, ratti **6** dhurra, pagoda, pollam **7** chinnam, chittak

Indian, American ***baby:*** **7** papoose ***ball game:*** **8** lacrosse ***carrier:*** **7** travois ***Central and South American:*** **3** Mam, Ona **4** Cuna, Inca, Maya **5** Arara, Aztec, Carib, Huave, Olmec, Taino, Yagua **6** Arawak, Aymara, Jivaro, Omagua, Toltec, Yahgan **7** Chibcha, Quechua, Zapotec **8** Tarascan, Yanomamo **10** Araucanian **11** Tupi-Guaraní ***food:*** **4** samp **5** maize **8** pemmican ***home:*** **5** hogan, lodge, tepee **6** pueblo, teepee, wigwam **7** wickiup ***leader:*** **4** Popé **6** Wovoka **7** Cochise, Osceola, Pontiac, Sequoia, Sequoya **8** Geronimo, Hiawatha, Powhatan, Sequoyah, Tecumseh **9** Black Hawk, Massasoit **10** Crazy Horse **11** Cornplanter, Sitting Bull ***money:*** **6** wampum ***North American:*** **3** Aht, Fox, Hoh, Kaw, Oto, Sac, Sia, Ute, Wea **4** Coos, Cora, Cree, Crow, Erie, Hopi, Hupa, Iowa, Otoe, Pima, Pomo, Sauk, Taos, Yuma, Zuni **5** Aleut, Caddo, Creek, Haida, Huron, Kansa, Kiowa, Maidu, Miami, Modoc, Omaha, Osage, Sioux, Uinta **6** Apache, Cayuga, Dakota, Lenape, Mandan, Micmac, Mohawk, Munsee, Navaho, Navajo, Nootka, Oglala, Ojibwa, Oneida, Paiute, Pawnee, Pueblo, Quapaw, Salish, Santee, Seneca, Siwash **7** Anasazi, Arapaho, Arikara, Bannock, Chilkat, Chinook, Choctaw, Dakotah, Esselen, Klamath, Kutenai, Mohican, Naskapi, Natchez, Ojibway, Pontiac, Shawnee, Tlingit **8** Cherokee, Cheyenne, Chippewa, Comanche, Delaware, Illinois, Iroquois, Kickapoo, Kwakiutl, Nez Percé, Onondaga, Powhatan, Seminole, Shoshoni **9** Blackfoot, Chickasaw, Menominee, Tsimshian, Tuscarora, Wampanoag, Winnebago **10** Assiniboin, Chiricahua, Gros Ventre, Potawatomi **11** Massachuset, Narraganset ***pipe:*** **7** calumet ***spirit:*** **5** totem **6** manitu **7** kachina, manitou

Indiana ***capital:*** **12** Indianapolis ***city:*** **4** Gary **6** Muncie **9** Fort Wayne, South Bend **10** Evansville, Terre Haute **11** Bloomington ***college, university:*** **6** DePauw, Purdue **9** Ball State, Notre Dame ***nickname:*** **7** Hoosier (State) ***river:*** **5** White **6** Wabash ***state bird:*** **8** cardinal ***state flower:*** **5** peony ***state tree:*** **5** tulip

Indian paintbrush **8** hawkweed **10** painted cup

indicate **4** bode, hint, mark, mean, show **5** augur, imply, point, prove **6** attest, convey, denote, evince, import, reveal **7** bespeak, betoken, connote, display, exhibit, express, presage, signify, suggest **8** disclose, evidence, foretell, manifest, register **9** designate **10** foreshadow, illustrate **11** demonstrate

indication **3** cue **4** clue, hint, mark, sign **5** proof, token, trace **6** augury, signal **7** gesture, inkling, portent, symptom **8** evidence, reminder, telltale **9** testimony **10** expression, suggestion **13** foreshadowing, manifestation

indicative **10** expressive, suggestive **11** evidentiary, symptomatic **12** illustrative **13** demonstrative

indicia **5** marks, signs **8** imprints, markings

indict **5** blame **6** accuse, charge **7** arraign, censure, impeach **9** criticize

indifference **6** apathy **9** aloofness, unconcern **10** detachment, dispassion **11** disinterest **12** carelessness, impartiality

indifferent **4** cold, cool, numb, so-so **5** aloof, blasé, stoic **6** casual, remote **7** average, neutral **8** careless, detached, mediocre, middling, moderate, ordinary, passable, unbiased, uncaring **9** apathetic, impartial, impassive, objective **10** nonchalant, unaffected **11** unconcerned, unemotional **12** uninterested, unprejudiced **13** disinterested, dispassionate

indigence 4 need, want **6** penury **7** poverty **9** neediness, pauperism, privation **11** deprivation, destitution

indigene 6 native **9** aborigine **10** aboriginal

indigenous 6 native **7** endemic, natural **10** aboriginal, congenital, connatural, unacquired **13** autochthonous

indigent 4 poor **5** broke, needy **9** destitute, penniless **11** impecunious, necessitous **12** impoverished

indigestion 9 dyspepsia, heartburn

indignant 3 mad **5** irate, riled, upset, vexed **6** galled, heated **7** annoyed **8** offended, outraged, provoked **9** affronted, irritated, resentful

indignation 5 pique **7** dudgeon **10** irritation, resentment

indignity 3 cut **4** slap **6** injury, insult, slight **7** affront, outrage **9** contumely, grievance **10** disrespect **11** humiliation **13** disparagement, embarrassment

indigo 4 anil, blue **8** deep blue

indigo bird 5 finch **7** bunting

Indira's father 5 Nehru (Jawaharlal)

indirect 7 devious, oblique, vagrant, winding **8** circular, sidelong, tortuous **9** deceitful, underhand, wandering **10** backhanded, circuitous, collateral, meandering, roundabout **11** duplicitous, underhanded

indiscreet 5 gabby **6** unwise **7** foolish, gossipy **8** tactless **9** impolitic, imprudent, untactful **10** ill-advised **11** loose-lipped

indiscretion 4 slip **5** folly, gaffe, lapse **7** blunder, faux pas, mistake, misstep **8** solecism **10** imprudence **11** impropriety

indiscriminate 5 mixed **6** hybrid, motley, random, varied **7** aimless, jumbled, vagrant **8** assorted, careless **9** arbitrary, desultory, haphazard, hit-or-miss, unplanned, wholesale **10** uncritical **11** promiscuous **12** conglomerate, multifarious, unrestrained **13** heterogeneous, miscellaneous

indispensable 5 basic, vital **6** needed **7** crucial, needful, pivotal **8** cardinal, critical **9** essential, necessary, requisite **10** imperative, obligatory **11** fundamental

indisposed 3 ill **4** down, sick **5** loath **6** ailing, averse, poorly, sickly, unwell **7** uneager **8** hesitant **9** reluctant, resistant, unwilling **11** disinclined

indisposition 6 malady **7** ailment, dislike, illness, malaise **8** aversion, disfavor, distaste, sickness, unhealth **10** affliction, reluctance

indisputable 4 sure, true **7** certain, evident, obvious **8** absolute, ironclad, positive **9** apodictic **10** undeniable **11** irrefutable, unequivocal **12** irrefragable, unassailable

indistinct 3 dim **4** hazy **5** faint, foggy, misty, murky, vague **6** bleary, blurry, cloudy **7** blurred, obscure, shadowy, unclear **8** confused **9** uncertain, undefined **12** undetermined

indistinguishable 4 same **5** alike, equal, vague **7** unclear **9** duplicate, identical **10** equivalent

indite 3 pen **5** write **6** record, scribe **7** compose, engross **10** transcribe

individual 3 one **4** body, lone, self, sole, soul, unit **5** being, human, party, thing **6** entity, mortal, person, proper, single **7** special **8** creature, discrete, distinct, peculiar, personal, separate, singular, solitary, specific **10** particular, respective **11** distinctive **13** idiosyncratic ***combining form:*** **4** idio

individualist 5 loner **6** hermit **8** lone wolf, maverick **13** nonconformist

individuality 4 self **7** essence, oneness **8** identity, selfhood **9** character **10** uniqueness **11** personality, singularity **12** idiosyncrasy, separateness

individualize 4 mark **7** specify **9** customize **10** specialize **11** distinguish, personalize, singularize **12** characterize **13** differentiate, particularize

Indochinese country 4 Laos **5** Burma **7** Myanmar, Vietnam **8** Cambodia, Thailand **9** Kampuchea

indoctrinate 5 teach, tutor **7** educate, program **8** convince, persuade **9** brainwash, inculcate

indolence 4 laze **5** sloth **7** inertia, languor **8** idleness, laziness, lethargy **9** torpidity **12** slothfulness, sluggishness **13** shiftlessness ***fruit of:*** **5** lotus

indolent 4 idle, lazy **6** torpid **8** fainéant, slothful, sluggish **9** lethargic, shiftless

indomitable 7 staunch **9** steadfast **10** invincible, unbeatable **11** impregnable **13** unconquerable

Indonesia *archipelago:* **5** Malay ***capital:*** **7** Jakarta **8** Djakarta ***city:*** **5** Medan **7** Bandung, Cilacap **8** Semarang, Surabaja, Surabaya **9** Palembang ***island group:*** **5** Sunda **8** Moluccas ***language:*** **6** Bahasa ***leader:*** **7** Suharto, Sukarno ***monetary unit:*** **6** rupiah ***regions:*** **4** Bali, Java **5** Ceram, Timor **6** Bangka, Borneo, Flores, Lombok, Madura

7 Celebes, Sumatra 8 Sulawesi 9 Irian Jaya *volcano:* 8 Krakatau, Krakatoa

indubitable 4 sure 6 patent 7 certain, evident, obvious 8 definite, ironclad, positive 9 apodictic, veritable 10 undeniable 11 irrefutable, self-evident, unequivocal 12 irrefragable

induce 5 cause 6 effect, elicit, prompt 7 actuate, procure 8 convince, engender, generate, motivate, occasion, persuade 9 encourage

inducement 4 bait, lure 6 come-on, motive 10 attraction, motivation 13 consideration

induct 4 lead 5 admit 6 enlist, enroll 7 appoint, install

inductance unit 5 henry

induction 8 entrance 9 accession, reasoning 10 enlistment 11 appointment 13 ratiocination

inductive 7 logical 9 prefatory, prelusive 11 a posteriori

indulge 3 pet 4 baby, bask 5 allow, favor, humor, spoil 6 cocker, coddle, cosset, oblige, pamper, permit, please, wallow 7 cater to, delight, gratify, satisfy 9 luxuriate 11 mollycoddle

indulgence 5 favor, mercy, treat 6 luxury 7 charity 8 clemency, courtesy, kindness, lenience, leniency 9 allowance, remission, tolerance 10 compassion, kindliness, permission, toleration 11 forbearance, forgiveness 12 dispensation, mercifulness 13 gratification

indulgence seller 5 Tezel (Johann) 6 Tetzel (Johann)

indulgent 4 easy, kind 7 clement, lenient 8 generous, merciful, tolerant 9 forgiving 10 charitable, permissive

indurate 6 harden 7 callous, confirm, congeal 8 hardened, solidify, stubborn 9 unfeeling 11 hard-hearted

industrialist 6 tycoon 7 magnate 12 manufacturer

industrious 4 busy 8 diligent, sedulous 9 assiduous, laborious

industry 4 work 5 labor 8 business, commerce 9 assiduity, diligence 10 enterprise

Indy 500 winner 4 Foyt (A. J.) 5 Mears (Rick), Unser (Al, Bobby) 8 Andretti (Mario)

inebriant see **intoxicant**

inebriate 3 sot 4 lush, soak 5 drunk, souse, tight, tipsy, toper 6 bibber, boozer 7 stupefy, tippler, tosspot 8 drunkard 10 intoxicate

inebriated 3 lit 5 drunk, lit up, oiled, stiff, tight, tipsy 6 blotto, juiced, loaded, plowed, potted, soused, stewed, tanked, wasted 7 crocked, pickled, pie-eyed, sloshed, smashed 8 polluted 9 plastered

inedible 9 poisonous 12 unappetizing

ineffable 5 taboo 9 forbidden 11 unspeakable, unutterable 13 undescribable

ineffaceable 7 lasting 8 enduring 9 indelible, permanent

ineffective 4 vain, weak 6 futile 7 useless 8 abortive, bootless, feckless, impotent 9 fruitless, powerless 10 emasculate, unavailing 12 unproductive, unsuccessful

ineffectiveness 8 futility 9 impotence

ineffectual see **ineffective**

inefficient 5 slack 6 clumsy 8 careless, slipshod, wasteful 9 negligent

inelastic 5 rigid, stiff 7 brittle 9 unbending 10 unyielding

inelegant 5 crass, crude, gross, rough 6 coarse, gauche, vulgar 7 awkward, uncouth 9 graceless, unrefined 10 uncultured, ungraceful 12 uncultivated

ineligible 5 unfit 8 unfitted, unworthy 10 unequipped, unsuitable 11 unqualified 12 disqualified

ineluctable 4 sure 5 bound, fated 6 doomed 7 certain 8 destined 9 necessary 10 inevitable, unevadable 11 unavoidable, unescapable 13 unpreventable

inept 5 unfit 6 clumsy, gauche, klutzy 7 artless, awkward, foolish, halting, unhandy 8 bumbling, bungling 9 all thumbs, ham-handed, maladroit, unskilled 10 malapropos, unskillful, unsuitable 11 heavy-handed, undexterous, unfortunate

inequality 8 imparity 9 disparity 10 unevenness 12 irregularity, variableness 13 disproportion, heterogeneity

inequitable 6 biased, unfair, unjust 7 partial 10 prejudiced 11 unjustified, unrighteous

inequity 4 bias 5 wrong 9 prejudice 10 unfairness, unjustness

ineradicable 6 innate 7 chronic 8 constant, inherent, stubborn 9 ingrained 10 deep-rooted, deep-seated, entrenched, inveterate 11 established, ever-present, never-ending

inert 4 calm, dead, idle 5 quiet, still 6 asleep, sleepy 7 dormant, passive 8 immobile, lifeless, sluggish 9 apathetic, lethargic 10 motionless

inert gas 4 neon 5 argon, radon, xenon 6 helium 7 krypton

inertia 5 sloth 6 apathy, stupor, torpor 7 languor 8 idleness, laziness, lethargy 9 indolence, inertness, lassitude, passivity, torpidity 10 immobility, inactivity 11 disinterest 12 listlessness, sluggishness

inescapable see **inevitable**

inessential see **unessential**
inestimable 9 priceless **11** measureless **12** immeasurable, unmeasurable, unfathomable
inevitable 4 sure **5** bound, fated **6** doomed **7** certain **8** destined **9** necessary **11** unavoidable, unescapable **12** foreordained **13** unpreventable
inevitably 8 perforce **10** willy-nilly **11** like it or not, unavoidably
inexcusable 6 guilty **8** blamable, culpable **9** untenable **10** censurable **11** blameworthy, condemnable **12** criticizable, unforgivable, unpardonable **13** reprehensible, unjustifiable
inexhaustible 8 tireless, untiring **9** unfailing, weariless **10** bottomless, unflagging **13** indefatigable
inexorable 5 rigid **6** strict **7** adamant **8** immobile, obdurate, stubborn **9** immovable, unbending **10** relentless, unyielding **11** unrelenting
inexpensive 3 low **5** cheap **7** cut-rate **8** moderate **10** reasonable
inexperience 7 naïveté, rawness **8** verdancy **9** freshness, greenness **10** callowness
inexperienced 3 raw **5** fresh, green, naive, young **6** callow **7** untried **8** unversed **9** unskilled, untrained, unworldly **10** amateurish, unseasoned
inexpert 9 maladroit, unskilled, untrained **10** amateurish
inexplicable 6 arcane, obtuse, opaque **7** cryptic **9** enigmatic **10** mysterious, mystifying, unsolvable **12** impenetrable, unfathomable **13** unaccountable, unexplainable
inexpressible 8 nameless **11** unspeakable, unutterable **13** undescribable, unexplainable
inexpressive 5 blank, stoic **6** stolid, vacant, wooden **7** deadpan **9** impassive **10** poker-faced **13** straight-faced
inextricable 9 insoluble **10** unsolvable
infallible 4 sure **5** exact **6** trusty **7** certain, correct, perfect **8** absolute, accurate, flawless, surefire, unerring **9** errorless, unfailing **10** dependable, impeccable **11** trustworthy **12** tried-and-true **13** unimpeachable
infamous 4 evil, vile **6** odious **7** hateful, heinous **8** flagrant, shameful **9** abhorrent, miscreant, nefarious, notorious **10** abominable, despicable, detestable, flagitious, scandalous, villainous **11** disgraceful, ignominious, opprobrious **12** contemptible, disreputable
infamy 5 odium, shame **7** obloquy **8** disgrace, dishonor, ignominy **9** disrepute, notoriety **10** opprobrium
infancy 6 nonage **8** babyhood **9** childhood
infant 4 babe, baby **5** bairn, child, green **7** bambino, neonate, newborn, papoose, toddler **8** bantling, immature, nursling **9** unfledged ***bed:* 4** crib **6** cradle **8** bassinet ***condition:* 5** colic ***food:* 3** pap **4** milk **7** pabulum ***room:* 7** nursery
infanta 8 princess
infantile 7 babyish, puerile **8** childish, immature
infantryman 7 dogface **8** doughboy **11** foot soldier ***Algerian:* 6** Zouave
infatuated 4 gaga **5** dotty, silly **7** foolish **8** besotted, enamored, obsessed **9** bewitched, rapturous **10** captivated, passionate
infatuation 4 rage **5** ardor, craze, crush, folly **7** passion, rapture **8** devotion **9** obsession, puppy love **11** fascination
infect 5 taint **6** defile, poison **7** corrupt, pollute **11** contaminate
infection 3 bug **6** sepses (plural), sepsis ***carrier:* 6** vector ***fungous:* 8** mycetoma
infectious 8 catching, epidemic, virulent **9** pestilent **10** contagious, corrupting **12** communicable **13** contaminating, transmittable
infelicitous 5 unapt, unfit **6** unmeet **7** awkward, unhappy **8** improper **9** imperfect **10** malapropos, unsuitable **11** regrettable, unfortunate
infer 5 judge **6** deduce, deduct, derive, gather, reason **7** collect, make out, suppose, surmise **8** conclude, construe **10** conjecture **11** extrapolate, hypothesize
inference 7 surmise **8** illation, sequitur **9** deduction **10** assumption, conclusion, conjecture, derivation **11** presumption, supposition
inferior 3 low **4** base, fair, hack, mean, poor, puny **5** cheap, lousy, lower, minor, petty, scrub, sorry, under, worse **6** common, deputy, feeble, impure, junior, lesser, nether, no-good, paltry, satrap, shoddy, sleazy, tawdry, tinpot, vassal **7** average, subject, unequal **8** declassé, low-grade, mediocre, middling, ordinary, unworthy, wretched **9** attendant, auxiliary, no-account, satellite, secondary, subaltern, subjacent, underling, worthless **10** inadequate, second-rate **11** substandard ***prefix:* 3** sub **4** demi **5** infra
infernal 6 Hadean **7** demonic, hellish, satanic **8** chthonic, damnable, demoniac, devilish, diabolic, plutonic **9** chthonian, plutonian, Tartarean **10** diabolical, sulphurous
inferno 3 pit **4** fire, hell **5** Hades, Sheol **6** blazes, Tophet **7** Gehenna **9** holocaust, perdition **10** underworld **11** netherworld **13** conflagration

Inferno ***division:*** **5** canto ***poet:*** **5** Dante (Alighieri) ***verse form:*** **9** terza rima

infertile **6** barren, effete **7** sterile **8** impotent **10** unfruitful **12** hardscrabble, unproductive

infest **4** teem **5** beset, swarm **6** plague **7** overrun **10** parasitize

infidel **5** pagan **7** atheist, heathen, heretic, skeptic **8** agnostic **10** unbeliever

infidelity **7** perfidy, treason **8** adultery, betrayal, cheating **9** disbelief, treachery **10** disloyalty **13** faithlessness

infinite **4** vast **7** endless, eternal, immense **8** unending **9** boundless, countless, limitless, perpetual, unlimited **11** everlasting, illimitable, measureless, sempiternal **12** immeasurable

infinity **8** eternity **10** perpetuity **11** endlessness **12** sempiternity **13** boundlessness, limitlessness

infirm **4** lame, sick, weak **5** frail **6** ailing, feeble, sickly **7** failing, fragile, unsound **8** decrepit, unstable **9** doddering **11** debilitated

infirmity **3** ill **4** flaw **5** decay **6** malady **7** ailment, disease, frailty, illness, malaise **8** debility, disorder, sickness, syndrome, weakness **9** complaint, condition **10** affliction, feebleness, sickliness **11** decrepitude **12** debilitation, enfeeblement

infix **4** root **5** embed, lodge **6** fasten, pierce **7** engrave, implant, impress

inflame **4** fire, gall, goad, rile, roil **5** anger, light, rouse **6** arouse, enrage, excite, foment, ignite, kindle, madden, redden, stir up **7** provoke **8** enkindle, irritate **9** aggravate **10** exacerbate, exasperate

inflammable **5** fiery **6** ardent **8** burnable, volatile **9** excitable, ignitable, irascible **11** combustible

inflammation **4** gout, sore **6** otitis, quinsy **7** catarrh, colitis **8** adenitis, bursitis, cystitis, neuritis, pleurisy, rachitis, swelling **9** arthritis, chilblain, gastritis, nephritis, phlebitis **10** bronchitis, cellulitis, combustion, dermatitis, gingivitis, laryngitis, tendinitis **12** encephalitis **13** poliomyelitis ***eye:*** **6** iritis **7** pinkeye **9** keratitis ***horse:*** **7** fistula, quittor ***intestines:*** **7** ileitis **9** enteritis ***suffix:*** **4** itis

inflammatory **8** exciting **9** explosive, seditious **11** provocative **13** rabble-rousing, revolutionary

inflate **4** fill **5** bloat, elate, swell **6** expand **7** amplify, distend **9** supersize **10** aggrandize

inflated **5** tumid, windy **6** turgid **7** bloated, swollen, verbose **9** bombastic, distended, dropsical, flatulent, overblown **10** heightened **11** exaggerated, pretentious

inflection **4** bend, tone **5** curve, pitch **6** accent, change, stress, timbre **8** emphasis, tonality **9** accidence **10** modulation

inflexible **3** set **4** grim, hard, iron **5** fixed, rigid, stiff **6** strict **7** adamant, die-hard **8** granitic, hard-line, ironclad, obdurate, stubborn **9** immovable, immutable, obstinate, steadfast, unbending **10** adamantine, brassbound, implacable, rock-ribbed, unbendable, unyielding **11** unalterable, unrelenting **12** unchangeable

inflict **5** visit, wreak **7** mete out, subject **8** dispense **10** administer

inflow **4** rush **7** arrival

influence **4** move, pull, sway **5** alter, bribe, clout, force, impel, lobby, touch **6** affect, compel, impact, modify, moment, strike, weight **7** command, control, impress, mastery **8** dominate, militate, persuade, prestige **9** authority, dominance

influenceable **8** gullible **9** malleable, receptive, tractable **11** persuadable, persuasible, suggestible

influential **6** potent **8** forceful, powerful **9** effective **10** persuasive **13** authoritative

influx **7** arrival **8** entrance, invasion **9** accession

inform **3** rat, tip **4** blab, clue, leak, post, tell, warn **5** brief, edify, endow, endue, imbue, teach **6** advise, betray, fill in, impart, leaven, notify, reveal, snitch, squeal, tattle, turn in, update **7** animate, apprise, caution, educate **8** acquaint, disclose, forewarn **9** advertise, enlighten **11** familiarize

informal **6** casual, dégagé, folksy **7** natural, offhand, relaxed **8** down-home, familiar, laid-back **9** easygoing **10** colloquial, unofficial **13** unceremonious

information **3** tip **4** data, fact, lore, news, poop, word **5** scoop **6** advice, notice, skinny, wisdom **7** lowdown, tidings **9** knowledge **12** intelligence ***manager:*** **9** cybrarian ***secondhand:*** **7** hearsay

information bureau ***abbreviation:*** **4** USIA, USIS

informative **8** edifying, exegetic **10** exegetical **11** educational, elucidative, explanatory **12** enlightening, illuminating

informed **4** wise **5** aware **6** au fait, versed **7** abreast, knowing **8** apprised, educated **9** au courant, cognizant **10** acquainted, conversant **11** enlightened **13** knowledgeable

informer **3** rat, spy **4** fink, mole, narc **5** stool **6** canary, gossip, snitch **7** rat fink, stoolie, tattler, tipster **8** squealer, telltale **10** deep throat, talebearer, tattletale **11** stool pigeon **13** whistle-blower

infra **5** after, below, later, under **7** beneath

infract 3 sin **6** breach, offend **7** violate **8** trespass **10** contravene, transgress
infraction 3 sin **4** foul **5** crime, error **6** breach **7** faux pas, misdeed, offense **8** trespass **9** violation **12** encroachment **13** contravention, transgression
infrastructure 4 base **5** basis **9** framework **10** foundation, groundwork, substratum **12** underpinning
infrequent 3 odd **4** rare **6** scarce, seldom **7** unusual **8** isolated, sporadic, uncommon, unwonted **10** occasional **11** exceptional
infringe 6 breach, impose, meddle, offend **7** disturb, obtrude, violate **8** encroach, entrench, trespass **10** transgress
infuriate 3 ire, mad **4** rile **5** anger, pique **6** enrage, madden, rankle **7** incense, inflame, outrage, provoke, steam up
infuse 4 fill, soak **5** imbue, steep **6** leaven **7** animate, implant, pervade, suffuse **8** permeate, saturate **10** impregnate
ingenious 5 acute, canny, sharp, smart, witty **6** adroit, clever, crafty **7** cunning, fertile **8** creative, original **11** imaginative, resourceful
ingenuity 5 knack, savvy, skill **6** acumen, smarts, talent **7** know-how, mastery **8** deftness, keenness **9** adeptness, handiness **10** adroitness, capability, cleverness, perception, shrewdness **11** proficiency **12** intelligence, skillfulness **13** inventiveness
ingenuous 4 open **5** naive **6** simple **7** artless, natural **8** innocent **9** childlike, guileless, unstudied **10** unaffected
ingest 3 eat **4** feed **6** devour **7** consume, partake, swallow
Inge work 6 Picnic **7** Bus Stop **18** Splendor in the Grass **19** Come Back Little Sheba
inglorious 8 shameful **11** disgraceful, ignominious, opprobrious **12** dishonorable, disreputable **13** discreditable, unrespectable
ingot 3 bar, pig, rod **4** mold **6** billet
ingrain 4 etch **5** imbue
ingrained 6 innate **8** inherent **9** essential **10** congenital, deep-rooted, deep-seated
ingratiating 5 silky **6** silken, smarmy **7** fawning **8** pleasing, unctuous **9** adulatory **10** flattering **11** sycophantic
ingredient 4 part **5** piece **6** factor **7** element **9** component **11** constituent
ingress 4 door **5** entry **6** access, entrée, portal **7** doorway, passage **8** entrance, entryway **9** admission, vestibule **10** admittance **11** entranceway
ingurgitate 4 bolt, cram, gulp, slop, wolf **5** gorge, scarf, stuff, swill **6** devour, gobble, guzzle **7** swallow
inhabit 4 live **5** dwell, haunt **6** occupy, people, settle, tenant **8** populate
inhabitant 5 liver **6** inmate, native **7** citizen, denizen, dweller, resider **8** indigene, resident **9** aborigine **10** autochthon ***foreign:*** **5** alien ***indigenous:*** **6** native **9** aborigine
inhale 7 breathe, consume, respire, swallow
inharmonious 6 atonal **7** jarring **9** dissonant, unmusical **10** discordant **11** cacophonous, conflicting, conflictive, disagreeing, quarrelsome, uncongenial **12** antagonistic
inhere 3 lie **5** dwell **6** belong, reside
inherent 4 born **5** basic, per se **6** inborn, native **7** built-in, connate, natural **8** immanent **9** elemental, essential, intrinsic **10** congenital, deep-seated **11** fundamental
inherit 7 acquire, receive, succeed
inheritance 3 DNA **4** gene, gift **6** devise, estate, legacy **7** bequest **8** heirloom, heritage **9** patrimony, tradition **10** birthright **13** primogeniture
inherited 6 native **7** connate, genetic, natural **10** bequeathed, congenital, connatural, handed-down, hand-me-down
inheritor 4 heir **7** heiress, legatee **11** beneficiary
inhibit 4 curb, slow **5** check **6** arrest, bridle, enjoin, fetter, hamper, hinder, hobble, impede **7** prevent, repress, trammel **8** hold back, obstruct, restrain, suppress, withhold **9** constrain **10** discourage
inhibition 4 curb **5** taboo **6** hang-up **7** barrier **9** hindrance, restraint, stricture **10** impediment, repression **11** suppression
inhuman 5 cruel, feral **6** brutal, savage **7** beastly, bestial, brutish **8** fiendish **9** barbarous, monstrous **10** diabolical
inhumane 4 fell, grim **5** cruel **6** brutal, fierce, malign, savage **8** ruthless, sadistic **9** barbarous, ferocious, heartless, merciless, truculent
inhumation 6 burial **9** interment, sepulture **10** entombment
inhume 4 bury **5** plant **6** entomb **7** put away **9** lay to rest
inimical 7 adverse, harmful, hostile **10** malevolent, unfriendly **11** belligerent, contentious **12** antagonistic, antipathetic
iniquitous 3 bad **4** base, evil, vile **5** wrong **6** sinful, unjust, wicked **7** immoral, vicious **9** nefarious
iniquity 3 sin **4** evil **5** crime, wrong **7** offense **9** turpitude **8** trespass **10** immorality, wickedness, wrongdoing **13** transgression
initial 5 first, prime **6** anlage, letter, maiden **7** approve, engrave, leading, opening, pri-

mary **8** earliest, foremost, monogram, original **9** beginning

initiate 4 open **5** begin, enter, set up, start **6** enroll, get off, induct, invest, launch, take up **7** install, kick off, usher in **8** commence **9** originate **10** inaugurate

initiation 5 debut **7** baptism **9** admission, beginning, induction **10** admittance **11** investiture, origination **12** commencement, introduction

initiative 4 push **5** drive, spunk **6** energy **8** ambition, aptitude, gumption **9** beginning **10** enterprise, get-up-and-go

inject 3 add **6** insert **7** implant, instill **9** inoculate, introduce, vaccinate

injection 3 fix **4** hypo, shot **5** serum **7** booster, vaccine **10** hypodermic **11** inoculation, vaccination

injudicious 4 rash **5** hasty **6** unwise **8** heedless, reckless **9** ill-judged, impolitic, imprudent **10** ill-advised, indiscreet **11** inexpedient **12** shortsighted

injunction 3 ban, bar **4** writ **5** order **6** behest, charge **7** bidding, command, dictate, mandate **9** direction **11** prohibition

injure 3 mar **4** foul, harm, hurt, maim **5** spoil, wound, wrong **6** blight, bruise, damage, deface, deform, impair, mangle **7** contort, cripple, disable, torture **8** maltreat, mutilate **9** disfigure **12** incapacitate

injurious 6 nocent **7** abusive, adverse, harmful, hurtful **8** damaging **9** offensive **10** defamatory **11** detrimental

injury 3 ill **4** harm, hurt **5** wound, wrong **6** bruise, damage, trauma **8** distress **9** detriment

injustice 4 tort **5** crime, wrong **6** breach, damage **7** outrage **8** inequity, trespass **9** grievance, violation **10** favoritism, wrongdoing

ink 3 dye, pen **4** sign **8** inscribe **9** autograph, signature, subscribe ***roller:*** **6** brayer

inkling 3 cue, tip **4** clue, hint, idea, lead, wind **5** hunch **6** notion, tip-off **8** telltale **9** suspicion **10** indication, intimation, suggestion

inky 3 jet **4** ebon **5** black, ebony, jetty, raven, sable **9** Cimmerian, pitch-dark **10** pitch-black

inlaid 5 piqué **6** boolle **7** hatched **8** enchased, nielloed **9** damascene, incrusted

Inland Empire 8 Illinois

inlet 3 arm, bay, ria **4** cove, gulf, loch **5** bayou, bight, creek, fiord, firth, fjord, sound **6** harbor, slough, strait **7** estuary ***Admiralties:*** **4** Kali ***Adriatic Sea:*** **5** Vlorë ***Aegean Sea:*** **7** Saronic ***Alaska:*** **4** Cook **5** Cross, Taiya **8** Chilkoot ***Aleutians:*** **5** Holtz, Nazan ***Angola:*** **5** Bengo, Tiger **6** Tigres ***Antarctica:*** **7** McMurdo **8** Amundsen **10** Shackleton ***Arabian Sea:*** **4** Qamr **5** Kamar ***Australia:*** **4** King **7** Repulse **10** Broad Sound ***Baffin Island:*** **9** Admiralty ***Baltic Sea:*** **6** Gdansk ***Barents Sea:*** **4** Kola **7** Pechora ***Bismarck Sea:*** **5** Kimbe ***Canada:*** **9** Howe Sound ***Cape Breton Island:*** **4** Mira ***Chile:*** **5** Otway ***Crete:*** **4** Suda **5** Canea ***Denmark:*** **3** Ise ***Djibouti:*** **6** Tajura **8** Tadjoura ***Ecuador:*** **5** Manta ***Florida:*** **10** Saint Lucie ***Georgia:*** **8** Altamaha ***Gulf of Alaska:*** **3** Icy **5** Woman ***Gulf of Mexico:*** **8** Suwannee **9** Matagorda **10** Terrebonne ***Hawaii:*** **11** Pearl Harbor ***Honshu:*** **3** Ise **5** Owari **6** Atsuta ***Iceland:*** **4** Axar, Eyja, Huna **5** Horna, Skaga, Vopna **8** Hunafloi ***Indonesia:*** **4** Bima **5** Saleh ***Ionian Sea:*** **7** Taranto ***Java:*** **4** Lada **5** Peper ***Kara Sea:*** **6** Enisei **7** Yenisei ***Labrador:*** **8** Hamilton ***Lake Erie:*** **8** Put-in-Bay, Sandusky ***Long Island:*** **8** Rockaway ***Madagascar:*** **8** Antongil ***Massachusetts:*** **9** Annisquam ***Massachusetts Bay:*** **10** Lynn Harbor ***Mediterranean Sea:*** **8** Valencia **9** Famagusta **10** Khalij Surt **11** Syrtis Major ***Mozambique:*** **5** Memba, Pemba ***Nantucket Sound:*** **5** Lewis ***New Guinea:*** **3** Oro **5** Berau, Hansa **11** McCluer Gulf ***New Jersey:*** **9** Little Egg ***New Zealand:*** **5** Hawke **6** Tasman ***North Carolina:*** **9** Albemarle ***Northern Ireland:*** **12** Belfast Lough ***North Sea:*** **4** Lyse **9** Hardanger ***Northwest Territories:*** **5** Wager **8** Bathurst, Franklin **9** Frobisher **12** Prince Albert ***Norway:*** **3** Tys **4** Bokn, Tana **5** Lakse, Sogne ***Norwegian Sea:*** **4** Nord, Salt, Stor, Vest **5** Ranen **8** Scoresby **9** Trondheim ***Ontario:*** **4** Owen ***Potomac:*** **10** Tidal Basin ***Philippines:*** **5** Baler, Pilar, Sogod **6** Butuan **9** Davao Gulf, Leyte Gulf, Panay Gulf ***Puget Sound:*** **4** Carr, Case ***Quebec:*** **6** Ungava ***Red Sea:*** **4** Foul ***Russia:*** **5** Chaun **8** Sakhalin ***Santa Cruz Islands:*** **8** Basilisk ***Solomon Islands:*** **4** Deep **8** Huon Gulf ***South Africa:*** **5** Table ***South Carolina:*** **4** Bull ***South China Sea:*** **4** Bias, Datu, Siam, Taya **5** Dasol **6** Brunei, Paluan **8** Lingayen ***Spitsbergen:*** **3** Ice **4** Bell **5** Kings ***Sumatra:*** **5** Bajur **10** Koninginne ***Wales:*** **5** Burry ***Washington:*** **11** Grays Harbor (see also **bay**)

inmate 7 convict **8** occupant, prisoner, resident **10** inhabitant

inmost part 4 core, pith **5** heart **6** center, depths, kernel, marrow **7** nucleus

inn 5 hotel, lodge, motel, serai **6** hostel, tavern **7** auberge, hospice, pension **8** hostelry **9** roadhouse **11** caravansary, public house **12** caravansarai **13** boardinghouse ***French:*** **7** auberge ***German:*** **7** Gasthof **8** Gasthaus

Spanish: **5** fonda **6** posada **7** parador *Turkish:* **6** imaret
innards **4** guts **5** belly **6** bowels, tripes **7** viscera **8** entrails, stuffing **10** intestines
innate see **inherent**
inner **3** gut **5** focal **6** hidden, middle, secret **7** central, nuclear, private **8** familiar, interior, internal, personal, visceral **9** concealed, essential *prefix:* **3** ent **4** ento
innervate **4** jolt, move **5** pique, rouse **6** excite **7** animate, provoke, quicken **8** motivate, vitalize **9** electrify, galvanize, stimulate
Innisfail **4** Eire, Erin **7** Ireland
innkeeper **4** host **8** boniface, hosteler, hotelier, landlord, publican
innocence **6** purity **7** naiveté **8** chastity **10** simplicity **11** artlessness, sinlessness
innocent **4** good, lamb, naïf, pure, void **5** clean, legal, licit, naive **6** chaste, devoid, lawful **7** artless, natural, unaware **8** harmless, ignorant, virtuous **9** blameless, childlike, exemplary, faultless, guileless, guiltless, ingenuous, innocuous, righteous, stainless, unstained, unsullied, untainted **10** inculpable, legitimate **12** unsuspecting
innocuous **5** banal, bland **6** pallid **7** insipid **8** harmless **11** inoffensive, unoffending **13** insignificant
innovation **6** change **7** novelty
innovative **3** new **5** novel **8** creative, original **9** inventive **10** newfangled **11** cutting-edge, leading-edge **12** trailblazing
innovator **9** architect, developer **10** originator **11** trailblazer **13** revolutionary
innuendo **4** clue, hint, slur **7** calumny **8** allusion **9** aspersion **10** backbiting, intimation **11** implication, insinuation
innumerable **4** many **6** legion, myriad, untold **7** umpteen **9** countless, uncounted **10** numberless **13** multitudinous
Ino *brother:* **9** Polydorus *father:* **6** Cadmus *grandfather:* **6** Agenor *husband:* **7** Athamas *mother:* **8** Harmonia *sister:* **5** Agave **6** Semele **7** Autonoë *son:* **8** Learchus, Palaemon **10** Melicertes
inobtrusive **4** meek **5** muted, quiet **6** modest **7** subdued **8** discreet, tasteful **10** restrained
inoculate **5** imbue, shoot, steep **6** infuse **7** implant, suffuse **9** vaccinate
inoffensive **5** bland **7** neutral **8** harmless **9** innocuous, peaceable
inopportune **8** ill-timed, mistimed, untimely **12** unseasonable
inordinate **5** undue **6** wanton **7** extreme **8** overmuch **9** excessive **10** exorbitant, gratuitous, immoderate, irrational **11** extravagant, intemperate, superfluous, uncalled-for **12** unreasonable **13** extraordinary
inorganic **7** mineral **10** artificial
in passing **5** aside **6** obiter **7** by the by **8** by the bye, by the way **12** incidentally
in perpetuum **4** ever **6** always **7** forever, for good **8** evermore, for keeps **9** eternally **10** enduringly **11** forevermore
input **4** data **6** advice, energy **7** comment, counsel, opinion **8** feedback, guidance, material, stimulus **11** information
inquest **5** probe **7** hearing, inquiry **11** examination **13** investigation
inquietude **5** angst **6** unease, unrest **7** anxiety, ferment, turmoil **8** distress **10** uneasiness **11** restiveness **12** restlessness **13** Sturm und Drang
inquire **3** ask, pry **4** seek **5** probe, query **7** examine **8** question **9** catechize **11** interrogate, investigate
inquiry **5** audit, probe, query **7** hearing **8** grilling, question, research, scrutiny **11** examination, questioning **13** investigation
inquisition **4** hunt **5** probe, quest, trial **6** search **7** inquiry **8** grilling, research **11** examination **13** interrogation, investigation
inquisitive **4** nosy **5** nosey **6** prying, snoopy **7** curious **8** meddling, snooping **9** intrusive **10** meddlesome **11** questioning
inquisitor **10** Torquemada (Tomás de)
in re **4** as to **5** about, as for **7** apropos **9** as regards, regarding **10** as respects, concerning, respecting **12** with regard to **13** with respect to
in respect to see **in re**
inroad **4** raid **5** foray **7** advance **8** invasion **9** incursion **12** encroachment
ins and outs **5** ropes **6** quirks **7** details **8** minutiae, oddities **11** incidentals, particulars **12** lay of the land
insane **3** mad, off **4** daft, nuts **5** batty, crazy, daffy, dotty, loony, manic, nutsy, nutty, rabid, silly, wacky **6** absurd, crazed, cuckoo, maniac, raving, schizo, screwy, teched **7** berserk, bonkers, cracked, haywire, lunatic, tetched, touched, unsound **8** demented, deranged, unhinged **9** eccentric, psychotic **10** disordered, irrational, moonstruck, unbalanced **11** harebrained **12** crackbrained, preposterous, unreasonable
insane asylum **6** bedlam **8** loony bin, madhouse, nuthouse, snake pit **10** sanatorium, sanitarium
insanity **5** folly, mania **6** frenzy, lunacy **7** madness **8** delirium, delusion, dementia, hysteria, illusion **9** craziness, dottiness, psychosis **11** derangement, psychopathy

insatiable 6 crying, greedy, urgent **7** exigent **8** pressing, ravenous **9** clamorous, demanding, voracious **10** quenchless **11** importunate **12** unappeasable, unquenchable

inscribe 4 etch, list **5** carve, enter, print, write **6** enroll, record **7** engrave, engross, impress, imprint **8** dedicate, enscroll, register

inscription 5 title **6** legend **7** epigram, epitaph, heading **8** epigraph **10** dedication ***Calvary:*** **4** INRI

inscrutable 6 arcane **7** deadpan **10** mysterious, poker-faced, sphinxlike, unknowable, unreadable **12** impenetrable, unfathomable

insect 3 bee, bug, fly **6** beetle ***adult:*** **5** imago ***antenna:*** **4** palp **6** feeler, palpus ***combining form:*** **5** entom **6** entomo ***covering:*** **6** chitin ***genus:*** **4** Nepa ***immature:*** **4** grub, pupa **5** larva, nymph **6** larvae (plural), maggot **8** wriggler **9** chrysalis **11** caterpillar ***kind:*** **3** ant, bee **4** flea, moth, wasp **5** aphid, scale **6** bedbug, beefly, beetle, cicada, earwig, hornet, mantid, mantis, mayfly **7** ant lion, cricket, firefly, June bug, katydid, ladybug, termite **8** honeybee, horsefly, housefly, lacewing, mosquito, stinkbug **9** bumblebee, butterfly, damselfly, dragonfly **10** silverfish, springtail **11** grasshopper **12** walkingstick ***luminous:*** **7** firefly **8** glowworm ***molt:*** **7** ecdysis ***moth:*** **4** luna **5** gypsy **6** miller, sphinx **7** noctuid, pyralid, tortrix, tussock **8** cecropia, cinnabar, forester, sphingid **9** clearwing, geometrid, saturniid, tortricid **10** Polyphemus ***multi-legged:*** **8** diplopod **9** centipede, millipede ***noisy:*** **6** cicada ***part:*** **4** palp **5** cerci (plural) **6** arista, cercus, labium, labrum, ocelli (plural), palpus, thorax **7** antenna, maxilla, ocellus **8** antennae (plural), mandible, maxillae (plural) **9** proboscis, spiracles **10** ovipositor **11** exoskeleton ***pest:*** **4** flea, lice (plural), mite **5** louse, midge, scale **7** blowfly, termite **8** horsefly, housefly, mealybug **9** cockroach, gypsy moth **10** boll weevil, Hessian fly, silverfish ***science:*** **10** entomology ***stage:*** **6** instar ***sucking:*** **5** aphid ***winged:*** **5** alate ***wingless:*** **4** flea, lice (plural) **5** louse **8** firebrat **10** silverfish, springtail **11** bristletail

insecticide 3 DDT **5** mirex, naled **6** aldrin, endrin **7** lindane, phorate **8** carbaryl, dieldrin, rotenone **9** chlordane, malathion, parathion **10** permethrin

insecure 5 shaky **6** unsafe, unsure, wobbly **7** anxious **8** unstable **9** uncertain **10** precarious **11** unconfident **12** apprehensive

inseminate 7 implant, instill **9** fertilize, pollinate **10** impregnate

insensate 4 dull, hard, numb **5** stony **6** brutal, numbed **7** callous **8** comatose **9** bloodless, heartless, impassive, unfeeling

insensibility 4 coma **6** apathy, torpor **8** lethargy, stoicism **12** indifference

insensible 4 cold, dead, dull, hard, numb, rapt **5** stoic **6** asleep, intent, numbed, obtuse, stolid **7** callous **8** absorbed, comatose, deadened, hardened, obdurate **9** apathetic, bloodless, engrossed, impassive, unfeeling **11** unconscious **12** anesthetized

insensitive 4 dull, hard, numb, rude **5** crass **6** numbed, obtuse, unkind **7** callous **8** benumbed, deadened, hardened, tactless, uncaring **9** bloodless, heartless, unfeeling **10** anesthetic, impossible **11** indifferent, unconcerned **12** anesthetized, unresponsive

insert 5 enter **7** implant, obtrude **9** interpose **10** interleave **11** intercalate, interpolate

insertion 8 addendum, addition **13** interpolation ***symbol:*** **5** caret

in short 7 briefly, tersely **9** concisely **10** succinctly

inside 6 closet, secret, within **7** private **8** hush-hush, interior **12** confidential ***combining form:*** **4** endo

insidious 3 sly **4** foxy, wily **6** artful, crafty, subtle, tricky **7** cunning, gradual **8** creeping, guileful **9** deceitful **13** surreptitious

insight 6 acumen, aperçu, wisdom **8** sagacity, sapience **9** intuition **11** discernment, penetration **13** understanding

insightful 4 keen, sage, wise **7** gnostic, knowing **9** intuitive, sagacious **10** discerning, perceptive **11** penetrating

insignia 4 mark, sign **5** badge **6** emblem **8** brassard **10** decoration

insignificant 4 mere, puny **5** dinky, minor, petty, small **6** casual, little, minute, paltry **7** minimal, trivial **8** nugatory, trifling **9** secondary, small-time **10** negligible **11** Mickey Mouse, minor-league, unimportant

insincere 5 false, lying, phony **6** double, forced, hollow, phoney, shifty, tricky **7** feigned **8** mala fide, slippery, spurious **9** deceitful, deceptive, dishonest, pretended, simulated **10** left-handed, mendacious, untruthful **11** dissembling, double-faced **12** hypocritical

insinuate 4 hint **5** imply **6** inject, insert, work in, worm in **7** implant, instill, suggest **9** introduce

insipid 4 drab, dull, mild, pale, thin, weak **5** banal, bland, vapid **6** jejune, watery **7** mundane, prosaic, tedious **8** bromidic, lifeless, ordinary **9** innocuous, tasteless **10** flavorless, monotonous, namby-pamby, wishy-washy **11** commonplace

insist **4** hold **5** argue, claim, swear **6** affirm, assert, demand, stress **7** certify, contend, declare, require, testify **8** maintain

insistent **6** crying, dogged, urgent **7** adamant, burning, clamant, exigent **8** emphatic, forceful, pressing, resolute **9** assertive, clamorous, obtrusive **10** determined, imperative, relentless **11** persevering

insolence **4** gall, guff, sass **5** brass, cheek, nerve **8** audacity, boldness, chutzpah, contempt, rudeness **9** arrogance, impudence **10** brazenness, disrespect, effrontery **11** haughtiness, presumption **12** impertinence

insolent **4** bold, flip, pert, rude **5** cocky, lofty, sassy, saucy **6** brazen, cheeky **7** haughty, uncivil **8** arrogant, cavalier, flippant, impolite, impudent, superior **9** audacious, barefaced, bold-faced **10** disdainful, peremptory **11** impertinent **12** contumelious, discourteous

insouciance **6** aplomb **9** disregard, unconcern **10** breeziness **11** disinterest, nonchalance **12** carelessness, heedlessness, indifference

insouciant **4** airy, flip **6** blithe, breezy, casual, jaunty **8** carefree, flippant, heedless **9** easygoing **10** nonchalant, untroubled **11** indifferent, thoughtless, unconcerned **12** devil-may-care, happy-go-lucky, lighthearted

inspect **3** con, vet **4** scan, view **5** audit, check, probe, study **6** review, size up, survey **7** canvass, examine, observe **8** appraise, check out, look over, question **9** check over **10** scrutinize **11** investigate

inspiration **4** idea, muse **6** animus, genius, vision **7** insight **8** afflatus **9** brainwave, influence **10** brainchild, brainstorm, creativity **13** enlightenment

inspire **4** fire, stir **5** elate, exalt, imbue, rouse **6** arouse, excite, foment, incite, prompt, strike **7** animate, enliven, impress, instill, quicken **8** motivate **9** encourage, galvanize, influence, stimulate **10** exhilarate

inspiring **6** moving **7** awesome, rousing **8** exalting, stirring **9** animating, uplifting **10** vitalizing

inspirit **4** fire, lift, spur, stir **5** cheer, elate, exalt, liven, rally, rouse, spark, steel **6** arouse, excite, incite, kindle, revive, uplift, vivify **7** animate, comfort, console, delight, enliven, gladden, hearten, nourish, quicken, refresh, restore **8** activate, embolden, energize, revivify, vitalize **9** encourage, stimulate **10** invigorate, strengthen

instability **8** fluidity **9** shakiness **10** insecurity, volatility **11** inconstancy **12** unsteadiness

install **4** seat, vest **5** put in, set up **6** induct, invest **8** ensconce, enthrone, entrench **9** establish

instance **4** case, cite, item **6** detail, ground, reason, sample **7** example **8** specimen **10** particular **12** illustration

instant **3** sec **4** wink **5** flash, jiffy, point, shake, trice **6** moment, second, urgent **7** current, exigent, present **8** existent, occasion, pressing **9** heartbeat, immediate, insistent, twinkling **10** imperative, present-day

instantaneous **4** fast **5** quick, rapid **9** immediate, ligntning, momentary **11** hair-trigger, split-second

instantly **3** now, PDQ **4** ASAP, stat **6** at once, pronto **8** directly **9** forthwith, right away **11** immediately

instead **4** else **6** in lieu, rather **11** alternately **13** alternatively

instigate **4** abet, fire, goad, plan, plot, prod, spur, urge **5** egg on, impel, raise **6** excite, foment, incite, stir up, whip up **7** provoke, suggest **8** motivate **9** stimulate **10** bring about

instill **5** imbue **6** impart, infuse, inject **7** implant, suffuse **8** engender **9** inculcate, introduce

instinct **4** nose **5** hunch, sense **7** feeling, impulse **8** aptitude, behavior **9** intuition **10** proclivity, sixth sense **11** gut reaction

instinctive **3** gut **6** inborn, innate, normal **7** natural **8** habitual, inherent, visceral **9** automatic, ingrained, intrinsic, intuitive, reflexive, unlearned **10** congenital, unprompted **11** involuntary, spontaneous, unmeditated

instinctual **6** reflex **7** natural, routine **8** habitual, knee-jerk, untaught **9** automatic, impulsive, intuitive, reflexive **10** mechanical, unthinking **11** involuntary, spontaneous, unconscious

institute **5** begin, found, set up, start **6** decree, launch, ordain **7** academy, pioneer, usher in **8** initiate, organize **9** establish, introduce, originate **10** inaugurate **12** organization

institution **4** firm, rite **5** habit **6** custom **9** enactment **10** foundation **13** establishment ***kind:*** **6** asylum, school **7** academy, college **8** hospital **10** sanatorium, sanitarium, sanitorium, university

instruct **4** show **5** coach, drill, guide, order, steer, teach, train, tutor **6** direct, enjoin, inform, school **7** apprise, command, counsel, educate, lecture **9** enlighten, prescribe

instruction **5** drill **6** advice, lesson **7** precept **8** coaching, guidance, teaching, training, tutelage **9** catechism, education, schooling

10 directions ***place of:*** **6** school **7** academe, academy, college **10** university
instructive 8 didactic, edifying, pedantic **9** pedagogic **11** educational, explanatory, explicative, informative **12** enlightening
instructor 3 don **4** guru **5** coach, guide, swami, tutor **6** mentor **7** teacher, trainer **8** educator, lecturer **9** pedagogue, preceptor
instrument 4 deed, gear, mean, tool **5** agent, means, organ **6** agency, device, gadget, medium **7** utensil, vehicle **9** apparatus, appliance, machinery, mechanism **11** contraption, contrivance **13** paraphernalia ***aircraft:*** **5** radar, radio **7** compass **9** altimeter, gyroscope **10** altazimuth, tachometer **11** transponder ***calculating:*** **6** abacus **8** computer **9** slide rule ***graphic:*** **6** camera **8** otoscope **9** telescope **10** binoculars, microscope **11** fluoroscope, stethoscope, stroboscope **12** bronchoscope, oscilloscope, spectrograph, spectroscope ***measuring:*** **4** gage **5** clock, gauge, radar, scale, sonar **7** alidade, ammeter, balance, caliper, sextant, transit **8** quadrant **9** altimeter, astrolabe, barometer, bolometer, manometer, pedometer, sonometer, voltmeter **10** anemometer, Fathometer, hydrometer, hygrometer, micrometer, radiometer, radiosonde, spirometer, tachometer, theodolite **11** chronometer, lie detector, range finder, seismograph, speedometer, thermometer **12** electroscope, galvanometer, oscillograph, oscilloscope **13** Geiger counter, potentiometer ***medical:*** **6** lancet, trocar **7** curette, forceps, specula (plural) **8** tenacula (plural) **9** tenaculum ***radiation-producing:*** **5** laser, maser (see also **implement; musical instrument; tool**)
instrumental 5 vital **6** useful **7** crucial, helpful **9** conducive, essential, necessary, requisite **10** imperative **13** indispensable
instrumentality 5 agent, force, means, organ **6** agency, energy, medium **7** channel, vehicle **8** ministry **9** mechanism
insubordinate 6 unruly **8** factious, mutinous **9** fractious, seditious **10** headstrong, rebellious, refractory **11** disobedient, intractable, uncompliant **12** contumacious, recalcitrant, ungovernable
insubstantial 4 airy, weak **5** frail **6** feeble, flimsy, jejune **7** fragile, tenuous **8** bodiless, ethereal **9** unfleshly **10** intangible **11** disembodied **12** apparitional
insufferable 10 unbearable **11** intolerable, unendurable **13** insupportable
insufficiency 4 lack **6** dearth **7** paucity, poverty **8** scarcity, shortage **10** deficiency, inadequacy, scantiness, scarceness **11** defalcation
insufficient 5 scant **6** scanty, scarce, skimpy **7** lacking, wanting **10** inadequate, incomplete
insular 5 local **6** narrow **7** bigoted, limited **8** confined, isolated, secluded **9** illiberal, parochial, sectarian, small-town **10** prejudiced, provincial, restricted
insulate 6 cut off, enisle **7** isolate **8** close off **9** segregate, sequester
insult 4 gibe, jeer, mock, slap, slur **5** abuse, fleer, scoff, scorn, shame, sneer, taunt **6** debase, deride, offend, revile **7** affront, disdain, obloquy, offense, outrage **8** derision, disgrace, ignominy, ridicule **9** contumely, humiliate **10** opprobrium **12** vituperation
insurance 8 guaranty, warranty **10** protection ***agency:*** **7** actuary **8** adjuster **11** underwriter ***term:*** **6** policy **7** annuity **8** coverage **9** bordereau **11** beneficiary ***type:*** **4** crop, fire **5** crime, flood, title **6** dental **7** no-fault **8** accident, casualty **9** liability **10** disability, homeowner's **11** workers' comp
insure 5 cinch, guard **6** shield **7** confirm, protect **9** guarantee, safeguard **10** underwrite
insurgent 5 rebel **6** anarch **8** factious, frondeur, mutineer, mutinous, revolter **9** anarchist, seditious **10** incendiary, rebellious **12** contumacious **13** insubordinate, revolutionary
insurrection 4 coup **6** mutiny, putsch, revolt, rising **8** uprising **9** rebellion
insurrectionist 5 rebel **6** anarch **8** frondeur, mutineer, revolter **10** malcontent
insusceptible 6 exempt, immune **9** resistant **10** impervious **11** unreceptive
intact 5 sound, whole **6** entire, unhurt, virgin **7** perfect **8** complete, unbroken, unmarred, virginal **9** undamaged, uninjured, untouched **10** unimpaired
intangible 4 airy **5** vague **7** elusive, ghostly **8** ethereal **10** evanescent, immaterial, impalpable **11** incorporeal
integer 4 unit **5** digit **6** entity, figure, number **7** numeral **11** whole number
integral 4 full **5** whole **6** entire **7** perfect **8** complete, inherent **9** composite, elemental, essential, necessary, requisite **11** constituent **13** indispensable
integrate 3 mix **4** fuse, join, link **5** blend, merge, unify, unite **6** embody, mingle **7** combine, conjoin **8** coalesce **9** harmonize, reconcile **10** amalgamate, assimilate, coordinate, synthesize **11** consolidate, desegregate
integrity 5 honor **6** virtue **7** honesty, probity **8**

cohesion **9** coherence, constancy, rectitude, soundness, wholeness **12** completeness
integument 4 coat **5** testa **7** coating, cuticle **8** covering, envelope
intellect 3 wit **4** mind **5** brain **6** acumen, brains, genius, reason, smarts **9** intuition, mentality **12** intelligence **13** comprehension, understanding
intellectual 5 brain **6** brainy, mental, pundit **7** bookish, egghead, erudite, psychic, thinker **8** academic, cerebral, highbrow, longhair **9** scholarly
intelligence 3 wit **4** dope, info, mind, news, word **5** brain, savvy, sense **6** acuity, acumen, brains, notice, reason, smarts, wisdom **7** hearsay, tidings **8** aptitude, judgment, learning, sagacity **9** knowledge, mentality, mother wit **10** brainpower, shrewdness
intelligent 4 keen, wise **5** acute, alert, aware, quick, sharp, smart, sound **6** adroit, astute, brainy, bright, clever, shrewd **7** cunning, knowing, logical **8** rational, sensible **9** brilliant, ingenious, sagacious **10** reasonable **11** quick-witted, ready-witted **13** perspicacious
intelligentsia 7 clerisy **8** literati, vanguard **10** avant-garde, illuminati
intelligible 5 clear, lucid, plain
intemperance 6 excess **7** license **9** depravity **10** debauchery, profligacy **11** dissipation, drunkenness **12** immoderation, incontinence
intemperate 5 harsh **6** bitter, brutal, severe **7** drunken, extreme, violent **8** bibulous **9** crapulous, dissolute, excessive **10** dissipated, exorbitant, gluttonous, immoderate, inordinate, profligate **12** unrestrained **13** overindulgent
intend 3 aim, try **4** mean, plan **5** essay, spell **6** assign, denote, design, scheme, strive **7** attempt, connote, propose, purpose, signify **8** endeavor **9** designate
intended 6 fiancé **7** engaged, fiancée **8** destined, plighted, promised, proposed **9** affianced, betrothed **10** calculated, deliberate
intense 4 keen **5** acute, vivid **6** ardent, fervid, fierce, severe, strong **7** extreme, fervent, furious, violent, zealous **8** powerful, vehement **9** assiduous, excessive, exquisite **10** heightened **12** concentrated
intensify 4 rise **5** mount, rouse **6** accent, heat up, stress **7** enhance, sharpen **8** escalate, heighten, increase, redouble **9** aggravate, emphasize **10** accentuate, aggrandize, exacerbate **11** concentrate
intensity 6 energy, fervor **7** passion **8** emphasis, ferocity, fervency, loudness **9** vehemence
intensive 6 all-out **7** zealous **8** sweeping, thorough **10** exhaustive **12** concentrated
pronoun: **6** itself, myself **7** herself, himself **8** yourself **9** ourselves **10** themselves, yourselves
intent 3 aim, set **4** bent, goal, plan, rapt, will **5** eager, fixed **6** design, import, object **7** decided, earnest, engaged, meaning, purport, purpose, riveted, wrapped **8** absorbed, conation, decisive, diligent, immersed, resolute, resolved, sedulous, volition **9** engrossed, objective, wrapped up **10** determined
intention 3 aim, end **4** goal, hope, plan, wish **6** design, desire, object **7** meaning, purpose **8** ambition **9** objective **10** aspiration
intentional 5 meant **7** advised, studied, willful, willing, witting **8** designed, proposed **9** voluntary **10** considered, deliberate **12** premeditated
intentionally 9 on purpose, purposely
inter 4 bury **5** plant **6** entomb, inhume **9** lay to rest
interact 9 cooperate **11** collaborate
interbreed 5 cross **9** hybridize **10** mongrelize
intercede 6 step in **7** mediate **9** arbitrate
intercept 4 grab **5** catch, seize, steal **6** cut off, hijack
intercessor 5 agent **6** broker **8** advocate, mediator **9** go-between, middleman
interconnect 4 join, link, mesh **5** unite **6** couple, hook up, link up
intercourse 3 sex **5** trade, truck **7** contact, dealing, traffic **8** business, commerce, dealings **9** communion **10** connection, networking **11** give-and-take **12** conversation **13** communication
intercross 9 hybridize **10** mongrelize
interdict 3 ban, bar **4** veto **5** block, taboo **6** cut off, enjoin, forbid, outlaw **7** censure, condemn, embargo **8** disallow, prohibit, sanction **9** proscribe **11** prohibition
interest 4 gain, grab, hook, lure, pull **5** pique, stake, tempt **6** appeal, arouse, behalf, engage, profit, regard **7** attract, concern, engross, involve, welfare **8** appeal to, intrigue **9** attention, curiosity, fascinate, tantalize, well-being **10** prosperity
interested 4 rapt **5** drawn **7** curious, partial **8** invested, partisan **9** attentive
interface 3 GUI **6** border **8** boundary **9** cooperate **11** communicate
interfere 6 butt in, horn in, meddle, step in **7** barge in, intrude
interim 3 gap **5** break, pause **6** acting, breach, hiatus, lacuna, pro tem **7** stopgap, time-out **8** downtime, meantime **9** makeshift, temporary **10** pro tempore **11** provisional

interior 3 gut **4** pith **5** belly, bosom, heart, inner **6** center, inland, inside, inward, marrow **8** visceral **9** heartland **10** hinterland
interject 3 add **6** fill in, insert **7** throw in
interjection *agreement:* 4 amen **5** roger **6** righto **7** right on ***attention-getter:* 3** hey **4** ahem, ahoy, psst **6** yoo-hoo ***cheer:* 3** rah, yay **5** wahoo **6** hooray, hurrah, hurray ***contempt:* 4** pooh **5** pshaw ***disappointment:* 4** rats **5** shoot **6** shucks ***disapproval:* 3** boo, fie ***disbelief:* 2** aw **3** huh ***disgust:* 3** bah, boo, pah, ugh **4** rats, yuck **5** faugh, yecch **6** phooey ***dismay:* 2** oy **4** oh no, uh-oh ***dismissal:* 3** git **4** shoo ***in golf:* 4** fore ***in hunting:* 6** yoicks ***in marching:* 3** hup, hut ***joy:* 4** whee **6** hooray, hurrah, hurray, yippee **7** hosanna, whoopee **8** alleluia **10** hallelujah ***mild apology:* 4** oops **6** whoops ***mild oath:* 3** gad **4** darn, drat, egad, geez, gosh, heck, jeez **5** egads, golly, zooks **6** jiminy, zounds **7** begorra, gee whiz, jeepers **8** gadzooks **13** gee whillikers ***O.K.:* 5** roger, wilco ***pain:* 2** ow **4** ouch ***regret:* 3** woe **4** alas **5** alack **8** lackaday ***relief:* 4** phew ***silence:* 2** sh **3** shh ***sneeze:* 5** achoo **6** atchoo **7** kerchoo ***sorrow:* 4** alas **5** alack **8** lackaday ***stop:* 4** whoa **5** avast ***surprise:* 2** ah, ho, lo, oh **3** aha, huh, oho, wow **4** gosh, oops **5** blimy, yikes, yipes, zowie **6** blimey ***triumph:* 3** aha, hah **6** eureka (see also **exclamation**)
interlace 3 mix **5** braid, plait, twine, weave **7** entwine **9** alternate
interlard 3 mix **6** mingle
interlock 4 mesh **5** unite **6** enmesh
interlocuter 4 host **5** emcee
interlope 6 butt in, horn in, meddle **7** intrude **8** encroach, infringe **9** interfere
interlude 4 halt, lull, rest **5** break, idyll, letup, pause, spell **6** hiatus, recess **7** episode, respite **8** breather, entr'acte, meantime, stoppage **9** meanwhile **10** suspension
intermediary 3 mid **4** mean **5** agent, envoy, organ **6** agency, broker, center, medium, middle, midway **7** central, channel, vehicle **8** delegate, emissary, mediator, ministry **9** go-between, middleman
intermediate 3 mid **4** fair, mean, so-so **5** mesne **6** broker, center, middle, midway, step in **7** arbiter, average, between, central, halfway **8** middling **9** arbitrate, go-between, middleman
intermediator 6 broker **7** arbiter, liaison, referee **9** go-between, middleman
interment 6 burial **9** sepulture **10** inhumation
intermesh 4 lock **6** engage **8** dovetail
interminable 7 endless, eternal, lasting **8** constant, infinite, unending **9** boundless, ceaseless, continual, limitless, permanent, perpetual, unceasing **10** protracted **11** everlasting, never-ending
intermission 4 lull, rest, stop **5** break, pause, spell **6** hiatus, recess **7** latency, respite, time-out **8** abeyance, dormancy, interval **10** quiescence, suspension **11** parenthesis
intermit 4 halt, stay **5** break, defer, delay **6** arrest, hold up, put off **7** suspend **8** postpone, prorogue **9** interrupt **11** discontinue
intermittent 6 broken, cyclic, fitful, serial **8** cyclical, metrical, periodic, seasonal, sporadic **9** irregular, recurrent, recurring, spasmodic, stop-and-go **10** occasional
intermix 4 meld **5** blend **6** mingle **8** comingle, compound **9** commingle, integrate **10** amalgamate
intermixture 4 brew **5** blend **7** amalgam **8** compound **9** composite, synthesis **12** amalgamation **13** miscegenation
intern 4 jail **6** immure **7** confine, impound, put away, trainee **8** imprison **11** incarcerate
internal 6 native **7** private **8** visceral **10** subjective ***concretion:* 9** gallstone ***prefix:* 5** intra
internal organs 4 guts **6** bowels, vitals **7** innards, viscera **8** entrails **10** intestines, penetralia
international organization 2 UN **3** FAO, IAM, ICJ, IFC, ILO, ITO, ITU, OAS, WHO, WMO, WTO **4** IAAF, IABA, IAEA, IARU, IATA, ICAO, IFIP, IMCO, NATO **5** ICFTU, SEATO **6** UNESCO, UNICEF
Internet forum 9 newsgroup
internuncio 5 envoy **6** bearer, legate **7** carrier, courier **8** delegate, emissary **9** go-between, messenger, middleman
interpolate 3 add **5** admit, annex, enter **6** append, fill in, inject, insert **7** throw in **9** introduce
interpose 6 butt in, fill in, insert, meddle, step in **7** intrude, mediate, obtrude, throw in **8** moderate **9** arbitrate, insinuate, introduce, negotiate **11** come between
interpret 5 gloss **6** decode **7** explain, expound **8** annotate, construe **9** elucidate, explicate **10** paraphrase
interpretation 5 gloss **7** meaning, reading, version **8** exegesis **9** construal, rendering **11** explanation, translation
interpretive 8 exegetic **10** diagnostic, exegetical, expository **11** explanatory, explicatory
interregnum 5 break, lapse, pause **6** hiatus **7** time-out
interrogate 3 ask **4** pump, quiz **5** grill, query **7** examine **8** question **9** catechize **12** cross-examine

interrupt 4 halt, stay, stop **5** abort, break, cut in **7** break in, chime in, suspend **8** cut short
interruption 3 gap **4** halt **5** break, pause, split **6** breach, cutoff, hiatus, lacuna, recess **7** caesura **8** stoppage
intersect 4 meet **5** cross **9** decussate **10** criss-cross
intersection 3 hub **4** node **8** crossing, junction, juncture **10** crossroads
intersperse 7 diffuse, scatter **8** sprinkle
interstice 3 gap **4** slit, slot, vent **5** chink, cleft, crack, space **6** breach, cavity, cranny **7** crevice, fissure, opening, orifice **8** aperture
intertwine 4 mesh **5** braid, plait, twist, weave **6** enlace **7** network **9** convolute **10** criss-cross
interval 3 gap **4** lull, wait **5** break, comma, delay, letup, pause, space **6** breach, hiatus, lacuna **7** caesura, interim, respite, time-out **8** downtime **9** pausation **11** parenthesis ***music:*** **4** rest
intervene 6 butt in, meddle, step in **7** intrude, mediate, obtrude
interweave 3 mix **4** fuse, join, knit, link, mesh **5** blend, plait, twine **6** enmesh **7** entwine, wreathe
intestinal 5 ileal **7** colonic, jejunal **8** duodenal
intestinal fortitude 4 grit, guts **5** nerve, pluck, spunk **6** mettle, spirit **7** courage **8** backbone **10** resolution
intestine 3 gut **4** tube **5** bowel, canal **7** viscera (plural) ***combining form:*** **4** coli, colo **6** entero ***part:*** **5** cecum, colon, ileum **7** jejunum **8** duodenum
in the same place 6 ibidem
intimacy 9 closeness **11** familiarity **12** acquaintance
intimate 3 gut **4** cozy, dear, fond, hint **5** amigo, close, crony, imply, inner, privy **6** attest, friend, impart, loving, secret **7** comrade, connote, devoted, nearest, suggest **8** familiar, inherent **9** close-knit, companion, confidant, ingrained, insinuate, intrinsic **12** confidential
intimation 3 cue **4** clue, hint **5** shade, tinge, trace **6** breath **7** inkling **8** telltale **10** suggestion
intimidate 3 awe, cow **4** bait **5** bully, chivy, daunt, scare **6** badger, coerce, hector **7** buffalo, overawe **8** browbeat, bulldoze, bullyrag **9** strong-arm, terrorize
intolerable 10 unbearable **11** unendurable **12** insufferable **13** insupportable
intolerant 6 biased, narrow **7** bigoted **8** dogmatic **9** hidebound, illiberal **10** inflexible, prejudiced **11** small-minded **12** narrow-minded
intonation 5 chant, pitch **6** accent, timbre **7** cadence **8** chanting **10** inflection, modulation, recitation
intone 5 chant, croon, drone **10** cantillate
in toto 3 all **6** wholly **7** all told, en masse **10** altogether
intoxicant 5 booze, drink, hooch, sauce **6** hootch, liquor, rotgut **7** alcohol, spirits **9** aqua vitae, firewater, moonshine
intoxicated 3 lit, wet **4** high **5** blind, drunk, fried, giddy, lit up, oiled, stiff, tight, tipsy **6** blotto, bombed, canned, elated, juiced, loaded, looped, potted, sodden, soused, stewed, stoned, tanked, tiddly, zonked **7** blitzed, crocked, drunken, excited, maudlin, muddled, pickled, pie-eyed, sloshed, smashed, sozzled **8** cockeyed, polluted, squiffed **9** crapulous, plastered **11** exhilarated
intoxication 3 joy **5** bliss **6** frenzy **7** ecstasy, elation, rapture **8** delirium, euphoria **9** transport **10** exaltation **11** drunkenness, inebriation
intractable 4 wild **5** balky **6** mulish, ornery, unruly **7** froward, willful **8** mutinous, obdurate, perverse, stubborn **9** fractious, obstinate, pigheaded, unbending **10** bullheaded, headstrong, inflexible, rebellious, refractory, unyielding **12** pertinacious, recalcitrant, ungovernable **13** undisciplined
intransigent 5 rigid, tough **7** willful **8** obdurate, perverse, resolute, stubborn **9** obstinate, unbending, unpliable **10** refractory, self-willed, unyielding **12** contumacious, pertinacious
intrepid 4 bold, game **5** brave, gutsy, hardy **6** daring, heroic **7** doughty, gallant, valiant **8** fearless, resolute, stalwart, unafraid, valorous **9** audacious, dauntless, undaunted **10** courageous **11** adventurous, temerarious
intricate 4 mazy **6** daedal, knotty **7** complex, gordian, tangled **8** abstruse, involved, tortuous **9** Byzantine, claborate **10** circuitous, convoluted **11** complicated **12** labyrinthine **13** sophisticated
intrigue 4 plot, wile **5** amour, cabal, cheat, pique, trick **6** affair, appeal, excite, scheme **7** attract, beguile, collude, connive, liaison, romance **8** cogitate, conspire, contrive, interest **9** machinate **10** conspiracy **11** machination
intriguing 8 enticing **9** absorbing, beguiling **10** engrossing, entrancing **11** captivating, fascinating, stimulating
intrinsic see **inherent**
intrinsically 5 per se **6** as such **7** at heart **10** inherently

introduce 5 begin, enter, found, set up **6** broach, fill in, insert, launch, unveil, work in **7** bring up, implant, install, instill, precede, preface, present, propose, throw in, usher in **8** initiate, innovate **9** insinuate, institute, interject, interpose, originate **10** inseminate

introduction 5 debut, proem **6** lead-in **7** introit, opening, preface, prelude **8** entrance, exordium, foreword, overture, preamble, prologue, protases (plural), protasis **12** prolegomenon

introductory 5 basic **7** initial, nascent, opening **8** proemial **9** beginning, prefatory **10** elementary **11** preliminary, preparatory

intrude 5 cut in **6** butt in, horn in, impose, invade, meddle **7** barge in, burst in, presume **8** encroach, infringe, trespass **9** interfere, interlope, interrupt

intrusive 4 busy, nosy **5** nosey **6** prying, snoopy **7** curious **8** meddling, snooping **9** officious **10** meddlesome **11** impertinent

in truth 6 indeed, really, verily **8** actually, candidly **9** veritably

intuit 5 infer, sense **6** deduce, divine **7** surmise

intuition 5 hunch **7** feeling, inkling, insight **8** instinct **10** sixth sense **11** second sight **12** presentiment

intuitive 6 innate **7** natural **8** unwilled, visceral **10** unthinking **11** instinctive, instinctual, involuntary, spontaneous, unconscious

Inuit 6 Eskimo

inundate 4 glut **5** drown, flood, swamp, whelm **6** deluge, engulf **7** overrun **8** overflow, submerge **9** overwhelm

inundation 5 flood, spate **6** deluge **7** Niagara, torrent **8** cataract, flooding, overflow **9** avalanche, cataclysm, landslide **10** cloudburst

inure 5 steel, train **6** harden, season **7** prepare, toughen **8** accustom **9** acclimate, habituate **10** discipline **11** familiarize

inutile 6 no-good **7** useless **8** unusable **9** valueless, worthless

invade 4 loot, raid **6** breach, occupy, ravage **7** overrun, pillage, plunder **8** encroach, infringe, trespass **9** penetrate

invader 8 intruder **10** encroacher, interloper, trespasser **11** infiltrator

invalid 3 bad **4** null, sick, void **5** false **6** ailing, infirm, shut-in, sickly **7** expired, unsound **8** baseless, disabled **9** bedridden, illogical, sophistic **10** fallacious, irrational **11** null and void **12** convalescent

invalidate 4 undo, void **5** annul, quash **6** cancel, offset, vacate **7** abolish, nullify **9** discredit, repudiate **10** counteract, disqualify, neutralize

invaluable 7 crucial **8** precious **9** essential, priceless **11** beyond price, inestimable **13** irreplaceable

invariable 4 same **5** fixed **6** static, steady **7** uniform **8** constant **9** continual, immovable, immutable, unfailing, unvarying **10** changeless, consistent, unchanging **11** inalterable, unalterable **12** unchangeable

invariably 4 ever **6** always **7** forever

invasion 4 raid **5** foray **6** attack, inroad **7** assault, offense **8** trespass **9** incursion, intrusion, offensive, onslaught **12** encroachment

invective 5 abuse **6** tirade **7** abusive, obloquy **8** diatribe, jeremiad **9** contumely, philippic, truculent **10** opprobrium, scurrility, scurrilous **11** opprobrious **12** billingsgate, contumelious, vituperation, vituperative

inveigh 4 kick, rail, rant **6** object **7** protest **8** complain **9** fulminate **11** expostulate, remonstrate

inveigle 4 coax, lure **5** decoy, snare, tempt **6** allure, cajole, entice, entrap, lead on, rope in, seduce, wangle **7** blarney, win over **8** blandish, butter up, maneuver, persuade

invent 4 coin, mint **6** cook up, create, design, devise, make up, patent, vamp up **7** concoct, dream up, fashion, hatch up, pioneer, think up **8** conceive, contrive, discover, engineer, envision **9** fabricate, formulate, originate

invention 7 coinage, fiction **8** creation **10** brainchild, innovation **11** contrivance

inventive 7 fertile, teeming **8** creative, fruitful, original **9** demiurgic, ingenious **10** innovative, innovatory **11** imaginative

inventor 5 maker **6** author, father, mother **7** creator, founder **8** engineer **9** architect, generator, innovator **10** discoverer, introducer, originator ***air brake:*** **12** Westinghouse (George) ***air conditioning:*** **7** Carrier (Willis) ***automobile:*** **7** Daimler (Gottlieb) ***ballpoint pen:*** **4** Loud (John) ***barbed wire:*** **7** Glidden (Joseph Farwell) ***barometer:*** **10** Torricelli (Evangelista) ***bifocal lens:*** **8** Franklin (Benjamin) ***camera:*** **7** Eastman (George) ***cash register:*** **5** Ritty (James) ***cotton gin:*** **7** Whitney (Eli) ***cylinder lock:*** **4** Yale (Linus) ***dirigible:*** **8** Zeppelin (Ferdinand von) ***dynamite:*** **5** Nobel (Alfred) ***electric battery:*** **5** Volta (Alessandro) ***electric fan:*** **7** Wheeler (George) ***electric organ:*** **7** Hammond (Laurens) ***electric razor:*** **6** Schick (Jacob) ***electric stove:*** **7** Hadaway (W. S.) ***elevator:*** **4** Otis (Elisha) ***fountain pen:*** **8** Waterman (Lewis) ***friction match:*** **6**

Walker (John) ***gyrocompass:*** **6** Sperry (Elmer) ***helicopter:*** **8** Sikorsky (Igor) ***hot-air balloon:*** **11** Montgolfier (Jacques, Joseph) ***incandescent lamp:*** **6** Edison (Thomas Alva) ***induction motor:*** **5** Tesla (Nikola) ***lawn mower:*** **5** Hills (Amariah) ***Linotype:*** **12** Mergenthaler (Ottmar) ***logarithm:*** **6** Napier (John) ***machine gun:*** **7** Gatling (Richard) ***microphone:*** **8** Berliner (Emile) ***microwave oven:*** **7** Spencer (Percy) ***movable type:*** **9** Gutenberg (Johannes) ***parachute:*** **9** Blanchard (Jean-Pierre) ***pendulum clock:*** **7** Huygens (Christiaan) ***phonograph:*** **6** Edison (Thomas Alva) ***photography:*** **6** Niepce (Nicéphore), Talbot (W. H. Fox) **8** Daguerre (Louis) ***piano:*** **10** Cristofori (Bartolomeo) ***radio:*** **7** Marconi (Guglielmo) ***reaper:*** **9** McCormick (Cyrus) ***revolver:*** **4** Colt (Samuel) ***rocket engine:*** **7** Goddard (Robert) ***safety pin:*** **4** Hunt (Walter) ***safety razor:*** **8** Gillette (King) ***sewing machine:*** **4** Howe (Elias) ***sleeping car:*** **7** Pullman (George) ***spinning jenny:*** **10** Hargreaves (James) ***steamboat:*** **5** Fitch (John) **6** Fulton (Robert), Miller (Patrick), Rumsey (James) **8** Jouffroy (Claude de) ***steam engine:*** **4** Watt (James) ***steam locomotive:*** **10** Stephenson (George) ***stethoscope:*** **7** Laënnec (René) ***submarine:*** **7** Holland (John Philip) ***synthesizer:*** **4** Moog (Robert) ***tank:*** **7** Swinton (Ernest) ***telegraph:*** **5** Morse (Samuel F. B.) ***telephone:*** **4** Bell (Alexander Graham) ***telescope:*** **10** Lippershey (Hans) ***television:*** **5** Baird (John) **6** Nipkow (Paul) **8** Zworykin (Vladimir) **10** Farnsworth (Philo) ***thermometer:*** **7** Galileo (Galilei) ***torpedo:*** **9** Whitehead (Robert) ***tractor:*** **5** Deere (John) ***transistor:*** **7** Bardeen (John) **8** Brattain (Walter), Shockley (William) ***vulcanized rubber:*** **8** Goodyear (Charles) ***writing for the blind:*** **7** Braille (Louis) ***zipper:*** **6** Judson (Whitcomb)

inventory 3 sum **4** fund, list **5** hoard, stock, store, tally **6** assets, digest, record, supply, survey **7** account, backlog, catalog, itemize, reserve, specify, summary **8** register, tabulate **9** catalogue, checklist, enumerate, reservoir, stockpile, summarize, synopsize

inverse 8 contrary, opposite

inversion 7 reverse **8** flipping, reversal, upending **9** about-face, turnabout, volte-face

invert 4 flip **5** upend **7** reverse **8** overturn, turn over **9** transpose

invertebrate 4 weak **5** timid **7** chicken, doormat, milksop **8** boneless, impotent, weakling **9** jellyfish, spineless **10** namby-pamby **11** ineffectual, milquetoast ***kind:*** **4** worm **6** insect, sponge **7** mollusc, mollusk **8** arachnid **9** arthropod **12** coelenterate

invest 4 gird, veil, wrap **5** adorn, array, dress, endow, imbue **6** clothe, confer, enfold, induct, infuse, ordain **7** empower, enclose, envelop, ingrain, install, suffuse

investigate 3 pry **4** sift **5** audit, probe, study **6** go into, search **7** dig into, examine, explore, inquire, inspect **8** check out, look into, muckrake, prospect, research **9** delve into **10** scrutinize **11** inquire into

investigation 5 audit, probe **6** survey **7** inquest, inquiry **8** research, scrutiny **11** fact-finding, inquisition

investigator 3 spy, tec **4** dick **5** hound **6** shamus, sleuth **7** gumshoe **8** hawkshaw, sherlock **9** detective **10** private eye

investiture 9 inaugural, induction **10** initiation, ordination **12** inauguration, installation, ratification

inveterate 3 old, set **5** fixed, sworn **6** rooted **7** abiding, chronic, settled **8** deep-dyed, enduring, habitual, hard-core, hardened, lifelong **9** confirmed, ingrained, perennial **10** continuing, deep-rooted, deep-seated, entrenched, habituated, persistent, persisting **11** established **12** incorrigible **13** dyed-in-the-wool

Invictus author 6 Henley (William Ernest)

invidious 7 envious, envying, jealous **9** green-eyed, obnoxious, resentful

invigorate 4 stir **5** brace, liven, pep up, rally, renew, rouse **6** perk up, vivify **7** animate, brace up, enliven, fortify, juice up, refresh, restore **8** energize, vitalize **9** reinforce, stimulate **10** rejuvenate, revitalize, strengthen

invincible 10 inviolable, unbeatable **11** impregnable, indomitable, insuperable **12** invulnerable, unassailable, undefeatable **13** unconquerable

in vino ____ 7 veritas

inviolable 4 safe **6** secure **10** impervious, sacrosanct **11** consecrated, impregnable **12** unassailable **13** incorruptible

invisible 6 hidden **9** concealed **10** intangible **12** unnoticeable **13** imperceptible

Invisible Man *author:* 5 Wells (H. G.) **7** Ellison (Ralph) ***character:*** **7** Griffin (Herbert)

invitation 4 call, lure **6** come-on **7** bidding, proffer **8** entreaty, proposal **10** enticement **11** proposition **12** solicitation

invite 3 ask, bid **4** call, lure **5** tempt **6** allure, call in, entice, summon **7** propose, request, solicit

inviting 8 engaging, enticing, tempting **9** appealing, beguiling, seductive **10** attractive, intriguing

invocation 6 appeal, prayer **8** entreaty, petition **11** conjuration, incantation **12** supplication

invoice 3 tab **4** bill, list **5** score **7** account **8** manifest **9** reckoning, statement **11** consignment

invoke 3 beg **4** pray **5** crave, plead **6** appeal, call on, effect **7** beseech, conjure, enforce, entreat, implore, solicit **8** call upon, petition **9** call forth, conjure up, implement, importune **10** supplicate

involuntary 6 forced, reflex **8** knee-jerk **9** automatic, impulsive, reflexive, unwitting **10** compulsory, unintended, unprompted **11** instinctive, spontaneous, unconscious, unmeditated **13** unintentional

involve 4 mire **6** affect, embody, engage, entail, take in **7** call for, concern, contain, embrace, embroil, include, require, subsume **8** comprise, entangle **9** encompass, implicate **10** complicate, comprehend **11** necessitate

involved 6 daedal, knotty **7** complex, gordian **8** confused **9** Byzantine, elaborate, intricate **10** convoluted **11** complicated **12** labyrinthine

invulnerable 6 immune, secure **10** impervious, invincible, unbeatable **11** impregnable, indomitable **12** unassailable

Io ***father:*** **7** Inachus ***guard:*** **5** Argus ***son:*** **7** Epaphus

iodine source 4 kelp

Iolanthe ***composer:*** **8** Sullivan (Arthur) ***librettist:*** **7** Gilbert (W. S.)

Iolcus king 5 Aeson **6** Pelias

Iole ***captor:*** **8** Heracles, Hercules ***father:*** **7** Eurytus ***husband:*** **6** Hyllus

ion 6 ligand ***kind:*** **5** anion **6** cation **8** thermion

Ion ***father:*** **6** Apollo ***mother:*** **6** Creusa ***stepfather:*** **6** Xuthus

Ionesco, Eugène ***play:*** **6** Chairs (The), Lesson (The) **10** Rhinoceros **11** Bald Soprano (The)

iota 3 bit, jot, ray **4** atom, hint, mite, whit **5** crumb, grain, ounce, scrap, shred, speck, trace **6** smidge, tittle **7** smidgen, smidgin **8** molecule, particle, smidgeon **9** scintilla

IOU 4 chit, debt ***part:*** **3** owe, you

Iowa ***capital:*** **9** Des Moines ***city:*** **4** Ames **7** Dubuque **8** Waterloo **9** Davenport, Sioux City **11** Cedar Rapids **13** Council Bluffs ***college, university:*** **5** Drake **8** Grinnell ***nickname:*** **7** Hawkeye (State) ***river:*** **9** Des Moines ***state bird:*** **9** goldfinch ***state flower:*** **15** wild prairie rose ***state tree:*** **3** oak

Iphicles ***brother:*** **8** Heracles, Hercules ***mother:*** **7** Alcmene ***son:*** **6** Iolaus

Iphigenia ***avenger:*** **12** Clytemnestra ***brother:*** **7** Orestes ***father:*** **9** Agamemnon ***mother:*** **12** Clytemnestra ***sister:*** **7** Electra

Iran ***ancient civilization:*** **4** Elam **5** Medes, Media **6** Persia ***capital:*** **6** Tehran **7** Teheran ***city:*** **3** Qom, Qum **6** Shiraz, Tabriz **7** Esfahan, Isfahan, Mashhad ***conqueror:*** **9** Alexander (the Great) ***gulf:*** **4** Oman **7** Persian ***island:*** **5** Qeshm ***language:*** **3** Tat **5** Farsi **7** Persian ***leader:*** **7** Pahlavi (Mohammad Reza, Reza Shah) **8** Khomeini (Ayatollah Ruholla) ***monetary unit:*** **4** rial ***mountain, range:*** **6** Elburz, Zagros **8** Damavand **9** Hindu Kush ***neighbor:*** **4** Iraq **6** Turkey **7** Armenia **8** Pakistan **10** Azerbaijan **11** Afghanistan **12** Turkmenistan ***river:*** **5** Atrek, Karun, Safid **7** Karkheh ***sea:*** **7** Caspian ***strait:*** **6** Hormuz

Iranian 7 Persian ***parliament:*** **6** Majlis ***religious movement:*** **5** Baha'i ***sect:*** **4** Shia ***sect member:*** **6** Shiite

Iraq ***ancient civilization:*** **5** Akkad, Sumer **8** Akkadian, Sumerian **9** Babylonia **10** Babylonian ***ancient name:*** **11** Mesopotamia ***capital:*** **7** Baghdad ***city:*** **5** Basra, Mosul, Najaf **6** Kirkuk **7** Falluja, Karbala **8** Fallujah ***conqueror:*** **9** Alexander (the Great) ***desert:*** **6** Syrian ***gulf:*** **7** Persian ***leader:*** **6** Faisal **7** Hussein (Saddam) ***monetary unit:*** **5** dinar ***neighbor:*** **4** Iran **5** Syria **6** Jordan, Kuwait, Turkey **11** Saudi Arabia ***port:*** **5** Basra **7** Umm Qasr ***river:*** **6** Tigris **9** Euphrates

irascible 4 tart **5** huffy, surly, testy **6** crabby, cranky, feisty, tetchy, touchy **7** bristly, grouchy, peevish, peppery, prickly **8** choleric, petulant, snappish **9** crotchety, fractious, irritable, querulous, splenetic **11** hot-tempered **12** cantankerous **13** quick-tempered

irate 3 mad **5** angry, livid, riled, vexed, wroth **6** fuming **7** enraged, furious, steamed **8** choleric, incensed, provoked, wrathful **9** indignant **10** infuriated

ire 4 fury, rage, rile **5** anger, wrath **6** choler, enrage, madden, temper **7** incense, steam up, umbrage **9** infuriate **10** exasperate **11** indignation **12** exasperation

Ireland 4 Eire, Erin **8** Hibernia ***capital:*** **6** Dublin ***city:*** **4** Cork **5** Kerry, Louth, Meath, Sligo **6** Galway **7** Donegal, Kildare, Wexford, Wicklow **8** Kilkenny, Limerick **9** Waterford **12** Dun Laoghaire ***county:*** **4** Cork, Mayo **5** Clare, Kerry, Louth, Meath, Sligo **6** Galway **7** Donegal, Kildare, Wexford **8** Limerick ***flag color:*** **5** green, white **6** orange ***flower:*** **8** shamrock ***island group:*** **4** Aran **8** Hibernia ***lake:*** **3** Ree (Lough) **4**

Derg (Lough) **5** Neagh (Lough) **6** Corrib (Lough) ***language:*** **4** Erse **5** Irish **6** Gaelic **7** English ***legislature:*** **4** Dail ***monetary unit:*** **4** euro ***nickname:*** **11** Emerald Isle ***province:*** **7** Munster **8** Connacht, Leinster ***river:*** **4** Erne, Nore **5** Boyne **6** Barrow, Liffey **7** Shannon ***symbol:*** **4** harp

Irene 3 Pax ***father:*** **4** Zeus **7** Jupiter ***mother:*** **6** Themis

irenic 4 calm **7** pacific **8** pacifist **9** peaceable, placative, placatory **10** nonviolent **12** conciliatory, propitiatory

iridescent 8 gleaming, lustrous **10** opalescent ***gem:*** **4** opal **5** pearl **7** apatite **8** ammolite **9** fire agate, moonstone ***shell:*** **7** abalone

iridium symbol 2 Ir

Iris ***father:*** **7** Thaumas ***mother:*** **7** Electra

Irish 4 Erse **6** Celtic, Gaelic ***accent:*** **6** brogue ***airline:*** **9** Aer Lingus ***cattle:*** **5** Kerry ***chief heir-elect:*** **6** tanist ***clan:*** **4** sept ***combining form:*** **7** Hiberno ***coronation stone:*** **7** Lia Fail ***cudgel:*** **9** shillalah **10** shillelagh ***death spirit:*** **7** banshee ***design:*** **8** claddagh ***dog:*** **6** setter **7** terrier ***elf:*** **10** leprechaun ***fortification:*** **4** liss ***girl:*** **4** lass **6** lassie **7** colleen ***god:*** **3** Ler **5** Dagda **6** Aengus ***goddess:*** **4** Badb, Bodb **6** Brigit **8** Morrigan ***hero:*** **9** Cuchulain **10** Cú Chulainn ***heroine:*** **7** Deirdre ***king:*** **9** Brian Boru ***lake:*** **5** lough ***language:*** **4** Erse ***militant force:*** **3** IRA ***nationalist:*** **4** Tone (Wolfe) **6** Pearse (Padraig) **7** Collins (Michael), Parnell (Charles) **8** De Valera (Eamon), O'Connell (Daniel) **9** Sarsfield (Patrick) ***nationalist society:*** **8** Sinn Fein ***patron saint:*** **7** Patrick ***police officer:*** **5** garda ***singer:*** **4** Enya **5** Makem (Tommy), Margo **6** Clancy (Bobby, Liam, Paddy, Patrick, Tom) **8** O'Donnell (Daniel) ***symbol:*** **4** harp ***theater:*** **5** Abbey ***writing system:*** **4** ogam **5** ogham (see also **Gaelic; Celtic**)

Irish moss 7 seaweed **9** carrageen

irk 3 try, vex **4** fret, gall, miff, pain, rile **5** annoy, peeve, pique, upset **6** abrade, bother, harass, nettle, ruffle, strain, stress **7** provoke, trouble **8** exercise, irritate **10** exasperate

irksome 6 vexing **7** tedious **8** annoying, rankling **9** provoking, upsetting, vexatious **10** bothersome, irritating, nettlesome, unpleasant **11** aggravating, troublesome, unpalatable

iron 4 firm, gyve, hard **5** press, rigid **6** fetter, strong **7** adamant, manacle, shackle **8** handcuff, obdurate **9** unbending **10** inexorable, inflexible ***combining form:*** **5** ferro **6** sidero ***German:*** **5** Eisen ***relating to:*** **6** ferric **7** ferrous **11** ferruginous ***symbol:*** **2** Fe

ironbound 5 harsh, rocky, rough, stern **6** craggy, jagged, rugged, severe, strict, uneven **7** scraggy **8** asperous, exacting, rigorous, scabrous **9** stringent **10** inflexible

Iron City 10 Pittsburgh

ironclad 5 fixed **7** binding **8** constant **9** immovable, immutable **10** inflexible, invariable **11** inalterable, irrefutable, unalterable **12** indisputable, irrefragable, unchangeable **13** unimpeachable

ironfisted 4 grim, hard, mean **5** harsh **6** brutal, severe, stingy **7** callous, miserly **8** pitiless, ruthless **9** penurious **10** implacable, unmerciful **11** hard-hearted, intractable, remorseless **12** unappeasable

ironhanded 5 harsh, rigid **6** severe, strict **8** despotic, rigorous **9** draconian, stringent **10** tyrannical **12** unpermissive

ironhearted 5 stony **7** callous **8** hardened, obdurate, ruthless **9** merciless, unfeeling **10** hard-boiled **11** cold-blooded **13** unsympathetic

iron horse 10 locomotive

ironic 3 wry **6** biting **7** caustic, cutting, cynical, mordant, satiric **8** sardonic **9** sarcastic, trenchant

iron ore 8 goethite, hematite, limonite, siderite, taconite **9** magnetite

Iron Pants 6 Patton (George)

irons 5 bonds, gyves **6** chains **7** bilboes, darbies, fetters **8** manacles, shackles

Iroquois tribe 6 Cayuga, Mohawk, Oneida, Seneca **8** Onondaga **9** Tuscarora

irradiate 4 beam, glow **5** edify, light, shine **6** uplift **7** light up **8** illumine **9** enlighten **10** illuminate

irrational 3 mad **5** crazy **6** absurd, insane **7** invalid **8** demented **9** cockamamy, illogical, senseless, sophistic **10** cockamamie, fallacious, ridiculous **12** preposterous, unreasonable ***number:*** **4** surd

irrefutable 4 sure **6** proven **7** certain **8** airtight, ironclad, positive **9** apodictic, veracious **10** conclusive, inarguable **11** indubitable **12** indisputable **13** incontestable

irregular 3 odd **5** erose, queer **6** fitful, patchy, random, spotty, uneven **7** aimless, erratic, unequal **8** aberrant, abnormal, atypical, informal, lopsided, peculiar, singular, sporadic, unstable, unsteady, variable **9** anomalous, desultory, divergent, eccentric, guerrilla, haphazard, hit-or-miss, spasmodic, unregular, unsettled **10** asymmetric, capricious, changeable, inconstant, off-balance, unbalanced, unofficial **11** exceptional, fluctuating **12** intermittent, unsystematic

irregularity 5 freak, quirk **6** oddity, vagary **7**

anomaly **8** deviance **9** deviation, roughness **10** aberration, inequality, unevenness **11** abnormality

irrelevant 5 inapt **9** unrelated **10** extraneous, immaterial, inapposite, peripheral **11** inessential, unessential, unimportant **12** inapplicable **13** insignificant

irreligious 6 unholy **7** godless, impious, profane, ungodly **11** blasphemous

irreparable 8 cureless, hopeless **9** incurable **11** immedicable **12** irredeemable, irremediable **13** irretrievable, unrecoverable

irreproachable 4 pure **8** flawless, innocent, spotless, virtuous **9** blameless, errorless, exemplary, faultless, guiltless, righteous **10** immaculate, impeccable, inculpable, unblamable

irresolute 5 shaky **6** fickle, unsure, wobbly **7** halting **8** doubtful, hesitant, unstable, waffling, wavering **9** equivocal, faltering, tentative, uncertain, undecided **10** ambivalent, changeable, inconstant, wishy-washy **11** fluctuating, half-hearted, vacillating

irresponsible 4 rash, wild **8** carefree, careless, feckless, reckless **10** incautious, unreliable **12** undependable **13** unaccountable, untrustworthy

irreverent 4 flip **7** impious, profane, ungodly **8** flippant **9** satirical **11** blasphemous **12** sacrilegious

irrevocable 4 firm **5** final **9** immutable **11** unalterable **12** irreversible, unchangeable **13** nonreversible

irrigate 3 wet **4** soak **5** flush, water

irrigation ditch 5 flume **6** sluice **7** acequia

irritability 5 pique **6** choler **8** edginess **9** petulance **10** crabbiness, impatience **11** fretfulness, peevishness ***abnormal:* 8** erethism

irritable 4 edgy, sour **5** cross, huffy, ratty, testy, waspy, whiny **6** crabby, cranky, crusty, grumpy, ornery, snappy, tetchy, touchy **7** fretful, grouchy, peevish, pettish, prickly, waspish **8** captious, choleric, petulant, snappish **9** crotchety, fractious, impatient, irascible, querulous, splenetic **12** cantankerous, disagreeable

irritant 4 itch, pest **5** nudge, peeve **6** bother, gadfly, noodge, nudnik, pester, plague **7** nudnick **8** headache, nuisance, vexation **9** annoyance **11** botheration

irritate 3 bug, irk, rub, vex **4** fret, gall, goad, rile, roil **5** anger, annoy, chafe, grate, peeve, pique, spite **6** abrade, badger, bother, burn up, harass, hector, madden, needle, nettle, offend, ruffle **7** inflame, provoke **9** aggravate, stimulate **10** exacerbate, exasperate

irritated 5 irate, testy **7** fretful, peevish **8** choleric **9** impatient, irascible

irritation 4 itch, pest, rash, sore **6** bother, plague **7** chagrin **8** nuisance, vexation **9** annoyance

irrupt 5 belch, eruct, surge **6** invade **7** intrude

irruption 4 raid **5** foray **6** inroad **7** upsurge **8** invasion **9** incursion, intrusion

I.R.S. employee 7 auditor **10** accountant

Irving novel 15 Cider House Rules (The) **17** Hotel New Hampshire (The) **20** World According to Garp (The)

Isaac *father:* 7 Abraham ***mother:* 5** Sarah ***son:* 4** Esau **5** Jacob ***wife:* 7** Rebekah

Isabella I *country:* 5 Spain ***home:* 7** Castile ***husband:* 9** Ferdinand

Isaiah 7 prophet ***father:* 4** Amoz

Iscah *brother:* 3 Lot ***father:* 5** Haran ***sister:* 6** Milcah

Iseult, Isolde *beloved:* 7 Tristan **8** Tristram ***husband:* 4** Mark

Ishbak *father:* 7 Abraham ***mother:* 7** Keturah

Ishbosheth's father 4 Saul

Ishmael 6 pariah **7** outcast **8** castaway, outsider **11** untouchable ***captain:* 4** Ahab ***father:* 7** Abraham ***mother:* 5** Hagar ***ship:* 6** Pequod

Ishtar *brother:* 7 Shamash ***father:* 3** Anu, Sin ***lover:* 6** Tammuz

Ishui's father 4 Saul **5** Asher

Isis *brother:* 6 Osiris ***father:* 3** Geb ***husband:* 6** Osiris ***mother:* 3** Nut ***son:* 4** Sept **5** Horus

Islam *adherent:* 6 Moslem, Muslim ***founder:* 8** Mohammed, Muhammad ***god:* 5** Allah ***holy city:* 5** Mecca ***holy month:* 7** Ramadan ***law:* 6** Sharia ***place of worship:* 6** mosque ***priest:* 4** imam ***scriptures:* 5** Koran, Quran ***sect:* 4** Shia, Sufi **5** Sunni **6** Salafi, Shiite, Sufism **7** Ismaili, Wahhabi **8** Salafism (see also **Muslim**)

island 3 ait, cay, key **4** holm **5** atoll, oasis **6** skerry **7** crannog ***Adriatic Sea:* 3** Vis **4** Brac, Cres, Hvar **5** Brach, Ciovo, Mljet, Solta **6** Lesina, Pharus ***Aegean Sea:* 4** Scio **5** Chios, Khios, Samos, Thira **6** Ikaria, Lemnos, Lesbos, Limnos **7** Nikaria **8** Mitilini, Mytilene, Santorin **10** Sakis-Adasi, Susam-Adasi ***Alaska:* 4** Adak, Atka, Attu, Kuiu **8** Wrangell ***American Samoa:* 3** Ofu, Tau **4** Rose **6** Swains ***Andaman Sea:* 4** Mali **5** Tavoy ***Antarctica:* 5** Scott, Young ***Arafura Sea:* 5** Dolak ***Arctic Archipelago:* 6** Baffin **8** Victoria ***Arctic Ocean:* 5** Senja ***Australian:* 5** Cocos **8** Tasmania ***Azores:* 4** Pico **5** Corvo, Faial ***Bahamas:* 3** Cat, Rum **4** Long **5** Abaco, Exuma **6** Andros, Inagua **7** Acklins, Crooked **8** Watlings **9** Eleuthera, Mayaguana **11** San Salvador ***Bahrain:*** **5** Sitra **8** Muharraq ***Baltic Sea:*** **4** Moon, Muhu **5** Faron, Mukhu, Rugen, Worms **6** Vormsi **7** Gotland **8** Bornholm, Gothland, Gottland ***Barents Sea:*** **4** Bear ***Bay of Naples:*** **5** Capri ***Bay of Panama:*** **4** Naos ***Bering Sea:*** **5** Medny **7** Nunivak **10** Big Diomede **13** Little Diomede ***Bismarck Archipelago:*** **5** Lihir **10** New Britain ***Bristol Channel:*** **5** Lundy ***Buzzards Bay:*** **9** Cuttyhunk ***Canadian:*** **5** Banks, Devon **6** Baffin **8** Bathurst, Melville, Somerset, Victoria **9** Anticosti, Ellesmere **10** Cape Breton **11** Axel Heiberg, Southampton **12** Newfoundland, Prince Edward ***Canaries:*** **6** Gomera **7** La Palma **8** Tenerife **9** Lanzarote ***Cape Verde:*** **4** Fogo, Maio, Mayo **5** Brava, Rombo ***Caribbean Sea:*** **4** Cuba **5** Aruba, Utila, Vache **6** Tobago **7** Antigua, Curaçao, Jamaica **8** Barbados, Dominica, Trinidad **10** Guadeloupe, Martinique, Puerto Rico (see also **Virgin group**) ***Carolines:*** **3** Uap, Yap **4** Truk **5** Chuuk, Nomoi, Sorol **6** Ponape **7** Hogoleu, Pohnpei **9** Ascension ***Chagos Archipelago:*** **11** Diego Garcia ***Chesapeake Bay:*** **4** Deal, Kent **5** Smith, Watts ***Chukchi Sea:*** **6** Herald ***Comoro group:*** **7** Mayotte ***Congo River:*** **4** Bamu ***Croatia:*** **3** Krk, Pag, Rab **5** Susak, Unije ***Cyclades:*** **3** Ios, Kea, Nio **4** Ceos, Keos, Milo **5** Delos, Melos, Milos, Naxos, Paros, Siros, Syros **6** Andros, Dhilos **7** Amorgos, Cythnos, Kithnos, Kythnos, Mykonos ***Denmark:*** **3** Als, Fyn, Mon **4** Aero, Fano, Moen, Mors **5** Alsen, Funen, Moers, Samso **8** Bornholm **9** Greenland **13** Fanum Fortunae ***East River:*** **5** Ward's **7** Welfare **9** Roosevelt ***England's:*** **7** Britain **9** Britannia **12** Great Britain ***English Channel:*** **5** Wight ***Fiji:*** **4** Koro **5** Mango, Vatoa ***French:*** **7** Corsica **12** New Caledonia ***French Polynesia:*** **4** Rapa, Reao, Ua Pu **5** Ua Pau ***Futunas:*** **5** Alofi ***Galápagos:*** **5** Pinta **7** Chatham, Isabela **8** Abingdon **10** Albermarle ***Georgia:*** **5** Tybee ***Germany:*** **4** Fohr **7** Fehmarn **9** Helgoland **10** Heligoland ***Greater Antilles:*** **4** Cuba **7** Jamaica **10** Hispaniola, Puerto Rico ***Greece:*** **4** Milo, Rodi **5** Creta, Crete, Hydra, Idhra, Kriti, Rodos, Tenos, Tinos **6** Euboea, Evvoia, Hydrea, Lesbos, Rhodes, Rhodus **9** Negropont **10** Negroponte ***Grenadines:*** **5** Union ***Gulf of Alaska:*** **6** Kodiak ***Gulf of Bothnia:*** **5** Karlö ***Gulf of Carpentaria:*** **5** Maria **6** Groote **7** Eylandt ***Gulf of Guinea:*** **7** Sao Tomé **8** Príncipe, Sao Thomé **11** Saint Thomas ***Gulf of Mexico:*** **3** Cat **5** Lobos ***Gulf of Panama:*** **3** Rey ***Gulf of St. Lawrence:*** **5** Brion ***Gulf of Thailand:*** **3** Kut **5** Samui ***Haiti:*** **6** Gonâve ***Hawaii:*** **4** Maui, Oahu **5** Kauai, Lanai **6** Niihau **7** Molokai **9** Kahoolawe ***Hudson Bay:*** **5** Coats ***Indian Ocean:*** **4** Mahé, Nias **5** Heard, Pemba **7** La Dique, Praslin, Réunion **8** Sri Lanka, Zanzibar **9** Mauritius **10** Madagascar ***Indonesia:*** **4** Bali, Biak, Java, Maja, Muna, Nias, Rhio, Riau, Roma, Roti, Savu, Sawu **5** Batam, Boano, Buton, Djawa, Japen, Lakor, Moena, Riouw, Rotti, Rupat, Sawoe, Solor, Sumba, Wetar, Wokam **6** Butung, Flores, Jappen, Lombok, Madura, Padang, Roepat, Romang, Soemba **7** Celebes, Madoera, Sumatra, Sumbawa **8** Boetoeng, Soembawa, Sulawesi **10** Bandanaira, Banda Neira, Sandalwood ***Iran:*** **5** Shahi ***Ireland:*** **4** Aran ***Irish Sea:*** **3** Man ***Italy:*** **4** Elba **6** Sicily **8** Sardinia ***Japan:*** **3** Iki, Uku **4** Naru, Yezo **5** Awaji, Fukae, Fukue, Hondo, Shodo **6** Honshu, Kyushu **7** Shikoku **8** Hokkaido **10** Shodoshima ***Java Sea:*** **4** Laut ***Kiribati:*** **6** Tarawa ***Lake Champlain:*** **5** Grand ***Lake Erie:*** **9** North Bass, South Bass **10** Middle Bass ***Lake Huron:*** **8** Drummond **10** Manitoulin ***Lake Michigan:*** **3** Hog **4** High **6** Beaver ***Lake Ontario:*** **5** Wolfe ***Lake Superior:*** **4** Sand **6** Royale **7** Manitou ***Lake Winnipeg:*** **5** Hecla ***largest:*** **9** Greenland ***Leeward group:*** **5** Nevis **7** Antigua, Barbuda, Redonda **8** Anguilla, Sombrero **10** Montserrat, Saint Kitts **13** St. Christopher ***legendary:*** **7** Cipango ***Lesser Sundas:*** **4** Alor **5** Ombai ***Long Island Sound:*** **4** City, Hart **5** Goose, Harts ***Malay Archipelago:*** **5** Kisar, Larat, Timor **6** Borneo **9** New Guinea ***Malaysia:*** **6** Penang, Pinang **13** Prince of Wales ***Malta:*** **4** Gozo ***Massachusetts:*** **9** Nantucket ***Mediterranean Sea:*** **4** Elba **5** Corfu, Crete, Malta **6** Cyprus, Euboea, Rhodes, Sicily **7** Corsica **8** Sardinia ***Moluccas:*** **4** Buru **5** Ambon, Ceram, Seram **6** Boeroe ***Mozambique channel:*** **10** Juan de Nova ***Myanmar:*** **5** Daung, Kadan, Lanbi ***Narragansett Bay:*** **5** Rhode **8** Prudence **9** Aquidneck, Conanicut ***Netherlands:*** **5** Texel **7** Ameland **8** Vlieland ***Netherlands Antilles:*** **7** Curaçao ***New York:*** **4** Fire, Long **5** Ellis **6** Staten **7** Liberty **9** Gardiners, Governors, Manhattan, Roosevelt ***New York Bay:*** **5** Ellis **6** Staten **7** Liberty **9** Governors, Manhattan ***New Zealand:*** **5** South, White **7** Chatham, Stewart **8** D'Urville ***Niagara River:*** **4** Goat ***Nile River:*** **4** Argo, Roda, Ruda **5** Rhoda **6** Rawdah **11** Elephantine ***North Channel:*** **3** Mew **8** Manihiki **9** Tongareva ***North Pacific:*** **4** Wake ***Northwest Territories:*** **5** Banks, Bylot, Devon **8** Bathurst, Melville **9** Ellesmere **10**

Cornwallis, Resolution **13** Prince of Wales ***Norwegian:*** **8** Jan Mayen ***Norwegian Sea:*** **5** Donna, Smola, Vikna ***Nova Scotia:*** **5** Sable **10** Cape Breton ***off Alaska:*** **4** Dall **5** Kayak ***off Albania:*** **5** Sazan **6** Saseno ***off Australia:*** **4** Dunk ***off Belize:*** **9** Ambergris ***off Brazil:*** **4** Apeu **5** Rocas ***off British Columbia:*** **4** King, Pitt **9** Vancouver ***off Cape Cod:*** **8** Muskeget **9** Nantucket ***off Chile:*** **5** Guafo, Mocha ***off China:*** **4** Amoy **5** Ma-tsu **6** Hainan, Quemoy, Taiwan ***off Crete:*** **3** Dia ***off Ecuador:*** **4** Puna ***off England:*** **3** Man **4** Sark **5** Wight **6** Jersey, Walney **8** Alderney, Guernsey ***off Florida:*** **3** Dog **4** Pine **6** Amelia **7** Pelican, Sanibel **9** Anastasia ***off French Guiana:*** **6** Devil's ***off Georgia:*** **10** Cumberland **11** Saint Simons ***off Germany:*** **4** Sylt ***off Greenland:*** **5** Disko ***off Guinea:*** **5** Tombo ***off Hispaniola:*** **5** Beata ***off Honduras:*** **5** Tigre ***off Iceland:*** **7** Surtsey ***off India:*** **5** Sagar ***off Ireland:*** **4** Tory **5** Clare, Clear ***off Kenya:*** **4** Lamu ***off Long Island:*** **7** Fishers ***off Louisiana:*** **5** Marsh ***off Maine:*** **4** Deer, Orrs **5** Swans **8** Monhegan **11** Mount Desert ***off Malay Peninsula:*** **6** Phuket **9** Singapore ***off Maryland:*** **10** Assateague ***off Massachusetts:*** **4** Plum **7** Naushon ***off Mexico:*** **7** Cozumel ***off Mississippi:*** **4** Horn, Ship ***off Mozambique:*** **3** Ibo ***off New Brunswick:*** **10** Campobello ***off Newfoundland:*** **4** Bell ***off Nigeria:*** **5** Lagos ***off North Carolina:*** **5** Bodie ***off Norway:*** **5** Bomlo, Froya, Hitra, Sotra, Stord, Vardo **8** Hitteren ***off Panama:*** **4** Naos **5** Coiba **6** Parida ***off Poland:*** **5** Wolin **6** Wollin ***off Puerto Rico:*** **4** Crab **7** Culebra, Vieques ***off Rhode Island:*** **5** Block ***off Scotland:*** **4** Bute, Iona, Jura **5** Arran, Islay ***off South Carolina:*** **5** North **6** Parris **10** Hilton Head ***off Sri Lanka:*** **5** Delft ***off Staten Island:*** **7** Hoffman ***off Sumatra:*** **3** Weh ***off Sweden:*** **5** Graso, Oland, Vaddo ***off Syria:*** **5** Arvad, Arwad, Rouad **6** Aradus ***off Tanzania:*** **5** Mafia, Pemba ***off Tasmania:*** **5** Bruni, Bruny ***off Tunisia:*** **5** Jerba **6** Djerba, Meninx ***off Venezuela:*** **5** Aruba **7** Bonaire **8** Buen Aire ***off Virginia:*** **5** Wreck ***off Wales:*** **5** Caldy **6** Caldey ***Orkneys:*** **3** Hoy ***Outer Hebrides:*** **5** Barra, Scarp ***Palmer Archipelago:*** **6** Anvers **7** Antwerp, Brabant ***Pearl Harbor:*** **4** Ford ***Persian Gulf:*** **4** Qeys **5** Kharg, Khark ***Philippines:*** **4** Buad, Cebu, Fuga, Ilin, Poro, Sulu **5** Balut, Batan, Bohol, Coron, Daram, Leyte, Luzon, Panay, Samal, Samar, Sugbu, Talim, Ticao, Verde **6** Negros **7** Masbate, Mindoro, Palawan, Paragua **8** Limasawa, Mindanao **10** Corregidor ***Puerto Rico:*** **4** Mona ***Quebec:*** **4** Alma ***Red Sea:*** **5** Tiran, Zugur, Zuqar ***Russia:*** **7** Wrangel ***St. Lawrence River:*** **4** Hare **5** Jesus **8** Montreal ***San Francisco Bay:*** **5** Angel ***Santa Cruz:*** **5** Anuda, Ndeni **6** Cherry ***Sea of Japan:*** **4** Sado **5** Rebun ***Sea of Marmara:*** **4** Avsa ***second largest:*** **9** New Guinea ***Senegal:*** **5** Gorée ***Seychelles:*** **4** Mahé **7** La Digue, Praslin ***Shetland archipelago:*** **4** Unst, Yell **5** Foula ***Sierra Leone:*** **5** Tasso ***South Atlantic:*** **5** Gough **6** Gough's **11** Saint Helena ***South Korea:*** **5** Cheju ***South of Tokyo:*** **3** Iwo **7** Iwo Jima, Naka Iwo ***South Orkneys:*** **10** Coronation ***South Pacific:*** **3** Hiu **4** Niue **5** Raoul **6** Savage, Sunday **7** Norfolk **8** Pitcairn ***Spitsbergen archipelago:*** **4** Edge ***Strait of Hormuz:*** **5** Qeshm, Qishm ***Sulu Archipelago:*** **4** Jolo **5** Lapac ***Svalbard:*** **4** Hope ***Sverdrup:*** **11** Axel Heiberg **12** Amund Ringnes ***Swedish:*** **3** Ven **4** Hven **5** Hveen, Orust ***Tanzania:*** **8** Zanzibar ***Texas:*** **5** Padre ***Thames River:*** **7** Sheppey ***third largest:*** **6** Borneo ***Tierra del Fuego:*** **5** Hoste ***Tonga:*** **3** Eua, Foa **4** Uiha **5** Haano ***Tuamotu Archipelago:*** **4** Anaa **5** Chain ***Turkish:*** **5** Imroz **6** Imbros ***Tuvalu:*** **7** Nanumea **9** Nukufetau ***Tyrrhenian Sea:*** **6** Ischia **11** Montecristo ***Vanuatu:*** **3** Api, Epi, Oba **4** Aoba, Gaua, Tana, Vate **5** Efate, Maewo, Tanna ***Venezuelan:*** **5** Patos **9** La Tortuga ***volcanic:*** **5** Tofua **7** Iwo Jima ***Wales:*** **8** Anglesea, Anglesey, Holyhead ***Weddell Sea:*** **4** Ross **6** Hearst ***Western Samoa:*** **5** Upolu **6** Savaii ***West Indies:*** **4** Mona, Saba, Salt **5** Nevis, Peter, Saona **6** Tobago, Tortue **7** Grenada, Tortuga **8** Trinidad **9** Santa Cruz **10** Concepción, Hispaniola, Montserrat, Saint Croix (see also **Bahamas; Greater Antilles; Leeward group; Virgin group; Windward group**) ***West of England:*** **7** Ireland ***West Pacific:*** **5** Dyaul, Fauro, Ocean **6** Banaba, Marcus **7** Iwo Jima, Kita Iwo **9** Minami Iwo ***with former penitentiary:*** **8** Alcatraz

island group ***Admiralty:*** **5** Manus ***Alaska:*** **3** Rat **8** Aleutian, Pribilof **9** Andreanof, Catherine ***Aleutians:*** **4** Near ***Aleutian:*** **3** Rat **4** Adak, Akun, Attu **5** Amlia, Kiska, Umnak **6** Kanaga, Tanaga, Unimak **8** Amchitka, Unalaska ***American Samoa:*** **5** Manua ***Apostle:*** **3** Oak **4** Long, Sand **5** Outer **8** Madeline, Michigan, Stockton ***Arabian Sea:*** **9** Laccadive ***Arctic Archipelago:*** **8** Sverdrup ***Arctic Ocean:*** **8** Svalbard **12** Novaya Zemlya ***Bahamas:*** **5** Berry, Exuma **6** Bimini ***Balearic:*** **5** Ibiza **7** Majorca, Menorca, Minorca **8** Mallorca ***Banda Sea:*** **5** Damar ***Bangladesh:*** **5** Hatia, Hatya ***Bay of Bengal:*** **7** Andaman, Nicobar ***between England and***

France: **7** Channel ***Bismarck Archipelago:*** **4** Feni **5** Tabar, Tanga ***Bismarck Sea:*** **4** Vitu ***British:*** **7** Bermuda ***Caribbean Sea:*** **4** Swan **5** Pearl **6** Cayman, Perlas, Pigeon **8** Pichones **10** Grenadines, West Indies ***Central Pacific Ocean:*** **4** Line **5** Samoa, Union **6** Danger, Midway **7** Phoenix, Tokelau **8** Manihiki **9** Polynesia **12** Northern Cook ***Channel:*** **4** Herm, Sark **5** Lihou, Sercq **6** Jersey **8** Guernsey ***Cook:*** **4** Atiu **5** Mauke ***Coral Sea:*** **4** Huon ***Cuba:*** **8** Camagüey ***Denmark:*** **6** Faroes **7** Faeroes ***D'Entrecasteaux:*** **8** Kaluwawa **9** Fergusson ***Dodecanese:*** **3** Coo, Cos, Kos **4** Caso, Lero, Simi, Syme **5** Kasos, Leros, Lipso, Lisso, Patmo, Telos **6** Calino, Lipsos, Nisiro, Patmos **7** Calimno, Nisiros, Nisyros **8** Kalymnos ***east of Philippines:*** **10** Micronesia ***East Siberian Sea:*** **4** Bear **8** Medvezhi ***Ecuador:*** **5** Colón **9** Galápagos ***England:*** **5** Farne ***Faeroes, Faroes:*** **4** Vago **5** Bordo, Sando ***Fiji:*** **3** Lau **7** Eastern ***Florida Keys:*** **4** Long, Vaca, West **5** Largo **7** Big Pine **9** Matecumbe, Sugarloaf ***Formosa Strait:*** **4** Hoko **6** Peng hu **10** Pescadores ***Fox:*** **5** Umnak **6** Akutan, Unimak **8** Unalaska ***France:*** **5** Salut **6** Safety **9** Kerguelen ***French Polynesia:*** **3** Low **6** Tubuai **7** Austral, Paumotu, Société, Society, Tuamotu **9** Marquesas, Touamotou ***Frisian:*** **3** Rom **4** Föhr, Sylt **5** Amrum, Juist, Mando, Texel **6** Borkum **7** Ameland **8** Langeoog, Pellworm, Vlieland **9** Helgoland, Norderney ***Germany:*** **8** Halligen ***Greece:*** **6** Aegean, Ionian **8** Cyclades **10** Dodecanese **11** Dodecanesus ***Hudson Bay:*** **7** Belcher ***Indian Ocean:*** **7** Aldabra ***Indonesia:*** **4** Asia, Batu, Pagi, Sula **5** Babar, Batoe, Pagai, Pageh, Penju, Spice, Wakde **6** Maluku ***Inner Hebrides:*** **4** Coll, Eigg, Iona, Jura, Muck, Mull, Skye **5** Canna, Gigha, Islay, Tiree, Tyree ***Ionian:*** **5** Corfu, Paxos, Zante **6** Cerigo, Ithaca, Leukas, Levkas **10** Santa Maura ***Ireland:*** **4** Aran ***Italy:*** **6** Lipari ***Japan:*** **5** Osumi ***Kuril:*** **4** Urup **5** Ketoi, Matua **6** Iturup **7** Etorofu, Matsuwa **8** Kunashir **9** Kunashiri ***largest:*** **5** Malay **8** Malaysia ***Lesser Antilles:*** **8** Windward ***Leti:*** **3** Moa **5** Lakor ***Line:*** **5** Flint **6** Malden, Vostok **7** Fanning, Palmyra **8** Starbuck **9** Christmas ***Loyalty:*** **3** Uea **4** Lifu, Maré, Uvea **5** Lifou ***Malay Archipelago:*** **5** Sunda **6** Soenda ***Marianas:*** **4** Maug, Rota **5** Pagan **6** Saipan ***Marquesas:*** **4** Eiào, Ua Pu **6** Hatutu, Hiva Oa, Ua Huka **7** Tahuata **8** Fatu Hiva, Nuku Hiva ***Marshall:*** **5** Wotho, Wotje **8** Eniwetok **9** Kwajalein ***Mediterranean Sea:*** **8** Baleares, Balearic ***Midway:*** **4** Sand **7** Eastern ***Moluccas:*** **3** Kai, Kei, Obi **4** Buru, Leti **5** Ambon, Banda, Letti, Seram **6** Boeroe **8** Tanimbar **9** Timorlaut ***New Caledonia:*** **7** Loyalty **9** Loyalties ***Northern Cook:*** **7** Penrhyn ***north of Australia:*** **9** Melanesia ***north of British Isles:*** **5** Faroe **7** Faeroes ***north off Fiji:*** **5** Hoorn **6** Futuna ***north of Madagascar:*** **7** Aldabra **8** Farquhar ***north of New Caledonia:*** **5** Belep ***north of New Guinea:*** **8** Bismarck **9** Admiralty **11** Admiralties ***Northwest Territories:*** **5** Parry ***off Alaska:*** **3** Fox ***off Alaska Peninsula:*** **8** Shumagin ***off Cape Cod:*** **9** Elizabeth ***off eastern Asia:*** **5** Kuril **6** Kurile ***off England:*** **6** Scilly ***off Florida:*** **11** Dry Tortugas ***off Guinea:*** **3** Los **4** Loos ***off Honduras:*** **5** Bahia ***off Morocco:*** **7** Madeira ***off New Guinea:*** **3** Aru **4** Aroe ***off Nicaragua:*** **4** Corn ***off northern Africa:*** **6** Canary **8** Canaries ***off northern Australia:*** **6** Wessel **7** Dampier ***off Sicily:*** **5** Egadi **8** Aegadian ***Okinawa:*** **4** Kume ***Outer Hebrides:*** **4** Uist ***Papua New Guinea:*** **5** Green ***Persian Gulf:*** **4** Tunb ***Philippines:*** **4** Cuyo **5** Tapul **6** Lubang **7** Basilan, Bisayas, Visayan ***Phoenix:*** **4** Hull, Mary **6** Birnie, Canton **9** Enderbury ***Portuguese:*** **6** Azores ***Quebec:*** **8** Magdalen **9** Madeleine ***Queen Charlotte:*** **7** Moresby ***Ryukyus:*** **5** Amami **7** Okinawa ***St. Lawrence River:*** **8** Thousand ***Sea of Japan:*** **3** Oki ***Sea of Marmara:*** **5** Kizil **7** Princes **11** Kizil Adalar ***Shumagin:*** **4** Unga ***Society:*** **5** Eimeo, Tahaa, Tahao, Taiti **6** Moorea, Tahiti **8** Otaheite ***Solomon:*** **4** Buka, Gizo, Savo **7** Malaita **11** Guadalcanal **12** Bougainville ***South Atlantic Ocean:*** **8** Falkland, Malvinas ***South China Sea:*** **6** Hirata **7** Paracel, Spratly ***south of New Zealand:*** **8** Auckland ***South Pacific:*** **11** Austronesia ***Sulu Sea:*** **7** Cagayan **9** Cagayanes ***Tonga:*** **5** Vavau ***Treasury:*** **4** Mono ***Truk:*** **3** Tol **4** Haru, Moen, Udot, Uman **5** Fefan ***Tyrrhenian Sea:*** **5** Ponza ***Venezuelan:*** **4** Aves, Bird **9** Los Roques ***Virgin, American:*** **9** Saint John **10** Saint Croix **11** Saint Thomas ***Virgin, British:*** **5** Peter **6** Norman **7** Anegada, Tortola **11** Jost Van Dyke ***West Europe:*** **12** British Isles ***West Indies:*** **6** Virgin **10** Guadeloupe ***west of French Polynesia:*** **4** Cook ***west of Scotland:*** **7** Western **8** Hebrides ***west Pacific Ocean:*** **4** Duff **5** Belau, Bonin, Mapia, Palau, Pelew **7** Ladrone, Mariana, Solomon, Vanuatu **8** Marshall, Treasury **9** Ogasawara **10** Saint David ***Windward:*** **10** Martinique

island nation ***Atlantic Ocean:*** **9** Cape Verde ***Indian Ocean:*** **8** Malagasy, Malgache, Sri Lanka **9** Mauritius **10** Madagascar, Seychelles ***Mediterranean Sea:*** **6** Cyprus ***Mo-***

zambique Channel: **6** Comoro **7** Comores ***off southern China:*** **6** Taiwan ***south of Greenland:*** **7** Iceland ***West Indies:*** **4** Cuba **7** Jamaica **8** Barbados **10** Saint Lucia ***West Pacific Ocean:*** **4** Fiji **5** Belau, Nauru, Palau, Samoa **6** Tuvalu **7** Vanuatu ***Windward group:*** **8** Dominica

island province 12 Prince Edward

island state 6 Hawaii

isle see **island**

Ismene *brother:* 9 Polynices **10** Polyneices ***father:*** **7** Oedipus ***mother:*** **7** Jocasta ***sister:*** **8** Antigone ***uncle:*** **5** Creon

isochronous 7 regular **8** cyclical, periodic, rhythmic **9** recurrent, recurring **10** periodical **12** intermittent

isolate 6 cut off, detach, enisle **7** seclude **8** close off, insulate, pinpoint, separate, set apart **9** segregate, sequester **10** quarantine

isolated 5 alone **6** random, remote, unique **7** unusual **8** solitary, sporadic **9** separated, withdrawn **11** exceptional, quarantined

Isolde see **Iseult**

Israel *airline:* 4 El Al ***ancient name:*** **4** Zion **5** Judea **6** Canaan, Judaea **9** Palestine ***capital:*** **9** Jerusalem ***city:*** **4** Acre **5** Haifa, Jaffa **7** Tel Aviv **9** Beersheba ***desert:*** **5** Negeb, Negev ***gulf:*** **5** Aqaba ***lake:*** **8** Tiberias **12** Sea of Galilee ***language:*** **6** Arabic, Hebrew ***monetary unit:*** **6** shekel ***neighbor:*** **5** Egypt, Syria **6** Jordan **7** Lebanon ***plain:*** **9** Esdraelon ***river:*** **6** Jordan ***sea:*** **4** Dead **13** Mediterranean

Israeli 5 sabra ***dance:*** **4** hora **5** horah ***gun:*** **3** Uzi

Israelite see **Hebrew; Jewish**

Issachar *father:* 5 Jacob ***mother:*** **4** Leah

issue 4 emit, flow, gush, pour, rise, seed, stem, vent **5** arise, birth, brood, child, empty, fruit, scion, topic **6** affair, appear, effect, emerge, get out, matter, put out, result, scions, sequel, source, spring, upshot **7** concern, debouch, descent, edition, emanate, give off, give out, outcome, problem, proceed, progeny, publish, release, subject **8** bulletin, children, question, throw off **9** come forth, offspring, originate, posterity **10** derive from, distribute, end product, promulgate **11** consequence, descendants, progeniture, publication

Istanbul *ancient name:* 9 Byzantium ***business section:*** **6** Galata ***country:*** **6** Turkey ***foreign quarter:*** **4** Pera **7** Beyoglu ***park:*** **8** Seraglio ***residential section:*** **7** Uskudar

isthmus *Africa-Asia:* 4 Suez ***America:*** **6** Panama ***Greece:*** **7** Corinth ***Malay Peninsula:*** **3** Kra

Italian *after:* 4 dopo ***against:*** **6** contro ***ahead:*** **6** avanti ***apple:*** **4** mela ***article:*** **2** il, la ***aunt:*** **3** zia ***automobile:*** **4** Fiat **6** Lancia **7** Ferrari **8** Maserati **9** Alfa Romeo **11** Lamborghini ***be:*** **6** essere ***book:*** **5** libro ***brandy:*** **6** grappa ***brother:*** **8** fratello ***cake:*** **5** torta ***cat:*** **5** gatto ***cathedral:*** **5** duomo ***cheers:*** **6** cin cin ***chicken:***5 pollo ***child:*** **7** bambino ***coffee:*** **5** caffè ***come:*** **6** venire ***day:*** **6** giorno ***deer:*** **5** cervo ***dialect:*** **6** Tuscan **8** Sicilian ***dictator:*** **9** Mussolini (Benito) ***die:*** **6** morire ***dinner:*** **6** pranzo ***do, make:*** **4** fare ***dog:*** **4** cane ***enough:*** **5** basta ***evening:*** **4** sera ***everyone:*** **5** tutti ***family:*** **4** Este **5** Cenci, Savoy **6** Borgia, Medici, Orsini, Pepoli, Savoia, Sforza **7** Colonna, Gonzaga, Spinola **8** Visconti ***fascist:*** **10** Blackshirt ***game:*** **5** bocce, bocci **6** boccie ***gentleman:*** **6** signor **7** signore ***give:*** **4** dare ***go:*** **6** andare ***goat:*** **5** capra ***good-bye:*** **4** ciao ***grape:*** **3** uva ***hear:*** **7** sentire ***hello:*** **4** ciao ***highway:*** **10** autostrada ***honey:*** **5** miele ***how much:*** **6** quanto ***ice cream:*** **6** gelato ***lady:*** **5** donna **7** signora **9** signorina ***leave:*** **7** partire ***magistrate:*** **7** podestà ***maybe:*** **5** forse ***meat:*** **5** carne **6** salami **8** pancetta **9** pepperoni, salsiccia **10** mortadella, prosciutto ***man:*** **4** uomo ***milk:*** **5** latte ***mountain soldier:*** **6** Alpino ***much:*** **5** molto ***mushroom:*** **5** fungo ***night:*** **5** notte ***nothing:*** **6** niente ***numbers:*** **3** due, sei, tre, uno **4** nove, otto **5** dieci, sette **6** cinque **7** quattro ***often:*** **6** spesso ***oil:*** **4** olio ***open:*** **6** aprire ***opera house:*** **7** La Scala ***over:*** **5** sopra ***patriot:*** **6** Cavour (Conte di), Rienzo (Cola di) **7** Mazzini (Giuseppe) **9** Garibaldi (Giuseppe) ***peach:*** **5** pesca ***pencil:*** **6** matita ***please:*** **9** per favore ***red:*** **5** rosso ***religious reformer:*** **10** Savonarola (Girolamo) ***resort:*** **4** Lido **5** Abano, Capri **8** Sorrento, Taormina ***road:*** **6** strada ***sandwich:*** **6** panino ***sell:*** **7** vendere ***shrimp:*** **6** scampi ***sing:*** **7** cantare ***sister:*** **7** sorella ***soldier:*** **7** soldato ***soup:*** **5** zuppa **10** minestrone ***speak:*** **7** parlare ***square:*** **6** piazza ***squid:*** **8** calamari ***star:*** **6** stella ***street:*** **3** via **5** corso ***summer:*** **6** estate ***sun:*** **4** sole ***tell, say:*** **4** dire ***thanks:*** **6** grazie ***think:*** **7** pensare ***toward:*** **5** verso ***uncle:*** **3** zio ***under:*** **5** sotto ***voice:*** **4** voce ***weight:*** **5** libra, oncia ***white:*** **6** bianco ***wine:*** **4** vino ***with:*** **3** con ***without:*** **5** senza ***write:*** **8** scrivere

Italy *bay:* 6 Naples ***capital:*** **4** Roma, Rome ***city:*** **4** Asti, Bari, Pisa **5** Aosta, Genoa, Milan, Padua, Parma, Siena, Turin **6** Genova, Mantua, Milano, Modena, Naples, Napoli, Padova, Torino, Venice, Verona **7** Bergamo, Bologna, Bolzano, Catania, Cremona, Firenze, Leghorn, Livorno, Mantova, Palermo, Perugia, Ravenna, Salerno, Taranto,

Trieste, Venezia **8** Florence, Siracusa, Syracuse ***enclave:*** **9** San Marino **11** Vatican City ***gulf:*** **5** Gaeta **7** Salerno, Taranto **11** Sant' Eufemia ***island, island group:*** **4** Elba, Lido **5** Capri **6** Ischia, Lipari, Sicily **7** Aeolian, Capraia **8** Sardinia ***lake:*** **4** Como **5** Garda **7** Bolsena **8** Maggiore **9** Bracciano ***leader:*** **9** Mussolini (Benito) ***monetary unit:*** **4** euro ***monetary unit, former:*** **4** lira **5** scudi (plural), scudo, soldi (plural), soldo ***mountain, range:*** **4** Alps, Etna **9** Apennines, Mont Blanc, Monte Rosa **10** Monte Corno ***neighbor:*** **6** France **7** Austria **8** Slovenia **11** Switzerland ***peninsula:*** **9** Salentina ***river:*** **4** Arno, Liri **5** Adige, Piave, Tiber **6** Isonzo, Tevere **8** Volturno ***sea:*** **6** Ionian **8** Adriatic, Ligurian **10** Tyrrhenian **13** Mediterranean ***strait:*** **7** Messina, Otranto ***volcano:*** **4** Etna **8** Vesuvius ***wine region:*** **4** Asti

itch 3 yen **4** ache, long, lust, pine, urge **5** crave, yearn **6** desire, hanker, hunger, thirst **7** craving, longing **8** appetite, pruritus, yearning **9** hankering

itchy 4 avid, edgy, keen **5** antsy, eager, jumpy **7** fidgety, restive **8** prurient, pruritic, restless **9** impatient

item 3 bit **5** entry, point, scrap, story, thing, topic **6** detail, matter **7** account, article, element, feature, product **8** clipping **9** commodity **10** particular

itemize 4 list **5** count, tally **6** number **7** catalog, run down, specify, tick off **8** document, spell out **9** catalogue, enumerate, inventory

iterate 5 drill, recap, renew **6** rehash, repeat, replay, retell **7** reprise, restate **12** recapitulate

Ithaca king 8 Odysseus

Ithamar's father 5 Aaron

itinerant 5 gypsy, nomad **6** roving **7** migrant, nomadic, roaming, vagrant **8** drifting, rambling, traveler, vagabond, wanderer **9** migratory, transient, unsettled, wandering, wayfaring **11** peripatetic

itty-bitty 3 wee **4** tiny **5** teeny, weeny **6** teensy **10** teeny-weeny **12** teensy-weensy

Ivanhoe *author:* **5** Scott (Walter) ***character:*** **5** Isaac **6** Cedric, Rowena, Ulrica **7** Rebecca, Wilfred **9** Robin Hood

Ivory Coast 11 Côte d'Ivoire ***capital:*** **7** Abidjan **12** Yamoussoukro ***city:*** **6** Bouaké ***language:*** **6** French ***monetary unit:*** **5** franc ***mountain:*** **5** Nimba ***neighbor:*** **4** Mali **5** Ghana **6** Guinea **7** Liberia **11** Burkina Faso ***river:*** **7** Bandama **9** Sassandra

ivory-tower 8 academic **11** conjectural, impractical, theoretical, unrealistic

Ivy League 4 Penn, Yale **5** Brown **7** Cornell, Harvard **8** Columbia **9** Dartmouth, Princeton **12** Pennsylvania

J

jab 3 hit **4** barb, blow, poke, prod, sock, stab **5** nudge, prick, punch **6** pierce, strike, thrust **8** puncture

jabber 3 gab, jaw, yak **6** babble, drivel, gabble **7** blather, chatter, prattle **8** nonsense **9** gibberish

jabberer 6 gabber, magpie **7** babbler, blabber, gabbler **8** prattler **9** chatterer **10** chatterbox

Jabberwocky author 7 Carroll (Lewis), Dodgson (Charles)

jabot 4 fall **5** frill **6** ruffle

____ jacet 3 hic

jack 3 tar **4** bird, card, fish, flag, hike, lift, move, salt **5** boost, brace, bread, dough, knave, knife, money, put up, raise **6** brandy, cheese, device, donkey, rabbit, sailor, seaman **7** laborer, mariner, servant **8** increase, standard **9** criticize, mechanism **10** take to task

jackal 4 dupe, pawn **5** agent, canid, patsy **6** canine, flunky, lackey, minion, stooge **7** cat's-paw **9** accessory, auxiliary **10** accomplice **11** stool pigeon ***god:*** **4** Anpu **6** Anubis

jackanapes 3 ape, imp **4** brat, fool **6** monkey

jackass 4 dolt, dope, fool, jerk **5** burro, dunce, idiot, schmo **6** donkey, nitwit **7** nebbish **8** bonehead, imbecile, numskull **9** blockhead, numbskull **10** nincompoop ***deer:*** **3** kob **8** antelope

jackdaw 7 grackle **9** blackbird

jacket 3 tux **4** Eton **5** parka, tunic **6** anorak, blazer, bolero, jerkin, reefer, sacque, tuxedo **7** doublet, Norfolk, peacoat, spencer **8** camisole **10** roundabout ***armored:*** **7** hauberk **9**

habergeon ***sleeveless:*** **4** vest **6** bolero, jerkin **9** waistcoat

jackhammer 5 drill **9** rock drill

jack-in-the-pulpit 4 arum

jackknife 4 dive **6** barlow ***game:*** **11** mumblety-peg

jackleg 6 make-do, novice **7** amateur, shyster, stopgap **9** dishonest, greenhorn, makeshift, temporary, unskilled **10** substitute **11** pettifogger **12** unscrupulous

jack-of-all-trades 6 tinker **7** go-to guy **8** factotum, handyman

jack-o'-lantern 6 fungus **7** pumpkin

jackpot 3 sum **4** pool **5** award, kitty, prize **6** reward, stakes **7** bonanza, success **8** windfall

jackrabbit 4 hare

jackstay 3 bar, rod **4** rope **7** rigging, support

Jacob *brother:* 4 Esau ***daughter:* 5** Dinah ***father:* 5** Isaac ***father-in-law:* 5** Laban ***mother:* 7** Rebekah ***new name:* 6** Israel ***son:* 3** Dan, Gad **4** Levi **5** Asher, Judah **6** Joseph, Reuben, Simeon **7** Zebulun **8** Benjamin, Issachar, Naphtali ***variant:* 5** James ***wife:* 4** Leah **6** Rachel

Jacobin 7 radical **9** Dominican, extremist

Jacob's ladder 4 herb **5** phlox **9** perennial

jade 3 gem, nag **4** bore, cloy, dull, minx, pall, tire, wear **5** color, drain, flirt, green, hussy, jewel, stone, tramp, weary, wench **6** wanton **7** fatigue, jezebel, mineral, trollop, wear out **8** gemstone, nephrite, strumpet, wear down

jaded 4 worn **5** blasé, bored, sated, tired, weary **6** dulled **7** cynical, wearied, worn-out **8** fatigued, satiated, worn down **9** apathetic, exhausted, surfeited **10** overworked

jaeger 4 skua **6** hunter **8** huntsman

Jael *husband:* 5 Heber ***victim:* 6** Sisera

jag 3 cut **4** barb, jerk, load, pink, tear **5** binge, notch, prick, spell, spree **6** bender, indent, thrill, thrust **7** serrate

jagged 5 erose, harsh, rough, sharp **6** broken, craggy, rugged, spiked, uneven **7** scraggy **8** serrated, unsmooth **9** irregular

Jaguar model 3 XKE

jai alai 6 pelota ***basket:* 5** cesta ***court:* 6** cancha **7** fronton

jail 3 can, jug, pen **4** coop, gaol, poky **5** clink, pokey **6** cooler, lockup, prison **7** confine, freezer, slammer **8** hoosegow, imprison, stockade **9** constrain **11** confinement, incarcerate

jailbird 3 con **5** felon, loser **7** convict **8** criminal, prisoner, repeater **10** recidivist

jailer 5 guard, screw **6** keeper, warden **7** turnkey **8** overseer

jakes 3 loo **5** privy **7** latrine **8** outhouse **9** backhouse

jalopy 3 car **4** auto, heap **5** crate, wreck **6** beater, junker **7** clunker, vehicle **10** automobile, rattletrap

jalousie 5 blind **6** window **7** shutter

jam 3 box, fix **4** bind, clog, cram, dunk, pack, push **5** block, crowd, crush, force, jelly, press, stuff, wedge **6** bruise, impede, plight, scrape, squash, squish **7** dilemma, squeeze **8** compress, conserve, obstacle, preserve **9** confiture, preserves **10** difficulty **11** predicament

Jamaica *capital:* 8 Kingston ***cay:* 5** Pedro **6** Morant ***city:* 10** Montego Bay **11** Spanish Town ***discoverer:* 8** Columbus (Christopher) ***location:* 10** West Indies ***mountain range:* 4** Blue **10** Dry Harbour ***sea:* 9** Caribbean

Jamaican *export:* 3 rum **5** sugar ***hair style:* 6** dreads **10** dreadlocks ***music:* 3** dub, ska **6** reggae ***musician:* 5** Cliff (Jimmy) **6** Marley (Bob, Ziggy) **7** Wailers ***nationalist:* 6** Garvey (Marcus)

jambalaya 4 olio **5** gumbo **6** medley **7** mélange, mixture **8** mishmash **10** hodgepodge, hotchpotch, salmagundi

jamboree 4 gala **5** revel **6** fiesta, frolic **7** carouse, shindig **8** carnival, festival, wingding **9** merriment **11** celebration **13** entertainment

James *brother:* 4 John **5** Jesus, Joses ***cousin:* 5** Jesus ***father:* 7** Zebedee **8** Alphaeus ***mother:* 4** Mary **6** Salome

James novel 8 American (The) **9** Europeans (The) **10** Bostonians (The), Confidence, Golden Bowl (The), Tragic Muse (The) **11** Ambassadors (The), Daisy Miller **14** Turn of the Screw (The), Wings of the Dove (The) **15** Portrait of a Lady (The) **16** Washington Square

James, P. D. *detective:* 9 Dalgliesh (Adam) ***novel:* 11** Original Sin

James Bond *actor:* 5 Craig (Daniel), Moore (Roger) **6** Dalton (Timothy) **7** Brosnan (Pierce), Connery (Sean), Lazenby (George) ***author:* 7** Fleming (Ian) ***cocktail:* 12** vodka martini ***film:* 4** Dr. No **9** GoldenEye, Moonraker, Octopussy **10** Goldfinger **11** Thunderball, View to a Kill (A) **12** Casino Royale **13** Die Another Day, License to Kill, Live and Let Die, Spy Who Loved Me (The) **15** For Your Eyes Only, Living Daylights (The), Quantum of Solace **16** World Is Not Enough (The), You Only Live Twice **17** Tomorrow Never Dies **18** Diamonds Are Forever, From Russia with Love

19 Man with the Golden Gun (The) 26 On Her Majesty's Secret Service *gun:* 7 Beretta, Walther 8 Lilliput *novel:* 4 Dr. No 9 Moonraker 10 Goldfinger 11 Thunderball 12 Casino Royale 13 Live and Let Die, Spy Who Loved Me (The) 15 For Your Eyes Only 16 You Only Live Twice 18 Diamonds Are Forever, From Russia with Love 19 Man with the Golden Gun (The) 26 On Her Majesty's Secret Service *secretary:* 10 Moneypenny (Miss) *villain:* 4 Drax (Sir Hugo), Dr. No, Khan (Kamal), King (Elektra) 5 Klebb (Rosa), Largo (Emilio), Mr. Big, Zorin 6 Carver (Elliot), Graves (Gustav), Renard 7 Blofeld (Ernst Stavro), Mr. White, Sanchez (Franz) 8 Gen. Orlov, Whitaker (Brad) 9 Dr. Kananga, Gen. Koskov, Kristados (Aristotle), Le Chiffre, Stromberg (Karl), Trevelyan (Alec) 10 Goldfinger (Auric), Scaramanga (Francisco)

Jammu and ____ 7 Kashmir

Jane Eyre *author:* 6 Brontë (Charlotte) *lover:* 9 Rochester

jangle 3 jar 4 ring 5 babel, clash 6 clamor, excite, hubbub 7 discord, quarrel 8 conflict 11 discordance, discordancy 12 disharmonize

jangling 5 harsh, noisy, tense 7 grating 9 dissonant 10 discordant, quarreling

janitor 5 super 6 porter 7 cleaner 9 caretaker, concierge, custodian 10 doorkeeper

japan 4 coat 7 coating, varnish 11 lacquerware

Japan 5 Nihon 6 Nippon *capital:* 3 Edo 5 Tokyo *city:* 4 Kobe 5 Kyoto, Osaka, Otaru 6 Nagoya 7 Fukuoka, Okinawa, Sapporo 8 Kawasaki, Nagasaki, Yokohama 9 Hiroshima *island:* 6 Honshu, Kyushu 7 Shikoku 8 Hokkaido *lake:* 4 Biwa 8 Chuzenji *monetary unit:* 3 yen *mountain:* 4 Fuji 8 Fujiyama

Japanese *aborigine:* 4 Ainu *art:* 6 bonsai, ukiyo-e 7 origami *baron:* 6 daimyo *battle cry:* 6 banzai *Buddha:* 5 Amida, Amita *business alliance:* 8 keiretsu *cartoons:* 5 anime *coin:* 2 bu *comics:* 5 manga *dancing girl:* 6 geisha *dish:* 4 miso, soba 5 gyoza, katsu, kombu, sushi 7 sashimi, tempura 8 sukiyaki, teriyaki *drama:* 3 Noh 6 Bugaku, Kabuki 7 Bunraku *drink:* 4 sake, saki *emperor:* 6 Mikado 7 Akihito 8 Hirohito *fencing:* 5 kendo *festival:* 3 Bon *fish:* 4 fugu *flower arrangement:* 7 ikebana *garment:* 6 kimono *gateway:* 5 torii *god:* 5 Ebisu, Hotei 7 Daikoku, Jurojin 8 Bishamon *goddess:* 6 Benten 9 Amaterasu *governor:* 6 shogun *grill:* 7 hibachi *honorific:* 3 san *immigrant:* 5 issei *instrument:* 4 biwa, koto 7 samisen 8 shamisen 10 shakuhachi *language:* 4 Ainu *martial art:* 4 judo 5 kendo 6 aikido, karate 7 jujitsu *martial artist:* 5 ninja *mat:* 6 tatami *measure:* 2 bu, ri *money:* 3 sen, yen *plum:* 6 loquat *poem:* 5 haiku, tanka *porcelain:* 5 imari *pottery:* 4 raku 7 satsuma *race:* 4 Ainu *radish:* 6 daikon *religion:* 6 Shinto 8 Buddhism 9 Shintoism *rice wine:* 4 sake, saki *robe:* 6 kimono *samurai clan:* 5 Taira 8 Minamoto *sash:* 3 obi *song:* 3 uta *suicide:* 7 seppuku 8 hara-kiri, hari-kari, kamikaze *theater:* 2 No 3 Noh 6 Bugaku, Kabuki 7 Bunraku *tidal wave:* 7 tsunami *vehicle:* 8 rickshaw *warrior:* 7 samurai *warrior code:* 7 bushido *weight:* 2 mo *wrestling:* 4 sumo *writing:* 4 kana 5 kanji 8 hiragana, katakana *zither:* 4 koto

Japanese-American 5 Issei, Nisei *second-generation:* 6 Sansei

jape 3 gag, kid, rib 4 gibe, jest, jibe, joke, mock, quip 5 crack, laugh, prank, tease 7 waggery 8 drollery 9 wisecrack, witticism

Japheth *brother:* 3 Ham 4 Shem *father:* 4 Noah *son:* 5 Gomer, Javan, Madai, Magog, Tiras, Tubal 7 Meshech

jar 4 bump, jolt, olla 5 cruse, quake, shake, shock, upset 6 jangle, jounce 7 tremble, vibrate 8 mismatch 9 container *ancient:* 6 krater 7 amphora, canopic

jardiniere 5 stand 6 holder 7 garnish

jargon 4 cant 5 argot, idiom, lingo, slang 6 patois, pidgin 7 dialect, lexicon, palaver 8 language 9 gibberish 10 mumbo-jumbo, vernacular, vocabulary 11 terminology *lawyer's:* 8 legalese *tinkers':* 6 shelta

jarl 4 earl 5 noble 8 nobleman 12 Scandinavian

jarring 5 harsh, rough 6 hoarse, jangly 7 grating, rasping, raucous 8 strident 9 dissonant 10 discordant, unsettling

jasmine 3 tea 4 vine 5 shrub 6 flower, yellow 7 perfume

Jason *father:* 5 Aeson *helper:* 5 Medea *lover:* 6 Creusa, Glauce, Glauke *quest:* 6 Fleece 12 Golden Fleece *ship:* 4 Argo *shipmate:* 8 Argonaut *teacher:* 6 Chiron 7 Cheiron *uncle:* 6 Pelias *wife:* 5 Medea

jasper 6 morlop, quartz 9 stoneware 10 chalcedony

jaundice 4 bias 7 disease, icterus 9 prejudice

jaundiced 6 biased, warped, yellow 7 colored, cynical, envious, hostile, jealous 9 distorted 10 suspicious

jaunt 4 ride, trip **5** drive, sally **6** junket, outing, ramble **7** journey **9** excursion
jaunty 4 airy, pert **5** fresh, light, peppy, perky **6** breezy, lively **7** buoyant **8** debonair **9** sprightly **10** nonchalant
java 6 coffee
Java *almond:* 7 talisay ***cotton:* 5** kapok ***jute:* 5** kenaf ***lake:* 4** Ijen **5** Dieng, Kelut ***plum:* 5** jaman **6** jambul **7** jambool ***strait:* 4** Bali **5** Sunda ***volcano:* 4** Gede, Kawi, Lawu **5** Bromo, Kelut, Raung **7** Ciremai
Javanese *civet:* 5 rasse ***orchestra:* 7** gamelan ***tree:* 4** upas
Javan squirrel 8 jelerang
javelin 5 lance, shaft, spear **7** assagai, assegai, harpoon
Javert's prey 7 Valjean (Jean)
jaw 3 gab, yak **4** chat, rail, talk **5** chops, clack, prate **6** babble, gabble **7** chatter, prattle **9** yakety-yak
jawbone 7 maxilla **8** arm-twist, mandible, persuade, talk into
jawbreaker 9 hard candy
jay 4 bird, blue, hick, rube **5** dandy **6** rustic **7** bumpkin, hayseed **9** chatterer, greenhorn
Jayhawker 9 guerrilla ***State:* 6** Kansas **8** Missouri
jazz 3 bop **4** guff, jive **5** bebop, swing **6** boogie **7** ragtime **8** malarkey, nonsense ***group:* 5** combo ***term:* 3** axe **4** blow, riff, scat, tune, vamp **5** bebop, chart, chops **6** bridge, groove, improv **7** changes **8** stop time **9** front line **10** broken time ***up:* 5** rouse **6** vivify **7** animate, enliven **9** stimulate
jazz musician 3 Ory (Kid) **4** Cole (Nat "King"), Getz (Stan), Hirt (Al), Mann (Herbie), Monk (Thelonious), O'Day (Anita), Rich (Buddy), Shaw (Artie) **5** Baker (Chet), Basie (Count), Brown (Clifford), Corea (Chick), Davis (Miles), Evans (Bill, Gil), Hines (Earl "Fatha"), James (Harry), Jones (Hank), Krall (Diana), Krupa (Gene), McRae (Carmen), Roach (Max), Smith (Jimmy), Sun Ra, Tatum (Art), Terry (Clark), Tormé (Mel), Young (Lester) **6** Bechet (Sidney), Blakey (Art), Burton (Gary), Carter (Benny, Betty), Dorsey (Jimmy, Tommy), Farmer (Art), Garner (Erroll), Gordon (Dexter), Herman (Woody), Hodges (Johnny), Jordan (Louis), Kenton (Stan), Miller (Glenn), Mingus (Charles), Morton (Jelly Roll), Oliver (King), Parker (Charlie "Bird"), Pepper (Art), Powell (Bud), Puente (Tito), Silver (Horace), Waller (Fats), Wilson (Teddy) **7** Brubeck (Dave), Coleman (Ornette), Connick (Harry), Goodman (Benny), Hampton (Lionel), Hancock (Herbie), Hawkins (Coleman), Holiday (Billie), Jarrett (Keith), Mehldau (Brad), Metheny (Pat), Rollins (Sonny), Rushing (Jimmy), Russell (Pee Wee), Shorter (Wayne), Vaughan (Sarah), Webster (Ben) **8** Adderley (Cannonball), Calloway (Cab), Coltrane (John), Eldridge (Roy), Marsalis (Wynton), Mulligan (Gerry), Peterson (Oscar), Williams (Mary Lou) **9** Armstrong (Louis), Blanchard (Terence), Christian (Charlie), Ellington (Duke), Gillespie (Dizzy), Grappelli (Stéphane), Henderson (Fletcher), Lunceford (Jimmie), Reinhardt (Django), Teagarden (Jack) **10** Fitzgerald (Ella), Montgomery (Wes), Washington (Dinah) **11** Beiderbecke (Bix)
jazzy 5 gaudy **6** brassy, flashy, glitzy, lively, rakish, sporty **7** raffish, splashy **8** animated, colorful, exciting, spirited **9** vivacious **10** flamboyant
jealous 5 green **7** envious **9** green-eyed, invidious, resentful **10** possessive
jeans brand 3 Lee **5** Levi's **8** Wrangler
jeer 4 gibe, jibe, mock **5** fleer, flout, scoff, scorn, sneer, taunt **6** deride, heckle, hector, insult **7** contemn, laugh at, mockery **8** derision, ridicule
Jeeves *creator:* 9 Wodehouse (P. G.) ***employer:* 7** Wooster (Bertie) ***position:* 5** valet **6** butler
jeez 4 gosh, heck **5** golly, shoot **6** shucks **7** jeepers
jefe 4 boss, head, lord **5** chief, ruler **6** honcho, leader **9** chieftain, commander
Jefferson, Thomas *home:* 10 Monticello ***lover:* 5** Sally (Hemings) ***state:* 8** Virginia
Jehoram *brother:* 7 Ahaziah ***father:* 4** Ahab **11** Jehoshaphat ***kingdom:* 5** Judah ***slayer:* 4** Jehu ***wife:* 8** Athaliah
Jehoshaphat *father:* 3 Asa **6** Ahilud, Nimshi, Paruah ***father-in-law:* 4** Ahab ***son:* 4** Jehu **7** Jehoram ***wife:* 8** Athaliah
Jehovah 3 God **6** Adonai, Elohim, Yahweh
Jehu 6 driver ***father:* 6** Hanani **11** Jehoshaphat ***grandfather:* 6** Nimshi ***son:* 8** Jehoahaz ***victim:* 5** Joram **7** Jehoram
jejune 4 dull, flat **5** banal, bland, empty, inane, silly, trite, vapid **7** insipid, puerile **8** lifeless **9** colorless **13** uninteresting
Jekyll's alter ego 4 Hyde (Mr.)
jell 3 set **4** form **6** cohere, gelate **7** congeal, thicken **8** coalesce **9** coagulate, take shape
jelly 3 set **4** mass **5** aspic **6** spread **7** congeal, thicken **9** coagulate
jellyfish 6 coward, medusa **7** doormat, medusan **8** medusoid, pushover, weakling **10**

ctenophore **12** coelenterate, invertebrate, siphonophore
jennet 3 ass **5** hinny, horse **6** donkey
jenny 4 bird **6** donkey, female
jeopardize 4 risk **5** peril **6** chance, expose, hazard **7** imperil **8** endanger
jeopardy 4 risk **5** peril **6** danger, hazard, menace **8** exposure **9** liability **12** endangerment
jeremiad 6 lament, screed, tirade **7** lecture **8** diatribe, harangue **9** complaint, philippic **11** declamation, lamentation
Jeremiah's scribe 6 Baruch
Jericho's conqueror 6 Joshua
jerk 3 ass, lug, tic, tug **4** dolt, dope, fool, jolt, pull, push, snap, twit, yank **5** brute, creep, idiot, lurch, ninny, spasm, twist, wrest **6** bounce, nitwit, thrust, twitch, wrench **7** jackass **8** preserve **10** nincompoop
jerkin 6 jacket
jerky 4 meat **5** inane **6** abrupt, stupid, sudden **7** foolish, idiotic, jolting **8** saccadic **9** senseless
Jerome's Bible 7 Vulgate
jersey 3 cow **6** fabric **7** sweater **8** pullover
Jerusalem 4 Sion, Zion **5** Salem **8** Holy City ***hill:* 4** Sion, Zion **6** Moriah ***mosque:* 4** Omar **6** Al-Aqsa **13** Dome of the Rock ***pool:* 6** Siloam **8** Bethesda
Jerusalem artichoke 5 tuber **8** girasole **9** sunflower
Jerusalem thorn 9 horsebean
jess 5 strap
Jesse *daughter:* 7 Abigail, Zeruiah ***father:* 4** Obed ***grandfather:* 4** Boaz ***son:* 4** Ozem **5** David, Eliab, Elihu **6** Raddai **7** Shammah **8** Abinadab, Nethanel ***youngest son:* 5** David
Jessica *father:* 7 Shylock ***husband:* 7** Lorenzo
jest 3 fun, gag, kid, rag, rib **4** butt, game, gibe, jape, jeer, joke, josh, mock, quip, razz **5** crack, fleer, flout, humor, prank, scoff, sneer, spoof, sport, tease **6** banter, gaiety **7** mockery, waggery **8** derision, drollery, ridicule **9** merriment, wisecrack, witticism
jester 3 wag, wit **4** fool **5** actor, clown, comic, joker **7** buffoon **8** comedian, funnyman, humorist, jokester, quipster **9** prankster **11** entertainer
Jesuit *founder:* 6 Loyola (Ignatius) ***leader:* 6** Xavier (St. Francis)
jet 4 coal, ebon, emit, gush, inky, Lear, rush, spew **5** black, ebony, plane, spout, spurt **6** engine, nozzle, squirt, stream, travel **7** current, jewelry **8** airplane **9** pitch-dark **10** pitch-black
Jethro *daughter:* 8 Zipporah ***son-in-law:* 5** Moses
jetsam 7 flotsam **8** wreckage **9** driftwood
jet set 5 A-list, elite **9** beau monde, haut monde **10** glitterati
jettison 4 drop, dump, junk, omit **5** eject, forgo, scrap **6** reject, remove **7** deep-six, discard **8** disposal, get rid of, throw out **9** sacrifice, throw away
jetty 4 dock, ebon, inky, pier, quay **5** black, ebony, groin, wharf **7** project, seawall **9** pitch-dark **10** breakwater, pitch-black
Jew 6 Essene, Hebrew, Semite **7** Israeli, Judaist **9** Israelite
jewel 3 gem **4** rock **5** adorn, bijou, ideal, prize, stone **7** bearing **8** gemstone, ornament, treasure **9** embellish
jeweler 8 lapidary ***famous:* 7** Cartier (Jacques, Louis, Pierre), Fabergé (Carl), Lalique (René), Tiffany (Charles Lewis)
jewelry 5 bling **10** bijouterie, bling-bling ***artificial:* 5** glass, paste **6** strass **7** costume ***piece:* 3** pin **4** ring **6** brooch **7** earring **8** bracelet, cufflink, necklace, tieclasp **9** lavaliere ***set:* 6** parure
Jewish *bread:* 5 matzo **6** matzoh ***ceremony:* 4** bris **8** havdalah **10** bar mitzvah, bas mitzvah, bat mitzvah ***combining form:* 5** Judeo **6** Judaeo ***credo:* 5** shema ***doctrine:* 6** Mishna **7** Mishnah ***New Year:* 12** Rosh Hashanah ***organization:* 8** Hadassah **9** B'nai B'rith ***prayer:* 7** kaddish, kiddush ***prayer book:* 6** siddur ***sabbath:* 8** Saturday ***scripture:* 5** Torah **6** Talmud ***synagogue:* 4** shul ***teacher:* 5** rabbi, rebbe **6** Hillel ***village:* 6** shtetl (see also **Hebrew**)
Jezebel 4 slut **5** hussy, tramp, trull, wench **6** wanton **7** trollop **8** slattern, strumpet ***father:* 7** Ethbaal ***home:* 5** Sidon ***husband:* 4** Ahab ***slayer:* 4** Jehu ***victim:* 6** Naboth
jib 3 arm, shy **4** balk, boom, sail, stop **5** demur **6** refuse **9** stop short
jibe 5 agree, fit in, match, shift, tally **6** accord, concur, square **7** conform **8** dovetail **9** harmonize **10** correspond, go together **12** change course
jiffy 3 sec **4** snap, tick, wink **5** flash, hurry, shake, trice **6** minute, moment, second **7** instant **11** split second
jig 4 fish, game, hoax, hook, jerk, play, ploy, ruse, sham, wile **5** catch, dance, feint, trick **6** device, gambit **7** gimmick **9** deception
jigger 4 jerk, mold, sail **5** alter, gismo, gizmo **6** device, dingus, doodad, gadget, widget **7** gimmick, machine, measure **9** doohickey, rearrange, shot glass, thingummy **10** manipulate
jiggle 4 jerk **5** shake **7** agitate **9** oscillate

jigsaw 3 cut **4** tool **6** puzzle **7** arrange, machine
jihad 3 war **6** strife **7** crusade, holy war **8** campaign, struggle
jilt 4 drop **5** ditch, leave **6** desert, reject **7** abandon, cast off, discard
jim-dandy 3 ace, gem, pip **4** A-one, lulu **5** doozy, great, ideal, nifty, peach, super, swell **6** doozie **7** perfect **8** knockout **9** excellent, first-rate, humdinger **11** outstanding
jimmy 3 bar, pry **4** open **5** crack, force, lever **7** crowbar **9** break open, force open
jimsonweed 6 datura **10** thorn apple
jingle 4 call, ring, song **5** clink, rhyme, sound, verse **6** tinkle
jingoistic 7 hawkish **11** belligerent **12** chauvinistic, militaristic **13** nationalistic
jinn 5 afrit, genie **6** afreet, spirit
jinx 3 hex **5** charm, curse, spell **6** plague, whammy **7** bad luck, evil eye **8** foredoom **10** affliction, misfortune
jitters 5 jumps, panic **6** nerves, shakes **7** anxiety, shivers, willies **9** whim-whams **11** nervousness, stage fright **13** heebie-jeebies
jittery 4 edgy **5** jumpy, nervy **6** goosey, spooky **7** anxious, fearful, fidgety, nervous, panicky **10** high-strung
jive 3 kid **4** fool, jazz, talk **5** dance, music, swing, tease **6** cajole, hot air, jargon
Joab ***brother:*** **6** Asahel **7** Abishai ***father:*** **7** Seraiah, Zeruiah ***slayer:*** **7** Benaiah ***uncle:*** **5** David ***victim:*** **5** Abner, Amasa
Joan of Arc ***birthplace:*** **7** Domremy ***epithet:*** **7** Pucelle (La) **13** Maid of Orléans ***king:*** **7** Charles (VII) ***victory:*** **7** Orléans
Joan's husband 5 Darby
Joash ***father:*** **4** Ahab **7** Ahaziah **8** Jehoahaz ***son:*** **6** Gideon **7** Amaziah **8** Jeroboam ***victim:*** **9** Zechariah
job 3 gig **4** duty, hire, item, post, role, spot, task, work **5** chore, stint, trade **6** effort, office **7** calling, posting, pursuit, robbery **8** business, function, position, vocation **9** situation **10** assignment, employment, engagement, livelihood, occupation, profession **11** undertaking
Job ***daughter:*** **6** Keziah **7** Jemimah ***father:*** **8** Issachar ***friend:*** **6** Bildad, Zophar **7** Eliphaz
jobber 6 broker, dealer, seller, trader **8** merchant **10** contractor, wholesaler
job-safety agency 4 OSHA
job-training program 4 JTPA
Jocasta ***daughter:*** **6** Ismene **8** Antigone ***husband:*** **5** Laius **7** Oedipus ***son:*** **7** Oedipus **8** Eteocles **9** Polynices **10** Polyneices
jock 5 pilot **7** athlete
jockey 4 play **5** rider, trick **7** beguile, exploit, finesse **8** maneuver **10** manipulate ***famous:*** **5** Baeza (Braulio), Krone (Julie) **6** Arcaro (Eddie), Bailey (Jerry), Murphy (Isaac), Pincay (Laffit) **7** Cauthen (Steve), Cordero (Angel), Hartack (Bill), Longden (Johnny), Stevens (Gary) **8** McCarron (Chris), McHargue (Darrel), Turcotte (Ron) **9** Shoemaker (Willie)
jocular 5 comic, funny, jolly, merry, witty **6** jocose, jocund, jovial, lively **7** amusing, comical, jesting, playful **8** cheerful, humorous **9** facetious
jocularity 3 fun, wit **4** glee **5** humor, mirth **6** gaiety **7** jollity **8** hilarity **9** joviality, merriment **11** high spirits, playfulness
jocund 3 gay **5** happy, jolly, merry **6** elated, jovial, lively **7** festive, gleeful, playful **8** mirthful **12** lighthearted
joe 3 guy **4** dude, java **6** coffee, fellow
jog 3 dig, jab, run **4** lope, move, pace, poke, prod, push, ride, stir, trot **5** nudge, punch, rouse, shake **6** bounce, change, jounce, prompt, remind
joggle 4 join, trot **5** dowel, joint, notch, shake, tooth **6** jostle
john 2 WC **3** lav, loo **4** head **5** jacks, privy **6** toilet **7** latrine **8** bathroom, lavatory **11** water closet
John Hancock 9 autograph, signature
Johnson, Samuel ***biographer:*** **7** Boswell (James) ***work:*** **8** Rasselas **10** dictionary
John the Baptist ***father:*** **9** Zacharias ***mother:*** **9** Elisabeth
John the Evangelist ***brother:*** **5** James ***father:*** **7** Zebedee ***mother:*** **6** Salome
joie de vivre 4 elan, zest **5** gusto **6** esprit **10** love of life
join 3 tie, wed **4** abut, ally, bind, bond, fuse, line, link, mate, yoke **5** affix, align, blend, marry, merge, piece, touch, unify, union, unite **6** attach, border, couple, engage, enlist, enroll, sign on, sign up, splice **7** combine, connect **8** compound, federate, side with **9** affiliate, associate, integrate **12** come together
joint 3 bar, ell, hip, tie **4** butt, crux, dive, knee, link, node, seam **5** ankle, elbow, hinge, nexus, union, wrist **6** common, mutual, public, shared, suture, united **7** hangout, knuckle, shiplap **8** abutment, combined, communal, conjunct, coupling, junction, juncture, shoulder **9** concerted, honky-tonk **10** collective, connection **11** cooperative **12** articulation ***combining form:*** **5** arthr **6** arthro, condyl **7** condylo ***disease:*** **9** arthritis **10** rheumatism
joist 4 beam **6** rafter, timber **7** support

joke 3 gag, kid, pun, rag, rib, yak **4** fool, jape, jest, josh, quip, razz **5** crack, humor, prank, sally **6** banter, corker, parody **7** mockery, sarcasm, waggery **8** drollery, one-liner **9** burlesque, wisecrack, witticism **11** monkeyshine ***hilarious:*** **12** sidesplitter ***stale:*** **8** chestnut

joker 3 guy, wag, wit **4** card, fool **5** catch, clown, comic, cutup **6** fellow, jester, kicker **7** proviso **8** comedian, humorist **9** condition **10** limitation **11** stipulation

jollity 3 fun **4** glee **5** cheer, mirth **6** gaiety, revels **7** revelry, whoopee **8** hilarity **9** festivity, jocundity, joviality, merriment **10** ebullience, jocularity **11** high spirits, merrymaking **12** cheerfulness, conviviality

jolly 3 fun, gay, kid **4** glad, jest, josh, very **5** humor, merry **6** banter, jocund, jovial, joyful, joyous **7** festive, gleeful, jocular, playful, roguish, waggish **8** cheerful, mirthful **9** convivial **10** frolicsome **12** lighthearted

Jolly Roger 4 flag **6** ensign ***user:*** **6** pirate

jolt 3 hit, jar **4** blow, bump, jerk, shot, slug, stun **5** check, clash, crash, knock, lurch, shake, shock, upset **6** impact, jounce, rattle **7** disturb, shake up, startle **8** astonish, surprise **9** collision

Jonah 7 prophet ***swallower:*** **4** fish **5** whale

Jonathan *brother:* **7** Johanan ***father:*** **4** Saul ***friend:*** **5** David

Jones, John Paul *ship:* **15** Bonhomme Richard ***victim:*** **7** Serapis

Jones novel 11 Thin Red Line (The) **15** Some Came Running **18** From Here to Eternity

jongleur 4 bard **6** singer **7** juggler **8** minstrel **10** troubadour **11** entertainer

jonquil 8 daffodil **9** narcissus, perennial

Jonson play 7 Volpone **9** Alchemist (The) **15** Bartholomew Fair

Joplin creation 3 rag **7** ragtime **11** Entertainer (The) **12** Maple Leaf Rag

Joram *brother:* **7** Ahaziah ***father:*** **3** Toi **4** Ahab **11** Jehoshaphat ***slayer:*** **4** Jehu ***son:*** **7** Ahaziah

Jordan *capital:* **5** Amman ***city:*** **5** Irbid, Zarqa ***gulf:*** **5** Aqaba ***language:*** **6** Arabic ***monarch:*** **7** Hussein **8** Abdullah ***monetary unit:*** **5** dinar ***mountain:*** **4** Ramm ***neighbor:*** **4** Iraq **5** Syria **6** Israel **11** Saudi Arabia ***sea:*** **4** Dead

jorum 3 cup, jug **6** vessel

Joseph *brother:* (see **Jacob** son) ***buyer:*** **8** Potiphar ***father:*** **5** Asaph, Jacob **9** Zacharias **10** Mattathias ***mother:*** **6** Rachel ***son:*** **5** Jesus **7** Ephraim **8** Manasseh ***wife:*** **4** Mary **7** Asenath

josh 3 kid, rag, rib **4** jest, joke, razz **5** chaff, jolly, tease **6** banter

Joshua's victory 7 Jericho

Joshua tree 5 yucca

joss 4 idol **5** image

Jo's sister 3 Amy, Meg **4** Beth

jostle 3 jar, jog **4** bump, push **5** crowd, elbow, nudge, press, shove **7** agitate, collide, compete, contend, vie with **8** shoulder

jot 3 bit **4** atom, iota, note, whit **5** grain, minim, speck, write **6** tittle **7** smidgen **8** particle

joule component 3 erg

jounce 3 bob, jar, jog **4** bump, jolt **5** shake, shock, thump **6** impact

journal 3 log **4** blog **5** diary, organ **6** ledger, record **7** account, gazette, minutes **8** magazine, register **9** chronicle, newspaper **10** periodical

journalist 3 Bly (Nellie) **4** Dowd (Maureen), Drew (Elizabeth), King (Larry), Pyle (Ernie), Reed (John), Rose (Charlie), Will (George F.), Zahn (Paula) **5** Baker (Russell), Brown (George), Cooke (Alistair), Dunne (Finley Peter), Evans (Rowland), Hersh (Seymour), Novak (Robert), Rowan (Carl), Royko (Mike), Safer (Morley), Smith (Hedrick), Stahl (Lesley), Stone (I. F.), Szulc (Tad), White (William Allen), Wolfe (Tom) **6** Arnett (Peter), Bierce (Ambrose), Broder (David), Brokaw (Tom), Couric (Katie), Ephron (Nora), Koppel (Ted), Gibson (Charles), Kuralt (Charles), Lehrer (Jim), Moyers (Bill), Murrow (Edward R.), Osgood (Charles), Rather (Dan), Reston (James), Reuter (Paul Julius), Rivera (Geraldo), Runyon (Damon), Safire (William), Shirer (William L.), Thomas (Helen, Lowell), Zenger (John Peter) **7** Blitzer (Wolf), Bradlee (Benjamin), Breslin (Jimmy), Cousins (Norman), Greeley (Horace), Gunther (John), Huntley (Chet), Kempton (Murray), McGrory (Mary), Mencken (H. L.), Pearson (Drew), Royster (Vermont), Russert (Tim), Tarbell (Ida), Trillin (Calvin), Wallace (Chris, Mike), Walters (Barbara) **8** Amanpour (Christiane), Anderson (Jack, Terry), Atkinson (Brooks), Brinkley (David), Cronkite (Walter), Garrison (William Lloyd), Jennings (Peter), Lippmann (Walter), Pulitzer (Joseph), Salinger (Pierre), Sevareid (Eric), Steffens (Lincoln), Thompson (Dorothy, Hunter), Williams (Brian), Winchell (Walter), Woodward (Bob) **9** Bernstein (Carl), Donaldson (Sam), Frederick (Pauline), Salisbury (Harrison), Schieffer (Bob)

journey 3 hie **4** hike, roam, tour, trek, trip **5** jaunt, quest **6** cruise, junket, safari, travel, voyage **7** caravan, odyssey, proceed, travels **8** progress **9** excursion **10** expedition, pilgrimage ***route:*** **9** itinerary ***stage:*** **3** leg

joust 4 duel, feud, spar, tilt **5** clash, fight **6** combat **7** contest **8** conflict **10** tournament ***arena:*** **5** lists **8** tiltyard

Jove see **Jupiter**

jovial 5 happy, jolly, merry **6** cheery **7** amiable **8** cheerful **9** convivial **11** good-humored, good-natured

jowl 3 jaw **5** cheek **6** dewlap, wattle **8** mandible

joy 4 glee **5** bliss, mirth **6** gaiety **7** delight, elation **8** felicity, fruition, gladness, pleasure **9** enjoyment, happiness, merriment **11** delectation

Joyce, James *birthplace:* 6 Dublin ***character:*** **5** Bloom (Leopold), Bloom (Molly) **7** Dedalus (Stephen) ***work:*** **6** Exiles **7** Ulysses **9** Dubliners **13** Finnegans Wake

joyful 3 gay **4** glad **5** happy, jolly, merry **6** elated, jocund **7** buoyant, gleeful, pleased **8** ecstatic, jubilant, mirthful **9** delighted, rapturous **12** lighthearted

jubilant 5 happy **6** elated, joyful, joyous **8** euphoric, exultant, exulting **9** cock-a-hoop, delighted, overjoyed, triumphal **10** triumphant

jubilate 5 exult, glory **7** delight, rejoice **9** celebrate

jubilation 3 joy **4** glee **7** ecstasy, rapture **8** euphoria, rhapsody **9** rejoicing, transport **10** exaltation, exultation, joyfulness, joyousness **11** celebration **12** exhilaration

jubilee 6 flambé **8** festival **9** festivity **10** indulgence **11** anniversary, celebration **13** commemoration

Judah *brother:* (see **Jacob** son) ***father:*** **5** Jacob ***king:*** **3** Asa **4** Ahaz, Amon **5** Joash **6** Abijam, Josiah, Jotham, Uzziah **7** Ahaziah, Amaziah, Jehoram **8** Hezekiah, Jehoahaz, Manasseh, Rehoboam, Zedekiah **9** Jehoiakim **10** Jehoiachin **11** Jehoshaphat ***mother:*** **4** Leah ***son:*** **4** Onan **6** Shelah

Judas 7 traitor **8** informer, turncoat ***father:*** **5** Simon **7** Chalphi **10** Mattathias ***replacement:*** **8** Matthias ***suicide place:*** **8** Aceldama, Akeldama

judge 3 ref, try, ump **4** call, deem, rate, rule, test **5** infer **6** critic, decide, deduce, jurist, reckon, settle, umpire **7** arbiter, justice, mediate, referee **8** assessor, critique, estimate, mediator **9** arbitrate, criticize, determine, moderator **10** adjudicate, arbitrator, chancellor, magistrate, negotiator **11** conciliator **12** intermediary ***bench:*** **4** banc ***chamber:*** **6** camera ***in Hades:*** **5** Minos **6** Aeacus **12** Rhadamanthus ***mallet:*** **5** gavel ***Muslim:*** **4** cadi, qadi **5** mufti

judgment 5 award, dicta (plural), sense **6** acumen, decree, dictum, ruling, result, wisdom **7** finding, insight, opinion, verdict **8** decision, sagacity, sentence **9** appraisal, deduction, good sense, inference **10** assessment, conclusion, discretion, estimation, evaluation, horse sense, punishment **11** common sense, discernment **13** determination

judgmental 7 carping **8** captious, critical **10** belittling, censorious, derogatory **11** disparaging, reproachful **12** disapproving, faultfinding **13** hypercritical

Judgment Day 8 doomsday

____ judicata 3 res

judicial *assembly:* 5 court ***document:*** **4** writ ***order:*** **10** injunction

judicious 3 apt **4** fair, just, sage, sane, wise **5** right, sound **6** astute **7** careful, prudent, sapient **8** accurate, discreet, rational, sensible **9** equitable, objective, sagacious **10** discerning, reasonable

Judith *father:* 5 Beeri ***home:*** **8** Bethulia ***husband:*** **4** Esau ***victim:*** **10** Holofernes

judo 10 martial art ***school:*** **4** dojo ***teacher:*** **6** sensei

Judy's husband 5 Punch

jug 3 jar, pen **4** coop, ewer, gaol, jail, olla, olpe, stew, stir, toby **5** clink, pokey **6** cooler, flagon, immure, intern, lockup, prison, vessel **7** confine, pitcher, slammer **8** demijohn, imprison **9** constrain, container **11** incarcerate

jug-band instrument 5 kazoo **6** bottle **7** washtub **9** stovepipe, washboard

juggernaut 11 steamroller

juggle 3 fix **4** fool, toss **5** bluff, trick **6** change, delude, doctor, handle, humbug, take in **7** balance, beguile, deceive, mislead, shuffle **9** rearrange **10** manipulate

juice 3 sap **4** fuel, must **5** fluid **7** current, essence **8** vitality **10** succulence **11** electricity ***fermented:*** **4** wine **5** cider, perry

juicy 4 racy **5** lusty **7** piquant **8** dripping **9** succulent **10** profitable **11** sensational

juju 4 luck **5** charm, magic **6** amulet, fetish, grigri, mascot **8** gris-gris, talisman **10** lucky charm

jujube 4 tree **5** fruit **7** gumdrop, lozenge

julep 5 drink

Juliet *betrothed:* 5 Paris ***father:*** **7** Capulet ***lover:*** **5** Romeo

July 14 11 Bastille Day

jumble 3 mix **4** cake, hash, mess, olio **5**

chaos, mix up, shake **6** cookie, medley, mess up, muddle, muss up **7** clutter, confuse, disturb, mélange, rummage, shuffle **8** disarray, disorder, mishmash, pastiche, scramble **9** confusion, patchwork, potpourri **10** assortment, hodgepodge, hotchpotch, miscellany

jumbo 4 huge, vast **5** giant **6** mighty **7** immense, mammoth, massive **8** colossal, enormous, gigantic, oversize **9** humongous, oversized **10** prodigious **11** elephantine

jump 3 hop **4** bolt, hike, leap, move, trip **5** avoid, begin, boost, bound, clear, flush, hurry, leave, put up, raise, shift, start, vault **6** attack, bounce, bustle, change, hurdle, hustle, jack up, pounce, spring **7** bail out, elevate, startle **8** increase, leap over

jumper 4 sled **5** dress, horse, smock **6** blouse, jacket

jumping-frog county 9 Calaveras

jumpy 4 edgy **6** on edge **7** anxious, jittery, nervous **9** excitable **10** high-strung

junction 4 seam **5** joint, union **7** joining, meeting **8** coupling **9** interface **10** confluence, connection, crossroads **12** intersection

juncture 4 seam **5** joint, point, union **6** crisis, moment **7** instant, joining **8** coupling **10** connection, crossroads **11** concurrence, convergence **12** turning point

jungle 3 web, zoo **4** hash, mash, maze **5** selva, snarl **6** jumble, morass, muddle, tangle **7** clutter, thicket **8** mishmash **9** labyrinth

Jungle Books, The ***author:*** **7** Kipling (Rudyard) ***bear:*** **5** Baloo ***boy:*** **6** Mowgli ***panther:*** **8** Bagheera ***python:*** **3** Kaa ***tiger:*** **9** Shere Khan ***wolf:*** **5** Akela

Jungle, The ***author:*** **8** Sinclair (Upton) ***locale:*** **7** Chicago **10** stockyards

junior 3 son **5** lower, minor, sonny, youth **6** lesser **7** student, younger **8** inferior, young man, youthful **9** secondary, youngster **11** subordinate

juniper 4 cade, cone **5** cedar, fruit, savin, shrub **7** conifer **9** evergreen

junk 4 boat, dope, drug, ship **5** scrap, trash, waste **6** debris, heroin, litter, refuse, reject **7** cashier, clutter, discard, rubbish, rummage **8** get rid of, jettison, throw out **9** narcotics, throw away ***e-mail:*** **4** spam

junker 4 heap **5** crate, wreck **6** beater, jalopy **10** rattletrap, rust bucket

junket 4 trip **5** feast, jaunt, spree **6** outing, picnic **7** banquet, dessert, journey **9** excursion

junk mail 4 spam

Juno ***bird:*** **7** peacock ***epithet:*** **6** Moneta ***Greek equivalent:*** **4** Hera ***husband:*** **7** Jupiter (see also **Hera**)

Junoesque 7 stately **10** curvaceous, statuesque

junta 5 cabal, group **7** council, faction **9** committee

Jupiter 4 Jove, Zeus ***angel:*** **7** Zadkiel ***cupbearer:*** **8** Ganymede ***daughter:*** **5** Venus **7** Minerva ***epithet:*** **6** Fidius, Fulgur, Stator, Tonans **7** Pluvius ***father:*** **6** Saturn ***lover:*** **6** Europa **8** Callisto ***mother:*** **3** Ops ***satellite:*** **6** Europa **8** Callisto, Ganymede ***son:*** **5** Arcas **6** Castor, Pollux ***temple:*** **7** Capitol ***wife:*** **4** Juno

juridical 5 legal **6** lawful **8** juristic **10** legalistic

jurisdiction 3 law, see **4** sway, zone **5** might, orbit, power, range, reach, scope, venue **6** county, domain, parish, sphere **7** circuit, command, compass, control, diocese, mastery, purview **8** dominion, hegemony, province **9** authority, bailiwick, territory **10** domination **11** supervision

jurisprudence 3 law

jurist 5 judge

jury 5 panel ***decision:*** **7** verdict

jury-rigged 6 make-do **7** stopgap **9** makeshift, temporary **10** improvised

just 3 apt, due, fit **4** even, fair, good, meet, only, true **5** equal, legal, right **6** barely, hardly, honest, lawful, proper, simply, square **7** correct, ethical, exactly, fitting, merited, precise, upright **8** accurate, deserved, rightful, suitable, unbiased **9** equitable, honorable, impartial, objective, requisite, righteous **10** legitimate, reasonable, scrupulous **11** appropriate, well-founded **12** unprejudiced

justice 3 law **5** court, judge, right **6** equity **7** honesty **8** evenness, fairness, fair play **10** lawfulness, magistrate **11** correctness **12** impartiality

justification 6 excuse, reason **7** account, apology, defense, grounds **8** apologia **9** rationale **10** validation **11** explanation, vindication

justify 5 argue, claim, prove **6** assert, defend, uphold, verify **7** account, bear out, confirm, contend, explain, support, warrant **8** maintain, make even, validate **9** vindicate **10** legitimate, legitimize **11** corroborate, rationalize **12** authenticate, legitimatize, substantiate

jut 4 hang, poke **5** bulge, pouch **6** beetle, thrust **7** project **8** extend up, overhang, protrude, stand out, stick out **9** extend out, extension **10** projection, protrusion **12** protuberance

jute 5 gunny **6** burlap **7** hessian, sacking

Juvenal **4** poet **5** Roman ***forte:*** **6** satire
juvenile **3** kid **5** actor, child, green, young, youth **6** callow, jejune, junior, moppet **7** preteen, puerile **8** childish, immature, youthful **9** childlike, fledgling, unfledged, youngling, youngster **11** undeveloped
juvenility **5** youth **9** childhood, greenness **10** immaturity, springtide, springtime **12** youthfulness
juxtaposed **4** next **8** abutting, adjacent, neighbor, proximal, touching **9** adjoining, bordering **10** appositive, contiguous, side-by-side **11** coterminous, neighboring **12** conterminous

K

kabob see **kebab**
kachina **4** doll **6** spirit **12** impersonator
kaddish **6** prayer
Kafka, Franz ***character:*** **4** Olga **6** Gregor (Samsa), Joseph (K.) ***novel:*** **5** Trial (The) **6** Castle (The) **7** Amerika ***story:*** **8** Judgment (The) **12** Hunger Artist (A) **13** Metamorphosis (The)
kaiser **5** ruler **7** emperor, monarch **8** autocrat **9** sovereign
kaka **6** parrot
kale **4** cash, cole **5** bucks, lucre, money, moola **6** moolah **7** cabbage **8** Brassica, colewort
kaleidoscopic **8** changing, colorful **10** variegated
Kali ***aspect:*** **5** Durga **7** Parvati ***husband:*** **4** Siva **5** Shiva
Kama ***god of:*** **4** love ***mount:*** **6** parrot **7** sparrow ***wife:*** **4** Rati
Kama ____ **5** Sutra
kamikaze **7** suicide **8** suicidal
kampong **6** hamlet **7** village
Kampuchea see **Cambodia**
kangaroo **6** hopper, leaper **7** wallaby **8** wallaroo **9** marsupial ***herd:*** **3** mob ***young:*** **4** joey
Kansas ***capital:*** **6** Topeka ***city:*** **4** Iola **6** Olathe, Salina **7** Abilene, Emporia, Shawnee, Wichita **8** Lawrence ***nickname:*** **9** Jayhawker (State), Sunflower (State) ***prison:*** **11** Leavenworth ***river:*** **8** Arkansas ***state bird:*** **10** meadowlark ***state flower:*** **9** sunflower ***state tree:*** **10** cottonwood
kaolin **4** clay
kaput **5** spent **6** ruined **7** done for, useless **8** defeated, finished, outmoded **9** destroyed
karakul **5** sheep **9** broadtail
karate ***level:*** **4** belt ***school:*** **4** dojo ***teacher:*** **6** sensei
karma **4** fate **7** destiny **9** emanation
kaross **3** rug **7** garment
kasha **5** grain **8** porridge **9** buckwheat
Katharina ***father:*** **8** Baptista ***suitor:*** **9** Petruchio
Katrina's suitor **9** Brom Bones **12** Ichabod Crane
katydid **3** bug **6** insect **11** grasshopper
katzenjammer **3** din **5** hoo-ha, noise **6** clamor, hoo-hah, hubbub, racket, rumpus **8** brouhaha, distress, foofaraw, hangover, headache **9** commotion
kava **5** shrub **6** pepper **8** beverage
kayo **6** defeat, finish **8** knockout **9** finish off **11** coup de grace
Kazakhstan ***capital:*** **6** Akmola, Astana ***city:*** **5** Semey **8** Pavlodar, Shymkent ***lake:*** **6** Tengiz **8** Balkhash ***language:*** **6** Kazakh **7** Russian ***monetary unit:*** **5** tenge ***mountain:*** **10** Khan-Tengri ***neighbor:*** **5** China **6** Russia **10** Kyrgyzstan, Uzbekistan **12** Turkmenistan ***river:*** **4** Ural **6** Irtysh **8** Syr Dar'ya ***sea:*** **4** Aral **7** Caspian
Kazantzakis hero **5** Zorba (Alexis)
kea **6** parrot
Keats poem **5** Lamia **8** Endymion, Hyperion, Isabella, To Autumn **11** Ode to Psyche **12** Eve of St. Agnes (The) **16** Ode on a Grecian Urn **17** Ode to a Nightingale
kebab **8** shashlik
kedge **6** anchor
keel **4** boat, lean, ship **5** barge, pitch, ridge, slump **6** carina **7** capsize **8** overturn **11** centerboard
keen **4** avid, fine, wail, yowl **5** acute, alert, eager, honed, mourn, neato, nifty, sharp, smart, super **6** ardent, astute, bewail, bright, clever, gung ho, intent, lament, peachy, shrewd **7** anxious, fervent, intense, whetted, zealous **8** animated, spirited **9** fine-edged,

impatient, sensitive, wonderful **10** perceptive, razor-sharp **11** lamentation, penetrating, quick-witted, sharp-witted **12** enthusiastic, sharp-sighted

keenness 3 wit **4** edge, zeal **6** acuity, acumen **10** enthusiasm **11** discernment, penetration **12** incisiveness, perspicacity

keep 3 own **4** hold, jail, mind, obey, save, stay, stet, tend **5** lodge, stock **6** castle, comply, detain, living, lockup, manage, prison, retain **7** abstain, conduct, confine, forbear, fulfill, possess, refrain, reserve **8** conserve, fortress, maintain, preserve, withhold **9** constrain **10** livelihood, sustenance **11** maintenance, subsistence

keep back 3 bar, dam **4** curb, hold, save, stay **6** detain, retain, retard, stifle **7** contain, inhibit, repress, reserve **8** restrain, restrict, suppress, withhold

keeper 5 guard **6** warden **7** big fish, curator **8** Cerberus, guardian, watchdog **9** custodian, protector

keeping 4 care, ward **5** aegis, trust **6** charge **7** custody, support **8** wardship **9** provision **10** caretaking, conformity, observance **11** maintenance **12** conservation, guardianship

keep on 4 last **5** abide **6** endure **7** persist **8** continue **9** hang tough, persevere

keep out 3 ban, bar **4** hold, stop **5** block, check, debar **6** forbid **7** embargo, exclude **8** prohibit, turn back **9** blackball

keepsake 5 token **6** trophy **7** memento **8** memorial, reminder, souvenir **11** remembrance

keep up 7 persist, prolong, sustain **8** continue, maintain, preserve **9** persevere

kef 3 pot **4** hash, hemp **5** grass **7** hashish **9** marijuana **10** dreaminess **12** tranquillity

keg 3 tun **4** butt, cask, pipe **6** barrel, firkin, vessel **8** hogshead **9** container

kegler 6 bowler

keister 3 bum, end **4** buns, butt, duff, rear, rump, seat, tail, tush **5** fanny **6** behind, bottom, heinie **8** backside, buttocks, derriere **9** posterior

keloid 4 scar

kelp 4 alga **7** seaweed

kelpie 3 dog **5** naiad, nixie **6** sprite

Kemo Sabe 10 Lone Ranger

ken 4 view **5** grasp, range, reach, scope, sight **7** horizon, purview **9** knowledge **10** perception **13** comprehension, understanding

kenaf 5 fiber **8** hibiscus

Kenilworth author 5 Scott (Walter)

Kennedy novel 8 Ironweed

kennel 4 pack **5** board **6** gutter **7** shelter **9** enclosure

keno 4 game ***similar to:*** **5** beano, bingo, lotto

Kentucky *capital:* 9 Frankfort ***city:*** **9** Lexington **10** Louisville **12** Bowling Green ***nickname:*** **9** Bluegrass (State) ***park:*** **11** Mammoth Cave ***racecourse:*** **14** Churchill Downs ***river:*** **4** Ohio ***state bird:*** **8** cardinal ***state flower:*** **9** goldenrod ***state tree:*** **11** tulip poplar

Kentucky bluegrass 3 Poa

Kenya *capital:* 7 Nairobi ***city:*** **6** Kisumu, Nakuru **7** Mombasa ***lake:*** **7** Turkana **8** Victoria ***monetary unit:*** **8** shilling ***mountain:*** **5** Elgon, Kenya ***neighbor:*** **5** Sudan **6** Uganda **7** Somalia **8** Ethiopia, Tanzania ***river:*** **4** Tana

kepi 3 cap

kerchief 6 hankie **7** bandana **8** babushka, bandanna, kaffiyeh ***Scottish:*** **5** curch

kerf 3 cut **4** nick, slit **5** cleft, notch **6** groove

kerfuffle 3 ado, row **4** flap, fuss, stir, to-do **5** hoo-ha **6** dust-up, hoo-hah, ruckus, rumpus **7** turmoil **8** foofaraw **9** commotion **11** disturbance

kermis 4 fair **8** carnival, festival

kernel 3 nub, nut **4** core, crux, gist, meat, pith, seed **5** grain **6** nubbin, upshot **7** essence, nucleus **9** substance

Kerouac novel 6 Big Sur **9** On the Road **10** Dharma Bums (The) **13** Subterraneans (The)

Kesey novel 21 Sometimes a Great Notion **25** One Flew over the Cuckoo's Nest

kestrel 4 bird, hawk **6** falcon **9** windhover

ketch 4 boat **6** vessel **8** sailboat **10** watercraft

ketone 7 acetone, camphor

kettle 3 pot **6** hollow, vessel **7** caldron, marmite, pothole **8** cauldron ***handle:*** **4** bail

kettledrum 5 naker **7** timpani (plural), timpano ***Moorish:*** **6** atabal

key 4 clue, isle, reef **5** basic, islet, vital **6** cotter, island, legend, master, opener, samara, spline, ticket, tip-off **7** central, crucial, digital, pivotal **8** critical, password, solution, tonality **9** essential, important **10** open sesame **11** fundamental ***combining form:*** **5** clavi, clavo ***notch:*** **4** ward ***type:*** **8** skeleton

keyboard 6 manual **7** clavier

key fruit 6 samara

Key Largo *director:* 6 Huston (John) ***star:*** **6** Bacall (Lauren), Bogart (Humphrey)

key man 5 chief **7** kingpin **9** locksmith

keynote 4 core, crux, gist, pith, tone **5** theme, tonic

keynoter 6 orator **7** speaker

Keystone Kops director 7 Sennett (Max)

Keystone State 12 Pennsylvania

khaki 3 tan **5** brown, cloth, color **7** garment, uniform

khamsin 4 wind

khan **5** chief, ruler **9** chieftain, sovereign **11** caravansary

khedive **5** ruler **7** viceroy

Khomeini **4** imam **9** ayatollah

Ki ***mother:*** **5** Nammu ***son:*** **5** Enlil

kiang **3** ass

kibble **4** meal **5** grain, grind **9** pulverize

kibbutz **4** co-op, farm **7** commune **10** collective, settlement **11** cooperative

kibe **4** heel, sore **8** swelling **9** chilblain

kibitz **4** chat **6** banter, butt in, meddle **7** comment, intrude, obtrude **9** interfere

kibitzer **7** meddler **8** busybody, observer **9** buttinsky, spectator **10** rubberneck

kibosh **3** hex **4** jinx, stop **5** check, curse

kick **4** bang, boot, punt **6** recoil, thrill, wallop

kicker **5** catch **6** clause, punter **9** condition, fine print

kick in **3** die, pay **4** give **5** begin, put up, start **6** donate, pony up **7** cough up, fork out **8** fork over, hand over **10** contribute

kick off **3** die **4** open **5** begin, croak, start **6** launch **8** commence, drop dead, embark on, initiate **10** inaugurate

kick out **2** ax **3** axe, can **4** fire, oust, sack **5** eject, evict, expel **6** bounce **7** cashier, dismiss **9** discharge

kickshaw **5** curio, goody, treat **6** bauble, dainty, gewgaw, morsel, tidbit, trifle **7** bibelot, trinket **8** delicacy **9** bagatelle

kid **3** guy, rag, rib **4** dupe, fool, gull, hoax, jest, joke, josh, razz **5** bairn, child, jolly, trick, youth **6** banter, befool, moppet, nipper **7** deceive, younger **8** flimflam, hoodwink, juvenile **9** bamboozle, youngling, youngster

kidnap **6** abduct, snatch **8** shanghai

kidney **3** ilk **4** kind, sort, type **5** gland, organ ***combining form:*** **4** reni, reno **5** nephr **6** nephro

kidney-shaped **8** reniform ***delicacy:*** **6** cashew

kielbasa **7** sausage

kilderkin **3** keg **4** cask **6** barrel

kilim **3** mat, rug **6** carpet

kill **2** ax **3** axe, end, ice, nix, off, zap **4** do in, prey, slay, stop, veto **5** creek, croak, erase, quash, scrag, snuff, waste **6** defeat, delete, finish, murder, quarry, stifle **7** bump off, butcher, channel, destroy, execute **8** blow away, carry off, dispatch, knock off, massacre **9** sacrifice, slaughter **10** annihilate **11** assassinate, exterminate

killer **5** bravo **6** gunman, hit man **7** butcher, torpedo **8** assassin, homicide ***combining form:*** **4** cide

Killer Angels author **6** Shaara (Michael)

killer whale **4** orca **8** cetacean

killing **5** blood, fatal **6** deadly, lethal, mortal, murder **7** carnage **8** butchery, foul play, homicide **9** bloodbath, bloodshed, slaughter **12** manslaughter ***of a race:*** **8** genocide ***of bacteria:*** **11** bactericide ***of a brother:*** **10** fratricide ***of a father:*** **9** patricide ***of a king:*** **8** regicide ***of a mother:*** **9** matricide ***of a relative:*** **9** parricide ***of a sister:*** **10** sororicide ***of oneself:*** **7** suicide ***of plants:*** **9** herbicide

killjoy **6** downer, grinch, grouch **7** spoiler **8** doomster, sourpuss **9** Cassandra, defeatist, doomsayer, gloomy Gus, pessimist, worrywart **10** spoilsport, wet blanket

Kilmer poem **5** Trees

kiln **4** oast, oven **7** furnace

kilt **5** skirt ***accessory:*** **7** sporran ***fabric:*** **5** plaid **6** tartan

kilter **4** trim **5** order, shape **6** fettle, repair **7** fitness **9** condition

kimono **4** gown, robe ***sash:*** **3** obi

kin **3** sib **4** clan, folk, sept **5** blood, flesh, house, stock, tribe **6** family **7** lineage, related **8** relation, relative

kind **3** ilk **4** good, like, sort, type, warm **5** breed, class, genre **6** benign, gentle, humane, loving, nature, stripe, tender **7** affable, amiable, clement, essence, feather, lenient, quality, species, variety **8** category, merciful, tolerant **9** character **10** altruistic, benevolent, charitable, forbearing, responsive **11** considerate, good-hearted, good-humored, good-natured, openhearted, softhearted, sympathetic, warmhearted

kindle **4** bear, fire, stir, wake, whet **5** light, rally, rouse, spark, start, waken **6** arouse, awaken, bestir, excite, foment, ignite, incite **7** inflame, provoke **8** activate **9** galvanize, instigate, stimulate **10** illuminate

kindliness **8** goodwill, sympathy **9** affection **10** solicitude **11** benevolence

kindly **6** benign, gentle **7** benefic **8** friendly, generous, gracious, pleasant **9** agreeable, benignant **10** beneficent, beneficial **11** considerate, good-hearted, sympathetic

kindness **5** favor, mercy **7** service **8** clemency, courtesy, goodwill, sympathy **10** compassion, generosity, indulgence **11** benevolence **13** consideration

kind of **5** quite **6** fairly, pretty, rather **8** passably, somewhat **9** tolerably **10** more or less, reasonably, relatively

kindred **3** sib **4** clan, folk, like, sept **5** alike, blood, flesh, house, stock, tribe **6** agnate, allied, family **7** cognate, connate, lineage, related, similar **9** relatives **10** affiliated, connatural **11** consanguine

king **3** rex **4** czar, tsar, tzar **5** mogul, ruler **6** tycoon **7** magnate, monarch **9** sovereign ***Albanian:*** **3** Zog **7** William ***Assyrian:*** **6** Sargon **11** Sennacherib, Shalmaneser ***Babylonian:*** **6** Sargon **9** Hammurabi **10** Belshazzar ***Belgian:*** **6** Albert **7** Leopold **8** Baudouin ***Bohemian:*** **9** Wenceslas **10** Wenceslaus ***Bulgarian:*** **5** Boris **6** Simeon ***Damascus:*** **8** Benhadad ***Danish:*** **4** Abel, Eric, Gorm, Hans, John, Olaf **5** Sweyn **6** Canute, Harold, Magnus **8** Nicholas, Waldemar **9** Christian, Frederick **11** Christopher ***Dutch:*** **7** William ***Egyptian:*** **3** Tut **4** Pepi, Seti **5** Khufu, Menes, Necho **6** Cheops, Ramses **7** Harmhab, Osorkon, Psamtik, Ptolemy **8** Ikhnaton, Thothmes, Thutmose **9** Amenhotep, Sesostris **11** Tutankhamen ***English:*** **4** John **5** Henry, James **6** Alfred, Canute, Edmund, Edward, Egbert, George, Harold **7** Charles, Richard, Stephen, William **8** Ethelred **9** Athelstan, Ethelbald, Ethelbert ***French:*** **3** Odo, roi **4** Jean, John **5** Henri, Henry, Louis, Pepin, Raoul **6** Philip, Robert, Rudolf **7** Charles, Francis, Lothair **8** François **9** Hugh Capet **11** Charlemagne ***German:*** **4** Carl, Karl **5** König, Louis **6** Lothar, Ludwig **7** Charles, Lothair ***Greek (modern):*** **4** Paul **6** George **9** Alexander **11** Constantine ***Hawaiian:*** **10** Kamehameha ***Hungarian:*** **6** Attila ***Indian:*** **4** raja **5** rajah ***Irish:*** **9** Brian Boru ***Italian:*** **7** Humbert, Umberto ***Jordanian:*** **5** Talal **7** Hussein **8** Abdullah ***Judah:*** (see at **Judah**) ***Judean:*** **5** Herod ***legendary:*** **3** Lud **4** Atli, Cole ***Lydian:*** **5** Gyges **7** Croesus **8** Alyattes ***Norwegian:*** **4** Eric, Erik, Inge, Olaf **5** Sweyn **6** Haakon, Harald, Harold, Magnus, Sigurd, Sverre ***Ostrogothic:*** **9** Theodoric ***Persian:*** **5** Cyrus **6** Darius, Xerxes ***Portuguese:*** **4** John **5** Henry, Louis, Peter **6** Carlos, Edward, Manuel, Sancho **7** Alfonso **9** Ferdinand, Sebastian ***Prussian:*** **7** Wilhelm, William **9** Frederick, Friedrich ***relating to:*** **5** regal, royal ***Saudi Arabian:*** **4** Saud **6** Faisal **9** Abdul-Aziz ***Scottish:*** **4** John **5** David, Edgar, James **6** Duncan **7** Macbeth, Malcolm, William **9** Alexander, Donalbane **10** David Bruce **11** Robert Bruce ***Spanish:*** **3** rey **5** Louis **6** Philip **7** Alfonso, Amadeus, Charles **9** Ferdinand **10** Juan Carlos ***Spartan:*** **8** Leonidas ***Swedish:*** **4** Eric, John **5** Oscar **6** Birger, Gustav, Haakon, Magnus **7** Charles **8** Gustavus, Waldemar **9** Frederick, Sigismund, Sten Sture ***Visigothic:*** **6** Alaric

King Arthur ***birthplace:*** **8** Tintagel ***chronicler:*** **8** Geoffrey (of Monmouth) ***court site:*** **7** Camelot **8** Caerleon ***deathplace:*** **6** Camlan ***father:*** **5** Uther ***father-in-law:*** **9** Laodogant, Leodegran **11** Leodegrance ***foster father:*** **5** Ector ***jester:*** **7** Dagonet ***knight:*** **3** Kay **4** Bors **5** Balan, Balin **6** Gareth, Gawain, Modred **7** Galahad, Geraint, Lamerok, Mordred, Tristan **8** Bedivere, Lancelot, Parsifal, Percival, Tristram **9** Launcelot ***lance:*** **3** Ron ***last abode:*** **6** Avalon ***last name:*** **9** Pendragon ***magician:*** **6** Merlin ***mother:*** **6** Ygerne **7** Igraine ***nephew:*** **6** Gareth, Modred **7** Mordred ***queen:*** **9** Guinevere ***shield:*** **7** Pridwin ***sister:*** **7** Morgain **11** Morgan le Fay ***slayer:*** **6** Modred **7** Mordred ***son:*** **6** Modred **7** Mordred ***steward:*** **3** Kay ***sword:*** **9** Excalibur ***victim:*** **6** Modred **7** Mordred ***wife:*** **9** Guinevere

king crab **7** limulus

kingdom **5** realm **6** domain, empire **7** demesne **8** monarchy

kingdom come **4** Zion **6** heaven **8** paradise **9** hereafter **10** afterworld

kingfish **4** boss **6** bigwig, honcho, master **7** big shot, croaker **8** mackerel

kingfisher **7** halcyon **10** kookaburra

King Kong ***character:*** **4** Dwan **6** Darrow (Ann), Denham (Carl), Wilson (Fred) **8** Driscoll (Jack), Prescott (Jack) ***director:*** **6** Cooper (Merian C.) **7** Jackson (Peter) **10** Guillermin (John) ***home:*** **11** Skull Island ***star:*** **4** Wray (Fay) **5** Black (Jack), Brody (Adrien), Cabot (Bruce), Lange (Jessica), Watts (Naomi) **6** Grodin (Charles) **7** Bridges (Jeff) **9** Armstrong (Robert)

King Lear ***actor:*** **3** Cox (Brian) **4** Holm (Ian) **5** Booth (Edwin), Jones (James Earl), Magee (Patrick) **7** Burbage (Richard), Garrick (David), Gielgud (John), Olivier (Laurence) **8** Scofield (Paul) ***author:*** **11** Shakespeare (William) ***daughter:*** **5** Regan **7** Goneril **8** Cordelia ***servant:*** **6** Oswald ***son:*** **5** Edgar **6** Edmund

kingly **5** regal, royal **6** august, lordly, regnal **7** exalted **8** imperial, majestic **9** imperious, masterful, monarchal, sovereign **10** monarchial **11** monarchical

King novel **6** Carrie **7** Shining (The) **8** Dead Zone (The) **9** Dark Tower (The), Green Mile (The), Salem's Lot **11** Firestarter, Pet Sematary

King Philip **9** Metacomet

kingpin **4** boss, guru, head **5** chief, mogul **6** bigwig, top dog **7** magnate **9** top banana **10** mastermind

Kings Peak range **5** Uinta

Kingu ***consort:*** **6** Tiamat ***slayer:*** **6** Marduk

kink **4** bend, curl, knot, whim **5** cramp, crick,

quirk, snarl, spasm, twist **6** tangle **11** peculiarity **12** eccentricity, imperfection
kinky 3 odd **4** bent **5** curly, outré, ultra, weird **6** curled, far-out, frizzy, quirky **7** bizarre, deviant, knotted, strange, twisted **9** eccentric **10** outlandish
kiosk 5 booth, stand **8** pavilion **9** newsstand **11** summerhouse
kip 3 bed, nap **4** hide, pelt, skin **5** sleep
Kipling work 3 Kim **6** L'Envoi **8** Gunga Din, Mandalay **10** Fuzzy Wuzzy **11** Jungle Books (The), Recessional **13** Just So Stories, Soldiers Three **15** Light That Failed (The), Puck of Pook's Hill **18** Captains Courageous
Kiribati ***capital:*** **6** Tarawa ***island, island group:*** **4** Line **6** Banaba **7** Gilbert, Phoenix ***location:*** **7** Oceania
kirk 6 church
kirsch 6 brandy, liquor
kirtle 4 coat, gown **5** dress, tunic **7** garment
Kish ***father:*** **3** Ner **4** Abdi **5** Abiel, Jeiel **6** Jehiel ***son:*** **4** Saul
kismet 3 lot **4** doom, fate, luck **5** weird **6** Moirai **7** destiny, fortune
kiss 4 buss, neck, peck **5** graze, smack, spoon **6** cookie, glance, smooch **7** lip-lock **8** osculate, pucker up **10** osculation
kisser 3 mug **4** face, lips **5** mouth
Kiss sculptor 5 Rodin (Auguste)
kit 3 set **4** gear, pelt **5** group **6** outfit, tackle, violin **7** package **8** caboodle **9** container **10** collection
kitchen 4 mess **6** galley **7** cuisine **8** scullery ***appliance:*** (see at **appliance**) ***boss:*** **4** chef (see also **cooking**)
kite 4 hawk, sail, soar **5** check, glede, hurry, mosey **7** saunter, take off **8** clear out, hightail, predator **9** spinnaker
kith 3 kin, sib **4** clan, folk **6** family **7** friends, kindred, kinfolk **9** neighbors, relatives
kitsch 4 camp, junk **9** vulgarity
kittenish 3 coy **6** elvish, frisky, impish **7** coltish, playful **10** frolicsome **11** mischievous
kitty 3 cat, pot **4** ante, fund, pool, puss **5** pussy **6** feline, stakes **7** jackpot
kiwi 4 bird **5** fruit **7** Apteryx **12** New Zealander
klatch 5 bunch, group **7** meeting **9** gathering **11** get-together
kleptomaniac 5 thief **7** booster **10** shoplifter
klutz 3 oaf **4** boob, clod, gawk, lout, lump **5** looby **6** lubber, lummox **7** bungler, palooka **8** shlemiel **9** schlemiel **10** stumblebum
klutzy 5 inept **6** clumsy **7** awkward **9** all thumbs, maladroit **10** blundering
knack 4 bent, gift, head **5** flair, forte, skill, trick **6** genius, talent **7** ability, aptness, command, faculty, know-how, mastery **8** aptitude, capacity, facility **9** dexterity, expertise, stratagem
knapsack 4 pack **8** backpack
knave 3 cad **4** heel, jack **5** fraud, rogue, scamp **6** rascal, varlet **7** bounder, lowlife, villain **8** scalawag, swindler **9** scoundrel **10** blackguard **11** rapscallion
knavery 5 fraud **6** deceit **8** mischief, trickery, villainy **9** chicanery, deception, rascality **10** dishonesty
knavish 5 lying **6** shifty, tricky **7** devious, roguish **8** rascally **9** deceitful, deceptive, dishonest **10** mendacious **12** unscrupulous
knead 4 form, mold, work **5** press, shape **7** massage **10** manipulate
knee 5 joint ***bend:*** **9** genuflect **12** genuflection ***bone:*** **7** patella
kneeler 5 stool **7** cushion **8** prie-dieu **9** footstool
knell 4 bong, peal, ring, toll **5** chime **6** summon **7** warning **8** announce, proclaim
knickknack 3 toy **4** dido **5** curio **6** bauble, gadget, gewgaw, trifle **7** bibelot, novelty, trinket, whatnot, whatsit **8** gimcrack, ornament, souvenir **9** bagatelle, bric-a-brac, objet d'art
knife 3 ulu **4** bolo, kris, shiv, snee **5** blade, bowie, panga, shank, sword **6** barong, cutter, dagger, lancet, parang, sickle **7** cleaver, machete, scalpel **8** stiletto, yataghan **11** switchblade ***case:*** **6** sheath ***handle:*** **4** haft, hilt ***maker:*** **6** cutler **7** grinder
knifelike 4 keen **5** acute, sharp **7** cutting **8** piercing, stabbing **11** penetrating
knight 3 dub, sir **5** eques **8** cavalier, chessman, horseman **9** caballero, chevalier ***code:*** **8** chivalry ***competition:*** **7** listing, tilting **8** jousting **10** tournament ***German:*** **6** Ritter ***servant:*** **4** page **5** valet **6** squire ***title:*** **3** sir ***wife:*** **4** lady
knighthood 8 chivalry
knightly 4 bold **5** brave, noble **6** heroic **7** gallant, valiant **10** chivalrous
Knight of the Round Table see **King Arthur**
Knight of the Rueful Countenance 10 Don Quixote
knit 4 bind, heal, join, link, mend, purl **5** plait, unite, weave **6** fabric, stitch **7** conjoin, crochet **8** contract **9** interlace **10** intertwine
knitting ***material:*** **4** yarn ***stitch:*** **3** rib **4** purl **6** garter ***tool:*** **6** needle
knob 3 bun, bur, nub **4** bump, burl, burr, dial, hill, hump, lump, node, umbo **5** bulge, gnarl, knoll, mound **6** button, finial, handle, nubble, pommel **7** hillock **12** protuberance

knobkerrie 3 bat **4** club, mace **5** billy **6** cudgel, weapon **7** war club **8** bludgeon **9** billy club, shillalah, truncheon **10** shillelagh

knock 3 bob, hit, rap, tap **4** bash, blow, bump, cuff, lick, swat **5** blame, clout, fault, pound, swipe, thump **6** strike **7** censure, condemn, setback **8** denounce, reversal **9** criticize **10** denunciate

knockabout 5 rough, rowdy, sloop, tough **7** roaming, vagrant **10** boisterous

knock down 4 drop, earn, fell, gain, raze **5** floor, level, lower **6** lay low, reduce **7** acquire, bring in, flatten **9** dismantle **11** disassemble

knocker 6 carper, critic **7** caviler **8** quibbler **10** complainer, criticizer **11** fault-finder

knock off 3 rob **4** copy, do in, halt, kill, quit, slay, stop **5** cease **6** deduct, defeat, desist, finish, murder **7** execute, imitate, take out, take ten **8** discount, overcome, subtract, take five **9** liquidate **11** assassinate, call it quits, counterfeit

knockout 2 KO **4** kayo, lulu **5** dandy, doozy, final **6** beauty, doozie, eyeful, looker, lovely **7** stunner **8** decisive, jim-dandy, striking, stunning **9** deathblow, finishing, humdinger **10** attractive **11** coup de grace, crackerjack

knock over 3 rob **4** down, drop, fell **5** amaze, floor, steal, upset **6** boggle, hijack, hold up, lay low, topple **7** flatten, stick up **9** bring down, eliminate, overpower, overthrow, overwhelm, prostrate

knoll 4 hill, knob, rise **5** mound **7** hillock

knot 3 bow, tie **4** bond, burr, link, loop, lump, node **5** bunch, gnarl, hitch, nexus **6** jungle, tangle **8** ligament, ligature, vinculum ***hair:*** **7** chignon ***in fiber:*** **3** nep ***kind:*** **4** bend, loop, slip **5** hitch **6** granny, splice, square **7** bowline **9** sheet bend **10** clove hitch, sheepshank

knotty 4 hard **6** sticky **7** complex, gnarled, Gordian **8** involved **9** byzantine, difficult, elaborate, intricate **10** formidable **11** complicated, problematic

knout 4 flog, lash, whip **7** scourge

know 3 wot **5** grasp **6** fathom, intuit **7** discern, realize **9** apprehend, recognize **10** comprehend, understand ***Scottish:*** **3** ken

knowable 9 graspable **10** cognizable, fathomable **12** intelligible **13** apprehensible

know-how 5 craft, knack, skill **6** talent **7** ability, cunning, faculty, mastery **8** aptitude **9** dexterity, expertise **10** adroitness, expertness **11** proficiency

knowing 3 hep, hip **4** sage, wise **5** aware, blasé, canny, savvy, smart **6** bright, clever **7** witting, worldly **8** sentient **9** cognizant, conscious, sagacious **10** conversant, discerning, insightful, perceptive **11** worldly-wise **13** sophisticated

know-it-all 6 smarty **7** wise guy **8** wiseacre **10** smart aleck **11** smarty-pants, wisenheimer

knowledge 3 ken **4** data, info, lore, news **5** facts **6** wisdom **7** science **8** learning **9** cognition, education, erudition **10** cognizance **11** information, scholarship **12** intelligence ***lack of:*** **9** ignorance ***mystical:*** **6** gnosis

knowledgeable 5 savvy **8** educated, informed

know-nothing 4 dolt, dope, fool **5** dummy, dunce, idiot, yahoo **6** dimwit **7** pinhead **8** agnostic, ignorant, numskull **9** benighted, blockhead, brainless, ignoramus, lamebrain, numbskull **10** illiterate, uneducated **11** empty-headed

knuckle 5 joint ***combining form:*** **6** condyl **7** condylo

knucklehead 4 dolt, dope, fool **5** dummy, dunce, idiot, yahoo **6** dimwit **8** clodpole, numskull **9** ignoramus, lamebrain, numbskull

knuckle under 3 bow **4** cave **5** yield **6** cave in, give in, submit **7** succumb **8** say uncle **9** surrender **10** capitulate

knurl 3 nub **4** bead, knob **5** ridge **12** protuberance

KO 8 knockout

koan 7 paradox

kobold 3 nis **5** dwarf, gnome **6** goblin, spirit, sprite

Kohinoor 3 gem **7** diamond

kohlrabi 7 cabbage **8** Brassica

kola 3 nut **4** tree

komatik 4 sled **6** sledge

kook 3 nut **5** crank, loony, wacko **6** cuckoo, weirdo **7** dingbat, lunatic, oddball **8** crackpot **9** ding-a-ling, fruitcake, screwball **10** crackbrain

kooky 4 bats, daft, nuts **5** batty, crazy, daffy, ditsy, ditzy, dotty, flaky, loony, nutty, silly, wacky, weird **6** freaky, fruity, insane, screwy **7** bizarre, idiotic, lunatic, offbeat, touched **8** demented **9** eccentric, fantastic **10** flipped out, freaked-out, off-the-wall, outlandish

kopeck 4 coin ***one hundred:*** **5** ruble

Koran *chapter:* **4** sura ***revealer of:*** **7** Gabriel ***scholar:*** **5** ulama, ulema

Korea, North *capital:* **9** P'yongyang ***city:*** **7** Hamhung **8** Ch'ongjin ***leader:*** **9** Kim Il-sung, Kim Jong Il **10** Kim Chong-Il ***monetary unit:*** **3** won ***mountain:*** **6** Paektu ***neighbor:*** **5** China **6** Russia **10** South Korea ***sea:*** **6** Yellow

Korea, South *captial:* **5** Seoul ***city:*** **5** Pusan,

Taegu **6** Inch'on, Taejon **7** Kwangju ***island:*** **5** Cheju ***monetary unit:*** **3** won ***neighbor:*** **10** North Korea ***river:*** **3** Han **7** Naktong ***sea:*** **5** Japan **6** Yellow

Korean *dynasty:* **5** Silla **7** Koguryo ***national dish:*** **6** kimchi

kosher **3** fit **4** pure **5** clean **6** proper **10** acceptable, legitimate, sanctioned **12** satisfactory ***not:*** **4** tref **7** terefah

Kosinski novel **5** Steps **10** Being There **11** Painted Bird (The)

Kosovo *capital:* **8** Priština ***city:*** **7** Prizren ***lake:*** **6** Badovc **8** Gazivoda ***monetary unit:*** **4** euro **5** dinar ***neighbor:*** **6** Serbia **7** Albania **9** Macedonia **10** Montenegro ***river:*** **3** Lab **4** Ibar **6** Erenik **7** Sitnica **9** White Drin

kowtow **3** bow **4** fawn **5** cower, defer, kneel, toady **6** cringe, grovel **7** honey up, truckle **8** bootlick **11** apple-polish

kraal **3** pen **6** corral **7** village **9** enclosure

kraken **5** squid **9** leviathan **10** giant squid, sea monster

krater **3** jar **4** vase **6** vessel

Kriemhild *brother:* **7** Gunther ***husband:*** **5** Etzel **6** Attila **9** Siegfried ***slayer:*** **10** Hildebrand ***victim:*** **5** Hagen

kris **6** dagger

Krishna *avatar of:* **6** Vishnu ***brother:*** **8** Balarama ***father:*** **8** Vasudeva ***mother:*** **6** Devaki ***uncle:*** **5** Kansa ***victim:*** **5** Kansa

Krupp works site **5** Essen

krypton symbol **2** Kr

Kubla Khan *author:* **9** Coleridge (Samuel Taylor) ***intruder's home:*** **7** Porlock ***palace:*** **6** Xanadu ***river:*** **4** Alph

kudos **4** bays, fame **5** award, glory, honor **6** honors, praise, renown **7** acclaim, bouquet, laurels **8** accolade, bouquets **10** compliment **11** distinction, recognition

kudu **8** antelope

kukri **5** sword

Kumin work **9** Up Country **12** Long Marriage (The)

kumquat **5** fruit ***kin:*** **6** orange

Kushner play **15** Angels in America

Kuwait *gulf:* **7** Persian ***island:*** **7** Bubiyan **8** Faylakah ***language:*** **6** Arabic **7** Persian ***monetary unit:*** **5** dinar ***neighbor:*** **4** Iraq **11** Saudi Arabia ***oasis:*** **8** Al-Jahrah

kvass **4** beer

kvetch **4** beef, crab, fret, fuss **5** gripe, whine **6** grouch, grouse **7** grumble **8** complain **9** bellyache

kyphosis **8** humpback **9** curvature, hunchback

Kyrgyzstan *capital:* **7** Bishkek ***city:*** **3** Osh ***conqueror:*** **9** Jöchi Khan ***lake:*** **8** Issyk-Kul ***language:*** **6** Kyrgyz **7** Russian ***monetary unit:*** **3** som ***mountain, range:*** **4** Alai **6** Pobedy **7** Victory **8** Tian Shan **10** Khan-Tengri **11** Kok Shaal-Tau ***neighbor:*** **5** China **10** Kazakhstan, Tajikistan, Uzbekistan ***river:*** **5** Naryn

L

Laadah *father:* **6** Shelah ***grandfather:*** **5** Judah

laager **4** camp **6** encamp **7** bivouac

lab see **laboratory**

Laban *daughter:* **4** Leah **6** Rachel ***father:*** **7** Bethuel ***grandfather:*** **5** Nahor ***sister:*** **7** Rebekah

label **3** tag **4** band, mark **6** marker, ticket **7** epithet, sticker **8** classify, hallmark, identify, insignia

labium **3** lip

La Bohème *composer:* **7** Puccini (Giacomo) ***librettist:*** **6** Illica (Luigi) **7** Giacosa (Giuseppe) ***role:*** **4** Mimi **6** Benoit **7** Colline, Musetta, Rodolfo **8** Marcello **9** Alcindoro, Schaunard ***setting:*** **5** Paris ***source author:*** **6** Murger (Henri)

labor **4** moil, task, toil, work **5** chore, grind, sweat **6** drudge, effort, strain, strive **7** slavery, travail **8** drudgery, endeavor, exertion, struggle **10** birth pangs, childbirth, donkeywork **12** childbearing ***camp:*** **5** gulag ***group:*** **3** AFL, CIO **5** ILGWU, union **6** AFL-CIO ***leader:*** **5** Hoffa (James, Jimmy), Lewis (John L.), Meany (George) **6** Chavez (Cesar) **7** Gompers (Samuel), Reuther (Walter), Sweeney (John J.) **8** Kirkland (Lane), Randolph (A. Philip)

laboratory *device:* **5** flask **6** beaker, mortar, pestle, retort **7** burette, pipette **8** crucible,

test tube **9** petri dish **12** Bunsen burner **13** proving ground
labored 4 hard **6** forced, taxing, tiring **7** arduous **8** strained **9** difficult, effortful, fatiguing, strenuous
laborer 4 esne, hack, hand, peon **5** grind, navvy, prole **6** coolie, menial **7** workman **10** roustabout, workingman ***Mexican:* 7** bracero
laborious 4 hard **6** tiring, uphill **7** arduous, onerous, operose **8** diligent, grueling, sedulous, toilsome **9** assiduous, difficult, effortful, strenuous **10** burdensome, unflagging **11** hardworking, industrious, persevering **12** backbreaking
La Brea 4 pits **7** tar pits ***fossil:* 7** mammoth **8** mastodon **10** saber-tooth
labyrinth 3 web **4** coil, knot, maze, mesh **5** skein, snarl **6** jungle, morass, tangle ***builder:* 8** Daedalus ***hero:* 7** Theseus ***monster:* 8** Minotaur
labyrinthine 4 mazy **6** daedal, knotty **7** complex, gordian **8** involved, mazelike, tortuous **9** Byzantine, elaborate, intricate **10** convoluted, perplexing **11** bewildering, complicated
lace 3 net, tat, tie **4** cord, trim **5** adorn, braid, frill, plait, twine **6** fasten, string **7** entwine, netting, tatting **8** filigree, openwork **9** embroider **10** embroidery, intertwine **11** needlepoint ***edge:* 5** picot ***fall:* 5** jabot ***ground:* 6** reseau ***into:* 5** abuse **6** attack **7** condemn ***kind:* 6** bobbin **7** Alençon, guipure, macramé, Maltese, Mechlin, torchon **8** Brussels, Venetian **9** Chantilly **11** needlepoint **12** Valenciennes ***make:* 3** tat ***pattern:* 5** toilé
Lacedaemon 6 Sparta
lacerate 3 cut, rip **4** gash, rend, tear **5** slash, wound **6** mangle, pierce **7** afflict, mangled, torment **8** distress
lacework 7 tatting
lachrymose 3 sad **5** teary, weepy **7** doleful, tearful, weeping **8** dolorous, mournful **11** tear-jerking
lack 4 need, want **6** dearth, defect **7** absence, default, deficit, failure, paucity, poverty, require **8** scarcity, shortage **9** privation **10** deficiency, inadequacy, scantiness **13** insufficiency
lackadaisical 4 idle, lazy, limp, slow **5** moony **6** dreamy **7** languid, passive **8** fainéant, indolent, listless, slothful **9** apathetic, enervated **10** languorous, spiritless **11** halfhearted
lackey 5 toady **6** fawner, flunky, minion, vassal **7** footman, servant **8** truckler **9** attendant, sycophant
lacking 3 shy **4** sans **5** minus, short **6** absent, flawed, needed **7** missing, needing, omitted, wanting, without **8** devoid of, impaired **9** defective, deficient **10** deprived of, inadequate, incomplete **11** halfhearted **12** insufficient
lackluster 3 dim **4** arid, blah, drab, dull, flat **5** blind, ho-hum, matte, muted, prosy, rusty, vapid **6** boring, leaden **7** prosaic **8** lifeless, mediocre **9** colorless, tarnished **10** uninspired **13** unimaginative
Laconian 7 Spartan ***king:* 5** Lelex, Myles **8** Menelaus
laconic 4 curt **5** bluff, blunt, brief, pithy, short, terse **7** brusque, concise **8** succinct
lacquer 5 glaze, gloss **6** enamel, finish **7** shellac, varnish
lacrosse *related game:* 7 jai alai ***term:* 5** clamp **6** crease, crosse, pocket **7** face-off ***team:* 3** ten
lactate 4 salt **5** ester, nurse **6** suckle **7** secrete **8** wet-nurse **10** breast-feed
lacteal 5 milky **6** cloudy, pearly
lacuna 3 gap, pit **4** void **5** blank, break, space **6** breach, cavity, hiatus **7** caesura **10** deficiency **12** interruption
lacy 4 fine **5** meshy **6** dainty **7** netlike **8** delicate, gossamer **9** filigreed
lad 3 boy, son, tad **4** tike, tyke **5** youth **6** shaver **9** shaveling, stripling ***Irish:* 4** boyo **5** bucko ***Scottish:* 5** chiel **7** callant
ladder 3 run **5** ranks, scale **6** series **7** ranking **9** hierarchy ***piece:* 4** rung **6** rundle
ladderlike 6 scalar, scaled **7** stepped **11** scalariform
lade 3 dip, tax **4** bail, load, pack, ship, stow **5** ladle, scoop **6** burden, saddle, weight **8** encumber
la-di-dah 6 chichi, too-too **7** elegant, genteel, stuck-up **8** affected, snobbish **9** conceited, grandiose, high-flown **10** hoity-toity **11** pretentious
ladies' man 4 stud, wolf **5** Romeo **7** amorist, Don Juan, gallant **8** lothario **9** womanizer
lading 4 haul, load **5** cargo, goods **6** burden **7** bailing, dipping, freight, loading, payload **8** shipment **11** consignment
ladle 3 dip **4** bail **5** scoop, spoon **6** dipper
Ladon 6 dragon ***father:* 7** Phorcus, Phorcys ***mother:* 4** Ceto ***slayer:* 8** Heracles, Hercules
lady 4 dame **5** madam, woman **6** female, matron ***French:* 4** dame ***German:* 4** Frau ***Italian:* 5** donna **7** signora ***Muslim:* 5** begum ***Spanish:* 4** doña **6** señora
lady ____ 4 luck **5** apple **6** beetle, chapel
ladybug 6 beetle ***Australian:* 7** vedalia
Lady Chatterley's Lover *author:* 8 Lawrence

(David Herbert) ***character:*** **6** Connie **7** Mellors (Oliver) **9** Constance

lady-killer 4 dude, hunk, roué, stud **7** playboy, seducer **8** Casanova, lothario **12** heartbreaker

Lady of the Lake, The 5 Ellen (Douglas), Nimue **6** Vivien ***author:*** **5** Scott (Walter)

Lady Windermere's Fan author 5 Wilde (Oscar)

Laertes *father:* 8 Acrisius, Polonius ***sister:*** **7** Ophelia ***son:*** **7** Ulysses **8** Odysseus ***victim:*** **6** Hamlet ***wife:*** **8** Anticlea

La Fontaine's forte 5 fable

lag 4 drag, flag, last, poke, slow, tire **5** dally, delay, tarry, trail **6** dawdle, linger, loiter **7** slacken **8** hang back, hindmost, interval **10** dillydally **13** procrastinate

lager 4 beer, brew, malt, suds **7** brewski

laggard 3 lax **4** slow **5** tardy **6** loafer **7** dawdler **8** dallying, dawdling, delaying, dilatory, flagging, lingerer, loiterer, slowpoke, sluggish, tarrying **9** apathetic, lazybones, lethargic, loitering, straggler **10** behindhand

La Gioconda 8 Mona Lisa ***composer:*** **10** Ponchielli (Amilcare) ***painter:*** **7** da Vinci (Leonardo) **8** Leonardo (da Vinci)

lagniappe 3 tip **4** gift, perk **5** bonus, extra **7** cumshaw, largess **8** dividend, gratuity **9** baksheesh, pourboire **10** perquisite

lagomorph 4 hare, pika **6** rabbit

lagoon 4 pond, pool **5** bayou, sound **6** strait **7** channel, narrows ***rim:*** **5** atoll

____ La Guardia 8 Fiorello

Lahmi *brother:* 7 Goliath ***slayer:*** **7** Elhanan

laid-back 4 cool **6** breezy, casual **7** relaxed **8** carefree, informal **9** easygoing, hang-loose **10** nonchalant

lair 3 den **4** cave **5** haunt, lodge **6** burrow, refuge **7** hideout, retreat **8** hideaway **9** sanctuary

Laius *father:* 8 Labdacus ***slayer, son:*** **7** Oedipus ***wife:*** **7** Jocasta

lake 4 loch, mere, pond, pool, tarn **5** lough **6** lagoon ***Adriatic:*** **6** Varano ***Alberta:*** **6** Louise ***Algeria:*** **5** Hodna ***Alps:*** **6** Annecy ***Arizona-Nevada:*** **4** Mead ***Armenia:*** **5** Sevan **6** Gokcha, Sevang **9** Lychnitis ***Aswan's:*** **6** Nasser ***Australia:*** **4** Eyre **5** Carey, Cowan, Frome, Wells **6** Barlee **7** Amadeus, Everard, Torrens **8** Gairdner ***Austria:*** **5** Atter, Traun **6** Kammer **8** Attersee **9** Kammersee ***Bolivia:*** **5** Poopó ***Botswana:*** **5** Ngami ***British Columbia:*** **4** Pitt **5** Atlin ***California:*** **4** Mono, Tule **5** Clear, Eagle, Honey ***Cambodia:*** **8** Tonle Sap ***Canada:*** **4** Dyke **8** Manitoba ***central Africa:*** **4** Kivu **5** Mweru **6** Albert ***Central America:*** **5** Guija ***central Europe:*** **5** Leman **6** Geneva, Lugano **7** Ceresio **8** Bodensee **9** Constance ***central North America:*** **5** Rainy ***Chile:*** **4** Laja **5** Ranco ***China:*** **6** Poyang **8** Dongting ***Colorado:*** **5** Grand ***Denmark:*** **5** Esrum ***east Africa:*** **6** Rudolf **7** Turkana ***east Asia:*** **6** Khanka **7** Xingkai **8** Hsingkai ***east central Africa:*** **8** Victoria **10** Tanganyika ***east China:*** **3** Tai **5** Dalai, Hulun ***Ethiopia:*** **4** Tana, Zwai **5** Abaya, Shala, Shamo, Tsana **8** Stefanie **9** Chew Bahir ***Finland:*** **5** Inari ***Florida:*** **5** Worth **10** Okeechobee ***Germany:*** **5** Ammer, Chiem **8** Ammersee, Chiemsee ***Ghana:*** **5** Volta ***Great:*** **4** Erie **5** Huron **7** Ontario **8** Michigan, Superior ***Greece:*** **5** Bolbe, Volvi ***Guatemala:*** **7** Atitlán ***Honduras:*** **5** Yojoa ***Honshu:*** **3** Omi **4** Biwa, Suwa, Yodo ***Hungary:*** **7** Balaton **10** Plattensee ***Idaho:*** **4** Waha **5** Grays **6** Priest **11** Coeur d'Alene, Pend Oreille ***India:*** **3** Dal **5** Wular **6** Chilka ***Indonesia:*** **4** Poso, Toba **5** Ranau ***Iowa:*** **5** Storm ***Iran:*** **5** Niriz, Shahi, Urmia **8** Matianus, Urumiyeh **9** Bakhtigan ***Ireland:*** **3** Gur, Ree **4** Conn, Derg, Mask **5** Allen, Arrow, Leane ***Israel:*** **12** Bahr Tabariya, Sea of Galilee ***Israel-Jordan:*** **7** Dead Sea ***Italy:*** **4** Como, Iseo, Nemi **5** Garda **6** Albano **7** Bolsena, Perugia **8** Maggiore **9** Trasimene ***Japan:*** **4** Imba **8** Imbanuma ***Kazakhstan:*** **7** Balqash **8** Balkhash ***Louisiana:*** **4** Soda **9** Catahoula **13** Pontchartrain ***Maine:*** **6** Sebago **9** Moosehead ***Mali:*** **4** Debo ***Manitoba:*** **4** Gods **5** Cedar, Moose **8** Winnipeg ***Mexico:*** **7** Chapala ***Michigan:*** **4** Burt ***Minnesota:*** **3** Red **4** Cass, Gull, Swan **5** Leech **6** Itasca **9** Mille Lacs **10** Minnetonka, of the Woods **11** Lac qui Parle ***Minnesota-Wisconsin:*** **5** Pepin ***Mongolian:*** **3** Har **5** Har Us, Khara **8** Khara Usu ***Montana:*** **8** Medicine ***mountain:*** **4** tarn ***Myanmar:*** **4** Inle ***Nevada:*** **4** Ruby **7** Pyramid ***New Hampshire:*** **5** Squam **13** Winnipesaukee ***New Jersey:*** **5** Union ***New York:*** **4** Long **5** Chazy, Keuka **6** Cayuga, George, Oneida, Otsego, Owasco, Placid, Seneca **7** Crooked, Saranac **8** Onondaga, Saratoga **9** Champlain **10** Chautauqua **11** Canandaigua, Skaneateles ***New Zealand:*** **4** Ohau **5** Hawea, Taupo **6** Pukaki, Wanaka **8** Wakatipu ***Nicaragua:*** **7** Managua ***North Africa:*** **4** Chad ***Northern Ireland:*** **5** Neagh ***Northwest Territories:*** **4** Gras **5** Baker, Garry, Pelly **9** Great Bear **10** Great Slave ***Norway:*** **5** Mjosa ***Nova Scotia:*** **7** Bras d'Or ***Ontario:*** **4** Rice, Seul **5** Trout ***Oregon:*** **5** Abert **6** Crater **7** Malheur, Wallowa ***Paraguay:*** **4** Ypoá ***Peru:*** **5** Junín **13** Chinchaycocha ***Philippines:*** **4** Bato, Taal **5** Lanao **6** Bombon ***Poland:*** **5** Mamry, Mauer ***Quebec:***

5 Minto, Payne ***Russia:*** **3** Seg **5** Chany, Ilmen, Lacha, Onega **6** Baikal, Ladoga **7** Rybinsk **10** Eltonskoye **11** Ladozhskoye ***Saskatchewan:*** **4** Cree **5** Ronge ***Scotland:*** **3** Ard, Awe **4** Doon, Earn, Ness, Oich, Shin, Sloy **5** Leven, Lochy, Maree, Morar, Shiel **6** Lomond ***Siberia:*** **6** Baikal, Baykal ***South Africa:*** **4** Kosi ***South America:*** **5** Merin, Mirim **8** Titicaca ***South Carolina:*** **7** Wateree ***South Dakota:*** **5** Andes ***southeast Africa:*** **5** Nyasa **6** Nyassa ***southwest Europe:*** **5** Ohrid **7** Okhrida ***Sweden:*** **5** Asnen, Roxen **6** Siljan, Vänern, Vetter **7** Malaren, Vattern ***Switzerland:*** **3** Zug **4** Biel, Joux **5** Zuger **6** Bieler, Bienne, Brienz, Sarnen, Sarner, Zurich **7** Lucerne, Lungern **8** Brienzer, Züricher **9** Neuchâtel, Zürichsee ***Tajikistan:*** **7** Karakul ***Tanzania:*** **5** Rukwa ***Texas-Louisiana:*** **5** Caddo ***Tibet:*** **4** Na-mu **6** Nam Tso, Tengri ***Turkey:*** **3** Tuz, Van **4** Bafa, Nice **5** Iznik, Sugla **6** Nicaea ***Uganda:*** **5** Kyoga ***Utah:*** **6** Powell, Sevier **9** Great Salt ***Vermont:*** **9** Champlain ***Wales:*** **4** Bala ***Washington:*** **4** Omak **5** Moses **6** Chelan **9** Wenatchee ***western China:*** **4** Ai-pi **6** Ebinur ***western United States:*** **4** Bear **5** Tahoe ***Wisconsin:*** **5** Green **9** Winnebago ***Yellowstone National Park:*** **5** Heart, Lewis **8** Shoshone ***Zaire:*** **5** Tumba ***Zambia:*** **9** Bangweolo, Bangweulu

lake group ***central North America:*** **5** Great ***Egypt:*** **5** Balah ***Maine:*** **8** Rangeley ***New York:*** **6** Finger ***Saskatchewan:*** **5** Quill ***Twin:*** **8** Washinee **9** Washining

lake herring 5 cisco

Lake poet 7 Southey (Robert) **9** Coleridge (Samuel Taylor) **10** Wordsworth (William)

Lake Wobegon Days author 7 Keillor (Garrison)

Lakmé ***aria:*** **8** Bell Song ***composer:*** **7** Delibes (Léo)

Lakshmi ***husband:*** **6** Vishnu ***son:*** **4** Kama

L. A. Law ***actor:*** **3** Dey (Susan) **5** Drake (Larry), Smits (Jimmy) **6** Dysart (Richard), Greene (Michele), Hamlin (Harry), Ruttan (Susan), Tucker (Michael) **7** Bernsen (Corbin), Rachins (Alan) **10** Eikenberry (Jill) ***character:*** **5** Kuzak (Michael) **6** Becker (Arnie), Kelsey (Ann), Melman (Roxanne) **7** Van Owen (Grace), Perkins (Abby) **8** Brackman (Douglas), McKenzie (Leland) **9** Markowitz (Stuart), Sifuentes (Victor) ***creator:*** **6** Bochco (Steven)

lam 3 hit **4** beat, blow, bolt, drub, flay, flee, flog, pelt, skip, whip **5** baste, paste, pound, scram, smack, split, whale **6** batter, beat it, buffet, cut out, decamp, escape, flight, hammer, pummel, strike, thrash, wallop **7** getaway, take off, vamoose **8** breakout, escaping **9** skedaddle

La Mancha's knight 10 Don Quixote

lamb 4 cade **5** sheep **6** cosset **8** yeanling ***leg of:*** **5** gigot ***parent:*** **3** ewe, ram

lambaste 3 pan **4** beat, drub, flay, flog, lash, lick, pelt, slam, slap, trim, whip **5** paste, pound, roast, scold, score, slash, smear **6** assail, attack, berate, cudgel, hammer, pummel, scathe, scorch, thrash, wallop **7** assault, blister, censure, clobber, reprove, scourge, shellac, upbraid **8** bludgeon, denounce, harangue, lash into **9** castigate, excoriate **10** tongue-lash

lambent 5 aglow **6** ardent, bright, lucent **7** beaming, glowing, radiant, shining **8** gleaming, luminous, lustrous **9** brilliant, effulgent, refulgent, twinkling **10** flickering, glittering, shimmering **12** incandescent

lamblike 4 meek **6** docile

lamb of God 5 Jesus **6** Christ **8** Agnus Dei

Lamb's pseudonym 4 Elia

lame 4 gimp, halt, limp **5** gimpy, stiff **6** feeble, flimsy **7** cripple, disable, halting, limping **8** crippled, disabled, hobbling, inferior **10** inadequate **11** ineffectual **12** contemptible, unconvincing

lamebrain 3 oaf **4** dolt, dope, goof, mutt, simp, yo-yo **5** chump, dummy, dunce, idiot, moron, ninny, noddy, stupe **6** dimwit, donkey, dum-dum, nitwit, noodle **7** airhead, dullard, pinhead, schnook **8** bonehead, clodpoll, dumbbell, dumbhead, imbecile, lunkhead, meathead, numskull **9** blockhead, ignoramus, numbskull, simpleton, thickhead **10** dunderhead, hammerhead, nincompoop **11** chowderhead, chucklehead, knucklehead

Lamech ***daughter:*** **6** Naamah ***father:*** **10** Methuselah ***son:*** **4** Noah **5** Jabal, Jubal **9** Tubalcain ***wife:*** **4** Adah **6** Zillah

lament 3 cry, rue **4** keen, moan, pine, wail, weep **5** dirge, elegy, mourn **6** bemoan, bewail, grieve, plaint, regret, repent, sorrow **7** deplore, elegize, wailing **8** jeremiad, threnody **9** complaint, ululation

lamentable 6 rueful, woeful **7** doleful, pitiful **8** dolorous, grievous, mournful **9** plaintive, sorrowful **10** afflictive, deplorable, lugubrious, melancholy **11** distressing, regrettable, unfortunate **13** heartbreaking

lamentation 5 elegy, grief **7** anguish, remorse, wailing **8** grieving, mourning, threnody **9** sorrowing, ululation

Lamerok ***father:*** **9** Pellinore ***lover:*** **8** Margawse ***slayer:*** **6** Gawain

lamia 3 hex **5** witch **7** hellcat, vampire **8** succubus **9** sorceress **11** enchantress
Lamia *country:* 5 Libya ***form:* 7** serpent ***lover:* 4** Zeus
lamina 5 blade, flake, layer, plate, scale
lamp 3 arc **4** bulb, davy **5** klieg, light, torch **7** lantern **10** candelabra **11** candelabrum ***floor:* 8** torchère **9** torchiere ***hanging:* 10** chandelier
lampblack 4 soot **6** carbon
Lampetia *father:* 6 Apollo, Helios ***husband:* 9** Asclepius ***mother:* 6** Neaera ***sister:* 9** Phaethusa
lampoon 4 mock **5** roast, spoof, squib **6** parody, satire, send-up **7** take off **8** ridicule, satirize **9** burlesque **10** caricature, pasquinade
lamprey 3 eel **8** nine-eyes
lanai 5 patio, porch **6** piazza **7** terrace, veranda
lance 4 gash, hurl, open **5** slash, spear **6** impale, pierce, skewer **7** javelin **8** transfix
Lancelot, Launcelot *father:* 3 Ban ***lover:* 6** Elaine **9** Guinevere ***son:* 7** Galahad ***victim:* 6** Gawain
lancer 10 cavalryman ***Prussian:* 5** uhlan
lancet 4 arch **5** blade, knife **6** cutter, window **7** scalpel
land 4 dirt, dock, gain, soil **5** acres, berth, earth, light, manor, shore, terra, tract **6** alight, estate, ground, obtain, pick up, secure **7** acquire, acreage, country, expanse, grounds, procure, set down, terrain, terrene **9** touch down **10** terra firma ***alluvial:* 5** delta ***barren:* 5** waste **6** desert ***cultivated:* 4** farm **5** glebe, tilth **7** tillage ***for grazing:* 3** lea, ley **5** range **6** meadow **7** pasture ***high:* 4** hill, mesa **7** plateau **8** mountain ***level:* 4** mesa **5** plain **7** plateau ***low:* 4** vale **6** valley **9** intervale ***measure:* 3** rod **4** acre ***open:* 3** lea **5** field, green, plain **6** meadow **7** pasture ***piece:* 3** lot **4** plot **5** tract **6** estate, parcel ***reclaimed:* 6** polder ***sloping:* 6** cuesta ***strip:* 7** isthmus ***wet:* 3** bog, fen **5** marsh, swamp **6** marish
land east of Eden 3 Nod
landed 4 alit
landlord 6 lessor, squire **9** innkeeper **10** freeholder
landmark 5 cairn, guide **9** benchmark, milestone, watershed **11** achievement **12** breakthrough, turning point
Land of Enchantment 9 New Mexico
Land of Lakes 8 Michigan
Land of Opportunity 3 USA **8** Arkansas **12** United States
Land of the Midnight Sun 6 Norway
landowner 6 squire, yeoman ***Anglo-Saxon:* 5** thane, thegn ***Dutch:* 7** patroon ***Scottish:* 5** laird
landscape 5 scene, vista **7** scenery, setting, terrain **8** backdrop, prospect
lane 3 way **4** path, road **5** aisle, alley, byway, track **6** street **7** pathway, roadway **8** footpath **10** passageway
Langland work 12 Piers Plowman
lang syne 4 past, yore **10** yesteryear
language 4 cant **5** argot, idiom, lingo, prose, slang **6** jargon, patois, speech, tongue **7** dialect, lexicon, palaver **10** vernacular, vocabulary **11** terminology ***ambiguous:* 8** newspeak **10** double-talk ***ancient:* 5** Greek, Latin **6** Hebrew **8** Etruscan, Sanskrit ***artificial:* 3** Ido **7** Volapük **9** Esperanto ***Bantu:* 3** Ila ***classical:* 5** Greek, Latin ***combining form:* 5** gloss, glott **6** glosso, glotto ***expert:* 8** linguist, polyglot ***informal:* 4** jive **5** lingo, slang ***meaningless:* 6** babble, jabber **7** blather **9** gibberish **10** mumbo-jumbo ***mixed:* 6** creole, pidgin ***pretentious:* 7** bombast, fustian **8** claptrap ***regional:* 7** dialect ***relating to:* 10** linguistic ***Romance:* 6** French **7** Catalan, Italian, Spanish **8** Romanian, Rumanian **10** Portuguese ***Scotch-Irish:* 4** Erse **6** Gaelic ***secret:* 4** cant, code **5** argot ***Siamese:* 3** Lao, Tai ***structure:* 6** syntax **7** grammar ***suffix:* 3** ese ***written:* 5** prose
languid 4 lazy, limp **5** inert **6** draggy, supine, torpid **8** drooping, flagging, inactive, listless, slothful, sluggish **9** apathetic, enervated, impassive, lethargic **10** languorous, phlegmatic, spiritless **13** lackadaisical
languish 4 fade, fail, pine, tire, wilt **5** brood, droop **6** weaken **7** decline **9** waste away
languishing 4 limp, weak **6** feeble, pining **7** languid **8** fainéant, indolent, listless, weakened **9** depressed, enervated, enfeebled **10** dispirited, spiritless **11** debilitated, devitalized **13** lackadaisical
languor 3 kef, kif **5** ennui **6** stupor, tedium, torpor **7** fatigue **8** doldrums, dullness, hebetude, lethargy **9** heaviness, inertness, lassitude, torpidity, weariness **10** exhaustion
languorous 4 lazy, limp **5** inert **6** draggy, supine, torpid **7** laggard, languid, passive, relaxed **8** dilatory, drooping, fainéant, flagging, inactive, indolent, indulged, listless, pampered, slothful, sluggard **9** apathetic, enervated, impassive, lethargic **10** phlegmatic, spiritless **13** lackadaisical
lank 4 bony, lean, thin **5** rangy, spare **6** gangly **7** angular, scraggy, slender **8** gangling
lanky 4 bony, lean, thin **5** gaunt, spare **6** gangly **7** scraggy, scrawny **8** gangling, rawboned

lanyard 4 cord, line, rope **7** cordage
Laocoön *city:* 4 Troy ***killer:* 8** serpents
Laodamia *father:* 7 Acastus ***husband:* 11** Protesilaus
Laomedon *daughter:* 7 Hesione ***father:* 4** Ilus ***kingdom:* 4** Troy ***mother:* 8** Eurydice ***slayer:* 8** Heracles, Hercules ***son:* 5** Priam **8** Tithonus
Laos *capital:* 9 Vientiane ***city:* 11** Savannakhet ***ethnic group:* 5** Hmong ***monetary unit:* 3** kip ***neighbor:* 5** Burma, China **7** Myanmar, Vietnam **8** Cambodia, Thailand **9** Kampuchea ***river:* 6** Mekong
lap 3 sip **4** fold, join, wind **5** drink **6** cuddle, splash, swathe **7** circuit, control, custody, shingle **9** imbricate
lapidary 6 cutter **7** elegant, jeweler **8** engraver, polisher
lapillus 4 lava **6** cinder
lapin 6 rabbit
Lapiths *foes:* 8 centaurs ***king:* 5** Ixion
lappet 4 flap, fold **5** lapel
lapse 3 err, gap, sin **4** fall, flub, goof, sink, slip, vice **5** boner, cease, error, fluff, gaffe, slide **6** breach, bungle, expire, foible, miscue **7** blooper, blunder, decline, failing, failure, faux pas, forfeit, frailty, mistake, screwup, subside **8** abeyance, apostasy, interval, trespass **9** backslide, deviation, oversight, violation **10** apostatize **11** backsliding, impropriety **12** indiscretion, interruption
lapsed 4 sunk **5** ended **6** ceased **7** expired **8** obsolete **9** forfeited
Laputan 6 absurd **9** visionary
Lar 3 god **6** spirit **12** household god
larboard 4 left, port **8** leftward
larcenist 5 thief **6** bandit, robber **7** burglar, filcher, stealer **8** pilferer **9** embezzler, plunderer, purloiner **10** pickpocket, shoplifter
larcenous 7 robbing **8** thieving **9** pilfering **10** plunderous **13** light-fingered
larceny 5 theft **7** looting, robbery **8** burglary, stealing, thievery, thieving ***kind:* 5** grand, petty
lard 3 fat **6** fatten, grease **10** shortening
larder 6 pantry
large 3 big, fat **4** bull, huge, vast **5** ample, bulky, giant, grand, great, gross, hefty, jumbo, major **6** goodly **7** copious, immense, mammoth, massive, outsize, sizable **8** colossal, enormous, gigantic, king-size, oversize, spacious, whopping **9** capacious, excessive, extensive, humongous, monstrous **10** exorbitant, large-scale, monumental, prodigious, stupendous, tremendous, voluminous **11** extravagant, substantial ***combining form:* 4** macr, mega **5** macro **6** megalo
largesse 4 alms, gift **6** bounty **7** bequest, charity, cumshaw, gifting, present **8** donation, gratuity **9** endowment, pourboire **10** almsgiving, generosity, liberality **11** benefaction, beneficence, benevolence, magnanimity, munificence **12** philanthropy
largo 4 slow **5** broad, tempo
lariat 4 bola, bolo, rope **5** lasso, noose, reata, riata ***user:* 6** cowboy, drover **10** cowpuncher
lark 4 bird, dido, romp **5** antic, caper, prank, shine, stunt, trick **6** frolic **7** rollick **8** escapade, songbird **9** diversion **10** tomfoolery **11** distraction, shenanigans **12** monkeyshines
larrup 3 tan **4** beat, cane, drub, dust, flay, flog, hide, lash, lick, whip, whup **5** pound, spank, whale **6** cudgel, lather, paddle, thrash, wallop **7** clobber, scourge, shellac, trounce **8** lambaste **10** flagellate
larva 3 bot **4** grub, worm **6** dobson, maggot **8** cercaria, hornworm, mealworm **10** casebearer **11** caterpillar **12** hellgrammite ***amphibian:* 7** tadpole ***crustacean:* 4** zoea ***flatworm:* 5** redia ***free-swimming:* 7** planula ***mollusk:* 7** veliger ***moth:* 8** leafworm ***tapeworm:* 6** measle
larynx 7 trachea **8** voice box
lasagna 5 pasta **7** noodles
lascivious 4 lewd **5** bawdy, loose, randy **6** carnal, coarse, rakish, wanton **7** fleshly, goatish, immoral, lustful, satyric **8** depraved, prurient **9** lecherous, libertine, lickerish, salacious **10** libidinous, licentious, lubricious, profligate **12** concupiscent
lash 4 beat, bind, dash, flay, flog, hide, whip **5** baste, birch, fling, pound, scold, slash, whale **6** assail, berate, buffet, pummel, scathe, strike, stripe, switch, thrash **7** blister, scarify, scourge, upbraid **8** lambaste **9** castigate, excoriate, horsewhip **10** flagellate
lass 3 gal **4** girl, maid **5** wench **6** damsel, maiden **7** colleen
lassitude 5 ennui, sloth **6** apathy, stupor, tedium, torpor **7** fatigue, languor **8** debility, doldrums, dullness, hebetude, laziness, lethargy **9** indolence, tiredness, torpidity, weariness **10** exhaustion **11** insouciance **12** heedlessness, indifference, listlessness, sluggishness
lasso see **lariat**
last 3 end, lag, nth **5** abide, final **6** endure, latest, latter, utmost **7** closing, extreme, perdure, persist **8** continue, crowning, eventual, farthest, furthest, hindmost, rearmost, remotest, terminal, ultimate **9** umpteenth, uttermost **10** concluding, conclusive **11** ter-

minating ***French:*** **7** dernier ***next to:*** **6** penult **11** penultimate

last-ditch 5 final **7** defiant **8** ultimate **9** desperate **10** concluding

lasting 6 stable **7** abiding, durable, undying **8** enduring, lifelong, long-term, longtime **9** continual, indelible, perennial, permanent, unceasing **10** continuing, continuous, perdurable, persisting **12** indissoluble, longstanding

Last of the Mohicans, The 5 Uncas ***author:*** **6** Cooper (James Fenimore) ***character:*** **4** Cora **5** Alice, Magua, Uncas **11** Natty Bumppo **12** Chingachgook

Last Supper, The ***painter:*** **7** da Vinci (Leonardo) **8** Leonardo (da Vinci) ***location:*** **5** Milan

latch 4 bolt, glom, hasp, hook **5** catch **6** fasten, secure **8** fastener ***British:*** **5** sneck

latchet 4 band, cord, lace **5** strap, thong **8** shoelace

late 4 dead, past, slow **5** tardy **6** former, recent, whilom **7** defunct, delayed, onetime, overdue, quondam **8** deceased, departed, sometime **9** preceding

latent 4 idle **5** inert **6** covert, fallow, hidden, innate, unripe **7** abeyant, dormant, lurking **8** immature, inactive, inherent **9** concealed, intrinsic, potential, quiescent

later 4 anon, soon **5** after, infra **6** behind **7** by and by, ensuing **9** afterward, following, posterior **10** subsequent, succeeding **12** subsequently

lateral 4 pass, side **6** branch **8** crabwise, flanking, sidelong, sideward, sideways, sidewise

laterally 8 crabwise, sideward, sideways, sidewise

latest 6 newest, red-hot **7** current **8** contempo **9** au courant **10** dernier cri **13** up-to-the-minute

latex 6 balata **8** emulsion ***product:*** **5** paint **6** chicle, rubber **11** gutta-percha

lath 4 slat **5** board, frame, stave, stick, strip

lather 4 flap, flog, foam, hide, lash, soap, stew, suds, whip **5** froth, spume, tizzy, yeast **6** dither, hoopla, pother, thrash, welter **7** scourge, turmoil **8** soapsuds

Latin 5 Roman **7** Italian **8** Hispanic ***after:*** **4** post ***always:*** **6** semper ***and:*** **2** et ***as directed:*** **6** ut dict ***be, being:*** **4** esse ***before:*** **4** ante, prae ***behold:*** **4** ecce ***believe:*** **5** credo ***book:*** **5** liber ***boy:*** **4** puer ***brother:*** **6** frater ***but:*** **3** sed ***day:*** **4** dies ***dog:*** **5** canis ***earth:*** **5** terra ***egg:*** **3** ova ***father:*** **5** pater ***foot:*** **3** pes ***friend:*** **6** amicus ***girl:*** **6** puella ***god:*** **4** deus ***goddess:*** **3** dea ***good-bye:*** **4** vale **5** salve ***grammarian:*** **7** Donatus (Aelius) ***greeting:*** **3** ave ***hail and farewell:*** **12** ave atque vale ***hand:*** **5** manus ***hello:*** **3** ave ***horse:*** **5** equus ***house:*** **5** domus ***is:*** **3** est ***law:*** **3** ius, jus, lex ***let it stand:*** **4** stet ***life:*** **4** vita ***light:*** **3** lux ***love:*** **3** amo **4** amas, amat, amor ***man:*** **4** homo ***mother:*** **5** mater ***moon:*** **4** luna ***night:*** **3** nox ***nothing:*** **5** nihil ***now:*** **4** nunc ***peace:*** **3** pax ***pronoun:*** **2** tu **3** ego, nos, vos ***road:*** **3** via ***same:*** **4** idem ***sea:*** **4** mare ***see:*** **4** vide ***sister:*** **5** soror ***step:*** **6** gradus ***sun:*** **3** sol ***that is:*** **5** id est ***thing:*** **3** res ***this:*** **3** hic, hoc **4** haec ***thus:*** **3** sic ***truth:*** **7** veritas ***war:*** **6** bellum ***welcome:*** **5** salve ***wife:*** **4** uxor ***woman:*** **6** femina ***year:*** **4** anno **5** annus

Latin American ***country:*** **4** Cuba, Peru **5** Chile **6** Belize, Brazil, Guyana, Mexico, Panama **7** Bolivia, Ecuador, Uruguay **8** Colombia, Honduras, Paraguay, Suriname **9** Argentina, Costa Rica, Guatemala, Nicaragua, Venezuela **10** El Salvador ***dance:*** **4** juba **5** conga, mambo, rumba, samba **6** maxixe, rhumba **7** carioca, lambada **8** capoeira, habanera, merengue **9** bossa nova ***revolutionary:*** **6** Castro (Fidel) **7** Bolívar (Simón), Guevara (Ché), Hidalgo (Father Miguel) **8** O'Higgins (Bernardo) **9** San Martín (José de)

Latinus ***daughter:*** **7** Lavinia ***father:*** **6** Faunus **8** Odysseus ***son-in-law:*** **6** Aeneas ***wife:*** **5** Amata

latitude 4 play, room **5** range, scope, space, width **6** leeway, margin **7** breadth, compass, freedom, liberty, license **9** elbowroom **10** discretion **12** independence

latke 7 pancake **13** potato pancake

Latona 4 Leto ***daughter:*** **5** Diana **7** Artemis ***father:*** **5** Coeus ***mother:*** **6** Phoebe ***son:*** **6** Apollo

Latter-day Saint 6 Mormon

lattice 4 grid, mesh **5** grate, grill **7** grating, network, trellis **12** reticulation

Latvia ***capital:*** **4** Riga ***city:*** **7** Liepaja **10** Daugavpils ***gulf:*** **4** Riga ***language:*** **7** Lettish ***monetary unit:*** **3** lat ***native:*** **4** Lett ***neighbor:*** **6** Russia **7** Belarus, Estonia **9** Lithuania ***river:*** **7** Daugava **12** Western Dvina ***sea:*** **6** Baltic

Latvian 4 Balt, Lett **7** Lettish

laud 5 adore, bless, cry up, extol, glory, honor **6** admire, praise, revere **7** acclaim, flatter, glorify, magnify, worship **8** eulogize, venerate **9** celebrate, reverence

laudable 6 worthy **9** admirable, deserving, estimable **11** commendable, meritorious, thankworthy **12** praiseworthy

laudatory 7 glowing **9** adulatory, approving

10 eulogistic, flattering 11 approbative, encomiastic, panegyrical 12 commendatory 13 complimentary

laugh 3 yuk 4 ha-ha, roar, yuck 5 tehee, whoop 6 cackle, giggle, guffaw, hee-haw, titter 7 chortle, chuckle, snicker 10 cachinnate

laughable 4 rich 5 comic, droll, funny, goofy, witty 6 absurd, jocose 7 amusing, comical, jocular, mocking, risible 8 derisive, derisory, farcical, humorous 9 ludicrous 10 ridiculous

Laugh-In ***cast:*** 4 Sues (Alan), Hawn (Goldie) 5 Buzzi (Ruth), Carne (Judy), Owens (Gary) 6 Dawson (Richard), Gibson (Henry), Tomlin (Lily) 7 Johnson (Arte) ***catch phrase:*** 10 sock it to me 12 go to your room ***guest:*** 6 Wilson (Flip) 7 Tiny Tim 8 Youngman (Henny) ***host:*** 5 Rowan (Dan) 6 Martin (Dick)

laughing 5 merry, riant 6 blithe 8 mirthful 9 sparkling

laughingstock 4 butt, dupe, fool, jest, joke, mark, mock 5 sport 6 target 7 mockery 8 derision

launch 4 boat, cast, fire, hurl 5 begin, debut, fling, heave, pitch, sling, start, throw 6 get off 7 jump off, kick off, lift off, release, take off, usher in 8 blast off, catapult, commence, embark on, initiate 9 inception, institute, introduce, motorboat, set afloat 10 inaugurate, initiation 12 inauguration

launder 4 wash 5 clean 6 trough 7 cleanse 8 sanitize, transfer

Laura's lover 8 Petrarch

laurels 4 bays, fame 5 award, honor, kudos, prize 6 awards, badges, honors, prizes, renown 7 acclaim 8 accolade, citation 9 accolades, citations 10 decoration, reputation 11 decorations, distinction 12 achievements, distinctions

laurel-tree nymph 6 Daphne

lava 2 aa 4 slag 5 magma 6 scoria 8 andesite, trachyte ***fragment:*** 8 lapillus ***stream:*** 4 flow 6 coulee

lavalava 5 cloth, skirt 6 sarong

lavaliere 7 pendant 8 necklace

lavatory 2 WC 3 loo 4 head, john 5 basin, jakes, potty, privy 6 johnny, toilet 7 latrine 8 bathroom, restroom, washroom 11 water closet

lave 4 pour, wash 5 bathe

Lavinia ***father:*** 7 Latinus ***husband:*** 6 Aeneas ***mother:*** 5 Amata

Lavinium's founder 6 Aeneas

lavish 4 lush, posh, pour 5 plush, spend, waste 6 swanky 7 liberal, opulent, profuse 8 effusive, prodigal, splendid, squander 9 bountiful, excessive, exuberant, luxuriant, luxurious, sumptuous 10 immoderate, inordinate, munificent 11 extravagant

law 3 act, lex 4 bill, code, rule 5 axiom, canon, edict, Torah 6 assize, decree, equity 7 dictate, justice, mandate, precept, statute, theorem 8 exigency 9 enactment, ordinance, principle 10 principium, regulation 11 commandment, fundamental 12 prescription ***body of:*** 4 code 7 pandect 12 constitution ***degree:*** 2 JD 3 LLB, LLD ***expert:*** 5 judge 6 jurist 7 justice ***practitioner:*** 6 lawyer 7 counsel 8 attorney 9 barrister, solicitor ***relating to:*** 5 jural, legal 7 canonic 8 forensic, juristic 9 judiciary ***violation of:*** 4 tort 5 crime 6 felony 11 misdemeanor

law-abiding 6 decent 7 duteous, dutiful, orderly, upright 8 obedient, obliging, straight 9 compliant, peaceable 10 forthright, respectful 11 respectable, well-behaved

Law & Order ***actor:*** 4 Röhm (Elisabeth) 6 Govich (Milena), Martin (Jesse), Orbach (Jerry) 7 Hendrix (Leslie) 8 Thompson (Fred) 9 Merkerson (S. Epatha), Waterston (Sam) ***character:*** 5 Green (Ed), McCoy (Jack) 6 Branch (Arthur) 7 Briscoe (Lennie), Cassady (Nina), Rodgers (Elizabeth) 8 Van Buren (Anita) 10 Southerlyn (Serena) ***creator:*** 4 Wolf (Dick)

lawbreaker 3 con 4 hood, thug 5 crook, felon 6 outlaw, sinner 7 convict, hoodlum, mobster 8 criminal, gangster, hooligan, jailbird, offender, scofflaw, violator 9 desperado, wrongdoer 10 malefactor, trespasser 12 transgressor

lawful 3 due 4 just 5 legal, legit, licit, valid 6 kosher 7 condign 8 bona fide, innocent, mandated, ordained 9 allowable, canonical, juridical, legalized 10 authorized, legitimate 11 permissible

lawgiver 5 Draco, Moses, solon 7 senator 8 alderman 10 councilman, legislator 11 congressman, thesmothete

lawlessness 5 chaos 6 strife 7 anarchy, discord, misrule, turmoil 8 conflict, disorder 9 mobocracy 10 illegality, misconduct, ochlocracy, unruliness, wrongdoing 11 criminality, pandemonium

lawman 7 marshal, officer, sheriff 9 policeman

Lawrence novel 7 Rainbow (The) 8 Kangaroo, Lost Girl (The) 9 Aaron's Rod 11 Women in Love 13 Plumed Serpent (The), Sons and Lovers

lawrencium symbol 2 Lr

lawsuit 4 case 5 cause, claim 6 action 8 replevin 9 assumpsit 10 litigation, proceeding 11 presentment, prosecution

lawyer 6 jurist, legist **7** counsel, pleader **8** advocate, attorney **9** barrister, counselor, solicitor ***dishonest:*** **7** shyster **11** pettifogger ***fictional:*** **5** Finch (Atticus) **7** Matlock (Ben), Rumpole (Horace) **10** Perry Mason ***French:*** **6** avocat ***title:*** **3** Esq. **7** Esquire

lax 5 loose, slack **6** casual, remiss, sloppy **7** lenient **8** careless, derelict, lacrosse **9** deficient, forgetful, negligent **10** neglectful, permissive **11** inattentive

lay 3 bet, put, set **5** apply, hatch, place, wager **6** assert, assign, ballad, charge, credit, devise, impute, settle, spread **7** amateur, arrange, ascribe, concoct, deposit, prepare, present **11** nonclerical

lay by 4 keep, save **5** amass, hoard, store **7** deposit, discard, store up **8** preserve, salt away, set aside **10** accumulate

lay down 3 set **4** rule **5** order, store, yield **6** assert, decree, define, give up, impose, ordain, record, resign **7** abandon, command, dictate, specify **8** hand over, preserve, proclaim **9** establish, prescribe, surrender **10** relinquish

layer 3 hen, ply **4** coat, film, seam, tier **5** paver, sheet **6** folium, lamina, strata (plural), veneer **7** coating, stratum **8** covering, laminate, membrane, sandwich, stratify ***inner:*** **6** lining ***of skin:*** **6** dermis **9** epidermis ***outer:*** **4** skin **6** veneer

lay for 6 ambush **8** surprise

lay in see **lay by**

layman 6 novice, oblate **7** amateur, secular **11** parishioner

lay off 4 fire, halt, quit, stop **5** avoid, cease, let go, lie by **6** desist **7** abstain, dismiss, measure, release **9** discharge, terminate **10** inactivity **11** discontinue

lay out 3 pay **4** give, plan **5** chart, dummy, place, spend **6** design, expend **7** arrange, display, exhibit, prepare **8** disburse

lay waste 4 ruin **5** wreck **6** ravage **7** destroy **8** desolate **9** devastate

lazar 5 leper

Lazarus' sister 4 Mary **6** Martha

laze 3 bum, lag **4** bask, hang, idle, loaf, loll **5** chill **6** dawdle, loiter, lounge, slouch **7** goof off, hang out **8** chill out **9** goldbrick **10** hang around

laziness 5 sloth **6** torpor **7** inertia, languor, laxness, loafing **8** idleness, lethargy, otiosity **9** indolence, lassitude, loitering, slackness **10** inactivity **11** languidness **12** listlessness

lazy 3 lax **4** idle **5** inert, slack **6** droopy, remiss, supine, torpid **7** languid, loafing, passive **8** fainéant, inactive, indolent, listless, slothful, sluggish **9** lethargic, negligent, shiftless, slowgoing **10** languorous

lazy Susan 4 tray **9** turntable

leach 4 drip, leak, ooze, perk, seep, suck, weep **5** bleed, drain, exude, issue **7** draw out, dribble, trickle **8** filtrate, perspire **9** discharge, lixiviate, percolate

lead 3 tip **4** head, hint, show, star **5** guide, metal, plumb, route, steer, trace, usher **6** bullet, ceruse, direct, escort, leader **7** captain, conduct, precede, preface **8** graphite, persuade, shepherd **9** spearhead **10** bellwether ***combining form:*** **5** plumb **6** plumbo ***ore:*** **6** galena **9** anglesite ***oxide:*** **6** sinter ***sounding:*** **5** plumb **7** plummet ***symbol:*** **2** Pb

lead astray 6 seduce **7** corrupt

leaden 4 drab, dull, flat, gray **5** heavy, inert **6** gloomy, somber **7** languid, weighty **8** dragging, lifeless, sluggish **9** ponderous

leader 4 boss, dean, duce, guru, head, jefe, lord **5** chief, guide, pilot **6** despot, honcho, rector **7** captain, foreman, general, headman, manager, warlord **8** chairman, director, hierarch, superior **9** chieftain, commander, conductor, demagogue, harbinger, precursor, president, principal, straw boss **10** bellwether, forerunner, pacesetter ***authoritarian:*** **10** Big Brother ***Cossack:*** **6** ataman, hetman ***German:*** **6** führer **7** fuehrer ***Japanese:*** **6** shogun ***military:*** **7** admiral, general, warlord **9** commander **12** field marshal ***Muslim:*** **3** aga **4** agha, amir, emir, imam **5** ameer **6** caliph, mullah ***national:*** **7** premier **9** president **12** chief of state

leading 4 arch, head, main **5** ahead, chief, first, major **6** famous, master **7** premier, primary **8** champion, foremost, headmost, peerless **9** paramount, principal, prominent, well-known **10** preeminent

lead on 3 con **4** bait, dupe, fool, gull, hoax, lure, scam, tole, toll, wile **5** cozen, flirt, tempt **6** allure, betray, cajole, coquet, delude, entice, entrap, humbug, seduce, suck in, take in, trifle **7** beguile, deceive, toy with **8** coquette, hoodwink, inveigle **9** bamboozle **11** string along

leaf 4 flip, foil, page, riff, scan, skim **5** blade, bract, folio, frond, petal, scale, sepal, thumb **6** browse, glance, riffle, spathe ***angle:*** **4** axil ***aperture:*** **5** stoma ***axis:*** **6** rachis ***combining form:*** **5** phyll **6** phyllo **7** phyllum ***edge:*** **9** crenation ***lily:*** **3** pad ***part:*** **4** lobe, vein **5** blade, costa, stoma **7** petiole, stipule, tendril ***pine:*** **6** needle ***vein:*** **5** costa

leafage 7 foliage, umbrage, verdure

leaflet 5 flier, flyer, pinna, sheet, tract **6** folder **7** handout **8** brochure, circular, handbill, pamphlet
leafy 4 lush **5** green, shady **6** shaded, wooded **7** foliate, verdant **8** foliated, laminate **9** verdurous
league 4 band, bond, club, crew **5** class, grade, group, guild, order, union, unite **6** circle **7** circuit, combine, society **8** alliance, category, division, grouping, sodality **9** coalition **10** conference, consortium, federation, fellowship, fraternity **11** association, brotherhood, confederacy **13** confederation
Leah *daughter:* 5 Dinah ***father:* 5** Laban ***husband:* 5** Jacob ***sister:* 6** Rachel ***son:* 4** Levi **5** Judah **6** Reuben, Simeon **7** Zebulun **8** Issachar
leak 4 drip, ooze, seep **5** break, crack, spill **6** escape, get out, reveal, source **7** come out, divulge, seepage **8** disclose **9** discharge **10** make public
leaky 6 broken, faulty, porous **7** cracked, damaged
lea, ley 4 veld **5** field, veldt **6** fallow, meadow **7** pasture **9** grassland, pasturage
lean 3 sag, tip **4** bend, bony, cant, heel, lank, list, slim, thin, tilt **5** gaunt, lanky, shift, slant, slope, spare **6** meager, meagre, skinny, slight, wasted **7** angular, deviate, haggard, incline, pinched, scraggy, scrawny, slender, stringy, wizened **8** gradient, rawboned **9** deficient **11** inclination
Leander's beloved 4 Hero
Leaning Tower site 4 Pisa
lean-to 3 hut **4** shed **5** shack **6** shanty **7** bivouac, shelter
leap 3 hop **4** buck, jump, loup, lutz, rise, soar **5** bound, caper, clear, mount, vault **6** ascend, gambol, hurdle, spring **7** saltate **8** capriole, surmount ***ballet:* 4** jeté **9** entrechat ***by a horse:* 7** gambado
Lear, King *daughter:* 5 Regan **7** Goneril **8** Cordelia ***son:* 5** Edgar **6** Edmund
learn 3 con **4** hear **5** grasp, study **6** attain, detect, master, pick up **7** acquire, catch on, discern, find out, realize, uncover, unearth **8** discover, memorize **9** apprehend, ascertain, determine **10** comprehend, understand **11** stumble onto
learned 4 sage, wise **6** expert, versed **7** bookish, erudite, sapient, studied **8** abstruse, academic, cultured, educated, esoteric, highbrow, lettered, pedantic, well-read **9** recondite, scholarly **10** cultivated, scholastic **12** intellectual
learner 4 tiro, tyro **5** pupil **6** novice, rookie **7** student, trainee **8** beginner, disciple, initiate, neophyte **9** greenhorn, postulant **10** apprentice, catechumen **11** abecedarian
learning 4 lore **6** wisdom **7** science, tuition **8** booklore, pedantry **9** education, erudition, knowledge **11** scholarship ***person of:* 7** egghead, scholar **9** professor **12** intellectual
lease 3 let **4** hire, rent **6** sublet **7** charter, compact **8** contract, covenant, document **11** continuance
leash 3 tie **4** bind, cord, curb, rein, rope **5** strap **6** bridle, fetter, hamper, tether **7** shackle, trammel **8** restrain **9** entrammel
least 6 fewest **7** minimal, minimum **8** smallest
leather 3 tan **4** hide, skin, whip **6** thrash ***kind:* 3** kid, kip, oak **4** bock, buff, calf, roan **5** crown, grain, mocha, strap, suede, whang **6** castor, latigo, oxhide, patent, roller, saddle, skiver **7** buffalo, chamois, morocco, ostrich, peccary **8** capeskin, cordovan, cordwain, shagreen ***maker:* 5** tawer **6** tanner **7** tannery ***piece:* 4** welt **5** strap, thong ***prepare:* 3** tan, taw **5** curry ***soft:* 5** mocha, suede **8** cabretta
leatherneck 6 marine
Leatherstocking Tales, The *author:* 6 Cooper (James Fenimore) ***hero:* 5** Natty (Bumppo) ***title:* 7** Prairie (The) **8** Pioneers (The) **10** Deerslayer (The), Pathfinder (The) **17** Last of the Mohicans (The)
leave 2 go **3** fly, let **4** blow, cede, exit, flee, move, part, quit, will **5** allow, scram, split **6** assent, assign, beat it, begone, commit, cut out, decamp, depart, desert, devise, escape, get off, legate, permit, resign, retire, set out, vacate **7** abandon, abscond, absence, consent, consign, entrust, forsake, get away, liberty, pull out, take off, vamoose **8** bequeath, clear out, farewell, furlough, hand down, transmit, vacation, withdraw **9** departure, disappear, surrender, terminate **10** permission, relinquish, sabbatical **13** authorization
leaved 5 green **7** foliate, verdant **8** foliated
leaven 5 imbue, steep, yeast **6** infuse, invest, modify, temper, vivify **7** enliven, ingrain, lighten, suffuse **8** moderate **9** alleviate, inoculate, sourdough **12** baking powder
leavening 5 yeast **9** sourdough **10** baking soda **12** baking powder
leave of absence 8 furlough
leave off 3 end **4** halt, quit, stop **5** cease **6** desist, give up **7** abstain **8** give over, surcease **9** terminate **11** discontinue
leave out 4 omit, skip **5** elide **7** exclude
Leaves of Grass author 7 Whitman (Walt)
leavings 4 lees, orts, rest **5** dregs, scrap **6** debris, grouts **7** balance, remains, remnant,

residue, rubbish **8** discards, oddments, remnants, residual, residuum **9** fragments, leftovers, remainder

Lebanon ***capital:*** **6** Beirut ***city:*** **4** Tyre **5** Sidon **6** Zahlah **7** Tripoli ***language:*** **6** Arabic, French ***monetary unit:*** **5** pound ***mountain:*** **6** Hermon ***neighbor:*** **5** Syria **6** Israel ***river:*** **6** Litani **7** Orontes ***sea:*** **13** Mediterranean ***valley:*** **5** Bekaa

Le Carré, John ***character:*** **6** Smiley (George) ***novel:*** **11** Russia House (The) **17** Little Drummer Girl (The) **22** Tinker Tailor Soldier Spy **23** Spy Who Came in from the Cold (The)

lecher **4** rake, roué, wolf **7** Don Juan, seducer **8** Casanova, lothario **9** debauchee, reprobate, libertine, womanizer **10** degenerate, profligate, voluptuary **11** philanderer

lecherous **4** lewd **5** bawdy, loose, randy **6** carnal, coarse, rakish, wanton **7** fleshly, goatish, immoral, lustful, satyric **8** depraved, prurient, scabrous **9** debauched, libertine, lickerish, salacious **10** lascivious, libidinous, licentious, lubricious, profligate **11** promiscuous **12** concupiscent

lectern **4** desk **5** podia (plural), stand **6** podium

lecture **4** talk **5** chide, scold, speak **6** berate, preach, rebuke, sermon, speech **7** address, declaim, expound, oration, reproof, reprove, upbraid **8** admonish, briefing, harangue, scolding **9** chalk talk, criticism, criticize, discourse, hold forth, reprimand, talking-to **10** allocution **12** disquisition, dressing-down

lecturer **3** don **6** docent, fellow, master, orator, reader **7** scholar, speaker, teacher, trainer **9** pedagogue, preceptor, professor **10** instructor **11** academician

Leda ***daughter:*** **5** Helen **12** Clytemnestra ***father:*** **8** Thestius ***husband:*** **9** Tyndareus ***lover:*** **4** swan, Zeus ***son:*** **6** Castor, Pollux

ledge **3** bar, rim **4** berm, lode, reef, sill, vein **5** bench, ridge, shelf **6** mantle **7** bedrock, molding **10** projection

ledger **4** book **5** tally **6** record **7** account, balance **8** notebook, register **9** reckoning

lee **5** haven **7** shelter **9** protected, sheltered

leech **4** milk, worm **5** bleed, drain **6** sponge, sucker **7** exhaust, sponger **8** barnacle, hanger-on, parasite **10** freeloader **11** bloodsucker **12** lounge lizard

leer **3** eye **4** ogle **5** fleer, gloat, smirk, sneer, stare **6** glance, goggle, squint **7** grimace

leery **4** wary **5** chary **6** unsure **7** dubious, guarded **8** cautious, doubtful, doubting **10** suspicious **11** circumspect, distrustful, mistrustful

lees **5** dregs **6** grouts, refuse **7** deposit, grounds, residue **8** leavings, residual, residuum, sediment **9** settlings **11** precipitate

leeward **8** downwind ***opposite:*** **8** windward

leeway **4** play, room **5** scope, space **6** margin **7** breadth, compass, freedom, liberty **8** latitude **9** elbowroom, tolerance

left **4** port **7** liberal, radical **8** departed, deserted, larboard, residual, sinister **9** abandoned, discarded, remaining, sinistral

left-handed **5** inept **6** clumsy, gauche **7** awkward, dubious **8** fumbling, southpaw **9** ambiguous, equivocal, insincere, maladroit **10** morganatic

left-hand page **5** verso

leftover **5** extra, spare **6** excess, unused **7** remnant, reserve, residue, surplus, uneaten, vestige **8** residual, unneeded **9** redundant, remainder, remaining **10** unconsumed **11** superfluous

leftovers see **leavings**

leftward **4** levo **5** aport ***go:*** **3** haw

leg **3** bow, gam **4** limb **5** shank, stage **6** branch **7** support, upright **8** cabriole **9** appendage, drumstick ***bone:*** **4** shin **5** femur, tibia **6** fibula **7** patella ***part:*** **4** calf, crus, foot, knee, shin **5** ankle, thigh

legacy **4** gift **5** trust **6** devise, estate **7** bequest **8** heirloom, heritage **9** endowment, patrimony, tradition **10** birthright **11** benefaction, inheritance

legal **5** legit, licit **6** lawful **7** allowed **8** innocent **9** juridical, statutory **10** legitimate, sanctioned ***matter:*** **3** res **4** case, suit ***order:*** **4** writ **7** summons **8** subpoena ***organization:*** **3** ABA ***party:*** **6** suitor **8** litigant **9** defendant, plaintiff ***restraint:*** **8** estoppel

legal tender **3** wad **4** cash **5** bread, dough, money, moola, notes **6** moolah, specie **7** coinage **8** banknote, currency **9** long green

legate **4** will **5** endow, envoy, grant, leave **6** bestow, commit, devise, deputy, devise, pass on **7** entrust, leave to **8** bequeath, delegate, emissary, hand down, transmit **10** ambassador

legatee **4** heir **7** devisee **9** inheritor

legato **5** fluid **6** smooth **7** flowing

legend **3** key **4** lore, myth, saga, tale, yarn **5** fable, motto, story **6** mythos **7** caption, fiction **8** epigraph, folklore, folktale, tall tale **9** mythology, tradition **11** inscription

legendary **5** famed **6** fabled, famous, mythic **7** fabular, fancied, fictive, storied **8** fabulous, mythical, renowned, supposed **9** well-

known **10** apocryphal, celebrated **11** illustrious, traditional **12** mythological
legerdemain 5 magic **8** prestige, trickery **9** chicanery, conjuring, deception **13** sleight of hand
leggings 5 chaps **7** puttees **9** gambadoes
leghorn 3 hat **4** fowl **5** straw **7** chicken
legible 5 clear **8** distinct, readable **12** decipherable, intelligible
legion 4 army, host, many, mass, rout **5** cloud, crowd, drove, flock, horde **6** myriad, scores, sundry, throng **7** phalanx, various **8** numerous, populous **9** countless, multitude **10** numberless
legislate 5 enact, order **6** codify, decree, ordain, permit, ratify **7** empower, mandate **8** legalize, regulate, sanction **9** establish
legislation 3 act, law **4** acts, bill, code, laws **5** bills, codes, rules **6** edicts **7** statute **8** charters, dictates, statutes **9** enactment, lawmaking **10** enactments, ordinances, regulation **11** regulations **12** codification
legislator 5 solon **7** senator **8** alderman, lawgiver, lawmaker **10** councilman **11** assemblyman, congressman, thesmothete
legislature 4 diet **5** house, junta **6** senate **7** council **8** assembly, congress **10** parliament ***Communist:* 6** soviet **9** politburo, presidium ***Danish:* 9** Folketing ***Finnish:* 9** Eduskunta ***German:* 9** Bundesrat, Bundestag ***Iceland:* 7** Althing ***Ireland:* 4** Dáil ***Israel:* 7** Knesset ***Norway:* 8** Storting ***one-house:* 10** unicameral ***Poland:* 4** Sejm ***Russian:* 4** duma ***Spain:* 6** Cortes ***Sweden:* 7** Riksdag ***two-house:* 9** bicameral ***Ukraine:* 4** Rada
legitimate 4 fair, just, true **5** legal, licit, sound, usual, valid **6** kosher, lawful, normal, proper **7** genuine, regular, typical **8** accepted, innocent, orthodox, rightful **9** allowable, authentic, canonical, customary **10** admissable, authorized, reasonable, recognized **11** justifiable, well-founded
Le Guin, Ursula K. *novel:* 7 Telling (The) **8** Solitude (The) **12** Dispossessed (The) **18** Left Hand of Darkness (The) ***series:* 8** Earthsea
legume 3 dal, pea, pod **4** bean, dhal, guar, seed **5** pulse **6** clover, lentil **7** soybean
leg up 3 aid **4** edge, lift **5** boost **6** assist **9** advantage, head start
lei 6 wreath **7** garland **8** necklace
Leibniz's invention 8 calculus
Leif Eriksson *discovery:* 7 Vinland ***father:* 4** Eric, Erik (the Red)
leisure 4 ease, rest, time **6** casual, chance, repose **7** freedom, liberty **8** downtime **10** relaxation **11** opportunity
leisurely 4 easy, slow **6** lazily, slowly **7** relaxed, restful **8** laid-back **9** unhurried
leitmotiv 4 idea **5** theme, topic **6** burden, motive, thesis **7** subject **8** idée fixe
lemma 5 bract, theme **7** heading, premise, theorem **8** argument **11** proposition
lemon 3 dud **4** bomb, bust, flop **5** fruit, loser, scent **6** flavor, yellow **7** failure
lemur 4 lori **5** indri, loris, potto **6** aye-aye, colugo, galago **7** tarsier **8** bush baby
lend 4 give, loan **5** allow, grant **6** afford, oblige, supply **7** advance, furnish, provide **11** accommodate
L'Engle novel 10 Many Waters **13** Wind in the Door (A), Wrinkle in Time (A)
length 4 span **5** ambit, range, reach, realm, scope **6** extent, radius **7** compass, expanse, measure, purview, section, stretch, yardage **8** distance, duration
lengthen 6 expand, extend, let out **7** draw out, prolong, spin out, stretch **8** elongate, increase, protract **9** string out ***Scottish:* 3** eke
lengthy 4 long **8** dragging, drawn-out, extended, overlong **9** elongated, prolonged **10** long-winded, protracted, voluminous **12** interminable
leniency 5 mercy **7** quarter **8** clemency **9** tolerance **10** indulgence, toleration **11** forbearance
lenient 4 easy, kind, mild, soft **6** benign, gentle, kindly **7** amiable, clement **8** merciful, obliging, tolerant **9** benignant, forgiving, indulgent **10** forbearing, permissive
lenity 5 mercy **7** quarter **8** clemency **9** tolerance **10** humaneness, indulgence **11** forbearance
lens 5 glass **6** lentil **8** meniscus ***kind:* 5** toric **6** convex **7** bifocal, concave **8** trifocal
lento 4 slow **5** tempo
Leofric's wife 6 Godiva
Leoncavallo opera 9 Pagliacci (I) **10** Chatterton
leonine 8 lionlike
Leonora 7 heroine ***alias:* 7** Fidelio ***husband:* 9** Florestan
leopard 3 cat **4** pard **5** ounce **7** panther
leper 6 pariah **7** Ishmael, outcast **8** castaway, derelict **9** incurable **10** Ishmaelite **11** untouchable ***hospital:* 9** lazaretto ***island:* 7** Molokai ***priest:* 6** Damien (Father)
Leper Priest 6 Damien (Father)
lepers' hospital 9 lazaretto
lepers' island 7 Molokai
lepidoptera 5 moths **8** skippers **11** butterflies **12** caterpillars
Leporello's master 11 Don Giovanni

leprechaun 3 elf **5** dwarf, fairy **6** sprite **7** brownie ***trade:* 8** cobbling
lepton 4 coin, muon **8** electron, neutrino
Lesage hero 7 Gil Blas
Lesbos poet 6 Sappho **7** Alcaeus
____ LeShan 3 Eda
lesion 3 cut **4** boil, flaw, harm, sore **5** ulcer, wound **6** injury **7** blister
Lesotho *capital:* 6 Maseru ***ethnic group:* 5** Sotho ***former name:* 10** Basutoland ***language:* 5** Sotho ***monetary unit:* 4** loti ***mountain:* 9** Ntlenyana ***neighbor:* 11** South Africa ***river:* 6** Orange **7** Caledon
less 5 lower, minus **7** reduced, without
lessen 3 cut **4** clip, crop, ease, thin, wane **5** abate, erode, lower, taper **6** dilute, impair, minify, recede, reduce, shrink, weaken **7** abridge, assuage, curtail, degrade, dwindle, lighten, relieve, subside **8** decrease, diminish, minimize, mitigate, taper off **9** attenuate
lessening 4 drop, fall **5** letup **8** decrease, slowdown **9** abatement, reduction **10** curtailing, diminution **11** degradation
lesser 5 lower, minor **7** smaller **8** inferior **9** secondary, small-time, subjacent **11** minor-league, subordinate **13** insignificant
lesson 4 text **5** chide, moral, study **6** rebuke **7** example, lecture, reading, reprove, warning **8** admonish, exercise, homework, reproach **9** reprimand **10** admonition, assignment **11** instruction
lessor 8 landlady, landlord **9** landowner **10** freeholder
let 4 make, rent **5** allow, grant, lease, leave **6** assign, permit, suffer **9** authorize **11** obstruction
letdown 5 slump **6** defeat **7** decline, descent, failure, reverse, setback **10** anticlimax, depression, misfortune **11** frustration
let go 3 can **4** boot, fire, free, sack **5** remit **6** unhand **7** dismiss, neglect, release, set free **8** liberate **9** discharge, terminate
lethal 4 fell **5** fatal **6** deadly, mortal, poison **7** baleful, deathly **8** poisoned, virulent **9** murderous, poisonous **11** destructive, devastating
lethargic 4 dull, idle, slow **5** dopey, heavy, inert **6** draggy, supine, torpid **7** dormant, laggard, languid, passive **8** comatose, dilatory, inactive, listless, slothful, sluggish **9** apathetic, impassive **10** languorous, phlegmatic, spiritless **11** indifferent **12** hebetudinous **13** lackadaisical
lethargy 5 sloth **6** apathy, phlegm, stupor, torpor **7** inertia, languor, slumber **8** dullness, hebetude, idleness, laziness **9** disregard, inanition, indolence, inertness, lassitude, torpidity **10** inactivity, supineness **11** impassivity, passiveness **12** listlessness
lethe 7 amnesia **8** oblivion **13** forgetfulness
Leto see **Latona**
let off 5 spare **6** excuse, exempt **7** absolve, relieve **8** dispense **9** discharge
let on 3 own **5** admit, allow, grant, own up, spill **6** betray, fess up, reveal **7** concede, confess, confirm, divulge, pretend **8** disclose, give away
let out 5 blurt, loose **6** exhale **7** release, set free, unloose **8** lengthen, liberate, set loose **9** discharge, turn loose
letter 2 ar, ef, el, em, en, ex **3** bee, cee, cue, dee, eff, ell, ess, gee, jay, kay, pee, tee, vee, wye, zed, zee **4** line, mail, memo, note, rune **5** aitch, print, vowel **6** report, screed, symbol **7** epistle, message, missive **8** dispatch, inscribe **9** consonant ***airmail:* 8** aerogram ***Anglo-Saxon:*** (see **Anglo-Saxon**) ***Arabic:*** (see **alphabet**) ***Greek:*** (see **alphabet**) ***Hebrew:*** (see **alphabet**) ***kind:* 4** open **5** chain, roman **6** italic, uncial **8** Dear John ***large:* 7** capital **9** majuscule, uppercase ***papal:* 4** bull **10** encyclical ***small:* 9** lowercase, minuscule ***start:* 4** Dear
lettuce 3 cos **4** Bibb, head **6** Boston **7** iceberg, romaine, Simpson **10** butterweed
let up 3 ebb **4** fall, stop, wane **5** abate, cease **6** lessen, relent **7** die away, die down, ease off, slacken, subside **8** decrease, diminish, moderate, taper off
letup 4 lull **5** break, pause **7** respite **9** abatement, cessation, lessening, reduction **10** slackening
levee 4 dike, dock, pier, quay **5** jetty, ridge, wharf **7** seawall **8** assembly, function **9** reception **10** breakwater, embankment, riverfront
level 3 aim, lay, par **4** calm, even, flat, raze, same, tier, true **5** equal, floor, flush, grade, plane **6** direct, ground, smooth, status, steady **7** aligned, flatten, mow down **8** balanced, bulldoze, demolish, equalize, parallel, smoothen, standing **9** bring down, intensity, knock down, magnitude **10** equivalent, horizontal, reasonable **11** equilibrium
lever 3 bar, pry **4** jack, tool **5** jimmy, peavy, prize **6** peavey, tappet **7** crowbar
leverage 5 clout, power **7** exploit **9** advantage, dominance, influence **11** superiority **13** effectiveness
leveret 4 hare
Levi *father:* 5 Jacob ***mother:* 4** Leah ***son:* 6** Kohath, Merari **7** Gershon
leviathan 4 huge **5** giant, jumbo, large, titan,

whale **7** Goliath, immense, mammoth, massive, monster, titanic **8** behemoth, colossal, colossus, enormous, gigantic **9** cyclopean, monstrous **10** formidable, gargantuan **11** elephantine, monstrosity

Leviathan author 6 Hobbes (Thomas)

levitate 4 lift, rise **5** float, raise **7** elevate, suspend

levity 5 folly, humor **8** buoyancy **9** absurdity, flippancy, frivolity, giddiness, lightness, silliness **10** jocularity, volatility

levy 3 tax **4** duty, toll, wage **5** exact, lay on **6** assess, charge, custom, enlist, impose, impost, tariff **7** carry on, collect **9** conscript **10** assessment, enlistment **12** conscription

lewd 5 bawdy, gross **6** coarse, ribald, smutty, vulgar **7** fleshly, goatish, lustful, obscene, satyric **8** depraved, improper, indecent, prurient, unchaste **9** debauched, lecherous, libertine, lickerish, salacious **10** indelicate, lascivious, libidinous, licentious, lubricious

Lewis and Clark interpreter 9 Sacagawea, Sacajawea

Lewis work 7 Babbitt **9** Dodsworth **10** Arrowsmith, Main Street **11** Elmer Gantry **16** Screwtape Letters (The) **18** Chronicles of Narnia (The)

lexicographer 8 compiler ***American:* 6** Porter (Noah) **7** Webster (Noah) **9** Worcester (Joseph) ***English:* 4** Wyld (Henry) **6** Fowler (Francis, Henry), Murray (James), Onions (Charles) **7** Craigie (William), Johnson (Samuel) **9** Partridge (Eric) ***French:* 6** Littré (Paul-Emile) **8** Larousse (Pierre) ***German:* 5** Grimm (Jakob, Wilhelm)

lexicon 4 cant **6** jargon **8** glossary, language, wordbook **9** inventory, word-hoard **10** dictionary, repertoire, vocabulary **11** terminology

liable 3 apt **4** open **5** given, prone **6** likely **7** exposed, subject **8** inclined **9** sensitive **10** answerable, assailable, vulnerable **11** accountable, responsible, susceptible

liaison 4 bond, link **5** amour, fixer **6** affair, broker, hookup **7** contact, romance **8** intrigue **9** go-between **10** connection **12** entanglement, intermediary, relationship **13** communication

liana 4 vine

liar 6 fibber **7** Ananias **8** fabulist, perjurer **9** falsifier **12** prevaricator ***female:* 8** Sapphira

libation 5 drink **6** liquid, liquor **7** potable **8** beverage, oblation, offering, potation

libel 4 slur **5** smear **6** defame, malign, vilify **7** asperse, calumny, obloquy, slander, traduce **8** bad-mouth, tear down **9** aspersion, denigrate **10** calumniate, defamation, scandalize **11** denigration

libelous 6 untrue **9** injurious, invidious, maligning, traducing, vilifying **10** backbiting, calumnious, defamatory, derogative, derogatory, detracting, detractive, malevolent, pejorative, scandalous, slanderous

liberal 4 full, open **5** ample, broad, loose **6** lavish **7** copious, profuse, radical **8** abundant, generous, prodigal, tolerant **9** bounteous, bountiful, indulgent, plentiful, unsparing **10** benevolent, bighearted, charitable, freehanded, munificent, openhanded, permissive, unorthodox **11** broad-minded

liberal arts *quadrivium:* 5 music **8** geometry **9** astronomy **10** arithmetic ***trivium:* 5** logic **7** grammar **8** rhetoric

liberate 4 free **5** loose **7** manumit, release, unchain **9** discharge, unshackle **10** commandeer, emancipate **11** appropriate, expropriate

liberator 6 savior **7** messiah **9** deliverer ***of Argentina:* 9** San Martín (José de) ***of Chile:* 8** O'Higgins (Bernardo) ***of Ecuador:* 5** Sucre (Antonio José de) ***of Scotland:* 5** Bruce (Robert the) ***of South America:* 7** Bolívar (Simón)

Liberia *capital:* 8 Monrovia ***coast:* 3** Kru **5** Grain ***neighbor:* 6** Guinea **10** Ivory Coast **11** Côte d'Ivoire, Sierra Leone

Liberian *language:* 3 Kwa ***native:* 3** Kru, Vai **4** Gola, Toma **5** Bassa, Grebo **6** Kruman

libertine 4 lewd, rake, roué **5** bawdy, loose, randy **6** carnal, rakish, wanton **7** Don Juan, lustful, raffish, satyric **8** Casanova **9** debauched, debauchee, dissolute, lecherous, salacious **10** degenerate, dissipated, lascivious, libidinous, licentious, profligate **11** promiscuous

liberty 4 risk **5** leave **6** chance **7** freedom, license **8** autonomy **9** franchise, privilege **10** permission **11** familiarity **12** emancipation, independence

libidinous 4 lewd **5** bawdy, loose, randy **6** carnal, rakish, wanton **7** fleshly, goatish, lustful, satyric **8** depraved, prurient **9** debauched, lecherous, libertine, lickerish, salacious **10** lascivious, licentious, lubricious, profligate **11** promiscuous **12** concupiscent

librarian 5 Dewey (Melvil)

library 7 archive **8** atheneum **9** athenaeum **11** bibliotheca ***desk:* 6** carrel

Libya *capital:* 7 Tripoli ***city:* 8** Benghazi ***desert:* 6** Sahara ***gulf:* 5** Sidra ***language:* 6** Arabic **7** Hamitic ***leader:* 7** Gadhafi, Qaddafi (Mu'ammar) ***monetary unit:* 5** dinar ***neigh-***

bor: 4 Chad 5 Egypt, Niger, Sudan 7 Algeria, Tunisia *sea:* 13 Mediterranean

lice 7 cooties

license 3 let, tag 5 allow, grant, leave 6 enable, laxity, permit, suffer, ticket 7 certify, empower, freedom, go-ahead, liberty 8 accredit, document, sanction, variance 9 authority, authorize, slackness 10 permission, profligacy 11 certificate, impropriety 12 carte blanche 13 authorization

licentious 4 lewd 5 bawdy, loose, randy 6 amoral, carnal, rakish, wanton 7 fleshly, goatish, immoral, lustful, satyric 8 depraved, prurient, scabrous 9 abandoned, debauched, dissolute, lecherous, libertine, salacious 10 lascivious, libidinous, lubricious, profligate 11 promiscuous 12 concupiscent

lichen 4 moss 6 archil, litmus 7 oakmoss *genus:* 5 Usnea

licit 4 okay 5 legal 6 lawful 7 allowed 8 approved, innocent, licensed 9 allowable, permitted 10 admissible, authorized, legitimate, sanctioned 11 permissible

lick 3 bit, dab, dig, hit, lap, rap, tan 4 beat, dash, deck, down, drub, hint, swat, whip, wipe 5 cream, pinch, pound, smack, smear, spank, taste, touch, trace, whiff 6 defeat, master, punish, thrash, tongue, wallop 7 clobber, conquer, shellac, trounce 8 lambaste, outstrip, overcome, surmount 9 overwhelm

lickerish see **libidinous**

lickety-split 4 fast 5 apace 6 presto, pronto 7 flat out, hastily, quickly, rapidly, swiftly 8 chop-chop, full tilt, headlong, pell-mell, speedily 9 posthaste 13 expeditiously, precipitately

licorice 4 root 5 candy *pill:* 6 cachou

lid 3 cap, top 5 cover 8 covering *moss:* 9 operculum

lie 3 fib 4 rest, tale 5 exist, fable, libel 6 belong, canard, covert, delude, extend, inhere, remain, repose, reside 7 consist, falsify, falsity, perjure, recline, untruth, whopper 8 misspeak, misstate, tall tale 9 dissemble, falsehood, fish story, mendacity 10 inaccuracy, taradiddle 11 prevaricate 12 misstatement

Liechtenstein *capital:* 5 Vaduz *language:* 6 German *monetary unit:* 4 euro *mountain range:* 4 Alps *neighbor:* 7 Austria 11 Switzerland *river:* 5 Rhein, Rhine

lied 4 song 7 art song

lief 4 fain, soon 6 freely, gladly 7 happily, readily 9 willingly 11 contentedly

liege 4 lord, true 5 loyal 6 ardent, master, vassal 7 abiding, staunch 8 constant, enduring, faithful, reliable, resolute, stalwart 9 dedicated, steadfast 10 dependable

lien 5 claim 6 charge, demand 8 interest, mortgage 10 imposition

lieu 5 place, stead

lieutenant 4 aide 5 looey, looie 6 backup, deputy 7 officer 9 assistant, coadjutor 10 aide-de-camp, coadjutant 11 subordinate

life 3 vim 4 brio, dash, élan, soul 5 verve 6 energy, esprit, spirit 8 vitality 9 animation, existence *animal:* 5 fauna *animal and plant:* 5 biota *combining form:* 3 bio *plant:* 5 flora *relating to:* 5 vital 8 biologic 10 biological *science:* 7 biology

life jacket 7 Mae West

lifeless 4 dead, drab, dull 5 inert 6 asleep, barren, torpid, wasted 7 defunct, extinct 8 comatose, deceased, departed 9 inanimate, inorganic, insensate 10 lackluster

lifelike 5 exact 7 natural, precise 8 accurate, faithful, veristic 9 realistic

life of ____ 5 Riley 8 the party

lift 4 heft, hike, jack, load, rear, rise 5 boost, exalt, filch, heave, hoist, pinch, raise, steal, swipe, theft 6 assist, pick up, pilfer, repeal, revoke, snitch, take up 7 elevate, purloin, rescind, reverse, support 8 levitate, stealing, thievery 10 plagiarize

lift-off 6 ascent, launch 7 takeoff 9 launching

ligament 3 tie 4 band, bond, link, yoke 5 nexus 8 ligature, vinculum 10 connection

ligature see **ligament**

Ligeia author 3 Poe (Edgar Allan)

light 4 airy, dawn, deft, easy, fair, fire, lamp, land, luck, neon 5 blond, flash, minor, perch, roost, sunny, torch 6 beacon, blithe, bright, candle, casual, facile, flimsy, fluffy, ignite, kindle, settle, simple, slight, strobe 7 lantern, sunrise, trivial 8 cheerful, daybreak, enkindle, illumine, luminous, trifling 9 frivolous, touch down 10 chandelier, effortless, illuminate *and shade interplay:* 11 chiaroscuro *combining form:* 4 luci, phot 5 lumin, photo 6 lumini, lumino *indicator:* 3 LED *measure:* 3 lux 4 phot 5 lumen 6 candle 7 candela *refractor:* 5 prism *relating to:* 6 photic *ring:* 4 halo 6 corona 7 aureola, aureole *science:* 6 optics *source:* 3 sun 4 lamp

light-emitting 6 lasing, lucent 7 beaming, fulgent, glowing, lambent, shining 8 luminous 9 effulgent, refulgent

lighten 4 dawn, ease, fade 5 allay, cheer 6 bleach, lessen, reduce 7 assuage, gladden, hearten, mollify, relieve 8 decrease, mitigate, unburden 9 alleviate, attenuate, extenuate 11 disencumber

light-headed 5 dizzy, faint, giddy, silly **6** swimmy **7** flighty **9** frivolous, slaphappy **10** unbalanced **11** disoriented, vertiginous
lighthearted 3 gay **4** glad **5** happy, jolly, merry, sunny **6** blithe, jocund, jovial, joyful, joyous, lively, upbeat **7** buoyant, festive, gleeful, playful **8** carefree, cheerful, mirthful, volatile **9** easygoing, expansive, sprightly, vivacious **10** blithesome, insouciant **12** effervescent, happy-go-lucky, high-spirited
lighthouse 6 beacon **7** warning
lighting crew member 6 gaffer
lightless 4 dark **5** unlit **7** aphotic, stygian **9** tenebrous, pitch-dark **10** caliginous, pitch-black **11** unillumined
lightness 6 bounce, gaiety, levity **8** buoyancy, vivacity **9** animation, frivolity **10** cheeriness, liveliness, resiliency, volatility **12** cheerfulness **13** effervescence
lightning bug 7 firefly
lignite 4 coal **9** brown coal
likable 4 nice **6** genial **7** affable, amiable, popular, winning, winsome **8** charming, engaging, friendly, pleasant, pleasing **9** agreeable, appealing, congenial **10** attractive, personable **11** good-natured
like 3 à la, dig **4** akin, same, such **5** close, enjoy, equal, match **6** admire, agnate, akin to, allied, prefer, relish **7** approve, cognate, kindred, related, similar, uniform **8** parallel, selfsame **9** analogous, consonant, identical **10** appreciate, comparable, comprehend, equivalent, resembling
likelihood 6 chance **8** prospect **11** eventuality, possibility, presumption, probability
likely 3 apt **5** given, prone **6** liable, odds-on **7** assumed **8** credible, inclined, possible, presumed, probable, probably, reliable, suitable **9** doubtless, plausible, promising **10** achievable, attractive, believable, presumably
liken 5 match **6** equate **7** compare **8** parallel **10** assimilate
likeness 4 copy, twin **5** clone, image **6** double, effigy **7** analogy, picture, replica **8** affinity, portrait, sameness **9** depiction, facsimile, look-alike, semblance **10** appearance, photograph, similarity, similitude, uniformity **11** resemblance
likewise 3 and, too **4** also **5** ditto **6** as well, withal **7** besides **8** moreover **9** similarly **10** in addition **11** furthermore
liking 4 bent **5** fancy, taste **6** desire **8** affinity, appetite, fondness, penchant, pleasure, soft spot, weakness **9** affection **10** attraction, partiality **11** inclination **12** appreciation, predilection
Lilith ***husband:*** **4** Adam ***successor:*** **3** Eve
lilliputian 3 wee **4** runt, tiny **5** dwarf, petty, pygmy, small **6** bantam, little, midget, peanut, peewee, shrimp **7** manikin **8** mannikin, pint-size, Tom Thumb **9** miniature, pint-sized, undersize **10** diminutive, homunculus
lilt 3 air **4** flow, purl, sing, song, tune **5** carol, pulse, swing, tempo **6** melody, rhythm **7** cadence **8** buoyancy
lily 3 pad **4** aloe, sego **5** calla, tiger, yucca **6** flower **7** leopard **8** mariposa ***genus:*** **4** Aloe
lily-livered 5 sissy, wimpy **6** craven, yellow **7** caitiff, chicken, fearful, gutless **8** cowardly, cowering, poltroon, recreant, timorous **9** spineless, spunkless, weak-kneed **12** fainthearted, poor-spirited **13** pusillanimous
lily-white 4 pure **6** chaste **7** upright **8** innocent, virtuous **9** blameless, estimable, exclusive, exemplary, guiltless, righteous, untainted **10** inculpable **11** uncorrupted
limb 3 arm, fin, gam, leg **4** lobe, twig, wing **5** bough, shoot, spray, sprig **6** branch, member, pinion **7** flipper **8** offshoot **9** appendage, dismember, extremity
limber 4 spry **5** agile, lithe, loose **6** nimble, pliant, supple **7** elastic, lissome, pliable, springy **8** flexible **9** lithesome, resilient
limbo 5 dance **7** neglect **8** oblivion **9** detention, purgatory **11** confinement, uncertainty
lime 4 tree **5** color, fruit, green **6** citrus, linden **7** calcium
limen 8 doorsill, doorstep **9** threshold
limerick 4 poem **5** verse ***writer:*** **4** Lear (Edward)
limestone 4 tufa, tuff **5** chalk **6** marble, oolite **7** coquina **10** travertine
lime tree 6 linden
limit 3 bar, cap, end, fix, max, set **4** curb **5** check, quota **6** border, bounds, curfew, define, extent, hinder, lessen **7** confine, curtail, enclose, extreme, mark out, measure **8** boundary, deadline, restrain, restrict **9** constrict, demarcate, determine, extremity, prescribe **12** circumscribe
limitless 4 vast **7** endless **8** infinite, wide-open **9** boundless, unbounded **10** indefinite **11** illimitable, innumerable, measureless **12** immeasurable, incalculable **13** inexhaustible
limn 4 draw **5** image, paint **6** depict, render, sketch **7** outline, picture, portray **8** describe **9** delineate, interpret, represent
Limoges product 5 china **9** porcelain
limp 3 lax **4** bent, halt, lame, wilt **5** hitch, loose, slack, spent, weary **6** dodder, droopy,

falter, hobble **7** flaccid, languid, shamble, shuffle, slumped **8** drooping **9** enervated, exhausted **10** spiritless

limpid 4 pure **5** clear, lucid **6** glassy, serene **8** pellucid **10** see-through, untroubled **11** crystalline, translucent, transparent **12** crystal clear

limping 4 halt, lame **5** gimpy **7** halting **8** hobbling, lameness **9** faltering **12** claudication

linchpin 8 backbone, mainstay

Lincoln ***assassin:*** **5** Booth (John Wilkes) ***biographer:*** **8** Sandburg (Carl) ***debater:*** **7** Douglas (Stephen) ***law partner:*** **7** Herndon (William) ***mother:*** **5** Nancy (Hanks) ***nickname:*** **9** Honest Abe **12** Railsplitter ***photographer:*** **5** Brady (Mathew) ***secretary of state:*** **6** Seward (William) ***secretary of war:*** **7** Stanton (Edwin) ***wife:*** **8** Mary Todd

Lindsay poem 5 Congo (The)

line 3 row **4** file, rank, rope **5** array, goods, queue, route **6** border, column, cordon, series, strain, string **7** contour, descent **8** business, pedigree, sequence **10** employment, occupation, succession ***curved:*** **3** arc ***mathematical:*** **6** vector ***metrical:*** **5** verse **6** verset **8** versicle ***of rulers:*** **7** dynasty ***weather map:*** **6** isobar

lineage 3 kin **4** clan, folk, race **5** birth, blood, breed, house, stirp, stock, tribe **6** family, origin, strain **7** descent, kindred **8** ancestry, breeding, pedigree **9** forebears, genealogy **10** derivation, extraction, succession **11** forefathers, progenitors

lineal 6 direct **8** familial **9** ancestral, inherited **10** bequeathed, hereditary

lineament 4 form **6** figure, relief **7** contour, feature, outline, profile **10** figuration, silhouette

lined 5 drawn, ruled **7** aligned, striate, striped **8** streaked, wrinkled

linen 4 lawn **5** cloth, toile **6** byssus, damask, fabric, napery, sheets **7** batiste, bedding, cambric, taffeta **8** cretonne, lingerie ***fiber:*** **3** tow ***source:*** **4** flax

lineup 6 roster

linger 3 lag **4** bide, drag, loll, mope, poke, stay, wait **5** abide, dally, delay, mosey, tarry **6** dawdle, loiter, put off, remain **7** saunter **10** dillydally **11** stick around **13** procrastinate

lingerie 8 negligee

lingo 4 cant **5** argot, idiom, slang **6** jargon, patois, patter, speech, tongue **7** dialect **10** vernacular, vocabulary

linguist 8 polyglot **11** philologist

linguistics 9 philology

liniment 3 oil **4** aloe, balm **5** salve **6** lotion **7** anodyne, unction, unguent **8** aloe vera, lenitive, ointment **9** demulcent **11** embrocation

lining 6 facing, insert **8** wainscot

link 3 tie **4** bind, bond, join, knot, ring, yoke **5** hitch, nexus, unite **6** attach, copula, couple, hookup, relate, splice **7** bracket, combine, conjoin, connect, contact, joining **8** catenate, division, vinculum **9** associate, conjugate **10** attachment, connection **11** association **12** relationship

linksman 6 golfer

linnet 5 finch

lint 3 fur, nap **4** down, fuzz, pile **5** floss, fluff **9** ravelings

lion 3 cat **4** puma **6** cougar **7** notable **8** eminence, luminary **9** carnivore, personage ***group:*** **5** pride ***young:*** **3** cub

lionhearted 4 bold **5** brave **6** heroic **7** valiant **8** fearless, intrepid, stalwart, unafraid, valorous **9** dauntless **10** courageous

lionize 4 fete **5** exalt, extol, honor **7** glorify **8** venerate **9** celebrate

Lion King, The ***character:*** **4** Nala, Scar, Zazu **5** Simba, Timon **6** Banzai, Mufasa, Pumbaa, Rafiki, Sarabi, Shenzi **8** Sarafina ***composer:*** **4** John (Elton) ***film score:*** **6** Zimmer (Hans) ***lyricist:*** **4** Rice (Tim) ***setting:*** **10** Pride Lands ***voice:*** **5** Irons (Jeremy), Jones (James Earl), Marin (Cheech) **8** Atkinson (Rowan), Goldberg (Whoopi) **9** Broderick (Matthew)

lion monkey 7 tamarin **8** marmoset

Lion of Judah 8 Selassie (Haile)

lip 3 rim **4** brim, edge, guff, kiss, sass **6** labium, labrum, margin **8** back talk ***relating to:*** **6** labial

lipid 3 fat, wax

lipped 7 labiate **9** bilabiate

liquefy 3 run **4** flux, melt, thaw **5** smelt **6** render **8** dissolve **10** deliquesce

liqueur 4 arak, ouzo, raki **5** crème **6** arrack, brandy, Kahlua, kirsch, kummel, pastis, Pernod **7** Campari, Cinzano, cordial, curaçao, ratafia, sambuca, sloe gin **8** absinthe, amaretto, anisette, Drambuie, Galliano, Tía Maria **10** Chartreuse, pousse-café

liquid 5 drink, fluid, sauce, water **6** watery **7** flowing **8** beverage, emulsion **11** mellifluous ***container:*** **3** cup, jug, keg, mug **4** vial **5** glass **6** bottle, goblet **7** pitcher, tumbler ***flammable:*** **3** gas, oil **5** ether, furan **6** butane, toluol **7** alcohol, toluene **8** gasoline, pyridine ***measure:*** **2** cc, ml, oz, pt, qt **3** cup, gal **4** pint **5** liter, litre, ounce, quart **6** gallon ***thick:*** **5** syrup **8** molasses

liquidate 3 pay **4** do in, kill **5** pay up, purge **6** murder, remove, rub out, settle, square **7**

bump off, convert, satisfy **8** amortize, dispatch, dissolve, knock off **9** eliminate, terminate **10** annihilate **11** assassinate

liquor 5 booze, drink, hooch **7** alcohol, potable, spirits **8** potation **9** firewater, inebriant **10** intoxicant ***add:*** **4** lace **5** spike ***Asian:*** **4** arak **6** arrack ***homemade:*** **5** hooch **9** moonshine **10** bathtub gin ***inferior:*** **5** hooch **6** redeye, rotgut ***Japanese:*** **4** sake, saki ***kind:*** **3** gin, rum, rye **5** vodka **6** brandy, geneva, scotch, whisky **7** aquavit, bourbon, schnaps, whiskey **8** schnapps, vermouth **9** aqua vitae **10** barley-bree ***malt:*** **3** ale **4** beer **5** nappy, stout **6** porter ***measure:*** **4** dram, shot **6** jigger **7** shooter ***Mexican:*** **5** sotol **6** mescal **7** tequila

lissome 5 agile, lithe **6** limber, nimble, supple, svelte **7** slender **8** flexible, graceful

list 3 tip **4** book, cant, file, heel, lean, menu, note, post, roll, tilt **5** arena, count, index, slant, slate, slope, tally **6** agenda, census, docket, lineup, record, roster **7** catalog, incline, itemize, specify **8** calendar, glossary, manifest, register, roll call, schedule, tabulate **9** chronicle, enumerate, inventory **13** particularize ***type:*** **3** hit **4** life, to-do, wish **5** punch, short **6** linked **7** laundry, mailing, waiting **8** shopping **10** best-seller

listen 4 hark, hear, heed, hist, note **5** audit **6** attend, harken **7** hearken, monitor **8** overhear **9** eavesdrop

listeners 8 audience

listless 4 dull, limp, weak **5** inert, slack **6** torpid, vacant **7** languid **8** indolent, sluggish **9** apathetic, enervated, lethargic, lymphatic **10** languorous, phlegmatic, spiritless **11** indifferent, languishing **13** lackadaisical

listlessness 6 apathy, stupor, torpor **7** fatigue, inertia, languor **8** doldrums, lethargy **9** indolence, lassitude, torpidity **10** enervation

litany 4 list **5** chant **6** prayer **7** account, listing, recital, refrain **8** petition, rogation **9** catalogue **10** invocation, recitation **11** enumeration **12** supplication

literal 4 bald, bare **5** blunt, exact, stark **6** actual, simple, strict **7** precise **8** accurate, bona fide, faithful, verbatim **9** authentic **11** unvarnished, word-for-word **13** unembellished

literally 5 truly **6** direct, indeed, openly, simply **7** plainly, totally, utterly **8** candidly, directly, verbatim **9** genuinely, virtually **11** word for word

literary 7 bookish, erudite, learned **8** lettered, well-read **9** authorial, scholarly **12** belletristic

literary work 4 book, opus, play, poem **5** drama, essay, novel **10** short story

literature 5 prose **6** poetry **7** fiction **13** belles-lettres

lithe 4 lean, slim **5** agile, spare **6** limber, supple, svelte **7** lissome, pliable, slender **8** flexible, graceful

lithium symbol 2 Li

lithographer 4 Ives (James Merritt) **7** Currier (Nathaniel)

Lithuania *capital:* 7 Vilnius ***city:*** **6** Kaunas **8** Klaipeda ***monetary unit:*** **5** litas ***neighbor:*** **6** Latvia, Poland, Russia **7** Belarus ***river:*** **5** Neman, Venta **7** Lielupe ***sea:*** **6** Baltic

litigant 4 suer **6** suitor **9** defendant, disputant, plaintiff

litigate 3 sue **6** indict **7** arraign, contest, dispute **9** prosecute

litigation 4 case, suit **7** lawsuit **11** prosecution, proceedings

litter 3 bed **4** cubs, junk **5** brood, couch, issue, strew, trash, waste, young **6** clutch, debris, refuse **7** bedding, clutter, garbage, kittens, piglets, progeny, puppies, rubbish, scatter **8** detritus **9** offspring, stretcher **10** scattering

little 3 bit, dab, toy, wee **4** dash, hint, mean, puny, tiny **5** brief, dinky, minor, petty, pinch, runty, short, small, taste, trace, young **6** bantam, meager, meagre, minute, narrow, paltry, petite, skimpy **7** limited, trivial **8** dwarfish, slightly, smallish, trifling **9** miniature, small-beer **10** diminutive, short-lived, undersized **11** microscopic, unimportant

Little Bighorn *state:* 7 Montana ***victim:*** **6** Custer (George Armstrong) ***victor:*** **11** Sitting Bull

little by little 6 slowly **8** inchmeal, steadily **9** gradually, piecemeal

Little Dipper *constellation:* 9 Ursa Minor ***star:*** **5** North **7** Polaris

Little Women *author:* 6 Alcott (Louisa May) ***character:*** **3** Amy, Meg **4** Beth **6** Laurie, Marmee ***surname:*** **5** March

littoral 5 beach, coast, shore **6** strand **7** coastal, seaside **8** seaboard, sea front, seashore **9** shoreline **10** oceanfront

liturgy 4 rite **6** ritual **7** service **8** ceremony **9** sacrament **10** ceremonial, observance, repertoire

livable 6 viable **8** adequate, bearable, passable **9** endurable, habitable, tolerable **11** inhabitable, supportable

live 4 fare, stay **5** abide, dwell, exist, on air, vital, vivid **6** actual, reside, thrive **7** breathe, current, subsist, survive

livelihood 3 job **4** game, keep, work **5** craft, trade **7** support **8** business, vocation **10** employment, handicraft, occupation, profession, sustenance **11** subsistence

liveliness 3 pep, zip **4** brio, élan, zing **5** verve, vigor **6** energy, hustle, spirit **8** dispatch, vibrance, vibrancy, vitality, vivacity **9** animation

lively 3 gay **4** busy, keen, pert, spry, yare **5** agile, alert, brisk, fresh, jazzy, jolly, merry, peppy, zippy **6** active, bouncy, bright, chirpy, frisky, jocund, nimble **7** animate, buoyant, chipper, intense, rousing **8** animated, bustling, hustling, spirited, vigorous, volatile **9** energetic, resilient, sparkling, sprightly, vivacious **11** stimulating

liven 5 pep up **6** jazz up, vivify **7** animate, freshen, quicken **8** energize, inspirit, vitalize **10** invigorate

liver 7 denizen **8** habitant, occupant, resident **10** inhabitant ***combining form:*** **5** hepat **6** hepato ***disease:*** **9** cirrhosis, hepatitis ***French:*** **4** foie ***lobster's:*** **8** tomalley

liverwort 8 hepatica **9** bryophyte

livestock 4 cows, hogs, pigs **5** bulls, goats, sheep **6** beasts, calves, cattle **7** animals ***feed:*** **6** silage **8** ensilage

live wire 6 dynamo **7** hustler, rustler **8** go-getter, promoter **9** energizer, generator **11** self-starter

livid 3 hot, mad, wan **4** ashy, pale **5** ashen, lurid, waxen **6** fuming, leaden, pallid, sultry **7** boiling, bruised, enraged, furious, reddish **8** blanched, contused, incensed **9** colorless **10** discolored, infuriated **12** black-and-blue **13** beside oneself

living 5 means, vital **6** extant, income **8** animated, existent **10** livelihood, sustenance ***combining form:*** **3** bio

living room 6 parlor **10** lebensraum

lizard 3 eft, Uta **4** gila, newt, uran **5** agama, anole, gecko, skink, teiid **6** dragon, goanna, iguana **7** monitor, reptile, saurian **8** basilisk, mosasaur, slowworm, squamate, whiptail **9** alligator, blindworm, chameleon, crocodile **10** chuckwalla, salamander ***combining form:*** **4** saur **5** saura, sauro

llama 7 camelid ***country:*** **4** Peru **7** Bolivia, Ecuador ***habitat:*** **5** Andes ***relative:*** **6** alpaca, vicuña **7** guanaco

Lloyd's business 9 insurance

lo 4 ecce, hark, heed, look, mark, mind **6** attend, behold **7** observe

load 3 tax **4** bias, copy, fill, haul, heap, lade, onus, pack, pile, stow, task **5** cargo, laden, swamp, weigh **6** burden, debase, doctor, dope up, eyeful, lading, saddle, weight **7** freight **8** encumber, shipment, transfer **9** liability, millstone, transport **11** consignment, encumbrance

loaded 4 full, high, rich **5** awash, doped **6** aboard, biased, filled, packed, stoned **7** boarded, brimful, crowded, wealthy **8** affluent, brimming, chockful, tripping, turned on **9** chock-full

loaf 3 bum, bun **4** idle, laze, lazy, loll **5** bread, dough **6** dawdle, lounge **7** goof off **8** lollygag **9** bum around, goldbrick **10** fool around

loafer 3 bum **4** shoe, slug **5** idler **6** slouch **7** goof-off, lounger **8** deadbeat, dolittle, fainéant, slugabed, sluggard **9** do-nothing, goldbrick, lazybones **11** beachcomber, lollygagger

loam 4 clay, dirt, sand, silt, soil **7** topsoil ***deposit:*** **5** loess

loan 3 pay **4** lend **6** credit **7** advance, imprest **9** grubstake ***figure:*** **3** APR

loan shark 6 lender, usurer **7** Shylock **10** pawnbroker **11** moneylender

loath 6 afraid, averse **8** hesitant **9** reluctant, unwilling **10** indisposed **11** disinclined **12** antipathetic

loathe 4 hate **5** abhor, scorn, spurn **6** detest, refuse, reject **7** despise **8** execrate **9** abominate

loathsome 4 foul, ugly, vile **5** gross, nasty **6** odious **7** beastly, hateful, hideous **8** horrible **9** abhorrent, execrable, obnoxious, offensive, repellent, repugnant, repulsive, revolting **10** abominable, deplorable, detestable, disgusting, nauseating

lob 4 loft, toss **5** chuck, fling, heave, pitch, sling, throw **6** propel

lobby 4 hall **5** foyer **7** promote **8** anteroom, corridor **9** influence, vestibule **10** passageway **11** waiting room

lobe 4 flap **7** pendant

lobo 4 wolf **8** gray wolf **10** timber wolf

lobster 8 crawfish **10** crustacean ***claw:*** **5** chela **6** pincer ***female:*** **3** hen ***male:*** **4** cock ***trap:*** **3** pot **5** creel

local 6 native **7** endemic, insular, topical **9** parochial **10** provincial

locale 4 area, belt, site, turf, ward **5** place, scene, venue **6** milieu, parish, region, sector **7** commune, quarter, setting **8** district, precinct, vicinage, vicinity **9** community, territory **11** mise-en-scène **12** neighborhood

locality 4 area, belt, city, site, turf, zone **5** block, field, haunt, place, tract **6** county, domain, hamlet, region, sector, sphere, square **7** habitat, section **8** district, environs, precinct, province, purlieus, township, vici-

nage, vicinity **9** bailiwick, situation, territory **12** neighborhood
localize 4 mass **5** amass, focus **7** cluster, collect **8** coalesce, pinpoint **10** accumulate **11** concentrate, consolidate **12** conglomerate
locate 3 fix, spy **4** espy, find, site, spot **5** dwell, place, trace **6** detect, reside, settle **7** nose out, situate, station, uncover **8** come upon, discover, pinpoint, position **9** establish, ferret out, search out **10** come across
location 4 area, site, post, spot **5** locus, place, point, scene, venue, where **7** bearing, habitat, setting **8** position **9** situation **11** mise-en-scène, whereabouts
loch 3 bay **4** lake
lock 4 bolt, curl, hank, hold, tuft **5** latch, tress **6** fasten, secure **7** ringlet **8** fastener **9** enclosure, fastening
lockjaw 7 tetanus, trismus
lock up 3 ice **4** seal **5** sew up **6** assure, clinch, ensure, ratify, secure, settle **7** confirm **8** complete, conclude, finalize, validate **9** guarantee
lockup 3 jug, pen **4** brig, cell, coop, gaol, jail, stir, tank **5** clink, pokey, pound **6** cooler, prison **7** slammer **8** bastille, hoosegow
loco 3 ape, mad **4** bats, nuts **5** balmy, batty, crazy, kooky, loony, nutty **6** crazed, insane, screwy **7** bananas, berserk, bonkers, cracked, flipped, lunatic **8** demented, deranged, frenzied, unhinged **10** flipped out
locomotive 5 cheer, dolly, train **6** engine ***small:* 5** dinky **6** dinkey ***type:* 5** steam **6** diesel **8** electric
locum tenens 3 sub **5** proxy **6** backup, fill-in, supply **7** stand-in **9** alternate, auxiliary, surrogate **10** substitute **11** pinch hitter, replacement, succedaneum
locus 3 hub **4** seat, site **5** focus, heart, stage **6** center **7** setting **8** cynosure, location, polestar **10** focal point **11** nerve center **12** headquarters
locust 4 tree, wood **5** carob **6** cicada, insect **11** grasshopper
locution 4 word **5** argot, idiom, lingo **6** jargon, patois, phrase **7** dialect **8** parlance, phrasing **9** utterance **10** expression **11** phraseology
lode 4 seam, vein **5** store **6** source, supply **7** deposit ***mother:* 7** bonanza
lodestar 4 guru **5** gauge, guide, ideal, model **6** beacon, leader, mentor **7** epitome **8** exemplar, paradigm **9** archetype, guidepost **11** inspiration
lodestone 6 magnet **9** magnetite
lodge 3 den, fix, inn **4** bunk, camp, club, file, lair, nest, root, stay **5** abide, abode, board, cabin, couch, dwell, embed, guild, hotel, house, motel, order, put up **6** billet, burrow, hostel, league, remain, shanty, tavern, wigwam **7** auberge, contain, cottage, deposit, hospice, quarter, receive, shelter **8** domicile, hostelry, sodality **9** gatehouse **10** fellowship **11** accommodate, brotherhood, caravansary, public house
lodger 5 guest **6** renter, roomer, tenant **7** boarder, resider
lodging 3 inn, pad **4** dorm, room **5** abode, hotel, motel, place **7** shelter **8** chambers, diggings, domicile, dwelling, quarters **9** apartment, residence **10** pied-à-terre **13** accommodation
loess 4 clay, loam, marl **7** deposit
loft 4 rise **5** attic, raise **6** dormer, garret, propel **7** gallery
loftiness 5 pride **6** height **7** disdain, hauteur, stature **8** altitude, eminence **9** aloofness, arrogance, elevation, pomposity, sublimity **11** haughtiness, superiority **13** condescension
lofty 4 airy, epic, high, tall **5** grand, noble, proud **6** aerial, august, raised, remote, superb **7** exalted, haughty, soaring, stately, sublime, utopian **8** arrogant, cavalier, elevated, eloquent, imposing, insolent, majestic, superior, towering **9** ambitious, grandiose, visionary **10** disdainful **11** overbearing, pretentious, skyscraping **12** supercilious
log 5 diary, tally **6** record, timber **7** journal **8** register ***cutter:* 8** chain saw ***mover:* 5** peavy **6** peavey **7** cant dog
loge 3 box **5** booth, stall **7** balcony **9** mezzanine
logger 9 lumberman **10** lumberjack, woodcutter ***legendary:* 10** Paul Bunyan
loggerhead 6 shrike, turtle
loggia 6 arcade **7** balcony, gallery, veranda
logic 6 reason **9** reasoning **10** syntactics ***specious:* 7** sophism **9** sophistry
logical 5 sound, valid **6** cogent **8** analytic, sensible **9** deducible, deductive, plausible **10** analytical, compelling, convincing, diagnostic, reasonable, scientific, systematic
logjam 5 crowd **7** impasse **8** blockage, deadlock, stoppage **11** obstruction
logo 5 badge, brand, motto **6** cipher, device, emblem, symbol **8** colophon, hallmark, monogram **9** trademark
logogriph 6 puzzle **7** anagram
logroll 4 birl
logy 4 dull, slow **5** dopey, heavy **6** drowsy, groggy, torpid **8** listless, sluggish
Lohengrin *composer:* 6 Wagner (Richard) ***father:* 8** Parsifal, Parzival ***wife:* 4** Elsa

loincloth 5 dhoti **11** breechcloth, breechclout
Loire city 5 Blois, Tours **6** Nantes **7** Orléans
loiter 3 bum, lag **4** drag, idle, laze, lazy, loaf, loll, poke **5** dally, delay, tarry, trail **6** dawdle, diddle, linger, lounge, put off, putter **8** lollygag **10** dillydally, fool around, hang around **11** screw around **13** procrastinate
Loki *father:* 8 Farbauti ***mother:* 3** Nal **6** Laufey ***offspring:* 3** Hel **4** Hela **6** Fenris **7** Midgard ***slayer:* 8** Heimdall ***victim:* 6** Balder, Baldur ***wife:* 5** Sigyn **9** Angurboda
Lolita *author:* 7 Nabokov (Vladimir) ***suitor:* 7** Humbert (Humbert)
loll 3 bum, lag **4** drag, idle, laze, lazy, loaf, poke **5** chill, dally, delay, droop, slump, tarry, trail **6** dawdle, diddle, linger, lounge, putter, slouch **8** chill out **10** dillydally, fool around, hang around **13** procrastinate
lollapalooza 4 lulu **5** beaut, doozy **6** doozie **8** knockout **9** humdinger
Lollards' leader 8 Wycliffe (John)
lollygag 4 idle, loaf, loll, poke, drag **5** chill **6** dawdle, diddle, loiter, piddle, putter **10** dilly-dally, fool around
Lombard 6 banker **11** moneylender ***king:* 5** Cleph **6** Alboin, Audoin **7** Aistulf, Aripert, Authari **9** Liudprand
London *attraction:* 3 Eye **5** Tower ***borough:* 5** Brent **6** Barnet, Bexley, Ealing, Harrow, Sutton **7** Barking, Bromley, Chelsea, Croydon, Enfield, Hackney, Lambeth **8** Haringey, Havering, Hounslow, Lewisham **9** Greenwich, Islington, Redbridge **10** Kensington **11** Westminster ***cathedral:* 7** St. Paul's ***clock:* 6** Big Ben ***district:* 4** Soho **5** Acton **7** Chelsea, Mayfair **9** Belgravia, Southwark ***gallery:* 4** Tate ***gardens:* 3** Kew ***policeman:* 5** bobby ***prison:* 7** Newgate ***river:* 6** Thames ***square:* 9** Leicester, Trafalgar ***street:* 4** Bond **5** Fleet **6** Strand **7** Downing **9** Whitehall **10** Piccadilly ***subway:* 4** tube
London novel 7 Sea Wolf (The) **8** Iron Heel (The) **9** White Fang **10** Martin Eden **13** Call of the Wild (The)
lone 4 only, sole, solo **5** alone **6** single, unique **8** deserted, forsaken, isolated, secluded, separate, singular, solitary **13** unaccompanied
lonely 4 left, lorn **5** alone **7** forlorn **8** deserted, forsaken, homesick, lonesome, rejected, solitary **9** abandoned
loneness 8 solitude **9** isolation **10** detachment **12** separateness, solitariness
loner 6 hermit **7** isolate, outcast, recluse **8** outsider, solitary **13** individualist
Lone Ranger, The *creator:* 7 Striker (Fran) ***companion:* 5** Tonto ***epithet:* 8** Kemo Sabe ***horse:* 6** Silver ***trademark:* 4** mask **12** silver bullet
Lone Star State 5 Texas
long 3 far, yen **4** ache, itch, pine, tall **5** wordy, yearn **6** hanker, hunger, prolix, thirst **7** endless, lengthy **8** dragging, drawn-out, extended, unending **9** extensive **10** full-length, protracted
long ago 4 yore
long-drawn-out 7 endless, lengthy **8** dragging, unending **10** protracted **12** interminable
Longfellow poem 8 Christus, Hiawatha, Hyperion, Kavanagh **10** Evangeline **11** My Lost Youth, Psalm of Life (A)
long for 4 want **5** covet, crave, mourn **6** desire, repine **8** aspire to
longing 3 yen **4** itch, lust, urge, wish **5** greed **6** desire, hunger, thirst **7** avidity, craving, passion **8** appetite
longshoreman 9 stevedore **10** roustabout
long-suffering 7 patient, stoical **8** enduring, resigned **9** compliant **10** forbearing, submissive **13** accommodating, uncomplaining
long suit 3 bag **4** gift **5** forte **6** métier, talent **8** strength **9** specialty
long-winded 5 wordy **6** prolix **7** diffuse, lengthy, verbose **8** rambling **9** garrulous, redundant **10** loquacious
loo 2 WC **3** lav **4** head, john **5** jakes, privy **6** toilet **7** latrine **8** bathroom, outhouse
look 3 air, eye **4** gape, gawk, gaze, leer, mien, ogle, peek, peep, peer, seem, view **5** glare, stare, watch **6** admire, appear, aspect, behold, expect, eyeful, glance, glower, goggle, regard, squint, survey, visage **7** bearing, examine, eyeball, glimpse, observe **8** demeanor, once-over **10** appearance, rubberneck
look after 4 mind, tend **5** nurse, serve, watch **6** attend, wait on **7** care for, husband **8** wait upon **9** watch over **10** provide for
look-alike 4 twin **5** clone **6** double **7** similar **8** matching **9** duplicate
look at 3 eye, see **4** face, ogle, scan, view **5** check **6** behold, ponder, regard **7** examine, inspect **8** confront, consider **11** investigate
look back 6 recall, review **7** reflect **8** remember **9** reminisce
look down on 5 abhor, scorn, scout, spurn **7** contemn, despise, disdain **8** dominate **9** tower over **10** tower above
looker 6 beauty, eyeful, lovely, vision **7** stunner, witness **8** knockout, ornament **9** bystander, sightseer, spectator **10** eyewitness
looker-on 5 gaper **6** viewer **7** watcher, witness **8** beholder, observer **9** bystander, spectator **10** eyewitness **12** rubbernecker

look for 4 seek **5** await **6** expect, plan on **9** search out **10** anticipate
looking glass 6 mirror **9** reflector
look into 5 check, probe, study **6** pursue, survey **7** examine, explore, inspect **8** check out, question, research **10** scrutinize **11** investigate
look out 4 mind **6** beware
lookout 4 aery, view **5** aerie, guard, scout, tower, vista, watch **6** cupola, picket, sentry **7** spotter **8** panorama, prospect, sentinel, watchman **9** belvedere, crow's nest, firetower **10** watchtower, widow's walk **11** observatory, perspective
look over 3 vet **4** read **5** check **6** review, size up **7** examine, inspect **8** appraise, evaluate
loom 4 brew, bulk, near, rear **5** hover, mount, tower **6** appear, come on, emerge, gather, impend **7** portend **8** approach, overhang, stand out, threaten **9** take shape ***part:*** **6** heddle **7** harness, shuttle, treadle, trundle
loon 3 nut, oaf **4** bird, clod, dodo, dolt, goof, lout, yo-yo **5** chump, dummy, dunce, ninny, noddy, stupe, yokel **6** dimwit, dum-dum, nitwit **7** airhead, buffoon, dullard, pinhead **8** bonehead, dumbbell, crackpot, imbecile, lunkhead, meathead, numskull **9** birdbrain, blockhead, ignoramus, lamebrain, numbskull, simpleton **10** dunderhead, nincompoop **11** chowderhead, chucklehead
loony 3 nut **4** bats, loco **5** balmy, batty, crazy, daffy, dippy, goofy, nutty, silly, wacky **6** absurd, insane, madman, screwy **7** fatuous, foolish, idiotic **8** demented **9** bedlamite, half-baked, ludicrous, senseless **10** ridiculous **11** harebrained **12** preposterous
loony bin 6 asylum, bedlam **8** bughouse, madhouse, nuthouse **9** funny farm **10** booby hatch, crazy house
loop 3 arc, eye **4** ansa, ring **5** curve, noose, picot **6** circle, eyelet, league, staple **7** circlet, circuit **8** doubling
looped 4 high **5** bowed, drunk, stiff **6** blotto, bombed, curved, juiced, loaded, potted, stewed, tanked, zonked **7** crocked, pickled, pie-eyed, sloshed, smashed **9** plastered **10** inebriated **11** curvilinear, intoxicated
loophole 3 out **6** escape, outlet **7** opening
loopy 4 bats, daft, nuts, wavy **5** arced, batty, bowed, crazy, daffy, dotty, flaky, nutty, silly, snaky, wacky **6** arched, curved, freaky, fruity, screwy, swirly **7** bizarre, idiotic, lunatic, offbeat, sinuous, touched **8** demented **9** eccentric **10** flipped out, off-the-wall, outlandish
loose 3 lax **4** easy, fast, free, lewd, limp **5** baggy, slack, untie, vague **6** flabby, wanton **7** flaccid, relaxed **8** flexible **9** debauched, desultory, dissolute, imprecise **10** disjointed, dissipated, ill-defined, licentious, unattached, unconfined **12** disconnected, unrestrained
loose end 6 detail **8** fragment
loose-lipped see **loquacious**
loosen 4 ease, free, undo **5** relax, slack, untie **6** unbind **7** ease off, manumit, release, slacken, unchain **8** liberate, unbuckle, unfasten **10** emancipate
loosen up 5 relax **6** unbend, unwind **7** ease off, stretch
loot 3 rob **4** haul, lift, pelf, raid, sack, swag **5** boost, booty, dough, lucre, money, moola, reave, rifle, spoil **6** boodle, moolah, ravish, spoils **7** despoil, pillage, plunder, ransack, stick up **9** knock over
looter 5 thief **7** brigand **8** marauder
lop 3 cut **4** chop, clip, crop, snip, trim **5** prune, sever **6** excise **8** amputate, truncate **9** dismember **10** guillotine
lope 3 jog, run **4** gait, romp, trot **5** amble **6** canter
lopsided 4 awry **5** askew **6** aslant, uneven **7** crooked, leaning, tilting **8** top-heavy **10** asymmetric, off-balance, unbalanced **12** asymmetrical **13** unsymmetrical
loquacious 5 gabby, talky, wordy **6** chatty, mouthy, prolix **7** verbose, voluble, yakking **8** babbling **9** garrulous, jabbering, talkative **10** blathering, chattering, long-winded **11** loose-lipped **12** motormouthed
Lorca play 5 Yerma **12** Blood Wedding
lord 3 sir **4** boss, duke, earl, peer **5** noble, ruler **6** master **7** marquis **8** governor, marquess, nobleman, viscount **9** sovereign, tyrannize ***feudal:*** **5** liege **8** seigneur, suzerain ***Muslim:*** **6** sayyid
Lord High Executioner 4 Koko
Lord Jim author 6 Conrad (Joseph)
lordly 5 grand, lofty, noble, proud **6** august, uppity **7** exalted, haughty, pompous, stately, swollen **8** affected, arrogant, cavalier, gracious, imposing, insolent, majestic, princely, snobbish, superior **9** dignified, egotistic, grandiose **10** disdainful, high-handed **11** dictatorial, magisterial, magnificent, overbearing, patronizing **12** aristocratic, supercilious **13** authoritarian, high-and-mighty
Lord of the Flies *author:* 7 Golding (William) ***character:*** **4** Jack **5** Piggy, Ralph
Lord of the Rings *author:* 7 Tolkien (J. R. R.) ***book:*** **9** Two Towers (The) **15** Return of the King (The) **19** Fellowship of the Ring (The) ***character:*** **3** Sam **5** Arwen, Frodo, Gimli **6**

Elrond, Gollum, Sauron **7** Aragorn, Baggins (Bilbo, Frodo), Boromir, Gandalf, Legolas, Saruman, Théoden **9** Galadriel, Treebeard ***film director:*** **7** Jackson (Peter) ***illustrator:*** **3** Lee (Alan) **4** Howe (John) ***race:*** **4** ents, orcs **5** wargs **6** huorns **7** hobbits **11** ringwraiths ***realm:*** **5** Arnor, Moria, Rohan **6** Gondor, Mordor **10** Lothlórien **11** Middle-earth **12** Undying Lands ***site:*** **5** Shire (The) **8** Isengard **9** Mount Doom, Rivendell ***star:*** **3** Lee (Christopher) **4** Hill (Bernard), Holm (Ian), Wood (Elijah) **5** Astin (Sean), Baker (Sala), Bloom (Orlando), Tyler (Liv) **6** Serkis (Andy) **7** Weaving (Hugo) **8** McKellen (Ian), Monaghan (Dominic) **9** Blanchett (Cate), Mortensen (Viggo) ***sword:*** **5** Sting **6** Narsil **7** Andúril **9** Glamdring

Lord's Prayer **9** Our Father **11** Paternoster

lore **6** mythos, wisdom **7** history **8** folkways, learning **9** knowledge, mythology, tradition **11** information **12** superstition

Lorelei **5** siren **9** temptress **10** seductress **11** femme fatale ***poet:*** **5** Heine (Heinrich) ***river:*** **5** Rhein, Rhine ***victim:*** **6** sailor **7** mariner

lorgnette **10** eyeglasses, spectacles **12** opera glasses

Lorna Doone ***author:*** **9** Blackmore (Richard) ***hero:*** **4** Ridd (John)

____ **Lorraine** **6** Alsace

lorry **3** rig, van **4** semi **5** truck

lose **4** miss, shed **5** evade, shake, waste, yield **6** escape, give up, mislay **7** destroy, forfeit, succumb **8** misplace, shake off, throw off **9** sacrifice, surrender

lose it **5** go ape **7** crack up, flip out, go crazy, run amok **8** freak out, run amuck

loser **3** dud **4** bomb, bust, flop **5** lemon **6** bummer, fiasco, misfit, turkey **7** also-ran, debacle, failure, washout **8** deadbeat **11** incompetent

loss **4** bath, harm, ruin **5** waste **6** damage, defeat, injury **7** deficit, failure, forfeit **8** casualty, decrease, fatality **9** depletion, privation, sacrifice, shrinkage **10** divestment, forfeiture, misfortune, misplacing **11** bereavement, deprivation, destruction

lost **4** asea, dead, gone, rapt **6** absent, astray, bygone, damned, doomed, futile, hidden, wasted **7** defunct, faraway, lacking, mislaid, missing **8** absorbed, departed, distrait, helpless, hopeless, vanished **9** condemned, desperate, destroyed **10** abstracted, insensible, overlooked **11** irrevocable, preoccupied **12** irredeemable, unregenerate

Lost Horizon ***author:*** **6** Hilton (James) ***character:*** **6** Conway (Hugh) ***land:*** **9** Shangri-La

lot **3** cut, ilk **4** doom, fate, heap, kind, mass, plat, yard **5** batch, block, bunch, field, moira, patch, quota, share, slice, tract, weird **6** assign, barrel, bundle, parcel, stripe **7** acreage, cluster, destiny, fortune, mete out, portion, species **8** allocate, clearing, frontage **9** aggregate, allowance, apportion

Lot ***father:*** **5** Haran ***sister:*** **5** Iscah **6** Milcah ***son:*** **4** Moab **5** Ammon ***uncle:*** **7** Abraham

lothario **4** lech, stud, wolf **5** letch, Romeo **6** lecher, tomcat **7** amorist, Don Juan, gallant, seducer **8** Casanova, paramour **9** debaucher, ladies' man, womanizer **10** lady-killer **11** philanderer

lotion **3** oil **4** balm **5** cream, salve **6** cerate **7** unguent **8** ablution, cosmetic, lenitive, liniment, ointment **9** demulcent **11** embrocation

lottery **6** raffle **7** drawing **11** sweepstakes

lotus-eater **7** dreamer **8** escapist, romantic **10** daydreamer **13** castle-builder

loud **5** forte, gaudy, noisy, showy **6** brassy, brazen, flashy, garish, glitzy, tawdry, vulgar **7** blaring, blatant, booming, chintzy, glaring, pealing, raucous, roaring **8** piercing, resonant, sonorous, strident **9** clamorous, deafening, obnoxious, obtrusive, offensive, tasteless **10** bigmouthed, boisterous, flamboyant, fortissimo, resounding, stentorian, thunderous, vociferous **12** earsplitting

loudmouth **6** ranter **7** stentor **8** blowhard, braggart **9** blusterer

loudspeaker **3** amp **6** Tannoy, woofer **7** tweeter **9** amplifier

Louisiana ***capital:*** **10** Baton Rouge ***city:*** **10** New Orleans, Shreveport ***college, university:*** **6** Tulane ***county:*** **6** parish ***lake:*** **13** Pontchartrain ***nickname:*** **7** Pelican (State) ***river:*** **11** Mississippi ***state bird:*** **12** brown pelican ***state flower:*** **8** magnolia ***state tree:*** **11** bald cypress

lounge **3** bar, bum, lie, pub, tap **4** idle, laze, loaf, loll, sofa **5** couch, dally, drift, lobby, relax **6** dawdle, loiter, parlor, repose, saloon **7** barroom, goof off, lie down, recline, taproom **8** restroom, kill time **10** living room

lounge lizard **3** fop **4** rake, toff **5** blade, dandy, leech **6** gigolo, sponge **9** ladies' man

Lourdes saint **10** Bernadette

louse **3** cad, cur, dog, rat **4** toad **5** aphid, creep, skunk, snake **6** cootie, psylla, rotter, slater, wretch **7** bounder, stinker ***egg:*** **3** nit

louse up **4** blow, flub, muff, ruin **5** botch, spoil, wreck **6** bobble, bollix, bumble, bungle, fumble

lousy **3** ill **4** poor, rife **5** awful **6** crummy, shoddy, rotten **7** replete, teeming **8** crawling, horrible, inferior, infested, terrible **9** miserable, repulsive **10** despicable **12** contemptible

lout 3 oaf **4** boob, boor, dolt, gawk, hick, rube **5** brute, chuff, churl, klutz, looby, scorn, yahoo, yokel **6** galoot, lubber, lummox, rustic **7** bumpkin, hayseed, palooka **9** simpleton **10** clodhopper

Louvre masterpiece 8 Mona Lisa **11** Venus de Milo

lovable 4 dear **5** sweet **6** cuddly **7** winning, winsome **8** adorable **9** appealing, endearing **11** embraceable

love 4 zeal **5** adore, ardor, crush, Cupid, prize, value **6** desire, dote on, fervor, revere **7** adulate, cherish, idolize, passion, romance, worship **8** devotion, fondness, idolatry, treasure, venerate, yearning **9** adoration, adulation, delight in **10** attachment **11** amorousness, infatuation ***combining form:*** **4** phil **5** philo, phily **6** philia ***French:*** **5** amour ***Italian:*** **5** amore ***tennis:*** **3** nil **4** zero **7** nothing

love apple 6 tomato

lovebird 6 budgie, parrot **10** budgerigar

love-bite 3 nip **6** hickey

love feast 5 agape

love god 4 Amor, Eros, Kama **5** Bhaga, Cupid

love goddess 5 Athor, Freya, Venus **6** Hathor, Inanna, Ishtar **7** Astarte **9** Aphrodite, Ashtoreth

love letter 8 mash note **9** valentine **10** billet-doux

lovely 4 fair **5** sweet, swell **6** comely, dainty, pretty **7** elegant **8** adorable, alluring, charming, delicate, engaging, graceful, knockout **9** beauteous, beautiful, exquisite **10** attractive, delightful, enchanting, entrancing **11** captivating, good-looking

love potion 7 philter, philtre **11** aphrodisiac

lover 3 fan **4** beau, buff **5** flame, leman, Romeo, swain **6** addict, steady, suitor, votary **7** amorist, darling, devotee, Don Juan, gallant, habitué, squeeze **8** fancy man, lothario, mistress, paramour **9** boyfriend, inamorata, inamorato **10** aficionado, girlfriend, sweetheart

lovey-dovey 5 mushy **6** doting **7** amorous **12** affectionate

loving 4 dear, fond **6** ardent, erotic, tender **7** amatory, amorous, cordial, devoted, fervent **8** attached, enamored, faithful **10** benevolent, infatuated, passionate, solicitous **11** impassioned **12** affectionate

low 3 moo **4** base, blue, dead, deep, flat, mean, neap **5** cheap **6** abject, ailing, humble, hushed, lesser, nether, poorly, sickly, sordid, unwell **7** cut-rate, reduced, scrubby **8** cast down, dejected, depleted, downcast, inferior, mediocre, wretched **9** declining, depressed, miserable, subnormal, woebegone **10** inadequate, indisposed **11** crestfallen, downhearted, unfavorable

lowbred 4 base, rude **6** coarse, oafish, vulgar **7** boorish, brutish, loutish, uncouth **8** churlish, cloddish, lubberly **11** uncivilized

low-cost 5 cheap **6** budget, cheapo **7** bargain, cut-rate **10** affordable, reasonable **11** inexpensive

low-down 4 base, mean, ugly, vile **6** grubby, odious, scurvy, sleazy, sordid **7** ignoble, squalid **8** shameful, wretched **9** abhorrent, worthless **10** despicable, disgusting **11** ignominious **12** contemptible

lowdown 4 dope, info **5** facts, goods, scoop, specs **6** skinny **8** briefing **11** information

lower 3 cut **4** clip, drop, fall, sink **5** frown, gloom, scowl, shave, slash, under **6** debase, demean, demote, humble, lesser, menace, nether, reduce **7** cut down, deflate, degrade, demerit, depress, descend, devalue, let down **8** inferior, mark down, overcast, submerge, threaten **9** devaluate, downgrade ***prefix:*** **5** infra

Lower Depths author 5 Gorki, Gorky (Maksim, Maxim)

lowest point 5 nadir ***in the U.S.:*** **11** Death Valley ***on earth's crust:*** **13** Mariana Trench ***on earth's surface:*** **7** Dead Sea

low-grade 4 hack **5** junky, lousy **6** cheesy, cruddy, shabby, shoddy, sleazy, tawdry **8** below par, déclassé, inferior, mediocre **9** deficient **10** second-rate **11** second-class, substandard **12** second-drawer

low-key 4 soft **5** muted, quiet **7** relaxed, subdued **8** laid-back, softened, tasteful **9** easygoing, minimized, temperate, toned down **10** played down, restrained **11** understated

lowland 4 flat, sump, vale **5** basin **6** bottom, slough, valley **7** bottoms ***Scottish:*** **6** lallan **7** lalland

lowlife 4 fink, heel **5** knave, rogue **6** no-good, outlaw, rascal, wretch **7** hoodlum, ruffian, villain **9** miscreant, reprobate, scoundrel **10** blackguard, black sheep, sleazeball **11** rapscallion, slimebucket **12** bottom-feeder

lowly 4 base, mean, meek **6** abject, humble, menial, modest **7** ignoble, mundane, obscure, prosaic, servile **8** baseborn, plebeian, unwashed

low-pressure 4 calm **6** casual, dégagé, folksy, mellow **7** relaxed **8** flexible, informal, laid-back **9** easygoing **10** nonchalant

low-spirited 3 sad **4** blue, down, glum **6** abject, droopy, gloomy, morose **7** doleful **8** cast down, dejected, downcast, saddened **9** bummed out, cheerless, depressed, woebegone **10** dispirited, melancholy **11** discouraged, downhearted **12** disheartened, heavyhearted

low tide 3 ebb **4** neap

loyal 4 firm, true **5** liege **6** ardent, trusty **7** devoted, dutiful, staunch **8** constant, faithful, resolute, true-blue **9** allegiant, steadfast, unfailing **10** dependable **11** trustworthy

loyalist 4 Tory **7** patriot **8** partisan **10** countryman **11** nationalist

loyalty 6 fealty **8** adhesion, devotion, fidelity **9** adherence, constancy **10** allegiance, attachment, dedication **11** staunchness **12** faithfulness **13** dependability, steadfastness

lozenge 4 pill **6** troche **7** diamond, rhombus **8** pastille

LSD 4 acid ***user:*** **8** acidhead

lubricate 3 oil **6** grease, smooth **7** moisten

lubricious 4 lewd, oily **5** slick **6** carnal, greasy, slippy, wanton **8** prurient, slippery, slithery, ticklish **9** lecherous, salacious **10** lascivious, libidinous **12** concupiscent

lucent 5 clear **6** bright, limpid **7** beaming, crystal, glowing, lambent, radiant, shining **8** clear-cut, luminous, pellucid **9** brilliant, effulgent, refulgent **11** unambiguous

Lucia di Lammermoor *character:* 7 Edgardo ***composer:*** **9** Donizetti (Gaetano) ***novelist:*** **5** Scott (Walter)

lucid 4 sane **5** clear **6** bright, limpid **7** crystal, lambent, radiant **8** clear-cut, knowable, luminous **9** brilliant, effulgent, graspable, refulgent, unblurred **10** articulate, fathomable **11** translucent, transparent, unambiguous **12** compos mentis, incandescent, intelligible, transpicuous

lucidity 6 acumen, sanity **7** clarity **8** sagacity, saneness **9** clearness, plainness, soundness **10** cognizance, perception **12** clairvoyance

Lucifer 5 devil, fiend, Satan, Venus **7** Old Nick **8** Apollyon **9** archfiend, Beelzebub **10** Old Scratch **13** Old Gooseberry

Lucinde *beloved:* 7 Leandre **9** Clitandre ***father:*** **7** Geronte **10** Sganarelle

luck 3 hap, hit **4** juju, meet **5** fluke, light **6** chance, happen, hazard, kismet **7** fortune, godsend, stumble **8** fortuity, occasion, windfall **9** advantage **11** opportunity ***token:*** **5** charm **6** amulet, clover, fetish, mascot **8** talisman **9** horseshoe **11** rabbit's foot

luckless 7 adverse, hapless, unhappy **8** ill-fated, untoward, wretched **9** miserable **10** ill-starred **11** star-crossed, unfavorable, unfortunate **12** misfortunate, unpropitious

lucky 6 golden, timely **7** favored **9** favorable, fortunate **10** auspicious, beneficial, felicitous, fortuitous, propitious **12** advantageous, providential **13** serendipitous ***Scottish:*** **5** canny

Lucky Jim author 4 Amis (Kingsley)

lucrative 6 paying **7** gainful **8** fruitful **10** high-income, productive, profitable, well-paying, worthwhile **11** moneymaking **12** advantageous, remunerative

lucre 3 pay **4** cash, gain, jack, loot, pelf, swag **5** booty, dough, green, money, moola **6** boodle, dinero, do-re-mi, moolah, profit, wampum **7** cabbage, revenue **9** long green **10** greenbacks

Lucrezia ____ 6 Borgia

Lucy's husband 4 Desi **5** Arnaz (Desi)

ludicrous 4 zany **5** antic, comic, droll, funny, goofy, nutty, silly **6** absurd **7** amusing, bizarre, comical, foolish, risible **8** farcical **9** fantastic, grotesque, laughable **10** off-the-wall, outlandish, ridiculous **11** incongruous **12** preposterous

Ludlum novel 14 Bourne Identity (The) **15** Bourne Supremacy (The) **16** Holcroft Covenant (The)

lug 3 nut, oaf, tow, tug **4** bear, buck, drag, draw, haul, hump, jerk, pull, tote **5** carry, ferry, shlep **6** convey, schlep **7** bruiser, schlepp **9** transport

luggage 4 bags, gear **7** baggage

lugubrious 3 sad **4** blue, dour, down, glum **5** bleak **6** dismal, dreary, gloomy, morose, rueful, somber, sullen, woeful **7** doleful, joyless **8** cast down, dejected, dolesome, downcast, mournful **9** cheerless, depressed, plaintive, saturnine, sorrowful, woebegone **10** depressing, despondent, lamentable, melancholy, oppressive **11** discouraged, dispiriting, downhearted **12** disconsolate

lukewarm 5 blasé, tepid **7** dubious, offhand **8** hesitant **9** uncertain, undecided **10** wishy-washy **11** halfhearted, indifferent

lull 3 ebb **4** balm, calm, hush, wane **5** letup, pause, quiet, still **6** becalm, pacify, soothe, temper **7** compose, decline, ease off, slacken **8** abeyance, interval **9** stillness **10** quiescence **11** tranquilize

lullaby 8 berceuse **10** cradlesong

lulu 3 ace, gem, pip **5** beaut, dandy, dilly, doozy, dream, honey **6** doozie, wonder **7** delight **8** jim-dandy, knockout **9** humdinger, sensation

lumber 3 tax **4** clog, lade, load, logs, plod, slog, wood **5** barge, clump, stump, weigh **6** burden, charge, rumble, saddle, timber, trudge **8** encumber

lumberjack see **logger**

luminance **10** brightness

luminary **3** sun, VIP **4** lion, name, star **5** celeb, light, nabob **6** leader, worthy **7** big name, notable **8** big-timer, eminence, somebody **9** celebrity, dignitary, superstar **10** notability **12** leading light

luminous **5** clear, lucid **6** bright, lucent **7** beaming, crystal, fulgent, lambent, radiant, shining **8** clear-cut, lustrous, pellucid **9** brilliant, effulgent, refulgent **11** illustrious, translucent, transparent **12** enlightening, incandescent

lummox **3** oaf **4** boor, clod, gawk, goon, hulk, lout **5** klutz, looby **6** lubber **7** palooka

lump **3** gob, lot, oaf, wad **4** blob, bulk, chip, clod, gawk, glob, heap, hunk, lout, mass, pile, welt **5** abide, batch, block, brook, bulge, bunch, chunk, hunch, klutz, knurl, looby, piece, scrap, stand, tumor **6** digest, endure, entire, lubber, morsel, nugget **7** handful, palooka, portion, stomach, swallow **8** swelling, totality **9** aggregate **10** protrusion, tumescence **12** protuberance

lumpy **5** crude, gawky, rough **6** choppy, clumsy, coarse, oafish **8** clumpish, unformed **9** roughhewn

lunacy **5** folly, mania **6** idiocy **7** fatuity, foolery, inanity, madness **8** delirium, dementia, insanity **9** absurdity, craziness, silliness, stupidity **10** imbecility **11** derangement, foolishness **13** senselessness

lunar ***dark area:*** **4** mare **5** maria (plural) ***valley:*** **4** rill **5** rille

lunatic **3** mad, nut **4** bats, daft, kook, loco, yo-yo, zany **5** balmy, batty, crank, crazy, nutty, raver, wacko, wacky **6** absurd, crazed, cuckoo, insane, madman, maniac, nitwit, psycho, screwy **7** bonkers, cracked, foolish **8** crackpot, demented, demoniac, deranged, frenzied, maniacal, paranoid, schizoid, unhinged **9** bedlamite, ding-a-ling, fruitcake, harebrain, screwball **10** crackbrain **11** nonsensical

lunch **3** eat **4** meal, nosh **5** snack

luncheonette **4** café **5** diner **6** bistro, eatery **7** beanery, canteen, tearoom **8** snack bar **9** cafeteria **10** coffee shop, restaurant **11** greasy spoon

lune **3** bow **5** curve **6** sickle **8** crescent, meniscus

lung ***combining form:*** **5** pneum, pulmo **6** pneumo, pulmon ***disease:*** **9** emphysema, pneumonia **10** byssinosis **12** tuberculosis

lunge **3** jab **4** dash, dive, stab **5** bound, drive, pitch, surge **6** charge, plunge, pounce, thrust

lunkhead **3** oaf **4** boob, clod, dodo, dolt, goof, yo-yo **5** booby, chump, dummy, dunce, idiot, moron, ninny, noddy, stupe **6** dimwit, dum-dum, nitwit **7** dullard **8** dumbbell, imbecile, numskull **9** birdbrain, ignoramus, lamebrain, numbskull, simpleton **10** nincompoop

lupine **5** feral **6** brutal, fierce **7** wolfish **8** ravening **9** predatory, rapacious **10** bluebonnet, sanguinary

lurch **3** bob, yaw **4** jerk, lean, list, reel, rock, roll, sway, tilt, toss **5** heave, pitch, slide, swing **6** bumble, careen, falter, plunge, seesaw, swerve, teeter, totter **7** blunder, stagger, stumble **8** flounder

lure **3** bag **4** bait, call, draw, fake, hook, pull, rope, toll, trap, wile **5** blind, catch, charm, decoy, snare, tempt, trick **6** appeal, cajole, come-on, draw in, draw on, entice, entrap, invite, lead on, seduce **7** attract, beguile, bewitch, capture, con game, enchant, ensnare, gimmick, wheedle **8** blandish, delusion, illusion, inveigle **9** captivate, fascinate, incentive, seduction, siren song **10** attraction, camouflage, enticement, inducement, seducement, temptation ***fishing:*** **3** fly **4** worm **5** spoon **6** minnow **8** bucktail

lurid **4** ashy, gory, gray, grim, pale **5** ashen, fiery, gross, livid, waxen **6** grisly, malign, sultry **7** baleful, ghastly, graphic, hideous, macabre, malefic, tabloid **8** blanched, gruesome, horrible, shocking, sinister, terrible **9** colorless **10** horrifying, maleficent, terrifying **11** sensational **12** melodramatic

Lurie novel **14** Foreign Affairs **18** War Between the Tates (The)

lurk **4** hide, slip **5** creep, prowl, skulk, slide, slink, sneak, snoop, steal **9** pussyfoot

luscious **4** rich, sexy **5** sapid, sweet, tasty, yummy **6** delish, divine, ornate, savory **7** opulent, piquant, sensual **8** sensuous **9** ambrosial, epicurean, exquisite, flavorful, luxurious, seductive, sumptuous, toothsome **10** delectable, delightful, flamboyant, flavorsome, voluptuous **11** scrumptious **13** mouth-watering

lush **3** sot **4** rank, rich, wino **5** dense, drink, drunk, yummy **6** bibber, boozer, deluxe, lavish, savory **7** fertile, opulent, profuse, sensual, teeming, tippler **8** abundant, drunkard, palatial, prodigal, sensuous, thriving **9** ambrosial, epicurean, exuberant, inebriate, luxuriant, luxurious, plentiful, sumptuous, toothsome **10** boozehound, delectable, delightful, profitable, prosperous, voluptuous **11** extravagant, flourishing

Lusitania **8** Portugal

lust **3** rut, yen **4** ache, itch, pine, urge, wish,

zeal, zest **5** ardor, crave, drive, greed, letch, yearn **6** desire, fervor, hanker, hunger, libido **7** avidity, craving, lechery, longing, passion **8** appetite, coveting, cupidity, lewdness, priapism, salacity, satyrism, yearning **9** carnality, eagerness, eroticism, lubricity, prurience, pruriency **10** enthusiasm, excitement, satyriasis, wantonness **11** nymphomania **13** concupiscence, lecherousness, salaciousness

luster 4 glow **5** glaze, gleam, glint, gloss, sheen, shine **6** polish **7** burnish, shimmer **8** lambency, radiance **9** afterglow **10** brightness, brilliance, brilliancy, effulgence, luminosity, refulgence **11** candescence, iridescence

lusterless 3 dim, wan **4** blah, drab, dull, flat, gray, matt **5** brown, dingy, dusky, faded, matte, muddy, muted, vapid **6** boring **10** uninspired

lustful 3 hot **4** lewd **5** bawdy, horny **6** carnal, erotic, wanton **7** burning, goatish, itching, ruttish, satyric **8** prurient **9** debauched, lecherous, libertine, lickerish, salacious **10** hot-blooded, lascivious, libidinous, licentious, lubricious, passionate **12** concupiscent

lustrate 5 purge **6** purify **7** cleanse

lustration 6 ritual **8** ablution **9** catharsis, cleansing, purgation **10** sprinkling **12** purification

lustrous 4 naïf **5** nitid, shiny **6** bright, gleamy, glossy, pearly, sheeny **7** fulgent, glowing, lambent, radiant, shining **8** gleaming, luminous, polished, splendid **9** brilliant, burnished, effulgent, refulgent **10** glimmering, glistening **11** resplendent **12** incandescent

lusty 4 hale **5** hardy, vital **6** brawny, hearty, mighty, potent, robust, strong, virile **7** dynamic, healthy, rousing **8** vigorous **9** energetic, strapping, strenuous **10** prodigious, red-blooded **12** enthusiastic

lute 4 clay, seal **5** grout **6** cement **7** bandora **8** mandolin **10** chitarrone, instrument ***Arabic:*** **3** oud ***Indian:*** **5** sitar ***Japanese:*** **4** biwa **7** samisen **8** shamisen ***Oriental:*** **3** tar ***two-necked:*** **7** theorbo

lutenist 5 Bream (Julian) **7** Dowland (John) **8** Gaultier (Denis)

Lutetia 5 Paris

Luxembourg ***capital:*** **10** Luxembourg ***monetary unit:*** **4** euro ***monetary unit, former:*** **5** franc ***mountain range:*** **8** Ardennes ***neighbor:*** **6** France **7** Belgium, Germany ***river:*** **4** Sûre **7** Alzette

luxuriant 4 lush, rank, rich **5** dense **6** fecund, lavish **7** copious, fertile, opulent, profuse, rampant, riotous, teeming **8** abundant, fruitful, luscious, prodigal, prolific **9** excessive, exuberant, sumptuous

luxuriate 4 bask **5** bloom, enjoy, feast, revel **6** abound, relish, thrive, wallow **7** delight, indulge **8** flourish

luxurious 4 lush, posh, rich **5** fancy, grand, plush, ritzy, showy **6** costly, deluxe, lavish, plushy **7** opulent, sensual, stately **8** imposing, majestic, palatial, splendid **9** elaborate, epicurean, expensive, grandiose, sumptuous **10** impressive **11** extravagant, magnificent ***situation:*** **7** fat city **10** bed of roses, easy street

luxury 5 frill, treat **6** dainty **7** amenity, comfort **8** delicacy, opulence **9** abundance, affluence **10** indulgence **11** superfluity **12** extravagance

lycée 6 school **10** high school

lyceum 4 hall **6** school **7** academy, chamber **9** institute

Lycidas author 6 Milton (John)

Lycomedes ***daughter:*** **8** Deidamia ***victim:*** **7** Theseus

Lycus ***brother:*** **7** Nycteus ***father:*** **7** Pandion ***slayer:*** **6** Zethus **7** Amphion ***wife:*** **5** Dirce

Lydian ***king:*** **5** Gyges **7** Croesus **8** Alyattes ***queen:*** **7** Omphale

lye 7 caustic **9** hydroxide

lynch 4 hang **5** scrag **6** gibbet, murder **7** execute **8** string up

Lynette see **Line**

lynx 4 puma **6** bobcat, cougar **7** caracal, wildcat **9** catamount

Lyra star 4 Vega

lyre 4 harp

lyric 3 ode **4** odic, poem **5** melic, verse **6** poetic **7** melodic, musical **8** operatic **9** exuberant, rhapsodic

lyrical 7 lilting, melodic, musical, songful, tuneful **8** operatic **9** melodious

lyricist 4 poet **10** librettist see **songwriter**

Lysander's beloved 6 Hermia

M

Maacah ***father:*** **5** Nahor **6** Talmai **7** Absalom ***husband:*** **5** David **6** Jehiel, Machir **8** Rehoboam ***son:*** **5** Hanan **6** Abijam, Achish **7** Absalom **10** Shephatiah

macabre **4** grim **5** lurid **6** grisly, horrid, morbid **7** deathly, ghastly, hideous **8** ghoulish, gruesome, horrible **9** deathlike **10** horrifying

macadam **3** tar **7** asphalt, roadway **8** pavement

macaque **6** monkey, rhesus

macaroni **3** fop **4** beau, buck, dude, toff **5** dandy, pasta, swell **7** coxcomb, gallant

macaw **3** Ara **6** parrot

Macbeth ***character:*** **4** Ross **5** Angus **6** Hecate, Lennox **7** Fleance ***slayer:*** **7** Macduff ***successor:*** **7** Malcolm ***title:*** **5** thane ***victim:*** **6** Banquo, Duncan

mace **4** club **5** baton, staff **6** cudgel, nutmeg **8** bludgeon

Macedonia ***capital:*** **6** Skopje ***city:*** **6** Tetovo ***monetary unit:*** **5** denar ***neighbor:*** **6** Greece, Serbia **7** Albania **8** Bulgaria ***part of:*** **7** Balkans ***peninsula:*** **6** Balkan

macerate **3** ret **4** soak **5** steep **6** drench, soften **7** immerse, suffuse **8** saturate

machete **4** bolo **5** knife **6** scythe

Machiavellian **4** wily **6** shrewd **7** cunning, devious **8** guileful, scheming **9** conniving, deceitful, insidious **10** conspiring **11** duplicitous, treacherous **12** unscrupulous

Machiavelli work **6** Prince (The) **8** Mandrake (The) **10** Mandragola (La)

machinate **4** plot **6** scheme **7** connive, finagle **8** conspire, intrigue, maneuver

machination **4** plot, ploy, ruse **5** cabal, dodge **6** gambit, scheme **8** artifice, intrigue, maneuver, scheming, trickery **9** chicanery, collusion, deception, dirty work, expedient, stratagem **10** hanky-panky, subterfuge **11** contrivance, skulduggery **12** gamesmanship, skullduggery

machine **6** device, engine, gadget **9** apparatus, appliance, automaton **11** contraption ***part:*** **3** cam **4** gear **5** lever, shaft, valve **6** caster, flange, router, switch **7** bearing

machine-gun **4** rake **6** strafe **8** enfilade **9** rapid-fire

machine-gun inventor **7** Gatling (Richard)

machinery **5** works **9** apparatus, equipment, mechanism

machismo **7** swagger **8** virility **9** manliness **11** masculinity

macho **4** stud **5** he-man, manly **6** virile **9** masculine

Machu Picchu resident **4** Inca

mackinaw **4** coat **5** cover, trout **7** blanket

mackintosh **7** slicker **8** raincoat

macrocosm **5** world **6** cosmos **8** creation, universe

mad **4** daft, nuts, rash, sore, wild **5** angry, crazy, irate, irked, kooky, livid, loony, loopy, nutty, rabid, upset, wacky **6** absurd, crazed, cuckoo, heated, insane, ireful, screwy **7** berserk, bonkers, cracked, enraged, foolish, frantic, furious, lunatic **8** choleric, demented, deranged, frenetic, frenzied, incensed, offended, outraged, seething, unhinged, worked up, wrathful **9** delirious, fanatical, fantastic, hilarious, illogical, senseless **10** distracted, infuriated, irrational, unbalanced

Madagascar ***capital:*** **10** Tananarive **12** Antananarivo ***channel:*** **10** Mozambique ***city:*** **9** Mahajanga, Toamasina ***language:*** **6** French **8** Malagasy ***monetary unit:*** **6** ariary ***mountain range:*** **9** Ankaratra

madame **3** Mrs. **4** wife **6** milady, missus ***German:*** **4** Frau ***Spanish:*** **3** Sra. **6** Señora

Madame Bovary ***author:*** **8** Flaubert (Gustave) ***character:*** **4** Emma (Bovary) **7** Charles (Bovary) **8** Rodolphe

Madame Butterfly ***character:*** **9** Cho-Cho-San, Cio-Cio-San, Pinkerton, Sharpless ***composer:*** **7** Puccini (Giacomo)

madcap **4** rash, wild, zany **5** antic **7** foolish **8** reckless **9** frivolous, hotheaded **10** capricious, incautious

Mad Cavalier **6** Rupert (Prince)

madden **3** ire, vex **4** goad **5** anger, craze **6** enrage **7** derange, incense, inflame, outrage, possess, steam up, unhinge **9** infuriate, unbalance

Madeira Islands ***capital:*** **7** Funchal ***export:*** **4** wine ***part of:*** **8** Portugal

mademoiselle 4 girl, Miss **6** maiden **9** governess **10** yellowtail **11** silver perch
made-to-order 6 custom **7** bespoke **10** customized **11** custom-built
made-up 5 bogus, faked, false, phony **6** phoney **7** painted **8** invented, mythical, specious **9** fictional, imaginary, pretended, trumped-up **10** apocryphal, fabricated, fictitious **11** make-believe **12** cosmeticized
madhouse 6 asylum, bedlam **8** loony bin **9** funny farm **10** booby hatch
madman 3 nut **4** kook, loon **5** loony, raver **6** cuckoo, maniac, psycho **7** lunatic, nutcase **9** bedlamite, psychotic, fruitcake
madness 4 rage **5** folly **6** lunacy **8** insanity **9** psychosis **11** derangement
Madonna initials 3 BVM
Madras 9 Tamil Nadu ***founder:*** **3** Day (Francis)
Madrid museum 5 Prado
madrigal 4 glee, poem, song **8** part-song
madrigalist *English:* 4 Byrd (William) **6** Morley (Thomas), Wilbye (John) **7** Tomkins (Thomas), Weelkes (Thomas) ***Flemish:*** **8** Willaert (Adriaan) ***Italian:*** **5** Lasso (Orlando di) **6** Lassus (Orlandus) **8** Marenzio (Luca) **10** Monteverdi (Claudio)
maelstrom 4 eddy **5** whirl, whorl **6** vortex **7** turmoil **9** whirlpool
maenad 9 bacchante, priestess ***cry:*** **4** evoe
maestro see **conductor**
Mafia 3 mob **4** ring **6** clique **7** rackets **8** gangland **9** Black Hand, syndicate **10** Cosa Nostra, underworld ***code:*** **6** omertà
mafioso 4 capo, goon **6** hit man **7** goombah, made man, mobster **8** gangster **9** racketeer
magazine 4 dump **5** cache, depot, organ, store **6** armory, digest, review, weekly **7** arsenal, gazette, journal, monthly **8** biweekly **9** bimonthly, quarterly, warehouse **10** depository, periodical, repository, storehouse **11** publication ***type:*** **3** box, pan **4** drum, news, tube **5** humor, trade **6** glossy, little, rotary **7** popular **8** literary
mage 6 priest **8** magician, sorcerer
maggot 3 bee **4** grub, whim **5** fancy, larva **6** megrim, vagary **7** caprice, conceit
Magi 6 Caspar, Gaspar **8** Melchior **9** Balthasar, Balthazar ***gift:*** **4** gold **5** myrrh **7** incense **12** frankincense
magic 4 juju **5** obeah, wicca **6** hoodoo, voodoo **7** alchemy, devilry, sorcery **8** satanism, witchery, witching, wizardry **9** conjuring, diablerie, diabolism, occultism, sortilege **10** hocus-pocus, mumbo jumbo, necromancy, witchcraft **11** abracadabra, bewitchment, enchantment, legerdemain, thaumaturgy
magical 5 runic **6** occult **8** wizardly **10** bewitching, entrancing **11** necromantic **12** thaumaturgic ***expression:*** **6** presto, shazam **8** alakazam **11** abracadabra
Magic Flute composer 6 Mozart (Wolfgang Amadeus)
magician 5 brujo, witch **6** shaman, wizard **7** Houdini, warlock **8** conjurer, satanist, sorcerer **9** diabolist, enchanter, trickster, voodooist **11** medicine man, necromancer, thaumaturge ***Arthurian:*** **6** Merlin ***Shakespearean:*** **8** Prospero ***stage:*** **5** Randi (James) **11** Copperfield (David), illusionist ***Tolkien's:*** **7** Gandalf
Magic Mountain, The *author:* 4 Mann (Thomas) ***character:*** **7** Castorp (Hans)
magisterial 6 lordly **7** pompous **8** dogmatic **9** imperious, masterful **10** high-handed **11** doctrinaire, domineering, overbearing **13** authoritative, self-important
Magister Ludi author 5 Hesse (Hermann)
magistrate 5 court, judge **7** bencher, justice **8** official ***ancient Greek:*** **5** ephor **6** archon ***ancient Roman:*** **6** aedile **7** duumvir, praetor, questor **8** quaestor ***Italian:*** **4** doge **7** podesta ***Scottish:*** **6** bailie
Magna Carta *king:* 4 John ***place signed:*** **9** Runnymede
magnanimous 5 noble **7** liberal **8** generous, princely **9** forgiving, unselfish **10** benevolent, bighearted, charitable, chivalrous, high-minded, munificent
magnate 5 baron, mogul, nabob **6** fat cat, prince, tycoon **9** personage, plutocrat
magnesium symbol 2 Mg
magnet 9 lodestone **10** attraction
magnetic 8 alluring **9** appealing, seductive **10** attractive **11** captivating, charismatic, fascinating **12** irresistible ***substance:*** **4** iron **7** ferrite
magnetism 4 draw, lure, pull **5** charm **6** allure, appeal **7** glamour **8** charisma **10** attraction **11** fascination
magnetize 4 draw, lure, wile **5** charm **6** seduce **7** attract, bewitch, enchant **9** captivate, fascinate
magnification unit 8 diameter
magnificence 4 pomp **7** majesty **8** grandeur, splendor **9** pageantry **13** sumptuousness
magnificent 5 grand, noble, regal, royal **6** august, lavish, lordly, superb **7** exalted, opulent, stately, sublime **8** glorious, imposing, majestic, palatial, princely, splendid **9** brilliant, grandiose, luxurious, sumptuous **11** extravagant, resplendent, splendorous **13** splendiferous

magnifier 4 lens **9** telescope ***jeweler's:* 5** loupe
magnify 4 hymn, laud **5** add to, boost, cry up, exalt, extol, swell **6** expand, extend, praise **7** amplify, augment, enhance, enlarge, ennoble, glorify, inflate **8** heighten, increase, maximize, multiply, overplay **9** aggravate, celebrate, embellish, embroider, intensify, overstate **10** aggrandize, exaggerate **13** overemphasize
magniloquent 5 tumid, windy **6** florid, turgid **7** aureate, flowery, fustian, orotund, pompous, swollen **8** sonorous **9** bombastic, high-flown, overblown, rhapsodic **10** euphuistic, rhetorical **11** declamatory
magnitude 4 size **5** order, range **6** extent, import, number, volume **7** bigness, caliber, measure, quality **8** enormity, hugeness, quantity, vastness **9** greatness, immensity, largeness **10** dimensions, importance, proportion **11** consequence
Magnolia State 11 Mississippi
magnum opus 7 classic **10** masterwork **11** chef d'oeuvre, masterpiece, tour de force
Magog's king 3 Gog
magpie 3 jay **4** bird **6** gabber, prater **7** blabber, hoarder **8** jabberer, prattler **9** chatterer, collector **10** chatterbox **12** blabbermouth
maguey 5 agave, fiber **7** cantala ***relative:* 4** aloe
magus 6 wizard **7** diviner, warlock **8** conjurer, magician, sorcerer **9** enchanter **10** astrologer **11** necromancer
Magyar 9 Hungarian ***leader:* 6** Attila
Mahalath *father:* 7 Ishmael **8** Jerimoth ***husband:* 4** Esau **8** Rehoboam
Mahfouz work 12 Cairo Trilogy
mah-jongg piece 4 tile
Mahlon *father:* 9 Elimelech ***mother:* 5** Naomi ***wife:* 4** Ruth
Maia *father:* 5 Atlas ***mother:* 7** Pleione ***sisters:* 8** Pleiades ***son:* 6** Hermes **7** Mercury
maid 4 girl, lass, miss **5** biddy, bonne, wench **6** au pair, damsel, lassie, live-in, virgin **7** servant **8** domestic **9** charwoman, hired girl **10** au pair girl ***Indian:* 4** ayah ***lady's:* 7** abigail ***stage:* 9** soubrette
maiden 3 gal **4** girl, lass, miss **5** first, fresh, missy, prime, wench **6** damsel, lassie, unused, virgin **7** initial, pioneer, primary **8** earliest, original, spinster, virginal **10** spinsterly ***Norse mythological:* 8** valkyrie
maidenhair tree 6 ginkgo
maidenhead 5 hymen **6** purity **9** virginity
maidenhood 9 virginity
Maid of Astolat 6 Elaine
Maid of Orleans, The 7 Pucelle (La) **9** Joan of Arc ***author:* 8** Schiller (Friedrich von)
mail 4 post **5** armor **7** hauberk, letters **8** messages
____ **mail 3** air **5** chain, snail
maim 4 maul **6** mangle **7** cripple, disable **8** mutilate, paralyze **9** disfigure
main 3 sea **5** chief, great, major, ocean, prime, trunk **7** central, high sea, leading, premier, primary **8** cardinal, foremost, high seas **9** paramount, principal **10** preeminent, prevailing **11** fundamental, outstanding, predominant
Maine *capital:* 7 Augusta ***city:* 6** Bangor **8** Lewiston, Portland ***college, university:* 5** Bates, Colby **7** Bowdoin ***lake:* 6** Sebago ***motto:* 6** Dirigo ***mountain:* 8** Cadillac, Katahdin ***nickname:* 8** Pine Tree (State) ***park:* 6** Acadia ***river:* 8** Kennebec **9** Penobscot ***state bird:* 9** chickadee ***state flower:* 22** white pine cone and tassel ***state tree:* 9** white pine
mainly 6 mostly **7** chiefly, largely **8** above all **9** primarily **10** especially **11** principally **13** predominantly
mainstay 4 prop **5** brace **6** pillar **7** bulwark, standby, support **8** backbone, buttress **9** supporter, sustainer
Main Street author 5 Lewis (Sinclair)
maintain 4 aver, avow **5** argue, claim **6** affirm, allege, assert, back up, defend, insist, keep up, manage, stress, uphold **7** care for, carry on, contend, declare, justify, persist, profess, support, sustain, warrant **8** continue, preserve **9** cultivate, emphasize, look after **10** provide for
maintenance 4 care, keep **6** living, upkeep **7** alimony, support **10** livelihood **11** subsistence **12** alimentation ***worker:* 7** janitor **9** custodian
maize 4 corn, milo **10** Indian corn
majestic 5 grand, noble, regal, royal **6** august, kingly, lordly, superb **7** exalted, stately **8** elevated, imperial, imposing, princely, splendid **9** dignified, grandiose **11** ceremonious, magnificent
majesty 4 pomp **5** glory **8** eminence, grandeur, splendor **9** greatness, loftiness **11** stateliness **12** magnificence
major 3 big **4** main, star **5** chief, grave, large **6** higher, larger **7** capital, greater, notable, primary, serious, sizable **8** sizeable, superior **9** principal, prominent **10** large-scale, preeminent **11** outstanding, predominant, significant **12** considerable
Major Barbara author 4 Shaw (George Bernard)

majority 4 bulk, edge **6** margin **13** preponderance

make 3 net **4** earn, form, mold **5** build, cause, erect, forge, frame, hatch, shape, spawn **6** create, effect, output **7** achieve, bring in, compose, fashion, prepare, produce **8** comprise, conclude, generate **9** construct, establish, fabricate, originate **10** constitute **11** manufacture, put together ***amends:*** **5** atone ***believe:*** **7** pretend ***certain:*** **6** assure **8** convince ***fast:*** **3** fix **4** gird **6** secure ***good:*** **7** succeed **9** indemnify ***known:*** **3** air **6** expose, reveal, spread **7** declare, divulge, uncover **8** announce, disclose, proclaim ***use of:*** **6** employ

make-believe 4 mock, sham **7** charade, fantasy, feigned, fiction **8** disguise, pretense **9** fictional, imaginary, insincere, pretended, simulated **10** fictitious

make do 4 cope **5** get by, get on, shift **6** endure, fake it, manage, wing it **7** survive **8** get along **9** improvise **11** extemporize **13** muddle through

make off 3 fly, run **4** flee, skip **5** leave, scoot, scram **6** decamp, depart, escape **7** abscond, run away **9** skedaddle

make out 3 pet, see **4** fare, neck **5** grasp, infer, spoon **6** accept, cuddle, deduce, derive, follow, gather, manage, take in, thrive **7** discern, prosper, succeed **8** conclude, flourish, get along, perceive **9** apprehend, determine, establish, interpret **10** comprehend, understand

make over 4 cede, deed **6** assign, convey, reform **7** remodel, reshape **8** renovate, transfer

maker 7 builder, creator **8** borrower, designer, inventor, producer **10** originator **11** constructor **12** manufacturer

makeshift 6 resort **7** stopgap **8** recourse, resource **9** expedient, temporary **10** expediency, jerry-built, jury-rigged, substitute **11** provisional **13** quick-and-dirty, rough-and-ready

make up 4 form **5** atone **6** devise, invent **7** arrange, compile, compose, concoct, fashion, prepare **8** comprise, contrive **9** apologize, construct, fabricate, formulate, improvise, reconcile **10** compensate

makeup 4 cast, form, kohl, mold **5** blush, fiber, gloss, grain, paint, rouge, shape, stamp, style **6** design, nature, powder, stripe, temper **7** blusher, mascara **8** eyeliner, lip gloss, war paint **9** character, eye shadow, formation **10** complexion, maquillage **11** arrangement, composition, disposition, greasepaint, personality, temperament **12** architecture, constitution, construction, organization

maladroit 5 inept **6** clumsy, gauche, klutzy **7** awkward, unhandy **8** bumbling, bungling, tactless **9** ham-handed, impolitic **10** blundering, ungraceful **11** heavy-handed **12** undiplomatic

malady 3 ill **7** ailment, disease, illness **8** disorder, sickness, syndrome **9** complaint, condition, infirmity **10** affliction

malaise 4 funk **5** dumps, ennui **8** debility, doldrums **10** enervation

Malamud, Bernard ***novel:*** **5** Fixer (The) **7** Natural (The) **9** Assistant (The) ***story:*** **11** Magic Barrel (The)

malapert 4 rude **5** brash, fresh, nervy, sassy, saucy, smart **6** brassy, brazen, cheeky **7** forward **8** impudent, insolent **12** presumptuous

Malaprop creator 8 Sheridan (Richard Brinsley)

malapropos 5 inapt, undue **8** improper, unseemly, untimely **10** unsuitable **11** inopportune **13** inappropriate, inopportunely

malaria 4 ague **6** miasma ***medicine:*** **7** quinine **8** Atabrine, cinchona **10** quinacrine ***mosquito:*** **9** anopheles

malarkey 4 bosh, bunk, guff **5** bilge, hokum, hooey, tripe **6** bunkum, drivel **7** baloney, eyewash, hogwash, rubbish, twaddle **8** nonsense, tommyrot **9** poppycock **10** balderdash **12** blatherskite

Malawi ***capital:*** **8** Lilongwe ***city:*** **8** Blantyre ***explorer:*** **11** Livingstone (David) ***former name:*** **9** Nyasaland ***lake:*** **5** Nyasa **6** Malawi ***language:*** **8** Chichewa ***monetary unit:*** **6** kwacha ***neighbor:*** **6** Zambia **8** Tanzania **10** Mozambique ***river:*** **5** Shire

Malaysia ***capital:*** **11** Kuala Lumpur ***city:*** **4** Ipoh **6** Penang **11** Johor Baharu ***island:*** **6** Borneo ***monetary unit:*** **7** ringgit ***neighbor:*** **8** Thailand **9** Indonesia ***peninsula:*** **5** Malay ***sea:*** **10** South China ***strait:*** **7** Malacca

malcontent 5 rebel **6** griper, grouch, unruly **8** agitator, factious, frondeur, grumbler, mutinous, restless **9** alienated **10** bellyacher, complainer, rebellious **11** disaffected, disgruntled **12** contumacious, dissatisfied

mal de mer 6 nausea **8** vomiting **10** queasiness **11** seasickness

Maldives ***capital:*** **4** Male ***language:*** **6** Divehi ***monetary unit:*** **7** rufiyaa

male 3 guy, tom **4** gent **5** macho, manly **6** manful, virile **7** manlike **9** masculine, staminate

malediction 4 jinx, oath **5** curse **7** malison **8** anathema **10** execration **11** imprecation

malefactor 5 felon, knave, rogue **6** sinner **8**

criminal, evildoer, offender **9** miscreant, reprobate, scoundrel, wrongdoer **10** blackguard, lawbreaker

maleficent **4** evil, vile **5** toxic **6** malign, sinful, wicked **7** baleful, baneful, beastly, harmful, noxious, vicious **8** damnable, sinister, virulent **9** execrable, injurious, nefarious, repugnant **10** pernicious, villainous **11** destructive

malevolence **4** evil **5** spite **6** grudge, malice, spleen **7** ill will **9** hostility, malignity **12** spitefulness **13** maliciousness

malevolent **4** evil **6** malign, wicked **7** baleful, hateful, hurtful, vicious **8** sinister, spiteful, venomous **9** injurious, malicious, malignant, poisonous

malfunction **6** glitch **7** misfire

Mali ***capital:*** **6** Bamako ***city:*** **5** Mopti, Ségou **7** Sikasso **8** Timbuktu **10** Tombouctou ***desert:*** **6** Sahara ***former name:*** **11** French Sudan ***language:*** **6** French ***monetary unit:*** **5** franc ***neighbor:*** **5** Niger **6** Guinea **7** Algeria, Senegal **10** Ivory Coast, Mauritania **11** Burkina Faso, Côte d'Ivoire ***river:*** **5** Niger

malice **4** bile, hate **5** spite, venom **6** animus, enmity, grudge, hatred, poison, spleen **7** ill will **8** meanness **9** animosity, antipathy **10** bitterness, resentment **11** hatefulness, malevolence **12** spitefulness **13** invidiousness

malicious **4** evil, mean **5** nasty, petty **6** wicked **7** baneful, hateful, heinous, jealous **8** spiteful, vengeful, venomous, virulent **9** poisonous, poison-pen, rancorous **10** malevolent

maliciousness see **malevolence**

malign **4** evil, soil **5** abuse, decry, libel, smear, stain, sully, taint **6** befoul, defame, defile, revile, smirch, vilify, wicked **7** asperse, baleful, baneful, blacken, detract, hateful, hostile, noxious, slander, tarnish, traduce, vicious **8** besmirch, derogate, inimical, sinister, spiteful, tear down, virulent **9** denigrate, disparage, injurious, rancorous **10** calumniate, depreciate, maleficent, malevolent, pernicious, scandalize, vituperate **11** deleterious, opprobriate **12** antagonistic, antipathetic

malignant **4** evil **5** fatal **6** deadly, lethal, wicked **7** baleful, hateful, vicious **8** devilish, fiendish, spiteful **9** injurious, rancorous **10** diabolical, malevolent

malison **5** curse **8** anathema **11** commination, imprecation, malediction

mall **4** lane **5** alley, plaza, strip **7** passage **9** concourse, esplanade, promenade **10** passageway **11** median strip

malleable **6** pliant, supple **7** ductile, plastic, pliable **8** flexible **9** adaptable

mallet **6** hammer

malodorous **4** foul, gamy, rank **5** fetid, fuggy, funky, fusty, musty, stale **6** frowsy, putrid, rancid, rotten, smelly, stinky **7** noisome, noxious, reeking, spoiled **8** mephitic, stinking **9** offensive **10** nauseating **11** ill-smelling **12** pestilential

Malraux novel **8** Man's Fate

Malta ***capital:*** **8** Valletta ***city:*** **5** Qormi **10** Birkirkara ***island:*** **4** Gozo **6** Comino ***language:*** **6** French **7** Maltese ***monetary unit:*** **4** lira ***sea:*** **13** Mediterranean

Maltese Falcon, The ***actor:*** **5** Astor (Mary), Lorre (Peter) **6** Bogart (Humphrey) **11** Greenstreet (Sydney) ***author:*** **7** Hammett (Dashiell) ***detective:*** **5** Spade (Sam) ***director:*** **6** Huston (John)

maltreat **5** abuse **6** ill-use, misuse, molest

Mamet, David ***film:*** **5** Heist **7** Verdict (The) **9** Wag the Dog **12** House of Games, Untouchables (The) ***play:*** **7** Oleanna, Romance **14** Boston Marriage **15** American Buffalo **17** Glengarry Glen Ross

mammal **2** ox **3** ass, bat, cat, cow, dog, elk, fox, pig, rat **4** bear, deer, goat, Homo, lion, mink, mole, oxen (plural), pika, seal, tahr, unau, urva, wolf **5** camel, civet, coati, fossa, genet, hippo, hyena, hyrax, koala, lemur, llama, moose, okapi, otter, panda, ratel, sable, sheep, shrew, sloth, takin, tapir, tiger, tigon, zebra **6** alpaca, badger, beaver, colugo, dassie, grison, jackal, marten, ocelot, rabbit, racoon, rodent, sifaka, tenrec, tiglon, vicuña, wombat **7** caracal, giraffe, guanaco, hyraces (plural), leopard, lioness, opossum, linsang, peccary, polecat, primate, raccoon, tigress **8** aardvark, aardwolf, edentate, elephant, hedgehog, kangaroo, kinkajou, mongoose, pangolin, pinniped, ruminant, squirrel, starnose, ungulate **9** armadillo, bandicoot **10** cacomistle **12** hippopotamus ***aquatic:*** **4** orca, seal **6** dugong, sea cow, walrus **7** cowfish, dolphin, grampus, manatee, narwhal, platypi (plural) **8** cetacean, platypus, porpoise, sirenian ***extinct:*** **6** quagga **8** mastodon, stegodon

mammon **4** pelf **5** lucre **6** riches, wealth **8** treasure **9** abundance, affluence **10** prosperity **11** possessions

mammoth **4** huge, vast **5** giant, jumbo **6** mighty **7** immense, massive, monster, titanic **8** colossal, enormous, gigantic **9** leviathan, monstrous **10** gargantuan, mastodonic, monumental **9** humongous **11** elephantine

man **2** Mr. **3** guy **4** buck, chap, cuss, dude,

gent, male **5** being, bloke **6** fellow, mister, mortal, person **7** husband **8** creature, paramour **9** boyfriend, mortality, personage **10** individual **11** Homo sapiens ***castrated:*** **6** eunuch ***combining form:*** **4** andr **5** andro, homin **6** homini ***common:*** **7** Joe Blow, John Doe **11** John Q. Public ***French:*** **5** homme ***Italian:*** **4** uomo ***Latin:*** **3** vir **4** homo ***old:*** **6** codger, geezer ***Spanish:*** **6** hombre ***Yiddish:*** **6** mensch

manage 3 run **4** cope, fare, head, keep, mind, tend **5** get by, get on, shift **6** afford, direct, effect, govern, handle **7** achieve, carry on, conduct, control, execute, finagle, operate, oversee, succeed **8** carry out, contrive, cope with, deal with, dominate, engineer, get along, maintain **9** cultivate, supervise **10** accomplish, administer, bring about **11** orchestrate, superintend

manageable 6 docile, pliant **8** amenable, bearable, biddable, passable **9** agreeable, compliant, endurable, tractable **10** responsive **11** cooperative, supportable, sustainable **13** accommodating

management 4 care **5** brass **6** charge **7** conduct, control, running **8** guidance, handling **9** direction, oversight **10** conducting **11** front office, supervising, supervision

manager 4 boss, exec **6** gerent **7** handler, officer **8** director, official, overseer, producer **9** conductor, executive **10** impresario, supervisor **13** administrator ***museum:*** **7** curator

mañana 7 someday **8** sometime, tomorrow

Man and Superman author 4 Shaw (George Bernard)

Manassas battle 7 Bull Run

Manasseh, Manasses *brother:* **7** Ephraim ***father:*** **6** Hashum, Joseph **8** Hezekiah **10** Pahathmoab ***grandfather:*** **5** Jacob ***grandson:*** **6** Gilead ***mother:*** **7** Asenath ***son:*** **6** Machir

man-at-arms 2 GI **7** fighter, soldier, warrior **10** serviceman

Mandalay author 7 Kipling (Rudyard)

mandarin 5 elder **6** orange **8** official **9** tangerine **10** bureaucrat, panjandrum

mandate 4 fiat, word **5** edict, order, ukase **6** behest, charge, decree **7** bidding, command, dictate **9** authority, directive **10** imperative, injunction **13** authorization

mandatory 6 forced **7** binding **8** required **9** de rigueur, necessary, requisite **10** compulsory, imperative, obligatory **11** involuntary

mandible 3 jaw **8** lower jaw

man-eater 4 lion, ogre **5** shark, tiger **8** cannibal **13** mackerel shark

Manette's daughter 5 Lucie

maneuver 3 ply **4** move, plan, plot, ploy, step **5** feint, trick, wield **6** design, device, gambit, handle, jockey, scheme, tactic, wangle **7** exploit, finagle, finesse **8** artifice, démarche, engineer, exercise, intrigue, movement, navigate **9** machinate, procedure, stratagem **10** manipulate, proceeding, subterfuge **11** contrivance, machination **12** manipulation

maneuvering room 8 latitude

Man for All Seasons, A *author:* **4** Bolt (Robert) ***subject:*** **4** More (Thomas)

manganese *ore:* **10** pyrolusite ***symbol:*** **2** Mn

manger 4 rack **6** cratch, feeder, trough

mangle 3 mar **4** iron, maim, maul **5** press **6** damage, deface, deform, impair, injure **7** butcher, contort, distort **8** lacerate, mutilate **9** disfigure

mangy 5 seedy **6** ragtag, shabby **7** scruffy, squalid **8** decrepit, tattered **9** moth-eaten **10** down-at-heel, threadbare

manhandle 5 abuse **6** batter **7** rough up **8** maltreat, mistreat **10** push around, slap around

Manhattan *building:* **8** Chrysler **11** Empire State ***district:*** **4** Soho **6** Harlem **7** Chelsea, Tribeca ***entertainment district:*** **11** Times Square ***financial district:*** **10** Wall Street ***museum:*** **3** Met **4** MOMA **7** Whitney **10** Guggenheim **12** Metropolitan ***opera house:*** **3** Met **12** Metropolitan ***purchaser:*** **6** Minuit (Peter) ***river:*** **4** East **6** Hudson ***school:*** **3** NYU **6** Hunter **8** Columbia **9** Juilliard

mania 4 rage, zeal **5** craze, fancy **6** frenzy, lunacy **7** madness, passion **8** fixation, idée fixe, insanity **9** cacoëthes, obsession **10** compulsion, enthusiasm **11** infatuation

maniac 3 bug, nut **4** loon **5** fiend, freak **6** madman, psycho, zealot **7** fanatic, lunatic, nutcase **8** crackpot **9** bedlamite **10** enthusiast

manifest 4 show **5** clear, overt, plain, shown, utter, voice **6** appear, embody, evince, expose, patent, reveal **7** display, evident, evinced, exhibit, express, invoice, obvious, visible **8** apparent, distinct, evidence, palpable, proclaim, revealed **9** evidenced, incarnate, objectify, prominent **10** illustrate, noticeable, observable **11** demonstrate, exteriorize, externalize, perceptible, unambiguous

manifestation 4 show, sign **5** proof **7** display, symptom **8** epiphany **10** appearance, revelation

manifesto 4 fiat, rule, writ **5** credo, creed, edict, ukase **6** decree, dictum, gospel, notice, policy, ruling **7** mandate **8** doctrine, document, platform **9** directive, statement, testament, testimony, ultimatum **10** deposi-

tion, injunction, resolution **11** declaration **12** announcement, notification, proclamation **13** pronouncement
manifold 7 diverse, various **8** compound, multiple, multiply, numerous **9** multiform, multiplex **10** multiphase **12** multifarious
manikin 4 runt **5** dummy, dwarf, gnome, model, pygmy **6** midget, peewee **8** Tom Thumb **10** homunculus
Manila *founder:* 7 Legazpi (Miguel López de) ***site:* 5** Luzon **11** Philippines ***victor:* 5** Dewey (George)
manioc 4 yuca **5** yucca **6** casava **7** cassava, tapioca
manipulate 3 ply, rig **4** play **5** steer, swing, tweak, wield **6** adjust, direct, doctor, handle, jockey, juggle, manage **7** beguile, conduct, control, exploit, finagle, finesse, massage **8** engineer, maneuver **9** machinate **10** tamper with
Man, Isle of *capital:* 7 Douglas ***cat:* 4** Manx ***possession of:* 7** Britain ***sea:* 5** Irish
Manitoba *capital:* 8 Winnipeg ***lake:* 8** Winnipeg **12** Winnipegosis ***mountain:* 5** Baldy ***provincial flower:* 13** prairie crocus ***river:* 6** Nelson **9** Churchill
mankind 6 humans, people **8** humanity **11** Homo sapiens
manlike 4 male **6** virile **8** hominoid, humanoid **9** masculine **10** anthropoid
manly 4 male **5** macho **6** virile **9** masculine
man-made 9 synthetic **10** artificial, factitious ***object:* 8** artefact, artifact
Mann character 6 Joseph **9** Leverkühn (Adrian) **10** Aschenbach (Gustav von), Felix Krull **11** Hans Castorp, Tonio Kröger
manner 3 air, way **4** form, kind, mien, mode, sort, vein, wont **5** habit, modus, style, usage **6** aspect, custom, method **7** bearing, conduct, fashion **8** behavior, demeanor, habitude, practice, presence **9** demeanour, etiquette, technique **10** consuetude, deportment **11** affectation, comportment **12** idiosyncrasy
mannered 7 stilted **8** affected, precious **10** artificial **13** self-conscious
mannerism 3 tic **4** pose **5** quirk **10** preciosity **11** affectation, peculiarity, singularity **12** eccentricity, idiosyncrasy **13** artificiality
mannerless 4 rude **6** coarse **7** boorish, ill-bred, uncivil, uncouth **8** impolite **12** discourteous
mannerly 5 civil **6** polite **7** genteel, refined **8** decorous, gracious, well-bred **9** civilized, courteous **10** respectful
Manon composer 8 Massenet (Jules)
Manon Lescaut *author:* 7 Prévost (Abbé) ***composer:* 7** Puccini (Giacomo) **8** Massenet (Jules) ***lover:* 9** des Grieux
manor 5 villa **6** estate, quinta **7** château, demesne **12** landed estate
manservant 5 valet **6** butler
mansion 4 hall **5** villa **6** palace **7** château
manslayer 6 killer **8** homicide, murderer
manta 3 ray **5** cloak, cloth, shawl **7** blanket
manteau 4 coat, robe, wrap **5** cloak **6** capote, domino, mantle, tabard
mantic 5 vatic **6** orphic **7** Delphic, fatidic **8** Delphian, oracular **9** prophetic, sibylline, vaticinal **10** divinatory
mantilla 4 cape, wrap **5** cloak, fichu, scarf, shawl **8** kerchief
mantle 4 cope, glow, pink, robe, rose **5** blush, cloak, color, cover, flush, rouge **6** capote, casing, pinken, redden **7** crimson
man-to-man 4 open **5** frank, plain **6** candid, direct, honest **10** forthright, unreserved **11** openhearted
mantra 2 om **5** chant, motto **6** prayer, slogan **9** watchword **10** invocation **11** incantation
manual 4 text **5** guide **6** primer **8** Baedeker, handbook, hornbook, textbook **9** guidebook, vade mecum **10** compendium **11** abecedarium, enchiridion ***religious:* 9** catechism ***worker:* 6** menial **7** laborer
manufacture 4 form, make **6** create**7** fashion, produce **8** assemble **9** construct, fabricate **11** put together
manumit 4 free **6** unbind **7** release, set free, unchain **8** liberate **9** unshackle **10** emancipate
manure 4 dung **6** ordure **7** excreta **9** excrement **10** fertilizer
manuscript 4 hand **6** scrawl **8** longhand **9** autograph **10** penmanship **11** calligraphy, handwriting ***ancient:* 5** codex **6** scroll **7** codices (plural) ***red part:* 6** rubric ***style:* 6** uncial ***symbol:* 6** obelus
many 5 scads **6** divers, legion, myriad, sundry **7** copious, diverse, umpteen, various **8** abundant, manifold, multiple, numerous **9** abounding, bounteous, bountiful, countless, multitude, plentiful **12** multifarious **13** multitudinous ***combining form:* 4** poly **5** multi, pluri
many-sided 7 diverse **8** all-round, talented **9** all-around, versatile **10** variegated **11** diversified **12** multifaceted, multifarious **13** comprehensive
Mao's successor 3 Hua (Guofeng, Kuo-feng) **4** Deng (Xiaoping), Teng (Hsiao-p'ing)
map 4 plan, plat **5** chart, draft, globe, graph **6** design, lay out, set out, sketch, survey **7** arrange, diagram, drawing, outline, tracing **9**

delineate ***collection:*** **5** atlas ***line:*** **6** isobar **7** contour, isogram, isohyet **8** isogloss, isogonic, isopleth, isotherm ***maker:*** **12** cartographer ***making:*** **11** cartography

maple ***genus:*** **4** Acer ***product:*** **5** syrup ***type:*** **3** red **5** sugar **8** box elder

map projection **5** conic **8** Mercator **9** polyconic **10** sinusoidal **12** orthographic **13** stereographic

maquillage **6** makeup

mar **4** ding, harm, hurt, scar, warp **5** spoil, stain **6** bruise, damage, deface, deform, impair, injure **7** blemish, scratch, tarnish, vitiate **9** disfigure

marabou **5** stork

Marat/Sade author **5** Weiss (Peter)

Marat, Jean-Paul ***colleague:*** **6** Danton (Georges) **11** Robespierre (Maximilien) ***slayer:*** **6** Corday (Charlotte)

maraud **4** loot, raid, sack **5** foray, harry **6** harass, ravage, ravish **7** despoil, pillage, plunder, ransack

marauder **6** bandit, pirate **7** brigand, spoiler, wrecker **9** buccaneer, desperado **10** freebooter

marble **3** mib, mig, taw **4** immy, migg **5** agate, aggie, alley, rance **6** blotch, miggle, mottle, streak **7** cipolin, glassie, steelie **9** limestone

marbled **6** veined **7** dappled, flecked, mottled **8** speckled, streaked

Marble Faun, The ***author:*** **9** Hawthorne (Nathaniel) ***character:*** **5** Hilda **6** Kenyon, Miriam **9** Donatello ***setting:*** **4** Rome

marcel **4** wave

march **3** hem, rim **4** abut, file, line **5** skirt **6** adjoin, border, parade **7** advance, headway, proceed **8** anabasis, boundary, frontier, outlands, progress, traverse **9** periphery **10** borderland

March ***date:*** **4** ides ***mother:*** **6** Marmee ***sisters:*** **3** Amy, Meg **4** Beth

March King **5** Sousa (John Philip)

Mardi Gras **8** carnival **10** Fat Tuesday ***city:*** **10** New Orleans

Marduk ***city:*** **7** Babylon ***consort:*** **8** Zarbanit, Zarpanit ***victim:*** **5** Kingu **6** Tiamat

mare **3** sea **5** horse **6** equine

mare's nest **3** con, din **4** hoax, scam **5** babel, cheat, fraud, put-on, spoof **6** bedlam, clamor, hubbub, humbug, racket, ruckus, tumult, uproar **7** swindle, turmoil **8** brouhaha, flimflam, illusion **9** confusion, imposture **10** hullabaloo **11** pandemonium

margarine **4** oleo

margin **3** hem, rim **4** brim, edge, join, line, play, room, side **5** bound, brink, frame, scope, shore, skirt, verge **6** border, fringe, leeway **7** minimum, outline, selvage **8** boundary, latitude, selvedge, surround, trimming **9** elbowroom, perimeter, periphery **13** circumference ***tiny:*** **4** hair

marginal **5** minor **7** limited, minimal **9** bordering **10** borderline, negligible, peripheral, subsidiary **13** insignificant

Marguerite's lover **5** Faust

Maria ____ **5** Elena **7** Stuarda

Marianas ***discoverer:*** **8** Magellan (Ferdinand) ***island:*** **4** Guam, Rota **5** Pagan **6** Guguan, Saipan, Tinian **7** Agrihan, Aguijan

marijuana **3** kef, kif, pot **4** hash, hemp, weed **5** bhang, grass **6** reefer **7** hashish **8** cannabis

marina **4** dock, pier, quay **5** basin, berth, wharf **8** boatyard

marinate **4** soak **5** steep **6** drench, pickle **7** immerse **8** macerate

marine **5** naval **7** abyssal, aquatic, deep-sea, oceanic, pelagic **8** nautical, seagoing, seascape **9** seafaring, thalassic **10** oceangoing **12** hydrographic **13** oceanographic ***crustacean:*** **6** shrimp **7** lobster **8** barnacle ***deposit:*** **5** coral ***plant:*** **4** kelp, nori **5** dulse **6** wakame **7** seaweed

mariner **3** gob, tar **4** jack, salt, swab **5** limey **6** hearty, rating, sailor, sea dog, seaman **7** jack-tar, old salt, swabbie **8** seafarer **9** sailorman, shellback, tarpaulin **10** bluejacket

marital **6** wedded **7** married, nuptial, spousal **8** conjugal, hymeneal **9** connubial

maritime **7** oceanic, pelagic **8** nautical **9** thalassic **12** navigational

mark **3** aim, jot, sap, tee **4** butt, dupe, fool, goal, gull, heed, look, nick, note, pick, show, sign, view **5** blaze, bound, brand, chart, chump, elect, grade, label, notch, stamp, token, trait **6** behold, choose, denote, evince, lay off, notice, object, opt for, rating, record, select, sucker, target, victim, virtue **7** betoken, delimit, discern, exhibit, fall guy, feature, gudgeon, indicia, initial, measure, observe, qualify, scratch, signify, symptom **8** function, indicate, perceive, register **9** attribute, character, designate, objective, single out **10** indication **11** differentia, distinction, distinguish **12** characterize ***distinctive:*** **7** indicia **8** indicium ***identifying:*** **4** logo, seal **6** emblem, signet, symbol **8** colophon, logotype ***of insertion:*** **5** caret ***of omission:*** **4** dele **8** ellipsis **10** apostrophe ***of retention:*** **4** stet ***over a vowel:*** **5** breve, haček **6** accent, macron, umlaut **8** dieresis **9** diaeresis **10** circumflex ***over n:*** **5** tilde ***punctuation:*** **4** dash **5** brace, colon, comma, slant, slash **6** hyphen, period **7**

bracket, solidus **9** backslash, guillemet, semicolon **10** apostrophe ***under a letter:*** **7** cedilla

Mark 6 Gospel ***cousin:*** **8** Barnabas ***mother:*** **4** Mary

mark down 3 cut **4** pare **5** shave, slash **6** reduce **7** devalue **8** discount **9** devaluate **10** depreciate, undervalue

marked 5 noted **6** patent, signal **7** evident, notable, obvious, pointed, salient **8** distinct, manifest, striking **9** arresting, prominent **10** noticeable, remarkable **11** conspicuous, outstanding **12** considerable **13** distinguished ***man:*** **4** Cain

marker 3 IOU, run **5** score **7** felt-tip

market 3 suq **4** fair, mall, sell, shop, souk, vend **5** store **6** bazaar, outlet, retail, rialto **8** emporium, exchange, showroom **9** advertise, traffic in, wholesale **11** merchandise ***kind:*** **4** flea **5** money, stock

marketable 5 sound **7** salable **8** vendible **10** commercial

marketplace 3 suq **4** mall, souk **5** agora **6** bazaar, rialto **8** emporium

marksman 4 shot **6** sniper **7** deadeye, shooter **12** sharpshooter

marl 4 clay, silt

marlin 8 billfish **9** spearfish

Marlowe play 8 Edward II **9** Dr. Faustus **10** Jew of Malta (The) **11** Tamburlaine **13** Doctor Faustus

marmot 6 rodent **9** woodchuck **10** prairie dog

maroon 3 red **6** claret, desert, strand **7** abandon, crimson, forsake, isolate, outcast **8** burgundy, castaway

Marquand character 4 Gray (Charles), Moto (Mr.) **5** Apley (George), Wayde (Willis) **6** Pulham (H.M.) **7** Goodwin (Melville)

Marquis, Don *cat:* 9 Mehitabel ***cockroach:*** **5** Archy

marriage 5 match, union **6** bridal **7** nuptial, spousal, wedding, wedlock **8** coupling, espousal, monogamy, nuptials, polygamy **9** matrimony **11** conjugality **12** connubiality ***combining form:*** **4** gamy **6** gamous ***notice:*** **5** banns ***outside a group:*** **7** exogamy ***within a group:*** **8** endogamy

marriageable 6 nubile **8** eligible

marriage broker 5 yenta **9** go-between **10** matchmaker

Marriage of Figaro composer 6 Mozart (Wolfgang Amadeus)

marrow 4 core, meat, pith, soul **5** heart, stuff **6** kernel **7** essence **12** quintessence

marry 3 tie, wed **4** join, link, mate, wive, yoke **5** hitch, merge, unite **6** couple, splice, spouse **7** combine, conjoin, espouse **9** conjugate

Mars 4 Ares **6** planet ***combining term:*** **4** areo ***feature:*** **4** face **5** basin **6** canyon, crater **7** volcano **8** polar cap ***lover:*** **5** Venus ***mission:*** **6** Viking **7** Mariner **10** Pathfinder ***moon:*** **6** Deimos, Phobos ***relating to:*** **7** martian (see also **Ares**)

Marseillaise composer 13 Rouget de Lisle (Claude-Joseph)

marsh 3 bog, fen **4** mire, ooze, quag **5** bayou, glade, swale, swamp **6** morass, muskeg, slough **7** wetland **8** quagmire **9** swampland

marshal 5 align, array, guide, order, rally, usher **6** deploy, direct, escort, muster **7** arrange, officer, round up **8** assemble, mobilize, organize, shepherd **9** methodize, systemize (see also **field marshal**)

Marshall Islands *atoll:* 6 Bikini **8** Enewetak **9** Kwajalein ***capital:*** **6** Majuro ***ethnic group:*** **11** Micronesian ***island chain:*** **5** Ralik, Ratak **6** Sunset **7** Sunrise **11** Marshallese

marshy 4 miry **5** boggy, mucky **6** quaggy, swampy **7** sloughy

marsupial 3 roo **4** euro **5** koala **6** possum, wombat **7** opossum, wallaby **8** kangaroo, wallaroo **9** bandicoot

marten 6 fisher, weasel

Martha *brother:* 7 Lazarus ***sister:*** **4** Mary

martial 7 warlike **8** militant, military, spirited **9** bellicose, combative, soldierly **11** belligerent **12** militaristic

martial art 4 judo **5** kendo **6** aikido, karate, kung fu, neijia, tai chi **7** shaolin **8** capoeira, jiujitsu **9** tae kwon do **11** tai chi chuan ***expert:*** **5** ninja ***school:*** **4** dojo ***teacher:*** **6** sensei

Martial's forte 7 epigram

Martin Chuzzlewit author 7 Dickens (Charles)

Martinique *capital:* 12 Fort-de-France ***department of:*** **6** France ***discoverer:*** **8** Columbus (Christopher) ***island group:*** **8** Windward ***location:*** **10** West Indies ***neighbor:*** **8** Dominica **10** Saint Lucia ***volcano:*** **5** Pelée

martyr 4 Paul, rack **5** Agnes, Alban, James, Peter, saint, wring **6** George, harrow, Justin **7** afflict, agonize, Clement, crucify, Cyprian, Stephen, torment, torture **8** Ignatius, Lawrence, Polycarp, sufferer **9** Joan of Arc, Sebastian **10** excruciate, Thomas More ***Protestant:*** **6** Ridley (Nicholas) **7** Cranmer (Thomas), Latimer (Hugh)

marvel 4 gape **6** wonder **7** miracle, portent, prodigy, stunner **9** curiosity, sensation **10** phenomenon **12** astonishment

marvelous 5 super, swell **6** divine **7** amazing, awesome, ripping **8** glorious, striking, stunning, superior, terrific, wondrous **9** excellent, wonderful **10** astounding, incredible, miraculous, phenomenal, prodigious, remarkable, staggering, stupendous, surprising **11** astonishing, exceptional, sensational, spectacular **12** awe-inspiring, supernatural **13** extraordinary

Marx brother 5 Chico, Gummo, Harpo, Zeppo **7** Groucho

Marxist 9 socialist **9** communist

Marx, Karl *book:* 7 Kapital (Das) ***collaborator:* 6** Engels (Friedrich)

Mary *husband:* 6 Clopas, Joseph **8** Alphaeus ***kinswoman:* 9** Elisabeth ***son:* 4** Mark **5** James, Jesus

Maryland *bay:* 10 Chesapeake ***capital:* 9** Annapolis ***city:* 9** Baltimore, Frederick ***college, university:* 6** Towson **7** Goucher **9** Annapolis **12** Johns Hopkins **12** Naval Academy (U.S.) ***fort:* 7** McHenry ***nickname:* 7** Old Line (State) ***river:* 7** Potomac **8** Patuxent ***state bird:* 15** Baltimore oriole ***state flower:* 14** black-eyed Susan ***state tree:* 8** white oak

mascot 4 juju **5** charm **6** amulet, fetish, symbol **8** gris-gris, talisman

masculine 4 male **5** macho, manly **6** manful, virile **7** manlike

masculinity 8 machismo, virility **9** manliness

Masefield work 7 Cargoes **8** Sea Fever

mash 4 pulp **5** crush, smash **6** squash, squish **7** squoosh **8** macerate **9** pulverize

masher 4 wolf **5** flirt **6** chaser **7** Don Juan, seducer **8** Casanova, lothario **9** ladies' man, womanizer **10** lady-killer **11** philanderer, skirt chaser

mash note 10 billet-doux, love letter

mask 4 hide, pose, sham, veil **5** cover, front, guard, guise, visor **6** facade, screen, vizard **7** dress up, frisket, pretext **8** coloring, disguise, pretense **9** dissemble, semblance **10** appearance, camouflage, false front, simulation **11** dissimulate

masonry 9 brickwork, stonework ***in a frame:* 7** nogging

masquerade 4 pose **6** facade **7** costume, posture **8** carnival, disguise **10** camouflage, masked ball **11** costume ball

mass 3 lot, sum, wad **4** bank, body, bulk, clot, core, glob, heap, hill, lump, pack, peck, pile **5** clump, mound **6** corpus, volume **7** expanse, globule, wadding **8** assemble, quantity **9** aggregate, stockpile, substance **11** aggregation **12** conglomerate ***compacted:* 4** cake ***for the dead:* 7** requiem ***of individuals:* 3** mob **4** host **5** crowd, crush, flock, horde, swarm **6** throng **12** congregation **13** agglomeration ***part:* 5** Kyrie **6** proper **8** Agnus Dei, ordinary

Massachusetts *cape:* 3 Ann, Cod ***capital:* 6** Boston ***city:* 6** Lowell, Quincy **9** Cambridge, Worcester **10** New Bedford **11** Springfield ***college, university:* 3** MIT **5** Clark, Smith, Tufts **7** Amherst, Berklee, Harvard, Wheaton **8** Brandeis, Williams **9** Hampshire, Holy Cross, Radcliffe, Wellesley **12** Mount Holyoke, Northeastern ***island:* 9** Nantucket **15** Martha's Vineyard ***mountain, range:* 8** Greylock **9** Berkshire ***nickname:* 3** Bay (State) **9** Old Colony (State) ***river:* 11** Connecticut ***state bird:* 9** chickadee ***state flower:* 9** mayflower ***state tree:* 3** elm (American) ***symbol:* 3** cod

massacre 4 kill **6** mangle, murder, pogrom **7** butcher, carnage **8** butchery, decimate, genocide, mangling, mutilate **9** bloodbath, bloodshed, slaughter **10** annihilate, blood purge, decimation, mutilation **11** exterminate **12** annihilation

massage 3 rub **5** knead **7** flatter, rubdown, shiatsu **8** blandish **10** manipulate

Massenet opera 5 Le Cid, Manon, Sapho, Thaïs **7** Werther

massive 4 huge, mega, vast **5** bulky, giant, jumbo, mondo, solid **6** mighty **7** hulking, immense, mammoth, weighty **8** colossal, cumbrous, enormous, gigantic, towering **9** humongous, monstrous **10** gargantuan, monumental, prodigious, stupendous, tremendous **11** elephantine, mountainous

master 4 best, boss, guru, head, lick, rule, tame **5** adept, bwana, chief, crack, learn, ruler, sahib, tutor **6** artist, expert, genius, honcho, leader, subdue, victor **7** captain, conquer, headman, maestro, padrone, prevail, skilled, triumph **8** dominant, dominate, employer, governor, overcome, overlord, overseer, regulate, skeleton, skillful, superior, surmount, virtuoso **9** authority, chieftain, conqueror, dominator, paramount, principal, sovereign **10** proficient **11** predominant ***of ceremonies:* 4** host **5** emcee **7** compere

masterful 4 deft **5** adept **6** adroit, expert **7** skilled **8** skillful **10** high-handed, proficient **11** magisterial **13** authoritative

masterly 5 adept, crack **6** adroit, expert **7** skilled **8** skillful **9** dexterous **10** proficient **11** crackerjack **12** accomplished

Master of Ballantrae, The 6 Durrie ***author:* 9** Stevenson (Robert Louis)

masterpiece 7 classic **10** magnum opus **11** chef d'oeuvre, tour de force
mastery 5 knack, skill **7** ability, command, control, know-how, prowess **8** dominion **9** authority, expertise **10** ascendancy, domination, expertness, virtuosity **11** proficiency, superiority
masticate 4 chaw, chew, pulp **5** champ, chomp, crush, munch **6** crunch **7** scrunch **8** macerate, ruminate **9** break down
mat 3 rug **4** felt **6** border, carpet, tatami
matador 6 torero **8** toreador **11** bullfighter ***adjunct:*** **6** muleta ***move:*** **4** pase **5** faena **8** veronica
Mata Hari 3 spy **10** seductress **11** femme fatale
match 3 pit **4** bout, game, meet, peer, suit, twin **5** array, equal, rival, touch, union **6** double, equate, oppose **7** compare, contest, counter, paragon, play off **8** alliance, analogue, marriage, opponent, parallel **9** adversary, correlate, duplicate, encounter, measure up, smackdown **10** antagonist, complement, coordinate, engagement, equivalent, reciprocal, supplement, tournament **11** counterpart **12** correspond to ***a bet:*** **3** see ***friction:*** **7** lucifer
matchless 6 unique **7** supreme **8** peerless, singular **9** nonpareil, unequaled, unrivaled **10** inimitable **12** incomparable, unparalleled
matchmaker see **marriage broker**
mate 3 bud, pal, tie, wed **4** chum, pair, twin **5** amigo, breed, buddy, crony, equal, hitch, marry **6** cohort, couple, double, fellow, friend, helper, splice, spouse **7** compeer, comrade, consort, partner **8** confrere, sidekick **9** associate, companion, copartner, duplicate, procreate **10** complement, equivalent, reciprocal **11** concomitant
maté 3 tea **5** holly **8** beverage
mater 3 mom, mum **6** mother **9** matriarch
____ **mater 4** alma
material 4 real, true **5** cloth, stuff **6** actual, fabric, matter, object **7** element, germane, worldly **8** palpable, physical, relevant, sensible, tangible **9** component, corporeal, essential, important, objective, pertinent, substance **10** applicable, ingredient, meaningful, phenomenal **11** appreciable, constituent, fundamental, perceptible, significant, substantial ***building:*** **5** adobe, brick **6** stucco **7** lagging, plaster, plywood, shingle **8** concrete
materialistic 7 secular, worldly **11** acquisitive
materialize 4 loom, rise **5** arise, issue **6** appear, embody, emerge, evolve, show up **7** develop, surface **8** manifest **9** come about, incarnate, take shape **12** substantiate
matériel 4 gear **5** stock **8** supplies **9** apparatus, equipment, machinery **10** provisions **13** accouterments, accoutrements, paraphernalia
maternal 8 motherly
matey 5 pally, tight **6** clubby **7** affable **8** amicable, familiar, friendly, intimate, sociable **9** congenial
mathematician *American:* **5** Wiles (Andrew) **6** Peirce (Charles S.), Veblen (Oswald), Wiener (Norbert) ***Austrian:*** **5** Gödel (Kurt) ***British:*** **6** Stokes (George) ***Dutch:*** **7** Huygens (Christiaan) ***English:*** **6** Newton (Isaac), Taylor (Brook), Turing (Alan), Wallis (John) **7** Pearson (Karl), Russell (Bertrand) **8** Hamilton (James Rowan) **9** Sylvester (James Joseph), Whitehead (Alfred North, Henry) ***French:*** **4** Weil (André) **5** Borel (Emile), Comte (Auguste), Viète (François) **6** Galois (Evariste), Pascal (Blaise), Picard (Charles-Emile) **7** Fourier (Jean-Baptiste), Laplace (Marquis de), Vernier (Pierre) **8** Painlevé (Paul), Poincaré (Jules-Henri) **9** Descartes (René) ***German:*** **5** Gauss (Carl Friedrich), Wolff (Freiherr von) **6** Staudt (Karl von) **7** Leibniz (Gottfried Wilhelm), Riemann (Georg) **11** Weierstrass (Karl) ***Greek:*** **6** Euclid **10** Archimedes, Pythagoras ***Hungarian:*** **5** Erdos (Paul) ***Italian:*** **8** Volterra (Vito) **10** Torricelli (Evangelista) ***Norwegian:*** **7** Stormer (Fredrik) ***Russian:*** **11** Lobachevsky (Nikolay) ***Scottish:*** **4** Tait (Peter) **6** Napier (John) **8** Stirling (James) ***Swiss:*** **5** Euler (Leonhard), Sturm (Jacques) **7** Steiner (Jakob)
mathematics *branch:* **4** trig **7** algebra **8** calculus, geometry, topology **10** arithmetic, statistics **12** trigonometry ***proven statement in:*** **7** theorem
____ **Mather 6** Cotton **7** Richard **8** Increase
mating arena 3 lek
matriarch 4 dame **6** mother **7** dowager **10** grande dame
matriculate 4 join **5** enter **6** enroll, sign on **8** register
matrimonial 6 bridal, wedded **7** marital, married, nuptial, spousal **8** conjugal, hymeneal **9** connubial **11** epithalamic
matrimony 7 wedlock **8** marriage **11** conjugality **12** connubiality
matrix 3 die, net, web **4** grid, mesh **5** array **6** cradle, gangue **7** complex, network **10** groundmass, truth table
matron 4 dame **7** dowager **8** chaperon **9** chaperone **10** grande dame
Mattathias *father:* **5** Simon **6** Ananos **7** Absalom, Boethus **10** Theophilus ***son:*** **8** Josephus

matter **4** body, core, gist, meat, pith, text **5** being, cause, order, point, sense, stuff, theme, thing, topic, value, weigh **6** affair, amount, burden, entity, import, object **7** concern, signify, subject **8** argument, material **9** grievance, magnitude, substance **11** constituent **12** circumstance

matter-of-fact **3** dry **5** plain, prose, sober, stoic **6** stolid **7** prosaic **9** impassive, objective, practical, pragmatic, realistic **10** hardboiled, hardheaded, impersonal, phlegmatic **11** down-to-earth **13** unimpassioned, unsentimental

mattress **3** pad **4** sack ***case:*** **4** tick ***fabric:*** **7** ticking ***straw:*** **6** pallet

mature **3** age, due **4** grow, ripe **5** adult, grown, owing, ready, ripen **6** flower, grow up, mellow, season, unpaid **7** advance, blossom, decline, develop, grown-up, overdue, payable, ripened **8** progress **9** developed, full-blown, full-grown **11** full-fledged

maudlin **5** gushy, mushy, silly, sappy, soppy **6** slushy, sticky **7** cloying, gushing, mawkish **8** bathetic **11** sentimental, tear-jerking

Maugham character **4** Kear, Liza **5** Carey, Rosie, Sadie **7** Mildred **8** Ashenden, Craddock **10** Strickland

maul **4** bang, bash, beat, club, drub, flog, whip **5** abuse, flail, pound **6** batter, bruise, buffet, cudgel, hammer, injure, mangle, molest, pummel, sledge, thrash **7** clobber, rough up **8** bludgeon, lambaste **9** manhandle

Mauna ____ **3** Kea, Loa

maunder **3** bat, gad **4** rove **5** drift, mooch, range **6** mumble, mutter, ramble, wander **7** blather, digress, traipse **8** divagate

Mauritania ***capital:*** **10** Nouakchott ***desert:*** **6** Sahara ***language:*** **5** Wolof **6** Arabic, Fulani **7** Soninke ***monetary unit:*** **7** ouguiya ***neighbor:*** **4** Mali **6** Guinea **7** Senegal **7** Algeria **13** Western Sahara ***river:*** **7** Senegal

Mauritius ***capital:*** **9** Port Louis ***island group:*** **9** Mascarene ***language:*** **6** Creole ***monetary unit:*** **5** rupee

mauve **5** lilac **6** purple, violet

maven **3** ace **4** buff, whiz **5** adept, freak, shark **6** addict, expert, master, savant **7** devotee, fanatic, hotshot **8** virtuoso **9** authority **10** enthusiast **11** connoisseur

maverick **5** rogue, stray **7** heretic **8** unmarked **9** dissident, unbranded **10** iconoclast **11** independent, loose cannon **13** nonconformist

maw **4** crop **5** chasm, mouth **6** cavity, gullet **7** stomach

mawkish **5** gushy, mushy, sappy, soppy **6** sloppy, slushy, sticky, syrupy **7** cloying, gushing, insipid, maudlin **8** bathetic, romantic **9** schmaltzy, sickening **10** lovey-dovey, nauseating **11** sentimental, tear-jerking

maxilla **3** jaw **4** bone

maxim **3** law, saw **4** rule **5** adage, axiom, gnome, moral, motto, tenet, truth **6** byword, dictum, saying, truism **7** precept, proverb, theorem **8** aphorism, apothegm **9** platitude, prescript, principle **11** commonplace

maximal **3** nth, top **6** utmost **7** highest, largest, supreme, topmost **8** complete, greatest, ultimate **9** paramount

maximum **3** nth, top **6** utmost **7** highest, largest, supreme, topmost **8** extremum, greatest, ultimate **9** paramount

may **5** might, shrub **6** spirea **8** hawthorn

maybe **7** perhaps **8** possibly **9** perchance **11** conceivably, uncertainty

Mayberry resident **4** Andy (Taylor), Opie (Taylor) **5** Gomer (Pyle) **6** Barney (Fife) **7** Aunt Bee

Mayflower ***document:*** **7** Compact ***passengers:*** **8** Pilgrims

mayhem **4** maim, riot **5** chaos, havoc **7** cripple, dislimb **8** mutilate **9** dismember **10** mutilation

mayor **11** burgomaster ***Boston:*** **6** Curley (James Michael) ***Chicago:*** **5** Daley (Richard) ***New York:*** **4** Koch (Edward) **6** Walker (Jimmy) **7** Lindsay (John) **8** Giuliani (Rudolph) **9** Bloomberg (Michael), La Guardia (Fiorello) ***Spanish:*** **7** alcalde

Mayor of Casterbridge, The ***author:*** **5** Hardy (Thomas) ***character:*** **8** Henchard (Michael)

maze **3** web **4** knot, mesh **5** skein, snarl **6** jungle, morass, tangle **7** confuse, network, perplex **8** bewilder, mishmash **9** labyrinth

Mazel ____! **3** tov

McCarthy novel **4** Road (The) **8** Crossing (The) **13** Blood Meridian **16** Cities of the Plain **18** All the Pretty Horses, No Country for Old Men

McCourt memoir **3** 'Tis **10** Teacher Man **12** Angela's Ashes

McCullers, Carson ***novel:*** **18** Ballad of the Sad Cafe (The) **18** Member of the Wedding (The) **20** Heart Is a Lonely Hunter (The) **23** Reflections in a Golden Eye

McCullough novel **10** Thorn Birds (The)

McEwan novel **8** Saturday **9** Amsterdam, Atonement, Black Dogs **12** Enduring Love

McMurtry novel **12** Buffalo Girls, Lonesome Dove **14** Horseman Pass By **15** Last Picture Show (The) **17** Terms of Endearment

McTeague author **6** Norris (Frank)

MD **3** doc **6** doctor, medico **8** sawbones **9** physician

mea culpa 5 error, fault **7** apology **9** admission **10** concession, confession
meadow 3 lea, ley **4** vega **5** field, green **7** pasture **9** grassland ***historic:* 9** Runnymede ***low-lying:* 5** haugh
meadow mushroom 6 agaric
meager 4 bare, bony, lean, mere, thin **5** gaunt, lanky, scant, short, spare **6** paltry, scanty, shabby, skimpy, skinny, slight, sparse **7** angular, minimum, scraggy, scrawny, scrimpy **8** exiguous, rawboned **9** deficient, miserable **10** inadequate **12** insufficient
meal 4 chow, fare, feed, grub **5** board, feast, lunch, snack **6** brunch, dinner, farina, picnic, repast, spread, supper **7** high tea, nooning **8** luncheon, victuals **9** breakfast, collation, elevenses, refection ***army:* 3** MRE **4** mess
mealy 6 spotty, uneven **11** farinaceous
mean 3 low, mid, par **4** base, fair, hint, norm, poor, want, wish **5** cheap, cruel, imply, lousy, lowly, mingy, petty, rough, small, snide, spell, tight, weigh **6** attest, center, common, denote, design, humble, intend, matter, medial, medium, middle, paltry, scummy, scurvy, shabby, shoddy, sleazy, stingy, unwell **7** average, betoken, connote, express, lowborn, miserly, pitiful, portend, propose, purport, signify, suggest, vicious **8** déclassé, indicate, inferior, mediocre, middling, midpoint, moderate, ordinary, pitiable, plebeian, stand for **9** designate, penurious, represent, symbolize **10** despicable, second-rate **11** closefisted, tightfisted **12** contemptible, intermediary, intermediate
meander 4 roam, rove, turn, wind **5** amble, drift, range, snake, stray, twist **6** ramble, wander **7** traipse, winding **8** vagabond **9** gallivant, labyrinth
meandering 5 snaky **7** sinuous **8** flexuous, tortuous **10** convoluted, serpentine **11** anfractuous
meaning 3 aim **4** gist, pith **5** drift, force, point, sense **6** effect, import, intent **7** essence, message, purport **9** intention, substance **10** definition, denotation, intimation **11** connotation, implication **12** significance **13** signification
meaningful 5 valid **7** pointed, serious, weighty **8** eloquent, material **9** important, momentous **10** expressive **11** sententious, significant, substantial **13** consequential
meaningless 5 empty, inane **6** absurd, futile, hollow, jejune **7** trivial **8** nugatory **11** nonsensical **13** insignificant
meanings *diverse:* 8 polysemy ***study of:* 9** semantics
means 5 funds, money **6** assets, avenue, income **7** backing, capital **8** finances, holdings, property, reserves **9** equipment, resources, substance **11** wherewithal
meantime 7 interim **8** interval
measly 4 poor, puny **5** petty, scant **6** meager, meagre, paltry, scanty, skimpy **7** pitiful, trivial **8** niggling, pathetic, picayune, piddling, trifling **9** miserable **10** picayunish **13** insignificant
measure 3 bar, ken **4** bill, size, step, test **5** bound, gauge, index, quota, scale, share, weigh **6** amount, bounds, effort, extent, figure, ration, reckon, resort, size up, survey **7** caliper, compute, delimit, mark out, portion **8** calliper, estimate, regulate, resource, standard **9** allotment, benchmark, calculate, calibrate, criterion, demarcate, determine, expedient, magnitude, yardstick **10** dimensions, indication, proportion, touchstone ***area:* 3** are, cho, mou, tan **4** acre **7** hectare ***capacity:* 3** cab, cor, pin, zak **4** fass, gill, peck, pint **5** liter, minim, quart, stere **6** bushel, gallon **8** fluidram **9** fluid dram **10** fluid ounce, milliliter ***cloth:* 3** ell ***combining form:* 6** metric **8** metrical ***depth:* 5** plumb, sound ***dry:* 4** peck **6** bushel ***electrical:* 3** amp, mho, ohm **4** volt, watt **6** ampere **7** coulomb ***energy:* 3** erg ***force:* 4** dyne ***horse height:* 4** hand ***interstellar space:* 6** parsec ***length:* 3** mil, pik, rod **4** alen, aune, foot, hiro, inch, link, mile, tsun, vara, yard **5** chain, cubit, meter **6** league **7** braccio, furlong **9** kilometer **10** centimeter, hectometer ***liquid:* 3** hin, tun **4** gill, pint **5** minim, quart **6** gallon ***mixed drinks:* 6** jigger ***of comparison:* 8** standard ***paper:* 4** ream ***printer's:* 2** em, en **4** pica **5** point ***radioactive decay:* 8** halflife ***rotation:* 5** angle ***strength of solution:* 7** titrate ***surface:* 3** are ***thermodynamic:* 7** entropy **8** enthalpy ***yarn:* 3** lea (see also **weight**)
measured 7 regular, stately **8** metrical **9** regulated, temperate, unhurried **10** calculated, controlled, deliberate, restrained **13** proportionate
Measure for Measure *character:* 6 Angelo, Juliet **7** Claudio, Mariana **8** Isabella **9** Vincentio ***setting:* 6** Vienna
measurement 4 area **6** degree **8** capacity, quantity **9** dimension, magnitude **11** calibration, mensuration
measure up to 3 tie **4** meet **5** equal, match, rival, touch **7** emulate **10** qualify for
measuring device 4 gage, tape **5** buret, gauge, ruler, scale, timer **7** burette, caliper, sextant, venturi **8** calipers **8** dipstick **9** al-

timeter, barometer, dosimeter, pedometer, yardstick **11** tensiometer, velocimeter

meat 4 core, food, gist, pith, pork, veal **5** flesh, jerky, steak **6** thrust, upshot **7** edibles **8** victuals **9** foodstuff, provender, substance **10** provisions **11** comestibles ***broth:*** **8** bouillon ***cake:*** **6** burger **9** hamburger ***cured:*** **7** biltong ***cut:*** **3** rib **4** loin, rump **5** chuck, flank, plate, round, shank **7** brisket, sirloin **8** rib roast **9** club steak, rump roast, short loin, short ribs **10** blade roast, flank steak, round steak, T-bone steak **12** sirloin steak ***dealer:*** **7** butcher ***deer:*** **7** venison ***dried:*** **5** jerky ***fastening pin:*** **6** skewer ***holding rod:*** **4** spit **10** rotisserie ***juices:*** **5** gravy ***packer:*** **5** Swift **6** Armour ***raw:*** **6** gobbet ***roasted:*** **8** barbecue ***roasting shop:*** **10** rotisserie ***seasoned:*** **7** sausage **8** pastrami, scrapple ***sheep:*** **6** mutton ***side:*** **8** sowbelly ***skewered:*** **5** kebab, kebob ***slice:*** **6** cutlet, rasher ***small portion:*** **6** collop ***tough part:*** **7** gristle

meat-eating 11 carnivorous

meathead 3 lug, oaf **4** clod, dodo, dolt, gawk, goon, lout **5** chump, klutz, looby **6** dimwit, lubber **7** bungler, palooka **8** dumbbell, numskull **9** birdbrain, ignoramus, lamebrain, numbskull **10** nincompoop

Mebd ***husband:*** **6** Ailill ***victim:*** **10** Cuchulainn

Mecca 4 goal ***country:*** **11** Saudi Arabia ***pilgrim:*** **5** hadji, hajji ***pilgrimage:*** **4** hadj, hajj ***port:*** **5** Jedda, Jidda **6** Jeddah, Jiddah ***shrine:*** **5** Kaaba

mechanic 7 artisan **9** machinist

mechanical 4 cold **7** cursory, pasteup, robotic **8** lifeless **9** automated, automatic, unfeeling **10** impersonal **11** emotionless, instinctive, involuntary, perfunctory, unemotional

mechanism 4 gear **5** gizmo, means, works **6** agency, doodad, jigger, medium, widget **7** whatsit **8** dohickey **9** apparatus, appliance, procedure, technique, thingummy **10** instrument **11** contraption, contrivance, thingamabob, thingamajig, thingumajig

medal 5 badge, honor, prize **6** reward **7** laurels **8** accolade **10** decoration **13** commemoration

meddle 3 pry **4** fool, nose **5** snoop **6** butt in, dabble, horn in, kibitz, monkey, putter, tamper, tinker **7** intrude, obtrude **8** trespass **9** interfere, interlope, intervene **10** mess around

meddler 5 snoop, yenta **7** snooper **8** busybody, intruder, kibitzer **9** buttinsky **12** troublemaker

meddlesome 4 busy, nosy **5** nosey **6** prying **9** intrusive, obtrusive, officious **11** impertinent, interfering

Medea 5 witch **9** sorceress **11** enchantress ***aunt:*** **5** Circe ***brother:*** **8** Absyrtus ***father:*** **6** Aeëtes ***husband:*** **5** Jason **6** Aegeus ***sister:*** **5** Circe ***son:*** **6** Medeus ***victim:*** **6** Creusa, Glauce, Glauke

medial 3 mid **4** mean **6** center, middle **7** average, central, halfway, midmost **8** middling, moderate **10** centermost, middlemost **11** equidistant **12** intermediary, intermediate

median see **medial**

mediate 5 judge **6** broker, convey, liaise, settle, step in, umpire **7** adjudge, referee, resolve **8** moderate, transmit **9** arbitrate, intercede, interfere, interpose, intervene, negotiate **10** conciliate

mediator 3 ref, ump **5** judge **6** broker, umpire **7** arbiter, liaison, referee **9** go-between, middleman **10** interceder, negotiator, peacemaker **11** intercessor

medical instrument 6 needle **7** forceps, scalpel, scanner, syringe **8** otoscope, speculum **9** endoscope **11** cardiograph, stethoscope

medical practitioner 2 PA, RN **3** doc, LPN **5** nurse **6** doctor, intern **7** interne, surgeon **9** physician

medicament 4 cure, pill **6** elixir, physic, remedy **7** nostrum **8** antidote, curative **10** palliative ***inert:*** **7** placebo

medicate 4 cure, dose, drug, heal **5** treat

medicinal 8 curative, remedial, salutary, sanative **9** healthful **12** health-giving, pharmaceutic

medicine 4 cure, pill **5** bromo **6** physic, remedy **7** anodyne, nostrum **8** busulfan, poultice **11** antipyretic ***African:*** **4** muti ***bottle:*** **4** vial ***branch:*** **7** surgery **8** oncology **9** neurology, pathology **10** bariatrics, cardiology, geriatrics, gynecology, nephrology, obstetrics, pediatrics, psychiatry ***cathartic:*** **8** evacuant **9** purgative ***combining form:*** **5** iatro **8** pharmaco ***quantity of:*** **4** dose **6** dosage ***shell:*** **7** capsule ***soothing:*** **7** anodyne **8** lenitive, narcotic, sedative **9** calmative, soporific

medicine man 6 doctor, kahuna, shaman **9** curandero

medieval study 5 logic **7** grammar, trivium **8** rhetoric **10** quadrivium

mediocre 4 dull, fair, hack, so-so **6** common **7** average, fairish **8** inferior, middling, moderate, ordinary, passable **9** tolerable **10** pedestrian, uninspired **11** commonplace, indifferent **12** run-of-the-mill **13** unexceptional

meditate 4 mull, muse **5** weigh **6** intend, pon-

der **7** purpose, reflect, revolve **8** cogitate, consider, mull over, ruminate, turn over **9** reflect on **10** deliberate **11** contemplate
meditative 6 broody **7** pensive **8** brooding **10** reflective, ruminative, thoughtful
meditator 4 yogi
Mediterranean 11 Mare Nostrum **12** Mare Internum ***coastal region:* 7** Riviera ***eastern shores:* 6** Levant ***island:*** (see at **island**) ***wind:* 7** mistral, sirocco **8** scirocco
medium 3 par **4** fair, mean, so-so **5** agent, organ **6** agency, métier, milieu, normal **7** ambient, average, channel, climate, culture, neutral, vehicle **8** ambience, middling, moderate, passable, standard **9** tolerable **10** atmosphere **11** clairvoyant, environment **12** run-of-the-mill ***of exchange:* 5** money **8** currency **11** legal tender
medley 4 brew, olio, stew **5** combo, gumbo **6** jumble, ragout **7** farrago, mélange, mixture **8** mishmash, pastiche **9** pasticcio, patchwork, potpourri **10** assortment, hodgepodge, hotchpotch, miscellany, salmagundi **11** gallimaufry
Medusa 6 Gorgon ***father:* 7** Phorcus, Phorcys ***hair:* 6** snakes ***mother:* 4** Ceto ***offspring:* 7** Pegasus **8** Chrysaor ***sister:* 6** Stheno **7** Euryale ***slayer:* 7** Perseus
medusa 9 jellyfish
meed 3 due **4** part **5** quota, share **6** amount, desert, ration, return, reward **7** guerdon, measure, portion **8** dividend **9** allotment, allowance **10** recompense
meek 3 shy **4** mild, tame **5** lowly, timid **6** docile, gentle, humble, modest **7** patient **8** tolerant **10** submissive, unassuming **11** deferential **13** long-suffering
meerschaum 4 pipe **9** sepiolite
meet 3 apt, fit **4** face, fair, fill, find, join, just, open, spot **5** cross, event, hit on, match, right, touch, unite **6** answer, chance, engage, oppose, proper, settle, take on **7** contest, convene, fitting, fulfill, hit upon, satisfy, stumble **8** approach, assemble, come upon, concours, conflict, confront, converge, suitable **9** encounter, measure up **10** congregate **11** competition ***a bet:* 3** see ***a need:* 7** suffice ***athletic:* 8** gymkhana **10** tournament ***by appointment:* 10** rendezvous
meeting 4 moot, talk **5** tryst **6** huddle, parley, powwow **7** session **8** assembly, conclave, concours, congress, junction **9** concourse, encounter, gathering, rencontre **10** conference, confluence, convention, rendezvous **11** competition, convocation, get-together **12** intersection ***Anglo-Saxon:* 5** gemot **6** gemote ***place:* 5** forum ***spiritual:* 6** séance
Mefistofele composer 5 Boito (Arrigo)
Megaera see **Erinyes**
megaphone 8 bullhorn **10** mouthpiece
Megara *father:* 5 Creon ***husband:* 8** Heracles, Hercules ***king:* 5** Nisus
megillah 5 story **7** account
megrim 3 bee **4** urge, whim **5** fancy, freak, humor **6** notion, vagary, whimsy **7** caprice, conceit, impulse, vertigo **8** crotchet, migraine **9** dizziness
Mehitabel 3 cat ***creator:* 7** Marquis (Don) ***friend:* 5** Archy
Mein Kampf author 6 Hitler (Adolf)
meiosis 7 litotes **12** cell division
Meissen 5 china **8** ceramics **9** porcelain
Meistersinger 5 Sachs (Hans) **9** Frauenlob
Meistersinger, Die *beloved:* 3 Eva ***composer:* 6** Wagner (Richard) ***hero:* 6** Walter ***mentor:* 5** Sachs (Hans)
melancholia 5 gloom **6** sorrow **7** despair, sadness **9** dejection, morbidity **10** depression, desolation, gloominess **11** despondency, dolefulness
melancholic 3 low, sad **4** blue, glum **6** gloomy, morose, triste **7** joyless **8** dejected, downcast, mournful **9** depressed, saddening **10** depressing, despondent, dispirited
melancholy 3 low, sad **4** blue, funk, glum **5** blues, dumps, ennui, gloom **6** dismal, dreary, gloomy, misery, morose, rueful, somber, tedium, triste, woeful **7** boredom, despair, doleful, joyless, sadness, unhappy **8** dejected, dolorous, downcast, funereal, mournful, saddened **9** black bile, dejection, depressed, plaintive, saddening, sorrowful **10** depressing, depression, despondent, dispirited, lachrymose, lugubrious **11** despondency, unhappiness **12** heavyhearted, wretchedness
mélange see **medley**
Melanippus *father:* 7 Theseus ***slayer:* 10** Amphiaraus ***victim:* 6** Tydeus
Melchior *companion:* 6 Caspar, Gaspar **9** Balthasar, Balthazar ***gift:* 4** gold
Melchizedek's kingdom 5 Salem
meld 3 mix **4** fuse **5** blend, merge **6** mingle **7** combine, mixture **8** compound **9** commingle, interfuse **10** amalgamate **11** intermingle
Meleager *beloved:* 8 Atalanta ***father:* 6** Oeneus ***mother:* 7** Althaea ***victim:* 4** boar
melee 3 row **4** fray, riot **5** brawl, broil, clash, fight, set-to **6** affray, fracas, ruckus, rumpus **7** scuffle **8** skirmish **9** scrimmage **10** donnybrook, free-for-all
meliorate 4 help **5** amend **6** better, soften **7** improve **8** mitigate, palliate
Mélisande's lover 7 Pelléas

melisma 7 cadenza, descant
mellifluous 5 sweet **6** dulcet, fluent, golden, liquid, smooth **7** flowing, honeyed, silvery **8** euphonic, soothing **10** euphonious **13** silver-tongued
mellow 3 age **4** aged, ripe **5** ripen **6** genial, golden, grow up, mature, season, smooth **7** honeyed, matured, ripened **8** laid-back, pleasant, seasoned **9** agreeable
melodic 5 sweet **6** dulcet **7** musical, songful, tuneful **8** canorous, euphonic **10** euphonious
melodious 5 lyric, sweet **6** dulcet **7** musical, songful, tuneful **8** euphonic **9** cantabile **10** euphonious
melody 3 air, lay **4** aria, lilt, song, tune **5** canto, music, theme **6** chorus, strain, warble **7** descant, refrain **11** tunefulness
melon 4 pepo **5** gourd **6** casaba, profit **8** crenshaw, honeydew, windfall **10** cantaloupe
Melpomene see **Muse**
melt 3 run **4** flux, fuse, thaw **6** relent, soften **7** liquefy **8** dissolve, liquesce, unfreeze **9** disappear **10** deliquesce ***down:*** **6** render ***together:*** **4** fuse
Melville, Herman ***character:*** **3** Pip **4** Ahab, Toby **5** Bembo, Chase **6** Cereno (Benito), Jermin, Pierre **7** Fayaway, Ishmael **8** Bartleby, Queequeg, Starbuck ***work:*** **4** Omoo **5** Mardi, Typee **6** Pierre **7** Redburn **8** Moby Dick **11** White-Jacket **12** Benito Cereno **13** Confidence-Man (The)
member 3 cut **4** part **5** piece **6** clause, parcel **7** portion, section, segment **8** division **9** appendage, component **10** ingredient ***Parliament:*** **2** MP ***political party:*** **4** Tory, Whig **7** Liberal **8** Democrat, Laborite **9** Labourite **10** Republican **12** Conservative ***service club:*** **3** Elk **4** Lion **8** Kiwanian, Rotarian
membrane 4 film, tela **5** velum **6** pleura **7** pleurae (plural) ***bodily:*** **6** serosa ***brain:*** **3** pia ***diffusion through:*** **7** osmosis ***dividing:*** **5** septa (plural) **6** septum ***ear:*** **8** tympanum ***enclosing:*** **5** tunic **8** indusium ***thin:*** **6** lamina **7** lamella, laminae (plural) **8** lamellae (plural) ***wing:*** **8** patagium
memento 5 relic, token, trace **6** trophy **7** vestige **8** keepsake, reminder, souvenir **11** remembrance
Memnon ***father:*** **8** Tithonus ***mother:*** **3** Eos **6** Aurora ***slayer:*** **8** Achilles
memoir 3 bio **4** life **5** diary **6** record, report, thesis **7** account, journal **8** anecdote **9** biography **11** confessions **12** recollection, reminiscence **13** autobiography
memoirist 7 Boswell, diarist **10** biographer
memorable 7 lasting, notable **8** historic **9** deathless, indelible, momentous, red-letter **10** noteworthy **11** significant **13** distinguished
memorandum 4 chit, note **6** minute, notice, record **7** tickler **8** notation, reminder **12** announcement
memorial 4 note **5** relic, token, trace **6** record, trophy **7** relique **8** keepsake, monument, reminder, souvenir **10** dedicatory **11** celebrative, remembrance **12** consecrative, remembrancer **13** commemoration, commemorative ***mound:*** **5** cairn
memorial park see **cemetery**
memorize 3 con, get **6** retain **8** remember
memory 6 recall **8** mind's eye, souvenir **9** anamnesis, awareness, flashback, retention **10** reflection **11** remembrance **12** recollection, reminiscence **13** retentiveness, retrospection ***assisting:*** **8** mnemonic ***loss:*** **7** amnesia ***trace:*** **6** engram ***unit:*** **3** meg
menace 4 risk **5** alarm, peril, scare **6** danger, hazard, threat **7** imperil, jeopard, torment **8** endanger, frighten, jeopardy, threaten **9** terrorize **10** intimidate, jeopardize
ménage 4 clan **5** house **6** family **8** quarters **9** household **12** housekeeping
menagerie 3 zoo **7** mixture
mend 3 fix, sew **4** cure, darn, heal, knit **5** patch, renew **6** cobble, doctor, look up, perk up, reform, remedy, repair, revamp **7** correct, improve, patch up, rebuild, rectify, redress, restore **8** overhaul, renovate **9** condition, refurbish **10** ameliorate, convalesce, recuperate **11** recondition, reconstruct
mendacious 5 false, lying **6** shifty **7** fibbing **9** deceitful, deceptive, dishonest, paltering **10** untruthful **11** dissembling **13** prevaricating
mendacity 3 lie **6** deceit **9** deception, duplicity, falsehood **10** dishonesty **12** equivocation **13** truthlessness
mendelevium symbol 2 Md
mendicancy 7 beggary, begging, bumming, cadging **8** mooching, sponging **11** panhandling
mendicant 5 friar **6** beggar **7** begging
Mending Wall author 5 Frost (Robert)
Menelaus ***brother:*** **9** Agamemnon ***father:*** **6** Atreus ***kingdom:*** **6** Sparta ***mother:*** **6** Aerope ***wife:*** **5** Helen
menial 4 dull **5** lowly **6** humble **7** servant, servile, slavish **8** obeisant, retainer **9** unskilled **10** obsequious **11** subservient, undignified
meniscus 4 lens **9** cartilage
Menlo Park inventor 6 Edison (Thomas Alva)
menopause 11 climacteric **12** change of life

menorah 10 candelabra
Menotti, Gian Carlo *character:* 5 Amahl ***opera:* 6** Consul (The), Medium (The) **9** Telephone (The)
men's store 12 haberdashery
mental 5 inner **7** psychic **8** cerebral, rational, thinking **9** reasoning, spiritual **10** immaterial, telepathic **11** intelligent **12** intellective, intellectual **13** psychological ***faculty:* 6** memory
mentalist 6 Geller (Uri) **7** Kreskin **8** Banachek
mentality 3 wit **5** sense **6** brains **7** mindset, outlook **9** intellect, mother wit **10** brainpower **12** intelligence
mention 4 cite, name, note **7** refer to, specify **8** advert to, allude to, citation, instance **9** reference
mentor 4 guru **5** coach, guide, tutor **7** teacher **9** counselor **10** counsellor
Mentor's pupil 10 Telemachus
menu 4 card, diet **5** carte **10** bill of fare **11** carte du jour ***item:* 4** soup **5** salad **6** entrée **7** dessert **9** appetizer
Mephibosheth *father:* 4 Saul **8** Jonathan ***mother:* 6** Rizpah
Mephistophelian 7 satanic **8** devilish, diabolic **10** diabolical
mephitic 4 rank **5** fetid, funky, musty **6** putrid, smelly **7** noisome, noxious, reeking **8** stinking **9** poisonous **10** malodorous
Merab *father:* 4 Saul ***husband:* 6** Adriel
mercenary 4 hack **5** ninja, ronin, venal **6** greedy **7** corrupt, soldier **8** hireling **10** gun for hire
merchandise 4 line, sell **5** cargo, goods, stock, trade, wares **6** deal in, job lot, market, retail **7** effects, promote, staples, traffic **8** products **9** publicize, vendibles **11** commodities
merchandiser 6 dealer, trader, vendor **8** retailer **9** tradesman **10** wholesaler **11** businessman **13** businesswoman
merchant 5 buyer **6** dealer, jobber, seller, trader, vendor **7** peddler **8** purveyor, retailer **9** tradesman **10** trafficker, wholesaler **11** businessman, storekeeper ***guild:* 5** Hansa, Hanse ***League:* 9** Hanseatic ***ship:* 5** oiler **6** argosy, coaler, galiot, packet, tanker, trader **7** collier, galliot, steamer **8** Indiaman **9** freighter ***wine:* 7** vintner
Merchant of Venice, The 7 Antonio ***character:* 6** Portia **7** Jessica, Lorenzo, Nerissa, Shylock **8** Bassanio
merciful 4 kind **6** benign, humane, kindly **7** clement, lenient **8** tolerant **9** forgiving, indulgent **10** charitable, forbearing **11** softhearted **13** compassionate
merciless 4 grim **5** cruel, harsh **6** brutal, savage, wanton **9** cutthroat, ferocious, unfeeling **10** gratuitous, implacable, ironfisted, unyielding **11** hardhearted, unrelenting **12** unappeasable
mercurial 5 flaky **6** fickle, mobile **7** erratic **8** unstable, variable, volatile **9** impulsive **10** capricious, changeable, inconstant **13** temperamental, unpredictable
mercury 5 azoth **11** quicksilver ***ore:* 8** cinnabar ***symbol:* 2** Hg
Mercury 6 planet (see also **Hermes**)
Mercutio *friend:* 5 Romeo ***slayer:* 6** Tybalt
mercy 4 pity, ruth **5** grace **6** lenity **7** caritas, charity **8** clemency, goodwill, kindness, leniency **9** benignity, tolerance **10** compassion, generosity, kindliness **11** benevolence, forbearance **13** commiseration ***petition for:* 5** kyrie **8** miserere
mere 4 bare, lake, pool, pure **6** meager, meagre, paltry **7** trivial **8** boundary, landmark, piddling **9** undiluted
merely 4 just, only **6** simply, solely, wholly
meretricious 4 loud, sham **5** gaudy, phony, showy **6** flashy, garish, glitzy, sleazy, tawdry, tinsel, trashy **7** chintzy **8** delusive, delusory, illusory **9** contrived, deceptive **10** misleading **11** counterfeit, pretentious
merganser 4 duck, smew
merge 3 mix **4** fuse, join **5** blend, unify, unite **6** mingle **7** combine **8** coalesce, compound **9** commingle, interfuse **10** amalgamate, assimilate **11** consolidate, intermingle
merger 5 union **6** fusion **7** melding **8** alliance, takeover **9** coalition **10** absorption **11** combination, unification **12** amalgamation **13** consolidation
meridian 4 acme, apex, peak **6** apogee, climax, summit, zenith **8** pinnacle
merit 3 due **4** earn, rate **5** arete, value, worth **6** virtue **7** caliber, deserts, deserve, entitle, justify, quality, stature, warrant **10** excellence, perfection, recompense **11** achievement
merited 3 due **4** fair, just **5** right **7** condign, fitting **8** deserved, rightful, suitable **9** justified, requisite **11** appropriate
meritorious 6 worthy **8** laudable **9** admirable, deserving, estimable, honorable **10** creditable **11** commendable, thankworthy **12** praiseworthy
Merlin 4 seer **5** augur, magus **6** shaman, wizard **7** prophet **8** magician **10** soothsayer **11** necromancer, thaumaturge
merlin 6 falcon **10** pigeon hawk

mermaid **3** nix **5** Ariel, nixie **7** manatee **8** sirenian **10** water nymph **11** water sprite

Merope ***father:*** **5** Atlas **8** Oenopion ***husband:*** **7** Polybus **8** Sisyphus **11** Cresphontes ***lover:*** **5** Orion ***mother:*** **7** Pleione ***sisters:*** **8** Pleiades ***son:*** **7** Aepytus, Glaucus

merriment **4** glee **5** mirth, revel **6** gaiety **7** jollity, revelry, whoopee **8** hilarity, reveling **9** festivity, jocundity, joviality **10** jocularity, jubilation **13** entertainment

merry **3** gay **4** glad **5** happy, jolly **6** blithe, jocund, jovial, joyful, joyous, lively **7** festive, gleeful **8** animated, cheerful, mirthful **9** hilarious, sprightly, vivacious **12** high-spirited, lighthearted

merry-andrew **4** fool, zany **5** clown, joker **6** jester, madcap **7** buffoon **9** harlequin **10** mountebank

merrymaker **7** partyer, reveler **8** carouser

merrymaking **5** party, revel **6** frolic, gaiety **7** jollity, revelry, whoopee **8** hilarity **9** festivity **12** conviviality

Merry Widow composer **5** Lehár (Franz)

Merry Wives of Windsor character **3** Nym **4** Ford, Page **5** Caius **6** Fenton, Pistol **7** Slender **8** Falstaff

mesa **5** bench, butte **7** plateau **9** tableland

mescal **5** agave **6** cactus, liquor, maguey, peyote

mesh **3** net, web **4** jibe, maze **5** skein, snare, snarl **6** engage, morass, tangle **7** entwine, netting, network **8** dovetail, entangle **9** harmonize, interlock, labyrinth **10** coordinate **12** reticulation

meshuga **3** mad **4** nuts **5** crazy, goofy, kooky, loony, nutty, wacky **6** insane, screwy **7** foolish

mesmeric **8** alluring, hypnotic **9** glamorous, seductive **10** bewitching, enchanting **11** captivating, fascinating

mesmerize **4** vamp **6** dazzle, seduce **7** bewitch **8** ensorcel, enthrall, entrance **9** captivate, ensorcell, fascinate, hypnotize, spellbind

Mesopotamia **4** Iraq ***civilization:*** **4** Elam **5** Akkad, Sumer **7** Assyria, Elamite **8** Akkadian, Assyrian, Sumerian **9** Babylonia **10** Babylonian ***river:*** **6** Tigris **9** Euphrates

mess **4** hash **5** botch, snafu **6** fright, jumble, muddle **7** eyesore **8** botchery, disarray, disorder, shambles, wreckage **9** confusion **10** hodgepodge, hotchpotch, miscellany ***around:*** **4** hang, idle **5** chill, dally **6** dawdle, doodle, fiddle, potter, putter **7** goof off, hang out **8** chill out, lollygag **10** dilly-dally ***up:*** **3** err **4** blow, flub, muff, ruin **5** botch, fluff, fudge, spoil, touse **6** bungle, fumble, tousle **7** butcher

message **4** note, post **5** sense, theme **6** letter, report **7** epistle, meaning, mission, missive, purport **8** bulletin, dispatch, telegram **9** directive, telegraph **10** communiqué **12** significance **13** communication, signification

Messalina's husband **8** Claudius

mess around **4** fool, idle **5** flirt **6** dabble, dawdle, fiddle, meddle, monkey, potter, putter, tamper, tinker **8** womanize **9** associate, interfere, interlope, philander

messenger **4** post **5** envoy **6** herald, runner **7** apostle, courier **8** emissary **9** go-between, harbinger **10** ambassador **11** internuncio **12** intermediary ***God's:*** **5** angel ***of the gods:*** **4** Iris **6** Hermes **7** Mercury ***Turkish:*** **6** chiaus

messiah **6** savior **7** saviour **8** defender **9** deliverer, liberator

Messiah composer **6** Handel (George Frideric)

messy **6** frowsy, frowzy, sloppy, unneat, untidy **7** chaotic, rumpled, unkempt **8** careless, confused, ill-kempt, slapdash, slipshod, slovenly **10** disheveled, disorderly **11** dishevelled ***abode:*** **3** sty **6** pigpen, pigsty

mestizo **5** métis **6** ladino **10** mixed-blood

Mestor ***father:*** **7** Perseus ***mother:*** **9** Andromeda

metal **4** gold, iron **5** steel **6** bronze ***alloy:*** (see **alloy**) ***casting mold:*** **5** ingot ***corrosion:*** **4** rust ***fuse:*** **6** solder ***in mass:*** **7** bullion ***layer:*** **7** plating ***lump:*** **6** nugget ***magnetic:*** **4** iron ***refuse:*** **4** slag **5** dross **6** scoria ***sheath:*** **5** armor ***source:*** **3** ore ***thin:*** **4** foil, leaf **5** plate ***worker:*** **5** smith **10** blacksmith

metallic element **3** tin **4** gold, iron, lead, zinc **6** barium, cobalt, copper, nickel, radium, silver, sodium **7** arsenic, bismuth, cadmium, calcium, lithium, mercury, uranium **8** aluminum, chromium, platinum, titanium, tungsten, vanadium **9** magnesium, manganese, potassium, strontium **10** molybdenum

metamere **6** somite **7** segment

metamorphic rock **5** slate **6** gneiss, marble, schist **9** quartzite, soapstone

metamorphose **6** change, mutate **7** convert, develop **9** transform, translate, transmute **11** transfigure **12** transmogrify

metamorphosis **6** change **8** changing, mutation **9** evolution, sea change **10** changeover **13** transmutation

Metamorphosis author **5** Kafka (Franz)

____ me tangere **4** noli

metaphor **5** trope **6** simile, symbol **7** analogy **8** allegory **10** comparison, similitude

metaphorical compound **7** kenning

metaphysical 8 bodiless, numinous **9** unearthly, unfleshly **10** immaterial, suprahuman **12** supermundane, supramundane, supranatural, transcendent **13** preternatural ***poet:*** **5** Donne (John) **6** Cowley (Abraham) **7** Crashaw (Richard), Herbert (George), Marvell (Andrew), Vaughan (Henry) **9** Cleveland (John)

mete 4 deal, dole, give **5** allot, bound **6** border, parcel, ration **7** portion **8** allocate, boundary, disburse, dispense **9** apportion **10** distribute

meteor 8 fireball **12** shooting star ***exploding:*** **6** bolide ***shower:*** **5** Lyrid **6** Leonid, Taurid **7** Aquarid, Geminid, Orionid, Perseid **10** Quadrantid

meteorite 8 aerolite **10** siderolite

meter 4 beat, scan **6** rhythm **7** cadence, measure, pattern

meter maid 4 Rita

metheglin 4 mead **8** beverage ***ingredient:*** **5** honey

method 3 way **4** mode, modi (plural), plan **5** means, modus, order, style **6** course, design, manner, schema, scheme, system **7** fashion, formula, pattern, process, routine, wrinkle **8** practice **9** procedure, technique **11** orderliness **13** modus operandi ***careful:*** **8** strategy ***of employing troops:*** **6** tactic **7** tactics ***of procedure:*** **4** game

methodical 5 exact **7** careful, logical, orderly, precise, regular **9** efficient, organized **10** deliberate, scrupulous, systematic, systemized **12** systematized

Methuselah *father:* **5** Enoch ***grandson:*** **4** Noah ***son:*** **6** Lamech

meticulous 5 exact, fussy, picky **6** strict **7** careful, finicky, precise **8** detailed, thorough **10** fastidious, nitpicking, pernickety, scrupulous **11** microscopic, painstaking, persnickety, punctilious **13** conscientious

métier 4 work **5** craft, field, forte, trade **7** calling, pursuit **8** business, strength, vocation **9** specialty **10** employment, occupation, profession

metrical foot 4 iamb **5** ionic, paeon **6** cretic, dactyl, iambic, iambus **7** anapest, pyrrhic, pyrrhus, spondee, triseme, trochee **8** bacchius, choriamb, dactylic, spondaic, tribrach, trochaic **9** anapestic **10** tribrachic

metric unit *area:* **3** are **7** hectare ***capacity:*** **5** liter, litre **9** decaliter, deciliter, kiloliter **10** centiliter, hectoliter, milliliter ***length:*** **5** meter **9** decameter, decimeter, dekameter, kilometer **10** centimeter, hectometer, millimeter ***mass and weight:*** **4** gram **7** quintal **8** decagram, decigram, dekagram, kilogram **9** centigram, hectogram, metric ton, milligram ***volume:*** **5** liter, litre

metro 4 tube **6** subway **11** underground

metropolis 4 city **7** capital

metropolitan 5 urban **6** urbane **7** primate **9** municipal **10** archbishop

mettle 4 fire, grit, guts **5** heart, moxie, nerve, pluck, spunk, steel, valor, vigor **6** daring, spirit, starch, temper **7** cojones, courage, resolve, stamina **8** backbone, boldness, tenacity, vitality **9** fortitude **10** resolution

mettlesome 4 bold, game **5** brave, fiery, gutsy **6** plucky, spunky **7** staunch, valiant **8** intrepid, resolute, spirited, vigorous **9** tenacious **10** courageous, determined

mew 3 hem, pen **4** cage, coop, gull **5** alley, fence **6** corral, immure, shut in, stable **7** enclose **8** hideaway

mewl 4 moan, pule **5** whine **6** snivel **7** whimper

Mexican *crop:* **5** sisal **8** henequen ***estate:*** **8** hacienda ***food:*** **4** masa, taco **5** chili, salsa **6** fajita, tamale **7** burrito, panocha, penuche, tostada **8** frijoles, tortilla **9** enchilada, guacamole **10** quesadilla **11** chimichanga ***hut:*** **5** jacal ***liquor:*** **6** mescal, mezcal **7** tequila

Mexico *ancient city:* **12** Tenochtitlán ***ancient culture:*** **4** Maya **5** Aztec, Mayan, Olmec **6** Toltec ***bay:*** **8** Campeche ***capital:*** **10** Mexico City ***city:*** **4** León **6** Juárez, Mérida, Oaxaca, Puebla **7** Nogales, Tijuana **8** Acapulco, Mexicali, Saltillo **9** Chihuahua, Matamoros, Monterrey **10** Cuernavaca **11** Guadalajara **12** Ciudad Juárez ***conqueror:*** **6** Cortés (Hernán, Hernando) ***discoverer:*** **7** Córdoba (Fernández de) ***emperor:*** **10** Maximilian ***gulf:*** **10** California ***island:*** **7** Cozumel ***island group:*** **13** Revillagigedo ***lake:*** **7** Chapala, Cuitzeo, Texcoco **9** Pátzcuaro ***language:*** **7** Spanish ***leader:*** **4** Díaz (Porfirio) **6** Juárez (Benito) **8** Carranza (Venustiano) ***monetary unit:*** **4** peso ***mountain, range:*** **8** Malinche **11** Sierra Madre ***neighbor:*** **6** Belize **9** Guatemala ***peninsula:*** **4** Baja **7** Yucatán ***port:*** **7** Tampico **8** Ensenada, Mazatlán, Veracruz ***resort:*** **6** Cancún **8** Acapulco ***revolutionist:*** **5** Villa (Pancho) **6** Zapata (Emiliano) **7** Hidalgo (Padre Miguel) ***river:*** **4** Mayo **5** Bravo, Yaquí **6** Balsas, Grande, Pánuco **7** Conchos **8** Grijalva, Río Bravo, Santiago **9** Rio Grande **10** Usumacinta ***ruined city:*** **5** Tulum, Uxmal **7** Mayapán **8** Palenque **11** Chichén Itzá ***state:*** **6** Oaxaca, Puebla, Sonora **7** Chiapas, Durango, Hidalgo, Tabasco, Yucatán **8** Veracruz ***sea:*** **9** Caribbean ***volcano:*** **6** Colima **9** Paricutín **11**

Ixtacihuatl **12** Citlaltépetl, Ixtaccihuatl, Popocatépetl

mezzanine 4 loge **5** story **7** balcony **8** entresol

mezzo 4 half **6** singer **7** soprano

mezzo-soprano ***American:*** **5** Elias (Rosalind), Horne (Marilyn), Jones (Sissieretta) **6** Bumbry (Grace), Gravès (Denyce) **7** Stevens (Risë), Verrett (Shirley) **8** Troyanos (Tatiana), von Stade (Frederica) ***Austrian:*** **6** Ludwig (Christa) ***English:*** **5** Baker (Janet) ***Italian:*** **7** Bartoli (Cecilia) **8** Cossotto (Fiorenza)

Miami ***bowl:*** **6** Orange ***chief:*** **12** Little Turtle ***county:*** **4** Dade ***stadium:*** **9** Joe Robbie ***team:*** **4** Heat **7** Marlins **8** Dolphins, Panthers

miasma 3 fog **4** haze, mist, murk, smog **5** brume, vapor **9** effluvium

mica 7 biotite **8** silicate **9** isinglass, muscovite

Michelangelo Buonarotti ***painting:*** **10** Holy Family (The) **12** Last Judgment (The) ***statue:*** **5** David, Moses, Pietà **7** Bacchus

Michener novel 5 Space, Texas **6** Hawaii, Poland, Source (The) **8** Caravans, Covenant (The), Drifters (The), Sayonara **10** Centennial, Chesapeake **13** Fires of Spring (The) **15** Bridges at Toko-Ri (The)

Michigan ***capital:*** **7** Lansing ***city:*** **5** Flint **7** Detroit, Pontiac **8** Ann Arbor, Dearborn **9** Kalamazoo **11** Grand Rapids **13** Sault Ste. Marie ***college, university:*** **6** Calvin **9** Kalamazoo **10** Wayne State ***lake:*** **4** Erie **5** Huron **8** Michigan, Superior ***nickname:*** **9** Wolverine (State) **10** Great Lakes (State) ***state bird:*** **5** robin ***state flower:*** **12** apple blossom ***state tree:*** **9** white pine

mickey 5 flask, split

Mickey Mouse 5 dinky, petty **7** trivial **8** trifling **9** pointless, small-time, worthless **10** irrelevant

microbe 3 bug **4** germ **5** virus **8** bacillus, pathogen **9** bacterium **13** microorganism see **microorganism**

microfilm sheet 5 fiche

Micronesia ***capital:*** **7** Palikir ***island, island group:*** **3** Yap **5** Chuuk **6** Kosrae **7** Pohnpei **8** Caroline

microorganism 3 bug **4** germ **5** ameba, virus **6** aerobe, amoeba **7** bacilli (plural), microbe, protist **8** bacillus, bacteria (plural), pathogen, protozoa (plural) **9** bacterium, protozoan, protozoon

microphone 3 bug **4** mike ***shield:*** **4** gobo

microscope 9 magnifier ***inventor:*** **11** Leeuwenhoek (Antoni van) ***part:*** **5** stage **6** mirror **8** eyepiece **9** objective

microscopic 4 tiny **5** small **6** minute **13** infinitesimal

Microsoft founder 5 Gates (Bill)

microwave 3 zap **4** nuke

Mid-Atlantic state 7 New York **8** Delaware, Maryland, Virginia **9** New Jersey **12** Pennsylvania, West Virginia

midday 4 noon, sext **8** high noon, noontide, noontime

middle 4 core, mean **5** mesne, waist **6** center, medial, median **7** average, central, halfway **8** interior **10** centermost **11** equidistant, intervening **12** intermediary, intermediate ***combining form:*** **3** mes **4** meso

Middle American country 4 Cuba **5** Haiti **6** Belize, Mexico, Panama **7** Bahamas, Grenada, Jamaica **8** Barbados, Dominica, Honduras **9** Costa Rica, Guatemala, Nicaragua **10** El Salvador

middlebrow 7 Babbitt

middle class 11 bourgeoisie

middle-class 9 bourgeois

middle ear ***bone:*** **5** incus **6** stapes **7** malleus ***membrane:*** **7** eardrum **8** tympanum

Middle Eastern country 4 Iran, Iraq, Oman **5** Egypt, Qatar, Sudan, Syria, Yemen **6** Cyprus, Israel, Jordan, Kuwait, Turkey **7** Bahrain, Lebanon **11** Saudi Arabia

Middle Kingdom 5 China

middleman 5 agent **6** broker **8** mediator **9** go-between **11** distributor, intercessor **12** intermediary, intermediate

Middlemarch author 5 Eliot (George), Evans (Mary Ann)

middle-of-the-road 7 neutral **8** moderate **9** impartial **11** nonpartisan

middling 4 fair, okay, so-so **6** decent, fairly, medium, rather **7** average, fairish, typical **8** adequate, mediocre, moderate, ordinary, passable **9** tolerable **10** moderately, second-rate **11** indifferent **12** intermediate, run-of-the-mill

midge 3 fly **4** gnat **6** punkie **7** no-see-um **8** dipteran **10** chironomid ***larva:*** **9** bloodworm

midget 4 runt **5** dwarf, pygmy **6** bantam, peewee **7** manikin **8** Tom Thumb **10** homunculus **11** hop-o'-my-thumb, Lilliputian

Midian ***father:*** **7** Abraham ***mother:*** **7** Keturah ***son:*** **5** Abida, Ephah, Epher **6** Eldaah, Hanoch

midpoint 3 par **4** mean, norm **6** center, median, middle **7** average, centrum, halfway **8** bull's-eye, standard

midwife 4 dhai **5** doula **6** granny, Lucina **10** accoucheur

mien **3** air, set **4** look **6** aspect, manner **7** address, bearing **8** carriage, demeanor, presence **9** mannerism **10** appearance, deportment, expression **11** comportment

miff **3** fit, irk, vex **4** beef, flap, spat **5** annoy, pique, run-in, upset **6** bother, fracas, nettle, offend, put out **7** dispute, provoke, quarrel, rhubarb **8** irritate, squabble **10** conniption, falling-out **11** altercation

might **3** may **4** sway **5** brawn, clout, force, means, power **6** energy, muscle **7** ability, command, control, mastery, potency **8** capacity, strength **9** authority, resources **12** forcefulness

mighty **4** huge, very **5** grand, great **6** heroic, potent, strong **7** eminent, immense, massive, titanic **8** enormous, forceful, gigantic, imposing, powerful, puissant **10** impressive, monumental, prodigious, stupendous, tremendous

Mignon composer **6** Thomas (Ambroise)

mignonette **4** herb **5** sauce **6** annual **6** reseda

migrant **5** exile, mover, nomad **7** drifter, nomadic, refugee **8** traveler, wanderer **9** itinerant, transient **10** expatriate

migrate **4** move, trek **5** drift, range, shift **6** wander **8** transfer

migration **6** exodus **8** diaspora ***of professionals:*** **10** brain drain

migratory **5** nomad **6** errant, mobile, moving, roving **7** nomadic, ranging **9** wandering

Mikado, The ***character:*** **4** Ko-Ko **6** Yum-Yum **7** Pooh-Bah **8** Nanki-Poo **9** Pitti-Sing ***composer:*** **8** Sullivan (Arthur) ***librettist:*** **7** Gilbert (W. S.)

milady **6** madame **10** noblewoman **11** gentlewoman

Milan ***family:*** **6** Sforza **8** Visconti ***opera house:*** **7** La Scala

Milcah ***brother:*** **3** Lot ***father:*** **5** Haran **10** Zelophehad ***husband:*** **5** Nahor ***son:*** **7** Bethuel

mild **4** calm, easy, meek, soft, tame **5** balmy, bland, faint, tepid **6** benign, docile, gentle, placid, serene, smooth, tender **7** amiable, clement, equable, insipid, lenient, patient, subdued **8** moderate, obliging **9** benignant, temperate **10** forbearing, submissive

mildew **4** mold, rust **6** fungus, growth

____ **mile** **7** country, statute **8** nautical

mileage recorder **8** odometer

milestone **5** event **6** marker **8** landmark, occasion

milieu **5** scene **6** medium, sphere **7** ambient, climate, setting **8** ambiance, ambience **10** atmosphere, background **11** environment, mise-en-scène **12** surroundings

militant **7** fighter, martial, warlike, warrior **8** activist, fighting **9** assertive, bellicose, combatant, combative, truculent **10** aggressive, pugnacious **11** belligerent, contentious, quarrelsome **12** gladiatorial

military **5** troop **6** forces, troops **7** martial, warlike **8** soldiery **9** soldierly **10** servicemen **11** armed forces, soldierlike ***alert protocol:*** **6** DEFCON ***alliance:*** **4** NATO ***base:*** **4** camp, fort, post **5** depot, field **6** billet **8** barracks, garrison, quarters **10** encampment ***officer:*** **5** major **7** captain, colonel, general **9** brigadier **10** lieutenant ***prisoner:*** **3** POW ***school:*** **3** OCS, OTS **4** ROTC, USMA **9** Annapolis, West Point ***sector:*** **10** combat zone, front lines **11** battlefront ***store:*** **2** BX, PX **10** commissary ***storehouse:*** **5** depot **6** armory **7** arsenal ***supplies:*** **8** matériel, ordnance ***unit:*** **5** corps, squad, troop **7** company, platoon **8** division, regiment **9** battalion **11** battle group ***vehicle:*** **4** jeep, tank **6** Abrams, Humvee **7** Bradley **9** Black Hawk, half-track

militate **4** tell **5** count, weigh **6** matter **11** carry weight

militia **7** reserve

milk **4** pump, rook, suck **5** drain, educe, empty, evoke, exact, mulct, nurse, wring **6** elicit, extort, fleece **7** exhaust, exploit, extract ***coagulated:*** **4** curd ***combining form:*** **4** lact **5** lacti, lacto ***curdled:*** **7** clabber ***fermented:*** **5** kefir **6** kumiss, yogurt **7** koumiss, yoghurt ***liquid part:*** **4** whey ***store:*** **5** dairy ***sugar:*** **7** lactose

milkfish **3** awa

milk shake **6** frappe **7** frosted

milky **4** fair, meek, mild, pale, tame **5** white **6** chalky, cloudy, gentle **7** lacteal, whitish **8** timorous ***lymph:*** **5** chyle

mill **5** grind, plant, shape, works **7** factory, machine **9** circulate, pulverize **11** manufactory

millenary **8** thousand

Miller, Arthur ***film:*** **7** Misfits (The) ***play:*** **5** Price (The) **9** All My Sons **8** Crucible (The) **12** After the Fall **16** Death of a Salesman **17** View from the Bridge (A) ***salesman:*** **5** Loman (Willy)

milliner **6** hatter

million ***combining form:*** **3** meg **4** mega

millionth ***combining form:*** **4** micr **5** micro

Mill on the Floss author **5** Eliot (George), Evans (Mary Ann)

millstone **4** duty, load, onus **6** burden, charge, weight **9** albatross **10** affliction, deadweight

Milne character **3** Roo **4** Pooh (Winnie the) **5** Kanga **6** Eeyore, Piglet, Tigger

milord 8 nobleman **9** gentleman, patrician **10** aristocrat **12** silk stocking
milquetoast see **milksop**
Miltiades' victory 8 Marathon
Milton work 5 Comus **7** Lycidas **8** L'Allegro **12** Areopagitica, Paradise Lost
mime 3 act **5** actor **6** act out **7** Marceau (Marcel) **9** performer, represent **11** impersonate **12** impersonator
mimic 3 act, ape, tui **4** aper, copy, mock, play **5** actor, enact **6** mummer, parody, parrot, player **7** copycat, imitate **8** resemble, simulate, travesty **9** burlesque, pantomime **11** impersonate **12** impersonator
mimicry 4 echo **6** parody **8** travesty **9** imitation, parroting **10** caricature **13** impersonation
minatory 4 dire, grim **7** baleful, baneful, direful, hostile, malefic, ominous **8** menacing, sinister **9** ill-boding **10** forbidding, foreboding, maleficent **11** frightening, threatening **12** intimidating
mince 4 chop, dice, hash **5** cut up, strut **6** prance, sashay, soften **8** moderate, restrain, tone down **9** euphemize
mincing 5 fussy **6** dainty, la-di-da, too-too **7** finical, finicky, stilted **8** affected, delicate **10** fastidious, pernickety **11** persnickety
mind 3 wit **4** mood, obey, soul, tend, will, wits **5** brain, fancy, watch, weigh **6** attend, belief, beware, brains, follow, memory, notice, psyche, reason, senses, spirit **7** care for, discern, dislike, feeling, observe, oversee, purpose **8** consider **9** intellect, intention, mentality, supervise **10** brainpower, gray matter **11** disposition, temperament **12** intelligence **13** consciousness ***combining form:*** **5** psych **6** psycho
mindful 5 alert, awake, aware **7** knowing **8** sensible, vigilant **9** attentive, cognizant, conscious, observant **10** conversant **13** conscientious
mindless 4 rash **5** ditsy, ditzy, inane, silly **6** jejune, simple, stupid **7** asinine, foolish, unaware, vacuous **9** nitwitted, oblivious **10** irrational, unthinking **13** unintelligent
mine 3 dig, pit, sap **4** fund, lode, vein, well **5** delve, drill, hoard, stock, store, trove **6** burrow, quarry, spring **7** bonanza, deposit, extract **8** eldorado, excavate, Golconda **10** excavation, wellspring **13** treasure trove ***coal:*** **8** colliery ***entrance:*** **4** adit
miner 6 pitman **7** collier
mineral 5 beryl, topaz, trona **6** augite, barite, garnet, iolite, pinite, rutile, sphene, spinel, sulfur, zircon **7** apatite, axinite, azurite, bornite, calcite, citrine, coesite, cyanite, jadeite, kernite, kunzite, olivine, zeolite **8** boracite, cinnabar, dolomite, epsomite, fayalite, feldspar, fluorite, hematite, lazulite, lazurite, siderite, sodalite, stibnite, triplite, wellsite **9** aragonite, celestite, cerussite, danburite, fosterite, kaolinite, lawsonite, magnetite, malachite, muscovite, phenakite, scapolite, tridymite, turquoise, wulfenite **10** chalcedony, orthoclase, pyrrhotite, tourmaline **11** alexandrite, chrysoberyl, melanterite **12** brazilianite, chalcopyrite, tincalconite **13** rhodochrosite ***flaky:*** **4** mica ***greasy:*** **4** talc **10** serpentine ***hard:*** **6** spinel **7** diamond **8** corundum ***iridescent:*** **4** opal ***nonmetallic:*** **5** boron **6** gypsum, halite **8** asbestos, graphite ***shiny:*** **4** gold **6** galena, pyrite, silver ***soft:*** **4** talc **6** gypsum **8** graphite ***transparent:*** **6** quartz
mineral water 7 seltzer **8** club soda
Minerva see **Athena**
mingle 3 mix **4** meld **5** blend, merge **6** commix **7** combine **8** intermix **9** associate, socialize
mingy 4 mean **5** cheap, tight **7** chintzy, miserly, scrimpy **8** grudging, ungiving **9** niggardly, penurious **10** pinchpenny **11** closefisted, tightfisted
miniature 3 wee **4** tiny **5** small, teeny, weeny **6** little, minute, petite, teensy **9** itsy-bitsy, itty-bitty **10** diminutive, small-scale, teeny-weeny **11** Lilliputian **12** illumination
minify 4 trim **6** lessen, shrink **7** abridge, curtail **8** decrease, diminish **10** abbreviate
minim 3 bit, jot **4** atom, iota **5** grain, speck **7** modicum, smidgen **8** particle ***music:*** **8** half note
minimal 5 basic, least, token **6** lowest **7** nominal **8** littlest, smallest **9** slightest
minimize 5 decry **6** reduce **7** run down **8** belittle, derogate, discount, downplay, play down **9** disparage, soft-pedal, underrate **10** depreciate **13** underestimate
minimum 3 dab, jot **4** iota, whit **5** least, speck **6** lowest, margin **7** smidgen **8** particle, pittance, smallest
minion 4 idol **5** toady **6** flunky, lackey, vassal, yes-man **7** devotee, flunkey, flunkie, spaniel **8** favorite, follower, parasite, truckler **9** sycophant, toadeater, underling **10** bootlicker **11** lickspittle, subordinate
minister 4 tend **5** agent, clerk, serve **6** cleric, curate, divine, parson **8** clerical, preacher, reverend **9** churchman, clergyman **10** ambassador **12** ecclesiastic ***of state:*** **10** chancellor ***plenipotentiary:*** **5** envoy **6** consul **8** diplomat, emissary
ministry 5 agent, organ **6** agency, clergy, me-

dium **7** cabinet **10** department, instrument **11** bureaucracy

mink kin 5 otter, skunk, stoat **6** ermine, ferret, fisher, weasel

Minnehaha's husband 8 Hiawatha

Minnesota *capital:* 6 St. Paul ***city:* 5** Edina **6** Duluth **9** Rochester **11** Minneapolis ***college, university:* 8** Carleton **9** Saint Olaf **10** Macalester ***nickname:* 6** Gopher (State) **9** North Star (State) ***park:* 9** Voyageurs ***river:* 7** St. Croix **9** Minnesota **11** Mississippi ***state bird:* 4** loon (common) ***state flower:* 12** lady's slipper ***state tree:* 7** red pine

minor 5 lower, petty, small, youth **6** casual, lesser, little, paltry, slight **7** trivial **8** inferior, mediocre, piddling, small-fry, trifling, underage **9** dependent, secondary, small-beer, small-time **10** bush-league, second-rate, shoestring **11** indifferent, unimportant **13** insignificant

minority 5 youth **6** nonage **7** infancy **9** childhood **10** immaturity

minor-league 5 small **6** lesser **9** secondary, small-time **11** unimportant

Minos *daughter:* 7 Ariadne, Phaedra ***father:* 4** Zeus **7** Jupiter ***kingdom:* 5** Crete ***monster:* 8** Minotaur ***mother:* 6** Europa ***son:* 9** Androgeos ***wife:* 8** Pasiphaë

Minotaur *father:* 4 bull ***home:* 9** labyrinth ***mother:* 8** Pasiphaë ***slayer:* 7** Theseus

minstrel 4 bard, wait **6** harper, singer **7** gleeman **8** jongleur **9** balladist **10** troubadour ***end man:* 5** Bones (Mr.), Tambo (Mr.) ***instrument:* 4** lute, lyre **5** naker, rebec, shawm, tabor **8** crumhorn, psaltery **9** krummhorn **10** tambourine

mint 3 pot **4** cast, coin, heap, pile, sage **5** basil, bugle, forge, issue, stamp, trove **6** boodle, bundle, create, intact, packet, savory, strike, unused **7** fortune, like-new, menthol, perfect, produce **8** brand-new, lavender, marjoram, original **9** blue curls, bugleweed, undamaged **10** pennyroyal

Minuit's purchase 9 Manhattan

minus 4 flaw, lack, less, sans **6** absent, defect **7** lacking, missing, wanting, without **8** drawback, negative, subtract **10** deficiency

minuscule 4 tiny **5** small **6** letter, little, minute **7** trivial **9** lowercase, miniature **10** negligible, small-scale **11** meaningless, microscopic **13** imperceptible, inappreciable, insignificant

minute 3 wee **4** jiff, memo, note, tiny **5** draft, flash, jiffy, small, teeny, weeny **6** little, moment, record, teensy **7** careful, instant, precise, trivial **8** detailed, itemized, thorough, trifling **9** itsy-bitsy, itty-bitty, miniature, minuscule **10** diminutive, memorandum, meticulous, scrupulous, teeny-weeny **11** Lilliputian, punctilious **13** infinitesimal

minutes 3 log **6** annals, record **7** summary **10** transcript **11** proceedings

minutiae 6 trivia **7** details **10** fine points, triviality **11** particulars

minx 4 bawd, moll, slut, tart **5** bimbo, tramp, wench, whore **6** floozy, harlot, hooker **7** hustler, trollop **8** strumpet **10** prostitute

miracle 4 boon, feat **6** marvel, wonder **7** godsend, portent, prodigy, stunner **8** windfall **9** sensation **10** phenomenon

miraculous 7 amazing **8** wondrous **9** marvelous, unearthly, wonderful **10** astounding, prodigious, superhuman **11** astonishing, spectacular **12** inexplicable, supernatural **13** preternatural

mirage 6 vision, wraith **8** delusion, illusion, phantasm **11** fata morgana, ignis fatuus **13** hallucination

Miranda *father:* 8 Prospero ***lover:* 9** Ferdinand

mire 3 bog, fen, mud **4** muck, ooze, sink, trap **5** delay, marsh, slush, swamp **6** detain, enmesh, entrap, hang up, morass, slough, tangle **7** bog down, embroil, ensnare, involve, set back **8** entangle **9** imbroglio, implicate, quicksand

Miriam's brother 5 Aaron, Moses

mirror 5 glass **6** embody, typify **7** reflect **8** speculum **9** exemplify, personify, reflector **10** illustrate **11** cheval glass **12** looking glass ***signaling:* 10** heliograph

mirth 3 fun, joy **4** glee **5** cheer **6** gaiety, levity **7** jollity, revelry **8** gladness, hilarity **9** festivity, frivolity, happiness, jocundity, joviality, merriment **10** jocularity **11** merrymaking **12** cheerfulness

mirthful 3 gay **5** jolly, merry, riant **6** jocund, jovial **7** festive **9** exuberant, hilarious **12** lighthearted

miry 4 oozy **5** boggy, mucky, muddy **6** marshy, slushy, swampy

misadventure 4 slip **5** boner, error, lapse **6** howler, mishap **7** blunder, faux pas **8** accident, calamity, casualty, disaster **9** cataclysm **10** misfortune **11** catastrophe

misanthrope 5 cynic, grump, loner **6** grinch **7** killjoy, recluse, scoffer **10** curmudgeon

misanthropic 7 cynical **10** antisocial

misappropriate 5 filch, steal **6** pilfer **7** purloin **8** embezzle, peculate **9** defalcate

misbegotten 7 bastard, illicit, natural **8** baseborn, deformed, spurious **10** fatherless, unfathered **12** contemptible, disreputable, ill-conceived, illegitimate

misbehave **5** act up, cut up, lapse, rebel, stray **6** act out, offend **7** carry on, disobey **8** trespass **10** roughhouse, transgress
misbehavior **7** misdeed **8** rudeness **9** high jinks **10** misconduct, wrongdoing **11** delinquency, dereliction, naughtiness **13** transgression
miscalculate **3** err **8** miscount, misgauge
miscarry **4** fail, flop **5** abort **6** fizzle **7** go wrong
miscellaneous **3** odd **5** mixed **6** motley, sundry, varied **7** diverse **8** assorted **9** different, disparate, scrambled **13** heterogeneous
miscellany **3** ana **4** hash, olio, stew **5** salad **6** jumble, medley, motley, muddle **7** farrago, mélange, mixture, omnibus **8** mixed bag, pastiche **9** anthology, congeries, pasticcio, patchwork, potpourri **10** assortment, hodgepodge, hotchpotch, salmagundi **11** aggregation, gallimaufry, odds and ends, olla podrida, smorgasbord
mischance **6** mishap **7** bad luck, tragedy **8** accident, casualty **9** adversity **10** misfortune **11** contretemps
mischief **3** ill **4** evil, harm **5** prank **6** damage, strife **7** devilry, roguery, trouble, waggery **8** deviltry, sabotage **9** devilment, diablerie, vandalism **10** wrongdoing **11** naughtiness, shenanigans **12** monkeyshines
mischief-maker **3** imp **4** puck **5** devil, knave, rogue, scamp **6** rascal **7** villain **8** agitator, scalawag **9** prankster, trickster **11** rapscallion **12** rabble-rouser
mischievous **3** sly **4** arch, foxy **5** antic, saucy **6** artful, bratty, impish, tricky, vexing **7** harmful, irksome, larkish, naughty, playful, puckish, roguish, tricksy, waggish **8** annoying, damaging, perverse, prankish, rascally, sportive **9** injurious, malicious **10** bothersome, frolicsome, ill-behaved
misconception **5** error **7** fallacy, mistake **8** delusion, illusion
misconduct **8** adultery **10** wrongdoing **11** dereliction, impropriety, malfeasance, malpractice, misbehavior **12** malversation **13** transgression
miscreant **4** heel **5** felon, knave, rogue **6** outlaw, rascal, sinner, wretch **7** corrupt, culprit, heretic, hoodlum, infidel, lowlife, vicious, villain **8** apostate, criminal, depraved, infamous, perverse **9** heretical, nefarious, scoundrel, unhealthy, wrongdoer **10** blackguard, degenerate, delinquent, unbeliever, villainous
miscue **4** goof, miss, slip, trip **5** error, fluff, lapse **6** slipup **7** blooper, blunder, mistake
misdeed **3** sin **5** crime, wrong **6** breach **7** offense **9** violation **10** infraction **13** transgression
misdoubt **4** fear **5** dread **7** suspect
mise-en-scène **3** set **4** site **6** locale, medium, milieu **7** ambient, climate, context, scenery, setting **8** ambiance, ambience, stage set **10** atmosphere, background **11** environment **12** stage setting, surroundings
miser **5** piker **7** hoarder, niggard, scrooge **8** tightwad **9** skinflint **10** cheapskate, pinchpenny
miserable **6** gloomy, meager, meagre, paltry, rueful, sordid, woeful **7** doleful, forlorn, piteous, pitiful, squalid **8** desolate, dolorous, downcast, hopeless, shameful, tortured, wretched **9** afflicted, destitute, sorrowful, worthless **10** despairing, despondent, melancholy
Miserables, Les ***author:*** **4** Hugo (Victor) ***character:*** **6** Javert (Inspector) **7** Cosette, Fantine, Valjean (Jean)
miserly **4** mean **5** close, tight **6** greedy, stingy **7** scrimpy **8** covetous, grasping **9** niggardly, penurious, scrimping **10** avaricious **11** closefisted, tightfisted **12** cheeseparing, parsimonious **13** penny-pinching
misery **3** woe **5** agony, dolor, grief **6** sorrow **7** anguish, squalor **8** calamity, distress **9** adversity, dejection, suffering **10** affliction, depression, desolation **11** despondency **12** wretchedness
misfit **6** oddity, weirdo **7** oddball **8** maverick **9** eccentric, screwball
misfortune **3** ill, woe **4** blow, harm, loss **5** cross, trial **7** reverse, setback, tragedy, trouble **8** accident, calamity, casualty, disaster, hardship **9** adversity, cataclysm **10** affliction, visitation **11** catastrophe, contretemps, tribulation
misgiving **4** fear **5** doubt, dread, qualm **6** unease **7** anxiety, scruple **8** distrust **9** suspicion **10** foreboding **11** premonition, trepidation **12** apprehension, presentiment
misguided **5** wrong **9** erroneous **10** ill-advised **11** injudicious **12** short-sighted
mishandle **4** flub **5** abuse, botch **6** bungle, fumble, mess up **7** rough up **8** maltreat **10** knock about, slap around
mishap **7** bad luck, tragedy **8** accident, casualty **9** adversity **11** contretemps
mishmash **4** olio, stew **6** jumble, litter, medley, motley, muddle **7** clutter, farrago, mélange, mixture, rummage **8** pastiche, scramble **9** pasticcio, patchwork, potpourri **10** hodgepodge, hotchpotch, salmagundi **11** gallimaufry
misidentify **5** mix up **7** confuse **8** confound

misinterpret 7 confuse, misread
mislay 4 lose
mislead 4 dupe, fool, gull, lure **5** bluff, cheat **6** betray, delude, entice, seduce, take in **7** beguile, deceive **8** hoodwink, inveigle **11** double-cross
misleading 5 false, wrong **8** delusive, delusory, specious **9** deceitful, deceptive **10** fallacious, inaccurate **11** casuistical, sophistical
mismatch 3 jar **5** clash **6** jangle **7** discord **8** conflict
misplace 4 lose
misprint 4 typo
misprision 5 scorn **7** despite, disdain, neglect **8** contempt, sedition **9** contumely, disregard **10** misconduct, negligence **11** concealment, dereliction, impropriety, malpractice
misrepresent 4 warp **5** twist **6** garble **7** distort, falsify, varnish **8** disguise **9** embellish, embroider **10** camouflage **11** counterfeit
misrepresentation 3 fib, lie **4** tale **5** story **6** canard **7** falsity, untruth **9** falsehood **10** distortion
miss 3 err, gal **4** fail, girl, lass, maid, omit, skip **5** avoid **6** damsel, escape, forget, ignore, lassie, maiden **7** failure, misfire, neglect **8** discount, leave out, overlook **9** disregard ***French:*** **4** Mlle. **12** Mademoiselle ***German:*** **8** Fräulein ***Spanish:*** **4** Srta. **8** Señorita
Missa Solemnis composer 9 Beethoven (Ludwig van)
misshape 4 warp **6** deform **7** contort, distort, torture **9** disfigure
missile 4 bolt, dart **5** arrow, shell, spear **6** bullet, rocket **10** cannonball, projectile ***shelter:*** **4** silo ***underwater:*** **7** torpedo (see also **guided missile**)
missing 4 AWOL, lost **6** absent
mission 3 aim, job **4** duty, goal, task **5** quest, recon **6** charge, errand, object, sortie **7** calling, embassy, purpose **8** legation, lifework, ministry, vocation **9** objective **10** assignment
missionary 7 apostle **8** emissary **10** evangelist, revivalist **12** propagandist, proselytizer
Mississippi *capital:* 7 Jackson ***city:*** **6** Biloxi **8** Gulfport **10** Greenville ***college, university:*** **12** Jackson State **8** Millsaps ***nickname:*** **8** Magnolia (State) ***river:*** **5** Pearl **11** Mississippi ***state bird:*** **11** mockingbird ***state flower:*** **8** magnolia ***state tree:*** **8** magnolia
missive 4 memo, note **6** letter, report **7** epistle, message **8** dispatch
Miss Julie author 10 Strindberg (August)
Miss Lonelyhearts author 4 West (Nathanael)
Missouri *capital:* 13 Jefferson City ***city:*** **7** St. Louis **10** Kansas City **11** Springfield **12** Independence ***college, university:*** **10** Washington ***lake:*** **15** Lake of the Ozarks ***nickname:*** **6** Show Me (State) ***river:*** **8** Missouri **11** Mississippi ***state bird:*** **8** bluebird ***state flower:*** **8** hawthorn ***state tree:*** **7** dogwood
misstate 4 warp **5** color, twist **6** garble **7** distort, falsify
misstatement 3 fib, lie **4** tale **7** falsity, untruth **9** falsehood **13** prevarication
misstep 4 flub, goof, slip **5** boner, error, fluff, gaffe, lapse **6** slipup **7** blooper, blunder, faux pas
mist 3 dim, fog **4** blur, film, haze, murk **5** befog, brume, cloud **7** becloud, obscure
mistake 4 flub, slip **5** boner, error, fluff, folly, gaffe, lapse, snafu **6** boo-boo, bungle, howler, slipup **7** blooper, blunder, confuse, faux pas, take for **8** confound **10** inaccuracy
mistaken 5 false, wrong **6** all wet, faulty, flawed, untrue **7** invalid **8** specious **9** defective, erroneous, incorrect, misguided, unfounded **10** fallacious, fraudulent, inaccurate **11** misinformed
mister 3 sir **7** husband ***French:*** **8** Monsieur ***German:*** **4** Herr ***Italian:*** **6** Signor ***Spanish:*** **5** Señor
mistreat 5 abuse **6** ill-use, molest **7** rough up **9** brutalize, manhandle
mistress 4 doxy, moll **5** lover, woman **7** hetaira **8** dulcinea, ladylove, paramour **9** concubine, courtesan, inamorata, kept woman **10** chatelaine, girlfriend ***of Charles II:*** **4** Gwyn (Nell) **8** Villiers (Barbara) ***of Edward III:*** **7** Perrers (Alice) ***of Henry II (England):*** **8** Clifford (Rosamund) ***of Henry II (France):*** **10** de Poitiers (Diane) ***of Louis XV:*** **9** Pompadour (Madame de) ***of Ludwig I:*** **6** Montez (Lola)
mistrust 5 doubt **7** concern, dispute, dubiety, surmise, suspect **8** wariness **9** apprehend, misgiving, suspicion **10** foreboding, skepticism **11** incertitude, uncertainty **12** apprehension
mistrustful 4 wary **5** leery **6** uneasy **7** dubious, jealous **8** doubting **9** skeptical **10** suspicious
misty 3 dim **4** hazy **5** foggy, vague **6** cloudy, vapory **7** blurred, obscure, tearful, unclear **8** confused, nebulous, vaporous **10** indistinct
misunderstanding 4 rift, spat, tiff **5** mix-up **6** breach **7** dispute, quarrel, rupture **8** squabble **10** falling-out **12** disagreement
misuse 5 waste ***of a word:*** **8** malaprop **11** malapropism

Mitchell novel 15 Gone with the Wind
mite 3 bit, jot **4** atom, iota **5** grain, minim, ounce, speck **6** acarid, tittle **7** chigger, modicum, smidgen **8** molecule, particle ***family:*** **8** oribatid
miter 5 crown, joint **9** headdress
mitigate 4 ease **5** abate, allay, relax, slake **6** lessen, soften, subdue, temper **7** assuage, lighten, mollify, relieve **8** palliate, moderate, tone down **9** alleviate, extenuate, meliorate
mitigation 4 ease **6** relief **8** easement
mitosis 12 cell division, karyokinesis ***stage:*** **8** anaphase, prophase **9** metaphase, telophase
mix 4 fuse, link, lump, meld, stir **5** blend, merge, unite **6** fusion, jumble, mingle, tangle, work in **7** amalgam, combine, concoct, confuse, conjoin **8** coalesce, compound, confound **9** associate, commingle, interfuse **10** amalgamate, crossbreed **11** intermingle **12** amalgamation
mixed 6 hybrid, impure, motley, sundry, varied **7** diluted, diverse, mongrel **8** assorted, compound **9** composite, crossbred, interbred, irregular **12** multifarious **13** heterogeneous, miscellaneous
mixed bag 4 hash, olio **5** gumbo, salad **6** jumble, medley **7** mélange **8** mishmash, pastiche **9** potpourri **10** assortment, hodgepodge, hotchpotch, miscellany, salmagundi **11** gallimaufry
mixed-up 5 fazed **6** addled **7** jumbled **8** confused **9** flustered, nonplused, perplexed **10** bewildered, disjointed, distracted, incoherent, nonplussed **12** disconcerted
mixologist 6 barman **7** tapster **9** barkeeper, bartender
mixture 4 brew, hash, olio, stew **5** alloy, blend, gumbo **6** fusion, hybrid, jumble, medley **7** amalgam, farrago, mélange **8** compound, mishmash, solution **9** composite, potpourri **10** concoction, confection, miscellany, salmagundi **11** combination **12** amalgamation
mix up 5 addle **6** fuddle, jumble, muddle **7** confuse, fluster, mistake **8** befuddle, bewilder, confound **10** disarrange, discompose **11** disorganize, misidentify
mix-up 4 hash, mess, muss **5** botch, chaos, error, melee **6** muddle, tangle **7** mistake **8** shambles **9** commotion, confusion
MKS unit 3 lux, ohm **4** mole, volt, watt **5** farad, henry, hertz, joule, lumen, meter, metre, tesla, weber **6** ampere, kelvin, newton, pascal, second **7** candela, coulomb, siemens **8** kilogram
Mnemosyne 6 Memory ***daughters:*** **5** Muses ***father:*** **6** Uranus ***lover:*** **4** Zeus ***mother:*** **4** Gaea
Moabite *city:* **3** Kir ***god:*** **7** Chemosh ***king:*** **5** Eglon, Mesha
Moab's father 3 Lot
moan 4 wail, weep **5** gripe, groan, whine **6** bewail, grieve, grouse, lament **7** deplore **8** complain
mob 3 jam **4** clan, gang, herd, pack, push, ring, riot **5** crowd, crush, horde, mafia, press, swarm **6** jostle, masses, rabble, throng **8** canaille, riffraff **9** hoi polloi, multitude **11** proletariat
mobile 5 fluid **6** moving **7** migrant, movable **8** cellular, moveable, variable **9** itinerant, migratory, unsettled, versatile **10** ambulatory **11** peripatetic
mobile home 4 tent **6** camper **7** trailer **9** Airstream
mobile-phone area 4 cell
mobilize 5 drive, impel, rally, ready, rouse **6** arouse, call up, muster, prompt, propel **7** actuate, animate, marshal **8** activate, assemble, organize **9** circulate
mobster 4 capo, goon, thug **6** hit man **7** goombah, made man, mafioso **8** criminal, gangster **9** godfather, racketeer
Moby Dick 5 whale **10** white whale ***author:*** **8** Melville (Herman) ***character:*** **3** Pip **6** Daggoo, Parsee **7** Ishmael **8** Queequeg, Starbuck, Tashtego ***pursuer:*** **4** Ahab ***ship:*** **6** Pequod
moccasin 6 loafer **7** slipper **8** larrigan
mock 3 ape **4** defy, fake, gibe, jape, jeer, razz, twit **5** bogus, chaff, dummy, false, feign, mimic, phony, quasi, sneer, taunt, tease **6** deride, ersatz, parody, pseudo, send up **7** deceive, feigned, imitate, lampoon, mislead **8** ridicule, satirize, so-called, spurious **9** imitation, simulated **10** artificial **11** counterfeit
mockery 4 sham **5** farce, scorn, sport **6** japery, parody, satire **7** take-off **8** contempt, derision, raillery, ridicule, travesty **9** burlesque, imitation **10** caricature **13** laughingstock
mocking 8 derisive, sardonic, scornful **9** sarcastic
mode 3 fad, way **4** chic, rage **5** state, style, vogue **6** custom, manner, method, status, system **7** fashion **9** condition, procedure, situation, technique **10** convention, dernier cri
model 4 copy, type **5** dummy, ideal, shape **6** design, effigy, mirror, mockup, symbol **7** classic, epitome, example, imitate, mani-

kin, paragon, pattern, perfect, replica, typical **8** ensample, exemplar, flawless, mannikin, maquette, nonesuch, paradigm, standard **9** archetype, beau ideal, blueprint, classical, criterion, exemplary, miniature, nonpareil **10** apotheosis, embodiment, prototypal, touchstone **12** paradigmatic, prototypical, reproduction ***famous:*** **4** Iman, Moss (Kate) **5** Banks (Tyra), Tiegs (Cheryl) **6** Hutton (Lauren), Parker (Suzy), Twiggy **8** Brinkley (Christie), Bündchen (Gisele), Campbell (Naomi), Crawford (Cindy), Schiffer (Claudia) **9** Shrimpton (Jean) **10** MacPherson (Elle), Turlington (Christy)

moderate 3 ebb **4** bate, curb, even, fair, mild, so-so, wane **5** abate, sober **6** lessen, medium, reduce, relent, soften, steady, subdue, temper **7** average, control, ease off, equable, lighten, limited, neutral, relieve, subside, trivial **8** centrist, constant, discreet, middling, mitigate, restrain **9** alleviate, constrain, temperate **10** abstemious, controlled, reasonable, restrained **11** indifferent **12** conservative

moderation 7 control, measure **9** restraint **10** abstinence, constraint, limitation, temperance **13** temperateness

moderator 5 judge **7** arbiter **8** chairman, examiner, governor, mediator **10** peacemaker **11** chairperson

modern 3 new **5** fresh, novel **6** recent **7** current **8** neoteric, up-to-date **10** newfangled, present-day **12** contemporary

modernize 4 redo **5** renew **6** update **7** remodel **8** renovate **9** refurbish **10** rejuvenate

modest 3 coy, shy **4** meek, prim **5** plain, timid **6** decent, demure, humble, proper, seemly, simple **7** bashful, prudish **8** decorous, discreet, moderate, reserved, reticent, retiring **9** diffident **10** unassuming **11** straitlaced, unassertive **12** self-effacing **13** unpretentious

Modest Proposal author 5 Swift (Jonathan)

modesty 7 decency, reserve **8** chastity, humility, timidity **9** propriety, reticence **10** diffidence

modicum 3 bit, jot, tad **4** atom, iota, mite, whit **5** grain, minim, ounce, pinch, scrap, speck, trace **7** smidgen, soupçon **8** particle

modify 4 vary **5** adapt, alter, amend, limit, tweak **6** adjust, change, mutate, revise, rework, temper **7** qualify **8** mitigate, moderate, restrain **9** refashion

modish 4 chic **5** smart, swank **6** chichi, trendy, with-it **7** dashing, stylish **11** fashionable

Modred *father:* 6 Arthur ***mother:* 8** Margawse ***slayer, victim:* 6** Arthur

module 4 item, unit **7** element **9** component **11** constituent

modulate 4 vary **5** tweak **6** adjust, attune, temper **8** fine-tune, regulate, restrain

modus operandi 5 style **6** custom, manner, method, system **7** process, program, routine **8** approach, practice, strategy **9** procedure, technique

modus vivendi 9 way of life

mogul 4 czar, king, lord **5** baron, nabob, ruler **6** bigwig, honcho, prince, sachem, top gun, tycoon **7** kingpin, magnate **9** plutocrat, potentate

Mohammed see **Muhammad**

Mohawk chief 5 Brant (Joseph) **8** Hiawatha

Mohican chief 5 Uncas

moiety 3 cut **4** half, part **5** piece **7** element, portion, section, segment **8** division **9** component

moil 3 tug, wet **4** grub, to-do, work **5** churn, dirty, drive, grind, labor, swirl **6** bustle, clamor, drudge, hubbub, lather, seethe, strain, strive, uproar **7** ferment, travail, trouble, wrangle **8** drudgery **9** agitation, commotion, confusion **10** hurly-burly, turbulence

moist 3 wet **4** damp, dank, dewy **5** humid **6** clammy, steamy, sticky **7** dampish, maudlin, tearful, wettish

moisten 3 wet **6** dampen **8** humidify, saturate

moisture 4 damp **5** vapor **7** wetness **8** humidity **13** precipitation

mojo 3 hex **4** jinx **5** charm, magic, power, spell **6** hoodoo, whammy

molar 5 tooth **7** grinder ***neighbor:* 6** canine

molasses 7 treacle **10** blackstrap

mold 3 die **4** cast, form, sort, type **5** forge, ingot, knead, shape, stamp **6** design, fungus **7** fashion, pattern **8** template **9** construct

moldable 6 pliant, supple **7** ductile, plastic, pliable **9** adaptable, malleable

molder 3 rot **5** decay, waste **7** crumble **9** break down, decompose **11** deteriorate **12** disintegrate

molding 4 bead, gula, ogee **5** congé, ogive, talon, torus **6** reglet **7** annulet, beading, cavetto, cornice, reeding **8** cincture **9** baseboard ***compound:* 4** beak, cyma, ogie **10** serpentine ***edge:* 5** arris ***flat:* 5** splay **6** fascia, fillet, listel, regula **7** chamfer ***simple curve:* 4** roll **5** flute, ovolo, torus **6** scotia **8** astragal

Moldova *capital:* 8 Chisinau, Kishinev ***former name:* 8** Moldavia ***language:* 8** Romanian ***monetary unit:*** **3** leu ***neighbor:*** **7** Romania, Ukraine ***river:*** **8** Dniester

moldy 5 dated, fusty, musty, passé **6** bygone, old hat **7** ancient, antique, archaic, outworn **8** mildewed, outdated **9** crumbling, moth-eaten **10** antiquated **12** old-fashioned

mole 3 spy **4** pier, quay **5** jetty, nevus **6** burrow, tunnel **9** birthmark **10** breakwater

molecule 3 bit, jot **4** iota **5** minim, speck **7** modicum **8** particle

molest 3 vex **4** bait **5** abuse, annoy, harry, tease **6** badger, bother, harass, heckle, hector, pester, plague **7** disturb, torment, trouble **9** persecute

Moll Flanders author 5 Defoe (Daniel)

mollify 4 calm, ease **5** allay **6** pacify, soften, soothe, temper **7** appease, assuage, lighten, placate, relieve, sweeten **8** mitigate **9** alleviate **10** ameliorate, conciliate, propitiate

mollusk 6 chiton ***bivalve:*** **4** clam **6** cockle, mussel, oyster, teredo **7** geoduck, scallop **8** shipworm ***cephalopod:*** **5** squid **7** octopus **8** argonaut, nautilus **10** cuttlefish ***part:*** **6** mantle, radula, siphon ***tooth shell:*** **9** dentalium ***univalve:*** **4** slug **5** conch, cowry, murex, snail, whelk **6** cowrie, limpet, triton **7** abalone **10** nudibranch, periwinkle

Molly ____ 7 Maguire, Pitcher

mollycoddle 3 pet **4** baby **5** humor, spoil **6** cocker, cosset, dandle, pamper **7** cater to, indulge, milksop **8** mama's boy **11** milquetoast

Moloch's pit 6 Tophet

molt 4 cast, shed, slip **6** change, slough **7** cast off, discard, ecdysis **9** slough off

molted skins 7 exuviae

molten 6 melted **7** glowing **9** liquefied

molten rock 4 lava **5** magma

molybdenum symbol 2 Mo

moment 3 sec **4** jiff **5** flash, jiffy, point, shake, trice **6** import, minute, second **7** instant **8** juncture, occasion **9** magnitude **10** importance **11** consequence, split second **12** significance

momentary 5 brief, quick **8** fleeting, fugitive **9** ephemeral, fugacious, transient **10** evanescent, short-lived, transitory

momentous 5 grave **7** epochal, fateful, serious, weighty **9** important **10** meaningful **11** significant, substantial **12** considerable **13** consequential

momentousness 6 import, weight **9** magnitude **10** importance **11** consequence, weightiness **12** significance

momentum 5 drive **6** energy, thrust **7** impetus, impulse **10** propulsion

Momo author 4 Ende (Michael)

momus 6 carper, critic, mocker **7** caviler **8** caviller **9** detractor **11** faultfinder

Monaco *commune:* **10** Monte Carlo ***language:*** **6** French ***monetary unit:*** **4** euro ***monetary unit, former:*** **5** franc ***neighbor:*** **6** France ***prince:*** **6** Albert **7** Rainier ***princess:*** **5** Grace **8** Caroline

monad 3 one **4** atom, unit **8** zoospore **9** protozoan

Mona Lisa 10 La Gioconda ***painter:*** **7** da Vinci (Leonardo) **8** Leonardo (da Vinci)

monarch 4 czar, king, raja, tsar, tzar **5** queen, rajah, ruler **6** kaiser, prince **7** emperor, empress, majesty **9** butterfly, potentate, sovereign ***daughter:*** **7** infanta **8** princess ***heir:*** **7** dauphin **11** crown prince ***son:*** **6** prince **7** infante

monarchical 5 regal, royal **6** kingly **8** imperial, kinglike, majestic **9** sovereign

monarchy 4 rule **5** realm, reign **7** kingdom **8** kingship **9** autocracy, monocracy **11** sovereignty

monastery 5 abbey **6** friary, priory **7** convent, nunnery **8** cloister ***Buddhist:*** **8** lamasery ***Eastern Orthodox:*** **5** laura ***head:*** **5** abbot, prior

monastic 4 abbé, monk **7** ascetic, brother **8** isolated, secluded **9** reclusive **10** cloistered **11** sequestered

____ Mondrian 4 Piet

monetary 6 fiscal **9** financial, pecuniary **10** numismatic

monetary rate 7 millage

monetary unit see at individual countries

money 4 cash, coin, gelt, jack, kale, loot, pelf, swag **5** bread, chips, dough, funds, lolly, lucre, moola, rhino, scrip **6** boodle, change, dinero, do-re-mi, mammon, moolah, riches, specie, wampum, wealth **7** cabbage, capital, coinage, lettuce, needful, scratch, stipend **8** bankroll, currency, finances, treasure **9** resources **10** greenbacks **11** filthy lucre, legal tender

moneyed 4 rich **5** flush **6** loaded **7** opulent, wealthy, well-off **8** affluent, well-to-do **10** prosperous, well-heeled

money-grubber 5 miser **7** hoarder, niggard, scrooge **8** tightwad **9** skinflint **10** cheapskate **12** penny-pincher

moneymaking 6 paying **7** gainful **9** lucrative **10** profitable, well-paying, worthwhile **12** advantageous, remunerative

monger 4 hawk, sell, vend **6** broker, dealer, hawker, peddle, trader, vendor **7** higgler, packman, peddler **8** huckster

Mongol *conqueror:* **9** Tamerlane **10** Kublai Khan **11** Genghis Khan, Tamburlaine ***peo-***

ples: **4** Daur, Olöt, Urat **5** Ordos **6** Bargut, Buryat, Buzawa, Chahar, Dorbet, Torgut **7** Karchin, Khalkha, Monguor

Mongolia *capital:* **9** Ulan Bator **11** Ulaanbaatar ***conqueror:*** **6** Ögödei **11** Genghis Khan ***desert:*** **4** Gobi ***lake:*** **6** Baikal ***monetary unit:*** **6** tugrik ***mountain range:*** **5** Altai, Altay **6** Kentai **7** Hentiyn **9** Altai Shan, Altay Shan ***neighbor:*** **5** China **6** Russia ***river:*** **4** Yalu **5** Orhun **7** Selenga

mongoose **4** urva

mongrel **3** cur **4** mule, mutt **5** cross **6** hybrid **7** bastard, mixture **8** half-bred **9** crossbred, half blood, half-breed **10** crossbreed

moniker **3** tag **4** name **6** handle **8** cognomen, nickname **9** sobriquet **11** appellation, designation

monish **4** warn

monition **6** caveat **7** caution, portent, warning **11** forewarning

monitor **4** test **5** check, watch **6** screen **7** adviser, observe, oversee **8** watchdog **11** keep track of

Monitor *designer:* **8** Ericsson (John) ***opponent:*** **8** Virginia **9** Merrimack

monitory **7** warning **8** advisory **10** cautionary

monk **4** abbé **5** friar **7** brother **8** cenobite, monastic **9** anchorite ***Buddhist:*** **4** lama **5** bonze ***Hindu:*** **8** sannyasi ***Roman Catholic:*** **8** Capuchin, Salesian, Trappist **9** Carmelite, Dominican **10** Carthusian, Cistercian, Franciscan **11** Augustinian ***room:*** **4** cell ***shaven crown:*** **7** tonsure ***title:*** **3** Dom, Fra **5** Padre

monkey **3** imp **4** mess **5** gamin **6** meddle, simian, tamper, urchin **8** busybody **9** interfere, interlope ***Ceylon:*** **4** maha ***Cochin China:*** **4** douc ***New World:*** **4** mico, saki, titi **6** howler, spider, uakari, woolly **7** sapajou, tamarin **8** capuchin, marmoset, squirrel **11** douroucouli ***Old World:*** **4** mona **5** Diana, drill **6** guenon, langur, rhesus, vervet **7** colobus, hanuman, macaque **8** mandrill, mangabey **9** proboscis **10** Barbary ape

monkeyshine **3** gag **4** dido, jape, lark **5** antic, caper, prank, stunt, trick **6** frolic **10** shenanigan, tomfoolery

monocratic **8** absolute, despotic **9** arbitrary, autarchic, tyrannous **10** autocratic, tyrannical

monogram **8** initials

monograph **5** study **6** thesis **8** tractate, treatise **9** discourse **12** disquisition, dissertation

monopolize **3** hog **5** sew up **6** absorb, corner **7** control, engross **8** dominate, take over

monopoly **5** trust **6** cartel, corner **7** control **9** ownership, syndicate **10** consortium, domination **11** exclusivity

monotone **5** drone, thrum **8** sameness

monotonous **4** blah, dull **6** boring, dreary **7** droning, humdrum, one-note, uniform **8** singsong, unvaried **9** unvarying **10** pedestrian, repetitive **11** repetitious

monotony **6** tedium **7** humdrum **8** flatness, sameness **10** uniformity

monsoon **6** deluge **8** downpour **9** rainstorm **10** cloudburst

monster **3** orc **4** ogre **5** beast, freak, giant, whale **6** mutant, ogress **8** behemoth, bogeyman, colossus, giantess **9** hellhound, leviathan, manticore ***biblical:*** **5** Rehab **8** Behemoth **9** Leviathan ***female:*** **6** Gorgon, Medusa, Scylla ***fire-breathing:*** **6** dragon, Typhon **7** Chimera **8** Chimaera ***fowl-dragon:*** **10** cockatrice ***French:*** **8** Tarasque ***Hebrew:*** **5** golem ***horse-fish:*** **11** hippocampus ***hundred-armed:*** **9** Enceladus ***hundred-eyed:*** **5** Argus ***hundred-handed:*** **8** Briareus ***lion-eagle:*** **7** griffin ***nine-headed:*** **5** Hydra ***serpent-headed:*** **6** gorgon ***study of:*** **10** teratology ***three-bodied:*** **6** Geryon ***three-headed dog:*** **8** Cerberus ***two-headed dog:*** **6** Orthos ***water:*** **6** kraken ***woman-bird:*** **5** Harpy ***woman-lion:*** **6** Sphinx ***woman-serpent:*** **7** Echidna (see also **dragon, giant**)

monstrosity **5** freak **6** horror **7** eyesore, outrage, prodigy **8** atrocity, enormity **11** abomination **12** malformation

monstrous **4** huge, vast **5** awful, giant, large **7** glaring, heinous, hellish, hideous, immense, inhuman, mammoth, massive, titanic **8** aberrant, abnormal, colossal, deformed, dreadful, enormous, fiendish, freakish, gigantic, god-awful, gruesome, horrible, infamous, shocking, towering **9** atrocious, egregious, fantastic, frightful, grotesque, humongous, loathsome, malformed, unnatural **10** diabolical, flagitious, gargantuan, horrendous, impressive, monumental, outrageous, prodigious, scandalous, stupendous, tremendous

montage **4** olio **6** jumble, medley **7** mélange, mixture **9** composite, patchwork, potpourri **10** assortment, miscellany **12** conglomerate

Montagues' enemies **8** Capulets

Montaigne's forte **5** essay

Montana *capital:* **6** Helena ***city:*** **5** Butte **7** Bozeman **8** Billings, Missoula **10** Great Falls ***lake:*** **8** Flathead ***motto:*** **9** Oro y plata ***mountain:*** **7** Granite (Peak) ***nickname:*** **8** Treasure (State) ***park:*** **7** Glacier ***river:*** **8** Missouri **11** Yellowstone ***state bird:*** **10** meadowlark ***state flower:*** **10** bitterroot ***state tree:*** **13** ponderosa pine

Montenegro *capital:* **7** Cetinje **9** Podgorica ***language:*** **7** Serbian ***monetary unit:*** **4** euro *park:* 8 Durmitor *river:* 3 Lim 4 Piva, Tara, Zita 6 Morača *sea:* 8 Adriatic

Monteverdi opera 5 Orfeo 7 Arianna

Montezuma *capital:* 12 Tenochtitlán *conqueror:* 6 Cortés, Cortéz (Hernán, Hernando) *people:* 6 Aztecs *revenge:* 8 diarrhea

month *Hindu:* 3 Pus 4 Asin, Jeth, Magh 5 Aghan, Chait, Sawan 6 Asargh, Bhadon, Kartik, Phagun 7 Baisakh *Jewish:* 2 Ab 4 Adar, Elul, Iyar 5 Nisan, Sivan, Tebet 6 Kislev, Shebat, Tammuz, Tishri 7 Heshvan *Muslim:* 4 Rabi 5 Rajab, Safar 6 Jumada, Sha'ban 7 Ramadan, Shawwal 8 Muharram 9 Dhu'l-Hijja, Dhu'l-Qa'dah

Montmartre church 10 Sacré Coeur

Montserrat *capital:* 8 Plymouth *discoverer:* 8 Columbus (Christopher) *location:* 10 West Indies *territory of:* 7 Britain *volcano:* 9 Soufrière

monument 5 cairn, stela, stupa 7 memento, tribute 8 archives, cenotaph, document, memorial 9 footstone, headstone, tombstone 10 gravestone 11 grave marker, testimonial *prehistoric:* 6 dolmen, menhir 8 cromlech, megalith

monumental 4 epic, huge, vast 6 mighty, mortal 7 awesome, immense, mammoth, massive 8 enormous, gigantic, historic, majestic, towering 9 monstrous 10 prodigious, stupendous, tremendous 11 mountainous, outstanding 12 overwhelming

mooch 3 bat, beg, bum 4 grub, roam, rove 5 amble, cadge, drift, range, slink, sneak, steal, stray 6 ramble, sponge, wander 7 maunder, meander, saunter 8 freeload, scrounge 9 panhandle

mooching 7 beggary 9 mendicity 10 mendicancy

mood 3 air 4 aura, feel, tone, whim 5 fancy, humor 6 spirit, temper, vagary 7 caprice, emotion, feeling, mind-set 8 ambiance, ambience 9 character, semblance 10 atmosphere 11 disposition, personality, temperament

moody 4 glum 5 mopey 6 fickle, gloomy 7 pensive 8 unstable 9 mercurial, whimsical 10 capricious, changeable, depressive, inconstant, melancholy 13 temperamental

moola 4 cash, coin, pelf, swag 5 bread, dough, money 6 dinero, specie, wampum 7 cabbage, scratch 9 long green

moon 4 gape, mope 5 dream 6 dawdle 8 languish 9 satellite *dark area:* 4 mare 5 maria (plural) 7 farside *god:* 3 Sin 5 Nanna 6 Meztli *goddess:* 4 Luna 5 Diana, Tanit 6 Hecate, Hekate, Selena, Selene, Tanith 7 Artemis, Astarte *period:* 5 phase *valley:* 4 rill *vehicle:* 3 LEM (see also **satellite**)

Moon and Sixpence author 7 Maugham (W. Somerset)

mooncalf 4 dolt, fool 5 dunce, ninny 7 jackass, tomfool 9 simpleton

moonfish 4 opah 5 platy

Moon River composer 7 Mancini (Henry)

moonshine 4 bosh, jake 5 hokum 6 bunkum, humbug 7 bootleg, eyewash, hogwash 8 homebrew, malarkey, nonsense, tommyrot 9 poppycock 10 balderdash, bathtub gin, contraband, flapdoodle 11 mountain dew 12 blatherskite

Moonstone, The *author:* 7 Collins (Wilkie) *detective:* 4 Cuff

moonstruck 4 daft, nuts 5 batty, corny, flaky, kooky, mushy, nutty, sappy, wacko, wacky 6 crazed, cuckoo, fruity, insane, screwy 7 berserk, bonkers, lunatic, maudlin, touched 8 romantic 9 nostalgic, schmaltzy 10 lovey-dovey, saccharine, unbalanced 11 sentimental

moor 3 bog, fen 4 dock, fell 5 berth, catch, tie up 6 anchor, Berber, fasten, Muslim, secure, tether 7 peat bog 8 make fast, Moroccan *fictional:* 7 Othello

moose 6 cervid *female:* 3 cow *male:* 4 bull *relative:* 3 elk 4 deer 6 wapiti 7 caribou 8 reindeer

moot 5 argue, plead 6 broach, debate 7 agitate, bring up, canvass, discuss, dispute, dubious, suggest, suspect 8 abstract, academic, arguable, disputed, doubtful 9 debatable, introduce, thrash out, uncertain, unsettled, ventilate 10 disputable, unresolved 11 problematic 12 questionable 13 controversial

mop 4 swab, wipe

mope 4 fret, idle, moon, pine, pout, sigh, stew, sulk 5 brood, drift, mosey 6 dawdle, linger 7 maunder, meander, saunter 8 languish

mopes 4 funk 5 blues, dumps, ennui, slump 7 dismals, malaise, sadness 8 dolefuls 10 depression, melancholy 11 unhappiness

mopey 3 low 4 blue, down, glum 6 broody, droopy, morose 7 doleful 8 cast down, dejected, downcast 9 depressed 10 dispirited, melancholy, spiritless

moppet 3 kid, tot 4 tike, tyke 5 chick, child 7 toddler 8 juvenile 9 youngster

mop up 4 beat, drub, dust, lick, whip 6 absorb, garner, gather 7 shellac, trounce 8 complete, lambaste 9 overwhelm

moral 3 saw 4 good, just, pure, rule 5 adage, axiom, gnome, maxim, noble, right 6 chaste, decent, dictum, honest, lesson, proper, saying, truism **7** epigram, ethical, preachy, precept, proverb, upright, virtual **8** aphorism, apothegm, didactic, elevated, sermonic, virtuous **9** honorable, righteous **10** high-minded, principled, scrupulous, upstanding **11** right-minded **13** conscientious

morale 4 mood **5** heart **6** esprit, mettle, spirit, temper **7** resolve **10** confidence **13** esprit de corps

moralistic 5 noble, pious **7** canting, ethical **8** didactic, virtuous **9** righteous **10** principled **11** pharisaical, right-minded **13** sanctimonious

morality 5 ethic, honor, mores **6** purity, virtue **7** decency, probity **8** goodness **9** integrity, rectitude, rightness **11** saintliness, uprightness **13** righteousness

moralize 6 preach **7** lecture **9** preachify, sermonize **11** pontificate

morals 5 mores **6** ethics, ideals **8** scruples **9** integrity, standards **10** principles

morass 3 bog, fen, web **4** knot, maze, mesh, mire, quag, trap **5** marsh, skein, snarl, swamp **6** jungle, muddle, tangle **8** quagmire **9** imbroglio

moratorium 3 ban **5** delay **8** interval **10** suspension

moray 3 eel

morbid 4 dark, sick **5** moody **6** gloomy, grisly, morose, sickly, sullen **7** unsound **8** diseased, gruesome **9** saturnine, unhealthy **11** melancholic, unwholesome **12** pathological

mordancy 7 acidity **8** acerbity, acridity, acrimony, asperity, pungency **9** harshness, sharpness **10** causticity, trenchancy **11** astringency

mordant 4 acid, keen **5** acerb, acrid, salty, sharp **6** biting **7** acerbic, burning, caustic, cutting, pungent **8** incisive, sardonic, scathing **9** sarcastic, trenchant

Mordecai *cousin:* 6 Esther ***father:* 4** Jair ***mother:* 6** Esther

more 3 new, too **4** also, else, plus **5** added, again, along, extra, fresh, older, other, spare **6** as well, better, nearer, withal **7** another, besides, farther, further, greater **8** likewise, moreover **9** increased **10** additional

More book 6 Utopia

more or less 5 about, circa **7** roughly **13** approximately

moreover 3 and, too **4** also **6** as well, withal **7** besides, further **8** likewise **10** in addition **11** furthermore **12** additionally

mores 6 ethics, habits, values **7** beliefs, customs, manners **8** folkways **9** amenities, etiquette **10** civilities **11** proprieties

Morgan le Fay 9 sorceress ***brother:* 6** Arthur (King)

moribund 5 dying **6** ebbing, fading **7** dormant, outworn **8** decaying, expiring, inactive **9** declining **11** obsolescent **13** deteriorating

Mormon Church *administrative unit:* 4 ward **5** stake ***founder:* 5** Smith (Joseph) ***leader:* 5** Young (Brigham) ***priest:* 5** elder

Mormon State 4 Utah

morning 4 dawn **5** sunup **6** aurora **7** dawning, sunrise **8** cockcrow, daybreak, daylight, forenoon ***moisture:* 3** dew **8** dewdrops ***song:* 6** aubade

Morocco *capital:* 5 Rabat ***city:* 3** Fès **6** Agadir, Meknès **7** Tangier **9** Marrakech, Marrakesh **10** Casablanca ***coast:* 7** Barbary ***language:* 6** Arabic, Berber ***monetary unit:* 6** dirham ***mountain, range:*3** Rif **5** Atlas **7** Toubkal ***neighbor:* 5** Spain **7** Algeria **13** Western Sahara ***sea:* 13** Mediterranean

moron 4 dodo, dolt, dope, fool **5** dummy, dunce, idiot **6** cretin, dimwit, stupid **7** dullard, half-wit **8** dumbbell, imbecile, numskull **9** ignoramus, lamebrain, numbskull, simpleton

moronic 4 dull, dumb **6** simple, stupid **8** backward, retarded **9** brainless, dim-witted, imbecilic **10** half-witted, slow-witted **12** feebleminded, simpleminded

morose 4 dour, glum, sour **5** moody, sulky **6** cranky, crusty, gloomy, morbid, sullen **7** crabbed, unhappy **9** depressed, saturnine **10** depressive, ill-humored, melancholy

morph 6 change, mutate **7** convert **9** transform, transmute **12** metamorphose, transmogrify

Morpheus *father:* 6 Hypnos ***god of:* 5** sleep

Morrison novel 4 Jazz, Love, Sula **7** Beloved **9** Bluest Eye (The) **13** Song of Solomon

Morse code *dash:* 3 dah ***dot:* 3** dit

morsel 3 bit, ort **4** bite **5** crumb, goody, piece, scrap, snack, taste, treat **6** dainty, nibble, tidbit **7** soupçon **8** delicacy, fragment, kickshaw, mouthful

mortal 3 man **5** awful, being, fatal, frail, human, party **6** deadly, lethal, person **7** deathly, earthly, extreme, fleshly, tedious, worldly **8** creature, ruthless, temporal **9** merciless, personage **10** implacable, individual, perishable **11** conceivable

mortality 5 flesh **7** mankind **8** fatality, humanity **9** death rate, humankind, lethality **10** deadliness

mortar 5 grout **6** binder, cannon, cement, vessel **7** plaster, sealant **8** howitzer, ordnance

Morte d'Arthur author 6 Malory (Thomas)

mortgage 4 hock, lien, pawn **6** pledge **10** obligation
mortician 8 embalmer **10** undertaker
mortified 6 shamed **7** ascetic, ashamed, austere **8** red-faced **9** chagrined **10** humiliated, shamefaced **11** embarrassed
mortify 5 abash, shame **6** deaden, dismay **7** chagrin, perturb **8** disgrace **9** discomfit, embarrass, humiliate
mortuary 8 funereal **10** sepulchral **11** funeral home
mosaic 5 inlay **7** chimera **8** terrazzo **9** composite, patchwork **12** tessellation ***piece:* 6** smalto **7** tessera **8** tesserae (plural)
Moscow *cathedral:* 8 St. Basil's **11** Saint Basil's ***citadel:* 7** Kremlin ***resident:* 9** Muscovite
Moses *brother:* 5 Aaron ***brother-in-law:* 5** Hobab ***deathplace:* 4** Nebo ***father-in-law:* 6** Jethro ***sister:* 6** Miriam ***son:* 7** Eliezer, Gershom ***spy:* 5** Caleb ***successor:* 6** Joshua ***wife:* 8** Zipporah
mosey 4 mope **5** amble, drift **6** dawdle, linger, ramble, stroll, wander **7** maunder, meander, saunter
mosh 4 slam **9** slam-dance
Moslem see **Muslim**
mosque 6 masjid ***niche:* 6** mihrab ***prayer caller:* 7** muezzin ***turret:* 7** minaret
mosquito 5 culex **7** skeeter ***eater:* 3** bat **4** bird, frog **9** dragonfly ***genus:* 5** Aëdes, Culex **9** Anopheles
moss 9 bryophyte ***kind:* 4** peat **8** sphagnum ***part:* 4** seta **7** capsule, rhizoid ***study of:* 8** bryology
mossback 4 fogy **6** fossil **10** fuddy-duddy **11** reactionary **12** antediluvian, conservative **13** stick-in-the-mud
mostly 6 mainly **7** chiefly, largely, overall, usually **9** generally, primarily **11** principally **13** predominantly
mote 3 bit, dot, jot **4** iota, whit **5** grain, point, speck, trace **8** flyspeck, particle
moth *immature:* 5 larva **6** larvae (plural) **11** caterpillar ***kind:* 4** luna **7** codling, tussock **8** Cecropia, silkworm **9** browntail ***order:* 11** Lepidoptera
moth-eaten 4 worn **5** dated, dingy, faded, mangy, moldy, musty, passé, ratty, seedy **6** bygone, old hat, patchy, shabby **7** antique, archaic, raggedy, run-down, unkempt **8** decrepit, outdated, outmoded, tattered, timeworn **10** antiquated, down-at-heel, threadbare **11** dilapidated
mother 2 ma **3** dam, mom **4** mama, root **5** fount, mammy, mater, momma, mommy, mummy, nurse **6** matrix, origin, source **7** care for, nurture **9** prototype, rootstock **10** provenance, wellspring ***combining form:* 4** matr **5** matri, matro ***French:* 4** mère ***German:* 6** Mutter ***Italian:* 5** madre ***Portuguese:* 3** mãe ***Spanish:* 5** madre
mother country 8 homeland **10** fatherland
Mother Courage author 6 Brecht (Bertolt)
motherly 8 maternal **9** nurturing **10** protective
mother-of-pearl 5 nacre
Mother of Presidents 8 Virginia
Mother of the Gods 3 Ops **4** Rhea **6** Cybele
motif 4 idea, text **5** point, theme, topic **6** design, device, figure, matter **7** pattern, subject **8** idée fixe **13** subject matter
motion 4 stir, sway **6** signal **7** gesture **8** movement, proposal, stirring **9** agitation
motionless 5 fixed, inert, still **6** frozen, static **7** stalled **8** becalmed, immobile, stagnant, unmoving **9** immovable, steadfast **10** stationary, stock-still
motion picture see **movie**
motivate 4 fire, goad, move, spur **5** impel, pique, rouse **6** arouse, excite, incite, induce, prompt **7** actuate, inspire, provoke, quicken, trigger **8** inspirit, persuade **9** galvanize, influence, stimulate
motivation 4 spur **5** drive **7** impetus, impulse **8** ambition, catalyst, stimulus **9** impulsion, incentive, stimulant **10** incitation, incitement **11** inspiration, instigation, provocation
motive 3 aim, end **4** spur **5** cause, point, theme, topic **6** design, device, figure, intent, matter, object, reason, spring **7** impulse, pattern, purpose, subject **8** stimulus **9** incentive, intention, rationale **10** incitement, inducement **11** inspiration
motley 4 olio, stew **5** mixed, salad **6** jumble, medley, varied **7** dappled, diverse, piebald **8** assorted, pastiche **9** disparate, multihued **10** assortment, hodgepodge, hotchpotch, miscellany, multicolor, salmagundi, variegated **11** gallimaufry, varicolored **12** conglomerate, multicolored, multifarious, parti-colored **13** heterogeneous, miscellaneous, polychromatic
motor 3 car **4** auto, ride **5** buggy, drive **6** cruise, engine **7** machine **10** automobile
motorboat 6 launch **7** cruiser, inboard **8** outboard, runabout **12** cabin cruiser
motorcycle 7 chopper **8** minibike **9** trail bike ***adjunct:* 7** sidecar
Motown 7 Detroit ***founder:* 5** Gordy (Berry) ***group:* 8** Four Tops, Miracles, Supremes **9** Vandellas **11** Temptations
mottle 4 spot **5** fleck **6** blotch, dapple, marble **7** spatter, speckle, stipple, splotch

mottled **5** tabby **7** blotchy, dappled, flecked, spotted **8** blotched, brindled, speckled **9** checkered **10** variegated

motto **3** cry **5** adage, axiom, maxim **6** byword, saying, slogan, war cry **7** precept, proverb **8** aphorism **9** battle cry, catchword, watchword **10** shibboleth **11** catchphrase

moue **3** mow, mug **4** face, pout **7** grimace

mound **4** bank, berm, cock, heap, hill, hump, mass, pile **5** cairn, drift, knoll, shock, stack **6** barrow, tumuli (plural) **7** bulwark, hillock, rampart, tumulus **9** elevation **10** embankment ***Buddhist:*** **5** stupa ***burial, Eastern Europe:*** **6** kurgan ***of detritus:*** **4** kame ***of sand:*** **4** dune ***of stones:*** **5** cairn

mount **3** alp, wax **4** lift, peak, rise, show, soar **5** arise, build, climb, frame, horse, put on, raise, rouse, scale, set up, stage, steed, swell **6** ascend, aspire, deepen, expand, launch, uprear **7** advance, augment, display, enhance, enlarge, install, magnify, produce, support, upsurge **8** bestride, escalade, escalate, heighten, increase, multiply, redouble **9** aggravate, intensify **10** promontory

mountain **3** alp, lot **4** bank, crag, dome, heap, hill, hulk, lump, mass, mesa, much, peak, pile, slew **5** bluff, butte, drift, mound, shock, stack **6** height, massif ***Adirondack:*** **9** Whiteface ***Africa's highest:*** **4** Kibo ***Alaska:*** **4** Bona **6** Denali **7** Foraker, Sanford **8** McKinley, Wrangell ***Alaska-Canada:*** **10** Saint Elias ***Alberta:*** **6** Castle **10** Eisenhower ***Alps:*** **4** Rosa (Monte) **5** Blanc, Eiger **8** Jungfrau **10** Matterhorn ***Andes:*** **4** Ruiz **5** Torrá ***Angola:*** **4** Moco ***Antarctica:*** **4** Mohl **6** Vinson (Massif) **7** Gardner **9** Elizabeth ***Apennines:*** **5** Amaro ***Appalachians:*** **8** Mitchell **10** Kittatinny **10** Washington **13** Clingmans Dome ***Argentina:*** **4** Azul **5** Negra, Payún **9** Aconcagua ***Asia Minor:*** **3** Ida ***Australia:*** **4** Ziel **5** Bruce **6** Cradle **9** Kosciusko ***Bavaria:*** **5** Arber ***Berkshires:*** **8** Greylock ***biblical:*** **5** Horeb, Sinai, Tabor **6** Ararat, Carmel, Gilboa, Gilead, Hermon, Moriah, Olivet, Pisgah **7** Lebanon **8** Har Tavor ***Black Hills:*** **6** Harney (Peak) **8** Rushmore ***Bolivia:*** **5** Cuzco, Tahua, Ubina **6** Sajama, Sorata **8** Illimani ***Borneo:*** **4** Raja **8** Kinabalu, Kinabulu ***California:*** **5** Guyot **6** Shasta, Sonora **7** Palomar, Whitney **8** Half Dome, Tuolumne **9** Excelsior **10** Buena Vista, Stanislaus ***Canada:*** **5** Keele, Logan ***Canaries:*** **5** Telde **8** Tenerife ***Carpathian:*** **4** Rysy ***Cascades:*** **7** Rainier ***Catskill:*** **6** Pisgah ***Caucasus:*** **5** Ushba **6** Elbrus ***Chile:*** **4** Mayo, Pili **5** Paine, Pular ***China:*** **4** Emei, Song ***Colombia:*** **4** Tama **5** Neiva ***Colorado:*** **3** Ute **5** Eolus, Pikes (Peak) **9** Purgatory (Peak) ***Costa Rica:*** **6** Blanco **14** Chirripó Grande ***Cuba:*** **8** Turquino ***Cyprus:*** **7** Olympus, Troodos ***depression:*** **3** col ***Dominican Republic:*** **6** Duarte **8** Trujillo ***Ecuador:*** **10** Chimborazo ***Egypt:*** **4** Musa **5** Sinai ***England:*** **11** Scafell Pike ***Ethiopia:*** **4** Guna **5** Holla ***Fiji:*** **8** Victoria **9** Tomaniivi ***foot:*** **8** piedmont ***France:*** **5** Blanc (Mont), Pilat ***French Guiana:*** **5** Amana ***Gabon:*** **8** Iboundji ***Georgia:*** **8** Springer **10** Oglethorpe ***Germany:*** **7** Zollern **9** Zugspitze **11** Fichtelberg ***Glacier National Park:*** **8** Kootenal ***Greece:*** **3** Ida **4** Ossa **5** Athos, Levka **6** Pelion **7** Helicon, Olympus **9** Parnassus, Psiloriti **10** Pendelikon, Pentelicus ***Greenland:*** **9** Gunnbjorn ***Himalayas:*** **3** Api **6** Khamet, Lhotse **7** Everest **9** Annapurna **10** Gasherbrum ***Honshu:*** **4** Yari **10** Yarigatake ***Idaho:*** **11** Pend Oreille ***India:*** **5** Japvo ***Indonesia:*** **4** Lawu **5** Kwoka, Lawoe, Raung **6** Raoeng, Semeru **7** Kerinci ***Iran:*** **8** Damavand ***Israel:*** **5** Meron **6** Carmel ***Italy:*** **4** Etna **8** Vesuvius ***Ivory Coast:*** **5** Nimba ***Japan:*** **4** Fuji, Sobo **5** Iwate, Oyama **7** Fujisan, Sobozan **8** Fujiyama ***Java:*** **5** Liman **6** Slamet ***Jordan:*** **3** Hor **5** Hārūn **6** Gilead ***Karakoram Range:*** **7** Dapsang **10** Masherbrum **12** Godwin Austen ***Maine:*** **8** Katahdin **10** Saddleback ***Malaysia:*** **5** Ophir, Tahan **6** Ledang ***Mediterranean entrance:*** **5** Calpe **9** Gibraltar ***Mexico:*** **7** Orizaba (Pico de) ***Montana:*** **8** Gallatin ***Nevada:*** **3** Ely ***Newfoundland:*** **9** Gros Morne ***New Hampshire:*** **9** Monadnock ***New York:*** **4** Bear **5** Marcy ***New Zealand:*** **3** Una **4** Cook **7** Aorangi **8** Aspiring ***North America's highest:*** **6** Denali **8** McKinley ***North Carolina:*** **8** Mitchell ***Oahu:*** **5** Kaala ***Oman:*** **4** Sham ***Oregon:*** **4** Hood ***Pakistan:*** **9** Tirich Mir ***Papua New Guinea:*** **7** Wilhelm **8** Victoria ***peak:*** **3** top **4** acme, apex, roof **5** crest, crown **6** summit, vertex, zenith **8** pinnacle ***Pennine Alps:*** **4** Rosa (Monte) **10** Matterhorn, Mont Cervin ***Philippines:*** **3** Apo, Iba **4** High, Labo **5** Silay ***Pyrenees:*** **11** de Vignemale ***ridge:*** **4** spur **5** arête, crest **7** sawbuck ***Romania:*** **11** Moldoveanul ***Russia's highest:*** **6** Elbrus ***Scotland:*** **8** Ben Nevis ***Sicily:*** **4** Etna ***South America:*** **7** Roraima **9** Aconcagua ***South Dakota:*** **6** Custer (Peak) ***Spain:*** **5** Yelmo **8** Mulhacén **11** Pico de Aneto ***Switzerland:*** **3** Dom **4** Dôle, Rosa (Monte), Tödi **5** Eiger, Mönch **6** La Dôle, Rusein **7** Pilatus **8** Jungfrau **10** Matterhorn ***Syria:*** **4** Druz **5** Duruz ***Tanzania:*** **11** Kilimanjaro ***Tasmania:*** **4** Ossa ***Tennessee:*** **13** Clingmans Dome ***Togo:*** **4**

Agou ***Turkey:*** **3** Ida ***Utah:*** **5** Kings ***Vermont:*** **8** Ascutney, Haystack, Stratton **9** Mansfield ***Vietnam:*** **8** Ngoo Linh ***Virginia:*** **6** Rogers ***Washington:*** **7** Olympus, Rainier **11** Saint Helens ***Western Hemisphere's highest:*** **9** Aconcagua ***White Mts.:*** **10** Washington ***world's highest:*** **7** Everest ***Wyoming:*** **3** Elk **5** Cloud **7** Gannett (Peak) **10** Grand Teton ***Yukon:*** **4** King **5** Logan

mountain climbing *equipment:* **2** ax **3** axe, nut **5** piton **7** crampon **9** carabiner ***maneuver:*** **6** rappel **10** rappelling

mountain dew see **moonshine**

mountain formation **7** orogeny **10** orogenesis

mountainous **4** huge, vast **6** alpine, mighty **7** immense, mammoth, massive **8** enormous, gigantic, towering **10** monumental, prodigious

mountain pass **3** col, gap ***Afghanistan-Pakistan:*** **6** Khyber ***Alps:*** **5** Gries ***California:*** **4** Muir **6** Sonora ***China-Myanmar:*** **5** Namni ***Colorado:*** **3** Ute **5** Mosca, Muddy, Music, Raton ***Europe:*** **8** Moravian ***Greece:*** **5** Rupel ***Hindu Kush Mts.:*** **5** Dorah, Durah ***Pakistan:*** **5** Bolan, Gomal, Gumal ***Sierra Nevada:*** **4** Mono ***Switzerland:*** **5** Furka, Gemmi **7** Grimsel **8** Lötschen ***Tunisia:*** **4** Faïd ***Ukrainian:*** **5** Uzhok ***Wyoming:*** **5** Union

mountain range ***Asia:*** **5** Altai, Altay **8** Himalaya, Tien Shan **9** Altai Shan, Altay Shan, Himalayan, Himalayas, Hindu Kush ***Australia:*** **8** Flinders ***Europe:*** **4** Alps **10** Carpathian ***Germany:*** **4** Harz **5** Hartz ***Greece:*** **4** Oeta ***India:*** **5** Ghats ***Iran:*** **6** Zagros ***Italy:*** **9** Apennines, Dolomites ***Mexico:*** **11** Sierra Madre ***North Africa:*** **5** Atlas ***North America:*** **5** Rocky **7** Rockies **11** Appalachian ***Russia:*** **4** Ural ***Scotland:*** **9** Grampians ***Sinai:*** **9** Gebel Musa ***Slovakia:*** **5** Tatra, Tatry **9** High Tatra ***South America:*** **5** Andes ***Spain:*** **8** Pyrenees ***Turkey:*** **3** Ida **6** Taurus **7** Kazdagi ***United States:*** **5** Rocky, White **6** Brooks **7** Cascade, Olympic, Rockies, Sawatch, Wasatch **8** Absaroka, Aleutian, Catskill, Wrangell **9** Blue Ridge, Wind River **10** Adirondack, Bitterroot, Black Hills, Clearwater, Grand Teton ***Zimbabwe:*** **6** Matopo (Hills) **7** Matoppo (Hills)

Mountain State **7** Montana **12** West Virginia

mountebank **5** quack **6** con man **8** swindler **9** charlatan **11** flimflammer, quacksalver **13** confidence man

Mount St. Helens **7** volcano

mourn **3** rue **6** bemoan, bewail, grieve, lament, sorrow **7** deplore, protest

mournful **3** sad **6** dismal, gloomy, rueful, triste, woeful **7** doleful, forlorn, unhappy **8** dejected, desolate, dolorous, funereal, grievous, wretched **9** dirgelike, plaintive **10** depressing, despondent, dispirited, lugubrious, melancholy **11** melancholic **12** heavy-hearted

mournfulness **5** blues, dumps, gloom **7** dismals, sadness **9** dejection **10** blue devils, depression, melancholy

mourning **5** grief **7** keening, remorse, wailing, weeping **8** grieving **9** lamenting, morbidity, sorrowing, ululation **10** heartbreak **11** bereavement, lamentation

Mourning Becomes Electra author **6** O'Neill (Eugene)

mourning period, Jewish **5** shiva **6** shivah

mourning symbol **7** armband

mouse **6** rodent, shiner **8** black eye ***meadow:*** **4** vole

mousy **3** shy **4** drab, dull **5** plain, quiet, timid **7** bashful **8** retiring, timorous **9** colorless, diffident, shrinking **11** unassertive **12** self-effacing

mouth **3** gob, maw **4** trap **5** chops **6** kisser **8** entrance **10** embouchure

mouthlike opening **5** stoma **7** stomata (plural)

mouthpiece **5** organ **6** puppet **7** speaker **8** front man **9** spokesman **10** figurehead **11** spokeswoman **12** spokesperson

mouthwatering **5** sapid, tasty, yummy **6** savory, toothy **9** delicious, palatable, succulent, toothsome **10** appetizing, delectable **11** good-tasting

mouthy **4** glib **5** gabby, talky, windy **7** verbose, voluble **8** effusive **9** bombastic, garrulous, talkative

movable **5** loose **6** mobile, motile, roving **8** portable **10** changeable

movables **5** goods **7** effects **8** chattels **10** belongings **11** furnishings

move **4** relo **5** budge, leave, march, shift, start, touch **6** affect, depart, incite, induce **7** advance, conduct, inspire, migrate, proceed, propose, request **8** dislodge, displace, motivate, persuade, progress, relocate, resettle, transfer, withdraw **9** influence, instigate, stimulate, transport **10** relocation

movement **4** flow, stir **5** tempo, trend **6** action, motion **7** crusade **8** activity, campaign, dynamism, maneuver, progress, stirring, tendency, velocity **9** migration ***music:*** **4** moto ***reflex:*** **5** taxis ***stimulated:*** **7** kinesis

movie **4** cine, film, show **5** flick **6** cinema, talkie **7** picture **9** photoplay **11** picture show **13** motion picture **7** western ***genre:*** **3** war **4** cult, epic **5** adult, anime, crime, oater **6** action, comedy, cowboy, family, horror, silent

7 cartoon, fantasy, Western **9** adventure, animation **11** documentary, martial arts **12** mockumentary ***short:*** **4** clip **8** newsreel

movie director *American:* **3** Lee (Spike), Ray (Nicholas) **4** Coen (Joel), Ford (John), Hill (George Roy), Mann (Anthony), Penn (Arthur), Ritt (Martin), Ross (Herbert), Sirk (Douglas), Wise (Robert) **5** Allen (Woody), Ashby (Hal), Brown (Clarence), Capra (Frank), Cukor (George), Demme (Jonathan), Donen (Stanley), Fosse (Bob), Hawks (Howard), Ivory (James), Jonze (Spike), Kazan (Elia), LeRoy (Mervyn), Logan (Joshua), Lucas (George), Lumet (Sidney), Lynch (David), Moore (Michael), Roach (Hal), Stone (Oliver), Vidor (King), Walsh (Raoul), Whale (James), Wyler (William), Zwick (Ed) **6** Altman (Robert), Beatty (Warren), Benton (Robert), Brooks (Richard), Burton (Tim), Cimino (Michael), Corman (Roger), Curtiz (Michael), Fuller (Samuel), Gibson (Mel), Hanson (Curtis), Howard (Ron), Huston (John), Kramer (Stanley), Malick (Terrence), Pakula (Alan), Parker (Alan), Seaton (George), Waters (John), Welles (Orson), Wilder (Billy) **7** Borzage (Frank), Cameron (James), Chaplin (Charlie), Coppola (Francis Ford, Sofia), Costner (Kevin), De Mille (Cecil B.), De Palma (Brian), Fleming (Victor), Gilliam (Terry), Jewison (Norman), Kubrick (Stanley), McCarey (Leo), Nichols (Mike), Pollack (Sydney), Redford (Robert), Siodmak (Robert), Stevens (George), Sturges (Preston), Van Sant (Gus), Wellman (William) **8** Avildsen (John), Eastwood (Clint), Flaherty (Robert), Friedkin (William), Griffith (David Wark), Grosbard (Ulu), Jarmusch (Jim), Levinson (Barry), Lubitsch (Ernst), Marshall (Penny), Minnelli (Vincente), Mulligan (Robert), Scorsese (Martin), Zemeckis (Robert) **9** Carpenter (John), Hitchcock (Alfred), Milestone (Lewis), Peckinpah (Sam), Preminger (Otto), Spielberg (Steven), Sternberg (Josef von), Streisand (Barbra), Tarantino (Quentin), Zinnemann (Fred) **10** Cassavetes (John), Heckerling (Amy), Mankiewicz (Joseph), Soderbergh (Steven) **11** Bogdanovich (Peter) **13** Frankenheimer (John) ***Australian:*** **4** Weir (Peter) **6** Noonan (Chris) **9** Armstrong (Gillian), Beresford (Bruce) ***Austrian:*** **4** Lang (Fritz) **8** Stroheim (Erich von) **9** Sternberg (Josef von) ***British:*** **4** Lean (David), Reed (Carol) **5** Leigh (Mike), Loach (Ken), Losey (Joseph), Reisz (Karel), Scott (Ridley) **6** Figgis (Mike), Frears (Stephen), Jordan (Neil), Newell (Mike), Parker (Alan), Powell (Michael) **7** Boorman (John), Branagh (Kenneth), Forsyth (Bill) **8** Anderson (Lindsay) **9** Hitchcock (Alfred) **10** Richardson (Tony) **11** Schlesinger (John) ***Chinese:*** **3** Lee (Ang) **4** Chen (Kaige) **5** Zhang (Yimou) ***French:*** **4** Demy (Jacques), Tati (Jacques), Vigo (Jean) **5** Malle (Louis) **6** Godard (Jean-Luc), Ophüls (Marcel), Renoir (Jean), Rohmer (Eric) **7** Bresson (Robert), Chabrol (Claude), Cocteau (Jean), Resnais (Alain), Rivette (Jacques) **8** Truffaut (François) ***German:*** **6** Herzog (Werner), Ophüls (Max) **7** Wenders (Wim) **8** Petersen (Wolfgang) **10** Fassbinder (Rainer Werner) **11** Riefenstahl (Leni), Schlöndorff (Volker) ***Italian:*** **5** Leone (Sergio) **6** De Sica (Vittorio) **7** Fellini (Federico) **8** Pasolini (Pier Paolo), Visconti (Luchino) **9** Antonioni (Michelangelo) **10** Bertolucci (Bernardo), Rossellini (Roberto), Wertmüller (Lina), Zeffirelli (Franco) ***Japanese:*** **3** Ozu (Yasujiru) **5** Itami (Juzo) **8** Kurosawa (Akira), Miyazaki (Hayao) **9** Mizoguchi (Kenji) ***Mexican:*** **6** Cuarón (Alfonso) ***New Zealand:*** **7** Campion (Jane) ***Polish*** **5** Wajda (Ardrzej) **7** Holland (Agnieszka) **8** Polanski (Roman) ***Russian:*** **9** Tarkovsky (Andrei) **10** Eisenstein (Sergei) ***Spanish:*** **6** Buñuel (Luis) **9** Almodóvar (Pedro) ***Swedish:*** **7** Bergman (Ingmar) **10** Zetterling (Mai)

movie producer *American:* **3** Fox (William) **4** Cohn (Jack) **5** Lasky (Jesse), Mayer (Louis B.), Zukor (Adolph) **6** Warner (Jack L.), Zanuck (Darryl, Richard) **7** Goldwyn (Samuel), Laemmle (Carl) **8** Selznick (David O.) **9** Weinstein (Bob, Harvey) ***Austrian:*** **9** Reinhardt (Max)

moving **5** astir **6** mobile **7** emotive, rousing **8** arousing, exciting, gripping, pathetic, poignant, stirring, touching **9** affecting, emotional, inspiring, transient **11** stimulating

moving stairs **9** escalator

mow **3** cut **4** clip, crop, fell, heap, moue, pile, raze, rick **5** level, shave, shear, stack **7** grimace **9** knock down

moxie **3** pep, vim, zip **4** grit, guts **5** brass, heart, nerve, oomph, pluck, savvy, spunk, vigor **6** energy, mettle, spirit, starch **7** cojones, courage, know-how **8** backbone **9** fortitude **10** get-up-and-go, resolution **13** determination

Mozambique *capital:* **6** Maputo ***language:*** **5** Bantu **7** Swahili **10** Portuguese ***monetary unit:*** **7** metical ***neighbor:*** **6** Malawi, Zambia **8** Tanzania, Zimbabwe **9** Swaziland **11**

South Africa ***river:*** **6** Ruvuma **7** Limpopo, Zambezi

Mozart, Wolfgang Amadeus ***birthplace:*** **8** Salzburg ***cataloger:*** **6** Köchel (Ludwig) ***deathplace:*** **6** Vienna ***opera:*** **8** Idomeneo **10** Magic Flute (The) **11** Don Giovanni, Il Rè Pastore **12** Così Fan Tutte **16** Marriage of Figaro (The)

MP's prey **4** AWOL **8** deserter

Mr. ***French:*** **8** Monsieur ***German:*** **4** Herr ***Italian:*** **6** Signor ***Spanish:*** **5** Señor

Mr. Moto star **5** Lorre (Peter)

Mrs. ***French:*** **3** Mme. **6** Madame ***German:*** **4** Frau ***Italian:*** **3** Sra. **7** Signora ***Spanish:*** **3** Sra. **6** Señora

Mrs. Grundy **4** prig **5** prude **7** puritan **8** bluenose

much **3** oft **4** long, many, most **5** often **6** highly, hugely, plenty **7** greatly, notably **8** abundant **9** eminently, extremely ***combining form:*** **4** poly **5** multi

Much Ado About Nothing character **4** Hero **7** Claudio, Don John **8** Beatrice, Benedick, Dogberry

muck **3** goo, mud **4** crap, crud, dirt, dung, glop, gook, goop, grub, gunk, junk, mess, mire, murk, plod, slog, slop, soil, toil **5** dirty, dreck, filth, grime, gumbo, slave, slime, swill, trash, waste **6** drudge, litter, manure, meddle, putter, sleaze, sludge, smirch, tinker **7** garbage, rubbish **8** nonsense **9** interfere

muckety-muck **3** VIP **5** nabob **6** bigwig, fat cat, honcho **7** big shot, kingpin, notable **8** kingfish, somebody **9** dignitary

mucky **4** foul **5** dirty, grimy, muddy, muggy, murky, nasty, soggy **6** cruddy, filthy, grubby, grungy **7** squalid, unclean

mucous **5** slimy **6** viscid

mud **4** dirt, mire, muck, ooze **5** dregs, slime **6** depths, sludge

muddle **3** mix **4** hash, mess, muck, rile, roil **5** addle, botch, mix up, snarl **6** ataxia, bungle, drivel, foul up, fumble, jumble, jungle, litter, mess up, tangle, tumble **7** clutter, confuse, fluster, perplex, rummage, shuffle, snarl up, stumble, stupefy **8** befuddle, bewilder, confound, disarray, disorder, distract, entangle, mishmash, scramble, shambles, throw off, unsettle **9** confusion, throw away **10** complicate, disarrange, discompose **11** disorganize

muddled **5** drunk, tight, tipsy, vague **7** mixed-up **8** inchoate **10** disjointed, disordered, incoherent, inebriated **11** intoxicated, unorganized

muddle through **4** cope, fare **5** get by, get on **6** manage **7** carry on, make out **8** get along

muddy **3** dim, fog **4** base, blur, drab, dull, fade, foul, hazy, oozy, roil, soil **5** befog, cloud, dingy, dirty, grime, grimy, murky **6** cloudy, gloomy, grubby, sordid, turbid **7** becloud, begrime, confuse, obscure, squalid, tarnish, unclean, unclear **8** confused

muff **4** blow, flub **5** botch, fluff **6** bobble, bollix, bungle, fumble, goof up, mess up **7** louse up, misplay, screw up **9** mishandle

muffle **3** gag **4** dull, mute, veil **5** shush **6** dampen, deaden, lessen, shroud, soften, stifle, subdue, wrap up **7** envelop, repress, silence, smother, squelch **8** bundle up, suppress, tone down

muffled **5** muted **6** dulled **7** stifled, subdued **8** deadened, obscured, silenced **9** distorted, enveloped **10** indistinct, suppressed

muffler **4** mask, veil **5** cloak, scarf

mug **3** cup, ham, mop, mow, rob **4** boob, dolt, dope, face, fool, moue, phiz, punk, puss, thug **5** dunce, idiot, mouth, rowdy, stein, tough **6** ambush, dimwit, kisser **7** assault, grimace, tankard **8** bullyboy, dumbbell, features, numskull **9** blockhead, bushwhack, ignoramus, roughneck

mugger **4** thug **6** robber **9** assailant, crocodile

muggy **4** damp **5** humid, moist **6** sticky, sultry **7** dampish

Muhammad ***adopted son:*** **3** Ali ***birthplace:*** **5** Mecca ***camel:*** **5** Kaswa ***daughter:*** **6** Fatima ***deathplace:*** **6** Medina ***deity:*** **5** Allah ***father:*** **8** Abdallah, Abdullah ***father-in-law:*** **7** Abu Bakr ***flight:*** **6** hegira, hejira ***follower:*** **6** Moslem, Muslim ***horse:*** **5** Buraq **7** Alborak ***religion:*** **5** Islam ***scripture:*** **5** Koran ***son:*** **7** Ibrahim ***son-in-law:*** **3** Ali ***successor:*** **6** caliph **7** Abu Bakr ***tribe:*** **7** Koreish, Quraysh ***uncle:*** **8** Abu Talib ***wife:*** **5** Aisha **6** Ayesha **7** Khadija

mulatto **5** métis, mixed **7** mestizo **9** half-breed, half-caste **10** crossbreed

mulberry **3** fig **10** breadfruit ***type:*** **6** banyan **11** India rubber, osage orange

mulct **4** fine, milk, rook **5** bleed, cheat, gouge **6** extort, fleece **7** deceive, defraud, forfeit, penalty, swindle **8** penalize **9** blackmail

mule **5** cross, scuff **6** bagman, hybrid **7** bastard, courier, mongrel **8** smuggler **9** crossbred, half blood, half-breed **10** crossbreed

mulish **8** contrary, perverse, stubborn **9** obstinate, pigheaded **10** bullheaded, headstrong, inflexible, refractory, unyielding **11** stiff-necked

mull **4** hash, muse **5** brood, think, weigh **6** ponder **7** reflect **8** cogitate, consider, medi-

tate, ruminate, turn over **9** pulverize **10** deliberate **11** contemplate
multicolored 4 pied **6** motley **7** dappled **9** prismatic **10** variegated **13** polychromatic
multifarious 5 mixed **6** motley, sundry, varied **7** diverse, various **8** assorted, manifold **13** heterogeneous, miscellaneous
multiform 6 sundry, varied **7** diverse, various **8** assorted, manifold **9** disparate **12** multifarious
multilateral 9 many-sided
multiple 4 many **6** shared, sundry **7** diverse, several, various **8** assorted, manifold, numerous **9** composite
multiplicity 3 lot **4** heap, load, mass, peck **5** flood, hoard, horde **6** barrel **7** variety **8** mountain, plethora **9** diversity, great deal, profusion
multiply 3 wax **4** rise **5** boost, breed, build, mount **6** expand, extend, spread **7** amplify, augment, enlarge, magnify **8** generate, heighten, increase **9** procreate, propagate, reproduce **10** aggrandize **11** proliferate
multitude 3 mob **4** army, herd, host, mass, slew **5** crowd, crush, drove, flock, horde, swarm **6** legion, myriad, public, throng **8** populace
multitudinous 4 many **6** legion, myriad, sundry **7** copious, various **8** abundant, manifold, numerous, populous **9** countless **10** numberless, voluminous **11** innumerable
mum 4 dumb, mute **5** quiet **6** silent **8** wordless **10** speechless, tongue-tied
mumble 6 murmur, mutter **7** maunder
mumbo jumbo 4 juju **6** fetish **9** gibberish **10** hocus-pocus **11** abracadabra **12** gobbledygook, superstition
mummer 4 mime **5** actor, mimic **12** impersonator
mummify 5 dry up, wizen **6** embalm, wither **7** shrivel **9** desiccate
munch 3 eat **4** chaw, chew **5** champ, chomp, snack **6** crunch **9** masticate
mundane 5 lowly **6** earthy, normal **7** earthly, humdrum, prosaic, routine, terrene, worldly **8** banausic, day-to-day, everyday, familiar, ordinary, telluric, workaday **9** practical, sublunary, tellurian **11** commonplace, terrestrial, uncelestial **13** materialistic
municipal 5 civic, local, urban **12** metropolitan
munificent 6 lavish **7** liberal **8** generous, handsome **9** bounteous, bountiful **10** benevolent, freehanded, openhanded **11** magnanimous **13** philanthropic
munitions maker 5 Krupp
muralist 4 Sert (José María) **6** Benton (Thomas Hart), Giotto, Orozco (José Clemente), Rivera (Diego) **7** La Farge (John) **9** Siqueiros (David Alfaro) **12** Michelangelo (Buonarotti)
murder 3 hit, off **4** do in, kill, slay **5** blood, lynch, scrag, snuff, waste **6** rub out **7** bump off, execute, garrote, killing, smother, take out **8** foul play, homicide, knock off, strangle **9** eradicate, liquidate, slaughter **10** annihilate, asphyxiate, decapitate, extinguish **11** assassinate, electrocute, exterminate **12** manslaughter ***brother:*** **10** fratricide ***father:*** **9** patricide ***king:*** **8** regicide ***mother:*** **9** matricide ***parent:*** **9** parricide ***sister:*** **10** sororicide
murderer 6 hit man, killer, slayer **7** butcher **8** assassin, homicide **9** cutthroat, manslayer **11** slaughterer
Murder in the Cathedral *author:* **5** Eliot (Thomas Stearns) ***character:*** **5** Henry (II) **6** Becket (Thomas à)
murderous 6 deadly, lethal **10** sanguinary **12** bloodthirsty
murk 3 fog **4** haze, mist **5** brume, gloom **6** miasma **8** darkness **9** obscurity
murky 3 dim **4** dark, dull, foul, gray **5** dirty, dusky, foggy, misty, muddy, roily, vague **6** cloudy, gloomy, opaque, somber, turbid **7** obscure **8** nebulous **9** ambiguous, equivocal, tenebrous **10** caliginous
murmur 3 hum **4** buzz, purr **5** drone, rumor **6** grouch, grouse, mumble, mutter, rumble **7** grumble, whisper **8** complain **9** grumbling, undertone **11** scuttlebutt, susurration
Muscat sultanate 4 Oman
muscle 4 beef, thew **5** brawn, force, might, power, sinew **6** energy **7** potency **8** strength **9** strong arm ***abdomen:*** **3** abs **7** abdomen ***arm:*** **3** bis **4** tris **6** biceps **7** triceps ***back:*** **4** lats **5** traps **9** trapezius ***buttock:*** **6** glutes ***calf:*** **6** soleus ***chest:*** **4** pecs **10** pectoralis ***jaw:*** **8** masseter ***kind:*** **6** flexor, tensor **7** dilator, evertor, levator, rotator **8** abductor, adductor, extensor ***leg:*** **4** hams ***loin:*** **5** psoas ***neck:*** **5** traps **8** platysma **9** trapezius ***shoulder:*** **5** delts **7** deltoid **10** deltoideus ***side:*** **4** lats ***stomach:*** **3** abs ***straight:*** **6** rectus ***study of:*** **7** myology ***thigh:*** **5** quads **8** gracilis **9** sartorius
muscle-bound 5 rigid, stiff **6** wooden
muscular 4 ropy **5** beefy, burly, husky **6** brawny, mighty, robust, sinewy, strong, sturdy **8** athletic, forceful, powerful, resolute, stalwart, vigorous **9** Herculean, strapping, well-built
muse 5 angel, brood, guide, think **6** genius, ponder, trance **7** reflect, reverie **8** cogitate,

meditate, mull over, ruminate, turn over **10** deliberate **11** contemplate

Muse ***father:*** **4** Zeus **7** Jupiter ***home:*** **7** Helicon ***leader:*** **6** Apollo ***mother:*** **9** Mnemosyne ***of astronomy:*** **6** Urania ***of choral song:*** **11** Terpsichore ***of comedy:*** **6** Thalia ***of dancing:*** **11** Terpsichore ***of epic poetry:*** **8** Calliope ***of history:*** **4** Clio ***of love poetry:*** **5** Erato ***of lyric poetry:*** **5** Erato ***of music:*** **7** Euterpe ***of pastoral poetry:*** **6** Thalia ***of sacred poetry:*** **8** Polymnia **10** Polyhymnia ***of tragedy:*** **9** Melpomene

museum **5** salon **7** archive, exhibit, gallery **8** atheneum **10** collection, repository ***famous:*** **3** Met **4** Fogg, MoMA, Tate **5** Field, Frick, Getty, Orsay, Prado **6** Louvre **7** Peabody, Walters, Whitney **9** Henry Ford, Hermitage, Hirshhorn **10** Guggenheim **11** Norton Simon, Smithsonian

mush **4** slop **5** grits, gruel, hokum **6** bathos, drivel, hominy **8** porridge, schmaltz

mushroom **4** grow **6** expand, spread **7** burgeon, explode, inflate **8** snowball **11** proliferate ***combining form:*** **3** myc **4** myco **5** mycet **6** myceto ***edible:*** **5** enoki, morel **6** bolete **7** cremini, crimini, porcini **8** shiitake **9** mousseron **10** champignon, portabella, portabello, portobello **11** chanterelle ***kind:*** **6** agaric, bolete **7** inky cap, russula ***part:*** **3** cap **4** gill, ring **5** stipe, volva **6** pileus **7** annulus **8** mycelium ***poisonous:*** **7** amanita **8** death cap **9** fly agaric, toadstool

mushy **4** soft **5** pulpy, soppy, vague **6** quaggy, spongy **7** amorous, maudlin, mawkish, squashy, squishy **8** bathetic, effusive, romantic, squooshy **9** schmaltzy **10** lovey-dovey, saccharine **11** sentimental

music ***abbreviation:*** **3** fff, ppp, sfz **5** cresc ***bass staff lines:*** **5** GBDFA ***bass staff spaces:*** **4** ACEG ***characteristic phrase:*** **9** leitmotif, leitmotiv ***chord:*** **5** major, minor, tonic **7** harmony **8** dominant **9** augmented **10** diminished ***closing:*** **4** coda ***embellishment:*** **3** run **4** turn **5** trill **7** cadenza, mordent, roulade **8** arpeggio, flourish **9** grace note ***for eight:*** **5** octet ***for five:*** **7** quintet ***for four:*** **7** quartet ***for nine:*** **5** nonet ***for one:*** **4** solo ***for seven:*** **6** septet ***for six:*** **6** sextet ***for three:*** **4** trio ***for two:*** **3** duo **4** a due, duet ***god:*** **6** Apollo ***hall:*** **5** odeum **7** cabaret, theater ***instrumental form:*** **3** jig, rag **4** jazz, reel **5** étude, fugue, gigue, march, polka, rondo, suite, waltz **6** minuet, pavane, sonata **7** bourrée, gavotte, mazurka, prelude, toccata **8** chaconne, concerto, courante, fantasia, galliard, nocturne, overture, rhapsody, ricercar, saraband, serenade, symphony, tone poem **9** allemande, polonaise ***morning:*** **6** aubade ***Muse:*** **7** Euterpe ***night:*** **8** nocturne, serenade ***note:*** **4** half **5** breve, minim, neume, whole **6** eighth, quaver **7** quarter **8** crotchet **9** sixteenth **10** semiquaver ***patron saint:*** **7** Cecilia ***period:*** **6** Modern, Rococo **7** Baroque **8** Medieval, Romantic **9** Classical ***symbol:*** **3** bar, key **4** clef, flat, note, rest, slur, turn **5** G clef, neume, sharp, staff **7** fermata, mordent **8** bass clef **9** alla breve **10** accidental, treble clef ***treble staff lines:*** **5** EGBDF ***treble staff spaces:*** **4** FACE ***vocal form:*** **3** air **4** aria, hymn, lied, mass, song **5** chant, motet, opera, round **6** anthem, ballad **7** cantata, chanson, chorale **8** cavatina, madrigal, operetta, oratorio, serenade **9** cabaletta

musical **4** show **5** revue **6** choral **7** lyrical, melodic, songful, tuneful **8** harmonic, operetta, zarzuela **9** melodious, symphonic **10** euphonious, harmonious ***famous:*** **4** Cats, Hair, Mame, Rent **5** Annie, Evita, Gypsy **6** Grease, Kismet, Les Miz, Oliver **7** Cabaret, Camelot, Candide, Chicago, Company, Follies **8** Carousel, Fiorello, Godspell, King and I (The), Lion King (The), Music Man (The), Oklahoma, Show Boat **9** Brigadoon, Funny Girl, Girl Crazy, On the Town, Over There, State Fair **10** Chorus Line (A), Dreamgirls, Hello Dolly, Kiss Me Kate, Miss Saigon, My Fair Lady, Pajama Game (The), She Loves Me **11** Damn Yankees, Of Thee I Sing, Sweeney Todd **12** Anything Goes, Bye Bye Birdie, Guys and Dolls, Into the Woods, Sound of Music (The), South Pacific, Sweet Charity **13** Les Misérables, Man of La Mancha, Silk Stockings, West Side Story, Wonderful Town **14** Finian's Rainbow, Flower Drum Song, Paint Your Wagon **15** Annie Get Your Gun **16** Fiddler on the Roof **17** Phantom of the Opera (The) **20** Jesus Christ Superstar

musical composition **4** aria, coda, hymn, lied, opus, song, trio **5** chant, canon, carol, dirge, étude, fugue, march, motet, opera, rondo, suite **6** anthem, ballad, sextet, sonata **7** cantata, chanson, chorale, prelude, quartet, quintet, requiem, scherzo, toccata **8** concerto, fantasia, madrigal, nocturne, operetta, oratorio, overture, postlude, serenade, sonatina, symphony **9** bagatelle, barcarole, cabaletta, interlude **10** intermezzo, recitative

musical direction ***accented:*** **7** marcato **8** sforzato **9** sforzando ***all:*** **5** tutti ***bowed:*** **4** arco ***brisk:*** **4** brio, vivo **6** vivace **7** allegro, animato ***connected:*** **6** legato ***detached:*** **8**

spiccato, staccato ***dignified:*** **8** maestoso ***disconnected:*** **8** staccato ***emotional:*** **12** appassionato ***emphatic:*** **7** marcato ***excited:*** **7** agitato ***fast:*** **4** vite, vivo **6** presto, veloce, vivace **7** allegro ***faster:*** **7** stretto **11** accelerando ***fluctuating tempo:*** **6** rubato ***forcefully:*** **7** furioso ***freely:*** **9** ad libitum ***from the beginning:*** **6** da capo ***gay:*** **7** giocoso ***gentle:*** **5** dolce **7** amabile, amoroso **10** affettuoso ***graceful:*** **8** grazioso ***half:*** **5** mezzo ***heavy:*** **7** pesante ***held firmly:*** **6** tenuto ***less:*** **4** meno ***little:*** **4** poco ***little by little:*** **9** poco a poco ***lively:*** **4** vite, vivo **6** vivace **7** allegro, animato, giocoso ***loud:*** **5** forte ***louder:*** **9** crescendo ***majestic:*** **8** maestoso ***moderate:*** **7** andante **8** moderato ***moderately loud:*** **10** mezzo forte ***moderately soft:*** **10** mezzo piano ***playful:*** **10** scherzando ***plucked:*** **9** pizzicato ***quick:*** **4** vite, vivo **6** presto, veloce, vivace **7** allegro ***quickening:*** **11** affrettando ***repeat:*** **3** bis **6** da capo ***run:*** **8** arpeggio **9** glissando ***sad:*** **7** dolente **8** doloroso ***separate:*** **6** divisi ***silent:*** **5** tacet ***singing:*** **9** cantabile ***sliding:*** **9** glissando ***slow:*** **5** grave, largo, lento **6** adagio **7** andante **9** larghetto ***slowing:*** **3** rit **6** ritard **10** ritardando **11** rallentando ***smooth:*** **6** legato ***soft:*** **5** dolce, piano ***softening:*** **10** diminuendo **11** decrescendo ***solemn:*** **5** grave ***spirited:*** **4** vivo **6** vivace **7** animato **9** spiritoso ***stately:*** **7** pomposo **8** maestoso ***sustained:*** **6** tenuto **9** sostenuto ***sweet:*** **5** dolce ***tender:*** **7** amabile, amoroso **10** affettuoso ***together:*** **4** a due **5** tutti ***very:*** **5** assai ***very fast:*** **11** prestissimo ***very loud:*** **10** fortissimo ***very soft:*** **10** pianissimo

musical drama **5** opera **8** operetta, zarzuela **9** singspiel

musical group **4** band, trio **5** choir, combo **6** chorus, sextet **7** quartet, quintet **8** ensemble, glee club **9** orchestra

musical instrument ***African:*** **5** mbira, rebab **7** kalimba ***ancient:*** **4** lyre, rote **5** crwth **6** syrinx **7** cithara, kithara, sistrum, timbrel **8** psaltery ***Arabic:*** **3** oud ***bagpipe:*** **7** musette, pibroch **8** psaltery ***brass:*** **4** horn, tuba **5** bugle **6** cornet **7** althorn, clarion, helicon, saxhorn, trumpet **8** trombone **10** flugelhorn, French horn, sousaphone ***Indian:*** **4** vina **5** sarod, sitar, tabla ***Japanese:*** **4** biwa, koto **7** samisen **8** shamisen **10** shakuhachi ***keyboard:*** **5** organ, piano **6** spinet **7** celesta, cembalo, clavier **8** calliope, melodeon, virginal **9** accordion **10** clavichord, concertina, pianoforte **11** harpsichord ***medieval:*** **4** lute **5** naker, rebab, rebec, shawm, tabor **7** gittern, mandola **8** cornetto, gemshorn, hornpipe, oliphant **9** monochord **10** hurdy-gurdy ***percussion:*** **4** bell, drum **5** anvil, güiro, piano **6** cymbal, maraca **7** maracas, marimba, timpani, tympani **8** bass drum, castanet, triangle **9** castanets, snare drum, xylophone **10** kettledrum, tambourine, vibraphone ***Persian:*** **6** santir ***reed:*** **4** oboe **7** bassoon **8** clarinet **9** harmonica, saxophone **11** English horn ***Renaissance:*** **4** viol **5** regal, shawm **6** curtal, spinet **7** bagpipe, bandora, cittern, rackett, sackbut, serpent, theorbo, vihuela, violone **8** crumhorn, recorder, virginal **9** krummhorn **10** chitarrone, colascione **11** harpsichord ***Russian:*** **9** balalaika ***stringed:*** **3** uke **4** harp, lute, lyre, viol **5** banjo, cello, piano, rebab, viola **6** fiddle, guitar, violin, zither **7** bandora, cittern, gittern, kantele, pandura, ukulele **8** autoharp, dulcimer, mandolin **10** contrabass, double bass **11** harpsichord, violoncello ***toy:*** **5** kazoo **7** ocarina ***woodwind:*** **4** oboe **5** flute **7** bassoon, piccolo **8** clarinet **9** saxophone **11** English horn

musical interval **5** fifth, major, minor, sixth, third **6** fourth, octave, second **7** perfect, seventh, tritone

musical syllable **2** do, fa, la, mi, re, si, ti, ut **3** sol

musician **4** bard **5** piper **6** player **7** jazzman, maestro **8** minstrel, virtuoso **9** performer **10** troubadour

muskeg **3** bog, fen **4** mire, quag **5** marsh, swamp **6** morass, slough **8** quagmire

musket **5** fusil **9** flintlock, matchlock **12** muzzleloader

Musketeer **5** Athos **6** Aramis **7** Porthos ***author:*** **5** Dumas (Alexandre) ***friend:*** **9** d'Artagnan

muskmelon **10** cantaloupe

Muslim ***ascetic:*** **4** Sufi **5** fakir **7** dervish **8** marabout ***body of scholars:*** **5** ulama, ulema ***branch:*** **4** Shia **5** Sunni **6** Shiite ***caller to prayer:*** **7** muezzin ***decree:*** **5** fatwa, irade ***devil:*** **5** Iblis ***garment:*** **5** burka, burqa **6** chador ***god:*** **5** Allah ***heavenly virgin:*** **5** houri ***holy city:*** **5** Mecca **6** Medina ***holy war:*** **5** jihad ***judge:*** **4** qadi **5** mufti ***lady:*** **5** begum ***law:*** **6** Sharia ***leader:*** **3** aga **4** agha, amir, emir, imam **5** ameer **6** caliph, sayyid, sultan **9** ayatollah ***lord:*** **5** omrah ***mendicant:*** **5** fakir ***messiah:*** **5** Mahdi ***month:*** (see at **month**) ***month of fasting:*** **7** Ramadan ***mosque:*** **6** masjid ***mystic:*** **4** Sufi ***official:*** **3** dey **6** mullah, vizier ***pilgrim:*** **5** hajji ***pilgrimage:*** **4** hadj, hajj **5** omrah ***prayer:*** **5** salat ***priest:*** **4** imam ***prophet:*** **8** Mohammed, Muhammad ***religion:*** **5** Islam ***scripture:*** **5**

Koran, Quran ***school:*** **7** madrasa **8** madrasah, madrassa **9** madrassah ***shrine:*** **5** Kaaba ***spirit:*** **4** jinn **5** djinn, jinni **6** djinni ***temple:*** **6** masjid, mosque ***theological student:*** **5** softa ***title:*** **3** aga **4** emir **6** caliph ***tradition:*** **5** sunna ***veil:*** **7** yashmak (see also **mosque; Muhammad**)

muss 3 row **4** mess **5** botch, chaos, mix-up, upset **6** jumble, mess-up, muddle, rumple, tousle **7** disrupt, rummage **8** disarray, dishevel, disorder, shambles **9** confusion **10** disarrange **11** disorganize

mussel 5 naiad ***genus:*** **4** Unio **7** Mytilus **8** Anodonta ***larva:*** **9** blackhead

Mussolini, Benito 4 Duce (Il) ***son-in-law:*** **5** Ciano (Galeazzo)

mussy 6 sloppy, untidy **7** tousled, unkempt **8** slovenly **9** cluttered **10** disheveled

must 4 duty, mold, need, want **5** gotta, juice, ought **6** devoir, should **9** condition, essential, necessity, requisite **10** obligation, sine qua non **11** requirement **12** precondition, prerequisite

muster 4 call, roll **5** crowd, group, raise, rally, rouse **6** enlist, enroll, gather, induce, invoke, join up, roster, sample, sign on, sign up, summon, work up **7** collect, convene, develop, include, marshal, produce **8** assemble, assembly, comprise, congress, generate, mobilize, organize, roll call, specimen **9** gathering, inventory, nose count **10** accumulate, assemblage, collection, congregate, rendezvous **12** accumulation, congregation

muster out 5 demob, let go **9** discharge **10** demobilize

musty 4 dank **5** funky, moldy, stale, tired, trite **6** frowsy, frowzy, old hat, smelly **7** airless, antique, mildewy, squalid **8** shopworn, timeworn **10** antiquated, malodorous, threadbare

Mut ***husband:*** **4** Amen, Amon ***son:*** **5** Chons **6** Chonsu, Khonsu

mutable 5 fluid **6** fickle, mobile, shifty **7** erratic, protean **8** slippery, unstable, unsteady, variable, volatile, wavering **9** changeful, mercurial, unsettled **10** capricious, changeable, inconstant **11** fluctuating, vacillating **12** inconsistent

mutate 4 vary **5** alter, morph **6** change, modify **9** refashion, transform, transmute **11** transfigure **12** metamorphose, transmogrify

mutation 5 sport **6** change **7** novelty **9** deviation, variation **10** alteration **11** vicissitude **12** modification **13** metamorphosis

mute 3 mum **4** dumb **5** quiet **6** dampen, deaden, muffle, muzzle, reduce, silent, soften, stifle, subdue **7** silence **8** silencer, wordless **9** voiceless **10** speechless, tongue-tied

muted 3 dim, mat **4** dull **6** low-key, silent **10** speechless

mutilate 3 mar **4** maim **6** damage, deface, injure, mangle **7** cripple **9** disfigure, dismember

mutineer 5 rebel

mutinous 6 unruly **8** factious **9** insurgent, seditious, turbulent **10** rebellious **12** contumacious **13** insubordinate

mutiny 5 rebel **6** revolt, rise up **8** uprising **9** rebellion **12** insurrection

mutt 3 cur, dog **4** mule **5** cross **6** hybrid **7** mixture, mongrel **9** half blood, half-breed **10** crossbreed

Mutt and ____ 4 Jeff

mutter 5 growl **6** grouch, grouse, mumble, murmur **7** grumble **9** undertone

muttonchops 9 burnsides, sideburns **10** sideboards **11** dundrearies **12** side-whiskers

mutual 5 joint **6** common, public, shared, united **7** related **8** communal, conjoint, conjunct **9** bilateral, connected **10** associated, reciprocal, respective ***prefix:*** **5** inter

muumuu 6 caftan

muzzle 3 gag **4** hush, mute, nose, phiz **5** snout **7** silence, squelch

muzzy 3 dim **4** dull, hazy **5** faint, vague **6** blurry, gloomy **7** blurred, muddled, unclear **8** confused, nebulous **9** imprecise

myalgia 4 ache, pain **5** cramp **6** strain **8** soreness

Myanmar 5 Burma ***bay:*** **6** Bengal ***capital:*** **6** Yangon **7** Rangoon ***monetary unit:*** **4** kyat ***neighbor:*** **4** Laos **5** China, India **8** Thailand **10** Bangladesh ***peninsula:*** **9** Indochina ***river:*** **7** Salween **9** Irrawaddy ***sea:*** **7** Andaman

My Antonia author 6 Cather (Willa)

My Last Duchess author 8 Browning (Robert)

My Lost Youth author 10 Longfellow (Henry Wadsworth)

Myra Breckenridge author 5 Vidal (Gore)

myriad 3 lot **4** heap, host, raft, slew **5** flood, horde, swarm **6** throng **9** countless, multitude **10** infinitude, numberless **11** innumerable **12** incalculable **13** multitudinous

myrmecology subject 3 ant **4** ants

myrmidon 6 minion **8** follower, retainer **9** attendant, underling **11** subordinate

Myron's statue 10 Discobolos, Discobolus **13** Discus Thrower (The)

Myrrha's son 6 Adonis

mysterious 6 arcane, mystic, occult, secret **7**

cryptic, obscure, strange **8** abstruse, esoteric, numinous **9** ambiguous, enigmatic, equivocal, recondite **10** cabalistic, unknowable **11** inscrutable **12** impenetrable, inexplicable, unfathomable **13** unaccountable

mystery 5 poser **6** enigma, puzzle, riddle, secret **7** arcanum, problem, stumper **8** whodunit **9** conundrum **10** closed book, perplexity, puzzlement **13** Chinese puzzle ***writer:* 3** Poe (Edgar Allan), Tey (Josephine) **5** Blake (Nicholas), Cross (Amanda), Doyle (Arthur Conan), Innes (Michael), James (P. D.), Lynds (Dennis), Marsh (Ngaio), Oates (Joyce Carol), Queen (Ellery), Stout (Rex), Waugh (Hillary) **6** Dexter (Colin), Parker (Robert B.), Peters (Ellis), Sayers (Dorothy) **7** Barnard (Robert), Collins (Michael, Wilkie), Gardner (Erle Stanley), Grafton (Sue), Hammett (Dashiell), MacLeod (Charlotte), Rendell (Ruth), Upfield (Arthur) **8** Chandler (Raymond), Christie (Agatha), Paretsky (Sara), Spillane (Mickey) **9** MacDonald (John D.), Macdonald (Ross) **10** Chesterton (G. K.)

mystic 4 seer **6** arcane, medium, occult, oracle, secret **7** obscure **8** anagogic, esoteric, hermetic, numinous **9** enigmatic, visionary **10** cabalistic, unknowable **11** inscrutable, necromantic **12** impenetrable, thaumaturgic **13** unaccountable

mystical 4 holy **6** arcane, covert, divine, occult, orphic, sacred, secret **7** cryptic, subrosa **8** anagogic, esoteric, hermetic, oracular, profound **9** recondite, spiritual **10** miraculous, symbolical **11** clandestine **12** supernatural, supranatural

mysticism 7 Orphism **8** cabalism, quietism **11** hermeticism

mystify 6 baffle, puzzle **7** confuse, obscure, perplex **8** befuddle, bewilder, confound **9** obfuscate

mystifying 7 cryptic, delphic **8** Delphian **9** enigmatic

mystique 4 aura **5** charm, magic **6** glamor **7** glamour **8** charisma **9** magnetism

myth 4 lore, saga, tale **5** fable, story **6** legend **7** fiction, figment, parable **8** allegory, folklore **9** tradition **11** fabrication

mythical 6 fabled, made-up, unreal **7** created, fictive **8** fabulous, fanciful, invented **9** fantastic, fictional, imaginary, legendary **10** apocryphal, fictitious

mythologist 4 Jung (Carl Gustav), Ovid **5** Tylor (Edward Burnett) **6** Eliade (Mircea), Frazer (James George), Müller (Friedrich Max) **8** Campbell (Joseph) **9** Euhemerus **10** Malinowski (Bronislaw)

N

Naamah *brother:* 9 Tubalcain ***father:* 6** Lamech ***husband:* 7** Solomon ***mother:* 6** Zillah ***son:* 8** Rehoboam

nab 4 grab **5** catch, pinch, run in, seize **6** arrest, clutch, collar, pick up, pull in, snatch **7** capture **9** apprehend

nabob 3 VIP **5** mogul, noble **6** bigwig, fat cat, tycoon **7** big shot, magnate, notable **8** big chief, eminence, governor **9** big cheese, dignitary, personage **10** notability

Nabokov novel 3 Ada **4** Gift (The), Pnin **6** Lolita **7** Defense (The), Despair **8** Pale Fire **14** King Queen Knave

nacre 13 mother-of-pearl

nada 3 nil, nix, zip **4** zero **5** zilch **6** naught **7** nothing, nullity **11** nothingness

nadir 4 base, foot **5** depth **6** bottom **8** low point ***opposite:* 6** zenith

nag 3 irk, vex **4** bait, carp, goad, ride **5** annoy, chivy, harry, horse, hound, shrew, worry **6** badger, bother, carp at, harass, heckle, hector, needle, peck at, pester, plague **7** henpeck, torment **8** complain, harangue, irritate

naiad 5 nymph

naïf 7 ingenue

nail 3 bag, get, nab **4** brad, grab, spad, stud, tack, trap **5** catch, clone, spike, sprig **6** arrest, collar, secure **7** capture **9** apprehend

naive 6 simple **7** artless, natural **8** gullible, innocent, wide-eyed **9** childlike, credulous, guileless, ingenuous, unstudied **10** self-taught, unaffected, unschooled **11** susceptible

naked 3 raw **4** bald, bare, mere, nude, pure **5** clear, sheer **6** peeled, scanty, simple, unclad

7 denuded, evident, exposed, obvious 8 revealed, starkers, stripped 9 au naturel, disclosed, unclothed, uncovered, undressed *combining form:* 4 gymn 5 gymno

Naked and the Dead author 6 Mailer (Norman)

namby-pamby 4 weak 5 banal, bland, inane, sissy, vapid 6 effete, jejune 7 insipid, milksop, nebbish 8 nebbishy, weakling 9 spineless 10 effeminate, indecisive, pantywaist, wishy-washy 11 milquetoast 12 milk-and-water 13 characterless

name 3 dub, nom, tab, tag, tap 4 cite, term 5 alias, label, nomen, title 6 finger, repute, rubric 7 appoint, baptize, epithet, moniker, specify 8 christen, identify, nominate 9 designate, incognito, sobriquet 10 denominate, reputation 11 appellation, appellative, designation *ancient Rome:* 7 agnomen 8 prenomen *assumed:* 5 alias 9 sobriquet *family:* 8 cognomen *fictitious:* 9 pseudonym *giver:* 6 eponym

nameless 6 unsung 7 obscure, unknown 9 anonymous 11 indefinable, unutterable 12 uncelebrated, unidentified

namely 3 viz. 5 id est, to wit 6 that is 8 scilicet 9 expressly, specially, videlicet 10 especially 12 particularly, specifically

Name of the Rose author 3 Eco (Umberto)

Namibia *capital:* 8 Windhoek *city:* 8 Oshakati, Rehoboth *desert:* 5 Namib 8 Kalahari *language:* 5 Bantu 6 German 9 Afrikaans *neighbor:* 6 Angola 8 Botswana 11 South Africa *river:* 6 Cunene, Orange 8 Okavango

nana 7 grandma 11 grandmother

Nana *author:* 4 Zola (Emile) *mother:* 8 Gervaise

Nancy Drew *aunt:* 6 Eloise *author:* 5 Keene (Carolyn) *boyfriend:* 3 Ned *creator:* 11 Stratemeyer (Edward) *dog:* 4 Togo *father:* 6 Carson *friend:* 4 Bess 5 Helen 6 George *housekeeper:* 6 Hannah

Nanna *brother:* 6 Nergal, Ninazu *father:* 5 Enlil *husband:* 6 Balder, Baldur *mother:* 6 Ninlil *son:* 3 Utu *wife:* 6 Ningal

nanny 5 nurse 9 caregiver, governess, nursemaid

Naomi 4 Mara *daughter-in-law:* 4 Ruth 5 Orpah *husband:* 9 Elimelech *son:* 6 Mahlon 7 Chilion

nap 4 doze, pile, rest, shag, wale, warp, weft, woof 5 sleep, weave 6 drowse, nod off, siesta, snooze 7 drop off, surface 10 forty winks

nape 6 scruff

Naphtali *brother:* 3 Dan *father:* 5 Jacob *mother:* 6 Bilhah *son:* 4 Guni 5 Jezer 7 Jahzeel, Jahziel, Shallum

naphtha 7 solvent 9 petroleum

napkin 5 cloth, doily, towel 9 serviette

napoleon 4 boot 6 pastry 8 card game 9 solitaire *bid:* 7 blucher 10 wellington

Napoleon *adversary:* 6 Nelson (Horatio) 7 Kutuzov (Mikhail) 10 Wellington (Duke of) *birthplace:* 7 Ajaccio, Corsica *brother:* 5 Louis 6 Jérome, Joseph, Lucien *brother-in-law:* 5 Murat (Joachim) *deathplace:* 8 St. Helena *defeat:* 7 Leipzig 8 Waterloo 9 Trafalgar *doctor:* 11 Antommarchi (Francesco) *father:* 5 Carlo *island of exile:* 4 Elba 8 St. Helena *marshal:* 3 Ney (Michel) 5 Murat (Joachim), Soult (Nicolas-Jean) 6 Suchet (Louis-Gabriel) *sister:* 5 Maria 8 Carlotta, Carolina *victory:* 3 Ulm 4 Jena, Lodi 5 Ligny 6 Abukir, Abu Qir, Arcole, Wagram 7 Bautzen, Dresden, Marengo 8 Borodino 10 Austerlitz *wife:* 9 Josephine 11 Marie Louise

narcissism 6 egoism, vanity 7 conceit, egotism 8 self-love, vainness 9 vainglory 11 egocentrism, self-conceit 13 conceitedness

narcissistic 4 vain 7 stuck-up 9 conceited, egotistic 10 self-loving 11 egotistical 12 self-absorbed, self-admiring, self-centered, vainglorious

Narcissus *admirer:* 4 Echo *father:* 9 Cephissus *mother:* 7 Liriope

narcotic 3 hop 4 dope, drug, junk 5 opium 6 heroin, opiate 7 anodyne, cocaine, hashish 8 hypnotic, morphine, nepenthe 9 somnolent, soporific 10 somnorific 11 somniferous *peddler:* 6 dealer, pusher

narrate 4 tell 5 state 6 detail, recite, relate, report 7 express, outline, recount 8 describe 9 chronicle

narrative 4 epic, myth, saga, tale, yarn 5 fable, story 6 legend, report 7 account, history, recital, version 8 anecdote 9 chronicle *medieval French:* 5 roman 7 romance *prose:* 5 novel 7 novella

narrator 6 teller 7 reciter 8 reporter 9 describer, performer 10 chronicler

narrow 5 close, small, taper 6 lessen, strait 7 bigoted, limited, precise, slender 8 contract, decrease, straiten 9 confining, constrict, hidebound, illiberal 10 brassbound, inflexible, intolerant, prejudiced, restricted

narrowly 6 barely 7 closely 8 scarcely, strictly

narrow-minded 5 petty 7 bigoted, insular 9 hidebound, illiberal 10 brassbound, intolerant, prejudiced, provincial

nasal 6 rhinal, twangy 9 nosepiece *combining form:* 4 rhin 5 rhino *sprayer:* 9 nebulizer

NASCAR champion 5 Busch (Kurt), Petty (Lee, Richard) **6** Gordon (Jeff), Martin (Mark), Newman (Ryan) **7** Jarrett (Dale), Johnson (Jimmie), Kenseth (Matt), Labonte (Bobby, Terry), Stewart (Tony) **9** Earnhardt (Dale)

nascency 5 birth **6** origin **7** genesis **8** birthing, creation, nativity **9** inception **11** parturition

nascent 7 budding, growing, newborn **8** emergent **9** beginning, embryonic, fledgling, incipient, sprouting **10** blossoming, burgeoning, initiative, initiatory

Naseby victor 7 Fairfax (Thomas) **8** Cromwell (Oliver)

____ **Nastase 4** Ilie

nasty 4 evil, foul, icky, mean, vile **5** awful, dirty, gross, snide **6** filthy, grubby, horrid, malign, odious, wicked **7** beastly, harmful, hateful, ill-bred, painful, raunchy, squalid, vicious **8** god-awful, indecent, spiteful **9** loathsome, malicious, malignant, obnoxious, offensive, repugnant, repulsive **10** disgusting, malevolent **11** distasteful **12** disagreeable

natant 8 floating, swimming

Nathan ***father:*** **4** Bani **5** Attai, David ***son:*** **5** Zabad

nation 4 race **5** realm, state, tribe **6** domain, people, polity **7** country, kingdom, society **8** dominion, populace, republic **11** sovereignty **12** commonwealth, principality ***Africa:*** **4** Chad, Mali, Togo **5** Benin, Congo, Egypt, Gabon, Ghana, Kenya, Libya, Niger, Sudan **6** Angola, Gambia, Guinea, Malawi, Rwanda, Uganda, Zambia **7** Algeria, Burundi, Comoros, Eritrea, Lesotho, Liberia, Morocco, Namibia, Nigeria, Senegal, Somalia, Tunisia **8** Botswana, Cameroon, Djibouti, Ethiopia, Tanzania, Zimbabwe **9** Cape Verde, Mauritius, Swaziland **10** Ivory Coast, Madagascar, Mauritania, Mozambique, Seychelles **11** Burkina Faso, Côte d'Ivoire, Sierra Leone, South Africa **12** Guinea-Bissau **16** Equatorial Guinea **18** São Tomé and Principe **22** Central African Republic ***Americas:*** **4** Peru **5** Chile **6** Belize, Brazil, Canada, Guyana, Mexico, Panama **7** Bolivia, Ecuador, Uruguay **8** Colombia, Honduras, Paraguay, Suriname **9** Argentina, Costa Rica, Guatemala, Nicaragua, Venezuela **10** El Salvador **12** United States ***Asia:*** **4** Laos **5** Burma, China, India, Japan, Korea, Nepal **6** Bhutan, Brunei, Ceylon, Taiwan **7** Armenia, Georgia, Myanmar, Vietnam **8** Cambodia, Malaysia, Maldives, Mongolia, Pakistan, Sri Lanka, Thailand **9** East Timor, Indonesia, Singapore **10** Azerbaijan, Bangladesh, Kazakhstan, Kyrgyzstan, North Korea, South Korea, Tajikistan, Timor-Leste **11** Afghanistan, Philippines **12** Turkmenistan ***Caribbean:*** **4** Cuba **5** Haiti **7** Bahamas, Grenada, Jamaica **8** Barbados, Dominica **10** Saint Lucia **15** St. Kitts and Nevis **17** Antigua and Barbuda, Dominican Republic, Trinidad and Tobago **18** Saint Kitts and Nevis **25** St. Vincent and the Grenadines **28** Saint Vincent and the Grenadines ***Europe:*** **5** Italy, Malta, Spain **6** Bosnia, Cyprus, France, Greece, Latvia, Monaco, Norway, Poland, Russia, Serbia, Sweden, Turkey **7** Albania, Andorra, Austria, Belarus, Belgium, Croatia, Denmark, Estonia, Finland, Germany, Hungary, Iceland, Ireland, Moldova, Romania, Ukraine **8** Bulgaria, Portugal, Slovakia, Slovenia **9** Lithuania, Macedonia, San Marino **10** Luxembourg, Montenegro, Yugoslavia **11** Netherlands, Switzerland **13** Czech Republic, Liechtenstein, United Kingdom ***Middle East:*** **3** UAE **4** Iraq, Iran, Oman **5** Qatar, Syria, Yemen **6** Israel, Jordan, Kuwait **7** Bahrain, Lebanon **11** Saudi Arabia **18** United Arab Emirates ***Oceania:*** **4** Fiji **5** Samoa, Tonga **7** Vanuatu **8** Kiribati **9** Australia **10** Micronesia, New Zealand **14** Papua New Guinea, Solomon Islands **15** Marshall Islands

national 6 native **7** citizen, federal, subject **8** resident **10** countryman **11** countrywide

National Basketball Association ***Atlanta:*** **5** Hawks ***Boston:*** **7** Celtics ***Charlotte:*** **7** Bobcats ***Chicago:*** **5** Bulls ***Cleveland:*** **9** Cavaliers ***Dallas:*** **9** Mavericks ***Denver:*** **7** Nuggets ***Detroit:*** **7** Pistons ***Golden State:*** **8** Warriors ***Houston:*** **7** Rockets ***Indiana:*** **6** Pacers ***Los Angeles:*** **6** Lakers **8** Clippers ***Memphis:*** **9** Grizzlies ***Miami:*** **4** Heat ***Milwaukee:*** **5** Bucks ***Minnesota:*** **12** Timberwolves ***New Jersey:*** **4** Nets ***New Orleans:*** **7** Hornets ***New York:*** **6** Knicks ***Oklahoma City:*** **7** Thunder ***Orlando:*** **5** Magic ***Philadelphia:*** **13** Seventy-sixers ***Phoenix:*** **4** Suns ***Portland:*** **12** Trail Blazers ***Sacramento:*** **5** Kings ***San Antonio:*** **5** Spurs ***Toronto:*** **7** Raptors ***Utah:*** **4** Jazz ***Washington:*** **7** Wizards

National Football League ***Arizona:*** **9** Cardinals ***Atlanta:*** **7** Falcons ***Baltimore:*** **6** Ravens ***Buffalo:*** **5** Bills ***Carolina:*** **8** Panthers ***Chicago:*** **5** Bears ***Cincinnati:*** **7** Bengals ***Cleveland:*** **6** Browns ***Dallas:*** **7** Cowboys ***Denver:*** **7** Broncos ***Detroit:*** **5** Lions ***Green Bay:*** **7** Packers ***Houston:*** **6** Texans ***Indianapolis:*** **5** Colts ***Jacksonville:*** **7** Jaguars ***Kansas City:***

6 Chiefs ***Miami:*** **8** Dolphins ***Minnesota:*** **7** Vikings ***New England:*** **8** Patriots ***New Orleans:*** **6** Saints ***New York:*** **4** Jets **6** Giants ***Oakland:*** **7** Raiders ***Philadelphia:*** **6** Eagles ***Pittsburgh:*** **8** Steelers ***St. Louis:*** **4** Rams ***San Diego:*** **8** Chargers ***San Francisco:*** **11** Forty-niners ***Seattle:*** **8** Seahawks ***Tampa Bay:*** **4** Bucs **10** Buccaneers ***Tennessee:*** **6** Titans ***Washington:*** **8** Redskins

National Hockey League ***Anaheim:*** **5** Ducks ***Atlanta:*** **9** Thrashers ***Boston:*** **6** Bruins ***Buffalo:*** **6** Sabres ***Calgary:*** **6** Flames ***Carolina:*** **10** Hurricanes ***Chicago:*** **10** Blackhawks ***Colorado:*** **9** Avalanche ***Columbus:*** **11** Blue Jackets ***Dallas:*** **5** Stars ***Detroit:*** **8** Red Wings ***Edmonton:*** **6** Oilers ***Florida:*** **8** Panthers ***Los Angeles:*** **5** Kings ***Minnesota:*** **4** Wild ***Montreal:*** **9** Canadiens ***Nashville:*** **9** Predators ***New Jersey:*** **6** Devils ***New York:*** **7** Rangers **9** Islanders ***Ottawa:*** **8** Senators ***Philadelphia:*** **6** Flyers ***Phoenix:*** **7** Coyotes ***Pittsburgh:*** **8** Penguins ***St. Louis:*** **5** Blues ***San Jose:*** **6** Sharks ***Tampa Bay:*** **9** Lightning ***Toronto:*** **10** Maple Leafs ***Vancouver:*** **7** Canucks ***Washington:*** **8** Capitals

nationalism **8** jingoism **10** chauvinism, patriotism

National League ***Arizona:*** **12** Diamondbacks ***Atlanta:*** **6** Braves ***Chicago:*** **4** Cubs ***Cincinnati:*** **4** Reds ***Colorado:*** **7** Rockies ***Florida:*** **7** Marlins ***Houston:*** **6** Astros ***Los Angeles:*** **7** Dodgers ***Milwaukee:*** **7** Brewers ***New York:*** **4** Mets ***Philadelphia:*** **8** Phillies ***Pittsburgh:*** **7** Pirates ***St. Louis:*** **9** Cardinals ***San Diego:*** **6** Padres ***San Francisco:*** **6** Giants ***Washington:*** **9** Nationals

national military park ***Alabama:*** **13** Horseshoe Bend ***Arkansas:*** **8** Pea Ridge ***Mississippi:*** **9** Vicksburg ***Pennsylvania:*** **10** Gettysburg ***South Carolina:*** **13** Kings Mountain ***Tennessee:*** **6** Shiloh

national monument ***Alabama:*** **11** Russell Cave ***Alaska:*** **9** Aniakchak ***Arizona:*** **5** Tonto **6** Navajo **7** Saguaro, Wupatki **8** Tuzigoot **10** Chiricahua, Pipe Spring, Tumacacori **11** Hohokam Pima **12** Sunset Crater, Walnut Canyon ***California:*** **8** Cabrillo, Lava Beds **9** Muir Woods, Pinnacles **10** Joshua Tree **11** Death Valley ***Colorado:*** **10** Yucca House ***Colorado-Utah:*** **8** Dinosaur **9** Hovenweep ***Florida:*** **12** Fort Matanzas **13** Fort Jefferson ***Georgia:*** **8** Ocmulgee **11** Fort Pulaski **13** Fort Frederica ***Iowa:*** **12** Effigy Mounds ***Louisiana:*** **12** Poverty Point ***Maryland:*** **11** Fort McHenry ***Minnesota:*** **9** Pipestone **12** Grand Portage ***Nebraska:*** **9** Homestead **11** Scotts Bluff ***New Mexico:*** **5** Pecos **7** El Morro **9** Bandelier, El Malpais, Fort Union **10** Aztec Ruins, White Sands ***New York:*** **11** Fort Stanwix **13** Castle Clinton ***South Carolina:*** **10** Fort Sumter **13** Congaree Swamp ***South Dakota:*** **9** Jewel Cave ***Utah:*** **11** Cedar Breaks **13** Rainbow Bridge ***Wyoming:*** **11** Devils Tower, Fossil Butte

national park ***Alaska:*** **6** Denali, Katmai **9** Lake Clark **10** Glacier Bay **11** Kenai Fjords, Kobuk Valley ***Angola:*** **4** Iona, Mupa ***Arizona:*** **11** Grand Canyon ***Arkansas:*** **10** Hot Springs ***Botswana:*** **5** Chobe ***California:*** **7** Redwood, Sequoia **8** Yosemite **11** King's Canyon ***Chad:*** **5** Manda ***Colombia:*** **5** Uraba ***Colorado:*** **9** Mesa Verde **13** Rocky Mountain ***eastern Africa:*** **10** Mount Kenya ***Florida:*** **8** Biscayne **10** Everglades ***Hawaii:*** **9** Haleakala ***India:*** **5** Kanha ***Japan:*** **5** Nikko ***Kentucky:*** **11** Mammoth Cave ***Kenya:*** **4** Meru **5** Tsavo **10** Royal Tsavo ***Lake Superior:*** **10** Isle Royale ***Maine:*** **6** Acadia ***Malaysia:*** **8** Kinabalu ***Minnesota:*** **9** Voyageurs ***Montana:*** **7** Glacier ***Nevada:*** **10** Great Basin ***Oregon:*** **10** Crater Lake ***Poland:*** **5** Ojcow, Tatra ***South Africa:*** **6** Kruger ***South Dakota:*** **8** Badlands, Wind Cave ***Sri Lanka:*** **4** Yala ***Sweden:*** **5** Sarek ***Tanzania:*** **5** Ruaha **9** Serengeti ***Texas:*** **7** Big Bend ***Utah:*** **4** Zion **6** Arches **11** Bryce Canyon, Canyonlands, Capitol Reef ***Virginia:*** **10** Shenandoah ***Washington:*** **7** Olympic **12** Mount Rainier **13** North Cascades ***Wyoming:*** **10** Grand Teton ***Wyoming-Idaho-Montana:*** **11** Yellowstone ***Zambia:*** **5** Kafue ***Zimbabwe:*** **13** Rhodes Inyanga, Victoria Falls

native **3** raw **4** wild **5** local **6** inborn, innate **7** connate, endemic, natural **8** domestic, indigene, inherent, internal, national **9** inherited **10** aboriginal, congenital, connatural, indigenous, unacquired ***Acadian Louisiana:*** **5** Cajun ***China:*** **3** Han **9** Celestial ***India:*** **5** sepoy ***Japan:*** **9** Nipponese ***London:*** **7** Cockney ***Mindanao:*** **3** Ata ***New England:*** **4** Yank **6** Yankee ***New York:*** **13** Knickerbocker

Native American see **Indian, American**

Native Son author **6** Wright (Richard)

Nativity **4** Noel, Xmas, yule **8** yuletide **9** Christmas ***scene:*** **6** crèche

nativity **5** birth, start **6** origin, outset **7** genesis **8** delivery **9** beginning, horoscope, inception **11** parturition

natter **3** gab, jaw, yak, yap **4** blab, buzz, chat, go on **5** prate, run on **6** babble, gabble, gossip, tattle **7** chatter, prattle, twaddle **8** chitchat, converse

natty **4** neat, tidy, trim **5** doggy, nobby, sassy, smart, swank **6** classy, dapper, jaunty, snazzy, spiffy, spruce, sprucy, swanky **7** bandbox, doggish, stylish **9** turned out **11** well-groomed

natural 4 pure, wild **5** naive, usual **6** candid, inborn, innate, native, normal, simple **7** artless, connate, organic **8** homespun, inherent, innocent **9** childlike, ingenuous, ingrained, primitive **10** congenital, indigenous, legitimate, unaffected **11** commonplace, instinctive, spontaneous

naturalist *American:* 4 Muir (John) **5** Gould (Stephen Jay), Hyatt (Alpheus) **6** Carson (Rachel) **7** Agassiz (Louis), Audubon (John James), Thoreau (H. D.), Verrill (Addison, Alpheus) **9** Burroughs (John) ***English:* 3** Ray (John) **5** White (Gilbert) **6** Darwin (Charles) **7** Wallace (Alfred Russel) **10** Williamson (William) ***French:* 5** Fabre (Jean-Henri) **7** Lamarck (Chevalier de), Réaumur (René-Antoine) ***German:* 8** Humboldt (Alexander von) ***Scottish:* 6** Wilson (Alexander) **10** Richardson (John)

nature 3 ilk, way **4** kind, sort, type **6** makeup, manner, stripe, temper **7** essence, scenery **8** creation, tendency, universe **9** character, landscape **10** complexion **11** description, disposition, personality, temperament **12** constitution

naught 3 nil, nix, zip **4** love, nada, zero **5** zilch **6** cipher **7** nothing, nullity **8** goose egg **11** nothingness

naughty 3 bad **4** lewd **5** bawdy **6** unruly, ribald, risqué, smutty, vulgar **7** froward, obscene, raunchy, wayward, willful **8** contrary, improper, perverse, rascally **10** ill-behaved **11** disobedient, mischievous **12** obstreperous, recalcitrant

Nauru *capital:* 5 Yaren ***former name:* 8** Pleasant (Island)

nauseate 5 repel **6** offend, sicken **7** disgust, repulse

nauseated 6 queasy **7** carsick **8** qualmish **9** disgusted, squeamish **10** grossed out

nauseating 6 putrid **7** noisome **9** loathsome, offensive, repellant, repugnant, repulsive, revolting, sickening **10** disgusting

Nausicaa *father:* 8 Alcinous ***mother:* 5** Arete

nautical 5 naval **6** marine **7** oceanic **8** maritime **12** navigational ***instrument:* 3** aba **7** compass, pelorus, sextant

Navajo dwelling 5 hogan

naval hero 5 Drake (Francis), Jones (John Paul), Perry (Matthew, Oliver Hazard) **6** Nelson (Horatio) **8** Farragut (David, George), Lawrence (James)

navel 6 middle **7** nombril **9** umbilicus **11** belly button ***combining form:* 6** omphal **7** omphalo ***type:* 5** innie, outie

navigate 4 helm, plot, sail **5** guide, pilot, steer **6** cruise **8** maneuver, traverse

navigation 8 piloting **10** seamanship **12** helmsmanship

navigational system 5 loran

navigator 5 flyer, pilot **6** airman **7** copilot ***Danish:* 6** Bering (Vitus) ***Dutch:* 6** Tasman (Abel) **7** Barents (Willem) ***English:* 4** Cook (Captain James) **5** Cabot (John, Sebastian), Drake (Francis) **6** Hudson (Henry) **7** Gilbert (Humphrey), Raleigh (Walter) **9** Vancouver (George) ***French:* 7** Cartier (Jacques) **9** La Perouse (Comte de) ***Italian:* 6** Caboto (Giovanni) **8** Columbus (Christopher), Vespucci (Amerigo) **9** Verrazano (Giovanni) **10** Verrazzano (Giovanni) ***Norwegian:* 4** Eric (the Red), Erik (the Red) **8** Ericsson (Leif), Eriksson (Leif) **12** Leif Ericsson, Leif Eriksson ***Portuguese:* 4** Dias (Bartolomeu, Dinis) **6** Cabral (Pedro Alvares), da Gama (Vasco) **8** Magellan (Ferdinand) ***Spanish:* 9** Fernández (Juan)

navy 4 blue **5** fleet **6** argosy, armada **8** flotilla ***officer:* 3** ADM, CWO, ENS **4** CAPT, LCDR, LTJG, RADM, VADM **6** ensign **7** admiral, captain **9** commander **10** lieutenant

Nazi 9 Hitlerite **10** brownshirt ***admiral:* 6** Dönitz (Karl), Raeder (Erich) **7** Doenitz (Karl) ***air force:* 9** Luftwaffe ***armed forces:* 9** Wehrmacht ***cheer:* 8** Siegheil ***collaborator:* 5** Laval (Pierre) **8** Quisling (Vidkun) ***concentration camp:* 6** Belsen, Dachau **9** Auschwitz, Treblinka **10** Buchenwald, Nordhausen ***field marshal:* 5** Model (Walter) **6** Keitel (Wilhelm), Paulus (Friedrich), Rommel (Erwin) **9** Rundstedt (Karl von) **10** Kesselring (Albert) ***greeting:* 4** heil **10** heil Hitler ***leader:* 3** Ley (Robert) **4** Hess (Rudolf), Röhm (Ernst) **5** Roehm (Ernst) **6** Führer, Göring (Hermann), Hitler (Adolf) **7** Fuehrer, Goering (Hermann), Himmler (Heinrich) **8** Goebbels (Joseph), Heydrich (Reinhard) **9** Rosenberg (Alfred) ***police:* 7** Gestapo ***propagandist:* 8** Goebbels (Joseph) ***submarine:* 5** U-boat ***surrender signer:* 4** Jodl (Alfred) **6** Keitel (Wilhelm) ***symbol:* 6** fylfot **8** swastika ***tactic:* 10** blitzkrieg ***tank:* 6** Panzer

NCO 3 cpl, sgt **8** corporal, sergeant

neap 3 low **4** tide

near 4 nigh **5** about, circa, close, round **6** almost, around **7** close by, close on **8** adjacent, approach **9** immediate, proximate **11** approximate

nearby 4 nigh **5** about, aside, close, handy **6**

around, beside **8** adjacent **9** adjoining, proximate **10** contiguous, convenient **11** neighboring
nearest 4 next **7** closest **8** adjacent, proximal **9** proximate **10** contiguous
nearsighted 6 myopic
neat 4 deft, nice, prim, snug, tidy, trig, trim **5** clean, clear, kempt **6** bovine, cattle, clever, smooth, spruce **7** orderly, precise, unmixed **8** straight, well-kept **9** shipshape, undiluted **10** methodical, systematic **11** spic-and-span, uncluttered, well-groomed **12** spick-and-span **13** unadulterated
neb 3 tip **4** beak, bill, nose, prow **5** snoot, snout **9** proboscis
Nebraska ***capital:*** **7** Lincoln ***city:*** **5** Omaha ***college, university:*** **9** Creighton ***nickname:*** **10** Cornhusker (State) ***river:*** **6** Platte **8** Missouri ***state bird:*** **10** meadowlark ***state flower:*** **9** goldenrod ***state tree:*** **10** cottonwood
nebula 6 galaxy
nebulous 4 hazy **5** vague **6** cloudy, turbid **7** clouded, obscure, unclear **9** ambiguous, amorphous, uncertain **10** indefinite, indistinct **13** indeterminate
necessary 5 basic, vital **6** needed **7** crucial, needful **8** cardinal, integral, required **9** de rigueur, essential, mandatory, requisite **10** compulsory, imperative, inevitable, obligatory, undeniable **11** fundamental, ineluctable, inescapable, unavoidable **12** all-important, prerequisite **13** indispensable
necessitate 5 cause, exact, force **6** compel, demand, entail **7** call for, involve, require **8** occasion
necessity 4 must, need **6** crisis, duress **7** poverty **8** exigency **9** essential, privation, requisite **10** compulsion, imperative, obligation, sine qua non **11** dire straits, needfulness, requirement **12** precondition, prerequisite
neck 3 pet **4** kiss **5** spoon **6** fondle, smooch ***back of:*** **4** nape **5** nucha, nuque **6** scruff ***ornament:*** **6** gorget, torque
necklace 5 chain **6** choker **7** rivière **8** carcanet ***floral:*** **3** lei
necktie 4 bolo **5** ascot **6** cravat **10** four-in-hand
necrology 4 obit **8** obituary
necromancy 4 juju, mojo **5** magic, vodun **6** hoodoo, voodoo **7** devilry, sorcery **8** witchery, wizardry **9** conjuring, diabolism, magicking **10** black magic, witchcraft **11** bewitchment, conjuration, enchantment, incantation, thaumaturgy
necropolis 8 boneyard, boot hill, cemetery, God's acre **9** graveyard **10** churchyard **12** memorial park, potter's field
necropsy 7 anatomy, autopsy **10** dissection, postmortem
née 4 born **10** originally
need 3 use **4** call, duty, lack, must, want **5** crave **6** demand, devoir, hunger, penury, thirst **7** poverty, require **8** distress, exigency, occasion, shortage **9** indigence, necessity, privation, requisite **10** compulsion, deficiency, obligation **11** deprivation, destitution, requirement
neediness 4 want **6** penury **7** poverty **9** essential, indigence, privation **11** deprivation, destitution **13** insufficiency
needle 3 rib **5** annoy, tease **6** harass, pester, plague **7** bedevil, hagride, obelisk, pricker, syringe **10** hypodermic ***case:*** **4** etui ***hole:*** **3** eye
needlefish 3 gar **8** pipefish
needlelike 7 styloid **8** belonoid ***part:*** **7** acicula
needlepoint 4 lace **7** alençon, crochet, tatting **8** bargello **10** embroidery **11** cross-stitch
needlework 4 lace **6** sewing **7** alençon, crochet, sampler, tatting **8** bargello, knitting **9** stitching **10** crocheting, embroidery **11** cross-stitch
needy 4 poor **5** broke **6** hard up **8** beggared, dirt-poor, indigent, strapped **9** destitute, penniless, penurious **10** down-and-out **11** impecunious, necessitous **12** impoverished
ne'er-do-well 3 bum, dud **5** loser **6** loafer, no-good **7** failure, wastrel **8** derelict, fainéant **9** shiftless **10** profligate, scapegrace
nefarious 4 evil, vile **6** savage, wicked **7** heinous, impious, noxious **8** depraved, dreadful, flagrant, infamous, perverse **9** execrable, miscreant, monstrous, offensive **10** abominable, degenerate, detestable, iniquitous, outrageous, villainous **11** opprobrious **13** reprehensible
negate 4 deny, undo, void **5** annul, belie, quash, rebut **6** cancel, impugn, refute, vacate **7** abolish, gainsay, nullify, redress, vitiate **8** abrogate, disallow, disprove, overturn, traverse **9** cancel out, disaffirm, repudiate **10** contradict, contravene, counteract, invalidate, neutralize
negative 2 no **3** nay, nix **4** deny, kill, veto **5** annul, cross, minus **6** impugn **7** adverse, gainsay, nullify, redress, refusal **8** abrogate, disprove, traverse **9** cancel out, frustrate **10** contradict, contravene, counteract, invalidate, neutralize **11** detrimental, unfavorable ***battery terminal:*** **5** anode ***ion:*** **5** anion ***Scottish:*** **3** nae ***sign:*** **5** minus
neglect 4 fail, omit **5** let go, shirk **6** forget, ignore, laxity, slight **7** failure, laxness **8** omission, overlook, overpass, pass over **9**

avoidance, disregard, oversight, pretermit **10** negligence **11** dereliction, inattention **12** carelessness
neglectful see **negligent**
negligee 4 gown **5** teddy **7** chemise, nightie **8** camisole, peignoir **9** nightgown
negligent 3 lax **5** slack **6** remiss **8** careless, derelict, heedless **9** forgetful, imprudent **10** delinquent, neglectful, nonchalant, regardless, unthinking **11** inattentive, pococurante, unconcerned **13** irresponsible, lackadaisical
negligible 4 puny, slim **5** minor, petty, small **6** meager, meagre, minute, remote, paltry, skimpy, slight **7** minimal, slender, trivial **8** nugatory, picayune, trifling **9** minuscule **11** meaningless, unimportant **13** imperceptible, insignificant
negotiable 8 passable **11** convertible **12** transferable
negotiate 4 cash **6** confer, dicker, hurdle, manage, parley, settle **7** arrange, bargain, develop, mediate, work out, wrangle **8** contract, covenant, moderate, surmount, transact, transfer **9** arbitrate **10** horse-trade
neigh 6 nicker, whinny
neighbor 4 abut **5** flank, frame, skirt, touch **6** adjoin, border **7** abutter **8** border on
neighborhood 4 area, nabe, turf, ward **5** block, range **6** parish **8** district, environs, locality, precinct, purlieus, vicinage, vicinity **9** community, proximity
neighborly 6 genial **7** amiable, cordial, helpful **8** amicable, friendly, obliging, sociable **9** congenial **10** gregarious, hospitable **11** considerate, cooperative, good-natured **13** accommodating
nematode 4 worm **7** eelworm **9** roundworm
Nemean predator 4 lion
nemesis 4 bane, doom **5** curse, enemy, rival **8** opponent **9** bête noire **11** retribution
neologism 7 coinage, new word
neon symbol 2 Ne
neophyte see **newcomer**
Neoptolemus 7 Pyrrhus ***father:*** **8** Achilles ***slayer:*** **7** Orestes ***victim:*** **5** Priam ***wife:*** **8** Hermione
neoteric 6 modern, recent
Nepal *capital:* **8** Katmandu **9** Kathmandu ***city:*** **7** Pokhara **8** Lalitpur ***monetary unit:*** **5** rupee ***mountain, range:*** **7** Everest **8** Himalaya **9** Himalayan, Himalayas **10** Dhaulagiri **11** Gauri Sankar **12** Kanchenjunga ***neighbor:*** **5** China, India ***river:*** **6** Ganges
nepenthe 6 opiate, potion **7** anodyne **8** lenitive, narcotic **9** analgesic **10** anesthetic, painkiller **11** anaesthetic
Nephthys *brother, husband:* **3** Set **4** Seth
nepotism 10 favoritism, partiality
Neptune 6 planet ***satellite:*** **6** Nereid, Triton (see also **Poseidon**)
nerd 4 drip, geek **5** dweeb **6** misfit, weenie **7** egghead, nebbish, oddball **10** pointy-head
Nereid 6 Thetis **7** Galatea **10** Amphitrite ***father:*** **6** Nereus ***mother:*** **5** Doris
Nereus *daughters:* **8** Nereides ***emblem:*** **7** trident ***father:*** **6** Pontus ***mother:*** **4** Gaea ***wife:*** **5** Doris
Nergal *brother:* **5** Nanna **6** Ninazu ***father:*** **5** Enlil ***mother:*** **6** Ninlil
Nero *birthplace:* **4** Rome ***mother:*** **9** Agrippina ***successor:*** **5** Galba ***tutor:*** **6** Seneca ***victim:*** **5** Lucan **6** Seneca **7** Octavia, Poppaea **9** Agrippina ***wife:*** **7** Octavia, Poppaea
Nero Wolfe creator 5 Stout (Rex)
nerve 4 face, gall, grit, guts **5** brass, cheek, crust, heart, moxie, spunk **6** daring **7** sciatic **8** audacity, backbone, boldness, chutzpah, temerity **9** assurance, brashness, fortitude, hardihood, hardiness **10** confidence, effrontery **11** presumption ***cell:*** **6** neuron ***cell group:*** **7** ganglia (plural) **8** ganglion ***cell part:*** **4** axon **8** dendrite, receptor ***combining form:*** **4** neur **5** neura, neuro ***cranial:*** **4** vagi (plural) **5** optic, vagus **8** abducens ***lesion:*** **8** neuritis
nerve center 3 hub **4** core, seat **5** focus, heart, locus **7** capital **8** cynosure, polestar **10** crossroads, focal point **12** headquarters
nerve gas 5 sarin, soman, tabun
nervous 4 edgy **5** antsy, jerky, jumpy, tense, timid **6** fitful, goosey, on edge, spooky, uneasy **7** erratic, fidgety, fretful, jittery, restive, twitchy, uptight **8** aflutter, agitated, skittery, skittish, spirited, twittery, unsteady, vigorous, volatile **9** excitable, irritable **10** high-strung **12** apprehensive
nervy 4 bold, edgy, flip, pert **5** brash, cocky, fresh, jerky, jumpy, sassy, tense **6** brassy, cheeky, goosey, plucky, uneasy **7** fidgety, forward, jittery, restive, twitchy, uptight **8** flippant, impudent, intrepid, twittery **9** excitable **10** high-strung **11** smart-alecky
ness 4 cape **8** foreland, headland **9** peninsula **10** promontory
Nessus' victim 8 Heracles, Hercules
nest 3 den **4** aery, home, lair, nidi (plural) **5** aerie, eyrie, nidus **7** hangout, shelter **11** aggregation ***eagle's:*** **4** aery **5** aerie, eyrie ***pheasant's:*** **4** nide ***wasp's:*** **8** vespiary
nest egg 5 cache, funds, hoard, kitty, stash **6** assets **7** reserve
nestle 4 snug **6** bundle, burrow, cuddle, huddle, nuzzle **7** snuggle
Nestor *father:* **6** Neleus ***kingdom:*** **5** Pylos

net **4** gain, gist, mesh **5** basic, catch, clear, seine, tulle, yield **6** maline **7** clean up, essence, malines ***conical:*** **5** trawl ***fishing:*** **5** seine ***hair:*** **5** snood

Nethanel ***brother:*** **5** David ***father:*** **5** Jesse **7** Pashhur **8** Obededom ***son:*** **8** Shemaiah

nether **3** low **4** down **5** below, lower, under **6** lesser **8** chthonic, inferior **9** subjacent **10** underworld **11** underground **12** subterranean

Netherlands **7** Holland ***capital:*** **9** Amsterdam ***city:*** **5** Hague (The) **7** Utrecht **8** The Hague **9** Rotterdam ***former inlet:*** **9** Zuider Zee ***island group:*** **11** West Frisian ***lake:*** **10** IJsselmeer ***language:*** **5** Dutch ***monetary unit:*** **4** euro ***monetary unit, former:*** **6** gulden, stiver **7** guilder ***neighbor:*** **7** Belgium, Germany ***river:*** **4** Maas **5** Meuse, Rhein, Rhine **7** Scheldt ***sea:*** **5** North

Netherlands Antilles ***capital:*** **10** Willemstad ***discoverer:*** **8** Columbus (Christopher) ***former name:*** **7** Curaçao ***island:*** **4** Saba **7** Bonaire **7** Curaçao ***location:*** **10** West Indies

netherworld **3** pit **4** hell **5** abyss, hades, Sheol **6** blazes, Tophet **7** Gehenna, inferno **8** hellfire **9** perdition **10** no-man's-land, underworld **11** underground

netlike **9** reticular **10** reticulate

nettle **3** irk, nag, vex **4** gall, huff, rile, roil **5** annoy, chafe, peeve, pique, upset **6** abrade, badger, harass, incite, put out, pester, ruffle, stir up **7** agitate, disturb, perturb, provoke **8** irritate **10** exasperate

nettle rash **5** hives **9** urticaria

nettlesome **5** pesky **6** vexing **7** galling, irksome, prickly **8** annoying, rankling **9** irritable, upsetting, vexatious **10** irritating

network **3** ABC, CBS, CNN, CTV, Fox, HBO, NBC, PBS, QVC, TBS, TNT, web **4** ESPN, grid, INHD, mesh, NESN, rete **8** gridiron, Internet **9** reticulum ***anatomical:*** **4** rete **5** retia (plural)

neurotic **6** phobic, touchy **7** anxious **8** abnormal, unstable **9** disturbed, obsessive **10** compulsive, disordered

neuter **3** fix **4** geld, spay **5** alter, unsex **7** sexless **8** castrate, mutilate **9** sterilize **11** desexualize **12** intransitive

neutral **7** hueless **8** detached, middling, unbiased **9** colorless, impartial, unaligned **10** achromatic, disengaged, even-handed, impersonal, nonaligned, pokerfaced **11** indifferent, nonpartisan **13** disinterested, dispassionate

neutralize **4** undo **5** annul **6** negate, offset **7** balance, nullify, redress, reverse **9** cancel out **10** counteract, invalidate **11** countervail **12** countercheck, counterpoise

Nevada ***capital:*** **10** Carson City ***city:*** **4** Elko, Reno **8** Las Vegas ***dam:*** **6** Hoover **7** Boulder ***lake:*** **4** Mead **5** Tahoe ***mountain:*** **8** Boundary (Peak) ***nickname:*** **6** Silver (State) ***river:*** **8** Humboldt ***state bird:*** **8** bluebird (mountain) ***state flower:*** **9** sagebrush ***state tree:*** **5** piñon **6** pinyon **15** bristlecone pine

névé **4** firn, snow

never-ending **7** eternal **8** immortal **9** ceaseless **11** everlasting

Never-Ending Story author **4** Ende (Michael)

nevertheless **3** but, yet **5** still **6** anyhow, anyway, though, withal **7** howbeit, however **8** after all **10** regardless **11** nonetheless, still and all

nevus **4** mole **9** birthmark

new **5** fresh, novel **6** modern, recent **7** another, revived **8** neoteric, pristine **9** fledgling **10** additional, unfamiliar **11** modernistic **12** contemporary ***combining form:*** **3** neo, nov **4** novo ***word:*** **7** coinage **9** neologism

New Age ***belief:*** **5** karma **6** cabala, holism, kabala **7** kabbala **8** kabbalah **9** occultism, pantheism, shamanism, theosophy, wholeness **10** numerology, soul travel **12** spiritualism **13** reincarnation, synchronicity ***community:*** **6** Esalen, Sedona, Totnes **7** Dornach **8** Byron Bay, Damanhur, Findhorn **9** Arcosanti, Auroville ***healing technique:*** **5** auras **8** Ayurveda, crystals **9** iridology **10** homeopathy **11** acupressure, acupuncture, biofeedback **12** aromatherapy ***practice:*** **4** yoga **5** reiki **7** fasting **10** channeling, meditation, syncretism ***teacher:*** **3** Orr (Leonard) **4** Dass (Ram), Long (Barry), Myss (Caroline) **5** Cohen (Andrew) **6** Chopra (Deepak), Walsch (Neale Donald), Wilber (Ken) **7** Kabbani (Hisham), Quanjer (Johan) **8** Cottrell (Douglas James), Rajneesh (Bhagwan Shree), Spangler (David) **9** Castaneda (Carlos), Helminski (Kabir) **10** Williamson (Marianne)

New Brunswick ***capital:*** **11** Fredericton ***city:*** **6** St. John **7** Moncton ***mountain:*** **8** Carleton ***provincial flower:*** **12** purple violet ***river:*** **9** Miramichi, Saint John **10** Nepisiguit **11** Restigouche

New Caledonia ***capital:*** **6** Nouméa ***department of:*** **6** France ***discoverer:*** **4** Cook (Capt. James) ***island:*** **7** Loyalty, Walpole **11** Isle of Pines

newcomer **4** colt, tiro, tyro **6** novice, rookie **7** trainee **8** beginner, freshman, initiate, neophyte **9** greenhorn, immigrant, novitiate **10** apprentice, tenderfoot

New Deal agency 3 CCC, NRA, REA, RFC, SEC, TVA, WPA **4** FDIC, NLRB

Newfoundland and Labrador *capital:* 7 St. John's ***mountain:* 8** Caubvick ***provincial flower:* 12** pitcher plant ***river:* 6** Gander **8** Exploits **9** Churchill

New Hampshire *capital:* 7 Concord ***city:* 6** Nashua **10** Manchester, Portsmouth ***college, university:* 9** Dartmouth ***motto:* 13** Live Free or Die ***mountain, range:* 5** White **10** Washington ***nickname:* 7** Granite (State) ***river:* 9** Merrimack **11** Connecticut ***state bird:* 11** purple finch ***state flower:* 11** purple lilac ***state tree:* 10** white birch

New Jersey *capital:* 7 Trenton ***city:* 6** Camden, Newark **7** Cape May **8** Paterson **9** Elizabeth **10** Jersey City ***college, university:* 4** Drew **7** Rutgers **9** Princeton, Seton Hall ***nickname:* 6** Garden (State) ***river:* 6** Hudson **7** Raritan **8** Delaware ***state bird:* 9** goldfinch ***state flower:* 6** violet ***state tree:* 6** red oak

New Mexico *capital:* 7 Santa Fe ***caverns:* 8** Carlsbad ***city:* 4** Taos **7** Roswell **9** Las Cruces, Los Alamos **10** Farmington **11** Albuquerque ***mountain, range:* 7** Wheeler (Peak) **14** Sangre de Cristo ***nickname:* 17** Land of Enchantment ***river:* 5** Pecos **9** Rio Grande ***state bird:* 10** roadrunner ***state flower:* 5** yucca ***state tree:* 5** piñon **6** pinyon

news 4 dope, poop, word **5** rumor **6** advice, gossip, report, tattle **7** lowdown, tidings **9** knowledge, speerings **11** information, scuttlebutt **12** announcement, intelligence ***agency:* 2** AP **3** AFP, UPI **4** TASS **7** Reuters **8** ITAR-TASS

newspaper 3 rag **5** daily, organ **6** review **7** gazette, journal, tabloid **8** magazine **10** periodical ***goof:* 4** typo ***publisher:* 6** Hearst (William Randolph) **7** Murdoch (Rupert) **11** Beaverbrook (Lord) ***section:* 4** arts, op-ed **6** comics, sports **8** business **10** classified

newt 3 eft **6** triton ***green:* 5** ebbet

New Testament see at **Bible**

New York *capital:* 6 Albany ***city:* 4** Rome, Troy **5** Utica **6** Elmira, Ithaca **7** Buffalo, Yonkers **8** Saratoga, Syracuse **9** Rochester ***college, university:* 3** RPI **4** Pace, CUNY, SUNY **5** Pratt, Siena **6** CW Post, Hunter, Vassar **7** Adelphi, Barnard, Colgate, Cornell, Fordham, Hofstra, St. Johns, Yeshiva **8** Columbia, Skidmore, Syracuse **9** Juilliard, West Point **13** Sarah Lawrence ***county:* 5** Tioga **6** Albany, Oneida, Queens **7** Clinton, Niagara **8** Dutchess, Onandaga ***island:* 4** Long, Fire ***lake, lake group:* 4** Erie **6** Cayuga, Finger, Oneida **7** Saranac **9** Champlain ***motto:* 9** Excelsior ***mountain, range:* 5** Marcy **8** Catskill **10** Adirondack ***nickname:* 6** Empire (State) ***prison:* 6** Attica ***river:* 6** Hudson **7** Niagara **10** St. Lawrence ***state bird:* 8** bluebird ***state flower:* 4** rose ***state tree:* 10** sugar maple

New York City 6 Gotham **8** Big Apple ***borough:* 5** Bronx **6** Queens **8** Brooklyn, Richmond **9** Manhattan **12** Staten Island ***neighborhood:* 4** Soho **6** Harlem **7** Tribeca

New Zealand *capital:* 10 Wellington ***city:* 8** Auckland **12** Christchurch ***ethnic group:* 5** Maori ***evergreen:* 4** tawa ***explorer:* 4** Cook (Capt. James) **6** Tasman (Abel) ***island:* 7** Chatham, Stewart ***island group:* 4** Cook **8** Manihiki **12** Northern Cook ***lake:* 5** Taupo ***language:* 5** Maori ***mountain, range:* 4** Cook **6** Egmont **12** Southern Alps ***native:* 4** Kiwi ***parrot:* 4** kaka ***shrub:* 4** tutu ***strait:* 4** Cook ***volcano:* 7** Ruapehu **9** Ngauruhoe

next 4 then **5** after, later **6** behind, beside, second **7** closest, ensuing, nearest **8** abutting, adjacent, touching **9** adjoining, afterward, alongside, following, proximate **10** contiguous, subsequent, succeeding **11** neighboring

next to 4 near **6** almost, beside **7** abreast, close by **8** abutting, adjacent, opposite, touching **9** adjoining, alongside, bordering **11** neighboring

nexus 3 tie **4** bond, knot, link, yoke **5** focus **6** center **8** ligament, ligature, vinculum **10** connection

Nez Percé chief 6 Joseph

Niagara 5 flood, spate **6** deluge **7** torrent **8** alluvion, cataract, flooding, overflow **9** cataclysm, waterfall **10** inundation

nib 3 tip **4** beak, bill, nose, prow **5** prong, snoot, snout, tooth **8** pen point **9** proboscis

nibble 3 eat, nip **4** bite, chew, crop, gnaw, nosh, peck, pick **5** graze, munch, snack, taste **6** morsel, tidbit

Nicaragua *capital:* 7 Managua ***city:* 4** León **6** Masaya **7** Grenada ***coast:* 8** Mosquito ***ethnic group:* 4** Maya **5** Mayan ***discoverer:* 8** Columbus (Christopher) ***language:* 7** Spanish ***monetary unit:* 7** córdoba ***neighbor:* 8** Honduras **9** Costa Rica ***sea:* 9** Caribbean

nice 4 fine, good, kind, mild, neat **5** right **6** benign, decent, polite, proper, seemly **7** affable, cordial, correct, fitting, refined **8** becoming, charming, decorous, obliging, pleasant, pleasing, suitable, virtuous, well-bred **9** admirable, agreeable, courteous,

congenial, enjoyable, favorable **10** attractive, personable **11** appropriate, respectable
niche 4 nook **6** alcove, corner, cranny, recess **7** calling **8** vocation **9** cubbyhole **11** compartment
Nicholas Nickleby author 7 Dickens (Charles)
nick 3 cut **4** chip, gash **5** cheat, notch, score **6** groove, record **10** overcharge **11** indentation
nickel symbol 2 Ni
nickname 3 tag **5** label **6** byword, handle **7** agnomen, epithet, moniker **8** cognomen **9** sobriquet **10** diminutive, hypocorism
Nicomede *conquest:* 10 Cappodocia ***dramatist:* 9** Corneille (Pierre) ***half-brother:* 6** Attale ***stepmother:* 7** Arsinoë
nictitate 3 bat **4** wink **5** blink **7** flutter, twinkle
nifty 4 cool, keen, neat **5** dandy, ducky, super, swell **6** clever, groovy, peachy **7** stylish **8** jim-dandy, splendid, terrific **9** ingenious
Niger *capital:* 6 Niamey ***city:* 6** Maradi, Zinder ***desert:* 5** Sahel **6** Sahara ***ethnic group:* 5** Hausa ***language:* 5** Hausa **6** Arabic, French ***monetary unit:* 5** franc ***neighbor:* 4** Chad, Mali **5** Benin, Libya **7** Algeria, Nigeria **11** Burkina Faso ***river:* 5** Niger
Nigeria *capital:* 5 Abuja, Lagos ***city:* 4** Kano **6** Ibadan, Ilorin **7** Oshogbo **9** Ogbomosho ***ethnic group:* 4** Igbo **5** Hausa **6** Fulani, Yoruba ***gulf:* 6** Guinea ***lake:* 4** Chad ***language:* 5** Hausa ***monetary unit:* 5** naira ***neighbor:* 4** Chad **5** Benin, Niger **8** Cameroon ***river:* 5** Benue, Niger **6** Kaduna
niggard 5 churl, miser, piker, screw **7** hoarder, scrooge **8** tightwad **9** skinflint **10** cheapskate, curmudgeon **12** money-grubber, penny-pincher
niggardly 5 tight **6** scanty, stingy **7** chintzy, miserly **9** penurious **10** begrudging **11** closefisted, tightfisted **12** cheeseparing, parsimonious **13** penny-pinching
niggling 5 minor, petty **6** measly, paltry, two-bit **7** trivial **8** picayune, piddling, tiresome, trifling **9** small-time **10** bothersome, picayunish **11** Mickey Mouse, small-minded
nigh 4 near **5** about, close, round **6** all but, almost, around, beside, nearby, nearly **7** close to **8** approach **9** immediate, just about, proximate, virtually **10** near at hand **11** practically
night blindness 10 nyctalopia
nightclub 5 disco **6** bistro, casino **7** cabaret **9** honky-tonk, speakeasy **11** discotheque
nightfall 3 eve **4** dusk, even **6** sunset **7** evening, sundown **8** eventide, gloaming, twilight
nighthawk 6 petrel **7** bullbat **10** goatsucker
nightjar 9 nighthawk **10** goatsucker **12** whip-poor-will
nightly 9 nocturnal
nightmare 5 dream, fancy, worry **6** fright, horror, ordeal, vision **7** bugbear, fantasy, incubus, torment **8** phantasm, phantasy, succubus **12** apprehension **13** hallucination
nightshade 6 tomato **7** henbane **8** eggplant **10** belladonna **11** bittersweet
nightstick 3 bat **4** club, mace **5** baton, billy, staff **6** cudgel **8** bludgeon **9** billy club, blackjack, shillalah, truncheon **10** shillelagh
Nike *father:* 6 Pallas ***goddess of:* 7** victory ***mother:* 4** Styx
nil 3 nix, zip **4** love, nada, wind, zero **5** zilch **6** naught **7** nothing
Nile 6 Al-Bahr ***dam:* 5** Aswan **6** Makwar **10** Gebel Aulia ***enclave:* 4** Lado ***explorer:* 5** Baker (Sir Samuel), Bruce (James), Grant (James Augustus), Speke (John Hanning) ***queen:* 4** Cleo **9** Cleopatra ***section:* 4** Abay **5** Abbai ***source lake:* 4** Tana
nilgai 8 antelope
nimble 4 deft, spry, yare **5** agile, alert, fleet, handy, light, quick, zippy **6** adroit, limber, lively **7** lissome **9** dexterous, sprightly **10** responsive **11** quick-witted
nimbus 4 aura, halo **5** glory **6** corona **7** aureole
Nimrod 6 hunter ***father:* 4** Cush
Nin, Anaïs *father:* 7 Joaquin ***friend:* 6** Miller (Henry)
Ninazu *brother:* 5 Nanna **6** Nergal ***father:* 5** Enlil ***mother:* 6** Ninlil
nincompoop 3 oaf **4** boob, clod, dodo, fool, goof, mutt, simp, yo-yo **5** chump, dummy, dunce, idiot, moron, ninny, noddy, stupe **6** dimwit, donkey, dum-dum, nitwit **7** airhead, dullard, pinhead, schnook, tomfool **8** bonehead, clodpoll, dumbbell, dumbhead, imbecile, lunkhead, meathead, numskull **9** birdbrain, blockhead, ignoramus, lamebrain, numbskull, simpleton, thickhead **10** dunderhead, hammerhead **11** chowderhead, chucklehead, knucklehead, ninnyhammer
nine 12 baseball team ***combining form:* 3** non **4** nona **5** ennea ***goddesses:* 5** Muses ***group:* 6** ennead ***inches:* 4** span ***instruments:* 5** nonet
nine-eyes 7 lamprey
Nine Worlds 3 Hel **6** Asgard **7** Alfheim, Midgard **8** Niflheim, Vanaheim **10** Jotunnheim **12** Muspellsheim **13** Svartalfaheim
ninny see **nincompoop**
Ninsum's son 9 Gilgamesh
Nintu *consort:* 4 Enki ***son:* 6** Ninsar

Ninurta ***father:*** **5** Enlil ***victim:*** **3** Kur
Ninus ***father:*** **5** Belus ***wife:*** **9** Semiramis
Niobe ***brother:*** **6** Pelops ***father:*** **8** Tantalus ***husband:*** **7** Amphion ***sister-in-law:*** **5** Aedon
nip 3 bit, nab, sip **4** bite, dart, dash, dram, drop, jolt, peck, shot, slug, swig **5** chill, clamp, hurry, pinch, sever, snort, steal **6** imbibe, snatch, thwart, tipple **7** cabbage, snifter, swallow **9** frustrate
nipper 3 kid **4** tike, tyke **5** child **6** moppet, shaver **7** pincers **9** youngling, youngster
nipple 3 pap **4** teat **7** mammila
Nippon 5 Japan
nippy 3 icy, raw **4** cold, cool **5** algid, chill, crisp, sharp **6** arctic, biting, bitter, chilly, frosty, wintry **7** caustic, glacial, numbing, shivery **8** chilling, freezing
nirvana 5 bliss, dream **6** heaven **7** Elysium, rapture **8** empyrean, euphoria, oblivion, paradise **9** Shangri-la
Nisus ***betrayer, daughter:*** **6** Scylla ***father:*** **7** Pandion
nitid 6 bright, glossy, lucent **7** fulgent, glowing, shining **8** gleaming, glinting, luminous, lustrous, polished **9** burnished
nitpick 4 carp **5** cavil **7** quibble **10** split hairs
nitrogen 5 azote ***combining form:*** **3** azo
nitty-gritty 4 core, gist, meat, pith **5** heart, stuff **6** burden, kernel **7** essence **9** substance **10** bottom line, brass tacks
nitwit 3 oaf **4** boob, clod, dodo, dolt, dope, goof, mutt, simp **5** chump, cluck, dummy, dunce, idiot, moron, ninny, noddy, stupe **6** donkey, dum-dum **7** airhead, dullard, pinhead, schnook **8** bonehead, clodpoll, dumbbell, imbecile, lunkhead, meathead, numskull **9** birdbrain, blockhead, ignoramus, lamebrain, numbskull, simpleton, thickhead **10** dunderhead, hammerhead, nincompoop **11** chowderhead, chucklehead, knucklehead
nix 2 no **3** nay, nil, zap **4** kill, nada, nope, veto, zero **5** quash **6** cancel, naught, reject, scotch, sprite **7** call off, nothing, nullify
Njord, Njorth ***daughter:*** **5** Freya ***son:*** **4** Frey ***wife:*** **6** Skadhi, Skathi
no 3 nay, nix **4** uh-uh **6** denial **7** refusal **8** negative **10** thumbs-down ***German:*** **4** nein ***Scottish:*** **3** nae
no-account see **no-good**
Noachian 3 old **4** aged **5** fusty, hoary **6** age-old **7** ancient, antique, archaic **8** timeworn **9** venerable **10** antiquated, oldfangled **12** antediluvian, old-fashioned **13** superannuated
Noah ***father:*** **6** Lamech **10** Zelophehad ***grandson:*** **4** Aram **6** Canaan ***great-grandson:*** **3** Hul ***landing place:*** **6** Ararat ***son:*** **3** Ham **4** Shem **6** Canaan **7** Japheth
Nobel Prize winner
chemistry:
1901: 8 van't Hoff (Jacobus) **1902: 7** Fischer (Emil) **1903: 9** Arrhenius (Svante) **1904: 6** Ramsay (William) **1905: 9** von Baeyer (Adolf) **1906: 7** Moissan (Henri) **1907: 7** Buchner (Eduard) **1908: 10** Rutherford (Ernest) **1909: 7** Ostwald (Wilhelm) **1910: 7** Wallach (Otto) **1911: 5** Curie (Marie) **1912: 8** Grignard (François), Sabatier (Paul) **1913: 6** Werner (Alfred) **1914: 8** Richards (Theodore) **1915: 11** Willstatter (Richard) **1918: 5** Haber (Fritz) **1920: 6** Nernst (Walther) **1921: 5** Soddy (Frederick) **1922: 5** Aston (Francis) **1923: 5** Pregl (Fritz) **1925: 9** Zsigmondy (Richard) **1926: 8** Svedberg (Theodor) **1927: 7** Wieland (Heinrich) **1928: 7** Windaus (Adolf) **1929: 6** Harden (Athur) **12** Euler-Chelpin (Hans von) **1930: 7** Fischer (Hans) **1931: 5** Bosch (Karl) **7** Bergius (Friedrich) **1932: 8** Langmuir (Irving) **1934: 4** Urey (Harold) **1935: 11** Joliot-Curie (Frédéric, Irene) **1936: 5** Debye (Peter) **1937: 6** Karrer (Paul) **7** Haworth (Walter) **1938: 4** Kuhn (Richard) **1939: 7** Ruzicka (Leopold) **9** Butenandt (Adolf) **1943: 6** Hevesy (Georg de) **1944: 4** Hahn (Otto) **1945: 8** Virtanen (Artturi) **1946: 6** Sumner (James) **7** Stanley (Wendell) **8** Northrop (John Howard) **1947: 8** Robinson (Robert) **1948: 8** Tiselius (Arne) **1949: 7** Giauque (William) **1950: 5** Alder (Kurt), Diels (Otto) **1951: 7** Seaborg (Glenn) **8** McMillan (Edwin) **1952: 5** Synge (Richard) **6** Martin (Archer) **1953: 10** Staudinger (Hermann) **1954: 7** Pauling (Linus) **1955: 10** du Vigneaud (Vincent) **1956: 7** Semenov (Nikolay) **11** Hinshelwood (Cyril) **1957: 4** Todd (Alexander) **1958: 6** Sanger (Frederick) **1959: 9** Heyrovsky (Jaroslav) **1960: 5** Libby (Willard) **1961: 6** Calvin (Melvin) **1962: 6** Perutz (Max) **7** Kendrew (John) **1963: 5** Natta (Giulio) **7** Ziegler (Karl) **1964: 7** Hodgkin (Dorothy) **8** Woodward (Robert) **1966: 8** Mulliken (Robert) **1967: 5** Eigen (Manfred) **6** Porter (George) **7** Norrish (Ronald) **1968: 7** Onsager (Lars) **1969: 6** Barton (Derek), Hassel (Odd) **1970: 6** Leloir (Luis) **1971: 8** Herzberg (Gerhard) **1972: 5** Moore (Stanford), Stein (William) **8** Anfinsen (Christian) **1973: 7** Fischer (Ernst) **9** Wilkinson (Geoffrey) **1974: 5** Flory (Paul) **1975: 6**

Prelog (Vladimir) **9** Cornforth (John) **1976: 8** Lipscomb (William) **1977: 9** Prigogine (Ilya) **1978: 8** Mitchell (Peter) **1979: 5** Brown (Herbert) **6** Wittig (Georg) **1980: 4** Berg (Paul) **6** Sanger (Frederick) **7** Gilbert (Walter) **1981: 5** Fukui (Kenichi) **8** Hoffmann (Roald) **1982: 4** Klug (Aaron) **1983: 5** Taube (Henry) **1984: 10** Merrifield (R. Bruce) **1985: 5** Karle (Jerome) **8** Hauptman (Herbert) **1986: 3** Lee (Yuan) **7** Polanyi (John) **10** Herschbach (Dudley) **1987: 4** Cram (Donald), Lehn (Jean-Marie) **8** Pedersen (Charles) **1988: 5** Huber (Robert) **6** Michel (Hartmut) **11** Deisenhofer (Johann) **1989: 4** Cech (Thomas) **6** Altman (Sidney) **1990: 5** Corey (Elias) **1991: 5** Ernst (Richard) **1992: 6** Marcus (Rudolph) **1993: 5** Smith (Michael) **6** Mullis (Kary) **1994: 4** Olah (George) **1995: 6** Molina (Mario) **7** Crutzen (Paul), Rowland (F. Sherwood) **1996: 4** Curl (Robert) **5** Kroto (Harold) **7** Smalley (Richard) **1997 4** Skou (Jens) **5** Boyer (Paul) **6** Walker (John) **1998: 4** Kohn (Walter) **5** Pople (John) **1999: 6** Zewail (Ahmed) **2000: 6** Heeger (Alan) **9** Shirakawa (Hideki) **10** MacDiarmid (Alan) **2001: 6** Noyori (Ryoji) **7** Knowles (William) **9** Sharpless (K. Barry) **2002: 4** Fenn (John) **6** Tanaka (Koichi) **8** Wüthrich (Kurt) **2003: 4** Agre (Peter) **9** MacKinnon (Roderick) **2004: 4** Rose (Irwin) **7** Hershko (Avram) **11** Ciechanover (Aaron) **2005: 6** Grubbs (Robert) **7** Chauvin (Yves), Schrock (Richard) **2006: 8** Kornberg (Roger) **2007: 4** Ertl (Gerhard) **2008: 5** Tsien (Roger) **7** Chalfie (Martin) **9** Shimomura (Osamu) **2009: 6** Steitz (Thomas), Yonath (Ada) **12** Ramakrishnan (Venkatraman) **2010: 4** Heck (Richard) **6** Suzuki (Akira) **7** Negishi (Ei-Ichi)

economics:

1969: 6 Frisch (Ragnar) **9** Tinbergen (Jan) **1970: 9** Samuelson (Paul) **1971: 7** Kuznets (Simon) **1972: 5** Arrow (Kenneth), Hicks (John) **1973: 8** Leontief (Wassily) **1974: 5** Hayek (Friedrich von) **6** Myrdal (Gunnar) **1975: 8** Koopmans (Tjalling) **11** Kantorovich (Leonid) **1976: 8** Friedman (Milton) **1977: 5** Meade (James), Ohlin (Bertil) **1978: 5** Simon (Herbert) **1979: 5** Lewis (Arthur) **7** Schultz (Theodore) **1980: 5** Klein (Lawrence) **1981: 5** Tobin (James) **1982: 7** Stigler (George) **1983: 6** Debreu (Gerard) **1984: 5** Stone (Richard) **1985: 10** Modigliani (Franco) **1986: 8** Buchanan (James) **1987: 5** Solow (Robert) **1988: 6** Allais (Maurice) **1989: 8** Haavelmo (Trygve) **1990: 6** Miller (Merton), Sharpe (William) **9** Markowitz (Harry) **1991: 5** Coase (Ronald) **1992: 6** Becker (Gary) **1993: 5** Fogel (Robert), North (Douglass) **1994: 4** Nash (John) **6** Selten (Reinhard) **8** Harsanyi (John) **1995: 5** Lucas (Robert) **1996: 7** Vickrey (William) **8** Mirrlees (James) **1998: 3** Sen (Amartya) **1999: 7** Mundell (Robert) **2000: 7** Heckman (James) **8** McFadden (Daniel) **2001: 6** Spence (Michael) **7** Akerlof (George) **8** Stiglitz (Joseph) **2002: 5** Smith (Vernon) **8** Kahneman (Daniel) **2003: 5** Engle (Robert) **7** Granger (Clive) **2004: 7** Kydland (Finn) **8** Prescott (Edward) **2005: 6** Aumann (Robert) **9** Schelling (Thomas) **2006: 6** Phelps (Edmund) **2007: 6** Maskin (Eric) **7** Hurwicz (Leonid), Myerson (Roger) **2008: 7** Krugman (Paul) **2009: 6** Ostrom (Elinor) **10** Williamson (Oliver) **2010: 7** Diamond (Peter) **9** Mortensen (Dale) **10** Pissarides (Christopher)

literature:

1901: 9 Prudhomme (Sully) **1902: 7** Mommsen (Theodor) **1903: 8** Bjornson (Bjornstjerne) **1904: 7** Mistral (Frédéric) **9** Echegaray (José) **1905: 11** Sienkiewicz (Henryk) **1906: 8** Carducci (Giosue) **1907: 7** Kipling (Rudyard) **1908: 6** Eucken (Rudolf) **1909: 8** Lagerlof (Selma) **1910: 5** Heyse (Paul) **1911: 11** Maeterlinck (Maurice) **1912: 9** Hauptmann (Gerhart) **1913: 6** Tagore (Rabindranath) **1915: 7** Rolland (Romain) **1916: 10** Heidenstam (Verner von) **1917: 9** Gjellerup (Karl) **11** Pontoppidan (Henrik) **1919: 9** Spitteler (Carl) **1920: 6** Hamsun (Knut) **1921: 6** France (Anatole) **1922: 9** Benavente (Jacinto) **1923: 5** Yeats (William Butler) **1924: 7** Reymont (Wladyslaw) **1925: 4** Shaw (George Bernard) **1926: 7** Deledda (Grazia) **1927: 7** Bergson (Henri) **1928: 6** Undset (Sigrid) **1929: 4** Mann (Thomas) **1930: 5** Lewis (Sinclair) **1931: 9** Karlfeldt (Erik Axel) **1932: 10** Galsworthy (John) **1933: 5** Bunin (Ivan) **1934: 10** Pirandello (Luigi) **1936: 6** O'Neill (Eugene) **1937: 12** Martin du Gard (Roger) **1938: 4** Buck (Pearl) **1939: 9** Sillanpää (Frans Eemil) **1944: 6** Jensen (Johannes) **1945: 7** Mistral (Gabriela) **1946: 5** Hesse (Hermann) **1947: 4** Gide (André) **1948: 5** Eliot (Thomas Stearns) **1949: 8** Faulkner (William) **1950: 7** Russell (Bertrand) **1951: 10** Lagerkvist (Pär) **1952: 7** Mauriac (François) **1953: 9** Churchill (Winston) **1954: 9** Hemingway (Ernest) **1955: 7** Laxness (Halldór) **1956: 7** Jiménez (Juan Ramón) **1957: 5** Camus (Albert) **1958: 9** Pasternak (Boris) **1959: 9** Quasimodo (Salvatore) **1960: 5** Perse (Saint-John) **1961: 6** Andric (Ivo) **1962: 9** Steinbeck (John) **1963: 7** Seferis (George) **1964: 6** Sartre (Jean-Paul) **1965: 9** Sholokhov (Mikhail) **1966: 5** Agnon (Shmuel Yosef), Sachs (Nelly) **1967: 8** Asturias (Miguel Angel) **1968: 8** Kawabata (Yasunari) **1969: 7** Beckett (Samuel) **1970: 12** Solzhenitsyn (Alexander) **1971: 6** Neruda (Pablo) **1972: 4** Böll (Heinrich) **1973: 5** White (Patrick) **1974: 7** Johnson (Eyvind) **9** Martinson (Edmund) **1975: 7** Montale (Eugenio) **1976: 6** Bellow (Saul) **1977: 10** Aleixandre (Vicente) **1978: 6** Singer (Isaac Bashevis) **1979: 6** Elytis (Odysseus) **1980: 6** Milosz (Czeslaw) **1981: 7** Canetti (Elias) **1982: 13** García Márquez (Gabriel) **1983: 7** Golding (William) **1984: 7** Seifert (Jaroslav) **1985: 5** Simon (Claude) **1986: 7** Soyinka (Wole) **1987: 7** Brodsky (Joseph) **1988: 7** Mahfouz (Naguib) **1989: 4** Cela (Camilo José) **1990: 3** Paz (Octavio) **1991: 8** Gordimer (Nadine) **1992: 7** Walcott (Derek) **1993: 8** Morrison (Toni) **1994: 2** Oe (Kenzaburo) **1995: 6** Heaney (Seamus) **1996: 10** Szymborska (Wislawa) **1997: 2** Fo (Dario) **1998: 8** Saramago (José) **1999: 5** Grass (Günter) **2000: 3** Gao (Xingjian) **2001: 7** Naipaul (V. S.) **2002: 7** Kertész (Imre) **2003: 7** Coetzee (J. M.) **2004: 7** Jelinek (Elfriede) **2005: 6** Pinter (Harold) **2006: 5** Pamuk (Orhan) **2007: 7** Lessing (Doris) **2008: 8** Le Clézio (J.-M. Gustave) **2009: 6** Müller (Herta) **2010: 11** Vargas Llosa (Mario)

peace:

1901: 5 Passy (Frédéric) **6** Dunant (Jean-Henri) **1902: 5** Gobat (Charles Albert) **8** Ducommun (Elie) **1903: 6** Cremer (William) **1905: 7** Suttner (Bertha von) **1906: 9** Roosevelt (Theodore) **1907: 6** Moneta (Ernesto) **7** Renault (Louis) **1908: 5** Bajer (Fredrik) **9** Arnoldson (Klas Pontus) **1909: 9** Beernaert (Auguste) **13** d'Estournelles (Paul) **1911: 5** Asser (Tobias), Fried (Alfred) **1912: 4** Root (Elihu) **1913: 10** La Fontaine (Henri) **1919: 6** Wilson (Woodrow) **1920: 9** Bourgeois (Léon) **1921: 5** Lange (Christian Louis) **8** Branting (Karl Hjalmar) **1922: 6** Nansen (Fridtjof) **1925: 5** Dawes (Charles) **11** Chamberlain (Austen) **1926: 6** Briand (Aristide) **10** Stresemann (Gustav) **1927: 6** Quidde (Ludwig) **7** Buisson (Ferdinand) **1929: 7** Kellogg (Frank) **1930: 9** Soderblom (Nathan) **1931: 6** Addams (Jane), Butler (Nicholas Murray) **1933: 6** Angell (Norman) **1934: 9** Henderson (Arthur) **1935: 9** Ossietzky (Carl von) **1936: 13** Saavedra Lamas (Carlos de) **1937: 5** Cecil (Robert) **1945: 4** Hull (Cordell) **1946: 4** Mott (John) **5** Balch (Emily Greene) **1949: 3** Orr (John Boyd) **1950: 6** Bunche (Ralph) **1951: 7** Jouhaux (Léon) **1952: 10** Schweitzer (Albert) **1953: 8** Marshall (George) **1957: 7** Pearson (Lester) **1958: 4** Pire (Dominique Georges) **1959: 9** Noel-Baker (Philip) **1960: 7** Luthuli (Albert John) **1961: 12** Hammarskjöld (Dag) **1962: 7** Pauling (Linus) **1964: 4** King (Martin Luther) **1968: 6** Cassin (René) **1970: 7** Borlaug (Norman) **1971: 6** Brandt (Willy) **1973: 8** Le Duc Tho **9** Kissinger (Henry) **1974: 4** Sato (Eisaku) **8** MacBride (Sean) **1975: 8** Sakharov (Andrey) **1976: 8** Corrigan (Mairead), Williams (Betty) **1978: 5** Begin (Menachem), Sadat (Anwar el-) **1979: 12** Mother Teresa **1980: 8** Esquivel (Adolfo Pérez) **1982: 6** Myrdal (Alva) **12** García Robles (Alfonso) **1983: 6** Walesa (Lech) **1984: 4** Tutu (Desmond) **1986: 6** Wiesel (Elie) **1987: 12** Arias Sánchez (Oscar) **1989: 9** Dalai Lama **1990: 9** Gorbachev (Mikhail) **1991: 13** Aung San Suu Kyi **1992: 6** Menchú (Rigoberta) **1993: 7** de Klerk (F. W.), Mandela (Nelson) **1994: 5** Peres (Shimon), Rabin (Yitzhak) **6** Arafat (Yasir) **1995: 7** Rotblat (Joseph) **1996: 10** Ramos-Horta (José) **11** Ximenes Belo (Carlos Felipe) **1997: 8** Williams (Jody) **1998: 4** Hume (John) **7** Trimble (David) **2000: 3** Kim (Dae-jung) **2001: 5** Annan (Kofi) **2002: 6** Carter (Jimmy) **2003: 5** Ebadi (Shirin) **2004: 7** Maathai (Wangari) **2005: 9** ElBaradei (Mohamed) **2006: 5** Yunus (Muhammad) **2007: 4** Gore (Al) **2008: 9** Ahtisaari (Martti) **2009: 5** Obama (Barack) **2010: 3** Liu (Xiaobo)

physics:

1901: 8 Roentgen (Wilhelm) **1902: 6** Zeeman (Pieter) **7** Lorentz (Hendrik Antoon) **1903: 5** Curie (Marie, Pierre) **9** Becquerel (Antoine-Henri) **1904: 6** Strutt (John) **8** Rayleigh (Lord) **1905: 6** Lenard (Philipp von) **1906: 7** Thomson (Joseph) **1907: 9** Michelson (Albert) **1908: 8** Lippmann (Gabriel) **1909: 5** Braun (Karl) **7** Marconi (Guglielmo) **1910: 11** van der Waals (Johannes) **1911: 4** Wien (Wilhelm) **1912: 5** Dalen (Nils) **1914: 4** Laue (Max von) **1915: 5** Bragg (William) **1917: 6** Barkla (Charles) **1918: 6** Planck (Max) **1919: 5** Stark (Johannes) **1920: 9** Guillaume (Charles) **1921: 8** Einstein (Albert) **1922: 4** Bohr (Niels) **1923: 8** Millikan (Robert) **1924: 8** Siegbahn (Karl) **1925: 5** Hertz (Gustav) **6** Franck (James) **1926: 6** Perrin (Jean-Baptiste) **1927: 6** Wilson (Charles) **7** Compton (Arthur) **1928: 10** Richardson (Owen) **1929: 7** Broglie (Louis-Victor de) **1930: 5** Raman (Chandrasekhara) **1932: 10** Heisenberg (Werner) **1933: 5** Dirac (Paul) **11** Schrödinger (Erwin) **1935: 8** Chadwick (James) **1936: 4** Hess (Victor) **8** Anderson (Carl) **1937: 7** Thomson (George) **8** Davisson (Clinton) **1938: 5** Fermi (Enrico) **1939: 8** Lawrence (Ernest) **1943: 5** Stern (Otto) **1944: 4** Rabi (Isidor Isaac) **1945: 5** Pauli (Wolfgang) **1946: 8** Bridgman (Percy) **1947: 8** Appleton (Edward) **1948: 8** Blackett (Patrick) **1949: 6** Yukawa (Hideki) **1950: 6** Powell (Cecil) **1951: 6** Walton (Ernest) **9** Cockcroft (John) **1952: 5** Bloch (Felix) **7** Purcell (Edward) **1953: 7** Zernike (Frits) **1954: 4** Born (Max) **5** Bothe (Walther) **1955: 4** Lamb (Willis) **5** Kusch (Polykarp) **1956: 7** Bardeen (John) **8** Brattain (Walter), Shockley (William) **1957: 3** Lee (Tsung Dao) **4** Yang (Chen Ning) **1958: 4** Tamm (Igor) **5** Frank (Ilya) **9** Cherenkov (Pavel) **1959: 5** Segrè (Emilio) **11** Chamberlain (Owen) **1960: 6** Glaser (Donald) **1961: 9** Mossbauer (Rudolf) **10** Hofstadter (Robert) **1962: 6** Landau (Lev) **1963: 5** Mayer (Maria) **6** Jensen (J. Hans), Wigner (Eugene) **1964: 5** Basov (Nikolay) **6** Townes (Charles) **9** Prochorov (Alexander) **1965: 7** Feynman (Richard) **8** Tomonaga (Shinichiro) **9** Schwinger (Julian) **1966: 7** Kastler (Alfred) **1967: 5** Bethe (Hans) **1968: 7** Alvarez (Luis) **1969: 8** Gell-Mann (Murray) **1970: 4** Néel (Louis) **6** Alfven (Hannes) **1971: 5** Gabor (Dennis) **1972: 6** Cooper (Leon) **7** Bardeen (John) **10** Schrieffer (John) **1973: 5** Esaki (Leo) **7** Giaever (Ivar) **9** Josephson (Brian) **1974: 4** Ryle (Martin) **6** Hewish (Antony) **1975: 4** Bohr (Aage) **9** Mottelson (Ben), Rainwater (L. James) **1976: 4** Ting (Samuel) **7** Richter (Burton) **1977: 4** Mott (Nevill) **8** Anderson (Philip), Van Vleck (John) **1978: 6** Wilson (Robert) **7** Kapitsa (Pyotr), Penzias (Arno) **1979: 5** Salam (Abdus) **7** Glashow (Sheldon) **8** Weinberg (Steven) **1980: 5** Fitch (Val) **6** Cronin (James) **1981: 8** Schawlow (Arthur), Siegbahn (Kai) **11** Bloembergen (Nicholaas) **1982: 6** Wilson (Kenneth) **1983: 6** Fowler (William) **13** Chandrasekhar (Subrahmanyan) **1984: 6** Rubbia (Carlo) **11** van der Meere (Simon) **1985: 8** Klitzing (Klaus von) **1986: 5** Ruska (Ernst) **6** Binnig (Gerd), Rohrer (Heinrich) **1987: 6** Müller (K. Alex) **7** Bednorz (J. Georg) **1988: 8** Lederman (Leon), Schwartz (Melvin) **11** Steinberger (Jack) **1989: 4** Paul (Wolfgang) **6** Ramsey (Norman) **7** Dehmelt (Hans) **1990: 6** Taylor (Richard) **7** Kendall (Henry) **8** Friedman (Jerome) **1991: 8** De Gennes (Pierre-Gilles) **1992: 7** Charpak (Georges) **1993: 5** Hulse (Russell) **6** Taylor (Joseph) **1994: 5** Shull (Clifford) **10** Brockhouse (Bertram) **1995: 4** Perl (Martin) **6** Reines (Frederick) **1996: 3** Lee (David) **8** Osheroff (Douglas) **10** Richardson (Robert) **3** Chu (Steven) **8** Phillips (William) **14** Cohen-Tannoudji (Claude) **1998: 4** Tsui (Daniel) **7** Störmer (Horst) **8** Laughlin (Robert) **1999: 6** 't Hooft (Gerardus) **7** Veltman (Martinus) **2000: 5** Kilby (Jack) **7** Alferev (Zhores), Kroemer (Herbert) **2001: 6** Wieman (Carl) **7** Cornell (Eric) **8** Ketterle (Wolfgang) **2002: 5** Davis (Raymond) **7** Koshiba (Masatoshi) **8** Giacconi (Riccardo) **2003: 7** Leggett (Anthony) **8** Ginzburg (Vitaly) **9** Abrikosov (Alexei) **2004: 5** Gross (David) **7** Wilczek (Frank) **8** Politzer (David) **2005: 4** Hall (John) **6** Hänsch (Theodor) **7** Glauber (Roy) **2006: 5** Smoot (George) **6** Mather (John) **2007: 4** Fert (Albert) **8** Grünberg (Peter) **2008: 5** Nambu (Yoichiro) **7** Maskawa (Toshihide) **9** Kobayashi (Makoto) **2009: 3** Kao (Charles K.) **5** Boyle (Willard), Smith (George) **2010: 4** Geim (Andre) **9** Novoselov (Konstantin)

physiology or medicine:

1901: 7 Behring (Emil von) **1902: 4** Ross (Ronald) **1903: 6** Finsen (Niels Ryberg) **1904: 6** Pavlov (Ivan) **1905: 4** Koch (Robert) **1906: 5** Golgi (Camillo) **11** Ramón y Cajal (Santiago) **1907: 7** Laveran (Alphonse) **1908: 7** Ehrlich (Paul) **11** Metchnikoff (Elie) **1909: 6** Kocher (Emil) **1910: 6** Kossel (Albrecht) **1911: 10** Gullstrand (Allvar) **1912: 6** Carrel (Alexis) **1913: 6** Richet (Charles) **1914: 6** Barany (Robert) **1919: 6** Bordet (Jules) **1920: 5** Krogh (August) **1922: 4** Hill (Archibald) **8** Meyerhof (Otto) **1923: 7** Banting (Frederick), Macleod (John) **1924: 9** Einthoven (Willem) **1926: 7** Fibiger (Johannes) **1927: 13**

Wagner-Jauregg (Julius) **1928: 7** Nicolle (Charles) **1929: 7** Eijkman (Christiaan), Hopkins (Frederick) **1930: 11** Landsteiner (Karl) **1931: 7** Warburg (Otto) **1932: 6** Adrian (Edgar) **11** Sherrington (Charles) **1933: 6** Morgan (Thomas) **1934: 5** Minot (George) **6** Murphy (William) **7** Whipple (George) **1935: 7** Spemann (Hans) **1936: 4** Dale (Henry) **5** Loewi (Otto) **1937: 12** Szent-Györgyi (Albert) **1938: 7** Heymans (Corneille) **1939: 6** Domagk (Gerhard) **1943: 3** Dam (Henrik) **5** Doisy (Edward) **1944: 6** Gasser (Herbert) **8** Erlanger (Joseph) **1945: 5** Chain (Ernst) **6** Florey (Howard) **7** Fleming (Alexander) **1946: 6** Muller (Hermann) **1947: 4** Cori (Carl, Gerty) **7** Houssay (Bernardo) **1948: 7** Mueller (Paul) **1949: 4** Hess (Walter) **5** Moniz (Antonio) **1950: 5** Hench (Philip) **7** Kendall (Edward) **10** Reichstein (Tadeus) **1951: 7** Theiler (Max) **1952: 7** Waksman (Selman) **1953: 5** Krebs (Hans) **7** Lipmann (Fritz) **1954: 6** Enders (John), Weller (Thomas) **7** Robbins (Frederick) **1955: 8** Theorell (Hugo) **1956: 8** Cournand (André), Richards (Dickinson) **9** Forssmann (Werner) **1957: 5** Bovet (Daniel) **1958: 5** Tatum (Edward) **6** Beadle (George) **9** Lederberg (Joshua) **1959: 5** Ochoa (Severo) **8** Kornberg (Arthur) **1960: 6** Burnet (Macfarlane) **7** Medawar (Peter) **1961: 6** Bekesy (Georg von) **1962: 5** Crick (Francis) **6** Watson (James) **7** Wilkins (Maurice) **1963: 6** Eccles (John), Huxley (Andrew) **7** Hodgkin (Alan) **1964: 5** Bloch (Konrad), Lynen (Feodor) **1965: 5** Jacob (Francois), Monod (Jacques) **5** Lwoff (André) **1966: 4** Rous (Francis) **7** Huggins (Charles) **1967: 4** Wald (George) **6** Granit (Ragnar) **8** Hartline (H. Keffer) **1968: 6** Holley (Robert) **7** Khorana (H. Gobind) **9** Nirenberg (Marshall) **1969: 5** Luria (Salvador) **7** Hershey (Alfred) **8** Delbruck (Max) **1970: 4** Katz (Bernard) **5** Euler (Ulf von) **7** Axelrod (Julius) **1971: 10** Sutherland (Earl) **1972: 6** Porter (Rodney) **7** Edelman (Gerald) **1973: 6** Frisch (Karl von), Lorenz (Konrad) **9** Tinbergen (Nikolaas) **1974: 4** Duve (Christian) **6** Claude (Albert), Palade (George) **1975: 5** Temin (Howard) **8** Dulbecco (Renato) **9** Baltimore (David) **1976: 8** Blumberg (Baruch), Gajdusek (D. Carlcton) **1977: 5** Yalow (Rosalyn) **7** Schally (Andrew) **9** Guillemin (Roger) **1978: 5** Arber (Werner), Smith (Hamilton) **7** Nathans (Daniel) **1979: 7** Cormack (Allan) **10** Hounsfield (Godfrey) **1980: 5** Snell (George) **7** Dausset (Jean) **10** Benacerraf (Baruj) **1981: 5** Hubel (David) **6** Sperry (Roger), Wiesel (Torsten) **1982: 4** Vane (John) **9** Bergstrom (Sune) **10** Samuelsson (Bengt) **1983: 10** McClintock (Barbara) **1984: 5** Jerne (Niels) **7** Koehler (Georges) **8** Milstein (Cesar) **1985: 5** Brown (Michael) **9** Goldstein (Joseph) **1986: 5** Cohen (Stanley) **14** Levi-Montalcini (Rita) **1987: 8** Tonegawa (Susumu) **1988: 5** Black (James), Elion (Gertrude) **9** Hitchings (George) **1989: 6** Bishop (J. Michael), Varmus (Harold) **1990: 6** Murray (Joseph), Thomas (E. Donnall) **1991: 5** Neher (Erwin) **7** Sakmann (Bert) **1992: 5** Krebs (Edwin) **7** Fischer (Edmond) **1993: 5** Sharp (Phillip) **7** Roberts (Richard) **1994: 6** Gilman (Alfred) **7** Rodbell (Martin) **1995: 5** Lewis (Edward) **9** Wieschaus (Eric) **15** Nüsslein-Volhard (Christiane) **1996: 7** Dohcrty (Peter) **11** Zinkernagel (Rolf) **1997: 8** Prusiner (Stanley) **1998: 5** Murad (Ferid) **7** Ignarro (Louis) **9** Furchgott (Robert) **1999: 6** Blobel (Günter) **2000: 6** Kandel (Eric) **8** Carlsson (Arvid) **9** Greengard (Paul) **2001: 4** Hunt (Tim) **5** Nurse (Paul) **8** Hartwell (Leland) **2002: 7** Brenner (Sydney), Horvitz (Robert), Sulston (John) **2003: 9** Lauterbur (Paul), Mansfield (Peter) **2004: 4** Axel (Richard), Buck (Linda) **2005: 6** Warren (J. Robin) **8** Marshall (Barry) **2006: 4** Fire (Andrew) **5** Mello (Craig) **2007: 5** Evans (Martin) **8** Capecchi (Mario), Smithies (Oliver) **2008: 9** zur Hausen (Harald) **10** Montagnier (Luc) **13** Barré-Sinoussi (Françoise) **2009: 7** Greider (Carol), Szostak (Jack) **9** Blackburn (Elizabeth) **2010: 7** Edwards (Robert)

Nobel's invention 8 dynamite

nobility 6 virtue **7** dignity, peerage, royalty **8** eminence, noblesse **9** loftiness **10** exaltation, excellence, worthiness **11** aristocracy, superiority, uprightness

noble 4 lord, peer **5** grand, lofty, moral **6** august, lordly, titled, worthy **7** courtly, eminent, exalted, notable, stately, sublime, upright **8** baronial, elevated, generous, gracious, highborn, highbred, imposing, magnific, majestic, princely, sterling, virtuous, wellborn **9** dignified, estimable, excellent, grandiose, honorable, righteous **10** high-minded, impressive, principled **11** illustrious, magnanimous, magnificent, outstanding, right-minded **12** aristocratic

nobleman 4 duke, earl, lord, peer **5** baron,

count **6** aristo, prince **7** baronet, marquis **8** marquess, viscount **10** aristocrat ***French:*** **5** comte **7** vicomte ***German:*** **4** Graf **8** margrave **9** landgrave ***Indian:*** **6** sardar, sirdar **8** maharaja **9** maharajah ***Islamic:*** **4** amir, emir **5** ameer ***Italian:*** **8** marchese ***Japanese (former):*** **6** daimyo ***Scandinavian:*** **4** jarl ***Spanish:*** **7** hidalgo

noblewoman 4 lady **7** duchess, peeress **8** baroness, countess, princess **11** marchioness, viscountess ***French:*** **7** baronne **8** marquise ***Italian:*** **8** marchesa

nobody 4 zero **6** cipher **7** nothing, nullity, upstart **9** nonentity **11** lightweight, small potato

nocturnal 7 nightly **9** nighttime

nocuous 3 bad **6** nocent **7** harmful, hurtful **8** damaging **9** injurious **11** deleterious, destructive, detrimental, mischievous

nod 3 bob, err **4** doze, okay **5** agree, droop, slump **6** assent, invite, signal **7** approve **8** approval **10** acceptance

nodding 6 casual, slight **7** passing **8** drooping **9** pendulous **11** superficial

noddle 3 nob, nut **4** bean, head, pate, poll **6** noggin

noddy 3 oaf **4** boob, clod, dodo, dolt, dope, fool, goof, mutt, simp, yo-yo **5** chump, dummy, dunce, moron, ninny, stupe **6** dimwit, donkey, dum-dum **7** airhead, dullard, pinhead, schnook **8** bonehead, clodpoll, dumbbell, dumbhead, imbecile, lunkhead, meathead, numskull **9** birdbrain, blockhead, ignoramus, lamebrain, numbskull, simpleton, thickhead **10** dunderhead, hammerhead, nincompoop **11** chowderhead, chucklehead, knucklehead

node 4 bump, burl, knob, knot, lump, mass **5** bulge, point **6** growth, vertex **8** swelling **11** enlargement, predicament **12** entanglement, protuberance

Noel 4 Xmas **5** carol **9** Christmas

nog 3 ale **4** beer, brew, malt, suds **5** lager, stout

noggin 3 cup, mug, nip, nob, nut **4** bean, gill, head, pate, poll **6** noddle, noodle

no-good 3 bum, dud **4** base, vile, worm **5** loser **6** scurvy, wretch **7** dirtbag, inutile, lowlife, rounder, wastrel **8** deadbeat, fainéant, shameful, unworthy, wretched **9** no-account, valueless, worthless **10** ne'er-do-well, profligate, scapegrace **11** ignominious **12** contemptible, disreputable **13** reprehensible

noise 3 din **4** blab, talk **5** babel, rumor, sound **6** clamor, gossip, hubbub, racket, ruckus, rumpus, tattle, uproar **7** ruction, sonance, stridor **8** resonant **11** pandemonium

noiseless 4 hush, mute **5** muted, quiet, still, whist **6** hushed, silent, stilly

noisemaker 4 horn **6** rattle **7** clapper, whistle

noisome 4 foul, rank, vile **5** fetid, funky, fusty, musty, nasty **6** filthy, horrid, putrid, rancid, smelly **7** harmful, noxious, squalid **8** stinking **9** obnoxious, offensive, repulsive, revolting, sickening **10** disgusting, malodorous, nauseating

noisy 4 loud **5** rowdy **7** blatant, booming, clamant, rackety, raucous, squeaky **8** clattery, strident **9** clamorous, deafening, turbulent **10** boisterous, chattering, clangorous, tumultuous, uproarious, vociferous **11** conspicuous **12** earsplitting, obstreperous

nomad 4 bedu, hobo **5** gipsy, gypsy, rover **6** beduin, Tuareg **7** bedouin, migrant, rambler, Touareg **8** vagabond, wanderer, wayfarer

nomadic 5 gipsy, gypsy **6** roving **7** roaming, vagrant **8** drifting, vagabond **9** itinerant, migratory, wandering, wayfaring **11** peripatetic **13** perambulatory

nom de plume see **pen name**

nomen 4 name **7** moniker **11** appellation, designation

nomenclature 4 list, name **7** catalog **8** glossary, taxonomy **11** appellation, designation, phraseology, terminology **12** codification

nominal 3 low **5** given, named, rated, small **6** formal, puppet **7** alleged, minimal, seeming, titular **8** apparent, so-called, trifling **9** pretended, professed **10** ostensible **11** approximate, inexpensive **12** satisfactory **13** insignificant

nominate 3 tap **4** call, name **5** offer, put up **7** appoint, propose, suggest **9** designate, recommend

nominee 6 choice **8** aspirant **9** candidate, contender **10** contestant

nonage 5 youth **7** infancy **8** minority **9** childhood **10** immaturity, juvenility

nonchalant 4 cool, easy **5** blasé **6** casual, mellow, serene **7** offhand **8** carefree, careless, cheerful, laid-back **9** easygoing **10** effortless, insouciant, untroubled **11** unconcerned, unflappable, unperturbed **12** lighthearted **13** lackadaisical

noncommittal 7 neutral **8** reserved **9** impassive **10** disengaged

nonconformist 5 loner, rebel **7** beatnik, heretic, oddball, offbeat, radical **8** bohemian, maverick **9** dissenter, dissident, eccentric, heretical, heterodox, protester, sectarian **10** schismatic, separatist, unorthodox **11** misbeliever, schismatist

nonconformity 6 heresy, schism **7** dissent **9** misbelief, recusancy **10** dissidence, hetero-

doxy, opposition **11** unorthodoxy **13** individualism
nonentity 4 zero **5** aught, zilch **6** cipher, nobody **7** nothing, nullity, whiffet **8** unperson **10** figurehead, mouthpiece
nonesuch 5 ideal **7** epitome, paragon, pattern **8** exemplar, paradigm, standard **9** archetype, beau ideal, matchless, nonpareil, unequaled, unrivaled **10** apotheosis
nonetheless 3 yet **5** still **6** anyway, though, withal **7** howbeit, however **8** although, after all **10** regardless **11** still and all
nonexistence 4 nada, void **7** nullity, vacuity **11** nothingness
nonflammable 9 fireproof **10** unburnable **13** incombustible
non-Hawaiian 5 haole
non-Jewish 3 goy **6** goyish **7** gentile
non-Muslim 6 giaour
no-nonsense 5 grave, sober **6** solemn **7** earnest, serious **8** resolute **9** pragmatic, realistic **10** hardheaded, sobersided **11** plainspoken **12** businesslike **13** unsentimental
nonpareil see **nonesuch**
nonpartisan 7 neutral **8** unbiased **9** equitable, impartial, objective, uncolored **10** nonaligned **11** independent **12** unprejudiced
nonplus 4 faze **5** stump **6** baffle, boggle, muddle, puzzle, rattle, stymie **7** buffalo, confuse, dilemma, flummox, fluster, mystify, perplex, stagger **8** bewilder, confound, distract, overcome, paralyze, quandary **9** discomfit, dumbfound, frustrate **10** disconcert
nonresistant 6 docile, pliant **7** passive, pliable **8** resigned, yielding **9** complying, malleable, tractable **10** conforming, submissive **11** acquiescent, conformable **13** accommodating
nonsense 3 rot **4** blah, bosh, bull, bunk, crap, gook, guff, jazz, punk, tosh **5** bilge, crock, drool, folly, fudge, Greek, hokum, hooey, trash, tripe **6** babble, blague, bunkum, drivel, hot air, humbug, jabber, piffle **7** baloney, blather, eyewash, flubdub, foolery, fooling, hogwash, inanity, rubbish, trifles, twaddle **8** buncombe, claptrap, falderal, folderol, flimflam, malarkey, pishposh, slipslop, tommyrot, trumpery **9** gibberish, moonshine, poppycock **10** applesauce, balderdash, double-talk, flapdoodle, tomfoolery **11** jabberwocky **12** blatherskite, fiddle-faddle, fiddlesticks **13** horsefeathers ***British:*** **10** codswallop
nonsensical 5 crazy, daffy, flaky, goofy, inane, kooky, loony, nutty, silly, wacky **6** absurd, screwy **7** foolish, idiotic, risible **9** illogical, laughable, ludicrous, senseless **10** irrational **12** preposterous, unreasonable
nonviolent 6 irenic **7** pacific **8** pacifist **9** peaceable **10** pacifistic
noodle 3 oaf **4** bean, boob, clod, dodo, dope, goof, head, mutt, poll, simp, yo-yo **5** chump, dummy, dunce, idiot, moron, ninny, noddy, stupe **6** dimwit, donkey, dum-dum, nitwit, noggin **7** airhead, dullard, pinhead, schnook **8** bonehead, clodpoll, dumbbell, dumbhead, imbecile, lunkhead, meathead, numskull **9** birdbrain, blockhead, ignoramus, lamebrain, numbskull, simpleton **10** dunderhead, hammerhead, nincompoop **11** chowderhead, chucklehead, knucklehead ***dish:*** **5** pasta **7** lasagna, lasagne **8** linguine, linguini **10** fettuccine, fettuccini **11** pappardelle
nook 3 bay **4** cove **5** hutch, niche **6** alcove, cavity, corner, cranny, recess **9** cubbyhole **11** compartment
noose 3 tie **4** bait, bind, hang, loop, lure, trap **5** lasso, snare **6** entrap, secure
norm 3 par **4** mean, rule, type **5** gauge, maxim, model **6** median **7** average, measure, pattern **8** paradigm, standard **9** benchmark, criterion **10** touchstone
Norma *composer:* 7 Bellini (Vincenzo) ***librettist:*** **6** Romani (Felice)
normal 4 sane **5** usual **6** common **7** average, general, natural, regular, typical **8** ordinary, standard **9** customary, prevalent **11** commonplace, traditional **12** conventional **13** perpendicular
Normandy's capital 5 Rouen
Norns 5 fates, Skuld, Urdur **9** Verthandi
Norris novel 3 Pit (The) **4** Blix **7** Octopus (The) **8** McTeague
Norse *abode of the dead:* 8 Niflheim ***alphabet:*** **5** Runic ***archer:*** **4** Egil ***bard:*** **5** scald, skald ***chieftain:*** **4** jarl, Rolf **5** Rollo ***demon:*** **4** Mara, Surt **5** Surtr ***dragon:*** **6** Fafnir **8** Nithhogg ***epic:*** **4** Edda ***explorer:*** **4** Eric, Erik, Leif **8** Ericsson (Leif), Eriksson (Leif) ***first man:*** **3** Ask **4** Askr ***first woman:*** **5** Embla ***giant:*** **4** Egil, Wade, Wate, Ymer, Ymir **5** Aegir, Egill, Hymir, Jotun, Mimir **6** Fafnir, Jotunn ***giantess:*** **4** Egia, Norn, Nott ***god:*** **3** Asa, Ass **4** Surt, Vali, Vili **5** Aesir (plural), Surtr, Vanir (plural) **6** Hoenir, Vithar **7** Vitharr **blind: 4** Hoth **5** Hoder, Hodur, Hothr **chief: 4** Oden, Odin **5** Othin, Wodan, Woden, Wotan **guardian: 7** Heimdal **8** Heimdall **9** Heimdallr **messenger: 6** Hermod **7** Hermodr **of beauty: 5** Baldr **6** Balder, Baldur **of evil: 4** Loke, Loki **of fertility: 4** Frey **5** Freyr **of fire: 4** Loke, Loki **of justice: 7** Forsete, Forseti **of light: 3** Dag **of peace: 5** Baldr **6**

Balder, Baldur **of poetry: 5** Brage, Bragi **of the hunt: 3** Ull **4** Ullr **of the seas: 5** Njord **6** Njoerd, Njorth **4** Hler **5** Aegir, Gymir **of the sky: 4** Odin **5** Othin, Wodan, Woden, Wotan **of thunder: 4** Thor **5** Donar **of war: 3** Tiu, Tiw, Tyr, Zio, Ziu **wolf: 6** Fenrir
goddess: **3** dis **4** Saga **5** disir (plural) **7** Asynjur **of fate: 3** Urd **4** Norn, Urth, Wyrd **5** Skuld **9** Verthandi **of healing: 3** Eir **of love: 5** Freya **of marriage: 5** Frigg **6** Frigga **of night: 4** Natt, Nott **of storms: 3** Ran **of the earth: 4** Erda **5** Joerd, Jorth **of the moon: 5** Nanna **of the sea: 3** Ran **of the sky: 5** Frigg **6** Frigga **of the underworld: 3** Hel **4** Hela **of youth: 4** Idun **5** Ithun **6** Ithunn ***gods' abode:*** **6** Asgard ***hall of heroes:*** **8** Valhalla ***king:*** **4** Atli, Olaf ***nobleman:*** **4** jarl ***patron saint:*** **4** Olaf ***poem:*** **4** rune ***poet:*** **5** scald, skald ***rainbow bridge:*** **7** Bifrost ***sea serpent:*** **4** Wade, Wate **6** kraken **7** Midgard ***smith:*** **6** Völund ***tale:*** **4** saga ***toast:*** **5** skoal ***watchdog:*** **4** Garm **5** Garmr ***world's destruction:*** **8** Ragnarok ***world tree:*** **8** Ygdrasil **10** Yggdrasill

north ***combining form:*** **4** arct **5** arcto

North African ***country:*** **5** Egypt, Libya **7** Algeria, Morocco, Tunisia ***fruit:*** **3** fig **4** date ***garment:*** **4** haik **7** burnous **8** burnoose ***grass:*** **4** alfa **7** esparto ***jackal:*** **4** dieb ***language:*** **6** Arabic, Berber ***Muslim sect:*** **6** Sanusi **7** Senussi ***people:*** **4** bedu **6** beduin, Berber, Hamite **7** bedouin ***seaport:*** **4** Oran, Sfax **6** Annaba **7** Tangier **10** Casablanca

North America ***country:*** **6** Belize, Canada, Mexico, Panama **8** Honduras **9** Costa Rica, Guatemala, Nicaragua **10** El Salvador **12** United States

North Carolina ***capital:*** **7** Raleigh ***city:*** **6** Durham **9** Asheville, Charlotte **10** Greensboro **12** Winston-Salem ***college, university:*** **4** Duke, Elon **10** Chapel Hill, Wake Forest ***mountain, range:*** **8** Mitchell **9** Blue Ridge **10** Great Smoky ***nickname:*** **7** Tar Heel (State) ***state bird:*** **8** cardinal ***state flower:*** **7** dogwood ***state tree:*** **4** pine

North Dakota ***capital:*** **8** Bismarck ***city:*** **5** Fargo, Minot **10** Grand Forks ***nickname:*** **5** Sioux (State) **11** Flickertail (State) ***river:*** **3** Red **8** Missouri ***state bird:*** **10** meadowlark ***state flower:*** **11** prairie rose ***state tree:*** **3** elm (American)

North Korea see **Korea, North**

northern 4 pike **6** boreal **11** hyperborean

Northern Ireland ***capital:*** **7** Belfast ***city:*** **5** Derry, Newry **6** Armagh **7** Lisburn ***conflict:*** **8** Troubles (The) ***county:*** **4** Down **6** Antrim, Armagh, Tyrone **9** Fermanagh **11** Londonderry ***lake:*** **10** Lough Neagh ***language:*** **3** BSL, ISL **5** Irish **11** Ulster Scots ***monetary unit:*** **5** pound ***mountains:*** **6** Mourne **7** Sperrin ***prison, former:*** **4** Maze ***province:*** **6** Ulster ***university:*** **6** Queens

Northern Mariana Islands ***commonwealth of:*** **12** United States ***discoverer:*** **8** Magellan (Ferdinand) ***island:*** **4** Rota **6** Saipan, Tinian

North Star State 9 Minnesota

Northwest Territories ***capital:*** **11** Yellowknife ***gulf:*** **8** Amundsen ***island:*** **5** Banks **8** Victoria ***lake:*** **9** Great Bear **10** Great Slave ***river:*** **9** Mackenzie ***sea:*** **8** Beaufort

north wind see at **wind**

Norway ***Arctic region:*** **7** Lapland ***cape:*** **7** Nordkyn ***capital:*** **4** Oslo ***city:*** **5** Hamar **6** Bergen **9** Stavanger, Trondheim ***inlet:*** **9** Skagerrak ***island:*** **5** Senja **6** Sørøya **8** Magerøya, Steinsøy **10** Nord-Kvaløy, Ringvassøy ***island group:*** **7** Lofoten **10** Vesterålen ***king:*** **4** Eric, Olaf, Olav **5** Oscar **6** Haakon, Harald, Magnus **7** Charles **9** Christian, Frederick **11** Christopher ***lake:*** **5** Mjøsa ***monetary unit:*** **5** krone ***mountain range:*** **6** Kjølen **11** Jotunheimen ***neighbor:*** **6** Russia, Sweden **7** Finland ***part of:*** **11** Scandinavia ***patron saint:*** **4** Olaf, Olav ***port:*** **5** Vardø **6** Tromsø **8** Kirkenes **10** Hammerfest ***river:*** **4** Tana **5** Glåma, Lågen **9** Dramselva ***sea:*** **5** North

Norwegian ***goblin:*** **5** nisse ***language:*** **5** Norse **6** Bokmal **7** Bokmaal, Nynorsk, Riksmal **8** Landsmal, Riksmaal **9** Landsmaal

nose 3 pry **4** beak, bent, bump, head, poke **5** aroma, flair, knack, scent, smell, sniff, snift, snoop, snoot, snout, snuff **6** muzzle, nuzzle, schnoz, talent **7** aptness, faculty, schnozz, smeller, sneezer **8** smell out **9** olfaction, proboscis, schnozzle ***combining form:*** **4** naso, rhin **5** rhino ***French:*** **3** nez ***kind:*** **3** pug **5** Roman **8** aquiline ***lengthener:*** **3** lie ***opening:*** **5** nares (plural) **7** nostril

nosebleed 9 epistaxis

nosedive 4 drop, fall **6** header, plunge **7** plummet

nosegay 4 posy **6** flower **7** bouquet, corsage **11** boutonniere

nosh 4 bite **5** graze, munch, snack **6** nibble

Nostradamus 4 seer **7** prophet ***birthplace:*** **6** St. Remy

Nostromo author 6 Conrad (Joseph)

nostrum 4 cure **6** elixir, remedy **7** cure-all, panacea **8** antidote, medicine **10** catholicon, corrective **11** restorative

nosy 6 prying, snoopy **7** curious, peeping **8**

snooping **9** intrusive **11** inquisitive, inquisitory
not 4 nary
notable 3 VIP **4** lion, star **5** celeb, chief, famed, mogul, nabob, power **6** big boy, biggie, big gun, bigwig, famous, fat cat, honcho, leader, prince, worthy **7** big name, big shot, eminent, magnate, pooh-bah **8** big chief, big-timer, big wheel, eminence, luminary, renowned, somebody, striking **9** big cheese, celebrity, character, chieftain, dignitary, distingué, personage, prominent, superstar **10** celebrated, celebrious, noteworthy, remarkable **11** conspicuous, heavyweight, illustrious, muckety-muck, personality **13** distinguished, high-muck-a-muck
notarize 7 certify, endorse **8** validate **12** authenticate
not at all 5 nohow, noway **6** noways, nowise
notch 3 cut, gap, jag **4** gash, kerf, mark, nick, nock, rung, slit, step **5** cleft, grade, score, stage **6** degree, groove, indent, rabbet, record **7** achieve, scratch **8** incision, undercut **11** indentation
notched 5 erose
note 3 jot **4** bond, chit, heed, mark, memo, show, sign, tone **5** catch, sound, token **6** letter, notice, record, regard **7** comment, discern, jotting, missive, observe, promise, set down **8** eminence, indicate, perceive, reminder **9** attention, knowledge **10** cognizance, memorandum, reputation **11** distinction, distinguish, observation
notebook 3 log **5** diary **7** journal
noted 5 famed **6** famous **7** eminent, leading, popular **8** esteemed, renowned, striking **9** acclaimed, prominent, well-known **10** celebrated, recognized, remarkable **11** illustrious **13** distinguished
noteworthy 7 salient **8** singular, striking **9** arresting, bodacious, memorable, prominent, red-letter **10** impressive, meaningful, remarkable **11** conspicuous, exceptional, high-profile, major-league, outstanding, significant **12** considerable **13** extraordinary
nothing 3 nil, nix, zip **4** nada, zero **5** aught, nihil, zilch **6** cipher, naught, nobody, nought, trifle **7** nullity, whiffet **8** goose egg, whipster **9** no-account, nonentity ***French:*** **4** rien ***German:*** **6** nichts ***Latin:*** **5** nihil ***Spanish:*** **4** nada
nothingness 4 nada, void **5** death **6** vacuum **7** nullity, vacuity **9** emptiness **12** nonexistence
notice 2 ad **3** eye, see **4** espy, heed, mark, memo **5** catch, sight **6** descry, regard, review **7** discern, observe, respect **8** handbill, perceive **9** attention, directive, recognize **10** cognizance, evaluation **11** declaration, information, observation **12** announcement, proclamation
noticeable 6 marked, patent, signal **7** evident, obvious, pointed, salient **8** apparent, manifest, striking **9** arresting, prominent **10** noteworthy, observable, remarkable **11** appreciable, conspicuous, eye-catching, outstanding, perceptible, significant **12** unmistakable
notify 3 cue **4** tell, warn **5** alert, brief **6** advise, clue in, fill in, inform **7** apprise **8** acquaint **9** enlighten
notion 4 clue, hint, idea, whim **5** fancy **6** belief, maggot, theory, vagary **7** caprice, conceit, concept, inkling, thought **8** crotchet **10** conception, impression, intimation, perception **11** inclination
notional 5 ideal **6** unreal **7** fancied, fictive **8** fanciful, illusory, imagined **9** imaginary, visionary, whimsical **10** capricious, conceptual **11** speculative, theoretical **12** hypothetical
notoriety 4 fame **6** infamy, renown **7** obloquy **9** disrepute **10** opprobrium, prominence **11** recognition
notorious 5 noted **6** famous **8** ill-famed, infamous **9** prominent, well-known **10** outrageous, scandalous **12** disreputable
Notus 6 Auster ***brother:*** **5** Eurus **6** Boreas **8** Zephyrus ***father:*** **6** Aeolus **8** Astraeus ***mother:*** **3** Eos
noun 4 name **7** nominal **11** substantive ***inflectional form:*** **4** case ***verbal:*** **6** gerund
nourish 4 feed, rear **5** nurse, raise **6** foster **7** bring up, build up, nurture, promote, support **8** maintain **9** cultivate, encourage **10** provide for, strengthen
nourishment 3 pap **4** diet, eats, feed, food, grub **6** viands **7** aliment, pabulum, vittles **8** victuals **9** nutriment, provender **10** sustenance
____ **nous 5** entre
nouveau riche 7 climber, parvenu, upstart **9** arriviste
Nova Scotia *capital:* 7 Halifax ***city:*** **9** Dartmouth ***island:*** **10** Cape Breton ***lake:*** **7** Bras D'Or ***provincial flower:*** **9** mayflower
novel 3 new, odd **4** book **5** fresh **6** unique **7** fiction, offbeat, unusual **8** atypical, original, peculiar, singular, uncommon **9** different, narrative **10** avant-garde, innovative, newfangled
novelist see **author**
Novello, ____ **4** Ivor
novelty 5 curio **6** bauble, gewgaw, oddity, trifle **7** bibelot, gimmick, newness, trinket,

whatnot **8** gimcrack, souvenir **9** bagatelle, curiosity, objet d'art **10** innovation, knick-knack

novice 3 cub **4** colt, punk, tyro **5** plebe **6** newbie, rookie **7** amateur, learner, recruit, student, trainee **8** aspirant, beginner, freshman, neophyte, newcomer, prentice **9** fledgling, greenhorn, novitiate, postulant **10** apprentice, tenderfoot **11** probationer

Novum Organum author 5 Bacon (Francis)

now 3 PDQ **4** ASAP, soon, stat **5** today **6** at once, pronto **7** anymore, present **8** directly, first off, promptly **9** forthwith, instanter, instantly, presently, right away, sometimes **11** immediately, straightway **12** straightaway

now and then 7 at times, betimes **9** sometimes **12** infrequently, occasionally, periodically, sporadically

Nox ***brother:*** **6** Erebus ***daughter:*** **3** Day **4** Eris **5** Light ***father:*** **5** Chaos ***husband:*** **6** Erebus ***son:*** **6** Charon, Hypnos **8** Thanatos

noxious 4 foul **5** fetid, toxic **6** deadly, putrid **7** baneful, harmful, noisome **8** stinking **9** dangerous, pestilent, poisonous, unhealthy **10** corrupting, pernicious **11** deleterious, destructive, detrimental, pestiferous **12** disagreeable, pestilential

nozzle 4 nose, vent **5** spout **7** channel

nth 4 last **6** utmost **7** extreme, highest, maximal, maximum, supreme **8** greatest, ultimate

nuance 4 hint **5** shade, tinge, touch, trace **6** nicety **7** shading, soupçon **8** overtone, subtlety **9** gradation, suspicion **10** refinement, suggestion **11** distinction

nub 4 bump, core, crux, gist, knob, knot, lump, meat, node, pith **5** bulge, point, short **6** kernel, upshot **8** swelling **9** substance **10** projection **12** protuberance

Nubian 5 Mahas **6** Birked, Kenuzi, Midobi **7** Dongola **8** Cushitic **9** Chari-Nile

nubile 4 ripe **10** attractive **12** marriageable

nuchal 4 nape

nuclear agency 3 AEC, NRC

nuclear particle 5 meson **6** proton **7** neutron

nucleus 3 bud **4** core, germ, head, kern, ring, seed **5** focus, spark **6** embryo ***material:*** **8** karyotin

nude 3 raw **4** bald, bare **5** naked, stark **6** barren, peeled, unclad **8** disrobed, starkers, stripped **9** au naturel, buck naked, unattired, unclothed, uncovered, undressed **10** stark naked

nudge 3 dig, jab, jog **4** near, poke, prod, push **5** elbow, shove **8** approach

nudnik 4 bore, drip, pest, pill, twit **8** nuisance

nugatory 4 idle, vain **5** empty, inane, vapid **6** futile, hollow, otiose **7** invalid, vacuous **8** trifling **9** fruitless, worthless **11** inoperative, meaningless

nugget 4 hunk, lump, plum **5** chunk **6** tidbit

nuisance 4 pain, pest, pill **6** bother, nudnik **7** nudnick **8** headache, irritant, pesterer, vexation **11** botheration

nuke 3 zap **4** bomb **5** crush, smash **6** attack **7** destroy **8** demolish **9** eradicate, microwave **10** annihilate **11** exterminate

null 4 void, zero **5** annul, empty **6** futile **7** invalid, useless **8** nugatory **9** worthless **10** invalidate, obliterate, unavailing **11** ineffective, ineffectual, inoperative

nullify 3 zap **4** undo, veto, void **5** abate, annul, limit, quash, scrub, trash **6** cancel, efface, negate, offset, repeal, revoke, squash **7** abolish, rescind, scratch, take out, wipe out **8** abrogate **10** annihilate, compensate, counteract, invalidate, neutralize **11** countervail

nullity 4 nada, zero **5** zilch **6** cipher, nobody **7** nothing, vacuity, whiffet **9** annulment, nonentity **11** nothingness **12** nonexistence

numb 5 chill, dazed **6** deaden, freeze **7** callous **8** deadened **9** insensate, paralyzed, stupefied, unfeeling **10** insensible, insentient **11** desensitize **12** anesthetized, desensitized

number 5 add up, count, digit, run to, sum to, tally, total **6** amount, cipher, figure **7** chiffer, include, integer, numeral, ordinal, several **8** cardinal, paginate **9** aggregate, enumerate ***added to another:*** **6** augend ***great:*** **4** army, host **5** horde **6** googol, legion **9** multitude **10** googolplex ***irrational:*** **4** surd ***resulting from division:*** **8** quotient ***resulting from multiplication:*** **7** product ***resulting from subtraction:*** **10** difference ***science:*** **11** mathematics

number one 3 top **4** best, main **5** chief, first, major **6** finest, Grade A, tip-top, top dog **7** capital, highest, leading, primary, stellar **8** dominant, five-star, foremost, superior **9** excellent, first-rate, front-rank, numero uno, principal, top-drawer **10** blue-ribbon, first-class, preeminent **11** first-string, outstanding, predominant

numbness 5 shock **6** stupor **10** anesthesia **11** anaesthesia **12** stupefaction ***combining form:*** **4** narc **5** narco

numeral 5 digit **6** cipher, figure, number **7** integer **11** whole number

numerate 4 list **5** count, tally **6** number **7** compute, itemize, tick off **8** tabulate **9** calculate

numerous 4 many **6** legion **7** profuse, umpteen **8** abundant, populous **9** plentiful **10** voluminous **13** multitudinous

Numitor ***brother:*** **7** Amulius ***daughter:*** **9** Rea

Silvia **10** Rhea Silvia ***grandson:*** **5** Remus **7** Romulus

numskull 3 oaf **4** boob, clod, dodo, dolt, dope, goof, mutt, simp **5** chump, dummy, dunce, idiot, moron, ninny, noddy, stupe **6** dimwit, donkey, dum-dum, nitwit **7** airhead, dullard, pinhead, schnook **8** bonehead, clodpate, clodpoll, dumbbell, dumbhead, imbecile, lunkhead, meathead **9** birdbrain, blockhead, ignoramus, lamebrain, simpleton, thickhead **10** dunderhead, hammerhead, nincompoop **11** chowderhead, chucklehead, knucklehead

nun 4 buoy **6** sister ***headcloth:*** **6** wimple

Nunavut *capital:* **7** Iqaluit ***island:*** **5** Devon **6** Baffin **9** Ellesmere **11** Southampton ***mountain:*** **7** Barbeau (Peak) ***peninsula:*** **7** Boothia **8** Melville ***provincial flower:*** **11** Arctic poppy

nunnery 7 convent **8** cloister **10** sisterhood ***head:*** **8** superior

nuptial 6 bridal, wedded **7** marital, married, spousal, wedding **8** conjugal, espousal, hymeneal, marriage **9** connubial **11** matrimonial

nurse 3 LPN, LVN **4** feed, nana, rear, suck **5** nanny, serve **6** attend, foster, pamper, suckle **7** care for, cherish, nourish, nurture **9** cultivate **10** minister to ***children's:*** **5** nanny ***English:*** **11** Nightingale (Florence) ***Indian:*** **4** ayah ***Chinese:*** **4** amah

nursemaid 4 nana **5** nanny **6** minder, sitter **9** governess **10** babysitter ***Indian:*** **4** ayah ***Chinese:*** **4** amah

nursery 6 crèche **7** brooder **8** hothouse **9** fosterage **10** greenhouse **12** conservatory

nurture 4 care, feed, rear, tend **5** nurse, raise, train **6** cradle, foster, parent, suckle **7** bring up, care for, develop, educate, nourish, rearing **8** breeding, instruct, training, tutelage **9** cultivate **10** upbringing

nut 3 bug **4** cola, kola, kook, loon, pili **5** acorn, betel, crank, fiend, freak, hazel, loony, pecan, piñon **6** almond, cashew, cuckoo, madman, maniac, walnut, zealot **7** buckeye, fanatic, filbert, hickory, lunatic **8** crackpot **9** bedlamite, ding-a-ling, macadamia, pistachio, screwball **10** enthusiast, Tom o' Bedlam ***of a violin bow:*** **4** frog, heel

Nut *consort:* **3** Geb, Keb ***daughter:*** **4** Isis **8** Nephthys ***son:*** **6** Osiris

nuthouse 6 asylum, bedlam **8** loony bin **9** funny farm **10** booby hatch **11** institution **12** insane asylum

Nutmeg State 11 Connecticut

nutria 5 coypu

nutriment 4 diet, fare, food, grub, keep **6** viands **7** aliment, pabulum **8** victuals **9** provender **10** provisions, sustenance **11** comestibles, nourishment, subsistence

nutrition 4 diet **7** vittles **8** victuals **10** sustenance **11** nourishment

nutritious 9 healthful, wholesome **10** alimentary, nourishing

nuts 3 mad **4** daft, keen, wild, zany **5** batty, crazy, dotty, kooky, loony, rabid, wacky **6** absurd, cuckoo, insane, screwy **7** bonkers, cracked, excited, foolish, idiotic **8** animated, demented, deranged **9** exuberant, fanatical, screwball **10** passionate, unbalanced **12** enthusiastic ***on forest floor:*** **4** mast

nutty see **nuts**

nuzzle 3 rub **4** root, snug **5** nudge **6** burrow, cuddle, nestle **7** snuggle

Nycteus *brother:* **5** Lycus ***daughter:*** **7** Antiope

nymph 3 nix **5** dryad, larva, naiad, nixie, oread, sylph **6** kelpie, maiden, sprite **7** mermaid ***changed into a bear:*** **8** Callisto ***changed into a laurel:*** **6** Daphne ***changed into a rock:*** **4** Echo ***mountain:*** **5** oread ***sea:*** **6** Nereid **7** Calypso ***water:*** **5** naiad **6** undine ***wood:*** **5** dryad

Nyx see **Nox** **mythology** see **myth**

O

oaf 3 ape, dub, lug **4** boob, boor, bull, clod, dodo, dolt, goof, goon, hulk, lout, lump, slob **5** booby, chump, clown, dummy, dunce, klutz **6** dum-dum, galoot, lubber, lummox **7** fathead, palooka **8** bonehead, lunkhead, meathead **9** blockhead, blunderer, lamebrain, simpleton

oafish 5 dense **6** clumsy, klutzy, rustic **7** boorish, doltish, loutish **8** bungling, churlish, clownish, lubberly

oak ***African:*** **7** turtosa ***fruit:*** **5** acorn ***genus:*** **7** Quercus ***kind:*** **3** bur, pin, red **4** bear, cork, holm, ilex, live **5** black, holly, roble, white **6** barren, cerris, encina **7** durmast, English, moss-cup, valonia **9** blackjack ***Mexican:*** **8** chaparro ***young:*** **8** flittern

oar 3 row **4** pole, pull **5** rower, scull **6** paddle **7** paddler ***part:*** **4** loom, palm **5** blade, shaft **6** button, collar ***pin:*** **5** thole

oarsman 3 bow **5** rower **6** stroke **7** sculler ***captain:*** **3** cox **8** coxswain

oasis 3 spa **4** wadi **6** refuge, relief ***ancient:*** **4** Merv ***Egypt:*** **4** Siwa **5** Gafsa **6** Dakhla **7** Farafra **8** Ammonium ***Libya:*** **5** Mizda, Sebha **6** Sabhah **7** Gadames **8** Ghudamis ***Niger:*** **5** Bilma ***Saudi Arabia:*** **5** Hofuf, Taima **7** Al-Hufuf

oast 4 kiln, oven

oat 5 grain, grass **6** cereal ***genus:*** **5** Avena ***Scottish:*** **3** ait

oater 7 western **10** horse opera

oath 3 vow **4** cuss **5** curse, swear **6** pledge **7** promise **8** cussword **9** expletive, profanity, swearword ***mild:*** **4** darn, drat, egad **6** jiminy, zounds

oatmeal 5 gruel **6** burgoo **8** porridge ***Scottish:*** **8** drammock

obdurate 3 set **4** firm, hard **5** harsh, rigid, stony **6** dogged, mulish **7** adamant, callous **8** stubborn **9** heartless, immovable, unbending, unfeeling **10** hard-boiled, inflexible, unshakable, unyielding **11** coldhearted, hardhearted, insensitive **12** intransigent, stonyhearted **13** unsympathetic

obeah 5 charm, magic ***relative:*** **5** vodun **6** vodoun, voodoo **8** Santeria **9** Candomblé

Obed ***father:*** **4** Boaz **6** Ephlal **8** Shemaiah ***mother:*** **4** Ruth ***son:*** **5** Jesse **7** Azariah

obedient 5 loyal **6** docile **7** devoted, duteous, dutiful, willing **8** amenable, biddable, obliging, yielding **9** compliant, tractable **10** law-abiding, manageable, respectful, submissive **11** acquiescent, cooperative, deferential, subservient

obeisance 3 bow **5** honor **6** curtsy, esteem, fealty, homage, kowtow, salaam **7** gesture, loyalty, respect **9** deference, reverence **10** allegiance, submission

obelisk 6 dagger, pillar, symbol

Oberon 9 fairy king ***messenger:*** **4** Puck ***wife:*** **7** Titania

obese 3 fat **5** bulky, gross, heavy, tubby **6** fleshy, portly **7** adipose, outsize, porcine **9** corpulent **10** overweight

obey 3 bow **4** heed, keep, mind **5** agree, defer, serve, yield **6** accede, accept, assent, comply, follow, regard, submit **7** abide by, conform, execute, fulfill, observe, satisfy **9** acquiesce

obfuscate 4 blur **5** cloud, muddy **6** darken **7** becloud, conceal, confuse, cover up, obscure **9** adumbrate

obi 4 sash

obiter dictum 4 note **6** remark **7** comment, opinion **10** commentary, incidental **11** observation

obituary 9 necrology **11** death notice

object 3 aim, end, use **4** goal, item, kick, view, wish **5** demur, focus, frown, point, thing **6** design, entity, except, intent, matter, motive, oppose, target **7** article, dissent, protest, purpose **8** complain, disagree, material **9** criticize, intention, something **10** disapprove

objection 5 demur **7** protest **8** argument, demurral, demurrer, question **9** challenge, complaint, exception **10** difficulty, opposition **11** disapproval **12** disagreement, remonstrance **13** remonstration

objectionable 5 unfit **8** unwanted **9** invidious, obnoxious, offensive, unwelcome **10** unpleasant **11** displeasing, distasteful, undesirable **12** disagreeable

objective 3 aim, end **4** fair, goal, just, lens, mark **6** actual, design, intent, target **7** mission, purpose **8** ambition, function, material, physical, sensible, unbiased **9** corporeal, equitable, impartial, intention **10** impersonal **11** independent, substantial **12** unprejudiced **13** dispassionate

objet d'art 5 curio, virtu (plural) **7** bibelot, novelty **8** kickshaw **10** knickknack

objurgate 5 chide, decry, scold **6** rebuke **7** censure, reprove, upbraid **8** admonish, reproach **9** castigate, reprimand

oblate 7 lay monk **9** flattened, religious

oblation 4 gift **6** corban **8** holy gift, offering **9** sacrifice **12** presentation

obligate 4 bind **7** require **8** encumber, restrict **9** constrain

obligated 5 bound, owing **6** liable **8** beholden, indebted **11** accountable, responsible

obligation 3 IOU, vow **4** bond, call, debt, dues, duty, need, oath **5** cause **6** burden, charge, pledge **7** promise **8** business, contract **9** committal, liability, necessity, restraint **10** commitment, compulsion, constraint **11** requirement **12** indebtedness

obligatory 7 binding **8** required **9** essential, mandatory, necessary, requisite **10** compulsory, imperative **11** unavoidable

oblige 3 aid **4** bind, help, make **5** avail, favor, force **6** assist, coerce, compel, please, profit

7 benefit, command, gratify, require 9 constrain 10 contribute 11 accommodate, necessitate
obliged 4 made 5 bound 6 forced 8 beholden, grateful, indebted, thankful 11 constrained 12 appreciative
obliging 4 kind 5 civil 7 amiable, helpful, willing 8 friendly, pleasant 11 complaisant, considerate, cooperative, good-humored, good-natured 12 good-tempered
oblique 6 sloped, tilted 7 devious, leaning, obscure, slanted, sloping, tilting 8 diagonal, inclined, indirect 9 inclining 10 roundabout
obliterate 4 raze, x out 5 erase 6 cancel, delete, efface, remove, rub out 7 blot out, destroy, expunge, wipe out 8 black out, cross out 9 extirpate, liquidate 10 annihilate
oblivion 5 lethe, limbo 7 amnesia, nirvana, nowhere 9 emptiness 11 nothingness 13 forgetfulness
oblivious 4 lost 5 blind 7 unaware 8 absorbed, heedless, ignorant 9 unknowing, unmindful, unwitting 10 unfamiliar, uninformed 11 incognizant, unconscious
oblong 4 oval 5 ovate 7 ellipse 8 elongate 9 elongated, rectangle 11 rectangular
obloquy 4 slam, slur 5 abuse, odium, shame 6 infamy, rebuke 7 calumny, censure 8 disgrace, dishonor, ignominy 9 aspersion, contumely, discredit, disrepute, invective, stricture 10 defamation, opprobrium, scurrility 11 disapproval 12 billingsgate, condemnation, vituperation
obnoxious 4 vile 5 awful 6 odious, rotten 7 hateful 9 abhorrent, invidious, loathsome, offensive, repellant, repellent, repugnant, revulsive, sickening 10 abominable, detestable, disgusting
oboe 4 reed 7 hautboy 8 hautbois, woodwind 10 double reed ***early:*** 5 shawm ***relative:*** 7 bassoon 10 cor anglais 11 English horn
O'Brian character 6 Aubrey (Jack) 7 Maturin (Stephen)
obscene 4 foul, lewd, rank, vile 5 bawdy, crude, dirty, gross, lurid, taboo 6 coarse, filthy, ribald, risqué, smutty, vulgar 7 immoral, noisome, profane, raunchy 8 indecent, scabrous 9 abhorrent, appalling, offensive, repellent, repugnant, repulsive, salacious 10 disgusting, lascivious, scurrilous 11 foulmouthed, unprintable 12 pornographic, scatological
obscure 3 dim 4 blur, hide, mask, veil 5 blind, cloak, cloud, cover, dusky, faint, minor, murky, shade, shady, vague 6 cloudy, darken, hidden, opaque, remote, screen, secret, shadow, shroud, veiled 7 clouded, conceal, cryptic, eclipse, removed, shadowy, unclear, unknown, unnoted 8 disguise, nameless, overcast, puzzling, secluded, shrouded 9 ambiguous, enigmatic, tenebrous, uncertain, undefined 10 camouflage, ill-defined, indefinite, indistinct, mysterious, overshadow 11 out-of-the-way, unimportant 12 inaccessible 13 inconspicuous
obscurity 3 fog 4 haze, mist, murk 5 gloom 6 enigma, miasma, puzzle 7 dimness, mystery, shadows 8 darkness 9 ambiguity
obsequies 4 rite 5 rites 6 burial 7 funeral 10 burial rite
obsequious 4 oily 6 abject, smarmy 7 fawning, fulsome, servile, slavish 8 obedient, obeisant, toadying, unctuous 9 parasitic 10 flattering, submissive 11 deferential, subservient, sycophantic
observance 4 rite, rule 6 custom, notice, regard, ritual 7 liturgy, service 8 ceremony, practice 9 adherence, attention, formality 10 ceremonial
observant 4 keen 5 alert, awake, aware, sharp 7 heedful, mindful 8 watchful 9 advertent, attentive 10 perceptive
observation 4 note 6 notice, record, remark 7 comment, finding, opinion 8 judgment, notation 9 attention, inference 10 commentary 12 obiter dictum
observatory 5 tower 7 lookout, outlook 8 overlook ***famous:*** 4 Lick 6 Wilson, Yerkes 7 Palomar ***instrument:*** 9 telescope
observe 3 eye, see 4 espy, keep, look, mark, mind, note, obey, twig, view 5 honor, opine, sight, state, study, watch 6 behold, comply, follow, look at, notice, remark 7 abide by, comment, conform, discern, respect 8 perceive 9 celebrate, solemnize 10 comply with 11 commemorate
obsess 5 beset, haunt, hound, rivet 6 absorb, plague 7 consume, possess 9 captivate, preoccupy
obsessed 6 dogged, driven, hipped, hooked 7 gripped, haunted, plagued 8 overcome, troubled 9 dominated, possessed 11 preoccupied 12 prepossessed
obsession 5 craze, mania 6 fetish, hang-up 8 fixation, idée fixe 11 infatuation 13 preoccupation
obsessive 5 rabid 8 frenetic, maniacal, neurotic 9 fanatical, possessed 10 passionate 11 preoccupied
obsolete 3 old 5 dated, passé, stale 6 old hat 7 disused, worn-out 8 outmoded, time-worn 9 out-of-date 10 antiquated, superseded 12 antediluvian, old-fashioned
obstacle 3 bar 4 bump, clog, snag 5 block,

catch, check, crimp, hitch **6** hurdle **7** barrier **8** handicap, hardship **9** hindrance, impedance, roadblock **10** difficulty, impediment **11** encumbrance, vicissitude **12** interference

obstinate 4 deaf, firm **5** balky, fixed **6** dogged, mulish, ornery **7** staunch, willful **8** obdurate, perverse, resolute, stubborn **9** pigheaded, resistant, unbudging, immovable **10** hardheaded, headstrong, inflexible, persistent, refractory, unyielding **11** intractable, stiff-necked, wrongheaded **12** intransigent, pertinacious, recalcitrant

obstreperous 4 loud **5** noisy, rowdy **6** unruly **7** blatant, raucous **8** strident **9** clamorous, insistent **10** boisterous, disorderly, vociferant, vociferous **11** disobedient, loudmouthed **12** rambunctious

obstruct 3 bar, dam **4** clog, hide, plug, stop **5** block, check, choke, close **6** cut off, hamper, hinder, impede, stymie, thwart **7** congest, occlude, prevent, shut off, shut out, trammel **9** interfere

obstruction 3 bar **4** snag **5** hitch **6** hamper, hurdle **7** barrier **8** blockage, obstacle, stoppage **9** hindrance, impedance **10** impediment

obtain 3 buy, get, win **4** earn, gain, have, reap **5** annex, reach **6** pick up, secure **7** achieve, acquire, chalk up, procure **8** purchase

obtrude 5 cut in **6** butt in, horn in, impose, meddle **7** presume, push out **8** chisel in, infringe **9** interfere, thrust out

obtrusive 4 nosy **5** pushy **6** prying **7** forward **8** meddling **9** bumptious, officious **10** meddlesome, protruding **11** impertinent, interfering

obtuse 4 dull, dumb, slow **5** blunt, dense, thick **6** stupid **7** rounded, unclear **11** insensitive

obverse 4 face, side **5** front **8** opposite **9** other side **10** complement **11** counterpart

obviate 4 ward **5** avert, deter, block **7** forfend, prevent, rule out **8** preclude, stave off **9** forestall, interfere, interpose, intervene **10** anticipate

obvious 5 clear, overt, plain **6** patent, simple **7** blatant, evident, glaring **8** apparent, clear-cut, distinct, manifest, palpable **10** undeniable **11** conspicuous, self-evident, transparent, unambiguous, unequivocal

oca 5 tuber **6** sorrel

O'Casey, Sean 9 dramatist **10** playwright ***plays:*** **17** Juno and the Paycock, Plough and the Stars (The)

occasion 4 call, need, shot, show, time **5** basis, break, cause, event **6** chance, demand, effect, excuse, ground, lead to, moment, reason **7** episode, instant, opening, produce **8** ceremony, incident, instance **9** condition, happening, necessity **10** bring about, foundation, occurrence **11** celebration, opportunity **12** circumstance **13** justification

occasional 3 few, odd **4** rare **6** casual, fitful, random, scarce, seldom **7** special, unusual **8** specific, sporadic, uncommon **9** irregular **10** incidental, infrequent

occasionally 7 at times

Occidental 7 Western **8** European **9** Westerner

occlude 4 clog, fill, hide, plug, stop **5** block, choke, close, cover **6** screen, stop up **7** close up, conceal, congest **8** block off, obstruct

occult 5 eerie, magic **6** arcane, orphic, secret **8** abstruse, esoteric, hermetic, mystical **9** recondite, unearthly **10** cabalistic, mysterious **12** supernatural

occupant 5 liver **6** inmate, tenant **7** denizen, dweller, resider **8** habitant, resident **10** inhabitant

occupation 3 job, use **4** line, work **5** trade **6** career, métier, office **7** calling, control, pursuit, seizure **8** activity, business, position, vocation **9** occupancy, residence **10** employment, habitation, possession, settlement

occupy 3 use **4** busy, fill, hold, take **5** seize, tie up **6** absorb, employ, engage, live in, people, take up, tenant **7** control, engross, immerse, inhabit, involve, possess **8** populate, reside in, take over

occur 3 hap **4** pass **5** arise, ensue, pop up **6** appear, befall, betide, chance, dawn on, happen, result, strike **7** come off, develop **9** take place, transpire

occurrence 3 hap **4** pass **5** event, state **7** episode **8** exigency, incident, juncture, occasion **9** adventure, condition, emergency, happening, situation

ocean 3 sea **4** blue, deep, main **5** brine, drink **6** Arctic, Indian **7** Pacific **8** Atlantic **9** Antarctic ***movement:*** **4** tide, wave

Oceania *country:* **4** Fiji **5** Belau, Nauru, Palau, Samoa, Tonga **6** Tuvalu **7** Vanuatu **8** Kiribati **9** Australia **10** New Zealand ***territory:*** **7** Tokelau **12** New Caledonia **13** American Samoa ***ethnic group:*** **6** Fijian, Papuan, Samoan **10** Melanesian, Polynesian **11** Micronesian ***language:*** **5** Maori **6** Fijian, Papuan, Pidgin, Samoan **10** Melanesian

oceanic 4 huge, vast **5** great **6** marine **7** immense, pelagic **8** enormous, maritime **9** saltwater, thalassic

Ocean State 11 Rhode Island

Oceanus ***daughter:*** **5** Doris **7** Oceanid **8** Eurynome ***father:*** **6** Uranus ***mother:*** **4** Gaea ***sister:*** **6** Tethys ***son:*** **6** Peneus **7** Alpheus ***wife:*** **6** Tethys

ocellus 3 eye **7** eyespot

ocelot 3 cat **7** wildcat

O'Connor novel 9 Wise Blood

octave 5 eight, scale **6** eighth, stanza **8** interval

Octavia ***brother:*** **8** Augustus ***grandson:*** **8** Caligula ***husband:*** **4** Nero **6** Antony

octopus 7 mollusc, mollusk **9** devilfish **10** cephalopod ***arm:*** **8** tentacle ***genus:*** **7** Polypus ***kin:*** **5** squid **10** cuttlefish

ocular 4 seen **5** optic **6** visual **7** eyelike, optical, visible **8** eyepiece, viewable **9** perceived

Odalisque painter 6 Ingres (Jean-Auguste-Dominique) **7** Matisse (Henri)

odd 4 lone, rare **5** extra, fluky, queer, rummy, weird **6** casual, chance, single, uneven **7** curious, erratic, strange, unusual **8** peculiar, singular **9** eccentric, unmatched **13** idiosyncratic

oddball 4 kook **5** kooky, weird **6** weirdo **7** bizarre, curious, offbeat, strange, unusual **8** original, peculiar **9** character, eccentric **10** outlandish **13** idiosyncratic

Odd Couple, The ***author:*** **5** Simon (Neil) ***character:*** **5** Felix, Oscar ***director:*** **4** Saks (Gene) **7** Nichols (Mike) ***star:*** **6** Carney (Art), Lemmon (Jack) **7** Klugman (Jack), Matthau (Walter), Randall (Tony)

oddity 5 freak, quirk **6** weirdo **7** anomaly **9** character, curiosity, departure, deviation, eccentric, weirdness **10** aberration, difference **11** abnormality, peculiarity, strangeness **12** eccentricity, idiosyncrasy, irregularity

odds 4 edge **5** favor, ratio **7** benefit, chances **8** handicap, variance **9** advantage, allowance, disparity **10** difference, likelihood, partiality **11** probability **12** disagreement

odds and ends 4 bits, olio **6** jumble, medley, motley, scraps **7** mélange, mixture **8** remnants, sundries **9** etceteras, leftovers, potpourri **10** assortment, hodgepodge, hotchpotch, miscellany **13** paraphernalia

ode 4 hymn, poem **5** lyric, psalm, verse ***part:*** **5** epode **7** strophe **11** antistrophe

Odets play 9 Golden Boy **11** Country Girl (The) **12** Awake and Sing **15** Waiting for Lefty

odeum 4 hall **7** theater **11** concert hall

Odin ***brother:*** **4** Vili ***daughter-in-law:*** **5** Nanna ***father:*** **3** Bor ***hall:*** **8** Valhalla ***horse:*** **8** Sleipnir ***maiden:*** **8** Valkyrie ***mansion:*** **9** Gladsheim ***mother:*** **6** Bestla ***raven:*** **5** Hugin, Munin ***ring:*** **8** Draupnir ***son:*** **3** Tyr **4** Thor, Vali **6** Balder, Baldur ***spear:*** **7** Gungnir ***sword:*** **4** Gram ***wife:*** **4** Fria, Rind **5** Frigg **6** Frigga ***wolf:*** **4** Geri **5** Freki

odious 4 foul, vile **6** horrid **7** hateful, heinous, noxious **8** horrible **9** abhorrent, execrable, invidious, loathsome, malicious, repellent, repugnant **10** abominable, despicable, detestable, disgusting

odium 4 hate, onus **5** shame **6** hatred, infamy, stigma **7** censure, obloquy **8** contempt, disgrace, dishonor, ignominy, loathing **9** disrepute **10** abhorrence, opprobrium **11** detestation **12** condemnation

odor 4 funk **5** aroma, scent, smell, stink, whiff **6** stench **7** bouquet, perfume **9** fragrance, redolence

odorous 5 heady, sweet **6** smelly, strong **7** pungent, scented **8** aromatic, fragrant, perfumed, redolent, unsavory **9** offensive

Odysseus 7 Ulysses ***dog:*** **5** Argos ***enchantress:*** **5** Circe ***father:*** **7** Laertes ***friend:*** **6** Mentor ***harasser:*** **8** Poseidon ***herb:*** **4** moly ***kingdom:*** **6** Ithaca ***mother:*** **8** Anticlea ***rescuer:*** **3** Ino **8** Nausicaa ***son:*** **9** Telegonus **10** Telemachus ***swineherd:*** **7** Eumaeus ***voyage:*** **7** odyssey ***wife:*** **8** Penelope

odyssey 4 trek **5** quest **6** voyage **7** journey **9** wandering **13** peregrination

Odyssey author 5 Homer

Oedipus ***brother-in-law:*** **5** Creon ***daughter:*** **6** Ismene **8** Antigone ***father:*** **5** Laius ***foster father:*** **7** Polybus ***foster mother:*** **8** Periboea ***kingdom:*** **6** Thebes ***mother:*** **7** Jocasta ***son:*** **8** Eteocles **9** Polynices **10** Polyneices ***victim:*** **5** Laius ***wife:*** **7** Jocasta

Oeneus ***kingdom:*** **7** Calydon ***son:*** **8** Meleager ***wife:*** **7** Althaea

Oenomaus ***charioteer:*** **8** Myrtilus ***daughter:*** **10** Hippodamia ***kingdom:*** **4** Pisa ***slayer:*** **6** Pelops

Oenone ***husband:*** **5** Paris ***rival:*** **5** Helen

oeuvre 4 work **6** corpus, output **8** lifework **10** collection **11** compilation

of ***German:*** **3** aus, von ***Italian:*** **5** degli, della, delle

off 4 away, kill, slay **5** aside **6** depart, murder, remote, slight **7** seaward, spoiled **8** dispatch **9** eccentric, incorrect

offal 4 guts **4** junk **5** gurry, trash, waste **6** debris, litter, refuse, spilth **7** carrion, garbage, innards, rubbish, viscera **8** entrails **9** sweepings **10** intestines

offbeat 3 odd **5** fresh, outré, weird **6** way out **7** bizarre, oddball, strange, unusual **8** bohemian, peculiar, singular, uncommon **9** different, eccentric, whimsical **10** outlandish, unorthodox **11** distinctive **13** idiosyncratic

off-color 3 ill, low **4** blue, racy **5** bawdy, broad, salty, shady **6** ailing, peaked, poorly, risqué, sickly, unwell **7** dubious, naughty **8** improper, indecent **10** indisposed, suggestive

offend 3 sin, vex **4** gall, hurt, miff, pain **5** anger, annoy, pique, repel, shock, upset **6** appall, breach, insult, nettle **7** affront, disturb, provoke, violate **8** aggrieve, distress, irritate **9** displease **10** antagonize, transgress

offender 5 felon **6** sinner **7** culprit **8** criminal, violator **9** wrongdoer **10** lawbreaker, malefactor **12** transgressor

offense 3 sin **4** huff, hurt, miff, tort, vice **5** crime, fault, pique, wrong **6** attack, breach, felony, injury, insult **7** affront, assault, dudgeon, misdeed, mistake, outrage, umbrage **9** indignity, onslaught, violation **10** aggression, infraction, resentment **11** misdemeanor

offensive 3 bad **4** foul, rank, vile **5** drive, onset **6** attack, odious **7** assault, fulsome, noisome, obscene, painful **8** nauseous, unsavory **9** loathsome, obnoxious, onslaught, repellent, repugnant, repulsive, sickening **10** aggression, aggressive, disgusting, nauseating, unpleasant **12** disagreeable, unappetizing **13** objectionable

offer 3 bid, try **4** seek, show **5** assay, essay, pitch, put up **6** afford, extend, submit, tender **7** advance, attempt, display, exhibit, hold out, present, propose, provide, suggest **8** endeavor, proposal, threaten **9** sacrifice **10** submission **11** proposition

offering 3 IPO **4** alms, gift **5** grant **6** course, corban **7** charity, present **8** donation, oblation **9** sacrifice **11** benefaction, beneficence **12** contribution

offhand 5 ad-lib **6** blithe, breezy, casual **8** informal **9** extempore, impromptu, unstudied **10** improvised, nonchalant, unprepared **11** extemporary, spontaneous, unrehearsed

office 3 job **4** duty **5** berth, suite **6** agency, billet, bureau **7** station **8** business, cube farm, function, province **9** situation, workplace **10** department ***head:*** **4** boss **7** manager ***holder:*** **9** incumbent **11** functionary ***machine:*** **3** fax **6** copier **7** printer **8** computer **10** calculator, fax machine **11** photocopier ***seeker:*** **9** candidate **10** politician ***without work:*** **8** sinecure ***worker:*** **5** clerk **6** typist **9** file clerk, secretary **10** bookkeeper

officer 3 cop **4** exec **6** noncom, police **7** John Law, manager **8** official **9** executive ***abbreviation:*** **2** Lt. **3** Adm., Col., Ens., Gen., Maj. **4** Capt., Cmdr. **5** Comdr., Lieut. ***army:*** **5** looey, looie, major **7** captain, colonel, general **10** lieutenant ***British:*** **9** brigadier ***court:*** **7** bailiff ***king's:*** **11** chamberlain ***law-enforcement:*** **3** cop **6** deputy, police **7** marshal, sheriff **9** constable, patrolman, policeman ***naval:*** **4** mate **6** ensign **7** admiral, captain **9** commander, commodore **10** lieutenant ***noncommissioned:*** **5** sarge **8** corporal, sergeant ***petty:*** **4** bos'n **5** bosun **6** yeoman **9** boatswain ***prison:*** **5** guard **6** warden

official 4 exec **7** cleared, manager **8** approved, bona fide, endorsed **9** authentic, canonical, cathedral, certified, executive **10** accredited, authorized, ex cathedra, magistrate, sanctioned **13** administrator, authoritative ***city or town:*** **5** mayor **8** alderman **9** councilor, selectman **10** councillor ***diplomatic:*** **5** envoy **6** consul **7** attaché **10** ambassador ***governmental:*** **6** syndic ***parish:*** **6** beadle ***sports:*** **3** ref, ump **6** umpire **7** referee **8** linesman ***university:*** **4** dean **6** bursar **7** provost **9** registrar **10** chancellor

officiate 5 chair, serve **6** direct, umpire **7** conduct, oversee, preside, referee **9** supervise **11** superintend

officious 4 busy, nosy **5** nosey, pushy **7** forward **8** meddling **9** assertive, intrusive, obtrusive **10** meddlesome **11** impertinent **13** self-important

offing 6 future **7** by-and-by **9** aftertime, hereafter **10** near future

off-key 3 odd **4** sour **7** jarring **9** anomalous, dissonant, unnatural **10** discordant **12** inharmonious

off-putting 8 daunting **9** dismaying, offensive, repellent **10** forbidding **11** distasteful **12** disagreeable, discouraging **13** disconcerting, disheartening, objectionable

offscouring 5 leper, trash **6** pariah, refuse, reject **7** outcast **8** castaway, derelict **11** untouchable

offset 6 square **7** balance **8** equalize **10** balance out, compensate, neutralize **11** counterpose, countervail **12** counterpoise, displacement

offshoot 4 twig **5** scion **6** branch **7** product, spin-off **9** affiliate, by-product, outgrowth **10** derivative, descendant

offspring 3 cub, kid **4** kids, seed **5** brood, child, hatch, issue, scion, spawn, swarm, young **7** produce, product, progeny **8** children **9** posterity **10** descendant **11** progeniture

off-the-wall 3 odd **5** kooky, weird **6** far-out, way-out **7** bizarre, oddball, unusual **8** freak-

ish **9** eccentric, fantastic, grotesque **10** outlandish
off-white 4 bone **5** cream, ivory **6** oyster, vellum **9** parchment
Of Human Bondage author 7 Maugham (W. Somerset)
Of Mice and Men *author:* 9 Steinbeck (John) ***character:* 6** George (Milton), Lennie (Small)
often 9 generally **10** frequently, habitually, repeatedly **11** recurrently
ogee 3 ess **4** arch **5** curve **7** molding
Ogier the ____ 4 Dane
ogive 3 rib **4** arch **5** graph
ogle 3 eye **4** gape, gaze, leer, look **5** stare **6** goggle **7** stare at **10** rubberneck
ogre 3 orc **5** bogey, giant, Shrek **6** Grinch **7** bugbear, monster **8** bogeyman **9** boogeyman ***Algonquian:* 7** wendigo, windigo
ogress 5 harpy, scold, shrew, vixen **6** amazon, virago **8** fishwife **9** termagant, Xanthippe
O'Hara novel 7 Pal Joey **16** Butterfield Eight **17** Ten North Frederick
Ohio *capital:* 8 Columbus ***city:* 5** Akron, Xenia **6** Canton, Dayton, Toledo **9** Cleveland **10** Cincinnati ***college, university:* 5** Miami **6** Kenyon **7** Antioch, Denison, Oberlin **9** Kent State **12** Bowling Green ***nickname:* 7** Buckeye (State) ***river:* 4** Ohio **6** Maumee **8** Sandusky ***state bird:* 8** cardinal ***state flower:* 16** scarlet carnation ***state tree:* 7** buckeye
Oholibamah *father:* 4 Anah ***husband:* 4** Esau
oil 3 fat, gas **4** balm, fuel, lube, oleo **5** oleum, slick **6** anoint, grease, pomade **7** blarney, incense, lanolin **8** flattery, soft soap **9** adulation, lubricant, lubricate, petroleum ***combining form:* 3** ole **4** olei, oleo ***company:* 3** Sun **4** Arco, Esso, Gulf, Hess, Hunt, Pure **5** ADNOC, Amoco, Citgo, Exxon, Getty, Mobil, Pemex, Shell, Sohio, Union, YUKOS **6** Aramco, Conoco, Lukoil, Sunoco, Texaco, Valero **7** Ashland, Chevron **8** Marathon, Pennzoil, Phillips, Sinclair, Standard **9** Petrobras **10** ExxonMobil, Occidental, PetroChina ***consecrated:* 6** chrism ***fragrant:* 5** attar **6** neroli ***fuel:* 3** gas **6** butane, petrol **7** benzene, propane **8** gasoline, kerosene ***relating to:* 5** oleic ***ship:* 6** tanker ***source:* 4** rape **5** olive, shale **6** canola **7** linseed **8** flaxseed, rapeseed **9** sunflower ***well:* 6** gusher
oilbird 8 guacharo
oily 5 fatty, slick, soapy, suave **6** greasy, smarmy, smooth **7** fulsome **8** slippery, unctuous **10** lubricious, obsequious, oleaginous
ointment 4 balm, nard **5** cream, salve **6** lotion **7** unction, unguent **8** calamine, liniment **9** emollient, spikenard **11** embrocation
OK, okay 3 aye, yea, yes **4** fine, good, safe, well, yeah **5** agree, allow, favor, licit **6** agreed, assent, decent, permit **7** approve, certify, endorse, support **8** accredit, adequate, all right, approval, blessing, high sign, passable, sanction, thumbs-up **9** authorize, hunky-dory **10** acceptable, permission **11** endorsement, permissible **12** satisfactory
Okinawa capital 4 Naha
Oklahoma *capital:* 12 Oklahoma City ***city:* 3** Ada **4** Enid **5** Tulsa **6** Norman ***college, university:* 11** Oral Roberts ***mountain:* 9** Black Mesa ***nickname:* 6** Sooner (State) ***river:* 3** Red **8** Arkansas, Canadian ***state bird:* 10** flycatcher ***state flower:* 9** mistletoe ***state tree:* 6** redbud
okra 4 soup **5** gumbo **6** mallow
old 4 aged, gray, late, past **5** dated, hoary, passé, stale **6** bygone, démodé, former, mature, senior, whilom **7** ancient, antique, archaic, elderly, lasting, onetime, overage, quondam, veteran **8** enduring, lifelong, Noachian, outmoded, timeworn **9** erstwhile, geriatric, long-lived, perennial, perpetual, primitive, venerable **10** antiquated, inveterate **13** superannuated ***Scottish:* 4** auld
old age 3 eld **6** dotage **8** caducity **10** senescence **11** decrepitude, elderliness, senectitude
Old Bailey 5 court
Old Colony State 13 Massachusetts
Old Curiosity Shop *author:* 7 Dickens (Charles) ***character:* 4** Nell **10** Little Nell
Old Dominion State 8 Virginia
Old Faithful 6 geyser
old-fashioned 4 aged **5** dated, dowdy, fusty, moldy, passé, stale, tired **6** bygone, démodé, quaint, stodgy **7** ancient, antique, archaic, outworn, vintage **8** obsolete, outdated, outmoded **9** out-of-date, unstylish **10** antiquated
old hand 3 pro, vet **6** expert, master **7** veteran **9** authority **10** past master, specialist
old hat 5 dated, passé, stale, tired, trite **6** démodé **7** antique, clichéd, vintage **8** outmoded, timeworn, well-worn **9** hackneyed, out-of-date **10** antiquated
Old Ironsides 12 Constitution (U.S.S.) ***poet:* 6** Holmes (Oliver Wendell)
Old Line State 8 Maryland
old maid 6 fusser **7** fusspot **8** spinster **10** fussbudget
Old North State 13 North Carolina

Old Rough and Ready 6 Taylor (Zachary)
Olds' car 3 Reo
old-time 5 dated **6** bygone **7** antique, vintage **10** antiquated **12** long-standing
old-timer 3 vet **5** elder **6** senior **7** ancient, antique, veteran
Old World 6 Europe
oleaginous see **oily**
oleaster 5 shrub **12** Russian olive
olecranon 9 funny bone
oleo 9 margarine
oleoresin 10 turpentine
oleum 3 oil
olfaction 5 sense, smell **8** smelling
olid 4 rank **5** fetid **6** putrid, rancid, rotten **7** stenchy **8** stinking **9** offensive **10** malodorous
olio 3 mix **4** hash, stew **5** gumbo, umble **6** medley **7** grab bag, mélange, mixture **8** mishmash, mixed bag **9** potpourri **10** assortment, collection, hodgepodge, hotchpotch, miscellany, salmagundi **11** gallimaufry
Oliver Twist *author:* 7 Dickens (Charles) ***character:* 5** Fagin, Nancy, Sikes (Bill) **6** Bumble (Mr.) **12** Artful Dodger
Ollie's partner 4 Stan
Olympian 3 god **5** lofty, noble **6** lordly **7** athlete, exalted, godlike **8** majestic, superior **10** competitor
Olympics site *1972:* 6 Munich **7** Sapporo ***1976:* 8** Montreal **9** Innsbruck ***1980:* 6** Moscow **10** Lake Placid ***1984:* 10** Los Angeles **8** Sarajevo ***1988:* 5** Seoul **7** Calgary ***1992:* 9** Barcelona **11** Albertville ***1994:* 11** Lillehammer ***1996:* 7** Atlanta ***1998:* 6** Nagano ***2000:* 6** Sydney ***2002:* 12** Salt Lake City ***2004:* 6** Athens ***2006:* 5** Turin **6** Torino ***2008:* 7** Beijing ***2010:* 9** Vancouver ***2012:* 6** London ***2016:*3** Rio **12** Rio de Janeiro
Oman *capital:* 6 Masqat, Muscat ***language:* 6** Arabic **7** Baluchi ***monetary unit:* 4** rial ***mountain range:* 7** Al-Hajar ***neighbor:* 5** Yemen **11** Saudi Arabia ***peninsula:* 7** Arabian ***sea:* 7** Arabian
Omar 4 poet **7** Khayyám ***country:* 6** Persia ***father:* 7** Eliphaz ***poem:* 8** Rubaiyat
omega 3 end **6** ending, finale, letter ***kin:* 3** zed, zee
omen 4 sign **5** augur, token **6** augury, boding **7** auspice, portent, presage, warning **8** bodement, prophecy **9** foretoken **10** foreboding, prediction, prognostic
ominous 4 dark, dire, grim **6** dismal **7** baleful, direful, doomful, fateful **8** alarming, lowering, menacing, sinister **9** ill-boding, prophetic **10** forbidding, foreboding, portentous **11** frightening, threatening **12** inauspicious, unpropitious
omission 3 cut, gap **4** lack, skip, slip **5** blank, break, chasm, error, lapse **6** hiatus, lacuna **7** elision, failure **8** eclipsis, ellipsis, overlook **9** exclusion ***mark:* 5** caret **8** ellipsis **10** apostrophe
omit 4 drop, fail, skip **5** elide **6** except, forget, ignore, slight **7** exclude, neglect **8** leave out, overlook, pass over
omnibus 3 ana **4** posy **5** album **7** garland **8** analects, treasury **9** anthology **10** miscellany **11** florilegium
omnipotent 6 divine **7** godlike, supreme **8** almighty **9** unlimited **11** all-powerful
omnipresent 7 allover, endless **8** infinite, unending **9** boundless, limitless, universal **10** ubiquitous
omniscient 4 wise **7** learned **9** know-it-all **10** all-knowing
omnium-gatherum see **olio**
Omphale *domain:* 5 Lydia ***slave:* 8** Heracles, Hercules
omphalos 3 hub **5** focus, navel **9** umbilicus **10** focal point **11** belly button
on 4 atop, over **5** above, along, going **7** working **9** operating **11** functioning
onager 3 ass **5** kiang **8** catapult
Onan's father 5 Judah
once 4 ever, late, past **5** at all **6** before, bygone, former, whilom **7** already, earlier, long ago, onetime, quondam **8** formerly, sometime
once-over 4 look **5** check **6** gander, glance, survey **10** inspection **11** examination
one 4 lone, only, sole, unit **5** monad **6** single, unique **7** numeral **8** separate, singular, solitary **9** undivided **10** individual, particular ***combining form:* 4** mono ***French:* 2** un **3** une ***German:* 3** ein **4** eine ***prefix:* 3** uni ***Scottish:* 2** ae **3** ane, yin ***Spanish:* 2** un **3** una, uno
one and a half *combining form:* 6 sesqui
one-eyed giant 7 Cyclops **10** Polyphemus
one-handed god 3 Tiu, Tyr
one-horse town 4 burg **5** thorp **6** hamlet, Podunk **7** village **11** whistle-stop
one hundred 6 centum ***years:* 7** century
O'Neill, Eugene *daughter:* 4 Oona ***heroine:* 4** Anna, Nina ***play:* 3** Ile **4** Gold **8** Hairy Ape (The) **12** Ah Wilderness, Anna Christie, Emperor Jones, Iceman Cometh (The) **13** Great God Brown (The), Marco Millions **16** Strange Interlude **18** Desire Under the Elms **22** Mourning Becomes Electra **24** Long Day's Journey into Night
oneiric 6 dreamy **8** anagogic **9** dreamlike

oneness 3 all **5** union, unity, whole **7** harmony **8** entirety, identity, sameness, totality **9** integrity, unanimity **10** singleness, uniformity **11** singularity, unification **13** individuality

onerous 4 hard **5** heavy, tough **6** taxing, trying **7** arduous, exigent, wearing, weighty **8** exacting, grievous, imposing, pressing, toilsome **9** demanding, difficult, laborious **10** burdensome, cumbersome, oppressive **11** troublesome

one-sided 6 biased, uneven **7** colored, partial, unequal **8** inclined, partisan, weighted **10** prejudiced, unbalanced, unilateral

onetime 3 old **4** once, past **6** bygone, former, whilom **7** quondam **8** previous **9** erstwhile

ongoing 7 current, growing **8** evolving **9** advancing, in process **10** continuing, continuous, developing, in progress, unfinished **11** progressing

on hand 4 here **5** ready **6** nearby **7** pending, present **9** available

onion 4 bulb **7** shallot ***bulb:*** **3** set ***genus:*** **6** Allium ***kin:*** **4** leek **6** garlic ***kind:*** **7** Bermuda, Danvers, Spanish ***roll:*** **5** bialy ***young:*** **8** scallion

online 5 wired **9** connected ***business:*** **5** e-tail ***guffaw:*** **3** LOL ***pages:*** **7** Web site ***system:*** **3** Web **8** Internet

onlooker 6 viewer **7** watcher, witness **8** beholder, kibitzer, observer **9** bystander, kibbitzer, spectator **10** eyewitness **12** rubbernecker

only 3 but, few, one, yet **4** just, lone, mere, save, sole, solo **5** alone **6** and yet, at most, except, merely, simply, single, solely, unique **7** however, utterly **8** entirely, singular, solitary **11** exclusively

onomasticon 7 lexicon **8** wordbook

onomatopoeic 5 mimic **6** echoic **7** mimetic **9** emulative, imitative **10** simulative

onset 4 dawn, rush **5** birth, get-go, start **6** attack, coming, origin **7** arrival, assault, dawning, offense, opening **8** invasion **9** beginning, inception, offensive **10** aggression **12** commencement

onslaught 5 blitz **6** attack, charge, deluge **7** assault, barrage, offense, torrent **8** invasion **9** offensive **10** aggression

on-target 3 apt, fit **5** exact, right **7** correct, perfect, precise **8** accurate **11** appropriate

Ontario *bay:* **8** Georgian ***capital:*** **7** Toronto ***city:*** **4** York **6** London, Ottawa **7** Markham, Windsor **8** Hamilton **9** Etobicoke, Kitchener, North York **10** Thunder Bay **11** Mississauga, Scarborough **13** Sault Ste. Marie ***lake:*** **4** Erie **5** Huron **7** Nipigon, Ontario **8** Superior ***provincial flower:*** **13** white trillium ***river:*** **5** Moose **6** Albany, Severn, Winisk

on the go 4 busy **6** active

on the house 4 free **6** comped, gratis **13** complimentary

on the nose 5 bingo **6** dead-on, spot-on **7** exactly **8** accurate **9** precisely **10** accurately

on the other hand 3 but **7** however **11** nonetheless **12** nevertheless

on the rocks 4 iced **7** with ice, wrecked

on the whole 6 mainly, mostly **7** usually **8** all in all **9** generally, in general, typically **10** altogether, by and large

onus 3 tax **4** duty, load, task **5** blame, brand, fault, guilt, odium, stain **6** burden, charge, stigma, weight **8** black eye **9** liability **10** obligation, oppression

onward 5 ahead, along, forth **7** forward **9** advancing

onyx 5 agate **10** chalcedony

oodles 4 gobs, lots, tons, wads **5** heaps, loads, piles, rafts, reams, scads **6** plenty

oolong 3 tea

oomph 3 pep, vim, zip **4** brio, dash, élan, push, zest, zing **5** drive, punch, verve, vigor **6** esprit, pizazz, spirit **7** pizzazz **8** strength, vitality **9** sex appeal

ooze 3 goo, mud **4** emit, goop, leak, seep, weep **5** bleed, exude, issue, marsh, slime, sweat **7** secrete, seepage **8** transude

opacity 9 murkiness, obscurity **10** obtuseness

opal 3 gem **5** jewel, stone **6** silica **7** girasol, hyalite **8** gemstone

opaque 3 dim **4** dull, hazy **5** dense, filmy, murky, vague **6** cloudy **7** clouded, obscure, unclear **8** abstruse

OPEC nation 3 UAE **4** Iran, Iraq **5** Libya, Qatar **6** Kuwait **7** Algeria, Nigeria **9** Indonesia, Venezuela **11** Saudi Arabia

open 4 ajar, bare, free, wide **5** frank, lance, overt, unzip **6** broach, candid, expand, expose, public, reveal, spread, unfold, unlock, unseal, unveil **7** convene, outdoor, uncover, unlatch **8** disclose, outdoors, unlocked, unsealed **9** available, uncovered, undecided **10** unfastened **11** susceptible, unconcealed, undisguised **12** unrestricted

open-air 7 outdoor, outside **8** alfresco, outdoors **9** out-of-door **10** out-of-doors

open-and-shut 4 easy **5** clear, plain **6** patent, simple **7** evident, obvious

openhanded 6 giving, lavish **7** liberal **8** generous **9** bounteous, bountiful, unselfish, unsparing **10** beneficent, bighearted, charitable, munificent **11** magnanimous

openhearted 4 kind, warm **5** frank, plain **6**

candid, honest **8** generous **10** responsive **11** sympathetic

opening 2 os **3** gap **4** dawn, door, gate, hole, pass, pore, slit, slot, vent **5** break, chasm, chink, cleft, crack, debut, intro, mouth, onset, start, stoma **6** breach, chance, lacuna, outlet, outset **7** crevice, dawning, fissure, orifice, pinhole **8** aperture, overture **9** beginning **11** opportunity ***ship's:*** **5** hatch **8** hatchway, porthole

open-minded 7 liberal **8** tolerant, unbiased **9** receptive **12** freethinking, unprejudiced

openmouthed 4 agog, awed, rapt **5** agape **6** amazed, gaping **7** stunned **9** astounded, surprised **10** astonished, speechless

open sesame 3 key **5** charm **6** ticket **8** passport, password

open up 4 fire, talk **5** shoot **6** reveal **7** cut into, divulge **8** disclose **9** make plain, spread out **11** communicate

opera *comic:* 5 buffa **6** bouffe ***glasses:*** **9** lorgnette ***house:*** **3** Met **7** La Scala **12** Covent Garden, Metropolitan ***kind:*** **4** soap **5** comic, grand, horse, space ***part:*** **3** act **4** aria **5** scena ***solo:*** **4** aria ***star:*** **4** diva **10** prima donna ***text:*** **8** libretto (see also individual titles and composers)

opera (famous) 4 Aida **5** Faust, Manon, Norma, Tosca **6** Carmen, Otello, Salome **7** Elektra, Fidelio, Macbeth, Nabucco, Walküre (Die), Wozzeck **8** Don Carlo, Falstaff, Idomeneo, La Bohème, Turandot **9** Don Carlos, Lohengrin, Rheingold (Das), Rigoletto, Siegfried **10** I Pagliacci, La Gioconda, La Traviata, Magic Flute (The), Prince Igor, Tannhäuser **11** Don Giovanni, William Tell **12** Così Fan Tutte, Manon Lescaut, Pearl Fishers (The) **14** Flying Dutchman (The) **15** Barber of Seville (The), Götterdämmerung, Madama Butterfly **16** Marriage of Figaro (The), Tristan und Isolde

operant 8 behavior **9** effective **10** measurable, observable, productive **12** conditioning

operate 3 act, run, use **4** work **5** drive, exert, steer **6** behave, direct, effect, handle, manage **7** carry on, conduct, control, perform, produce **8** function, maneuver **9** influence **10** manipulate

operation 3 use **4** step **6** action **7** concern, mission, process, surgery **8** activity, business, exercise, exertion, function, maneuver **9** procedure **10** employment, engagement, enterprise **11** performance, transaction

operative 3 key **5** agent, alive **6** active, moving, usable **7** dynamic, in force, running, working **8** relevant **9** effective **10** functional **11** efficacious, secret agent

operator 4 user **5** agent, fixer, pilot **6** doctor, driver **7** schemer, surgeon **9** conductor

operculum 3 lid **4** flap **8** covering

operetta composer 5 Friml (Rudolf), Lehár (Franz), Suppé (Franz von) **6** Straus (Oscar) **7** Herbert (Victor), Romberg (Sigmund), Strauss (Johann) **8** Sullivan (Arthur) **9** Offenbach (Jacques)

operose 4 dull **6** boring, tiring **7** tedious **8** tiresome, toilsome, weariful **9** difficult, laborious, wearisome

Ophelia *beloved:* 6 Hamlet ***brother:*** **7** Laertes ***father:*** **8** Polonius

ophidian 5 snake **9** snakelike

opiate 4 dope, drug **7** anodyne **8** hypnotic, narcotic, nepenthe, sedative **9** analgesic, soporific **10** anesthetic, painkiller **11** somniferous **12** somnifacient, tranquilizer ***type:*** **7** codeine **8** morphine

opine 4 aver, deem, hold, view **5** claim, judge, state, think **6** advise, assert **7** believe, express, suppose **8** point out **9** recommend

opinion 4 idea, view **5** tenet **6** belief, notion, theory **7** feeling, thought **8** attitude, estimate, judgment, reaction **9** sentiment **10** assumption, conclusion, conjecture, conviction, estimation, hypothesis, persuasion **11** speculation, supposition ***express an:*** **4** vote **5** judge **9** criticize

opium 4 dope, drug **8** narcotic ***derivative:*** **6** heroin **7** codeine **8** laudanum, morphine **9** paregoric ***source:*** **5** poppy

opossum 9 marsupial ***kin:*** **8** kangaroo

opponent 3 con, foe **4** anti **5** enemy, rival **6** muscle **7** nemesis **9** adversary, assailant, combatant **10** antagonist, challenger, competitor **12** counteragent

opportune 3 apt, fit **6** timely **8** suitable **9** favorable, well-timed **10** auspicious, convenient, felicitous, propitious **11** appropriate

opportunity 4 turn **5** break, space, spell **6** chance **7** opening **8** juncture, occasion, prospect **12** circumstance

oppose 4 buck, defy, deny, duel **5** cross, fight, repel **6** attack, combat, debate, differ, object, refute, resist **7** assault, contest, counter, dispute, prevent, protest **8** confront, contrast, disagree, obstruct **9** withstand **10** contradict, contravene, controvert, disapprove

opposed 3 con **4** agin, anti **6** contra **7** adverse, against **11** adversarial **12** antagonistic, antipathetic

opposite 4 foil **5** polar **6** contra, facing **7** antonym, counter, inverse, obverse, opposed, reverse **8** antipode, antipole, contrary, contrast, converse **9** antipodal, diametric **10** antipodean, antithesis **11** contrasting, counterpole **12** antithetical, counterpoint **13** contradictory ***prefix:*** **3** dis **5** retro **6** contra **7** counter

opposition **3** con, foe **5** enemy **7** rivalry **8** conflict, defiance **9** adversary, animosity, hostility **10** antagonism, antithesis, resistance **11** contrariety, disapproval

oppress **5** abuse, crush, wrong **6** burden, injure, sadden, subdue **7** afflict, torment, torture, trouble **8** aggrieve, distress, overload **9** persecute, subjugate, weigh down

oppressive **5** harsh, heavy **6** brutal, dismal, gloomy, severe, somber, sombre, taxing **7** exigent, onerous, weighty **8** crushing, exacting, grievous, stifling **9** demanding **10** burdensome, depressing, tyrannical **11** dispiriting, overbearing, suffocating **12** discouraging, overwhelming ***force:*** **4** onus, yoke **6** burden, weight

oppressor **5** bully **6** despot, tyrant **8** autocrat, dictator **9** strongman

opprobrious **4** evil, vile **6** odious, vulgar **7** abusive, hateful **8** infamous **9** notorious, truculent **10** despicable, scurrilous **11** disgraceful, ignominious **12** contemptible, contumelious, vituperative

opprobrium **5** abuse, blame, odium, scorn, shame **6** infamy **7** obloquy **8** contempt, disgrace, dishonor, ignominy, reproach **9** contumely, discredit, disesteem, disrepute **10** scurrility **12** vituperation

oppugn **5** argue, fight **6** battle, combat **7** contend, contest, dispute **8** question

Ops **4** Rhea ***consort:*** **6** Cronus, Saturn ***daughter:*** **5** Ceres **7** Demeter

opt **3** tap **4** pick **5** elect, favor **6** choose, decide, prefer, select

optical **6** ocular, visual **8** visional ***debris:*** **7** floater ***instrument:*** **4** lens **5** scope **7** transit **9** magnifier, periscope, telescope **10** microscope

optimal **4** best **5** ideal **6** choice, finest **7** perfect, supreme **8** choicest

optimist **4** bull **5** hoper **7** dreamer **8** idealist, Micawber **9** Pollyanna **10** positivist

optimistic **4** rosy **5** happy, merry, sunny **6** bright, hoping, upbeat **7** assured, buoyant, hopeful, roseate **8** cheerful, positive, sanguine, trusting **9** confident, promising **11** rose-colored **12** Pollyannaish

option **4** pick **5** claim, extra, grant, right **6** choice **7** license **8** contract, election **9** accessory, privilege, selection **10** preference **11** alternative, prerogative

optional **4** free **5** extra **8** elective **9** voluntary **11** alternative **13** discretionary ***item:*** **5** add-on, extra

opulence **4** luxe **6** bounty, luxury, plenty, riches, wealth **7** fortune **9** abundance, affluence, plenitude, profusion **10** luxuriance **12** extravagance

opulent **4** lush, rich **5** plush, showy, swank **6** deluxe, lavish **7** moneyed, profuse, wealthy **8** affluent, palatial **9** luxuriant, luxurious, plentiful, sumptuous **11** extravagant **12** ostentatious

opuntia **6** cactus

opus **4** work **5** piece **6** oeuvre **7** product **8** creation **11** composition

or **4** else, gold **6** golden, yellow **9** otherwise

oracle **4** sage, seer **5** augur, sibyl **6** augury, medium, Pythia, vision **7** prophet **8** haruspex, prophecy **10** apocalypse, revelation, soothsayer ***site:*** **6** Claros, Delphi, Didyma, Dodona **7** Olympia **9** Epidaurus

oracular **5** vatic **6** mantic, orphic **7** cryptic, Delphic, fatidic, obscure **8** Delphian, dogmatic **9** ambiguous, arbitrary, prophetic, sibylline, vaticinal

oral **4** exam **5** vocal **6** spoken, verbal, voiced **8** narrated, viva voce **9** unwritten **11** examination

orange **6** citrus ***brownish:*** **6** Titian ***deep:*** **11** bittersweet ***gem:*** **7** jacinth ***genus:*** **6** Citrus ***kin:*** **4** lime **5** lemon **7** kumquat, satsuma **8** mandarin **9** tangerine **10** grapefruit ***kind:*** **4** sour **5** blood, chino, navel, Osage, sweet **7** Seville **8** bergamot, mandarin, Valencia ***oil:*** **6** neroli ***seed:*** **3** pip ***skin:*** **4** rind

orangutan **3** ape **6** pongid **7** primate **10** anthropoid

Oranjestad island **5** Aruba

orate **4** rant **5** mouth, speak, spiel **6** preach **7** address, declaim, lecture **8** bloviate, harangue, perorate **9** discourse, sermonize, speechify **11** pontificate

oration **6** homily, sermon, speech **7** address, lecture **9** discourse ***funeral:*** **6** eulogy

orator **7** speaker ***American:*** **4** Clay (Henry) **5** Bryan (William Jennings), Henry (Patrick) **7** Calhoun (John C.), Douglas (Stephen), Webster (Daniel) ***British:*** **5** Burke (Edmund) **8** Disraeli (Benjamin) **9** Churchill (Winston), Gladstone (William) ***French:*** **8** Mirabeau (Comte de) ***Greek:*** **5** Corax **8** Pericles **11** Demosthenes ***Roman:*** **6** Cicero

oratory **6** chapel, speech **7** bombast **8** rhetoric **9** discourse, elocution, eloquence **10** expression **11** exhortation, speechcraft

orb **3** eye **4** ball **5** globe, round **6** circle, sphere

orbit **4** path **5** ambit, range, reach, scope, sweep, track **6** extent, radius **7** ellipse ***farthest point:*** **4** apse **5** apsis **6** apogee **8** aphelion ***nearest point:*** **4** apse **5** apsis **7** perigee **10** perihelion

orchard **5** trees **10** plantation

orchestra **4** band **7** gamelan **8** ensemble, symphony **12** philharmonic ***instrument:*** **4** harp, oboe, tuba **5** cello, flute, viola **6** chimes, violin **7** bassoon, cymbals, piccolo, timpani, trumpet **8** bass drum, clarinet, triangle, trombone **9** castanets, snare drum, xylophone **10** double bass, French horn, tambourine **11** English horn, violoncello **12** glockenspiel ***leader:*** **9** conductor ***section:*** **5** brass **6** string **7** brasses, strings **8** woodwind **9** woodwinds **10** percussion

orchestrate **5** blend, score, unify **6** manage **7** arrange, compose **8** organize **9** harmonize, integrate **10** coordinate

orchid ***genus:*** **4** Disa ***kind:*** **7** calypso, pogonia **8** cattleya, oncidium **9** cymbidium **11** cypripedium ***petal:*** **3** lip **8** labellum ***product:*** **5** salep ***tuber:*** **5** salep

ordain **4** will **5** enact, order **6** decree, direct, impose, invest **7** appoint, command, conduct, destine, dictate, install, lay down **9** establish, prescribe, pronounce **10** predestine

ordeal **4** test **5** agony, cross, trial **7** calvary, torment, trouble **8** crucible **9** suffering **10** affliction, difficulty, visitation **11** tribulation

order **4** book, fiat, rank **5** array, caste, class, genre, range **6** decree, lineup, method, scheme, series, system **7** command, harmony, mandate, marshal, pattern, reserve **8** classify, neatness, position, shipment, tidiness **9** directive, hierarchy, procedure, structure **10** injunction, regularity **11** progression ***lack of:*** **5** chaos **6** ataxia **7** anarchy, clutter **9** confusion **11** pandemonium ***of business:*** **6** agenda, docket ***of preference:*** **8** priority

orderly **4** aide, calm, neat, tidy, trim **6** batman **7** correct, precise, regular, soldier, uniform **8** methodic, peaceful **9** attendant, organized, peaceable, regulated, shipshape **10** methodical, systematic **11** uncluttered, well-behaved **12** businesslike

ordinance **3** law **4** code, rule **5** edict **6** decree **7** precept, statute **9** direction, prescript **10** regulation

ordinary **4** so-so **5** banal, cheap, judge, plain, trite, usual **6** common, normal **7** average, humdrum, mundane, natural, popular, prelate, prosaic, regular, routine, typical **8** everyday, familiar, inferior, mediocre, workaday **9** clergyman, customary, quotidian **10** uneventful, unoriginal **11** commonplace

ordnance **4** arms, guns **6** cannon **7** weapons **8** armament, supplies, weaponry **9** artillery, munitions **10** ammunition

ore **4** gold, rock **5** metal **6** copper, silver **7** mineral **8** platinum ***analysis:*** **5** assay ***deposit:*** **4** lode, vein ***excavation:*** **5** stope ***iron:*** **5** ocher, ochre **8** goethite, hematite, limonite ***lead:*** **6** galena ***process:*** **8** leaching, smelting ***refuse:*** **4** slag **5** dross, matte **6** scoria ***smelted:*** **7** regulus

oread **5** nymph

Oregon ***capital:*** **5** Salem ***city:*** **4** Bend **6** Eugene **7** Coos Bay, Medford **8** Portland ***college, university:*** **4** Reed ***lake:*** **6** Crater ***mountain, range:*** **4** Hood **7** Cascade ***nickname:*** **6** Beaver (State) ***river:*** **5** Snake **8** Columbia ***state bird:*** **10** meadowlark ***state flower:*** **11** Oregon grape ***state tree:*** **10** Douglas fir

Orestes ***father:*** **9** Agamemnon ***friend:*** **7** Pylades ***mother:*** **12** Clytemnestra ***sister:*** **7** Electra **9** Iphigenia ***victim:*** **9** Aegisthus **12** Clytemnestra ***wife:*** **8** Hermione

organ **5** agent, means **6** agency, medium, review **7** channel, journal, vehicle **8** magazine, ministry **9** newspaper **10** instrument, periodical ***ancient:*** **9** hydraulus ***barrel:*** **10** hurdy-gurdy ***bodily:*** **3** ear, eye **4** lung, nose, skin **5** gland, heart, liver **6** kidney, larynx, spleen, tongue, tonsil, viscus **9** intestine ***displacement:*** **8** prolapse ***mouth:*** **9** harmonica ***part:*** **4** pipe, reed, stop **5** pedal, valve **6** blower **7** console, tremolo **8** keyboard **9** wind chest ***reed:*** **8** melodeon **9** harmonium ***stop:*** **4** oboe, sext **5** gamba, quint, viola **6** dulcet **7** bassoon, celesta, melodia, subbass, tertian **8** carillon, diapason, dulciana, gemshorn ***tactile:*** **6** feeler **8** tentacle

organ cactus **7** saguaro

organic **5** basic **6** innate **7** natural, primary **8** inherent, integral **9** essential **10** structural **11** fundamental

organism **5** being, plant **6** animal ***disease-producing:*** **4** germ **5** virus **8** pathogen **9** bacterium ***single-celled:*** **5** monad **6** amoeba **9** protozoan

organist ***American:*** **3** Fox (Virgil) **5** Biggs (E. Power) **6** Newman (Anthony) ***Dutch:*** **9** Sweelinck (Jan) ***English:*** **6** Wesley (Samuel) **7** Gibbons (Christopher, Edward, Ellis, Orlando) ***French:*** **5** Alain (Marie-Claire), Widor (Charles) **6** Franck (César) **8** Messiaen (Olivier) **10** Schweitzer (Albert) ***German:*** **4** Bach (Johann Sebastian) **6** Handel (George Frideric), Walcha (Helmut) **7**

Richter (Anton, Ernst, Ferdinand, Johann, Karl) ***Swiss:*** **4** Rogg (Lionel)

organization 4 body, club, unit **5** group, guild, setup **6** agency, system **7** pattern **9** framework, structure **11** arrangement, association, corporation, institution **13** establishment ***college:*** **4** frat **8** sorority **10** fraternity ***criminal:*** **3** Mob **4** gang **5** Mafia ***fraternal:*** (see **fraternal society**) ***government:*** (see **government agency**) ***lack of:*** **5** chaos ***political:*** **4** bloc **5** party **7** apparat, machine ***service:*** **3** USO, VFW

organize 4 form **5** array, group, order, rally, set up, start **6** create, line up **7** arrange **8** classify, unionize **9** construct, establish, institute, integrate **10** constitute, coordinate **11** put together

orgulous 5 proud

orgy 4 rite **5** binge, revel, spree **7** blowout, carouse, debauch, rampage, revelry, splurge **8** carousal **9** bacchanal **10** indulgence, saturnalia **11** bacchanalia

oriel 3 bay **6** window

orient 3 set **4** face **5** adapt, align, pearl, sheen **6** adjust, direct, inform, locate, luster **7** arrange **8** acquaint, lustrous **9** sparkling **11** accommodate, familiarize

Orient 4 Asia, East **7** Far East

Oriental 3 rug **5** Asian **6** carpet **7** Eastern **10** Far Eastern

orientation 7 bearing **8** location, position **9** alignment, direction **10** adjustment **11** arrangement

orifice see **opening**

oriflamme 4 flag **5** ideal **6** banner, pennon, symbol **7** pendant, pennant **8** standard, streamer

origami 12 paper folding ***bird:*** **5** crane

origin 4 root, seed, well **5** birth, blood, start **6** source **7** descent, genesis, lineage **8** ancestry, fountain, pedigree **9** beginning, inception, maternity, parentage, paternity **10** derivation, extraction, provenance, wellspring

original 3 new **5** first, model, novel, prime **6** native, unique **7** initial, pattern, pioneer, primary **8** creative, earliest **9** archetype, ingenious, innovator, inventive, precursor, primitive, prototype **10** archetypal, forerunner, innovative, primordial

originally 5 first **7** at first **8** formerly **9** initially, primarily

originate 4 coin, flow, hail, make, rise, stem **5** arise, begin, found, hatch, issue, set up, start **6** create, derive, invent, launch, spring **7** emanate, proceed, produce, think up **8** commence, generate, initiate, innovate **9** institute, introduce

originator 5 maker **6** author **7** creator, founder, planner **8** inventor, producer **9** initiator, innovator **10** institutor, introducer

oriole 4 bird **8** troupial ***European:*** **6** loriot ***genus:*** **7** Icterus ***golden:*** **6** loriot ***kind:*** **6** golden **7** orchard **8** Bullock's **9** Baltimore

Orion 6 hunter **13** constellation ***beloved:*** **3** Eos ***belt:*** **7** Ellwand ***father:*** **7** Hyrieus **8** Poseidon ***slayer:*** **5** Diana **7** Artemis ***star:*** **5** Rigel **9** Bellatrix **10** Betelgeuse

orison 6 prayer **8** entreaty, petition **12** supplication

Orithyia *lover:* **6** Boreas ***son:*** **5** Zetes **6** Calais

Orlando author 5 Woolf (Virginia)

Orlando Furioso author 7 Ariosto (Ludovico)

Orléans heroine 9 Joan of Arc

orlop 4 deck

ormolu 5 brass **6** bronze

ornament 3 gem **4** bead, deck, trim **5** adorn, jewel **6** bedeck, finial, tassel **7** dress up, garnish, jewelry, pendant, whatnot **8** beautify, decorate, filigree **9** embellish, embroider, lavaliere ***Christmas tree:*** **4** bulb **5** angel **6** tinsel ***lip:*** **6** labret ***shoulder:*** **7** epaulet

ornamental case 4 etui

ornate 4 lush, rich **5** fancy, gaudy, showy **6** florid, frilly, gilded, glitzy, rococo **7** baroque, flowery, opulent **8** overdone **9** elaborate, luxuriant, sumptuous **10** flamboyant

ornery 5 balky, cross, testy **6** crabby, cranky, crusty, grumpy **7** bearish, froward, grouchy **8** contrary, perverse, stubborn, vinegary **9** crotchety, difficult, irascible, irritable **10** inflexible, vinegarish **12** cantankerous

ornithic 5 avian **8** birdlike

ornithologist *American:* **4** Bond (James) **7** Audubon (John James), Bartram (William) **8** Peterson (Roger Tory) ***English:*** **5** Gould (John) ***Scottish:*** **6** Wilson (Alexander)

orotund 4 full, loud **5** round **7** flowery, fustian, pompous, ringing **8** resonant, sonorous **9** bombastic, high-flown, overblown **10** euphuistic, oratorical, resounding, rhetorical, stentorian **11** declamatory **12** magniloquent **13** grandiloquent

Orpah *husband:* **7** Chilion ***sister-in-law:*** **4** Ruth

orphan 4 waif **5** Annie, gamin, stray **6** bereft, gamine, urchin **7** cast-off, ignored **8** forsaken, homeless **9** abandoned, foundling, neglected **10** motherless, parentless

Orpheus *father:* **6** Apollo **7** Oeagrus ***home:*** **6** Thrace ***instrument:*** **4** lyre ***mother:*** **8** Calliope ***wife:*** **8** Euridice

orphic 6 arcane, mystic, occult **7** cryptic,

Delphic, obscure **8** abstruse, Delphian, esoteric, hermetic, mystical, oracular, profound **9** enigmatic, recondite

ort 3 bit **4** bite **5** crumb, piece, scrap **6** morsel **7** remnant **8** leftover

orthodox 6 proper **8** accepted, approved, official, received, standard **9** canonical, customary **10** conformist, recognized, sanctioned **11** established, traditional **12** acknowledged, conservative, conventional **13** authoritative

orthography 7 writing **8** spelling

ortolan 7 bunting

Orwell novel 10 Animal Farm **18** Nineteen Eighty-four

oryx 7 gemsbok **8** antelope

os 3 ora (plural) **4** bone, ossa (plural) **5** mouth **7** orifice

Osborne play 6 Luther **11** Entertainer (The) **15** Look Back in Anger

oscillate 3 wag **4** sway, vary **5** swing, waver **6** change, seesaw **7** vibrate **9** alternate, fluctuate

oscillation 4 sway **5** swing **9** variation, vibration **10** undulation **11** fluctuation, periodicity

osculate 3 lip **4** buss, kiss, peck **5** smack **6** smooch

osculation 4 buss, kiss, peck **6** smooch **7** liplock

osier 3 rod **6** willow **7** dogwood

Osiris *brother:* 3 Set **4** Seth ***father:* 3** Geb, Keb, Seb ***mother:* 3** Nut ***scribe:* 5** Thoth ***sister:* 4** Isis ***slayer:* 3** Set **4** Seth ***son:* 5** Horus **6** Anubis ***wife:* 4** Isis

osmium symbol 2 Os

osmosis 4 flow **8** transfer **9** diffusion **10** absorption **12** assimilation **13** incorporation

osprey 4 hawk **8** fish hawk

osseous 4 bony **8** bonelike

ossicle 4 bone **5** incus **6** stapes **7** malleus

ossify 3 set **6** harden **7** stiffen **8** solidify **9** fossilize

osso ____ 4 buco

ossuary 4 tomb **5** vault **8** boneyard, cemetery **9** sepulcher, sepulchre

ostensible 6 stated **7** alleged, seeming **8** apparent, asserted, illusive, illusory, so-called, supposed **9** pretended, professed, purported, semblable **11** superficial

ostentation 4 pomp, show **5** flash, swank **7** display **9** pomposity, showiness, vainglory **10** flashiness, pretension **11** flamboyance

ostentatious 4 loud **5** gaudy, showy, swank **6** flashy, garish, swanky **7** pompous, splashy **8** overdone, peacocky **10** flamboyant, peacockish **11** pretentious **12** vainglorious

ostiole 4 pore **7** orifice **8** aperture

ostracism 5 exile **7** removal **9** exclusion **10** banishment, relegation **11** deportation

ostracize 3 bar, cut **4** shun, snub **5** exile **6** banish, deport **7** exclude, keep out, shut out **8** throw out **9** blackball **10** expatriate **12** cold-shoulder

ostrich 4 rhea **6** ratite

Ostrogoth king 9 Theodoric

Oswego tea 7 bee balm

otalgia 7 earache

Otello composer 5 Verdi (Giuseppe) **7** Rossini (Gioacchino)

O tempora! O ____! 5 mores

Othello *ancient / ensign:* 4 Iago ***author:* 11** Shakespeare (William) ***lieutenant:* 6** Cassio ***maid:* 6** Emilia ***victim, wife:* 9** Desdemona

others 4 rest **9** remainder ***and:* 4** et al **6** et alia, et alii **7** et aliae

other than 3 but **4** save **6** except **7** besides **9** apart from, aside from, except for, excepting, excluding

otherwise 3 not **4** else **5** if not **6** or else **7** changed **9** different **11** differently **12** anything else **13** alternatively

otic 5 aural **8** auditory **9** auricular

otiose 4 idle, vain **5** empty **6** futile, hollow **7** surplus, useless **8** nugatory **9** fruitless, pointless, worthless **11** ineffective, purposeless, superfluous **12** functionless **13** supernumerary

Ottawa chief 7 Pontiac

ottoman 4 seat **5** couch **6** fabric **9** footstool

Ottoman 4 Turk **7** Turkish ***council:* 5** divan ***governor:* 3** bey ***official:* 3** aga, dey **6** vizier ***ruler:* 3** bey **5** Osman, Selim **8** Suleiman, Süleyman

Otus 5 giant ***brother:* 9** Ephialtes ***father:* 6** Aloeus **8** Poseidon ***mother:* 9** Iphimedia ***slayer:* 6** Apollo

ouch 5 bezel, jewel **6** brooch, buckle **7** setting **8** ornament **11** exclamation

ounce 3 bit, cat **4** dram **5** pinch, scrap, shred **6** amount, splash, weight **7** measure, modicum, smidgen **8** fraction, particle **11** snow leopard

our *French:* 5 notre ***Italian:* 6** nostra ***Spanish:* 7** nuestro

Our Town author 6 Wilder (Thornton)

oust 4 fire, sack **5** eject, evict, expel **6** banish, deport, remove, topple, unseat **7** boot out, cast out, deprive, dismiss, kick out **8** displace, drive out, force out, relegate, supplant, take away, throw out **10** dispossess

ouster 7 removal **8** ejection, eviction **9** discharge, dismissal, expulsion **10** banishment

out 4 away, exit **5** forth, loose **6** absent, excuse ***of control:*** **4** amok, wild **5** amuck **7** chaotic ***of gas:*** **5** tired **7** drained **9** exhausted ***of line:*** **4** awry, rude **5** askew, fresh ***of place:*** **13** inappropriate ***of sorts:*** **5** cross **7** grouchy, peevish **9** irritable ***of the ordinary:*** **3** odd **7** bizarre, strange, unusual

outage 4 loss **5** break **7** failure **8** blackout **12** interruption

out-and-out 5 gross, sheer, total, utter **7** perfect **8** absolute, complete, positive **9** downright **10** consummate **11** unmitigated, unqualified **13** thoroughgoing

outback 4 bush **6** sticks **7** boonies **9** boondocks **10** hinterland, wilderness

Outback call 5 cooee

outboard 4 boat **5** motor **6** engine

outbreak 4 rash, rise, rush **5** burst, flare, spike, surge **6** attack, blowup, plague, revolt **7** flare-up **8** epidemic, eruption, increase, uprising **9** rebellion **12** insurrection

outbuilding 4 barn, shed

outburst 3 fit **4** gush, gust **5** flare, sally, scene, spasm, storm, surge **6** frenzy, tirade **7** flare-up, tantrum, torrent **8** eruption, paroxysm, upheaval **9** explosion

outcast 4 hobo **5** exile, leper, tramp **6** pariah **7** Ishmael, vagrant **8** castaway, derelict, vagabond **9** reprobate **10** expatriate, Ishmaelite **11** offscouring, untouchable

outclass 3 top **4** best **5** excel **6** exceed **7** surpass

outcome 3 end **5** event, fruit, issue **6** effect, result, sequel, upshot **9** aftermath **10** conclusion **11** aftereffect, consequence, development

outcrop 4 rock **5** ledge **6** appear **7** project **8** protrude **10** projection, protrusion **12** protuberance

outcry 3 hue **4** yell **5** noise, shout **6** clamor, tumult, uproar **7** auction, ferment, protest **8** upheaval **9** commotion, objection **11** exclamation

outdated 3 old **5** passé **6** bygone, démodé, old hat **7** antique, archaic, vintage **10** antiquated, old-fangled **12** old-fashioned

outdistance 3 top **4** beat, best, pass **5** excel, trump **6** better, exceed **7** eclipse, surpass

outdo 3 top **4** beat, best, pass **5** excel, trump **6** better, defeat, exceed **7** eclipse, surpass, triumph **8** overcome **9** transcend

outdoor 7 open-air **8** alfresco

outer 6 remote **7** surface **8** exoteric, exterior, external **9** extrinsic **10** extraneous **11** superficial

outermost 4 last **5** final **6** far-off **7** distant, extreme **8** farthest, furthest, remotest

outfit 3 kit, rig, set **4** band, firm, gear, suit, team, togs, unit **5** corps, dress, equip, getup, group, squad, troop **6** clothe, supply, tackle, troupe **7** appoint, company, concern, costume, furnish **8** accouter, accoutre, business, clothing, ensemble, matériel, tackling **9** equipment, provision **10** enterprise **12** organization **13** accouterments, accoutrements, establishment

outflank 5 evade **6** bypass **9** get around **10** circumvent

outflow 6 efflux **8** drainage, effluent **9** effluence

out-front 4 open **5** frank **6** candid, honest **10** forthright

outgoing 4 open **7** affable **8** friendly, sociable **9** departing, expansive **10** gregarious, responsive **11** extroverted

outgrowth 6 effect, result **7** product, spin-off **8** offshoot **9** by-product, offspring **10** derivative **11** aftereffect, consequence

outhouse 5 jakes, privy **7** latrine

outing 4 spin, trip **5** drive, jaunt, sally **6** junket, picnic **9** excursion **10** appearance, disclosure

outlandish 3 odd **4** wild **5** alien, outré, ultra, weird **6** exotic **7** bizarre, curious, extreme, foreign, offbeat, strange, uncouth, unusual **8** peculiar, singular **9** eccentric, fantastic, tasteless **10** ridiculous, unorthodox **11** extravagant

outlast 6 endure **7** survive, weather **9** withstand

outlaw 3 ban, con **4** wild **5** crook **6** bandit, banned, enjoin, forbid **7** exclude, illegal **8** criminal, disallow, fugitive, prohibit, renegade, restrict **9** desperado, interdict, proscribe **10** illegalize, rebellious

outlay 3 pay, tab **4** cost, give **5** spend **6** amount, expend **7** expense, payment **8** disburse **11** expenditure **12** disbursement

outlet 4 exit, hole, mart, shop, vent **5** issue, store **6** avenue, egress, escape, market **7** channel, opening, passage, release **8** aperture **10** discounter, receptacle

outline 4 edge, form, limn, plan **5** brief, draft, shape, trace **6** bounds, border, précis, schema, sketch **7** contour, profile, summary **8** abstract, boundary, skeleton, syllabus, synopsis **9** delineate, summarize **10** figuration, silhouette **11** skeletonize

outlive 7 survive, weather

outlook 4 side, view **5** angle, scope, sight, slant, vista **6** aspect, future **7** promise **8** attitude, forecast, position, prospect **9** direction, viewpoint **10** standpoint **11** expectation, observatory, perspective, point of view

outlying 3 far **6** far-off, remote **7** distant, faraway, removed **8** far-flung
outmoded 4 dead **5** dated, passé, tired **6** old hat **7** antique, archaic **8** obsolete **9** moth-eaten, unstylish **10** oldfangled **11** obsolescent **12** old-fashioned
Out of Africa author 7 Dinesen (Isak)
out-of-date 3 old **4** past **5** passé, stale **6** démodé, old hat, square **7** antique, archaic, old-time, vintage **8** obsolete **9** unstylish **10** antiquated, oldfangled **12** old-fashioned
out of it 4 lost **5** dazed, spacy **6** addled, spacey **7** muddled **8** confused, demented **10** bewildered
out-of-the-way 4 rare **6** remote **7** distant, obscure, removed, unusual **8** secluded, uncommon
outpost 4 base **6** branch, colony **7** station **8** foothold **10** detachment, settlement
outpouring 4 flow, gush, rush **5** burst, flood, spate, spurt **6** deluge, stream **7** torrent **8** effusion
output 4 crop, gain, take **5** power, yield **6** amount, profit **7** harvest, produce, product **10** production **11** achievement, information
outrage 4 fury, rape **5** abuse, shock, wrong **6** injury, insult, offend **7** affront, incense, violate **8** aggrieve, atrocity, ill-treat, mischief, violence **9** brutality, infuriate **10** resentment, scandalize
outrageous 5 awful, gross **6** horrid, insane, odious, unholy, wicked **7** beastly, ghastly, heinous, ignoble, obscene **8** dreadful, flagrant, horrible, indecent, shocking, terrible **9** atrocious, egregious, excessive, fantastic **10** abominable, inordinate, scandalous **11** intolerable
outré 3 odd **5** ultra **6** far-out **7** bizarre, extreme, offbeat, strange **8** peculiar **9** eccentric **10** off-the-wall
outrigger 4 boat, beam, prau, proa, spar
outright 4 pure **5** total, utter, whole **6** entire **7** perfect **8** absolute, complete, entirely, positive **9** on the spot **10** completely, consummate **11** unequivocal, unmitigated, unqualified **13** thoroughgoing
outrun 3 top **4** beat, pass **6** exceed **7** surpass
outset 4 dawn **5** birth, get-go, start **7** opening **9** beginning, inception **12** commencement
outshine 3 top **4** beat, best **5** excel **6** better, exceed **7** eclipse, surpass
outside 5 alien **7** foreign, open-air **8** alfresco, exterior, external ***combining form:* 3** ect, exo **5** extra
outsider 5 alien **7** inconnu **8** newcomer, stranger **9** foreigner
outsmart see **outwit**
outspoken 4 free, open **5** blunt, frank, plain, vocal **6** candid, direct, honest **7** up front **8** explicit **10** forthright, point-blank, unreserved **11** unequivocal
outstanding 3 due **4** A-one, star **5** boffo, noted, owing, socko **6** signal, superb, tip-top, unpaid **7** capital, eminent, notable, salient, stellar **8** dominant, striking, superior, top-notch **9** arresting, excellent, first-rate, prominent, unsettled **10** noticeable, preeminent, remarkable, unresolved **11** conspicuous, distinctive, exceptional, magnificent, superlative, uncollected **13** extraordinary
outstrip 3 top **4** beat, best, pass **5** excel **6** better, exceed **7** surpass **8** distance, go beyond, overtake **9** transcend **11** leave behind
outward 5 overt **7** evident, visible **8** apparent, exterior, external **10** noticeable, ostensible **11** superficial
outweigh 6 exceed **8** overbear **10** overshadow **11** overbalance **12** preponderate
outworn see **outmoded**
ouzel 6 dipper, thrush **9** blackbird
oval 5 track **6** oblong **7** ellipse **8** elliptic **9** egg-shaped, racetrack **10** elliptical **11** ellipsoidal
ovation 5 kudos **6** homage, praise **7** acclaim, tribute **8** applause, approval, cheering, clapping, plaudits **11** acclamation
oven 4 kiln, oast **5** range, stove
over 4 anew, atop, done, past, upon **5** above, again, aloft, ended **6** across, beyond **8** done with, finished, once more ***French:* 3** sur ***German:* 4** über ***prefix:* 3** epi, sur **5** extra, hyper, super, supra ***Spanish:* 5** sobre
overabundance 4 glut **6** excess **7** surfeit, surplus **8** plethora **10** surplusage **11** superfluity
overact 3 ham, mug **4** rant **5** emote **10** exaggerate
overage 6 excess **7** surplus
overall 5 smock, total **6** global, mainly, mostly **7** chiefly, general, largely **8** as a whole, sweeping **9** generally, inclusive, in general, primarily **10** far and wide **11** principally **13** comprehensive, predominantly
overalls 5 pants **8** trousers
over and above 4 also **6** as well, beyond **7** besides **8** as well as **10** in addition
over and over 3 oft **5** often **8** ofttimes **10** frequently, oftentimes, repeatedly **11** continually, recurrently
overbearing 5 bossy **6** lordly **7** haughty, pompous **8** absolute, arrogant, despotic, dominant, imperial, insolent, scornful, superior **9** imperious, tyrannous **10** autocratic, disdainful, dominating, high-handed, oppressive, peremptory, tyrannical **11** dictato-

rial, domineering, magisterial **12** supercilious **13** high-and-mighty
overblown **6** turgid **7** flowery, hyped up, orotund, pompous **8** inflated **9** bombastic, excessive, high-flown **10** euphuistic, oratorical, rhetorical **11** declamatory, exaggerated, pretentious **12** magniloquent **13** grandiloquent
overcast **3** sew **4** dull, gray, hazy **5** cloud, cover **6** cloudy, darken, shadow **7** becloud, blanket, clouded, obscure **8** covering, lowering **9** adumbrate
overcharge **3** pad **4** bilk, clip, rook, skin, soak **5** cheat, stick **6** fleece **7** inflate
overcoat **5** paint **6** capote, raglan, ulster **7** surtout **9** balmacaan, outerwear **12** chesterfield
overcome **4** beat, best, lick **5** drown, throw **6** defeat, hurdle, master **7** conquer, prevail, triumph **8** surmount **9** prostrate
overconfident **4** rash **5** brash, cocky, pushy **8** arrogant, cocksure, reckless **9** hubristic, presuming **12** presumptuous
overdo **7** exhaust, fatigue, wear out **9** embellish **10** exaggerate
overdue **4** late **5** owing, tardy **6** behind, unpaid **7** belated, delayed, payable **8** dilatory **9** unsettled **10** behindhand, delinquent, unpunctual **11** outstanding
overemphasize **7** magnify **8** heighten **9** dramatize, embellish **10** exaggerate
overflow **4** pour **5** cover, drown, flood, slosh, spate, spill, swamp **6** deluge, engulf, excess, outlet **7** surfeit, surplus, torrent **8** flooding, inundate, spillage, submerge **10** inundation, surplusage **11** superfluity
overgrown **4** lush **5** dense, thick **6** brushy **7** hulking **8** ungainly **9** excessive, ponderous **10** junglelike
overhang **3** jut **4** loom **5** bulge **6** beetle, extend, impend **7** project **8** protrude, stick out, threaten **10** projection
overhaul **3** fix **4** mend, redo **5** patch, renew **6** doctor, remake, repair, revamp, revise **7** rebuild, restore **8** renovate **11** recondition, reconstruct
overhead **4** atop **5** above, aloft, smash **7** ceiling, expense **8** expenses
overheated **5** fiery **7** fervent **8** inflated **9** perfervid **11** impassioned
overindulgence **6** excess **7** surfeit **8** gluttony **11** dissipation **12** immoderation, intemperance
overjoyed **6** elated **7** gleeful **8** blissful, ecstatic, euphoric, exultant, jubilant, thrilled **9** rapturous **11** transported
overkill **4** glut **6** excess **7** surfeit, surplus, too much **8** plethora **10** obliterate, redundancy, surplusage **11** superfluity
overlap **7** shingle **9** imbricate
overlay **3** cap **4** coat **5** cover, glaze **6** finish, veneer **7** blanket, coating, lacquer, varnish **8** covering **11** superimpose **12** transparency
overload **4** glut **5** stuff **6** burden, excess, pile on, strain **7** surfeit
overlook **4** fail, miss, omit, skip **5** check, let go **6** excuse, forget, ignore, pass by, slight, slip up, survey, wink at **7** blink at, condone, forgive, inspect, let pass, neglect **8** discount, dominate, surmount **9** disregard, supervise **11** superintend
overlord **4** czar, tsar, tzar **5** chief, mogul, ruler **6** tycoon **7** magnate **8** suzerain **9** potentate, sovereign
overly **3** too **6** too-too, unduly **11** exceedingly, excessively **12** immoderately, inordinately
overpass **5** cross **6** bridge **8** crossing, traverse **9** traversal **11** interchange
overplay **4** hype **6** expand **7** enlarge, inflate, magnify, point up, stretch **8** maximize **9** dramatize **10** exaggerate **11** hyperbolize
overpower **4** rout **5** crush, swamp, whelm **6** defeat, master, subdue **7** conquer **8** vanquish **9** prostrate, subjugate **11** steamroller
overreach **3** con **4** beat, bilk **5** cheat, outdo **6** defeat, outfox, outwit **7** defraud **8** flimflam, outsmart **10** exaggerate **11** outmaneuver
override **4** veto **5** annul **6** cancel **7** nullify **10** counteract, neutralize
overriding **3** key **4** main **5** chief, major, prime, vital **7** central, crucial, pivotal, primary, supreme **8** cardinal, dominant, foremost **9** paramount, principal
overrule **4** undo, veto **5** upset **6** negate, revoke **7** reverse **8** set aside **11** countermand
overrun **4** beat, raid, teem, whip **5** swamp, swarm **6** defeat, excess, infest, invade, occupy, ravage, spread, thrash **7** clobber, conquer
overseas **6** abroad **11** transmarine, ultramarine **12** transoceanic, transpacific **13** transatlantic
oversee **3** run **4** boss, tend **5** watch **6** direct, manage, survey **7** command, examine, inspect **9** supervise **11** superintend
overseer **4** boss, exec, head **5** chief **7** foreman, manager **8** director **9** executive **10** supervisor **13** administrator
overshadow **4** veil **5** cloud, dwarf, shade **6** darken, exceed **7** becloud, eclipse, obscure, surpass **8** dominate, outshine, outweigh **9** adumbrate

overshoe 4 boot **6** arctic, galosh, patten, rubber
oversight 4 care, slip **5** aegis, check, error, lapse **6** charge, slip-up **7** control, failure, mistake, neglect **8** omission **10** intendance, management **11** supervision
overspread 3 cap **5** beset, cover, flood, swarm **6** infest, invade **7** blanket, obscure, pervade **8** permeate
overstate 3 pad **7** amplify, enlarge, magnify **9** embellish, embroider **10** exaggerate
overstep 6 exceed, offend **7** surpass, violate **8** infringe, trespass **10** transgress
overstock 4 glut **5** extra **6** excess **7** surplus **9** remainder **10** surplusage
overstress 7 magnify **8** maximize **10** exaggerate
overt 4 open **5** clear **6** patent **7** evident, obvious, outward, visible **8** apparent, manifest **10** observable
overtake 4 pass **5** catch **6** pass by **7** outpace, surpass **8** come upon, outstrip **11** outdistance
Over the Rainbow ***composer:*** **5** Arlen (Harold) ***lyricist:*** **7** Harburg (E. Y.) ***movie:*** **10** Wizard of Oz (The) ***singer:*** **7** Garland (Judy)
over there 3 yon **6** yonder
over-the-top 5 outré **7** extreme **8** reckless **9** egregious, excessive **10** exorbitant, flamboyant, outrageous **11** extravagant
overthrow 4 fell, oust, rout **5** evert, purge, upset **6** defeat, depose, remove, topple, unseat **7** conquer **8** dethrone, downfall **9** bring down
overtone 4 hint **5** sense **8** coloring, harmonic **9** inference **10** suggestion **11** association, connotation, implication **12** undercurrent
overture 3 bid **5** proem **7** advance, preface, prelude, present **8** approach, foreword, preamble, prologue, proposal **9** prelusion **10** initiative **11** proposition **12** introduction, presentation
overturn 3 tip **4** flip, void **5** upend, upset **6** topple, tumble **7** capsize, nullify, reverse **8** set aside **10** invalidate
overused 5 banal, musty, stale, tired, trite **7** clichéd, worn-out **9** hackneyed **10** threadbare
overview 6 aperçu, précis, survey **7** epitome, summary **10** conspectus
overweening 5 brash, pushy **6** lordly, uppish, uppity **7** forward **8** arrogant **9** conceited, presuming **10** immoderate **11** exaggerated **12** presumptuous
overweight 3 fat **5** beefy, burly, dumpy, gross, heavy, husky, obese, plump, pudgy, stout **6** chubby, chunky, flabby, fleshy, portly, rotund **7** outsize **8** heavyset, thickset **9** corpulent
overwhelm 4 beat, bury, rout, ruin, sink, whip **5** crush, drown, flood, swamp, upset, wreck **6** boggle, defeat, deluge, engulf, thrash **7** conquer, destroy, oppress, shatter, shellac, smother **8** inundate, submerge **9** devastate, prostrate **10** demoralize **11** steamroller, subordinate
overwhelmed 6 aghast **7** shocked, stunned, touched **8** defeated, helpless **10** distressed **13** thunderstruck
overwhelming 4 huge **5** great **7** extreme **8** numerous
overwrought 5 hyper, upset **7** anxious, frantic, wound up **8** agitated, frenetic, stressed, troubled **9** disturbed, emotional **10** distracted, freaked out, high-strung, hysterical **11** discomposed
Ovid work 5 Fasti **6** Amores **7** Tristia **8** Heroides **13** Metamorphoses
ovine 5 sheep **9** sheeplike
ovoid 9 egg-shaped
ovule 3 egg ***fertilized:*** **4** seed
ovum 3 egg **6** gamete **7** egg cell **11** macrogamete
owing 3 due **6** in debt, mature, unpaid **7** overdue, payable **9** unsettled **11** outstanding
owing to 4 over **7** through **9** because of **10** by reason of **11** on account of
owl ***cry:*** **4** hoot ***genus:*** **4** Bubo, Otus ***kind:*** **3** elf **4** barn, gray, lulu **5** eagle, gnome, madge, pygmy, snowy **6** barred, horned **7** saw-whet, screech **9** long-eared **10** short-eared **11** great horned
Owl and the Pussycat author 4 Lear (Edward)
own 4 avow, have, hold **5** admit, allow, enjoy, grant, let on **6** accept, fess up, retain **7** concede, confess, possess **8** disclose **9** recognize **11** acknowledge
owner 6 holder **8** landlady, landlord **9** possessor, purchaser **10** proprietor
ownership 4 hand **5** title **8** dominion, property **10** possession **11** proprietary ***perpetual:*** **8** mortmain
ox 3 yak **4** anoa, gaur, musk, zebu **5** bison, steer **6** bovine **7** banteng, buffalo ***Asian:*** **4** zebu ***attachment:*** **4** yoke ***extinct:*** **4** urus **7** aurochs ***family:*** **7** Bovidae ***relating to:*** **6** bovine ***wild:*** **4** anoa, gaur **7** banteng
oxeye 5 daisy **6** flower
oxford 4 shoe **5** cloth, sheep **6** cotton, fabric
oxide ***calcium:*** **4** lime **9** quicklime ***ferric:*** **4** rust ***sodium:*** **4** soda
oxidize 4 rust
oxygen 3 air, gas **5** ozone **7** element ***discov-***

erer: **9** Lavoisier (Antoine) ***form:*** **5** ozone ***liquid:*** **3** lox

oyster 7 bivalve, mollusc, mollusk ***bed:*** **4** park **6** claire, cultch ***eggs:*** **5** spawn ***genus:*** **6** Ostrea ***lining:*** **5** nacre ***Long Island:*** **9** bluepoint ***product:*** **5** pearl ***shell:*** **4** test **5** shuck ***young:*** **4** spat

oyster plant 7 salsify

Oz 9 Australia, Down Under ***creator:*** **4** Baum (L. Frank) ***inhabitant:*** **8** Munchkin ***princess:*** **4** Ozma

Ozark State 8 Missouri

Ozem *brother:* **5** David ***father:*** **5** Jesse **9** Jerahmeel

Ozymandias author 7 Shelley (Percy Bysshe)

P

pabulum 3 pap **4** food **7** aliment **8** nutrient **9** blandness, nutriment **10** insipidity, sustenance **11** nourishment

paca 4 cavy

pace 3 set **4** beat, clip, gait, lead, rate, step, time, walk **5** speed, tempo, tread, troop **6** motion, stride, timing **7** example, fluency, measure, precede, proceed, routine, step off **8** ambulate, antecede, movement, progress, regulate

pachyderm 8 elephant

pacific 4 calm, mild **6** gentle, irenic, placid, serene **8** dovelike, peaceful, soothing, tranquil **9** peaceable, temperate **12** conciliatory

Pacific *island:* **3** Yap **4** Wake **6** Easter, Jarvis, Saipan, Tahiti, Tarawa **7** Iwo Jima, Tokelau **8** Pitcairn, St. Helena **11** Guadalcanal ***nation:*** **4** Fiji **5** Belau, Japan, Nauru, Palau, Tonga **6** Tuvalu **7** Vanuatu **8** Kiribati

Pacificator, Great 4 Clay (Henry)

Pacific Ocean discoverer 6 Balboa (Vasco Núñez de)

pacifist 4 dove **6** irenic **8** appeaser, peaceful, peacenik **9** peaceable **10** nonviolent **11** peacemonger

pacify 4 calm, cool, ease, lull **5** allay, quell, quiet, still **6** disarm, settle, soften, soothe, subdue, temper **7** appease, assuage, mollify, placate **9** subjugate **10** conciliate, propitiate

pack 3 jam, kit, lot, lug, ram, set, wad **4** band, bear, cram, deck, fill, gang, heap, load, lump, mass, pile, stow, tamp, tote, unit **5** bunch, carry, cover, crowd, ferry, group, store, stuff, troop **6** bundle, charge, clique, convey, depart, gather **7** possess **8** assemble, compress, knapsack **9** container, equipment, influence, transport **10** collection, congregate

package 3 box **4** bale, deal, unit, wrap **5** array, combo, whole **6** bundle, parcel **7** enclose, present, wrapper **8** shipment **9** container **10** collection **11** combination

pack animal 3 ass **4** mule **5** burro, camel, horse, llama **6** donkey **7** jackass **13** beast of burden

packed 4 full **5** awash, dense, flush **6** filled, jammed **7** brimful, crowded, stuffed **8** brimming **9** chock-full **10** compressed

packet 3 wad **4** boat, mass, pile **5** group **6** bundle, parcel **7** cluster

pact 4 bond, deal **6** accord, treaty **7** bargain, concord **8** alliance, contract, covenant **9** agreement

pad 3 bed, mat, wad **4** foot, mute **5** fudge, guard, paper, stuff **6** buffer, expand, muffle, shield, tablet **7** augment, bolster, cushion, stretch **8** dressing, increase **9** embellish, embroider, overstate **10** exaggerate, overcharge

paddle 3 oar, row **4** beat, stir **5** spank **6** propel, thrash

paddock 5 field **7** pasture **9** enclosure

paddy wagon 10 Black Maria

padre 3 Fra **6** father, priest **8** chaplain, minister **9** clergyman, confessor

paean 4 hymn, song **6** anthem, eulogy, praise **7** tribute **8** accolade, encomium **9** panegyric

page 4 book, call, leaf **5** folio, sheet **6** locate, summon **7** bellhop, equerry ***left-hand:*** **5** verso ***right-hand:*** **5** recto

pageant 4 sham, show **7** charade, display, tableau **8** pretense **9** spectacle **10** exhibition

pageantry 4 pomp, show **7** display, panoply **8** flourish, splendor **9** spectacle **10** exhibition **11** flamboyance, ostentation **12** magnificence

Pagliacci, I *character:* **5** Canio, Nedda, Tonio

6 Silvio ***composer:*** 11 Leoncavallo (Ruggero)

pagoda 2 ta **6** temple

pail 3 hod **6** bucket, piggin, vessel **7** scuttle

pain 3 irk **4** ache, care, hurt, pang **5** agony, cramp, grief, throe, upset **6** grieve, harass, stitch, twinge **7** afflict, anguish, torture, travail, trouble **8** aggrieve, distress **9** suffering **10** affliction, discomfort ***back:*** **7** lumbago ***muscular:*** **7** myalgia

painful 3 raw **4** hard, sore **5** acute, sharp **6** aching, trying **7** arduous, irksome **8** annoying, piercing, stinging **9** agonizing, difficult, laborious, torturous, upsetting, vexatious **10** afflictive, tormenting

painkiller 4 drug **6** opiate **7** anodyne, codeine **8** morphine, narcotic **9** analgesic **10** anesthetic

painstaking 5 exact **7** careful, heedful **8** diligent, exacting, thorough **9** assiduous, diligence, laborious **10** meticulous, scrupulous **11** punctilious

paint 4 coat, daub, limn, swab, tint **5** adorn, brush, color, cover, horse, pinto, rouge, stain **6** depict, makeup **7** coating, pigment, portray, produce, touch up **8** cosmetic, decorate **9** delineate, represent **10** maquillage

painter 6 artist ***American:*** **4** Cole (Thomas), Haas (Richard), West (Benjamin), Wood (Grant) **5** Abbey (Edwin Austin), Davis (Stuart), Gorky (Arshile), Grosz (George), Henri (Robert), Hicks (Edward), Homer (Winslow), Johns (Jasper), Kline (Franz), Kroll (Leon), Marin (John), Marsh (Reginald), Moses (Grandma), Peale (Anna, Charles Willson, James, Raphaelle, Rembrandt, Sarah, Titian), Ryder (Albert Pinkham), Shahn (Ben), Sloan (Eric, John), Weber (Max), Wyeth (Andrew, Jamie, Newell Convers) **6** Albers (Josef), Benton (Thomas Hart), Catlin (George), Church (Frederick Edwin), Coburn (Alvin Langdon), Copley (John Singleton), Durand (Asher), Eakins (Thomas), Hassam (Childe), Hopper (Edward), Inness (George), Leutze (Emanuel), Martin (Agnes, Homer), Newman (Barnett), Rivers (Larry), Rothko (Mark), Stella (Frank), Stuart (Gilbert), Tanguy (Yves), Thorpe (Thomas), Warhol (Andy) **7** Allston (Washington), Bearden (Romare), Bellows (George), Bingham (George Caleb), Cassatt (Mary), Duchamp (Marcel), Harnett (William), Hartley (Marsden), Kinkade (Thomas), La Farge (John), O'Keeffe (Georgia), Parrish (Maxfield), Pollock (Jackson), Sargent (John Singer), Sheeler (Charles), Tiffany (Louis Comfort), Tworkov (Jack), Wiggins (Carleton) **8** Basquiat (Jean-Michel), Melchers (Gari), Rockwell (Norman), Sullivan (Patrick), Trumbull (John), Whistler (James McNeill) **9** Bierstadt (Albert), de Kooning (Willem), Feininger (Lyonel), Reinhardt (Ad), Remington (Frederic), Twachtman (John Henry), Vanderlyn (John), Walkowitz (Abraham) **10** Motherwell (Robert), Whittredge (Thomas) **12** Lichtenstein (Roy), Rauschenberg (Robert) ***Austrian:*** **5** Klimt (Gustav) **9** Kokoschka (Oskar) ***Belgian:*** **5** Ensor (James) **6** Campin (Robert) **8** Magritte (René) ***Canadian:*** **4** Kane (Paul) **6** Harris (Lawren), Watson (Homer) **7** Jackson (Alexander Young), Thomson (Tom) **9** MacDonald (James Edward Hervey) ***Chinese:*** **4** Wu Li **6** Ma Yüan **7** Wang Wei **8** Yen Li-pen ***Dutch:*** **3** Dou (Gerrit) **4** Hals (Frans), Lely (Peter), Maas (Nicolas) **5** Bosch (Hieronymus), Hooch (Pieter de), Steen (Jan) **6** Potter (Paul) **7** de Hooch (Pieter), de Witte (Emanuel), Hobbema (Meindert), van Gogh (Vincent), Vermeer (Jan) **8** Mondrian (Piet), Ruisdael (Jacob van, Salomon), Ruysdael (Salomon), Terborch (Gerard) **9** de Kooning (Willem), Rembrandt (van Rijn), Wouwerman (Philips) **11** Terbrugghen (Hendrik) ***English:*** **4** Hunt (William Holman), John (Augustus), Lear (Edward) **5** Bacon (Francis), Blake (William), Brown (Ford Madox), Lewis (Wyndham), Watts (George Frederick) **6** Fuseli (Henry), Romney (George), Stubbs (George), Turner (Joseph Mallord William), Wilson (Richard), Wright (Joseph) **7** Hockney (David), Hogarth (William), Kneller (Godfrey), Millais (John), van Dyke (Anthony) **8** Landseer (Edwin), Lawrence (Thomas), Reynolds (Joshua), Rossetti (Dante Gabriel) **9** Constable (John), Nicholson (Ben, William) **10** Alma-Tadema (Lawrence), Burne-Jones (Edward) **12** Gainsborough (Thomas) ***Finnish:*** **9** Järnefelt (Edvard) ***Flemish:*** **4** Eyck (Hubert van, Jan van), Goes (Hugo van der) **6** Rubens (Peter Paul), Weyden (Rogier van der) **7** Memling (Hams), Teniers (David), Van Dyck (Anthony), van Eyck (Hubert, Jan) **8** Breughel, Brueghel (Abraham, Ambrose, Jan, Pieter) ***French:*** **3** Arp (Hans) **4** Doré (Gustave), Dufy (Raoul), Erté, Gros (Antoine-Jean) **5** Corot (Camille), David (Jacques-Louis), Degas (Edgar), Léger (Fernand), Manet (Edouard), Monet (Claude), Redon (Odilon), Vouet (Simon) **6**

Braque (Georges), Breton (André), Claude (of Lorrain), Clouet (François, Jean), Gérôme (Jean-Léon), Greuze (Jean-Baptiste), Ingres (Jean-Auguste-Dominique), Le Brun (Charles), Le Nain (Antoine, Louis, Mathieu), Millet (Jean-François), Renoir (Pierre-Auguste), Seurat (Georges), Sisley (Alfred), Tanguy (Yves), Vernet (Carle, Horace, Joseph) **7** Balthus, Bonheur (Rosa), Bonnard (Pierre), Boucher (François), Cézanne (Paul), Chagall (Marc), Chardin (Jean-Baptiste), Courbet (Gustave), Daumier (Honoré), Duchamp (Gaston, Marcel), Gauguin (Paul), Matisse (Henri), Morisot (Berthe), Poussin (Nicolas), Rouault (Georges), Utrillo (Maurice), Watteau (Antoine) **8** Dubuffet (Jean), Magritte (René), Pissarro (Camille), Rousseau (Henri, Théodore), Vlaminck (Maurice de), Vuillard (Edouard) **9** Delacroix (Eugène), Fragonard (Jean-Honoré), Géricault (Théodore), Laurencin (Marie) **10** Bouguereau (William), Meissonier (Jean-Louis) **11** Caillebotte (Gustave) **13** Claude Lorrain ***German:*** **5** Dürer (Albrecht), Ernst (Max), Grosz (George), Nolde (Emil) **6** Albers (Josef), Müller (Friedrich "Maler") **7** Cranach (Lucas), Holbein (Hans), Lochner (Stefan), Richter (Gerhard), Schwind (Moritz von), Zoffany (Johann) **8** Kirchner (Ernst), Kollwitz (Käthe) **9** Grünewald (Matthias), Kandinsky (Wassily) **10** Schongauer (Martin), Wohlgemuth (Michael) ***Greek:*** **6** Zeuxis **7** Apelles **10** Polygnotus ***Irish:*** **5** Yeats (Jack, John Butler) ***Italian:*** **4** Reni (Guido), Rosa (Salvator), Tura (Cosme) **5** Campi (Antonio, Bernardino, Giulio, Vincenzo), Lippi (Fra Filippo, Filippino, Lorenzo), Piero (della Francesca, di Cosimo), Sarto (Andrea del) **6** Andrea (del Sarto), Cosimo (Agnolo di, Piero di), Giotto, Romano (Giulio), Sodoma (Il), Titian, Vasari (Giorgio) **7** Bellini (Gentile, Giovanni, Jacopo), Chirico (Giorgio De), Cimabue, da Vinci (Leonardo), Fiesole (Giovanni da), Martini (Simone), Orcagna, Peruzzi (Baldassare), Raphael, Tiepolo (Giovanni), Uccello (Paolo), Zuccari (Taddeo) **8** del Sarto (Andrea), Fabriano (Gentile da), Giordano (Luca), Leonardo (da Vinci), Mantegna (Andrea), Masaccio, Montagna (Bartolommeo), Perugino, Pontorno (Jacopo da), Severini (Gino), Veronese (Paolo), Vivarini (Alvise, Antonio, Bartolomeo) **9** Carpaccio (Vittore), Correggio, Francesca (Piero della) **10** Caravaggio, Modigliani (Amedeo), Signorelli (Luca), Tintoretto, Verrocchio (Andrea del), Zuccarelli (Francesco) **11** Ghirlandaio (Domenico), Ghirlandajo (Domenico) **12** Michelangelo (Buonarotti), Parmigianino ***Japanese:*** **5** Korin **6** Sesshu ***Lithuanian:*** **7** Soutine (Chaim) ***Mexican:*** **6** Orozco (José Clemente), Rivera (Diego), Tamayo (Rufino) **9** Siqueiros (David Alfaro) ***Norwegian:*** **5** Munch (Edvard) ***Russian:*** **7** Chagall (Marc), Roerich (Nikolay) **9** Kandinsky (Wassily) ***Scottish:*** **6** Ramsay (Allan) **7** Nasmyth (Alexander), Raeburn (Henry) ***Spanish:*** **4** Dalí (Salvador), Goya (Francisco), Gris (Juan), Miró (Joan), Sert (José Maria) **6** Ribera (José), Rincón (Antonio del), Tapiés (Antonio) **7** El Greco, Herrera (Francisco de), Murillo (Bartolomé Esteban), Picasso (Pablo), Zuloaga (Ignacio) **8** Zurbarán (Francisco de) **9** Velázquez (Diego) ***Swedish:*** **4** Zorn (Anders) **6** Roslin (Alexander) ***Swiss:*** **4** Klee (Paul), Witz (Konrad) **6** Fuseli (Henry)

painting **3** oil **7** acrylic, picture **10** watercolor ***circular:*** **5** tondo ***one-color:*** **8** monotint **10** monochrome ***plaster:*** **5** secco **6** fresco ***style:*** **4** Dada **5** fauve **6** cubism, cubist, Gothic, pop art, rococo **7** baroque, Bauhaus, dadaism, fauvism, fauvist, realism, realist **8** Barbizon, futurism, futurist, romantic **9** Byzantine, geometric, mannerism, mannerist **10** classicism, classicist, surrealism, surrealist **11** romanticism **13** expressionism, expressionist, impressionism, impressionist ***technique:*** **3** oil **6** fresco, pastel **7** gouache, polymer, tempera **9** encaustic **10** watercolor ***tool:*** **5** brush, easel, knife, paint **6** canvas **7** palette ***wall:*** **5** mural

pair **3** duo, two **4** dyad, item, join, mate, span, team, twin, yoke **5** brace, match, twins, unite **6** couple **7** doublet, twosome **8** geminate

Pakistan ***capital:*** **9** Islamabad ***city:*** **6** Lahore, Multan **7** Karachi **9** Hyderabad **10** Faisalabad, Rawalpindi ***language:*** **4** Urdu ***leader:*** **6** Bhutto (Benazir) **9** Musharraf (Pervez) ***monetary unit:*** **5** rupee ***mountain, range:*** **8** Himalaya **9** Himalayan, Himalayas **11** Nanga Parbat ***neighbor:*** **4** Iran **5** China, India **11** Afghanistan ***sea:*** **7** Arabian

pal **3** bud **4** chum, mate, pard **5** amigo, buddy, crony **6** comate, friend **7** comrade, partner **9** companion

palace **5** court, manor, manse **6** castle **7** alcazar, château, mansion **8** seraglio

paladin **6** leader **8** advocate, champion, defender, official

Palamedes ***brother:*** **6** Sforza **8** Achilles ***fa-***

ther: 8 Nauplius *slayer:* 7 Corinda, Ulysses 8 Odysseus

palatable 5 sapid, tasty 6 savory 8 pleasing, savorous, tasteful 9 agreeable, appealing, delicious, toothsome 10 acceptable, appetizing 12 satisfactory

palate 5 taste 6 liking 6 relish

palatial 4 rich 5 grand, large, noble, plush, regal 6 deluxe, ornate 7 opulent, stately 8 imposing, majestic, splendid 9 grandiose, luxuriant, luxurious, sumptuous 10 impressive 11 magnificent

Palau *capital:* 5 Koror *former name:* 5 Pelew *island:* 5 Koror 6 Angaur 7 Eli Malk 10 Babelthuap, Urukthapel *language:* 7 Palauan

palaver 3 gas, yak 4 blab, cant, chat, guff, talk 6 babble, cajole, hot air, jargon, parley, powwow, speech 7 chatter, prattle 8 colloquy, converse, dialogue 10 conference, discussion, rap session 12 conversation

pale 3 dim, wan 4 area, ashy, dull, fade, sick, weak 5 ashen, faded, faint, fence, field, light, livid, pasty, stake, waxen 6 anemic, blanch, chalky, doughy, feeble, pallid, picket, sallow, sickly, weaken, whiten 7 enclose, ghastly, insipid 8 blanched, district, encircle 9 bloodless, colorless, enclosure

palindrome 3 aha, bib, dad, dud, DVD, eke, ere, eve, ewe, eye, gag, gig, huh, mem, mom, mum, nun, pap, PCP, pep, pip, pop, pup, sis, SOS, tat, TNT, tot, tut, wow 4 deed, kook, ma'am, noon, peep, poop, toot 5 alula, civic, imami, kayak, Kazak, level, madam, minim, put-up, radar, refer, rotor, stats, Tebet, tenet, we few 6 pull-up, terret 7 deified, race car, reviver, top spot 9 Malayalam, never even 11 borrow or rob, drawn inward, Kinnikinnik, Madam I'm Adam

palinode 10 retraction 11 recantation

pall 4 bore, cloy, damp, jade, sate, tire 5 cloak, cloth, cloud, drape, ennui, gloom, weary 6 coffin, damper, mantle, shadow 7 dwindle, satiate, surfeit 8 covering

palladium 9 safeguard *symbol:* 2 Pd

Pallas 6 Athena *brother:* 6 Aegeus *father:* 7 Pandion *slayer:* 7 Theseus *wife:* 4 Styx (see also **Athena**)

palliate 4 ease, help 5 cover, salve 6 excuse, lessen, reduce, soften, soothe, temper 7 assuage, cover up, lighten 8 mitigate, moderate 9 alleviate, sugarcoat, whitewash 10 ameliorate

pallid 3 wan 4 ashy, dull, pale, weak 5 ashen, pasty, waxen 6 anemic, doughy, sickly 8 blanched, lifeless 9 bloodless, colorless

pallor 8 lividity, paleness 9 pastiness, whiteness 10 etiolation 12 glaucousness

pally 4 cozy 5 close, matey 6 chummy 7 devoted 8 familiar, friendly, intimate

palm 5 prize, steal, swipe 6 trophy 7 conceal, triumph, victory *beverage:* 4 nipa *fiber:* 4 bass, bast, coir 8 piassava *fruit:* 4 date 7 coconut 11 coquilla nut *kind:* 3 fan, wax 4 atap, coco, date, doom, hemp, nipa, sago 5 areca, betel, ivory, royal, sabal 6 miriti, raffia, rattan 7 cabbage, feather, palmyra 8 carnauba, palmetto, piassava 12 Washingtonia *leaf:* 4 olla 5 frond *lily:* 2 ti *starch:* 4 sago *vine:* 6 rattan

palmer 7 pilgrim

Palmetto State 13 South Carolina

palmistry 6 augury 8 prophecy 10 divination 11 soothsaying

palm off 5 foist 7 deceive, pretend 8 disguise

palmy 6 golden 7 booming, halcyon, opulent 8 affluent, thriving 10 prospering, prosperous 11 flourishing

Palmyra's queen 7 Zenobia

palooka 3 oaf 4 boob, dolt, goon, lout, lump 5 boxer, klutz 6 baboon, galoot, lummox 7 bruiser

palpable 4 real, sure 5 clear, plain 6 patent 7 certain, evident, obvious, tactile 8 apparent, concrete, definite, distinct, manifest, material, positive, tangible 10 noticeable 11 discernible, perceptible, unequivocal

palpate 4 feel 5 touch 6 finger 7 examine

palpitate 4 beat 5 pulse, throb 6 quiver 7 flutter, pulsate 12 pitter-patter

palsy-walsy 4 cozy 5 close, thick, tight 6 chummy 8 intimate 10 buddy-buddy

palter 3 fib, lie 5 evade 6 dicker, haggle 7 bargain, chaffer, deceive, falsify, wrangle 10 equivocate 11 prevaricate 12 misrepresent

paltry 3 low 4 base, mean, poor, puny, vile 5 cheap, petty, tatty 6 meager, measly, narrow, shabby, shoddy, sleazy, trashy 7 lowdown, pitiful, trivial 8 beggarly, inferior, picayune, piddling, rubbishy, trifling 9 worthless 10 despicable, picayunish 11 unimportant 12 contemptible 13 insignificant

paludal place 3 fen 5 marsh

Pamela author 10 Richardson (Samuel)

pampa 5 plain 7 prairie 9 grassland

pamper 3 pet 4 baby 5 humor, spoil 6 caress, cocker, coddle, cosset, cuddle, dandle, fondle 7 cater to, cherish, gratify, indulge 9 spoon-feed 11 mollycoddle

pamphlet 5 flier, flyer, tract 6 folder 7 leaflet 8 brochure, circular 9 throwaway 10 broadsheet

pan 3 pot, rap 4 slam, wash 5 basin, knock, roast, trash 6 attack, vessel 7 censure, con-

demn, skillet **8** denounce, ridicule **9** betel leaf, container, criticism, criticize **10** receptacle
Pan 5 Inuus **6** Faunus ***father:* 6** Hermes ***invention:* 6** syrinx ***lower part:* 4** goat ***mother:* 8** Penelope ***pipe:* 6** syrinx ***seat of worship:* 7** Arcadia ***son:* 7** Silenus
panacea 4 cure **6** elixir, remedy **7** cure-all, nostrum **10** catholicon
Panacea's father 9 Asclepius **11** Aesculapius
panache 4 brio, dash, élan, tuft, zest **5** ardor, crest, flair, style, verve, vigor **6** esprit, polish, spirit **8** aigrette, flourish, vivacity **11** flamboyance
panama 3 hat
Panama *discoverer:* 6 Balboa (Vasco Núñez de) **8** Columbus (Christopher) ***gulf:* 7** San Blas **8** Mosquito ***language:* 7** Spanish ***leader:* 7** Noriega (Manuel) ***monetary unit:* 6** balboa ***neighbor:* 8** Colombia **9** Costa Rica ***peninsula:* 6** Azuero ***sea:* 9** Caribbean ***volcano:* 8** Chiriquí
pancake 8 flapjack, slapjack ***chain:* 4** IHOP ***French:* 5** crepe ***Jewish:* 5** latke **6** blintz **7** blintze ***Russian:* 4** blin **5** blini
Pandarus 6 archer **8** procuror ***father:* 6** Lycaon ***slayer:* 8** Diomedes
pandect 4 code, laws **8** treatise **10** compendium **11** compilation
pandemic 4 rife **7** general, rampant **9** contagion, extensive, prevalent **10** contagious, widespread **11** wide-ranging
pandemonium 3 din **5** babel, chaos, furor **6** bedlam, clamor, hubbub, tumult, uproar **7** anarchy, discord, inferno, misrule, turmoil **8** disorder **9** confusion **10** hullabaloo
pander 4 pimp **5** cater **9** exploiter, go-between
Pandion *daughter:* 6 Procne **9** Philomela ***son:* 6** Pallas
Pandora *creator:* 10 Hephaestus ***husband:* 10** Epimetheus
pane 4 side **5** sheet **7** section
panegyric 6 eulogy, praise **7** tribute **8** citation, encomium **9** laudation **10** compliment **12** commendation
panegyrical 8 praising **9** laudative, laudatory **10** eulogistic **11** encomiastic **12** commendatory **13** complimentary
panel 4 jury **5** board, frame **6** hurdle **7** console, section **9** dashboard
panfry 5 sauté
pang 4 ache, pain, stab **5** agony, prick, spasm, throe **6** stitch, twinge **7** anguish, torment **8** distress
Pangloss's pupil 7 Candide
panhandle 3 beg, bum, tap **5** cadge, hit up, touch **6** hustle **7** solicit
panhandler 6 beggar
panic 4 fear, riot, rush **5** alarm, scare **6** dismay, frenzy, fright, horror, terror **7** anxiety, terrify **8** frighten, hysteria, stampede
pannier 4 hoop, pack **6** basket, hamper **9** overskirt
panoply 4 pomp, show **5** armor, array **6** attire **7** display, fanfare **9** trappings
panorama 4 view **5** range, reach, scene, scope, sweep, vista **7** display, expanse, picture, purview **12** presentation
panoramic 8 sweeping, synoptic **12** all-inclusive, unobstructed **13** comprehensive
pan out 4 work **5** click, prove, score **7** come off, succeed
pant 4 blow, gasp, gulp, huff, puff **5** chuff, heave **6** wheeze
Pantagruel 5 giant ***companion:* 7** Panurge ***father:* 9** Gargantua ***mother:* 7** Badebec
pantaloon 7 buffoon, trouser
Pantaloon's daughter 9 Columbine
pantheon 4 gods **5** Aesir **6** temple **9** hierarchy **10** hall of fame
panther 4 pard, puma **6** cougar, jaguar **7** leopard **12** mountain lion
pantomime 5 drama, mimic **6** act out, ballet, dancer **7** charade **12** harlequinade ***clown:* 7** Pierrot
pantry 6 closet, larder **7** buttery **9** storeroom
pants 5 jeans **6** slacks **7** drawers, garment **8** breeches, britches, knickers, trousers
Panurge's companion 10 Pantagruel
Paolo's lover 9 Francesca
pap 4 food, mash, mush **7** aliment, pabulum **8** soft food **9** blandness, nutriment **10** sustenance **11** nourishment
papal 8 pontific **9** apostolic **10** pontifical ***court:* 5** Curia ***decree:* 8** decretal ***envoy:* 6** nuncio ***letter:* 4** bull **10** encyclical
paper 5 essay, sheet, theme **6** letter, report **7** article **8** document **9** monograph, newsprint **10** memorandum **11** composition, publication **12** dissertation ***measure:* 4** ream **5** quire ***roll:* 6** scroll ***scrap:* 4** chad ***size:* 3** cap **5** atlas, crown, folio, legal, royal, sexto, sixmo **6** octavo, quarto **7** emperor **8** elephant, foolscap, imperial ***stiff:* 7** bristol **9** cardboard **12** bristol board ***strong:* 5** kraft **6** manila ***thin:* 6** tissue **9** onionskin ***transparent:* 8** glassine ***writing:* 3** rag **6** vellum **9** parchment
paper folding 7 origami
paperwork 7 red tape
papillon 7 spaniel **9** butterfly
Papua New Guinea *archipelago:* 8 Bismarck

capital: **11** Port Moresby ***city:*** **3** Lae ***island:*** **12** Bougainville ***language:*** **4** Motu **8** Tok Pisin ***monetary unit:*** **4** kina ***neighbor:*** **9** Indonesia, Irian Jaya

par 4 mean, norm **5** equal, score, usual **6** median, normal **7** average, typical **8** equality, standard

parable 4 myth, tale **5** fable, moral, story **7** example **8** allegory

parachute 7 bailout, skydive ***part:*** **5** riser **6** canopy **7** harness, ripcord

Paraclete 9 Holy Ghost **10** Holy Spirit

parade 4 brag, pomp **5** array, boast, flash, march, shine, strut **6** expose, flaunt, review **7** display, exhibit, fanfare, marshal, panoply, show off **8** brandish, ceremony, proclaim **9** advertise, cavalcade, pageantry, promenade **10** masquerade, procession

paradigm 5 ideal, model **6** mirror **7** example, pattern **8** exemplar, standard **9** archetype, beau ideal, framework, prototype

paradise 4 Eden, Zion **5** bliss **6** heaven, utopia **7** arcadia, elysium, nirvana **8** empyrean **9** Shangri-la **10** wonderland **12** New Jerusalem, promised land

Paradise Lost author 6 Milton (John)

paragon 3 gem **4** tops **5** champ, cream, ideal, jewel, match, model, peach, saint **6** beauty **7** compare, epitome **8** champion, exemplar, last word, nonesuch, parallel, ultimate **9** archetype, beau ideal, nonpareil **10** apotheosis

Paraguay *capital:* **8** Asunción ***lake:*** **4** Ypoá ***language:*** **7** Guarani, Spanish ***monetary unit:*** **7** guarani ***neighbor:*** **6** Brazil **7** Bolivia **9** Argentina ***river:*** **9** Pilcomayo

parallel 4 akin, copy, even, like **5** agree, align, alike, along, equal, liken, match **6** double, equate, line up **7** aligned, compare, similar **8** analogue **9** alongside, analogous, companion, consonant, corollary, correlate, duplicate **10** comparable, comparison, correspond, equivalent, similarity **11** coextensive, counterpart, duplication, resemblance **13** correspondent, corresponding

parallelogram 5 rhomb **6** oblong, square **7** rhombus **8** rhomboid **9** rectangle **13** quadrilateral

paralysis 5 palsy **7** inertia **9** impotence

paralyze 3 awe **4** daze, numb, stun **6** benumb, deaden, dismay **7** cripple, disable, nonplus, petrify, stupefy **8** shut down **10** immobilize **12** incapacitate

paramount 5 chief, ruler **6** master **7** capital, leading, primary, regnant, supreme **8** cardinal, crowning, dominant, foremost, headmost, superior **9** principal, sovereign, uppermost **10** commanding, preeminent **11** predominant

paramour 5 lover, Romeo **7** Don Juan, gallant **8** Casanova, lothario, mistress **9** courtesan, inamorata, inamorato

parapet 4 wall **7** bastion, bulwark, rampart **10** battlement, breastwork ***part:*** **6** merlon **12** crenellation

paraphernalia 4 gear **5** items **6** outfit, tackle **7** effects **8** property **9** equipment, trappings **10** belongings **11** accessories, furnishings **13** accouterments, accoutrements, appurtenances

paraphrase 6 reword **7** restate, version **9** interpret, rendering, translate **11** restatement, translation

parasite 5 leech, toady **6** sponge, sucker **7** sponger **8** barnacle, deadbeat, hanger-on **9** dependent, exploiter, sycophant **10** freeloader, self-seeker **11** bloodsucker

parasitic 8 sponging, toadying **9** leechlike **11** freeloading, sycophantic **12** bloodsucking ***flatworm:*** **5** fluke **9** trematode

parasol 8 umbrella

____ paratus 6 semper

Parcae 5 Fates, Norns **6** Moirai ***name:*** **4** Nona **5** Morta **6** Decuma

parcel 3 box, cut, lot **4** deal, dole, land, mete, pack, part, plot, wrap **5** allot, array, batch, bunch, group, share, tract **6** assign, bundle, divide, packet, ration **7** package, partial, portion, prorate, section, segment **8** allocate, disburse, disperse, division **9** apportion, partition **10** distribute

parch 3 dry **4** burn, sear **5** dry up, roast, toast **6** dry out, scorch **7** shrivel **9** dehydrate, desiccate

parched 3 dry **4** arid, sere **5** dusty **7** bone-dry, thirsty **8** scorched, withered **9** shriveled, waterless **10** dehydrated

parchment 4 skin **5** paper **6** vellum **7** diploma **8** document

pardon 4 free **5** remit, spare **6** excuse, let off **7** absolve, amnesty, condone, forgive, release **8** liberate, reprieve, tolerate **9** acquittal, exculpate, indemnity, remission **10** absolution, indulgence **11** exculpation, exoneration, forgiveness

pardonable 6 venial **9** allowable, excusable **11** permissible

pare 3 cut **4** clip, crop, peel, trim **5** lower, prune, shave **6** reduce, remove **7** curtail, cut back, cut down, trim off, whittle **8** diminish

parent 4 make, rear **5** beget, cause, hatch, raise, spawn **6** author, create, father, mother, origin **7** bring up, care for, produce

8 begetter, generate **9** originate, procreate **10** progenitor

parenthetically 7 by the by **8** by the bye, by the way **9** in passing **12** incidentally

parentless 6 orphan **8** orphaned

par excellence 3 top **5** prime **6** superb **7** premier, supreme **8** foremost, peerless, superior **9** matchless, number one, unmatched **10** first-class, preeminent **11** outstanding

pariah 5 leper **7** Ishmael, outcast **8** castaway **10** Ishmaelite **11** offscouring, untouchable ***Japanese:*** **3** eta

Paris ***airport:*** **4** Orly ***ancient name:*** **7** Lutetia ***avenue:*** **13** Champs-Elysées ***basilica:*** **10** Sacré Coeur ***cathedral:*** **9** Notre Dame ***city hall:*** **12** Hôtel de Ville ***college:*** **8** Sorbonne ***garden:*** **9** Tuileries **10** Luxembourg ***island:*** **11** Île de la Cité ***museum:*** **5** Cluny **6** Louvre ***palace:*** **6** Louvre **7** Bourbon ***patron saint:*** **9** Geneviève ***racecourse:*** **7** Auteuil ***river:*** **5** Seine ***section:*** **8** Left Bank **9** Right Bank **10** Montmartre, Rive Gauche **12** Latin Quarter ***stock exchange:*** **6** Bourse ***subway:*** **5** Métro ***tower:*** **6** Eiffel

Paris ***beloved:*** **5** Helen ***betrothed:*** **6** Juliet ***father:*** **5** Priam ***mother:*** **6** Hecuba ***slayer:*** **11** Philoctetes ***wife:*** **6** Oenone

parish 6 county **8** district **9** community **12** congregation, neighborhood

Parisina ***author:*** **5** Byron (Lord) ***husband:*** **3** Azo ***lover:*** **4** Hugo ***slayer:*** **3** Azo

parity 8 equality, sameness, symmetry **10** similarity, similitude **11** equivalence, equivalency, parallelism

park 4 stop **5** green, plaza **7** deposit, funfair, reserve **8** carnival, preserve **9** esplanade **11** reservation

parka 6 anorak, jacket **7** garment **8** pullover **9** outerwear

park designer 4 Vaux (Calvert) **6** Paxton (Joseph) **7** Alphand (Jean), Le Nôtre (André), Olmsted (Frederick Law)

parlance 4 cant, talk **5** argot, idiom, lingo, style, usage **6** jargon, patois, phrase, speech **7** wording **8** language, locution, phrasing **9** verbalism **11** phraseology

parlay 3 bet **4** risk **5** bid up, boost, stake, wager **6** expand, extend, hazard **7** build up, enhance, enlarge, exploit, venture **8** increase, leverage **9** transform

parley 4 talk **5** speak **6** confab, confer, huddle, powwow **7** discuss, meeting **8** colloquy, converse, dialogue **9** discourse, negotiate **10** conference, discussion **11** confabulate **12** conversation **13** confabulation

parliament see **legislature**

parlor 4 room **5** salon **11** drawing room **13** reception room

parlous 5 dicey, hairy, risky **6** chancy, touchy, tricky, unsafe **8** critical, ticklish **9** dangerous, hazardous **10** precarious

Parnassian 4 poet **6** poetic

parochial 5 local **6** narrow **7** insular, limited **9** sectarian, small-town **10** provincial, restricted

parody 3 rib **4** mock **5** mimic, spoof **6** satire **7** imitate, lampoon, mockery, takeoff **8** ridicule, travesty **9** burlesque, imitation **10** caricature

parole 4 free, word **6** let out, pledge **7** promise, release **9** discharge, probation, watchword **11** performance

paronomasia 3 pun **11** play on words

paroxysm 3 fit **4** bout **5** spasm, throe **6** attack, frenzy **7** flare-up, seizure **8** eruption, outbreak, outburst **9** explosion **10** conniption, convulsion

parrot 3 ape **4** aper, copy, echo **5** mimic **6** repeat **7** chatter, copycat, imitate ***kind:*** **3** ara, kea **4** jako, kaka, lory **5** macaw **6** Amazon, budgie, kakapo **8** cockatoo, lorikeet, lovebird, parakeet **9** cockatiel **10** budgerigar **11** African gray

parrot fever 11 psittacosis

parry 4 duck, fend **5** avert, avoid, block, dodge, elude, evade **7** counter, deflect, evasion, fend off, prevent, respond, ward off **8** sidestep, stave off **9** turn aside **10** circumvent

parse 4 scan **7** analyze, dissect, examine, resolve **8** construe **9** anatomize, explicate, interpret

Parsi 11 Zoroastrian

Parsifal ***composer:*** **6** Wagner (Richard) ***magician:*** **8** Klingsor ***quest:*** **5** Grail ***son:*** **9** Lohengrin ***temptress:*** **6** Kundry

parsimonious 4 mean **5** cheap, close, tight **6** frugal, stingy **7** chintzy, miserly, sparing, thrifty **9** penurious **10** restrained **11** closefisted, tightfisted **12** cheese-paring **13** penny-pinching

parsley 4 herb **7** garnish ***family:*** **6** carrot ***piece:*** **5** sprig

parson 6 cleric, pastor, rector **8** clerical, minister, preacher, reverend **9** clergyman **12** ecclesiastic

parsonage 5 manse **7** rectory

part 3 bit, cut **4** chip, role, unit **5** chunk, piece, quota, scrap, sever, share, slice **6** detail, divide, member, moiety, ration, sector **7** element, measure, portion, quantum, quarter, section, segment **8** division, fraction, fragment, function, separate **9** component

partake of 3 eat **5** savor, share **6** accept, sample **7** acquire, consume, receive **9** enter into **11** participate

Parthenon *sculptor:* 7 Phidias **8** Pheidias ***sculpture:* 6** frieze ***site:* 9** Acropolis

partial 6 biased, unfair, warped **7** colored, half-way **8** inclined, one-sided **9** jaundiced **10** fractional, incomplete, prejudiced **11** fragmentary, predisposed

partiality 4 bent, bias **5** favor, taste **6** liking **7** leaning **8** affinity, fondness, tendency **10** favoritism, preference **11** inclination **12** one-sidedness, predilection

participant 5 party **6** fellow, member, player, sharer **7** partner, sharing **11** contributor, shareholder

participate 4 join, play **5** share **6** engage, join in **7** partake **8** take part

particle 3 ace, bit, dab, dot, jot, ort, tad **4** atom, doit, dram, drop, hint, hoot, iota, mite, mote, spot, whit **5** atomy, crumb, fleck, grain, minim, ounce, scrap, shred, speck **6** morsel, tittle **7** granule, modicum, smidgen, smidgin, soupçon **8** fragment, smidgeon **9** scintilla ***atomic:* 3** ion **5** anion **6** baryon, cation ***elementary:* 3** psi, tau **4** kaon, muon, pion **5** boson, meson **6** baryon, hadron, lambda, lepton, photon, proton **7** fermion, hyperon, neutron, nucleon, upsilon **8** electron, mesotron, neutrino, positron ***hypothetical:* 5** gluon, quark **6** parton **8** graviton ***virus:* 6** virion ***with negative charge:* 8** electron ***with positive charge:* 6** proton **8** positron

particular 4 fact, full, item **5** exact, fussy, picky, point **6** detail, minute, single, unique **7** careful, correct, element, feature, finicky, precise, special, unusual **8** accurate, detailed, distinct, especial, exacting, itemized, separate, solitary, specific **10** fastidious, individual, meticulous, pernickety, scrupulous **11** distinctive, exceptional, persnickety, punctilious **12** circumstance

particularize 4 list **6** detail **7** catalog, itemize, specify **8** spell out **9** enumerate, inventory **13** individualize

parting 4 last **5** adieu, break, congé, final **6** good-by **7** good-bye **8** division, farewell **10** divergence, separation **11** leave-taking, valedictory

partisan 6 backer, biased, warped **7** devotee, die-hard, fanatic, patriot, sectary **8** adherent, advocate, disciple, follower, guerilla, one-sided, stalwart, upholder **9** factional, guerrilla, irregular, satellite, sectarian, supporter

partition 4 wall **6** divide, screen **7** divider, section, wall off **8** disunion, division, fence off, separate **10** separation

partner 4 ally, chum, mate **5** buddy, crony **6** cohort, fellow **7** comrade **8** confrere, sidekick **9** assistant, associate, colleague, companion **10** accomplice **11** confederate

partnership 4 axis, firm **5** union **7** cahoots, company, sharing **8** alliance, business, marriage, relation **11** affiliation, association, combination **12** consociation, togetherness **13** participation

parturient 6 gravid, parous **8** enceinte, pregnant **9** expecting

parturition 5 birth **8** delivery **10** childbirth **12** childbearing

party 4 ball, band, bash, bevy, bloc, crew, fete, gala, luau, orgy, rave, side **5** actor, corps, covey, feast, group, revel, troop **6** fiesta, frolic, kegger, mortal, person, social, soiree, troupe **7** blowout, carouse, faction, roister, shindig **8** carousal, litigant, wingding **9** bacchanal, gathering, make merry, raise hell **10** detachment, individual, saturnalia **11** bacchanalia, celebration, participant

parvenu 7 upstart **9** arriviste **12** nouveau riche

Pascal essay 6 Pensée

pasha 3 dey

Pasiphaë *daughter:* 7 Ariadne, Phaedra ***husband:* 5** Minos ***son:* 8** Minotaur

pass 3 bye, die, end **4** fare, hand **5** cease, enact, get by, lapse, occur, relay, spend, while **6** crisis, depart, elapse, exceed, expire, hand on, happen, permit, push on, slight, slip by, strait **7** come off, develop, journey, proceed, succumb **8** bequeath, fork over, hand down, juncture, outshine, outstrip, transmit **9** while away ***Afghanistan:* 5** Murgh ***Afghanistan-Pakistan:* 6** Khyber ***Alaska:* 5** White ***Alps:* 5** Cenis, Loibl **7** Brenner, Ljubelj, Simplon **9** St. Bernard ***California:* 5** Cajon ***China-India:* 9** Karakoram ***Colorado:* 3** Ute ***mountain:* 3** col, gap **4** ghat **5** notch ***Pakistan:* 5** Kilik ***Russian:* 12** Caspian Gates ***Tennessee:* 10** Cumberland ***Turkey:* 13** Cilician Gates

passable 4 okay, open, so-so **6** decent **8** adequate, all right **9** tolerable, unblocked **10** accessible, good enough **12** satisfactory

passably 6 enough **8** all right, somewhat **10** moderately

passage 3 way **4** exit, fare, hall, iter, path, text **5** route, shift **6** access, arcade, avenue, course, egress, strait, travel, tunnel, voyage **7** channel, excerpt, hallway, journey, transit **8** corridor, transfer, traverse **9** enactment, quotation **10** transition **11** transmittal **12** transference, transmission ***air:*** **7** windway ***arched:*** **6** arcade ***Atlantic-Pacific:*** **9** Northwest ***narrow:*** **3** gut ***roofed:*** **6** arcade **9** breezeway

Passage to India author 7 Forster (E. M.)

pass away 3 die, end **6** demise, depart, elapse, expire, perish **7** decease, succumb **9** disappear

pass by 4 miss, omit **6** forget, ignore **7** neglect **8** overlook **9** disregard

passé 4 dead **5** dated, stale **6** démodé, old hat **7** demoded, disused, extinct, outworn **8** obsolete, outdated, outmoded **9** out-of-date **10** antiquated, oldfangled, superseded **12** old-fashioned

passel 3 lot **4** heap, pack **5** bunch **6** bundle **9** multitude

passenger 4 fare

passing 5 brief, death, quick **6** demise, highly **7** cursory, decease **8** fleeting **9** ephemeral, fugacious, extremely, momentary, transient **10** evanescent, short-lived, transitory **11** exceedingly, superficial

passion 4 fire, heat, itch, love, lust, zeal **5** agony, amour, ardor, craze, crush, drive **6** desire, fervor, hunger **7** avidity, craving, ecstasy, emotion, rapture **8** appetite, devotion, yearning **9** eagerness, suffering, transport **10** enthusiasm, excitement **11** amorousness, infatuation

passionate 3 hot **5** angry, fiery **6** ardent, fervid, heated **7** amorous, aroused, blazing, burning, excited, fervent, furious, intense **8** incensed, vehement **9** impetuous, steamed up **10** hot-blooded, stimulated **11** hot-tempered **12** enthusiastic **13** quick-tempered

passive 4 idle **5** inert **6** docile, latent **8** enduring, immobile, inactive, listless, resigned, yielding **9** apathetic, compliant, lethargic, quiescent **10** motionless, nonviolent, phlegmatic, submissive **11** acquiescent, complaisant, indifferent, unresistant

pass out 3 die **5** faint, swoon **7** divvy up **8** disburse, keel over **10** distribute

pass over 4 miss, omit, skip **6** forget, ignore **7** dismiss, neglect **8** discount, leave out **9** disregard

Passover 5 Pasch **6** Pesach ***bread:*** **5** matzo **6** matzoh ***meal:*** **5** seder

pass up 5 forgo **6** refuse, reject **7** decline

past 3 ago, old **4** gone, late, once, yore **5** above, after, prior **6** beyond, bygone, former, whilom **7** onetime, quondam **8** anterior, foretime, lang syne, previous, sometime **9** antiquity, erstwhile, foregoing, precedent, preceding, yesterday **10** antecedent, yesteryear

pasta 5 dough ***kind:*** **4** orzo, ziti **5** penne, ruote **6** rotini **7** fusilli, gemelli, gnocchi, lasagna, lasagne, mafalda, noodles, ravioli **8** farfalle, linguine, linguini, macaroni, rigatoni **9** canneloni, capellini, cavatappi, fettucine, fettucini, manicotti, radiatore, spaghetti, tubettini **10** cannelloni, conchiglie, fettuccine, fettuccini, tortellini, vermicelli **11** cappelletti, orecchiette, pappardelle

paste 3 fix, hit **4** beat, clay, drub, food, glue, sock **5** affix, dough, pound, stick, stuff **6** adhere, attach, cement, defeat, fasten, thrash, wallop **7** trounce **8** adhesive, material

Pasternak character 4 Lara **7** Zhivago (Dr.)

pastiche 4 olio **6** jumble, medley **7** farrago, mélange, mixture **8** mishmash **9** potpourri **10** assortment, hodgepodge, hotchpotch, miscellany, salmagundi **11** gallimaufry

pastime 4 game **5** hobby, sport **9** amusement, diversion **10** recreation **13** entertainment

past master 3 ace, pro, wiz **4** whiz **5** adept, maven **6** expert, wizard **8** virtuoso **9** authority

pastor 5 padre **6** cleric, parson **8** minister, preacher, reverend, sky pilot **9** clergyman

pastoral 4 idyl **5** idyll, rural **6** rustic **7** bucolic, country, crosier, idyllic **8** agrarian, clerical, innocent, peaceful **10** campestral

pastor's assistant 6 curate

pastry 3 bun, pie **4** baba, cake, flan, tart **5** torte **6** cornet, Danish, éclair, gâteau **7** baklava, beignet, bouchée, dariole, gâteaux (plural), palmier, savarin, strudel, tartlet **8** napoleon, papillon, piroshki, pirozhki, turnover **9** barquette, cream puff, madeleine, petit four, vol-au-vent **10** cheesecake **11** profiterole **12** millefeuille ***kind:*** **4** filo, puff **5** flaky **6** phyllo ***shell:*** **7** timbale **8** meringue

pasture 3 lea, ley **4** feed, land **5** field, grass, graze **6** browse, meadow **9** grassland

pasty 3 wan **4** pale **6** doughy, pallid, sickly **7** meat pie **8** turnover **9** unhealthy

pat 3 apt, dab, set **4** firm **5** fixed, slice, stiff, trite **6** dead-on **7** apropos, fitting **8** apposite, standard, suitable **9** contrived, pertinent, rehearsed

patch 3 bit, fix **4** area, fill, mend, plot **5** cover, piece, scrap, spell **6** doctor, emblem, fill up, repair, shield **7** connect, plaster **8** material **10** connection

patchwork 4 olio **5** quilt **6** jumble **7** mixture **8**

covering, mishmash, mixed bag **10** assortment, hodgepodge, hotchpotch, miscellany, salmagundi

patchy 6 fitful, random, spotty, uneven **7** erratic **8** sporadic **9** haphazard, hit-or-miss, irregular **12** intermittent

pate 4 bean, dome, head, poll **5** brain, crown **6** noddle, noggin, noodle

patella 7 kneecap, kneepan

patent 4 open **5** clear, plain, right **6** secure **7** evident, license, obvious, visible **8** apparent, distinct, manifest **9** exclusive, privilege, prominent, protected **11** proprietary

paternal 8 fatherly ***relative:* 6** agnate

paternity 7 lineage **8** ancestry **10** fatherhood, provenance **11** progenitors

Pater Noster 9 Our Father **11** Lord's Prayer

path 3 way **4** lane, line, road, tack, walk **5** byway, orbit, route, track, trail **6** avenue, bridle, course **7** passage, walkway **9** direction **10** trajectory

pathetic 3 sad **4** poor **5** sorry **6** absurd, moving, paltry **7** piteous, pitiful, risible, useless **8** inferior, pitiable, poignant, touching **9** affecting, laughable, miserable **10** lamentable, ridiculous

Pathfinder, The *author:* 6 Cooper (James Fenimore) ***hero:* 6** Bumppo (Natty)

pathogen 4 germ **5** E. coli, virus **9** bacterium

pathological 7 deviant **8** aberrant, abnormal, diseased, maniacal, schizoid **9** psychotic

pathos 4 pity **7** emotion **8** sympathy **9** poignance, poignancy

pathway 4 line, walk **5** route, track, trail **6** course **7** channel, conduit, network, passage

patience 4 cool **8** calmness, stoicism **9** composure, endurance **10** equanimity, sufferance **11** forbearance, resignation, self-control

Patience *composer:* 8 Sullivan (Arthur) ***librettist:* 7** Gilbert (W. S.)

patient 4 case, meek **8** enduring **9** easygoing **10** persistent **11** susceptible **13** long-suffering ***man:* 3** Job

patina 4 aura, coat, film **6** finish, polish **7** coating **8** covering **10** appearance, coloration

patio 5 atria (plural), court **6** atrium **7** terrace **9** courtyard

patois 4 cant **5** argot, lingo, slang **6** jargon **7** dialect **10** colloquial, vernacular

patriarch 4 sire **6** father, nestor **7** creator, founder **9** architect, graybeard ***biblical:* 5** David, Isaac, Jacob **7** Abraham

patrician 5 noble **6** aristo **9** blue blood, gentleman **10** aristocrat, upper-class

patriciate 5 elite **6** gentry **9** blue blood, gentility **10** upper crust **11** aristocracy

patrimony 6 estate, legacy **8** heritage **9** endowment **10** birthright **11** inheritance

patriot 5 jingo **8** jingoist, loyalist **9** flag-waver **10** chauvinist **11** nationalist

patriotism 8 jingoism **10** chauvinism **11** nationalism

Patroclus *friend:* 8 Achilles ***slayer:* 6** Hector

patrol 5 guard, round, scout, troop, watch **7** protect **8** sentinel **9** keep watch

patrolman 3 cop **5** guard **6** police **7** officer

patrol wagon see **paddy wagon**

patron 5 angel **6** backer, client **7** sponsor **8** customer, guardian **9** protector, supporter **10** benefactor

patronage 4 help **5** aegis, trade **6** custom **7** backing, subsidy, support, traffic **8** activity, advocacy, auspices, business, cronyism **9** clientage, clientele, influence **10** pork barrel, protection **11** benefaction, sponsorship **12** guardianship

patronize 3 aid, use **4** back **5** deign, favor **6** assist, shop at **7** protect, support **8** frequent **10** condescend

patron saint *of beggars, cripples:* 5 Giles ***of children:* 8** Nicholas ***of England:* 6** George ***of fishermen:* 5** Peter ***of France:* 5** Denis ***of Ireland:* 7** Patrick ***of lawyers:* 4** Ives ***of musicians:* 7** Cecilia ***of Norway:* 4** Olaf ***of physicians:* 4** Luke ***of sailors:* 4** Elmo **8** Nicholas ***of Scotland:* 6** Andrew ***of shoemakers:* 7** Crispin ***of Spain:* 5** James **8** Santiago ***of travelers:* 11** Christopher ***of Wales:* 5** David ***of winegrowers:* 7** Vincent ***of workers:* 6** Joseph

patsy 3 sap **4** dupe, fool, mark **5** chump **6** pigeon, sucker, victim **8** easy mark, pushover

patter 4 cant **5** argot, lingo, slang, spiel **6** babble, jargon, patois **7** chatter, prattle

pattern 4 copy, form, plan **5** guide, ideal, model, motif, order, plaid, shape **6** argyle, design, figure, floral, follow, method, mirror, system **7** diagram, emulate, example, imitate, paisley **8** exemplar, grouping, paradigm, standard, template **9** archetype, incidence, prototype **10** flight path, stereotype **11** arrangement, orderliness **12** distribution **13** configuration

paucity 4 lack, want **6** dearth **7** poverty **8** scarcity, shortage **9** scantness, smallness **10** deficiency, meagerness, meagreness **13** insufficiency

Paul the Apostle *birthplace:* 6 Tarsus ***companion:* 5** Silas, Titus **7** Artemas, Timothy **8** Barnabas ***original name:* 4** Saul ***place of conversion:* 8** Damascus ***prosecutor:* 9**

Tertullus ***teacher:*** **8** Gamaliel ***tribe:*** **8** Benjamin

paunch 3 gut, pot **5** belly, tummy **7** abdomen, stomach **8** potbelly **9** bay window, beer belly **11** breadbasket, corporation

paunchy 3 fat **5** beefy, plump, tubby **6** chunky, portly, rotund **8** thickset **10** overweight, potbellied

pauper 6 beggar **7** have-not **8** bankrupt, indigent **9** mendicant

pauperism 4 need, ruin, want **6** penury **7** beggary, poverty **9** indigence, neediness, privation **11** destitution

pause 3 gap **4** halt, hush, lull, rest, stop, wait **5** break, comma, delay, lapse, letup **6** hiatus, linger, recess **7** caesura, respite, take ten, time out **8** breather, hesitate, inaction, interval, take five **9** cessation, interlude **10** hesitation, suspension **12** intermission, interruption

pave 3 lay, tar **5** cover **7** asphalt, surface **8** blacktop, concrete

pavement 6 tarmac **7** asphalt, macadam, surface **8** concrete, sidewalk

pavilion 4 tent **5** kiosk **6** canopy, gazebo **9** belvedere **11** summerhouse

paw 4 feel, foot, grab, hand, mitt **5** grope, touch **6** fondle, handle, molest, scrape

pawn 4 hock, tool **6** pledge, puppet, stooge, victim **7** deposit, hostage, warrant **8** guaranty, security **9** guarantee **10** chess piece, instrument

pax 5 peace **6** tablet

Pax ____ 3 Dei **6** Romana **10** Britannica

pay 3 fee **4** ante, wage **5** remit, serve, spend **6** answer, ante up, defray, expend, kick in, lay out, pony up, profit, render, salary, settle, tender, reward **7** benefit, bring in, cough up, forfeit, fork out, satisfy, stipend **8** disburse, earnings, shell out **9** discharge, emolument, indemnify, reimburse **10** compensate, recompense, remunerate **12** compensation, remuneration

payable 3 due **4** owed **5** owing **6** mature, unpaid **7** overdue **9** unsettled **10** obligatory **11** outstanding, uncollected

paycheck 5 wages **6** salary

payload 4 haul **5** cargo, goods **6** burden, lading, weight **7** freight, tonnage **8** shipment

payment 3 fee **4** dues **5** award, money **6** amends, outlay, return, reward **7** penance **8** defrayal, requital **11** restitution **12** compensation, remuneration, satisfaction

payoff 3 fix **5** bribe **6** climax, profit, result, reward, upshot **7** outcome **8** clincher, decisive **10** conclusion, conclusive, denouement **11** retribution

payola 5 bribe

PDQ 4 ASAP, stat **6** at once, pronto **8** directly, right now, right off **9** forthwith, instanter, instantly, right away **11** immediately, straightway **12** straightaway

peace 3 pax **4** calm, ease, pact **5** amity, order, quiet **6** accord, repose **7** concord, harmony, silence **8** serenity **11** tranquility **12** tranquillity

peaceable 6 dovish, irenic **7** amiable, pacific **8** amicable, friendly, pacifist, tranquil **10** nonviolent **11** complaisant **12** conciliatory

peaceful 4 calm **5** still, quiet **6** irenic, placid, serene **7** equable, halcyon, pacific **8** composed, tranquil **9** unruffled **10** harmonious, nonviolent, untroubled

peacemaker 7 arbiter **8** mediator, pacifier, placater **10** arbitrator, negotiator **11** conciliator, pacificator

peace officer 3 cop **6** police **9** policeman **11** policewoman

peach 3 ace, pip, rat **4** blab, lulu, tree **5** fruit, honey **6** betray, inform, reveal, snitch, squeal **7** Elberta **8** knockout **9** freestone, humdinger, nectarine **10** clingstone **11** crackerjack ***family:*** **4** rose

Peach State 7 Georgia

peachy 4 fine, good, neat, nice **5** dandy, neato, nifty, super, swell **8** pleasant, pleasing **9** excellent, hunky-dory, marvelous, wonderful

peacockish 5 showy, swank **6** chichi, flashy, swanky **7** splashy **8** show-offy **10** flamboyant **11** pretentious **12** ostentatious

peak 3 top **4** acme, apex, roof **5** crest, crown **6** summit, vertex, zenith **8** pinnacle ***Arizona:*** **9** Humphreys ***Bighorn Mtns.:*** **5** Cloud ***Black Hills:*** **6** Harney ***California:*** **6** Lassen **9** Telescope ***Cascade Range:*** **6** Lassen ***Colorado:*** **5** Grays, Longs, Pikes **6** Blanca **7** La Plata **11** Uncompahgre ***Idaho:*** **5** Borah ***Kyrgyzstan:*** **5** Lenin **6** Pobeda ***Montana:*** **7** Granite **8** Electric ***Nevada:*** **7** Wheeler **8** Boundary **10** Charleston ***New Mexico:*** **7** Truchas, Wheeler **12** Sierra Blanca ***South Dakota:*** **6** Harney ***Sri Lanka:*** **5** Adam's **8** Samanala ***Tajikistan:*** **5** Lenin **9** Communism ***Utah:*** **5** Kings ***White Mtns.:*** **8** Boundary ***Wyoming:*** **5** Cloud **6** Franks **7** Gannett (see also **mountain**)

peaked 3 ill, wan **4** ashy, pale, sick **5** acute, ashen, drawn, sharp **6** ailing, pallid, sickly **7** pointed **9** emaciated

peal 4 bell, bong, ring, toll **5** chime, knell, sound **7** ring out, ringing **8** ding-dong

peanut 4 mani **6** goober, legume, peewee, shrimp **9** pipsqueak

Peanuts ***character:*** **4** Lucy (van Pelt) **5** Linus, Patty (Peppermint), Rerun, Sally (Brown), Spike **6** Frieda, Marcie, Pig-Pen, Snoopy **8** Franklin **9** Schroeder, Woodstock **12** Charlie Brown ***creator:*** **6** Schulz (Charles M.) ***expression:*** **4** rats ***forerunner:*** **8** Li'l Folks

pear **4** Bosc, pome **5** Anjou, Hardy **6** Comice, Garber, Seckel **7** Kieffer, LeConte **8** Bartlett ***cider:*** **5** perry

pearl **3** gem **4** dear **5** jewel **7** paragon **8** treasure

Pearl Mosque site **4** Agra

pearly **8** lustrous, nacreous, precious **10** iridescent, opalescent

pear-shaped **8** pyriform

peasant **4** carl, kern, peon, serf **5** churl **6** rustic **7** bumpkin, hayseed, villein ***Arab:*** **6** fellah ***Indian:*** **4** ryot ***Latin-American:*** **9** campesino ***Philippine:*** **3** tao ***Russian:*** **5** mujik **6** moujik, muzhik

peccary **8** javelina ***genus:*** **7** Tayassu

peck **3** lot, nag **4** buss, carp, fuss, heap, kiss, load, mess, pile, poke **6** carp at, nibble, pick at, pick up, pierce, strike **8** quantity

pecking order **6** ladder **7** pyramid **9** food chain, hierarchy

peculate **5** steal **8** embezzle **9** defalcate **11** appropriate

peculiar **3** odd **4** rare **5** queer, weird **6** unique **7** bizarre, curious, oddball, offbeat, special, strange, unusual **8** abnormal, singular, specific, uncommon **9** eccentric **10** individual, particular **11** distinctive

peculiarity **3** tic **4** mark **5** quirk, trait **6** oddity **7** feature, quality **8** property **9** attribute, character, mannerism **12** eccentricity, idiosyncrasy

pecuniary **6** fiscal **8** economic, monetary **9** financial

pedagogue **5** tutor **6** pedant **7** teacher **8** educator **12** schoolmaster

pedagogy **8** teaching **9** education

pedal **5** lever **7** bicycle, treadle ***digit:*** **3** toe

pedant **7** teacher **9** formalist **10** schoolmarm **12** precisionist

pedantic **3** dry **4** arid, dull **6** stodgy **7** bookish, donnish, erudite, learned, tedious **8** academic, didactic, priggish **9** ponderous **10** pedestrian, scholastic **11** pedagogical **13** unimaginative

peddle **4** hawk, push, sell, vend **5** pitch **6** monger **8** huckster

peddler **6** coster, dealer, hawker, monger, vendor **8** huckster, merchant, promoter **9** tradesman **12** costermonger

pedestal **4** base, foot **5** stand **7** footing, support **10** foundation **12** underpinning ***part:*** **4** dado **6** plinth **7** subbase

pedestrian **4** blah, dull **5** banal **6** dreary, stodgy, walker **7** humdrum, mundane, prosaic **8** everyday, ordinary **11** commonplace **13** unimaginative ***crossing:*** **5** zebra **10** footbridge

pedigree **6** origin, purity **7** descent, history, lineage **8** ancestry, purebred **9** bloodline, genealogy **10** background, extraction, family tree

peduncle **4** stem **5** stalk **7** pedicel

peek **3** spy **4** look **6** glance **7** glimpse

peel **4** bark, pare, rind, skin **5** flake, scale, strip **7** take off **8** flake off **9** break away, exfoliate

peeled **4** bare, open **5** naked **7** denuded, exposed **8** stripped **9** uncovered

peep **3** see, spy **4** look **5** chirp, tweet, watch **6** glance, squeak **7** glimpse, twitter **9** sandpiper

Peeping Tom **5** snoop **6** voyeur **7** prowler, snooper

peer **3** pry **4** gaze, lord **5** equal, glare, noble, stare **6** goggle, squint **9** associate ***British:*** **4** duke, earl **5** baron **7** marquis **8** marquess, viscount

Peer Gynt ***author:*** **5** Ibsen (Henrik) ***beloved:*** **7** Solveig ***character:*** **6** Anitra ***composer:*** **5** Grieg (Edvard) ***mother:*** **3** Ase **4** Aase

peerless **4** best **6** unique **7** perfect, supreme **8** superior **9** matchless, nonpareil, paramount, unequaled, unmatched, unrivaled **12** incomparable, unparalleled

peeve **3** bug, irk, vex **4** miff, rile **5** anger, annoy, pique **6** bother, nettle, put out **7** disturb, provoke **8** irritate, nuisance, vexation **9** aggravate, annoyance, grievance **10** exasperate **11** aggravation

peevish **4** sour **5** cross, testy **6** cranky, grumpy, ornery **7** fretful, whining **8** petulant **9** fractious, irritable, obstinate, querulous **11** ill-tempered

peewee **4** runt, tike, tyke **5** dwarf, pigmy, pygmy, small **6** midget, shaver, shrimp, squirt **9** miniature **10** diminutive, flycatcher **11** lilliputian

peg **3** fix, pin, tee **4** mark, plug, step **5** dowel, prong, stake, throw **6** attach, fasten, marker **7** pin down, pretext, support **8** identify

Pegasus **5** horse, steed ***rider:*** **11** Bellerophon

pejorative **7** adverse **8** critical, debasing **9** slighting **10** belittling, derogatory, detractive **11** denigrating, deprecatory, disparaging, opprobrious, unfavorable **12** depreciatory

pelagic **6** marine **7** oceanic **8** maritime

Peleus ***brother:*** **7** Telamon ***father:*** **6** Aeacus ***half brother:*** **6** Phocus ***son:*** **8** Achilles ***victim:*** **8** Eurytion ***wife:*** **6** Thetis

pelf 4 loot, swag **5** booty, lucre, money, moola **6** boodle, moolah, riches, spoils **7** plunder

Pelias ***country:*** **6** Iolcus ***father:*** **8** Poseidon ***half brother:*** **5** Aeson ***son:*** **7** Acastus

Pelican State 9 Louisiana

Pelléas ***beloved:*** **9** Mélisande ***brother, slayer:*** **6** Golaud

Pelles ***daughter:*** **6** Elaine ***grandson:*** **7** Galahad

pellet 3 wad **4** ball, shot **6** sphere **10** projectile

Pellinore ***slayer:*** **6** Gawain ***son:*** **5** Torre **6** Dornar **7** Lamerok **8** Percival **9** Agglovale

pell-mell 5 chaos, snarl **6** muddle, rashly **7** chaotic, clutter, hastily **8** confused, disarray, disorder, headlong, reckless **9** confusion, haphazard, hurriedly **10** carelessly, heedlessly **11** hurry-scurry **13** helter-skelter

pellucid 5 clear, plain, sheer **6** limpid **7** crystal, evident, obvious **8** clear-cut, luminous **9** unblurred **10** see-through **11** crystalline, transparent

Pelops ***father:*** **8** Tantalus ***son:*** **6** Atreus **8** Pittheus, Thyestes ***wife:*** **10** Hippodamia

pelota 4 ball **7** jai alai

pelt 3 fur, run **4** beat, blow, dash, drub, hide, hurl, rush, skin, whop **5** hurry, pound, scoot, speed, strip, throw, whack **6** assail, batter, pepper, pummel, strike, wallop **7** bombard, hotfoot

pen 3 sty **4** cage, coop, jail, swan **5** pound, quill, write **6** cooler, corral, indite, prison, shut in, stylus, writer **7** close in, confine, enclose, fence in **9** ballpoint, enclosure

penal 8 punitive **12** correctional, disciplinary

penalize 4 dock, fine **5** mulct **6** punish **7** deprive **8** handicap **10** discipline **12** disadvantage

penalty 4 fine, loss **5** mulct **7** damages, forfeit **8** hardship **10** amercement, forfeiture, punishment **12** disadvantage

penance 4 rite **7** penalty **8** hardship **9** atonement **10** punishment

penchant 4 bent **5** taste **6** liking **7** leaning **8** affinity, fondness, tendency **9** inclining **10** partiality, proclivity, propensity **11** inclination **12** predilection

pendant 4 flag, jack, rope **7** fixture **8** lavalier, ornament **10** supplement

pendent 7 hanging **9** suspended, undecided, unsettled **11** overhanging **12** undetermined

pending 6 during **8** awaiting, imminent **9** undecided, unsettled **12** undetermined

____ **Pendragon 5** Uther

pendulous 7 hanging **8** dangling, drooping, wavering **9** faltering, suspended, tentative, uncertain **10** hesitating, indecisive **11** vacillating

Penelope ***father:*** **7** Icarius ***father-in-law:*** **7** Laertes ***husband:*** **7** Ulysses **8** Odysseus ***mother:*** **8** Periboea ***son:*** **10** Telemachus ***suitor:*** **7** Agelaus

penetrable 6 porous **8** pervious **9** permeable

penetrate 3 jab **4** bore, go in, stab **5** break, drive, enter, probe, touch **6** affect, charge, invade, pierce **7** pervade **8** discover, encroach, perceive, permeate, puncture, saturate **9** percolate, perforate **10** understand

penetrating 4 keen **5** acute, sharp **6** astute, shrewd **8** incisive, piercing **9** trenchant **10** discerning, insightful, perceptive **11** quick-witted, sharp-witted **12** sharp-sighted

Peneus ***daughter:*** **6** Daphne ***father:*** **7** Oceanus ***mother:*** **6** Tethys

penguin type 6 Adélie

____ **Penh 5** Phnom

peninsula 4 neck **10** chersonese ***Alaska:*** **5** Kenai **6** Seward ***Australia:*** **6** Tasman ***Barents Sea:*** **5** Kanin ***British colony:*** **9** Gibraltar ***Canada:*** **5** Bruce, Gaspé **6** Ungava **8** Labrador ***Chile:*** **5** Swett ***China:*** **8** Shandong ***Costa Rica:*** **3** Osa ***Croatia:*** **6** Istria ***Denmark:*** **7** Jutland ***eastern United States:*** **8** Delmarva ***Estonia:*** **5** Sorve ***Florida:*** **8** Pinellas **9** Canaveral ***France:*** **5** Giens ***Greece:*** **4** Acte **10** Chalcidice **11** Peloponnese **12** Peloponnesus ***Guam:*** **5** Orote ***Hong Kong:*** **7** Kowloon ***Honshu:*** **3** Izu **5** Miura ***Massachusetts:*** **7** Cape Ann, Cape Cod ***Mexico:*** **4** Baja **7** Yucatan **14** Baja California ***Michigan:*** **8** Keweenaw ***Middle East:*** **5** Sinai ***New Guinea:*** **4** Huon ***New Jersey:*** **9** Sandy Hook ***New Zealand:*** **5** Banks, Mahia ***Nunavut:*** **7** Boothia **8** Melville ***Ontario:*** **5** Bruce ***Persian Gulf:*** **9** Ras Tanura ***Quebec:*** **5** Gaspé ***Russia:*** **4** Kola **5** Taman, Yamal **6** Kolski, Taimyr **9** Kamchatka ***Scotland:*** **7** Kintyre ***South Australia:*** **4** Eyre **5** Yorke ***Southeast Asia:*** **5** Malay **9** Indochina ***southeastern Europe:*** **6** Balkan ***southwestern Asia:*** **6** Arabia **7** Arabian ***southwestern Europe:*** **7** Iberian ***Texas:*** **9** Matagorda ***Tierra del Fuego:*** **5** Mitre ***Turkey:*** **8** Anatolia **9** Asia Minor ***Ukraine:*** **5** Kerch **6** Crimea **7** Crimean ***Wales:*** **5** Gower, Lleyn ***Washington:*** **7** Olympic ***Wisconsin:*** **4** Door

Peninsular State 7 Florida

penitence 3 rue **4** ruth **6** regret, sorrow **7** anguish, remorse **8** distress, humbling **10** con-

trition, repentance **11** compunction, self-reproof **12** self-reproach
penitent 5 sorry **6** rueful **8** contrite **9** regretful, repentant **10** apologetic, remorseful
penitentiary see **prison**
penman 5 clerk **6** author, scribe, writer **7** copyist **9** scrivener **12** calligrapher
penmanship 4 hand **5** style **6** script **7** writing **11** calligraphy, chirography, handwriting
pen name 6 anonym **9** pseudonym **10** nom de plume ***Addison, Joseph:*** **4** Clio ***Arouet, François-Marie:*** **8** Voltaire ***Beyle, Marie-Henri:*** **8** Stendhal ***Blair, Eric:*** **12** George Orwell ***Blixen, Karen:*** **11** Isak Dinesen ***Brontë, Anne:*** **9** Acton Bell ***Brontë, Charlotte:*** **10** Currer Bell ***Brontë, Emily:*** **9** Ellis Bell ***Clemens, Samuel:*** **9** Mark Twain ***Dickens, Charles:*** **3** Boz ***Dodgson, Charles Lutwidge:*** **12** Lewis Carroll ***Dupin, Amandine-Aurore:*** **10** George Sand ***Evans, Mary Ann:*** **11** George Eliot ***Faust, Frederick:*** **8** Max Brand ***Franklin, Benjamin:*** **11** Poor Richard ***Geisel, Theodore:*** **7** Dr. Seuss ***Glidden, Frederick:*** **9** Luke Short ***Lamb, Charles:*** **4** Elia ***Lederer, Esther:*** **10** Ann Landers ***Munro, Hector Hugh:*** **4** Saki ***Poquelin, Jean-Baptiste:*** **7** Molière ***Porter, William Sidney:*** **6** O. Henry ***Ramé, Maria Louise:*** **5** Ouida ***Thibault, J.-A.-F.:*** **13** Anatole France ***Viaud, L.-M.-J.:*** **10** Pierre Loti ***Wofford, Chloe Anthony:*** **12** Toni Morrison
pennant 4 flag, jack **5** color **6** banner, ensign **8** standard, streamer **9** banderole **12** championship
penniless 4 poor **5** broke, needy **8** bankrupt, indigent **9** destitute, insolvent **11** impecunious
pennon 4 flag, jack, wing **5** color **6** banner, ensign **8** bannerol, gonfalon, streamer **9** banderole, oriflamme
Pennsylvania *capital:* **10** Harrisburg ***city:*** **4** Erie **7** Reading **8** Scranton **9** Allentown **10** Pittsburgh **12** Philadelphia ***college, university:*** **6** Drexel, Lehigh, Temple **7** LaSalle **8** Bryn Mawr, Bucknell **9** Dickinson, Haverford, Lafayette, Penn State, Villanova **10** Swarthmore **14** Carnegie Mellon ***mountain range:*** **6** Pocono ***nickname:*** **8** Keystone (State) ***river:*** **9** Allegheny **10** Schuylkill **11** Monongahela, Susquehanna ***state bird:*** **12** ruffed grouse ***state flower:*** **14** mountain laurel ***state tree:*** **7** hemlock
penny-pincher 5 miser **7** niggard, scrooge **8** tightwad **9** skinflint **10** cheapskate
penny-pinching 4 mean **6** frugal, stingy, thrift **7** miserly, thrifty **9** frugality, niggardly, parsimony, penurious **11** tightfisted **12** cheeseparing, parsimonious
penny-wise 5 canny, tight **6** frugal, stingy **7** prudent, sparing, thrifty **9** provident **10** economical **12** parsimonious
pen point 3 neb, nib
pension 3 inn **5** hotel, lodge **6** hostel, reward **7** annuity, auberge, payment, stipend **8** gratuity **9** allowance **12** room and board, roominghouse **13** boardinghouse
pensioner 7 retiree
pensive 3 sad **6** dreamy, musing **7** wistful **10** meditative, melancholy, reflective, ruminative, thoughtful **11** preoccupied **13** contemplative
Pentateuch 5 Torah ***books:*** **6** Exodus **7** Genesis, Numbers **9** Leviticus **11** Deuteronomy
Penthesilea *queen of:* **7** Amazons ***slayer:*** **8** Achilles
Pentheus *grandfather:* **6** Cadmus ***king of:*** **6** Thebes ***mother:*** **5** Agave
penumbra 4 veil **5** cover, shade **6** fringe, screen, shadow, shroud **7** curtain
penurious 4 mean, poor **5** needy, tight **6** frugal, stingy **7** miserly **8** indigent, stinting **9** destitute, niggardly **11** impecunious, tightfisted **12** impoverished, parsimonious **13** penny-pinching
penury 4 need, want **7** beggary, poverty **8** distress **9** indigence, privation, pauperism **11** destitution, needfulness
peon 4 serf **5** prole, slave **6** drudge, toiler, worker **7** laborer, peasant **11** galley slave ***Anglo-Saxon:*** **4** esne
peonage 4 yoke **6** thrall **7** bondage, helotry, serfdom, slavery **9** servitude, thralldom, villenage **11** enslavement
people 3 kin **4** folk **5** folks, peeps, plebs **6** public **7** society **8** populace **9** commoners, community, plebeians **10** commonalty **11** inhabitants, rank and file, third estate ***combining form:*** **5** ethno
pep 3 vim, zip **4** brio, dash **5** gusto, moxie, punch, verve, vigor **6** energy, spirit **7** sparkle **8** vitality, vivacity **10** get-up-and-go, liveliness **11** high spirits
pepo 5 gourd, melon **6** squash **7** pumpkin **8** cucumber
pepper 4 kava, pelt **5** chili **6** season, shower **7** cayenne, paprika, pimento, tabasco **8** capsicum, cascabel, chipotle, habanero, jalapeño, pimiento, sprinkle **9** condiment, seasoning **12** Scotch bonnet
peppery 3 hot **5** cross, fiery, sharp, spicy, testy, zesty **6** biting, lively, snappy, touchy **7** piquant, pungent **8** choleric, poignant,

seasoned, stinging **9** irascible, irritable **11** hot-tempered **13** quick-tempered

peppy 4 spry **5** alert, perky **6** active, bright, lively **7** vibrant **8** animated, spirited, vigorous **9** energetic, sprightly, vivacious

Pequod ***cabin boy:*** **3** Pip ***captain:*** **4** Ahab ***harpooner:*** **6** Daggoo **8** Queequeg, Tashtego ***mate:*** **8** Starbuck ***seaman:*** **7** Ishmael

per 3 via **4** a pop, each, with **6** apiece **7** by way of, for each, through **9** by means of **12** individually

perambulate 4 walk **6** ramble, stroll **8** traverse **9** promenade

per capita 4 each **6** apiece, by each **7** equally, for each

perceive 3 see **4** espy, feel, know, mark, note **5** grasp, seize, sense **6** detect, notice, remark **7** discern, observe, realize **8** identify **9** apprehend, recognize **10** comprehend, understand

percentage 3 cut **4** part **5** piece, share, slice **6** profit **7** portion **9** advantage **10** commission, proportion **11** probability

perceptible 5 clear **6** marked **7** visible **8** apparent, definite, distinct, palpable, sensible, tangible **10** detectable, noticeable, observable **11** appreciable, discernible **12** recognizable

perception 3 ken **4** idea **5** grasp, image **6** acumen, notion **7** concept, feeling, insight, thought **9** awareness, cognition **10** impression **11** discernment, observation

perceptive 4 keen, sage, wise **5** acute, alert, aware, sharp **7** knowing **9** intuitive, observant, sagacious, sensitive **10** discerning, insightful, responsive **13** understanding

perch 3 bar, peg, set **4** fish, land, rest, seat **5** light, roost, sit on **6** alight, settle **7** set down, sit atop, sit down

perchance 5 maybe **6** mayhap **7** perhaps **8** possibly **11** conceivably

percipience 6 acumen **8** keenness **9** cognition, intuition **10** astuteness **11** discernment **12** appreciation, perspicacity **13** comprehension

percolate 4 drip, ooze, seep **5** exude, leach **6** charge, filter, simmer, spread **7** pervade, trickle **9** penetrate

percussion 3 jar **4** bump, jolt **5** clash, crash, shock **6** impact **9** collision **10** concussion ***instrument:*** (see at **musical instrument**)

Perdita ***father:*** **7** Leontes ***mother:*** **8** Hermione

perdition 4 hell **5** hades **7** inferno **9** damnation **10** underworld **11** netherworld

Père Goriot author 6 Balzac (Honoré de)

peregrination 4 trek, trip, walk **7** journey, travels **9** traversal **10** expedition

peremptory 5 bossy, final **7** haughty **8** absolute, arrogant, decisive, dogmatic, imperial **9** imperious, masterful **10** autocratic, commanding, disdainful, high-handed, imperative **11** dictatorial, domineering, magisterial, overbearing

perennial 7 durable **8** constant, enduring, lifelong **9** continual, long-lived, permanent, perpetual, recurrent, unceasing **10** continuing, persistent, persisting, unchanging **11** long-lasting

Perez ***brother:*** **5** Zerah ***father:*** **5** Judah ***mother:*** **5** Tamar

perfect 4 full, pure **5** exact, ideal, model, right, sound, total, utter, whole **6** entire, expert, intact, polish, proper, refine **7** correct, improve, precise **8** absolute, accurate, complete, finished, flawless, peerless, spotless, unbroken, unflawed **9** downright, excellent, faultless, matchless, stainless, unalloyed, undiluted **10** consummate, impeccable, proficient **11** unequivocal, unmitigated, unqualified

perfection 4 acme **5** ideal **6** purity, virtue **7** paragon **9** integrity, wholeness **10** excellence, excellency **12** flawlessness

perfectly 5 fully, quite **6** wholly **7** to a turn, utterly **8** entirely **10** altogether, completely, thoroughly

perfidious 5 false **6** untrue **8** disloyal **9** deceitful, dishonest, faithless **10** treasonous, traitorous, unfaithful, unreliable **11** treacherous

perfidy 6 deceit **7** falsity, sellout, treason **8** betrayal **9** falseness, treachery **10** disloyalty, infidelity **13** faithlessness

perforate 3 pit **4** bore **5** drill, prick, punch **6** pierce **8** puncture **9** penetrate

perform 2 do **3** act **4** play, work **5** enact **6** behave, comply, effect **7** achieve, execute, fulfill, operate, playact, present, satisfy **8** bring off, carry out, complete, function **9** discharge, entertain, implement **10** accomplish

performance 3 act **4** deed, feat, show, work **6** acting, action **7** conduct, display **8** behavior, efficacy, exercise **9** discharge, execution, operation **10** efficiency, exhibition **11** achievement, fulfillment **12** presentation

performer 4 doer, mime **5** actor, mimic **6** mummer, player **7** actress, artiste, trouper **8** thespian **9** playactor **12** impersonator

perfume 4 balm **5** aroma, cense, scent, smell, spice **6** sachet **7** bouquet, incense, odorize **9** aromatize, fragrance, redolence ***source:*** **4** musk **5** attar, myrrh, orris **8** bergamot

perfumer 4 Dior (Christian), Nose (The) **5** Estée **6** Chanel (Coco), Lanvin, Lauder **8** Guerlain (Aimé, Jacques), Guichard (Aurelien, Jean)
perfunctory 7 cursory, routine **8** careless **9** automatic **10** impersonal, mechanical **11** superficial
pergola 5 arbor, bower **7** trellis
perhaps 5 maybe **8** feasibly, possibly **9** perchance **11** conceivably
periapt see **amulet**
Pericles ***father:*** **10** Xanthippus ***mistress:*** **7** Aspasia ***mother:*** **8** Agariste
peril 4 risk **6** danger, hazard, menace **8** exposure, jeopardy **9** liability **12** endangerment
perilous 5 hairy, risky **6** chancy, unsafe **7** unsound **9** dangerous, desperate, hazardous, uncertain **11** treacherous
____ **Perilous 5** Siege
perimeter 4 edge **5** limit, verge **6** border, bounds, margin **8** boundary
period 3 age, end, era **4** span, stop, term, time **5** cycle, phase, point, spell, stage **6** extent **8** division, duration, interval, sentence
periodic 6 cyclic, fitful **7** regular **8** cyclical, repeated, sporadic **9** recurrent, recurring **10** occasional **11** fluctuating **12** intermittent
periodical 3 mag **5** organ **6** cyclic, review **7** journal **8** cyclical, magazine **9** alternate, newspaper, recurrent, recurring **10** isochronal **11** isochronous, publication **12** intermittent
peripatetic 6 moving, roving **7** nomadic, walking **8** ambulant, vagabond **9** itinerant, traveling, wayfaring **10** ambulatory, pedestrian, travelling **13** perambulatory
peripheral 6 remote **7** lateral, surface **8** far-flung, marginal, outlying **9** auxiliary, secondary **10** borderline, tangential **11** out-of-the-way **13** supplementary
perish 3 die, end **4** pass **5** cease **6** be lost, demise, depart, expire, vanish **7** decease, decline, go under, succumb **8** collapse, pass away **9** disappear
perjure 3 lie **6** delude **7** deceive, distort, falsify, mislead **8** forswear **9** misinform **10** equivocate **11** prevaricate
perk 4 gain, mend, plus **5** bonus, cheer, extra **7** benefit, freshen, improve, refresh, smarten **8** brighten
perky 5 alert, cocky, happy **6** bouncy, bubbly, cheery, chirpy, frisky, jaunty, lively, upbeat **7** buoyant, chipper **8** animated, cheerful, spirited, sportive **9** energetic, sparkling, sprightly, vivacious **12** effervescent, high-spirited
permanent 5 fixed **6** stable **7** abiding, durable, lasting **8** constant, enduring, hair wave **9** continual, perennial **10** changeless, invariable, unchanging **11** established, everlasting **12** imperishable
permeable 6 porous, spongy **8** pervious **9** absorbent, diffusive **10** penetrable
permeate 5 imbue **6** drench, infuse, spread **7** diffuse, pervade, suffuse **8** saturate **9** penetrate, percolate **10** impregnate, infiltrate **11** pass through
permissible 4 okay **5** legal **7** allowed **8** approved **9** allowable, tolerable, tolerated **10** acceptable, authorized, sanctioned
permission 5 leave **6** assent, permit **7** consent, license **8** approval, sanction **9** agreement, allowance **11** approbation, endorsement **12** acquiescence **13** authorization
permissive 3 lax **4** open **7** lenient, liberal **8** tolerant **9** easygoing, forgiving, indulgent **10** forbearing **11** acquiescent, complaisant
permit 3 let **4** okay, pass **5** agree, allow, grant, leave **6** accede, enable, say yes, suffer **7** consent, license, warrant **8** sanction, tolerate **9** allowance, authorize, give leave **10** permission **13** authorization
permutation 6 change **7** variety, version **9** variation **10** alteration, innovation **11** arrangement, vicissitude **12** modification
pernicious 4 evil **5** fatal, toxic **6** deadly, lethal, malign, wicked **7** baleful, baneful, harmful, hurtful, killing, malefic, noxious, ruinous **8** damaging, sinister, virulent **9** injurious, malignant, offensive, poisonous **10** maleficent **11** deleterious, destructive, detrimental, devastating
Pernod flavor 5 anise **8** licorice
perorate 5 speak **7** declaim, lecture **8** bloviate, harangue, proclaim **9** hold forth, speechify
perpend 5 study, weigh **6** ponder **7** examine, reflect **8** consider, think out **9** reflect on, think over **10** excogitate, think about **11** contemplate
perpendicular 5 plumb, sheer, steep **7** upright **8** straight, vertical **11** precipitate, precipitous
perpetrate 6 commit, effect **7** inflict, execute, perform **8** carry out **10** bring about
perpetual 7 endless, eternal, undying **8** constant, unending **9** ceaseless, continual, incessant, perennial, recurrent, unceasing **10** continuous **11** everlasting, unremitting
perpetuate 7 sustain **8** conserve, continue, eternize, maintain, preserve **9** keep alive **10** eternalize **11** immortalize
perplex 5 befog, mix up, stump **6** baffle, be-

muse, muddle, puzzle **7** buffalo, confuse, mystify, nonplus, perturb **8** befuddle, bewilder, confound, distract, entangle **9** dumbfound **10** discompose

perplexed 7 at a loss, mixed up, puzzled **8** confused

Perry Mason *author:* 7 Gardner (Erle Stanley) ***character:* 5** Drake (Paul), Drumm (Lt. Steve), Mason (Perry), Tragg (Lt. Arthur) **6** Burger (Hamilton), Street (Della) **8** Anderson (Lt. Andy) ***TV star:* 4** Burr (Raymond), Hale (Barbara)

perquisite 3 tip **4** gain **5** right **6** profit **7** benefit, payment **8** gratuity **9** privilege

per se 6 as such, solely **8** in itself **11** essentially **13** intrinsically

persecute 4 bait, ride **5** annoy, harry, hound, worry, wrong **6** badger, harass, hector, injure, molest, pester, pick on, plague, punish, pursue **7** afflict, oppress, torment, torture **8** aggrieve

Persephone 4 Kore **10** Proserpina ***father:* 4** Zeus **7** Jupiter ***husband:* 5** Hades, Pluto ***mother:* 5** Ceres **7** Demeter

Perseus *father:* 4 Zeus **7** Jupiter ***grandfather:* 8** Acrisius ***mother:* 5** Danaë ***victim:* 6** Medusa **8** Acrisius ***wife:* 9** Andromeda

perseverance 8 tenacity **9** diligence, endurance **10** dedication **11** persistence **13** steadfastness

persevere see **persist**

Persia 4 Iran

Persian *ancient:* 4 Mede ***fairy:* 4** peri ***governor:* 6** satrap ***language:* 5** Farsi, Parsi ***mystic:* 4** sufi ***New Year's:* 6** Nowruz ***poet:* 4** Omar **5** Hafez, Hafiz **7** Firdusi **8** Ferdowsi, Firdausi, Firdawsi, Firdousi **11** Omar Khayyám ***prophet:* 9** Zoroaster ***robe:* 6** caftan ***sacred books:* 6** Avesta ***sun-god:* 7** Mithras ***title:* 4** shah ***writing:* 9** cuneiform

persiflage 6 banter, joking **7** jesting, kidding, ribbing **8** badinage, raillery, repartee

persist 4 go on, last **5** abidc **6** cndure, hang on, keep on, linger **7** carry on, prevail **8** continue **9** persevere

persistence 8 duration **9** endurance **10** continuity **11** continuance **12** continuation

persistent 6 dogged **7** lasting **8** enduring, obdurate, stubborn **9** continual, steadfast, tenacious **10** continuing, determined, relentless, unshakable **11** persevering, unremitting

persnickety 5 fussy, picky **6** choosy **7** finicky **8** exacting **10** fastidious, particular

person 3 guy **4** self, soul **5** being, human **6** entity, mensch, mortal **8** creature, specimen **10** individual

personable 4 nice **6** genial **7** affable, amiable **8** charming, friendly, pleasant, pleasing **9** appealing, congenial **10** attractive

personage 3 VIP **5** human, mogul **6** bigwig, figure, honcho **7** big shot, magnate, notable **8** creature, luminary, somebody **9** celebrity, character, dignitary **10** individual

personal 3 own **5** privy **7** private, special **8** peculiar **10** individual, particular

personal effects 5 stuff **10** belongings **11** possessions

personality 3 ego, VIP **4** self **6** makeup, nature, temper **7** notable **8** identity, selfhood **9** celebrity, character **10** complexion **11** disposition, singularity, temperament **13** individuality

personate 3 act **4** play **5** enact **6** embody, typify **7** perform **9** epitomize, exemplify, represent **10** illustrate

personify 6 embody, typify **8** stand for **9** actualize, epitomize, exemplify, incarnate, represent, symbolize **11** emblematize

perspective 4 view **5** angle, scene, slant, vista **7** outlook **8** position, prospect **9** viewpoint **10** standpoint **11** point of view

perspicacious 4 keen **5** acute, quick, savvy, sharp **6** astute, clever, shrewd **9** observant, sagacious **10** discerning, insightful, perceptive **11** penetrating

perspicacity 6 acumen **7** insight **8** keenness **10** astuteness, shrewdness **11** discernment, penetration, percipience

perspicuous 5 clear, lucid, plain **6** lucent, simple **7** crystal, precise **8** clear-cut, pellucid **11** unambiguous

perspiration 5 sweat

perspire see **sweat**

persuadable 4 open **7** willing **9** receptive **11** suggestible, susceptible

persuade 3 win **4** coax, lead, sell, sway, urge **5** argue **6** entice, induce, prompt **7** convert, impress, win over **8** convince **9** influence, prevail on **11** bring around

persuasion 4 kind, mind, sort, type, view **5** group **6** belief, school **7** faction, opinion **8** argument **9** character, prejudice, sentiment **10** connection, conviction **11** affiliation, description

Persuasion author 6 Austen (Janc)

persuasive 6 cogent **7** telling, winning **8** credible **10** compelling, convincing **11** influential

pert 4 bold, chic, flip, trim **5** alert, cocky, fresh, lippy, sassy, saucy, smart **6** brazen, bright, cheeky, jaunty, lively **7** forward **8** animated, flippant, spirited **9** audacious, sprightly, vivacious

pertain 5 apply, refer **6** affect, bear on, belong, regard, relate **7** concern **8** bear upon **9** touch upon
pertinacious 4 firm **5** fixed **6** dogged, mulish **7** willful **8** resolute, stubborn **9** obstinate, tenacious **10** inflexible, persistent, unshakable, unyielding
pertinent 3 apt, fit **5** ad rem **7** apropos, fitting, germane **8** apposite, material, relevant **10** applicable **11** appropriate
perturb 5 upset, worry **6** bother **7** agitate, disturb, fluster, trouble **8** disorder, disquiet, unsettle **10** discompose, disconcert
Peru *ancient civilization:* 4 Inca ***capital:* 4** Lima ***city:* 5** Cusco, Cuzco **6** Callao **8** Arequipa, Trujillo ***conqueror:* 7** Pizarro (Francisco) ***ethnic group:* 7** Quechua ***lake:* 8** Titicaca ***language:* 6** Aymara **7** Quechua, Spanish ***leader:* 8** Fujimori (Alberto) ***monetary unit:* 3** sol ***mountain, range:* 5** Andes **9** Huascarán ***neighbor:* 5** Chile **6** Brazil **7** Bolivia, Ecuador **8** Colombia ***river:* 6** Amazon **7** Marañón ***volcano:* 5** Misti **7** El Misti **8** Yucamani
peruse 4 read, scan **5** study **6** survey **7** examine **8** consider, look over, pore over
Peruvian singer 5 Sumac (Yma)
pervade 5 imbue **6** spread **7** diffuse **8** permeate, saturate **9** penetrate, percolate, transfuse **10** impregnate
perverse 5 balky **6** cranky, mulish, ornery **7** corrupt, deviant, froward, peevish, wayward, willful **8** contrary, depraved, improper, stubborn **9** incorrect, irritable, obstinate **10** degenerate, headstrong, refractory **11** stiff-necked, wrongheaded **12** crossgrained, unreasonable
pervert 4 ruin, skew, warp **5** abuse, twist **6** debase, divert, garble, misuse **7** corrupt, debauch, deprave, distort, deviant, falsify, vitiate **8** misstate, mistreat **9** misdirect
pervious 4 open **6** porous **9** permeable **10** accessible, penetrable
pesky 6 vexing **7** irksome **8** annoying **9** vexatious **10** bothersome **11** troublesome
pessimist 5 cynic **9** Cassandra, defeatist, doomsayer, worrywart **11** misanthrope
pessimistic 6 gloomy, morose **7** cynical **10** despairing **11** distrustful **12** misanthropic
pest 4 bane **5** trial, worry **6** bother, nudnik, plague, vermin **7** nudnick, trouble **8** irritant, nuisance, vexation **9** annoyance, tormentor
pester 3 bug, irk, nag **4** ride **5** annoy, harry, tease, worry **6** badger, bother, harass, hassle, plague **7** bedevil, disturb, torment **8** irritate
pestiferous 7 baneful, noxious **8** annoying, infected **9** infective, pestilent **10** pernicious **11** troublesome
pestilence 5 curse **6** plague **7** scourge
pestilential 5 fatal **6** deadly, lethal, vexing **7** baneful, deathly, noxious, ruinous **8** annoying **10** pernicious
pestle 4 mano **6** muller ***vessel:* 6** mortar
pet 3 cat, dog, hug **4** dear, kiss, love, neck, pout, sulk **5** loved, spoon **6** caress, cosset, dandle, fondle, pamper, stroke **7** beloved, cherish, darling, indulge **8** favorite, treasure **9** cherished
petcock 3 tap **5** valve **6** faucet, spigot
Peter Grimes composer 7 Britten (Benjamin)
peter out 4 fade, wane **5** abate, cease **6** lessen, recede, run dry **7** dwindle **8** decrease, diminish, taper off **9** drain away
Peter Pan *author:* 6 Barrie (James) ***character:* 5** Wendy **7** Michael **9** Tiger Lily **10** Tinker Bell ***dog:* 4** Nana ***family:* 7** Darling ***pirate:* 4** Hook, Smee
Peter the Apostle *brother:* 6 Andrew ***father:* 5** Jonah ***original name:* 5** Simon
Peter the Great *father:* 6 Alexis ***mother:* 8** Nataliya ***wife:* 7** Eudoxia **9** Catherine
petite 5 small **6** little **8** smallish **10** diminutive
petition 3 ask **4** plea **5** plead **6** appeal **7** beseech, entreat, implore, request, solicit **8** entreaty **10** supplicate **11** application **12** supplication
Petrarch's beloved 5 Laura
Petrified Forest author 8 Sherwood (Robert)
petrify 4 daze, numb, stun **5** chill, scare **6** benumb, deaden, harden **7** startle **8** confound, frighten, paralyze
Petruchio's wife 9 Katharina, Katharine
pettifogger 7 shyster **8** quibbler **9** nitpicker
petty 4 mean **5** minor, small **6** measly, narrow, paltry **7** trivial **8** niggling, picayune, piddling, trifling **9** frivolous, secondary **10** irrelevant, negligible **11** small-minded, subordinate, unimportant **13** insignificant
petty officer 6 noncom
petulant 5 huffy, moody, sulky, testy, whiny **6** touchy **7** grouchy, peevish **8** snappish **9** irascible, irritable, querulous **10** ill-humored
pew 3 row **4** seat **5** bench
peyote 6 cactus, mescal ***drug:* 9** mescaline
Phaedra *father:* 5 Minos ***husband:* 7** Theseus ***mother:* 8** Pasiphaë ***sister:* 7** Ariadne ***stepson:* 10** Hippolytus
Phaëthon's father 6 Helios **7** Phoebus
phalanx 4 army, host, mass **5** horde **6** myriad, throng **6** troops

phantasm 5 dream, fancy, ghost **6** spirit, vision **7** fantasy, fiction, figment, specter, spectre **8** daydream, delusion, illusion **9** invention **10** apparition **11** fabrication **13** hallucination

phantom 5 dummy, ghost, shade, spook **6** goblin, shadow, spirit, vision **7** bugbear, chimera, eidolon, specter, spectre **8** illusory, spectral **9** imaginary **10** apparition, fictitious **12** will-o'-the-wisp

pharaoh 3 Tut **4** Seti **5** Menes, ruler **6** Ahmose, Ramses, tyrant **7** Harmhab **8** Ikhnaton, Thutmose **9** Amenhotep, Merneptah **11** Tutankhamen, Tutankhaten

pharisee 9 hypocrite

pharmacist 8 druggist **10** apothecary ***British:*** **7** chemist

pharos 6 beacon **10** lighthouse

Pharsalus, battle of *vanquished:* 6 Pompey ***victor:*** **6** Caesar (Julius)

phase 4 part, side, view **5** point, stage, state **6** adjust, aspect **7** conduct **8** carry out, position **9** condition, situation, viewpoint **10** appearance

PhD exam 5 orals

Phèdre author 6 Racine (Jean)

phenomenal 6 actual **7** unusual **8** material, physical, sensible, singular, tangible, uncommon **9** corporeal, fantastic, objective **10** astounding, remarkable **11** astonishing, exceptional, outstanding, perceivable, perceptible, substantial **13** extraordinary

phenomenon 4 fact **5** event **6** marvel, object, rarity, wonder **7** miracle, reality **9** actuality, sensation **10** experience, uniqueness **11** peculiarity, singularity

philander 8 womanize

philanthropic 6 giving, humane **8** generous **10** altruistic, benevolent, bighearted, charitable **11** magnanimous **12** eleemosynary, humanitarian

philanthropist *American:* 5 Gates (Bill) **6** Cooper (Peter), Girard (Stephen), Mellon (Andrew) **7** Buffett (Warren), Cornell (Ezra), Eastman (George), Packard (David), Whitney (Gertrude Vanderbilt) **8** Carnegie (Andrew), Stanford (Leland) **9** Rosenwald (Julius) **10** Vanderbilt (Cornelius) **11** Rockefeller (J. D.) ***English:*** **11** Wilberforce (William) ***Swedish:*** **5** Nobel (Alfred)

Philemon's wife 6 Baucis

philharmonic 8 symphony **9** orchestra, symphonic

Philip of Macedonia *father:* 7 Amyntas ***son:*** **9** Alexander

philippic 4 rant **6** tirade **8** diatribe, harangue, jeremiad **12** condemnation

Philippics author 6 Cicero

Philippines *capital:* 6 Manila ***city:*** **4** Cebu **5** Davao **10** Quezon City ***discoverer:*** **8** Magellan (Ferdinand) ***guerrilla:*** **3** Huk **10** Hukbalahap ***island:*** **4** Cebu **5** Leyte, Luzon, Panay, Samar **6** Negros **7** Masbate, Mindoro, Palawan **8** Mindanao ***language:*** **7** Ilocano, Tagalog **8** Filipino, Pilipino ***leader:*** **6** Aquino (Corazon), Marcos (Ferdinand) ***liberator:*** **9** MacArthur (Douglas) ***patriot:*** **5** Rizal (José) ***monetary unit:*** **4** peso ***people:*** **3** Ati **4** Moro ***sea:*** **4** Sulu **5** Samar **7** Celebes, Sibuyan, Visayan **8** Mindanao **10** Philippine, South China ***volcano:*** **4** Taal **5** Mayon

Philippi victor 6 Antony (Marc, Mark) **8** Octavian

Philip the Tetrarch *father:* 5 Herod ***mother:*** **9** Cleopatra

philistine 4 boob **7** Babbitt **9** bourgeois, vulgarian **10** capitalist **11** materialist

Philistine *champion:* 7 Goliath ***city:*** **4** Gath, Gaza **5** Ekron **6** Ashdod **8** Ashkelon ***foe:*** **5** David **6** Samson ***god:*** **5** Dagon

Philoctetes *father:* 5 Poeas ***victim:*** **5** Paris

Philomela 11 nightingale ***father:*** **7** Pandion ***ravisher:*** **6** Tereus ***sister:*** **6** Procne

philosopher *American:* 5 Adler (Mortimer), Dewey (John), James (William), Quine (Willard), Rorty (Richard), Royce (Josiah) **6** Langer (Susanne), Peirce (C. S.) **7** Marcuse (Herbert), Mumford (Lewis), Strauss (Leo) **9** Santayana (George) ***Arab:*** **8** Averroës, Avicenna ***Austrian:*** **6** Popper (Karl) **12** Wittgenstein (Ludwig) ***Chinese:*** **5** Laoxi **6** Lao-tsu **7** Dai Zhen, Mencius, Tai Chen **9** Confucius ***Danish:*** **11** Kierkegaard (Soren) ***Dutch:*** **7** Erasmus (Desiderius), Spinoza (Baruch de) ***English:*** **4** Ayer (A. J.), Joad (C. E. M.), Mill (John Stuart), More (Henry, Thomas), Watt (James) **5** Bacon (Francis), Burke (Edmund), Locke (John), Moore (G. E.), Occam (William of), Paine (Thomas) **6** Berlin (Isaiah), Hobbes (Thomas), Huxley (Thomas), Ockham (William), Popper (Karl) **7** Bentham (Jeremy), Russell (Bertrand), Spencer (Herbert), Whewell (William) **9** Whitehead (Alfred North) **12** Wittgenstein (Ludwig) ***Finnish:*** **11** Westermarck (Edward) ***French:*** **4** Weil (Simone) **5** Comte (Auguste), Taine (Hippolyte) **6** Pascal (Blaise), Sartre (Jean-Paul), Valéry (Paul) **7** Abelard (Peter), Bergson (Henri), Derrida (Jacques), Diderot (Denis), Fourier (Charles) **8** Foucault

(Michel), Maritain (Jacques), Rousseau (Jean-Jacques), Voltaire **9** Descartes (René), Montaigne (Michel de) **10** Saint-Simon (Comte de) **11** Montesquieu (Baron de) **12** Merleau-Ponty (Maurice) ***German:*** **4** Kant (Immanuel), Marx (Karl) **5** Frege (Gottlob), Hegel (Georg Wilhelm Friedrich), Wolff (Christian von) **6** Carnap (Rudolf), Fichte (Immanuel, Johann), Herder (Johann von) **7** Husserl (Edmund), Jaspers (Karl), Leibniz (Gottfried) **8** Spengler (Oswald) **9** Heidegger (Martin), Nietzsche (Friedrich), Schelling (Friedrich von) **12** Schopenhauer (Arthur) **14** Albertus Magnus ***Greek:*** **4** Zeno **5** Plato, Timon **6** Thales **7** Gorgias, Proclus **8** Diogenes, Epicurus, Longinus, Socrates **9** Aristotle, Epictetus **10** Anaxagoras, Democritus, Empedocles, Heraclitus, Parmenides, Protagoras, Pythagoras, Xenocrates, Xenophanes **11** Anaximander **12** Theophrastus ***Irish:*** **8** Berkeley (George) ***Italian:*** **5** Croce (Benedetto) **6** Ficino (Marsilio) **11** Machiavelli (Niccolo) ***Jewish:*** **5** Buber (Martin), Philo **10** Maimonides (Moses) **12** Philo Judaeus ***Roman:*** **6** Seneca (Lucias Annaeus) **8** Boethius (Anicius), Plotinus **9** Lucretius ***Scottish:*** **4** Hume (David), Mill (James), Reid (Thomas) **7** Stewart (Dugald) ***Spanish:*** **6** Suárez (Francisco) **7** Unamuno (Miguel de) **13** Ortega y Gasset (José) ***Swedish:*** **10** Swedenborg (Emanuel)

philosopher's stone 3 key **6** elixir

philosophical 4 calm **7** stoical **8** composed, rational, resigned **9** unruffled **10** thoughtful

philosophy 6 system, theory, values **7** beliefs, inquiry **8** attitude, calmness **10** discipline ***component:*** **5** logic **6** ethics **10** aesthetics **11** metaphysics **12** epistemology

philter 4 drug **5** charm, tonic **6** potion **9** stimulant **10** love potion **11** aphrodisiac, restorative

Phineas *beloved:* **9** Andromeda ***tormentors:*** **7** Harpies ***wife:*** **9** Cleopatra

phlegm 5 humor, mucus **6** apathy **8** calmness, coolness, dullness **9** composure, sangfroid **10** equanimity **11** impassivity, nonchalance **12** indifference

phlegmatic 4 calm, cool, dull **5** aloof, stoic **6** stolid **8** detached **9** apathetic, impassive, lethargic **11** indifferent, unconcerned

Phlegyas *daughter:* **7** Coronis ***father:*** **4** Ares, Mars ***son:*** **5** Ixion

phobia see **fear**

Phobos 4 moon **9** satellite ***brother:*** **6** Deimos ***father:*** **4** Ares, Mars

Phocus *father:* **6** Aeacus **8** Ornytion ***half brother:*** **6** Peleus **7** Telamon ***mother:*** **8** Psamathe ***slayer:*** **6** Peleus **7** Telamon ***wife:*** **7** Antiope

Phoebe 5 Diana **7** Artemis ***daughter:*** **4** Leto ***father:*** **9** Leucippus ***mother:*** **4** Gaea

Phoebus see **Apollo**

Phoenician *city:* **4** Acre, Tyre **5** Sidon ***colony:*** **8** Carthage ***god:*** **4** Baal **6** Eshmun ***goddess:*** **6** Baltis **7** Astarte

Phoenix *pupil:* **8** Achilles ***sister:*** **6** Europa ***team:*** **4** Suns **7** Coyotes **9** Cardinals **12** Diamondbacks

phony 4 fake, sham **5** bogus, cheat, faker, false, fraud **6** ersatz, humbug, pseudo **8** impostor, specious, spurious **9** charlatan, dishonest, pretender **10** ficticious, suspicious **11** counterfeit **12** hypocritical

photograph 3 pic **4** film, snap **5** shoot **6** glossy **7** picture, tintype **8** snapshot ***color:*** **5** sepia ***three-dimensional:*** **8** hologram

photographer 8 photoist **9** cameraman **10** shutterbug ***famous:*** **3** Ray (Man) **4** Capa (Cornell, Robert), Haas (Ernst), Hine (Lewis), Penn (Irving), Riis (Jacob) **5** Adams (Ansel), Arbus (Diane), Atget (Eugène), Brady (Mathew), Evans (Frederick, Walker), Frank (Robert), Horst (Horst Peter), Karsh (Yousuf), Lange (Dorothea), Model (Lisette), Nadar, Parks (Gordon), Ritts (Herb), Smith (W. Eugene), Weber (Bruce), White (Clarence, Minor) **6** Abbott (Berenice), Avedon (Richard), Beaton (Cecil), Brandt (Bill), Coburn (Alvin), Curtis (Edward S.), Newton (Helmut), Porter (Eliot), Rowell (Galen), Siegel (Eliot), Strand (Paul), Talbot (William Henry Fox), Weegee, Wegman (William), Weston (Brett, Edward) **7** Brassaï, Cameron (Julia Margaret), Emerson (Peter), Halsman (Philippe), Jackson (William Henry), Kertész (André), Salomon (Erich), Siskind (Aaron), Snowdon (Earl of), Thomson (John), Watkins (Carleton) **8** Callahan (Harry), Cosindas (Marie), Daguerre (Louis-Jacques-Mandé), Kasebier (Gertrude), Scavullo (Francesco), Steichen (Edward), Steinert (Otto) **9** Caponigro (Paul), Feininger (Andreas), Leibovitz (Annie), Meyrowitz (Joel), Muybridge (Eadweard), O'Sullivan (Timothy), Rejlander (Oscar), Rothstein (Arthur), Stieglitz (Alfred), Winogrand (Garry) **10** Cunningham (Imogen), Heartfield (John), Moholy-Nagy (Laszlo) **11** Bourke-White (Margaret), Eisenstaedt (Alfred) **12** Mapplethorpe (Robert)

photographic 5 exact, vivid **7** graphic **8** accurate, detailed **9** pictorial **11** picturesque

solution: **4** hypo **5** fixer, toner **7** reducer **9** developer

phrase 5 couch, frame, idiom **6** slogan **7** diction, express, styling, wording **8** locution, verbiage **9** catchword, formulate, verbalism, watchword **10** expression

Phrygian *god:* 4 Atys **5** Attis ***goddess:* 6** Cybele ***king:* 5** Midas **7** Gordius

phthisis 2 TB **11** consumption **12** tuberculosis

phylactery 5 charm **6** amulet **7** periapt **8** talisman

physic 4 cure, heal **5** purge **6** remedy **8** medicine **9** cathartic, purgative **10** medication

physical 4 real **5** lusty, rough **6** actual, bodily, carnal, sexual **7** fleshly, natural, somatic **8** concrete, corporal, material, sensible, tangible **9** corporeal, objective **10** phenomenal **11** perceivable, perceptible, substantial

physician 2 MD **3** doc **5** medic **6** doctor, medico **7** surgeon **8** sawbones ***American:* 4** Koop (C. Everett), Rush (Benjamin), Salk (Jonas) **5** Minot (George), Spock (Benjamin), Still (Andrew) **6** Jarvik (Robert), Murphy (John), Weller (Thomas) **7** Huggins (Charles), Robbins (Frederick), Theiler (Max) **8** Richards (Dickinson) **9** Sternberg (George Miller) ***Arab:* 8** Avicenna ***Canadian:* 5** Osler (William) ***English:* 4** Ross (Ronald) **6** Harvey (William), Jenner (Edward, William), Willis (Thomas) **8** Sydenham (Thomas) ***French:* 5** Widal (Fernand) **7** Laveran (Charles) **10** Schweitzer (Albert) ***German:* 7** Sylvius (Franciscus) ***Greek:* 5** Galen **11** Hippocrates ***Italian:* 7** Galvani (Luigi) ***organization:* 3** AMA ***South African:* 7** Barnard (Christiaan) ***Swiss:* 10** Paracelsus (see also **Nobel Prize winner** *physiology or medicine;* **surgeon**)

physicist *American:* 4 Rabi (I. I.), Ting (Samuel) **5** Fermi (Enrico), Gibbs (J. Willard), Kusch (Polykarp), Mayer (Maria-Goeppert), Pauli (Wolfgang), Pupin (Michael), Segré (Emilio), Smyth (Henry DeWolf), Stern (Otto) **6** Teller (Edward), Townes (Charles), Wigner (Eugene) **7** Alvarez (Luis), Feynman (Richard), Goddard (Robert), Purcell (Edward) **8** Einstein (Albert), Gell-Mann (Murray), McMillan (Edwin), Millikan (Clark, Robert), Mulliken (Robert), Shockley (William), Van Allen (James) **9** Michelson (Albert), Schwinger (Julian) **11** Oppenheimer (J. Robert) ***Austrian:* 4** Mach (Ernst) **7** Doppler (Christian) **11** Schrödinger (Erwin) ***British:* 4** Snow (C. P.) **5** Dirac (B. A. M.), Jeans (James), Joule (James) **6** Dalton (John), Kelvin (Baron), Newton (Isaac), Powell (Cecil), Stokes (George) **7** Faraday (Michael), Hodgkin (Dorothy), Thomson (George, Joseph, William) **7** Tyndall (John) **8** Rayleigh (Lord), Robinson (Robert), Thompson (Benjamin, Silvanus) **9** Wollaston (William) **10** Richardson (Owen), Rutherford (Ernest), Wheatstone (Charles) ***Chinese:* 4** Yang (Chen-Ning) ***Danish:* 4** Bohr (Aage, Niels) ***Dutch:* 6** Zeeman (Pieter) **7** Huygens (Christian), Lorentz (Hendrik), Zernike (Frits) **11** Van der Waals (Johannes) ***French:* 4** Néel (Louis) **5** Arago (François) **6** Ampère (André-Marie), Perrin (Jean-Baptiste) **7** Coulomb (Charles-Augustin de), Kastler (Alfred), Réaumur (René-Antoine de) **8** Lippmann (Gabriel) ***German:* 3** Ohm (Georg) **4** Laue (Max von), Wien (Wilhelm) **5** Hertz (Gustav, Heinrich), Stark (Johannes), Weber (Wilhelm) **6** Jensen (Hans), Lenard (Philipp), Nernst (Walther), Planck (Max) **7** Meitner (Lise) **8** Roentgen (Wilhelm) **9** Helmholtz (Hermann von), Kirchhoff (Gustav), Mossbauer (Rudolf) **10** Fahrenheit (Daniel), Hofstadter (Robert) ***Indian:* 5** Raman (Chandrasekhara) ***Irish:* 6** Walton (Ernest) ***Italian:* 5** Rossi (Bruno), Volta (Alessandro) **7** Galileo (Galilei), Galvani (Luigi) **10** Torricelli (Evangelista) ***Japanese:* 6** Yukawa (Hideki) **8** Tomonaga (Shinichiro) ***Mexican:* 8** Vallarta (Manuel) ***Russian:* 4** Tamm (Igor) **6** Landau (Lev) **9** Prokhorov (Aleksandr) ***Scottish:* 4** Tait (Peter) **6** Wilson (Charles) **7** Maxwell (James Clerk) ***Swedish:* 7** Rydberg (Johannes) **8** Angstrom (Anders), Siegbahn (Kai, Karl) ***Swiss:* 6** Zwicky (Fritz) **7** Piccard (Auguste) (see also **Nobel Prize winner** *physics*)

physiognomy 3 mug **4** face **5** front **6** aspect, visage **7** profile **8** features **9** character **10** lineaments **11** countenance, temperament

physiologist *English:* 8 Starling (Ernest) ***German:* 5** Weber (Ernst), Wundt (Wilhelm) **7** Schwann (Theodor) **9** Helmholtz (Hermann von) ***Italian:* 11** Spallanzani (Lazzaro) (see also **Nobel Prize winner** *physiology or medicine*)

physique 3 bod **4** body, form **5** build, shape **6** figure, makeup **7** anatomy **9** structure **12** constitution

pianist *American:* 4 Nero (Peter), Tesh (John), Wild (Earl) **5** Janis (Byron), Watts (André) **6** Duchin (Peter), Joplin (Scott), Serkin (Peter, Rudolf) **7** Cliburn (Van), Istomin (Eugene), Ohlsson (Garrick), Perahia (Murray), Winston (George) **8** Graffman

(Gary), Horowitz (Vladimir), Pennario (Leonard) **9** Fleischer (Leon) **10** Johannesen (Grant), Rubinstein (Arthur) ***Argentinian:*** **8** Argerich (Martha) **9** Barenboim (Daniel) ***Austrian:*** **6** Czerny (Karl) **7** Brendel (Alfred) **8** Schnabel (Artur) ***Bulgarian:*** **11** Weissenberg (Alexis) ***Canadian:*** **5** Gould (Glenn) ***Chilean:*** **5** Arrau (Claudio) ***Cuban:*** **5** Bolet (Jorge) ***English:*** **4** Hess (Myra) **5** Ogdon (John) **6** Curzon (Clifford) ***French:*** **6** Cortot (Alfred) **7** Cziffra (Gyorgy) **9** Casadesus (Robert), Entremont (Philippe) **10** Saint-Saëns (Camille) ***German:*** **6** Kempff (Wilhelm) **8** Schumann (Clara) **9** Gieseking (Walter) ***Hungarian:*** **5** Liszt (Franz) **7** Cziffra (Gyorgy) ***Italian:*** **6** Busoni (Ferruccio) **7** Pollini (Maurizio) **8** Clementi (Muzio) ***Japanese:*** **6** Uchida (Mitsuko) ***Polish:*** **6** Chopin (Frédéric) **7** Hofmann (Josef) **10** Paderewski (Ignacy), Rubinstein (Arthur) ***Romanian:*** **4** Lupu (Radu) **7** Lipatti (Dinu) ***Russian:*** **6** Berman (Lazar), Gilels (Emil), Kissin (Evgeny) **7** Richter (Sviatoslav) **8** Horowitz (Vladimir), Pachmann (Vladimir von) **9** Ashkenazy (Vladimir) **10** Rubinstein (Anton) **12** Rachmaninoff (Sergey) ***Spanish:*** **6** Iturbi (José) **8** Granados (Enrique) **10** de Larrocha (Alicia) ***Swiss:*** **4** Anda (Geza) (see also **jazz musician**)

piano **5** grand **6** softly, spinet **7** quietly, upright **9** baby grand ***builder:*** **5** Knabe (William), Stein (Johann), Zumpe (Johann) **7** Baldwin (Dwight) **8** Steinway (Henry) **9** Bechstein (Friedrich) **10** Chickering (Jonas), Silbermann (Johann) ***inventor:*** **10** Cristofori (Bartolomeo) ***keys:*** **7** ivories ***pedal:*** **6** damper **9** sostenuto

piazza **5** patio, plaza, porch **6** square **7** balcony, gallery, portico, terrace, veranda **9** courtyard

picaro **5** rogue, rover, thief **6** pirate **7** brigand, corsair **8** bohemian, sea rover **9** buccaneer **10** freebooter

picayune **5** petty **6** measly, paltry, trifle **7** trivial **8** piddling **11** small-minded **13** insignificant

pick **3** rob, tap **4** best, carp, cull, open, pull, take, tool **5** elect, pluck, probe, prize **6** choice, choose, chosen, option, pierce, pilfer, remove, select, unlock **7** harvest, provoke **8** selected **9** exclusive, single out

picket **4** pale, post **5** fence, guard, stake, watch **6** sentry, tether **7** enclose, lookout, protest **8** palisade, sentinel, watchman **11** demonstrate

pickle **3** fix, jam **4** dill, spot **5** brine, treat **6** plight, scrape **7** dilemma, gherkin, trouble **8** marinate, preserve **10** difficulty **11** predicament

pick on **5** bully, harry, taunt, tease **6** hector, pester **9** criticize, single out

pick out **4** espy, name, spot **6** choose, descry, detect, select, take in **7** discern **8** identify, perceive **9** apprehend, ascertain, recognize **11** distinguish

pickpocket **3** dip **5** thief **6** dipper **8** cutpurse

pick up **3** buy, get **4** cull, gain, earn, land, lift, tidy **5** catch, glean, hoist, learn, raise, run in **6** arrest, detain, gather, notice, obtain, pull in, resume, revive **7** acquire, clean up, collect, restart **8** perceive **9** apprehend **10** appreciate, understand

pickup **3** ute **5** truck **9** detention **10** hitchhiker **11** improvement **12** acceleration

picky **5** fussy **6** choosy **7** finicky **10** fastidious, particular, pernickety **11** persnickety

picnic **4** snap **5** cinch **6** breeze, outing **7** cookout **8** cakewalk **11** piece of cake

picture **4** limn, show **5** image, photo, pinup **7** drawing, tableau **8** describe, painting, portrait **9** depiction, portrayal **10** simulacrum **11** delineation, description **13** spitting image ***stand:*** **5** easel

picturesque **5** vivid **6** quaint, scenic **8** artistic, charming

piddling **4** puny **5** petty **6** meager, meagre, measly, paltry **7** trivial **8** picayune, trifling **11** Mickey Mouse, unimportant **13** insignificant

pie **4** flan, tart **5** pasty **6** pastry **7** cobbler, dessert **8** turnover

piebald **5** mixed **6** motley **7** mottled **10** multicolor, variegated

piece **4** part **5** patch, slice **6** member, parcel **7** firearm, portion, section, segment **8** division, fraction, fragment **9** allotment **10** allocation

pièce de résistance **8** main dish **9** showpiece **11** centerpiece, chef d'oeuvre, masterpiece

piecemeal **5** apart **6** slowly **7** gradual **8** bit by bit **9** by degrees, gradually **11** fragmentary

piece of cake **4** snap **5** cinch **6** breeze, picnic, shoo-in **8** duck soup, kid stuff, pushover

pied **6** motley **7** blotchy, brindle, dappled, mottled **8** brindled, speckled **9** multihued **10** variegated **11** varicolored **12** parti-colored

pier **4** anta, dock, quay, slip **5** berth, jetty, levee, wharf **6** column, pillar **8** pilaster ***architectural:*** **4** anta

pierce **3** cut **4** stab **5** probe, spear **6** impale, incise, skewer **8** puncture **9** penetrate, perforate **10** run through

piercing 4 high, keen 5 acute, sharp 6 piping, shrill 8 shooting, stabbing, strident 9 knifelike 12 earsplitting ***tool:*** 3 awl

piety 6 fealty 7 loyalty 8 devotion, fidelity, sanctity 9 reverence 10 allegiance, dedication, devoutness 12 faithfulness

piffle 4 bosh, bunk 5 bilge, hokum, hooey 6 bunkum, drivel 7 baloney, eyewash, hogwash, rubbish, twaddle 8 malarkey, nonsense, tommyrot 9 poppycock 10 balderdash, codswallop

pig 3 hog 4 Babe, slob 5 Porky, shoat, swine 6 farrow, piglet, porker 7 casting, glutton ***breed:*** 5 Duroc 8 Tamworth 9 Berkshire, Hampshire, Yorkshire ***female:*** 3 sow 4 gilt ***feral:*** 9 razorback ***litter:*** 6 farrow ***male:*** 4 boar 6 barrow ***meat:*** 3 ham 4 pork 5 bacon 7 sausage 8 chitlins 12 chitterlings ***sound:*** 3 wee ***wild:*** 4 boar 7 peccary, warthog 8 babirusa

pigeon 3 Nun, sap 4 dupe, fool, gull, mark 5 chump, decoy, patsy 6 culver, stooge, sucker 7 fall guy, stoolie 8 rock dove ***genus:*** 7 Columba ***house:*** 4 cote, loft ***kind:*** 4 barb, rock 5 homer 6 homing, pouter, roller 7 carrier, crowned, fantail, tumbler ***relative:*** 4 dove ***young:*** 5 squab

pigeon hawk 6 merlin

pigeonhole 4 slot, sort 5 class, cubby, grade, group, niche 6 recess, shelve 7 catalog 8 category, classify, grouping 10 categorize 11 compartment

piggish 6 greedy 7 selfish, swinish 10 gluttonous

pigheaded 5 rigid 6 dogged, mulish 7 willful 8 contrary, perverse, stubborn 9 obstinate 10 inflexible, unyielding

piglet 5 shoat

pigment 3 dye 4 tint 5 color, paint, stain 8 colorant, dyestuff, tincture ***black:*** 9 lampblack ***blue:*** 4 cyan 5 azure, smalt 6 indigo 7 cyanine 8 cerulean 9 verdigris 11 ultramarine ***brown:*** 5 sepia ***umber:*** 6 bister, sienna ***combining form:*** 5 chrom 6 chromo ***dark:*** 7 melanin ***green:*** 7 celadon 8 viridian 10 biliverdin ***orange:*** 7 realgar 8 carotene ***red:*** 4 lake 5 eosin ***toxic:*** 8 gossypol ***yellow:*** 5 ocher, ochre 6 flavin, lutein 7 flavine, xanthin

pigpen 3 sty 4 dump, mess 5 hovel

pigskin 6 saddle 8 football

pike 4 dive, Esox, fish 5 spear 7 highway 8 pickerel

piker 5 miser 7 scrooge 8 tightwad 9 skinflint 10 cheapskate 12 penny-pincher

pilaster 4 pier 6 column, pillar

pilchard 7 herring, sardine

pile 3 fur, lot, nap 4 coat, fill, heap, hill, load, mass, much, pack, peck, pyre, rick 5 amass, crowd, drive, mound, stack 6 bundle, column, jumble 7 collect, fortune, reactor 8 quantity 9 great deal 10 assemblage, collection 11 aggregation 12 accumulation

pileup 4 mass 5 crash, smash 8 accident 9 collision 12 accumulation

pilfer 3 rob 4 lift, take 5 filch, pinch, steal, swipe 6 finger, snitch, thieve 7 purloin 11 appropriate

pilgarlic 4 butt 8 baldhead 13 laughingstock

Pilgrim 5 Alden (John) 6 Carver (John) 7 Puritan, Winslow (Edward) 8 Bradford (William), Brewster (William), Standish (Myles) ***interpreter:*** 7 Squanto ***ship:*** 9 Mayflower

pilgrim 5 hadji, hajji 6 palmer 8 traveler, wanderer, wayfarer

pilgrimage 4 hadj, hajj, trip 7 journey ***destination:*** 5 Mecca 6 Assisi, Delphi, Dodona, Fátima, Medina 7 Lourdes 8 Bodh Gaya 10 Canterbury, Kusinagara

Pilgrim's Progress 8 allegory ***author:*** 6 Bunyan (John) ***hero:*** 9 Christian

pill 4 ball, bore, pain, pest 5 bolus 6 pellet 7 capsule, lozenge 8 medicine, nuisance 9 annoyance

pillage 4 lift, loot, sack 5 booty, prize, reave, reive, spoil, steal 6 maraud, ravage, thieve 7 despoil, plunder, purloin 8 spoliate 9 depredate, desecrate

pillar 4 pier, post, prop 5 pylon, shaft, stela, stele 6 column, stelae (plural) 7 obelisk, support, upright 8 backbone, mainstay, pedestal, pilaster

pillory 6 stocks

pillow 3 pad 4 rest 7 bolster, cushion, support

pillowcase 4 sham

pilot 3 ace 4 lead, show, tool 5 drive, flier, guide, steer 6 airman, direct, leader 7 aviator, conduct, guiding, tracing 8 aviatrix, helmsman, shepherd ***seat:*** 7 cockpit

pimple 3 dot, zit 4 acne, boil, spot, stud 6 papule 7 blemish, blister, pustule, speckle 8 sprinkle, swelling

pin 3 leg, peg 4 clip, hold, join 5 affix, blame, rivet, stake 6 attach, broach, brooch, cotter, emblem, fasten, secure, trifle 8 fastener, hold down, ornament, restrain

pinafore 5 apron, dress, frock

pinch 3 bit, nab, nip 4 dash, lift, pain, take 5 filch, press, prune, run in, skimp, steal, swipe, taper, theft, tweak 6 arrest, crisis, narrow, pilfer, snatch, stress 7 confine, deficit, larceny, squeeze, straits 8 compress, exigency, hardship, juncture, pressure, stealing, straiten **9** apprehend, constrict, emergency, privation, tight spot **10** substitute

pinchbeck 4 fake, sham **5** alloy, bogus, false, phony **6** pseudo **8** spurious **9** brummagem **11** counterfeit

pinch hitter 3 sub **6** backup, fill-in, relief **7** stand-in **9** alternate, surrogate **10** substitute **11** alternative, replacement

pinchpenny 4 mean **5** cheap, close, mingy, tight **6** stingy **7** chintzy, costive, miserly, scrimpy **9** niggardly, penurious **11** close-fisted, tightfisted **12** parsimonious

Pindar *home:* 6 Thebes ***poem:* 3** ode

pine 4 ache, long, mope, sigh, tree, wish, wood **5** brood, crave, dream, yearn **6** desire, grieve, hanker, hunger, lament, thirst **7** conifer **8** languish **9** evergreen ***textile screw:* 3** ara **4** hala **7** lauhala

Pine Tree State 5 Maine

pinhead 4 dolt, dope, fool **5** dunce **6** dimwit, doofus, nitwit **7** dullard **8** dumbbell **9** bird-brain

pinion 3 cog **4** bind, gear, wing **5** quill, tie up, truss **6** fetter, tether **7** disable, feather, shackle **8** cogwheel, restrain **9** hamstring

pink 3 cut **4** best, peak, stab **5** blush **6** flower, height, pierce **7** excited, paragon **9** perforate

pinna 3 ear, fin **4** wing **7** feather, leaflet

pinnacle 3 top, tor **4** acme, apex, peak **5** crest, crown, serac, spire **6** apogee, climax, height, summit, zenith **7** steeple **8** capsheaf, meridian **11** culmination

pinniped 4 seal **6** walrus

Pinocchio author 7 Collodi (Carlo) **9** Lorenzini (Carlo)

pinochle *card:* 3 ace, ten **4** jack, king, nine **5** queen ***term:* 4** meld **5** widow **7** auction ***two-handed:* 7** goulash

pinpoint 3 aim, fix **4** spot, tiny **5** exact, place **6** locate **7** precise **8** identify, stand out **9** determine, highlight, recognize **11** distinguish

Pinter play 8 Betrayal **9** Caretaker (The) **10** Homecoming (The)

pinto 4 pied, pony **5** horse, paint **7** mottled, piebald **8** skewbald

pint-size 3 wee **5** dwarf, small **6** midget, pocket **9** miniature **10** diminutive

pioneer 5 first, prime **6** maiden **7** explore, founder, initial, primary, settler **8** colonist, earliest, explorer, original **9** innovator **10** avant-garde, pathfinder **11** trailblazer **12** frontiersman ***famous:* 5** Boone (Daniel), Bowie (Jim), Clark (William), Lewis (Meriwether) **6** Carson (Kit), Colter (John) **7** Bridger (Jim), Chapman (John), Frémont (John C.), Whitman (Marcus) **8** Crockett (Davy)

pious 4 holy **5** godly **6** devout, worthy **7** devoted, dutiful **8** reverent, virtuous **9** hypocrite, pietistic, prayerful, religious **10** devotional **12** hypocritical

pip 3 dot **4** blip, peep, seed, spot **5** speck **9** break open

pipe 3 keg, tun **4** butt, cask, duct, flue, hose, tube **5** briar **6** barrel, convey, funnel, siphon **7** channel, conduct, conduit **8** aqueduct, hogshead **10** meerschaum ***ceremonial:* 7** calumet ***part:* 4** bowl, stem

pipe down 4 hush **5** dry up, quiet **6** shut up **7** be quiet

pipe dream 4 wish **7** chimera, fantasy **8** illusion

pipeline 5 works **6** system **7** channel, conduit, process **8** activity, supplier **10** connection

pipsqueak 6 shaver, squirt **7** tadpole **8** half-pint, small fry

piquancy 4 zest **5** gusto **6** relish

piquant 4 racy, tart **5** sharp, spicy, tangy, zesty **6** biting, lively, savory, snappy **7** peppery, pungent **8** poignant, spirited **9** flavorful, sparkling **10** appetizing **11** provocative, stimulating

pique 3 irk, vex **4** huff, miff, move **5** anger, annoy, peeve, pride, rouse **6** arouse, excite, nettle, offend, put out **7** dudgeon, offense, provoke, quicken **8** irritate, motivate, vexation **9** aggravate, annoyance, challenge, stimulate **10** exasperate, irritation, resentment

piracy 5 theft **7** lifting, looting, pillage, plunder, robbery **8** stealing, thievery **10** plagiarism

piranha 6 caribe

pirate 5 rover **6** looter, picaro, raider, robber, sea dog **7** brigand, corsair, sea wolf **8** marauder, picaroon, pillager, sea rover **9** buccaneer, plunderer, privateer, sea robber **10** freebooter ***address:* 5** matey ***English:* 4** Read (Mary) **5** Bonny (Anne), Teach (Edward) **6** Morgan (Henry) **7** Dampier (William) **10** Blackbeard ***flag:* 10** Jolly Roger ***French:* 7** Laffite (Jean), Lafitte (Jean) ***Scottish:* 4** Kidd (William)

Pirates of Penzance, The *composer:* 8 Sullivan (Arthur) ***librettist:* 7** Gilbert (W. S.)

pirogue 5 canoe **6** dugout

pirouette 4 spin, turn **5** twirl, wheel, whirl

piscator 6 angler **9** fisherman

pismire 3 ant

pistol 3 gat, rod **4** Colt **5** Glock, Luger **6** Magnum, Mauser, roscoe **7** bulldog, handgun **8** revolver, small arm **9** derringer, pepperbox ***case:*** **7** holster

pit 3 vie **4** dent, hell, hole, scar **5** arena, hades, match, shaft, stone **6** cavity, hollow, oppose **7** counter, play off **8** pockmark **11** indentation

Pit and the Pendulum author 3 Poe (Edgar Allan)

pitch 3 dip, set **4** buck, dive, drop, fall, hurl, line, play, plug, tilt, tone, toss **5** erect, fling, heave, lurch, put up, resin, slant, sling, slope, spiel, throw **6** encamp, go down, plunge **7** discard, incline, present, promote, sidearm **8** distance **9** advertise, declivity **13** advertisement ***uneven:*** **3** rub

pitch-dark 3 jet **4** ebon, inky **5** black, ebony, jetty

pitcher 4 ewer, olla, olpe, toby **5** cruse **6** beaker, flagon **7** creamer ***area:*** **5** mound ***handle:*** **3** ear **4** ansa see also **baseballer**

pitch in 3 aid **4** help **5** begin, set to, start **6** fall to **8** commence, get going, start off **9** subscribe, volunteer **10** contribute

piteous 3 sad **4** poor **8** pathetic **9** affecting **10** lamentable **11** distressing

pitfall 4 risk, snag, trap **5** catch, peril, snare **6** danger, hazard **9** booby trap **10** difficulty **12** entanglement

pith 3 nub **4** core, kill, meat, pulp **5** focus, heart **6** center, import, kernel **7** essence, nucleus **9** substance **10** importance **12** significance

pith helmet 4 topi **5** topee

pithy 5 brief, crisp, meaty, short, terse **6** cogent **7** compact, concise, pointed **8** succinct **12** epigrammatic **13** short and sweet

pitiable 4 poor **5** cheap, sorry **8** shameful **10** deplorable, lamentable **12** contemptible

pitiful 3 sad **4** mean, poor **5** cheap, sorry **6** meager, meagre, paltry, shabby **7** forlorn **8** beggarly, pathetic, wretched **9** miserable **10** despicable, inadequate **12** contemptible **13** heartbreaking

pitiless 4 cold, hard **5** cruel, harsh, stony **6** brutal **8** inhumane, uncaring **9** barbarous, unfeeling **10** unmerciful **11** coldhearted, hardhearted

pittance 4 wage **5** scrap, trace **6** trifle **7** modicum, peanuts **9** allowance

pity 3 rue **4** ache, ruth **5** mercy **6** regret, sorrow **7** empathy, feel for, sadness **8** distress, sympathy **10** compassion, condolence, sympathize **11** commiserate **13** commiseration

pivot 3 pin **4** slew, slue, turn **5** hinge, shaft, swing, wheel **6** center, swivel

pivotal 3 key **5** chief, vital **7** central, crucial **8** critical, decisive **9** essential, important

pixie 3 elf, fay, imp **5** antic, fairy, scamp **6** elvish, impish, rascal, sprite **7** brownie, coltish, playful, puckish **8** prankish **11** mischievous

pixilated 3 fey **7** bemused, erratic, flighty, muddled, touched **9** eccentric, whimsical **10** capricious

Pizarro, Francisco *brother:* **7** Gonzalo ***city founded:*** **4** Lima ***conquest:*** **4** Peru ***victims:*** **5** Incas **9** Atahualpa **10** Atahuallpa

pizzazz 3 pep, vim, zip **4** bang, brio, dash, élan, snap, zest, zing **5** éclat, flair, flash, gusto, moxie, oomph, punch, verve **6** dazzle, energy, hoopla, sizzle, spirit **7** glamour, panache **8** vitality **10** excitement

placard 4 bill, post **6** notice, plaque, poster **7** affiche **8** handbill

placate 4 calm, ease **6** pacify, soothe **7** appease, assuage, comfort, mollify, satisfy, sweeten, win over **10** conciliate, propitiate

place 3 lay, put, set **4** area, lieu, loci (plural), post, rank, site, spot, zone **5** locus, point, stead, tract **6** region, status **7** situate, station **8** district, identify, locality, location, pinpoint, position, standing **9** establish, recognize ***combining form:*** **3** top **4** loco, topo, topy

placid 4 calm, easy, mild **5** quiet, still **6** gentle, serene **7** halcyon **8** composed, peaceful, tranquil, waveless, windless **9** unruffled **10** complacent, unagitated, untroubled **11** undisturbed **13** imperturbable

plagiarize 4 copy, crib **5** steal **6** pirate **11** appropriate

plague 3 vex **4** bane, evil, pest **5** annoy, beset, curse, harry, hound, smite, trial, worry **6** blight, bother, infest, harass, hassle, hector, pester **7** afflict, bedevil, disease, disturb, scourge, torment, trouble **8** calamity, distress, epidemic, invasion, irritant, irritate, nuisance, outbreak, pandemic **9** annoyance, beleaguer **10** affliction, black death, pestilence **11** infestation

plaid 6 tartan

plain 3 lea **4** bald, bare, open, pure, veld **5** blunt, clear, field, frank, llano, pampa, usual, veldt **6** candid, common, homely, modest, pampas, patent, severe, simple, steppe, tundra **7** expanse, evident, obvious, prairie, savanna **8** apparent, distinct, everyday, homespun, manifest, ordinary, savannah, straight **9** outspoken, unadorned **10** absolutely, forthright, unaffected **11** undecorated, unvarnished **13** uncomplicated

plainclothesman 3 tec **4** dick **6** shamus,

sleuth **7** gumshoe **8** hawkshaw **9** detective **12** investigator

plainness 6 candor, purity **7** clarity, honesty **8** lucidity **10** simplicity

plainsong 5 chant **12** cantus firmus

plainspoken 4 open **5** frank **6** candid, direct, honest **8** straight, truthful **10** forthright **11** undisguised, unvarnished

plaintive 3 sad **4** glum **6** woeful **7** doleful, piteous, pitiful **8** dolorous, downcast, mournful **9** sorrowful **10** dispirited, lamentable, lugubrious, melancholy

plait 4 fold **5** braid, pleat, weave **7** pigtail **10** intertwine, interweave

plan 3 aim, map, way **4** cast, goal, idea, mean, plot **5** chart, frame **6** design, devise, intend, intent, lay out, map out, method, scheme, set out **7** arrange, diagram, drawing, outline, pattern, program, project, propose, purpose, work out **8** contrive, engineer, organize, strategy, think out **9** blueprint, formulate, intention, procedure **11** arrangement, formulation

plane 3 fly **4** even, flat, tool, tree **5** flush, level **6** smooth (see also **airplane**)

planet 4 Mars **5** Earth, Venus **6** Saturn, Uranus **7** Jupiter, Mercury, Neptune ***dwarf:* 4** Eris **5** Ceres, Pluto ***path:* 5** orbit ***satellite:* 4** moon ***shadow:* 5** umbra ***small:* 8** asteroid

planetary 4 vast **6** global **7** erratic, immense **8** colossal, enormous **9** universal, wandering, worldwide **11** terrestrial

plangent 7 orotund, ringing, vibrant **8** resonant, sonorous **9** consonant, plaintive **10** expressive, resounding **11** reverberant

plank 4 item, wood **5** board, floor **6** lumber, timber **7** article, support

plant 3 fix, pot, set, sow **4** bury, grow, hide, mill, park, root, seed, tomb **5** cache, cover, imbed, inter, place, plunk, put in, stash, works **6** entomb, inhume, occult, screen **7** conceal, factory, install, lay away, put away, secrete **8** colonize, populate **9** cultivate ***angiosperm:* 5** dicot **7** monocot ***aquatic:* 4** reed **5** lotus, sedge **7** awlwort, cattail, fanwort, papyrus **8** duckweed, eelgrass, hornwort, pondweed **9** water lily **10** watercress **11** bladderwort **12** pickerelweed ***aromatic:* 4** nard **6** lovage **9** spikenard ***Australian:* 6** mallee **7** banksia **8** blackboy **10** eucalyptus ***body:* 4** stem **7** thallus ***bulbous:* 4** Ixia, lily **5** camas, onion, tulip **7** jonquil **8** hyacinth **9** narcissus ***carnivorous:* 6** sundew **10** butterwort **12** pitcher plant, Venus flytrap ***cell layer:* 7** phellem ***climbing:* 3** ivy **4** vine **5** betel, liana, vetch **6** bryony, derris, smilax **7** creeper, jasmine **8** bignonia, fumitory, moonseed, scammony, wisteria **12** morning glory ***coloring agent:* 8** carotene **11** chlorophyll, xanthophyll ***combining form:* 4** phyt **5** phyto ***cone-bearing:* 3** fir, yew **4** pine **5** cedar, cycad **6** ginkgo, spruce **7** conifer, cypress, redwood **10** arborvitae, gymnosperm ***desert:* 4** aloe **5** agave **6** cactus, cholla **8** mesquite, ocotillo **9** paloverde **11** brittlebush ***disease:* 3** rot **4** gall, mold, rust, scab, smut, wilt **5** ergot **6** blight, mildew, mosaic **7** blister **8** clubroot **9** black spot **10** black heart ***extinct:* 8** calamite ***flowerless:* 4** alga, fern, kelp, moss **5** algae (plural), fungi (plural) **6** fungus, lichen **7** seaweed **8** clubmoss **9** bryophyte, equisetum, horsetail, liverwort ***fluid:* 3** gum, sap **4** milk **5** latex, resin ***gland:* 7** nectary ***hallucinogenic:* 4** hemp **5** poppy **6** mescal **8** cannabis **9** marijuana ***hard-to-grow:* 5** miffy ***largest:* 7** sequoia ***life:* 5** flora ***marine:* 4** kelp, nori **5** dulse, fucus **6** wakame **7** seaweed **8** gulfweed **10** sea lettuce ***marsh:* 4** reed **5** carex, sedge **7** bogbean, bulrush, calamus, cattail **8** red maple, sphagnum **10** rose mallow **11** loosestrife ***medicinal:* 4** aloe, sage **5** poppy, senna, tansy **6** catnip, fennel, garlic, hyssop, ipecac, nettle **7** aconite, boneset, burdock, camphor, comfrey, ginseng, hemlock, henbane, juniper, lobelia, mullein, mustard, parsley **8** camomile, capsicum, cinchona, feverfew, licorice, pilewort, plantain, wormwood **9** asafetida, chamomile, dandelion, echinacea, fenugreek, monkshood **10** asafoetida, goldenseal, peppermint ***microscopic:* 4** mold **6** diatom **7** euglena **8** bacteria (plural) **9** bacterium ***oldest:* 11** bristlecone ***onion-like:* 4** leek **5** chive **7** shallot **8** scallion ***opening:* 5** stoma **7** stomata (plural) ***parasitic:* 6** dodder, fungus **7** pinesap **8** gerardia **9** broomrape, mistletoe, rafflesia, witchweed **10** beechdrops ***part:* 3** bud, nut, sap **4** bark, bulb, cell, cone, corm, leaf, pome, root, seed, stem, wood **5** bract, drupe, fruit, grain, spore, stool, thorn, tuber, xylem **6** catkin, flower, nectar, phloem, raceme, spadix **7** rhizome **8** lenticel **9** cellulose, cotyledon **11** chlorophyll, chloroplast **13** inflorescence ***pepper:* 3** ava **4** kava ***pest:* 5** aphid, scale **6** chafer, thrips, weevil **7** cutworm **8** fruit fly, wireworm **9** gypsy moth **10** cankerworm, leafhopper, phylloxera **11** codling moth ***poisonous:* 4** poke, upas **5** sumac **6** castor, croton, datura **7** amanita, cassava, cowbane, henbane, lobelia, tobacco **8** foxglove, larkspur, locoweed, mayapple, oleander, pokeweed **9** baneberry, monkshood **10** belladonna, jimsonweed, manchineel, nightshade ***saprophytic:*** **5** fungi (plural) **6** fungus **7** pinesap **9** pinedrops, snow plant **10** beechdrops, Indian pipe ***succulent:*** **4** aloe **5** agave **6** cactus **10** bitterroot ***thorny:*** **4** rose **5** briar **6** cactus, nettle, teasel **7** caltrop, thistle **9** cocklebur ***tissue:*** **5** xylem **6** phloem **7** cambium, medulla **8** meristem ***young:*** **5** scion, shoot **6** sprout **7** cutting **8** seedling

plantain 5 fruit **6** banana

plantation 5 manor **6** colony, estate, quinta **7** acreage, demesne **8** hacienda **10** encampment, habitation, settlement

plant louse 5 aphid

plaque 4 film **5** badge, patch **6** brooch, lesion, tablet **7** tribute **8** bacteria, memorial **13** commemoration

plaster 3 dab **4** coat **5** affix, cover, gesso **6** stucco **7** coating, conceal, overlay **8** dressing ***of paris:*** **5** gesso **6** gypsum

plastered 3 lit **4** high **5** drunk, lit up, oiled **6** bashed, blotto, bombed, juiced, potted, soaked, soused, stewed, stoned, tanked, wasted, zonked **7** crocked, drunken, pickled, pie-eyed, sloshed, smashed, sottish **10** inebriated, liquored up **11** intoxicated

plastic 4 soft **5** vinyl **6** pliant, supple **7** ductile, pliable **8** creative, flexible, moldable, workable **9** adaptable, formative, malleable, synthetic **10** artificial, credit card, sculptural

plat 3 lot, map **4** plan **5** chart, tract **6** parcel **7** quadrat

plate 4 base, coat, disc, dish, disk, gild, tile **5** layer, paten, scute, slice **6** enamel, fascia, lamina, plaque **7** anodize, lamella, overlay

plateau 4 mesa **5** table **6** upland **9** altiplano, tableland ***arid:*** **4** puna ***barren:*** **5** field **6** paramo ***dry:*** **5** karoo **6** karroo

platform 3 map **4** bank, base, dais, deck, plan **5** bimah, forum, ledge, riser, shelf, stage, stump **6** design, pallet, perron, podium, pulpit, scheme **7** balcony, pattern, rostrum **8** hustings, scaffold **9** banquette, manifesto **11** declaration ***temporary:*** **7** staging **8** scaffold ***wooden:*** **9** boardwalk

Plath, Sylvia *novel:* 7 Bell Jar (The) ***poem:*** **5** Ariel, Daddy

platinum symbol 2 Pt

platitude 6 cliché, truism **7** bromide **8** banality, prosaism **10** shibboleth

Plato *father:* 7 Ariston ***literary form:*** **6** dialog **8** dialogue ***original name:*** **10** Aristocles ***school:*** **7** Academy ***work:*** **3** Ion **4** Meno **5** Crito, Lysis **6** Laches, Phaedo **7** Apology, Gorgias **8** Phaedrus, Republic (The) **9** Charmides, Symposium

platter 5 plate **6** record **8** trencher

platypus 8 duckbill

plaudits 5 kudos **6** cheers, praise **7** acclaim, ovation **8** applause, approval, encomium **9** accolades **11** acclamation

plausible 8 credible, specious **10** believable, convincing, creditable, persuasive, reasonable

play 3 act, fun **4** game, jest, joke, romp **5** drama, feint, serve, sport, treat, trick, wager **6** cavort, comedy, fiddle, frolic, gambit, gambol, leeway, margin **7** delight, disport, perform **8** latitude, pleasure **9** amusement, diversion, enjoyment, stratagem **10** manipulate, recreation ***an instrument:*** **3** bow **4** beat, blow, pick **5** pluck, sound, strum **6** strike **7** squeeze ***kind:*** **5** farce **6** comedy **7** musical, tragedy **8** one-acter **9** melodrama, pantomime ***part:*** **3** act **5** scene **8** epilogue, prologue ***passionate:*** **9** melodrama ***site:*** **8** stage set

playact 5 put on **7** perform, posture, pretend **9** personate **11** impersonate, make believe

playboy 4 rake, roué **7** swinger **8** hedonist, lothario **9** bon vivant, libertine

play down 8 minimize **9** deprecate, soft-pedal, underrate **11** de-emphasize

player 5 actor **6** mummer **7** actress, athlete, trouper **8** musician, thespian **9** contender, performer **10** competitor, contestant **11** participant ***reserve:*** **11** benchwarmer

player piano 7 Pianola **10** Disklavier

play for time 5 stall

playful 5 antic, jolly, ludic, merry, pixie **6** elvish, frisky, impish, jocund, joking, jovial, lively **7** coltish, jocular, puckish, waggish **8** humorous, sportive **9** kittenish, sprightly **10** frolicsome

play off 3 pit, vie **5** match **6** oppose **7** counter **8** contrast

plaything 3 toy

play up 6 stress **7** feature **9** dramatize, emphasize, highlight, overstate, underline **10** accentuate, exaggerate, underscore

playwright 9 dramatist **10** dramaturge (see also **dramatist**)

plaza 6 circus, common, square, zocalo **9** carrefour **11** marketplace

plea 4 suit **5** alibi **6** appeal, excuse, orison, prayer **7** apology, defense, pretext, request **8** entreaty, overture, petition **11** application, imploration **12** supplication ***defendant's:*** **4** nolo **6** guilty **8** innocent **9** not guilty

plead 3 beg **4** pray **5** argue **6** allege, answer, appeal **7** beseech, entreat, implore **8** advocate, maintain **9** importune **10** supplicate

pleasant 4 fair, fine, good, nice **5** clear, sunny, sweet **6** cheery, genial, pretty **7** amiable, clarion, likable, welcome **8** amicable, charming, cheerful, engaging, gracious, grateful, likeable, pleasing, sunshine, sunshiny **9** agreeable, appealing, cloudless, congenial, convivial, enjoyable, favorable, unclouded **10** delightful, gratifying

pleasantry 3 fun **4** jest, joke **6** banter, levity **8** badinage, repartee **9** wittiness **10** jocularity

please 4 like, suit, wish **5** agree, amuse, enjoy, serve **6** choose **7** content, delight, gladden, gratify, indulge, satisfy ***French:*** **12** s'il vous plait ***German:*** **5** bitte ***Spanish:*** **8** por favor

pleasing 4 good, nice **6** pretty **7** welcome **8** suitable **9** agreeable, congenial, favorable, palatable **10** attractive, delightful, gratifying **12** satisfactory

pleasure 3 fun, joy **4** will **5** bliss, fancy **6** desire, liking, relish **7** delight, gladden, gratify **8** felicity, gladness, hedonism **9** amusement, diversion, enjoyment, happiness, merriment **11** inclination

pleat 4 fold **5** crimp **6** crease

plebe 5 frosh **8** freshman

plebeian 3 low **4** base **5** crude, lowly **6** coarse, common, humble, menial **8** commoner, everyday, ordinary **10** lower-class

plebiscite 4 vote

plectrum 4 pick

pledge 3 vow **4** bail, bind, bond, gage, hock, oath, pawn, seal, sign, word **5** drink, swear, toast, token **6** parole, plight, surety **7** chattel, earnest, promise, warrant **8** bailment, contract, covenant, guaranty, security, warranty **9** agreement, assurance, certainty, guarantee, undertake **11** hypothecate

pledget 3 pad **8** compress

Pleiades 4 Maia **6** Merope **7** Alcyone, Celaeno, Electra, Sterope, Taygeta **8** Asterope ***brightest star:*** **7** Alcyone

plenary 4 full **5** whole **6** entire **7** general **8** absolute, complete **9** inclusive **11** unqualified **12** unrestricted

plenitude 4 glut **6** excess **7** satiety, surfeit **8** fullness **9** abundance, profusion, repletion **11** copiousness, sufficiency, superfluity **12** completeness

plenteous 7 fertile **8** abundant, fruitful, prolific **9** abounding **10** productive

plentiful 4 full, rich, rife **5** ample, flush **7** copious, profuse **8** abundant, affluent, generous **9** abounding, bounteous, unstinted **10** sufficient

plenty 3 lot **4** heap, lots, pack, peck, pile **6** stacks, wealth **8** adequacy, fullness, mountain **9** abundance, affluence, great deal **10** cornucopia

pleonasm 8 verbiage **9** prolixity, tautology, verbosity, wordiness **10** redundancy **11** periphrasis, superfluity

plethora 4 glut **5** flood **6** excess **7** overrun, surfeit, surplus **8** fullness, overflow **9** abundance, profusion, repletion **11** superfluity **13** overabundance

plexus 4 rete **7** network

pliable 6 supple **7** plastic **9** adaptable **10** adjustable **11** complaisant, manipulable

pliant 5 lithe **6** limber, supple **7** ductile, plastic, springy **8** flexible, moldable, workable, yielding **9** adaptable, malleable, tractable **10** manageable

plica 4 fold **6** crease, groove

plight 3 fix, jam, vow **4** hole, spot, word **5** swear **6** engage, pickle, pledge, scrape **7** betroth, dilemma, promise **8** quandary **9** betrothal **10** difficulty, engagement **11** predicament

plod 4 slog, toil **5** grind, slave, tramp, tread, tromp **6** drudge, lumber, trudge **8** plug away

plot 3 map **4** area, land, mark, note, plan, ruse **5** cabal, chart, story, tract **6** design, devise, invent, lay out, locate, parcel, scheme **7** collude, compact, connive, diagram, outline **8** conspire, contrive, intrigue, scenario **9** collusion, conniving, machinate **10** complicity, connivance, conspiracy **11** machination

plover 5 pewit, stilt **6** peewit **7** lapwing **8** dotterel, killdeer ***relative:*** **9** sandpiper, turnstone

plow 3 dig **4** till, turn **5** break **6** furrow, harrow, trench **8** turn over **9** cultivate ***part:*** **4** beam, frog **5** share **7** coulter **8** landside **9** moldboard

ploy 4 ruse, scam, wile **5** feint, trick **6** device, frolic, gambit, tactic **7** gimmick **8** artifice, escapade, maneuver **9** stratagem **11** contrivance

pluck 3 rob, tug **4** grit, guts, pick, pull, yank **5** cheek, grasp, heart, moxie, nerve, spunk **6** daring, fleece, mettle, remove, snatch, spirit, tweeze **7** bravery, courage, pull out

plucky 4 bold, game **5** brave **6** feisty, spunky **7** doughty **8** fearless, spirited, unafraid **9** dauntless **10** courageous

plug 3 tap **4** bung, clog, core, cork, fill, hype, pack, push, stop, tout **5** block, blurb, boost, choke, close, cry up, shoot, spile **6** device, remedy **7** congest, fitting, hydrant, promote, stopper **8** obstruct **9** advertise, publicity, publicize **10** connection

plug-ugly 4 goon, thug **5** bully, rowdy, tough

7 goombah, hoodlum, ruffian 8 enforcer 9 roughneck

plum 5 prize 6 purple, reward 7 guerdon, premium 8 dividend ***dried:*** 5 prune ***kind:*** 6 damson 7 bullace 9 greengage ***spiny:*** 4 sloe 10 blackthorn

plumage 8 feathers ***early:*** 4 down

plumb 5 delve, probe, sound 6 fathom, weight 7 examine, explore, install, measure 8 vertical 10 vertically 13 perpendicular

plume 4 tail 5 array, preen, pride, prize 6 column 7 feather 8 aigrette

plummet 4 dive, drop, fall 5 crash 6 plunge, tumble 8 collapse, nose-dive 11 precipitate

plump 3 fat 4 drop, fall, full 5 ample, buxom, favor, pudgy, round, stout, tubby 6 chubby, portly, rotund, zaftig 7 rounded, support 8 roly-poly 9 pneumatic 10 Rubenesque

plumply 7 frankly, plainly 8 candidly 12 forthrightly

plunder 3 rob 4 loot, sack, swag, take 5 booty, prize, seize, spoil, steal, strip 6 boodle, rapine, spoils 7 despoil, pillage, ransack, relieve, stick up 9 pillaging

plunge 3 bet, ram, run 4 dive, drop, fall, jump, rush, sink, stab, swim 5 drive, lunge, pitch, stick 6 charge, gamble, hasten, hurtle, thrust, topple, tumble 7 descend, immerse, plummet 8 nose-dive, submerge 9 penetrate

plus 3 and 4 also, more, perk 5 added, asset, bonus, boost, extra 6 excess 7 benefit 8 addition, increase, positive

plush 4 full, rich 6 deluxe, fabric, lavish, velvet 7 opulent 8 luscious, palatial 9 expensive, luxuriant, luxurious, sumptuous

Pluto 3 Dis 5 Hades ***brother:*** 4 Zeus 7 Jupiter, Neptune 8 Poseidon ***father:*** 6 Cronus, Saturn ***mother:*** 3 Ops 4 Rhea ***wife:*** 10 Persephone, Proserpina

plutocrat 5 mogul 6 fat cat, tycoon 7 magnate 9 financier, moneybags 10 capitalist

plutonian 8 infernal 10 underworld

plutonium symbol 2 Pu

Plutus ***father:*** 6 Iasion ***god of:*** 6 riches, wealth ***mother:*** 5 Ceres 7 Demeter

ply 3 use 4 bias, sail 5 apply, exert, layer, wield 6 employ, handle, strand, supply, travel, voyage 7 furnish, perform 8 maneuver, practice 11 inclination

pneuma 4 soul 5 anima 6 psyche, spirit

pneumatic 4 airy 5 ample, buxom, plump 6 aerial, zaftig 9 spiritual 10 curvaceous 11 atmospheric

poach 4 cook 5 steal 6 coddle, simmer 7 intrude 8 encroach, trespass 9 interlope 11 appropriate

Pocahontas ***father:*** 8 Powhatan ***husband:*** 5 Rolfe (John)

pock 3 pit 4 hole, spot 7 pustule

pocket 3 bag 4 lift, sack 5 filch, pinch, pouch, purse, steal, swipe 6 cavity 7 capsule, dead end, impasse 8 cul-de-sac 9 condensed 10 blind alley ***billiards:*** 4 pool

pocketbook 3 bag 4 poke 5 purse 6 clutch, income, wallet 7 handbag 8 billfold 9 clutch bag

pocket bread 4 pita 5 pitta

pocket money 6 change 9 petty cash 11 small change

pocket-size 4 tiny 5 small 9 miniature 10 diminutive

pod 3 bag, gam, sac 4 boll, case, hull, husk, skin 5 shell, shuck 6 cocoon 7 capsule, silique 8 seedcase ***plant:*** 3 pea 4 bean, okra 5 chili, gumbo 6 cassia, cowpea, legume, lentil, peanut, pepper 8 capsicum, mesquite, milkweed 9 lespedeza

pod-bearing tree 5 carob 6 locust 7 catalpa

podiatry 9 chiropody

podium 4 dais 6 pulpit 7 lectern, rostrum 8 platform

____ **podrida** 4 olla

Poe, Edgar Allan ***detective:*** 5 Dupin (C. Auguste) ***poem:*** 5 Bells (The), Raven (The) 6 Lenore 7 Israfel, To Helen, Ulalume 8 Eldorado, For Annie 10 Annabel Lee ***tale:*** 6 Ligeia, Shadow 7 Gold-Bug (The), Morella, Silence 8 Black Cat (The) 13 Tell-tale Heart (The) 15 Purloined Letter (The) 17 Cask of Amontillado (The), Pit and the Pendulum (The) 19 Masque of the Red Death (The) 21 Fall of the House of Usher (The)

poem 3 ode 4 epic, epos, idyl, rime, rune, song 5 ditty, elegy, epode, idyll, lyric, rhyme, verse 6 ballad, epopee, jingle, rondel, sonnet 7 eclogue, rondeau 8 limerick, madrigal ***closing:*** 5 envoi, envoy ***division:*** 4 foot, line 5 canto, epode, stich, verse 6 stanza 7 refrain 8 epilogue, prologue ***Japanese:*** 5 haiku, tanka ***of eight lines:*** 6 octave 7 triolet ***of four lines:*** 8 quatrain ***of fourteen lines:*** 6 sonnet ***of three lines:*** 7 triplet ***pastoral:*** 7 eclogue, georgic ***short:*** 5 ditty 7 epigram

poet 4 bard, muse, scop 5 skald 6 lyrist 7 elegist 8 idyllist, lyricist 9 balladist, sonneteer 10 Parnassian ***American:*** 3 Poe (Edgar Allan) 4 Dove (Rita), Hass (Robert), Nash (Ogden), Read (Thomas), Rich (Adrienne), Ryan (Kay), Tabb (John Banister), Tate (Allen) 5 Auden (Wystan Hugh), Benét (Stephen Vincent), Crane (Hart), Field (Eugene), Frost (Robert), Guest (Edgar), Moore (Marianne), Plath (Sylvia), Pound (Ezra), Riley (James Whitcomb), Wylie (Elinor) **6** Barlow (Joel), Bishop (Elizabeth), Brooks (Gwendolyn), Bryant (William Cullen), Ciardi (John), Dickey (James), Dunbar (Paul Laurence), Hughes (Langston), Kilmer (Joyce), Lanier (Sidney), Lowell (Amy, James Russell, Robert), McKuen (Rod), Millay (Edna St. Vincent), Pinsky (Robert), Ransom (John Crowe), Seeger (Alan), Strand (Mark), Taylor (Edward), Warren (Robert Penn), Wilbur (Richard) **7** Angelou (Maya), Ashbery (John), Collins (Billy), Emerson (Ralph Waldo), Freneau (Philip), Halleck (Fitz-Greene), Jeffers (Robinson), Lindsay (Vachel), Markham (Edwin), Merrill (James), Nemerov (Howard), Roethke (Theodore), Shapiro (Karl), Stevens (Wallace), Whitman (Walt) **8** Berryman (John), Cummings (E. E.), Ginsberg (Allen), MacLeish (Archibald), Robinson (Edwin Arlington), Sandburg (Carl), Teasdale (Sara), Wheatley (Phillis), Whittier (John Greenleaf), Williams (C. K., William Carlos) **9** Dickinson (Emily), Santayana (George) **10** Bradstreet (Anne), Longfellow (Henry Wadsworth) **12** Wigglesworth (Michael) ***Anglo-Saxon:*** **7** Caedmon, Cynwulf **8** Cynewulf, Kynewulf ***Arab:*** **5** Jarir **6** Hariri **8** al-Hariri ***Australian:*** **8** Paterson (Andrew Barton) ***Belgian:*** **11** Maeterlinck (Maurice) ***Canadian:*** **5** Pratt (Edwin John) **6** Hébert (Anne) **7** Roberts (Charles G. D.), Service (Robert) **8** Drummond (William Henry) **9** Fréchette (Louis-Honoré) ***Chilean:*** **6** Neruda (Pablo) **7** Mistral (Gabriela) ***Chinese:*** **4** Li Po, Tu Fu **7** Wang Wei ***Danish:*** **4** Rode (Helge) **5** Ewald (Johannes) ***English:*** **3** Gay (John) **4** Gray (Thomas), Owen (Wilfred), Pope (Alexander), Rowe (Nicholas), Tate (Nahum), Wyat (Thomas) **5** Blake (William), Byron (Lord), Carew (Thomas), Clare (John), Donne (John), Eliot (Thomas Stearns), Gower (John), Hardy (Thomas), Keats (John), Noyes (Alfred), Wilde (Oscar), Wyatt (Thomas), Young (Edward) **6** Arnold (Matthew), Austin (Alfred), Belloc (Hilaire), Brooke (Rupert), Butler (Samuel), Clough (Arthur Hugh), Cowper (William), Dryden (John), Graves (Robert), Larkin (Philip), Milton (John), Savage (Richard), Sidney (Philip), Surrey (Earl of), Symons (Arthur), Waller (Edmund), Warton (Thomas), Watson (William), Wotton (Henry) **7** Bridges (Robert), Campion (Thomas), Chaucer (Geoffrey), Gilbert (W. S.), Herbert (George), Herrick (Robert), Hopkins (Gerard Manley), Housman (A. E.), Kipling (Rudyard), Layamon, Marvell (Andrew), Patmore (Coventry), Quarles (Francis), Shelley (Percy Bysshe), Skelton (John), Southey (Robert), Spender (Stephen), Spenser (Edmund) **8** Betjeman (John), Browning (Elizabeth Barrett, Robert), de la Mare (Walter), Langland (William), Lovelace (Richard), Meredith (George), Rossetti (Christina, Dante Gabriel), Suckling (John), Tennyson (Alfred Lord), Thompson (Francis) **9** Coleridge (Samuel Taylor), Masefield (John), Swinburne (Algernon Charles) **10** Chatterton (Thomas), FitzGerald (Edward), Wordsworth (William) **11** Shakespeare (William) ***Finnish:*** **8** Runeberg (Johan Ludvig) ***French:*** **5** Marot (Clément) **6** Musset (Alfred de), Valéry (Paul), Villon (François) **7** Bourget (Paul), Chénier (André de, Marie-Joseph), Gautier (Théophile), Rimbaud (Arthur), Ronsard (Pierre de) **8** Malherbe (François de), Mallarmé (Stéphane), Verlaine (Paul) **9** Lamartine (Alphonse de) **10** Baudelaire (Charles) **11** Apollinaire (Guillaume) ***German:*** **5** Heine (Heinrich), Rilke (Rainer Maria), Sachs (Hans), Storm (Theodor) **6** Brecht (Bertolt), Goethe (Johann Wolfgang von), Uhland (Ludwig) **7** Walther (von der Vogelweide), Wolfram (von Eschenbach) **8** Schiller (Friedrich von) **9** Klopstock (Friedrich Gottlieb) **10** Tannhäuser ***Greek:*** **5** Arion, Homer **6** Elytis (Odysseus), Erinna, Hesiod, Pindar, Ritsos (Yannis), Sappho **7** Agathon, Alcaeus, Orpheus, Seferis (George), Thespis **8** Anacreon **9** Simonides **10** Apollonius, Theocritus ***Hindu:*** **5** Naidu (Sarojini) **6** Tagore (Rabindranath) **8** Kalidasa, Tulsidas ***Hungarian:*** **6** Petofi (Sandor), Zrinyi (Miklos) ***Irish:*** **5** Moore (Thomas), Wolfe (Charles), Yeats (William Butler) **6** Heaney (Seamus) **7** Dunsany (Lord), Muldoon (Paul) **8** Drummond (William Henry), MacNeice (Louis) ***Italian:*** **4** Rosa (Salvator), Vida (Marco) **5** Dante (Alighieri), Tasso (Torquato) **7** Ariosto (Ludovico), Manzoni (Alessandro), Montale (Eugenio) **8** Carducci (Giosuè), Leopardi (Giacomo), Petrarch **9** Boccaccio (Giovanni), D'Annunzio (Gabriele), Marinetti (Filippo Tommaso), Quasimodo (Salvatore), Ungaretti (Giuseppe) ***Japanese:*** **5** Basho **6** Matsuo ***medieval:*** **8** minstrel, trouvère **10** troubadour ***Mexican:*** **3** Paz (Octavio) ***nonsense:*** **4**

Lear (Edward) **7** Dr. Seuss ***Norwegian:*** **8** Bjornson (Bjornstjerne), Welhaven (Johan) **9** Wergeland (Henrik) ***Persian:*** **4** Sadi **5** Attar, Hafez, Hafiz **11** Omar Khayyám ***Roman:*** **4** Ovid **6** Horace, Vergil, Virgil **7** Juvenal, Martial, Statius **8** Catullus, Tibullus **9** Lucretius ***Russian:*** **4** Blok (Aleksandr) **7** Brodsky (Joseph), Pushkin (Aleksandr), Yesenin (Sergey) **9** Akhmatova (Anna), Kheraskov (Mikhail), Pasternak (Boris), Tsvetaeva (Marina) **10** Mandelstam (Osip), Mayakovsky (Vladimir) **11** Yevtushenko (Yevgeny) ***Saint Lucian:*** **7** Walcott (Derek) ***Scottish:*** **4** Hogg (James), Muir (Edwin) **5** Burns (Robert), Scott (Alexander, Walter) **6** Dunbar (William), Ramsay (Allan) **7** Thomson (James) **10** MacDiarmid (Hugh) ***Spanish:*** **5** Lorca (Federico García) **7** Jiménez (Juan Ramón) **8** Figueroa (Francisco) **10** Aleixandre (Vicente) **11** García Lorca (Federico) ***Swedish:*** **5** Sachs (Nelly) **6** Tegner (Esaias) **8** Snoilsky (Carl Johan) **9** Karlfeldt (Erik Axel) ***Swiss:*** **5** Amiel (Henri Frédéric) **9** Spitteler (Carl) ***Welsh:*** **6** Thomas (Dylan) **7** Aneurin, Watkins (Vernon)

poetic **5** lyric **6** dreamy **8** romantic **9** aesthetic, beautiful ***word:*** **3** ere, e'er, thy **4** dost, doth, hast, hath, kine, ne'er, thee, thou, wert, wilt **5** thine **8** forsooth **9** beauteous

poet laureate ***British:*** **3** Pye (Henry) **4** Rowe (Nicholas), Tate (Nahum) **6** Austin (Alfred), Cibber (Colley), Dryden (John), Hughes (Ted), Jonson (Ben), Motion (Andrew) **7** Bridges (Robert), Southey (Robert) **8** Betjeman (John), Davenant (William), Day-Lewis (Cecil), Shadwell (Thomas), Tennyson (Alfred) **9** Masefield (John), Whitehead (William) **10** Wordsworth (William) ***American:*** **4** Dove (Rita), Hall (Donald), Hass (Robert) **5** Glück (Louise) **6** Kooser (Ted), Kunitz (Stanley), Merwin (W. S.), Pinsky (Robert), Strand (Mark), Warren (Robert Penn), Wilbur (Richard) **7** Brodsky (Joseph), Collins (Billy), Nemerov (Howard), Van Duyn (Mona)

poetry **5** verse

poetry term **4** iamb, mora, scan **5** arsis, canto, envoi, ictus, ionic, paeon, rhyme, stave, stich **6** dactyl, septet, sestet, stanza, thesis **7** anapest, cadence, elision, euphony, quintet, refrain, spondee, strophe, trochee **8** chiasmus, choriamb, cinquain, end rhyme, eye rhyme, quatrain, rhopalic **9** decameter, dithyramb, hexameter, near rhyme, octameter, terza rima **10** enjambment, fourteener, heptameter, ottava rima, rhyme royal **11** Alexandrine, antistrophe, heroic verse, rhyme scheme, shaped verse **12** sprung rhythm

Pogo creator **5** Kelly (Walt)

poi **4** taro

poignancy **6** pathos **7** emotion, sadness **9** sentiment

poignant **3** sad **4** keen **5** acute, sharp **6** biting, moving **7** painful, piquant, pointed, pungent **8** incisive, piercing, stirring, touching **9** affecting

point **3** aim, dot, end, jag, nib, tip **4** apex, crux, item, mark, show, site, spot, step, tine, turn, unit **5** motif, place, stage, theme, topic, trace, verge **6** detail, direct, intent, moment, motive, object, period, reason **7** decimal, essence, instant, meaning, purpose, subject **8** headland, juncture, locality, location, particle, position **9** direction **10** promontory **12** significance

pointed **5** acute, sharp **6** barbed, marked, signal **7** salient **8** incisive, striking **9** arresting, pertinent, prominent **11** conspicuous, penetrating

pointer **3** dog, tip **4** clue, hint **5** arrow, guide **6** gundog **9** indicator **10** suggestion

pointillist **6** Seurat (Georges), Signac (Paul) **8** Pissarro (Camille)

pointless **4** idle, vain **5** inane, silly **6** futile **7** useless **8** bootless **9** fruitless, senseless, worthless **10** immaterial, irrelevant, unavailing, unfruitful **11** meaningless **12** unprofitable

point of view **5** angle, slant **7** outlook **8** position, prospect **11** perspective

poise **4** ease, hang, tact **5** brace, grace, hover, skill **6** aplomb, steady **7** address, balance, bearing, dignity, support, suspend **8** carriage, elegance, serenity **9** assurance, composure, diplomacy, sangfroid **10** confidence, equanimity **11** delicatesse, equilibrium, savoir faire, tactfulness

poised **4** calm **6** at ease, serene, steady **7** assured, equable **8** composed, tranquil **9** collected, confident **13** self-possessed

poison **4** bane, upas **5** toxin, venom **6** toxoid **7** arsenic, botulin, cyanide, envenom **8** toxicant **9** botulinum, contagion **10** strychnine **13** contamination ***arrow:*** **4** inée, upas **6** curare **7** ouabain ***combining form:*** **3** tox **4** toxi, toxo **6** toxico

poisoning ***food:*** **8** botulism ***lead:*** **8** plumbism

poisonous **5** toxic **7** baneful, miasmal, nocuous, noxious **8** mephitic, venomous, virulent **9** pestilent **10** pernicious

poke **3** dig, hit, jab, jut, lag, pry **4** cuff, nose, prod, push, sock, stab, stir, urge **5** bulge, dally, delay, elbow, nudge, punch, snoop, tarry **6** dawdle, meddle, pierce, putter, thrust **7** intrude, project, rummage **8** stick out **9** interfere, interject, interpose

poker ***bet total:*** **3** pot ***bullet:*** **3** ace ***form:*** **4** stud ***hand:*** **4** pair **5** flush **8** straight **9** full house **10** royal flush **13** straight flush ***ploy:*** **5** bluff ***stake:*** **4** ante ***term:*** **3** see **4** call, draw, open **5** raise ***token:*** **4** chip

poker-faced **5** blank, staid **7** deadpan, neutral **9** impassive **11** inscrutable, noncommital **12** inexpressive

pokey **3** can, jug, pen **4** brig, coop, jail, stir **5** clink **6** cooler, prison **7** slammer **9** calaboose

poky **4** slow **5** dingy, seedy **6** dreary, shabby **7** cramped, laggard, run-down **8** dilatory, plodding, sluggish

Poland ***capital:*** **6** Warsaw ***city:*** **4** Lódz **6** Gdansk, Kraków, Poznan **7** Wroclaw **8** Katowice, Szczecin ***leader:*** **6** Walesa (Lech) ***monetary unit:*** **5** zloty ***mountain range:*** **10** Carpathian ***national hero:*** **10** Kosciuszko (Thaddeus) ***neighbor:*** **6** Russia **7** Belarus, Germany, Ukraine **8** Slovakia **9** Lithuania **13** Czech Republic ***river:*** **4** Oder **7** Vistula ***sea:*** **6** Baltic

polar **6** arctic **7** pivotal **8** opposite **9** diametric

pole **3** rod **4** punt, spar **5** anode, shaft, staff, stick, stilt **7** cathode ***Indian:*** **5** totem ***Scottish:*** **5** caber

polecat **5** fitch, skunk **6** ferret **7** fitchet

polemic **6** attack, debate, screed, tirade **7** defense, dispute **8** argument, diatribe, harangue, jeremiad **9** assertion, philippic **10** contention, refutation **11** controversy, disputation **12** denunciation, remonstrance

polemical **11** contentious, opinionated **12** disputatious **13** argumentative, controversial

polestar **3** hub **5** focus, guide **10** focal point

police **3** law, man **4** fuzz, heat **6** govern, patrol **7** control, monitor **8** regulate ***officer:*** **3** cop **4** flic, fuzz, heat **5** bobby **6** copper, lawman, peeler **7** John Law, sheriff, trooper **8** bluecoat, Dogberry, flatfoot, gendarme **9** constable, patrolman **11** carabiniere

policy **4** plan **6** course, method, number **7** lottery, program **8** contract, practice **9** procedure **10** management

polio vaccine developer **4** Salk (Jonas) **5** Sabin (Albert)

polish **3** rub, wax **4** buff **5** glaze, glint, gloss, sheen, shine **6** luster, refine, smooth, soften **7** burnish, culture, enhance, improve, perfect, touch up **8** brighten **10** refinement

Polish ***dumpling:*** **6** pirogi **7** pierogi ***leader:*** **6** Walesa (Lech) ***patriot:*** **9** Kosciusko (Thaddeus) ***pope:*** **8** John Paul ***sausage:*** **8** kielbasa, kielbasy ***soldier:*** **7** Pulaski (Casimir)

polish off **5** eat up **6** devour **7** consume, put away **8** dispatch **9** dispose of

polite **5** civil **7** courtly, genteel, refined **8** cultured, mannerly, polished, well-bred **9** attentive, courteous **10** thoughtful **11** considerate **12** well-mannered

politeness **7** manners **8** civility, courtesy **10** refinement

politic **4** wise **5** suave **6** adroit, shrewd, smooth **7** prudent, tactful **8** tactical **9** advisable, expedient, judicious, sagacious **10** diplomatic

political ***meeting:*** **6** caucus ***party:*** **3** GOP **10** Democratic, Republican ***system:*** **7** fascism **9** communism, democracy, socialism

poll **4** cast, clip, crop, head, nape, pate **5** count, shear, tally, votes **6** noggin, record, sample, survey **7** canvass, pollard **8** question **9** interview **10** canvassing ***type:*** **4** exit **5** straw

pollack **4** fish **6** saithe **8** bluefish ***family:*** **3** cod

pollard **3** top **4** crop, tree **7** cut back

pollen-producing organ **6** stamen

pollex **5** thumb

____ polloi **3** hoi

pollster **5** Zogby (John) **6** Gallup (George), Harris (Lou)

pollute **4** foul, soil **5** dirty, spoil, stain, sully, taint **6** befoul, damage, debase, defile **7** corrupt, profane **10** adulterate **11** contaminate

pollution **4** smog **5** abuse **8** impurity **10** defilement

Pollux **10** Polydeuces ***brother:*** **6** Castor ***father:*** **4** Zeus ***mother:*** **4** Leda ***sister:*** **5** Helen **12** Clytemnestra

Pollyanna **8** optimist ***author:*** **6** Porter (Eleanor)

Pollyannaish **6** blithe, cheery, upbeat **8** cheerful, positive **10** optimistic **11** rose-colored

pollywog **7** tadpole

Polonius ***daughter:*** **7** Ophelia ***hiding place:*** **5** arras ***slayer:*** **6** Hamlet ***son:*** **7** Laertes

poltergeist **5** ghost **6** spirit

poltroon **6** coward, craven, yellow **7** chicken, dastard, gutless **8** cowardly **9** dastardly **11** lily-livered

Polydorus ***father:*** **5** Priam **6** Cadmus ***mother:*** **6** Hecuba **8** Harmonia ***slayer:*** **8** Achilles **10** Polymestor **11** Polymnestor

polygon ***eight-sided:*** **7** octagon ***five-sided:*** **8** pentagon ***four-sided:*** **8** tetragon ***nine-sided:*** **7** nonagon ***seven-sided:*** **8** heptagon ***six-sided:*** **7** hexagon ***ten-sided:*** **7** decagon

three-sided: **8** triangle ***twelve-sided:*** **9** dodecagon

Polyhymnia 4 Muse ***invention:*** **4** lyre

polymer 5 amber, nylon **6** rubber, Teflon **7** shellac **8** Bakelite, silicone

Polynesian 5 Maori **6** Samoan, Tongan **8** Hawaiian, Tahitian **9** Marquesan

Polynices *brother:* 8 Eteocles ***father:*** **7** Oedipus ***mother:*** **7** Jocasta ***wife:*** **5** Argia **6** Argeia

polyp 5 tumor, zooid **6** growth **7** hydroid ***freshwater:*** **5** hydra

Polyphemus 7 Cyclops ***beloved:*** **7** Galatea ***father:*** **8** Poseidon ***victim:*** **4** Acis

pome 4 pear **5** apple, fruit

pommel 4 knob **6** handle

pomp 4 show **5** array **6** parade, ritual **7** display, fanfare, panoply **8** ceremony, grandeur, splendor **9** pageantry, vainglory **11** ostentation

pompano 4 fish **8** carangid **10** butterfish

Pompeii's volcano 8 Vesuvius

pompous 4 vain **5** proud, showy **6** lordly, ornate, stuffy **7** stuck-up **8** arrogant, boastful, inflated **9** bombastic, conceited, important, overblown **10** egocentric, flamboyant, pontifical **11** magisterial, pretentious **12** ostentatious, vainglorious

pond 4 mere, pool, tarn **5** stank **6** lagoon ***growth:*** **4** scum **5** algae

ponder 4 mull, muse **5** study, think, weigh **6** reason **7** examine, perpend, reflect **8** appraise, cogitate, consider, evaluate, meditate, mull over, ruminate **9** reflect on, speculate **10** deliberate, think about **11** contemplate

ponderous 4 dull **5** heavy **6** clumsy, dreary, stodgy, wooden **7** labored, massive, weighty **8** cumbrous, lifeless, plodding, unwieldy **9** lumbering **10** burdensome, cumbersome, oppressive

poniard 6 dagger

Ponte Vecchio *city:* 8 Florence ***river:*** **4** Arno

Pontiac 5 chief ***tribe:*** **6** Ottawa

pontiff 4 pope

pontifical 7 pompous **8** dogmatic **9** episcopal **11** magisterial

pony 4 crib, trot **5** horse **6** bronco, cayuse **7** mustang ***breed:*** **6** Exmoor **8** Shetland

pony up 3 pay **6** lay out, pay out **7** dish out, dole out, fork out **8** hand over, shell out, turn over **10** compensate, remunerate

pooch 3 dog, pup **4** tyke **5** hound, puppy **6** bowwow, canine

Pooh *creator:* 5 Milne (A. A.) ***friend:*** **5** Kanga **6** Eeyore, Piglet, Tigger ***illustrator:*** **7** Shepard (Ernest)

pooh-bah 3 VIP **4** czar, king, star, tsar, tzar **5** baron, heavy, mogul **6** big gun, bigwig, honcho, kahuna, prince, worthy **7** big name, big shot, kingpin, magnate, notable **8** big wheel, eminence, luminary **9** big cheese, personage, superstar **11** heavyweight

pooh-pooh 5 scorn **6** deride **7** disdain, dismiss, sneer at **8** minimize, play down

pool 3 pot **4** mere, pond, tarn **5** chain, group, kitty, merge, trust **6** cartel, lagoon, laguna, puddle **7** combine, jackpot **9** syndicate ***player:*** **7** Mosconi (Willie) **13** Minnesota Fats (see also **billiards**)

poop 4 dirt, info, tire **7** fatigue

poor 4 base, mean **5** broke, needy, scant, skimp, spare **6** humble, meager, meagre, paltry, scanty, skimpy, sparse **8** bankrupt, beggarly, indigent, strapped **9** destitute, insolvent, penniless, penurious **10** down-and-out, pauperized, stone-broke **11** impecunious, necessitous

poorly 3 ill, low **4** sick **5** badly **6** ailing, sickly, unwell **10** indisposed **11** imperfectly

pop 3 dad, dot, gun, hit, try **4** dada, dart, ding, shot, slap, slog, sock, soda **5** catch, crack, daddy, drink, fling, shoot, whack, whirl **6** attack, bug out, effort, father, strike **7** assault, attempt, explode **8** backfire

pop artist 5 Blake (Peter), Johns (Jasper) **6** Warhol (Andy) **7** Hockney (David), Indiana (Robert) **9** Oldenburg (Claes), Wesselman (Tom) **10** Rosenquist (James) **12** Lichtenstein (Roy) (see also **pop singer**)

pope 3 Leo **4** John, Mark, Paul, Pius **5** Caius, Conon, Donus, Felix, Gaius, Lando, Linus, Peter, Soter, Urban **6** Adrian, Agatho, Fabian, Julius, Lucius, Martin, Sixtus, Victor **7** Anterus, Clement, Damasus, Gregory, Hadrian, Hyginus, Marinus, Paschal, Pontian, Romanus, Sergius, Stephen, Zosimus **8** Agapetus, Anicetus, Benedict, Boniface, Calixtus, Eugenius, Eusebius, Formosis, Gelasius, Hilarius, Honorius, Innocent, John Paul, Liberius, Nicholas, Pelagius, Siricius, Theodore, Vigilius, Vitalian **9** Adeodatus, Alexander, Anacletus, Callistus, Celestine, Cornelius, Densdedit, Dionysius, Eutychian, Evaristus, Hormisdas, Marcellus, Miltiades, Severinus, Silverius, Silvester, Sisinnius, Sylvester, Symmachus, Valentine, Zacharias **10** Anastasius, Melchiades, Sabinianus, Simplicius, Zephyrinus **11** Christopher, Constantine, Eleutherius, Eutychianus, Marcellinus, Telesphorus

Pope poem 7 Dunciad (The) **10** Essay on Man (An) **13** Rape of the Lock (The)

Popeye *accessory:* 4 pipe ***baby:* 7** Swee'Pea **8** Sweet Pea ***creator:* 5** Segar (E. C.) ***energizer:* 7** spinach ***friend:* 5** Wimpy **8** Olive Oyl ***occupation:* 6** sailor ***rival:* 5** Bluto

pop in 4 call **5** visit **6** drop by, look up, stop by **8** come over

popinjay 3 fop **4** toff **5** dandy, swell **7** peacock **8** macaroni

poplar 5 abele, alamo, aspen **6** balsam **9** tulip tree **10** cottonwood **12** balm of Gilead

Poppaea's husband 4 Nero

poppycock 3 rot **4** bosh, bunk, guff **5** bilge, hokum, hooey **6** bunkum **7** baloney **8** malarkey, nonsense, tommyrot **10** balderdash

pop singer 3 Lee (Brenda), Ray (Johnnie), Vee (Bobby) **4** Cher, Como (Perry), Enya, Gore (Lesley), Joel (Billy), Page (Patti), Ross (Diana) **5** Abdul (Paula), Aiken (Clay), Arden (Toni), Cline (Patsy), Lopez (Trini), Simon (Carly, Paul), Valli (Frankie) **6** Avalon (Frankie), Brewer (Teresa), Crosby (Bing), Fisher (Eddie), Martin (Dean, Tony), Mathis (Johnny), Midler (Bette), Murray (Billy), Pitney (Gene), Spears (Britney), Summer (Donna), Vallee (Rudy), Vinton (Bobby) **7** Bennett (Tony), Buffett (Jimmy), Diamond (Neil), Estefan (Gloria), Francis (Connie), Houston (Whitney), Jackson (Michael), Loggins (Kenny), Madonna, Rodgers (Jimmie), Simpson (Jessica), Sinatra (Frank), Warwick (Dionne) **8** Aguilera (Christina), Williams (Andy) **9** Streisand (Barbra)

populace 5 plebs **6** masses, people, public **9** citizenry, commonage, commoners, plebeians **10** commonalty **11** commonality, rank and file, third estate

popular 5 cheap, noted **6** common, famous **7** admired, current, favored, general, leading **8** accepted, approved, favorite, ordinary **9** preferred, prevalent, prominent, well-known, well-liked **10** democratic, prevailing, widespread **11** inexpensive

populate 6 occupy, people, settle **7** inhabit

populous 6 packed **7** crowded, teeming **8** numerous **9** congested **13** multitudinous

porcelain *Chinese:* 9 Lowestoft ***English:* 3** Bow **5** Derby, Spode **6** Minton **7** Aynsley, Belleek, Bristol, Chelsea **8** Caughley, Wedgwood ***French:* 6** Sèvres **7** Limoges ***German:* 7** Dresden, Meissen ***ingredient:* 6** kaolin ***Italian:* 6** Doccia ***Japanese:* 5** Imari

porch 4 deck **5** lanai **6** piazza **7** gallery, veranda **8** verandah

porcupine 8 hedgehog

pore 6 outlet **7** opening, orifice, reflect **8** meditate **10** interstice

pore over 4 read, scan **5** study **6** peruse **10** scrutinize

porgy 3 tai **4** fish, scup **6** sparid **8** menhaden

Porgy and Bess *composer:* 8 Gershwin (George) ***librettist:* 7** Heyward (DuBose) **8** Gershwin (Ira)

Po River city 5 Milan, Padua, Turin **6** Milano, Padova, Torino, Verona **7** Brescia

pork 3 ham, pig **5** bacon, swine **8** sowbelly ***cut:* 3** ham **4** jowl, loin, side **7** fatback **8** forefoot, hind foot, spare rib **9** picnic ham **10** Boston butt

pork-barreling 9 patronage

pornographic 7 obscene

porous 5 leaky **6** spongy **8** pervious **9** permeable **10** penetrable

porpoise 5 whale **7** dolphin

porridge 4 mush **5** gruel, kasha **6** burgoo, cereal, congee, pablum, sowens **7** oatmeal, pabulum **8** flummery, loblolly **9** stirabout

port 4 hole, jack, left, wine **5** cover, haven **6** harbor, refuge **7** bearing, opening, retreat, shelter **8** larboard, left side **9** anchorage, harborage, roadstead, sanctuary **11** comportment ***opposite:* 9** starboard

portable 5 handy **6** mobile, wieldy

portal 4 door, gate **5** entry **7** doorway, gateway **8** approach, entrance, entryway

portcullis 4 gate **5** orgue **7** grating, lattice

portend 4 bode **5** augur **6** signal **7** betoken, predict, presage, promise, signify **8** forebode, forecast, foretell, indicate, prophesy **9** adumbrate, foretoken **10** foreshadow, vaticinate

portent 4 omen, sign **6** augury, boding **7** presage, prodigy **9** foretoken, sensation **10** foreboding, indication **11** premonition

portentous 5 grave **6** solemn **7** ominous, pompous, serious, weighty **8** inflated **9** marvelous, momentous, ponderous **10** prodigious

porter 5 hamal, stout **6** bearer, redcap, skycap **7** bellboy, bellhop, carrier **9** transport **10** doorkeeper

Porter novel 11 Ship of Fools

Portia 6 lawyer ***husband:* 6** Brutus **8** Bassanio ***maid:* 7** Nerissa

portico 4 stoa **9** colonnade

portion 3 cut, lot **4** bite, part **5** dower, moira, piece, quota, share, slice **6** moiety, parcel **7** measure, quantum, segment **8** division ***largest:* 10** lion's share ***unused:* 8** leftover

portly 3 fat **5** bulky, heavy, large, stout **6** fleshy **7** rotound, stately, weighty **8** imposing **9** corpulent **10** overweight

portmanteau 7 holdall **8** carryall, suitcase
portrait 4 bust **5** image **6** figure, statue **7** picture **8** painting **9** depiction
portray 4 draw, limn, play **5** enact, paint **6** depict, render **7** picture **8** describe **9** delineate, interpret, represent
portrayal 5 image **7** account, picture **8** likeness, painting **9** depiction **11** delineation, description, performance **12** illustration
Portugal ***capital:*** **6** Lisbon ***city:*** **5** Porto **6** Oporto **7** Amadora ***former colony:*** **3** Goa **5** Macao **6** Angola, Brazil ***former name:*** **9** Lusitania ***island group:*** **6** Azores **7** Madeira ***leader:*** **4** Luís **7** Salazar (Antonio de) ***monetary unit:*** **4** euro ***monetary unit, former:*** **6** escudo ***neighbor:*** **5** Spain ***peninsula:*** **6** Iberia **7** Iberian ***river:*** **5** Tagus
pose 3 act, air, ask, set, sit **4** airs, fake, role, sham **5** feign, front, offer, place, stand, state, strut **6** affect, assume, pass as, stance **7** pass for, pass off, present, pretend, show off, suggest **8** attitude, pretense, set forth **9** mannerism **10** pretension **11** affectation
Poseidon 7 Neptune ***brother:*** **4** Zeus **5** Hades, Pluto **7** Jupiter ***consort:*** **4** Tyro **6** Medusa **7** Demeter ***father:*** **6** Cronus ***mother:*** **4** Rhea ***offspring:*** **7** Pegasus ***son:*** **5** Orion **6** Neleus, Pelias, Triton **7** Antaeus **10** Polyphemus ***weapon:*** **7** trident ***wife:*** **10** Amphitrite
poser 6 puzzle, riddle **7** problem **9** conundrum **11** brainteaser
poseur 4 fake **5** bluff, decoy, fraud, phony, pseud, quack **6** phoney **7** bluffer **8** deceiver, imposter **9** charlatan, hypocrite, pretender **10** mountebank **11** masquerader **12** impersonator
posh 4 chic, rich, tony **5** fancy, grand, smart, swank **7** elegant, stylish **9** exclusive, expensive, luxurious **11** fashionable, highfalutin, pretentious
posit 3 fix **5** offer **6** affirm, assert, assume **7** premise, present, presume, propose, suggest **9** postulate
position 3 job **4** rank, site, spot **5** locus, place, point, situs, stand, state **6** belief, locate, stance **7** emplace, footing, stature **8** attitude, capacity, location, prestige, standing **10** standpoint ***without work:*** **8** sinecure
positive 4 firm, real, sure **6** actual, useful **7** assured, certain, decided, factual, genuine, reality **8** absolute, complete, definite, forceful, outright **9** confident, doubtless, effective, favorable **10** beneficial, inarguable, optimistic, undeniable **11** categorical, irrefutable, unequivocal, unqualified **12** indisputable, unmistakable **13** incontestable
possess 3 own **4** have, hold, keep **5** carry **6** retain **7** acquire, control
possessed 3 mad **6** crazed, hooked **8** frenzied **9** bewitched
possession 7 control **8** property **9** occupancy, ownership **10** occupation
possessive 7 jealous **8** watchful **10** protective **11** proprietary
possibility 2 if **4** odds **6** chance **8** instance **9** potential **10** likelihood **11** contingency, feasibility
possible 6 doable, likely, viable **7** earthly **8** feasible **9** expedient, potential **10** imaginable, realizable **11** practicable
possibly 5 maybe **7** perhaps **8** by chance **9** perchance **11** conceivably
post 3 set **4** camp, mail, pole, ride, send, spot, stem, task **5** affix, after, hurry, newel, place, put up, score, stage, stake **6** advise, column, fill in, inform, notify, office, pillar **7** apprise, express, placard, publish, station **8** announce, denounce, position **9** advertise **10** assignment
poster 4 bill, sign **6** notice **7** affiche, placard **9** broadside, signboard **12** announcement **13** advertisement
posterior 4 back, butt, hind, rear, rump, seat, tail **5** after, fanny, later **6** behind, caudal, dorsal, heinie, hinder **7** ensuing, rear end, tail end **8** backside, buttocks, derriere, hindmost, rearward **9** following **10** subsequent
posterity 6 future **7** progeny **8** children **9** offspring **11** descendants
posthaste 4 fast **6** at once, pronto **7** fleetly, quickly, rapidly, swiftly **8** promptly, speedily **11** immediately
Postimpressionist painter 6 Seurat (Georges) **7** Cezanne (Paul), Gauguin (Paul), Van Gogh (Vincent) **8** Pissarro (Camille), Rousseau (Henri)
postmortem 7 autopsy **8** necropsy
postpone 5 defer, delay, table **6** hold up, put off, shelve **7** hold off, lay over, suspend **8** hold over, prorogue
postulate 5 axiom, claim **6** assert, assume, demand, thesis **7** premise, suppose **10** assumption, hypothesis, presuppose **11** hypothesize, presumption, supposition
posture 4 mode, pose **5** state **6** affect, assume, manner, stance, status **7** bearing, outlook **8** attitude, carriage, position **9** condition, situation **12** attitudinize
posy 5 bloom **6** flower **7** blossom, bouquet, corsage, nosegay **9** sentiment
pot 3 bet, pan, wad **4** ante, hemp, olla, weed **5** grass, kitty, stake, wager **6** boodle, bun-

dle, pipkin **7** marmite **8** cannabis **9** marijuana

potable 5 clean, drink, fresh **6** liquid, liquor **8** beverage **9** drinkable

potassium ore 7 sylvite

potato 3 yam **4** spud **5** tater ***bud:*** **3** eye

pot-au-____ 3 feu **5** creme

potbelly 3 gut **5** stove **6** paunch **9** bay window, spare tire **11** corporation

Potemkin mutiny site 6 Odessa

potency 3 pep **5** force, might, power, vigor **6** energy, muscle **8** strength **9** influence, puissance **10** capability **13** effectiveness

potent 4 rich **6** mighty, robust, strong, virile **7** dynamic **8** forceful, forcible, powerful **9** effective **10** persuasive **11** influential

potential 6 latent, likely **7** ability, promise **8** capacity, possible **9** plausible, promising **10** imaginable **11** conceivable, possibility

pother 3 ado **4** flap, fret, fuss, stir, to-do **5** furor, whirl, worry **6** bustle, flurry, furore, hassle, hubbub, tumult, uproar **7** fluster, turmoil **9** agitation, annoyance, commotion, confusion

potion 6 liquid **7** mixture, philter, philtre **8** medicine **10** concoction

Potiphar's slave 6 Joseph

Potiphera ***daughter:*** **7** Asenath ***son-in-law:*** **6** Joseph

Potok novel 6 Chosen (The) **16** My Name Is Asher Lev

potpourri 4 olio **5** blend **6** medley, sachet **7** grab bag, mélange, variety **8** mishmash, pastiche **10** assortment, collection, hodgepodge, hotchpotch, miscellany, salmagundi **11** gallimaufry

potshot 3 cut, dig **4** barb, gibe, jibe **5** crack, shoot, swipe **6** attack, insult **9** criticism

potter see **putter**

Potter character 5 Mopsy, Mr. Tod **6** Flopsy, Jemima (Puddleduck) **10** Cotton-tail, Hunca Munca **11** Peter Rabbit **12** Jeremy Fisher

potter's field 8 cemetery, God's acre **9** graveyard

pottery 4 raku **5** delft, Imari **7** redware **8** ceramics, clayware, slipware **10** lusterware, terra-cotta, yellowware **11** earthenware

pouch 3 bag, sac **4** sack **5** bulge, bursa, burse **6** pocket **7** saccule **8** sacculus

pouf 5 quilt **7** ottoman **9** comforter

poultry 4 fowl ***type:*** **4** duck, swan **5** goose, quail **6** grouse, pigeon, turkey **7** chicken, ostrich, peacock **8** pheasant **9** partridge

pounce 5 seize, swoop, talon **6** attack, powder **7** assault, stencil

pound 4 bang, bash, beat, slam, slug, sock **5** drive, money, smite, stamp, throb, thump, tramp **6** batter, buffet, hammer, pummel, strike, thrash, wallop **7** belabor, impress, pulsate **9** enclosure

Pound work 6 Cantos (The)

poupée 4 doll

pour 4 flow, gush, rain, rill, rush, teem **5** flood, issue, skink, spate, surge, swarm **6** decant, deluge, drench, sluice, spring, stream **7** cascade, torrent **8** inundate, overflow

pourboire 3 tip **7** cumshaw **8** gratuity **9** baksheesh

pout 3 pet **4** fish, moue, sulk **5** grump **8** protrude **10** expression, protrusion

poverty 4 need, want **6** dearth, penury **7** beggary, paucity **8** hardship, poorness, scarcity, shortage **9** indigence, neediness, pauperism, privation **10** mendicancy, scarceness **11** destitution **13** pennilessness

POW camp 6 stalag

powder 4 bray, dust, talc **5** crush **6** talcum **8** sprinkle **9** comminute, pulverize, triturate **10** besprinkle

power 3 vis **4** sway **5** force, might, sinew, steam, vigor, vires (plural) **6** energy, muscle **7** command, ability, control, potency, voltage **8** dominion, dynamism, imperium, strength **9** authority, influence, privilege, puissance, strong arm **10** ascendancy, domination **11** prerogative, sovereignty, superiority **12** jurisdiction, potentiality ***combining form:*** **5** dynam **6** dynamo ***unit:*** **4** watt

powerful 5 great **6** mighty, potent, strong **7** dynamic **8** dominant, puissant, vigorous **9** energetic, strenuous **10** convincing, impressive, invincible, persuasive

powerless 4 weak **5** inert **6** feeble, unable **7** passive **8** impotent **9** incapable **11** incompetent, ineffective

powwow 4 chat, talk **6** confab, confer, huddle, parley **7** discuss, meeting **8** ceremony **9** gathering **10** discussion **11** confabulate, get-together

practicable 5 utile **6** doable, likely, usable, useful **8** feasible, possible **9** operative **10** functional

practical 5 handy, utile **6** active, useful, versed **7** applied, skilled, trained, virtual **8** sensible **9** pragmatic, realistic **10** functional **11** down-to-earth, experienced **12** businesslike

practically 5 about **6** all but, almost, near to, nearly **7** close to **8** in effect **9** in essence, just about

practice 3 ply, use, way **4** form, mode, wont **5** drill, habit, usage **6** custom, manner, method, repeat, system, tryout, warm up **7** perform, process, workout **8** drilling, engage in, exercise, habitude, rehearse **9** procedure, rehearsal **10** convention

pragmatic 7 factual, logical **8** rational **9** practical, realistic **11** down-to-earth

prairie 4 veld **5** pampa, plain, veldt **6** pampas **7** plateau **9** grassland

prairie chicken 6 grouse

prairie wolf 6 coyote

praise 4 hail, hymn, laud, puff **5** bravo, cry up, exalt, extol, honor, kudos **6** belaud, kudize **7** acclaim, adulate, applaud, commend, flatter, glorify, hosanna, magnify, ovation, plaudit, puffery **8** accolade, applause, approval, citation, encomium, eulogize, flattery **9** celebrate, laudation, panegyric, recommend **10** aggrandize, compliment, panegyrize **11** acclamation **12** commendation

praiseworthy 8 laudable **9** admirable, deserving, estimable **11** commendable, meritorious

prance 4 step **5** mince, strut **6** sashay, spring **8** cakewalk

prank 3 gag **4** deck, dido, lark, whim **5** adorn, antic, caper, fancy, spiff, sport, trick **6** doll up, frolic, gambol, levity, shavie, vagary, whimsy **7** caprice, deck out, doll out, dress up, garnish, rollick, spiff up **8** beautify, decorate, escapade, ornament, spruce up **9** embellish, frivolity, horseplay, smarten up **10** shenanigan, tomfoolery **11** monkeyshine

prankster 3 wag **5** cutup, joker

prate 3 gab, jaw, yak **4** blab, chat, go on **5** run on **6** babble, gabble, jabber **7** blabber, blather, chatter **9** yakety-yak

prater 5 yenta **6** gossip, magpie **10** chatterbox **12** blabbermouth

pratfall 6 mishap, tumble **7** blunder, stumble **11** humiliation

prattle 3 gab **4** blab **5** prate **6** babble, gabble, jabber, natter **7** blabber, chatter

prawn 6 shrimp **11** langoustine ***French:*** **8** crevette

praxis 5 habit **6** action, custom, manner **7** conduct **8** exercise, habitude, practice

Praxiteles statue 5 Satyr **6** Hermes **9** Aphrodite

pray 3 ask, beg **5** plead **6** appeal **7** beseech, entreat, implore, request **8** petition **10** supplicate

prayer 4 plea, suit **6** appeal, litany, orison **7** angelus, begging, worship **8** blessing, devotion, entreaty, petition, pleading, rogation **9** adoration **11** application, imploration, imprecation **12** supplication ***beads:*** **6** rosary ***ending:*** **4** amen ***for the dead:*** **7** requiem ***Jewish:*** **7** kaddish, kiddush ***period:*** **6** novena **7** triduum ***shawl:*** **7** tallith

prayer book 6 missal, siddur **8** breviary

prayerful 4 holy **5** godly, pious **6** devout **7** earnest, sincere

preach 4 urge **6** exhort **7** address, deliver, lecture **8** admonish, advocate, moralize **9** sermonize **10** evangelize

preacher 5 padre **6** cleric, divine, parson, pastor **8** chaplain, clerical, minister, reverend **9** churchman, clergyman **10** evangelist, sermonizer **12** ecclesiastic

preaching friar 9 Dominican

preachy 4 smug **7** donnish **8** didactic, pedantic, sermonic, unctuous **9** homiletic, hortative, pedagogic, pietistic **10** moralizing **11** exhortative, sermonizing **13** sanctimonious, self-righteous

preamble 5 intro, proem **8** exordium, foreword, overture, prologue **12** introduction

precarious 4 iffy **5** dicey, risky, shaky **6** chancy, touchy, tricky, unsafe **7** dubious **8** delicate, doubtful, insecure, ticklish, unstable **9** dangerous, hazardous, sensitive, uncertain **10** unreliable

precaution 4 care **8** prudence **9** foresight, insurance, provision, safeguard **11** forethought

precede 4 lead, rank **5** usher **6** herald **7** forerun, outrank, surpass **8** announce, antedate, go before **9** introduce

precedence 5 order **8** priority **9** seniority

precedent 4 past, rule **5** model, prior **6** former **7** earlier, example **8** anterior **9** foregoing **10** convention

preceding 4 past **5** prior **6** before, former **7** ahead of, prior to **8** anterior, hitherto **9** erstwhile **10** heretofore **11** in advance of ***prefix:*** **4** ante

precept 3 law **4** rule **5** axiom, edict, order, tenet **6** behest, decree **7** bidding, command **8** doctrine **9** principle **10** injunction, regulation **11** fundamental

preceptive 8 didactic

preceptor 4 head **5** tutor **7** teacher **9** principal **10** headmaster

precinct 4 area **6** domain, region, sector, sphere **7** quarter, section **8** district, division, township **9** bailiwick, enclosure

precious 3 pet **4** dear, nice, rare, rich, very **5** fussy, great, loved, showy **6** adored, choice, costly, la-di-da, prized **7** beloved, darling **8** affected, esteemed, favorite, valuable **9** cherished, exquisite, extremely, priceless **10** invaluable

precipice 5 brink, cliff **8** overhang

precipitancy **4** rush **5** haste, hurry **9** hastiness **10** abruptness, suddenness **11** hurriedness

precipitate **4** fall, hurl **5** hasty, sheer, steep, throw **6** abrupt, madcap, sudden, upshot **7** bring on, deposit, grounds, hurried, outcome, product **8** condense, headlong, sediment, separate **9** breakneck, impatient **10** unexpected, unforeseen **11** consequence

precipitation **4** hail, mist, rain, snow **5** sleet **7** deposit **8** sediment

precipitous **4** rash **5** hasty, sheer, steep **6** abrupt, sudden **7** hurried, rushing **8** headlong, heedless, plunging **9** breakneck **13** perpendicular

précis **6** digest, survey **7** summary **8** abstract, overview, syllabus **10** abridgment, compendium **11** abridgement **12** condensation

precise **4** nice **5** exact, fixed, right **6** narrow, strict **7** correct, limited **8** accurate, clear-cut, definite, rigorous, specific **9** clocklike, stringent **10** particular

precisely **4** just **5** right **7** exactly **8** strictly

precision **4** care **5** rigor **6** nicety **8** accuracy **9** exactness **10** exactitude, refinement **11** correctness

preclude **5** avert, deter **7** forfend, obviate, prevent, rule out **8** prohibit, stave off **9** forestall

precocious **5** smart **6** brainy, bright, mature **7** forward **8** advanced

precondition **4** must, need **7** proviso **9** essential, necessity, provision, requisite **10** sine qua non **11** requirement, stipulation

precursor **6** herald **8** ancestor, forebear **9** harbinger, indicator, prototype **10** antecedent, forerunner

predator **6** hunter, preyer, raptor **7** stalker **8** devourer **9** destroyer **10** bird of prey

predatory **6** greedy **8** ravening, ravenous **9** pillaging, rapacious **10** plundering **12** exploitative

predecessor **8** ancestor, forebear **9** precursor, prototype **10** antecedent, forerunner

predicament **3** fix, jam **4** bind, hole, spot **5** pinch, state **6** corner, muddle, pickle, plight, puzzle, scrape, strait **7** dilemma, impasse, trouble **8** hardship, nuisance, quagmire **9** condition, situation **10** difficulty

predicate **4** aver, avow, base, rest **5** found, imply **6** affirm, assert, avouch **7** declare, profess **9** establish

predict **5** augur, guess, infer **6** expect **7** forbode, foresee, portend, surmise **8** announce, conclude, forebode, forecast, foretell, indicate, prophesy, soothsay **10** conjecture, vaticinate **13** prognosticate

prediction **6** augury **8** forecast, prophecy **9** prognosis **10** expectancy **11** expectation

predilection **4** bent, bias **5** fancy, taste **6** liking **7** leaning **8** fondness, penchant, tendency **9** inclining **10** partiality, proclivity, propensity **11** inclination

predispose **4** bend, bias, tend, sway **5** prime **6** affect **7** incline **9** influence

predisposed **5** prone, ready **6** biased **7** partial, willing **8** inclined **11** susceptible

predisposition **4** bent, bias **7** leaning **8** penchant, tendency **9** inclining **10** partiality, proclivity, propensity **11** inclination

predominant **3** top **4** main **5** chief, major **6** master, ruling **7** capital, general, leading, primary, supreme **8** reigning, superior **9** number one, paramount, principal, sovereign **10** prevailing **11** outstanding

predominate **4** rule **5** reign **6** govern, master **7** command, control, prevail **8** outweigh

preeminence **6** renown **7** primacy **8** dominion, prestige **9** supremacy **10** ascendancy, domination, excellence, importance **11** distinction, superiority

preeminent **3** top **4** main **5** chief, first **7** capital, stellar, supreme **8** dominant, foremost, peerless, towering, ultimate **9** matchless, number-one, paramount, principal, unrivaled **10** surpassing, unrivalled **11** outstanding, unmatchable **12** incomparable, transcendent ***prefix:*** **4** arch

preempt **4** bump, take **5** annex, seize, usurp **6** assume **7** acquire, replace **8** arrogate **9** forestall **10** confiscate, substitute **11** appropriate, expropriate

preen **5** gloat, groom, pride, primp, swell **6** smooth

preface **4** lead, open **5** begin, intro, proem, usher **6** herald **8** exordium, foreword, overture, preamble, prologue **9** introduce **11** preliminary **12** introduction

prefatory **7** opening **8** proemial **12** introductory

prefect **7** head boy, monitor **8** head girl **10** magistrate

prefer **5** elect, favor **6** choose, opt for, select **7** advance, elevate, promote, upgrade

preferable **5** finer **6** better **8** superior, worthier

preference **4** pick **6** choice, option **8** election, priority **9** advantage, elevation, promotion, selection, upgrading **10** favoritism, partiality

prefigure **4** hint **7** foresee **8** indicate **9** adumbrate **10** foreshadow

pregnancy **9** gestation, gravidity

pregnant **4** full, rich **5** heavy **6** gravid, parous

7 teeming, weighty 8 eloquent, enceinte, profound 9 expectant, expecting, gestating, inventive, momentous, with child 10 expressive, meaningful, parturient 11 significant

prehensile 8 grasping

prejudice 3 mar 4 bias, harm, hurt, sway 5 color, favor 6 damage, injure, injury, racism, sexism 7 bigotry, leaning 8 aversion 9 antipathy, hostility, influence 10 partiality 11 intolerance 12 one-sidedness

prejudicial 6 biased 7 bigoted 8 damaging 9 injurious 11 deleterious, detrimental

prelate 5 abbot 6 bishop 7 primate 8 cardinal, diocesan 9 patriarch 10 archbishop 12 ecclesiastic

preliminary 4 heat 5 basic, match, trial 7 initial, opening 8 proemial 9 beginning 10 qualifying 11 fundamental 12 introductory

prelude 5 intro, proem 7 opening 8 exordium, foreword, overture, prologue 12 introduction, prolegomenon

premature 5 early 8 untimely 10 beforehand

premeditated 5 set up 7 planned, studied, willful 8 designed, intended 9 conscious 10 calculated, considered, deliberate, thought-out 11 intentional

premier 4 head, main 5 chief, first 7 leading, primary 8 earliest, foremost, original 9 principal 13 prime minister

premiere 5 debut 7 opening 8 earliest, original 9 beginning 10 first night

premise 4 base 5 posit 6 assume, thesis 8 building, property, set forth 9 postulate 10 assumption 11 postulation, proposition, supposition

premium 4 agio 5 bonus, extra, prize 6 reward 8 dividend, superior 9 excellent 10 recompense 11 exceptional

premonition 4 omen 9 misgiving, suspicion 10 foreboding 11 forewarning 12 apprehension, presentiment

preoccupied 4 deep, lost, rapt 6 absent, intent 7 engaged, faraway, worried 8 absorbed, immersed 9 concerned, engrossed, wrapped up 10 abstracted, distracted 11 inattentive 12 absentminded

prep 5 basic, coach, drill, equip, groom, prime, ready, train, trial 8 get ready 11 preliminary 12 introductory

preparation 4 base, plan 5 study 7 fitness, measure 8 compound, medicine, training 9 alertness, foresight, readiness 10 background, concoction

preparatory 5 basic 11 preliminary, rudimentary 12 introductory

prepare 3 fit, fix, set 4 gird 5 draft, groom, prime, ready, train 6 draw up, make up, outfit 7 fortify, furnish 9 formulate

prepared 3 set 4 up on 5 fixed, ready 6 primed 7 treated 9 processed

preponderance 4 bulk 8 dominion, majority, main part 9 ascendant, dominance, supremacy 10 ascendancy, domination 11 superiority

preponderant 7 supreme 8 dominant, superior 9 paramount 10 prevailing

preponderate 4 rule 5 reign 6 exceed 7 command, dictate, outrank, prevail 8 dominate, outweigh

preposition 2 at, by, in, of, on, to, up 3 for, off 4 down, from, into, like, near, onto, over, past, upon, with 5 about, above, after, along, among, below, since, under, until 6 across, around, before, behind, beside, during, except, inside, toward, within 7 against, beneath, between, outside, through, without

prepossess 4 bias, sway 5 favor 6 absorb, engage, occupy 7 engross, immerse, involve 9 influence

prepossessing 7 likable 9 appealing 10 attractive

preposterous 4 wild 5 crazy, wacky 6 absurd, insane 7 asinine, foolish, idiotic 9 fantastic, laughable, senseless 10 irrational, ridiculous 11 harebrained 12 unreasonable

prerequisite 4 must, need 5 vital 8 required 9 condition, essential, mandatory, necessary, necessity 10 imperative, sine qua non 11 requirement 13 indispensable

prerogative 5 power, right 8 appanage, immunity 9 authority, exemption, privilege 10 birthright, perquisite

presage 4 bode, omen, warn 5 augur, sense 6 augury, boding, herald, intuit 7 portend, portent, predict, promise, warning 8 announce, forebode, forecast, foretell, forewarn, indicate, prophesy, soothsay 9 foretoken, harbinger, intuition, misgiving 10 foreboding, foreshadow, prediction, prognostic, vaticinate

presbyter 5 elder 6 priest

prescience 9 foresight 12 anticipation, clairvoyance 13 foreknowledge

prescribe 3 fix, set 4 rule 5 guide, order 6 assign, choose, decide, decree, define, direct, impose, ordain, select 7 dictate, lay down, pick out, require, specify 9 designate, determine, stipulate

prescript 3 law 4 rule 5 edict, order 6 decree 10 regulation

prescription 3 med 4 drug, rule 5 claim,

right, title **6** custom, remedy **8** medicine **9** direction **10** medication

presence 3 air **4** look, mien **5** poise **6** aspect, spirit **7** address, bearing **8** carriage, demeanor **9** composure

present 3 act, aim, now **4** boon, gift, give, here, pose, show **5** award, bring, favor, offer, point, stage, tense, today **6** at hand, bestow, confer, convey, direct, donate, extend, in view, modern, render, submit, tender **7** hand out, largess, perform, proffer **8** existing, nominate **9** introduce **12** contemporary

presentable 3 fit **6** decent, proper **8** becoming **9** befitting **10** acceptable **11** appropriate **12** satisfactory

present-day 6 living, recent **7** current, ongoing, popular, topical **8** contempo, existent, existing, pressing, up-to-date **9** prevalent, surviving **10** prevailing **12** contemporary

presently 3 now **4** anon, soon **5** today **6** in time, one day **7** by and by **9** forthwith, these days **10** before long

preservation 4 care **6** saving, shield **7** defense, keeping **8** pickling **10** husbanding, protection **11** conservancy, maintenance, safekeeping

preserve 3 can, jam **4** save **5** jelly, put up **6** embalm, ensile, keep up, pickle **7** protect, shelter, sustain **8** keep safe, maintain **9** confiture

preside 3 run **4** head, lead **5** chair **6** direct, handle, manage **7** conduct, control, operate, oversee **8** moderate **9** officiate

president, U. S. 3 Abe, DDE, FDR, HST, Ike, JFK, LBJ, RMN **4** Bush (George, George W.), Ford (Gerald R.), Polk (James K.), Taft (William H.) **5** Adams (John, John Quincy), Grant (Ulysses S.), Hayes (Rutherford B.), Nixon (Richard M.), Obama (Barack), Tyler (John) **6** Arthur (Chester A.), Carter (Jimmy), Hoover (Herbert), Monroe (James), Pierce (Franklin), Reagan (Ronald), Taylor (Zachary), Truman (Harry S.), Wilson (Woodrow) **7** Clinton (Bill), Harding (Warren), Jackson (Andrew), Johnson (Andrew, Lyndon), Kennedy (John F.), Lincoln (Abraham), Madison (James) **8** Buchanan (James), Coolidge (Calvin), Fillmore (Millard), Garfield (James), Harrison (Benjamin, William Henry), McKinley (William), Van Buren (Martin) **9** Cleveland (Grover), Jefferson (Thomas), Roosevelt (Franklin D., Theodore) **10** Eisenhower (Dwight D.), Washington (George)

presidential nominee 4 Dole (Robert J.), Gore (Albert) **5** Dewey (Thomas), Kerry (John) **6** McCain (John) **7** Dukakis (Michael), Mondale (Walter) **8** Humphrey (Hubert), McGovern (George) **9** Goldwater (Barry), Stevenson (Adlai)

presidio 4 fort **7** bastion, citadel **8** fastness, fortress, garrison **10** stronghold **13** fortification

Presley, Elvis 4 King (The) **6** Pelvis (The) ***daughter:*** **9** Lisa Marie ***manager:*** **6** Parker (Col. Tom) ***middle name:*** **4** Aron **5** Aaron ***property:*** **9** Graceland ***wife:*** **9** Priscilla

press 3 hug, jam, ram **4** cram, iron, mass, pack, pile, push, rush, urge **5** clasp, crowd, crush, drive, force, horde, hurry, media, shove **6** demand, hustle, insist, jostle, propel, squash, stress, throng, thrust **7** beseech, entreat, imprint, printer, squeeze **9** constrain, influence, multitude

pressing 5 acute, vital **6** urgent **7** crucial, earnest, exigent, serious **8** critical **9** immediate, important, insistent **10** compelling, imperative

pressure 4 push, rush **5** drive, impel **6** burden, coerce, strain, stress **7** tension **10** constraint ***combining form:*** **5** piezo ***instrument:*** **9** barometer ***unit:*** **3** bar **6** pascal

prestige 4 fame, rank, sway **5** power **6** cachet, credit, esteem, regard, renown, repute, status, weight **7** dignity, stature **8** eminence, position, standing **9** authority, influence **10** importance, prominence **11** consequence, distinction

prestigious 5 famed, great **6** famous **7** eminent, honored, notable **8** esteemed, renowned **9** prominent, respected **10** celebrated **11** influential **13** distinguished

presto 4 fast **7** hastily, quickly, rapidly **8** suddenly **9** posthaste **11** immediately

presumably 6 likely, surely **8** probably **9** doubtless

presume 4 dare **5** guess, imply, infer, think, trust **6** expect, gather, impose, reason **7** believe, intrude, suppose, surmise, venture **8** infringe **9** postulate **10** conjecture

presumption 4 gall **5** brass, cheek, nerve **6** belief, daring, ground, reason, thesis **7** conceit **8** audacity, chutzpah, evidence **9** brashness, inference, postulate **10** confidence, effrontery

presumptuous 4 bold, smug **5** brash, fresh, pushy **6** cheeky, uppity **7** forward **8** arrogant **9** audacious, confident **11** overweening, self-assured

presuppose 5 posit **6** assume, expect **7** imagine, require, surmise **9** postulate

pretend 3 act **4** fake, pose, sham **5** bluff, claim, false, feign, guess, put on **6** affect, assume, delude, invent **7** deceive, imitate,

mislead, playact, profess, purport, suppose, surmise **8** simulate **9** imaginary **11** counterfeit, make-believe
pretender 4 fake, sham **5** actor, faker, fraud, phony **6** humbug **8** claimant, impostor **9** hypocrite
pretense 3 act, air **4** face, fake, mask, pose, sham **5** claim, cloak, cover, front, guise **6** deceit, facade, humbug **7** charade, fiction **8** disguise **9** deception, false show, imposture **10** masquerade, simulation **11** affectation, make-believe, ostentation
pretension 5 claim, right **6** vanity **8** ambition **10** allegation, aspiration **11** affectation
pretentious 4 arty **5** lofty, put-on, showy **6** chichi, la-de-da, la-di-da, too-too **7** pompous, stilted **8** affected, inflated, lah-de-dah, lah-di-dah, puffed up, snobbish, specious **9** bombastic, conceited, grandiose, lah-dee-dah, overblown **10** euphuistic, rhetorical **11** highfalutin **12** high-sounding, magniloquent, vainglorious
preternatural 7 psychic, unusual **8** abnormal, atypical **9** anomalous, unearthly, untypical **10** mysterious **12** inexplicable, supernatural **13** extraordinary
pretext 4 mask, ploy **5** alibi, cloak, cover, front, guise **6** device, excuse **7** apology **10** subterfuge
pretty 4 cute, fair **5** bonny, quite **6** comely, fairly, lovely, rather, sort of **7** cunning **8** graceful, pleasant, pleasing, somewhat **9** appealing, beautiful **10** attractive, more or less **11** good-looking **12** considerable
prevail 4 beat, rule **5** reign **6** master **7** conquer, impress, persist, triumph **8** convince, dominate, domineer, overcome, override, persuade **9** influence
prevalent 4 rife **6** ruling **7** favored, popular, regnant **8** accepted, dominant, superior **9** ascendant, customary, paramount, sovereign **10** accustomed, widespread
prevaricate 3 fib, lie **5** avoid, evade **6** palter **7** confuse, deceive, distort, falsify, quibble **12** misrepresent
prevarication 3 fib, lie **4** tale **5** lying, story **6** canard, deceit **7** falsity **9** deception, falsehood
prevent 3 bar, dam **4** balk, foil, ward **5** avert, avoid, block, check, debar, deter, estop **6** arrest, baffle, forbid, hinder, impede, thwart **7** forfend, head off, inhibit, obviate **8** obstruct, preclude, prohibit, stave off **9** forestall, frustrate, interdict **10** anticipate
previous 4 fore, past **5** early, prior **6** before, former **7** earlier, onetime **8** anterior **9** erstwhile, foregoing, in advance **10** antecedent, beforehand
previously 4 once **5** afore, ahead **6** before **7** already, earlier **8** formerly **9** erstwhile **10** heretofore
prewar 10 antebellum
prey 4 feed, game, mark **5** chase **6** quarry, target, victim **8** casualty, distress
Priam ***daughter:*** **6** Creusa **8** Polyxena **9** Cassandra ***father:*** **8** Laomedon ***grandfather:*** **4** Ilus ***kingdom:*** **4** Troy **5** Ilium ***slayer:*** **7** Pyrrhus **11** Neoptolemus ***son:*** **5** Paris **6** Hector, Lycaon **7** Helenus, Troilus **9** Deiphobus, Polydorus ***wife:*** **6** Arisbe, Hecuba
Priapus ***father:*** **7** Bacchus **8** Dionysus ***mother:*** **5** Venus **9** Aphrodite
price 3 fee, fix, tab **4** cost, fare, rate, toll **6** amount, assess, charge, figure, outlay, reward, tariff **7** expense, payment **8** appraise
priceless 4 rare, rich **5** droll, funny, witty **6** absurd, costly, prized, valued **7** amusing **8** precious, valuable **9** cherished, treasured **10** invaluable
pricey 4 dear **5** steep **6** costly **9** expensive
prick 3 jab **4** goad, mark, prod, spur, urge **5** egg on, point, sting, thorn **6** affect, excite, exhort, pierce, prompt **7** pinhole **8** puncture **9** perforate
prickly 5 burry, sharp, spiny **6** briary, thorny, tetchy, tingly, touchy, trying **7** brambly, waspish **8** annoying, nettling, snappish, stinging **9** difficult, fractious, irritable, vexatious **10** bothersome, irritating, nettlesome **11** troublesome
pride 3 ego, top **4** best, brag, pack, pick **5** boast, cream, elite, exult, group, preen, prime, prize, vaunt **6** choice, egoism, hubris, vanity **7** conceit, delight, elation, dignity, disdain, egotism **8** smugness, treasure **9** arrogance, cockiness, vainglory **10** self-esteem, self-regard **11** self-respect **12** congratulate
Pride and Prejudice author 6 Austen (Jane)
prideful 6 elated **7** haughty **8** exultant **10** disdainful
prier 5 snoop **7** meddler **8** busybody, quidnunc **9** buttinsky
priest 5 padre **6** cleric, divine, father, rector **8** chaplain **9** clergyman, presbyter ***ancient Roman:*** **6** flamen **8** pontifex ***Biblical:*** **3** Eli ***Buddhist:*** **4** lama ***Celtic:*** **5** druid ***French:*** **4** abbé, curé ***Muslim:*** **4** imam ***prop:*** **4** bell, book **6** candle ***tribal:*** **6** shaman
priestly 8 clerical, hieratic **10** sacerdotal
prig 5 prude, thief **6** pedant **8** bluenose **9** Mrs. Grundy **10** goody-goody
priggish 5 fussy **6** stuffy **7** genteel, pompous,

prudish **8** affected, pedantic **11** puritanical, straitlaced

prim 4 neat, nice, snug, tidy, trig **5** stiff **6** formal, proper, strict, stuffy, wooden **7** correct, genteel, orderly, precise, prudish **8** decorous, priggish **11** straitlaced

prima donna 4 diva, snob, star **7** artiste **9** chanteuse **10** narcissist **11** leading lady

prima facie 4 true **5** valid **8** apparent **11** self-evident

primal 5 basic **6** age-old **7** ancient, premier **8** cardinal, original **9** atavistic, paramount, primitive **10** preeminent **11** prehistoric

primary 4 main **5** basal, basic, chief, first **6** direct **7** initial, pioneer, radical **8** cardinal, earliest, original **9** elemental, essential, firsthand, immediate, number-one, paramount, principal **10** aboriginal, underlying **11** fundamental, rudimentary **12** foundational, introductory ***combining form:*** **4** prot **5** proto ***prefix:*** **4** arch **5** archi

primate 3 ape, man **5** human, lemur, loris **6** aye-aye, bishop, bonobo, monkey **7** gorilla **10** anthropoid, archbishop, chimpanzee, human being **11** Homo sapiens ***nocturnal:*** **5** loris **7** tarsier ***small:*** **6** galago

prime 3 top **4** best, dawn, fill, load, morn, peak, pick, rate **5** coach, cream, elite, first, paint, sunup, tonic, youth **6** choice, excite, height, spring, symbol **7** capital, highest, initial, morning, prepare, provoke, quicken **8** earliest, motivate, original, superior **9** excellent, first-rate, principal, stimulate **10** first-class

primer 4 book **5** guide **6** manual, reader **8** hornbook

primeval 7 ancient **8** earliest, original **10** aboriginal

primitive 3 raw **4** rude **5** basic, crude, early **6** savage **7** archaic, Spartan **8** barbaric, original, primeval **9** atavistic, barbarian, barbarous, elemental, essential, unevolved **10** elementary, primordial, underlying **11** fundamental, preliterate, uncivilized, undeveloped **12** uncultivated ***combining form:*** **5** palae, paleo **6** archae, archeo, palaeo **7** archaeo ***prefix:*** **4** arch **5** arche, archi

primogenitor 4 sire **8** ancestor, forebear **9** precursor **10** forefather

primordial 5 basic, early, first **7** ancient **8** earliest, original

primp 4 fuss **5** adorn, dress, fix up, preen **7** dress up

prince ***Anglo-Saxon:*** **8** atheling ***Arab:*** **4** amir, emir **5** ameer ***Austrian:*** **8** archduke ***Ethiopian:*** **3** ras ***Indian:*** **4** raja, rana **5** rajah ***of demons:*** **9** Beelzebub ***of Monaco:*** **6** Albert **7** Rainier ***of the church:*** **8** cardinal ***of Wales:*** **7** Charles

Prince and the Pauper author 5 Twain (Mark) **7** Clemens (Samuel)

Prince Edward Island ***capital:*** **13** Charlottetown ***provincial flower:*** **12** lady's slipper

Prince Igor composer 7 Borodin (Aleksandr)

princely 5 grand, noble, royal **8** generous, imposing, majestic **9** dignified **11** magnificent

princess 7 infanta ***fictional:*** **3** Ida, Mia **4** Aura, Leia, Miyu, Ozma, Xena **5** Ariel, Belle, Fiona, She-Ra, Storm, Vespa, Zelda **6** Anelle, Aurora, Kadiya **7** Camilla, Jasmine **8** Angelica, Starfire **9** Belphoebe, Blackfire, Britomart, Buttercup, Gwenevere, Snow White **10** Bradamante, Cinderella, Pocahontas **11** Casamassima ***mythical:*** **3** Ino **5** Medea ***of Monaco:*** **5** Grace

Prince Valiant ***artist:*** **6** Foster (Hal) ***son:*** **3** Arn ***wife:*** **5** Aleta

principal 4 arch, dean, head, main, star **5** chief, first, major, prime **6** assets **7** capital, leading, premier, primary, stellar **8** cardinal, champion, dominant, foremost **9** paramount **10** headmaster, preeminent **11** outstanding, predominant ***combining form:*** **4** prot **5** proto ***prefix:*** **4** arch **5** archi

principium 3 law **5** axiom, basis **7** element, theorem **10** foundation **11** fundamental

principle 3 law **4** code, form, rule **5** axiom, basis, canon, ethic, tenet **6** ground, origin, source **7** conduct, faculty, precept **8** doctrine, polestar, rudiment **10** assumption, convention, foundation **11** fundamental

principled 5 moral, noble **6** honest **7** ethical, upright **8** virtuous **9** righteous **10** moralistic

print 4 type **5** issue, litho, stamp, write **7** engrave, impress, publish, typeset **10** impression ***style:*** **4** bold **5** roman **6** italic **7** cursive **8** boldface

printer ***English:*** **6** Caxton (William) ***German:*** **9** Gutenberg (Johann, Johannes) ***Italian:*** **6** Bodoni (Giambattista) **8** Manutius (Aldus)

printing 7 edition, reissue **10** impression ***measure:*** **4** pica **5** agate ***plate:*** **10** stereotype ***process:*** **4** roto **7** gravure **11** lithography ***tool:*** **6** brayer

priority 4 lead **5** order **8** ordering **9** supremacy **10** importance, precedence, preference

prison 3 can, pen **4** brig, coop, jail, keep **5** clink **6** cooler, lockup **7** dungeon, slammer **8** bastille, big house, stockade **9** calaboose **11** reformatory **12** penitentiary ***British:*** **4** gaol ***California:*** **8** Alcatraz **10** San Quentin ***New York:*** **6** Attica **8** Sing Sing **12** Rikers

Island ***Northern Ireland:*** **4** Maze ***resident:*** **6** inmate **7** convict **8** jailbird ***Russian:*** **5** gulag
prisoner 7 captive, convict, hostage **8** criminal, detainee, jailbird
prissy 5 picky **7** finicky, precise, prudish **8** exacting **10** fastidious, particular **11** straitlaced
pristine 4 pure **5** clean, fresh **8** earliest, original **9** unspoiled
privacy 6 secret **7** retreat, secrecy **9** seclusion **11** concealment
private 5 inner **6** secret **7** soldier **8** eyes-only, hush-hush, intimate, personal **9** concealed **10** closed-door, restricted, unofficial **11** independent, sequestered **12** confidential
privateer 4 ship **6** pirate **7** gunship **9** mercenary
private eye 3 spy, tec **4** tail **6** sleuth, shamus **7** gumshoe **8** sherlock **9** detective **12** investigator
privately 7 sub rosa **8** covertly, in camera, in secret, secretly
privation 4 lack, loss, need, want **6** dearth, penury **7** absence, poverty **8** distress **9** indigence, neediness, suffering
privilege 4 boon **5** favor, grant, right **7** license **8** appanage **9** allowance, exemption **10** birthright, concession, perquisite **11** entitlement, opportunity, prerogative ***pope-granted:*** **6** indult
privy 2 WC **3** can, loo **4** head, john **5** jakes **6** secret, toilet **7** latrine **8** bathroom, informed, lavatory, outhouse, personal **9** concealed, withdrawn **11** water closet
prize 3 pry, top **4** best, loot, pick, plum, rate, swag **5** award, booty, cream, elite, force, lever, purse, spoil, value **6** choice, esteem, reward, spoils, trophy **7** capture, cherish, jackpot, plunder, premium **8** treasure **10** appreciate **11** outstanding
prizefighting 6 boxing **8** pugilism
pro 3 for **6** expert, master **8** skillful **9** authority, in favor of **11** affirmative ***opposite:*** **3** con **4** anti
probable 6 likely **7** seeming **8** apparent, credible, expected, feasible, rational, reliable **10** reasonable
probe 4 poke, quiz, test **5** query, sonde, study **6** search **7** dig into, examine, explore, feel out, inquest, inquire, inquiry **8** check out, look into, research, sound out **9** delve into, penetrate **11** exploration, investigate, reconnoiter **13** investigation
probity 5 honor **6** virtue **7** honesty **8** fairness, goodness **9** integrity, rectitude **11** uprightness
problem 4 mess, snag **5** hitch, issue, poser **6** enigma, hassle, puzzle, riddle **7** dilemma, example, mystery, puzzler, trouble **8** hardship, headache, question **10** difficulty
problematic 4 iffy, moot, open **7** dubious **8** arguable, doubtful **9** debatable, uncertain, unsettled **10** precarious **12** questionable
proboscis 4 beak, nose **5** snoot, snout, trunk
procedure 4 plan, step **6** course, custom, method, policy, system **7** formula, measure, routine **8** protocol **9** operation **11** instruction
proceed 2 go **4** flow, move, rise, stem, wend **5** arise, get on, issue, segue **6** emerge, push on, spring, travel **7** advance, carry on, emanate, journey **8** continue **9** originate
proceedings 8 goings-on ***recorded:*** **4** acta **6** annals **7** minutes
proceeds 4 gain, take **5** yield **6** profit, result, return **8** earnings
process 3 way **4** mode, wise **5** modus, treat **6** handle, manner, method, refine, system **7** fashion, prepare, recycle, routine **8** workings **9** evolution, operation, outgrowth, procedure, technique **11** development ***nerve cell:*** **4** axon
procession 5 march, order, train **6** parade, series, string **7** caravan, cortege **8** sequence **9** cavalcade, march-past, motorcade **11** consecution
proclaim 5 extol **6** assert, insist **7** declare, exhibit, glorify, publish **8** announce, evidence, manifest **9** advertise, broadcast, make known **10** annunciate, bruit about
proclivity 4 bent **5** taste **6** liking **7** leaning **8** affinity, fondness, penchant, tendency **9** proneness **11** inclination **12** predilection
Procne ***father:*** **7** Pandion ***husband:*** **6** Tereus ***sister:*** **9** Philomela ***son:*** **4** Itys
procrastinate 5 dally, delay **6** dawdle
procreate 5 beget, breed **7** produce **8** conceive, generate, multiply **9** reproduce
Procris' husband 8 Cephalus
Procrustean ____ 3 bed
proctor 7 monitor, oversee **9** supervise **10** supervisor
procure 3 buy, get **4** gain **6** obtain, pick up **7** achieve, acquire **8** purchase **10** bring about
prod 3 dig, jab, jog **4** goad, poke, push, spur, stir, urge **5** egg on, elbow, nudge, point, prick, rouse **6** excite, exhort, incite, thrust **8** motivate **9** stimulate **10** incitement
prodigal 4 lush **6** lavish **7** opulent, profuse, riotous, spender, wastrel **8** reckless, wasteful **9** exuberant, luxuriant **10** profligate, squanderer **11** extravagant, spendthrift
prodigious 4 huge, vast **6** mighty, unreal **7** amazing, immense, mammoth, massive, strange, unusual **8** colossal, enormous, gi-

gantic **9** fantastic, marvelous, wonderful **10** astounding, impressive, monumental, phenomenal, remarkable, staggering, stupendous, surprising **11** astonishing **13** extraordinary

produce 4 bear, form, grow, make, show, sire **5** beget, breed, build, cause, erect, frame, hatch, mount, put on, raise, spawn, stage, yield **6** create, effect, father, output, parent, secure, work up **7** deliver, fashion, turn out **8** engender, generate, multiply **9** construct, fabricate, originate, procreate, propagate **10** bring about **11** manufacture, put together

product 5 fruit, issue, yield **6** effect, legacy, output, result, upshot **7** harvest, outcome, turnout **8** artifact, creation, multiple, offshoot **9** handiwork, outgrowth **11** consequence, manufacture ***combining form:*** **3** gen

production 5 fruit, yield **6** output **7** staging, turnout **8** artifact, assembly, creation **9** execution, handiwork, rendering **11** achievement, manufacture, realization

productive 4 rich **6** fecund, useful **7** fertile **8** abundant, fruitful, prolific **9** rewarding **10** beneficial

proem 5 intro **7** preface, prelude **8** exordium, foreword, overture, prologue **11** preliminary **12** introduction

profane 3 lay **4** damn, foul **5** abuse, dirty, pagan **6** coarse, debase, defile, filthy, impure, unholy, vulgar **7** impious, obscene, secular **8** indecent, temporal, unsacred **9** desecrate **10** irreverent, unhallowed **11** blasphemous, irreligious **12** sacrilegious, unsanctified

profanity 4 oath **5** abuse, curse **7** cursing, cussing **8** swearing **9** blasphemy, sacrilege **10** execration **11** imprecation, irreverence

profess 4 aver, avow **5** claim, teach **6** affirm, allege, assert, avouch **7** declare, pretend, protest, purport **8** maintain, practice

profession 3 art, job, vow **5** craft, trade **6** avowal, career, métier **7** calling **8** business, vocation **9** assertion, specialty, statement, testimony **10** handicraft, occupation, walk of life **11** affirmation

professional 4 paid **6** expert, master **7** learned, skilled **9** authority **10** proficient, specialist **11** experienced **12** businesslike

professor 3 don **6** expert **7** teacher **8** academic, educator

proffer 4 give, pose **6** extend, submit, tender **7** hold out, present, suggest **10** invitation, suggestion

proficiency 5 savvy, skill **7** ability, advance, mastery, prowess **8** facility, progress **9** adeptness, dexterity, expertise, knowledge **10** competence

proficient 4 able **5** adept **6** expert **7** capable, skilled **8** advanced, masterly, skillful **9** authority, competent, effective, masterful, qualified **11** crackerjack, experienced **12** accomplished

profile 3 bio **5** chart **6** sketch, survey **7** contour, diagram, outline **8** exposure, portrait, side view **9** biography **10** silhouette **11** description

profit 3 net **4** gain, take **5** serve, yield **6** excess, income, payoff, return **7** benefit, receipt **8** earnings, proceeds **10** percentage **12** compensation ***sudden:*** **7** killing

profitable 6 paying, useful **7** gainful **8** fruitful **9** lucrative, rewarding **10** beneficial, well-paying, worthwhile **11** moneymaking **12** advantageous, remunerative

profligate 4 wild **6** waster **7** immoral, spender, wastrel **8** prodigal, reckless, wasteful **9** abandoned, dissolute, indulgent, reprobate **10** dissipated, immoderate, licentious, squanderer **11** extravagant, promiscuous, spendthrift **13** self-indulgent

profound 4 deep, wise **5** heavy, total, utter **7** abysmal, intense **8** absolute, abstruse, complete, esoteric, thorough **9** intensive **10** deep-seated, insightful

profundity 5 depth **6** wisdom **7** insight **8** deepness **12** abstruseness

profuse 4 lush **6** lavish **7** copious, fulsome, liberal, opulent **8** abundant, generous, prodigal **9** abounding, bounteous, bountiful, excessive, exuberant, luxuriant, plentiful **10** munificent **11** extravagant

profusion 4 glut, riot **5** flood, spate, surge **6** bounty, deluge, excess, wealth **7** nimiety, satiety, surfeit, surplus, torrent **8** overflow, overload, plethora **9** abundance, plenitude **10** lavishness, luxuriance, oversupply, plentitude, redundancy **11** copiousness, prodigality, sufficiency, superfluity **12** extravagance **13** overabundance

progenitor 4 sire **6** author, father, mother **8** ancestor, forebear **9** initiator, precursor **10** antecessor, forefather, forerunner, originator **11** predecessor

progeny 4 line **5** issue **6** litter, result, scions **7** outcome, product **8** children **9** offspring, posterity **11** descendants

prognosis 8 estimate, forecast, prophecy **9** prevision **10** estimation, prediction **11** expectation **12** anticipation

prognostic 4 omen, sign **6** augury **7** portent, presage **10** foreboding, indication

prognosticate 6 divine **7** foresee, predict, presage **8** forecast, foretell, prophesy
program 4 bill, book, plan, show **5** plans, slate **6** agenda, course, docket, lineup, policy **7** listing **8** calendar, playbill, schedule, syllabus **9** broadcast, procedure, timetable **10** bill of fare, curriculum
programming language 3 SQL **4** DASL, JADE, Java, LISP, Perl, Thue **5** Algol, BASIC, COBOL, CORAL **6** Euclid, Groovy, Inform, Pascal, Prolog, Python, Scheme, Simula **7** FORTRAN, Haskell, Miranda **10** JavaScript, PostScript **11** Visual Basic
progress 4 fare, gain, grow **5** get on, march **6** course, growth **7** advance, headway, passage, proceed **8** anabasis, get along, momentum **9** evolution, flowering, unfolding **11** advancement, development, improvement ***planned:* 7** telesis
progressing 5 afoot **7** en route **8** under way
progression 4 path **5** chain **6** course, growth, series **7** advance **8** sequence **9** evolution, unfolding **10** trajectory **11** development
progressive 6 modern **7** growing, liberal, radical **8** advanced, tolerant **9** advancing **10** developing, increasing
prohibit 3 ban, bar **4** stop **5** block, debar **6** enjoin, forbid, outlaw **7** prevent **8** preclude **9** interdict
prohibited 4 tabu **5** taboo **6** banned, barred **7** illegal, illicit **8** verboten **9** forbidden
prohibition 3 ban, bar **5** taboo **7** embargo **8** sanction **9** interdict **10** constraint, forbidding, injunction **12** disallowance, interdiction, proscription
prohibitive 5 steep **6** costly **7** sky-high **9** excessive **10** exorbitant, forbidding **11** restrictive
project 3 jut **4** cast, feat, plan **5** bulge **6** affair, design, devise, extend, intend, scheme, vision **7** arrange, concern, emprise, exploit, feature, imagine, propose, purpose, venture **8** business, conceive, envisage, envision, game plan, overhang, protrude, stand out, stick out, strategy **9** blueprint, visualize **10** enterprise **11** proposition, undertaking
projection 3 jut **4** bump, knob, view **5** bulge **7** display **8** estimate, forecast, overhang, scheming, swelling **9** extension **10** jutting out, perception **11** expectation ***vaulted:* 4** apse
prolapse 3 sag
proletariat 6 masses **7** workers **8** laborers **9** commoners, hoi polloi **12** working class
prolific 4 rich **6** fecund, gifted, lavish **7** fertile **8** abundant, creative, fruitful **9** abounding, bountiful, inventive **10** generating, generative **11** reproducing **12** reproductive
prolix 4 long **5** windy, wordy **7** diffuse, lengthy, tedious, verbose **8** drawn out, rambling, tiresome **9** redundant, wearisome **10** long-winded
prologue 7 opening, preface, prelude **8** exordium, foreword, overture, preamble **9** beginning **12** introduction
prolong 6 extend **7** drag out, draw out, spin out, stretch **8** continue, elongate, lengthen
prolonged 7 lasting, lengthy **8** drawn-out **9** lingering **10** continuing, persistent, persisting
prom 4 ball, fete, gala **5** dance **6** formal
promenade 4 deck, walk **6** parade, stroll **9** boardwalk
Prometheus ***brother:* 5** Atlas **9** Menoetius **10** Epimetheus ***creation:* 3** man **7** mankind ***father:* 7** Iapetus ***gift:* 4** fire ***mother:* 7** Clymene ***muralist:* 6** Orozco ***rescuer:* 8** Heracles, Hercules ***tormentor:* 5** eagle
prominence 4 crag, fame, rise, spur **5** bulge **6** height, renown, status **8** eminence, headland, prestige, salience, standing **9** celebrity, elevation **10** importance, projection **11** distinction
prominent 5 famed, great, noted **6** famous, marked, signal **7** eminent, jutting, leading, notable, popular, salient **8** renowned, striking **9** arresting, notorious, well-known **10** celebrated, noticeable, pronounced, remarkable **11** conspicuous, eye-catching, illustrious, outstanding **13** distinguished ***person:* 3** VIP **4** BMOC, lion **5** mogul, nabob **6** bigwig, honcho **7** big shot, grandee **8** luminary, mandarin, somebody **9** dignitary **13** high-muck-a-muck
promiscuous 5 mixed **6** casual, random, varied **7** immoral **8** careless **9** haphazard, hit-or-miss, irregular **10** licentious **11** unselective **12** unrestrained
promise 3 vow **4** bode, bond, oath, word **5** agree, augur, swear, vouch **6** assure, engage, ensure, expect, insure, parole, pledge, plight **7** betroth, compact, consent, declare, outlook, portend, presage, suggest **8** contract, covenant, indicate **9** assurance, betrothal, potential, undertake **11** declaration, expectation
promised land 4 Zion **6** Canaan, heaven **8** paradise **11** kingdom come
promising 6 likely **7** hopeful **9** favorable **10** auspicious **11** encouraging
promissory note 3 IOU
promontory 4 beak, bill, cape, head, ness **5** bulge, point **8** foreland, headland

promote 3 aid **4** help, hype, plug, puff, push, sell, tout **5** boost, favor, raise **6** foster, launch, prefer **7** advance, build up, elevate, endorse, forward, further, nurture, present, support **8** advocate, champion **9** advertise, encourage, publicize, recommend
promotion 6 step up **7** advance, buildup, puffery **9** elevation, publicity, upgrading **10** preference, preferment **11** advancement, advertising, improvement **13** advertisement
prompt 3 apt, cue, jog **4** fast, goad, help, hint, move, spur, urge **5** alert, quick, rapid, ready **6** assist, incite, induce, on time, remind, speedy, stir up, timely **7** suggest **8** convince, persuade, punctual, reminder **10** responsive
promulgate 5 issue **6** decree **7** declare, publish **8** announce, proclaim **9** advertise, broadcast **10** annunciate **11** disseminate
prone 3 apt **4** flat, open **5** given, level **6** liable, likely, supine **7** subject, tending, willing **8** disposed, facedown, inclined **9** lying down, reclining, prostrate, recumbent **10** horizontal **11** predisposed, susceptible
prong 4 barb, fang, fork, spur, stab, tine **5** point, thorn **6** pierce
pronghorn 8 antelope
____ pro nobis 3 ora
pronoun ***archaic:*** **2** ye **3** thy **4** thou **5** thine ***demonstrative:*** **4** that, this **5** these, those ***indefinite:*** **3** all, any, few, one **4** both, each, none, some **5** no one, other **6** anyone, either, nobody **7** another, anybody, neither, nothing, someone **8** anything, somebody **9** everybody, something **10** everything ***personal:*** **2** he, it, my, we **3** her, him, she, you **4** them, they ***possessive:*** **2** my **3** her, his, its, our **4** hers, mine, ours, your **5** their, yours **6** theirs ***reflexive:*** **6** itself, myself **7** herself, himself, oneself, ourself **8** yourself **9** ourselves **10** themselves, yourselves ***relative:*** **3** who **4** that, what, whom **5** which, whose, whoso **6** whomso **7** whoever **8** whatever, whomever **9** whichever, whosoever **10** whatsoever, whomsoever **11** whichsoever
pronounce 3 say **5** judge, sound, speak, state, utter **6** affirm, assert, decree, recite **7** declare **9** enunciate **10** articulate
pronounced 5 clear **6** marked, strong **7** assured, decided, evident, obvious **8** clear-cut, definite, distinct **12** unmistakable
pronouncement 5 edict **6** decree **9** manifesto, statement **11** declaration, publication **12** notification
pronto 3 now, PDQ **4** ASAP, fast, stat **6** at once **7** quickly **8** directly **9** forthwith, instanter, instantly, posthaste, right away **11** immediately
pronunciation ***distinctive:*** **4** burr, lilt **5** drawl, twang **6** accent, brogue ***study:*** **8** orthoepy **9** phonetics
proof 4 test **5** facts, goods, repro **6** galley **8** argument, evidence **9** testament, testimony **10** impression **11** attestation **12** confirmation
proofreaders' mark 4 dele, stet **5** caret
prop 4 stay **5** brace, shore **6** buoy up, hold up **7** bolster, shore up, support, sustain **8** buttress **10** strengthen **12** underpinning
propaganda 4 hype **8** agitprop, lobbying
propagandize 4 tout **5** boost, extol **7** advance, promote, trumpet **9** brainwash, catechize, inculcate **10** promulgate **11** proselytize **12** indoctrinate
propagate 5 beget, breed, raise, strew **6** extend, spread **7** diffuse, publish, radiate **8** disperse, generate, increase, multiply, transmit **9** circulate, cultivate, publicize, reproduce **10** distribute **11** disseminate
propel 4 goad, move, push, spur, urge **5** drive, egg on, power, shoot, shove **6** exhort, launch, thrust **7** actuate **8** activate
propellant 3 gas **4** fuel, spur **7** impetus, impulse **8** catalyst, stimulus **9** explosive, incentive, stimulant **10** motivation
propensity 7 leaning **8** penchant **10** preference **11** inclination
proper 3 apt, due, fit **4** good, just, meet, nice, prim, true **5** exact, right **6** au fait, decent, prissy, seemly, useful **7** correct, desired, fitting, genteel **8** becoming, decorous, priggish, rightful, rigorous, suitable **9** befitting **10** felicitous **11** appropriate, comme il faut, distinctive ***combining form:*** **4** orth **5** ortho
property 4 land, mark **5** acres, trait, worth **6** assets, estate, realty, riches, virtue, wealth **7** acreage, chattel, effects, feature, fortune, quality **8** chattels, dominion, hallmark, holdings, premises **9** attribute, ownership, resources, substance **10** belongings, possession, real estate ***conveyor:*** **7** alienor ***recipient:*** **7** alienee ***seller:*** **7** Realtor ***transfer:*** **8** alienate
prophecy 6 vision **8** forecast **10** divination, prediction **11** foretelling
prophesy 5 augur **6** divine, preach **7** foresee, portend, predict, presage **8** forecast, foretell, instruct, soothsay **9** adumbrate, prefigure **10** vaticinate **13** prognosticate
prophet 4 seer **5** augur, sibyl **6** auspex, oracle **7** diviner, seeress **8** foreseer, haruspex **9** predictor **10** forecaster, foreteller, prophesier, soothsayer **11** Nostradamus **13** fortune-

teller ***Arthurian:*** **6** Merlin ***Major:*** **6** Daniel, Isaiah **7** Ezekiel **8** Jeremiah ***Minor:*** **4** Amos, Joel, Osee **5** Hosea, Jonah, Micah, Nahum **6** Haggai **7** Malachi, Obadiah **8** Habakkuk **9** Zechariah, Zephaniah
Prophet author 6 Gibran (Khalil)
prophetess 5 sibyl **6** Pythia **7** Deborah **9** Cassandra
prophetic 5 vatic **6** orphic **7** Delphic **8** Delphian, oracular **9** presaging, prescient, sibylline, vaticinal **10** predictive, revelatory **11** apocalyptic, foretelling
propinquity 7 kinship **8** nearness **9** closeness, proximity **10** contiguity
propitiate 5 adapt, atone **6** adjust, pacify, soothe **7** appease, assuage, gratify, mollify, placate, satisfy **9** intercede, reconcile **10** conciliate
propitious 4 good, rosy **5** lucky **6** benign, bright **7** benefic, helpful **8** favoring **9** favorable, fortunate, opportune, promising **10** auspicious, beneficent, beneficial, benevolent **12** advantageous
proponent 6 backer **8** advocate, champion, defender **9** expounder, supporter **10** enthusiast
proportion 4 rate, size **5** allot, ratio, quota, share **6** adjust, divide **7** balance, conform, harmony **8** symmetry **9** dimension **10** percentage **12** relationship
proportional 5 scale **7** in scale, pro rata **8** relative **9** equalized **10** contingent, equivalent, reciprocal **11** correlative, symmetrical **12** commensurate **13** commensurable, corresponding
proposal 3 bid **4** idea, plan **6** motion, scheme **7** outline, proffer, project **8** scenario **10** invitation, suggestion **11** proposition ***final:*** **9** ultimatum
propose 3 aim, ask, put **4** name, plan, pose **5** offer **6** design, intend, submit, tender **7** advance, move for, present, request, solicit, suggest **8** nominate, put forth, set forth, theorize **9** recommend **10** put forward
proposition 4 plan **5** offer **6** scheme, thesis **7** premise, suggest, theorem **8** proposal **10** invitation, suggestion
propound 3 put **4** pose **5** offer **7** present, suggest **8** put forth
proprietor 5 owner **8** landlord **9** possessor
propriety 7 aptness, decency, decorum, manners **8** behavior, civility, good form **9** etiquette, rightness **10** seemliness **11** correctness, fittingness, suitability **12** decorousness
propulsion 4 fuel, push **5** drive, force, power **6** energy, thrust
prorate 5 allot, divvy, quota, share, split **6** assess, divide, parcel, ration **7** divvy up, portion **9** apportion, partition **10** distribute
prorogue 3 end **4** rise, stay **5** defer, delay **6** hold up, put off, recess, shelve **7** adjourn, hold off, suspend **8** dissolve, hold over, postpone **9** terminate
prosaic 4 dull, flat **5** banal, prose, prosy, trite, vapid **6** boring, common **7** factual, literal, mundane, tedious **8** everyday, lifeless, ordinary, workaday **9** colorless **10** lackluster, uneventful **11** commonplace **13** unimaginative
proscenium 5 frame, stage **9** forestage **10** foreground
proscribe 3 ban **4** damn **6** enjoin, forbid, outlaw **7** condemn **8** prohibit, sentence **9** interdict
proscription 3 ban **4** tabu **5** taboo **8** sanction **11** prohibition **12** condemnation, interdiction
prosecute 3 sue **4** wage **5** press **6** charge, indict, pursue **7** carry on, perform **8** continue **9** bring suit, persevere
prosecutor 2 DA
proselyte 7 convert, recruit **8** neophyte
proselytize 5 draft **6** enlist, enroll, sign up **7** convert, recruit, win over **8** convince **9** brainwash, catechize **11** prevail upon **12** indoctrinate
____ prosequi 5 nolle
prospect 4 mine, view **5** scene, vista **6** chance, survey, vision **7** dig into, explore, lookout, outlook **8** customer, exposure **9** candidate **10** expectancy **11** expectation, possibility **12** anticipation
prospective 6 coming, future, likely **7** awaited, ensuing, nearing, pending, planned, would-be **8** destined, eventual, expected, hoped-for, intended, proposed, soon-to-be **9** impending, looked-for, potential, scheduled **10** consequent, succeeding **11** anticipated, approaching, predestined, forthcoming
prospectus 4 list, plan **6** design, layout, précis **7** epitome, outline, program, summary **8** bulletin, synopsis **9** catalogue, timetable **10** projection **11** description **12** announcement
prosper 5 score, yield **6** arrive, do well, thrive **7** make out, produce, succeed, turn out **8** flourish, grow rich
prosperity 4 ease **6** riches, wealth **7** success **8** thriving **9** abundance, advantage, affluence, well-being
Prospero *daughter:* 7 Miranda ***servant:*** **5** Ariel ***slave:*** **7** Caliban
prosperous 4 rich, well **5** happy, lucky **6** ro-

bust, strong **7** booming, halcyon, opulent, wealthy, well-off **8** affluent, thriving, well-to-do **9** desirable, favorable, fortunate, promising, well-fixed **10** auspicious, successful, well-heeled **11** comfortable, flourishing

prostitute **4** bawd, doxy, drab, moll **5** abuse, B-girl, madam, quean, whore **6** callet, debase, floozy, harlot, hooker, misuse, wanton **7** chippie, cocotte, corrupt, cyprian, floozie, hustler, Paphian **8** call girl, meretrix, strumpet **9** courtesan, party girl **11** fille de joie, nightwalker **12** camp follower, streetwalker ***reformed:*** **8** magdalen **9** magdalene

prostitution **8** harlotry, whoredom **13** streetwalking ***house of:*** **4** crib, stew **6** bagnio **7** brothel, lupanar **8** bordello, cathouse **10** bawdy house **13** sporting house

prostrate **4** fell, flat **5** abase, level, prone **6** humble, lay low, submit, supine **7** exhaust, wear out **8** helpless, overcome **9** decumbent, exhausted, overpower, overwhelm, powerless, recumbent **10** procumbent, submissive

protagonist **4** hero, lead, star **5** actor **6** leader **7** heroine, sponsor **8** advocate, champion **9** principal

protean **6** mobile, varied **7** diverse, mutable **8** variable **9** adaptable, versatile **10** changeable

protect **4** save **5** cover, guard **6** defend, screen, secure, shield **7** shelter **8** preserve, restrict **9** safeguard

protection **4** care **5** aegis, armor, bribe, graft, guard **6** safety, shield **7** bulwark, defense, shelter, support **8** armament, coverage, immunity, security **9** extortion, insurance, safeguard **11** supervision

protector **5** armor, guard **6** patron, regent, shield **8** guardian **9** caretaker

protégé **4** ward **5** pupil **7** student, trainee **8** disciple

protein **4** zein **5** actin, opsin **6** avidin, enzyme, fibrin, globin **7** albumin, elastin, fibroin, histone, keratin, legumin, sericin **8** creatine, globulin, glutelin, prolamin, protamin, proteose, vitellin ***complex:*** **6** mucoid ***derivative:*** **7** peptide, peptone ***poisonous:*** **5** abrin, ricin

pro tem **6** acting **7** interim **9** ad interim, temporary

protest **4** aver, avow, beef **5** sit-in **6** affirm, assert, avouch, except, object, oppose, picket, resist **7** declare, dissent, profess **8** maintain **9** challenge, complaint, objection **10** disapprove **11** demonstrate, disapproval **13** demonstration

Protestant **5** Amish **6** Mormon, Quaker, Shaker **7** Baptist, Lollard, Pilgrim, Puritan **8** Anglican, Lutheran, Moravian **9** Adventist, Mennonite, Methodist, Unitarian **11** Pentecostal **12** Episcopalian, Presbyterian ***Bohemian:*** **7** Hussite ***French:*** **8** Huguenot

protocol **4** code, form, rule **6** custom, ritual **7** compact, conduct, decorum, manners **8** courtesy **9** concordat, etiquette, politesse, propriety **11** conventions, formalities

prototype **4** norm **5** model, pilot **6** design **7** example, pattern **8** original, paradigm, standard

prototypical **5** ideal, model **7** classic **9** classical, exemplary **10** archetypal

protozoan **4** cell **5** ameba **6** amoeba **7** ciliate, stentor **10** flagellate, paramecium

protract **6** drag on, extend **7** drag out, draw out, prolong, stretch **8** continue

protrude **3** jut **4** poke, pout **5** bulge **6** jut out **7** project **8** overhang, stand out, stick out

protrusion **3** jut, nub **4** bump **5** bulge **8** swelling **10** projection

protuberant **5** bulgy **7** bulging **9** prominent **11** conspicuous

proud **4** vain **5** huffy, lofty, noble **6** lordly, stuffy, superb **7** haughty, pleased, pompous, stuck-up, stately **8** arrogant, exultant, glorious, scornful, snobbish, spirited, splendid, superior, vigorous **9** conceited, delighted, imperious **10** disdainful, high-handed **11** magnificent, pretentious, resplendent **12** ostentatious, supercilious

Proulx novel **9** Postcards **12** Shipping News (The)

Proust character **5** Swann (Charles) **6** Marcel, Odette (Swann) **7** Charlus (Baron de) **8** Gilberte (Swann) **9** Albertine

prove **3** try **4** show, test **5** argue, check **6** attest, pan out, verify **7** bear out, certify, confirm, examine, explain, turn out **8** document, indicate, validate **9** determine, establish **11** corroborate, demonstrate **12** substantiate

provenance **4** root, well **6** origin, source **7** history **9** inception **10** derivation

provender **4** feed, food **8** victuals **10** provisions

proverb **3** saw **5** adage, axiom, maxim **6** byword, saying **7** epigram **8** aphorism

provide **4** give, hand **5** endow, endue, equip, serve, state **6** afford, outfit, render, supply **7** deliver, furnish, prepare, specify, support **8** dispense, hand over, maintain **9** stipulate

provided **5** given **6** if only **8** equipped, supplied

providence **4** care **6** thrift **7** caution, economy **8** prudence **9** foresight, frugality **11** forethought, thriftiness

provident 5 canny, chary **6** frugal, saving **7** careful, prudent, sparing, thrifty **8** prepared **10** economical, unwasteful **11** foresighted

providential 5 happy, lucky **9** benignant, fortunate **10** auspicious, fortuitous

province 4 area, duty, role, work **5** field, shire **6** canton, county, domain, office, region, sphere **7** demesne, pursuit, terrain **8** district, dominion, function **9** bailiwick, champaign, territory **10** department **12** jurisdiction

provincial 5 local, rural **6** narrow, rustic, simple **7** country, insular, limited **8** pastoral **9** parochial, sectarian, small-town **11** countrified

proving ground 10 laboratory, White Sands

provision 5 stock, store **6** supply **9** condition **11** preparation, requirement, reservation, stipulation

provisional 5 stamp **6** acting, pro tem **9** temporary **10** contingent **11** conditional

provisions 4 feed, food, grub **5** stock **6** viands **7** aliment, edibles, nurture, vittles **8** supplies, victuals **9** provender **10** sustenance **11** comestibles ***dealer:*** **8** chandler

proviso 6 clause **7** article **9** condition **11** stipulation

provocation 5 cause, wrong **7** offense **8** stimulus, vexation **9** annoyance, incentive **10** incitement **11** instigation

provocative 4 edgy **5** heady **8** alluring, annoying, arousing, exciting **9** offensive **10** intriguing **11** challenging, stimulating

provoke 3 bug, irk, vex **4** abet, rile, stir, wake **5** anger, annoy, cause, evoke, pique, rouse, upset, waken **6** arouse, awaken, bother, excite, foment, harass, incite, induce, kindle, nettle, stir up, whip up **7** incense, inflame, inspire, outrage, quicken **8** generate, irritate, motivate, occasion **9** challenge, galvanize, instigate, stimulate

provost 4 head **6** keeper **7** marshal **8** director **10** magistrate **13** administrator

prow 3 bow **4** stem **5** front **10** projection

prowess 5 skill, valor **7** bravery, command, courage, heroism, mastery **9** expertise, gallantry **10** excellence

prowl 4 hunt, roam **5** skulk, slink, sneak, steal **6** search, wander

proximate 4 near, next **5** close **6** nearby **8** adjacent, imminent **9** following, immediate, preceding **10** near-at-hand **11** forthcoming

proximity 8 nearness, vicinity **9** adjacency, closeness, immediacy **10** contiguity **11** propinquity

proxy 5 agent **6** deputy **7** stand-in **8** attorney **9** surrogate **10** substitute

pro ____ 3 tem **4** bono, rata **5** forma, tanto **7** tempore

prude 4 prig **7** old maid, Puritan **8** bluenose **9** Mrs. Grundy

prudence 4 care **5** skill **6** acumen, reason, thrift, wisdom **7** caution, economy **8** sagacity **9** foresight, frugality **10** astuteness, discretion, expediency, precaution, providence, shrewdness **11** calculation, forethought, thriftiness

prudent 4 sage, sane, wary, wise **5** canny, chary **6** frugal **7** careful, politic **8** cautious, discreet, sensible **9** expedient, judicious **11** circumspect

prudish 4 prim **5** stern **6** narrow, prissy, proper, severe, strict, stuffy **7** austere, genteel **8** affected, decorous, priggish **11** puritanical, straitlaced

prune 3 cut, lop **4** clip, crop, pare, plum, thin, trim **5** shear **6** cut off, reduce, remove **7** cut away, cut back, shorten **8** pare down, truncate

prurience 4 lust **6** desire, libido **7** lechery, passion **8** cupidity **9** carnality, eroticism **11** lustfulness **13** concupiscence

prurient 4 lewd **5** bawdy **6** erotic **7** goatish, lustful, satyric, sensual **9** lickerish **10** lascivious, libidinous, passionate **12** concupiscent

pruritic 5 itchy

Prussian *aristocrat:* 6 Junker **12** Hohenzollern ***prime minister:*** **8** Bismarck (Otto von) ***ruler:*** **7** Wilhelm **9** Frederick (the Great)

pry 4 nose, open, poke **5** jimmy, lever, snoop **6** meddle **7** inquire **9** interfere

prying 4 nosy **6** snoopy **7** curious **8** meddling, snooping **9** intrusive, obtrusive, officious **10** meddlesome **11** impertinent, inquisitive

psalm 3 ode **4** hymn, poem, song **5** paean ***book:*** **7** psalter ***selection:*** **6** Hallel ***word:*** **5** selah

psalmist 4 poet **5** Asaph, David **6** cantor

pseudo 4 fake, mock, sham **5** bogus, false, phony **7** pretend **8** spurious **9** imitation **10** artificial **11** counterfeit

pseudonym 5 alias **7** pen name **9** falsc name, stage name **10** nom de plume **11** nom de guerre

psyche 4 mind, soul **5** anima **6** animus, pneuma, spirit ***part:*** **2** id **3** ego **8** superego

Psyche's beloved 4 Eros **5** Cupid

psychiatrist 6 shrink **8** alienist **11** neurologist ***American:*** **3** May (Rollo) **5** Reich (Wilhelm) **6** Kramer (Peter), Rogers (Carl) **7**

Erikson (Erik) **8** Sullivan (Harry Stack) **9** Menninger (Karl) ***Austrian:*** **5** Adler (Alfred), Freud (Anna, Sigmund), Reich (Wilhelm) ***British:*** **5** Laing (R. D.) ***French:*** **5** Lacan (Jacques) ***German:*** **5** Fromm (Erich) **6** Horney (Karen) ***Swiss:*** **4** Jung (Carl) **9** Rorschach (Hermann)

psychic **4** seer **6** medium, mental, occult **8** cerebral **9** mentalist, prophetic, spiritual **10** mind reader, telepathic **11** clairvoyant, telekinetic **12** intellectual, supersensory ***American:*** **5** Cayce (Edgar), Dixon (Jeane) **10** Montgomery (Ruth) ***power:*** **3** ESP

psycho **3** nut **5** crazy, sicko, wacko **6** madman, maniac, mental, schizo, weirdo **7** berserk, haywire, lunatic, nutcase **8** crackpot, demented, deranged, head case **9** fruitcake, screwball, sociopath

psychoanalyst **4** Jung (Carl Gustav), Rank (Otto) **5** Adler (Alfred), Freud (Sigmund), Fromm (Erich), Klein (Melanie), Kohut (Heinz), Lacan (Jacques) **6** Horney (Karen) **7** Erikson (Erik) **8** Ferenczi (Sandor)

psychologist **6** shrink **9** therapist ***American:*** **5** James (William) **6** Terman (Lewis), Watson (John), Yerkes (Robert) **7** Skinner (B. F.) **9** Thorndike (Edward L.) ***English:*** **4** Ward (James) **8** Spearman (Charles), Tichener (Edward) ***German:*** **5** Wundt (Wilhelm) **6** Müller (Georg), Stumpf (Carl) **10** Wertheimer (Max)

psychotic **3** mad **5** crazy **6** insane **8** demented, deranged, schizoid **13** schizophrenic

ptarmigan **6** grouse

ptomaine **6** poison

pub **3** bar, inn **4** dive **5** joint **6** tavern **7** barroom, gin mill, taproom **8** grogshop **9** roadhouse **11** rathskeller

puberty **11** adolescence

public **4** open **5** civic, civil, state **6** common, mutual, people, shared, social **7** general, popular, society **8** communal, national, populace **9** community, municipal, universal **10** accessible, government

publican **7** barkeep **8** landlord, licensee, taverner **9** bartender, collector, innkeeper **12** tax collector

publication **4** book **7** article, journal **8** magazine, pamphlet **9** broadside, newspaper **10** periodical ***list:*** **12** bibliography

public house **3** bar, inn **6** hostel, saloon, tavern **7** auberge, hospice **8** hostelry

publicity **3** ink **4** hype, plug **5** blurb, press, promo **6** hoopla, notice **7** billing, fanfare, write-up **8** ballyhoo **9** attention, promotion **11** advertising **12** announcement **13** advertisement

publicize **3** air **4** bill, hype, plug, puff, push, tout **5** boost **7** promote, trumpet **8** announce **9** advertise, broadcast **10** press-agent, promulgate

publish **3** air **5** issue, print **6** get out, inform, put out, report **7** release **8** announce, bring out, proclaim **9** advertise, broadcast, make known **10** distribute, promulgate **11** disseminate

Puccini opera **5** Tosca **7** Le Villi **8** La Bohème, Turandot **12** Manon Lescaut **15** Madame Butterfly

puck **3** elf, imp **4** disk **5** fairy **6** spirit, sprite **9** hobgoblin, prankster

pucker **4** fold **5** purse **6** cockle, crease **7** wrinkle **8** compress, contract **9** constrict

puckish **5** antic, elfin, larky, pixie **6** elvish, impish **7** playful **8** prankish **9** whimsical **11** mischievous

Puck's master **6** Oberon

pudding **4** duff **6** burgoo **7** custard, tapioca ***baked:*** **5** kugel **10** brown Betty

pudgy **3** fat **5** plump, round, stout, tubby **6** chubby, chunky, flabby, rotund **8** plumpish, roly-poly

pueblo **4** town **7** village **8** dwelling ***ceremonial room:*** **4** kiva

Pueblo tribe **3** Zia **4** Hopi, Taos, Zuñi **5** Acoma, Jemez, Keres, Tigua **6** Laguna **7** Cochiti

puerile **5** inane, silly **6** jejune **7** foolish **8** childish, immature, juvenile

Puerto Rico ***capital:*** **7** San Juan ***city:*** **5** Ponce **7** Bayamon **8** Mayagüez ***discoverer:*** **8** Columbus (Christopher) ***language:*** **7** Spanish ***location:*** **10** West Indies

puff **3** pad **4** blow, brag, crow, drag, emit, huff, pant, plug, pouf, push, tout, waft **5** blurb, boast, boost, elate, expel, quilt, swell, vaunt, whiff **6** exhale, pastry, praise **7** flatter, inflate **8** swelling **9** advertise, comforter, publicize **10** exaggerate

puffer **8** blowfish **9** globefish, swellfish

puffery **4** buzz, hype, plug **7** fanfare **8** ballyhoo **9** promotion, publicity **11** advertising **12** exaggeration, press-agentry

puffin **4** bird **7** seabird **9** sea parrot **10** shearwater ***cousin:*** **3** auk

puffy **7** swollen **8** inflated

pug **3** bun, dog **4** nose **5** boxer, track **9** footprint

Puget Sound port **6** Tacoma **7** Seattle

pugilism **6** boxing **13** prizefighting

pugilist **5** boxer **7** fighter **12** prizefighter

pugnacious **7** defiant, scrappy **8** brawling,

fighting, militant **9** bellicose, combative, truculent **10** aggressive, rebellious **11** belligerent, contentious, quarrelsome **13** argumentative
pugnacity 9 hostility **10** aggression, truculence, truculency **12** belligerence **13** combativeness
puisne 6 junior **8** inferior
puissance 5 force, might, power **6** energy **7** potency **8** strength
puissant 6 mighty, potent, strong **8** forceful, powerful
pukka 4 real, tops **7** genuine **8** bona fide **9** authentic **10** first-class
pule 3 cry **4** mewl **5** whine **7** whimper
Pulitzer Prize fiction winner ***1918:*** **5** Poole (Ernest) ***1919:*** **10** Tarkington (Booth) ***1921:*** **7** Wharton (Edith) ***1922:*** **10** Tarkington (Booth) ***1923:*** **6** Cather (Willa) ***1924:*** **6** Wilson (Margaret) ***1925:*** **6** Ferber (Edna) ***1926:*** **5** Lewis (Sinclair) ***1927:*** **9** Bromfield (Louis) ***1928:*** **6** Wilder (Thornton) ***1929:*** **8** Peterkin (Julia) ***1930:*** **7** La Farge (Oliver) ***1931:*** **6** Barnes (Margaret) ***1932:*** **4** Buck (Pearl) ***1933:*** **9** Stribling (T. S.) ***1934:*** **6** Miller (Caroline) ***1935:*** **7** Johnson (Josephine) ***1936:*** **5** Davis (Harold) ***1937:*** **8** Mitchell (Margaret) ***1938:*** **8** Marquand (John) ***1939:*** **8** Rawlings (Marjorie Kinnan) ***1940:*** **9** Steinbeck (John) ***1942:*** **7** Glasgow (Ellen) ***1943:*** **8** Sinclair (Upton) ***1944:*** **6** Flavin (Martin) ***1945:*** **6** Hersey (John) ***1947:*** **6** Warren (Robert Penn) ***1948:*** **8** Michener (James) ***1949:*** **7** Cozzens (James Gould) ***1950:*** **7** Guthrie (A. B.) ***1951:*** **7** Richter (Conrad) ***1952:*** **4** Wouk (Herman) ***1953:*** **9** Hemingway (Ernest) ***1955:*** **8** Faulkner (William) ***1956:*** **6** Kantor (MacKinlay) ***1958:*** **4** Agee (James) ***1959:*** **6** Taylor (Robert Lewis) ***1960:*** **5** Drury (Allen) ***1961:*** **3** Lee (Harper) ***1962:*** **7** O'Connor (Edwin) ***1963:*** **8** Faulkner (William) ***1965:*** **4** Grau (Shirley Ann) ***1966:*** **6** Porter (Katherine Anne) ***1967:*** **7** Malamud (Bernard) ***1968:*** **6** Styron (William) ***1969:*** **7** Momaday (N. Scott) ***1970:*** **8** Stafford (Jean) ***1972:*** **7** Stegner (Wallace) ***1973:*** **5** Welty (Eudora) ***1975:*** **6** Shaara (Michael) ***1976:*** **6** Bellow (Saul) ***1978:*** **9** McPherson (James Alan) ***1979:*** **7** Cheever (John) ***1980:*** **6** Mailer (Norman) ***1981:*** **5** Toole (John Kennedy) ***1982:*** **6** Updike (John) ***1983:*** **6** Walker (Alice) ***1984:*** **7** Kennedy (William) ***1985:*** **5** Lurie (Alison) ***1986:*** **8** McMurtry (Larry) ***1987:*** **6** Taylor (Peter) ***1988:*** **8** Morrison (Toni) ***1989:*** **5** Tyler (Anne) ***1990:*** **8** Hijuelos (Oscar) ***1991:*** **6** Updike (John) ***1992:*** **6** Smiley (Jane) ***1993:*** **6** Butler (Robert Olen) ***1994:*** **6** Proulx (E. Annie) ***1995:*** **7** Shields (Carol) ***1996:*** **4** Ford (Richard) ***1997:*** **10** Millhauser (Steven) ***1998:*** **4** Roth (Philip) ***1999:*** **10** Cunningham (Michael) ***2000:*** **6** Lahiri (Jhumpa) ***2001:*** **6** Chabon (Michael) ***2002:*** **5** Russo (Richard) ***2003:*** **9** Eugenides (Jeffrey) ***2004:*** **5** Jones (Edward P.) ***2005:*** **8** Robinson (Marilynne) ***2006:*** **6** Brooks (Geraldine) ***2007:*** **8** McCarthy (Cormac) ***2008:*** **4** Diaz (Junot) ***2009:*** **6** Strout (Elizabeth) ***2010:*** **7** Harding (Paul)
pull 3 oar, row, tow, tug **4** drag, draw, haul, lure, root, yank **5** clout, draft, drive, force, pluck, put on, wrest **6** appeal, assume, entice **7** attract, draw out, extract, stretch **9** advantage, influence **10** attraction
pull back 6 rein in **7** retreat **8** withdraw
pull down 4 draw, earn, raze, ruin **5** lower, wreck **6** reduce **7** depress, destroy **8** demolish, overcome **9** dismantle
pullet 3 hen **5** chick **7** chicken
pulley 5 wheel **6** sheave ***watch's:*** **5** fusee
pull in 3 nab **4** stop **5** check, pinch **6** arrest, arrive, collar, detain, pick up **7** inhibit **8** hold back, restrain **9** apprehend
pulling 6 towage **7** draught, haulage **8** traction ***cable:*** **7** towline
Pullman 3 car **7** sleeper **8** suitcase **11** railroad car
pull off 6 attain, manage **7** achieve, succeed **8** carry out **10** accomplish
pull out 4 exit, quit **5** leave **6** depart **7** abandon, retreat, take off **8** shove off, withdraw
pull through 5 rally **7** get over, recover, ride out, survive, weather **9** get better
pullulate 4 teem **5** breed, crawl, swarm **6** abound, sprout **7** produce **9** germinate
pull up 4 halt, stop **5** check **6** rebuke **8** draw even **9** reprimand
pulp 4 mash, pith **5** crush **6** bruise, squash **7** tabloid **8** soft part
pulpit 4 ambo, dais **6** podium **7** lectern, rostrum **8** ministry, platform
pulpy 4 soft **5** cheap, juicy, lurid, mushy **6** spongy **11** sensational
pulsate 4 beat, pump **5** pound, throb **7** vibrate **9** oscillate, palpitate
pulse 4 beat **5** throb **6** rhythm
pulverize 4 beat, ruin **5** crush, grind, smash, wreck **6** crunch, powder **7** atomize, destroy **8** demolish **9** micronize **10** annihilate
puma 3 cat **6** cougar **7** panther **12** mountain lion
pummel 3 hit **4** beat, drub **5** pound, punch **6** batter, buffet, hammer, thrash, wallop **7** belabor

pump 4 draw, shoe, quiz **5** exert, grill, heart, raise **6** device, elicit **7** operate **8** energize, question
pumpernickel 3 rye **5** bread
pumpkin 4 pepo **6** orange, squash **12** jack-o'-lantern ***family:*** **5** gourd
pump up 4 fill **6** excite, expand **7** enthuse, inflate **8** energize, increase, motivate **9** stimulate
pun 4 joke **11** paronomasia, play on words **13** double meaning
punch 3 box, cut, die, dig, hit, jab, jog, pep **4** bang, blow, cuff, poke, prod, push, snap, sock **5** clout, drive, notch, smack, vigor **6** buffet, emboss, energy, impact, pummel, strike, thrust **8** uppercut, vitality **9** emphasize, perforate
punch bowl 8 monteith
punch-drunk 5 dazed, dizzy, woozy **6** addled, groggy **8** unsteady **9** befuddled, slaphappy **10** staggering **11** disoriented
puncheon 3 log **4** cask, slab, tool **6** timber
puncher 5 boxer **6** cowboy
Punch's wife 4 Judy
punchy 5 dazed, dizzy, vivid **6** addled, lively **7** dynamic, vibrant **8** forceful, spirited, vigorous **9** befuddled, energetic, slaphappy **11** light-headed
punctilious 5 exact, fussy **7** careful, precise **9** attentive, observant **10** meticulous, particular, scrupulous **11** painstaking
punctual 5 ready **6** on time, prompt, timely
punctuate 4 mark **5** point **6** accent, divide, stress **8** separate **9** emphasize, interrupt **10** accentuate
punctuation mark 4 dash **5** brace, colon, comma, slant, slash **6** hyphen, parens, period **7** bracket, solidus, virgule **8** diagonal, ellipsis **9** backslash, guillemet, semicolon **10** apostrophe **11** parenthesis
puncture 3 jab **4** bore, flat, hole, stab **5** burst, drill, prick, punch **6** blow up, debunk, pierce, riddle **7** deflate, explode **8** disprove **9** discredit, perforate **11** perforation
pundit 4 guru, sage **5** maven, swami **6** critic, expert **7** teacher, wise man **9** authority, columnist **11** talking head
pungency 4 bite **5** sting **8** piquancy **9** intensity, sharpness
pungent 5 acrid, acute, harsh, sharp, spicy, tangy, zesty **6** barbed, biting **7** caustic, cutting, intense, mordant, painful, peppery, piquant, pointed **8** exciting, incisive, poignant, stinging **9** trenchant **10** irritating **11** provocative, stimulating
punish 4 fine, hurt **5** mulct, spank **6** amerce, avenge **7** chasten, correct, put down, reprove, revenge, scourge, torture **8** chastise, penalize **9** castigate, criticize **10** discipline
punishment 3 rod **4** fine **5** lumps, mulct **7** penalty, reproof **10** amercement, chastening, correction, discipline **11** castigation, comeuppance, just deserts **12** chastisement ***instrument:*** **7** scourge
punitive 5 penal **11** castigating, vindicative **12** correctional, disciplinary
punk 4 hood, thug **5** cholo, rowdy, tough **6** novice, rookie, tinder **7** hoodlum, ruffian, toughie **8** beginner, gangster, inferior **9** roughneck **10** delinquent ***rock group:*** **7** Ramones **10** Sex Pistols
punkah 3 fan
punt 4 boat, boot, kick, play **6** gamble, propel
Punta del ____ 4 Este
puny 4 weak **5** dinky, petty, small **6** feeble, little, measly, paltry, slight **7** trivial **8** inferior, niggling, picayune, piddling, trifling
pupa 9 chrysalid, chrysalis
pupil 5 cadet, tutee **7** learner, scholar, student **8** disciple **9** schoolboy **10** apprentice, schoolgirl ***French:*** **5** élève
puppet 4 doll, dupe, pawn, tool **6** figure, stooge **10** figurehead, marionette
puppy 3 dog **5** whelp
Purcell opera 13 Dido and Aeneas
purchase 3 buy **4** hold **6** obtain, pay for **7** acquire, procure **9** advantage **11** acquisition
pure 5 clean, fresh, plain, sheer, total, utter **6** chaste, decent **7** a priori, genuine, perfect, unmixed **8** absolute, abstract, innocent, spotless, virtuous **9** authentic, continent, exemplary, inviolate, stainless, unalloyed, undiluted, untainted **10** immaculate **11** theoretical, unblemished, unmitigated, unqualified **13** unadulterated
purebred 8 pedigree **9** full-blood, pedigreed **10** registered **11** full-blooded
puree 4 soup **5** paste
purely 4 just **5** quite **6** merely, simply, wholly **7** exactly, totally, utterly **8** entirely **10** altogether, completely **11** exclusively
purfle 4 trim **6** border **8** decorate, ornament
purgation 9 catharsis, cleansing **10** lustration
purgative 5 jalap **7** lustral **9** cathartic
purge 3 rid **4** oust **5** clear, expel **6** purify, remove **7** cleanse, wipe out **8** get rid of, lustrate **9** eliminate, liquidate
purification 8 ablution **9** catharsis, cleansing, expiation, purgation **10** absolution, lustration **11** expurgation **12** regeneration ***sacrament:*** **7** baptism
purify 5 clean, purge **6** filter, refine **7** clarify, cleanse
Purim 11 Feast of Lots ***queen:*** **6** Esther

puritan 4 prig **5** prude **8** bluenose **9** Mrs. Grundy
puritanical 4 prim **5** rigid **6** severe, strict **7** ascetic, austere, prudish **8** priggish **9** bluenosed **11** straitlaced
purity 8 chastity **9** innocence
purl 4 eddy, edge, knit **5** swirl, whirl **6** border, murmur, stitch **9** embroider
purlieu 5 haunt **7** hangout
purlieus 6 bounds, limits **7** suburbs **8** boundary, confines, environs **9** outskirts, precincts **12** neighborhood
purloin 3 nip **4** lift, take **5** filch, pinch, steal, swipe **6** pilfer, remove, rip off, snitch **11** appropriate
purloiner 5 crook, thief **8** larcener **9** larcenist
purple 4 plum, robe **5** cloth, grape, lilac, mauve, regal **6** florid, maroon, orchid, ornate, turgid, violet **7** flowery, pigment, pompous **8** imperial, lavender **9** bombastic, high-flown, overblown **10** rhetorical
Purple Heart 5 award, medal **10** decoration
purport 4 gist, mean **5** claim, drift, sense, tenor **6** allege, intend, thrust **7** meaning, message, profess, purpose **8** maintain **9** substance **11** connotation, implication **12** significance, significancy
purported 7 alleged, reputed, seeming **8** apparent, so-called, supposed **9** professed **10** ostensible
purpose 3 aim, end, use **4** goal, plan **5** point **6** action, design, intent, object **7** meaning, mission, resolve, subject **8** ambition, function, proposal **9** direction, intention, objective **10** aspiration, resolution **13** determination
purposeful 5 telic **6** driven, intent **7** earnest, planned, studied, willful **8** resolute **9** conscious, dedicated **10** calculated, considered, deliberate, determined **11** intentional **12** premeditated
purposeless 6 random **9** desultory, haphazard, hit-or-miss, irregular, unplanned
purposely 9 expressly **10** explicitly **12** deliberately **13** intentionally
purr 3 hum **6** murmur
purse 3 bag, sum **4** knit **5** money, pouch, prize **6** pucker, wallet **7** handbag **8** reticule **9** clutch bag **10** pocketbook, prize money ***Scottish:*** **7** sporran
pursue 3 woo **4** hunt, seek **5** chase, haunt, hound, stalk, track, trail **6** badger, follow **7** afflict, go after, proceed **8** continue, engage in **9** persecute, persevere
pursuit 3 job **4** hunt, work **5** chase, quest, trade **6** search **8** activity, business, vocation **9** avocation, following **10** employment, occupation, profession
purvey 6 obtain, peddle, supply **7** furnish, provide **9** provision
purview 3 ken **5** ambit, limit, orbit, range, reach, scope, sweep **6** extent **8** boundary
push 3 pep **4** goad, plug, prod, sell, spur, urge **5** boost, drive, elbow, exert, force, impel, press, punch, shove, vigor **6** attack, effort, energy, expand, peddle, propel, throng, thrust **7** advance, assault, impetus, promote **8** ambition, pressure, vitality **9** incentive, influence, offensive **10** enterprise, get-up-and-go, initiative
Pushkin, Alexander *novel:* **12** Eugene Onegin ***play:*** **10** Stone Guest (The) **12** Boris Godunov ***story:*** **13** Queen of Spades (The)
push off 4 exit **5** leave, start **6** depart, set out
push on 6 travel **7** advance, journey, proceed **8** continue, progress
pushover 4 snap **5** chump, cinch, softy **6** breeze, picnic, stooge, sucker **9** soft touch
pushy 4 bold **5** brash, nervy **7** forward **8** forceful **9** assertive, obnoxious **10** aggressive **12** presumptuous
pusillanimous 5 timid **6** coward, craven **7** chicken, gutless **8** cowardly, poltroon, timorous **9** spineless **11** lily-livered
puss 3 cat, mug **4** face **6** kisser, kitten
pussycat 5 sissy, softy **6** softie **8** pushover, weakling **9** soft touch **10** namby-pamby **13** bleeding heart
pussyfoot 5 creep, dodge, evade, glide, skulk, slink, sneak, steal **6** tiptoe **10** equivocate
pustule 4 boil **6** pimple **7** abscess, blister **8** furuncle **9** carbuncle
put 3 lay, set **4** park **5** place **8** position
putative 7 assumed, reputed **8** accepted, believed, presumed, supposed **11** conjectural **12** hypothetical
put away 3 eat **4** stow **5** eat up, swill **6** commit, devour, lock up **7** confine, consume **9** polish off **11** incarcerate
put by 4 save **5** lay in, store **7** lay away **8** lay aside, salt away
put down 5 crush, quash, quell **6** demean, demote, depose, squash, subdue **7** squelch **8** belittle, suppress **9** criticize, disparage, downgrade, humiliate
put forth 5 issue **6** assert **7** present, propose
put off 5 defer, delay **7** suspend **8** hold over, postpone
put on 3 act, don, kid **4** fake **5** apply, bluff, feign, mount, stage **6** affect, assume **7** mislead, perform, pretend, produce
put-on 3 act **4** fake, sham, show **5** faked, phony, spoof **6** parody **7** assumed, feigned

8 affected, disguise 9 pretended 10 artificial, false front

put out **3** vex **4** gall **5** annoy, douse, evict, issue, upset **6** bother, quench **7** disturb, produce, publish, trouble **8** irritate **9** aggravate, displease, embarrass **10** disconcert, exasperate, extinguish **13** inconvenience

putrefy **3** rot **5** decay, spoil, taint **6** molder **7** corrupt **9** break down, decompose

putrid **4** foul **5** fetid **6** rancid, rotten **7** corrupt, decayed, noisome, spoiled

putsch **4** coup **6** revolt **8** takeover, uprising **9** coup d'état, overthrow, rebellion **10** usurpation

putter **4** club, idle **6** fiddle, golfer, tinker **8** golf club

putting area **5** green

putto **5** cupid **6** cherub **8** amoretto

put together **4** form, join, make **5** build, unite **7** combine, connect, fashion, produce **8** assemble **9** construct, fabricate

putty **3** mud **4** clay **6** cement

put up **4** bunk **5** board, build, erect, house, lodge, raise **6** billet, harbor **7** quarter **8** domicile **9** construct

put up with **4** bear **5** stand **6** endure **8** tolerate

Puzo novel **6** Omerta **7** Last Don (The) **8** Fools Die, Sicilian (The) **9** Godfather (The)

puzzle **3** why **4** foil, koan **5** poser, rebus **6** baffle, enigma, fuddle, muddle, riddle **7** anagram, confuse, mystery, mystify, nonplus, paradox, perplex, problem, tangram **8** acrostic, befuddle, bewilder, confound **9** conundrum, crossword, dumbfound, frustrate **10** disconcert **11** brainteaser ***number:*** **6** Sudoku

puzzle out **5** solve **6** answer, decode **7** clarify, clear up, explain, unravel **8** decipher, unriddle

puzzling **6** knotty **7** cryptic **8** baffling **9** confusing, difficult, enigmatic **10** mystifying, perplexing **11** bewildering, paradoxical **12** inexplicable

Pygmalion ***beloved:*** **7** Galatea ***character:*** **5** Eliza (Doolittle) **7** Higgins (Henry) ***father:*** **5** Belus ***musical:*** **10** My Fair Lady ***playwright:*** **4** Shaw (George Bernard) ***sister:*** **4** Dido ***victim:*** **8** Sichaeus

pygmy **4** tiny **5** dwarf **6** bantam, little, midget **8** dwarfish **10** diminutive, homunculus **11** lilliputian

Pylades ***companion:*** **7** Orestes ***father:*** **9** Strophius ***wife:*** **7** Electra

pylon **4** post **5** tower **6** marker **7** gateway

Pym's creator **3** Poe (Edgar Allan)

Pynchon novel **13** Mason and Dixon **15** Gravity's Rainbow

pyramid builder **5** Khufu **6** Cheops

Pyramus' beloved **6** Thisbe

pyre **4** heap, pile

pyretic **3** hot **7** burning, febrile, fevered **8** feverish

pyromaniac **5** torch **8** arsonist **10** incendiary

pyrosis **9** heartburn

pyrotechnics **7** display **9** fireworks, spectacle

Pyrrha's husband **9** Deucalion

Pyrrhonist **7** doubter, skeptic **10** unbeliever

Pyrrhus ***kingdom:*** **6** Epirus ***victory:*** **7** Asculum

Pythias' friend **5** Damon

python **3** boa **5** snake ***slayer:*** **6** Apollo

pyx **3** box **4** case **6** vessel **9** container **10** receptacle

Q

Qatar ***capital:*** **4** Bida, Doha ***gulf:*** **7** Persian ***language:*** **6** Arabic ***monetary unit:*** **4** rial **5** riyal ***neighbor:*** **11** Saudi Arabia ***peninsula:*** **7** Arabian

QED word **4** erat, quod **13** demonstrandum

q.t., on the **7** sub rosa **8** covertly, secretly **13** under the table

quack **3** cry **4** honk, sham **6** con man, humbug **7** shammer **9** charlatan **10** mountebank **12** saltimbanque

quackery **4** hoax, scam **5** fraud, hokum **6** deceit **8** flimflam, pretense **9** deception, duplicity, imposture **11** dissembling

quad see **quadrangle**

quadrangle **4** yard **5** close, court, patio **6** square **7** polygon **9** courtyard, curtilage, enclosure

quadrant **3** arc **6** fourth **9** one-fourth **10** instrument

quadratic **4** boxy **6** square **7** boxlike **10** four-square

quadriga **7** chariot

quadrille 5 dance, ombre **8** card game **11** square dance
quadrivium subject 5 music **8** geometry **9** astronomy **10** arithmetic
quaestor 6 bursar **8** official **9** paymaster, treasurer
quaff 3 sip **4** swig, toss **5** drink, sup up **6** guzzle, imbibe, sup off **7** carouse, swallow
quagga 3 ass
quaggy 4 soft **5** boggy, mushy, pulpy **6** flabby, marshy, spongy **7** flaccid, squashy, squishy **8** squooshy, yielding
quagmire 3 bog, fen, fix, jam **4** mire **5** marsh, pinch, swamp **6** morass, pickle, plight, scrape, slough **7** dilemma **8** quandary **9** imbroglio, marshland, swampland **11** predicament
quahog 4 clam **7** mollusc, mollusk **9** shellfish **11** cherrystone
quail 5 cower, wince **6** blanch, blench, cringe, flinch, recoil, shrink **7** shudder, squinch, tremble **8** bobwhite ***flock of:*** **4** bevy
quaint 3 odd **5** funny, queer **7** antique, archaic, curious, oddball, strange, unusual **8** peculiar, singular **9** different, eccentric, whimsical **10** antiquated, unfamiliar **12** old-fashioned
quake 5 shake, waver **6** dither, quaver, quiver, shiver, tremor **7** shudder, temblor, tremble, twitter, vibrate **8** trembler
Quaker 6 Friend ***city:*** **12** Philadelphia ***colonizer:*** **4** Penn (William) ***color:*** **4** gray ***founder:*** **3** Fox (George) ***poet:*** **6** Barton (Bernard) **8** Whittier (John Greenleaf) ***pronoun:*** **3** thy **4** thee, thou **5** thine ***State:*** **12** Pennsylvania
qualification 6 caveat **7** ability, fitness **8** adequacy, aptitude, capacity, standard **9** condition, criterion **10** capability, competence **11** requirement, restriction, stipulation
qualified 3 fit **4** able **6** au fait, proper, proved, proven, tested **7** capablc, limited, partial, skilled, trained **8** eligible, modified, reserved **9** competent **10** restricted **11** conditional **12** accomplished
qualify 3 fit **5** limit **6** lessen, modify, reduce, soften, temper **7** certify, entitle, license, mollify, prepare **8** describe, mitigate, moderate **9** authorize **12** characterize
quality 4 rank **5** class, elite, grade, merit, prime, savor, state, trait, value, worth **6** factor, flower, gentry, status, virtue **7** caliber, element, feature, stature **8** position, property, standing **9** attribute, blue blood, character, gentility, parameter **10** excellence, patriciate, perfection
qualm 4 fear **5** demur, doubt **6** nausea, unease **7** illness, scruple **8** mistrust **9** faintness, misgiving, objection **10** conscience, foreboding, reluctance, uneasiness **11** compunction, nervousness, uncertainty **12** apprehension, remonstrance **13** unwillingness
qualmish 3 ill **4** sick **6** queasy, uneasy, unwell **8** hesitant, nauseous **9** nauseated, reluctant, squeamish, uncertain **10** scrupulous **12** apprehensive
quandary 3 fix, jam **4** bind, hole, spot **5** pinch **6** pickle, plight, scrape **7** dilemma **8** quagmire **10** difficulty **11** predicament
quantity 4 body, bulk, dose **5** total **6** amount, degree, volume **9** abundance, aggregate, magnitude ***fixed:*** **8** constant ***small:*** **3** bit **7** modicum, smidgen
quantum 5 quota, share, total **6** amount, budget, ration **7** measure, portion **9** aggregate, allotment, allowance, increment **13** apportionment ***of gravity:*** **8** graviton ***of radiant energy:*** **6** photon ***of vibrational energy:*** **6** phonon ***theory originator:*** **6** Planck (Max)
quarantine 6 detain **7** confine, isolate **8** restrain **9** isolation, restraint **10** detainment **11** confinement
quarrel 3 row **4** beef, bolt, dust, fray, fuss, miff, spar, spat, tiff **5** argue, arrow, brawl, broil, clash, fight, melee, run-in, scrap, set-to **6** affray, battle, bicker, differ, dustup, fracas, ruckus, squall, strife **7** brabble, discord, dispute, dissent, fall out, rhubarb, ruction, scuffle, wrangle **8** argument, catfight, conflict, disagree, skirmish, squabble **9** altercate, bickering, brannigan, lock horns, imbroglio, scrimmage **10** contention, difference, dissension, falling-out **11** altercation, embroilment **12** disagreement
quarrelsome 6 brawly **7** adverse, counter, hostile, scrappy, warlike **8** brawling, choleric, inimical, militant **9** bellicose, combative, irascible, irritable, rancorous, truculent **10** pugnacious **11** bad-tempered, belligerent, contentious **12** cantankerous, disputatious **13** argumentative
quarry 3 dig, pit **4** game, mine, pane, prey **5** chase, delve **6** source, victim **8** excavate **10** excavation
quarter 4 area, bunk, part **5** board, house, lodge, mercy, put up **6** barrio, billet, canton, fourth, ghetto, harbor, sector **7** barrack, section, shelter **8** clemency, district, division, locality, precinct, quadrant ***circle:*** **8** quadrant ***note:*** **8** crotchet ***pint:*** **4** gill ***ship's:*** **6** fo'c'sle **10** forecastle
quarterback 4 boss, head, lead **6** direct, leader, player **7** athlete, oversee **8** director,

overseer **9** supervise **10** footballer, supervisor

quartet 4 four **5** group **6** tetrad **8** ensemble, foursome **10** quadruplet, quaternion **11** composition

quart, metric 5 liter, litre

quartz 4 onyx, sard **5** agate **6** jasper **7** citrine, mineral **8** amethyst, sardonyx **9** cairngorm, carnelian **10** chalcedony

quash 2 ax **3** axe, nix **4** undo, veto, void **5** annul, crush, quell **6** defeat, negate, quench, stifle, subdue **7** abolish, nullify, put down, repress, smother, squelch **8** abrogate, dissolve, suppress **10** extinguish, invalidate

quasi 6 almost **7** nominal, seeming, virtual **8** apparent

Quasimodo 9 hunchback ***creator:*** **4** Hugo (Victor) ***occupation:*** **10** bell ringer ***residence:*** **5** Paris **9** Notre Dame

quaver 4 note **5** quake, shake, trill, waver **6** dither, shiver, tremor **7** shudder, tremble, twitter **10** eighth note

quay 4 dock, pier, slip **5** berth, jetty, levee, wharf **6** marina **7** moorage

quean 4 bawd, slut, tart **5** tramp, wench, whore **6** harlot, hooker **7** chippie, hustler **8** strumpet **9** courtesan **10** prostitute **12** streetwalker

queasy 3 ill **4** sick **6** qualmy, uneasy, unwell **7** dubious **8** delicate, doubtful, hesitant, nauseous, qualmish, troubled **9** hazardous, nauseated, reluctant, squeamish

Quebec province *capital:* **6** Quebec ***city:*** **5** Laval **8** Montreal **9** Longueuil ***island:*** **9** Anticosti ***mountain:*** **9** Tremblant **10** D'Iberville ***peninsula:*** **5** Gaspé ***provincial flower:*** **10** fleur-de-lys **11** madonna lily ***river:*** **10** St. Lawrence

Queeg's ship 5 Caine

queen *Austria-Hungary:* **12** Maria Theresa ***Belgian:*** **6** Astrid ***Danish:*** **8** Margaret, Margrete ***Egyptian:*** **9** Cleopatra **10** Hatshepsut ***English:*** **4** Anne, Mary **8** Victoria **9** Elizabeth ***French and English:*** **7** Eleanor ***Netherlands:*** **7** Beatrix, Juliana **10** Wilhelmina ***of Carthage:*** **4** Dido ***of heaven:*** **4** Mary, moon **7** Astarte ***of Isles:*** **6** Albion ***of Ithaca:*** **8** Penelope ***of Navarre:*** **8** Margaret ***of Scots:*** **4** Mary ***of Sheba:*** **6** Balkis ***of the Adriatic:*** **6** Venice ***of the Antilles:*** **4** Cuba ***of the East:*** **7** Zenobia ***of the fairies:*** **3** Mab **7** Titania ***of the gods:*** **4** Hera, Juno, Sati ***of the Nile:*** **9** Cleopatra ***of the North:*** **9** Edinburgh ***of the underworld:*** **3** Hel **4** Hela **10** Persephone, Proserpina ***Spanish:*** **7** Isabela **8** Isabella ***Spartan:*** **4** Leda ***Swedish:*** **9** Christina

Queen Anne's lace 6 carrot **10** wild carrot

Queen of Spades *author:* **7** Pushkin (Alexander) ***composer:*** **11** Tchaikovsky (Peter Ilyich)

Queensland *capital:* **8** Brisbane ***explorer:*** **4** Cook (Captain James)

queer 3 odd **5** bogus, weird **7** bizarre, curious, deviant, dubious, oddball, strange, touched, unusual **8** doubtful, peculiar, singular **9** eccentric, worthless **10** homosexual, outlandish, suspicious **11** counterfeit

quell 4 calm, stop **5** allay, check, crush, quash, quiet **6** pacify, quench, squash, subdue **7** conquer, put down, squelch **8** overcome, suppress, vanquish **9** overwhelm, subjugate **10** extinguish

Quemoy's neighbor 4 Amoy **5** Matsu

quench 4 sate **5** allay, douse, quash, quell, slake **6** lessen, put out, reduce **7** appease, assuage, gratify, lighten, put down, relieve, satiate, satisfy **8** mitigate, suppress **9** alleviate, eliminate **10** extinguish

quenelle 8 dumpling, meatball **9** forcemeat

quern 4 mill

querulous 5 whiny **7** fretful, peevish, pettish, whining **8** petulant **9** lamenting **10** whimpering **11** complaining

query 3 ask **4** quiz **5** doubt, grill **7** dubiety, inquire, inquiry **8** question **9** catechize **11** interrogate **13** interrogation

quest 4 hunt **5** probe **6** pursue, search **7** delving, inquire, inquiry, probing, pursuit, seeking **8** research **9** pursuance **11** inquisition **13** investigation ***object:*** **5** grail

question 3 ask, pry **4** poll, pump, quiz **5** doubt, grill, issue, probe, query **6** chance, matter **7** debrief, dispute, examine, inquire, inquiry, problem, suspect **8** distrust, mistrust **9** catechize, challenge, objection **10** difficulty, puzzle over **11** interrogate, possibility **13** interrogation, interrogatory

questionable 4 iffy, moot **5** shady, vague **6** unsure **7** dubious, obscure, suspect **8** arguable, doubtful, unproven **9** debatable, equivocal, refutable, uncertain **10** disputable, fly-by-night, improbable, unreliable **11** problematic **12** undependable

questioning 5 probe, query **6** show-me **7** delving, dubious, inquiry, probing **8** doubtful, grilling **9** inquiring, quizzical, skeptical, uncertain **11** incredulous, inquisitive, unbelieving **12** disbelieving **13** interrogation, interrogatory, investigative

quetzal 4 bird, coin **6** trogon

queue 3 row **4** file, line, rank, wait **5** braid **6** column **8** sequence

quibble 4 carp **5** argue, cavil **6** argufy, bicker, niggle, object **7** dispute, evasion, nitpick, wrangle **8** squabble **9** criticism, criticize, objection **10** split hairs

quick 4 core, deft, fast, keen, pith, root **5** acute, adept, agile, brisk, fleet, hasty, rapid, sharp, smart, swift **6** abrupt, bright, clever, nimble, prompt, speedy, sudden **7** hurried **9** breakneck, impetuous **10** harefooted **11** expeditious **12** lickety-split ***combining form:* 5** tachy

quick bread 6 muffin **7** biscuit

quicken 4 goad, grow, move, spur, stir, wake **5** hurry, liven, pique, rouse, speed **6** arouse, awaken, excite, hasten, incite, induce, kindle, revive, step up, vivify **7** actuate, animate, enliven, provoke, shake up, sharpen, speed up **8** activate, energize, motivate, vitalize **9** galvanize, stimulate **10** accelerate, exhilarate, invigorate

quickly 5 apace **6** at once, pronto **9** forthwith, posthaste **12** straightaway

quickness 5 haste, speed **8** alacrity, celerity, dispatch, legerity, rapidity, velocity **9** fleetness, rapidness, swiftness **10** promptness

quicksand 3 bog **4** mire **6** morass

quicksilver 7 mercury **9** mercurial **10** inconstant

quick-tempered 5 cross, fiery, ratty, testy **6** cranky, touchy **7** peppery **8** choleric, petulant **9** irascible, irritable, splenetic **10** passionate

quick-witted 3 apt **4** keen **5** acute, agile, alert, canny, ready, sharp, smart **6** astute, brainy, bright, clever, prompt **9** brilliant **10** perceptive **11** intelligent, penetrating

quid 3 cut, wad **4** chew, coin **5** money, pound **9** sovereign

quiddity 3 nub **4** gist, meat, pith **6** trifle **7** essence, quibble **8** crotchet **12** eccentricity, quintessence

quidnunc see **rumormonger**

quiescent 4 calm **5** quiet, still **6** benign, hushed, latent, placid, serene, stilly **7** abcyant, dormant, halcyon, lurking **8** inactive, tranquil **10** untroubled

quiet 4 calm, hush, idle, lull, mute, stop **5** abate, allay, inert, muted, shush, still, whist **6** asleep, becalm, gentle, hushed, lessen, placid, serene, settle, silent, soothe, subdue **7** compose, halcyon, pacific, passive, restful, silence, subdued **8** decrease, inactive, peaceful, reserved, secluded, taciturn, tranquil **9** noiseless, soundless, stillness, unruffled **11** tranquility, tranquilize, unobtrusive **12** tranquillity

quietus 3 end **5** death, sleep **6** damper, demise, finish **7** decease, passing, silence **8** curtains **10** inactivity, settlement **11** termination

quill 3 pen **5** float, shaft, spine, spool **6** bobbin **7** feather, spindle

quilt 4 pouf, puff **5** duvet **8** coverlet **9** comforter, eiderdown **11** counterpane ***design:* 8** trapunto

quince 3 bel

quintessence 4 gist, meat, pith, soul **5** ideal, model, stuff **6** marrow **7** epitome **8** exemplar, last word, quiddity, ultimate **9** substance **10** apotheosis **12** essentiality

quintessential 5 ideal, model **7** classic, typical **8** ultimate **9** classical, exemplary **10** archetypal, consummate, prototypal **12** prototypical

quintillionth combining form 4 atto

quintuple 8 fivefold

quip 3 dig, gag, kid **4** gibe, gird, jape, jeer, jest, jibe, joke **5** crack, fleer, sally, scoff, sneer, tease **6** banter, oddity, retort, zinger **7** quibble **8** drollery, repartee **9** wisecrack, witticism **12** equivocation

quipster 3 wag, wit **4** card **5** clown, comic, droll, joker **6** jester **8** comedian, funnyman, humorist, jokester **11** wisecracker

quirk 3 tic **4** bend, kink, quip, whim **5** crook, curve, twist **6** groove, oddity, vagary **7** caprice **8** accident, crotchet **9** mannerism **11** peculiarity **12** idiosyncrasy

quirky 3 odd **7** erratic, offbeat **8** peculiar **9** eccentric, irregular, whimsical **10** capricious **13** idiosyncratic

quirt 4 lash, whip

quisling 5 Judas, rebel **7** traitor **8** apostate, betrayer, defector, turncoat **10** copperhead **11** backstabber **12** collaborator

quit 3 end, pay **4** drop, free, halt, stop **5** cease, chuck, leave **6** depart, desert, desist, give up, resign, retire, settle **7** abandon, drop out, forsake, release, relieve, satisfy **8** knock off, leave off, released, renounce, withdraw **9** discharge, liquidate, surrender, terminate **10** relinquish **11** discontinue

quite 3 all **4** just, very, well **5** fully, in all **6** in toto, purely, rather, wholly **7** exactly, totally, utterly **8** entirely **9** perfectly **10** absolutely, altogether, completely, positively, thoroughly **12** considerably

quittance 6 amends **7** redress **8** reprisal, requital **9** atonement, discharge, expiation, repayment **10** recompense, reparation **11** restitution **12** compensation

quitter 4 funk **6** coward, craven **7** chicken, dastard **8** poltroon, recreant **9** defeatist **11** yellowbelly

quiver 4 beat, case **5** pulse, quake, shake,

throb, waver **6** arrows, dither, jitter, quaver, shiver, tremor **7** pulsate, shudder, tremble, twitter, vibrate **9** palpitate, vibration

qui vive 5 alert **7** lookout

Quixote see **Don Quixote**

quixotic 7 foolish **8** fanciful, illusory, romantic **9** fantastic, imaginary, visionary **10** capricious, chimerical, idealistic **11** impractical

quiz 3 ask **4** exam, test **5** grill, query **7** examine, inquire **8** question **9** catechize **11** interrogate **12** cross-examine

quizzical 3 odd **5** queer **6** quaint, show-me **7** curious, dubious, mocking, probing, puzzled, teasing **8** doubtful, doubting, sardonic **9** inquiring, skeptical **11** incredulous, inquisitive, questioning, unbelieving **12** disbelieving

quodlibet 5 issue, point **6** debate, medley **7** mélange **8** fantasia, question **11** disputation

quoin 5 angle, block, wedge **6** corner **8** keystone, voussoir

quoit 4 hoop, ring **6** circle

quoits peg 3 hob

quondam 4 late, once, past **6** bygone, former, whilom **7** defunct, onetime **8** sometime **9** erstwhile **10** occasional

quorum 4 body **5** group **7** council **8** majority

quota 3 cut, lot **4** bite, meed, part **5** share, slice, whack **6** amount, parcel, ration **7** measure, portion, quantum **9** allotment, allowance **10** allocation, percentage, proportion

quotation 3 bid **5** offer, price **7** excerpt, extract, passage **8** citation

quotation mark, French 9 guillemet

quote 3 bid **4** cite, list **5** blurb, offer, price, refer **6** adduce, borrow, repeat **7** excerpt, extract, passage **8** citation

quotidian 5 daily, plain, usual **6** common **7** average, diurnal, prosaic, regular, routine, vanilla **8** day-to-day, everyday, ordinary, workaday **9** circadian **11** commonplace **12** unremarkable

quotient 5 ratio, share **7** caliber, portion **9** allotment, magnitude **10** percentage, proportion

Quo Vadis *author:* 11 Sienkiewicz (Henryk) ***character:* 4** Nero **5** Lygia, Peter **8** Vinicius **9** Petronius

R

Ra *son:* 6 Khonsu ***wife:* 3** Mut

Raamah *father:* 4 Cush ***son:* 5** Dedan, Sheba

Rabbi Ben Ezra author 8 Browning (Robert)

rabbit 4 cony, hare **5** bunny, coney ***female:* 3** doe ***fictional:* 5** Fiver, Hazel, Mopsy, Peter **6** Flopsy, Harvey **7** Thumper **8** Crusader, Ricochet **9** Bugs Bunny **10** Cotton-tail **11** Easter Bunny ***food:* 5** salad **6** carrot **7** lettuce ***neutered:* 5** lapin ***tail:* 4** scut

rabble 3 mob **4** mass, rout **5** crush, horde **6** masses **8** canaille, populace, riffraff, unwashed **9** hoi polloi **10** lower class **11** proletariat, rank and file

rabble-rouser 7 inciter **8** agitator, fomenter **9** demagogue **10** incendiary **12** troublemaker

Rabelais character 7 Panurge **9** Gargantua **10** Pantagruel

rabid 3 mad **4** wild **5** crazy, ultra **6** crazed, insane **7** extreme, fanatic, frantic, furious, radical, zealous **8** demented, deranged, frenetic, frenzied, obsessed, ultraist **9** delirious, extremist **10** corybantic **11** hydrophobic

rabies 11 hydrophobia

raccoon 8 ringtail ***dog:* 6** tanuki ***relative:* 5** civet, coati, panda **8** civet cat, kinkajou **10** cacomistle, coatimundi

race 3 rev **4** bolt, dart, dash, gill, lash, meet, rush, tear, type **5** brook, chase, creek, fling, hurry, match, rally, relay, shoot, speed, spurt **6** charge, course, gallop, runnel, scurry, sprint, stream **7** channel, contest, rivalry, rivulet, scamper **8** marathon **9** grand prix **11** competition, watercourse ***zigzag:* 6** slalom

race car 4 Elva, Lola, Ralt **5** Lotus, March, Swift **6** Abarth, Cooper, Merlyn, Royale, Turner **7** Avenger, Brabham, Chevron, Crosslé, Ferrari, Mallock, McLaren, Reynard, TransAm, Triumph **8** Corvette **9** Van Diemen **12** Austin Healey

racecourse 4 oval, turf **5** track **8** speedway

racehorse 5 Alsab, Kelso **6** Forego **7** Assault, Barbaro, Man O' War **8** Affirmed, Citation **9** Riva Ridge, War Emblem **10** War Admiral

11 Forward Pass, Seattle Slew, Secretariat, Smarty Jones **12** Native Dancer
Rachel ***father:*** **5** Laban ***husband:*** **5** Jacob ***servant:*** **6** Bilhah ***sister:*** **4** Leah ***son:*** **6** Joseph **8** Benjamin
rachis **4** back **5** chine, spine **8** backbone **12** spinal column
rachitic **5** shaky **6** wobbly **7** rackety, rickety, tenuous **9** tremulous **10** ramshackle, rattletrap
____ **Rachmaninoff** **6** Sergei, Sergey
racing enthusiast **8** railbird
racism **7** bigotry, jim crow **9** apartheid, prejudice **11** segregation
racist **4** nazi **5** bigot **7** bigoted **10** intolerant, prejudiced **11** supremacist
rack **3** bed **4** buck, bunk, pace, pain, sack, scud **5** frame, wring **6** harass, harrow, martyr, strain, wrench **7** afflict, agonize, antlers, crucify, ratchet, sawbuck, stretch, torment, torture **8** distress, sawhorse **9** framework, persecute **10** excruciate
racket **3** con, din **4** game **5** babel, fraud, hooha, noise **6** clamor, hubbub, rattle, scheme, tumult, uproar **7** pursuit, swindle **8** ballyhoo, brouhaha, foofaraw **10** hullabaloo **11** pandemonium
racketeer **7** goombah, mafioso, mobster **8** extorter, gangster **9** godfather ***law:*** **4** RICO (Act)
rack up **3** win **4** gain **5** reach, score **6** attain **7** achieve, realize **10** accomplish
raconteur **11** storyteller
racy **4** blue, gamy **5** bawdy, broad, juicy, salty, spicy, vampy, zesty **6** purple, risqué, smutty, snappy, vulgar, wicked **7** piquant, pungent **8** indecent, off-color, vigorous **10** suggestive
Radames' beloved **4** Aïda
radar image **3** pip **4** blip, spot **5** trace
Raddai ***brother:*** **5** David ***father:*** **5** Jesse
radiance **3** ray **4** glow **5** glory, shine **6** luster **7** aureola, aureole **8** splendor **10** brightness, brilliance
radiant **4** glad **5** aglow, beamy, shiny **6** bright, cheery, lucent **7** beaming, fulgent, glowing, lambent **8** cheerful, luminous, lustrous **9** brilliant, effulgent **10** effulgence **12** incandescent
radiate **4** beam, glow **5** gleam, shine, strew **6** spread **7** diverge **8** illumine **10** illuminate
radiation unit **3** rad, rem, rep **7** langley, sievert **8** roentgen
radiator **6** cooler, heater **9** convector **11** transmitter **13** heat exchanger
radical **4** acyl, root **5** basal, basic, rebel, ultra **7** extreme, fanatic, primary **8** agitator, cardinal, inherent, militant, ultraist **9** anarchist, essential, extremist, intrinsic **10** subversive, underlying **11** fundamental **12** foundational, iconoclastic **13** revolutionary ***mathematical:*** **4** surd
radicle **4** root **5** radix **9** hypocotyl
radio **4** AM-FM **8** wireless ***frequency range:*** **8** waveband ***shortwave:*** **3** ham **7** amateur
radioactive **3** hot **7** nuclear
radium ***discoverer:*** **5** Curie (Marie, Pierre) ***symbol:*** **2** Ra
radius **5** ambit, orbit, range, reach, sweep **6** extent **7** compass, purview **9** extension
radix **4** base, root **6** source
radon symbol **2** Rn
raffish **6** coarse, jaunty, rakish, sporty, vulgar **9** dissolute **12** devil-may-care
raffle **7** drawing, lottery
raft **3** lot, ton **4** heap, mess, pile, scad, slew **5** balsa, float **6** bundle ***Maori:*** **4** moki
rafter **4** balk, beam, viga
rag **3** jaw, kid, rib **4** bait, jive, josh, rail, razz, rock **5** baste, cloth, scold, tease **6** berate, harass, hector, needle, pester **7** tabloid, torment **9** newspaper
ragamuffin **3** bum **4** hobo, waif **5** gamin, tramp **6** beggar, gamine, orphan, urchin **7** wastrel **8** vagabond **9** scarecrow **11** guttersnipe
rage **3** cry, fad, ire, mad, wax **4** chic, fume, fury, mode, rant **5** anger, craze, fancy, furor, go ape, mania, storm, style, vogue, wrath **6** blow up, frenzy, furore, lose it, seethe **7** fashion, madness, passion **8** boil over, hysteria, violence **10** dernier cri **11** indignation
ragged **4** rent, torn **5** seedy **6** frayed, jagged, shabby, uneven **7** unkempt, worn-out **8** frazzled, straggly, tattered **10** threadbare
raging **4** wild **6** stormy **7** furious, extreme, intense, violent **8** blustery **9** ferocious, turbulent **10** blustering **11** tempestuous
ragout **4** stew **5** salmi **6** burgoo, jumble, medley **7** farrago, goulash, mélange, mixture **8** mishmash **9** potpourri **10** hodgepodge, salmagundi **11** gallimaufry
rags **4** duds, garb **5** dress **6** attire, shreds **7** apparel, clothes, raiment, threads **8** clothing **10** attirement **11** habiliments
ragtag see **rabble**
ragwort **7** senecio **9** cineraria, groundsel **10** butterweed
raid **4** bust, loot, sack **5** foray, harry **6** attack, forage, harass, inroad, invade, maraud, ravage, sortie **7** assault, despoil, overrun, plunder **8** invasion, spoliate **9** incursion, onslaught
raider **6** pirate **10** freebooter

rail 3 bar, jaw **5** fence, scold, track **6** berate, revile **7** barrier, inveigh, upbraid **8** banister **10** tongue-lash, vituperate
rail bird 4 coot, sora **5** crake **7** clapper **8** marsh hen, water hen ***extinct:* 4** moho
railing 8 banister **10** balustrade ***part:* 8** baluster
raillery 5 scorn **6** banter **7** mockery, teasing **8** badinage, derision, ridicule, taunting **10** lampoonery, persiflage
railroad *branch:* 6 siding ***car:* 5** coach, diner, stock **6** hopper **7** caboose, gondola, Pullman ***engine:* 10** locomotive ***locomotive:* 9** iron horse ***station:* 5** depot ***underground:* 4** tube **5** metro **6** subway ***worker:* 6** porter **7** fireman **8** brakeman, engineer **9** conductor **11** gandy dancer
raiment 4 duds, garb, gear, togs **5** array, dress **6** attire **7** apparel, clothes, threads, vesture **8** clothing, garments, glad rags, vestiary **9** caparison, vestments **10** attirement **11** habiliments
rain 4 spit **6** deluge, mizzle, shower **7** drizzle **8** downpour, sprinkle **10** cloudburst **13** precipitation
rainbow 3 arc **4** irid, iris **5** array, gamut **7** fantasy **8** illusion, spectrum **9** pipe dream ***bridge:* 7** Bifrost ***chaser:* 9** visionary ***goddess:* 4** Iris
rainbow fish 5 guppy, trout **6** wrasse
raincoat 3 mac **4** mack **6** poncho, trench **7** oilskin, slicker **10** mackintosh
rain leader 9 downspout
rain tree 9 monkeypod
raise 2 up **4** ante, grow, hike, jack, jump, lift, pump, rear **5** boost, breed, erect, exalt, hoist, put up **6** foment, incite, jack up, leaven, muster, uplift **7** augment, bring up, collect, elevate, enhance, inflate, produce **8** heighten, increase **9** construct, cultivate, increment, propagate
raisin 5 grape **7** currant, sultana **10** dried grape
Raisin in the Sun author 9 Hansberry (Lorraine)
raison d' ____ 4 état, être
raja 4 king **5** chief, ruler **6** prince **9** dignitary
rake 3 rip **4** comb, roué, scan **5** angle, blood, pitch, rifle, scamp, scour, slope **6** forage, glance, lecher, rascal, scrape, search, strafe **7** incline, playboy, ransack, rummage, scratch **8** enfilade, lothario **9** debauchee, libertine **10** profligate
rakehell 4 fast, wild **5** blood, rogue, scamp **6** rascal, sporty **7** playboy, raffish **8** lothario, rascally **9** debauchee, dissolute, lecherous, libertine **10** licentious, profligate
rake-off 3 cut **4** bite, take **5** chunk, share **7** portion **9** baksheesh, lagniappe **10** commission, percentage
rake's look 4 leer, ogle
Rake's Progress artist 7 Hogarth (William)
rakish see **rakehell**
rally 4 race, stir, wake **5** harry, renew, rouse, waken **6** arouse, awaken, bestir, kindle, muster, perk up, pick up, repair, volley **7** convene, enliven, marshal, rebound, recover **8** assemble, clambake, comeback, mobilize, recovery **9** challenge, re-collect **10** invigorate, reorganize
rallying cry 5 motto **6** byword, slogan **9** watchword **10** shibboleth **11** catchphrase
ram 5 Aries, crash, crowd, drive, pound, sheep, stuff **6** batter, plunge, strike, thrust **7** warship
Rama's wife 4 Sita
ramble 3 gad **4** roam, rove **5** drift, range, run on, stray, troll **6** stroll, wander **7** blather, digress, diverge, maunder, meander, saunter, traipse **8** divagate, straggle **9** gallivant
rambler 4 rose **5** gypsy, hiker, nomad, rover **6** roamer, walker **7** drifter, vagrant **8** stroller, vagabond, wanderer **9** itinerant **10** ranch house
rambunctious 5 rowdy **6** unruly **7** raucous, willful **10** boisterous, headstrong **11** intractable **12** recalcitrant, ungovernable
ramification 5 shoot **6** branch, offset **8** offshoot **9** outgrowth, offspring **11** consequence
ramify 6 branch, divide, extend **7** develop, radiate **9** branch out, propagate **11** proliferate
Ramona author 7 Jackson (Helen Hunt)
ramose 8 branched
ramp 5 apron **7** incline
rampage 4 rage, riot, tear **5** binge, fling, spree, storm
rampageous 4 wild **6** unruly **7** riotous
rampant 4 rank, rife, wild **7** rearing, regnant **9** prevalent, unbridled **10** widespread **12** uncontrolled, unrestrained
rampart 4 wall **5** ridge **7** bulwark, parapet **9** barricade **10** breastwork
ramshackle 6 flimsy **7** rickety, run-down **8** decrepit **10** tumbledown **11** dilapidated
ram's mate 3 ewe
ranch 5 finca **6** quinta, spread **8** estancia, hacienda ***worker:* 6** cowboy, gaucho **7** cowgirl, cowhand, cowpoke **10** cowpuncher
rancher 6 cowboy **7** breeder **9** cattleman
rancid 4 high, rank, sour **5** fetid **6** putrid, skunky, smelly **7** noisome, spoiled **8** stinking **9** offensive **10** malodorous
rancor 4 gall **6** animus, enmity, hatred **7** ill

will **9** animosity, antipathy, hostility **10** antagonism, bitterness

rancorous 6 bitter **7** hateful, hostile **8** spiteful, venomous **9** malicious, malignant, vitriolic **10** malevolent **11** acrimonious **12** antagonistic

Rand, Ayn *novel:* 6 Anthem **12** Fountainhead (The) **13** Atlas Shrugged

random 6 casual **7** aimless **8** slapdash **9** arbitrary, desultory, haphazard, hit-or-miss, unplanned **10** accidental, contingent, hit-and-miss, incidental **11** purposeless

randy 4 lewd **5** bawdy, lusty **7** lustful, satyric **9** lecherous, libertine, lickerish, salacious **10** lascivious, libidinous, licentious

range 3 row, run **4** area, band, roam, rove, shot, site, sort, span, vary **5** align, ambit, carry, drift, field, gamut, orbit, order, reach, realm, ridge, scale, scope, space, stove, stray, sweep, width **6** assort, domain, extent, length, limits, ramble, sierra, sphere, spread, wander **7** compass, earshot, expanse, eyeshot, habitat, meander, purview, stretch **8** confines, distance, latitude, locality, panorama, province, stovetop, traverse, vicinity **9** amplitude, extension, gallivant, magnitude, territory **12** distribution

range finder 9 telemeter

ranger 3 spy **5** scout **6** lawman, patrol, warden **8** overseer **9** caretaker, protector

rangy 4 lean **5** lanky **6** gangly **7** spindly **8** gangling

rani's mate 4 raja **5** rajah

rank 3 row **4** file, foul, lush, rate, seed, sort, tier **5** class, fetid, funky, grade, gross, humid, order, place, queue **6** assort, cachet, coarse, filthy, lavish, putrid, rancid, rating, smelly, status **7** arrange, dignity, echelon, footing, noisome, profuse, rampant, reeking, station, stature **8** classify, evaluate, flagrant, outright, position, standing, stinking **9** downright, egregious, loathsome, luxuriant, overgrown, repulsive **10** consummate, malodorous **11** conspicuous, unmitigated

rank and file 5 plebs **6** people, plebes **8** populace **9** commonage, commoners, plebeians **10** commonalty **11** enlisted men

rankle 3 irk, vex **4** rile **5** annoy **6** bother, fester, nettle, seethe **8** embitter, irritate **9** aggravate **10** exasperate

ransack 3 rob **4** comb, grub, loot, rake **5** rifle, scour **6** forage, ravage **7** plunder, rummage

Ran's husband 5 Aegir

ransom 3 buy **4** free **6** redeem, regain, rescue **7** deliver, recover **8** liberate **13** consideration

rant 3 jaw, rag **4** huff, rage, rail, rate, rave **5** mouth, scold **6** screed, tirade **7** bluster, bombast, declaim, fustian **8** bloviate, harangue, perorate **10** vituperate **11** rodomontade

ranula 4 cyst

rap 3 hit, tap **4** blow, chat, swat, talk, wipe **5** blame, chide, knock, swipe **6** charge, patter, rebuke **7** censure, condemn, reproof **8** causerie, denounce, reproach, sentence **9** criticize, criticism, reprehend, reprimand, reprobate **10** discussion **12** conversation

rapacious 6 greedy **8** covetous, grasping, ravening, ravenous **9** predatory, raptorial, voracious **10** gluttonous, predaceous

rapacity 5 greed **7** avarice, avidity **8** cupidity, voracity **10** greediness **12** covetousness, ravenousness

rape 4 ruin **5** colza, force, spoil **6** canola, defile, ravage, ravish **7** assault, debauch, despoil, outrage, plunder, violate **9** violation **10** ravishment, spoliation

Rape of the Lock, The *author:* 4 Pope (Alexander) ***heroine:* 7** Belinda

Raphael *birthplace:* 6 Urbino ***subject:* 7** Madonna ***teacher:* 8** Perugino

rapid 4 fast **5** brisk, chute, fleet, hasty, quick, swift **6** speedy **7** hurried **9** breakneck **11** expeditious

rapidity 5 haste, hurry, speed **8** celerity, velocity

rapids 5 chute **8** cataract **10** white water

rapier 4 épée **5** blade, sword

rapine 4 loot, pelf, swag **5** booty, prize, spoil **6** boodle, spoils **7** pillage, plunder **10** spoliation

Rappaccini's Daughter 8 Beatrice ***author:* 9** Hawthorne (Nathaniel)

rapper 3 DMX, Eve, GZA, Jin **4** Ice T, Jay-Z **5** Cee-Lo, Rakim **6** Eminem, Heavy D, KRS-ONE, Mac Dre, Mos Def, Run DMC, Twista **7** Caushun, LL Cool J, OutKast **8** Ludacris, Melle Mel, Paul Wall **9** Kanye West, Method Man, Snoop Dogg **10** Kool Moe Dee, Lupe Fiasco, Spoonie Gee, Vanilla Ice **11** Busta Rhymes, Public Enemy

rapport 5 unity **6** accord **7** concord, harmony **8** affinity **9** communion **13** communication

rapscallion see **rascal**

rap session 6 confab, parley **7** palaver **8** colloquy **10** discussion

rapt 6 intent **7** engaged **8** absorbed, immersed **9** engrossed **10** enthralled **11** carried away, preoccupied, transported

raptor 3 owl **4** hawk **5** eagle **6** condor, falcon, merlin, osprey **7** kestrel, vulture **9** gyrfalcon **10** bird of prey **11** deinonychus

rapture 5 swoon **6** heaven **7** delight, ecstasy,

nirvana **9** transport **10** exaltation **13** seventh heaven

rara ____ 4 avis

rare 3 few, red **4** pink, thin **6** choice, dainty, exotic, scarce, seldom, select **7** elegant, unusual **8** delicate, singular, sporadic, superior, uncommon, unwonted **9** exquisite, recherché, underdone **10** infrequent, occasional **11** distinctive, exceptional **13** extraordinary

rarefied 4 fine, thin **7** tenuous **8** esoteric **10** attenuated

rarefy 4 thin **6** refine **9** attenuate

rarely 6 little, seldom **9** extremely, unusually **12** infrequently

raring 4 avid, keen **5** eager **6** gung-ho **12** enthusiastic

rarity 5 curio **6** oddity **7** curiosa **8** scarcity **9** curiosity **10** aberration **11** collectible

rascal 3 imp **4** rake **5** devil, knave, rogue, scamp **7** lowlife, villain, wastrel **8** scalawag **9** miscreant, reprobate, scoundrel, skeezicks **10** blackguard **11** rapscallion ***Irish:* 8** spalpeen

rash 5 hasty, heady **6** abrupt, brazen, daring, madcap, plague, sudden, unwary, unwise **7** foolish **8** careless, epidemic, eruption, headlong, heedless, outbreak, reckless **9** audacious, daredevil, foolhardy, hotheaded, impetuous, imprudent, impulsive **10** ill-advised, incautious, indiscreet, unthinking **11** injudicious, precipitate, temerarious, thoughtless

rasp 4 file, fret **5** annoy, chafe, grate **6** abrade, scrape **7** scratch **8** irritate

raspberry 7 catcall **8** blackcap **10** Bronx cheer

raspy 3 dry **5** harsh, rough **6** hoarse **7** grating, jarring, raucous **8** scrabbly, scratchy

rat 4 blab, fink, heel, scab, sing **5** louse **6** defect, desert, inform, rodent, snitch, squeak, squeal, tattle **7** stoolie **8** apostate, defector, informer, recreant, renegade, squealer, turncoat **9** bandicoot, repudiate, turnabout **11** stool pigeon **12** tergiversate ***female:* 3** doe

ratchet 4 pawl **6** detent

rate 3 fee, set, tab **4** cost, earn, rank **5** assay, class, grade, merit, price, scale, set at, value **6** amount, assess, charge, degree, esteem, regard, survey, tariff **7** apprize, deserve, valuate **8** appraise, classify, consider, estimate, evaluate, price tag **9** valuation **10** proportion

rather 4 a bit **5** quite **6** fairly, in lieu, kind of, pretty, sort of **7** instead **8** somewhat **10** more or less, preferably **11** alternately **13** alternatively

rathskeller 3 bar, inn, pub **4** dive **6** saloon, tavern **7** barroom, taproom **8** alehouse, basement

ratify 4 seal **5** enact **7** approve, certify, confirm, endorse, license **8** accredit, sanction, validate

rating 4 mark, rank **5** class, grade **6** number **8** estimate, standing

ratio 5 scale **7** percent **8** fraction, quotient **10** percentage, proportion

ratiocination 8 judgment, sequitur **9** inference, reasoning **10** conclusion

ration 4 dole, food, meal, mete **5** allot, divvy, quota, share **6** divide, parcel **7** measure, mete out, prorate **8** allocate **9** allotment, allowance **10** provisions **13** apportionment

rational 4 calm, cool, sane **5** lucid, sober, sound **6** stable **7** logical, prudent **8** sensible, thinking **9** judicious **10** consequent, reasonable **11** circumspect, intelligent, level-headed **12** intellectual

rationale 5 basis, logic **6** reason **7** grounds **9** reasoning **11** explanation **13** justification

rationalize 7 explain, justify **10** account for **11** externalize

ratite 3 emu, moa **4** kiwi, rhea **7** ostrich

rattail 3 cod **9** grenadier

rattan 4 cane, palm **6** switch **7** malacca

Rattigan play 10 Winslow Boy (The) **14** Separate Tables

rattle 3 gab, jaw, yak **4** chat, faze, rale **5** abash, addle, clack, noise, rouse, run on, upset **6** babble, gabble, jangle, racket **7** chatter, clatter, confuse, disturb, flummox, perplex, unnerve **8** bewilder, confound, distract **9** discomfit, embarrass **10** disconcert, noisemaker

rattlebrained 5 dizzy, giddy, silly **7** flighty **8** skittish **9** frivolous

rattling 4 very **5** brisk, quick **6** damned, lively, mighty **8** whacking, whopping **9** energetic, extremely **11** exceedingly

ratty 4 mean **5** dowdy, dumpy, seedy, tacky **6** cheesy, scurvy, shabby **7** unkempt **8** slovenly **9** irritable **10** despicable **11** treacherous **12** contemptible

raucous 4 loud **5** harsh, noisy, rough, rowdy **6** hoarse, unruly **7** grating, jarring, squawky **8** rowdyish, strident **9** termagant, turbulent **10** boisterous, disorderly, stridulent, stridulous, tumultuous **11** cacophonous **12** rambunctious

raunchy 4 foul **5** dirty, nasty **6** coarse, filthy, sloppy, smutty, vulgar **7** obscene **8** indecent **9** salacious

ravage 4 loot, raze, ruin, sack **5** foray, harry, spoil, strip, waste, wreck **6** forage, invade, ravish **7** despoil, overrun, pillage, plunder, ransack, scourge **8** desolate, spoliate **9** depredate, desecrate, devastate

rave 4 gush, rant **5** storm **6** babble, jabber **7** enthuse **10** rhapsodize

ravel 3 run **4** fray **5** snarl **6** muddle, tangle **7** perplex, untwine **8** entangle **9** extricate **10** complicate **11** disentangle

ravelings 4 lint **7** threads

Ravel work 6 Boléro **7** La Valse **14** Daphnis et Chloé **17** Rapsodie espagnole

raven 3 jet **4** ebon, inky, prey **5** black, ebony, jetty, sable **7** despoil, plunder **9** pitch-dark **10** pitch-black ***relative:*** **3** jay **4** crow **6** magpie **7** blue jay

Raven, The *author:* **3** Poe (Edgar Allan) ***lost love:*** **6** Lenore ***refrain:*** **9** Nevermore

ravenous 6 greedy, hungry **7** starved **8** edacious, famished, starving **9** rapacious, voracious **10** gluttonous

ravine 3 cut, gap **4** gulf, pass, wadi **5** abyss, chasm, cleft, clove, flume, gorge, gulch, gully, notch **6** arroyo, canyon, clough, coulee, defile, gutter, nullah **7** crevice, fissure **8** barranca, crevasse ***Mt. Washington's:*** **9** Tuckerman

raving 3 mad **5** manic, rabid, upset **6** crazed **7** frantic, lunatic, unglued **8** demented, deranged, frenetic, frenzied, maniacal, obsessed, unhinged, worked up **9** ravishing **10** distraught, flipped out, hysterical, irrational **11** overwrought

ravish 4 rape **5** force, spoil **6** defile **7** assault, despoil, outrage, pillage, plunder, violate **8** deflower, entrance, overcome **9** enrapture, transport

raw 4 cold, nude, rude **5** bleak, chill, crass, crude, fresh, green, naked, rough, young **6** callow, coarse, impure, native, unclad, unripe, vulgar **7** uncouth **8** immature, uncooked, unformed **9** au naturel, inelegant, irritated, run-of-mine, unbridled, unclothed, undressed, unrefined **10** unfinished, unpolished **13** inexperienced

rawboned 4 bony, lank, lean **5** gaunt, gawky, lanky, spare **6** skinny **7** angular, scraggy, scrawny

ray 4 beam **5** gleam, manta, shaft, skate, trace **6** radius, streak, stream **7** radiate, sawfish, sunbeam, torpedo **8** moonbeam **9** devilfish, thornback **10** guitarfish

raze 4 ruin **5** level **7** destroy **8** demolish, pull down, tear down

razor 4 Atra **6** shaver

razz 3 rag, rib **4** bait, josh, mock, twit **5** scout, taunt **6** badger, banter, deride, heckle, hector **8** ridicule (see also **raspberry**)

RBI 11 run batted in **12** runs batted in

re 4 as to **5** about, as for **7** apropos **9** apropos of, as regards, regarding **10** as respects, concerning, relating to, respecting **12** with regard to **13** with respect to

reach 4 beat, gain, pass, span, tack **5** carry, get at, get to, grasp, level, range, scope, sweep, touch **6** arrive, attain, extend, extent, rack up, thrust **7** achieve, contact, horizon, project, stretch **9** encompass, influence **10** accomplish, get through

____ reaction 4 dark **5** alarm, chain, light **7** nuclear **8** chemical

reactivate 5 renew **6** revive **8** rekindle, revivify **9** resurrect **10** revitalize **11** resuscitate

read 4 scan, skim **6** peruse **8** pore over ***inability to:*** **8** dyslexia

readable 7 legible

reader 6 lector, primer **7** proofer, scanner **8** bookworm **9** anthology

readily 4 well **6** easily, freely **7** lightly **9** willingly **12** effortlessly

readiness 4 ease **5** skill **6** DEFCON **7** aptness **8** alacrity, dispatch, facility **9** dexterity, quickness **10** promptness **11** inclination, promptitude **12** preparedness

reading 6 lesson **7** lection, version, vulgate **9** rendition **10** recitation

ready 3 set **4** prep, ripe, yare **5** equip **6** active, gear up, make up, primed, prompt **7** prepare **8** inclined, prepared **9** available

real 4 true, very **5** pukka, sound, valid **6** actual, honest **7** certain, genuine, sincere **8** bona fide, concrete, existent, tangible **9** authentic, undoubted, veridical **10** sure-enough, undeniable **11** substantive **12** indisputable

real-estate abbreviation 3 ARM, apt, flr, gar, gdn, kit, lux, mbr, MLS, TLC, vic **4** bsmt, bdrm, frpl, FSBO, furn, HVAC, PITI, util, wbfp **5** RESPA

realism 6 verism **7** verismo **10** naturalism, pragmatism **11** objectivism, objectivity

realistic 4 sane **5** sober, sound **7** genuine, natural **8** lifelike, rational, sensible, veristic **9** practical, pragmatic **10** bottom-line, hard-boiled, hardheaded, reasonable, unromantic **11** down-to-earth **12** matter-of-fact **13** unsentimental

reality 4 fact, true **5** being, sooth, truth **9** actuality, existence, substance **13** flesh and blood

realize 4 gain, reap **5** grasp, reach, score **6** attain, rack up **7** achieve, feature, imagine, reflect **8** conceive, envisage, envision **9** actualize, recognize **10** accomplish, comprehend

really 4 very **5** truly **6** indeed, verily **7** awfully, clearly **8** actually, honestly **9** assuredly, certainly, decidedly, genuinely **10** definitely, positively **11** exceedingly, indubitably, undoubtedly **12** unmistakably

realm 5 orbit, range, scope, sweep **6** domain, empire, estate, extent, radius, sphere **7** compass, demesne, kingdom, purview **8** dominion

ream 4 load, scad **5** widen **7** enlarge **11** countersink

reanimation 7 rebirth, revival **10** renascence, resurgence **11** reawakening, renaissance **12** risorgimento

reap 3 cut **4** earn, gain **5** glean, shear **6** garner, gather, obtain, sickle, thresh **7** harvest

rear 3 aft **4** back, butt, hind, lift, ramp, rump, seat, tail **5** after, breed, build, erect, fanny, hoist, nurse, put up, raise, set up, stern **6** behind, bottom, fledge, foster, heinie, uphold **7** bring up, caboose, elevate, nurture **8** backside, buttocks, hindmost **9** construct, posterior

rear end 3 bum, bun, can **4** butt, duff, moon, rump, seat, tail, tush **5** booty, fanny, stern **6** behind, bottom, heinie **7** caboose, keister **8** backside, buttocks, derriere **9** posterior

rearmost 3 end **4** last **5** final **8** terminal, ultimate

rearrange see **readjust**

rearward 3 aft **4** back **6** behind **8** backward **9** posterior **10** retrograde

Rea Silvia ***father:*** **7** Numitor ***son:*** **5** Remus **7** Romulus

reason 3 why, wit **4** mind, nous **5** basis, cause, infer, proof, think **6** excuse, ground, motive, sanity, senses **7** account, reflect **8** argument, cogitate, conceive, persuade **9** inference, intellect, rationale, soundness, speculate, wherefore **10** deliberate **11** explanation **12** intelligence **13** consideration, justification, ratiocination, understanding

reasonable 4 fair, just **5** cheap, level, sound **6** modest **7** logical, low-cost, tenable **8** credible, feasible, moderate, rational, sensible **9** equitable, plausible **10** acceptable, affordable, restrained **11** inexpensive, intelligent

reasoning 4 case **5** logic **8** argument **9** deduction

reasonless 7 invalid **8** baseless **9** illogical, senseless, unfounded **10** fallacious, groundless, irrational **11** meaningless, purposeless

reawaken 5 renew **6** revive **7** refresh **8** revivify **9** reanimate **10** regenerate **12** reinvigorate

rebate 6 lessen, refund, return **8** decrease, diminish, give back **9** deduction, reduction

Rebecca ***beloved:*** **7** Ivanhoe ***father:*** **5** Isaac

Rebekah ***brother:*** **5** Laban ***father:*** **7** Bethuel ***husband:*** **5** Isaac ***nurse:*** **7** Deborah ***son:*** **4** Esau **5** Jacob

rebel 6 anarch, mutiny, resist, revolt **7** disobey **8** frondeur, mutineer **9** insurgent **10** malcontent **13** revolutionary, revolutionist

rebellion 6 émeute, mutiny, revolt, rising **8** defiance, intifada, sedition, uprising **10** insurgence, insurgency, resistance, revolution **12** insurrection

rebellious 6 unruly **8** mutinous, stubborn **9** insurgent **10** refractory **11** disaffected, disobedient **12** contumacious, unmanageable **13** insubordinate

rebirth 7 revival **9** awakening **10** conversion, renascence, resurgence **11** reanimation, reawakening, renaissance **12** resurrection, risorgimento

rebound 5 rally **6** bounce, reecho, recoil, repeat **7** recover **8** comeback, recovery, ricochet, snap back **10** convalesce

rebozo 5 scarf, shawl

rebuff 4 slap, snub **5** repel **6** reject **7** fend off, repulse, ward off **8** turn away

rebuild 6 repair, revamp **7** remodel, restore **8** overhaul, renovate, retrofit **9** modernize, refurbish **11** recondition, reconstruct **12** rehabilitate

rebuke 3 rap **4** snub **5** chide, scold, scorn **6** berate, earful, lesson, rebuff **7** bawl out, lecture, reproof, reprove **8** admonish, call down, reproach, scolding **9** reprimand, talking-to **10** tongue-lash **11** comeuppance, objurgation **12** admonishment, dressing-down **13** tongue-lashing

rebut 5 repel **6** refute, reject **7** confute, fend off, repulse, ward off **8** confound, disprove, stave off **10** controvert, disconfirm

rebuttal 5 reply **6** answer, retort **7** defense, riposte **8** argument, comeback, response **9** rejoinder **10** refutation **11** repudiation

recalcitrant 6 unruly **7** froward, willful **8** contrary, perverse, stubborn, untoward **9** fractious, obstinate, resistant **10** headstrong **11** intractable **12** ungovernable, unmanageable

recall 4 stir **5** evoke, renew, rouse, waken **6** arouse, awaken, cancel, memory, remind, repeal, revive, revoke **7** bethink, rescind, restore, retract, reverse **8** callback, remember, resemble, take back, withdraw **9** anamnesis, recollect, reinstate, reminisce, represent, reproduce **10** revocation **11** bring to mind, countermand, remembrance **12** recollection, reminiscence

recant 5 unsay **6** abjure, revoke **7** retract **8**

forswear, renounce, take back, withdraw **9** backtrack, repudiate
recap 5 sum up **6** précis, résumé, review **7** reprise, retread, summary **8** overview **9** summarize **10** retrograde
recapitulate 5 sum up **6** resume, review **9** summarize **10** retrograde
recapitulation 5 sum-up **6** précis, résumé, review **7** epitome, reprise, summary **9** summing-up
recede 3 ebb **4** back **5** abate, taper **6** lessen, reduce, retire **7** dwindle, regress, retract, retreat **8** decrease, diminish, fall back, withdraw **10** retrograde, retrogress
receipts 4 gate, take **5** sales **6** income **7** revenue, takings **8** earnings, proceeds
receive 4 host **5** admit, catch, greet **6** accept, endure, suffer, take in **7** acquire, sustain, welcome **10** experience
received 5 plain, sound **6** common **7** popular **8** accepted, familiar, ordinary, orthodox **12** acknowledged, conventional
receiver 4 dish **5** donee, fence, pager **6** aerial **7** antenna, catcher, scanner **9** recipient, treasurer
recent 3 new **4** late **5** fresh, novel **6** latest, modern **8** neoteric
receptacle 6 hamper, holder, hopper, trough, vessel **9** container **10** repository
receptive 4 open **7** passive **8** amenable **9** sensitive **10** accessible, hospitable, open-minded, responsive **11** persuadable, persuasible, suggestible, susceptible
recess 4 cove, nook **5** break, cleft, niche **6** alcove, grotto, hiatus **7** adjourn **8** prorogue **9** prorogate, terminate **11** indentation
Recessional author 7 Kipling (Rudyard)
recessive 3 shy **8** retiring **9** reclusive, withdrawn **10** unsociable
recherché 4 rare **5** novel **6** choice, dainty, exotic, select **7** elegant, unusual **8** affected, delicate, original, superior, uncommon **9** exquisite **11** pretentious
recipe 7 formula **9** procedure **12** prescription
recipient 5 donee **7** grantee **8** receiver **11** beneficiary
reciprocal 4 mate, twin **5** match **6** double, fellow, mutual **8** requited **9** bilateral, companion, duplicate **10** coordinate **11** interactive ***prefix:* 5** inter
reciprocate 5 repay **6** retort, return **7** requite **8** exchange **9** retaliate **10** compensate, recompense **11** interchange
recital 5 story **6** soiree **7** concert, reading **9** discourse, narration **10** recounting **11** enumeration, performance
recite 4 tell **5** chant, count, state **6** detail, number, relate, repeat, report, set out **7** declaim, narrate, recount, reel off **8** describe, rehearse **9** pronounce
reckless 4 rash, wild **5** brash, hasty **6** daring, madcap **8** carefree, heedless **9** audacious, daredevil, foolhardy, hotheaded **10** ill-advised, incautious **11** harebrained, temerarious, thoughtless **12** devil-may-care **13** irresponsible
reckon 3 sum **5** count, gauge, guess, judge, opine, tally, total **6** cipher, figure, number, regard **7** account, compute, suppose, surmise **8** consider, estimate **9** calculate, enumerate **10** conjecture **11** approximate
reckoning 3 tab **4** bill **5** tally, score **7** account, invoice **9** statement **10** arithmetic, estimation **11** calculation, computation
reclaim 4 save, tame **6** redeem, reform, rescue **7** deliver, recover, restore **9** restitute **11** recondition, reconstruct **12** rehabilitate
recline 3 lie **4** rest, tilt **5** couch, slant, slope **6** lounge, repose **7** lie down **10** stretch out
reclining 4 flat **5** prone **6** supine **9** decumbent, prostrate, recumbent
recluse 5 loner **6** hermit, shut-in **7** eremite **8** cenobite, solitary **9** anchorite ***female:* 7** ancress **9** anchoress
reclusive 8 eremitic, hermetic, reserved, solitary **9** withdrawn **10** antisocial, eremitical, unsociable **12** misanthropic
recognition 6 credit, esteem, notice **9** attention, awareness, gratitude **10** cognizance, perception **11** realization **12** appreciation
recognize 4 note, spot **5** admit **6** notice **7** observe, realize **8** accredit, diagnose, identify **9** apprehend **10** appreciate **11** acknowledge, determinate, distinguish
recoil 4 balk, kick **5** cower, dodge, quail, start, wince **6** blench, cringe, flinch, shrink **7** rebound, retract, squinch **8** reaction
recollect 5 evoke **6** recall, remind, revive **7** bethink **8** remember **9** reminisce
recollection 6 memory, recall **9** anamnesis, flashback **11** remembrance **12** reminiscence
recommence 5 renew **6** pick up, reopen, resume, take up **7** restart **8** continue
recommend 4 tout **6** advise, praise, prefer **7** acclaim, commend, counsel, endorse, entrust, propose, suggest **8** advocate
recommendation 4 plug **5** pitch **6** advice **7** counsel **11** endorsement, testimonial
recompense 3 pay **4** wage **5** repay **6** amends, reward **7** guerdon, premium, redress, requite **8** gratuity, requital **9** indemnify, indemnity, quittance, reimburse, repayment **10** compensate, remunerate, reparation **11** reciprocate, restitution, retribution **12** com-

pensation, remuneration **13** consideration, gratification
reconcile 4 suit, tune **5** adapt **6** accept, accord, adjust, attune, make up, resign, settle, square, submit, tailor **7** conform, get over, resolve **9** harmonize, integrate **10** conciliate, coordinate **11** accommodate
recondite 4 deep **6** arcane, hidden, mystic, occult, orphic, secret **7** cryptic, erudite, learned, obscure **8** abstruse, academic, esoteric, hermetic, profound **9** concealed, difficult, enigmatic, scholarly
recondition 3 fix **4** mend **6** doctor, repair, revamp **7** rebuild, restore **8** make over, overhaul, retrofit **9** restitute **10** rejuvenate **12** rehabilitate
reconnoiter 5 scout **6** survey
reconsider 6 review, revise **7** rethink, reweigh **8** reassess **9** reexamine **10** reevaluate **13** think better of
reconstruct 6 recast, re-form, remake, revamp **7** rebuild, reclaim, remodel, restore **8** make over, overhaul, readjust, renovate **9** refashion, restitute **10** reassemble, reorganize
record 4 disc, disk, tape **5** album **6** annals, enroll **7** archive, journal, platter **8** archives, document, register **9** chronicle **10** transcript ***of a meeting:*** **7** minutes ***of proceedings:*** **4** acta ***ship's:*** **3** log **7** logbook
recorder 4 TiVo **5** flute **9** registrar ***flight:*** **8** black box
record player 4 hi-fi **5** phono **8** Victrola **9** turntable **10** gramophone, phonograph
recount 4 tell **5** state **6** recite, relate, report, retail **7** narrate **8** describe, rehearse **9** enumerate
recoup 6 regain **7** get back, reclaim, recover **8** retrieve **9** repossess
recourse 6 backup, refuge, resort **7** standby, stopgap, support **8** resource **9** expedient, makeshift
recover 4 heal, mend **5** evict, rally, renew **6** recoup, redeem, regain, revive **7** get back, get over, improve, rebound, reclaim, recycle, restore **8** retrieve, snap back **9** come round, reacquire, recapture, re-collect, repossess, restitute **10** bounce back, convalesce, recuperate
recreant 3 rat **5** false **6** coward, craven, untrue **7** chicken, dastard, unloyal **8** apostate, cowardly, defector, deserter, disloyal, poltroon, renegade, turncoat **9** dastardly, faithless, turnabout **10** perfidious, traitorous, unfaithful **13** pusillanimous
recreate 4 play **5** evoke, renew **7** freshen, refresh, restore **11** reconstruct
recreation 4 play **5** hobby, sport **7** leisure, pastime **8** activity **9** avocation, diversion **10** relaxation **13** entertainment
recrudesce 5 recur **6** return, revert, revive **7** reoccur **8** break out
recruit 4 boot, hire **5** raise **6** engage, enlist, enroll, muster, novice, rookie **7** draftee **8** beginner, enlistee, freshman, headhunt, neophyte, newcomer **9** conscript, fledgling, reinforce, replenish **10** apprentice, tenderfoot
rectifier 4 tube **5** diode **8** detector, ignitron
rectify 3 fix **4** mend **5** amend, emend **6** adjust, remedy, repair **7** correct
rectitude 6 virtue **7** honesty, probity **8** morality **9** rightness **11** uprightness **13** righteousness
rector 6 parson, pastor, priest **9** clergyman **10** headmaster
rectory 5 manse **8** benefice **9** parsonage
recumbent 4 flat **5** prone **6** supine **7** leaning, resting **8** reposing **9** lying down, prostrate, reclining
recuperate 4 heal, mend **5** rally **6** regain, revive **7** rebound, recover **8** snap back **10** convalesce
recur 5 cycle, haunt **6** repeat, resort, return **7** iterate, revolve **8** turn back
recurring 7 chronic **8** periodic **10** continuous, isochronal, periodical, persistent **11** isochronous **12** intermittent
red 4 puce, ruby **5** coral, gules, rouge, ruddy **6** cerise, claret, florid, maroon **7** carmine, crimson, flushed, glowing, magenta, oxblood, scarlet, vermeil **8** burgundy, sanguine **9** vermilion ***combining form:*** **4** rhod **5** rhodo
Red 6 Bolshy, commie **7** Bolshie, comrade **9** Bolshevik, Communist
redact 4 edit **6** censor, revise
Red and the Black author 8 Stendhal
red ape 9 orangutan
red arsenic 7 realgar
red-backed sandpiper 6 dunlin
Red Badge of Courage, The *author:* 5 Crane (Stephen) ***hero:*** **7** Fleming (Henry)
red-bellied snipe 9 dowitcher
redbird 7 tanager **8** cardinal **13** summer tanager
red blood cell 11 erythrocyte
red-blooded 5 juicy, lusty, manly **6** hearty, robust, virile **8** vigorous **9** energetic
redbreast 4 knot **5** robin **7** sunfish
red-breasted snipe 9 dowitcher
Redburn author 8 Melville (Herman)
red carp 8 goldfish
red cobalt 9 erythrite

red copper ore 7 cuprite
Red Cross *founder:* 6 Barton (Clara), Dunant (Henri) ***Knight:* 6** George
redden 5 blush, color, flush, rouge **6** mantle, ruddle **11** incarnadine
red dog 5 blitz
redecorate 4 redo **5** fix up **9** refurbish
redeem 4 free, save **5** atone, loose, renew **6** offset, pay off, ransom, reform, rescue **7** expiate, reclaim, recover, restore **9** exonerate
redeemer 5 Jesus **6** Christ, savior **7** messiah, saviour
redemption 6 ransom **7** release **9** atonement, expiation, salvation **11** deliverance
red-eye 5 hooch **6** flight, rotgut **7** whiskey **8** home brew, rock bass **9** moonshine
red-faced 5 ruddy **6** florid, shamed **7** abashed, flushed, glowing **8** blushing, rubicund, sanguine, sheepish **9** mortified **11** embarrassed
red felt hat 3 fez
redfish 4 bass, drum **5** perch **6** salmon **10** ocean perch **11** channel bass
red hickory 6 pignut
red-hot 5 fiery **6** ardent, fervid **7** blazing, boiling, burning, fervent, flaming, glowing **8** brand-new, scalding, sizzling **9** scorching **10** blistering, passionate, sweltering **11** impassioned
red Indian paint 9 bloodroot **11** sanguinaria
red ink 7 arrears, deficit **8** shortage
red inkberry 8 pokeweed
red ironbark 8 eucalypt **10** eucalyptus
red iron ore 5 ocher, ochre **8** hematite
red lauan 8 mahogany
red-legged crow 6 chough
red-legged sandpiper 9 turnstone
red-letter 7 notable **8** historic **9** important, memorable **10** noteworthy, observable, remarkable **11** significant
red-light district 5 stews **10** tenderloin
red mite 7 chigger
redneck 4 clod, hick, rube **5** Bubba, yahoo, yokel **6** rustic **7** bumpkin, hayseed **9** hillbilly **10** clodhopper, good old boy, good ole boy
redo 5 renew **6** repeat, revamp **7** remodel, restyle **8** make over, overhaul, refinish, renovate **9** refurbish **10** redecorate
red ocher 8 hematite
redolence 4 balm, odor **5** aroma, attar, scent, spice **7** bouquet, incense, perfume **9** fragrance
redolent 5 balmy, spicy, sweet **7** odorous, scented **8** aromatic, fragrant, perfumed **9** ambrosial, evocative **10** suggestive **11** reminiscent
redouble 4 dupe **7** dualize, enhance, magnify **8** heighten **9** duplicate, intensify, reinforce **10** strengthen
redoubt 4 fort **7** bastion, citadel **8** fastness, fortress **10** stronghold
redoubtable 5 famed, great **6** famous, mighty **7** awesome, eminent **8** imposing, puissant, renowned **9** prominent **10** celebrated, formidable, impressive **11** illustrious **12** intimidating, overwhelming **13** distinguished
redound 6 accrue, recoil **7** conduce, reflect **10** contribute
red pigment 4 lake **5** eosin, ocher, ochre **6** ruddle
Red Planet 4 Mars
redpoll 5 finch **6** linnet
redraft 6 revamp, revise, rework **7** restyle, rewrite **8** make over, overhaul, rescript, revision, work over **9** recension
redress 4 heal **6** amends, avenge, negate, offset, relief, remedy **7** correct **8** reprisal, requital **9** cancel out, indemnity, quittance, vindicate **10** compensate, counteract, correction, neutralize, recompense, reparation **11** restitution, retribution **12** compensation
red roe 5 coral **6** caviar
redroot 7 alkanet, pigweed **9** bloodroot **12** New Jersey tea
red sable 8 kolinsky
red silver ore 9 proustite
red squirrel 9 chickaree
reduce 2 ax **3** axe, cut **4** cull, diet, melt, pare **5** abate, force, lower, shade, shave, slash, smelt **6** humble, lessen, recede, weaken **7** abridge, curtail, cut back, cut down, dwindle, liquefy, squeeze **8** boil down, compress, contract, decrease, diminish, discount, mark down, minimize, simplify, taper off **10** depreciate, slenderize **11** consolidate
reductio ad ____ 8 absurdum
reduction 6 digest, précis, rebate **7** cutback, cutdown, epitome, summary **8** abstract, discount, markdown, synopsis **9** abatement **10** shortening **11** curtailment **12** condensation
redundancy 6 excess **7** nimiety, surfeit **8** pleonasm **9** abundance, profusion, prolixity, tautology **10** repetition **11** periphrasis, reiteration, superfluity **13** supernumerary
redundant 5 extra, spare, windy, wordy **6** de trop, prolix **7** surplus, verbose **9** duplicate, excessive, iterative **11** duplicative, reiterative, repetitious, superfluous, tautologous **13** supernumerary
redux 7 revived **8** restored
redwing 6 thrush **9** blackbird
redwood 7 amboyna, sequoia **8** mahogany

reed **4** di mo, pipe **5** arrow, grass
reed instrument **3** sax **4** dizi, oboe **5** shawm **6** curtal **7** bagpipe, bassoon, dulcian **8** bagpipes, clarinet, crumhorn, melodeon **9** accordion, harmonica, krummhorn, saxophone **10** concertina **11** English horn
reedy **4** thin **6** skinny, stalky, twiggy **7** spindly
reef **3** bar, cay, key **4** lode, vein **5** atoll, ledge **6** reduce, skerry **7** sandbar
reek **4** funk **5** fetor, smell, stink **6** stench **9** effluvium
reeking **4** rank **5** fetid, funky, fusty **6** putrid, rancid, smelly, stinky **7** noisome, stenchy **10** malodorous
reel **4** spin, sway, turn **5** lurch, spool, weave, whirl **6** bobbin, careen, teeter, totter, waggle, wobble **7** stagger, stumble **8** fall back
reestablish **5** renew **6** revive **7** restore **9** reinstate **10** reinscribe **11** reintroduce
reevaluate **6** review **7** rethink, reweigh **8** reassess **9** reexamine **10** reconsider
reeve **4** ruff **6** thread **9** sandpiper **10** magistrate
reexamine see **reevaluate**
refashion **5** alter **6** change, modify, recast, remake, revamp **7** remodel **8** make over, overhaul **9** transmute
refection **4** feed, meal **6** repast **11** nourishment, refreshment
refectory **7** commons **10** dining hall
refer **6** advert, allude, assign, relate, submit **7** ascribe **9** attribute
referee **3** ump **5** judge **6** umpire **7** adjudge, arbiter, mediate **8** mediator **9** arbitrate, officiate **10** adjudicate, arbitrator
reference **6** credit, source **7** meaning, mention **8** allusion, citation, innuendo, relation, resource **11** testimonial ***guide:*** **5** index **12** bibliography ***work:*** **5** atlas, bible, guide **6** manual **7** almanac **8** handbook **9** directory, guidebook, thesaurus **10** dictionary **11** enchiridion **12** encyclopedia
referendum **4** poll, vote **10** plebiscite
refine **5** prune, smelt **6** polish, purify, smooth **7** elevate, improve, perfect, process **8** civilize **9** cultivate
refined **4** pure **6** subtle, urbane **7** elegant, genteel, raffiné **8** cultured, elevated, ladylike, raffinée, well-bred **9** civilized **10** cultivated, fastidious **13** sophisticated
refinement **5** couth, grace, taste **6** finish, polish **7** culture, finesse, suavity **8** breeding, civility, courtesy, elegance, subtlety, urbanity **9** politesse **10** politeness **11** cultivation **12** civilization, distillation, purification **13** clarification
reflect **4** echo, pore, show **5** weigh **6** bounce, mirror, ponder, reason, return **7** redound **8** chew over, cogitate, consider, ruminate **9** cerebrate **10** deliberate, retrospect **11** contemplate, demonstrate
reflection **4** slur **5** image **6** musing **7** replica, thought **8** reproach **9** aspersion **10** cogitation, meditation, rumination, simulacrum **11** cerebration **12** deliberation, reproduction **13** animadversion, consideration, contemplation
reflective **7** pensive **9** reflexive **10** cogitative, indicative, meditative, ruminative, thoughtful **12** deliberative **13** contemplative
reflux **3** ebb **4** GERD **8** backflow
reform **5** amend, emend **6** redeem, revise **7** correct, improve, reclaim, shape up **8** make over **10** correction, houseclean, regenerate
Reformation leader **4** Knox (John) **6** Calvin (John), Luther (Martin) **7** Zwingli (Huldrych)
reformatory **3** pen **6** prison **7** borstal **8** big house, remedial **10** corrective **12** penitentiary
refractory **6** mulish, unruly **7** froward, restive **8** contrary, perverse, stubborn **9** obstinate **10** bullheaded, headstrong, rebellious, unyielding **11** intractable, stiff-necked **12** unmanageable
refrain **4** fa-la, keep, la-la, stop **5** eieio, tra-la **6** burden, chorus, fa-la-la, shrink **7** abstain, forbear, tra-la-la **8** hold back
refresh **5** renew **6** revive **7** animate, enliven, quicken, restore **8** irrigate, recreate, renovate **9** replenish, stimulate **10** rejuvenate
refresher **5** drink, tonic **6** bracer **8** reminder **9** stimulant **11** restorative
refreshing **5** brisk, tonic **7** bracing **8** reviving **9** analeptic, animating **10** delightful, energizing **11** restorative, stimulating **12** invigorating, rejuvenating
refrigerant **3** ice **5** freon **7** coolant, cryogen **12** fluorocarbon **13** sulfur dioxide
refrigerator **6** cooler, fridge, icebox, walk-in **9** condenser **10** Frigidaire
refuge **3** den **4** lair, port **5** cover, haven **6** asylum, covert, harbor, resort **7** hideout, protect, retreat, shelter **8** hideaway, recourse, resource **9** expedient, harborage, sanctuary, safe house
refugee **2** DP **5** exile **6** émigré **7** evacuee **8** emigrant, fugitive **10** boat person, expatriate
refulgent **6** bright **7** glowing, radiant **8** luminous **9** brilliant
refund **5** repay **6** rebate **8** give back **9** reimburse, repayment, restitute **11** restitution
refurbish **4** redo **5** fix up, renew **6** revamp **7**

restore **8** make over, overhaul, renovate, retrofit **10** redecorate, rejuvenate **11** recondition

refusal 4 veto **6** denial **7** regrets **8** negative, negation **9** disavowal **10** abnegation, thumbs-down **11** declination, repudiation

refuse 3 jib, nix **4** chum, deny, junk, scum **5** dreck, dross, offal, spurn, swill, trash, waste **6** debris, litter, reject, scraps, spilth **7** decline, garbage, residue, rubbish **8** disallow, leavings, remnants, turn down, withhold **9** reprobate, repudiate, sweepings **10** disapprove

refutation 8 disproof, elenchus, rebuttal

refute 4 deny **5** rebut **7** confute **8** confound, disprove **10** controvert, disconfirm

regain 6 recoup **7** get back, recover **8** reoccupy, retrieve **9** recapture, repossess ***possession:*** **7** replevy **8** replevin

regal 5 grand **6** august, kingly, purple **7** queenly, stately, sublime **8** glorious, imperial, imposing, kinglike, majestic, princely, splendid **9** monarchal, sovereign **10** monarchial **11** magnificent, monarchical, resplendent

regale 4 feed **5** amuse, feast **6** dinner, divert, spread **7** banquet **9** entertain

regalia 5 array **6** finery **8** frippery, insignia **9** caparison, full dress, trappings **10** decoration **11** habiliments

Regan *father:* 4 Lear ***husband:*** **8** Cornwall ***sister:*** **7** Goneril **8** Cordelia

regard 4 deem, heed, mark, note, rate, view **5** assay, favor, honor, judge, value **6** admire, assess, esteem, homage, liking, look at, notice, reckon, repute **7** account, concern, respect **8** approval, consider, devotion, estimate, fondness **9** attention **10** admiration, cognizance, estimation, observance, solicitude **11** approbation, contemplate, observation **12** appreciation, satisfaction **13** consideration

regardful 7 heedful **8** watchful **9** advertent, attentive, observant **10** perceptive, respectful

regarding 4 as to, in re **5** about, anent, as for **7** apropos **8** touching **9** apropos of **10** as respects, concerning, relative to, respecting **11** in respect to **13** with respect to

regatta 4 race ***site:*** **6** Henley **10** Argenteuil

regenerate 5 renew **6** reform, revive **7** rebirth, restore **8** recreate **9** reproduce

regent 5 ruler **6** warden **8** governor **9** protector

regicide's victim 4 king **7** monarch

regime 4 rule, term **5** reign **6** empire, tenure **7** dynasty **10** government, leadership

regimen 4 diet, plan, rule **6** course **10** government

region 4 area, belt, part, zone **5** field, tract **6** domain, locale, sector, sphere **7** demesne, terrain **8** locality, province, vicinity **9** bailiwick, territory **12** neighborhood

regional 5 local **9** localized, sectional **10** provincial **11** territorial

register 4 file, list, note, roll, till **5** enter, range, tally **6** annals, docket, enroll, ledger, record, roster **7** catalog, check in, express **8** indicate **9** catalogue

regnant 4 rife **6** ruling **7** current, popular **8** dominant, reigning **9** paramount, prevalent, sovereign **10** prevailing, widespread

regress 6 revert **9** backslide **10** retrograde

regret 3 rue, woe **4** care **5** grief, mourn **6** bemoan, bewail, excuse, grieve, lament, repent, sorrow **7** anguish, apology, deplore, remorse **9** heartache, penitence **10** contrition, heartbreak **11** compunction

regretful 5 sorry **6** rueful **8** contrite, mournful, penitent **9** repentant, sorrowful **10** apologetic, remorseful **11** penitential

regrettable 3 sad **6** too bad, woeful **8** grievous **10** lamentable **11** distressing, unfortunate **13** heartbreaking

regular 3 due, set **4** even **5** fixed, usual **6** common, normal, steady **7** average, equable, general, natural, orderly, typical, uniform **8** complete, constant, everyday, methodic, ordinary, standard **9** clocklike, customary, prevalent **10** methodical, systematic **11** commonplace **12** run-of-the-mill

regulate 5 order, scale **6** adjust, direct, govern, police, square, temper **7** arrange, control **8** organize **9** methodize, systemize **11** systematize

regulation 3 law **4** rule **5** canon, edict, order **6** decree **7** precept, statute **9** ordinance, prescript **11** restriction **12** codification

regulator 8 governor

rehabilitate 4 cure, heal **7** reclaim, recover, restore **8** renovate **9** reeducate, restitute **11** recondition

rehash 5 reuse **6** repeat, review, rework **7** restate, version **8** chew over, rehearse, talk over **9** rendering, rendition, rewording **11** restatement **12** recapitulate

rehearsal 5 trial **6** dry run, tryout **7** recital **8** dummy run, practice **10** run-through, simulation **11** reiteration **12** woodshedding

rehearse 5 drill, train **6** repeat **7** run over **8** exercise, practice **10** run through

Rehoboam *father:* 7 Solomon ***kingdom:*** **5** Judah **6** Israel ***mother:*** **6** Naamah

reign 4 rule, sway **6** govern **7** prevail **8** dominate, dominion **11** predominate, sovereignty

reimburse 3 pay **5** repay **6** recoup, refund **7**

pay back, requite **9** indemnify **10** compensate, remunerate

rein 4 curb, stem **5** check **6** bridle **7** compose, control, repress **8** hold back, restrain, suppress

reinforce 4 prop **5** brace **7** augment, bolster, enlarge, fortify, recruit, sustain **8** buttress, increase, redouble **10** invigorate, strengthen

reinstate 6 recall **7** restore **11** reestablish, reintroduce **12** rehabilitate

reintroduce 6 recall, revive **7** restore **9** reinstate **11** reestablish

reinvestment 4 DRIP **8** plowback

reiterate 5 renew, resay **6** repeat, resume, retell **7** reprise

reject 3 nix **4** jilt, junk, shed **5** debar, scorn, scrap, spurn **6** abjure, pariah, pass up, rebuff, refuse **7** cashier, castoff, decline, discard, dismiss, exclude, outcast, repulse, shut out **8** castaway, jettison, throw out, turn away, turn down **9** eliminate, repudiate, shoot down, throw away **10** disapprove

rejoice 5 cheer, exult, glory **7** delight, gladden **8** jubilate

rejoinder 5 reply **6** answer, retort **8** comeback, rebuttal, repartee, response

rejuvenate 5 green, renew **7** refresh **8** renovate **9** modernize **10** revitalize

rekindle 5 renew **6** revive **7** restart **8** reawaken, reignite, revivify **10** reactivate, revitalize

relate 4 link, tell **5** apply, refer **6** assign, detail, recite, report **7** connect, express, narrate, pertain, recount **8** describe, disclose, interact, rehearse **9** appertain, chronicle

related 4 akin **5** alike, enate **6** agnate, allied **7** cognate, connate, germane, kindred **8** incident **9** analogous, connected, identical, pertinent **10** associated, connatural, homologous **11** consanguine

relation 3 kin **6** agnate **7** hinship, kinsman **8** affinity **9** kinswoman, reference **11** propinquity

relationship 3 tie **4** bond, link **5** ratio, tie-in, union **6** affair **7** analogy, contact, liaison **8** affinity, alliance **10** connection **11** affiliation, association **13** confederation, consanguinity

relative 2 ma, pa **3** mom, pop, sib, sis, son **4** aunt, mama, papa **5** blood, madre, mamma, momma, niece, pappy, pater, poppa, uncle **6** agnate, cousin, father, mother, nephew, parent, sister **7** apropos, brother, cognate, germane, kinsman, sibling **8** ancestor, daughter, grandson, relation, relevant **9** ascendant, dependent, kinswoman, pertinent **10** applicable, collateral, descendant, grandchild **11** comparative, conditional, grandfather, grandmother, grandparent **13** granddaughter

relatives 3 kin **4** kith **5** folks **7** kindred, kinfolk **8** kinfolks **9** relations

relax 4 bask, ease, laze, loaf, loll, rest **5** chill, let go, loose, remit **6** loosen, lounge, modify, unbend, unkink, unwind **7** slacken **8** chill out, kick back, loosen up, unbuckle, wind down **9** untighten **10** decompress

relaxation 3 fun **4** ease, rest **5** hobby **6** repose **7** leisure, pastime **9** amusement, diversion, enjoyment **10** recreation

relaxed 5 loose, slack **6** casual, dégagé, mellow **8** informal **9** easygoing **11** low-pressure

release 4 emit, free, vent **5** issue, let go, loose, untie, yield **6** acquit, let out, loosen, pardon, ransom, unbind, uncage **7** give off, give out, manumit, set free, unchain, unleash **8** liberate, unfetter **9** acquittal, discharge, exculpate, exonerate, surrender **10** emancipate **11** manumission **12** emancipation ***conditional:*** **6** parole

relegate 5 exile, expel **6** assign, banish, charge, commit, demote, resign **7** commend, confide, consign, entrust **8** delegate, hand over, transfer, turn over

relent 3 ebb **4** cave, ease, wane **5** abate, let up, yield **6** give in, submit **7** die away, die down, ease off, slacken, subside **8** moderate **9** acquiesce **10** capitulate

relentless 5 cruel, rigid, stern **6** dogged **7** adamant, nonstop **8** constant, obdurate, rigorous, unabated **9** ferocious, incessant, stringent **10** implacable, inexorable, inflexible, unyielding **11** remorseless, unfaltering

relevant 3 apt, fit **5** ad rem **6** cogent **7** apropos, germane **8** apposite, material, relative **9** pertinent **10** admissible, applicable **11** applicative, appropriate **12** proportional

reliable 4 safe, sure **5** solid, sound, tried, valid **6** proven, secure, trusty **7** bedrock, certain **8** constant, verified **9** foolproof, validated **10** dependable **11** trustworthy **12** tried-and-true

reliance 4 hope **5** faith, stock, trust **10** dependence

relic 5 token **6** corpse **7** antique, memento, remains, remnant, vestige **8** artifact, fragment, keepsake, memorial, reminder, souvenir **11** remembrance

relict 5 widow **8** survivor

relief 3 aid **4** ease, fret, hand, help, lift **5** break, cameo **6** assist, raised, remedy, succor **7** comfort, redress, respite, support, welfare **8** breather, fretwork, repoussé **9** abatement, diversion **10** assistance, mitigation **11** alleviation, deliverance ***pitcher:*** **6** closer **7** fireman, stopper

relieve 3 rid **4** calm, ease, free, help, quit, vent **5** allay, relax, spell **6** assist, exempt, lessen, loosen, reduce, remedy, soften, solace, soothe, succor, supply **7** absolve, assuage, comfort, deprive, lighten, mollify, release **8** diminish, dispense, mitigate, moderate, palliate, unburden **9** alleviate

religion 4 cult, Jain, sect, Sikh **5** Baha'i, cause, creed, dogma, faith, Hindu, Islam **6** belief, church, Jewish, Mormon, Muslim, Shinto **7** Friends, Jainism, Judaism, Quakers, Sikhism **8** Buddhism, Buddhist, devotion, doctrine, Hinduism **9** Christian, Mormonism, Shintoism **11** Zoroastrian **12** Christianity

religious 3 nun **4** holy, monk **5** friar, godly, pious **6** devout, priest, sacred, votary **7** staunch, upright **8** cenobite, faithful, monastic, priestly, reverent **9** pietistic, prayerful, spiritual, steadfast **10** scriptural, scrupulous, worshipful

relinquish 4 cede, quit, shed **5** forgo, leave, waive, yield **6** desert, give up, resign **7** abandon, discard, lay down, release **8** abdicate, hand over, renounce **9** quitclaim, sacrifice, surrender

relish 4 like, tang, zest **5** enjoy, fancy, flair, gusto, savor, taste **6** flavor, liking, palate **7** chutney, delight **8** chowchow, fondness, penchant, pleasure, sapidity **9** appetizer, condiment, enjoyment **10** appreciate, piccalilli **11** delectation, hors d'oeuvre

relucent 6 bright **7** glaring, radiant, shining **10** reflecting

reluctant 3 shy **4** wary **5** chary, loath **6** afraid, averse **8** cautious, grudging, hesitant **9** unwilling **10** indisposed **11** disinclined ***prophet:*** **5** Jonah

rely 3 bet **4** bank, plan **5** count **6** depend, gamble, reckon

rely on 5 trust **6** expect **10** anticipate

remain 4 bide, last, live, stay, wait **5** abide, stand, tarry **6** endure, linger, loiter **7** persist, survive **8** continue **10** hang around **11** stick around

remainder 4 rest **5** dregs, trace **6** excess **7** balance, residue, remnant, surplus, vestige **8** leavings, leftover, residual, residuum

remains 4 body **5** ashes, bones, ruins **6** corpse, debris, relics **7** balance, cadaver, carcass, flotsam **8** leavings, remnants **9** reliquiae

remand 8 send back

remark 4 gibe, note **5** aside, crack **7** comment, mention **9** utterance, wisecrack, witticism **10** annotation **11** observation **12** obiter dictum

remarkable 4 rare **5** great **6** signal, unique **7** salient, strange, unusual **8** singular, striking, uncommon **9** arresting, bodacious, momentous, prominent **10** impressive, noteworthy, noticeable **11** conspicuous, exceptional, outstanding, significant **13** extraordinary

remarkably 4 unco

remedial 8 curative, salutary, sanative **9** medicinal **10** corrective **11** restorative, therapeutic **12** recuperative

remedy 3 fix **4** cure, drug, heal **5** salve, solve **6** elixir, relief, repair **7** correct, cure-all, nostrum, panacea, rectify, redress, relieve **8** antidote, medicine, specific **9** alleviate, treatment **10** corrective, medicament, medication

remember 5 educe, evoke **6** recall, record, relive, retain, reward **7** bethink **9** flash back, recollect, reminisce **10** bear in mind **11** commemorate, memorialize

remembrance 4 gift **5** favor, relic, token **6** déjà vu, memory, recall, trophy **7** memento, present, thought **8** keepsake, memorial, reminder, souvenir **9** anamnesis, flashback **12** recollection, reminiscence

remind 6 advise, prompt **7** bethink **8** admonish

reminder 4 hint, memo **5** relic, token **6** prompt, trophy **7** memento **8** keepsake, memorial, monument, souvenir **9** refresher **10** admonition, memorandum **11** remembrance

reminisce see **remember**

reminiscence 6 memory, recall **8** anecdote **9** anamnesis, flashback **11** remembrance **12** recollection

remise 4 cede, deed **5** alien, grant **6** assign, convey **8** make over, transfer **9** quitclaim

remiss 3 lax **4** lazy **5** slack **8** careless, derelict, heedless, indolent, slothful **9** negligent **10** delinquent, neglectful, slatternly **11** inattentive

remit 4 send, ship, stay, stop **5** abate, defer, delay, relax **6** desist, hold up, pardon, put off, remand, shelve **7** condone, consign, forgive, forward, hold off **8** dispatch, moderate, postpone

remnant 3 end **4** heel, husk, part, rest, rump **5** relic, trace, wrack **6** fag end, relict **7** balance, oddment, residue **8** leavings, leftover, residuum **9** remainder

remodel 4 redo **6** recast, revamp **8** make over, overhaul, redesign **9** refashion **11** reconstruct

remonstrance 5 demur **7** protest **8** demurral, demurrer, scolding **9** challenge, objection
remonstrate 5 argue, demur, plead, scold **6** combat, object, oppose, reason **7** protest **9** challenge
remora 4 clog, drag **6** sucker **9** hindrance **10** impediment **11** encumbrance, shark sucker
remorse 3 rue **4** ruth **5** guilt, smart **6** regret, sorrow **9** penitence **10** contrition, repentance **11** compunction **12** self-reproach
remorseful see **regretful**
remote 3 far, off **4** slim **5** aloof **6** far-off, slight **7** distant, faraway, obscure, outside, slender **8** detached, far-flung, frontier, isolated, lonesome, off-lying, outlying, secluded **9** backwoods, withdrawn **10** negligible **11** godforsaken, out-of-the-way ***combining form:*** **3** tel **4** tele
remotest 6 utmost **7** extreme, outmost **8** farthest **9** outermost, uttermost **11** furthermost
remove 4 doff, skim **5** purge **6** delete, unseat **7** extract, take off, take out **8** dislodge, evacuate, take away, withdraw **9** clear away, eliminate ***from office:*** **6** depose ***hair:*** **8** depilate ***surgically:*** **6** resect
removed 5 aloof, apart **6** far-off, remote **7** devious, distant, faraway, obscure **8** detached, far-flung, isolated, outlying, separate **10** distracted **11** unconnected
remunerate 3 pay **5** repay **7** requite **9** indemnify, reimburse **10** compensate, recompense
remunerative 6 paying **7** gainful, payable **9** lucrative **10** productive, profitable **11** moneymaking
Remus *brother:* **7** Romulus ***father:*** **4** Mars ***mother:*** **9** Rea Silvia **10** Rhea Silvia ***slayer:*** **7** Romulus
renaissance see **rebirth**
renal 7 nephric **9** nephritic
rend 3 rip **4** rive, tear **5** split **6** cleave, divide
render 3 pay **4** cede, limn **5** yield **6** depict, give up, impart, return, submit **7** deliver, execute, pay back, picture, portray, present, proffer, provide, restore **8** carry out, describe, hand over, turn over **9** delineate, interpret, represent, translate, transpose **10** administer, relinquish **12** administrate
rendering 4 copy **7** version **9** depiction **10** paraphrase **11** description, performance, restatement, translation **12** reproduction
rendezvous 4 date **5** haunt, tryst **6** gather, muster **7** collect, hangout, meeting **8** assemble **10** congregate, engagement **11** appointment, assignation, get-together
rendition 7 reading, version **10** adaptation **11** performance, translation
renegade 3 rat **5** rebel **6** outlaw **7** heretic **8** apostate, defector, deserter, maverick, recreant, turncoat **9** turnabout **10** schismatic
renege 4 deny **5** welch, welsh **6** cry off, recall, recant, revoke **7** back off, back out, retract **8** renounce, withdraw **9** backpedal
renew 6 redeem, reform, revamp, revive **7** freshen, refresh, remodel **8** make over, overhaul, recharge, recreate, rekindle, renovate, revivify **9** refurbish, resurrect **10** reactivate, recommence, regenerate, rejuvenate, revitalize
rennet 8 abomasum
renounce 4 deny, quit **5** demit **6** abjure, defect, desert, give up, recant, renege, resign **7** abandon, decline, forsake, put away, retract **8** abdicate, abnegate, disclaim, forswear, swear off **9** repudiate, sacrifice **10** apostatize
renovate 4 redo **5** renew **6** remake, repair, revamp, revive **7** furbish, refresh, restore **8** overhaul, revivify **9** modernize, refurbish, resurrect **10** rejuvenate, revitalize **12** rehabilitate
renown 4 fame **5** éclat, glory, kudos **6** repute **7** acclaim **8** eminence, prestige **9** celebrity, notoriety **10** prominence, reputation **11** distinction
renowned 5 famed, great, noted **6** fabled, famous **7** eminent, notable **8** extolled **9** acclaimed, legendary, notorious, prominent, well-known **10** celebrated **11** illustrious, outstanding **13** distinguished
rent 3 let, rip **4** hire, rift, tear, torn **5** lease, split **6** breach, sublet **7** charter, fissure, rupture **8** fracture
rental 4 hire **7** tenancy
renter 6 lessee, tenant **11** leaseholder
renunciation 6 denial **7** refusal **8** apostasy, eschewal, forgoing **9** disavowal, sacrifice, surrender **10** abdication, abnegation, disclaimer, self-denial **11** abandonment, forswearing, repudiation, resignation
reorder 5 shift **7** permute **9** rearrange, reshuffle
reorganization 7 shake-up **8** turnover
repair 3 fix **4** mend **5** patch **6** cobble, doctor **7** fitness, service **8** overhaul **9** condition **11** recondition
reparations 6 amends **7** redress **9** indemnity, quittance **10** recompense, settlement **11** restitution **12** satisfaction
repartee 4 quip **6** banter, retort **7** riposte **8** backchat, badinage, comeback **9** cross talk, rejoinder **10** persiflage
repast 3 eat **4** feed, meal **5** feast **9** refection
repay 6 offset, return, reward **7** requite **9** in-

demnify, reimburse **10** compensate, recompense, remunerate **11** get even with
repeal 4 lift, null, void **5** annul **6** recall, revoke **7** abandon, abolish, nullify, rescind, reverse **8** abrogate, renounce
repeat 4 copy, echo **5** recap, recur, rerun, resay **6** go over, parrot, reecho, recite, rehash, relate, retell **7** imitate, iterate, reprise, restate **9** duplicate, reiterate, replicate **11** reduplicate **12** recapitulate
repeater 7 firearm **10** recidivist
repeating 7 iterant **9** perennial, recurrent **11** reiterative, repetitious
repel 5 rebut **6** rebuff, reject, revolt, sicken **7** disgust, fend off, hold off, repulse, ward off **8** nauseate, stave off
repellent 4 foul, vile **5** nasty **7** noisome **8** aversive **9** abhorrent, loathsome, obnoxious, offensive, repulsive, revolting **10** forbidding, disgusting, off-putting **11** rebarbative
repent 3 rue **6** regret
repentance 3 rue **4** ruth **6** sorrow **7** remorse **10** contrition **11** compunction
repentant see **regretful**
repetition 4 copy, echo **5** rerun **7** recital, reprise **11** duplication
rephrase 6 recast, reword **7** restate
repine 4 beef, fuss, kick, long, moan, wail **5** gripe, yearn **6** grouse, hanker, murmur **7** grumble **8** complain
replace 7 put back, restore **8** exchange, supplant **9** supersede **10** substitute
replacement 3 sub **6** fill-in, loaner, makeup **7** stand-in **9** alternate, surrogate, temporary **10** substitute **11** locum tenens, pinch hitter, succedaneum
replenish 4 fill **5** renew, stock **6** refill **7** refresh, restock, restore
replete 4 full, rife **5** awash, lousy **6** packed **7** brimful, crammed, stuffed **8** brimming **9** chock-full **11** overflowing
replica 4 copy, dupe, fake **5** clone, ditto **6** carbon **9** duplicate, facsimile, imitation **10** carbon copy, simulacrum **12** reproduction
replicate 4 copy **5** clone **6** repeat **9** reproduce
reply 4 echo, RSVP **6** answer, rejoin, retort **7** respond **8** comeback, repartee, response **9** rejoinder
report 4 bang, boom, news, tell **5** crack, relay, rumor, study **6** record, relate, return, review, show up **7** account, article, check in, hearsay, narrate, recount, rundown **8** advisory, bulletin, describe, dispatch **9** broadcast, chronicle, narrative, statement **11** compte rendu
reporter 7 newsman **8** pressman **9** newshound, newswoman **10** journalist ***inexperienced:*** **3** cub
repose 3 lie **4** calm, rest **5** peace, poise, quiet, sleep **7** lie down, recline **8** quietude **9** composure, stillness **10** inactivity, quiescence, relaxation **11** restfulness, tranquility **12** tranquillity
repository 3 ark **5** depot, store **7** archive, arsenal **8** magazine, treasury **10** storehouse
repossess see **regain**
reprehend 3 rap **4** rate, skin **5** blame, chide, fault, knock, scold **6** berate, rebuke **7** censure, condemn, upbraid **8** admonish, denounce **9** criticize **10** denunciate
reprehensible 4 base, evil **6** guilty, sinful, unholy, wicked **8** blamable, criminal, culpable **10** censurable **11** blameworthy, disgraceful
represent 3 act **6** denote, depict, embody, mirror, recall, relate, render, sketch, typify **7** display, exhibit, express, hold out, imitate, make out, narrate, outline, picture, portray, present, protest, realize, signify, suggest **8** describe, stand for **9** delineate, epitomize, exemplify, interpret, personify, symbolize **10** constitute, illustrate, substitute **11** emblematize, impersonate
representation 5 draft, image **6** effigy, symbol **7** picture **8** likeness **9** portrayal, statement **10** caricature, delegation
representative 5 agent, envoy, model, proxy **6** deputy, sample **7** burgess, example, typical **8** delegate, emissary, sampling, specimen **9** exemplary, spokesman **10** ambassador, legislator, prototypal, substitute **11** congressman **12** illustrative, prototypical **13** congresswoman
repress 4 curb **5** check, sit on **6** bridle, muffle, stifle, subdue **7** smother, squelch, swallow **8** keep down, restrain, suppress
repression 4 curb **7** amnesia, control **8** stifling **9** clampdown, crackdown, restraint **10** constraint
reprieve 4 stay **5** grace **7** respite, suspend
reprimand 3 rap **4** rate, ream, task **5** chide, scold **6** rebuke **7** bawl out, censure, chew out, reproof, reprove **8** admonish, call down, reproach, scolding **9** reprimand, talking-to **10** admonition **12** admonishment, dressing-down **13** tongue-lashing
reprisal 7 redress, revenge **8** revanche **9** vengeance **11** counterblow, retaliation, retribution
reprise 5 recap **6** repeat **9** reiterate **10** recurrence, repetition
reproach 3 rap **4** rail **5** blame, chide, scold **6** berate, rebuke **7** bawl out, censure, chew out, remorse, reprove, upbraid **8** admonish,

call down **9** reprimand **10** admonition, opprobrium **12** admonishment
reprobate 3 rap **4** skin **5** blame, scamp, spurn **6** refuse, reject, sinner **7** censure, condemn, lowlife, villain **8** denounce, scalawag **9** miscreant, scoundrel **10** blackguard, degenerate
reproduce 4 bear, copy, sire **5** beget, breed, spore **7** imitate **8** multiply **9** duplicate, procreate, propagate, replicate **10** regenerate **11** reduplicate
reproduction see **replica**
reproductive cell 3 egg **4** ovum **5** sperm, spore **6** gamete **12** spermatozoid, spermatozoon
reproof 3 rap **6** rebuke **7** censure, lecture **8** scolding **9** criticism, reprimand **10** admonition **11** castigation **12** admonishment, reprehension **13** remonstration
reprove 5 chide, scold **6** rebuke **7** censure, chasten **8** admonish, call down, lambaste, reproach **9** criticize, dress down, reprimand
reptile 4 croc **5** gator, skink, snake **6** caiman, cayman, gavial, iguana, lizard, turtle **7** tuatara **8** tortoise **9** alligator, crocodile, sphenodon ***combining form:*** **6** herpet **7** herpeto ***extinct:*** **8** dinosaur
republic 5 state **6** nation **9** democracy
Republican Party 3 GOP ***symbol:*** **8** elephant
Republic author 5 Plato
repudiate 4 deny **5** spurn **6** abjure, disown, recant, refuse, reject **7** decline, disavow, dismiss **8** disclaim, renounce **9** disaffirm **10** apostatize, disapprove
repugnance 6 horror **7** disgust **8** aversion, loathing **9** repulsion, revulsion **10** abhorrence, antagonism, odiousness **11** abomination, detestation
repugnant 4 foul, vile **5** nasty, yucky **6** creepy, horrid, skanky **7** noisome **8** aversive, gruesome **9** abhorrent, loathsome, obnoxious, offensive, repulsive, revolting **10** disgusting
repulse 5 rebut, repel, spurn **6** rebuff, reject, revolt, sicken **7** disgust, fend off, hold off, ward off **8** nauseate, stave off
repulsion see **repugnance**
repulsive see **repugnant**
reputable 7 eminent, upright **8** esteemed **9** estimable, honorable **10** creditable, legitimate, recognized, sanctioned **11** respectable, trustworthy **13** well-thought-of
reputation 4 fame, name, note **5** éclat, honor **6** esteem, renown, report **8** position, prestige, standing **9** celebrity, character, notoriety
reputed 6 honest **7** alleged **8** putative, supposed **9** estimable, purported **10** creditable, ostensible **11** respectable **12** hypothetical
request 3 ask, dun, sue **4** pray, seek, wish **5** plead, press **6** appeal, ask for, demand, invite **7** entreat, solicit **8** entreaty, petition **10** invitation
Requiem for a Nun author 8 Faulkner (William)
require 3 ask, beg **4** lack, need, want **5** claim, crave **6** demand, desire **7** call for, dictate, mandate, solicit **8** insist on **11** necessitate
required 3 due **5** vital **7** crucial **9** essential, mandatory, necessary, requisite **10** compulsory, obligatory **11** fundamental
requirement 4 must, need, want **5** claim **6** charge, demand **9** condition, essential, necessity, requisite **10** imperative, sine qua non **11** stipulation
requisite 3 due **4** must **5** vital **7** crucial, needful **8** cardinal **9** condition, essential, necessity **10** imperative, sine qua non **11** fundamental **12** precondition **13** indispensable
requisition 4 call **5** claim, exact **6** demand **7** solicit **11** application
requite 3 pay **5** repay **6** return **7** revenge, satisfy **9** indemnify, reimburse **10** compensate, recompense, remunerate **11** reciprocate
reredos 6 screen **9** partition
rescind 4 lift **5** annul **6** cancel, recall, repeal, revoke **7** retract, reverse **8** roll back, take back
rescue 4 free, save **6** ransom, redeem **7** bailout, deliver, reclaim, recover, release, salvage **8** liberate, preserve **9** extricate **11** deliverance
rescuer 6 savior **7** saviour
research 5 probe, study **7** inquest, inquiry **8** look into **9** delve into **10** experiment **11** examination, inquisition, investigate **13** investigation
resect 6 cut out, excise **8** amputate **9** extirpate
resemblance 7 analogy **8** likeness **9** alikeness **10** comparison, similarity, similitude **11** parallelism
resemble 5 favor **6** recall **8** look like, simulate **9** take after **11** approximate
resembling 3 à la **4** like **6** akin to
resentful 4 sore **6** bitter, piqued, sullen **7** envious
resentment 5 pique **6** animus, grudge, malice, rancor **7** dudgeon, offense, umbrage **9** animosity **11** indignation
reservation 5 doubt **7** booking, enclave, proviso **8** homeland, preserve **9** condition, misgiving, sanctuary **10** limitation
reserve 4 book, fund, hold, keep **5** hoard, put by, stash, stock, store, tract **6** retain, supply

7 nest egg, savings, standby 8 contract, distance, fallback, hold back, postpone, set aside, squirrel, withhold 9 inventory, restraint, reticence, stockpile 10 constraint, discretion, diffidence 13 qualification

reserved 4 cool 5 aloof, stiff 6 demure, formal, remote 7 distant 8 reticent, retiring, taciturn 9 diffident, reclusive, secretive, withdrawn 10 unsociable 11 tight-lipped 12 closemouthed 13 self-contained

reservoir 5 hoard, stock, store 6 supply 7 nest egg 9 inventory, stockpile

reside 3 lie 4 hive, live, stay 5 dwell, exist 6 inhere 7 consist

residence 4 home, stay 5 abode, house 7 address 8 domicile, dwelling 9 occupancy 10 habitation

resident 5 liver 6 inmate, lodger, native, tenant 7 citizen, denizen, dweller, present 8 inherent, occupant 10 inhabitant 11 householder

residential area 9 community 12 neighborhood

residual 7 balance, payment, remnant 8 leavings, leftover 9 remainder

residue 3 ash 4 heel, lees, marc, rest, silt, slag 5 ashes, dregs, grout 6 debris, excess, scraps 7 balance, grounds, remains, remnant, surplus 8 leavings, remnants, residuum 9 leftovers, remainder, scourings

resign 4 cede, quit 5 demit, leave, yield 6 give up, retire, submit 7 abandon, consign 8 abdicate, hand over, relegate, renounce, step down 9 reconcile, surrender 10 relinquish

resignation 8 meekness 9 demission, surrender 10 abdication, compliance, submission 12 acquiescence, renunciation

resigned 9 compliant 10 submissive 11 acquiescent, complaisant

resile 6 recede, recoil, spring 7 rebound, retract, retreat 8 draw back, snap back

resilient 6 bouncy, supple, whippy 7 buoyant, elastic, springy 8 flexible, stretchy 9 adaptable

resin 4 balm 5 copal, damar, roset 6 dammar 7 acrylic, copaiba ***aromatic:*** 6 balsam, mastic 8 sandarac ***fragrant:*** 5 elemi 6 storax, styrax 7 ladanum 8 labdanum ***gum:*** 5 myrrh 7 benzoin ***medicinal:*** 6 guaiac 8 guaiacum ***of an insect:*** 3 lac ***synthetic:*** 8 phenolic ***used by bees:*** 8 propolis

resist 4 buck, defy, kick 5 rebel 6 baffle, combat, oppose, revolt 7 contest, counter, gainsay 8 traverse 10 contradict, contravene

resistance 7 dissent 8 defiance, variance 10 dissension, dissidence, opposition 11 contrariety, obstruction

resistance unit 3 ohm

resistor 8 rheostat, varistor 10 thermistor

resolute 3 set 4 bent, bold, fast, firm, true 6 intent, steady, sturdy 7 decided, staunch 8 constant, decisive, faithful, intrepid, stubborn 9 obstinate, steadfast, tenacious, undaunted 10 determined, persistent 12 pertinacious, single-minded

resolution 4 guts 5 heart, nerve, pluck, spunk 6 mettle, spirit 7 courage, outcome 8 decision, firmness, tenacity 10 conclusion 12 perseverance 13 determination, steadfastness

resolve 5 clear, crack 6 decide, settle 7 clear up, iron out, unravel, work out 8 boldness, conclude, decipher, firmness 9 breakdown, determine, intention, reconcile 10 unscramble 13 determination, steadfastness

resonant 4 deep, full, rich 6 silver 7 booming, echoing, orotund, vibrant 8 powerful, sonorous 11 reverberant

resonate 4 echo, peal, ring 7 resound, vibrate 11 reverberate

resort 3 spa 4 lido 5 haven, hotel, lodge, shift 6 harbor, refuge 7 retreat, riviera, stopgap 8 recourse 9 expedient, makeshift 10 substitute ***last:*** 8 pis aller

resound 4 boom, echo, peal, ring 11 reverberate

resounding 7 booming, echoing, orotund, vibrant 8 emphatic, sonorous 10 clangorous, resonating, thunderous 11 unequivocal

resource 3 aid 5 asset, means, shift 6 supply 7 standby

resourceful 5 adept 6 adroit, artful, clever, shrewd 7 capable, cunning 8 creative, skillful 9 ingenious, inventive 10 innovative 11 imaginative 12 enterprising

resources 5 funds, means, money, purse 6 assets, riches, wealth 7 capital, fortune, reserve 8 bankroll, finances, property, reserves 9 substance 11 wherewithal

respect 3 awe 5 favor, honor, props 6 admire, detail, devoir, esteem, homage, regard, revere 7 account, concern 8 venerate 9 deference 10 admiration, estimation, particular, veneration

respectable 4 fair 5 ample 6 decent, proper, worthy 8 adequate 9 admirable, estimable, honorable 10 sufficient 11 appropriate, presentable 12 satisfactory 13 well-thought-of

respectful 5 civil 6 polite 8 obeisant, reverent 9 courteous 11 deferential, reverential

respecting 3 per 4 as to, in re 5 about 7 apro-

pos **9** as regards, regarding **10** as concerns, concerning, relating to **11** considering
respire 7 breathe
respite 4 lull, rest **5** break, delay, pause, spell, truce **6** hiatus, recess, relief **8** breather, reprieve, surcease **12** intermission
resplendent 5 regal **7** glowing, shining **8** glorious, gorgeous **9** brilliant, refulgent **11** magnificent
respond 5 react, reply **6** answer, rejoin, retort **8** come back
response 5 reply **6** answer, retort, return **7** riposte **8** antiphon, comeback, reaction **9** rejoinder ***involuntary:*** **6** reflex **7** tropism
responsibility 4 buck, duty, onus **5** blame, brief, fault **6** burden, charge, devoir **10** obligation **11** reliability
responsible 6 liable **8** amenable, reliable **10** answerable, chargeable, dependable **11** accountable, trustworthy
responsive 4 open **8** sentient **9** sensitive **11** susceptible, sympathetic
rest 3 nap, sit **4** calm, ease, laze, loaf, loll, lull, stay **5** let up, pause, peace, quiet, relax, spell **6** catnap, depend, excess, lounge, repose **7** balance, leisure, lie down, recline, remains, remnant, surplus **8** breather, leavings, vacation **9** interlude, predicate, remainder
restate 4 echo **6** reword **8** rephrase **9** translate **10** paraphrase **12** recapitulate
restatement 10 paraphrase **11** translation
restaurant 4 café **5** diner **6** eatery **7** beanery **9** brasserie, cafeteria **10** coffee shop **11** coffeehouse, greasy spoon ***price:*** **8** à la carte, prix fixe **10** table d'hôte ***worker:*** **4** chef, cook **6** busboy, server, waiter **7** maître d', waitron **8** waitress **10** dishwasher, headwaiter, waitperson **12** maître d'hôtel
restful 4 calm **5** quiet **6** placid **8** peaceful, tranquil
restitute 6 refund, return **7** reclaim, recover, restore **8** give back **11** recondition, reconstruct **12** rehabilitate
restitution 6 amends, refund, return **7** redress **8** reprisal **9** indemnity, quittance **10** recompense, reparation **11** restoration **12** remuneration, satisfaction
restive 4 edgy **5** balky, nervy, tense **6** ornery, uneasy **7** fidgety, froward, uptight, wayward **8** contrary, perverse, skittish
restiveness 7 anxiety, ferment, turmoil **8** disquiet **9** balkiness **10** inquietude, perversity **11** contrariety, disquietude, waywardness **12** contrariness
restless 5 antsy, itchy, jumpy **6** fitful, uneasy **7** anxious, fidgety, fretful, jittery, nervous, unquiet **8** agitated, troubled **9** disturbed, perturbed, unsettled **12** discontented, dissatisfied
restorative 4 balm **5** tonic **7** healing **8** curative, remedial, sanative **12** recuperative
restore 4 cure, heal, mend, stet **5** amend, remit, renew, right **6** recall, recoup, reform, remedy, render, repair, return, revive **7** get back, improve, reclaim, recover, rectify, refresh, replace **8** give back, recreate, renovate, revivify **9** refurbish, reinstate, replenish, restitute **10** regenerate, rejuvenate **11** recondition, reestablish **12** rehabilitate
restrain 3 bit, gag **4** bate, curb, rein **5** check, leash **6** arrest, bridle, halter, hamper, hinder, hold in, impede, muzzle, temper **7** collect, control, harness, inhibit, repress **8** hold back, hold down, moderate, suppress
restrained 4 cool **6** low-key **5** canny, quiet **6** modest **7** subdued **8** discreet, reserved, reticent, retiring, tasteful **9** contained, inhibited, temperate **10** controlled, reasonable
restraint 5 stint **6** bridle **7** durance, embargo, reserve **8** estoppel, pullback **9** hindrance **10** deterrence, inhibition, limitation, moderation **11** confinement, forbearance **12** straitjacket
restrict 3 bar, tie **4** bind, curb **5** hem in, limit **6** hamper, hobble, impede, narrow, shrink **7** confine, curtail, delimit, inhibit, trammel **8** hold back, prelimit **10** delimitate **12** circumscribe ***a will:*** **6** entail
restriction 4 curb **5** check, limit, stint **7** control **9** restraint **10** constraint, limitation, regulation **11** confinement, prohibition **12** proscription **13** qualification
restyle 4 redo **6** revamp, revise, rework **8** make over
result 3 end **4** flow, stem **5** close, ensue, fruit, issue **6** effect, emerge, finish, follow, payoff, sequel, upshot **7** outcome, product **8** sequence, solution **9** aftermath, come about, eventuate **10** conclusion, denouement, production **11** aftereffect, consequence, eventuality ***incidental:*** **7** spinoff
resume 4 go on **5** renew **6** pick up, reopen **7** carry on, proceed, restart **8** continue **10** recommence
résumé 2 CV **4** vita **5** sum-up **6** précis **7** summary **9** summation, summing-up
resurgence 5 rally **7** rebirth, revival **8** comeback, recovery **10** renascence **11** renaissance **12** risorgimento
resurrect 5 raise, renew **6** come to, revive **8** retrieve, revivify **10** reactivate
resurrection 7 rebirth, revival **10** renascence **11** renaissance **12** risorgimento

resuscitate see **resurrect**
retail 4 sell, tell, vend **6** market **7** narrate **11** merchandise
retailer 6 dealer, seller, trader, vendor **8** merchant **9** tradesman **10** shopkeeper **11** storekeeper **12** merchandiser
retain 3 own **4** hire, hold, keep **6** detain **7** reserve **8** hold over, preserve, remember, withhold
retainer 3 fee **6** lackey, menial, minion, yeoman **7** deposit, servant **8** employee, follower **9** bite plate, dependent, pensioner
retaliate 7 get back, get even **10** strike back
retaliation see **reprisal**
retaliatory 8 punitive, vengeful **10** vindictive
retard 4 clog, mire, slow **5** delay, stunt **6** detain, fetter, hamper, hang up, hinder, impede, slow up **7** set back, slacken **8** decrease, hold back, restrain **10** decelerate
retarded 3 dim **4** dull, dumb, slow **6** opaque, simple, stupid **8** backward **9** dim-witted **10** half-witted, slow-witted **11** exceptional
retch 3 gag **4** barf, hurl, puke, spew **5** heave, vomit **6** spit up **7** bring up, throw up, upchuck **8** disgorge
retention 6 memory **7** storage
reticent see **reserved**
reticulate 4 vein **5** veiny **6** meshed, netted **7** netlike **10** crisscross
retinue 4 band, tail **5** suite, train **6** livery **7** company, cortege **9** entourage, following
retire 4 exit, quit **5** leave, yield **6** bow out, depart, recede, resign, turn in **7** dismiss, pension **8** step down, withdraw **9** discharge, strike out, terminate **10** relinquish
retired person 7 emerita **8** emeritus **9** pensioner
retiree 6 senior **9** pensioner **10** golden-ager **13** senior citizen
retirement allowance 3 SEP **7** pension
retiring 3 shy **5** mousy, timid **6** demure, modest **7** bashful **8** reserved **9** diffident, withdrawn **11** unassertive
retool 7 reequip **10** reengineer
retort 5 reply, sally **6** answer, rejoin **7** counter, respond, riposte **8** comeback, repartee, response **9** rejoinder, retaliate, wisecrack
retouch 5 alter, emend, renew **6** repair **7** correct, enhance, improve, restore
retract 4 deny **5** unsay **6** abjure, recall, recant, recede, renege, resile, revoke **7** disavow, rescind, retreat, swallow **8** forswear, renounce, take back, withdraw
retreat 3 den, ebb **4** flee, quit **5** cover, haven, leave **6** ashram, asylum, bow out, covert, decamp, depart, escape, recede, recoil, refuge, shrink, vacate **7** abandon, back off, back out, pull out, shelter **8** back down, draw back, evacuate, fall back, hideaway, withdraw **9** backtrack, climb down, sanctuary **10** give ground, withdrawal
retrench 3 cut **4** pare **5** slash **6** excise, lessen, reduce **7** abridge, curtail **9** economize
retribution 6 return, reward **7** deserts, revenge **8** avenging, reprisal, requital, revanche **9** vengeance **10** punishment, recompense **11** counterblow, retaliation ***goddess of:* 3** Ate **4** Fury **7** Nemesis
retrieve 5 fetch **6** recall, recoup, redeem, rescue **7** get back, recover, restore, salvage **9** resurrect
retro 5 campy **7** antique, revival, vintage **9** nostalgic **12** old-fashioned
retrograde 4 back **7** inverse, reverse **8** backward, inverted, rearward
retrogress see **revert**
retrospect 9 hindsight **12** recollection **13** reexamination
retrospective 6 review **8** backward **10** exhibition, reflective, ruminative
return 5 recur, repay, reply, yield **6** answer, rebate, regain, rejoin, render, repeat, retort, revert **7** bring in, get back, rebound, recover, reprise, requite, respond, reverse, riposte **8** comeback, dividend, earnings, give back, proceeds, reappear, response **9** rejoinder, repayment, reversion **10** recompense, recurrence **11** reciprocate, restitution
Return of the Native *author:* 5 Hardy (Thomas) ***character:* 4** Clym (Yeobright) **8** Eustacia (Vye)
Reuben *brother:* 6 Joseph ***father:* 5** Jacob ***mother:* 4** Leah ***son:* 5** Carmi **6** Hanoch, Hezron, Phallu
Réunion *capital:* 7 St.-Denis ***city:* 6** St.-Paul **7** St.-Louis **8** St.-Pierre ***department of:* 6** France ***ethnic group:* 6** Creole ***former name:* 7** Bourbon **9** Bonaparte ***island group:* 9** Mascarene
revamp 4 redo **5** renew **6** remake, repair, revise, rework **7** remodel, restyle, rewrite **8** make over, overhaul, redesign, renovate **9** refurbish **11** recondition
reveal 4 bare, blab, jamb, leak, open, show, tell **5** admit, let on, peach, spill **6** betray, evince, expose, impart, unmask, unveil **7** confess, declare, display, divulge, exhibit, publish, uncover, undress **8** announce, decipher, disclose, discover, give away, unclothe **9** broadcast, made known **11** acknowledge, communicate **12** bring to light
revel 4 bask, orgy, riot **5** binge, feast, party, spree **6** boogie, frolic, gaiety, hoopla, wallow **7** carouse, delight, indulge, jollity, rois-

ter, rollick, wassail, whoopla **8** carnival, carousal, festival **9** bacchanal, celebrate, festivity, luxuriate, merriment, whoop-de-do **11** bacchanalia, celebration, merrymaking

revelation 6 kicker **8** epiphany, giveaway, prophecy, surprise **9** discovery **10** apocalypse, disclosure **13** manifestation

reveler 7 orgiast **8** bacchant, carouser **9** bacchante, wassailer **10** merrymaker

revelry 4 orgy, riot **6** gaiety **7** carouse, jollity, wassail, whoopee, whoopla **8** carousal, partying **9** festivity, high jinks, merriment, whoop-de-do **10** whoop-de-doo **11** merrymaking

revenant 5 ghost, haunt, shade, spook **6** shadow, spirit, undead, wraith, zombie **7** phantom, specter, spectre **8** phantasm, prodigal, visitant **10** apparition

revenge 5 right **6** defend **7** get back, get even, redress, requite **8** reprisal, requital, revanche **9** retaliate, vindicate **11** retaliation, retribution

revenue 4 rent **5** gains, issue, yield **6** income, profit, return **7** comings **8** earnings, interest, proceeds, receipts, taxation

reverberant 6 hollow **7** booming, echoing **8** resonant **10** resounding

reverberate 4 echo, gong, ring **6** reecho **7** resound

revere 4 laud **5** adore, exalt, extol, honor, prize, value **6** admire, esteem, regard **7** cherish, magnify, respect, worship **8** treasure, venerate **10** appreciate

revered 6 sacred **9** estimable, venerable

reverence 3 awe **5** adore, dread, honor, piety **6** esteem, fealty, homage **7** loyalty, respect, worship **8** devotion, venerate **9** deference, obeisance, solemnity **10** veneration ***gesture of:*** **3** bow **6** kowtow **8** kneeling **12** genuflection

reverend 4 abbé, holy **5** clerk, vicar **6** clergy, cleric, deacon, divine, parson, rector **8** chaplain, clerical, minister, preacher **9** churchman, clergyman **11** clergywoman **12** ecclesiastic

reverent 5 godly, pious **6** devout **7** dutiful **9** prayerful **10** God-fearing, respectful, worshipful

reverie 4 muse **5** dream **6** trance, vision **7** fantasy **8** daydream **10** absorption, brown study, meditation **11** abstraction **13** woolgathering

reversal 4 turn **5** U-turn **6** double, switch **7** setback, undoing **8** backfire, flip-flop **9** about-face, inversion, turnabout, volte-face **10** switcheroo **12** solarization **13** change of heart

reverse 4 lift, undo **6** change, contra, defeat, invert, recall, repeal, revoke **7** capsize, counter, rescind, setback **8** antipode, backward, contrary, disaster, exchange, opposite, overrule, overturn **9** about-face, backwards, diametric, overthrow, transpose, turnabout, volte-face **10** antithesis, misfortune

reversion 4 turn **5** lapse **6** return **7** atavism, escheat **9** about-face, throwback, turnabout, volte-face **10** regression, succession

revert 4 turn **6** return **7** decline, devolve, escheat, inverse, regress **8** turn back **9** backslide **10** degenerate, retrograde, retrogress

revetment 4 berm **6** bunker, riprap **9** barricade, earthwork **10** embankment

review 4 scan **5** audit, recap, study **6** assess, go over, parade, report, revise, survey **7** analyze, journal, rethink **8** analysis, critique, magazine, revision, scrutiny, talk over **9** criticism, reexamine, refresher **10** evaluation, inspection, periodical, reconsider, reevaluate **11** examination **13** reexamination, retrospective

revile 4 rail, rate **5** abuse, scold **6** attack, berate, defame, malign, vilify **7** asperse, bawl out, chew out, upbraid **8** belittle, disgrace, execrate **9** blaspheme **10** tongue-lash, vituperate

revise 4 edit **5** alter, amend, emend, proof, renew **6** change, polish, redraw, reform, retool, revamp, rework **7** correct, improve, redraft, restore, restyle, rewrite **8** overhaul, redesign, work over **9** red-pencil **10** blue-pencil

revision 6 change, revamp, update **7** redraft **8** facelift, overhaul, updating **10** alteration, correction, emendation **11** overhauling **12** modification

revitalize see **revive**

revival 7 rebirth, renewal **8** comeback **10** renascence, resurgence **11** reanimation, renaissance, restoration **12** regeneration, rejuvenation, resurrection, risorgimento **13** recrudescence, resuscitation

revive 4 wake **5** rally, renew, rouse **6** arouse, awaken, come to, recall **7** bring to, enliven, freshen, quicken, refresh, restore **8** reawaken, rekindle, renovate, retrieve **9** reanimate, resurrect **10** reactivate, recuperate, regenerate, rejuvenate **11** bring around, reintroduce, resuscitate **12** reinvigorate

revoke 4 lift, void **5** annul, erase **6** abjure, cancel, recall, recant, renege, repeal **7** abolish, nullify, rescind, retract, reverse **8** abrogate, call back **10** invalidate **11** countermand

revolt 4 riot **5** rebel, repel, shock **6** mutiny, resist, sicken **7** disgust, repulse **8** nauseate, outbreak, uprising **9** jacquerie, rebellion **10** insurgence, insurgency **12** insurrection

revolter 5 rebel **6** anarch **8** frondeur, mutineer **9** anarchist, insurgent **10** malcontent

revolting 4 foul, ugly, vile **5** nasty **6** horrid **7** hideous, noisome, obscene **8** shocking **9** atrocious, loathsome, repellent, repugnant, repulsive **10** disgusting, nauseating

revolution 4 gyre, reel, riot, roll, spin, turn **5** cycle, orbit, twirl, wheel, whirl **6** mutiny **7** circuit **8** gyration, rotation, uprising **9** pirouette, rebellion **10** barrel roll, changeover, somersault **12** insurrection

revolutionary 5 rebel, ultra **7** extreme, radical **8** mutineer, rotating, ultraist **9** extremist, insurgent ***American:*** **4** Hale (Nathan), Reed (John) **5** Adams (Samuel), Allen (Ethan), Henry (Patrick), Shays (Daniel) **6** Revere (Paul) ***English:*** **5** Paine (Thomas) ***French:*** **5** Marat (Jean-Paul) **6** Danton (Georges) **8** Mirabeau (Comte de) **9** Saint-Just (Louis) **11** Robespierre (Maximilien) ***Irish:*** **4** Tone (Wolfe) **6** Pearse (Padraig, Patrick) **7** Collins (Michael), Parnell (Charles Stewart) **8** Casement (Roger), de Valera (Eamon), Griffith (Arthur), O'Connell (Daniel) ***Mexican:*** **5** Villa (Pancho) **6** Zapata (Emiliano) **7** Hidalgo (Padre Miguel) ***Russian:*** **5** Kirov (Sergey), Lenin (Vladimir Ilyich) **7** Trotsky (Leon) **8** Kerensky (Aleksandr) **9** Kropotkin (Pyotr)

revolutionize 9 transform **11** transfigure

revolve 4 spin, turn **5** twirl, wheel, whirl **6** circle, gyrate, rotate

revolver 3 gat, gun, rod **4** Colt **5** Glock, Luger, Ruger **6** Magnum, pistol, six-gun **7** firearm, handgun, shooter, sidearm **10** six-shooter

revue 4 show **9** burlesque **10** production, vaudeville **13** entertainment

revulsion 4 hate **6** hatred, horror **7** disgust **8** aversion, loathing **10** abhorrence, repugnance **11** abomination, detestation

reward 5 bonus, booty, crown, medal, price, prize **6** bounty, carrot, payoff, trophy **7** guerdon, jackpot, premium **8** dividend **10** compensate, honorarium, recompense, remunerate **12** compensation, remuneration

rewarding 7 gainful **8** edifying, fruitful, valuable **9** lucrative **10** beneficial, fulfilling, gratifying, productive, profitable, satisfying, worthwhile **12** advantageous, remunerative

reword see **restate**

rework 6 revamp, revise **7** restyle, rewrite

Reynard 3 fox

rhadamanthine 3 due **4** just **5** right **6** strict **7** condign, fitting, merited **8** deserved, rigorous, rightful, suitable **9** requisite, stringent **11** appropriate

Rhadamanthus 5 judge ***brother:*** **5** Minos ***father:*** **4** Zeus **7** Jupiter ***mother:*** **6** Europa

rhapsodic 5 lyric **8** ecstatic, effusive **9** emotional, exuberant

rhapsodize 4 gush, rave **5** drool **6** effuse **7** enthuse

Rhea 3 Ops ***daughter:*** **4** Hera, Juno **5** Ceres, Vesta **6** Hestia **7** Demeter ***father:*** **6** Uranus ***husband:*** **6** Cronus, Saturn ***mother:*** **4** Gaea ***son:*** **4** Zeus **5** Hades, Pluto **7** Jupiter, Neptune **8** Poseidon

Rheingold, Das *character:* **4** Loge, Loki **5** Freya, Wotan **6** Fafner, Fafnir, Fasolt **8** Alberich ***composer:*** **6** Wagner (Richard)

rheostat 8 resistor

rhesus 6 monkey **7** macaque

rhetoric 4 rant **6** speech **7** bombast, fustian, oratory **8** rhapsody **9** elocution, eloquence, verbosity **11** rodomontade, speechcraft ***term:*** **6** aporia, simile **7** litotes **8** metaphor **10** apostrophe, digression **12** alliteration, onomatopoeia

rhetorical 4 glib **5** gassy, grand, tumid, windy **6** florid, fluent, ornate, purple, turgid **7** aureate, flowery, orotund, pompous, stilted **8** eloquent, forensic, inflated, overdone, sonorous **9** bombastic, grandiose, high-flown, overblown, tumescent **10** euphuistic, flamboyant, oratorical **11** declamatory, highfalutin, overwrought, pretentious **12** high-sounding, magniloquent **13** grandiloquent

rhetorician 6 orator, writer **7** speaker ***Roman:*** **10** Quintilian

Rhine River *city:* **4** Bonn, Köln **5** Basel, Mainz **7** Coblenz, Cologne, Koblenz **8** Duisburg, Mannheim **9** Rotterdam, Wiesbaden **10** Düsseldorf ***nymph:*** **7** Lorelei ***tributary:*** **3** Aar, Ill, Lek **4** Aare, Lahn, Main, Ruhr, Waal

rhizome 4 root **5** tuber

Rhode Island *bay:* **12** Narragansett ***capital:*** **10** Providence ***city:*** **7** Newport, Warwick **9** Pawtucket ***college, university:*** **4** RISD **5** Brown ***island:*** **5** Block ***nickname:*** **5** Ocean (State) **11** Little Rhody ***river:*** **8** Pawtuxet ***state bird:*** **14** Rhode Island red ***state flower:*** **6** violet ***state tree:*** **8** red maple

Rhodesia 8 Zimbabwe

rhombus 7 diamond, lozenge **13** parallelogram

rhonchus 5 snore

Rhône River ***city:*** **4** Lyon **5** Arles, Lyons **6** Geneva **7** Avignon ***lake:*** **6** Geneva ***mountain range:*** **4** Jura ***tributary:*** **5** Isère, Saône

rhubarb 3 row **4** flap **5** run-in **6** ruckus, tangle **7** dispute, quarrel, wrangle **8** argument, pieplant **11** altercation, controversy

rhyme 4 poem, song **5** agree, ditty, verse **6** accord, jingle, poetry **7** conform **8** dovetail **9** harmonize **10** coordinate, correspond ***scheme:*** **4** ABAB

rhymer 4 bard, poet **5** odist **7** metrist **8** lyricist **9** poetaster, rhymester, sonneteer, versifier

rhythm 4 beat, flow, lilt, time **5** meter, pulse, swing **6** accent, groove **7** cadence, measure, pattern **8** sequence

rhythmic 7 pulsing, regular **8** measured, metrical

rialto 6 market **8** district, exchange **11** marketplace

riant 3 gay **5** jolly, merry **6** blithe, bright, jocund, jovial **7** buoyant, gleeful **8** cheerful, mirthful **10** blithesome

riata 4 rope **5** lasso **6** lariat

rib 3 fun, kid, rag **4** band, bone, dike, fool, jape, jest, joke, josh, purl, razz, stay, wale **5** chaff, costa, ridge, tease **6** banter, costae (plural), lierne, needle

ribald 3 raw **4** blue, racy, rude, sexy **5** bawdy, crude, dirty, salty, spicy **6** coarse, earthy, filthy, purple, risqué, smutty, vulgar **7** naughty, obscene, profane, raunchy **8** indecent, off-color **9** offensive, reprobate, salacious **10** suggestive

ribbon 3 bow **4** band, tape **5** braid, shred, strip **6** cordon, fillet, stripe, tatter **7** bandeau

rice 7 arborio, basmati, risotto ***dish:*** **5** pilaf **6** congee **7** risotto **9** jambalaya ***drink:*** **4** sake, saki **5** mirin **6** arrack ***field:*** **5** paddy ***husk:*** **5** lemma

rich 4 dear, lush, oily, posh **5** ample, fatty, flush, grand, heavy, plush, swank, vivid **6** costly, creamy, deluxe, fecund, gilded, lavish, loaded, monied, ornate, potent, rococo **7** baroque, copious, elegant, fertile, filling, moneyed, opulent, orotund, profuse, wealthy, well-off **8** abundant, affluent, eloquent, fruitful, palatial, well-to-do **9** abounding, bountiful, elaborate, luxuriant, luxurious, plentiful, sumptuous, well-fixed **10** productive, prosperous, well-heeled **11** extravagant ***person:*** **4** have **5** Midas, mogul, nabob **6** fat cat **7** Croesus, magnate **9** moneybags, plutocrat

Richardson work 6 Pamela **8** Clarissa

Richelieu's successor 7 Mazarin

riches 4 gold, pelf **5** booty, lucre, worth **6** mammon, wealth **7** fortune **8** opulence, property, treasure **9** resources ***demon of:*** **6** Mammon

rick 4 cock, heap, pile **5** shock, stack

rickety 4 weak **5** shaky **6** flimsy, wobbly **7** unsound **8** decrepit, insecure, rachitic, unstable, unsteady **10** ramshackle, rattletrap

ricochet 4 ping, skim, skip **5** carom **6** bounce, glance **7** rebound **9** boomerang

rid 6 divest **7** relieve **8** unburden **11** disencumber

riddle 5 rebus **6** enigma, puzzle **7** mystery, perplex, problem **9** conundrum, perforate **10** closed book, puzzlement **11** brainteaser

ride 4 spin, tour, trip **5** drive, jaunt, mount **6** travel **7** journey **8** carousel **9** excursion

ride out 6 endure **7** outlast, survive, weather **9** withstand

rider 6 clause, cowboy, jockey **7** codicil **8** addendum, addition, appendix, horseman, reinsman **9** amendment **10** equestrian, horsewoman, supplement

ridge 3 rib, top **4** bank, berm, brow, fold, keel, reef, roll, ruck, seam, wave **5** arête, arris, chine, crest, esker, knurl, plica, spine **6** crease, divide, furrow, rimple, saddle, summit **7** annulet, breaker, crinkle, hogback, wrinkle **8** shoulder **9** razorback **11** corrugation ***gravelly:*** **5** esker ***on the skin:*** **4** wale, weal, welt ***sharp:*** **7** hogback

ridicule 3 pan, rib **4** gibe, haze, jape, jeer, mock, razz, ride, twit **5** chaff, flout, mimic, roast, scoff, scout, sneer, squib, taunt **6** deride, satire **7** lampoon, mockery, pillory, sarcasm **8** derision, raillery, satirize, travesty **9** burlesque **10** caricature ***god of:*** **5** Momus ***object of:*** **4** butt **13** laughingstock

ridiculous 5 comic, daffy, dotty, goofy, silly, wacky **6** absurd, insane **7** bizarre, comical, foolish, risible **8** derisory, farcical **9** cockamamy, fantastic, grotesque, laughable, ludicrous, monstrous, senseless **10** cockamamie, outrageous **11** for the birds, harebrained **12** preposterous, unbelievable

riding ***academy:*** **6** manège ***costume:*** **5** habit ***pants:*** **8** jodhpurs ***whip:*** **3** bat **4** crop **5** quirt

Rienzi composer 6 Wagner (Richard)

rife 4 full **5** flush **6** common **7** replete, teeming **8** abundant, swarming **9** abounding, plentiful, prevalent **10** widespread **11** overflowing

riff 4 flip, leaf, scan, skim **5** theme, thumb **6** browse **8** ostinato

riffle 4 flip, leaf, fret, scan, skim, wave **5** shoal, thumb **6** browse, sluice **7** shallow, shuffle **10** interstice

riffraff 3 mob **5** trash, waste **6** debris, kelter,

litter, masses, rabble, refuse **7** garbage, rubbish **8** canaille, unwashed **9** hoi polloi, multitude **11** proletariat
rifle 3 arm, gun, rob **4** loot, sack **5** steal **6** burgle, groove, weapon **7** carbine, despoil, firearm, pillage, plunder, ransack, rummage **9** chassepot ***accessory:*** **6** ramrod ***attachment:*** **5** scope **8** silencer ***kind:*** **6** Garand, Mauser **7** Enfield **8** Browning **9** Remington **10** Winchester **11** Springfield
rift 3 gap **4** rent **5** break, chasm, chink, cleft, crack, fault, space, split **6** breach, cleave, divide, hiatus, schism **7** fissure, opening, rupture **8** crevasse, division, fracture, interval **9** fault line **10** separation **12** estrangement
rig 3 arm, fit, fix **4** fake, gear, semi **5** dress, equip, getup, trick **6** adjust, clothe, doctor, outfit, tackle **7** apparel, arrange, costume, derrick, furnish, turn out **8** accouter, accoutre, clothing, equipage **9** apparatus, construct, equipment **10** manipulate
rigging 3 net **4** duds, gear, togs **5** dress, lines, ropes **6** attire, chains, tackle, things **7** apparel, clothes, raiment **8** clothing **9** apparatus, equipment
right 3 apt, due, fit **4** fair, just, sane, true, well **5** amend, amply, claim, droit, emend, exact, sound, title **6** at once, common, decent, dexter, direct, equity, honest, lawful, proper, square, strict **7** condign, correct, exactly, fitting, freedom, genuine, healthy, liberty, license, merited, old-line, rectify, redress **8** accurate, bona fide, orthodox, smack-dab, suitable **9** authentic, befitting, equitable, privilege, veracious, veritable **10** perquisite **11** appropriate, correctness, prerogative ***combining form:*** **4** orth, rect **5** dextr, ortho, recti **6** dextro ***feudal:*** **4** soke ***legal:*** **5** droit **8** usufruct ***royal:*** **7** regalia (plural)
right away 3 now **6** at once, pronto **8** directly, promptly **9** forthwith, instanter, instantly **11** immediately, straight off, straightway **12** then and there
righteous 4 good, holy, just, pure **5** godly, moral, noble, pious **6** devout, worthy **7** ethical, genuine, sinless, upright **8** innocent, virtuous **9** blameless, guiltless **10** inculpable, principled
righteousness 5 honor **6** equity, virtue **7** honesty, justice, probity **8** holiness, morality **9** integrity, rectitude
rightful 3 apt, due, fit **4** fair, just, true **5** legal **6** honest, lawful, proper **7** condign, fitting **8** deserved, suitable **9** befitting, equitable, impartial **10** applicable, legitimate **11** appropriate
right-handed 6 dexter **7** dextral **9** clockwise
right-hand page 5 recto
rightist 4 tory **11** reactionary **12** conservative
right-minded 5 moral, noble **6** decent, honest **7** ethical **8** virtuous **10** upstanding
Rights of Man author 5 Paine (Thomas)
rigid 3 set **4** firm, hard, taut **5** fixed, stiff, tense **6** severe, strict **7** austere, precise, hard-set **8** cast-iron, ironclad, obdurate, rigorous **9** draconian, immovable, inelastic, rockbound, stringent, unbending **10** adamantine, brassbound, inflexible, relentless, unyielding **11** unbudgeable **13** rhadamanthine
rigidity 6 turgor **7** buckram **8** hardness **9** stiffness ***muscular:*** **8** myotonia
rigmarole 6 bunkum, drivel, ramble **7** blather **8** nonsense **9** gibberish, procedure **10** balderdash, mumbo jumbo **12** gobbledygook
Rigoletto *composer:* **5** Verdi (Giuseppe) ***daughter:*** **5** Gilda ***setting:*** **6** Mantua
rigor 7 cruelty **8** asperity, hardness, hardship, severity **9** austerity, exactness, harshness, roughness, sharpness, sternness **10** affliction, difficulty, exactitude, strictness **11** tribulation **13** inflexibility
rigorous 5 exact, harsh, rigid, rough, stern, stiff **6** bitter, brutal, proper, rugged, severe, strict **7** ascetic, drastic, onerous, precise **8** accurate, exacting **9** draconian, ironbound, stringent **10** burdensome, inflexible, ironhanded, oppressive **11** punctilious **13** rhadamanthine
rile 3 bug, rub, vex **4** roil **5** anger, annoy, grate, muddy, peeve, pique, upset **6** muddle, nettle, put out, rankle **7** agitate, disturb, fluster, inflame, perturb, provoke **8** disorder, disquiet, irritate **9** aggravate **10** discompose, exasperate
rill 3 run **4** burn, purl **5** bourn, brook, creek **6** runnel, stream, valley **7** freshet, rivulet **8** brooklet **9** streamlet **11** watercourse
rim 3 hem, lip **4** bank, boss, brim, edge, ring **5** bezel, bezil, bound, brink, skirt, verge **6** border, flange, fringe, margin, shield **7** annulus, horizon, outline **8** boundary, surround **9** perimeter, periphery ***of a basket:*** **4** hoop ***of a cask:*** **5** chime ***of an insect's wing:*** **6** termen ***of a spoked wheel:*** **5** felly **6** felloe
Rimbaud work 12 Season in Hell (A) **13** Illuminations (Les)
rime 3 ice **4** hoar **5** crust, frost **7** coating, encrust **9** hoarfrost, Jack Frost **12** incrustation
Rinaldo *beloved:* **8** Angelica ***cousin:*** **7** Orlando ***father:*** **5** Aymon ***horse:*** **6** Bayard

mother: **3** Aya ***sister:*** **10** Bradamante ***uncle:*** **11** Charlemagne
rind 4 bark, husk, peel, skin **5** crust **9** crackling
ring 3 eye, hem, rim **4** band, bloc, bong, echo, gird, gyre, hoop, loop, peal, toll **5** arena, bezel, cabal, chime, clang, cycle, group, knell, knoll, round, sound **6** circle, clique, collar, girdle, staple **7** annulus, clangor, combine, compass, resound, vibrate **8** bracelet, cincture, encircle, surround **9** coalition, encompass **11** combination, reverberate ***around sun or moon:*** **6** corona ***curtain:*** **3** eye ***for a compass:*** **6** gimbal ***harness:*** **3** dee **6** button, terret ***heraldic:*** **7** annulet ***in a hinge:*** **7** gudgeon ***of chain:*** **4** link ***of color:*** **8** stocking ***of leaves or flowers:*** **6** wreath **7** garland ***of light:*** **4** halo **5** glory **6** corona, nimbus **7** aureole **8** halation ***of rope or metal:*** **4** hank **6** becket **7** garland, grommet, thimble ***of two hoops:*** **6** gimmal ***relating to:*** **7** annular ***used as a valve or diaphragm:*** **5** wafer ***wedding:*** **4** band
Ring and the Book author 8 Browning (Robert)
ringed 8 annulate, bordered **9** encircled **10** surrounded
ringer 4 fake, spit **5** clone, image **6** double **7** clapper, picture **8** impostor, portrait **10** simulacrum **13** spitting image
ringing 7 orotund, vibrant **8** decisive, emphatic, plangent, resonant, sonorous **10** clangorous, resounding **11** reverberant, unequivocal
ringleader 4 boss **5** chief **6** honcho, top dog **7** kingpin **9** godfather, top banana **10** head honcho, instigator, mastermind
ringlet 4 curl, lock **5** crimp, tress **7** circlet, earlock, tendril
Ring of the Nibelung composer 6 Wagner (Richard)
ringworm 5 tinea
rinse 4 dunk, lave, wash **5** bathe, douse, swill **6** shower, sluice **7** cleanse ***the mouth:*** **6** gargle
riot 5 brawl, broil, melee, revel, spree **6** bedlam, émeute, jumble, revolt, tumult, uproar **7** carouse, debauch, rampage, revelry, roister, wassail **8** carousal, disorder, uprising **9** commotion **10** debauchery, donnybrook, revolution **11** disturbance
riotous 4 lush, wild **6** stormy, unruly, wanton **7** bacchic, profuse, untamed **8** abundant **9** abounding, clamorous, exuberant, luxuriant, plentiful, turbulent, unchecked **10** boisterous **11** saturnalian, tempestuous **12** unrestrained
rip 4 gash, hole, rend, rent, rive, spit, tear **5** shred, slash, split **6** attack, cleave **7** current, sputter **8** lacerate, undertow **9** criticize, disparage **12** undercurrent ***into:*** **5** go for **6** assail, attack **8** lambaste ***off:*** **3** con, rob **4** copy **5** cheat, steal, theft **7** defraud, imitate, swindle **9** imitation
ripe 4 aged, full, late **5** adult, grown, ready, ruddy, plump **6** mature, mellow, smelly, timely **7** grown-up **8** prepared, suitable **9** developed, full-blown, full-grown, offensive, opportune **10** seasonable **11** appropriate, full-fledged
ripen 3 age **4** cure, grow **6** better, grow up, mature, mellow, season **7** develop, enhance, improve, perfect **8** heighten, maturate
rip off 3 con, rob **4** copy **5** cheat, steal **7** defraud, imitate, swindle
rip-off 4 copy, scam **5** fraud, theft **7** swindle **8** stealing **9** deception, imitation **12** exploitation
riposte 5 parry, reply **6** retort, return, thrust **8** back talk, comeback, repartee **13** counterattack
ripping 4 fine **5** grand, nifty, super, swell **6** divine, peachy **7** capital **8** glorious, splendid, terrific **9** admirable, delicious, excellent, fantastic, marvelous, wonderful **10** delightful, delectable, remarkable **11** scrumptious, sensational
ripple 3 lap **4** curl, fret, riff, wave **6** cockle, dimple, lipper, popple, ruffle, spread, wimple **7** crinkle, wavelet, wrinkle **8** undulate
rip-roaring 5 noisy **6** lively **8** exciting **9** hilarious **10** boisterous, rollicking, uproarious
ripsnorter 3 ace, pip **4** lulu **5** dandy, doozy **6** doozie, hummer **8** jim-dandy, knockout **9** humdinger **11** crackerjack
riptide 7 current **8** undertow **12** undercurrent
Rip Van Winkle ***author:*** **6** Irving (Washington) ***dog:*** **4** Wolf
rise 3 wax **4** grow, hill, lift, rear, soar **5** awake, get up, issue, mount, stand, surge, swell **6** ascend, ascent, awaken, emerge, expand, growth, origin, spring, uprear **7** advance, augment, develop, emanate, enhance, enlarge, hilltop, stand up, succeed, surface, upsurge **8** eminence, heighten, increase **9** ascension, beginning, increment, intensify, originate, terminate ***above:*** **8** surmount ***again:*** **7** resurge **9** resurrect ***against:*** **5** rebel **6** mutiny, revolt ***and fall:*** **4** tide **5** heave **6** welter ***and shine:*** **5** get up ***gradually:*** **4** loom
Rise of Silas Lapham author 7 Howells (William Dean)
riser 4 dais, step **8** platform

risible **4** rich **5** comic, droll, funny, jokey **6** absurd **7** comical **8** farcical **9** laughable, ludicrous **10** ridiculous

risk **4** ante, dare, defy **5** peril, stake, throw, wager **6** chance, danger, gamble, hazard, menace, stakes **7** imperil, jeopard, venture **8** endanger, exposure, jeopardy **9** adventure, encounter, liability **10** jeopardize

risky **4** bold **5** dicey, hairy **6** chancy, daring, touchy, tricky **7** parlous, unsound **8** delicate, perilous, ticklish **9** dangerous, hazardous, unhealthy **10** jeopardous, precarious **11** adventurous, speculative, treacherous

risqué **4** blue, lewd, racy, sexy **5** broad, crude, dirty, salty, spicy, vampy **6** coarse, daring, earthy, purple, ribald, vulgar **7** naughty, obscene, raunchy **8** indecent, off-color, scabrous **9** salacious **10** indecorous, indelicate, suggestive

rite **6** office **7** liturgy, mystery, service **8** ceremony **9** formality, ordinance, sacrament, solemnity **10** ceremonial, initiation, observance **11** celebration, sacramental ***funeral:*** **6** exequy **7** obsequy **8** exequies **9** obsequies ***Jewish:*** **4** bris ***of initiation or purification:*** **7** baptism ***of knighthood:*** **8** accolade (see also **sacrament**)

ritual see **rite**

ritzy **4** posh **5** fancy, swank **6** chichi, classy, modish, snazzy, swanky **7** elegant, high-hat, stylish **9** au courant, exclusive, expensive, luxurious **11** fashionable **12** ostentatious

rival **3** tie, try, vie **4** even, peer, side **5** equal, match **6** strive **7** attempt, compete, contend, contest, emulate **8** approach, opponent **9** adversary, competing, contender, measure up **10** antagonist, competitor, contending, contestant **11** comparative, competition

rivalry **6** strife **7** contest, warfare **8** conflict, jealousy, tug-of-war **9** emulation **10** contention, opposition **11** competition

rive **3** rip **4** rend, tear **5** break, burst, crack, sever, smash, split **6** cleave, divide, shiver, sunder **7** fissure, shatter **8** fracture, fragment, lacerate, separate, splinter

river ***Afghanistan:*** **5** Kabul ***Africa:*** **4** Bomu, Juba, Nile, Uele **5** Chari, Congo, Shari, Tsavo, Zaire **6** Atbara, Mbomou, Songwe, Ubangi **7** Aruwimi, Limpopo, Zambesi, Zambezi **9** Astaboras, Crocodile ***Alabama:*** **5** Coosa **6** Mobile **7** Conecuh, Perdido **9** Tombigbee **10** Tallapoosa ***Alaska:*** **5** Kobuk **6** Copper, Noatak, Tanana **7** Koyukuk, Susitna **9** Kuskokwim ***Albania:*** **4** Drin **5** Drini ***Argentina:*** **5** Negro **6** Paraná **7** Matanza ***arm:*** **6** branch **9** tributary ***Asia:*** **3** Ili **4** Amur, Lena, Oxus **5** Indus **6** Jayhun, Sutlej **7** Oedanes **8** Amu Darya **9** Dyardanes **11** Brahmaputra ***Australia:*** **4** Daly **5** Roper, Yarra **6** Barwon, Culgoa, Dawson, DeGrey, Murray **7** Darling, Fitzroy, Lachlan **8** Victoria **10** Yarra Yarra ***Austria:*** **4** Enns ***bank:*** **5** levee ***Belgium:*** **4** Leie, Yser **5** Rupel, Senne, Weser **6** Dender, Dindar, Ourthe **8** Visurgis ***Bolivia:*** **4** Beni **5** Abuná **6** Mamoré ***Borneo:*** **5** Kajan ***bottom:*** **3** bed ***Brazil:*** **3** Ica **4** Pará, Paru **5** Negro, Xingu **6** Paraná **7** Madeira, Tapajos, Tapajoz ***British Columbia:*** **6** Skeena **10** Bella Coola ***Burma:*** **4** Pegu **7** Irawadi **8** Chindwin **9** Irrawaddy ***California:*** **3** Eel, Pit **4** Kern, Yuba **6** Merced **7** Feather, Salinas, Trinity **8** Tuolumne ***Cambodia:*** **8** Tonle Sap ***Canada:*** **3** Bow **4** Back **5** Moose, Peace, Slave **6** Beaver, Fraser, Nelson **8** Gatineau, Saguenay **9** Athabasca, Great Fish, Mackenzie, Richelieu **11** Assiniboine ***Carolinas:*** **7** Catawba ***central United States:*** **3** Fox **5** Grand **6** Neosho, Platte, Wabash **8** Keya Paha, Missouri, Niobrara **9** Tennessee, Verdigris **10** Republican, Saint Croix **11** Mississippi ***channel:*** **6** alveus ***Chile:*** **3** Loa **5** Itata, Maule **6** Bío-Bío **8** Valdivia ***China:*** **3** Bei, Han, Hun, Nen, Wei **4** Amur, Dong **5** Baihe, Chang, Huang, Tarim **6** Yellow **7** Kashgar, Yangtze ***China-North Korea:*** **4** Yalu ***Colombia:*** **4** Meta, Tomo **6** Atrato **9** Magdalena ***Colorado:*** **5** Yampa **8** Gunnison ***Connecticut:*** **6** Thames **7** Niantic, Shepaug **9** Naugatuck **10** Farmington, Housatonic, Quinnipiac **11** Willimantic ***Crimea:*** **4** Alma ***crossing:*** **4** ford ***current:*** **4** eddy **6** rapids ***Czech Republic:*** **4** Iser **6** Jizera, Moldau, Vltava ***dam:*** **4** weir ***Denmark:*** **4** Stor ***dried bed:*** **4** wadi ***East Asia:*** **4** Yalu **5** Amnok **7** Oryokko ***Ecuador:*** **4** Napo **10** Esmeraldas ***England:*** **3** Esk, Exe, Nen, Ure **4** Aire, Avon, Eden, Nene, Ouse, Tees, Tyne, Wear, Yare **5** Swale, Trent **6** Mersey, Ribble, Thames ***Ethiopia:*** **3** Omo **4** Baro, Dawa ***Europe:*** **4** Eger, Elbe, Labe, Oder, Ohre, Saar **5** Albis, Meuse, Saale **6** Danube, Ticino ***Florida:*** **6** Indian **9** Kissimmee **10** Saint Johns **12** Apalachicola ***Foster's:*** **6** Swanee ***France:*** **3** Ain, Lot, Lys, Var **4** Aire, Aude, Cher, Eure, Gers, Loir, Oise, Orne, Saar, Tarn, Yser **5** Adour, Aisne, Drôme, Indre, Isère, Loire, Marne, Rhône, Saare, Sâone, Seine, Somme, Yonne **6** Allier, Ariège, Scarpe, Vienne **7** Durance, Garonne, La Riège, Moselle **8** Charente, Dordogne ***Georgia:*** **6** Etowah, Oconee **8** Altamaha, Ocmulgee **13** Chattahoochee ***Germany:*** **3** Ems, Rur **4** Eder, Eger, Elbe,

Isar, Main, Rems, Ruhr, Saar **5** Hunte, Lippe, Mosel, Rhine, Spree, Werra, Weser **6** Neckar ***Germany-Poland:*** **4** Oder ***Ghana:*** **5** Volta ***god:*** **7** Alpheus, Inachus **8** Achelous ***Greece:*** **3** Iri **4** Arta **5** Lerna, Lerne **7** Alpheus, Eurotas **8** Achelous **9** Arakhthos ***Honduras:*** **4** Ulúa **5** Aguán **6** Patuca ***Iberian:*** **5** Douro, Duero ***Idaho:*** **5** Lemhi ***Illinois:*** **8** Mackinaw ***India:*** **4** Sind **5** Sindh, Tapti **6** Chenab, Ganges, Jhelum, Kaveri, Kistna **7** Cauvery, Krishna **8** Acesines, Godavari ***inlet:*** **5** bayou **6** slough ***Iran:*** **3** Kor **4** Mand, Mund **5** Karun **8** Safid Rud, Sefid Rud ***Ireland:*** **3** Lee **4** Deel, Erne, Suir **5** Boyne, Clare, Foyle **6** Barrow, Liffey **7** Shannon ***Italy:*** **4** Adda, Arno, Liri, Nera **5** Adige, Arnus, Etsch, Liris, Oglio, Padus, Piave, Tiber **6** Ollius, Rapido, Tevere, Trebia **7** Athesis, Rubicon, Secchia, Tiberis, Trebbia **8** Rubicone, Volturno ***Kansas:*** **6** Pawnee ***Kazakhstan-Russia:*** **4** Emba, Ural **5** Tobol **6** Irtysh ***Kenya:*** **4** Athi, Tana ***Kubla Khan's:*** **4** Alph ***land:*** **4** holm **5** flats **7** bottoms ***Latvia:*** **5** Gauja ***Latvia-Lithuania:*** **7** Lielupe ***Lebanon:*** **6** Litani ***Little Rock's:*** **8** Arkansas ***living on the bank of:*** **8** riparian ***longest:*** **4** Nile ***Louisiana:*** **11** Atchafalaya ***Maine:*** **8** Kennebec **9** Aroostook, Penobscot ***Malaysia:*** **9** Trengganu ***Maryland:*** **8** Monocacy, Patapsco, Patuxent **9** Nanticoke ***Massachusetts:*** **7** Charles, Taunton **9** Merrimack, Westfield **10** Housatonic ***Mexico:*** **6** Pánuco, Sonora **7** Tabasco **8** Grijalva ***Michigan:*** **4** Cass **5** Huron **7** Saginaw **8** Manistee, Muskegon **9** Cheboygan, Kalamazoo **10** Michigamme, Shiawassee ***Mississippi:*** **5** Pearl, Yazoo **10** Pascagoula ***Moldova-Ukraine:*** **8** Dneister ***Missouri:*** **5** Osage ***mouth:*** **5** delta ***Myanmar:*** **4** Pegu **7** Irawadi **8** Chindwin **9** Irrawaddy ***Nebraska:*** **4** Loup **6** Nemaha, Platte **7** Elkhorn ***Netherlands:*** **4** Maas, Waal **5** Issel, Yssel **6** Amstel, IJssel **7** Vahalis ***New England:*** **4** Saco **6** Nashua **9** Merrimack **10** Blackstone **11** Connecticut **12** Androscoggin ***New Jersey:*** **6** Rahway **7** Passaic, Raritan **8** Tuckahoe ***New York:*** **5** Tioga **6** Hudson, Mohawk, Oneida, Oswego, Seneca **7** Chemung, Niagara **8** Chenango ***New Zealand:*** **7** Waikato ***Nicaragua:*** **4** Coco **7** Segovia ***Nigeria:*** **5** Benin ***North Carolina:*** **3** Haw, Tar **5** Neuse **6** Chowan **8** Alamance ***northeast United States:*** **4** Ohio **6** Hoosic **7** Genesee, Hocking **8** Delaware, Mahoning **9** Allegheny **11** Monongahela, Susquehanna ***Northern Ireland:*** **4** Bann **6** Mourne ***North Korea:*** **4** Yalu **5** Daido **7** Taedong ***northwest United States:*** **5** Snake **7** Klamath **8** Columbia **11** Pend Oreille ***Norway:*** **4** Otra, Tana, Teno ***nymph:*** **5** naiad ***of fire:*** **10** Phlegethon ***of forgetfulness:*** **5** Lethe ***of ice:*** **7** glacier ***of woe:*** **7** Acheron ***Ohio:*** **5** Miami **8** Cuyahoga, Sandusky **9** Muskingum **10** Tuscarawas ***Oklahoma:*** **8** Cimarron ***Oregon:*** **5** Rogue **6** Owyhee **7** Malheur **8** McKenzie **9** Clackamas, Deschutes **10** Willamette ***Nevada:*** **7** Truckee ***Pakistan:*** **4** Ravi ***Panama:*** **5** Tuira **7** Chagres ***Papua New Guinea:*** **3** Fly **5** Sepik ***Paraguay:*** **3** Apa **9** Pilcomayo ***Pennsylvania:*** **6** Lehigh **10** Schuylkill ***Peru:*** **5** Rímac, Santa **7** Marañón **8** Apurímac, Huallaga, Urubamba ***Philippines:*** **4** Abra, Agno **5** Pasig **7** Cagayan **8** Cotabato, Mindanao, Pampanga ***Poland:*** **3** San **7** Vistula ***Portugal:*** **4** Sado **7** Mondego ***relating to:*** **7** fluvial ***Rhode Island:*** **7** Seekonk **8** Sakonnet **10** Providence ***Romania:*** **5** Arges ***Russia:*** **3** Don, Oka, Ufa, Usa **4** Kama, Kara, Lena, Msta, Neva, Sura, Svir **5** Onega, Terek, Volga **6** Anadyr, Angara, Belaya, Kolima, Kolyma, Ussuri, Vyatka **7** Dnieper, Pechora, Yenisey **8** Barguzin, Kostroma, Voronezh, Vychegda ***Russia-Ukraine:*** **6** Donets ***sacred:*** **6** Ganges ***Scotland:*** **3** Dee, Don, Esk, Tay **4** Doon, Nith, Spey, Tyne **5** Afton, Annan, Clyde, Forth, Tweed **6** Teviot **7** Deveron **8** Findhorn ***Shanghai's:*** **7** Huangpu, Hwang Pu ***Sicily:*** **5** Salso **6** Simeto ***siren:*** **7** Lorelei ***Slovakia:*** **3** Vag, Vah **4** Gran, Hron, Waag **5** Garam, Nitra **6** Neutra, Nyitra ***South Africa:*** **4** Vaal **6** Orange ***South America:*** **3** Apa **6** Amazon **8** Amazonas, Orellana **9** Pilcomayo ***South Carolina:*** **6** Saluda, Santee **7** Wateree **8** Congaree ***South Dakota:*** **3** Bad ***Southeast Asia:*** **6** Dza-chu, Mekong **7** Salween **8** Lan-ts'ang ***southeast United States:*** **6** Pee Dee **7** Noxubee, Washita **8** Escambia, Ouachita, Suwannee **10** Okanoxubee ***southern United States:*** **6** Sabine ***South Korea:*** **3** Kum ***southwest United States:*** **3** Red **4** Gila, Zuni **5** Pecos **8** Canadian, Colorado ***Spain:*** **4** Ebro **5** Tagus **6** Aragon **12** Guadalquivir ***Sweden:*** **4** Göta **5** Kalix ***Switzerland:*** **3** Aar **4** Aare **5** Reuss **7** Obringa ***Syria:*** **6** Khabur **7** Orontes ***Tasmania:*** **4** Huon ***Tbilisi's:*** **4** Kura ***Texas:*** **5** Llano **6** Brazos, Nueces **7** San Saba, Trinity **9** Guadalupe ***Texas-Mexico:*** **8** Rio Bravo **9** Rio Grande ***tidal:*** **7** estuary ***Tokyo's:*** **6** Sumida ***Turkey:*** **4** Aras **5** Araks **6** Seihun, Seyhan ***Ukrainian:*** **3** Bug **4** Alma, Styr ***underworld:*** **4** Styx **5** Lethe **7** Acheron, Cocytus **10** Phlegethon ***Uruguay:*** **5** Negro ***Utah:*** **5** Provo, Uinta, Weber **6** Jordan,

Sevier ***valley:*** **6** strath ***Venezuela:*** **5** Apure, Caura **6** Caroní **7** Orinoco ***Vermont:*** **3** Mad **5** Onion, White **8** Winooski ***Virginia:*** **3** Dan **5** James **7** Rapidan **9** Nansemond **10** Appomattox, Shenandoah **12** Chickahominy, Rappahannock ***wailing:*** **7** Cocytus ***Wales:*** **4** Dyfi **5** Clwyd, Dovey, Teifi ***Washington:*** **6** Skagit, Yakima **9** Klickitat, Snohomish, Wenatchee ***West Africa:*** **5** Niger **6** Gambia **7** Senegal ***western United States:*** **7** Laramie **8** Columbia, Flathead **11** Yellowstone ***West Virginia:*** **7** Kanawha ***Wisconsin:*** **8** Kickapoo **9** Menominee ***Wyoming:*** **8** Shoshone **10** Gros Ventre **11** Medicine Bow

Rivera's wife 5 Kahlo (Frida)

river duck 4 teal **6** wigeon **7** dabbler, mallard, widgeon **8** shoveler **9** greenwing

river horse 5 hippo **12** hippopotamus

riverine 8 riparian

river island 3 ait **4** eyot

rivet 3 fix, pin **4** bolt, brad, stud **5** affix **6** absorb, attach, clinch, fasten **7** engross **8** fastener

Riviera city 4 Nice **6** Cannes, Monaco **7** Antibes, San Remo **8** St. Tropez **10** Monte Carlo

rivulet 3 run **4** beck, burn, gill, race, rill **5** bourn, brook, creek **6** runlet, runnel, stream **9** streamlet

Rizpah ***father:*** **4** Aiah ***lover:*** **4** Saul ***son:*** **6** Armoni **12** Mephibosheth

roach 3 hog **6** shiner **7** sunfish

road 3 way **4** fare, lane, line, path **5** drive, going, route, track **6** artery, avenue, career, causey, course, street **7** highway, journey, passage **8** causeway, chaussée, crossway, highroad, pavement, speedway, turnpike **9** boulevard **12** thoroughfare ***along a cliff:*** **8** corniche ***around a city:*** **6** bypass **7** beltway ***bend:*** **7** hairpin ***edge:*** **4** berm **8** shoulder ***French:*** **6** chemin ***Irish:*** **6** boreen ***machine:*** **5** paver **6** grader **9** bulldozer ***Roman:*** **3** via **4** iter ***shoulder:*** **4** berm ***side:*** **6** branch **8** shunpike ***Spanish:*** **6** camino ***surface:*** **3** tar **6** gravel **7** asphalt, macadam **8** pavement

roadblock 7 barrier **8** blockade **9** barricade **11** obstruction

road book 3 map **5** atlas **9** gazetteer, itinerary

roadhouse 3 bar, inn **4** dive **5** hotel, lodge **6** tavern **9** nightclub

roadrunner 6 cuckoo **13** chaparral cock

road rut 6 kettle **7** pothole **9** chuckhole

roam 3 bat, bum, gad, run **4** rove, walk **5** drift, prowl, range, stray **6** ramble, stroll, travel, wander **7** meander, traipse **8** straggle, vagabond **9** gallivant

roamer 3 bum **5** gipsy, gypsy, nomad, rover **6** ranger, walker **7** drifter, prowler, rambler, vagrant **8** marauder, stroller, traveler, vagabond, wanderer **11** nightwalker

roar 3 din **4** bawl, bell, boom, bray, howl, yell **5** shout **6** bellow, clamor, outcry **7** bluster **10** vociferate ***bullring:*** **3** olé

roast 4 bake, mock, rack, sear **5** broil, grill, joint, parch **6** scathe, scorch **7** banquet, blister, mockery, swelter **8** barbecue, ridicule **9** criticize

rob 3 cop, mug **4** lift, loot, nick, raid, roll, sack **5** boost, filch, heist, pinch, pluck, reave, steal **6** burgle, fleece, hijack, hold up, pilfer, rip off, snitch, thieve **7** defraud, deprive, despoil, pillage, plunder, purloin, ransack, stick up, swindle **8** knock off **9** knock over **10** burglarize

robber 4 yegg **5** crook, thief **6** bandit, looter, mugger, pirate, reiver **7** brigand, burglar, footpad, rustler **8** hijacker, swindler **9** holdup man **10** cat burglar, highwayman, sandbagger, stickup man **12** housebreaker ***grave:*** **5** ghoul

robbery 5 heist, theft **6** holdup, piracy **7** larceny, mugging, stickup **8** banditry

robe 3 aba **4** cape, gown, wrap **5** cloak, habit **6** caftan, mantle **7** garment, manteau **8** covering, dalmatic, vestment ***baptismal:*** **7** chrisom ***bishop's:*** **7** chimere ***of Roman emperors:*** **6** purple ***Turkish:*** **6** dolman

Robin Goodfellow 4 Puck **6** sprite

Robinson Crusoe ***author:*** **5** Defoe (Daniel) ***character:*** **6** Friday

robot 5 droid, golem **7** android **8** automata (plural) **9** automaton

Rob Roy author 5 Scott (Walter)

robust 4 hale, rude **5** hardy, husky, lusty, rough, sound, stout **6** hearty, potent, rugged, sinewy, strong, sturdy **7** healthy **8** athletic, muscular, vigorous **9** energetic, strapping **10** boisterous, red-blooded, full-bodied, prosperous

robustious 4 rude **5** lusty, rough, rowdy, wooly **6** rugged **7** boorish, ill-bred, loutish **8** churlish, clownish **9** unrefined **10** boisterous, unpolished

rock 4 crag, reel, roll, sway, toss **5** geode, pitch, quake, shake, swing **6** totter **7** boulder, breccia **8** astonish, convulse, undulate **9** oscillate ***basaltic:*** **5** wacke ***cavity:*** **3** vug ***combining form:*** **4** lite, lith, lyte, petr **5** clast, petri, petro ***decomposed:*** **6** gossan ***fissile:*** **5** shale ***formation:*** **4** sill **5** butte, nappe **6** pluton **7** rimrock, terrane **8** isocline, syncline ***fragment:*** **8** xenolith ***igneous:*** **4** lava, sial, sima **5** magma **6** basalt, gabbro, pumice **7** diabase, diorite, granite **8** eruptive, felstone, obsidian, porphyry, traprock **10** travertine ***layer:*** **10** mantlerock ***mass:*** **5** scree **9** batholith ***metamorphic:*** **5** slate **6** gneiss, marble, schist **9** quartzite, soapstone ***molten:*** **4** lava ***sedimentary:*** **4** clay, coal **5** chalk, chert, coral, flint, shale **8** mudstone **9** limestone, sandstone, siltstone ***volcanic:*** **4** tuff **6** basalt

rock band 3 REM, Who (The) **4** Cure (The) **5** Byrds (The), Clash (The), Cream, Doors (The), Kinks (The), Queen **6** Eagles (The), Pixies (The), Police (The) **7** Animals (The), Beatles (The), Bee Gees (The), Blondie, Bon Jovi, Chicago, Nirvana, Ramones (The), Rascals (The), Santana **8** Coldplay, Drifters (The), Green Day, Megadeth, Pearl Jam, Platters (The), Supremes (The), Van Halen **9** Aerosmith, Alice Cooper, Beach Boys (The), Metallica, Pink Floyd, Radiohead, Steely Dan, Yardbirds (The) **10** Deep Purple, Duran Duran, Jethro Tull, Moody Blues, Sex Pistols (The), Spice Girls **11** Four Seasons (The), King Crimson, Led Zeppelin **12** Black Sabbath, Fleetwood Mac, Grateful Dead (The), Talking Heads (The) **13** Nine Inch Nails, Rolling Stones (The)

rock bass 7 sunfish

rock-bottom 4 root **6** lowest **8** cheapest **9** lowermost **11** fundamental

rocket 3 fly, zip **4** soar, whiz, zoom **5** mount **6** ascend, bullet **7** missile, shoot up **8** firework, starship **10** projectile ***European:*** **6** Ariane ***landing:*** **7** reentry **10** splashdown ***launcher:*** **7** bazooka ***launching:*** **7** liftoff **8** blastoff ***scientist:*** **5** Braun (Wernher von) **7** Goddard (Robert) ***section:*** **5** stage

rockfish 4 cony, hind **5** coney **7** grouper, jewfish, sea bass **8** bocaccio **10** scorpaenid **11** striped bass

Rockies resort 4 Vail **5** Aspen **8** Snowmass **9** Telluride

____ **Rockne 5** Knute

rock rabbit 4 cony, pika **5** coney, hyrax **6** dassie

rock-ribbed 5 rigid **8** dogmatic, obdurate **9** unbending **10** inflexible, unyielding

rock star 3 J. Lo, Pop (Iggy) **4** Bono, Cher, Crow (Sheryl), Dion (Celine), Flea, Gaga (Lady), Joel (Billy), John (Elton), King (Carole), Love (Courtney), Moon (Keith), Rose (Axl), Roth (David Lee) **5** Abdul (Paula), Berry (Chuck), Bowie (David), Haley (Bill), Harry (Debbie), Holly (Buddy), Lewis (Jerry Lee), Lopez (Jennifer), Paige (Jimmy), Plant (Robert), Seger (Bob), Smith (Patti), Starr (Ringo), Tyler (Stephen), Wyman (Bill), Young (Neil) **6** Burdon (Eric), Cobain (Kurt), Cooper (Alice), Domino (Fats), Eminem, Garcia (Jerry), Jagger (Mick), Joplin (Janis), Lennon (John), Manson (Marilyn), Prince, Spears (Britney), Vaughn (Stevie Ray), Vedder (Eddie) **7** Bon Jovi (Jon), Clapton (Eric), Cochran (Eddie), Daltrey (Roger), Diddley (Bo), Fogerty (John), Hendrix (Jimi), Lavigne (Avril), Madonna, Mercury (Freddie), Michael (George), Perkins (Carl), Presley (Elvis), Shannon (Del), Stefani (Gwen), Stewart (Rod), Vincent (Gene), Winwood (Steve) **8** Costello (Elvis), Harrison (George), Morrison (Jim, Van), Osbourne (Ozzy), Richards (Keith), Van Halen (Eddie) **9** Boy George, McCartney (Paul), Townshend (Pete) **10** Mellencamp (John) **11** Springsteen (Bruce) **13** Little Richard

rockweed 5 algae, fucus **7** seaweed **12** bladder wrack

rocky hill 3 tor **5** kopje

rococo 4 busy **5** showy **6** florid, frilly, ornate **7** baroque, elegant, opulent **9** elaborate, intricate **10** decorative, flamboyant **11** overwrought

rod 3 bar, gat **4** cane, pole, wand **5** baton, dowel, spoke, staff, stave, stick **6** pistol **7** scepter **8** revolver **10** correction, discipline, punishment **11** castigation **12** chastisement ***bundle of:*** **6** fasces

rodent 3 rat **4** cavy, cony, mole, paca, pika, vole **5** cavie, coney, coypu, mouse, shrew **6** agouti, beaver, gerbil, gopher, jerboa, marmot, murine, nutria, rabbit **7** hamster, lemming, leveret, muskrat **8** capybara, chipmunk, dormouse, squirrel, tuco tuco, viscacha, vizcacha, water rat **9** guinea pig, porcupine **10** chinchilla, field mouse, prairie dog **11** kangaroo rat, meadow mouse, pocket mouse **12** pocket gopher ***aquatic:*** **5** coypu **6** beaver, nutria **7** muskrat **8** musquash ***burrowing:*** **4** mole, paca **6** gerbil, gopher **7** hamster **8** viscacha, vizcacha ***family:*** **5** murid **6** murine **7** sciurid ***genus:*** **3** Mus **5** Lepus ***tropical:*** **6** agouti

rodeo 7 contest, roundup **9** enclosure **10** exhibition **11** competition ***animal:*** **5** horse, steer **10** Brahma bull ***event:*** **10** calf roping **11** bulldogging **12** bronco riding ***performer:*** **5** clown **6** cowboy

____ **Rodin 7** Auguste

rodomontade 4 blow, brag, rant **5** boast, swash, vaunt **7** bluster, swagger **9** gasconade **11** braggadocio

Rodomonte ***beloved:*** **8** Doralice ***slayer:*** **8** Ruggiero

Rodrigo Díaz de Bivar 5 El Cid
rod-shaped 7 virgate **8** bacillar **9** bacillary
roe 4 deer, eggs **6** beluga, caviar, osetra **7** sevruga
Roentgen's discovery 4 X-ray
Roethke work 6 Waking (The) **8** Far Field (The)
rogation 6 litany, prayer **8** entreaty, petition **10** beseeching **12** supplication
____ **Rogers 3** Roy **4** Carl, Fred, Will **6** Ginger, Robert
rogue 5 cheat, gypsy, knave, scamp **6** rascal **7** lowlife, sharper, villain **8** picaroon, scalawag, swindler **9** defrauder, miscreant, reprobate, scoundrel, skeezicks, trickster **10** blackguard, mountebank **11** rapscallion ***relating to:*** **10** picaresque
roguery 5 fraud **7** devilry, knavery, waggery **8** deviltry, mischief, trickery **9** devilment, diablerie **11** waggishness **12** sportiveness
roguish 3 sly **4** arch **6** impish, wicked **7** knavish **8** devilish, espiègle, scampish **10** picaresque **11** mischievous
roil 3 mud, vex **4** foul, rile, romp **5** annoy, dirty, grate, muddy, peeve, upset **6** befoul, muddle, nettle, stir up **7** agitate, disturb **8** disorder, irritate **9** aggravate **10** exasperate
roily 5 muddy, riley **6** turbid **9** turbulent
roister 4 riot **5** revel **6** frolic **7** carouse, reveler, wassail **9** wassailer
Roland 7 Orlando ***battle site:*** **9** Roncevaux **12** Roncesvalles ***beloved:*** **4** Aude ***betrayer:*** **4** Gano **7** Ganelon ***friend:*** **6** Oliver **7** Olivier ***horn:*** **7** Olivant ***sword:*** **8** Durandal, Durendal ***uncle:*** **11** Charlemagne
role 3 bit **4** duty, lead, part, pose **5** cameo, cloak, guise, niche **6** aspect, office **7** quality **8** capacity, function, position **9** character **13** impersonation
roll 3 bun, rob **4** bolt, coil, flow, furl, gyre, list, pour, rock, toss, turn, wind, wrap **5** heave, pitch, surge **6** bundle, roster, rotate, stream, swathe, wallow, wrap up **7** biscuit, brioche, envelop, revolve, swaddle, trundle **8** involute, register, schedule, turn over ***ring-shaped:*** **5** bagel
roll about 6 wallow, welter
roll back 5 lower **6** reduce, repeal **7** curtail, rescind
roller 3 rod **4** bowl, drum, wave **6** canary, caster, platen **7** breaker, carrier, tumbler **8** cylinder
Roller Derby round 3 jam
rollick 4 lark, play, romp **5** caper, frisk, party, revel, sport **6** cavort, frolic, gambol **7** disport, skylark **8** escapade **9** merriment
rollicking 4 wild **5** antic, merry **6** frisky, lively **8** sportive **10** boisterous, frolicsome **12** high-spirited
rolling stock 4 cars **7** coaches, engines **8** cabooses, Pullmans, sleepers, trailers **11** locomotives
rolling stone 4 hobo **5** gipsy, gypsy, nomad, rover, tramp **6** roamer **7** drifter, rambler, vagrant **8** vagabond, wanderer
Rolling Stones 4 Wood (Ron) **5** Jones (Brian), Watts (Charlie), Wyman (Bill) **6** Jagger (Mick), Taylor (Dick, Mick) **7** Stewart (Ian) **8** Richards (Keith)
roly-poly see **rotund**
Roman 5 Latin **7** Italian ***amphitheater:*** **9** Colosseum ***assembly:*** **5** forum **6** senate **7** comitia ***building:*** **5** Forum **6** Circus **8** basilica, Pantheon ***clan:*** **4** gens ***comedy writer:*** **7** Plautus (Titus), Terence ***conspirator:*** **6** Brutus (Marcus Junius) **7** Cassius (Gaius) **8** Catiline ***date:*** **4** Ides **7** calends, kalends ***Doric:*** **6** Tuscan ***emperor:*** **4** Nero, Otho **5** Galba (Servius Sulpicius), Nerva (Marcus Cocceius), Titus, Verus (Lucius Aurelius) **6** Julian, Trajan **7** Hadrian, Maximus (Magnus Clemens, Marcus Clodius, Petronius), Severus (Lucius Septimius) **8** Augustus, Caligula, Claudius, Commodus (Lucius Aelius), Domitian, Tiberius, Valerian **9** Caracalla, Vespasian **10** Diocletian, Theodosius **11** Constantine, Valentinian ***entrance hall:*** **5** atria (plural) **6** atrium ***epic:*** **6** Aeneid ***epigrammatist:*** **7** Martial ***family:*** **7** Gracchi ***Fates:*** **4** Nona **5** Morta **6** Decuma, Parcae ***festival:*** **10** Saturnalia ***founder:*** **5** Remus **7** Romulus ***fountain:*** **5** Trevi **6** Triton ***garment:*** **4** toga **5** tunic ***general:*** **5** Sulla (Lucius Cornelius), Titus **6** Antony (Marc), Marius (Gaius), Scipio (Publius Cornelius) **8** Agricola (Gnaeus Julius)
god: **3** Lar **4** deus **blind: 6** Plutus **chief: 4** Jove **7** Jupiter **messenger: 7** Mercury **of agriculture: 6** Saturn **of animals: 6** Faunus **of death: 4** Mors **of dreams: 8** Morpheus **of fire: 6** Vulcan **of gates and doors: 5** Janus **of healing: 9** Asclepius **11** Aesculapius **of heaven: 6** Uranus **of households: 3** Lar **5** Lares **7** Penates **of love: 4** Amor **5** Cupid **of medicine: 9** Asclepius **11** Aesculapius **of mirth: 5** Comus **of regeneration: 7** Priapus **of sleep: 6** Somnus **of the sea: 6** Pontus **7** Neptune, Proteus **of the sun: 3** Sol **6** Apollo **of the underworld: 3** Dis **5** Orcus, Pluto **8** Dispater **of the wind: 5** Eurus, Notus **6** Aeolus, Aquilo, Auster, Boreas **8** Favonius, Zephyrus **of war: 4** Mars **8** Quirinus **of**

wealth: 6 Plutus of wine: 7 Bacchus of woods: 6 Faunus two-faced: 5 Janus *goddess:* 3 dea of agriculture: 5 Ceres of beauty: 5 Venus of dawn: 6 Aurora *of death:* 5 Morta of flowers: 5 Flora of handicrafts: 7 Minerva of harvests: 3 Ops of health: 7 Minerva of hope: 4 Spes of hunting: 5 Diana of justice: 7 Astraea of love: 5 Venus of marriage: 4 Juno of night: 3 Nox of peace: 3 Pax of springs: 7 Juturna of strife: 9 Discordia of the earth: 5 Terra 6 Tellus of the hearth: 5 Vesta of the moon: 4 Luna of the sea: 10 Amphitrite of the underworld: 10 Proserpina of victory: 6 Vacuna of war: 7 Bellona of wisdom: 7 Minerva of womanhood: 4 Juno *greeting:* 3 ave *hero:* 6 Caesar (Julius) 11 Cincinnatus (Lucius Quinctius) *hill:* 7 Caelian, Viminal 8 Aventine, Palatine, Quirinal 9 Esquiline 10 Capitoline *historian:* 4 Livy 5 Nepos 7 Sallust, Tacitus 9 Suetonius *king:* 7 Romulus, Servius, Tullius 12 Ancus Martius 13 Numa Pompilius *marketplace:* 5 agora *military formation:* 3 ala 6 alares (plural) 7 phalanx *miltary unit:* 6 cohort, legion 7 maniple *officer:* 9 centurion *official:* 5 augur, edile 6 aedile, censor, consul, lictor 7 praetor, prefect, tribune 8 quaestor 9 proconsul *people:* 5 Laeti, plebs 6 populi (plural) 7 populus, Sabines 9 plebeians *philosopher:* 4 Cato 6 Seneca 8 Apuleius 9 Epictetus, Lucretius *physician:* 9 Asclepius 11 Aesculapius *port:* 5 Ostia *procurator:* 6 Pilate (Pontius) *province:* 4 Asia 5 Lycia, Syria 6 Achaea, Africa, Arabia, Cyprus, Raetia 7 Baetica, Belgica, Galatia, Numidia, Sicilia, Thracia 8 Aegyptus, Dalmatia 9 Aquitania, Britannia, Lusitania 10 Cappadocia, Mauretania *racecourse:* 6 circus *road:* 4 iter *slave:* 9 Spartacus *statesman:* 4 Cato 5 Pliny 6 Caesar, Cicero, Pompey, Seneca 7 Agrippa 8 Augustus, Gracchus, Maecenas 9 Flaminius *symbol of authority:* 6 fasces

roman à ____ 4 clef

romance 3 woo 4 gest, love 5 amour, court, fling, geste, novel 6 affair 7 fantasy, fiction 8 stardust 10 love affair 12 bodice ripper

Romance language 6 French 7 Catalan, Italian, Spanish 8 Romanian, Rumanian 9 Sardinian 10 Portuguese

romance writer 4 Holt (Victoria), Robb (J. D.) 5 Brown (Sandra), Chase (Loretta), Clark (Mary Higgins), Heyer (Georgette), Steel (Danielle) 6 Dailey (Janet), Graham (Heather), Howard (Linda), Krantz (Judith), Krentz (Jayne Ann), Putney (Mary Jo), Stuart (Anne) 7 Baldwin (Faith), Collins (Jackie), Cookson (Catherine), Coulter (Catherine), Estrada (Rita Clay), Garwood (Julie), Hatcher (Robin Lee), Maxwell (Anne), Osborne (Maggie), Roberts (Nora), Spencer (LaVyrle), Stewart (Mary), Whitney (Phyllis) 8 Bradford (Barbara Taylor), Cartland (Barbara), Deveraux (Jude), Gabaldon (Diana), McNaught (Judith), Phillips (Susan Elizabeth) 9 Alsobrook (Rosalyn), Evanovich (Janet), Woodiwiss (Kathleen)

Romania *capital:* 9 Bucharest *city:* 4 Iasi 6 Brasov, Galati 7 Craiova 9 Constanta, Timisoara *monetary unit:* 3 leu 4 bani *mountain range:* 10 Carpathian *neighbor:* 6 Serbia 7 Hungary, Moldova, Ukraine 8 Bulgaria *part of:* 7 Balkans *peninsula:* 6 Balkan *river:* 5 Siret, Tisza 6 Danube *sea:* 5 Black

romantic 5 gauzy, ideal, idyll, mushy 6 ardent, dreamy, exotic, gothic, poetic, unreal 7 amorous, maudlin, mawkish 8 fanciful, quixotic 9 fantastic, imaginary, visionary 10 idealistic, lovey-dovey 11 sentimental

Romany 5 Gipsy, Gypsy

Romeo 5 lover, swain 7 amorist, Don Juan, gallant 8 Casanova, lothario, paramour *beloved:* 6 Juliet *enemy:* 6 Tybalt *father:* 8 Montague *friend:* 8 Mercutio

Rommel, Erwin 9 Desert Fox

romp 4 lark, play 5 caper, frisk, sport 6 cavort, frolic, gambol, hoyden 7 rollick, runaway, skylark 8 escapade

Romulus *brother:* 5 Remus *father:* 4 Mars *mother:* 9 Rea Silvia 10 Rhea Silvia *victim:* 5 Remus

rondure 3 arc, orb 4 arch, ball, ring 5 curve, globe, round 6 circle, sphere 9 curvature

rood 5 cross 8 crucifix

roof 3 hip, top 4 apex, peak 5 cover, crest, crown 6 summit 7 ceiling 8 covering, housetop *material:* 3 tar, tin 4 tile 5 slate, straw, terne 6 copper, thatch 7 shingle *of a cavern:* 4 dome *of the mouth:* 6 palate *part:* 3 hip 4 eave 5 eaves 6 soffit 8 overhang 9 ridgepole *structure:* 9 penthouse *type:* 5 gable 6 hipped 7 gambrel, lamella, mansard 9 butterfly *vaulted:* 4 dome

roofer 5 tiler

rook 4 bilk, colt, crow, scam, tyro 5 cheat, mulct, raven, stick 6 castle, fleece, novice 7 amateur, defraud, recruit, swindle, trainee 8 beginner, flimflam, freshman, neophyte, newcomer 10 apprentice, tenderfoot

rookery 5 roost 6 colony

rookie 4 colt, tyro **5** plebe **6** novice **7** amateur, recruit, trainee **8** beginner, freshman, neophyte, newcomer **10** apprentice, tenderfoot

room 3 den **4** cell, hall, play, rein **5** divan, house, lodge, put up, salon, scope, space **6** alcove, billet, leeway, margin, reside, studio **7** chamber, cubicle, expanse, gallery, lodging **9** clearance ***ancient Roman:* 5** atria (plural) **6** atrium ***eating:* 4** nook **6** alcove **7** commons, kitchen **8** mess hall **9** refectory ***food storage:* 6** larder, pantry ***for paintings:* 7** gallery ***in a harem:* 3** oda ***in a monastery:* 4** cell **9** refectory **11** calefactory ***in a prison:* 4** cell ***on a ship:* 5** cabin **6** galley ***round:* 7** rotunda

roomer 5 guest **6** lodger, renter, tenant **7** boarder

roomy 4 wide **5** ample, broad, large **8** spacious **9** capacious **10** commodious

Roosevelt, Franklin D. *birthplace:* 8 Hyde Park ***dog:* 4** Fala ***message:* 12** fireside chat ***mother:* 4** Sara ***predecessor:* 6** Hoover (Herbert) ***program:* 7** New Deal ***successor:* 6** Truman (Harry) ***vacation home:* 10** Campobello ***wife:* 7** Eleanor

roost 3 sit **4** land, nest, rest **5** perch **6** alight, settle **7** rookery **8** dovecote

rooster 4 cock **5** capon **8** cockerel, gamecock **10** cockalorum **11** chanticleer

root 3 dig, fix **4** base, bulb, core, grub, pith, stem, well **5** basis, cheer, embed, grout, lodge, plant, radix, tuber **6** bottom, etymon, ground, marrow, origin, settle, source **7** applaud, bedrock, essence, footing, radical **8** radicate **9** beginning, establish, inception **10** foundation ***aromatic:* 7** ginseng ***edible:* 3** oca, yam **4** beet, taro, yuca **5** yucca **6** carrot, daikon, ginger, jicama, manioc, potato, radish, turnip **7** burdock, cassava, parsnip, salsify **8** celeriac, kohlrabi, rutabaga, tuckahoe **11** horseradish ***fragrant:* 5** orris **7** vetiver ***main:* 7** taproot ***medicinal:* 5** jalap **7** ginseng ***relating to:* 7** radical ***starch:* 4** arum **7** tapioca ***word:* 6** etymon

rootlet 7 radicle, rhizoid

root out 4 grub **9** eradicate, extirpate **10** deracinate

Roots *author:* 5 Halcy (Alcx) ***character:* 3** Lea (George, Tom) **4** Toby **5** Haley (Alex, Simon Alexander) **6** Bertha, Waller (Bell, John, Kizzy, Dr. William) **7** Cynthia, Matilda **8** Kintango **9** Missy Anne **10** Kunta Kinte

rope 3 guy, tie **4** bind, cord, line, stay **5** belay, bight, brace, cable, chord, lasso, riata, sheet **6** binder, fasten, halter, hawser, lariat, marlin, shroud, strand, string, tether **7** halyard, lashing, marline, painter, towline **8** buntline, lifeline ***fiber:* 4** coir, hemp, jute **5** abaca, sisal **6** Manila **8** henequen ***loop:* 7** cringle ***mooring:* 6** hawser ***ship's:* 4** vang **5** sheet **6** marlin, parral, parrel, shroud **7** lanyard, marline, ratline **9** mainsheet

ropedancer 11 funambulist

rope off 6 cordon

ropes 10 ins and outs, procedures, techniques

ropy 4 wiry **6** sinewy **7** stringy, viscous **8** muscular

roque 7 croquet

rorqual 5 whale **7** finback **8** fin whale **11** baleen whale

Rosalind's beloved 7 Orlando

rosary 5 beads **7** chaplet **8** beadroll, devotion **11** prayer beads

rose 4 glow, pink **5** blush, color, flush, rouge **6** mantle, pinken, redden **7** crimson **10** erysipelas ***Chinese:* 8** Cherokee ***cotton:* 7** cudweed ***feature:* 5** thorn ***kind:* 4** moss **5** Peace, Vogue **6** Circus, damask **7** Fashion, Granada, Iceberg, New Dawn, Pascali, Tiffany **8** Rubaiyat **9** Floradora, Montezuma, polyantha, Tropicana **10** Floribunda **11** grandiflora, Mount Shasta **12** Crimson Glory

roseate see **rosy**

rose-colored see **rosy**

Rosenkavalier composer 7 Strauss (Richard)

rose of ____ 6 Sharon

rose oil 5 attar

Rose Tattoo author 8 Williams (Tennessee)

rosette 7 cockade **8** ornament

Rosinante's master 7 Quixote (Don)

Rosmersholm author 5 Ibsen (Henrik)

____ Rossetti 5 Dante (Gabriel) **9** Christina ***work:* 8** Sing-Song **11** Annus Domini, House of Life (The), Seek and Find, Sister Helen **12** Beata Beatrix, Goblin Market

Rossini opera 6 Otello **8** Tancredi **11** Cenerentola (La), William Tell **14** Siege of Corinth (The) **15** Barber of Seville (The)

Rostand hero 6 Cyrano (de Bergerac)

roster 4 list, roll, rota **5** slate **6** muster, scroll **8** register, roll call, schedule **9** honor roll **10** muster roll **11** waiting list

rostrum 4 dais **5** bimah **6** pulpit **7** lectern, tribune **8** platform

rosy 3 red **4** pink **5** sunny **6** bright, upbeat **7** beamish **8** cheerful, sanguine **10** optimistic

rot 4 bosh, bull, mold **5** decay, hooey, spoil, taint, trash **6** fester, molder **7** corrupt, crapola, crumble, eyewash, garbage, hogwash, putrefy, rubbish **8** gangrene, nonsense **9** break down, decompose, poppycock **10** balderdash, degenerate **11** deteriorate, putrescence **12** disintegrate, putrefaction **13** decomposition

rotary 6 circle **8** gyratory, spinning, whirling **10** roundabout **11** vertiginous **13** traffic circle

rotate 4 gyre, roll, spin, turn **5** pivot, twirl, wheel, whirl **6** gyrate, swivel **7** revolve, trundle **9** alternate, pirouette ***a log:*** **4** birl

rotation 4 gyre, loop, turn **5** cycle, orbit, pivot, round, wheel, whirl **7** circuit, turning **8** gyration **10** revolution, succession

rote 5 crowd, grind **6** custom, groove, memory **7** routine **8** practice **9** automatic, treadmill **10** mechanical, repetition **12** memorization

Roth novel 11 Call It Sleep **15** Goodbye Columbus **16** American Pastoral **17** Portnoy's Complaint

rotten 4 foul **5** fetid, lousy **6** crummy, putrid **7** corrupt, decayed, spoiled, tainted **9** nefarious, offensive, putrified **10** decomposed, degenerate, putrescent

rotter 3 cad, cur **4** heel, lout **5** creep, louse **7** bounder **9** scoundrel **10** blackguard

rotund 3 fat **5** obese, plump, podgy, pudgy, round, stout, thick, tubby **6** chubby, chunky, portly, stocky **7** rounded **8** heavyset, roly-poly, thickset **9** corpulent **10** potbellied

roué 4 lech, rake, wolf **6** lecher **7** amorist, Don Juan, gallant, seducer, swinger **8** Casanova, lothario, sybarite **9** bon vivant, debauchee, libertine, womanizer **10** sensualist, voluptuary **11** philanderer

rouge 3 red **4** glow, pink, rose **5** blush, color, flush **6** mantle, pinken, redden **7** crimson

rough 3 raw **4** rude, wild **5** brute, bumpy, crass, crude, hairy, harsh, raspy, rowdy, yahoo **6** choppy, coarse, craggy, crusty, hoarse, jagged, rugged, stormy, uneven **7** cragged, grating, jarring, rasping, raucous, ruffian, scraggy, uncivil, uncouth **8** bullyboy, churlish, impolite, scabrous, unformed **9** difficult, imperfect, strenuous, turbulent, unrefined **10** boisterous, tumultuous, unfinished, unpolished **11** approximate, tempestuous

rough-and-ready 5 crude **6** make-do **7** stopgap **8** slapdash **9** expedient, impromptu, makeshift **10** improvised **11** provisional **13** quick-and-dirty

rough-hewn 4 rude **5** crude, plain **10** unfinished, unpolished **12** uncultivated

roughly 5 about, circa **9** virtually **10** more or less **13** approximately

roughneck see **ruffian**

rough out 5 block, chalk, draft **6** sketch **7** outline **9** adumbrate **11** skeletonize

rough up 4 beat, maul **6** batter, pummel **8** maltreat **9** brutalize, manhandle **10** slap around

roulette *bet:* **4** noir, trio **5** rouge, split **7** six-line **10** straight up ***term:*** **5** passe, tiers **6** impair, manque, mucker **7** orphans **8** croupier **9** house edge

round 4 gyre, tour, turn **5** bowed, cycle, globe, wheel **6** circle, curved, rotund **7** annular, circuit **8** circular, globular, roly-poly, rotation, sequence **9** orbicular, spherical **10** conglobate

roundabout 6 circle, detour, rotary **7** circuit, compass, curving, devious, oblique, winding **8** circular, indirect **10** circuitous, meandering **13** traffic circle

rounded 5 bowed, plump **6** arched, convex, curved, rotund, zaftig **7** concave **9** developed **10** curvaceous, Rubenesque **13** well-developed

rounder 4 rake, roué, waif **6** no-good, waster **7** wastrel **8** prodigal, vagabond **9** libertine **10** ne'er-do-well, profligate

roundly 4 well **5** fully, quite **6** widely, wholly **7** bluntly, sharply, smartly, utterly **8** candidly, entirely **9** brusquely **10** altogether, completely, rigorously, scathingly, thoroughly, vigorously

round off 3 cap, top **5** crown **6** climax, finish **8** conclude **9** culminate

round-robin 6 appeal, letter, series **7** protest **8** petition, sequence **9** statement **10** tournament

round trip 4 tour **7** circuit **9** excursion

round up 4 herd **5** drive, group **6** gather **7** cluster, collect **8** assemble

rouse 3 jog **4** call, goad, rock, stir, wake, whet **5** alarm, awake, pique, rally, roust, waken **6** awaken, bestir, excite, foment, incite, kindle, muster, rattle, recall, revive, vivify, work up **7** agitate, animate, commove, disturb, enliven, provoke, quicken **8** motivate **9** aggravate, challenge, galvanize, instigate, stimulate

rousing 5 brisk, peppy **6** lively **8** animated, exciting, spirited, stirring **9** inspiring **11** stimulating **12** exhilarating, intoxicating

Rousseau work 5 Émile

roustabout 4 hand **6** worker **7** laborer, workman **8** deckhand **10** workingman **12** longshoreman, troublemaker

route 3 way **4** path, road, send, ship **5** guide, pilot, steer, track, trail **6** avenue, bypass, course, detour, direct, divert, escort, flyway, seaway, skyway **7** channel, circuit, conduct, consign, forward, highway, journey, passage, portage, sea-lane **8** corridor, dispatch, transmit, traverse **9** direction, itinerary

routine 3 act, bit, rut **4** dull, pace, rote **5** chore, drill, grind, habit, ho-hum, plain, round, trial, usual **6** course, groove, improv, shtick, wonted **7** chronic, formula, program, regimen, regular, utility **8** accepted, everyday, habitual, ordinary, standard, workaday **9** customary, monologue, procedure, quotidian, treadmill **10** accustomed, donkeywork, mechanical **11** commonplace, cut-and-dried, perfunctory **12** housekeeping, unremarkable

rove 3 gad **4** roam **5** drift, range, stray **6** ramble, wander **7** meander, traipse **8** straggle, vagabond **9** gallivant

rover 5 gipsy, gypsy, nomad, stray **6** picaro, pirate, roamer, viking **7** corsair, drifter, floater, rambler, vagrant **8** picaroon, runabout, traveler, vagabond, wanderer **9** buccaneer, meanderer **10** freebooter **12** rolling stone

roving 6 errant, mobile **7** movable, nomadic, vagrant **8** straying, vagabond **9** itinerant, migratory, wayfaring **11** peripatetic

row 3 oar, way **4** bank, crew, file, fray, fuss, line, muss, rank, spat, tier, tiff **5** align, brawl, broil, chain, fight, melee, order, queue, range, run-in, scrap, scull, strip, swath **6** bicker, clamor, column, dustup, fracas, kickup, paddle, propel, ruckus, series, string, stroke **7** brabble, dispute, quarrel, rhubarb, wrangle **8** argument, diagonal, sequence, squabble **9** commotion **10** falling-out, single file, succession **11** altercation, disturbance, progression

rowdy 4 punk, rude **5** bully, crude, rough, yahoo **6** unruly **7** hoodlum, rackety, raffish, raucous, ruffian **8** bullyboy, hooligan **9** roughneck **10** boisterous, disorderly, robustious **11** rumbustious **12** rambunctious

Rowena *father:* 7 Hengist ***guardian:* 6** Cedric ***husband:* 7** Ivanhoe **9** Vortigern

Rowling character 3 Ron (Weasley) **5** Harry (Potter), Snape (Severus) **6** Malfoy (Draco), Sirius (Black) **8** Hermione (Granger) **9** Voldemort (Lord) **10** Dumbledore (Albus)

Roxana *husband:* 9 Alexander ***rival:* 7** Statira

royal 5 grand, noble, regal **6** kingly, lordly **7** stately **8** glorious, imperial, imposing, majestic, princely, splendid **9** grandiose, monarchal, sovereign **10** monarchial **11** magnificent, monarchical

rub 4 buff **5** chafe, grate, shine **6** abrade, polish, smooth, stroke **7** burnish, massage

Rubaiyat author 4 Omar (Khayyám)

rubber 4 buna **5** crepe **6** caucho, eraser **10** caoutchouc ***basis:* 5** latex ***hard:* 7** ebonite ***synthetic:* 8** neoprene ***tree:* 3** Ule **4** Para

Rubber City 5 Akron

rubberneck 3 eye **4** gape, gawk, gaze **5** snoop, stare **6** goggle **8** sightsee

rubber-stamp 2 OK **4** okay **7** approve, certify, endorse **9** authorize

rubbish 3 rot **4** bosh, crap, crud, junk, muck, slop, tosh **5** bilge, dreck, hooey, offal, trash, truck, waste **6** debris, litter, refuse, raffle, rubble, spilth **7** crapola, garbage, hogwash **8** nonsense, riffraff, tommyrot **9** poppycock, sweepings **11** foolishness

rubbishy 5 cheap, tatty **6** paltry, shoddy, sleazy, trashy **9** worthless

rubble 5 ruins, scree **6** debris, litter **8** detritus, wreckage

rube 4 boor, hick, naïf **5** churl, cluck, swain, yahoo, yokel **6** rustic **7** bumpkin, hayseed, redneck **9** greenhorn, hillbilly **10** clodhopper **12** apple-knocker, backwoodsman

rubicund 3 red **5** flush, ruddy **6** florid **7** glowing, reddish **8** sanguine **11** full-blooded, incarnadine

rubidium symbol 2 Rb

____ Rubik 4 Erno

rub out 3 ice, off, zap **4** do in, kill, slay **5** erase, smoke, waste, whack **6** finish, murder **7** bump off, destroy, put away **8** dispatch, knock off **9** liquidate, terminate **10** extinguish, obliterate **11** assassinate

rubric 4 name, rule **5** canon, class, gloss, style, title **6** custom **7** concept, heading **8** category, headline **9** tradition **11** appellation, designation **13** interpolation

ruck 3 mob **4** fold, heap, mass, pile **5** crimp, crowd, group, purse, ridge **6** cockle, crease, furrow, gather, jumble, pucker, rumple **7** crinkle, crumple, scrunch, wrinkle **10** generality **11** corrugation

rucksack 4 pack **6** kit bag **7** musette **8** backpack

ruckus 3 ado, row **4** fuss, to-do **5** brawl, melee, scrap **6** fracas, furore, hassle, pother, rumpus, shindy, uproar **7** dispute, quarrel, rhubarb, shindig, wrangle **8** squabble **9** commotion **10** falling-out **11** altercation, controversy, disturbance

ruddle see **redden**

ruddy 3 red **4** ripe, rosy **5** flush **6** blowsy, florid **7** flushed, glowing **8** rubicund, sanguine **11** full-blooded, incarnadine

rude 3 raw **4** curt **5** crass, gross, gruff, harsh, rough, rowdy, surly **6** abrupt, callow, clumsy, coarse, crusty, robust, rugged, rustic, sturdy, unhewn, vulgar **7** boorish, brusque, ill-bred, loutish, lowbred, uncivil, uncouth **8** arrogant, churlish, clownish, impolite, tactless **9** barbarian, barbarous, elemental, inelegant, primitive, rough-hewn, unrefined **10** ungracious, unmannered, unmannerly, unpolished **11** ill-mannered, impertinent, uncivilized **12** discourteous, uncultivated **13** disrespectful

rudimentary **5** basal, basic **6** simple **7** initial, primary **8** simplest **9** beginning, elemental, vestigial **10** elementary **11** fundamental, undeveloped **12** introductory

rudiments **4** ABCs **6** basics **10** essentials **12** fundamentals

rue **3** woe **4** pity, ruth **5** dolor, grief, mourn, prick **6** grieve, lament, regret, repent, sorrow **7** anguish, deplore, remorse **8** sympathy **9** heartache, penitence **10** affliction, compassion, contrition, heartbreak, repentance **11** compunction

rueful **5** sorry **6** woeful **8** contrite, penitent **9** regretful, sorrowful **10** remorseful

ruff **5** frill, perch, trump **6** collar, fringe **9** sandpiper **11** pumpkinseed ***female:*** **5** reeve

ruffian **4** goon, hood, punk, thug **5** beast, brute, bully, rowdy, tough, yahoo **6** Apache, hector **7** gorilla, hoodlum **8** bullyboy, hooligan **9** muscleman, roughneck, swaggerer

ruffle **3** bug, irk, rub, vex **4** fret, gall, wear **5** annoy, brawl, chafe, frill, graze, jabot, pleat, ruche **6** abrade, bother, nettle, ripple **7** agitate, bristle, disturb, flounce, provoke, trouble, wrinkle **8** drumbeat, furbelow, irritate, skirmish **9** commotion

rug **3** mat **6** carpet, runner, toupee **7** laprobe ***kind:*** **3** rag, rya **6** hooked **7** braided, dhurrie, drugget, flokati, Persian **8** Aubusson, bearskin, Oriental **10** Savonnerie

rugby ***formation:*** **5** scrum **9** scrummage ***goal:*** **7** dropped, penalty ***period:*** **4** half ***player:*** **6** center, hooker, winger **8** standoff **9** scrum half ***scoring:*** **3** try **4** goal **10** conversion ***team:*** **7** fifteen ***term:*** **4** heel **5** match **7** convert, dribble, hand off, knock on **9** fair catch ***time-out:*** **8** stoppage ***version:*** **5** union **6** league

rugged **5** burly, hardy, harsh, heavy, husky, rough, tough **6** brawny, coarse, craggy, jagged, robust, severe, stable, stormy, strong, sturdy, uneven **7** arduous, austere, scraggy **8** leathery, muscular, rigorous, scabrous, stalwart, vigorous **9** difficult, inclement, strenuous, unrefined, weathered **10** formidable, unpolished **11** tempestuous

Ruggiero ***guardian:*** **7** Atlante ***sister:*** **7** Marfisa ***slayer:*** **11** Tisaphernes ***wife:*** **10** Bradamante

rug rat **3** tot **4** tyke **6** moppet **7** toddler

Ruhr city **5** Essen **8** Dortmund

ruin **4** bane, bust, dash, do in, doom, fall, loss, rape, raze, sack, undo **5** decay, havoc, smash, spoil, trash, use up, waste, wrack, wreck **6** beggar, finish, pauper, perish, ravage **7** corrupt, deplete, despoil, destroy, exhaust, failure, nemesis, pillage, shatter, undoing, wipe out **8** bankrupt, collapse, decimate, demolish, downfall, spoliate **9** depredate, devastate, disrepair, overthrow, pauperize, shipwreck **10** desolation, impoverish **11** destruction, devastation, dissolution **12** degeneration **13** deterioration

ruination **4** bane, loss, rack **5** havoc **7** undoing **8** calamity, disaster, downfall **10** decimation **11** destruction, devastation

ruinous **5** fatal **7** baneful **10** calamitous, disastrous, pernicious **11** cataclysmic, destructive **12** catastrophic

rule **3** law, Raj **4** lead, sway **5** axiom, bylaw, canon, edict, habit, judge, maxim, moral, order, reign **6** assize, custom, decree, deduce, dictum, direct, govern, regime, truism **7** brocard, command, control, precept, prevail, regency, regimen, resolve, statute **8** decretum, doctrine, dominate, domineer, dominion **9** authority, determine, etiquette, ordinance, principle, procedure **10** regulation ***absolute:*** **7** autarky **8** autarchy ***by a god:*** **8** theonomy

Rule Britannia composer **4** Arne (Thomas)

rule out **3** bar **5** block, debar **6** forbid, refuse, reject **7** dismiss, exclude, forfend, head off, obviate, prevent **8** preclude, prohibit, stave off **9** eliminate

ruler **4** king, lord **5** queen **6** archon, dynast, ferule, gerent, prince, regent, satrap, sultan **7** emperor, monarch, viceroy **8** governor, hierarch, oligarch, pentarch, princess, theocrat **9** dominator, imperator, matriarch, patriarch, potentate, sovereign **12** straightedge ***absolute:*** **6** despot, tyrant **8** autocrat, dictator, overlord ***Arab:*** **4** amir, emir **5** ameer, sheik **6** sharif, sheikh, sultan ***Asian:*** **4** khan ***Byzantine Empire:*** **6** exarch ***Egyptian:*** **7** pharaoh ***family:*** **7** dynasty ***Iranian:*** **4** shah ***one of four:*** **8** tetrarch ***one of seven:*** **8** heptarch ***one of three:*** **7** triarch **8** triumvir ***Persian:*** **6** satrap ***Russian:*** **4** czar, tsar, tzar ***Turkish:*** **3** bey, dey **6** sultan

ruling **3** law **4** call **5** chief, edict, order, ukase **6** decree **7** current, finding, popular, regnant, verdict **8** decision, judgment **9** directive, judgement, prevalent, statement **10** prevailing, widespread **11** predominant **12** adjudication

Rumania see **Romania**

rumble 4 buzz, roar, roll **5** brawl, drone, fight, growl, rumor **6** murmur, report **7** hearsay, quarrel, resound, thunder **8** feedback **9** complaint **11** altercation, disturbance, reverberate, scuttlebutt
ruminant 3 Bos, cow, yak **4** deer, goat, tahr **5** bison, camel, llama, okapi, serow, sheep, takin **6** alpaca, cattle, musk ox, vicuña **7** buffalo, chamois, chewing, giraffe, guanaco **8** antelope **9** pronghorn ***stomach:*** **5** rumen **6** omasum **8** abomasum **9** reticulum
ruminate 4 chew, mull, muse **5** champ, chomp, weigh **6** ponder **7** reflect **8** cogitate, consider, meditate **9** masticate **10** deliberate **11** contemplate
ruminative 7 pensive **8** thinking **9** pondering **10** cogitative, meditative, reflective, thoughtful **11** speculative **13** contemplative, introspective
rummage 4 comb, fish, grub, hash, hunt, poke, rake, rout, seek **5** delve, scour **6** ferret, forage, jumble, litter, search **7** clutter, ransack **8** mishmash **9** potpourri **10** hodgepodge, hotchpotch, miscellany
rummy 3 gin, odd, sot **4** lush, soak, wino **5** drunk, souse, toper **6** boozer **7** bizarre, canasta, curious, guzzler, strange, swiller, tippler, tosspot **8** drunkard, peculiar **9** eccentric, inebriate **10** boozehound
rumor 4 blab, buzz, talk **5** bruit, noise, story **6** canard, gossip, murmur, mutter, report, rumble, tattle **7** hearsay, tidings, whisper **9** grapevine **11** scuttlebutt, susurration ***personified:*** **4** Fama
rumormonger 5 yenta **6** gossip **8** gossiper, informer, quidnunc, telltale **9** whisperer **10** talebearer, tattletale
rump 3 can **4** beam, butt, duff, hind, rear, tush **5** fanny **6** behind, bottom, breech, heinie **7** keester, keister, rear end **8** backside, buttocks, derriere, haunches **9** posterior
rumple 4 fold, muss, ruck **5** crimp, screw, touse **6** pucker, tousle **7** crimple, crinkle, scrunch, wrinkle **8** dishevel, disorder
rumpus see **ruckus**
run 3 fly, hie, jog **4** bolt, dart, dash, flee, flow, race, rush, scud, tear **5** chase, haste, hurry, scoot, skirr, speed **6** career, gallop, hasten, scurry, sprint, streak, stream **7** scamper, scuttle, smuggle **9** skedaddle
run across 4 meet **8** bump into, discover **9** encounter, stumble on
runagate 4 hobo **5** gipsy, gypsy, nomad, tramp **6** outlaw **7** drifter, floater, lamster, vagrant, wastrel **8** bohemian, fugitive, rapparee, vagabond, wanderer **11** guttersnipe
run along 2 go **5** leave, scram **6** beat it, begone, cut out, depart **7** buzz off, get lost, skiddoo, take off, vamoose **8** shove off **9** skedaddle **10** make tracks
runaround 4 duck, slip **5** dodge **7** elusion, evasion
run away 4 bolt, flee, skip **5** elope, leave, scram, skirr, split, steal **6** depart, desert, escape **7** abscond, make off **8** clear out, light out, stampede **9** skedaddle **10** make tracks
runaway 4 romp, wild **5** loose **6** outlaw **7** escapee, lamster **8** deserter, fugitive **10** delinquent **12** uncontrolled
run down 3 hit, ram, tag **5** catch, knock, trace **6** pursue **7** decline **8** belittle, derogate, diminish **9** apprehend, disparage **10** depreciate **11** catch up with
run-down 5 dingy, seedy, tacky, tired **6** beat-up, bushed, shabby **7** rickety, ruinous, worn-out **8** decrepit, tattered, untended **9** burned-out, exhausted, neglected **10** bedraggled, down-at-heel, ramshackle, uncared-for **11** dilapidated
rundown 4 dope, poop **5** recap, scoop **6** report, review, skinny, update **7** outline, summary **8** briefing, synopsis
runes 4 ogam **5** ogham **7** futhark
rung 3 bar **4** step **5** grade, notch, round, spoke, staff, stage, stair, tread **6** degree, rundle **10** crosspiece
run-in 3 row **4** tiff **5** brush, fight, set-to **6** hassle, scrape, tangle **7** dispute, quarrel, rhubarb, wrangle **8** skirmish, squabble **9** encounter **10** falling-out **11** altercation
run into 3 hit, ram **4** meet **9** encounter, stumble on **11** collide with
runner 3 rug **5** gofer, miler, racer **6** carpet, stolon **7** carrier, courier, tendril **8** smuggler, sprinter **9** go-between, messenger **10** marathoner **11** ballcarrier see **track star**
running 6 active, fluent **7** cursive, dynamic, flowing, working **9** operative **10** continuous **11** functioning
run-of-the-mill 4 dull, so-so **5** usual **6** common, normal **7** average, humdrum, regular, typical **8** everyday, familiar, mediocre, middling, moderate, ordinary **9** prevalent **10** monotonous **11** commonplace, indifferent **12** intermediate **13** unexceptional
run on 3 gab, yak **4** blab **5** clack **6** babble, cackle, gabble, jabber, ramble, rattle **7** chatter, prattle **8** continue
run out of 5 use up **6** finish **7** exhaust
run over 5 spill **6** exceed, repeat **7** examine **8** overfill, overflow, rehearse
runt 5 dwarf, pygmy **6** midget, peanut, peewee, shrimp, squirt **7** manikin **8** mannikin,

Tom Thumb **10** homunculus **11** hop-o'-my-thumb, lilliputian
run through 3 jab **4** blow, gore, read, scan, stab **5** spend, use up, waste **6** expend, finish, impale, pierce **7** consume, examine, exhaust **8** rehearse, squander, transfix
runty 3 wee **4** puny **6** peewee **7** stunted **8** dwarfish **10** diminutive, undersized
run up 5 build, erect, mount **6** expand **7** augment, enlarge **8** increase, multiply **9** construct **10** accumulate
runway 4 duct, path **5** strip, track, trail **6** sluice, tarmac **7** channel, conduit **8** airstrip, platform
rupture 4 rend, rent, rift, rive **5** break, burst, cleft, sever, split **6** breach, cleave, hernia, schism, sunder **7** blowout, break up, disrupt, divorce, fissure, parting, split-up **8** division, fracture, separate **9** partition **10** separation **11** dissolution **12** estrangement
R.U.R. ***author:*** **5** Capek (Karel) ***character:*** **5** robot
rural 6 rustic **7** bucolic, country, idyllic **8** agrarian, arcadian, down-home, pastoral **10** campestral **11** countrified
ruse 3 con, jig **4** hoax, ploy, wile **5** dodge, feint, fraud, stall, trick **6** deceit, gambit **7** gimmick, swindle **8** artifice, maneuver, trickery **9** deception, stratagem **10** subterfuge **13** double-dealing
rush 3 fly, rip, run **4** boil, bolt, dart, dash, flit, flow, hurl, lash, race, roar, scud, tear, tide, whiz **5** blitz, break, carry, chase, court, daily, flash, haste, hurry, lunge, onset, sally, scoot, sedge, shoot, spate, speed, storm, surge **6** attack, barrel, beat it, bustle, career, charge, course, hasten, hurtle, hustle, irrupt, plunge, streak, stream, thrill, whoosh **7** assault, cattail, current, rampage, torrent **8** stampede **9** whirlwind, wire grass **13** precipitation
Rushdie novel 5 Shame **13** Satanic Verses (The) **17** Midnight's Children
rushing 5 hasty **6** abrupt, sudden **7** hurried **8** headlong **9** impetuous **11** precipitate, precipitous
rusk 7 biscuit **8** biscotto
Russia ***capital:*** **6** Moscow ***city:*** **3** Ufa **4** Omsk, Orel, Perm' **5** Kazan', Kursk **6** Grozny, Samara **7** Groznyy, Izhevsk, Ivanovo **8** Murmansk **9** Leningrad, Volgograd **10** Stalingrad **11** Chelyabinsk, Novosibirsk, Vladivostok **12** St. Petersburg **13** Yekaterinburg ***czar:*** **4** Ivan **5** Basil, Boris (Godunov), Peter (the Great) **6** Alexis, Dmitry, Feodor, Vasily **7** Dimitri, Godunov (Boris), Michael (Romanov), Romanov (Michael) **8** Nicholas, Romanoff, Theodore **9** Alexander ***empress:*** **4** Anna (Ivanovna) **9** Catherine (the Great), Elizabeth (Petrovna) ***ethnic group:*** **7** Cossack ***island:*** **8** Sakhalin ***island group:*** **5** Kuril **6** Kurile ***lake:*** **5** Il'men', Onega **6** Baikal, Ladoga ***leader:*** **5** Lenin (Vladimir), Putin (Vladimir) **6** Stalin (Joseph) **7** Trotsky (Leon) **8** Brezhnev (Leonid) **10** Khrushchev (Nikita) ***legislature:*** **4** Duma ***monetary unit:*** **5** kopek, ruble **6** kopeck ***mountain, range:*** **4** Ural **5** Altai, Altay, Sayan **6** Elbrus, Kolyma, Koryak **8** Caucasus, Stanovoy ***neighbor:*** **5** China **6** Latvia, Norway **7** Belarus, Estonia, Finland, Georgia, Ukraine **8** Mongolia **9** Kazakstan **10** Azerbaijan, Kazakhstan, North Korea ***peninsula:*** **4** Kola **5** Gydan, Kanin, Yamal **6** Taymyr **7** Chukchi **9** Kamchatka ***region:*** **7** Siberia **9** Circassia **11** Golden Horde ***revolution:*** **9** Bolshevik ***river:*** **3** Don **4** Amur, Lena, Neva, Ural **5** Desna, Dvina, Vitim, Volga **6** Belaya, Kolyma, Vilyui, Vilyuy **7** Pechora, Yenisey **9** Indigirka ***sea:*** **4** Azov, Kara **5** Black, White **6** Laptev **7** Barents, Caspian, Chukchi, Okhotsk ***secret police:*** **3** KGB, MVD **4** NKVD ***strait:*** **6** Bering
Russian ***aristocrat:*** **5** boyar ***caviar:*** **6** beluga ***comrade:*** **8** tovarich, tovarish ***country house:*** **5** dacha ***dog:*** **6** borzoi **7** Samoyed ***drink:*** **5** kvass, vodka ***family:*** **7** Romanov **9** Stroganov ***farmer:*** **5** kulak ***forest:*** **5** taiga ***grandmother:*** **8** babushka ***instrument:*** **9** balalaika ***monk:*** **8** Rasputin ***no:*** **4** nyet ***pancakes:*** **5** blini ***peasant:*** **5** kulak, mujik **6** moujik, muzhik ***republic:*** **6** oblast ***saint:*** **15** Alexander Nevsky ***urn:*** **7** samovar ***vehicle:*** **6** troika ***villa:*** **5** dacha
rustic 4 hick, rube, rude **5** churl, clown, plain, rough, rural, swain, yokel **6** farmer **7** bucolic, bumpkin, country, granger, hayseed, peasant, plowboy, plowman, redneck, uncouth **8** agrarian, pastoral **9** chawbacon, hillbilly **10** campestral, clodhopper, countryman, husbandman **11** countrified **12** apple-knocker, backwoodsman
rustle 5 haste, hurry, speed, steal, swish **6** forage, swoosh **7** crackle, crinkle **8** susurrus
rustler 5 thief **6** duffer, robber **7** forager **8** marauder
Rustum's son 6 Sohrab
rusty 4 slow **6** bygone, creaky **7** outworn **8** outdated, outmoded **10** antiquated, discolored **12** old-fashioned
rut 5 gouge, grind, track **6** furrow, groove **7** channel, routine **9** treadmill
rutabaga 5 swede **6** turnip

ruth **3** rue, woe **4** pity **5** grief, mercy **6** regret, sorrow **7** anguish, remorse, sadness **8** distress, sympathy **9** attrition, penitence **10** compassion, contrition, repentance **11** compunction **13** commiseration
Ruth ***husband:*** **4** Boaz **6** Mahlon ***mother-in-law:*** **5** Naomi ***son:*** **4** Obed
ruthful **6** woeful **7** doleful **8** dolorous, wretched **9** miserable, sorrowful
ruthless **4** hard **5** cruel, harsh **6** brutal, savage **7** inhuman **8** pitiless **9** barbarous, cutthroat, dog-eat-dog, ferocious, heartless, merciless, unsparing **10** implacable, ironfisted **11** cold-blooded
ruttish **4** lewd **5** lusty, randy **6** wanton **7** goatish, lustful, satyric **9** lecherous, lickerish, salacious **10** lascivious, libidinous **12** concupiscent
Rwanda ***capital:*** **6** Kigali ***ethnic group:*** **4** Hutu **5** Tutsi ***language:*** **6** French, Rwanda ***monetary unit:*** **5** franc ***neighbor:*** **5** Congo **6** Uganda **7** Burundi **8** Tanzania

S

____ Saarinen **4** Eero **5** Eliel
Sabatini novel **11** Scaramouche **12** Captain Blood
sabbatical **4** rest **5** leave **7** time off **8** vacation
saber **5** sword **7** cutlass **8** scimitar
sabertooth **3** cat **5** tiger
sable **3** fur **4** dark, inky **5** black, ebony, raven **6** gloomy, somber, sombre, weasel **8** mourning
sabot **4** clog, shoe **10** wooden shoe
sabotage **5** wreck **6** damage, hamper, hinder **7** cripple, disable, subvert, torpedo **8** obstruct, wreckage, wrecking **9** frustrate, undermine, vandalize **10** subversion **11** undermining
Sabra ***father:*** **7** Ptolemy ***rescuer:*** **8** St. George ***son:*** **3** Guy **5** David **9** Alexander
sac **4** caul, cyst **5** pouch **7** vesicle
saccharine **5** mushy, sweet **6** sugary, syrupy **7** candied, cloying, honeyed, maudlin, mawkish, sugared **9** oversweet, schmaltzy **11** sentimental, sugar-coated **12** ingratiating
sacerdotal **8** hieratic, pastoral, priestly **10** priestlike **11** ministerial
sachem **4** boss **5** chief **6** leader
sachet **3** bag **6** powder **7** perfume **9** potpourri
sack **2** ax **3** axe, bag, bed, can **4** bunk, drop, fire, loot, raid, wine **5** expel, pouch, strip, waste **6** pocket, ravage, tackle **7** boot out, cashier, despoil, dismiss, hammock, kick out, pillage, plunder **8** desolate, spoliate **9** container, depredate, desecrate, devastate, white wine
sackbut **8** trombone
sacque **6** jacket
sacrament **4** rite **6** ritual **7** baptism, penance **8** ceremony, marriage **9** Communion, Eucharist, matrimony **10** holy orders **12** confirmation
sacrarium **6** chapel, shrine **7** oratory, piscina **8** sacristy **9** sanctuary
sacred **4** holy **5** godly **6** divine, immune **7** angelic, blessed, saintly **8** hallowed, numinous **9** inviolate, spiritual **10** inviolable, sacrosanct, sanctified **11** consecrated, sacramental ***combining form:*** **4** hagi, hier, sacr **5** hagio, hiero, sacro ***monkey:*** **6** baboon, rhesus **7** hanuman ***place:*** **7** sanctum ***song:*** **4** hymn ***weed:*** **7** vervain
sacrifice **4** bunt, cede, lamb, lose, loss **5** forgo, yield **6** devote, donate, eschew, give up, martyr, victim **7** forfeit, offer up **8** dedicate, hecatomb, immolate, oblation, offering **12** renunciation
sacrilege **6** heresy **7** impiety, offense **9** blasphemy, violation **11** desecration, irreverence, profanation
sacrilegious **7** impious, profane, ungodly **10** irreverent **11** blasphemous
sacristan **6** sexton
sacristy **6** vestry
sacrosanct **9** inviolate **10** inviolable
sad **4** blue, down, glum **5** sorry **6** dismal, dreary, gloomy, morose, triste, woeful **7** doleful, joyless, piteous, pitiful, unhappy **8** dejected, desolate, dolorous, downbeat, downcast, grieving, mournful, pathetic, pitiable **9** depressed, sorrowful, woebegone **10** depressing, dispirited, lamentable, melancholy **11** melancholic **12** heavyhearted
sadden **7** depress, oppress, trouble **8** aggrieve, dispirit **9** weigh down **10** discourage

saddle 3 tax **4** lade, load, task **5** weigh **6** burden, charge, hamper, impede, impose, weight **7** aparejo, inflict **8** encumber, restrict ***adjunct:* 7** stirrup ***part:* 6** cantle, pommel ***strap:* 5** cinch, girth **6** latigo **7** harness
sadness 3 woe **4** funk **5** blues, dolor, dumps, gloom, grief, mopes **6** misery, sorrow **7** dismals, megrims **8** doldrums, glumness, mourning **9** dejection, dysphoria, heartache **10** blue devils, depression, desolation, melancholy **11** despondency, melancholia, unhappiness
safari 4 hunt, trek, trip **7** caravan, journey **10** expedition
safe 4 snug, wary **5** chary **6** secure, unhurt **7** careful, guarded **8** cautious, defended, shielded, unharmed **9** innocuous, protected, sheltered, strongbox, uninjured, unscathed **10** inviolable, sheltering **11** impregnable **12** invulnerable, unassailable
safecracker 4 yegg **8** picklock **9** cracksman
safeguard 4 ward **6** convoy, defend, escort, shield, surety **7** bulwark, defense, protect **8** armament, preserve **10** precaution, protection
safety 6 asylum, refuge **7** defense, shelter **8** immunity, security **9** assurance, sanctuary **10** protection **13** inviolability
sag 3 dip **4** bend, drop, flag, flap, flop, hang, sink, slip, wilt **5** droop, slide, slump **6** dangle, hollow, slouch **7** decline, drop off, falloff, sinkage, sinking **8** downturn, prolapse, settling, sinkhole **9** concavity, downswing **10** depression
saga 4 Edda, epic, myth, tale **5** story **6** legend **9** chronicle, narrative **12** Heimskringla
sagacious 4 keen, wise **5** acute, smart **6** astute, clever, shrewd **7** knowing, prudent, sapient **8** critical **9** far-seeing, judicious **10** discerning, insightful, perceptive **11** intelligent **13** perspicacious
sagacity 5 grasp **6** acuity, acumen, wisdom **7** insight **8** judgment, keenness, prudence, sapience **10** perception, shrewdness **11** discernment, penetration, percipience, perspicuity **12** perspicacity **13** comprehension, judiciousness, understanding
sagamore 5 chief **6** sachem
Sagan work 6 Cosmos **16** Bonjour tristesse
sage 4 Bias, guru, mint, wise **5** Solon, Vyasa **6** Buddha (Gautama), Chilon, expert, Gandhi (Mohandas), Lao Tzu, master, Narada, Nestor, nestor, pundit, savant, shrewd, Thales **7** gnostic, knowing, learned, prudent, sapient, scholar, Solomon, Valmiki, wise man **8** polymath, profound, sensible **9** Confucius, judicious **10** discerning, insightful, perceptive **11** penetrating, philosophic ***Hindu:* 6** pandit, pundit **7** mahatma
Sage of Chelsea: 7 Carlyle (Thomas) ***of Concord:* 7** Emerson (Ralph Waldo) ***of Emporia:* 5** White (William Allen) ***of Ferney:* 8** Voltaire ***of Monticello:* 9** Jefferson (Thomas) ***of Pylos:* 6** Nestor
Sagebrush State 6 Nevada
Sagittarius 6 archer **7** centaur **13** constellation
sago 4 palm **6** starch
saguaro 6 cactus
sahib 3 sir **6** master **9** gentleman
sail 3 fly **4** dart, flit, scud, skim, wing **5** fleet, float, shoot, skirr, sweep **6** cruise, mizzen **7** spencer **9** spinnaker ***into wind:* 4** luff ***support:* 4** mast ***triangular:* 3** jib **5** genoa
sailing term 3 aft, bow, lee, yaw **4** alee, beam, boom, port, tack, trim **5** abaft, abeam, aloft, belay, brale, stern **6** astern, adrift, fouled, pay out **7** cast off, heading, rigging, sea room **8** downhaul, overhaul, sounding, underway **9** starboard **10** batten down, Cunningham, lubber line, scandalize **11** self-tacking
sailing vessel 4 bark, brig, moth, yawl **5** xebec, yacht **6** barque, cutter **7** clipper, frigate, galleon **8** schooner, skipjack **10** barkentine, brigantine **11** barquentine
sailor 3 gob, tar **4** jack, mate, salt, swab **6** hearty, sea dog, seaman **7** jack-tar, mariner, matelot, old salt, swabbie **8** flatfoot, seafarer, shipmate, water dog **9** shellback, tarpaulin, yachtsman **10** bluejacket ***British:* 5** limey ***East Indian:* 6** lascar ***fictional:* 6** Sinbad ***patron saint:* 4** Elmo ***song:* 6** chanty **7** chantey **9** barcarole
saint 7 paragon ***biography:* 11** hagiography ***list:* 9** hagiology ***Muslim:* 3** pir (see also **patron saint**)
Saint, The 12 Simon Templar ***creator:* 9** Charteris (Leslie)
Saint Anthony's cross 3 tau
Saint Elmo's Fire 9 corposant
Saint Helena *capital:* 9 Jamestown ***colony of:* 7** Britain ***island:* 9** Ascension
Saint Joan author 4 Shaw (George Bernard)
Saint John's bread 5 carob
Saint Kitts and Nevis *capital:* 10 Basseterre ***island group:* 7** Leeward ***location:* 10** West Indies
Saint Louis attraction 11 Gateway Arch
Saint Lucia *capital:* 8 Castries ***island group:* 8** Windward ***location:* 10** West Indies ***volcano:* 8** Quilabou
saintly 4 holy, pure **5** godly, pious **6** devout,

worthy **7** angelic, blessed, upright **8** beatific, seraphic, virtuous **9** righteous
Saint Paul's architect 4 Wren (Christopher)
Saint Peter's Basilica *architect:* 7 Bernini (Gian Lorenzo) **12** Michelangelo (Buonarotti) ***sculpture:* 5** Pietà
Saint-Pierre and Miquelon *capital:* 8 St.-Pierre ***department of:* 6** France
Saint Teresa birthplace 5 Avila
Saint Vincent and the Grenadines *capital:* 9 Kingstown ***island group:* 8** Windward ***location:* 10** West Indies ***volcano:* 9** Soufrière
Saint Vitus' dance 6 chorea
sake 3 end **4** good **5** drink **7** benefit, purpose, welfare
Saki 5 Munro (H. H.)
salaam 3 bow **6** kowtow **8** greeting **9** obeisance
salacious 4 blue, fast, lewd, racy **5** bawdy **6** erotic, ribald, risqué, smutty **7** lustful, obscene, satyric **8** indecent, off-color, prurient **9** lecherous, libertine **10** lascivious, libidinous, licentious
salad *item:* 3 egg, udo **4** bean, cuke, herb **5** cress, olive, onion, pasta **6** carrot, celery, cheese, endive, pepper, potato, radish, tomato **7** anchovy, arugula, cabbage, crouton, lettuce, mesclun, niçoise, parsley, spinach **8** chickpea, cucumber, garbanzo, mushroom, scallion **9** radicchio **10** watercress ***dressing:* 5** ranch **6** French **7** Italian, Russian **10** blue cheese, buttermilk, gorgonzola **11** vinaigrette ***type:* 4** Cobb **5** chef's **6** Caesar **7** Waldorf **8** coleslaw
salamander 3 eft, olm **4** newt **7** urodele **8** mud puppy, water dog **10** hellbender ***Mexican:* 7** axolotl
salary 3 pay **4** take, wage **6** income **7** stipend **8** earnings **9** emolument **10** recompense **12** compensation, remuneration
sale 6 bazaar, demand **7** auction **8** closeout, disposal, transfer **9** clearance **11** transaction
salesperson 3 rep
salient 6 marked, signal **7** obvious, weighty **8** striking **9** arresting, important, obtrusive, pertinent, prominent **10** impressive, noticeable, projecting, pronounced, remarkable **11** conspicuous, outstanding, significant
saline 5 briny, salty **8** brackish
Salinger, J. D. *character:* 4 Esmé **6** Holden (Caulfield) ***novel:* 14** Franny and Zooey **15** Catcher in the Rye
saliva 4 spit **6** slaver, sputum **7** spittle
salivate 5 drool **6** drivel, slaver **7** slobber
____ Salk 5 Jonas
sallow 3 wan **4** pale, waxy **5** pasty **6** pallid, sickly, willow, yellow **7** bilious **9** jaundiced
sally 3 gag **4** gust, jape, jest, joke, quip **5** blast, burst, crack, jaunt **6** depart, junket, outing, set out, sortie, volley, zinger **7** barrage, flare-up **8** drollery, eruption, outbreak, outburst, paroxysm **9** discharge, excursion, explosion, wisecrack, witticism
salmagundi see **hodgepodge**
salmon 3 dog **4** chum, coho, kelt, parr, pink **5** smolt **6** grilse, Sebago **7** chinook, sockeye **9** brandling ***cured:* 4** nova **7** gravlax **8** gravlaks ***male:* 6** kipper ***smoked:* 3** lox
Salome *composer:* 7 Strauss (Richard) ***father:* 5** Herod ***husband:* 6** Philip **7** Zebedee **11** Aristobulus ***mother:* 8** Herodias ***son:* 4** John **5** James ***victim:* 4** John (the Baptist)
salon 4 hall, shop **5** suite **6** parlor **7** gallery **9** apartment, reception **10** exhibition
saloon 3 bar, pub **6** tavern **7** barroom, cantina, gin mill, taproom **9** beer joint **12** watering hole
salt 3 gob, tar **4** jack, keep, NaCl, swab **5** brine, limey **6** sailor, saline, sea dog, seaman **7** jack-tar, mariner **8** salinize, seafarer **9** sailorman
salt away 4 bank, save **5** hoard, lay by, lay up, put by, stash, store **7** deposit **8** lay aside, squirrel
saltpeter 5 niter, nitre
salty 4 blue, racy **5** briny, crude, spicy, tangy **6** earthy, purple, risqué, saline **7** caustic, mordant, pungent **8** brackish, off-color, scathing **9** trenchant
salubrious 5 tonic **7** bracing, healthy **8** hygienic, salutary **9** healthful, wholesome **10** beneficial **11** restorative **12** invigorating
Salus see **Hygeia**
salutary 5 tonic **6** benign **7** bracing, healing **8** curative, remedial, sanative **9** analeptic, healthful, vulnerary, wholesome **10** beneficial, salubrious **11** restorative, therapeutic **12** advantageous, health-giving
salutation 2 hi **4** hail **5** hello, howdy **7** welcome **8** greeting ***Arab:* 6** salaam ***French:* 5** salut ***Hawaiian:* 5** aloha ***Italian:* 4** ciao ***Latin:* 3** ave ***Spanish:* 4** hola
salute 4 hail **5** greet, honor **6** praise **7** address, commend **8** greeting **12** congratulate
salvage 4 save **6** ransom, recoup, redeem, regain, rescue **7** deliver, reclaim, recover **8** retrieve
salvation 6 saving **7** keeping **10** redemption **11** deliverance **12** conservation, preservation
Salvation Army founder 5 Booth (General William)
salve 4 balm **5** cream, quiet **6** cerate, chrism,

lotion, remedy **7** assuage, unction, unguent **8** ointment **9** emollient

salver 4 tray

salvo 4 hail **5** burst, spray, storm **6** attack, shower, volley **7** barrage, proviso **9** broadside, cannonade, discharge, fusillade **11** bombardment

Samaritan 6 helper **10** benefactor

same 4 idem, like, very **5** equal, exact **7** coequal, similar **8** constant **9** duplicate, identical, unvarying **10** consistent, equivalent, invariable, unchanging ***combining form:*** **3** hom **4** homo

Samoa *capital:* **4** Apia ***island:*** **5** Upolu **6** Savai'i ***monetary unit:*** **4** tala

samovar 3 urn

samp 6 cereal, hominy

sampan 4 boat **5** skiff

sample 3 try **4** case, part, test, unit **5** piece, taste **7** dip into, element, example, excerpt, portion, segment **8** fragment, instance, specimen **10** indication **11** case history, constituent **12** illustration

Samson *betrayer:* **7** Delilah ***birthplace:*** **5** Zorah ***deathplace:*** **4** Gaza ***father:*** **6** Manoah ***tribe:*** **3** Dan

Samson Agonistes author 6 Milton (John)

Samuel *father:* **7** Elkanah ***grandson:*** **5** Heman ***mentor:*** **3** Eli ***mother:*** **6** Hannah

samurai code 7 Bushido

San Antonio *team:* **5** Spurs ***landmark:*** **5** Alamo

sanatorium 3 spa **8** hospital, rest home

sanctify 5 bless **6** hallow, ordain, purify **8** dedicate **10** consecrate

sanctimonious 5 pious **7** canting, preachy **8** unctuous **9** pharisaic **11** pharisaical **12** hypocritical, Pecksniffian **13** self-righteous

sanction 2 OK **4** fiat, okay **5** bless, leave **6** assent, decree, permit, ratify **7** approve, backing, boycott, certify, consent, embargo, endorse, license, penalty, support **8** accredit, approval **9** allowance, authorize **10** commission, permission, sufferance **11** approbation, endorsement **12** confirmation, ratification **13** authorization, encouragement

sanctity 8 holiness **9** godliness **11** saintliness, uprightness **13** inviolability, righteousness

sanctuary 5 haven, oasis **6** asylum, covert, harbor, refuge, shrine, temple **7** reserve, retreat, shelter **8** preserve **9** holy place

sanctum 4 lair **6** shrine **7** retreat, shelter **9** holy place, sanctuary

sand 3 tan **4** buff, ecru, fawn, grit **5** beach, beige, camel, grind, khaki, scour, shore **6** gravel, polish, smooth **7** burnish **8** granules

sandal 4 clog, zori **5** sabot, thong **6** patten **8** flip-flop, huarache **10** espadrille

sandbag 3 hit **4** stun **6** ambush, waylay **7** deceive

sandbar 4 reef, spit **7** tombolo

Sandburg, Carl *biographical subject:* **7** Lincoln (Abraham) ***work:*** **9** People Yes (The) **12** Chicago Poems, Harvest Poems **13** Smoke and Steel **16** Rootabaga Stories

Sand County Almanac author 7 Leopold (Aldo)

sandpiper 4 knot, ruff **5** reeve **6** dunlin **9** shorebird

sandstone deposit 6 flysch

sandwich 3 BLT, sub **4** club, gyro, hero, roti **5** butty, Cuban, po'boy **6** Denver, hoagie, Reuben **7** grinder, Western **9** submarine **10** muffuletta ***shop:*** **4** deli

sandy 4 fair **5** blond **6** blonde, grainy, gritty

sane 3 fit **4** good, hale, sage, well, wise **5** lucid, right, sober, sound **6** cogent, normal **7** healthy, logical, prudent, sapient **8** all there, balanced, oriented, rational, sensible **9** judicious, wholesome **10** reasonable **11** levelheaded **12** compos mentis

San Francisco *hill:* **3** Nob **7** Russian ***tower:*** **4** Coit

sangfroid 4 calm **5** poise **6** aplomb, phlegm **8** serenity **9** composure **10** equanimity **11** self-control

sanguinary 4 gory **6** bloody **9** homicidal, murdering, murderous **12** bloodstained, bloodthirsty

sanguine 4 gory **5** flush, ruddy **6** bloody, florid, secure, upbeat **7** assured, buoyant, flushed, glowing, hopeful **8** bloodred, cheerful, rubicund **9** confident, homicidal, murdering, murderous **10** optimistic **11** self-assured **12** blood-stained, bloodthirsty, Pollyannaish **13** self-confident

sanitary 5 clean **7** sterile **8** hygienic **9** healthful **10** antiseptic, salubrious

sanitize 5 clean, purge **6** bleach, censor, purify **7** cleanse, launder **8** black out **9** disinfect, expurgate, sterilize **10** bowdlerize

sanity 6 health, reason **7** balance **8** lucidity, prudence **9** normality, soundness, stability

San Marino *capital:* **9** San Marino ***monetary unit:*** **4** euro ***monetary unit, former:*** **4** lira ***neighbor:*** **5** Italy

sans 7 lacking, missing, wanting, without

Sanskrit *dialect:* **4** Pali ***epic:*** **8** Ramayana ***Scripture:*** **4** Veda **6** Purana

Santa Lucia composer 5 Denza (Luigi)

São Tomé and Príncipe *capital:* **7** São Tomé ***language:*** **10** Portuguese ***location:*** **12** Gulf of Guinea ***monetary unit:*** **5** dobra

sap 4 dupe, fool, gull, mark **5** chump, drain, ninny **6** pigeon, sucker, weaken **7** cripple, deplete, disable, exhaust, fall guy **8** enervate, enfeeble **9** attenuate, schlemiel, undermine **10** debilitate ***pine:*** **5** resin, rosin

sapid 5 tasty **6** savory **9** delicious, flavorful, palatable, toothsome **10** appetizing **11** scrumptious

sapience see **sagacity**

sapient see **sagacious**

sapling 4 tree **5** child, youth **9** youngster

Sapphira's husband 7 Ananias

Sappho *forte:* 6 poetry ***island:* 6** Lesbos ***student:* 6** Erinna

sappy 5 ditzy, flaky, mushy, silly, soupy **6** drippy, slushy, sticky, syrupy **7** cloying, foolish, maudlin, mawkish **8** bathetic **11** sentimental

Saracen hero 9 Rodomonte

Sarah *husband:* 7 Abraham ***maid:* 5** Hagar ***son:* 5** Isaac

sarcasm 3 wit **4** gibe **5** irony, scorn **6** satire **7** mockery **8** acerbity, mordancy, ridicule, sneering **10** causticity

sarcastic 4 acid, tart **5** acerb, sharp **6** biting, ironic **7** acerbic, caustic, cutting, cynical, jeering, mocking, mordant, satiric **8** sardonic, scathing, scornful, stinging **9** corrosive

sarcophagus 4 tomb **6** coffin

sardine 4 sild **7** anchovy, herring **8** pilchard

Sardinia *capital:* 8 Cagliari ***neighbor:* 7** Corsica

sardonic 3 wry **6** ironic **7** caustic, cynical, jeering, mocking, satiric **8** derisive, scornful, sneering **9** corrosive, sarcastic **10** disdainful **12** contemptuous

sarong 5 skirt **7** garment

Sarpedon *brother:* 5 Minos **12** Rhadamanthus ***father:* 4** Zeus **7** Jupiter ***mother:* 6** Europa **8** Laodamia

Sartor ____ 8 Resartus

Sartre work 4 Wall (The) **5** Flies (The) **6** Nausea, No Exit **8** Huis Clos **10** Saint Genet

sash 3 obi **4** belt **6** girdle **8** ceinture, cincture **9** waistband **10** cummerbund

sashay 5 mince, strut **6** prance **7** flounce, saunter, swagger

Saskatchewan *capital:* 6 Regina ***city:* 8** Moose Jaw **9** Saskatoon **12** Prince Albert ***mountain range:* 12** Cypress Hills ***provincial flower:* 7** red lily **11** prairie lily ***river:* 9** Churchill **11** Assiniboine

sass 3 lip **4** guff **5** brass, cheek, mouth, sauce **8** back talk **9** impudence, insolence **12** impertinence

sassy 4 bold, flip, pert, wise **5** fresh, lippy, nervy, smart **6** brazen, cheeky **7** forward **8** flippant, impudent, insolent, malapert **9** audacious, unabashed **11** smart-alecky

Satan 5 demon, devil, fiend **6** diablo **7** Lucifer, Old Nick, serpent, villain **9** archfiend, Beelzebub **10** Old Scratch

satanic 4 evil **6** wicked **7** demonic, hellish **8** demoniac, devilish, diabolic, fiendish, infernal

satanism 9 diabolism

satchel 3 bag **4** case, tote **5** pouch **6** valise **7** handbag **9** briefcase

sate 4 cloy, fill, glut, jade, pall **5** gorge, stuff **6** stodge **7** appease, overeat, placate, surfeit **8** overfill **9** overstuff **10** conciliate

sated 4 full **6** filled, gorged **7** glutted, overfed, replete, stuffed **8** appeased, chockful **9** chock-full, surfeited

satellite 4 moon **5** toady **6** cohort, minion **7** Sputnik **8** adherent, disciple, follower, henchman, partisan **9** attendant, supporter, sycophant, tributary ***of Jupiter:* 6** Europa **8** Callisto, Ganymede ***of Mars:* 6** Deimos, Phobos ***of Neptune:* 6** Nereid, Triton ***of Saturn:* 4** Rhea **5** Dione, Janus, Mimas, Titan **6** Phoebe, Tethys **7** Iapetus **8** Hyperion **9** Enceladus ***of Uranus:* 5** Ariel **6** Oberon **7** Miranda, Titania, Umbriel

satiate see **sate**

satire 3 wit **5** irony, spoof, squib **6** parody **7** lampoon, mockery, takeoff **8** raillery, ridicule, spoofery, travesty **9** burlesque **10** caricature, lampoonery, pasquinade, persiflage

satiric 6 ironic **7** mocking **8** farcical, ironical

satirist *American:* 5 Twain (Mark) **6** Bierce (Ambrose) ***English:* 4** Pope (Alexander) **5** Swift (Jonathan), Waugh (Evelyn) **7** Marston (John) ***French:* 7** Molière **8** Rabelais (François), Voltaire ***Greek:* 8** Menippus **12** Aristophanes ***Italian:* 7** Aretino (Pietro) ***Roman:* 6** Horace **7** Juvenal, Martial, Persius **8** Apuleius **9** Petronius

satirize 4 mock **5** spoof **6** parody, send up **7** lampoon **8** ridicule **10** caricature

satisfaction 6 amends **7** redress **8** pleasure, serenity **9** atonement **10** reparation **11** contentment, fulfillment, restitution, vindication **12** propitiation **13** gratification

satisfactory 4 fair, good, okay **5** sound **6** decent **7** alright **8** adequate, all right, passable **9** agreeable, competent, tolerable **10** acceptable, sufficient **13** unexceptional

satisfy 3 pay **4** fill, meet, sate, suit **5** clear, humor, pay up, serve **6** answer, assure, dispel, pacify, please, settle, square **7** appease, content, fulfill, gladden, gratify, indulge, placate, satiate, suffice, win over **8** convince, persuade **9** conform to, discharge, indemnify **10** comply with

satori 12 illumination **13** enlightenment

satrap 5 ruler **6** cohort **7** viceroy **8** governor, henchman, sidekick **11** subordinate

saturate 3 sop, wet **4** fill, soak **5** bathe, douse, imbue, souse, steep **6** charge, drench, infuse **7** pervade, suffuse **8** permeate, waterlog **9** transfuse

Saturday Night Live ***cast member:*** **3** Fey (Tina) **4** Sanz (Horatio) **5** Chase (Chevy), Myers (Mike), Short (Martin), Vance (Danitra) **6** Carvey (Dana), Curtin (Jane), Dratch (Rachel), Farley (Chris), Kattan (Chris), Morgan (Tracy), Murphy (Eddie), Murray (Bill), Nealon (Kevin), Newman (Laraine), Radner (Gilda), Rocket (Charles) **7** Aykroyd (Dan), Belushi (John), Crystal (Billy), Ferrell (Will), Franken (Al), Hammond (Darrell), Hartman (Phil), Meadows (Tim), Parnell (Chris), Rudolph (Maya), Sandler (Adam), Shearer (Harry) **9** MacDonald (Norm), O'Donoghue (Michael) ***creator:*** **8** Michaels (Lorne)

Saturn ***moon:*** **4** Rhea **5** Dione, Janus, Mimas, Titan **6** Phoebe, Tethys **7** Iapetus **8** Hyperion **9** Enceladus see also **Cronus**

saturnalia 4 orgy **5** party, revel **6** excess **7** debauch **9** bacchanal **11** bacchanalia, dissipation

saturnine 4 dour, glum, grim **5** sulky, surly **6** gloomy, moping, morose, somber, sombre, sullen **7** crabbed **8** funereal, sardonic

satyr 4 faun, goat, lech, rake, wolf **5** letch **6** lecher **8** Casanova, lothario **9** butterfly

satyric 4 lewd **5** randy **6** wanton **7** goatish, lustful **8** prurient **9** lecherous, libertine, lickerish, salacious **10** lascivious, libidinous, licentious, lubricious **11** promiscuous **12** concupiscent

sauce 3 lip **4** guff, sass **5** mouth **6** relish **7** topping **8** back talk **9** condiment, impudence ***kind:*** **3** soy **4** hard, mole, roux **5** aioli, chili, curry, gravy, melba, pesto, ponzu, salsa **6** Mornay, panada, tamari, tartar **7** chutney, marengo, Newburg, piquant, soubise, tartare, velouté **8** béchamel, duxelles, marinara, matelote, noisette, normande **9** béarnaise, lyonnaise, rémoulade **10** bordelaise, Provençale **11** hollandaise, vinaigrette

saucy see **sassy**

Saudi Arabia ***capital:*** **6** Riyadh ***city:*** **5** Jedda, Jidda, Mecca **6** Jeddah, Jiddah, Medina ***desert:*** **7** Arabian **10** Rub Al-Khali **12** Empty Quarter ***gulf:*** **7** Persian ***monetary unit:*** **4** rial **5** riyal ***neighbor:*** **3** UAE **4** Iraq, Oman **5** Qatar, Yemen **6** Jordan ***peninsula:*** **7** Arabian ***sea:*** **3** Red

Saul ***concubine:*** **6** Rizpah ***cousin:*** **5** Abner ***daughter:*** **5** Merab **6** Michal ***father:*** **4** Kish ***general:*** **5** Abner ***son:*** **8** Jonathan ***successor:*** **5** David ***uncle:*** **3** Ner ***wife:*** **7** Ahinoam

saunter 4 mope, roam, rove **5** amble, drift, mosey **6** loiter, ramble, sashay, stroll, wander **7** meander, traipse

sausage 5 wurst **6** banger, kishke, salami, Vienna, wiener **7** baloney, bologna, boloney, chorizo, saveloy **8** cervelat, kielbasa, kielbasy **9** andouille, bratwurst, frankfurt, pepperoni, Thuringer **10** knackwurst, knockwurst, liverwurst, mortadella **11** frankfurter

sauté 3 fry **4** sear **5** brown, grill **6** sizzle **7** frizzle

savage 4 grim, wild **5** brute, cruel, feral **6** bloody, brutal, fierce, Gothic, rugged **7** bestial, brutish, inhuman, untamed, vicious, wolfish **8** barbaric, inhumane, primeval, ravenous, unbroken **9** barbarian, barbarous, ferocious, heartless, murderous, primitive, rapacious, truculent, voracious **10** implacable, relentless **11** uncivilized **12** bloodthirsty, uncontrolled, uncultivated, unsocialized

savagery 7 cruelty **8** atrocity **9** barbarity, brutality, depravity **10** bestiality, inhumanity **11** abomination, monstrosity, viciousness **12** ruthlessness

savanna 4 veld **5** plain, veldt **9** grassland

savant 4 sage **7** scholar, thinker, wise man

save 3 bar, but, yet **4** bank, keep, only, stow **5** amass, avoid, cache, guard, hoard, lay by, lay in, lay up, put by, set by, skimp, spare, store **6** defend, except, gather, keep up, manage, ransom, redeem, rescue, scrimp, shield, unless **7** barring, besides, collect, deliver, deposit, however, husband, lay away, protect, reclaim, reserve, salvage, set free, store up **8** conserve, lay aside, liberate, maintain, preserve, salt away, set aside, squirrel **9** aside from, economize, excluding, safeguard, stash away, stockpile **10** accumulate

savior 7 messiah, paladin, rescuer **8** defender **9** deliverer, liberator, preserver, protector, salvation **11** white knight

savoir faire 4 tact **5** grace, poise **6** aplomb **7** address, dignity, finesse, manners **8** urbanity **10** confidence, refinement **13** self-assurance

savor 4 odor, tang **5** enjoy, scent, smack,

smell, spice, taste, tinge **6** flavor, relish, season **8** sapidity

savory **5** sapid, spicy, tangy, tasty **7** piquant **9** flavorful, palatable, toothsome **10** appetizing

savvy **4** deft **5** adept, craft, handy, knack, skill **6** clever, talent **7** ability, know-how, skilled **8** deftness **9** adeptness, expertise, handiness, ingenuity **10** capability, cleverness, competence

saw **3** cut, hew **5** adage, axiom, maxim **6** byword, cliché, cutter, saying **7** precept, proverb **8** aphorism, apothegm

____ **saw** **3** bow, jig, pit, rip **4** band, buck, buzz, fret, hack, whip **5** chain, crown, saber **6** coping, scroll **7** compass, keyhole **8** circular, crosscut

sawbones **3** doc **6** doctor **7** surgeon **9** physician

sawbuck **6** tenner **7** trestle

sawhorse see **sawbuck**

saw-toothed **7** serrate, serried **8** serrated **11** denticulate

Saxon ***assembly:*** **4** moot **5** gemot **6** gemote ***nobleman:*** **8** atheling ***serf:*** **4** esne **6** thrall ***warrior:*** **5** thane

say **4** talk, tell **5** mouth, speak, state, utter, voice **6** affirm, assert, assume, recite, remark **7** comment, declare, express **8** announce, proclaim **9** enunciate, pronounce **10** articulate

Sayers character **6** Wimsey (Lord Peter)

saying **3** mot, saw **5** adage, axiom, maxim, motto **6** byword, dictum, truism **7** precept, proverb **8** aphorism, apothegm

scab **5** crust **6** eschar **8** blackleg **13** strikebreaker

scabbard **6** sheath

scabrous **4** lewd **5** bawdy, harsh, rough, salty, scaly **6** craggy, crusty, grubby, jagged, knobby, knotty, ribald, rugged, scurfy, sordid, uneven **7** bristly, prickly, scraggy, squalid **8** indecent, prurient **9** salacious **10** scandalous

scads **4** gobs, lots, tons, wads **5** heaps, loads, piles, rafts, reams **6** oodles, plenty **8** slathers **10** quantities

scaffold **5** stage, truss **7** staging **8** platform **9** framework

Scala, La ***city:*** **5** Milan **6** Milano ***production:*** **5** opera

scalawag see **scamp**

scald **4** boil, burn **6** scorch

scale **4** peel, rate, skin **5** climb, flake, gamut, gauge, mount, ratio, scute, strip **6** ascend, degree, extent, ladder, lamina, scutum, squama **7** measure, ranking **8** escalade, flake off, spall off **9** exfoliate, hierarchy **10** desquamate, proportion **11** decorticate ***auxiliary:*** **7** vernier ***earthquake:*** **7** Richter ***musical:*** **2** do, fa, la, mi, re, ti, ut **3** sol ***temperature:*** **6** Kelvin **7** Celsius, Réaumur **10** centigrade, Fahrenheit ***wind:*** **8** Beaufort

scallion **4** leek **5** onion **7** shallot **10** green onion

scalp **4** flay, skin **5** cheat **6** resell, trophy

scam **3** con, gyp **4** bilk, dupe, fool, hoax **5** cheat, fraud, stick, trick **6** delude, diddle, take in **7** beguile, deceive, defraud, swindle **8** flimflam, hoodwink, phishing **11** double-cross

scamp **3** imp **4** brat, rake, tyke **5** devil, joker, knave, rogue **6** rascal, urchin **7** hellion **8** scalawag, slyboots **9** prankster, scoundrel, skeezicks **11** rapscallion

scamper **3** run **4** dash, skip **5** scoot **6** scurry **7** scuttle

scan **3** eye, MRI **4** skim, view **5** audit, check **6** browse, review, survey **7** examine, eyeball, inspect **8** glance at **10** run through, scrutinize

scandal **5** rumor **6** gossip, infamy **7** calumny, obloquy, offense, slander **8** disgrace, dishonor, reproach **9** aspersion, discredit, disrepute **10** backbiting, defamation, detraction, opprobrium

scandalize **5** libel, shock, smear **6** defame, malign **7** asperse, slander **9** denigrate **10** calumniate

scandalmonger **6** gossip **8** busybody, gossiper, quidnunc, telltale **9** backbiter, muckraker **10** talebearer

scandalous **7** heinous **8** infamous, libelous, shameful, shocking **9** notorious, offensive **10** defamatory, outrageous, scurrilous **11** disgraceful

Scandinavian see **Norse**

Scandinavian country **6** Norway, Sweden **7** Denmark, Finland, Iceland

scant **5** short, skimp, spare, stint, tight **6** meager, meagre, paltry, scarce, scrimp, skimpy, slight, sparse **7** scrimpy, wanting **8** exiguous **10** inadequate **12** insufficient

scantiness **4** lack **6** dearth **7** deficit, paucity **8** scarcity, shortage, sparsity **10** deficiency, inadequacy, scarceness, sparseness **13** insufficiency

scanty see **scant**

scapegoat **6** target, victim **7** fall guy **9** sacrifice **11** whipping boy

scapegrace **5** knave, rogue, scamp **6** bad egg, rascal, sinner **7** ruffian, varmint, villain **8** hooligan, recreant, scalawag **9** miscreant, reprobate, scoundrel **10** blackguard, black sheep, delinquent **11** rapscallion

Scapin 5 rogue, valet **6** rascal ***author:* 7** Molière ***employer:* 7** Léandre

scar 3 mar **4** flaw **5** score **6** deface, defect, keloid **7** blemish, scratch **8** cicatrix, pockmark **9** cicatrize, disfigure ***on a seed:* 5** hilum

scarab 6 beetle

scaramouch see **scamp**

scarce 3 few **4** rare **5** scant **6** barely, hardly, scanty, sparse **7** limited, wanting **8** sporadic, uncommon **9** deficient **10** inadequate, infrequent, occasional **12** insufficient

scarcity see **scantiness**

scare 5 alarm, panic, spook **6** fright **7** horrify, petrify, shake up, startle, terrify **8** frighten, paralyze **9** terrorize

scaredy-cat 4 wimp, wuss **5** mouse, sissy **6** coward **7** chicken, dastard **8** alarmist, poltroon **11** milquetoast, yellowbelly

scare up 4 find, snag **5** rally **6** corral, gather, locate, obtain, secure **7** acquire, collect, procure, unearth **8** smoke out **9** ferret out, track down

scarf 3 boa **4** gulp, wolf **5** ascot, fichu, plaid, shawl, stole **6** cravat, devour, gobble, inhale **8** babushka, liripipe, mantilla, puggaree **10** lambrequin ***Mexican:* 6** rebozo

Scarlet Letter, The *author:* 9 Hawthorne (Nathaniel) ***character:* 5** Pearl **6** Hester (Prynne) **10** Dimmesdale (Arthur) **13** Chillingworth (Roger)

Scarlet Pimpernel author 5 Orczy (Baroness Emmuska)

Scarlett's home 4 Tara

scary 6 creepy, spooky **8** chilling **9** frightful ***cry:* 3** boo

scathe 4 burn, flay, flog, harm, lash, sear **5** roast, slash **6** assail, berate, scorch, thrash **7** blister, scarify, scourge, upbraid **8** lambaste **9** castigate, excoriate

scathing 6 biting, brutal **7** caustic, mordant **8** stinging **9** trenchant

scatter 3 sow, ted **4** cast, part, shed **5** strew **6** divide, spread **7** bestrew, break up, diffuse, disband, diverge **8** disperse, sprinkle **9** broadcast, dissipate **10** besprinkle, distribute **11** disseminate

scatterbrained 5 dizzy, giddy, silly **7** flighty, foolish **8** heedless **9** frivolous

scattering 8 diaspora **10** dispersion

scavenger 5 hyena **6** jackal **7** vulture

scenario 4 plot **6** script **7** outline **8** libretto, synopsis **10** screenplay

scene 3 row, set **4** fuss, site, spot, view **5** arena, field, place, sight, vista **6** locale, milieu, sphere **7** episode, outlook, setting, tableau, tantrum **8** backdrop, locality, location, stage set **9** commotion, landscape, situation **10** background **11** environment **12** stage setting

scenery 3 set **5** decor, props **7** setting **8** stage set **10** properties **11** furnishings **12** stage setting

scent 4 nose, odor **5** aroma, smell, sniff, snuff, whiff **7** bouquet, essence, incense, odorize, perfume **9** aromatize, fragrance, redolence

scepter 4 mace **5** baton, staff **11** sovereignty

schedule 4 list, roll **5** chart, slate, table **6** agenda, docket, record, roster **7** catalog, program, reserve **8** calendar, register, roll call **9** catalogue, timetable

scheme 4 plan, plot, ploy, ruse **5** bunco, bunko, cabal, order **6** design, device, devise **7** collude, connive, diagram, program, project **8** cogitate, conspire, contrive, game plan, intrigue, proposal, strategy **9** blueprint, expedient, machinate **10** conspiracy, strategize **11** arrangement, contrivance, machination ***type:* 5** Ponzi **7** pyramid

schism 4 rent, rift **5** break, chasm, cleft, split **6** breach, divide, heresy **7** discord, dissent, fissure, rupture **8** cleavage, division, fracture **10** disharmony, dissidence, divergence, falling-out, heterodoxy, separation **11** unorthodoxy **12** estrangement

schlemiel 4 fool **5** chump, klutz **7** bungler

schlep 3 lug, tow **4** drag, haul, hump, plod, pull, slog, tote **5** carry, truck **6** trudge **7** shamble, shuffle **8** straggle

schlock 4 junk, mean **5** cheap, dreck, gaudy, junky, tacky, tatty **6** cheesy, common, kitsch, shoddy, sleazy, tawdry, trashy **8** inferior, low-grade **11** second-class, substandard

schmaltzy 5 mushy, soppy **6** drippy **7** maudlin, mawkish **11** sentimental, tear-jerking

schmo 4 dolt, dope, dork, fool, goof, jerk, mutt, simp, twit, yo-yo **5** brute, chump, idiot, moron, ninny, noddy, scamp **6** dimwit, donkey, dumdum, nitwit, noodle, nudnik, rascal **7** dullard, halfwit, jackass, schmuck, schnook **8** bonehead, clodpoll, imbecile, lunkhead, meathead, numskull **9** birdbrain, blockhead, ignoramus, lamebrain, numbskull, thickhead **10** dunderhead, hammerhead, nincompoop **11** chowderhead, chucklehead, knucklehead

schmooze 3 gab, yak **4** chat **6** chat up **8** converse

schnoz 4 beak, nose **5** snout **6** honker

scholar 4 sage, wonk **5** pupil **6** savant **7**

bookman, egghead, student, wise man **8** bookworm, polymath **12** intellectual ***Hindu:*** **6** pandit, pundit ***Muslim:*** **5** ulama, ulema

scholarly 7 bookish, erudite, learned **8** academic, educated, studious **10** scholastic **12** intellectual

scholarship 5 award, grant **7** stipend **8** learning **9** education, erudition, knowledge **11** learnedness

scholastic 7 bookish, erudite, learned **8** academic, lettered, literary, pedantic **9** scholarly ***life:*** **8** academia

school 3 gam, pod **5** shoal, teach, train, tutor **7** academy, college, educate **8** instruct **9** alma mater, institute **10** discipline, university ***English:*** **4** Eton **6** Harrow ***French:*** **5** école, lycée ***grounds:*** **6** campus ***Jewish:*** **5** heder **7** yeshiva ***judo:*** **4** dojo ***organization:*** **3** PTA, PTO ***religious:*** **8** seminary ***term:*** **7** quarter **8** semester **9** trimester ***type:*** **4** coed

schoolbook 4 text **6** primer, reader **7** speller

School for Scandal author 8 Sheridan (Richard Brinsley)

schooner 4 ship **5** stoup **6** goblet, seidel **7** tumbler **8** sailboat

Schubert forte 4 lied, song

science *of agriculture:* **8** agronomy ***of animals:*** **7** zoology ***of criminal punishment:*** **8** penology ***of environment:*** **7** ecology ***of fermentation:*** **8** zymology ***of health:*** **7** hygiene **9** hygienics ***of heredity:*** **8** genetics ***of human behavior:*** **10** psychology ***of measuring time:*** **8** horology **11** chronometry ***of motion:*** **8** kinetics ***of mountains:*** **7** orology ***of plants:*** **6** botany ***of projectiles:*** **10** ballistics ***of the earth:*** **7** geology

scientific classification 8 taxonomy

sci-fi writer 3 Lem (Stanislaw) **4** Card (Orson Scott), Dick (Philip K.), Pohl (Frederik) **5** Disch (Thomas M.), Lewis (C. S.), Niven (Larry), Verne (Jules), Wells (H. G.) **6** Aldiss (Brian), Asimov (Isaac), Bester (Alfred), Bishop (Michael), Butler (Octavia), Clarke (Arthur C.), Delany (Samuel), Farmer (Philip José), Gibson (William), Le Guin (Ursula), Leiber (Fritz), Miller (Walter), Norton (Andre) **7** Ballard (J. G.), Clement (Hal), Ellison (Harlan), Herbert (Frank), Hubbard (L. Ron), Van Vogt (A. E.), Zelazny (Roger) **8** Anderson (Poul), Bradbury (Ray), Heinlein (Robert A.), Sterling (Bruce), Sturgeon (Theodore), Vonnegut (Kurt) **9** Gernsback (Hugo), Kornbluth (C. M.) **10** Silverberg (Robert)

scimitar 5 saber, sabre, sword **7** cutlass

scintilla 3 bit, jot **4** atom, iota, whit **5** grain, spark, speck, trace **7** smidgen **8** particle

scintillate 5 flash, gleam, glint, spark **6** glance **7** glimmer, glisten, glitter, shimmer, sparkle, twinkle **9** coruscate

scion 4 heir **5** child, graft, issue **7** progeny **8** offshoot **9** inheritor, offspring, successor **10** descendant

scoff at 4 mock, twit **5** fleer, scorn **6** deride **7** contemn, disdain **8** belittle, pooh-pooh, ridicule

scold 3 rag **4** chew, lash, rail, rant **5** baste, blame, chide, grill, harpy, hound, shrew, vixen **6** berate, grouch, grouse, harass, murmur, mutter, rebuke, revile, virago **7** bawl out, blister, censure, chasten, chew out, grumble, lecture, reprove, tell off, upbraid **8** admonish, execrate, fishwife, lambaste, reproach, Xantippe **9** criticize, dress down, excoriate, objurgate, reprehend, reprimand, termagant, Xanthippe **10** tongue-lash, vituperate

scoop 3 dig, dip **4** bail, beat, lift **5** gouge, ladle, spade **6** dig out, pick up, shovel **8** excavate **9** exclusive

scoot 3 fly, run, zip **4** dash, flee, race, rush, skip **5** hurry, scram, skirr, slide **6** hustle, scurry, sprint **7** scamper **9** skedaddle

scope 3 ken **4** area, room **5** ambit, gamut, orbit, range, reach, sweep **6** extent, leeway, margin, radius **7** breadth, compass, purview **8** capacity, fullness, latitude **9** amplitude, extension

Scopes trial lawyer 5 Bryan (William Jennings) **6** Darrow (Clarence)

scorch 4 bake, burn, char, flay, sear **5** broil, roast, singe **6** scathe **7** blacken, blister, scarify, scourge, swelter **8** lambaste **9** castigate, excoriate

score 3 cut, tab, win **4** bill, gain, goal, line, mark, nick, slit **5** cleft, count, notch, reach, tally, total **6** attain, furrow, groove, grudge, rack up, record, thrive, twenty **7** account, achieve, invoice, prosper, scratch, succeed **8** flourish **9** reckoning **10** accomplish

scorn 4 gibe, jeer, mock **5** abhor, flout, scoff, spurn, taunt **6** deride **7** contemn, despise, despite, disdain, jeering, mockery **8** contempt, derision, ridicule, scoffing, taunting **9** contumely

Scorpius star 7 Antares

Scot 4 Celt, Gael

Scotch cocktail 6 Rob Roy **9** Rusty Nail

scoter 7 sea coot, sea duck

Scotland *capital:* **9** Edinburgh ***church:*** **11** the Auld Kirk ***city:*** **6** Dundee **7** Glasgow **8** Aberdeen **9** Inverness **11** Dunfermline ***emblem:*** **7** thistle ***firth:*** **5** Clyde, Forth, Moray **6** Solway ***former capital:*** **5** Perth ***island, is-***

land group: **4** Iona, Jura, Mull, Skye, Uist **5** Arran, Islay **7** Orkneys **9** Shetlands **8** Hebrides ***lake:*** **8** Loch Ness **10** Loch Lomond ***mountain, range:*** **8** Ben Nevis **9** Grampians ***patron saint:*** **6** Andrew ***river:*** **3** Dee, Esk **5** Clyde

Scott, Sir Walter ***novel:*** **5** Abbot (The) **6** Rob Roy **7** Ivanhoe **8** Talisman (The), Waverley **9** Woodstock **10** Kenilworth **11** Redgauntlet **12** Old Mortality **14** Quentin Durward ***poem:*** **7** Marmion **13** Lady of the Lake (The)

____ Scott case **4** Dred

Scottish **4** Erse **6** Gaelic ***cap:*** **3** tam **9** glengarry **11** tam-o'-shanter ***child:*** **5** bairn ***coin:*** **6** bawbee ***dance:*** **4** reel **5** fling **10** strathspey ***Gaelic:*** **4** Erse ***guide:*** **6** gillie ***hero:*** **5** Bruce (Robert) **7** Wallace (William) ***hill:*** **4** brae ***lake:*** **4** loch ***landowner:*** **5** laird ***language:*** **4** Erse **6** Gaelic ***no:*** **3** nae ***outlaw:*** **6** Rob Roy ***plaid:*** **6** tartan ***pudding:*** **6** haggis ***skirt:*** **4** kilt ***spirit:*** **6** kelpie **7** banshee ***sword:*** **8** claymore ***trousers:*** **5** trews

scoundrel **3** cad **4** heel **5** knave, rogue, scamp **6** bad guy, rascal **7** lowlife, villain **9** miscreant, reprobate **10** blackguard

scour **4** comb, rake **5** erode, purge, range, scrub **6** forage, search **7** corrode, eat away, ransack, rummage **8** wear away **9** ferret out

scourge **4** bane, flay, flog, hide, lash, whip, whop **5** curse, flail, slash, whale **6** plague, ravage, scathe, stripe, thrash **7** afflict, blister, despoil, pillage, scarify **8** chastise, lambaste **9** castigate, depredate, desecrate, devastate, excoriate **10** affliction, flagellate, pestilence

Scourge of God **6** Attila

scout **3** spy **6** ranger, survey **7** explore, lookout **8** searcher, watchman **11** investigate, reconnoiter

scouting group **3** BSA, GSA

scow **3** hoy **5** barge **6** garvey **7** lighter

scowl **5** frown, glare, lower **6** glower

scrabble **5** grope **6** scrawl **7** clamber **8** flounder

scraggly **6** ragged, shaggy, uneven **7** unkempt **9** irregular

scraggy **4** bony, lank, lean **5** gaunt, harsh, lanky, rocky, rough **6** jagged, rugged, skinny, uneven **7** angular, scrawny, spindly, unlevel **8** gangling, rawboned, scabrous

scram **3** git **4** scat, shoo **5** scoot, split **6** beat it, begone, get out **7** buzz off, get lost, skiddoo, take off, vamoose **8** clear out **9** skedaddle

scramble **4** hash **6** jumble, jungle, muddle, scurry, tumble **7** clamber, clutter, rummage, scuttle, shuffle **8** mishmash, scrabble, straggle **9** confusion

scrambled **7** chaotic, jumbled, mixed-up **8** confused **9** corrupted **10** disordered, disorderly

scrap **3** bit, jot, ort, row **4** chip, dump, fray, iota, junk, spat, tiff, whit **5** abort, brawl, chuck, crumb, fight, melee, piece, set-to, shred, speck **6** bicker, fracas, reject, sliver, tittle **7** brabble, cutting, discard, fall out, quarrel, scuffle, smidgen, wrangle **8** fragment, jettison, leftover, particle, squabble, throw out **9** throw away

scrape **3** fix, jam, rub **4** mess, rasp, spot **5** chafe, fight, grate, graze, pinch, scour, scuff, shave, skimp, spare, stint **6** abrade, pickle, plight, scrimp **7** dilemma, scratch, trouble **8** abrasion, struggle **11** predicament

scrappy **6** feisty **8** brawling **9** combative, truculent **10** pugnacious **11** belligerent, contentious, quarrelsome

scratch **4** claw, rake, rasp **5** grate, money, score, scrup **6** scotch, scrape, scrawl **7** call off **8** scrabble, scribble

scratchy **5** rough **6** gritty **7** itching, prickly, rasping **8** abrasive, granular, tingling **10** irritating

scrawl **6** doodle **7** scratch **8** scrabble, scribble

scrawny **4** bony, lank, lean **5** gaunt, lanky **6** skinny **7** scraggy **8** rawboned

scream **3** cry **4** riot, yell, yowl **5** shout **6** screak, shriek, shrill, squeal **7** screech

screech **6** screak, scream, shriek, shrill, squeal

screed **4** rant **5** level, spiel **6** letter, tirade **8** diatribe, harangue, jeremiad **9** discourse, philippic **11** disputation **12** disquisition

screen **4** cull, hide, sift, veil **5** blind, sieve **6** facade, filter, movies, shroud, winnow **7** conceal, obscure, pick out **9** partition **10** camouflage ***Japanese:*** **5** shoji

screw **9** propeller

screwball **3** nut, wag **4** kook, zany **5** clown, crazy, cutup, flake, flaky, freak, gonzo, joker, kooky, loony, loopy, nutty, silly, wacko, wacky **6** madcap, weirdo **7** buffoon, dingbat, farceur **8** crackpot, jokester **9** ding-a-ling, eccentric, fruitcake, whimsical

Screwtape Letters author **5** Lewis (C. S.)

screwy **3** mad **4** daft, nuts **5** batty, crazy, goofy, loony, nutty, wacky **6** absurd, insane **7** bizarre, cracked, lunatic **9** eccentric **10** unbalanced

scribble **5** write **6** scrawl **7** scratch **8** squiggle

scribe **5** clerk, write **6** author, penman, writer **7** copyist **9** scrivener, secretary **10** amanuensis

scrimmage 4 fray **5** brawl, broil, clash, fight, melee, scrap, scrum, set-to **6** battle, fracas, ruckus, rumpus **7** scuffle **8** skirmish **10** donnybrook, free-for-all
scrimp 4 save **5** stint **6** save up, scrape **8** conserve **9** economize
script 4 hand, text **5** write **8** longhand, scenario **10** penmanship, screenplay **11** calligraphy, chirography, handwriting, orchestrate
scrivener 5 clerk **6** notary, scribe, writer **7** copyist **10** amanuensis
scrooge 5 miser **7** niggard **8** tightwad **9** skinflint **10** cheapskate **12** moneygrubber
scrounge 3 beg, bum, tap **4** grub, hunt, loot **5** cadge, filch, mooch, pinch, steal, swipe, touch **6** forage, hustle, pilfer, snitch, sponge, thieve **7** finagle, solicit, wheedle **8** freeload **9** panhandle
scroungy 5 dirty, seedy **6** grubby, grungy, scurvy, scuzzy, shabby, sleazy, sordid **7** scruffy, squalid, unkempt **8** slovenly **10** slatternly
scrub 3 rub **4** buff, drop, wash **5** abort, brush, scour **6** cancel, mallee, maquis, polish **7** abandon, call off, cleanse, scratch **9** chaparral, eliminate
scrubby 4 drab, mean **5** dingy, dowdy, runty **6** paltry, ragged, shabby, shoddy **7** rundown, runtish, stunted **8** inferior **9** neglected **10** bedraggled, broken-down
scruff 4 nape, neck
scruffy 5 mangy, seedy, tacky **6** frowsy, frowzy, shabby, shaggy **7** run-down, scrubby, unkempt **8** slovenly, tattered **10** down-at-heel, threadbare
scrumptious 5 tasty, yummy **8** heavenly, luscious **9** ambrosial, delicious, succulent, toothsome **10** delectable, delightful **13** mouthwatering
scruple 3 bit, jot **4** balk, iota **5** demur, doubt, grain, qualm, scrap, shred, worry **7** concern, modicum **8** particle, question **9** hesitancy **11** compunction
scrupulous 5 exact, fussy **6** honest, minute, strict **7** careful, heedful, upright **8** critical, punctual, rigorous **9** honorable **10** fair-minded, fastidious, meticulous, principled, upstanding **11** painstaking, punctilious **12** conscionable **13** conscientious
scrutinize 4 comb, scan **5** audit, probe, study **6** peruse **7** analyze, canvass, dig into, dissect, examine, eyeball, inspect **8** look over, pore over **9** check over **11** contemplate, investigate
scrutiny 4 scan **5** audit **6** review, survey **7** perusal **8** analysis **10** inspection **11** examination **12** surveillance
scuba diver 7 frogman **8** aquanaut
scud 3 fly **4** race, rain, rush, sail, skim **5** brume, froth, scoot, speed, spray, spume **6** clouds, scurry, shower
scuff 6 scrape **7** scratch, shamble, shuffle
scuffle 3 row **4** fray **5** brawl, broil, fight, scrap, set-to **6** affray, fracas, hubbub, tussle **7** bobbery, grapple, shamble, shuffle, wrestle **10** roughhouse
scull 3 oar, row **4** boat **5** shell **6** propel
sculpt 3 hew **5** carve, shape **6** chisel
sculptor ***American:*** **3** Lin (Maya) **4** Gabo (Naum), Judd (Donald), Taft (Lorado) **5** Andre (Carl), Koons (Jeff), Pratt (Bela), Segal (George), Serra (Richard), Smith (David), Story (William) **6** Aitkin (Robert), Calder (Alexander), Fraser (James Earle), French (Daniel Chester), Powers (Hiram), Zorach (William) **7** Borglum (Gutzon), Cornell (Joseph), Noguchi (Isamu) **8** Lachaise (Gaston), Lipchitz (Jacques), Nadelman (Elie), Nevelson (Louise) **9** Bourgeois (Louise), Mestrovic (Ivan), Oldenburg (Claes), Remington (Frederic) **12** Saint-Gaudens (Augustus) ***Czech:*** **6** Stursa (Jan) ***Danish:*** **11** Thorvaldsen (Bertel), Thorwaldsen (Bertel) ***Dutch:*** **6** Sluter (Claus) ***English:*** **5** Moore (Henry), Watts (George) **7** Epstein (Jacob), Flaxman (John) **8** Hepworth (Barbara) ***French:*** **3** Arp (Hans, Jean) **4** Bloc (André) **5** Rodin (Auguste) **6** Dubois (Paul), Houdon (Jean-Antoine) **7** Maillol (Aristide), Pevsner (Antoine) **9** Bartholdi (Frédéric-Auguste), Roubillac (Louis-François) ***German:*** **5** Hesse (Eva) ***Greek:*** **5** Myron **7** Phidias **8** Pheidias **10** Polyclitus, Praxiteles **11** Polycleitus ***Italian:*** **5** Leoni (Leone), Salvi (Niccolò, Nicola) **6** Canova (Antonio), Pisano (Andrea, Nino), Robbia (Andrea, Giovanni, Girolamo, Luca della) **7** Bernini (Gian Lorenzo), Cellini (Benvenuto), da Vinci (Leonardo), Orcagna, Quercia (Jacopo della) **8** Ghiberti (Lorenzo), Leonardo (da Vinci), Vittoria (Alessandro) **9** Donatello, Sansovino (Jacopo) **10** Giocometti (Alberto), Verrocchio (Andrea del) **12** Michelangelo (Buonarroti) ***Rhodian:*** **9** Polydorus ***Romanian:*** **8** Brancusi (Constantin) ***Russian:*** **7** Zadkine (Ossip) ***Swedish:*** **6** Milles (Carl) **9** Oldenburg (Claes) ***Swiss:*** **10** Giacometti (Alberto)
scum 5 algae, dregs, dross **6** refuse, vermin **8** riffraff
scummy 3 low **4** base, mean, vile **5** dirty,

mucky, slimy **6** grubby, odious, sleazy, sordid **7** squalid **10** despicable **12** contemptible
scurrilous 4 foul **5** dirty, gross, nasty **6** coarse, filthy, vulgar **7** abusive, obscene, profane **8** indecent **9** insulting, offensive **10** outrageous **11** opprobrious **12** contumelious, vituperative
scurry 3 run **4** dart, dash **5** scoot, shoot **6** bustle **7** scamper, scuffle, scuttle
scurvy see **scummy**
scut 4 tail
scuttle 3 run **4** hole, pail, sink **5** abort, scrap, wreck **6** basket, scurry **7** destroy, opening
scuttlebutt 4 buzz, talk **5** rumor **6** gossip, report **7** chatter, hearsay **9** grapevine
Scylla 4 rock ***counterpart:* 9** Charybdis ***father:* 5** Nisus ***lover:* 5** Minos
scythe handle 5 snath **6** snathe
sea 4 blue, deep, main **5** brine, drink, ocean ***Antarctica:* 4** Ross **5** Davis **7** Weddell **8** Amundsen ***Arctic:* 4** Kara **7** Chukchi **8** Beaufort, Karskoye **9** Chuckchee, Norwegian **11** Chukotskoye **12** East Siberian ***Asia-Europe:* 5** Black ***Asia Minor:* 7** Icarian ***Atlantic:* 5** North **7** Weddell **9** Caribbean ***Australia-Indonesia:* 7** Arafura ***Balkan Peninsula-Italy:* 8** Adriatic ***Bay of Bengal:* 7** Andaman ***China-Korea:* 5** Huang, Hwang **6** Yellow ***combining form:* 3** mer **4** mari **5** pelag **6** pelago **7** thalass **8** thalasso ***Corsica-Italy:* 10** Tyrrhenian ***Denmark-Norway:* 9** Skagerrak ***Denmark-Sweden:* 8** Kattegat ***England-Ireland:* 5** Irish ***Fiji:* 4** Koro ***France-Italy:* 8** Ligurian ***Greece:* 5** Crete ***Greece-Italy:* 6** Ionian ***Greece-Turkey:* 6** Aegean **8** Thracian ***Honshu:* 6** Sagami ***Indian Ocean:* 5** Timor **7** Arabian ***Indonesia:* 4** Bali **6** Flores ***inland:* 3** Red **4** Aral **7** Caspian ***Japan:* 3** Suo **6** Inland ***Kazakhstan:* 4** Aral ***Malay Archipelago:* 5** Banda ***Mexico:* 6** Cortés ***Netherlands:* 6** Wadden ***North Atlantic:* 8** Sargasso ***Northern Europe:* 6** Baltic, Ostsee **8** Suevicum ***North Pacific:* 6** Bering ***off Scotland:* 8** Hebrides ***off Sweden:* 5** Aland ***Pacific:* 4** Java **5** China, Coral **6** Maluku **7** Celebes, Eastern, Molucca, Solomon **9** East China **10** South China ***Philippine:* 4** Sulu ***Russia:* 5** White **7** Okhotsk ***Russia-Ukraine:* 4** Azov ***South Pacific:* 4** Ross **6** Tasman **8** Amundsen ***Turkey:* 7** Marmara **9** Propontis ***Uzbekistan:* 4** Aral ***West Pacific:* 5** Ceram, Japan **8** Bismarck **10** Philippine
sea anemone 5 polyp
seabird see **bird** *aquatic*
seacoast 5 beach, coast, shore **6** strand **8** littoral **9** shoreline
sea cucumber 7 trepang **11** holothurian
sea dog see **sailor**
sea duck 5 eider, scaup **6** scoter **9** merganser
sea eagle 4 erne **6** osprey **8** fish hawk
seafarer 3 tar **4** salt **6** sailor **7** jack-tar, mariner
seafood dish 4 clam, crab **5** clams, squid **6** cockle, mussel, oyster, scampi, shrimp **7** ceviche, lobster, mussels, oysters, scallop, seviche **8** calamari, scallops
seagoing 8 maritime, nautical
seal 5 sigil, stamp **6** cachet, signet **7** sticker ***female:* 3** cow ***herd:* 3** pod **5** patch ***joint:* 6** gasket ***young:* 3** pup
sealant 4 lute **5** caulk, grout **6** luting, mastic **8** caulking
sea lily 7 crinoid
seam 4 bond **5** joint, union **8** coupling, juncture **10** connection
seaman see **sailor**
sea monster 3 Orc **6** kraken **9** leviathan
seamount 5 guyot
seamy 5 dirty, rough, seedy **6** sordid **7** squalid **12** disreputable
séance 7 meeting, session, sitting ***holder:* 6** medium
seaport *Alaska:* 6 Juneau **9** Anchorage ***Albania:* 5** Vlorë **6** Durres, Valona ***Algeria:* 4** Bône, Oran **6** Annaba ***Angola:* 6** Lobito, Luanda **7** Cabinda **8** Benguela ***Argentina:* 11** Buenos Aires, Mar del Plata ***Australia:* 4** Eden **5** Bowen, Perth **6** Darwin, Hobart, Sydney **8** Brisbane **9** Melbourne **10** Wollongong ***Azores:* 5** Horta ***Balearic:* 5** Ibiza ***Belgium:* 6** Ostend **7** Antwerp ***Benin:* 7** Cotonou **9** Porto-Novo ***Black Sea:* 5** Varna **6** Burgas, Odessa **9** Constanta ***Brazil:* 3** Rio **4** Pará **5** Bahia, Belém, Natal **6** Recife, Santos **7** Vitoria **8** Salvador **9** Fortaleza **10** Pernambuco **11** Pôrto Alegre, São Salvador **12** Rio de Janeiro ***Bulgaria:* 5** Varna **6** Burgas ***Cameroon:* 6** Douala ***Canaries:* 8** Arrecife **9** Las Palmas ***Chile:* 5** Arica **8** Coquimbo **10** Valparaíso ***China:* 4** Amoy **6** Dalian, Fuzhou, Lüshun, Xiamen **7** Foochow, Hsiamen, Qingdao, Tianjin **8** Shanghai, Shenzhen, Tientsin, Tsingtao **9** Guangzhou, Zhenjiang **10** Chen-chiang, Port Arthur ***Colombia:* 6** Lorica **9** Cartagena **12** Barranquilla ***Corsica:* 5** Calvi **7** Ajaccio ***Costa Rica:* 5** Limón **10** Puntarenas ***Crimean:* 5** Kerch, Yalta **10** Sebastopol, Sevastopol ***Croatia:* 5** Rieka, Split **6** Rijeka **9** Dubrovnik ***Cuba:* 6** Havana **8** La Habana, Matanzas, Santiago ***Cyprus:* 9** Famagusta ***Denmark:* 5** Arhus **6** Aarhus, Alborg **7** Aalborg **8** Elsinore **10** Copenhagen ***Ecuador:* 9** Guayaquil ***Egypt:* 4** Said **10** Alexandria

England: **4** Hull **5** Dover **9** Liverpool **10** Portsmouth **11** Southampton ***Equatorial Guinea:*** **4** Bata ***Eritrea:*** **4** Aseb ***Estonia:*** **5** Pärnu **7** Tallinn ***Finland:*** **3** Abo **4** Kemi, Oulu, Pori, Vasa **5** Hango, Kotka, Rauma, Turku, Vaasa **6** Vyborg ***Florida:*** **5** Miami, Tampa **9** Pensacola **12** Apalachicola, Jacksonville ***France:*** **4** Nice **5** Brest, Havre **6** Calais, Cannes, Toulon **7** Dunkirk, Le Havre **8** Bordeaux, Boulogne **9** Cherbourg, Dunkerque, Marseille **10** Marseilles ***French Polynesia:*** **7** Papeete ***Georgia:*** **8** Savannah **9** Brunswick ***Georgia, Republic of:*** **4** Pot'i ***Germany:*** **4** Kiel **5** Emden **6** Bremen, Lübeck, Wismar **7** Hamburg, Rostock **8** Cuxhaven **11** Bremerhaven ***Ghana:*** **4** Tema **5** Accra ***Greece:*** **5** Pylos, Syros, Volos **7** Piraeus ***Guatemala:*** **7** San José **10** Livingston ***Haiti:*** **5** Cayes **10** Cap Haitien ***Honduras:*** **7** La Ceiba **8** Trujillo ***India:*** **3** Goa **4** Puri **5** Marud **6** Bombay, Madras, Mumbai, Old Goa **7** Calicut, Chennai **8** Calcutta **9** Jagannath **10** Trivandrum ***Iran:*** **4** Jask **7** Bushehr ***Iraq:*** **5** Basra ***Ireland:*** **4** Cork **5** Sligo **6** Dingle, Dublin, Galway, Tralee **8** Drogheda, Limerick **9** Waterford **10** Balbriggan ***Israel:*** **4** Acre, Akko, Elat, Yafo **5** Accho, Eilat, Haifa, Jaffa, Joppa **6** Ashdod **8** Ashqelon ***Italy:*** **4** Bari **5** Anzio, Gaeta, Genoa **6** Genova, Naples, Napoli, Pesaro, Rimini, Venice **7** Leghorn, Livorno, Marsala, Messina, Rapallo, Salerno, Taranto, Trieste, Venezia **8** Brindisi, Siracusa, Sorrento, Syracuse ***Ivory Coast:*** **5** Tabou **7** Abidjan ***Jamaica:*** **8** Kingston **10** Montego Bay ***Japan:*** **4** Kobe, Oita **5** Kochi, Osaka, Rumoi, Ujina, Uraga **6** Sasebo **7** Fukuoka **8** Nagasaki, Yokohama **9** Hiroshima ***Java:*** **5** Tegal, Tuban **7** Cilacap, Jakarta **8** Semarang, Surabaya ***Jordan:*** **5** Aqaba, Elath **6** Aelana ***Latvia:*** **4** Riga ***Lebanon:*** **4** Tyre **5** Saida, Sidon **6** Beirut **7** Tripoli ***Libya:*** **6** Tobruk **7** Tripoli **8** Benghazi ***Lithuania:*** **5** Memel **8** Klaipeda ***Madagascar:*** **8** Tamatave ***Maine:*** **7** Belfast **8** Portland ***Malaysia:*** **4** Miri, Weld **5** Pekan **6** Melaka, Pinang **7** Malacca **10** George Town ***Massachusetts:*** **6** Boston **9** Fall River **10** New Bedford ***Mauritius:*** **9** Port Louis ***Mediterranean:*** **4** Gaza, Oran **5** Genoa, Haifa, Jaffa **6** Beirut, Naples, Venice **7** Algiers, Bizerte, Catania, Palermo, Piraeus, Tripoli **8** Benghazi, Port Said **9** Barcelona, Marseille **10** Alexandria, Marseilles ***Mexico:*** **7** Tampico **8** Acapulco, Mazatlán, Veracruz ***Minorca:*** **5** Mahón ***Moluccas:*** **5** Ambon ***Montenegro:*** **5** Kotor ***Morocco:*** **4** Safi, Salé **5** Ceuta **6** Agadir **7** Tangier, Tétouan **10** Casablanca ***Mozambique:*** **5** Beira, Pemba **6** Amelia, Maputo, Xai Xai **11** Porto Amelia ***New Hampshire:*** **10** Portsmouth ***New Zealand:*** **8** Auckland **10** Wellington ***Nicaragua:*** **5** Brito ***Nigeria:*** **5** Lagos **8** Harcourt ***Niger mouth:*** **5** Bonny ***North Korea:*** **4** Yuki **5** Nampo, Unggi **6** Wonsan ***Norway:*** **4** Bodo, Moss **5** Vadso **6** Bergen, Tromso **9** Stavanger, Trondheim **11** Fredrikstad ***Oman:*** **6** Masqat, Muscat **7** Salalah ***Pakistan:*** **5** Pasni **6** Gwadar **7** Karachi ***Papua New Guinea:*** **3** Lea ***Peru:*** **3** Ilo **4** Eten **5** Paita, Pisco **6** Callao ***Philippines:*** **4** Cebu **5** Davao, Laoag **6** Aparri, Cavite, Iloilo, Manila **7** Legaspi **8** Tacloban **9** Zamboanga ***Poland:*** **6** Danzig, Gdansk, Gdynia **7** Stettin **8** Szczecin ***Portugal:*** **4** Faro **5** Porto **6** Oporto **7** Funchal, Setúbal ***Puerto Rico:*** **5** Ponce **7** Arecibo, San Juan **8** Mayagüez ***Russia:*** **6** Vyborg **8** Murmansk **11** Kaliningrad, Vladivostok ***Ryukyu:*** **4** Naha, Nawa ***Sakhalin Island:*** **8** Korsakov ***Saudi Arabia:*** **5** Jedda, Jidda, Yanbu, Yenbo **6** Jeddah, Jiddah, Jubail ***Scotland:*** **3** Ayr **5** Leith, Leven **6** Dundee **7** Glasgow **8** Aberdeen ***Sicily:*** **7** Catania, Marsala, Messina, Palermo **8** Syracuse ***Slovenia:*** **5** Kopar, Koper, Piran ***Somalia:*** **7** Berbera **9** Mogadishu ***South Africa:*** **5** Natal **6** Durban **8** Cape Town ***South Carolina:*** **8** Savannah **10** Charleston ***South Korea:*** **5** Masan, Mokpo, Pusan **6** Inchon **7** Incheon, Masampo ***Spain:*** **4** Vigo **5** Cádiz, Gijón **6** Abdera, Málaga **8** Alicante **9** Algeciras, Barcelona, Cartagena, Las Palmas ***Sri Lanka:*** **7** Colombo **10** Batticaloa ***Sumatra:*** **5** Medan **6** Padang **9** Banda Aceh ***Sweden:*** **4** Umea **5** Gavle, Lulea, Malmö, Pitea, Ystad **8** Göteborg **9** Stockholm **10** Gothenburg **11** Helsingborg ***Tanzania:*** **5** Lindi, Tanga **8** Zanzibar **11** Dar es Salaam ***Thailand:*** **4** Trat **8** Bang Phra ***Tunisia:*** **4** Sfax **5** Gabès **6** Sousse **7** Bizerta, Bizerte ***Turkey:*** **4** Rize **5** Izmir, Sinop **6** Samsun, Smyrna **7** Antalya **8** Istanbul ***Ukraine:*** **5** Kerch, Yalta **6** Odessa **7** Kherson ***Vanuatu:*** **4** Vila **8** Port-Vila ***Vietnam:*** **3** Hue **6** Da Nang **7** Tourane **8** Haiphong, Nha Trang ***Virginia:*** **7** Norfolk **10** Portsmouth ***Yemen:*** **4** Aden **5** Mocha

seaport capital **4** Aden, Apia, Dili, Lomé, Suva **5** Accra, Adana, Dakar, Lagos **6** Banjul, Belize, Bissau, Dublin, Havana, Kuwait, Lisbon, Maputo, Masqat, Muscat, Roseau **7** Algiers, Batavia, Colombo, Jakarta, Moresby, San Juan **8** Castries, Djakarta, Freetown, Hamilton, Helsinki, Honolulu, Kingston, Monrovia, Valletta **9**

Mogadishu, Nuku'alofa, Porto-Novo, Reykjavík, Singapore **10** Bridgetown, Daressalem, Libreville, Mogadiscio, Paramaribo **11** Dar es Salaam, Port of Spain **12** Port-au-Prince

sear 3 dry **5** brand, parch, singe **6** burn up, scorch, sizzle **7** shrivel **9** cauterize, dehydrate, desiccate

search 4 beat, comb, grub, hunt, scan, seek **5** chase, check, delve, frisk, grope, quest, rifle, scour **6** ferret, forage, google **7** fossick, hunting, manhunt, pursuit, ransack, rummage, run down **8** finecomb, scavenge, scout out **9** cast about, ferret out **10** scrutinize

searing 3 hot **5** harsh **6** severe **7** blazing, burning, intense **8** scathing **9** agonizing, scorching **10** blistering **12** excruciating

sea robber 5 rover **6** pirate **7** corsair **8** picaroon **9** buccaneer **10** freebooter

seasickness 6 nausea **8** mal de mer

season 3 fit **4** fall, term, time, Yule **5** spice, train, treat **6** autumn, flavor, harden, pepper, period, school, spring, summer, winter **7** prepare, toughen **8** marinade, marinate **9** acclimate, Christmas **10** case-harden, discipline **11** acclimatize

seasonable 3 apt **6** timely **7** welcome **9** favorable, opportune, pertinent, well-timed **10** auspicious, convenient, propitious **11** appropriate

seasoned 6 inured, mature, tested, versed **7** adapted, matured, veteran **8** flavored, hardened **9** flavorful, practiced **10** acclimated, habituated **11** experienced **12** acclimatized, accomplished

seasoning 3 bay **4** dill, herb, mace, sage, salt **5** anise, basil, chili, clove, cumin, spice, thyme **6** cloves, fennel, garlic, ginger, nutmeg, pepper, savory **7** cayenne, chervil, mustard, oregano, paprika, parsley, saffron **8** allspice, cardamom, cinnamon, rosemary, tarragon, turmeric **9** condiment, coriander

seat 3 hub **4** base, beam, duff, rear, rest, rump **5** basis, chair, place, usher **6** behind, bottom, center, settee **7** fulcrum **8** backside, buttocks, derriere **9** fundament, posterior **10** foundation ***church:*** **3** pew ***on a camel or elephant:*** **6** howdah ***upholstered:*** **9** banquette

sea urchin 7 echinus **8** echinoid

seaweed 4 agar, alga, kelp, limu, nori, tang, ulva **5** dulse, fucus, kombu **6** fucoid, wakame **8** sargasso **9** carrageen, Irish moss **12** bladder wrack

Sea Wolf, The ***author:*** **6** London (Jack) ***captain:*** **10** Wolf Larsen ***ship:*** **5** Ghost

Sebastian ***brother:*** **6** Alonso ***sister:*** **5** Viola

secco 3 dry **8** painting, staccato

secede 4 quit **5** leave **8** separate, withdraw

seclude 4 hide **6** closet, immure, retire, screen **7** confine, enclose, isolate, shut off **8** cloister, separate, withdraw **9** sequester

secluded 6 hidden, remote **7** private, recluse, shut off **8** hermetic, isolated, screened, solitary **9** concealed, reclusive, withdrawn **10** cloistered, tucked away **11** out-of-the-way, quarantined, sequestered

seclusion 7 privacy **8** solitude **9** isolation **10** separation, withdrawal

second 4 wink **5** flash, jiffy, place, trice **6** moment **7** endorse, instant, support **9** twinkling

secondary 3 sub **6** lesser **7** derived **8** borrowed, inferior **9** resultant, tributary **10** collateral, derivative, subsequent **11** subordinate, subservient

second-class 6 common **8** déclassé, inferior, low-grade, mediocre

secondhand 4 used, worn **7** derived **8** borrowed **10** derivative

second-string 3 sub **6** backup **9** alternate **10** substitute

secrecy 7 silence, stealth **10** covertness, subterfuge **11** concealment, furtiveness

secret 5 sneak **6** arcane, closet, covert, hidden, occult **7** cryptic, furtive, obscure, subrosa **8** abstruse, backdoor, discreet, hermetic, hush-hush, stealthy **9** concealed, recondite **10** classified, restricted, undercover **11** clandestine, out-of-the-way, underhanded **12** confidential, hugger-mugger **13** surreptitious, under-the-table ***combining form:*** **5** crypt, krypt **6** crypto, krypto

secret agent 3 spy **8** emissary

secretary 4 aide, desk **5** clerk **6** scribe **9** assistant **10** amanuensis, escritoire ***king's:*** **10** chancellor

Secretary-General 3 Ban (Ki-moon), Lie (Trygve) **4** Jebb (Gladwyn) **5** Annan (Kofi), Thant (U) **8** Waldheim (Kurt) **12** Boutros-Ghali (Boutros), Hammarskjöld (Dag)

secrete 4 bury, emit, hide **5** cache, exude, plant, stash **6** screen **7** conceal, deposit, emanate

secretion 3 pus **5** mucus

secretive 7 furtive **8** reticent, taciturn **10** backstairs, buttoned-up **11** tight-lipped **12** close-mouthed **13** unforthcoming

secretly 7 sub rosa **9** furtively **10** stealthily

secret police ***East Germany:*** **5** Stasi ***Soviet Union:*** **3** KGB, MGB, MVD **4** NKVD, OGPU **5** Cheka

secret society 3 KKK **4** tong **5** cabal, Mafia, Triad **6** Mau Mau, Yakuza **7** camorra **9** camarilla, Carbonari **10** Cosa Nostra, Freemasons, Ku Klux Klan

sect 4 cult **5** creed, party **7** faction **8** division, religion **12** denomination

sectarian 5 local **8** splinter **9** dissident, heretical, heterodox, parochial **10** provincial, schismatic, unorthodox **13** nonconformist

sectary 5 rebel **7** heretic **8** adherent, disciple, follower, partisan **9** dissenter, dissident **10** schismatic, separatist **13** nonconformist, revolutionary

section 3 cut **4** area, belt, part, unit, zone **5** chunk, piece, slice, tract **6** member, moiety, parcel, region, sector, sphere **7** portion, quarter, segment **8** district, division, locality, precinct **11** subdivision

sector 4 area, zone **7** quarter, section **8** district, precinct **11** subdivision

secular 3 lay **4** laic **7** earthly, profane, worldly **8** temporal, unsacred **11** nonclerical, terrestrial **12** nonreligious

secure 3 fix, ice, tie **4** bind, fast, firm, gain, land, lock, moor, nail, safe, seal **5** catch, cinch, clamp, cover, fixed, guard, solid, sound, tried **6** anchor, assure, cement, clinch, defend, effect, ensure, fasten, insure, obtain, shield, stable **7** acquire, assured, capture, procure, protect, tie down **8** reliable, sanguine **9** confident, safeguard **10** batten down, bring about **11** established, impregnable

security 4 bail, bond, pawn **5** guard, T-note, token **6** pledge, safety, shield, surety **7** defense, earnest, warrant **8** guaranty, immunity, warranty **9** assurance, guarantee, safeguard, soundness, stability **10** collateral, protection, steadiness **13** certification

sedate 4 calm **5** grave, sober, staid **6** placid, proper, seemly, serene, steady **7** earnest, serious **8** composed, decorous, tranquil **9** collected, dignified, unruffled **10** sobersided **13** dispassionate, imperturbable

sedative 4 balm **6** downer, Valium **7** calmant, Librium, Miltown, Seconal **8** barbital, hyoscine, Nembutal **9** calmative, soporific **10** depressant **11** barbiturate **12** sleeping pill, tranquilizer **13** tranquillizer

sedentary 4 lazy **6** seated **7** alluvia, settled, sitting **8** inactive **10** stationary

sediment 4 lees, silt **5** dregs, dross **7** bottoms, deposit, grounds, heeltap, residue **8** residuum **9** settlings **11** precipitate ***layer:*** **5** varve

sedition 4 coup **6** mutiny, putsch, revolt, strike **7** protest, treason **8** intrigue, uprising **9** coup d'état, rebellion **10** revolution **12** insurrection

seditious 8 disloyal, factious, mutinous **9** dissident, insurgent **10** rebellious, traitorous **11** treacherous

seduce 4 bait, coax, lure **5** decoy, tempt **6** allure, betray, delude, entice, entrap, lead on, ravish **7** corrupt, debauch, deceive **8** entrance, inveigle

seducer 4 rake, roué, vamp **7** Don Juan, playboy **8** Casanova, lothario **9** libertine, womanizer **11** philanderer

seduction 4 lure **8** conquest **9** siren song **10** allurement, attraction, ravishment, temptation

seductive 5 siren **8** alluring, magnetic, tempting **9** beguiling **10** attractive, bewitching, enchanting **11** captivating

seductress 5 siren **7** Lorelei **9** temptress **11** femme fatale

sedulous 8 diligent, tireless **9** assiduous, laborious **10** persistent **11** industrious, persevering, unremitting

see 4 call, espy, gaze, look, mark, peer, scan, view **5** sight, watch **6** behold, descry, divine, notice, take in **7** discern, find out, glimpse, make out, observe, realize **8** consider, envisage, envision, perceive **9** apprehend, ascertain, recognize, visualize

seed 3 pip, sow **4** core, germ **5** brood, grain, issue, ovule, plant, spark, spawn, spore **6** embryo, kernel, notion **7** concept, nucleus, progeny **8** children **9** offspring **11** descendants ***aromatic:*** **5** anise **6** fennel ***coating:*** **5** testa **6** testae (plural) ***covering:*** **4** aril ***of a bean:*** **7** haricot ***of a vine:*** **6** peanut ***poisonous:*** **10** castor bean ***poppy:*** **3** maw ***scar:*** **5** hilum ***small:*** **3** pip ***vessel:*** **3** pod **5** fruit, pyxis **7** silicle, silique

seedcase 3 pod **4** aril

seedy 5 dingy, faded, mangy, ratty, tired **6** droopy, frowsy, frowzy, shabby, used up, wilted **7** run-down, scruffy, squalid, unkempt, wilting **8** decaying, decrepit, drooping, flagging, inferior, slovenly, tattered **9** neglected, overgrown **10** bedraggled, down-at-heel, threadbare **12** disreputable

seek 3 try **4** fish, hunt, root **5** assay, delve, essay, offer, quest, sniff **6** pursue, strive **7** attempt, inquire, look for, request **8** endeavor, smell out **9** search for, search out, undertake

seem 3 act **4** look **5** imply **6** appear, behave **7** suggest **8** resemble

seemly 3 fit **6** decent, proper, suited **7** apropos, correct, fitting **8** becoming, decorous, suitable **9** befitting, congenial, congruous **10** compatible, conforming **11** appropriate, comme il faut

seep 4 drip, leak, ooze, weep **5** bleed, exude,

leech, sweat **6** filter, strain **7** diffuse, dribble, trickle **8** transude **9** percolate

seer 5 augur, sibyl **6** oracle **7** diviner, prophet **8** foreseer, haruspex **9** predictor **10** forecaster, foreteller, soothsayer **11** clairvoyant, Nostradamus, vaticinator **13** fortune-teller

seesaw 3 yaw **4** rock, veer **5** lurch, pitch, swing **6** teeter **7** bascule **8** flip-flop **9** alternate, fluctuate, oscillate **11** teeterboard **12** teeter-totter

seethe 3 sop **4** boil, burn, foam, fret, fume, rage, soak, stew **5** churn, erupt, froth, souse, steam, steep **6** bubble, drench, simmer, sizzle **7** bristle, ferment, parboil, smolder **8** saturate, smoulder, waterlog

see-through 5 clear **6** limpid **8** pellucid **11** translucent, transparent

segment 3 bit, cut, lap, leg **4** clip, part **5** phase, piece **6** divide, member, moiety **7** portion, section **8** division, fragment, separate **10** categorize

sego 4 lily

segregate 6 enisle, select **7** isolate **8** separate **9** sequester **10** disconnect

segregation 9 apartheid, isolation **10** jim crowism, separatism **13** ghettoization

segue 7 proceed **8** continue **10** transition **11** progression

seidel 5 stoup **8** schooner

seine 3 net **5** trawl

Seine tributary 4 Oise **5** Marne, Yonne

seismologist 7 Richter (Charles)

seize 3 bag, nab **4** glom, grab, take **5** annex, catch, clasp, grasp, usurp **6** abduct, arrest, clinch, clutch, kidnap, occupy, secure, snatch **7** capture, grapple, impound **8** arrogate, carry off **9** apprehend, sequester **10** commandeer, confiscate **11** appropriate, expropriate

seizure 3 fit **4** turn **5** spasm, spell, throe **6** access, attack, taking **7** capture **8** paroxysm, takeover **9** breakdown **10** annexation, convulsion, usurpation **12** confiscation

seldom 6 hardly, rarely **8** scarcely **10** hardly ever **12** infrequently, occasionally, sporadically

select 4 best, cull, fine, pick, rare **5** A-list, cream, elite, prime **6** choice, choose, chosen, culled, opt for, picked **7** favored, pick out **8** screened, superior **9** exclusive, exquisite, preferred, recherché, single out

selection 6 choice **7** culling, excerpt, picking **8** choosing **10** assortment, preference

selective 5 fussy, picky **6** choosy **7** choosey, finicky **8** specific **10** discerning, particular, scrupulous **11** persnickety

Selene 4 Luna **6** Hecate **7** Artemis ***beloved:*** **8** Endymion ***brother:*** **6** Helios ***father:*** **8** Hyperion ***mother:*** **4** Thea ***sister:*** **3** Eos

selenium symbol 2 Se

self 3 ego ***combining form:*** **3** aut **4** auto

self-absorbed 4 smug **8** egoistic **9** conceited, egotistic **10** complacent, egocentric **11** egotistical, introverted **12** narcissistic **13** inner-directed

self-acting 9 automatic

self-assertive 4 bold **5** brash, pushy **6** cheeky **7** forward **8** cocksure, militant **9** audacious, obtrusive, officious **10** aggressive **11** impertinent, overweening **12** presumptuous

self-assurance 5 poise **6** aplomb **8** coolness **9** composure, sangfroid **10** confidence, equanimity **13** collectedness

self-assured 4 smug **6** poised **8** sanguine **9** confident

self-centered 9 conceited, egotistic **10** egocentric **11** egotistical **12** narcissistic

self-composed 4 calm **6** poised, serene **7** assured **9** collected, confident, possessed **10** controlled

self-confidence 5 poise **6** aplomb **9** assurance

self-confident 5 cocky **6** jaunty, poised **7** assured **8** sanguine

self-conscious 4 prim **5** stiff **6** formal, uneasy **7** awkward, stilted, studied **8** affected, mannered **9** contrived, ill at ease **10** artificial

self-contained 6 closed, formal **7** built-in **8** composed, enclosed, reserved, reticent **9** exclusive **10** restrained **11** independent

self-control 7 balance, dignity, reserve **9** restraint, stability, willpower **10** abstinence, constraint, discipline, temperance **11** forbearance

self-defense art 4 judo **6** aikido, karate, kung fu **7** jujitsu **9** tai kwan do

self-destruction 7 seppuku, suicide **8** felo-de-se, hara-kiri, hari-kari

self-discipline 4 will **8** stoicism **9** willpower **10** abstinence

self-educated 12 autodidactic

self-effacing 3 shy **5** timid **6** modest **7** bashful **8** retiring, sheepish **9** diffident, unassured **11** unassertive

self-esteem 5 pride **6** vanity **7** conceit, dignity, egotism **10** narcissism **11** amour propre

self-evident 5 clear, plain **6** patent **7** obvious **8** manifest, palpable **10** prima facie, undeniable **12** demonstrable, unmistakable ***truth:*** **5** axiom

self-explanatory 5 clear, plain **7** evident, ob-

vious **8** manifest **11** perspicuous, transparent
self-governing 7 popular **9** sovereign **10** autonomous, democratic
self-importance 3 ego **5** pride **6** egoism, hubris **7** conceit, egotism **9** arrogance, pomposity, vainglory
self-important 4 smug, vain **6** lordly **7** bloated, haughty, pompous **8** arrogant **9** conceited, egotistic **10** pontifical **11** magisterial, pretentious
self-indulgent 9 libertine, sybaritic **10** hedonistic
self-interest 6 egoism
selfish 6 stingy **8** egoistic **9** egotistic **10** egocentric, ungenerous **11** egomaniacal **12** self-centered **13** self-indulgent
selfless 8 generous **10** altruistic, benevolent, charitable
self-love 6 egoism, vanity **7** conceit, egotism **8** vainness **9** vainglory **10** narcissism **11** amour propre **13** conceitedness
self-possessed 4 calm **6** poised, serene **7** equable **8** composed, sanguine **9** collected, unruffled **11** unflappable **13** imperturbable
self-proclaimed 8 so-called **9** soi-disant **10** self-styled
Self-Reliance author 7 Emerson (Ralph Waldo)
self-respect 5 pride **7** dignity **11** amour propre
self-restraint 8 chastity, sobriety **9** willpower **10** abnegation, abstention, abstinence, continence, discipline **11** forbearance
self-righteous 5 pious **7** canting, preachy **8** unctuous **9** pharisaic **10** complacent, goody-goody **11** pharisaical **12** hypocritical, pecksniffian **13** sanctimonious
self-sacrificing 8 generous, selfless **9** unselfish
self-satisfied 4 smug **8** priggish **10** complacent
self-seeking 6 greedy **7** selfish **8** egoistic **9** egotistic **10** egocentric **11** egotistical
self-serving see **self-seeking**
self-starter 7 hustler **8** go-getter
self-styled 7 nominal, would-be **8** so-called **9** soi-disant
self-taught 12 autodidactic
sell 4 hawk, vend **5** trade **6** barter, deal in, hustle, market, peddle, retail, unload **7** auction **8** exchange
sell out 4 dump, move **6** betray, turn in, unload **7** deceive **8** inform on **11** double-cross
selvage, selvedge 3 hem **4** edge **6** border
semblance 3 air **4** face, look, mask, pose, show, veil **5** front, guise, image **6** aspect, facade, simile, veneer **7** analogy, feeling, modicum **8** affinity, disguise, likeness, pretense **10** apparition, appearance, comparison, false front, masquerade, similarity, similitude, simulacrum **11** countenance
Semele *father:* 6 Cadmus ***mother:* 8** Harmonia ***sister:* 3** Ino **5** Agave **7** Autonoë ***son:* 7** Bacchus **8** Dionysus
semi 3 rig **4** demi, half, hemi **5** truck **6** partly
seminar 5 forum **8** colloquy **10** colloquium, conference, roundtable
Seminole chief 7 Osceola
Semiramis *husband:* 5 Ninus ***kingdom:* 7** Babylon
Semite 3 Jew **4** Arab **6** Hebrew **7** Moabite **8** Akkadian, Assyrian **9** Canaanite **10** Babylonian, Phoenician
Senapo *daughter:* 8 Clorinda ***kingdom:* 8** Ethiopia
senate 7 chamber, council **8** assembly **11** legislature
senator 5 solon **8** lawmaker **10** legislator
send 4 mail, post, ship **5** relay, remit, route **6** commit, export, launch **7** address, advance, airmail, consign, forward, traject **8** dispatch, transmit ***back:* 6** remand
Sendak book 17 In the Night Kitchen **21** Where the Wild Things Are
send in 6 submit
send-up 5 roast, spoof **6** parody, satire **7** lampoon, takeoff **9** burlesque **10** caricature, pasquinade
Senegal *capital:* 5 Dakar ***enclave:* 6** Gambia ***ethnic group:* 5** Wolof **6** Fulani **7** Malinke ***language:* 6** French ***monetary unit:* 5** franc ***neighbor:* 4** Mali **6** Guinea **10** Mauritania **12** Guinea-Bissau ***river:* 6** Gambia
senescence 6 old age **8** caducity **11** elderliness, senectitude
senility 6 dotage
senior 5 doyen, elder, older, prior **7** ancient, doyenne, oldster **8** higher-up, old-timer, superior **10** golden-ager
Sennacherib *domain:* 7 Assyria ***father:* 6** Sargon ***kingdom:* 7** Assyria ***slayer, son:* 8** Sharezer **11** Adrammelech
sensation 4 bomb **5** éclat **6** marvel, tingle, wonder **7** feeling, miracle, prodigy, stunner **8** response **9** bombshell **10** impression, perception, phenomenon **13** consciousness
sensational 3 hot **5** boffo, juicy, lurid **6** purple, vulgar **7** tabloid **8** dramatic, exciting, fabulous, glorious, slambang, smashing, stunning **9** hunky-dory, marvelous, thrilling **10** astounding, impressive, incredible, remarkable, scandalous **11** astonishing, ex-

travagant, outstanding, spectacular **12** electrifying
sense 3 wit **4** feel **5** sight, smell, taste, touch **6** divine, intuit, pick up **7** believe, discern, feeling, hearing, meaning, message, realize **8** consider, judgment, perceive, prudence **9** awareness, foresight, intuition **10** anticipate, cognizance, discretion, perception **12** intelligence, significance **13** comprehension, consciousness, understanding ***sixth:* 3** ESP
Sense and Sensibility author 6 Austen (Jane)
senseless 4 cold, numb **5** silly **6** absurd, numbed, simple, stupid **7** fatuous, foolish, idiotic, moronic, trivial, witless **8** benumbed, comatose, deadened, mindless **9** brainless, pointless **10** irrational **11** meaningless, purposeless, unconscious
senselessness 5 folly **7** inanity **8** insanity **9** absurdity, stupidity **12** illogicality
sense organ 3 ear, eye **4** nose, skin **6** tongue **8** receptor
sensibility 5 taste **7** emotion, feeling, insight **8** judgment, keenness **9** affection, awareness, sensation **11** discernment, penetration **12** appreciation
sensible 4 sage, sane, wise **5** solid, sound **6** astute, shrewd **7** logical, prudent, sapient **8** rational **9** judicious, objective, sagacious **10** reasonable
sensitive 4 keen, sore **5** aware, prone **6** liable, tender, touchy, tricky **7** feeling, nervous **8** delicate, sensible, sentient, ticklish **9** emotional **10** high-strung, perceptive, precarious, responsive **11** susceptible **13** understanding
sensitive plant 6 mimosa ***family:* 3** pea
sensual 4 lush **6** animal, carnal, earthy **7** fleshly, mundane, worldly **8** temporal **9** epicurean, luxurious, sybaritic **10** hedonistic, voluptuous **11** irreligious, unspiritual
sensuality 4 lust **6** desire, luxury **7** lechery, license **8** hedonism, lewdness, pleasure **9** carnality, depravity, eroticism, prurience **10** debauchery, degeneracy, immorality, indulgence, perversion, profligacy, sybaritism **11** dissipation **13** dissoluteness, gratification, salaciousness
sensuous 4 lush **6** carnal **7** fleshly **8** luscious **9** epicurean, luxurious, sybaritic **10** hedonistic, voluptuous **13** self-indulgent
sentence 3 rap **4** damn, doom **5** blame, judge **6** dictum, ordain, punish **7** adjudge, condemn, convict, verdict **8** decision, denounce, judgment, penalize **10** adjudicate, punishment
sententious 5 crisp, pithy, terse **7** concise, piquant, pointed **8** eloquent, pregnant, succinct **10** aphoristic, expressive, meaningful, moralistic, moralizing
sentient 5 alert, aware, savvy **7** knowing **8** sensible **9** attentive, cognizant, conscious, receptive, sensitive **10** conversant, discerning, perceptive, percipient, responsive **12** appreciative
sentiment 4 view **5** ethos **6** belief **7** emotion, feeling, leaning, opinion, passion, posture **8** penchant, position, tendency **9** affection, inclining, sensation **10** conception, conviction, partiality, persuasion, propensity **11** disposition, inclination, sensibility
sentimental 4 soft **5** corny, gooey, gushy, mushy, sappy, soupy, sweet **6** dreamy, drippy, slushy, sticky, sugary, syrupy, tender **7** cloying, gushing, insipid, maudlin, mawkish **8** bathetic, effusive, romantic **9** misty-eyed, nostalgic, schmaltzy **10** idealistic, lovey-dovey, moonstruck, namby-pamby, saccharine, soft-boiled **11** tear-jerking **12** affectionate
sentimentality 4 mush **8** schmaltz
sentinel see **sentry**
sentry 5 guard, watch **6** picket **7** lookout **8** sentinel, watchman
separate 4 comb, only, part, sift, sole, sort **5** apart, sever, split **6** cut off, detach, divide, single, unique **7** asunder, diverse, divided, divorce, isolate, several, split up, unravel, various **8** alienate, detached, discrete, disjoint, distinct, insulate, isolated, solitary, splinter, uncouple **9** different, divergent, extricate, segregate **11** compartment, distinctive, distinguish, independent, unconnected **12** disconnected, discriminate **13** differentiate
separation 3 gap **4** rift **5** break, split **6** schism **7** breakup, divorce, parting, rupture, split-up **8** disunion, disunity, division **9** apartheid, dichotomy, partition **11** disjunction, dissolution, segregation **12** dissociation, estrangement **13** disconnection, sequestration
separatism 9 apartheid **11** segregation
separatist 10 schismatic **12** secessionist
sepia 3 ink **5** brown, umber **6** sienna
sepulchral 4 grim **5** bleak, grave **6** dismal, gloomy, solemn, somber **7** doleful, macabre **8** funereal, ghoulish, mortuary **9** tenebrous
sepulchre 4 tomb **5** grave, vault **9** mausoleum
sequel 3 end **5** close **6** effect, ending, finish, result, upshot **7** closing, outcome **8** epilogue **9** aftermath **10** succession **11** aftereffect, consequence, development,

eventuality, progression, termination **12** continuation

sequence 3 row, run, set **4** flow **5** chain, order, train **6** course, series, string **8** disposal, ordering **9** placement **10** procession, succession **11** arrangement, disposition, progression **12** distribution

sequential 6 serial **9** succedent **10** continuous, succeeding, successive **11** consecutive **12** successional **13** chronological

sequester 4 hide, take **5** annex, seize **6** attach, cut off, enisle **7** impound, isolate, preempt, seclude, secrete **8** accroach, arrogate, cloister, close off, insulate, separate, set apart, withdraw **9** segregate **10** commandeer, confiscate, dispossess **11** appropriate, expropriate

sequoia 7 big tree, redwood **12** coast redwood

seraglio 5 harem

serape 5 shawl

seraph 5 angel **8** guardian **9** messenger

seraphic 4 pure **7** angelic, sublime **8** beatific, cherubic, ethereal

Serbia ***capital:*** **8** Belgrade ***city:*** **3** Bar, Niš **7** Novi Sad, Pancevo **10** Kragujevac ***former leader:*** **9** Miloševi⊠ (Slobodan) ***monetary unit:*** **4** euro **5** dinar ***neighbor:*** **6** Bosnia, Kosovo **7** Albania, Croatia, Hungary, Romania **8** Bulgaria **9** Macedonia **10** Montenegro ***part of:*** **7** Balkans ***peninsula:*** **6** Balkan ***province:*** **9** Vojvodina ***province, former:*** **6** Kosovo ***river:*** **4** Sava **6** Danube ***sea:*** **8** Adriatic

sere 3 dry **4** arid **5** dried **7** parched, thirsty **8** withered **9** shriveled, unwatered

serenade 7 lullaby **8** shivaree **9** charivari

serene 4 calm **5** quiet, still **6** limpid, placid, poised, sedate **7** halcyon **8** composed, tranquil **9** unruffled **10** untroubled

serenity 4 calm **5** peace **8** calmness, quietude **9** composure, placidity, stillness **10** equanimity **11** contentment, tranquility **12** peacefulness, tranquillity

serf 4 esne, peon **5** churl, helot, slave **6** thrall **7** bondman, villein ***freeborn:*** **7** colonus

sergeant 3 NCO **6** noncom

serial 4 soap **10** sequential, successive **11** consecutive, installment

series 3 row, run, set **4** list, tier **5** chain, range, scale, train **6** catena, column, parade, sequel, string **8** sequence **9** cavalcade, gradation **10** procession, succession **11** progression **12** continuation

serious 4 grim, hard **5** grave, heavy, major, sober, staid, stern, tough **6** intent, sedate, severe, solemn, somber, sombre, steady **7** austere, earnest, intense, pensive, sincere, unfunny, weighty **8** funereal, menacing, resolute, sobering **9** difficult, humorless, important, laborious, strenuous, unamusing **10** determined, formidable, meditative, no-nonsense, poker-faced, purposeful, reflective, sobersided, thoughtful, unhumorous **11** significant, threatening **12** businesslike **13** contemplative

sermon 6 homily, speech, tirade **7** address, lecture, oration **8** harangue **9** preaching **10** preachment **11** exhortation

sermonize 5 orate **6** dilate, exhort, preach **7** dissert, lecture **8** moralize **9** discourse, expatiate, preachify **10** dissertate, evangelize **11** pontificate

serpent 5 fiend, Satan, snake ***fabled:*** **8** basilisk ***mythical:*** **10** cockatrice ***sound:*** **4** hiss

serpentine 4 rock, wily **5** snaky **6** snakey **7** cunning, devious, mineral, sinuous, winding **8** flexuous, tempting, tortuous **9** snakelike **10** circuitous, convoluted, meandering

serrated 7 notched, toothed **8** saw-edged, sawtooth **10** saw-toothed **11** denticulate

servant 4 maid, peon **5** slave, valet **6** butler, flunky, helper, lackey, menial **7** famulus, footman **8** domestic, handmaid, hireling, houseboy **9** attendant **11** chamberlain, chambermaid ***India:*** **4** syce ***kitchen:*** **8** scullion ***Wodehouse:*** **6** Jeeves

serve 3 act, fit, use **4** help, make, play, suit, work **5** avail, nurse, spend, treat **6** foster, handle, wait on **7** advance, benefit, care for, present, promote, provide, satisfy, suffice, work for **8** deal with, function **9** encourage, officiate **10** minister to

service 3 use **4** duty, help, rite **5** favor **6** employ, repair, ritual **7** account, benefit, fitness, liturgy **8** ceremony, courtesy, disposal, maintain **10** active duty, assistance, ceremonial, observance, usefulness **11** maintenance **12** dispensation

serviceable 5 handy, utile **6** decent, usable, useful **7** durable, helpful **8** adequate, suitable **9** efficient, practical **10** acceptable, beneficial, convenient, dependable, functional **11** utilitarian **12** satisfactory

servile 6 abject, craven, humble, menial **7** fawning, slavish **8** obedient, obeisant **9** groveling **10** obsequious, submissive **11** subservient

servility 7 bondage, helotry, peonage, serfdom, slavery **9** thralldom **11** enslavement

serving 6 dollop **7** helping, portion

servitude 5 labor **6** corvée, thrall **7** bondage, helotry, peonage, serfdom, slavery **9** captivity, indenture, thralldom, villenage **10** subjection **11** enslavement **12** enthrallment

sesame 3 til **4** teel ***grass:*** **4** gama ***seed paste:*** **6** tahini

Sesame Street *human character:* 3 Bob, Tom **4** Alan, Gabi, Luis **5** David, Linda, Maria, Miles, Susan **6** Gordon, Savion **8** Mr. Hooper (Harold) ***Muppet:*** **3** Zoe **4** Abby, Bert, Biff, Elmo **5** Count (The), Ernie, Oscar, Sully, Telly **6** Fluffy, Grover, Kermit, Rosita, Slimey, Snuffy **7** Barkley, Big Bird **9** Guy Smiley, Miss Piggy **13** Cookie Monster, Count von Count ***puppeteer:*** **6** Henson (Jim)

sessile 5 fixed **6** rooted **7** settled **8** attached **11** established

session 6 assize, séance **7** meeting, sitting

set 3 aim, dry, fix, gel, lay, lot, put **4** firm, jell **5** array, batch, bunch, fixed, group, place, put on, ready, rigid, scene **6** belong, harden, impose, placed, rooted, secure, stated **7** arrange, certain, cluster, congeal, decided, deposit, dictate, jellify, lay down, located, prepare, scenery, situate, specify, station **8** prepared, resolute, resolved, situated, solidify, specific **9** confirmed, designate, establish, prescribe, specified, stipulate, tenacious **10** assortment, determined, gelatinize, inflexible, positioned, prescribed, stipulated **11** established, mise-en-scène ***a gem:*** **6** collet ***right:*** **7** redress

set aside 4 void **5** annul **7** discard, dismiss, reserve **8** overrule

set back 4 mire **5** delay **6** detain, hang up, hinder, retard, slow up

setback 4 snag **5** check, hitch **6** defeat, glitch, holdup, rebuff **7** reverse **8** obstacle, reversal **9** hindrance **10** impediment, regression

set down 4 land **5** light, perch, roost **6** alight, record **9** establish, touch down

set fire to 4 burn **5** light, spark **6** ignite, kindle **7** emblaze, inflame **8** enkindle, touch off

set forth 4 cite **5** state **6** adduce, affirm, allege, avouch, depart, embark, launch, submit **7** advance, declare, express, present, proffer, propose, take off **8** proclaim, spell out **9** introduce **10** account for

set free 5 loose **6** redeem, rescue, unbind **7** deliver, manumit, unchain, unloose **8** liberate, unloosen **9** unshackle **10** emancipate

Seth *brother:* 4 Abel, Cain ***father:*** **4** Adam ***mother:*** **3** Eve ***son:*** **4** Enos

set out 5 start **6** embark, intend **7** take off **9** undertake

Set *brother:* 6 Osiris ***mother:*** **3** Nut ***opponent:*** **5** Horus ***victim:*** **6** Osiris

settee 4 seat, sofa **5** bench, divan **6** lounge

setting 5 scene **7** context, scenery **8** ambience **10** background **11** mise-en-scène ***for a stone:*** **4** ouch

settle 3 fix, lay, pay, put **4** calm, sink **5** allay, judge, light, pay up, perch, place, quiet, roost, still **6** alight, clinch, decide, soothe, square, verify, wind up **7** arrange, clarify, compose, confirm, dispose, install, mediate, resolve, satisfy, work out **8** colonize, conclude, ensconce, nail down **9** determine, discharge, establish, negotiate, reconcile, touch down

settlement 4 deal, mise **6** colony, hamlet **7** outpost, quietus, village **8** decision **9** agreement **10** conclusion, encampment, habitation, resolution **11** arrangement **13** determination ***Israeli:*** **6** moshav

settler 7 pioneer **8** colonist, squatter **9** colonizer

set-to 3 row **4** fray, spat **5** brawl, broil, brush, fight, run-in, scrap **6** affray, blowup, fracas, tussle **7** dispute, quarrel, rhubarb, scuffle **8** argument, skirmish **9** encounter **10** falling-out **11** altercation

set up 4 open **5** erect, found, raise, start **6** create, launch **7** arrange, install **8** assemble, generate, initiate, organize **9** construct, establish, institute, originate

setup 4 plan, trap **5** array, trick **6** layout, scheme, shoo-in **7** pattern, project, setting **8** assembly, carriage, position, slam dunk **9** alignment, apparatus, structure, sure thing **11** arrangement, preparation **12** constitution

Seuss, Dr. 6 Geisel (Theodore) ***character:*** **6** Grinch, Horton, Sam-I-Am, Yertle ***work:*** **11** Cat in the Hat (The) **15** Green Eggs and Ham, Horton Hears a Who, Yertle the Turtle

seven *combining form:* 4 hept, sept **5** hepta, septi ***group of:*** **6** heptad **8** hebdomad

seventeenth century 8 seicento

sever 3 cut, lop **4** part, rend **5** slice, split **6** cleave, cut off, detach, divide, lop off, sunder **7** break up, divorce **8** amputate, disjoint, separate

several 4 a few, many, some **6** divers, plural, sundry, varied **7** certain, diverse, various **8** assorted, discrete, distinct, manifold, numerous, separate, specific **9** different **10** respective

severe 4 dour, grim, hard **5** acute, grave, harsh, heavy, rigid, sober, stern, tough **6** bitter, brutal, rugged, strict **7** arduous, ascetic, austere, extreme, intense, onerous,

serious, weighty **8** exacting, pitiless, rigorous **9** demanding, difficult, laborious, strenuous, stringent, unbending **10** forbidding, implacable, inflexible, iron-willed, oppressive, unyielding **11** disciplined, heavy-handed
severity 5 rigor **7** gravity, urgency **8** exigency, grimness, obduracy, rigidity **9** austerity, harshness, intensity, plainness, privation, restraint, spareness, starkness, sternness **10** strictness, stringency **11** seriousness
sew 4 darn, mend, seam **5** baste **6** needle, stitch, suture
Seward's Folly 6 Alaska
sewer 4 duct **5** ditch, drain **6** tailor **7** cesspit, conduit **8** cesspool, stitcher
sewing *aid:* 7 thimble ***case:* 4** etui ***kit:* 9** housewife
sewing-machine inventor 4 Howe (Elias)
sew up 3 ice **4** darn, mend, seal **5** patch **6** clinch, decide, ensure, secure, settle, stitch, tailor **7** confirm **8** complete, conclude, finalize, nail down **9** determine
sexless 6 neuter **7** epicene **8** neutered
sex manual 9 Kama-sutra
sexton 6 deacon **9** custodian, sacristan
sexual 4 blue, lewd, racy **6** carnal, erotic, ribald, risqué, smutty **7** obscene **8** venereal **9** salacious **12** pornographic
sexual desire 4 eros, lust **6** libido
sexy 4 blue, racy **5** bawdy, spicy **6** erotic, purple, ribald, risqué, steamy, sultry **7** naughty **8** alluring, off-color, sensuous **9** appealing, salacious, seductive **10** attractive, suggestive
Seychelles *capital:* 8 Victoria ***island:* 4** Mahé **7** La Digue, Praslin ***language:* 6** Creole, French ***monetary unit:* 5** rupee
Sganarelle *brother:* 6 Ariste ***daughter:* 7** Lucinde ***ward:* 7** Leonore **8** Isabelle ***wife:* 7** Martine
shabby 5 dingy, dowdy, faded, mangy, ratty, seedy, sorry, tacky, tatty, tired **6** frayed, scurvy, shoddy, sleazy, sordid **7** outworn, rickety, run-down, scrubby, scruffy, squalid, worn-out **8** beggarly, decaying, decrepit, dog-eared, tattered **9** miserable, motheaten, neglected, worm-eaten **10** bedraggled, down-at-heel, ramshackle, threadbare **11** dilapidated **12** deteriorated, disreputable **13** deteriorating, unrespectable
shack 3 cot, hut **4** camp, shed **5** cabin, hovel, lodge **6** shanty **7** cottage
shackle 4 gyve **5** bilbo, chain, leash, strap **6** fetter, hobble, hog-tie, impede, pinion, secure **7** enchain, leg-iron, manacle, trammel **8** handcuff **9** entrammel
shad 7 clupeid, herring
shade 3 bit, hue, tad **4** cast, tint, tone, veil **5** ghost, tinge, trace, umbra **6** awning, darken, nuance, screen **7** dimness, eclipse, phantom, shelter, specter, spectre, umbrage **8** darkness, penumbra, phantasm, tincture **9** gradation, intensity, obscurity **10** apparition **11** distinction
shadow 3 dim, dog, tag **4** haze, hint, tail **5** cloud, shade, tinge, touch, trace, trail, umbra **6** screen, spirit, wraith **7** eidolon, obscure, phantom, specter, umbrage, vestige **8** overcast, penumbra, phantasm, revenant, tincture **9** inumbrate, overcloud, suspicion **10** apparition, intimation, suggestion **11** adumbration
shadowy 3 dim **4** dark **5** dusky, faint, murky, vague **6** gloomy, shaded **7** ghostly, obscure **9** tenebrous **10** indistinct
shady 4 dark **5** bosky, dusky, fishy **6** purple, shabby, shoddy **7** clouded, dubious, suspect **8** doubtful, screened **9** equivocal, sheltered, uncertain **10** suggestive, suspicious, umbrageous, unreliable **12** disreputable
Shaffer play 5 Equus **7** Amadeus
shaft 3 jab, ray, rod **4** axle, barb, beam, dart, pole, stem **5** arrow, lance, shoot, spear, stalk, thill **6** thrust **7** chimney, spindle **8** short end
shag 3 nap, rug **4** pile **5** chase, fetch **7** thicket, tobacco **9** cormorant
shaggy 5 bushy **7** unkempt **8** uncombed
shake 3 jar, jog, rid **4** deal, jerk, jolt, lose, rock, roil, sway **5** avoid, churn, daunt, elude, jiffy, quake, shock, waver, worry **6** escape, frappe, jiggle, joggle, quaver, quiver, shimmy, shiver, tremor **7** agitate, shingle, shudder, temblor, tremble, unnerve, vibrate **8** brandish, convulse, unsettle **9** palpitate **10** earthquake
shake down 5 frisk, gouge, screw, wrest, wring **6** coerce, extort, fleece, search **7** squeeze **9** blackmail
shakedown 3 bed **4** test **5** dance, trial **6** pallet, search, tryout **7** pursuit, testing **8** exaction **9** blackmail, extortion **10** inspection
Shaker leader 3 Lee (Ann) **9** Mother Ann
Shakespearean actor 4 Kean (Edmund) **5** Booth (Edwin), Dench (Judi), Evans (Maurice), Terry (Ellen) **6** Irving (Henry), Jacobi (Derek) **7** Branagh (Kenneth), Burbage (Richard), Garrick (David), Gielgud (John), Olivier (Laurence), Siddons (Sarah) **8** Ashcroft (Peggy), Macready (William), McKellen (Ian), Redgrave (Michael), Scofield

(Paul) **9** Barrymore (Ethel, John, Lionel, Maurice) **10** Richardson (Ralph)

Shakespeare, William 4 bard ***character:* 3** Hal **4** Doll (Tearsheet), Hero, Iago, Kent, Lear, Puck **5** Ariel, Edgar, Feste, Harry, Percy (Henry), Poins (Ned), Regan, Romeo, Timon, Titus (Andronicus), Viola **6** Antony, Banquo, Bottom, Brutus, Caesar, Cassio, Duncan, Edmund, Emilia, Fabian, Hamlet, Hecate, Hermia, Jaques, Juliet, Oberon, Olivia, Orsino, Pistol, Portia **7** Antonio, Caliban, Cassius, Claudio, Fleance, Goneril, Horatio, Hotspur, Jessica, Laertes, Lavinia, Macbeth, Macduff, Malcolm, Miranda, Ophelia, Orlando, Othello, Perdita, Shylock, Sir Toby (Belch), Theseus, Titania, Troilus **8** Bassanio, Beatrice, Benedick, Claudius, Cordelia, Cressida, Dogberry, Falstaff (Sir John), Gertrude, Hermione, Lysander, Malvolio, Mercutio, Mortimer, Pericles, Polonius, Prospero, Rosalind **9** Cleopatra, Cymbeline, Demetrius, Desdemona, Hippolyta, Katherine, Petruchio, Sir Andrew (Aguecheek), Vincentio **10** Fortinbras, Holofernes **11** Bolingbroke, John of Gaunt, Lady Macbeth, Lady Macduff, Peter Quince **13** Queen Gertrude, Queen Margaret ***contemporary:* 6** Jonson (Ben) **7** Marlowe (Christopher) ***forest:* 5** Arden ***mother:* 9** Mary Arden ***play:* 6** Hamlet, Henry V **7** Henry IV, Henry VI, Macbeth, Othello, Tempest (The) **8** King John, King Lear, Pericles **9** Cymbeline, Henry VIII, Richard II **10** Coriolanus, Richard III **11** As You Like It, Winter's Tale (The) **12** Julius Caesar, Twelfth Night **13** Timon of Athens **14** Comedy of Errors (The), Romeo and Juliet **16** Love's Labour's Lost, Merchant of Venice (The), Taming of the Shrew (The) **17** Measure for Measure **18** Antony and Cleopatra **19** Much Ado About Nothing **20** All's Well That Ends Well, Midsummer Night's Dream (A) ***theater:* 5** Globe ***wife:* 12** Anne Hathaway

shaky 4 weak **6** infirm, unsure, wobbly **7** aquiver, dubious, jittery, quaking, rackety, rickety, suspect, trembly, unsound **8** doubtful, insecure, rachitic, unstable, unsteady, wavering **9** quivering, tottering, trembling, tremulous, uncertain, unsettled **10** indecisive, precarious, rattletrap, unreliable **11** problematic, vacillating

shale 4 rock **5** slate

shallot 4 herb **5** onion **10** green onion

shallow 4 idle, vain **5** petty, shoal **7** cursory, sketchy, trivial **8** trifling **9** depthless, frivolous **11** perfunctory, superficial

shallows 6 lagoon, shoals

Shallum *father:* 5 Shaul, Zadok **6** Jabesh, Josiah, Sismai, Tikvah **8** Colhozeh, Naphtali **9** Hallohesh ***mother:* 6** Bilhah ***nephew:* 8** Jeremiah ***slayer:* 7** Menahem ***son:* 6** Mibsam **7** Hilkiah **8** Maaseiah ***victim:* 9** Zechariah

shalom 5 peace

sham 3 act, ape **4** fake, hoax, mock **5** bluff, bogus, bunco, cheat, dummy, false, farce, feign, fraud, phony, pseud, put on, spoof **6** deceit, ersatz, facade, fakery, forged, invent, pseudo **7** assumed, feigned, forgery, imitate, mislead, mockery, pretend **8** affected, flimflam, simulate, spurious, travesty **9** brummagem, burlesque, deception, hypocrisy, imitation, imposture, pinchbeck, simulated **10** artificial, caricature, false front, fictitious, fraudulent, sanctimony, substitute **11** counterfeit, make-believe **12** pecksniffery ***combining form:* 5** pseud **6** pseudo

shaman 6 healer, priest, wizard **7** diviner **8** conjurer, conjuror, magician, sorcerer **9** enchanter, priestess **10** high priest, soothsayer **11** faith healer, necromancer, thaumaturge, witch doctor

Shamash 6 sun-god ***father:* 3** Sin ***sister:* 6** Ishtar ***wife:* 3** Aya

shamble see **shuffle**

shambles 4 mess **5** chaos **6** jumble, muddle **8** disarray, disorder, wreckage **9** confusion

shame 4 pity **5** abash, guilt, odium **6** infamy, stigma **7** chagrin, mortify, obloquy, remorse, scandal **8** disgrace, dishonor, ignominy **9** disrepute, embarrass, humiliate, ill repute **10** opprobrium **11** humiliation **12** self-reproach **13** embarrassment, mortification

shamefaced 7 abashed **8** blushing, sheepish **9** mortified **10** humiliated **11** crestfallen, embarrassed

shameless 6 arrant, brazen, wanton **7** blatant, immoral **8** depraved, flagrant, immodest, impudent **9** abandoned, bald-faced, barefaced, dissolute, unabashed **10** outrageous, profligate, unblushing **11** brazen-faced, disgraceful **12** presumptuous

Shammah *brother:* 5 David ***father:* 4** Agee **5** Jesse, Reuel ***grandfather:* 4** Esau **7** Ishmael ***son:* 7** Jonadab **8** Jonathan

Shammua *father:* 5 David, Galal **6** Bilgah, Zaccur ***mother:* 9** Bathsheba ***son:* 4** Abda

shamus 3 cop **4** dick, tail **6** copper, shadow, sleuth **7** gumshoe **8** flatfoot, sherlock **9** constable, detective, operative, policeman **10** private eye **12** investigator **13** police officer

shanghai 6 abduct, hijack, kidnap
Shangri-la 5 Tibet **6** utopia **7** arcadia **8** paradise **9** Cockaigne, fairyland **10** wonderland
shank 3 leg **4** shin, stem **5** stalk, tibia
shanty 3 cot, hut **4** camp, shed **5** cabin, hovel, lodge, shack **7** cottage
shape 3 fit **4** case, cast, form, mold, plan, trim **5** forge, frame, state, whack **6** aspect, devise, fettle, figure, kilter, repair, sculpt, tailor, work up **7** contour, fitness, outline, pattern, profile **8** assemble **9** condition, construct, fabricate, semblance **10** appearance, silhouette **12** conformation **13** configuration ***combining form:*** **5** morph **6** morpho ***dark:*** **6** shadow **10** silhouette
shapeable 6 pliant, supple **7** ductile, plastic, pliable **8** flexible **9** tractable
shapeless 8 inchoate, unformed **9** amorphous
shapely 4 trim **5** buxom **9** Junoesque **10** curvaceous, statuesque, well-turned **11** clean-limbed
shard 4 chip **5** chunk, scale, scrap, shell **6** sliver **7** elytron **8** carapace, fragment
share 3 cut, lot **4** part **5** chunk, claim, quota, slice, stake **6** divide, parcel, ration **7** dole out, give out, helping, partake, portion, prorate, quantum **8** dispense, fraction, interest, quotient **9** allotment, allowance, apportion **10** experience, percentage, proportion **11** participate
shared 5 joint **6** common, mutual, public **8** communal, conjoint, conjunct **9** concerted **10** collective **11** cooperative
Sharezer *father, victim:* 11 Sennacherib
shark 5 cheat **8** swindler ***kind:*** **4** gata, mako, sand, tope **5** nurse, tiger **7** basking, dogfish, leopard **8** mackerel, man-eater, thresher **9** porbeagle **10** great white, hammerhead ***skin:*** **8** shagreen
sharp 3 sly **4** acid, keen, tony, trig **5** acerb, acrid, acute, alert, canny, crisp, honed, quick, slick, smart, swank **6** astute, biting, brainy, bright, clever, jagged, nimble, peaked, shrewd, shrill, snappy, snazzy **7** caustic, dashing, intense, pointed, prickly, stylish, whetted **8** clean-cut, clear-cut, incisive **9** brilliant, ingenious, knifelike, vitriolic **10** astringent, perceptive **11** intelligent, penetrating, quick-witted, resourceful
sharpen 4 edge, file, hone, whet **5** grind, strop
sharper 6 con man **7** diddler **8** chiseler, swindler **9** defrauder, trickster **10** mountebank **12** double-dealer
sharp-eyed 4 keen **5** alert **8** vigilant, watchful **9** attentive, observant **10** discerning, perceptive
sharpie see **sharper**
sharpness 4 edge **6** acuity, acumen **9** precision
sharpshooter 6 sniper **7** deadeye **8** marksman
sharp-sighted 8 hawk-eyed, lynx-eyed **9** eagle-eyed
sharp-witted 4 keen **5** acute, canny, quick, smart **6** astute, clever, shrewd **11** intelligent
shatter 4 dash **5** break, burst, crush, smash **6** shiver **8** demolish, fragment, splinter **9** pulverize **10** annihilate **11** fragmentize **12** disintegrate
shatterable 7 brittle, fragile **9** breakable, frangible
shave 3 cut **4** clip, crop, pare, peel, skim, trim **5** lower, plane, prune, shear, skive **6** barber, cut off, deduct, reduce, scrape, sliver **7** cut back, whittle **8** mark down
shaver 3 boy, kid, lad, tad **4** tike, tyke **5** child, razor **6** barber, laddie, squirt **9** stripling, youngster
shawl 4 wrap **5** fichu, manta **6** afghan, chador, serape **7** tallith **8** mantilla
shawm's descendant 4 oboe
Shawnee chief 8 Tecumseh, Tecumtha **9** Cornstalk
Shaw play 6 Geneva **7** Candida **9** Pygmalion, Saint Joan **11** Misalliance **12** Major Barbara **13** Arms and the Man
shay 6 chaise **8** carriage
shear 3 cut, mow **4** clip, crop, pare, snip, trim **5** prune, shave, skive **6** barber
shears 8 scissors
shearwater 4 bird **6** petrel **7** skimmer
sheath 4 case, skin **5** cover **7** holster **8** scabbard
sheathe 4 case, clad, face, side, skin, wrap **5** cover, panel **6** encase, jacket
Sheba *father:* 6 Bichri ***queen:* 6** Balkis
shebang 4 mess **6** affair **7** schmear **8** business, caboodle **9** ball of wax, enchilada
shed 3 hut **4** cast, doff, drop, emit, molt **5** exude, hovel, hutch, scrap, shack, stall **6** divest, lean-to, reject, slough **7** cast off, diffuse, discard, radiate, take off **8** jettison, throw out **9** throw away
sheen 5 glaze, gleam, glint, gloss, shine **6** finish, luster, lustre, polish **7** burnish, glitter, shimmer **8** radiance **9** shininess **10** brightness
sheeny see **shiny**
sheep 5 ovine ***breed:*** **5** Tunis **6** Dorper, Dorset, Exmoor, Merino, Navajo, No-Tail, Oxford, Panama, Romney **7** Cheviot, Colbred,

Karakul, Lincoln, Ryeland, Suffolk **8** Columbia, Cotswold, Polwarth **9** Hampshire, Leicester, Montadale, Southdown **10** Corriedale, Debouillet **11** Rambouillet ***coat:*** **4** wool **6** fleece ***disease:*** **3** gid, orf ***female:*** **3** ewe ***genus:*** **4** Ovis ***male:*** **3** ram **6** wether ***meat:*** **6** mutton ***relating to:*** **5** ovine ***Scottish:*** **9** blackface ***sound:*** **5** bleat ***tender:*** **8** shepherd ***wild:*** **3** sha **5** urial **6** aoudad, argali, bharal **7** bighorn, mouflon ***young:*** **4** lamb

sheepish 4 meek **5** timid **7** abashed, ashamed, bashful **8** timorous **9** diffident **10** shamefaced **11** embarrassed

sheepskin 4 roan **6** mouton **7** diploma **9** parchment ***prepare:*** **3** taw

sheer 4 pure, skew, thin, turn, veer **5** filmy, gauzy, steep, utter **6** abrupt, arrant, flimsy, simple, swerve **7** chiffon, deflect, deviate, perfect, unmixed **8** absolute, complete, gossamer, outright **9** out-and-out, unalloyed, undiluted **10** diaphanous, see-through **11** precipitate, precipitous, transparent, unmitigated

sheet 3 ply **4** film, leaf, page, sail, slab **5** cover, linen, paper **6** lamina, veneer **8** membrane **9** newspaper

sheet ____ 3 ice **4** film **5** glass, metal, music **6** anchor

shelf 3 hob **4** bank, edge, reef, sill **5** ledge, shoal **6** mantel **7** counter **8** sandbank

shell 3 pod **4** boat, bomb, case, hull, husk, rake, skin **5** blitz, conch, shuck **6** pepper **7** bombard, capsule, grenade, mollusc, mollusk **8** carapace **9** cannonade, cartridge ***defective:*** **3** dud ***explosive:*** **4** bomb ***layer:*** **5** nacre ***ornamental:*** **6** cowrie ***study:*** **10** conchology

shellac 4 beat, drub, flay, lick, rout, trim, whap, whip, whop, whup **5** resin, smear, whomp **6** defeat, thrash **7** clobber, smother, trounce **8** lambaste, vanquish

Shelley, Percy Bysshe ***friend:*** **5** Byron (Lord), Keats (John) ***poem:*** **5** Cloud (The) **7** Adonais, Alastor **8** Queen Mab **10** Ozymandias, To a Skylark **16** Ode to the West Wind ***wife:*** **4** Mary

shellfish 4 clam, crab **5** conch, cowry, prawn, snail, whelk **6** cockle, limpet, mussel, oyster, quahog, triton **7** abalone, crawdad, geoduck, lobster, mollusc, mollusk, scallop **8** barnacle, crayfish, escargot **10** crustacean, periwinkle

shell out 3 pay **4** give **5** spend **8** fork over, hand over

shell-shaped 6 spiral **9** cochleate

shelter 3 den, hut, lee **4** cote, fold, hide, port, roof, shed, tent **5** bower, cloak, cover, haven, house, shack **6** asylum, burrow, covert, defend, harbor, refuge, shield **7** defense, foxhole, hideout, hospice, housing, lodging, pillbox, protect, retreat **8** hideaway, hidy-hole, security **9** dwellings, hermitage, hidey-hole, sanctuary ***for aircraft:*** **6** hangar ***for cows:*** **4** barn, byre ***toward:*** **4** alee

shelve 4 dish, drop, stay, tilt **5** defer, delay, slope, stock, waive **6** freeze, give up, hold up, put off **7** hold off, suspend **8** hold over, mothball, postpone, prorogue, set aside

Shem ***brother:*** **3** Ham **7** Japheth ***father:*** **4** Noah

Shema's father 4 Joel **6** Hebron

Shemida's father 6 Gilead

shenanigan 4 dido, lark **5** antic, caper, prank, stunt, trick **6** frolic **8** escapade, mischief **10** tomfoolery **11** monkeyshine

Sheol see **hades**

shepherd 4 lead, show, tend **5** guide, pilot, route, steer, watch **6** direct, escort, leader **7** conduct **8** guardian ***dog:*** **6** collie **12** border collie ***stick:*** **5** crook, staff

Sheridan, Richard Brinsley ***character:*** **8** Bob Acres, Malaprop (Mrs.) **10** Lady Teazle **13** Lady Sneerwell, Lydia Languish ***play:*** **6** Critic (The), Rivals (The) **7** Pizarro **16** School for Scandal (The)

sheriff 5 reeve **6** lawman **7** marshal, officer ***aide:*** **6** deputy

sherlock 4 dick, tail **5** snoop **6** shadow, shamus, sleuth **7** gumshoe **8** hawkshaw **9** detective **10** private eye **12** investigator

Sherlock Holmes ***address:*** **11** Baker Street ***creator:*** **5** Doyle (Arthur Conan) ***sidekick:*** **6** Watson (Dr.)

sherry 4 fino, wine **7** oloroso **10** manzanilla **11** amontillado

shibboleth 3 saw, tag **5** axiom, maxim **6** byword, cliché, phrase, saying, slogan, truism **7** bromide **8** banality, chestnut, password, prosaism **9** catchword, platitude, watchword **11** catchphrase, commonplace

shield 4 fend, roof, ward **5** aegis, armor, cover, guard, haven, house, pavis **6** buffer, defend, harbor, screen, secure **7** buckler, bulwark, defense, protect, shelter **8** defilade **9** safeguard **10** escutcheon ***band:*** **4** fess ***bullfighter's:*** **9** burladero ***light:*** **5** targe ***part:*** **4** boss, umbo **7** bordure ***Roman:*** **7** testudo

shield-like 7 peltate

shift 3 yaw **4** bend, bout, move, stir, tack, time, tour, turn, vary, veer **5** alter, budge, get by, spell, stint, trick **6** change, make do, manage, remove, resort, swerve **7** deviate, replace, shuffle, stopgap **8** get along, relocate, resource, transfer **9** deviation, expedient, fluctuate **10** alteration, changeover, conversion, transition **11** fluctuation

shiftless 4 idle, lazy **5** inept **8** feckless, indolent, slothful **11** inefficient

shifty 3 sly **4** foxy, wily **5** cagey, lying, shady, slick **6** crafty, sneaky, tricky **7** cunning, devious, elusive, evasive, furtive **8** guileful, slippery, sneaking **9** conniving, deceitful, deceptive, dishonest, insidious, underhand **10** inconstant, untruthful **11** duplicitous, underhanded **12** equivocating

shill 5 blind, decoy, pitch **6** capper **8** promoter **10** accomplice, sales pitch

shillelagh 3 bat **4** club, cosh, mace **5** baton, billy, stick **6** cudgel **8** bludgeon **9** bastinado, billy club, blackjack, truncheon **10** nightstick

shilling 3 bob

shilly-shally 5 fudge, hedge, stall, waver **6** dawdle, dither, waffle **7** whiffle **8** hesitate **9** temporize, vacillate **11** prevaricate **12** tergiversate

Shimea *brother:* 5 David ***father:* 5** David, Jesse ***son:* 7** Jonadab **8** Jonathan

shimmer 5 flash, gleam, glint, sheen **6** luster, lustre **7** glimmer, glisten, glitter, spangle, sparkle, twinkle **9** coruscate **11** coruscation, scintillate **13** scintillation

shimmy 5 dance, shake **6** quiver, shiver, tremor **7** chemise, shudder, tremble, vibrate **9** vibration

shin 3 run **4** dash **5** scoot, tibia **6** scurry, sprint **7** scamper

shindig 4 ball, bash, fête, gala **5** binge, dance, party, revel **6** affair, frolic **7** blowout **8** wingding

shine 3 ray, rub **4** beam, buff, burn, glow **5** blaze, flare, flash, glare, glaze, gleam, glint, gloss, sheen **6** luster, lustre, polish **7** burnish, glimmer, glisten, glitter, radiate, shimmer, sparkle, twinkle **9** luminesce **10** incandesce

shiner 4 fish **8** black eye, cyprinid

shingle 5 beach, coast, shore **7** haircut, overlap, overlay **8** detritus **9** signboard

shiny 6 agleam, bright, glossy **7** fulgent, radiant **8** dazzling, gleaming, lustrous, polished **9** burnished, effulgent **10** glistening

ship 4 boat, send **5** remit, route **6** export **7** consign, forward, freight **8** dispatch, transfer, transmit ***ancient:* 6** bireme, galley **7** galleon, trireme ***attendant:* 7** steward ***beam:* 7** keelson ***berth:* 4** dock, slip ***boat:* 6** dinghy **7** lighter ***body:* 4** hull ***cabin:* 9** stateroom ***commercial:* 5** liner, oiler **6** argosy, tanker, trader **9** freighter ***crew member:* 4** hand, mate **6** sailor ***deck:* 4** boat, main, poop **5** orlop **6** bridge **10** forecastle ***fishing:* 6** lugger **7** trawler ***fleet:* 6** armada ***floor:* 4** deck ***front:* 3** bow **4** prow, stem **8** cutwater ***hoister:* 4** boom **5** davit **7** capstan ***kitchen:* 6** galley ***left side:* 4** port **8** larboard ***military:* 6** cutter, PT boat **7** carrier, cruiser **9** destroyer, submarine ***officer:* 4** mate **5** bosun **6** purser **7** captain, steward **9** boatswain ***part:* 3** bow **4** beam, deck, helm, hold, hull, keel, mast, skeg, stem **5** bilge, hatch, stern **6** bridge, rudder **7** scupper ***partition:* 7** bulwark **8** bulkhead ***personnel:* 4** crew ***platform:* 9** crow's nest, gangboard, gangplank ***poetic:* 4** bark ***post:* 4** bitt, mast **7** bollard ***prison:* 4** brig ***projection:* 7** sponson ***rear:* 5** stern ***record:* 3** log ***right side:* 9** starboard ***room:* 4** brig **5** cabin **6** galley ***rope:* 4** line **5** sheet **7** halyard ***sailing:* 3** hoy **4** brig, dhow, prau, proa, yawl **5** ketch, sloop, xebec, yacht **6** lugger **7** caravel, galleon **8** schooner ***steerer:* 4** helm **6** tiller ***storage area:* 4** hold ***to the rear of:* 3** aft **5** abaft **6** astern ***valve:* 7** seacock ***window:* 4** port **8** porthole

shipment 5 cargo **6** lading **7** freight, payload **8** delivery **11** consignment

Ship of Fools author 6 Porter (Katherine Anne)

Shipping News author 6 Proulx (Annie)

ships, group of 4 navy **5** fleet, flota **6** armada **8** flotilla

shipshape 4 neat, snug, tidy, trig, trim **7** orderly **11** spic-and-span, uncluttered **12** spick-and-span

shipworm 6 teredo

shire 5 horse **6** county **8** district **10** draft horse

shirk 4 duck, lurk, shun **5** avoid, creep, dodge, elude, evade, skulk, slink, sneak, steal **8** sidestep

shirker see **slacker**

shirt 3 tee **4** polo, sark **5** dress, kurta, sport **6** blouse, jersey **9** guayabera

shirty 3 mad **5** angry, cross, irate **6** heated, ireful **7** annoyed **8** choleric, incensed, offended **9** indignant, irritated

shiv 5 blade, knife, shank **6** dagger **8** stiletto

Shiva *consort:* 3 Uma **4** Devi, Kali **5** Durga, Gauri **6** Ambika, Chandi **7** Parvati **9** Haimavati ***son:* 6** Ganesa, Ganesh, Skanda **7** Ganesha **10** Karttikeya

shiver 5 burst, quake, shake, smash **6** quaver, quiver, tremor **7** shatter, shudder, tremble, twitter **8** fragment, splinter, splitter

shlep see **schlep**

shoal 3 bar **4** bank, hook, reef, spit **6** school

7 barrier, sandbar, shallow, tombolo **8** sandbank, sand reef

shoat 3 hog, pig **4** gilt **5** swine **6** piglet, porker

Shobab *father:* 5 Caleb, David ***mother:* 6** Azubah **9** Bathsheba

shock 3 jar **4** blow, bump, daze, jolt, pile, rick, stun **5** amaze, clash, crash, mound, quake, shake, sheaf **6** appall, dismay, impact, insult, offend, trauma, tremor **7** astound, disgust, horrify, outrage, stagger, startle, stupefy, temblor **8** astonish, surprise **9** collision, electrify **10** concussion, earthquake, percussion, scandalize, traumatize **11** flabbergast **12** stupefaction

shock absorber 6 spring **7** dashpot, snubber

shocker 4 blow **7** stunner **8** surprise, thriller **9** bombshell, eye-opener, sensation **11** showstopper

shocking 5 awful, lurid **6** horrid **7** glaring, heinous **8** dreadful, horrible, horrific, shameful, terrible **9** appalling, atrocious, frightful, monstrous, revolting, traumatic **10** outrageous, scandalous **11** disgraceful, distressing, unspeakable

shoddy 4 base, mean, poor **5** cheap, dingy, gaudy, junky, seedy, tacky, tatty **6** cheesy, common, flimsy, paltry, shabby, sleazy, tawdry, trashy **7** run-down, scruffy **8** inferior, rubbishy, shameful **9** makeshift **10** broken-down, down-at-heel, jerry-built, jury-rigged **11** dilapidated, disgraceful, ignominious, pretentious **12** dishonorable, disreputable **13** discreditable

shoe 3 pac **4** boot, clog, geta, mule, pump **5** sabot, wedge **6** brogan, brogue, buskin, gaiter, galosh, gillie, loafer, oxford, patten, sandal, slip-on **7** chopine, ghillie, slipper, sneaker **8** balmoral, moccasin, platform, plimsoll **10** clodhopper, espadrille ***armored:* 8** solleret ***athlete's:* 7** sneaker ***form:* 4** last, tree ***kind:* 8** elevator, open-toed **10** high-heeled ***part:* 3** tip, toe **4** arch, heel, lace, lift, sole, vamp **5** cleat, shank, upper **6** box toe, collar, foxing, insole, lining, throat, tongue **7** counter, outsole **8** backstay ***protective:* 6** galosh, rubber ***shiner:* 6** polish **9** bootblack ***wooden:* 5** sabot **7** chopine

shoelace tip 5 aglet

shoeless 6 unshod **8** barefoot **9** discalced

shoemaker 7 cobbler ***patron saint:* 7** Crispin ***Scottish:* 6** souter

Shogun author 7 Clavell (James)

Sholem Aleichem character 5 Golde, Tevye, Yente

shoo 4 scat **5** drive, leave, scare, scram, split **6** beat it, begone, bug off, skidoo **7** buzz off, get lost, skiddoo, vamoose **8** clear out **9** skedaddle, take a hike **10** hit the road

shoo-in 6 winner **7** sure bet **8** slam dunk **9** sure thing

shoot 3 bud, fly, gun, ray **4** beam, bolt, dart, dash, fire, lash, race, rush, sail, scud, skim, spew, tear **5** blast, chase, fling, photo, plink, shaft, skirr, snipe, spurt **6** branch **7** project **9** discharge **10** photograph

shoot down 3 pan, rap **4** bash, kill, slam **5** blast, decry, knock, scorn, trash **6** assail, deride, dump on, reject, squash **7** deflate, squelch, torpedo **8** bad-mouth, belittle, derogate, discount, disprove, puncture, ridicule **9** discredit

shooting 4 keen **5** acute, sharp **7** gunplay **8** piercing, stabbing

shooting star 6 meteor **8** fireball

shoot up 4 soar **6** inject, rocket **7** burgeon **8** mushroom **9** skyrocket

shop 4 hunt **5** store **6** browse, market, outlet, search **8** boutique, emporium, showroom

shoplift 3 bag, cop **4** lift, palm **5** boost, filch, pinch, steal, swipe **6** pilfer, rip off, snitch

shop owner 8 merchant, retailer **9** tradesman **10** proprietor

shopworn 5 banal, faded, stale, tired, trite **6** cliché, soiled **7** clichéd **8** overused **9** hackneyed **10** threadbare

shore 4 bank, prop, stay **5** beach, brace, brink, coast **6** bear up, strand, uphold **7** bolster, shingle, support, sustain **8** buttress, littoral, seacoast **9** coastland, coastline, riverbank, riverside, waterside **10** embankment, waterfront

shorebird see at **bird**

short 3 shy **4** curt **5** blunt, brief, crisp, scant, skimp, spare, squat, stint, terse **6** abrupt, meager, meagre, scanty, scarce, skimpy, stubby **7** brusque, compact, concise, lacking, laconic, stunted, wanting **8** abridged, succinct **9** deficient **10** inadequate **11** abbreviated **12** insufficient

shortage 4 lack **5** pinch **6** dearth, ullage **7** deficit, paucity **8** scarcity **10** deficiency, inadequacy, scantiness

shortcoming 3 bug, sin **4** flaw, lack **5** fault, lapse **6** defect **7** demerit, failing **8** weakness **9** weak point **10** deficiency **12** imperfection

shortcut 5 macro **6** bypass, cutoff

shorten 3 bob, cut **4** clip, dock **5** elide, slash **6** lessen, reduce, shrink **7** abridge, curtail, cut back, cut down, excerpt **8** boil down, compress, condense, contract, decrease, diminish, minimize, truncate **10** abbreviate

shorthand 11 stenography ***method:* 5** Gregg **6** Pitman

shorthanded 7 wanting **11** undermanned **12** understaffed
short-lived 5 brief **7** passing **8** fleeting **9** ephemeral, fugacious, momentary, temporary **10** evanescent, transitory
shortly 4 anon, soon **6** pronto **7** briefly, by and by, in brief, quickly, tersely **8** directly **9** concisely, presently **10** succinctly **11** laconically
shortness 7 brevity **9** concision
shortsighted 6 myopic **8** heedless, reckless **10** astigmatic
short-spoken 4 curt **5** bluff, blunt, brief, gruff, terse **6** abrupt, crusty, snippy **7** brusque **8** snippety
short-tempered 5 testy **6** touchy **7** prickly **8** snappish **9** irascible, irritable
Shoshone chief 8 Washakie **9** Pocatello
shot 3 nip, pop, try **4** dose, dram, drop, jolt, stab **5** blast, break, carom, crack, fling, guess, ounce, photo, range, reach, snort, swipe, whack, whirl **6** chance, effort, stroke **7** attempt, snifter **8** marksman, occasion **9** discharge **11** opportunity
shoulder 4 bear, edge, push, side **5** elbow, press, shove **6** assume, hustle, jostle, take on **8** bulldoze ***bone:* 7** scapula **8** clavicle ***covering:* 6** tippet **8** scapular ***muscle:* 7** deltoid ***relating to:* 7** humeral **8** scapular
shoulder blade 7 scapula
shout 3 cry **4** bark, bawl, bray, call, roar, yell **5** blare, whoop **6** bellow, clamor, holler, scream **7** exclaim **10** vociferate
shove 3 dig, jab, jam **4** cram, prod, push **5** crowd, drive, elbow, press **6** jostle, propel, thrust **8** bulldoze, shoulder
shovel 3 dig **4** grub **5** delve, scoop, spade **6** dig out, dredge, trowel **8** excavate
shoveler 4 duck **9** broadbill
shove off 2 go **3** git **4** blow, exit **5** leave, scoot, scram, split **6** beat it, cut out, decamp, depart, move on **7** move out, pull out, vamoose **8** clear out, run along
show 4 fair, film, lead, pomp, sham **5** array, flick, front, guide, mount, movie, offer, prove, revue, sport, stage **6** appear, arrive, direct, effect, evince, expose, flaunt, lay out, parade, reveal, set out, submit, unveil **7** conduct, display, divulge, exhibit, explain, fanfare, panoply, picture, present, produce, project, trot out **8** brandish, disclose, evidence, illusion, indicate, instruct, manifest, proclaim **9** determine, establish, pageantry, represent, semblance, spectacle **10** appearance, exhibition, exposition, illustrate, production **11** demonstrate, materialize, performance **13** demonstration, manifestation
Show Boat *author:* 6 Ferber (Edna) ***composer:* 4** Kern (Jerome) ***lyricist:* 11** Hammerstein (Oscar)
showcase 6 flaunt, parade **7** cabinet, exhibit, feature, vitrine
shower 4 hail, rain, wash **5** bathe, burst, party, salvo, spray, storm **6** deluge, lavish, volley **7** barrage, cascade, shatter, spatter **8** cataract, downpour, fountain, rainfall **9** broadside, cannonade, fusillade **10** cloudburst **11** bombardment
showman 8 producer, promoter **10** impresario ***famous:* 4** Cody (William F.) **6** Barnum (Phineas T.)
Show Me State 8 Missouri
show off 4 brag **5** boast, flash, model, strut, vaunt **6** expose, flaunt, hotdog, parade **7** display, exhibit, swagger, trot out **8** brandish **10** grandstand
show-off 3 ham **6** hotdog **7** boaster, hotshot, peacock **8** blowhard, braggart **9** swaggerer **13** exhibitionist
showpiece 3 gem **5** jewel, prize **10** magnum opus, masterwork **11** chef d'oeuvre, masterpiece
show up 4 come **6** appear, arrive, debunk, expose, reveal, unmask **8** discover **9** discredit, embarrass **10** invalidate **11** materialize
showy 4 loud **5** gaudy, jazzy **6** flashy, garish, ornate, sporty, tawdry **7** opulent, splashy **8** gorgeous, overdone, striking **9** luxurious, sumptuous **10** flamboyant **11** overwrought, pretentious, resplendent, sensational **12** meretricious, orchidaceous, ostentatious
shred 3 bit, dag, jot, rag **4** chip, iota, whit **5** crumb, grain, grate, ounce, scrap, shave, speck, trace **6** sliver, tatter **7** modicum, smidgen, snippet **8** demolish, fragment, particle **9** scintilla
shrew 3 erd, nag **4** mole **5** harpy, scold, vixen, witch **6** dragon, gorgon, ogress, rodent, virago **7** hellcat **8** battle-ax, fishwife, harridan, she-devil, spitfire, Xantippe **9** battle-axe, termagant, Xanthippe
shrewd 3 sly **4** cagy, foxy, keen, wily, wise **5** acute, cagey, canny, savvy, sharp, slick, smart **6** artful, astute, clever, crafty, smooth **7** knowing, prudent **8** sensible **9** ingenious, judicious, sagacious **10** discerning **11** intelligent, penetrating, quick-witted **13** perspicacious
shrewish 5 cross, testy **6** cranky, snappy **7** nagging, peevish, peppery **8** choleric, petulant **9** crotchety, fractious, irascible, splenetic **10** ill-natured **11** contentious,

intractable, quarrelsome **12** disputatious **13** quick-tempered, short-tempered

shriek 3 cry **4** yell **6** screak, scream, shrill, squawk, squeal **7** screech

shrill 4 keen **5** acute, sharp **6** piping **8** piercing, strident **9** deafening **12** earsplitting

shrimp 4 runt **5** prawn **6** peanut, peewee, scampi, shorty **9** pipsqueak **10** crustacean

shrine 5 altar **6** temple **7** sanctum **9** reliquary, sacrarium, sanctuary ***Buddhist:*** **4** tope **5** stupa **7** chorten

shrink 3 shy **4** wane **5** cower, quail, slink, start, wince **6** blench, boggle, cringe, flinch, huddle, recede, recoil, wither **7** analyst, dwindle, refrain **8** compress, condense, contract, draw back, withdraw **9** constrict, shrivel up, therapist, waste away **12** psychiatrist, psychologist

shrinking 3 shy **5** mousy, timid **7** bashful **8** retiring, skittish **9** withdrawn

shrive 5 purge **6** pardon, purify **7** absolve, confess, expiate **8** lustrate

shrivel 4 wilt **5** dry up, parch, wizen **6** shrink, wither **7** dwindle, wrinkle **9** dehydrate, desiccate

Shropshire Lad author 7 Housman (A. E.)

shroud 4 hide, rope, veil, wrap **5** cloak, cover, shade **6** enfold, enwrap, screen **7** conceal, enclose, envelop, obscure **8** cerement, obstruct **9** cerecloth **12** winding-sheet

shrouded 5 privy **6** covert, hidden, secret **7** obscure **10** mysterious

shrub 4 bush **5** elder, erica, hazel **6** muskit, privet **7** arboret, dyeweed, guayule **8** barberry, bluewood, boxthorn, inkberry, ironweed, rosebush **9** bearberry **10** bladdernut ***Asian:*** **4** bago **6** kerria **8** caragana, japonica ***desert:*** **4** jhow **7** ephedra **8** tamarisk ***dwarf:*** **6** bonsai ***East Indian:*** **3** aal **4** sunn ***European:*** **4** cade **8** woodbine ***evergreen:*** **3** box, kat, yew **4** ilex, khat, titi **5** furze, heath, holly, pyxie, savin, taxus **6** kalmia, laurel, myrtle, nandin, protea, sabine, savine **7** boxwood, heather, jasmine, juniper, rosebay **8** lambkill, oleander, rosemary, tamarisk ***flowering:*** **5** ribes, tiara, wahoo **6** daphne, laurel, myrtle, spirea **7** chamise, chamiso, mahonia, maybush, rhodora, spiraea, weigela **8** magnolia, mezereon, ninebark, oleander, oleaster, shadblow, shadbush, snowball, snowbush, tornillo, viburnum, wisteria ***genus:*** **3** Iva **4** Ilex, Inga, Itea, Rhus, Rosa, Ulex **7** Solanum **8** Euonymus ***hardwood:*** **4** pelu **6** cornel, kowhai ***Mexican:*** **8** ocotillo ***New Zealand:*** **4** tutu ***ornamental:*** **6** privet **7** syringa **9** bluebeard ***pasture:*** **8** cowberry ***prickly:*** **4** Ulex **5** briar, chico, furze, gorse **7** bramble **8** hawthorn, mesquite **9** buckthorn ***thicket:*** **6** maquis **7** macchia **9** chaparral ***tropical:*** **4** kava, Sida **5** henna **7** lantana **8** buddleia **10** frangipani ***West Indian:*** **4** anil **7** acerola

shrug off 8 belittle, downplay, minimize

shtick 3 act, bag, bit **5** spiel **6** number **7** routine **9** specialty **11** performance

Shuah *father:* **7** Abraham ***mother:*** **7** Keturah

shuck 3 pod **4** case, cast, hull, husk, junk, peel, shed, skin **5** ditch, scrap, shell, strip **6** reject, remove, slough **7** discard, peel off, take off **8** jettison **11** decorticate

shudder 5 quake, shake **6** quaver, quiver, shimmy, shiver, tremor **7** frisson, tremble, twitter, vibrate

shuffle 3 mix **4** hash **5** dodge, evade, hedge, scuff, shift **6** jumble, mess up, muddle, weasel **7** clutter, reorder, rummage, shamble **8** disarray, disorder, intermix, mishmash **9** rearrange **10** disarrange, equivocate **11** disorganize

shun 3 cut **4** duck, snub **5** avoid, dodge, elude, evade, scorn **6** escape, eschew, refuse, reject **7** decline, disdain

shunt 4 turn **5** avert, shift **6** change, divert, switch **7** deflect, shuttle **8** transfer **9** sidetrack

shush 4 hush **5** quiet, still **6** muffle, muzzle, shut up, stifle **7** repress, silence, squelch **8** suppress

shut 3 bar **4** lock, seal, slam **5** close **6** fasten **9** close down **10** batten down

Shute novel 10 On the Beach

shut in 3 hem, mew, pen **4** cage, coop, wall **5** fence **6** coop up, immure **7** confine, enclose **8** imprison

shut-in 7 invalid **8** confined **9** withdrawn **12** convalescent

shut out 3 bar **6** screen **7** exclude **9** ostracize

shutter 5 blind **6** screen

shuttle 5 ferry, shunt **6** bobbin **7** commute, spindle **9** alternate

shuttlecock 4 bird **5** bandy

shut up 3 gag, mew, pen **4** cage, hush, jail, mute **5** burke, choke, quiet, shush, still **6** muzzle, stifle **7** confine, enclose, impound, silence, squelch **8** choke off, imprison, pipe down, suppress **9** quiet down **11** incarcerate

shy 3 coy **4** balk, duck, meek, shun, wary **5** avoid, chary, elude, evade, mousy, quail, scant, short, timid **6** averse, blench, demure, modest, recoil, scanty, scarce, shrink **7** bashful, fearful, lacking, wanting **8** hesitant, reserved, reticent, retiring, sheepish, timorous **9** diffident, withdrawn **11** introverted, unassertive **12** apprehensive, insufficient, self-effacing **13** self-conscious

Shylock 6 usurer **9** loan shark ***daughter:* 7** Jessica

shyster 11 pettifogger

Siam see **Thailand**

sib 3 bro, kin, sis **4** akin **6** sister **7** brother, kindred, kinsman, related **8** relation, relative **9** relatives

Sibelius composition 9 Finlandia **11** Valse Triste

Siberian *dog:* 5 husky **7** Samoyed ***native:* 5** Tatar, Yakut **6** Tartar, Tungus **7** Chukchi **9** Mongolian ***plain:* 6** steppe ***tent:* 4** yurt

sibilate 4 buzz, fizz, hiss, whiz **6** fizzle, sizzle **7** whisper

sibling 3 bro, sis **6** sister **7** brother

sibyl 4 seer **6** oracle **7** prophet **10** prophetess, soothsayer **13** fortune-teller

sic 3 set **4** thus **5** chase **6** attack

Sicilian secret organization 5 Mafia **10** Cosa Nostra

Sicily *capital:* 7 Palermo ***city:* 4** Enna **7** Catania, Messina **8** Siracusa, Syracuse, Taormina ***volcano:* 4** Etna

sick 3 ill **5** fed up, tired, weary **6** ailing, laid up, morbid, peaked, rotten, unwell, wobbly **7** fevered, invalid **8** confined, diseased **9** bedridden, defective, disgusted, unhealthy **10** indisposed **11** debilitated

sicken 5 upset **7** afflict, disgust, fall ill **8** nauseate

sickle 5 blade, mower **6** scythe **8** crescent

sickle-shaped 7 falcate

sickly 3 ill, low, wan **4** puny, weak **5** frail **6** ailing, anemic, feeble, infirm, morbid, peaked, poorly, unwell **8** delicate, diseased **9** unhealthy **10** indisposed **11** unhealthful, unwholesome **12** insalubrious

sickness 3 bug **6** malady **7** ailment, disease, illness **8** disorder, syndrome **9** complaint, condition, infirmity **10** affliction **13** indisposition

sick-out 7 blue flu

sic transit gloria ____ 5 mundi

side 4 clad, team **5** angle, facet, flank **6** aspect **9** direction **10** standpoint ***combining form:* 5** later **6** lateri, latero ***exposed:* 8** windward ***of a coin:* 7** obverse, reverse ***sheltered:* 3** lee

sideboard 5 table **6** buffet **8** credence, credenza ***for wine:* 8** cellaret **10** cellarette

sideburns 9 burnsides **10** sideboards **11** dundrearies, muttonchops

sidekick 3 pal **4** chun **5** buddy, crony **7** partner **9** assistant, companion **10** accomplice

sideline 5 eject, hobby **6** injure **7** disable, pastime, take out **9** avocation, diversion **10** recreation **11** distraction **12** incapacitate

sidereal 6 astral, starry **7** stellar

side road 5 byway **8** bystreet, shunpike

sideshow 9 diversion **11** distraction

sidestep 4 duck **5** avoid, burke, dodge, evade, hedge, skirt **6** bypass, swerve, weasel **10** circumvent, equivocate **12** tergiversate

sideswipe 5 brush, carom, graze, shave **6** glance, scrape

sidetrack 5 shunt **6** divert, switch **7** deflect

sidewhiskers see **sideburns**

side with 4 back **5** favor **6** second, uphold **7** endorse, support **8** backstop, champion

sidle 4 edge, inch, slip

siege 4 bout **5** spell **6** attack **7** assault, seizure **8** blockade **9** onslaught

Siegfried *composer:* 6 Wagner (Richard) ***lover:* 8** Brunhild ***mother:* 9** Sieglinde ***slayer:* 5** Hagen ***sword:* 7** Balmung ***vulnerable spot:* 4** back **8** shoulder ***wife:* 9** Kriemhild

Sienkiewicz novel 8 Quo Vadis

sierra 3 saw **4** fish **5** range **8** mackerel **13** mountain range

Sierra ____ 4 Club **5** Ancha, Leone, Madre **6** Blanca, Nevada

Sierra Leone *capital:* 8 Freetown ***ethnic group:* 5** Mende, Temne ***language:* 4** Krio **7** English ***monetary unit:* 5** leone ***neighbor:* 6** Guinea **7** Liberia

Sierra Nevada lake 5 Tahoe

siesta 3 nap **4** doze **5** sleep **6** catnap, snooze **10** forty winks

sieve 4 sift **6** filter, screen, winnow **8** colander, filtrate, strainer

Sif's husband 4 Thor

sift 3 pan **4** comb, cull, sort **5** glean, sieve **6** filter, screen, strain, winnow **8** filtrate, separate

sigh 3 sob **4** gasp, long, moan, pine **5** groan, sough, whine, yearn **6** exhale, grieve, hanker, murmur **7** breathe, respire, suspire

sight 3 aim, eye, spy **4** espy, view **5** scene, vista **6** notice, vision **7** make out, outlook ***relating to:* 5** optic **6** ocular, visual **7** optical

sightseer 7 tourist **10** rubberneck **12** rubbernecker

sign 3 cue, ink **4** flag, hint, mark, omen **5** index, proof, token, trace **6** motion, signal, symbol **7** endorse, gesture, indicia, initial, symptom, vestige, warning **8** evidence, exponent, reminder **9** autograph, indicator **10** expression, indication, suggestion ***box office:* 3** SRO ***magic:* 4** rune ***directional:* 5** arrow ***of the zodiac:*** (see **zodiac sign**)

signal **3** cue, nod **4** flag **5** alarm, alert **6** beckon, wigwag **7** gesture **8** high sign **9** indicator, semaphore ***distress:*** **3** SOS **6** Mayday

signature **4** name **9** autograph **11** John Hancock ***flourish:*** **6** paraph

signet **4** ring, seal **5** stamp **6** device **8** hallmark, intaglio

significance **4** pith **5** merit, point, sense **6** credit, import, moment, weight **7** gravity, meaning **9** authority, magnitude **10** importance **11** consequence, weightiness

significant **5** major, sound, valid **7** notable, telling, weighty **8** material, powerful **9** important, momentous **10** compelling, convincing, meaningful, noteworthy **11** substantial **12** considerable **13** consequential

signification **4** gist **5** point, sense **6** import **7** essence, meaning, message, purport **9** substance **10** intendment **11** implication **12** notification **13** understanding

signify **4** mean, show **5** count, imply, spell, weigh **6** convey, denote, intend, matter **7** add up to, bespeak, connote, express, purport, suggest **8** indicate

sign on **4** book, hire, join **5** draft **6** engage, enlist, enroll, induct, join up, retain, secure **7** recruit **9** conscript

sign over **4** cede, deed **5** alien, grant **6** assign, convey, remise **7** consign **8** alienate, transfer

sign up **4** join **5** enrol, enter **6** enlist, enroll, muster

Sigurd ***horse:*** **5** Grani ***slayer:*** **5** Hogni ***victim:*** **6** Fafner, Fafnir ***wife:*** **6** Gudrun

Sigyn's husband **4** Loki

Sikhism ***deity:*** **4** Akal ***founder:*** **5** Nanak **9** Guru Nanak ***leader:*** **5** Arjan **9** Guru Arjan **11** Gobind Singh ***scripture:*** **9** Adi Granth ***shrine:*** **12** Golden Temple

silage **6** fodder

silence **3** gag **4** calm, hush, lull, mute **5** quash, quell, quiet, shush, still **6** dampen, deaden, muffle, muzzle, shut up, squash, stifle **7** secrecy, squelch **8** choke off, muteness, quietude, suppress **9** quietness, reticence, stillness

silent **3** mum **4** dumb, mute **5** muted, quiet, still, tacit, whist **6** hushed, stilly **8** reticent, taciturn, unspoken, wordless **9** noiseless, soundless, voiceless **10** speechless **11** close-lipped, tight-lipped **12** closemouthed, tight-mouthed

Silent Night writer **4** Mohr (Joseph) **6** Gruber (Franz)

silhouette **6** shadow **7** contour, outline, profile **9** lineament, lineation **10** figuration **11** delineation

silicon symbol **2** Si

Silicon Valley city **7** San Jose **8** Palo Alto

silk **5** fiber **7** foulard **8** sarcenet, sarsenet ***fabric:*** **4** gros **5** caffa, ninon, Pekin, satin, surah, tulle **6** mantua, pongee, samite, sendal, tussah **7** taffeta ***factory:*** **8** filature ***hat:*** **6** topper ***maker:*** **4** worm ***raw:*** **6** greige ***source:*** **6** cocoon ***waste:*** **4** noil **5** floss ***wild:*** **6** tussah

sill **5** bench, ledge, shelf **9** threshold

silliness **5** folly **6** idiocy **7** inanity **9** absurdity, stupidity

silly **4** daft **5** balmy, crazy, daffy, dippy, dizzy, funny, giddy, inane, loony, sappy, wacky **6** absurd, simple **7** asinine, fatuous, flighty, foolish, idiotic, vacuous, witless **9** brainless, frivolous, ludicrous, nitwitted, senseless **10** irrational, ridiculous, weak-minded **11** empty-headed, harebrained, light-headed **12** preposterous, simple-minded **13** rattlebrained

silt **4** marl **5** dregs **7** deposit, residue **8** alluvium, sediment

silver **4** coin **5** money, shiny **6** argent, dulcet **7** bullion, element **8** flatware, lustrous, sterling **9** argentine, tableware ***relating to:*** **9** argentine ***symbol:*** **2** Ag

silverfish **6** insect, tarpon

silversmith **6** Revere (Paul) **11** metalworker

silver-tongued **4** glib **6** fluent **7** voluble **8** eloquent

silvery **6** argent **7** shining **9** argentine, brilliant **10** glittering, shimmering

Silvia's beloved **9** Valentine

____ Simbel **3** Abu

Simenon character **7** Maigret (Inspector)

Simeon ***father:*** **5** Jacob ***mother:*** **4** Leah ***son:*** **4** Ohad **6** Nemuel

simian **3** ape **5** chimp, lemur, loris **6** baboon, bonobo, galago, monkey **7** apelike, gorilla, primate, tarsier **9** orangutan **10** anthropoid, chimpanzee, monkeylike

similar **4** akin, like **5** alike **6** agnate **7** uniform **8** parallel, suchlike **9** analogous, consonant **10** comparable, reciprocal **11** correlative **13** complementary, corresponding

similarity **6** parity **7** analogy, harmony, kinship **8** affinity, likeness, parallel, sameness **9** alikeness, closeness, congruity, semblance **10** conformity, congruence **11** coincidence, correlation, homogeneity, parallelism, resemblance

similarly **8** likewise

simile **7** analogy **8** affinity, likeness, metaphor **9** alikeness, semblance **10** comparison

11 correlation, resemblance ***word:*** **2** as **4** like

similitude 4 copy **5** image **6** double **7** analogy, kinship, replica **8** affinity, likeness, metaphor, relation, sameness **9** alikeness, congruity, semblance **10** comparison, similarity **11** correlation, counterpart, equivalence, resemblance

simmer 4 boil, fret, fume, stew, stir **5** churn **6** bubble, seethe **7** ferment, smolder

simmer down 5 relax

Simon *brother:* 5 Jesus **6** Andrew ***father:* 5** Jonah ***new name:* 5** Peter ***son:* 5** Judas, Rufus **9** Alexander

Simon ____ 5 Magus **6** Legree **8** of Cyrene **9** the Zealot

Simon Maccabaeus *father:* 10 Mattathias ***nickname:* 6** Thassi ***slayer:* 7** Ptolemy

Simon play 9 Odd Couple (The) **10** Chapter Two, Plaza Suite **11** Biloxi Blues **12** Sunshine Boys (The) **13** Lost in Yonkers **16** Come Blow Your Horn **17** Barefoot in the Park **20** Brighton Beach Memoirs **21** Last of the Red Hot Lovers **22** Prisoner of Second Avenue (The)

simp 4 dope **5** dunce, idiot, moron **6** dimwit, nitwit **7** pinhead **8** bonehead, imbecile, lunkhead, numskull **9** blockhead, lamebrain, numbskull **10** nincompoop

simple 4 easy, mere, pure **5** basic, lucid, naive, plain, sheer **6** modest **7** artless, natural, unmixed **8** absolute, trusting **9** childlike, credulous, ingenuous, unadorned **10** effortless, elementary, unaffected **11** fundamental, undecorated, unelaborate **13** unpretentious ***combining form:* 4** hapl **5** haplo

simpleminded 4 dull, slow **5** naive **6** stupid **7** foolish, idiotic, moronic **8** gullible, retarded **9** dim-witted, imbecilic **10** half-witted, slow-witted

simpleton 4 dolt, dope, fool **5** dummy, dunce, idiot, moron **6** cretin, dimwit, nitwit **7** dullard, half-wit, pinhead **8** bonehead, dumbbell, imbecile, lunkhead **9** blockhead, ignoramus, lamebrain **10** nincompoop

simplify 4 ease **7** clarify, clear up **8** boil down **10** facilitate, streamline, unscramble **11** disentangle **13** straighten out

simply 4 just, only **6** merely

Simpsons, The *catchphrase:* 3 d'oh **12** don't have a cow ***character:* 3** Abe, Apu, Moe **4** Bart, Lisa **5** Homer, Marge, Patty, Selma, Snake **6** Barney, Krusty, Maggie, Martin, Willie **7** Bouvier, Mr. Burns, Skinner (Principal Seymour) **8** Chalmers (Supt.), Milhouse, Smithers **9** Dr. Hibbert, Joe Quimby (Mayor) **11** Chief Wiggum (Clancy), Ned Flanders, Nelson Muntz, Sideshow Bob, Sideshow Mel, Troy McClure **12** Kent Brockman, Mrs. Krabappel ***creator:* 8** Groening (Matt) ***Lisa's instrument:* 3** sax **9** saxophone ***setting:* 11** Springfield ***voice:* 5** Smith (Yeardley) **6** Azaria (Hank), Kavner (Julie) **10** Cartwright (Nancy) **12** Castellaneta (Dan)

simulacrum 4 copy **5** clone, ditto, guise, image, trace **6** double, ersatz, mirror, ringer **7** picture, replica **8** likeness, portrait **9** facsimile, imitation, semblance **10** appearance **12** reproduction **13** impersonation, spitting image

simulate 3 ape **4** fake, sham **5** feign, mimic **6** embody, mirror, parody, parrot **7** imitate **8** resemble **9** incarnate **11** counterfeit

simulated 4 fake, mock, sham **5** bogus, dummy, false, phony **6** ersatz **8** spurious **9** imitation, insincere, pretended **10** artificial, fictitious, substitute **11** counterfeit

simultaneous 6 coeval **10** coexistent, coexisting, coincident, coinciding, concurrent, synchronic **11** synchronous **12** contemporary

simultaneously 6 at once **7** jointly **8** together **9** meanwhile

sin 3 err **4** debt, evil, no-no, tort, vice **5** crime, fault, guilt, lapse, misdo, stray, wrong **6** offend **7** demerit, misdeed, offense **8** hamartia, iniquity, trespass **10** deficiency, peccadillo, transgress, wickedness, wrongdoing **11** shortcoming **12** imperfection ***deadly:* 4** envy, lust **5** anger, greed, pride, sloth **8** gluttony **12** covetousness

Sin 7 moon-god ***daughter:* 6** Ishtar ***son:* 7** Shamash ***wife:* 6** Ningal

since 3 ago **5** after **6** behind **7** because, whereas **8** as long as **9** following **10** inasmuch as **11** considering ***Scottish:* 4** syne

sincere 4 real, true **5** frank, plain **6** actual, candid, devout, honest **7** artless, earnest, genuine, serious **8** bona fide, truthful **9** authentic, heartfelt, ingenuous, unfeigned **10** aboveboard, forthright **12** wholehearted **13** unpretentious

sincerity 6 candor **7** honesty **8** goodwill, openness **9** frankness, good faith **11** artlessness, earnestness

Sinclair novel 6 Jungle (The)

sine qua non 4 must **9** condition, essential, necessity, requisite **11** requirement **12** precondition, prerequisite

sinew 6 tendon

sinewy 4 ropy, wiry **5** tough **6** brawny **7** fibrous, stringy **8** muscular

sinful 3 bad **4** base, evil, vile **5** wrong **6** guilty, unholy, wicked **7** immoral, peccant, vicious **8** blamable, culpable, damnable, depraved, shameful **9** reprobate **10** iniquitous **11** blameworthy, disgraceful **13** reprehensible

sing 3 rat **4** fink, hymn **5** carol, chant, chirp, croon, troll, yodel **6** inform, intone, snitch, squeal, warble **7** confess, descant, lullaby **8** serenade, vocalize **10** cantillate

singe 4 burn, char, sear **6** scorch

singer 4 alto, bass **5** mezzo, tenor **6** canary **7** crooner, soloist, soprano **8** baritone, choirboy, songbird, songster, vocalist **9** balladeer, chorister, contralto **10** troubadour **12** mezzo-soprano ***cabaret:*** **11** chansonnier ***female:*** **9** chanteuse ***opera:*** **4** diva **10** cantatrice, prima donna ***religious:*** **6** cantor (see also **alto, baritone, bass, folksinger, mezzo-soprano, pop singer, rock star, soprano**)

singing *exercise:* 7 solfège ***group:*** **5** choir **6** chorus **7** chorale **8** glee club

single 3 hit, odd, one **4** free, lone, only, sole **5** unwed **6** maiden, unique **7** base hit, unitary **8** distinct, isolated, separate, solitary, specific **9** exclusive, unmarried **10** individual, particular, unattached ***combining form:*** **3** mon **4** hapl, mono **5** haplo ***prefix:*** **3** uni

single-minded 5 rigid **6** dogged, driven, intent **7** adamant, devoted, diehard **8** hellbent, obdurate, resolute, resolved, stubborn **9** dedicated, steadfast, unbending **10** brassbound, determined, inexorable, inflexible, purposeful, relentless, unyielding

single out 4 cull, mark, pick **5** elect, favor **6** choose, opt for, select **9** designate **11** distinguish

singsong 4 cant

singular 3 odd **4** lone, only, rare, sole, solo **5** weird **6** unique **7** bizarre, oddball, strange, unusual **8** peculiar, solitary, uncommon **9** exclusive **10** individual, outlandish, particular, unexampled **11** exceptional **13** extraordinary

singularity 5 quirk, unity **6** oddity **7** anomaly, oneness **8** identity **9** exception **11** peculiarity, personality **12** idiosyncrasy **13** individuality, particularity

singularize 4 mark **11** distinguish, individuate **12** characterize **13** differentiate, individualize

sinister 4 dark, dire, evil, left **6** creepy, malign **7** baleful, fateful, malefic, ominous **8** lowering, menacing **9** ill-omened, malicious **10** foreboding, maleficent, portentous **11** apocalyptic, threatening **12** inauspicious, unpropitious

sink 3 dip, pit, sag **4** bore, bury, dive, drop, fall, sump, wane **5** basin, drill, droop, lower, sewer, slope, slump, stoop, swamp **6** hollow, invest, plunge, settle, thrust, worsen **7** capsize, cesspit, decline, depress, descend, founder, go under, immerse, let down, scuttle, subside, torpedo **8** cesspool, hellhole, submerge, submerse **9** concavity, disappear **10** depression

sinker 3 bob **5** plumb **6** weight **8** doughnut, fastball, plumb bob

sinkhole 3 dip, sag **4** bowl **5** basin **6** hollow **8** cesspool **9** concavity **10** depression

sinless 4 pure **6** chaste **8** innocent **9** righteous **10** impeccable

sinner 5 rogue, scamp **6** bad egg, outlaw, rascal, wretch **7** lowlife, villain **8** criminal, evildoer, offender **9** libertine, miscreant, reprobate, scoundrel, wrongdoer **10** black sheep, delinquent, profligate, malefactor **11** rapscallion

Sinn ____ 4 Fein

sinuous 4 wavy **5** lithe, snaky **7** winding **8** flexuous, tortuous **10** convoluted, meandering, serpentine **11** anfractuous, snake-shaped

sinus 6 cavity, hollow, recess

Sioux 6 Dakota ***chief:*** **8** Red Cloud **10** Crazy Horse **11** Sitting Bull ***language:*** **6** Dakota, Lakota ***people:*** **3** Ofo **4** Crow **6** Biloxi, Tutelo **7** Catawba, Hidatsa **9** Winnebago

sip 5 drink, savor, taste **6** imbibe

siphon 3 tap **4** draw, pipe, pump **5** draft, drain **6** convoy, divert, funnel **7** channel, conduct, draw off **8** transmit

sir 4 lord **5** title **6** knight, mister **9** gentleman

sire 4 lord **5** beget, breed, hatch, spawn **6** father, parent **7** founder **8** engender **9** patriarch, procreate, propagate, reproduce **10** forefather

siren 4 vamp **5** alarm **7** Lorelei **9** temptress **10** seductress **11** femme fatale ***film:*** **4** Bara (Theda)

Siren 5 Ligea **8** Leucosia **10** Parthenope ***German:*** **7** Lorelei

sirenian 6 dugong, sea cow **7** manatee

siren song 4 lure **5** decoy, snare **6** come-on **10** allurement, enticement, temptation

Sirius 7 Dog Star

sister 3 nun **7** sibling ***French:*** **5** soeur ***Latin:*** **5** soror ***Spanish:*** **7** hermana

Sister Carrie author 7 Dreiser (Theodore)

sisterly 7 sororal

Sisyphus *brother:* 7 Athamas **9** Salmoneus ***father:*** **6** Aeolus ***mother:*** **7** Enarete ***son:*** **7** Glaucus

sit 4 pose **5** perch, roost

Sita ***abductor:*** **6** Ravana ***husband, rescuer:*** **4** Rama

sitarist 7 Shankar (Ravi)

sitcom 3 ALF **4** MASH, Mr. Ed, Soap **5** Ellen, Maude **6** Cheers **7** Frasier, Friends, Jetsons (The), Newhart **8** Get Smart, Love Boat (The), Mister Ed, Munsters (The), Roseanne, Seinfeld, Simpsons (The) **9** Bewitched, Cosby Show (The), Full House, Happy Days, I Love Lucy, Odd Couple (The) **10** Brady Bunch (The), Green Acres, Jeffersons (The), Night Court **11** Flintstones (The), Golden Girls (The), Murphy Brown, My Three Sons, Wonder Years (The) **12** Addams Family (The), Barney Miller, Fawlty Towers, Hogan's Heroes, Honeymooners (The), King of Queens (The), Mork and Mindy, Will and Grace **13** One Day at a Time, Our Miss Brooks, Sanford and Son, Three's Company **14** All in the Family **15** Diff'rent Strokes, Father Knows Best, Gilligan's Island, Home Improvement, I Dream of Jeannie, Leave It to Beaver, Ozzie and Harriet **17** Are You Being Served, Laverne and Shirley, My Favorite Martian, Petticoat Junction **18** Beverly Hillbillies (The) **19** Married with Children **20** Keeping Up Appearances **21** Everybody Loves Raymond

site 3 dig **4** home, spot **5** haunt, locus, place, point, scene, venue **6** locale **7** station **8** locality, location, position

sit-in 7 protest

sitting 6 séance **7** session ***prolonged:*** **8** sederunt

Sitting Bull's tribe 5 Sioux **6** Dakota

sitting duck 4 butt, mark **6** target

situate 3 put, set **5** place **6** locate **7** install **8** position

situation 3 job **4** post, rank **5** point, state **6** plight, status **7** footing, setting, station **8** location, position, standing **9** condition **13** circumstances

situs 5 place, venue **6** locale

Siva see **Shiva**

six ***combining form:*** **3** hex, sex **4** hexa, sexi **5** sexti ***group of:*** **6** sestet, sextet **9** sextuplet ***relating to:*** **6** senary

sixfold 8 sextuple

six-pack 3 abs

six-shooter 3 gun **6** pistol **8** revolver

sixth sense 3 ESP **5** hunch **7** insight **9** intuition, telepathy **12** clairvoyance

sizable 3 big **5** ample, hefty, large, major, roomy **8** spacious **9** capacious, extensive **10** commodious, large-scale **11** substantial **12** considerable

size 2 sm, xl **3** lge, med **4** area, bulk, mass **5** range, scope, width **6** extent, height, length, spread, volume **7** bigness, breadth, caliber, expanse, measure, stature **9** amplitude, dimension, extension, greatness, largeness, magnitude **10** dimensions, proportion **11** measurement, proportions

size up 3 peg **4** rate, read **5** assay, gauge, judge, value **6** assess, review, survey **7** adjudge, dope out **8** appraise, estimate, evaluate **9** figure out

sizzle 3 fry **4** buzz, fizz, hiss, whiz **5** grill **6** hoopla, seethe **7** pizzazz **8** sibilate **10** excitement

sizzling 3 hot **6** red-hot, torrid **7** burning **8** scalding, white-hot **9** scorching

skald 4 bard, poet

Skanda 6 war-god ***brother:*** **6** Ganesa, Ganesh **7** Ganesha ***father:*** **4** Siva **5** Shiva

skate 3 nag, ray **4** skid, skim **5** glide, skirr, slide **8** glissade ***blade:*** **6** runner ***kind:*** **6** figure, hockey, in-line **11** Rollerblade

skateboard maneuver 3 air **4** bail, hang **5** carve, grind, ollie, pivot **8** kickflip

skater see **ice skater**

skating ***area:*** **10** kiss and cry ***game:*** **8** ringette **9** broomball, ice hockey **12** in-line hockey, roller hockey ***site:*** **3** ice **4** rink ***term:*** **3** COP **4** axel, lobe, lutz, quad **5** T-stop **6** Mohawk, rocker, spiral **7** bracket, choctaw, gliding, salchow, sit spin, swizzle, toe loop, twizzle **8** heel stop, star lift, striding, stroking, toe picks **9** camel spin, crossover, free dance, free skate, waltz jump, Zayak Rule **11** death spiral, falling leaf, hydrant lift ***type:*** **3** ice **5** trail **6** in-line, roller

skedaddle 3 run **4** bolt, flee, skip **5** scoot, scram, split **6** beat it, begone, bug off, cut out, decamp, get out **7** make off, run away, scamper, skiddoo, take off, vamoose **8** clear out **10** make tracks

skein 4 coil, hank **5** flock, snarl, twist **6** tangle **12** entanglement

skeletal 4 bony **5** gaunt **6** wasted **7** angular, scraggy, starved **8** rawboned **9** emaciated **10** cadaverous

skeleton 5 bones, draft, frame **6** sketch **7** diagram, outline **9** bare bones, framework ***marine:*** **5** coral, shell

skeptic 5 cynic **7** doubter, scoffer **8** agnostic **10** Pyrrhonist, questioner, unbeliever **11** disbeliever

skeptical 4 wary **5** leery **6** show-me **7** cynical, dubious **8** doubtful, doubting **9** quizzical **10** dissenting, suspicious **11** mistrustful, questioning, unbelieving **12** disbelieving, freethinking

skepticism 5 doubt **7** dubiety **8** distrust, mistrust, wariness **9** dubiosity, misgiving, suspicion **11** incertitude, uncertainty
skerry 4 isle, reef **6** island
sketch 4 draw, plot **5** draft, rough, trace **6** depict, design, doodle, lay out, map out, précis **7** develop, diagram, outline, portray **8** block out, chalk out, rough out **9** blueprint, delineate **12** characterize
sketchy 4 iffy **5** crude, rough, vague **6** skimpy, slight **7** cursory, shallow **8** skeletal **10** incomplete **11** preliminary, superficial **12** questionable
skew 4 bias, veer **5** angle, fudge, slant, slide **6** swerve **7** distort
skewer 3 rod **4** spit **5** lance, spear, spike **6** impale, pierce **8** puncture, ridicule, transfix **9** brochette, criticize
ski 5 glide, slide ***lift:*** **4** J-bar, T-bar **5** chair **7** gondola
skid 5 glide, skate, slide **6** pallet, runner **7** spinout **8** sideslip
skiddoo 4 scat **5** leave, scram, split **6** beat it, begone, bug off, decamp, depart, vacate **7** buzz off, take off, vamoose **8** clear out, shove off **9** skedaddle, take a hike **10** hit the road, make tracks
skid row 6 bowery
skier *American:* 3 Moe (Tommy) **4** Kidd (Billy) **5** Mahre (Phil, Steve) **6** Miller (Bode) **7** Johnson (Bill) ***Austrian:* 5** Maier (Hermann) **6** Proell (Annemarie), Sailer (Toni) **7** Klammer (Franz), Schranz (Karl) **10** Girardelli (Marc) **11** Moser-Proell (Annemarie) ***French:* 5** Killy (Jean-Claude) ***Italian:* 5** Tomba (Alberto) **6** Thoeni (Gustavo) ***Luxembourg:* 10** Girardelli (Marc) ***Swedish:* 8** Stenmark (Ingemar) ***Swiss:* 10** Zurbriggen (Pirmin)
skiff 4 boat **7** rowboat
skiing *area:* 3 run **5** slope ***cross-country:* 7** touring ***event:* 6** schuss, slalom **8** downhill **11** giant slalom ***horse-drawn:* 9** skijoring ***kind:* 6** Alpine, Nordic ***position:* 7** vorlage ***technique:* 6** wedeln **8** snowplow, traverse ***turn:* 7** christy **8** christie
skill 3 art **5** craft, knack **7** ability, address, command, cunning, finesse, know-how, mastery, prowess, sleight **8** deftness, facility **9** dexterity, expertise, ingenuity, readiness, technique **10** adroitness, competence **11** proficiency
skilled 3 apt **4** able **5** adept **6** expert **7** capable, trained **8** masterly, talented **9** competent, masterful, practiced **10** proficient **12** accomplished
skillet 3 pan **6** spider **9** frying pan
skillful 4 able, deft **5** adept, crack, handy **6** adroit, clever, daedal, expert **7** skilled **8** masterly **9** competent, dexterous, masterful, practiced, workmanly **10** proficient **11** crackerjack, workmanlike **12** accomplished
skim 4 sail, scan, scud, skip **5** brush, carom, glide, graze, skirr **6** browse **8** embezzle, ricochet
skimp 4 save **5** pinch, scant, spare, stint **6** meager, scanty, scrape, sparse **7** slender **8** begrudge, conserve, retrench, withhold **9** economize
skimpy 5 scant, spare **6** meager, meagre, paltry, scanty, scarce, sparse **7** limited, wanting **8** exiguous **9** deficient **10** inadequate **12** insufficient
skim through 4 scan **6** browse
skin 3 fur, gyp, pod, rap **4** clad, clip, flay, husk, hide, pare, peel, pelt, rind, soak **5** blame, cheat, cover, scale, shell, stiff, strip **6** fleece, sheath, slough **7** censure, condemn, sheathe **8** denounce **9** epidermis, sheathing **10** integument, overcharge **11** decorticate ***animal:* 4** coat, hide, pelt **6** hackle, peltry ***beaver:* 4** plew ***combining form:* 3** cut **4** cuti, derm **5** derma, dermo, dermy **6** dermat, dermia, dermis **7** cutaneo, dermata (plural), dermato, epiderm **8** epidermo ***depression:* 6** dimple ***disease:* 4** acne **5** hives, mange **6** eczema, herpes, tetter **8** ringworm **10** dermatitis ***dry:* 5** scurf ***fold:* 5** plica ***layer:* 5** derma **6** corium, dermis **7** cuticle **9** epidermis ***opening:* 4** pore ***protuberance:* 3** tag, wen **4** mole, wart **6** pimple ***rabbit:* 5** coney ***relating to:* 6** dermal **9** cuticular, epidermal ***spot:* 7** freckle
skin-deep 7 shallow, trivial **11** superficial
skinflint 5 miser **7** niggard, scrooge **8** tightwad **10** cheapskate, pinchpenny
skin game 3 con **4** scam **5** bunco, bunko, cheat, fraud, sting, trick **6** hustle, racket **7** swindle **8** flimflam
skink 4 adda **6** lizard
skinny 4 bony, dope, info, lank, lean, thin **5** gaunt, lanky, scoop, spare, weedy **6** twiggy **7** angular, lowdown, scraggy, scrawny **8** rawboned, skeletal **9** emaciated
Skin of Our Teeth author 6 Wilder (Thornton)
skip 3 hop, run **4** flee, jump, leap, omit, trip **5** bound, caper, carom, frisk, leave, scoot, skirr **6** cavort, gambol, ignore, pass up, spring **7** abscond, misfire, scamper, skitter **8** leave out, overlook, pass over, ricochet **9** skedaddle
skipjack 4 boat, fish, tuna **8** bluefish, ladyfish, sailboat

skipper **5** pilot **6** leader **7** captain **9** butterfly, commander
ski resort ***Austrian:*** **9** Kitzbühel ***Canadian:*** **5** Banff **8** Big White, Sun Peaks, Whistler **9** Tremblant (Mont) **10** Lake Louise ***French:*** **8** Chamonix ***Italian:*** **7** Cortina ***Swiss:*** **5** Davos **6** Gstaad **7** Verbier, Zermatt **8** St. Moritz **9** Engelberg, Sugarloaf ***U. S.:*** **4** Alta, Taos, Vail **5** Aspen, Stowe **6** Big Sky **8** Snowbird, Snowmass **9** Camelback, Lake Tahoe, Snowbasin, Sun Valley, Telluride **10** Killington **11** Jackson Hole, Squaw Valley **12** Breckenridge
skirmish **3** row **4** fray **5** broil, brush, clash, melee, run-in, scrap, set-to **6** affray, battle, fracas **7** assault, dispute **8** conflict, struggle **9** encounter, scrimmage
skirr **3** run **4** bolt, flee, sail, scud, skim, skip **5** float, scoot, shoot **7** make off, scamper **9** skedaddle
skirt **3** hem, rim **4** brim, duck, edge **5** avoid, bound, brink, burke, dodge, elude, evade, hedge, verge **6** border, bypass, define, detour, escape, fringe, ignore, margin **8** sidestep, surround **9** perimeter, periphery **10** circumvent ***ballet:*** **4** tutu ***feature:*** **3** hem **4** slit ***long:*** **4** maxi ***Polynesian:*** **5** pareo, pareu ***Scottish:*** **4** kilt ***short:*** **4** mini ***style:*** **5** A-line **6** sheath **9** crinoline ***support:*** **11** farthingale
skit **6** shtick, sketch **9** burlesque ***show:*** **5** revue
skitter **3** hop **4** flit, skip, trip **6** scurry, spring **7** scamper
skittery see **skittish**
skittish **3** coy, shy **4** edgy, wary **5** chary, dizzy, jumpy, leery **6** fickle **7** bashful, fidgety, flighty, nervous, rabbity, restive **8** unstable, volatile **9** excitable, frivolous, impulsive, mercurial, whimsical **10** capricious, unreliable
skive **4** pare **5** carve, shave, slice
skivvies **9** underwear
skoal **5** toast **6** health
skua **4** bird **6** jaeger **7** seabird
skulduggery **5** fraud **8** foul play, trickery **9** chicanery, duplicity **10** hanky-panky
skulk **4** lurk, slip **5** creep, prowl, shirk, slink, sneak, steal
skull **4** head, mind **5** brain **7** cranium **8** brainpan **9** braincase ***back of:*** **7** occiput ***bone:*** **5** vomer **6** zygoma **7** ethmoid, frontal **8** parietal, sphenoid, temporal ***jawless:*** **9** calvarium ***joint:*** **6** suture ***part:*** **3** jaw **5** inion
skullcap **6** beanie, pileus **7** calotte **8** yarmulke **9** calvarium, zucchetto
skunk **4** beat, drub, lick, scum, whip, whup **6** thrash, wallop **7** clobber, polecat, shellac, stinker, trounce **8** civet cat, lambaste **9** overwhelm, slaughter ***genus:*** **8** Mephitis
sky **5** azure **6** heaven, welkin **7** heavens **8** empyrean **9** firmament
sky-blue **5** azure **8** cerulean
skylarking **5** revel **7** revelry, whoopee **9** high jinks, horseplay, rowdiness, whoop-de-do **10** roughhouse **12** roughhousing
skylight **6** window
skyline **7** horizon, outline
sky pilot **5** padre **6** cleric, parson, pastor **8** chaplain, minister, preacher **9** churchman, clergyman
skyrocket **4** rise, soar **7** shoot up **8** catapult
sky sighting **3** UFO
slab **5** block, chunk, slice, strip **8** pavement
slack **3** lax **4** lazy, slow, soft **5** inert, loose, relax **6** remiss **7** ease off, laggard, passive, relaxed **8** careless, derelict, dilatory, inactive, indolent, slothful, sluggish, stagnant **9** leisurely, lethargic, negligent **10** neglectful
slacken **3** ebb, lax **4** ease, slow, wane **5** abate, let up, loose, relax **6** detain, ease up, lessen, loosen, relent, retard, slow up **7** die down, dwindle, ease off, subside **8** diminish, moderate, slow down **9** untighten **10** decelerate
slacker **3** bum **4** slug **5** idler, sloth **6** loafer **7** goof-off, shirker, wastrel **8** deadbeat, layabout, slugabed, sluggard **9** goldbrick, lazybones **10** delinquent **11** couch potato
slag **4** lava **5** dross **6** cinder, debris, scoria
slake **5** allay **6** deaden, quench **7** crumble, hydrate, relieve, satisfy **9** alleviate
slam **3** bat, hit, jab, pan, rap **4** bang, bash, beat, belt, blow, boom, dash, drub, flay, slug, slur, swat, wham **5** blast, crack, crash, fling, knock, pound, slash, smack, smash, swipe, whack **6** batter, cudgel, hammer, scathe, strike, thwack, wallop **7** clobber, potshot **8** lambaste **9** castigate
slam-dance **4** mosh
slam dunk **5** cinch, setup **6** shoo-in **7** safe bet **9** certainty, sure thing
slammer **3** can, jug, pen **4** brig, coop, jail, stir **5** clink, pokey **6** cooler, lockup, prison **9** calaboose **12** penitentiary
slander **4** slur, tale **5** libel, slime, smear, sully **6** defame, malign, smirch, vilify **7** asperse, calumny, scandal, tarnish, traduce **8** besmirch **9** denigrate **10** backbiting, calumniate, defamation, detraction, scandalize **11** mud-slinging **12** back-stabbing
slang **4** cant, jive **5** argot, lingo **6** jargon, patois, patter **7** dialect **10** vernacular
slant **3** tip **4** bank, bias, cant, heel, lean, list, skew, tilt, veer, warp **5** angle, aside, bevel, grade, slope, splay **7** distort, incline, lean-

ing, outlook **8** gradient **9** prejudice, viewpoint **10** standpoint **11** inclination **12** predilection ***combining form:*** **4** clin **5** clino

slap 3 hit, pop **4** bash, blow, cuff, shot, slam, swat **5** clout, smack, spank, whack **6** buffet, insult, rebuff, strike **7** affront, putdown **8** brickbat, lambaste, penalize **9** castigate

slapdash 5 hasty, messy **6** random, sloppy **7** cursory **8** careless, slipshod **9** half-baked, haphazard, hit-or-miss, makeshift

slap down 5 quell **6** kibosh **7** squelch **8** prohibit, suppress

slaphappy 5 dazed, dizzy, woozy **6** punchy **10** punch-drunk

slash 3 cut **4** clip, gash, hack, pare, slit **5** lower, shave, slice **6** reduce, scathe, scorch **7** abridge, blister, curtail, cut back, cut down, scarify, scourge, shorten **8** lacerate, lambaste, mark down **9** castigate, excoriate **10** abbreviate

slat 4 lath **5** board, stave, strip **6** louver, louvre **7** airfoil

slate 4 gray, list, rock, tile **6** lineup, record, tablet, ticket **7** shingle **8** schedule **9** designate

slather 5 smear **6** spread **8** squander

slattern 4 bawd, moll, slut, tart **5** hussy, tramp, wench **6** floozy, harlot **7** chippie, jezebel, trollop **8** strumpet **10** prostitute **11** painted lady **12** scarlet woman, streetwalker

slaughter 4 kill, slay **6** murder **7** butcher, carnage, killing, wipe out **8** butchery, decimate, demolish, hecatomb, massacre **9** bloodbath, bloodshed, liquidate **10** annihilate, butchering **11** destruction, exterminate, liquidation **12** annihilation

slaughterhouse 8 abattoir, shambles

Slav 4 Pole, Serb, Sorb, Wend **5** Croat, Czech **6** Bulgar, Slovak **7** Russian, Serbian, Slovene **8** Bohemian, Croatian, Moravian **9** Bulgarian, Ruthenian, Ukrainian

slave 4 grub, help, peon, plod, serf, slog, toil **5** grind, helot, swink **6** drudge, menial, thrall, toiler, vassal **7** bondman, chattel, servant ***feudal:*** **4** serf ***harem:*** **9** odalisque ***liberated:*** **8** freedman ***Muslim:*** **6** Mamluk **8** Mameluke ***Spartan:*** **5** helot

slave driver 6 tyrant **7** foreman **8** martinet, overseer **10** taskmaster **11** Simon Legree

slaver 4 spit **5** drool, froth **6** drivel, saliva **7** dribble, slobber, spittle **8** salivate

slavery 6 thrall **7** bondage, helotry, peonage, serfdom **9** indenture, servitude, thralldom **11** subjugation

Slavic apostle 5 Cyril **9** Methodius

slavish 6 abject, menial **7** servile **8** obeisant, wretched **9** groveling, imitative, laborious **10** obsequious, unoriginal **11** subservient

slay 4 do in, kill **6** murder **7** bump off, butcher, execute, put away **8** dispatch, knock off **9** liquidate, slaughter **11** assassinate

slayer 7 butcher **11** executioner

sleazy 3 low **5** cheap, dingy, seedy, tacky, tatty **6** cheesy, flimsy, shabby, shoddy, trashy **7** run-down, squalid **8** gimcrack **10** down-at-heel **11** dilapidated **12** disreputable

sled 4 luge, pung **6** sleigh **7** coaster, travois **8** toboggan ***Russian:*** **6** troika

sled dog 5 husky **8** malamute

sledge 4 maul **6** hammer, sleigh ***Eskimo:*** **7** komatik ***Lapp:*** **5** pulka

sleek 4 oily **6** glassy, glossy, smooth **7** elegant, stylish **8** lustrous, polished **10** glistening

sleep 3 nap **4** doss, doze, rest **6** catnap, repose, siesta, snooze **7** shut-eye, slumber **11** slumberland ***bringer:*** **7** sandman ***combining form:*** **4** hypn, narc **5** hypno, narco, somni ***god:*** **6** Hypnos, Somnus ***noise:*** **5** snore

sleeper 3 tie **4** beam, mole **7** Pullman **8** long shot **11** double agent, stringpiece

sleeping 7 dormant **8** comatose ***disease:*** **10** narcolepsy

sleepless 7 wakeful **8** vigilant **9** insomniac

sleeplessness 8 insomnia

sleepwalker 12 somnambulist

sleepy 4 dozy **6** drowsy **7** nodding **9** somnolent **10** slumberous

sleigh 4 pung **6** sledge

sleight 4 ploy, ruse, wile **5** skill, trick **7** gimmick, prowess **8** artifice, deftness, maneuver **9** dexterity, stratagem **10** adroitness

sleight of hand 11 legerdemain

slender 4 lean, slim, thin, trim **5** lithe, reedy, spare **6** skinny, slight, svelte, twiggy **7** spindly, willowy

sleuth 4 dick, Drew (Nancy) **5** Brown (Encyclopedia, Father), Hardy (Frank, Joe), Kojak (Theo), Lupin (Arsène), McGee (Travis), Morse, Queen (Ellery), Saint (The), snoop, Spade (Sam), Tracy (Dick), Vance (Philo), Wolfe (Nero) **6** Alleyn (Roderick), Archer (Lew), Belden (Trixie), Hammer (Mike), Holmes (Sherlock), Marple (Miss), Poirot (Hercule), shamus, Wimsey (Peter) **7** Cadfael (Brother), Columbo, Fansler (Kate), gumshoe, Maigret, Marlowe (Philip), Rawlins (Easy), Templar (Simon "The Saint") **8** Drummond (Bulldog), hawkshaw, Millhone (Kinsey), Rockford (Jim), sherlock **9** Dalgliesh (Adam), detective, Scarpetta (Kay), Wallander (Kurt) **10** private eye, Warshawski (V. I.) **12** investigator

slew 3 lot, mob, ton **4** army, heap, host, load, mess, pile, raft, skid, turn, veer **5** batch, bunch, crowd, flock, pivot, twist **6** myriad, passel, swerve, throng **9** abundance, multitude

slice 3 cut **4** gash, slit **5** allot, carve, divvy, quota, sever, share, slash, split, wedge **6** cleave, divide, incise, sample **7** dissect, portion, segment **8** allocate **9** allotment, allowance

slick 4 film, glib, oily, slip, wily **5** sharp, sleek, soapy **6** crafty, glossy, greasy, shrewd, smarmy, smooth, tricky **7** cunning **8** slippery, slithery, unctuous **10** lubricious, oleaginous

slicker 4 dude **5** dandy, shark **6** con man **7** cheater, diddler, grifter, oilskin, sharper **8** raincoat, swindler **9** trickster **11** flimflammer

slide 3 dip, sag **4** flow, ramp, skid, slip **5** chute, coast, chute, drift, glide, skate, slump, spill **6** scooch, stream **7** decline, slither **8** downturn **9** downswing, downtrend **12** transparency

slight 4 omit, skip, slim, snub, thin **5** frail, reedy, scorn, small **6** flimsy, ignore, meager, meagre, modest, offend, paltry, remote, skinny **7** contemn, neglect, outside, putdown, slender, tenuous, trivial **8** brush-off, delicate, discount, overlook, smallish, trifling **9** disregard, pint-sized **10** disrespect, negligible

slightly 4 a bit, a tad **6** a touch **7** a little

slim 4 thin **5** lithe, reedy, small, spare **6** meager, meagre, minute, narrow, paltry, remote, skinny, slight, svelte, twiggy **7** lissome, outside, slender, tenuous **9** lithesome **10** negligible

slim down 4 diet, fast **6** reduce **10** slenderize

slime 3 goo, mud **4** glop, gook, guck, gunk, muck, ooze, scum **5** filth **6** sleaze, sludge **7** slander

slimy 4 oozy **6** mucous **7** viscous

sling 3 lob **4** cast, fire, hang, hurl, sock, toss **5** chuck, heave, march, pitch, throw **6** dangle, launch **7** suspend **8** catapult

slink 4 lurk **5** creep, prowl, skulk, slide, sneak, steal **7** gumshoe

slinky 4 sexy **5** lithe, sleek **6** svelte **7** furtive, lissome, sinuous, slender, willowy **8** graceful, sensuous, stealthy

slip 3 sag **4** dock, drop, fall, flow, flub, goof, lurk, shed, sink, skid **5** berth, boner, creep, error, fluff, gaffe, glide, lapse, slide, slink, slump, sneak, steal **6** escape **7** blooper, blunder, decline, drop off, fall off, faux pas, mistake, slither **8** downturn, throw off **9** downswing, downtrend

slipper 4 mule, shoe **5** scuff **6** bootee, bootie, sandal **8** flip-flop, pantofle

slippery 3 icy **4** eely, oily **5** slick **6** greasy, shifty, smooth **7** devious, evasive **8** illusive, slithery **10** lubricious

slipshod 6 blowsy, blowzy, flimsy, frowsy, frowzy, shabby, shoddy, sloppy, untidy **7** rumpled, scrubby, scruffy, unkempt **8** careless, ill-kempt, slapdash, slovenly, tattered **9** haphazard, makeshift, negligent **10** bedraggled, disheveled, down-at-heel

slipup 4 goof **5** boner, error, fluff, lapse **6** bungle, glitch, miscue, mishap **7** blooper, blunder, faux pas, misstep, mistake, setback, stumble **8** accident **9** mischance, oversight **10** misfortune **11** misjudgment

slit 3 cut, gap **4** gash, rent **5** chink, crack, slash, slice **6** cranny, incise **7** crevice, fissure, opening

slither 4 slip **5** creep, glide, sidle, slide, slink, snake, sneak, steal **7** wriggle **8** undulate

slithery see **slippery**

sliver 5 scrap, shard, shave, shred, slice **6** paring **7** shaving, snippet **8** splinter

slob 3 oaf **4** boor, clod, goon, lout **6** galoot, sloven

slobber 4 gush **5** drool, froth **6** drivel, effuse, slaver **7** dribble, enthuse **8** salivate

sloe 4 plum **10** blackthorn

slog 4 grub, moil, plod, plug, toil **5** chore, grind, labor, shlep, slave, sweat **6** drudge, schlep, trudge **7** schlepp

slogan 5 maxim, motto **6** byword **9** battle cry, catchword, watchword **10** shibboleth **11** catchphrase

sloop 4 boat **5** yacht **8** sailboat

slop 3 mud, pap **4** gush, muck **5** douse, dreck, dregs, offal, slosh, slush, spill, swill **6** guzzle, pablum, refuse, splash, sludge **7** garbage, pabulum, rubbish **8** splatter

slope 3 tip **4** bend, brae, cant, heel, lean, list, rise, skew, swag, sway, tilt **5** grade, pitch, scarp, slant **6** ascent, glacis **7** descent, incline, leaning, recline **8** gradient **9** acclivity, declivity, obliquity **11** inclination ***combining form:*** **5** cline **6** clinal

sloppy 5 dowdy, gushy, messy **6** slushy, untidy **7** gushing, unkempt **8** careless, effusive, ill-kempt, slapdash, slipshod, slovenly **10** bedraggled, disheveled **11** dishevelled

slosh 4 gush, slop, wash **5** churn, swash **6** gurgle, splash **8** flounder, splatter

slot 4 vent **5** niche, notch **6** groove, keyway **7**

keyhole, opening, passage **8** aperture **10** pigeonhole

sloth 4 laze, unau **5** idler **6** acedia, apathy, idling, lazing, loafer, slouch, torpor **7** goof-off, languor, loafing, slacker **8** idleness, laziness, lethargy **9** heaviness, indolence, lassitude, lazybones, torpidity **11** couch potato **12** listlessness, sluggishness **13** shiftlessness ***three-toed:*** **2** ai

slothful 4 idle, lazy **8** fainéant, indolent **9** shiftless

slouch 3 bum, oaf, sag **4** laze, loaf, loll, lout, mope, slug **5** droop, idler, sloth, slump, stoop **6** loafer, loiter, lounge **7** saunter, shamble, shuffle **8** fainéant, slugabed, sluggard **9** do-nothing, lazybones

slough 3 bog, fen **4** cast, mire, molt, quag, shed, sump **5** inlet, marsh, scrap, swamp **6** morass, reject **7** discard **8** jettison, quagmire, throw out **9** backwater, marshland, swampland, throw away

Slovakia *capital:* 10 Bratislava ***city:*** **6** Kosice ***monetary unit:*** **6** koruna ***mountain range:*** **10** Carpathian ***neighbor:*** **6** Poland **7** Austria, Hungary, Ukraine **13** Czech Republic ***river:*** **3** Váh **4** Hron **6** Danube, Morava

Slovenia *capital:* 9 Ljubljana ***city:*** **7** Maribor ***monetary unit:*** **4** euro ***monetary unit, former:*** **5** tolar ***neighbor:*** **5** Italy **7** Austria, Croatia, Hungary ***part of:*** **7** Balkans ***peninsula:*** **6** Balkan

slovenly 5 dingy, messy, mussy, seedy, slack **6** frowsy, frowzy, grubby, grungy, scuzzy, shabby, skanky, sleazy, sloppy, untidy **7** squalid, unkempt **8** careless, slapdash, slipshod **10** bedraggled, slatternly

slow 4 late, poky **5** brake, check, lento, pokey, tardy **6** adagio, hinder, impede, leaden, retard, torpid **7** halting, lagging, slacken **8** dilatory, dragging, plodding, sluggish, stagnant **9** leisurely, snaillike, unhurried **10** decelerate, snail-paced, straggling

slowpoke 5 snail **6** lagger **7** dawdler, laggard **8** lingerer, loiterer **9** straggler

sludge 3 mud **4** crud, gook, guck, gunk, mire, muck, ooze, slop **5** slime **6** sewage **8** sediment

slug 3 bum, hit, nip, tot **4** bash, belt, dram, drop, jolt, shot, slam, swat **5** blast, clout, idler, larva, pound, punch, smack, smash, snail, snort, thump **6** buffet, bullet, loafer, slouch, thwack, wallop **7** clobber, goof-off, slacker **8** fainéant, toothful **9** do-nothing, lazybones **11** couch potato ***genus:*** **5** Limax

slugfest 4 bout **5** brawl, set-to **6** rumble **8** dogfight **10** donnybrook, prizefight

sluggard 3 bum **5** idler **6** loafer, slouch **7** dawdler, goof-off, laggard, shirker, slacker **8** deadbeat, fainéant, slowpoke **9** do-nothing, goldbrick, lazybones

slugger 5 boxer **6** batter, hitter **7** palooka

sluggish 4 lazy, logy, slow **5** inert, slack **6** draggy, leaden, stupid, torpid **7** lumpish **8** dragging, indolent, listless, slothful **9** apathetic, lethargic

sluice 4 duct, flow, gush, pour, race, wash **5** flush, surge **6** trough **7** channel **8** spillway **9** floodgate

slum 6 ghetto **7** skid row

slumber 3 nap **4** doze **5** sleep **6** catnap, drowse, snooze, stupor, torpor **8** dormancy, hebetude, lethargy **9** lassitude, torpidity

slumberous see **sleepy**

slumgullion 4 stew **6** burgoo, ragout **7** goulash

slump 3 dip, sag **4** drop, fall, flag, funk, loll, sink, slip **5** droop, hunch, slide **6** slouch, trough **7** decline, drop off, falloff **8** collapse, downturn **9** downslide, downswing, downtrend, recession **10** depression, stagnation

slur 4 blot, blur, lisp, onus, slam, spot **5** brand, knock, libel, odium, smear, stain **6** befoul, defame, insult, malign, stigma, vilify **7** blacken, calumny, obloquy, obscure, slander, spatter, traduce **8** black eye, brickbat, innuendo, tear down **9** aspersion, bespatter, denigrate, discredit, disparage **10** accusation, calumniate

slurp 3 lap **4** gulp, suck **5** lap up, swill **6** guzzle

slush 3 mud **4** mire, muck, slop **6** drivel **8** schmaltz

sly 4 arch, foxy, wily **5** cagey, saucy, shady, slick **6** artful, clever, crafty, shifty, shrewd, smooth, sneaky, subtle, tricky **7** cunning, devious, furtive, roguish, vulpine **8** guileful, scheming, slippery, stealthy **9** designing, insidious, underhand **11** mischievous, underhanded

slyboots see **scamp**

slyness 4 wile **5** guile **7** cunning **8** caginess, foxiness, wiliness **9** canniness **10** craftiness

smack 3 bat, bop, box **4** bang, bash, belt, biff, blow, buss, chop, clip, cuff, dash, hint, kiss, peck, reek, slam, slap, sock, tang, whop **5** clout, crack, plumb, punch, right, savor, smell, spang, spank, stink, taste, tinge, trace, whack **6** buffet, heroin, relish, smooch, square, strike, thwack **7** clobber, soupçon

smack-dab 4 bang, just **5** plumb, right, spang

6 square **7** exactly **8** squarely **9** perfectly, precisely

small 3 wee **4** mean, mini, puny, tiny **5** bitty, dinky, dwarf, micro, minor, petty, runty, short, teeny **6** bantam, little, meager, meagre, minute, monkey, narrow, paltry, petite, slight, teensy **7** cramped, stunted, trivial **8** picayune, piddling, pint-size, trifling **9** miniature, minuscule, pint-sized **10** diminutive, negligible, undersized **11** ineffectual, unimportant ***combining form:*** **4** micr, mini **5** micro

small fry 4 kids, tots **8** children **10** youngsters

small-minded 4 mean **5** petty **6** narrow **7** bigoted **9** hidebound, illiberal, parochial **10** brassbound, intolerant, provincial

smallpox 7 variola

small talk 4 chat **6** banter **7** chatter, palaver, prattle **8** badinage, chitchat, raillery, repartee **10** persiflage

small-time 5 minor, petty **6** paltry, two-bit **7** trivial **8** picayune, piddling, trifling **10** bush-league, negligible, shoestring **11** minor-league, unimportant **13** insignificant

smalt 4 blue

smarmy 4 glib, oily **5** slick **6** sleazy **7** buttery, fawning, fulsome **8** unctuous **10** obsequious, oleaginous **12** ingratiating

smart 3 apt **4** ache, chic, keen **5** acute, alert, canny, fresh, natty, nobby, quick, sassy, saucy, savvy, sharp, slick, sting, swank, throb **6** brainy, bright, cheeky, clever, dapper, shrewd, spiffy, spruce, suffer **7** dashing, stylish **8** impudent **11** fashionable, intelligent, quick-witted, ready-witted, sharp-witted

smart aleck 7 show-off, wise guy **8** wiseacre **9** know-it-all **11** wisecracker, wisenheimer

smart-alecky 4 wise **5** fresh, sassy, saucy **6** cheeky **8** impudent, insolent **9** bold-faced **11** impertinent

smart set 5 elect, elite **6** bon ton, gentry **7** in crowd, quality, society, who's who **9** beau monde, haut monde **10** blue bloods, upper crust **11** aristocracy, Four Hundred, high society

smarty-pants 7 wise guy **9** know-it-all, swellhead **11** wisenheimer

smash 3 hit, jar **4** bang, bash, belt, blow, boom, clap, jolt, raze, ruin, slam, slug, sock, wham, whop **5** blast, boffo, burst, clash, crack, crash, crush, shock, whack, wreck **6** batter, impact, pileup, shiver, wallop **7** clobber, crack-up, debacle, destroy, shatter, success **8** collapse, decimate, demolish, knockout, overhand, splinter **9** breakdown, collision, pulverize, sensation, succès fou **10** annihilate **12** disintegrate

smashup 5 crash, wreck **6** fiasco, pileup **7** crack-up, debacle **8** accident, collapse, disaster **9** breakdown, collision

smattering 3 few **7** handful **10** sprinkling

smear 3 dab, tar **4** beat, coat, daub, drub, lick, slur, soil, whip **5** cover, libel, stain, sully, taint **6** befoul, defame, defile, malign, smirch, smudge, spread, thrash, vilify **7** asperse, blacken, calumny, plaster, shellac, slander, tarnish, traduce **8** besmirch **9** bespatter, denigrate **10** calumniate

smell 4 funk, nose, odor, reek **5** aroma, scent, sense, smack, sniff, snuff, stink, trace, whiff **6** detect, stench **7** bouquet, perfume **9** fragrance, redolence ***rotten egg:*** **6** sulfur

smell, sense of 9 olfaction

smelly 4 rank **5** fetid, funky, reeky **6** foetid, putrid, rancid, stinky **7** noisome, reeking, stenchy **8** mephitic, stinking **10** malodorous

smelt 4 flux, fuse, slag **6** reduce, refine, tomcod **8** sparling **9** sand lance, whitebait

smidgen 3 bit, dab, jot **4** atom, iota, mite **5** crumb, speck, touch **6** morsel

smile 4 beam, grin **5** smirk **6** simper

smirch see **smudge**

smirk 4 grin, leer **5** fleer, sneer **6** simper **7** grimace

smite 3 hit **4** belt, kill, sock **5** clout, whack **6** assail, attack, strike **7** afflict, assault, clobber, torment

smithereens 4 bits **6** pieces **9** fragments, particles

smitten 4 gaga **5** taken **6** hooked **8** besotted, enamored **9** enamoured, enchanted, entranced **10** captivated, enraptured, infatuated **11** intoxicated

smock 5 apron, dress, frock **8** pinafore

smoke 4 cure, fume **5** fumes, vapor **8** fastball, fumigate **9** cigarette

smoky 4 fumy, gray, hazy **5** murky, sooty **6** turbid **7** reeking **10** caliginous, smoldering

smolder 4 fume, glow, stew **5** churn **6** bubble, seethe, simmer **7** ferment **9** fulminate

smooch 4 buss, kiss, neck, peck **5** smack **8** osculate

smooth 4 easy, even, flat, oily **5** fluid, flush, level, plane, sleek, slick, suave **6** facile, fluent, glassy, glossy, polish, urbane **7** cursive, flatten, flowing, running **8** glabrous, hairless, soothing, unbroken **10** effortless, unwrinkled

smooth-spoken 4 glib **6** fluent **8** eloquent **10** articulate **13** silver-tongued

smorgasbord 4 hash, olio **6** buffet, jumble, medley **7** farrago, grab bag, mélange **8**

mishmash, mixed bag, pastiche **9** potpourri **10** hodgepodge, hotchpotch, miscellany, salmagundi **11** gallimaufry

smother 5 choke, douse, quell **6** hush up, muffle, quench, stifle **7** blanket, repress, squelch **8** inundate, restrain, suppress **9** overwhelm, suffocate **10** asphyxiate

smudge 3 dab **4** blot, blur, daub, foul, soil **5** dirty, smear, stain, sully, taint **6** bedaub, blotch, defile, smirch **7** begrime, besmear, blacken, blemish, splotch, tarnish **8** besmirch

smug 8 priggish **9** conceited **10** complacent **13** self-satisfied

smuggle 3 run **7** bootleg

smut 4 porn **5** filth **9** obscenity **11** pornography

smutty 4 blue, foul, lewd, racy **5** bawdy, dirty, nasty, sooty **6** coarse, filthy, risqué, vulgar **7** obscene, raunchy **8** indecent, off-color, prurient **9** salacious **12** pornographic, scatological

Smyrna 5 Izmir

snack 3 tea **4** bite, nosh, tapa **6** morsel, nibble **11** refreshment

snaffle 3 bit, cop **4** lift **5** filch, pinch, swipe **6** pilfer, pocket **7** purloin

snafu 5 botch, error, mix-up, snarl **6** bungle, foul up, mess up, muddle **7** chaotic, screwup **9** confusion

snag 3 nab **4** curb, grab, hook, nail, tear **5** catch, hitch **6** glitch, holdup, hurdle, obtain, secure **7** capture **8** drawback, obstacle **9** apprehend **10** impediment **11** obstruction

snail 5 whelk **6** limpet **7** mollusc, mollusk **8** escargot, ramshorn, slowpoke **9** gastropod **10** periwinkle

snake 3 boa **4** fink **5** crawl, creep, racer, slide **6** python, writhe **7** hognose, serpent, slither **8** anaconda, ophidian, undulate ***genus:*** **4** Eryx ***poisonous:*** **3** asp **5** adder, cobra, coral, krait, mamba, viper **6** elapid, taipan **7** rattler **8** pit viper **10** bushmaster, copperhead, fer-de-lance **11** cottonmouth **13** water moccasin

snakebird 6 darter **7** anhinga

snake-eater 8 mongoose **13** secretary bird

snakelike 7 sinuous **8** ophidian **10** serpentine

snakeroot 7 bugbane **10** wild ginger **11** blazing star

snakeweed 7 bistort **13** poison hemlock

snaky 7 sinuous, winding **8** flexuous, tortuous **10** convoluted, meandering, serpentine **11** anfractuous

snap 4 bang, bark **5** break, cinch, crack **6** breeze, lose it, picnic **7** crackle **8** duck soup, kid stuff, pushover **10** child's play

snap back 6 revive **7** rebound, recover **10** convalesce, recuperate

snappy 4 edgy, fast, tart **5** brisk, hasty, huffy, natty, quick, rapid, sharp, smart, swank, swift, testy **6** lively, prompt, speedy, touchy **7** dashing, stylish, waspish **8** animated, petulant, vigorous **9** breakneck, fractious, irritable, vivacious

snapshot 4 view **5** image, photo **6** précis, sketch, visual **7** picture **8** overview, synopsis **10** shadow copy

snare 3 bag, get, net **4** bait, hook, lure, trap **5** catch, decoy, noose, tempt **6** come-on, enmesh, entice, entrap, seduce, tangle **7** capture, catch up, chicane, embroil, ensnare, ensnarl, involve, mantrap, pitfail, trammel **8** entangle, inveigle **9** chicanery, deception **10** enticement, temptation

snarl 3 jam, web **4** bark, gnar, knot, maze, mesh **5** chaos, growl, ravel, skein **6** jungle, morass, muddle, tangle **7** perplex **8** disarray, disorder, entangle, gridlock, mishmash **9** confusion, labyrinth **10** complexity, complicate **12** complication, entanglement

snatch 3 bit, nab **4** grab, jerk, take, yank **5** catch, pluck, seize, swipe **6** abduct, clutch, kidnap, wrench **8** fragment

snazzy 4 chic **5** fancy, gaudy, jazzy, nobby, ritzy, sassy, sharp, smart, showy, swank **6** chichi, classy, flashy, garish, glitzy, jaunty, spiffy, swanky **7** elegant

sneak 3 cur, pad **4** lurk, slip, worm **5** crawl, creep, glide, mooch, prowl, shirk, skulk, skunk, slide, slink, steal **6** covert, secret, tiptoe, weasel **7** furtive, gumshoe, slither, smuggle **8** hush-hush, slyboots, stealthy **9** pussyfoot, scoundrel **10** undercover **11** clandestine

sneaky 4 foxy **6** shifty, tricky **7** devious, furtive **8** guileful, indirect, slippery, stealthy **9** underhand **11** duplicitous, underhanded

sneer 4 gibe, jeer **5** fleer, scoff, smirk **7** grimace, snigger

sneeze 5 achew, achoo **6** ahchoo ***cause:*** **5** snuff **6** dander, pollen **7** allergy **8** dust mite ***French:*** **7** atchoum ***German:*** **7** hatschi ***Spanish:*** **6** atchís

snicker 5 laugh **6** giggle, titter **7** chortle, chuckle

snide 4 mean **5** nasty **8** spiteful **9** malicious **11** insinuating

sniff 4 jeer, nose **5** scent, scoff, smell, snoop **6** inhale

sniffy 4 smug **5** aloof, lofty **6** lordly, snooty, uppity **7** haughty, pompous, stuck-up **8** scornful, superior **10** disdainful, hoity-toity **12** contemptuous, supercilious

snifter 3 nip, sip, tot **4** dram, drop, jolt, shot, slug **5** glass, snort **6** finger, goblet
snip 3 bit, cut **4** clip, crop, trim **5** notch, scrap **8** fragment
snipe 4 carp **9** sandpiper
sniper 6 gunman, killer **7** shooter **8** marksman, rifleman **12** sharpshooter
snippety see **snippy**
snippy 4 curt, tart **5** bluff, blunt, brief, gruff, short, terse **6** abrupt, crusty **7** brusque **8** snappish
snit 3 fit **4** flap, fume, huff, stew **5** panic, pique, sweat, tizzy **6** dither, frenzy, lather, pother, swivet **10** conniption
snitch 3 cop, nip, rat **4** beak, blab, fink, hook, lift, palm, sing, tell **5** filch, peach, pinch, spill, steal, swipe **6** inform, pilfer, pocket, squeal, tattle **7** purloin, rat fink, stoolie, tattler, tipster **8** betrayer, informer, squealer **11** stool pigeon
snivel 3 sob **4** weep **5** cower, whine **6** cringe, whinge **7** blubber, snuffle, whimper
snob 5 snoot **6** poseur **7** parvenu
snobbish 6 la-de-da, la-di-da, snooty, uppity **7** elitist, haughty, high-hat, stuck-up **8** lah-de-dah, lah-di-dah **9** lah-dee-dah **10** hoity-toity **11** patronizing, pretentious **12** supercilious **13** condescending
snook 5 cobia **6** robalo **12** sergeant fish
snooker 3 con **4** dupe, fool, hoax, pool **5** trick **6** delude **7** beguile, deceive, defraud **8** flimflam, hoodwink **9** bamboozle **11** hornswoggle
snoop 3 pry, spy **4** nose, peek, peep, peer, poke **5** prier, pryer **6** ferret, meddle, sleuth **7** gumshoe, intrude, meddler **8** busybody, quidnunc **9** detective, inspector, interfere **10** rubberneck
snooper 3 spy **9** detective, inspector **12** investigator
snoopy 4 nosy **6** prying **7** curious **8** meddling **9** intrusive **10** meddlesome **11** inquisitive
snoot see **snout**
snooty see **snobbish**
snooze 3 kip, nap **4** doze **5** sleep **6** catnap, drowse, nod off, siesta **7** drop off, slumber **10** forty winks
snore 8 rhonchus
snort 3 nip, tot **4** dram, drop, jolt, shot, slug **5** scoff, snarl **6** exhale, inhale **7** snifter
snout 3 neb **4** beak, nose **6** muzzle, schnoz **7** schnozz **9** proboscis
snow ***glacial:*** **4** firn, névé ***melted:*** **5** slush ***pellet:*** **7** graupel ***ridge:*** **8** sastruga
snow apple 8 mushroom
snowball 5 mount, run up **6** expand **7** augment, burgeon, explode, inflate **8** increase, multiply, mushroom, viburnum **10** accumulate **11** proliferate
snowbird 5 finch, junco **6** thrush **7** bunting **9** fieldfare, ivory gull
Snow-Bound author 8 Whittier (John Greenleaf)
snow finch 9 brambling
snow grouse 9 ptarmigan
snow leopard 5 ounce
Snow Leopard author 11 Matthiessen (Peter)
snowstorm 8 blizzard
snub 3 cut **4** shun **5** blunt, scorn, spite, spurn **6** rebuff, rebuke, slight, stubby **7** put down **9** ostracize, repudiate **12** cold-shoulder
snuff 3 ice, off **4** kill, nose **5** pinch, scent, smell **6** murder, rappee **7** execute **10** extinguish **11** exterminate
snug 4 cozy, neat, taut, tidy, trim **5** comfy, cushy, tight **6** burrow, cuddle, nestle, nuzzle, secure **7** orderly **9** sheltered, shipshape **11** comfortable
snuggle 5 spoon **6** burrow, cuddle, curl up, huddle, nestle, nuzzle
so 3 sae **4** ergo, then, thus, true **5** hence **6** indeed **9** similarly, therefore **11** accordingly **12** consequently
soak 3 ret, sop, sot, wet **4** bilk, clip, lush, skin, swig, wino **5** douse, drink, gouge, imbue, souse, steep **6** boozer, drench, fleece, infuse, rip off, seethe **7** drinker, guzzler, immerse **8** drunkard, permeate, saturate, submerge **9** alcoholic, penetrate **10** boozehound, impregnate, overcharge ***flax:*** **3** ret
soap 4 suds **6** stroke **7** flatter, wheedle **8** blandish, butter up, inveigle **9** sweet-talk ***hard:*** **7** castile ***ingredient:*** **3** lye, oil **5** scent **9** fragrance
soapbox 4 dais **6** podium **7** rostrum **8** hustings, platform, scaffold
soap plant 5 amole
soapstone 4 talc **8** steatite
soapwort 7 cowherd **11** bouncing bet
soar 3 fly **4** lift, rise **5** arise, climb, glide, hover, mount, shoot **6** ascend, rocket **7** shoot up **8** increase **9** skyrocket
sob 3 cry **4** bawl, blub, wail, weep **7** blubber, whimper
sober 4 calm, cool **5** grave, staid **6** low-key, proper, sedate, solemn **7** austere, earnest, serious, subdued **8** composed, low-keyed, moderate, rational, reserved **9** abstinent, collected, practical, pragmatic, realistic, temperate **10** abstaining, abstemious, controlled, hardheaded, no-nonsense, reasonable, restrained **11** disciplined, down-to-earth **12** matter-of-fact **13** imperturbable, self-possessed

sobriety 7 gravity **10** abstinence, continence, sedateness, temperance **11** seriousness
sobriquet 3 tag **5** alias **6** byname **7** epithet, moniker **8** cognomen, nickname **10** hypocorism
so-called 6 formal **7** alleged, nominal, titular **8** supposed **9** pretended, professed, purported **10** ostensible, self-styled
soccer *cup:* 5 World ***official:* 7** referee **8** linesman ***player:* 6** booter, goalie, kicker, winger **7** forward, link man, striker, sweeper **8** defender, fullback, halfback **10** goalkeeper ***star:* 4** Hamm (Mia), Pelé **5** Akers (Michelle), Henry (Thierry), Klose (Miroslav) **6** Zidane (Zinedine) **7** Beckham (David), Ronaldo **8** Chastain (Brandi), Maradona (Diego) **10** Ronaldinho **11** Beckenbauer (Franz) ***term:* 3** net **4** boot, chip, kick, trap **6** corner, header, tackle, volley **7** dribble, kickoff, throw-in **8** back-heel, free kick, goal kick, goal line **9** touchline **10** center spot, corner flag, corner kick **11** dropped ball, halfway line, penalty kick, penalty spot
sociable 5 close **6** genial **7** affable, amiable, cordial **8** familiar, gracious **9** clubbable, congenial, convivial **10** gregarious, hospitable **11** good-natured
social 5 civic, civil **8** communal **9** clubbable, convivial **10** collective, gregarious, hospitable **11** extroverted **13** companionable ***class:* 5** caste
Social Contract author 8 Rousseau (Jean-Jacques)
socialist *American:* 4 Debs (Eugene) **6** Ripley (George), Thomas (Norman) ***British:* 4** Owen (Robert, Robert Dale), Webb (Beatrice, Sidney) **6** Morris (William) ***French:* 7** Fourier (Charles), Viviani (René) **10** Saint-Simon (Henri de) ***German:* 4** Marx (Karl) **6** Engels (Friedrich) **9** Luxemburg (Rosa) **10** Liebknecht (Wilhelm)
socialize 3 mix **5** party, visit **6** hobnob, mingle **7** consort **9** associate **10** fraternize
social worker 4 Riis (Jacob), Wald (Lillian D.) **6** Addams (Jane) **7** Alinsky (Saul), Lathrop (Julia C.)
society 4 club **5** elite, guild **6** gentry, league, people, public **7** company, quality, who's who **8** populace, sodality **9** beau monde, community, haut monde **10** fellowship, fraternity, upper class, upper crust **11** aristocracy, association, brotherhood **13** companionship ***branch:* 7** chapter
sociologist *American:* 4 Bell (Daniel), Ward (Lester Frank) **5** Balch (Emily Green), Whyte (William H.) **6** Du Bois (W. E. B.), Glazer (Nathan), Sumner (William Graham) **7** Johnson (Charles Spurgeon), Riesman (David) ***English:* 7** Spencer (Herbert) ***French:* 8** Durkheim (Emile) ***German:* 5** Weber (Max) ***Italian:* 6** Pareto (Vilfredo) ***Swedish:* 6** Myrdal (Alva, Gunnar)
sock 3 bop, box, hit **4** bash, belt, blow, chop, cuff, ding, slap, slog **5** clout, punch, smack, smash, whack **6** argyle, buffet, strike, thwack, wallop **7** clobber **8** stocking
sock away 4 bank, save, stow **5** cache, hoard, lay by, put by, stash **8** lay aside
socks 4 hose **7** hosiery
Socrates *birthplace:* 6 Athens ***poison:* 7** hemlock ***pupil:* 5** Plato ***wife:* 8** Xantippe **9** Xanthippe
Socratic 8 maieutic
sod 4 land, peat, turf **5** earth, grass **6** ground
soda 3 pop **4** cola **5** tonic **7** seltzer
sodality 4 club **5** guild, lodge, order, union **6** league **7** society **9** community **10** fellowship, fraternity **11** association, brotherhood
sodden 3 wet **5** soggy, soppy **6** soaked, soused **7** soaking, sopping **8** drenched, dripping **9** saturated **11** waterlogged, wringing-wet
sodium symbol 2 Na
Sodom and ____ 8 Gomorrah ***visitor:* 3** Lot
sofa 5 couch, divan **7** ottoman **9** banquette, davenport
so far 3 yet **5** as yet, still **6** to date **7** till now **8** hitherto, until now **10** heretofore
Sofia native 6 Bulgar **9** Bulgarian
soft 4 cozy, easy, mild, snug **5** balmy, comfy, cushy, downy, faint, mushy, silky **6** doughy, flabby, gentle, low-key, pliant, satiny, silken, simple, smooth, spongy, tender **7** cottony, lenient, pillowy, pliable, squashy, squishy, subdued, velvety **8** cushiony, workable, yielding **9** malleable **11** comfortable
softcover 9 paperback
soften 4 ease, tame **5** abate, allay, relax **6** dampen, lessen, mellow, soothe, subdue, temper, weaken **7** assuage, lighten, mollify **8** diminish, mitigate, moderate, palliate, tone down **9** alleviate
soft hail 7 graupel
softhearted 4 kind, warm **6** humane, kindly, tender **7** lenient **10** responsive **11** sympathetic **13** compassionate
soft palate 5 velum
soft-pedal 4 mute **6** dampen, hush up, muffle, subdue **8** minimize, play down, suppress, tone down **9** underplay **11** de-emphasize
soft-soap 3 con **4** coax **6** cajole, soothe, wan-

gle **7** blarney, flatter, wheedle **8** blandish, butter up, inveigle **9** sweet-talk

soggy 3 wet **6** doughy, soaked, sodden **7** soaking, sopping **8** drenched, dripping **9** saturated **10** bedraggled **11** waterlogged

Sohrab and Rustum author 6 Arnold (Matthew)

soi-disant 7 alleged **8** putative, so-called, supposed **9** pretended, professed, purported **10** ostensible, self-styled

soil 3 mud, tar **4** daub, dirt, foul, land, loam, mess, muck, murk **5** dirty, earth, grime, muddy, smear, stain, sully, taint **6** defile, ground, smirch, smudge **7** begrime, blacken, country, pollute, tarnish **8** besmirch, discolor, homeland **10** fatherland, motherland, terra firma **11** contaminate ***aggregate:*** **3** ped ***clay:*** **5** gault ***combining form:*** **3** geo **4** agro ***dark:*** **9** chernozem ***deposit:*** **5** loess **7** eluvium ***infertile:*** **6** podzol ***layer:*** **4** gley, sola (plural) **5** solum ***rich:*** **6** hotbed ***tropical:*** **7** latosol

soiree 4 fete, gala **5** party **6** affair, social **7** evening, shindig **8** function **9** festivity, reception **11** celebration **13** entertainment

sojourn 4 bide, stay, stop **5** abide, lodge, tarry, visit **6** linger **7** layover **8** stopover

Sol 3 sun **7** daystar, phoebus ***horse:*** **4** Eous **5** Ethon **9** Erythreos (see also **Helios**)

solace 5 allay, amuse, cheer **6** buck up **7** comfort, console, hearten **8** inspirit **10** condolence

solar disk 4 Aten, Aton

solarium 7 sunroom

solar-system model 6 orrery

solder 4 fuse, weld **5** braze

soldier 2 GI **5** grunt, sepoy **7** dogface, draftee, fighter, private, recruit, trooper, veteran, warrior **8** bluecoat, doughboy, fusilier, rifleman **9** free lance, guerrilla, man-at-arms, mercenary **10** carabineer, carabinier, serviceman **11** condottiere, infantryman ***ancient Greece:*** **7** hoplite ***British:*** **5** Tommy **7** redcoat ***cavalry:*** **6** hussar **8** chasseur ***Confederate:*** **3** reb ***French:*** **5** poilu **6** Zouave ***German:*** **5** jerry ***irregular:*** **8** guerilla **9** guerrilla ***Prussian:*** **5** uhlan ***Turkish:*** **9** janissary

sole 3 one **4** lone, only **5** alone **6** bottom, single, unique **8** flatfish, singular **9** exclusive

solecism 4 goof, slip **5** boner, error, gaffe, lapse **6** misuse **7** blooper, blunder, faux pas, mistake **9** barbarism, indecorum, vulgarism **11** impropriety

solemn 5 grand, grave, sober, staid, stern **6** august, formal, ritual, sedate, somber, sombre **7** earnest, plenary, serious, stately, weighty **8** funereal, imposing, majestic **9** dignified **10** ceremonial, impressive, no-nonsense, sobersided **11** ceremonious, magnificent

solemnize 4 keep **5** bless, honor **6** hallow **7** dignify, observe **8** venerate **9** celebrate, ritualize **10** consecrate **11** commemorate

solicit 3 ask, beg **4** lure, tout, urge **5** apply **6** demand, drum up, entice **7** beseech, bespeak, canvass, entreat, implore, request **8** petition **9** importune **11** proposition, requisition

solicitor 6 jurist, lawyer, suitor **7** pleader **8** advocate, attorney **9** counselor

solicitous 4 avid, keen **5** eager, fussy **6** ardent, tender **7** anxious, careful, devoted, fearful, finicky, worried **8** rigorous **9** assiduous, attentive, concerned, impatient **10** fastidious, meticulous, scrupulous **11** considerate, punctilious, sympathetic **12** apprehensive **13** conscientious

solicitude 4 care, heed **5** qualm, worry **6** unease **7** anxiety, concern, scruple **9** attention, vigilance **10** uneasiness **11** compunction **12** watchfulness **13** consideration

solid 4 firm, hard **5** dense, sound, valid **6** cogent, secure, stable, sturdy, united **7** compact **8** reliable, unbroken **9** steadfast, unanimous, undivided **10** convincing **11** substantial

solidarity 5 union, unity **6** cement, esprit **7** concord, oneness **8** cohesion **9** integrity **10** singleness **12** cohesiveness, togetherness **13** esprit de corps

solidify 3 dry, fix, gel, set **4** cake, jell **6** freeze, harden, secure **7** compact, congeal **8** compress, contract, indurate **11** consolidate

solitary 4 lone, lorn, only, solo **5** alone **6** hermit, lonely, single, unique **7** recluse **8** derelict, deserted, desolate, eremitic, forsaken, isolated, lonesome, separate, singular **9** abandoned, reclusive, withdrawn **10** antisocial, particular, unsociable **11** standoffish **12** misanthropic **13** unaccompanied

solitude 7 privacy **8** loneness **9** aloneness, isolation, seclusion **10** detachment, loneliness, quarantine, retirement, withdrawal **11** confinement **12** separateness

solo 4 aria, lone **5** alone **6** single **7** unaided **8** solitary **13** independently, unaccompanied

Solomon ***brother:*** **8** Adonijah ***daughter:*** **7** Taphath **8** Basemath ***father:*** **5** David ***kingdom:*** **6** Israel ***mother:*** **9** Bathsheba ***son, successor:*** **8** Rehoboam ***victim:*** **4** Joab **8** Adonijah

Solomon Islands ***capital:*** **7** Honiara ***ethnic group:*** **10** Melanesian ***island:*** **7** Florida,

Malaita, Rennell **8** Choiseul **11** Guadalcanal, Santa Isabel **12** San Cristóbal
solon 8 lawgiver **10** legislator
so long 4 by-by, ciao, ta-ta **5** adieu, adios **6** bye-bye, good-by **7** cheerio, good-bye, toodles **8** farewell, Godspeed, toodle-oo
solution 6 answer, result ***salt:* 6** saline
solve 3 fix **5** break, crack **6** decode, reveal, settle **7** clarify, clear up, dope out, explain, unravel, work out **8** construe, decipher, unriddle, untangle **9** elucidate, figure out, interpret, puzzle out **11** disentangle
Somalia *capital:* 9 Mogadishu ***gulf:* 4** Aden ***language:* 6** Arabic, Somali ***location:* 12** Horn of Africa ***monetary unit:* 8** shilling ***neighbor:* 5** Kenya **8** Djibouti, Ethiopia
somatic 6 bodily, carnal **7** fleshly **8** corporal, parietal, physical **9** corporeal
somber 3 dim **4** dark, drab, dull, grim **5** bleak, dusky, grave, heavy, murky, staid **6** dismal, dreary, gloomy, sedate, solemn **7** doleful, joyless, obscure, serious, weighty **8** funereal, mournful **9** tenebrous **10** caliginous, depressing, depressive, lugubrious, melancholy, sepulchral, sobersided, tenebrific **11** dispiriting
somersault 4 flip
somewhat 4 a bit, a tad **5** quite **6** fairly, kind of, rather, sort of **7** a little **8** slightly **9** partially, tolerably **10** moderately
sommelier's offering 4 wine
____ Sommer 4 Elke
somniferous see **sleepy**
somnolent see **sleepy**
Somnus *brother:* 4 Mors ***god of:* 5** sleep ***mother:* 3** Nox
son *French:* 4 fils ***Italian:* 6** figlio ***Spanish:* 4** hijo
song 3 air, lay **4** aria, glee, hymn, lied, tune **5** carol, chant, ditty, lyric, paean **6** ballad, melody, number **7** chanson **8** madrigal ***biblical:* 8** canticle ***boat:* 9** barcarole **10** barcarolle ***French:* 7** chanson ***German:* 4** lied **6** lieder (plural) ***lamentation:* 5** dirge **8** threnode, threnody ***medieval:* 8** sirvente **9** sirventes ***morning:* 6** aubade ***of joy:* 5** paean ***operatic:* 4** aria **7** arietta **8** cavatina **9** cabaletta ***Portuguese:* 4** fado ***sacred:* 5** psalm ***sailor's:* 6** chanty, shanty **7** chantey ***short:* 8** canzonet ***wedding:* 8** hymeneal
song and dance 5 pitch, spiel
songbird see at **bird**
Song of Myself author 7 Whitman (Walt)
Song of Solomon 9 Canticles
songwriter 8 composer, lyricist ***famous:* 3** Ebb (Fred) **4** Anka (Paul), Bock (Jerry), Cahn (Sammy), Duke (Vernon), Hart (Lorenz), Kern (Jerome), King (Carole), Nyro (Laura), Webb (Jimmy), Wolf (Hugo) **5** Arlen (Harold), Berry (Chuck), Byrne (David), Cohan (George M.), Cohen (Leonard), Cooke (Sam), David (Hal), Dietz (Howard), Dylan (Bob), Evans (Ray), Green (Adolph), Holly (Buddy), Loewe (Frederick), Simon (Carly, Paul), Styne (Jule), Waits (Tom), Weill (Kurt) **6** Berlin (Irving), Comden (Betty), Coward (Noel), Denver (John), Dozier (Lamont), Fields (Dorothy), Foster (Stephen), Goffin (Gerry), Herman (Jerry), Kander (John), Leiber (Jerry), Lennon (John), Lerner (Alan Jay), Lovett (Lyle), McHugh (Jimmy), Mercer (Johnny), Nelson (Willie), Newman (Randy), Parton (Dolly), Porter (Cole), Sedaka (Neil), Seeger (Pete), Taupin (Bernie), Taylor (James), Travis (Merle), Warren (Harry), Wonder (Stevie) **7** Diamond (Neil), Guthrie (Woody), Harburg (E. Y.), Harnick (Sheldon), Holland (Brian, Eddie), Loesser (Frank), Mancini (Henry), Manilow (Barry), Novello (Ivor), Orbison (Roy), Rodgers (Richard), Romberg (Sigmund), Spector (Phil), Stoller (Mike), Youmans (Vincent) **8** Costello (Elvis), Gershwin (George, Ira), Hamlisch (Marvin), Mayfield (Curtis), Mitchell (Joni), Morrison (Van), Robinson (Smokey), Schubert (Franz), Schwartz (Arthur), Sondheim (Stephen) **9** Bacharach (Burt), Donaldson (Walter), McCartney (Paul), Strayhorn (Billy), Von Tilzer (Albert, Harry), Van Heusen (Jimmy) **10** Carmichael (Hoagy) **11** Hammerstein (Oscar), Springsteen (Bruce)
Sonja ____ 5 Henie
Sonnambula composer 7 Bellini (Vincenzo)
sonnet *developer:* 8 Petrarch ***part:* 5** octet **6** octave, sestet
sonorous 7 ringing, vibrant **8** resonant **10** oratorical, resounding, rhetorical **11** declamatory **12** magniloquent **13** grandiloquent
Sons and Lovers hero 5 Morel (Paul)
Sontag novel 9 In America **12** Volcano Lover (The)
soon 4 anon **6** any day, pronto **7** betimes, by and by, quickly, rapidly, shortly **8** directly, promptly, speedily **9** forthwith, presently, right away **10** before long
Sooner State 8 Oklahoma
soothe 4 balm, calm, ease, hush, lull **5** allay, quiet, salve, still **6** becalm, pacify, settle, solace, subdue **7** appease, assuage, comfort, compose, console, massage, mollify, placate, relieve **8** calm down, reassure **9** alleviate **10** conciliate, propitiate **11** tranquilize

soothsay **5** augur **8** prophesy **9** adumbrate **10** vaticinate **13** prognosticate

soothsayer **4** seer **5** sibyl **6** oracle **7** diviner, prophet **8** foreseer **9** predictor **10** forecaster, foreteller ***ancient Roman:*** **5** augur **6** auspex **8** haruspex ***blind:*** **8** Tiresias (see also **prophet**)

sop **3** wet **4** gift, soak **5** bribe, douse, goody, souse, steep **6** deluge, drench, reward, seethe **7** douceur **8** gratuity, saturate, waterlog **9** incentive, lagniappe, sweetener **10** enticement

sophism see **sophistry**

sophistic **5** false, phony **7** invalid, seeming, unsound **8** delusive, illusory, spurious **9** beguiling, casuistic, deceptive, plausible **10** fallacious, fraudulent, misleading, ostensible

sophisticated **5** blasé, jaded, suave **6** smooth, svelte, urbane **7** complex, knowing, refined, worldly **8** cultured, involved, schooled, seasoned **9** Byzantine, elaborate, intricate, practiced **10** world-weary **11** complicated, experienced, worldly-wise **12** cosmopolitan

sophistry **9** casuistry **12** equivocation **13** dissimulation, prevarication

Sophocles play **4** Ajax **7** Electra **8** Antigone **10** Oedipus Rex

Sophonisba ***brother:*** **8** Hannibal ***father:*** **9** Hasdrubal ***husband:*** **6** Syphax

soporific **4** dozy **6** drowsy, opiate, sleepy **7** anodyne, calming, numbing **8** hypnotic, narcotic, sedative **9** calmative, deadening, somnolent **10** anesthetic, slumberous **11** somniferous **12** somnifacient **13** tranquilizing

soprano ***American:*** **4** Pons (Lily) **5** Costa (Mary), Gluck (Alma), Moffo (Anna), Moore (Grace), Price (Leontyne), Sills (Beverly) **6** Arroyo (Martina), Battle (Kathleen), Callas (Maria), Curtin (Phyllis), Donath (Helen), Farrar (Geraldine), Garden (Mary), Munsel (Patrice), Norman (Jessye), Peters (Roberta), Piazza (Marguerite), Resnik (Regina), Upshaw (Dawn) **7** Farrell (Eileen), Fleming (Renée), Kirsten (Dorothy), Stevens (Risë), Traubel (Helen) **8** Ponselle (Rosa) ***Australian:*** **5** Melba (Nellie) **10** Sutherland (Joan) ***Austrian:*** **4** Popp (Lucia) **7** Rysanek (Leonie) **8** Sembrich (Marcella) ***Canadian:*** **7** Stratas (Teresa) ***French:*** **7** Crespin (Régine) ***German:*** **6** Leider (Frida) **7** Lehmann (Lilli, Lotte) **11** Schwarzkopf (Elisabeth) ***Italian:*** **5** Freni (Mirella), Grisi (Giuditta, Giulia), Patti (Adelina) **6** Scotto (Renata) **7** Bartoli (Cecilia), Tebaldi (Renata) **10** Tetrazzini (Luisa) **11** Ricciarelli (Katia) ***Korean:*** **6** Sumi Jo ***Mexican:*** **8** Cruz-Romo (Gilda) ***New Zealand:*** **8** Te Kanawa (Kiri) ***Norwegian:*** **8** Flagstad (Kirsten) ***Romanian:*** **8** Cotrubas (Ileana) ***Russian:*** **8** Netrebko (Anna) ***Spanish:*** **7** Caballé (Montserrat) **8** Berganza (Teresa) **12** de los Angeles (Victoria) ***Swedish:*** **4** Lind (Jenny) **7** Nilsson (Birgit) (see also **mezzo-soprano**)

sorcerer **4** mage **5** magus **6** wizard **7** warlock **8** conjurer, conjuror, magician **9** enchanter **11** necromancer, thaumaturge **13** thaumaturgist

sorceress **3** hag, hex **5** Circe, witch

sorcery **5** magic **8** diablery, wizardry **9** conjuring **10** necromancy, witchcraft **11** bewitchment, enchantment, thaumaturgy ***West Indian:*** **5** obeah

sordid **3** low **4** base, foul, mean, vile **5** dirty, nasty, seamy, shady, venal **6** blowsy, blowzy, filthy, frowsy, frowzy, grubby, scurvy, shabby, sleazy **7** ignoble, lowdown, squalid, unclean **8** degraded, shameful, wretched **9** loathsome, mercenary **10** despicable, scandalous, slatternly **11** disgraceful **12** contemptible, disreputable **13** reprehensible

sore **3** raw **4** achy, boil **5** angry, irked, ulcer, upset, vexed **6** aching, bitter, canker, peeved, tender **7** abscess, chancre, hurting, painful **8** inflamed, smarting **9** chilblain, irritated, rancorous, resentful, sensitive **10** affliction

sorehead **4** crab **5** grump **6** griper, grouch **7** grouser **8** grumbler, sourpuss **10** bellyacher, complainer, crosspatch, malcontent

sorrel **3** oca **4** dock **8** chestnut, sourwood

sorrow **3** rue, sob, woe **4** moan, ruth **5** dolor, grief, mourn **6** grieve, lament, misery, regret **7** anguish, remorse, sadness **8** distress, grieving, mourning **9** dejection, heartache, suffering **10** affliction, heartbreak, melancholy **11** lamentation, unhappiness **12** mournfulness

sorrowful **3** sad **6** rueful, triste, woeful **7** doleful, forlorn, piteous, ruthful, unhappy **8** dolorous, downcast, grieving, mournful, tristful, wretched **9** afflicted, miserable, plaintive, woebegone **10** lamentable, lugubrious, melancholy **11** heartbroken **12** disconsolate

sorry **3** bad, sad **4** mean, poor **5** cheap **6** cheesy, paltry, scummy, scurvy, shabby, shoddy **7** scruffy, unhappy **8** beggarly, contrite, mournful, penitent, pitiable, saddened, trifling, wretched **9** miserable, regretful, repentant **10** apologetic, despicable, inadequate, melancholy, remorseful **11** disgraceful, penitential **12** contemptible, heavyhearted

sort 3 ilk, lot, set **4** comb, cull, kind, pick, sift, type **5** class, order **6** choose, screen, select, stripe, winnow **7** arrange, catalog, species, variety **8** classify, separate **9** catalogue, character **10** categorize, pigeonhole

sortie 4 dash, raid **5** foray, sally **7** assault, mission **9** excursion **10** expedition

sortilege 6 augury **7** sorcery **8** divining, witchery **10** divination, necromancy, witchcraft **11** thaumaturgy

so-so 4 fair, okay **6** decent, enough, fairly, medium, rather **7** average, fairish **8** adequate, mediocre, middling, moderate, passable, passably **9** tolerably **10** moderately **11** indifferent **12** run-of-the-mill

sot 4 lush, wino **5** drunk, souse **6** bibber, boozer **7** guzzler, tippler, tosspot **8** drunkard **9** alcoholic, inebriate **10** boozehound

sotto voce 3 low **5** aside **6** softly **7** faintly, mutedly, quietly **9** privately

souchong 3 tea

sough 4 sigh **7** suspire, whisper

soul 4 pith **5** anima, being, heart, stuff **6** animus, breast, marrow, pneuma, psyche, spirit **7** essence **9** élan vital, substance **10** conscience, vital force **12** quintessence ***combining form:*** **5** psych **6** psycho

soulful 6 moving, tender **7** emotive, fervent **8** poignant, stirring, touching **9** affecting, emotional **11** impassioned, sentimental

soul singer 4 Gaye (Marvin) **5** Bland (Bobby), Brown (James), Cooke (Sam), Flack (Roberta), Green (Al), Hayes (Isaac) **6** Butler (Jerry), Knight (Gladys), Sledge (Percy) **7** Charles (Ray), Pickett (Wilson), Redding (Otis) **8** Franklin (Aretha), Mayfield (Curtis)

sound 3 fit **4** firm, hale, kyle, safe, sane **5** audio, legit, noise, plumb, probe, right, sober, solid, valid, whole **6** cogent, fathom, intact, secure, stable, sturdy, unhurt **7** correct, earshot, healthy, logical, prudent **8** rational, reliable, sensible, unharmed **9** judicious, resonance, undamaged, vibration, wholesome **10** convincing, reasonable **11** well-founded **12** satisfactory, well-grounded **13** reverberation ***combining form:*** **3** son **4** phon, soni, sono **5** audio, audit, phone, phono, phony **6** audito, phonia ***gentle:*** **6** rustle ***high-pitched:*** **4** ping, ting ***pleasant:*** **7** euphony ***quality:*** **6** timbre ***repeating:*** **7** rat-a-tat **8** rataplan **10** rat-a-tat-tat ***science:*** **6** sonics **7** phonics **9** acoustics

Sound *Alaska:* **5** Cross ***Antarctica:*** **7** McMurdo ***Australia:*** **4** King **5** Broad ***Bahamas:*** **5** Exuma ***Canada:*** **4** Howe **6** Nansen ***Connecticut-New York:*** **10** Long Island ***English Channel:*** **8** Plymouth ***Georgia:*** **8** Altamaha ***Greenland:*** **5** Smith ***Gulf of Mexico:*** **8** Suwannee **11** Mississippi ***Massachusetts:*** **8** Vineyard **9** Nantucket ***New England:*** **11** Block Island ***North Carolina:*** **4** Core **5** Bogue **7** Pamlico, Roanoke **9** Albemarle, Currituck ***Northwest Territories:*** **4** Peel **8** Melville **9** Lancaster **12** Prince Albert ***Norwegian Sea:*** **8** Scoresby ***Ontario:*** **4** Owen ***Scotland:*** **3** Hoy **4** Jura, Mull **5** Inner ***Spitsbergen:*** **4** Bell ***Washington:*** **5** Puget

Sound and the Fury, The *author:* **8** Faulkner (William) ***character:*** **5** Benjy (Compson), Caddy (Compson), Jason (Compson) **6** Dilsey **7** Quentin (Compson)

soundness 6 health, sanity **7** balance **8** lucidity, prudence, security, solidity, strength **9** integrity, stability **11** reliability **12** practicality

sound off 7 speak up **8** speak out

soup *beet:* **6** borsch **7** borscht ***bowl:*** **6** tureen ***clear:*** **5** broth **8** bouillon, consommé, julienne ***cold:*** **8** gazpacho **11** vichyssoise ***curry:*** **12** mulligatawny ***okra:*** **5** gumbo ***seafood:*** **7** chowder ***soy:*** **4** miso ***thick:*** **5** gumbo, puree **6** bisque, burgoo, potage ***vegetable:*** **10** minestrone

soupçon see **particle**

soupy 5 foggy, gooey, gushy, murky, mushy **6** drippy, slushy, smoggy **7** cloying, maudlin, mawkish **8** cornball **9** schmaltzy **10** saccharine **11** sentimental, tear-jerking

sour 4 acid, dour, tart **5** acerb, acrid, tangy, testy **6** acidic, bitter, crabby, cranky, curdle, grumpy, morose, rancid, rotten, sullen, turned **7** acerbic, grouchy, peevish, prickly, spoiled, unhappy **8** embitter, vinegary **9** acidulous, fermented **12** disagreeable

source 4 font, root, well **5** basis, cause, fount, model, onset, start **6** mother, origin, spring **7** dawning, genesis **8** begetter, fountain, wellhead **9** beginning, inception, informant, precursor, prototype, reference, rootstock **10** antecedent, authorship, birthplace, derivation, originator, progenitor, provenance, wellspring **11** origination, provenience **12** fountainhead

sourness 7 acidity **8** acerbity, asperity

sourpuss 4 crab **5** crank, grump **6** griper, grouch **7** grouser, killjoy **8** grumbler, sorehead **10** bellyacher, complainer, crosspatch, curmudgeon **11** misanthrope

souse 3 dip, sop, sot **4** lush, soak, wino **5**

binge, drown, steep **6** boozer, drench, pickle, plunge, seethe **7** immerse **8** drunkard, inundate, marinate, preserve, saturate, submerge, submerse **9** alcoholic, immersion, inebriate **10** boozehound, intoxicate **11** dipsomaniac

soused 3 lit **4** high **5** drunk, lit up, oiled **6** bashed, blotto, bombed, juiced, potted, soaked, soused, stewed, stoned, tanked, wasted, zonked **7** crocked, drunken, pickled, pie-eyed, sloshed, smashed, sottish **8** polluted **9** plastered **10** inebriated, liquored up **11** intoxicated

south *combining form:* 5 austr **6** austro ***French:* 3** sud ***Spanish:* 3** sur

South Africa *capital:* 8 Cape Town, Pretoria **12** Bloemfontein ***city:* 6** Durban **12** Johannesburg ***desert:* 8** Kalahari ***enclave:* 7** Lesotho ***grassland:* 4** veld **5** veldt ***language:* 5** Bantu **7** English **9** Afrikaans ***monetary unit:* 4** rand ***mountain range:* 11** Drakensberg ***native:* 3** San **4** Khoi, Zulu **5** Pondo, Sotho, Swazi, Venda, Xhosa **6** Tswana **7** Bushmen, Khoisan **9** Hottentot ***neighbor:* 7** Namibia **8** Botswana **9** Swaziland **10** Mozambique, Zimbabwe ***plateau:* 5** Karoo **6** Karroo ***province:* 7** Gauteng **8** Northern **9** Free State **10** Mpumalanga ***river:* 6** Molopo, Orange ***settlers:* 5** Boers

South America *country:* 4 Peru **5** Chile **6** Brazil, Guyana **7** Bolivia, Ecuador, Uruguay **8** Colombia, Paraguay, Suriname **9** Argentina, Venezuela ***ethnic group:* 6** Aymara, Creole, Indian **7** mestizo, mulatto, Quechua, Spanish **10** Amerindian, Portuguese ***language:* 6** Aymara **7** Guaraní, Quechua, Spanish **10** Portuguese

South Carolina *capital:* 8 Columbia ***city:* 10** Charleston, Greenville ***college, university:* 7** Citadel, Clemson ***fort:* 6** Sumter ***island, island group:* 3** Sea **6** Edisto, Parris **10** Hilton Head ***nickname:* 8** Palmetto (State) ***river:* 6** Edisto, Pee Dee, Santee **7** Tugaloo **8** Savannah ***state bird:* 12** Carolina wren ***state flower:* 13** yellow jasmine ***state tree:* 8** palmetto

South Dakota *capital:* 6 Pierre ***city:* 9** Rapid City **10** Sioux Falls ***mountain:* 6** Harney (Peak) **8** Rushmore **10** Black Hills ***nickname:* 6** Coyote (State) **10** Mt. Rushmore (State) ***park:* 8** Badlands, Wind Cave ***river:* 8** Missouri **11** Belle Forche ***state bird:* 18** ring-necked pheasant ***state flower:* 12** pasqueflower ***state tree:* 6** spruce

southerly 7 austral

South Korea see **Korea, South**

southpaw 5 lefty

South-West Africa 7 Namibia

south wind see at **wind**

souvenir 5 relic, token **6** trophy **7** memento **8** keepsake, memorial, reminder **11** remembrance

sovereign 4 coin, czar, free, king, tsar **5** queen, regal, royal, ruler **6** kingly, ruling **7** emperor, empress, highest, monarch, regnant, supreme **8** absolute, autarkic, autocrat, dominant, imperial, kinglike, majestic **9** ascendant, autarchic, monarchal, number one, paramount, potentate **10** autonomous, monarchial **11** independent, monarchical, predominant **12** self-governed

soviet 7 council **9** committee

Soviet Union 4 CCCP, USSR

sow 4 seed, toss **5** drill, fling, plant, strew **7** bestrew, scatter **9** broadcast **11** disseminate

soybean paste 4 miso

spa 5 baths, hydro, wells **6** hot tub, resort, spring, waters **7** springs **13** watering place ***Czech:* 6** Bilina **8** Karlsbad ***English:* 4** Bath **6** Buxton **9** Harrogate ***French:* 3** Dax **5** Evian ***German:* 3** Ems **5** Baden **6** Bad Ems **9** Kissingen

space 3 gap **4** area, room **5** blank, ether, plena (plural), scope **6** cavity, extent, plenum, spread, volume **7** breadth, expanse, stretch **8** capacity, distance, interval, universe **9** amplitude, expansion

spaced-out 4 high **5** doped **6** stoned, zonked **7** drugged **8** hopped-up, turned on

space station 3 Mir **6** Salyut, Skylab

spacious 3 big **4** vast, wide **5** ample, large, roomy **7** immense **8** enormous, extended **9** boundless, capacious, cavernous, expansive, extensive **10** commodious, voluminous

spade 3 dig, loy **4** grub **5** dig up, scoop **6** dig out, shovel **8** excavate

Spade, Sam 4 dick **6** shamus, sleuth **7** gumshoe **9** detective **10** private eye ***creator:* 7** Hammett (Dashiell) ***novel:* 13** Maltese Falcon (The)

Spain *ancient name:* 8 Hispania ***capital:* 6** Madrid ***city:* 6** Málaga **7** Seville **8** Pamplona, Valencia, Zaragoza **9** Barcelona, Saragossa ***island group:* 6** Canary **8** Balearic ***king:* 10** Juan Carlos ***leader:* 6** Franco (Francisco) ***monetary unit:* 4** euro ***monetary unit, former:* 4** real **6** peseta ***mountain:* 8** Mulhacén **11** Pico de Aneto ***mountain range:* 8** Pyrenees ***neighbor:* 6** France **8** Portugal ***peninsula:* 7** Iberian ***region:* 6** Aragon, Murcia **7** Galicia **8** Valencia **9** Andalusia, Catalonia ***river:* 4** Ebro **12**

Guadalquivir ***sea:*** **13** Mediterranean ***strait:*** **9** Gibraltar

spall **4** chip **5** flake **7** shaving **8** fragment **9** exfoliate

span **4** arch, term, time **5** cross, reach **6** extent, length, period, spread **7** compass, measure, stretch **8** duration, interval, lifetime, straddle, traverse

spangle **4** trim **5** flash, gleam **6** sequin **7** glitter, shimmer, sparkle, twinkle **9** coruscate **11** scintillate

Spaniard **9** Castilian

Spanish ***aunt:*** **3** tia ***bay:*** **5** bahia ***bed:*** **4** cama **5** lecho ***bird:*** **6** pájaro ***boss:*** **7** cacique ***bread:*** **3** pan ***bridge:*** **6** puente ***bull:*** **4** toro **6** el toro ***chaperone:*** **6** duenna ***church:*** **7** iglesia ***combining form:*** **7** hispano ***crossword puzzle:*** **10** crucigrama ***dance:*** **4** jota **5** baile, salsa **6** bailar **8** fandango, flamenco **9** zapateado ***devil:*** **6** diablo ***dictator:*** **8** caudillo ***door:*** **6** puerta ***dress:*** **7** vestido ***folksong:*** **6** tonada ***fortress:*** **7** alcazar ***game:*** **5** juego ***garrison:*** **8** presidio ***gift:*** **6** regalo ***gold:*** **3** oro ***good-bye:*** **5** adiós ***hello:*** **4** hola ***hors d'oeuvre:*** **4** tapa ***house:*** **4** casa ***husband:*** **6** esposo, marido ***ice cream:*** **6** helado ***inn:*** **6** posada ***journey:*** **5** viaje ***library:*** **10** biblioteca ***light:*** **3** luz ***mayor:*** **7** alcalde ***milk:*** **5** leche ***money:*** **5** plata **6** dinero ***movie:*** **8** pelicula ***movies:*** **4** cine ***number:*** **3** dos, uno **4** diez, doce, ocho, once, seis, tres **5** cinco, nueve, siete **6** cuatro ***national hero:*** **3** Cid (El) **5** El Cid ***nobleman:*** **7** grandee ***operetta:*** **8** zarzuela ***penal settlement:*** **8** presidio ***plain:*** **4** vega **5** llano, pampa ***plantation:*** **8** hacienda ***please:*** **8** por favor ***princess:*** **7** infanta ***ranch:*** **5** finca **8** estancia ***river:*** **3** rio ***room:*** **4** sala **6** cuarto ***saint:*** **7** Dominic **8** Ignatius ***sale:*** **5** venta ***scarf:*** **7** pañuelo **8** mantilla ***school:*** **7** colegio, escuela ***shawl:*** **6** rebozo, serape ***shirt:*** **6** camisa ***shoe:*** **6** zapato **7** calzado ***singer:*** **8** cantante ***skirt:*** **5** falda ***soccer:*** **6** fútbol ***street:*** **5** calle ***thank you:*** **7** gracias ***title:*** **3** don, Sra. **4** doña, Srta. **5** señor **6** señora **8** señorita ***tree:*** **5** árbol ***trousers:*** **10** pantalones ***uncle:*** **3** tío ***wife:*** **6** esposa ***wine:*** **4** sack **6** sherry

Spanish fly **9** cantharis

spank **4** cane, flog, lash, slap **5** smack **6** larrup, paddle, punish, thrash **7** scourge **8** chastise

spar **3** box, vie **4** pole **5** joust, sprit, stall **7** dispute, wrangle **8** longeron ***ship's:*** **4** boom, gaff, mast, yard **7** yardarm **8** bowsprit

spare **4** lank, lean, pity, save, slim **5** avoid, extra, gaunt, lanky **6** backup, excess, excuse, exempt, let off, meager, meagre, pardon, scanty, scrape, scrimp, skimpy, skinny, slight, unused **7** absolve, relieve, reserve, scrawny, scrimpy, surplus **8** leftover **10** additional **11** superfluous

sparing **4** bare, wary **5** canny, chary, tight **6** frugal, meager, meagre, saving, stingy **7** prudent, thrifty **9** provident **10** economical, restrained, unwasteful **11** tightfisted **12** parsimonious

spark **3** woo **5** court, ember, glint **6** foment, incite, kindle, set off **7** provoke, trigger **8** activate, touch off **9** instigate, scintilla

sparkle **4** zing **5** flash, gleam, glint, verve **7** glimmer, glisten, glitter, shimmer, twinkle **8** vivacity **9** animation, coruscate **10** effervesce, liveliness **11** coruscation, scintillate **13** scintillation

sparkling **6** bubbly, lively **8** animated, bubbling **9** brilliant **12** effervescent

Spark novel **11** Memento Mori **21** Prime of Miss Jean Brodie (The)

sparse **4** rare, thin **5** scant **6** meager, meagre, scanty, scarce, skimpy **7** limited, scrimpy **8** exiguous, sporadic, uncommon **9** dispersed, scattered **10** inadequate, infrequent, occasional **12** insufficient

Sparta **10** Lacedaemon ***country:*** **7** Laconia ***king:*** **8** Leonidas, Menelaos ***opponent:*** **6** Athens ***queen:*** **4** Leda

Spartacus ***author:*** **4** Fast (Howard) ***slayer:*** **7** Crassus

spasm **3** fit, tic **4** pang **5** burst, crick, throe **6** twitch **8** paroxysm **10** convulsion ***muscular:*** **6** clonus

spasmodic **5** jerky **6** fitful, spotty **7** erratic **8** sporadic **9** desultory, excitable **10** convulsive **12** intermittent

spat **3** row **4** flap, miff, tiff **5** fight, scene, scrap **6** bicker, gaiter, hassle, oyster **7** brabble, dispute, fall out, quarrel, rhubarb, wrangle **8** argument, outburst, squabble **10** falling-out **11** altercation

spate **4** flow, flux, gush, pour, rain, rush, tide **5** flood, river, spurt, surge **6** deluge, series, shower, stream **7** current, freshet, torrent **8** cataract, outburst, overflow **10** inundation, outpouring

spatter **4** slop, slur, spit **5** douse, fleck, plash, slosh, smear, spray, spurt, swash **6** befoul, defame, malign, splash, splosh, vilify **7** asperse, blacken, handful, slander, speckle, splurge, stipple, traduce **8** besmirch, sprinkle **9** denigrate, disparage

spawn **4** eggs, sire **5** beget, breed, brood, hatch, issue **6** create, father, parent **7** produce, product, progeny, provoke **8** engender, generate **9** offspring, originate, procreate, propagate, reproduce, stimulate

speak 3 gab, jaw, say, yak **4** blab, chat, chin, talk **5** blurt, drawl, mouth, orate, spiel, spout, utter, voice **6** assert, convey, intone, mumble, murmur, mutter, parley **7** address, declaim, declare, lecture, phonate, whisper **8** converse, dilate on, perorate, vocalize **9** discourse, enunciate, expatiate, hold forth, verbalize ***combining form:*** **4** phon ***confusedly:*** **7** stammer, stutter **8** splutter ***for:*** **7** testify

speaker 5 voice **6** orator **9** spokesman **10** mouthpiece **12** spokesperson

spear 3 gig **4** pike, spit **5** gouge, lance, spike **6** impale, pierce, skewer **7** assagai, assegai, harpoon, leister, trident **8** puncture, transfix **9** penetrate

spearhead 4 lead **5** front **6** direct

spear-thrower 6 atlatl **7** woomera

special 4 rare **6** unique **7** express, notable, unusual **8** peculiar, uncommon **10** designated, individual, noteworthy, particular **11** distinctive, exceptional, outstanding

species 4 kind, sort, type **5** breed, class, order

specific 3 set **5** exact **6** strict, unique **7** express, limited, precise, special **8** clean-cut, clear-cut, definite, distinct, especial, explicit **10** individual, particular **11** categorical, unambiguous

specify 3 fix, set **4** cite, list, name **6** detail **7** itemize, mention, pin down, tick off **8** instance, spell out **9** determine, enumerate, establish, inventory, stipulate **13** particularize

specimen 4 case, sort, type **6** sample **7** example, neotype, variety **8** exemplar, holotype, instance, sampling **12** illustration

specious 5 empty, false **6** hollow **8** spurious **9** casuistic, plausible, sophistic **10** misleading, ostensible **11** sophistical

speciousness 7 sophism **9** casuistry, sophistry

speck 3 bit, dot, jot **4** atom, iota, mite, mote, spot, tick, whit **5** crumb, fleck, grain, point, shred, trace **7** freckle, smidgen **8** molecule, particle, pinpoint

speckle 3 dot **4** spot **5** flake, fleck **6** dapple, pepper **7** stipple **8** sprinkle

spectacle 4 pomp, show **5** drama, sight **6** parade **7** display, pageant, panoply, tableau **10** exhibition, exposition **12** extravaganza

spectacular 5 stagy **7** amazing, pageant **8** dazzling, dramatic, striking, wondrous **9** marvelous, thrilling, wonderful **10** astounding, eye-popping, histrionic, miraculous, phenomenal, prodigious, staggering, stupefying, stupendous, theatrical **11** astonishing, sensational **12** extravaganza

spectator 5 gazer **6** viewer **7** watcher, witness **8** beholder, observer, onlooker **9** bystander **10** eyewitness

Spectator author 6 Steele (Richard) **7** Addison (Joseph)

specter 5 ghost, shade **6** shadow, spirit, wraith **7** eidolon, phantom **8** phantasm, revenant, visitant **10** apparition

spectral 6 spooky **7** ghastly, ghostly, phantom **9** ghostlike, unearthly **10** shadowlike **11** disembodied, phantomlike

spectrum 5 ambit, gamut, range, scale, sweep **7** compass **8** diapason **9** continuum ***producer:*** **5** prism

speculate 4 muse **5** study, think, weigh **6** ponder, reason, review, wonder **7** reflect **8** cogitate, consider, meditate, ruminate, theorize **9** cerebrate **10** conjecture, deliberate **11** contemplate

speculation 5 guess, hunch **6** gamble, review, theory **7** surmise **9** brainwork **10** conjecture

speculative 5 risky **7** curious, pensive **8** academic **10** thoughtful **11** conjectural, theoretical **12** hypothetical

speech 4 talk **5** idiom, spiel, voice **6** debate, homily, parley, sermon, tirade, tongue **7** address, dialect, diction, lecture, monolog, oration, palaver **8** dialogue, diatribe, harangue, language, parlance, rhetoric **9** discourse, monologue, utterance **10** allocution, expression, vernacular **11** declamation **12** articulation, disquisition, vocalization **13** verbalization ***defect:*** **4** lisp **7** stutter

speechcraft 7 oratory **8** rhetoric **9** elocution

speechless 3 mum **4** dumb, mute **6** silent **7** aphonic **10** dumbstruck, tongue-tied

speed 3 fly, hie, run, zip **4** clip, gait, pace, race, rush, tear, whiz **5** chase, haste, hurry, tempo **6** barrel, burn up, career, hasten, hustle, whoosh **7** quicken **8** alacrity, celerity, dispatch, expedite, highball, legerity, momentum, rapidity, velocity **9** fleetness, quickness, swiftness **10** accelerate, cannonball, facilitate, promptness

speed skater see **ice skater**

speedway 5 track **8** turnpike **9** racetrack **10** racecourse

speedy 4 fast **5** brisk, fleet, hasty, quick, rapid, swift **6** nimble, prompt **8** headlong **9** breakneck **11** expeditious

spell 3 hex **4** bout, jinx, mojo, rune, time, tour, turn **5** charm, hitch, shift, stint, throe, while **6** attack, period, streak, voodoo **7** relieve, stretch **11** conjuration, incantation

spellbind 3 hex **4** grip, vamp **5** charm **7** bewitch, catch up, enchant **8** enthrall, entrance **9** enrapture, fascinate, hypnotize, mesmerize
spelling 11 orthography ***bad:*** **10** cacography
spell out 7 clarify, explain, expound **8** construe, set forth **9** elucidate, explicate, interpret
spelunker 5 caver
spend 3 pay **4** blow, drop, pass **5** use up, waste **6** lavish, lay out, outlay **7** consume, exhaust, fork out, hand out, splurge **8** disburse, shell out, squander **9** dissipate, go through, throw away, while away **10** contribute, run through
spender 7 wastrel **8** prodigal **10** high roller, profligate, squanderer **11** scattergood
spendthrift see **spender**
Spenser poem 11 Faerie Queen (The)
spent 4 shot **5** all in **6** effete, pooped, used-up, wasted **7** drained, worn-out **8** burnt out, consumed, depleted, washed-up **9** exhausted, washed-out
spew 4 gush, ooze **5** belch, eject, eruct, erupt, expel, exude, flood, heave, shoot, spray, vomit **6** irrupt, spit up, squirt **7** throw up, upchuck **8** disgorge
sphagnum 4 moss
sphere 3 orb **4** area, ball, star, turf, zone **5** arena, field, globe, range, realm, round, scope **6** circle, domain, planet **7** demesne, rondure, terrain **8** dominion, province **9** bailiwick, territory **12** jurisdiction
spherical 5 round **6** global **7** globose **8** globular **9** orbicular
Sphinx *builder:* 6 Khafre ***father:* 6** Typhon ***mother:* 7** Echidna ***query:* 6** riddle ***site:* 4** Giza **6** Thebes
spice 3 pep, zip **4** kick, mace, tang, zest **5** anise, aroma, clove, cumin, poppy, savor, scent, smack, smell, taste **6** cloves, fennel, ginger, nutmeg, pepper, relish, sesame **7** bouquet, caraway, perfume **8** cardamom, cinnamon, piquancy **9** fragrance, redolence, seasoning
Spice Islands 8 Moluccas
spick-and-span 3 new **4** mint, neat, snug, tidy, trig, trim **5** clean, fresh **6** spruce **7** orderly **8** brand-new, spotless **9** shipshape **10** immaculate **11** well-groomed
spicy 3 hot **4** racy **5** bawdy, fiery, salty, tangy, zesty **6** lively, purple, ribald, risqué, savory, snappy, wicked **7** gingery, peppery, piquant, pungent, scented, zestful **8** aromatic, fragrant, off-color, perfumed, redolent, seasoned, spirited **9** flavorful, salacious **10** scandalous, suggestive **11** titillating
spider 6 Aranea, frypan **7** skillet **8** arachnid **9** frying pan **10** black widow
spiel 4 jive, line **5** pitch **6** patter **12** song and dance
Spielberg film 4 Hook, Jaws **6** Always, Munich **7** Amistad **8** Terminal (The) **9** Lost World (The) **11** Color Purple (The) **12** Jurassic Park, Twilight Zone (The) **14** Empire of the Sun, Minority Report, Schindler's List, War of the Worlds **15** Catch Me if You Can **16** Sugarland Express (The) **17** Saving Private Ryan **19** Raiders of the Lost Ark
spieler 4 tout **6** barker, hawker, talker **8** huckster
spigot 3 tap **4** cock, gate **5** valve **6** faucet **7** hydrant, petcock, shutoff **8** stopcock
spike 3 pin **4** brob, heel, lace, nail **5** lance, piton, spear **6** antler, impale, needle, skewer **7** spindle **8** increase, mackerel, puncture, transfix
spile 4 bung **5** spout
spill 4 blab, drip, drop, fall, flow, slop, tell **5** spray **6** betray, inform, reveal, splash, squeal, tattle **7** divulge, dribble, run over, spatter **8** disclose, overflow
Spillane detective 10 Mike Hammer
spilth 5 dregs, dross, swill, trash, waste **6** debris, refuse, scraps **7** garbage, rubbish **8** leavings
spin 4 gyre, reel, ride, swim, turn **5** dizzy, swirl, twirl, wheel, whirl **6** gyrate, rotate **7** revolve **8** rotation **9** pirouette, whirligig **10** revolution ***a log:* 4** birl ***out:* 4** draw **6** extend **7** prolong, stretch **8** elongate, lengthen, protract **10** prolongate
spinal column 5 chine **6** rachis ***curvature:* 8** lordosis ***part:* 8** vertebra (see also **spine**)
spindle 3 pin, rod **5** newel, shaft, spike **6** impale, rachis
spindly 5 frail, lanky, rangy, shaky, weedy **6** flimsy, gangly, skinny, twiggy, wobbly **7** fragile, rickety, tottery **8** gangling, skeletal, unsteady **9** emaciated **10** jerry-built
spine 4 back **6** rachis **7** spicule **8** backbone **9** vertebrae
spineless 5 timid **8** cowardly, timorous **9** weak-kneed **10** weak-willed **12** invertebrate
spin-off 8 offshoot **9** by-product, outgrowth **10** derivative, descendant
____ **Spinoza 6** Baruch
spinster 7 old maid **10** maiden lady
spiny 6 barbed, thorny **7** prickly **8** echinate **10** nettlesome
spiral 4 coil, curl, wind **5** helix, twine, twist **6** volute **7** helical, helices (plural) **8** gyroidal, volution **9** cochleate, corkscrew ***combining form:* 3** gyr **4** gyro **5** helic **6** helico

spire 4 coil **5** twist, whorl **7** steeple **8** pinnacle

spirit 3 pep, vim, zip **4** brio, dash, élan, gimp, grit, guts, life, mood, snap, soul, zeal, zest, zing **5** anima, ardor, drive, force, heart, moxie, oomph, pluck, shade, spunk, tenor, verve, vigor **6** animus, daimon, energy, esprit, fervor, ginger, mettle, morale, pneuma, psyche, starch, temper, wraith **7** courage, passion, phantom, specter, spectre **8** phantasm, revenant, vitality **9** animation, élan vital, substance **10** apparition, enthusiasm, get-up-and-go, liveliness ***away:*** **6** abduct, kidnap, snatch ***bottled:*** **5** genie ***evil:*** **3** ker **4** aitu **5** afrit, demon **6** afreet **7** erlking, shaitan ***female:*** **5** nymph **7** banshee ***Hopi:*** **7** kachina ***of a place:*** **10** genius loci ***Persian:*** **4** peri

spirited 4 bold, game, keen **5** eager, fiery, peppy **6** ardent, gritty, lively, plucky, spunky **7** chipper, fervent, gingery, peppery, valiant, zealous **8** animated, cheerful, intrepid, resolute **9** audacious, dauntless, energetic, sprightly, vivacious **10** courageous, mettlesome, passionate **12** enthusiastic

spirits 5 booze, drink **6** liquor, tipple **9** aqua vitae, firewater ***low:*** **5** blues, dumps, ennui **8** doldrums **10** blue devils, depression, melancholy

spiritual 6 sacred **7** saintly **8** churchly, mystical, numinous, platonic **9** religious **10** high-minded, immaterial, unphysical **11** disembodied, incorporeal, nonmaterial, nonphysical **12** metaphysical, supernatural, transcendent

spiritualist 6 medium, mystic **7** psychic

spit 5 spear **6** impale, saliva, skewer, slaver, sputum **7** spatter, sputter **8** splutter **9** brochette **11** expectorate

spite 5 venom **6** grudge, malice, rancor, spleen **7** ill will, revenge **9** pettiness, vengeance **11** malevolence **13** maliciousness

spiteful 4 mean **5** catty, nasty, snide **6** malign, wicked **7** vicious, waspish **8** venomous **9** malicious, malignant, rancorous **10** malevolent, vindictive

spitfire 4 fury **5** harpy, shrew, vixen **6** dragon, virago **7** hellcat, tigress **8** fishwife, harridan **9** termagant

spitting image 4 twin **5** clone **6** double, ringer **9** duplicate **10** carbon copy, dead ringer, simulacrum

spittoon 8 cuspidor

splash 3 sop, wet **4** slop, soak **5** douse, slosh, spray, swash **6** drench **7** spatter **8** sprinkle

splashy 5 gaudy, jazzy, showy **6** flashy, garish, glitzy, tawdry **7** blatant, dashing **8** colorful, dazzling, striking **10** flamboyant, theatrical **11** sensational **12** meretricious, ostentatious

splatter 4 slop **5** douse, plash, slosh, spray, swash **6** splash **8** sprinkle

splay 4 cant, tilt **5** angle, bevel, gawky, slant, slope **6** clumsy, extend, spread **7** awkward, incline **8** ungainly **9** expansion **11** inclination

spleen see **spite**

splendid 4 fine **5** grand, showy **6** superb **7** elegant, shining **8** glorious, gorgeous **9** brilliant, excellent, marvelous, wonderful **10** first-class, impressive **11** illustrious, magnificent, outstanding **12** transcendent

splendor 4 pomp **5** glory **6** dazzle **7** panoply **8** grandeur, richness **9** pageantry, spectacle **10** brilliance, brilliancy **12** magnificence

splenetic 5 cross, surly **6** fuming **8** incensed, spiteful **9** malicious **10** ill-natured, malevolent **11** ill-tempered

splice 3 tie **4** join, mate, mesh **5** braid, graft, plait, unite

splint 5 brace, strip **7** support **10** immobilize

splinter 4 rive **5** burst, smash **6** shiver, sliver **7** faction, shatter **8** fragment **12** disintegrate

split 3 rip **4** part, rend, rent, rift, rima, rime, rive, tear **5** break, carve, chasm, chink, cleft, crack, sever, slice **6** breach, cleave, cloven, divide, schism, sunder **7** break up, disjoin, dissect, diverge, divorce, divvy up, fission, fissure, rupture **8** cleavage, dissever, fracture, separate **11** dichotomize ***combining form:*** **5** schiz **6** schizo **7** schisto

splotch 4 blob, blot, spot **5** fleck, stain **6** smudge

splurge 4 orgy **5** binge, fling, spree **7** blowout, rampage **10** indulgence **12** extravagance

splutter 4 spit **6** babble, jabber **7** stammer

spoil 3 mar, rob, rot **4** baby, harm, prey, ruin, sack **5** decay, humor, taint, waste, wreck **6** coddle, cosset, curdle, damage, defile, impair, molder, pamper, ravish **7** blemish, cater to, destroy, indulge, pillage, putrefy, tarnish, vitiate **8** demolish **9** break down, decompose **11** mollycoddle

spoiled 4 rank, sour **6** putrid, rancid, rotten, ruined **7** coddled, decayed, gone bad **8** impaired, indulged, pampered **9** indulgent

spoils 4 haul, loot, swag **5** booty **7** pillage, plunder

spoilsport 7 killjoy

spoken 4 oral, said, told **6** verbal, voiced **7** uttered **8** phonetic, viva voce **9** delivered, unwritten **11** articulated

sponge 4 grub **5** cadge, leech, mooch **6** absorb, loofah 7 moocher 8 freeload, parasite, scrounge 10 freeloader ***material:*** 8 mesoglea ***opening:*** 6 oscula (plural) 7 osculum, ostiole

sponger 5 leech 7 moocher 8 parasite 10 freeloader

spongy 4 soft 5 mushy, pulpy 6 porous, quaggy 7 squashy, squishy 9 absorbent

sponsor 4 back, fund 5 angel, stake 6 backer, patron, surety 7 endorse, finance 8 advocate, bankroll, champion, Maecenas, mainstay, promoter, vouch for 9 grubstake, guarantee, guarantor, patronize, subsidize, supporter 10 benefactor, underwrite 11 underwriter

sponsorship 5 aegis 7 backing, support 8 advocacy, auspices 9 patronage

spontaneous 5 ad-lib 7 natural, offhand 8 ad-libbed, unforced 9 automatic, extempore, impromptu, impulsive, unstudied 10 improvised, off-the-cuff, unprompted 11 instinctive, unmeditated 13 unconstrained

spontoon 4 pike 5 lance, spear

spoof 4 sham 5 farce, put-on 6 parody, satire, send-up 7 lampoon, takeoff 8 travesty

spook 3 spy 5 agent, alarm, ghost, haunt, scare 7 specter, spectre, startle, terrify 8 frighten

spooky 5 eerie, weird 6 creepy 7 ghostly, ominous, uncanny 8 eldritch 9 unearthly

spool 4 reel, wind 6 bobbin

spoon 3 pet, woo 4 neck 5 court, ladle, scoop 6 cuddle

spoonbill 4 ibis 8 shoveler 9 ruddy duck 10 paddlefish

Spoon River poet 7 Masters (Edgar Lee)

spoony 5 mushy, silly 6 simple, slushy, syrupy 7 fatuous, foolish, mawkish, smitten, witless 9 schmaltzy 10 saccharine 11 sentimental

spoor 5 scent, trace, track, tract, trail 7 vestige 8 footstep 9 droppings, footprint

sporadic 4 rare 6 catchy, fitful, random, scarce, sparse, spotty 7 erratic 8 episodic, isolated, uncommon 9 desultory, irregular, scattered, spasmodic 10 infrequent, occasional

sport 3 fun 4 game, jest, joke, mock, play 6 frolic, racing, trifle 7 mockery, show off 9 diversion, high jinks, horseplay 10 recreation ***indoor:*** 6 boxing, hockey, squash 7 bowling 8 handball 9 wrestling 10 acrobatics, basketball, gymnastics 11 racquetball, table tennis ***Olympic:*** 4 judo 6 boxing, diving, hockey, rowing 7 archery, cycling, fencing, shot put 8 canoeing, football, high jump, long jump, marathon, shooting, swimming, yachting 9 decathlon, pole vault, water polo, wrestling 10 basketball, gymnastics, pentathlon, triple jump, volleyball 11 discus throw, hammer throw 12 javelin throw, steeplechase 13 weightlifting ***water:*** 6 diving, rowing 7 sailing, surfing 8 canoeing, swimming, yachting ***winter:*** 4 luge 6 hockey, skiing 7 curling, lugeing, skating 8 biathlon, sledding 10 ski jumping 11 bobsledding, tobogganing

sporting house 6 bagnio 7 brothel 8 bordello

sportive 5 antic 6 frisky, impish 7 playful, roguish, waggish 10 frolicsome 11 mischievous

sportiveness 7 devilry, roguery, waggery 8 deviltry, mischief 9 devilment, rascality

sporty 4 fast 5 peppy 6 breezy, casual, jaunty, lively 7 dashing, relaxed 8 debonair, informal 10 insouciant 11 streamlined

spot 3 fix, jam, nip, pip, see 4 espy, post, site 5 fleck, hit on, locus, place, point, speck 6 blotch, detect, pickle, plight, scrape 7 dilemma, smidgen, spatter, speckle 8 diagnose, flyspeck, identify, location, pinpoint, position 9 recognize, situation 11 predicament

spotless 4 pure 5 clean 6 chaste 8 hygienic, sanitary, unsoiled 9 undefiled, unstained, unsullied 10 immaculate 11 unblemished

spotlight 5 focus 6 notice 7 feature, point up 8 interest, point out 9 attention, emphasize, public eye, publicity 10 illuminate 12 illumination

spotted 4 seen 6 calico, motley 7 brindle, dappled, flecked, piebald 8 brindled, speckled, stippled

spouse 4 mate, wife 5 bride, groom, hubby 7 consort, husband

spout 3 jet 4 gush 5 chute, eject, spray, spurt 6 nozzle, squirt

sprain 4 pull, tear, turn 5 twist 6 wrench 7 stretch

sprawl 4 flop, loll 5 drape, slump 6 extend, lounge, slouch, spread 7 stretch 11 spread-eagle

spray 3 fog 4 hose, mist 6 shower, spritz 7 aerosol, atomize, diffuse, spatter 8 atomizer, droplets, fumigate, nebulize 9 spindrift

spread 3 jam, lay, set, sow, ted 4 deal, oleo, open, pâté, push 5 apply, feast, jelly, space, splay, strew, sweep 6 butter, expand, extend, fan out, pass on, retail 7 banquet, breadth, diffuse, expanse, overrun, pervade, radiate, scatter, slather, stretch, suffuse 8 bedcover, coverlet, dispense, disperse, mushroom, permeate 9 amplitude, broadcast, circulate, diffusion, dissipate, expansion, extension, profusion, propagate, radiation **10** dispersion, distribute, outstretch **11** counterpane, disseminate **12** transmission **13** proliferation

spree 3 jag **4** bash, bust, lark, orgy, riot, tear **5** binge, drunk, fling, revel **6** bender, frolic **7** blowout, carouse, rampage, splurge **8** carousal, wingding **10** indulgence **11** bacchanalia

sprig 4 brad, heir, twig **5** scion, shoot **7** pintail **9** ruddy duck

sprightly 3 gay **4** keen, spry, yare **5** agile, alert, antic, brisk, peppy, perky, zesty, zingy, zippy **6** active, breezy, chirpy, frisky, jaunty, lively, nimble **7** animate, chipper, coltish, piquant, playful, pungent **8** animated, cheerful, spirited, sportive **9** energetic, vivacious **10** frolicsome, rollicking

spring 3 hop **4** flow, free, jump, leap, lope, rise, root, skip, stem, trip, well **5** arise, begin, bound, cause, fount, issue, start **6** appear, bounce, emerge, hurdle, pounce, reason, source, uncoil, vernal **7** come out, emanate, proceed, rebound, startle **8** commence, fountain, stimulus, wellhead **9** originate **10** incitement, resilience **12** fountainhead ***back:*** **6** resile ***mineral:*** **3** spa

springe 4 trap **5** noose, snare **7** pitfall **9** booby trap

springlike 6 vernal

springy 6 supple **7** elastic **8** flexible, stretchy **9** recoiling, resilient

sprinkle 3 dot **4** rain, spot **5** shake, speck, spray, strew **6** pepper, powder, spritz **7** asperse, drizzle, freckle, scatter, speckle, stipple **9** bespeckle

sprint 3 run **4** dart, dash, race, shin, tear **5** scoot **6** gallop, hurtle, scurry **7** scamper

sprite 3 elf, fay, nix **4** puck **5** dryad, fairy, naiad, nixie, nymph, oread, pixie, sylph **6** kelpie **7** brownie **9** hamadryad, hobgoblin

spritz 3 jet **5** spray, spurt **6** shower, squirt

sprout 3 bud **4** grow **5** scion, shoot **6** ratoon, sucker **7** burgeon **8** offshoot **9** germinate

spruce 4 trim **5** natty, sassy, spiff **6** dapper, spiffy **11** well-groomed

spry 4 yare **5** agile, brisk, sound, zesty, zippy **6** active, lively, nimble, robust **7** healthy **8** animated, spirited, vigorous **9** energetic, vivacious

spud 5 tater **6** potato

____ **Spumante 4** Asti

spume 4 fizz, foam, head, scum, suds **5** froth, spray, yeast **6** lather

spunk 4 grit, guts **5** heart, moxie, nerve, pluck **6** mettle, spirit, tinder **7** cojones, courage **8** backbone, gumption **9** fortitude, toughness **10** liveliness, resolution

spunky 4 bold **5** brave, fiery **6** daring **7** doughty, gingery, peppery **8** fearless, spirited **9** dauntless **10** courageous, mettlesome **12** high-spirited

spur 4 goad, prod, stir, urge **5** egg on, impel, prick, rally, rouse, spine **6** arouse, branch, exhort, motive, prompt, propel **7** impetus, impulse **8** buttress, catalyst, excitant, stimulus **9** actuation, incentive, instigate, stimulant, stimulate **10** incitement, inducement, motivation, projection ***part:*** **5** rowel

spurious 4 fake, mock, sham **5** bogus, dummy, false, phony, put-on **6** ersatz, pseudo **7** assumed, feigned, pretend **8** affected **9** brummagem, imitation, pinchbeck, pretended, simulated **10** apocryphal, artificial, substitute **11** counterfeit, make-believe **12** illegitimate ***combining form:*** **5** pseud **6** pseudo

spurn 4 snub **5** flout, scoff, scorn, scout, sneer **6** rebuff, refuse, reject **7** contemn, decline, despise, disdain, dismiss, repulse **8** turn down **9** disregard, reprobate, repudiate **10** disapprove **12** cold-shoulder

spurt 3 jet **4** gush, jump **5** burst, expel, spout, surge **6** shower, spritz, squirt **7** upsurge **8** eruption, increase **9** discharge

sputter 4 fizz, fume, rage, rant, rave, spew, spit **6** gibber, jabber **7** bluster, stammer

spy 5 agent, scout, snoop, spook **6** beagle, sleuth **7** gumshoe **8** informer, saboteur **9** detective **12** investigator **13** undercover man ***name:*** **4** Ames (Aldrich), Boyd (Belle) **5** André (John), Blunt (Anthony), Fuchs (Klaus) **6** Philby (Kim), Smiley (George) **7** Burgess (Guy), Hanssen (Robert), Maclean (Donald), Pollard (Jonathan) **8** Mata Hari

spyglass 9 telescope

spying 9 espionage

Spyri's heroine 5 Heidi

squab 5 couch **6** pigeon **7** cushion

squabble 3 row **4** miff, spat, tiff **5** argue **6** bicker, dustup **7** brabble, dispute, quarrel, wrangle

squad 4 crew, side, team, unit **5** cadre **6** detail, lineup, patrol

squalid 3 low **4** base, foul, mean, vile **5** dingy, dirty, nasty, seedy **6** filthy, frowsy, frowzy, grubby, scurvy, shabby, shoddy, sleazy, slummy, sordid **7** ignoble, low-down, run-down, scrubby, unclean, unkempt **8** slovenly, wretched **10** despicable, disheveled **11** dilapidated **12** disreputable

squall 3 caw, row, yap, yip **4** bark, bawl, beef, feud, fuss, gust, howl, roar, tiff, wail, yawp, yell, yelp, yowl **5** brawl, fight, hoo-ha, shout **6** bellow, clamor, flurry, fracas, hubbub, ruckus, rumpus, scream, shriek, squeal, yammer **7** dispute, flare-up, quarrel, rhubarb, screech **8** brouhaha, squabble **9** bickering, caterwaul, commotion **10** falling-out, hullabaloo **11** altercation

squalor 5 filth **6** misery **7** neglect, poverty **8** baseness, iniquity **9** depravity, dirtiness **10** sordidness **11** degradation **12** wretchedness

squander 4 blow **5** spend, waste **7** consume, exhaust, fritter, scatter **9** dissipate, throw away **10** trifle away **11** fritter away

squanderer see **spender**

square 3 fit, fix **4** bang, boxy, even, fair, jibe, just, tied **5** adapt, agree, align, clear, equal, exact, match, pay up, plaza, sharp, spang, tally **6** accord, adjust, settle **7** balance, conform, satisfy, settled **8** check out, dovetail, orthodox, quadrate, smack-dab, straight, unbiased **9** equitable, liquidate, objective, quadratic, reconcile, rectangle

squash 3 jam **4** cram, mash, pepo, pulp **5** crush, gourd, press, quell **7** flatten, put down, squeeze, squelch **8** suppress ***variety:*** **5** acorn **6** cushaw, Sibley, turban **7** Hubbard, scallop **8** pattypan, zucchini **9** butternut, crookneck **10** Marblehead

squat 3 low **5** dumpy, hunch, stoop, stout, thick **6** chunky, crouch, hunker, stocky, stubby **8** heavyset, thickset **10** hunker down **11** thick-bodied

squawfish 4 chub **8** cyprinid **10** pikeminnow

squawk 3 caw, yap, yip **4** beef, crab, fuss, yawp **5** bleat, gripe **6** yammer **7** protest, screech **8** complain **9** bellyache, complaint

squeak 3 rat **4** blab, fink, peep, pipe, sing **5** cheep, creak **6** escape, inform, snitch, tattle **10** tattletale

squeal 3 rat, yip **4** blab, howl, sing, yell, yelp, yowl **5** bleat, creak, grate, gripe, peach **6** inform, screak, scream, shriek, shrill, snitch, squawk, tattle **7** protest, screech **8** complain **10** tattletale

squealer 3 rat **4** fink **6** canary, snitch, weasel **7** ratfink, stoolie, tattler, tipster **8** betrayer, informer **10** talebearer, tattletale **11** stool pigeon

squeamish 5 fussy, upset **6** queasy **7** finical, finicky **8** nauseous **9** nauseated **10** fastidious, particular, pernickety **11** persnickety

squeeze 3 hug, jam **4** bind, cram, grip, milk, pack, push **5** clasp, crowd, crush, exact, gouge, juice, pinch, press, screw, wring **6** clutch, coerce, compel, crunch, eke out, enfold, extort, jostle, squash, squish **7** dilemma, embrace, extract **8** compress, contract, pressure, quandary **9** shake down **11** compression, predicament

squelch 5 quell, shush, sit on **6** muffle, muzzle, squash, squish, stifle, subdue **7** repress, silence, smother **8** strangle, suppress **10** extinguish

squib 4 fire **6** filler **7** lampoon **8** shoot off **9** detonator **11** firecracker

squid 7 mollusc, mollusk **8** calamari, calamary **10** cephalopod ***kin:*** **7** octopus **10** cuttlefish

squiggle 4 worm **6** doodle, scrawl, squirm, writhe **7** scratch **8** curlicue, scrabble, scribble

squinch 5 quail, start, wince **6** blench, crouch, recoil, shrink

squint 4 peek, peep, peer **10** hagioscope, strabismus

squire 6 attend, escort, lawyer **7** consort, gallant **8** cavalier, chaperon **9** accompany, landowner

squirm 4 worm **6** fidget, wiggle, writhe **7** wriggle

squirrel 4 stow **5** cache, hoard, stash **7** secrete ***red:*** **9** chickaree

squirt 3 jet, kid, pup, tot **4** brat, tyke **5** sprat, spray, spurt, twerp **6** shaver, shrimp, splurt, spritz **7** spatter

squish 3 jam **4** cram, mash, mush, pack, push **5** crush, press, quash, smash **7** flatten, scrunch, squeeze, squelch, trample

squishy 4 soft **6** flabby, quaggy, slushy, spongy

Sri Lanka ***aborigine:*** **5** Vedda ***bay:*** **6** Bengal ***capital:*** **7** Colombo ***city:*** **5** Kandy **8** Moratuwa ***ethnic group:*** **9** Sinhalese ***former name:*** **6** Ceylon ***language:*** **5** Tamil **9** Sinhalese ***monetary unit:*** **5** rupee ***shoals:*** **11** Adam's Bridge ***strait:*** **4** Palk

SRO 7 sellout

SS chief 7 Himmler (Heinrich)

S-shaped 7 sigmoid ***arch, molding:*** **4** ogee

stab 3 dig, pop, try **4** pang, poke, shot **5** crack, drive, fling, guess, prick, spear, stick, whack, whirl **6** effort, pierce, thrust, twinge **7** attempt **8** puncture **9** penetrate

Stabat ____ 5 Mater

stabile 6 steady **9** sculpture **10** stationary

stabilize 3 fix, set **4** prop **5** brace, poise **6** cement, firm up, fixate, prop up, secure, settle, steady **7** balance, ballast, support, sustain **8** solidify **9** reinforce

stable 3 set **4** barn, fast, firm, mews, safe, sure **5** fixed, solid, sound **6** secure, steady, sturdy **7** abiding, durable, lasting, staunch **8** balanced, constant, enduring, resolute **9** immutable, permanent, steadfast, unvarying

10 perdurable, stationary, unchanging, unshakable
stack 4 cock, heap, hill, load, mass, pile, pipe, rick **5** mound, sheaf **7** chimney, pyramid
stack up 3 add **5** equal, total **6** equate, gather **7** compare, measure
stadium 4 bowl, dome, rink, ring **5** arena **6** garden **8** coliseum **10** hippodrome **12** amphitheater ***level:*** **4** tier
staff 3 rod **4** cane, club, prop, rung, team, wand **5** baton, billy **6** cudgel **7** faculty, support **9** personnel ***bishop's:*** **7** crosier, crozier ***medical:*** **8** caduceus ***of office:*** **4** mace
stag 4 male, solo **5** alone
stage 3 lot **4** dais, play, rung, show, step **5** grade, level, mount, notch, phase, put on **6** degree, period, status **7** execute, perform, present, produce **8** platform ***direction:*** **4** exit **5** enter **6** exeunt ***scenery:*** **3** set **8** backdrop ***show:*** **4** play **5** drama, revue **7** musical **9** burlesque **10** vaudeville ***signal:*** **3** cue ***whisper:*** **5** aside
stage set 5 decor, scene **7** scenery **8** backdrop **11** mise-en-scène
stagger 4 daze, reel, stun, sway **5** amaze, floor, lurch, pitch, stump, waver, weave **6** boggle, careen, dither, falter, teeter, topple, totter, wobble, zigzag **7** astound, nonplus, perplex, shatter, stumble, stupefy **8** astonish, bowl over **9** dumbfound, overwhelm, vacillate **11** flabbergast
stagnant 5 musty, stale **6** static **8** immobile, unmoving **10** motionless, stationary
stagnate 4 idle **5** stall **6** fester **8** languish, stultify, vegetate
stagy 10 artificial, histrionic, theatrical **11** pretentious **12** melodramatic
staid 5 grave, sober **6** formal, sedate, solemn, somber, sombre, stuffy **7** earnest, serious, starchy **8** composed, decorous, priggish **9** dignified
stain 3 dye, tar **4** blot, daub, onus, slur, soil, spot **5** brand, color, odium, shame, smear, sully, taint, tinge **6** blotch, defile, embrue, imbrue, smirch, smudge, stigma **7** blemish, pigment, tarnish **8** besmirch, colorant, discolor, dishonor, dyestuff, tincture
staircase ***handrail:*** **8** banister **9** bannister ***outdoor:*** **6** perron ***post:*** **5** newel **8** baluster
stake 3 bet, lay, pot, set **4** ante, back, game, pale, play, post, risk **5** claim, put on, share, wager **6** gamble, paling, picket, pledge, tether **7** finance **8** bankroll, interest **10** capitalize, investment
stalag 7 POW camp **10** prison camp
stale 5 banal, dusty, faded, fusty, moldy, musty, passé, tired, trite **7** clichéd, tedious, worn-out **8** overused, shopworn, stagnant, timeworn **9** hackneyed, tasteless **11** commonplace, stereotyped
stalemate 3 tie **4** draw **7** impasse **8** deadlock, gridlock, standoff
stalk 4 hunt, prey **5** chase, track **6** ambush, follow, pursue, stride **8** flush out ***flower:*** **8** peduncle ***leaf:*** **7** petiole ***short:*** **5** stipe
stall 3 bay, pew **4** halt **5** booth, brake, check, delay, hedge, kiosk, stand **6** arrest, put off **7** conk out, counter, hold off **8** obstruct **9** stonewall **10** filibuster **11** compartment, prevaricate
stalwart 4 bold **5** brave, gutsy, hardy, husky, stout, tough **6** brawny, robust, sinewy, strong, sturdy **7** valiant **8** fearless, intrepid, unafraid, valorous, vigorous **9** dauntless, tenacious, undaunted **10** courageous
stamen part 6 anther **8** filament
stamina 8 tenacity **9** endurance, fortitude, tolerance **11** persistence **12** staying power
stammer 6 gibber, jabber **7** sputter, stutter **8** hesitate, splutter
stamp 3 ilk, lot **4** etch, kind, mark, mint, mold, seal, sort, type **5** clomp, clump, pound, print, tromp **6** hammer, stripe **7** impress, imprint, trample **8** hallmark, inscribe **9** character **10** impression **12** characterize
stampede 4 bolt, dash, rout, rush, tear **5** crush, panic, rodeo **6** charge
stamps 7 postage
stance 4 pose **7** bearing, posture **8** attitude, carriage, position **10** deportment
stanch 4 stem, stop **5** check **6** stop up **8** hold back
stanchion 4 post, prop **5** brace **7** support
stand 4 bear **5** abide, booth, brook, kiosk, stall, treat **6** endure, handle, suffer **7** counter, stomach, swallow, weather **8** attitude, platform, position, tolerate ***artist's:*** **5** easel ***three-legged:*** **6** tripod, trivet ***ornamental:*** **7** étagère
standard 3 law, par **4** flag, jack, mean, norm, rule **5** color, gauge, ideal, model, stock, usual **6** banner, common, ensign, median, normal, pennon **7** average, classic, example, general, labarum, measure, pattern, pennant, regular, typical, uniform **8** accepted, everyday, exemplar, familiar, ordinary, orthodox, paradigm **9** archetype, benchmark, criterion, customary, principle, yardstick **10** recognized, regulation, touchstone **11** established, fundamental
standardize 6 adjust **7** conform **8** regulate **9** reconcile
stand for 4 bear, mean **5** allow **6** denote, per-

mit **7** signify **8** indicate, tolerate **9** put up with, represent, symbolize

stand-in 3 sub **5** proxy **6** backup, second **9** alternate, surrogate **10** substitute, understudy **11** pinch hitter, replacement **12** impersonator

standing 4 rank, term **5** erect, fixed, place **6** cachet, credit, repute, status **7** dignity, footing, station, stature, upright **8** capacity, duration, eminence, position, prestige, stagnant **9** character, permanent, situation **10** estimation, reputation **11** consequence, established

standoff see **stalemate**

standoffish 5 aloof **6** chilly **7** distant, haughty **8** detached, reserved **9** reclusive, withdrawn **10** unfriendly, unsociable **12** misanthropic

stand out 3 jut **4** bulk, loom **5** bulge **7** project **8** protrude

standpatter 4 fogy, tory **5** fogey **7** diehard **8** mossback **11** bitter-ender **12** conservative

standpoint 4 side **5** angle, slant **7** outlook **9** direction **11** perspective

standstill 4 halt, stop **5** check, pause **7** impasse **8** deadlock, dead stop **9** cessation, stalemate

Stanford site 8 Palo Alto

Stanley Kowalski's wife 6 Stella

Stanleys' car 7 steamer

Stan's partner 5 Ollie

stanza 7 strophe ***combining form:* 5** stich ***final:* 5** envoi ***of eight lines:* 6** octave ***of four lines:* 6** ballad **8** quatrain ***of six lines:* 6** sestet ***of three lines:* 6** tercet **7** triplet ***Persian:* 8** rubaiyat

star 4 icon, idol, lead, main, nova **5** actor, chief, major **6** étoile **7** actress, capital **8** asterisk, dominant, luminary **9** celebrity, headliner, principal **10** preeminent **11** outstanding ***bright:* 4** Vega **5** Algol, Deneb, Rigel, Spica **6** Altair, Castor, Pollux, Sirius **7** Antares, Canopus, Capella, Polaris, Procyon, Regulus **8** Arcturus **9** Aldebaran, Archernar, Fomalhaut **10** Beta Crucis, Betelgeuse **11** Alpha Crucis **12** Beta Centauri **13** Alpha Centauri ***combining form:* 4** astr **5** aster, astro **6** astero, sidero ***envelope:* 6** corona ***exploding:* 4** nova ***five-pointed:* 8** pentacle, stellate **9** pentagram ***giant:* 10** Betelgeuse ***North:* 7** Polaris ***six-pointed:* 8** hexagram

starch 3 pep **4** push, snap **5** drive, moxie, punch, spunk, vigor **7** stiffen **8** gumption, vitality **9** formality ***combining form:* 4** amyl **5** amylo

starchy 4 prim **5** aloof, stiff **6** doughy, formal, wooden **7** stilted

star-crossed 6 doomed **7** hapless, unlucky **8** ill-fated, luckless **10** ill-starred **11** unfortunate **12** misfortunate

Stardust composer 10 Carmichael (Hoagy)

stare 3 eye **4** gape, gawk, gaze, ogle, peer **6** goggle **10** rubberneck

stark 3 raw **4** bare, nude, pure **5** bleak, blunt, clear, harsh, naked, quite, rigid, sheer, utter **6** barren, strict, unclad, vacant, wholly **8** absolute, complete, desolate, stripped **9** au naturel, out-and-out **10** absolutely

starry 6 astral **7** stellar **8** sidereal

starry-eyed 6 dreamy, unreal **7** utopian **8** ecstatic **9** rapturous, visionary **11** impractical, unrealistic **13** impracticable

Star-Spangled Banner writer 3 Key (Francis Scott)

start 4 bolt, dawn, draw **5** arise, begin, crank, found, get-go, issue, onset, quail, react, set up, wince **6** blench, create, embark, flinch, launch, outset, recoil, shrink, spring, take up **7** actuate, genesis, infancy, kickoff, opening, trigger **8** activate, commence, embark on, initiate, organize, reaction **9** beginning, establish, institute, originate **10** inaugurate **12** commencement

startle 4 jolt, jump **5** alarm, scare, shock, spook **8** astonish, frighten, surprise

Star Trek *captain:* 4 Kirk (James T.) **5** Sisko (Benjamin) **6** Archer (Jonathan), Picard (Jean-Luc) **7** Janeway (Kathryn) ***character:* 3** Dax (Jadzia), Kim (Harry), Nog, Odo, Rom, Yar (Natasha) **4** Data, Kurn, Lore, Sulu, Troi (Deanna, Lwaxana), Worf **5** Adami (Kai Winn), Dukat, Duras (Lursa, B'Etor), McCoy ("Bones"), Nerys (Kira), Paris (Tom), Quark, Riker (Will), Sarek, Scott, Spock, Tuvok, Uhura **6** Bashir (Julian), Chekov, Doctor (The), Guinan, Gowron, O'Brien (Keiko, Miles), Torres (B'Elanna), Weyoun **7** Crusher (Dr. Beverly, Wesley), La Forge (Geordi) **8** Chakotay **9** Borg Queen **11** Seven of Nine ***creator:* 11** Roddenberry (Gene) ***fan:* 7** Trekker, Trekkie ***race:*4** Borg, Gorn, Voth **5** Breen, Human, Trill, Vorta **6** Lurian, Pakled, Terran, Vulcan **7** Bajoran, Ferengi, Iconian, Klingon, Romulan, Tribble **8** Andorian, Betazoid, El-Aurian, Jem'Hadar **9** Nausicaan, Tellarite **10** Cardassian, Changeling ***actor:* 5** Nimoy (Leonard), Takei (George) **6** Kelley (DeForest) **7** Mulgrew (Kate), Shatner (William), Stewart (Patrick) **8** Fletcher (Louise), Goldberg (Whoopi) **11** Auberjonois (René) ***starship:* 10** Enterprise

starved 6 hungry **8** famished, ravenous, underfed

Star Wars 3 SDI ***actor:* 3** Lee (Christopher) **4** Ford (Harrison) **5** Jones (James Earl) **6** Fisher (Carrie), Hamill (Mark), Neeson (Liam) **7** Jackson (Samuel L.), Portman (Natalie) **8** Guinness (Alec), McGregor (Ewan), Williams (Billy Dee) **9** McDiarmid (Ian) ***character:* 4** Fett (Boba, Jango), Jinn (Qui-Gon), Leia (Princess), Maul (Darth), Solo (Han), Yoda (Master) **5** Binks (Jar Jar), Dooku (Count), Vader (Darth) **8** Grievous (General) **9** Chewbacca, Palpatine (Senator, Chancellor, Emperor), Skywalker (Anakin, Luke) **10** Calrissian (Lando) **12** Jabba the Hutt ***composer:* 8** Williams (John) ***creator:* 5** Lucas (George) ***film:* 7** New Hope (A) **13** Phantom Menace (The) **15** Return of the Jedi **16** Revenge of the Sith **17** Attack of the Clones, Empire Strikes Back (The) ***group:* 4** Jedi, Sith **5** Ewoks **6** Clones, Droids **8** Wookiees **13** Rebel Alliance ***parody:* 6** Troops **10** Spaceballs **12** Hardware Wars ***planet:* 4** Hoth **5** Naboo **7** Dagobah **8** Alderaan, Tatooine **9** Coruscant ***threat:* 9** Death Star

stash 4 bury, hide, pile **5** cache, hoard, plant, store **7** conceal, lay away, nest egg, secrete **8** lay aside, sock away, squirrel **9** stockpile

stasis 7 balance, inertia **9** equipoise **10** immobility, stagnation **11** equilibrium

stat 3 now, PDQ **4** ASAP **6** at once, pronto

state 3 air, put, say **4** aver, mode, rank, tell, vent **5** utter **6** affirm, assert, recite, relate, report **7** declare, dignity, explain, expound, express, posture, recount **8** attitude, capacity, describe, position, set forth, standing **9** condition, enunciate, situation, ventilate ***subdivison:* 6** county

state *easternmost:* 5 Maine ***largest:* 6** Alaska ***smallest:* 11** Rhode Island ***southernmost:* 6** Hawaii

state abbreviation *Alabama:* 3 Ala. ***Alaska:* 4** Alas. ***Arizona:* 4** Ariz. ***Arkansas:* 3** Ark. ***California:* 3** Cal. **5** Calif. ***Colorado:* 3** Col. **4** Colo. ***Connecticut:* 4** Conn. ***Delaware:* 3** Del. ***Florida:* 3** Fla. ***Idaho:* 3** Ida. ***Illinois:* 3** Ill. ***Indiana:* 3** Ind. ***Kansas:* 3** Kan. **4** Kans. ***Kentucky:* 3** Ken. ***Massachusetts:* 4** Mass. ***Michigan:* 4** Mich. ***Minnesota:* 4** Minn. ***Mississippi:* 4** Miss. ***Montana:* 4** Mont. ***Nebraska:* 3** Neb. **4** Nebr. ***Nevada:* 3** Nev. ***New Mexico:* 4** N. Mex. ***North Carolina:* 4** N. Car. ***North Dakota:* 4** N. Dak. ***Oklahoma:* 4** Okla. ***Oregon:* 3** Ore. **4** Oreg. ***Pennsylvania:* 4** Penn. **5** Penna. ***South Carolina:* 4** S. Car. ***South Dakota:* 4** S. Dak. ***Tennessee:* 4** Tenn. ***Texas:* 3** Tex. ***Vermont:* 4** Verm. ***Virginia:* 4** Virg. ***Washington:* 4** Wash. ***West Virginia:* 3** W. Va. ***Wisconsin:* 3** Wis. **4** Wisc. ***Wyoming:* 3** Wyo.

stately 5 grand, lofty, noble, regal, royal **6** august, formal, kingly, lordly, solemn **7** courtly, elegant, gallant, haughty **8** gracious, imperial, imposing, majestic, palatial, princely **9** dignified **10** ceremonial, impressive, monumental **11** ceremonious, magnificent

statement 3 tab **4** bill **5** score **6** avowal, charge, dictum, remark, report **7** account, comment, invoice, recital **8** averment **9** affidavit, assertion, manifesto, narrative, reckoning, testimony, utterance **10** deposition, expression **11** description ***introductory:* 7** preface **8** foreword, prologue

stateroom 5 cabin

statesman 10 politician ***American:* 3** Hay (John Milton) **4** Clay (Henry), Hull (Cordell), Otis (James), Root (Elihu) **5** Adams (Samuel), Henry (Patrick), Lodge (Henry Cabot), Vance (Cyrus) **6** Bunche (Ralph), Bunker (Ellsworth), Dulles (John Foster), Kennan (George F.), Morris (Gouverneur), Powell (Colin), Sumner (Charles) **7** Acheson (Dean), Hancock (John), Kellogg (Frank B.), Lansing (Robert), Sherman (John, Roger), Stimson (Henry L.), Webster (Daniel) **8** Franklin (Benjamin), Hamilton (Alexander), Harriman (Averell), Pinckney (Charles, Thomas), Randolph (Edmund Jennings, John, Payton), Rutledge (John), Trumbull (Jonathan, Joseph) **9** Kissinger (Henry), Stevenson (Adlai) **10** Stettinius (Edward Reilly) ***Australian:* 9** Wentworth (William Charles) ***Austrian:* 6** Renner (Karl) **7** Kaunitz (Wenzel von) **8** Dollfuss (Engelbert) **10** Metternich (Klemens von) **13** Schwarzenberg (Felix zu) ***Canadian:* 4** King (W. L. Mackenzie) **7** Laurier (Wilfrid) **8** Thompson (John Sparrow) **9** Macdonald (John Alexander, John Sandfield), Mackenzie (Alexander, William Lyon) ***Chinese:* 3** Yen (Hsishan) **4** Deng (Xiaoping), Kung (Hsiang-hsi), Teng (Hsiao-p'ing), Wang (Anshih, Chingwei), Yuan (Shih-kai) **9** Sun Yat-Sen ***Dutch:* 6** de Witt (Johan de) **7** Grotius (Hugo), Stikker (Dirk) ***East German:* 8** Ulbricht (Walter) ***English:* 3** Fox (Charles, Henry) **4** Eden (Anthony, George, William), More (Thomas), Peel (Arthur, Robert, William), Pitt (William), Vane (Henry) **5** Cecil (Robert, William), North (Francis, Frederick, Roger) **6** Morley (John), Sidney (Algernon, Henry, Philip, Robert), Temple (Henry, William), Wolsey (Thomas) **7** Halifax (Earl of), Reading (Marquis of), Russell

(John, William), Stanley (Edward George, Edward Henry), Stewart (Robert), Warwick (Earl of) **8** Cromwell (Oliver, Thomas), Disraeli (Benjamin), Robinson (George Frederick Samuel), Villiers (George) **9** Cavendish (Spencer, William), Churchill (Randolph, Winston), Gladstone (William), Salisbury (Earl, Marquis of), Strafford (Earl of), Wellesley (Arthur, Richard Colley) **10** Palmerston (Lord), Rockingham (Marquis of), Sunderland (Earl of), Walsingham (Francis), Wellington (Duke of) **11** Chamberlain (Austen, Joseph, Neville), Shaftesbury (Earl of) **12** Chesterfield (Earl of) ***Finnish:*** **9** Stahlberg (Kaarlo Juho) ***French:*** **5** Sully (Duc de) **6** Guizot (François-Pierre-Guillaume), Thiers (Louis-Adolphe), Turgot (Anne-Robert-Jacques) **7** Herriot (Edouard), Mazarin (Jules), Schuman (Robert), Viviani (René) **8** Hanotaux (Gabriel) **9** Lafayette (Marquis de), Millerand (Alexandre), Richelieu (Duc de) **10** Clemenceau (Georges) **11** Tocqueville (Alexis de) ***German:*** **5** Wirth (Joseph) **10** Stresemann (Gustav) ***German-Danish:*** **9** Struensee (Johann Friedrich) ***Greek:*** **6** Zaimis (Alexandros) **8** Pericles **9** Aristides **11** Cleisthenes, Demosthenes **12** Themistocles ***Israeli:*** **4** Eban (Abba) **5** Begin (Menachem), Dayan (Moshe), Peres (Shimon), Rabin (Yitzhak) **7** Sharett (Moshe) **9** Ben-Gurion (David) ***Italian:*** **6** Cavour (Conte di), Crispi (Francesco) **7** Orlando (Vittorio Emanuele) **11** Machiavelli (Niccolo) ***Japanese:*** **3** Ito (Hirobumi) **5** genro, Kanoe **6** Kanoye ***Norwegian:*** **6** Nansen (Fridtjof) ***Polish:*** **7** Zaleski (August) **9** Pilsudski (Jozef) **10** Paderewski (Ignacy) ***Prussian:*** **5** Stein (Karl) ***Roman:*** **4** Cato (Marcus Porcius) **6** Cicero (Marcus Tullius), Pompey, Seneca (Lucius Annaeus) **7** Agrippa (Marcus Vipsanius) **8** Gracchus (Gaius, Tiberius), Maecenas (Gaius) **9** Symmachus (Quintus Aurelius) ***Russian:*** **5** Witte (Sergey) **7** Molotov (Vyacheslav) **8** Potemkin (Grigory) **9** Vyshinsky (Andrey) ***Scottish:*** **4** Knox (John) ***South American:*** **7** Bolívar (Simón) **9** San Martín (José de) ***Swiss:*** **4** Ador (Gustave) **5** Welti (Emil)

static **5** fixed, inert **6** stable, steady **7** stabile, stalled, stopped **8** constant, immobile, inactive, stagnant, unmoving **9** immovable, unvarying **10** changeless, unchanging

station **4** post, rank, site, spot **5** depot, locus, place, point **6** assign **7** footing **8** capacity, standing **9** character **10** white noise

stationary **5** fixed **6** static **8** immobile, stagnant, unmoving **9** immovable **10** motionless, stock-still

statue ***base:*** **6** plinth **8** pedestal ***gigantic:*** **8** Colossus ***Greek:*** **5** atlas **7** telamon **8** caryatid ***religious:*** **5** Pietà ***small:*** **8** figurine

stature see **status**

status **4** rank **5** merit, place, worth **6** cachet, rating, renown **7** caliber, dignity, footing, posture, quality **8** capacity, eminence, position, prestige, standing **9** character, condition, situation **10** prominence **11** consequence, distinction

statute **3** act, law **4** bill **5** canon, edict **9** enactment, ordinance

staunch **4** fast, firm, sure, true **5** liege, loyal, solid, sound **6** secure, stable, strong, trusty **8** constant, faithful, reliable, resolute, stalwart **9** steadfast **10** dependable **11** substantial, trustworthy

stave off **4** foil **5** avert, block, deter, dodge, elude, parry, rebut, repel **6** rebuff, thwart **7** forfend, obviate, prevent, repulse **8** preclude **9** forestall **10** circumvent

stay **3** guy, lag **4** bide, halt, prop, rest, stop, wait **5** abide, brace, check, defer, delay, dwell, lodge, tarry, visit **6** linger, put off, remain **7** sojourn, support, suspend **8** hold over, postpone, stop over **9** interrupt **10** suspension **11** stick around

stead **4** lieu **5** place **9** advantage

steadfast **4** firm, sure, true **5** fixed, liege, loyal **7** abiding, adamant, patient, staunch **8** constant, enduring, faithful, immobile, reliable, resolute, stubborn **9** immovable, unbending, unmovable **10** dependable, unwavering, unyielding **11** unfaltering, unflinching **12** never-failing, single-minded, wholehearted **13** unquestioning

steady **3** set **4** beau, even, fast, firm, sure **5** fixed, liege, loyal, sober **6** stable, static **7** abiding, ballast, certain, durable, equable, nonstop, regular, stabile, staunch, uniform **8** constant, enduring, faithful, habitual, reliable, resolute, unbroken, unshaken **9** ceaseless, incessant, stabilize, unvarying **10** changeless, consistent, continuous, dependable, persistent, sweetheart, unchanging, unswerving, unwavering **11** unfaltering **12** unchangeable, wholehearted

steak **4** club, cube, loin **5** chuck, flank, round, T-bone **6** rib eye **7** brisket, sirloin **9** Delmonico, hamburger, Salisbury **10** tenderloin **11** filet mignon, London broil, porterhouse **13** chateaubriand

steal **3** bag, cop, nab, nip, rob **4** glom, grab, hook, kite, lift, loot, lurk, slip, take **5** boost, creep, filch, glide, heist, pinch, poach, prowl, seize, shirk, sidle, skulk, slide, slink, sneak, swipe **6** burgle, fleece, hijack, pilfer, pocket, snatch, snitch, thieve, tiptoe **7** bargain, pillage, plunder, purloin **8** embezzle, shanghai, shoplift **9** pussyfoot **10** burglarize, plagiarize **11** appropriate ***a vehicle:*** **6** hijack **8** highjack

stealing 5 theft **6** piracy **7** larceny, robbery **8** burglary

stealthy 3 sly **4** wily **6** covert, crafty, feline, secret, shifty, silent, slinky, sneaky **7** catlike, cunning, furtive, sub-rosa **8** hush-hush, skulking, slinking, sneaking **9** noiseless **10** undercover **11** clandestine **13** surreptitious

steam 3 gas, pep, zip **4** foam, fume, mist, rage **5** anger, force, might, power, vapor **6** energy, seethe **8** momentum

steam bath 5 sauna

steamboat structure 5 texas

steamer 4 boat, clam, ship

steam organ 8 calliope

steamy 3 hot **5** humid, muggy **6** erotic, sticky, sultry, torrid **8** stifling

steed 5 horse, mount **7** charger

steel 4 gird **5** brace, nerve, rally **6** buck up, harden **7** fortify, hearten, stiffen **8** embolden, inspirit **9** reinforce **10** strengthen

steep 3 sop **4** high, soak **5** bathe, dizzy, imbue, sheer **6** abrupt, drench, infuse **7** arduous, extreme, immerse, suffuse **8** elevated, marinate, saturate **9** excessive **10** exorbitant, immoderate, impregnate, inordinate **11** precipitate, precipitous

steeple 5 spire, tower **6** flèche

steer 4 helm, lead **5** guide, pilot, point, route **6** direct, escort, tip-off **7** channel, conduct, skipper **8** shepherd ***a ship:*** **4** conn, helm, luff

steersman 3 cox **7** captain **8** coxswain

Stegner novel 13 Angle of Repose, Spectator Bird (The) **20** Big Rock Candy Mountain (The)

stein 3 mug **5** stoup **6** goblet **7** tankard

Steinbeck novel 5 Pearl (The) **10** Cannery Row, East of Eden **12** Of Mice and Men, Tortilla Flat **13** Grapes of Wrath (The)

Stein's companion 6 Toklas (Alice B.)

Steinway product 5 piano

stellar 6 astral, starry **7** leading, shining **8** sidereal, standout, starlike **10** preeminent **11** outstanding, predominant, superlative

stem 4 flow, head, rise, stop **5** abate, arise, check, issue **6** arrest, derive, spring, stanch **7** control, develop, emanate, proceed **8** peduncle **9** originate ***plant:*** **4** axis **5** haulm ***underground:*** **5** tuber **7** rhizome

stench 4 funk, reek **5** smell, stink

stentorian 4 loud **7** blaring, booming, orotund, raucous, roaring **8** sonorous, strident **9** clamorous, deafening **10** thundering **12** earsplitting

step 4 hoof, pace, rung, walk **5** grade, level, notch, stage, stair, stile, track, tread **6** degree **7** measure, traipse **8** footfall **9** gradation ***dance:*** **3** pas

step-by-step 7 gradual **9** piecemeal

steppe 5 plain **6** tundra

Steppenwolf author 5 Hesse (Hermann)

stereotype 4 mold **5** plate **7** pattern **10** categorize, pigeonhole **11** standardize

stereotypical 4 hack **5** banal, stale, trite **7** clichéd **8** shopworn, timeworn **9** hackneyed **11** commonplace

sterile 4 arid, bare, vain **6** barren, fallow **7** aseptic, worn-out **8** desolate, hygienic, impotent, lifeless, sanitary **9** fruitless, infertile **10** antiseptic, unfruitful, uninspired **11** disinfected **12** unproductive

sterilize 3 fix **4** geld, spay **5** alter **6** neuter, purify **7** cleanse **8** sanitize **9** disinfect **10** emasculate

sterilized 7 aseptic

sterling 4 pure, true **5** noble **6** worthy **8** virtuous **9** estimable, exemplary, honorable

stern 4 grim **5** harsh, rigid, sober, stony **6** gloomy, severe, strict **7** ascetic, austere **8** obdurate **10** forbidding, implacable, inexorable, inflexible **11** unrelenting

Sterne novel 14 Tristram Shandy

sternutation 8 sneezing

sternward 3 aft **5** abaft

Sterope *father:* **5** Atlas ***mother:*** **7** Pleione ***sisters:*** **8** Pleiades

Stevenson, Robert Louis *character:* **3** Jim (Hawkins) **4** Hyde (Mr.) **5** David (Balfour) **6** Jekyll (Dr.), Silver (Long John) ***novel:*** **9** Kidnapped **14** Treasure Island

stew 4 boil, brew, flap, fret, fume, fuss, hash, olio, olla, snit **5** daube, gumbo, salmi, sweat, tizzy, worry **6** burgoo, dither, jumble, lather, medley, menudo, pother, ragout, seethe, simmer, swivet, tumult **7** brothel, goulash, mélange, mixture, parboil, swelter, turmoil **8** bordello, mishmash, mulligan, pot-au-feu **9** Brunswick, cassoulet, commotion, confusion, pasticcio, potpourri **10** hodgepodge, hotchpotch, miscellany, turbulence **11** gallimaufry, olla podrida, ratatouille, slumgullion **13** bouillabaisse

steward 6 manage **7** manager **8** overseer **10** supervisor

stewed 3 lit **4** high **5** drunk, lit up, oiled **6** bashed, blotto, bombed, cooked, juiced, potted, soaked, soused, stewed, stoned, tanked, wasted, zonked **7** crocked, drunken, pickled, pie-eyed, sloshed, smashed, sottish **8** simmered **9** plastered **10** inebriated, liquored up **11** intoxicated

Stheno see **Gorgon**

stick 3 put, rod **4** glue, pole, stab **5** affix, baton, cling **6** adhere, attach, cleave, cohere, fasten **7** scruple **10** overcharge

stick around 4 bide, stay, wait **5** abide, dally, tarry **6** linger, remain

sticker 3 pin **4** barb, seal, shiv, spur **5** decal, point, prong, shank, spike, spine, stamp **6** dagger **8** stiletto

stick-in-the-mud 4 fogy **5** fogey **6** fossil **8** mossback **10** fuddy-duddy

stick out 3 jut **5** bulge **6** beetle **7** project **8** overhang, protrude

stick up 3 mug, rob **6** waylay **7** project **8** protrude

sticky 5 gluey, gooey, gummy, humid, muggy, mushy, soggy, tacky **6** clammy, knotty, slushy, sultry, thorny, viscid **7** awkward, cloying, maudlin, mawkish, viscous **8** adhesive, bathetic, clinging, romantic **9** difficult **11** problematic, sentimental, tear-jerking

stiff 3 lit, set **4** body, firm, hard, lush **5** cheat, drunk, harsh, oiled, rigid, stark, steep, stick, tense, tight, tipsy **6** buzzed, corpse, frozen, jelled, juiced, person, plowed, potent, potted, severe, soused, stewed, wooden **7** cadaver, carcass, sloshed, starchy, stilted **8** hardened, reserved, stubborn **9** cardboard, inelastic, petrified, plastered, unbending **10** inflexible, mechanical, unyielding **11** intoxicated, intractable

stiffen 5 tense **6** harden **7** thicken **8** rigidify, solidify **9** stabilize **10** immobilize

stifle 3 gag **4** hush, mute **5** burke, choke, deter **6** dampen, deaden, hush up, muffle, muzzle **7** repress, silence, smother, squelch **8** stultify, suppress **9** suffocate **10** asphyxiate, discourage

stigma 4 blot, onus, spot **5** brand, odium, shame, stain, taint **6** smudge, smutch **8** black eye, disgrace, dishonor, petechia, tainting

stigmatize 5 brand, label, stamp

still 3 but, yet **4** calm, even, hush, lull **5** allay, inert, quiet, shush, whist **6** even so, hushed, placid, serene, settle, silent, though, withal **7** alembic, halcyon, silence **8** peaceful, stagnant, tranquil **9** noiseless, quietness, soundless **10** motionless, stationary **11** furthermore, nonetheless, tranquility **12** nevertheless

stilt 4 bird, pile, pole **8** longlegs **9** shorebird

stilted 4 prim **5** stiff **6** formal, wooden **7** pompous, starchy **8** affected **9** cardboard

stilt-like bird 6 avocet

Stimpy's pal 3 Ren

stimulant 4 goad, spur **5** tonic **7** impetus, impulse **8** caffeine, catalyst, excitant **9** analeptic, energizer, incentive **10** incitement, motivation

stimulate 4 fire, goad, move, prod, spur, urge, whet **5** impel, pique, rouse, set up, spark **6** arouse, excite, fire up, foment, incite, prompt, vivify, work up **7** agitate, enliven, inspire, provoke, quicken, trigger **8** activate, energize, motivate, vitalize **9** galvanize **10** exhilarate

stimulus 4 goad, kick, push, spur **5** boost, cause **6** charge, motive **7** impetus, impulse **8** catalyst **9** incentive **10** incitement, inducement, motivation **11** instigation, provocation **13** encouragement

sting 3 con **4** scam, trap **5** cheat, prick, smart, snare **6** hustle, tingle **7** con game **8** skin game

stinging 8 aculeate

stingy 4 mean **5** close, tight **6** frugal, narrow, paltry, skimpy **7** chintzy, costive, miserly, niggard, scrimpy, sparing, thrifty **8** grudging **9** niggardly, penny-wise, penurious **10** economical, ironfisted, pinchpenny, ungenerous **11** tightfisted **12** cheeseparing, parsimonious **13** penny-pinching

stink 4 flap, funk, fuss, reek **5** smell **6** stench **7** malodor

stinker 3 dog, dud **4** bomb, bust, flop **5** lemon, loser, skunk **6** petrel, turkey **7** wash-out

stinking see **smelly**

stinky see **smelly**

stint 3 job **4** bout, task, time, tour, turn **5** chore, cramp, pinch, scant, share, shift, skimp, spare, spell **6** amount, scrape, scrimp **8** quantity, restrict **9** allotment, stricture **10** assignment, limitation **11** restriction

stipend 3 fee, pay **4** hire, wage **5** award **6** salary **7** payment **9** allowance, emolument **13** consideration

stipple 3 dot **5** fleck, speck **6** pepper **7** freckle, speckle **8** sprinkle

stipulate 5 state **6** detail **7** specify **8** contract, spell out **13** particularize

stipulation 5 limit, terms **7** proviso, strings **9** condition, provision **11** requirement

stir 3 ado, din, mix **4** fuss, rout, to-do, wake, whet **5** blend, budge, churn, impel, rally, rouse, roust, spark, waken **6** arouse, bustle, excite, flurry, foment, hubbub, incite, kindle, pother, seethe, simmer, tumult, whip

up **7** agitate, disturb, ferment, inspire, provoke, quicken **8** activity **9** agitation, commotion, galvanize, stimulate **11** disturbance
stirrup 6 stapes **8** footrest
stithy 5 anvil
stoat 6 ermine, weasel
stock 4 butt, fund, hope, race **5** brace, carry, faith, goods, hoard, store, talon, trunk, trust **6** family, supply **7** furnish, lineage **8** pedigree, reliance **9** inventory, selection **10** confidence, dependence **11** merchandise
stockade 4 jail **5** fence **6** paling, prison **8** palisade **9** enclosure, guardroom
stock exchange 4 AMEX, FTSE, NYSE **6** bourse, NASDAQ
stockings 4 hose **5** socks **7** hosiery
stockpile 4 bank, heap, mass **5** amass, cache, hoard, lay up, store **6** garner, supply **7** backlog, collect, nest egg, reserve, store up **9** inventory, reservoir **10** accumulate, repository
stocky 3 fat **5** beefy, burly, dumpy, husky, plump, pudgy, squat, stout, thick **6** chunky, stubby, stumpy **8** heavyset, thickset **9** corpulent
stodge 4 fill, sate **5** gorge, stuff **7** overeat, surfeit
stodgy 5 fusty **6** stuffy **9** hidebound, out-of-date **12** old-fashioned
stogie 4 shoe **5** cigar **6** brogan
stoic 4 Zeno **6** stolid **7** Spartan **9** apathetic, impassive **10** phlegmatic **11** indifferent, unconcerned
stoicism 9 stolidity **11** impassivity ***founder:*** **4** Zeno
stoke 3 fan **4** feed, fuel, poke, stir, tend **6** supply
Stoker novel 7 Dracula
stolid 3 dry **4** dull, flat **5** stoic **6** wooden **8** rocklike **9** apathetic, impassive, unruffled **10** phlegmatic **11** unemotional
stomach 3 gut, maw **4** bear, craw **5** abide, belly, brook, stand, taste, tummy **6** digest, endure, paunch, venter **7** abdomen, swallow **8** appetite, tolerate ***combining form:*** **5** gastr **6** gastro, ventri, ventro ***enzyme:*** **6** pepsin, rennin ***muscle:*** **7** pylorus ***ruminant:*** **6** omasum **8** abomasum **9** reticulum ***Scottish:*** **4** kyte
stomachache 5 colic, gripe **12** collywobbles
stomp 5 clomp, clump, pound, tramp, tromp **7** trample
stone 3 gem **4** rock **5** lapis **6** pebble **7** boulder ***base:*** **6** plinth ***block of:*** **8** monolith ***carving:*** **7** epitaph ***chip:*** **5** spall ***combining form:*** **4** lite, lith, lyte ***cosmic:*** **6** meteor **9** chondrite, meteorite ***facing:*** **6** ashlar ***for grinding grains:*** **6** metate ***fruit:*** **5** drupe ***memorial:*** **5** cairn, stela **7** obelisk ***monument:*** **6** dolmen **8** megalith ***of a fruit:*** **3** pit ***paving:*** **3** set **4** sett
____ Stone 7 Blarney, Rosetta
Stone novel 11 Lust for Life **18** Agony and the Ecstasy (The)
stonecrop 5 sedum
stoned 3 lit **4** high **5** boozy, doped, drunk, fried, oiled, tight, tipsy **6** buzzed, canned, juiced, loaded, plowed, potted, soused, stewed, tanked, wasted, zonked **7** crocked, drugged, muddled, pickled, pie-eyed, sloshed, smashed **8** hopped-up, turned on, wiped out **9** pixilated, plastered, spaced-out, strung out **10** inebriated, tripped out **11** intoxicated
stonewall 5 delay, stall **6** hamper, hinder, impede, stymie **8** obstruct
stooge 3 act, sap **4** dupe, foil, gull, mark, pawn, tool **5** chump, dummy, patsy, proxy **6** puppet, sucker, victim **7** fall guy **8** sidekick **9** represent **11** stool pigeon, straight man **12** second banana
Stooge 3 Moe (Howard) **5** Curly (Howard), Larry (Fine)
stool pigeon 3 rat **4** fink, nark **5** decoy **6** canary, snitch **7** ratfink, tipster **8** informer
stoop 3 dip **4** bend, duck, sink **5** deign, hunch, porch, slump **6** resort, slouch **7** descend, portico, veranda **8** stairway **10** condescend
stop 3 bar, can, dam, end **4** clog, fill, halt, plug, quit, stay, stem **5** block, brake, cease, check, close, stall, tarry **6** arrest, desist, ending, kibosh, stanch **7** disrupt, occlude, prevent, sojourn, suspend **8** knock off, obstruct **9** cessation, interrupt, terminate **10** conclusion, standstill **11** discontinue, termination ***up:*** **4** cork, plug **7** occlude
stopgap 5 shift **6** resort **8** recourse, resource **9** expedient, makeshift **10** expediency, substitute
stopover 4 stay **5** visit **7** sojourn
stoppage 4 halt **6** cutoff, strike **7** walkout **8** shutdown **10** standstill **11** obstruction
Stoppard play 7 Jumpers **9** Real Thing (The) **10** Travesties **13** Coast of Utopia (The)
stopper 4 bung, cork, fill, plug **5** close
store 3 bin **4** fund, mart, pack, shop, stow, tank **5** amass, cache, depot, hoard, lay up, stash **6** ensile, garner, market, outlet, shoppe, supply **7** arsenal, backlog, bootery, deposit, reserve **8** boutique, cumulate, emporium, mothball, showroom, squirrel **9** abundance, chandlery, inventory, reservoir, stockpile, warehouse **10** accumulate, depository, five-and-ten, repository **11** five-and-

dime **12** accumulation ***display:*** **6** endcap **8** showcase

storehouse 5 depot **7** arsenal, granary **8** magazine **9** stockpile **10** depository, repository

storekeeper 8 merchant, retailer **9** tradesman

storeroom 6 larder, pantry **7** buttery

storm 3 row **4** fury, gale, hail, rage, rant, rave, roar, rush, to-do **5** beset, blast, blitz, burst, furor, onset, salvo **6** assail, attack, charge, clamor, fall on, flurry, furore, hubbub, outcry, pother, racket, shower, squall, tumult **7** assault, bluster, cyclone, monsoon, ruction, tempest, thunder, tornado, turmoil, twister, typhoon **8** blizzard, downpour, fall upon, outbreak, outburst, paroxysm, upheaval **9** broadside, commotion, discharge, hurricane, nor'easter, onslaught **10** cloudburst, hurly-burly **11** northeaster, northwester

storm trooper 10 brownshirt

stormy 4 foul **5** rainy, rough **6** raging **7** furious **8** blustery **9** turbulent **10** tumultuous **11** tempestuous, threatening

story 3 fib, lie **4** epic, saga, tale, yarn **5** conte, fable **6** canard, legend, report **7** account, fiction, märchen, parable, version **8** allegory, anecdote, folktale, megillah, tall tale **9** chronicle, fairy tale, narration, narrative **11** description, fabrication

storyteller 4 liar **6** fibber **8** fabulist **9** raconteur

stoup 4 font **5** basin **6** flagon, goblet **7** chalice, tankard

stout 3 ale, fat **4** brew **5** beefy, bulky, burly, heavy, husky, obese, plump, thick **6** fleshy, porter, portly, strong, sturdy **9** corpulent **10** overweight

Stout detective 5 Wolfe (Nero)

stouthearted 4 bold, game **5** brave, gutsy **7** doughty, gallant, valiant **8** fearless, intrepid, resolute, stalwart, stubborn, unafraid **9** audacious, dauntless, undaunted **10** courageous

stove 4 kiln, oven **5** range **8** Franklin, potbelly

stow 3 bin **4** lade, load, pack **5** stash, store **7** arrange, deposit

stower 9 stevedore

Stowe work 4 Dred

strabismus 6 squint

straddle 4 span **6** sprawl **8** bestride **11** spread-eagle

strafe 4 rake **6** attack **8** enfilade **10** machine-gun

straggle 3 lag **4** poke, roam, rove **5** drift, range, stray **6** dawdle, loiter, ramble, wander **7** maunder, meander **8** trail off **9** string out

straight 4 even, fair, neat, pure, true **5** erect, plain, plumb, right **6** at once, candid, direct, honest, linear, square **7** unmixed, upright **8** orthodox **9** bourgeois, forthwith, undiluted **10** aboveboard, button-down, forthright **12** conventional **13** unadulterated ***combining form:*** **4** orth, rect **5** ortho, recti

straightaway 3 now **6** at once **7** stretch **8** directly, first off, promptly **9** forthwith, instanter **11** immediately

straighten 4 even, tidy **5** align **6** neaten, unbend, uncurl **7** rectify

straightforward 5 frank, lucid **6** candid, direct, honest **7** genuine, precise, sincere **8** clear-cut **9** outspoken **10** forthright **11** undeviating

strain 3 air, tax, try **4** hint, kind, pull, sort, toil, tune, vein **5** exert, stock, sweat, tinge, touch, trace, twist **6** filter, melody, screen, streak, stress, strive, wrench **7** lineage, overtax, tension, trouble **8** ancestry, exertion, overwork, pedigree, pressure, struggle **9** overexert

strait 4 bind, kyle, pass **5** pinch **6** crisis, plight **7** channel, dilemma, narrows, squeeze **8** exigency, hardship, juncture **9** crossroad, emergency **10** difficulty **11** contingency ***Adriatic Sea-Ionian Sea:*** **7** Otranto ***Alaska:*** **3** Icy ***Alaska-Russia:*** **6** Bering ***Albania-Greece:*** **5** Corfu ***Asia-Europe:*** **11** Dardanelles ***Atlantic-Baffin Island:*** **5** Davis ***Atlantic-Mediterranean:*** **9** Gibraltar ***Atlantic-Nantucket Sound:*** **8** Muskeget ***Atlantic-North Sea:*** **7** English ***Atlantic-Pacific:*** **5** Drake **8** Magellan ***Atlantic-Saint Lawrence:*** **5** Cabot ***Baffin Island-Quebec:*** **6** Hudson ***Bering Sea-Sea of Okhotsk:*** **5** Kuril **6** Kurile ***Bismarck Sea-Solomon Sea:*** **6** Vitiaz ***Canada:*** **3** Rae **5** Dease ***East China Sea:*** **5** Korea **8** Tsushima ***East China-South China:*** **6** Taiwan **7** Formosa ***England-France:*** **5** Dover ***Flores Sea-Indian Ocean:*** **4** Sape ***Flores Sea-Savu Sea:*** **4** Alor ***Indian Ocean-Java Sea:*** **5** Sunda ***India-Sri Lanka:*** **4** Palk ***Indonesia:*** **4** Alas, Alor, Bali **5** Tioro **6** Lombok **7** Dampier **8** Macassar, Makassar, Surabaya ***Inner Hebrides:*** **5** Tiree ***Iran-Oman:*** **6** Hormuz ***Italy:*** **7** Messina ***Japan:*** **4** Yura **5** Bungo, Kitan **7** Hayasui ***Japan-Sakhalin Island:*** **4** Soya ***Lake Huron:*** **10** Mississagi ***Lake Huron-Lake Michigan:*** **8** Mackinac ***Malay Archipelago:*** **5** Wetar ***Malaysia-Singapore:*** **6** Johore ***Malay-Sumatra:*** **7** Malacca ***New Jersey-Staten Island:*** **7** van Kull ***New South Wales-Tasmania:*** **4** Bass

New Zealand: **4** Cook ***Northwest Territories:*** **6** Barrow **8** Franklin, Victoria **13** Prince of Wales ***Nova Scotia:*** **5** Canso ***Pacific-San Francisco Bay:*** **10** Golden Gate ***Pacific-South China Sea:*** **5** Luzon ***Philippines:*** **5** Bohol, Tanon **6** Iloilo **7** Basilan ***Russia:*** **4** Kara ***Suvu Sea-Timor Sea:*** **4** Roti ***Sea of Azov-Black Sea:*** **5** Kerch **7** Enikale ***Sea of Japan:*** **5** Tatar ***Solomon Islands:*** **12** Bougainville ***South China Sea:*** **7** Mindoro **9** Singapore ***Turkey:*** **8** Bosporus **9** Bosphorus, Karadeniz ***Vancouver-Washington:*** **10** Juan de Fuca ***Wales:*** **5** Menai ***Washington Sound:*** **4** Haro

straitened **7** lacking, pinched, wanting **8** deprived, strapped **9** deficient, destitute **10** distressed, inadequate **12** impoverished

straitlaced **4** prim **5** staid, stiff **6** formal, narrow, prissy, strict, stuffy **7** genteel, prudish, starchy, stilted **8** priggish **9** hidebound, Victorian **11** puritanical

strand **4** bank **5** beach, coast, fiber, leave, shore, wreck **6** desert, maroon, thread **7** abandon, shingle **8** cast away, filament, littoral, seacoast, seashore **9** shipwreck **10** run aground, waterfront

strange **3** odd **5** alien, crazy, eerie, fishy, funny, kinky, kooky, nutty, outré, queer, weird **6** exotic, far-out, freaky **7** bizarre, curious, oddball, offbeat, uncanny, unknown, unusual **8** aberrant, abnormal, atypical, peculiar, singular **9** eccentric, fantastic, grotesque **10** mysterious, off-the-wall, outlandish, unfamiliar **11** exceptional **12** unaccustomed

Strange Interlude author **6** O'Neill (Eugene)

stranger **5** alien, guest **7** visitor **8** newcomer, outsider, wanderer **9** auslander, foreigner, immigrant, transient

strangle **5** burke, choke, shush **6** muffle, quelch, stifle **7** garotte, garrote **8** suppress, throttle **10** asphyxiate

strap **4** band, beat, belt, bind, rein **5** leash **6** attach, punish, secure, suffer **7** binding, leather **8** distress **9** constrict

strapping **5** beefy, burly, hardy, husky **6** brawny, robust, rugged, sturdy **8** muscular, vigorous **10** able-bodied

stratagem **4** play, plot, ploy, ruse, wile **5** feint, trick **6** device, gambit, scheme, tactic **8** artifice, intrigue, maneuver **10** conspiracy, subterfuge **11** machination

strategy **4** plan **6** design, method, scheme **7** project, tactics **8** game plan **9** blueprint

stratum **3** bed **4** rank **5** class, grade, layer, level

Strauss, Richard ***opera:*** **6** Salome **7** Elektra **13** Rosenkavalier (Der) **15** Ariadne auf Naxos **16** Frau ohne Schatten (Die) ***tone poem:*** **7** Don Juan **10** Don Quixote **11** Heldenleben (Ein) **20** Thus Spake Zarathustra **23** Death and Transfiguration

straw **3** hay **5** blond **6** flaxen, golden, thatch ***braided:*** **6** sennit ***mat:*** **6** tatami ***plaited:*** **7** leghorn

straw man **4** dupe, foil, sham

stray **3** err, gad **4** lost, roam, rove, waif **5** drift, range **6** depart, errant, ramble, random, wander **7** deviate, digress, diverge, erratic, meander, runaway, traipse, vagrant **8** divagate, homeless, sporadic **9** gallivant

streak **4** hint, vein **5** fleck, tinge, trace **6** dapple, marble, mottle, strain, stripe **7** striate **8** tincture **9** suspicion, variegate **10** intimation, suggestion

streaked **5** upset **7** brindle, marbled, striped **8** brindled, grizzled **9** disturbed

stream **3** run **4** beck, burn, flow, flux, gill, gush, pour, race, rill, rush, sike, tide **5** bourn, brook, creek, spate, surge **6** bourne, branch, rindle, runnel, sluice **7** current, freshet, rivulet, torrent **8** affluent

streambed **4** wadi, wash **5** gully

streamer **4** flag, jack **6** banner, burgee, ensign, pennon **7** pennant **8** banderol, bannerol, standard **9** banderole

streamline **7** contour **8** organize, simplify **9** modernize

street **3** way **4** drag, road, wynd **5** alley, drive **6** artery, avenue **7** roadway **9** boulevard **12** thoroughfare ***border:*** **4** curb **7** curbing ***material:*** **6** cobble **7** asphalt, macadam **11** cobblestone ***name:*** **3** Elm **4** Main, Park **5** Maple, State

streetcar **4** tram **7** trolley

Streetcar Named Desire, A ***author:*** **8** Williams (Tennessee) ***character:*** **6** Stella (Kowalski) **7** Blanche (DuBois), Stanley (Kowalski)

Street Scene author **4** Rice (Elmer)

strength **5** brawn, force, forte, might, power, sinew, vigor **6** energy, muscle **7** potency **8** firmness, security **9** fortitude, intensity, soundness, stability, toughness **10** steadiness, sturdiness

strengthen **4** gird **5** brace, steel **6** anneal, beef up, harden, prop up **7** bolster, enhance, fortify, support, toughen **8** buttress, embolden, energize **9** intensify, reinforce, undergird **10** invigorate, rejuvenate

strenuous **4** hard **5** tough **6** taxing, uphill **7** arduous, operose **9** demanding, difficult, effortful, Herculean, laborious **12** backbreaking

Strephon 8 shepherd ***beloved:*** **5** Chloe **6** Urania

stress 6 accent, burden, import, play up, strain, weight **7** anxiety, feature, tension, trouble, urgency **8** emphasis, pressure **9** emphasize, italicize, underline **10** accentuate, underscore **12** accentuation ***in poetry:*** **5** ictus

stretch 4 area, draw, time **5** crane, range, reach, scope, space, spell, sweep, tract, while **6** extend, extent, length, limber, region, spread **7** breadth, compass, draw out, expanse, magnify, prolong, purview, spin out, tighten **8** distance, elongate, lengthen, protract **9** embellish, embroider, expansion, overstate **10** exaggerate ***on a frame:*** **6** tenter ***out:*** **6** sprawl **7** lie down, recline

stretchable 7 ductile, elastic, tensile

stretched 4 taut

stretcher 4 yarn **6** gurney, litter **8** tall tale

strew 3 sow **4** dust **5** cover **6** pepper, spread **7** scatter **8** disperse, sprinkle **9** broadcast, circulate, propagate **10** distribute **11** disseminate

stricken 3 hit, ill **4** hurt, sick **6** bereft **7** injured, wounded **9** afflicted **11** overwhelmed

strict 4 firm **5** exact, harsh, rigid, stern, tough **6** narrow, severe **7** precise **8** exacting, faithful, rigorous **9** draconian, stringent, unsparing **10** inflexible, ironhanded, meticulous, scrupulous **11** punctilious

stricture 5 cramp, stint **7** censure, reproof **8** reproach **9** aspersion, criticism, reprimand **10** constraint, limitation **11** restriction **13** animadversion

stride 4 gait, pace, step **5** march, stalk **7** advance **8** straddle

strident 4 loud **5** harsh **6** shrill **7** grating, jarring, rasping, raucous, squawky **8** piercing **9** clamorous, insistent, obtrusive **10** boisterous, discordant, stentorian, vociferous **11** loudmouthed **12** earsplitting, obstreperous

strife 4 fray **5** broil, fight **6** battle, combat **7** discord, dispute, dissent, quarrel, rivalry, warfare, wrangle **8** argument, conflict, disunity, friction, struggle, tug-of-war **10** contention, difference, dissension, dissidence **11** altercation, competition, controversy

strike 3 hit, pop, rap **4** bash, beat, find, poke, slam, slap, slug, sock, swat, whap, whop **5** clout, knock, punch, smack, smite, swipe, thump, whack **6** affect, assail, attack, cudgel, delete, hammer, pummel, thrash **7** assault, impress, inflict, inspire, wildcat **8** discover, stoppage

strike out 4 dele **5** elide **6** delete, efface **7** expunge

striking 5 showy, vivid **6** cogent, marked, signal **7** salient, telling **8** forceful **9** arresting, prominent **10** compelling, noticeable, remarkable **11** conspicuous, outstanding

Strindberg play 6 Easter, Father (The) **8** Comrades **9** Creditors (The), Dream Play (A), Miss Julie **10** Master Olaf **11** Ghost Sonata (The) **12** Dance of Death (The), Gustavus Vasa

string 3 row **4** file, line, rank, tier **5** chain, order, queue, train, twine **6** sequel, series **7** echelon **8** recourse, resource, sequence **10** succession ***together:*** **4** bead ***up:*** **4** hang **5** noose, scrag **6** gibbet

stringent see **strict**

stringy 4 lean, ropy, wiry **6** sinewy **7** fibrous **8** muscular

strip 4 band, bare, doff, flay, husk, peel, sack, skin **5** scale **6** billet, denude, divest, expose, fillet, ravage, ribbon **7** bandeau, deprive, disrobe, pillage, uncover, undress **8** unclothe ***leather:*** **5** thong ***of wood:*** **4** lath, slat ***skin, blubber:*** **5** scarf **6** flense

stripe 3 ilk **4** band, kind, lash, sort, type **5** order **6** strake, streak **7** banding, chevron, lineate, striate, variety

stripling 3 boy, lad **5** youth **9** youngster **10** adolescent

stripper 6 peeler, teaser **9** ecdysiast

stripteaser see **stripper**

strive 3 try, vie **4** seek **5** labor **6** strain **7** attempt, contend **8** endeavor, struggle **9** undertake

stroke 3 fit, hit, pet, rub **4** blow, hone, whet **5** swing **6** attack, caress, fondle, soothe **7** flatter **8** apoplexy, ischemia **9** heartbeat

stroll 4 rove, turn, walk **5** amble, drift, mosey, paseo **6** cruise, linger, ramble, wander **7** saunter, traipse **9** promenade

stroller 4 pram **6** go-cart **8** carriage **12** baby carriage, perambulator

strong 4 fast, firm, hard **5** burly, hardy, lusty, solid, sound, stout, tough **6** brawny, hearty, heroic, mighty, potent, robust, rugged, secure, sinewy, stable, sturdy **7** durable, intense, staunch **8** forceful, muscular, powerful, stalwart, vigorous **9** resilient, strapping, tenacious **10** able-bodied, full-bodied, spirituous **12** concentrated

strong-arm 5 bully **6** bounce, coerce, hector, lean on **7** assault, dragoon **8** browbeat, bulldoze, bullyrag **9** terrorize **10** intimidate

strongbox 4 arca, safe **5** chest **6** coffer **9** reliquary **13** treasure chest

stronghold 4 fort **7** bastion, bulwark, citadel, redoubt **8** fastness, fortress

strongman 4 Amin (Idi), Tito **5** Assad

(Hafez), Perón (Juan) **6** Castro (Fidel), Chávez (Hugo), despot, Marcos (Ferdinand), Mobutu (Sese Seko), Samson, Taylor (Charles), tyrant **7** Batista (Fulgencio), Hussein (Saddam), Noriega (Manuel), Suharto **8** caudillo, Pinochet (Augusto) **9** Milošević (Slobodan), Mussolini (Benito)

strong point 5 forte **6** métier

strong suit see **strong point**

strontium symbol 2 Sr

strophe 5 verse **6** stanza

struck 3 hit **5** smote

structure 4 form **5** frame **6** format, makeup, system **7** anatomy, complex, edifice, network **8** building, erection, skeleton **9** framework **10** morphology **11** arrangement, composition

struggle 3 try, vie **4** agon **5** trial **6** battle, effort, hassle, strain, strife, strive, tussle **7** attempt, compete, contend, contest, grapple, scuffle **8** endeavor, exertion, flounder, skirmish, striving **9** undertake **11** undertaking

strumpet 4 bawd, jade, slut, tart **5** hussy, tramp, trull, wench **6** floozy, harlot, hooker, wanton **7** jezebel, trollop **8** slattern

strut 6 flaunt, parade, prance, sashay **7** flounce, peacock, show off, swagger

stub 3 end **4** butt, tail **5** stump **6** put out, strike **7** remnant **10** extinguish

stubborn 5 balky, rigid **6** cussed, dogged, mulish, ornery **7** adamant, lasting, willful **8** obdurate, perverse **9** obstinate, pigheaded, steadfast, unbending **10** bullheaded, determined, headstrong, inexorable, inflexible, persistent, rebellious, refractory, relentless, unyielding **11** intractable **12** contumacious, pertinacious, single-minded

stubby 5 dumpy, short, squat, stout **6** stocky, stumpy **8** heavyset, thickset

stuck 5 clung, glued **6** jammed, wedged **7** adhered, baffled, blocked, saddled, stabbed, stopped, stumped **8** attached, held fast **11** overcharged

stuck-up 4 vain **6** sniffy, snippy, snooty **7** haughty **8** snobbish **9** conceited **12** narcissistic, supercilious

stud 3 guy **4** dude, hunk, male, nail, post **5** cleat, he-man, himbo, macho **6** button, pillar **7** earring, speckle, upright **8** sprinkle, stallion

student 4 tiro, tyro **5** pupil, tutee **6** novice **7** protégé, scholar **8** disciple, neophyte **10** apprentice ***college:*** **9** undergrad **13** undergraduate ***female:*** **4** coed ***first-year:*** **5** frosh **8** freshman ***fourth-year:*** **6** senior ***French:*** **5** élève **8** étudiant ***military:*** **5** cadet, middy **10** midshipman ***second-year:*** **4** soph **9** sophomore ***third-year:*** **6** junior ***wandering:*** **7** goliard

studio 4 shop **7** atelier **8** workroom, workshop

studious 7 bookish, learned **9** scholarly

Studs Lonigan creator 7 Farrell (James T.)

study 3 con, den, vet **4** case, cram, muse **5** étude **6** ponder, survey **7** analyze, examine, inspect, reverie **8** consider **9** attention, think over **10** excogitate, scrutinize

stuff 3 jam, ram **4** cram, fill, glut, junk, pack, sate, tamp **5** crowd, gorge, shove **6** matter, things **7** essence, jam-pack, squeeze, surfeit **8** material, overfill **9** substance **11** possessions

stuffy 4 dull, prim **5** close, fuggy, heavy, humid, stale, thick **6** narrow, stodgy **7** airless, bloated, genteel, humdrum, pompous, prudish, stilted **8** priggish, stagnant, stifling **9** hidebound, Victorian **10** oppressive, pontifical **11** puritanical, suffocating **12** narrow-minded **13** self-important, self-righteous

stultify 4 dull **6** deaden, impair, stifle, weaken **7** inhibit, nullify, repress, smother, trammel **8** restrain, stagnate, suppress **9** suffocate **10** discourage, invalidate

stumble 3 err **4** reel, slip, trip **5** error, fluff, gaffe, lapse, lurch **6** falter, muddle, slipup, totter **7** blunder, faux pas, mistake, stagger, stammer **8** flounder

stump 3 end **4** beat, butt, dare, defy, plod, stub **5** barge, clomp, clump, stick **6** baffle, outwit, puzzle, stymie, trudge **7** buffalo, flummox, galumph, mystify, nonplus, perplex **8** bewilder, campaign, confound, hustings, politick **9** barnstorm, challenge **11** electioneer

stun 4 daze **5** amaze, floor, shock **6** dazzle **7** astound, nonplus, stagger, stupefy **8** astonish, bewilder, bowl over, knock out, paralyze **9** dumbfound **11** flabbergast

stunning 6 superb **7** amazing, awesome **8** gorgeous, striking **9** excellent, wonderful **10** astounding, impressive, remarkable, staggering, surprising **11** astonishing

stunt 4 curb, feat **5** antic, caper, check, dwarf, prank, trick **6** hinder, impair, retard **8** escapade, hold back, suppress

stupefy 4 daze, dull, faze, stun **5** addle, amaze **6** muddle, rattle **7** astound, nonplus, petrify, stagger **8** astonish, bewilder, paralyze **9** disorient, dumbfound **11** flabbergast

stupendous 4 huge **7** amazing, awesome, massive, titanic **8** colossal, enormous, gigantic, stunning, towering, wondrous **9** fantastic, humongous, marvelous, monstrous, wonderful **10** astounding, miraculous, monumental, phenomenal, prodigious, staggering, tremendous **11** astonishing, spectacular **12** breathtaking, mind-boggling, overwhelming

stupid 3 dim **4** dull, dumb, slow **5** dense, dopey, inane, silly, thick **6** oafish, obtuse, simple, torpid **7** asinine, brutish, doltish, fatuous, foolish, idiotic, moronic, witless **8** backward, ignorant, mindless, retarded **9** brainless, fatheaded, imbecilic, laughable, ludicrous, pinheaded, senseless, vexatious **10** half-witted, slow-witted **11** blockheaded, thickheaded, thick-witted **12** exasperating **13** chuckleheaded

stupor 6 torpor, trance **7** languor **8** dullness, hebetude, lethargy, narcosis **9** lassitude, torpidity **10** anesthesia, somnolence **13** insensibility ***combining form:*** **4** narc **5** narco

sturdy 5 hardy, solid, sound, stout, tough **6** robust, rugged, secure, strong **7** durable, healthy, staunch **8** stalwart, vigorous **9** strapping

sturgeon 6 beluga ***roe:*** **6** caviar

Sturm und Drang 5 angst **6** unease, unrest **7** anxiety, ferment, turmoil **8** disquiet **9** agitation **10** inquietude, turbulence **11** disquietude, restiveness **12** restlessness

St. Vitus' ____ 5 dance

sty 3 pen **4** coop, cyst **6** pigpen **7** piggery

stygian 4 dark **6** gloomy **7** hellish, sunless **8** infernal, plutonic **9** Cimmerian, plutonian

style 3 fad, way **4** chic, élan, mode, rage, vein **5** craze, decor, flair, trend, vogue **6** manner **7** fashion, panache **10** dernier cri **11** savoir-faire ***hair:*** **4** coif **8** coiffure

stylish 3 mod **4** chic, posh, tony, trig **5** doggy, natty, ritzy, sassy, sharp, showy, sleek, slick, smart, swank, swell **6** chichi, dapper, dressy, modern, modish, snappy, snazzy, spiffy, trendy, with-it **7** à la mode, dashing, doggish **8** spiffing, up-to-date **10** newfangled **11** fashionable

stymie 4 stop **5** block **6** hamper, hinder, impede, thwart **7** flummox, prevent **8** confound, obstruct **9** frustrate, hamstring

Stymphalides' slayer 8 Heracles, Hercules

Styron novel 13 Sophie's Choice **22** Confessions of Nat Turner (The)

Styx *father:* 7 Oceanus ***ferryman:*** **6** Charon ***location:*** **5** Hades ***mother:*** **6** Tethys

Styx's counterpart 5 Lethe **7** Acheron, Cocytus **10** Phlegethon

suave 4 oily **5** slick **6** smarmy, smooth, urbane **7** cordial, courtly, gallant, politic, refined, tactful, worldly **8** debonair, gracious, polished, unctuous, well-bred **9** courteous **10** cultivated, diplomatic **12** ingratiating **13** sophisticated

sub 5 below, proxy, under **6** backup, fill-in **7** stand-by, stand-in **8** pinch-hit **9** alternate, secondary, surrogate **10** understudy **11** locum tenens, pinch hitter, replacement

subaltern 8 inferior **9** secondary, underling

subdue 4 curb, tame **5** crush, quash, quell **6** defeat, master, quench **7** conquer, control, put down, repress, squelch **8** beat down, overcome, suppress, tone down, vanquish **9** overpower, overthrow, subjugate

subdued 4 soft, tame **5** muted, quiet, sober **6** low-key, mellow, subtle **7** neutral, serious **8** low-keyed, softened, tasteful, tempered **9** moderated, toned down **10** controlled, restrained, submissive **11** unobtrusive

subjacent 3 low **5** lower, under **6** lesser, nether **8** inferior

subject 3 apt **4** core, open **5** liege, motif, point, prone, theme, topic **6** expose, liable, likely, matter, motive, vassal **7** citizen, exposed, lay open, problem **8** argument, inferior, material, question **9** dependent, leitmotif, secondary, sensitive, subjugate, substance, tributary **11** subordinate, subservient, susceptible

subjective 6 biased **10** prejudiced

subjugate see **subdue**

sublime 4 holy **5** ideal, lofty, noble, proud **6** august, divine, sacred, superb **7** blessed, exalted **8** elevated, glorious, heavenly, majestic, splendid **9** celestial, spiritual **11** magnificent, resplendent **12** transcendent

submarine 4 hero **5** po'boy, U-boat **6** hoagie **7** grinder ***detector:*** **5** sonar

submerge 3 dip **4** duck, dunk, sink **5** drown, flood, swamp **6** deluge, engulf, plunge **7** founder, go under, immerse **8** inundate, overflow

submerse see **submerge**

submissive 4 meek, tame **6** abject, docile, pliant **7** servile, slavish, subdued **8** amenable, obedient, obeisant, yielding **9** compliant, tractable **10** obsequious **11** acquiescent, deferential, subservient, unresisting **12** nonresisting

submit 3 bow **4** cave, fold, obey **5** defer, offer, yield **6** accede, comply, give in, hand in, relent, send in, tender **7** concede, deliver, go under, present, proffer, provide, subject, succumb, suggest **9** acquiesce, surrender **10** capitulate **11** buckle under **12** knuckle under

subordinate 5 minor, scrub, under **6** junior **7** adjunct, subject **8** inferior **9** accessory, ancillary, auxiliary, dependent, secondary, subaltern, tributary, underling **10** collateral, submissive, subsidiary **11** subservient

sub rosa 6 covert, secret **7** furtive, private **8** covertly, in camera, secretly, stealthy **9** by stealth, furtively, privately, secretive, underhand **10** stealthily **11** clandestine, underhanded **13** clandestinely, surreptitious

subscribe 3 ink **4** sign **5** agree **6** accede, adhere, assent, attest, pledge **7** approve, consent, endorse, support **8** sanction **9** acquiesce

subsequent 4 next **5** after, later **6** serial **7** ensuing **9** following, resultant, resulting **10** sequential, succeeding, successive **11** consecutive ***prefix:*** **4** post

subsequently 4 next, then **5** after, later, since **9** afterward **10** afterwards, thereafter

subservient 6 abject, docile **7** fawning, ignoble, servile, slavish **8** adjuvant, obeisant **9** accessory, ancillary, auxiliary, compliant, truckling **10** collateral, obsequious, submissive **11** acquiescent, deferential, subordinate, sycophantic

subside 3 die, ebb **4** ease, fall, lull, sink, wane **5** abate, let up, taper **6** ease up, recede, settle **7** decline, descend, die away, die down, dwindle, ease off, slacken **8** decrease, diminish, moderate

subsidiary 5 minor **6** backup, branch **7** subject **8** adjuvant **9** accessory, ancillary, auxiliary, secondary, tributary **10** collateral **11** subordinate **12** supplemental **13** supplementary

subsidize 4 back, fund **5** endow, stake **7** finance, promote, sponsor, support **8** bankroll **9** grubstake **10** underwrite

subsidy 4 gift **5** grant **6** reward **10** subvention **13** appropriation

subsistence 4 keep, salt **5** bread, means **6** income, living **7** support **9** resources **10** livelihood, sustenance **11** maintenance, wherewithal **12** alimentation

substance 3 nub **4** bulk, core, crux, gist, mass, meat, pith, soul **5** being, drift, focus, heart, point, sense, stuff, tenor **6** amount, burden, entity, import, kernel, marrow, matter, nubbin, object, thrust, upshot, wealth **7** essence, meaning, nucleus, purport **8** material, property, sum total **9** resources **12** essentiality, quintessence

substantial 3 big **4** full **5** ample, hefty, large, meaty, solid **6** strong, sturdy **7** massive, sizable, weighty **8** abundant, concrete, material, physical, sensible, tangible **9** corporeal, important, objective **10** meaningful, phenomenal **11** significant **12** considerable

substantiate 5 prove **6** embody, evince, verify **7** bear out, confirm, justify **8** evidence, manifest, validate **9** establish, incarnate, objectify, vindicate **11** corroborate, demonstrate **12** authenticate

substantive 4 firm, noun, real **5** solid **8** definite **9** essential

substitute 4 mock, sham, swap **5** dummy, locum, proxy, trade **6** acting, backup, deputy, double, ersatz, fill-in, refuge, resort, second, switch **7** replace, reserve, standby, stand-in, stopgap **8** exchange, recourse, resource, spurious **9** alternate, expedient, imitation, makeshift, simulated, surrogate, temporary **10** artificial, expediency, understudy **11** alternative, locum tenens, pinch hitter, replacement, succedaneum

substratum 4 base **5** basis **6** bottom, ground **7** bedrock, footing **10** foundation, groundwork **12** underpinning

substructure 4 base, seat **5** basis **6** bottom **7** footing **10** foundation, groundwork **12** underpinning

subsume 6 embody, take in **7** contain, embrace, include, involve **8** comprise **9** encompass **10** comprehend

subterfuge 4 ploy, ruse, scam, sham **5** cheat, feint, fraud **6** deceit, dupery **7** chicane **8** trickery **9** chicanery, deception **10** dishonesty

subterranean 11 underground

subtle 4 fine **5** faint **6** artful, astute **7** cunning, refined **8** delicate, finespun, guileful, skillful **9** insidious **10** indistinct **13** inconspicuous

subtract 6 deduct, remove **7** take off **8** discount, knock off, take away, withdraw, withhold

subtraction 6 rebate **8** discount **9** abatement, deduction **10** diminution, withdrawal ***term:*** **7** minuend **9** remainder **10** subtrahend

suburb 5 slurb **8** edge city

suburbs 7 fringes **8** environs, purlieus **9** outskirts

subversion 8 sabotage **11** undermining **12** undercutting

subvert 5 upset **6** debase **7** corrupt, deprave, vitiate **8** overturn, sabotage **9** overthrow, undermine

subway *British:* 4 tube **11** underground ***French:*** **5** métro

succeed 3 win **4** boom **5** click, ensue, go far, score **6** arrive, follow, go over, make it, pan out, thrive, win out **7** catch on, come off, make out, prevail, prosper, replace, triumph **8** displace, flourish, get ahead, make good, supplant **9** supervene

succes ____ 3 fou **7** d'estime
success 3 hit **4** fame **5** smash, éclat **6** wealth **7** arrival, fortune, killing, triumph, victory **8** fruition **10** attainment, prosperity **11** achievement, fulfillment
successful 5 boffo, smash, socko **7** booming **8** fruitful, thriving **9** effective, lucrative **10** prosperous, triumphant, victorious **11** flourishing
succession 3 row **5** chain, cycle, march, order, round, suite, train **6** course, sequel, series, string **8** sequence **11** progression
successive 4 next **7** ensuing **9** following **10** subsequent
successor 4 heir **8** claimant, follower **9** inheritor **11** beneficiary
succinct 4 curt **5** blunt, brief, pithy, short, terse **7** brusque, compact, concise, laconic, summary **11** compendious
succor 3 aid **4** help, lift **6** assist, relief **7** comfort, relieve, support **10** assistance, sustenance
succulent 5 juicy **8** luscious ***plant:*** **4** aloe, hoya **5** agave, ficus, yucca **6** cactus, cereus, hoodia, viscum **7** begonia
succumb 3 bow, die **4** cave, fold, wilt **5** defer, yield **6** accede, buckle, cave in, expire, give in, perish, relent, resign, submit **7** give out, go under, knuckle **8** collapse **9** break down, surrender **10** capitulate **11** buckle under **12** knuckle under
sucker 3 con, gyp, sap **4** bilk, dupe, fool, gull, mark, rook **5** cheat, chump, patsy, shoot **6** diddle, pigeon **7** defraud, fall guy, swindle **8** hoodwink, pushover **9** bamboozle
suckle 5 nurse **7** nourish, nurture **10** breastfeed
Sudan *capital:* 8 Khartoum ***desert:*** **6** Libyan ***language:*** **6** Arabic ***monetary unit:*** **5** dinar ***neighbor:*** **4** Chad **5** Congo, Egypt, Kenya, Libya **6** Uganda **7** Eritrea **8** Ethiopia ***river:*** **4** Nile ***sea:*** **3** Red
sudden 4 rash **5** hasty, swift **6** abrupt, prompt **7** hurried **8** headlong **9** impetuous, impromptu, impulsive **10** unexpected, unforeseen **11** precipitant, precipitate, precipitous
suddenly 5 aback **7** hastily, shortly, unaware **8** abruptly, promptly, unawares **9** all at once **10** by surprise **12** unexpectedly
suds 4 beer, fizz, foam, head, soap **5** froth, spume **6** lather
sue 8 litigate
suer 8 litigant
suet 3 fat **4** lard **6** tallow
Suez Canal *builder:* 7 Lesseps (Ferdinand de) ***city:*** **8** Ismailia, Port Said
suffer 4 ache, bear, lump **5** abide, admit, allow, brook, leave, stand, yield **6** accept, endure, permit, submit **7** agonize, anguish, stomach, sustain, swallow, undergo **8** tolerate **10** experience **11** countenance
sufferer 6 victim
suffering 4 ache **5** agony, dolor **6** misery, ordeal **7** anguish, passion, torment, torture **8** distress **10** affliction, misfortune
suffice 5 avail, serve
sufficient 3 due **5** ample **6** common, decent, enough, plenty **8** adequate, all right **9** competent, tolerable **10** acceptable **11** comfortable **12** commensurate, satisfactory **13** commensurable, proportionate ***poetic:*** **4** enow
suffocate 5 burke, choke **6** stifle **7** smother **8** snuff out, strangle **10** asphyxiate
suffrage 4 vote **5** voice **6** ballot **9** franchise
suffragist 4 Catt (Carrie Chapman), Howe (Julia Ward), Mott (Lucretia), Paul (Alice) **5** Stone (Lucy) **7** Anthony (Susan B.), Bloomer (Amelia), Stanton (Elizabeth Cady) **8** Woodhull (Victoria Claflin) **9** Pankhurst (Emmeline)
suffuse 4 fill **5** bathe, flush, imbue, steep **7** pervade **8** permeate, saturate **10** impregnate
sugar 6 aldose, fucose, ribose, xylose **7** glucose, lactose, maltose, mannose, pentose, sorbose, sucrose, sweeten **8** fructose, furanose, levulose **10** saccharose ***burnt:*** **7** caramel ***combining form:*** **4** gluc, glyc, sucr **5** gluco, glyco, sucro **7** sacchar **8** sacchari, saccharo ***from palm sap:*** **7** jaggery ***Mexican:*** **7** panocha, penuche ***source:*** **4** beet, cane, corn **5** maple
sugarcane refuse 7 bagasse
sugarcoat 5 candy **6** veneer **7** sweeten, varnish **8** palliate **9** extenuate, gloss over, gloze over, whitewash
sugary 6 syrupy **7** cloying, honeyed, mawkish **10** saccharine **11** sentimental
suggest 4 hint **5** evoke, imply **6** submit **7** connote, propose, signify **8** indicate, intimate **9** adumbrate, insinuate
suggestion 3 cue **4** clue, hint **5** shade, smack, tinge, trace **6** advice **7** inkling **8** allusion, innuendo, overtone, proposal, reminder **9** suspicion, undertone **10** indication, intimation **11** implication, insinuation
suggestive 4 racy **5** salty, spicy **6** ribald, risqué **8** off-color **9** evocative **10** indicative **11** reminiscent
suicidal pilot 8 kamikaze
suicide 8 felo-de-se **10** self-murder **13** self-slaughter ***Japanese:*** **7** seppuku **8** hara-kiri, hari-kari

suit 3 fit **4** case, jibe, plea **5** adapt, agree, befit, cause, check, serve, tally **6** accord, action, adjust, appeal, become, go with, please, prayer, square, tailor **7** conform, enhance, flatter, lawsuit, request, satisfy **8** entreaty, petition **9** agree with, reconcile **10** go together **11** accommodate, application, imploration, imprecation **12** solicitation, supplication ***card:*** **5** clubs **6** hearts, spades **8** diamonds ***type:*** **4** zoot **6** monkey, vested **9** paternity **10** pin-striped **11** class-action

suitable 3 apt, due, fit **4** just, meet **5** right **6** proper, seemly, useful **7** condign, fitting **8** apposite, becoming, deserved, eligible **9** pertinent, qualified, requisite **10** acceptable, felicitous **11** appropriate

suitcase 3 bag **4** grip **6** valise **7** carry-on, holdall **8** carryall

suite 3 lot, row, set **4** flat **5** array, group, rooms, staff, train **6** sequel, series, string **7** lodging, retinue **8** chambers, sequence **9** apartment, entourage, following

suitor 4 beau **5** lover, spark, swain, wooer **7** admirer, gallant, sparker **8** cavalier, paramour **9** boyfriend **10** petitioner

sulfur 9 brimstone

sulk 4 mope, pout **5** brood, gloom

sulky 4 cart, dour, glum **5** moody **6** gloomy, morose, sullen **7** crabbed **9** saturnine

sullen 4 dour, glum, mean, sour **5** moody, pouty, surly **6** crabby, dismal, gloomy, grumpy, morose, somber, sombre **7** crabbed, pouting **8** lowering, scowling **9** glowering, saturnine **10** ill-humored **11** pessimistic

Sullivan's partner 7 Gilbert (William Schwenk)

sully 3 tar **4** soil **5** dirty, shame, smear, stain, taint **6** defame, defile, malign, vilify **7** asperse, blacken, pollute, slander, tarnish, traduce **8** besmirch, disgrace, dishonor **9** denigrate

Sultan of Swat 8 Babe Ruth

sultry 3 hot **4** sexy **5** close, humid, muggy **6** steamy, sticky, stuffy, torrid **7** airless **8** stifling **9** seductive **10** passionate, sweltering, voluptuous

sum 3 add, all, tot **4** mass, tote **5** gross, total, whole **6** amount, digest, entity, figure, resumé **7** epitome **8** entirety, integral, nutshell, totality **9** aggregate, epitomize

Sumatra *country:* 9 Indonesia ***highest peak:*** **7** Kerinci **8** Kerintji ***largest city:*** **5** Medan ***shrew:*** **4** tana

Sumerian *city:* 4 Kish, Umma **5** Erech **6** Lagash, Nippur ***dragon:*** **3** Kur ***god:*** **3** Abu, Kur, Utu **4** Enki **5** Enlil, Lahar, Nanna, Nintu **6** Dumuzi, Nergal, Ninazu **7** Enkimdu ***goddess:*** **6** Ningal, Ninlil

summarize 5 recap **6** digest **7** abridge, outline **8** boil down, condense **9** epitomize, synopsize **11** encapsulate **12** recapitulate

summary 5 recap **6** aperçu, digest, précis, résumé, review, wrap-up **7** compend, epitome, outline, roundup, rundown **8** abstract, overview, scenario, synopsis **9** inventory **10** abridgment, compendium, conspectus **11** abridgement **12** condensation

summer *French:* 3 été ***Spanish:*** **6** verano

summerhouse 6 alcove, gazebo, pagoda **9** belvedere

summery 7 estival

summit 3 top **4** acme, apex, peak, roof **5** crest, crown **6** apogee, climax, height, vertex, zenith **8** capstone, meridian, pinnacle **11** culmination

summon 3 bid **4** call, cite **5** evoke, order **6** beckon, call in, invite, muster **7** arraign, command, conjure, convene, convoke, send for **8** assemble, subpoena

sump 4 sink **8** cesspool

sumptuous 4 lush, rich **5** grand **6** costly, deluxe, lavish, superb **7** opulent **8** gorgeous, luscious, palatial, splendid **9** grandiose, luxurious **11** extravagant, resplendent **12** awe-inspiring

sun 3 orb, Sol **4** bask, star **7** daystar, phoebus **8** daylight, luminary, radiance **9** radiation ***combining form:*** **4** heli **5** helio ***disk:*** **4** Aten ***god:*** **3** Lug, Sol, Tem, Utu **4** Amen, Atmu, Atum, Inti, Lleu, Llew, Lugh, Utug **5** Horus, Sunna, Surya **6** Apollo, Babbar, Helios, Marduk **7** Khepera, Ninurta, Phoebus, Shamash **8** Hyperion, Merodach

Sun Also Rises, The *author:* 9 Hemingway (Ernest) ***character:*** **6** Ashley (Brett), Barnes (Jake)

sunder 3 cut **4** rend, rive **5** break, sever, slice, split **6** cleave, divide **8** dissever, disunite, separate

sundial part 6 gnomon

sundown 4 dusk **7** evening **8** eventide, gloaming, twilight

sundries 7 notions **8** oddments **9** etceteras **11** odds and ends

sundry 4 many, some **6** varied **7** diverse, several, various **8** assorted, manifold, numerous **9** different, disparate **12** multifarious **13** miscellaneous, multitudinous

sunfish 4 opah **7** pompano **8** bluegill **11** pumpkinseed

Sunflower State 6 Kansas

sun-god see at **sun**

Sun King 8 Louis XIV

sunny **4** fair, fine, warm **5** clear, happy **6** blithe, bright, cheery, chirpy, golden **7** beaming, clarion, radiant **8** cheerful, pleasant, rainless **9** brilliant, cloudless, unclouded **10** optimistic

sunrise **4** dawn, morn **6** aurora **7** dawning, morning **8** cockcrow, daybreak, daylight ***goddess:*** **3** Eos **6** Aurora

sunroom **8** solarium

sunset **3** eve **4** dusk **7** evening **8** gloaming, twilight

Sunset State **6** Oregon

Sunshine State **7** Florida

sunup see **sunrise**

sup **3** eat **4** dine **5** feast

super **4** very **5** great **8** powerful, splendid, terrific **9** excellent, extremely, fantastic, first-rate, wonderful **11** outstanding

superannuated **4** aged **5** hoary, passé **6** bygone **7** ancient, archaic, elderly, outworn **8** obsolete, outdated, outmoded **9** out-of-date **10** antiquated **11** obsolescent **12** old-fashioned

superb **4** A-one, rich **5** grand, lofty, noble, prime, primo, super **7** elegant, exalted, optimal, optimum, opulent, stately, sublime, supreme **8** glorious, gorgeous, imposing, majestic, peerless, splendid, standout **9** excellent, marvelous, matchless, wonderful **11** magnificent, outstanding, resplendent, sensational, splendorous **13** splendiferous

supercilious **5** lofty **6** lordly, sniffy, snippy **7** haughty, stuck-up **8** cavalier, snobbish, superior **10** disdainful **11** patronizing **13** condescending, high-and-mighty

superficial **5** hasty **6** breezy, casual, slight **7** cursory, shallow, sketchy, surface, trivial **8** external, skin-deep **9** depthless, frivolous **11** perfunctory

superfluity **4** glut **5** frill **6** excess **7** nimiety, overrun, surfeit, surplus **8** overflow, overkill, overload, overmuch, overplus, plethora **10** oversupply, redundancy, surplusage **11** prodigality **12** extravagance **13** overabundance

superfluous **5** extra, spare **6** de trop, excess, otiose **7** surplus **8** needless **9** excessive, redundant **10** gratuitous **11** uncalled-for, unnecessary

superintend **4** boss **6** direct, manage **7** control, oversee **10** administer

superintendence **4** care **6** charge **7** conduct, running **8** handling **9** authority, direction, oversight **10** management

superior **4** rare **5** above, lofty, major, prime, proud, upper **6** better, choice, higher, lordly, select, sniffy, snippy, snooty **7** capital, greater, haughty, premium, stuck-up **8** arrogant, brass hat, cavalier, dominant, higher-up, insolent **9** excellent, first-rate, marvelous **10** disdainful, first-class, preeminent, preferable, remarkable **11** exceptional, overbearing, patronizing, predominant **13** condescending, high-and-mighty

superiority **9** advantage, dominance, seniority, supremacy, upper hand **10** ascendancy

superjacent **4** over **6** higher **7** greater **9** overlying

superlative **3** ace **4** A-one, best **8** peerless, standout **9** matchless **10** consummate **11** magnificent, outstanding

Superman **9** Clark Kent ***actor:*** **4** Alyn (Kirk), Cain (Dean) **5** Reeve (Christopher), Routh (Brandon) **6** Reeves (George) **7** Collyer (Bud) ***bane:*** **10** kryptonite ***birthplace:*** **7** Krypton ***creator:*** **7** Shuster (Joe) ***employer:*** **11** Daily Planet (The) ***father:*** **5** Jor-El ***foe:*** **3** Zod (General) **6** Luthor (Lex) **7** Bizarro **8** Brainiac, Darkseid, Doomsday, Mxyzptlk (Mr.) ***friend:*** **5** Olsen (Jimmy) ***girlfriend:*** **8** Lois Lane ***mother:*** **4** Lara ***original name:*** **5** Kal-El

supernatural **5** magic **6** divine, mystic **7** magical, psychic, uncanny **8** heavenly **9** celestial, unearthly **10** miraculous, paranormal, phenomenal **12** metaphysical, transcendent **13** extraordinary

supernatural being **3** elf, fay, god, hob, imp, nix **4** jinn, ogre, peri, puck **5** afrit, angel, bogle, deity, demon, fairy, gnome, jinni, lamia, naiad, nixie, nymph, pixie, satyr, sylph, Titan, troll **6** afreet, goblin, kelpie, seraph, spirit, sprite **7** banshee, brownie, bugbear, goddess, incubus, silenus, vampire, wendigo, windigo **8** bogeyman, demiurge, succubus **9** boogeyman, hobgoblin **10** leprechaun

supernumerary **5** extra, spare **6** de trop, excess, walk-on **7** reserve, surplus **8** leftover **9** redundant

supersede **5** usurp **7** replace, succeed **8** displace, supplant

supervene **5** ensue, occur **6** befall, follow, result **7** succeed **9** eventuate, transpire

supervise **3** run **4** boss **5** steer **6** direct, govern, manage **7** conduct, control, monitor, oversee, proctor, referee **8** chaperon, overlook **10** administer

supervision **4** care **6** charge **7** control, running **8** auspices, handling **9** direction, oversight **10** intendance, management **11** stewardship

supervisor **7** foreman, manager **8** director, overseer **13** administrator

supine 5 inert, prone, slack **7** passive **8** inactive, indolent **9** prostrate, recumbent **10** horizontal **12** outstretched
supper club 6 nitery **7** cabaret **9** night spot
supplant 4 oust **5** usurp **6** cut out, unseat **7** replace, succeed **8** crowd out, displace, force out **9** overthrow, supersede
supple 5 agile, lithe, withy **6** limber, nimble, pliant, whippy **7** ductile, elastic, lissome, plastic, pliable, springy, willowy **8** flexible, graceful, moldable **9** adaptable, malleable, resilient
supplement 3 add, pad **4** coda **5** rider **6** append, beef up, enrich, extend, sequel **7** adjunct, augment, codicil, enhance, fill out, fortify **8** addendum, addition, appendix, buttress, increase **9** accessory, reinforce **10** postscript, strengthen
suppliant 5 asker **6** beggar, suitor **9** solicitor **10** petitioner
supplicant see **suppliant**
supplicate 3 ask, beg, sue **4** pray **5** crave, plead **6** appeal, invoke **7** beseech, entreat, implore, solicit **8** petition **9** importune
supplication 4 plea, suit **6** appeal, orison, prayer **8** entreaty, petition **11** application
supplies 6 stores **8** matériel **9** equipment, materials **10** provisions
supply 3 man **4** feed, fund, hand, help **5** cache, equip, hoard, stock, store **6** afford, outfit, purvey **7** deliver, fulfill, furnish, provide, reserve, satisfy, surplus **8** dispense, hand over, transfer, turn over **9** inventory, provision, reservoir, stockpile **10** contribute **12** accumulation
support 3 aid **4** back, base, bear, hand, help, lift, prop, root, side, stay **5** abide, adopt, boost, brace, bread, brook, carry, favor, shore, strut, truss **6** anchor, assist, bear up, buoy up, column, crutch, defend, endure, girder, pillar, prop up, second, suffer, uphold, verify **7** alimony, applaud, approve, backing, bolster, comfort, confirm, embrace, endorse, espouse, fortify, fulcrum, nourish, nurture, pull for, shore up, stiffen, sustain, trestle **8** abutment, advocate, backstop, buttress, champion, mainstay, maintain, sanction, side with, tide over, underpin **9** encourage, reinforce, underprop **10** assistance, foundation, livelihood, provide for, strengthen, sustenance **11** corroborate, hand-holding, maintenance, subsistence **12** underpinning
supporter 3 fan **4** ally **6** patron **7** booster, sectary **8** adherent, advocate, champion, disciple, exponent, follower, henchman, partisan **9** proponent
suppose 4 deem **5** allow, guess, infer, opine, posit, think **6** assume, expect, gather, reckon **7** believe, imagine, presume, pretend, surmise, suspect **8** consider **9** postulate, speculate **10** conjecture **11** hypothesize
supposed 7 alleged, seeming **8** apparent, putative **10** ostensible
supposition 2 if **5** guess, hunch, posit **6** notion, theory, thesis **7** premise, surmise **9** postulate **10** assumption, conjecture, hypothesis **11** postulation, presumption, speculation
supposititious 6 unreal **7** dubious, fictive, reputed **8** doubtful, fanciful, illusory, putative, spurious **9** fantastic, fictional, imaginary, pretended, simulated **10** chimerical, fictitious, fraudulent **11** conjectural **12** hypothetical, illegitimate, questionable
suppress 4 curb, stop **5** burke, check, choke, crush, drown, quash, quell, shush, spike, stunt **6** arrest, censor, cut off, hush up, muffle, muzzle, quench, retard, squash, stifle, subdue **7** abolish, collect, conceal, control, prevent, put down, silence, smother, squelch, swallow **8** prohibit, restrain, snuff out, withhold **9** overthrow **10** extinguish
suppurate 6 fester
supra 5 above
supremacy 7 control, mastery **8** dominion **9** authority, dominance **10** ascendancy, domination, mastership, prepotency **11** preeminence, sovereignty **12** predominance **13** preponderance
supreme 4 best **5** chief, final, prime **6** superb, utmost **7** highest, leading, maximum, perfect **8** absolute, cardinal, crowning, foremost, greatest, peerless, towering, ultimate **9** matchless, paramount, principal, sovereign, unequaled, unmatched, unrivaled **10** preeminent, surpassing **11** culminating, predominant, superlative, unmatchable, unsurpassed **12** incomparable, transcendent, unparalleled **13** unsurpassable
Supreme Being 3 God **5** Allah **7** creator, Jehovah **8** Almighty ***belief in:*** **5** deism
Supreme Court justice 3 Jay (John) **4** Taft (William Howard) **5** Alito (Samuel), Black (Hugo), Chase (Salmon P.), Kagan (Elena), Stone (Harlan Fiske), Story (Joseph), Taney (Roger B.) **6** Breyer (Stephen G.), Burger (Warren), Holmes (Oliver Wendell), Hughes (Charles Evans), Scalia (Antonin), Souter (David), Thomas (Clarence), Vinson (Fred), Warren (Earl) **7** Brennan (William), Cardozo (Benjamin), Douglas (William O.), O'Connor (Sandra Day), Roberts (John G.), Stevens (John Paul), Kennedy (An-

thony M.) **8** Blackmun (Harry), Brandeis (Louis), Ginsburg (Ruth Bader), Marshall (John, Thurgood) **9** Rehnquist (William), Sotomayor (Sonia) **11** Frankfurter (Felix)

surcease 3 end **4** halt, quit, rest, stay, stop **6** desist **7** refrain, respite, suspend **8** knock off, leave off, postpone, stoppage **9** cessation, remission **10** suspension **11** discontinue **12** postponement

sure 3 set **4** fast, firm, safe **5** fixed **6** indeed, secure, stable, steady, strong **7** certain, staunch **8** absolute, definite, enduring, positive, reliable, unerring **9** confident, convinced, steadfast **10** convincing, dependable, inevitable, infallible, undeniable, unshakable, unwavering **11** indubitable, trustworthy, unequivocal, unfaltering **12** indisputable **13** incontestable, unquestioning

surefire 7 assured, certain **8** reliable **10** dependable, guaranteed

sure thing 6 shoo-in, winner **9** certainty

surety 4 bail, bond **5** angel **6** backer, patron, pledge **7** sponsor **8** guaranty, security, warranty **9** certainty, certitude, guarantee, guarantor **10** confidence, conviction

surf 4 scan, skim **6** browse **9** bodyboard, kneeboard

surfing term 4 deck, tube **5** leash **6** A-frame, barrel, drop in, hollow, turtle **7** bail out, carving, cutback, grommet, hang ten, snaking, wipeout **8** backdoor, blown out **9** goofy foot **10** impact zone **12** kneeboarding

surface 3 top **4** face, pave, rise, skin **5** cover **6** appear, come up, emerge, facade, facing, finish, patina, show up, veneer **7** outside **8** covering, exterior **11** superficial

surfeit 4 cloy, fill, glut, jade, pall, sate **5** gorge, stuff **6** excess **7** replete, satiate, surplus **8** overfill, overflow, overkill, overmuch, overplus, plethora **10** surplusage **11** overindulge, superfluity **13** overabundance

surge 4 flow, gush, pour, rise, roll, rush, soar, tide, wave **5** flood, swell **6** billow, deluge, sluice, stream **7** torrent

surgeon 8 sawbones ***American:*** **4** Mayo (Charles, William), Reed (Walter) **6** Thorek (Max) **7** Cushing (Harvey), DeBakey (Michael) **8** McDowell (Ephraim) ***English:*** **5** Paget (James) **6** Lister (Joseph) ***French:*** **4** Paré (Ambroise) **5** Broca (Paul) ***South African:*** **7** Barnard (Christiaan)

surgery 9 operation ***instrument:*** **5** clamp, curet, laser **6** gorget, lancet, splint, stylet, trocar **7** forceps, scalpel

surgical removal 8 ablation ***combining form:*** **6** ectomy

Suriname *capital:* **10** Paramaribo ***former name:*** **11** Dutch Guiana **6** Sranan ***monetary unit:*** **7** guilder ***mountain range:*** **10** Tumac-Humac ***neighbor:*** **6** Brazil, Guyana **12** French Guiana ***river:*** **6** Maroni **8** Suriname **10** Courantyne

surly 4 dour, glum **5** cross, gruff, sulky **6** crusty, grumpy, morose, sullen **7** bearish, crabbed, grouchy **8** churlish, menacing, snappish **9** irritable, saturnine **10** ungracious **11** ill-mannered, threatening **12** discourteous

surmise see **suppose**

surmount 3 cap, top **4** best, down, leap, lick **5** clear, climb, crest, crown, excel, outdo, vault **6** better, hurdle, master **7** conquer, surpass **8** outstrip, overcome, vanquish **9** negotiate, transcend

surpass 3 cap, top **4** beat, best **5** excel, outdo, trump **6** better, exceed, outrun **7** eclipse, outpace **8** go beyond, outclass, outshine, outstrip, outweigh, overstep **9** transcend **10** overshadow

surplice 5 cotta, ephod **8** vestment

surplus 5 extra, spare **6** excess **7** overage, overrun, reserve, surfeit **8** leftover, overflow, overkill, overmuch, plethora **9** overstock, remainder **10** oversupply **11** superfluity, superfluous

surprise 4 faze, stun **5** amaze, floor **6** ambush, dismay, rattle, waylay, wonder **7** astound, capture, nonplus, stagger, startle, stupefy **8** astonish, bewilder, bowl over **9** amazement, dumbfound, overpower, take aback **11** flabbergast **12** astonishment, stupefaction

surreal 5 weird **7** bizarre **9** dreamlike, fantastic **10** outlandish **12** unbelievable

surrealist 3 Arp (Jean), Ray (Man) **4** Dalí (Salvador), Népo **5** Ernst (Max) **6** Breton (André), Tanguy (Yves) **8** Magritte (René) **9** de Chirico (Giorgio)

surrender 4 cave, cede, fold **5** waive, yield **6** cave in, give in, give up, resign, submit **7** abandon, concede, succumb **8** cry uncle, hand over **10** abdication, capitulate, relinquish, submission **12** capitulation ***sign:*** **7** hands up **9** white flag

surreptitious see **stealthy**

surrogate 3 sub **5** proxy **6** acting, deputy, fill-in **7** stand-in, stopgap **9** makeshift **10** substitute **11** locum tenens, pinch hitter, replacement

surround 3 hem, rim **4** edge, gird, loop, ring **5** beset, bound, hem in, limit, round, skirt, verge **6** border, circle, fringe, girdle, margin **7** besiege, compass, confine, enclose, en-

velop, outline **8** encircle **9** encompass **12** circumscribe
surrounding 5 about **7** ambient **12** circumjacent ***prefix:* 4** peri **6** circum
surroundings 6 milieu **7** ambient **8** ambience **11** environment
surveillance 3 eye, tab **4** tail **5** vigil, watch **7** lookout **8** scrutiny, stakeout **9** vigilance **11** supervision
survey 3 con, vet **4** case, poll, scan, view **5** assay, audit **6** assess, précis, review, size up **7** canvass, examine, inspect, pandect, perusal, preview **8** analysis, appraise, estimate, evaluate, look over, overlook, overview, scrutiny, syllabus **9** check over **10** scrutinize **11** reconnoiter
survive 4 keep, last **6** endure **7** carry on, hold out, outlast, outlive, outwear, persist, recover, ride out, weather **8** continue, live down **9** withstand **11** come through, live through, pull through
Surya 6 sun-god ***son:* 4** Manu, Yama **5** Karna **6** Asvins ***temple site:* 7** Konarak
susceptible 4 open **5** naive, prone **6** liable **7** exposed, pliable, subject **8** disposed, inclined, sensible **9** malleable, receptive, sensitive **10** responsive, vulnerable **11** impressible, persuadable
suspect 5 doubt, fishy, guess **6** assume, unsure **7** believe, dubious, imagine, suppose, surmise **8** distrust, doubtful, mistrust **9** doubtable, uncertain **10** disbelieve **11** problematic
suspend 3 bar **4** bate, halt, hang, stay, stop **5** debar, defer, delay, hover, sling **6** dangle, depend, hold up, put off, shelve **7** adjourn, hold off **8** intermit, postpone, prorogue **9** eliminate **11** discontinue
suspended 6 frozen **7** hanging, pendant, pendent, stopped **8** dangling, swinging **9** pendulous
suspenders 6 braces **8** galluses
suspense 7 anxiety, mystery, tension **10** expectancy **11** expectation, uncertainty **12** apprehension
suspension 4 halt, stay, stop **5** delay, letup, pause **6** cutoff, freeze **7** latency, respite, time-out **8** abeyance, dormancy, stoppage **9** remission **10** moratorium, quiescence **11** cold storage, withholding **12** intermission, interruption, postponement
suspicion 4 hint **5** doubt, dread, guess, hunch, qualm, shade, smell, tinge, touch, trace, whiff **7** concern, dubiety, surmise **8** distrust, mistrust, wariness **9** chariness, misgiving **10** foreboding, intimation, skepticism, suggestion **11** incertitude, premonition, supposition, uncertainty
suspicious 4 wary **5** chary, fishy, leery **7** dubious, jealous, suspect **8** doubtful, watchful **9** doubtable, skeptical **11** distrustful, mistrustful, problematic **12** apprehensive, questionable
suspire 4 sigh **5** sough
sustain 4 bear, feed, prop, save **5** brace, carry, stand **6** bear up, buoy up, endure, foster, hold up, keep up, succor, suffer, uphold **7** bolster, confirm, nourish, nurture, prolong, relieve, shore up, support, undergo **8** buttress, preserve
sustenance 3 pap **4** food, keep, meat **5** bread, means **6** living, viands **7** aliment, alimony, pabulum, support **8** victuals **9** nutriment, provender **10** livelihood, provisions **11** maintenance, nourishment, subsistence, wherewithal
susurration 4 purr **6** mumble, murmur, mutter, rustle **7** whisper **9** undertone
suture 3 sew **4** seam **6** stitch
suzerain 5 ruler **8** overlord **9** sovereign
svelte 4 slim **5** lithe, sleek, suave **6** smooth, urbane **7** elegant, slender **8** graceful
swab 3 mop **4** Q-Tip **5** clean **6** sponge
swaddle 4 roll, wrap **5** drape **6** enfold, swathe, wrap up **7** blanket **8** enshroud, enswathe
swag 3 sag, yaw **4** loot, sway, tilt **5** booty, droop, lurch, money, prize **6** boodle, spoils **7** festoon, garland, pillage, plunder **10** contraband
swagger 4 brag **5** boast, bully, strut, swank, swash, swell **6** sashay **7** bluster, bravado, peacock, saunter **9** arrogance, cockiness, gasconade **11** braggadocio, swashbuckle
swagman 4 hobo **5** rover, tramp **7** drifter, vagrant **8** vagabond, wanderer
swain 4 beau **5** lover, spark, wooer **6** rustic, suitor **7** admirer **8** shepherd **9** boyfriend
swallow 3 buy, sip **4** bear, belt, bolt, down, gulp, swig, take, toss, wolf **5** abide, brook, drink, quaff, slurp, stand, swill **6** absorb, accept, digest, endure, guzzle, imbibe, ingest, inhale **7** believe, consume, fall for, repress, retract, stomach **8** chugalug, take back, tolerate **11** ingurgitate
swamp 3 bog, fen **4** holm, mire, moss, muck, quag **5** drown, flood, glade, marsh, whelm **6** deluge, engulf, morass, muskeg, slough **7** bottoms **8** inundate, overcome, overflow, quagmire, submerge **9** everglade, marshland, overwhelm ***Everglades:* 10** Big Cypress ***Georgia:* 10** Okefenokee ***North Carolina-Virginia:* 6** Dismal

swamped **5** awash **7** brimful, flooded, overrun **8** engulfed **9** inundated, submerged **11** overflowing, overwhelmed

Swamp Fox **6** Marion (Francis)

swan ***female:*** **3** pen ***genus:*** **4** Olor **6** Cygnus ***male:*** **3** cob **4** cobb ***young:*** **6** cygnet

swank **4** posh, tony, trig **5** boast, fancy, ritzy, sharp, showy, smart, swell, swish **6** chichi, classy, dapper, deluxe, lavish, plushy, snappy, trendy **7** elegant, peacock, show off, splashy, stylish, swagger **8** peacocky **9** glamorous, luxurious **10** flamboyant, peacockish

Swan Lake ***character:*** **5** Odile **6** Odette **9** Siegfried (Prince) **11** Von Rothbart ***composer:*** **11** Tchaikovsky (Pyotr Ilyich)

swap **5** trade, truck **6** barter, change, switch **7** bargain, traffic **8** exchange **10** substitute

swarm **3** jam, mob **4** army, bevy, herd, host, mass, pack, push, shin, teem **5** crawl, crowd, crush, drove, flock, group, horde, mount, press **6** abound, gather, myriad, throng **7** climb up, cluster, overrun **9** multitude, pullulate **10** congregate

swarthy **4** dark **5** dusky, sooty **6** brunet **8** bistered

swash **3** lap **4** brag, dash, gush, rush, slop **5** boast, churn, douse, froth, plash, slosh **6** bubble, burble, gurgle, seethe, splash **7** bluster, channel, saunter, spatter, splurge, swagger

swat **3** bat, box, hit, rap **4** bash, belt, blow, cuff, lick, slap, slog, slug, sock **5** blast, clout, homer, knock, smack, smash, smite, swipe, whack **6** buffet, larrup, strike, wallop **7** clobber

swath **4** belt, path **5** strip, sweep **6** stroke

swathe see **swaddle**

sway **4** bend, bias, rock, rule **5** lurch, range, reach, scope, sweep, swing, waver, weave **6** affect, careen, direct, govern, totter, wobble **7** command, control, dispose, impress, incline, mastery, stagger, win over **8** dominate, dominion, overrule, persuade, undulate **9** authority, dominance, fluctuate, influence, oscillate, vacillate **10** domination, predispose

Swaziland ***capital:*** **7** Lobamba, Mbabane ***language:*** **5** Swazi ***monetary unit:*** **9** lilangeni ***neighbor:*** **10** Mozambique **11** South Africa ***river:*** **5** Usutu **6** Komati **8** Umbeluzi

swear **3** vow **4** avow, bind, cuss, damn, oath, rail, rant **5** abuse, curse, vouch **6** adjure, affirm, assert, attest, depone, depose, pledge, plight **7** declare, promise, testify, warrant **8** covenant, maintain **9** blaspheme, imprecate **10** asseverate

swearword **4** cuss, oath **5** curse **9** expletive, obscenity

sweat **4** emit, glow, moil, ooze, seep, toil, weep **5** exude, grind, labor **6** strain, swivet **7** excrete **8** perspire, transude **12** perspiration

sweater **8** cardigan, pullover, slipover **10** turtleneck

sweaty **6** clammy, sticky **7** glowing **10** perspiring

Sweden ***Arctic region:*** **7** Lapland ***capital:*** **9** Stockholm ***city:*** **5** Malmö **8** Göteborg ***gulf:*** **7** Bothnia **8** Kattegat ***island:*** **5** Öland **7** Gotland ***lake:*** **6** Vänern **7** Mälaren, Vättern **9** Hjälmaren ***monetary unit:*** **5** krona ***mountain range:*** **5** Kölen ***neighbor:*** **6** Norway **7** Finland ***part of:*** **11** Scandinavia ***river:*** **3** Dal ***sea:*** **6** Baltic

Swedish Nightingale **4** Lind (Jenny)

Swedish pop group **4** ABBA

sweep **3** arc, fly, mop, win **4** flit, sail, scud, skim, wing **5** ambit, broom, brush, clean, clear, curve, drive, orbit, range, reach, scope, surge, whisk **6** extent, radius, search **7** compass, purview, victory **9** extension

sweeping **5** broad **6** all-out **7** blanket, general, overall, radical **8** thorough, whole-hog **9** extensive, inclusive, out-and-out, universal, wholesale **11** far-reaching **12** all-embracing

sweepings **4** dust **5** trash, waste **6** debris, litter, refuse **7** garbage, residue, rubbish **8** detritus

sweet **5** candy, honey **6** bonbon, dulcet, lovely, sugary, syrupy **7** angelic, cloying, dessert, melodic, scented, sugared, winning, winsome **8** aromatic, fragrant, heavenly, luscious, perfumed **9** ambrosial, delicious **10** delectable, saccharine ***combining form:*** **4** glyc **5** glyco

Sweet ____ **7** Adeline, Charity **8** Caroline **12** Georgia Brown

sweeten **5** candy, honey, sugar **6** soften **7** appease, assuage, enhance, mollify, placate **9** sugarcoat, sugar over **10** conciliate, propitiate

sweetheart **3** gra **4** dear, love **5** flame, honey **7** beloved, darling, tootsie **10** heartthrob, honeybunch

sweetmeat **5** candy **6** comfit **8** delicacy, preserve **10** confection

sweet potato **3** yam **7** boniato

sweet-talk **4** coax **5** charm **6** banter, cajole, wangle **7** blarney, flatter, wheedle **8** blandish, butter up, inveigle, soft-soap

swell **4** fine, grow, keen, neat, pout, puff **5** bloat, bulge, dandy, neato, nifty, pouch, super, surge, swank **6** abound, billow, blow up, dilate, expand, groovy, peachy **7** amplify, augment, balloon, distend, enlarge, inflate, peacock, swagger, upsurge **8** increase, jim-dandy, terrific **9** crescendo, marvelous, wonderful ***British:*** **3** nob **4** toff

swelled head 5 pride **6** egoism, vanity **7** conceit, egotism **8** smugness **9** arrogance, vainglory **10** narcissism **11** amour propre, self-conceit

swelling 3 sty **4** boil, bubo, bump, corn, gall, node **5** bulge, edema, tumid, tumor **6** bunion, growth, nodule **7** gibbous **8** tubercle **9** carbuncle, chilblain, expansion, tumescent **10** tumescence **11** excrescence **12** inflammation, protuberance

sweltering 3 hot **5** fiery **6** baking, sultry, torrid **7** burning **8** broiling, roasting, sizzling **9** scorching

swerve 3 yaw **4** skew, turn, veer **5** sheer, shift, stray, waver **6** depart, wander **7** deflect, deviate

swift 4 fast **5** fleet, hasty, quick, rapid, ready **6** prompt, snappy, speedy, sudden **8** full-tilt, headlong **9** breakneck

____ Swift 3 Tom **8** Jonathan ***character:*** **8** Gulliver

swiftness 4 gait, pace **5** haste, hurry, speed **6** hustle **8** celerity, dispatch, legerity, rapidity, velocity

swig 4 belt, down, drag, gulp, pull, slug **5** booze, draft, drain, drink, quaff, swill **6** guzzle, imbibe, tipple **7** swallow, swizzle

swill 4 bolt, gulp, slop, swig, tope, wolf **5** booze, draft, drink, gorge, scarf, scoff, slops **6** debris, gobble, guzzle, inhale, spilth, tank up, tipple **7** consume, garbage, hogwash, rubbish, swizzle

swim 3 dip **4** reel, spin, turn **5** bathe, crawl, float, swoon, whirl **9** dizziness, dog-paddle

swimmingly 6 easily **8** smoothly **10** splendidly

swimming stroke 5 crawl **7** dolphin, trudgen **9** butterfly, dog paddle

swindle 3 con, gyp **4** bilk, clip, dupe, fake, hoax, rook, scam, sell, sham, skin, soak **5** bunco, bunko, cheat, cozen, fraud, gouge, phony, rogue, shaft, skunk, sting **6** chouse, diddle, fleece, humbug, hustle, take in **7** con game, defraud **8** flimflam, hoodwink **9** bamboozle, imposture, victimize **11** hornswoggle

swindler 5 cheat, crook, ganef, gonif, shark **6** con man, goniff **7** sharper, shyster **8** deceiver **9** charlatan, defrauder **10** mountebank

swine see **hog**

swing 4 jive, slew, slue, sway, veer **5** flail, lurch, pivot, twirl, waver, weave, whirl, wield **6** dangle, divert, rhythm, rotate, seesaw, stroke, swerve, switch **7** revolve, suspend **8** brandish **9** alternate, fluctuate, oscillate, vacillate

swinish 5 feral **6** coarse **7** beastly, bestial, porcine

swipe 3 cop, hit, nab, rap **4** blow, clip, conk, grab, hook, lick, lift, nick, sock, swat, wipe **5** clout, filch, heist, knock, pinch, smack, steal **6** pilfer, snatch, snitch, strike, wallop

swirl 4 eddy, purl, roil **5** curve, twist, whirl, whorl **6** swoosh, vortex **9** whirlpool **11** convolution

swish 4 buzz, chic, fizz, hiss, posh, tony, whiz **5** ritzy, smart, swank, whisk **6** classy, dressy, sizzle, trendy, whoosh **7** elegant, stylish **8** sibilate

Swiss Family Robinson author 4 Wyss (Johann David)

switch 3 rod, wag **4** beat, flay, flog, lash, swap, veer, wand, whip **5** shift, shunt, trade, whisk **6** change, strike, waggle **7** scourge **8** exchange, flip-flop, reversal **9** about-face, sidetrack **10** substitute **12** substitution

Switzerland *canton:* 3 Uri, Zug **4** Jura, Vaud **5** Berne **6** Geneva, Ticino, Valais ***capital:*** **4** Bern **5** Berne ***city:*** **5** Basel **6** Geneva, Zürich **8** Lausanne ***lake:*** **6** Geneva, Wallen **7** Lucerne **9** Constance, Neuchâtel, Thunersee, Zürichsee ***language:*** **6** French, German **7** Italian ***monetary unit:*** **5** franc ***mountain, range:*** **4** Alps, Jura **9** Monte Rosa ***neighbor:*** **5** Italy **6** France **7** Austria, Germany **13** Liechtenstein ***resort:*** **5** Davos, Vevey **7** Zermatt **8** Montreux, St. Moritz **10** Interlaken ***river:*** **3** Aar **4** Aare **5** Rhine, Rhône ***state:*** **6** canton

swivel 4 spin, turn **5** pivot, swing, twirl, whirl **6** rotate **7** revolve **9** pirouette

swivet see **snit**

swizzle 3 mix **4** stir **5** swill **6** guzzle, tipple

swollen 5 puffy, tumid **6** turgid **7** bloated, bulbous, bulging, pompous **8** enlarged, inflated, varicose **9** bombastic, distended, tumescent **10** rhetorical

swoon 4 coma, daze, fade **5** droop, faint **6** torpor **7** pass out, rapture, syncope **8** black out

swoosh 4 eddy, gush, purl, rush **5** swirl, whirl, whorl

sword 4 épée, foil **5** saber, sabre **6** barong, bilboa, rapier, Toledo **7** cutlass **8** claymore, falchion, scimitar, yataghan

sword-shaped 6 ensate **8** ensiform

sworn 6 avowed **7** devoted **8** affirmed **9** committed, confirmed **10** deep-rooted, deep-seated, entrenched, inveterate

sybarite 7 epicure **8** hedonist **9** libertine **10** sensualist, voluptuary

sybaritic 6 carnal **7** sensual **8** sensuous **9** epicurean, libertine, luxurious **10** hedonistic, voluptuous

sycophancy 7 fawning **8** flattery, toadying **9** truckling **11** bootlicking

sycophant 5 leech, toady **6** flunky, lackey, minion, yes-man **8** groveler, hanger-on, parasite, truckler **9** easy rider, flatterer, toadeater **10** bootlicker, self-seeker **11** lickspittle **13** apple-polisher

sycophantic 7 fawning, servile, slavish **8** toadying, unctuous **9** groveling, kowtowing, parasitic, truckling **10** obsequious **11** bootlicking

Sycorax's son 7 Caliban

syllable ***deletion:*** **7** apocope ***last:*** **6** ultima ***lengthening of:*** **7** ectasis ***musical:*** **2** do, fa, la, mi, re, si, ti, ut **3** sol ***next to last:*** **6** penult ***shortening:*** **7** elision, systole ***stressed:*** **5** arsis

syllabus 6 aperçu, digest, précis, sketch, survey **7** epitome, outline, pandect, summary **8** abstract, headnote, synopsis **10** compendium

sylph 5 fairy, nymph **6** sprite

sylvan 5 bosky, woody **6** rustic, wooded ***deity:*** **3** Pan **4** Faun **5** dryad, satyr **6** Faunus **7** Silenus **8** Arethusa, Silvanus, Sylvanus

symbol 4 icon, logo, mark, sign **5** badge, glyph, motif, stamp, token **6** design, device, emblem, mascot ***chemical:*** see individual element ***musical:*** **4** clef, flat, hold, note, rest, turn **5** shake, sharp **7** fermata, mordent, natural

symbolic 5 token **10** emblematic **11** allegorical

symbolist poet 7 Rimbaud (Arthur) **8** Mallarmé (Stéphane), Verlaine (Paul)

symbolize 4 mean **6** embody, mirror, typify **7** signify **8** stand for **9** epitomize, exemplify, personify, represent **10** illustrate **11** emblematize

symmetrical 5 equal **7** regular **8** balanced

symmetry 5 order **6** parity **7** balance, harmony **8** equality, evenness **9** agreement, congruity **10** conformity, proportion, regularity **11** arrangement

sympathetic 4 kind, warm **6** benign, caring, humane, kindly, tender **8** amenable, friendly **9** agreeable, approving, benignant, congenial, congruous, consonant, favorable, receptive **10** compatible, consistent, responsive **11** considerate, kindhearted, softhearted, warmhearted

sympathize 4 pity **7** condole **11** commiserate

sympathy 4 pity, ruth **5** heart **6** accord, solace, warmth **7** comfort, harmony, rapport **8** affinity, kindness **9** agreement **10** benignancy, compassion, condolence, kindliness, tenderness **11** consolation, sensitivity **13** commiseration

symphonic 10 orchestral

symphony 9 orchestra **12** philharmonic ***movement:*** **5** rondo **6** minuet

symposium 5 forum **7** meeting, seminar **9** gathering **10** conference, discussion

symptom 4 mark, sign **5** index, token **8** evidence **10** indication

symptoms 7 indicia **8** syndrome

synagogue 4 shul **6** temple ***platform:*** **5** bimah

sync 4 jibe **5** agree, match **7** harmony **8** coincide **9** harmonize **10** concurrent **12** simultaneous

synchronize 5 agree **6** concur **8** coincide

synchronous 6 coeval **10** coetaneous, coexistent, coexisting, coincident, concurrent **11** concomitant **12** contemporary, simultaneous **13** geostationary

syncope 4 coma **5** faint, swoon **8** blackout

syndicate 3 mob **4** pool **5** chain, group, mafia, trust, union **6** cartel, league **7** combine **11** association, partnership **12** conglomerate, organization

syndrome 3 ill **6** malady **7** ailment, disease **8** disorder, sickness **9** complaint, condition, infirmity

synergic 5 joint **6** shared **8** coacting, coactive, conjoint **9** collusive, concerted **11** cooperating, cooperative, coordinated

synod 4 body, diet **7** council, meeting **8** assembly, conclave, congress **10** conference, convention **11** convocation

synopsis 5 brief, recap **6** aperçu, digest, précis, review **7** capsule, epitome, outline, rundown, summary **8** abstract, breviary, syllabus **10** abridgment, compendium, conspectus **12** condensation

synopsize 5 recap, sum up **6** digest **7** outline, summate **8** abstract, boil down, compress, condense **9** epitomize, inventory, summarize

synthesis 5 blend, union **6** fusion, merger **7** amalgam **8** blending, compound **9** composite **11** combination **12** amalgamation **13** incorporation

synthesize 4 fuse, meld **5** blend, merge, unify **7** combine **8** compound **9** harmonize, integrate **10** amalgamate **11** incorporate

synthetic 6 ersatz **7** man-made, plastic **9** imitation, unnatural **10** artificial, fabricated **11** counterfeit ***fiber:*** **3** PBI, PLA **5** Modal, Mylar, Nomex, nylon, Orlon, saran, Zylon **6** Kevlar, olefin, sulfar, Twaron, vinyon **7** acetate, acrylic, lyocell, spandex, vectran, vinalon **9** polyester **10** modacrylic

Syria *capital:* 8 Damascus ***city:*** **4** Homs **6** Aleppo ***language:*** **6** Arabic, French ***monetary unit:*** **5** pound ***neighbor:*** **4** Iraq **6** Israel, Jordan, Turkey **7** Lebanon

syringe 4 hypo **6** needle **10** hypodermic

Syrinx 5 nymph ***pursuer:*** **3** Pan

syrinx 7 panpipe **8** panpipes

syrup 6 orgeat **9** grenadine

syrupy 5 gooey, mushy, sappy, sweet **6** drippy, dulcet, slushy, sticky, sugary **7** cloying, maudlin, mawkish **9** schmaltzy **10** saccharine **11** sentimental

system 3 way **4** mode, plan **5** modus, order, setup **6** entity, manner, method, scheme **7** complex, network, pattern, process, regimen, routine **8** strategy **9** procedure, structure, technique

systematic 7 logical, ordered, orderly, regular **8** arranged **9** organized **10** analytical, methodical

systematize 5 array, order **6** codify **7** arrange, catalog, dispose, marshal **8** classify, organize, regiment **9** catalogue, methodize

system of weights 4 troy **11** avoirdupois **12** apothecaries

T

tab 4 bill, cost, flap, list, loop, rate **5** check, count, price, score **6** charge, record **7** account, invoice **8** eagle eye, price tag, scrutiny **9** appendage, designate, extension, reckoning, statement **12** surveillance

tabard 4 cape, coat **5** tunic **10** coat of arms

tabby 3 cat **6** feline, cement **8** brindled

tabernacle 4 tent **5** hovel **6** church, temple

tabes 7 atrophy, wasting **12** degeneration

Tabitha's Greek name 6 Dorcas

table 4 fare, list **5** bench, board, chart, defer, stand **6** buffet, put off, record, shelve, teapoy **7** counter **8** mahogany, postpone **9** sideboard ***ornament:*** **7** epergne **11** centerpiece ***writing:*** **4** desk **9** secretary **10** escritoire

table d' ____ 4 hôte

tableland 4 mesa **5** butte **6** upland **7** plateau ***Alabama-West Virginia:*** **10** Cumberland ***Arizona:*** **5** Kanab **6** Kaibob ***England:*** **8** Dartmoor ***India:*** **5** Malwa (see also **plateau**)

tablet 3 bar, pad **4** cake, disk, pill, slab **5** panel, slate **6** pellet, plaque, troche **7** lozenge, notepad **8** steno pad

tableware 4 cups **5** bowls, china, forks **6** dishes, knives, plates, silver, spoons **7** glasses, saucers **8** settings, utensils **9** stainless

tabloid 3 rag **5** lurid, pulpy **6** digest **7** summary **9** condensed, newspaper **11** sensational **12** scandal sheet

taboo 3 ban **4** no-no **6** banned, enjoin, forbid, outlaw **7** inhibit, obscene **9** forbidden, ineffable, interdict, off-limits, restraint **10** inhibition **11** restriction, unspeakable **12** interdiction

tabor 4 drum

tabulate 4 list **5** count, order **6** codify, figure, record **7** arrange **9** enumerate **11** systematize

tabulation 4 list **5** chart, tally **6** record **7** account

tabula ____ 4 rasa

tacit 6 silent, unsaid **7** assumed, implied **8** implicit, inferred, unspoken **9** intimated, suggested **10** subtextual, undeclared, underlying, understood **11** acquiescent, unexpressed **12** inarticulate

taciturn 4 dumb **6** silent **7** laconic **8** reserved, reticent, wordless **9** secretive **11** tight-lipped **12** closemouthed

Tacitus work 7 Annales **8** Dialogus, Germania **9** Historiae

tack 3 pin, yaw **4** beat, brad, gear, join, nail, stay, turn **5** baste, reach, shift **6** attach, course, double, stitch, swerve, turn up, zigzag **7** tangent **8** put about **9** come about, deviation **10** alteration, deflection, digression, sea biscuit **11** ship biscuit **12** pilot biscuit

tackle 3 cat, rig **4** gear, sack **6** outfit, take on, take up **7** halyard, lineman, rigging **8** set about **9** apparatus, equipment, machinery, undertake **10** footballer, linebacker, plunge into **13** paraphernalia

tacky 5 cheap, crude, dingy, dowdy, gaudy, messy, seedy, ratty, tatty **6** blowsy, frowsy, frumpy, kitsch, shabby, sleazy, sloppy, sticky, frumpy, tawdry, untidy, vulgar **7** run-down, unkempt **8** adhesive, frumpish, slovenly **9** inelegant, tasteless, unstylish **10** down-at-heel, threadbare

tact 5 poise, touch **6** acumen **7** address, finesse, suavity **8** civility, courtesy, delicacy, urbanity **9** diplomacy, politesse **10** adroitness, politeness, smoothness **11** savoir faire, sensitivity

tactful 5 civil, suave **6** adroit, urbane **7** politic **8** delicate, discreet, polished **9** courteous, sensitive **10** diplomatic, perceptive, thoughtful **11** considerate

tactic 4 hoax, plan, play, ploy, ruse, scam **5** dodge, feint, means, stunt, trick **6** device, gambit, method **7** sleight **8** approach, artifice, maneuver, strategy **9** procedure, stratagem

tactical 7 politic, prudent **9** advisable, expedient, strategic

tactics 4 plan **6** method, scheme **8** maneuver, playbook, strategy **9** stratagem

tactile 8 palpable, tangible **9** touchable

taction 4 feel **5** touch **7** contact **9** palpation

tactless 4 rude **5** blunt, crude, inept **6** candid, clumsy, gauche **7** awkward **8** impolite **9** impolitic, maladroit **10** indiscreet **11** insensitive

tad 3 bit, boy, lad, son **4** lick, mite, snap, spot, whit **5** child, crumb, shade, sonny, speck **6** laddie, nipper, shaver **7** smidgen **8** fraction

tadpole 8 polliwog, pollywog

taffy 5 candy **8** flattery

tag 3 bit, dog, end **4** cost, flag, game, logo, mark, name, tail **5** aglet, brand, label, price, trail **6** append, charge, follow, select, shadow, slogan, tassel, tatter, ticket **7** license, run down **8** graffito, identify, insignia

tagline 5 motto **6** byword, slogan

Tahiti ***city:*** **7** Papeete ***painter:*** **7** Gauguin (Paul) ***war god:*** **3** Oro

tail 3 dog, end, tag **4** butt, rear **5** hound, stalk **6** follow, pursue, shadow **7** hind end, rear end **8** backside, buttocks **9** posterior ***bone:*** **6** coccyx ***relating to:*** **6** caudal ***short:*** **4** scut

tailed 7 caudate

tailor 3 fit, hem, sew **4** suit **5** adapt, alter, style **7** fashion **8** clothier, seamster **11** haberdasher

tailor-made 6 fitted, suited **7** bespoke, fitting **8** suitable **10** well-suited **11** appropriate

taint 3 rot **4** blot, blur, foul, harm, hurt, smut, soil, spot, turn, vice **5** brand, cloud, color, decay, dirty, fault, smear, spoil, stain, sully, touch **6** befoul, darken, defile, poison, smudge, smutch **7** blacken, blemish, corrupt, pollute, putrefy, tarnish **8** besmirch, discolor **9** discredit **10** adulterate, stigmatize **11** contaminate

taipan 5 snake **8** merchant **11** businessman

Taiwan 7 Formosa ***capital:*** **6** Taipei ***channel:*** **5** Bashi ***city:*** **6** T'ai-nan **8** Pan-ch'iao, T'ai-chung **9** Kao-hsiung ***language:*** **8** Mandarin ***leader:*** **13** Chiang Kai-shek ***mountain:*** **6** Yü Shan

Tajikistan ***capital:*** **8** Dushanbe ***monetary unit:*** **5** diram **6** somoni ***monetary unit, former:*** **5** ruble, tanga ***mountain, range:*** **6** Pamirs **9** Communism (Peak), Trans Alai **10** Revolution (Peak) ***neighbor:*** **5** China **10** Kyrgyzstan, Uzbekistan **11** Afghanistan ***river:*** **8** Amu Dar'ya, Syr Dar'ya

Taj Mahal 9 mausoleum ***builder:*** **9** Shah Jahan ***site:*** **4** Agra

take 3 cop, get, nab **4** glom, grab **5** annex, catch, seize, steal, swipe **6** endure, gather, obtain, secure **7** capture, receive **8** proceeds, receipts ***account of:*** **6** notice ***advantage of:*** **5** abuse **7** exploit ***after:*** **6** follow **8** resemble ***apart:*** **7** analyze, dissect **9** dismantle ***care:*** **6** beware ***care of:*** **3** fix **4** tend **5** nurse **6** attend ***exception:*** **6** object ***five:*** **4** rest **5** break, relax ***from:*** **7** deprive, detract **8** subtract ***it easy:*** **5** relax ***on the:*** **7** corrupt, crooked ***part:*** **4** join **5** share **11** participate ***place:*** **5** occur **6** happen ***to task:*** **5** scold **7** reprove ***turns:*** **9** alternate ***unawares:*** **8** surprise

take away 4 grab **5** wrest **6** arrest, commit, deduct, detach, detain, remove, revoke **7** deprive, detract **8** diminish, discount, minimize, subtract, withdraw

take back 5 unsay **6** abjure, recall, recant, return, revoke **7** replace, restore, retract, swallow **8** forswear, withdraw **9** repossess

take down 4 note **5** lower, write **6** humble, record, reduce **7** deflate **8** dismount **9** dismantle **11** disassemble

take in 3 con **4** dupe, fool, furl, jail **5** admit, bluff, board, house, trick **6** absorb, accept, arrest, attend, betray, delude, embody **7** beguile, compass, contain, deceive, embrace, include, involve, mislead, observe, receive, shelter, snooker, subsume **8** flimflam, hoodwink, perceive **9** apprehend, bamboozle, encompass, four-flush **10** assimilate, comprehend, understand **11** double-cross

take off 2 go **4** doff, exit, quit, soar **5** leave,

scram **6** begone, deduct, depart, remove, set out **7** pull out, skiddoo, vamoose **8** clear out, discount, hightail, light out, subtract, withdraw **9** skedaddle

takeoff 5 spoof **6** launch, parody, satire, send-up **7** lampoon **8** travesty **9** burlesque **10** caricature ***area:*** **3** pad **6** runway

take on 3 don **4** face, hire, meet **5** adopt, annex, fight **6** accept, append, assume, attack, battle, employ, engage, strike, tackle **7** contest, embrace, espouse, venture **8** endeavor, set about **9** encounter, undertake

take out 4 date, dele, kill, omit **5** loose, whack **6** deduct, excise, remove **7** destroy, release, unleash **8** discount, knock off, separate, subtract, withdraw, withhold **9** eliminate **10** annihilate

take over 5 seize, spell, usurp **6** assume **7** capture, relieve

take up 3 use **4** fill, open **5** adopt, begin, enter, raise, renew, set to, start **6** absorb, accept, assume, gather, occupy, resume, shrink, tackle **7** embrace, espouse, kick off, restart, shorten, tighten **8** commence, continue, initiate **10** recommence

talc 6 powder **8** steatite **9** soapstone

tale 3 fib, lie **4** myth, saga, yarn **5** fable, rumor, story **6** canard, legend **7** fiction **8** anecdote **9** narration, narrative

talebearer 3 rat **4** fink **5** yenta **6** canary, gossip, snitch **7** rat fink, tattler **8** busybody, gossiper, informer, quidnunc, squealer, telltale **9** informant **10** newsmonger, tattletale **11** rumormonger, stool pigeon **12** blabbermouth **13** scandalmonger

talent 4 bent, gift, head, nose **5** craft, dowry, flair, forte, knack, skill **6** genius **7** ability, aptness, faculty **8** aptitude **9** endowment, expertise

talented 4 able **6** clever, expert, gifted **8** skillful

Tale of Two Cities, A *author:* 7 Dickens (Charles) ***character:*** **5** Lucie (Manette) **6** Carton (Sidney), Darnay (Charles) **7** Defarge (Madame), Manette (Alexander)

Tales of a Traveller author 6 Irving (Washington)

Tales of a Wayside Inn author 10 Longfellow (Henry Wadsworth)

Tales of Hoffman composer 9 Offenbach (Jacques)

talisman 4 juju, luck **5** charm **6** amulet, fetish, grigri, mascot, scarab **7** periapt **8** grisgris **10** phylactery

Talisman author 5 Scott (Walter)

talk 3 gab, rap, yak **4** blab, buzz, chat, chin, yarn **5** prate, rumor, run on, speak, utter, voice **6** babble, gabble, gossip, parley, patter, report, speech **7** address, chatter, declaim, hearsay, lecture, prattle **8** colloquy, converse, dialogue, harangue **9** discourse, utterance **10** discussion **12** conversation ***about:*** **7** discuss ***back:*** **4** sass ***empty:*** **3** gas **6** hot air **7** bombast ***foolish:*** **4** bunk **6** babble **7** chatter, palaver ***indistinctly:*** **6** mumble, mutter ***over:*** **7** discuss ***shop:*** **5** argot ***slowly:*** **5** drawl ***small:*** **6** banter **8** chitchat **10** persiflage ***wildly:*** **4** rant, rave

talkative 4 glib **5** gabby, vocal **6** chatty, fluent **7** gossipy, voluble **9** garrulous **10** loquacious **13** communicative

talk over 6 debate **7** discuss, hash out **8** consider **9** thrash out **10** deliberate

talky 5 gabby, windy, wordy **6** chatty, prolix **7** verbose, voluble

tall 4 high, long **5** lanky, large, lofty, rangy **6** absurd **7** pompous **8** towering **9** high-flown **10** far-fetched **11** skyscraping **12** altitudinous

tallow 3 fat **4** lard, suet **6** grease

tally 3 tab **4** jibe, list, tale **5** agree, count, match, score, total **6** accord, census, number, reckon, square **7** account, balance, catalog, compute, conform, itemize **8** check off, register, tabulate **9** agreement, catalogue, enumerate, harmonize, inventory, reckoning **10** complement, correspond

talon 4 claw, hand **5** stock **6** finger

talus 5 ankle, scree, slope **9** anklebone **10** astragalus

tam 3 cap

Tamar *brother:* 7 Absalom ***father:*** **5** David **7** Absalom ***father-in-law:*** **5** Judah ***half brother:*** **5** Amnon ***seducer:*** **5** Amnon ***son:*** **5** Perez, Zerah

tamarisk 9 salt cedar

tambour 3 cup **4** drum **9** embroider **10** embroidery

Tamburlaine the Great author 7 Marlowe (Christopher)

tame 4 bust, dull, meek, mild **5** break, train, vapid **6** bridle, docile, gentle, humble, soften, subdue **7** harness, insipid, reclaim, subdued **8** domestic, familiar, obedient **9** tractable **10** housebreak, submissive **11** domesticate, housebroken **12** domesticated

Taming of the Shrew, The *character:* 6 Bianca **8** Baptista **9** Katharina, Petruchio ***locale:*** **5** Padua

Tammany boss 5 Tweed (William)

Tammuz's lover 6 Ishtar

tam-o'-shanter 3 cap

tamp 3 ram **4** pack **5** pound, press, stuff

tampion 4 plug **5** cover

tan 3 sun, taw **4** beat, ecru, flog, whip **5**

beige, brown, taupe, tawny, toast **6** bronze, darken, thrash **7** biscuit

Tan novel 11 Joy Luck Club (The) **15** Kitchen God's Wife (The) **19** Bonesetter's Daughter (The)

tanager 7 redbird

Tancred, Tancredi *beloved:* 8 Clorinda ***composer:* 7** Rossini (Gioacchino) ***father:* 3** Odo ***mother:* 4** Emma ***victim:* 8** Clorinda

tandem 4 pair **7** bicycle, concert **8** carriage

tang 3 nip **4** bite, fang, odor, ring, zest **5** aroma, clang, prong, sapor, savor, shank, smack, taste, trace **6** flavor, relish **8** piquancy, pungency, sapidity **9** spiciness

tangible 4 real **7** tactile **8** concrete, material, palpable, physical, sensible **9** corporeal, touchable **10** detectable, observable, phenomenal **11** appreciable, discernible, perceptible, substantial

tangle 3 mat, web **4** foul, knot, maze, mesh, shag **5** ravel, skein, snare, snarl **6** entrap, hamper, jumble, jungle, morass, muddle, pileup, raffle **7** dispute, embroil, ensnare, ensnarl, involve, thicket **8** obstruct **9** implicate **10** complicate **11** altercation, predicament **12** complication

Tanglewood Tales author 9 Hawthorne (Nathaniel)

tango 5 dance **8** circuity **11** indirection **13** deceitfulness

tangy 5 sharp **6** lively **7** piquant, pungent, zestful **9** flavorful

tank 3 vat **5** basin **7** cistern **8** aquarium **9** reservoir ***American:* 6** Abrams **7** Bradley, Sherman ***German:* 6** panzer ***part:* 6** turret

tankard 3 mug **5** stein, stoup **6** flagon **9** blackjack

tanked 3 lit **4** high, lost **5** drunk, lit up, oiled **6** bashed, blotto, bombed, failed, gave up, juiced, potted, soaked, soused, stewed, stoned, tanked, wasted, zonked **7** crocked, drunken, pickled, pie-eyed, sloshed, smashed, sottish **9** collapsed, plastered **10** inebriated, liquored up **11** intoxicated

tanker 4 ship **5** oiler

Tannhäuser *character:* 5 Venus **9** Elisabeth ***composer:* 6** Wagner (Richard) ***locale:* 8** Wartburg **9** Venusberg

tantalize 3 rag **4** bait, lure **5** tease, tempt **6** entice, needle **7** torment **9** frustrate

Tantalus *daughter:* 5 Niobe ***father:* 4** Zeus ***son:* 6** Pelops

tantamount 4 same **5** alike, equal **8** parallel, selfsame **9** duplicate, identical **10** equivalent **12** commensurate

tantara 5 blare **7** fanfare

tantivy 3 run **6** gallop

tantrum 3 fit **6** blowup **8** outburst, paroxysm **9** hysterics **10** conniption

Tanzania *capital:* 6 Dodoma **11** Dar es Salaam ***city:* 6** Arusha ***former name:* 10** Tanganyika ***island:* 5** Mafia, Pemba **8** Zanzibar ***lake:* 5** Rukwa **6** Malawi **8** Victoria **10** Tanganyika ***language:* 7** Swahili ***monetary unit:* 8** shilling ***mountain:* 11** Kilimanjaro ***neighbor:* 5** Congo, Kenya **6** Malawi, Rwanda, Uganda, Zambia **7** Burundi **10** Mozambique ***plain:* 9** Serengeti ***river:* 6** Kagera, Rufiji, Ruvuma **7** Pangani ***volcano:* 6** Lengai

Taoism founder 5 Laozi **6** Lao-tzu

tap 3 hit, pat **4** cock, draw, flap, name, plug, tick **5** chuck, draft, drain, nudge, touch, valve **6** faucet, select, siphon, spigot, strike **7** appoint, draw off, hydrant, percuss, petcock **8** drumbeat, half sole, nominate, stopcock **9** designate

tape 4 band, belt, bind **5** strip **6** fillet, ribbon **7** bandage ***kind:* 5** inkle **6** ferret **7** masking **8** adhesive ***machine:* 4** deck **8** recorder

taper 4 wane, wick **5** abate, close, draft, pinch, spire **6** candle, lessen, narrow, reduce **7** dwindle, glimmer **8** decrease, diminish

tapering 5 conic, spiry **6** spired, terete **7** conical **8** ensiform, fusiform, napiform, subulate **9** acuminate, attenuate **10** lanceolate

tapestry 5 arras, kilim **6** dossal **7** curtain, Gobelin, hanging ***pattern:* 7** cartoon ***subject:* 4** hunt **7** unicorn

Taphath's father 7 Solomon

tapioca 4 yuca **5** yucca **6** manioc **7** cassava, farinha, pudding

tapir 4 anta

taproom 3 bar, pub **4** café **6** bodega, saloon, tavern **7** cantina **8** dramshop **9** roadhouse

tapster 6 barman **7** barkeep, barmaid, skinker **9** barkeeper, bartender **10** mixologist

tar 3 gob **4** jack, salt, soil, swab **5** pitch, smear, stain, sully, taint **6** defile, hearty, sailor, seaman **7** asphalt, besmear, mariner, shipman **8** besmirch, creosote, deckhand, flatfoot **9** shellback

taradiddle 3 fib, lie **5** hooey, story, trash **6** bunkum, canard **7** baloney, falsity **8** claptrap, nonsense **9** falsehood **10** balderdash **13** prevarication

tarantella 5 dance

tarantula 6 spider **10** wolf spider

Taras Bulba author 5 Gogol (Nikolai)

tarboosh 3 fez, hat

tardy 4 dull, late, lazy, slow **7** belated, delayed, laggard, overdue **8** dilatory, sluggish **10** behindhand, delinquent, unpunctual

tare 4 seed, weed **5** vetch, weigh **6** darnel, weight **11** undesirable **13** counterweight

target **3** aim **4** butt, goal, mark, prey **5** aim at **6** object, quarry, victim **9** objective **11** sitting duck ***center:*** **8** bull's-eye ***shooter's:*** **10** clay pigeon

Tar Heel State **13** North Carolina

tariff **3** tax **4** cost, duty, levy, rate **5** price **6** charge, impost **7** tribute **10** assessment

Tarkington character **6** Penrod **10** Alice Adams

tarn **4** lake, pool

tarnish **3** dim, mar **4** dull, foul, harm, hurt, soil **5** dirty, muddy, smear, spoil, stain, sully, taint **6** damage, darken, defile, injure, smirch, smudge, smutch **7** begrime, besmear, blemish, vitiate **8** besmirch, discolor

taro **3** yam **4** eddo **5** aroid **6** yautia **7** dasheen, malanga ***product:*** **3** poi ***root:*** **4** eddo

tarpaulin **3** gob **4** jack, salt, swab **5** cover, sheet **6** hearty, sailor, seaman **7** mariner, shipman **9** shellback

tarpon **8** ladyfish **10** silverfish

tarry **3** lag **4** bide, drag, stay, wait **5** abide, dally, delay, visit **6** dawdle, linger, loiter, pitchy, remain **7** sojourn

tarsus **5** ankle

tart **3** pie **4** acid, bawd, moll, slut, sour **5** acerb, quean, sharp, tramp, trull, whore **6** biting, harlot, pastry **7** acerbic, cutting, piquant, pungent, tootsie **8** chess pie, strumpet **10** prostitute

tartar **5** argol **6** plaque **8** calculus

Tartar see **Tatar**

Tartuffe author **7** Molière

Tarzan ***chimpanzee:*** **7** Cheetah ***creator:*** **9** Burroughs (Edgar Rice) ***mate:*** **4** Jane ***son:*** **3** Boy **4** Jack **5** Korak

task **3** job **4** duty, lade, load, post, slog, toil, work **5** chare, chore, labor, stint **6** assign, burden, charge, detail, devoir **7** mission, project **8** business, encumber, function **9** challenge, dress down, reprimand **10** assignment, commission **11** undertaking **12** dressing-down

Tasmanian **4** wolf **5** devil ***capital:*** **6** Hobart ***pine:*** **4** Huon

tassel **3** tag **4** tuft **5** adorn **6** fringe **7** pendant, tzitzit **8** ornament **13** inflorescence

Tasso, Torquato ***patron:*** **4** Este (Alfonso II d') ***work:*** **6** Aminta **7** Rinaldo **18** Jerusalem Delivered

taste **3** eat, sip, try **4** tang, zest **5** savor, smack **6** flavor, liking, palate, relish **7** stomach **8** appetite, elegance, fondness, sapidity, soft spot, weakness **10** experience, partiality, preference, refinement **11** inclination ***kind:*** **4** salt, sour **5** sweet **6** bitter ***organ:*** **3** bud

tasteful **4** fine **7** elegant, genteel, refined, stylish **8** artistic, becoming **9** aesthetic

tasteless **4** dull, flat **5** bland, crass, gaudy, showy, stale, tacky, vapid **6** vulgar **7** insipid **8** off-color, unsavory **9** inelegant, savorless, unrefined **10** flavorless

tasty **5** sapid, yummy **6** dainty, delish, savory **8** luscious **9** delicious, flavorful, palatable, succulent, toothsome **10** appetizing, delectable, flavorsome **11** scrumptious

Tatar **6** Mongol, Turkic **7** Turkish **9** Mongolian ***leader:*** **4** Vatu

tattered **4** torn **5** dingy, seedy **6** frayed, ragged, ripped, shabby **7** raggedy, rundown, worn-out **10** bedraggled, threadbare **11** dilapidated

tattle **3** rat, wag, yak **4** blab, buzz, dish, talk, tell **5** clack, prate, rumor **6** gossip, inform, report, snitch, squeal **7** chatter, hearsay, prattle **8** chitchat **9** grapevine **11** scuttlebutt

tattletale see **talebearer**

tatty **5** cheap, dingy, dowdy, dumpy, seedy, tacky **6** beat-up, cheesy, paltry, scuzzy, shabby, shoddy, sleazy, trashy **7** run-down, scrubby **8** rubbishy **10** threadbare **11** dilapidated

taunt **3** jab **4** gibe, jeer, mock, quip, razz, skit, twit **5** scout, tease **6** deride, insult **7** affront, provoke **8** reproach, ridicule **9** challenge

taurine **6** bovine **8** bull-like

Taurus **4** bull ***star:*** **9** Aldebaran

taut **4** firm, snug, trim **5** rigid, tense, tight **6** corded **10** high-strung

tautology **8** iterance, pleonasm **9** iteration **10** redundancy, repetition

tavern **3** bar, inn, pub **4** café, dive **6** bistro, bodega, saloon **7** barroom, cantina, gin mill, taproom **8** alehouse, pothouse, wineshop **9** roadhouse **11** public house, rathskeller **12** watering hole **13** watering place

taverner **7** barkeep **8** boniface, publican **9** barkeeper, bartender, innkeeper **12** saloonkeeper

taw **3** tan **6** marble **7** partner

tawdry **4** loud **5** cheap, gaudy, tacky **6** brazen, flashy, garish, tinsel **7** chintzy, glaring, ignoble **9** brummagem, dime-store **12** meretricious

tawny **3** tan **4** buff **5** beige, brown, sandy **6** copper, tanned

tax **4** cess, duty, lade, levy, load, onus, scot, toll **5** drain, tithe **6** assess, burden, cumber, impost, saddle, strain, tariff, weight **7** tribute **8** encumber **10** imposition ***agency:*** **3** IRS ***feudal:*** **7** scutage, tallage ***kind:*** **4** geld **5** sales, tithe **6** excise, income **8** property **9** ad valorem, surcharge ***on salt:*** **7** gabelle ***rate:*** **10** assessment

taxi 3 cab, car **4** hack **5** cyclo

taxi driver 5 cabby **6** cabbie, hackie **7** hackman

taxing 5 tough **6** trying **7** exigent, onerous, wearing **8** exacting, grievous, grueling **9** demanding, difficult **10** burdensome, oppressive

Taygeta *father:* 5 Atlas ***mother:* 7** Pleione ***sisters:* 8** Pleiades

tazza 3 cup **4** vase

Tchaikovsky, Pyotr Ilyich *ballet:* 8 Swan Lake **10** Nutcracker (The) **14** Sleeping Beauty ***opera:* 12** Eugene Onegin **13** Queen of Spades (The)

tea 5 party **6** repast **8** beverage **9** reception ***black:* 5** bohea, pekoe **8** souchong ***box:* 5** caddy ***cake:* 6** cookie ***genus:* 4** Thea ***herbal:* 6** ptisan, tisane ***kind:* 4** herb, Java **5** Assam, black, bohea, green, hyson, pekoe **6** Ceylon, congou, oolong **7** cambric, rooibos **8** Earl Grey, souchong **9** chamomile, sassafras **10** Darjeeling

teach 5 coach, edify, guide, train, tutor **6** impart, school **7** educate, instill, profess **8** instruct **9** enlighten, inculcate **12** indoctrinate

teacher 4 guru, prof **5** coach, guide, tutor **6** docent, master, mentor, pedant **7** maestro, trainer **8** educator **9** pedagogue, preceptor, professor **10** instructor **12** schoolmaster ***Hindu:* 5** swami ***Jewish:* 5** rabbi, rebbe ***Muslim:* 6** mullah ***organization:* 3** NEA ***religious:* 9** catechist **10** mystagogue

Tea for Two composer 7 Youmans (Vincent)

team 4 band, club, crew, gang, join, pair, side, yoke **5** group, squad, troop, wagon **6** stable, troupe **8** carriage ***baseball:* 4** nine ***basketball:* 4** five **7** quintet ***football:* 6** eleven ***kind:* 2** JV **6** jayvee **7** varsity

teamster 6 driver **7** trucker

tear 3 cry, cut, fly, rip, run **4** bolt, claw, dash, drop, flaw, gash, hole, lash, pull, race, rend, rift, rive, rush, slit, snag, weep **5** chase, hurry, shoot, shred, slash, speed, split, spree **6** career, charge, course, sunder, tatter, wrench **7** droplet, fissure, rupture **8** lacerate **10** laceration

tear down 4 raze, ruin, slur **5** knock, smash, smear, wreck **6** defame, malign, vilify **7** asperse, traduce, destroy, shatter, slander **8** demolish **9** denigrate, disparage, take apart **10** annihilate, calumniate **11** disassemble

tearful 3 sad **5** misty, moist, weepy **6** crying, watery, woeful **7** bawling, sobbing, weeping **8** mournful, pathetic **9** lamenting, sniveling, sorrowful **10** blubbering, lachrymose

tear-jerking 5 mushy **6** drippy, sticky **7** maudlin, mawkish **8** touching **9** schmaltzy **11** sentimental

teary-eyed 5 blear, moist

tease 3 bug, kid, rag, rib, rip **4** bait, coax, comb, gibe, jive, josh, ride, tear, twit **5** annoy, chaff, chivy, harry, shred, taunt, worry **6** cajole, harass, needle, pester, pick on, plague **7** bedevil, torment **8** ridicule **9** tantalize

teaser 4 lure **5** promo **7** preview

teched 3 mad **4** daft **5** batty, crazy **6** insane **7** cracked, lunatic **8** demented

technicality 6 detail **8** loophole

technique 4 mode **5** modus **6** method, system **8** approach **9** procedure **13** modus operandi

ted 5 strew **6** spread **7** scatter

tedious 3 dry **4** dull **5** ho-hum, stale **6** boring, dreary, trying **7** irksome, operose **8** drudging, tiresome **9** dryasdust, wearisome **10** monotonous **11** mind-numbing **13** uninteresting

tedium 4 yawn **5** ennui **7** boredom **8** doldrums, dullness, monotony, sameness

teem 4 flow, pour **5** crawl, empty, swarm **6** abound, bustle **7** produce **9** pullulate

teeming 4 lush, rife **5** alive **6** aswarm **7** replete **8** abundant, swarming, thronged **9** abounding **11** overflowing

teen 5 youth **10** adolescent

tee off 4 open **5** begin, drive, enter, start **8** commence, initiate

teeter 4 rock, sway **5** waver **6** falter, seesaw, wobble **9** vacillate

telamon 5 atlas ***counterpart:* 8** caryatid

Telamon *brother:* 6 Peleus ***father:* 6** Aeacus ***half-brother:* 6** Phocus ***son:* 4** Ajax **6** Teucer

Telegonus *father:* 7 Ulysses **8** Odysseus ***mother:* 5** Circe

telegraph 4 wire **5** cable **6** signal ***code:* 5** Morse ***inventor:* 5** Morse (Samuel F. B.)

Telemachus *father:* 7 Ulysses **8** Odysseus ***mother:* 8** Penelope

telephone 4 buzz, call, cell, dial, ring **6** mobile, ring up **8** cordless, landline ***inventor:* 4** Bell (Alexander Graham)

Telephus *father:* 8 Heracles, Hercules ***mother:* 4** Auge

telescope 5 glass **6** finder **7** compact **8** compress, condense, contract, spyglass **9** reflector, refractor

television 2 TV **4** tube **5** video **8** boob tube, idiot box ***antenna:* 10** rabbit ears ***award:* 4** Emmy ***British:* 5** telly ***children's:* 6** kidvid ***frequency:* 3** UHF, VHF ***interference:* 4** snow ***network:* 3** ABC, BBC, CBS, Fox, HBO, NBC, NET, PBS, QVC, TNT **4**

ESPN, INHD ***pioneer:*** **5** Baird (John Logie) **8** De Forest (Lee), Goldmark (Peter Carl), Zworykin (Vladimir) **10** Farnsworth (Philo T.) ***program:*** **4** news **5** pilot, rerun **6** series, sitcom **7** western **8** game show, talk show **9** broadcast, docudrama, soap opera **11** infomercial ***tube:*** **9** kinescope

tell 3 rat, say **4** blab, clue **5** count, mound, order, spill, state, utter **6** advise, betray, fill in, inform, notify, relate, report, retail, reveal, tattle **7** confess, declare, divulge, narrate, recount **8** disclose, give away **9** come clean

teller 5 clerk **6** banker **7** cashier, counter **8** informer, narrator **12** communicator

telling 5 solid, sound, valid **6** cogent **7** weighty **8** powerful **9** effective **10** convincing, expressive

tell off 4 flay, rate, ream **5** chide, scold **6** berate, rebuke **7** bawl out, chew out, reprove, upbraid **8** admonish, call down **9** dress down, excoriate, reprimand **10** take to task, tongue-lash, vituperate

tell on 6 inform, snitch, tattle

telltale 3 cue **4** clue, fink, lead, sign **5** proof **6** canary, gossip, signal, snitch, tip-off **7** rat fink, tattler **8** evidence, gossiper, informer, quidnunc, signpost, squealer **9** indicator **10** indication, newsmonger **12** blabbermouth, gossipmonger **13** scandalmonger

telluric 6 earthy **7** earthly, mundane, terrene, worldly **9** sublunary **11** terrestrial

tellurium symbol 2 Te

temblor 5 quake, shake, shock **6** tremor **8** upheaval **10** aftershock, earthquake

temerarious 4 rash **6** daring **8** heedless, reckless **9** audacious, daredevil, foolhardy, venturous **11** adventurous, venturesome **13** adventuresome

temerity 4 gall **5** cheek, nerve **6** daring **8** audacity, chutzpah, rashness **9** assurance, brashness, hardihood, hardiness **10** effrontery **12** recklessness **13** foolhardiness

temper 4 heat, mean, mind, mood, tone, vein **5** admix, alloy, anger, blood, grain, humor, trend **6** anneal, attune, dander, dilute, govern, hackle, makeup, medium, season, soften, spirit, strain **7** courage, mollify, passion, quality, toughen **8** hardness, moderate, modulate, restrain **9** character, composure, condition **10** resilience, resiliency **11** disposition, personality

temperament 4 mood **5** humor **6** manner, makeup, mettle, nature **9** character **10** complexion **11** disposition, personality

temperamental 5 moody **6** ornery, touchy **7** erratic **8** contrary, ticklish, unstable, variable, volatile **9** mercurial **10** capricious, changeable, high-strung, inconstant **13** unpredictable

temperance 8 sobriety **9** austerity, restraint **10** abstinence, continence, moderation, self-denial **11** self-control ***advocate of:*** **6** Nation (Carry) **7** Willard (Frances)

temperate 4 calm, even, mild, soft **5** balmy, sober **6** modest, steady **7** clement **8** discreet, moderate **9** abstinent, continent **10** abstemious, controlled, reasonable, restrained **11** abstentious

temperature 4 heat, mood **5** fever **6** degree, warmth **7** hotness **8** coldness **9** intensity

tempered 7 diluted, treated **8** adjusted, hardened, softened **9** mitigated, moderated, qualified **12** strengthened

tempest 3 din **4** blow, gale, rage, wind **5** furor, hurly, storm **6** hubbub, squall, tumult, uproar **8** brouhaha, foofaraw **9** commotion, hurricane **10** hullabaloo, hurly-burly

Tempest character 5 Ariel **6** Alonso **7** Caliban, Miranda **8** Prospero **9** Ferdinand

tempestuous 4 wild **5** roily, rough **6** raging, stormy **7** furious, moiling, violent **8** blustery **9** turbulent **10** tumultuous

temple 4 fane **6** church **9** synagogue **10** tabernacle ***ancient:*** **8** pantheon ***Aztec:*** **8** teocalli ***Buddhist:*** **2** ta **3** wat ***Eastern:*** **6** pagoda ***Greek:*** **9** Parthenon ***sanctuary:*** **4** naos **5** cella, Nemea **6** adytum **10** penetralia

tempo 4 pace, rate, time **5** speed **6** rhythm ***fast:*** **6** presto, vivace **7** allegro ***moderate:*** **7** andante ***slow:*** **5** grave, lento **6** adagio

temporal 3 lay **5** civil **6** carnal **7** earthly, mundane, profane, secular, worldly **13** chronological, synchronistic

temporary 6 acting **7** Band-Aid, interim **8** fleeting **9** ad interim, makeshift, transient **10** short-lived, substitute, transitory **11** provisional

temporize 5 delay, stall, yield **6** palter **7** draw out **8** gain time **10** equivocate **11** prevaricate

tempt 3 woo **4** bait, lure, risk, sway **5** court, decoy **6** allure, entice, entrap, invite, lead on, seduce **7** provoke **8** inveigle **9** tantalize

temptation 4 bait, lure, trap **5** decoy, siren, snare **6** allure, come-on **9** seduction **10** attraction, enticement

tempting 8 alluring **9** appealing, delicious, seductive **10** attractive, come-hither

temptress 4 vamp **5** siren **7** Lorelei **10** seductress **11** femme fatale

ten *cents:* **4** dime ***combining form:*** **3** dec, dek **4** deca, deka **5** decem ***dollars:*** **7** sawbuck ***mills:*** **4** cent ***thousand:*** **6** myriad ***years:*** **6** decade

tenable 5 sound **8** rational **10** defendable, defensible, reasonable **12** maintainable
tenacious 3 set **4** fast, firm, true **5** fixed, stout **6** dogged, secure, sturdy **8** adhesive, clinging, resolute, stalwart, stubborn **9** obstinate, steadfast **10** persistent **11** persevering
tenacity 4 grit, guts **5** moxie, pluck, spunk **6** mettle, spirit **7** courage **8** firmness **10** resolution **11** persistence **13** determination
tenant 6 holder, lessee, lodger, renter **7** boarder, dweller **8** occupant ***feudal:*** **6** vassal
tenantable 7 livable **9** habitable **11** inhabitable
Ten Commandments 9 Decalogue ***director:*** **7** DeMille (Cecil B.)
tend 4 lean, mind, till, work **5** guard, labor, nurse, serve, watch **6** foster **7** babysit, care for, conduce, incline, nurture, oversee **8** minister **9** cultivate, look after, watch over
tendency 4 bent, bias **5** drift, tenor, trend **7** current, leaning **8** penchant **10** partiality, proclivity, propensity **11** disposition, inclination **12** predilection
tendentious 6 biased **7** colored, partial **8** one-sided, partisan **10** prejudiced
tender 3 bid **4** fond, mild, soft, sore, warm **5** green, money, mushy, offer **6** extend, gentle, humane, loving, submit, touchy **7** fragile, lenient, painful, present, proffer, propose **8** delicate, proposal **9** sensitive, succulent **11** considerate, warmhearted **12** affectionate **13** compassionate
tenderfoot 4 colt, punk, tiro, tyro **6** novice, rookie **7** amateur **8** beginner, freshman, neophyte, newcomer **9** cheechako, fledgling, greenhorn, novitiate **10** apprentice
tenderhearted 6 kindly **11** sympathetic **13** compassionate
Tender Is the Night author 10 Fitzgerald (F. Scott)
tendon 4 band, cord **5** nerve, sinew **6** leader **9** hamstring
tendril 4 curl, vine **6** cirrus, spiral **7** ringlet
tenebrific 4 dark, glum, gray, grim **5** black, bleak, sable **6** dismal, dreary, gloomy, somber, sombre **8** desolate, funereal **10** depressing, oppressive **11** dispiriting
tenebrous 3 dim **4** dark, deep, dusk, hazy **5** dusky, foggy, muddy, murky, vague **6** cloudy, gloomy **7** cryptic, obscure, shadowy, unclear **9** ambiguous, lightless **10** caliginous
tenement 4 flat **6** rental, walk-up, warren **7** lodging, rookery **8** building **9** apartment, residence
tenet 3 ism **5** canon, creed, dogma **6** belief **7** paradox **8** doctrine **9** principle **10** empiricism
tenfold 7 decuple
Tennessee *capital:* **9** Nashville ***city:*** **7** Memphis **9** Knoxville **11** Chattanooga ***college, university:*** **10** Vanderbilt ***mountain, range:*** **7** Lookout **10** Great Smoky **13** Clingmans Dome ***nickname:*** **9** Volunteer (State) ***public works:*** **3** TVA **9** Norris Dam ***river:*** **9** Tennessee **11** Mississippi ***state bird:*** **11** mockingbird ***state flower:*** **4** iris ***state tree:*** **11** tulip poplar
tennis *award:* **8** Davis Cup ***item:*** **3** net **4** ball **6** racket **7** racquet ***kind:*** **5** table **7** doubles, singles **8** platform ***score:*** **4** ad-in, love **5** add-in, ad-out, deuce **6** add-out ***serve:*** **3** acc ***shoe:*** **7** sneaker ***stroke:*** **3** cut, lob **4** chop, drop **5** serve, slice **6** volley **8** backhand, forehand ***term:*** **3** let, set **5** court, fault **7** service **9** advantage, backcourt
tennis champ 4 Ashe (Arthur), Borg (Bjorn), Cash (Pat), Graf (Steffi), King (Billie Jean), Noah (Yannick), Wade (Virginia) **5** Budge (Don), Chang (Michael), Court (Margaret Smith), Evert (Chris), Gómez (Andres), Henin (Justine), Laver (Rod), Lendl (Ivan), Nadal (Rafael), Perry (Fred), Safin (Marat), Seles (Monica), Stich (Michael), Vilas (Guillermo), Wills (Helen) **6** Agassi (André), Austin (Tracy), Becker (Boris), Casals (Rosie), Edberg (Stefan), Fraser (Neale), Gibson (Althea), Hewitt (Lleyton), Hingis (Martina), Kramer (Jack), Muster (Thomas), Pierce (Mary), Stolle (Fred), Tilden (Bill) **7** Connors (Jimmy), Courier (Jim), Emerson (Roy), Federer (Roger), Lacoste (René), McEnroe (John), Nastase (Ilie), Novótna (Jana), Sampras (Pete) **8** Connolly (Maureen), González (Pancho), Martínez (Conchita), Newcombe (John), Rosewall (Ken), Sabatini (Gabriela), Wilander (Mats), Williams (Serena, Venus) **9** Davenport (Lindsay), Goolagong (Evonne) **10** Mandlikova (Hana) **11** Navratilova (Martina)
Tennyson poem 4 Maud **7** Ulysses **8** Princess (The), Tiresias **10** Enoch Arden, In Memoriam **12** Locksley Hall **23** Charge of the Light Brigade (The)
tenor 4 mood, tone **5** drift, voice **6** singer **7** meaning, purport **8** tendency **9** substance ***American:*** **5** Lanza (Mario) **6** Hadley (Jerry), Peerce (Jan), Tucker (Richard) **9** McCracken (James) ***Belgian:*** **6** Maison (René) ***Canadian:*** **7** Vickers (Jon) ***Czech:*** **6** Slezak (Leo) ***Danish:*** **8** Melchior (Lauritz) ***English:*** **5** Pears (Peter) ***German:*** **10** Wun-

derlich (Fritz) ***Irish*** **9** McCormack (John) ***Italian:*** **5** Gigli (Beniamino) **6** Alagna (Roberto), Caruso (Enrico) **7** Bocelli (Andrea), Corelli (Franco) **8** Bergonzi (Carlo) **9** del Monaco (Mario), di Stefano (Giuseppe), Pavarotti (Luciano) ***Spanish:*** **5** Kraus (Alfredo) **7** Domingo (Plácido) **8** Carreras (José) ***Swedish:*** **5** Gedda (Nicolai) **8** Björling (Jussi) **9** Bjoerling (Jussi)

tenpins 7 bowling

tense 4 edgy, taut **5** nervy, rigid, tight, wired **6** uneasy **7** anxious, jittery, nervous, restive, uptight **8** strained, stressed **10** high-strung ***grammatical:*** **4** past **6** future **7** perfect, present **8** preterit **9** preterite **10** pluperfect **11** progressive

tension 5 state, steam **6** nerves, strain, stress, unease **7** anxiety, balance **8** edginess, pressure, tautness **9** agitation, hostility, stiffness **10** discomfort, opposition, uneasiness **11** nervousness, uptightness

tent 4 camp **6** canopy, encamp, laager **7** bivouac, shelter ***kind:*** **3** ger, pup **4** yurt **5** Baker, tepee **6** teepee **7** marquee **8** pavilion, umbrella ***maker:*** **4** Omar ***material:*** **6** canvas ***part:*** **3** fly, guy, peg **4** pole **5** stake

tentacle 3 arm **6** barbel, feeler

tentative 4 test **5** chary, loath, probe, trial **6** averse **7** halting **8** hesitant, insecure **9** diffident, makeshift, reluctant, uncertain, undecided, unsettled **10** irresolute **11** conditional, disinclined, problematic, provisional

tenth 5 tithe ***combining form:*** **4** deci

tenuous 4 slim, thin, weak **5** reedy, shaky **6** feeble, flimsy, slight, stalky **7** fragile, sketchy, slender **8** gossamer **10** precarious **11** implausible **13** insubstantial, unsubstantial

tenure 4 term **6** estate **10** incumbency ***feudal:*** **7** burgage

tepid 4 mild, warm **7** warmish **8** lukewarm **9** apathetic **11** halfhearted, indifferent

tequila source 5 agave

terbium symbol 2 Tb

Terentia's husband 6 Cicero

Tereus *son:* 4 Itys ***wife:*** **6** Procne

tergiversate 3 haw, hem, rat **5** dodge, evade, hedge **6** defect, desert, waffle, weasel **7** abandon, shuffle **8** renounce, sidestep **9** pussyfoot, repudiate **10** apostatize, equivocate

term 3 dub, end **4** call, name, span, tour, word **5** label, spell, stint, title **6** detail, period, tenure **7** quarter, session **8** duration, semester **9** designate **10** conclusion, denominate, expression, limitation, particular **11** appellation, designation

termagant 5 harpy, scold, shrew, vixen **6** ogress, virago **8** fishwife, harridan **9** Xanthippe

terminable 6 finite

terminal 3 end, lag **4** last **5** anode, depot, fatal, final **6** finial, latest, latter, lethal **7** cathode, closing, extreme, station **8** eventual, hindmost, junction, ultimate **9** extremity **10** concluding ***negative:*** **7** cathode ***positive:*** **5** anode

terminate 2 ax **3** end **4** boot, drop, fire, halt, kill, quit, sack, stop **5** abort, cease, close, issue, leave **6** cut off, finish, wind up **7** abolish, dead-end, dismiss **8** complete, conclude, dissolve **9** determine, discharge **10** extinguish **11** assassinate, discontinue

terminology 4 cant **5** argot, idiom, lingo **6** jargon, patois **7** lexicon **8** language, shoptalk **10** vernacular, vocabulary **12** nomenclature

termite 5 alate **8** white ant

ternary 5 third **6** triple **9** threefold

Terpsichore see **Muse**

terrace 4 bank, deck, mesa, park, roof, step **5** bench, porch, shelf **6** street **7** balcony, sundeck **8** platform **9** promenade

terra-cotta 4 clay **7** pottery

terra firma 4 dirt, land, soil **5** earth **6** ground

terrain 4 area, land, turf **5** field **6** domain, ground, milieu, sphere **8** province **9** bailiwick, territory **10** topography **11** environment

terrapin 6 turtle

terrestrial 4 land **6** earthy, ground **7** earthly, mundane, worldly **8** everyday, ordinary, telluric, workaday **9** earthlike, planetary, sublunary **10** earthbound

terrible 4 dire **5** awful, dread **6** grisly, horrid **7** dreaded, fearful, ghastly, heinous, hideous, intense, macabre, vicious, violent **8** dreadful, gruesome, horrible, horrific, shocking, vehement **9** abhorrent, appalling, atrocious, frightful, harrowing, loathsome, monstrous **10** disastrous, formidable, horrendous, horrifying

terrier 3 dog ***kind:*** **3** fox **4** blue, bull, Skye **5** cairn, Irish, Welsh **6** Boston **8** Airedale, Lakeland **9** Yorkshire

terrific 5 boffo, socko, super, swell **6** superb **7** amazing, awesome **8** dreadful, dynamite, glorious **9** appalling, fantastic, frightful, marvelous, upsetting, wonderful **10** formidable, incredible **11** magnificent, sensational **13** extraordinary

terrify 5 alarm, scare **7** scarify, startle **8** affright, frighten **10** intimidate
terrifying 4 grim **5** scary **6** grisly, horrid **7** ghastly, hideous, macabre **8** alarming, dreadful, fearsome, gruesome, horrible, horrific, terrible **9** frightful **10** formidable, horrifying
territory 4 area, belt, land, turf, zone **5** field, route, state, tract **6** domain, region, sphere **7** country, demesne, terrain **8** conquest, district, dominion, province **9** bailiwick **10** borderland **12** jurisdiction
terror 4 fear **5** alarm, dread, panic, worry **6** dismay, fright, horror **7** scourge **9** nightmare **11** fearfulness, trepidation
terrorize 3 cow **5** alarm, bully, scare **6** coerce, fright, menace **7** scarify **8** browbeat, bulldoze, frighten, threaten **9** strong-arm **10** intimidate
terry 4 loop **5** cloth **6** fabric **12** Turkish towel
terse 4 curt **5** brief, crisp, pithy, short **6** abrupt **7** brusque, compact, concise, elegant, laconic, summary **8** polished, succinct **11** compendious, sententious, telegraphic **12** monosyllabic
tertiary 5 third
terza ____ 4 rima
tessera 3 die **4** tile **6** tablet, ticket
test 3 try **4** exam, quiz **5** assay, check, essay, final, proof, prove, taste, touch, trial, try on **6** sample, tryout, verify **7** confirm, examine, midterm **8** evaluate, gut check, sounding, trial run **9** benchmark, criterion **10** evaluation, experiment, touchstone **11** examination
testa 6 cupule **7** coating **8** envelope, seed coat, tegument **10** integument
testament 4 will **5** credo, creed, proof **7** tribute, witness **8** evidence **9** scripture **11** attestation **12** confirmation
tester 4 coin **6** canopy, prover **7** analyst, assayer **8** examiner **12** investigator
testifier 7 witness **8** deponent
testify 5 prove, swear **6** affirm, attest, depone, depose, evince **7** certify, witness **11** certificate
testimonial 5 proof **6** salute **7** tribute, witness **8** evidence, memorial, monument **9** affidavit, character, reference **11** attestation **12** appreciation, commendation, confirmation **13** commemoration
testimony 5 proof **6** avowal **7** witness **8** evidence **9** affidavit, authority **10** deposition, profession **11** affirmation, attestation, declaration **12** confirmation **13** corroboration, documentation
testy 4 edgy **5** cross, fussy, hasty **6** cranky, ornery, tetchy, touchy **7** fretful, grouchy, peevish **8** choleric **9** crotchety, irascible, irritable **10** ill-humored, out of sorts **12** cantankerous **13** quick-tempered
tetanus 7 lockjaw, trismus
tetchy see **testy**
tête-à-tête 4 chat, talk **5** à deux **7** private, vis-à-vis **8** causerie **10** face-to-face **12** conversation
tether 3 tie **4** bind, rope **5** cable, chain, stake **6** fasten, fetter, lariat, picket **8** restrain **9** restraint
Tethys ***daughters:*** **9** Oceanides ***father:*** **6** Uranus ***husband:*** **7** Oceanus ***mother:*** **4** Gaea **5** Terra
tetrad 4 four **7** quartet **8** foursome **10** quaternion
Teutonic 6 German **8** Germanic ***language:*** **5** Dutch **6** Danish, German, Gothic **7** English, Flemish, Frisian, Swedish **9** Afrikaans, Norwegian
Texas ***capital:*** **6** Austin ***city:*** **4** Waco **6** Dallas, El Paso **7** Houston **8** Amarillo **9** Arlington, Fort Worth **10** San Antonio ***college, university:*** **3** SMU **4** Rice **5** Lamar **6** Baylor **9** Texas Tech ***island:*** **5** Padre ***mountain:*** **9** Guadalupe (Peak) ***nickname:*** **8** Lone Star (State) ***park:*** **7** Big Bend ***river:*** **3** Red **5** Pecos **6** Brazos **8** Colorado **9** Rio Grande ***state bird:*** **11** mockingbird ***state flower:*** **10** bluebonnet ***state tree:*** **5** pecan
text 6 script
textbook 6 primer
textile 5 cloth **6** fabric ***dealer:*** **6** mercer ***machine:*** **8** calender ***pattern:*** **7** paisley **11** houndstooth ***shop:*** **7** mercery ***starch:*** **4** sago ***treat:*** **9** mercerize
texture 3 web **4** feel, hand, wale, woof **5** weave **6** fabric
Thackeray novel 9 Pendennis **10** Vanity Fair **11** Barry Lyndon, Henry Esmond
Thailand ***capital:*** **7** Bangkok ***city:*** **9** Chiang Mai ***former name:*** **4** Siam ***island:*** **6** Phuket ***monetary unit:*** **4** baht ***neighbor:*** **4** Laos **5** Burma **7** Myanmar **8** Cambodia, Malaysia ***river:*** **10** Chao Phraya ***sea:*** **7** Andaman
Thaïs 7 hetaera, hetaira **9** courtesan ***author:*** **6** Francc (Anatolc) ***composer:*** **8** Massenet (Jules) ***husband:*** **7** Ptolemy ***lover:*** **9** Alexander (the Great)
thalassic 6 marine **7** oceanic **8** maritime
Thalia see **Graces; Muse**
thallium symbol 2 Tl
Thanatopsis author 6 Bryant (William Cullen)
Thanatos 5 death ***brother:*** **6** Hypnos ***mother:*** **3** Nyx

thankful **4** glad **8** grateful **12** appreciative
thanks **5** grace **8** blessing **9** gratitude **11** benediction **12** appreciation, gratefulness
Thanksgiving **5** feast **7** holiday ***first celebrant:*** **6** Indian **7** Pilgrim ***food:*** **6** turkey
thatch **3** mop **4** hair, roof **5** cover
that is *Latin:* **5** id est
Thaumas ***daughter:*** **4** Iris **5** Aello, Harpy **7** Celaeno, Ocypete ***daughters:*** **7** Harpies ***father:*** **6** Pontus ***mother:*** **4** Gaea ***wife:*** **7** Electra
thaumaturgic **5** magic **6** Magian, mystic, witchy **7** magical **8** wizardly **9** marvelous **10** miraculous **11** necromantic **12** supernatural
thaumaturgy **5** magic **7** sorcery **8** cabbalah, kabbalah, witchery, wizardry **10** necromancy
thaw **4** melt **5** deice, relax **6** unbend **7** defrost, liquefy **8** dissolve, unfreeze **10** condescend, deliquesce
the **7** article ***French:*** **2** la, le, un **3** les, une ***German:*** **3** das, der, die, ein **4** eine ***Italian:*** **2** il, la **3** una, uno ***Spanish:*** **2** el, la, un **3** las, los, una, uno
Thea ***daughter:*** **6** Selene ***father:*** **6** Uranus ***husband:*** **8** Hyperion ***mother:*** **4** Gaea
theater **4** nabe **5** drama, stage **6** boards **9** playhouse **10** footlights ***award:*** **4** Obie, Tony ***district:*** **6** rialto ***drop:*** **5** scrim ***entrance:*** **5** foyer, lobby ***Greek:*** **5** odeum ***movie:*** **6** cinema **8** cineplex, megaplex **9** multiplex ***outdoor:*** **7** drive-in ***part:*** **3** box, pit **4** loge **5** apron, stage, wings **6** stalls **7** balcony, parquet **8** parterre **9** greenroom, mezzanine, orchestra **10** proscenium **11** dress circle, grand circle, royal circle, upper circle
theatrical **5** stagy **6** staged **8** dramatic, thespian **10** artificial, flamboyant, histrionic **11** dramaturgic **12** melodramatic ***agent:*** **6** Morris (William) ***device:*** **4** prop ***group:*** **6** troupe
Theban Eagle **6** Pindar
Thebes ***founder:*** **6** Cadmus ***king:*** **5** Laius **7** Oedipus ***queen:*** **5** Niobe **7** Jocasta
Theda ____ **4** Bara
theft **5** heist, pinch **6** holdup, piracy **7** break-in, larceny, robbery **8** burglary, stealing, thievery **9** pilferage ***combining form:*** **5** klept **6** klepto
theme **4** stem, text, tune **5** essay, lemma, motif, paper, point, topic, topos **6** burden, matter, melody, mythos, thesis **7** article, conceit, message, subject **8** argument **11** composition **12** dissertation
Themis ***father:*** **6** Uranus ***goddess of:*** **3** law **7** justice ***husband:*** **4** Zeus **7** Jupiter ***mother:*** **4** Gaea
then **4** also, anon, ergo, next, thus, when **5** again, hence, later **7** besides, further **8** moreover **9** therefore, thereupon **10** in addition **11** accordingly, furthermore **12** additionally, consequently
thence **4** away **7** thereof **9** from there, therefrom
Theogony poet **6** Hesiod
theologian ***American:*** **6** Merton (Thomas) **7** Edwards (Jonathan), Niebuhr (Reinhold), Tillich (Paul), Walther (Carl) ***Dutch:*** **6** Jansen (Cornelis) ***English:*** **4** Bede (Venerable) **5** Pusey (Edward), Watts (Isaac) **6** Alcuin, Wesley (John) **7** Langton (Stephen) **8** Pelagius, Wycliffe (John) ***French:*** **6** Calvin (John) **7** Abelard (Peter), William (of Auvergne, of Auxerre) **8** Maritain (Jacques), Sabatier (Auguste), Teilhard (de Chardin, Pierre) ***German:*** **6** Rahner (Karl) **7** Eckhart (Meister) **8** Albertus (Magnus) **9** Niemöller (Martin) **10** Bonhoeffer (Dietrich) ***Greek:*** **9** Zygomalas (Theodore) ***Italian:*** **6** Thomas (Aquinas) **7** Aquinas (Thomas), Socinus (Fausto, Laelius) ***Scottish:*** **10** Duns Scotus (John) ***Spanish:*** **6** Suárez (Francisco) **7** Vitoria (Francisco de) **8** Servetus (Michael) ***Swedish:*** **9** Soderblom (Nathan) ***Swiss:*** **4** Küng (Hans) **5** Barth (Karl), Vinet (Alexandre-Rodolphe) **6** Calvin (John), Cauvin (Jean)
theological ***school:*** **8** seminary ***virtue:*** **4** hope **5** faith **7** charity
____ Theologica **5** Summa
theorbo **4** lute
theorem **3** law **4** rule **5** axiom **7** formula, inverse, stencil **8** converse **9** principle **10** principium **11** fundamental, proposition
theoretical **4** pure **5** ideal **8** abstract, academic, notional, unproved **11** conjectural, speculative **12** hypothetical **13** problematical, suppositional
theorize **5** guess **6** submit **7** suggest **9** formulate, postulate, speculate **10** conjecture **11** hypothesize
theory **7** perhaps, premise, surmise **8** supposal **10** conjecture, hypothesis **11** speculation, supposition ***astronomical:*** **7** big bang ***suffix:*** **3** ism
therapeutic **5** tonic **7** healing, helpful **8** curative, remedial, salutary, sanative **9** healthful, medicinal, vulnerary, wholesome **10** beneficial, corrective **11** restorative **12** health-giving
therapy **9** treatment

therefore **4** ergo, then, thus **5** hence **6** hereat, thence **11** accordingly **12** consequently
therefrom **4** away **6** thence
thereupon **4** ergo, then, thus **6** at once, at that, thence **8** directly **9** right away, therefore, wherefore **11** accordingly, straightway **12** consequently
thermal unit **3** Btu **6** degree **7** calorie
thermometer **5** gauge **9** indicator ***kind:*** **7** Celsius, Réaumur **10** centigrade, Fahrenheit
thermos **5** dewar **10** Dewar flask
Theroux work **9** Saint Jack **13** Mosquito Coast (The) **14** Half Moon Street **18** Great Railway Bazaar (The)
Thersites' slayer **8** Achilles
thesaurus editor **5** Roget (Peter Mark)
Theseus ***beloved:*** **7** Ariadne ***father:*** **6** Aegeus ***mother:*** **6** Aethra ***slayer:*** **9** Lycomedes ***son:*** **10** Hippolytus ***victim:*** **6** Sciron **8** Minotaur **10** Procrustes ***wife:*** **7** Phaedra
thesis **5** essay, point, theme **6** belief **7** premise **8** downbeat, position, tractate, treatise **9** discourse, monograph, postulate, synthesis **10** contention, exposition **11** postulation, proposition, supposition **12** disquisition, dissertation
thespian **5** actor **6** mummer, player **7** actress, trouper **8** dramatic **9** performer **10** histrionic, theatrical **11** dramaturgic **12** impersonator, melodramatic
Thespis' forte **5** drama **7** tragedy
Thessalian hero **5** Jason **8** Achilles
Thetis **6** Nereid ***father:*** **6** Nereus ***husband:*** **6** Peleus ***mother:*** **5** Doris ***son:*** **8** Achilles
theurgist **5** witch **7** warlock **8** magician, sorcerer **12** wonder-worker
thew **4** beef **5** brawn, might, power, sinew, vigor **6** muscle **8** strength, vitality
thick **3** fat **4** wide **5** broad, bulky, burly, close, dense, dumpy, husky, squat, stout **6** chummy, chunky, packed, stocky **7** compact, crammed, crowded, viscous **8** familiar, heavyset, intimate **11** inspissated
thicken **3** set **4** blur, clot, jell **6** curdle **7** broaden, compact, congeal **8** condense **9** coagulate **10** inspissate **11** concentrate
thicket **4** bosk, bush, shaw, wood **5** clump, copse, grove, hedge **6** bosket, covert, mallee, tangle **7** boscage, bosquet, coppice, spinney **8** hedgerow, quickset **9** brushwood, canebrake, chaparral
thickness **3** ply **4** bulk, loft **5** depth, gauge, layer, sheet **7** density **9** viscosity
thickset **5** bulky, burly, heavy, husky, plump, pudgy, stout, tubby **6** chubby, chunky, portly, stocky, sturdy **7** compact **9** corpulent
thief **3** dip **4** prig, yegg **5** ganef, gonif **6** bandit, goniff, lifter, looter, pirate, rascal, robber **7** booster, burglar, filcher, stealer **8** hijacker, larcener, pilferer, water rat **9** larcenist, purloiner **10** cat burglar, highwayman, pickpocket, shoplifter **12** housebreaker
thieve **3** rob **4** hook, lift, pick, roll **5** boost, filch, pinch, pluck, steal, swipe **6** hijack, hold up, pilfer, rip off, snitch **7** purloin **8** knock off **9** knock over
thievery see **theft**
thievish **7** corrupt, crooked **9** larcenous **13** light-fingered
thigh **3** ham **5** flank **6** gammon ***bone:*** **5** femur ***relating to:*** **6** crural **7** femoral
thimble **3** cup **5** cover
thin **4** fine, lank, lean, slim **5** gaunt, lanky, reedy, scant, sharp, sheer, spare **6** dilute, flimsy, meager, meagre, rarefy, scanty, skimpy, skinny, slight, sparse, stalky, treble, twiggy, watery **7** diluted, scraggy, scrawny, slender, spindly, squinny, subtile, tenuous **8** rarefied, skeletal **9** attenuate, extenuate **10** attenuated **11** watered-down **13** unsubstantial
thing **4** item, unit **5** being, event **6** entity, matter, object **7** article, concern, element **10** occurrence, phenomenon ***in law:*** **3** res
thingamajig **5** gismo, gizmo **6** dingus, doodad, gadget, hickey, jigger, widget **7** whatsit **9** doohickey
things **4** gear **5** goods, stock, stuff **7** baggage, clothes, effects, luggage **8** chattels, clothing, matériel, movables, property, supplies **10** belongings, provisions **11** impedimenta, merchandise **13** accoutrements, paraphernalia
think **4** mull, muse **5** brood, study, weigh **6** ideate, ponder, reason **7** believe, imagine, reflect, suppose, surmise **8** cogitate, consider, meditate, ruminate **9** cerebrate, speculate **10** conjecture, deliberate, excogitate **11** contemplate
Thinker sculptor **5** Rodin (Auguste)
Thin Man, The ***actor:*** **3** Loy (Myrna) **6** Powell (William), Skippy **9** O'Sullivan (Maureen) ***author:*** **7** Hammett (Dashiell) ***character:*** **4** Nick (Charles), Nora (Charles) **6** Wynant (Clyde, Dorothy) ***dog:*** **4** Asta
third **4** show **8** tertiary ***combining form:*** **3** tri ***power:*** **4** cube
third degree **7** torture **8** grilling **11** inquisition, questioning **13** interrogation
third estate **5** plebs **6** people, plebes **8** populace **9** commonage, commoners, plebeians **10** commonalty **11** rank and file
Third Man author **6** Greene (Graham)
Third of May painter **4** Goya (Francisco)

thirst 3 yen **4** itch, long, lust, pine **5** crave, yearn **6** desire, hanker, hunger **7** craving, dryness, longing **8** appetite

thirsty 3 dry **4** arid, avid **5** eager **6** ardent **7** anxious, bone-dry, parched **8** droughty **9** absorbent, waterless

this and that 8 oddments, sundries **9** etceteras **11** miscellanea, odds and ends

Thisbe's lover 7 Pyramus

This Side of Paradise author 10 Fitzgerald (F. Scott)

thistle 4 weed **7** caltrop ***Russian:*** **10** tumbleweed

thistlebird 9 goldfinch

thither 3 yon **5** there **6** yonder

thole 3 peg, pin **6** endure

Thomas à ____ 6 Becket, Kempis

Thomas's Greek name 7 Didymus

Thomas opera 6 Mignon

____ Thompson 4 Emma **5** Sadie **6** Hunter **7** Dorothy, Francis, J. Walter **8** Benjamin

thong 4 band, lace, lash, rein, zori **5** lasso, strap, strip, whang **6** sandal **7** latchet **8** flip-flop

Thor 5 Donar ***father:*** **4** Odin **5** Wotan ***god of:*** **7** thunder ***hammer:*** **8** Mjollnir ***mother:*** **5** Jordh, Jorth

thorax 5 chest, trunk **6** pereon

Thoreau, Henry David *friend:* 7 Emerson (Ralph Waldo) ***pond:*** **6** Walden ***town:*** **7** Concord ***work:*** **6** Walden

thorium symbol 2 Th

thorn 4 barb **5** briar, spike, spine **7** prickle, spinule **9** annoyance **10** irritation

thorny 5 sharp, spiny **6** briary, touchy, tricky **7** awkward, prickly, spinous **8** ticklish **9** difficult, vexatious **10** nettlesome **11** troublesome

thorough 4 full **6** minute **7** careful, in-depth **8** complete, detailed, diligent, whole-hog **9** downright **10** blow-by-blow, exhaustive, meticulous **11** painstaking **13** conscientious

thoroughbred 5 racer **8** pedigree, purebred **9** pedigreed, pureblood **10** bloodstock **11** full-blooded

thoroughfare 3 way **4** road **5** track **6** artery, avenue, street **7** highway, parkway **8** corridor **9** boulevard

thoroughgoing 5 utter **6** all-out **7** extreme **8** absolute, complete, outright, whole-hog **9** out-and-out **10** consummate, exhaustive **11** straight-out, unmitigated **13** dyed-in-the-wool

thou 3 you **5** grand ***French:*** **5** mille

though 3 yet **5** still, while **6** albeit **7** however, whereas **8** after all **11** nonetheless **12** nevertheless

thought 4 idea **6** notion, reason **7** concept, opinion **8** ideation **9** brainwork **10** cogitation, conception, meditation, reflection, rumination **11** cerebration, speculation **12** deliberation, intellection **13** contemplation

thoughtful 6 polite **7** gallant, heedful, mindful, pensive, serious **8** gracious, studious, thinking **9** attentive, courteous **10** cogitative, meditative, reflective, ruminative, solicitous **11** considerate **12** deliberative, intellectual **13** contemplative

thoughtless 4 rash, rude **5** brash, hasty **6** madcap **7** selfish **8** careless, feckless, heedless, impolite, reckless, uncaring **9** insensate **10** incautious, ungracious **12** discourteous **13** inconsiderate

thousand *combining form:* 4 kilo ***cubed:*** **7** billion ***dollars:*** **5** grand ***squared:*** **7** million ***years:*** **10** millennium

thousandth 10 millesimal ***combining form:*** **5** milli

thrall 4 peon, serf, yoke **5** helot, slave **7** bondage, bondman, helotry, peonage, serfdom, slavery, villein **9** servitude, villenage **10** absorption **11** enslavement

thrash 3 tan **4** beat, belt, drub, flog, hide, lash, lick, maul, pelt, trim, whip **5** baste, flail, pound, smear, swing, thump, whale, whang **6** batter, buffet, larrup, pummel, stripe, wallop **7** scourge, shellac, trounce **8** flounder, lambaste, work over **10** flagellate

thrash out 4 moot **5** argue **6** debate **7** discuss, dispute **10** deliberate, kick around

thread 4 line, vein, yard **5** fiber, trail, weave **6** strand, stream, string **8** filament ***ball of:*** **4** clew ***dental:*** **5** floss ***holder:*** **6** bobbin ***kind:*** **4** silk, yarn **5** floss, lisle **6** cotton **8** surgical ***loose:*** **8** raveling **9** ravelling ***surgical:*** **6** catgut, suture

threadbare 4 hack, worn **5** dingy, faded, seedy, stale, tacky, tatty, tired, trite **6** beat-up, cheesy, cliché, frayed, ragged, shabby, shoddy **7** clichéd, run-down, tedious, worn-out **8** shopworn, slipshod, tattered, time-worn, well-worn **9** destitute, hackneyed **10** down-at-heel **11** commonplace, dilapidated, down-at-heels, stereotyped **13** down-at-the-heel

threadlike 6 filate **11** filamentous

threads 4 duds **7** clothes **8** clothing, garments

threat 6 danger, duress, menace **7** assault, warning **8** big stick, coercion **11** thunderbolt

threaten 3 cow **4** warn **5** augur, lower **6** coerce, menace **7** caution, portend, presage **8** endanger, forebode, forewarn, overhang **10** intimidate

three 4 trey **5** crowd ***combining form:* 3** ter, tri
threefold 5 trine **6** thrice, treble, trinal, triple **7** triplex
Three Musicians artist 7 Picasso (Pablo)
Three Musketeers 5 Athos **6** Aramis **7** Porthos ***author:* 5** Dumas (Alexandre) ***friend:* 9** D'Artagnan
Threepenny Opera, The *author:* 6 Brecht (Bertolt) ***composer:* 5** Weill (Kurt)
threescore 5 sixty
Three Sisters, The 4 Olga **5** Irina, Masha ***author:* 7** Chekhov (Anton)
threesome 4 trio **5** triad, trine **6** triple, triune, troika **7** trinity **8** triangle **11** triumvirate
three-wheeler 5 cycle, trike **7** pedicab **8** tricycle **10** velocipede
threnody 5 dirge, elegy **6** lament
thresh 3 lam, tan **4** beat, belt, drub, flog, hide, lash, lick, pelt, trim, wave, whip **5** baste, forge, flail, pound, slate, smear, swing, thump, whale, whang **6** batter, buffet, larrup, pummel, strike, stripe, wallop, winnow **7** scourge, shellac, trounce **8** lambaste, work over **10** flagellate
threshold 3 eve **4** door, edge, gate, sill **5** brink, limen, verge **6** outset **8** boundary
thrift 6 saving **7** economy, sea pink **8** prudence **9** frugality, parsimony
thrifty 5 canny **6** frugal, saving **7** sparing **9** provident **10** economical **12** cheeseparing, parsimonious **13** penny-pinching
thrill 3 wow **4** bang, boot, kick, rush, send **5** blast, throb **6** charge, excite, shiver, tingle, wallop **7** frisson, tremble, vibrate **9** electrify **10** excitement **11** titillation
thriller 6 gothic **7** chiller, mystery, shocker **8** whodunit **9** dime novel **10** hair-raiser **13** penny dreadful
thrive 4 boom, grow **7** advance, burgeon, develop, prosper, succeed **8** flourish, get ahead
throat 3 maw **4** tube **5** gorge **6** groove, gullet **7** channel, weasand ***infection:* 5** strep **12** epiglottitis ***inflammation:* 5** croup **6** angina, quinsy **10** laryngitis **11** pharyngitis ***relating to:* 8** guttural ***warmer:* 5** scarf
throaty 5 gruff, husky, thick **6** hoarse **8** gravelly, guttural
throb 4 ache, beat, drum **5** pound, pulse **6** thrill **7** pulsate, vibrate **9** palpitate
throe 3 fit **4** pain, pang **5** agony, spasm **6** attack **7** seizure **9** suffering **10** convulsion **11** contraction
thrombus 4 clot **8** blockage, coagulum
throne 4 seat **5** chair, crown, power, reign **8** cathedra, dominion **11** sovereignty
throng 3 jam, mob **4** host, pack, push, rout **5** bunch, crowd, crush, drove, flock, group, horde, press, scrum, shoal, swarm **6** resort **9** multitude **10** assemblage
throttle 3 gun **5** choke **6** throat **7** garrote, trachea **8** strangle, suppress **11** accelerator, strangulate
through 3 per, via **4** done, past **5** due to, ended **6** direct **7** by way of, done for, nonstop, owing to **8** by dint of, complete, finished, washed-up **9** because of, by means of, completed, concluded **10** by virtue of, terminated, throughout ***prefix:* 3** dia, per
throughout 3 mid **4** amid **5** midst **6** during **7** all over, overall **10** everywhere, far and near, far and wide, high and low
Through the Looking Glass *author:* 7 Carroll (Lewis) ***character:* 5** Alice
throve 9 burgeoned, prospered **10** flourished
throw 3 lob, peg, put **4** cast, fire, hurl, toss **5** chuck, fling, heave, pitch, sling **6** afghan, launch, propel **7** buck off, project ***in the towel:* 4** quit **6** give up
throw away 4 blow, cast, junk, shed **5** scrap, waste **7** discard, fritter **8** jettison, squander
throwback 7 atavism **9** reversion **11** anachronism
throw off 4 lose, shed **5** addle, shake **7** confuse, fluster **8** befuddle, bewilder, distract ***the track:* 6** derail **7** confuse, mislead
throw out 4 emit, junk, shed **5** chuck, eject, evict, scrap **6** reject **7** discard **8** jettison
throw up 4 barf, cast, hurl, lose, puke, quit, spew, toss **5** heave, retch, vomit **7** upchuck **8** disgorge **11** regurgitate
thrush 4 omao **5** mavis, ouzel, robin, veery **6** mistle **8** bluebird **9** blackbird, fieldfare, mistletoe **11** nightingale
thrust 3 dig, jab, ram **4** barb, butt, core, cram, dash, dive, duck, gist, hurl, kick, pith, poke, prod, push, stab, tilt **5** barge, crowd, cut in, drive, force, lunge, press, punch, sense, shoot, shove, spear, stick, stuff **6** burden, extend, insert, pierce, plunge, propel, upshot **7** assault, obtrude, project, purport, riposte **8** pressure **9** substance
thud 3 jar **4** bump, jolt, plop **5** clunk, throb, thump **6** impact **10** concussion
thug 3 mug **4** goon, hood, punk **5** bully, rough, rowdy, tough **6** Apache, Capone, gunman, hit man **7** hoodlum, mobster, ruffian **8** enforcer, gangster, hooligan, plug-ugly **9** cutthroat, roughneck
thulium symbol 2 Tm
thumb 4 leaf, turn **5** digit, hitch, ovolo **6** pollex, riffle **8** pollices (plural) **9** hitchhike

thumbs-up 3 AOK, nod **4** okay **7** go-ahead **10** green light
thumb through 4 scan **6** browse, riffle **7** dip into
thump 3 bop, hit **4** bash, beat, belt, blow, drub, jolt, pelt, whip, whup **5** knock, paste, pound, punch, shock, smack, sound, whack **6** batter, buffet, defeat, impact, pummel, strike, thrash, thwack, wallop **7** clobber, endorse, promote, shellac, trounce **8** advocate
thunder 4 bang, boom, clap, peal, roar **6** rumble **7** resound **8** rumbling **9** fulminate
thunderbolt 9 lightning
thunder lizard 11 apatosaurus **12** brontosaurus
thunderstruck 5 agape **6** amazed **7** shocked, stunned **8** dismayed **9** astounded, staggered **10** astonished, bewildered, confounded **11** dumbfounded **13** flabbergasted
Thurber character 5 Mitty (Walter)
thurible 6 censer
thus 3 sic **4** ergo, then **5** hence **9** therefore **11** accordingly **12** consequently ***French:* 5** ainsi
Thus Spake Zarathustra author 9 Nietzsche (Friedrich)
thwack 3 bop **4** belt, biff, blow, pelt, sock, whop **5** crack, pound, smack, thump, whack **6** wallop **7** clobber
thwart 4 balk, beat, dash, foil **5** bench, block, deter **6** baffle, hamper, hinder, oppose, scotch, stymie **7** flummox, prevent **8** confound, obstruct **9** checkmate, frustrate **10** circumvent, contravene, disappoint
Thyestes *brother:* 6 Atreus ***daughter:* 7** Pelopia ***father:* 6** Pelops ***mother:* 10** Hippodamia ***son:* 9** Aegisthus
Tiamat *husband:* 4 Apsu ***slayer:* 6** Marduk
tiara 5 crown **6** diadem **8** headband
Tibetan *animal:* 3 yak **5** takin ***capital:* 5** Lhasa ***coin:* 5** tanga ***dog:* 5** Lhasa **9** Lhasa apso ***monk:* 4** lama ***people:* 6** Bhotia, Sherpa
tibia 8 shinbone
tic 5 quirk, spasm **6** twitch **9** twitching
tick 5 check **8** arachnid, parasite **9** checkmark **11** bloodsucker
ticker 4 bomb **5** clock, heart, watch
ticket 3 key, tag **4** comp, pass, vote **5** slate **6** ballot **7** receipt **8** passport, password **10** open sesame ***seller:* 7** scalper
tickle 4 stir **5** amuse, tease, touch **6** arouse, excite, please, tingle **7** delight, gratify, provoke **9** stimulate, titillate
tickled 5 happy **6** amused **7** pleased **9** delighted
ticklish 5 dicey **6** tender, thorny, touchy, tricky **8** delicate, unstable **9** sensitive **10** precarious **13** oversensitive
tick off 3 ire, irk **5** anger **6** rankle **7** incense, provoke **9** aggravate
tidal flood 4 bore
tidbit 3 ort **4** bite **5** goody, treat **6** dainty, morsel, nugget
tide 4 flow, flux, rush **5** drift, flood, spate, surge **6** stream **7** current, holiday ***type:* 3** ebb, low **4** high, neap **5** flood **6** spring
tidings 4 news, word **6** advice **7** message **11** information **12** intelligence
tidy 4 fair, neat, smug, snug, trim **5** kempt **6** pick up **7** clean up, orderly, precise **9** shipshape **10** acceptable, methodical **11** respectable, spic-and-span, substantial, uncluttered, well-groomed **12** satisfactory, spick-and-span
tie 3 guy, rod **4** band, bind, bolo, bond, cord, draw, gird, join, knit, knot, lash, link, moor, rope, yoke **5** equal, leash, match, truss **6** attach, clip-on, cravat, fasten, fetter, hamper, oxford, ribbon, secure **7** connect, harness, shackle **8** dead heat, deadlock, fastener, ligament, ligature, restrain, shoelace, standoff, vinculum **9** constrain, stalemate **10** attachment, four-in-hand
tied 4 even **5** bound **6** joined, united **8** attached, fastened **9** connected
tier 3 row **4** bank, deck, file, line, rank **5** class, grade, group, story **6** league **7** echelon **8** category, grouping
tie-up 3 jam **4** snag **5** crimp, delay, hitch, snarl **6** glitch **7** problem **8** gridlock, slowdown, stoppage **10** connection, traffic jam **11** association
tiff 3 row **4** fuss, spat **5** run-in, scrap **6** bicker **7** brabble, dispute, quarrel, wrangle **8** argument, squabble **10** falling-out **11** altercation **12** disagreement
tiffany 5 gauze **11** cheesecloth
tiger 3 cat **6** feline **9** carnivore ***young:* 3** cub
tight 4 fast, firm, snug, taut, trim **5** cheap, close, drunk, fixed, tipsy **6** firmly, secure, stingy **7** compact, crowded, drunken, miserly **8** intimate **9** difficult, tenacious **10** inebriated **11** closefisted, intoxicated **12** cheeseparing, parsimonious **13** penny-pinching
tighten 4 bind **5** choke, close, cramp, pinch, screw **6** clench, fasten, narrow, secure, shrink **8** compress, restrict **9** clamp down, constrict
tightfisted see **stingy**
tight-lipped 6 silent **8** reserved, reticent, taciturn **12** closemouthed

tightwad **5** miser, piker **7** niggard, scrooge **9** skinflint **10** cheapskate **12** penny-pincher

tile **5** plate, slate **6** domino **7** tessera **8** linoleum

till **3** hoe, sow **4** disk, plow, tend, turn, up to, work **6** before, harrow **7** prior to **9** cultivate **11** in advance of **12** cash register

tillable **6** arable **10** cultivable **12** cultivatable

tillage **4** farm, land **5** tilth **7** culture **11** cultivation

tiller **4** helm **5** stalk **6** farmer, sprout **7** planter, steerer **9** sodbuster **10** cultivator

tilt **3** tip **4** bank, bent, bias, cant, cock, heel, lean, list, toss **5** grade, joust, level, lurch, pitch, slant, slope, speed **6** attack, charge, thrust **7** dispute, incline, leaning, recline **8** gradient **11** inclination

timbal **4** drum **10** kettledrum

timber **3** log **4** balk, beam, stud, tree, wood **5** board, joist, plank, trees, woods **6** forest, girder, lumber, rafter **8** woodland ***uncut:*** **8** stumpage ***wolf:*** **4** lobo

timbre **4** tone **6** temper **7** quality **9** resonance, tone color

timbrel **4** drum **10** tambourine

time **3** age, era **4** bout, date, hour, pace, span, term **5** clock, epoch, shift, space, spell, stint, tempo, while **6** moment, period, season **7** instant, stretch **8** duration, occasion **11** opportunity ***abbreviation:*** **3** CDT, CST, EDT, EST, MDT, MST, PDT, PST ***combining form:*** **5** chron **6** chrono ***gone by:*** **3** ago **4** past **9** yesterday **10** yesteryear **12** auld lang syne ***long:*** **3** age, eon, era **4** aeon ***of day:*** **4** dawn, dusk, noon **5** night **6** sunset **7** evening, morning, sunrise **8** daybreak, twilight **9** afternoon ***olden:*** **4** yore **10** yesteryear ***period:*** **3** age, day, eon, era **4** aeon, hour, week, year **5** epoch, month **6** decade, minute, moment, second **7** century, instant **9** fortnight **10** millennium ***present:*** **3** now ***relating to:*** **8** temporal ***short:*** **5** jiffy **6** moment, second **7** instant ***to come:*** **6** future **8** tomorrow ***waste:*** **4** loaf **5** dally **6** loiter

time and again **3** oft **5** often **6** hourly **8** commonly, ofttimes **10** constantly, frequently, oftentimes, repeatedly **11** continually, over and over **12** periodically

Time founder **4** Luce (Henry R.) **6** Hadden (Briton)

timeless **7** ageless, eternal, unaging **8** unageing **9** atemporal, perpetual **11** everlasting

timely **5** early **6** prompt, proper **8** punctual, suitable **9** opportune **10** seasonable **11** appropriate

Time Machine author **5** Wells (H. G.)

time-out **4** rest **5** break, pause **6** hiatus, recess **7** respite **8** breather **9** interlude **12** interruption

timepiece **5** clock, watch **7** sundial **8** horologe **9** clepsydra, metronome, stopwatch **10** water clock **11** chronograph, chronometer

timetable **6** agenda, docket **7** program **8** calendar, schedule

timeworn **3** old **4** aged, hack **5** hoary, stale, trite **6** age-old **7** ancient **8** dog-eared, Noachian **9** hackneyed **10** threadbare

time zone **7** Central, Eastern, Pacific **8** Mountain

timid **3** shy **4** wary **5** chary, mousy **6** afraid, yellow **7** bashful, chicken, fearful, halting, nervous, panicky **8** cowardly, retiring, timorous **9** diffident, tentative, trepidant, uncertain **11** unassertive **12** apprehensive, fainthearted

timidity **4** fear **7** modesty, shyness **8** meekness **9** hesitancy, reticence **10** diffidence, hesitation

Timon's servant **7** Flavius

timorous **4** wary **5** timid **6** afraid **7** fearful **8** retiring **9** shrinking, tremulous **12** apprehensive

Timothy's associate **4** Paul **5** Titus

tin **3** box, can **5** metal **7** element **9** container ***mining region:*** **8** stannary ***relating to:*** **7** stannic **8** stannous ***sheet:*** **6** latten ***symbol:*** **2** Sn

tincture **3** dye **4** cast, hint, tint **5** color, shade, smack, stain, tinge, touch, trace **6** iodine, streak **8** colorant, dyestuff, laudanum **9** paregoric **10** intimation, suggestion

tinder **4** punk **5** spunk **8** kindling

tine **5** point, prong, spike **6** branch

tinge **3** dye, hue **4** cast, hint, tint, tone **5** color, imbue, shade, stain, tinct, touch **8** tincture **10** intimation

tingle **5** sting **6** thrill **7** prickle **9** sensation

tinker **3** fix **4** mend, mess, muck, play **5** gypsy **6** adjust, diddle, fiddle, mender, potter, putter, repair **7** bungler, twiddle **9** repairman

tinkle **4** ring, ting **5** chink, clink, plink **6** jingle

tinny **4** thin **5** cheap, harsh **8** metallic

tinsel **5** gaudy **6** flashy, garish, tawdry **7** chintzy, glaring, trinket **8** ornament, specious **9** clinquant **11** superficial **12** meretricious

tint **3** dye, hue **4** cast, tone, wash **5** color, shade, tinge, touch **8** tincture **10** coloration **12** pigmentation

tiny **3** wee **4** itsy **5** bitsy, bitty, elfin, micro, pygmy, teeny, weeny **6** minute, peewee, pocket, teensy, weensy **8** pint-size **9** itsy-bitsy, itty-bitty, miniature, minuscule **10** diminutive, pocket-size, teeny-weeny **11** lilliputian, microscopic **12** teensy-weensy **13** infinitesimal

tip 3 cap, cue, top **4** apex, cant, clue, cusp, heel, hint, lean, list, peak, perk, tilt **5** point, slant, slope, steer, upset **6** advice, topple **7** cumshaw, incline **8** gratuity, overturn, turn over **9** baksheesh, lagniappe, pourboire **11** information

tip off 4 warn **5** alert

tip-off 4 clue, hint, sign **6** advice **7** pointer, red flag, warning **8** giveaway, jump ball **10** indication

Tippecanoe and ____ too 5 Tyler

tippet 4 cape **5** scarf **8** liripipe

tipple 3 bib, sip **4** swig, tope **5** booze, drink **6** guzzle, imbibe **7** swizzle **8** liquor up

tippler 3 sot **4** lush, soak **5** drunk, toper **6** bibber, boozer **7** tosspot **8** drunkard **9** inebriate

tipstaff 7 bailiff

tipster 4 fink, tout **6** canary, snitch **7** adviser, rat fink, stoolie, tattler **8** informer, squealer **11** stool pigeon

tipsy 3 lit **4** high **5** askew, drunk, lit up, oiled, tight **7** drunken, fuddled, sloshed **8** unsteady **10** inebriated **11** intoxicated

tiptoe 5 creep, skulk, slink, sneak, steal **9** pussyfoot

tirade 4 rant **6** screed **8** diatribe, harangue, jeremiad **9** philippic **12** denunciation, vituperation **13** tongue-lashing

tire 3 sap **4** bore, fail, flag, jade, pall, poop, wear **5** drain, droop, ennui, weary, wheel **6** tucker, weaken **7** exhaust, fatigue, wear out **8** enervate, wear down ***airless:* 4** flat **7** blowout ***kind:* 4** bias, snow **6** radial **7** retread **9** whitewall

tired 4 worn **5** spent, weary **6** done in **7** drained, run-down, worn out **8** fatigued, flagging **9** enervated, exhausted

tiredness 7 fatigue **8** collapse **9** lassitude **10** enervation, exhaustion **11** prostration

tireless 10 unflagging **13** indefatigable, inexhaustible

Tiresias 4 seer **10** soothsayer

tiresome 4 dull **5** stale **6** boring **7** irksome, lumpish, operose, tedious

Tirol *capital:* 9 Innsbruck ***country:* 7** Austria ***mountains:* 4** Alps

Tisiphone see **Erinyes**

tissue 3 web **4** film, mesh **5** fiber, gauze, paper **6** fabric ***anatomical:* 4** tela **5** fiber **6** diploe **8** ganglion **10** epithelium ***connective:* 4** tela **6** stroma, tendon **9** cartilage ***kind:* 3** fat **5** nerve **6** muscle **7** nervous **8** muscular **10** connective ***layer:* 6** dermis **7** stratum ***plant:* 4** bast, wood **5** xylem **6** phloem

titan 5 giant **8** colossus

Titan *father:* 6 Uranus ***female:* 4** Rhea **6** Tethys, Themis ***male:* 6** Cronus **7** Iapetus, Oceanus ***mother:* 4** Gaea

Titan author 7 Dreiser (Theodore)

Titania's husband 6 Oberon

titanic 4 huge, vast **5** great **6** mighty **7** immense, mammoth, massive **8** colossal, enormous, gigantic **9** cyclopean, Herculean, monstrous **10** gargantuan, tremendous

Titanic *actor:* 4 Zane (Billy) **5** Bates (Kathy) **6** Stuart (Gloria) **7** Winslet (Kate) **8** DiCaprio (Leonardo) ***director:* 7** Cameron (James) ***last U. S. survivor:* 7** Asplund (Lillian) ***line:* 9** White Star ***rescuing vessel:* 9** Carpathia ***sister ship:* 7** Olympic **9** Britannic

titanium symbol 2 Ti

tithe 3 tax **4** levy **5** tenth **12** contribution

Tithonus *beloved by:* 3 Eos ***father:* 8** Laomedon

Titian painting 5 Danaë **8** Ecce Homo **10** Assumption (The), Holy Family (The) **12** Rape of Europa (The) **13** Maltese Knight, Medea and Venus, Venus and Cupid **14** Worship of Venus (The) **17** Bacchus and Ariadne

titillate 6 arouse, excite, stir up, thrill, tickle **9** stimulate

title 3 dub, due **4** call, deed, dibs, name, term **5** claim, merit, nomen **7** baptize, caption, heading **8** cognomen **9** designate **10** denominate **11** appellation, appellative, designation **12** championship, compellation, denomination ***academic:* 4** dean, Prof. **7** provost **9** president, professor ***Dutch:* 7** mynheer ***ecclesiastic:* 3** Rev. **5** abbot **6** bishop **8** cardinal, reverend **10** archbishop ***Etruscan:* 3** lar ***feminine:* 2** Ms. **3** Mrs. **4** dame, lady, ma'am, miss **5** madam **6** abbess, madame, milady, missus **8** mistress ***French:* 6** madame **8** monsieur **12** mademoiselle ***German:* 4** Frau, Herr **8** Fräulein ***Hindu:* 4** babu, raja, rani **5** baboo, rajah, ranee ***holder:* 5** noble **8** champion ***Indian:* 3** sri **5** sahib ***Islamic:* 4** amir, emir, imam **5** ameer, hadji, hajji **6** sayyid **9** ayatollah ***Italian:* 5** donna **6** signor **7** signora **9** signorina ***masculine:* 2** Mr. **6** mister ***monk's:* 3** fra **7** brother ***of nobility:* 3** sir **4** duke, earl, king, lady, lord, sire **5** baron, count, queen **6** prince **7** baronet, duchess, marquis **8** Archduke, baroness, countess, marchesa, marchese, marquise, princess, viscount **11** marchioness, viscountess ***Oriental:* 4** khan

Persian: **5** mirza ***Portuguese:*** **3** dom **4** dona **6** senhor **7** senhora **9** senhorita ***Spanish:*** **3** don **4** doña ***Turkish:*** **3** aga, bey

titmouse 4 bird **6** tomtit **7** bushtit **9** chickadee

Tito 4 Broz (Josip)

titter 5 laugh **6** giggle **7** chortle, chuckle, snicker, snigger

tittle 3 bit, jot **4** atom, iota, mite **5** minim, speck **7** smidgen **8** particle **9** diacritic

titular 5 legal **6** titled **7** nominal **8** so-called **11** designative

Tityus *father:* 4 Zeus ***slayer:* 6** Apollo

Tiu see **Tyr**

tizzy 4 flap, fume, snit, stew **5** sweat **6** dither, swivet, uproar

T-man 5 agent **8** revenuer

to (Scottish) 3 tae

toad 4 agua **6** anuran, peeper **8** truckler **9** amphibian, brownnose, sycophant **10** batrachian, bootlicker **11** lickspittle ***genus:* 4** Bufo, Hyla

toady 4 fawn **5** cower, leech **6** cringe, flunky, grovel, kowtow, lackey, sponge **7** truckle **8** bootlick, parasite, truckler **9** brownnose, sycophant **10** bootlicker **11** apple-polish, lickspittle

toast 5 bread, drink, salud, singe, skoal **6** cheers, health, l'chaim, pledge, prosit, salute **7** wassail **8** mazel tov **9** celebrate ***kind:*** **5** melba **6** French **8** zwieback

toastmaster 2 MC **5** emcee

To a Waterfowl author 6 Bryant (William Cullen)

tobacco 4 leaf, weed ***cask:* 8** hogshead ***chewing:* 4** chaw, quid ***ingredient:* 3** tar **8** nicotine ***juice:* 6** ambeer ***kind:* 4** shag **5** flake, snuff **6** burley **7** caporal, latakia, perique, Turkish **8** Virginia **9** broadleaf, mundungus ***pipe:* 4** heel **6** dottle ***rolled:* 5** cigar **9** cigarette ***Turkish:* 7** latakia

Tobacco Road author 8 Caldwell (Erskine)

to be *Latin:* 4 esse

to be sure 6 indeed **7** granted **9** certainly

Tobias *father:* 5 Tobit ***son:* 8** Hyrcanus

toby 3 jug, mug **7** pitcher

tocsin 3 SOS **5** alarm, alert **6** signal

today 3 now **9** currently, presently

toddler 3 tot **4** tike, tyke **6** rug rat

to-do 4 fuss, rout, stir **5** hoo-ha, rouse, stink, whirl **6** bother, bustle, clamor, furore, hoohah, hubbub, hurrah, pother, ruckus, rumpus, tumult, uproar **7** turmoil **8** foofaraw **9** agitation, commotion **10** hurly-burly **11** disturbance

toe 5 digit ***big:* 6** hallux ***combining form:* 6** dactyl

toehold 7 footing

toff 3 fop **4** beau **5** blade, dandy, swell **7** coxcomb, peacock **8** macaroni, popinjay **9** exquisite **12** clotheshorse

toga 4 gown, robe, wrap

together 5 as one **6** at once, joined, united **7** jointly **8** mutually **10** conjointly **11** concertedly **12** coincidently, collectively, concurrently ***prefix:* 3** col, com, con, cor, sym, syn

togetherness 5 union **7** cahoots **8** alliance **10** connection, solidarity **11** affiliation, association, combination, conjunction, partnership

toggle 3 pin **6** fasten, switch **9** alternate **10** crosspiece

Togo *capital:* 4 Lomé ***language:* 3** Ewe **6** French ***monetary unit:* 5** franc ***neighbor:* 5** Benin, Ghana **11** Burkina Faso

togs 3 rig **4** duds, suit **5** dress **6** attire, outfit **7** apparel, clothes, raiment, rigging, threads **8** clothing, ensemble, garments

To His Coy Mistress author 7 Marvell (Andrew)

toil 3 fag, net, tug **4** grub, plod, plug, slog, trap, work **5** grind, labor, slave, snare, sweat **6** drudge **7** slavery, travail **8** drudgery

toiler 4 peon **5** slave **6** drudge, slavey **9** workhorse

toilet 3 loo **4** head, john **5** bidet, potty, privy **6** johnny **7** latrine **8** bathroom, lavatory **11** water closet

toilsome 4 hard **5** heavy **6** uphill **7** arduous, labored **9** difficult, effortful, laborious, strenuous

Tokay 4 wine

token 4 buck, chip, gift, mark, note, sign **5** badge, check, favor, index, piece, plume, prize, relic, scrip **6** copper, emblem, pledge, symbol, ticket, trophy **7** earnest, gesture, memento, symptom, warrant **8** evidence, keepsake, memorial, reminder, security, souvenir **9** indicator **10** expression, indication **11** perfunctory, remembrance

To Kill a Mockingbird *author:* 3 Lee (Harper) ***character:* 3** Jem (Finch), Tom (Robinson) **4** Dill (Harris) **5** Ewell (Bob), Scout (Finch) **7** Atticus (Finch), Mayella (Ewell) **9** Boo Radley, Calpurnia **10** Cunningham (Walter) ***town:* 7** Maycomb

Tokyo *formerly:* 3 Edo ***island:* 6** Honshu

tolerable 2 OK **4** fair, okay **6** common, decent **7** livable **8** adequate, all right, bearable, passable **9** endurable **10** acceptable, sufferable **11** respectable **12** satisfactory

tolerably 4 so-so **5** quite **6** fairly, pretty, rather **8** passably **9** averagely **10** moderately

tolerance 6 leeway **8** patience **9** allowance, endurance, deviation, fortitude, variation **10**

indulgence, resistance, sufferance **11** forbearance, habituation

tolerant 4 easy **5** broad **7** lenient, liberal **8** placable **9** easygoing, eurytopic, forgiving, indulgent, tractable **10** open-minded, permissive **11** broad-minded, sympathetic **13** understanding

tolerate 4 bear, bide, hack **5** abide, allow, brook, stand **6** accept, endure, pardon, permit, suffer **7** condone, stomach, swallow **8** bear with, live with **9** put up with **11** countenance

Tolkien creature 3 Ent, Orc **4** Warg **5** Ainur, Huorn, Troll **6** Balrog, Hobbit, Nazgul, Shelob **9** Oliphaunt **10** Ringwraith

toll 3 fee, tax **4** bell, bong, cost, levy, peal, ring **5** chime, knell, price, sound **6** charge, summon, tariff **7** expense **8** casualty **10** assessment

tollbooth 11 customhouse

Tolstoy work 8 Cossacks (The) **11** War and Peace **12** Anna Karenina **16** Death of Ivan Ilich (The)

tomato 9 love apple

tomb 5 crypt, grave **6** burial **9** mausoleum, sepulcher, sepulchre, sepulture ***ancient Egyptian:*** **7** mastaba ***empty:*** **8** cenotaph

tomboy 6 gamine, hoyden

tombstone 4 slab **8** memorial, monument **11** grave marker ***inscription:*** **3** RIP **8** hic jacet

tome 4 book **6** volume

tomfool 3 ass **4** dolt, fool, jerk **5** crazy, idiot, loony, ninny, silly, wacky **6** absurd, donkey, stupid **7** doltish, foolish, jackass **8** clodpoll, dummkopf, imbecile **9** blockhead, fantastic, horse's ass, thickhead **10** dunderhead, nincompoop **11** chowderhead, chucklehead, harebrained **12** preposterous

tomfoolery 4 dido, lark **5** antic, caper, prank, shine, trick **6** frolic **8** escapade, fandango **9** high jinks **10** shenanigan **11** monkeyshine

Tom Jones author 8 Fielding (Henry)

tommyrot 4 bosh, bull, bunk **5** bilge, hooey, trash **7** baloney, eyewash, hogwash, rubbish **8** claptrap, nonsense **9** poppycock **10** balderdash **13** horsefeathers

Tom o'Bedlam 3 nut **4** loon **5** loony **6** madman, maniac **7** lunatic

tomorrow 6 future, mañana

Tom Sawyer *author:* 5 Twain (Mark) **7** Clemens (Samuel) ***character:*** **5** Becky (Thatcher) **8** Huck Finn, Injun Joe **9** Aunt Polly **10** Muff Potter

Tom Thumb 4 runt **5** dwarf, pygmy **6** midget, peanut, peewee **7** manikin **8** half-pint, mannikin **10** homunculus **11** lilliputian

ton 3 lot **4** chic **5** bunch, style, trend, vogue **6** bundle **7** fashion

tone 3 hue **4** cast, mode, mood, note, tint, vein **5** color, pitch, shade, sound, style, tinge **6** accent, manner, spirit, strain, temper, timbre **7** fashion **10** inflection

toned 3 cut, fit **4** buff, firm, trim **6** buffed **7** defined **8** muscular

toned down 4 mute, soft **5** muted, quiet, sober **6** low-key, mellow **7** subdued **8** laid-back, low-keyed, softened **10** restrained **11** understated

Tonga *capital:* 9 Nuku'alofa ***ethnic group:*** **10** Polynesian ***explorer:*** **4** Cook (Capt. James) **6** Tasman (Abel) ***island group:*** **5** Vava'u **6** Haapai **9** Tongatapu ***monetary unit:*** **6** pa'anga

tongue 4 lick, pole, tang **6** glossa, lingua, speech **7** clapper, dialect, languet **8** language **10** vernacular ***combining form:*** **4** glot **5** gloss, lingu **6** glossa, glosso, lingua, lingui, linguo **7** glossia

tongue-lash 4 lash, rail **5** chide, scold **6** berate, rebuke, revile **7** bawl out, chew out, tell off, reprove, upbraid **8** admonish, call down, reproach **9** castigate, reprimand **10** vituperate

tongue-lashing 6 rebuke, tirade **7** censure, reproof **8** scolding **9** reprimand, talking-to **11** castigation **12** dressing-down

tongue-tied 3 mum, shy **4** mute **6** silent **7** bashful **9** diffident **10** speechless **12** inarticulate

tonic 3 pop **4** cola, soda **5** brisk **7** bracing, soda pop **8** curative, salutary **10** refreshing **11** restorative, stimulating **12** exhilarating, invigorating ***extract:*** **4** cola **9** berberine

tons 4 gobs, lots **5** heaps, loads, piles, reams, scads **6** oodles

tony 4 chic, posh **5** smart, swank, swish **6** classy, modish, uptown **7** à la mode, elegant, stylish **9** exclusive **11** fashionable

too 4 also, ever, over, very **5** along **6** as well, overly, unduly, withal **7** awfully, besides, further, greatly **8** likewise, moreover, overmuch **9** extremely, immensely **10** in addition, remarkably, strikingly **11** exceedingly, excessively, furthermore **12** additionally, exorbitantly, immoderately, inordinately **13** exceptionally

tool 4 pawn **5** means **6** puppet, rimmer, stooge **7** cat's-paw, hayfork, machine, rounder, utensil **8** picklock **9** appliance, implement, mechanism **10** instrument ***axlike:*** **3** adz **4** adze ***boring:*** **5** auger, drill ***carving:*** **6** veiner ***cleaving:*** **4** froe ***cobbler's:*** **3** awl ***cooper's:*** **3** adz **4** adze ***cutting:*** **2** ax **3** adz, axe, saw **4** adze **5** edger, knife **6** shears **8** billhook ***digging:*** **4** pick **5** spade **6** shovel **7** mattock ***engraving:*** **5** burin ***farm:*** **6** seeder ***filing:*** **4** rasp **7** riffler ***garden:*** **3** hoe **4** rake **5** spade **6** trowel, weeder ***grasping:*** **6** pincer **7** tweezer **8** tweezers ***mining:*** **3** gad **6** trepan ***piercing:*** **3** awl ***prehistoric:*** **6** eolith ***pruning:*** **6** shears **9** secateurs ***rubbing:*** **9** burnisher ***scooping:*** **6** router ***toothed:*** **3** saw **7** rippler ***woodworking:*** **3** adz, saw **4** adze **5** bevel, plane **6** chisel, hammer

toot 3 bat, jag **4** bout, bust, honk, tear **5** binge, blast, drunk, snort, sound, souse, spree **6** bender **7** carouse

tooth 5 molar **7** incisor **8** bicuspid, premolar ***combining form:*** **4** dent **5** denti, dento ***cuspid:*** **6** canine **8** dogtooth, eyetooth ***cutting:*** **10** carnassial ***decay:*** **6** caries ***doctor:*** **7** dentist ***gear:*** **3** cog ***horse:*** **4** tush ***material:*** **4** pulp **6** dentin, enamel **8** cementum ***pointed:*** **4** fang **6** canine, cuspid ***small:*** **8** denticle

toothless 7 useless **8** edentate **10** edentulous **11** ineffective, ineffectual

toothsome 5 sapid, tasty **6** delish, savory **8** luscious, pleasant, pleasing, tasteful **9** agreeable, delicious, palatable, succulent **10** appetizing, attractive **11** scrumptious

too-too 6 la-di-da **7** extreme **8** affected, overdone, overmuch, precious **9** excessive **10** hoity-toity, inordinate **11** exaggerated, overrefined, pretentious

tootsie 3 pet **4** dear **5** honey, sugar **7** beloved, darling, sweetie **10** sweetheart, sweetie pie

top 3 cap, tip **4** acme, apex, best, cusp, head, peak, pick, roof **5** cream, crest, crown, elite, point, prime, prize **6** apical, choice, climax, height, summit, utmost, vertex **7** capital, highest, maximal, maximum, surface **8** five-star, loftiest, pinnacle, superior **9** first-rate, uppermost **10** first-class **11** culmination

tope 3 nip **4** soak **5** booze, drink, shark, stupa **6** guzzle, imbibe, tipple **7** swizzle **8** liquor up

toper 3 sot **4** lush, soak, wino **5** drunk, rummy, souse **6** bibber, boozer **7** tippler, tosspot **8** drunkard **9** inebriate **10** boozehound

Tophet 4 hell **5** hades, Sheol **6** blazes **7** Gehenna, inferno **9** perdition **10** underworld

topic 4 talk, text **5** issue, motif, point, score, theme **6** burden, matter, motive, thread **7** content, subject **8** argument **11** proposition

topical 5 local **7** current, nominal **8** regional **9** temporary **11** superficial

topmost 7 highest, leading, supreme **8** crowning, ultimate **9** paramount, principal **10** consummate, preeminent **11** culminating

top-notch 4 A-one **5** prime, primo **6** choice **7** capital **8** five-star, superior **9** excellent, first-rate **10** first-class **11** first-string

top off 3 cap **5** crown **6** climax, finish, refill **8** complete, conclude, resupply **9** culminate

topography 7 surface, terrain **8** features

topple 3 tip **4** drop, fall **5** crash, lurch, pitch, slump, upset **6** defeat, falter, plunge, totter, tumble **8** collapse, keel over, overturn **9** overthrow

tops 4 A-one, best **5** primo **6** at most **7** highest, supreme **8** peerless, superior **9** at the most, first-rate, matchless, nonpareil **11** outstanding

topsy-turvy 7 chaotic, jumbled, mixed-up **8** cockeyed, confused, inverted **10** disjointed, disordered, upside down

toque 3 cap, hat

tor 4 crag, hill, peak **5** butte, cliff, mound, talus

Torah 10 Pentateuch

torch 4 fire **5** flame, light **6** ignite **7** firebug **8** arsonist, flambeau, guidance **10** flashlight, incendiary

toreador 6 torero **7** matador **11** bullfighter

torero see **toreador**

torment 3 rag, try, vex **4** bait, bane, hell, hurt, pain, pang, rack **5** abuse, agony, curse, grill, harry, tease, worry, wring **6** harass, harrow, heckle, misery, molest, needle, plague **7** afflict, agonize, anguish, bedevil, crucify, distort, hagride, torture, travail, trouble **8** distress **9** persecute, tantalize **10** affliction, excruciate

torn 4 rent **5** split **6** ragged, ripped, unsure **7** mangled **8** tattered, wrenched **9** lacerated, uncertain, undecided

tornado 6 funnel **7** cyclone, twister **9** windstorm, whirlwind

toro 4 bull

torpedo 3 gun, ray **4** mine, thug **5** blast, bravo, smash, wreck **6** gunman, gunsel, hit man, killer, weapon **7** destroy, nullify, scuttle **8** assassin, firework **9** explosive, shoot down **10** hatchet man, projectile, triggerman **11** electric ray

torpid 4 dull, lazy, numb **5** dopey, inert **6** sodden, stupid **7** dormant **8** comatose, inactive, sluggish **9** apathetic, lethargic **12** hebetudinous

torpor 4 coma, daze **5** swoon **6** apathy, stupor **7** languor **8** dopiness, dullness, hebetude, lethargy **9** lassitude, passivity, stolidity **10** stagnation **12** listlessness

torque 5 twist

torrent 4 rush **5** flood, spate **6** deluge, stream **7** cascade, Niagara **8** cataract, flooding **9** cataclysm **10** inundation, outpouring
torrid 3 hot **5** fiery **6** ardent, fervid, heated, red-hot, sultry **7** boiling, burning, flaming, parched **8** broiling, white-hot **9** scorching **10** hot-blooded, passionate, sweltering **11** impassioned
tort 5 crime, wrong **7** offense **10** wrongdoing
tortilla dish 4 taco **6** flauta **7** burrito, chalupa, tostada **9** enchilada **10** quesadilla **11** chimichanga
Tortilla Flat author 9 Steinbeck (John)
tortoise 6 turtle **8** terrapin **9** chelonian ***beak:*** **3** neb ***shell:*** **8** carapace
tortuous 5 snaky **6** cranky, tricky **7** crooked, devious, sinuous, winding **8** flexuous, indirect, involute, involved **9** meandrous **10** circuitous, convoluted, meandering, serpentine **11** anfractuous, vermiculate **12** labyrinthine
torture 4 pain, rack, warp **5** agony, wring **6** harrow, martyr **7** afflict, agonize, anguish, crucify, torment **9** martyrdom **10** excruciate **11** third degree
tortured 4 bent **6** racked, warped **7** twisted **8** deformed **9** distorted
tory 5 right **7** old-line **8** loyalist, old guard, orthodox, rightist, royalist **12** conservative
Tosca *character:* 5 Mario (Cavaradossi) **7** Scarpia (Baron) ***composer:*** **7** Puccini (Giacomo)
tosh 3 rot **4** bosh, bunk **5** bilge, hooey **6** bunkum, drivel, humbug **7** baloney, eyewash, hogwash, twaddle **8** malarkey, nonsense, tommyrot, trumpery
toss 4 cast, flap, flip, hurl, rock, roll **5** chuck, drink, fling, heave, match, pitch, quaff, sling, surge, throw, vomit **6** imbibe, tumble, welter, writhe **7** discard **9** knock back, throw away
tosspot see **tippler**
tot 3 add, kid, nip, sum **4** dram, shot, slug, tike, tyke **5** child, snort **6** figure, infant, nipper, shaver, squirt **7** snifter, toddler
total 3 add, all, sum **4** foot, full **5** add up, equal, gross, run to, smash, sum to, utter, whole, wreck, yield **6** all-out, amount, entire, figure, number **7** crack up, destroy, overall, perfect, quantum **8** absolute, complete, demolish, entirety, outright, quantity **9** aggregate, full-blown, full-scale, inclusive, unlimited **10** consummate, unreserved **11** unmitigated **13** comprehensive, thoroughgoing
totalitarian 8 absolute, despotic **10** autocratic **11** dictatorial **13** authoritarian
totality 3 all, sum **4** lump **5** whole **7** oneness **8** entirety **9** aggregate, wholeness **12** completeness
totalize 3 add, sum **5** sum up **6** figure **7** summate
tote 3 lug **4** cart, haul, load, pack **5** carry, ferry, shlep, sum up **6** burden, convey, figure, schlep, shlepp **7** schlepp, summate **9** transport **10** pari-mutuel
totem 6 emblem, symbol
To the Lighthouse author 5 Woolf (Virginia)
totter 4 reel, sway **5** lurch, shake, waver **6** falter, toddle, topple, wobble **7** stagger
touch 3 dab, tad **4** abut, feel, meet, move, stir **5** brush, graze **6** adjoin, border, caress, finger, stroke **7** contact, palpate, smidgen **9** palpation, tactility
touchable 7 tactile **8** palpable, tangible
touch down 4 land **5** light, perch, roost **6** alight, settle
touched 3 odd, off **5** batty, crazy, moved **7** stirred **8** affected **9** emotional
touching 4 as to, in re **5** about, anent, as for **6** moving, tender **7** against, apropos, emotive, meeting, piteous, pitiful, tangent **8** abutting, adjacent, pathetic, pitiable, poignant, stirring **9** adjoining, affecting, apropos of, as regards, bordering, immediate, impinging, regarding **10** as respects, back-to-back, concerning, contiguous, respecting, tangential **11** coterminous **12** conterminous
touch off 5 erupt, spark, start **6** ignite, incite, kindle **7** explode, inflame, provoke, trigger **8** initiate **9** instigate **11** precipitate
touchstone 4 test **5** check, gauge, proof, trial **7** measure **8** standard **9** barometer, benchmark, criterion, yardstick
touch up 3 fix **5** patch **6** rework **7** improve, perfect
touchy 5 dicey, huffy, risky, testy **6** tender, tricky **7** peppery **8** delicate, ticklish **9** explosive, hazardous, irascible, irritable, sensitive **10** precarious **11** inflammable, quarrelsome, thin-skinned **13** oversensitive, temperamental, unpredictable
tough 3 mug **4** goon, hard, hood, lout, punk, thug **5** bully, hardy, harsh **6** rugged, severe, unruly **7** arduous, hoodlum, onerous, ruffian **8** bullyboy, hooligan, obdurate **9** arbitrary, demanding, difficult, effortful, hard-nosed, hidebound, laborious, resistant, roughneck, strenuous **10** hard-bitten, hardboiled, hardheaded, refractory **11** unbreakable
toughen 5 inure **6** anneal, harden, season, temper **9** acclimate, habituate **10** strengthen **11** acclimatize

toughie 4 goon, hood, lout, punk, thug **5** poser, rowdy **7** hoodlum, ruffian, stumper **8** bullyboy, hooligan, plug-ugly **9** roughneck
toupee 3 rug, wig **6** peruke, wiglet **7** periwig **8** postiche **9** hairpiece
tour 4 bout, trip, turn **5** jaunt, round, shift, spell, stint **6** junket, period, travel, troupe **7** circuit, journey **8** progress **9** barnstorm, excursion **10** expedition, rubberneck
tour de force 4 deed, feat **7** classic, display, exploit **10** magnum opus, masterwork **11** achievement, chef d'oeuvre, masterpiece
Tour de France winner 4 Riis (Bjarne) **5** Roche (Stephen) **6** Fignon (Laurent), Landis (Floyd), LeMond (Greg), Sastre (Carlos) **7** Delgado (Pedro), Hinault (Bernard), Pantani (Marco), Pereiro (Oscar), Ullrich (Jan) **8** Contador (Alberto), Induráin (Miguel) **9** Armstrong (Lance)
tour guide 8 cicerone
tourist 7 tripper, visitor **8** traveler **9** sightseer, traveller **10** day-tripper, rubberneck, vacationer **12** excursionist, globe-trotter
tournament 4 meet, open, tilt **5** pro-am **6** jousts, series **7** contest, tourney **8** carousel **10** round-robin **11** competition **12** championship
tourney 4 meet **5** event, games, match **7** compete, contest **8** concours **11** competition
tousle 4 mess, muss **6** rumple **8** dishevel, disorder
tout 3 spy, tip **4** brag, hype, laud, plug **5** watch **6** blow up, peddle, praise, talk up **7** acclaim, crack up, promote, solicit **8** ballyhoo, persuade, proclaim **9** publicize
tovarich 7 comrade
tow 3 lug, tug **4** drag, draw, haul, pull, rope, yarn **5** chain, trail **6** hawser ***truck:*** **7** wrecker
towel word 3 his **4** hers
tower 4 loom **5** spire **6** turret **8** overlook ***biblical:*** **4** Edar **5** Babel ***on a mosque:*** **7** minaret
towering 4 high, tall **5** grand, lofty **6** aerial **7** soaring **8** imposing, majestic **9** excessive, grandiose **10** monumental, prodigious **11** magnificent, skyscraping **12** altitudinous, overwhelming
towhee 5 finch **7** chewink
to wit 3 viz **6** namely, that is **8** scilicet **9** c'est-à-dire, videlicet
town 4 burg **6** hamlet, podunk **7** borough, village ***medieval:*** **5** bourg
town and ____ 4 gown **7** country
townsman 7 burgher, citizen
town square 5 plaza ***Italian:*** **6** piazza
toxic 6 poison **7** harmful, noxious **8** venomous, virulent **9** poisonous **10** infectious
toxin 5 venom **6** poison
toy 3 top **4** fool, play, yo-yo **5** antic, curio, dally, flirt, knack, mouse, tease **6** bauble, caress, coquet, diddle, fiddle, gewgaw, puzzle, rattle, Slinky, trifle **7** bibelot, Frisbee, foot bag, novelty, pastime, trinket, whatnot **8** gimcrack **9** plaything, pogo stick **10** diminutive, Erector Set, knickknack, Silly Putty, sock monkey, Spirograph, View-Master **11** jumping jack **12** kaleidoscope
trace 3 jot, ray, run, tug **4** blip, echo, hint, iota, mark, path, scan, wisp **5** relic, shade, spoor, tinge, trail, tread **6** derive, detect, nuance, shadow, strain, streak **7** outline, remains, remnant, run down, soupçon, symptom, vestige **8** discover, tincture, traverse **9** delineate, footprint, remainder, scintilla, suspicion **10** intimation, suggestion
trachea 6 larynx, throat, vessel **7** weasand **8** throttle, windpipe
track 3 way **4** drag, oval, path, rail, road, sign, slot, step, tail **5** chase, cover, print, spoor, trace, trail, tread **6** artery, follow, pursue, shadow, travel **7** footway, imprint, monitor, pathway, vestige **8** footpath, footstep **9** footprint **10** racecourse ***cycle:*** **9** velodrome
track-and-field event 4 dash **5** relay **6** discus **7** javelin, hurdles, shot put **8** footrace, high jump, long jump **9** broad jump, decathlon, pole vault **10** heptathlon, triple jump **11** discus throw **12** steeplechase
track star 3 Coe (Sebastian) **4** Nool (Erki) **5** Flo-Jo, Jones (Marion), Lewis (Carl), Moses (Edwin), Nurmi (Paavo), Ovett (Steve), Owens (Jesse), Pérec (Marie-José), Viren (Lasse) **6** Beamon (Bob), Devers (Gail), Jenner (Bruce), O'Brien (Dan), Oerter (Al), Sebrie (Roman), Toomey (Bill) **7** Johnson (Michael, Rafer), Mathias (Bob), Rudolph (Wilma), Shorter (Frank), Zátopek (Emil) **8** Thompson (Daley), Zaharias (Babe Didrikson) **9** Bannister (Roger), Didrikson (Babe) **12** Joyner-Kersee (Jackie)
tract 3 lot **4** area, belt, farm, land, plat, plot, zone **5** block, claim **6** parcel, region **7** leaflet, portion, terrain **8** pamphlet, preserve **9** territory
tractable 4 tame **6** docile, gentle, pliant **7** ductile, plastic, pliable **8** amenable, biddable, flexible, obedient, workable **9** adaptable, breakable, malleable **10** manageable
tractate 5 summa **6** memoir, thesis **7** pandect **8** hornbook, monument, treatise **9** discourse, monograph **10** commentary **12** disquisition, dissertation, introduction

traction 4 drag, pull **5** force **7** drawing, tension **8** friction
tractor maker 4 Case **5** Deere (John) **6** Kubota **7** Farmall
trade 4 deal, sell, swap **5** craft, truck **6** barter, change, custom, market, métier, peddle, switch **7** bargain, calling, pursuit, traffic **8** business, commerce, exchange, industry, vocation **10** employment, occupation, profession, substitute **11** merchandise, transaction ***illicit:* 11** black market
trademark 3 tag **4** logo **5** brand, label, stamp **6** patent, symbol **8** colophon, logotype **9** brand name
trader 4 ship **6** broker, dealer, vendor **8** merchant
trade route 7 sea-lane
trade show 4 expo **10** exhibition, exposition
tradition 4 lore, myth **5** habit **6** belief, custom, legacy, legend, mythos, rubric **7** folkway **8** folklore, heredity, heritage, practice **9** mythology **10** convention **12** old wives' tale
traditional 4 oral **5** usual **6** common, spoken, verbal **7** classic, old-line, popular **8** habitual, orthodox **9** classical, customary, old-school, unwritten **10** button-down **11** established **12** acknowledged, buttoned-down, conservative, conventional
traditionalist 6 purist **12** conservative
traditionalistic 4 tory **7** die-hard, old-line **8** orthodox, standpat **12** conservative
traduce 4 slur **5** libel, smear, wrong **6** betray, breach, defame, malign, vilify **7** asperse, slander, violate **8** disgrace, tear down **9** denigrate **10** calumniate
Trafalgar commander 6 Nelson (Horatio)
traffic 4 deal **5** cargo, fence, trade, truck **6** barter, custom **7** bootleg, freight **8** commerce, dealings, exchange, movement **9** patronage, transport **11** black-market ***circle:* 6** rotary **10** roundabout ***cone:* 5** pylon ***jam:* 5** tie-up **6** holdup **8** blockage, gridlock **10** bottleneck
trafficker 6 dealer, trader
tragedy 3 woe **6** mishap, plague **8** calamity, disaster **9** cataclysm, mischance **10** misfortune **11** catastrophe **12** misadventure
trail 3 dog, lag, tag **4** drag, flag, path, plod, poke **5** chase, dally, delay, tarry, trace, track **6** dawdle, follow, linger, pursue, shadow **7** draggle, gumshoe, pathway, traipse **8** footpath, footwalk **10** bridle path ***emigrant:* 6** Oregon ***Florida:* 7** Tamiami ***Georgia-Maine:* 11** Appalachian ***Indian:* 5** Great
trailer 5 truck **7** preview **9** motor home, transport **10** mobile home
trailer truck 4 semi
train 2 el **3** row **4** file, tame **5** coach, drill, teach, track **6** column, convoy, course, school, sequel, series, thread **7** caravan, cortege, educate, prepare, retinue **8** exercise, instruct, sequence **9** cultivate, entourage, following, habituate **10** succession **11** progression
trainee 4 tiro, tyro **6** novice **7** learner **8** beginner, neophyte **10** apprentice
training 7 tuition **8** teaching, tutelage **9** education, schooling **11** instruction ***horse:* 6** manège
traipse 3 gad **4** hoof, pace, roam, rove, step, walk **5** amble, range, trail, tramp, tread **6** ramble, stroll, wander **7** maunder, meander **8** ambulate **9** gallivant
trait 4 mark **5** point, quirk, touch, trace **6** oddity, stroke **7** feature, quality **8** hallmark, property, specific **9** attribute
traitor 3 rat **5** Judas **8** apostate, betrayer, defector, deserter, quisling, renegade, turncoat **9** turnabout
traitorous 5 Punic **8** apostate, disloyal, mutinous, recreant, renegade **9** faithless **10** perfidious, rebellious, unfaithful **11** treacherous
traject 4 beam, pass, pipe, send **5** carry **6** convey, render **7** conduct, forward, impress **8** hand down, transfer, transmit **9** broadcast, transfuse
trajectory 3 arc **4** path **5** curve **11** progression
tram 3 car **7** trolley **9** streetcar
trammel 3 tie **4** bind, curb **5** check, gauge, leash **6** fetter, hamper, hobble **7** compass, confine, ensnare, manacle, pothook, shackle **8** entangle, handcuff **9** restraint
tramontane 8 outsider **9** foreigner, outlander **11** transalpine
tramp 3 bum **4** hike, hobo, jade, plod, slog, thud **5** bimbo, caird, clump, gipsy, gypsy, march, stamp, stiff, stomp, tread **6** ramble, stroll, travel, trudge, wander **7** chippie, drifter, floater, saunter, traipse, vagrant **8** clochard, derelict, footslog, homeless, stroller, vagabond, wanderer **10** prostitute
trample 4 mash **5** crush, pound, stamp, stomp, tread, tromp
trance 4 daze, muse **5** swoon **7** ecstasy, rapture, reverie **8** hypnosis **9** catalepsy, enrapture **10** absorption, brown study **11** abstraction
tranquil 4 calm, easy **5** quiet, still **6** dreamy, placid, poised, serene **7** restful **8** composed, peaceful **10** untroubled **13** self-possessed
tranquilize 4 calm, hush, lull **5** quiet, relax, still **6** becalm, pacify, sedate, settle, soothe, subdue **7** compose, mollify

tranquilizer 6 downer **8** diazepam, pacifier, sedative **10** depressant **11** barbiturate
tranquillity 4 calm **5** peace, quiet **8** calmness, serenity **9** composure, placidity
transaction 4 deal **5** trade **7** bargain, dealing **8** contract, covenant **9** agreement
transcend 3 top **4** beat, best **5** excel, outdo **6** better, exceed **7** surpass **8** outshine, outstrip, overcome, surmount
transcendent 5 ideal **7** perfect, sublime, supreme **8** abstract, immanent **10** consummate, surpassing
Transcendentalist 6 Alcott (Bronson), Fuller (Margaret) **7** Emerson (Ralph Waldo), Thoreau (Henry David)
transcribe 4 copy **5** write **6** record **8** transfer **9** translate, write down **13** transliterate
transfer 4 cede, deed, hand, pass, ship **5** carry, grant, shift **6** assign, convey, remove, supply **7** consign, convert, deliver, devolve, dispose **8** alienate, hand over, make over, relocate, turn over **9** carry over **10** assignment, conveyance **11** disposition
transfix 4 spit **5** lance, spear, spike, stick **6** impale, skewer **7** spindle **8** entrance **9** fascinate, hypnotize, mesmerize
transform 5 alter, morph **6** change, mutate **7** commute, convert **12** metamorphose
transformation 8 reaction **10** changeover, conversion **13** metamorphosis
transfuse 5 endue, imbue **7** pervade, suffuse, traject **8** permeate, saturate **9** penetrate, percolate **10** impregnate
transgress 3 err, sin **6** breach, exceed, offend **7** violate **8** infringe, overpass, overstep, trespass **10** contravene
transgression 3 sin **5** crime, error, wrong **6** breach **7** misdeed, offense **9** violation **12** infringement
transient 4 hobo **5** brief, tramp **7** drifter, migrant, passing **8** fleeting, flitting, fugitive, volatile **9** ephemeral, fugacious, momentary, temporary **10** evanescent, fly-by-night, short-lived **11** impermanent
transit 7 passage **8** traverse **10** conveyance
transition 4 leap **5** segue, shift **6** change **7** passage **10** conversion **13** metamorphosis
transitory see **transient**
translate 6 render **7** convert **9** interpret, reproduce **10** paraphrase
translation 9 rendition **10** conversion, paraphrase
transmarine 7 oversea **8** overseas
transmission 7 gearbox **8** handover **9** broadcast, infection
transmit 3 air **4** beam, hand, pass, pipe, send **6** convey, hand on, impart, pass on, render, signal **7** channel, conduct, consign, diffuse, forward, traject **8** bequeath, dispatch, hand down **9** broadcast
transmogrify see **transform**
transmute see **transform**
transoceanic message 4 wire **5** cable **9** cablegram
transparent 5 clear, filmy, gauzy, sheer **6** limpid **7** crystal **8** clear-cut, gossamer, pellucid **10** diaphanous, see-through **11** crystalline
transpire 3 hap **4** leak **5** exude, occur, sweat **6** chance, emerge, happen **7** develop **9** come about, take place **11** come to light
transplant 8 relocate, resettle
transport 3 bus, fly, lag, lug, wow, zap, zip **4** haul, hump, lift, pack, pass, send, ship, taxi, tote **5** carry, ferry, motor, truck **6** convey, excite, ravish, remove, thrill **7** delight, ecstasy, freight, rapture, sealift, trundle, vehicle **8** carriage, displace, railroad, rhapsody **9** carry away, chauffeur, troopship **10** conveyance, helicopter
transportation 6 moving **7** freight, hauling, removal, vehicle **8** carriage, carrying **10** conveyance **12** displacement
transpose 6 invert **7** convert, permute, reorder, reverse **9** rearrange **11** interchange
transude 4 ooze, reek, seep, weep **5** bleed, sweat **7** diffuse, give off **8** permeate **9** transfuse
transverse 5 cross **6** across, lintel, thwart **7** transom **8** crossbar, crossing **9** crossbeam, crosswise **10** crosspiece
trap 3 bag, net **4** bait, snag **5** catch, decoy, set up, snare **6** ambush, enmesh, tangle **7** ensnare, pitfall **8** birdlime, deadfall, entangle, quagmire **9** ambuscade
trappings 4 gear **5** dress **6** finery **8** equipage, ornament **9** adornment, caparison, equipment **10** decoration **11** habiliments **13** accouterments, accoutrements, embellishment, paraphernalia
Trappist 4 monk ***writer:*** **6** Merton (Thomas)
trash 3 rag, rot **4** bosh, bunk, junk, ruin, scum, slop **5** bilge, blast, dreck, dregs, hokum, offal, spoil, tripe, waste, wreck **6** bunkum, debris, insult, litter, refuse, rubble **7** clutter, destroy, garbage, hogwash, put down, rubbish **8** claptrap, malarkey, nonsense, tommyrot **9** disparage, poppycock, throw away, vandalize **10** balderdash **11** guttersnipe, proletariat
trash can 7 dustbin
trashy 5 bawdy, cheap, tatty **6** cruddy, shoddy, sleazy, smutty, vulgar **8** rubbishy **9** third-rate

trauma 4 blow, pain **5** shock, upset, wound **6** crisis, injury, stress **8** collapse **9** suffering
travail 4 grub, moil, task, toil, work **5** grind, labor, pains **6** drudge, effort **7** slavery, torment **8** drudgery, struggle
travel 4 fare, pass, roam, tour, trek, trip, wend **5** jaunt, range, tramp **6** junket, push on, voyage **7** explore, journey, passage, proceed, traffic, transit **8** movement, traverse **9** gallivant **10** hit the road ***term:*** **3** ETA **4** fare **9** all aboard
traveler 5 gipsy, gypsy, nomad, rover **7** drummer, tourist **8** runabout, runagate, salesman, vagabond **9** itinerant, sightseer **10** journeyman **11** peripatetic **12** rolling stone
traveling library 10 bookmobile
traverse 4 ride, span, walk **5** cover, cross, march, route, trace, track **6** course, thwart, travel, voyage **7** examine, transit **8** crossing, navigate, obstacle, pass over **9** adversity **10** crisscross, pass across **11** perambulate, peregrinate
travesty 3 ape **4** mock, sham **5** farce, mimic, spoof **6** parody **7** imitate, lampoon, mimicry, mockery, take off **8** ridicule **9** burlesque **10** caricature, distortion ***satanic:*** **9** Black Mass
Traviata, La *character:* **7** Alfredo (Germont), Germont **8** Violetta (Valéry) ***composer:*** **5** Verdi (Giuseppe)
trawl 3 net **4** fish **7** setline
tray 6 salver, server **7** platter **8** teaboard ***revolving:*** **9** lazy Susan
treacherous 5 false, Punic, risky **6** chancy, tricky **7** unsound **8** disloyal, perilous, recreant **9** dangerous, deceptive, faithless, hazardous, insidious **10** perfidious, traitorous, unfaithful, unreliable
treachery 7 perfidy, treason **8** bad faith, betrayal **9** duplicity **10** disloyalty, infidelity **11** double-cross **13** dastardliness, double-dealing, faithlessness
treacle 4 mush **5** slush, syrup **6** bathos **8** molasses, schmaltz **11** golden syrup
tread 4 hoof, pace, plod, step, walk **5** dance, march, stamp, stomp, trace, track, tramp, tromp, troop **6** follow, stride **7** footing, traipse, trample **8** footstep
treadle 5 lever, pedal
treadmill 3 rut **4** rote **5** chore, grind **6** groove **7** routine **8** drudgery, turnspit
treason 7 perfidy **8** betrayal, sedition **9** treachery **10** disloyalty, misprision **11** lèse-majesté
treasure 4 haul, save **5** adore, cache, hoard, pearl, prize, trove, value **6** esteem, revere, riches, wealth **7** apprize, cherish, idolize, worship **8** conserve, preserve, venerate **9** reverence **10** appreciate
Treasure Island *author:* **9** Stevenson (Robert Louis) ***character:*** **7** Ben Gunn **8** Long John (Silver) ***narrator:*** **10** Jim Hawkins
treasurer 6 bursar, purser **7** curator **8** receiver **11** chamberlain
Treasure State 7 Montana
treasure trove 4 find, mine **7** bonanza, pay dirt **8** El Dorado, Golconda, gold mine
treasury 4 fisc, mine **5** cache, chest, hoard **6** argosy, coffer, museum **7** bonanza, gallery, omnibus **8** archives, El Dorado, Golconda, gold mine, war chest **9** anthology, exchequer **10** depositary, depository, repository, storehouse
treat 5 goody, nurse **6** bonbon, dainty, doctor, goodie, handle, manage, morsel, tidbit **7** care for **8** deal with, delicacy, medicate **10** minister to ***animals:*** **3** vet ***leather:*** **3** tan, taw **7** tanning
treatise 6 thesis **8** tractate **9** discourse, monograph **10** exposition **12** disquisition, dissertation
treatment 4 care **7** therapy
treaty 4 pact **6** accord **7** charter, compact, concord **8** alliance, contract, covenant **9** agreement, concordat **10** convention
treble 4 high **6** shrill, triple **7** descant, soprano **9** threefold **11** high-pitched
tree 3 apa, ash, box, dao, dar, elm, eng, fir, koa, kou, lin, oak, sal, ule, yew **4** ague, atle, copa, dhak, kaki, lime, linn, mora, neem, pine, poon, tawa, teak, teil, titi, tung, upas, wych **5** aalii, abele, alamo, alder, athel, beech, birch, carob, cedar, ebony, holly, larch, lemon, maire, maple, osier, pipal, roble, rowan, sauch, saugh, sumac, taxus, yulan **6** arbute, banyan, cherry, cornel, deodar, ginkgo, kamala, linden, loquat, lychee, mallee, medlar, mimosa, myrtle, orange, poplar, redbud, sapota, spruce, tan oak, tupelo **7** arariba, arbutus, camphor, conifer, cypress, deodara, dogwood, hemlock, inkwood, juniper, kumquat, lentisk, madrona, madrone, murmast, redwood, sequoia, seringa, wallaba, zelkova **8** basswood, bergamot, black gum, bluejack, cinchona, corkwood, laburnum, loblolly, longleaf, magnolia, mahogany, sourwood, sweetgum, sycamine, sycamore, tamarisk **9** balsam fir, sassafras **10** candlewood, chinaberry, chinquapin **11** bald cypress **12** balm of Gilead, rhododendron ***African:*** **4** akee, cola, shea **5** limba, sassy **6** baobab **7** avodire, bubinga **8** sasswood **9** berberine ***Australian:*** **4** toon, yate **5** wilga **7** blue gum **8** lacewood, quan-

dong **9** casuarina **10** eucalyptus **11** bottlebrush ***branch:*** **5** bough ***combining form:*** **3** dry **4** dryo **5** arbor, dendr **6** arbori, dendra (plural), dendro ***genus:*** **4** Acer, Cola, Maba, Olea, Para **5** Abies **11** Callistemon ***palm:*** **4** coco, nipa **5** ratan **6** pinang, raffia, rattan **7** coquito **8** carnauba ***tropical:*** **3** ake, ama **4** akee, copa, dita, ohia, palm, pili, sago, teak, upas, yaya **5** areca, assai, balsa, cacao, ceiba, cycad, lehua, mamey **6** acajou, balata, baobab, bataan, citrus **7** genipap, logwood, majagua, palmyra, quassia, soursop **8** allspice, barbasco, mahogany, mangrove, milkwood, palmetto, rosewood, soapbark, sweetsop, tamarind **9** candlenut, jacaranda, sapodilla **10** breadfruit, calamondin, manchineel **11** candleberry, coconut palm ***trunk:*** **4** bole ***young:*** **7** sapling

trefoil **4** leaf **6** clover **8** ornament ***part:*** **3** arc

trek **4** hike, trip **6** travel, trudge **7** journey **9** migration **10** expedition

trellis **5** arbor **6** screen **7** lattice, pergola **8** espalier **11** latticework

tremble **5** quake, shake **6** dither, quaver, quiver, shiver **7** shudder, twitter, vibrate

tremblor see **temblor**

tremendous **4** huge, vast **6** mighty **7** awesome, immense, massive, titanic **8** colossal, enormous, fearsome, gigantic, terrific, towering **9** fantastic, monstrous **10** formidable, gargantuan, incredible, monumental, prodigious, stupendous **13** extraordinary

tremolo **7** vibrato

tremor **5** quake, shake, shock **6** quaver, quiver, shiver **7** shudder, temblor **10** earthquake ***muscular:*** **8** dystaxia

tremulous **5** shaky, timid **6** afraid **7** aquiver, fearful, quaking, shivery **8** timorous **9** quivering, shivering

trench **4** sink **5** ditch, fosse, gully, verge **6** border, furrow, trough ***Caribbean:*** **6** Cayman ***Pacific:*** **7** Mariana

trenchant **4** acid, keen **5** acerb, crisp, sharp **6** biting **7** acerbic, caustic, cutting, mordant, probing, satiric **8** clear-cut, distinct, incisive, sardonic, scathing **9** sarcastic **11** penetrating

trencher **4** tray **7** platter

trencherman **5** eater **7** glutton **8** gourmand

trend **3** fad, run **4** flow, mode **5** curve, drift, shift, style, swing, tenor, vogue **6** course, temper **7** current, fashion, incline **8** approach, movement, tendency **9** direction

trendy **3** hep, hip, hot **4** cool, tony **5** faddy **6** groovy, modish, with-it **7** à la mode, faddish, stylish **8** downtown, nouvelle, up-todate **11** fashionable, ultramodern

trepang **10** bêche-de-mer **11** sea cucumber

trepidation **4** fear **5** alarm, dread **6** dismay **7** anxiety **12** apprehension **13** consternation

trespass **3** err, sin **4** debt **5** lapse, poach **6** breach, invade, offend **7** impinge, intrude **8** encroach, entrench, infringe **9** interlope, violation **10** infraction, transgress **12** encroachment, infringement **13** transgression

tress **4** curl, lock **5** braid, plait

trestle **4** buck **5** frame **6** bridge **7** sawbuck, support **8** sawhorse **9** framework

trey **5** three

triad **4** trio **5** chord **6** triple, troika **7** harmony, trinity **9** threesome **11** triumvirate

trial **3** woe **4** care, test **5** cross, essay, rigor, worry **6** dry run, hassle, misery, ordeal, sorrow, tryput **7** anguish, attempt, contest, trouble **8** crucible, distress, endeavor, gauntlet, hardship, struggle, vexation **9** adversity, rehearsal, suffering **10** affliction, coup d'essai, difficulty, experiment, misfortune, proceeding, temptation **11** preliminary, tribulation **12** experimental

trial balloon **6** feeler, tryout

trial run **4** test **5** essay **7** break-in **10** experiment

triangle type **5** acute, right **6** obtuse **7** scalene **9** isosceles **11** equilateral

tribal unit **6** moiety **7** phratry

tribe **4** clan, folk, race **5** house, phyle, stock **6** family **7** kindred, lineage

tribulation **3** woe **5** cross, trial **6** burden, ordeal **9** adversity **10** affliction, oppression, visitation **11** persecution

tribunal **3** bar **4** dais, rota **5** bench, court **8** platform **10** consistory **12** court of honor

tributary **5** bayou, creek **6** branch, feeder, stream **7** subject **8** affluent, influent **9** backwater, confluent, dependent, satellite **12** contributory

tribute **5** paean, toast **6** eulogy, homage **8** citation, encomium **9** panegyric **10** salutation **11** recognition, testimonial **12** appreciation

trice **4** lash, wink **5** blink, flash, jiffy, shake **6** moment, second, secure **7** instant **8** eyeblink **9** twinkling **11** split second

trick **3** jig **4** bilk, dido, dupe, fool, gull, hoax, hose, lark, play, ploy, ruse, scam, sham **5** antic, caper, dodge, feint, fraud, prank, stunt **6** gambit, outwit, scheme **7** chicane, finagle, gimmick, sleight **8** escapade, flimflam, hoodwink **9** bamboozle, deception, stratagem, victimize **10** red herring, shenanigan, tomfoolery **11** hornswoggle, monkeyshine **13** practical joke

trickery **4** scam, wile **5** cheat, fraud **6** deceit **7** chicane, dodgery **8** jugglery **9** chicanery, deception **10** subterfuge **11** double cross **13** double-dealing, jiggery-pokery, sharp practice

trickle 4 drip, seep **5** creep, trill **7** dribble

trickster 5 cheat, shark **6** con man **7** cheater, diddler, grifter, sharper **8** conjurer, deceiver, magician, swindler **9** defrauder **11** flimflammer, illusionist **12** double-dealer

tricksy 5 rough **6** trying **7** arduous **8** prankish

tricky 3 sly **4** foxy, wily **5** dodgy **6** catchy, clever, crafty, shifty, sticky, thorny, touchy, trying **7** cunning, knavish **8** delusive, guileful, slippery, ticklish, tortuous, unstable **9** deceptive, difficult, dishonest, ingenious, intricate **10** misleading, nettlesome, precarious, unreliable **11** complicated, treacherous, troublesome **12** undependable

trident 5 spear

tried 6 proved, proven, secure, tested, trusty **7** staunch **8** approved, faithful, reliable, stalwart, true-blue **9** certified, steadfast **10** dependable **11** trustworthy

tried and true 5 loyal **6** proven, secure, steady, tested, trusty **8** faithful, reliable, stalwart **9** steadfast **10** dependable **11** trustworthy

trifle 3 bob, fig, pin, toy **4** doit, fool, mess, play **5** curio, dally, flirt, sport, waste **6** bauble, coquet, diddle, doodle, fiddle, fidget, footle, frivol, gewgaw, monkey, niggle **7** bibelot, conceit, fribble, fritter, novelty, trinket, twiddle, whatnot **8** folderol, gimcrack, kickshaw, nonsense, squander **9** bagatelle, cream puff, dalliance **10** knickknack, triviality **11** small change

trifling 4 tiny **5** petty **6** measly, paltry, piddly, slight **7** trivial **8** niggling, nugatory, picayune, piddling, piffling **9** frivolous, worthless **10** negligible **11** Mickey Mouse, unimportant **13** insignificant

trifolium 6 clover **8** shamrock

trig 4 chic, neat, prim, snug, tidy, trim **5** sharp, smart, swank, trick **6** classy, modish, snappy **7** chipper, dashing, orderly, precise, stylish **9** shipshape

trigger 4 fire **5** cause, spark, start **6** ignite, kindle, set off **7** actuate, release **8** activate, initiate, touch off

triggerman 3 gun **5** bravo **6** gunsel, killer **7** torpedo **8** assassin **9** cutthroat, pistolero

trigonometric function see at **function**

trill 4 burr, drop, roll **5** chirr, shake, twirl **6** quaver, warble **7** dribble, revolve, trickle, twitter, vibrato

trillion combining form 4 tera, treg **5** trega

trillionth combining form 4 pico

trim 3 cut, fit **4** buff, clip, crop, deck, neat, pare, snug, tidy, trig **5** adorn, order, prune, shape, shave, shear, skive, toned **6** barber, dapper, fettle, kilter, repair, spruce **7** chipper, dress up, garnish, orderly, shapely **8** clean-cut, decorate, manicure **9** shipshape **11** spic-and-span, streamlined, well-groomed **12** spick-and-span ***a tree:*** **5** prune **7** pollard

Trinidad and Tobago *capital:* **11** Port of Spain ***monetary unit:*** **6** dollar ***sea:*** **9** Caribbean

trinity see **triad**

trinket 3 toy **5** curio, jewel **6** bauble, doodad, gewgaw, trifle **7** bibelot, novelty, whatnot **8** gimcrack, kickshaw **9** bagatelle, plaything, tchotchke **10** knickknack

trinkets 10 bijouterie

trio of goddesses 5 Fates **6** Furies, Graces

trip 3 hop, run **4** fall, ride, skip, slip, step, tour, trek **5** boner, caper, dance, error, lapse **6** bungle, junket, outing, sashay, travel, tumble, voyage **7** blooper, blunder, journey, mistake, misstep, stumble **9** excursion **10** expedition

tripe 4 guts **5** bilge, trash **6** menudo, waffle, viscus **7** innards, viscera (plural) **8** entrails, stuffing **9** internals

triple 4 trio **5** triad, trine **6** treble, triune, troika **7** triform, trilogy, trinity **8** trifecta **9** threefold, threesome **11** three-bagger, triumvirate

Triple Crown winner *1919:* **9** Sir Barton ***1930:*** **10** Gallant Fox ***1935:*** **5** Omaha ***1937:*** **10** War Admiral ***1941:*** **9** Whirlaway ***1943:*** **10** Count Fleet ***1946:*** **7** Assault ***1948:*** **8** Citation ***1973:*** **11** Secretariat ***1977:*** **11** Seattle Slew ***1978:*** **8** Affirmed

Triple Crown site 7 Pimlico **11** Belmont Park **14** Churchill Downs

tripped out 4 high **5** doped **6** stoned, zonked **7** drugged **8** hopped-up, turned on, wiped out **9** spaced-out **10** freaked-out

Tristan's beloved 6 Iseult, Isolde

Tristan und Isolde composer 6 Wagner (Richard)

triste 3 sad **5** sorry **7** doleful, pensive, wistful **8** mournful **9** depressed, sorrowful **10** melancholy **11** melancholic

Tristram Shandy author 6 Sterne (Laurence)

trite 3 pat, set **4** dull, flat, hack **5** banal, corny, musty, slick, stale, stock, tired, vapid **6** cliché, jejune, old-hat **7** prosaic, worn-out **8** bathetic, bromidic, flyblown, ordinary, shopworn, timeworn, well-worn **9** hackneyed **10** threadbare **11** commonplace, stereotyped **13** platitudinous, stereotypical

triton 5 conch **7** mollusc, mollusk **9** shellfish

Triton 6 merman ***attribute:* 5** conch ***father:* 7** Neptune **8** Poseidon ***mother:* 10** Amphitrite

triturate 4 bray **5** crush, grind **6** powder **9** comminute, pulverize

triumph 3 joy, win **4** crow, palm **5** exult, glory, vaunt **6** master **7** conquer, prevail, succeed, success, victory **8** conquest, overcome, surmount **10** exultation, jubilation

triumphant 8 exultant, exulting, jubilant **10** conquering, victorious

triumvirate see **triad**

Triumvirate member 6 Antony (Marc), Caesar (Julius), Pompey (the Great) **7** Anthony (Mark), Crassus (Marcus Licinius), Lepidus (Marcus Aemilius) **8** Octavius (Gaius)

trivet 4 rack **5** stand **6** tripod

trivia 8 factoids, minutiae **9** small beer **11** small change **13** small potatoes

trivial 5 dinky, light, minor, petty, small **6** casual, measly, paltry, piddly, slight **8** nugatory, picayune, piddling, piffling, trifling **9** small-beer **10** negligible **11** Mickey Mouse, unimportant **13** insignificant

troche 6 tablet **7** lozenge **8** pastille **9** cough drop

troglodyte 6 hermit **7** caveman, recluse **11** cave dweller

Troilus *beloved:* 8 Cressida, Criseyde ***father:* 5** Priam ***mother:* 6** Hecuba ***slayer:* 8** Achilles

Trojan *horse builder:* 5 Epeus ***king:* 5** Priam ***priest:* 7** Laocoön ***queen:* 6** Hecuba ***soothsayer:* 7** Helenus **9** Cassandra ***warrior:* 5** Paris **6** Aeneas, Agenor, Hector **7** Glaucus **8** Sarpedon **9** Euphorbus, Polydamas

Trojan Horse builder 5 Epeus **6** Epeius

troll 4 fish, lure, sing, spin **5** angle, dwarf, prowl **6** goblin, search

trolley 3 car **4** cart, tram **8** carriage **9** streetcar

Trollope novel 10 Claverings (The) **11** Ayala's Angel, Phineas Finn **12** Phineas Redux **12** Way We Live Now (The) **15** Eustace Diamonds (The) **16** Barchester Towers

trombone 7 sackbut

tromp 4 beat, drub, hike, pelt, slog, walk, whup **5** pound, stamp, stomp, stump, tread **6** batter, buffet, pummel, thrash, trudge, wallop **7** belabor, clobber, trample **8** lambaste

troop 4 army, band, crew, host, pace, step, walk **5** corps, crowd, flock, tread **6** legion, outfit **7** brigade, company, soldier, traipse **8** assembly **9** associate, battalion, gathering, multitude **10** collection

trooper 3 cop **5** actor, horse **7** soldier **9** policeman **10** cavalryman

trope 6 cliché, simile **8** metaphor, metonymy **10** synecdoche

Trophonius *brother:* 8 Agamedes ***temple site:* 6** Delphi

trophy 3 cup **5** award, prize, relic, scalp, token **6** spoils **7** memento **8** hardware, keepsake, memorial, reminder, souvenir **9** loving cup **11** remembrance

tropical 3 hot **4** lush, warm **5** balmy, humid **6** jungly, steamy, sultry, torrid **10** equatorial

tropical storm see **typhoon**

Tropic of Cancer author 6 Miller (Henry)

Tros' son 4 Ilus **8** Ganymede

trot 3 jog **4** gait, lope, pony, rack **5** amble, hurry **7** setline **11** translation

troth 6 commit, engage, pledge **7** loyalty **8** affiance, contract, espousal, fidelity **10** engagement **12** faithfulness

trot out 4 show **6** expose, parade **7** display, disport, exhibit, show off

Trotsky, Leon *associate:* 5 Lenin (Vladimir) ***rival:* 6** Stalin (Joseph)

troubadour 4 bard, poet **6** singer **8** jongleur, minstrel, musician **9** balladist **10** folksinger

trouble 3 ado, ail, ill, irk, vex, woe **4** care, pain **5** annoy, beset, Dutch, grief, harry, haunt, pains, trial, upset, worry **6** bother, effort, harass, kiaugh, misery, pester, plague, ruffle, strain, stress, unrest **7** afflict, agitate, ailment, bedevil, concern, disturb, oppress, perturb, torment **8** aggrieve, disquiet, distress, hardship, hot water, irritate, vexation **9** suffering **10** difficulty, disconcert **11** disturbance, predicament

troubled 6 uneasy **7** anxious, worried **9** concerned, disturbed **10** distressed

troublemaker 7 hellion **8** agitator **9** firebrand **10** instigator **11** provocateur **12** rabble-rouser

troublesome 5 pesky **6** thorny, tricky, trying, vexing **7** carking, onerous, prickly **8** annoying **9** difficult, upsetting, vexatious **10** bothersome, burdensome, cumbersome, disturbing **11** disquieting, importunate, pestiferous

troublous 5 pesky **6** rugged, stormy **7** onerous **9** turbulent, vexatious **10** tumultuous **11** tempestuous

trough 3 hod **4** bowl, tank **5** basin, drain **6** vessel **7** channel **10** depression

trounce 4 beat, drub, lick, rout, whip, whup **5** crush, whomp **6** defeat, larrup, punish, thrash, thresh, wallop **7** clobber, shellac **9** overwhelm

troupe 4 band **5** corps, party **6** outfit **7** company

trouper 4 mime **5** actor, mimic **6** mummer,

player **7** actress, artiste **8** thespian **9** performer **11** entertainer
trousers 5 pants **6** slacks **7** drawers **8** breeches, britches ***tartan:*** **5** trews
trout *kind:* **3** sea **4** char, lake **5** brook, brown, river **7** rainbow **8** speckled **9** steelhead
Trovatore, Il *character:* **7** Azucena, Leonora, Manrico **11** Count di Luna ***composer:*** **5** Verdi (Giuseppe)
trove 4 find, haul **5** hoard, store **8** treasure **10** collection **11** aggregation **12** accumulation
Troy 5 Ilium ***epic of:*** **5** Iliad ***excavator:*** **10** Schliemann (Heinrich) ***founder:*** **4** Ilus ***modern site:*** **9** Hissarlik **11** Dardanelles (see also **Trojan**)
truant 4 idle **5** shirk **7** shirker, slacker **8** shirking **10** delinquent
truce 4 lull **5** letup, pause, peace **6** accord **7** respite **9** armistice, cease-fire
truck 3 ute, van **4** semi, swap **5** lorry, trade **6** barter, handle, peddle, retail **7** bargain, traffic **8** commerce, dealings, exchange ***military:*** **6** camion
Truckee River city 4 Reno
truckle 4 fawn **5** cower, defer, toady **6** cringe, grovel, kowtow **8** bootlick **11** apple-polish
truckler 5 leech, toady **6** lackey, sponge **7** spaniel **8** parasite **9** sycophant **10** bootlicker **11** lickspittle **13** apple-polisher
truculent 4 fell, grim **5** cruel, harsh, rough, sharp **6** brutal, deadly, fierce, savage, severe **7** abusive, warlike **9** barbarous, bellicose, combative, ferocious **10** pernicious, pugnacious **11** belligerent, contentious, destructive, opprobrious, quarrelsome
trudge 4 plod, slog, trek **5** march, tramp, tromp **8** footslog
true 4 real, very **5** valid **6** actual, honest, trusty **7** factual, genuine, staunch, upright **8** accurate, bona fide, constant, faithful, resolute, rightful **9** authentic, honorable, steadfast, undoubted, veracious, veritable **10** dependable, legitimate, undeniable **11** indubitable, trustworthy **12** indisputable **13** authoritative
true-blue 5 loyal **6** proven, steady, trusty **7** genuine **8** bona fide, constant, faithful, reliable, stalwart **9** steadfast **10** unswerving
truism 3 saw **4** rule **5** adage, axiom, gnome, maxim, moral **6** cliché, dictum, gospel, saying, verity **8** aphorism, apothegm **9** platitude **10** shibboleth **11** commonplace
Truk Island 3 Tol **4** Moen, Udot, Uman **5** Fefan **6** Dublon
truly 4 well **6** easily, indeed, really, surely, verily **7** de facto **8** actually **9** doubtless, genuinely, sincerely, veritably **10** absolutely, definitely, positively, truthfully, undeniably **11** confidently, doubtlessly, undoubtedly
Truman, Harry S *birthplace:* **5** Lamar **8** Missouri ***predecessor:*** **3** FDR ***successor:*** **3** DDE ***wife:*** **4** Bess
trump 3 cap, top **4** beat, best, pass, ruff **5** excel, outdo **6** better **7** manille, surpass **8** clincher, jew's harp, outstrip, override, spadille ***up:*** **6** invent **7** concoct **9** fabricate **11** manufacture
trumpery 4 bosh, junk, muck, slop, tosh **5** bilge, cheap, dreck, hokum, trash **6** bunkum, cheesy, common, humbug, paltry, piffle, shoddy, trashy **7** baloney, twaddle **8** claptrap, flimflam, malarkey, nonsense, rubbishy, tommyrot **10** double-talk
trumpet 4 horn, tout **6** herald **7** clarion **8** ballyhoo ***call:*** **6** sennet ***ram's horn:*** **6** shofar
trumpeter 4 Hirt (Al), swan **5** André (Maurice), Baker (Chet), Botti (Chris), Brown (Clifford), Davis (Miles), James (Harry) **6** Alpert (Herb), Balsom (Alison), Bolden (Buddy), Farmer (Art), Voisin (Roger) **7** Schwarz (Gerard) **8** advocate, Eldridge (Roy), eulogist, Marsalis (Wynton), Masekela (Hugh), Sandoval (Arturo) **9** Armstrong (Louis), encomiast, Gillespie (Dizzy), spokesman **10** mouthpiece, panegyrist, Severinsen (Doc)
truncate 3 lop, top **4** crop, trim **5** prune, shear **6** cut off **7** abridge, shorten **10** abbreviate
truncheon 3 bat **4** club **5** baton, billy **6** cudgel, warder **8** bludgeon **9** billy club **10** nightstick, shillelagh
trundle 3 bed, tub **4** cart, haul, roll, spin **5** churn, wheel **6** rotate **7** revolve **9** transport
trunk 3 box **4** body, bole, case, stem **5** chest, torso **7** channel, circuit, luggage ***elephant:*** **9** proboscis ***tree:*** **4** bole **5** stump
truss 3 tie **4** band, bind **5** brace **7** bandage, bracket, support **9** framework, supporter **10** strengthen
trust 4 hope, pool, rely **5** faith, stock **6** assume, bank on, belief, cartel, charge, commit, credit, rely on **7** build on, combine, confide, consign, count on, custody, keeping, presume **8** bank upon, credence, depend on, reckon on, reliance, rely upon **9** assurance, certainty, certitude, syndicate **10** confidence, conviction, dependence, depend upon **11** safekeeping **12** conglomerate
trustee 8 guardian **9** custodian, protector **10** supervisor
trustworthy 4 sure, true **5** tried, valid **6** honest, proven, secure **8** accurate, credible, faithful, reliable, stalwart, true-blue **9** authentic, realistic, steadfast, veracious **10** de-

pendable **11** responsible **12** tried and true **13** authoritative

trusty 4 true **5** tried **6** proven, secure, stable, steady **7** certain, convict **8** faithful, reliable **9** steadfast, truepenny **10** dependable **11** responsible **12** tried and true

truth 5 axiom, maxim, sooth **6** candor, gospel, verity **7** lowdown, reality, veritas **8** veracity **9** rightness **11** genuineness **12** authenticity ***goddess:*** **4** Maat ***serum:*** **11** scopolamine

truthful 5 frank **6** candid, honest **7** factual, sincere **8** accurate **9** realistic, veracious, veridical

truthfulness 6 candor, verity **7** honesty **8** veracity

try 3 aim, tax, vex **4** seek, shot, stab, test **5** annoy, assay, essay, judge, offer, prove, study, whack, whirl, worry **6** aspire, harass, harrow, sample, strain, stress, strive **7** afflict, adjudge, attempt, trouble **8** endeavor, struggle **9** undertake **10** adjudicate, experiment

trying 6 taxing, thorny, tricky, vexing **7** arduous, onerous **8** annoying, exacting, grueling **9** demanding, difficult, strenuous, vexatious **10** irritating

try out 4 test **5** check, prove **6** verify **7** confirm **8** audition

tryst 4 date **7** meeting **10** engagement, rendezvous **11** appointment, assignation

tsar see **czar**

tsunami 9 tidal wave

tub 3 vat **4** boat **9** container ***hot:*** **3** spa **7** Jacuzzi

tuba 7 helicon **9** bombardon, euphonium **10** sousaphone

tubby 3 fat **5** plump, podgy, porky, pudgy **6** chubby, chunky, rotund **8** roly-poly

tube 2 TV **4** duct, flue, hose, pipe **5** buret **6** siphon, subway, tunnel, vessel **7** burette, channel, conduit, cuvette, pipette, syringe **8** cylinder, pipeline **10** television ***anatomical:*** **3** vas **4** duct, vasa (plural) **7** salpinx **9** salpinges (plural)

tuber 3 oca, set **4** bulb, corm, root, stem, taro, yamp, yuca **5** salep, yucca **6** manioc, potato **7** cassava, rhizome **10** prominence

tuberculosis 8 phthisis, scrofula **11** consumption

tucker out 4 do in, poop, tire **5** drain, weary **7** exhaust

tuft 5 clump, mound **7** cluster ***of feathers:*** **7** panache ***ornamental:*** **6** pom-pom ***vascular:*** **6** glomus

tufted 7 crested

tug 3 tow **4** drag, draw, haul, moil, pull, toil **5** labor **6** strain, strive

tug-of-war 5 match **6** strife **7** contest, grapple, rivalry **8** conflict, struggle **11** competition

tuition 3 fee **6** charge **8** teaching, training, tutelage **9** education, schooling **11** instruction ***collector:*** **6** bursar

tumble 4 drop, fall, trip **5** upset **6** plunge, topple **8** collapse, keel over **9** bring down, overthrow

tumbledown 8 decrepit **10** ramshackle **11** dilapidated

tumbler 5 glass **6** roller **7** acrobat, gymnast **11** cartwheeler

tumbrel 4 cart **5** wagon **7** tipcart

tumescent 6 turgid **7** aureate, bloated, bulging, flowery, swollen **8** inflated, swelling **9** bombastic, dropsical, overblown **10** euphuistic, rhetorical

tummy 3 gut **5** belly **6** paunch **7** abdomen, stomach **8** potbelly **9** bay window **11** breadbasket

tumult 3 din **4** flap, riot, to-do **5** babel, broil, hoo-ha, hurly, noise, whirl **6** clamor, dither, hoo-haw, hubbub, lather, outcry, pother, racket, strife, uproar **7** ferment, tempest, turmoil **8** disorder, foofaraw, outburst, paroxysm, upheaval **9** agitation, commotion, confusion, kerfuffle, maelstrom **10** convulsion, hullabaloo, hurly-burly, turbulence

tumultuous 5 rowdy **6** stormy, unruly **7** raucous, riotous **9** clamorous, turbulent **10** boisterous, disorderly **11** rumbustious, tempestuous **12** rambunctious

tumulus 5 grave, knoll, mound **6** barrow **7** hillock

tun 3 keg, vat **4** butt, cask, pipe **6** barrel **8** hogshead, puncheon

tuna 3 ahi **4** pear **6** bigeye, bonito **7** bluefin **8** albacore, skipjack **9** scombroid, yellowfin

tune 3 air **4** dial, lilt, song **5** theme, tweak **6** accord, adjust, amount, attune, extent, jingle, melody, strain, temper **7** descant **8** modulate, regulate

tuneful 5 sweet **6** dulcet **7** melodic **9** melodious

tungsten 7 wolfram **9** scheelite **10** wolframite

tunic 4 jama **5** jupon **6** kirtle **7** hauberk ***Greek:*** **6** chiton

tunicate 4 salp **8** ascidian, chordate **9** sea squirt **11** urochordate

Tunisia *capital:* **5** Tunis ***city:*** **4** Sfax **6** Ariana ***island:*** **5** Jerba ***language:*** **6** Arabic ***monetary unit:*** **5** dinar ***neighbor:*** **5** Libya **7** Algeria ***ruins:*** **8** Carthage

tunnel 4 tube **6** burrow **7** conduit **8** crawlway ***Alps:*** **7** Simplon **11** Loetschberg ***France:*** **4** Rove ***Hudson river:*** **7** Holland, Lincoln ***Nevada:*** **5** Sutro ***railroad:*** **6** Hoosac **7** Cascade

Turandot ***character:*** **3** Liu **5** Calaf ***author:*** **5** Gozzi (Carlo) ***composer:*** **6** Busoni (Ferruccio) **7** Puccini (Giacomo)

turban 7 bandana, pugaree **8** bandanna **9** headdress

turbid 4 dark **5** dense, mucky, muddy, murky, riley, roily, smoky, thick **6** cloudy, opaque, roiled **7** clouded, obscure

turbot 8 flatfish

turbulence 3 din **4** flap, stew **5** babel, fight, hoo-ha **6** dither, fracas, lather, pother, tumult, uproar **7** turmoil **8** foofaraw **9** agitation, commotion

turbulent 4 wild **5** bumpy, roily, rough, rowdy **6** raging, stormy, unruly **7** furious, moiling, raucous, riotous, roaring **8** agitated, blustery, swirling **9** clamorous **10** boisterous, tumultuous

tureen 3 pot **4** bowl **5** crock **6** vessel **9** casserole

turf 3 sod **4** area, peat **5** grass, sward, track **6** domain, region **7** terrain **9** racetrack, territory **11** horse racing **12** neighborhood

turgid see **tumescent**

Turkey ***capital:*** **6** Ankara ***city:*** **5** Adana, Bursa, Izmir, Konya **8** Istanbul ***enclave:*** **8** Naxçivan ***lake:*** **3** Van ***leader:*** **7** Atatürk (Kemal) ***monetary unit:*** **4** lira ***mountain, range:*** **6** Ararat, Taurus ***neighbor:*** **4** Iran, Iraq **5** Syria **6** Greece **7** Armenia, Georgia **8** Bulgaria ***peninsula:*** **6** Balkan **9** Asia Minor ***river:*** **6** Tigris **8** Menderes **9** Euphrates ***sea:*** **6** Aegean **7** Marmara **13** Mediterranean

turkey ***buzzard:*** **7** vulture ***disease:*** **9** blackhead ***head growth:*** **5** snood **7** dewbill ***male:*** **3** tom **7** gobbler ***throat pouch:*** **6** wattle ***young:*** **5** poult

Turkish ***cavalryman:*** **5** spahi ***empire:*** **7** Ottoman ***governor:*** **4** vali ***inn:*** **4** kahn **6** imaret ***soldier:*** **5** nizam **9** janissary ***sultan:*** **5** Ahmed, Selim **7** Bajazet, Bayezid, Ilderim ***sword:*** **8** yataghan ***title:*** **3** aga, bey **4** agha **5** pasha **6** vizier **7** effendi

Turkmenistan ***capital:*** **8** Ashgabat **9** Ashkhabad ***desert:*** **7** Kara-Kum ***monetary unit:*** **5** manat, tenne ***neighbor:*** **4** Iran **10** Kazakhstan, Uzbekistan **11** Afghanistan ***river:*** **6** Murgab **7** Murghab **8** Amu Dar'ya ***sea:*** **7** Caspian

Turks and Caicos Islands ***capital:*** **9** Grand Turk ***location:*** **10** West Indies ***passage:*** **6** Caicos **8** Mouchoir ***territory of:*** **7** Britain

turmeric 3 dye **4** herb **5** spice **6** ginger **8** dyestuff

turmoil 4 coil, flap, moil, riot, stew, stir, to-do **5** chaos, whirl **6** clamor, dither, hassle, hubbub, lather, pother, strife, tumult, unease, unrest, uproar, welter **7** ferment **8** disorder, upheaval **9** agitation, commotion, confusion **10** disruption, hurly-burly, turbulence, uneasiness **11** pandemonium **13** helter-skelter, Sturm und Drang

turn 3 yaw, zag, zig **4** bend, bias, bout, cast, grow, gyre, reel, spin, tack, tour, veer, whip, wind **5** angle, curve, pivot, refer, shunt, spell, stint, swirl, train, twirl, whirl **6** detour, divert, gyrate, mutate, revert, rotate, switch, swivel **7** circuit, convert, deflect, deviate, digress, diverge, reverse, revolve **8** gyration, rotation **9** about-face, deviation, pirouette, volte-face

turnabout 3 rat **6** coward **7** reverse **8** apostate, defector, recreant, reversal **9** about-face, reversion, volte-face **11** retaliation **12** merry-go-round

turn aside 4 veer, shun, sway, veer **5** avert, repel, shunt, stave **6** divert, refuse, reject, swerve **7** deflect, deviate, digress, dismiss, diverge, fend off, reflect, ward off **9** sidetrack

turncoat 3 rat, spy **5** Judas **7** traitor **8** apostate, betrayer, defector, deserter, quisling, recreant, renegade **9** traitress, turnabout **13** tergiversator

turn down 4 jilt, veto **5** spurn **6** rebuff, refuse, reject **7** decline, dismiss **9** repudiate **10** disapprove

turned on 4 high **5** doped **6** stoned, zonked **7** aroused, drugged, excited **8** hopped-up, tripping **9** activated, spaced-out, zonked-out **10** passionate **12** enthusiastic

turn in 5 crash, rat on **6** betray, inform, rat out, retire, submit **7** deliver, produce, sack out **8** hand over **9** hit the hay **10** hit the sack, relinquish

turning point 4 cusp **5** pivot **6** climax, crisis **8** landmark **11** climacteric

turn inside out 5 evert

turnip 5 swede **8** rutabaga ***Scottish:*** **4** neep

turnip-shaped 8 napiform

turnkey 6 jailer

turn left 3 haw

Turn of the Screw, The ***author:*** **5** James (Henry) ***character:*** **5** Flora, Miles **10** Peter Quint ***composer:*** **7** Britten (Benjamin)

turn on 5 start **6** excite, ignite **7** start up **8** activate, motivate **9** stimulate, titillate

turn over 4 plow, roll **5** upend, upset **6** assign, commit, give up, rotate **7** capsize, consign, deliver, entrust, furnish, provide, revolve **8** delegate, transfer **9** overthrow, surrender **10** relinquish

turnpike 7 highway

turn right 3 gee

turn up 4 find **6** appear, arrive, reveal **7** uncover, unearth **8** discover **9** encounter **11** materialize

Turow work 4 One L **16** Presumed Innocent

turpentine 7 galipot, solvent, thinner ***ingredient:*** **6** pinene ***tree:*** **4** pine **9** terebinth

turret 5 tower **6** cupola, louver, louvre **7** mirador **8** bartizan **9** belvedere

turtle 8 terrapin, tortoise **9** chelonian ***edible part:*** **7** calipee **8** calipash ***genus:*** **4** Emys ***sea:*** **6** ridley **8** hawkbill ***shell:*** **8** carapace ***shell part:*** **8** plastron

Tuscany *city:* **4** Pisa **8** Florence ***river:*** **4** Arno ***tower:*** **4** Pisa ***wine:*** **7** chianti

tusk 4 fang **5** ivory, tooth

tusker 6 dugong, walrus **7** mammoth, muntjac, narwhal, warthog **8** elephant, musk deer **11** barking deer

tussle 4 spar **5** scrap, scrum **6** hassle, scrape **7** scuffle, wrangle, wrestle **8** argument, skirmish, struggle **9** scrimmage **11** controversy

tussock 4 tuft **5** clump, mound **7** cluster

tutelage see **tuition**

tutor 3 don **5** coach, teach **6** docent, mentor **7** teacher **9** pedagogue, preceptor **10** instructor

Tut's tomb discoverer 6 Carter (Howard)

tutti 3 all **8** everyone **9** everybody

Tuvalu *capital:* **8** Funafuti ***ethnic group:*** **10** Polynesian ***former name:*** **6** Ellice (Islands)

TVA dam 5 Ocoee

twaddle 3 jaw, yak **4** bosh, bull, bunk, chat, guff, muck, talk, tosh **5** clack, drool, hooey, prate, run on **6** babble, bunkum, burble, drivel, gabble, hot air, humbug, jabber, tattle **7** baloney, blabber, blarney, blather, chatter, hogwash, prattle, rubbish **8** claptrap, malarkey, nonsense, tommyrot, trumpery **9** poppycock **10** applesauce, balderdash **12** blatherskite

Twain character 3 Jim **5** Becky (Thatcher) **8** Huck Finn, Injun Joe **9** Aunt Polly, Joe Harper, Tom Sawyer

tweak 4 jerk, mock, pull, zing **5** annoy, pinch, pluck **6** adjust, bother, modify, twitch **8** fine-tune **9** poke fun at

tweet 4 call, note **5** cheep, chirp **7** chirrup, twitter

Twelfth Night character 5 Viola **6** Olivia, Orsino (Duke) **7** Antonio, Cesario **8** Malvolio **9** Sebastian, Toby Belch

twelve *combining form:* **5** dodec **6** dodeca

twenty 5 score ***combining form:*** **4** icos **5** icosa, icosi

twerp 4 brat, drip, fool, jerk, nerd, twit **6** squirt

twibil 2 ax **3** axe

twice 3 bis **7** twofold ***combining form:*** **3** bis ***prefix:*** **3** dis

twice a day 3 b.i.d. **8** bis in die **11** semidiurnal

twice a year 8 biannual **10** semiannual, semiyearly

twig 5 shoot, sprig, withe **6** branch ***bundle of:*** **5** fagot **6** faggot

twiggy 4 slim, thin **5** reedy **6** skinny, slight, stalky **7** slender **9** sticklike

twilight 3 eve **4** dusk **5** gloam, gloom **6** sunset **7** decline **8** gloaming **9** nightfall **10** crepuscule

Twilight of the Gods 8 Ragnarok ***composer:*** **6** Wagner (Richard)

twill 5 chino, cloth, serge, toile, tweed, weave **6** fabric **7** cheviot **8** dungaree **9** bombazine, gabardine **11** herringbone

twin 4 dual, like, mate **5** clone, match **6** bifold, binary, double, fellow, paired **7** matched, similar, twofold **8** matching **9** companion, duplicate, identical **10** coordinate, reciprocal

Twin Cities 6 St. Paul **11** Minneapolis

twine 4 coil, cord, curl, wind, wrap **5** twist, weave **6** spiral, string **7** embrace, meander, wreathe **8** entangle **9** interlace **10** interweave

twinge 4 ache, pain, pang, stab **5** pluck, shoot, throe, twang, tweak **6** stitch

twinkle 3 bat **4** flit, wink **5** blink, flash, flirt, gleam, glint, light, shake, shine, trice **7** flicker, flutter, glimmer, glisten, glitter, shimmer, sparkle **9** coruscate, nictitate **11** coruscation, scintillate

twin stars 6 Castor, Pollux

twirl 4 coil, gyre, spin **5** pitch, trill, whirl, whorl **6** gyrate **7** revolve **9** pirouette

twist 3 wry **4** coil, curl, skew, turn, warp, wind **5** belie, gnarl, pivot, twine, twirl, wring **6** garble, spiral, sprain, squirm, torque, wrench, writhe **7** contort, distort, entwine, falsify, pervert, wriggle

twisted 3 wry **4** awry, sick **5** askew, kinky **6** swirly, warped **9** perverted

twister 6 funnel **7** tornado **9** dust devil, whirlwind **10** waterspout

twit 4 dolt, fool, gibe, jeer, jive, josh, mock, quiz, razz **5** chide, rally, scout, taunt, tease, twerp **6** deride **8** bonehead, numskull, ridicule **9** blockhead, numbskull **10** nincompoop

twitch 3 tic **4** jerk, pang, pull, yank **5** pluck, spasm, throe, tweak **6** quiver **10** quack grass

twitter 4 chat, peep **5** cheep, chirp, quake, tweet **6** cackle, giggle, jargon, quiver, shiver, titter, tremor, warble **7** chatter, chirrup, tremble

twittery 6 giggly **8** chattery **9** flustered, tremulous

two 3 duo **4** duet, pair **5** twain **6** couple ***combining form:*** **3** bis, duo, dyo ***divide into:*** **4** fork **6** bisect **9** bifurcate ***prefix:*** **3** twi

two-faced 9 deceitful, dishonest, insincere **11** duplicitous **12** hypocritical **13** double-dealing ***god:*** **5** Janus

twofold 4 dual, twin **5** binal, duple **6** binary, double, duplex, dyadic, paired **9** dualistic

two-footed 7 bipedal

Two Gentlemen of Verona *author:* **11** Shakespeare (William) ***character:*** **5** Julia **6** Silvia, Thurio **7** Proteus **9** Valentine

two-sided 9 bilateral

twosome 3 duo **4** dyad, item, pair **5** brace **6** couple **7** doublet

two-time 4 dupe **6** betray, delude, humbug, take in **7** beguile, cheat on, deceive, mislead **9** bamboozle **11** double-cross

two-wheeler 4 bike **5** cycle **7** bicycle, scooter **10** motorcycle

Tybalt *cousin:* **6** Juliet ***family:*** **7** Capulet ***slayer:*** **5** Romeo ***victim:*** **8** Mercutio

tycoon 5 mogul, nabob **7** magnate

tyke 3 dog, kid **5** child, hound, puppy **6** canine, moppet, nipper, shaver **7** mongrel

tympanum 7 eardrum **9** middle ear

Tyndareus *kingdom:* **6** Sparta ***wife:*** **4** Leda

type 3 cut, ilk, key, lot, way **4** cast, form, kind, mold, sort **5** breed, class, genre, order, print, serif, stamp **6** kidney, nature, stripe **7** feather, species, variety **8** category, keyboard ***bar:*** **4** slug ***font:*** **5** Arial, Goudy **6** Bodoni **7** Antigua, Century, Courier **8** Garamond, Palatino, Perpetua **9** Helvetica **10** Times Roman ***measure:*** **2** em, en **4** pica **5** point ***set:*** **7** compose ***setter:*** **10** compositor ***size:*** **4** pica **5** agate, elite, pearl ***stroke:*** **5** serif ***style:*** **4** bold **5** roman, serif **6** Gothic, italic **7** Fraktur **8** boldface **9** lightface, sans serif ***tray:*** **6** galley

Typee *author:* **8** Melville (Herman) ***character:*** **4** Toby

typewriter *part:* **3** key **6** platen, spacer ***type size:*** **4** pica **5** elite

Typhon 3 Set **7** monster **8** Typhoeus ***offspring:*** **6** Sphinx **7** Chimera **8** Cerberus, Chimaera ***wife:*** **7** Echidna

typhoon 7 cyclone **9** hurricane **13** tropical storm

typical 5 ideal, model, usual **6** common, normal **7** classic, general, natural, regular **8** symbolic

typify 6 embody, mirror **9** epitomize, exemplify, personify, represent, symbolize **10** illustrate **11** emblematize **12** characterize

typo 5 error **7** erratum **8** misprint **11** corrigendum

typographer 7 printer **10** compositor

Tyr 3 Tiu ***brother:*** **4** Thor ***father:*** **4** Odin **5** Woden ***god of:*** **3** war ***mother:*** **5** Jordh, Jorth

tyrannical 8 absolute, despotic **9** arbitrary **10** absolutist, autocratic, oppressive **11** dictatorial

tyrannize 7 oppress **8** dominate, domineer, overbear

tyrannous 5 harsh **6** brutal, severe **8** absolute, despotic **9** arbitrary, fascistic **10** autocratic **11** dictatorial

tyranny 7 cruelty, fascism **9** autocracy, despotism, monocracy **10** absolutism, domination, oppression **12** dictatorship

tyrant 4 czar, duce, tsar, tzar **5** ruler **6** despot, führer **7** fuehrer, pharaoh, usurper **8** autocrat, dictator **9** oppressor, strongman **10** absolutist

Tyrian ____ 6 purple

tyro 4 punk **6** novice, rookie **7** amateur, dabbler, student **8** beginner, freshman, neophyte, newcomer **9** novitiate **10** apprentice, dilettante, tenderfoot **11** abecedarian

Tyrol see **Tirol**

tzar see **czar**

tzigane 3 Rom **5** gypsy **6** Romany

U

übermensch 8 superman

ubiquitous 7 allover **9** pervasive, universal **10** everywhere, wall-to-wall, widespread **11** omnipresent

U-boat 3 sub **7** pigboat **9** submarine

Uganda *capital:* **7** Kampala ***falls:*** **5** Ripon ***lake:*** **5** Kyoga **6** Albert, Edward, George **8** Victoria ***leader:*** **4** Amin (Idi) ***monetary unit:*** **8** shilling ***mountain:*** **5** Elgon ***mountain range:*** **9** Ruwenzori ***neighbor:*** **5**

Congo, Kenya, Sudan **6** Rwanda **8** Tanzania ***river:*** **4** Nile
ugly 4 vile **7** hideous **8** deformed **9** loathsome, misshapen, offensive, repugnant, repulsive, unsightly **10** disfigured **12** unattractive
Ugly Duckling author 8 Andersen (Hans Christian)
ukase 4 fiat **5** edict, order **6** decree, dictum, ruling **7** command, dictate, mandate **9** directive **10** injunction **12** proclamation **13** pronouncement
Ukraine *capital:* 4 Kiev ***city:*** **4** Lviv, Lvov **5** Yalta **6** Odessa **7** Kharkiv **9** Chernobyl ***ethnic group:*** **7** Cossack ***monetary unit:*** **6** hryvny ***mountain range:*** **10** Carpathian ***neighbor:*** **6** Poland, Russia **7** Belarus, Hungary, Moldova **8** Slovakia ***peninsula:*** **5** Kerch **6** Crimea **7** Crimean ***river:*** **3** Bug **5** Tisza **6** Donets **7** Dnieper **8** Dniester ***sea:*** **4** Azov **5** Black
Ulalume author 3 Poe (Edgar Allan)
ulcer 4 sore **6** fester **7** corrupt ***kind:*** **6** peptic **8** duodenal ***mouth:*** **10** canker sore
ulna 7 forearm
Ulster hero 6 Fergus **7** Deirdre **9** Conchobar, Cuchulain, Cuchullin **10** Cú Chulainn
ulterior 5 privy **6** covert, future, hidden, latent **7** further, obscure, remoter **9** ambiguous, concealed **10** subsequent, succeeding **11** undisclosed
ultimate 3 end, nth **4** acme, last, peak **5** basic, final, utter **6** summit, utmost, zenith **7** closing, epitome, extreme, maximum, primary, supreme, topmost **8** absolute, deciding, decisive, eventual, farthest, furthest, greatest, original, terminal **9** elemental, paramount **10** apotheosis, concluding, conclusive, consummate, preeminent **11** categorical, fundamental, furthermost, indivisible **12** incomparable, quintessence
ultimatum 5 order **6** demand, threat **7** mandate **9** challenge **12** notification
ultra 5 kinky, outré, rabid **6** beyond, far-out, too-too **7** extreme, fanatic, radical **9** excessive, extremist, fanatical **10** outlandish **11** extravagant
ultraconservative 11 reactionary
ultraist 5 rabid **6** zealot **7** extreme, fanatic, radical **9** extremist
ultramarine 7 oversea, sea-blue **8** overseas **11** lapis lazuli
ululate 3 bay **4** howl, wail, yowl
Ulysses *author:* 5 Joyce (James) ***character:*** **5** Bloom (Leopold), Molly (Bloom) **6** Blazes (Boylan) **7** Dedalus (Stephen) ***last word:*** **3** yes (see also **Odysseus**)
umber 5 brown, sepia, shade **6** darken, shadow
umbilicus 3 hub **4** core **5** heart, hilum, navel **6** center
umbra 5 shade **6** shadow
umbrage 4 hint, huff **5** anger, pique, shade **6** shadow **7** chagrin, dudgeon, foliage, leafage, offense **9** annoyance, suspicion **10** irritation, resentment **11** displeasure, indignation **12** exasperation
umbrageous 5 shady **6** shaded, touchy **7** shadowy **8** shadowed **9** defensive, sensitive
umbrella 5 cover, guard, shade **6** brolly, pileus, screen **7** parasol, protect, shelter **8** sunshade **10** protection **11** bumbershoot
umph see **oomph**
umpire 3 ref **5** judge **6** decide, settle **7** arbiter, referee **9** arbitrate **10** arbitrator ***call:*** **3** out **4** balk, ball, safe **6** strike
unabashed 5 blunt, brash, frank, naked, overt **6** arrant, brassy, brazen, candid **7** blatant, forward **8** outright **9** audacious, barefaced, shameless, undaunted **10** unblushing **11** undisguised, unmitigated **12** unapologetic
unabbreviated see **unabridged**
unable 5 inept, unfit **8** helpless, impotent **9** incapable, maladroit, powerless, unskilled **10** unequipped **11** incompetent, unqualified **13** incapacitated
unabridged 5 uncut, whole **6** entire, intact **8** complete **10** full-length **11** uncondensed **13** unabbreviated
unacceptable 8 unwanted **9** unwelcome **10** unsuitable **11** intolerable, undesirable **12** inadmissible **13** exceptionable, inappropriate, insupportable, objectionable
unaccompanied 4 lone, sole, solo, stag **5** alone, apart **6** single **8** detached, solitary **9** a cappella **10** unattended, unescorted
unaccountable 6 arcane, mystic **7** strange **8** baffling, puzzling **9** enigmatic **10** mysterious, mystifying, unknowable, unreliable **12** impenetrable, inexplicable, undependable, unfathomable **13** irresponsible, unexplainable
unaccustomed 3 new **5** alien, novel **6** unused **7** strange, unusual **8** singular, uncommon, unwonted **10** unexpected, unfamiliar
unadorned 4 bald, bare **5** naked, plain, spare, stark **6** rustic, severe, simple **7** artless, austere, natural, spartan **11** undecorated **13** unembellished, unembroidered, unpretentious
unadulterated 4 neat, pure **5** sheer, utter **7** genuine, unmixed **8** absolute, straight **9** unalloyed, undiluted **11** unmitigated, unqualified

unaffected **5** naive **6** candid, simple **7** artless, callous, genuine, natural, sincere, unmoved **9** guileless, impassive, ingenuous, unaltered, unchanged, unstudied, untouched **10** hard-boiled, impervious **13** unpretentious

unalloyed **4** pure **5** sheer, total **7** genuine, unmixed **8** absolute, straight **9** authentic, out-and-out, undiluted **11** unmitigated, unqualified **13** thoroughgoing, unadulterated

unalterable **5** fixed **7** binding, bounden, certain, decided **8** constant, required **9** immutable, mandatory, necessary **10** compulsory, invariable **12** unchangeable **13** predetermined

unambiguous **5** clear, lucid, plain **6** patent **7** evident, express, obvious, precise **8** apparent, clean-cut, clear-cut, decisive, definite, distinct, explicit, manifest, specific, univocal **10** definitive, forthright **11** categorical, translucent, transparent, unequivocal **12** transpicuous

unanimous **5** as one **6** united **8** communal, univocal **9** unopposed **10** collective **11** uncontested **13** consentaneous

unanimously **5** as one **6** wholly **7** en masse **10** altogether

unanticipated **9** unplanned **10** surprising, unexpected, unforeseen **12** out of the blue

unappeasable **4** grim **7** adamant **8** obdurate, resolute **9** insatiate, unbending **10** implacable, insatiable, relentless, unyielding **11** unrelenting **12** unquenchable

unappetizing **4** icky **5** gross, yucky **7** insipid **8** unsavory **9** repugnant **11** unappealing, unpalatable **12** unattractive

unapproachable **5** aloof **6** remote, offish **7** distant **8** reserved **10** unfriendly, unsociable **11** standoffish, unreachable **12** inaccessible, unattainable

unasked **7** willing **8** unbidden, unsought, unwanted **9** uninvited, unwelcome, voluntary **10** gratuitous, unprompted **11** spontaneous, uncalled-for, unrequested, voluntarily

unassailable **6** secure **8** airtight **10** invincible, inviolable, undeniable **11** impregnable, irrefutable **12** indisputable, invulnerable **13** incontestable, unconquerable

unassertive **3** shy **4** meek **5** mousy, timid **6** modest, mousey **7** bashful **8** backward, reticent, retiring, sheepish, timorous **9** diffident, shrinking **10** submissive **12** self-effacing

unassuming **3** shy **6** humble, modest, simple **8** ordinary, retiring **9** diffident **11** unassertive **12** self-effacing **13** unpretentious

unattached **4** free **5** loose **6** single **8** separate **9** unmarried **10** unassigned **11** uncommitted, unconnected **12** disconnected, freestanding, unassociated

unattainable **7** elusive **10** impossible **12** inaccessible

unattractive **4** drab, dull, ugly **5** dowdy, plain **6** homely **8** frumpish **10** unalluring, unsuitable **11** unappealing, undesirable **12** unflattering

unauthentic **4** fake, mock, sham **5** bogus, dummy, faked, false, phony **6** ersatz, forged, pseudo **7** feigned **8** affected, spurious **9** contrived, imitation, pretended, simulated **10** apocryphal, artificial **11** counterfeit, make-believe **12** illegitimate

unavailable **4** busy **6** absent, tied up **7** missing **8** occupied

unavailing **4** idle, vain **5** empty **6** barren, futile **7** useless **8** abortive, bootless **9** fruitless, pointless **11** ineffective, ineffectual **12** unproductive

unavoidable **5** fated **7** certain **8** destined **9** impending, necessary **10** compulsory, inevitable, obligatory **11** ineluctable, inescapable

unavoidably **8** perforce **10** helplessly, inevitably, willy-nilly **11** inescapably, necessarily, whether or no

unaware, unawares **5** aback **7** unready **8** abruptly, heedless, ignorant, off guard, suddenly **9** oblivious, unknowing, unmindful, unwitting **10** by surprise, unfamiliar, uninformed, unprepared **12** unacquainted, unexpectedly

unbalance **11** destabilize

unbalanced **3** mad **4** daft **5** batty, nutty **6** crazed, insane, uneven, wobbly **7** unequal, unsound **8** demented, deranged, lopsided, unhinged, unstable **9** psychotic **10** disordered, moonstruck

unbearable **11** intolerable, unendurable **12** excruciating, insufferable

unbeautiful **4** ugly **5** plain **6** homely **8** uncomely, unlovely **9** unsightly **10** ill-favored, unbecoming, uninviting **12** unattractive

unbecoming **8** improper, unlovely, unseemly, untimely, untoward, unworthy **9** inelegant, tasteless, unfitting **10** indecorous, indelicate, malapropos, unsuitable **11** disgraceful **12** unattractive **13** inappropriate

unbelievable **7** amazing, awesome **8** fabulous **9** fantastic **10** astounding, improbable, incredible, phenomenal, staggering, stupendous **11** astonishing, implausible, spectacular **12** unconvincing, unimaginable **13** extraordinary, inconceivable

unbeliever **5** pagan **6** giaour **7** atheist, doubter, gentile, heathen, heretic, infidel, scoffer, skeptic **8** agnostic **10** Pyrrhonist **11** freethinker

unbelieving 5 leery **6** show-me **8** agnostic, apostate, doubting **9** quizzical, skeptical **10** dissenting, suspicious **11** incredulous, mistrustful, questioning

unbending 4 iron **5** rigid, stern, stiff **6** severe **8** hard-line, obdurate, resolute **9** inelastic **10** brassbound, inexorable, inflexible, unyielding

unbiased 4 fair, just **5** equal **7** neutral **8** detached, tolerant **9** equitable, impartial, objective, unbigoted **10** even-handed, open-minded **11** broad-minded, uncommitted **12** unprejudiced **13** disinterested, dispassionate

unbidden 7 unasked, willing **8** unsought, unwanted **9** impromptu, uninvited, unwelcome, voluntary **10** gratuitous, unprompted **11** spontaneous, unrequested

unbind 4 free, undo **5** loose, untie **6** detach, loosen **7** manumit, release, unchain, unloose **8** dissolve, liberate, unfasten, unloosen **9** discharge, disengage, unshackle **10** emancipate

unblemished 4 pure **7** perfect **8** flawless, spotless, unmarred, virtuous **9** exemplary, faultless, stainless, undefiled, unspotted, unsullied **10** immaculate **11** untarnished

unbosom 4 bare, open, tell **6** betray, expose, reveal, unveil **7** divulge, express, uncover **8** disclose

unbound 4 free **5** freed, loose **6** loosed **10** unattached, unconfined, unfastened

unbounded 4 open **6** untold **7** endless **8** infinite, unending **9** excessive, limitless, unchecked, unlimited **10** immoderate, indefinite, inordinate **11** extravagant, measureless **12** immeasurable, incalculable, uncontrolled, unrestrained

unbreakable 7 durable, lasting **10** unyielding **11** everlasting

unbridled 4 free **5** loose **6** madcap **8** reckless, uncurbed **9** dissolute, unchecked **10** immoderate, licentious, unconfined, unfettered, ungoverned **11** spontaneous, uninhibited, unrepressed **12** uncontrolled, unrestrained, unrestricted **13** unconstrained

unbroken 5 solid, sound, whole **6** entire, intact, single **8** complete, constant, enduring **9** ceaseless, steadfast, unceasing, undamaged, undivided, unsubdued, unvarying **10** continuous, unimpaired **13** uninterrupted

unburden 3 rid **4** dump, ease, lose **5** shake **6** reveal, unload **7** cast off, confess, confide, off-load, relieve **8** shake off, throw off **9** discharge **10** relinquish **11** disencumber

uncalled-for 8 baseless, needless **9** officious, unfounded **10** gratuitous, groundless **11** unessential, unjustified, unnecessary, unwarranted **13** unjustifiable

uncanny 5 eerie, weird **6** creepy, spooky **7** ghostly, strange **9** unearthly, unnatural **10** mysterious, mystifying, superhuman **11** supernormal, supranormal **12** supernatural

uncared-for 5 dingy **6** beat-up, shabby **7** rickety, run-down, worn-out **8** decrepit, derelict, deserted, desolate, forsaken, tattered, untended **9** neglected **10** broken-down, down-at-heel, ramshackle, tumble-down **11** dilapidated

uncaring 4 cold **7** callous **9** heartless, negligent, oblivious, unfeeling, unheeding **11** coldhearted, hard-hearted, indifferent, insensitive, thoughtless, unconcerned **13** inconsiderate, unsympathetic

unceasing 7 abiding, endless, eternal, nonstop, undying **8** constant, enduring, unbroken, unending **9** continual, perennial, perpetual **10** continuous **11** amaranthine, everlasting, unremitting **12** imperishable, interminable **13** uninterrupted

unceremonious 4 curt, rude **5** bluff, blunt, frank, hasty, sharp, short, terse **6** abrupt, breezy, casual, sudden **7** brusque, hurried, offhand **8** familiar, informal **10** ungracious **11** precipitate, precipitous

uncertain 4 hazy, iffy, moot **5** vague **6** chancy, fitful, unsure, wobbly **7** dubious, erratic, halting, unclear **8** arguable, doubtful, insecure, slippery, unstable, unsteady, variable **9** ambiguous, debatable, undecided, unsettled **10** ambivalent, disputable, inconstant, indefinite, precarious **11** problematic, speculative **12** questionable, undependable **13** indeterminate, problematical, unforeseeable, unpredictable, untrustworthy

uncertainty 5 doubt **7** dubiety **8** distrust, mistrust **9** ambiguity, suspicion **10** indecision, perplexity, puzzlement, skepticism, uneasiness **11** ambivalence **12** doubtfulness, irresolution

unchain 4 free **5** loose **6** loosen, unbind **7** manumit, release **8** liberate, unfasten, unfetter **9** discharge, unshackle **10** emancipate **11** disenthrall

unchangeable 3 set **4** firm **5** fixed **7** settled **8** constant **9** immutable, permanent **10** continuing, inflexible, invariable **11** established, inalterable

unchanging 5 fixed **6** stable, static, steady **7** abiding, equable, eternal, settled, stabile, uniform **8** constant, enduring **9** immutable, steadfast, unvarying **10** consistent, continuing, invariable

unchaste 4 easy, lewd **5** bawdy, loose **6** impure, vulgar, wanton **7** immoral, lustful, obscene, scarlet, unclean **8** depraved, prurient **9** debauched, dissolute, lecherous, salacious **10** adulterous, lascivious, libidinous, licentious, profligate **11** promiscuous

unchecked 5 loose **7** rampant **9** spreading, unbounded, unbridled **10** widespread **11** uninhibited **12** unrestrained, unrestricted

uncivil 4 rude **5** crass, crude **6** coarse, savage, vulgar **7** boorish, ill-bred, uncouth **8** barbaric, impolite **9** barbarous **10** indecorous, uncultured, ungracious **11** ill-mannered, uncourteous **12** discourteous **13** disrespectful

uncivilized 4 rude, wild **5** crude **6** brutal, coarse, Gothic, savage **7** boorish, Hunnish, ill-bred, loutish, lowbred, uncouth **8** barbaric, churlish **9** barbarian, barbarous, primitive, unrefined **10** mannerless, uncultured, unmannerly, unpolished **12** uncultivated **13** unenlightened

unclad see **unclothed**

uncle *cry:* 6 give up **9** surrender ***Dutch:* 6** critic **7** advisor ***French:* 5** oncle ***Scottish:* 3** eme ***Spanish:* 3** tío ***U.S. symbol:* 3** Sam

unclean 4 foul **5** dingy, dirty, grimy **6** filthy, grubby, grungy, impure, soiled, sordid **7** corrupt, defiled, immoral, obscene, squalid, stained, sullied, tainted **8** befouled, indecent, polluted, unchaste **9** tarnished **10** besmirched, desecrated **12** contaminated

unclear 3 dim **4** hazy **5** murky, vague **6** bleary, blurry, cloudy, opaque, unsure **7** clouded, cryptic, dubious, obscure, shadowy **8** doubtful, nebulous, overcast, puzzling **9** ambiguous, enigmatic, tenebrous, unsettled **10** ill-defined, indistinct, indefinite, inexplicit **13** indeterminate

Uncle Remus creator 6 Harris (Joel Chandler)

Uncle Tom's Cabin *author:* 5 Stowe (Harriet Beecher) ***character:* 5** Eliza, Topsy **6** Legree (Simon) **9** Little Eva

Uncle Vanya author 7 Chekhov (Anton)

unclothe 5 strip **6** denude, divest, expose, unveil **7** display, disrobe, uncloak, uncover, undress

unclothed 4 bare, nude **5** naked **6** peeled, unclad **7** denuded, exposed **8** in the raw, stripped **9** au naturel, buck-naked, undressed **10** stark naked

unclouded 4 fair **5** clear, lucid, sunny **6** bright **7** halcyon **8** rainless, sunshiny

uncluttered 4 neat, tidy, trig, trim **7** orderly **9** organized, shipshape **11** spic-and-span, well-ordered **12** spick-and-span

uncombed 5 messy, mussy **6** matted, mussed **7** ruffled, snarled, tangled, tousled, unkempt **10** disheveled

uncommon 3 odd **4** rare **5** novel **6** choice, scarce, unique **7** special, unusual **8** esoteric, especial, singular, sporadic, unwonted **10** infrequent, noteworthy, remarkable **11** distinctive, exceptional **12** unaccustomed **13** extraordinary

uncommunicative 3 mum **4** dumb **5** aloof **6** offish, silent **7** distant, guarded, private **8** reserved, reticent, taciturn **9** reclusive, secretive, withdrawn **10** antisocial, poker-faced, speechless, tongue-tied, unsociable **11** inscrutable, standoffish, tight-lipped **12** closemouthed, tight-mouthed, unresponsive **13** unforthcoming

uncompassionate 4 cold, hard **5** stony **7** callous **8** obdurate, pitiless, uncaring **9** heartless, unfeeling **10** hard-boiled **11** coldhearted, hardhearted, insensitive **12** stonyhearted **13** unsympathetic

uncomplicated 4 easy **5** basic, clear, plain **6** simple **8** clear-cut **10** effortless, elementary, manageable, uninvolved

uncomplimentary 7 adverse **8** critical **9** degrading **10** belittling, derogatory, pejorative **11** deprecatory, disparaging, unfavorable **12** depreciative, depreciatory, unflattering

uncompromising 4 firm **5** rigid **8** hard-line, obdurate, resolute, stubborn **9** hard-nosed, immovable, insistent, unbending **10** brass-bound, determined, inexorable, inflexible, unshakable, unyielding **12** intransigent, single-minded

unconcealed 4 bald, bare, open **5** frank, naked, overt, plain **6** candid **7** blatant, evident, exposed, express, obvious, visible **8** apparent, explicit, manifest, palpable **10** forthright **11** openhearted, transparent, undisguised, unvarnished

unconcern 6 apathy **7** neglect **9** aloofness, disregard **10** alienation, detachment, dispassion **11** disinterest, inattention, insouciance, nonchalance **12** carelessness, heedlessness, indifference **13** preoccupation

unconcerned 4 cool **6** remote **7** unmoved **8** careless, detached, heedless **9** alienated, apathetic, oblivious, unmindful, unruffled **10** insouciant, neglectful, untroubled **11** inattentive, indifferent, unperturbed **12** uninterested **13** disinterested, dispassionate

unconditional 5 sheer, total, utter **8** absolute, definite, explicit, outright **9** downright, out-

and-out **10** unreserved **11** unequivocal, unqualified **12** unrestricted **13** thoroughgoing
unconfined 4 free, vast **5** loose **7** at large **9** at liberty, boundless, limitless, unlimited **12** unrestrained, unrestricted
uncongenial 6 at odds **8** unfitted **9** repellent, repugnant, unlikable **10** discordant, unsociable, unsuitable **11** conflicting, displeasing **12** antipathetic, disagreeable, incompatible, unattractive **13** unsympathetic
unconnected 5 alone, apart **8** discrete, detached, disjoint, disjunct, distinct, inchoate, rambling, separate **9** unrelated **10** unattached **11** independent **12** unassociated **13** discontinuous, noncontinuous
unconquerable 10 invincible, inviolable, unbeatable **11** bulletproof, impregnable, indomitable, insuperable **12** invulnerable, unassailable
unconscionable 5 undue **6** unfair, unholy, unjust, wanton, wicked **7** immoral, ungodly **8** barbaric, criminal **9** barbarous, unethical **10** exorbitant, inordinate, outrageous **11** inexcusable, uncivilized **12** unprincipled, unscrupulous
unconscious 3 out **6** asleep, chance **7** out cold, stunned, unaware **8** comatose **9** insensate, passed out, unplanned, unwitting **10** blacked out, insensible, knocked out **11** inadvertent, instinctual, involuntary **12** uncalculated **13** unintentional
unconsciousness 4 coma **5** faint **6** stupor, torpor, trance **7** syncope **13** obliviousness
unconsidered 4 rash **5** brash, hasty **6** casual **7** offhand **8** careless, reckless, slapdash **9** desultory, haphazard, hit-or-miss, hotheaded, impetuous, unplanned **10** ill-advised, incautious, unthinking **11** thoughtless
unconstrained 4 free, open **6** blithe, dégagé, wanton **7** buoyant, gushing, relaxed **8** animated, carefree, effusive, informal, outgoing **9** easygoing, expansive, liberated **10** expressive, nonchalant, unreserved
uncontrollable 4 wild **6** unruly **7** wayward, willful **9** fractious **10** headstrong, refractory, self-willed **11** intractable **12** overwhelming, recalcitrant, ungovernable, unmanageable **13** irrepressible, undisciplined
uncontrolled 4 free, wild **5** loose **6** wanton **9** automatic, excessive, unbounded, unlimited, unmanaged **10** autonomous, immoderate, licentious, ungoverned **11** independent, instinctual, involuntary, unconscious, uninhibited, unregulated **12** disorganized, unrestrained **13** self-governing
unconventional 3 odd **4** beat, boho **5** kinky, kooky, outré **6** casual, far-out, freaky, quirky, unique, way-out, weirdo **7** bizarre, deviant, oddball, offbeat, unusual, wayward **8** aberrant, abnormal, atypical, bohemian, freakish, original, peculiar **9** anomalous, eccentric, irregular **10** avant-garde, unexpected, unorthodox **11** uncustomary **13** idiosyncratic
unconvinced 5 leery **6** unsure **7** dubious **8** doubtful **9** skeptical, undecided **10** suspicious
unconvincing 4 lame **6** feeble, flimsy, forced **7** dubious, suspect **8** doubtful, strained **10** farfetched, improbable, incredible **11** implausible, unrealistic **12** unbelievable **13** unsubstantial
uncooked 3 raw
uncouple 4 part **6** detach, divide **7** disjoin, divorce, unhitch **8** separate, unfasten **9** disengage **10** disconnect, dissociate **12** disaffiliate
uncouth 3 odd, raw **4** rude **5** crass, crude, gross, rough **6** clumsy, coarse, rugged, vulgar **7** awkward, bizarre, boorish, ill-bred, loutish, strange, uncivil **8** barbaric, clownish, impolite, ungainly **9** eccentric, graceless, inelegant, unrefined **10** outlandish, uncultured, unpolished **11** ill-mannered, uncivilized **12** discourteous, uncultivated ***person:*** **3** oaf **4** boor, dolt, lout **5** clown **7** bumpkin **9** barbarian
uncover 4 bare **5** strip **6** betray, detect, divest, expose, remove, reveal, unmask, unveil **7** display, divulge, unearth **8** disclose
uncritical 5 naive **9** credulous **11** perfunctory
unction 3 oil **4** balm **5** cream, salve **6** balsam, cerate, chrism **7** suavity, unguent **8** liniment, ointment **9** emollient **11** embrocation
unctuous 4 oily **5** fatty, slick, soapy, suave **6** greasy, smarmy **7** cloying, fawning, fulsome **8** slippery **9** wheedling **10** flattering, oleaginous, saccharine **11** sycophantic
uncultivated 4 wild **5** crass, crude, gross **6** coarse, desert, fallow, savage, vulgar **7** boorish, lowbrow, uncouth **8** barbaric, unplowed, untilled **9** barbarian, barbarous, inelegant, unrefined **10** unpolished **11** uncivilized
uncultured 3 raw **4** rude **5** crass, crude, gross, rough **6** coarse, vulgar **7** artless, boorish, ill-bred, loutish, lowbred, lowbrow, natural, uncouth **8** barbaric, churlish, cloddish **9** barbarian, barbarous, benighted, inelegant, unrefined **10** unpolished **11** uncivilized **13** unenlightened
uncustomary 4 rare **7** special, strange, un-

usual **8** aberrant, abnormal, atypical, singular, uncommon **9** anomalous **10** surprising, unfamiliar, unorthodox **11** exceptional **13** extraordinary

uncut 5 whole **6** entire, intact **8** complete **9** undiluted **10** full-length, unabridged **11** uncondensed **13** unabbreviated

undamaged 5 sound, whole **6** intact, unhurt **8** unbroken, unmarred **9** uninjured, unscathed **10** unimpaired **11** unblemished

undaunted 4 bold **5** brave **6** daring, heroic **7** doughty, Spartan, valiant **8** fearless, intrepid, resolute, unafraid, valorous **9** audacious **10** courageous **11** lionhearted, unconquered, unflinching **12** stouthearted

____ und Drang 5 Sturm

undeceive 8 disabuse **11** disillusion

undecided 4 iffy, moot, open **6** unsure **7** dubious, pending **8** doubtful, wavering **9** equivocal, tentative, uncertain, unsettled **10** ambivalent, indefinite, unresolved **12** undetermined

undeclared 5 tacit **6** unsaid **7** assumed, implied **8** accepted, implicit, inferred, presumed, unspoken, unstated **10** understood

undecorated 4 bare **5** plain, stark **6** homely, severe, simple **8** no-frills **9** unadorned **12** unornamented **13** unembellished, unembroidered

undefiled 4 pure **6** chaste, intact, vestal, virgin **8** innocent, spotless, virginal, virtuous **9** stainless, unstained, unsullied, untainted **10** immaculate **11** unblemished, untarnished

undefined 3 dim **4** hazy **5** faint, vague **6** bleary **7** obscure, shadowy, unclear **8** inchoate, nebulous, unformed **9** amorphous, shapeless **10** indistinct **12** undetermined

undemonstrative 4 calm, cold, cool **5** aloof, chill **7** aseptic, distant, laconic **8** reserved, retiring **9** contained, inhibited, shrinking, withdrawn **10** restrained, unsociable **11** emotionless, passionless, standoffish, unemotional **12** matter-of-fact, unresponsive **13** self-contained

undeniable 6 patent **7** certain, evident, genuine, obvious **8** manifest **9** veridical **10** inarguable **11** indubitable, irrefutable, unequivocal **12** indisputable **13** incontestable

undependable 6 fickle, tricky, unsafe **7** erratic **10** capricious, fly-by-night, inconstant, unreliable **12** inconsistent, questionable **13** irresponsible, unpredictable, untrustworthy

under 3 low, sub **4** down, less **5** below, lower, short **6** lesser **7** beneath, covered, subject **8** downward, inferior **9** dependent, receiving, secondary, subjacent **11** subordinate ***prefix:*** **3** hyp, sub **4** hypo

undercarriage 5 frame **9** framework **11** landing gear

undercover 6 covert, hidden, secret **7** furtive, stealth, sub-rosa **8** hush-hush, stealthy **11** clandestine **12** confidential **13** surreptitious ***person:*** **3** spy **4** mole **5** agent, spook **6** sleuth **9** detective, operative **10** counterspy **11** double agent, secret agent **12** counteragent

undercroft 5 crypt, vault **7** chamber **8** catacomb

undercut 7 subvert **8** sabotage

underdeveloped 4 poor **7** dwarfed, stunted **8** backward, immature **9** unevolved **10** third-world

underdog 5 loser **6** victim **7** also-ran, fall guy, wannabe **9** dark horse

underdone 3 raw, red **4** rare

underestimate 6 slight **7** dismiss **8** belittle, discount, disprize, minimize **9** deprecate, disparage, sell short **10** depreciate

undergarment 3 bra **4** BVDs, slip **5** teddy **6** bikini, bodice, briefs, corset, girdle, shorts, undies **7** chemise, drawers, panties, stammel, step-ins **8** lingerie, pretties, Skivvies, woollies **9** brassiere, jockstrap, long johns, petticoat, underwear **10** foundation

undergo 4 bear, face **5** abide, brave, brook **6** endure, suffer **7** sustain, weather **8** submit to, tolerate **9** withstand **10** experience

undergraduate 4 coed, soph **5** frosh **6** junior, senior **8** freshman **9** collegian, sophomore

underground 4 tube **5** metro, train **6** buried, hidden, nether, secret, subway **7** illegal, offbeat, railway **8** hypogeal, hypogean **10** undercover **11** alternative, clandestine **12** subterranean **13** surreptitious

underhanded 3 sly **4** wily **5** shady **6** covert, crafty, secret, shifty, sneaky, tricky **7** cunning, devious, elusive, evasive, furtive, subrosa **8** guileful, sneaking, stealthy **9** deceitful, deceptive **10** circuitous **11** clandestine, duplicitous **13** surreptitious

underlie 4 bear **6** prop up **7** subtend, support **8** buttress

underline 4 mark **6** play up, stress **9** emphasize, italicize **10** accentuate, underscore

underling 4 aide, peon, serf **5** gofer, scrub, slave **6** flunky, gopher, lackey, menial, minion **7** fall guy **8** inferior **9** assistant, attendant, subaltern **11** subordinate

underlying 4 root **5** basal, basic **7** primary **8** implicit **9** elemental, essential **11** fundamental

Under Milk Wood author 6 Thomas (Dylan)

undermine **3** sap **4** foil **5** blunt, erode **6** impair, thwart, weaken **7** cripple, disable, subvert **8** sabotage **9** attenuate, frustrate **10** debilitate, demoralize
undermost **6** bottom, lowest **9** lowermost **10** bottommost, nethermost, rock-bottom
underneath **4** sole **5** below, lower **6** bottom **7** covered
underpin **4** back, base, prop, root **5** brace **6** uphold **7** bolster, justify, shore up, support **8** buttress, validate **10** strengthen **11** corroborate
underpinning **4** base, prop, root, stay **5** basis, brace **7** bedrock, footing, seating, support **8** buttress **10** foundation, groundwork **12** substructure
underprivileged **4** poor **5** needy **7** hapless, unlucky **8** deprived **11** handicapped, unfortunate **13** disadvantaged
underrate **7** devalue **8** discount, mark down, minimize, write off **9** devaluate, write down **10** depreciate
underscore **6** accent, play up, stress **9** emphasize, italicize **10** accentuate
underside **4** sole **6** bottom **7** reverse
undersized **3** toy **4** baby, mini, puny **5** dinky, dwarf, pygmy, runty, short, small **6** bantam, little, pocket, slight **7** scrubby, stunted **9** miniature **10** diminutive **11** Lilliputian
understand **3** con, dig, ken, see **4** grok, know **5** grasp, guess, infer, savvy, sense, think **6** accept, assume, deduce, expect, fathom, figure, follow, gather, reason, reckon, take in, take it **7** believe, discern, imagine, presume, realize, suppose, surmise, suspect, suss out **8** conceive, conclude, consider, perceive **9** apprehend, interpret **10** appreciate, comprehend, conjecture
understandable **5** clear, lucid, plain **8** clear-cut, coherent, knowable **9** excusable, graspable, plausible **10** articulate, believable, defensible, fathomable, reasonable **11** justifiable, perceivable, unambiguous **12** intelligible **13** apprehensible
understanding **3** ken, wit **4** deal, pact **5** grasp, sense **6** accord, humane, kindly **7** compact, empathy, entente, insight, mastery **8** sympathy **9** agreement, awareness, knowledge, tolerance **10** acceptance, impression, perception **11** considerate, discernment, explanation, sympathetic **12** apprehension, relationship **13** comprehension
understatement **7** litotes
understood **5** tacit **7** assumed, implied **8** accepted, implicit, inferred, unspoken
understudy **6** double, backup, fill-in **7** standby, stand-in **9** surrogate **10** substitute **11** replacement
undertake **3** try **4** dare **5** assay, begin, essay, start **6** accept, assume, pledge, strive, tackle, take on, take up **7** attempt, certify, execute, perform, promise, warrant **8** commence, contract, covenant, endeavor, set about, set forth, shoulder **9** guarantee
undertaker **8** embalmer **9** mortician
undertaking **3** job **4** task **6** affair, charge, effort **7** calling, emprise, exploit, mission, project, pursuit, venture **8** endeavor **9** adventure, guarantee, operation **10** enterprise **11** proposition, transaction
under-the-table **6** covert, hidden, secret, sneaky **7** furtive, on the q.t., sub-rosa **8** hush-hush, stealthy **9** concealed, underhand **10** undercover **11** clandestine **13** surreptitious
undertone **3** hue, hum **4** buzz, cast, hint, tint **5** drone, shade **6** mumble, murmur, mutter, rumble **7** inkling **10** suggestion **11** association, connotation, implication
undertow **4** eddy **7** current, riptide, sea puss
undervalue see **underrate**
underwater **9** submarine **10** subaquatic, subaqueous ***breathing apparatus:*** **5** scuba ***captain:*** **4** Nemo ***chamber:*** **7** caisson ***device:*** **8** paravane ***missile:*** **7** torpedo ***sound detector:*** **5** sonar
underwear see **undergarment**
underwood **5** brush, copse, hedge, scrub **7** boscage, coppice, thicket **9** shrubbery
underworld **4** hell **5** hades, Sheol **6** Erebus, Tophet **7** Gehenna, inferno **8** gangland **9** antipodes **11** Pandemonium ***boatman:*** **6** Charon ***deity:*** **3** Dis **4** Bran **5** Pluto **6** Osiris ***goddess:*** **6** Hecate **10** Persephone ***organization:*** **4** tong **5** Mafia, Triad **6** Yakuza **10** Cosa Nostra ***relating to:*** **8** chthonic ***watchdog:*** **8** Cerberus
underwrite **4** back, fund, sign **5** endow, stake **6** assure, insure, pay for, secure **7** agree to, endorse, finance, sponsor, support **8** bankroll **9** grubstake, guarantee **11** subscribe to
undesigning **5** frank **6** candid, honest **7** artless, earnest, genuine, sincere **9** guileless, ingenuous, unfeigned **10** aboveboard, forthright
undesirable **8** annoying, unwanted **9** offensive, unwelcome **10** ill-favored, unpleasant, unsuitable **11** displeasing, inadvisable, troublesome **12** disagreeable, unacceptable, unattractive **13** inappropriate, objectionable
undesired **8** needless, unsought, unwanted **9** uninvited, unwelcome **10** gratuitous **11** uncalled-for, unnecessary **12** nonessential

undetermined **5** vague **7** dubious, obscure, pending, unclear **8** doubtful **9** ambiguous, equivocal, uncertain, undecided, undefined, unsettled **10** ill-defined, indefinite, indistinct **12** inconclusive

undeveloped **5** crude, green, rough **6** latent **8** backward, immature, inchoate **9** embryonic, incipient, primitive, unevolved **10** unfinished

undiluted **4** neat, pure **5** sheer, utter **7** genuine, unmixed **8** absolute, straight **9** authentic, unalloyed **11** unmitigated, unqualified **13** unadulterated

undiplomatic **4** rash, rude **5** brash, cocky **6** brazen, cheeky **8** impudent, tactless **9** audacious, hotheaded, impolitic, impulsive, maladroit, untactful **10** ill-advised, indiscreet **11** impertinent, injudicious, insensitive, thoughtless **12** presumptuous

undisciplined **4** wild **6** unruly, wanton **7** froward, restive, wayward, willful **8** contrary, untoward **9** fractious **10** disorderly, rebellious, refractory **11** intractable **12** contumacious, noncompliant, obstreperous, recalcitrant, ungovernable, unmanageable

undisclosed **6** hidden, sealed, secret **7** unknown, unnamed **8** ulterior, withheld **9** anonymous **10** unreported, unrevealed **11** clandestine, unmentioned, unspecified **12** confidential, undesignated, unidentified

undisguised **4** bald, open, pure **5** frank, naked, overt, sheer, stark **6** candid, patent **7** obvious **8** apparent, explicit, manifest, palpable **9** barefaced **11** openhearted, unconcealed, unvarnished

undistinguished **5** cheap, stock **6** common **7** humdrum, obscure, routine **8** déclassé, everyday, inferior, low-grade, mediocre, middling, ordinary, workaday **10** second-rate **11** commonplace, nondescript, second-class **12** run-of-the-mill **13** insignificant

undisturbed **6** in situ

undivided **3** one **4** full **5** fixed, total, whole **6** entire, intact, united **8** complete, unbroken **9** unanimous **10** continuous, unswerving **11** indivisible **12** concentrated, undistracted

undo **4** free, open, ruin, veto **5** annul, loose, untie, upset, wrack, wreck **6** cancel, defeat, loosen, negate, stymie, unbind, unsnap **7** abolish, destroy, nullify, release, reverse, vitiate, wipe out **8** abrogate, disallow, overturn, unfasten, unloosen **9** disengage **10** contravene, invalidate **11** disentangle, outmaneuver

undoing **4** bane, doom, ruin, slip **5** shame **7** misstep **8** downfall, reversal **9** destroyer, overthrow, ruination **10** misfortune **11** destruction, humiliation

undoubted **4** real, sure, true **7** certain, genuine **8** definite, positive **9** authentic **10** undisputed

undoubtedly **5** truly **6** indeed, really, surely **7** clearly **8** of course **9** assuredly, certainly **10** definitely, positively, presumably, undeniably **11** indubitably

undress see **unclothe**

undressed **4** nude, rude **5** naked **6** unclad **7** exposed **8** in the raw, stripped **9** au naturel, unclothed

undue **5** inapt **7** extreme **8** ill-timed, improper, needless, untimely **9** excessive, unfitting **10** immoderate, indecorous, inordinate, unsuitable **11** extravagant, uncalled-for, unnecessary, unwarranted **12** unreasonable **13** inappropriate, unjustifiable

undulant fever **11** brucellosis

undulate **4** roll, swag, sway, wave **5** heave, snake, swell, swing **6** billow, ripple **7** slither **9** fluctuate, oscillate

unduly **3** too **6** overly **9** extremely, immensely **11** excessively **12** immoderately, inordinately, unreasonably **13** unnecessarily

undying **7** abiding, ageless, endless, eternal **8** enduring, immortal, unending **9** continual, deathless, perennial, perpetual, unceasing **10** continuing **11** amaranthine, everlasting **12** imperishable, unquenchable

unearth **4** find, show **5** dig up, learn **6** exhume, expose, reveal **7** exhibit, find out, root out, uncover **8** come upon, disclose, discover, dredge up, excavate **9** ascertain, determine **10** come across

unearthly **5** eerie, weird **6** absurd, insane, spooky **7** awesome, ghostly, uncanny, ungodly **8** abnormal, ethereal, heavenly, numinous, spectral **9** appalling, fantastic **10** miraculous, mysterious, outlandish, superhuman, suprahuman **12** preposterous, supermundane, supernatural **13** preternatural

unease **4** care, fear **5** agita, angst, worry **6** strain, stress, unrest **7** anxiety, concern, tension **8** disquiet, distress **9** abashment, confusion, misgiving **10** discomfort, discontent, solicitude **11** disquietude, fretfulness, nervousness, uncertainty, uptightness **12** apprehension, discomfiture, discomposure **13** embarrassment

uneasy **4** edgy **5** jumpy, tense **6** afraid **7** anxious, awkward, fearful, fidgety, fretful, nervous, restive, unquiet, uptight, worried **8** agitated, doubtful, insecure, restless, unstable **9** ambiguous, concerned, difficult, disturbed, perturbed, uncertain, unsettled **10**

disquieted, precarious, solicitous **11** embarrassed **12** apprehensive **13** uncomfortable

uneducated 5 crude, rough **8** ignorant, untaught **9** benighted, untutored **10** illiterate, unlettered, unschooled **12** uncultivated, uninstructed

unembellished 4 bald, bare **5** blunt, plain, spare, stark **6** severe **7** austere **9** essential, unadorned **11** undecorated, unelaborate, ungarnished, unvarnished **12** unornamented **13** unembroidered, unpretentious

unemotional 4 cold, cool **5** chill, stoic, stony **6** frigid, sedate, serene **7** deadpan, equable, glacial, stoical **8** composed, obdurate, reserved, reticent **9** apathetic, impassive **10** hard-boiled, phlegmatic **11** insensitive, passionless, unexcitable **12** intellectual, thick-skinned, unresponsive **13** dispassionate

unemployed 4 idle **5** fired **6** otiose, unused **7** jobless, laid.off, loafing **8** inactive, leisured, workless **10** unoccupied

unending 7 eternal, undying **8** constant, immortal, infinite, timeless **9** boundless, ceaseless, continual, incessant, limitless, perennial, perpetual, unceasing **10** continuous **11** amaranthine, everlasting, unremitting **12** interminable **13** uninterrupted

unenlightened 5 naive **6** unread **7** heathen, unaware **8** backward, ignorant, nescient **9** benighted, unknowing **10** uneducated, uninformed **11** uninitiated **12** uncultivated

unenthusiastic 4 cool **5** tepid **8** grudging, listless, lukewarm **9** apathetic, unexcited **10** lackluster, lacklustre, spiritless **11** half-hearted, indifferent, perfunctory **12** uninterested

unequal 3 odd **6** uneven, unfair **7** diverse **8** inferior, lopsided, one-sided **9** different, disparate, divergent, irregular **10** asymmetric, dissimilar, inadequate, mismatched, off-balance **12** insufficient

unequaled 6 unique **7** supreme **8** foremost, nonesuch, peerless **9** matchless, paramount, unmatched, unrivaled **10** preeminent, surpassing **12** incomparable, transcendent, unparalleled **13** unprecedented

unequivocal 5 clear **6** direct, patent **7** certain, evident **8** apparent, definite, distinct, explicit, manifest, palpable **10** undeniable **11** categorical, indubitable, unambiguous **12** indisputable, undisputable

unerring 5 exact **6** dead-on **7** certain, correct, perfect, precise **8** accurate, reliable **9** faultless, unfailing **10** dependable, infallible **11** trustworthy

unessential 8 marginal, needless, unneeded **9** redundant **10** expendable, gratuitous, irrelevant, peripheral, unrequired **11** dispensable, superfluous, uncalled-for, unimportant, unnecessary

unethical 5 venal, wrong **7** corrupt, crooked, immoral **9** dishonest, reprobate **12** disreputable, unprincipled, unscrupulous

uneven 3 odd **4** wavy **5** bumpy, erose, harsh, jaggy, rough **6** craggy, jagged, patchy, ragged, random, rugged, spotty **7** scraggy, unequal, varying **8** lopsided, scabrous, scraggly, variable **9** haphazard, hit-or-miss, irregular **10** asymmetric, imbalanced, unbalanced

unevenness 4 bump, wave **7** anomaly **8** asperity, imparity **9** disparity, imbalance, roughness, variation **10** inequality **12** irregularity, lopsidedness **13** disproportion

uneventful 5 usual **6** placid **7** humdrum, prosaic, routine **8** ordinary **10** unexciting **11** commonplace **12** unremarkable

unexampled 4 lone, only, sole, solo **5** alone **6** unique **8** singular, solitary **9** matchless, unequaled, unmatched, unrivaled **10** consummate, inimitable, sui generis, unequalled, unrivalled **12** incomparable, unparalleled **13** unprecedented

unexcited 4 calm **5** blasé, stoic **6** placid, sedate, serene **7** relaxed, stoical **8** composed, tranquil **9** apathetic, collected, unruffled **10** nonchalant **11** indifferent **12** uninterested **13** dispassionate

unexciting 4 arid, dull, tame **5** banal, bland, ho-hum **6** boring, stodgy **7** humdrum, insipid, prosaic, tedious **8** lifeless, tiresome **10** monotonous **11** commonplace

unexpected 10 surprising, unforeseen **11** unpredicted **13** unanticipated

unexpectedly 5 aback, short **6** sudden **7** unaware **8** abruptly, suddenly, unawares **9** forthwith **11** unwittingly **12** accidentally **13** inadvertently

unexpended 5 saved **7** reserve, surplus **8** left over, reserved **9** remaining

unexpired 5 valid **9** operative

unexpressed 5 tacit **6** silent, unsaid **7** assumed, implied **8** implicit, presumed, unspoken, wordless **9** unuttered **10** undeclared, understood

unfailing 4 fast, sure **7** certain, devoted **8** constant, faithful, reliable, resolute, surefire, unerring **9** steadfast, unvarying **10** consistent, dependable, infallible, invariable, persistent, unchanging, unflagging, unwavering **11** everlasting, persevering, unrelenting **12** tried-and-true **13** inexhaustible

unfair 4 foul **5** wrong **6** biased, shabby, uneven, unjust **7** unequal **8** wrongful **9** arbitrary, dishonest, unethical **10** prejudiced **11** inequitable, underhanded, unrighteous

unfaithful 5 false **6** untrue **8** cheating, disloyal, recreant, turncoat **9** faithless, two-timing **10** adulterous, inaccurate, perfidious, traitorous **11** treacherous **13** untrustworthy

unfaltering 3 set **4** firm **6** steady **7** abiding **8** constant, enduring, resolute, tireless **9** steadfast, unfailing **10** continuous, unflagging, unwavering **11** persevering **12** never-failing, wholehearted

unfamiliar 3 new, odd **5** alien, novel, weird **6** exotic **7** foreign, strange, unaware, unknown, unusual **8** abnormal, peculiar **11** incognizant, out-of-the-way **12** unaccustomed, unacquainted

unfashionable 5 dated, dowdy, passé, stale **6** bygone, démodé, old-hat, shabby **7** outworn **8** outdated, outmoded **9** out-of-date, unstylish **10** antiquated, oldfangled

unfasten 4 free, open, undo **5** loose, unbar, unfix, unpin, untie **6** detach, loosen, unbind, unbolt, unlace, unlock, unsnap **7** release, unclasp, unhitch, unlatch, unleash, unloose, unstrap **8** unbuckle, unfetter, unloosen, untether **9** disengage

unfathomable 7 abysmal, obscure **8** profound **9** boundless, enigmatic, unplumbed **10** bottomless, fathomless, unknowable **11** inscrutable **12** immeasurable, impenetrable

unfavorable 3 bad, ill **4** poor **6** averse, unfair, unkind **7** adverse, hostile, opposed **8** contrary, damaging, inimical, negative **9** disliking, troubling **11** detrimental, displeasing **12** antagonistic, disapproving, inauspicious ***prefix:* 3** dys

unfavorably 4 awry **5** amiss, badly **6** astray, poorly **7** wrongly **10** negatively, unsuitably **13** unfortunately

unfeasible 8 quixotic **9** visionary **10** chimerical, impossible, unworkable **11** impractical, speculative, theoretical, unrealistic **12** unattainable, unrealizable **13** impracticable

unfeeling 4 cold, hard, numb **5** cruel, harsh, stern, stony **6** brutal, leaden, marble, numbed, severe, stolid, unkind **7** callous **8** benumbed, deadened, hardened, obdurate, pitiless, ruthless, uncaring **9** apathetic, heartless, indurated, insensate, senseless **10** hardboiled, insensible, insentient **11** cold-blooded, coldhearted, hardhearted, insensitive, unemotional **12** anesthetized **13** unsympathetic

unfeigned 4 real, true **6** actual, hearty, honest **7** artless, earnest, genuine, natural, sincere **8** innocent **9** guileless, heartfelt, ingenuous **12** wholehearted

unfinished 3 raw **5** crude, rough **7** sketchy **9** imperfect, roughhewn, undressed **10** incomplete, unpolished

Unfinished Symphony composer 8 Schubert (Franz)

unfit 4 sick, weak **5** inapt, inept **6** faulty **7** deprive, disable, unsound, useless **8** disabled, improper, unsuited **9** ill-suited, incapable, maladroit **10** disqualify, ill-adapted, inadequate, ineligible, unsuitable **11** ill-equipped, incompetent, unqualified **12** disqualified, incompatible **13** inappropriate, incapacitated

unfitting 5 inapt **8** improper, unseemly **9** imprudent **10** ill-advised, inapposite, malapropos, unbecoming, unsuitable **11** inadvisable **13** inappropriate

unfix 4 part, undo **5** loose, sever **6** cut off, detach, loosen, sunder, unbind **7** unloose **8** uncouple, unfasten, unloosen **9** disengage **10** disconnect, dissociate

unflagging 6 steady **7** staunch **8** constant, tireless, untiring **9** unceasing, unfailing, unwearied **11** persevering, unfaltering, unrelenting, unremitting **13** indefatigable, inexhaustible

unflappable 4 calm **6** poised, serene **7** assured, equable **8** composed, laid-back **9** collected, unruffled **10** deliberate, nonchalant **11** self-assured **13** imperturbable, self-possessed

unfledged 5 green, young **6** callow, jejune, unripe **7** puerile **8** immature, juvenile **10** unseasoned **11** undeveloped, unfeathered **13** inexperienced

unflinching 4 firm, grim **6** dogged **7** doughty, staunch, valiant **8** fearless, intrepid, resolute **9** dauntless, steadfast **10** courageous, relentless, unwavering, unyielding **11** unfaltering, unrelenting **12** stouthearted

unfold 4 open **6** deduce, evolve, expand, expose, extend, flower, mature, reveal, unwrap **7** blossom, burgeon, clear up, develop, display, dope out, exhibit, explain, resolve **8** decipher, disclose, evidence, manifest **9** elaborate, explicate, figure out, puzzle out, transpire **10** effloresce, outstretch **11** come to light

unforced 4 easy **7** natural, willing, witting **8** elective, optional **9** available, easygoing, voluntary **10** deliberate, volitional **11** intentional **12** unprescribed **13** discretionary, noncompulsory

unforeseeable 9 uncertain, unplanned **10** accidental

unforeseen 6 chance **8** surprise **10** accidental,

surprising, unexpected **11** unlooked-for, unpredicted **13** unanticipated

unforgivable 9 untenable **10** censurable, inexpiable, outrageous **11** blameworthy, inexcusable, intolerable **12** indefensible, unacceptable, unpardonable **13** insupportable, reprehensible, unjustifiable

unformed 4 rude **5** crude, rough, vague **6** callow **8** immature, inchoate, nebulous, unshaped **9** amorphous, roughhewn, shapeless **10** indefinite, unfinished, unpolished **11** undeveloped, unfashioned **12** unstructured **13** indeterminate

unfortunate 3 bad, sad **4** dire, poor **6** woeful, wretch **7** adverse, awkward, hapless, unhappy, unlucky **8** grievous, ill-fated, luckless, untoward, wretched **9** desperate, graceless, ill-chosen, miserable **10** afflictive, calamitous, deplorable, disastrous, ill-starred, lamentable, unsuitable **11** distressing, regrettable, star-crossed, unfavorable **12** disagreeable, inauspicious, infelicitous, unsuccessful **13** heartbreaking

unfounded 4 idle, vain **5** false **8** baseless, spurious, unproven **9** deceptive, dishonest, untenable **10** fabricated, fallacious, gratuitous, groundless, mendacious, misleading, untruthful **11** uncalled-for, unsupported, unwarranted

unfriendly 4 cold, cool **5** alien, aloof, chill, gruff, surly **6** chilly, frosty, remote **7** distant, grouchy, hostile, opposed, warlike **8** inimical, unsocial **10** antisocial, censorious, inimicable, unsociable **11** ill-disposed, uncongenial **12** antagonistic, disagreeable, inhospitable, misanthropic, unneighborly **13** unsympathetic

unfruitful 4 arid, idle **5** empty, waste **6** barren, desert, effete, fallow, futile, wasted **7** parched, sterile, useless **8** abortive, bootless, depleted, impotent **9** infertile, pointless **10** unavailing **11** ineffective, ineffectual **12** impoverished, unproductive, unprofitable

unfurl 4 open **6** expose, reveal, spread, unfold, unroll, unwind **7** develop, display, exhibit, uncover **8** disclose **9** elaborate, spread out

unfurnished 4 bare **5** empty **6** vacant

unfussy 5 loose **6** breezy, casual, common, dégagé, folksy, mellow **7** cursory, relaxed **8** familiar, informal, laid-back **9** easygoing **10** unreserved **11** low-pressure, pococurante, unconcerned **12** unparticular **13** unceremonious, uncomplicated

ungainly 5 gawky, lanky, splay **6** clumsy, klutzy, oafish **7** awkward, boorish, hulking, loutish, lumpish, uncouth **8** bungling, clownish, lubberly, unwieldy **9** lumbering, maladroit **10** blundering

ungarnished 5 plain **6** modest, simple **9** unadorned **11** undecorated, unelaborate **12** unornamented **13** unembellished, unembroidered

ungenerous 4 mean **5** petty, tight **6** paltry, shabby, skimpy, stingy **7** chintzy, miserly **8** grudging, picayune, ungiving **9** illiberal, niggardly, penurious **10** pinchpenny **11** closefisted, tightfisted **12** parsimonious **13** penny-pinching

ungodly see **unholy**

ungovernable 4 wild **6** unruly **7** froward, lawless, willful **8** mutinous, untoward **9** fractious, turbulent, unbridled **10** disorderly, headstrong, rebellious, refractory, tumultuous **11** intractable **12** recalcitrant, uncontrolled, unmanageable **13** irrepressible, undisciplined

ungraceful 5 crude, gawky, inept, stiff **6** clumsy, gauche, klutzy, oafish, wooden **7** artless, awkward, halting, labored, stilted **8** bumbling, bungling, ungainly, untoward **9** all thumbs, inelegant, lumbering, maladroit **10** blundering

ungracious 4 rude **5** gruff **6** crusty **7** brusque, uncivil **8** churlish, impolite **9** offensive **10** unmannerly **11** disobliging, ill-mannered, impertinent, thoughtless, uncalled-for **12** disagreeable, discourteous **13** disrespectful, inconsiderate, unceremonious

ungraspable 6 opaque **7** obscure **8** baffling **9** enigmatic **10** unknowable **12** impenetrable, inexplicable, unfathomable

ungrateful 9 thankless

unguarded 5 frank, hasty **6** candid, direct, unwary **7** offhand **8** careless, heedless, reckless **9** impolitic, imprudent, impulsive **10** incautious, indiscreet, unthinking **11** defenseless, thoughtless, unprotected

unguent 4 balm **5** cream, salve **6** balsam, cerate, chrism, lotion **8** ointment **9** emollient, lubricant **11** embrocation

ungulate 3 hog, pig **4** deer **5** horse, tapir **6** hoofed **8** elephant **10** rhinoceros

unhallowed 4 evil **6** impure, unholy, wicked **7** immoral, impious, profane, ungodly **8** infernal **9** nefarious **10** desecrated, iniquitous, irreverent **13** unconsecrated

unhampered 4 free, open **5** frank, loose **6** direct **8** uncurbed **9** unbridled, unchecked, unimpeded, unlimited **10** unhindered **11** uninhibited, untrammeled **12** unrestrained, unrestricted, unobstructed **13** unconstrained

unhand 5 let go **7** release

unhandy **5** bulky, inept **6** clumsy, gauche, klutzy **7** awkward, halting, hulking **8** bumbling, bungling, cumbrous, unwieldy **9** all thumbs, ham-handed, maladroit, ponderous **10** cumbersome, unskillful **12** inconvenient

unhappiness **3** woe **5** blues, dolor, dumps, gloom, grief, worry **6** misery, mishap, sorrow **7** anxiety, sadness **8** distress **9** dejection **10** depression, desolation, discontent, heartbreak, melancholy **11** despondency, dolefulness **12** mournfulness, wretchedness **13** cheerlessness

unhappy **3** sad **4** down, glum, grim **5** sorry **6** dismal, dreary, gloomy **7** joyless **8** dejected, downcast, mournful, saddened, troubled, wretched **9** cheerless, depressed, sorrowful, woebegone **10** despondent, dispirited, melancholy **11** melancholic, unfortunate **12** disconsolate, heavyhearted

unharmed **4** safe **5** sound **6** intact, secure, unhurt **8** unbroken, unmarred **9** protected, undamaged, undefiled, uninjured, unscathed **10** unimpaired **11** unblemished

unhealthiness **7** ailment, disease, illness, malaise **8** debility, sickness **9** infirmity **10** affliction, sickliness **11** decrepitude **13** indisposition

unhealthy **3** ill **4** sick **6** ailing, infirm, sickly, unwell **7** baneful, noisome, noxious, unsound **8** diseased **9** injurious **11** deleterious, unwholesome **12** insalubrious

unheard-of **3** new **6** unique **7** obscure, unknown, unnoted **8** nameless **10** phenomenal, unrenowned **12** uncelebrated **13** extraordinary, unprecedented

unhesitating **7** assured, earnest **8** decisive, positive, resolute **9** confident, immediate, unchecked **10** determined, forthright, purposeful **11** unflinching **12** wholehearted

unhinge **5** addle, craze **6** madden, ruffle **7** derange **9** unbalance

unhinged **3** mad **4** daft, loco, nuts **5** balmy, crazy, loony, wacky **6** insane **7** lunatic, unglued **8** demented, deranged **9** disturbed **10** unbalanced

unholy **4** base, evil, vile **6** impure, sinful, wicked **7** heinous, immoral, impious, profane, ungodly **8** dreadful, fiendish, godawful, shocking **9** atheistic, barbarous **10** iniquitous, irreverent, outrageous, scandalous, unhallowed **11** irreligious, unbelieving **12** sacrilegious, unsanctified **13** reprehensible

unhorse **5** pitch, throw **6** topple, tumble, unseat **7** buck off **8** dislodge, dismount, overturn, unsaddle **9** overthrow

unhurried **4** easy, slow **6** casual **7** laggard, relaxed **8** dilatory, laid-back **9** easygoing, leisurely **10** deliberate **11** low-pressure

unhurt **4** safe **5** sound, whole **6** entire, intact **7** perfect **8** unbroken, unharmed, unmarred **9** undamaged, uninjured, unscathed, untouched **10** unimpaired **11** unblemished

unification **5** union **6** fusion, hookup, merger **7** amalgam, joining, linkage, melding, merging **8** alliance, coupling **9** coalition **10** connection, federation **11** affiliation, coalescence, combination **12** amalgamation **13** confederation, consolidation

uniform **4** even, like, suit **5** alike, dress, equal, level **6** attire, outfit, stable, steady **7** ordered, orderly, regular, similar, stabile **8** constant, unvaried **9** consonant, unvarying **10** comparable, consistent, invariable, unchanging **11** homogeneous **13** unfluctuating ***combining form:*** **3** iso ***type:*** **3** BDU **5** blues, habit, khaki **6** livery, whites

uniformity **6** parity **7** oneness **8** equality, evenness, identity, monotony, sameness **9** agreement, congruity, constancy **11** consistency **13** invariability

uniformly **6** always, evenly **7** equally **8** smoothly **10** comparably **11** analogously, identically **12** equivalently

unify **3** tie, wed **4** bind, bond, fuse, knit, link, mesh **5** blend, marry, merge, unite **6** cement, couple **7** combine, conjoin **8** coalesce, compound, federate **9** integrate **10** amalgamate, centralize, synthesize **11** concatenate, consolidate

unimaginable **10** incredible, unknowable **11** unthinkable **12** mind-boggling, unbelievable **13** extraordinary, inconceivable, indescribable

unimaginative **4** dull, flat **5** banal, bland, trite, vapid **6** common **7** literal, prosaic, routine, vanilla **8** bromidic **10** derivative, pedestrian, uncreative, uninspired **11** commonplace

unimpaired **4** safe **5** sound **6** intact, unhurt **7** perfect **8** unbroken, unharmed, unmarred **9** undamaged, uninjured, unscathed **11** unblemished

unimpassioned **4** calm, cool **5** sober, stoic **6** placid, remote, stolid **7** deadpan **8** detached, lukewarm, reserved, tranquil **9** impassive, temperate **10** phlegmatic, spiritless **11** cold-blooded, emotionless **12** matter-of-fact

unimpeachable **5** valid **7** correct **8** flawless, reliable, virtuous **9** blameless, exemplary, faultless, unspotted, unsullied **10** conclusive, impeccable, undisputed **11** unblemished, untarnished **13** authoritative

unimportant **4** mere **5** minor, petty **6** casual,

minute, paltry **7** trivial **8** piddling **9** small-beer, worthless **10** expendable, immaterial, irrelevant, negligible **11** dispensable, meaningless, superfluous **13** insignificant

uninformed 7 unaware **8** ignorant, nescient **9** oblivious, unknowing, unwitting **10** unfamiliar **11** incognizant, superficial **12** unacquainted, undiscerning

uninhabited 5 empty, waste **6** barren, vacant **7** vacated **8** deserted, desolate, forsaken **9** abandoned, evacuated **10** unoccupied

uninhibited 3 lax **4** free **5** loose **8** uncurbed **9** expansive, fancy-free, liberated, unbridled **10** boisterous, ungoverned, unhampered, unreserved **11** spontaneous, unrepressed, untrammeled **12** unrestrained, unsuppressed **13** unconstrained

uninjured 4 safe **5** sound, whole **6** intact, unhurt **8** unharmed, unmarred **9** undamaged, undefiled, unscathed, untouched **10** unimpaired

uninspired 4 blah, drab, dull **5** banal, stock, trite, vapid **6** boring, leaden, old-hat, stodgy **7** humdrum, insipid, plastic, sterile, vanilla **8** bromidic, lifeless, ordinary **9** colorless **10** lackluster, lacklustre, pedestrian, uncreative, unoriginal **11** commonplace **13** unimaginative

unintelligent 4 dumb **5** dense **6** obtuse, stupid **7** asinine, brutish, doltish, fatuous, foolish, moronic, vacuous, witless **8** mindless **9** brainless, ludicrous **10** half-witted, ill-advised, irrational, ridiculous, weak-minded **11** harebrained, lamebrained **12** feeble-minded

unintentional 6 chance, random **9** haphazard, unplanned, unwitting **10** accidental, fortuitous, incidental, unexpected, unforeseen, unthinking **11** inadvertent, unconscious, unlooked-for **12** adventitious, coincidental

uninterested 5 aloof, blasé, bored, jaded **9** apathetic, incurious, unexcited **10** uninvolved **11** indifferent, unconcerned

uninteresting 3 dry **4** arid, blah, drab, dull, flat **5** banal, dusty, ho-hum, stale **6** boring, jejune **7** humdrum, insipid, prosaic, tedious **8** bromidic, plodding, tiresome **9** colorless, dryasdust, wearisome **10** monotonous, pedestrian, uneventful, unexciting

uninterrupted 6 direct **7** endless, nonstop **8** constant, unbroken, unending **9** ceaseless, continual, incessant, perpetual, sustained, unceasing **10** continuous **11** undisturbed, unremitting

uninvited 7 unasked **8** unbidden, unsought **9** intruding **10** gratuitous **11** uncalled-for, unrequested, unsolicited **12** presumptuous

union 4 bloc, bond, club **5** alloy, artel, group, guild, joint **6** fusion, league, merger **7** amalgam, joining, melding, merging, society **8** alliance, congress, coupling, junction, juncture, marriage, sodality **9** coalition **10** connection, federation, fellowship **11** association, brotherhood, coalescence, combination, confederacy, cooperative, unification **13** confederation, consolidation ***branch:*** **5** local ***labor:*** **3** AFL, CIO, UAW, UMW **5** ILGWU

unique 3 odd, one **4** lone, only, sole, solo **5** alone, novel **6** single **8** peculiar, peerless, singular, solitary, uncommon, unwonted **9** anomalous, exclusive, matchless, unequaled, unmatched, unrivaled **10** inimitable, particular, sui generis, unequalled, unexampled, unrivalled **11** distinctive, exceptional **12** incomparable, unparalleled, unrepeatable **13** extraordinary, idiosyncratic, unprecedented

uniqueness 8 identity **10** singleness **11** singularity **13** individuality

____**-Unis 5** Etats

unit 3 arm, one **4** area, item, part, wing **5** digit, group, monad, piece, whole **6** entity **7** element, measure **8** molecule **9** component **10** individual **11** constituent ***administrative:*** **6** agency, bureau, sector **8** district ***boy scout:*** **5** troop ***educational:*** **6** course ***military:*** (see at **military**) ***of acceleration:*** **3** gal ***of action:*** **7** episode ***of advertising space:*** **4** line **6** column ***of an element:*** **4** atom **8** molecule ***of angular measure:*** **6** radian ***of area:*** **3** are **4** acre **6** morgen **7** hectare **9** square rod **10** square mile, square yard ***of astronomical distance:*** **6** parsec **9** light-year ***of brightness:*** **7** lambert ***of capacitance:*** **5** farad ***of capacity:*** **2** cc, ml **3** cup, tun **4** cord, dram, gill, peck, pint **5** liter, litre, minim, ounce, quart **6** barrel, bushel, firkin, gallon ***of computer information:*** **3** bit, gig, meg **4** byte **8** gigabyte, megabyte ***of conductance:*** **3** mho **7** siemens ***of distance:*** **4** mile, yard **5** meter **6** league **7** furlong ***of electricity:*** **3** amp **4** volt, watt **6** ampere **7** coulomb ***of energy:*** **3** erg **5** joule **7** quantum **8** watt-hour ***of explosive force:*** **7** megaton ***of fineness:*** **5** carat, karat ***of force:*** **4** dyne **6** newton **7** poundal ***of frequency:*** **5** hertz **7** fresnel ***of grain:*** **5** sheaf ***of heat:*** **3** BTU **5** therm **7** calorie ***of illumination:*** **3** lux **5** lumen ***of inductance:*** **5** henry ***of length:*** **3** mil, rod **4** foot, hand, inch, mile, rood, yard **5** chain, fermi, meter **6** fathom, micron **7** furlong **9** kilometer **historic: 5** cubit ***of loudness:*** **4** sone **7** decibel ***of lumber:***

9 board foot ***of magnetic flux:*** **5** gamma, gauss, tesla, weber **7** maxwell ***of magnetic intensity:*** **7** oersted ***of magnetomotive force:*** **7** gilbert ***of pressure:*** **3** bar, psi **4** torr **6** pascal **10** atmosphere ***of radiation:*** **3** rad **8** roentgen ***of radioactivity:*** **5** curie ***of resistance:*** **3** ohm ***of solar radiation:*** **7** langley ***of sound absorption:*** **5** sabin ***of speech:*** **4** word **6** toneme **7** phoneme **8** morpheme, syllable ***of speed:*** **3** CPS, MPH, RPM **4** knot ***of temperature:*** **6** degree, kelvin ***of time:*** **3** age, day, eon **4** beat, bell, hour, week, year **5** month **6** minute, season, second **8** svedberg ***of viscosity:*** **5** poise ***of volume:*** **5** stere **9** cubic foot, cubic yard **10** cubic meter ***of weight:*** **3** cwt, ton **4** dram, gram, tael **5** carat, grain, ounce, pound, tonne **6** drachm **7** gigaton, kiloton, quintal, scruple **8** kilogram, millieme **9** metric ton, microgram, milligram ***historic:*** **3** tod **5** gerah, libra ***Indian:*** **4** tola ***Russian:*** **4** pood ***of work:*** **3** erg **5** ergon, joule ***social:*** **4** clan **5** tribe **6** family **7** chapter

unitary 5 whole **9** undivided **11** indivisible

unite 3 mix, tie, wed **4** ally, band, bind, bond, fuse, join, knit, link, meld, pool, weld **5** blend, graft, marry, merge, unify **6** cement, couple, gather, league, mingle, splice **7** combine, conjoin, connect **8** assemble, coadjute, coalesce, compound, federate **9** affiliate, aggregate, commingle **10** amalgamate, federalize **11** confederate, incorporate

united 3 one, wed **5** joint **6** allied, linked, merged, wedded **7** made one **8** agreeing, combined, in accord **10** harmonious

United Arab Emirates *capital:* 8 Abu Dhabi ***city:*** **5** Dubai **6** Dubayy ***coast:*** **6** Pirate **7** Trucial ***emirate:*** **5** Dubai **6** Dubayy **8** Abu Dhabi ***former name:*** **13** Trucial States ***gulf:*** **4** Oman **7** Persian ***monetary unit:*** **6** dirham ***neighbor:*** **4** Oman **11** Saudi Arabia ***peninsula:*** **7** Arabian ***strait:*** **6** Hormuz

United Kingdom *capital:* 6 London ***city:*** **3** Ely **4** Bath **5** Derby, Dover, Leeds **6** Exeter, Oxford **7** Bristol, Cardiff, Glasgow, Paisley **8** Bradford, Brighton, Coventry, Plymouth **9** Cambridge, Edinburgh, Leicester, Liverpool, Newcastle, Sheffield **10** Birmingham, Manchester, Nottingham **11** Bournemouth ***colony:*** **8** Falkland (Islands) ***component:*** **5** Wales **7** England **8** Scotland **12** Great Britain ***conqueror:*** **6** Caesar (Julius) **7** William (the Conqueror) ***county:*** **4** Kent **5** Devon, Essex **6** Dorset, Surrey, Sussex **7** Norfolk, Suffolk **8** Cornwall, Somerset **9** Berkshire, Wiltshire, Yorkshire ***island:*** **3** Man **4** Jura, Skye **5** Islay, Lewis, Wight **6** Jersey **8** Anguilla, Guernsey, Mainland ***island group:*** **6** Orkney **7** Channel **8** Hebrides, Shetland ***language:*** **5** Welsh **6** Gaelic ***leader:*** **8** Cromwell (Oliver) **9** Churchill (Winston) ***monarch:*** **4** Anne, Mary **5** Henry, James **6** Alfred (the Great), Edward, George **7** Charles, Richard, William **8** Victoria **9** Elizabeth ***monetary unit:*** **5** pence, penny, pound ***monetary unit, former:*** **3** bob **5** crown, groat **6** florin, guinea **7** ha'penny **8** farthing, shilling, sixpence **9** halfpenny **10** threepence ***mountain, range:*** **7** Scafell (Peak), Snowdon **8** Ben Nevis, Cumbrian, Grampian **12** Cheviot Hills ***peninsula:*** **7** Kintyre ***prehistoric site:*** **7** Avebury **9** Skara Brae **10** Stonehenge ***river:*** **3** Dee, Exe, Wye **4** Aire, Avon, Ouse **5** Clyde **6** Mersey, Severn, Thames ***sea:*** **5** Irish, North **6** Celtic ***territory:*** **8** Anguilla

United Nations secretary-general 3 Ban (Ki-moon), Lie (Trygve) **5** Annan (Kofi), Thant (U) **8** Waldheim (Kurt) **12** Boutros-Ghali (Boutros), Hammarskjöld (Dag)

United States *desert:* 6 Mojave **7** Sonoran **8** Colorado ***highest point:*** **6** Denali (Mt.) **8** McKinley (Mt.) ***island:*** **6** Hawaii, Kodiak, Unimak **7** Nunivak **9** Admiralty, Chichagof **10** St. Lawrence **13** Prince of Wales ***island group:*** **3** Fox **6** Hawaii **8** Aleutian, Pribilof, Thousand ***lowest point:*** **11** Death Valley ***mountain range:*** **5** Coast, Green, Ozark, Rocky, White **7** Cascade, Olympic **8** Catskill **9** Blue Ridge **10** Adirondack, Great Smoky **11** Appalachian **12** Sierra Nevada ***national park:*** **4** Zion **6** Denali **7** Glacier, Olympic, Redwood, Sequoia **8** Badlands, Carlsbad, Wind Cave, Yosemite **9** Mesa Verde, Mt. Rainier **10** Everglades, Grand Teton, Hot Springs, Isle Royale, Shenandoah **11** Dry Tortugas, Grand Canyon, Kenai Fjords, Mammoth Cave, Yellowstone ***possession:*** **10** Puerto Rico ***state:*** **4** Iowa, Ohio, Utah **5** Idaho, Maine, Texas **6** Alaska, Hawaii, Kansas, Nevada, Oregon **7** Alabama, Arizona, Florida, Georgia, Indiana, Montana, New York, Vermont, Wyoming **8** Arkansas, Colorado, Delaware, Illinois, Kentucky, Maryland, Michigan, Missouri, Nebraska, Oklahoma, Virginia **9** Louisiana, Minnesota, New Jersey, New Mexico, Tennessee, Wisconsin **10** California, Washington **11** Connecticut, Mississippi, North Dakota, Rhode Island, South Dakota **12** New Hampshire, Pennsylvania, West Virginia **13** Massachusetts, North Carolina,

South Carolina ***territory:*** **4** Guam **13** American Samoa, Virgin Islands

unity 5 union **6** accord **7** concord, harmony, oneness **8** identity, soleness **9** agreement, consensus **10** continuity, singleness, solidarity

universal 3 all **5** broad, total, whole **6** common, cosmic, entire, global **7** general, generic **8** catholic **9** extensive, planetary, unlimited, worldwide **10** ecumenical, ubiquitous **11** omnipresent **12** all-embracing, all-inclusive, cosmopolitan **13** comprehensive ***combining form:*** **4** omni

universe 3 all **5** whole, world **6** cosmos, system **8** creation **9** macrocosm

unjust 5 wrong **6** biased, shabby, unfair **7** partial, unequal **8** one-sided, improper, wrongful **9** inequable **10** prejudiced, undeserved **11** inequitable, unrighteous

unjustifiable 5 undue **7** invalid **8** baseless **9** unfounded, untenable **10** groundless **11** inexcusable, unsupported, unwarranted **12** indefensible

unkempt 5 messy **6** frowsy, frowzy, ragtag, shaggy, sloppy, untidy **7** ruffled, rumpled, scruffy, tousled **8** scraggly, slipshod, slovenly, uncombed **10** bedraggled, disarrayed, disheveled, disordered, unpolished **11** disarranged

unkind 4 mean, vile **5** cruel, harsh, rough, stern **6** severe **7** callous **8** uncaring **9** inclement, malicious **10** ungenerous, ungracious **11** insensitive, thoughtless, unfavorable **12** uncharitable **13** unsympathetic

unknowable 6 arcane, hidden, mystic, occult, secret **7** cryptic **8** mystical, numinous **9** enigmatic, recondite **10** mysterious **11** inscrutable, ungraspable **12** impenetrable, unfathomable

unknowing 6 unwary **7** unaware **8** heedless, ignorant **9** oblivious, unmindful, unwitting **10** insensible, unfamiliar, uninformed **11** incognizant **12** unsuspecting

unknown 6 hidden, nobody, secret **7** obscure, strange **8** nameless **9** anonymous, incognito

unlawful 6 banned **7** bootleg, corrupt, crooked, illegal, illicit, immoral **8** criminal, outlawed, verboten, wrongful **9** forbidden, felonious, nefarious **10** contraband, flagitious, indictable, iniquitous, prohibited, proscribed, unlicensed **11** black-market **12** illegitimate, unauthorized

unlearned 5 naive **6** unread **7** unaware **8** ignorant, nescient, untaught **10** illiterate, uneducated, unlettered, unschooled **11** instinctive **13** unenlightened

unleash 4 free, vent **5** let go, loose, untie, visit, wreak **6** unbind **7** inflict, release **8** carry out, liberate **10** bring about

unless 3 but **4** save **6** except, saving **7** barring, but that, without **9** excepting, excluding

unlettered see **uneducated**

unlikable 9 obnoxious, offensive, repellent **10** unpleasant **11** displeasing, distasteful **12** disagreeable

unlike 5 mixed **6** varied **7** diverse, unequal, various **8** assorted **9** different, disparate, divergent **10** dissimilar **11** contrasting, distinctive, diversified **13** heterogeneous

unlikely 5 faint, unfit **6** remote, slight **7** distant, dubious **8** doubtful **10** farfetched, improbable, unsuitable **11** implausible, unpromising **12** questionable

unlimited 4 full, vast **5** total **6** untold **7** endless, immense **8** absolute, infinite, wide-open **9** boundless, countless, unbounded, universal **10** unconfined, unfettered **11** unqualified, untrammeled **12** immeasurable, interminable, unrestrained, unrestricted **13** comprehensive, unconditional, unconstrained

unlit 4 dark, inky **6** gloomy **7** shadowy **9** lightless, tenebrous

unload 4 drop, dump, junk **5** chuck, ditch, empty **6** debark, remove **7** confess, confide, deep-six, deliver, discard, divulge, lighten, relieve **8** disclose, disgorge, jettison **9** disburden, discharge, disembark, eighty-six, stevedore **11** disencumber

unloose 4 free, undo **5** let go, relax, untie **6** detach, unbind **7** break up, manumit, release, set free, slacken **8** liberate, uncouple, unfasten **9** disengage, extricate, untighten **10** disconnect

unlucky 6 jinxed **7** hapless, ominous **8** ill-fated, untoward **9** ill-boding **10** ill-starred **11** detrimental, inopportune, regrettable, star-crossed, unfavorable, unfortunate **12** inauspicious, unpropitious

unmanageable 4 wild **5** balky, bulky **6** unruly **7** awkward **8** contrary, cumbrous, perverse, stubborn, unwieldy **9** fractious **10** cumbersome, disorderly, headstrong, rebellious, refractory **11** intractable **12** obstreperous, recalcitrant, ungovernable **13** uncooperative, undisciplined

unmannered 4 rude **5** crude, rough **6** coarse, gauche **7** boorish, ill-bred, loutish **8** impolite **10** indecorous, ungracious **12** discourteous **13** disrespectful

unmarred 5 sound, whole **6** intact, unhurt **7** perfect **8** pristine, unflawed, unharmed **9**

undamaged, undefiled, unscathed, unstained **10** unimpaired **11** unblemished, untarnished

unmask 6 debunk, detect, expose, reveal, show up **7** deflate, uncover **8** disclose, discover, disprove **9** demystify

unmatched 3 odd **4** only **5** alone **6** unique **8** peerless, singular **9** unequaled, unrivaled **10** inimitable, unequalled, unrivalled **11** exceptional **12** incomparable, unparalleled

unmerciful 5 cruel, harsh **6** brutal **7** callous, extreme **8** inhumane, pitiless, ruthless, uncaring, vengeful **9** heartless, unfeeling, unsparing **10** relentless

unmindful 7 unaware **8** careless, heedless **9** forgetful, negligent, oblivious, unheeding, unwitting **10** abstracted, distracted, neglectful **11** inattentive

unmistakable 5 clear, frank, plain **6** patent **7** certain, decided, evident, express, obvious **8** apparent, definite, distinct, explicit, manifest, palpable **11** unambiguous, unequivocal

unmitigated 4 pure, rank **5** gross, sheer, utter **6** arrant **7** perfect, unmixed **8** absolute, clearcut, complete, outright **9** downright, out-and-out, unalloyed, undiluted **10** consummate, unmodified, unrelieved **11** straight-out, unqualified **13** thoroughgoing

unmixed 4 mere, neat, pure **5** plain, sheer, utter **6** simple **7** perfect, sincere **8** absolute, straight **9** unalloyed, unblended, undiluted, undivided **11** unmitigated, unqualified **13** unadulterated

unmoved 4 calm, cool, firm **5** aloof, stony **6** in situ, stolid **7** adamant, callous, stoical **8** obdurate **9** impassive, untouched **10** insensible, untroubled **11** unconcerned, unemotional, unimpressed **12** unresponsive

unnamed 5 incog **6** secret **7** obscure, unknown **9** anonymous, incognito **11** unspecified **12** unidentified

unnatural 7 uncanny **8** aberrant, abnormal **9** anomalous, contrived, irregular, synthetic **10** artificial, fabricated, factitious

unnecessary 6 excess **7** surplus **8** needless, optional, prodigal **9** avoidable, redundant **10** expendable, extraneous, gratuitous **11** dispensable, inessential, superfluous, uncalled-for, unessential **12** nonessential

unnerve 5 daunt, shake, throw, upset, worry **6** dismay, rattle **7** agitate, disturb, fluster, perturb, trouble, unhinge **8** bewilder, confound, distress **9** undermine **10** disconcert, discourage, dishearten, intimidate

unobstructed 4 open **5** clear **8** passable **9** unblocked, unimpeded **10** unhampered, unhindered **12** unrestricted

unobtrusive 5 quiet **6** modest **7** subdued **8** reserved, retiring, tasteful **10** restrained **13** inconspicuous

unoccupied 4 free, idle **5** empty **6** vacant **7** jobless, vacated **8** deserted **9** abandoned, available **10** employable, unemployed **11** uninhabited

unofficial 7 pirated, private, wildcat **8** informal **9** irregular **10** unapproved, unorthodox **12** unauthorized, unsanctioned

unorganized 7 aimless, chaotic, muddled **8** confused, inchoate, nebulous, rambling, unformed **9** amorphous, arbitrary, haphazard, shapeless, unplanned **10** disjointed, disordered, incoherent, incohesive **11** spontaneous

unoriginal 5 banal, stock **6** copied, old-hat **7** clichéd, humdrum, prosaic, sterile **8** borrowed, ordinary **9** hackneyed, imitative **10** derivative, uninspired **11** commonplace, plagiarized **12** conventional **13** unimaginative

unornamented 4 bare **5** plain, spare, stark **6** chaste, modest, severe, simple **7** austere **9** unadorned **11** unelaborate, ungarnished **13** unembellished, unembroidered

unorthodox 3 odd **5** kinky, novel, weird **6** far-out **7** offbeat, strange, unusual **8** abnormal, maverick **9** different, dissident, eccentric, heretical, irregular, sectarian **10** schismatic, unexpected **13** nonconformist

unorthodoxy 6 heresy, schism **7** dissent **8** variance **9** ingenuity, recusancy **10** contention, dissidence, innovation **13** nonconformism, nonconformity

unpaid 3 due **5** owing **6** mature **7** donated, overdue, payable, pro-bono **8** freewill, honorary, wageless **9** unsettled, voluntary, volunteer **10** delinquent, gratuitous, receivable **11** contributed, outstanding

unpalatable 8 unsavory **10** flavorless **11** distasteful **12** unappetizing

unparalleled 6 unique **8** peerless, singular **9** matchless, unequaled, unmatched, unrivaled **10** inimitable, unequalled, unrivalled **11** exceptional **12** incomparable

unplanned 5 fluky **6** chance, random **7** aimless **9** desultory, haphazard, hit-or-miss **10** accidental, unexpected, unforeseen, unintended **11** inadvertent **12** adventitious, coincidental, unconsidered **13** unintentional

unpleasant 4 sour **5** seamy **7** painful **8** annoying **9** offensive, troubling **10** disturbing, irritating **11** displeasing, distasteful, distressing **12** disagreeable **13** objectionable

unpolished 4 rude **5** crude, gruff, rough **6** crusty, vulgar **7** brusque, uncivil, uncouth **8**

homespun **9** inelegant, roughhewn, unrefined **10** amateurish, uncultured, unfinished, ungracious **11** ill-mannered, uncivilized

unpredictable 4 iffy **5** dicey, fluky **6** chancy, fickle, random, touchy **7** erratic, mutable **8** unstable, variable, volatile **9** arbitrary, mercurial, uncertain, whimsical **10** capricious, changeable **13** unforeseeable

unprejudiced 4 fair, just **5** equal **8** balanced, unbiased **9** equitable, impartial, objective, unbigoted, uncolored **10** even-handed, fair-minded, open-minded **11** nonpartisan **12** uninfluenced **13** disinterested, dispassionate

unpressed 7 rumpled, wrinkly **8** crinkled, puckered, wrinkled

unpretentious 5 frank, plain **6** candid, honest, modest, simple **7** genuine **8** ordinary **9** unadorned **10** forthright, unaffected, unassuming **11** plain-spoken

unprincipled 5 venal **7** corrupt, crooked, immoral **9** deceitful, dishonest, dissolute, mercenary, reprobate, unethical **10** inconstant, iniquitous, profligate, unfaithful **11** underhanded **12** unscrupulous

unproductive 4 vain **6** barren, futile **7** sterile, useless **8** bootless, depleted, feckless, impotent **9** fruitless, infertile **10** unavailing **11** ineffectual **12** hardscrabble

unprofitable 4 idle, vain **6** barren, futile **7** useless **8** bootless **9** fruitless **10** unavailing **11** ineffective **12** unproductive, unsuccessful

unprogressive 8 orthodox **9** illiberal **11** traditional **12** conservative

unpropitious 4 grim **5** bleak **7** ominous, unlucky **9** ill-boding, ill-omened **10** foreboding **11** inopportune, threatening, unfavorable **12** discouraging

unprosperous 4 poor **5** needy **8** strapped **9** penurious **11** impecunious

unprotected 6 unsafe **7** exposed **8** helpless, insecure **9** unguarded **10** endangered, undefended, unshielded, vulnerable **11** defenseless, susceptible, unsheltered

unproved 7 untried **8** untested **10** postulated **11** conjectural, preliminary, provisional, speculative, theoretical **12** experimental, hypothetical

unpunctual 4 late **5** tardy **6** remiss **7** belated, delayed, overdue **10** behindhand, delinquent

unqualified 4 firm, rank **5** sheer, total, unfit, utter **7** express **8** absolute, explicit, unfitted **9** incapable, out-and-out, steadfast, unalloyed, undiluted, unskilled **10** ineligible, unequipped, unreserved, unsuitable **11** ill-equipped, incompetent, unmitigated **12** wholehearted **13** unadulterated, unconditional

unquenchable 7 exigent **9** demanding, insatiate, insistent **10** insatiable **12** effervescent, unrestrained **13** irrepressible, unconstrained

unquestionable 4 real, sure, true **7** certain, genuine **8** absolute, bona fide **9** authentic, undoubted **10** sure-enough, undeniable **11** established, indubitable, self-evident, well-founded **12** indisputable, well-grounded **13** authoritative, incontestable, unimpeachable

unquestioning 4 firm, sure **5** fixed **6** steady **7** abiding **8** enduring, gullible, resolute, trusting, unshaken **9** accepting, believing, credulous, steadfast **10** uncritical, unshakable, unwavering **11** unfaltering, unqualified **12** never-failing, unsuspecting

unravel 4 fray **5** break, solve **6** answer, decode, unknit, unwind **7** clear up, dope out, explain, resolve, unsnarl **8** decipher, dissolve, untangle **9** elucidate, extricate, figure out, interpret, puzzle out, translate **11** disentangle

unreadable 7 deadpan **9** illegible **10** poker-faced **11** inscrutable **12** hieroglyphic **13** cacographical

unreal 4 fake **5** bogus, false **6** fabled **7** fictive **8** chimeric, fanciful, illusory, mythical **9** fantastic, fictional, imaginary, imitation **10** artificial, chimerical, fictitious, improbable, incredible **11** nonexistent **12** unbelievable
combining form: **5** pseud **6** pseudo

unrealistic 7 blue-sky, idyllic, utopian **8** fanciful, quixotic, romantic **9** distorted, idealized, overblown **10** farfetched, ivory-tower, overstated, starry-eyed, unworkable **11** exaggerated, extravagant, impractical, sensational

unreasonable 5 undue **6** absurd **7** invalid **9** arbitrary, excessive, illogical, senseless **10** exorbitant, fallacious, headstrong, immoderate, inordinate, irrational, peremptory, ridiculous **11** extravagant, incongruous, uncalled-for, unwarranted **12** preposterous **13** unjustifiable

unreasoned 7 invalid, unsound **9** deceptive, illogical, sophistic, unfounded **10** fallacious, ill-founded, irrational, misleading, ungrounded **11** nonrational

unrefined 3 raw **4** rude **5** crass, crude, rough, tacky **6** coarse, earthy, impure, vulgar **7** natural, uncouth **9** graceless, inelegant, maladroit, roughhewn **10** uncultured, unpolished **11** ill-mannered, uncivilized, unprocessed **12** uncultivated

unreflective 6 casual **7** offhand **8** careless, feckless, heedless, mindless **9** imprudent, impulsive, oblivious, unheeding **10** indiscreet, nonchalant, unthinking **11** inadvertent, perfunctory, thoughtless **13** ill-considered

unrehearsed 5 ad-lib **7** offhand **8** ad-libbed, informal **9** extempore, impromptu, unstudied **10** improvised, off-the-cuff, unprepared **11** extemporary, spontaneous **12** extemporized

unrelated 8 discrete, separate **9** different, disparate **10** dissimilar, extraneous, irrelevant **11** independent

unrelenting 3 set **4** grim **5** stern **7** adamant, endless **8** constant, resolute, ruthless, tireless **9** ceaseless, continual, hard-nosed, incessant, tenacious, unbending, unsparing **10** continuous, determined, implacable, inexorable, inflexible, persistent, unflagging, unshakable, unwavering, unyielding **12** unappeasable

unreliable 6 fickle, shifty, tricky, unsafe **7** dubious **8** fallible, slippery, two-faced **9** deceitful, deceptive, faithless, trustless, uncertain **10** capricious, fly-by-night, inaccurate, inconstant, perfidious, unfaithful **11** vacillating **12** falsehearted, questionable, unconvincing, undependable **13** irresponsible, unpredictable, untrustworthy

unremarkable 4 so-so **5** plain, usual **6** common, decent, normal **7** average, mundane, prosaic, routine **8** adequate, everyday, familiar, habitual, mediocre, ordinary, workaday **9** customary, quotidian **11** commonplace, nondescript **12** run-of-the-mill **13** unexceptional

unremitting 7 abiding, chronic, endless, lasting, nonstop, ongoing **8** constant, enduring, unending **9** ceaseless, continual, incessant, perennial, perpetual, sustained, unceasing **10** continuous, persistent, persisting, relentless **12** interminable **13** uninterrupted

unrepentant 10 impenitent **11** remorseless **12** unregenerate

unrepresentative 7 deviant, unusual **8** aberrant, abnormal, atypical **9** anomalous, divergent, eccentric, irregular, untypical **11** exceptional, heteroclite **13** nonconforming

unreserved 4 open **5** frank, plain **6** candid **8** effusive, explicit, outgoing, outright **9** expansive, talkative **10** definitive **11** forthcoming, openhearted, unconcealed, undisguised, unqualified **13** demonstrative, unconstrained

unresolved 4 moot **7** pending **8** hesitant, wavering **9** faltering, tentative, uncertain, undecided, unsettled **10** ambivalent, hesitating, indecisive, irresolute, unanswered **11** vacillating

unrespectable 3 low **5** shady **6** shabby, shoddy **8** shameful, unworthy **10** inglorious **11** disgraceful, ignominious **12** dishonorable, disreputable **13** discreditable

unresponsive 4 cold **5** aloof, stoic **6** frigid, remote, stolid **7** distant, passive **8** detached, reserved **9** inhibited, withdrawn **10** forbidding, insentient **11** insensitive, passionless, unemotional **12** uninterested **13** insusceptible, unsusceptible

unrest 6 strife, tumult **7** anarchy, anxiety, ferment, tension, turmoil **8** disorder, disquiet, distress, edginess, upheaval **9** agitation, commotion, confusion **10** inquietude, turbulence, uneasiness **11** disquietude, disturbance, instability **12** perturbation **13** Sturm und Drang

unrestrained 6 wanton **7** rampant **8** uncurbed **9** audacious, excessive, unbridled **10** immoderate, inordinate, ungoverned, unhampered **11** extravagant, intemperate, spontaneous, uninhibited, untrammeled **12** uncontrolled **13** demonstrative, irrepressible, overindulgent

unrestricted 4 free, full, open **9** boundless, extensive, unlimited **10** accessible, unconfined, unfettered, unhampered **11** far-reaching, unqualified, wide-ranging **12** unobstructed **13** unconditional

unripe 3 raw **5** green, young **6** callow, jejune **7** untried **8** emergent, immature, juvenile, unformed, youthful **9** unfledged, untrained **10** unprepared, unseasoned **11** undeveloped **13** inexperienced

unrivaled 4 only, sole **5** alone **6** unique **7** leading, stellar, supreme **8** champion, foremost, greatest, peerless **9** matchless, paramount, principal, unequaled, unmatched **10** inimitable, preeminent, unequalled **11** outstanding, predominant **12** incomparable, unparalleled

unroll 6 expose, extend, reveal, unfurl, unwind **7** exhibit, open out **8** disclose **9** spread out

unromantic 5 sober **8** sensible **9** practical, pragmatic, realistic **10** hard-boiled, hardheaded **11** down-to-earth, level-headed, utilitarian **12** businesslike, matter-of-fact **13** unsentimental

unruffled 4 calm, cool **6** poised, placid, serene, smooth **7** equable, unmoved **8** composed, tranquil **9** collected, unexcited **10** nonchalant, untroubled **11** unconcerned, undisturbed, unflappable **13** imperturbable, self-possessed

unruly **4** wild **5** rowdy **7** froward, raucous, wayward, willful **8** contrary, perverse, untoward **9** fractious, obstinate, turbulent **10** boisterous, disorderly, headstrong, ill-behaved, rebellious, refractory, tumultuous **11** disobedient, intractable **12** contumacious, incorrigible, obstreperous, rambunctious, recalcitrant, ungovernable, unmanageable **13** undisciplined

unsafe **5** risky, shaky **6** chancy **7** erratic, harmful, parlous, rickety, tottery, unsound **8** insecure, perilous, slippery, unstable **9** dangerous, hazardous, uncertain **10** precarious, ramshackle, unreliable, vulnerable **11** threatening, treacherous **12** undependable

unsaid **5** known, tacit **6** silent **7** assumed, implied **8** accepted, implicit, indirect, inferred, presumed, unspoken, unstated, wordless **9** customary, unuttered **10** insinuated, undeclared, understood **11** traditional, unexpressed

unsatisfactory **3** bum **4** lame **8** mediocre **9** defective, deficient **10** inadequate **11** displeasing, substandard **12** unacceptable **13** disappointing

unsavory **4** rank **5** gross, shady **7** insipid **9** repugnant, repulsive, sickening, tasteless **11** distasteful, ill-flavored **12** disagreeable, unappetizing

unsay **4** lift, void **6** abjure, cancel, disown, recall, recant, revoke **7** nullify, rescind, retract, reverse, suspend **8** abnegate, abrogate, disclaim, forswear, renounce, take back, withdraw **11** countermand

unscathed **4** safe **5** sound, whole **6** intact, unhurt **8** unharmed **9** uninjured, unscarred, untouched **11** unscratched

unscented **8** odor-free, odorless

unschooled **5** naive **7** artless, natural, vacuous **8** ignorant **9** ingenuous, unstudied **10** illiterate, unaffected, uneducated, unlettered **11** empty-headed

unscramble **5** solve, untie **6** decode, unwind **7** clarify, clear up, resolve, restore, sort out, unravel, untwine **8** decipher, untangle **9** extricate, figure out **11** disentangle **12** disembarrass

unscrupulous **5** shady, venal **7** corrupt, crooked, knavish **8** scheming, wrongful **9** deceitful, dishonest, mercenary, shameless, underhand, unethical **11** underhanded **12** exploitative, unprincipled

unseasonable **8** ill-timed, untimely **12** inconvenient

unseasoned **3** raw **4** flat **5** bland, fresh, green, young **6** callow **7** untried **8** immature **9** credulous, tasteless, unfledged, untrained **10** flavorless **11** unpracticed **13** inexperienced

unseat **3** axe, can **4** boot, buck, fire, oust, sack **5** eject, pitch, purge, throw **6** depose, recall, remove **7** buck off, dismiss, unhorse **8** dethrone, dislodge, displace **9** ostracize

unseemliness **8** solecism **9** barbarism, gaucherie, immodesty, impudence, indecency, vulgarity **10** imprudence, incivility, indelicacy **11** impropriety **12** indiscretion

unseemly **8** improper, untoward **9** inelegant, unrefined **10** indecorous, indelicate, malapropos, unbecoming, unsuitable **11** unbefitting **13** inappropriate

unseen **6** hidden **9** concealed, invisible, unnoticed **10** overlooked, unobserved **11** unsuspected

unsentimental see **unromantic**

unserviceable **7** useless **10** inoperable, unfeasible, unworkable **11** impractical, unrealistic **13** impracticable, nonfunctional

unsettle **3** vex **4** faze **5** spook, upset **6** bother, flurry, jumble, rattle, ruffle **7** agitate, disturb, fluster, perturb, trouble, unhinge, unnerve **8** bewilder, confound, disarray, disorder, disquiet **9** discomfit **10** discompose, disconcert

unsettled **4** open **5** fluid, owing, shaky **6** mobile, queasy, shaken, uneasy, unpaid **7** anxious, dubious, mutable, overdue, payable, pending, restive **8** agitated, bothered, doubtful, frontier, restless, troubled, unstable, unsteady, variable **9** disturbed, uncertain, undecided **10** changeable, unbalanced, unresolved **11** outstanding, problematic **12** undetermined

unsex **3** fix **4** geld, spay **5** alter **6** change, neuter **8** castrate **9** sterilize **10** emasculate

unshackle **4** free **5** loose **6** loosen, unbind **7** manumit, release, unchain **8** liberate, unfetter **10** emancipate

unshakable **4** firm, sure **5** fixed **6** stable, steady **7** abiding, adamant, settled, staunch **8** resolute **9** steadfast, tenacious **10** determined, persistent, unwavering, unyielding **11** unfaltering **12** never-failing

unshaped **5** vague **7** nascent **8** formless, inchoate, unformed **9** amorphous, embryonic **10** incoherent **11** preliminary

unshared **4** sole **6** single, unique **7** private **8** singular **9** exclusive, undivided **10** individual **11** distinctive

unshod **8** barefoot, shoeless **9** discalced **10** barefooted

unsightly **4** ugly **5** gross **6** grisly **7** hideous **9** repulsive **10** ill-favored **12** unattractive

unskillful **5** inept **6** clumsy, gauche **7** awkward, unhandy **8** bumbling, bungling, inexpert **9** ham-handed, incapable, maladroit, stumbling, untrained

unsnarl see **untangle**

unsociable 3 shy **4** cool **5** aloof, timid **6** offish, remote, shut-in **7** distant **8** reserved, secluded, solitary **9** diffident, reclusive, withdrawn **10** unfriendly **11** introverted, standoffish **12** inaccessible, unneighborly

unsoiled 5 clean **8** spotless **9** unspotted, unstained, unsullied, untainted **10** immaculate **11** unblemished, untarnished

unsophisticated 5 corny, green, naive **6** callow, folksy, rustic, simple **7** artless, natural, sincere, uncouth **8** gullible, innocent **9** childlike, ingenuous, unrefined, unworldly

unsorted 5 mixed **6** divers, motley, sundry, varied **7** diverse, jumbled, mingled **9** disparate, scrambled, unmatched, unrefined **10** variegated **11** diversified **12** multifarious **13** heterogeneous, miscellaneous

unsought 7 unasked, willing **8** unbidden, unwanted **9** undesired, uninvited, unwelcome, voluntary **10** gratuitous **11** spontaneous, unsolicited

unsound 3 mad **4** weak **5** frail, shaky, wrong **6** faulty, flawed, flimsy, infirm, insane, sickly, untrue **7** damaged, fragile, invalid **8** decrepit, specious **9** defective, erroneous, imperfect, incorrect, unhealthy **13** insubstantial

unsparing 5 ample, harsh, stern, tough **6** lavish, severe, strict **7** copious, liberal, onerous, profuse **8** abundant, exacting, generous, prolific, rigorous, ruthless **9** bounteous, bountiful, demanding, plenteous **10** freehanded, munificent, openhanded, unmerciful **11** magnanimous

unspeakable 4 dire, evil **5** awful **6** grisly **7** beastly, ghastly, hateful, heinous, hideous **8** dreadful, ghoulish, gruesome, horrific, shocking **9** appalling, atrocious, execrable, frightful, loathsome, monstrous, obnoxious, repugnant, repulsive, revolting **10** abominable, detestable, disgusting, horrendous, outrageous, scandalous **11** unutterable **13** inexpressible

unspoiled 5 ideal **6** intact, virgin **7** halcyon, idyllic, perfect, untamed **8** arcadian, pastoral, pristine, virginal **9** idealized, undefiled, untouched **10** unimpaired **11** unblemished, uncorrupted

unspoken 4 mute **5** tacit **6** hinted, silent, unsaid **7** assumed, implied **8** implicit, inferred, presumed, unstated, wordless **9** intimated, suggested, unuttered **10** undeclared, understood **11** unexpressed

unstable 5 fluid, shaky **6** fickle, shifty, tricky, wobbly **7** dubious, rickety, suspect **8** insecure, slippery, unsteady, variable, volatile, wavering **9** ambiguous, changeful, fluctuant, irregular, mercurial, teetering, uncertain, unsettled **10** capricious, inconstant, precarious **11** vacillating **13** temperamental, unpredictable

unstated 5 tacit **6** latent, unsaid **7** assumed, implied **8** implicit **10** understood

unsteady 5 rocky, shaky, tippy **6** uneven, wobbly **7** erratic, mutable, rickety, varying **8** shifting, unstable, variable **9** changeful, irregular, tottering **10** changeable, inconstant ***British:*** **5** wonky

unstudied 5 naive **6** casual **7** artless, natural, offhand **8** careless, informal, unforced, unversed **9** extempore, guileless, impromptu, ingenuous, makeshift, unplanned **10** improvised, nonchalant, unaffected, unpolished **11** extemporary, spontaneous, unrehearsed **13** improvisatory

unstylish 4 drab, dull **5** dated, dowdy, fusty, passé, ratty, tacky **6** démodé, frumpy, old-hat, shabby, stodgy **7** vintage **8** outdated, outmoded **9** inelegant, moth-eaten, out-of-date **10** antiquated, oldfangled **12** old-fashioned **13** unfashionable

unsubstantial 4 thin **5** frail, shaky **6** feeble, flimsy, infirm **7** fragile, shadowy, tenuous **8** ethereal, illusory **9** dreamlike, imaginary **10** immaterial, impalpable, intangible **11** implausible, incorporeal, nonmaterial, nonphysical

unsuitable 5 inapt, undue, unfit **7** awkward, jarring **8** ill-timed, improper, unfitted, unseemly, untimely **9** ill-suited **10** ill-adapted, inadequate, inapposite, malapropos, mismatched, unbecoming **11** inadvisable, inopportune, unbefitting, unqualified **12** incompatible, infelicitous, unacceptable, unseasonable **13** inappropriate

unsullied 4 pure **5** clean **6** chaste **8** flawless, spotless, unsoiled **9** blameless, exemplary, guiltless, stainless, taintless, undefiled **10** immaculate **11** unblemished, untarnished

unsure 5 dicey, shaky **6** wobbly **7** dubious, unclear **8** doubtful, insecure, unstable, wavering **9** fluctuant, skeptical, uncertain, undecided **10** ambivalent, indecisive, irresolute, unreliable **11** unconvinced, vacillating **12** questionable, undependable **13** untrustworthy

unsurpassable 7 supreme **8** ultimate **9** matchless **10** consummate, preeminent **12** transcendent

unsusceptible 6 immune, inured **8** hardened

9 impassive, resistant **10** impervious **11** insensitive **12** invulnerable, unresponsive

unsuspecting 5 naive **6** unwary **8** gullible, trustful, trusting **9** confiding, credulous, imprudent **10** incautious

unswerving see **unfaltering**

unsympathetic 4 cold, cool **5** chill, stony **6** averse **7** callous, unmoved **8** detached **9** apathetic, unfeeling, unpitying **10** hard-boiled **11** coldhearted, hardhearted, indifferent, insensitive, unconcerned **12** stonyhearted **13** disinterested

untactful 4 flip, rash, rude **5** brash **6** brazen **8** flippant, insolent **9** audacious, impolitic, imprudent, maladroit **10** indiscreet **11** impertinent, thoughtless **12** presumptuous, undiplomatic

untamed 4 wild **5** brute, feral **6** carnal, fierce, savage **7** bestial, brutish **8** barbaric **9** primitive **11** uncivilized

untangle 5 solve **7** clear up, explain, resolve, unravel, unsnarl, untwine, untwist **9** elucidate, extricate, interpret **10** disembroil, disentwine, straighten, unscramble **11** disencumber **12** disembarrass

untaught 5 naive **7** natural **8** ignorant, nescient **9** intuitive, untrained, untutored **10** uneducated, unlettered, unschooled **11** empty-headed, instinctual, spontaneous

untempered 6 wanton **7** extreme **9** excessive **10** gratuitous, immoderate, inordinate **11** extravagant **12** unrestrained

untenable 5 wrong **6** faulty, flimsy **10** inadequate **12** indefensible

untended 5 seedy **7** rickety, run-down **8** decrepit, derelict, deserted, forsaken, tattered **9** neglected **10** ramshackle, tumbledown, uncared-for **11** dilapidated

Unter den ____ 6 Linden

untested 6 intact, unused **7** untried **8** unproved, unproven **11** unpracticed

unthinkable 10 impossible, incredible, outlandish **12** preposterous, unimaginable **13** extraordinary, inconceivable, unprecedented

unthinking 8 careless, feckless, habitual, heedless, knee-jerk **9** automatic, reflexive, unheeding, unmindful **10** distracted, unintended **11** inattentive, inadvertent, instinctive, instinctual, involuntary, perfunctory, spontaneous, thoughtless **12** unreflective

unthrifty 6 lavish, wanton **7** ruinous **8** prodigal, wasteful **9** imprudent **10** profligate **11** extravagant, improvident **12** uneconomical

untidy 5 messy **6** sloppy **7** chaotic, jumbled, unkempt **8** confused, littered, slapdash, slipshod, slovenly **9** cluttered **10** disheveled, disordered, disorderly, topsy-turvy **11** disarranged, dishevelled **12** disorganized

untie 5 let go **6** loosen, unbind, unknot, unlace, unlash **7** release, resolve, set free **8** unstring **9** extricate **11** disencumber, disentangle **12** disembarrass

until 4 up to **6** before **7** prior to **11** in advance of

untimely 5 early, undue **9** premature **10** malapropos **11** ill-seasoned, inopportune **12** unseasonable

untiring 7 devoted, patient **8** diligent, enduring **9** assiduous, ceaseless, dedicated, energetic, unceasing **10** determined, persistent, unflagging, unwavering, unwearying **11** persevering, unfaltering **13** indefatigable, inexhaustible

untold 4 huge, vast **7** immense **8** enormous, gigantic **9** countless **10** prodigious **11** innumerable, uncountable **12** incalculable **13** indescribable

untouchable 5 dalit, leper **6** pariah **7** harijan, outcast **8** outcaste

Untouchables leader 4 Ness (Eliot) **5** Stack (Robert) **7** Costner (Kevin)

untouched 4 pure **5** sound, whole **6** intact, virgin **7** unmoved **8** flawless, pristine, unharmed, unmarred, untapped, virginal **9** undamaged, unspoiled **10** unaffected **11** unblemished, unconcerned, unimpressed

untoward 7 adverse, awkward, froward, unlucky **8** ill-fated, improper, indecent, luckless, unseemly **9** unfitting, vexatious **10** ill-starred, indecorous, indelicate, unbecoming **11** intractable, unfortunate **12** inconvenient, recalcitrant, ungovernable, unmanageable, unpropitious

untrained see **unskilled**

untrammeled 8 uncurbed **9** unimpeded **10** unconfined, unfettered, ungoverned, unhampered **11** uninhibited **12** unobstructed, unrestrained, unrestricted

untried 3 raw **5** fresh, green **6** callow, rookie **8** unproved, untested **10** innovative, pioneering, unseasoned **11** unpracticed **13** inexperienced, unprecedented

untroubled 4 calm **5** still **6** blithe, placid, serene **7** halcyon **8** carefree, composed, peaceful, tranquil **9** easygoing, unruffled **10** insouciant, nonchalant **11** unconcerned, unperturbed **12** lighthearted

untrue 4 fake **5** false, wrong **8** disloyal, specious **9** erroneous, faithless, incorrect **10** fictitious, inaccurate, unfaithful ***combining form:* 5** pseud **6** pseudo

untrustworthy 5 shady **6** shifty, unsafe, unsure **7** devious, dubious **8** disloyal, slippery, two-faced **9** deceptive, negligent, two-timing **10** fly-by-night, unreliable **11** duplicitous **12** questionable, undependable **13** double-dealing, irresponsible

untruth 3 fib, lie **4** sham **5** error **6** canard, deceit **7** blarney, fallacy, falsity, fiction, hogwash **9** deception, duplicity, falsehood, falseness, hypocrisy, mendacity **11** fabrication, insincerity **12** misstatement **13** prevarication

untruthful 4 sham **5** bogus, false, lying, phony **7** knavish **8** specious **9** deceitful, dishonest, erroneous, incorrect **10** fictitious, inaccurate, mendacious

untutored see **unschooled**

unusable 7 outworn, useless **8** obsolete **9** worthless **10** inoperable, unavailing, unworkable **11** impractical, unrealistic **12** inapplicable **13** nonfunctional

unused 3 new **4** idle **5** fresh **6** excess **7** dormant, surplus **8** leftover, residual **9** untouched

unusual 3 odd **4** rare **5** outré **6** quaint, unique **7** bizarre, curious, special, strange **8** aberrant, abnormal, peculiar, singular, uncommon, atypical, unwonted **9** anomalous, different, eccentric, irregular **11** exceptional **13** extraordinary

unusually 4 very **5** extra **6** highly, rarely, seldom **8** markedly **9** curiously, extremely, strangely **10** abnormally, especially, peculiarly, remarkably, strikingly, uncommonly **11** exceedingly **12** infrequently, particularly

unutterable 5 taboo **7** awesome **9** ineffable **11** unspeakable **13** indescribable, inexpressible

unvaried 4 like, same **5** alike **7** uniform **9** identical **10** consistent, unchanging **11** undeviating

unvarnished see **undisguised**

unvarying see **unchanging**

unveil see **uncover**

unversed 3 raw **5** green **6** callow **7** untried **8** inexpert **9** unfledged **10** unfamiliar, unseasoned **11** uninitiated, unpracticed **13** inexperienced

unwanted see **unwelcome**

unwarranted 5 undue **8** baseless **9** misguided, unfounded **10** gratuitous, groundless, immoderate, unprovoked **11** extravagant, inexcusable, injudicious, uncalled-for, unjustified **12** unreasonable **13** insupportable, unjustifiable, unsupportable

unwary 5 brash, hasty **8** careless, gullible, heedless, reckless **9** credulous, impetuous, imprudent, unguarded **10** ill-advised, incautious, indiscreet **11** thoughtless **12** unsuspecting

unwavering see **unfaltering**

unwelcome 7 unasked **8** unsought, unwanted **9** undesired, uninvited **11** undesirable **12** unacceptable **13** objectionable

unwell 3 ill **4** sick **5** frail, shaky **6** ailing, feeble, infirm, offish, peaked, queasy, sickly, wobbly **8** diseased, stricken **9** afflicted, enfeebled, unhealthy **10** indisposed **11** debilitated

unwholesome 4 foul **5** toxic **6** sickly **7** adverse, corrupt, harmful, immoral, noisome, noxious, unsound **8** diseased **9** injurious, loathsome, offensive, unhealthy **10** pernicious, subversive **11** deleterious, detrimental, unhealthful **12** insalubrious

unwieldy 5 bulky **7** awkward, massive **8** cumbrous **9** ponderous **10** burdensome, cumbersome **12** unmanageable

unwilling 5 loath **6** averse **8** grudging, hesitant **9** obstinate, reluctant **10** indisposed **11** disinclined

unwind 4 rest, undo **5** let go, relax **6** loosen, unbend, uncoil, unfold, unreel, unroll **7** ease off, slacken, unravel **8** calm down, kick back, loosen up

unwise 4 rash **5** silly **6** stupid **7** asinine, fatuous, foolish, idiotic, witless **8** reckless **9** brainless, foolhardy, ill-judged, imbecilic, impolitic, imprudent, ludicrous, misguided, senseless **10** ill-advised, indiscreet, ridiculous **11** impractical, injudicious, thoughtless, undesirable, unfortunate **13** unintelligent

unwitting 6 chance **7** unaware **8** ignorant, innocent **9** haphazard, oblivious, unknowing, unmindful, unplanned **10** unfamiliar, uninformed, unintended **11** inadvertent **12** unacquainted

unwonted 4 rare **6** signal, unique **7** notable, unusual **8** singular, uncommon **10** remarkable, unexpected **11** exceptional **12** unaccustomed **13** extraordinary

unworkable 7 useless **8** quixotic **9** half-baked **10** impossible, infeasible, inoperable, unfeasible **11** impractical, unrealistic **12** inapplicable **13** impracticable, nonfunctional

unworldly 5 naive **6** astral, dreamy, simple **7** artless, natural **8** ethereal, innocent, trusting **9** celestial, ingenuous, spiritual, unearthly, visionary **11** impractical **13** inexperienced

unworthy 6 no-good **7** ignoble **8** shameful, unseemly **9** no-account, unmerited, worthless **10** unbecoming **11** disgraceful, inexcusable, undeserving

unwrap see **uncover**

unwritten 4 oral **5** blank, tacit **6** latent, spoken, verbal **7** assumed **8** accepted, implicit

10 understood **11** traditional, word-of-mouth **12** conventional

unyielding 4 firm, grim, hard, iron **5** fixed, rigid, stern, stiff, stony, tough **6** dogged, mulish **7** adamant **8** hard-core, obdurate, stubborn **9** hard-nosed, immovable, insistent, obstinate, pigheaded, steadfast, unbending **10** determined, headstrong, implacable, inexorable, inflexible, persistent, relentless, unshakable **11** intractable, unrelenting **12** pertinacious, single-minded, unappeasable

up 4 hike, jump, lift, rise **5** above, ahead, arise, astir, boost, built, mount, raise, risen **6** ascend, arisen, lifted, versed **7** abreast, promote **8** familiar, increase, informed, positive **9** au courant, northward **10** acquainted, conversant ***prefix:*** **3** ana, sur

up-and-coming 7 go-ahead, hot-shot **8** aspiring **9** promising **11** presumptive, prospective **12** enterprising

upbeat 4 rosy **5** arsis **6** cheery **7** buoyant, hopeful **8** cheerful, positive, sanguine **9** confidant, expectant, promising **10** heartening, optimistic **12** Pollyannaish

upbraid 3 rap **4** lash, rate **5** chide, scold **6** berate, rail at, rebuke, revile, scorch **7** bawl out, censure, chasten, chew out, reprove, scourge, tell off **8** admonish, chastise, reproach **9** castigate, criticize, dress down, reprimand **10** tongue-lash, vituperate

upbringing 7 nurture, rearing **8** training **9** schooling

upchuck 4 barf, hurl, puke, spew, toss **5** heave, retch, vomit **6** spit up **7** bring up, throw up **8** disgorge **11** regurgitate

upcoming 7 looming, nearing, pending **8** expected, foreseen, imminent **9** advancing, impending, onrushing **11** anticipated, approaching, forthcoming, prospective

up-country 4 bush **6** inland, sticks, upland **7** outback **8** backland, frontier, interior, outlying, woodland **9** backwater, backwoods, boondocks **10** hinterland, timberland

update 5 amend, brief, renew **6** inform, revamp, revise, revive **7** apprise, enhance, improve, refresh, restore, rundown, upgrade **8** renovate **9** modernize, refurbish **10** rejuvenate

Updike, John *character:* 6 Rabbit (Angstrom) ***novel:*** **7** Centaur (The), Couples **9** Rabbit Run **11** Rabbit Redux **12** Rabbit at Rest, Rabbit Is Rich **17** Witches of Eastwick (The)

upend 4 beat, best, drub, flip, lick, skin, trim, whip **5** cream, crush, upset **6** invert, subdue, thrash, topple, unseat, wallop **7** capsize, clobber, conquer, overrun, shellac, trounce **8** dethrone, lambaste, overcome, overturn, vanquish **9** overpower, overwhelm, subjugate

upgrade 4 hike, rise **5** boost, raise **6** prefer **7** advance, elevate, enhance, improve, promote **8** increase **9** promotion **10** betterment **11** advancement, improvement **12** breakthrough

upheaval 6 clamor, outcry, tumult, upturn **7** ferment, turmoil **8** churning, disaster, disorder **9** cataclysm, commotion **10** alteration, convulsion, disruption **11** catastrophe

uphill 4 hard **6** rising, rugged, taxing **7** arduous, labored, operose, tedious **8** climbing, grucling, toilsome **9** ascending, difficult, effortful, gruelling, laborious, punishing, strenuous, wearisome

uphold 3 aid **4** back, help, lift, prop **5** brace, carry, hoist, raise **6** assist, back up, bear up, buoy up, defend, second **7** bolster, elevate, justify, shore up, support, sustain **8** advocate, backstop, buttress, champion, maintain, side with **9** vindicate

upkeep 4 cost **7** expense **8** overhead **11** expenditure, maintenance

upland 4 mesa **5** table **7** plateau

uplift 4 buoy **5** cheer, edify, hoist, raise **6** take up **7** animate, elevate, enliven, gladden, hearten **8** brighten, embolden, inspirit **9** encourage **10** exhilarate, strengthen

upon 4 atop ***prefix:*** **3** epi

upper class 4 rank **5** elite **6** gentry **7** peerage, quality, society, who's who **8** affluent, nobility, noblesse, well-to-do **9** blue blood, gentility, haut monde **10** patricians, patriciate **11** aristocracy **13** carriage trade, Establishment

upper hand 4 edge, sway **5** leg up **7** control, mastery **8** leverage **9** advantage, dominance **10** ascendancy **11** superiority **12** predominance

uppermost 3 top **6** apical **7** highest **8** loftiest

uppity 4 smug **5** aloof, brash **6** lordly, sniffy, snippy, snooty, snotty **7** forward, haughty, pompous **8** arrogant, cavalier **9** conceited, egotistic, imperious, know-it-all, presuming **10** disdainful, high-handed **11** overweening, pretentious **12** contemptuous, presumptuous, supercilious **13** self-asserting, self-assertive, self-important

upright 4 fair, good, just, pure, true **5** erect, moral, noble, piano **6** honest, raised **7** correct, ethical **8** elevated, goalpost, standing, vertical, virtuous **9** equitable, exemplary, honorable, impartial **10** principled, scrupulous **13** conscientious, perpendicular

uprightness 5 honor **6** repute, virtue **7** honesty, probity **8** morality, nobility **9** character, integrity, rectitude **13** righteousness
uprising 4 riot **6** mutiny, revolt **8** upheaval **9** rebellion **10** insurgence, revolution **12** insurrection
uproar 3 din, row **4** coil, fuss, to-do, riot **5** babel, brawl, broil, chaos, furor, hoo-ha, melee, whirl **6** bedlam, clamor, fracas, furore, hassle, hoo-hah, hubbub, mayhem, pother, racket, ruckus, rumpus, shindy, tumult **7** shindig, turmoil **8** brouhaha, disorder, foofaraw **9** commotion, confusion **10** hullabaloo, hurly-burly, turbulence **11** pandemonium
uproarious 5 noisy, rowdy **7** comical, rackety, raucous, riotous **8** brawling, clattery, mirthful, strident **9** clamorous, hilarious **10** clangorous, hysterical, resounding, rollicking, tumultuous **12** obstreperous **13** sidesplitting
uproot 4 grub, move, weed **8** displace, overturn, supplant **9** eradicate, extirpate, overthrow, supersede **10** annihilate, transplant **11** exterminate
upset 3 ail, ill, irk, vex **4** rile, roil **5** annoy, evert, worry **6** bother, defeat, dismay, invert, jumble, muddle, topple, tumble **7** afflict, agitate, capsize, disturb, fluster, invalid, jittery, jumbled, muddled, perturb, rattled, reverse, shook up, tip over, toppled, trouble, unnerve, worried **8** agitated, bewilder, bothered, confound, confused, disarray, dismayed, disorder, distress, overturn, troubled, turn over, unnerved **9** afflicted, confusion, disturbed, flustered, knock over, overthrow, perturbed **10** bewildered, confounded, disconcert, disordered, distracted, distressed, indisposed, invalidate, overthrown, overturned, tipped over **11** overwrought **12** apprehensive, disconcerted
upshot 5 issue **6** burden, climax, effect, ending, finish, result **7** outcome, purport **9** substance **10** conclusion, denouement **11** consequence, culmination, termination **12** significance
upside-down 7 chaotic, haywire, jumbled **8** backward, confused, inverted, pell-mell, reversed **10** disordered, overturned, topsy-turvy **13** helter-skelter
upstanding see **upright**
upstart 5 comer **7** parvenu **8** outsider **9** arriviste, pretender **12** nouveau riche **13** social climber
upsurge 4 gain, jump, rise, rush, tide, wave **5** boost, flood, spurt, swell **6** deluge, growth **7** advance **8** increase
uptight 4 edgy **5** riled, tense **6** uneasy **7** anxious, nervous, restive, worried **8** stressed **10** high-strung
up to 4 till **5** until **6** before **11** in advance of
up-to-date 6 modern, modish, timely, trendy, with-it **7** abreast, à la mode, current, stylish **8** advanced, brand-new, contempo **9** au courant, plugged-in **10** avant-garde **11** cutting-edge, fashionable **12** contemporary **13** state-of-the-art
upturn 4 jump, rise **6** growth **8** increase **11** improvement
Urania see **Muse**
Uranus 6 planet ***moon:*** **5** Ariel **6** Oberon **7** Titania ***mother, wife:*** **4** Gaea ***offspring:*** **6** Titans **8** Cyclopes ***overthrower, son:*** **6** Cronus
urban 9 municipal **12** metropolitan
urbane 5 suave **6** poised, smooth **7** elegant, genteel, politic, refined **8** cultured, debonair, gracious, polished **9** civilized, distingué **10** cultivated, diplomatic **12** cosmopolitan **13** sophisticated
urbanize 6 citify
urchin 3 imp **4** brat **5** child, gamin, scamp **10** ragamuffin
Urdur see **Norn**
urge 3 egg, sic, yen **4** coax, goad, itch, lust, prod, push, spur, wish **5** drive, egg on, impel, press, prick, set on, tar on **6** adjure, cajole, compel, demand, desire, exhort, incite, induce, needle, prompt, propel **7** beseech, conjure, craving, entreat, implore, impulse, inspire, longing, passion, promote, propose, provoke, solicit, wheedle **8** advocate, appetite, blandish, pressure, yearning **9** encourage, instigate, stimulate **12** high-pressure
urgency 5 haste **6** duress, stress **8** exigence, exigency, pressure **9** necessity **10** compulsion, insistence
urgent 5 vital **6** crying **7** burning, clamant, crucial, driving, exigent, instant, present **8** critical, pressing **9** clamorous, demanding, immediate, impelling, insistent, momentous **10** compelling, imperative **11** importunate
Uriel 9 archangel
Uris novel 3 Haj (The) **5** QB VII **6** Exodus **7** Trinity **9** Battle Cry, Mitla Pass **10** Angry Hills (The), Redemption
urn 4 vase **6** vessel **7** samovar ***Greek:*** **7** amphora
Ursa Major 9 Great Bear **11** Great Dipper
Ursa Minor 10 Little Bear **12** Little Dipper ***star:*** **7** Polaris **8** polestar **9** North Star
Uruguay *capital:* **10** Montevideo ***language:*** **7** Spanish ***monetary unit:*** **4** peso ***neighbor:*** **6**

Brazil **9** Argentina ***river:*** **7** La Plata **8** Río Negro

usable 6 liquid **7** running, working **9** adaptable, available, operative **10** accessible, applicable, employable, expendable, functional, marketable, negotiable **11** exploitable, functioning, operational, serviceable

usage 3 way **4** form, mode, wont **5** habit, sense **6** action, amount, custom, manner, method, praxis **7** process **8** habitude, practice **9** formality, procedure **10** convention

use 3 ply **4** wont, work **5** apply, avail, habit, serve, treat, value, wield, worth **6** custom, demand, employ, handle, liking, manage, manner **7** benefit, exploit, operate, purpose, service, utility, utilize **8** deal with, exercise, exertion, function, impose on, occasion, practice, regulate **9** advantage, habituate, objective, relevance **10** employment, manipulate **11** application

used 8 pre-owned, shopworn **10** secondhand

used up 5 all in, spent **6** bleary, effete, sapped, wasted **7** drained, emptied, fargone, worn-out **8** consumed, depleted **9** exhausted, washed-out

useful 3 fit **4** meet **5** handy, utile **7** helpful **8** fruitful, suitable, valuable **9** favorable, practical **10** beneficial, convenient, functional, productive, profitable, propitious, worthwhile **11** appropriate, practicable, serviceable, utilitarian **12** advantageous

usefulness 5 value, worth **7** fitness, service, utility **8** function **9** advantage, relevance, substance **10** expedience, expediency **12** practicality **13** applicability

useless 4 idle, vain **5** inept **6** futile **7** inutile **8** bootless, hopeless, unusable **9** fruitless, pointless, worthless **10** unavailing, unworkable **11** impractical, ineffective, ineffectual, inoperative **12** unproductive, unprofitable **13** impracticable, nonfunctional

user 5 buyer **6** addict **8** consumer, customer, utilizer

use up 5 drain, spend **6** devour, expend **7** consume, deplete, exhaust **8** draw down **10** run through

usher 4 lead, seat **5** guide **6** escort **7** conduct, precede **9** conductor **10** doorkeeper

usher in 5 begin, greet, start **6** launch **7** kick off, trumpet, welcome **8** announce, commence, initiate, proclaim **9** institute, introduce, originate **10** inaugurate

usual 5 stock, typic **6** common, kosher, normal, wonted **7** average, regular, routine, typical, vanilla **8** accepted, everyday, expected, familiar, habitual, ordinary, orthodox, standard, workaday **9** customary, prevalent, quotidian **10** accustomed, prevailing **11** commonplace, established **12** conventional, unremarkable

usually 6 mainly, mostly **7** as a rule **8** commonly, normally **9** generally, routinely **10** habitually, ordinarily **11** customarily

usurer 7 Shylock **9** loan shark **11** moneylender

usurp 4 take **5** seize, wrest **6** assume **7** preempt **8** arrogate, displace, supplant **10** commandeer **11** appropriate

Utah *capital:* 12 Salt Lake City ***city:*** **4** Orem **5** Ogden, Provo ***college, university:*** **12** Brigham Young ***lake:*** **6** Powell **9** Great Salt ***motto:*** **8** Industry ***mountain:*** **5** Kings (Peak) ***nickname:*** **7** Beehive (State) ***park:*** **4** Zion **5** Bryce **6** Arches **11** Canyonlands ***river:*** **5** Green **6** Sevier ***state bird:*** **14** California gull ***state flower:*** **8** sego lily ***state tree:*** **10** blue spruce

utensil 3 pan, pot **4** fork, tool **5** knife, spoon **6** device, vessel **8** saucepan, teaspoon **9** implement **10** instrument

uterus 4 womb

Uther Pendragon *son:* 6 Arthur ***wife:*** **6** Ygerne **7** Igraine

utile 5 handy **6** useful **7** working **9** available, operative, practical **10** accessible, convenient, dependable, functional **11** practicable, serviceable

utilitarian 6 useful **9** practical, pragmatic **10** functional ***philosopher:*** **4** Mill (John Stuart) **7** Bentham (Jeremy)

utility 3 use **7** benefit, fitness, service **8** function **9** advantage, relevance **10** efficiency, usefulness **12** practicality **13** applicability

utilize 3 use **5** apply, spend **6** bestow, deploy, employ, handle, occupy **7** exploit **8** exercise **11** appropriate

utmost 3 nth, top **4** acme, apex, best, peak **6** height, zenith **7** extreme, highest, maximal, maximum, supreme **8** farthest, furthest, greatest, pinnacle, remotest, ultimate **9** damnedest, extremity

utopia 4 Eden, Zion **5** bliss **6** heaven **7** Elysium **8** paradise **9** Cockaigne, dreamland, Shangri-la **10** dreamworld **12** promised land **13** Elysian fields

Utopia author 4 More (Thomas)

utopian 5 ideal, lofty **6** edenic **7** dreamer **8** arcadian, fanciful, idealist, quixotic **9** grandiose, ideologue, visionary **10** chimerical, idealistic, impossible, millennial, unfeasible **11** impractical **12** otherworldly **13** castle-builder, impracticable

utter 3 say **4** damn, dang, darn, rank, talk, tell

5 sheer, speak, stark, state, total, voice 6 arrant, dashed, deuced, reveal 7 blasted, blessed, declare, deliver, divulge, express, flat-out 8 absolute, bring out, complete, crashing, disclose, infernal, outright, positive, throw out 9 downright, out-and-out, pronounce, verbalize 10 articulate, confounded, consummate 11 come out with, straight-out, unmitigated, unqualified 13 thoroughgoing

utterance 4 rant, vent, word 5 voice 6 speech 7 oration 8 delivery, speaking 9 assertion, discourse, statement 10 expression, revelation 11 declaration 12 announcement, articulation 13 pronouncement, verbalization

utterly 4 just 5 plumb, quite 6 in toto 7 totally 8 entirely 9 perfectly 10 absolutely, altogether, completely, thoroughly

uttermost 4 last 5 final 7 extreme, outmost 8 farthest, furthest, remotest

Utu see **Shamash**

Uzbekistan ***capital:*** 8 Tashkent ***city:*** 7 Bokhara, Bukhara 9 Samarkand, Samarqand ***desert:*** 8 Kyzyl Kum ***enclave:*** 10 Karakalpak ***monetary unit:*** 3 som 5 tiyin ***neighbor:*** 9 Kazakstan 10 Kazakhstan, Kyrgyzstan, Tajikistan 11 Afghanistan 12 Turkmenistan ***river:*** 8 Amu Dar'ya, Syr Dar'ya 9 Zeravshan ***sea:*** 4 Aral

V

vacancy 4 void 6 vacuum 7 opening 8 idleness 9 blankness, emptiness

vacant 4 bare, free, idle, open, void 5 blank, clear, empty, inane, stark 6 unused 7 deadpan, vacuous 8 deserted, unfilled 9 abandoned, impassive 10 tenantless, unoccupied 11 empty-headed 12 inexpressive

vacate 4 quit, void 5 annul, clear, empty, leave 6 bow out, give up, repeal, revoke 7 abandon, rescind, retract, reverse 8 abrogate, check out, dissolve, evacuate 9 discharge 10 relinquish

vacation 4 rest, trip 5 break, leave 6 recess 7 holiday, leisure, respite, time off 8 furlough, interval 10 sabbatical 12 intermission

vacationer 7 tourist, tripper 9 weekender 10 rubberneck 12 holidaymaker

vaccination 4 shot 7 booster 9 injection 11 inoculation

vaccine 4 shot 5 serum 9 antiserum 11 preparation ***inventor:*** 4 Salk (Jonas), Zhou (Jian) 5 Cohen (Joe), Sabin (Albert) 6 Frazer (Ian), Jenner (Edward), Talwar (Gursaran) 8 Hilleman (Maurice)

vacillate 4 sway, yo-yo 5 waver 6 dither, falter, seesaw, teeter, waffle, waggle 7 swither, whiffle 8 hesitate 9 alternate, fluctuate, oscillate 10 equivocate 12 shilly-shally

vacillating 4 weak 6 fickle, unsure, wobbly 8 hesitant, shifting, unstable, unsteady 9 fluctuant, tentative, uncertain, undecided, unsettled 10 changeable, inconstant, indecisive, irresolute 12 shilly-shally

vacillation 5 doubt 8 to-and-fro, wavering 9 hesitancy 10 fickleness, indecision 12 irresolution, shilly-shally

vacuity 4 hole, void 6 cavity, hollow, vacuum 7 inanity 9 black hole, blankness, ditsiness, ditziness, emptiness, stupidity 10 hollowness 11 nothingness

vacuous 4 idle, void 5 blank, empty, inane, silly 6 stupid, vacant 7 foolish, shallow 11 birdbrained, empty-headed, superficial

vacuum 4 void 5 space 7 suction 9 emptiness 11 nothingness ***bottle:*** 5 dewar 7 thermos

vacuum tube 5 diode 6 triode 7 tetrode ***casing:*** 4 bulb

vade mecum 5 guide 6 manual 8 Baedeker, handbook 9 guidebook 11 enchiridion

____ Vadis 3 Quo

vagabond 3 bum 4 hobo 5 gipsy, gypsy, idler, nomad, rogue, rover, tramp 6 picaro, roamer 7 drifter, floater, migrant, nomadic, vagrant, wastrel 8 bohemian, clochard, picaroon, runabout, runagate, traveler, wanderer 9 itinerant, transient, wandering 11 peripatetic

vagarious 6 fickle 7 erratic, flighty, mutable, wayward 8 unstable, volatile 9 impulsive, mercurial, whimsical 10 capricious, inconstant 13 unpredictable

vagary 3 bee 4 whim 5 crank, fancy, freak,

humor, quirk **6** megrim, whimsy **7** caprice, fantasy **8** crotchet

vagrancy 6 roving **7** roaming **8** drifting, nomadism, rambling **9** wandering **10** itinerancy

vagrant see **vagabond**

vague 3 dim **4** hazy **5** blear, faint, foggy, fuzzy, gauzy, misty, muddy, woozy **6** bleary, blurry, cloudy, dreamy, slight, vacant **7** inexact, obscure, shadowy, unclear **8** confused, nebulous, vaporous **9** ambiguous, dreamlike, enigmatic, imprecise, uncertain **10** diaphanous, ill-defined, indefinite, indistinct **13** indeterminate, unsubstantial

vain 4 idle **5** empty, proud **6** futile, hollow, otiose **7** foppish, haughty, stuck-up, trivial, useless **8** abortive, arrogant, boastful, bootless, nugatory **9** conceited, fruitless, valueless, worthless **10** egocentric, profitless, sophomoric, unavailing **11** egotistical, ineffective, ineffectual **12** narcissistic, unproductive, unprofitable, unsuccessful **13** self-important

vainglorious 8 arrogant, boastful, bragging, puffed-up, vaunting **9** conceited, egotistic **10** swaggering **11** egotistical **12** supercilious

vainglory 4 pomp **5** pride **6** egoism, vanity **7** conceit, egotism **9** arrogance **10** pretension **11** haughtiness **12** boastfulness

valance 5 drape **6** pelmet **7** curtain, drapery **10** lambrequin

vale 4 dale, dell, glen **5** combe **6** dingle, hollow, valley

valediction 5 adieu **7** good-bye **8** farewell **11** leave-taking

valedictory see **valediction**

valentine 4 card, dear, love **7** beloved, darling, tribute **10** sweetheart

valet 7 servant **9** attendant **10** manservant

valiant 4 bold **5** brave **6** heroic, plucky **7** doughty, gallant, valiant **8** fearless, intrepid **9** dauntless **10** chivalrous, courageous **11** lionhearted **12** greathearted, stouthearted

valid 4 just, true **5** legal, solid, sound **6** cogent, lawful, potent, proven **7** binding, in force, logical, telling **8** attested, bona fide, credible, forceful **9** effective, effectual, operative **10** acceptable, compelling, convincing, legitimate, persuasive **11** justifiable, trustworthy **12** well-grounded

validate 5 prove **6** affirm, ratify, verify **7** approve, bear out, certify, confirm, endorse, justify, probate **8** legalize, sanction **10** legitimate, legitimize **11** corroborate, rubber-stamp **12** authenticate, substantiate

validity 5 force, proof **7** cogency, potency **8** efficacy **9** soundness **10** lawfulness **13** effectiveness

valise 3 bag **4** grip **6** kit bag, suiter **7** handbag, Pullman **8** gripsack, suitcase **9** gladstone, two-suiter **10** weekend bag **11** portmanteau **12** overnight bag, traveling bag **13** traveling case

Valjean's pursuer 6 Javert

Valkyrie 6 maiden **8** Brynhild ***mother:*** **4** Erda

valley 4 dale, dell, dene, glen, vale, wadi **5** basin, combe, gulch, gully, swale **6** canyon, dingle, hollow, ravine **10** depression ***Africa-Asia:*** **4** Rift **9** Great Rift ***Alps:*** **11** Grindelwald ***ancient Greece:*** **5** Nemea ***Asia:*** **7** Fergana ***California:*** **3** Noe **4** Napa **5** Death, Squaw **7** Central **8** Imperial, Yosemite **10** San Joaquin **11** San Fernando ***Dead Sea area:*** **6** Arabah ***Dominican Republic:*** **5** Cibao ***Egypt:*** **6** Kharga ***England:*** **5** Doone ***Germany:*** **4** Ruhr ***Greece:*** **5** Tembi, Tempe ***India:*** **4** Kulu **7** Kashmir (Vale of) ***Ireland:*** **5** Avoca, Ovoca ***Israel:*** **4** Elah ***Lebanon:*** **4** Biqa **5** Bekaa ***moon:*** **4** rill **5** rille ***New York:*** **12** Sleepy Hollow ***Pennsylvania:*** **7** Nittany ***Scotland:*** **7** Glen Roy ***Switzerland:*** **5** Hasli **8** Engadine **11** Grindelwald ***Virginia:*** **10** Shenandoah ***Washington:*** **11** Grand Coulee

Valmiki's epic 8 Ramayana

valor 4 guts **6** mettle, spirit, virtue **7** bravery, courage, heroism, prowess, stomach **8** chivalry, valiance, valiancy **9** fortitude, gallantry **10** resolution

valorous see **valiant**

valse 5 waltz

valuable 4 dear **5** utile **6** costly, prized, useful, worthy **8** precious **9** expensive, important, rewarding, treasured **10** satisfying, worthwhile

valuate 4 rate **5** assay, price **6** assess, survey **7** adjudge **8** appraise, estimate

valuation 4 cost, rate **5** price, worth **6** rating **7** opinion **8** estimate, judgment **9** appraisal **10** assessment, estimation **12** appreciation

value 4 cost, rate **5** assay, gauge, judge, price, prize, scale, worth **6** assess, assign, charge, esteem, figure, reckon, regard, return, survey **7** account, apprize, care for, cherish, compute, quality, respect, utility **8** appraise, estimate, evaluate, quantity, treasure **9** appraisal, principle **10** appreciate, assessment, equivalent, importance **11** market price **12** denomination

valve 3 tap **4** cock, flap, gate **6** device, faucet, poppet, spigot **7** hydrant, petcock, shutoff **8** stopcock **9** regulator ***cardiac:*** **6** mitral **8** bicuspid

vamoose 3 git **4** scat **5** leave, scram, split **6**

beat it, begone, cut out, decamp, depart, get out **7** run away, skiddoo, take off **8** clear out **9** skedaddle

vamp 3 fix **4** fake, lure, mend, wile **5** ad-lib, flirt, intro, patch, siren, tempt **6** cook up, entice, groove, lead-in, make up, repair, seduce **7** beguile, charmer, rebuild **8** inveigle **9** fabricate, formulate, improvise, refurbish, temptress **10** gold digger, seductress **11** enchantress, extemporize, femme fatale ***famous:*** **4** Bara (Theda) **5** Negri (Pola) **6** Golden (Eve), Harlow (Jean), Lamarr (Hedy), Salome **7** Delilah, Jezebel **8** Dietrich (Marlene), Mata Hari **9** Cleopatra

vampire 3 bat **5** lamia **6** Lestat, undead **7** Dracula **9** Nosferatu **11** bloodsucker ***novelist:*** **4** Rice (Anne) **6** Stoker (Bram)

van 3 car **4** head, lead, wing **5** front, truck, wagon **7** minibus **9** forefront **11** cutting edge, leading edge

vandal 3 Hun **5** yahoo **6** looter **8** pillager **9** despoiler, destroyer, plunderer, spoliator

vandalize 5 smash, trash, wreck **6** damage, deface, ravage, tear up **7** destroy **8** demolish, sabotage

Vandal king 8 Gaiseric, Genseric

Vandyke 5 beard **6** border, collar, edging, goatee

vane 3 web **7** feather, wind tee **8** vexillum **10** bellwether **11** weathercock

Van Gogh, Vincent ***brother:*** **4** Theo ***friend:*** **7** Gauguin (Paul) ***residence:*** **5** Arles ***subject:*** **10** sunflowers

vanguard 4 lead **5** front **9** forefront **11** cutting edge, leading edge

vanilla 4 tame **5** beige, cream, plain **7** extract **8** ordinary **9** innocuous **10** white-bread **12** conventional **13** garden-variety

vanish 3 die, fly **4** fade, flee, melt **5** clear **8** dissolve, evanesce **9** disappear, dissipate, evaporate **13** dematerialize

vanity 3 ego **5** pride **6** egoism **7** conceit, egotism **8** self-love, smugness **9** vainglory **10** narcissism, pretension **13** dressing table

Vanity Fair author 9 Thackeray (William Makepeace)

vanquish 4 beat, best, drub, lick, rout **5** cream, crush, quell **6** defeat, humble, subdue, thrash **7** clobber, conquer, destroy, smother, trounce **8** surmount **9** overpower, overthrow, subjugate **10** annihilate

vantage 4 edge, odds **8** handicap **9** head start, upper hand ***point:*** **3** POV **5** perch **7** lookout, outlook **8** position **10** watchtower

Vanuatu ***capital:*** **8** Port-Vila ***ethnic group:*** **10** Melanesian ***explorer:*** **4** Cook (Capt. James) ***former name:*** **11** New Hebrides ***island:*** **3** Epi **5** Efate, Maéwo, Tanna **6** Ambrim **8** Aneityum, Malekula **9** Erromango, Pentecost **13** Espíritu Santo ***language:*** **6** French ***monetary unit:*** **4** vatu

vapid 4 dull, flat, weak **5** banal, bland, ditsy, ditzy, inane, silly **6** jejune **7** fatuous, insipid, sapless, vacuous **9** brainless, colorless, innocuous **10** namby-pamby, wishy-washy **13** uninteresting

vapor 3 fog, gas **4** brag, haze, mist, smog **5** brume, cloud, smoke, steam **6** breath, miasma, nimbus **7** bluster **8** phantasm ***condensed:*** **3** dew ***frozen:*** **4** hoar, rime **5** frost **9** hoarfrost

vaporize 5 steam **6** ablate **8** disperse, dissolve, evanesce **9** dissipate, evaporate

vaporous 4 airy, hazy **5** foggy, misty, vague, wispy **6** cloudy, unreal **7** gaseous **8** ethereal, illusory, volatile **10** evanescent **13** unsubstantial

vaquero 5 waddy **6** cowboy, gaucho, herder, waddie **7** cowpoke **8** buckaroo, herdsman, wrangler **10** cowpuncher

varia 6 medley **7** mélange, mixture, omnibus **8** treasury **9** anthology **10** compendium, miscellany **11** compilation

variable 5 fluid **6** fickle, fitful, mobile, symbol **7** mutable, protean **8** unstable, unsteady, volatile **9** irregular, mercurial, uncertain, unsettled, versatile **10** capricious, changeable, inconstant **13** temperamental

variance 3 war **4** odds **6** change, strife **7** discord, dispute, dissent **8** conflict, disunity, division **9** variation **10** contention, difference, dissension, dissidence **11** fluctuation **12** disagreement

variation 4 riff **5** shade, shift **6** change, nuance **7** partita **8** mutation **9** disparity **10** alteration, difference, divergence **11** fluctuation, declination, discrepancy, oscillation **12** modification **13** dissimilarity

varicolored see **variegated**

varicose 7 bulging, dilated, swollen

varied 5 mixed **6** motley, sundry **7** diverse, various **8** assorted **9** different, disparate, divergent **10** dissimilar **12** multifarious **13** heterogeneous, kaleidoscopic, miscellaneous

variegated 4 pied **5** mixed, pinto **6** calico, motley **7** checked, dappled, diverse, mottled, piebald, spotted **8** skewbald, stippled, streaked **9** checkered, multihued **10** multicolor, parti-color, polychrome **12** multicolored, parti-colored **13** kaleidoscopic, polychromatic

variety 3 ilk **4** kind, mode, sort, type **5** array, breed **6** flavor, medley, nature, stripe **8**

mixed bag **9** diversity, variation **10** assortment, collection, miscellany, subspecies **12** multiformity, multiplicity

various 4 some **5** mixed **6** divers, sundry, unlike **7** diverse, several, unalike **8** assorted, separate **9** different, disparate, divergent, unsimilar **10** dissimilar **12** multifarious **13** heterogeneous, miscellaneous

varlet 3 cur **4** page **5** knave, rogue, skunk **6** menial, rascal, wretch **8** coistrel **9** attendant, miscreant, scoundrel **10** blackguard

varmint 4 pest **5** knave, rogue, scamp, skunk, sneak **6** rascal **7** critter **9** scoundrel

varnish 4 coat **5** adorn, cover, glaze, gloss, japan **6** veneer **7** coating, conceal, cover up, shellac **8** covering **9** embellish, gloss over, sugarcoat, whitewash ***component:*** **5** elemi, resin

vary 5 alter, range **6** change, depart, differ, modify, mutate **7** deviate, digress, diverge **8** modulate **9** diversify

vase 3 urn **5** tazza **6** crater, krater, vessel **7** amphora

Vashni's father 6 Samuel

Vashti's husband 6 Xerxes **9** Ahasuerus

vassal 4 leud, serf **5** helot, liege, slave **6** tenant **7** bondman, homager, peasant, servant, subject **8** bondsman, liege man **9** dependent, underling **11** subordinate **12** feudal tenant ***high-ranking:*** **7** vavasor **8** vavasour

vast 4 huge, mega **5** giant, great, jumbo **6** untold **7** immense, mammoth, oceanic, titanic **8** colossal, enormous, gigantic, spacious, whopping **9** boundless, expansive, humongous **10** gargantuan, tremendous, widespread **12** astronomical

vastness 5 sweep **8** enormity, hugeness **9** immensity, magnitude **13** expansiveness

vat 3 tub, tun **4** beck, butt, cask, kier, tank **5** keeve, kieve **6** barrel, liquor, vessel **7** cistern **8** cauldron ***cheese:*** **7** chessel

vatic 6 mantic **7** fatidic **8** oracular **9** fatidical, prophetic, sibylline **10** predictive **11** apocalyptic

Vatican City 10 papal state ***army:*** **11** Swiss Guards ***chapel:*** **7** Sistine ***church:*** **11** Saint Peter's ***court:*** **4** Rota ***ruler:*** **4** Pope ***site:*** **4** Rome

vaticinal see **vatic**

vaticinate 5 augur **6** divine **7** portend, predict, presage **8** forebode, forecast, foretell, prophesy, soothsay **9** adumbrate **13** prognosticate

vaudeville 5 revue **9** burlesque, music hall **11** variety show **12** song and dance

vaudevillian 11 entertainer

vault 3 pit, sky **4** arch, cave, dome, jump, leap, room, safe, tomb **5** bound, crypt **6** cavern, cellar, cupola, hurdle, spring, welkin **7** archway, dungeon **8** catacomb, overleap **9** firmament **10** undercroft

vaulting 4 arch, dome **7** emulous **8** aspiring **9** ambitious **12** enthusiastic **13** opportunistic

vaunt 4 blow, brag, crow, puff, rant **5** boast, strut **6** flaunt, parade **7** bluster, display, exhibit, show off **8** brandish **9** gasconade **11** rodomontade

veal 4 calf ***cutlet:*** **9** schnitzel ***roasted:*** **10** fricandeau ***shank:*** **8** osso buco

vector 5 agent **7** carrier **9** direction **10** pollinator

Vedic religion ***country:*** **5** India ***god:*** **4** Agni, deva, Soma **5** Indra **6** Varuna ***language:*** **8** Sanskrit ***priest:*** **7** Brahman ***treatise:*** **9** Upanishad ***writing:*** **7** Rig Veda, Samhita

veer 3 yaw **4** cast, chop, slew, sway, turn **5** fetch, sheer, shift, trend **6** depart, swerve **7** deflect, deviate, digress, diverge

vegetable 3 pea, soy, udo, yam **4** bean, beet, corn, kale, leek, okra, soya, spud, taro, wort **5** chard, chive, cress, green, onion, plant **6** carrot, celery, cowpea, endive, garlic, legume, lentil, peanut, pepper, potato, radish, sorrel, squash, tomato, turnip **7** cabbage, chayote, dullard, lettuce, mustard, parsley, parsnip, pumpkin, rhubarb, salsify, shallot, soybean, spinach **8** broccoli, collards, cucumber, eggplant, kohlrabi, lima bean, rutabaga, scallion, snap bean **9** artichoke, asparagus, muskmelon **10** watermelon **11** cauliflower, horseradish, sweet potato ***bog:*** **6** muskeg ***covering:*** **4** peel, rind, skin ***dish:*** **5** salad ***mold:*** **5** humus ***seller:*** **6** grocer **7** grocery **12** costermonger ***sponge:*** **5** luffa **6** loofah ***spread:*** **4** oleo **9** margarine

vegetarian 9 herbivore **11** herbivorous

vegetate 4 idle, laze, loaf, loll **5** chill, slack **6** loiter, lounge **7** goof off, hang out **8** chill out, languish, lollygag, slack off, stagnate **9** goldbrick, hibernate

vegetation 5 flora **6** growth, plants **7** verdure **8** greenery **9** plant life ***floating:*** **4** sudd **8** pleuston

vehement 3 hot **4** wild **5** fiery, rabid **6** ardent, bitter, fervid, fierce, heated **7** excited, fervent, vicious, violent, zealous **8** forceful, powerful **9** perfervid **10** passionate **11** impassioned **12** antagonistic

vehicle 3 ATV, bus, cab, car, SUV, van **4** auto, bike, taxi, tool **5** agent, buggy, means, organ, plane, sedan, train, truck, wagon **6** agency, binder, medium, vector **7** bicycle, carrier, channel, machine, solvent, travois **8** airplane, ministry **9** ambulance, implement, motor home, transport **10** automobile, conveyance, instrument, motorcycle ***baby's:*** **4** pram **8** carriage, stroller **9** baby buggy ***child's:*** **5** trike **7** scooter **8** tricycle ***farm:*** **4** wain **7** tractor ***horse-drawn:*** **4** cart, dray **5** buggy, lorry, sulky, wagon **6** hansom, landau, troika **7** calèche, phaeton **8** carriage **9** buckboard ***military:*** **4** jeep, tank **6** Humvee ***one-wheeled:*** **8** unicycle ***passenger:*** **3** bus, cab, car **4** auto, taxi **7** ricksha **8** cable car, rickshaw ***public:*** **3** bus **4** tram **5** train **6** subway **7** omnibus, trolley ***Roman:*** **7** chariot ***winter:*** **4** sled **6** sleigh **8** snowplow **10** snowmobile

veil **4** caul, hide, mask, wrap **5** cloak, cloth, cloud, cover, velum **6** chador, mantle, screen, shield, shroud **7** conceal, cover up, curtain, obscure, secrete, yashmak **8** covering, disguise, enshroud **10** camouflage, false front ***chalice:*** **3** aer ***Muslim:*** **7** yashmak ***netting:*** **6** maline **7** malines

vein **3** bed, way **4** line, lode, mind, mode, mood, seam, tone, tube **5** style, tenor **6** manner, nature, spirit, strain, streak, vessel **7** channel, fashion, pattern, quality, stratum **8** aptitude **11** blood vessel ***combining form:*** **3** ven **4** veni, veno ***deposit:*** **3** ore ***fluid:*** **5** blood ***heart:*** **8** vena cava ***leaf:*** **3** rib ***leg:*** **7** saphena **9** saphenous ***neck:*** **7** jugular ***small:*** **6** venule ***varicose:*** **5** varix

velar **8** guttural ***nasal consonant:*** **3** eng **4** agma

veld **7** prairie **9** grassland

velleity **4** bent, wish **5** fancy **6** desire, liking **7** leaning **10** propensity **11** inclination

velocipede **4** bike **5** cycle, trike **6** tandem **7** bicycle, pedicab **8** tricycle

velocity **4** pace **5** haste, speed, tempo **7** headway **8** celerity, rapidity **9** quickness, swiftness **12** acceleration

velum **4** caul, veil **8** membrane **10** soft palate

velvet **4** gain, mild, rich, soft **5** cloth **6** fabric, profit, smooth **8** winnings **10** antler skin

velvety **4** mild, soft **5** plush **6** smooth

venal **4** paid **6** sordid **7** corrupt **8** bribable **9** mercenary, unethical **11** corruptible, purchasable **12** unprincipled, unscrupulous

vend **4** hawk, sell, toot **6** market, monger, peddle, retail **8** huckster **9** advertise, broadcast

vendee **5** buyer **6** client **8** customer **9** purchaser

vendetta **4** feud **7** rivalry **9** blood feud

vendible **7** salable **8** sellable **10** marketable **12** merchantable

vendor **6** dealer, duffer, hawker, seller **7** packman, peddler **8** huckster, merchant, retailer, salesman

vendue **4** sale **7** auction **10** public sale

veneer **3** ply **4** burl, coat, face, mask, show, veil **5** cover, front, gloss, layer, plate **6** facade, facing **7** conceal, overlay **8** disguise

venerable **3** old **4** aged **5** hoary **6** sacred **7** ancient, antique, elderly, honored, revered, stately **8** esteemed **9** admirable, dignified, estimable, honorable, respected

venerate **5** adore, honor, prize **6** admire, esteem, revere **7** cherish, idolize, respect, worship **8** treasure **9** reverence

veneration **3** awe **5** honor **6** esteem, homage **7** respect, worship **9** adoration, reverence **10** admiration **11** hero worship

venery **3** sex **4** game, prey **5** chase **7** hunting

venesection **10** phlebotomy

Venetian ***boat:*** **7** gondola ***boatman:*** **9** gondolier ***product:*** **5** glass **9** glassware ***ruler:*** **4** doge ***school:*** **6** Titian **7** Bellini, Tiepolo **8** Veronese **9** Giorgione **10** Tintoretto ***street:*** **5** canal ***suburb:*** **6** Murano

Venezuela ***capital:*** **7** Caracas ***city:*** **8** Valencia **9** Maracaibo **12** Barquisimeto ***island:*** **9** Margarita ***lake:*** **8** Valencia **9** Maracaibo ***language:*** **7** Spanish ***monetary unit:*** **7** bolívar ***mountain, range:*** **5** Andes **6** Parima (Serra, Sierra) **7** Bolívar (Pico) **9** Pacaraima **11** Pico Bolívar, Serra Parima **12** Sierra Parima ***neighbor:*** **6** Brazil, Guyana **8** Colombia ***peninsula:*** **9** Paraguaná ***river:*** **7** Orinoco ***sea:*** **9** Caribbean ***waterfall:*** **10** Angel Falls

Venezuelan ***herdsman:*** **7** llanero ***liberator:*** **7** Bolívar (Simón) ***people:*** **5** Carib **6** Timote

vengeance **6** payoff **7** payback, redress, revenge **8** reprisal, revanche **9** repayment **10** punishment **11** retaliation, retribution

vengeful **8** punitive **10** vindictive **11** retaliatory

venial **5** minor **7** trivial **8** harmless, trifling **9** allowable, excusable, tolerable **10** condonable, forgivable, pardonable, remissible, remittable **13** insignificant

Venice of the East **7** Bangkok, Udaipur

Venice of the North **6** Bruges, Brugge **9** Amsterdam, Stockholm **12** St. Petersburg

Veni, Creator ____ **8** Spiritus

venison **4** deer

veni, vidi, ____ **4** vici

venom **4** bane, hate **5** spite **6** malice, poison, rancor **7** ill will, vitriol **8** embitter **9** contagion, malignity, virulence **11** malevolence

venomous **5** toxic **6** deadly, malign, poison **7** baneful, malefic, noxious **8** spiteful, viperish, viperous, virulent **9** malicious, malignant, poisonous **10** malevolent, pernicious **12** vituperative

vent 3 air **4** emit, flue, hole, pipe, pour, slit **5** burst, expel, issue, loose, utter, voice **6** broach, nozzle, outlet **7** chimney, exhaust, express, give off, opening, orifice, release, take out, unleash, volcano **8** breather, fumarole, spiracle **9** discharge **11** black smoker

venter 3 gut **5** belly **6** paunch **7** abdomen, stomach

ventilate 3 air **5** state, utter **6** aerate, expose **7** discuss, express **9** advertise, broadcast, circulate, verbalize **11** investigate

ventral area 7 abdomen, stomach

ventricle 6 cavity **7** chamber

ventriloquist 9 performer **11** entertainer ***companion:*** **5** dummy ***famous:*** **6** Bergen (Edgar)

venture 3 bet, try **4** dare, face, feat, gest, risk **5** brave, peril, stake, wager **6** chance, expose, gamble, hazard **7** attempt, daresay, emprise, exploit **8** endanger, jeopardy, long shot, make bold **9** challenge, crapshoot, speculate **10** enterprise **11** speculation, undertaking

venturesome 4 bold, rash **5** brave **6** daring **8** reckless **9** audacious, daredevil, foolhardy **11** adventurous, temerarious

venue 4 site **5** arena, forum, place, scene **6** locale, outlet **7** setting **8** locality

Venus 6 planet, Vesper **7** daystar, Lucifer **8** Hesperus ***husband:*** **6** Vulcan ***son:*** **4** Amor **5** Cupid **6** Aeneas (see also **Aphrodite**)

Venus de ____ 4 Milo

____ vera 4 aloe

veracious 4 just, true **5** exact, frank, right, valid **6** candid, honest **7** correct, factual, sincere **8** accurate, truthful

veracity 4 fact **5** truth **6** candor **7** honesty **8** accuracy, trueness **9** actuality, exactness **11** correctness **12** truthfulness

veranda 5 lanai, porch, stoop **6** piazza **7** gallery, portico

verb *auxiliary:* 3 are, can, did, had, has, may, was **4** have, must, were, will, word **5** could, might, shall, would **6** should ***form:*** **6** active, gerund **7** passive **10** infinitive, participle ***kind:*** **10** transitive **12** intransitive ***linking:*** **6** copula ***mood:*** **8** optative **10** imperative, indicative **11** subjunctive ***tense:*** **4** past **6** aorist, future **7** perfect, present **9** predicate **10** pluperfect

verbal 4 oral **5** wordy **6** gerund, spoken **7** literal **9** unwritten **10** infinitive, participle, rhetorical **11** word-for-word

verbalism 4 term **6** phrase **7** wording **8** phrasing **9** prolixity, windiness, wordiness **11** phraseology

verbalization 4 talk **6** speech **8** speaking **9** discourse, utterance **12** articulation, vocalization

verbalize 3 air, say **4** talk **5** speak, state, utter, voice, write **6** broach **7** express **8** bloviate, vocalize **9** ventilate

verbatim 5 exact **6** direct **7** exactly, literal, precise **8** directly **9** literally, literatim, precisely **10** accurately **11** word-for-word

verbiage 4 talk **6** phrase **7** diction, wording **8** parlance, phrasing, pleonasm **9** wordiness **10** redundancy **11** phraseology

verbose 5 gassy, windy, wordy **6** prolix **7** diffuse **9** garrulous, redundant, talkative **10** loquacious, pleonastic **11** tautologous

verbosity 9 prolixity, windiness, wordiness **10** redundancy

verboten 5 taboo **6** banned **7** illegal **8** outlawed **9** forbidden **10** prohibited

verdant 4 lush **5** green, leafy, naive **6** grassy, unripe

verdict 6 assize, ruling **7** finding, opinion **8** decision, judgment **9** judgement

Verdi opera 4 Aïda **6** Ernani, Oberto, Otello **7** Nabucco **8** Don Carlo, Falstaff, Lombardi (I), Traviata (La) **9** Don Carlos, Rigoletto, Trovatore (Il) **15** Simon Boccanegra

verdure 7 foliage **8** greenery **9** greenness **10** vegetation

verge 3 hem, lip, rim **4** abut, cusp, edge, sink **5** bound, brink, skirt, staff, touch **6** adjoin, border, fringe, margin **7** selvage **8** approach, shoulder **9** threshold **10** borderline

veridical see **veracious**

verifiable 4 true **6** proven **7** certain **8** provable **9** undoubted

verification 5 proof **10** validation **11** attestation **12** confirmation **13** corroboration

verify 4 aver, test **5** check, prove, vouch **6** attest, settle **7** bear out, confirm **8** document, validate **9** establish, fact-check **11** corroborate, demonstrate **12** authenticate, substantiate

verily 5 truly **6** indeed **7** in truth **9** assuredly, certainly **11** confidently, undoubtedly

veritable 4 real, true **6** actual **7** factual, genuine **8** bona fide **9** authentic, undoubted **10** sure-enough **11** indubitable

verity 5 truth **6** gospel, truism **7** honesty, reality **9** actuality **12** truthfulness

vermiform 8 wormlike

vermilion 3 red

vermin 4 lice, mice, pest, rats, scum **5** fleas, pests, trash **7** bedbugs, varmint

Vermont *capital:* **10** Montpelier ***city:*** **5** Barre,

Stowe **7** Rutland **10** Burlington ***college, university:*** **7** Norwich **8** Marlboro **10** Bennington, Middlebury ***mountain, range:*** **5** Green **9** Mansfield ***nickname:*** **13** Green Mountain (State) ***river:*** **11** Connecticut ***state bird:*** **12** hermit thrush ***state flower:*** **9** red clover ***state tree:*** **10** sugar maple

vernacular 4 cant **5** argot, idiom, lingo, slang **6** common, jargon, patois, patter, speech, tongue, vulgar **7** dialect, vulgate **8** language **9** dialectal **10** colloquial **12** mother tongue

vernal 5 fresh, green **6** spring **8** youthful **10** springlike

Verne, Jules *character:* 4 Fogg (Phileas), Nemo (Captain) **12** Passepartout ***submarine:*** **8** Nautilus ***work:*** **16** Mysterious Island (The) **21** From the Earth to the Moon **26** Around the World in Eighty Days **28** Journey to the Center of the Earth

versant see **conversant**

versatile 5 handy **6** adroit, facile **7** protean **8** variable **9** all-around, competent, many-sided **10** changeable **11** well-rounded **12** ambidextrous

verse 3 lay, ode **4** epic, poem, rune **5** lyric, poesy, rhyme **6** ballad, jingle, poetry, sonnet, stanza **7** passage **8** acquaint **11** composition, familiarize ***amateurish:*** **8** doggerel ***analysis:*** **8** scansion ***four-line:*** **8** quatrain ***free:*** **5** blank **8** unrhymed ***humorous:*** **8** limerick ***six-line:*** **6** sestet ***three-line:*** **6** tercet ***two-line:*** **7** couplet ***writer:*** **4** poet

versed 5 adept **6** au fait **7** abreast, skilled, veteran **8** familiar, informed, seasoned **9** au courant, competent, practiced **10** acquainted **11** experienced **13** knowledgeable

versifier 4 bard, poet **6** rhymer **9** poetaster, rhymester, sonneteer

version 4 copy **5** draft, model **6** flavor, remake **7** account, edition, reading, variant **8** revision **9** iteration, narrative, redaction, rendition, rewording **10** adaptation, paraphrase **11** arrangement, description, incarnation, restatement, translation

versus 4 anti **6** contra **7** against, vis-à-vis **11** over against

vertebra 7 segment ***kind:*** **6** dorsal, lumbar, sacral **8** cervical, thoracic **9** coccygeal

vertebrae 4 back **5** spine **6** coccyx, rachis, sacrum **8** backbone, tailbone **12** spinal column

vertebrate 6 animal ***characteristic:*** **5** spine **7** cranium **12** spinal column ***kind:*** **4** bird, fish, frog **6** mammal **7** reptile **9** amphibian

vertex 3 cap, top **4** acme, apex, peak **5** crest, crown **6** apogee, summit, tip-top, zenith

vertical 5 erect, plumb, sheer, steep **7** upright **8** straight **10** lengthwise, straight-up **13** perpendicular

vertiginous 5 dizzy, giddy, woozy **6** fickle, rotary **11** light-headed

vertigo 6 megrim **9** dizziness, giddiness

verve 3 pep, vim, zip **4** brio, dash, élan, fire, life, zest, zing **5** flair, gusto, moxie, oomph, style, vigor **6** bounce, energy, esprit, spirit, spring **7** panache **8** vitality, vivacity **10** enthusiasm, liveliness **13** sprightliness

very 3 too **4** bare, mere, most, much, pure, real, same, true **5** exact, ideal, model, plain, quite, sheer, super, truly, utter **6** actual, ever so, highly, hugely, mighty, really, simple **7** awfully, genuine, greatly, notably, perfect, precise, special **8** absolute, actually, bona fide, selfsame, terribly **9** authentic, decidedly, extremely, genuinely, identical, undoubted **10** absolutely, particular **11** exceedingly ***French:*** **4** très ***German:*** **4** sehr ***Italian:*** **5** assai, molto ***Scottish:*** **3** gey ***Spanish:*** **3** muy

vesicle 3 sac **4** cell, cyst **5** bulla **6** cavity **7** blister, vacuole

Vespasian's son 5 Titus

vespertilion 7 bat-like

vespers 8 evensong

____ **Vespucci 7** Amerigo

vessel 3 can, cup, jar, pan, pot, tub, urn **4** boat, bowl, cask, drum, duct, ewer, olla, pail, ship, tank, tube, vase, vein **5** canal, churn, craft, cruse **6** artery, barrel, bottle, bucket, censer, firkin, flagon, kettle, krater, pottle **7** cresset, pitcher **8** crucible **9** container **10** receptacle, watercraft ***Arab:*** **4** dhow ***combining form:*** **3** vas **4** angi, vaso **5** angio ***drinking:*** **3** cup, mug **4** toby **5** flask, glass, gourd, stein, stoup **6** goblet, seidel **7** tankard, tumbler ***Indian:*** **4** lota **5** lotah ***Scottish:*** **6** quaich, quaigh

vest 6 weskit **9** waistcoat

Vesta see **Hestia**

vestal 4 pure **6** chaste, virgin **8** celibate, virginal, virtuous

vestibule 5 entry, foyer, lobby **6** cavity **7** hallway, narthex, passage **8** anteroom, entrance, entryway **10** antechapel **11** antechamber

vestige 4 echo **5** dregs (plural), relic, scrap, stump, trace, track **6** shadow **7** memento, remains, remnant **8** leftover **9** remainder **10** hide or hair **11** hide nor hair

vestment 3 alb **4** cope, garb, gown, robe **5** amice, cotta, dress, fanon, habit, orale, stole, tunic **6** attire, rochet **7** apparel, cassock, garment, maniple, pallium, tunicle **8** chasuble, cincture, clothing, covering, dalmatic, parament, surplice ***ancient Hebrew:*** **5** ephod **11** breastplate

vestry 6 closet **8** sacristy **9** sacrarium

vesture 4 robe **6** clothe **7** apparel, garment **8** clothing **10** habiliment

Vesuvius 7 volcano

vet 5 check **6** go over, review **7** analyze, examine, inspect **8** appraise, check out, evaluate, look over **10** old soldier

vetch 3 ers **4** herb, tare **6** legume ***type:*** **4** milk (vetch) **5** crown (vetch), hairy (vetch)

veteran 4 ex-GI **5** adept **6** expert, master **7** old hand, skilled **8** old-timer, warhorse **9** practiced, shellback **10** past master **11** experienced

veto 2 ax **3** axe, nix **4** kill, void **5** quash **6** defeat, forbid, refuse, reject **7** decline, nullify **8** abrogate, disallow, negative, prohibit **9** blackball **10** disapprove **11** prohibition **12** interdiction

vex 3 bug, irk **4** fret, gall, itch, roil **5** annoy, chafe, gripe, harry, rowel, tease, worry **6** badger, baffle, bother, harass, harrow, nettle, pester, plague, puzzle, rankle, ruffle **7** chagrin, torment, trouble **8** bullyrag, distress, irritate

vexation 4 fret, sore **5** chafe, trial **6** bother **7** problem, torment **8** distress, headache **9** annoyance, troubling **10** affliction, harassment, irritation **11** aggravation, bedevilment, provocation

vexatious 5 pesky **7** prickly **8** annoying, tiresome **9** troublous **10** bothersome, irritating **11** distressing, troublesome **12** exasperating

vexed 6 sticky, touchy **7** debated, weighty **8** ticklish **9** difficult, discussed, troubling

vexing 5 tough **7** irksome **8** annoying **9** difficult, harassing, upsetting **10** bothersome, irritating **11** distressing, troublesome

via 3 per **4** over, with **5** along **7** by way of, through **9** by means of

viable 6 doable **7** capable **8** feasible, possible, workable **11** practicable, sustainable

vial 6 ampule **7** ampoule

viands 4 eats, fare, feed, food, grub **7** aliment, edibles, vittles **8** victuals **9** provender **10** provisions **11** comestibles

vibrant 5 alive, vital, vivid **6** bright, lively, punchy **7** ringing **8** resonant **9** consonant, pulsating **10** resounding **11** oscillating **12** effervescent

vibrate 3 jar **4** ring **5** quake, shake, swing, throb, waver **6** quiver, shimmy, thrill, tremor **7** flutter, pulsate **8** undulate **9** fluctuate, oscillate, vacillate

vibration 4 aura **5** quake, shake, trill **6** motion, quaver, quiver, shimmy, spirit, tremor **7** flutter, shaking **8** fremitus, wavering **9** emanation, trembling **11** fluctuation, oscillation, vacillation

vicar 6 pastor, priest **8** minister, reverend **9** clergyman

Vicar of Wakefield, The *author:* 9 Goldsmith (Oliver) ***character:*** **8** Primrose

vice 3 sin **4** evil, flaw **5** crime, fault **6** defect **7** devilry, failing, frailty, offense, scandal **8** iniquity **9** deformity, depravity, indecency **10** corruption, debauchery, immorality, perversion, wickedness **11** shortcoming

vice-president 4 veep **6** deputy **7** officer **9** executive ***American:*** **4** Burr (Aaron), Bush (George), Ford (Gerald), Gore (Albert), King (William) **5** Adams (John), Agnew (Spiro), Biden (Joseph), Dawes (Charles), Gerry (Elbridge), Nixon (Richard), Tyler (John) **6** Arthur (Chester), Cheney (Richard), Colfax (Schuyler), Curtis (Charles), Dallas (George), Garner (John Nance), Hamlin (Hannibal), Hobart (Garret), Morton (Levi), Quayle (Dan), Truman (Harry), Wilson (Woodrow) **7** Barkley (Alben), Calhoun (John Caldwell), Clinton (George), Johnson (Andrew, Lyndon Baines, Richard Mentor), Mondale (Walter), Sherman (James Schoolcraft), Wallace (Henry), Wheeler (William) **8** Coolidge (Calvin), Fillmore (Millard), Humphrey (Hubert Horatio), Marshall (Thomas), Tompkins (Daniel), Van Buren (Martin) **9** Fairbanks (Charles), Hendricks (Thomas), Jefferson (Thomas), Roosevelt (Theodore), Stevenson (Adlai) **11** Rockefeller (Nelson) **12** Breckinridge (John)

viceroy 5 nabob **6** exarch, satrap **7** khedive **8** alderman, governor **9** butterfly **11** stadtholder

vice versa 10 conversely **12** contrariwise

vicinity 4 area, nabe **5** range **6** extent, locale, region, shadow **7** suburbs **8** ballpark, district, environs, locality, nearness, precinct **9** closeness, magnitude, proximity **12** neighborhood

vicious 4 evil, mean, vile **5** cruel **6** fierce, malign, savage, sinful, wicked **7** brutish, corrupt, hateful, immoral, noxious, violent **8** depraved, horrible, perverse, spiteful **9** barbarous, ferocious, malicious, malignant, monstrous, nefarious, reprobate **10** degenerate, flagitious, iniquitous, malevolent, villainous, vindictive

vicissitude 5 rigor, trial **6** chance, change **7** weather **8** hardship, mutation, reversal **9** adversity, mischance **10** affliction, difficulty, misfortune, mutability **11** fluctuation, permutation, progression, tribulation

victim 4 butt, dupe, gull, mark, prey **5** chump, patsy **6** pigeon, martyr, quarry, sucker **7** fall guy **8** casualty, fatality, offering, underdog **9** sacrifice

victimize 4 dupe, fool, gull, hoax **5** cheat, cozen, trick **6** prey on **7** deceive, swindle **8** flimflam, hoodwink **9** bamboozle, sacrifice **11** hornswoggle

victor 5 champ **6** top dog, winner **7** subduer **8** champion **9** conqueror **10** vanquisher

Victorian 4 prim **6** prissy, stuffy **7** prudish **8** priggish **11** puritanical, straitlaced **12** old-fashioned

Victoria, Queen *family:* 7 Hanover ***father:* 6** Edward ***husband:* 6** Albert ***prime minister:* 8** Disraeli (Benjamin) **9** Gladstone (William), Melbourne (Lord) ***son:* 6** Edward

victory 3 win **4** rout **5** sweep **6** defeat **7** mastery, success, triumph **8** conquest, walkaway, walkover **10** overcoming **11** superiority ***costly:* 7** Pyrrhic ***easy:* 4** romp **7** runaway **8** cakewalk, walkaway ***monument:* 4** arch **13** Arc de Triomphe ***reward:* 6** spoils ***sign:* 3** vee ***symbol:* 4** flag **6** laurel, wreath

Victory author 6 Conrad (Joseph)

victuals 4 chow, eats, feed, food, grub, prog **6** viands **7** edibles, vittles **9** provender **10** provisions **11** comestibles

____ **Vidal 4** Gore

videlicet 3 viz **5** to wit **6** namely, that is **8** scilicet **11** that is to say

video game 4 Doom, Myst **6** Tetris **7** SimCity **10** Donkey Kong **12** Mortal Kombat ***maker:* 3** THQ **4** Sega **5** Atari, Namco, Raven, Shaba, Z-Axis **6** Capcom, Konami **7** Ubisoft, Vivendi **8** Luxoflux, Nintendo, Treyarch, Williams **9** Neversoft **10** Activision, Square Enix

vie 3 pit **5** match **6** oppose, strive **7** compete, contend, contest, counter **8** struggle

Viennese *city hall:* 7 Rathaus ***family:* 8** Habsburg, Hapsburg ***palace:* 7** Hofburg ***park:* 6** Prater ***river:* 6** Danube

Vietnam *capital:* 5 Hanoi ***city:* 3** Hue **6** Da Nang, Saigon **8** Haiphong **13** Ho Chi Minh City ***delta:* 6** Mekong ***gulf:* 6** Tonkin **8** Thailand ***monetary unit:* 4** dong ***mountain:* 8** Fan-si-pan ***neighbor:* 4** Laos **5** China **8** Cambodia **9** Kampuchea ***river:* 3** Red **6** Mekong ***sea:* 10** South China

Vietnamese New Year 3 Tet

view 3 eye, see **4** espy, look, plan, scan **5** scene, sight, vista, watch **6** behold, belief, look at, notice, notion, regard, review, survey **7** close-up, examine, inspect, lookout, observe, opinion, outlook, picture, scenery, vantage **8** judgment, panorama, perceive, prospect, scrutiny, snapshot **10** conviction, inspection, scrutinize **11** contemplate, examination

viewer 7 witness **8** looker-on, onlooker **9** bystander, spectator **10** eyewitness

viewing instrument 5 glass, scope **6** binocs **7** glasses **9** telescope **10** binoculars, microscope **12** field glasses ***combining form:* 5** scope

viewpoint 3 eye **5** angle, slant, stand **6** stance **7** outlook **8** attitude, position **9** direction **11** perspective

vigil 4 wake **5** watch **7** lookout, prayers **9** devotions **10** deathwatch **11** wakefulness **12** surveillance, watch and ward

vigilance 5 watch **9** alertness **12** surveillance, watchfulness

vigilant 4 keen, wary **5** alert, awake, aware, chary, sharp **7** careful, jealous, on guard **8** cautious, open-eyed, watchful **9** attentive, sharp-eyed, wide-awake

vignette 5 scene **6** sketch **7** glimpse, picture **8** ornament

vigor 3 pep, vim, zip **4** brio, push, snap, tuck **5** ardor, drive, force, gusto, moxie, oomph **6** energy, mettle, muscle, spirit, starch **7** potency **8** dynamism, strength, tonicity, virility, vitality **9** hardihood, lustiness, puissance **10** get-up-and-go, robustness, sturdiness

vigorous 5 brisk, hardy, lusty, stout, tough, vital **6** active, hearty, lively, potent, robust, strong, sturdy, virile **7** dashing, driving, dynamic, healthy **8** athletic, forceful, muscular, powerful, spirited, youthful **9** energetic, strenuous **10** mettlesome, red-blooded

Viking see **Norse**

vile 4 base, evil, foul, mean, ugly **5** gross, nasty, slimy **6** filthy, horrid, sordid, vulgar, wicked **7** low-down, noisome, obscene, squalid **8** depraved, wretched **9** abhorrent, loathsome, obnoxious, offensive, perverted, repugnant, repulsive, revolting **10** despicable, disgusting **12** contemptible

vilify 5 abuse, libel, smear **6** assail, attack, berate, defame, malign **7** asperse, run down, slander, spatter, traduce **8** denounce, tear down **9** denigrate, disparage **10** calumniate

villa 5 dacha, manor **6** estate, quinta **7** château, mansion **9** residence

village 4 burg, town **5** bourg, thorp **6** hamlet **7** townlet ***African:* 4** dorp **5** kraal ***Indian:* 6** pueblo ***Japanese:* 4** mura ***Jewish:* 6** shtetl ***Malay:* 7** kampong ***Russian:* 3** mir

Village Blacksmith author 10 Longfellow (Henry Wadsworth)

villain 4 boor, heel, ogre **5** demon, devil, heavy, knave, rogue **6** bad guy, rascal, sinner **7** lowlife **8** antihero, criminal, evildoer, offender, scalawag **9** character, miscreant, reprobate, scoundrel **10** blackguard, malefactor ***classic:*** **4** Iago **5** Judas (Iscariot) **6** Brutus (Marcus Junius) **8** Quisling (Vidkun)

villainous 4 evil **6** rotten, wicked **7** corrupt, debased, heinous, vicious **8** depraved, wretched **9** atrocious, felonious, miscreant, nefarious **10** detestable, diabolical, flagitious, iniquitous, perfidious, traitorous **11** treacherous

villainy 4 vice **5** crime **8** evilness **9** depravity, treachery, turpitude **10** corruption, wickedness

villein 7 peasant **8** villager

villenage 4 yoke **6** tenure, thrall **7** bondage, serfdom **9** servitude, thralldom

vim 3 zip **4** brio, dash, élan, gimp, zing **5** gusto, oomph, verve, vigor **6** bounce, energy, esprit, spirit **7** vinegar **9** animation **10** enthusiasm, razzmatazz

____ vincit omnia 4 Amor

vinculum 3 tie **4** bond, knot, link, yoke **5** nexus **8** ligament, ligature

vindicable 7 tenable **9** excusable **10** condonable, defendable, defensible, pardonable **11** justifiable, warrantable

vindicate 4 free **5** clear, guard, prove, right **6** acquit, avenge, defend, excuse, refute, shield, uphold, verify **7** absolve, bear out, confirm, deliver, justify, redress, revenge, support, warrant **8** maintain **9** exculpate, exonerate, safeguard **11** corroborate **12** substantiate

vindictive 5 catty, nasty **6** malign **7** hateful, hurtful, vicious **8** punitive, spiteful, vengeful, venomous **9** malicious, malignant, poisonous

vine 3 aka, hop, ivy, iyo, pea **5** grape, kudzu, liana, liane, maile, plant **6** maypop **7** chayote, climber, creeper **8** catbrier, clematis **11** bittersweet ***Asian:*** **6** pikake ***East Indian:*** **4** soma

vinegar 3 pep, vim **6** liquid **8** ill humor, sourness **9** condiment **12** preservative ***relating to:*** **10** acetic acid ***steep in:*** **6** pickle

vinegarish 4 sour **6** bitter, cranky, ornery **7** bearish, waspish **8** snappish **9** crotchety, irascible **12** cantankerous, cross-grained, disagreeable

Vinegar Joe 8 Stilwell (Joseph)

vineyard ***French:*** **3** cru **7** château, domaine

Vinland discoverer 4 Leif (Ericsson, Eriksson) **12** Leif Ericsson, Leif Eriksson

vintage 3 age, old **4** crop, wine **5** yield **7** antique, classic, harvest **8** outdated **9** classical **10** antiquated **12** old-fashioned

Viola ***brother:*** **9** Sebastian ***husband:*** **6** Orsino ***play:*** **12** Twelfth Night

viola da ____ 5 gamba

violate 4 rape **5** break, wrong **6** breach, defile, offend, ravish **7** disturb, outrage, profane, traduce **8** fracture, infringe, trespass **9** desecrate, disregard **10** contravene, transgress

violation 4 foul, rape **5** break, crime, wrong **6** breach, injury **7** offense, outrage, perjury, scandal **8** trespass **9** blasphemy, injustice, sacrilege **10** illegality, infraction, ravishment **11** desecration, disturbance, misdemeanor, profanation **12** encroachment, infringement, interruption **13** contravention, transgression

violence 4 fury, riot **5** clash **6** frenzy, mayhem **7** assault, outrage, rampage **8** foul play, savagery **9** onslaught **10** distortion, roughhouse

violent 5 cruel, harsh, rabid **6** fierce, raging, savage, stormy **7** berserk, furious, intense, vicious **8** slam-bang, vehement **9** explosive, ferocious **10** hellacious **11** acrimonious, destructive

violet 5 mauve **6** purple **8** amethyst, lavender **10** heliotrope

violin 6 fiddle **10** instrument ***kind:*** **5** Amati, Strad **8** Guarneri **10** Guarnerius, Stradivari **12** Stradivarius ***part:*** **3** bow, nut, peg **4** neck **6** bridge, scroll, string **8** chin rest **9** tailpiece **10** soundboard **11** fingerboard ***precursor:*** **5** rebec **6** rebeck

violinist ***American:*** **4** Hahn (Hilary) **5** Elman (Mischa), Fodor (Eugene), Ricci (Ruggiero), Stern (Isaac) **6** Midori, Powell (Maud) **7** Heifetz (Jascha), Menuhin (Yehudi) **8** Kreisler (Fritz), Milstein (Nathan) **9** Zimbalist (Efrem) ***Belgian:*** **5** Ysayë (Eugene) **8** Grumiaux (Arthur) ***Czech:*** **3** Suk (Josef) ***Dutch:*****4** Rieu (André) ***English:*** **7** Kennedy (Nigel), Menuhin (Yehudi) ***French:*** **9** Grappelli (Stéphane) **12** Francescatti (Zino) ***German:*** **6** Mutter (Anne-Sophie) ***Hungarian:*** **4** Auer (Leopold) **7** Joachim (Joseph), Szigeti (Joseph) ***Israeli:*** **6** Shaham (Gil) **7** Perlman (Itzhak) **8** Zukerman (Pinchas) ***Italian:*** **6** Viotti (Giovanne Battista) **7** Corelli (Arcangelo), Vivaldi (Antonio) **8** Paganini (Niccolo) **9** Geminiani (Francesco) ***Japanese:*** **6** Midori (Goto) ***Korean:*** **5** Chang (Sarah) ***Latvian:*** **6** Kremer (Gidon) ***Roma-***

nian: 6 Enescu (George) ***Russian:*** 8 Oistrakh (David, Igor)

violin maker 4 Salò (Gasparo da) 5 Amati (Andrea, Antonio, Girolamo, Nicolo) 7 Maggini (Giovanni Paolo), Stainer (Jacob) 8 Guarneri (Andrea, del Gesù, Giuseppe, Pietro) 10 Guarnerius (Andrea, Giuseppe, Pietro), Stradivari (Antonio, Francesco, Omobono) 12 Stradivarius (Antonio, Francesco, Omobono)

VIP 3 CEO 4 BMOC, lion 5 celeb, mogul, nabob 6 big gun, biggie, bigwig, fat cat, honcho 7 big shot, notable, someone 8 big wheel, luminary, mandarin, somebody 9 big cheese, celebrity, dignitary 10 panjandrum 13 high-muck-a-muck

viper 3 asp 5 adder, snake 7 serpent 10 bushmaster, copperhead, fer-de-lance 11 rattlesnake 13 water moccasin

virago 3 hag 5 harpy, scold, shrew, vixen 6 amazon, dragon, gorgon, ogress 8 battle-ax, fishwife, harridan, Xantippe 9 battle-axe, termagant, Xanthippe

Virgil 4 poet 5 guide 6 orator 8 cicerone ***epic:*** 6 Aeneid ***hero:*** 6 Aeneas ***poems:*** 8 Eclogues, Georgics

virgin 3 new 4 pure 5 first, fresh, unwed 6 chaste, intact, maiden, modest, unused, vestal 7 initial 8 celibate, innocent, primeval, pristine, spotless 9 abstinent, undefiled, unmarried, unspoiled, unsullied, untouched 10 immaculate

virginal 4 pure 5 fresh 6 chaste, intact, maiden, spinet 8 pristine, virtuous 9 undefiled, unspoiled, unsullied, untouched

Virgin Goddess 5 Diana 6 Hestia 7 Artemis

Virginia ***capital:*** 8 Richmond ***city:*** 7 Norfolk, Roanoke 10 Alexandria 11 Newport News 13 Virginia Beach ***college, university:*** 3 VMI 7 Hampton 10 Sweet Briar 11 George Mason, Old Dominion 12 James Madison 13 Randolph-Macon 14 William and Mary ***historical site:*** 10 Monticello 11 Mount Vernon 12 Williamsburg ***mountain, range:*** 6 Rogers 9 Blue Ridge ***nickname:*** 11 Old Dominion ***river:*** 5 James 7 Potomac 10 Shenandoah ***state bird:*** 8 cardinal ***state flower:*** 7 dogwood (American) ***state tree:*** 7 dogwood (American)

Virginian, The ***author:*** 6 Wister (Owen) ***character:*** 7 Trampas

Virgin Island 5 Peter 6 Norman, St. John 7 Anegada, St. Croix, Tortola 8 St. Thomas

Virgin Islands (U.S.) ***capital:*** 15 Charlotte Amalie ***island:*** 6 St. John 7 St. Croix 8 St. Thomas ***location:*** 10 West Indies ***territory of:*** 12 United States

Virgin Islands, British ***capital:*** 8 Road Town ***island:*** 5 Peter 6 Norman 7 Anegada, Tortola 11 Jost Van Dyke, Virgin Gorda ***location:*** 10 West Indies

virginity 6 purity 8 celibacy, chastity 10 chasteness, maidenhead, maidenhood

Virgin Queen 9 Elizabeth

Virgo star 5 Spica

virgule 5 comma, slant, slash 7 solidus 8 diagonal

viridity 5 green 7 naïveté 9 freshness, greenness, innocence

virile 4 male 5 macho, manly 6 manful, potent, robust 7 manlike 8 forceful, vigorous 9 energetic, masculine

virtual 5 moral, tacit 7 de facto 8 implicit 9 essential, practical 10 electronic 11 fundamental

virtuality 4 core, pith, soul 5 being, juice, stuff 6 effect, marrow, nature 7 essence, makings 8 quiddity 9 substance 10 capability 12 essentiality, quintessence, potentiality

virtually 4 nigh 6 all but, almost, fairly, nearly, next to 7 morally 8 as good as, in effect, well-nigh 9 basically, in essence, literally 10 implicitly 11 effectively, essentially, practically 13 approximately, fundamentally, substantially

virtue 5 merit, power, right, trait, valor, value, vigor, worth 7 courage, feature, potency, probity, quality 8 chastity, goodness, morality, strength 9 attribute, character, puissance, rectitude, rightness 10 excellence, excellency, perfection 11 uprightness ***cardinal:*** 4 hope, love 5 faith 7 charity, justice 8 prudence 9 fortitude 10 temperance

virtuosic 5 showy 6 expert, flashy 7 hotshot, skilled 9 brilliant, masterful 10 consummate, prodigious 12 razzle-dazzle

virtuoso 4 whiz 6 expert, master, savant, wizard, wonder 7 artiste, hotshot, maestro, prodigy 10 past master, wunderkind

virtuous 4 good, pure 5 moral, noble, pious, right 6 chaste, decent, modest, proper 7 ethical, sinless 8 innocent, spotless 9 blameless, faultless, guiltless, righteous, unsullied, untainted 10 inculpable, moralistic 11 respectable, right-minded, untarnished

virulent 5 harsh, toxic 6 biting, bitter, malign, poison 7 cutting, hateful, hostile, noxious 8 scathing, spiteful, venomous 9 malicious, malignant, pestilent, poisonous, rancorous, vitriolic 10 pathogenic

virus 3 bug 8 pathogen 9 contagion, infection

vis 5 force, might, power

visage 3 mug, pan **4** cast, face, look, mien, phiz, puss **6** aspect, kisser **8** features **9** semblance **10** expression **11** countenance
vis-à-vis 4 date **6** escort, facing, toward, versus **7** against **8** fronting, opposite, together **9** tête-à-tête **10** compared to, face-to-face **11** counterpart
visceral 3 gut **4** deep **5** inner **8** internal, intimate **9** intuitive **10** intestinal **11** instinctive, instinctual
viscid see **viscous**
viscount 4 lord, peer **8** nobleman
viscous 4 limy, ropy **5** gluey, gooey, gummy, limey, slimy, thick **9** glutinous, semifluid **10** gelatinous **12** mucilaginous
vise 5 clamp, screw **7** squeeze
Vishnu 4 Hari ***avatar:*** **4** Rama **5** Kurma **6** Buddha, Matsya, Vamena, Varaha **7** Krishna **9** Narasinha ***consort:*** **3** Sri **4** Shri **7** Lakshmi ***home:*** **4** Meru
visible 6 patent **7** obvious **8** apparent, viewable **9** available, well-known **10** detectable, observable **11** conspicuous, discernible, macroscopic, perceivable, perceptible **12** recognizable
Visigoth *conquest:* **4** Rome ***king:*** **6** Alaric
vision 3 eye **5** dream, fancy, image, sense, sight **6** beauty, seeing **7** concept, fantasy, feature, picture, specter **8** daydream, eyesight, phantasm, presence, prophecy **9** foresight, nightmare **10** apparition, perception, phenomenon, revelation **13** manifestation ***combining form:*** **4** opto **5** opsis ***deceptive:*** **6** mirage ***relating to:*** **5** optic **6** visual **7** optical
visionary 4 seer **5** ideal, lofty, noble **6** unreal **7** blue-sky, dreamer, utopian **8** fanciful, idealist, illusory, quixotic, romantic **9** ambitious, ideologue, imaginary **10** abstracted, daydreamer, idealistic, starry-eyed **11** impractical
visionless 5 blind
visit 3 gam, see **4** call, chat, stay, talk, tour **5** pop in, run in **6** call on, come by, drop by, drop in, look in, look up, stay at, stop by, stop in **7** force on, sojourn **8** come over, converse, stay with, stopover **10** social call
visitation 3 woe **4** wake **5** cross, trial **6** misery, ordeal, plague **8** calamity **9** martyrdom **10** affliction **11** tribulation
visitor 5 alien, guest **6** caller, drop-in **7** company, invitee **8** stranger, visitant **9** transient **10** houseguest
visor 4 bill, mask **6** domino **8** eyeshade, disguise, face mask, sunshade
vista 4 view **5** scene, sight **7** lookout, outlook **8** panorama, prospect **9** landscape **11** perspective
visual 5 optic **6** ocular **7** graphic, optical, seeable **8** viewable **9** pictorial **11** discernible, perceivable, perceptible
visualize 3 see **4** view **5** fancy, image **6** call up **7** feature, imagine, picture **8** conceive, envisage, envision **9** conjure up
vital 4 dire **5** alive **6** lively, living, mortal, urgent **7** animate, crucial, pivotal **8** animated, cardinal, critical, decisive, integral, pressing, required, vigorous **9** essential, important, necessary, requisite **10** imperative, red-blooded **11** fundamental, life-or-death **12** invigorating **13** indispensable
vitality see **vigor**
vitalize 5 liven **6** arouse, excite, infuse, perk up, spirit, vivify **7** animate, enliven, quicken **8** energize **9** encourage, galvanize, stimulate **10** invigorate
vitals see **viscera**
vitamin 6 biotin, niacin **7** choline, folacin, retinal, retinol **8** thiamine **9** carnitine, cobalamin, folic acid **10** calciferol, pyridoxine, riboflavin, tocopherol **12** ascorbic acid
Vita Nuova author 5 Dante (Alighieri)
vitelline 5 yolky **6** yellow
vitiate 3 mar **4** harm, soil, undo **5** annul, spoil, sully, taint **6** damage, debase, defile, impair, negate **7** blemish, corrupt, debauch, deprave, nullify, pervert, tarnish **8** abrogate **9** undermine **10** bastardize, demoralize, invalidate
vitreous 6 glassy
vitriol 4 acid, bile **5** spite, venom **6** malice, rancor **7** sulfate **8** acrimony **9** virulence **12** sulfuric acid
vitriolic 4 acid **5** acrid **7** acerbic, caustic, cutting, mordant **8** scathing, stinging, virulent **9** rancorous, truculent
vituperate 3 rag **4** lash, rail, rant, rate **5** abuse, baste, curse, scold, score **6** berate, malign, revile, scorch **7** asperse, bawl out, chew out, condemn, cuss out, upbraid **8** lambaste **9** castigate **10** tongue-lash
vituperation 5 abuse **6** rebuke **7** censure, obloquy, reproof **8** scolding **9** contumely, invective **10** scurrility **11** fulmination, mudslinging **12** billingsgate **13** tongue-lashing
vituperative 7 abusive, railing, scurril **8** scathing, scolding, scurrile, venomous, viperish **9** invective **10** censorious, scurrilous **11** opprobrious **12** contumelious
vivace 5 brisk **6** lively **8** animated, spirited
vivacious 3 gay **4** airy, pert **5** perky, spicy, sunny, zesty **6** bouncy, breezy, bubbly, jaunty, lively, sparky **7** buoyant, chipper **8**

animated, pixieish, spirited **9** ebullient, sprightly **12** effervescent, high-spirited
vivacity see **verve**
Vivaldi epithet 9 Red Priest (the)
____ vivant 3 bon
vivarium 9 terrarium
viva voce 4 oral **6** orally, spoken **11** word-of-mouth
viverrid 5 civet, fossa, genet **7** linsang
vivid 5 alive, sharp **6** bright, garish, lively, punchy, visual **7** graphic, intense, vibrant **8** animated, colorful, eloquent, lifelike **9** chromatic, pictorial **10** expressive **11** picturesque
vivify 5 liven, renew **6** excite, infuse, kindle, revive **7** animate, enliven, quicken, refresh, restore **9** stimulate
vixen 3 fox, nag **5** harpy, scold, shrew **6** ogress, virago **8** fishwife, harridan, Xantippe **9** termagant, Xanthippe
viz 5 to wit **6** namely, that is **8** scilicet **9** videlicet **12** in other words
vizard 4 face, mask **5** guise, visor **6** domino **8** disguise
vocabulary 4 cant **5** argot, lingo, slang, words **6** jargon, patois **7** lexicon **8** glossary **9** word-hoard **10** vernacular **11** terminology
vocal 4 oral **5** blunt, frank **6** phonic, spoken, voiced **7** uttered **8** eloquent **9** outspoken **10** articulate, expressive, free-spoken
vocalic 5 vowel
vocalist 4 diva **6** belter, canary, singer **7** crooner, warbler, yodeler **8** minstrel, songbird **9** balladeer, chanteuse, chorister **10** cantatrice, prima donna
vocalization 4 song **5** voice **6** speech **7** diction **8** speaking **9** utterance **11** enunciation **12** articulation **13** pronunciation
vocalize 3 air, hem **4** sing, talk **5** chant, croon, speak, state, utter, voice **6** warble **7** express **9** enunciate, pronounce
vocal organ 6 larynx **8** voice box ***bird:*** **6** syrinx
vocation 3 art, job **4** call, work **5** craft, trade **6** career, métier **7** calling, mission, pursuit **8** business, lifework **10** employment, handicraft, occupation, profession
vociferate 3 bay, cry **4** bark, bray, call, roar, yawp, yell **5** shout **6** bellow, clamor, holler **7** thunder
vociferous 4 loud **5** noisy **6** shrill **7** blatant, clamant, raucous **8** strident **9** clamorous **11** openmouthed **12** obstreperous
vodka *brand:* 5 Stoli **7** Absolut **8** Smirnoff **11** Stolichnaya ***source:*** **3** rye **4** corn **5** wheat **6** barley, potato
vogue 3 cry, fad, ton **4** chic, mode, pose, rage **5** craze, favor, furor, style, trend **6** furore **7** fashion **10** dernier cri, popularity **11** stylishness
voice 3 put, say **4** part, talk, tell, vent **5** say-so, sound, speak, state, utter **6** assert, choice, medium, singer, speech **7** declare, express, opinion, present **8** vocalize **9** condition, enunciate, formulate, pronounce, statement, utterance, verbalize **10** articulate, expression, instrument ***female:*** **4** alto **5** mezzo **7** soprano **9** contralto ***high:*** **5** tenor **7** soprano **8** falsetto ***in grammar:*** **6** active **7** passive ***Latin:*** **3** vox ***male:*** **4** bass **5** tenor **8** baritone ***quality:*** **5** pitch **6** timbre ***quiet:*** **7** whisper ***relating to:*** **5** vocal **8** phonetic ***without:*** **4** dumb, mute
voice box 6 larynx
voiced 4 oral **5** vocal **6** sonant, spoken **7** uttered **8** phonated **9** expressed
voiceless 3 mum **4** dumb, mute, surd **6** silent **8** breathed **12** inarticulate
void 3 gap, nix **4** emit, hole, idle, lack, null, undo **5** abyss, annul, blank, clear, empty, inane, quash **6** bereft, cancel, cavity, hollow, negate, remove, vacant, vacate, vacuum **7** absence, give off, negated, nullify, rescind, reverse, vacuity, vacuous **8** abrogate, deserted, evacuate **9** black hole, discharge, eliminate, emptiness **10** extinguish **11** nothingness
voilà 4 ta-da **5** ta-dah, there
volant 4 fast, spry, yare **5** agile, fleet, quick, zippy **6** flying, lively, nimble **9** dexterous, sprightly
volar 6 palmar
volatile 5 flaky **6** fickle, flakey, flying, lively **7** erratic, essence, flighty **8** fleeting, fugitive, skittery, skittish, unstable, variable, volcanic **9** ephemeral, explosive, fugacious, mercurial, momentary, transient **10** capricious, changeable, evanescent, inconstant, short-lived, transitory **11** impermanent **13** temperamental
volatility 10 fickleness **11** flightiness, inconstancy, instability **13** changeability
volcanic 7 violent **8** volatile **9** explosive ***crater:*** **4** maar ***explosion:*** **8** eruption ***glass:*** **8** obsidian ***matter:*** **3** ash **4** lava, tufa, tuff **5** magma **6** scoria ***mound:*** **4** cone ***passage:*** **6** throat **7** conduit ***vent:*** **8** fumarole **9** solfatara
volcano 4 hill, vent **8** mountain ***Alaska:*** **6** Katmai (Mount) **8** Wrangell (Mount) **9** Aniakchak (Crater) ***Andes:*** **5** Omate **12** Huaina Putina ***Antarctica:*** **6** Erebus (Mount) ***Azores:*** **4** Alto (Pico) ***California:*** **6** Lassen (Peak) ***Canaries:*** **5** Teide (Pico de), Teyde (Pico de) **8** Tenerife (Pico de) ***Co-***

lombia: **5** Huila (Nevado del), Pasto **6** Purace **7** Galeras ***Costa Rica:*** **4** Poás **5** Barba, Irazú ***Ecuador:*** **6** Sangay **8** Antisana, Cotopaxi ***extinct:*** **4** Popa (Mount) **5** Iriga, Kenya (Mount) **8** Mauna Kea **9** Haleakala (Crater) ***Guatemala:*** **4** Agua **5** Fuego **7** Atitlán ***Hawaii:*** **7** Kilauea **8** Mauna Kea, Mauna Loa ***Honshu:*** **4** Nasu **5** Asama, Azuma **6** Bandai **8** Nasudake **9** Asamayama ***Iceland:*** **5** Askja, Hecla, Hekla ***Indonesia:*** **3** Awu (Gunung) **5** Agung (Gunung) **7** Tambora (Gunung) ***island:*** **5** Thera, Thira **8** Krakatau, Krakatoa, Santorin **9** Santorini ***Italy:*** **8** Vesuvius **9** Stromboli ***Iwo Jima:*** **9** Suribachi (Mount) ***Japan:*** **3** Aso **5** Unzen **6** Asosan ***Java:*** **4** Gede (Gunung) **5** Bromo, Gedeh (Gunung), Kelud (Gunung), Salak (Gunung) ***Madeira:*** **5** Ruivo (Pico) ***Martinique:*** **5** Pelée (Mount) ***Mexico:*** **6** Colima **7** Orizaba **9** Paricutín **12** Popocatepetl ***mud:*** **5** salse ***New Zealand:*** **7** Ruapehu (Mount) **9** Ngauruhoe, Tongariro ***Peru:*** **5** Misti (El) ***Philippines:*** **3** Apo (Mount) **4** Taal **5** Mayon (Mount) **8** Pinatubo (Mount) ***Sicily:*** **4** Etna ***Solomons:*** **5** Balbi ***South America:*** **5** Lanín, Maipo, Maipu ***Sumatra:*** **5** Dempo (Gunung) **7** Kerinci **8** Kerintji ***type:*** **6** shield **10** cinder cone ***Washington:*** **11** Saint Helens (Mount) ***West Indies:*** **9** Soufrière

____ volente **3** Deo

volition **4** will **6** choice, desire, intent, option **8** decision, election **9** selection **10** preference

volley **4** hail, shot **5** burst, round, salvo, storm **6** return, shower **7** barrage **8** drumfire **9** broadside, cannonade, discharge, fusillade

volplane **5** glide

Volpone **3** Fox (The) ***author:*** **6** Jonson (Ben) ***servant:*** **5** Mosca

Volsung ***grandson:*** **6** Sigurd **9** Siegfried ***great-grandfather:*** **4** Odin ***son:*** **7** Sigmund

voltage **5** power **6** energy **9** intensity

Voltaire ***drama:*** **5** Zaïre **6** Alzire, Brutus, Mèrope, Oedipe **7** Mahomet **8** Tancrède ***novel:*** **5** Zadig **7** Candide ***real name:*** **6** Arouet (François Marie)

volte-face **5** U-turn **8** flip-flop, reversal, turnover **9** about-face, inversion, turnabout **10** switcheroo **13** change of heart

voluble **4** glib **5** gabby, talky, windy **6** chatty, fluent, mouthy, prolix **7** verbose **8** effusive, vocative **9** garrulous, talkative **10** long-winded, loquacious

volume **4** body, book, bulk, mass, size, tome **5** album, flood, folio, space **6** amount, scroll **7** content **8** capacity, loudness, quantity **9** aggregate **12** displacement

voluminous **4** full **5** bulky **6** legion, prolix **7** copious **8** numerous, prolific **9** capacious **10** convoluted **13** multitudinous

Volumnia's son **10** Coriolanus

voluntary **4** free **7** willful, willing, witting **8** elective, freewill, optional **10** autonomous, deliberate, volitional **11** independent, intentional, spontaneous **13** discretionary

volunteer **5** offer **6** enlist, join up, sign up **7** present, propose, suggest ***hospital:*** **12** candy striper

Volunteer State **9** Tennessee

voluptuous **4** sexy **5** ample, buxom **6** wanton **7** languid, sensual **8** luscious, sensuous **9** bodacious, luxurious **10** curvaceous

volute **5** helix, shell **6** scroll, spiral **7** mollusc, mollusk **8** curlicue

vomit **3** gag **4** barf, cast, gush, hurl, lose, puke, spew, toss **5** expel, retch **6** spit up **7** bring up, throw up, upchuck **8** disgorge **11** regurgitate

vomiting **6** emesis

Vonnegut work **9** Galapagos, Timequake **10** Cat's Cradle, Hocus Pocus **11** Player Piano **13** Sirens of Titan (The) **18** Slaughterhouse Five **20** Breakfast of Champions **22** Happy Birthday Wanda June

voodoo **3** hex **4** jinx, juju, mojo **5** charm, magic, spell, vodun **6** amulet, whammy **7** bewitch, enchant, sorcery **8** ensorcel, wizardry **9** ensorcell **10** hocus-pocus, mumbo jumbo, necromancy, witchcraft **11** abracadabra, implausible, unrealistic ***relative:*** **5** obeah **8** santeria **9** Candomblé

voracious **4** avid **5** eager **6** ardent, greedy, hungry **7** piggish, starved **8** edacious, famished, ravenous, starving **9** rapacious **10** gluttonous, insatiable, omnivorous, quenchless

vortex **4** eddy, gyre **5** swirl **7** tornado **9** hurricane, maelstrom, whirlpool, whirlwind **11** tourbillion

votary **3** bug, fan, nut **4** buff **5** lover **6** addict, zealot **7** admirer, apostle, devotee, groupie, habitué **8** adherent, advocate, believer, disciple, follower **9** worshiper **10** aficionado, enthusiast, worshipper

vote **3** opt **4** poll **5** elect, judge, offer **6** ballot, choice, choose, decide, ratify, select, ticket **7** adjudge, declare, endorse, express, opinion, propose, suggest, verdict **8** election, suffrage **9** franchise **10** expression ***affirmative:*** **3** aye, nod, yea, yes **6** placet ***kind:*** **5** proxy, straw, voice **6** secret **7** write-in **8** absentee **10** plebiscite, referendum ***negative:*** **2** no **3** nay ***right to:*** **8** suffrage **9** franchise

votive **8** grateful **10** devotional

vouch 5 prove **6** affirm, assert, assure, attest, uphold, verify **7** certify, confirm, support, witness **8** accredit **9** guarantee **11** corroborate **12** substantiate

voucher 3 IOU **4** chit **5** proof **6** coupon, surety **7** receipt **9** affidavit, indenture **10** credential **11** certificate **13** authorization

vouchsafe 4 give **5** award, favor, grant **6** accord, bestow, confer, oblige **7** concede, furnish

vow 4 aver, oath, word **5** swear, troth **6** assert, attest, pledge, plight **7** confirm, declare, promise, warrant **8** covenant **9** assertion, guarantee **10** obligation **11** declaration

vowel 6 letter, symbol **11** speech sound ***kind:*** **4** high, long **5** glide, schwa, short **9** diphthong **11** monophthong ***omission:*** **7** aphesis **11** contraction ***variation:*** **6** ablaut, umlaut

voyage 4 sail, trek, trip **5** jaunt **6** cruise, junket, outing, travel **7** journey, odyssey, set sail **8** traverse **9** excursion **10** expedition, pilgrimage

voyeur 6 peeper **10** peeping Tom

Vronski's lover 12 Anna Karenina

Vulcan see **Hephaestus**

vulgar 3 low, raw **4** base, lewd, loud, rude, vile **5** crass, crude, gaudy, gross, rough, showy, tacky **6** coarse, earthy, flashy, garish, ribald, sordid, tawdry **7** chintzy, kitschy, lowbred, lowbrow, obscene, profane, uncouth **8** churlish, improper, indecent, off-color, unseemly **9** barbarous, graceless, low-minded, offensive, tasteless, unrefined **10** indecorous, indelicate, scurrilous, unpolished, vernacular **11** pretentious

vulgate 10 vernacular

Vulgate translator 6 Jerome

vulnerability 8 exposure, soft spot, weakness **10** underbelly **12** Achilles' heel

vulnerable 4 open, weak **6** liable **7** exposed **10** assailable **11** susceptible

vulnerary 4 balm **5** salve, tonic **7** healing, unguent **8** curative, ointment, remedial, salutary, sanative **9** medicinal, wholesome **10** salubrious **11** restorative, therapeutic **12** healthgiving

vulpine 3 sly **4** foxy, wily **5** slick **6** artful, astute, crafty, shrewd, tricky **7** cunning, foxlike **8** guileful

vulture 4 bird **6** condor **11** lammergeier, lammergeyer ***food:*** **7** carrion ***relative:*** **4** hawk **5** eagle **6** falcon **7** buzzard

vulturine 8 ravenous **9** predatory, rapacious, raptorial **10** predaceous, predacious, scavenging

W

wacky 3 fey, mad **4** daft, nuts **5** batty, daffy, crazy, flaky, kooky, loony, loopy, silly **6** absurd, fruity, insane, screwy **7** bonkers, cracked, foolish, idiotic, lunatic, offbeat **8** crackers, demented **9** eccentric **10** irrational **11** harebrained **12** preposterous

wad 3 gob, jam **4** chaw, cram, lump, mint, pile, plug, quid, roll, swab **5** chunk, stuff **6** boodle, bundle, packet, pellet **7** fortune **8** bankroll

waddle 6 toddle

waddy 4 club, cosh **6** cowboy, cudgel **7** rustler **8** bludgeon

wade 4 ford, plod **5** labor **6** drudge, plodge, trudge ***into:*** **5** set to **6** attack, plunge, tackle **9** undertake

wadi 3 bed **4** wash **5** gully **6** arroyo, coulee, course, ravine **9** streambed **10** depression **11** watercourse

wafer 4 chip, disk, host **5** matzo, obley, slice **6** matzoh **7** cracker

waffle 4 yo-yo **5** tripe, waver **6** dither, drivel, seesaw **7** blather **8** flip-flop **9** fluctuate, vacillate **10** equivocate

waft 4 flag, gust, puff, waif, wave **5** carry, drift, float, hover **7** pennant

wag 3 bob, nod, wit **4** card, lash, wave **5** clown, cutup, joker, shake, swing, whisk **6** kidder, switch, twitch, waddle **8** brandish, comedian, funnyman, jokester

wage 3 fee, pay **6** income, reward, salary **7** carry on, payment, stipend **8** earnings, pittance, receipts **9** emolument **10** recompense **12** compensation, remuneration

wager 3 bet, lay, pot **4** ante, game, risk **5** stake **6** chance, gamble, hazard **7** venture

waggery 3 gag **4** jest, joke **5** prank, sport **7** devilry, kidding, roguery **8** deviltry, droll-

ery, mischief **10** impishness, pleasantry **11** roguishness **12** sportiveness **13** practical joke
waggish 4 arch, pert **5** antic, comic, droll, saucy, witty **6** impish, jocose **7** comical, jocular, playful, puckish, roguish **8** humorous, prankish, sportive **9** facetious **10** frolicsome **11** mischievous
waggle 3 bob **4** reel, sway
Wagner, Richard ***birthplace:*** **7** Leipzig ***father-in-law:*** **5** Liszt (Franz) ***festival site:*** **8** Bayreuth ***opera:*** **4** Ring **6** Rienzi **7** Walküre (Die) **8** Parsifal **9** Lohengrin, Rheingold (Das), Siegfried **10** Die Walküre, Tannhäuser **12** Das Rheingold **13** Meistersinger (Die) **14** Flying Dutchman (The) **15** Götterdämmerung **16** Tristan und Isolde **17** Ring of the Nibelung (The) ***patron:*** **6** Ludwig ***recurring theme:*** **9** leitmotif, leitmotiv ***wife:*** **5** Minna **6** Cosima
wagon 3 van **4** cart, dray, tram, trek, wain **7** caravan, coaster, hayrack **9** Conestoga
wahoo 3 ono **8** mackerel **9** winged elm **11** burning bush
waif 5 gamin, stray **6** gamine, orphan, urchin **8** wanderer **9** foundling **10** ragamuffin **11** guttersnipe
wail 3 bay, cry **4** bawl, blub, fuss, howl, keen, weep, yowl **5** mourn, whine **6** bemoan, lament, plaint, repine **7** blubber, ululate **8** complain **9** complaint **11** lamentation
wain 5 wagon **9** Big Dipper
wainscot 4 dado
waistband 3 obi **4** belt, sash **6** girdle **8** ceinture, cincture **10** cummerbund
waistcoat 4 vest **5** gilet **6** jerkin, weskit
wait 4 bide, idle, lurk, stay **5** abide, dally, delay, serve, tarry, watch **6** expect, hold on, linger, remain **8** hang fire, mark time, sit tight **10** anticipate **11** stick around
waiter 4 tray **6** carhop, garçon, salver, server **7** servant **9** attendant
Waiting for ____ 5 Godot, Lefty
wait on 4 tend **5** serve **6** attend, tend to **7** care for, cater to **9** look after
waive 4 cede, stay **5** allow, defer, delay, forgo, table, yield **6** give up, hold up, put off, shelve **7** abandon, concede, dismiss, hold off, suspend **8** hand over, hold over, postpone **9** surrender **10** relinquish
wake 4 path, stir, wash **5** alert, arise, get up, rally, rouse, track, vigil, watch **6** arouse, bestir, excite, kindle, stir up **7** roll out **8** activate, backwash **9** aftermath, stimulate
wakeful 5 alert **8** restless, vigilant **9** insomniac, sleepless
waken see **wake**
Walden author 7 Thoreau (Henry David)
wale 3 rib **4** bend, welt **5** brace, ridge **6** strake
Wales ***capital:*** **7** Cardiff ***city:*** **6** Bangor **7** Newport, Swansea **8** St. David's ***island:*** **8** Anglesey ***mountain:*** **7** Snowdon ***patron saint:*** **5** David ***river:*** **3** Dee ***strait:*** **5** Menai ***symbol:*** **4** leek **6** dragon **8** daffodil (see also **Cymric**)
walk 3 pad **4** gait, hike, hoof, pace, path, plod, roam, slog, step, trip **5** alley, amble, clump, mince, paseo, stave, strut, stump, trail, tramp, tread, troop **6** hoof it, prance, ramble, sashay, stride, stroll, toddle, trudge, waddle, wander **7** saunter, shamble, shuffle, stumble, swagger, traipse **8** ambulate, traverse **9** promenade **11** base on balls, perambulate, peregrinate
walkaway 4 romp, rout
walking shorts 8 Bermudas
walking stick 4 cane **5** staff **6** crutch, insect **7** phasmid, whangee
walk out 5 leave **6** strike
walk out on 5 leave **6** desert **7** abandon, forsake
Walküre composer 6 Wagner (Richard)
walkway 4 path **7** passage **9** promenade
wall 3 bar, hem **4** side, stop **5** block, close, fence, hedge **6** immure **7** barrier, close in, enclose **8** blockade, surround **9** barricade, enclosure, roadblock, structure ***bearing:*** **7** support ***hanging:*** **8** tapestry ***painting:*** **5** mural **6** fresco ***protective:*** **7** parapet, rampart ***top of:*** **6** coping
wallaby 8 kangaroo
wallet 5 funds **6** folder **8** billfold **9** accessory, resources **10** pocketbook
Wallis and Futuna Islands ***capital:*** **7** Matautu ***island:*** **4** Uvéa ***territory of:*** **6** France
wallop 3 bop, hit **4** bang, bash, beat, belt, blow, boil, bust, clip, drub, lick, pelt, slam, slug, sock, whip, whop, whup **5** baste, paste, pound, punch, smack, whack **6** buffet, pummel, thrash, thwack **7** shellac, trounce **8** lambaste
walloping 4 huge **5** giant **7** immense, mammoth, monster **8** colossal, enormous, gigantic, smashing **10** gargantuan, impressive, incredible, prodigious
wallow 4 bask, roll **5** enjoy, revel **6** billow, welter **7** delight, indulge **9** luxuriate
Wall Street debut 3 IPO
____ Walpole 4 Hugh **6** Horace
____ Walton 3 Sam **5** Izaak
waltz 5 dance, valse
Waltz King 7 Strauss (Johann)
Wampanoag chief 9 Massasoit, Metacomet **10** King Philip

wampum 4 peag **5** beads, money **6** shells
wan 3 dim **4** ashy, gray, pale, waxy, weak, worn **5** ashen, faint, livid, lurid, pasty, waxen **6** anemic, doughy, feeble, infirm, pallid, peaked, sallow, sickly **7** ghastly, languid **8** blanched **9** bloodless, colorless, washed-out **10** cadaverous, white-faced
wand 3 rod **4** pole, tube **5** baton, staff
wander 3 bat, bum, gad **4** mill, roam, rove, swan **5** amble, dally, drift, float, gypsy, mooch, prowl, range, stray, tramp **6** ramble, stroll **7** deviate, digress, diverge, maunder, meander, saunter, traipse **8** divagate, straggle, vagabond **9** expatiate, gallivant **10** kick around
wanderer 4 waif **5** gypsy, nomad, rover, stray **7** pilgrim, vagrant **8** runabout, vagabond
wandering 7 erratic, migrant, nomadic, vagrant **8** vagabond **9** itinerant, migratory, walkabout, wayfaring **10** roundabout **11** peripatetic
wane 3 dim, ebb **4** fail, fall **5** abate, let up **6** lessen, recede, reduce, relent, shrink, weaken **7** decline, dwindle, slacken, subside **8** decrease, diminish, moderate, slack off, taper off
wangle 6 scheme **7** finagle, wheedle **8** inveigle, scrounge **10** manipulate
wannabe 5 clone **7** also-ran, copycat, hopeful, wishful **8** apparent, aspiring, desiring, desirous **9** ambitious, look-alike, potential
want 4 lack, like, need, void, wish **5** covet, crave, fault **6** dearth, desire, penury **7** absence, poverty, require **8** exigency **9** indigence, necessity, neediness, privation **10** deficiency, desiderate, inadequacy, scantiness **11** destitution, requirement **13** insufficiency
wanting 4 away, less, sans **5** minus, scant, short **6** absent, scanty, scarce **7** lacking, missing, without **9** deficient **10** inadequate, incomplete **12** insufficient
wanton 4 doxy, jade, lewd, minx, rank, slut **5** bawdy, cruel, hussy, loose, tramp, trull, wench **6** coquet, floozy, harlot, lavish, trifle, unruly **7** baggage, cyprian, immoral, jezebel, lustful, obscene, Paphian, sensual, trollop, wayward **8** inhumane, pitiless, ruthless, slattern, spiteful, sportive, strumpet **9** dissolute, luxuriant, malicious, merciless **10** gratuitous, lascivious, malevolent, outrageous, prostitute **11** extravagant, mischievous, uncalled-for
wapiti 3 elk **4** stag **7** red deer
war 4 feud, odds **5** fight **6** battle, combat, strife **7** contest **8** conflict, struggle, variance **9** hostility **10** antagonism **11** competition ***German:*** **5** Krieg **10** blitzkrieg ***god:*** **3** Tiu, Tyr **4** Ares, Mars, Odin **5** Woden, Wotan ***goddess:*** **4** Enyo **5** Anath **6** Inanna, Ishtar **7** Bellona ***Latin:*** **6** bellum ***Muslim:*** **5** jehad, jihad ***relating to:*** **7** martial
War and Peace *author:* **7** Tolstoy (Leo) ***character:*** **6** Andrey (Prince), Pierre (Bezukhov) **7** Natasha (Rostova) ***composer:*** **9** Prokofiev (Sergey)
warble 4 sing **5** carol, chirp, trill, tweet **6** gadfly, maggot, quaver **7** descant, melisma, twitter
warbler 4 bird **6** singer **7** kinglet **8** songster **9** blackpoll **11** gnatcatcher ***European:*** **10** chiffchaff
____ **Warbucks 5** Daddy
war casualties group 3 DAV
war cry 5 motto **6** slogan ***Greek:*** **5** alala ***Japanese:*** **6** banzai
ward 4 care **5** aegis, stave **6** barrio, charge **7** custody, defense, keeping **8** district, division, precinct, security **9** bishopric **10** protection **11** safekeeping **12** guardianship
warden 6 jailer, keeper, regent **7** provost **8** governor, guardian, official **9** castellan, constable, custodian, protector **10** commandant, supervisor
ward off 5 avert, parry, rebut, repel **6** divert **7** deflect **8** turn away **9** forestall
wardrobe 5 trunk **6** closet **7** apparel, armoire, clothes **8** clothing **9** garderobe **12** clothespress ***assistant:*** **7** dresser
warehouse 4 stow **5** depot, lodge, stock, store **7** confine, deposit, shelter, storage, stowage **8** building **9** stockroom, storeroom **10** depository, repository **11** accommodate ***oriental:*** **6** godown
wares 4 line **5** goods, stock **9** vendibles **11** commodities, marketables, merchandise
warfare 6 battle, combat, strife **8** conflict, struggle **10** operations **11** hostilities ***type:*** **4** germ **6** trench **10** biological
warhorse 4 hack **5** steed **7** charger, courser, veteran **8** chestnut, standard
warlike 7 hawkish, martial **8** militant, military **9** bellicose, combative, truculent **10** aggressive, pugnacious **11** belligerent
warlock 3 wiz **4** mage **5** magus **6** wizard **8** conjurer, conjuror, magician, satanist, sorcerer **9** diabolist, enchanter **11** necromancer
warm 4 bask, heat, kind **5** angry, fresh **6** ardent, genial, heated, heat up, loving, reheat, secure, tender **7** affable, cordial, excited, fervent, sincere **8** friendly, gracious, spirited **9** heartfelt **10** passionate, responsive **11** kindhearted, sympathetic **12** affectionate,

enthusiastic, wholehearted **13** compassionate *air:* **7** thermal
warmed-over 5 banal, stale, tired, trite **6** old-hat **7** clichéd **8** shopworn, timeworn **9** hackneyed
warmhearted 4 kind **6** benign, kindly, loving, tender **7** cordial **8** generous **9** benignant, unselfish **10** benevolent **11** magnanimous, sympathetic **12** affectionate **13** compassionate
warmth 4 glow, heat **7** comfort **8** fondness **9** affection **10** cordiality
warmup 5 run-up **6** lead-in, opener **7** kickoff, preface, prelude, preview **8** overture, preamble, prologue **9** countdown **11** preliminary **12** introduction
warn 3 tip **4** clew, clue **5** alert **6** advise, inform, notify, tip off **7** apprise, caution, counsel **8** admonish
warning 3 tip **4** hint **5** alarm, alert **6** caveat, notice, signal, tip-off **7** caution, counsel, summons **8** monition, monitory **10** admonition, cautionary **12** admonishment *legal:* **6** caveat
War of the Worlds author 5 Wells (H. G.)
warp 4 base, bend, cast, kink, rope, wind **5** color, curve, twist **6** buckle, debase, deform, wrench **7** confuse, contort, corrupt, deflect, distort, pervert, torture, vitiate **10** bastardize **12** misrepresent
warrant 4 pawn, writ **5** proof, prove, token **6** affirm, assert, assure, attest, avouch, ensure, ground, insure, pledge, secure **7** certify, contend, declare, justify, precept **8** guaranty, maintain, mittimus, sanction, security **9** assurance, authority, authorize, guarantee **10** foundation **11** certificate **12** confirmation **13** justification
warranty 4 bail, bond **6** surety **8** covenant, security **9** guarantee
warren 4 maze **7** network, rabbits **8** tenement
Warren novel 14 All the King's Men
warrior 2 GI **4** hero **7** battler, fighter, soldier **8** champion **9** combatant **10** serviceman *female:* **6** Amazon *Japanese:* **5** ronin **7** samurai *princess:* **4** Xena **7** Lawless (Lucy)
Warsaw *castle:* **5** Zamek *river:* **7** Vistula
wart 4 flaw **6** defect, growth **7** blemish, verruca **11** excrescence
wary 5 alert, cagey, canny, chary, leery **7** careful, dubious, guarded, mindful **8** cautious, skittish, vigilant, watchful **10** suspicious **11** circumspect, distrustful
wash 3 lap, pan, tub **4** hose, lave, suds, wadi **5** bathe, clean, creek, douse, drift, float, flush, gully, marsh, scrub, slosh, swill **6** drench, shower, sluice, splash **7** cleanse, coating, launder, laundry, shampoo, suffuse **8** backwash
washed-out 4 beat **5** all in, faded, spent, tired, weary **6** bushed, effete, sapped, used-up, wasted **7** drained **8** depleted **9** exhausted
washed-up 4 beat, done **5** kaput, spent **6** done in **7** also-ran, defunct, done for, through **8** finished
washing 4 bath **6** lavage **7** laundry **8** ablution, lavation *ceremonial:* **6** lavabo
Washington *capital:* **7** Olympia *city:* **6** Tacoma **7** Seattle, Spokane **9** Vancouver **10** Walla Walla *college, university:* **7** Gonzaga, Whitman **9** Evergreen *dam:* **11** Grand Coulee *mountain, range:* **7** Cascade, Olympic, Rainier **8** St. Helens *nickname:* **9** Evergreen (State) *river:* **6** Yakima **8** Columbia *state bird:* **9** goldfinch *state flower:* **12** rhododendron *state tree:* **7** hemlock
Washington, D.C., designer 7 L'Enfant (Pierre-Charles)
Washington, George *home:* **11** Mount Vernon *wife:* **6** Martha
Washington Square author 5 James (Henry)
wasp 5 mason **6** digger, hornet, vespid **8** braconid **9** ichneumon, mud dauber **12** yellow jacket
waspish 5 testy **6** snappy, snarky, snippy, touchy **7** peevish, vespine **8** petulant, snappish, vinegary **9** crotchety, fractious, irritable, querulous **10** vinegarish **12** cantankerous, cross-grained
wassail 5 binge, carol, drink, revel, spree, toast **6** bender **7** carouse, revelry, roister **8** carousal, drinking
Wasserstein play 15 Heidi Chronicles (The) **17** Sisters Rosenzweig (The)
waste 4 arid, fail, kill, loss, ruin, sack, wild **5** empty, offal, scrap, trash **6** barren, damage, debris, desert, devour, litter, ravage, refuse, sewage, shrink, weaken **7** badland, consume, despoil, destroy, fritter, garbage, pillage, plunder, rubbish **8** decrease, desolate, emaciate, enfeeble, misspend, prodigal, spoilage, squander, wear away, wildland **9** devastate, dissipate, excrement, sweepings, throw away **10** desolation, wilderness **11** prodigality **12** extravagance, extravagancy *maker:* **5** haste *time:* **5** dally **6** dawdle, footle, piddle, trifle
waste away 4 fade, fail **6** molder, shrink **7** atrophy, decline, dwindle, shrivel **10** degenerate
wasted 3 lit **4** high **5** drunk, gaunt **6** peaked, sickly, stoned **7** elapsed, ravaged **8** skeletal

9 emaciated **10** cadaverous, skeletonic **11** intoxicated

wasteful 6 lavish **8** prodigal **9** throwaway **10** profligate, thriftless, uneconomic **11** extravagant, improvident, inefficient, spendthrift

wastefulness 6 excess **10** lavishness **11** prodigality **12** extravagance, immoderation

wasteland 4 wild **5** heath **6** barren **10** desolation, wilderness

Waste Land author 5 Eliot (T. S.)

wastrel 3 rip **4** rake, roué **7** rounder, spender **8** prodigal **9** fritterer, libertine **10** dissipater, high roller, ne'er-do-well, profligate, squanderer **11** scattergood, spendthrift

watch 3 eye, see, spy **4** bide, look, mind, tend, tout, wait, wake, ward **5** guard, shift, vigil **6** attend, follow, look at, notice, sentry **7** care for, lookout, monitor, observe, surveil **8** bulletin, eagle eye, scrutiny, sentinel, watchman **9** attention, timepiece, vigilance **10** duty period, observance **11** chronometer, observation **12** surveillance ***chain:*** **3** fob ***maker:*** **10** horologist

watchdog 5 guard **6** keeper **8** Cerberus, guardian **9** custodian, protector

watcher 6 viewer **7** guarder, lookout **8** beholder, follower, guardian, observer, onlooker **9** spectator

watchful 4 wary **5** alert, chary **7** on guard, wakeful **8** cautious, vigilant **9** attentive, observant, sleepless, wide-awake **10** unsleeping ***Scottish:*** **5** tenty **6** tentie

watchman 5 guard, scout **6** patrol, picket, sentry, warder **7** lookout **8** sentinel

watch out 6 beware **8** take care

watchtower 6 turret **7** lookout **8** barbican, bartizan **10** lighthouse

watchword 3 cry **5** motto **6** mantra, parole, signal, slogan **8** password **9** principle **10** shibboleth **11** catchphrase, countersign

water 4 hose, soak, thin, tide **5** drink, fluid, spray **6** dilute, liquid, supply **7** moisten **8** irrigate, moisture, snowmelt, sprinkle **10** excellence **13** amniotic fluid ***body:*** **3** bay, sea **4** gulf, lake, pool **5** ocean **6** lagoon, strait **9** reservoir ***combining form:*** **4** aqui, aquo, hydr **5** hydro ***French:*** **3** eau ***goddess:*** **4** Nina **7** Anahita, Anaitis ***Latin:*** **4** aqua ***Spanish:*** **4** agua

water buffalo 4 arna **5** bovid **7** carabao ***female:*** **5** arnee

water clock 9 clepsydra

water closet 2 WC **3** loo **4** head, john **5** privy **6** toilet **7** latrine **8** bathroom, lavatory

watercourse 4 dike, duct **5** bayou, canal, ditch **6** arroyo **7** channel, conduit **8** aqueduct, headrace, tailrace **9** streambed

water cow 6 dugong **7** manatee

watered-down 5 washy **6** dilute **7** diluted

waterfall 5 chute, sault, shoot **7** cascade **8** cataract ***Brazil:*** **6** Iguaçú (Falls), Iguazú (Falls) ***California:*** **8** Yosemite (Falls) ***Canada:*** **5** Grand (Falls) **8** Takkakaw **9** Churchill (Falls) ***Canada-U.S.:*** **7** Niagara (Falls) ***Congo:*** **6** Boyoma (Falls) **7** Stanley (Falls) ***former Nile:*** **4** Owen (Falls) **5** Ripon (Falls) ***Kentucky:*** **10** Cumberland (Falls) ***New Zealand:*** **10** Sutherland (Falls) ***Niagara:*** **8** American, Canadian **9** Horseshoe ***Norway:*** **6** Rjukan (Falls) ***Oregon:*** **9** Multnomah (Falls) ***South Africa:*** **6** Tugela (Falls) ***Snake River:*** **4** Twin (Falls) **8** Shoshone (Falls) ***Venezuela:*** **5** Angel (Falls) ***Washington:*** **10** Snoqualmie (Falls) ***world's highest:*** **5** Angel (Falls) ***Wyoming:*** **11** Yellowstone (Falls) ***Zambezi River:*** **8** Victoria (Falls)

water finder 6 dowser **11** divining rod

waterfront 8 seacoast **9** lakeshore, riverside

water hole 5 oasis

watering hole 3 bar, pub **4** café **5** oasis **6** lounge, nitery, resort, saloon, tavern **7** barroom, cabaret, gin mill, taproom **9** nightclub, nightspot, roadhouse **10** supper club **11** rathskeller

waterless 3 dry **4** arid, sere **7** bone-dry, parched **8** droughty **9** anhydrous **10** dehydrated

waterlog 8 saturate

waterloo 4 ruin **6** defeat **7** failure **8** disaster, downfall

water nymph 3 nix **4** lily **5** naiad, nixie **6** mayfly, Nereid **7** Oceanid **9** dragonfly

water oscillation 6 seiche

water pipe 4 bong **5** spout **6** hookah **8** narghile, nargileh **12** hubble-bubble

water plant 7 aquatic, seaweed **8** duckweed, wild rice **9** arrowhead, tape grass **10** hydrophyte, manna grass **11** bladderwort

water rat 6 nutria

watershed 6 crisis, divide **12** turning point

water spirit 3 nix **5** nixie, nymph **6** sprite, undine

water tank 7 cistern

watery 4 pale, thin, weak **5** banal, bland, vapid, washy **6** dilute, serous **7** diluted, insipid

wattle 4 gill, grid, jowl **5** frame **8** caruncle **9** framework, interlace **10** interweave

wattle and ____ 4 daub

wave 3 wag **4** flag, flap **5** heave, ridge, surge, sweep, swell **6** comber, influx, marcel, motion, period, ripple, signal, waggle **7** breaker, dismiss, flutter, gesture, upsurge **8**

activity, brandish, flourish, undulate **9** disregard ***large:*** **7** tsunami

waver **4** reel, sway **5** swing, weave **6** dither, falter, quaver, quiver, teeter, totter, wobble **7** flicker, stagger, whiffle **8** hesitate, undulate **9** oscillate, vacillate **12** shilly-shally

wavering **4** weak **5** shake, shaky **6** unsure, wobbly **7** halting **8** doubtful, insecure, to-and-fro, unstable **9** equivocal, faltering, fluctuant, hesitancy, undecided, vibration, whiffling **10** hesitating, hesitation, indecision, irresolute **11** fluctuating, vacillating, vacillation **12** irresolution, shilly-shally

Waverley novels **6** Rob Roy **7** Ivanhoe **10** Kenilworth **14** Quentin Durward ***author:*** **5** Scott (Walter)

wavy **4** ondé, undé **7** rolling **8** rippling, swelling **9** fluctuant **10** undulating **11** fluctuating

wavy pattern **5** moiré **8** squiggle **10** undulation **11** crenulation

wax **4** come, grow, rise **5** boost, build, mount **6** become, expand, record **7** augment, enlarge **8** heighten, increase, multiply, paraffin, simonize **9** secretion, substance ***Chinese:*** **4** pela

waxen **3** wan **4** ashy, pale **5** ashen, livid **6** pallid, smooth **7** pliable **8** blanched, moldable **9** colorless

way **3** ilk **4** door, kind, mode, much, path, road, sort, type, very **5** entry, habit, means, order, route, state, style, usage **6** access, artery, action, avenue, course, custom, degree, manner, method, street **7** ability, fashion, feature, ingress, opening, outcome, respect **8** distance, entrance, practice **9** boulevard, condition, direction, procedure, technique **11** opportunity, possibility **12** thoroughfare

wayfarer **4** hobo **5** gipsy, gypsy, hiker, nomad, rover, tramp **7** rambler **8** traveler, vagabond **9** itinerant, journeyer, traveller

wayfaring **6** roving **7** nomadic, vagrant **8** vagabond **9** itinerant, traveling, wandering **10** travelling **11** peripatetic **13** perambulatory

waylay **4** jump **5** brace **6** ambush, attack **8** surprise **9** bushwhack, still-hunt

Wayne's World ***actor:*** **5** Myers (Mike) **6** Carvey (Dana) ***character:*** **5** Garth, Wayne

Way of All Flesh author **6** Butler (Samuel)

Way of the World author **8** Congreve (William)

wayward **5** balky **6** fickle, unruly **7** froward, restive, vagrant, willful **8** contrary, perverse, untoward **9** whimsical **10** capricious, headstrong **11** intractable, wrongheaded **12** ungovernable **13** unpredictable

we ***French:*** **4** nous ***German:*** **3** wir ***Italian:*** **3** noi ***Spanish:*** **8** nosotros

weak **3** dim, wan **4** puny, soft, thin **5** faint, frail, shaky, timid **6** dilute, feeble, flimsy, infirm, sickly, unsure, watery, wobbly **7** brittle, diluted, fragile, rickety, spindly, tenuous, unsound **8** decrepit, delicate, helpless, impotent, inferior, insecure, timorous, unstable, wavering **9** deficient, enfeebled, inaudible, powerless, spineless, uncertain **10** improbable, inadequate, unreliable, unstressed **11** debilitated, implausible, ineffective, ineffectual, vacillating, watered-down **12** unconvincing, undependable **13** insubstantial, unsubstantial

weaken **3** lag, sap **4** fail, flag, thin, wane **5** abate **6** damage, dilute, impair, lessen, reduce, soften **7** corrode, decline, disable, dwindle, subvert, unbrace **8** enervate, enfeeble, moderate **9** attenuate, grind down, honeycomb, undermine **10** debilitate, demoralize, invalidate

weak-kneed **5** timid **6** wobbly **7** gutless **8** cowardly, wavering **9** faltering, uncertain, whiffling **10** irresolute **11** lily-livered, vacillating **12** fainthearted, shilly-shally **13** pusillanimous

weakling **4** wimp, wuss **5** mouse, sissy **7** doormat, milksop, sad sack **8** pushover **9** jellyfish **10** namby-pamby **11** milquetoast, mollycoddle **12** invertebrate

weakness **4** flaw, hole, vice **5** crack, fault, taste **6** defect, desire, liking, relish **7** failing, frailty **8** appetite, debility, fondness, soft spot **9** infirmity **10** feebleness **11** decrepitude, shortcoming **12** Achilles' heel

weal **4** welt **5** ridge **7** welfare **9** well-being

weald **5** woods **6** forest **8** woodland **10** timberland, wilderness

wealth **5** goods, worth **6** assets, estate, mammon, plenty, riches **7** capital, fortune **8** holdings, opulence, property **9** abundance, affluence, profusion, resources **11** possessions

Wealth of Nations author **5** Smith (Adam)

wealthy **4** rich **5** flush **6** loaded **7** moneyed, opulent, well-off **8** affluent, well-to-do **9** well-fixed **10** prosperous, well-heeled **12** silk-stocking

wean **4** free, part **5** alien **6** detach **8** accustom, estrange, separate

weapon **3** bow, gun **4** bill, bolo, bomb, club, dart, dirk, mace, nuke, pike, shiv **5** A-bomb, arrow, H-bomb, knife, lance, prick, rifle, saber, sabre, sling, spear, steel, sword **6** dagger, Magnum, musket, pistol, poleax, rapier, rocket **7** bazooka, broadax, car bomb, carbine, firearm, gisarme, halberd, handgun, javelin, machete, missile, shotgun, sidearm, stun gun, torpedo, war club **8** battle-ax, bludgeon, broadaxe, catapult, crossbow, death ray, nerve gas, nunchaku, partisan, partizan, petronel, revolver, spontoon, tomahawk **9** battle-axe, blackjack, boomerang, derringer, slingshot **10** atomic bomb, machine gun, projectile **11** blunderbuss, depth charge, nuclear bomb **12** quarterstaff **13** brass knuckles

weapons 4 arms **7** arsenal, battery **8** ordnance **9** armaments, artillery, munitions **13** armamentarium

wear 3 rub **4** fray, tire **5** chafe, dress, erode, grind **6** abrade, attire, endure, impair **7** corrode, exhibit, fatigue, fashion **8** abrasion, clothing ***and tear:* 12** depreciation ***thin:* 4** fray **5** chafe **6** tatter **7** hackney

wear down 5 drain, erode, grind **6** abrade, weaken **7** corrode, degrade, exhaust, fatigue

weariness 5 ennui **7** boredom, fatigue, languor **8** lethargy **9** lassitude **10** enervation, exhaustion **12** taedium vitae

wearing 6 taxing, tiring, trying **9** difficult, fatiguing

wearisome see **tiresome**

wear out 3 fag **4** bust, do in, fray, poop, tire **5** drain **6** efface, tucker **7** consume, deplete, exhaust, frazzle **8** overstay

weary 4 beat, jade, limp, tire, worn **5** drain, jaded, spent, tired **6** bushed, done in, pooped, tucker, wasted **7** drained, fatigue, worn-out **8** dog-tired, fatigued, tiresome **9** apathetic

weasand 6 gullet, throat **7** trachea **8** windpipe **9** esophagus

weasel 5 dodge, evade, hedge, slink, sneak, stoat **6** ermine, escape, ferret, mammal **7** sneaker **8** sidestep **9** pussyfoot **10** equivocate ***Scottish:* 8** whittret

weather 4 rain **5** storm **6** bear up, endure, expose **7** climate, ride out, undergo **9** withstand ***forecasting:* 11** meteorology

weathercock 4 vane

weathered 8 hardened, seasoned, tempered

weave 4 cane, lawn, leno, spin, sway **5** braid, cloth, lurch, twine, waver **6** careen, fabric, pleach, raddle, wobble, zigzag **7** pattern, stagger, textile, texture **8** contrive **9** interlace **10** crisscross, intertwine

weaver 4 loom **7** Arachne, webster

web 3 net **4** mesh, vane **5** snare, snarl **6** enmesh, fabric, tangle **7** ensnare, netting, network **8** entangle **10** enmeshment **12** entanglement

Weber opera 6 Oberon **9** Euryanthe **10** Freischütz (Der)

____ **Webster 4** Noah **6** Daniel

Web vending 5 e-tail **9** e-commerce

wed 4 join, link, mate, yoke **5** hitch, marry, merge, unite **6** splice **7** combine, conjoin, connect, espouse **10** tie the knot

wedded 7 marital, nuptial **8** conjugal, hymeneal **9** connubial **11** matrimonial

wedding 5 union **6** bridal **7** spousal **8** espousal, marriage, nuptials ***words:* 3** I do

wedding anniversary *fifteenth:* 7 crystal ***fifth:* 6** wooden ***fiftieth:* 6** golden ***first:* 5** paper ***seventy-fifth:* 7** diamond ***tenth:* 3** tin ***twentieth:* 5** china ***twenty-fifth:* 6** silver

wedge 4 shim **5** chock, stuff **8** golf club, golf shot, keystone **10** force apart

wedge-shaped 7 cuneate **8** cottered, sphenoid **9** cuneiform ***mark:* 5** caret

wedlock 4 knot, yoke **8** espousal, marriage **9** matrimony **11** conjugality **12** connubiality

wee 4 tiny **5** bitsy, bitty, early, small, teeny **6** little, minute, teensy **9** itty-bitty, miniature **10** diminutive, teeny-weeny **11** Lilliputian, little bitty **12** teensy-weensy

weed 4 dock, tare **5** chess, clear, plant **6** cockle, darnel, dodder, nettle, remove **7** burdock, burseed, ragweed, ruderal **8** amaranth, charlock, purslane **9** chickweed, cocklebur, dandelion, knotgrass, marijuana, poison ivy, poison oak, stickseed **10** cheatgrass, lady's thumb, sow thistle ***biblical:* 4** tare ***European:* 6** spurry **7** spurrey ***killer:* 8** paraquat **9** herbicide ***Western:* 4** loco

weedy 4 lean, thin **5** lanky **6** skinny **7** scrawny, stringy, willowy **8** untended **9** overgrown

week 6 period **8** hebdomad ***two weeks:* 9** fortnight

weep 3 cry, sob **4** drip, moan, ooze, tear, wail **5** bleed, exude, sweat **6** lament **7** blubber, dribble, trickle **8** transude

weepy 5 misty, moist, teary **7** tearful **10** lachrymose

weevil 7 billbug **8** curculio

weft 3 web **4** pick, woof, yarn **6** fabric, thread

weigh 3 way **4** heft, rate, tare **5** count, judge, scale, study **6** burden, ponder **7** balance, measure, oppress, perpend **8** appraise, bear down, consider, evaluate, militate **11** contemplate

weigh down 4 load **5** press **6** burden, sadden **7** depress, oppress **8** encumber **10** discourage, overburden

weight 3 tax **4** heft, lade, load, mass, onus, task **5** class, force, power **6** amount, assign, burden, charge, credit, import, moment, saddle **7** oppress, potency, quality **8** encumber, poundage, pressure, prestige, quantity **9** authority, influence, magnitude **10** corpulence, importance **11** consequence **12** significance ***allowance:*** **4** tare ***apothecary:*** **4** dram **5** grain, pound **7** scruple ***Asian:*** **4** tael **5** catty ***gem:*** **5** carat ***measure of:*** **3** fun, kin, kip, oke, tan, tod, ton, vis, yin **4** dram, gram, mina, rotl **5** grain, libra, ounce, picul, pound **7** long ton, scruple **8** kilogram, short ton **9** metric ton ***system:*** **3** net **4** troy **6** metric **10** apothecary **11** avoirdupois

weightiness **4** pith **6** import, moment **7** dignity, gravity **9** heaviness, magnitude, solemnity **10** importance **11** consequence, massiveness **12** significance **13** momentousness

weight lifting term **4** curl, pull, push **5** clean, press, shrug, squat **6** snatch **8** deadlift **12** clean and jerk

weightlifter **4** Kono (Tommy), Tang (Gonghong) **5** Dimas (Pyrros), Mutlu (Halil) **6** Weller (Ronny) **7** Krastev (Antonio) **8** Alexeyev (Vasily), Pechalov (Nikolay) **9** Chemerkin (Andrei), Reza Zadeh (Hossein), Taranenko (Leonid) **10** Schemansky (Norbert)

weighty **3** fat **5** grave, gross, heavy, hefty, obese, sober, staid **6** fleshy, portly, sedate, severe, solemn, somber **7** massive, serious, telling **8** cumbrous, grievous, powerful **9** corpulent, effective, important, momentous, ponderous **10** burdensome, convincing, cumbersome **11** significant, substantial **12** considerable **13** consequential

weir **3** dam **5** stank

weird **3** odd **5** eerie, queer **6** creepy, freaky, spooky **7** bizarre, curious, oddball, strange, uncanny **8** freakish, peculiar, singular, sinister **9** eccentric, fantastic, unearthly **10** mysterious **11** inscrutable **12** supernatural **13** preternatural

weirdo **4** geek, kook, loon **5** freak **7** nutcase, oddball **8** crackpot **9** eccentric, screwball

welcome **4** hail **5** cheer, greet, hello, howdy **6** accept, invite, salute **7** embrace, invited, receive **8** greeting, pleasant, pleasing **9** agreeable, favorable, reception **10** gratifying, hospitable **11** hospitality, pleasurable

weld **4** bond, fuse, join **5** braze, joint, merge, unite **6** solder

welfare **3** aid **4** dole, help, weal **5** pogey **6** health, relief, succor **7** benefit, fortune, success, support **8** interest **9** advantage, happiness, well-being **10** assistance, commonweal, prosperity

welkin **3** sky **5** ether, vault **6** heaven **7** heavens **8** empyrean **9** firmament

well **3** far, fit, pit **4** easy, emit, hale, hole, pool, rise, sane **5** amply, clear, cured, fully, quite, shaft, sound, truly **6** easily, freely, healed, indeed, justly, kindly, likely, nicely, origin, rather, really, source, spring, wholly **7** clearly, healthy, perhaps, readily, rightly **8** entirely, expertly, pleasing, possibly, probably, properly, sensibly, smoothly, suitably **9** advisable, correctly, desirable, elegantly, favorably, fittingly, fortunate, perfectly, wholesome

well-being **4** weal **6** health **7** welfare **8** thriving **9** happiness **10** prosperity

well-bred **6** urbane **7** genteel, refined **8** cultured, highborn, polished **9** civilized, patrician **10** cultivated **11** blue-blooded, gentlemanly

well-built **4** buff **5** hunky, solid **8** muscular **9** strapping

well-developed **5** curvy **7** fulsome, rounded, shapely **8** advanced **9** Junoesque **10** curvaceous

well-disposed **7** amiable **8** friendly **9** favorable, receptive **11** sympathetic **13** understanding

Welles movie **5** Trial (The) **7** Macbeth, Othello **8** Jane Eyre, Stranger (The), Third Man (The) **11** Citizen Kane, Touch of Evil **15** Journey into Fear **16** Chimes at Midnight, Lady from Shanghai (The) **20** Magnificent Ambersons (The)

well-favored **4** fair **5** bonny **6** comely, lovely, pretty **7** winsome **8** gorgeous, handsome **9** beauteous, beautiful **10** attractive **11** good-looking

well-fixed see **well-to-do**

well-founded **5** sound, valid **6** cogent **8** rational **9** justified **10** convincing

well-groomed **4** neat, snug, tidy, trig, trim **5** natty, smart **6** dapper, snappy, spiffy, spruce, sprucy **7** orderly **8** clean-cut **9** shipshape

well-heeled see **well-to-do**

Wellington **4** duke **7** general **8** Iron Duke ***horse:*** **10** Copenhagen ***original name:*** **9** Wellesley (Arthur) ***victory:*** **7** Vitoria **8** Talavera, Waterloo **9** Salamanca

well-known **5** famed, noted **6** famous **7** big-name, eminent, popular **8** renowned **9** notorious, prominent **10** celebrated **11** illustrious

well-liked **7** beloved, favored, popular **8** favorite **9** cherished, preferred

well-mannered **5** civil, suave **6** poised, polite, proper, urbane **7** genteel, tactful **9** courteous **10** diplomatic

well-nigh 6 all but, almost, fairly, nearly, next to **8** as good as **9** just about, virtually **11** essentially, practically
well-off see **well-to-do**
well-paying 7 gainful **9** lucrative, rewarding **10** profitable, worthwhile **11** moneymaking **12** advantageous, remunerative
Wells novel 11 Time Machine (The) **12** Invisible Man (The) **14** War of the Worlds (The)
wellspring 4 font, root **5** fount **6** origin, source **7** genesis **8** fountain **10** provenance **11** provenience **12** fountainhead
well-thought-of 6 valued, worthy **7** admired, reputed **9** estimable, reputable **10** creditable **11** respectable
well-timed 6 timely **7** apropos, fitting, timeous **9** favorable, opportune **10** auspicious, felicitous, fortuitous, propitious, seasonable
well-to-do 4 rich **5** flush **6** loaded, monied **7** moneyed, upscale, wealthy **8** affluent **10** prosperous **11** comfortable
well-turned 4 trim **5** plump **7** rounded, shapely **10** curvaceous, felicitous, Rubenesque, statuesque **11** clean-limbed
well-worn 5 banal, musty, stale, stock, tired, trite **6** frayed, old-hat, shabby **7** clichéd **8** bromidic, cobwebby, dog-eared, overused **9** hackneyed **10** threadbare **11** commonplace, stereotyped
Welsh see **Cymric**
welsh 5 dodge **6** renege, resile **7** back out, default
welt 4 blow, edge, seam, wale, weal **5** ridge, wheal, whelk **6** insert
welter 4 coil, moil, toss **5** chaos, churn, steep, surge **6** flurry, hassle, hubbub, jumble, lather, ruckus, seethe, thrash, wallow, writhe **7** ferment, turmoil **8** disorder **9** confusion
____ **Welty 6** Eudora
wen 4 bleb, cyst **5** blain **6** growth **7** vesicle **11** excrescence
wench 3 gal **4** girl, jade, lass, maid, minx, miss, puss, slut, tart **5** hussy, nymph, tramp, trull, whore, woman **6** damsel, gamine, harlot, hoyden, lassie, maiden, wanton **7** jezebel, servant, trollop **8** slattern, strumpet
wend 3 hie **4** fare, pass **6** direct, push on, repair, travel **7** journey, proceed
werewolf 9 loup-garou **11** lycanthrope
Werther's beloved 5 Lotte **9** Charlotte
Wesleyan 9 Methodist
West 8 Occident
western 5 oater **9** Hesperian **10** horse opera, occidental ***hemisphere:* 8** Americas, New World
Western novelist 4 Grey (Zane), Ross (Dana Fuller) **5** Brand (Max), Faust (Frederick), Short (Luke) **6** Judson (E. Z. C.), L'Amour (Louis), Patten (Lewis), Wister (Owen) **7** Guthrie (A. B.), Leonard (Elmore) **8** Buntline (Ned), McMurtry (Larry)
West Indies *country:* 4 Cuba **5** Haiti **7** Bahamas, Grenada, Jamaica **8** Barbados, Dominica **10** Guadeloupe, Martinique, Puerto Rico, Saint Lucia **17** Dominican Republic ***island group:* 6** Virgin (Islands) **7** Bahamas, Leeward (Islands) **8** Antilles (Greater, Lesser), Windward (Islands)
West Point *father of:* 6 Thayer (Sylvanus) ***freshman:* 5** plebe ***student:* 5** cadet
West Side Story *composer:* 9 Bernstein (Leonard) ***heroine:* 5** Maria ***lyricist:* 8** Sondheim (Stephen)
West Virginia *capital:* 10 Charleston ***city:* 8** Wheeling **10** Huntington ***mountain:* 10** Spruce Knob ***nickname:* 8** Mountain (State) ***river:* 4** Ohio ***state bird:* 8** cardinal ***state flower:* 12** rhododendron ***state tree:* 10** sugar maple
west wind see at **wind**
wet 3 sop **4** damp, dank, rain, soak, wash, weak **5** douse, drown, drunk, humid, moist, rainy, soggy, soppy, souse, water **6** dampen, drench, soaked, sodden, soused, sweaty, watery **7** moisten, raining, soaking, sopping **8** drenched, dripping, humidify, irrigate, moisture, saturate, slippery **9** saturated, spineless ***combining form:* 4** hygr **5** hygro
wet blanket 6 grinch **7** killjoy **8** sourpuss **9** pessimist **10** spoilsport **11** party pooper
wether 4 goat **5** sheep
wetland 3 bog, fen **4** mire, quag **5** marsh, swamp **6** morass, muskeg, slough
whack 3 bat, hit, pop, try **4** bash, belt, biff, blow, chop, cuff, kill, pelt, shot, sock, stab, wham, whap, whop **5** crack, punch, smack, smash **6** attack, defeat, murder, strike, wallop **7** bump off **8** knock off, lambaste ***up:* 4** part **5** divvy, split **6** divide **7** portion **9** apportion
whale 3 hit **4** beat, cete, flog, hide, lash, whip **5** giant **6** defeat, strike, stripe, thrash **7** mammoth **8** cetacean, behemoth **9** leviathan **10** flagellate ***arctic:* 7** bowhead ***group:* 3** gam, pod ***killer:* 4** orca ***kind:* 3** sei **4** blue **5** right, sperm **6** baleen, beluga, killer **7** narwhal, rorqual **8** cachalot ***novel:* 8** Moby Dick ***toothed:* 5** pilot (whale) **9** blackfish ***white:* 4** huso ***young:* 4** calf
whalebone 9 scrimshaw
wham 3 hit **4** bang, beat, blow, boom, clap, slam **5** blast, burst, crack, crash, smash, whack **6** impact, propel, strike **7** explode

whammy 3 hex, zap **4** jinx, juju **5** curse, spell **6** hoodoo, voodoo **7** evil eye
wharf 4 dock, pier, quay **5** jetty, levee
Wharton novel 10 Buccaneers (The), Ethan Frome **12** House of Mirth (The) **14** Age of Innocence (The) **18** Custom of the Country (The)
whatever 5 at all **9** in any case
whatnot 7 étagère
wheal 4 lump, welt **5** ridge, whelk
wheat 4 crop **5** emmer, flour, grain, grass, spelt **6** cereal **7** einkorn ***beard:*** **3** awn ***beat:*** **6** thresh ***chaff:*** **4** bran ***crushed:*** **6** bulgur ***disease:*** **4** rust, smut ***type:*** **4** club **5** durum
wheedle 3 con **4** coax **5** cozen **6** cajole, entice, seduce **7** blarney, flatter **8** blandish, inveigle, scrounge, soft-soap **9** sweet-talk
wheel 3 VIP **4** auto, gyre, move, reel, spin, turn **5** cycle, drive, motor, pilot, pivot, round, whirl **6** bigwig, circle, gyrate, league, rotate, totter, travel **7** big shot, circuit, revolve **8** rotation **9** about-face, volte-face ***part:*** **3** hub, rim **4** tire **5** felly, spoke ***shaft:*** **4** axle ***spoke:*** **6** radius ***toothed:*** **3** cog **4** gear
wheeze 3 saw, yuk **4** gasp, hiss, joke, puff, rasp **5** adage, cough **6** saying **7** proverb, whistle **8** chestnut, rhonchus
whelk 4 wale, weal, welt **5** wheal
whelm 4 bury, sink **5** cover, drown, flood, swamp **6** deluge, engulf **8** bear down, inundate, overbear, overcome, submerge **9** devastate
whelp 3 cub, kid, pup **4** bear **5** child, puppy **9** youngster
whereas 5 since, while **6** seeing, though **7** howbeit **8** although **11** considering
wherefore 3 why **4** thus **5** proof **6** ground, reason, whence **8** argument **11** explanation
wherewithal 5 funds, means, money **9** resources
wherry 4 boat **5** barge, scull **7** lighter, rowboat
whet 4 edge, goad, hone **5** drink, rally, rouse, waken **6** arouse, awaken, excite, kindle **7** sharpen, starter **8** aperitif **9** appetizer, challenge, stimulate **10** incitement **11** hors d'oeuvre
whiff 3 fan **4** blow, gust, hint, puff, waft **5** expel, smoke, tinge, trace **6** breath, exhale, inhale **7** soupçon, whisper **9** strikeout **10** indication, inhalation
whiffet 6 nobody, squirt **9** nonentity
whiffle 4 blow, gust, puff **5** waver **6** dither, falter **9** fluctuate, vacillate **12** shilly-shally
while 4 pass, time, when **5** spell **6** albeit, moment, though **7** howbeit, stretch, whereas **8** although, as long as, so long as
whilom 4 past **6** bygone, former **7** onetime, quondam **8** formerly, previous, sometime **9** erstwhile
whim 3 bee **4** idea, kink **5** dream, fancy, freak, humor **6** maggot, megrim, notion, vagary **7** caprice, capstan, conceit, thought **8** crotchet
whimper 3 cry **4** fret, mewl, pule, wail **5** bleat, whine **6** snivel
whimsical 4 iffy, zany **5** ditsy, ditzy, droll, fancy, flaky **6** chancy, fickle, fitful, flakes, quirky, random **7** erratic, flighty, mutable, puckish, wayward **8** fanciful, freakish, volatile **9** eccentric, impulsive, mercurial, pixilated, screwball, uncertain, vagarious **10** capricious, pixillated **13** unpredictable
whimsy 3 bee **4** play **5** dream, fancy, freak, humor **6** levity, maggot, megrim, notion, vagary **7** caprice, conceit, fantasy **9** capriccio, frivolity
whim-wham 4 dido **5** curio, fancy, frill **6** bauble, gewgaw, ruffle, trifle **7** bibelot, flounce, trinket, whatnot **8** furbelow, gimcrack, kickshaw **9** objet d'art **10** knickknack
whine 3 cry **4** cant, fret, fuss, kick, moan, pule, wail **5** bleat, gripe **6** grouse, repine, snivel, whinge, yammer **7** grumble, snuffle, whimper **8** complain **9** bellyache
whinny 5 neigh **6** nicker **7** whicker
whiny 5 fussy **7** fretful, grouchy, peevish **8** petulant **9** irritable, querulous
whip 3 cut, hem, set, tan **4** beat, cane, crop, dash, flog, hide, jerk, lash, lick, pull, rout, wind, wrap **5** abuse, mop up, quirt, spank, sting, whale, whisk **6** defeat, lather, snatch, strike, stroke, subdue, switch, thrash, urge on **7** agitate, dessert, provoke, rawhide, shellac, trounce, utensil **8** coachman, lambaste, overcome, vanquish **9** instigate, overwhelm **10** flagellate **13** cat-o'-nine-tails ***braided:*** **10** blacksnake
whippersnapper see **whiffet**
whipping boy 4 goat **5** patsy **7** fall guy **9** scapegoat
whippy 6 supple **7** elastic, springy **8** flexible **9** resilient
whir 3 fly, hum **4** burr, buzz, whiz **5** chirr, churr, drone, whizz **7** revolve, vibrate **9** bombinate
whirl 3 ado, gig, pop, try **4** eddy, flit, fuss, gyre, moil, reel, shot, spin, stab, stir, swim, turn, veer **5** hurry, pivot, swirl, whack, wheel **6** bustle, circle, gyrate, hassle, hubbub, pother, rotate **7** circuit, dervish, tur-

moil **8** ballyhoo, gyration, rotation **9** commotion, pirouette **10** revolution

whirligig 4 gyre, spin **6** beetle, gyrate **8** carousel **9** pirouette **12** merry-go-round

whirlpool 3 ado **4** eddy, fuss **6** bustle, flurry, furore, tumult, vortex **7** turmoil **8** vortices (plural) **9** commotion, maelstrom ***bath:* 6** hot tub **7** Jacuzzi

whirlwind 2 oe **4** rush, stir, to-do **5** hasty, spout, swift **6** bustle **7** cyclone, tornado, twister, typhoon **8** headlong **9** commotion, dust devil, dust storm, hurricane **10** waterspout **11** tourbillion

whish 4 fizz, hiss **6** fizzle **8** sibilate

whisk 3 mix, nip, wag, zip **4** beat, flit, whip **5** broom, brush, fluff, hurry, speed **6** switch

whisker 4 hair **7** bristle **8** filament, vibrissa **9** outrigger **11** hairbreadth

whiskered 5 hairy **6** pilose **7** bearded, bristly, hirsute **8** stubbled, unshaven

whiskers 5 beard **6** goatee **7** stubble, weepers **8** bristles **9** burnsides, peach fuzz, sideburns **11** dundrearies, muttonchops

whiskey 3 rye **6** liquor, Scotch **7** alcohol, bourbon ***with beer chaser:* 11** boilermaker

whisper 4 buzz, hint, hiss, whiz **5** rumor, shade, tinge, touch, trace, whiff **6** breath, gossip, murmur, mutter **8** sibilate, susurrus **9** suspicion, undertone **11** susurration

whist 4 game, hush **5** quiet, still **6** silent **9** noiseless, soundless

whistle 4 pipe, toot **5** flute, whiff **6** signal, tootle, wheeze

whistle-stop 5 stump **8** campaign, politick **9** barnstorm **11** electioneer

whit 3 bit, fig, jot, rap **4** atom, damn, hoot, iota, mite **5** crumb, scrap, shred, speck, whoop **7** dribble, modicum, smidgen **8** molecule, particle

white 4 pure **5** cream, ivory, livid, milky, snowy **6** albino, blanch, bleach, pallid **7** silvery **9** colorless ***combining form:* 4** leuc, leuk **5** leuco, leuko ***egg's:* 5** glair **6** glaire **7** albumen

White novel 12 Stuart Little **13** Charlotte's Web

white cliffs of ____ 5 Dover

White Fang author 6 London (Jack)

White House *designer:* 5 Hoban (James) ***first occupant:* 5** Adams (Abigail, John)

white lightning 5 hooch **7** bootleg, whiskey **9** moonshine **10** bathtub gin **11** mountain dew

whiten 4 fade, pale **5** frost **6** blanch, bleach, blench **8** etiolate **10** decolorize

white plague 2 TB **8** phthisis **11** consumption **12** tuberculosis

whitewash 6 parget **7** cover up **9** gloss over, gloze over, sugarcoat

whither 5 where **7** whereto **9** whereunto

whiting 3 cod **4** hake **10** silver hake

Whitman work 13 Leaves of Grass

Whitsunday 9 Pentecost

Whittier poem 9 Snow-Bound **10** Maud Muller **11** Barefoot Boy **16** Barbara Frietchie

whittle 3 hew **4** chip, form, fret, pare, trim **5** carve, shape, shave, skive **6** reduce, sculpt **8** diminish

whiz 3 fly, hum, zip **4** buzz, flit, hiss, zoom **5** hurry, speed, swish, whirl **6** expert, fizzle, genius, phenom, rotate, whoosh **8** virtuoso **10** wunderkind

whoa 3 hey **4** slow, stop **6** hold up

whole 3 all, fit, sum **4** full, hale, sane **5** sound, total, uncut, unity **6** entire, entity, healed, intact, system, unhurt **7** healthy, perfect, plenary **8** complete, entirely, entirety, flawless, restored, totality, unbroken, unmarred ***combining form:* 3** hol, pan **4** holo

wholehearted 6 ardent **7** devoted, earnest, fervent, sincere **8** bona fide **9** committed, heartfelt, steadfast, unfeigned **10** passionate, unwavering **11** impassioned **12** enthusiastic **13** unquestioning

whole-hog 6 all-out, gung-ho **8** complete, thorough **9** full-scale **11** straight-out **13** thoroughgoing

wholeness 7 oneness **8** entirety, totality **9** integrity, soundness **10** intactness, perfection

whole note 9 semibreve

whole number 5 digit **6** cipher **7** integer, numeral

wholesome 3 fit **4** good, hale, safe, sane, well **5** right, sound **6** benign **7** healthy **8** hygienic, salutary **9** favorable, healthful **10** beneficial, salubrious

wholly 3 all **4** only **6** in toto, singly, solely, purely **7** totally **8** entirely **10** altogether, completely **11** exclusively

whomp 3 hit **4** beat, drub, slap, whip, whup **5** crash, thump **6** crunch, strike, thrash, wallop **7** clobber, shellac, trounce **8** lambaste

whomp up 4 stir **5** rouse, spark **6** arouse, excite, foment

whoopee 3 fun **5** revel, yahoo **6** gaiety, hoopla, hooray, yippee **7** jollity, revelry, wassail, whoopla **8** hilarity **9** festivity, high jinks, merriment **10** hurly-burly **11** merrymaking

whoopla see **hoopla**

whop 3 bat, bop **4** bash, beat, biff, blow, drub, lick, sock **5** baste, pound, smack, thump, whack **6** batter, buffet, defeat, hammer, pummel, strike, thrash, thwack, wallop **7** trounce **8** lambaste

whopper 3 lie **4** lulu **5** beaut, doozy, whale **6** doozie **8** knockout, tall tale **9** humdinger

whopping 4 huge, vast **6** mighty **7** amazing, immense, massive **8** colossal, enormous, gigantic, whacking **9** bodacious, humongous, monstrous **10** gargantuan, incredible, prodigious **13** extraordinary

whorl 4 coil, eddy, turn **5** swirl **6** spiral

why 5 cause **6** enigma, motive, puzzle, reason, riddle **7** mystery, problem, what for **9** conundrum, rationale, therefore, wherefore **10** puzzlement **11** explanation

wicked 4 evil, mean, very, vile **5** awful, black, wrong **6** fierce, malign, sinful, unholy **7** corrupt, hateful, heinous, immoral, naughty, ungodly, vicious **8** depraved, devilish, fiendish **9** atrocious, barbarous, dangerous, extremely, hazardous, injurious, malicious, malignant, nefarious **10** iniquitous, malevolent, outrageous **11** treacherous

wickedness 3 sin **4** evil, vice **7** devilry **8** enormity, iniquity, satanism **9** depravity **10** corruption, immorality **12** devilishness, fiendishness

wicker 4 twig **5** osier, withe **6** branch

wicket 4 arch, door, gate, hoop **6** window ***sticky:*** **3** fix, jam **4** knot **7** toughie **9** conundrum, tight spot

wide 4 vast **5** broad, fully **8** extended, spacious, straying, sweeping **9** deviating, expansive, extensive, inclusive **10** completely **13** comprehensive

widen 4 ream **6** dilate, expand, extend, open up, spread **7** broaden, distend, enlarge

widespread 4 rife, vast **6** common **7** current, general, popular, rampant, regnant **8** far-flung **9** extensive, pervasive, prevalent **10** far-ranging, ubiquitous

widget 5 gismo, gizmo **6** device, dingus, doodad, gadget, hickey, jigger **7** gimmick, whatsit **9** doohickey, thingummy **11** contraption, thingamabob, thingamajig, thingumajig

width 4 gape, kerf, span **5** depth, range **6** spread **7** breadth **9** extension

wield 3 use **5** exert **6** handle **7** control **8** brandish, exercise **10** manipulate ***the gavel:*** **7** preside

wiener 3 dog **5** frank **6** hot dog **7** sausage **11** frankfurter **13** Vienna sausage

Wiesel work 4 Dawn **5** Night **8** Fifth Son (The) **9** Testament (The)

wife 3 Mrs. **4** mate **5** bride, woman **6** female, matron, missis, missus, spouse **7** consort, partner **8** helpmate, helpmeet ***Latin:*** **4** uxor ***of a rajah:*** **4** rani **5** ranee

wifely 7 uxorial

wig 3 jaw, rap, rug **4** flip, rail, rate **5** chide, freak, scold **6** berate, peruke, rebuke, revile, toupee **7** bawl out, chew out, reproof, upbraid **8** postiche, reproach **9** hairpiece, reprimand **10** tongue-lash

wiggle 4 jerk **5** shake, twist **6** fidget, squirm, writhe ***Scottish:*** **5** hotch

wight 3 man **5** human **6** animal, mortal, person **7** critter **8** creature **10** human being, individual

wild 3 mad **4** fast **5** crazy **6** barren, raging, savage, stormy, unruly **7** erratic, frantic, furious, natural, untamed, vicious **8** barbaric, blustery, desolate, frenetic, frenzied, reckless **9** barbarian, barbarous, delirious, fantastic, turbulent, wasteland **10** incautious, outlandish **11** extravagant, intractable, sensational, tempestuous, uncivilized, uninhabited **12** preposterous, uncontrolled, uncultivated, ungovernable, unmanageable **13** irresponsible, undisciplined

wild ass 5 kiang **6** onager

wildcat 4 eyra, lynx **6** ocelot, strike **10** jaguarundi

Wild Duck author 5 Ibsen (Henrik)

wildebeest 3 gnu

wilderness 4 bush **5** heath, waste **6** barren, desert **9** backlands, wasteland **10** hinterland **11** backcountry

Wilder play 7 Our Town **10** Matchmaker (The) **14** Skin of Our Teeth (The)

wild-eyed 6 raving **7** blue-sky, radical **9** visionary

wile 4 ploy, ruse, vamp **5** charm, feint, guile, trick **6** allure, deceit, entice, gambit **7** attract, beguile, bewitch, chicane, cunning, enchant, gimmick **8** artifice, inveigle, maneuver, trickery **9** captivate, chicanery, fascinate, magnetize, stratagem **10** subterfuge

wiliness 5 guile **7** cunning

will 4 like, wish **5** cause, elect, leave, order **6** choice, choose, decree, desire, direct, intend, intent, liking, option, ordain, please **7** bequest, consent, control, passion, purpose **8** appetite, bequeath, pleasure, volition **9** intention, testament **10** discipline **11** disposition, inclination, self-control **13** determination, self-restraint ***addition:*** **7** codicil ***maker:*** **8** testator **9** testatrix ***without:*** **9** intestate

willful 5 heady **6** dogged, mulish, ornery, unruly **7** froward, wayward **8** perverse, stubborn **9** obstinate, pigheaded, voluntary **10** deliberate, hardheaded, headstrong, purposeful, self-willed **11** intentional, intractable, wrongheaded **12** contumacious, pertinacious, ungovernable

Williams play 10 Camino Real, Rose Tattoo (The) **14** Glass Menagerie (The), Summer and Smoke **16** Cat on a Hot Tin Roof, Night of the Iguana (The), Sweet Bird of Youth **18** Suddenly Last Summer **20** Streetcar Named Desire (A)

William Tell *canton:* 3 Uri ***composer:* 7** Rossini (Gioacchino)

willies 6 creeps, shakes **7** jimjams, jitters, shivers **9** whim-whams **10** goose bumps **13** heebie-jeebies

willing 3 apt **4** fain, game, glad, open **5** prone, ready **6** minded **7** forward, witting **8** amenable, disposed, inclined, obliging, unforced **9** agreeable, compliant, favorable, receptive, voluntary **10** deliberate, volitional **11** intentional, predisposed

williwaw 4 gust, wind **5** blast **8** outburst, paroxysm **9** commotion

will-o'-the-wisp 7 fantasy, figment, phantom **8** daydream, delusion **11** ignis fatuus

willow 5 osier, salix **6** sallow **10** cricket bat ***flower cluster:* 6** catkin ***kind:* 5** crack, pussy, white **6** basket **7** weeping ***Virginia:* 4** Itea

willowy 4 tall **5** lithe **6** pliant, supple, svelte **7** lissome, pliable, slender **8** graceful

Wilson play 6 Fences **11** Piano Lesson (The) **12** Talley's Folly **13** Hot l Baltimore (The) **20** Ma Rainey's Black Bottom

wilt 3 sag **4** swag **5** droop, dry up, wizen **6** wither **7** shrivel **8** languish

wily 3 sly **4** cagy, foxy **5** cagey, canny, slick **6** artful, astute, clever, crafty, shrewd, tricky **7** cunning, devious, vulpine **8** guileful, scheming **10** serpentine

wimble 4 bore **5** auger, borer, brace, drill **6** gimlet

Wimbledon's game 6 tennis

wimp 4 nerd, wuss **5** sissy **6** weenie **7** doormat, nebbish **9** jellyfish **11** milquetoast

wimple 4 bend, veil, wrap **5** cover, curve **6** ripple ***wearer:* 3** nun

wimp out 6 beg off, cave in, give in **8** back down

wimpy 4 lame, puny, weak **5** dinky, inept, timid **6** craven, feeble **7** gutless **8** cowardly, feckless, impotent, pathetic **9** spineless **10** namby-pamby, wishy-washy **11** ineffective, ineffectual

win 3 get **4** beat, earn, gain, kayo **5** reach, score **6** attain, defeat, obtain, secure **7** achieve, acquire, conquer, procure, produce, realize, succeed, success, triumph, victory **8** conquest, persuade **9** influence **10** accomplish ***over:* 6** disarm, induce **8** convince, persuade, talk into **9** prevail on

wince 5 cower, quail, start **6** blanch, blench, cringe, flinch, recoil, shrink **7** squinch

wind 3 air, dry, fan, gas **4** bend, blow, clue, coil, curl, gale, gird, gust, haul, hint, reel, rest, talk, turn, warp, wrap **5** cover, crank, curve, force, hoist, raise, sound, spool, twine, twist **6** breath, breeze, circle, enlace, girdle, notion, zephyr **7** enclose, entwine, envelop, inkling, involve, monsoon, nothing, tighten **8** easterly, encircle, entangle, surround, tendency, westerly **9** direction, idle words, influence, insinuate **10** indication, intimation, suggestion ***Adriatic:* 4** bora ***cold:* 4** bora **7** mistral, pampero **8** williwaw ***combining form:* 4** anem **5** anemo, venti, vento ***gentle:* 6** breeze, zephyr ***god:* 6** Boreas (north) **8** Favonius, Zephyrus (west) ***hot:* 6** simoom **7** sirocco **8** scirocco ***instrument:* 4** vane **10** anemometer **11** weather vane ***into:* 8** aweather ***measure of speed:* 4** knot ***Mediterranean:* 4** bora **7** sirocco **8** levanter, libeccio, scirocco ***scale:* 8** Beaufort ***stormy:* 4** gale **7** cyclone, tornado, twister **9** hurricane **11** northeaster ***warm:* 4** föhn **5** foehn **7** chinook

windbag 6 gabber **7** blabber **8** bigmouth, blowhard, braggart

windfall 4 boon, gain **5** break **7** jackpot **8** fortuity

winding 4 curl, kink **5** snaky **6** spiral **7** coiling, curving, devious, sinuous **8** flexuous, indirect, tortuous, twisting **9** meandrous **10** circuitous, convoluted, meandering, roundabout, serpentine **11** anfractuous **12** labyrinthine

wind instrument 3 sax **4** horn, oboe, pipe, tuba **5** flute, shawm **6** cornet **7** bagpipe, bassoon, panpipe, piccolo, sackbut, trumpet **8** bagpipes, clarinet, crumhorn, recorder, trombone **9** krummhorn, saxophone **10** cor anglais, flugelhorn, French horn, sousaphone **11** English horn

windmill 4 spin **5** wheel **7** machine ***fighter:* 10** Don Quixote

window 3 eye **4** pane **7** opening **8** aperture, casement, jalousie ***cover:* 5** blind **7** curtain, shutter ***French:* 7** fenêtre ***over a door:* 7** transom **8** fanlight ***part:* 4** pane, sash, sill **5** frame ***projecting:* 3** bay **5** oriel ***roof's:* 6** dormer **7** lucarne **8** skylight ***round:* 5** oxeye ***Scottish:* 7** winnock ***ship's:* 4** port **8** porthole

windpipe 7 trachea ***combining form:* 6** trache **7** tracheo

windrow **4** bank, heap, hill, mass, pile **5** mound, ridge, stack

wind up **3** end **4** halt **5** close **6** finish, settle **8** complete, conclude **9** terminate

windup **3** end **5** close **6** ending, finale, finish **9** backswing **10** completion, conclusion **11** termination

windy **4** airy **5** blowy, gassy, gusty, inane, tumid, wordy **6** breezy, prolix, stormy, turgid **7** diffuse, orotund, pompous, verbose **8** blustery, inflated **9** bombastic, overblown **11** tempestuous **13** grandiloquent, unsubstantial

wine **4** vino **5** drink, juice **8** beverage ***aromatized:*** **8** vermouth **9** hippocras ***beverage:*** **5** negus, punch **6** bishop, cooler **7** sangria **8** sangaree, spritzer **9** hippocras ***bottle:*** **6** fiasco, magnum **8** decanter, jeroboam **10** methuselah ***cabinet:*** **8** cellaret ***cask:*** **3** tun, vat **4** butt, pipe ***cellar:*** **6** bodega ***combining form:*** **3** eno, oen **4** oeno ***discoverer:*** **4** Noah ***distillate:*** **6** brandy, cognac ***dry:*** **3** sec **4** brut ***flavor:*** **4** mull ***fortified:*** **4** port **5** Tokay **6** Malaga, Muscat, sherry **7** Madeira, marsala, oloroso **8** muscatel ***fragrance:*** **4** nose **7** bouquet ***lover:*** **9** oenophile **11** oenophilist ***maker:*** **7** vintner **8** vigneron **10** winegrower **13** viticulturist ***merchant:*** **7** vintner ***pink:*** **4** rosé **5** blush ***red:*** **4** port **5** Gamay, Macon, Medoc, Rioja **6** Barolo, Beaune, claret, merlot, Shiraz **7** Chianti **8** Bordeaux, Burgundy, cabernet, Sancerre **9** Lambrusco, Pinot Noir, St. Emilion, zinfandel **10** Beaujolais, Sangiovese **11** Petite Sirah **12** Valpolicella ***region:*** **3** Ahr **4** Asti, Cuzo, Jura, Nahe, Napa, Saar, Toro **5** Baden, Douro, Jerez, Loire, Mosel, Pfalz, Rhône, Ruwer **6** Alsace, Sonoma, Veneto **7** Mendoza, Tuscany **8** Bordeaux, Burgundy, Rheingau **9** Champagne **10** Napa Valley **11** Finger Lakes, Rheinhessen ***relating to:*** **6** vinous ***residue:*** **4** marc ***rice:*** **4** sake ***richness:*** **4** body ***sediment:*** **4** lees **5** dregs ***shop:*** **6** bistro, bodega, tavern ***sparkling:*** **4** Asti **7** Vouvray **8** cold duck, sparkler, Spumante **9** champagne, Lambrusco ***specialist:*** **9** enologist **10** oenologist ***spiced:*** **5** negus **6** mulled (wine) **9** hippocras ***steward:*** **9** sommelier ***study of:*** **7** enology **8** oenology ***sweet:*** **4** port **5** Tokay **6** canary, Malaga, muscat **7** Catawba, Madeira, malmsey, marsala, oloroso, Vouvray **8** Malvasia, muscatel, sauterne **9** Sauternes **11** scuppernong ***sweeten:*** **4** mull ***vessel:*** **7** chalice ***white:*** **4** hock **5** Rhine, Soave **7** Catawba, Chablis, Moselle, Orvieto, Vouvray **8** Bordeaux, muscadet, Riesling, Semillon, vermouth **9** champagne, Hermitage, Meursault, pinot gris **10** chardonnay, Montrachet **11** Chenin Blanc, pinot grigio, scuppernong **13** liebfraumilch **14** sauvignon blanc ***year:*** **7** vintage

wing **3** ala, arm, ell, fly **4** sail, unit, vane **5** annex, flank, fleet, pinna, wound **6** flight **7** airfoil, faction, flanker, section **9** appendage, expansion, extension, improvise ***combining form:*** **3** ali **4** pter **5** ptero ***relating to:*** **4** alar **5** alary

wingding **4** bash, fete, gala **5** binge, party **7** blowout, shindig **9** festivity

winged **5** alate, fleet, rapid, swift **7** soaring **8** elevated ***deity:*** **4** Amor, Eros, Nike **5** Cupid **6** Hermes **7** Mercury ***horse:*** **7** Pegasus ***monster:*** **5** harpy

wingless **8** apterous

winglike **4** alar **5** alary ***part:*** **3** ala **4** alae (plural)

wink **3** bat, nap **5** flash, jiffy, shake, trice **6** moment, second, signal **7** connive, flicker, instant, twinkle **9** nictitate, twinkling **11** split second

winner **3** ace **4** lulu **5** beaut, doozy **6** doozie, top dog, victor **7** success **8** champion **9** conqueror, humdinger **11** titleholder

Winnie-the-Pooh ***author:*** **5** Milne (A. A.) ***character:*** **3** Roo **5** Kanga **6** Eeyore, Piglet, Tigger

winning **8** charming, engaging, pleasing **9** agreeable **10** delightful, successful, triumphant, victorious **11** captivating **13** prepossessing

winnow **3** fan **4** blow, cull, pare, sift, sort **6** delete, filter, narrow, reduce, remove, screen, select **8** separate

winsome **5** sweet **6** dulcet, lovely **8** charming, cheerful, engaging, pleasing **9** easygoing **12** lighthearted

winter **6** season **9** hibernate ***French:*** **5** hiver ***Spanish:*** **8** invierno

Winter's Tale, A ***author:*** **11** Shakespeare (William) ***character:*** **7** Camillo, Leontes, Paulina, Perdita **8** Florizel, Hermione **9** Antigonus, Autolycus, Polixenes

wintry **3** icy **4** cold **5** bleak, hoary, nippy, snowy **6** frigid, frosty **8** chilling, freezing, hibernal **12** bone-chilling

wipe **3** dry, rub **4** swab **5** towel, whisk **6** napkin, smudge, sponge **8** squeegee

wipe out **4** rout **5** crash, erase, smear, sweep **6** efface **7** blot out, destroy, expunge **8** decimate **9** eradicate, extirpate **10** annihilate, obliterate

wipeout **4** fall, rout **5** crash **8** drubbing **11** destruction **12** annihilation

wire 3 rod **4** cord, line, send **5** cable, metal **6** thread **7** message **8** meshwork, telegram **9** cablegram, telegraph **10** finish line ***measure:*** **3** mil **5** gauge
wiry 4 lean, ropy **6** sinewy, supple **7** fibrous, stringy
Wisconsin *capital:* **7** Madison ***city:*** **6** Racine **7** Kenosha **8** Green Bay **9** Milwaukee ***college, university:*** **5** Ripon **6** Beloit **9** Marquette ***lake:*** **7** Mendota ***motto:*** **7** Forward ***nickname:*** **6** Badger (State) ***peninsula:*** **4** Door ***river:*** **7** St. Croix **9** Menominee, Wisconsin **11** Mississippi ***state bird:*** **5** robin ***state flower:*** **6** violet ***state tree:*** **10** sugar maple
wisdom 5 sense **7** insight, science **8** judgment, learning, sagacity, sageness, sapience **9** good sense, knowledge **10** horse sense **11** common sense, information
wise 4 sage **5** brash, cagey, canny, cocky, fresh, nervy, sassy **6** astute, cheeky, crafty, fill in, inform, notify, shrewd, sophic **7** gnostic, knowing, politic, prudent, sapient **8** discreet, flippant, impudent, insolent, sensible, tactical **9** advisable, expedient, judicious, sagacious, scholarly **10** discerning, insightful, perceptive, thoughtful **11** foresighted, impertinent, intelligent, smart-alecky **13** contemplative, knowledgeable, perspicacious ***old man:*** **6** Nestor ***person:*** **4** sage **6** savant **7** scholar
wiseacre see **wise guy**
wisecrack 3 dig, gag **4** barb, gibe, jape, jest, joke, quip **5** sally **6** zinger **9** witticism
wise guy 6 smarty **7** mobster **8** gangster, smart-ass **9** know-it-all, swellhead **10** smart aleck **11** smarty-pants, wisenheimer
wise man 4 guru, sage **5** magus **6** Nestor, savant
Wise Men see **Magi**
wish 3 bid **4** care, goal, like, long, lust, want **5** covet, crave, fancy, foist, order, yearn **6** desire, impose **7** request **10** desiderate
wishbone 7 furcula
wishful 5 eager **7** anxious, hopeful, longing **8** desirous
wishy-washy 4 lame, weak **5** banal, bland, vapid, wimpy **6** jejune, watery **7** insipid, languid **10** namby-pamby **11** ineffective, ineffectual **13** characterless
wisp 3 bit **5** shred, strip, trace **6** sliver, snatch, streak **7** smidgen, snippet **8** fragment **9** scintilla
wispy 4 slim **5** frail **6** flimsy, slight **7** slender, tenuous **8** fleeting, nebulous **10** evanescent
Wister novel 9 Virginian (The)
wistful 3 sad **6** dreamy, triste **7** longing, pensive **8** yearning **9** nostalgic **10** melancholy
wit 3 wag **5** brain, comic, droll, humor, irony, joker **6** banter, esprit, jester, reason, satire, wisdom **7** farceur, punster **8** banterer, comedian, funnyman, judgment, humorist, jokester, quipster, repartee **9** alertness, ingenuity, intellect **10** cleverness, persiflage
witch 3 hag, hex **5** crone, dowse, spell **6** voodoo, Wiccan **7** charmer **8** magician, sorcerer **9** sorceress **11** enchantress ***companion:*** **3** cat ***group:*** **5** coven ***male:*** **6** wizard **7** warlock ***meeting:*** **6** sabbat **7** sabbath ***town:*** **5** Endor ***vehicle:*** **5** broom
witchcraft 5 magic, wicca **6** hoodoo, voodoo **7** devilry, hexerei, sorcery **8** wizardry **9** diablerie, sortilege, voodooism **10** black magic, hocus-pocus, mumbo jumbo, necromancy **11** abracadabra, thaumaturgy
witch hazel 5 shrub **6** lotion
witchy 6 Wiccan **7** magical **8** wizardly **9** sorcerous **11** necromantic **12** thaumaturgic
with 3 for, per, pro, via **4** over, upon **5** about **6** having **7** against, by way of, through **8** as well as **9** by means of, in favor of **10** by virtue of ***French:*** **4** avec ***German:*** **3** mit ***Italian, Spanish:*** **3** con ***Latin:*** **3** cum
withal 3 too, yet **4** also **5** still **6** as well, though **7** besides, howbeit, however **8** after all, moreover **11** furthermore, nonetheless **12** additionally, nevertheless
withdraw 4 exit, quit **5** demit, leave, unsay **6** depart, bow out, call in, cash in, desert, detach, recall, recant, recede, recoil, retire, secede, shrink **7** back out, drop out, pull out, retract, retreat, scratch, take off, take out **8** back down, evacuate, fall back, pull away, push back, separate, take back, turn away **9** disengage, stand down **10** disconnect, give ground
withdrawal 4 exit **6** exodus **7** exiting, pullout, removal, retreat **9** departure **10** alienation, detachment, retirement, retraction, revocation
withdrawn 4 cool **5** aloof **6** casual, remote **7** distant, removed **8** detached, isolated, reserved, retiring, solitary **9** incurious, unaffable, uncurious **10** unsociable **11** indifferent, introverted, standoffish, unconcerned, unexpansive **12** uninterested, unresponsive
wither 3 age, dry **4** fade, sear, wilt **5** dry up, parch, quail, wizen **6** scorch **7** mummify, shrivel
withered 4 sere **7** sapless **8** shrunken, wrinkled **9** shriveled
withhold 4 deny **5** check **6** deduct, detain, re-

fuse, retain **7** abstain, deprive, forbear, inhibit, refrain, reserve **8** restrain, subtract **9** constrain

within 4 into **5** among **6** inside **7** indoors, inwards **8** enclosed, interior, inwardly **10** inner place ***prefix:*** **3** ent **4** endo, ento **5** infra, intra, intro

with-it 6 modern, modish, trendy **7** à la mode, current, faddish, stylish **8** up-to-date **9** au courant **11** fashionable **12** contemporary

without 4 less, open, past, sans **5** minus **6** absent **7** lacking, open air, outside, wanting **8** outdoors **10** externally, out-of-doors ***Latin:*** **4** sine

with respect to 2 re **4** as to, in re **5** as for **7** apropos **8** touching **9** as regards, regarding **10** concerning

withstand 4 bear, buck, defy **5** fight, repel **6** endure, oppose, resist, suffer **7** hold off, survive, sustain **8** tolerate, traverse

withy 4 twig **5** osier **6** branch, willow **8** flexible **9** resilient

witless 3 mad **4** daft, nuts **5** crazy, daffy, dotty, nutty, silly **6** insane, simple, stupid **7** asinine, cracked, foolish, idiotic **8** demented, deranged, mindless **9** bedlamite, brainless, senseless **10** weak-minded, unbalanced

witlessness 5 folly **6** idiocy, lunacy **7** inanity **8** insanity **9** absurdity, stupidity

witness 3 see **4** note, sign, view **5** proof, vouch **6** attest, depone, depose, notice, viewer **7** bear out, confirm, betoken, certify, testify, watcher **8** attester, beholder, deponent, evidence, looker-on, observer, onlooker **9** bystander, spectator, testament, testifier, testimony **11** affirmation, attestation, corroborate, testimonial **12** confirmation

witticism 3 dig, gag, mot **4** gibe, jape, jest, jibe, joke, quip **5** crack, sally **6** bon mot **8** one-liner, repartee **9** throwaway, wisecrack

witting 5 aware **7** knowing, willful **8** sensible, sentient **9** cognizant, conscious, voluntary **10** deliberate **11** intentional

witty 5 funny **6** clever, jocose **7** amusing, jocular **8** humorous **9** facetious **13** scintillating

wiz 3 ace **5** adept, fiend **6** artist, expert, phenom **7** artiste **8** virtuoso

wizard 3 ace **4** mage **5** adept, druid, fiend, magus **6** expert, phenom **7** warlock **8** conjurer, magician, sorcerer, virtuoso **9** enchanter **10** past master **11** necromancer, thaumaturge **13** thaumaturgist

wizardly 5 magic **6** mystic, witchy **7** magical **9** sorcerous **10** mysterious **11** necromantic **12** thaumaturgic

Wizard of Menlo Park 6 Edison (Thomas Alva)

Wizard of Oz *author:* 4 Baum (L. Frank) ***character:*** **6** Tin Man **7** Dorothy **9** Scarecrow **11** Tin Woodsman **12** Cowardly Lion ***dog:*** **4** Toto

wizardry 5 magic **6** voodoo **7** sorcery **8** witchery **9** diablerie, sortilege **10** black magic, necromancy, witchcraft **11** bewitchment, conjuration, enchantment

wizen 3 dry **4** sere, wilt **5** dry up **6** shrink, wither **7** dried-up, shrivel, wrinkle

wizened 4 aged, sere **5** dried **6** shrunk **7** pinched **8** shrunken, withered, wrinkled

wobble 4 reel, rock, sway **5** quake, shake, waver, weave **6** dither, falter, quaver, teeter, totter **7** stagger, stumble, tremble **8** nutation **9** vacillate

wobbly 4 weak **5** rocky, shaky **6** unsure **7** rackety, rickety **8** insecure, rachitic, unstable, unsteady, wavering **9** faltering, teetering, tottering **10** nutational **11** vacillating

Wodehouse, P. G. *castle:* 9 Blandings ***character:*** **6** Bertie (Wooster), Gussie (Fink-Nottle), Jeeves, Psmith **7** Wooster (Bertie) **8** Emsworth (Lord), Mulliner (Mr.) **10** Threepwood (Clarence, Freddie) **12** Lord Emsworth ***club:*** **6** Drones

Woden see **Odin**

woe 3 rue **4** bale, bane, care **5** grief **6** misery, regret, sorrow **7** anguish, sadness, trouble **8** calamity **9** heartache **10** affliction, heartbreak **11** lamentation, unhappiness **12** wretchedness

woebegone 3 low, sad **4** blue, down, worn **6** shabby **7** doleful, forlorn, ruthful **8** dejected, dolorous, downcast, wretched **9** depressed, miserable, sorrowful **10** despondent, melancholy **11** crestfallen, downhearted, low-spirited

woeful 3 sad **5** heavy, sorry **6** dismal, rueful, tragic, triste **7** ruthful **8** dejected, dolorous, downcast, grievous, mournful, stricken, tortured, wretched **9** afflicted, aggrieved, depressed, heartsick, miserable, plaintive, sorrowful **10** deplorable, lamentable, lugubrious, melancholy **11** distressing, downhearted, low-spirited **12** disconsolate

wolf 4 bolt, lobo, rake, roué **5** canid **6** canine, coyote, devour, gobble, masher **7** Don Juan, poverty **8** Casanova, lothario **10** starvation ***genus:*** **5** Canis ***group:*** **4** pack ***young:*** **5** whelp

Wolfe novel 17 Look Homeward Angel, Of Time and the River **18** You Can't Go Home Again **20** Bonfire of the Vanities (The)

wolfish 4 wild **5** cruel, feral **6** fierce, lupine,

savage **7** bestial, brutish, vicious **9** ferocious
wolverine ***European:*** **7** glutton ***genus:*** **4** Gulo
Wolverine State 8 Michigan
woman 4 dame, lady **5** madam **6** female, matron **8** mistress **10** girlfriend ***attractive:*** **5** belle, vixen **6** beauty, eyeful, looker **7** stunner **8** knockout ***combining form:*** **4** gyny **5** gynec **6** gynaec, gyneco, gynous **7** gynaeco ***courageous:*** **7** heroine ***dignified:*** **6** matron **7** dowager **10** grande dame ***dowdy:*** **5** frump ***English:*** **6** milady ***first, biblical:*** **3** Eve ***first, mythological:*** **7** Pandora ***French:*** **5** femme ***German:*** **4** Frau **8** Fräulein ***Hawaiian:*** **6** wahine ***Indian:*** **5** squaw ***Italian:*** **5** donna **7** signora ***old:*** **3** hag **4** dame **5** crone **6** beldam, carlin, gammer, granny ***Polynesian:*** **6** wahine ***pregnant:*** **7** gravida ***resembling:*** **8** gynecoid ***royal:*** **5** queen **8** princess ***sailor:*** **4** Wave ***servant:*** **4** maid ***soldier:*** **3** Wac ***Spanish:*** **4** doña **5** mujer **6** señora ***strong:*** **6** amazon, virago ***surfer:*** **6** wahine ***unmarried:*** **4** miss **6** maiden **8** spinster ***young:*** **4** girl, lass **6** lassie, maiden **7** ingenue
womanize 4 wolf **9** gallivant, philander **10** fool around, mess around
womanizer 4 rake, roué, stud, wolf **6** masher **7** Don Juan, gallant, playboy **8** Casanova, lothario **9** ladies' man, mack daddy **10** ladykiller **11** philanderer
womb 6 uterus ***combining form:*** **6** hyster **7** hystero
women ***hatred of:*** **8** misogyny ***organization of:*** **3** DAR, NOW **8** sorority ***seclusion of:*** **6** purdah
wonder 3 awe **4** muse **5** doubt **6** marvel **7** dubiety, miracle, portent, prodigy **8** mistrust, question **9** amazement, speculate, suspicion **10** admiration, skepticism **12** astonishment
wonderful 4 keen **5** grand, great, nifty, super, swell **6** divine, groovy, peachy, spiffy **7** amazing, strange, too much, topping **8** dynamite, fabulous, glorious, spiffing, terrific **9** admirable, excellent, marvelous, wunderbar **10** astounding, delightful, miraculous, out-of-sight, stupendous **11** astonishing, outstanding
wondrous 6 mystic **7** amazing, awesome, strange **9** marvelous **10** astounding, formidable, miraculous, portentous, prodigious, remarkable, stupendous, surprising **11** astonishing, spectacular **13** extraordinary
wonk 4 dork, geek, nerd, swot **5** dweeb, grind
wonky 4 awry **5** geeky, nerdy, shaky **7** bookish **8** unsteady
wont 3 apt **4** used **5** habit, usage **6** custom, manner **8** accustom, habitude, inclined, practice **10** accustomed, consuetude
wonted 5 usual **7** routine **8** habitual, ordinary **9** customary **10** accustomed
woo 3 sue **5** court **6** pursue **7** address, entreat
wood 5 weald **6** forest, lumber, timber **8** golf club ***combining form:*** **3** xyl **4** lign, xylo **5** ligni, ligno ***decayed:*** **4** punk ***eater:*** **7** termite ***for burning:*** **5** fagot **6** tinder **8** kindling ***fragrant:*** **5** cedar ***golf:*** **6** driver ***hard:*** **3** ash, elm, oak **4** ebon, rata, teak **5** aalii, alder, aspen, beech, birch, ebony, maple **6** cherry, poplar, walnut **7** hickory **8** chestnut, hornbeam, ironwood, mahogany, sycamore ***imperfection:*** **4** knot **5** gnarl ***light:*** **5** balsa **8** corkwood ***made of:*** **5** treen ***measure:*** **4** cord **5** stere ***pattern in:*** **5** grain **6** figure ***product:*** **3** tar **5** paper **10** turpentine ***soft:*** **3** fir, yew **4** pine **5** cedar, larch **6** spruce **7** cypress, hemlock, redwood
wood alcohol 6 methyl **8** carbinol, methanol
woodchuck 6 marmot **9** groundhog
wood coal 7 lignite
wooded 5 bosky, treed **6** sylvan **8** forested, timbered
wooden 5 rigid, stiff **6** clumsy **7** awkward, stilted **8** ligneous **10** inflexible
wooden shoe 4 clog **5** sabot
woodland 5 copse, taiga, weald **6** forest, pinery **7** coppice ***deity:*** **3** Pan **4** faun **5** satyr **6** Faunus **7** silenus
wood nymph 5 dryad
woodpecker 4 bird **7** flicker, wryneck **9** sapsucker ***genus:*** **5** Picus ***kind:*** **5** downy, green, hairy **8** imperial, pilcated **9** redheaded **11** ivory-billed
woodsman 6 logger **8** forester **10** bushranger
wood sorrel 3 oca **6** oxalis **8** shamrock **9** carambola
woodsy 6 rustic, sylvan
woodwind 3 sax **4** oboe, reed **5** flute, shawm **7** bassoon, piccolo **8** clarinet **9** saxophone **10** cor anglais, instrument **11** English horn **13** contrabassoon
woodworker 9 carpenter **12** cabinetmaker
woody 8 ligneous **12** station wagon
wooer 4 beau **5** lover, spark, swain **6** suitor **7** admirer, gallant, sparker
woof 4 bark, crow, weft, yarn **5** boast, weave **6** fabric, thread **7** texture
wool 3 fur **4** coat, hair **6** fabric, fleece ***cut:*** **5** shear ***fabric:*** **4** felt **5** baize, crepe, serge, tweed **6** covert, duffel, duffle, kersey, mohair, poplin, shoddy, velour **7** flannel, worsted **8** cashmere, chenille **9** gabardine **10** broadcloth ***fat:*** **7** lanolin ***kind:*** **4** hogg **6** angora, hogget, virgin ***low-quality:*** **5** mungo **6**

shoddy ***musk-ox:*** **6** qiviut ***process:*** **7** carding ***short fiber:*** **4** noil ***source:*** **4** goat, lamb **5** camel, llama, sheep **6** alpaca

Woolf, Virginia ***home:*** **10** Bloomsbury ***husband:*** **7** Leonard ***novel:*** **5** Waves (The), Years (The) **7** Orlando **11** Mrs. Dalloway **13** Room of One's Own (A) **15** To the Lighthouse

woolly **5** fuzzy, hairy, nappy **6** fleecy, shaggy **7** hirsute

woozy **4** hazy, sick, weak **5** dazed, dizzy, faint, fuzzy, muzzy, vague **6** addled, blurry, groggy, punchy **8** confused **9** slaphappy **11** light-headed

word **3** vow **4** oath, term **5** logos **6** pledge **7** promise **8** locution **9** utterance **10** expression ***connective:*** **11** conjunction ***group:*** **6** clause, phrase **8** sentence ***last:*** **4** Amen ***misused:*** **8** malaprop **11** malapropism ***naming:*** **4** noun ***new:*** **7** coinage **9** neologism ***of action:*** **4** verb ***of honor:*** **4** oath **7** promise ***origin:*** **9** etymology ***part:*** **8** syllable ***root:*** **6** etymon ***scrambled:*** **7** anagram ***shortened:*** **11** contraction **12** abbreviation ***square:*** **10** palindrome ***ultimatum:*** **4** else ***with opposite meaning:*** **7** antonym ***with same meaning:*** **7** synonym ***with same pronunciation:*** **7** homonym **9** homophone ***with same spelling:*** **7** homonym **9** homograph

wordbook **5** vocab **7** lexicon **8** glossary **9** thesaurus **10** dictionary, vocabulary

word-for-word **7** literal **8** ad verbum, verbally, verbatim

wordiness **8** verbiage **9** logorrhea, prolixity, verbosity **10** bloviation

word-of-mouth **4** oral **6** spoken, verbal **8** viva voce **9** unwritten

Wordsworth, William ***friend:*** **9** Coleridge (Samuel T.) ***poem:*** **7** Prelude (The) ***sister:*** **7** Dorothy

wordy **5** windy **6** prolix, verbal **7** diffuse, verbose **9** dictional, garrulous, iterative, redundant, vocabular **10** long-winded, logorrheic, loquacious, rhetorical

work **3** act, fix, job, run, use **4** duty, line, opus, task, tend, till, toil **5** chore, craft, drive, forge, grind, guide, labor, shape, solve, sweat, trade **6** effect, effort, métier, result, strain, strive **7** arrange, calling, control, fashion, operate, perform, product, provoke, pursuit, resolve, travail **8** activity, business, contrive, drudgery, exertion, function, vocation **10** assignment, employment, occupation, profession ***unit:*** **3** erg **5** joule

workaday **5** plain, usual **7** mundane, prosaic, routine **8** ordinary **9** quotidian **11** commonplace

worker **4** doer, hand, serf **5** prole **6** toiler, wallah **7** artisan, laborer **8** employee, mechanic, operator **9** operative **11** proletarian ***fellow:*** **7** comrade, partner **9** colleague ***group:*** **4** crew, gang **5** artel, shift, staff, union ***hard:*** **5** slave **6** beaver, drudge ***insect:*** **3** ant, bee **4** wasp **7** termite ***itinerant:*** **6** boomer **7** migrant ***unskilled:*** **4** peon **7** jackleg, laborer

working **4** busy, live **6** active, useful, viable **7** dynamic, engaged, running **8** employed, occupied **9** operative **11** functioning ***not:*** **5** kaput **6** broken

work out **3** fix **5** solve, train **6** devise, settle **7** arrange, develop, resolve **8** exercise

workout **4** test **5** drill **8** exercise, practice **10** daily dozen

work over **4** beat, redo **5** scrag, study **6** beat up, mess up, redraw, rehash, revamp, revise **7** examine, redraft, restyle, rewrite, rough up **9** manhandle

workroom **3** lab **4** shop **6** studio **7** atelier **10** laboratory

Works and Days author **6** Hesiod

world **5** class, earth, globe, realm **6** career, cosmos, nature, planet, public, sphere, system **7** kingdom, society **8** creation, division, everyone, renowned, universe **9** human race, macrocosm, microcosm **13** distinguished ***combining form:*** **4** cosm **5** cosmo

worldly **5** blasé **6** carnal, earthy, urbane **7** earthly, fleshly, mundane, profane, secular, sensual, terrene **8** material, telluric, temporal **9** sublunary **11** terrestrial **12** cosmopolitan **13** sophisticated

worldly-wise **12** cosmopolitan **13** sophisticated

World Series winner ***1990:*** **4** Reds ***1991:*** **5** Twins ***1992, 1993:*** **8** Blue Jays ***1995:*** **6** Braves ***1996, 1998, 1999, 2000:*** **7** Yankees ***1997, 2003:*** **7** Marlins ***2001:*** **12** Diamondbacks ***2002:*** **6** Angels ***2004:*** **6** Red Sox ***2005:*** **8** White Sox ***2006:*** **9** Cardinals ***2007:*****6** Red Sox ***2008:*****8** Phillies ***2009:*****7** Yankees ***2010:*****6** Giants

World War I ***battle:*** **5** Aisne, Marne, Somme, Ypres **6** Isonzo, Verdun **7** Jutland **9** Caporetto **10** Tannenberg **11** Dardanelles ***battle line:*** **9** Siegfried ***general:*** **4** Foch (Ferdinand), Haig (Douglas) **6** Joffre (Joseph), Pétain (Philippe) **7** Allenby (Edmund) **8** Pershing (John) **10** Hindenburg (Paul von), Ludendorff (Erich) ***hero:*** **4** York (Alvin) **8** Red Baron (The) **10** Richthofen (Manfred von) **12** Rickenbacker (Eddie) ***treaty:*** **10** Versailles

World War II ***admiral:*** **6** Dönitz (Karl), Halsey (William "Bull"), Nimitz (Chester), Nimitz

(Chester) **8** Yamamoto (Isoroku) ***alliance:*** **4** Axis **6** Allies ***battle:*** **4** St.-Lô **5** Anzio, Bulge **6** Bataan, Midway, Tarawa, Warsaw **7** Britain, Iwo Jima, Okinawa, Saint-Lô **8** Coral Sea, Normandy **9** El Alamein, Leyte Gulf **10** Stalingrad **11** Guadalcanal ***general:*****4** Jodl (Alfred), Tojo (Hideki) **5** Clark (Mark) **6** Arnold (Hap), Keitel (Wilhelm), Patton (George), Rommel (Erwin), Zhukov (Georgy) **7** Bradley (Omar) **8** Marshall (George) **9** MacArthur (Douglas), Rundstedt (Gerd von) **10** Eisenhower (Dwight David), Kesselring (Albert), Montgomery (Bernard) ***hero:*** **6** Murphy (Audie) ***journalist:*** **4** Pyle (Ernie) ***weapon:*** **5** A-bomb **6** rocket **8** buzz bomb

world-weary 5 blasé, jaded **7** cynical **9** apathetic, exhausted

worldwide 6 cosmic, global **8** catholic **9** planetary, universal **10** ecumenical **12** cosmopolitan

worm 3 cad, cur **4** grub, lout **5** borer, creep, fluke, leech, louse, screw, treat **6** edge in, maggot, no-good, squirm, thread, wiggle, wretch, writhe **7** extract, triclad, wriggle **8** helminth, nematode, squiggle **9** planarium, trematode ***African:*** **3** Loa ***marine:*** **6** nereid **7** annelid, tubifex ***parasitic:*** **5** fluke, leech **7** ascarid, ascaris, cestode, filaria **8** helminth, trichina **9** strongyle

worn 3 old, wan **4** aged, beat **5** drawn, jaded, tatty, tired, weary **6** eroded, frayed, ragged, shabby **7** haggard **8** fatigued **9** woebegone **10** threadbare

worn-out 4 beat **5** all in, spent, tired, weary **6** bleary, bushed, ragged, used-up **7** drained, run-down **8** decrepit, depleted, fatigued, overused **9** exhausted, worm-eaten **10** broken-down, threadbare, tumbledown **11** debilitated, dilapidated

worried 6 afraid, on edge **7** anxious, nervous **8** bothered, distrait, troubled **9** concerned, tormented **10** distracted, distraught, distressed

worry 3 nag, try, vex **4** care, fret, fuss, gnaw, goad, pain, stew, test **5** angst, annoy, beset, shake, tease, trial, upset **6** assail, attack, bother, harass, needle, pester, plague, pull at, uncase **7** afflict, anguish, anxiety, concern, disturb, oppress, torment, trouble **8** aggrieve, distress, irritate **9** agitation, annoyance, misgiving

worrywart 7 fusspot **9** Cassandra, doomsayer, pessimist **10** fussbudget

worse 8 inferior

worsen 4 sink **7** decline **10** degenerate **11** deteriorate

worship 4 love **5** adore, honor **6** admire, dote on, homage, revere **7** idolize, lionize, liturgy, respect **8** devotion, idolatry, venerate **9** adoration, affection, reverence **10** admiration, veneration ***object of:*** **3** god **4** icon, idol ***place of:*** **5** altar **6** church, mosque, shrine, temple **9** cathedral, synagogue **10** tabernacle

worshipper 3 fan **6** votary **7** admirer, devotee **8** adherent, believer, disciple **10** enthusiast

worsted 4 yarn **5** stuff **6** caddis, fabric **7** cheviot, etamine, flannel, lasting **8** shalloon **9** bombazine, sharkskin **10** broadcloth

worth 4 rate **5** merit, price, value **6** regard, riches, wealth **7** caliber, calibre, fortune, quality, stature **9** resources, substance, valuation **10** excellence

worthless 4 vain **6** futile, no-good, otiose **7** inutile **8** nugatory **9** no-account

worthwhile 6 paying **7** gainful **9** estimable, honorable, lucrative **10** profitable, well-paying

worthy 4 good **5** noble **8** laudable, standout **9** admirable, deserving, desirable, estimable, honorable **10** acceptable, creditable **11** commendable, meritorious

Wotan see **Odin**

Wouk novel 10 Winds of War (The) **11** Caine Mutiny (The)

would-be 7 hopeful, wishful **8** apparent, aspiring, desiring, desirous **9** ambitious, potential

wound 3 cut **4** blow, harm, hurt, pain, rift **6** damage, injure, injury, insult, lesion, trauma **8** lacerate **10** laceration ***sign:*** **4** scab, scar **5** blood **7** blister

wow 3 hit **4** boff, grab **5** amaze, boffo, smash **6** dazzle **7** astound, impress, success **8** bedazzle

Wozzeck composer 4 Berg (Alban)

wrack 4 kelp, raze, ruin **5** smash, total **7** destroy, flotsam, remnant, seaweed **8** decimate, demolish, shambles, wreckage **11** destruction

wraith 5 ghost, shade, spook **6** double, shadow, spirit **7** phantom, specter, spectre **8** phantasm **10** apparition

wrangle 3 row **4** spar, spat, tiff **5** argue, brawl, fight, scrap **6** bicker, fracas, haggle, hassle **7** brabble, dispute, fall out, finagle, quarrel, quibble **8** squabble **11** altercation

wrangler 6 cowboy **8** buckaroo **9** ranch hand

wrap 3 fur **4** bind, cape, cere, coat, roll **5** cloak, drape, shawl, stole **6** bundle, clothe, enfold, invest, jacket, mantle, muffle, parcel, shroud, swathe **7** bandage, blanket, conceal, dress up, embrace, enclose, engross, envelop, involve, package, swaddle **8** bundle up, enshroud

wrapped up 4 deep **6** intent **7** engaged **8** absorbed, consumed, immersed **9** engrossed **11** preoccupied
wrapper 5 cover **6** jacket **10** dust jacket **12** dressing gown
wrap up 6 muffle **8** close out, complete, conclude **9** summarize
wrap-up 4 coda **5** close **6** capper, closer, finale, report **7** closing **8** epilogue **9** summation **10** denouement
wrath 3 ire **4** fury, rage **5** anger **6** choler **8** ferocity **9** vengeance **10** punishment **11** retribution
wrathful 3 mad **5** angry, irate **6** heated, raging **7** enraged, furious **8** choleric, incensed, inflamed **10** infuriated
wreak 5 cause, exact, visit **6** effect, impose **7** inflict
wreath 3 bay, lei **5** crown **6** anadem, laurel **7** chaplet, circlet, coronal, coronet, garland, laurels
wreathe 4 coil, curl, wind **5** twine, twist **6** spiral **7** entwine **9** corkscrew **10** interweave
wreck 4 do in, heap, hulk, raze, ruin **5** beach, crack, crash, cream, smash, total, trash **6** beater, damage, jalopy, junker, pileup, ravage, strand **7** clunker, crack-up, destroy, scuttle, smashup, torpedo **8** decimate, demolish **9** vandalize
wreckage 5 wrack **6** debris **7** flotsam **8** detritus, shambles **11** destruction
wrecker 8 salvager, tow truck
wrench 4 jerk, pull, rack, tool, turn, warp, yank **5** force, twist, wrest, wring **6** change, injure, injury, snatch, socket, sprain, strain **7** disable, distort, pervert, squeeze **8** distress, twisting ***kind:*** **6** monkey **7** ratchet
wrest 4 rend, rive **5** exact, twist, wring **6** elicit, extort, snatch, wrench **7** extract, squeeze
wrestle 6 combat, strain, strive, tussle **7** contend, grapple, scuffle **8** struggle
wrestling *champion:* **4** Ladd (Ernie), Race (Harley) **5** Gagne (Verne), Hogan (Hulk), Studd (Big John) **7** Ventura (Jesse) **8** Kowalski (Killer) **9** Slaughter (Sgt.) **13** André the Giant ***hold:*** **4** lock **6** nelson **8** headlock, scissors ***kind:*** **4** sumo ***term:*** **3** pin **4** fall **5** throw **8** takedown
wretch 3 cur, dog **4** scum, toad, worm **5** devil, knave, louse, rogue, skunk, snake **6** rascal, rotter **7** caitiff, hangdog, lowlife, outcast, rat fink, stinker, villain **8** scalawag, stinkard **9** scoundrel **10** blackguard, sleazeball **11** rapscallion
wretched 3 low, sad **4** base, foul, mean, vile **6** abject, dismal, horrid, scurvy, sordid, woeful **7** abysmal, doleful, forlorn, ignoble, ruthful, servile, squalid, unhappy **8** dejected, dolorous, hopeless, inferior **9** afflicted, execrable, miserable, sorrowful **10** despairing, despicable, deplorable
wretchedness 3 woe **6** misery **7** anguish **8** distress
wriggle 4 worm **5** slink **6** squirm, writhe
Wright, Richard *character:* **6** Bigger (Thomas) ***novel:*** **8** Black Boy **9** Native Son
wring 3 wry **5** choke, exact, screw, twist, wrest **6** extort, squirm, wrench, writhe **7** afflict, draw out, extract, squeeze, torment ***the neck:*** **5** scrag
wringing-wet 5 soppy **6** soaked, sodden, soused **7** soaking, sopping **8** drenched, dripping **9** saturated
wrinkle 4 fold, ruck, ruga, seam **5** crimp, crisp, plica, ridge, wizen **6** cockle, crease, furrow, pucker, rumple **7** crumple, scrunch, shrivel **9** corrugate, crow's-foot, worry line **11** corrugation
wrinkled 5 lined **6** rugose, rumply **7** creased **8** puckered, rugulose
wrist 5 joint **6** carpus ***bone:*** **6** carpal, hamate **8** pisiform
writ 5 brief, order **6** assize, capias, decree, elegit, extent **7** mandate, process, summons, warrant **8** detainer, document, mandamus, mittimus, praecipe, replevin, subpoena **9** execution **10** attachment, certiorari, court order, injunction **11** fieri facias, scire facias, supersedeas **12** habeas corpus, venire facias
write 3 ink, jot, pen **4** note **5** chalk, draft, print, score, spell **6** answer, author, byline, draw up, indite, ordain, pencil, record, scrawl, scribe **7** compose, dissert, engross, fire off, put down, scratch, set down **8** inscribe, scribble, spell out **9** autograph, transpose **10** correspond
write down 4 note **6** record, reduce **10** transcribe
write off 6 cancel **7** dismiss, expense **8** amortize, discount **9** eliminate **10** depreciate
write-off 4 debt, loss **7** expense **8** donation **9** allowance, deduction, reduction
writer 4 poet **6** author, penman, scribe **8** composer, novelist **9** scribbler, wordsmith ***bad:*** **4** hack (see also **author**)
write-up 5 blurb, story **7** account, article
writhe 4 curl, worm **5** twist **6** squirm, suffer, wallow, welter, wiggle, wrench **7** agonize, contort, distort, wriggle **8** convolve, squiggle
writing 4 book, hand, note **5** essay, paper, print, prose, style, words **6** letter, notice, record, script **8** document, longhand **10** literature, penmanship **11** calligraphy, composition, inscription ***character:*** **6** letter **9**

cuneiform **10** hieroglyph ***combining form:*** **4** gram **6** grapho, graphy ***for the blind:*** **7** braille ***instrument:*** **3** pen **5** chalk, quill **6** pencil, stylus ***sacred:*** **5** Bible, Koran, Quran **6** Talmud, Tantra **9** scripture ***surface:*** **5** board, paper, slate **6** scroll **9** parchment

wrong 3 bad, ill, off, sin **4** awry, evil, harm, hurt, tort **5** abuse, amiss, badly, crime, false, inapt, unfit **6** afield, astray, injure, injury, malign, offend, sinful, unfair, unjust, untrue **7** defraud, immoral, oppress, outrage, violate **8** aggrieve, ill-treat, improper, inequity, iniquity, mistaken, opposite **9** erroneous, grievance, incorrect, injustice, misguided, unethical, violation

wrongdoer 5 felon **6** sinner **8** criminal, offender **9** miscreant, reprobate **10** accomplice, delinquent, malefactor **12** transgressor

wrongdoing 3 sin **4** evil **5** crime **7** misdeed, offense **8** iniquity **10** misconduct **11** malefaction, malfeasance, misbehavior

wrongful 6 unjust, unfair **7** illegal, illicit, lawless **8** criminal, improper, unlawful **12** illegitimate

wrongheaded 6 mulish **7** froward **8** contrary, perverse **9** obstinate

wrought 4 made **6** formed, shaped, worked **7** created **8** finished, hammered **9** decorated, fashioned ***up:*** **7** excited, stirred

wry 4 bent **5** askew, twist, wrest **6** ironic, wrench **7** crooked, twisted **8** humorous, sardonic

wryneck 10 woodpecker **11** torticollis

wurst 7 sausage

Wuthering Heights *author:* **6** Brontë (Emily) ***character:*** **5** Cathy **9** Catherine **10** Heathcliff ***family:*** **6** Linton **8** Earnshaw

Wycliffite 7 Lollard

Wyoming *capital:* **8** Cheyenne ***city:*** **6** Casper **7** Laramie ***mountain, range:*** **5** Rocky **7** Gannett (Peak) **9** Wind River **10** Grand Teton ***nickname:*** **8** Equality (State) ***river:*** **5** Green, Snake **6** Powder **7** Bighorn ***state bird:*** **10** meadowlark ***state flower:*** **16** Indian paintbrush ***state tree:*** **10** cottonwood

x 3 chi, ten **4** kiss **5** annul, cross, erase, error, times, wrong **6** cancel, delete, efface **7** mistake, unknown **8** abscissa **9** signature

Xanthippe 3 nag **5** scold, shrew **6** nagger **9** termagant ***husband:*** **8** Socrates

xenon symbol 2 Xe

Xenophon work 8 Anabasis **9** Cyropedia, Hellenica

xerophyte 6 cactus

Xerxes *crossing site:* **10** Hellespont ***defeat:*** **7** Plataea, Salamis ***father:*** **6** Darius ***kingdom:*** **6** Persia ***mother:*** **6** Atossa ***victory:*** **11** Thermopylae

Xmas 4 Noel, yule **8** Nativity, yuletide

X-ray *discoverer:* **8** Roentgen (Wilhelm) ***science:*** **9** radiology

xylophone relative 7 marimba **9** xylorimba **10** vibraphone

yacht 4 race, sail **6** cruise **7** cruiser **8** sailboat **12** cabin cruiser

yahoo 3 hun, yay **4** boor, clod, dolt, hood, lout, punk, thug **5** brute, chuff, churl, clown, rough, rowdy, tough **6** hoorah, hooray, hurrah, savage, terror, vandal, yippie **7** buffoon, bumpkin, hoodlum, ruffian, toughie **8** bullyboy, hooligan **9** roughneck **10** clodhopper

Yahweh 3 God **6** Adonai, Elohim **7** Jehovah

yak 2 ox **3** gab, jaw **4** blab, chat **5** clack, prate **6** babble, gabble, jabber, natter, yammer **7** blabber, blather, chatter, palaver, prattle **11** confabulate

Yale student 3 Eli

Yalta participant 6 Stalin (Joseph) **9** Churchill (Winston), Roosevelt (Franklin Delano)

yam 4 taro **7** boniato **11** sweet potato

yammer 3 cry **4** bawl, crab, fuss, moan, wail, yawp, yell **5** bleat, gripe, whine **6** babble, bellow, clamor, gabble, grouch, grouse, jabber, natter, snivel, squawk **7** blather, prattle, whimper **8** complain **9** bellyache, caterwaul

yank 3 tug **4** grab, jerk, pull, tear **5** hoick **6** snatch, wrench **7** extract

yap 3 gab **4** bark, hick **5** mouth, prate **6** babble, bowwow, gabble, jabber, natter, rustic, yammer **7** blather, bumpkin, chatter, hayseed, prattle **9** hillbilly **10** clodhopper

yard 3 pen **4** herd, quad, spar, unit **5** court, garth, glass **6** length **7** grounds, measure **9** curtilage, enclosure **10** playground, quadrangle ***five and one-half:*** **3** rod ***part of:*** **4** foot ***two hundred and twenty:*** **7** furlong

yardstick 4 norm, test **5** basis, gauge, model **7** measure, pattern **8** paradigm, standard **9** barometer, benchmark, criterion, guideline **10** touchstone

yare 4 deft, spry **5** agile, brisk, handy, lithe, quick, ready, zippy **6** lively, nimble, volant **7** lissome **9** sprightly

yarn 4 tale, talk **5** fiber, story **6** caddis, cotton, crewel, strand, thread **7** account, caddice **8** anecdote, tall tale **9** adventure, narration, narrative ***ball of:*** **4** clew ***coil:*** **5** skein **6** skeane ***cotton:*** **10** candlewick ***for fastening a sail:*** **6** roband ***metallic:*** **6** tinsel ***woolen:*** **6** crewel **7** worsted **8** shetland

yaw 4 rock, swag, veer **5** lurch **6** swerve **7** deviate **9** alternate, deviation **10** deflection

yawn 3 gap **4** bore, gape **5** ennui **6** cavity, tedium **7** boredom, bromide **10** dullsville

yawning 4 deep **5** agape **6** gaping **7** abyssal **9** cavernous

yawp 3 bay, cry, nag **4** bark, bawl, beef, crab, fuss, gape, wail **5** bleat, gripe **6** clamor, outcry, squall, squawk, yammer **8** complain **9** bellyache

yaws 9 frambesia

yclept 5 named **6** called

yea 3 aye, too **4** also, amen, even, more, okay **5** truly **6** agreed, assent, as well, indeed, really, verily **7** besides, granted **8** likewise, moreover, positive **9** certainly **10** definitely **11** affirmation, affirmative **12** additionally

yeanling 3 kid **4** lamb

year 4 time **5** cycle **6** period ***academic division:*** **4** term **7** quarter, session **8** semester **9** trimester ***French:*** **5** année ***kind:*** **4** leap **5** solar **6** fiscal **8** academic, calendar, sidereal ***Latin:*** **5** annus ***Scottish:*** **7** towmond ***Spanish:*** **3** año

yearbook 5 annal **6** annual **7** almanac

yearling 4 colt, foal **5** filly

Yearling, The *author:* **8** Rawlings (Marjorie Kinnan) ***character:*** **4** Jody ***fawn:*** **4** Flag

yearly 6 annual **8** annually

yearn 4 ache, burn, itch, long, lust, pant, pine, sigh, wish **5** dream, spoil **6** hanker, hunger, thirst

yearning 4 wish **5** ardor, drive, eager **6** desire, thirst **7** craving, wistful **8** appetite **10** aspiration

years 3 age, era ***five:*** **7** lustrum **12** quinquennial, quinquennium ***four:*** **11** quadrennial, quadrennium ***one hundred:*** **7** century **9** centenary **10** centennial ***one thousand:*** **10** millennium ***ten:*** **6** decade **9** decennial, decennium ***three:*** **9** triennial, triennium ***two:*** **8** biennial, biennium

yeast 4 barm, foam, suds **5** froth, spume **6** lather, leaven **7** ferment

yeasty 5 dizzy, giddy, light **6** frothy **7** flighty **8** immature, restless, seething **9** exuberant, frivolous, unsettled **11** light-headed

Yeats, William Butler *beloved:* **9** Maud Gonne ***birthplace:*** **6** Dublin ***play:*** **7** Deirdre **9** Herne's Egg (The) **16** Countess Cathleen (The) ***poetry:*** **5** Tower (The) **12** Second Coming (The) **16** Wild Swans at Coole (The) **18** Sailing to Byzantium ***theater:*** **5** Abbey

yegg 5 thief **6** robber **7** burglar **8** picklock **11** safecracker

yell 3 cry **4** bawl, call, howl, roar, wail **5** cheer, hallo, hollo, shout, whoop **6** bellow, clamor, holler, outcry, scream, shriek, squall **10** vociferate

yellow 3 age **4** buff, mean, weak, yolk **5** amber, blond, color, lemon, straw, tawny, topaz **6** canary, coward, craven, flaxen, golden, sallow **7** citrine, gutless, ignoble, jasmine, mustard, saffron **8** cowardly, discolor **9** dastardly, jaundiced, spunkless **11** sensational **12** dishonorable **13** pusillanimous ***brownish:*** **3** dun **5** amber, ocher ***dye:*** **7** annatto ***greenish:*** **5** olive **6** acacia **10** chartreuse

yellowhammer 5 finch **7** bunting, flicker

yelp 3 cry, yap **4** bark **6** outcry, squeal

Yemen *capital:* **4** Sana **5** Sanaa ***city:*** **4** Aden **5** Ta'izz ***desert:*** **10** Rub' al-Khali ***gulf:*** **4** Aden ***island:*** **7** Socotra ***island group:*** **7** Kamaran ***language:*** **6** Arabic ***monetary unit:*** **4** rial ***neighbor:*** **4** Oman **11** Saudi Arabia ***peninsula:*** **7** Arabian ***sea:*** **3** Red **7** Arabian

yen 4 ache, itch, long, lust, pine, sigh, urge **5** taste, yearn **6** desire, hanker, hunger, thirst **7** craving, longing, passion **8** appetite, yearning **9** hankering

yeoman 5 clerk **6** farmer **7** freeman **8** retainer **9** attendant, beefeater, landowner **10** freeholder **11** homesteader

yeomanly 5 loyal **6** sturdy **8** faithful

Yerby novel 13 Foxes of Harrow (The)

yes 3 aye, yea, yeh, yep, yup **4** okay, yeah **5** agree **6** agreed, assent, gladly **7** consent, exactly **8** all right **9** assuredly, certainly, willingly **11** affirmation, affirmative, undoubtedly ***French:*** **3** oui ***German:*** **2** ja ***Italian:*** **2** si ***Russian:*** **2** da ***Spanish:*** **2** si

yeshiva 6 school **8** seminary

yes-man 5 toady **6** lap dog, minion, stooge **7** spaniel **8** groveler, truckler **9** flatterer, sycophant **10** bootlicker **13** apple-polisher

yesterday 4 past, yore **8** recently **10** recent time ***French:*** **4** hier ***Spanish:*** **4** ayer

yesteryear 4 past, yore **7** history **8** foretime, lang syne **12** auld lang syne

yet 3 but, too **4** also, even, more, only, save **5** so far, still **6** as well, though, withal **7** besides, earlier, finally, howbeit, however, someday, thus far **8** after all, hitherto, moreover, sometime **10** eventually, ultimately **11** furthermore, nonetheless, still and all **12** additionally, nevertheless

Yevtushenko poem 7 Babi Yar, Baby Yar

Ygerne see **Igraine**

Yiddish *bit:* 5 shtik **6** shtick **7** schtick ***bargain:*** **7** metziah ***bore:*** **6** nudnik **7** nudmick ***burst:*** **5** plotz ***cash:*** **6** mezuma ***celebration:*** **6** simcha ***comment:*** **6** kibitz **7** kibbitz ***converse:*** **7** shmooze **8** schmooze ***craziness:*** **8** meshugas, mishegas ***crazy:*** **7** meshuga **8** meshugge ***crazy person:*** **11** meshuggener ***drag:*** **5** shlep **6** schlep, shlepp **7** schlepp ***fool:*** **10** shmendrick ***go away:*** **7** gay avek ***go to sleep:*** **10** gay shlafen ***grandpa:*** **5** zayde ***gripe:*** **6** kvetch ***knickknack:*** **9** tchotchke ***long story:*** **8** megillah ***loser:*** **6** nebish ***man of integrity:*** **6** mensch ***matchmaker:*** **8** shadchen ***meddler:*** **5** yenta ***money:*** **4** gelt ***munch:*** **4** nosh ***nerve, gall:*** **7** chutzpa **8** chutzpah ***pleasure, pride:*** **6** noches ***rejoice:*** **5** kvell ***subhuman:*** **5** golem ***unlucky person:*** **9** shlemazel

yield 3 bow, net, pay **4** bear, bend, cave, cede, crop, earn, fold **5** defer, grant, waive **6** accede, bounty, buckle, comply, impart, output, profit, relent, render, resign, return, reward, submit, supply, tender **7** abandon, bring in, concede, consent, deliver, furnish, harvest, produce, product, proffer, provide, revenue, succumb **8** abdicate, collapse, generate, hand over **9** acquiesce, surrender **10** bring forth, capitulate, production, relinquish

yielding 4 soft **6** docile, pliant, supple **7** bearing, passive, pliable **8** flexible **9** adaptable, malleable, tractable **10** manageable, productive, submissive **11** acquiescent, unresistant

yikes 3 gee, wow **4** gosh, uh-oh

yin and ____ 4 yang

yip 3 cry **4** bark, yelp

yippee 3 yay **6** hoorah, hooray, hurrah, hurray **10** hallelujah

yoga posture 5 asana

yoke 3 bar, tie, wed **4** bond, join, link, pair, span, team **5** clamp, frame, hitch, marry, unite **6** attach, couple, inspan **7** bondage, connect, control, harness, peonage, serfdom, slavery **8** marriage **9** servitude **10** crosspiece, oppression ***combining form:*** **3** zyg **4** zygo ***part:*** **5** oxbow

yokel 3 oaf, yap **4** boor, clod, hick, rube **5** churl, swain **6** rustic **7** bucolic, bumpkin, hayseed **9** chawbacon, hillbilly **10** clodhopper, countryman

yolk 4 food **6** yellow

yon see **yonder**

yonder 5 there **7** farther, further, thither **8** outlying

yore 3 old **7** history **8** foretime, lang syne **9** antiquity, yesterday **10** yesteryear

you 2 ye **3** one **4** thee, thou ***French:*** **2** tu **4** vous ***German:*** **2** du **3** Sie ***Spanish:*** **2** tu **5** usted **7** ustedes

young 3 fry, new **4** baby, tyro **5** brood, fresh, green **6** babies, callow, infant, junior, litter, tender, unripe **7** untried **8** childish, immature, juvenile, unformed, youthful **9** unfledged **10** unfinished, unseasoned **11** unpracticed **13** inexperienced ***animal:*** **3** cub, fry, kid, kit, pup **4** calf, colt, fawn, foal, joey **5** puppy **6** kitten, heifer, piglet ***bird:*** **5** chick **7** gosling ***bring forth:*** **3** ean **4** yean ***hare:*** **7** leveret ***sheep, goat:*** **4** lamb **8** yeanling

younger 6 junior

youngster 3 boy, cub, kid, lad, tad, tot **4** girl, lass, tike, tyke **5** chick, child **6** moppet, shaver, squirt **8** juvenile **9** fledgling

your 3 thy

youth 3 lad **5** prime **6** period, spring **8** juvenile, preadult, teenager **9** stripling **10** adolescent, springtide, springtime **12** inexperience ***ancient Greek:*** **6** ephebe **7** ephebus ***goddess of:*** **4** Hebe ***mythological:***

6 Adonis, Apollo, Icarus **8** Ganymede ***time of:*** **9** salad days

youthful 5 fresh, green, young **6** boyish, callow, maiden, unripe **7** puerile **8** immature, juvenile, virginal **9** beardless, unfledged

yowl 3 bay, cry **4** bawl, howl, wail **6** scream, squall, squeal **7** ululate **9** caterwaul

yucca 7 cassava **9** bear grass

Yugoslav leader 4 Tito (Josip Broz)

Yukon *bay:* 9 Mackenzie ***capital:*** **10** Whitehorse ***city:*** **6** Dawson ***mountain:*** **5** Logan ***river:*** **5** Yukon **8** Klondike

yule 4 Noel, Xmas **8** Nativity **9** Christmas **13** Christmastide

Z

Zambia *capital:* 6 Lusaka ***city:*** **5** Kitwe, Ndola **11** Livingstone ***lake:*** **5** Mweru **9** Bangweulu **10** Tanganyika ***monetary unit:*** **6** kwacha ***mountain range:*** **8** Muchinga ***neighbor:*** **5** Congo **6** Angola, Malawi **7** Namibia **8** Tanzania, Zimbabwe **10** Mozambique ***river:*** **5** Kafue **7** Luangwa, Zambezi ***waterfall:*** **13** Victoria Falls

zany 3 nut, wag **4** card, fool, kook **5** antic, campy, clown, comic, crazy, cutup, dotty, goofy, idiot, joker, kooky, loony, nutty, wacky **6** jester, madcap **7** buffoon, farceur, half-wit **8** clowning, clownish, comedian, funnyman, jokester **9** harlequin, prankster, screwball, simpleton, trickster **11** merry-andrew

zap 3 hit **4** blow, kill, nuke **5** blast, snuff **6** attack **7** destroy, wipe out **8** dissolve **9** eliminate, irradiate, liquidate **10** annihilate

Zauberflöte composer 6 Mozart (Wolfgang Amadeus)

zeal 4 brio, fire, zest **5** ardor, drive, mania **6** desire, energy, esprit, fervor, spirit **7** avidity, passion, urgency **8** devotion, dynamism, keenness **9** eagerness, intensity, vehemence **10** enthusiasm, fanaticism, fierceness

zealot 3 bug, fan, nut **4** buff **5** fiend, freak **6** maniac, votary **7** devotee, fanatic, sectary **8** partisan **10** aficionado, enthusiast **12** true believer

zealous 4 avid, keen **5** afire, eager, fiery, fired, nutty, rabid **6** ardent, fervid, gung-ho **7** devoted, fanatic, fervent **8** frenetic, obsessed, wild-eyed **9** dedicated, fanatical, possessed **10** passionate **11** impassioned **12** enthusiastic

zebra 6 equine **7** referee **9** crosswalk ***extinct:*** **6** quagga ***type:*** **6** Grevy's **8** mountain **9** Burchell's

zebu 4 oxen

Zebulun 9 lost tribe ***brother:*** **4** Levi **5** Judah **6** Simeon ***father:*** **5** Jacob ***mother:*** **4** Leah

zecchino 6 sequin

Zechariah 7 prophet

Zedekiah 9 Mattaniah ***father:*** **6** Josiah

zenana 5 harem, serai **8** seraglio

zenith 3 top **4** acme, apex, peak **6** apogee, height, summit, vertex **8** capstone, pinnacle **11** culmination **12** highest point ***opposite:*** **5** nadir

Zenobia *husband:* 9 Odenathus ***kingdom:*** **7** Palmyra

Zeno follower 5 Stoic

Zephaniah 7 prophet **9** Sophonias

zephyr 6 breeze **8** west wind

Zephyrus *father:* 8 Astraeus ***mother:*** **3** Eos **6** Aurora

zeppelin 5 blimp **7** airship **9** dirigible

zero 2 oh **3** aim, nil, nix, zip **4** love, nada, none, null, void **5** aught, nadir, zilch **6** cipher, naught, nobody **7** nothing, nullity **8** goose egg **9** nonentity

zest 4 élan, peel, tang, zeal **5** gusto, taste **6** flavor, relish **7** delight, passion, sparkle **8** appetite, piquancy, pleasure **9** eagerness, enjoyment **10** enthusiasm

zesty 4 racy, tart **5** brisk, sharp, spicy, tangy **6** biting, lively, savory, snappy **7** peppery, piquant, pungent **8** exciting, poignant, seasoned, spirited **9** flavorful

Zetes *brother:* 6 Calais ***father:*** **6** Boreas ***mother:*** **8** Orithyia ***slayer:*** **8** Heracles, Hercules

Zethus *brother:* 7 Amphion ***father:*** **4** Zeus **7** Jupiter ***mother:*** **7** Antiope

Zeus 7 Jupiter ***brother:*** **5** Hades **8** Poseidon ***daughter:*** **3** Ate **4** Hebe **5** Helen **6** Athena **7** Artemis **9** Aphrodite **10** Persephone, Proserpina ***father:*** **6** Cronus ***home:*** **7** Olympus

(Mt.) ***lover:*** **4** Leda, Leto, Maia **5** Danaë, Dione, Metis **6** Aegina, Europa, Latona, Semele, Themis **7** Alcmene, Antiope, Demeter **8** Callisto, Eurynome ***mother:*** **4** Rhea ***nurse:*** **9** Almathaea ***oracle:*** **6** Dodona ***shield:*** **5** aegis ***sister:*** **4** Hera, Juno ***son:*** **4** Ares **5** Arcas, Argus, Minos **6** Aeacus, Apollo, Hermes, Zethus **7** Amphion, Perseus **8** Dionysus, Heracles, Hercules, Sarpedon, Tantalus ***tree:*** **3** oak ***wife:*** **4** Hera, Juno ***weapon:*** **11** thunderbolt

zigzag **4** tack, turn **5** angle, crank, weave **6** jagged **7** chevron **8** flexuous, indirect, serrated ***course:*** **6** slalom

zilch **3** nil, zip **4** nada, zero **5** aught, squat **6** cipher, diddly, naught, nobody **7** nothing, nullity **8** goose egg **9** nonentity **11** diddly-squat

Zimbabwe ***capital:*** **6** Harare ***city:*** **5** Gweru **6** Kwekwe, Mutare **8** Bulawayo, Maxvingo **11** Chitungwiza ***dictator:*** **6** Mugabe (Robert) ***ethnic group:*** **5** Shona **7** Ndebele ***former name:*** **8** Rhodesia ***lake:*** **6** Kariba ***language:*** **5** Bantu ***neighbor:*** **6** Zambia **8** Botswana **10** Mozambique **11** South Africa ***river:*** **4** Sabi **7** Limpopo, Zambezi ***waterfall:*** **13** Victoria Falls

zinc **7** element ***ingot:*** **7** spelter ***ore:*** **6** blende **10** sphalerite ***symbol:*** **2** Zn

zing **3** pan, pep, rap, vim, zap, zip **4** brio, dash, élan, slam, snap, zeal **5** ardor, flair, oomph, verve, vigor **6** energy, esprit, fervor, spirit **7** panache, passion, sparkle **8** dynamism, vitality **9** animation, eagerness **10** ebullience, enthusiasm

zinger **3** dig **4** barb, gibe, jibe, slam **6** retort **7** riposte

Zion **5** bliss **6** heaven, Israel **7** Elysium **8** eternity, paradise **12** New Jerusalem, promised land

Zionist ***American:*** **5** Szold (Henrietta) ***English:*** **7** Sokolow (Nahum) **8** Zangwill (Israel) ***German:*** **6** Nordau (Max Simon) ***Hungarian:*** **5** Herzl (Theodor) ***Israeli:*** **5** Buber (Martin) **8** Weizmann (Chaim)

zip **3** fly, nil, nix, pep, run, vim **4** brio, dash, hiss, rush, nada, snap, tear, whiz, zero, zest, zing, zoom **5** drive, gusto, hurry, oomph, speed, squat, whisk, zilch **6** bustle, energy, hasten, hustle **7** nothing **8** vitality **10** excitement, liveliness **11** diddly-squat

zippy **4** keen, spry, yare **5** agile, alert, brisk, peppy, quick, ready **6** lively, nimble, snappy, speedy **7** dynamic **8** spirited **9** sprightly

zircon **6** jargon **7** jargoon, mineral ***variety:*** **7** jacinth **8** hyacinth

zirconium symbol **2** Zr

zit **6** pimple

zither **10** instrument ***Chinese:*** **3** kin **4** ch'in ***Japanese:*** **4** koto ***relative:*** **8** autoharp, dulcimer

zodiac sign **3** Leo (the Lion) **5** Aries (the Ram), Libra (the Balance, the Scales), Virgo (the Virgin) **6** Cancer (the Crab), Gemini (the Twins), Pisces (the Fishes), Taurus (the Bull) **7** Scorpio (the Scorpion) **8** Aquarius (the Water Bearer) **9** Capricorn (the Goat) **11** Sagittarius (the Archer)

Zola work **4** Nana **7** J'accuse **8** Drunkard (The), Germinal **9** La Débâcle **10** L'Assommoir **13** Thérèse Raquin

zombie **5** robot **8** cocktail **9** automaton

zone **4** area, band, belt **5** layer, tract **6** region, sector **7** portion, quarter, section, segment, stretch **8** district, division, encircle, surround **9** partition, territory

zonked **4** high **5** dazed, doped, drunk, tight **6** ripped, stoned **7** drugged, drunken, smashed **8** hopped-up, tripping, turned on, wiped out **9** spaced-out, strung out, stupefied **10** inebriated, tripped out **11** intoxicated

zoologist ***American:*** **5** Clark (Eugenie), Hyatt (Alpheus) **6** Carson (Rachel), Fossey (Dian), Osborn (Henry Fairfield), Yerkes (Robert) **7** Agassiz (Alexander), Ditmars (Raymond), Merriam (Clinton) **8** Hornaday (William) ***Austrian:*** **6** Frisch (Karl von) ***British:*** **6** Darwin (Charles), Huxley (Julian, Thomas) **7** Goodall (Jane), Medawar (Peter) **9** Lankester (Edwin) ***Dutch:*** **10** Swammerdam (Jan) ***French:*** **6** Buffon (G.-L. Leclerc), Cuvier (Georges) ***German:*** **7** Haeckel (Ernst) ***Norwegian:*** **6** Nansen (Fridtjof) ***South African:*** **5** Broom (Robert) ***Swedish:*** **8** Linnaeus (Carolus)

zoom **3** hum, zip **4** buzz, dash, whiz, zero **5** focus, speed, whizz **6** streak **7** shoot up **9** skyrocket

zoophyte **5** coral **6** sponge **8** bryozoan **9** gorgonian **10** sea anemone

Zoroastrian ***demon:*** **4** deva ***god:*** **10** Ahura Mazda ***sacred writings:*** **6** Avesta

zounds **3** gad **4** egad **8** gadzooks **11** odd's bodkins

zucchetto **7** calotte **8** skullcap

zwieback **5** toast **7** biscuit

zygomatic bone **5** malar **9** cheekbone

zygote **4** cell **6** oocyst